internships
2003

23rd EDITION

THOMSON

PETERSON'S

Australia • Canada • Mexico • Singapore • Spain • United Kingdom • United States

CONTENTS

Getting the Most Out of Your Internship Experience

by Joel F. Clark, Ph.D.

Joel Clark is Assistant Professor of Government and Co-Director of Internships at George Mason University and Director of Michigan State University's Washington Program. Professor Clark's book, *Intern to Success*, was published in 2002. For more advice on internships, visit www.internsuccess.com.

The Value of Internships Today

Each year thousands of interns work in a wide variety of places, including corporations, law firms, government agencies, media organizations, interest groups, clinics, labs, museums, and historical sites. How popular are internships? Consider the recent trends. In the early 1980s, only 1 in 36 students completed an internship or other experiential learning program. Compare this to 2000, where one study found that approximately 86 percent of college students had completed internships, with 69 percent reporting having had two or more.[1]

By definition, internships are a way to learn by doing, so you shouldn't be expected to know everything about them before you start. At the same time, intern success is not automatic. You must work to make it happen. An old saying applies here: "Success is a combination of preparation and luck." A stroke of luck gets you only so far if you are not prepared to maximize the opportunity. But preparation alone is insufficient for success. Good things must also happen to you. The trick is to increase the chances that good things will happen.

The Employer's Perspective

Students are obviously responding to the needs of employers in deciding to complete at least one internship. A survey by the National Association of Colleges and Employers, for example, reported that 70 percent of employers require new hires to have had internships or other on-the-job training, with 61 percent of respondents offering summer internships to provide that experience.[2]

Employers consider internships a good option in both healthy and ailing economies. In healthy economies, managers often struggle to fill their positions with eager workers who can adapt to changing technologies. Internships offer a low-cost way to get good workers into "the pipeline" without offering them a full-time position up front. In struggling economies, on the other hand, downsizing often requires employers to lay off workers without thinking about who will cover their responsibilities. Internships offer an inexpensive way to offset position losses resulting from these disruptive layoffs.

The Intern's Perspective

If you are looking to begin a career, change your career, or supplement your formal education with practical training, internships are a good bet for several reasons.

Internships offer a relatively quick way to gain work experience and develop job skills. Try this exercise. Scan the Sunday want ads of your newspaper. Choose a range of interesting advertisements for professional positions that you would consider taking. List the desired or required job skills and work experiences specified in the ads. How many of these skills and experiences do you have? Chances are, if you are still in school or a recent graduate, you don't have most of the skills and experience employers require of their new hires. What do you do?

You now face a dilemma confronted by numerous people before you. Although you are mentally prepared to start near the bottom of your chosen career, you don't even meet the prerequisites for the entry level! More than a few students have said in despair: "I know I must pay my dues to develop job skills and attain real work experience. But if no one will hire me with my current qualifications, how do I get those skills and experiences?" Good question.

The growing reality is that many entry-level positions require skills and experiences that schools and part-time jobs don't provide. Sure, you know your way around an office computer. You have some customer service experience. You may even have edited the college newspaper or organized a charity event for your sorority. But you still lack the relevant skills and on-the-job experiences that many hiring managers require.

A well-chosen internship can offer a way out of this common dilemma by providing you job training and accumulated hours in an actual career field. Internships help you take your existing knowledge and skills and apply them in ways that will help you compete for good jobs. As Alan Goodman, Director of Career Services at Catholic University explains, "When you apply for a position and can explain during your interview what you did and what kinds of skills you gained, those are the things that employers really value."[3]

Internships offer a relatively risk-free way to explore a possible career path. Believe it or not, the best internship may tell you what you <u>don't</u> want to do for the next ten or twenty years. Think about it. If you put all your eggs in one basket, what happens if your dream

---

[1] Kristin Grimsley, "For Today's College Grads, It Isn't Just About Money," *Washington Post,* 5 May 2000, sec. H, p.1.

[2] Survey by the National Association of Colleges and Employers, reported in Steven Ginsberg, "Schools Out, Work's In," *Los Angeles Times,* 23 June 1997, sec. DD, p. 29.

[3] Quoted in Pat D'Angelo, "First Career Step: Good Internships Provide Students With Meaningful Work Experiences," *Washington Times,* 10 April 2000, sec. F, p. 8.

job turns out to be the exact opposite of what you want or who you are? This is what a student of mine who interned at a prestigious Washington, D.C., public relations firm told me recently. Unfortunately (or fortunately, depending on how you look at it), her story is quite common.

I liked my coworkers and learned a lot about advertising and events management. But I learned that I don't have a passion for it. People work very long hours, and it always seems to be "crunch time." My last year's internship at a nonprofit women's advocacy group is looking a lot better in comparison. While the money may not be as good, they seem to be making a real difference in people's lives.

The point here is that internships offer a relatively low-cost opportunity to "try out" a career field to see if it's right for *you*. Of course, it's still important to complete one or more career assessments, which are readily available at your school's career center or through online educational resources. But a thorough career exploration should also include direct exposure to the fields you are considering. As Mary Wills, Career Center Director at Fresno Pacific University, puts it, internships provide a chance "to experience the good, the bad, and the ugly" of a career field.[4]

Internships offer real opportunities to do career networking and can significantly increase your chances of landing a good full-time position. Have you heard the saying: "It's not what you know, but who you know"? For good or ill, the reality is that who you know (or who knows you) can make a big difference in your job search. Studies show fewer than 20 percent of job placements occur through traditional application methods, including newspaper and trade journal advertisements, employment agencies, and career fairs. Instead, 60 to 90 percent of jobs are found through personal contacts and direct application.[5]

What's going on here? Put yourself in the place of a busy supervisor who must fill a vacant position. You can advertise the position, which requires a formal job announcement, review of resumes, and several interviews. Or you can rely on colleagues and subordinates to identify capable prospective applicants. Usually you will favor applicants who are referred to you by someone you know or those you personally know yourself. Even employers who must advertise a position don't always conduct a thorough review of all applicants. Instead, they employ "coping mechanisms" to streamline the process. One way to cope is to seriously consider only those applicants who have worked for you in the past or who are currently working as interns or part-time employees.

Career "networking" is a necessary strategy to break into this hidden hiring process. Simply put, networking is the exchange of information with others for mutual benefit. Your career network can tell you where the jobs are and help you compete for them. Isn't it better to develop your networking skills now, when the stakes aren't as high, than later when you are competing with everyone else for full-time jobs? The internship hiring process and the weeks you actually spend on the job provide excellent opportunities to talk with various people about careers, your skills, and ways to succeed.

---

[4] Quoted in Darina K. Lazo, "Learning By Doing. For Graduates Wanting to Work After Graduation, Internships Are Key," *The Fresno Bee*, 5 June 2000, sec. E, p. 1.

[5] Reported in *Moving On: A Guide for Career Planning and Job Search*, George Mason University Career Services, 1997, p. 43.

Choosing the Right Internship for You

Because internships today are so plentiful, chances are good that you will get hired somewhere. Finding an internship that is right for *you,* however, will take more effort. Unfortunately, too many people accept the first internship offer without seriously considering their goals, their personal values, and the broad range of available choices. Why leave to chance the choice of an internship where you will work part-time or full-time for several weeks, or months, or even longer? As you review numerous job listings, keep this thought in mind: *There is no "best" internship. There are only better and worse internships depending on my values, needs, and goals.*

An important step in developing your short list of internship choices is to learn about the range of jobs available to you. The internship universe is broad indeed, as you will soon see.

Workplace Size and Status

Workplaces vary greatly in their size, status, and overall mission. Obviously, your main consideration should be your basic interest in the job. But as you gather information to create a short list of possibilities, you might also consider the potential differences between high- and low-profile, and small and large workplaces.

What are high-profile workplaces? You should consider a workplace "high-profile" if most people have heard about it and, consequently, more interns want to work there. For example, high-profile government departments or agencies include the U.S. State Department, the White House, and the FBI. High-profile media organizations include ABC, NBC, CBS, and CNN.

As a general rule, high-profile workplaces tend to be more competitive. Typically, many more people apply for these internships than there are positions to fill. If you have personal contacts at a high-profile organization, talk to them about your application and the odds of getting hired. If you don't have contacts, expect your resume to land on a stack of dozens or even hundreds of others. Generally, applicants without personal contacts face more serious, although not insurmountable, hiring barriers.

High-profile internships often have more rigorous and lengthy application procedures, including letters of recommendation and writing samples. For example, the State Department's application process usually takes a minimum of nine months. So if you are interested in working at a high-profile internship, plan to spend more time and effort compiling your application materials.

You might now be thinking: "I know it's harder to land a high-profile internship. But shouldn't I strive for the best?" Of course you should. There is nothing inherently wrong with these places in that most offer excellent opportunities. But keep in mind that for every high-profile choice, there may be dozens of lesser-known workplaces that offer similar or better opportunities for some interns. For example, if your goal is to produce television documentaries, a smaller production company like Heintz Media Productions in Arlington, Virginia, could be a good alternative should the Discovery Channel not call you back. If you can't get hired at the United Nations or Amnesty International, the lesser-known Human Rights Watch is a great alternative. Usually these lower profile organizations are only lesser known to the general public. Employers in a particular field will likely know them because it's their job to know them.

Workplace size is also something to consider. Many large workplaces offer some obvious advantages. First, large workplaces tend to be more high profile. People are more likely to know about the larger workplace and be impressed that you worked there. Who cares if you spent your days answering phones, filing, and sorting mail? You DID work there. If your primary goal is to add impressive-sounding names to your resume, a large workplace could do the trick.

Second, internships at larger workplaces might be more integrated within the organization's personnel structure. This is good if you seek formal mentoring arrangements or training programs. Many larger workplaces provide more opportunities for getting hired in a paid position at your internship's completion, if that's what you seek. It's simple logic that the more employees and offices within an organization, the greater the chance of getting hired into a permanent position.

While larger workplaces can be good choices, they may have some downsides. For example, you could find the bureaucratic structure in a large workplace stifling. Or you may feel like a cog in a large wheel that has little or no connection to the organization's "end product." This might be tolerable if you can still develop your skills and make good contacts. But what if there is little real work because the office has too many interns? In this case your career portfolio will be quite thin at your internship's conclusion.

To thoroughly explore all your options, consider some possible merits of smaller (and lower profile) workplaces. Because smaller workplaces are generally less known, their internships are usually less competitive. Smaller workplaces often have streamlined application procedures, so you could get hired in a matter of days or weeks, not the months it often takes for larger organizations. Some smaller workplaces might even provide better opportunities to interact with supervisors and to be treated as a regular employee might. As Susan Bing-hamton, owner of a small political consulting firm explains, "I offer hands-on experience. I also refer my interns to other employers and go the extra mile for them in helping get them jobs."[1]

On the downside, a smaller workplace might offer fewer opportunities for structured interaction among interns and supervisory staff. There may be fewer mentoring opportunities simply because there are fewer employees. Also, the management may be less inclined to hold formal training sessions or provide enrichment activities, such as luncheon talks or in-service training.

These possible differences between workplaces are very rough guideposts. Obviously, organizations that fall within these categories will vary greatly. Make sure you investigate your internship choices thoroughly and prepare to ask specific questions about these issues during your job interviews.

Paid Versus Unpaid Internships

Given the choice, everyone would choose a paid over an unpaid internship, all else being equal. This is entirely understandable. After spending years in school and sacrificing your short-term monetary interests for long-term educational and career goals, why shouldn't you get paid for your labor? The problem is that rarely is all else equal in choosing between internships. In some cases a paid internship is a better choice for you, but in many cases it isn't. Internship compensation should be weighed among many factors.

The good news is that more internships are paid now than in the past. This trend reflects the increasing competition employers face in attracting good workers, especially in healthy economies. However, salary should not be your most important consideration if you can afford to temporarily work for free or very cheap. Remember you are interning to gain work experience and career-building opportunities, not to get rich.

The issue of compensation should also be considered alongside other recent changes in the career marketplace. Corporate recruiters report that college graduates rank salary lower on their list of job priorities than before. Less quantifiable "quality of life" factors, including the workplace mission, flex-time options, educational tuition support, and vacation time are increasingly important considerations for new recruits.[2] In choosing an internship, and ultimately a paid job, you should consider all these factors. And since this is your life we're talking about, the relative importance you assign to each should reflect your personal preferences, not those of your teachers, friends, or even relatives.

[1] Comments made at "Getting the Most Out of Your Internship," Career Panel II, George Mason University, 1997.

[2] Grimsley, "It Isn't Just About Money," 2000.

How to Apply for Internships

For many people, perfecting their application materials is a daunting process. Prospective interns are notorious for creating their resumes and cover letters at the last minute—and it shows. Since there are numerous resources available to help you do it right, there is no excuse for sending out flawed materials.

Your resume and cover letter won't get you hired. A job interview is usually necessary to secure the job. At the same time, well-crafted resumes and cover letters will help you get interviews, while flawed ones will certainly decrease your chances of advancing to the interview stage. When writing resumes and cover letters, aim for clarity and brevity. Your resume and cover letter should not exceed one page each.

Resumes

There are two basic types of resume: chronological and functional. *Chronological resumes* list your education, work, and extracurricular experiences separately in reverse chronological order (most recent first). *Functional resumes,* in contrast, group all your skills and experiences under broad functional categories. This format allows individuals who are changing careers to emphasize their most marketable attributes, while de-emphasizing problems such as long unemployment or specific jobs that didn't work out. Most individuals seeking internships don't fit the applicant profile for functional resumes and will therefore use the chronological resume.

Before you start crafting your resume, track down basic information, including the actual time periods you spent in schools and on jobs and the exact titles of clubs, organizations, and awards. You should also inventory your most important skills and experiences. The more you can place your skills in specific contexts, the more effective your resume will be.

As you complete the following steps, keep in mind the employers who will read your resume. They will quickly scan your resume, so make it easy to pick out your best qualifications and the contact information they need to arrange a job interview.

All resumes should contain certain categories of information. These are your personal contact information, your objective, your education, your work experience, any pertinent additional information that doesn't fit in these standard categories, and an offer to provide references upon request.

Your personal contact information. Write your name in capital letters, centered horizontally on the page, about one inch from the top. Use your formal name (not nickname) and include your middle initial to add some formality. You may choose to type your name in bold face or slightly increase the font. But don't get too carried away with this.

Enter your school address and phone number on the left-hand margin and your permanent home address and phone number (if different from your school address) on the right-hand margin, two or three lines below your name. If you only have one address, center it under your name or place it on the left-hand margin. If you will be traveling during the job search process, be sure to list the address and phone number of someone who always knows where to reach you. Employers who can't reach you right away might contact another applicant. Include the e-mail address that you check regularly.

Your objective statement. Your objective is important because it describes the type of internship you seek. Since you are applying for an internship, not a full-time job, your objective should balance your general employment goals with specific learning objectives. You should develop several objective statements for different internships. Here are some examples:

OBJECTIVE: A full-time internship in advertising to develop copywriting and administrative skills.

OBJECTIVE: A part-time internship at a nonprofit organization with opportunities to learn about grassroots mobilization.

OBJECTIVE: An internship in federal legislative affairs that builds on my volunteer work for the Michigan State Senate.

Education. From most recent back, list your degrees completed (e.g., A.A., A.S., B.A., B.S.), major programs of study, institution(s) attended, minors or concentrations, and any noteworthy seminars, course work, projects, or study-abroad experiences. If your course work or projects don't add to your qualifications, don't include them. List your grade point average (GPA) if it's higher than 3.0 and any other relevant academic honors such as dean's list or honors program. If you are still pursuing a degree, use the phrase "Candidate for the degree of . . . ." If you have already graduated, use "Awarded the degree of . . . ."

If you have not graduated and are not currently pursuing a degree, simply list the dates you attended school and possibly several courses completed. If you transferred from one school to another, you may want to list the prior school depending on how long you attended and whether you achieved significant honors.

Work history. In reverse chronological order, list the following: your position title, name of organization, location of work (city, state), and years of work. Then describe your work responsibilities and other relevant factors in succinct, active phrases. Unlike passive phrases ("assured attainment of balanced budgets in two consecutive years"), active phrases are crisp, action-oriented descriptions of the same tasks ("balanced the budget in two consecutive years"). List your most important responsibilities first and describe them more fully than less significant tasks. Emphasize your personal achievements rather than the activities themselves. For example, saying "security guard for clothing store" doesn't distinguish you from other security guards. Instead, emphasize what you accomplished as a security guard: "Supervised a team of 3 store security personnel, implemented new security training program, and achieved 30 percent drop in stolen merchandise as lead security guard." Note the use of action verbs: *supervised, created, implemented,* and *achieved.*

Additional activities. Optional categories such as "skills," "activities and interests," or "awards and honors" can group information that doesn't fit neatly in the above categories. A *skills* category lists any specialized skills you have, including computer skills (e.g., HTML, Lotus 123, PowerPoint, Excel), foreign language skills, or working knowledge of research programs (e.g., LexisNexis). Many employers value an applicant's specific office skills more than their major or academic achievements, so be sure to highlight your skills in ways that distinguish you from other applicants.

An ***activities and interests*** category is a good place for applicants to round out their personal profile. Activities that include community service, club involvement, or campus leadership can strengthen your resume, especially when they are linked to specific skills. Special interests that round out your "personality type" might include sports activities or hobbies.

An ***awards and honors*** category is useful for significant honors beyond those listed in other categories. For example, "Rotary Club Young Citizen Award" or "Eagle Scout Award" should be listed here, while things like "dean's list" or "employee achievement award" should be listed in the education or experience sections.

References. It's best to just put "References available on request." Most career experts advise applicants not to list specific references on their resume because they should know when their references are called, and prospective employers won't hesitate to ask for them anyway. Make sure you have a list of at least 3 references (with updated contact information) should employers ask.

In describing your education, experiences, and achievements, always strive for accurate and concise action-oriented phrases. Cut out nonessential words and transitions, and consistently use past tense for everything except what you are currently doing. Avoid overinflating your achievements and NEVER lie. It's okay to sell yourself but don't reinvent the truth. For example, if your job title was Office Receptionist, don't rename it Office Communications Facilitator. If you are not proficient in certain skills, don't say you are. Finally, avoid using inflated terms like "expert," or "full knowledge." Few people in this world are true experts on anything. Claiming you are will raise doubts about your other claims and your general maturity. A White House official once complained to me that a student applicant described himself as an "expert" on Middle East politics. Instead, he should have simply indicated that his concentration was Middle East politics.

Cover Letters

Your cover letter is just as important as your resume. In fact, these two documents should always work together. A good cover letter will accomplish three things: (1) explain why you are interested in the job and organization; (2) give the recipient a reason to be interested in you; and (3) lay the groundwork for further contact. This is a lot to ask of a one-page letter but, with careful editing, it can be done.

The following is an outline of a standard cover letter:

Your mailing address
Your phone number/e-mail

Date

Mr./Ms./Dr. A. Recipient
Title
Company Name
Company Address

Dear Mr./Ms./Dr. A Recipient. Avoid addressing your letter "To whom it may concern." Make the extra effort to find out the name and title of the person who will review your letter and resume and be sure to get the spelling right. This personal touch can make a big difference.

Introduce yourself. Your lead paragraph should clarify who you are, the intern position you seek, and, if possible, how the job will help promote your larger goals. For example: "Currently, I am a senior marketing major at Smith College who seeks an internship in Kent and Associates's advertising department. Since my ultimate goal is to be an account executive, an advertising internship can help me gain some necessary skills." If there isn't an identifiable internship position, describe what you seek in more general terms. Make sure you also mention how you learned of the position. Be as specific as you can. For example, if you spoke with someone over the phone, mention his or her name. Or if you learned about the internship through school or on a Web site, briefly describe the circumstances.

Highlight your most relevant skills and experiences. In your letter, refer specifically to the most relevant educational and work experiences listed on your resume and the useful skills you possess. For example: "As my resume states, last summer I gained advertising experience while working part-time at the San Francisco Symphony." In addition, describe briefly what you hope to gain from the internship. You might also mention your good personality traits or work ethic but keep it brief. The cover letter's purpose is to get your resume read, not list everything in it.

Set yourself up for the interview. Offer to come in for an interview or make yourself available for a phone interview if a personal visit is impractical. For example, you may want to say something like: "I am very interested in learning more about your internship position and DynaCorp's excellent work with defense contractors. You can reach me at [phone number and e-mail]. I will follow up with a phone call next week to arrange a meeting with you or another DynaCorp representative."

Sincerely,
Your signature
Type your formal name.

Use proper English and avoid slang and abbreviations. Keep your sentences short and use action verbs. Also, keep your total length to a single page. It's best if the actual text of the letter does not exceed a half page in length. This kind of brevity takes work, so keep drafting until you get it just right!

Students usually make the same simple mistakes on their resumes and cover letters. Employers often complain about typographical errors, passive voice, and inflated claims of knowledge or experience. Do you think your current drafts are perfect? Although you have scanned your materials numerous times for errors, you probably have missed one or more mistakes. To avoid sending out flawed application materials, be sure to have several trusted friends and family members read over your drafts. Also, have a professor or career guidance counselor review your work.

Interviews

You should take internship interviews seriously for several reasons. First, some intern positions are highly coveted and therefore highly competitive. Also, since most employers rely heavily on interns to help them accomplish their mission, they take the hiring process seriously. If they sense you are unprofessional or uncommitted, they will pass you over for someone else. Your job is to convince them that you are the best "fit" out of all applicants.

You should begin preparing for job interviews before you start scheduling them. Think carefully about what you bring to the internship and what you hope to gain from the experience. Before you contact your short list of employers, make sure you have the latest information on them and can use it to distinguish yourself from other applicants.

- What is the organization's mission?
- What are the principal products or services the organization provides?
- Who are the organization's principal clients, customers, and partners?
- What job positions are currently being offered?
- What are the organization's sales or other recent performance indicators?

Ideally, you will be able to speak to one or two current interns in the office. Tactfully try to find out about the workplace, the person who will interview you, and any special attributes they are looking for in an intern. During the interview, try to weave in comments that show you did your homework.

In addition to doing research, review the three basic job interview types: factual, situational, and conversational. In each instance your goal is to showcase your skills and experiences and to convey that you are a mature, personable, and trainable applicant.

Factual interviews focus on facts associated with grades, work, and experiences. A typical question might be: "So, you are a history major and economics minor. What does a minor in economics require?" In answering this type of question, aim to succinctly provide the information asked for and then steer your answer toward one of your major strengths. Your response might go something like this:

My economics minor required Micro- and Macroeconomics, Economic Theory and Practice, and three upper-level economics courses of my choosing. [*Note:* A weak answer might stop here.] For my electives I chose Political Economy, Monetary Policy, and International Markets because I am very interested in the economic and political dimensions of globalization. My economics minor also required me to do hands-on projects and analysis using economic forecasting methods. So I think it really complemented my history major, which was much more fact-based.

Just because your interviewer emphasizes facts in her questions doesn't mean you should take the interview lightly. Factual questions can be easily mishandled. A question like "Why do you want to intern at Sharpe Industries?" presents both traps and opportunities. Avoid answers that betray a poor understanding of what the company does or a haphazard way of choosing to apply for an internship there. For example, avoid saying things like "My friend Jim is also applying here, and we thought it would be cool to work in the same place this summer." Instead, be prepared to show that you have carefully researched the company and thought about your short- and long-term goals. For example:

In my career research, I kept coming across Sharpe Industries as a global leader in corporate management services, and I was impressed with the way Sharpe encourages its employees to constantly update their skills and training. I have already attained some experience with computer networks by working part-time at GlobeCom. While I learned a lot at GlobeCom, I also want to work in an industry leader to confirm my interest in management consulting as a career field.

Situational interviews often start with factual questions but move on to questions about how you would respond to certain (usually difficult) situations. For example: "Our interns at New Horizons interview youths locked up in county juvenile halls. How would you handle a situation where a male youth only wanted to talk about your dating life?" The point of this question is not to determine whether you read the training manual (you wouldn't be expected to), but instead how mature and tactful you are in responding to awkward situations. A good answer might go something like this:

> I would remind the individual that we were talking for a specific purpose, and that his participation in the New Horizons program was a privilege that could be revoked if he didn't take the interview process seriously. If the youth persisted, I would terminate the interview and notify my supervisor immediately about what happened.

Like situational interviews, *conversational interviews* usually start out as factual ones. But instead of remaining a formal question-and-answer session, this interview quickly becomes an unstructured conversation between you and the interviewer about such things as the internship, the organization, your background, and any other topic that comes up. Often the style is relaxed—and even fun. While this interview is less stressful, don't take it any less seriously than the other two. Whether you realize it or not, your interviewer is still assessing your character, poise, articulation, and ability to relate to other people.

In a conversational interview you should adjust your style to better fit your interviewer's style. But don't get too chummy or informal, and avoid saying things that reflect badly on you as an applicant. For example, don't say things like the following, even in very light moments:

- I am really bored by school.
- Most of my professors are clueless.
- Nobody works because they like to, but because they have to.
- My main goals are to make money and retire early.
- I am a born leader.
- I'm not a morning person.

Even interview pros can be rattled by certain questions, so prepare as much as you can. You should avoid quick yes and no answers as well as rambling monologues. Instead, try to answer in succinct statements that put your record and personal attributes in the best light. For example: "Tell me about yourself" may seem easy. But for many applicants it's a minefield. If you are a "spontaneous" person, do you say so? Spontaneity may indicate flexibility in adapting to new situations, but it might also suggest you lack deliberation and the ability to follow through when things get tough. So be prepared to explain why your spontaneous personality is an asset.

At some point you will likely be asked if you have any questions. Make sure you always have some questions. In fact, you should interview them as much as they interview you. Now is the time to clarify what you will do, whom you will work for, and other benefits of the internship program.

Here are some possible questions to consider:

- Who would be my direct supervisor?
- What would be my primary tasks?
- How much interaction will I have with full-time staff?
- Will I have opportunities to take on more responsibilities?
- Is there a formal training program?
- Are there opportunities to do job shadowing?
- Will I be able to attend policy meetings or go to conferences?
- Is the internship paid? If not, are stipends available to offset my travel costs?
- How will I be evaluated?
- Is it possible to apply for a full-time job at the internship's conclusion?
- Have past interns been hired by the organization?

It is understandable that at this stage you are eager to please. But be careful not to promise your interviewers too much. As Michelle Rupp, a four-time intern, cautions: "Don't commit to something you can't do. Be realistic to yourself in terms of time. You don't want to have to stop your internship midway through."[1]

Punctuality and appearance are crucial to making good first impressions. So plan to arrive early. If you find you are very early, take a walk around the block. Review your resume. Clear your mind. If you are running late, make the best of a bad situation by calling ahead and informing your interviewer. Good personal grooming is just as important as finding the right outfit, so make sure your clothes fit and they, and you, are clean. Be sure to bring the right accessories. A briefcase

---

[1] "Getting the Most Out of Your Internship," Career Panel II, 1997.

or folder with extra copies of your resume, a pen, and writing paper are standard items.

Body language is also critical to interview success. Smile and offer a firm handshake. Maintain good posture and eye contact. Don't fidget or constantly shift your sitting position. Speak clearly and be a good listener. Instead of searching for complex words or phrases, stick to language you are comfortable with. Back up statements with brief personal anecdotes about real situations. Throughout the interview convey an attitude of interest in the job and an eagerness to work hard.

Telephone interviews. Many students intern away from home, which makes a phone interview necessary. Most tips for in-person interviews apply here, except visual cues. Since your job will likely include answer-ing the office phones, you are probably being evalu-ated on your phone demeanor. So make sure you listen carefully to each question and modulate your voice so that you can be heard clearly without speaking too loudly.

Scheduling is a major challenge for phone interviews, so make yourself as available as possible. Because employers are very busy, they will likely call another applicant if they can't complete your interview. Be will-ing to work around their schedule, and free up a suf-ficient block of time in case the interview is delayed or runs over.

For all interviews, be sure to send a typed or writ-ten thank-you letter within a day or two. Thank them for meeting with you and reaffirm your interest in working for the organization.

Making the Most of Your Internship Experience

Once you land your dream internship, how do you make the most of it? In my experience working with hundreds of interns, one point has proven true time and again: Intern success is not automatic; you must *work* at it. Remember, you—not your teachers, program administrators, or workplace supervisors—are primarily responsible for your internship success. Since all workplaces are different, you won't have the full picture until you actually start the job. Once you begin, it's up to you to evaluate your surroundings and adapt accordingly.

The Early Stage of Your Internship

Your internship program will usually require a written learning contract. This document covers the terms of your employment and identifies your learning objectives. It is best if you can sit down with your supervisor and complete the contract together. Think carefully about the skills and experiences you hope to gain, and encourage your supervisor to be specific about planned projects and activities.

If your workplace provides a formal orientation or training program for its interns, take it seriously. However, don't be surprised if your workplace doesn't provide any formal training. In their study of internship practices, for example, Cathy Ryan and Roberta Krapels found that most interns receive no formal training at all. Instead, they are expected to "learn the ropes" through informal means, such as reviewing workplace literature and anticipating the needs of their supervisors.[1] Obviously, this situation can be very disorienting if you are used to detailed directions provided by your teachers or work supervisors.

The vast majority of interns find their overall work experiences challenging and rewarding. But for many, the first week on the job is less than satisfying. Because you have built up high expectations about your internship, you may feel somewhat let down once you start work. Perhaps the workplace isn't as glamorous as you thought. Or maybe the office staffers are not outwardly enthusiastic about your arrival. As you experience feelings of doubt, keep in mind that most people feel uncomfortable starting a new job, whether it's their first job or fifth. Your challenge is to handle these early doubts with enthusiasm and grace. If you find yourself with little or nothing to do, don't panic. Keep yourself busy by studying your workplace training manual and other forms of literature, finding your way around and introducing yourself, and asking people if they need help.

Intern Dos and Don'ts

Here are general internship dos and don'ts that you should follow from day one. First, the "don'ts."

Don't be late or abuse your breaks. This seems obvious. But employers frequently complain about interns who show up late or not at all. Just because you are not paid doesn't mean you can set your own hours. No matter what else you do effectively on the job and how personable and otherwise competent you are, your consistent tardiness will become a serious mark against you, even if your supervisor doesn't seem to notice.

Don't make personal phone calls or e-mails and don't play on the computer. Personal phone calls and personal computer use are pet peeves for many employers, even if they don't confront you on it right away. Workplaces are tightening their policies on these activities and monitoring their employees more closely. Don't find this out the hard way!

Don't dress inappropriately. Workplace dress codes vary widely. A general rule-of-thumb is to emulate existing office standards. Sloppy dress and grooming are never good practices; they convey the impression that you may also be sloppy in how you approach your job and life. Instead, aim for neat clothes that don't detract from who you are and what you do.

Don't disrespect other people's workspaces. Always leave the office workspaces cleaner than when you found them, even in very messy offices. If you use someone else's desk, clean up after yourself. This seems obvious, but you would be surprised at how often this simple rule is broken.

Don't be a complainer or a slacker. Bosses resent complainers because it's clear they are not team players. They are viewed as spoiled individuals who are not ready for the responsibilities of a real job. Interns who start out with an inflated belief in their worth as employees are bound to become resentful and disgruntled. Realistic expectations are the key to your whole experience. If you expect to make policy, supervise others, or land the big account, you are bound to be disappointed. Instead of complaining about mundane tasks from the very beginning, strive to complete them quickly and efficiently. When you demonstrate that you can cover the basics well, better projects should follow.

Don't be a "know-it-all." There is a fine line between being confident and assertive and knowing everything. At times you may know more than your coworkers or even your boss. However, no one likes to work with someone who thinks they have all the answers. It's okay to have opinions, even strong ones at times. But be sure to express them only when appropriate. Sometimes a better strategy is to hold back

---

[1] "Organizations and Internships," *Business Communications Quarterly* 60, no. 4. (1997): 126–131.

and quietly assess a situation before blurting out the most obvious answer. You may actually learn something. And you will avoid those simple yet costly gaffes that know-it-alls frequently make.

Don't be afraid to ask questions or speak up at the right time. If you have a legitimate question or need clarification, ask someone. Your bosses will appreciate your attempt to closely follow their instructions. A well-timed question can also help you avoid mistakes or costly delays in completing your tasks. Remember, as an intern you are not expected to fully understand everything you are asked to do on the first try.

The following "dos" are some best practices that can significantly improve your chances for intern success.

Do be an active and enthusiastic learner. Try to make a learning experience out of everything, even the most mundane tasks. Are you sorting and distributing mail? Try to learn who frequently contacts your organization and what they want. When you are photocopying, try to absorb the information contained in the originals. Elena Mayberry, an intern coordinator at the Smithsonian and a former intern herself, suggests that "intellectual sparkle" is what distinguishes a great intern from a mediocre one. This is "a desire to learn, a curiosity about a lot of things, and an enthusiasm for what you do."[2]

Do give your internship some time to develop before concluding there are problems. Interns often experience a lull in their jobs once the "honeymoon" period is over but before they gain more challenging tasks. How you handle this lull is crucial to your overall internship experience. If you become cynical, chances are you will sabotage your opportunities to gain better responsibilities. Instead, try to handle these challenges with patience. It is likely that your bosses are still assessing whether you can handle more.

After a few weeks, go back and review your learning contract and notes from your job interview and initial meetings with your supervisors or staff members. Did they promise that more substantial duties and projects would follow? Have they? If not, tactfully offer to take on more while still covering your basic responsibilities. As Bruce Craig, Communications Manager at the Smithsonian's Office of Museum Studies, explains, interns should "stand up for their rights and make sure they are not being taken advantage of." At the same time, they should also "make sure they work on the projects they were hired to."[3]

Do actively seek out opportunities to create your own projects. As you cover your basic tasks, look around the office to see where improvements can be made. Is the filing system a disaster? Are boxes of unrecorded data lying on the storage room floor? Is the company Web site horribly out of date? Instead of ignoring these problems, the savvy intern will try to fix them. Be sure to get permission before you start. This is also a good way to show that you are indispensable to the workplace. As Will Stone, Chief of Staff for U.S. Representative David Obey, says: "Look for the void, and ask about it. See if you can build a better mousetrap."[4]

There are other ways to expand your responsibilities. You can ask to "shadow" a regular employee on service calls or to meetings outside the office. Or you can seek feedback on your existing work. Ask how you could improve that summary report or letter to a client, or how you might have handled that rude caller differently. Asking for feedback shows that you want to improve yourself and do a good job for the benefit of the organization.

Do go the "extra mile" at times to demonstrate your willingness to pitch in and be a team player. Are there certain "crunch times" in your office? Instead of always dropping your work and leaving at 5 p.m., it's sometimes better to stay and finish the day's project or pitch in to help others finish theirs. Steve Selby, a Principal at Squier Knapp Dunn, looks for interns who can meet the challenges of working in a fast-paced political consulting firm. According to Selby: "The kind of people we like to hire are those who show some initiative and extra hustle. When it comes to hiring, those interns stand out in our mind."[5]

The more you look and act like a regular employee, the more likely you will be treated like one. Do you put in an honest day's work? Do you attend regular staff meetings (if allowed) and participate when you have something to contribute? Do you sit with other employees during lunch, even occasionally? Although you are still "just an intern," most supervisors and staff will treat you like a regular employee when you act like one. They may even decide they can't afford to let you go. That's what happened to Kristin Watkins. She is a former intern and now a full-time employee at Wider Opportunities, a national nonprofit association that creates employment opportunities for low-income women. According to Watkins, "Once you make yourself indispensable, it's very hard for the organization to let you go. They feel they have an investment in you."[6]

Do actively seek mentor relationships with supervisors and coworkers when appropriate. A frequent benefit of interning is the willingness of someone to mentor you. Mentors are more senior staff members and supervisors who take a special interest

---

[2] Comments made at "Getting the Most Out of Your Internship," Career Panel III, George Mason University, 1998.

[3] Comments made at "Getting the Most Out of Your Internship," Career Panel I, George Mason University, 1996.

[4] Comments made at Michigan State University's Washington Internship Seminar, 31 January 2001.

[5] Comments made at Michigan State University's Washington Internship Seminar, 10 April 2002.

[6] "Getting the Most Out of Your Internship," Career Panel III, 1998.

in your career aspirations and are willing to help you advance your career when they can. Often these mentors were interns themselves just a few short years ago and seek to help someone the way they were helped. Listen closely to successful people when they discuss their career histories; a mentor invariably shows up at critical points in their rise to the top.

Gaining a mentor may be one of the most important things you do at your internship. Once again, who you know is more important than what you know. While your immediate supervisors are good mentor candidates, don't neglect lower-level staff or contacts you make outside your office.

Do share your career aspirations with supervisors, coworkers, and those you encounter outside the workplace. This suggestion closely relates to the last one. Although you know what your immediate and long-term goals are, others don't unless you tell them. At appropriate times, you should make your goals known. This provides those who may want to help with the information they need to help you in the right way.

Try to take advantage of networking possibilities wherever they arise. When you network, you seek out and develop connections with others for mutual benefits. Networking is a socially acceptable practice, and all successful professionals do it. Begin with your friends and coworkers. Talk with them about their jobs and career paths. Ask them how they like their jobs, what their typical day is like, and what advice they have for someone who is considering a career in that field. You may be surprised at how helpful people can be.

Networking is not just talking about yourself but also being sincerely interested in others and what they do. A good networker is polite, personable, and genuine. To help you remember the names of contacts, be sure to exchange business cards. If your contact suggests you call or e-mail her later, do it. She may have a job lead or further contact in mind or genuinely want to help you in some other way.

Do build your own workplace portfolio. Employers are often impressed when job applicants can provide concrete examples of their work experiences and skill development. Providing them an actual copy of the newsletter you created at your internship, for example, will bolster your claim to "effective writing and organizational skills." What should go into your portfolio? The best strategy at this point is to save everything and decide later what you will actually keep. This includes letters and memos you wrote, research findings, reports you created, and newsletters you edited. Your academic assignments should also be included.

Do be open to learning from people whose backgrounds are different from yours. An underappreciated value of internships is that they can expose you to people with different backgrounds or life experiences. Try to meet and talk with as many people

as possible. Listen carefully to what they say and learn from them. Just because someone didn't go to college doesn't mean he or she doesn't have valuable wisdom to impart. In some instances, you may learn more from lower-placed staff than from your supervisors.

Ending Your Internship

How you end an internship is just as important as how you begin one. Your last days on the job are a time for personal satisfaction, honest evaluation, and looking forward.

Most academic internship programs require a written *work evaluation.* When possible, arrange personal meetings with your supervisors and possibly more senior staff to discuss the evaluation. While most interns receive good evaluations, some supervisors will indicate specific areas where you need improvement. Don't become defensive or resentful if you receive constructive criticism. Instead, take such advice for what it's worth and move on.

Final meetings with supervisors and regular staff members provide great opportunities to reemphasize your academic and career goals. If you are looking for a full-time job, now is a good time to reaffirm your interests. In some cases it's appropriate to directly ask for a job. In others, it isn't. If in doubt, just ask something like: "What can someone like me do to further prepare for a career in this field?"

Final meetings are also a good time to ask for a *letter of recommendation* for an existing job, for a future job, or for graduate school. Since you have worked for free or cheap for several weeks or months, it's not too much to ask of your employer. If you are not yet applying for jobs or graduate school, try to get a generic letter of recommendation. While a generic letter isn't great, it's better than nothing. Many employers are willing to revise a generic letter later when you do apply for jobs.

Your last days on the job are also a good time for *personal evaluation.* Take an inventory of what you accomplished and what remains to be done. Think about what you learned about the career field. Have your personal and work values been reinforced by your internship experience, or have they changed somewhat as a result of what you learned? Keep in mind that most people (even those who love their jobs) don't like something about their chosen career field. Try to realistically weigh the pros and cons of your internship experience.

An important part of intern success is *knowing when to leave.* Some interns become too comfortable with their position and decide to stay even though they have exhausted all the opportunities the internship offered. Your employer might even offer you a stipend to stay on. If so, be honest with yourself in deciding whether or not to take it. Often it's better to do two or three separate internships at different organizations than to remain at the same internship for a long period of time.

If you are disappointed with your internship experience, resist the temptation to burn your bridges. While that might make you feel good temporarily, it can hurt you in the long run. Also, interns who leave on a bad note may make it harder for future intern applicants who may be more suited to the organization.

Keep in touch with your former colleagues after you leave. A job position or other opportunity may open up later, or one of your network contacts may have a lead for you. A short e-mail to your contacts every couple of months can keep you on their radar screen.

Remember that it's primarily up to you to get the most out of your internship. Countless interns before you have achieved success, and you can too! Good luck.

International Applicants for U.S. Internships

by Elizabeth Chazottes

Elizabeth Chazottes is the Executive Director and CEO of the Association for International Practical Training and has written numerous articles on international training, overseas employment, and international human resources issues.

International Applicants for U.S. Internships

Nothing is more exciting and rewarding than an international internship in the United States. International participants have been coming to the United States for years to learn American methods of business, to perfect their English skills, and to make international connections that last a lifetime. There are more opportunities today than ever before, but you must be well informed. Take the time to learn about your options and which program will best meet your needs. The better prepared you are, the more successful your experience will be. All international students interested in coming to the U.S. for an internship or international program should make sure they are clear on what they can and cannot do in the workplace and on the type of visa they receive to come to the U.S.

In an effort to provide guidance that is as accurate as possible for students from outside the United States, each employer listed in *Internships 2003* has been asked if applications will be accepted from international students. Peterson's has also asked if the employer is willing to undertake the necessary steps—either directly with the U.S. Immigration and Naturalization Service (INS) or through an educational exchange organization—to make it possible for the student to secure a proper U.S. visa that will allow them to complete the internship and legally receive a salary or stipend, if applicable, while in the United States.

There are significant penalties for employers who hire foreign nationals illegally. Foreign nationals can be deported and barred from returning to the United States for violating their visa status. If an employer in the United States offers you an internship, make certain that both you *and* the employer know and follow the requirements of U.S. law *before* you leave home.

Passports

In order to get a U.S. visa that permits employment in an internship, you must have a valid passport from your own country. Your passport must be valid for six months beyond the date on which you expect to leave the United States. A number of countries have special "passport validity" agreements with the United States under which a passport is considered to be valid for six months beyond the expiration date stated in the passport. In order to avoid last-minute problems, you should contact U.S. consular officials as early as possible to determine the exact requirement for your country.

Visas

Unlike many countries, the United States does not issue work permits or residence permits or require police registration. Instead, what an individual may or may not do while in the United States depends entirely on the specific type of visa granted. As a result, the United States has the world's most complex visa system—there are currently forty-six different kinds of nonimmigrant visas! Please note that although an individual may be a full-time student in his or her own country, a "student" visa for admission to the United States applies only to people attending an American school for full-time study. Therefore, the three kinds of student visas (F-1, J-1, and M) cannot be used by a student coming to the United States uniquely for an internship experience.

As a general rule, there are only two U.S. visas that are likely to be suitable for students coming to the United States for employment in an internship:

J-1 "Exchange Visitor": J-1 visa programs are managed by approved organizations or sponsors, such as U.S. government agencies, schools and universities, hospitals, companies, and private nonprofit educational exchange organizations. The Bureau of Educational and Cultural Affairs of the U.S. Department of State, formerly the U.S. Information Agency, has authority over these programs. There are fourteen different J-1 categories, each with its own specific rules and regulations. Among these categories are those that permit international high school students, university students, trainees, au pairs, and researchers to participate in programs in the U.S. Each sponsor is granted a "program description" that specifies the activities that are permitted for participants in the sponsor's program.

Of the fourteen J-1 categories, the "trainee" category is suitable for most international students coming to the U.S. for paid internships. J-1 trainees can come to the U.S. to receive training in their field for periods of up to eighteen months. A detailed training program must be prepared by the U.S. host employer, specifying the objectives and skills to be learned as well as the length of time required to complete the program. A trainee cannot replace a U.S. worker but comes to the U.S. to acquire skills and knowledge in U.S. methodology.

The number of trainee programs has grown over the years. Two of the long-standing trainee exchange organizations for students are the International Association of Students in Economics and Business Management (AIESEC)—for business and economics students—and the International Association for the Exchange of Students for Technical Experience (IAESTE)—for students in technical fields. The Council on International Educational Exchange (CIEE) is the largest of the student trainee programs, followed by the Association for International Practical Training (AIPT), which brings in students and professionals from some eighty countries annually. Other programs are also available that deal primarily with trainees from specific countries or regions of the world or specific industries. Some U.S. universities also run trainee programs.

There are three additional J-1 categories that may also be of interest to students who desire a work experience in the U.S.: Summer Travel/Work, Camp Counselor, and Au Pair.

Several organizations have been granted J-1 authorizations for "summer travel/work" programs. These permit university students to work in any job they may find during the summer months (November to February for students from the Southern Hemisphere). No extensions of visas are permitted, and changes to other J-1 visa categories are not allowed. Pre-placement is required for 50 percent of the participants, and students should check with the U.S. sponsoring organization about specific requirements. The Council on International Educational Exchange is the largest of these programs, but several other programs also operate summer travel/work programs.

The second type of J-1 visa is for placements in summer camps for camp counselor experience. Participants must be at least 18 years old. Placements are limited to a maximum of four months and must be for genuine camp counseling assignments in accredited U.S. camps. The YMCA, Camp America, Summer Camp USA, and InterExchange operate several of the better-known camp counselor programs.

The third is the au pair category. Au pair programs allow participants to live with and participate in the home life of an American host family while providing child-care services and attending a U.S. postsecondary educational institution. The au pair participant cannot provide child-care services for more than 45 hours per week. All participants must register and attend classes offered by an accredited U.S. postsecondary institution. Au pairs must be between the ages of 18 and 26, be secondary school graduates or the equivalent, and be proficient in spoken English.

In some cases, an individual coming to the United States on the J-1 visa may be subject to something called the "two-year foreign residence requirement." Some countries have asked the U.S. government to establish a "skills list" for its citizens. If the person's field is included on the skills list for his or her country, that means that this particular skill is greatly needed in the home country, and it will generally be necessary for the individual to return to his or her country after completing their program in the U.S. Someone subject to this residence requirement must return to his or her home country for a minimum of two years before coming back to the United States on most of the nonimmigrant visas or as a "permanent resident." Most European countries do not have skills lists, but many other countries do. If the ability to return to the United States within a two-year period after training is of concern,

you should get specific information regarding this from U.S. consular officials. Also, participants who receive funding from the sending foreign government or the U.S. government may also be subject to the two-year residency requirement.

J-1 Program Sponsors

Trainee Exchange Programs

Aiesec/US
135 West 50th Street, 17th Floor
New York, NY 10020
212-757-3774
Fax: 212-757-4062
E-mail: jimk@aiesecus.org
www.us.aiesec.org

American-Scandinavian Foundation
58 Park Avenue
New York, NY 10016
212-879-9779
Fax: 212-879-9779
E-mail: info@amscan.org
www.amscan.org

Association for International Practical Training (AIPT)
10400 Little Patuxent Parkway, Suite 259
Columbia, MD 21044-3519
410-997-2200
410-997-2883
Fax: 410-992-3924
E-mail: aipt@aipt.org
www.aipt.org

CDS International
871 United Nations Plaza
New York, NY 10017-1814
212-497-3500
Fax: 212-497-3535
E-mail: info@cdsintl.org
www.cdsintl.org

Council on International Educational Exchange (CIEE)
633 Third Avenue
New York, NY 10017
800-Council
Fax: 212-822-2649
E-mail: info@councilexchanges.org
www.ciee.org

InterExchange, Inc.
161 Sixth Avenue
New York, NY 10013
212-924-0446
Fax: 212-924-0575
E-mail: info@interexchange.org
www.interexchange.org

YMCA International Program Services
71 West 23rd Street, Suite 1904
New York, NY 10010
212-727-8800
888-477-9622 (toll-free)
Fax: 212-727-8814

E-mail: ips@ymcanyc.org
www.ymcanyc.org

Agricultural and Agribusiness Trainee Programs

MAST International
395 VoTech Building
1954 Buford Avenue
St. Paul, MN 55108-6197
612-624-3740
Fax: 612-625-7031
E-mail: mast@tc.umn.edu
Web: mast.coafes.umn.edu

Summer Travel / Work Programs

Council on International Educational Exchange, CIEE
(see address in previous list)

InterExchange, Inc.
(see address in previous list)

YMCA International Program Services
(see address in previous list)

Au Pair Programs

Au Pair in America
River Plaza
9 West Broad Street
Stamford, CT 06902-3788
800-727-2437
203-869-9090
Fax: 203-863-6180
www.aifs.org

EF Au Pair
EF Center Boston
One Memorial Drive
Cambridge, MA 02142
617-619-1100
E-mail: aupair.ww@ef.com
www.ef.com/US/ap

InterExchange Au Pair
(see address for InterExchange, Inc. in previous list)

Camp Counselor Programs

Camp America
9 West Broad Street
Stamford, CT 06902-3788
800-727-2437
Fax: 203-399-5590
www.aifs.com/camp

InterExchange—Camp USA Program
(see address in previous list)

International Camp Counselor Program—YMCA
(see address in previous list)

Summer Camp USA (formerly BUNAC)
P.O. Box 430
Southbury, CT 06488
800-GO BUNAC
203-264-0901

Q "International Cultural Exchange Visitor": The "Q" visa allows the U.S. employer to apply to INS for permission to hire a person over 18 years of age from another country for a period of not more than fifteen months. The purpose of the program is for the international participant to work or train and to share or demonstrate his or her own culture with Americans. A frequently cited example of a major Q employer is the EPCOT Center at Walt Disney World in Florida. Another example would be a museum or a department of a museum devoted to the art and culture of the student's home country.

The "cultural component" must be an integral part of the employment or training offered. The employer must demonstrate that the individual to be hired is fully able to communicate with Americans about his or her culture as well as being fully qualified for the work aspects of the position. Substantial documentation is required as part of the employer's application.

Visa Procedures

If an employer's applications for a Q visa are successful, the District Office of the Immigration and Naturalization Service will advise the U.S. Embassy in the student's country. The student can then obtain the visa and travel to the U.S. In the case of the J-1 visa, the sponsoring organization that is arranging the program issues a U.S. government document called an IAP-66 (a Certificate of Eligibility). The IAP-66, which is sent to the student, is used to apply for the J-1 visa in his or her own country.

When Q visa holders enter the United States, the admitting Immigration Inspector issues a Form I-94 (Arrival/Departure Record) that notes the specific visa granted and the date when the "Permit to Stay" expires. When J-1 visa holders enter, they are issued a Permit to Stay with the notation "D/S" (for duration of status). This means that J-1 trainees may remain in the U.S. as long as they are engaged in their training program or until the end date of their IAP-66, plus thirty days. The I-94 form (and IAP-66 for the J-1 trainee) is the only documentation needed for the student to proceed to the workplace and take up the assignment.

Employment Eligibility Verification

U.S. law requires employers to examine documentation proving that persons hired are either citizens of the United States or noncitizens legally authorized for employment during their stay in the United States.

Essentially, the law requires that within three business days after a person is hired, the employer must *physically examine* documentation that (a) establishes proof of the new employee's identity and (b) establishes that the person is either a U.S. citizen or is a noncitizen who has the legal right to be employed in the United States. The law requires that a record of the verification process be maintained in the employer's files for a period of three years after the date of hiring. For this purpose, the INS has developed the I-9 form.

Virtually all kinds of employment are covered, from a full-time job with a large employer such as IBM to selling hamburgers part-time at the local McDonald's. Certainly, all of the jobs listed in *Internships 2003* will require you and your employer to complete the I-9 form. The I-9 form is in two parts. The top half must be filled out by the employee—you. You then present the form, together with your documentation, to your employer, who will complete the bottom half of the form.

Social Security Number

In most cases, you will need to obtain a Social Security number. It is widely used in the United States as a basic identification number—and in most automated payroll systems, in university enrollment systems, and for transactions such as opening a bank account.

Individuals entering the U.S. on the F, J, M, and Q visas are usually exempt from the U.S. Social Security tax. But even if you are exempt from paying Social Security tax, you will still need to obtain a Social Security number. Social Security regulations require that you apply in person, and it is advised that you do this shortly after arrival. Normally, numbers are issued within a few weeks.

It will be important for you to provide full documentation that clearly shows you have a visa that permits employment. The Social Security official to whom you submit your application will want to see your passport, your I-94 form, visa documents (such as the triplicate copy of the IAP-66), and any documents related to your work placement. If you do not present the proper documentation, a Social Security card marked "Not Valid for Employment" will be issued. If this happens, you will not be able to receive a salary or stipend during your internship. If you have any problems getting your Social Security card, you should contact your sponsoring organization for assistance.

Income Tax

As a general rule, individuals coming to the United States on any of the visas discussed in this article will be subject to U.S. income tax (and possibly state and local income tax) on the money they earn while in the country, and they must file an income tax return. Between January 1 and April 15 of the year following your employment, you will have to submit an income tax return (Form 1040EZ or Form 1040) to the IRS. The 1040EZ is used if you have no dependents, earned less than $50,000 of income, and have no travel expense deductions. If you have remained in the country from one year to the next, you also must submit a Form 8843 to verify your nonresident status. Tax regulations and procedures are not simple, and you should seek help from your employer and/or your sponsoring organization if you are partici-

pating in a J-1 program. You may also wish to secure a copy of IRS Publication 519, *U.S. Tax Guide for Aliens*, which is available free of charge from the Internal Revenue Service. Forms are available online at www.irs.ustreas.gov/prod/forms_pubs/.

Full-Time Students at U.S. Schools

Individuals enrolled at U.S. colleges and universities for full-time academic study are usually admitted on the basis of the F-1 (student), M-1 (student), or student category of the J-1 visa. In each case, internship employment may be possible before graduation, after graduation, or both. When such employment may take place, the length of time allowed, and what the employment is called (practical training, curricular practical training, academic training) depend on the specific visa and circumstances of the individual student. A number of schools in the United States offer academic courses—usually known as cooperative education programs—that combine periods of study with periods of practical training employment. Under certain conditions, students from other countries who are enrolled as regular, full-time students in a cooperative education program are allowed to undertake the practical training assignments (usually paid) in the same manner as American students. For information on enrollment in cooperative education programs and the American colleges and universities that offer these opportunities, contact:

Cooperative Education & Internship Association
4190 S. Highland Dr., Suite 211
Salt Lake City, UT 84124
Telephone: 801-984-2026
Fax: 801-984-2027
E-mail: sher@ceiainc.org
www.ceia.org

Whether or not the student is enrolled in a cooperative education program, whether it is before or after graduation, and regardless of the type of visa (M-1, F-1, or J-1), the student remains under the legal sponsorship of his or her college, university, or (in the case of some J-1 students) Exchange Visitor Program sponsor. Therefore, students should seek assistance from the international student adviser at their school.

Visa Violations or Overstays

In recent years, U.S. immigration laws have become more restrictive. All international visitors, trainees, and temporary work visa holders should make sure that they fully understand their responsibilities under the particular visa they use to enter the U.S. It is extremely important that you know exactly what you are permitted to do on the type of visa you have been granted and how long you are permitted to remain in the United States. If you have any questions about this, please check with your program sponsor, employer, or the INS.

If your program ends early, you are not permitted to remain in the United States. You must either return home upon completion of your internship or work program or take the steps necessary to legally remain in the United States. There are severe penalties for foreign nationals who overstay their visas or who violate their status. You could be barred from returning to the U.S. for ten years or longer if you violate your visa status, even unintentionally.

In Conclusion

Most countries of the world have very strict regulations regarding employment for noncitizens in order to protect job opportunities for their own citizens. The United States is no different. What is different, however, is the U.S. system of visas and the rules and regulations that apply to each type (and subtype) of visa. The process of acquiring the proper visa takes a good deal of time (sometimes as long as four to six months) and can often be frustrating and confusing. Therefore, it is important to plan ahead and contact prospective employers as early as possible so that the employer has sufficient time to undertake the paperwork involved. If you have applied to or have been accepted by a "trainee" program, make sure that the employer knows the name of the organization, because each sponsoring organization has its own internal procedures that must be followed. Prepare well in advance, ask lots of questions, and make sure you understand what needs to be done. If you do your research and begin early, you will soon be on your way to a fulfilling internship experience in the United States.

What Sponsors Seek in an Intern

by Jay Heflin and Richard Thau

Jay Heflin and Richard Thau are freelance business writers from New York City.

What Sponsors Seek in an Intern

Graduating students usually discover that choosing a job is bewildering and aggravating. And to make matters worse, some students find themselves with jobs that they know very little about. But there is something that can teach a student the fundamentals of career life: an internship.

"College graduates who have served internships receive, on average, higher starting salaries and more job offers than those with no internship experience," says Maury Hanigan, president of New York–based Hanigan Consulting Group, a firm that studies the internship programs of Fortune 500 companies.

Indeed, internships can be the most impressive item

David Reynolds, Human Resource Specialist, Wolf Creek Nuclear Operating Corporation, Burlington, Kansas

"We look for candidates who have a unique interest in power generation," states David Reynolds, Human Resources Specialist with Wolf Creek Nuclear Operating Corporation, a commercial nuclear electric power generating station. His company employs, at about $10.50 an hour, junior and senior college students for one semester.

But interest is not the only requirement to secure an internship at Wolf Creek, as Mr. Reynolds explains. "Grades and the student's major are also important. We look for engineering students who have a GPA above a 2.5 or 2.7, something above average."

on a student's resume. It shows real experience and the ability to accomplish more than digesting college classroom theories. In some instances, participating in an internship will put a particular person ahead of the competition and can be the deciding factor in securing paid employment later.

Corporations know the advantages of hiring interns. In today's competitive economy, companies can no longer afford to spend valuable recruiting time on unknown entities. Internships allow a company to "test" a prospective employee nearly risk-free. A lot more can be learned about a person's work habits and attitudes within a semester internship than in a number of half-hour

Amy Leahy, Intern Coordinator, Omicon Cable, Hamtramck, Michigan

"Enthusiastic" is the way Amy Leahy describes the interns she hires. "Experience is something we give them [the interns] in return," she adds. Ms. Leahy works with Omicon Cable, a public-access cable company. Her company employs local programming interns of college or even high school level.

"We want to show the person interested in pursuing this career that it is not a 9 to 5 job and also that it could be for anyone," says Leahy. Interns who work at Omicon Cable are not paid for the first semester; if they decide to stay on, they receive a small monthly stipend.

interviews. It is common to find companies hiring 80 to 90 percent of their interns for full-time positions after graduation.

Companies also favor interns because they help to improve the bottom line. While most interns are paid a nominal stipend, their take-home pay is usually nowhere near what it would cost a company to employ someone full-time. "Some companies find investing in summer internships more cost effective than straight recruiting," stated Roger Muller, Placement Director at Northwestern University.

What do sponsors seek in an intern? The answer to this question is simple: It varies. Seemingly there are just as many different, specific qualifications needed

Catherine Councill, President, Maryland Film Office, Baltimore, Maryland

Catherine Councill at the Maryland Film Office believes in giving high school graduates a chance to learn a career. Her company markets the state of Maryland to film companies, enticing them to do their shooting there. "We like to bring the people on board who show the greatest amount of enthusiasm during the interview," she says.

But being a high school graduate isn't the only qualification required to interview with Ms. Councill's company. "Normally we like to have interns who are studying marketing or communication. That way they know the lingo that accompanies the marketing field."

Marya Warshaw, Director, Gowanus Arts Exchange, Brooklyn, New York

For Marya Warshaw at the Gowanus Arts Exchange, experience is needed to fill one of her internship slots. "For our arts administration intern," she explains, "we look for someone who has worked before. Especially on the technical side, it's hard to teach someone all that needs to be done and still get a show off the ground."

Gowanus' internships are as short as eight weeks or as long as a full year. The longer "experience required" positions are paid. "We try to be very accommodating [on both the time availability and salary] because having interns on our crew is very valuable, for us as well as for them."

to land an internship as there are companies within the broad scope of corporate America. No single criterion, such as grades, job experience, or major, can encapsulate what companies seek in their prospective interns. Each corporation has specific needs, and those needs must be filled by interns with specific skills.

Interest, Not Just Grades

"Good grades and related job experience are important. But we also look at what school activities they [prospective interns] participate in," said Kim Hendershot, personnel specialist at Burns and McDonnell in Kansas City, Missouri, an engineering consulting firm that hires about 30 paid interns each year.

Hendershot said the company considers school activities so important because they give insight about a student: "Belonging to the Greek system or being a member of an organization that is related to their discipline can often tell us more about a student than can be reflected in their grades or job experience."

Another company that considers school activities and personal interests in addition to grades and related job experience is *The Nation* magazine. "Grades and majors aren't as big a deal as interest in progressive causes and knowledge of such current events," said Sandy Wood, a staffer at *The Nation* in charge of recruiting interns.

The Nation employs 7 interns in New York and 1 in Washington, D.C. While at the magazine, interns must complete four "assignments" that require that they assist the publication's editors and columnists. "Their tasks on the assignments vary widely," said Mr. Wood. "There are some secretarial duties and research to be done. But the biggest part they play is fact checking and assisting the publicity director with news releases."

Desire, Experience, and Grades

Still, there are companies that consider a candidate's grade point average as important as interpersonal skills and interests.

Jennifer Craig, the marketing director at Union Station, a mall in Indianapolis, said, "Careful attention to detail and a grade point average of at least 3.0" are required to intern with her company. Responsibilities for an intern include implementing special events, creating press releases, and assisting with programs that will enhance gross sales.

Craig went on to say that "qualified individuals for an internship program at Union Station should display a high drive, a willingness to be flexible, and related experience." Union Station employs 2 interns each year. Each intern is paid a weekly stipend of about $100.

Just as Craig said a related background in the field of marketing is important to becoming an intern in her company, so did Jeanine Triolo, marketing manager with *Vibe* magazine in New York City. "If they're majoring in marketing, I'd be more inclined to hire them," she said. "They are taught the fundamentals of marketing in school and are ready to apply what they've learned. I don't have to teach them anything; we can get right to work on projects that need to be accomplished for the magazine."

Triolo also sees availability of the intern's time as a crucial factor when considering who to hire. "I need someone for at least three or four days a week. We have

THE MEXICAN MUSEUM

Yalonda Perez, Intern Coordinator, Mexican Museum, San Francisco, California

At the Mexican Museum in San Francisco, California, possessing previous experience with the correct educational background can help secure an internship position. "Our interns are usually undergraduates majoring in art history or Latino history or graduate students with work experience," says Ms. Perez, an employee with the Museum.

Her museum accepts students into a wide range of internship programs. They range from curatorial to outreach programs. These positions are not paid, but the work completed does count toward college credit for the intern.

Council for Court Excellence

Priscilla Skillman, Program Analyst, Council for Court Excellence, Washington, D.C.

To be an intern at the Council for Court Excellence, the student has to be a triple threat: interested, experienced, and knowledgeable. "We require that our interns have an interest in public policy, a strong academic background, and be able to provide writing samples of past work," reports Priscilla Skillman, Program Analyst for the firm. Her group is a nonprofit, nonpartisan civic organization working to improve the administration of justice in local and federal courts.

Interns are not paid, but the experienced gained is immeasurable. "Our interns are usually with us for one semester," says Ms. Skillman, "but we would be delighted to have them stay longer." Skillman's firm accepts 1 to 3 interns per semester to assist in the development of selected projects.

---

projects lasting between fourteen and twenty days, and for [the interns] to get the best education possible about life in the marketing world, they have to see the project through all the way, from beginning to deadline."

The Universal Trait

Amid numerous company needs and intern qualifications, there was one universal trait that all internship sponsors hoped to see in internship candidates: a winning attitude. Possessing the desire to succeed is key to unlocking any door of opportunity.

How to Use This Book

Internships 2003 is a comprehensive directory of internship opportunities across the United States and abroad. The guide provides detailed, pertinent, annually updated information on tens of thousands of short-term positions available in numerous career areas.

Listings are categorized according to the type of company or organization that sponsors the internship. Most sponsors offer positions in career areas that extend beyond their specific field, so you should use the **Field of Interest Index** to find the types of programs that interest you. For example, this index will allow you to find a public relations position at an accounting firm or an accounting position at a public relations firm.

To help you make the most effective use of *Internships 2003*, entries contain the following groups of information:

What You'll Find in the Profiles

1. General Information
In this section you will find a brief description of the organization and its purpose and data on its size and the number of internship applications received each year.

2. Internships Available
Provides information about the type and number of positions available, basic job descriptions, duration of the internships, salaries, training, eligibility requirements, and whether international applicants are accepted.

3. Benefits
Provides information about the benefits available to interns, including training, housing, meal plans, health plans, whether an intern may arrange for college credit* through his or her own college or university, permanent employment opportunities, and placement services.

4. International Internships
Provides location of organization's internship placement opportunities outside the United States.

5. Contact
Includes the name, address, telephone number, and, when available, fax number, e-mail and World Wide Web addresses of the contact for the organization's internship program. Make special note of any application directions listed here to increase your chances for a positive response from the internship sponsor.

*College credit arrangements must be made prior to the student's participation in the internship.

GENERAL COMPANY
123 Main Street
Urban Center, NJ 08543

❶ **General Information** Entrepreneurial database publishing and communications company specializing in education and career reference books. Established 1966. Number of employees: 200. Division of Unified Corporation, Atlanta, Georgia. Number of internship applications received each year: 50.

❷ **Internships Available** ▶ *2 public relations interns:* responsibilities include drafting and disseminating press releases, establishing media contacts. Duration is 8 weeks. Paid. Candidates should have word processing skills, either Apple or IBM. Open to college sophomores, college juniors, college seniors. ▶ *35 data editors:* responsibilities include reviewing survey data for internal consistency, resolving discrepant data with respondents over the phone, data entry. Duration is 6 months. $6 per hour. Open to college sophomores. International applications accepted.

❸ **Benefits** Formal training, opportunity to attend seminars/workshops, and free parking. Sponsor is willing to complete any necessary paperwork required for an intern to receive educational credit. Possibility of full-time employment. Placement assistance provided, including letters of recommendation, names of contacts. Housing provided at $95 per week. Meals provided at no cost.

❹ **International Internships** Available in Paris, France; Madrid, Spain.

❺ **Contact** Call or write to Internship Coordinator, P.O. Box 2123, Urban Center, New Jersey 08543. In-person interview required. Phone: 609-555-1212. Fax: 609-555-0923. E-mail: coord@gc.com. World Wide Web: http://www.gc.com. Application deadline: May 15.

A Note on International Internships

"Exciting Jobs Overseas," "Hundreds of Positions Worldwide: All Fields"—the ads sound great. Do your thing in another country. See the world. Maybe—but before you've gone too far, a closer look might be in order. What is an "international" career and what do *you* want from it? Are you interested in business, government, the United Nations, nonprofit voluntary groups? Do you want to teach, undertake research, be a part of management, or assist in the needs of developing countries? And, perhaps most important of all, do you want to advance your career in the

United States, or do you want to pursue an international career in the fullest sense of the word by spending most of your working life in other countries? If you are honest with yourself in answering questions such as these, you will be a long way toward realizing your goal.

Far too many people seem to think that a strong interest in international work or some past foreign travel experience is sufficient to launch an international career. Unfortunately, this thinking can lead to a rude awakening.

First of all, you should think about the potential international applications of your chosen profession. Then, in addition to the training and preparation necessary to do your job, you should think about the additional preparation needed for an international career. What kind of language skills will you need? Do you have the ability to work with people of many different cultural backgrounds?

Use the listings in the **International Internships Index** and be a bit creative by making use of the **Employer Index.** While the opportunities listed in the **International Internships Index** are exclusively international in nature, many other employers listed in *Internships 2003* offer experiences with an international dimension. You can also find international opportunities in the **Field of Interest Index** under the International category.

The international dimension of every field of human endeavor expands as the world grows more interdependent, and challenging opportunities exist for the individual interested in an international career. Whether one's working life develops in a single country overseas, in a series of assignments in different countries, or in the United States with only occasional overseas travel, one or more international internship experiences will give you that all-important head start on an international career.

Some organizations accept interns of any age or academic level. Others limit their internships based on the academic level of the applicant. The **Academic Level Required Index** identifies organizations that have indicated the academic level(s) that are required for their internships. These may or may not be minimum requirements. An organization may indicate one or all of the options available, from high school student through college graduate.

If you are looking for an internship so that you have relevant experience to put on your resume, but whether you are going to be paid is still a concern, use the **Paid Internships Index** to find all of the organizations that are willing to pay for your talents and skills. Keep in mind that an unpaid internship will still give you valuable experience and will enhance your resume.

If you already have enough experience to know that you are on the right career path, check out the **Possibility of Permanent Employment Index** to find organizations that indicate they have an interest in keeping their best interns on the job on a full-time basis.

About the Data

The information in these listings was collected during the winter of 2001 and the spring of 2002 through questionnaire mailings and telephone interviews with representatives of each of the sponsoring organizations. For those few organizations that failed to respond to Peterson's survey in time to meet publication deadlines, information was drawn from Web sites. Although every entry has been completely updated, you should be aware that changes in the data may occur after the publication of the book; contact the sponsors directly for the most current information on their internship program.

Peterson's does not make any claim concerning the hiring policies or practices of sponsoring organizations in this book.

ACCOMMODATIONS AND FOODSERVICES

GENERAL

AMELIA ISLAND PLANTATION
PO Box 3000
Amelia Island, Florida 32035-3000

General Information 1,350 acre internationally recognized, gated resort/residential community located in northeast Florida offering miles of sandy beach and many amenities. Established in 1974. Number of employees: 1,100. Number of internship applications received each year: 500.

Internships Available ▶ *3–10 commercial recreation interns:* responsibilities include social recreation and corporate recreation interns split duties in program design, implementation and evaluation or children's programs and group events, guest relations, major projects, pool maintenance, and minor facilities upkeep. Candidates should have ability to work with others, college courses in field, knowledge of field, self-motivation, own transportation, fluency in conversational English (speaking, reading, writing, and comprehension), and customer service skills; first aid, CPR, and life saving certificates preferred. Duration is minimum of 16 weeks. $225 per week housing stipend. Open to college juniors, college seniors, graduate students. ▶ *3–6 culinary/pastry interns:* responsibilities include gaining hands-on experience in a wide variety of culinary situations through a rotation that includes banquets, pastry, and restaurants. Candidates should have ability to work independently, ability to work with others, college courses in field, knowledge of field, plan to pursue career in field, own transportation, knife skills, customer service skills, fluency in conversational English (speaking, reading, writing, and comprehension). Duration is flexible. $7.50 per hour plus $1.00 per hour worked upon successful completion of internship. Open to college juniors, college seniors, graduate students. ▶ *1–2 environmental interpretation interns:* responsibilities include assisting nature science program manager in providing social and group guests, club members, property owners, employees and the community with nature programs; working closely with local animal sanctuaries in animal rescues on property; assisting with main nature displays and retail operations. Candidates should have college courses in field, knowledge of field, oral communication skills, personal interest in the field, self-motivation, own transportation, customer service skills, fluency in conversational English (speaking, reading, writing, and comprehension). Duration is minimum of 16 weeks. $225 per week housing stipend. Open to college juniors, college seniors, graduate students. ▶ *4–8 golf level I and turf management interns:* responsibilities include working as a golf level I intern (assisting guests, members, owners, and employees in golf experience) or as a turf management intern (mowing greens, collars, tees, fairways and roughs, raking sand bunkers, and changing cups). Candidates should have ability to work independently, knowledge of field, plan to pursue career in field, strong interpersonal skills, own transportation, customer service skills, valid driver's license, a good driving record, basic knowledge of golf, fluency in conversational English (speaking, reading, writing, and comprehension). Duration is 16–32 weeks. $5.15 per hour plus tips. Open to college juniors, college seniors, graduate students. ▶ *2–4 lodging and housekeeping interns:* responsibilities include working as either a lodging intern (rotating through transportation, front desk/reservations departments) or housekeeping intern (assisting with daily activities including inspecting rooms and public areas, ordering supplies, and other duties). Candidates should have college courses in field, experience in the field, self-motivation, strong interpersonal skills, must have own transportation, customer service skills, valid driver's license, good driving record, fluency in conversational English (speaking, reading, writing, and comprehension). Duration is minimum of 16 weeks. $225 per week housing stipend. Open to college juniors, college seniors, graduate students. ▶ *1 marketing intern:* responsibilities include working closely with the marketing, public relations, promotions and graphics departments in implementation of new promotions, programs, events, by creating and distributing flyers, and preparing articles and press releases. Candidates should have ability to work independently, declared college major in field, knowledge of field, oral communication skills, self-motivation, strong interpersonal skills, written communication skills, good time-management and problem-solving skills, valid driver's license, own transportation, knowledge of QuarkXpress, fluency in conversational English (speaking, reading, writing, and comprehension). Duration is minimum of 16 weeks. $225 per week housing stipend. Open to college juniors, college seniors. ▶ *1–2 tennis interns:* responsibilities include court maintenance, pro shop duties, tennis instruction, racquet stringing, organization, and implementation of tournaments. Candidates should have ability to work independently, college courses in field, knowledge of field, plan to pursue career in field, own transportation, customer service skills, 4.5 level of tennis playing ability, ability to string racquets, fluency in conversational English (speaking, reading, writing, and comprehension). Duration is 16–32 weeks. $5.15 per hour; additional pay for giving lessons. Open to college juniors, college seniors, graduate students.

Benefits Formal training, free meals, job counseling, on-the-job training, opportunity to attend seminars/workshops, possible full-time employment, willing to act as a professional reference, willing to complete paperwork for educational credit, willing to provide letters of recommendation, assistance in locating housing, use of amenities/property at a discounted rate.

Contact Write, call, fax, e-mail, or through World Wide Web site Barbara Ross, Internship Coordinator. Phone: 904-277-5904. Fax: 904-491-4345. E-mail: intern@aipfl.com. Telephone interview required. Applicants must submit a formal organization application, letter of interest, resume, 2 academic and 2 professional references, 3 writing samples for marketing positions. Applications are accepted continuously. World Wide Web: http://www.aipfl.com.

AMERICAN HOSPITALITY ACADEMY
PO Box 7832
Hilton Head, South Carolina 29938

General Information Company providing resorts with year-round recreational activities programs as well as food and beverage, front-desk staff, and theme park internships. Established in 1986. Number of employees: 800. Number of internship applications received each year: 2,000.

Internships Available ▶ *500–750 interns:* responsibilities include working in one of the following areas: resort activities, front office, food service, or theme park. Candidates should have ability to

American Hospitality Academy (continued)

work with others, knowledge of field, oral communication skills, personal interest in the field, self-motivation, ability to live and train with people from a diversity of cultures. Duration is 3–12 months. $300 per month. Open to college freshmen, college sophomores, college juniors, college seniors, recent college graduates, individuals 18-30 years old. International applications accepted.

Benefits Formal training, free housing, job counseling, on-the-job training, opportunity to attend seminars/workshops, possible full-time employment, willing to act as a professional reference, willing to complete paperwork for educational credit, willing to provide letters of recommendation, shuttled transportation to and from training site, local telephone, all utilities, cable television, weekly grocery trips, cultural nights, and quarterly socials, rewards and recognition programs.

Contact Write, call, fax, e-mail, or through World Wide Web site Human Resources. Phone: 800-864-6762. Fax: 843-785-4368. E-mail: aha@americanhospitalityacademy.com. Telephone interview required. Applicants must submit a formal organization application, letter of interest, resume, three personal references, letters of recommendation and college/university documentation of internship requirements may be requested. Application deadline: at least 4 months in advance of desired start date. World Wide Web: http://www.americanhospitalityacademy.com.

BONAVENTURE HOTEL & SUITES
404 South Figueroa Street
Los Angeles, California 90071

General Information Hotel. Established in 1961. Number of employees: 850. Unit of Interstate Hotel Corporation, Pittsburgh, Pennsylvania. Number of internship applications received each year: 75.

Internships Available ▶ *MIS interns.* Duration is minimum of 3 months. Unpaid. Open to college freshmen, college sophomores, college juniors, college seniors, recent college graduates, graduate students, individuals reentering the workforce. ▶ *Accounting interns:* responsibilities include assisting the department with general office work, compiling and researching information, and attending department meetings. Candidates should have ability to work with others, computer skills, knowledge of field, office skills, oral communication skills, organizational skills, personal interest in the field, self-motivation. Duration is minimum of 3 months. Unpaid. Open to college freshmen, college sophomores, college juniors, college seniors, recent college graduates, graduate students, individuals reentering the workforce. ▶ *Catering department interns:* responsibilities include assisting in the planning of events, completing general office work, compiling and researching information. Candidates should have ability to work with others, computer skills, office skills, oral communication skills, organizational skills, research skills, written communication skills, major in hotel management, business, or communications (preferred). Duration is minimum of 2 eight-hour shifts for 10- to 15-week school-year program; minimum of 3 eight-hour shifts for 12- to 15-week summer program. Unpaid. Open to college freshmen, college sophomores, college juniors, college seniors, recent college graduates, graduate students, individuals re-entering the workforce and career changers only if enrolled in a college program. ▶ *Convention services department interns:* responsibilities include communicating with customers, planning events, and compiling and researching information. Candidates should have ability to work with others, computer skills, office skills, oral communication skills, organizational skills, research skills, written communication skills, major in hotel management, business, or communications (preferred). Duration is minimum of 2 eight-hour shifts for 10- to 15-week school-year program; minimum of 3 eight-hour shifts for 12- to 15-week summer program. Unpaid. Open to college freshmen, college sophomores, college juniors, college seniors, recent college graduates, graduate students, individuals re-entering the workforce and career changers only if enrolled in a college program. ▶ *Culinary interns.* Duration is minimum of 3 months. Unpaid. Open to college freshmen, college sophomores, college juniors, college seniors, recent college graduates, graduate students, individuals reentering the workforce. ▶ *Food and bever-*

age interns: responsibilities include assisting outlet managers with organizing and implementing marketing concepts, developing new marketing and promotional strategies, and researching and tracking; sales promotion and follow-up to generate new business. Candidates should have office skills, oral communication skills, organizational skills, research skills, written communication skills, marketing skills and some knowledge of food and beverage required; major in hotel restaurant management, business, or communications preferred. Duration is minimum of 2 eight-hour shifts for 10- to 15-week school-year program; minimum of 3 eight-hour shifts for 12- to 15-week summer program. Unpaid. Open to college freshmen, college sophomores, college juniors, college seniors, recent college graduates, graduate students, individuals re-entering the workforce and career changers only if enrolled in a college program. ▶ *Front-office interns.* Duration is minimum of 3 months. Unpaid. Open to college freshmen, college sophomores, college juniors, college seniors, recent college graduates, graduate students, individuals reentering the workforce. ▶ *Human resources interns:* responsibilities include helping plan and coordinate hotel-sponsored events, creating and implementing incentive programs for associates, screening applicants and checking references for recruitment, managing associate accounts, and coordinating associate benefits including discounts or worker's compensation. Candidates should have computer skills, office skills, oral communication skills, organizational skills, strong interpersonal skills, written communication skills, major in hotel management, business, or communications preferred. Duration is minimum of 2 eight-hour shifts for 10- to 15-week school-year program; minimum of 3 eight-hour shifts for 12- to 15-week summer program. Unpaid. Open to recent high school graduates, college freshmen, college sophomores, college juniors, college seniors, recent college graduates, graduate students, individuals re-entering the workforce and career changers only if enrolled in a college program. ▶ *Sales and marketing interns:* responsibilities include attending weekly sales meetings; researching competitive analyses; telemarketing to potential clients; accessing group sales files; reviewing group sales, tour, travel, and corporate files for potential business; creating sales flyers. Candidates should have computer skills, office skills, oral communication skills, organizational skills, research skills, strong interpersonal skills, written communication skills, good marketing skills; aptitude for sales; major in hotel management, business, communications, sociology, or psychology (preferred). Duration is minimum of 2 eight-hour shifts for 10- to 15-week school-year program; minimum of 3 eight-hour shifts for 12- to 15-week summer program. Unpaid. Open to college freshmen, college sophomores, college juniors, college seniors, recent college graduates, graduate students, individuals re-entering the workforce and career changers only if enrolled in a college program. International applications accepted.

Benefits Formal training, free meals, on-the-job training, opportunity to attend seminars/workshops, possible full-time employment, travel reimbursement, willing to act as a professional reference, willing to complete paperwork for educational credit.

International Internships Available.

Contact Write, call, fax, or e-mail Putri Sarnadi, Employment Coordinator, 404 South Figueroa Street, Los Angeles, California 90071. Phone: 213-612-4844. Fax: 213-612-4849. E-mail: putri.sarnadi@westin.com. Telephone interview required. Applicants must submit a letter of interest, resume, three personal references. Applications are accepted continuously.

THE CLUB AT SEABROOK ISLAND
1002 Landfall Way
Johns Island, South Carolina 29455

General Information Private residential resort community. Established in 1971. Number of employees: 300. Number of internship applications received each year: 30.

Internships Available ▶ *7 recreation interns:* responsibilities include working in all areas of the Recreation Department, including Kids Club, rental office and fitness center, lifeguarding, teen and family programs, and poolside activities. Candidates should have knowledge of field, organizational skills, personal interest in the

field, self-motivation, strong interpersonal skills, strong leadership ability. Duration is May to September. $400 per month. Open to college seniors.
Benefits Formal training, free housing, free meals, job counseling, names of contacts, on-the-job training, opportunity to attend seminars/workshops, possible full-time employment, willing to act as a professional reference, willing to complete paperwork for educational credit, willing to provide letters of recommendation.
Contact Write, fax, e-mail, or through World Wide Web site Scott D. Raisley, Director of Recreation, 1002 Landfall Way, Johns Island, South Carolina 29455. Phone: 800-845-2475. Fax: 843-768-7524. E-mail: sirec@bellsouth.net. In-person interview recommended (telephone interview accepted). Applicants must submit a letter of interest, resume, three personal references. Applications are accepted continuously. World Wide Web: http://www.seabrookresort.com.

CROWNE PLAZA RESORT
130 Shipyard Drive
Hilton Head Island, South Carolina 29928

General Information Resort hotel. Established in 1993. Number of employees: 300. Division of Six Continents Hotels & Resorts, Atlanta, Georgia. Number of internship applications received each year: 150.
Internships Available ▶ *100 rooms division/F&B/leisure activities/culinary interns:* responsibilities include hands-on operation training in resort hotel. Candidates should have ability to work independently, computer skills, declared college major in field, knowledge of field, oral communication skills, plan to pursue career in field, self-motivation, strong interpersonal skills, strong leadership ability, written communication skills. Duration is flexible. $7.25–$7.50 per hour. Open to college sophomores, college juniors, college seniors, recent college graduates. International applications accepted.
Benefits Formal training, housing at a cost, job counseling, meals at a cost, on-the-job training, opportunity to attend seminars/workshops, possible full-time employment.
Contact Write, call, fax, or e-mail Melissa Love Snyder, Assistant Director of Human Resources, 130 Shipyard Drive, Hilton Head, South Carolina 29928. Phone: 843-842-2400 Ext. 7634. Fax: 843-785-4879. E-mail: melissa.snyder@6c.com. In-person interview recommended (telephone interview accepted). Applicants must submit a formal organization application, resume, three personal references. Applications are accepted continuously.

KIAWAH ISLAND RESORT
12 Kiawah Beach Drive
Kiawah, South Carolina 29455

General Information 10,000-acre resort that caters to business groups and family vacationers. Number of employees: 350. Number of internship applications received each year: 50.
Internships Available ▶ *14–20 recreation interns:* responsibilities include working in 5 different areas of recreation department, completing a special project, meeting with department heads/supervisors, and going on a field trip. Candidates should have ability to work with others, oral communication skills, organizational skills, self-motivation, strong leadership ability, major in recreation preferred. Duration is 12–15 weeks. $175 per week. Open to college juniors, college seniors, recent college graduates, graduate students. International applications accepted.
Benefits Formal training, free housing, free meals, job counseling, names of contacts, on-the-job training, possible full-time employment, willing to act as a professional reference, willing to complete paperwork for educational credit, willing to provide letters of recommendation.
Contact Write, call, fax, e-mail, or through World Wide Web site Debbie Cheesman, Recruiting Manager. Phone: 843-768-2880. Fax: 843-768-6022. E-mail: debbie_cheesman@kiawahresort.com. Telephone interview required. Applicants must submit a letter of interest, resume, personal reference, 3 professional or academic references. Application deadline: April 20 for summer, July 20 for fall interns, December 20 for spring. World Wide Web: http://www.kiawahresort.com.

RADISSON SUITE BEACH RESORT
600 South Collier Boulevard
Marco Island, Florida 34145

General Information Hotel resort. Number of employees: 185. Affiliate of Meristar Hotels & Resorts, Washington, District of Columbia. Number of internship applications received each year: 350.
Internships Available ▶ *Food and beverage division interns:* responsibilities include learning all food and beverage positions including those of bartender, host, cashier and banquet server. Candidates should have ability to work with others, computer skills, oral communication skills, organizational skills, written communication skills. Duration is 12–18 months. $7 per hour. Open to recent high school graduates, college sophomores, college juniors, college seniors, recent college graduates, individuals reentering the workforce. ▶ *Rooms division interns:* responsibilities include front desk duties, including checking guests in and out; learning computer system; housekeeping duties, including supervising room attendants, working the desk in housekeeping, inspecting rooms. Candidates should have ability to work with others, computer skills, oral communication skills, organizational skills, self-motivation, written communication skills. Duration is 12–18 months. $7 per hour. Open to college freshmen, college sophomores, college juniors, college seniors, individuals reentering the workforce. International applications accepted.
Benefits Formal training, free meals, housing at a cost, on-the-job training, opportunity to attend seminars/workshops, willing to provide letters of recommendation.
Contact Write, fax, or e-mail June Drew, Human Resources Manager. Fax: 941-394-4312. E-mail: june.drew@meristar.com. No phone calls. Telephone interview required. Applicants must submit a letter of interest, resume. Applications are accepted continuously.

SNOW MOUNTAIN RANCH
PO Box 169
Winter Park, Colorado 80482

General Information YMCA conference center and family resort. Established in 1907. Number of employees: 250. Branch of YMCA of the Rockies, Estes Park, Colorado. Number of internship applications received each year: 15.
Internships Available ▶ *2–10 adventure education instructors:* responsibilities include facilitating adventure/outdoor based programs, including low/high elements challenge course, environmental education, climbing wall, day hike interpretations, snowshoeing, and cross-country skiing. Candidates should have ability to work with others, knowledge of field, oral communication skills, organizational skills, plan to pursue career in field, self-motivation, strong leadership ability, current first aid and adult/child CPR certification required. Duration is 1–3 semesters. Position available as unpaid or at $155 per week. Open to college sophomores, college juniors, college seniors, recent college graduates, graduate students, individuals reentering the workforce. ▶ *1 chaplain's assistant:* responsibilities include supporting the office of the chaplain in providing leadership in the development of the religious and spiritual life and activities at Snow Mountain Ranch for guests and staff. Candidates should have ability to work independently, ability to work with others, computer skills, declared college major in field, knowledge of field, office skills, oral communication skills, organizational skills, personal interest in the field, self-motivation, strong leadership ability, writing skills, driver's license; previous experience leading and participating in church activities; musical background preferred. Duration is 1–2 semesters. Position available as unpaid or at $155 per week. Open to college seniors, recent college graduates, graduate students. ▶ *1–2 conference associates:* responsibilities include managing and administrating conference resources to the effect of efficient communication and negotiation of services to meet group needs. Candidates should have ability to work with others, computer skills, office skills, oral communication skills, organizational skills, personal interest in the field, self-motivation, strong leadership ability, driver's license and acceptable driving record. Duration is 1–3 semesters. Position available as unpaid or at $155 per week. Open to college juniors, college seniors, recent college graduates, graduate students, career changers, individuals reenter-

Snow Mountain Ranch (continued)

ing the workforce. ▶ *1 craft shop supervisor:* responsibilities include providing supervision and guidance to staff and guests, and teaching crafts to the guests and staff who visit the craft shop; will include training of new employees. Candidates should have ability to work independently, ability to work with others, experience in the field, oral communication skills, organizational skills, personal interest in the field, self-motivation, strong leadership ability. Duration is May to August/September. Position available as unpaid or at $170 per week. Open to college juniors, college seniors, recent college graduates, graduate students, career changers, individuals reentering the workforce. ▶ *2 family programs assistants:* responsibilities include developing, marketing, and implementing family programs for the guests of Snow Mountain Ranch. Candidates should have ability to work independently, ability to work with others, college courses in field, experience in the field, oral communication skills, organizational skills, plan to pursue career in field, self-motivation, strong leadership ability, written communication skills, guitar skills helpful; first aid and CPR certification required. Duration is summer (May to August). Position available as unpaid or at $155 per week. Open to college juniors, college seniors, recent college graduates. ▶ *1–5 food and beverage interns:* responsibilities include working on various assignments. Candidates should have ability to work independently, experience in the field, organizational skills, personal interest in the field, self-motivation, strong interpersonal skills, strong leadership ability. Duration is 1–3 semesters. Position available as unpaid or at $155 per week. Open to college sophomores, college juniors, college seniors, recent college graduates. ▶ *11 front-desk attendants:* responsibilities include ensuring the satisfaction of all potential and actual guests over the telephone and in person; accounting for all income during assigned shift; checking guests in and out; and operating computer and switchboard. Candidates should have college courses in field, computer skills, office skills, oral communication skills, organizational skills, plan to pursue career in field, strong interpersonal skills, strong leadership ability, fundamental math skills. Duration is 1–2 semesters. Position available as unpaid or at $155 per week. Open to college sophomores, college juniors, college seniors, recent college graduates, graduate students, career changers, individuals reentering the workforce. ▶ *1–2 human resources associates:* responsibilities include assisting with the daily operations of the human resources office by completing secretarial, receptionist, and driving duties. Candidates should have ability to work independently, computer skills, knowledge of field, office skills, oral communication skills, organizational skills, plan to pursue career in field, self-motivation, strong interpersonal skills, strong leadership ability, written communication skills, driver's license and acceptable driving record. Duration is 1–2 semesters. Position available as unpaid or at $155 per week. Open to college juniors, college seniors, recent college graduates, graduate students. ▶ *1 recreation supervisor:* responsibilities include training, scheduling, and general supervision of recreation staff and facilities. Candidates should have ability to work independently, knowledge of field, oral communication skills, organizational skills, personal interest in the field, self-motivation, strong interpersonal skills, strong leadership ability, writing skills, current certifications in Lifeguard Training, First Aid, and CPR; minimum 3 years lifeguarding and pool supervisory experience (preferred). Duration is 1–3 semesters. Position available as unpaid or at $170–$180 per week. Open to college sophomores, college juniors, college seniors, recent college graduates, graduate students. ▶ *2 staff activities coordinators:* responsibilities include developing, implementing, and evaluating activities for co-workers on their time off. Candidates should have ability to work independently, ability to work with others, knowledge of field, oral communication skills, organizational skills, personal interest in the field, self-motivation, strong leadership ability, written communication skills, driver's license and acceptable driving record. Duration is 1–2 semesters. Position available as unpaid or at $155 per week. Open to college juniors, college seniors, recent college graduates, graduate students, law students.

Benefits Formal training, free housing, free meals, job counseling, on-the-job training, opportunity to attend seminars/workshops, possible full-time employment, willing to act as a professional reference, willing to complete paperwork for educational credit, will-

ing to provide letters of recommendation, free use of recreation facilities on-site and downhill ski benefits at nearby Winter Park Resort.

Contact Write, call, fax, e-mail, or through World Wide Web site Jeni Fuqua, Human Resources Director. Phone: 877-562-7962. Fax: 303-449-6781. E-mail: hroffice@snowmtnranch.org. Telephone interview required. Applicants must submit a formal organization application, letter of interest, resume, 3 reference forms (form provided by YMCA). Applications are accepted continuously. World Wide Web: http://www.ymcarockies.org.

SOUTH SEAS RESORT
PO Box 194
Captiva Island, Florida 33924

General Information Full-service destination resort property. Established in 1970. Number of employees: 750. Division of MeriStar Hotels and Resorts, Washington, District of Columbia. Number of internship applications received each year: 300.

Internships Available ▶ *5–15 culinary interns:* responsibilities include working with chefs in three restaurants. Candidates should have ability to work independently, ability to work with others, experience in the field, oral communication skills, organizational skills, self-motivation. Duration is 6 months. $8.25 per hour. Open to recent high school graduates, college freshmen, college sophomores, college juniors, college seniors, recent college graduates, graduate students, law students, career changers, individuals reentering the workforce. ▶ *1 fitness intern:* responsibilities include assisting guests in proper use of equipment; coordinating and implementing fitness programs; registering and assisting guests at check-in; general customer service and fitness center support. Candidates should have college courses in field, oral communication skills, plan to pursue career in field, strong interpersonal skills, written communication skills, CPR certification; additional fitness certification helpful. Duration is 7–15 weeks. $50 per week stipend. Open to college sophomores, college juniors, college seniors. ▶ *5–8 front desk/lodging interns.* Candidates should have ability to work independently, analytical skills, computer skills, editing skills, experience in the field, oral communication skills, organizational skills, research skills, self-motivation, strong interpersonal skills, writing skills. Duration is 9 months. $8 per hour plus commissions. Open to recent high school graduates, college freshmen, college sophomores, college juniors, college seniors, recent college graduates, graduate students, law students, career changers, individuals reentering the workforce. ▶ *15–20 housekeeping interns:* responsibilities include servicing and cleaning resort units. Candidates should have ability to work independently, ability to work with others, knowledge of field, oral communication skills, organizational skills, self-motivation. Duration is 9 months (minimum). $7 per hour. Open to recent high school graduates, college freshmen, college sophomores, college juniors, college seniors, recent college graduates, graduate students, law students, career changers, individuals reentering the workforce. ▶ *5–10 landscaping interns:* responsibilities include manicuring and taking care of greenhouse, nursery stock, trees, and shrubs; maintaining interiorscapes; cleaning streets and grounds. Candidates should have ability to work independently, experience in the field, oral communication skills, personal interest in the field, self-motivation, strong interpersonal skills. Duration is 9 months (minimum). $7–$9 per hour. Open to recent high school graduates, college freshmen, college sophomores, college juniors, college seniors, recent college graduates, graduate students, career changers, individuals reentering the workforce. ▶ *1–6 recreation interns:* responsibilities include assisting in the planning and implementation of daily activities and special events, general office support, and completion of a major project. Candidates should have ability to work with others, college courses in field, personal interest in the field, self-motivation, strong leadership ability. Duration is 4 months or 1 semester. $750 per semester. Open to college juniors, college seniors, recent college graduates, graduate students. ▶ *20–50 server interns:* responsibilities include carrying trays and waiting on guests. Candidates should have ability to work independently, oral communication skills, organizational skills, self-motivation, strong interpersonal skills, strong leadership ability. Duration is 6 months. $7.75 per hour. Open to recent high school graduates, college freshmen, college sophomores, college juniors, college seniors, recent college graduates, graduate students, law students, career changers, individuals reentering the workforce. International applications accepted.

Benefits Job counseling, names of contacts, on-the-job training, opportunity to attend seminars/workshops, possible full-time employment, willing to complete paperwork for educational credit, willing to provide letters of recommendation, attendance at AHMA management classes, guest service and alcohol certification training, housing provided at $75–$150 biweekly, meals provided at a small cost.

Contact Write, call, fax, or e-mail Bonnie Zeidler, Human Resources Director. Phone: 941-472-7588. Fax: 941-472-7648. E-mail: bonnie.zeidler@meristar.com. In-person interview recommended (telephone interview accepted). Applicants must submit a formal organization application, letter of interest, resume. Applications are accepted continuously. World Wide Web: http://www. southseasresort.com.

STARWOOD HOTELS & RESORTS
1111 Westchester Avenue, 4th Floor
White Plains, New York 10604

General Information Largest hotel company in the world with more than 725 hotels in 80 countries. Established in 1997. Number of employees: 450. Subsidiary of Starwood Hotels & Resorts Worldwide, Inc., White Plains, New York. Number of internship applications received each year: 25.

Internships Available ▶ *1 public relations intern:* responsibilities include writing news releases, fact sheets, and executive biographies; handling media requests for information; organizing special events and programs; minor administrative duties. Candidates should have ability to work independently, ability to work with others, computer skills, editing skills, office skills, oral communication skills, organizational skills, plan to pursue career in field, self-motivation, writing skills, college courses in communications or public affairs (preferred). Duration is 1 semester. Position available as unpaid or at $5.50–$6.50 per hour. Open to college freshmen, college sophomores, college juniors, college seniors, recent college graduates. International applications accepted.

Benefits Possible full-time employment, willing to complete paperwork for educational credit, willing to provide letters of recommendation.

Contact Write, fax, or e-mail Mark Ricci, Public Relations Manager. Fax: 914-640-8458. E-mail: mark.ricci@starwoodhotels.com. No phone calls. In-person interview recommended (telephone interview accepted). Applicants must submit a resume, three writing samples, three personal references, cover letter. Application deadline: June 15. World Wide Web: http://www.starwood.com.

WILD DUNES RESORT
5801 Palmetto Drive
Isle of Palms, South Carolina 29451

General Information Resort. Established in 1976. Number of employees: 450. Unit of Lowe Enterprises (Destination Hotels & Resorts), Boulder, Colorado. Number of internship applications received each year: 100.

Internships Available ▶ *2–16 recreation interns:* responsibilities include programming and implementing activities and programs. Candidates should have college courses in field, oral communication skills, personal interest in the field, strong interpersonal skills, strong leadership ability, written communication skills. Duration is 1 semester. $250 per month. Open to college juniors, college seniors. International applications accepted.

Benefits Free housing, names of contacts, on-the-job training, opportunity to attend seminars/workshops, possible full-time employment, willing to act as a professional reference, willing to complete paperwork for educational credit, willing to provide letters of recommendation, employee discounts, access to all amenities, nationally accredited internship site through Resort and Commercial Recreation Association (RCRA); 20% discount at any of resort's restaurants; free meals on days of camp work.

International Internships Available.

Contact Write, call, fax, or e-mail Kyle Markgraf, Recreation Manager. Phone: 800-845-8880 Ext. 2292. Fax: 843-886-2195. E-mail: recreation@wilddunes.com. Telephone interview required. Applicants must submit a formal organization application, resume, three personal references, cover letter. Applications are accepted continuously. World Wide Web: http://www.wilddunes.com.

ADMINISTRATIVE AND SUPPORT SERVICES

EMPLOYMENT SERVICES

AMERICAN ASSOCIATION OF OVERSEAS STUDIES
9933 65th Road
New York, New York 11374

General Information International placement service working with over 200 universities and 150 preparatory and high schools to place 100 students annually in business, law, theater, communications/media, sciences, journalism, politics, arts/ museums, psychology, women's studies, music, fashion, and food and wine areas. Established in 1984. Number of employees: 1. Affiliate of Anglo International Education Consultants, London, United Kingdom. Number of internship applications received each year: 50.

Internships Available ▶ *60–100 interns:* responsibilities include various duties according to the internship; positions available in New York or London. Candidates should have ability to work independently, computer skills, office skills, oral communication skills, organizational skills, personal interest in the field, self-motivation, strong interpersonal skills, writing skills, enthusiasm, willingness to help. Duration is 1–3 months. Unpaid. Open to high school seniors, recent high school graduates, college freshmen, college sophomores, college juniors, college seniors, recent college graduates, graduate students, law students. International applications accepted.

Benefits Housing at a cost, job counseling, names of contacts, opportunity to attend seminars/workshops, willing to act as a professional reference, willing to complete paperwork for educational credit, willing to provide letters of recommendation.

International Internships Available in London, United Kingdom.

Contact Write, call, fax, e-mail, or through World Wide Web site Ms. Janet Kollek Evans, Director, 51 Drayton Gardens, London SW10 9EX United Kingdom. E-mail: aaos2000@hotmail.com. Telephone interview required. Applicants must submit a formal organization application, personal reference, letter of recommendation. Applications are accepted continuously. Fees: $200. World Wide Web: http://www.worldwide.edu/uk/aaos/.

ASSOCIATION FOR INTERNATIONAL PRACTICAL TRAINING (AIPT), CAREER DEVELOPMENT PROGRAMS/IAESTE UNITED STATES
10400 Little Patuxent Parkway, Suite 250
Columbia, Maryland 21044-3519

General Information International practical training exchange organization that arranges on-the-job training exchanges for students and young professionals in a variety of fields in more than 70 countries. Established in 1950. Number of employees: 50. Number of internship applications received each year: 4,000.

Internships Available ▶ *50–150 Career Development/IAESTE United States interns:* responsibilities include training in a field of choice ranging from technical fields to hospitality/tourism. Candidates should have ability to work independently, college courses in field, experience in the field, self-motivation, international interest. Duration is 1–18 months. Paid. Open to college freshmen, college sophomores, college juniors, college seniors, graduate students, law students. International applications accepted.

Benefits Formal training, health insurance, housing at a cost, meals at a cost, on-the-job training, opportunity to attend seminars/ workshops, willing to complete paperwork for educational credit.

International Internships Available.

Contact Write, call, fax, e-mail, or through World Wide Web site Katie McDonough, Customer Service Representative. Phone: 410-997-2200. Fax: 410-992-3924. E-mail: aipt@aipt.org. Telephone interview required. Applicants must submit a formal organization application, letter of interest, resume, academic transcripts, portfolio, personal reference, essay. Application deadline: January 1. Fees: $25. World Wide Web: http://www.aipt.org.

BOSTON UNIVERSITY INTERNATIONAL PROGRAMS
232 Bay State Road
Boston, Massachusetts 02215

General Information Programs offering internships in China, England, Spain, Russia, France, Australia, Germany, Ireland, Israel, and Washington, DC; programs combine academic course work with a full-time internship and each program awards 16-20 semester hours of credit. Established in 1984. Number of employees: 16. Division of Boston University, Boston, Massachusetts. Number of internship applications received each year: 800.

Internships Available ▶ *15–25 interns (Beijing, China):* responsibilities include working in any of the following fields: advertising and public relations, the arts, business and economics, health and human services, hospitality administration, journalism, film and television, politics, and prelaw. Candidates should have oral communication skills, personal interest in the field, self-motivation, written communication skills, four semesters or equivalent of college-level Chinese. Duration is 1 semester. Unpaid. Open to college juniors, college seniors, recent college graduates. ▶ *10–30 interns (Dresden, Germany):* responsibilities include working in any of the following fields: business and economics, engineering, film and television, health and human services, and journalism. Candidates should have oral communication skills, personal interest in the field, self-motivation, written communication skills, five semesters or equivalent of college-level German. Duration is 1 semester. Unpaid. Open to college juniors, college seniors, recent college graduates. ▶ *15–25 interns (Dublin, Ireland):* responsibilities include working in any of the following fields: advertising and public relations, the arts, business and economics, health and human services, hospitality administration, journalism, film and television, politics, and prelaw. Candidates should have oral communication skills, personal interest in the field, self-motivation, written communication skills. Duration is 1 semester. Unpaid. Open to college juniors, college seniors, recent college graduates. ▶ *5–20 interns (Haifa, Israel):* responsibilities include working in any of the following fields: archaeology, business, computer technologies, education, international trade, medical services, public relations, social work, and women's studies. Candidates should have oral communication skills, personal interest in the field, self-motivation, written communication skills. Duration is 1 semester. Unpaid. Open to college sophomores, college juniors, college seniors, recent college graduates. ▶ *175–230 interns (London, England):* responsibilities include working in any of the following fields: advertising, marketing and public relations, the arts, film and television, journalism, management and finance, economics, prelaw, politics and international relations, psychology, and social policy. Candidates should have oral communication skills, personal interest in the field, self-motivation, written communication skills. Duration is 1 semester. Unpaid. Open to college sophomores, college juniors, college seniors, recent college graduates. ▶ *15–25 interns (Madrid, Spain):* responsibilities include working in any of the following fields: advertising and public relations, the arts, business and economics, health and human services, hospitality administration, journalism, film, and television, politics, prelaw, and Teaching English to Speakers of Foreign Languages (TEFL). Candidates should have oral communication skills, personal interest in the field, self-motivation, written communication skills, five semesters or equivalent of college-level Spanish. Duration is 1 semester. Unpaid. Open to college juniors, college seniors, recent college graduates. ▶ *10–30 interns (Moscow, Russia Federation):* responsibilities include working in any of the following fields: advertising and public relations, the arts, business and economics, health and human services, hospitality administration, journalism, film and television, politics, and prelaw. Candidates should have oral communication skills, personal interest in the field, self-motivation, written communication skills, four semesters or equivalent of college-level Russian. Duration is 1 semester. Unpaid. Open to college sophomores, college juniors, college seniors, recent college graduates. ▶ *40–60 interns (Paris, France):* responsibilities include working in any of the following fields: advertising and public relations, the arts, business and economics, health and human services, hospitality administration, journalism, film and television, politics, and prelaw. Candidates should have oral communication skills, personal interest in the field, self-motivation, written communication skills, four semesters or equivalent of college-level French. Duration is 1 semester. Unpaid. Open to college sophomores, college juniors, college seniors, recent college graduates. ▶ *70 interns (Sydney, Australia):* responsibilities include working in any of the following fields: advertising and public relations, the arts, business and economics, health and human services, hospitality administration, journalism, film and television, and politics. Candidates should have oral communication skills, personal interest in the field, self-motivation, written communication skills. Duration is 1 semester. Unpaid. Open to college juniors, college seniors, recent college graduates. ▶ *30–50 interns (Washington, D.C.):* responsibilities include working in any of the following fields: advertising and public relations, the arts, business and economics, health and human services, hospitality administration, journalism, film and television, politics, and prelaw. Candidates should have oral communication skills, personal interest in the field, self-motivation, written communication skills. Duration is 1 semester. Unpaid. Open to college juniors, college seniors. International applications accepted.

Benefits Formal training, willing to complete paperwork for educational credit, academic credit for internship.

International Internships Available in Sydney, Australia; Beijing, China; Paris, France; Dresden, Germany; Dublin, Ireland; Haifa, Israel; Moscow, Russian Federation; Madrid, Spain; London, United Kingdom.

Contact Write, call, fax, e-mail, or through World Wide Web site Division of International Programs. Phone: 617-353-9888. Fax: 617-353-5402. E-mail: abroad@bu.edu. Applicants must submit a formal organization application, academic transcripts, two letters of recommendation, approval of participation from home institution, 1-2 writing samples (depending on program), in-person interview (telephone acceptable) recommended for some programs. Application deadline: March 15 for fall, March 1 for summer, October 15 for spring. Fees: $45. World Wide Web: http://www.bu.edu/abroad.

CENTER FOR CULTURAL INTERCHANGE
17 North Second Avenue
St. Charles, Illinois 60174

General Information Nonprofit student and adult exchange organization that sends American college-age students and recent graduates abroad for internship opportunities. Established in 1985. Number of employees: 14. Number of internship applications received each year: 20.

Internships Available ▶ *Up to 100 interns:* responsibilities include working in business, accounting/finance, travel/tourism, social service, or other fields, depending on the intern's educational background and destination. Candidates should have college courses in field, office skills, personal interest in the field, language skills may be necessary. Duration is 1–3 months. Unpaid. Open to college juniors, college seniors, recent college graduates, graduate students.

Benefits Health insurance, housing at a cost, meals at a cost, names of contacts, on-the-job training, opportunity to attend seminars/workshops, willing to act as a professional reference, willing to complete paperwork for educational credit, willing to provide letters of recommendation.

International Internships Available in France; Dublin, Ireland; Florence, Italy; Spain; London, United Kingdom.

Contact Write, call, fax, e-mail, or through World Wide Web site Jacqui Metcalf, Outbound Programs Director. Phone: 888-227-6231. Fax: 630-377-2307. E-mail: jacqui@cci-exchange.com. Applicants must submit a formal organization application, letter of interest, resume, letter of recommendation, language interview may be necessary. Applications are accepted continuously. World Wide Web: http://www.cci-exchange.com.

COLLEGE WORKS PAINTING
1505 East 17th Street, Suite 210
Santa Ana, California 92705

General Information Organization providing training and financial support to organize and operate an independent house-painting business. Established in 1997. Number of employees: 2,000. Division of National Services Group, Santa Ana, California. Number of internship applications received each year: 8,000.

Internships Available ▶ *600–800 branch managers:* responsibilities include recruiting and training a 6-9 person team; marketing, pricing, and selling services; production, quality and cost control; collections; and promoting ethical business practices; positions available across U.S. Candidates should have ability to work independently, ability to work with others, analytical skills, oral communication skills, organizational skills, self-motivation, strong leadership ability. Duration is April-September (part-time in spring, full-time in summer). Average pay of $7200 per internship. Open to college freshmen, college sophomores, college juniors, college seniors, recent college graduates. International applications accepted.

Benefits Formal training, free meals, job counseling, names of contacts, on-the-job training, opportunity to attend seminars/workshops, possible full-time employment, tuition assistance, willing to complete paperwork for educational credit, willing to provide letters of recommendation, scholarships, trips to Cabo San Lucas, special training workshops for top producers, multiple business contacts.

Contact Write, call, fax, e-mail, or through World Wide Web site Matthew Stewart, Vice President, 1505 East 17th Street, Suite 210, Santa Ana, California 92705. Phone: 714-564-7900. Fax: 714-564-8725. E-mail: swpainting@aol.com. Telephone interview required. Applicants must submit a formal organization application, resume, 3 in-person interviews. Application deadline: April 1. World Wide Web: http://www.nationalservicesgroup.com.

DYNAMY, INTERNSHIP YEAR
27 Sever Street
Worcester, Massachusetts 01609

General Information Nine-month internship program for students exploring their career interests; interns complete a three-week Outward Bound course and a series of three 9-week internships during the program. Established in 1969. Number of employees: 14. Number of internship applications received each year: 60.

Internships Available ▶ *40 interns:* responsibilities include completing 1 to 3 internships (areas include business, education, government, radio, TV, theater, social service, fine arts, medicine, restaurant/hotel management, retail, and environmental science), meeting weekly with a Dynamy Internship year adviser, and participating in community service activities and a 3-week outdoor education program. Candidates should have ability to work

Dynamy, Internship Year (continued)
independently, oral communication skills, self-motivation, strong interpersonal skills, strong leadership ability. Duration is 4–9 months. Unpaid. Open to recent high school graduates, college freshmen, college sophomores, college juniors, college seniors, individuals ages 17-22. International applications accepted.
Benefits Formal training, housing at a cost, job counseling, on-the-job training, opportunity to attend seminars/workshops, tuition assistance, willing to act as a professional reference, willing to provide letters of recommendation, up to 12 college credits available through Clark University.
Contact Write, call, fax, e-mail, or through World Wide Web site Mr. Keith Robichaud, Director of Admissions. Phone: 508-755-2571. Fax: 508-755-4692. E-mail: krobichaud@dynamy.org. In-person interview recommended (telephone interview accepted). Applicants must submit a formal organization application, academic transcripts, two writing samples, three letters of recommendation, $35–$50 application fee. Applications are accepted continuously. World Wide Web: http://www.dynamy.org.

EDUCATIONAL PROGRAMMES ABROAD (EPA)
350 East Michigan Avenue, Suite 225
Kalamazoo, Michigan 49007

General Information Educational organization that offers academic internships in London, Bonn, Berlin, Brussels, Madrid, Paris, Melbourne, and Edinburgh. Established in 1977. Number of employees: 2. Division of Educational Programmes Abroad, London, United Kingdom. Number of internship applications received each year: 600.
Internships Available ► *Interns:* responsibilities include working in national or regional government, various businesses, social services, health administration, medical research, media, or environmental organizations in London, Bonn, Berlin, Brussels, Madrid, Paris, Melbourne, or Edinburgh. Candidates should have ability to work independently, knowledge of field, personal interest in the field, self-motivation, strong interpersonal skills, written communication skills. Duration is 1 semester or summer. Unpaid. Open to college juniors, college seniors, recent college graduates, graduate students, law students. International applications accepted.
Benefits Housing at a cost, meals at a cost, willing to complete paperwork for educational credit.
International Internships Available in Melbourne, Australia; Brussels, Belgium; Paris, France; Bonn and Berlin, Germany; Madrid, Spain; London and Edinburgh, United Kingdom.
Contact Write, call, fax, e-mail, or through World Wide Web site U.S. Director. Phone: 616-382-0139. Fax: 616-382-5222. E-mail: epainterns@aol.com. Applicants must submit a formal organization application, resume, academic transcripts, writing sample, personal reference, letter of recommendation. Application deadline: March 1 for summer, May 1 for fall, November 15 for spring. World Wide Web: http://www.studyabroad.com/epa/.

HANDS ON ATLANTA
1605 Peachtree Street, Suite 100
Atlanta, Georgia 30309

General Information Nonprofit, volunteer organization that organizes more than 250 flexible volunteer opportunities per month and matches 20,000 volunteer members to these opportunities. Established in 1989. Number of employees: 50. Affiliate of City Cares of America, New York, New York. Number of internship applications received each year: 50.
Internships Available ► *2–4 development interns:* responsibilities include assisting with grant writing, individual and corporate giving, and special events related to fund-raising. Candidates should have ability to work independently, ability to work with others, analytical skills, computer skills, editing skills, oral communication skills, organizational skills, personal interest in the field, research skills, self-motivation, writing skills. Duration is 10 weeks. Unpaid. ► *7–12 program management interns:* responsibilities include working directly with volunteers to meet critical community needs; interns can choose among program areas including education, homelessness, or housing. Candidates should have ability to work

independently, computer skills, editing skills, oral communication skills, organizational skills, personal interest in the field, self-motivation, strong interpersonal skills, writing skills. Duration is 10 weeks. Unpaid. ► *2 special events interns:* responsibilities include assisting in planning and implementing special events including event logistics, public relations, and advertising. Candidates should have computer skills, editing skills, oral communication skills, organizational skills, personal interest in the field, self-motivation, strong interpersonal skills, writing skills. Duration is 10 weeks. Unpaid. Open to college freshmen, college sophomores, college juniors, college seniors, recent college graduates, graduate students, law students, career changers, individuals reentering the workforce. International applications accepted.
Benefits Formal training, on-the-job training, opportunity to attend seminars/workshops, possible full-time employment, willing to act as a professional reference, willing to complete paperwork for educational credit, willing to provide letters of recommendation.
Contact Write, call, fax, e-mail, or through World Wide Web site Tamala Fortson, Human Resources Supervisor. Phone: 404-879-2753. Fax: 404-872-2251. E-mail: tfortson@handsonatlanta.com. In-person interview required. Applicants must submit a letter of interest, resume, two writing samples, two personal references. Applications are accepted continuously. World Wide Web: http://www.handsonatlanta.com.

INTERN AMERICA, INC.
308 East 85th Street
New York, New York 10028

General Information Professional placement organization that provides unpaid internships in the United States to international and U.S. candidates. Established in 1997. Number of employees: 2.
Internships Available ► *Interns:* responsibilities include working in a tailor-made internship based on individual's education or experience; fields include architecture, art, communications, computers, education, engineering, entertainment, fashion, finance, government, hospitality, import/export, health care, international trade, law, marketing, public affairs, public relations, social work, and travel/tourism. Candidates should have ability to work independently, college courses in field, computer skills, knowledge of field, office skills, oral communication skills, personal interest in the field, research skills, self-motivation, strong interpersonal skills, written communication skills, advanced-level English language skills for international students. Duration is minimum of 4 weeks. Unpaid. Open to college freshmen, college sophomores, college juniors, college seniors, recent college graduates, graduate students, law students, career changers, junior professionals. International applications accepted.
Benefits Job counseling, on-the-job training, willing to act as a professional reference, willing to complete paperwork for educational credit, willing to provide letters of recommendation, information on housing provided, packet awarded at end of internship with new resume including internship experience, letters of reference from Intern America and the host company, certificate of completion.
Contact Write, call, fax, e-mail, or through World Wide Web site Shannon Randolph, Executive Director, 308 East 85th Street, New York, New York 10028. Phone: 212-517-6510. Fax: 212-517-6866. E-mail: contact@internamerica.com. In-person interview recommended. Applicants must submit a formal organization application, letter of interest, resume, writing sample, $950 fee for a minimum of four weeks and $150 for each additional week (upon acceptance). Applications are accepted continuously. World Wide Web: http://www.internamerica.com.

INTERN EXCHANGE INTERNATIONAL LTD.
1858 Mallard Lane
Villanova, Pennsylvania 19085

General Information Organization offering travel to London and the opportunity to participate in career-based internships, arts activities, special interest activities, and cultural trips/tours. Established in 1987. Number of employees: 1. Number of internship applications received each year: 225.

Internships Available ▶ *15–20 resident assistants (London):* responsibilities include supervising interns studying in London. Candidates should have college courses in field, plan to pursue career in field, self-motivation, strong interpersonal skills, strong leadership ability, background in journalism, theater, film/video, photography, psychology, business, fashion and design, fine arts, or Web site design. Duration is 31 days in June-July. Stipend. Open to college seniors, recent college graduates, graduate students, teachers; must be at least 20 years of age. ▶ *150–240 student travel interns (London):* responsibilities include interning in any of the following academic areas: archaeology, architecture, art history/appreciation, business (banking/finance, marketing), communications, government and politics, health sciences, journalism, prelaw, premed, social services, film, photography, fashion and design, and community service. Candidates should have ability to work independently, oral communication skills, personal interest in the field, self-motivation, strong interpersonal skills, strong leadership ability. Duration is 30 days in June-July. Unpaid. Open to individuals ages 16-18. International applications accepted.
Benefits On-the-job training, willing to complete paperwork for educational credit, willing to provide letters of recommendation, cultural trips available, housing provided for resident assistants.
International Internships Available in London, United Kingdom.
Contact Write, call, fax, e-mail, or through World Wide Web site Nina Miller Glickman, Director, 130 Harold Road, Woodmere, New York 11598. Phone: 516-374-3939. Fax: 516-374-2104. E-mail: internexchange@compuserve.com. Applicants must submit a formal organization application, letter of interest, academic transcripts, fee of approximately $5495 and deposit of $450 upon acceptance for student-travel interns only, 1-2 letters of recommendation (depending on field). Applications are accepted continuously. Fees: $50. World Wide Web: http://www.internexchange.com.

INTERNSHIPS INTERNATIONAL
1612 Oberlin Road, #5
Raleigh, North Carolina 27608

General Information Placement service for quality unpaid internships in locations worldwide. Established in 1994. Number of employees: 2. Number of internship applications received each year: 50.
Internships Available ▶ *Interns:* responsibilities include working in all fields as requested by interns. Duration is 8 weeks to 3 months. Unpaid. Open to college seniors, recent college graduates, graduate students, law students, career changers. International applications accepted.
Benefits On-the-job training, willing to act as a professional reference, willing to provide letters of recommendation.
International Internships Available in Melbourne, Australia; Santiago, Chile; Paris, France; Dresden, Germany; Budapest, Hungary; Dublin, Ireland; Florence, Italy; Capetown, South Africa; Bangkok, Thailand; Glasgow, United Kingdom; London, United Kingdom.
Contact Write, call, fax, e-mail, or through World Wide Web site Judy Tilson, Director. Phone: 919-832-1575. Fax: 919-832-8980. E-mail: intintl@aol.com. In-person interview recommended (telephone interview accepted). Applicants must submit a formal organization application, letter of interest, resume, academic transcripts, two letters of recommendation, photo; program fee of $800 ($1000 for London placement; $1500 for Dublin placement). Applications are accepted continuously. World Wide Web: http://www.rtpnet.org/~intintl.

JEWISH VOCATIONAL SERVICE/ KOHN SUMMER INTERN PROGRAM
77 Geary Street, Suite 401
San Francisco, California 94108

General Information Vocational, career, and employment specialists. Established in 1985. Number of employees: 60. Number of internship applications received each year: 100.
Internships Available ▶ *30 Kohn interns:* responsibilities include political advocacy, journalism, Web site development, event coordinator, curriculum development, or marketing or public

relations. Candidates should have oral communication skills, organizational skills, personal interest in the field, strong interpersonal skills, strong leadership ability, written communication skills. Duration is June 17 to August 9. $1800 per duration of internship. Open to Jewish undergraduate freshmen, sophomores, and juniors; freshmen must have completed school year.
Benefits On-the-job training, opportunity to attend seminars/workshops, willing to act as a professional reference, willing to complete paperwork for educational credit, willing to provide letters of recommendation.
Contact Write, call, fax, e-mail, or through World Wide Web site Rebecca Bassin, Kohn Program Coordinator. Phone: 415-782-6223. Fax: 415-391-3617. E-mail: rbassin@jvs.org. In-person interview recommended (telephone interview accepted). Applicants must submit a formal organization application, two personal references. Application deadline: April 1 for summer. World Wide Web: http://www.jvs.org.

JOB CORPS
200 Constitution Avenue, NW, N-4507
Washington, District of Columbia 20210

General Information Employment and training center. Established in 1964. Number of employees: 35. Division of United States Department of Labor, Washington, District of Columbia. Number of internship applications received each year: 50.
Internships Available ▶ *4–6 associates:* responsibilities include acting as knowledgeable consultants in working with professional staff. Candidates should have ability to work independently, analytical skills, computer skills, knowledge of field, oral communication skills, research skills, self-motivation, strong interpersonal skills, written communication skills, interest in youth programs. Duration is one year to 18 months. $29,966 to $54,699 per year depending on work experience and education. Open to recent college graduates, graduate students.
Benefits Names of contacts, on-the-job training, opportunity to attend seminars/workshops, travel reimbursement, willing to complete paperwork for educational credit, willing to provide letters of recommendation.
Contact Write, call, or fax Curtis Massey, Associate Program Coordinator. Phone: 202-693-3102. Fax: 202-693-2767. In-person interview recommended (telephone interview accepted). Applicants must submit a formal organization application, letter of interest, resume, academic transcripts, two personal references, three letters of recommendation. Applications are accepted continuously. World Wide Web: http://www.jobcorps.org.

MOGPA (MINNESOTA ORGANIZATION FOR GLOBAL PROFESSIONAL ASSIGNMENTS)
2345 Rice Street, Suite 200
St. Paul, Minnesota 55113

General Information Organization that provides bilingual college students or recent graduates, pursuing a career in business, engineering, science or technology, with 6-12 month internships in Asia with American, Japanese, and Chinese companies. Established in 1993. Number of employees: 6. Affiliate of University of Minnesota, Twin Cities Campus, Minneapolis, Minnesota. Number of internship applications received each year: 100.
Internships Available ▶ *Business-related fields interns (Japan or China):* responsibilities include entry-level work for American, Japanese, or Chinese company in Japan or China in the fields of business administration, international business, accounting, finance, management, marketing, etc. Candidates should have college courses in field, experience in the field, oral communication skills, plan to pursue career in field, written communication skills, ability to speak fluent English and either Japanese or Mandarin. Duration is 6–12 months. $700 to $1600 per month (negotiated with individual companies). ▶ *Computer-related fields interns (China or Japan):* responsibilities include entry-level work for an American, Japanese, or Chinese company located in Japan or China in the fields of information systems/technology, computer science, computer programming, software, etc. Candidates should have college courses in field, computer skills, experience in the field,

MOGPA (Minnesota Organization for Global Professional Assignments) (continued)
oral communication skills, plan to pursue career in field, written communication skills, ability to speak fluent English and either Japanese or Mandarin. Duration is 6–12 months. $700 to $1600 per month (negotiated with individual companies). ▶ *Engineering-related fields interns (Japan or China):* responsibilities include entry-level work for an American, Japanese, or Chinese company in Japan or China in the fields of chemical engineering, mechanical engineering, electrical engineering, etc. Candidates should have college courses in field, experience in the field, oral communication skills, plan to pursue career in field, written communication skills, ability to speak fluent English and either Japanese or Mandarin; marketing skills (preferred). Duration is 6–12 months. $700 to $1600 per month (negotiated with individual companies). Open to college juniors, college seniors, recent college graduates, graduate students, U.S. citizens and some permanent residents.
Benefits Housing at a cost, job counseling, possible full-time employment, willing to complete paperwork for educational credit, assistance in obtaining visas and housing.
International Internships Available in China; Japan.
Contact Write, call, fax, e-mail, or through World Wide Web site Heidi Henderson, Communications Director, 2345 Rice Street, Suite 200, St. Paul, Minnesota 55113. Phone: 651-481-0583. Fax: 651-481-0592. E-mail: recruiter@interninasia.com. In-person interview recommended (telephone interview accepted). Applicants must submit a formal organization application, letter of interest, resume, academic transcripts, 2 short essays, demonstrated proficiency in an Asian language through a 5-minute video. Applications are accepted continuously. Fees: $75. World Wide Web: http://www.interninasia.com.

MOUNTBATTEN INTERNSHIP PROGRAMME
50 East 42nd Street, Suite 2000
New York, New York 10017-5405

General Information Exchange visitor program providing one-year professional internships for British, New Zealand, and Australian citizens in New York and for U.S. citizens only in London, UK. Established in 1984. Number of employees: 14. Number of internship applications received each year: 1,250.
Internships Available ▶ *25–35 internships in London:* responsibilities include general entry-level work in various fields including finance, marketing, banking, commerce, legal, and information technology. Duration is 12 months beginning in October (some beginning in March). Approximately 1100 British pounds per month. Open to recent college graduates, graduate students, law students, career changers, only those who are U.S. citizens. ▶ *150–160 internships in New York:* responsibilities include general entry-level work in management, business, commerce, and finance with clerical, administrative, research, paralegal, analytical, and information technology duties. Duration is 1 year beginning in January, May, or September. $960 per month. Open to recent college graduates, graduate students, law students, career changers, only those who are citizens of Great Britain, Australia, or New Zealand (no U.S. citizens). Candidates for all positions should have computer skills, office skills, oral communication skills, self-motivation, strong interpersonal skills, written communication skills. International applications accepted.
Benefits Formal training, free housing, health insurance, job counseling, on-the-job training, opportunity to attend seminars/workshops, willing to act as a professional reference, willing to complete paperwork for educational credit, willing to provide letters of recommendation.
International Internships Available in London, United Kingdom.
Contact Write, call, fax, e-mail, or through World Wide Web site Ellen S. Lautz, Administrative Director, 50 East 42nd Street, Suite 200, New York, New York 10017-5405. Phone: 212-557-5380. Fax: 212-557-5383. E-mail: elautz@mountbatten.org. In-person interview required. Applicants must submit a formal organization application, resume, academic transcripts, three personal references, three letters of recommendation, personal statement (essay form). Application deadline: May 31 for internships in London. Fees: $50. World Wide Web: http://www.mountbatten.org.

NATIONAL CONSORTIUM FOR GRADUATE DEGREES FOR MINORITIES IN ENGINEERING AND SCIENCE, INC.
PO Box 537
Notre Dame, Indiana 46556

General Information Organization that matches students who are interested in graduate degrees in engineering and science with employer sponsors; over 75 companies and over 80 universities participate. Established in 1976. Number of employees: 8. Number of internship applications received each year: 800.
Internships Available ▶ *40 PhD fellowships in engineering and science (20 each):* responsibilities include working on engineering and science projects. Duration is 1-3 summers. $14,000 living stipend per year towards graduate school tuition and fees. Open to students obtaining PhD in either engineering or science. ▶ *200 master's fellowships in engineering:* responsibilities include working on engineering projects. Candidates should have enrollment in engineering degree program; undergraduates must intend to pursue masters' degree in engineering. Duration is 1-3 summers. $10,000 living stipend per year towards graduate school tuition and fees. Open to college juniors, college seniors, graduate students.
Benefits Housing at a cost, on-the-job training, travel reimbursement.
Contact Write, call, fax, e-mail, or through World Wide Web site Saundra Johnson, Executive Director. Phone: 574-631-7771. Fax: 574-287-1486. E-mail: gem.l@nd.edu. Applicants must submit a formal organization application, resume, academic transcripts, two letters of recommendation. Application deadline: December 1. World Wide Web: http://www.gemfellowship.org.

OFFICE OF INTERNSHIPS AND EXPERIENTIAL EDUCATION
Taft Hall, The University of Rhode Island
Kingston, Rhode Island 02881

General Information Internship office that administers full-time and part-time internships for academic credit. Internship opportunities are available nationwide as well as in Dublin, Ireland. Established in 1975. Number of employees: 3. Unit of University of Rhode Island, University College, Kingston, Rhode Island. Number of internship applications received each year: 250.
Internships Available ▶ *600 interns.* Candidates should have ability to work independently, oral communication skills, plan to pursue career in field, self-motivation, strong interpersonal skills, written communication skills, 60 credits completed, with a 2.5 GPA. Duration is 1 semester or summer, full- or part-time. Unpaid. Open to college juniors, college seniors. International applications accepted.
Benefits Job counseling, on-the-job training, opportunity to attend seminars/workshops, willing to act as a professional reference, willing to complete paperwork for educational credit, willing to provide letters of recommendation, interviewing assistance.
International Internships Available in Dublin, Ireland.
Contact Write, call, fax, e-mail, or through World Wide Web site Moira Keating, Ph.D., Intern Advisor. Phone: 401-874-2160. Fax: 401-874-4573. E-mail: intern@etal.uri.edu. In-person interview required. Applicants must submit a formal organization application, academic transcripts, 1-2 letters of recommendation, telephone interview acceptable for non-URI students. Application deadline: April 1 for summer, June 1 for fall, November 1 for spring. World Wide Web: http://www.uri.edu/univco/internships.

PUBLIC SERVICE CORPS, NEW YORK CITY, DEPARTMENT OF CITYWIDE ADMINISTRATIVE SERVICES
1 Centre Street, Room 2435
New York, New York 10007

General Information Agency that provides internship opportunities throughout city agencies. Established in 1966. Number of employees: 8. Division of New York Department of Citywide Administrative Services, New York, New York. Number of internship applications received each year: 1,600.

Internships Available ▶ *1,000 Federal Work-Study Program interns:* responsibilities include working in a broad range of fields including government administration, creative arts, social work, health care, research, education, computer science, economic development, finance, accounting, labor relations, transportation, and management. Duration is to be determined by each school. $5.90–$12.48 per hour. Open to undergraduates, graduate students, and law students who are eligible for Federal Work-Study Program. ▶ *Academic credit/volunteer interns:* responsibilities include working in a broad range of fields including government administration, creative arts, social work, health care, research, education, computer science, economic development, finance, accounting, labor relations, transportation, and management. Duration is flexible. Unpaid. Open to college freshmen, college sophomores, college juniors, college seniors, graduate students, law students. Candidates for all positions should have specific college courses and/or skills by internship.
Benefits On-the-job training, opportunity to attend seminars/workshops, willing to complete paperwork for educational credit, experience in public service; credit can be arranged with college approval.
Contact Write, call, fax, or e-mail Dr. Marjorie Jelin, Director. Phone: 212-669-3255. Fax: 212-669-3633. E-mail: mjelin@dcas.nyc.gov. In-person interview required. Applicants must submit a formal organization application. Applications are accepted continuously. World Wide Web: http://www.nyc.gov.

RHODE ISLAND STATE GOVERNMENT INTERN PROGRAM
Room 8AA, State House Building
Providence, Rhode Island 02903

General Information Program that places college, graduate, and law students in Rhode Island's government agencies for internships. Established in 1969. Number of employees: 5. Number of internship applications received each year: 450.
Internships Available ▶ *200 interns:* responsibilities include working in a state government agency such as the Department of Health, the Department of Education, or the Attorney General's office. Duration is 8–12 weeks. Position available as unpaid or at $20 per day for Rhode Island residents; work-study available for out-of-state residents. Open to high school seniors, college freshmen, college sophomores, college juniors, college seniors, law students, career changers. International applications accepted.
Benefits Job counseling, names of contacts, opportunity to attend seminars/workshops, possible full-time employment, willing to complete paperwork for educational credit, willing to provide letters of recommendation.
Contact Call, fax, or e-mail Mr. Robert W. Gemma, Executive Director. Phone: 401-222-6782. Fax: 401-222-6142. E-mail: rgemma@rilin.state.ri.us. In-person interview required. Applicants must submit a letter of interest, resume, writing sample (law students only). Application deadline: May 15 for summer. World Wide Web: http://www.rilin.state.ri.us.

RHODE ISLAND STUDENT EMPLOYMENT NETWORK
560 Jefferson Boulevard
Warwick, Rhode Island 02886

General Information Statewide year-round clearinghouse for student employment and experiential education. Established in 1971. Number of employees: 55. Unit of Rhode Island Higher Education Assistance Authority, Warwick, Rhode Island. Number of internship applications received each year: 800.
Internships Available ▶ *300–500 Rhode Island interns:* responsibilities include various duties depending on where the intern is placed. Duration is 1–2 semesters. Position available as unpaid or paid. Open to college freshmen, college sophomores, college juniors, college seniors, graduate students, law students, Rhode Island residents or those attending school in Rhode Island.
Benefits Job counseling, names of contacts, willing to complete paperwork for educational credit, willing to provide letters of recommendation.

Contact Write, call, e-mail, or through World Wide Web site Deanna DiIorio, Education Assistance Technician. Phone: 401-736-1180. Fax: 401-732-3541. E-mail: ddiiorio@riheaa.org. In-person interview recommended (telephone interview accepted). Program registration. Applications are accepted continuously. World Wide Web: http://www.riheaa.org.

SMITHSONIAN INSTITUTION, OFFICE OF FELLOWSHIPS & GRANTS
750 9th Street NW, Suite 9300
Washington, District of Columbia 20560-0902

General Information Office that offers fellowships and internships for research and study in fields that are actively pursued by the museums and research organizations of the Institution.
Internships Available ▶ *James E. Webb Minority Graduate interns:* responsibilities include interning in the areas of business and public administration. Duration is 10 weeks. $400 per week. ▶ *Minority Internship Program interns:* responsibilities include participating in research or museum-related activities in one of the many museums or departments of the Smithsonian Institution. Duration is 10 weeks. $350 per week. ▶ *Native American Internship Program interns:* responsibilities include participating in research or museum activities related to Native American studies. Duration is 10 weeks. $350 per week.
Benefits Opportunity to attend seminars/workshops, travel reimbursement, willing to complete paperwork for educational credit, willing to provide letters of recommendation.
Contact Write, call, e-mail, or through World Wide Web site Ms. Pamela Hudson, Program Manager, 750 9th Street, NW, Suite 9300, Washington, District of Columbia 20560-0902. Phone: 202-275-0655. Fax: 202-275-0489. E-mail: siofg@ofg.si.edu. Application deadline: January 15 for James E. Webb Minority Graduate and Minority Internship Program, February 1 for summer Native American Program, June 1 for fall Native American Program, October 1 for spring Native American Program. World Wide Web: http://www.si.edu/research+study.

UNITED STATES ARMY RECRUITING COMMAND
1307 Third Avenue
Fort Knox, Kentucky 40121-2726

General Information Unit that conducts recruiting of health-care professionals for the Army Medical Department. Number of employees: 30. Unit of United States Department of the Army, Washington, District of Columbia. Number of internship applications received each year: 65.
Internships Available ▶ *60 advanced general dentistry interns.* Candidates should have ability to work with others, oral communication skills, research skills, strong leadership ability, written communication skills. Duration is October 1 to September 30. $3400 per month. Open to senior dental students, dental school graduates within 3 years after graduation. ▶ *5–10 clinical psychology interns.* Candidates should have analytical skills, college degree in related field, oral communication skills, strong interpersonal skills, strong leadership ability, written communication skills. Duration is 1 year. $35,000–$40,000 per year. Open to graduate students. ▶ *10 dietetics interns.* Candidates should have computer skills, oral communication skills, strong interpersonal skills, strong leadership ability, written communication skills. Duration is September to May. $2400 per month. Open to college seniors, recent college graduates, graduate students. ▶ *6 occupational therapy interns.* Candidates should have computer skills, oral communication skills, strong interpersonal skills, strong leadership ability, written communication skills. Duration is 7 months. $2400 per month. Open to college seniors, recent college graduates, graduate students.
Benefits Formal training, health insurance, meals at a cost, opportunity to attend seminars/workshops, possible full-time employment, travel reimbursement, tuition assistance, willing to complete paperwork for educational credit, on-post housing or housing allowance, subsistence allowance.
Contact Write, call, fax, e-mail, or through World Wide Web site Maj. Tanya Beecher, RA Operations Officer, 1307 Third Avenue, Fort Knox, Kentucky 40121. Phone: 502-626-0367. Fax: 502-626-

0923. E-mail: tanya.beecher@usarec.army.mil. In-person interview required. Applicants must submit a formal organization application, letter of interest, resume, academic transcripts, three letters of recommendation, other materials as specified by specific position; physical exam required (paid for by employer). Applications are accepted continuously. World Wide Web: http://www.healthcare.goarmy.army.com.

VOLUNTEERS FOR PEACE
1034 Tiffany Road
Belmont, Vermont 05730

General Information Placement service that places North Americans in 1500 work camps worldwide. Established in 1981. Number of employees: 3. Number of internship applications received each year: 600.
Internships Available ▶ *1,200–1,400 international work campers:* responsibilities include living with an international group of 12-20 persons and becoming involved in a community service project. Candidates should have organizational skills, self-motivation, strong interpersonal skills, intercultural experience. Duration is 2 to 3 weeks each program; interns normally register for multiple camps. Unpaid. Open to individuals age 15 or over. International applications accepted.
Benefits Free housing, meals at a cost, opportunity to attend seminars/workshops, willing to complete paperwork for educational credit, inexpensive international experience.
International Internships Available.
Contact Write, call, fax, e-mail, or through World Wide Web site Amy Bannon, Outgoing Placement Director. Phone: 802-259-2759. Fax: 802-259-2922. E-mail: vfp@vfp.org. Applicants must submit a formal organization application, $200 for room and board upon acceptance. Applications are accepted continuously. World Wide Web: http://www.vfp.org.

THE WASHINGTON CENTER FOR INTERNSHIPS AND ACADEMIC SEMINARS
2301 M Street, NW, Fifth Floor
Washington, District of Columbia 20037-1427

General Information Center that provides off-campus full-time internships and 1–2 week academic seminars in all fields for students from more than 750 colleges and universities. Established in 1975. Number of employees: 50. Number of internship applications received each year: 1,500.
Internships Available ▶ *50 College Plus One interns:* responsibilities include varied duties depending on student's interests and expertise. Candidates should have analytical skills, office skills, oral communication skills, plan to pursue career in field, self-motivation, written communication skills. Duration is 10–12 weeks. Position available as unpaid or paid. Open to recent college graduates, graduate students, law students. ▶ *50 Law Plus One interns:* responsibilities include varied law-related duties depending upon student's interests. Candidates should have analytical skills, knowledge of field, office skills, oral communication skills, plan to pursue career in field, written communication skills. Duration is 10 weeks in the summer. Position available as unpaid or paid. Open to law students. ▶ *30 North American Free Trade Agreement (NAFTA) Program interns:* responsibilities include varied duties related to bi- or tri-lateral trade issues between U.S., Canada, and Mexico. Candidates should have analytical skills, knowledge of field, office skills, oral communication skills, personal interest in the field, written communication skills. Duration is 10–15 weeks. Minimum $2000 financial assistance guaranteed and applied toward housing. Open to college juniors, college seniors, graduate students. ▶ *50–75 diversity in Congress program interns:* responsibilities include being placed in congressional offices; general staff work. Candidates should have ability to work with others, analytical skills, office skills, oral communication skills, self-motivation, written communication skills. Duration is 10–15 weeks. $2000 minimum guaranteed financial assistance applied toward housing. Open to college juniors, college seniors, graduate students. ▶ *25–75 diversity leaders interns:* responsibilities include variety of tasks for students in any major field, with an emphasis on quantitative

and analytical skills. Candidates should have analytical skills, office skills, oral communication skills, self-motivation, strong leadership ability, written communication skills. Duration is 10–15 weeks. Housing fees paid (minimum value of $2775). Open to college juniors, college seniors, graduate students. ▶ *50–75 environment interns:* responsibilities include varied duties related to environmental issues. Candidates should have analytical skills, knowledge of field, office skills, oral communication skills, self-motivation, written communication skills, major in any field related to environment. Duration is 10–15 weeks. Guaranteed minimum financial assistance of $1000 applied toward housing. Open to college juniors, college seniors, graduate students. ▶ *10–25 federal government interns:* responsibilities include working for federal government agencies, such as Commerce, Interior, and EPA on various projects and initiatives. Candidates should have computer skills, oral communication skills, organizational skills, research skills, written communication skills. Duration is 10–15 weeks. Position available as unpaid or at $4500–$6000 per semester. Open to college juniors, college seniors. ▶ *500 main program interns:* responsibilities include working in American studies, arts management, business, communications, computer science, consumer advocacy, environment, government affairs, health and science, international relations/studies, labor relations/studies, law, politics/public policy, public administration, social work, urban studies, or women's studies. Candidates should have analytical skills, office skills, oral communication skills, organizational skills, self-motivation, written communication skills. Duration is 10–15 weeks. Position available as unpaid or at $1000–$6000 per semester depending on placement. Open to college juniors, college seniors, recent college graduates, graduate students, law students. ▶ *50–75 mass communications interns:* responsibilities include working in journalism, public relations, public affairs, or advertising. Candidates should have college courses in field, knowledge of field, oral communication skills, plan to pursue career in field, self-motivation, written communication skills. Duration is 10–15 weeks. Guaranteed financial assistance of $1000 minimum applied toward housing. Open to college juniors, college seniors, graduate students. ▶ *50–75 nonprofit leaders interns:* responsibilities include working for a nonprofit organization, such as an advocacy group, or trade or professional associations. Candidates should have ability to work with others, analytical skills, office skills, oral communication skills, self-motivation, written communication skills. Duration is 10–15 weeks. Guaranteed financial assistance of $1000 minimum applied toward housing. Open to college juniors, college seniors, graduate students. ▶ *50 study abroad in DC interns:* responsibilities include varied duties with an international component possibly involving the use of foreign language and cultural skills. Candidates should have office skills, oral communication skills, organizational skills, self-motivation, written communication skills. Duration is 10–15 weeks. Position available as unpaid or paid. Open to college juniors, college seniors, graduate students. ▶ *50–75 women leaders interns:* responsibilities include varied duties related to public policy. Candidates should have ability to work independently, ability to work with others, analytical skills, office skills, oral communication skills, self-motivation, written communication skills. Duration is 10–15 weeks. Guaranteed financial assistance of $1000 (minimum) applied toward housing. Open to college juniors, college seniors, graduate students. International applications accepted.

Benefits Formal training, housing at a cost, names of contacts, opportunity to attend seminars/workshops, possible full-time employment, willing to act as a professional reference, willing to complete paperwork for educational credit, willing to provide letters of recommendation, financial aid available in certain fields.

Contact Write, call, fax, e-mail, or through World Wide Web site Dr. Eugene J. Alpert, Senior Vice President, 2301 M Street NW, Fifth Floor, Washington, District of Columbia 20037-1427. Phone: 800-486-8921. Fax: 202-336-7609. E-mail: info@twc.edu. Applicants must submit a formal organization application, resume, academic transcripts, two letters of recommendation, short essay on topic related to internship request area. Application deadline: March 15 for summer, June 15 for fall, November 15 for spring. Fees: $60. World Wide Web: http://www.twc.edu.

Y.E.S. TO JOBS
PO Box 3390
Los Angeles, California 90078

General Information Program designed to introduce minority high school students to career opportunities behind the scenes in the entertainment industry. Established in 1987. Number of employees: 3. Number of internship applications received each year: 800.

Internships Available ▶ *150–250 interns:* responsibilities include various duties as entry-level assistants working in the entertainment industry. Candidates should have computer skills, oral communication skills, personal interest in the field, self-motivation, strong interpersonal skills, written communication skills. Duration is 10 weeks. Paid. Open to high school students, individuals 16-18 years old.

Benefits Formal training, job counseling, names of contacts, on-the-job training, opportunity to attend seminars/workshops, willing to complete paperwork for educational credit, willing to provide letters of recommendation.

Contact Write, e-mail, or through World Wide Web site Marsha Cole, Program Coordinator. E-mail: yestojobs@aol.com. No phone calls. In-person interview required. Applicants must submit a formal organization application, letter of interest, resume, academic transcripts, letter of recommendation. Application deadline: April 1 for summer. World Wide Web: http://www.yestojobs.org.

YMCA TRAINING ALLIANCE
11 East Adams Street, Suite 300
Chicago, Illinois 60603

General Information Nonprofit organization that helps individuals achieve economic and career advancement by providing opportunities to enhance skills and self-esteem through job training and placement, literacy education, and referral services; also works with coalitions on issues relating to economic advancement and community development. Established in 1976. Number of employees: 40. Unit of YMCA of Metropolitan Chicago, Chicago, Illinois. Number of internship applications received each year: 12.

Internships Available ▶ *2 IT support interns:* responsibilities include assisting staff with desktop problems, providing technical support to instructors with new applications, developing program to provide legacy equipment for trainee graduates. Candidates should have ability to work independently, ability to work with others, experience in the field, office skills, oral communication skills, organizational skills, personal interest in the field, knowledge of common office applications and network software. Duration is flexible (minimum 8 weeks). Unpaid. Open to college juniors, college seniors, recent college graduates, technical school seniors. ▶ *1–2 employment interns:* responsibilities include assisting individuals in making career decisions and overcoming barriers to employment. Candidates should have computer skills, oral communication skills, organizational skills, self-motivation, strong interpersonal skills, strong leadership ability. Duration is flexible. Unpaid. Open to college sophomores, college juniors, college seniors, recent college graduates, graduate students, career changers. ▶ *1 fund-raising administration intern:* responsibilities include assisting in researching/writing grant proposals. Candidates should have ability to work independently, computer skills, editing skills, research skills, self-motivation, writing skills. Duration is flexible. Unpaid. Open to college juniors, college seniors, recent college graduates, graduate students, career changers. ▶ *1 literacy volunteer coordinator:* responsibilities include assisting with recruitment, referral to training and placement, and scheduling of students with literacy volunteers. Candidates should have ability to work with others, office skills, oral communication skills, organizational skills, self-motivation, written communication skills. Duration is flexible. Unpaid. Open to college seniors, recent college graduates, graduate students, career changers. ▶ *1 research and development intern:* responsibilities include gathering data and participating in preparing reports to study the effects of training

and pre-employment activities on the economic self-sufficiency of low-income individuals. Candidates should have ability to work independently, ability to work with others, analytical skills, computer skills, editing skills, organizational skills, research skills, writing skills. Duration is flexible. Unpaid. Open to college juniors, college seniors, recent college graduates, graduate students, law students, career changers. ▶ *1 technology intern for rollouts:* responsibilities include assisting in planning rollout of w2k desktop software in mixed environment, test applications, troubleshooting connectivity problems, documentation, and training staff. Candidates should have ability to work independently, ability to work with others, analytical skills, computer skills, knowledge of field, oral communication skills, organizational skills, personal interest in the field, some familiarity with Windows 2000 Server and Active Directory. Duration is 3 months. Unpaid. Open to college juniors, college seniors, recent college graduates, technical college seniors and graduates. ▶ *1 working knowledge intern:* responsibilities include tutoring, helping with curriculum development, and publishing a student-written journal. Candidates should have ability to work with others, computer skills, oral communication skills, personal interest in the field, self-motivation, written communication skills. Duration is flexible. Unpaid. Open to college juniors, college seniors, recent college graduates, career changers. International applications accepted.

Benefits Job counseling, possible full-time employment, travel reimbursement, willing to complete paperwork for educational credit, willing to provide letters of recommendation.

Contact Write, call, or fax Mr. Syd Lines, Technology and Volunteer Resources Manager. Phone: 312-913-2150 Ext. 25. Fax: 312-913-2157. In-person interview recommended (telephone interview accepted). Applicants must submit a letter of interest, resume. Applications are accepted continuously.

ZIP HOLDINGS, INC.
507 Capitol Court, NE, Suite 300
Washington, District of Columbia 20002

General Information Human resources consulting/staffing company. Established in 2000. Number of employees: 15. Number of internship applications received each year: 40.

Internships Available ▶ *Up to 5 business development interns:* responsibilities include assisting in developing a marketing plan, calling clients and following up on calls, coordinating and attending networking events, and coordinating with human resources administrator. Candidates should have ability to work independently, ability to work with others, knowledge of field, office skills, oral communication skills, organizational skills, personal interest in the field, self-motivation, strong leadership ability. Duration is 1 semester. Position available as unpaid or at stipend awarded at end of semester. ▶ *1–2 financial interns:* responsibilities include assisting in administering all accounting functions, maintaining ledgers, paperwork, and research as needed. Candidates should have ability to work independently, ability to work with others, analytical skills, college courses in field, computer skills, knowledge of field, office skills, organizational skills, research skills, self-motivation, Microsoft Excel. Duration is 1 semester. Position available as unpaid or at Stipend awarded at end of semester. Open to college juniors, college seniors. International applications accepted.

Benefits Names of contacts, on-the-job training, opportunity to attend seminars/workshops, possible full-time employment, willing to act as a professional reference, willing to complete paperwork for educational credit, willing to provide letters of recommendation, opportunity to attend networking events.

Contact Write Claudine Hawthorne, Internship Coordinator. No phone calls. In-person interview recommended (telephone interview accepted). Applicants must submit a formal organization application, letter of interest, resume, academic transcripts, two personal references, one to two writing samples. Application deadline: April 30 for summer, July 30 for fall, November 15 for spring. World Wide Web: http://www.tempzone.com.

ARTS, ENTERTAINMENT, AND RECREATION

GENERAL

ABRAMS ARTIST AGENCY
9200 Sunset Boulevard, 11th Floor
Los Angeles, California 90069

General Information Talent agency. Established in 1986. Number of employees: 43. Number of internship applications received each year: 150.
Internships Available ▶ *Interns:* responsibilities include assisting agents and staff in all aspects of operations in order to learn how a talent agency works; screening calls; pulling submissions; script coverage; contact with all departments: MP/TV, Commercial, Voice Over, Hosting, and Business Affairs. Candidates should have ability to work independently, ability to work with others, oral communication skills, self-motivation, written communication skills. Duration is flexible. Unpaid. Open to high school seniors, recent high school graduates, college freshmen, college sophomores, college juniors, college seniors, recent college graduates, graduate students, law students, career changers, individuals reentering the workforce. International applications accepted.
Benefits Willing to complete paperwork for educational credit.
Contact Write or fax Internship Coordinator, 9200 Sunset Boulevard, Eleventh Floor, Los Angeles 90069. Fax: 310-276-6193. No phone calls. In-person interview required. Applicants must submit a letter of interest, resume. Applications are accepted continuously.

ABRAMS ARTIST AGENCY
275 7th Avenue, 26th Floor
New York, New York 10001

General Information Talent agency. Established in 1977. Number of employees: 39. Number of internship applications received each year: 20.
Internships Available ▶ *5 assistant agents.* Candidates should have ability to work with others, office skills, oral communication skills, organizational skills, personal interest in the field, writing skills. Duration is flexible. Unpaid. Open to college freshmen, college sophomores, college juniors, college seniors, graduate students, law students. International applications accepted.
Benefits Possible full-time employment, willing to complete paperwork for educational credit, willing to provide letters of recommendation, opportunity to attend NY theater, $10 per day travel reimbursement.
Contact Write, fax, or e-mail Mary Guzowski, Agent Assistant. Fax: 646-486-0100. E-mail: mary.guzowski@abramsart.com. No phone calls. In-person interview required. Applicants must submit a letter of interest, resume. Applications are accepted continuously.

ALL STARS PROJECT, INC./CASTILLO THEATRE
500 Greenwich Street, #201
New York, New York 10013

General Information Independent multicultural arts center housing off-off-Broadway Castillo Theatre, a laboratory for developmental theater and extensive inner-city youth programs. Established in 1983. Number of employees: 25. Number of internship applications received each year: 75.

Internships Available ▶ *4–6 All Stars Project/nonprofit management interns:* responsibilities include assisting in cultivation, research, volunteer program management, marketing, special events, and fund-raising. Candidates should have ability to work independently, ability to work with others, computer skills, office skills, oral communication skills, personal interest in the field, plan to pursue career in field, self-motivation. Duration is minimum 3 months (preferred); one weeknight or daytime weekend shift per week. Unpaid. Open to college freshmen, college sophomores, college juniors, college seniors, recent college graduates, graduate students, law students, career changers, individuals reentering the workforce. ▶ *2–4 All Stars Project/public relations interns:* responsibilities include working with skilled, public relations director promoting off-off-Broadway theater and nonprofit development programs for inner-city youth; hands-on experience dealing with major media outlets in the largest media market in the U.S. Candidates should have ability to work independently, computer skills, office skills, oral communication skills, personal interest in the field, strong interpersonal skills, English language skills required. Duration is minimum 3 months (preferred) including weekday hours. Unpaid. Open to college freshmen, college sophomores, college juniors, college seniors, recent college graduates, graduate students, career changers, individuals reentering the workforce. ▶ *3–6 theater costume design/construction and wardrobe interns:* responsibilities include working with resident designer at the Castillo Theatre; costume construction, makeup, wardrobe; qualified interns may participate in design; house staff shift part of internship requirement. Candidates should have ability to work independently, ability to work with others, oral communication skills, personal interest in the field, self-motivation. Duration is minimum 3 months; evenings and weekends preferred. Unpaid. Open to college freshmen, college sophomores, college juniors, college seniors, recent college graduates, graduate students, career changers, individuals reentering the workforce. ▶ *3–6 theater lighting design interns:* responsibilities include working with resident designer to produce lighting for Castillo Theatre; electrics; qualified interns may assist in design; weekly house staff shift part of internship requirement. Candidates should have ability to work independently, ability to work with others, knowledge of field, oral communication skills, personal interest in the field, self-motivation. Duration is minimum 3 months (preferred) evenings and weekends only. Unpaid. Open to recent high school graduates, college freshmen, college sophomores, college juniors, college seniors, recent college graduates, graduate students, career changers, individuals reentering the workforce. ▶ *3–6 theater management/theater assistant interns:* responsibilities include working with managing director of growing off-off-Broadway theater; hands-on experience in theatrical and event production, scheduling, budget management, staff development, and audience building. Candidates should have ability to work independently, ability to work with others, computer skills, office skills, organizational skills, personal interest in the field, self-motivation. Duration is minimum 3 months (preferred); flexible am/pm hours. Unpaid. Open to recent high school graduates, college freshmen, college sophomores, college juniors, college seniors, recent college graduates, graduate students, law students, career changers, individuals reentering the workforce. ▶ *4–8 theater production assistants/stage hands:* responsibilities include assisting producers and stage managers at the Castillo Theatre; attendance at rehearsals required. Candidates should have ability to work independently, ability to work with others, oral communication skills, organizational skills, personal interest in the field. Duration is minimum 3 months (preferred); evenings and some weekends. Unpaid. Open to college freshmen, college sophomores, college juniors, college seniors, recent college graduates, graduate students, career changers, individuals reentering the workforce. ▶ *2–4 theater set construction and scenic painting interns:* responsibilities include working with resident designer to produce sets for Castillo Theatre productions: research, construction, scenic painting; qualified interns may assist in design; weekly house staff shift part of internship requirement. Candidates should have ability to work independently, ability to work with others, knowledge of field, oral communication skills, personal interest in the field, self-motivation, theater experience preferred. Duration is minimum 3 months (preferred); flexible hours including evenings. Unpaid. Open to recent high school graduates, college freshmen, college sophomores, college juniors, college seniors, recent college graduates, career changers, individuals reentering the workforce. ▶ *2–4 theater sound design interns:* responsibilities include working with resident designer at Castillo Theatre; research, sound engineering; weekly house staff shift part of internship requirement. Candidates should have ability to work independently, ability to work with others, oral communication skills, personal interest in the field, self-motivation. Duration is minimum 3 months (preferred); flexible hours evenings and weekends. Unpaid. Open to college freshmen, college sophomores, college juniors, college seniors, recent college graduates, graduate students, career changers, individuals reentering the workforce. International applications accepted.

Benefits Formal training, names of contacts, on-the-job training, opportunity to attend seminars/workshops, willing to act as a professional reference, willing to complete paperwork for educational credit, willing to provide letters of recommendation, credit available for most positions.

Contact Write, call, fax, e-mail, or through World Wide Web site Gail Elberg, Director, Volunteer and Intern Programs, 500 Greenwich Street, #201, New York, New York 10013. Phone: 212-941-9400. Fax: 212-941-8340. E-mail: gailelberg@aol.com. In-person interview recommended (telephone interview accepted). Applicants must submit a letter of interest, resume. Applications are accepted continuously. World Wide Web: http://www.allstars.org.

AMELIA WELLNESS CENTER
869 Sadler Road, Suite 5
Fernandina Beach, Florida 32034

General Information Health and fitness club. Established in 1987. Number of employees: 25. Subsidiary of Amelia Island Plantation, Amelia Island, Florida. Number of internship applications received each year: 75.

Internships Available ▶ *1–2 interns:* responsibilities include acting as manager-on-duty, group fitness leader, and customer service representative; fitness assessment, exercise prescription, promotion, advertising and selling fitness programs offered by club. Candidates should have computer skills, oral communication skills, organizational skills, plan to pursue career in field, self-motivation, strong interpersonal skills, strong leadership ability, writing skills. Duration is generally 3 to 4 months, but will accommodate to meet semester requirements. $300–$600 per month. Open to college seniors, recent college graduates, graduate students. International applications accepted.

Benefits Formal training, job counseling, names of contacts, on-the-job training, opportunity to attend seminars/workshops, possible full-time employment, willing to act as a professional reference, willing to complete paperwork for educational credit, willing to provide letters of recommendation.

Contact Write, call, fax, e-mail, or through World Wide Web site Krissy Michaels, Intern Coordinator, 869 Sadler Road, Suite 5, Fernandina Beach, Florida 32034. Phone: 904-261-0557. Fax: 904-261-5671. E-mail: awc@net-magic.net. Telephone interview required. Applicants must submit a letter of interest, resume, three personal references. Application deadline: April 1 for summer, December 1 for spring. World Wide Web: http://www.ameliawellness.nu.

APERTURE FOUNDATION
20 East 23rd Street
New York, New York 10010-4463

General Information Not-for-profit organization devoted to the promotion of photography as a unique form of expression through publication, exhibition, and educational programs. Established in 1952. Number of employees: 30. Number of internship applications received each year: 500.

Internships Available ▶ *2 Paul Strand archive interns:* responsibilities include maintaining ongoing file of Strand material in print and other related material; organizing, cataloging and preserving Aperture collection of artwork and photographs; inventorying and organizing book library; exhibition preparation work (Burden Gallery and Traveling Exhibitions); administration of copyright and permissions for use of photographs by Paul Strand; assembly, distribution, and recordkeeping of limited editions and portfolios; darkroom and on-camera copy work. Candidates should have ability to work independently, ability to work with others, office skills, organizational skills, personal interest in the field, research skills. Duration is minimum of 6 months. $250 per month. Open to college seniors, recent college graduates, graduate students. ▶ *2 design interns:* responsibilities include preparing files for color output, creating mechanicals, sizing art, scanning and placing photographs, conceptual design on selected projects, and general office support. Candidates should have ability to work independently, computer skills, experience in the field, office skills, personal interest in the field, strong interpersonal skills. Duration is minimum of 6 months. $250 per month. Open to college seniors, recent college graduates, graduate students. ▶ *2 development interns:* responsibilities include compilation of proposal packets (research, writing, and editing), updating donor listings, assisting with the annual appeal, assisting with board and donor relations, assisting with special events, maintaining the development database, assisting with the coordination of Work-Scholar Program. Candidates should have oral communication skills, organizational skills, personal interest in the field, research skills, strong interpersonal skills, writing skills. Duration is minimum of 6 months. $250 per month. Open to college seniors, recent college graduates, graduate students. ▶ *2 director's office interns:* responsibilities include acting as liaison between Director's office and other departments; locating and requesting review copies of books, periodicals, and videos; maintaining the library; maintaining a database; and assisting with the preparation of important meetings. Candidates should have ability to work independently, office skills, oral communication skills, organizational skills, strong interpersonal skills, writing skills. Duration is minimum of 6 months. $250 per month. Open to college seniors, recent college graduates, graduate students. ▶ *4 editorial interns:* responsibilities include researching pictures and texts, reviewing manuscripts and portfolios, contacting outside sources to request artwork for reproduction, proofreading, compiling copy for catalogues and book jackets, some darkroom work, some development and publicity support, and registering copyrights. Candidates should have ability to work independently, editing skills, experience in the field, organizational skills, strong interpersonal skills, writing skills. Duration is minimum of 6 months. $250 per month. Open to college seniors, recent college graduates, graduate students. ▶ *2 foreign rights interns:* responsibilities include interfacing with foreign distributors and publishers, assisting with contracts and licensing agreements, arranging coeditions of Aperture books with publishers worldwide, identifying new publishing partners, preparing for the Frankfurt Book Fair, organizing pricing of books for potential foreign copublications. Candidates should have ability to work independently, computer skills, office skills, organizational skills, personal interest in the field, writing skills. Duration is minimum of 6 months. $250 per month. Open to college seniors, recent college graduates, graduate students. ▶ *2 image resource interns:* responsibilities include gathering information for licensing program, maintaining research library, assisting in creation of photographer lists and mailing information packets, and general support as needed. Candidates should have computer skills, personal interest in the field, research skills, knowledge of contemporary photography, attention to details. Duration is minimum of 6 months. $250 per month. Open to college seniors,

recent college graduates, graduate students. ▶ *2 information technology/systems interns:* responsibilities include assisting with client server and variety of other applications; assisting staff with daily computing functions as needed. Candidates should have interest in pursuing degree in information systems/technology, experience with Microsoft systems (preferred). Duration is minimum of 6 months. $250 per month. Open to college seniors, recent college graduates, graduate students. ▶ *2 marketing and circulation interns:* responsibilities include preparing sales materials, updating and mailing media kits, maintaining contact with distributors and sales representatives, creating and placing advertisements, selling ad space, maintaining the database, and producing direct mail. Candidates should have ability to work independently, computer skills, office skills, organizational skills, personal interest in the field, writing skills. Duration is minimum of 6 months. $250 per month. Open to college seniors, recent college graduates, graduate students. ▶ *2 production interns:* responsibilities include acting as liaison with outside companies, checking quotes and mechanicals, writing purchase orders, organizing and packaging original materials for transport, assisting with color corrections and some designing, and organizing information for invoicing, distribution, and billing. Candidates should have knowledge of field, office skills, organizational skills, plan to pursue career in field, strong interpersonal skills. Duration is minimum of 6 months. $250 per month. Open to college seniors, recent college graduates, graduate students. ▶ *2 publicity interns:* responsibilities include maintaining publicity books, assisting in the preparation of materials, creating first draft press releases, circulating reviews to sales representatives, updating files and mailing lists, research, assisting in promotion projects, and permissions. Candidates should have ability to work independently, office skills, organizational skills, personal interest in the field, strong interpersonal skills, writing skills. Duration is minimum of 6 months. $250 per month. Open to college seniors, recent college graduates, graduate students, law students. ▶ *2 traveling exhibition/gallery interns:* responsibilities include maintaining files on correspondence and venues contacted, researching potential venues, keeping the mailing list of potential venues up to date, assisting in the creation of exhibition kits, and mailing the kits to potential venues, coordinating exhibitions, maintaining the museum/gallery database, assisting with Burden Gallery openings and other gallery activities. Candidates should have ability to work independently, oral communication skills, organizational skills, personal interest in the field, research skills, strong interpersonal skills, writing skills. Duration is minimum of 6 months. $250 per month. Open to college seniors, recent college graduates, graduate students. International applications accepted.
Benefits On-the-job training, possible full-time employment, willing to act as a professional reference, willing to complete paperwork for educational credit, willing to provide letters of recommendation, limited edition print upon completion of internship.
Contact Write, call, fax, or e-mail Maria Decsey, Work-Scholar Coordinator. Phone: 212-505-5555 Ext. 336. Fax: 212-475-8790. E-mail: mdecsey@aperture.org. In-person interview recommended (telephone interview accepted). Applicants must submit a letter of interest, resume, two writing samples. Applications are accepted continuously. World Wide Web: http://www.aperture.org.

ARTISTS SPACE
38 Greene Street, 3rd Floor
New York, New York 10013

General Information Nonprofit organization that supports emerging artists in the visual arts, including video, performance, architecture, and design. Established in 1973. Number of employees: 7. Number of internship applications received each year: 150.
Internships Available ▶ *1 artists file intern:* responsibilities include assisting artist file coordinator through updating database of artists, conducting appointments in the file, troubleshooting with the database, and possible Web site assistance if applicable. Candidates should have computer skills, personal interest in the field, self-motivation, strong interpersonal skills, strong art

background and Macintosh skills. Duration is flexible. Unpaid.
▶ *1 curatorial intern:* responsibilities include working closely with curator and artists, reviewing artists' work, and assisting with events and exhibitions. Candidates should have ability to work independently, computer skills, personal interest in the field, self-motivation, strong art background. Duration is flexible. Unpaid.
▶ *Operations interns:* responsibilities include assisting with day-to-day operations of the gallery, working with intern coordinator, participating in special projects, and dealing with past and present exhibitions. Candidates should have ability to work independently, computer skills, organizational skills, personal interest in the field, self-motivation, strong interpersonal skills. Duration is flexible. Unpaid. Open to college freshmen, college sophomores, college juniors, college seniors, recent college graduates, graduate students. International applications accepted.
Benefits Job counseling, on-the-job training, willing to act as a professional reference, willing to complete paperwork for educational credit, willing to provide letters of recommendation, possibility of exhibiting samples of work, access to many NYC galleries and museums.
Contact Write, call, fax, e-mail, or through World Wide Web site Ms. Liz Campbell, Coordinator. Phone: 212-226-3970. Fax: 212-966-1434. E-mail: artspace@artistsspace.org. In-person interview recommended (telephone interview accepted). Applicants must submit a formal organization application, letter of interest, resume, two personal references. Applications are accepted continuously. World Wide Web: http://www.artistsspace.org.

ARTNET.COM
61 Broadway, 23rd Floor
New York, New York 10006-2701

General Information Company specializing in the buying, selling, and researching of fine art online; Online Gallery Network is largest of it's kind with over 1,300 galleries, 36,000 works, and 13,000 artists from around the globe.
Internships Available ▶ *Online Gallery Netwok interns (production):* responsibilities include involvement in creation and maintenance of individual gallery Web sites and artist information within online network and general administrative duties associated with network. Candidates should have familiarity with Adobe PhotoShop (recommended); attention to detail, dedication to accuracy required; basic HTML knowledge helpful but not required. Unpaid.
▶ *Online Gallery Network sales interns:* responsibilities include coordinating art fairs, updating gallery/artist databases, preparing media kits, and general administrative duties. Candidates should have computer skills, oral communication skills, organizational skills, personal interest in the field, written communication skills, foreign language speaking ability (a plus). Unpaid.
Benefits $10 daily stipend to cover expenses.
Contact E-mail Internship Coordinator. Phone: 212-497-9700. Fax: 212-497-5007. E-mail: cruch@artnet.com. Word-formatted resume and brief cover letter. Applications are accepted continuously. World Wide Web: http://www.artnet.com.

ARTS AND ENTERTAINMENT TASK FORCE OF STREAMING MEDIA ALLIANCE
55 Perry Street, #1M
New York, New York 10014

General Information Trade organization that assists Alliance members doing business with Hollywood, Broadway, and the performing arts at large. Established in 2000. Number of employees: 3. Number of internship applications received each year: 70.
Internships Available ▶ *1–2 assistants to chairman:* responsibilities include research in streaming media, maintaining membership records, organizing events, taking minutes at meetings, updating Web site. Candidates should have computer skills, office skills, oral communication skills, personal interest in the field, strong interpersonal skills, writing skills. Duration is 1–2 semesters. Unpaid. Open to college juniors, college seniors, law students.
Benefits Opportunity to attend seminars/workshops, willing to act as a professional reference, willing to complete paperwork for educational credit, willing to provide letters of recommendation.

Contact E-mail Internship Coordinator. E-mail: metro@nytheatrewire.com. No phone calls. Applicants must submit a letter of interest, resume. Applications are accepted continuously.

ASIAN AMERICAN ARTS CENTRE
26 Bowery, 3rd Floor
New York, New York 10013

General Information Multipurpose facility that offers ongoing visual arts exhibitions of contemporary Asian-Americans as well as one folk exhibit a year. Established in 1974. Number of employees: 4. Number of internship applications received each year: 5.

Internships Available ▶ *1 curatorial intern:* responsibilities include working closely with the director, researching and organizing exhibits. Candidates should have college courses in field, editing skills, knowledge of field, oral communication skills, personal interest in the field, strong interpersonal skills, written communication skills. Duration is 3 months. Unpaid. Open to college freshmen, college sophomores, college juniors, college seniors, recent college graduates, graduate students. ▶ *1 development assistant:* responsibilities include researching funding resources, writing grant proposals, and assisting in preparing grants. Candidates should have editing skills, research skills, strong interpersonal skills, strong leadership ability, writing skills. Duration is 3 months. Unpaid. Open to college freshmen, college sophomores, college juniors, college seniors, recent college graduates, graduate students. ▶ *1 gallery assistant:* responsibilities include various tasks depending on intern's abilities and interests. Candidates should have computer skills, knowledge of field, organizational skills, personal interest in the field, strong interpersonal skills, writing skills. Duration is 3 months. Unpaid. Open to college freshmen, college sophomores, college juniors, college seniors, recent college graduates, graduate students. ▶ *1–2 research assistants:* responsibilities include examining and archiving materials. Candidates should have computer skills, knowledge of field, oral communication skills, research skills, self-motivation, strong interpersonal skills, writing skills. Duration is 3 months. Unpaid. International applications accepted.

Benefits On-the-job training, willing to complete paperwork for educational credit, willing to provide letters of recommendation, general training, opportunity to learn working processes in all areas of exhibition and art administration and development.

Contact Write or e-mail Mr. Robert Lee, Director. E-mail: aaartsctr@aol.com. In-person interview required. Applicants must submit a resume, letter of interest, specifying which position desired, one-page writing sample. Applications are accepted continuously. World Wide Web: http://www.artspiral.org.

BARBARA STRASEN
1724 South Pacific Avenue
San Pedro, California 90731

General Information Freelance visual artist who makes paintings (often combined with photography, mixed media, and installations) for exhibit and sale to galleries and museums nationally and internationally. Number of employees: 2. Number of internship applications received each year: 10.

Internships Available ▶ *1–3 studio assistants/interns:* responsibilities include painting under tutelage, canvas building, preparation imagery research, literary research, professional correspondence, framing and presenting artwork, and manufacturing 2-D and 3-D components of artwork. Candidates should have ability to work independently, ability to work with others, college courses in field, oral communication skills, personal interest in the field, research skills, self-motivation. Duration is flexible. Unpaid. Open to college seniors, recent college graduates, graduate students, career changers. International applications accepted.

Benefits Formal training, job counseling, names of contacts, on-the-job training, willing to act as a professional reference, willing to complete paperwork for educational credit, willing to provide letters of recommendation, use of research facilities.

Contact Write or e-mail Ms. Barbara Strasen, Artist. E-mail: bstrasen@earthlink.net. No phone calls. In-person interview recom-

mended (telephone interview accepted). Applicants must submit a letter of interest, resume, three letters of recommendation. Applications are accepted continuously.

BETSEY JOHNSON
498 Seventh Avenue, 21st Floor
New York, New York 10018

General Information Fashion designer showroom. Established in 1978. Number of employees: 50. Number of internship applications received each year: 100.

Internships Available ▶ *3–4 design interns:* responsibilities include assisting design team with fabric resourcing, arts and crafts, and running errands. Candidates should have ability to work independently, ability to work with others, knowledge of field, personal interest in the field. Duration is flexible. Unpaid. ▶ *4–5 sales interns:* responsibilities include assisting sales executives and customer relations, compiling sketch and swatch booklets, typing line sheets and letters, filing, and running errands. Candidates should have ability to work independently, ability to work with others, office skills, organizational skills, self-motivation, written communication skills. Duration is flexible. Unpaid. Open to recent high school graduates, college freshmen, college sophomores, college juniors, college seniors, recent college graduates, graduate students. International applications accepted.

Benefits Possible full-time employment, willing to complete paperwork for educational credit, willing to provide letters of recommendation.

Contact Write, call, or fax Jesika Homeijer, Sales. Phone: 212-244-0843. Fax: 212-244-0855. In-person interview required. Applicants must submit a letter of interest, resume. Applications are accepted continuously. World Wide Web: http://www.betseyjohnson.com.

BLAZING ADVENTURES
Box 5068, 48 Upper Village Mall
Snowmass Village, Colorado 81615

General Information Organization providing outdoor adventure tours. Established in 1969. Number of employees: 100. Number of internship applications received each year: 12.

Internships Available ▶ *1–2 group services interns:* responsibilities include working with conference coordinators to develop and manage active adventures and tour programs. Candidates should have ability to work independently, ability to work with others, computer skills, oral communication skills, organizational skills, personal interest in the field, self-motivation, strong leadership ability, written communication skills. Duration is May 15–August 31 (minimum 12 weeks). $150 per week plus 2% sales commission. ▶ *4–5 main office summer interns:* responsibilities include assisting guests with reservations in a knowledgeable and professional manner, resolving customer service issues and any operational problems, and utilizing the telephones and computers extensively to perform these responsibilities (all under the supervision of the office manager). Candidates should have ability to work independently, computer skills, office skills, oral communication skills, organizational skills, self-motivation. Duration is May 15-August 31. $150 per week plus 2% sales commission. ▶ *3–5 outdoor recreation guides:* responsibilities include training for a specific department and utilizing gained knowledge while providing professional service to guests. Candidates should have ability to work independently, ability to work with others, oral communication skills, personal interest in the field, self-motivation, strong leadership ability. Duration is May 5–August 31. Paid. Open to college freshmen, college sophomores, college juniors, college seniors, recent college graduates, graduate students, law students, career changers, individuals reentering the workforce.

Benefits Formal training, housing at a cost, job counseling, on-the-job training, possible full-time employment, willing to act as a professional reference, willing to complete paperwork for educational credit, willing to provide letters of recommendation.

Contact Write, call, fax, e-mail, or through World Wide Web site Laurie Harris, Manager. Phone: 970-923-4544. Fax: 970-923-4994. E-mail: blazing@rof.net. Telephone interview required. Applicants must submit a formal organization application, resume, personal reference, letter of recommendation. Application deadline: May

Blazing Adventures (continued)
1 for priority deadline; however, applications are accepted on a continuous basis. World Wide Web: http://www.blazingadventures. com.

BLOOMINGTON PARKS AND RECREATION
109 East Olivo
Bloomington, Illinois 61704

General Information Parks and recreation program providing recreation for individuals of all ages plus open space for passive involvement. Established in 1968. Number of employees: 250. Unit of City of Bloomington, Bloomington, Illinois. Number of internship applications received each year: 10.
Internships Available ▶ *1 marketing intern:* responsibilities include marketing recreation programs; working with local newspaper, radio, and cable TV. Candidates should have ability to work with others, oral communication skills, self-motivation, written communication skills. Duration is semester-basis/fitting requirements of school granting credit for internship. Position available as unpaid or paid. ▶ *2 recreation leaders:* responsibilities include planning, implementing and evaluating recreation programs; learning about marketing, budgeting, staffing and more. Candidates should have ability to work with others, experience in the field, oral communication skills, self-motivation, strong leadership ability. Duration is semester-basis/fitting requirements of school granting credit for internships. $80 per week. Open to college seniors, graduate students. International applications accepted.
Benefits On-the-job training, opportunity to attend seminars/workshops, possible full-time employment, willing to act as a professional reference, willing to complete paperwork for educational credit, willing to provide letters of recommendation.
Contact Write, call, or e-mail Barb Wells, Superintendent of Recreation. Phone: 309-434-2260. Fax: 309-434-2483. E-mail: bwells@cityblm.org. In-person interview recommended (telephone interview accepted). Applicants must submit a formal organization application, letter of interest, resume. Applications are accepted continuously. World Wide Web: http://www.cityblm.org/parks.

BOSTON PHOTO COLLABORATIVE
67 Brookside Avenue
Jamaica Plain, Massachusetts 02130

General Information Nonprofit community photography organization that brings photography to people traditionally without access to the medium. Established in 1991. Number of employees: 5. Number of internship applications received each year: 30.
Internships Available ▶ *Interns:* responsibilities include positions available in fund-raising and special events, publicity, exhibits, program development, education, technology and web design, and computer mentoring; most likely, interns will work in several areas at once, rather than one area exclusively. Candidates should have ability to work independently, ability to work with others, editing skills, office skills, oral communication skills, organizational skills, personal interest in the field, research skills, self-motivation, writing skills, creative thinking and problem-solving abilities; Mac-based computer skills; word-processing, design, database, Internet. Duration is flexible; available throughout year, full- or part-time, days or evenings. Unpaid. Open to high school students, recent high school graduates, college freshmen, college sophomores, college juniors, college seniors, recent college graduates, graduate students, law students, career changers, individuals reentering the workforce. International applications accepted.
Benefits On-the-job training, opportunity to attend seminars/workshops, possible full-time employment, willing to act as a professional reference, willing to complete paperwork for educational credit, willing to provide letters of recommendation.
Contact Write, call, fax, or e-mail Alisa Dichter, Associate Director. Phone: 617-524-7729. Fax: 617-524-4357. E-mail: bosphoto@ channell.com. In-person interview recommended (telephone interview accepted). Applicants must submit a formal organization application, letter of interest, resume. Applications are accepted continuously. World Wide Web: http://www.bostonphoto. org.

BRICK WALL MANAGEMENT
648 Amsterdam Avenue, Suite 4A
New York, New York 10025

General Information Music artist management company. Established in 1996. Number of employees: 3. Number of internship applications received each year: 100.
Internships Available ▶ *1–3 general interns:* responsibilities include general office administration. Candidates should have ability to work independently, computer skills, office skills, oral communication skills, organizational skills, personal interest in the field, plan to pursue career in field, research skills, strong interpersonal skills, writing skills. Duration is 3–5 months. Unpaid. Open to college freshmen, college sophomores, college juniors, college seniors, recent college graduates, career changers. International applications accepted.
Benefits On-the-job training, willing to act as a professional reference, willing to complete paperwork for educational credit, willing to provide letters of recommendation.
Contact Write, call, fax, or e-mail Jason Pachter, Internship Coordinator. Phone: 212-501-0748. Fax: 212-724-0849. E-mail: jason@brickwallmgmt.com. In-person interview required. Applicants must submit a letter of interest, resume. Applications are accepted continuously. World Wide Web: http://www.brickwallmgmt.com.

BRISTOL-MYERS SQUIBB–CENTER FOR HEALTH AND FITNESS
1 Squibb Drive
New Brunswick, New Jersey 08903

General Information Corporate employee health and fitness center. Established in 1994. Number of employees: 2. Number of internship applications received each year: 6.
Internships Available ▶ *1–2 health and fitness interns:* responsibilities include working with participants to complete fitness assessments and exercise prescriptions, assisting in operation of facility and opening/closing routines. Candidates should have ability to work independently, college courses in field, computer skills, oral communication skills, personal interest in the field, self-motivation, strong interpersonal skills, CPR certification. Duration is 1 semester. Unpaid. Open to college freshmen, college sophomores, college juniors, college seniors, recent college graduates. International applications accepted.
Benefits Names of contacts, on-the-job training, possible full-time employment, willing to act as a professional reference, willing to complete paperwork for educational credit, willing to provide letters of recommendation.
Contact Write, call, or e-mail Sharon Combes-Kelemen, Supervisor of Health and Fitness, 1 Squibb Drive, New Brunswick, New Jersey 08903. Phone: 732-519-3900. Fax: 732-519-1727. E-mail: fitness.center@bms.com. In-person interview required. Applicants must submit a resume, academic transcripts. Applications are accepted continuously.

BRYNWOOD COUNTRY CLUB
6200 West Good Hope Road
Milwaukee, Wisconsin 53223

General Information Private country club with 18–hole golf course, tennis courts, swimming pool, banquet facility, fine dining room, and mens and ladies locker rooms. Established in 1928. Number of employees: 100. Number of internship applications received each year: 100.
Internships Available ▶ *1–3 interns:* responsibilities include working in facets of the club that need the most help for different time periods; primarily in food and beverage. Candidates should have ability to work independently, ability to work with others, oral communication skills, plan to pursue career in field, strong leadership ability, written communication skills. Duration is 3 to 6 months, one semester, one year, or 18 months. $7.50 per hour. Open to recent high school graduates, college freshmen, college sophomores, college juniors, college seniors, recent college graduates, graduate students, must be 18 or older. International applications accepted.

college freshmen, college sophomores, college juniors, college seniors, recent college graduates, graduate students, career changers. International applications accepted.
Benefits Formal training, free housing, job counseling, names of contacts, on-the-job training, willing to act as a professional reference, willing to complete paperwork for educational credit, willing to provide letters of recommendation.
Contact Write, call, or fax Ms. Karen Rosga, Chief of Interpretation, RR1, Box 60 AA, Custer, South Dakota 57730. Phone: 605-673-2288. Fax: 605-673-3294. Telephone interview required. Applicants must submit a formal organization application, letter of interest, resume, academic transcripts may be required; 2-3 personal references. Application deadline: March 25 for summer, July 25 for fall. World Wide Web: http://www.nps.gov/jeca.

THE JEWISH MUSEUM
1109 5th Avenue
New York, New York 10128

General Information Museum of Jewish interest and of art. Established in 1904. Unit of Jewish Theological Seminary of America, New York, New York. Number of internship applications received each year: 50.
Internships Available ▶ *1–5 interns:* responsibilities include clerical support to Museum department heads, including phone, light research, and some computer work (data entry, word processing). Candidates should have ability to work independently, ability to work with others, analytical skills, computer skills, knowledge of field, office skills, oral communication skills, organizational skills, personal interest in the field, research skills, writing skills. Duration is 8–20 weeks. Unpaid. Open to high school seniors, recent high school graduates, college freshmen, college sophomores, college juniors, college seniors, recent college graduates, graduate students, law students, career changers, individuals reentering the workforce. International applications accepted.
Benefits On-the-job training, opportunity to attend seminars/workshops, possible full-time employment, willing to act as a professional reference, willing to complete paperwork for educational credit, willing to provide letters of recommendation.
Contact Write, call, fax, or e-mail Patricia Gurevich, Internship Coordinator. Phone: 212-423-2308. Fax: 212-423-3232. E-mail: pgurevich@thejm.org. In-person interview required. Applicants must submit a formal organization application, letter of interest, resume. Applications are accepted continuously. World Wide Web: http://thejewishmuseum.org.

JOHN F. KENNEDY PRESIDENTIAL LIBRARY AND MUSEUM
Columbia Point
Boston, Massachusetts 02125

General Information Presidential library. Established in 1964. Number of employees: 55. Unit of National Archives and Records Administration, College Park, Maryland. Number of internship applications received each year: 60.
Internships Available ▶ *3–5 audiovisual archives interns:* responsibilities include assisting staff in cataloging historic films/video/audio tapes, and still photos; duties include copying, data entry, researching answers to questions from the public, assisting researchers with operation of audio/video/film equipment, identifying scenes in films, and simple preservation practices involving film, photos, and magnetic media. Candidates should have ability to work independently, ability to work with others, analytical skills, oral communication skills, research skills, self-motivation, written communication skills. Duration is flexible (minimum of 8 weeks). $10 per hour. Open to college freshmen, college sophomores, college juniors, college seniors, graduate students. ▶ *1–3 museum collections and exhibits interns:* responsibilities include assisting in collections processing, inventory and care of objects, group and independent projects, contributing to the documentation, preservation, and exhibition of the collection. Candidates should have ability to work independently, ability to work with others, oral communication skills, organizational skills, personal interest in the field, college courses in museum studies, history, or American studies. Duration is flexible (minimum of 10 weeks). $10 per hour.

Open to college juniors, college seniors, recent college graduates, graduate students, career changers, individuals reentering the workforce. ▶ *2–3 research room interns:* responsibilities include assisting research room archivist with handling reference queries from the public from phone, fax, e-mail, or in person; involves registering researchers, retrieving archival materials from stack areas, data entry, and answering telephones. Candidates should have ability to work independently, ability to work with others, office skills, oral communication skills, research skills, written communication skills. Duration is flexible (minimum of 8 weeks). $10 per hour. Open to college freshmen, college sophomores, college juniors, college seniors, graduate students. ▶ *5–7 textual archives interns:* responsibilities include assisting in the processing and cataloging of collections of historic papers; involves photocopying, data entry, some moderate lifting. Candidates should have ability to work independently, ability to work with others, analytical skills, research skills, self-motivation, written communication skills. Duration is flexible (minimum of 8 weeks). $10 per hour. Open to college freshmen, college sophomores, college juniors, college seniors, graduate students. International applications accepted.
Benefits Formal training, on-the-job training, opportunity to attend seminars/workshops, willing to complete paperwork for educational credit, willing to provide letters of recommendation.
Contact Write, call, fax, e-mail, or through World Wide Web site Intern Coordinator. Phone: 617-929-4534. Fax: 617-929-4538. E-mail: kennedy.library@nara.gov. In-person interview recommended (telephone interview accepted). Applicants must submit a formal organization application, letter of interest, resume, academic transcripts, letter of recommendation. Application deadline: February 28 for summer; continuous for other positions. World Wide Web: http://www.jfklibrary.org.

THE J. PAUL GETTY TRUST
1200 Getty Center Drive
Los Angeles, California 90049-1687

General Information Art museum of European art; research institute for the history of art and humanities; conservation institute; grant program. Established in 1953. Number of employees: 1,200. Number of internship applications received each year: 200.
Internships Available ▶ *20 Getty graduate interns:* responsibilities include working in one of the Getty programs. Candidates should have ability to work with others, college degree in related field, knowledge of field, plan to pursue career in field, research skills, writing skills. Duration is 8–12 months. $17,296 for 8 months; $25,000 for 12 months. Open to graduate students. International applications accepted.
Benefits Health insurance, on-the-job training, opportunity to attend seminars/workshops, willing to provide letters of recommendation, educational travel stipend of $1200.
Contact Write, call, e-mail, or through World Wide Web site Elliott Kai-Kee, Administrator, Graduate Intern Program, Education Department, 1200 Getty Center Drive, Los Angeles, California 90049-1687. Phone: 310-440-7222. E-mail: interns@getty.edu. In-person interview recommended (telephone interview accepted). Applicants must submit a formal organization application, letter of interest, academic transcripts, two letters of recommendation. Application deadline: early January. World Wide Web: http://www.getty.edu/about/opportunities/intern.html.

KANSAS STATE HISTORICAL SOCIETY
6425 Southwest Sixth Avenue
Topeka, Kansas 66615-1099

General Information Society that collects, preserves, and interprets Kansas history. Established in 1875. Number of employees: 140. Number of internship applications received each year: 10.
Internships Available ▶ *1 Lela Barnes intern:* responsibilities include managing archives and manuscript records. Candidates should have ability to work independently, computer skills, organizational skills, plan to pursue career in field, research skills, written communication skills. Duration is 10 weeks. $1800 per duration of internship. ▶ *3–5 interns:* responsibilities include working in the

Kansas State Historical Society (continued)

archaeology, archives, or education department, the historical preservation office, or the Kansas Museum of History. Candidates should have ability to work independently, ability to work with others, computer skills, oral communication skills, research skills, written communication skills. Duration is 6–10 weeks. Unpaid. Open to college juniors, college seniors, graduate students. International applications accepted.
Benefits Job counseling, names of contacts, possible full-time employment, willing to complete paperwork for educational credit, willing to provide letters of recommendation.
Contact Write, call, fax, e-mail, or through World Wide Web site Dr. David A. Haury, Associate Director. Phone: 785-272-8681 Ext. 209. Fax: 785-272-8682. E-mail: dhaury@kshs.org. In-person interview recommended (telephone interview accepted). Applicants must submit a formal organization application, letter of interest, resume, academic transcripts, letter of recommendation. Application deadline: April 15 for summer, June 15 for fall, November 15 for spring. World Wide Web: http://www.kshs.org.

KRESGE ART MUSEUM
Michigan State University
East Lansing, Michigan 48824

General Information Art museum that collects, preserves, exhibits, and interprets works of art of all periods. Established in 1959. Number of employees: 7. Unit of Michigan State University, East Lansing, Michigan. Number of internship applications received each year: 30.
Internships Available ▶ *1 museum intern:* responsibilities include learning all facets of museum work including exhibit development, grant writing, registration, and publicity. Candidates should have ability to work independently, ability to work with others, college degree in related field, computer skills, oral communication skills, written communication skills. Duration is 10 months. $13,000 per duration of internship. International applications accepted.
Benefits Health insurance, job counseling, names of contacts, opportunity to attend seminars/workshops, travel reimbursement, willing to provide letters of recommendation, inexpensive faculty housing.
Contact Write Ms. Carol Fisher, Education Coordinator. Telephone interview required. Applicants must submit a letter of interest, three personal references. Application deadline: March 15. World Wide Web: http://www.msu.edu/unit/kamuseum.

LASSEN VOLCANIC NATIONAL PARK
PO Box 100, 38050 Highway 36 East
Mineral, California 96063-0100

General Information National park with the mission of preserving and protecting the park's natural resources and providing for the continued enjoyment of the land. Established in 1916. Number of employees: 130. Number of internship applications received each year: 40.
Internships Available ▶ *1 cultural resources assistant:* responsibilities include assisting with museum cataloging and curatorial tasks of historical, archival, and botanical collections; assisting with cataloging and organizing photo, slide, and library collections. Candidates should have ability to work independently, ability to work with others, computer skills, knowledge of field, organizational skills, personal interest in the field, research skills, written communication skills. Duration is flexible. Unpaid. Open to recent high school graduates, college freshmen, college sophomores, college juniors, college seniors, recent college graduates, graduate students, career changers, individuals reentering the workforce. ▶ *1–3 resource management aides:* responsibilities include working either independently of or in direct support of resource management staff on defined field project work, computer database entry, and other projects. Candidates should have ability to work independently, ability to work with others, knowledge of field, personal interest in the field, self-motivation. Duration is 3 months in summer (June through August). Unpaid. Open to college juniors, college seniors, recent college graduates, graduate students, career changers. ▶ *1 sign mapping technician:* responsibilities include

updating park sign inventory, sign mapping, and photo editing. Candidates should have ability to work independently, computer skills, experience in the field, organizational skills, personal interest in the field, self-motivation. Duration is May 1 to October 1. Unpaid. Open to college juniors, college seniors, recent college graduates, graduate students, career changers. ▶ *1–4 spring and summer interpretive aides:* responsibilities include supporting junior ranger, living history, and field interpretive programs and helping in the visitor center. Candidates should have ability to work independently, oral communication skills, personal interest in the field, self-motivation, strong interpersonal skills, written communication skills. Duration is February or March through early June and June through August. Unpaid. Open to recent high school graduates, college freshmen, college sophomores, college juniors, college seniors, recent college graduates, graduate students, career changers, individuals reentering the workforce. ▶ *1–2 winter interpretive aides:* responsibilities include assisting with winter interpretive programs; working with slide, photo, and museum collections; and recording wildlife sightings. Candidates should have ability to work independently, oral communication skills, personal interest in the field, self-motivation, strong interpersonal skills, strong leadership ability, written communication skills. Duration is January through March. Unpaid. Open to recent high school graduates, college freshmen, college sophomores, college juniors, college seniors, recent college graduates, graduate students, career changers, individuals reentering the workforce. International applications accepted.
Benefits Formal training, free housing, names of contacts, on-the-job training, willing to complete paperwork for educational credit, willing to provide letters of recommendation, possible reimbursement for some expenses.
Contact Write, call, fax, or e-mail Nancy Bailey, Volunteers in Parks Coordinator. Phone: 530-595-4444 Ext. 5133. Fax: 530-595-3408. E-mail: nancy_bailey@nps.gov. In-person interview recommended (telephone interview accepted). Applicants must submit a formal organization application, two personal references. Application deadline: March 1 for summer, October 1 for winter, December 1 for spring.

LIBRARY OF CONGRESS–CAROLINE AND ERWIN SWANN FOUNDATION FOR CARICATURE AND CARTOON
101 Independence Avenue, SE
Washington, District of Columbia 20540-4730

General Information Foundation that promotes caricature and cartoon through scholarship, publication, exhibition, cataloging, and preservation. Established in 1967. Number of employees: 4. Unit of Library of Congress, Washington, District of Columbia. Number of internship applications received each year: 21.
Internships Available ▶ *1 Swann Foundation fellowship:* responsibilities include making use of the collections of the Library of Congress for at least two weeks during fellowship, giving a public lecture on work in progress, giving Library of Congress a copy of any publication produced as a result of fellowships for Swann Foundation Archives. Duration is September through June. $15,000 per duration of internship. Open to graduate students, students who have received MA or PhD within three years of application. International applications accepted.
Benefits Willing to complete paperwork for educational credit, access to collections of the Library of Congress, public lectures.
Contact Write, call, e-mail, or through World Wide Web site Martha Kennedy, Curatorial Assistant, Prints and Photographs Division, Washington 20540-4730. Phone: 202-707-9115. E-mail: swann@loc.gov. Applicants must submit a formal organization application, resume, academic transcripts, writing sample, three letters of recommendation, accompanying visual materials (slides or photocopies). Application deadline: February 15 for fall. World Wide Web: http://lcweb.loc.gov/rr/print/swann/swann_foundation.html.

LIBRARY OF CONGRESS JUNIOR FELLOWS PROGRAM
Library of Congress, LM-642
Washington, District of Columbia 20540-4600

General Information Library that collects and preserves material from a wide range of disciplines including history, area studies, film, fine arts, literature, and music. Established in 1800. Number of employees: 5,000. Unit of United States Federal Government, Washington, District of Columbia.

Internships Available ► *6 junior fellows:* responsibilities include assisting in selected divisions to reduce arrearage, producing finding aids and bibliographic records, preparing materials for preservation and service, and doing bibliographical research; positions available in music division, rare book and special collections, American history and literature; cataloging; photography; film, television, and radio; sound recordings; American popular culture; librarianship; preservation. Duration is 2-3 months in summer (40 hours per week). $300 per week. Open to college juniors, college seniors, recent college graduates, graduate students. International applications accepted.

Contact Write, call, fax, or e-mail Junior Fellows Program Coordinator, Library Services. Phone: 202-707-5330. Fax: 202-707-6269. E-mail: jrfell@loc.gov. Applicants must submit academic transcripts, letter of recommendation, cover letter indicating area(s) of interest, resume or Application for Federal Employment (SF 171). Application deadline: April 15. World Wide Web: http://lcweb.loc.gov/rr/jrfell/.

LONGWOOD GARDENS
PO Box 501
Kennett Square, Pennsylvania 19348

General Information Display garden promoting the art and enjoyment of horticulture for the public, while providing opportunities for research and learning. Established in 1954. Number of employees: 350. Number of internship applications received each year: 150.

Internships Available ► *2 arboriculture interns:* responsibilities include assisting the arborist crew in maintaining the tree collection; further responsibilities described on Web site. Candidates should have arboriculture/urban forestry experience (preferred). Duration is 3–12 months. $6.50 per hour. ► *1 continuing education intern:* responsibilities include assisting with continuing education program; refer to Web site. Candidates should have ability to work independently, computer skills, office skills, oral communication skills, strong interpersonal skills, writing skills. Duration is 1 year. $6.50 per hour. Open to college freshmen, college sophomores, college juniors, college seniors, recent college graduates. ► *1 curatorial intern:* responsibilities include assisting curator in daily activities; refer to Web site. Candidates should have ability to work with others, computer skills, oral communication skills, self-motivation, written communication skills, familiarity with plant nomenclature. Duration is 1 year. $6.50 per hour. Open to college freshmen, college sophomores, college juniors, college seniors, recent college graduates. ► *4 greenhouse production interns:* responsibilities include working with production crops and unusual crop; refer to Web site. Candidates should have ability to work independently, ability to work with others, knowledge of field, personal interest in the field, self-motivation. Duration is 3–12 months. $6.50 per hour. Open to college freshmen, college sophomores, college juniors, college seniors, recent college graduates. ► *2 integrated pest management interns:* responsibilities include assisting integrated pest manager; refer to Web site. Candidates should have ability to work independently, ability to work with others, oral communication skills, personal interest in the field, self-motivation, written communication skills. Duration is 3–12 months. $6.50 per hour. Open to college freshmen, college sophomores, college juniors, college seniors, recent college graduates. ► *1 landscape design intern:* responsibilities include various duties; refer to Web site. Candidates should have computer skills, knowledge of field, oral communication skills, personal interest in the field, plan to pursue career in field, self-motivation, strong interpersonal skills, written communication skills, CAD experience. Duration is 6–12 months. $6.50 per hour. Open to

college freshmen, college sophomores, college juniors, college seniors, recent college graduates. ► *1 library science intern:* responsibilities include helping maintain horticultural library collection; refer to Web site. Candidates should have ability to work with others, computer skills, office skills, organizational skills, personal interest in the field, self-motivation. Duration is 1 year. $6.50 per hour. Open to college freshmen, college sophomores, college juniors, college seniors, recent college graduates. ► *2 nursery interns:* responsibilities include general nursery work; refer to Web site. Candidates should have ability to work independently, ability to work with others, college courses in field, knowledge of field, personal interest in the field, plan to pursue career in field. Duration is 3–9 months. $6.50 per hour. Open to college freshmen, college sophomores, college juniors, college seniors, recent college graduates. ► *8 outdoor display or groundskeeping interns:* responsibilities include maintenance of annuals and perennials; working with herbs, ground covers, vegetables, fruits, and roses; or various groundskeeping duties; refer to Web site. Candidates should have ability to work independently, ability to work with others, knowledge of field, personal interest in the field, plan to pursue career in field, self-motivation. Duration is 3–12 months. $6.50 per hour. Open to college freshmen, college sophomores, college juniors, college seniors, recent college graduates. ► *2 performing arts interns (administrative or technical):* responsibilities include assisting with publicity/marketing for 350-event program; refer to Web site. Candidates should have ability to work independently, oral communication skills, personal interest in the field, self-motivation, written communication skills. Duration is 1 year. $6.50 per hour. Open to college freshmen, college sophomores, college juniors, college seniors, recent college graduates. ► *1 research intern:* responsibilities include assisting in care and evaluation of plant materials; refer to Web site. Candidates should have ability to work independently, ability to work with others, knowledge of field, organizational skills, personal interest in the field, research skills, self-motivation. Duration is 3–12 months. $6.50 per hour. Open to college freshmen, college sophomores, college juniors, college seniors, recent college graduates. ► *5 special display/indoor display interns:* responsibilities include assisting in development of floral and special displays and maintaining display garden; refer to Web site. Candidates should have ability to work independently, ability to work with others, personal interest in the field, plan to pursue career in field, self-motivation. Duration is 3–12 months. $6.50 per hour. Open to college freshmen, college sophomores, college juniors, college seniors, recent college graduates. ► *2 student programs interns:* responsibilities include working with students; refer to Web site. Candidates should have ability to work independently, computer skills, office skills, oral communication skills, organizational skills, self-motivation, strong interpersonal skills, strong leadership ability, writing skills. Duration is 1 year. $6.50 per hour. Open to college freshmen, college sophomores, college juniors, college seniors, recent college graduates. ► *2 visitor education interns:* responsibilities include interpreting gardens; refer to Web site. Candidates should have computer skills, office skills, oral communication skills, organizational skills, strong interpersonal skills, writing skills. Duration is 9–12 months. $6.50 per hour. Open to college freshmen, college sophomores, college juniors, college seniors, recent college graduates. International applications accepted.

Benefits Formal training, free housing, job counseling, names of contacts, on-the-job training, opportunity to attend seminars/workshops, possible full-time employment, willing to act as a professional reference, willing to complete paperwork for educational credit, willing to provide letters of recommendation.

Contact Write, call, fax, e-mail, or through World Wide Web site Bill Simeral, Student Programs Coordinator. Phone: 610-388-1000 Ext. 508. Fax: 610-388-2908. E-mail: studentprograms@longwoodgardens.org. Applicants must submit a formal organization application, resume, academic transcripts, two letters of recommendation, statement of professional objectives. Application deadline: February 1 for summer and fall, November 1 for winter and spring. World Wide Web: http://www.longwoodgardens.org.

LOS ANGELES MUNICIPAL ART GALLERY
4804 Hollywood Boulevard
Los Angeles, California 90027

General Information   City-run gallery supporting the southern California art community and its artists. Established in 1971. Number of employees: 45. Division of Cultural Affairs Department, Los Angeles, California. Number of internship applications received each year: 30.

Internships Available   ▶ *3–6 education interns:* responsibilities include working as gallery educators while evaluating and exploring the potential of art galleries and museums as educational sources. Candidates should have ability to work independently, college courses in field, computer skills, oral communication skills, personal interest in the field, research skills, self-motivation, strong interpersonal skills, writing skills. Duration is 3–4 months. Unpaid. Open to recent high school graduates, college freshmen, college sophomores, college juniors, college seniors, recent college graduates, graduate students, career changers, individuals reentering the workforce, college graduates who are interested in museum education. International applications accepted.

Benefits   Names of contacts, opportunity to attend seminars/workshops, willing to act as a professional reference, willing to complete paperwork for educational credit, willing to provide letters of recommendation, formal training in museum education.

Contact   Write, call, fax, or e-mail Ms. Ida Blaine, Education Coordinator. Phone: 213-473-8436. In-person interview recommended (telephone interview accepted). Applicants must submit a formal organization application, letter of interest, resume. Application deadline: May 1 for summer, August 1 for fall, December 1 for spring.

THE MARITIME AQUARIUM AT NORWALK
10 North Water Street
Norwalk, Connecticut 06854

General Information Aquarium, maritime museum, and educational center that encourages and excites appreciation of science and the interrelationship of global ecology and natural and cultural events as they relate to Long Island Sound. Established in 1988. Number of employees: 80. Number of internship applications received each year: 300.

Internships Available   ▶ *5 college interns:* responsibilities include opportunities to work in Education, Animal Husbandry, Volunteer, Marketing or Exhibit departments; interns required to complete a project related to their internship. Candidates should have ability to work independently, computer skills, oral communication skills, personal interest in the field, research skills, self-motivation, strong interpersonal skills, writing skills. Duration is 1 month (minimum). Unpaid. Open to college freshmen, college sophomores, college juniors, college seniors, recent college graduates, graduate students. ▶ *5 high school interns:* responsibilities include a rotation through 3 different departments (Education, Aquarium, and Volunteers), participating in a variety of jobs from preparing seal food to helping teach educational programs. Candidates should have ability to work independently, oral communication skills, personal interest in the field, research skills, self-motivation, strong interpersonal skills, strong leadership ability, writing skills. Duration is minimum of 6 weeks. Unpaid. Open to high school students, recent high school graduates, individuals at least 16 years old. International applications accepted.

Benefits   Names of contacts, on-the-job training, possible full-time employment, willing to act as a professional reference, willing to complete paperwork for educational credit, willing to provide letters of recommendation.

Contact   Write, fax, e-mail, or through World Wide Web site Amy Ferland, Internship Coordinator. Fax: 203-838-5416. E-mail: internships@maritimeaquarium.org. No phone calls. In-person interview recommended (telephone interview accepted). Applicants must submit a formal organization application, letter of interest, resume, academic transcripts, three letters of recommendation. Applications are accepted continuously. World Wide Web: http://maritimeaquarium.org.

MEADOWSIDE NATURE CENTER
5100 Meadowside Lane
Rockville, Maryland 20855

General Information   Nature center located within a 2700-acre regional park outside of Washington, D.C. Established in 1927. Number of employees: 5. Unit of Maryland National Capital Park and Planning Commission, Department of Parks, Silver Spring, Maryland. Number of internship applications received each year: 20.

Internships Available   ▶ *1–2 naturalist interns:* responsibilities include developing and presenting interpretive programs for diverse audiences including conservation clubs and special events; assisting with field studies and maintenance of wildlife and heritage gardens, rehabilitated animal display, and other exhibits. Candidates should have college courses in field, oral communication skills, personal interest in the field, self-motivation, strong interpersonal skills, ability to deal with the general public. Duration is 14–16 weeks. Position available as unpaid or at hourly minimum wage or a little higher, as funds are available. Open to college juniors, college seniors, recent college graduates, graduate students, career changers, individuals reentering the workforce.

Benefits   Formal training, on-the-job training, opportunity to attend seminars/workshops, willing to act as a professional reference, willing to complete paperwork for educational credit, willing to provide letters of recommendation, outings to other park facilities, park housing available at cost.

Contact   Write, call, or fax Sara Staples, Intern Coordinator. Phone: 301-924-4141. Fax: 301-924-1034. In-person interview recommended. Applicants must submit a letter of interest, resume, academic transcripts, evidence of academic coursework. Application deadline: March 1 for summer, June 1 for winter, November 1 for spring.

MEMPHIS BROOKS MUSEUM OF ART, INC.
1934 Poplar Avenue, Overton Park
Memphis, Tennessee 38104

General Information   Fine arts museum whose collection spans from the ancient to the contemporary. Established in 1916. Number of employees: 59. Number of internship applications received each year: 20.

Internships Available   ▶ *1–2 curatorial interns:* responsibilities include assisting curator with research of collections and exhibitions. Candidates should have ability to work independently, college courses in field, computer skills, knowledge of field, plan to pursue career in field, research skills, writing skills. Duration is 1 semester. Unpaid. Open to college juniors, college seniors, recent college graduates, graduate students. ▶ *1–2 media/public relations interns:* responsibilities include writing press releases, assisting in media outreach/contact, and supporting public relations staff. Candidates should have ability to work independently, computer skills, oral communication skills, self-motivation, strong interpersonal skills, written communication skills. Duration is June to August. Unpaid. Open to college juniors, college seniors, recent college graduates. ▶ *Membership interns:* responsibilities include promotion of memberships, outreach, researching and identifying potential new members, and helping design membership information and recruitment plan. Candidates should have ability to work independently, oral communication skills, organizational skills, self-motivation, strong interpersonal skills, written communication skills. Duration is June to August. Unpaid. Open to college juniors, college seniors, recent college graduates. ▶ *1 registrar's office intern:* responsibilities include assisting in general office work, helping upkeep collections, and preparing exhibits. Candidates should have ability to work independently, computer skills, declared college major in field, plan to pursue career in field, research skills. Duration is 1 semester. Unpaid. Open to college seniors, recent college graduates, graduate students. International applications accepted.

Benefits   On-the-job training, willing to complete paperwork for educational credit, willing to provide letters of recommendation.

Contact   Write or e-mail Ruth O'Donnell, Human Resources Administrator. Fax: 901-725-4071. E-mail: brooks@brooksmuseum.org. No phone calls. In-person interview required. Applicants must submit a letter of interest, resume, writing sample. Applications are accepted continuously. World Wide Web: http://www.brooksmuseum.org.

THE METROPOLITAN MUSEUM OF ART
1000 Fifth Avenue
New York, New York 10028-0198

General Information Art museum that emphasizes encyclopedic collection of master works of art. Established in 1870. Number of employees: 2,500. Number of internship applications received each year: 450.
Internships Available ▶ *Interns:* responsibilities include varied duties for college and graduate students interested in art museum and related careers. Both full- and part-time positions are available for the summer as well as the academic year. Please contact the Education Department for further information. Candidates should have ability to work with others, computer skills, oral communication skills, written communication skills, background in art history, knowledge of foreign languages. Duration is 10 weeks to 12 months. Position available as unpaid or paid. Open to college freshmen, college sophomores, college juniors, college seniors, recent college graduates, graduate students. International applications accepted.
Benefits Meals at a cost, on-the-job training, willing to complete paperwork for educational credit, letters of recommendation provided if appropriate.
Contact Write, call, e-mail, or through World Wide Web site Internship Program. Phone: 212-570-3710. E-mail: mmainterns@metmuseum.org. In-person interview required. Applicants must submit a letter of interest, resume, academic transcripts, two letters of recommendation, essay of not more than 500 words which states reason for application and career goals, list of art history and other relevant courses taken. Application deadline: contact "Internship Programs" for exact dates. World Wide Web: http://www.metmuseum.org/.

MILWAUKEE PUBLIC MUSEUM
800 West Wells Street
Milwaukee, Wisconsin 53233

General Information Natural and human history museum. Established in 1882. Number of employees: 260. Number of internship applications received each year: 200.
Internships Available ▶ *1–3 anthropology interns:* responsibilities include collections work in the following areas: American Indian, Africa, Pacific Islands, and Central and South America. Candidates should have ability to work independently, ability to work with others, analytical skills, college courses in field, computer skills, office skills, organizational skills, plan to pursue career in field, research skills, self-motivation, writing skills. Duration is 1–3 months. Unpaid. Open to college sophomores, college juniors, college seniors, recent college graduates, graduate students. ▶ *1–2 botany interns:* responsibilities include assisting with collections management, lab work, and local fieldwork. Candidates should have ability to work independently, analytical skills, college courses in field, computer skills, organizational skills, plan to pursue career in field. Duration is 1–3 months. Unpaid. Open to college juniors, college seniors, recent college graduates, graduate students. ▶ *1–2 development interns:* responsibilities include assisting in the coordination, development, and implementation of special events and programs at the museum. Candidates should have ability to work independently, office skills, organizational skills, self-motivation, strong interpersonal skills. Duration is 1–6 months. Unpaid. Open to college juniors, college seniors, recent college graduates, graduate students. ▶ *1–3 education interns:* responsibilities include presenting educational programs to groups and performing collection research and program development. Candidates should have ability to work independently, college courses in field, oral communication skills, organizational skills, personal interest in the field, self-motivation, strong interpersonal skills. Duration is 1–3 months. Unpaid. Open to college sophomores, college juniors, college seniors, recent college graduates, graduate students. ▶ *1–3 exhibit programs interns:* responsibilities include assisting in the production of various components of permanent and temporary exhibits, the installation of special exhibits, and upkeep of exhibits.

Candidates should have ability to work independently, college courses in field, experience in the field, plan to pursue career in field. Duration is 1–2 semesters. Unpaid. Open to college juniors, college seniors, recent college graduates. ▶ *1–2 geology interns:* responsibilities include assisting with collections management, lab work, and local fieldwork. Candidates should have ability to work independently, analytical skills, college courses in field, organizational skills, plan to pursue career in field, research skills. Duration is 1–3 months. Unpaid. Open to college juniors, college seniors, recent college graduates, graduate students. ▶ *1–2 history interns:* responsibilities include working on collections from colonial America, European societies, North Africa, Middle East, classical civilizations, Asia, and specific areas in textiles and military weapons. Candidates should have ability to work independently, analytical skills, college courses in field, computer skills, editing skills, office skills, organizational skills, plan to pursue career in field, research skills, self-motivation, writing skills. Duration is 1–3 months. Unpaid. Open to college seniors, graduate students. ▶ *1–3 marketing interns:* responsibilities include working in public relations, communications, advertising, and journalism. Candidates should have ability to work independently, college courses in field, computer skills, editing skills, knowledge of field, office skills, oral communication skills, organizational skills, self-motivation, strong interpersonal skills, writing skills. Duration is 1–3 months. Unpaid. Open to college sophomores, college juniors, college seniors, recent college graduates. ▶ *1–2 zoology interns:* responsibilities include assisting with collections maintenance, lab work, and local fieldwork. Candidates should have ability to work independently, analytical skills, college courses in field, computer skills, knowledge of field, plan to pursue career in field, research skills, self-motivation, written communication skills. Duration is 1–3 months. Unpaid. Open to college juniors, college seniors, recent college graduates, graduate students. International applications accepted.
Benefits Job counseling, names of contacts, on-the-job training, opportunity to attend seminars/workshops, willing to complete paperwork for educational credit, willing to provide letters of recommendation.
Contact Write, call, fax, or e-mail Ms. Dawn Scher Thomae, Museum Internship Coordinator. Phone: 414-278-6157. Fax: 414-278-6100. E-mail: thomae@mpm.edu. In-person interview recommended (telephone interview accepted). Applicants must submit a letter of interest, resume. Application deadline: March 1 for summer, November 1 for spring. World Wide Web: http://www.mpm.edu.

THE MINNEAPOLIS INSTITUTE OF ARTS
2400 Third Avenue, South
Minneapolis, Minnesota 55404

General Information Art museum that emphasizes collection of master works of art in the areas of painting; sculpture; decorative arts; prints; drawings; photography; textiles; and Asian, African, Oceanic, and Native-American arts. Established in 1883. Number of employees: 200. Number of internship applications received each year: 75.
Internships Available ▶ *1–2 curatorial interns:* responsibilities include assisting in preparation of object files and occasionally researching and writing gallery and catalog materials. Candidates should have ability to work with others, college courses in field, organizational skills, research skills, writing skills. Duration is dependent on project requirements. Unpaid. Open to college freshmen, college sophomores, college juniors, college seniors, recent college graduates, graduate students, career changers, individuals reentering the workforce. ▶ *2–3 development interns:* responsibilities include assisting department in various capacities relating to fund-raising. Candidates should have computer skills, knowledge of field, office skills, oral communication skills, research skills, written communication skills. Duration is dependent on project requirements. Unpaid. Open to college freshmen, college sophomores, college juniors, college seniors, recent college graduates, graduate students. ▶ *5–10 education interns:* responsibilities include assisting in preparation of teaching materials for use in schools and researching and writing gallery and catalog materials. Candidates should have ability to work independently, computer skills, editing skills, plan to pursue career in field,

The Minneapolis Institute of Arts (continued)

research skills, writing skills. Duration is dependent on project requirements. Unpaid. Open to college freshmen, college sophomores, college juniors, college seniors, recent college graduates, graduate students. ▶ *3–5 library interns:* responsibilities include working on various projects relating to library exhibits including museum object files. Candidates should have college courses in field, computer skills, experience in the field, organizational skills, strong interpersonal skills, written communication skills. Duration is dependent on project requirements. Unpaid. Open to college freshmen, college sophomores, college juniors, college seniors, recent college graduates, graduate students, career changers, individuals reentering the workforce. ▶ *1–2 marketing/communications interns:* responsibilities include compiling press clippings and other various duties and opportunities. Candidates should have ability to work with others, college courses in field, computer skills, editing skills, experience in the field, written communication skills. Duration is dependent on project requirements. Unpaid. Open to college freshmen, college sophomores, college juniors, college seniors. ▶ *1 registration intern:* responsibilities include working on various projects including inventory of parts of a collection. Candidates should have ability to work with others, college courses in field, experience in the field, office skills, organizational skills, plan to pursue career in field. Duration is dependent on project requirements. Unpaid. Open to college freshmen, college sophomores, college juniors, college seniors, recent college graduates, graduate students. International applications accepted.
Benefits Names of contacts, opportunity to attend seminars/workshops, possible full-time employment, willing to complete paperwork for educational credit, willing to provide letters of recommendation.
Contact Write, call, fax, e-mail, or through World Wide Web site Treden P. Wagoner, Intern Coordinator. Phone: 888-642-2787 Ext. 3189. Fax: 612-870-3004. E-mail: twagoner@artsmia.org. Applicants must submit a formal organization application, letter of interest, resume, academic transcripts, two letters of recommendation, writing samples and interviews may be required. Application deadline: March 1 for summer, June 1 for fall/winter, October 1 for winter/spring. World Wide Web: http://www.artsMIA.org.

MINNESOTA MUSEUM OF AMERICAN ART
75 West Fifth Street, Landmark Center, Suite 505
St. Paul, Minnesota 55102

General Information Art museum that collects, preserves, enriches, and educates the community on 19th- and 20th-century American art. Established in 1927. Number of employees: 8. Number of internship applications received each year: 50.
Internships Available ▶ *1 curatorial assistant:* responsibilities include assisting curator with didactics, gallery installation, and research. Candidates should have computer skills, knowledge of field, research skills, writing skills. Duration is 3 months. Unpaid. Open to college seniors, recent college graduates, graduate students. ▶ *1 education assistant:* responsibilities include assisting director of education with educational materials for use by museum visitors, volunteers, and docents. Candidates should have computer skills, knowledge of field, office skills, research skills, self-motivation, writing skills. Duration is 3–12 months. Unpaid. Open to college seniors, recent college graduates, graduate students. ▶ *1 public relations/marketing assistant:* responsibilities include assisting PR coordinator with writing and distributing press releases and other publications. Candidates should have ability to work independently, computer skills, editing skills, knowledge of field, office skills, oral communication skills, organizational skills, self-motivation, writing skills. Duration is 3 months. Unpaid. Open to college juniors, college seniors, recent college graduates, graduate students, career changers. International applications accepted.
Benefits Opportunity to attend seminars/workshops, willing to complete paperwork for educational credit, willing to provide letters of recommendation, complimentary museum membership.
Contact Write, call, fax, e-mail, or through World Wide Web site Tami Miller, Visitor Services Coordinator. Phone: 651-292-4395. Fax: 651-292-4340. E-mail: tmiller@mmaa.org. In-person interview

recommended (telephone interview accepted). Applicants must submit a formal organization application, letter of interest, resume, academic transcripts. Applications are accepted continuously. World Wide Web: http://www.mmaa.org.

THE MINNESOTA ZOO
13000 Zoo Boulevard
Apple Valley, Minnesota 55124

General Information Conservation organization and facility whose goal is to help people realize the importance of animals and their impact on the world. Established in 1977. Number of employees: 300. Number of internship applications received each year: 80.
Internships Available ▶ *10–30 animal management interns:* responsibilities include caring for exotic and domestic animals, preparing diets, cleaning exhibits; learning techniques of zoo animal management, observing, reporting, and evaluating animal behavior; responding to animal emergencies, observing medical procedures, and effectively communicating with visitors on animal-related questions. Candidates should have college courses in field, oral communication skills, strong interpersonal skills. Duration is 10-14 weeks (30-40 hours per week). Unpaid. Open to college juniors, college seniors. ▶ *1 butterfly hoop house/garden entomologist/interpretive naturalist:* responsibilities include daily maintenance of insect collection and butterfly hoop house; interaction with zoo guests and volunteers while staffing butterfly garden; providing interpretive information to zoo volunteers and guests; monitoring hoop house area to prevent damage, butterfly/moth escapes, and pest problems; accurate recordkeeping; assisting in developing and implementing a conservation message or project; replying to pertinent correspondence; assisting with reference work or additional tasks as needed. Candidates should have ability to work independently, college courses in field, plan to pursue career in field, self-motivation, strong interpersonal skills. Duration is May to September. Unpaid. Open to college juniors, college seniors. ▶ *2–4 education interns:* responsibilities include teaching in the informal setting of a zoo, handling animals for interpretive demonstrations, developing effective presentations, responding to questions from diverse audiences, structuring lesson plans, developing curriculum, working effectively with students and zoo education staff, and becoming environmental interpreters. Candidates should have college courses in field, oral communication skills, plan to pursue career in field, strong interpersonal skills, written communication skills. Duration is 10-14 weeks (30-40 hours per week). Unpaid. Open to college juniors, college seniors. ▶ *2 farmkeepers:* responsibilities include assisting with cleaning and maintenance of animal pens and exhibits; groundskeeping and horticulture maintenance; interpreting various farm animals to the public; assisting with demonstrations and domestic animal training. Candidates should have ability to work independently, college courses in field, plan to pursue career in field, self-motivation, strong interpersonal skills. Duration is two 3-month positions available: April to July or July to October. Unpaid. Open to college juniors, college seniors. ▶ *1–2 horticulture interns:* responsibilities include assisting with horticulture projects throughout the Zoo, and assisting in maintenance of greenhouse plants. Candidates should have ability to work independently, college courses in field, plan to pursue career in field, self-motivation, strong interpersonal skills. Duration is 10-14 weeks (30-40 hours per week). Unpaid. Open to college juniors, college seniors, second-year technical college students.
Benefits Willing to act as a professional reference, willing to complete paperwork for educational credit, willing to provide letters of recommendation.
Contact Write, call, fax, e-mail, or through World Wide Web site Jill Wallin, Personnel Aide. Phone: 952-431-9219. Fax: 952-431-9211. E-mail: jill.wallin@state.mn.us. In-person interview recommended (telephone interview accepted). Applicants must submit a formal organization application, letter of interest, resume, academic transcripts, letter of recommendation. Application deadline: March 1 for summer, August 1 for fall, October 1 for winter, December 1 for spring. World Wide Web: http://www.mnzoo.com.

MISSOURI BOTANICAL GARDEN
PO Box 299
St. Louis, Missouri 63166-0299

General Information Botanical garden and research center that provides educational programs. Established in 1859. Number of employees: 350. Number of internship applications received each year: 50.

Internships Available ▶ *5–6 horticulture interns.* Candidates should have college courses in field, plan to pursue career in field, ability to work outside in heat and humidity. Duration is 12 weeks. $6.24 per hour. Open to college freshmen, college sophomores, college juniors, college seniors.

Benefits Job counseling, names of contacts, on-the-job training, possible full-time employment, willing to complete paperwork for educational credit, willing to provide letters of recommendation. **Contact** Write, call, fax, or e-mail Dr. Shannon Smith, Director of Horticulture. Phone: 314-577-5190. Fax: 314-577-9465. E-mail: lisa.francis@mobot.org. Applicants must submit a formal organization application, letter of interest, resume, three letters of recommendation, additional materials available on Web site. Application deadline: February 1 for horticulture interns; call or visit Web site for information regarding other departmental internships. World Wide Web: http://www.mobot.org/hort/.

MONTANA FISH, WILDLIFE, AND PARKS, REGION 7, MAKOSHIKA STATE PARK
PO Box 1242
Glendive, Montana 59330

General Information State park that preserves and protects an area of natural scenic beauty and ecological significance for the benefit of the public. Established in 1901. Number of employees: 4. Division of Montana Department of Fish, Wildlife, and Parks, Helena, Montana. Number of internship applications received each year: 5.

Internships Available ▶ *1–2 interpreter/paleontologists:* responsibilities include performing general duties related to park management; developing trails and campfire lectures; and educating young visitors about dinosaurs. Candidates should have college courses in field, computer skills, oral communication skills, writing skills, student at Montana university or other Montana college only. Duration is 480 hours. $8 per hour. Open to college sophomores, college juniors, college seniors, must be student at Montana college or university.

Benefits On-the-job training, possible full-time employment, willing to complete paperwork for educational credit, willing to provide letters of recommendation.

Contact Write, call, or e-mail Dale Carlson, Park Manager. Phone: 406-365-6256. Fax: 406-365-8043. E-mail: makoshikapark@mcn.net. Telephone interview required. Applicants must submit a letter of interest, resume, academic transcripts. Application deadline: March 15 for summer.

THE MONTCLAIR ART MUSEUM
3 South Mountain Avenue
Montclair, New Jersey 07042

General Information Art museum with a permanent collection spanning 3 centuries of American art with strengths in 19th-century American landscapes, Hudson River School, and American impressionist paintings, in addition to a Native American collection of almost 4000 objects which represent nearly every North American indigenous culture. Established in 1914. Number of employees: 30. Number of internship applications received each year: 30.

Internships Available ▶ *Summer interns:* responsibilities include assisting staff in various areas including communications, curatorial, education, development, library, volunteer, exhibit design and installation, museum store, or Yard School of Art. Candidates should have ability to work with others, computer skills, oral communication skills, personal interest in the field, strong leadership ability, written communication skills. Duration is 3 months. Unpaid. Open to high school seniors, college freshmen, college sophomores, college juniors, college seniors, recent college graduates.

Benefits Names of contacts, willing to complete paperwork for educational credit, willing to provide letters of recommendation. **Contact** Write, fax, or e-mail Rachel Wynne, Assistant Educator. Fax: 973-746-0536. E-mail: rachel@montclair-art.org. No phone calls. Applicants must submit a letter of interest, resume. Application deadline: May 15.

MONTSHIRE MUSEUM OF SCIENCE
One Montshire Road
Norwich, Vermont 05055

General Information Science museum that uses materials and devices, natural objects, exhibits, live animals, and indoor/outdoor settings as catalysts in experiencing science and encouraging observation, curiosity, intuition, problem-solving, and imagination. Established in 1974. Number of employees: 26. Number of internship applications received each year: 16.

Internships Available ▶ *1 Internet and education intern:* responsibilities include developing bibliography of global Internet resources. Candidates should have ability to work independently, computer skills, experience in the field, oral communication skills, strong interpersonal skills. Duration is 15 weeks. $600 stipend. Open to college juniors, college seniors, recent college graduates, graduate students, career changers. ▶ *4 environmental education interns:* responsibilities include planning, development, and teaching in environmental day camps. Candidates should have ability to work with others, personal interest in the field, ability to work with children. Duration is 10 weeks in summer. $1000 stipend. Open to college freshmen, college sophomores, college juniors, college seniors, recent college graduates, graduate students. ▶ *1–2 exhibit/design fabrication interns:* responsibilities include researching, designing, constructing, and refining exhibits. Candidates should have ability to work independently, oral communication skills, research skills, written communication skills. Duration is 15 weeks. $600 stipend. Open to college juniors, college seniors, recent college graduates, graduate students, career changers. ▶ *1 land management intern:* responsibilities include following master plan and management objectives for 100-acre property, doing trail and grounds work. Candidates should have ability to work independently, personal interest in the field, self-motivation, ability to operate chain saw. Duration is 15 weeks. $600 stipend. Open to college juniors, college seniors, recent college graduates, graduate students, career changers. ▶ *1 membership and development intern:* responsibilities include development and coordination of annual fund, major gifts, and planned giving programs; working with Montshire Associates, a local forum for business, education, and government; providing support for family and individual members. Candidates should have ability to work independently, oral communication skills, organizational skills, strong interpersonal skills, written communication skills. Duration is 15 weeks. $600 stipend. Open to college juniors, college seniors, recent college graduates, graduate students, career changers. ▶ *1 public relations intern:* responsibilities include working in the various avenues of communication. Candidates should have editing skills, oral communication skills, plan to pursue career in field, research skills, strong interpersonal skills, written communication skills. Duration is 15 weeks. $600 stipend. Open to college juniors, college seniors, recent college graduates, graduate students, career changers. ▶ *1–4 science education interns:* responsibilities include teaching a variety of science and ecology classes to preschoolers, school children, teachers, and families; participating in environmental camps, overnights, and demonstrations; developing curricula; interpreting exhibits, outreach programs, teacher workshops, and courses. Candidates should have ability to work independently, personal interest in the field, strong interpersonal skills, interest in working with children and adults. Duration is 15 weeks. $600 stipend. Open to college juniors, college seniors, recent college graduates, graduate students, career changers.

Benefits Free housing, on-the-job training, willing to act as a professional reference, willing to complete paperwork for educational credit, willing to provide letters of recommendation.

Contact Write, call, fax, e-mail, or through World Wide Web site Lou-Anne Conrow, Intern Coordinator. Phone: 802-649-2200. Fax: 802-649-3637. E-mail: montshire@montshire.net. In-person interview recommended (telephone interview accepted). Applicants must

Montshire Museum of Science (continued)

submit a formal organization application, letter of interest, resume, writing and art sample for exhibit/design interns, writing sample for public relations interns. Applications are accepted continuously. World Wide Web: http://www.montshire.net.

MOORES CREEK NATIONAL BATTLEFIELD
40 Patriots Hall Drive
Currie, North Carolina 28435

General Information Preserves the site of the Revolutionary War Battle of Moores Creek. Established in 1926. Number of employees: 6. Unit of United States National Park Service, Washington, District of Columbia. Number of internship applications received each year: 4.

Internships Available ► *1–4 visitor use assistants:* responsibilities include performing interpretation, managing resources, and conducting historical research. Candidates should have computer skills, knowledge of field, oral communication skills, personal interest in the field, strong interpersonal skills. Duration is year-round. Unpaid. Open to recent high school graduates, college freshmen, college sophomores, college juniors, college seniors, must be 18 and accepted for college study. International applications accepted.

Benefits Names of contacts, travel reimbursement, willing to complete paperwork for educational credit, experience in a national park.

Contact Write, call, fax, or e-mail Linda L. Brown, Lead Park Ranger. Phone: 910-283-5591. Fax: 910-283-5351. E-mail: linda_brown@nps.gov. In-person interview recommended (telephone interview accepted). Applicants must submit a resume, two personal references. Applications are accepted continuously. World Wide Web: http://www.gov.nps.mocr.

MORRIS ARBORETUM OF THE UNIVERSITY OF PENNSYLVANIA
9414 Meadowbrook Avenue
Philadelphia, Pennsylvania 19118

General Information University arboretum that emphasizes teaching, research, and outreach programs. Established in 1932. Number of employees: 55. Unit of University of Pennsylvania, Philadelphia, Pennsylvania. Number of internship applications received each year: 50.

Internships Available ► *1 arborist intern:* responsibilities include working in all phases of tree care. Candidates should have ability to work with others, personal interest in the field, climbing experience. Duration is 1 year. $7.80 per hour. Open to college juniors, college seniors, recent college graduates. ► *1 education intern:* responsibilities include working closely with education staff and volunteer guides to develop workshops for experienced guides and training sessions to recruit new guides; supervising school tour program, running special programs for school children, and developing specialized tours for the public; and helping coordinator prepare adult-education course brochures by selecting course topics and instructors and writing promotional copy for the brochures. Candidates should have ability to work independently, college courses in field, computer skills, editing skills, experience in the field, oral communication skills, self-motivation, strong interpersonal skills, written communication skills. Duration is 1 year. $7.80 per hour. Open to college seniors, recent college graduates, graduate students, career changers, individuals reentering the workforce. ► *1 flora of Pennsylvania intern:* responsibilities include working in a major herbarium and creating a modern flora using computerized systems. Candidates should have ability to work independently, analytical skills, college courses in field, computer skills, knowledge of field, personal interest in the field, plan to pursue career in field, research skills, self-motivation, written communication skills. Duration is 1 year. $7.80 per hour. Open to college seniors, recent college graduates, graduate students, career changers, individuals reentering the workforce. ► *1 flower garden intern:* responsibilities include working with experienced horticulturist to plan, plant, and maintain Arboretum's rose garden display. Candidates should have ability to work independently, ability to work with others, college courses in field, knowledge of

field, personal interest in the field, self-motivation. Duration is 1 year. $7.80 per hour. Open to college juniors, college seniors, recent college graduates, graduate students, career changers, individuals reentering the workforce. ► *1 horticultural intern:* responsibilities include assisting arboretum horticulturists in all phases of garden development and care and supervising gardening activities of volunteers and part-time staff. Candidates should have ability to work independently, college courses in field, knowledge of field, organizational skills, personal interest in the field, self-motivation, strong interpersonal skills. Duration is 1 year. $7.80 per hour. Open to college juniors, college seniors, recent college graduates, graduate students, career changers, individuals reentering the workforce. ► *1 plant protection intern:* responsibilities include assisting the arboretum's plant pathologist with the Integrated Pest Management (IPM) program. Candidates should have ability to work independently, analytical skills, college courses in field, personal interest in the field, research skills, self-motivation. Duration is 1 year. $7.80 per hour. Open to college seniors, recent college graduates, graduate students, career changers, individuals reentering the workforce. ► *1 propagation intern:* responsibilities include assisting propagator in the development of plant production and propagation schemes. Candidates should have ability to work independently, ability to work with others, college courses in field, knowledge of field, organizational skills, personal interest in the field, self-motivation. Duration is 1 year. $7.80 per hour. Open to college seniors, recent college graduates, graduate students, career changers, individuals reentering the workforce. ► *1 urban forestry intern:* responsibilities include working on community landscape consultation projects. Candidates should have college courses in field, computer skills, editing skills, oral communication skills, organizational skills, personal interest in the field, self-motivation, strong interpersonal skills, written communication skills. Duration is 1 year. $7.80 per hour. Open to college seniors, recent college graduates, graduate students, career changers, individuals reentering the workforce. International applications accepted.

Benefits Formal training, health insurance, on-the-job training, opportunity to attend seminars/workshops, tuition assistance, willing to act as a professional reference, willing to complete paperwork for educational credit, willing to provide letters of recommendation, vacation and dental benefits.

Contact Write, call, fax, e-mail, or through World Wide Web site Ms. Jan McFarlan, Education Coordinator. Phone: 215-247-5777 Ext. 156. Fax: 215-247-7862. E-mail: jlm@pobox.upenn.edu. Telephone interview required. Applicants must submit a letter of interest, resume, academic transcripts, three letters of recommendation. Application deadline: February 15 for June start date. World Wide Web: http://www.morrisarboretum.org.

MOUNT DESERT ISLAND HISTORICAL SOCIETY
373 Sound Drive, PO Box 653
Mount Desert, Maine 04660

General Information Society that manages a museum and archive, offers educational programs, acts as a voice for historic preservation on Mount Desert Island, and publishes an annual history journal. Established in 1931. Number of employees: 2. Number of internship applications received each year: 15.

Internships Available ► *1 museum assistant:* responsibilities include assisting with tours of museum, cataloging, collection care, research assistance, and program development assistance. Candidates should have ability to work independently, computer skills, oral communication skills, personal interest in the field, research skills, strong interpersonal skills, written communication skills. Duration is 3 months (June 1 to August 31). $1000 stipend. Open to college freshmen, college sophomores, college juniors, college seniors, recent college graduates, graduate students. International applications accepted.

Benefits Free housing, willing to act as a professional reference, willing to complete paperwork for educational credit, willing to provide letters of recommendation, opportunity to gain basic experience in small museum management.

Contact Write, call, or e-mail Jaylene Roths, Executive Director. Phone: 207-276-9323. Fax: 207-276-4204. E-mail: mdihistory@

downeast.net. Telephone interview required. Applicants must submit a letter of interest, resume. Application deadline: February 1. World Wide Web: http://www.mdihistory.org.

MOUNT RUSHMORE NATIONAL MEMORIAL
PO Box 268
Keystone, South Dakota 57751-0268

General Information National Park Service site that commemorates the first 150 years of American democracy with a mountain carving of four important Presidents' faces. Established in 1925. Number of employees: 70. Unit of National Park Service, Washington, District of Columbia. Number of internship applications received each year: 10.
Internships Available ▶ *1–2 interpretation interns:* responsibilities include developing and presenting interpretive talks and guided walks, staffing information desk, performing informal roving interpretation, assisting speaker at evening program, and assisting with special events and museum curator research. Candidates should have ability to work with others, oral communication skills, personal interest in the field, self-motivation, written communication skills. Duration is 12 to 16 weeks in fall, winter, and spring, (possibly in summer, if housing is available). Stipend of $75 per week. Open to college students in a related field. ▶ *1 museum intern:* responsibilities include accessioning and cataloging, database management, preventive conservation, museum storage and security, exhibit planning, and possibly collections research. Candidates should have ability to work with others, college courses in field, organizational skills, plan to pursue career in field, research skills, self-motivation, written communication skills. Duration is 12 to 16 weeks in fall, winter, and spring. Stipend of $75 per week. Open to recent college graduates, graduate students, career changers, college students actively enrolled in museum studies for academic credit. ▶ *2–3 resource management and visitor protection interns:* responsibilities include assisting with visitor services and monitoring trails, climbing areas, and boundaries. Candidates should have ability to work independently, ability to work with others, oral communication skills, personal interest in the field, self-motivation. Duration is 12–16 weeks. Stipend of $75 per week. Open to college freshmen, college sophomores, college juniors, college seniors. International applications accepted.
Benefits Formal training, job counseling, meals at a cost, on-the-job training, willing to act as a professional reference, willing to complete paperwork for educational credit, willing to provide letters of recommendation, potential seasonal job opportunities with the National Park Service, limited reimbursement for some expenses, free housing (if available).
Contact Write, call, fax, or e-mail Bruce Mellberg, Volunteer Coordinator. Phone: 605-574-3151. Fax: 605-574-2307. E-mail: bruce_mellberg@nps.gov. Telephone interview required. Applicants must submit a letter of interest, resume, three personal references. Applications are accepted continuously. World Wide Web: http://www.nps.gov/moru.

MUSA HERITAGE GALLERY
Musa Building, Bamfem Quarters, PO Box 21
Kumbo-Nso, NW Province Cameroon

General Information Museum with focus on the arts and crafts of the Cameroon grassfields. Established in 1996. Number of employees: 2. Number of internship applications received each year: 20.
Internships Available ▶ *1 museum attendant:* responsibilities include escorting visitors and serving as an assistant in running the Museum. Candidates should have ability to work independently, oral communication skills, organizational skills, personal interest in the field, self-motivation, written communication skills. Duration is 3 months. Unpaid. Open to recent high school graduates, college freshmen, college sophomores, college juniors, college seniors, recent college graduates. International applications accepted.
Benefits Free housing, free meals.
International Internships Available.
Contact Write or e-mail Peter Musa, Director, PO Box 21, Kumbo-Nso Cameroon. E-mail: musape@yahoo.com. Applicants must submit a letter of interest. Applications are accepted continuously. World Wide Web: http://btinternet.com/~mulamba.

MUSEUM OF ARTS AND SCIENCES
1040 Museum Boulevard
Daytona Beach, Florida 32114

General Information Museum of art, science, and history that emphasizes the conservation of and education about its permanent collections in the areas of American art, Cuban art, African art, French art, Chinese art, decorative arts, Indian and Persian miniatures, as well as the prehistory of Florida. Established in 1954. Number of employees: 23. Number of internship applications received each year: 20.
Internships Available ▶ *1–2 anthropology interns:* responsibilities include assisting in coordinating anthropological/archaeological programming and materials; artifact interpretation, identifying, and exhibition. Candidates should have college courses in field, computer skills, knowledge of field, organizational skills, research skills, writing skills. Duration is minimum 6 weeks; 2-month commitment preferred. Unpaid. Open to college freshmen, college sophomores, college juniors, college seniors, recent college graduates, graduate students. ▶ *1–3 collections department/registrar assistants:* responsibilities include research, cataloging, object handling; specialized projects may be developed based on personal interest. Candidates should have college courses in field, computer skills, organizational skills, personal interest in the field, research skills, self-motivation. Duration is year-round (minimum 6 weeks). Unpaid. Open to college sophomores, college juniors, college seniors, recent college graduates, graduate students. ▶ *1–2 decorative art curatorial interns:* responsibilities include researching decorative arts objects on display and preparing short summaries which will be entered into an interactive computer database in gallery. Candidates should have college courses in field, computer skills, organizational skills, personal interest in the field, research skills, writing skills, Macintosh knowledge (a plus). Duration is minimum 6 weeks; 2-month commitment preferred. Unpaid. Open to college juniors, college seniors, recent college graduates, graduate students. ▶ *1–4 environmentalist assistants:* responsibilities include coordination and development of environmental and educational programming and materials; guest services; special activities; and basic upkeep of environmental/historical sites. Candidates should have college courses in field, computer skills, knowledge of field, organizational skills, research skills, writing skills. Duration is minimum 6 weeks; 2-month commitment preferred. Unpaid. Open to college freshmen, college sophomores, college juniors, college seniors, recent college graduates, graduate students. ▶ *1–2 fine art curatorial interns:* responsibilities include research, cataloging, object handling; specialized projects may be developed based upon personal interests. Candidates should have college courses in field, computer skills, organizational skills, personal interest in the field, research skills, writing skills. Duration is minimum 6 weeks; 2-month commitment preferred. Unpaid. Open to college sophomores, college juniors, college seniors, recent college graduates, graduate students. ▶ *2–3 museum education interns:* responsibilities include curriculum development, research, and tours. Candidates should have ability to work with others, computer skills, oral communication skills, personal interest in the field, research skills, writing skills. Duration is minimum 6 weeks; 2-month commitment preferred. Unpaid. Open to college freshmen, college sophomores, college juniors, college seniors, recent college graduates, graduate students. ▶ *1–2 museum store assistants:* responsibilities include creating marketing plans and merchandising programs for store. Candidates should have knowledge of field, oral communication skills, organizational skills, self-motivation, written communication skills. Duration is flexible (2-month commitment preferred). Unpaid. Open to college juniors, college seniors, recent college graduates, graduate students. ▶ *1–3 paleontology interns:* responsibilities include assisting in coordinating archaeological programming and materials; artifact identification, interpretation, and exhibition; development of curriculum; and cataloging. Candidates should have college courses in field, computer skills, knowledge of field, organizational skills, research skills, writing skills. Duration is minimum 6 weeks; 2-month commitment preferred. Unpaid. Open to college fresh-

Museum of Arts and Sciences (continued)

men, college sophomores, college juniors, college seniors, recent college graduates, graduate students. ▶ *1 public relations assistant:* responsibilities include writing, editing and distributing news releases on a variety of museum events and programs; organizing and archiving museum photos and slides. Candidates should have declared college major in field, editing skills, organizational skills, writing skills. Duration is 1 semester. Unpaid. Open to college juniors, college seniors. International applications accepted.

Benefits Formal training, names of contacts, possible full-time employment, willing to complete paperwork for educational credit, willing to provide letters of recommendation.

Contact Write, call, fax, e-mail, or through World Wide Web site Holly Keris, Curator of Collections. Phone: 386-255-0285. Fax: 386-255-5040. E-mail: hollymoas@aol.com. In-person interview required. Applicants must submit a letter of interest, resume, three personal references. Application deadline: May 1 for summer, October 1 for spring. World Wide Web: http://www.moas.org.

MUSEUM OF CONTEMPORARY ART
220 East Chicago Avenue
Chicago, Illinois 60611

General Information Contemporary art museum focusing on international, multimedia work from 1945 to present; maintains permanent collection of over 2000 works and over 3000 artist books. Established in 1967. Number of employees: 190. Number of internship applications received each year: 200.

Internships Available ▶ *1–3 collections and exhibitions interns:* responsibilities include assisting director with daily operations of collections management, exhibition organization and tours, research, contracts, and budget management. Candidates should have ability to work independently, ability to work with others, computer skills, office skills, organizational skills, research skills. Duration is 3 months (16 hours per week). Unpaid. ▶ *3–4 curatorial interns:* responsibilities include assisting curatorial staff with research, preparing artists' biographies, handling correspondence, general research inquiries, and daily departmental activities. Candidates should have ability to work independently, knowledge of field, organizational skills, personal interest in the field, research skills, writing skills. Duration is 3 months (16 hours per week). Unpaid. ▶ *1–2 development interns:* responsibilities include conducting research, developing lists of prospects, sending proposals in the area of restricted fund-raising, and assisting with grant writing. Candidates should have office skills, organizational skills, personal interest in the field, research skills, self-motivation, written communication skills. Duration is 3 months (16 hours per week). Unpaid. ▶ *1–2 editorial interns:* responsibilities include assisting museum editor and designer in all phases of production of museum gallery and working on invitations and calendar, including proofreading and basic editing. Candidates should have computer skills, editing skills, knowledge of field, organizational skills, written communication skills. Duration is 3 months (16 hours per week). Unpaid. ▶ *2–3 education interns:* responsibilities include assisting in art historical research and providing on-site support for outreach program, public lectures, and docent training sessions. Candidates should have computer skills, office skills, oral communication skills, organizational skills, research skills, strong interpersonal skills. Duration is 3 months (16 hours per week). Unpaid. ▶ *1–3 graphic design interns:* responsibilities include developing and producing materials related to MCA's graphic needs, including exhibition catalogues, gallery signage, and brochures. Candidates should have ability to work independently, ability to work with others, college courses in field, computer skills, knowledge of field, organizational skills. Duration is 3 months (16 hours per week). Unpaid. ▶ *1–2 library interns:* responsibilities include organizing library resources by sorting and labeling books. Candidates should have ability to work independently, computer skills, office skills, organizational skills, personal interest in the field, written communication skills. Duration is 3 months (16 hours per week). Unpaid. ▶ *3–4 marketing interns:* responsibilities include conducting research on prospective audience markets, assisting in analysis of demographic admissions, and working in database. Candidates should have oral communication skills, organizational skills, personal interest in the field, research skills,

strong interpersonal skills, writing skills. Duration is 3 months (16 hours per week). Unpaid. ▶ *2–4 performance programs interns:* responsibilities include participating in various aspects of developing and producing MCA programs in performance art, dance, music, literature, and video/film, maintaining resource files, completing marketing and administrative tasks, and assisting with artists and house management at performances. Candidates should have ability to work with others, college courses in field, knowledge of field, oral communication skills, organizational skills. Duration is 3 months (16 hours per week). Unpaid. ▶ *1–3 photo archives interns:* responsibilities include assisting library staff in the slide library by sorting, relabeling, and organizing. Candidates should have computer skills, knowledge of field, office skills, organizational skills, personal interest in the field, self-motivation. Duration is 3 months (16 hours per week). Unpaid. ▶ *3–4 public relations interns:* responsibilities include assisting in planning and implementing publicity; writing press releases, public service announcements, and media alerts, and conducting visitor surveys. Candidates should have ability to work independently, office skills, oral communication skills, organizational skills, personal interest in the field, written communication skills. Duration is 3 months (16 hours per week). Unpaid. ▶ *1–3 special events/hospitality interns:* responsibilities include maintaining special events calendar, organizing on-site problem solving, offering creative input, and assisting with planning and coordinating events. Candidates should have ability to work with others, computer skills, knowledge of field, oral communication skills, organizational skills. Duration is 3 months (16 hours per week). Unpaid. Open to college freshmen, college sophomores, college juniors, college seniors, recent college graduates, graduate students. International applications accepted.

Benefits Formal training, opportunity to attend seminars/workshops, willing to complete paperwork for educational credit, willing to provide letters of recommendation, opportunity to attend staff events, receptions, meetings, lecture series, access to MCA job boards.

Contact Write, call, fax, or through World Wide Web site Lauren Cumbia, Internship Coordinator. Phone: 312-280-2660. Fax: 312-397-4095. In-person interview recommended (telephone interview accepted). Applicants must submit a formal organization application, letter of interest, resume, two letters of recommendation. Application deadline: March 15 for summer, July 15 for fall, November 15 for winter/spring. World Wide Web: http://www.mcachicago.org.

MUSEUM OF FINE ARTS, DEPARTMENT OF EDUCATION
465 Huntington Avenue
Boston, Massachusetts 02115

General Information Nonprofit organization whose mission is to educate the public about the MFA. Established in 1876. Number of employees: 45. Division of Museum of Fine Arts, Boston, Boston, Massachusetts. Number of internship applications received each year: 60.

Internships Available ▶ *Interns:* responsibilities include assisting with teaching art classes for community groups; working on services for disabled visitors; promoting lectures, concerts, and programs; some clerical work. Candidates should have ability to work with others, computer skills, office skills, oral communication skills, organizational skills, personal interest in the field, self-motivation. Duration is 1 semester. Unpaid. Open to college juniors, college seniors, recent college graduates, graduate students. International applications accepted.

Benefits Opportunity to attend seminars/workshops, willing to act as a professional reference, willing to complete paperwork for educational credit, willing to provide letters of recommendation, discounts in museum store and free admission to the museum at all times.

Contact Write Karen Strangfeld, Internship Coordinator. Fax: 617-267-9328. No phone calls. In-person interview recommended (telephone interview accepted). Applicants must submit a formal organization application, letter of interest, two letters of recommendation. Applications are accepted continuously. World Wide Web: http://www.mfa.org.

THE MUSEUM OF FINE ARTS, HOUSTON
PO Box 6826
Houston, Texas 77265-6826

General Information Museum dedicated to serving all people by pursuing excellence in art through collection, exhibition, and education. Established in 1900. Number of employees: 500. Number of internship applications received each year: 100.
Internships Available ▶ *5 summer interns:* responsibilities include working in various curatorial and administrative departments. Candidates should have personal interest in the field, research skills, writing skills. Duration is 10 weeks. $2500 per duration of internship. Open to college sophomores, college juniors, college seniors. International applications accepted.
Benefits Health insurance, job counseling, names of contacts, on-the-job training, possible full-time employment, willing to act as a professional reference, willing to complete paperwork for educational credit, willing to provide letters of recommendation.
Contact Write, call, fax, or through World Wide Web site Rebecca Seabaugh, Administrative Assistant. Phone: 713-639-7320. Fax: 713-639-7707. In-person interview required. Applicants must submit a letter of interest, resume, academic transcripts, letter of recommendation, one-page essay describing applicant's interest in internship. Application deadline: January 18. World Wide Web: http://www.mfah.org.

MUSEUM OF SCIENCE
Science Park
Boston, Massachusetts 02114

General Information Museum designed to stimulate interest in science and technology and to further understanding of their importance to individuals and society. Established in 1830. Number of employees: 450. Number of internship applications received each year: 500.
Internships Available ▶ *Interns:* responsibilities include writing and editing print materials, working with the public and school groups, and serving in a variety of departments within the Museum. Candidates should have personal interest in the field, strong interpersonal skills. Duration is 3-12 months in winter/spring and summer/fall periods. Position available as unpaid or at $6.75–$7 per hour. Open to recent high school graduates, college freshmen, college sophomores, college juniors, college seniors, recent college graduates, graduate students, career changers, individuals reentering the workforce, high school seniors who have volunteered at the museum.
Benefits Names of contacts, on-the-job training, opportunity to attend seminars/workshops, possible full-time employment, willing to act as a professional reference, willing to complete paperwork for educational credit, meals at a discount, informal job counseling.
Contact Write, call, fax, e-mail, or through World Wide Web site Daniel Gomez-Palacio, Internship Program Coordinator. Phone: 617-589-0314. Fax: 617-589-0454. E-mail: interncoordinator@mos.org. In-person interview recommended (telephone interview accepted). Applicants must submit a letter of interest, resume, 2 writing samples for publication and media relations positions. Application deadline: April 6 for summer; continuous for fall/spring positions. World Wide Web: http://www.mos.org.

THE MUSEUM OF TELEVISION AND RADIO
25 West 52nd Street
New York, New York 10019

General Information Museum that collects, preserves, and exhibits radio and television programs. Established in 1975. Number of employees: 180. Number of internship applications received each year: 1,000.
Internships Available ▶ *2–4 curatorial department interns:* responsibilities include compiling information about programs and individuals significant in the history of the media, listening to and reviewing programs in the museum's collection, and drafting correspondence. Candidates should have ability to work independently, editing skills, office skills, organizational skills, research skills, self-motivation, writing skills, knowledge of field (helpful). Duration is flexible. Unpaid. Open to high school seniors, college freshmen, college sophomores, college juniors, college seniors, recent college graduates, graduate students. ▶ *1 development department intern:* responsibilities include researching sources of corporate/individual underwriting, coordinating department activities, and preparing press kits. Candidates should have ability to work independently, computer skills, oral communication skills, organizational skills, research skills, written communication skills. Duration is May to August. Unpaid. Open to high school seniors, college freshmen, college sophomores, college juniors, college seniors, recent college graduates, graduate students, career changers, individuals reentering the workforce. ▶ *1–2 education department interns:* responsibilities include assisting in the research, preparation, and teaching of group presentations and scheduling groups for education programs. Candidates should have computer skills, oral communication skills, personal interest in the field, strong interpersonal skills, written communication skills. Duration is according to need. Unpaid. Open to college freshmen, college sophomores, college juniors, college seniors, recent college graduates, graduate students, career changers. ▶ *1–4 library services department interns:* responsibilities include watching videotapes, listening to audio tapes, using microfilm and reference sources to research facts, and indexing. Candidates should have ability to work independently, computer skills, editing skills, office skills, research skills, self-motivation, writing skills. Duration is flexible. Unpaid. Open to high school seniors, college freshmen, college sophomores, college juniors, college seniors, recent college graduates, graduate students, career changers, individuals reentering the workforce. ▶ *1–2 public relations department interns:* responsibilities include working closely with the staff on routine duties (typing, filing, photocopying) and long-term projects (press releases, telephone projects, organization of exhibition openings, and press conferences). Candidates should have ability to work independently, computer skills, office skills, organizational skills, personal interest in the field, research skills, self-motivation, strong interpersonal skills, writing skills. Duration is flexible. Unpaid. Open to college freshmen, college sophomores, college juniors, college seniors, recent college graduates, graduate students, career changers, individuals reentering the workforce. ▶ *Research services interns:* responsibilities include assisting in organization of extensive print information received daily; assisting in all aspects of television and communications; working on special projects as needed. Candidates should have ability to work independently, computer skills, editing skills, office skills, organizational skills, research skills, written communication skills. Duration is flexible. Unpaid. Open to college freshmen, college sophomores, college juniors, college seniors, recent college graduates. ▶ *1–2 special events/membership interns.* Candidates should have ability to work independently, computer skills, office skills, organizational skills, research skills. Duration is May to August. Unpaid. Open to high school seniors, college freshmen, college sophomores, college juniors, college seniors, recent college graduates, graduate students, career changers, individuals reentering the workforce. ▶ *Special projects intern (vice president's office):* responsibilities include independent and creative thinking for the vice president's current project. Candidates should have ability to work independently, office skills, oral communication skills, research skills, writing skills, telephone etiquette. Unpaid. Open to college juniors, college seniors, recent college graduates, graduate students, career changers.
Benefits Formal training, opportunity to attend seminars/workshops, willing to complete paperwork for educational credit, willing to provide letters of recommendation.
Contact Call, fax, or e-mail Shannon Slon Simon, Internship Coordinator. Phone: 212-621-6615. Fax: 212-621-6700. E-mail: ssimon@mtr.org. In-person interview recommended (telephone interview accepted). Applicants must submit a formal organization application, letter of interest, resume, two letters of recommendation. Application deadline: April 1 for priority summer deadline; however, applications are accepted on a continuous basis. World Wide Web: http://www.mtr.org.

MUSKEGON MUSEUM OF ART
296 West Webster Avenue
Muskegon, Michigan 49440

General Information Art museum that collects and exhibits ancient through contemporary American, European, and Asian artwork including paintings, prints, drawings, sculpture, glass, and photography. Established in 1911. Number of employees: 13. Unit of Muskegon Public Schools, Muskegon, Michigan. Number of internship applications received each year: 10.

Internships Available ▶ *2 collections management interns:* responsibilities include working with the registrar to learn aspects of collection data management, data entry, inventory, label production, condition reports, exhibit installation, loans, and art accessions. Candidates should have ability to work independently, ability to work with others, computer skills, editing skills, office skills, oral communication skills, organizational skills, research skills, self-motivation. Duration is flexible. Unpaid. Open to recent high school graduates, college freshmen, college sophomores, college juniors, college seniors, recent college graduates, career changers, individuals reentering the workforce. ▶ *1–2 curatorial interns:* responsibilities include conducting in-depth research on selected areas of the permanent collection and exhibition training. Candidates should have ability to work independently, analytical skills, computer skills, editing skills, oral communication skills, organizational skills, research skills, self-motivation, strong interpersonal skills, writing skills. Duration is flexible. Unpaid. Open to college juniors, college seniors, recent college graduates, career changers. ▶ *1–2 education interns:* responsibilities include interpretation of selected portions of the permanent collection; writing didactic labels, exhibit brochures, and family gallery guides; organizing programming and art education stations; working with the Museum Docent program in-museum tours and classroom outreach. Candidates should have computer skills, editing skills, oral communication skills, research skills, strong interpersonal skills, writing skills. Duration is flexible. Unpaid. Open to recent high school graduates, college freshmen, college sophomores, college juniors, college seniors, recent college graduates, career changers, individuals reentering the workforce. ▶ *1 gift shop intern:* responsibilities include working with manager, buying and selling museum merchandise, doing inventory and budget, creating design and layout, and working on some advertising. Candidates should have computer skills, oral communication skills, personal interest in the field, self-motivation, strong interpersonal skills. Duration is flexible. Unpaid. Open to college freshmen, college sophomores, college juniors, college seniors, recent college graduates, career changers, individuals reentering the workforce. ▶ *1 public relations and development intern:* responsibilities include coordinating communications, media relations, general museum communications, visitor services, marketing, special projects, grant preparation, and campaign and membership development. Candidates should have computer skills, editing skills, oral communication skills, organizational skills, personal interest in the field, research skills, strong interpersonal skills, writing skills. Duration is flexible. Unpaid. Open to college juniors, college seniors, recent college graduates, career changers. International applications accepted.

Benefits Job counseling, on-the-job training, opportunity to attend seminars/workshops, willing to act as a professional reference, willing to complete paperwork for educational credit, willing to provide letters of recommendation, assistance with preparing job applications.

Contact Write, call, fax, or e-mail Art Martin, Registrar. Phone: 231-720-2570. Fax: 231-720-2585. E-mail: artjmartin@yahoo.com. In-person interview required. Applicants must submit a formal organization application, resume, academic transcripts, letter of recommendation. Applications are accepted continuously. World Wide Web: http://www.muskegon.k12.mi.us/mma/index.html.

NATIONAL BUILDING MUSEUM
401 F Street, NW
Washington, District of Columbia 20001

General Information Museum whose exhibits and educational programs interpret the worlds of engineering and architectural design, environmental and urban planning, building crafts and materials, and historic preservation. Established in 1980. Number of employees: 75. Number of internship applications received each year: 50.

Internships Available ▶ *8–15 student interns:* responsibilities include working in one of the following departments: exhibits, collections, education, public affairs, development, or administration. Candidates should have ability to work independently, ability to work with others, editing skills, oral communication skills, personal interest in the field, self-motivation, writing skills. Duration is flexible. Unpaid. Open to college freshmen, college sophomores, college juniors, college seniors, recent college graduates, graduate students. International applications accepted.

Benefits Names of contacts, opportunity to attend seminars/workshops, possible full-time employment, willing to act as a professional reference, willing to complete paperwork for educational credit, willing to provide letters of recommendation, weekly intern enrichment program for summer interns, complimentary member benefits.

Contact Write, call, fax, e-mail, or through World Wide Web site Michael Kruelle, Director of Volunteer and Visitor Services. Phone: 202-272-2448. Fax: 202-272-2564. E-mail: mkruelle@nbm.org. In-person interview recommended (telephone interview accepted). Applicants must submit a formal organization application, academic transcripts, writing sample, two letters of recommendation. Applications are accepted continuously. World Wide Web: http://www.nbm.org.

NATIONAL MUSEUM OF AMERICAN HISTORY
14th Street and Constitution Avenue, NW, Room 1040
MRC 0605
Washington, District of Columbia 20560-0605

General Information Museum that investigates, interprets, collects, preserves, exhibits, and honors the heritage of the American people. Established in 1964. Number of employees: 400. Unit of Smithsonian Institution, Washington, District of Columbia. Number of internship applications received each year: 400.

Internships Available ▶ *35–150 interns:* responsibilities include assisting in scholarly research, museum practices, and developing professional skills in a variety of career fields; contact office for list of current projects. Candidates should have personal interest in the field, various skills (depending on project). Duration is 8 weeks minimum, up to 1 year. Unpaid. Open to recent high school graduates, college freshmen, college sophomores, college juniors, college seniors, recent college graduates, graduate students, law students, career changers, individuals reentering the workforce, minimum age of 16 years and at least a high school junior. International applications accepted.

Benefits Formal training, job counseling, names of contacts, opportunity to attend seminars/workshops, willing to complete paperwork for educational credit, willing to provide letters of recommendation.

Contact Write, call, fax, or e-mail Suzanne McLaughlin, Intern Coordinator. Phone: 202-357-1606. Fax: 202-786-2851. E-mail: intern@nmah.si.edu. In-person interview recommended (telephone interview accepted). Applicants must submit a formal organization application, academic transcripts, two letters of recommendation, personal essay as outlined on the application. Application deadline: February 15 for summer, July 1 for fall, October 15 for spring. World Wide Web: http://www.si.edu/nmah/interns.

NATIONAL MUSEUM OF WOMEN IN THE ARTS
1250 New York Avenue, NW
Washington, District of Columbia 20005

General Information Art museum whose permanent collection (renaissance to present), temporary exhibits, and education programs recognize the achievements of women artists. Established in 1981. Number of employees: 96. Number of internship applications received each year: 100.

Internships Available ▶ *1 Coca-Cola intern:* responsibilities include working in any of the following departments: accounting, administration, development, curatorial, education, exhibit design and production, library and resource center research, national programs, publications, public relations, registrar, retail operations, special events, information technology, member services. Candidates should have college courses in field, knowledge of field, oral communication skills, organizational skills, personal interest in the field, research skills, strong interpersonal skills, written communication skills, plan to pursue museum career, prior experience (exhibit design and production), minimum GPA of 3.25. Duration is 1 summer (June to August); 1 fall; 1 winter (12 weeks). $1500 per duration of internship. Open to college juniors, college seniors, recent college graduates, graduate students. ▶ *1 Exxon Mobile Institutional Advancement intern:* responsibilities include working with the director and key members of an interdepartmental team to conduct research, strategize, plan, implement and administer current and new fund-raising programs for individual, corporate, and foundation donors. Candidates should have ability to work independently, oral communication skills, research skills, strong interpersonal skills, writing skills, minimum GPA of 3.2. Duration is June-August (8 weeks). $2000 per duration of internship. Open to college freshmen, college sophomores, college juniors. ▶ *1 Lebovitz intern:* responsibilities include working in any of the following departments: accounting, administration, development, curatorial, education, exhibit design and production, library and resource center research, national programs, publications, public relations, registrar, retail operations, special events, member services. Candidates should have ability to work with others, computer skills, editing skills, knowledge of field, oral communication skills, personal interest in the field, research skills, self-motivation, writing skills, plan to pursue career in art, prior experience (exhibition design and production), minimum GPA of 3.25. Duration is June-August (12 weeks, full-time). $1500 per duration of internship. Open to college juniors, college seniors, recent college graduates. ▶ *12–14 general interns:* responsibilities include working in any of the following departments: accounting, administration, development curatorial, education, exhibit design and production, library and resource center research, national programs, publications, public relations, registrar, retail operations, special events, information technology, member services. Candidates should have ability to work with others, computer skills, knowledge of field, oral communication skills, organizational skills, personal interest in the field, research skills, writing skills, prior experience (exhibit design and production), minimum GPA of 3.0. Duration is 12 weeks. Unpaid. Open to college juniors, college seniors, graduate students. International applications accepted.

Benefits Formal training, opportunity to attend seminars/workshops, possible full-time employment, willing to complete paperwork for educational credit, willing to provide letters of recommendation, art history course on women artists (fall and winter only), tours of exhibits at other museums in Washington, DC featuring women artists.

Contact Write, call, fax, e-mail, or through World Wide Web site Sallie E. Altizer, Manager of Volunteer and Visitor Services. Phone: 800-222-7270. Fax: 202-393-3234. E-mail: saltizer@nmwa.org. Applicants must submit a letter of interest, resume, academic transcripts, personal reference, letters of recommendation including one personal letter and one academic letter; applicants for Coca-Cola, Lebovit and publications/PC internships must submit one writing sample (1-2 pages) in addition to other requirements. Application deadline: March 15 for summer, June 15 for fall, October 15 for winter. World Wide Web: http://www.nmwa.org.

NATIONAL PARK SERVICE OZARK NATIONAL SCENIC RIVERWAYS
PO Box 490
Van Buren, Missouri 63965

General Information Park that conserves outstanding examples of the natural and cultural resources of the United States for the benefit and enjoyment of present and future generations. Established in 1964. Number of employees: 100. Unit of United States National Park Service, Washington, District of Columbia. Number of internship applications received each year: 5.

Internships Available ▶ *1–2 archival assistants:* responsibilities include assisting in cataloging and organizing archival material. Duration is flexible. Unpaid. ▶ *1 landscape architect:* responsibilities include updating public land records; developing public sign

proposals, plans, and drawings for public park facilities, and trails, reviewing scenic easements, rights of way, and park boundaries. Duration is May-September. Unpaid. ▶ *2 natural resources interns:* responsibilities include assisting in monitoring waterways, conducting bacteria sampling, lab work, and other natural resource duties. Duration is flexible. Position available as unpaid or paid. Open to college juniors, college seniors, recent college graduates, graduate students. International applications accepted.

Benefits Formal training, job counseling, willing to complete paperwork for educational credit, willing to provide letters of recommendation.

Contact Write, call, or fax Debbie Wisdom, Personnel Specialist. Phone: 573-323-4236. Fax: 573-323-4140. In-person interview recommended (telephone interview accepted). Applicants must submit a resume. Applications are accepted continuously. World Wide Web: http://www.nps.gov/ozar/.

THE NAVAL HISTORICAL CENTER
805 Kidder Breese Street, SE
Washington Navy Yard, District of Columbia 20374-5060

General Information Museum that undertakes historical research and writing, archival management, documentary editing, museum exhibits, educational and public programs, collections management, and library services for the Navy and the public. Established in 1801. Number of employees: 90. Unit of Department of the Navy, Washington, District of Columbia. Number of internship applications received each year: 50.

Internships Available ▶ *1–6 archival interns:* responsibilities include processing and cataloging documents, answering public inquiries, and assisting researchers. Candidates should have ability to work independently, analytical skills, organizational skills, personal interest in the field, research skills, self-motivation. Duration is 120–800 hours. Position available as unpaid or at $400 per duration of internship. Open to college freshmen, college sophomores, college juniors, college seniors, recent college graduates, graduate students, career changers, individuals reentering the workforce. ▶ *1–4 art curator interns:* responsibilities include supporting the organizing of the Navy's art collection as well as researching and writing for the collection's exhibit program. Candidates should have ability to work with others, college courses in field, computer skills, knowledge of field, research skills, written communication skills. Duration is 120–800 hours. Position available as unpaid or at $400 per duration of internship. Open to college freshmen, college sophomores, college juniors, college seniors, recent college graduates, graduate students, career changers, individuals reentering the workforce. ▶ *1–4 conservation interns:* responsibilities include assisting with conservation projects and independent artifact care. Candidates should have ability to work independently, ability to work with others, organizational skills, personal interest in the field, appreciation of artifacts. Duration is 120–800 hours. Position available as unpaid or at $400 per duration of internship. Open to individuals majoring in conservation. ▶ *1–4 copyediting interns:* responsibilities include editing publications for printed products of the branches, including books, booklets, brochures, and magazines. Candidates should have ability to work independently, computer skills, editing skills, organizational skills, self-motivation, written communication skills. Duration is 120–800 hours. Position available as unpaid or at $400 per duration of internship. Open to college juniors, college seniors, recent college graduates, graduate students, career changers. ▶ *1–10 curator interns:* responsibilities include assisting the museum curator with research and developing an exhibition script or text for publications. Candidates should have ability to work independently, research skills, strong interpersonal skills, writing skills. Duration is 120–800 hours. Position available as unpaid or at $400 per duration of internship. Open to high school seniors, recent high school graduates, college freshmen, college sophomores, college juniors, college seniors, recent college graduates, graduate students, career changers, individuals reentering the workforce. ▶ *1–5 design interns:* responsibilities include making models, preparing shop drawings, type design, graphic photography, photo silkscreening, mounting photographs, and assisting in matting, framing, and installation. Candidates should have ability to work with others, computer skills, experience in the field. Duration is 120–800

The Naval Historical Center (continued)

hours. Position available as unpaid or at $400 per duration of internship. Open to high school seniors, recent high school graduates, college freshmen, college sophomores, college juniors, college seniors, recent college graduates, graduate students, career changers, individuals reentering the workforce. ▶ *1–4 education interns:* responsibilities include working independently and with the director of education to conceive, develop, and implement education programs directly relating to the museum's collection. Candidates should have ability to work independently, personal interest in the field, research skills, strong interpersonal skills, written communication skills. Duration is 120–800 hours. Position available as unpaid or at $400 per duration of internship. Open to college juniors, college seniors, recent college graduates, graduate students, career changers, individuals reentering the workforce. ▶ *3–20 historian interns:* responsibilities include historical research and writing for the branches dealing with post-1945 U.S. Naval history, U.S. commissioned ships, and aviation history of the U.S. Navy. Candidates should have ability to work independently, analytical skills, college courses in field, research skills, writing skills. Duration is 120–800 hours. Position available as unpaid or at $400 per duration of internship. Open to college freshmen, college sophomores, college juniors, college seniors, recent college graduates, graduate students, career changers, individuals reentering the workforce. ▶ *2 library interns:* responsibilities include all aspects of library work. Candidates should have ability to work independently, ability to work with others, computer skills, organizational skills, personal interest in the field, research skills. Duration is 120–800 hours. Position available as unpaid or at $400 per duration of internship. Open to college freshmen, college sophomores, college juniors, college seniors, recent college graduates, graduate students, career changers. ▶ *1–6 public relations interns:* responsibilities include writing press releases and public service announcements, developing mailing lists, and creating and implementing strategies to increase local and national awareness of The Navy Museum. Candidates should have ability to work independently, editing skills, oral communication skills, organizational skills, writing skills. Duration is 120–800 hours. Position available as unpaid or at $400 per duration of internship. Open to college freshmen, college sophomores, college juniors, college seniors, recent college graduates, graduate students, career changers, individuals reentering the workforce. ▶ *2–10 registrarial interns:* responsibilities include collections management of the Navy's artifact collection, including accessioning, cataloging, and identifying artifacts. Candidates should have ability to work independently, ability to work with others, computer skills, organizational skills, research skills, self-motivation. Duration is 3–10 weeks. Position available as unpaid or at $400 per duration of internship. Open to high school seniors, recent high school graduates, college freshmen, college sophomores, college juniors, college seniors, recent college graduates, graduate students, career changers, individuals reentering the workforce. International applications accepted.

Benefits On-the-job training, opportunity to attend seminars/workshops, willing to act as a professional reference, willing to complete paperwork for educational credit, willing to provide letters of recommendation, small stipend.

Contact Write, call, fax, or e-mail Dr. Edward M. Furgol, Curator. Phone: 202-433-6901. Fax: 202-433-8200. E-mail: furgol.edward@nhc.navy.mil. In-person interview recommended (telephone interview accepted). Applicants must submit a formal organization application, academic transcripts, writing sample, letter of recommendation, portfolio for design interns. Applications are accepted continuously. World Wide Web: http://www.history.navy.mil.

NEW ENGLAND AQUARIUM
Central Wharf
Boston, Massachusetts 02110-3399

General Information Aquarium dedicated to presenting, promoting, and protecting the world of water. Established in 1969. Number of employees: 230. Number of internship applications received each year: 800.

Internships Available ▶ *12–15 aquarist interns:* responsibilities include caring for fish, birds, and herps; pen cleaning; feeding; collecting, record keeping and observing. Candidates should have ability to work independently, ability to work with others, analytical skills, college courses in field, knowledge of field, personal interest in the field. Duration is 12 weeks (212 hours). Unpaid. Open to college freshmen, college sophomores, college juniors, college seniors, recent college graduates, career changers, individuals reentering the workforce. ▶ *Communication assistants:* responsibilities include activity in media relations, promotions, and special events; arranging promotional events with radio stations and local organizations; some general office duties. Candidates should have oral communication skills, personal interest in the field, strong interpersonal skills, written communication skills. Unpaid. Open to college freshmen, college sophomores, college juniors, college seniors, recent college graduates, graduate students. ▶ *1–3 conservation associates:* responsibilities include researching policies and programs; evaluating and tracking legislation and regulatory proposals; drafting comments on legislation and reports. Candidates should have editing skills, office skills, writing skills. Duration is 12 weeks (212 hours). Unpaid. Open to college seniors, recent college graduates, graduate students, law students, career changers. ▶ *Corporate relations interns:* responsibilities include assisting corporate relations staff in managing relationships with the major corporations that support the aquarium. Candidates should have computer skills, office skills, oral communication skills, organizational skills, strong interpersonal skills. Unpaid. Open to college freshmen, college sophomores, college juniors, college seniors, recent college graduates, graduate students, law students. ▶ *Hospitality interns:* responsibilities include supervising and training volunteers and evaluating programs and performance; providing information on other local attractions, restaurants, and activities around Boston; studying visitor interactions and museum systems. Candidates should have ability to work with others, analytical skills, oral communication skills, hospitality or tourism background (preferred). Unpaid. Open to college sophomores, college juniors, college seniors, recent college graduates, graduate students. ▶ *2–4 lobster rearing facility/aquaculture interns:* responsibilities include assisting with daily husbandry and maintenance, recording of all relevant data, and preparing diet. Candidates should have declared college major in field, knowledge of field, personal interest in the field, research skills, biological lab skills. Duration is 12 weeks (212 hours). Unpaid. Open to college freshmen, college sophomores, college juniors, college seniors, recent college graduates, graduate students, career changers, individuals reentering the workforce. ▶ *7–10 penguin colony associates:* responsibilities include assisting with basic animal husbandry; cleaning animal environment, food preparation, feeding and recording eating patterns/behaviors. Candidates should have knowledge of field, oral communication skills, personal interest in the field, self-motivation, strong interpersonal skills, swimming ability. Duration is 12 weeks (212 hours). Unpaid. Open to recent high school graduates, college freshmen, college sophomores, college juniors, college seniors, recent college graduates, graduate students, law students, career changers, individuals reentering the workforce. ▶ *Promotions assistants:* responsibilities include pitching letters, press releases, media advisories, fact sheets, and project backgrounders; researching, compiling, and updating mailing and faxing lists. Candidates should have office skills, oral communication skills, personal interest in the field, strong interpersonal skills, writing skills. Unpaid. Open to college freshmen, college sophomores, college juniors, college seniors, recent college graduates, graduate students. ▶ *Retail interns:* responsibilities include merchandise planning, presentation, and development; assessing merchandise needs and inventory; data entry. Candidates should have ability to work with others, computer skills, oral communication skills, organizational skills. Unpaid. Open to college freshmen, college sophomores, college juniors, college seniors, recent college graduates, graduate students. ▶ *Special events interns:* responsibilities include coordinating committees, resource theme elements, event favors, and talent; assisting with mailing, phone follow-ups, signage, and seating arrangements. Candidates should have analytical skills, organizational skills, personal interest in the field, strong interpersonal skills, strong leadership ability. Unpaid. Open to college sophomores, college juniors, college seniors, graduate students. ▶ *5–10 visitor* *programs interns:* responsibilities include educating public on marine environment, giving prepared presentations, and supervising volunteers. Candidates should have ability to work with others, oral communication skills, strong interest in marine science. Duration is 12 weeks (212 hours). Unpaid. Open to college freshmen, college sophomores, college juniors, college seniors, recent college graduates, graduate students, career changers, individuals reentering the workforce. ▶ *2–5 water quality analysts:* responsibilities include collecting water samples from various exhibits and assisting with chemical and microbiological analysis of samples. Candidates should have ability to work independently, ability to work with others, analytical skills, computer skills, oral communication skills, organizational skills, personal interest in the field, self-motivation, written communication skills, at least a high-school sophomore-level understanding of chemistry. Duration is 12 weeks (212 hours). Unpaid. Open to recent high school graduates, college freshmen, college sophomores, college juniors, college seniors, recent college graduates, graduate students, law students, career changers, individuals reentering the workforce. International applications accepted.

Benefits Formal training, job counseling, names of contacts, on-the-job training, opportunity to attend seminars/workshops, possible full-time employment, willing to complete paperwork for educational credit, formal training in marine science, free passes, discounts.

Contact Write, fax, e-mail, or through World Wide Web site Volunteer and Internship Office. Fax: 617-973-6552. E-mail: vols@neaq.org. No phone calls. In-person interview recommended (telephone interview accepted). Applicants must submit a formal organization application, letter of interest, resume, portfolio for design positions, writing sample for communications positions; academic transcripts and letters of recommendation (optional but helpful). Application deadline: February 13 for summer; continuous for fall and spring, November 28 for January term/winter term. World Wide Web: http://www.neaq.org.

NEW YORK BOTANICAL GARDEN
200th Street and Kazimiroff Boulevard
Bronx, New York 10458-5126

General Information Internationally recognized center for botanical research, dedicated to environmental education and the conservation of plant diversity; operations at this facility include scientific research, horticulture, and education. Established in 1891. Number of employees: 560. Number of internship applications received each year: 80.

Internships Available ▶ *2–3 Bronx green-up interns:* responsibilities include implementing programs in community gardening and composting, and supporting the development of school garden lessons and curriculum. Candidates should have ability to work independently, knowledge of field, oral communication skills, personal interest in the field, self-motivation, strong interpersonal skills. Duration is variable (according to funding). Salary depends on funding. Open to college freshmen, college sophomores, college juniors, college seniors, recent college graduates. ▶ *5–7 Everett Public Service Internship Program positions:* responsibilities include working on community outreach, research, education projects. Candidates should have college courses in field, computer skills, knowledge of field, oral communication skills, personal interest in the field, plan to pursue career in field, research skills, strong interpersonal skills, strong leadership ability. Duration is 8–10 weeks. $200 per week. Open to college freshmen, college sophomores, college juniors, college seniors, recent college graduates, graduate students. ▶ *1–7 botanical science interns:* responsibilities include working side by side with prominent scientists in areas such as economic botany, systematic botany, molecular systematics, and the Harding Laboratory, Library, and Herbarium, (the largest in the Western Hemisphere, containing six million plant specimens). Candidates should have college courses in field, knowledge of field, personal interest in the field, plan to pursue career in field, research skills. Duration is variable (according to funding). Salary depends on funding. Open to college freshmen, college sophomores, college juniors, college seniors, recent college graduates, graduate students. ▶ *16 horticulture interns:* responsibilities include assisting gardeners, curators, and manag-

ers in the care of plants, gardens, collection, and records. Candidates should have ability to work independently, college courses in field, knowledge of field, plan to pursue career in field, self-motivation, strong interpersonal skills. Duration is 6–8 months. Position available as unpaid or at $7.50 per hour. Open to college freshmen, college sophomores, college juniors, college seniors, recent college graduates, career changers. ▶ *8–10 instructors:* responsibilities include assisting with children's gardening programs, interpreting hands-on exhibits at interactive Children's Garden; presenting science activities to children and adults. Candidates should have ability to work with others, oral communication skills, personal interest in the field, self-motivation, strong leadership ability. Duration is 4–8 months. $8.50–$10.50 per hour. Open to high school students, recent high school graduates, college freshmen, college sophomores, college juniors, college seniors, recent college graduates, graduate students. International applications accepted.

Benefits On-the-job training, opportunity to attend seminars/workshops, possible full-time employment, willing to act as a professional reference, willing to complete paperwork for educational credit, willing to provide letters of recommendation.

Contact Write, call, fax, or e-mail Claribel Irizarry, Human Resources Representative. Phone: 718-817-8872. Fax: 718-220-6504. E-mail: hr2@nybg.org. In-person interview recommended (telephone interview accepted). Applicants must submit a formal organization application, letter of interest, resume, academic transcripts, three personal references. Application deadline: March 31 for horticulture positions and Everett positions; continuous for other positions. World Wide Web: http://www.nybg.org.

NORLANDS LIVING HISTORY CENTER
290 Norlands Road
Livermore, Maine 04253

General Information Museum that brings to life the daily activities of 19th-century rural New England through role playing, hands-on experience, and demonstrations performed in historic buildings. Established in 1974. Number of employees: 23. Unit of Washburn-Norlands Foundation, Livermore, Maine. Number of internship applications received each year: 12.

Internships Available ▶ *2–4 agricultural interns:* responsibilities include performing 19th-century farm activities, working with school groups, working with livestock, and maintaining site. Candidates should have ability to work independently, oral communication skills, personal interest in the field, self-motivation, strong interpersonal skills. Duration is 2 to 6 months (possibly longer depending on organization's needs). $50 per week; increases to $75 a week after 3 months, to $100 a week after 6 months. Open to recent high school graduates, college freshmen, college sophomores, college juniors, college seniors, recent college graduates, graduate students, law students, career changers, individuals reentering the workforce, individuals with farming backgrounds. ▶ *1 archival intern:* responsibilities include researching, organizing, and maintaining the archives; working with visiting scholars. Candidates should have ability to work independently, computer skills, organizational skills, personal interest in the field, research skills, self-motivation. Duration is dependent on the amount of time needed to complete projects. $50 per week; increases to $75 a week after 3 months, to $100 a week after 6 months. Open to college juniors, college seniors, graduate students, law students, career changers, librarians and teachers. ▶ *1 curatorial intern:* responsibilities include working in an 1870s mansion that has recently undergone major restoration and maintaining collections. Candidates should have ability to work independently, ability to work with others, computer skills, organizational skills, research skills, self-motivation. Duration is 2–6 months. $50 per week; increases to $75 a week after 3 months, to $100 a week after 6 months. Open to college juniors, college seniors, recent college graduates, graduate students, career changers. ▶ *2–4 interpretation/education interns:* responsibilities include guiding tours and groups, working as living-history interpreter for hands-on educational programs, possibility of working with lifestock and site maintenance. Candidates should have oral communication skills, organizational skills, personal interest in the field, self-motivation, strong interpersonal

Norlands Living History Center (continued)

skills, strong leadership ability. Duration is 2-6 months (may be extended longer than 6 months). $50 per week; increases to $75 a week after 3 months, to $100 a week after 6 months. Open to college juniors, college seniors, recent college graduates, graduate students, law students, career changers, individuals reentering the workforce, retired teachers, history buffs, and individuals with farming backgrounds. International applications accepted.
Benefits Free housing, possible full-time employment, willing to act as a professional reference, willing to complete paperwork for educational credit, willing to provide letters of recommendation.
Contact Write, call, fax, or e-mail Judith Bielecki, Executive Director. Phone: 207-897-4366. Fax: 207-897-4963. E-mail: norlands@ctel.net. In-person interview recommended (telephone interview accepted). Applicants must submit a formal organization application, letter of interest, resume, 2-page essay, 3 letters of recommendation or personal references. Applications are accepted continuously. World Wide Web: http://www.norlands.org.

NORTH CAROLINA STATE PARKS AND RECREATION, CLIFFS OF THE NEUSE STATE PARK
345-A Park Entrance Road
Seven Springs, North Carolina 28578

General Information Park serving the people of North Carolina and protecting a unique area of scientific value and scenic beauty. Established in 1945. Number of employees: 8. Unit of North Carolina State Park System, Raleigh, North Carolina. Number of internship applications received each year: 6.
Internships Available ▶ *1 museum/librarian/researcher:* responsibilities include working in park museum cataloging slides, conducting research on cliff deposits, and writing papers on findings. Duration is 4 months. Unpaid. Open to college juniors, college seniors, recent college graduates, graduate students. ▶ *Researchers:* responsibilities include collecting and cataloging a plant collection of flora found in the park to be stored in the park's herbarium. Duration is 4 months. Unpaid. Open to college seniors, recent college graduates, graduate students. Candidates for all positions should have ability to work independently, college courses in field, knowledge of field, oral communication skills, personal interest in the field, research skills. International applications accepted.
Benefits Free housing, names of contacts, possible full-time employment, willing to complete paperwork for educational credit, willing to provide letters of recommendation.
Contact Write or call Mr. Daniel G. Smith, Park Superintendent. Phone: 919-778-6234. In-person interview required. Applications are accepted continuously.

NORTH CAROLINA STATE PARKS AND RECREATION, HANGING ROCK STATE PARK
PO Box 278
Danbury, North Carolina 27016

General Information State park that strives to preserve and protect an area of scenic and natural beauty and provide a recreational area for the public. Established in 1936. Number of employees: 11. Unit of North Carolina Division of Parks and Recreation, Raleigh, North Carolina. Number of internship applications received each year: 5.
Internships Available ▶ *1 assistant ranger:* responsibilities include park operations and interpretation. Candidates should have college courses in field, knowledge of field, oral communication skills, self-motivation, strong interpersonal skills. Duration is 7 months. Position available as unpaid or at $7.25 per hour. Open to college freshmen, college sophomores, college juniors, college seniors, recent college graduates. ▶ *1 lifeguard:* responsibilities include lifeguarding lake. Candidates should have knowledge of field, oral communication skills, self-motivation, strong interpersonal skills, American Red Cross certification. Duration is 3 months. $7.15 per hour. Open to high school seniors, recent high school graduates, college freshmen, college sophomores, college juniors, college seniors, recent college graduates. ▶ *1 naturalist/interpreter:* responsibilities include presenting natural and cultural interpretive programs to park visitors. Candidates should have ability to

work independently, college courses in field, knowledge of field, oral communication skills, strong interpersonal skills. Duration is 3-6 months (40 hours per week). Unpaid. Open to college juniors, college seniors, recent college graduates, graduate students. ▶ *1 park attendant:* responsibilities include maintaining and operating campgrounds and resource management. Candidates should have knowledge of field, oral communication skills, personal interest in the field, self-motivation, strong interpersonal skills. Duration is 6 months. Position available as unpaid or at $6 per hour. Open to college freshmen, college sophomores, college juniors, college seniors. ▶ *1 resource management specialist:* responsibilities include working on assigned resource management problems and issues; some research may be involved. Candidates should have ability to work independently, declared college major in field, experience in the field, research skills, strong interpersonal skills, written communication skills. Duration is 3-6 months (40 hours per week). Unpaid. Open to college juniors, college seniors, recent college graduates, graduate students. International applications accepted.
Benefits Housing at a cost, names of contacts, possible full-time employment, willing to complete paperwork for educational credit, willing to provide letters of recommendation.
Contact Write, call, fax, or e-mail Mr. Tommy R. Wagoner, Park Superintendent. Phone: 336-593-8480. Fax: 336-593-9166. E-mail: hangingrock@mindspring.com. In-person interview recommended (telephone interview accepted). Applicants must submit a formal organization application, resume. Application deadline: February 1 for summer, December 1 for spring.

NORTH CAROLINA STATE PARKS AND RECREATION, JOCKEY'S RIDGE STATE PARK
West Carolina Drive
Nags Head, North Carolina 27959

General Information Park providing high-quality management of scenic, ecological, and cultural values for public benefit. Established in 1975. Number of employees: 16. Unit of North Carolina State Park System, Raleigh, North Carolina. Number of internship applications received each year: 50.
Internships Available ▶ *2-3 assistant rangers:* responsibilities include planning and providing public education. Candidates should have ability to work independently, knowledge of field, oral communication skills, personal interest in the field, research skills, self-motivation, strong interpersonal skills. Duration is 3 months for 2 assistants and 9 months for other assistant. $7.25 per hour. ▶ *2 volunteer/ naturalist interns:* responsibilities include planning and providing public education. Candidates should have ability to work independently, college courses in field, knowledge of field, oral communication skills, personal interest in the field, research skills, self-motivation, strong interpersonal skills. Duration is flexible. Unpaid. Open to high school students, recent high school graduates, college freshmen, college sophomores, college juniors, college seniors, recent college graduates, graduate students, law students, career changers, individuals reentering the workforce. International applications accepted.
Benefits Names of contacts, on-the-job training, possible full-time employment, willing to act as a professional reference, willing to complete paperwork for educational credit, willing to provide letters of recommendation, free housing for volunteers working over 16 hours per week.
Contact Write, call, or fax Mr. John Fullwood, Park Ranger II, PO Box 592, Nags Head, North Carolina 27959. Phone: 252-441-7132. Fax: 252-441-8416. In-person interview recommended (telephone interview accepted). Applicants must submit a formal organization application, letter of interest. Application deadline: March 1 for summer, July 1 for fall.

NORTH CAROLINA STATE PARKS AND RECREATION, JORDAN LAKE STATE RECREATION AREA
280 State Park Road
Apex, North Carolina 27502

General Information Park that preserves a unique area of scenic significance, natural beauty, and provides recreational enjoyment.

Established in 1980. Number of employees: 31. Unit of North Carolina State Park System, Raleigh, North Carolina. Number of internship applications received each year: 1.
Internships Available ▶ *1–4 assistant park rangers:* responsibilities include providing information to guests, registering campers, supervising other summer help and ticket booth operations, and performing all tasks necessary in park operations. Candidates should have ability to work independently, college courses in field, oral communication skills, plan to pursue career in field, self-motivation, strong interpersonal skills. Duration is 4–6 months. Position available as unpaid or at $7.25 per hour. Open to college freshmen, college sophomores, college juniors, college seniors, recent college graduates, individuals reentering the workforce.
Benefits Formal training, names of contacts, possible full-time employment, willing to complete paperwork for educational credit, willing to provide letters of recommendation.
Contact Write or call Mr. Mike Seigh, Park Superintendent. Phone: 919-362-0586. In-person interview required. Applicants must submit a formal organization application, resume. Application deadline: March 1 for summer.

NORTH CAROLINA STATE PARKS AND RECREATION, MOUNT JEFFERSON STATE PARK
Jefferson, North Carolina 28694

General Information State park that preserves and protects an area of scenic beauty and environmental and ecological significance. Established in 1956. Number of employees: 8. Unit of North Carolina State Park System, Raleigh, North Carolina. Number of internship applications received each year: 15.
Internships Available ▶ *1 archaeological researcher:* responsibilities include researching archaeology of the river area. Candidates should have ability to work independently, ability to work with others, analytical skills, college courses in field, computer skills, editing skills, knowledge of field, personal interest in the field, research skills, self-motivation, writing skills. Duration is flexible. Position available as unpaid or at $6.75 per hour. Open to college juniors, college seniors, recent college graduates, graduate students. ▶ *1 bird surveyor:* responsibilities include developing accurate bird list in printed form and on the Internet, conducting PIF, conducting Golden Winged and Cerulean Warbler Atlas projects. Candidates should have ability to work independently, analytical skills, computer skills, editing skills, knowledge of field, organizational skills, personal interest in the field, research skills, self-motivation, strong interpersonal skills, writing skills. Duration is June to mid-August. $6.75 per hour. Open to college juniors, college seniors, graduate students. ▶ *1 geological researcher:* responsibilities include conducting geological investigations of Mount Jefferson State Natural Area to gain an understanding of complete geological history of the area; preparing a written report to be filed with state park unit and district interpretation and education specialist; producing a geologic map using GIS software. Candidates should have ability to work independently, analytical skills, computer skills, editing skills, knowledge of field, organizational skills, personal interest in the field, research skills, self-motivation, strong interpersonal skills, writing skills. Duration is flexible. Position available as unpaid or at $6.75 per hour. Open to college juniors, college seniors, graduate students. ▶ *1 interpretive specialist:* responsibilities include developing programs for schools and evening visitors and making field identifications. Candidates should have ability to work independently, analytical skills, college courses in field, computer skills, editing skills, knowledge of field, office skills, oral communication skills, organizational skills, personal interest in the field, research skills, self-motivation, strong interpersonal skills, writing skills. Duration is flexible. Position available as unpaid or at $6.75 per hour. Open to college sophomores, college juniors, college seniors, recent college graduates, graduate students, career changers. ▶ *1 natural heritage researcher:* responsibilities include floristics inventory, documenting endangered species, and identifying species recognized as endangered. Candidates should have ability to work independently, analytical skills, college courses in field, computer skills, editing skills, knowledge of field, organizational skills, personal interest in the field, research skills, self-motivation, strong interpersonal skills, writing skills. Duration is flexible. Position available as unpaid

or at $6.75 per hour. Open to college juniors, college seniors, recent college graduates, graduate students, career changers. ▶ *1 park photographer:* responsibilities include photographing flora and fauna of the park. Candidates should have ability to work independently, knowledge of field, personal interest in the field, self-motivation, strong interpersonal skills. Duration is flexible. Unpaid. Open to recent high school graduates, college freshmen, college sophomores, college juniors, college seniors, recent college graduates, graduate students, career changers. International applications accepted.
Benefits Free housing, names of contacts, possible full-time employment, willing to complete paperwork for educational credit, willing to provide letters of recommendation, paid positions for North Carolina residents only.
Contact Write, call, fax, or e-mail Mr. Jay Wild, Superintendent, PO Box 48, Jefferson, North Carolina 28640. Phone: 336-982-2587. Fax: 336-982-3943. E-mail: moje@skybest.com. In-person interview recommended (telephone interview accepted). Applicants must submit a letter of interest, resume. Application deadline: January 31 for paid interns; continuous for volunteer interns. World Wide Web: http://www.ncsparks.net.

NORTH CAROLINA STATE PARKS AND RECREATION, NEW RIVER STATE PARK
1477 Wagoner Access Road, PO Box 48
Jefferson, North Carolina 28640

General Information Recreational park that seeks to preserve and protect an area of scenic beauty and environmental and ecological significance. Established in 1976. Number of employees: 22. Unit of North Carolina State Park System, Raleigh, North Carolina. Number of internship applications received each year: 15.
Internships Available ▶ *1–3 archaeological researchers:* responsibilities include researching and documenting archaeology of the river area. Candidates should have ability to work independently, ability to work with others, analytical skills, college courses in field, computer skills, editing skills, knowledge of field, personal interest in the field, research skills, self-motivation, writing skills. Duration is 4–10 months. Unpaid. Open to college juniors, college seniors, recent college graduates, graduate students. ▶ *1 bird surveyor:* responsibilities include developing accurate bird lists, conducting PIF and Birds in Forested Landscapes study, conducting Warbler Atlas Project. Candidates should have ability to work independently, analytical skills, computer skills, editing skills, knowledge of field, organizational skills, personal interest in the field, research skills, self-motivation, strong interpersonal skills, writing skills. Duration is 8–10 weeks. Position available as unpaid or at $6.75 per hour. Open to college juniors, college seniors, graduate students. ▶ *1 botanical surveyor of New River State Park:* responsibilities include organizing botanical information previously gathered; gathering new information on plants and plant communities within the park; mapping plant communities. Candidates should have ability to work independently, analytical skills, computer skills, knowledge of field, organizational skills, personal interest in the field, research skills, self-motivation, strong interpersonal skills. Duration is 8–10 weeks. $6.75 per hour. Open to college juniors, college seniors, graduate students. ▶ *1–2 butterfly study interns:* responsibilities include identifying different species of butterflies within park boundaries, preparing a list of different species and noting rare findings, and producing butterfly brochure for the use of the public. Candidates should have ability to work independently, ability to work with others, computer skills, knowledge of field, office skills, personal interest in the field, research skills, self-motivation, writing skills. Duration is 3–4 months. Position available as unpaid or at $6.75 per hour. Open to college juniors, college seniors, recent college graduates, graduate students. ▶ *1 canoe trail specialist:* responsibilities include conducting a natural and historical investigation of the New River in order to create a 26.5-mile self-guided canoe trail; information in the guide should include local history, ecology, and geology, as well as provide basic stewardship principles. Candidates should have ability to work independently, analytical skills, computer skills, editing skills, knowledge of field, organizational skills, personal interest in the field, research skills, self-motivation,

North Carolina State Parks and Recreation, New River State Park (continued)

strong interpersonal skills, writing skills. Duration is 3 months. Position available as unpaid or at $6.75 per hour. Open to college juniors, college seniors, graduate students. ► *2–4 exhibit and publications specialists:* responsibilities include design, layout, and construction of new exhibits and publications for park interpretive programs and materials. Candidates should have ability to work independently, analytical skills, college courses in field, computer skills, editing skills, knowledge of field, organizational skills, personal interest in the field, research skills, self-motivation, strong interpersonal skills, writing skills, desktop publishing skills (preferred). Duration is 3–10 months. Position available as unpaid or at $6.75 per hour. Open to college freshmen, college sophomores, college juniors, college seniors, recent college graduates, individuals reentering the workforce. ► *1–4 interpretive specialists:* responsibilities include developing school and evening group programs and identifying species in the field. Candidates should have ability to work independently, analytical skills, college courses in field, computer skills, editing skills, knowledge of field, office skills, oral communication skills, organizational skills, personal interest in the field, research skills, self-motivation, strong interpersonal skills, writing skills. Duration is 3–10 months. Position available as unpaid or at $6.75 per hour. Open to college sophomores, college juniors, college seniors, recent college graduates, graduate students, career changers. ► *1–4 mapping interns:* responsibilities include mapping the state park using GIS software and GPS devices. Candidates should have ability to work independently, analytical skills, college courses in field, computer skills, editing skills, knowledge of field, organizational skills, personal interest in the field, research skills, self-motivation, strong interpersonal skills, writing skills. Duration is 4–6 months. Position available as unpaid or at $6.75 per hour. Open to college juniors, college seniors, recent college graduates, graduate students, career changers. ► *1–2 natural heritage researchers:* responsibilities include identifying and documenting endangered species and performing floristics or faunal inventory. Candidates should have ability to work independently, analytical skills, college courses in field, computer skills, editing skills, knowledge of field, organizational skills, personal interest in the field, research skills, self-motivation, strong interpersonal skills, writing skills. Duration is 3–12 months. Position available as unpaid or at $6.75 per hour. Open to college juniors, college seniors, recent college graduates, graduate students, career changers. ► *1–2 park photographers:* responsibilities include photographing flora and fauna of the state park. Candidates should have ability to work independently, knowledge of field, personal interest in the field, self-motivation, strong interpersonal skills. Duration is 3 months. Unpaid. Open to recent high school graduates, college freshmen, college sophomores, college juniors, college seniors, recent college graduates, graduate students, career changers. ► *1–3 river user surveyors:* responsibilities include conducting survey of river water levels to ensure safe use by rafters and canoers. Candidates should have ability to work independently, analytical skills, college courses in field, computer skills, knowledge of field, office skills, personal interest in the field, research skills, self-motivation, strong interpersonal skills, writing skills. Duration is 3–6 months. Position available as unpaid or at $6.75 per hour. Open to college juniors, college seniors, recent college graduates, graduate students. ► *5–10 trails construction technicians:* responsibilities include design, layout, and construction of hiking trails using hand tools and natural materials; supervision of volunteer and court-assigned laborers. Candidates should have ability to work independently, personal interest in the field, self-motivation, strong interpersonal skills. Duration is 3–10 months. Position available as unpaid or at $6.75 per hour. Open to recent high school graduates, college freshmen, college sophomores, college juniors, college seniors, recent college graduates, graduate students, career changers, individuals reentering the workforce. International applications accepted.

Benefits Free housing, job counseling, names of contacts, possible full-time employment, willing to act as a professional reference, willing to complete paperwork for educational credit, willing to provide letters of recommendation, paid internships for North Carolina residents only.

Contact Write, call, fax, or e-mail Mr. Jay Wild, Superintendent. Phone: 336-982-2587. Fax: 336-982-3943. E-mail: neri@skybest.

com. In-person interview recommended (telephone interview accepted). Applicants must submit a resume, academic transcripts, three personal references, letter of recommendation. Application deadline: January 31 for paid interns; continuous for volunteer interns. World Wide Web: http://www.ncsparks.net.

NORTH CAROLINA STATE PARKS AND RECREATION, PETTIGREW STATE PARK
2252 Lakeshore Road
Creswell, North Carolina 27928

General Information State park whose goal is to preserve and protect unique state natural areas and provide public enjoyment. Established in 1939. Number of employees: 9. Unit of North Carolina Division of Parks and Recreation, Raleigh, North Carolina. Number of internship applications received each year: 5.

Internships Available ► *1–2 general utility workers:* responsibilities include working with the administrative staff, maintenance staff, and generally doing what needs to be done. Candidates should have ability to work independently, ability to work with others, personal interest in the field. Duration is March to September (40 hours per week). $6.75 per hour. Open to recent high school graduates, college freshmen, college sophomores, college juniors, college seniors, individuals reentering the workforce, must be 18 years or older. ► *1–2 naturalists:* responsibilities include conducting aquatic plant surveys, rare plant species surveys, and new plant experimentation. Candidates should have personal interest in the field, plan to pursue career in field. Duration is flexible. Unpaid. Open to college sophomores, college juniors, college seniors. ► *1 park attendant:* responsibilities include maintaining grounds and facilities. Candidates should have ability to work independently, ability to work with others, personal interest in the field, plan to pursue career in field, valid driver's license. Duration is 3 months in summer. $6 per hour. Open to recent high school graduates, must be 18 years or older. ► *1 volunteer:* responsibilities include performing various duties around the park. Candidates should have ability to work independently, ability to work with others, personal interest in the field, plan to pursue career in field, self-motivation. Duration is flexible. Unpaid. Open to college freshmen, college sophomores, college juniors, college seniors, recent college graduates, graduate students. International applications accepted.

Benefits Names of contacts, possible full-time employment, willing to act as a professional reference, willing to complete paperwork for educational credit, willing to provide letters of recommendation, free camping.

Contact Write, call, fax, or e-mail Internship Coordinator. Phone: 252-797-4475. Fax: 252-797-7405. E-mail: pettigrew_sp@coastalnet. com. In-person interview recommended (telephone interview accepted). Applications are accepted continuously. World Wide Web: http://ils.unc.edu/parkproject/ncparks.html.

NORTH CAROLINA STATE PARKS AND RECREATION, RAVEN ROCK STATE PARK
3009 Raven Rock Road
Lillington, North Carolina 27546

General Information State park that conserves and protects natural resources and provides opportunities for recreation and environmental education. Established in 1916. Number of employees: 5. Unit of North Carolina Department of Environment and Natural Resources, Raleigh, North Carolina. Number of internship applications received each year: 1.

Internships Available ► *1 facilities and grounds intern:* responsibilities include assisting in the routine maintenance of park facility and grounds. Candidates should have ability to work independently, ability to work with others, self-motivation. Duration is 3–4 months. Unpaid. ► *1 natural resource interpreter:* responsibilities include utilizing interpretive materials on a rotating basis to provide information on the park's natural resources. Candidates should have ability to work independently, oral communication skills, personal interest in the field, research skills, self-motivation, written communication skills. Duration is flexible. Unpaid. ► *1 trail maintenance intern:* responsibilities include assisting staff in maintenance of

hiking and bridle trails, trimming overgrowth and fallen trees from trail path, and maintaining water bars, footbridges, trail blazes, signs, and markers. Candidates should have ability to work independently, ability to work with others, self-motivation. Duration is 3–4 months. Unpaid. Open to recent high school graduates, college freshmen, college sophomores, college juniors, college seniors, recent college graduates, graduate students, law students, career changers, individuals reentering the workforce. International applications accepted.
Benefits Names of contacts, possible full-time employment, willing to complete paperwork for educational credit, willing to provide letters of recommendation.
Contact Write, call, fax, or e-mail Eric Folk, Park Ranger 1. Phone: 910-893-4888. Fax: 910-814-2200. E-mail: ravenroc@infi.net. In-person interview required. Applicants must submit a formal organization application. Applications are accepted continuously. World Wide Web: http://ils.unc.edu/parkproject/ncparks.htm.

OFFICE OF HISTORIC ALEXANDRIA
PO Box 178, City Hall
Alexandria, Virginia 22313

General Information Office involved with the preservation of historic sites, artifacts, records, and the enhancement and preservation of the cultural diversity of Alexandria; provides programs to bring people and business to the city. Established in 1983. Number of employees: 70. Unit of City of Alexandria, Alexandria, Virginia. Number of internship applications received each year: 40.
Internships Available ▶ *6–8 Alexandria archaeology interns:* responsibilities include assisting with archaeological field work, exhibits, artifact analysis, and public programs. Candidates should have ability to work independently, ability to work with others, computer skills, personal interest in the field, self-motivation. Duration is 4–12 weeks. Unpaid. Open to high school students, college freshmen, college sophomores, college juniors, college seniors, recent college graduates, graduate students. ▶ *1 Archives and Records Center intern :* responsibilities include preparing and finding records and cataloging the collection of archival materials relating to history of the city. Candidates should have ability to work independently, ability to work with others, analytical skills, college courses in field, computer skills, knowledge of field, office skills, organizational skills, plan to pursue career in field, self-motivation, writing skills. Duration is 6–8 weeks. Position available as unpaid or at hourly rate if funding is available. Open to college juniors, college seniors, recent college graduates, graduate students. ▶ *4 Black History Resource Center interns:* responsibilities include assisting with interpretation and public programs. Candidates should have oral communication skills, plan to pursue career in field, strong interpersonal skills, written communication skills. Duration is 6–8 weeks. Unpaid. Open to high school students, college freshmen, college sophomores, college juniors, college seniors, recent college graduates, graduate students, career changers. ▶ *1–2 Ft. Ward Museum interns:* responsibilities include cataloging. Candidates should have editing skills, knowledge of field, plan to pursue career in field, research skills, writing skills. Duration is 8 weeks (minimum). Unpaid. Open to college sophomores, college juniors, college seniors, recent college graduates, graduate students. ▶ *4 Gadsby's Tavern Museum interns:* responsibilities include assisting with interpretation and public programs. Candidates should have knowledge of field, oral communication skills, plan to pursue career in field, writing skills. Duration is 6–8 weeks. Unpaid. Open to high school seniors, college freshmen, college sophomores, college juniors, college seniors, recent college graduates, graduate students. ▶ *1–3 Lyceum interns:* responsibilities include assisting with exhibits and public programs. Candidates should have ability to work independently, oral communication skills, personal interest in the field, self-motivation, strong interpersonal skills, written communication skills. Duration is 6–8 weeks. Unpaid. Open to high school seniors, college freshmen, college sophomores, college juniors, college seniors, recent college graduates, graduate students, individuals reentering the workforce. International applications accepted.
Benefits Formal training, job counseling, names of contacts, on-the-job training, opportunity to attend seminars/workshops,

willing to act as a professional reference, willing to complete paperwork for educational credit, willing to provide letters of recommendation.
Contact Write, call, fax, e-mail, or through World Wide Web site Ms. Jean Taylor Federico, Director. Phone: 703-838-4554. Fax: 703-838-6451. E-mail: jean.federico@ci.alexandria.va.us. In-person interview recommended (telephone interview accepted). Applicants must submit a letter of interest, resume, three personal references, three letters of recommendation. Applications are accepted continuously. World Wide Web: http://ci.alexandria.va.us/oha.

OLYMPIC NATIONAL PARK
600 East Park Avenue
Port Angeles, Washington 98362

General Information National park managing 923,000 acres of coast, rainforest, and mountains. Established in 1938. Number of employees: 140. Unit of United States National Park Service, Washington, District of Columbia. Number of internship applications received each year: 75.
Internships Available ▶ *8–9 backcountry rangers:* responsibilities include assisting park rangers with various tasks including visitor contacts, providing information to the public, patrolling trails and roads, operating backcountry stations, minor trail maintenance, various resource management projects, light maintenance, and search-and-rescue operations. Candidates should have ability to work independently, ability to work with others, oral communication skills, personal interest in the field. Duration is 1–3 months. $50 per month. Open to college freshmen, college sophomores, college juniors, college seniors, recent college graduates, graduate students, law students, career changers, individuals reentering the workforce. ▶ *14 campground hosts:* responsibilities include assisting area park rangers with operations and light maintenance of campgrounds in a designated location within the park. Candidates should have ability to work independently, ability to work with others, oral communication skills, personal interest in the field, access to recreation vehicle or trailer. Duration is usually June to Labor Day. Position available as unpaid or at $50 per month. Open to college seniors, recent college graduates, graduate students, career changers, individuals reentering the workforce. ▶ *4–8 education rangers:* responsibilities include assisting with daily operations of a major visitor center, providing environmental education programs to local schools, conducting nature walks and talks, planning exhibits, and assisting with search-and-rescue. Candidates should have ability to work independently, computer skills, oral communication skills, strong interpersonal skills, strong leadership ability, written communication skills. Duration is 3–4 months. $100 per month. Open to college freshmen, college sophomores, college juniors, college seniors, recent college graduates, graduate students. ▶ *4–6 natural resource management interns:* responsibilities include aiding park scientists and resource managers in a variety of projects, including fish and other wildlife studies, wilderness revegetation, conducting plant ecology research, monitoring programs, and collecting and inputting resource data. Candidates should have ability to work independently, ability to work with others, college courses in field, oral communication skills, personal interest in the field, written communication skills. Duration is 2–5 months. $50–$100 per month. Open to college freshmen, college sophomores, college juniors, college seniors, recent college graduates, graduate students. ▶ *1–3 wilderness information center interns:* responsibilities include developing a working knowledge of park wilderness destinations, regulations, and "Leave No Trace" outdoor skills; issuing camping reservations and permits; answering phone and mail. Candidates should have ability to work independently, ability to work with others, oral communication skills, strong leadership ability, written communication skills. Duration is April to September. $50 per month. Open to college freshmen, college sophomores, college juniors, college seniors, recent college graduates, graduate students, law students, career changers, individuals reentering the workforce. International applications accepted.
Benefits Free housing, job counseling, names of contacts, opportunity to attend seminars/workshops, willing to complete paperwork for educational credit, willing to provide letters of recommendation.

Olympic National Park (continued)

Contact Write, call, fax, or e-mail Volunteer Coordinator. Phone: 360-565-3000. Fax: 360-565-3015. E-mail: olym_mail_room@nps.gov. Applicants must submit a formal organization application, resume. Application deadline: March 15 for natural resource management, campground host, and summer education rangers, October 1 for winter education rangers; continuous for all other positions. World Wide Web: http://www.nps.gov/olym.

ORLANDO MUSEUM OF ART
2416 North Mills Avenue
Orlando, Florida 32803

General Information Museum featuring public programs and activities that interpret its permanent collections and special exhibits. Established in 1924. Number of employees: 40. Number of internship applications received each year: 20.

Internships Available ▶ *3 education interns:* responsibilities include performing activities tailored to the needs of the department that plans museum programs. Candidates should have ability to work independently, computer skills, oral communication skills, organizational skills, strong interpersonal skills, knowledge of pre-Columbian, African, or contemporary American art (helpful). Duration is minimum of 2 months. Unpaid. Open to college sophomores, college juniors, college seniors, recent college graduates, graduate students.

Benefits Formal training, names of contacts, on-the-job training, opportunity to attend seminars/workshops, willing to complete paperwork for educational credit, willing to provide letters of recommendation.

Contact Write or e-mail Ms. Susan Rosoff, Curator of Education. E-mail: srosoff@omart.org. No phone calls. In-person interview recommended (telephone interview accepted). Applicants must submit a letter of interest, resume, letter of recommendation. Applications are accepted continuously. World Wide Web: http://www.omart.org.

PASADENA HISTORICAL MUSEUM
470 West Walnut Street
Pasadena, California 91103

General Information Museum operating exhibition galleries, an historic 1906 mansion, a museum of Finnish folk art, and a library archive. Established in 1924. Number of employees: 13. Number of internship applications received each year: 5.

Internships Available ▶ *1 assistant educator:* responsibilities include assisting with ongoing educational programs, exhibition development, and updating docent training materials. Candidates should have ability to work independently, office skills, oral communication skills, organizational skills, personal interest in the field, strong interpersonal skills. Duration is flexible. Unpaid. Open to high school students, recent high school graduates, college freshmen, college sophomores, college juniors, college seniors, recent college graduates, graduate students, law students, career changers, individuals reentering the workforce. ▶ *1 assistant manager of membership:* responsibilities include data entry, mailings, scheduling of meetings and organizing events; some clerical work. Candidates should have ability to work independently, computer skills, office skills, organizational skills, self-motivation, written communication skills. Duration is flexible. Unpaid. Open to recent high school graduates, college freshmen, college sophomores, college juniors, college seniors, recent college graduates, graduate students, law students, career changers, individuals reentering the workforce. ▶ *1 collections intern:* responsibilities include assisting with research and care of extensive collection of circa 1900 art and antiques. Candidates should have ability to work independently, computer skills, knowledge of field, organizational skills, personal interest in the field, research skills. Duration is summer (two to three months). $3000 per duration of internship. Open to college freshmen, college sophomores, college juniors, college seniors, recent college graduates, graduate students, law students, career changers, individuals reentering the workforce. ▶ *1 facilities/operations assistant manager:* responsibilities include working with committees to schedule set-up of meetings and events; maintenance and organizing. Candidates should have ability to work independently,

ability to work with others, organizational skills, self-motivation. Duration is flexible. Unpaid. Open to recent college graduates, graduate students, career changers, individuals reentering the workforce. ▶ *1 public relations intern:* responsibilities include developing/producing ads, flyers, promotional materials, database and news clippings; possible presentations. Candidates should have computer skills, editing skills, oral communication skills, personal interest in the field, strong interpersonal skills, writing skills. Duration is flexible. Unpaid. Open to recent high school graduates, college freshmen, college sophomores, college juniors, college seniors, individuals reentering the workforce. ▶ *1–3 research library interns:* responsibilities include assisting researchers in use of library; conservation of documents, books, and photographs; researching reference questions; and assisting in cataloging library and archival materials. Candidates should have ability to work with others, analytical skills, computer skills, office skills, research skills, self-motivation. Duration is 3–12 months. Unpaid. Open to high school seniors, recent high school graduates, college freshmen, college sophomores, college juniors, college seniors, recent college graduates, graduate students, law students, career changers, individuals reentering the workforce. International applications accepted.

Benefits Formal training, names of contacts, on-the-job training, willing to act as a professional reference, willing to complete paperwork for educational credit, willing to provide letters of recommendation.

Contact Write, fax, or e-mail Ardis Willwerth, Director of Exhibitions. Fax: 626-577-1662. E-mail: awillwerth@pasadenahistory.org. No phone calls. In-person interview required. Applicants must submit a letter of interest, resume, two personal references, two letters of recommendation. Application deadline: May 15 for summer. World Wide Web: http://www.pasadenahistory.org.

PEABODY ESSEX MUSEUM
East India Square
Salem, Massachusetts 01970

General Information Museum of art, architecture, and culture. Established in 1799. Number of employees: 120. Number of internship applications received each year: 100.

Internships Available ▶ *9–15 museum education interns:* responsibilities include assisting with educational programming; helping to produce the Museum's most popular public program "Eerie Events". Candidates should have ability to work independently, computer skills, knowledge of field, oral communication skills, strong interpersonal skills, writing skills. Duration is by arrangement. Position available as unpaid or at $1000 for 3-month internship. Open to college freshmen, college sophomores, college juniors, college seniors, recent college graduates, graduate students. International applications accepted.

Benefits Formal training, job counseling, names of contacts, opportunity to attend seminars/workshops, possible full-time employment, willing to act as a professional reference, willing to complete paperwork for educational credit, willing to provide letters of recommendation.

Contact Write, call, fax, or e-mail Donna McDermott-Thorland, Manager of Interpretive Programs, East India Square, Salem, Massachusetts 01970. Phone: 978-745-9500 Ext. 3017. Fax: 978-740-3636. E-mail: donna_mcdermott-thorland@pem.org. In-person interview recommended (telephone interview accepted). Applicants must submit a letter of interest, resume, academic transcripts. Applications are accepted continuously. World Wide Web: http://www.pem.org.

PENNSBURY MANOR
400 Pennsbury Memorial Road
Morrisville, Pennsylvania 19067

General Information Historic site of William Penn's reconstructed home. Established in 1939. Number of employees: 20. Unit of Pennsylvania Historical and Museum Commission, Harrisburg, Pennsylvania. Number of internship applications received each year: 10.

Internships Available ▶ *1 Alice Hemenway Memorial intern:* responsibilities include doing curatorial/research work, developing educational programs, or doing horticultural work. Candidates should have personal interest in the field, plan to pursue career in field. Duration is flexible. Paid. Open to college juniors, college seniors, recent college graduates, graduate students, career changers, individuals reentering the workforce. ▶ *1 PHMC intern:* responsibilities include doing research/curatorial work, developing educational programs, or doing horticultural work. Candidates should have college courses in field, knowledge of field, personal interest in the field, plan to pursue career in field. Duration is 12-15 weeks in summer. $6.50 per hour. Open to those who live in or attend school in Pennsylvania; must have student status for the semester before and after internship. ▶ *Interns (for credit or experience):* responsibilities include doing curatorial/research work, developing educational programs, or doing horticultural work. Candidates should have personal interest in the field. Duration is flexible. Unpaid. International applications accepted.

Benefits On-the-job training, willing to act as a professional reference, willing to complete paperwork for educational credit, willing to provide letters of recommendation.

Contact Write Mary Ellyn Kunz, Museum Educator. In-person interview recommended (telephone interview accepted). Applicants must submit a formal organization application, letter of interest, resume, academic transcripts. Application deadline: December 15 for summer positions; continuous for others. World Wide Web: http://www.Pennsburymanor.org.

PENNSYLVANIA HISTORICAL AND MUSEUM COMMISSION
Commonwealth Keystone Building, Plaza Level, 400 North Street
Harrisburg, Pennsylvania 17120-0053

General Information Public history and museum agency for the Commonwealth of Pennsylvania. Established in 1945. Number of employees: 500. Number of internship applications received each year: 100.

Internships Available ▶ *45–50 interns:* responsibilities include completing a variety of assignments in history, historic preservation, museums, archives, architecture, communications, and related fields. Candidates should have ability to work independently, ability to work with others, analytical skills, oral communication skills, research skills, written communication skills. Duration is 10–15 weeks. $7 per hour. Open to college freshmen, college sophomores, college juniors, college seniors, graduate students, Pennsylvania residents or students attending a Pennsylvania college (applicants must be returning to class at conclusion of internship). International applications accepted.

Benefits Job counseling, names of contacts, on-the-job training, opportunity to attend seminars/workshops, possible full-time employment, travel reimbursement, willing to act as a professional reference, willing to complete paperwork for educational credit, willing to provide letters of recommendation, pre-professional experience, willing to provide supervision for academic credit.

Contact Write, call, fax, e-mail, or through World Wide Web site Linda Shopes, Historian and Internship Coordinator, Commonwealth Keystone Building, Plaza Level; 400 Norton Street, Harrisburg, Pennsylvania 17120-0053. Phone: 717-772-3257. Fax: 717-214-2989. E-mail: lshopes@state.pa.us. In-person interview required. Applicants must submit a formal organization application, academic transcripts, writing sample, letter of recommendation. Application deadline: December 15 for summer. World Wide Web: http://www.phmc.state.pa.us.

PICTURED ROCKS NATIONAL LAKESHORE
PO Box 40
Munising, Michigan 49862-0040

General Information Recreation area that strives to protect natural and cultural resources. Established in 1966. Number of employees: 30. Unit of United States National Park Service, Washington, District of Columbia. Number of internship applications received each year: 20.

Internships Available ▶ *1 biological technician:* responsibilities include researching and documenting flora, fauna, and other natural resources. Candidates should have ability to work

independently, computer skills, knowledge of field. Duration is 4–5 months. Unpaid. Open to college seniors, recent college graduates, graduate students. ▶ *1 sociological researcher:* responsibilities include conducting research and surveys on visitor use, impacts, and preferences in the lakeshore. Candidates should have ability to work independently, ability to work with others, knowledge of field, oral communication skills, self-motivation. Duration is May 1-October 1. Unpaid. Open to college juniors, college seniors, recent college graduates, graduate students. International applications accepted.

Benefits Free housing, job counseling, names of contacts, on-the-job training, willing to complete paperwork for educational credit, willing to provide letters of recommendation.

Contact Write, call, or fax Administrative Manager. Phone: 906-387-2607. Fax: 906-387-4025. Applicants must submit a letter of interest, resume, academic transcripts, three personal references. Application deadline: February 1 for summer. World Wide Web: http://www.nps.gov/piro.

REYNOLDA HOUSE MUSEUM OF AMERICAN ART
2250 Reynolda Road, PO Box 11765
Winston-Salem, North Carolina 27116-1765

General Information Historic house/art museum emphasizing interdisciplinary learning in American art, music, and literature; collection includes American paintings, prints, and sculpture. Established in 1964. Number of employees: 49. Affiliate of Wake Forest University, Winston-Salem, North Carolina. Number of internship applications received each year: 75.

Internships Available ▶ *1 education assistant:* responsibilities include assisting coordinator of education in scheduling, leading tours, development and implementation of public programs, special research projects and planning trips. Candidates should have ability to work independently, college degree in related field, experience in the field, oral communication skills, plan to pursue career in field, strong interpersonal skills, written communication skills. Duration is September through August. Stipend of $15,000. Open to recent college graduates, graduate students. ▶ *3–4 education interns:* responsibilities include leading school tours, performing general research and an independent research project, assisting with operation of education department. Candidates should have ability to work independently, college courses in field, oral communication skills, personal interest in the field, research skills, written communication skills. Duration is 1 semester. Unpaid. Open to college juniors, college seniors, recent college graduates, graduate students. ▶ *1 public relations assistant:* responsibilities include assisting in writing, editing and mailing press releases on museum events and exhibits; maintaining press kits; serving as liaison with local publications and organizations, and providing assistance to the public relations department. Candidates should have ability to work independently, computer skills, organizational skills, personal interest in the field, strong interpersonal skills, written communication skills. Duration is September to August. Stipend of $15,000. Open to recent college graduates, graduate students. ▶ *1 public relations intern (summer):* responsibilities include writing copy and conducting program outreach. Candidates should have computer skills, oral communication skills, organizational skills, personal interest in the field, self-motivation, written communication skills. Duration is one summer. Unpaid. Open to college juniors, college seniors, recent college graduates, graduate students, individuals reentering the workforce. International applications accepted.

Benefits Job counseling, names of contacts, opportunity to attend seminars/workshops, willing to act as a professional reference, willing to complete paperwork for educational credit, willing to provide letters of recommendation.

Contact Write, call, fax, or e-mail Ms. Kathleen Hutton, Coordinator of Education. Phone: 336-725-5325. Fax: 336-725-7475. E-mail: khutton@reynoldahouse.org. In-person interview recommended (telephone interview accepted). Applicants must submit a formal organization application, letter of interest, resume, two letters of recommendation. Application deadline: May 1 for 1-year paid position, July 1 for fall, November 1 for January position, December 1 for spring. World Wide Web: http://www.reynoldahouse.org.

RHODE ISLAND HISTORICAL SOCIETY
110 Benevolent Street
Providence, Rhode Island 02906

General Information   History museum that collects Rhode Island objects, documents, memorabilia, and plans exhibits about Rhode Island history. Established in 1822. Number of employees: 35. Number of internship applications received each year: 25.

Internships Available   ▶ *1–2 assistant copy editors:* responsibilities include modifying, assembling, and preparing publications sent to RIHS and sending to peer reviewers for comment and review; proofreading manuscripts at all stages of production; preparing index for upcoming quarterly magazines. Candidates should have ability to work independently, analytical skills, computer skills, editing skills, knowledge of field, oral communication skills, organizational skills, personal interest in the field, research skills, self-motivation, strong interpersonal skills, writing skills, one year minimum experience in editing or writing; college major in journalism or English. Duration is flexible. Unpaid. Open to college juniors, college seniors, recent college graduates, graduate students, career changers. ▶ *1–3 collections care interns (for museum):* responsibilities include cataloging, preparing for storage, and inventorying museum collections as needed by department; researching family or business history as related to artifacts in the collections; learning the most appropriate methods to store artifacts. Candidates should have ability to work independently, analytical skills, college courses in field, computer skills, knowledge of field, oral communication skills, organizational skills, personal interest in the field, research skills, self-motivation, strong interpersonal skills, strong leadership ability, writing skills, must be working toward at least BA in history, art history, or related field. Duration is flexible. Unpaid. Open to college juniors, college seniors, recent college graduates, graduate students, career changers. ▶ *1–2 collections management in manuscripts interns:* responsibilities include cataloging, storing, and working generally with patrons requiring retrieval of manuscript materials; simple preservation methods for paper-based materials will be learned and employed. Candidates should have ability to work independently, analytical skills, college courses in field, computer skills, oral communication skills, organizational skills, personal interest in the field, research skills, self-motivation, strong interpersonal skills, writing skills, knowledge of history and libraries. Duration is flexible. Unpaid. Open to college juniors, college seniors, recent college graduates, graduate students, career changers. ▶ *1–2 interns for Goff Institute for Ingenuity and Enterprise:* responsibilities include researching data about RI companies and businesses and working with other staff to plan lectures, seminars, and workshops. Candidates should have ability to work independently, computer skills, knowledge of field, oral communication skills, organizational skills, personal interest in the field, research skills, self-motivation, strong interpersonal skills, writing skills, major in history. Duration is flexible. $7.50 per hour. Open to college juniors, college seniors, recent college graduates, graduate students, career changers. ▶ *Interns in collection management in graphics:* responsibilities include researching and cataloging photographs or cartographic objects; entering data into database; learning basic preservation techniques and how to properly store paper-based materials. Candidates should have ability to work independently, analytical skills, computer skills, editing skills, knowledge of field, office skills, oral communication skills, organizational skills, personal interest in the field, research skills, self-motivation, strong interpersonal skills, writing skills, college courses in library science or history. Duration is flexible. Unpaid. Open to college juniors, college seniors, recent college graduates, graduate students, career changers. ▶ *1–2 interns in nonprofit administration development:* responsibilities include working with development department staff on Friends' Campaign fund-raising; assisting in coordination of calling team, mailings, and volunteer appreciation; and assisting in preparing materials to be mailed. Candidates should have ability to work independently, analytical skills, computer skills, office skills, oral communication skills, organizational skills, self-motivation, strong interpersonal skills, writing skills. Duration is September-December (minimum 8 hours per week). Unpaid. Open to college juniors, college seniors, recent college graduates, graduate students, career changers. ▶ *1–2 research interns:* responsibilities include research

on RI history topics for major exhibition to open in approximately 2006. Candidates should have computer skills, declared college major in field, editing skills, knowledge of field, oral communication skills, plan to pursue career in field, strong interpersonal skills, writing skills, prefer research experience. Duration is fall and/or spring semester; (preference for entire academic year). Position available as unpaid or at $7.5 per hour dependent upon grant funding. Open to college seniors, recent college graduates, graduate students. International applications accepted.

Benefits   Formal training, on-the-job training, opportunity to attend seminars/workshops, willing to act as a professional reference, willing to complete paperwork for educational credit, willing to provide letters of recommendation.

Contact   Write, call, or fax Ms. Linda Eppich, Chief Curator. Phone: 401-331-8575. Fax: 401-751-2307. In-person interview recommended (telephone interview accepted). Applicants must submit a formal organization application, letter of interest, resume, writing sample, letter of recommendation. Application deadline: April 1 for summer; at least 2 months prior to start of internship for academic year positions, December 15 for spring semester. World Wide Web: http://rihs.org.

ROCK BRIDGE MEMORIAL STATE PARK
5901 South Highway 163
Columbia, Missouri 65203

General Information   Recreational state park of 2273 acres known for its cave systems, hiking and biking trails, and wild area. Established in 1967. Number of employees: 15. Unit of Department of Natural Resources, Division of State Parks, Jefferson City, Missouri. Number of internship applications received each year: 1.

Internships Available   ▶ *1–3 naturalists:* responsibilities include leading tours and programs and conducting research. Candidates should have ability to work independently, oral communication skills, organizational skills, self-motivation, strong interpersonal skills. Duration is 3 months. Position available as unpaid or at $6 to $8 per hour or stipend. Open to recent high school graduates, college freshmen, college sophomores, college juniors, college seniors, recent college graduates, graduate students, law students, career changers, individuals reentering the workforce. ▶ *Park aides:* responsibilities include helping with general maintenance duties, greeting visitors, and performing light office duties. Candidates should have ability to work independently, computer skills, editing skills, office skills, oral communication skills, personal interest in the field, self-motivation, strong interpersonal skills, strong leadership ability, writing skills. Duration is flexible. Unpaid. Open to high school students, recent high school graduates, college freshmen, college sophomores, college juniors, college seniors, recent college graduates, graduate students, law students, career changers, individuals reentering the workforce. ▶ *1–10 stewardship interns:* responsibilities include removing old fences and cedar trees and prescribed burning in the park. Candidates should have ability to work with others, research skills. Duration is flexible. Position available as unpaid or at $6 per hour. Open to high school students, recent high school graduates, college freshmen, college sophomores, college juniors, college seniors, recent college graduates, graduate students, law students, career changers, individuals reentering the workforce. ▶ *1 volunteer coordinator:* responsibilities include coordinating volunteers working in park, including those who work with the Friends of Rock Bridge. Candidates should have oral communication skills, self-motivation, strong interpersonal skills, strong leadership ability, ability to handle responsibility for up to 10 people's safety in adverse wilderness conditions. Duration is flexible. Position available as unpaid or at $6 to $8 per hour or stipend. ▶ *3–8 wild cave tour leaders:* responsibilities include leading groups on tours of wild caves. Duration is 6 to 7 months per year (3-year commitment). Unpaid. Open to college freshmen, college sophomores, college juniors, college seniors, recent college graduates, graduate students, law students. International applications accepted.

Benefits   Possible full-time employment, willing to complete paperwork for educational credit, willing to provide letters of recommendation.

Contact Write, fax, or e-mail Mr. Scott W. Schulte, Superintendent. Fax: 573-442-2249. E-mail: dsprock@mail.dnr.state.mo.us. No phone calls. In-person interview recommended (telephone interview accepted). Applicants must submit a letter of interest, resume, three personal references. Applications are accepted continuously.

ROTUNDA GALLERY
33 Clinton Street
Brooklyn, New York 11201

General Information Contemporary visual art gallery. Established in 1981. Number of employees: 4. Unit of Brooklyn Information and Culture (BRIC), Brooklyn, New York. Number of internship applications received each year: 5.
Internships Available ▶ *5 interns.* Candidates should have ability to work independently, office skills, oral communication skills, personal interest in the field, self-motivation, strong interpersonal skills. Duration is 1 semester. Unpaid. Open to college juniors, college seniors, recent college graduates, graduate students, individuals reentering the workforce, working artists. International applications accepted.
Benefits On-the-job training, willing to act as a professional reference, willing to complete paperwork for educational credit, willing to provide letters of recommendation.
Contact Write, call, fax, or e-mail Meridith McNeal, Director of Education. Phone: 718-875-4047 Ext. 13. Fax: 718-488-0609. E-mail: rotunda@brooklynx.org. In-person interview recommended (telephone interview accepted). Applicants must submit a letter of interest, resume. Applications are accepted continuously. World Wide Web: http://www.brooklynx.org.

SAGAMORE INSTITUTE, INC.
PO Box 146, Sagamore Road
Raquette Lake, New York 13436

General Information Nonprofit National Landmark offering public tours and programs in regional culture and outdoor and environmental education. Established in 1972. Number of employees: 25. Number of internship applications received each year: 150.
Internships Available ▶ *3 acting/performance interpretation interns:* responsibilities include performing play (4 performances per week), interpreting camp's history, and leading public tours in character. Candidates should have ability to work with others, analytical skills, oral communication skills, acting skills, experience, and liberal arts education. Duration is June 15-September 5 and/or September 5-October 31. $150 per week. Open to college juniors, college seniors, recent college graduates, graduate students, career changers. ▶ *3 historic interpreters:* responsibilities include leading public tours of National Landmark; interpreting architectural, socio-economic, regional, and national land-use history. Candidates should have analytical skills, college courses in field, oral communication skills, strong interpersonal skills, strong leadership ability, writing skills. Duration is June 15-September 5 and/or September 5-October 31. $150 per week. Open to college juniors, college seniors, recent college graduates, graduate students, career changers, individuals reentering the workforce. ▶ *2 management interns:* responsibilities include assisting innkeeper, registrar and bookshop/craft shop. Candidates should have ability to work independently, office skills, oral communication skills, organizational skills, strong interpersonal skills, retail experience desirable. Duration is June 15-September 5 and/or September 5-October 31. $150 per week. Open to college freshmen, college sophomores, college juniors, college seniors, recent college graduates, graduate students. ▶ *1 oral historian:* responsibilities include managing and developing archives of resident artisans and families and assisting with public interpretation. Candidates should have ability to work independently, declared college major in field, knowledge of field, oral communication skills, research skills, strong interpersonal skills. Duration is June 15-September 5 and/or September 5-October 31. $150 per week. Open to college juniors, college seniors, recent college graduates, graduate students. ▶ *2 outdoor environmental educators:* responsibilities include assisting guiding staff with environmental education program for wide variety of ages. Candidates should have college courses in field, experience in the field, oral communication skills, strong

interpersonal skills, strong leadership ability, first aid/CPR certifications; water safety instruction/wilderness first responder certification (desirable). Duration is June 15-September 5 and/or September 5-October 31. $150 per week. Open to college juniors, college seniors, recent college graduates, graduate students. ▶ *1 theater technician intern:* responsibilities include managing visitor's center performance space for multiple use, lighting/sound design and run, and some changeovers. Candidates should have ability to work independently, computer skills, experience in the field, oral communication skills, strong interpersonal skills, basic lighting and sound design/run skills, liberal arts education (preferred). Duration is June 15 to September 5 and/or September 5 to October 15. $150 per week. Open to college sophomores, college juniors, college seniors, recent college graduates, graduate students, career changers. ▶ *1 tour supervisor:* responsibilities include managing tours and training. Candidates should have analytical skills, college degree in related field, oral communication skills, strong interpersonal skills, strong leadership ability, writing skills, teaching/interpretive experience. Duration is June 15-September 5 and/or September 5-October 31. $150 per week. Open to recent college graduates, graduate students, career changers. International applications accepted.
Benefits Formal training, free housing, free meals, job counseling, on-the-job training, opportunity to attend seminars/workshops, willing to act as a professional reference, willing to complete paperwork for educational credit, willing to provide letters of recommendation.
Contact Write, call, fax, e-mail, or through World Wide Web site Michael S. Wilson, Sagamore Associate Director, 9 Kiwassa Road, Saranac Lake, New York 12983. Phone: 518-891-1718. Fax: 518-891-2561. E-mail: mwilson@northnet.org. In-person interview recommended (telephone interview accepted). Applicants must submit a letter of interest, resume, three personal references, one expository writing sample. Application deadline: May 1 for summer (mid-June to early September), July 31 for fall (September to October). World Wide Web: http://www.sagamore.org.

THE SAINT LOUIS ART MUSEUM
1 Fine Arts Drive, Forest Park
St. Louis, Missouri 63110-1380

General Information Comprehensive, free public art museum with diverse collection from cultures worldwide, strong educational programs, and a regular schedule of special exhibits. Established in 1879. Number of employees: 200. Number of internship applications received each year: 30.
Internships Available ▶ *1 Romare Bearden Minority Museum Fellow:* responsibilities include working primarily with elementary students, as well as giving public lectures, researching and writing on collection and/or special exhibits, and other responsibilities contingent upon the Fellow's background and the Museum's current programs. Candidates should have ability to work with others, oral communication skills, plan to pursue career in field, research skills, major and/or at least 1 year graduate work in art education, art history, anthropology, museum studies, area studies, archaeology, or related field (no studio artists, except as an undergraduate field with graduate work in qualifying area). Duration is 1 year. $23,000 per year. Open to career changers, those with at least one year of graduate school by starting date. ▶ *3–4 summer interns:* responsibilities include researching, giving public gallery talks, writing synopses of works in the collection for public use, conducting visitor surveys, preparing teacher workshop materials, researching potential acquisitions and future exhibitions, attending staff meetings, and performing various responsibilities in the education and curatorial departments and museum library. Candidates should have research skills, self-motivation, writing skills, major in art education, art history, anthropology, museum studies, archaeology, or related field (no studio artists). Duration is 2 months full- or part-time, in June and July. Unpaid. Open to college seniors, graduate students, recent college graduates planning to attend graduate school, St. Louis city or county residents. International applications accepted.
Benefits Names of contacts, opportunity to attend seminars/workshops, willing to complete paperwork for educational credit,

The Saint Louis Art Museum (continued)

willing to provide letters of recommendation, assistance with resume preparation, health benefits, and travel reimbursement (Romare Bearden fellowships only).
Contact Write, call, fax, e-mail, or through World Wide Web site Stephanie Sigala, Acting Director of Education. Phone: 314-655-5264. Fax: 314-721-4911. E-mail: athena@slam.org. Applicants must submit a letter of interest, resume, academic transcripts, 1 writing sample in a humanities area (research positions), cover letter indicating exact dates and times of availability to work, names and phone numbers of 3 professional or academic references. Application deadline: February 1 for summer, March 1 for Bearden fellows. World Wide Web: http://www.slam.org.

THE SMITHSONIAN ASSOCIATES
1100 Jefferson Drive, SW, Room 3077
Washington, District of Columbia 20560-0701

General Information Educational and cultural outreach arm of the Smithsonian Institution that creates and administers special programs and educational activities as well as providing membership services. Number of employees: 100. Unit of Smithsonian Institution, Washington, District of Columbia. Number of internship applications received each year: 75.
Internships Available ▶ *Interns:* responsibilities include researching and planning educational programs for children and adults or working in any of the other departments including public affairs, national outreach, marketing/membership, study tours, young associates, Discovery Theater, or administration. Candidates should have strong interest in TSA's mission and in educational programming. Duration is flexible. Unpaid. Open to college freshmen, college sophomores, college juniors, college seniors, graduate students. International applications accepted.
Benefits Opportunity to attend seminars/workshops, willing to complete paperwork for educational credit, hands-on learning experience.
Contact Write, call, e-mail, or through World Wide Web site Volunteer Coordinator. Phone: 202-786-3234. E-mail: volunof@tsa.si.edu. In-person interview recommended (telephone interview accepted). Applicants must submit a formal organization application, writing sample, cover letter explaining areas of interest and proposed dates of availability, 2 letters of recommendation from professors. Applications are accepted continuously. World Wide Web: http://www.si.edu/tsa/rap.

SMITHSONIAN INSTITUTION, ANACOSTIA MUSEUM AND CENTER FOR AFRICAN AMERICAN HISTORY AND CULTURE
1901 Fort Place SE, MRC 520
Washington, District of Columbia 20020

General Information Museum and center devoted to increasing public understanding and awareness of the historical experiences and cultural expressions of people of African descent and heritage living in the Americas. Established in 1967. Number of employees: 25. Division of Smithsonian Institution, Washington, District of Columbia. Number of internship applications received each year: 60.
Internships Available ▶ *3–6 education, research, and public programs interns:* responsibilities include research, database acquisition, interacting with visitors, working Internet, online word processing, and occasional site visitation in Washington, D.C. area. Candidates should have ability to work independently, ability to work with others, analytical skills, computer skills, oral communication skills, organizational skills, research skills, self-motivation, written communication skills. Duration is 6 weeks to 2 months. Unpaid. Open to college sophomores, college juniors, college seniors, graduate students. International applications accepted.
Benefits Names of contacts, on-the-job training, opportunity to attend seminars/workshops, willing to complete paperwork for educational credit, willing to provide letters of recommendation.
Contact Write, call, fax, or e-mail Toni Brady, Public Program Specialist, 1901 Fort Place, SE, Washington, District of Columbia 20020. Phone: 202-610-3370. Fax: 202-287-3183. E-mail: bradyt@am.si.edu. Applicants must submit a formal organization applica-

tion, letter of interest, resume, academic transcripts, three letters of recommendation, statement of interest. Applications are accepted continuously. World Wide Web: http://www.si.edu.

SMITHSONIAN INSTITUTION, ARCHITECTURAL HISTORY AND HISTORIC PRESERVATION
Arts and Industries Building, Room 2263, MRC 417
Washington, District of Columbia 20560

General Information Office that integrates the architectural history of Smithsonian buildings with their preservation, conducts research on history of all Institution buildings, reviews proposed changes which affect historical integrity of buildings, and possesses holdings and records relating to the design and construction of Institution buildings. Established in 1986. Number of employees: 6. Division of Smithsonian Institution, Washington, District of Columbia. Number of internship applications received each year: 40.
Internships Available ▶ *1–2 architectural history interns:* responsibilities include integrating original documentation, such as correspondence and memoranda, architectural drawings, photographs, and other architectural materials to explore history of the Smithsonian buildings. Candidates should have ability to work independently, analytical skills, college courses in field, research skills, writing skills. Duration is 10 weeks. Position available as unpaid or paid. Open to college freshmen, college sophomores, college juniors, college seniors, recent college graduates, graduate students. International applications accepted.
Benefits Job counseling, names of contacts, opportunity to attend seminars/workshops, willing to act as a professional reference, willing to complete paperwork for educational credit, willing to provide letters of recommendation.
Contact Write, call, or e-mail Sabina Wiedenhoeft, Intern Coordinator. Phone: 202-357-2571. E-mail: ahhpmx@sivm.si.edu. Applicants must submit a letter of interest, resume, academic transcripts, writing sample, two letters of recommendation. Application deadline: January 1 for spring, April 1 for summer. World Wide Web: http://www.si.edu.

SMITHSONIAN INSTITUTION ARCHIVES
Arts and Industries Building, 900 Jefferson Drive, SW, Room 2135
Washington, District of Columbia 20560-0414

General Information Repository for documents of historic value about the Smithsonian. Established in 1846. Number of employees: 25. Unit of Smithsonian Institution, Washington, District of Columbia.
Internships Available ▶ *Interns:* responsibilities include working as an apprentice to a staff specialist in the areas of archiving, institutional history, oral history, or national collections. Candidates should have prior course work in American history, humanities, museum studies, collections management, or the sciences (desirable, but not a pre-requisite). Duration is 10 weeks. Position available as unpaid or paid. Open to college freshmen, college sophomores, college juniors, college seniors, graduate students. International applications accepted.
Benefits Formal training, on-the-job training, opportunity to attend seminars/workshops, willing to act as a professional reference, willing to complete paperwork for educational credit, willing to provide letters of recommendation, possible stipend.
Contact Write, call, fax, e-mail, or through World Wide Web site Tracy Elizabeth Robinson, Internship Coordinator, Arts and Industries Building, 900 Jefferson Drive, SW, Room 2135, Washington, District of Columbia 20560-0414. Phone: 202-357-1420 Ext. 33. Fax: 202-357-2395. E-mail: osiaref@osia.si.edu. Applicants must submit a formal organization application, academic transcripts, two letters of recommendation, essay, application (which can be downloaded from Web site). Application deadline: March 15 for summer, July 1 for fall, November 1 for spring. World Wide Web: http://www.si.edu/archives.

SMITHSONIAN INSTITUTION, JOSEPH HENRY PAPERS
Arts and Industries Building 2188, 900 Jefferson Drive, SW
Washington, District of Columbia 20024

General Information Historical documentary editing project preparing a 11-volume selective letterpress edition of the papers of Joseph Henry (1797-1878), an eminent American physicist, professor at Princeton University, and the first Secretary of the Smithsonian Institution. Established in 1967. Number of employees: 4. Division of Smithsonian Institution, Washington, District of Columbia. Number of internship applications received each year: 25.

Internships Available ▶ *1–3 research interns:* responsibilities include conducting historical research on selected or assigned topics relating to documents or themes to be treated in current or future volumes of *The Papers of Joseph Henry.* Candidates should have ability to work independently, ability to work with others, personal interest in the field, research skills, self-motivation, written communication skills. Duration is 2–3 months. Unpaid. Open to college sophomores, college juniors, college seniors, recent college graduates, graduate students, career changers. International applications accepted.

Benefits Health insurance, job counseling, opportunity to attend seminars/workshops, willing to act as a professional reference, willing to complete paperwork for educational credit, willing to provide letters of recommendation, use of research facilities, 20% discount at museum store; stipends may be available.

Contact Write, call, fax, e-mail, or through World Wide Web site Mr. Marc Rothenberg, Internship Coordinator/Editor, PO Box 37012, Washington, District of Columbia 20013-7012. Phone: 202-357-1421 Ext. 18. Fax: 202-786-2878. E-mail: rothenbergm@osia.si.edu. Applicants must submit a formal organization application, academic transcripts, writing sample, letter of recommendation. Application deadline: April 1 for summer. World Wide Web: http://www.si.edu/archives/ihd/jhp.

SMITHSONIAN INSTITUTION LIBRARIES
NHB 26A, MRC 154, 10th and Constitution Avenue, NW
Washington, District of Columbia 20560

General Information System of branch libraries that contains hard-bound volumes, rare books, current journals, and manuscripts. Unit of Smithsonian Institution, Washington, District of Columbia. Number of internship applications received each year: 50.

Internships Available ▶ *Collection management interns.* Duration is flexible. Unpaid. ▶ *Planning and administration interns.* Duration is flexible. Unpaid. ▶ *Research services interns.* Duration is flexible. Unpaid. ▶ *Systems and technical services interns.* Duration is flexible. Unpaid. Open to college freshmen, college sophomores, college juniors, college seniors, recent college graduates, graduate students. International applications accepted.

Benefits Job counseling, names of contacts, opportunity to attend seminars/workshops, willing to complete paperwork for educational credit, willing to provide letters of recommendation.

Contact Write, call, fax, e-mail, or through World Wide Web site Internship Coordinator. Phone: 202-357-1851. Fax: 202-357-4532. E-mail: averav@sil.si.edu. In-person interview recommended (telephone interview accepted). Applicants must submit a formal organization application, letter of interest, resume, academic transcripts. Applications are accepted continuously. World Wide Web: http://www.sil.si.edu.

SMITHSONIAN INSTITUTION, NATIONAL MUSEUM OF AFRICAN ART
950 Independence Avenue, SW
Washington, District of Columbia 20560-0708

General Information Major research and reference center and the only national museum in the United States dedicated to the collection, exhibition, conservation, and study of African art. Established in 1978. Number of employees: 55. Unit of Smithsonian Institution, Washington, District of Columbia. Number of internship applications received each year: 50.

Internships Available ▶ *Interns:* responsibilities include assisting museum staff in the following departments: administration, conservation, curatorial, education, exhibition and design, photo archives, public affairs, or registration. Candidates should have ability to work with others, plan to pursue career in field, research skills, self-motivation, writing skills, background in art history, museum studies, anthropology, or related disciplines. Duration is 10-week minimum (20 hours per week) in fall, spring or summer. Unpaid. Open to college juniors, college seniors, recent college graduates, graduate students, individuals interested in exploring museum professions. International applications accepted.

Benefits On-the-job training, willing to complete paperwork for educational credit, willing to provide letters of recommendation.

Contact Write, call, fax, or e-mail Dr. Veronika Jenke, Internship Coordinator, PO Box 37012, National Museum of African Art, 0708, Washington, District of Columbia 20013-7012. Phone: 202-357-4600 Ext. 225. Fax: 202-357-4879. E-mail: jenkev@nmafa.si.edu. Telephone interview required. Applicants must submit a formal organization application, letter of interest, resume, academic transcripts, personal reference, two letters of recommendation, essay. Application deadline: February 15 for summer, June 15 for fall, October 15 for spring. World Wide Web: http://www.si.edu/nmafa/.

SMITHSONIAN INSTITUTION, NATIONAL MUSEUM OF NATURAL HISTORY
10th Street and Constitution Avenue, NW
Washington, District of Columbia 20560-0166

General Information Museum that employs curatorial and scientific staff to collect specimens and conduct research and field observations in the natural sciences. Established in 1910. Number of employees: 550. Branch of Smithsonian Institution, Washington, District of Columbia. Number of internship applications received each year: 200.

Internships Available ▶ *Natural science interns:* responsibilities include beginning and completing a project assigned and supervised by curator or museum specialist. Candidates should have ability to work independently, ability to work with others, analytical skills, computer skills, knowledge of field, oral communication skills, plan to pursue career in field, research skills, self-motivation, written communication skills. Duration is 1–12 months. Unpaid. Open to college freshmen, college sophomores, college juniors, college seniors, recent college graduates. International applications accepted.

Benefits Names of contacts, on-the-job training, opportunity to attend seminars/workshops, willing to act as a professional reference, willing to complete paperwork for educational credit, willing to provide letters of recommendation.

Contact Write, fax, e-mail, or through World Wide Web site Mary Sangrey, Program Director, Room CE 214, 10th Street and Constitution Avenue, NW, Washington, District of Columbia 20560-0166. Phone: 202-357-4548. Fax: 202-786-2563. E-mail: sangrey.mary@nmnh.si.edu. In-person interview recommended (telephone interview accepted). Applicants must submit a formal organization application, two letters of recommendation, cover letter, academic transcripts (desirable). Application deadline: February 1. World Wide Web: http://www.nmnh.si.edu/rtp/.

SMITHSONIAN INSTITUTION, NATIONAL PORTRAIT GALLERY
PO Box 37012, Victor Building, Suite 8300, MRC 973
Washington, District of Columbia 20013-7012

General Information Free public museum for the exhibition and study of portraiture and statuary depicting men and women who have made significant contributions to the history, development, and culture of the people of the United States and the artists who created such works. Established in 1962. Number of employees: 100. Unit of Smithsonian Institution, Washington, District of Columbia. Number of internship applications received each year: 30.

Internships Available ▶ *15–20 interns:* responsibilities include assistance with varied projects depending on needs of the departments as well as intern's skills and interests. Candidates should have computer skills, editing skills, knowledge of field, oral communication skills, research skills, writing skills. Duration is 2-3 months (20 hours per week). Unpaid. Open to college freshmen, college sophomores, college juniors, college seniors, graduate students. International applications accepted.

Benefits Opportunity to attend seminars/workshops, willing to complete paperwork for educational credit, willing to provide letters of recommendation.

Contact Write, call, fax, or e-mail Shirlee Lampkin, Intern Coordinator, Education Department, PO Box 37012, Victor Building, Suite 8300 MRC 973, Washington, District of Columbia 20013-7012. Phone: 202-275-1811. Fax: 202-275-1904. E-mail: lampkins@npg.si.edu. Applicants must submit a formal organization application, resume, academic transcripts, two personal references, 500-1000 word essay. Application deadline: April 30 for summer; continuous for other times of year. World Wide Web: http://www.npg.si.edu/.

SMITHSONIAN INSTITUTION, NATIONAL POSTAL MUSEUM
MRC 570
Washington, District of Columbia 20560-0570

General Information One of the largest and most comprehensive collections of stamps and philatelic materials in the world, housing six major galleries. Established in 1993. Number of employees: 25. Unit of Smithsonian Institution, Washington, District of Columbia. Number of internship applications received each year: 24.

Internships Available ► *10 interns:* responsibilities include working with professional staff on current projects relating to exhibits, education, collections, curatorship, and membership/public affairs. Candidates should have ability to work with others, computer skills, office skills, oral communication skills, personal interest in the field, research skills. Duration is flexible. Unpaid. Open to college freshmen, college sophomores, college juniors, college seniors, graduate students, some high school students. International applications accepted.

Benefits Job counseling, names of contacts, opportunity to attend seminars/workshops, willing to complete paperwork for educational credit.

Contact Write, fax, or through World Wide Web site Intern Coordinator, Education Department—MRC 570, Washington, District of Columbia 20560-0570. Fax: 202-633-9393. No phone calls. Applicants must submit a formal organization application, academic transcripts, personal reference, essay. Applications are accepted continuously. World Wide Web: http://www.si.edu/postal/.

SMITHSONIAN INSTITUTION, OFFICE OF IMAGING, PRINTING, AND PHOTOGRAPHIC SERVICES
American History Building, Room LB054, MRC 644
Washington, District of Columbia 20560-0644

General Information Central photographic unit in support of the Smithsonian's research and publications, for museum's collections, for documenting the Institution's history, and for the needs of the public. Established in 1846. Number of employees: 25. Division of Smithsonian Institution, Washington, District of Columbia. Number of internship applications received each year: 30.

Internships Available ► *Electronic imaging interns:* responsibilities include assisting staff in scanning photographic images and cataloging them into the master database, digital restoration, retouching, printing, and conversion of photo CD images. Candidates should have ability to work independently, analytical skills, editing skills, office skills, oral communication skills, personal interest in the field, research skills, strong interpersonal skills, strong leadership ability, writing skills, knowledge of professional cameras and lighting equipment, knowledge of Internet, America Online, and PhotoShop. Duration is 4–9 weeks. Unpaid. Open to high school seniors, recent high school graduates, college freshmen, college sophomores, college juniors, college seniors, recent

college graduates, graduate students, law students, career changers, individuals reentering the workforce. ► *Photo studio assistants:* responsibilities include assisting photographers in studio, special event, or electronic photo assignments; working on preparation, execution, and post-production of all projects. Candidates should have ability to work independently, analytical skills, computer skills, editing skills, knowledge of field, office skills, oral communication skills, organizational skills, personal interest in the field, research skills, self-motivation, strong interpersonal skills, strong leadership ability, writing skills, basic camera equipment of their own (camera, lenses and flash). Duration is 6–8 weeks. Unpaid. Open to college freshmen, college sophomores, college juniors, college seniors, recent college graduates, graduate students, law students, career changers, individuals reentering the workforce. International applications accepted.

Benefits Job counseling, on-the-job training, opportunity to attend seminars/workshops, willing to act as a professional reference, willing to complete paperwork for educational credit, willing to provide letters of recommendation.

Contact Write, call, fax, or e-mail Lorie Aceto, Deputy Director. Phone: 202-786-2707. Fax: 202-786-2756. E-mail: acetolh@oipp.si.edu. Applicants must submit a formal organization application, academic transcripts, portfolio, personal reference. Application deadline: February 1 for summer, October 1 for winter. World Wide Web: http://www.photo2.si.edu.

THE SOCIETY FOR THE PRESERVATION OF NEW ENGLAND ANTIQUITIES
141 Cambridge Street
Boston, Massachusetts 02114

General Information Museum of cultural history that preserves, interprets, and collects buildings, landscapes, and objects reflecting New England life from the 17th-century to the present. Established in 1910. Number of employees: 100. Number of internship applications received each year: 100.

Internships Available ► *2–6 interns:* responsibilities include working with collections, archaeology, archives, education, public relations, and research departments on current and special projects in museum interpretation, social history, architectural history, and landscape and agricultural history. Candidates should have ability to work independently, analytical skills, college courses in field, knowledge of field, personal interest in the field, research skills. Duration is flexible. Unpaid. Open to college freshmen, college sophomores, college juniors, college seniors, recent college graduates, graduate students, career changers, individuals reentering the workforce. International applications accepted.

Benefits Opportunity to attend seminars/workshops, willing to complete paperwork for educational credit, willing to provide letters of recommendation.

Contact Write, fax, e-mail, or through World Wide Web site Ms. Susan L. Porter, Research Manager. Fax: 617-227-3956. E-mail: susanporter@spnea.org. No phone calls. In-person interview recommended (telephone interview accepted). Applicants must submit a formal organization application, letter of interest, resume, three personal references, three letters of recommendation. Application deadline: May 1 for summer; continuous for other times of year. World Wide Web: http://www.spnea.org.

SOUTHERN OHIO MUSEUM AND CULTURAL CENTER
PO Box 990, 825 Gallia Street
Portsmouth, Ohio 45662

General Information Art museum that presents 11-month schedule of temporary exhibits, primarily in the visual arts in addition to performing arts and films; offers classes, workshops, and special programs. Established in 1979. Number of employees: 11. Number of internship applications received each year: 2.

Internships Available ► *1 exhibit curator:* responsibilities include assisting in organizing exhibits, making contacts, and following up with paperwork. Candidates should have computer skills, oral communication skills, organizational skills, research skills, strong interpersonal skills, written communication skills. Duration is 3 months minimum. Unpaid. Open to recent college graduates,

graduate students. ▶ *1 public relations assistant:* responsibilities include assisting in publicizing museum programs, preparation of newsletters and news releases, and some graphic arts work. Candidates should have computer skills, editing skills, oral communication skills, strong interpersonal skills, writing skills. Duration is 3 months minimum. Unpaid. Open to college juniors, college seniors, recent college graduates, graduate students. International applications accepted.
Benefits Names of contacts, on-the-job training, opportunity to attend seminars/workshops, possible full-time employment, willing to complete paperwork for educational credit, willing to provide letters of recommendation.
Contact Write, fax, or e-mail Ms. Kay Bouyack, Administrative Director. Fax: 740-354-4090. E-mail: museum82@falcon1.com. No phone calls. In-person interview required. Applicants must submit a letter of interest, resume, two personal references, letter of recommendation. Applications are accepted continuously.

SOUTH STREET SEAPORT MUSEUM
207 Front Street
New York, New York 10038

General Information Maritime history museum, located in a 12-block historic district in downtown Manhattan, that interprets the role of the seaport in the development of the city, the state, and the nation through education programs, exhibitions, and the preservation of buildings and ships. Established in 1967. Number of employees: 100. Number of internship applications received each year: 150.
Internships Available ▶ *1–2 collections management interns:* responsibilities include artifact cataloguing, re-housing and research, maintaining artifact files and home computer work. Candidates should have ability to work independently, ability to work with others, computer skills, organizational skills, personal interest in the field, research skills. Duration is flexible (one or more days per week). Unpaid. Open to college seniors, recent college graduates, graduate students, career changers. ▶ *1–2 development interns:* responsibilities include providing research support to busy fund-raising office; assisting with grant applications and reports. Candidates should have ability to work independently, ability to work with others, office skills, personal interest in the field, research skills, written communication skills. Duration is flexible (2-3 half days per week). Unpaid. Open to college juniors, college seniors, recent college graduates, graduate students, career changers, individuals reentering the workforce. ▶ *Interns:* responsibilities include working in any of the following areas: archaeology, education, fund-raising/development, maritime crafts, marketing/special events, printing and stationers shop, schooner *Lettie G. Howard*, ship restoration and maintenance, collections management, exhibit research, library, membership, publications, tour marketing, schooner *Pioneer*, boat building, volunteer department, and Elderhostel. Candidates should have ability to work independently, ability to work with others, computer skills, office skills, personal interest in the field, written communication skills. Duration is flexible. Unpaid. Open to high school students, recent high school graduates, college freshmen, college sophomores, college juniors, college seniors, recent college graduates, graduate students, career changers, individuals reentering the workforce, must be 16 years old or over. ▶ *1–4 schooner crew interns:* responsibilities include acting as deck hands on one or both of the vessels including deckwork underway duties; and watch keeping; ship maintenance. Candidates should have personal interest in the field, strong interpersonal skills. Duration is flexible. Unpaid. Open to high school students, recent high school graduates, college freshmen, college sophomores, college juniors, college seniors, recent college graduates, graduate students, law students, career changers, individuals reentering the workforce, must be 16 years old or over. ▶ *2–4 wet lab interns:* responsibilities include guiding visitors through wet lab during open hours; feeding and care of animals; and maintenance of wet lab aquarium. Candidates should have ability to work independently, oral communication skills, personal interest in the field, knowledge of biology helpful. Duration is April 15 to October 15 (flexible). Unpaid. Open to high school students, recent high school graduates, college freshmen, college sophomores, college juniors, college seniors, recent college

graduates, any individual willing to be trained (must be 16 years old or over). International applications accepted.
Benefits Formal training, on-the-job training, opportunity to attend seminars/workshops, possible full-time employment, willing to act as a professional reference, willing to complete paperwork for educational credit, willing to provide letters of recommendation.
Contact Write, call, fax, or e-mail Richard Dorfman, Director of Volunteers and Community Outreach. Phone: 212-748-8727. Fax: 212-748-8610. E-mail: rdorfman@southstseaport.org. In-person interview required. Applicants must submit a resume. Applications are accepted continuously. World Wide Web: http://www. southstseaport.org.

SPRINGFIELD ARMORY NATIONAL HISTORIC SITE
1 Armory Square
Springfield, Massachusetts 01105-1299

General Information Site commemorating the critical role Springfield Armory played in the nation's military history; preserves, researches, and interprets the firearms collection, archives, library, and structures; provides the story of technological developments of the Armory complex and their impacts on civilization. Established in 1974. Number of employees: 14. Unit of National Park Service, Washington, District of Columbia. Number of internship applications received each year: 10.
Internships Available ▶ *1–2 archives summer interns:* responsibilities include organizing, boxing, and cataloging archives; housekeeping and environmental monitoring. Candidates should have analytical skills, computer skills, oral communication skills, organizational skills, research skills, written communication skills. Duration is 12 weeks (minimum of 30 hours per week). Unpaid. Open to college freshmen, college sophomores, college juniors, college seniors. ▶ *1–2 collections management interns:* responsibilities include environmental monitoring; housekeeping, including cleaning exhibits; using the collection management database, Automated National Catalog System (ANCS). Candidates should have ability to work with others, computer skills, editing skills, self-motivation, writing skills. Duration is 2 semesters (minimum of 240 hours). Position available as unpaid or paid. Open to college juniors, college seniors, recent college graduates, graduate students, law students, career changers, individuals reentering the workforce. ▶ *1–2 conservation interns:* responsibilities include rehousing archaeological collection; cleaning and housing paper, metal, and wood materials. Candidates should have ability to work with others, computer skills, editing skills, self-motivation, writing skills. Duration is 1 semester. Position available as unpaid or paid. Open to college juniors, college seniors, recent college graduates, graduate students, law students, career changers, individuals reentering the workforce. ▶ *1–3 interpretive program assistants:* responsibilities include assisting with development of museum exhibits and public programs, testing curriculum-based education programs. Candidates should have ability to work independently, oral communication skills, self-motivation, strong interpersonal skills, writing skills. Duration is 120 hours. Position available as unpaid or paid. Open to college juniors, college seniors, recent college graduates, graduate students, law students, career changers, individuals reentering the workforce. ▶ *4–6 library/archives interns:* responsibilities include cataloging new books, rehousing archives, participating in housekeeping, and making phase boxes for historic books. Candidates should have analytical skills, computer skills, oral communication skills, organizational skills, research skills, written communication skills. Duration is 1 semester (minimum of 120 hours). Unpaid. Open to college juniors, college seniors, recent college graduates, graduate students, law students, career changers, individuals reentering the workforce. ▶ *1–2 maintenance resource evaluators:* responsibilities include gathering and entering data into the inventory assessment program, entering reports and evaluating the maintenance program. Candidates should have ability to work with others, computer skills, editing skills, self-motivation, writing skills. Duration is 8–10 weeks. Position available as unpaid or paid. Open to college juniors, college seniors, recent college graduates, graduate students, law students, career changers, individuals reentering the workforce. ▶ *1 market plan developer:* responsibilities include creating a plan

Springfield Armory National Historic Site (continued)

to publicize the Historic Site and available services and programs. Candidates should have oral communication skills, organizational skills, strong interpersonal skills, strong leadership ability, writing skills. Duration is flexible (minimum of 10 hours per week). Position available as unpaid or paid. Open to college juniors, college seniors, recent college graduates, graduate students, law students, career changers, individuals reentering the workforce. ▶ *4–6 oral history interns:* responsibilities include transcribing, compiling, and cataloging information on the 100 oral histories into the parks database; intern will need to read *Transcribing and Editing Oral History* by Willa K. Baum. Candidates should have ability to work independently, computer skills, editing skills, knowledge of field, organizational skills, ability to understand elderly voices on audio tape. Duration is 1 semester (minimum of 120 hours). Unpaid. Open to college juniors, college seniors, recent college graduates, graduate students, law students, career changers, individuals reentering the workforce. ▶ *1 pre-program intern (art conservation):* responsibilities include practicing a group of completed conservation treatments, including all relevant documentation materials, organized for portfolio presentation. Candidates should have ability to work with others, analytical skills, computer skills, knowledge of field, plan to pursue career in field, research skills, written communication skills. Duration is 8–10 weeks. Unpaid. Open to applicants to graduate programs in art conservation. ▶ *1 promotional development intern:* responsibilities include creating brochures, flyers, and other non-personal materials for the public and schools; researching and developing concepts with park rangers. Candidates should have ability to work independently, computer skills, knowledge of field, personal interest in the field, strong leadership ability, writing skills. Duration is flexible (minimum of 10 hours per week). Unpaid. Open to college juniors, college seniors, recent college graduates, graduate students, law students, career changers, individuals reentering the workforce. ▶ *1–2 research assistants:* responsibilities include researching publications, archives, microfilm, or newspapers for park staff or outside researchers. Candidates should have ability to work independently, ability to work with others, analytical skills, computer skills, research skills, written communication skills. Duration is 1 semester (minimum of 120 hours). Unpaid. Open to college juniors, college seniors, recent college graduates, graduate students, law students, career changers, individuals reentering the workforce. ▶ *1 summer intern (art conservation):* responsibilities include full participation in the routine activities of a small objects conservation cab; emphasis will be on treatment, documentation and preventive conservation; research opportunities also possible. Candidates should have ability to work independently, ability to work with others, computer skills, declared college major in field, plan to pursue career in field, written communication skills. Duration is 8–10 weeks. Unpaid. Open to graduate students in art conservation. International applications accepted.

Benefits Formal training, names of contacts, on-the-job training, opportunity to attend seminars/workshops, willing to act as a professional reference, willing to complete paperwork for educational credit, willing to provide letters of recommendation, worker's compensation, local travel expenses (mileage).

Contact Write, call, fax, e-mail, or through World Wide Web site Joanne Gangi, Chief of Visitor Services, Volunteer Parks Program Coordinator. Phone: 413-734-8551. Fax: 413-747-8062. E-mail: joanne_gangi@nps.gov. In-person interview recommended (telephone interview accepted). Applicants must submit a letter of interest, resume, writing sample, two personal references, security background check required. Application deadline: July 1 for fall and January winter break, November 1 for spring and summer. World Wide Web: http://www.nps.gov/spar.

SPRINGFIELD LIBRARY AND MUSEUMS
220 State Street
Springfield, Massachusetts 01103

General Information Administrative organization for the Springfield libraries and 4 separate museums. Established in 1857. Number of employees: 275. Number of internship applications received each year: 10.

Internships Available ▶ *1–4 Springfield Art Museums education assistants:* responsibilities include assisting in preparation of Museum's Art Discovery Center and developing hands-on art projects for Museum visitors of all ages. Candidates should have ability to work independently, ability to work with others, organizational skills, personal interest in the field, self-motivation. Duration is flexible. Unpaid. Open to college freshmen, college sophomores, college juniors, college seniors, career changers. ▶ *1–2 Springfield Science Museum education assistants (investigation station):* responsibilities include assisting with the creation of hands-on science activities which will be developed for use in the Museum's Investigation Station. Candidates should have ability to work independently, college courses in field, knowledge of field, organizational skills, personal interest in the field, research skills, self-motivation. Duration is flexible. Unpaid. Open to college freshmen, college sophomores, college juniors, college seniors, recent college graduates, career changers, individuals reentering the workforce. ▶ *1–3 Springfield Science Museum education assistants (school programs):* responsibilities include attending training sessions and becoming familiar with science program materials in preparation for conducting tours and teaching science programs to children visiting the Museum. Candidates should have ability to work independently, ability to work with others, oral communication skills, personal interest in the field, self-motivation. Duration is flexible. Unpaid. Open to college freshmen, college sophomores, college juniors, college seniors, recent college graduates, career changers, individuals reentering the workforce. ▶ *1 curatorial assistant (art):* responsibilities include assisting in various duties depending on intern's interest. Candidates should have ability to work independently, ability to work with others, computer skills, declared college major in field, knowledge of field, oral communication skills, plan to pursue career in field, research skills, written communication skills. Duration is one semester (flexible). Unpaid. Open to college seniors, graduate students. ▶ *1 curatorial assistant (science):* responsibilities include cataloguing natural history collections, exhibit preparation, possibly some animal care. Candidates should have ability to work independently, ability to work with others, computer skills, declared college major in field, knowledge of field, plan to pursue career in field. Duration is 1 semester. Unpaid. Open to college juniors, college seniors, graduate students. ▶ *1–2 development interns:* responsibilities include grant research and grant writing; corporate sponsor research and proposal drafting; assistance with mailings, membership solicitations, and special fund-raising event. Candidates should have ability to work independently, research skills, strong interpersonal skills, writing skills. Duration is January-May, possibly June-August. Unpaid. Open to college freshmen, college sophomores, college juniors, college seniors, recent college graduates, graduate students, career changers, individuals reentering the workforce. ▶ *1 drawings into Delta Cad intern (Science Museum):* responsibilities include transferring hand-drawn museum floor layouts into computer generated drawings using the Delta Cad program. Candidates should have ability to work independently, computer skills, oral communication skills, personal interest in the field, written communication skills. Duration is flexible. Unpaid. Open to college freshmen, college sophomores, college juniors, college seniors, recent college graduates, graduate students, career changers. ▶ *1–4 education assistants:* responsibilities include assisting in developing hands-on activities, developing materials for tours, and conducting tours in museums. Candidates should have ability to work independently, ability to work with others, organizational skills, personal interest in the field, research skills, self-motivation. Duration is flexible. Unpaid. Open to college freshmen, college sophomores, college juniors, college seniors, recent college graduates, career changers. ▶ *1–2 museum preparation interns (Science Museum):* responsibilities include assisting the exhibit preparator in museum work ranging from permanent exhibit maintenance to traveling exhibition installation. Candidates should have ability to work with others, oral communication skills, personal interest in the field, self-motivation. Duration is flexible. Unpaid. Open to college freshmen, college sophomores, college juniors, college seniors, recent college graduates, graduate students, career changers. ▶ *1 public relations intern:* responsibilities include writing press releases, writing for a variety of audiences, and performing various other publicity-related duties. Candidates should have ability to work independently, ability to work with others, college courses in field, computer skills, editing skills, oral communication skills, organizational skills, plan to pursue career in field, research skills, writing skills. Duration is 1 semester. Unpaid. Open to college seniors, graduate students.

Benefits Job counseling, on-the-job training, willing to act as a professional reference, willing to complete paperwork for educational credit, willing to provide letters of recommendation.

Contact Write Ms. Sara Orr, Publicist. Phone: 413-263-6800. Fax: 413-263-6807. E-mail: sorr@spfldlibmus.org. In-person interview required. Applicants must submit a letter of interest, resume, academic transcripts, writing sample may be required. Application deadline: March 1 for summer, June 1 for fall, November 1 for spring. World Wide Web: http://www.quadrangle.org.

SQUAM LAKES NATURAL SCIENCE CENTER
PO Box 173
Holderness, New Hampshire 03245

General Information Center whose mission is to advance understanding of ecology by exploring New Hampshire's natural world. Established in 1966. Number of employees: 35. Number of internship applications received each year: 40.

Internships Available ▶ *1 island caretaker and education intern:* responsibilities include caretaking, working with visitors, natural history interpretation. Candidates should have ability to work independently, oral communication skills, personal interest in the field, self-motivation, strong interpersonal skills, ability to deal with unusual living arrangement (on island for most of summer). Duration is mid-June to Labor Day (minimum of 5 nights per week on island). $100 per week. ▶ *4–5 summer education/animal care interns:* responsibilities include 15-minute animal presentations ("mini-talks") to general public; some work on special events and projects; helping care for live animal collection; working with docents; rotation in Science Center Day Camp. Candidates should have ability to work independently, ability to work with others, oral communication skills, personal interest in the field, self-motivation, courses in environmental education, education, or natural sciences. Duration is June 1 to August 30 (some flexibility). $100 per week. Open to college juniors, college seniors, recent college graduates, graduate students, career changers, individuals reentering the workforce.

Benefits Free housing, names of contacts, on-the-job training, opportunity to attend seminars/workshops, willing to act as a professional reference, willing to complete paperwork for educational credit, willing to provide letters of recommendation, opportunity to work with live animals.

Contact Write, fax, e-mail, or through World Wide Web site Amy Yeakel, Director of Education. Fax: 603-968-2229. E-mail: amy.yeakel@nhnature.org. No phone calls. In-person interview recommended (telephone interview accepted). Applicants must submit a formal organization application, letter of interest, resume, personal reference, two letters of recommendation. Application deadline: February 15 for summer (June 1 to August 30). World Wide Web: http://www.nhnature.org.

STATEN ISLAND INSTITUTE OF ARTS AND SCIENCES
75 Stuyvesant Place
Staten Island, New York 10301-1998

General Information Organization that focuses on Staten Island and its people and has strong collections in these subjects. Established in 1881. Number of internship applications received each year: 50.

Internships Available ▶ *2 archival assistants:* responsibilities include working on special research projects requiring direct involvement with original material (including artifacts and archival holdings such as oral and written personal histories, documents, photographs, leaflets, fliers, and memoirs); identifying and locating appropriate artifacts, archival holdings, and materials relating to the material culture and contributions of working-class people on Staten Island. Candidates should have ability to work independently, ability to work with others, personal interest in the field, research skills, self-motivation, writing skills. Duration is

15 weeks. Unpaid. Open to high school seniors, recent high school graduates, college freshmen, college sophomores, college juniors, college seniors, recent college graduates, individuals reentering the workforce. ▶ *1 art collections intern:* responsibilities include inventorying, cataloging, and storing art collection objects, entering art collection objects into database, marking museum objects with permanent identification numbers, tracking incoming donations to the permanent collection, completing condition reports for incoming loans, updating incoming loan files, assisting with installation and removal of exhibits, and other assigned collections-related duties. Candidates should have ability to work independently, ability to work with others, organizational skills, personal interest in the field, research skills, self-motivation. Duration is flexible, 2 days per week (4 hours per day preferred). Unpaid. Open to college freshmen, college sophomores, college juniors, college seniors. ▶ *1 marketing intern:* responsibilities include assisting in preparation of media and newsletter mailings, distribution of printed materials, and direct marketing of group programs and public events through contact with tourism professionals and community groups. Candidates should have ability to work with others, computer skills, editing skills, organizational skills, personal interest in the field, self-motivation, writing skills. Duration is flexible. Unpaid. Open to college freshmen, college sophomores, college juniors, college seniors, recent college graduates, graduate students, career changers, individuals reentering the workforce. ▶ *2 science assistants:* responsibilities include performing various duties within the science department; possible areas of work include archaeology collection, entomology, botany, zoology, data entry, geology, Staten Island paleontology, mounted bird collection, herbarium, and myxomycete collection. Candidates should have ability to work independently, college courses in field, computer skills, knowledge of field, personal interest in the field, research skills, self-motivation. Duration is flexible. Unpaid. Open to college freshmen, college sophomores, college juniors, college seniors, recent college graduates. International applications accepted.

Benefits Formal training, job counseling, on-the-job training, opportunity to attend seminars/workshops, possible full-time employment, willing to act as a professional reference, willing to complete paperwork for educational credit, willing to provide letters of recommendation.

Contact Write, call, fax, or e-mail Bart Bland, Director of Exhibitions. Phone: 718-727-1135. Fax: 718-273-5683. E-mail: bartbland@aol.com. In-person interview required. Applicants must submit a letter of interest, resume, academic transcripts. Applications are accepted continuously. World Wide Web: http://www.siiasmuseum.com.

STATEN ISLAND ZOO, EDUCATION DEPARTMENT
614 Broadway
Staten Island, New York 10310

General Information Zoological park focusing on the goals of conservation, education, and recreation in order to present exotic animals to the public. Established in 1936. Number of employees: 50. Unit of Staten Island Zoo, Staten Island, New York. Number of internship applications received each year: 50.

Internships Available ▶ *1 camp art teacher:* responsibilities include teaching art programs and creating curriculum. Candidates should have ability to work independently, experience in the field, plan to pursue career in field, strong interpersonal skills, college courses in education or art. Duration is 3 months. $250 per week. Open to college juniors, college seniors. ▶ *1 camp recreation teacher:* responsibilities include teaching recreation and creating curriculum. Candidates should have ability to work independently, experience in the field, personal interest in the field, strong interpersonal skills. Duration is 3 months. $250 per week. Open to college juniors, college seniors, recent college graduates. ▶ *1 camp science teacher:* responsibilities include teaching science programs and creating curriculum. Candidates should have ability to work with others, experience in the field, oral communication skills, plan to pursue career in field, ability to work with animals. Duration is 3 months. $250 per week. Open to college juniors, college seniors, recent college graduates. ▶ *1 zoomobile teacher:* responsibilities include teaching outreach programs with live animals and

Arts, Entertainment, and Recreation **121**

Peterson's ■ *Internships 2003*

www.petersons.com

Staten Island Zoo, Education Department (continued)
feeding and taking care of animals in education department. Candidates should have ability to work independently, college degree in related field, experience in the field, strong interpersonal skills, ability to work with animals. Duration is 9 months. $375 per week. Open to recent college graduates, graduate students. International applications accepted.
Benefits Formal training, job counseling, names of contacts, on-the-job training, opportunity to attend seminars/workshops, willing to act as a professional reference, willing to complete paperwork for educational credit, willing to provide letters of recommendation.
Contact Write, call, or fax Karin Jakubowsti, Assistant Director of Education. Phone: 718-442-3101 Ext. 37. Fax: 718-981-8711. In-person interview recommended (telephone interview accepted). Applicants must submit a letter of interest, resume. Application deadline: April 30 for summer, July 15 for fall. World Wide Web: http://www.statenislandzoo.org.

STONES RIVER NATIONAL BATTLEFIELD
3501 Old Nashville Highway
Murfreesboro, Tennessee 37129-3094

General Information Organization dedicated to preserving the natural and cultural features of the national battlefield site and providing for the study and interpretation of the Battle of Stones River. Established in 1927. Number of employees: 19. Unit of United States National Park Service, Washington, District of Columbia. Number of internship applications received each year: 75.
Internships Available ▶ *1 clerical assistant:* responsibilities include performing office work, including filing and data entry. Candidates should have computer skills, editing skills, knowledge of field, office skills, organizational skills. Duration is 8–10 weeks. Unpaid. Open to recent high school graduates, college freshmen, college sophomores, college juniors, college seniors, recent college graduates, graduate students, career changers, individuals reentering the workforce. ▶ *1 historian:* responsibilities include conducting historical research. Candidates should have college courses in field, computer skills, knowledge of field, oral communication skills, research skills, writing skills. Duration is flexible. Unpaid. Open to recent college graduates, graduate students, career changers, individuals reentering the workforce. ▶ *1 interpreter:* responsibilities include preparing and presenting interpretive programs and operating the visitor's center. Candidates should have ability to work with others, knowledge of field, oral communication skills, personal interest in the field, research skills, writing skills. Duration is flexible. Unpaid. Open to recent high school graduates, college freshmen, college sophomores, college juniors, college seniors, recent college graduates, graduate students, career changers, individuals reentering the workforce. ▶ *1 library assistant:* responsibilities include cataloging and classifying library. Candidates should have computer skills, knowledge of field, office skills, organizational skills. Duration is flexible. Unpaid. Open to college juniors, college seniors, recent college graduates, graduate students, career changers, individuals reentering the workforce. ▶ *1 maintenance worker:* responsibilities include maintaining trails, including spreading woodchips and clearing debris. Candidates should have ability to work independently, knowledge of field, organizational skills, personal interest in the field, self-motivation. Duration is flexible. Unpaid. Open to recent high school graduates, college freshmen, college sophomores, college juniors, college seniors, recent college graduates, graduate students, career changers, individuals reentering the workforce. ▶ *1 museum technician:* responsibilities include caring for museum collection. Candidates should have analytical skills, computer skills, knowledge of field, organizational skills, research skills. Duration is flexible. Unpaid. Open to college juniors, college seniors, recent college graduates, graduate students, career changers, individuals reentering the workforce. ▶ *1 natural resource management technician:* responsibilities include biological monitoring, taking plant census, and eradicating exotic species. Candidates should have ability to work independently, analytical skills, college courses in field, research skills, self-motivation. Duration is flexible. Unpaid. Open

to college juniors, college seniors, recent college graduates, graduate students, career changers, individuals reentering the workforce.
Benefits Formal training, job counseling, on-the-job training, opportunity to attend seminars/workshops, willing to complete paperwork for educational credit, willing to provide letters of recommendation, worker's compensation.
Contact Write, call, fax, or e-mail Bettie C. Cook, Volunteer Coordinator. Phone: 615-893-9501. Fax: 615-893-9508. E-mail: stri_information@nps.gov. In-person interview recommended (telephone interview accepted). Applicants must submit a formal organization application, two personal references. Applications are accepted continuously. World Wide Web: http://www.nps.gov/stri.

STRONG MUSEUM
1 Manhattan Square
Rochester, New York 14607

General Information Public educational institution that collects, preserves, and interprets historic artifacts, manuscripts, and other materials that depict everyday life in America after 1820, emphasizing the Northeast during the era of industrialization. Established in 1982. Number of employees: 300. Number of internship applications received each year: 25.
Internships Available ▶ *2 summer interns:* responsibilities include working in one of the following: collections, research, conservation, or education departments. Candidates should have ability to work independently, analytical skills, computer skills, declared college major in field, oral communication skills, organizational skills, plan to pursue career in field, research skills, strong interpersonal skills, writing skills. Duration is 12 weeks. $5200 per duration of internship. Open to college seniors, recent college graduates, graduate students. ▶ *1–20 volunteer interns:* responsibilities include working in one of the following: collections, library, research, administration, conservation, education or guest services. Candidates should have ability to work with others, oral communication skills, research skills, self-motivation, writing skills. Duration is 10–12 weeks. Unpaid. Open to college sophomores, college juniors, college seniors, recent college graduates, graduate students, career changers.
Benefits Job counseling, names of contacts, on-the-job training, opportunity to attend seminars/workshops, possible full-time employment, willing to act as a professional reference, willing to complete paperwork for educational credit, willing to provide letters of recommendation.
Contact Write, call, fax, or e-mail Kathleen S. Dengler, Vice President for Human Resources. Phone: 585-263-2701 Ext. 267. Fax: 585-263-3598. E-mail: kdengler@strongmuseum.org. In-person interview required. Applicants must submit a formal organization application, letter of interest, resume, three writing samples, two personal references, letter of recommendation. Application deadline: December 15 for summer. World Wide Web: http://www.strongmuseum.org.

SUNSET CRATER VOLCANO, WALNUT CANYON, AND WUPATKI NATIONAL MONUMENTS
Route 3, Box 149
Flagstaff, Arizona 86004

General Information Three national monuments managed by the National Park Service including a volcano, cliff dwellings, and pueblo archaeological sites; provides for visitor enjoyment, education, and resource protection. Number of employees: 50. Unit of Flagstaff Area National Monuments, Flagstaff, Arizona. Number of internship applications received each year: 100.
Internships Available ▶ *10–20 environmental education/interpretation/visitor services interns:* responsibilities include staffing visitor center; developing and conducting interpretive programs for park visitors; developing and conducting environmental education programs for school groups; creating educational displays and publications; roving trails and making visitor contacts to discourage theft and vandalism of natural and cultural resources; preparing equipment for wildfire management; assisting in first aid and emergency situations. Candidates should have oral communication skills, personal interest in the field, self-motivation, strong interpersonal

skills, written communication skills. Duration is 3–6 months. Unpaid. Open to recent high school graduates, college freshmen, college sophomores, college juniors, college seniors, recent college graduates, graduate students, career changers, individuals reentering the workforce. ▶ *1–2 maintenance interns:* responsibilities include providing maintenance of park facilities including janitorial services, trail maintenance, trash collection, painting, minor repairs, and other physical labor duties as skills allow. Candidates should have ability to work independently, ability to work with others, experience in the field, personal interest in the field, self-motivation, ability to do physical labor. Duration is 3–6 months. Unpaid. Open to high school seniors, recent high school graduates, college freshmen, college sophomores, college juniors, college seniors, recent college graduates, graduate students, career changers, individuals reentering the workforce. ▶ *1–5 resource management interns:* responsibilities include assisting in studying and protecting cultural and natural resources; performing curatorial work, roving archaeological sites, conducting scientific studies, assisting in planning efforts, entering data on computer, and assisting interpretive staff in preparing educational material. Candidates should have analytical skills, knowledge of field, personal interest in the field, research skills, self-motivation. Duration is 3–6 months. Unpaid. Open to college freshmen, college sophomores, college juniors, college seniors, recent college graduates, graduate students, individuals reentering the workforce. International applications accepted.
Benefits Formal training, free housing, job counseling, names of contacts, on-the-job training, opportunity to attend seminars/workshops, willing to act as a professional reference, willing to complete paperwork for educational credit, willing to provide letters of recommendation, coverage for on-the-job injury or tort claim, uniform provided.
Contact Write, call, fax, or e-mail Kris Cole, Volunteer Coordinator. Phone: 928-526-0502. Fax: 928-714-0565. E-mail: flag_vip@nps.gov. Telephone interview required. Applicants must submit a formal organization application, letter of interest, resume, three personal references. Applications are accepted continuously. World Wide Web: http://www.nps.gov/sucr.

SUPREME COURT OF THE UNITED STATES, OFFICE OF THE CURATOR
1 First Street, NE
Washington, District of Columbia 20543

General Information Office that preserves the history of the Supreme Court; creates the historical exhibits in the building; develops, catalogues, and preserves the collections of the Supreme Court; and offers private tours and lectures. Established in 1973. Number of employees: 7. Unit of Supreme Court of the United States, Washington, District of Columbia. Number of internship applications received each year: 150.
Internships Available ▶ *2–8 curatorial interns:* responsibilities include conducting lectures and tours for visitors and assisting with curatorial projects which may include cataloging photographs, papers, and memorabilia; assisting with the development and installation of exhibits; researching and responding to public information requests. Candidates should have computer skills, office skills, oral communication skills, research skills, strong interpersonal skills, written communication skills. Duration is minimum of 24 hours per week for 12 weeks; or 3 weeks, mid-December to first week in January. Position available as unpaid or at $10 per hour for summer positions; academic credit for other positions. Open to college freshmen, college sophomores, college juniors, college seniors, recent college graduates, graduate students. International applications accepted.
Benefits Willing to complete paperwork for educational credit, willing to provide letters of recommendation, training in curatorial work, museum procedures, and public speaking; reimbursement for some commuting expenses.
Contact Write, call, or fax Trisha Brooks, Visitor Programs Coordinator. Phone: 202-479-2940. Fax: 202-479-2926. In-person interview recommended (telephone interview accepted). Applicants must submit a formal organization application, letter of interest, resume, three personal references, three letters of recommendation. Application deadline: March 1 for summer (May-August), July 1

for fall (September-December), October 1 for winter (mid-December to 1st week of January), November 1 for winter (January-May). World Wide Web: http://www.supremecourtus.gov.

THEODORE ROOSEVELT NATIONAL PARK
315 Second Avenue, PO Box 7
Medora, North Dakota 58645

General Information National park preserving the Little Missouri Badlands and 70,000 acres that are home to a variety of plants, wildlife including bison, elk, wild horses, and almost 200 species of birds. Established in 1947. Number of employees: 80. Number of internship applications received each year: 20.
Internships Available ▶ *2–3 biological science technicians:* responsibilities include performing resource management duties including exotic pest control and wildlife surveys. Candidates should have ability to work independently, ability to work with others, oral communication skills, research skills, self-motivation, written communication skills. Duration is 2–3 months. Position available as unpaid or paid. Open to college freshmen, college sophomores, college juniors, college seniors, recent college graduates, graduate students, career changers, individuals reentering the workforce. ▶ *3–5 interpretive volunteers:* responsibilities include working at the information desk, presenting information to the public at talks and formal evening programs, leading guided nature hikes, and undertaking special projects that employ the skills of the volunteer. Candidates should have ability to work independently, ability to work with others, oral communication skills, organizational skills, self-motivation, written communication skills. Duration is 2–3 months. Unpaid. Open to college freshmen, college sophomores, college juniors, college seniors, recent college graduates, graduate students, individuals reentering the workforce. International applications accepted.
Benefits Formal training, free housing, job counseling, names of contacts, on-the-job training, willing to complete paperwork for educational credit, willing to provide letters of recommendation, subsistence pay.
Contact Write or call Bruce M. Kaye, Chief of Interpretation. Phone: 701-623-4466. E-mail: bruce_kaye@nps.gov. Telephone interview required. Applicants must submit a letter of interest, resume, two personal references. Application deadline: February 15 for spring/summer, June 15 for fall. World Wide Web: http://www.nps.gov/thro.

TIMPANOGOS CAVE NATIONAL MONUMENT
RR 3, Box 200
American Fork, Utah 84003

General Information National monument encompassing 250 acres, consisting of 3 caves linked by manmade tunnels in the canyon walls of American Fork Canyon. Established in 1922. Number of employees: 10. Unit of United States National Park Service, Washington, District of Columbia. Number of internship applications received each year: 25.
Internships Available ▶ *1 administrative support intern:* responsibilities include answering phones, typing, filing, and performing other office work. Candidates should have ability to work with others, experience in the field, office skills, oral communication skills, self-motivation, written communication skills. Duration is flexible. Unpaid. Open to college sophomores, college juniors, college seniors. ▶ *1 cave management/interpretation intern:* responsibilities include conducting tours of caves, maintaining the area, gathering data on the caves, and mapping and surveying caves. Candidates should have ability to work with others, college courses in field, knowledge of field, oral communication skills, self-motivation, written communication skills. Duration is flexible. Unpaid. Open to college sophomores, college juniors, college seniors, recent college graduates, graduate students. ▶ *1 visitor center intern:* responsibilities include greeting visitors, conducting interpretive programs, providing information, and operating cash register. Candidates should have knowledge of field, oral communication skills, self-motivation, strong interpersonal skills, written communication skills. Duration is 4 months. Unpaid. Open to college sophomores, college juniors, college seniors. International applications accepted.

Timpanogos Cave National Monument (continued)

Benefits Formal training, job counseling, names of contacts, on-the-job training, willing to act as a professional reference, willing to complete paperwork for educational credit, willing to provide letters of recommendation, necessary equipment/supervision provided.
Contact Write, call, fax, e-mail, or through World Wide Web site Mr. Michael Gosse, Chief Ranger. Phone: 801-756-5239. Fax: 801-756-5661. E-mail: michael_gosse@nps.gov. In-person interview recommended (telephone interview accepted). Applicants must submit a letter of interest, resume. Application deadline: March 15 for summer. World Wide Web: http://www.nps.gov.

TONGASS NATIONAL FOREST, ADMIRALTY NATIONAL MONUMENT
8461 Old Dairy Road
Juneau, Alaska 99801

General Information National monument and wilderness dedicated to preserving natural, cultural, geological, historical, scientific, recreational, wildlife, and wilderness resources and monitoring and protecting a coastal, temperate rain forest. Established in 1978. Number of employees: 15. Unit of United States Forest Service, Washington, District of Columbia. Number of internship applications received each year: 10.
Internships Available ▶ *1–2 wilderness rangers:* responsibilities include backcountry monitoring of wilderness campsites, cabins, and recreation sites; conducting campsite cleanup; and assisting with visitor contact and wilderness education. Candidates should have ability to work with others, oral communication skills, personal interest in the field, self-motivation. Duration is April 23 to August 25. Unpaid. Open to college juniors, college seniors, recent college graduates, graduate students, law students, career changers. International applications accepted.
Benefits Free housing, free meals, job counseling, names of contacts, travel reimbursement, willing to complete paperwork for educational credit, willing to provide letters of recommendation.
Contact Write, call, fax, or e-mail Mr. John Neary, Wilderness Assistant. Phone: 907-790-7481. Fax: 907-586-8795. E-mail: jneary@fs.fed.us. In-person interview recommended (telephone interview accepted). Applicants must submit a formal organization application. Application deadline: March 31. World Wide Web: http://www.fs.fed.us/r10/chatham/anm.

TRAILSIDE MUSEUMS AND WILDLIFE CENTER
Palisades Interstate Park Commission
Bear Mountain, New York 10911

General Information Large park and recreational facility that promotes conservation of natural resources and provides space for outdoor recreation, home to non-releasable native New York wildlife; also performs wildlife rehabilitation. Established in 1927. Number of employees: 15. Number of internship applications received each year: 10.
Internships Available ▶ *4 zookeeper assistants:* responsibilities include providing care for permanently injured or orphaned park wildlife in zoo setting under the supervision of a park ranger/zookeeper. Candidates should have ability to work independently, ability to work with others, oral communication skills, plan to pursue career in field, self-motivation, animal-related experience helpful, but will train. Duration is mid-May to mid-August (2 positions) or end of August to mid- November (2 positions). Unpaid. Open to college freshmen, college sophomores, college juniors, college seniors. International applications accepted.
Benefits Formal training, names of contacts, on-the-job training, possible full-time employment, willing to act as a professional reference, willing to complete paperwork for educational credit, willing to provide letters of recommendation, payment for pre-exposure rabies shots ($300 value) at conclusion of internship.
Contact Write, call, fax, or e-mail Ms. Jennifer Verstraete, Park Ranger/Zookeeper. Phone: 845-786-2701 Ext. 263. Fax: 845-786-0496. E-mail: uncl@icu.com. In-person interview recommended (telephone interview accepted). Applicants must submit a resume. Application deadline: May 1 for summer, August 31 for fall. World Wide Web: http://www.bearmountainzoo.org.

UCR/CALIFORNIA MUSEUM OF PHOTOGRAPHY
University of California, Riverside
Riverside, California 92501

General Information Facility that promotes understanding of photography and related media through collections, research, exhibition, and instruction. Established in 1973. Number of employees: 10. Unit of University of California, Riverside, Riverside, California. Number of internship applications received each year: 75.
Internships Available ▶ *3–5 museum assistants:* responsibilities include assisting with educational programs and exhibitions installation and performing administrative, collections, curatorial, marketing, and publications duties. Candidates should have ability to work independently, computer skills, oral communication skills, personal interest in the field, written communication skills. Duration is minimum of 3 months. Unpaid.
Benefits Job counseling, willing to complete paperwork for educational credit, willing to provide letters of recommendation.
Contact Write, fax, e-mail, or through World Wide Web site Jennifer Stratton, Museum Store Assistant. Fax: 909-787-4797. E-mail: jenstrat@pop.ucr.edu. No phone calls. In-person interview recommended (telephone interview accepted). Applicants must submit a letter of interest, resume, portfolio. Applications are accepted continuously. World Wide Web: http://www.cmp.ucr.edu.

U.S. HOLOCAUST MEMORIAL MUSEUM
100 Raoul Wallenberg Place, SW
Washington, District of Columbia 20024-2126

General Information Leading institution for the documentation, study, and interpretation of Holocaust history. Established in 1993. Number of employees: 600. Branch of United States Holocaust Memorial Council, Washington, District of Columbia. Number of internship applications received each year: 200.
Internships Available ▶ *Academic publications interns:* responsibilities include reviewing submitted memoirs, articles, and books for possible publication and assisting in production of the museum's journal *Holocaust and Genocide Studies.* Candidates should have ability to work independently, editing skills, research skills, writing skills, European language skills. Duration is 12 weeks. Position available as unpaid or paid. Open to college sophomores, college juniors, college seniors, recent college graduates, graduate students, career changers, individuals reentering the workforce.
▶ *Archives interns:* responsibilities include translating and summarizing wartime trial records. Candidates should have college courses in field, computer skills, knowledge of field, research skills, writing skills, European language skills. Duration is 10–12 weeks. Position available as unpaid or paid. Open to college sophomores, college juniors, college seniors, recent college graduates, graduate students, career changers, individuals reentering the workforce.
▶ *Collections interns:* responsibilities include assisting with research projects and catalog holdings of the museum's collections. Candidates should have ability to work independently, ability to work with others, computer skills, research skills, writing skills. Duration is 10–12 weeks. Position available as unpaid or paid. Open to college sophomores, college juniors, college seniors, recent college graduates, graduate students, career changers.
▶ *Education interns:* responsibilities include assisting with the development of various educational projects including teacher resources. Candidates should have ability to work independently, ability to work with others, computer skills, knowledge of field, research skills, writing skills. Duration is 10–12 weeks. Position available as unpaid or paid. Open to college sophomores, college juniors, college seniors, recent college graduates, graduate students, career changers. ▶ *International programs interns:* responsibilities include assisting with the development of programs sponsored by the museum throughout the world. Candidates should have computer skills, knowledge of field, oral communication skills, strong interpersonal skills, written communication skills, knowledge of eastern European language helpful. Duration is 10–12 weeks. Position available as unpaid or paid. Open to college sophomores, college juniors, college seniors, recent college graduates, graduate students, career changers. ▶ *2–3 legal interns:* responsibilities include preparing briefs, researching, editing. Candidates should have analytical skills, college courses in field, knowledge of field,

research skills, writing skills. Duration is 10–12 weeks. Position available as unpaid or paid. Open to recent college graduates, law students. ▶ *Membership interns:* responsibilities include assisting with the development and maintenance of the membership program. Candidates should have computer skills, office skills, oral communication skills, strong interpersonal skills, written communication skills. Duration is 10–12 weeks. Position available as unpaid or paid. Open to college sophomores, college juniors, college seniors, recent college graduates, graduate students, career changers. ▶ *Photo archive department interns:* responsibilities include maintaining archives of Holocaust photographs. Candidates should have ability to work independently, ability to work with others, analytical skills, computer skills, organizational skills, research skills. Duration is 10–12 weeks. Position available as unpaid or paid. Open to college sophomores, college juniors, college seniors, recent college graduates, graduate students, career changers. ▶ *Research interns:* responsibilities include assisting senior research scholars. Candidates should have ability to work independently, ability to work with others, computer skills, editing skills, research skills, writing skills. Duration is 10–12 weeks. Position available as unpaid or paid. Open to college sophomores, college juniors, college seniors, recent college graduates, graduate students, law students, career changers, individuals reentering the workforce. ▶ *Volunteer services interns:* responsibilities include assisting with the development of a volunteer program for a diverse constituency. Candidates should have ability to work independently, computer skills, oral communication skills, strong interpersonal skills, writing skills. Duration is 10–12 weeks. Position available as unpaid or paid. Open to college sophomores, college juniors, college seniors, recent college graduates, graduate students, career changers. International applications accepted.
Benefits Formal training, job counseling, names of contacts, on-the-job training, opportunity to attend seminars/workshops, willing to act as a professional reference, willing to complete paperwork for educational credit, willing to provide letters of recommendation.
Contact Write, call, fax, or through World Wide Web site Internship Coordinator. Phone: 202-479-9738. Fax: 202-488-6568. Telephone interview required. Applicants must submit a formal organization application, letter of interest, resume, academic transcripts, two letters of recommendation. Application deadline: March 15 for summer, June 15 for fall, October 15 for winter/spring. World Wide Web: http://www.ushmm.org.

VIRGINIA MUSEUM OF FINE ARTS
2800 Grove Avenue
Richmond, Virginia 23221-2466

General Information State supported museum that houses a collection of original works of art and sponsors a variety of art programs. Established in 1936. Number of employees: 193. Number of internship applications received each year: 70.
Internships Available ▶ *1–2 art reference librarians:* responsibilities include assisting staff in implementation of auxiliary services provided to museum staff, scholars, students, and the public. Candidates should have ability to work with others, computer skills, knowledge of field, organizational skills, personal interest in the field, self-motivation. Duration is 1 semester. Unpaid. Open to college juniors, college seniors, recent college graduates, graduate students. ▶ *1–2 arts administration interns:* responsibilities include assisting in the research, planning, and coordination of a variety of ongoing educational programs, resources, and services. Candidates should have ability to work independently, computer skills, organizational skills, research skills, self-motivation, writing skills. Duration is 1 semester. Unpaid. Open to college juniors, college seniors, recent college graduates, graduate students. ▶ *1–4 curatorial interns:* responsibilities include researching, cataloging, and working on permanent and special exhibits. Candidates should have ability to work independently, college courses in field, computer skills, organizational skills, research skills, self-motivation, writing skills. Duration is 1 semester. Unpaid. Open to college seniors, recent college graduates, graduate students. ▶ *1 docent program intern:* responsibilities include assisting staff with administration and collections research needs in the tour services office. Candidates should have ability to work with others, computer skills,

oral communication skills, organizational skills, research skills, self-motivation, writing skills. Duration is 1 semester. Unpaid. Open to college juniors, college seniors, recent college graduates, graduate students. ▶ *1 grants and research intern:* responsibilities include assisting with researching sources for funding and developing proposals to foundations and corporations. Candidates should have ability to work independently, computer skills, organizational skills, plan to pursue career in field, research skills, writing skills. Duration is 1 semester. Unpaid. Open to college juniors, college seniors, recent college graduates. ▶ *1–2 marketing and public affairs interns:* responsibilities include assisting staff with publicizing and marketing special exhibits, programs, and events. Candidates should have computer skills, declared college major in field, office skills, self-motivation, writing skills. Duration is 1 semester. Unpaid. Open to college juniors, college seniors, recent college graduates, graduate students. ▶ *1–2 membership interns:* responsibilities include assisting staff with general operating services, activities, and benefits. Candidates should have ability to work with others, computer skills, office skills, oral communication skills, organizational skills, self-motivation. Duration is 1 semester. Unpaid. Open to college juniors, college seniors, recent college graduates, graduate students. ▶ *1 photographic resources intern:* responsibilities include assisting staff with documentation of works of art from permanent collection and various daily operational services. Candidates should have computer skills, knowledge of field, organizational skills, research skills, self-motivation, strong interpersonal skills. Duration is 1 semester. Unpaid. Open to college juniors, college seniors, recent college graduates, graduate students. ▶ *1–2 research projects interns:* responsibilities include researching museum's collection and producing new or updating existing documentation. Candidates should have ability to work independently, ability to work with others, college courses in field, computer skills, research skills, writing skills. Duration is 1 semester. Unpaid. Open to college juniors, college seniors, recent college graduates, graduate students. ▶ *6–7 school and family programs interns:* responsibilities include researching and producing materials for school and adult activities and working on special events and programs. Candidates should have ability to work with others, computer skills, office skills, oral communication skills, organizational skills, plan to pursue career in field, research skills, self-motivation, writing skills. Duration is 1 semester. Unpaid. Open to college juniors, college seniors, recent college graduates, graduate students. ▶ *1 statewide educational resources intern:* responsibilities include assisting staff with the development of traveling exhibits, research, inspection and repair of media resources, and general office support. Candidates should have ability to work independently, ability to work with others, computer skills, office skills, organizational skills, research skills, self-motivation, writing skills. Duration is 1 semester. Unpaid. Open to college juniors, college seniors, recent college graduates, graduate students. ▶ *2–3 visitor services interns:* responsibilities include assisting with staffing information and special events ticket desks; providing customer services related to permanent galleries. Candidates should have computer skills, office skills, oral communication skills, organizational skills, strong interpersonal skills, writing skills. Duration is 1 semester. Unpaid. Open to college juniors, college seniors, recent college graduates. International applications accepted.
Benefits Willing to act as a professional reference, willing to complete paperwork for educational credit, willing to provide letters of recommendation.
Contact Write, call, e-mail, or through World Wide Web site David Pittman, Internship Coordinator. Phone: 804-204-2662. Fax: 804-204-2675. E-mail: dpittman@vmfa.state.va.us. In-person interview recommended (telephone interview accepted). Applicants must submit a letter of interest, resume, academic transcripts, writing sample, two letters of recommendation. Application deadline: March 15 for summer, August 15 for fall, November 15 for spring. World Wide Web: http://www.vmfa.state.va.us.

WADSWORTH ATHENEUM MUSEUM OF ART
600 Main Street
Hartford, Connecticut 06103-2990

General Information Fine arts museum housing a collection with strengths in 19th-century American painting, Renaissance

Wadsworth Atheneum Museum of Art (continued)

and Baroque European painting, European and American decorative arts, the Amistad Foundation Collection of African-American art and artifacts, and the Nutting Collection of Colonial American furniture. Established in 1842. Number of employees: 150. Number of internship applications received each year: 100.

Internships Available ▶ *1 Amistad Foundation intern:* responsibilities include providing general curatorial support, writing label copy, research, and cataloging. Candidates should have ability to work independently, analytical skills, computer skills, organizational skills, self-motivation, written communication skills. Unpaid. Open to college seniors, recent college graduates, graduate students. ▶ *1 business office intern:* responsibilities include performing office duties. Candidates should have ability to work with others, computer skills, office skills, organizational skills, self-motivation. Duration is flexible. Unpaid. Open to college freshmen, college sophomores, college juniors, college seniors, recent college graduates, graduate students, career changers, individuals reentering the workforce. ▶ *1 curatorial intern:* responsibilities include conducting research on permanent collection, labeling objects, and cataloging entries. Candidates should have ability to work independently, ability to work with others, computer skills, knowledge of field, research skills, self-motivation, written communication skills. Duration is flexible. Unpaid. Open to college freshmen, college sophomores, college juniors, college seniors, recent college graduates, graduate students, career changers, individuals reentering the workforce. ▶ *1 design and installation intern:* responsibilities include assisting with 2- and 3-dimensional designs within the organization. Candidates should have ability to work independently, ability to work with others, knowledge of field, personal interest in the field, self-motivation. Duration is flexible. Unpaid. Open to college freshmen, college sophomores, college juniors, college seniors, recent college graduates, graduate students, career changers, individuals reentering the workforce. ▶ *1 development intern:* responsibilities include fund-raising, writing grants, learning how to solicit corporate contributions/individual patrons, conducting market research, and building databases. Candidates should have ability to work independently, ability to work with others, computer skills, office skills, organizational skills, self-motivation. Duration is flexible. Unpaid. Open to college freshmen, college sophomores, college juniors, college seniors, recent college graduates, graduate students, career changers, individuals reentering the workforce. ▶ *1 education intern:* responsibilities include assisting in implementing public programs including lectures, concerts, films, symposia, teachers' workshops, and children's programs; writing educational material including gallery handouts and slide programs; grant writing; and surveying educational programs. Candidates should have ability to work independently, computer skills, office skills, organizational skills, research skills, written communication skills. Duration is flexible. Unpaid. Open to college freshmen, college sophomores, college juniors, college seniors, recent college graduates, graduate students, career changers, individuals reentering the workforce. ▶ *1 library intern:* responsibilities include serving museum staff and the public. Candidates should have ability to work independently, ability to work with others, computer skills, office skills, organizational skills, self-motivation. Duration is flexible. Unpaid. Open to college freshmen, college sophomores, college juniors, college seniors, recent college graduates, graduate students, career changers, individuals reentering the workforce. ▶ *1 membership intern:* responsibilities include assisting in membership drives, organizing membership activities and exhibit openings, and coordinating publication of membership materials. Candidates should have computer skills, office skills, oral communication skills, strong interpersonal skills, written communication skills. Duration is flexible. Unpaid. Open to college freshmen, college sophomores, college juniors, college seniors, recent college graduates, graduate students, career changers, individuals reentering the workforce. ▶ *1 museum shop intern:* responsibilities include assisting in retail facility within museum. Candidates should have ability to work with others, oral communication skills, organizational skills, self-motivation. Duration is flexible. Unpaid. Open to college freshmen, college sophomores, college juniors, college seniors, recent college graduates, graduate students, career changers, individuals reentering the workforce. ▶ *1 photographic services intern:* responsibilities

include maintaining museum's extensive slide holdings, handling all slide loans to staff and public, processing all requests regarding rights and reproductions, planning photo shoots, and filing and maintaining photographic archives. Candidates should have ability to work independently, ability to work with others, office skills, organizational skills, research skills, self-motivation. Duration is flexible. Unpaid. Open to college freshmen, college sophomores, college juniors, college seniors, recent college graduates, graduate students, career changers, individuals reentering the workforce. ▶ *1 public information intern:* responsibilities include assisting public relations staff with writing press releases. Candidates should have ability to work with others, computer skills, editing skills, self-motivation, written communication skills. Duration is flexible. Unpaid. Open to college freshmen, college sophomores, college juniors, college seniors, recent college graduates, graduate students, career changers, individuals reentering the workforce. ▶ *1 registrar intern:* responsibilities include maintaining provenance files on permanent collections, making accession cards, and researching objects for inventory. Candidates should have ability to work with others, computer skills, office skills, oral communication skills, self-motivation, written communication skills. Duration is flexible. Unpaid. Open to college freshmen, college sophomores, college juniors, college seniors, recent college graduates, graduate students, career changers, individuals reentering the workforce. International applications accepted.

Benefits Job counseling, names of contacts, opportunity to attend seminars/workshops, possible full-time employment, willing to complete paperwork for educational credit, willing to provide letters of recommendation, opportunity to attend all museum education programs.

Contact Write, call, fax, or e-mail Dana Engstrom DeLoach, Assistant Curator of Public Programs. Phone: 860-278-2670 Ext. 3121. Fax: 860-249-7780. E-mail: dana.deloach@wadsworthatheneum.org. In-person interview recommended (telephone interview accepted). Applicants must submit a letter of interest, resume, academic transcripts, writing sample, two letters of recommendation. Application deadline: March 15 for summer, July 15 for fall/winter, November 1 for spring. World Wide Web: http://www.wadsworthatheneum.org.

WHITE SANDS NATIONAL MONUMENT
PO Box 1086
Holloman A.F.B., New Mexico 88330

General Information National monument that preserves the world's largest gypsum dunefield. Established in 1933. Number of employees: 24. Unit of United States National Park Service, Washington, District of Columbia. Number of internship applications received each year: 4.

Internships Available ▶ *1 environmental interpretation intern:* responsibilities include performing interpretive ranger duties, developing and presenting talks, conducting nature walks, staffing information desk, and performing roving interpretation on foot. Candidates should have college courses in field, oral communication skills, self-motivation, strong interpersonal skills, written communication skills. Duration is 12-14 weeks in spring, fall, or winter. Unpaid. Open to college juniors, college seniors, recent college graduates, graduate students, career changers. ▶ *1 geology interpretation intern:* responsibilities include performing interpretive ranger duties; developing and presenting programs on geology and ecology of the dunes; staffing information desk; developing exhibits/informational brochures. Candidates should have oral communication skills, self-motivation, strong interpersonal skills, written communication skills, major in geology or earth science education. Duration is 12-14 weeks in summer. Unpaid. Open to college juniors, college seniors, graduate students. International applications accepted.

Benefits Formal training, free housing, job counseling, names of contacts, on-the-job training, travel reimbursement, willing to act as a professional reference, willing to complete paperwork for educational credit, willing to provide letters of recommendation, $50 per week food reimbursement for environmental interpretation positions.

Contact Write, call, fax, e-mail, or through World Wide Web site Mr. John Mangimeli, Volunteer Coordinator. Phone: 505-679-

2599 Ext. 230. Fax: 505-479-4333. E-mail: john_mangimeli@nps.gov. Applicants must submit a formal organization application, resume, academic transcripts, two letters of recommendation, materials through Student Conservation Association application process (603)543-1700. Application deadline: January 1 for spring (March to late May), March 1 for summer (mid-May to mid-August), August 1 for fall (October to December), October 15 for winter (late December to mid-March). World Wide Web: http://www.nps.gov/whsa.

WHITNEY MUSEUM OF AMERICAN ART
945 Madison Avenue
New York, New York 10021

General Information Museum dedicated to collecting, preserving, and interpreting 20th and 21st century American art. Established in 1930. Number of employees: 193. Number of internship applications received each year: 125.
Internships Available ▶ *Interns:* responsibilities include working in a variety of areas including curatorial, branch museums, communications, education, film and video, library, registration, marketing, development, publications, and new media. Candidates should have ability to work with others, college courses in field, computer skills, office skills, research skills, self-motivation. Duration is 2–4 months. Position available as unpaid or paid. Open to college sophomores, college juniors, college seniors, graduate students. International applications accepted.
Benefits On-the-job training, opportunity to attend seminars/workshops, possible full-time employment, willing to complete paperwork for educational credit, willing to provide letters of recommendation, discounts at museum and facilities, stipends of $500–$600 for summer program.
Contact Write or e-mail Lisa Dowd, Human Resources Manager. Fax: 212-606-0210. E-mail: hr@whitney.org. No phone calls. In-person interview required. Applicants must submit a letter of interest, resume, academic transcripts, personal reference, letter of recommendation, one-page statement of purpose saying what the intern hopes to gain from the internship and what he/she hopes to contribute to the organization. Application deadline: March 1 for summer; continuous for academic-year placements. World Wide Web: http://www.whitney.org.

WILDLIFE PRAIRIE STATE PARK
3826 North Taylor Road, RR 2, Box 50
Peoria, Illinois 61615

General Information Zoological and botanical park that encompasses 2000 acres of grazing land, lakes, and woodlands, presenting the wild animals once native to Illinois. Established in 1978. Number of employees: 50. Number of internship applications received each year: 50.
Internships Available ▶ *3–4 education interns:* responsibilities include greeting school groups and assisting with various interpretive programs including day camps, guiding tours, presenting daily interpretive programs to the general public, assisting with special events, performing certain opening and closing procedures, trail monitoring, and completing a special project. Candidates should have ability to work independently, oral communication skills, strong interpersonal skills, biology and/or environmental interests. Duration is 12 weeks or longer. Position available as unpaid or paid. Open to college juniors, college seniors, recent college graduates, graduate students. International applications accepted.
Benefits On-the-job training, possible full-time employment, willing to act as a professional reference, willing to complete paperwork for educational credit, willing to provide letters of recommendation, leadership skills, possibility of free housing.
Contact Write, call, fax, or e-mail Rebecca Rees, Internship Coordinator. Phone: 309-676-0998 Ext. 6758. Fax: 309-676-7783. E-mail: wppnat@aol.com. In-person interview recommended (telephone interview accepted). Applicants must submit a letter of interest, resume, three personal references. Applications are accepted continuously. World Wide Web: http://www.wildlifepark.org.

WIND CAVE NATIONAL PARK
RR1 Box 190
Hot Springs, South Dakota 57747

General Information National park that preserves and protects an exceptional maze-cave with a rare cave formation called "boxwork", and maintains a beautiful mixed-grass prairie complete with representative wildlife. Established in 1903. Number of employees: 60. Unit of United States National Park Service, Washington, District of Columbia. Number of internship applications received each year: 50.
Internships Available ▶ *2–4 interpretation park rangers:* responsibilities include preparing and presenting interpretive programs including cave tours, visitor center demonstrations, and prairie hikes. Candidates should have ability to work independently, oral communication skills, personal interest in the field, self-motivation, strong interpersonal skills. Duration is 3–5 months. $50–$75 per week. Open to college sophomores, college juniors, college seniors, recent college graduates, graduate students, law students, career changers. International applications accepted.
Benefits Formal training, free housing, job counseling, names of contacts, on-the-job training, travel reimbursement, willing to complete paperwork for educational credit, willing to provide letters of recommendation, uniform allowance, meal stipend.
Contact Write, call, fax, or e-mail Phyllis Cremonini, Assistant Chief of Interpretation, RR1, Box 190, Hot Springs, South Dakota 57747. Phone: 605-745-4600. Fax: 605-745-4207. E-mail: phyllis_cremonini@nps.gov. Telephone interview required. Applicants must submit a letter of interest, resume, academic transcripts. Application deadline: March 15 for summer, August 1 for fall, November 1 for spring. World Wide Web: http://www.nps.gov/wica.

WINTERTHUR MUSEUM, GARDEN AND LIBRARY
Winterthur, Delaware 19735

General Information Complete community for the presentation, preservation, and exploration of American arts and historic structures; naturalistic garden; research library and academic center. Established in 1951. Number of employees: 613. Number of internship applications received each year: 30.
Internships Available ▶ *1 arborist intern:* responsibilities include assisting arborists in maintaining health and vigor of the trees throughout Winterthur garden; learning good arboricultural techniques and safety practices. Duration is 2 months (June to August). $9.50 per hour. ▶ *7 horticulture interns:* responsibilities include assisting the horticulturist of a particular garden and/or plant group; working with a horticulturist or production supervisor in maintaining the design of the garden or plant group by practicing good horticulture techniques. Duration is 2 months (June to August). $9.50 per hour. Candidates for all positions should have ability to work with others, knowledge of field, personal interest in the field. Open to college freshmen, college sophomores, college juniors, college seniors. International applications accepted.
Benefits Meals at a cost, opportunity to attend seminars/workshops, possible full-time employment, willing to complete paperwork for educational credit, willing to provide letters of recommendation, field trips, safety training.
Contact Write, call, fax, or e-mail Kay Collins, Employment Manager. Phone: 302-888-4830. Fax: 302-888-4956. E-mail: kcolli@winterthur.org. In-person interview required. Applicants must submit a formal organization application, letter of interest, resume. Application deadline: March 31.

WOMEN'S HISTORY AND RESOURCE CENTER
1734 N Street, NW
Washington, District of Columbia 20036

General Information Archives and library devoted to women's history with an emphasis on women in volunteerism. Established in 1984. Number of employees: 25. Unit of General Federation of Women's Clubs, Washington, District of Columbia. Number of internship applications received each year: 100.
Internships Available ▶ *Interns:* responsibilities include working with books and archival materials, researching answers to refer-

ence inquiries, assisting researchers, receiving training for archival computer project tasks, and archival processing and cataloging. Candidates should have ability to work independently, ability to work with others, college courses in field, computer skills, office skills, organizational skills, research skills, strong interest in archives, women's history, and volunteerism. Duration is fall, spring, or summer (flexible hours). Unpaid. Open to college freshmen, college sophomores, college juniors, college seniors, graduate students, individuals reentering the workforce. International applications accepted.

Benefits Willing to act as a professional reference, willing to complete paperwork for educational credit, willing to provide letters of recommendation, small stipend at completion of internship.

Contact Write, fax, or e-mail Suzanne Gould, Director, 1734 N Street, NW, Washington, District of Columbia 20036. Fax: 202-835-0246. E-mail: whrc@gfwc.org. In-person interview required. Applicants must submit a resume. Applications are accepted continuously. World Wide Web: http://www.gfwc.org/whrc.htm.

YESHIVA UNIVERSITY MUSEUM
15 West 16th Street
New York, New York 10011

General Information Museum that preserves, exhibits, and interprets Jewish life, art history, and culture through multidisciplinary exhibitions, contemporary shows, and scholarly catalogs. Established in 1973. Number of employees: 10. Unit of Yeshiva University, New York, New York. Number of internship applications received each year: 25.

Internships Available ▶ *1 curatorial intern:* responsibilities include research, cataloging, and exhibitions. Candidates should have ability to work independently, ability to work with others, computer skills, editing skills, office skills, research skills, writing skills. Duration is 3 months minimum. Unpaid. Open to high school students, recent high school graduates, college freshmen, college sophomores, college juniors, college seniors, recent college graduates, graduate students, individuals reentering the workforce. ▶ *2 education interns:* responsibilities include conducting youth programs and art workshops for visiting school groups (after training). Candidates should have ability to work independently, ability to work with others, office skills, oral communication skills, written communication skills. Duration is 2–12 months. Unpaid. Open to high school students, college freshmen, college sophomores, college juniors, college seniors, graduate students, individuals reentering the workforce. ▶ *1 registration intern:* responsibilities include collections research and recordkeeping. Candidates should have ability to work independently, ability to work with others, computer skills, editing skills, office skills, research skills, writing skills. Duration is minimum of 3 months. Unpaid. Open to high school students, college freshmen, college sophomores, college juniors, college seniors, graduate students, individuals reentering the workforce. International applications accepted.

Benefits Job counseling, names of contacts, opportunity to attend seminars/workshops, willing to complete paperwork for educational credit, willing to provide letters of recommendation.

Contact Write or fax Ms. Randi Glickberg, Administrator. Phone: 212-294-8338. Fax: 212-294-8335. E-mail: rglickberg@yum.cjh.org. In-person interview required. Applicants must submit a letter of interest, resume, 2 personal references/letters of recommendation. Applications are accepted continuously. World Wide Web: http://www.yu.edu/museum/.

ZOO NEW ENGLAND
One Franklin Park Road
Boston, Massachusetts 02121

General Information Private nonprofit organization that manages the Franklin Park Zoo and Stone Zoo. Established in 1911. Number of employees: 230. Number of internship applications received each year: 12.

Internships Available ▶ *1–6 animal care interns:* responsibilities include assisting the animal care staff at the Franklin Park Zoo (Boston) and/or Stone Zoo (Stoneham). Candidates should have ability to work independently, ability to work with others, oral

communication skills, organizational skills, plan to pursue career in field, self-motivation. Duration is 12 weeks (full-time). Unpaid. Open to college juniors, college seniors, recent college graduates, graduate students, career changers. ▶ *1 animal records assistant:* responsibilities include assisting with animal and library records. Candidates should have ability to work independently, computer skills, office skills, organizational skills, research skills, written communication skills. Duration is 6 months or 1 semester. Unpaid. Open to recent high school graduates, college freshmen, college sophomores, college juniors, college seniors, recent college graduates, graduate students, career changers. ▶ *2–3 education assistants:* responsibilities include assisting with or leading programs for school-aged children; gathering program materials for classes; interpreting exhibits. Candidates should have ability to work independently, college courses in field, editing skills, knowledge of field, office skills, oral communication skills, organizational skills, personal interest in the field, self-motivation, strong interpersonal skills, strong leadership ability, writing skills. Duration is 3–4 months. Unpaid. Open to college juniors, college seniors, recent college graduates, graduate students. ▶ *1–3 horticulture interns:* responsibilities include assisting with the preparation, installation, and maintenance of extensive plant collection at Franklin Park Zoo (Boston) or Stone Zoo (Stoneham). Candidates should have ability to work independently, ability to work with others, knowledge of field, personal interest in the field, research skills, self-motivation. Duration is 1 semester. Unpaid. Open to college sophomores, college juniors, college seniors, recent college graduates, graduate students, career changers. ▶ *1 marketing intern:* responsibilities include assisting with special events, promotions, marketing, and administrative tasks. Candidates should have office skills, oral communication skills, organizational skills, personal interest in the field, strong interpersonal skills, writing skills. Duration is 1 semester. Unpaid. Open to college sophomores, college juniors, college seniors, recent college graduates, graduate students, career changers. ▶ *2 youth programs coordinators (ZooTeen program):* responsibilities include recruitment, orientation, development, training and supervision of the ZooTeen Program, including managing payroll, scheduling, and maintaining records and daily logs; evaluating teens, planning special events, assessing the program, creating and implementing curriculum and coordinating professional developmental workshops. Candidates should have ability to work independently, computer skills, declared college major in field, editing skills, experience in the field, office skills, oral communication skills, organizational skills, personal interest in the field, plan to pursue career in field, self-motivation, strong interpersonal skills, strong leadership ability, writing skills. Duration is 4 months (full-time). $2000 per duration of internship. Open to college sophomores, college juniors, college seniors, recent college graduates, graduate students. International applications accepted.

Benefits Formal training, job counseling, meals at a cost, on-the-job training, opportunity to attend seminars/workshops, possible full-time employment, willing to act as a professional reference, willing to complete paperwork for educational credit, willing to provide letters of recommendation, free entrance to zoos anywhere in U.S., reimbursement for project expenses.

Contact Write, call, fax, or e-mail James L. Brantley, III, Director of Community Relations and Volunteer Services. Phone: 617-989-2017. Fax: 617-541-0732. E-mail: jbrantley@zoonewengland.com. In-person interview recommended (telephone interview accepted). Applicants must submit a formal organization application, letter of interest, resume, academic transcripts, personal reference, two letters of recommendation, TB test required. Applications are accepted continuously. World Wide Web: http://www.zoonewengland.com.

PERFORMING ARTS COMPANIES

THE ACTING COMPANY–GROUP I ACTING COMPANY, INC.
690 Eighth Avenue, 3rd Floor
New York, New York 10036

General Information Professional touring classical repertory theater. Established in 1972. Number of employees: 11. Number of internship applications received each year: 30.

Internships Available ▶ *2 development interns:* responsibilities include performing administrative fund-raising duties. Candidates should have ability to work independently, ability to work with others, computer skills, oral communication skills, organizational skills, self-motivation. Duration is 1–2 semesters. $50 per week. Open to college freshmen, college sophomores, college juniors, college seniors, recent college graduates. ▶ *2 marketing interns:* responsibilities include working with publicity outlets, performing venues, archives and board directors on a variety of public relations/marketing tasks. Candidates should have ability to work independently, ability to work with others, computer skills, oral communication skills, organizational skills, personal interest in the field, written communication skills. Duration is 1–2 semesters. $50 per week. Open to college freshmen, college sophomores, college juniors, college seniors, recent college graduates. ▶ *1–2 office interns:* responsibilities include performing administrative duties. Candidates should have ability to work independently, computer skills, organizational skills, personal interest in the field, self-motivation, written communication skills. Duration is 1–2 semesters. $50 per week. Open to recent high school graduates, college freshmen, college sophomores, college juniors, college seniors, recent college graduates, graduate students. ▶ *1 production intern:* responsibilities include assisting production manager in mounting two full-stage productions and one educational workshop. Candidates should have ability to work independently, ability to work with others, computer skills, knowledge of field, organizational skills, personal interest in the field. Duration is 4 months (mid-September to mid-January). $50 per week. Open to recent high school graduates, college freshmen, college sophomores, college juniors, college seniors, recent college graduates, graduate students. ▶ *1–2 stage management interns:* responsibilities include assisting with rehearsals. Candidates should have ability to work independently, computer skills, oral communication skills, organizational skills, personal interest in the field, plan to pursue career in field, written communication skills. Duration is 4 months (mid-September to mid-January). $100 per week. Open to college freshmen, college sophomores, college juniors, college seniors, recent college graduates, graduate students. International applications accepted.

Benefits Job counseling, names of contacts, on-the-job training, possible full-time employment, willing to act as a professional reference, willing to complete paperwork for educational credit, willing to provide letters of recommendation.

Contact Write, fax, or e-mail Mr. Robert Hoyt, Associate Producing Director, PO Box 898, Times Square Station, New York, New York 10108-0898. Fax: 212-944-5524. E-mail: intern@theactingcompany.org. In-person interview recommended (telephone interview accepted). Applicants must submit a letter of interest, resume, letter of recommendation, 1-2 personal references. Applications are accepted continuously. World Wide Web: http://www.theactingcompany.org.

ACTOR'S THEATRE OF LOUISVILLE
316 West Main Street
Louisville, Kentucky 40202

General Information Regional repertory theater that produces 30 or more shows a season including three major festivals. Established in 1964. Number of employees: 200. Number of internship applications received each year: 100.

Internships Available ▶ *1 apprentice/intern company intern:* responsibilities include curriculum development; recruiting; updating and maintaining library and archives. Candidates should have ability to work independently, computer skills, organizational skills, self-motivation, strong interpersonal skills, attention to detail. Duration is late August to early June. Unpaid. Open to college freshmen, college sophomores, college juniors, college seniors, recent college graduates, graduate students, career changers, individuals reentering the workforce. ▶ *1 casting and company management intern:* responsibilities include weekly attendance at rehearsals; maintaining communication with artists, designers, and other regional theaters; research, scheduling general auditions, arranging local casting needs, maintaining resume files, and performing reference checks. Candidates should have experience in the field, office skills, strong interpersonal skills, sense of humor; computer skills a plus. Duration is last August to early June. Unpaid. Open to college freshmen, college sophomores, college juniors, college seniors, recent college graduates, graduate students, career changers, individuals reentering the workforce. ▶ *1 company and volunteer management intern:* responsibilities include initiating contact with contracted artists; coordinating transportation and housing needs; assisting Development Board with audience recruitment. Candidates should have oral communication skills, organizational skills, strong interpersonal skills, sense of humor, discretion; computer skills a plus. Duration is late August to early June. Unpaid. Open to college freshmen, college sophomores, college juniors, college seniors, recent college graduates, graduate students, career changers, individuals reentering the workforce. ▶ *4–6 costume interns:* responsibilities include working with the staff in one of the following areas: assistant to the designer, technical costume/shop management, wardrobe, or wigs. Candidates should have oral communication skills, organizational skills, strong interpersonal skills, design skills (for some positions). Duration is late August to early June. Unpaid. Open to college freshmen, college sophomores, college juniors, college seniors, recent college graduates, graduate students, career changers, individuals reentering the workforce. ▶ *1 festival management intern:* responsibilities include events and project coordination, producing numerous publications and flyers, setting up exhibits and merchandise displays, coordinating travel and lodging arrangements for guests, coordinating volunteers. Candidates should have computer skills, oral communication skills, organizational skills, strong interpersonal skills, experience with word processing, database management, and desktop publishing (helpful). Duration is January to April. Unpaid. Open to college freshmen, college sophomores, college juniors, college seniors, recent college graduates, graduate students, career changers, individuals reentering the workforce. ▶ *1 lighting intern:* responsibilities include production work (hanging and focusing, etc.); drafting, paperwork, assisting professional lighting designers. Candidates should have computer skills, experience in the field. Duration is late August to early June. Unpaid. Open to college freshmen, college sophomores, college juniors, college seniors, recent college graduates, graduate students, career changers, individuals reentering the workforce. ▶ *2 literary management interns:* responsibilities include attending rehearsals, assisting with playwright residencies, library research, reading new plays, writing articles for ATL publications, administrative support for various literary projects, dramaturgy. Candidates should have ability to work with others, oral communication skills, organizational skills, research skills, self-motivation, written communication skills. Duration is late August to early June. Unpaid. Open to college freshmen, college sophomores, college juniors, college seniors, recent college graduates, graduate students, career changers, individuals reentering the workforce. ▶ *Properties interns:* responsibilities include working with full-time staff in props shop. Candidates should have ability to work with others, knowledge of field, personal interest in the field, self-motivation. Duration is late August to early June (40 hours per week). Unpaid. ▶ *2 public relations/marketing interns:* responsibilities include media relations, single ticket and subscription audience development, promotions, writing press releases. Candidates should have ability to work with others, analytical skills, oral communication skills, organizational skills, written communication skills. Duration is late August to early June. Unpaid. Open to college freshmen, college sophomores, college juniors, college seniors, recent college graduates, graduate students, career changers, individuals reentering the workforce. ▶ *1 scenic design intern:* responsibilities include working as a

Actor's Theatre of Louisville (continued)

member of the theater's design staff. Candidates should have ability to work independently, experience in the field, personal interest in the field, self-motivation. Duration is late August to early June. Unpaid. Open to college freshmen, college sophomores, college juniors, college seniors, recent college graduates, graduate students, career changers, individuals reentering the workforce. ▶ *1 sound intern:* responsibilities include running sound board during performances; assisting sound engineer; assistant design opportunities. Candidates should have ability to work independently, personal interest in the field. Duration is 1/2 season or full season. Unpaid. Open to college freshmen, college sophomores, college juniors, college seniors, recent college graduates, graduate students, career changers, individuals reentering the workforce. ▶ *3 stage management interns:* responsibilities include assisting at rehearsals; running mainstage productions; keeping track of props; preshow and post-show duties for mainstage production. Candidates should have experience in the field, organizational skills, strong interpersonal skills. Duration is late August to early June. Unpaid. Open to college freshmen, college sophomores, college juniors, college seniors, recent college graduates, graduate students, career changers, individuals reentering the workforce. ▶ *1 volunteer and audience relations intern:* responsibilities include front-of-house activities; assisting with volunteer programs and Audience (Accessible) Services. Candidates should have ability to work independently, oral communication skills, organizational skills, strong interpersonal skills. Duration is late August to early June (approximately 20 hours per week). Unpaid. Open to college freshmen, college sophomores, college juniors, college seniors, recent college graduates, graduate students, career changers, individuals reentering the workforce. International applications accepted.
Benefits Names of contacts, on-the-job training, opportunity to attend seminars/workshops, possible full-time employment, willing to act as a professional reference, willing to complete paperwork for educational credit, willing to provide letters of recommendation.
Contact Write, call, fax, e-mail, or through World Wide Web site Carnessa Ottelin, Director of the Apprentice/Intern Company. Phone: 502-584-1265. Fax: 502-561-3300. E-mail: cottelin@ actorstheatre.org. In-person interview required. Applicants must submit a formal organization application, letter of interest, resume, academic transcripts, portfolio, two letters of recommendation. Application deadline: April 15. World Wide Web: http://www. actorstheatre.org.

ALLEY THEATRE
615 Texas Avenue
Houston, Texas 77002

General Information Theater presenting plays of merit performed by a company of actors for a subscription audience. Established in 1947. Number of employees: 100. Number of internship applications received each year: 75.
Internships Available ▶ *1–3 company management interns:* responsibilities include assisting with management of actors, including travel and housing arrangements. Candidates should have office skills, oral communication skills, organizational skills, self-motivation, strong interpersonal skills, written communication skills. Duration is 10–16 weeks (full or part-time). Unpaid. Open to college freshmen, college sophomores, college juniors, college seniors, recent college graduates, graduate students, career changers. ▶ *1–3 costumes/wigs interns:* responsibilities include assisting shop manager and wigmaster. Candidates should have ability to work independently, knowledge of field, plan to pursue career in field, research skills, self-motivation, strong interpersonal skills. Duration is 10–16 weeks (full or part-time). Position available as unpaid or at $200 per week. Open to college freshmen, college sophomores, college juniors, college seniors, recent college graduates, graduate students, career changers. ▶ *1–3 development interns:* responsibilities include fund-raising, special events, development office support. Candidates should have computer skills, office skills, oral communication skills, organizational skills, personal interest in the field, self-motivation, strong interpersonal skills, writing skills. Duration is 10–16 weeks (full or part-time). Unpaid. Open to high school seniors, college freshmen, college sophomores, col-

lege juniors, college seniors, recent college graduates, graduate students, career changers. ▶ *1–3 dramaturgy interns:* responsibilities include reading new plays and performing literary research. Candidates should have ability to work independently, analytical skills, computer skills, editing skills, oral communication skills, personal interest in the field, research skills, self-motivation, strong interpersonal skills, writing skills. Duration is 10–16 weeks (full or part-time). Unpaid. Open to college freshmen, college sophomores, college juniors, college seniors, recent college graduates, graduate students, career changers. ▶ *1–3 education and community outreach interns:* responsibilities include assisting with outreach programming. Candidates should have computer skills, office skills, organizational skills, strong interpersonal skills, written communication skills. Duration is 10–16 weeks (full or part-time). Unpaid. Open to college freshmen, college sophomores, college juniors, college seniors, graduate students. ▶ *1–3 lighting and sound interns:* responsibilities include operating Prestige 3000 lighting system. Candidates should have ability to work independently, ability to work with others, college courses in field, computer skills, knowledge of field, self-motivation. Duration is 10–16 weeks (full or part-time). Position available as unpaid or at $200 per week. Open to college freshmen, college sophomores, college juniors, college seniors, recent college graduates, graduate students, career changers. ▶ *1–3 marketing interns:* responsibilities include devising advertising strategies. Candidates should have computer skills, knowledge of field, office skills, oral communication skills, organizational skills, personal interest in the field, research skills, self-motivation, strong interpersonal skills, writing skills. Duration is 10–16 weeks (full or part-time). Unpaid. Open to college freshmen, college sophomores, college juniors, college seniors, recent college graduates, graduate students, career changers. ▶ *1–3 production management interns:* responsibilities include production and theater management. Candidates should have ability to work independently, computer skills, office skills, oral communication skills, organizational skills, plan to pursue career in field, writing skills. Duration is 10–16 weeks (full or part-time). Unpaid. Open to high school seniors, recent high school graduates, college freshmen, college sophomores, college juniors, college seniors, recent college graduates, graduate students, career changers. ▶ *1–3 props interns.* Candidates should have ability to work independently, analytical skills, knowledge of field, personal interest in the field, research skills, self-motivation, strong interpersonal skills. Duration is 10–16 weeks (full or part-time). Position available as unpaid or at $200 per week. Open to college freshmen, college sophomores, college juniors, college seniors, recent college graduates, graduate students, career changers, individuals reentering the workforce. ▶ *1–3 public relations interns:* responsibilities include writing press releases. Candidates should have computer skills, editing skills, office skills, oral communication skills, organizational skills, personal interest in the field, research skills, self-motivation, strong interpersonal skills, writing skills. Duration is 10–16 weeks (full or part-time). Unpaid. Open to high school seniors, college freshmen, college sophomores, college juniors, college seniors, recent college graduates, graduate students, career changers. ▶ *1–3 scenery interns:* responsibilities include carpentry, painting scenery, and assisting technical director. Candidates should have ability to work with others, college courses in field, experience in the field, organizational skills, plan to pursue career in field, self-motivation. Duration is 10–15 weeks. Unpaid. Open to college freshmen, college sophomores, college juniors, college seniors, recent college graduates, graduate students. ▶ *1–3 stage management interns:* responsibilities include assisting stage managers with preparation for rehearsals and performances. Candidates should have computer skills, experience in the field, oral communication skills, organizational skills, plan to pursue career in field, strong interpersonal skills. Duration is 10–15 weeks. Unpaid. Open to college freshmen, college sophomores, college juniors, college seniors, recent college graduates, graduate students.
Benefits Names of contacts, on-the-job training, possible full-time employment, willing to act as a professional reference, willing to complete paperwork for educational credit, willing to provide letters of recommendation, flexible hours.
Contact Write, call, fax, or e-mail Joe Angel Babb, Education and Community Outreach Coordinator. Phone: 713-227-5156 Ext. 6. Fax: 713-227-7116. E-mail: joeab@alleytheatre.org. In-person

interview recommended (telephone interview accepted). Applicants must submit a letter of interest, resume, two letters of recommendation. Application deadline: April 15 for summer, July 15 for fall, October 30 for spring. World Wide Web: http://www.alleytheatre.org.

ALLIANCE THEATRE COMPANY
1280 Peachtree Street, NE
Atlanta, Georgia 30309

General Information   Theater company offering a diverse 8-play season of contemporary plays, musical theater, world and regional premieres, and classics in its 784-seat mainstage and 200-seat studio theaters; also offers 2 children's theater productions. Established in 1966. Number of employees: 100. Division of Woodruff Arts Center, Atlanta, Georgia. Number of internship applications received each year: 30.

Internships Available   ▶ *4 stage management apprentices:* responsibilities include performing clerical work, maintaining rehearsal halls during rehearsal, assisting with all rehearsals, preparation and distribution of rehearsal and performance notes, operating backstage positions. Candidates should have ability to work with others, experience in the field, office skills, oral communication skills, organizational skills, plan to pursue career in field. Duration is 8–9 months. $250 per week plus overtime after 40 hours. Open to recent college graduates, graduate students.

Benefits   Job counseling, names of contacts, on-the-job training, possible full-time employment, willing to act as a professional reference, willing to provide letters of recommendation.

Contact   Write or fax Mr. Rixon Hammond, Production Manager. Fax: 404-733-4773. No phone calls. In-person interview recommended (telephone interview accepted). Applicants must submit a formal organization application, letter of interest, resume, three personal references, two letters of recommendation. Application deadline: May 20. World Wide Web: http://www.alliancetheatre.org.

AMERICAN CONSERVATORY THEATER
30 Grant Avenue
San Francisco, California 94108

General Information   One of the nation's largest and most active resident professional theaters. Established in 1967. Number of employees: 500. Number of internship applications received each year: 75.

Internships Available   ▶ *1–3 artistic department interns:* responsibilities include working with the directors and artistic staff in the artistic, casting, and literary departments; projects include new play development, visiting artist support, artistic planning, and script evaluation. Candidates should have ability to work independently, analytical skills, computer skills, editing skills, experience in the field, office skills, oral communication skills, organizational skills, plan to pursue career in field, research skills, self-motivation, strong interpersonal skills, writing skills. Duration is 2–10 months. $6.75 per hour. Open to college freshmen, college sophomores, college juniors, college seniors, recent college graduates, graduate students, career changers. ▶ *1 arts management intern:* responsibilities include assisting managing director and front of house manager with budget projections, research, general administration, event coordination, and volunteer coordination. Candidates should have computer skills, experience in the field, office skills, oral communication skills, organizational skills, plan to pursue career in field, research skills, strong interpersonal skills, strong leadership ability. Duration is 2–10 months. $6.75 per hour. Open to college juniors, college seniors, recent college graduates, graduate students. ▶ *1 costume rental intern:* responsibilities include maintaining large stock of period costumes; organizing and creating a unified look for business, personal, and theatrical rentals; and furnishing rehearsal costumes for mainstage theater productions. Candidates should have ability to work independently, college courses in field, computer skills, experience in the field, office skills, oral communication skills, organizational skills, plan to pursue career in field, research skills, self-motivation, strong interpersonal skills, written communication skills. Duration is 9–10 months. $6.75 per hour. Open to college freshmen, college sophomores, college juniors, college seniors, recent college graduates, graduate students, career changers, individuals reentering the workforce. ▶ *1 costume shop intern:* responsibilities include assisting in costume shop, shopping, stitching, and various costume building; duties as determined by the shop manager. Candidates should have ability to work independently, ability to work with others, college courses in field, computer skills, editing skills, experience in the field, office skills, oral communication skills, organizational skills, plan to pursue career in field, research skills, self-motivation, strong leadership ability, writing skills. Duration is 9–10 months. $6.75 per hour. Open to college freshmen, college sophomores, college juniors, college seniors, recent college graduates, individuals reentering the workforce. ▶ *1 lighting design intern:* responsibilities include assisting the lighting design associate in maintaining all records necessary for upkeep of the repertory plot and inventory, drafting designs for special effects, assisting the designers in hanging and focusing lights, and supervising technical rehearsals. Candidates should have ability to work independently, ability to work with others, college courses in field, computer skills, experience in the field, office skills, oral communication skills, organizational skills, plan to pursue career in field, research skills, self-motivation, strong leadership ability, written communication skills. Duration is 9–10 months. $6.75 per hour. Open to college seniors, recent college graduates, graduate students. ▶ *1 makeup and wig construction intern:* responsibilities include working under the direction of the theater's wigmaster in the repertory shop and on special projects. Candidates should have ability to work independently, ability to work with others, analytical skills, knowledge of field, oral communication skills, organizational skills, plan to pursue career in field, research skills, self-motivation, practical experience in related field; college degree in related field preferred. Duration is 9–10 months. $6.75 per hour. Open to college freshmen, college sophomores, college juniors, college seniors, recent college graduates, graduate students, individuals reentering the workforce. ▶ *1 marketing/public relations intern:* responsibilities include learning day-to-day operations, writing, proofreading, photo production, developing and executing signage and posters, and maintaining the database. Candidates should have ability to work independently, analytical skills, college courses in field, computer skills, editing skills, experience in the field, office skills, oral communication skills, organizational skills, plan to pursue career in field, research skills, self-motivation, strong interpersonal skills, strong leadership ability, written communication skills. Duration is 2 months (minimum). $6.75 per hour. Open to college sophomores, college juniors, college seniors, recent college graduates, graduate students. ▶ *1 production management intern:* responsibilities include assisting the production management team in operation of production departments; learning about season schedule, budget planning, contracts, design development, and day-to-day production operations. Candidates should have ability to work independently, analytical skills, college courses in field, computer skills, editing skills, experience in the field, office skills, oral communication skills, organizational skills, plan to pursue career in field, research skills, self-motivation, strong interpersonal skills, written communication skills. Duration is 8–10 months. $6.75 per hour. Open to college seniors, recent college graduates, graduate students, career changers. ▶ *1 properties intern:* responsibilities include creation and fabrication of hand props and set dressings for mainstage productions. Candidates should have ability to work independently, analytical skills, college courses in field, experience in the field, office skills, oral communication skills, organizational skills, plan to pursue career in field, research skills, self-motivation, strong interpersonal skills, written communication skills. Duration is 9–10 months. $6.75 per hour. Open to college freshmen, college sophomores, college juniors, college seniors, recent college graduates, graduate students, career changers. ▶ *1 sound design intern:* responsibilities include assisting the repertory designer in mounting each production. Candidates should have ability to work independently, college courses in field, computer skills, experience in the field, office skills, oral communication skills, organizational skills, plan to pursue career in field, research skills, self-motivation, strong interpersonal skills, writing skills. Duration is 9–10 months. $6.75 per hour. Open to college seniors, recent college graduates, graduate students. ▶ *2–3 stage management interns:* responsibilities include

American Conservatory Theater (continued)

assisting by becoming an integral member of stage management team on specifically assigned mainstage shows. Candidates should have ability to work independently, analytical skills, college courses in field, computer skills, editing skills, experience in the field, office skills, oral communication skills, organizational skills, plan to pursue career in field, research skills, self-motivation, strong interpersonal skills, strong leadership ability, written communication skills. Duration is 8–10 months. $6.75 per hour. Open to college freshmen, college sophomores, college juniors, college seniors, recent college graduates, graduate students, career changers, individuals reentering the workforce. ▶ *1 technical design intern:* responsibilities include working under the direction of the design associate and the technical supervisor to learn the specific techniques and construction methods developed by the theater staff; emphasis on drafting and mold building. Candidates should have ability to work independently, ability to work with others, college courses in field, computer skills, knowledge of field, office skills, oral communication skills, organizational skills, plan to pursue career in field, research skills, written communication skills. Duration is 9–10 months. $6.75 per hour. Open to college juniors, college seniors, recent college graduates, graduate students.
Benefits Formal training, job counseling, names of contacts, on-the-job training, opportunity to attend seminars/workshops, possible full-time employment, willing to act as a professional reference, willing to provide letters of recommendation, assistance with resume preparation.
Contact Write or through World Wide Web site Jennifer Caleshu, Internship Coordinator, 30 Grant Avenue, San Francisco, California 94108-5800. No phone calls. In-person interview recommended (telephone interview accepted). Applicants must submit a formal organization application, letter of interest, resume, portfolio, writing sample, three letters of recommendation. Application deadline: April 15 for production positions; continuous for artistic and administrative positions. Fees: $15. World Wide Web: http://www.act-sfbay.org.

THE AMERICAN PLACE THEATRE
111 West 46th Street
New York, New York 10036

General Information Theater producing the work of American writers that strives for an uncompromising commitment to unconventional and daring plays. Established in 1963. Number of employees: 28. Number of internship applications received each year: 400.
Internships Available ▶ *4 administrative assistants:* responsibilities include assisting staff with day-to-day functions of office. Candidates should have ability to work independently, computer skills, editing skills, office skills, oral communication skills, organizational skills, self-motivation, strong interpersonal skills, writing skills. Duration is flexible. Position available as unpaid or paid. Open to college juniors, college seniors, recent college graduates, graduate students. ▶ *1 assistant to artistic director:* responsibilities include assisting artistic director in script evaluations, fund-raising, correspondence, and daily maintenance of activities schedule. Candidates should have ability to work independently, analytical skills, college courses in field, computer skills, editing skills, knowledge of field, office skills, oral communication skills, organizational skills, plan to pursue career in field, research skills, self-motivation, strong interpersonal skills, writing skills. Duration is one academic year. Position available as unpaid or paid. Open to college seniors, recent college graduates, graduate students, career changers, individuals reentering the workforce. ▶ *3 education interns:* responsibilities include assisting education directors in the coordination and creative planning of 3 education programs: Urban Writes, Literature to Life, and Teacher's Place. Candidates should have ability to work independently, analytical skills, college courses in field, computer skills, knowledge of field, office skills, oral communication skills, organizational skills, self-motivation, strong interpersonal skills, writing skills, interest in production/stage management. Duration is one academic year. Position available as unpaid or paid. Open to college seniors, recent college graduates, graduate students. ▶ *1–2 fund-raising interns:* responsibilities include assist-

ing the director of development in tracking funders and writing grants. Candidates should have ability to work independently, ability to work with others, computer skills, editing skills, office skills, organizational skills, personal interest in the field, research skills, writing skills. Duration is 1 semester. Position available as unpaid or paid. Open to college seniors, recent college graduates, graduate students, individuals reentering the workforce. ▶ *2–4 literary interns:* responsibilities include assisting artistic director in reading and processing incoming submissions and with new play development programs. Candidates should have ability to work independently, ability to work with others, analytical skills, college courses in field, computer skills, office skills, oral communication skills, organizational skills, personal interest in the field, research skills, self-motivation, writing skills, interest in playwriting or dramaturgy. Duration is 1 semester. Position available as unpaid or paid. Open to college juniors, college seniors, recent college graduates, graduate students. ▶ *2 production interns:* responsibilities include assisting production manager in rehearsal and running of productions. Candidates should have ability to work independently, ability to work with others, college courses in field, computer skills, experience in the field, office skills, oral communication skills, organizational skills, plan to pursue career in field, self-motivation, written communication skills. Position available as unpaid or paid. Open to college juniors, college seniors, recent college graduates, graduate students. International applications accepted.
Benefits Job counseling, names of contacts, on-the-job training, opportunity to attend seminars/workshops, possible full-time employment, travel reimbursement, willing to act as a professional reference, willing to complete paperwork for educational credit, willing to provide letters of recommendation.
Contact Write, fax, or e-mail Internship Director. Fax: 212-391-4019. E-mail: pfontana@americanplacetheatre.org. No phone calls. In-person interview recommended (telephone interview accepted). Applicants must submit a letter of interest, resume, three letters of recommendation. Applications are accepted continuously. World Wide Web: http://www.americanplacetheatre.org.

AMERICAN REPERTORY THEATRE AND INSTITUTE FOR ADVANCED THEATRE TRAINING
64 Brattle Street
Cambridge, Massachusetts 02138

General Information Fully professional resident theater company at Harvard University's Loeb Drama Center in Cambridge that produces a 5-play mainstage season, a New Stages series, and a number of special events using a permanent ensemble of actors, directors, designers, technicians, and administrators. Established in 1979. Number of employees: 60. Unit of Harvard University, Cambridge, Massachusetts. Number of internship applications received each year: 20.
Internships Available ▶ *1 artistic management intern:* responsibilities include assisting in company management/casting office. Candidates should have ability to work independently, office skills, oral communication skills, organizational skills, self-motivation, strong interpersonal skills, written communication skills, some background or interest in casting (helpful). Duration is variable periods from September through June (minimum 20 hours per week). Unpaid. Open to college freshmen, college sophomores, college juniors, college seniors, graduate students. ▶ *1 box office intern:* responsibilities include assisting staff in the sale and processing of subscription and individual ticket orders and performing general customer services and computer work. Candidates should have ability to work independently, computer skills, office skills, strong interpersonal skills. Duration is flexible. Unpaid. Open to college freshmen, college sophomores, college juniors, college seniors, recent college graduates, graduate students. ▶ *1 costumes intern:* responsibilities include assisting in all phases of construction process. Candidates should have ability to work independently, knowledge of field, organizational skills, self-motivation. Duration is 12 weeks; summer position not available. Unpaid. Open to college freshmen, college sophomores, college juniors, college seniors, graduate students. ▶ *1 fund-raising/development or financial management intern:* responsibilities include fund-raising/development position involves researching prospects, working with

volunteer committees, maintaining records, and helping with special events and telethons; financial management entails working with comptroller and staff on all aspects of financial operations and assisting with maintenance of general accounting records. Candidates should have computer skills, office skills, oral communication skills, personal interest in the field, strong interpersonal skills, written communication skills. Duration is flexible. Unpaid. Open to college freshmen, college sophomores, college juniors, college seniors, recent college graduates, graduate students, career changers, individuals reentering the workforce. ▶ *1 house management intern:* responsibilities include assisting in front-of-house operations and event planning, company management, and building operations. Candidates should have ability to work independently, office skills, oral communication skills, self-motivation, strong interpersonal skills. Duration is flexible. Unpaid. Open to recent high school graduates, college freshmen, college sophomores, college juniors, college seniors, recent college graduates, individuals reentering the workforce. ▶ *1 lighting intern:* responsibilities include hands-on experience working with electricians and designers for a production; assisting lighting staff in special projects, electrics load-ins, and focusing and tech of shows. Candidates should have some basic knowledge of theater lighting and electrics. Duration is flexible; summer position not available. ▶ *1 literary management intern:* responsibilities include assisting with events, dramaturgical research, critical evaluation of scripts, and gathering research material. Candidates should have ability to work independently, computer skills, office skills, self-motivation, writing skills, familiarity with the major dramatic authors and with theatrical production process; fast, accurate typing ability (preferred). Duration is flexible. Unpaid. Open to college freshmen, college sophomores, college juniors, college seniors, recent college graduates, graduate students, career changers. ▶ *1 marketing/public relations intern:* responsibilities include assisting in planning and execution of audience studies and ticket sales initiatives. Candidates should have office skills, oral communication skills, strong interpersonal skills, writing skills, experience in business, general management, sales, marketing, or public relations (preferred). Duration is 12 weeks. Unpaid. Open to college freshmen, college sophomores, college juniors, college seniors, recent college graduates, graduate students. ▶ *1 movement and dance intern:* responsibilities include assisting movement coach and following the movement for actors and movement composition classes for directors within the Institute. Candidates should have minimum 2 years experience in teaching and theater, strong background in two or more of the following: Alexander, Feldenkrais, Rolfing, Sensory Awareness, Grotowski, Commedia dell'Arte, Fitzmaurice Voicework, Meyerhold's Biomechanics, Yoga, Tai Chi, Modern Dance, Classical Dance, Theatre and Jazz Dance, acrobatics, circus techniques, stage combat, choreography, directing. Duration is 6-10 week full-time commitment between September and June. ▶ *1 paint intern:* responsibilities include assisting scenic artist in the realization of set designs using a variety of paint techniques; obtaining practical experience in the translation of the design into large-scale finished set pieces from color mixing through installation. Candidates should have some knowledge of scenic art or fine art (preferred). Duration is minimum 12 weeks (16 hours per week); summer position not available. ▶ *1 production management intern:* responsibilities include working closely with production manager; small projects specific to each production; general office duties, research for props and scenery, providing rehearsal support, assisting with budgeting; other production-related tasks. Candidates should have ability to work independently, oral communication skills, organizational skills, self-motivation, strong interpersonal skills, written communication skills. Duration is flexible; summer position not available. Unpaid. Open to college freshmen, college sophomores, college juniors, college seniors, recent college graduates, graduate students. ▶ *1 running crew intern:* responsibilities include assisting with stage management, lighting, wardrobe, sound, or properties. Candidates should have strong interpersonal skills, broad background in technical theatre as well as some experience backstage. Duration is 2 to 3 months; summer position not available. Unpaid. Open to college freshmen, college sophomores, college juniors, college seniors, recent college graduates, graduate students. ▶ *1 scenery intern:* responsibilities include assisting in budgeting, schedul-

ing, construction, finishing, and installation of scenery and property. Candidates should have ability to work independently, oral communication skills, self-motivation, strong interpersonal skills, written communication skills. Duration is 12 weeks (minimum); 16 hours per week; summer position not available. Unpaid. Open to college freshmen, college sophomores, college juniors, college seniors, recent college graduates, graduate students. ▶ *1 stage management intern:* responsibilities include assisting in all aspects of the production process. Candidates should have ability to work independently, ability to work with others, organizational skills, self-motivation, strong leadership ability, some knowledge of theater production and some stage management experience (preferred). Duration is 8 to 12 weeks; summer position not available. Position available as unpaid or paid. Open to college freshmen, college sophomores, college juniors, college seniors, recent college graduates, graduate students. ▶ *1 voice and speech intern:* responsibilities include observing and assisting the head of voice ands peech in teaching classes, coaching actors, coaching students, and preparing productions. Candidates should have college courses in field, knowledge of field, personal interest in the field, strong background in two or more of the following: Fitzmaurice Voicework, Linklater, Lessac, or Roy Hart techniques; Alexander for Feldenkrais training; stage dialects, phonetics, or speech science; previous coaching, directing, or acting experience (highly recommended). Duration is 6- to 10- week full- time commitment between September and June. Unpaid. Open to recent college graduates, graduate students. International applications accepted.

Benefits Names of contacts, on-the-job training, willing to act as a professional reference, willing to complete paperwork for educational credit, willing to provide letters of recommendation, stipends to cover basic living expenses may be available for running crew, scenery, properties, and paint interns.

Contact Write or through World Wide Web site Internship Director. In-person interview recommended (telephone interview accepted). Applicants must submit a formal organization application, letter of interest, resume, two personal references, see Web page for details. Application deadline: May 1 for voice and speech position; movement and dance position; continuous for all other positions; summer internships are not available. World Wide Web: http://www.amrep.org.

AMERICAN STAGE
211 Third Street South
St. Petersburg, Florida 33731

General Information Nonprofit residential professional theater mandated as an arts agency to provide theater productions and related educational and outreach programs to the citizens of west central Florida. Established in 1977. Number of employees: 15. Number of internship applications received each year: 25.

Internships Available ▶ *1–2 administrative interns:* responsibilities include performing general administrative, fund-raising, and box office work. Candidates should have ability to work with others, computer skills, editing skills, office skills, oral communication skills, research skills, self-motivation, writing skills. Duration is 1 semester. Position available as unpaid or paid. Open to college freshmen, college sophomores, college juniors, college seniors, recent college graduates, graduate students. ▶ *1–4 education interns:* responsibilities include teaching curriculum for summer theater camp for children ages 6-16. Candidates should have ability to work independently, analytical skills, oral communication skills, organizational skills, plan to pursue career in field, research skills, self-motivation, strong interpersonal skills, strong leadership ability, writing skills. Duration is May 15 to August 15. $150–$250 per week. Open to college juniors, college seniors, recent college graduates, graduate students, career changers, individuals reentering the workforce. ▶ *1–2 performance/production interns:* responsibilities include understudying mainstage productions, assisting with staged readings and auditions, and serving as assistant stage manager for mainstage productions. Candidates should have ability to work independently, ability to work with others, computer skills, experience in the field, oral communication skills, organizational skills, research skills, self-motivation, written communication skills. Duration is 1 semester. $150 per week (housing occasionally offered in lieu of stipend). Open to recent high

American Stage (continued)

school graduates, college freshmen, college sophomores, college juniors, college seniors, recent college graduates, graduate students, career changers. ▶ *2–4 technical interns:* responsibilities include working in carpentry and costume shops and running shows. Candidates should have ability to work independently, ability to work with others, analytical skills, knowledge of field, oral communication skills, organizational skills, personal interest in the field, self-motivation. Duration is 1 semester. $150–$225 per week. Open to recent high school graduates, college freshmen, college sophomores, college juniors, college seniors, recent college graduates, graduate students, career changers, individuals reentering the workforce. International applications accepted.

Benefits Formal training, job counseling, names of contacts, on-the-job training, opportunity to attend seminars/workshops, willing to complete paperwork for educational credit, willing to provide letters of recommendation.

Contact Write Toni Wright, Education Coordinator, PO Box 1560, St. Petersburg, Florida 33731. Fax: 727-821-2444. E-mail: tw1554@yahoo.com. No phone calls. In-person interview recommended (telephone interview accepted). Applicants must submit a letter of interest, resume, portfolio, three personal references, three letters of recommendation, 5 writing samples. Application deadline: March 1 for summer, July 1 for fall, December 1 for spring. World Wide Web: http://www.americanstage.org.

AMERICAN STAGE FESTIVAL (THE YOUNG COMPANY)
14 Court Street
Nashua, New Hampshire 03060

General Information Nationally-recognized professional theater in southern New Hampshire with a 500-seat house producing 5 mainstage and 5 children's shows and staged readings from May to September. Established in 1971. Number of employees: 18. Number of internship applications received each year: 500.

Internships Available ▶ *2 administrative/marketing interns:* responsibilities include assisting company manager and management staff. Candidates should have knowledge of field, oral communication skills, organizational skills, plan to pursue career in field, written communication skills. Duration is June 1 to August 31. Stipend. ▶ *1 costumer:* responsibilities include designing and constructing costumes. Candidates should have knowledge of field, plan to pursue career in field. Duration is June 1 to August 31. Stipend. ▶ *2 directing interns:* responsibilities include assisting with mainstage. Candidates should have knowledge of field, oral communication skills, plan to pursue career in field, strong interpersonal skills, written communication skills. Duration is June 1 to August 31. Stipend. ▶ *1 lighting intern:* responsibilities include assisting with mainstage shows and design. Candidates should have knowledge of field, plan to pursue career in field. Duration is June 1 to August 31. Stipend. ▶ *1 properties intern:* responsibilities include assisting property master on all shows, acting as property manager for Young Company. Candidates should have knowledge of field, plan to pursue career in field. Duration is June 1 to August 31. Stipend. ▶ *4 stage managers:* responsibilities include assisting stage managers of mainstage and Young Company. Candidates should have ability to work with others, knowledge of field, oral communication skills, plan to pursue career in field. Duration is June 1 to August 31. Stipend. Open to recent high school graduates, college freshmen, college sophomores, college juniors, college seniors, recent college graduates. International applications accepted.

Benefits Free housing, on-the-job training, opportunity to attend seminars/workshops, willing to act as a professional reference, willing to complete paperwork for educational credit, willing to provide letters of recommendation, stipend ($75–$100 per week depending on position); EMC credit for stage managers.

Contact Write, fax, or e-mail Ms. Allison Szklarz, Managing Director. Fax: 603-889-2336. E-mail: amstagefest@aol.com. No phone calls. Telephone interview required. Applicants must submit a letter of interest, resume. Application deadline: April 15. World Wide Web: http://www.americanstagefestival.org.

APPEL FARM ARTS AND MUSIC CENTER
457 Shirley Road
Elmer, New Jersey 08318

General Information Fine and performing arts center concentrating on 3 areas: presenting arts (music, dance, theater) to the local community; providing affordable meeting and work space for artists and art organizations; and offering arts education for children through a summer camp. Established in 1960. Number of employees: 18. Number of internship applications received each year: 50.

Internships Available ▶ *1 assistant events coordinator:* responsibilities include house manager for Evening and Family Matinee Series in a 250-seat house, assisting with coordination of 2,000-seat Country Music events and 10,000-seat Arts and Music Festival, assisting with Community Arts Outreach program, and miscellaneous other office duties. Candidates should have ability to work independently, oral communication skills, organizational skills, self-motivation, strong interpersonal skills, strong leadership ability. Duration is 3–9 months. $300 per month. ▶ *1–2 marketing associates/box office coordinators:* responsibilities include box office management for 16 plus shows (250-seat house), 3 plus shows (2,000-seat house), 1 show (10,000-seat house); assisting with marketing to radio, press, and audience; tabulating audience surveys and selling ads for program book. Candidates should have ability to work independently, ability to work with others, oral communication skills, organizational skills, self-motivation, written communication skills. Duration is 3–9 months. $300 per month. ▶ *1 outreach coordinator:* responsibilities include coordinating and executing outreach programs with schools and artists, maintaining surveys and records of program, and other miscellaneous office duties. Candidates should have ability to work independently, oral communication skills, organizational skills, strong interpersonal skills, written communication skills. Duration is 3–9 months. $300 per month. Open to college seniors, recent college graduates, graduate students, individuals reentering the workforce.

Benefits Free housing, free meals, names of contacts, on-the-job training, possible full-time employment, willing to act as a professional reference, willing to complete paperwork for educational credit, willing to provide letters of recommendation.

Contact Write, call, fax, e-mail, or through World Wide Web site Ms. Heather A. Yelle, Internship Coordinator, PO Box 888, Elmer, New Jersey 08318. Phone: 856-358-2472. Fax: 856-358-6513. E-mail: appelarts@aol.com. Telephone interview required. Applicants must submit a formal organization application, letter of interest, resume, three letters of recommendation. Applications are accepted continuously. World Wide Web: http://www.appelfarm.org.

ARDEN THEATRE COMPANY
40 North Second Street
Philadelphia, Pennsylvania 19106

General Information Nonprofit professional theater company whose mission is to tell the greatest stories by the greatest storytellers of all time, stories that arouse, provoke, illuminate, and inspire. Established in 1988. Number of employees: 35. Number of internship applications received each year: 300.

Internships Available ▶ *6 apprentices:* responsibilities include working in every aspect of operations including artistic direction, marketing, box office, development, production (load-in/strike, run crew, prop/set/costume building), stage management, finance, and general management. Candidates should have ability to work with others, oral communication skills, plan to pursue career in field, self-motivation. Duration is one season (August to June). $275 per week plus full health benefits. Open to college seniors, recent college graduates, graduate students, law students, career changers, individuals reentering the workforce. ▶ *1 artistic assistant:* responsibilities include assisting artistic office staff. Candidates should have office skills, oral communication skills, organizational skills, strong interpersonal skills. Duration is flexible. Unpaid. Open to high school seniors, recent high school graduates, college freshmen, college sophomores, college juniors, college seniors, recent college graduates, law students, career changers, individuals reentering the workforce. ▶ *1–2 development assistants:* responsibilities include assisting development staff in all areas of fund-raising. Candidates should have computer skills, office skills, oral communication skills, strong interpersonal skills, written communication skills. Duration is flexible. Unpaid. Open to high school seniors, recent high school graduates, college freshmen, college sophomores, college juniors, college seniors, recent college graduates, graduate students, law students, career changers, individuals reentering the workforce. ▶ *1–3 front-of-house interns:* responsibilities include assisting in all front-of-house responsibilities including house management and box office. Candidates should have oral communication skills, strong interpersonal skills. Duration is flexible during September-June season. Unpaid. Open to recent high school graduates, college freshmen, college sophomores, college juniors, college seniors, recent college graduates. ▶ *1–2 marketing assistants:* responsibilities include assisting staff in all areas of marketing. Candidates should have computer skills, office skills, strong interpersonal skills. Duration is flexible. Unpaid. Open to high school seniors, recent high school graduates, college freshmen, college sophomores, college juniors, college seniors, recent college graduates, graduate students, law students, career changers, individuals reentering the workforce. ▶ *15–20 production assistants:* responsibilities include running crew and assistants, working in areas of lighting, sound, props, costumes, and sets. Candidates should have ability to work with others, personal interest in the field. Duration is show-by-show for season of 7 shows. Position available as unpaid or at $80–$175 per week. Open to high school seniors, recent high school graduates, college freshmen, college sophomores, college juniors, college seniors, recent college graduates, law students, career changers, individuals reentering the workforce. International applications accepted.

Benefits Job counseling, names of contacts, on-the-job training, opportunity to attend seminars/workshops, possible full-time employment, willing to act as a professional reference, willing to complete paperwork for educational credit, willing to provide letters of recommendation.

Contact Write, fax, or through World Wide Web site Intern or Apprentice Coordinator. Fax: 215-922-7011. No phone calls. In-person interview recommended (telephone interview accepted). Applicants must submit a letter of interest, resume. Application deadline: May 1 for Arden Professional Apprentice Program; continuous for other positions. World Wide Web: http://www.ardentheatre.org.

ARENA STAGE
1101 Sixth Street, SW
Washington, District of Columbia 20024

General Information One of the country's leading resident theater companies consisting of a core of resident artists, craftspeople, theater technicians, and administrators who seek to illuminate the American spirit through the highest professional standard of theater art; 8-play season runs mid-August through mid-June. Established in 1950. Number of employees: 180. Number of internship applications received each year: 300.

Internships Available ▶ *7–11 artistic interns:* responsibilities include assisting in directing, literary management, casting/production, or community engagement/education. Candidates should have analytical skills, college courses in field, experience in the field, organizational skills, research skills, writing skills. Duration is flexible (full-time); may follow production cycle (6-8 weeks). $120 per week. ▶ *14–20 arts administration interns:* responsibilities include assisting the executive director, external affairs office, or finance/personnel office; or working with communications/marketing/media relations, development (fund-raising and special events), information systems, casting/production office, or sales office. Candidates should have knowledge of field, office skills, oral communication skills, organizational skills, strong interpersonal skills, writing skills. Duration is flexible (full-time). $120 per week. ▶ *4–6 community engagement interns:* responsibilities include assisting in administrative management or production of Living Stage (social outreach theater). Candidates should have knowledge of field, personal interest in the field, strong interpersonal skills, written communication skills, commitment to children and theater for social change. Duration is flexible (full-time). $120 per week. ▶ *10–20 technical/production interns:* responsibilities include assisting with costumes, lighting, production management, properties, scene painting/set construction, sound, or stage management.

Candidates should have ability to work independently, college courses in field, experience in the field, plan to pursue career in field, strong interpersonal skills. Duration is flexible (full-time); not available in summer. $120 per week. Open to college freshmen, college sophomores, college juniors, college seniors, recent college graduates, graduate students, career changers. International applications accepted.

Benefits Job counseling, names of contacts, opportunity to attend seminars/workshops, possible full-time employment, willing to act as a professional reference, willing to complete paperwork for educational credit, willing to provide letters of recommendation, modest stipend, minority fellowships available.

Contact Write, call, fax, e-mail, or through World Wide Web site Intern Program Coordinator. Phone: 202-554-9066. Fax: 202-488-4056. E-mail: interns@arenastage.org. Applicants must submit a letter of interest, resume, academic transcripts, statement of how internship matches career objective; 2 letters of recommendation (one academic, one professional); mandatory interview in person or by phone; a critical writing sample (directing and administrative applicants only); see Web site for details. Application deadline: March 1 for summer, April 1 for minority fellowships, May 1 for fall, October 1 for winter/spring. World Wide Web: http://www.arenastage.org.

ASH LAWN OPERA FESTIVAL
1941 James Monroe Parkway
Charlottesville, Virginia 22902-8722

General Information Summer festival producing 2 operas and 1 musical theater production for a total of 28 performances; hosts additional musical and theatrical productions for all ages. Established in 1978. Number of employees: 60. Unit of The College of William and Mary, Williamsburg, Virginia. Number of internship applications received each year: 20.

Internships Available ▶ *1 administrative intern:* responsibilities include maintaining databases, organizing fund-raising mailings, designing summer festival programs, providing general office support. Candidates should have computer skills, office skills, organizational skills, self-motivation, writing skills. Duration is flexible. Unpaid. Open to high school seniors, recent high school graduates, college freshmen, college sophomores, college juniors, college seniors, recent college graduates, graduate students. ▶ *1 arts management intern:* responsibilities include working in administrative office, with production staff, and in the costume shop and box office. Candidates should have ability to work with others, computer skills, office skills, organizational skills, self-motivation. Duration is flexible. Unpaid. Open to college freshmen, college sophomores, college juniors, college seniors, recent college graduates, graduate students. ▶ *1 development intern:* responsibilities include composing development materials and fund-raising strategies and expanding and maintaining databases. Candidates should have ability to work independently, ability to work with others, computer skills, organizational skills, research skills, self-motivation, writing skills. Duration is flexible. Unpaid. Open to college juniors, college seniors, recent college graduates, graduate students. ▶ *1 marketing intern:* responsibilities include developing marketing strategies and contacts; researching, organizing, and updating grant information; and assisting with grant writing. Candidates should have ability to work with others, computer skills, office skills, organizational skills, research skills, self-motivation, writing skills. Duration is flexible. Unpaid. Open to college freshmen, college sophomores, college juniors, college seniors, recent college graduates, graduate students. ▶ *1 press intern:* responsibilities include composing press releases and calendar listings; organizing press databases; and developing contacts with area newspapers, magazines and radio and television stations. Candidates should have ability to work independently, ability to work with others, computer skills, organizational skills, self-motivation, writing skills. Duration is one summer. Unpaid. Open to college freshmen, college sophomores, college juniors, college seniors, recent college graduates, graduate students. ▶ *1 production intern:* responsibilities include scene painting, scene shifting, lighting design, theatrical sewing, and carpentry. Candidates should have ability to work independently, ability to work with others, knowledge of field, self-motivation. Duration is one summer. Unpaid. Open to high

Ash Lawn Opera Festival (continued)

school seniors, recent high school graduates, college freshmen, college sophomores, college juniors, college seniors, recent college graduates, graduate students. International applications accepted.

Benefits Free housing, job counseling, names of contacts, willing to complete paperwork for educational credit, willing to provide letters of recommendation, hands-on experience in the operation and production of professional opera company.

Contact Write, call, fax, e-mail, or through World Wide Web site Assistant to the General Director. Phone: 434-293-4500. Fax: 434-293-0736. E-mail: opera@avenue.org. Applicants must submit a letter of interest, resume. Application deadline: February 1 for spring, April 1 for summer. World Wide Web: http://www.ashlawnopera.org.

ATLANTIC THEATER COMPANY
336 West 20th Street
New York, New York 10011

General Information Nonprofit off-Broadway acting ensemble dedicated to producing new theater and featuring a distinctive acting technique. Established in 1985. Number of employees: 11. Number of internship applications received each year: 25.

Internships Available ► *2–4 development/marketing interns:* responsibilities include marketing, fund-raising, and organizing development and benefits. Candidates should have ability to work independently, ability to work with others, computer skills, organizational skills, personal interest in the field, self-motivation, writing skills. Duration is flexible. Unpaid. Open to college freshmen, college sophomores, college juniors, college seniors, recent college graduates, graduate students. ► *3 office interns:* responsibilities include managing house and box office, and performing general office work. Candidates should have editing skills, office skills, oral communication skills, organizational skills, self-motivation, strong interpersonal skills, writing skills. Duration is September 1-May 31. Unpaid. Open to college freshmen, college sophomores, college juniors, college seniors, recent college graduates. ► *3 production interns:* responsibilities include working on lighting, sets, props, costumes, and running crew for all productions. Candidates should have knowledge of field. Duration is flexible. Unpaid. Open to college freshmen, college sophomores, college juniors, college seniors, recent college graduates. International applications accepted.

Benefits Names of contacts, on-the-job training, opportunity to attend seminars/workshops, willing to complete paperwork for educational credit, willing to provide letters of recommendation.

Contact Write or fax Internship Coordinator. Fax: 212-645-8755. No phone calls. In-person interview recommended (telephone interview accepted). Applicants must submit a letter of interest, resume. Applications are accepted continuously. World Wide Web: http://www.atlantictheater.org.

BARROW GROUP
312 West 36th Street
New York, New York 10018

General Information Theater performing full-length new works. Established in 1986. Number of employees: 5. Number of internship applications received each year: 20.

Internships Available ► *1–3 development interns:* responsibilities include grant writing, fund-raising, and publicity. Candidates should have ability to work independently, computer skills, editing skills, oral communication skills, organizational skills, research skills, self-motivation, writing skills. Duration is 3–6 months. Unpaid. Open to college juniors, college seniors, recent college graduates, graduate students, career changers. ► *1–4 general management interns:* responsibilities include assisting the managing director in all aspects of production, fund-raising, Web site management, and Board of Trustees relationship. Candidates should have computer skills, office skills, oral communication skills, organizational skills, self-motivation, written communication skills. Duration is flexible. Unpaid. Open to recent high school graduates, college freshmen, college sophomores, college juniors, college seniors, recent college graduates, graduate students, career

changers. ► *1–3 literary management interns:* responsibilities include reading and responding to scripts, helping organize reading series, recommending projects for production. Candidates should have ability to work independently, computer skills, editing skills, knowledge of field, oral communication skills, organizational skills, personal interest in the field, self-motivation, writing skills. Duration is 3–6 months. Unpaid. Open to recent high school graduates, college freshmen, college sophomores, college juniors, college seniors, recent college graduates, graduate students. ► *1–3 production interns:* responsibilities include assisting director and/or stage manager; helping with box office, house/stage management, and running crew. Candidates should have ability to work with others, personal interest in the field, plan to pursue career in field, self-motivation. Duration is one fall or spring. Unpaid. Open to high school students, recent high school graduates, college freshmen, college sophomores, college juniors, college seniors, recent college graduates, individuals reentering the workforce.

Benefits On-the-job training, opportunity to attend seminars/workshops, possible full-time employment, travel reimbursement, willing to complete paperwork for educational credit, willing to provide letters of recommendation.

Contact Write, e-mail, or through World Wide Web site Eric Paeper, Managing Director. E-mail: barrowgroup@earthlink.net. In-person interview recommended (telephone interview accepted). Applicants must submit a letter of interest, resume. Applications are accepted continuously. World Wide Web: http://www.barrowgroup.org.

BATTERY DANCE COMPANY
380 Broadway, 5th Floor
New York, New York 10013-3518

General Information Dance company that tours internationally, works extensively in the public schools, and produces an annual free public dance festival in New York City's financial district; also organizes domestic tours by foreign dance troupes. Established in 1976. Number of employees: 15. Number of internship applications received each year: 60.

Internships Available ► *2 administrative assistants:* responsibilities include performing office management duties. Candidates should have ability to work independently, ability to work with others, computer skills, office skills, oral communication skills, personal interest in the field, self-motivation, written communication skills. Duration is flexible. Unpaid. ► *1 intern:* responsibilities include coordinating contracts and publicity, acting as site liaison, assisting in ad campaign, and administration. Candidates should have ability to work independently, ability to work with others, oral communication skills, personal interest in the field, self-motivation, written communication skills. Duration is flexible. Unpaid. Open to high school students, recent high school graduates, college freshmen, college sophomores, college juniors, college seniors, recent college graduates, graduate students, law students, career changers, individuals reentering the workforce. International applications accepted.

Benefits Job counseling, names of contacts, on-the-job training, possible full-time employment, willing to act as a professional reference, willing to complete paperwork for educational credit, willing to provide letters of recommendation, opportunity to attend seminars/workshops and performances.

Contact Write, call, fax, e-mail, or through World Wide Web site Mr. Ronald Knoth, Managing Director. Phone: 212-219-3910. Fax: 212-219-3911. E-mail: knoth@bway.net. In-person interview recommended (telephone interview accepted). Applicants must submit a letter of interest, resume, writing sample, applications by e-mail encouraged. Applications are accepted continuously. World Wide Web: http://www.batterydanceco.com.

BERKELEY REPERTORY THEATRE
2025 Addison Street
Berkeley, California 94704

General Information Professional, nonprofit theater company that produces mainstage, short-run, and school touring productions. Established in 1968. Number of employees: 125. Number of internship applications received each year: 200.

Internships Available ▶ *1 costumes intern:* responsibilities include participating in costume construction, crafts, repairs, and alterations; assisting with makeup, hair, and wigs; working on stock maintenance; and running wardrobe for some major productions. Candidates should have ability to work independently, ability to work with others, knowledge of field, personal interest in the field, plan to pursue career in field, self-motivation, sewing skills. Duration is August/September to June/July. $400 per month. Open to college juniors, college seniors, recent college graduates, graduate students. ▶ *1 development intern:* responsibilities include assisting with fund-raising campaigns and donations, including direct mail, telefunding, special events, and administration. Candidates should have computer skills, knowledge of field, plan to pursue career in field, research skills, self-motivation, strong interpersonal skills, writing skills, basic experience in area of application. Duration is August/September to June/July. $400 per month. Open to college juniors, college seniors, recent college graduates, graduate students. ▶ *1 education intern:* responsibilities include assisting the planning of school touring production, arranging student matinees, assisting at teacher in-service seminars and teacher artist workshops, and providing administrative help on curriculum study guides. Candidates should have computer skills, oral communication skills, plan to pursue career in field, research skills, self-motivation, strong interpersonal skills, written communication skills, basic experience in area of application. Duration is August/September to June/July. $400 per month. Open to college juniors, college seniors, recent college graduates, graduate students. ▶ *1 lighting/electrics intern:* responsibilities include assisting master electrician in all phases of technical electrics production, including maintenance and repair of the lighting system, hanging and focusing, testing special effects, and lighting. Candidates should have ability to work independently, ability to work with others, knowledge of field, personal interest in the field, plan to pursue career in field, self-motivation, basic experience in area of application. Duration is August/September to June/July. $400 per month. Open to college juniors, college seniors, recent college graduates, graduate students. ▶ *1 literary/dramaturgy intern:* responsibilities include reading and critiquing plays under consideration for the season; assisting the literary manager with processing new scripts; occasionally writing and/or editing materials for programs, newsletters, and study guides; maintaining script library; and possibly serving as production dramaturg. Candidates should have ability to work independently, computer skills, editing skills, knowledge of field, plan to pursue career in field, research skills, writing skills, basic experience in area of application. Duration is August/September to June/July. $400 per month. Open to college juniors, college seniors, recent college graduates, graduate students. ▶ *1–2 marketing/public relations/graphic design interns:* responsibilities include working with single ticket and subscription campaigns, telemarketing, direct mail projects, and community outreach. Candidates should have computer skills, editing skills, knowledge of field, organizational skills, plan to pursue career in field, research skills, self-motivation, writing skills, basic experience in area of application. Duration is August/September to June/July. $400 per month. Open to college juniors, college seniors, recent college graduates, graduate students. ▶ *1 production management intern:* responsibilities include assisting in overseeing technical departments; contracting; designers; hiring; technical staff; scheduling; tracking expenses and payroll. Candidates should have computer skills, knowledge of field, office skills, oral communication skills, personal interest in the field, plan to pursue career in field, self-motivation, strong interpersonal skills, written communication skills, basic experience in area of application. Duration is August/September to June/July. $400 per month. Open to college juniors, college seniors, recent college graduates, graduate students. ▶ *1 properties intern:* responsibilities include working in prop shop and procuring or building all properties for a show. Candidates should have ability to work independently, knowledge of field, plan to pursue career in field, research skills, self-motivation, strong interpersonal skills, basic experience in area of application. Duration is August/September to June/July. $400 per month. Open to college juniors, college seniors, recent college graduates, graduate students. ▶ *1 scenic construction intern:* responsibilities include working with woods, metals, and plastics, and acting as builder, welder, and draftsperson. Candidates should

have ability to work independently, ability to work with others, analytical skills, knowledge of field, plan to pursue career in field, self-motivation, ability to use craftmaking tools. Duration is August/September to June/July. $400 per month. Open to college juniors, college seniors, recent college graduates, graduate students. ▶ *1 scenic painting intern:* responsibilities include developing craft projects using sculpting, texture, color matching, and a variety of scenic painting techniques; assisting scenic artists with all productions; and assisting scenic designers in dressing sets. Candidates should have ability to work independently, ability to work with others, knowledge of field, plan to pursue career in field, self-motivation, basic experience in area of application. Duration is August/September to June/July. $400 per month. Open to college juniors, college seniors, recent college graduates, graduate students. ▶ *1 sound intern:* responsibilities include working with audio technician on sophisticated sound system designing, recording, and digital sampling and installing; maintaining and repairing the sound system. Candidates should have ability to work independently, ability to work with others, knowledge of field, plan to pursue career in field, research skills, self-motivation, basic experience in area of application. Duration is August/September to June/July. $400 per month. Open to college juniors, college seniors, recent college graduates, graduate students. ▶ *1–2 stage management interns:* responsibilities include assisting stage managers in all aspects of their work, including rehearsal process, technical rehearsals, and possibly working with a production through the completion of the run. Candidates should have computer skills, knowledge of field, plan to pursue career in field, self-motivation, strong interpersonal skills, strong leadership ability, basic experience in area of application. Duration is August/September to June/July. $400 per month. Open to college juniors, college seniors, recent college graduates, graduate students. ▶ *1 theater administration intern:* responsibilities include assisting in contracting artists, house management, and assorted projects as needed. Candidates should have computer skills, office skills, plan to pursue career in field, strong interpersonal skills, strong leadership ability, writing skills. Duration is August/September to June/July. $400 per month. Open to college seniors, recent college graduates, graduate students, law students, career changers. International applications accepted.

Benefits Formal training, job counseling, names of contacts, on-the-job training, opportunity to attend seminars/workshops, possible full-time employment, willing to act as a professional reference, willing to complete paperwork for educational credit, willing to provide letters of recommendation, housing provided for a limited number of interns.

Contact Write, fax, or e-mail Intern Coordinator. Fax: 510-647-2929. E-mail: internship@berkeleyrep.org. No phone calls. In-person interview recommended (telephone interview accepted). Applicants must submit a letter of interest, resume, three personal references, three letters of recommendation, 2 writing samples if applying for the literary internship. Application deadline: April 1. World Wide Web: http://www.berkeleyrep.org.

BILINGUAL FOUNDATION OF THE ARTS
421 North Avenue 19
Los Angeles, California 90031

General Information Bilingual Spanish-English theater company that performs plays by Hispanic and Hispanic-American playwrights and also has a touring children's theater company and teen theater. Established in 1973. Number of employees: 14. Number of internship applications received each year: 10.

Internships Available ▶ *1–2 development/marketing interns:* responsibilities include fund-raising and development. Candidates should have college courses in field, computer skills, knowledge of field, personal interest in the field, research skills, self-motivation, strong interpersonal skills, strong leadership ability, writing skills. Duration is 3–12 months. Unpaid. ▶ *1–2 marketing interns/development grantwriters, researchers:* responsibilities include performing data entry, compiling statistical data, preparing audience surveys, reporting survey results, assisting in preparation of marketing plan; writing grants to request supporting funds and researching new funding sources. Candidates should have college courses in field, computer skills, knowledge of field, office skills, organizational

Bilingual Foundation of the Arts (continued)
skills, personal interest in the field, research skills, self-motivation, strong interpersonal skills, writing skills. Duration is flexible. Unpaid. Open to college seniors, recent college graduates, graduate students, career changers, individuals reentering the workforce.
Benefits On-the-job training, possible full-time employment, willing to provide letters of recommendation.
Contact Write, fax, or e-mail Aracely Alvarez, Managing Director. Fax: 323-225-1250. E-mail: bfa99@earthlink.net. No phone calls. In-person interview required. Applicants must submit a letter of interest, resume, three personal references, two letters of recommendation. Applications are accepted continuously. World Wide Web: http://www.bfatheatre.org.

BOND STREET THEATRE
2 Bond Street
New York, New York 10012

General Information Theater focusing on original work having a physical style; tours internationally performing socially relevant material with minimal use of language. Established in 1976. Number of employees: 5. Number of internship applications received each year: 100.
Internships Available ▶ *1 acting intern:* responsibilities include acting as understudy for all roles, standing-in for actors as necessary in rehearsals, attending all rehearsals (as possible), learning all skills (musical, physical). Candidates should have experience in the field, plan to pursue career in field, self-motivation, strong interpersonal skills, strong physical training or capability of physical training (dance, gymnastics); musical skills are a plus. Duration is open. Position available as unpaid or paid. Open to college freshmen, college sophomores, college juniors, college seniors, recent college graduates, graduate students. ▶ *1 business intern:* responsibilities include helping to design, implement, and produce company projects with artistic director and managing director. Candidates should have ability to work independently, ability to work with others, computer skills, organizational skills, personal interest in the field, writing skills. Duration is open. Position available as unpaid or paid. Open to college freshmen, college sophomores, college juniors, college seniors, recent college graduates, graduate students, career changers, individuals reentering the workforce. ▶ *1 costume design intern.* Candidates should have ability to work independently, knowledge of field, personal interest in the field, research skills, self-motivation, strong interpersonal skills. Duration is open. Position available as unpaid or paid. Open to college freshmen, college sophomores, college juniors, college seniors, recent college graduates, graduate students, career changers, individuals reentering the workforce. ▶ *1 development intern:* responsibilities include identifying and drafting applications for grants, foundations, and awards. Candidates should have ability to work independently, computer skills, personal interest in the field, research skills, self-motivation, writing skills. Duration is open. Position available as unpaid or paid. Open to college freshmen, college sophomores, college juniors, college seniors, recent college graduates, graduate students, career changers, individuals reentering the workforce. ▶ *1 directing intern:* responsibilities include assisting the director and dramaturgical functions. Candidates should have oral communication skills, personal interest in the field, plan to pursue career in field, research skills, strong interpersonal skills, writing skills. Duration is open. Position available as unpaid or paid. Open to college freshmen, college sophomores, college juniors, college seniors, recent college graduates, graduate students. ▶ *1 general management intern:* responsibilities include general office management and management/coordination of company projects. Candidates should have ability to work independently, computer skills, office skills, organizational skills, self-motivation, written communication skills. Duration is open. Position available as unpaid or paid. Open to college freshmen, college sophomores, college juniors, college seniors, recent college graduates, graduate students, career changers, individuals reentering the workforce. ▶ *1 press/marketing intern:* responsibilities include primarily marketing productions to festivals and other venues, both in USA and globally; some press work also. Candidates should have computer skills, oral communication skills, personal interest in the field, self-motivation,

strong interpersonal skills, writing skills. Duration is open. Position available as unpaid or paid. Open to college freshmen, college sophomores, college juniors, college seniors, recent college graduates, graduate students, career changers, individuals reentering the workforce. ▶ *1 production intern:* responsibilities include all around production assistance. Candidates should have ability to work independently, organizational skills, strong interpersonal skills, versatility, a wide range of interests and abilities in the field. Duration is open. Position available as unpaid or paid. Open to college freshmen, college sophomores, college juniors, college seniors, recent college graduates, graduate students, career changers, individuals reentering the workforce. ▶ *1 set design intern.* Candidates should have ability to work independently, knowledge of field, personal interest in the field, research skills, self-motivation, strong interpersonal skills. Duration is open. Position available as unpaid or paid. Open to college freshmen, college sophomores, college juniors, college seniors, recent college graduates, graduate students, career changers, individuals reentering the workforce. ▶ *1 stage management intern.* Candidates should have ability to work independently, ability to work with others, knowledge of field, organizational skills, personal interest in the field, self-motivation. Duration is open. Position available as unpaid or paid. Open to college freshmen, college sophomores, college juniors, college seniors, recent college graduates, graduate students, career changers. International applications accepted.
Benefits Formal training, on-the-job training, opportunity to attend seminars/workshops, willing to complete paperwork for educational credit, willing to provide letters of recommendation, possibility of international travel, possible stipend.
Contact Write, call, fax, e-mail, or through World Wide Web site Joanna Sherman, Artistic Director. Phone: 212-254-4614. Fax: 212-254-4614. E-mail: info@bondst.org. In-person interview recommended (telephone interview accepted). Applicants must submit a letter of interest, resume, photo (recommended) for acting interns. Applications are accepted continuously. World Wide Web: http://www.bondst.org.

CENTER STAGE
700 North Calvert Street
Baltimore, Maryland 21202

General Information Professional regional theater whose artistic goal is to explore a wide range of dramatic literature and production approaches, from fresh visions of the classics to active support for contemporary writing. Established in 1963. Number of employees: 110. Number of internship applications received each year: 100.
Internships Available ▶ *1 company management intern:* responsibilities include assisting with all aspects of company and facilities management, including actor, director, and other theater consultants' contacts, travel arrangements, and accommodations; auditions; management of all theater-owned housing units; and attending to the needs and requirements of visiting artists. Candidates should have ability to work independently, ability to work with others, computer skills, oral communication skills, organizational skills, self-motivation. Duration is August/September to May/June. $85 per week. Open to recent college graduates, students willing to take a year off from school. ▶ *1 costumes/wardrobe intern:* responsibilities include assisting in costume shop with construction, shopping for shows, and maintenance of stock, as well as assisting with running crew and daily wardrobe maintenance as needed; opportunities to learn more about crafts or wig maintenance also available. Candidates should have ability to work with others, knowledge of field, oral communication skills, self-motivation, fast and accurate sewing skills. Duration is August/September to May/June. $85 per week. Open to recent college graduates, career changers, students willing to take a year off from school. ▶ *1 development/fund-raising intern:* responsibilities include active participation in all fund-raising activities, including the annual direct mail and telefunding campaigns, special events, funding research, special projects, and day-to-day booking and acknowledgement of gifts. Candidates should have computer skills, office skills, oral communication skills, organizational skills, self-motivation, strong interpersonal skills. Duration is August/September to May/June. $85 per week. Open to recent college graduates, career chang-

ers, students willing to take a year off from school. ▶ *1 education/ Theater for a New Generation intern:* responsibilities include assisting in scheduling workshops and other programs for middle and high schools, universities, and colleges; facilitating theater artists' school visits; developing educational and outreach activities and materials; and other special projects. Candidates should have college degree in related field, computer skills, oral communication skills, organizational skills, self-motivation, strong interpersonal skills. Duration is August/September to May/June. $85 per week. Open to recent college graduates, students willing to take a year off from school. ▶ *1 electrics intern:* responsibilities include assisting electricians with hanging and focusing, creation of special effects, maintenance of lighting equipment, and running of each show. Candidates should have ability to work with others, computer skills, knowledge of field, oral communication skills, self-motivation. Duration is August/September to May/June. $85 per week. Open to recent college graduates, career changers, students willing to take a year off from school. ▶ *1 marketing intern:* responsibilities include assisting with market research and ticket promotions, coordinating complimentary gift certificate program, distributing marketing materials, and working with the on-campus sales team. Candidates should have computer skills, knowledge of field, office skills, oral communication skills, self-motivation, strong interpersonal skills, written communication skills. Duration is August/September to May/June. $85 per week. Open to recent college graduates, students willing to take a year off from college. ▶ *1 properties intern:* responsibilities include assisting in all aspects of procuring and creating props for each production; this includes carpentry, sculpting, metalwork, sewing, upholstery, painting, drawing, and research. Candidates should have ability to work with others, experience in the field, oral communication skills, research skills, self-motivation. Duration is August/September to May/June. $85 per week. Open to recent college graduates, career changers, students willing to take a year off from school. ▶ *1 public relations intern:* responsibilities include managing the student critics program, generating publicity for the theater's educational programs, producing the in-house newsletter, and assisting with publications, press relations, advertising, and promotions. Candidates should have computer skills, knowledge of field, office skills, oral communication skills, self-motivation, strong interpersonal skills, writing skills. Duration is August/September to May/June. $85 per week. Open to recent college graduates, students willing to take a year off from college. ▶ *1 scenic art intern:* responsibilities include assisting the charge painter in the painting and occasional sculpting of all scenic elements. Candidates should have ability to work with others, experience in the field, oral communication skills, personal interest in the field, self-motivation, painting and drawing skills. Duration is August/September to May/June. $85 per week. Open to recent college graduates, career changers, students willing to take a year off from school. ▶ *1 scenic carpentry intern:* responsibilities include working in the scene shop on construction of scenery for six mainstage productions. Candidates should have ability to work independently, ability to work with others, oral communication skills, self-motivation, experience with wood construction and standard shop tools. Duration is August/September to May/June. $85 per week. Open to recent college graduates, students willing to take a year off from college. ▶ *1 sound intern:* responsibilities include assisting audio engineers in maintaining and installing equipment and with the running of each show. Candidates should have ability to work with others, computer skills, knowledge of field, oral communication skills, self-motivation. Duration is August/September to May/June. $85 per week. Open to recent college graduates, career changers, students willing to take a year off from school. ▶ *2 stage management interns:* responsibilities include working in all aspects of stage management, with primary duties in the rehearsal hall and as part of the running crew. Candidates should have computer skills, experience in the field, oral communication skills, organizational skills, self-motivation, strong interpersonal skills. Duration is August/September to May/June. $105 per week. Open to recent college graduates, career changers, students willing to take a year off from school. ▶ *1 volunteer services intern:* responsibilities include assisting the director of volunteer services in all aspects of the management of a volunteer corps of nearly 850 volunteers performing a variety of activities in support of production,

administrative and artistic departments. Duration is August/September to May/June. $85 per week. Open to recent college graduates, students willing to take a year off from college.
Benefits Free housing, job counseling, names of contacts, on-the-job training, opportunity to attend seminars/workshops, possible full-time employment, willing to act as a professional reference, willing to complete paperwork for educational credit, willing to provide letters of recommendation, assistance with resume and interview preparation, free e-mail, complimentary tickets, opportunities to supplement living allowance.
Contact Write, call, fax, or through World Wide Web site Katharyn Davies, Internship Coordinator. Phone: 410-685-3200 Ext. 330. Fax: 410-539-3912. Telephone interview required. Applicants must submit a formal organization application, letter of interest, resume, two letters of recommendation, portfolio or writing sample may be required. Application deadline: April 15 for upcoming season. World Wide Web: http://www.centerstage.org.

CENTRAL PARK SUMMERSTAGE
830 Fifth Avenue
New York, New York 10021

General Information New York's premier free performing arts festival that presents productions of superior artistic caliber. Established in 1983. Number of employees: 15. Subsidiary of City Parks Foundation, New York, New York. Number of internship applications received each year: 200.
Internships Available ▶ *1–3 Web interns:* responsibilities include Web site maintenance, acting as liaison to Web development firm, developing content for bi-weekly newsletter, handling e-mail requests. Candidates should have ability to work independently, ability to work with others, experience in the field, research skills, writing skills, basic knowledge (advanced preferred) of HTML, JAVAScript, computer specialists, Web environments. Duration is 1-2 semesters or 1 summer. Unpaid. Open to college freshmen, college sophomores, college juniors, college seniors, recent college graduates, career changers. ▶ *2–3 community outreach interns:* responsibilities include developing and executing grassroots marketing plans for various ethnic/socioeconomic communities in NYC. Candidates should have ability to work independently, oral communication skills, self-motivation, awareness of community issues; second language (preferred). Duration is spring or summer semester. Unpaid. Open to college freshmen, college sophomores, college juniors, college seniors, recent college graduates, career changers. ▶ *1–2 production interns:* responsibilities include assisting production manager with all duties including handling technical riders, liaisoning between production and office staff, working on-site during shows, and scheduling crew. Candidates should have experience in the field, office skills, oral communication skills, strong interpersonal skills, production knowledge, dedication. Duration is 2–3 months. $150–$200 per week. Open to college freshmen, college sophomores, college juniors, college seniors, recent college graduates, individuals reentering the workforce. ▶ *1–3 programming interns:* responsibilities include assisting in talent research, maintenance of artist files, developing agency contacts, preparing and maintaining press materials, and organizing video archive. Candidates should have office skills, oral communication skills, writing skills, strong knowledge of music industry recommended. Duration is 1-2 semesters or 1 summer. Unpaid. Open to college freshmen, college sophomores, college juniors, college seniors, recent college graduates, career changers. ▶ *1–2 sponsorship/development interns:* responsibilities include assisting sponsorship and development managers in researching foundations, corporations, and other funding sources; writing grant/sponsorship proposals; and maintaining member benefits. Candidates should have office skills, research skills, strong interpersonal skills, writing skills. Duration is 1-2 semesters or 1 summer. Unpaid. Open to college freshmen, college sophomores, college juniors, college seniors, recent college graduates, career changers. International applications accepted.
Benefits Names of contacts, possible full-time employment, travel reimbursement, willing to act as a professional reference, willing to complete paperwork for educational credit, willing to provide letters of recommendation.

Central Park SummerStage (continued)

Contact Write, fax, e-mail, or through World Wide Web site Internship Coordinator. Fax: 212-360-2754. E-mail: info@ summerstage.org. No phone calls. Telephone interview required. Applicants must submit a letter of interest, resume, two writing samples. Application deadline: February 25 for spring, April 25 for summer, September 20 for fall. World Wide Web: http://www. summerstage.org.

THE CHILDREN'S THEATRE COMPANY
2400 Third Avenue South
Minneapolis, Minnesota 55404

General Information North America's largest professional theater for young people and adults dedicated to producing excellence in theater for audiences in the Twin Cities and nationwide. Established in 1965. Number of employees: 270. Number of internship applications received each year: 100.

Internships Available ▶ *3–4 costume construction interns:* responsibilities include working as assistant draper, painter/dyer, milliner, design assistant, or general shop. Candidates should have ability to work independently, ability to work with others, declared college major in field, experience in the field, oral communication skills, organizational skills. Duration is 3 months minimum. Unpaid. Open to college juniors, college seniors, recent college graduates, graduate students. ▶ *1–2 development interns:* responsibilities include focusing on the process of networking, fund-raising, grant writing, building and maintaining databases, and research on funding sources. Candidates should have ability to work independently, computer skills, knowledge of field, organizational skills, research skills, writing skills. Duration is 3 months minimum (20 hours per week minimum). Unpaid. Open to college juniors, college seniors, recent college graduates, graduate students. ▶ *1–2 directing interns:* responsibilities include assisting during the rehearsal process as an in-house critic and dramaturg as well as being an active participant in the development and direction of the plays. Candidates should have ability to work with others, analytical skills, experience in the field, office skills, organizational skills, research skills. Duration is 3 months. Unpaid. Open to college seniors, recent college graduates, graduate students. ▶ *1–2 education outreach interns:* responsibilities include working directly with students and teachers to coordinate and schedule summer programs; school partnership programs; teacher training workshops; assisting staff in creating curriculum. Candidates should have ability to work independently, ability to work with others, computer skills, declared college major in field, experience in the field, office skills, organizational skills, plan to pursue career in field, research skills, strong leadership ability. Duration is 3 months. Position available as unpaid or paid. Open to college seniors, recent college graduates, graduate students. ▶ *2–3 lighting and sound interns:* responsibilities include duties based on intern's abilities and department needs. Candidates should have ability to work independently, ability to work with others, experience in the field, oral communication skills, organizational skills, plan to pursue career in field. Duration is 3 months minimum. Unpaid. Open to college juniors, college seniors, recent college graduates, graduate students. ▶ *1–2 marketing interns:* responsibilities include helping create the institution's public persona; areas of focus include media relations, database maintenance, and departmental organization. Candidates should have computer skills, editing skills, knowledge of field, office skills, organizational skills. Duration is 3 months minimum. Unpaid. Open to college juniors, college seniors, recent college graduates, graduate students. ▶ *6–8 performing apprentices:* responsibilities include acting in productions, classes, and studio theater production. Candidates should have college courses in field, oral communication skills, plan to pursue career in field, self-motivation, strong interpersonal skills. Duration is 11 months. Stipend. Open to college juniors, college seniors, recent college graduates, graduate students. ▶ *1 properties apprentice.* Candidates should have ability to work independently, declared college major in field, experience in the field, oral communication skills, plan to pursue career in field. Duration is 3 months minimum. Stipend. Open to college seniors, recent college graduates, graduate students. ▶ *2–3 properties construction interns:* responsibilities include learning basic techniques for building both hard and soft props;

hand and large props construction, furniture building, and welding techniques. Candidates should have ability to work independently, declared college major in field, experience in the field, oral communication skills, plan to pursue career in field, self-motivation. Duration is 3 months minimum. Unpaid. Open to college juniors, college seniors, recent college graduates, graduate students. ▶ *1 stage management apprentice:* responsibilities include assisting with preproduction and rehearsals, run of 3–4 mainstage and/or tour productions, and stage managing 1–3 studio theater projects. Candidates should have computer skills, declared college major in field, experience in the field, organizational skills, plan to pursue career in field, strong leadership ability. Duration is 8–10 weeks. Stipend. Open to college juniors, college seniors, recent college graduates, graduate students. ▶ *4–5 stage management interns:* responsibilities include learning Actor's Equity Association rules and regulations and becoming an integral part of the rehearsal and performance process. Candidates should have ability to work with others, experience in the field, office skills, organizational skills, plan to pursue career in field, strong leadership ability. Duration is 3 months minimum. Unpaid. Open to college juniors, college seniors, recent college graduates, graduate students. International applications accepted.

Benefits Formal training, names of contacts, possible full-time employment, willing to complete paperwork for educational credit, willing to provide letters of recommendation.

Contact Write, fax, or e-mail Lisa Kneller, Education Department Manager. Fax: 612-874-8119. E-mail: education@ childrenstheatre.org. No phone calls. In-person interview recommended (telephone interview accepted). Applicants must submit a letter of interest, resume, portfolio, two letters of recommendation. Applications are accepted continuously. World Wide Web: http:// www.childrenstheatre.org.

CHILD'S PLAY TOURING THEATRE
2518 West Armitage Avenue
Chicago, Illinois 60647

General Information Professional touring children's theater that performs stories and poems written by children and adapted by professional actors and musicians. Established in 1978. Number of employees: 16. Number of internship applications received each year: 50.

Internships Available ▶ *1–3 administrative/public relations interns:* responsibilities include producing newsletter and assisting general manager and office manager. Candidates should have ability to work with others, computer skills, office skills, oral communication skills, research skills, written communication skills. Duration is flexible. Position available as unpaid or paid. ▶ *1–3 assistants to executive director/producer:* responsibilities include all aspects of running a theater, including board development, fund-raising, and marketing. Candidates should have computer skills, oral communication skills, organizational skills. Duration is flexible. Position available as unpaid or paid. ▶ *1–3 development interns:* responsibilities include researching funding sources and assisting with proposal preparation. Candidates should have computer skills, oral communication skills, research skills, self-motivation, strong interpersonal skills, writing skills. Duration is flexible. Position available as unpaid or paid. ▶ *1–3 special project interns:* responsibilities include overseeing various aspects of Writing Our World (WOW) project. Candidates should have computer skills (Internet and Web site updates). Duration is flexible. Position available as unpaid or paid. ▶ *3 story readers/coordinators:* responsibilities include reading, categorizing, culling, filing young authors' works, contacting young authors, and helping to script stories. Candidates should have computer skills, office skills, oral communication skills, organizational skills, personal interest in the field, written communication skills. Duration is flexible. Position available as unpaid or paid. ▶ *2–6 technical interns:* responsibilities include assisting production manager with sets, props, and costumes. Candidates should have ability to work with others, knowledge of field, personal interest in the field, self-motivation. Duration is flexible. Position available as unpaid or paid. International applications accepted.

Benefits Names of contacts, on-the-job training, opportunity to attend seminars/workshops, possible full-time employment, will-

ing to act as a professional reference, willing to complete paperwork for educational credit, willing to provide letters of recommendation, reimbursement of work-related travel expenses, lunch allowance (for those who work 20 hours or more per week); occasional stipends.

Contact Write, call, fax, or e-mail Ms. June Podagrosi, Executive Director and Producer. Phone: 773-235-8911. Fax: 773-235-5478. E-mail: interns@cptt.org. In-person interview recommended (telephone interview accepted). Applicants must submit a formal organization application, letter of interest, resume, portfolio, personal reference, letter of recommendation, 1 or 2 writing samples. Applications are accepted continuously. World Wide Web: http://www.cptt.org.

THE CHORAL ARTS SOCIETY OF WASHINGTON
5225 Wisconsin Avenue, NW, Suite 603
Washington, District of Columbia 20015-2016

General Information 200-member symphonic chorus that performs a season subscription series at the Kennedy Center in addition to concerts with the National Symphony Orchestra, international tours, and recordings. Established in 1965. Number of employees: 12. Number of internship applications received each year: 50.

Internships Available ▶ *1 development intern:* responsibilities include assisting with fund-raising activities including donor tracking and recognition, silent auction tracking, funder research, proposal coordination, and other duties as assigned. Candidates should have computer skills, editing skills, office skills, oral communication skills, organizational skills, research skills, self-motivation, strong interpersonal skills, written communication skills. Duration is flexible. Unpaid. Open to college sophomores, college juniors, college seniors, recent college graduates, graduate students. ▶ *1 education/outreach coordinator:* responsibilities include assisting Director of Education in coordinating a choral tribute to Dr. Martin Luther King, Jr.; arranging preconcert lectures for students; and providing area students with complimentary tickets for concerts. Candidates should have ability to work independently, office skills, oral communication skills, organizational skills, self-motivation, strong interpersonal skills, written communication skills. Duration is flexible. Unpaid. Open to college sophomores, college juniors, college seniors, recent college graduates, graduate students. ▶ *1 production intern:* responsibilities include assisting production department in administrative tasks including arranging concert season, chorus management, cataloging scores and music library, and other tasks as assigned. Candidates should have ability to work independently, ability to work with others, computer skills, editing skills, office skills, oral communication skills, organizational skills, research skills, self-motivation, written communication skills. Duration is flexible. Unpaid. Open to college sophomores, college juniors, college seniors, recent college graduates. ▶ *1 public relations/marketing intern:* responsibilities include writing press releases, designing brochures, assisting with marketing research and group sales, designing and editing the quarterly newsletter, updating press lists, and photographing and assisting with special events. Candidates should have computer skills, oral communication skills, organizational skills, self-motivation, strong interpersonal skills, written communication skills. Duration is flexible. Unpaid. Open to college sophomores, college juniors, college seniors, recent college graduates, graduate students. International applications accepted.

Benefits Formal training, job counseling, names of contacts, on-the-job training, opportunity to attend seminars/workshops, possible full-time employment, willing to act as a professional reference, willing to complete paperwork for educational credit, willing to provide letters of recommendation.

Contact Write, call, fax, e-mail, or through World Wide Web site Kevin Zarcone, Director of Audience Services. Phone: 202-244-3669. Fax: 202-244-4244. E-mail: kevinzarcone@choralarts.org. In-person interview required. Applicants must submit a letter of interest, resume, three personal references, writing sample upon request for certain positions. Applications are accepted continuously. World Wide Web: http://www.choralarts.org.

CINCINNATI PLAYHOUSE IN THE PARK
Box 6537
Cincinnati, Ohio 45206

General Information Live theater company that presents professional theater productions to the Cincinnati region; member of the League of Regional Theaters. Established in 1960. Number of employees: 60. Number of internship applications received each year: 150.

Internships Available ▶ *Production interns.* Candidates should have ability to work with others, computer skills, organizational skills, personal interest in the field. Duration is flexible. Unpaid. ▶ *3–5 stage management interns:* responsibilities include helping union stage management staff run rehearsals and performances, possible opportunity to stage manage outreach touring show. Candidates should have ability to work with others, analytical skills, organizational skills, knowledge of stage management techniques. Duration is part of or all 2002–2003 season. $185 per week. Open to college freshmen, college sophomores, college juniors, college seniors, recent college graduates, graduate students. International applications accepted.

Benefits Possible full-time employment, willing to complete paperwork for educational credit, willing to provide letters of recommendation.

Contact Write, call, fax, e-mail, or through World Wide Web site Bruce Coyle, Production Stage Manager. Phone: 513-345-2242. Fax: 513-345-2254. E-mail: bruce.coyle@cincyplay.com. In-person interview required. Applicants must submit a letter of interest, resume. Applications are accepted continuously. World Wide Web: http://www.cincyplay.com.

CIRCA '21 DINNER PLAYHOUSE
1828 Third Avenue
Rock Island, Illinois 61201

General Information Theater that produces a year-round season of musicals, modern comedies, a series of children's plays, and special guest artist concerts as well as national tours. Established in 1977. Number of employees: 65. Number of internship applications received each year: 15.

Internships Available ▶ *Marketing/sales interns:* responsibilities include participating in marketing campaigns and sales program. Candidates should have ability to work independently, ability to work with others, computer skills, oral communication skills, written communication skills. Duration is minimum of 6 weeks. Unpaid. Open to recent high school graduates, college juniors, college seniors, graduate students. ▶ *1–2 public relations interns:* responsibilities include writing copy for ads and press releases; creating flyers, promotional materials, and mailing lists; assisting with group sales. Candidates should have college courses in field, computer skills, personal interest in the field, self-motivation, strong interpersonal skills, written communication skills, artistic skills helpful. Duration is flexible. Unpaid. Open to college juniors, college seniors, recent college graduates. ▶ *1 stage management intern:* responsibilities include assisting resident stage manager with rehearsal duties and functioning as a running crew member. Candidates should have declared college major in field, experience in the field, organizational skills, personal interest in the field, strong interpersonal skills, strong leadership ability. Duration is linked to the production schedule. Unpaid. Open to college juniors, college seniors, recent college graduates, graduate students. ▶ *1–2 technical interns:* responsibilities include assisting in building of scenery and/or painting, maintaining the show, and functioning as a running crew member. Candidates should have ability to work independently, ability to work with others, college courses in field, experience in the field, organizational skills, technical skills. Duration is linked to the production schedule. Unpaid. Open to college sophomores, college juniors, college seniors, recent college graduates. International applications accepted.

Benefits Job counseling, names of contacts, on-the-job training, possible full-time employment, tuition assistance, willing to act as a professional reference, willing to complete paperwork for educational credit, willing to provide letters of recommendation, possible reimbursement for academic credit.

Circa '21 Dinner Playhouse (continued)

Contact Write or e-mail Mr. Dennis Hitchcock, Producer. Fax: 309-786-4119. E-mail: dpjh@circa21.com. No phone calls. In-person interview recommended (telephone interview accepted). Applicants must submit a letter of interest, resume, two letters of recommendation. Applications are accepted continuously. World Wide Web: http://www.circa21.com.

CLASSIC STAGE COMPANY
136 East 13th Street
New York, New York 10003

General Information Nonprofit 178-seat theater dedicated to the reimagination of classics for an American audience; produces a season of 4 plays committed to new directorial or authorial perspectives on the classics. Established in 1967. Number of employees: 54. Number of internship applications received each year: 25.

Internships Available ▶ *2 audience services interns:* responsibilities include assisting in member solicitation, tracking, and related clerical work. Candidates should have ability to work with others, office skills, oral communication skills, customer service experience preferred. Duration is 2–3 months. Position available as unpaid or paid. Open to college freshmen, college sophomores, college juniors, college seniors, recent college graduates, graduate students. ▶ *3 marketing/development interns:* responsibilities include assisting in research, grant compilation, and related clerical work. Candidates should have ability to work independently, analytical skills, knowledge of field, research skills, writing skills. Duration is 1 semester. Unpaid. Open to college seniors, recent college graduates, graduate students. ▶ *4 production/management interns:* responsibilities include assisting with budget research, acquisition of production needs, actual production work, company and facilities management. Candidates should have ability to work with others, experience in the field, office skills, oral communication skills, organizational skills, self-motivation. Duration is 1 semester. Unpaid. Open to college freshmen, college sophomores, college juniors, college seniors, recent college graduates, graduate students.

Benefits Formal training, job counseling, names of contacts, opportunity to attend seminars/workshops, possible full-time employment, willing to act as a professional reference, willing to complete paperwork for educational credit, willing to provide letters of recommendation, complimentary tickets to off-Broadway productions.

Contact Write, fax, e-mail, or through World Wide Web site Ms. Rachel M. Tischler, General Manager. Fax: 212-477-7504. E-mail: rachel.tischler@classicstage.org. No phone calls. In-person interview recommended (telephone interview accepted). Applicants must submit a letter of interest, resume, two personal references. Application deadline: May 1 for summer, August 1 for fall, November 20 for spring. World Wide Web: http://www.classicstage.org.

THE CLEVELAND PLAY HOUSE
8500 Euclid Avenue
Cleveland, Ohio 44106

General Information Theater dedicated to the presentation of new and classical plays. Established in 1915. Number of employees: 60. Number of internship applications received each year: 200.

Internships Available ▶ *1–8 assistant directors:* responsibilities include assisting directors during rehearsals. Duration is 6–8 weeks. Unpaid. ▶ *1 business intern:* responsibilities include helping in all areas of business office. Duration is 8–10 weeks. Unpaid. ▶ *2 development interns:* responsibilities include grant writing, telemarketing, and fund-raising. Duration is 2–12 months. Unpaid. ▶ *2 literary interns:* responsibilities include reading and evaluating scripts and assisting dramaturg. Duration is 6 weeks to 9 months. Unpaid. ▶ *4 marketing interns:* responsibilities include assisting in all aspects of marketing. Duration is 2–12 months. Unpaid. ▶ *1 playwriting intern:* responsibilities include assisting literary manager. Duration is 6 weeks to 9 months. Unpaid. ▶ *2 production assistants:* responsibilities include assisting stage managers in rehearsal and performance. Duration is 6 weeks to 9 months.

Unpaid. ▶ *6 shop interns:* responsibilities include working with costumes, lights, sound, and props. Duration is 2–9 months. Unpaid. Open to recent college graduates, graduate students.

Benefits Job counseling, possible full-time employment, willing to act as a professional reference, willing to complete paperwork for educational credit, willing to provide letters of recommendation.

Contact Write, call, fax, or e-mail Mr. David Colacci, Director of Apprentice Program. Phone: 216-795-7000 Ext. 205. Fax: 216-795-7005. E-mail: dcolacci@clevelandplayhouse.com. Applicants must submit a letter of interest, resume, photo. Applications are accepted continuously. World Wide Web: http://www.clevelandplayhouse.com.

COLLEGE LIGHT OPERA COMPANY
Highfield Theatre, PO Drawer 906
Falmouth, Massachusetts 02541

General Information Summer stock music theater serving as training ground for all aspects of theater performance, production, and management. Established in 1969. Number of employees: 80. Number of internship applications received each year: 400.

Internships Available ▶ *1 assistant business manager:* responsibilities include assisting business manager in various tasks, maintaining mailing lists, and supervising snack bar operation. Candidates should have ability to work independently, computer skills, experience in the field, office skills, oral communication skills, writing skills. Duration is June to August. $1600 per duration of internship. Open to college freshmen, college sophomores, college juniors, college seniors, recent college graduates. ▶ *2 box office treasurers:* responsibilities include managing box office. Candidates should have ability to work independently, ability to work with others, experience in the field, office skills, oral communication skills, organizational skills, written communication skills. Duration is June to August. $1600 per duration of internship. Open to high school seniors, recent high school graduates, college freshmen, college sophomores, college juniors, college seniors, graduate students. ▶ *1 cook:* responsibilities include menu planning, food buying and cooking for 80 people in co-op setting. Candidates should have ability to work independently, ability to work with others, knowledge of field, organizational skills, personal interest in the field, self-motivation, strong leadership ability. Duration is June to August. $5000 per duration of internship. Open to college freshmen, college sophomores, college juniors, college seniors, recent college graduates, career changers, individuals reentering the workforce. ▶ *6 costume crew interns:* responsibilities include assisting with making costumes. Candidates should have ability to work independently, ability to work with others, sewing skills. Duration is June to August. $2000 per duration of internship. Open to high school seniors, recent high school graduates, college freshmen, college sophomores, college juniors, college seniors, recent college graduates, graduate students. ▶ *1 costume designer:* responsibilities include designing or pulling from stock costumes for 9 musicals. Candidates should have ability to work with others, college courses in field, experience in the field, organizational skills, strong leadership ability, costume design and building skills. Duration is June to August. $4000 per duration of internship. Open to college sophomores, college juniors, college seniors, recent college graduates, graduate students. ▶ *18 orchestra musicians:* responsibilities include performing in 9 musicals. Candidates should have ability to work with others, experience in orchestra work. Duration is June to August. $1000 per duration of internship. Open to high school seniors, recent high school graduates, college freshmen, college sophomores, college juniors, college seniors, recent college graduates, graduate students. ▶ *1 publicity director:* responsibilities include writing press releases, distributing literature and posters, preparing weekly programs, maintaining theater bulletin boards, house managing, and supervising ushers. Candidates should have ability to work independently, ability to work with others, computer skills, editing skills, experience in the field, oral communication skills, organizational skills, self-motivation, writing skills. Duration is June to August. $1600 per duration of internship. Open to college freshmen, college sophomores, college juniors, college seniors, recent college graduates. ▶ *32 singers/actors:* responsibilities include performing in 9 musicals. Candidates should have ability to work with others, personal interest in the

field, self-motivation, strong singing/acting skills. Duration is June to August. Unpaid. Open to college freshmen, college sophomores, college juniors, college seniors, recent college graduates, graduate students. ▶ *6 stage crew interns:* responsibilities include assisting with building scenery. Candidates should have ability to work independently, ability to work with others, knowledge of field, experience in set construction, set painting, and lighting. Duration is June to August. $2000 per duration of internship. Open to high school seniors, recent high school graduates, college freshmen, college sophomores, college juniors, college seniors, recent college graduates. ▶ *1 stage set designer:* responsibilities include designing and building stage sets and lights for 9 musicals using a crew of 6 stage hands. Candidates should have ability to work independently, ability to work with others, college courses in field, experience in the field, organizational skills, strong leadership ability, skills in designing and building stage scenery. Duration is June to August. $4000 per duration of internship. Open to college juniors, college seniors, recent college graduates, graduate students. International applications accepted.
Benefits Formal training, free housing, free meals, job counseling, names of contacts, on-the-job training, willing to act as a professional reference, willing to complete paperwork for educational credit, willing to provide letters of recommendation.
Contact Write, call, fax, e-mail, or through World Wide Web site Mr. Robert A. Haslun, Producer, 162 South Cedar Street, Oberlin, Ohio 44074. Phone: 440-774-8485. Fax: 440-775-8642. E-mail: bob.haslun@oberlin.edu. Applicants must submit a formal organization application, resume, two letters of recommendation, audition tape for orchestra and vocal company. Application deadline: March 15 for summer; continuous after March 15 if openings remain. World Wide Web: http://www.collegelightopera.com.

CORTLAND REPERTORY THEATRE, INC.
37 Franklin Street
Cortland, New York 13045

General Information Professional summer stock theater whose mission is to bring affordable cultural opportunities to a primarily rural area. Established in 1972. Number of employees: 2. Number of internship applications received each year: 250.
Internships Available ▶ *6 performing interns:* responsibilities include acting in productions and doing shop duties. Candidates should have ability to work with others, college courses in field, knowledge of field, personal interest in the field, self-motivation. Duration is up to 14 weeks in summer. $90 per week. Open to college freshmen, college sophomores, college juniors, college seniors, graduate students. ▶ *4 production interns:* responsibilities include performing, props, scenery, costume, light, sound duties, and running crews. Candidates should have ability to work with others, college courses in field, knowledge of field, oral communication skills, self-motivation. Duration is up to 14 weeks in summer. $90 per week. Open to college freshmen, college sophomores, college juniors, college seniors, recent college graduates, graduate students. International applications accepted.
Benefits Formal training, free housing, on-the-job training, opportunity to attend seminars/workshops, willing to provide letters of recommendation.
Contact Write, fax, or e-mail Kerby Thompson, Producing Director. Fax: 607-753-0047. E-mail: cortlandrep@hotmail.com. No phone calls. In-person interview required. Applicants must submit a letter of interest, resume, three personal references, 3 professional references, audition for performing internships. Application deadline: April 1 for summer. World Wide Web: http://www.cortlandrep.org.

COURT THEATRE (THE PROFESSIONAL THEATRE AT THE UNIVERSITY OF CHICAGO)
5535 South Ellis Avenue
Chicago, Illinois 60637

General Information Professional residence Equity theater company located on the University of Chicago campus. Established in 1954. Number of employees: 25. Unit of University of Chicago, Chicago, Illinois. Number of internship applications received each year: 50.

Internships Available ▶ *1 casting intern:* responsibilities include developing schedules, assisting with organizational research, setting up auditions, and processing new actor pictures and resumes. Candidates should have knowledge of field, oral communication skills, organizational skills, personal interest in the field, plan to pursue career in field, self-motivation, written communication skills. Duration is flexible. Unpaid. Open to college juniors, college seniors, recent college graduates. ▶ *1 costume shop intern:* responsibilities include researching, shopping for, and coordinating costume and prop elements. Candidates should have experience in the field, knowledge of field. Duration is 4 months. Unpaid. Open to college juniors, college seniors, graduate students. ▶ *1–3 dramaturgy interns:* responsibilities include researching and writing playnotes. Candidates should have computer skills, editing skills, research skills, writing skills. Duration is 6–14 weeks. Unpaid. Open to college juniors, college seniors, graduate students. ▶ *1–3 production assistants:* responsibilities include developing projects with various staff members. Candidates should have knowledge of field, personal interest in the field, plan to pursue career in field. Duration is flexible. Unpaid. Open to college juniors, college seniors, graduate students. ▶ *2 stage management interns:* responsibilities include working directly with stage manager and assistant stage manager in all areas of preparation and the rehearsal process, including the technical rehearsal; may lead to a paid position. Candidates should have computer skills, knowledge of field, office skills, organizational skills, personal interest in the field, self-motivation. Duration is 6–14 weeks. Unpaid. Open to college seniors, recent college graduates, graduate students.
Benefits On-the-job training, opportunity to attend seminars/workshops, possible full-time employment, willing to act as a professional reference, willing to complete paperwork for educational credit, willing to provide letters of recommendation.
Contact Write Executive Assistant to Managing Director. Fax: 773-834-1897. E-mail: directors@courttheatre.org. No phone calls. In-person interview recommended (telephone interview accepted). Applicants must submit a letter of interest, resume, two personal references, two letters of recommendation. Applications are accepted continuously. World Wide Web: http://www.courttheatre.org.

CREEDE REPERTORY THEATRE
124 North Main Street
Creede, Colorado 81130

General Information Nonprofit theater striving to raise standards of practice, to make the performing arts more accessible to the public, and to promote greater understanding of the performing arts. Established in 1966. Number of employees: 60. Number of internship applications received each year: 500.
Internships Available ▶ *1 business intern:* responsibilities include working with bookkeeping and in advertising, payroll, fund-raising, box office, and front-of-house duties. Candidates should have computer skills, office skills, oral communication skills, organizational skills, personal interest in the field, self-motivation, strong interpersonal skills, strong leadership ability, written communication skills. Duration is 4 months. $175 per week. ▶ *3 costume interns:* responsibilities include sewing and maintaining costumes and dressing actors. Candidates should have ability to work independently, personal interest in the field, self-motivation, strong interpersonal skills. Duration is late May to late August. $175 per week. Open to recent high school graduates, college freshmen, college sophomores, college juniors, college seniors, recent college graduates, graduate students, law students, career changers, individuals reentering the workforce. ▶ *1 light/sound intern:* responsibilities include assisting technical director in hanging and changing light plans and designing and assisting lighting designer during shows and set changeovers. Candidates should have ability to work independently, ability to work with others, analytical skills, knowledge of field, organizational skills, personal interest in the field, self-motivation. Duration is late May to late August. $175 per week. Open to recent high school graduates, college freshmen, college sophomores, college juniors, college seniors, recent college graduates, graduate students, law students, career changers, individuals reentering the workforce. ▶ *2–3 shop/set interns:* responsibilities include building, painting, and assembling

Creede Repertory Theatre (continued)

sets; conducting set changeovers and backstage scene changes; and running shows by performing crew work. Candidates should have ability to work independently, analytical skills, personal interest in the field, plan to pursue career in field, self-motivation, strong interpersonal skills, strong leadership ability. Duration is mid-May to late August. $175 per week. Open to recent high school graduates, college freshmen, college sophomores, college juniors, college seniors, recent college graduates, graduate students, law students, career changers, individuals reentering the workforce. ▶ *1 stage management intern:* responsibilities include assisting stage manager, functioning as stage manager for 1 show, scheduling, typing, and working backstage. Candidates should have ability to work independently, experience in the field, oral communication skills, organizational skills, self-motivation, strong interpersonal skills, strong leadership ability, written communication skills. Duration is mid-May to late August. $175 per week. Open to recent high school graduates, college freshmen, college sophomores, college juniors, college seniors, recent college graduates, graduate students, law students, career changers, individuals reentering the workforce. International applications accepted.

Benefits Free housing, names of contacts, on-the-job training, possible full-time employment, willing to act as a professional reference, willing to complete paperwork for educational credit, willing to provide letters of recommendation.

Contact Write, call, fax, e-mail, or through World Wide Web site Mr. Maurice LaMée, Executive Director, 124 North Main Street, PO Box 269, Creede, Colorado 81130. Phone: 719-658-2540. Fax: 719-658-2343. E-mail: crt@creederep.com. In-person interview recommended (telephone interview accepted). Applicants must submit a formal organization application, letter of interest, resume, three personal references. Application deadline: March 1. World Wide Web: http://www.creederep.com.

DALLAS THEATER CENTER
3636 Turtle Creek Boulevard
Dallas, Texas 75219

General Information Theater committed to supporting the work of the most exciting, daring, and uncompromising artists as well as serving the community through the plays presented and special programs offered. Established in 1959. Number of employees: 75. Number of internship applications received each year: 100.

Internships Available ▶ *1–3 arts administrators:* responsibilities include working in the areas of fund-raising, marketing, development, and general management; assisting department heads in daily operations, special events, and planning. Candidates should have ability to work independently, analytical skills, computer skills, editing skills, office skills, oral communication skills, organizational skills, personal interest in the field, self-motivation, strong interpersonal skills, writing skills. Duration is August to May. Minimum wage. Open to college freshmen, college sophomores, college juniors, college seniors, recent college graduates, graduate students. ▶ *1 company manager:* responsibilities include assisting in all areas required to maintain efficient company operations, including booking travel, housing, and hospitality arrangements for visiting artists. Candidates should have ability to work independently, computer skills, office skills, oral communication skills, organizational skills, personal interest in the field, self-motivation, strong interpersonal skills, strong leadership ability, written communication skills. Duration is August to May. Minimum wage. Open to college freshmen, college sophomores, college juniors, college seniors, recent college graduates, graduate students. ▶ *2 director/literary managers:* responsibilities include assisting mainstage productions, directing workshop production, reading new scripts, gathering and organizing research for mainstage productions, attending local productions, maintaining correspondence with playwrights, and providing administrative assistance. Candidates should have ability to work independently, computer skills, knowledge of field, office skills, oral communication skills, organizational skills, plan to pursue career in field, research skills, self-motivation, strong interpersonal skills, strong leadership ability, written communication skills. Duration is August to May. Minimum wage. Open to college juniors, college seniors,

recent college graduates, graduate students. ▶ *1 education and community programs intern:* responsibilities include assisting the director of education in overseeing all education and community programs; serving as teaching assistants for school outreach programs; communicating with other departments including artistic, production and marketing, and DISD schools to gather information and facilitate scheduling. Candidates should have computer skills, office skills, oral communication skills, self-motivation, strong interpersonal skills, written communication skills. Duration is August to May. Minimum wage. Open to college juniors, college seniors, recent college graduates, graduate students. ▶ *6–8 production interns:* responsibilities include assisting with props, costumes, electrics, sound, carpentry, scenic art, wardrobe, and stage operations. Candidates should have ability to work independently, ability to work with others, college courses in field, experience in the field, plan to pursue career in field, self-motivation. Duration is August to May. Minimum wage. Open to college freshmen, college sophomores, college juniors, college seniors, recent college graduates, graduate students, career changers. ▶ *1 production management intern:* responsibilities include assisting producing manager in overseeing all production-related concerns, including scheduling and the facilitation of communication between production departments and visiting artists. Candidates should have ability to work independently, ability to work with others, computer skills, office skills, oral communication skills, organizational skills, personal interest in the field, self-motivation. Duration is August to May. Minimum wage. Open to college juniors, college seniors, recent college graduates, graduate students. ▶ *2 stage managers:* responsibilities include working with Equity stage managers in all aspects of their work and being involved in production from the beginning of the rehearsal process through the run of mainstage productions. Candidates should have ability to work independently, computer skills, editing skills, experience in the field, oral communication skills, organizational skills, self-motivation, strong interpersonal skills, strong leadership ability. Duration is August to May. Minimum wage. Open to college freshmen, college sophomores, college juniors, college seniors, recent college graduates, graduate students, career changers. International applications accepted.

Benefits On-the-job training, opportunity to attend seminars/workshops, possible full-time employment, willing to act as a professional reference, willing to complete paperwork for educational credit, willing to provide letters of recommendation.

Contact Write, call, fax, or through World Wide Web site Lisa Lawrence Holland, Director of Education and Community Programs. Phone: 214-252-3916. Fax: 214-521-7666. E-mail: lisa. holland@dallastheatercenter.org. Applicants must submit a formal organization application, letter of interest, resume, three letters of recommendation. Application deadline: June 1. World Wide Web: http://www.dallastheatercenter.org.

DENVER CENTER THEATRE COMPANY
1050 13th Street
Denver, Colorado 80204

General Information Nonprofit regional theater producing 12 productions in four theaters and tour productions locally, nationally, and internationally. Established in 1978. Number of employees: 400. Division of Denver Center for the Performing Arts, Denver, Colorado. Number of internship applications received each year: 100.

Internships Available ▶ *1–2 administration interns:* responsibilities include assisting in various aspects of administration for nonprofit regional theater. Candidates should have ability to work independently, computer skills, office skills, oral communication skills, organizational skills, personal interest in the field, self-motivation, strong interpersonal skills, written communication skills. Position available as unpaid or paid. Open to recent college graduates, graduate students, law students. ▶ *1–2 costume/wigs/wardrobe interns:* responsibilities include running crew assignment involving costume and accessories maintenance and quick change techniques. Candidates should have ability to work independently, oral communication skills, personal interest in the field, self-motivation, strong interpersonal skills, flexibility for long working hours. Duration is 6–8 weeks. Position available as unpaid or at $8–$10 per hour. Open to high school seniors, recent high school graduates, college freshmen, college sophomores, college juniors, college seniors, recent college graduates, graduate students, law students, career changers, individuals reentering the workforce. ▶ *1 lighting design intern:* responsibilities include working with resident and guest professional staff members during the season with a focus on drafting, equipment maintenance, electrics, special effects, and special projects. Candidates should have ability to work independently, ability to work with others, knowledge of field, personal interest in the field, plan to pursue career in field, self-motivation. Duration is September to May. Position available as unpaid or paid. Open to high school students, college sophomores, college juniors, college seniors, recent college graduates. ▶ *Marketing interns:* responsibilities include assisting in various aspects of marketing and communication for nonprofit regional theater. Candidates should have ability to work independently, computer skills, office skills, personal interest in the field, self-motivation, written communication skills. Duration is 1–2 semesters. Position available as unpaid or paid. Open to college seniors, recent college graduates, graduate students. ▶ *1 properties intern:* responsibilities include using techniques in welding, vacuforming plastics, painting, carving, furniture construction and upholstery, and other crafts. Candidates should have ability to work with others, knowledge of field, personal interest in the field. Position available as unpaid or paid. Open to college juniors, college seniors, recent college graduates, graduate students. ▶ *1 scene design intern:* responsibilities include drafting, model building, design and technical research in scenic and prop areas, and scene painting. Candidates should have ability to work independently, computer skills, knowledge of field, oral communication skills, plan to pursue career in field, self-motivation, strong interpersonal skills. Duration is 8–40 weeks. Position available as unpaid or paid. Open to college juniors, college seniors, recent college graduates, graduate students. ▶ *1 scene painting intern:* responsibilities include using traditional methods and innovative techniques, assisting the DCTC scenic artists in painting and finishing scenery and technical effects for productions. Candidates should have ability to work with others, knowledge of field, personal interest in the field. Position available as unpaid or paid. Open to high school seniors, recent high school graduates, college juniors, college seniors, recent college graduates, graduate students, career changers, individuals reentering the workforce. ▶ *1 sound intern:* responsibilities include assisting sound designers in fabrication of show recordings, including recording and editing of music and sound effects; setting up sound recording, reproducing, amplification, and communication equipment for rehearsals and performances; maintaining sound department equipment, libraries, and facilities; and other related activities as may be required for the actualization of theater sound. Candidates should have ability to work independently, ability to work with others, computer skills, knowledge of field, oral communication skills, personal interest in the field, written communication skills. Position available as unpaid or paid. Open to high school seniors, recent high school graduates, college freshmen, college sophomores, college juniors, college seniors, recent college graduates, graduate students. ▶ *1–3 stage management/production interns:* responsibilities include organizing daily schedules, conducting rehearsals, attending design and production meetings, and focusing on the detail work surrounding productions. Candidates should have ability to work independently, knowledge of field, oral communication skills, plan to pursue career in field, self-motivation, strong interpersonal skills. Duration is 10–38 weeks. Unpaid. Open to college freshmen, college sophomores, college juniors, college seniors, recent college graduates, graduate students, law students, career changers. ▶ *1 technical production intern:* responsibilities include working in a master/apprentice relationship with the technical director, learning a variety of disciplines, ranging from fiscal management to high tech invention of scenic solutions. Candidates should have ability to work independently, ability to work with others, college courses in field, knowledge of field, organizational skills, personal interest in the field, plan to pursue career in field. Position available as unpaid or paid. Open to college seniors, recent college graduates, graduate students. International applications accepted.

Benefits Formal training, names of contacts, on-the-job training, possible full-time employment, willing to act as a professional reference, willing to complete paperwork for educational credit, willing to provide letters of recommendation, limited stipends and free housing may be available in some departments.
Contact Write, call, fax, or e-mail Rick Barbour, Production Manager, 1101 13th Street, Denver, Colorado 80204. Phone: 303-572-4445. Fax: 303-825-2117. E-mail: barbour@dcpa.org. In-person interview recommended (telephone interview accepted). Applicants must submit a letter of interest, resume. Applications are accepted continuously. World Wide Web: http://www.denvercenter.org.

DODGER THEATRICAL HOLDINGS, INC.
1501 Broadway, Suite 1904
New York, New York 10036

General Information Theatrical partnership that produces Broadway plays and musicals. Established in 1983. Number of employees: 45. Number of internship applications received each year: 50.
Internships Available ▶ *1 administrative intern:* responsibilities include providing office assistance and clerical support; pre-production planning, contractual arrangements, inventory, and client services. Candidates should have computer skills, office skills, organizational skills, personal interest in the field, strong interpersonal skills, telephone and reception skills. Duration is 1 semester. Paid. ▶ *1 manufacturing intern:* responsibilities include helping to manufacture large period shows for clients. Candidates should have college courses in field, knowledge of field, oral communication skills, organizational skills, research skills, strong interpersonal skills, strong background in costume history and construction; creative, motivated individuals planning a career in costume design or manufacturing are preferred. Duration is 1 semester. Paid. ▶ *1 rental intern:* responsibilities include pulling together large period shows for clients. Candidates should have college courses in field, oral communication skills, organizational skills, personal interest in the field, research skills, strong interpersonal skills, strong background in costume history or fashion; creative, motivated individuals planning a career in costume or production design (preferred). Duration is 1 semester. Paid. Open to college freshmen, college sophomores, college juniors, college seniors.
Benefits Possible full-time employment, willing to complete paperwork for educational credit, full-time interns are eligible to receive a nominal stipend on a weekly basis.
Contact Write or fax Serina Hollis, Human Resources Manager, 21-07 41st Avenue, Long Island City, New York 11101. Fax: 718-729-5118. No phone calls. In-person interview required. Applicants must submit a letter of interest, resume. Applications are accepted continuously.

DORSET THEATRE FESTIVAL
Box 510
Dorset, Vermont 05251-0510

General Information Professional nonprofit Equity theater company producing summer seasons of 5 mainstage plays and children's play. Established in 1976. Number of employees: 76. Program of American Theatre Works Inc., Dorset, Vermont. Number of internship applications received each year: 50.
Internships Available ▶ *3–4 arts management interns:* responsibilities include helping with fund-raising, publicity, box office duties, special events planning, and related managerial tasks. Candidates should have experience in the field, organizational skills, plan to pursue career in field, self-motivation, strong interpersonal skills, writing skills. Duration is 3-4 months in summer. $100–$125 per week. Open to college freshmen, college sophomores, college juniors, college seniors, recent college graduates, graduate students, career changers, individuals reentering the workforce. ▶ *3–5 technical theater interns:* responsibilities include working closely with designers on costumes, props, sets, and lighting. Candidates should have ability to work independently, ability to work with others, college courses in field, knowledge of field, plan to pursue career in field. Duration is 3-4 months in summer. $100–$125 per week. Open to college freshmen, college sophomores, college juniors,

college seniors, recent college graduates, graduate students, individuals reentering the workforce. International applications accepted.

Benefits Free housing, names of contacts, on-the-job training, opportunity to attend seminars/workshops, willing to act as a professional reference, willing to complete paperwork for educational credit, willing to provide letters of recommendation.

Contact Write, call, fax, e-mail, or through World Wide Web site Barbara Ax, General Manager. Phone: 802-867-2223. Fax: 802-867-0144. E-mail: theatre@sover.net. In-person interview recommended (telephone interview accepted). Applicants must submit a letter of interest, resume, two personal references. Application deadline: April 15. World Wide Web: http://www.theatredirectories.com.

THE DRAMA LEAGUE
165 West 46th Street, Suite 601
New York, New York 10036

General Information Organization whose purpose is to develop and administer programs that foster the growth of artists and audiences. Established in 1916. Number of employees: 6. Number of internship applications received each year: 50.

Internships Available ▶ *1 administrative intern:* responsibilities include daily mail, receptionist work, special projects (including archival work), and sending out mailings. Candidates should have ability to work independently, office skills, oral communication skills, organizational skills, personal interest in the field, research skills, self-motivation, strong interpersonal skills, writing skills, MS Word, Excel, QuarkXpress, and ACCESS. Duration is 12 weeks. $50 per 20-hour week. Open to college freshmen, college sophomores, college juniors, college seniors.

Benefits Job counseling, names of contacts, opportunity to attend seminars/workshops, possible full-time employment, travel reimbursement, willing to complete paperwork for educational credit, willing to provide letters of recommendation.

Contact Write, fax, or e-mail Jane Ann Crum, Executive Director. Fax: 212-302-2254. E-mail: jacrum@dramaleague.org. No phone calls. In-person interview recommended (telephone interview accepted). Applicants must submit a letter of interest, resume. Application deadline: January 1 for spring, April 1 for summer, July 1 for fall, October 1 for winter. World Wide Web: http://www.dramaleague org.

EDEN THEATRICAL WORKSHOP, INC.
1570 Gilpin Street
Denver, Colorado 80218

General Information Community theater organization that focuses primarily on social issues-oriented dramas. Established in 1963. Number of employees: 1. Number of internship applications received each year: 6.

Internships Available ▶ *1 administrative assistant:* responsibilities include assisting in every aspect of program including paperwork and artistic projects. Candidates should have ability to work independently, ability to work with others, editing skills, oral communication skills, self-motivation, writing skills, interest in small nonprofit organizations. Duration is flexible. Unpaid. Open to college freshmen, college sophomores, college juniors, college seniors, recent college graduates, graduate students, career changers, retirees. International applications accepted.

Benefits Free meals, job counseling, names of contacts, willing to complete paperwork for educational credit, willing to provide letters of recommendation, reimbursement of incidental expenses.

Contact Write or call Ms. Lucy M. Walker, President/Executive Director. Phone: 303-321-2320. In-person interview recommended (telephone interview accepted). Applicants must submit a letter of interest, resume. Applications are accepted continuously.

FAIRFAX SYMPHONY ORCHESTRA
PO Box 1300
Annandale, Virginia 22003

General Information Nonprofit professional symphony orchestra that performs year-round in northern Virginia and greater metropolitan Washington, D.C. Established in 1956. Number of employees: 4. Number of internship applications received each year: 30.

Internships Available ▶ *1 administrative intern:* responsibilities include assisting executive director and acting as board liaison. Candidates should have ability to work independently, computer skills, office skills, oral communication skills, organizational skills, self-motivation, strong interpersonal skills, writing skills. Duration is 8–12 weeks. Unpaid. Open to college juniors, college seniors, recent college graduates, graduate students, individuals reentering the workforce. ▶ *1 marketing intern:* responsibilities include assisting with press relations and promotional projects. Candidates should have ability to work independently, ability to work with others, computer skills, editing skills, experience in the field, office skills, oral communication skills, organizational skills, self-motivation, writing skills. Duration is 8–24 weeks. Unpaid. Open to college seniors, recent college graduates, graduate students, career changers, individuals reentering the workforce.

Benefits Job counseling, on-the-job training, opportunity to attend seminars/workshops, possible full-time employment, willing to complete paperwork for educational credit, willing to provide letters of recommendation, tickets to concerts.

Contact Write, fax, or e-mail Rachel M. Garrity, Executive Director. Fax: 703-642-7205. E-mail: rgarrity@fairfaxsymphony.org. In-person interview recommended (telephone interview accepted). Applicants must submit a letter of interest, resume, personal reference. Applications are accepted continuously. World Wide Web: http://www.fairfaxsymphony.org.

52ND STREET PROJECT
500 West 52nd Street, 2nd Floor
New York, New York 10019

General Information Nonprofit organization that serves inner-city children by putting them together with adult actors to create original theater. Established in 1981. Number of employees: 8. Number of internship applications received each year: 40.

Internships Available ▶ *1–3 theater interns:* responsibilities include working with staff in the areas of marketing, development, business, production, and teaching. Candidates should have computer skills, office skills, oral communication skills, personal interest in the field, self-motivation, strong interpersonal skills, strong leadership ability, written communication skills, love working with children. Duration is flexible. Unpaid. Open to high school seniors, recent high school graduates, college freshmen, college sophomores, college juniors, college seniors, recent college graduates, graduate students. International applications accepted.

Benefits Names of contacts, willing to complete paperwork for educational credit, willing to provide letters of recommendation, weekend or week-long trips to the country with children.

Contact Write, call, fax, e-mail, or through World Wide Web site George R. Babiak, Production Manager. Phone: 212-333-5252. Fax: 212-333-5598. E-mail: project52@aol.com. In-person interview recommended (telephone interview accepted). Applicants must submit a letter of interest, resume, 3 personal references or 3 letters of recommendation. Applications are accepted continuously. World Wide Web: http://www.52project.org.

FIJI COMPANY/PING CHONG AND COMPANY
47 Great Jones Street
New York, New York 10012

General Information Center focusing on contemporary avant-garde theater and art. Established in 1975. Number of employees: 4. Number of internship applications received each year: 10.

Internships Available ▶ *1 general management intern:* responsibilities include duties tailored to intern's abilities and center's needs. Candidates should have office skills, oral communication skills, personal interest in the field, research skills, strong interpersonal skills, written communication skills. Duration is flexible (at least 3 months preferred). Unpaid. Open to college freshmen, college sophomores, college juniors, college seniors, recent college graduates, graduate students, individuals reentering the workforce. International applications accepted.

Benefits Job counseling, willing to complete paperwork for educational credit, willing to provide letters of recommendation, small stipend available.

Contact Write, fax, or e-mail Sachiko Willis, General Manager. Fax: 212-529-1703. E-mail: pingchong@earthlink.net. No phone calls. In-person interview recommended (telephone interview accepted). Applicants must submit a letter of interest, resume. Applications are accepted continuously. World Wide Web: http://www.pingchong.org.

FLAT ROCK PLAYHOUSE
PO Box 310
Flat Rock, North Carolina 28731

General Information Theater that produces ten shows annually from May through December. Established in 1952. Number of employees: 70. Number of internship applications received each year: 30.

Internships Available ▶ *15–18 apprentices/interns:* responsibilities include learning through practical experience and exposure to as many facets of theatre as possible, including acting, technical/design, improvisation, scene design, lighting, costumes, and resume preparation (apprentices). Candidates should have ability to work with others, experience in the field, plan to pursue career in field, self-motivation. Duration is 10–30 weeks. Position available as unpaid or at $175 per week. Open to recent high school graduates, college freshmen, college sophomores, college juniors, college seniors, recent college graduates, graduate students, individuals reentering the workforce.

Benefits Free housing, free meals, on-the-job training, opportunity to attend seminars/workshops, willing to act as a professional reference, willing to complete paperwork for educational credit, willing to provide letters of recommendation, Equity Membership Candidacy Program.

Contact Write, call, fax, e-mail, or through World Wide Web site Dennis C. Maulden, Director of Educational Programs. Phone: 828-693-0403 Ext. 18. Fax: 828-693-6795. E-mail: frp@flatrockplayhouse.org. Applicants must submit a formal organization application, resume, two personal references, in-person audition recommended (video tape acceptable). Application deadline: April 1 for summer. World Wide Web: http://www.flatrockplayhouse.org.

FLORIDA GRAND OPERA
1200 Coral Way
Miami, Florida 33145

General Information Grand opera producing company presenting 35 performances of 5 grand operas each session in addition to a small-scale touring production and various other performance programs. Established in 1942. Number of employees: 25. Number of internship applications received each year: 100.

Internships Available ▶ *10–12 Young Artist Studio Singers:* responsibilities include studying, training, and giving frequent professional and educational outreach performances. Candidates should have ability to work with others, oral communication skills, plan to pursue career in field. Duration is September to April. $180 weekly stipend plus additional compensation for chorus participation.
▶ *1 Young Artist Studio coach/accompanist:* responsibilities include working extensively with the resident and visiting musical staff; duties include coaching the Young Artists, taking part in school and community performances, accompanying chorus rehearsals, and preparing and calling titles (projected English, translations). Duration is September to April. $180 weekly stipend plus additional remuneration for calling titles. International applications accepted.

Benefits Free housing, health insurance, opportunity to attend seminars/workshops, possible full-time employment, willing to complete paperwork for educational credit, willing to provide letters of recommendation, utilities (except phone), round-trip transportation to Miami.

Contact Write, call, or fax Internship Coordinator. Phone: 305-854-1643. Fax: 305-856-1042. E-mail: auditions@fgo.org. Application (available in summer 2002); to be placed on mailing list e-mail: auditions@fgo.org. Application deadline: October 27. World Wide Web: http://www.fgo.org.

FLORIDA STUDIO THEATRE
1241 North Palm Avenue
Sarasota, Florida 34236

General Information Professional nonprofit theater that runs a mainstage season of contemporary plays October through August under Actor's Equity Contract, a cabaret club theater with a three-show mainstage program, November through May, and various new play festivals. Established in 1973. Number of employees: 75. Number of internship applications received each year: 500.

Internships Available ▶ *3–4 children's education interns:* responsibilities include organizing and teaching children's acting programs and performing on children's tour. Candidates should have oral communication skills, personal interest in the field, strong interpersonal skills. Duration is October to May. $75–$100 per week. Open to recent college graduates. ▶ *2–3 development or marketing administration interns:* responsibilities include working box office or concessions, development, or marketing. Candidates should have ability to work independently, ability to work with others, computer skills, office skills, oral communication skills, organizational skills, written communication skills. Duration is summer (late May to late August); or year (September to May). $75–$100 per week. Open to recent high school graduates, college freshmen, college sophomores, college juniors, college seniors, recent college graduates. ▶ *2 literary management interns:* responsibilities include providing literary assistance to the new play program, script analysis and evaluation, and general clerical support. Candidates should have ability to work independently, computer skills, office skills, organizational skills, research skills, writing skills. Duration is May to August and September to June. $75–$100 per week. Open to recent high school graduates, college freshmen, college sophomores, college juniors, college seniors, recent college graduates. ▶ *2–3 production interns:* responsibilities include building sets, working with props and costumes, and loading and running shows. Candidates should have ability to work independently, ability to work with others, experience in the field, organizational skills, personal interest in the field, self-motivation. Duration is 3–12 months. $75 per week. Open to recent high school graduates, college freshmen, college sophomores, college juniors, college seniors, recent college graduates. ▶ *3–4 stage management interns:* responsibilities include assisting Equity stage managers with rehearsals and running mainstage productions and cabarets. Candidates should have analytical skills, knowledge of field, organizational skills, strong interpersonal skills, strong leadership ability. Duration is October to May; summer position also available. $75–$100 per week. Open to recent high school graduates, college freshmen, college sophomores, college juniors, college seniors, recent college graduates. International applications accepted.

Benefits Formal training, free housing, on-the-job training, possible full-time employment, willing to act as a professional reference, willing to complete paperwork for educational credit, willing to provide letters of recommendation.

Contact Write, call, fax, e-mail, or through World Wide Web site James Ashford, Casting and Literary Coordinator. Phone: 941-366-9017. Fax: 941-955-4137. E-mail: james@fst2000.org. Telephone interview required. Applicants must submit a formal organization application, letter of interest, resume, 2-3 personal references, 2-3 letters of recommendation, audition required for children's education interns. Applications are accepted continuously. World Wide Web: http://www.fst2000.org.

FOOLS COMPANY, INC.
423 West 46th Street
New York, New York 10036-3510

General Information Not-for-profit cultural and educational organization whose mission is to produce and present innovative and unconventional works and workshops in all areas of the performing arts. Established in 1970. Number of employees: 5. Number of internship applications received each year: 50.

Internships Available ▶ *5 administration interns:* responsibilities include working in funding, publicity, and public relations for performing arts productions and workshops. Duration is 3 months. Unpaid. ▶ *2 production interns:* responsibilities include assisting

Fools Company, Inc. (continued)

with company productions and workshops. Duration is 3–6 months. Unpaid. Candidates for all positions should have ability to work independently, oral communication skills, self-motivation, strong interpersonal skills, written communication skills. Open to high school seniors, recent high school graduates, college freshmen, college sophomores, college juniors, college seniors, recent college graduates, graduate students, law students, career changers, individuals reentering the workforce. International applications accepted.

Benefits Formal training, job counseling, names of contacts, on-the-job training, opportunity to attend seminars/workshops, possible full-time employment, willing to act as a professional reference, willing to complete paperwork for educational credit, willing to provide letters of recommendation.

Contact Write, call, or e-mail Ms. Jill Russell, Executive Director. Phone: 212-307-6000. E-mail: foolsco@nyc.rr.com. In-person interview required. Applicants must submit a letter of interest, resume, telephone interview acceptable for international applicants only. Applications are accepted continuously.

GEVA THEATRE
75 Woodbury Boulevard
Rochester, New York 14607

General Information Theater that strives to present and advance the art of theater so that its artists, audience, and the community can celebrate the human experience through an active participation in this art form. Established in 1972. Number of employees: 75. Number of internship applications received each year: 35.

Internships Available ▶ *1 literary intern:* responsibilities include script analysis and heavy duty play development work. Candidates should have computer skills, knowledge of field, organizational skills, personal interest in the field, writing skills. Duration is 9 months. Unpaid. ▶ *2 stage management apprentices:* responsibilities include assisting in running shows. Candidates should have computer skills, experience in the field, oral communication skills, organizational skills, plan to pursue career in field, self-motivation. Duration is 10 months. $206–$250 per week. Open to recent college graduates, graduate students.

Benefits Job counseling, names of contacts, possible full-time employment, willing to complete paperwork for educational credit, willing to provide letters of recommendation.

Contact Write, e-mail, or through World Wide Web site Skip Greer, Director of Education. Fax: 716-232-4031. E-mail: sgreer@gevatheatre.org. No phone calls. In-person interview recommended (telephone interview accepted). Applicants must submit a letter of interest, resume. Applications are accepted continuously. World Wide Web: http://www.gevatheatre.org.

GLIMMERGLASS OPERA
PO Box 191
Cooperstown, New York 13326

General Information Summer opera festival. Established in 1975. Number of employees: 300. Number of internship applications received each year: 300.

Internships Available ▶ *18 administrative interns:* responsibilities include duties in one of the following areas: accounting/finance, box office, development, house management, housing and transportation, marketing/public relations, and operations/special events, general administration. Candidates should have computer skills, oral communication skills, organizational skills, personal interest in the field, strong interpersonal skills. Duration is May to August. $210 per week. Open to college freshmen, college sophomores, college juniors, college seniors, recent college graduates, graduate students. ▶ *6 artistic interns:* responsibilities include duties in one of two areas: music (locating and copying music, transporting instruments, orchestra pit set-up), Young American Artist Program Administration (acting as liaison between young artists and Director of Artistic Administration). Candidates should have computer skills, knowledge of field, oral communication skills, organizational skills, strong interpersonal skills, driver's license. Duration is May to August. $210 per week. Open to col-

lege juniors, college seniors, recent college graduates, graduate students, career changers, individuals reentering the workforce. ▶ *32 production interns:* responsibilities include duties in the following areas: audio/video, costume construction or crafts, costume shop management, electrics, hair and make-up, projected titles, properties, scene painting, scenery construction, shop management, stage operations, or wardrobe, production shop management, stage management. Candidates should have ability to work with others, experience in the field, oral communication skills. Duration is May to August. $210 per week. Open to college freshmen, college sophomores, college juniors, college seniors, recent college graduates, graduate students. International applications accepted.

Benefits Free housing, on-the-job training, opportunity to attend seminars/workshops, possible full-time employment, willing to act as a professional reference, willing to complete paperwork for educational credit, willing to provide letters of recommendation.

Contact Write, call, fax, e-mail, or through World Wide Web site Internship Coordinator. Phone: 607-547-5704. Fax: 607-547-6030. E-mail: interns@glimmerglass.org. Telephone interview required. Applicants must submit a letter of interest, resume, two personal references. Application deadline: March 8. World Wide Web: http://www.cooperstown.net/glimmerglass.

GOODMAN THEATRE
170 North Dearborn
Chicago, Illinois 60601

General Information Oldest and largest nonprofit theater in Chicago producing classic, contemporary, and new works. Established in 1925. Number of employees: 100. Number of internship applications received each year: 150.

Internships Available ▶ *1 arts administration intern:* responsibilities include providing clerical and special project assistance to the assistants to the artistic director, executive director, and associate producer; attending staff meetings and assisting with preparations for board meetings; planning and organizing intern forum. Candidates should have computer skills, oral communication skills, organizational skills, personal interest in the field, strong interpersonal skills, written communication skills. Duration is 3–5 months. Stipend (varies from season to season). Open to college juniors, college seniors, recent college graduates, graduate students. ▶ *Business administration interns:* responsibilities include assisting with a variety of activities, including routine accounting, travel and housing arrangements for guest artists, and special projects. Candidates should have ability to work with others, oral communication skills, plan to pursue career in field, written communication skills, basic knowledge of business and clerical procedures. Duration is 3–5 months. Stipend (varies from season to season). Open to college seniors, recent college graduates, graduate students. ▶ *1 casting intern:* responsibilities include scheduling and monitoring auditions, corresponding with actors and agents, and maintaining actor files. Candidates should have ability to work independently, computer skills, office skills, plan to pursue career in field, strong interpersonal skills, written communication skills. Duration is 3–5 months. Stipend (varies from season to season). Open to college juniors, college seniors, recent college graduates, graduate students. ▶ *1 costuming intern:* responsibilities include general costume construction and assisting with office clerical tasks. Candidates should have ability to work independently, ability to work with others, experience in the field, organizational skills, plan to pursue career in field. Duration is 2 to 3 months in fall/winter only (20 hours per week minimum). Stipend (varies from season to season). Open to college juniors, college seniors, recent college graduates, graduate students. ▶ *1 development intern:* responsibilities include researching prospective contributors and grants, writing for newsletters and the annual report, developing fund-raising campaigns, and writing solicitation letters. Candidates should have ability to work with others, computer skills, knowledge of field, oral communication skills, plan to pursue career in field, written communication skills. Duration is 3-5 months; special, short-term placements are an option. Stipend (varies from season to season). Open to college juniors, college seniors, recent college graduates, graduate students. ▶ *1 dramaturgy intern:* responsibilities include researching various subjects for newsletter articles and program notes, assisting with preparation of scripts for rehearsals, maintaining in-house library, working on script changes once play is in production, and assisting with new script reading and evaluation. Candidates should have ability to work independently, computer skills, editing skills, organizational skills, research skills, written communication skills. Duration is 3–5 months. Stipend (varies from season to season). Open to college juniors, college seniors, recent college graduates, graduate students. ▶ *1 education and community programs intern:* responsibilities include assisting with student matinee performances, writing articles or exercises for study guides, compiling information from student and teacher evaluations, helping to coordinate high school teacher seminars, corresponding with school groups or other community organizations, and assisting with organization of archival material. Candidates should have ability to work independently, computer skills, oral communication skills, organizational skills, personal interest in the field, written communication skills. Duration is 3–5 months. Stipend (varies from season to season). Open to college juniors, college seniors, recent college graduates, graduate students. ▶ *1 electrics intern:* responsibilities include hanging and focusing lights, helping to create special effects, equipment maintenance. Candidates should have ability to work independently, experience in the field, organizational skills, plan to pursue career in field, strong interpersonal skills, knowledge of computerized lighting systems (a plus). Duration is 2 to 3 months in fall/winter only (20 hours per week minimum). Stipend (varies from season to season). Open to college juniors, college seniors, recent college graduates, graduate students. ▶ *1 literary management intern:* responsibilities include assisting in solicitation and recording of new manuscripts; maintaining extensive script library; analyzing and evaluating solicited manuscripts; corresponding with playwrights, agents, theaters, and play development programs; and researching playwright production histories. Candidates should have ability to work independently, computer skills, editing skills, organizational skills, research skills, written communication skills. Duration is 3–5 months. Stipend (varies from season to season). Open to college juniors, college seniors, recent college graduates, graduate students. ▶ *1 properties intern:* responsibilities include assisting with researching, purchasing, creating, and maintaining scenic elements for a variety of period and contemporary productions. Candidates should have ability to work independently, ability to work with others, knowledge of field, organizational skills, plan to pursue career in field. Duration is 2 to 3 months in fall/winter only (20 hours per week minimum). Stipend (varies from season to season). Open to college juniors, college seniors, recent college graduates, graduate students. ▶ *1 public relations intern:* responsibilities include assisting in areas of marketing and advertising, proofreading newsletter and program copy, compiling audience survey results, distributing promotional materials, and facilitating special events. Candidates should have ability to work with others, knowledge of field, office skills, plan to pursue career in field, written communication skills. Duration is 3–5 months. Stipend (varies from season to season). Open to college juniors, college seniors, recent college graduates, graduate students. ▶ *1 scenery intern:* responsibilities include building and installing scenery. Candidates should have ability to work with others, experience in the field, organizational skills, plan to pursue career in field, self-motivation. Duration is 2 to 3 months in fall/winter only (20 hours per week minimum). Stipend (varies from season to season). Open to college juniors, college seniors, recent college graduates, graduate students. ▶ *Sound interns:* responsibilities include helping to create sound scores for mainstage and studio productions, and learning advanced procedures for installing, operating, and maintaining sound equipment. Candidates should have ability to work with others, experience in the field, plan to pursue career in field, self-motivation. Duration is 2 to 3 months in fall/winter only; 20 hours per week minimum. Stipend (varies from season to season). ▶ *1–2 stage management interns:* responsibilities include assisting stage managers with preproduction preparation and continuing through technical rehearsals, preview weeks, and opening nights. Candidates should have computer skills, experience in the field, organizational skills, plan to pursue career in field, strong interpersonal skills. Duration is 6-8 weeks or length of production. Stipend (varies from season to season). Open to college seniors, recent college graduates,

graduate students. ▶ *1 ticket services intern:* responsibilities include learning the art of customer service, operating the box office computer system, and assisting with the planning of special events. Candidates should have ability to work with others, computer skills, knowledge of field, office skills, plan to pursue career in field. Duration is 3–5 months. Stipend (varies from season to season). Open to college juniors, college seniors, recent college graduates, graduate students. International applications accepted.
Benefits Job counseling, names of contacts, on-the-job training, opportunity to attend seminars/workshops, willing to act as a professional reference, willing to complete paperwork for educational credit, willing to provide letters of recommendation.
Contact Write, call, e-mail, or through World Wide Web site Ms. Julie Massey, Intern Coordinator. Phone: 312-443-3813. Fax: 312-443-7448. E-mail: juliemassey@goodman-theatre.org. In-person interview recommended (telephone interview accepted). Applicants must submit a formal organization application, letter of interest, resume, two letters of recommendation. Application deadline: March 1 for summer, June 1 for fall, October 1 for winter. World Wide Web: http://www.goodman-theatre.org.

GOODSPEED MUSICALS
Box A
East Haddam, Connecticut 06423

General Information Professional, award-winning theater with a 30-year history of producing musical theater. Established in 1963. Number of employees: 100. Number of internship applications received each year: 200.
Internships Available ▶ *2 carpentry interns:* responsibilities include running crew and building sets. Candidates should have ability to work independently, college courses in field, oral communication skills, personal interest in the field, strong interpersonal skills. Duration is 1–2 semesters. Weekly stipend. Open to college freshmen, college sophomores, college juniors, college seniors, graduate students. ▶ *2 electric interns:* responsibilities include running follow spots for production and helping shop build shows. Candidates should have ability to work independently, college courses in field, oral communication skills, personal interest in the field, strong interpersonal skills. Duration is 1–2 semesters. Weekly stipend. Open to college freshmen, college sophomores, college juniors, college seniors, graduate students. ▶ *2 props interns:* responsibilities include running crew and building props. Candidates should have ability to work independently, college courses in field, oral communication skills, personal interest in the field, strong interpersonal skills. Duration is 1–2 semesters. Weekly stipend. Open to college freshmen, college sophomores, college juniors, college seniors, graduate students. ▶ *1 scenic art intern:* responsibilities include helping the scenic artists paint scenery. Candidates should have ability to work independently, college courses in field, oral communication skills, personal interest in the field, strong interpersonal skills. Duration is 1–2 semesters. Weekly stipend. Open to college freshmen, college sophomores, college juniors, college seniors, recent college graduates. ▶ *2–4 stage management interns:* responsibilities include assisting stage manager during rehearsals and performances. Candidates should have ability to work independently, college degree in related field, computer skills, editing skills, knowledge of field, office skills, oral communication skills, organizational skills, plan to pursue career in field, self-motivation, strong interpersonal skills, strong leadership ability, writing skills. Duration is 4–16 weeks. Stipend of $200 per week. Open to recent college graduates. ▶ *2 wardrobe interns:* responsibilities include working in the costume shop and running wardrobe. Candidates should have ability to work independently, college courses in field, oral communication skills, personal interest in the field, strong interpersonal skills. Duration is 1–2 semesters. Weekly stipend. Open to college freshmen, college sophomores, college juniors, college seniors, graduate students. International applications accepted.
Benefits Free housing, names of contacts, on-the-job training, opportunity to attend seminars/workshops, willing to complete paperwork for educational credit, willing to provide letters of recommendation.
Contact Write, fax, e-mail, or through World Wide Web site Carrie Smith, Assistant Production Manager, Box A, East Haddam,

Goodspeed Musicals (continued)
Connecticut 06243. Fax: 860-873-2480. E-mail: csmith@goodspeed. org. No phone calls. Telephone interview required. Applicants must submit a formal organization application, letter of interest, resume, three personal references, proof that credit will be received from educational institution. Applications are accepted continuously. World Wide Web: http://www.goodspeed.org.

HARTFORD STAGE
50 Church Street
Hartford, Connecticut 06103

General Information Regional theater company that produces top-quality professional theater for Connecticut's capital city and its surrounding communities; under the direction of Michael Wilson since April 1998, Hartford Stage has deepened its commitment to new works and reinterpretations of classic plays. Established in 1964. Number of employees: 50. Number of internship applications received each year: 50.
Internships Available ▶ *1–3 AETNA Fellowships:* responsibilities include apprenticing in various departments including artistic administration, production, literary management, education, and stage management. Candidates should have ability to work independently, analytical skills, college degree in related field, computer skills, editing skills, office skills, oral communication skills, organizational skills, plan to pursue career in field, research skills, self-motivation, strong interpersonal skills, strong leadership ability, writing skills. Duration is 5–9 months. Paid. Open to individuals of color who are graduate students or recent college graduates. ▶ *5–7 interns:* responsibilities include performing tasks related to available positions in administration (business, communications, and development), production, stage management, production management, company management, literary management, dramaturgy, and education. Candidates should have ability to work independently, college courses in field, computer skills, experience in the field, office skills, oral communication skills, organizational skills, plan to pursue career in field, research skills, self-motivation, strong interpersonal skills, writing skills. Duration is flexible. Unpaid. Open to college juniors, college seniors, recent college graduates, graduate students. International applications accepted.
Benefits On-the-job training, willing to act as a professional reference, willing to complete paperwork for educational credit, willing to provide letters of recommendation.
Contact Write, fax, or e-mail Edward Duran, Internship Coordinator. Fax: 860-525-4420. E-mail: eddieduran@hartfordstage.org. No phone calls. In-person interview recommended (telephone interview accepted). Applicants must submit a formal organization application, letter of interest, resume, three letters of recommendation. Application deadline: April 1 for summer, November 1 for spring. World Wide Web: http://www.hartfordstage.org.

HORSE CAVE THEATRE
Box 215
Horse Cave, Kentucky 42749

General Information Nonprofit repertory theater bringing professional theater to the area at an affordable price while promoting educational outreach programs and student theater workshops. Established in 1976. Number of employees: 10. Number of internship applications received each year: 12.
Internships Available ▶ *6–9 apprentices:* responsibilities include assisting with lighting, scene shop, costumes, props, box office management, sound, or administration. Candidates should have ability to work independently, ability to work with others, knowledge of field, personal interest in the field, self-motivation. Duration is 6 months. $50–$75 per week. Open to recent high school graduates, college freshmen, college sophomores, college juniors, college seniors, recent college graduates, graduate students. International applications accepted.
Benefits Free housing, on-the-job training, opportunity to attend seminars/workshops, willing to act as a professional reference, willing to complete paperwork for educational credit, willing to provide letters of recommendation.

Contact Write, call, fax, or e-mail Lynn Gilcrease, Education Associate. Phone: 270-786-1200. Fax: 270-786-5298. E-mail: hctstaff@ scrtc.com. In-person interview recommended (telephone interview accepted). Applicants must submit a formal organization application, resume, two letters of recommendation. Application deadline: April 1. World Wide Web: http://www.horsecavetheatre.org.

INDIANA REPERTORY THEATRE
140 West Washington Street
Indianapolis, Indiana 46204

General Information Theater company that produces 6 mainstage and 3 upperstage productions in a season that operates from September to May. Established in 1972. Number of employees: 175. Number of internship applications received each year: 20.
Internships Available ▶ *3–4 administrative interns:* responsibilities include assisting professional staff in a variety of areas including marketing/sales, education, public relations, or development. Candidates should have computer skills, office skills, oral communication skills, organizational skills, plan to pursue career in field, research skills, written communication skills. Duration is minimum of 3 months. Unpaid. ▶ *5–6 production interns:* responsibilities include working in various areas including stage management, costume shop, properties, company management, production management, scene shop, scenic art, and electrics/sound; working side-by-side with professional staff. Candidates should have ability to work with others, oral communication skills, organizational skills, personal interest in the field, plan to pursue career in field, self-motivation. Duration is minimum of 3 months. Unpaid. Open to college freshmen, college sophomores, college juniors, college seniors.
Benefits Names of contacts, possible full-time employment, willing to complete paperwork for educational credit, willing to provide letters of recommendation.
Contact Write or e-mail Josh Friedman, Production Supervisor. E-mail: jfriedman@indianarep.com. No phone calls. In-person interview recommended (telephone interview accepted). Applicants must submit a formal organization application, letter of interest, resume, three letters of recommendation. World Wide Web: http://www.indianarep.com.

JENNIFER MULLER/THE WORKS
131 West 24th Street
New York, New York 10011

General Information New York City-based contemporary dance company that does extensive international touring. Established in 1974. Number of employees: 5. Number of internship applications received each year: 15.
Internships Available ▶ *1 accounting intern:* responsibilities include working on general ledger and bookkeeping tasks. Candidates should have computer skills. Duration is flexible. Unpaid. Open to college freshmen, college sophomores, college juniors, college seniors, recent college graduates, graduate students, dancers. ▶ *2 administration interns:* responsibilities include assisting managers in day-to-day operations, special events, and fund-raising. Duration is flexible. Unpaid. Open to college freshmen, college sophomores, college juniors, college seniors, recent college graduates, graduate students. ▶ *1 tour planning intern:* responsibilities include contacting sponsors; travel and hotel bookings. Duration is flexible. Unpaid. Open to college freshmen, college sophomores, college juniors, college seniors, recent college graduates, graduate students, dancers. International applications accepted.
Benefits Job counseling, possible full-time employment, willing to complete paperwork for educational credit, willing to provide letters of recommendation.
Contact Write Ms. Lynette Muller, Office Manager. Phone: 212-691-3803. Fax: 212-206-6630. E-mail: theworksnyc@compuserve. com. In-person interview recommended (telephone interview accepted). Applications are accepted continuously.

JOHN DREW THEATER OF GUILD HALL
158 Main Street
East Hampton, New York 11937

General Information Performing arts presenter and Equity theater associated with art museum. Number of employees: 14. Unit of Guild Hall of East Hampton, East Hampton, New York. Number of internship applications received each year: 50.

Internships Available ▶ *Intern (Executive Director's Office):* responsibilities include computer trouble shooting, Web site update, and special projects. Candidates should have ability to work independently, computer skills, office skills, oral communication skills, strong interpersonal skills, writing skills. Duration is flexible. Position available as unpaid or at $8 per hour. Open to high school seniors, recent high school graduates, college freshmen, college sophomores, college juniors, college seniors, recent college graduates, individuals reentering the workforce. ▶ *1 marketing/PR intern:* responsibilities include researching/drafting press releases; media list maintenance; administrative duties; distribution and organization of materials. Candidates should have ability to work independently, computer skills, editing skills, organizational skills, personal interest in the field, self-motivation, writing skills. Duration is June to mid-August (10–15 hours per week). Unpaid. Open to recent high school graduates, college freshmen, college sophomores, college juniors, college seniors, recent college graduates, graduate students, career changers, individuals reentering the workforce. ▶ *1 production management intern:* responsibilities include assisting production manager. Candidates should have theater background. Duration is one summer. Unpaid. Open to college freshmen, college sophomores, college juniors, college seniors. ▶ *1–2 technical interns:* responsibilities include completing general backstage assignments. Candidates should have personal interest in the field. Duration is one summer. Unpaid. Open to high school seniors, college freshmen, college sophomores, college juniors, college seniors. International applications accepted.

Benefits Job counseling, names of contacts, willing to complete paperwork for educational credit, willing to provide letters of recommendation, academic credit can be arranged.

Contact Write, call, fax, or through World Wide Web site Josh Gladstone, Artistic Director. Phone: 631-324-4051. Fax: 631-324-2722. E-mail: joshgladstone@guildhall.org. In-person interview required. Applicants must submit a letter of interest, resume. Applications are accepted continuously. World Wide Web: http://www.GuildHall.org.

LINCOLN CENTER FOR THE PERFORMING ARTS
70 Lincoln Center Plaza
New York, New York 10023-6583

General Information Producer and presenter of 300 events annually and manager of the Lincoln Center complex. Established in 1956. Number of employees: 500. Number of internship applications received each year: 80.

Internships Available ▶ *2 arts management interns:* responsibilities include providing assistance on projects to be chosen by the intern in consultation with senior staff members. Candidates should have ability to work independently, analytical skills, computer skills, oral communication skills, plan to pursue career in field, written communication skills. Duration is 12 weeks in fall. $500 per week. Open to graduate students, recent graduate-level graduates. International applications accepted.

Benefits Names of contacts, possible full-time employment, willing to complete paperwork for educational credit, willing to provide letters of recommendation, tickets to performances.

Contact Write, fax, or e-mail Jay D. Spivack, Director of Human Resources and Administrative Services. Fax: 212-875-5185. E-mail: humanresources@lincolncenter.org. No phone calls. In-person interview required. Applicants must submit a resume, cover letter. Application deadline: July 31. World Wide Web: http://www.lincolncenter.org.

MABOU MINES
150 First Avenue
New York, New York 10009

General Information Avant-garde theater company emphasizing the creation of new theater pieces from original texts and the theatrical use of existing texts staged from a specific point of view. Established in 1970. Number of employees: 4. Number of internship applications received each year: 75.

Internships Available ▶ *1–3 administrative interns:* responsibilities include assisting in maintaining archives, preparing promotional materials, running errands, handling telephone calls, general filing, computer input, and general office maintenance. Duration is 1 semester. Unpaid. Open to college freshmen, college sophomores, college juniors, college seniors, recent college graduates, priority given to those familiar with company's work. International applications accepted.

Benefits Job counseling, opportunity to attend seminars/workshops, willing to complete paperwork for educational credit, willing to provide letters of recommendation, opportunity to accompany artistic directorate to art events.

Contact Write, call, fax, or e-mail Company Manager. Phone: 212-473-0559. Fax: 212-473-2410. E-mail: office@maboumines.org. In-person interview required. Applicants must submit a letter of interest, resume. Applications are accepted continuously. World Wide Web: http://www.maboumines.org.

MAINE STATE MUSIC THEATRE
14 Maine Street, Suite 109
Brunswick, Maine 04011

General Information Theater dedicated to polishing, preserving, and producing musical plays and training young theater professionals. Established in 1959. Number of employees: 60. Number of internship applications received each year: 1,000.

Internships Available ▶ *4 administrative interns:* responsibilities include working with company management, marketing, box office, and house management. Candidates should have ability to work independently, computer skills, office skills, oral communication skills, organizational skills, strong interpersonal skills. Duration is May to August. $60 per week. Open to recent high school graduates, college freshmen, college sophomores, college juniors, college seniors, recent college graduates, graduate students, must be 18 years old. ▶ *8 performers.* Candidates should have ability to work with others, experience in the field, organizational skills, plan to pursue career in field, self-motivation. Duration is May to August. $60 per week. Open to recent high school graduates, college freshmen, college sophomores, college juniors, college seniors, recent college graduates, graduate students. ▶ *12 technicians:* responsibilities include working in stage management, painting, scenery, props, electrics, and costumes; and building and installing sets. Candidates should have ability to work independently, ability to work with others, experience in the field, plan to pursue career in field, self-motivation. Duration is May to August. $60 per week. Open to recent high school graduates, college freshmen, college sophomores, college juniors, college seniors, recent college graduates, graduate students, must be 18 years old.

Benefits Free housing, free meals, names of contacts, on-the-job training, opportunity to attend seminars/workshops, willing to complete paperwork for educational credit, willing to provide letters of recommendation, 8 Actors Equity membership candidate points (for performers and technical interns).

Contact Write, call, fax, or e-mail Kathi Kacinski, Company Manager. Phone: 207-725-8769. Fax: 207-725-1199. E-mail: msmtjobs@blazenetme.net. In-person interview recommended (telephone interview accepted). Applicants must submit a formal organization application, resume, two letters of recommendation. Application deadline: March 1. World Wide Web: http://www.msmt.org.

MANHATTAN CLASS COMPANY
120 West 28th Street, 2nd Floor
New York, New York 10001

General Information   Off-Broadway theater. Established in 1983. Number of employees: 10. Number of internship applications received each year: 20.

Internships Available   ▶ *1 arts in education intern:* responsibilities include assisting the Education Department with special projects, correspondence, Youth Theater Company meetings, general office help, errands, and filing. Candidates should have computer skills, office skills, oral communication skills, personal interest in the field, strong interpersonal skills, written communication skills. Duration is flexible. Unpaid. Open to high school seniors, recent high school graduates, college freshmen, college sophomores, college juniors, college seniors, recent college graduates, graduate students, career changers, individuals reentering the workforce. ▶ *1 box office intern:* responsibilities include assisting ticketing and marketing manager with database entry, ticketing, research, special projects, mailings, and general office duties. Candidates should have ability to work independently, computer skills, office skills, oral communication skills, personal interest in the field, written communication skills. Duration is flexible. Unpaid. Open to high school seniors, recent high school graduates, college freshmen, college sophomores, college juniors, college seniors, recent college graduates, graduate students, career changers, individuals reentering the workforce. ▶ *1 development intern:* responsibilities include correspondence, working in database, working on special projects including the Annual Benefit, research, data entry, and running errands. Candidates should have ability to work with others, computer skills, office skills, oral communication skills, personal interest in the field, written communication skills. Duration is flexible. Unpaid. Open to recent high school graduates, college freshmen, college sophomores, college juniors, college seniors, recent college graduates, career changers, individuals reentering the workforce. ▶ *2–3 general management interns:* responsibilities include running errands, filing, copying, assisting with mailings and correspondence, and working on special projects. Candidates should have ability to work independently, computer skills, office skills, oral communication skills, strong interpersonal skills, writing skills. Duration is based on applicant's availability. Unpaid. Open to recent high school graduates, college freshmen, college sophomores, college juniors, college seniors, recent college graduates, graduate students, career changers, individuals reentering the workforce. ▶ *1 house management intern:* responsibilities include assisting house manager with general theater management duties during run of show. Candidates should have ability to work independently, oral communication skills, personal interest in the field, self-motivation, strong interpersonal skills. Duration is flexible. Unpaid. Open to high school seniors, recent high school graduates, college freshmen, college sophomores, college juniors, college seniors, recent college graduates, graduate students. ▶ *1–2 production interns:* responsibilities include assisting with production of a not-for-profit theater. Candidates should have knowledge of field, office skills, oral communication skills, personal interest in the field, strong interpersonal skills, writing skills. Duration is based on applicant's availability. Unpaid. Open to high school seniors, recent high school graduates, college freshmen, college sophomores, college juniors, college seniors, recent college graduates, graduate students, career changers, individuals reentering the workforce. International applications accepted.

Benefits   Names of contacts, travel reimbursement, willing to complete paperwork for educational credit, willing to provide letters of recommendation.

Contact   Write, fax, e-mail, or through World Wide Web site Philip Mann, Office Manager, 120 West 26t Street, 2nd Floor, New York, New York 10001. Phone: 212-727-7722. Fax: 212-727-7780. E-mail: info@mcctheater.org. In-person interview required. Applicants must submit a letter of interest, resume, two personal references. Applications are accepted continuously. World Wide Web: http://www.mcctheater.com/mcc/.

MANHATTAN THEATRE CLUB
311 West 43rd Street, 8th Floor
New York, New York 10036

General Information   Major off-Broadway theater with a commitment to developing and producing new works; sponsors a variety of special events including readings of plays-in-progress and Writers-in-Performance series. Established in 1970. Number of employees: 70. Number of internship applications received each year: 500.

Internships Available   ▶ *15–18 theater/management interns:* responsibilities include working in the following departments: artistic casting, development/fund-raising, executive producing, general management, business, education, literary, marketing, musical theater, production management, and Writers-in-Performance. Candidates should have ability to work independently, ability to work with others, office skills, oral communication skills, personal interest in the field, written communication skills. Duration is 1–3 semesters. $185 per week. Open to college freshmen, college sophomores, college juniors, college seniors, recent college graduates, graduate students, career changers. International applications accepted.

Benefits   On-the-job training, opportunity to attend seminars/workshops, possible full-time employment, willing to complete paperwork for educational credit, willing to provide letters of recommendation, free and discounted tickets to cultural events in New York City.

Contact   Write, fax, e-mail, or through World Wide Web site Jamie Beth Cohen, Assistant Education Director and Coordinator, Paul A. Kaplan Theatre Management Program. Fax: 212-399-4329. E-mail: interns@mtc-nyc.org. No phone calls. In-person interview recommended (telephone interview accepted). Applicants must submit a formal organization application, letter of interest, resume, two letters of recommendation. Application deadline: March 15 for summer, July 15 for fall, November 15 for winter/spring. World Wide Web: http://www.ManhattanTheatreClub.com.

McCARTER THEATRE–CENTER FOR THE PERFORMING ARTS
91 University Place
Princeton, New Jersey 08540

General Information   Performing arts center producing and presenting world-class artists in drama, music, dance, and special events; received 1994 Tony Award for outstanding regional theater. Established in 1963. Number of employees: 150. Number of internship applications received each year: 150.

Internships Available   ▶ *1 company/production management intern:* responsibilities include coordinating artists' travel and housing arrangements, scheduling use of company car, and tracking company management expenses, and providing administrative support to the business office. Candidates should have ability to work independently, office skills, organizational skills, self-motivation, strong interpersonal skills, strong leadership ability. Duration is 9–10 months. $75 weekly stipend. Open to college juniors, college seniors, recent college graduates, career changers, individuals reentering the workforce. ▶ *1 costumes/wardrobe intern:* responsibilities include planning, building, and maintaining costumes. Candidates should have ability to work independently, ability to work with others, college courses in field, knowledge of field, organizational skills, personal interest in the field, research skills, self-motivation. Duration is 9–10 months. $75 weekly stipend. Open to college juniors, college seniors, recent college graduates, graduate students, career changers, individuals reentering the workforce. ▶ *1 development intern:* responsibilities include involvement with government, corporate, foundation, and individual solicitations for support; compiling statistics, donor record management, gift entry, and acknowledgement and special event operations. Candidates should have ability to work independently, office skills, organizational skills, personal interest in the field, research skills, self-motivation, writing skills. Duration is 9–10 months. $75 weekly stipend. Open to college juniors, college seniors, recent college graduates, graduate students, career changers, individuals reentering the workforce. ▶ *2 directing/producing interns:* responsibilities include administrative work for the office of the Artistic Director, assisting with in-house casting, NY/NJ production coverage, reading of new material for the artistic team, serving as assistant to the director on mainstage production (subject to the Artistic Director's discretion). Candidates should have experience in the field, organizational skills, personal interest in the field, plan to pursue career in field, self-motivation, strong interpersonal skills, strong leadership ability, written communication skills. Duration is 9–10 months. $75 weekly stipend. Open to college juniors, college seniors, recent college graduates, graduate students, career changers, individuals reentering the workforce. ▶ *1 education intern:* responsibilities include assisting with school contacts, coordinating staffing of student performances, traveling with in-school tours, serving as assistant instructor, and team teaching one or more Creative Drama and Youth Theater programs. Candidates should have college courses in field, computer skills, experience in the field, office skills, oral communication skills, personal interest in the field, strong interpersonal skills. Duration is 9–10 months. $75 weekly stipend. Open to recent college graduates, graduate students, individuals reentering the workforce. ▶ *1 house management/special events intern:* responsibilities include full front-of-house management responsibilities including managing service and concessions areas, coordinating usher schedules, assisting receptions, benefits, dinners, and lobby rentals. Candidates should have oral communication skills, organizational skills, strong interpersonal skills, strong leadership ability. Duration is 9–10 months. $75 weekly stipend. Open to college juniors, college seniors, recent college graduates, graduate students, career changers, individuals reentering the workforce. ▶ *1 literary management intern:* responsibilities include participating in the administration of the Literary Office, script reading, planning and coordinating McCarter's new play festival, organizing playreadings, and occasional dramaturgical research. Candidates should have ability to work with others, editing skills, knowledge of field, oral communication skills, research skills, writing skills. Duration is 9–10 months. $75 weekly stipend. Open to college juniors, college seniors, recent college graduates, graduate students, career changers, individuals reentering the workforce. ▶ *1 marketing/special events intern:* responsibilities include assisting with press and publicity management, publications management, audience development, and group sales, assisting with parties and receptions, and house management responsibilities for all student matinees. Candidates should have ability to work with others, computer skills, oral communication skills, organizational skills, self-motivation, written communication skills. Duration is 9–10 months. $75 weekly stipend. Open to college juniors, college seniors, recent college graduates, graduate students, career changers, individuals reentering the workforce. ▶ *1 producing intern:* responsibilities include participating in the artistic activities of the theater including casting, script reading, correspondence, NY/NJ production coverage, and play reading, including a substantial amount of artistic administrative work. Candidates should have ability to work with others, computer skills, knowledge of field, office skills, oral communication skills, organizational skills, self-motivation. Duration is 9–10 months. $75 weekly stipend. Open to college juniors, college seniors, recent college graduates, graduate students, career changers, individuals reentering the workforce. ▶ *1 properties intern:* responsibilities include participating in the procurement, construction, set-up, running, and maintenance of props, beginning with the design process and continuing through to strike. Candidates should have ability to work independently, ability to work with others, knowledge of field, organizational skills, personal interest in the field, self-motivation. Duration is 9–10 months. $75 weekly stipend. Open to college juniors, college seniors, recent college graduates, graduate students, career changers, individuals reentering the workforce. ▶ *1 stage management intern:* responsibilities include preparing for and attending rehearsal with shared responsibility for organizing and tracking production needs, communicating with various departments, and maintaining a work environment conducive to the best artistic efforts. Candidates should have college courses in field, knowledge of field, oral communication skills, organizational skills, plan to pursue career in field, self-motivation, strong interpersonal skills, strong leadership ability. Duration is 9–10 months. $75 weekly stipend. Open to college juniors, college seniors, recent college graduates, graduate students, career changers, individuals reentering the workforce. ▶ *1 technical direction/scene shop intern:* responsibili-

ties include working in all aspects of scenery development for a large proscenium stage operating on a repertory schedule, and participating on changeover and running crews. Candidates should have analytical skills, college courses in field, knowledge of field, organizational skills, self-motivation, strong interpersonal skills, strong leadership ability. Duration is 9–10 months. $75 weekly stipend. Open to college juniors, college seniors, recent college graduates, graduate students, career changers, individuals reentering the workforce. International applications accepted.
Benefits Free housing, names of contacts, opportunity to attend seminars/workshops, possible full-time employment, willing to act as a professional reference, willing to complete paperwork for educational credit, willing to provide letters of recommendation.
Contact Write, fax, e-mail, or through World Wide Web site Grace Shackney, Intern Coordinator. Phone: 609-258-6502. Fax: 609-497-0369. E-mail: gshackney@mccarter.org. In-person interview recommended (telephone interview accepted). Applicants must submit a formal organization application, letter of interest, resume, two personal references, two letters of recommendation, writing samples for literary and marketing internships. Application deadline: March 31 for fall interns. World Wide Web: http://www.mccarter.org.

MERRIMACK REPERTORY THEATRE
50 East Merrimack Street
Lowell, Massachusetts 01852

General Information Professional theater producing 7 quality productions from September through June. Established in 1979. Number of employees: 20. Number of internship applications received each year: 30.
Internships Available ▶ *2 administrative interns:* responsibilities include assisting administrative staff with special projects, data entry, answering phones, bulk mailings, and typing. Candidates should have ability to work independently, computer skills, organizational skills, personal interest in the field, self-motivation, strong interpersonal skills. Duration is flexible (at least 12 weeks). Unpaid. ▶ *4 production interns:* responsibilities include assisting production staff in areas of stage management, electrics, and scenery. Candidates should have ability to work independently, knowledge of field, personal interest in the field, self-motivation, strong interpersonal skills. Duration is 9 months. Position available as unpaid or paid. Open to high school students, recent high school graduates, college freshmen, college sophomores, college juniors, college seniors, recent college graduates, graduate students. International applications accepted.
Benefits Possible full-time employment, willing to act as a professional reference, willing to complete paperwork for educational credit, willing to provide letters of recommendation, 2 free tickets to each production.
Contact Write, call, fax, or e-mail Linda Trudel, Office Manager. Phone: 978-454-6324 Ext. 224. Fax: 978-934-0166. E-mail: info@merrimackrep.org. In-person interview recommended (telephone interview accepted). Applicants must submit a resume, three personal references. Applications are accepted continuously. World Wide Web: http://www.merrimackrep.org.

MILWAUKEE REPERTORY THEATER
108 East Wells Street
Milwaukee, Wisconsin 53202

General Information Major regional theater producing a broad range of classical and contemporary theater pieces. Established in 1953. Number of employees: 150. Number of internship applications received each year: 75.
Internships Available ▶ *14–16 actors:* responsibilities include acting and understudying on projects. Candidates should have college courses in field, knowledge of field, plan to pursue career in field, self-motivation, strong interpersonal skills. Duration is 1 full season (August to May). Position available as unpaid or at $50 per week. Open to college seniors, recent college graduates, graduate students, individuals reentering the workforce, semi-professional actors. ▶ *3 directing interns:* responsibilities include assisting directors with projects, running understudy rehearsals, and directing readings of new materials. Candidates should have ability to work independently, knowledge of field, oral communica-

Milwaukee Repertory Theater (continued)

tion skills, organizational skills, personal interest in the field, plan to pursue career in field, research skills, strong interpersonal skills, strong leadership ability, writing skills. Duration is 1 full season (August to May). Position available as unpaid or at $50 per week. Open to college seniors, recent college graduates, graduate students, individuals reentering the workforce, early career directors. ▶ *1 literary intern:* responsibilities include reading new scripts, researching projects, and assisting with research for specific productions. Candidates should have ability to work independently, editing skills, knowledge of field, organizational skills, personal interest in the field, research skills, self-motivation, writing skills. Duration is 1 full season (August to May). Position available as unpaid or at $50 per week. Open to college seniors, recent college graduates, graduate students, individuals reentering the workforce, semi-professional dramaturgs or literary managers. ▶ *1 production apprentice (lights and sound):* responsibilities include assisting light and sound supervisor in the preparation of designs for shows at the Milwaukee Repertory; intern will also run "A Christmas Carol" crew. Candidates should have analytical skills, declared college major in field, experience in the field, organizational skills, plan to pursue career in field, self-motivation, strong interpersonal skills. Duration is August 1 to May 12. $7.50 per hour. Open to recent college graduates, graduate students. ▶ *2 production apprentices (A Christmas Carol):* responsibilities include assignment in specific areas of production including electrics, sound, paint, and running the production of "A Christmas Carol" at the Pabst Theater. Candidates should have declared college major in field, experience in the field, personal interest in the field, self-motivation, strong interpersonal skills. Duration is November 4 to December 27. $225 per week. Open to high school seniors, recent college graduates, graduate students. International applications accepted.

Benefits Free housing, job counseling, opportunity to attend seminars/workshops, willing to act as a professional reference, willing to complete paperwork for educational credit, willing to provide letters of recommendation, points toward an Actors Equity status.

Contact Write, call, or e-mail Sandy Ernst, Intern Company Director. Phone: 414-224-1761 Ext. 374. Fax: 414-224-9097. E-mail: sernst@milwaukeerep.com. In-person interview recommended (telephone interview accepted). Applicants must submit a formal organization application, resume, writing sample, three personal references, three letters of recommendation, auditions required for acting internships. Application deadline: April 1 for acting interns. World Wide Web: http://www.milwaukeerep.com.

MONTE BROWN DANCE
1170 Broadway
New York, New York 10001

General Information International 9-member contemporary touring dance company. Established in 1981. Number of employees: 9. Number of internship applications received each year: 5.

Internships Available ▶ *1 administrative intern:* responsibilities include assisting with duties related to fund-raising, booking, financial management, programming, marketing, attending staff and board meetings, taking turns with the management staff in the general upkeep of the office/studio. Candidates should have interest in arts administration. Duration is one summer or 1-2 semesters. Unpaid. Open to college juniors, college seniors, recent college graduates, graduate students.

Benefits Names of contacts, opportunity to attend seminars/workshops, willing to complete paperwork for educational credit, willing to provide letters of recommendation, 3 hours of credit if arranged by student in advance of internship.

Contact Write, call, fax, or e-mail Managing Director. Phone: 212-251-0789. Fax: 212-251-0743. E-mail: montebrowndance@earthlink.net. In-person interview required. Applicants must submit a letter of interest, resume. Applications are accepted continuously. World Wide Web: http://www.montebrowndance.org.

THE NEW CONSERVATORY THEATRE CENTER
25 Van Ness Avenue, Lower Lobby
San Francisco, California 94102

General Information Nonprofit theater school and performing arts company for children ages 7-18 emphasizing new and socially aware plays for family audiences; offers seven educational theater touring companies for youths in grades K-12; school provides theater and musical theater training as well as performance opportunities for youth ages 7-18. Established in 1981. Number of employees: 20. Number of internship applications received each year: 25.

Internships Available ▶ *3 Pride Season interns:* responsibilities include working in production (stage management, design, or with assistant directors); program is designed to feature work for and by gay and lesbian artists. Candidates should have ability to work independently, analytical skills, office skills, oral communication skills, personal interest in the field, self-motivation, strong interpersonal skills. Duration is flexible (evening hours). Position available as unpaid or at $5.75–$7 per hour. Open to college freshmen, college sophomores, college juniors, college seniors. ▶ *1 development intern.* Candidates should have ability to work independently, analytical skills, computer skills, editing skills, office skills, oral communication skills, organizational skills, plan to pursue career in field, research skills, self-motivation, strong interpersonal skills, strong leadership ability, writing skills. Duration is 3–6 months. Position available as unpaid or at $5.75–$9 per hour. Open to high school students, recent high school graduates, college freshmen, college sophomores, college juniors, college seniors, recent college graduates, graduate students. ▶ *2 general audience interns:* responsibilities include working in production or audience development and marketing. Candidates should have ability to work independently, office skills, oral communication skills, organizational skills, strong interpersonal skills, strong leadership ability. Duration is flexible (evening hours). Position available as unpaid or at $5.75–$7 per hour. Open to recent high school graduates, college freshmen, college sophomores, college juniors, college seniors, recent college graduates. ▶ *1 marketing and promotion intern.* Candidates should have ability to work independently, college courses in field, computer skills, knowledge of field, office skills, oral communication skills, personal interest in the field, research skills, self-motivation, strong interpersonal skills, strong leadership ability, writing skills. Duration is 3–9 months. Position available as unpaid or at $7–$9 per hour. Open to college freshmen, college sophomores, college juniors, college seniors, recent college graduates, graduate students. ▶ *3 teaching assistants.* Candidates should have oral communication skills, strong interpersonal skills, strong leadership ability. Duration is 1–9 months. Position available as unpaid or at $5.75–$6.75 per hour. Open to recent high school graduates, college freshmen, college sophomores, college juniors, college seniors, recent college graduates, graduate students, must be at least 18 years old. ▶ *1 touring program intern:* responsibilities include providing technical assistance for Youth Aware program, a 7-production touring program that travels to schools in northern California. Candidates should have ability to work with others, analytical skills, computer skills, office skills, oral communication skills, organizational skills, personal interest in the field, research skills, self-motivation, strong leadership ability, writing skills. Duration is 3–9 months. Position available as unpaid or at $5.75–$7 per hour. Open to recent high school graduates, college freshmen, college juniors, college seniors, career changers. International applications accepted.

Benefits On-the-job training, opportunity to attend seminars/workshops, possible full-time employment, travel reimbursement, willing to provide letters of recommendation.

Contact Write or through World Wide Web site Mr. Ed Decker, Executive Director. No phone calls. In-person interview recommended (telephone interview accepted). Application deadline: April 1 for summer, July 1 for fall. World Wide Web: http://www.nctcsf.org.

NEW JERSEY SHAKESPEARE FESTIVAL
36 Madison Avenue
Madison, New Jersey 07940

General Information Actor's Equity theater devoted to producing the works of Shakespeare and other classic masterworks. Established in 1962. Number of employees: 250. Number of internship applications received each year: 500.

Internships Available ▶ *2 box office interns:* responsibilities include functioning as junior staff members, dealing with the public, and learning the important and intricate workings of ticketing procedures. Candidates should have ability to work independently, computer skills, knowledge of field, office skills, oral communication skills, organizational skills, strong interpersonal skills. Duration is flexible. Unpaid. ▶ *3–5 costume design interns:* responsibilities include assisting costume shop supervisor and designers for the productions. Candidates should have ability to work independently, ability to work with others, college courses in field, knowledge of field, oral communication skills, personal interest in the field, plan to pursue career in field. Duration is summer (late May through August) or fall (mid-August through December). Unpaid. ▶ *5 directing interns:* responsibilities include assisting on mainstage productions, coaching apprentices on scenes and monologues, and directing projects with non-equity company members. Candidates should have ability to work independently, college courses in field, knowledge of field, oral communication skills, plan to pursue career in field, research skills, self-motivation, strong interpersonal skills, strong leadership ability, written communication skills. Duration is flexible. Unpaid. ▶ *1–2 house management interns:* responsibilities include functioning as house manager for the festival, reporting to the managing director, and dealing with the public. Candidates should have ability to work independently, analytical skills, experience in the field, office skills, oral communication skills, organizational skills, self-motivation, strong interpersonal skills, strong leadership ability, written communication skills. Duration is flexible. Unpaid. ▶ *3 lighting design interns:* responsibilities include assisting with mainstage productions and working under the supervision of the master electrician. Candidates should have ability to work independently, college courses in field, computer skills, knowledge of field, personal interest in the field, strong interpersonal skills. Duration is flexible. Unpaid. ▶ *2 production interns:* responsibilities include assisting with logistical operations, including transporting actors, pricing and purchasing supplies, theater maintenance, and load-ins. Candidates should have ability to work independently, analytical skills, computer skills, office skills, oral communication skills, organizational skills, personal interest in the field, research skills, self-motivation, strong interpersonal skills, written communication skills. Duration is flexible. Unpaid. ▶ *2 props interns:* responsibilities include coordinating and acquiring props for each show and acting as properties manager throughout the season. Candidates should have experience in the field, oral communication skills, personal interest in the field, research skills, strong interpersonal skills, painting and craftwork experience. Duration is flexible. Unpaid. ▶ *3–4 set design interns:* responsibilities include assisting with the construction and painting of sets and props for each show. Candidates should have ability to work independently, college courses in field, knowledge of field, plan to pursue career in field, research skills, strong interpersonal skills, painting skills, carpentry skills. Duration is summer (May through August) or fall (August through December). Unpaid. ▶ *1–2 sound design interns:* responsibilities include working directly with resident sound designer and taking responsibility for the operation of sound for each show. Candidates should have ability to work independently, ability to work with others, computer skills, editing skills, knowledge of field, oral communication skills, research skills. Duration is flexible. Unpaid. ▶ *6 stage management interns:* responsibilities include assisting Equity stage managers for each show. Candidates should have analytical skills, computer skills, knowledge of field, office skills, oral communication skills, organizational skills, personal interest in the field, plan to pursue career in field, strong interpersonal skills, written communication skills. Duration is summer (May through August) or fall (August through December). Unpaid. ▶ *2–4 technical production interns:* responsibilities include working as part of the team that builds and mounts productions for the festival. Candidates should have ability to work independently, analytical skills, knowledge of field, organizational skills, personal interest in the field, research skills, strong interpersonal skills, drafting skills (preferred). Duration is flexible. Unpaid. ▶ *6 theater administration interns:* responsibilities include working in publicity, development, general management, and/or casting divisions. Candidates should have ability to work independently, computer skills, editing skills, office skills, oral communication skills, organizational skills, personal interest in the field, research skills, strong interpersonal skills, writing skills, experience in specific area (preferred). Duration is summer (May through August) or fall (August through December). Unpaid. Open to college freshmen, college sophomores, college juniors, college seniors, recent college graduates, graduate students, law students, career changers, individuals reentering the workforce. International applications accepted.

Benefits Formal training, housing at a cost, job counseling, names of contacts, opportunity to attend seminars/workshops, possible full-time employment, travel reimbursement, willing to act as a professional reference, willing to complete paperwork for educational credit, willing to provide letters of recommendation, stipend for returning interns.

Contact Write, fax, or e-mail Jake Berger, Education Associate. Fax: 973-408-3361. E-mail: jberger@njshakespeare.org. No phone calls. In-person interview recommended (telephone interview accepted). Applicants must submit a formal organization application, letter of interest, resume, portfolio, three personal references, work samples if applicable to area of interest. Application deadline: May 15 for summer, September 1 for fall. Fees: $25. World Wide Web: http://www.njshakespeare.org.

NEW YORK STATE THEATRE INSTITUTE
Russell Sage Campus, 37 First Street
Troy, New York 12180

General Information Professional theater company and statewide arts-in-education program that develops one new musical theater production a season for family audiences, and performs a range of classical, modern, contemporary, and new works for school, family, and general audiences. Established in 1976. Number of employees: 32. Number of internship applications received each year: 100.

Internships Available ▶ *20–30 interns:* responsibilities include working in areas of technical theater, arts management, performance, and arts-in-education; participating in the operation of a professional theater. Candidates should have theater skills. Duration is 5 months. Unpaid. Open to high school seniors, recent high school graduates, college freshmen, college sophomores, college juniors, college seniors, recent college graduates, graduate students, career changers, individuals reentering the workforce. International applications accepted.

Benefits Formal training, job counseling, names of contacts, opportunity to attend seminars/workshops, travel reimbursement, tuition assistance, willing to complete paperwork for educational credit, willing to provide letters of recommendation, academic credit granted by State University of New York at Albany and Russell Sage College.

Contact Write, call, fax, e-mail, or through World Wide Web site Ms. Arlene Leff, Intern Program Administrator/Education Director. Phone: 518-274-3573. Fax: 518-274-3815. E-mail: nysti@capital. net. In-person interview recommended (telephone interview accepted). Application deadline: June 1 for summer, December 1 for spring. World Wide Web: http://www.nysti.org.

NORTH SHORE MUSIC THEATRE
62 Dunham Road, PO Box 62
Beverly, Massachusetts 01915-0062

General Information Professional theater dedicated to the American musical and programs for young audiences, serving over 300,000 patrons from April through December. Established in 1955. Number of employees: 100. Unit of North Shore Community Arts Foundation, Beverly, Massachusetts. Number of internship applications received each year: 100.

Internships Available ▶ *2 company management interns:* responsibilities include assisting company manager with housing, transporta-

North Shore Music Theatre (continued)

tion, and services for Equity companies and concert road groups. Candidates should have office skills, self-motivation, strong interpersonal skills. Duration is 4–8 months. $200 per week. Open to individuals 21 years of age and older. ▶ *2–4 electrics interns:* responsibilities include hanging and focusing instruments and running follow spots for musicals and concerts. Candidates should have strong interpersonal skills, no fear of heights. Duration is 4–8 months. $200 per week. Open to individuals 18 years of age and older. ▶ *6–8 production assistants:* responsibilities include working within various departments to gain basic understanding and assisting in various departments with show runs. Candidates should have strong interpersonal skills. Duration is 4–8 months. $200 per week. Open to individuals 18 years of age and older. ▶ *1 scenic art intern:* responsibilities include scenic painting for musicals and concerts; emphasis is on painting 3-dimensional units. Candidates should have ability to work independently, ability to work with others, experience in the field, personal interest in the field. Duration is 4–8 months. $200 per week. Open to individuals 18 years of age and older. ▶ *2 sound interns:* responsibilities include maintaining equipment, sound setup, and operating wireless microphones for musicals and concerts. Candidates should have knowledge of field, personal interest in the field, plan to pursue career in field, strong interpersonal skills. Duration is 4–8 months. $200 per week. Open to individuals 18 years of age and older. ▶ *1–2 stage management interns:* responsibilities include assisting Equity stage manager or running crew supervisor in rehearsing and running musicals and children's shows. Candidates should have knowledge of field, personal interest in the field, self-motivation, strong interpersonal skills, strong leadership ability. Duration is 4–8 months. $200 per week. Open to individuals 18 years of age and older. ▶ *1–2 wardrobe interns:* responsibilities include providing fitting, maintenance, and dressing needs for musicals and concerts. Candidates should have knowledge of field, strong interpersonal skills, sewing skills. Duration is 4–8 months. $200 per week. Open to individuals 18 years of age and older. International applications accepted.

Benefits Names of contacts, opportunity to attend seminars/workshops, possible full-time employment, willing to complete paperwork for educational credit, willing to provide letters of recommendation, educational stipend.

Contact Write, fax, or e-mail Associate Production Manager. Fax: 978-922-0768. E-mail: amignone@nsmt.org. No phone calls. In-person interview recommended (telephone interview accepted). Applicants must submit a formal organization application, letter of interest, resume, three personal references. Applications are accepted continuously. World Wide Web: http://www.nsmt.org.

OPERA COMPANY OF PHILADELPHIA
1420 Locust Street, Suite 210
Philadelphia, Pennsylvania 19102

General Information Company presenting performances of grand opera in the original language of composition with internationally acclaimed performers and rising young talent, staged at the Academy of Music. Established in 1975. Number of employees: 30. Number of internship applications received each year: 20.

Internships Available ▶ *1 box office intern:* responsibilities include taking subscription and single ticket orders, performing data entry, answering phones, and filing. Candidates should have ability to work with others, computer skills, office skills, oral communication skills. Duration is flexible. Unpaid. ▶ *1 business office intern:* responsibilities include data entry, accounting, filing, and typing. Candidates should have computer skills, experience in the field, office skills. Duration is flexible. Unpaid. ▶ *1 development intern:* responsibilities include typing and data entry, filing, recordkeeping, planning special events, scheduling, and acknowledging donors. Candidates should have computer skills, knowledge of field, office skills. Duration is flexible. Unpaid. ▶ *1–3 education office interns:* responsibilities include coordinating dress rehearsal attendance, corresponding, entering data, maintaining teacher contact, coordinating special events, assisting with general clerical and administrative tasks, researching opera background for educational materials, and some public relations duties. Candidates should

have computer skills, editing skills, office skills, personal interest in the field, research skills, writing skills. Duration is flexible. Unpaid. Open to anyone with the desire to work with the Company. ▶ *1 general administration intern:* responsibilities include answering phones, typing, and filing. Candidates should have ability to work with others, computer skills, office skills, organizational skills, personal interest in the field. Duration is flexible. Unpaid. ▶ *1 marketing intern:* responsibilities include creating target marketing mailings, researching possible audience members, and designing advertisements. Candidates should have computer skills, office skills, oral communication skills, personal interest in the field, written communication skills. Duration is flexible. Unpaid. ▶ *1 public relations intern:* responsibilities include assisting with mass mailings; editing and producing press releases, media packages, and newsletters; scheduling press and artists' interviews and conferences; and filing. Candidates should have computer skills, editing skills, office skills, organizational skills, personal interest in the field. Duration is flexible. Unpaid. International applications accepted.

Benefits Names of contacts, possible full-time employment, willing to complete paperwork for educational credit, willing to provide letters of recommendation, work-study granted to in-state residents (when possible).

Contact Write, call, fax, or e-mail Judy L. Williams, Assistant Director of Education. Phone: 215-893-3600 Ext. 216. Fax: 215-893-7801. E-mail: williams@operaphilly.com. In-person interview recommended (telephone interview accepted). Applicants must submit a letter of interest, resume. Applications are accepted continuously. World Wide Web: http://www.operaphilly.com.

PAN ASIAN REPERTORY THEATRE
47 Great Jones Street
New York, New York 10012

General Information Professional theater celebrating Asian-American expressiveness, producing new plays, Asian masterworks in translation, and Western classics in non-traditional settings. Established in 1977. Number of employees: 3. Number of internship applications received each year: 50.

Internships Available ▶ *Administrative interns.* Candidates should have ability to work with others, college courses in field, knowledge of field, oral communication skills, personal interest in the field, self-motivation. Duration is 3 months (minimum). Paid. ▶ *1 marketing intern.* Candidates should have ability to work with others, college courses in field, knowledge of field, self-motivation. Duration is 3 months (minimum). Paid. ▶ *Production interns.* Candidates should have ability to work with others, college courses in field, knowledge of field, personal interest in the field, self-motivation. Duration is flexible. Paid. Open to college freshmen, college sophomores, college juniors, college seniors, recent college graduates, graduate students. International applications accepted.

Benefits Names of contacts, willing to complete paperwork for educational credit, willing to provide letters of recommendation, small stipend for transportation.

Contact Write, call, fax, or e-mail Erika Hirokawa, Educational Marketing Coordinator. Phone: 212-505-5655. Fax: 212-505-6014. E-mail: panasian@aol.com. Applicants must submit a letter of interest, resume. Applications are accepted continuously. World Wide Web: http://www.panasianrep.org.

THE PEARL THEATRE COMPANY
80 Saint Mark's Place
New York, New York 10003

General Information Nonprofit classical theater company. Established in 1982. Number of employees: 9. Number of internship applications received each year: 100.

Internships Available ▶ *1 administrative intern:* responsibilities include assisting in all administrative departments including marketing, development, finance, production, and artistic direction. Candidates should have ability to work independently, computer skills, knowledge of field, office skills, oral communication skills, personal interest in the field, plan to pursue career in field, self-motivation, strong interpersonal skills, writing skills. Duration is 5-10 months, from August through June. $175 weekly stipend.

Open to college juniors, college seniors, recent college graduates, career changers. ▶ *1 costume intern:* responsibilities include assisting costume designer on 5 classical plays and wardrobe maintenance. Candidates should have ability to work independently, ability to work with others, plan to pursue career in field, self-motivation, positive attitude, reasonable background in theatrical costumes. Duration is 5-10 months (full-time), from August through June. $175 weekly stipend. Open to recent college graduates. ▶ *2 stage management interns:* responsibilities include assisting stage manager with 3 to 5 productions, scheduling, prompting, blocking, production meetings, light board, sound, and floor managing. Candidates should have ability to work independently, analytical skills, knowledge of field, oral communication skills, organizational skills, plan to pursue career in field, self-motivation, strong interpersonal skills. Duration is 6 to 10 months (full-time), from August through June. $175 weekly stipend. Open to recent college graduates. International applications accepted.

Benefits Job counseling, names of contacts, on-the-job training, possible full-time employment, willing to act as a professional reference, willing to complete paperwork for educational credit, willing to provide letters of recommendation, Equity membership candidacy points for stage management interns.

Contact Write, fax, or e-mail Meghan Beals, Programs Manager. Fax: 212-505-3404. E-mail: mbeals@pearltheatre.org. No phone calls. In-person interview recommended (telephone interview accepted). Applicants must submit a letter of interest, resume, two writing samples, three personal references. Applications are accepted continuously. World Wide Web: http://www.pearltheatre.org.

PENINSULA PLAYERS
W4351 Peninsula Players Road
Fish Creek, Wisconsin 54212-9799

General Information Professional resident summer theater. Established in 1935. Number of employees: 40. Number of internship applications received each year: 40.

Internships Available ▶ *2–4 administrative interns:* responsibilities include assisting with box office operation, promotion and publicity, accounting, and house management. Candidates should have office skills, oral communication skills, personal interest in the field, strong interpersonal skills, written communication skills. Duration is 1 summer, June 1 to Labor Day. $75 per week. ▶ *6 production interns:* responsibilities include working in areas of costume, carpentry, electrical, design, props, and stage management. Candidates should have ability to work with others, knowledge of field, personal interest in the field, self-motivation. Duration is 1 summer, June 1 to Labor Day. $75 per week. Open to high school seniors, recent high school graduates, college freshmen, college sophomores, college juniors, college seniors, recent college graduates, graduate students, career changers. International applications accepted.

Benefits Free housing, free meals, possible full-time employment, travel reimbursement, willing to act as a professional reference, willing to complete paperwork for educational credit, willing to provide letters of recommendation.

Contact Write or call Mr. Todd Schmidt, General Manager. Phone: 920-868-3287. Telephone interview required. Applicants must submit a formal organization application, letter of interest, resume, two letters of recommendation. Application deadline: May 1. World Wide Web: http://www.peninsulaplayers.com.

PIONEER PLAYHOUSE
840 Stanford Road
Danville, Kentucky 40422

General Information Summer stock theater that produces plays. Established in 1950. Number of employees: 30. Number of internship applications received each year: 50.

Internships Available ▶ *5–10 acting and technical interns:* responsibilities include assisting in all aspects of play productions. Candidates should have ability to work with others, plan to pursue career in field, self-motivation, strong leadership ability. Duration is June to September. Unpaid. Open to high school students, recent high school graduates, college freshmen, college sophomores, college juniors, college seniors, recent college graduates, graduate students, law students, career changers, individuals reentering the workforce, must be between the ages of 14 and 60. International applications accepted.

Benefits Housing at a cost, meals at a cost, names of contacts, on-the-job training, opportunity to attend seminars/workshops, possible full-time employment, tuition assistance, willing to act as a professional reference, willing to complete paperwork for educational credit, willing to provide letters of recommendation.

International Internships Available.

Contact Write, call, or fax Col. Eben-Henson, Production Manager. Phone: 859-236-2747. Fax: 859-236-2341. E-mail: pioneer@mis.net. In-person interview recommended. Applicants must submit a letter of interest, $947 tuition includes room and board (high school students); $500 tuition (college students) includes room and board. Application deadline: May 1. World Wide Web: http://www.pioneerplayhouse.com.

PITTSBURGH CIVIC LIGHT OPERA
719 Liberty Avenue
Pittsburgh, Pennsylvania 15222

General Information Producer of Broadway-scale, professional musicals in a 2,837-seat theater during the summer. Established in 1946. Number of employees: 20. Number of internship applications received each year: 50.

Internships Available ▶ *1–2 Gene Kelly Awards interns:* responsibilities include coordinating award ceremony, patterned after Tony Awards for Allegheny County High Schools, marketing to production. Candidates should have computer skills, oral communication skills, personal interest in the field, self-motivation, strong interpersonal skills, strong leadership ability, writing skills. Duration is 3–4 months. $50 per week. ▶ *1 summer development intern.* Candidates should have ability to work independently, computer skills, office skills, oral communication skills, organizational skills, strong interpersonal skills, written communication skills. Duration is 8–10 weeks. $75 per week. ▶ *1 summer education and outreach intern:* responsibilities include performing general duties including data entry and assisting with a variety of outreach programs. Candidates should have computer skills, office skills, oral communication skills, organizational skills, strong interpersonal skills, written communication skills. Duration is 8–10 weeks. $75 per week. ▶ *1 summer general administration intern:* responsibilities include working for the executive director and handling a full range of administrative tasks in company office. Candidates should have ability to work independently, computer skills, office skills, oral communication skills, organizational skills, research skills, self-motivation, strong interpersonal skills, written communication skills. Duration is 8–10 weeks. $75 per week. ▶ *1 summer hair/wig intern:* responsibilities include assisting wig and hair designer with preparation, styling, and maintaining of performers' hair and wigs. Candidates should have ability to work independently, knowledge of field, personal interest in the field, self-motivation, strong interpersonal skills. Duration is 8–10 weeks. $75 per week. ▶ *1 summer promotion/marketing intern:* responsibilities include performing a broad range of tasks including writing press releases, distributing flyers and posters; and escorting stars on interviews. Candidates should have ability to work independently, college courses in field, computer skills, editing skills, office skills, oral communication skills, organizational skills, personal interest in the field, self-motivation, strong interpersonal skills, writing skills. Duration is 8–10 weeks. $75 per week. ▶ *1–8 technical interns:* responsibilities include hands-on experience in technical aspects of theater, including sound, lighting, properties, stage management and production management. Candidates should have ability to work independently, college courses in field, computer skills, knowledge of field, oral communication skills, personal interest in the field, self-motivation, strong interpersonal skills, strong leadership ability, written communication skills. Duration is 8–10 weeks. $75 per week. Open to recent high school graduates, college freshmen, college sophomores, college juniors, college seniors. International applications accepted.

Benefits Names of contacts, on-the-job training, willing to act as a professional reference, willing to complete paperwork for educational credit, willing to provide letters of recommendation.

Pittsburgh Civic Light Opera (continued)

Contact Write, call, fax, e-mail, or through World Wide Web site Teresa Silvestri, Education Programs Manager, Penn Avenue Place, 130 CLO Academy Way, 8th Floor, Pittsburgh, Pennsylvania 15222. Phone: 412-281-2234 Ext. 2. Fax: 412-281-2232. E-mail: tsilvestri@pittsburghclo.org. In-person interview recommended (telephone interview accepted). Applicants must submit a formal organization application, letter of interest, resume, two personal references. Application deadline: March 9 for summer, December 20 for spring. World Wide Web: http://www.pittsburghCLO.org.

PLAYHOUSE ON THE SQUARE
51 South Cooper
Memphis, Tennessee 38104

General Information Nonprofit professional theater with a mission to create challenging, truthful, entertaining, and culturally diverse high-quality theater that reflects, improves, and reaches the present and future community. Established in 1969. Number of employees: 23. Number of internship applications received each year: 300.

Internships Available ▶ *7 acting interns:* responsibilities include acting and technical or administrative work. Candidates should have ability to work with others, knowledge of field, plan to pursue career in field, self-motivation. Duration is 1 year. $100 per week. Open to recent college graduates. ▶ *1 administrative intern:* responsibilities include assisting with clerical duties, box office, house management, and subscription drive. Candidates should have ability to work independently, computer skills, knowledge of field, oral communication skills, self-motivation, strong leadership ability. Duration is 1 year. $100 per week. Open to recent college graduates. ▶ *1 costumes intern:* responsibilities include assisting with costuming. Candidates should have college courses in field, knowledge of field, organizational skills, plan to pursue career in field, self-motivation. Duration is 1 year. $100 per week. Open to recent college graduates. ▶ *1 props intern:* responsibilities include gathering, building, renting, buying, run, and organizing properties. Candidates should have ability to work independently, ability to work with others, experience in the field, plan to pursue career in field, self-motivation. Duration is 1 year. $100 per week. Open to recent college graduates. ▶ *2 stage management interns:* responsibilities include assisting with management and technical tasks. Candidates should have ability to work independently, ability to work with others, knowledge of field, organizational skills, self-motivation, strong leadership ability. Duration is 1 year. $100 per week. Open to recent college graduates. ▶ *1 technical/set design intern:* responsibilities include assisting with set construction. Candidates should have ability to work with others, knowledge of field, organizational skills, personal interest in the field, self-motivation. Duration is 1 year. $100 per week.

Benefits Free housing, health insurance, job counseling, names of contacts, on-the-job training, possible full-time employment, willing to act as a professional reference, willing to complete paperwork for educational credit, willing to provide letters of recommendation, free utilities, local phone, laundry facilities.

Contact Write Jackie Nichols, Executive Producer. Phone: 901-725-0776. Fax: 901-272-7530. In-person interview required. Applicants must submit a resume, two letters of recommendation. Applications are accepted continuously. World Wide Web: http://playhouseonthesquare.org.

PORTLAND STAGE COMPANY
PO Box 1458
Portland, Maine 04104

General Information Resident professional theater producing a 6-play mainstage season and providing numerous other educational and cultural services. Established in 1974. Number of employees: 30. Number of internship applications received each year: 100.

Internships Available ▶ *1–3 directing/dramaturgy interns:* responsibilities include assisting directors on mainstage productions, conducting dramaturgical research, and assisting artistic staff on day-to-day administrative activities. Candidates should have knowledge of field, plan to pursue career in field, research skills, self-motivation, strong interpersonal skills, writing skills. Duration is September to May. $65 per week. Open to recent high school graduates, college freshmen, college sophomores, college juniors, college seniors, recent college graduates, graduate students. ▶ *1 literary/education intern:* responsibilities include assisting literary staff with reading and evaluating scripts, playwright correspondence, researching and preparing educational resource guides, and assisting with student matinees, school workshops and discussions. Candidates should have ability to work independently, computer skills, oral communication skills, organizational skills, research skills, writing skills. Duration is September to May. $65 per week. Open to college freshmen, college sophomores, college juniors, college seniors, recent college graduates, graduate students. ▶ *2 marketing/development interns:* responsibilities include assisting with publicity, media relations, fund-raising, grant research, ticket promotions, press releases, and all aspects of promoting a regional theater. Candidates should have ability to work independently, computer skills, knowledge of field, personal interest in the field, self-motivation, writing skills. Duration is September to May. $65 per week. Open to college freshmen, college sophomores, college juniors, college seniors, recent college graduates, graduate students. ▶ *3–5 production interns:* responsibilities include working in all production departments, with areas of specialization in carpentry/props, costumes/wardrobe, electrics/sound; assisting construction and maintenance; and serving on run crew. Candidates should have ability to work independently, ability to work with others, knowledge of field, plan to pursue career in field, self-motivation. Duration is September to May. $65 per week. Open to recent high school graduates, college freshmen, college sophomores, college juniors, college seniors, recent college graduates, graduate students. ▶ *2 stage management interns:* responsibilities include assisting Equity stage managers in all areas of production and preproduction. Candidates should have ability to work with others, knowledge of field, organizational skills, plan to pursue career in field, self-motivation. Duration is September to May. $65 per week. Open to recent high school graduates, college freshmen, college sophomores, college juniors, college seniors, recent college graduates, graduate students. International applications accepted.

Benefits Formal training, free housing, on-the-job training, opportunity to attend seminars/workshops, possible full-time employment, willing to act as a professional reference, willing to complete paperwork for educational credit, willing to provide letters of recommendation.

Contact Write, call, fax, e-mail, or through World Wide Web site Lindsay Cummings, Education Manager. Phone: 207-774-1043. Fax: 207-774-0576. E-mail: portstage@aol.com. Telephone interview required. Applicants must submit a formal organization application, letter of interest, resume, writing sample, two letters of recommendation. Application deadline: April 30 for full-season positions; continuous for partial-season positions. World Wide Web: http://www.portlandstage.com.

PRIMARY STAGES
131 West 45th Street, 2nd Floor
New York, New York 10036

General Information Producer of new American plays. Established in 1985. Number of employees: 6. Number of internship applications received each year: 75.

Internships Available ▶ *1–4 literary interns:* responsibilities include reading and analysis of play submissions, upkeep of database, correspondence with agents/playwrights, participation in attending workshops/readings in New York City. Candidates should have analytical skills, computer skills, office skills, personal interest in the field, self-motivation, written communication skills. Duration is 9 weeks or more. Unpaid. Open to college juniors, college seniors, recent college graduates, graduate students, career changers. ▶ *1–4 production interns:* responsibilities include assisting the set, lighting, costume, or sound designer in research and implementation of production design. Candidates should have ability to work with others, knowledge of field, oral communication skills, personal interest in the field, self-motivation. Duration is 5 weeks or more. Unpaid. Open to college freshmen, college sophomores, college juniors, college seniors, recent college graduates, graduate students, career changers, individuals reentering the workforce. ▶ *1–4 publicity and marketing interns:* responsibilities include assisting publicity/marketing staff in marketing production, special events, and subscription campaigns. Candidates should have oral communication skills, self-motivation, strong interpersonal skills, writing skills. Duration is flexible. Unpaid. Open to college freshmen, college sophomores, college juniors, college seniors, recent college graduates, graduate students, career changers, individuals reentering the workforce. ▶ *1–4 stage management interns:* responsibilities include assisting the manager in rehearsals and serving as running crew backstage. Candidates should have knowledge of field, oral communication skills, personal interest in the field, self-motivation, strong interpersonal skills. Duration is 9 weeks or more. Unpaid. Open to college freshmen, college sophomores, college juniors, college seniors, recent college graduates, graduate students, career changers, individuals reentering the workforce.

Benefits Job counseling, names of contacts, on-the-job training, opportunity to attend seminars/workshops, willing to complete paperwork for educational credit, willing to provide letters of recommendation.

Contact Write, fax, or e-mail Tyler Marchant, Associate Artistic Director. Fax: 212-840-9725. E-mail: tyler@primarystages.com. No phone calls. In-person interview recommended (telephone interview accepted). Applicants must submit a letter of interest, resume, two personal references. Applications are accepted continuously.

PULSE ENSEMBLE THEATRE
432 West 42nd Street
New York, New York 10036

General Information Ensemble theater company that produces mainstage shows, Bare Bones Classic Season (a studio season), and readings of new plays. Established in 1989. Number of employees: 8. Number of internship applications received each year: 60.

Internships Available ▶ *12–20 acting interns:* responsibilities include playing small parts in shows and providing general assistance in the preparation of shows. Candidates should have acting experience or training. Duration is 6 months. Unpaid. Open to recent high school graduates, college freshmen, college sophomores, college juniors, college seniors, recent college graduates, graduate students, law students, career changers, individuals reentering the workforce. ▶ *2–4 business management interns.* Candidates should have college courses in field, computer skills, knowledge of field, personal interest in the field, plan to pursue career in field. Duration is flexible. Unpaid. Open to college juniors, college seniors, recent college graduates, graduate students, law students, career changers. ▶ *2–4 directing interns:* responsibilities include assisting the director in taking a play from casting through to performance. Candidates should have ability to work independently, ability to work with others, experience in the field, oral communication skills, research skills, strong leadership ability. Duration is 6–8 weeks. Unpaid. Open to recent high school graduates, college students, recent college graduates, graduate students, individuals reentering the workforce. ▶ *2–6 fund-raising interns:* responsibilities include finding funding sources, helping to complete grant applications, and helping at fund-raising events. Candidates should have ability to work independently, computer skills, knowledge of field, organizational skills, research skills, writing skills. Duration is 3–12 months. Unpaid. Open to recent college graduates, graduate students, law students, career changers. ▶ *2–4 management interns:* responsibilities include assisting the general manager, organizing volunteer groups, and assisting at the box office. Candidates should have ability to work independently, computer skills, organizational skills, personal interest in the field, research skills, writing skills. Duration is 6 months. Unpaid. Open to high school seniors, recent high school graduates, college freshmen, college sophomores, college juniors, college seniors, recent college graduates, graduate students, law students, career changers, individuals reentering the workforce. ▶ *2–4 marketing interns:* responsibilities include typing and distributing publicity and making promotional telephone calls. Candidates should have ability to work independently, computer skills, office skills, organizational skills, research skills, writing skills. Duration is 3 months minimum.

Unpaid. Open to high school seniors, recent high school graduates, college freshmen, college sophomores, college juniors, college seniors, recent college graduates, graduate students, law students, career changers, individuals reentering the workforce. ▶ *2–3 production interns:* responsibilities include setting up scenery, working on sound tapes, and running lighting boards. Candidates should have ability to work independently, knowledge of field, organizational skills, personal interest in the field, research skills, written communication skills. Duration is 3 months minimum. Unpaid. Open to recent high school graduates, college freshmen, college sophomores, college juniors, college seniors, recent college graduates, graduate students, law students, career changers, individuals reentering the workforce. ▶ *1–3 stage management interns:* responsibilities include operating shows and sound and light equipment and setting props. Candidates should have computer skills, editing skills, experience in the field, oral communication skills, personal interest in the field, writing skills. Duration is 2 months minimum. Unpaid. Open to high school seniors, recent high school graduates, college freshmen, college sophomores, college juniors, college seniors, recent college graduates, graduate students, law students, career changers, individuals reentering the workforce. International applications accepted.

Benefits Formal training, job counseling, on-the-job training, opportunity to attend seminars/workshops, possible full-time employment, willing to act as a professional reference, willing to complete paperwork for educational credit, willing to provide letters of recommendation, reimbursement for job-related travel.

Contact Write, e-mail, or through World Wide Web site Alexa Kelly, Artistic Director. E-mail: intern@pulseensembletheatre.org. No phone calls. In-person interview required. Applicants must submit a letter of interest, resume, two letters of recommendation, headshot, audition (for acting interns). Application deadline: June 1 for fall, December 1 for spring. World Wide Web: http://www.pulseensembletheatre.org.

QUEENS THEATER IN THE PARK
PO Box 520069
Flushing, New York 11352

General Information Performing arts center. Established in 1989. Number of employees: 51. Number of internship applications received each year: 20.

Internships Available ▶ *1–3 office interns.* Candidates should have computer skills, office skills, oral communication skills, organizational skills, self-motivation, strong interpersonal skills. Duration is 1 semester. Unpaid. ▶ *1–3 stage production interns:* responsibilities include performing work for theater, assisting stage manager, production manager, and other production personnel. Candidates should have computer skills, knowledge of field, organizational skills, personal interest in the field, self-motivation, strong interpersonal skills. Duration is 1 semester. Unpaid. Open to high school students, recent high school graduates, college freshmen, college sophomores, college juniors, college seniors, recent college graduates, graduate students, law students, career changers, individuals reentering the workforce. International applications accepted.

Benefits On-the-job training, possible full-time employment, willing to act as a professional reference, willing to complete paperwork for educational credit, willing to provide letters of recommendation.

Contact Write, call, fax, or e-mail Ms. Gail Koelln, Development Director. Phone: 718-760-0686. Fax: 718-760-5092. E-mail: qtipgail@aol.com. In-person interview required. Applicants must submit a letter of interest, resume. Applications are accepted continuously. World Wide Web: http://www.queenstheatre.org.

REPERTORIO ESPANOL
138 East 27th Street
New York, New York 10016

General Information Spanish language theater company that presents plays from Spain's Golden Age, contemporary Latin-American classics, and works by new playwrights. Established in 1968. Number of employees: 12. Number of internship applications received each year: 1.

Repertorio Espanol *(continued)*
Internships Available ▶ *Interns:* responsibilities include performing duties in the areas of community affairs, media relations, and fund development; preparing press packages for groups and responding to inquiries; arranging rehearsals, changing sets, helping with various production activities. Candidates should have ability to work independently, ability to work with others, computer skills, knowledge of field, office skills, oral communication skills, plan to pursue career in field, writing skills. Duration is flexible. Unpaid. Open to recent high school graduates, college freshmen, college sophomores, college juniors, college seniors, recent college graduates. International applications accepted.
Benefits Names of contacts, possible full-time employment, willing to complete paperwork for educational credit, willing to provide letters of recommendation, free tickets to performances.
Contact Write, call, fax, or e-mail Allison Astor-Vargas, Special Projects Manager. Phone: 212-889-2850. Fax: 212-686-3732. E-mail: repertorio@mindspring.com. In-person interview recommended (telephone interview accepted). Applicants must submit a letter of interest, resume. Applications are accepted continuously. World Wide Web: http://www.repertorio.org.

ROUNDABOUT THEATRE COMPANY, INC.
231 West 39th Street
New York, New York 10018

General Information Nonprofit Broadway theater presenting revivals of classic plays. Established in 1965. Number of employees: 95. Number of internship applications received each year: 100.
Internships Available ▶ *1 business office intern:* responsibilities include assisting with income and expense controls, clerical duties, and daily operations. Candidates should have computer skills, organizational skills, accounting experience (helpful). Duration is flexible. $10–$40 per day. Open to high school students, recent high school graduates, college freshmen, college sophomores, college juniors, college seniors, recent college graduates, graduate students, law students, career changers. ▶ *3 development interns:* responsibilities include assisting with clerical duties, researching potential donors, and performing specific fund-raising projects. Candidates should have computer skills, oral communication skills, organizational skills, strong interpersonal skills, written communication skills. Duration is flexible. $10–$40 per day. Open to recent high school graduates, college freshmen, college sophomores, college juniors, college seniors, recent college graduates, graduate students. ▶ *1 education intern:* responsibilities include assisting with research and writing of newsletter articles, study guides, and lobby display; assisting with school visits; clerical duties. Candidates should have oral communication skills, organizational skills, research skills, written communication skills, attention to detail. Duration is flexible. $10–$40 per day. Open to high school students, recent high school graduates, college freshmen, college sophomores, college juniors, college seniors, recent college graduates, graduate students, career changers, individuals reentering the workforce. ▶ *1 management intern:* responsibilities include assisting with processing and management of contracts and maintaining company files of past productions. Candidates should have analytical skills, declared college major in field, oral communication skills, organizational skills, self-motivation, written communication skills. Duration is flexible. $10–$40 per day. Open to recent college graduates, graduate students, career changers. ▶ *1 marketing intern:* responsibilities include assisting with clerical duties, ticket sales, press coverage, public relations, subscriber services, and special events. Candidates should have computer skills, oral communication skills, organizational skills, strong interpersonal skills. Duration is flexible. $10–$40 per day. Open to high school students, recent high school graduates, college freshmen, college sophomores, college juniors, college seniors, recent college graduates, graduate students, law students, career changers. ▶ *Production interns:* responsibilities include assisting technicians and carpenters with construction, installation, and maintenance of scenery, props, and lighting equipment; assisting in related office work. Candidates should have ability to work with others, experience in the field, organizational skills. Duration is flexible. $10–$40 per day. Open to high school seniors, recent high school graduates, college freshmen, college sophomores,

college juniors, college seniors, recent college graduates, graduate students, career changers. ▶ *2 ticket services interns:* responsibilities include clerical duties, large mailings, some data entry and phone calls. Candidates should have ability to work independently, oral communication skills, organizational skills. Duration is flexible. $10–$40 per day. Open to high school students, recent high school graduates, college freshmen, college sophomores, college juniors, college seniors, recent college graduates, individuals reentering the workforce.
Benefits Job counseling, names of contacts, on-the-job training, opportunity to attend seminars/workshops, possible full-time employment, travel reimbursement, willing to complete paperwork for educational credit, willing to provide letters of recommendation, stipend available.
Contact Write or fax Philip Alexander, Education Program Manager. Phone: 212-642-9629. Fax: 212-944-8214. In-person interview required. Applicants must submit a letter of interest, resume. Application deadline: March 1 for summer (suggested), August 1 for fall (suggested), November 1 for spring/January term (suggested). World Wide Web: http://www.roundabouttheatre. org.

SAN FRANCISCO OPERA
301 Van Ness Avenue
San Francisco, California 94102

General Information Opera producing a season of international opera and regularly presenting premiers of new operas and commissioned works. Established in 1932. Number of employees: 1,120. Number of internship applications received each year: 100.
Internships Available ▶ *1–2 artistic and musical administration interns:* responsibilities include acting as liaison with artists, managers, and other theaters; conducting research, entering computer data about auditions; organizing audition material; filing confidential artistic information. Candidates should have ability to work independently, computer skills, office skills, organizational skills, personal interest in the field, strong interpersonal skills. Duration is open. Unpaid. Open to recent high school graduates, college freshmen, college sophomores, college juniors, college seniors, recent college graduates, graduate students, individuals reentering the workforce. ▶ *1–2 costume shop interns:* responsibilities include running errands, shopping for fabrics and materials, maintaining notion inventory, sorting fabric samples, recording and arranging trimmings, pulling and replacing costumes from stock. Candidates should have ability to work with others, knowledge of field, oral communication skills, personal interest in the field, self-motivation, good physical stamina in order to move heavy boxes and costumes, as well as freedom from colorblindness and vertigo. Duration is open. Unpaid. Open to recent high school graduates, college freshmen, college sophomores, college juniors, college seniors, recent college graduates, graduate students, career changers, individuals reentering the workforce. ▶ *1–2 development interns:* responsibilities include individual and institutional gifts fund-raising, assisting with grant writing, prospect research, fund-raising systems, planned giving, telefunding, and preparation of collateral materials design, and copy writing. Candidates should have office skills, oral communication skills, self-motivation, strong interpersonal skills, writing skills. Duration is open. Unpaid. Open to recent high school graduates, college freshmen, college sophomores, college juniors, college seniors, recent college graduates, graduate students, career changers. ▶ *1–2 finance/accounting interns:* responsibilities include filing and organizing financial documents, reconciling and analyzing accounts, and assisting with special projects. Candidates should have ability to work with others, analytical skills, computer skills, knowledge of field, organizational skills, self-motivation. Duration is open. Unpaid. Open to recent high school graduates, college freshmen, college sophomores, college juniors, college seniors, recent college graduates, graduate students, career changers, individuals reentering the workforce. ▶ *1–2 guild activities and events interns:* responsibilities include working with the board of directors; assisting with special events, education and outreach program, volunteer management, and fund-raising development. Candidates should have ability to work with others, computer skills, office skills, oral

communication skills, organizational skills, self-motivation, written communication skills. Duration is open. Unpaid. Open to recent high school graduates, college freshmen, college sophomores, college juniors, college seniors, recent college graduates, graduate students, career changers, individuals reentering the workforce.
▶ *1–2 human resources/labor relations interns:* responsibilities include assisting with recruiting/hiring, health and safety fair, employee training and development, managing personnel records, compensation and benefit coordination, and policies and procedures administration. Candidates should have ability to work independently, ability to work with others, computer skills, editing skills, office skills, oral communication skills, organizational skills, self-motivation, writing skills. Duration is open. Unpaid. Open to recent high school graduates, college freshmen, college sophomores, college juniors, college seniors, recent college graduates, graduate students, career changers, individuals reentering the workforce.
▶ *1–2 information systems interns:* responsibilities include assisting with data backup and maintenance, equipment and software inventory management, conducting Internet research and file searches, routine network and hardware maintenance, and with Sybase, C++, Powerbuilder, Access, and RPG programming. Candidates should have ability to work independently, ability to work with others, computer skills, knowledge of field, office skills, personal interest in the field, research skills. Duration is open. Unpaid. Open to recent high school graduates, college freshmen, college sophomores, college juniors, college seniors, recent college graduates, graduate students, career changers, individuals reentering the workforce. ▶ *1–2 marketing interns:* responsibilities include composing collateral copy, collecting art/images for brochures, compiling information from a variety of sources, editing/proofreading documents and coordinating proofreading throughout organization; placing advertisements or event-related media; assisting with budgeting, sales reporting, and compiling statistics. Candidates should have ability to work with others, computer skills, editing skills, oral communication skills, organizational skills, writing skills. Duration is open. Unpaid. Open to recent high school graduates, college freshmen, college sophomores, college juniors, college seniors, recent college graduates, graduate students, career changers, individuals reentering the workforce. ▶ *1–2 opera center interns:* responsibilities include assisting with events and performances, preparations for Western Opera Theater (national touring company), public relations and marketing, artist services, and with various aspects of the Merola Opera Program (11-week training for young artists). Candidates should have ability to work with others, computer skills, oral communication skills, personal interest in the field, written communication skills. Duration is open. Unpaid. Open to recent high school graduates, college freshmen, college sophomores, college juniors, college seniors, recent college graduates, graduate students, career changers, individuals reentering the workforce. ▶ *1–2 orchestra administration interns:* responsibilities include providing general assistance to the orchestra manager by assisting with musicians' employment records, assisting with engaging substitute and extra musicians, assisting with rehearsals and performances, tracking attendance and breaks, and assisting with financial reports. Candidates should have computer skills, oral communication skills, personal interest in the field, strong interpersonal skills, written communication skills. Duration is open. Unpaid. Open to recent high school graduates, college freshmen, college sophomores, college juniors, college seniors, recent college graduates, graduate students, individuals reentering the workforce. ▶ *1–2 public relations interns:* responsibilities include assisting members of public relations team with daily activities, assisting with mailings and photo distribution; maintaining photo and artist files; assisting during performances, events, and conferences when necessary; maintaining press database. Candidates should have ability to work with others, computer skills, editing skills, knowledge of field, office skills, oral communication skills, organizational skills, personal interest in the field, self-motivation, written communication skills. Duration is open. Unpaid. Open to recent high school graduates, college freshmen, college sophomores, college juniors, college seniors, recent college graduates, graduate students, career changers, individuals reentering the workforce. ▶ *1–2 special events interns:* responsibilities include producing and coordinating 75-125 donor recognition and cultivation events per year; development

and management of event budgets and timelines; coordinating event logistics, such as catering, decor, seating, guest check-in; training and supervising volunteers; production of printed materials, such as programs and invitations; enlisting the support of and communicating with the opera's executive office, artistic and production staff, and development and marketing departments. Duration is open. Unpaid. Open to recent high school graduates, college freshmen, college sophomores, college juniors, college seniors, recent college graduates, graduate students, individuals reentering the workforce. ▶ *1–2 technical production interns:* responsibilities include participating in production meetings, assisting with the design and management of productions from scene shop to stage, creating and manipulating information on department network. Candidates should have ability to work with others, computer skills, personal interest in the field. Duration is open. Unpaid. Open to recent high school graduates, college freshmen, college sophomores, college juniors, college seniors, recent college graduates, graduate students, individuals reentering the workforce. International applications accepted.
Benefits Possible full-time employment, willing to act as a professional reference, willing to complete paperwork for educational credit, willing to provide letters of recommendation, opportunity to attend dress rehearsals and performances.
Contact Write, call, fax, e-mail, or through World Wide Web site Erin Johnson, Human Resources Assistant/Internship Coordinator. Phone: 415-861-4008. Fax: 415-551-6297. E-mail: ejohnson@sfopera.com. In-person interview recommended (telephone interview accepted). Applicants must submit a formal organization application, resume, 2-3 personal references. Applications are accepted continuously. World Wide Web: http://www.sfopera.com.

SEACOAST REPERTORY THEATRE
125 Bow Street
Portsmouth, New Hampshire 03801

General Information Year-round professional theater that presents 9 mainstage shows, 9 children's shows, and classes. Established in 1987. Number of employees: 15. Number of internship applications received each year: 10.
Internships Available ▶ *1–2 administrative interns.* Candidates should have knowledge of field, office skills, oral communication skills, organizational skills, strong interpersonal skills, computer literacy and knowledge of graphics a plus. Duration is June to September. Position available as unpaid or paid. Open to high school students, recent high school graduates, college freshmen, college sophomores, college juniors, college seniors, recent college graduates, graduate students, career changers, individuals reentering the workforce. ▶ *2–6 stage management interns:* responsibilities include attending rehearsals; helping with props, electrics, sound, carpentry, paint, costumes, and running of shows; helping with general upkeep of workspaces; phone calls. Candidates should have ability to work independently, ability to work with others, oral communication skills, organizational skills, self-motivation, strong leadership ability. Duration is 6–52 weeks. Position available as unpaid or paid. Open to high school students, recent high school graduates, college freshmen, college sophomores, college juniors, college seniors, recent college graduates, graduate students, law students, career changers, individuals reentering the workforce. ▶ *4–8 technical interns:* responsibilities include physical building and painting of sets and props; working with sound and electrics; general upkeep of workspace; possible running of shows; working with costumes. Candidates should have ability to work with others, oral communication skills, organizational skills, self-motivation, knowledge of field helpful. Duration is 6–52 weeks. Position available as unpaid or paid. Open to high school students, recent high school graduates, college freshmen, college sophomores, college juniors, college seniors, recent college graduates, graduate students, law students, career changers, individuals reentering the workforce. International applications accepted.
Benefits On-the-job training, possible full-time employment, willing to act as a professional reference, willing to provide letters of recommendation, possible free housing.
Contact Write or fax Eileen Rogosin, Associate Producer. Fax: 603-431-7818. E-mail: info@seacoastrep.org. No phone calls.

Seacoast Repertory Theatre (continued)

In-person interview recommended (telephone interview accepted). Applicants must submit a formal organization application, letter of interest, resume, two letters of recommendation. Application deadline: April 15 for summer positions; continuous for other positions. World Wide Web: http://www.seacoastrep.org.

SEATTLE OPERA
PO Box 9248
Seattle, Washington 98109

General Information Opera company producing 5 full-scale operas per season, plus one educational outreach show. Established in 1964. Number of employees: 65. Number of internship applications received each year: 30.
Internships Available ▶ *3 assistant direction interns:* responsibilities include observing rehearsals, keeping a "blocking book," walking roles for absent performers, and other duties as determined by the stage director. Candidates should have ability to work independently, knowledge of field, oral communication skills, personal interest in the field, plan to pursue career in field, strong interpersonal skills. Duration is 4 weeks. Unpaid. Open to college seniors, recent college graduates, graduate students, career changers, individuals reentering the workforce. ▶ *5 costume interns:* responsibilities include assisting the costume shop manager in shopping and other duties based on the ability of the intern. Candidates should have ability to work independently, knowledge of field, oral communication skills, personal interest in the field, strong interpersonal skills, ability to sew at an intermediate level. Duration is 6 weeks. Unpaid. Open to recent high school graduates, college freshmen, college sophomores, college juniors, college seniors, recent college graduates, graduate students, career changers, individuals reentering the workforce, individuals studying fashion design or college theater costume design/construction. ▶ *5 hair and make-up interns.* Candidates should have ability to work independently, knowledge of field, oral communication skills, personal interest in the field, strong interpersonal skills, previous experience in make-up application for stage. Duration is 3 weeks. Unpaid. Open to recent high school graduates, college freshmen, college sophomores, college juniors, college seniors, recent college graduates, graduate students, career changers, individuals reentering the workforce, those studying wig and make-up application for theater and opera or those studying at salon schools. ▶ *5 music library interns:* responsibilities include working directly with the music librarian, marking scores, and performing other duties as determined by the music librarian. Candidates should have ability to work independently, ability to work with others, knowledge of field, personal interest in the field, self-motivation, ability to read music well and in different clefs. Duration is 6–10 weeks. Unpaid. Open to recent high school graduates, college freshmen, college sophomores, college juniors, college seniors, recent college graduates, graduate students, career changers, individuals reentering the workforce, high school seniors over 18 years of age. ▶ *5 stage management interns:* responsibilities include working as part of the stage management team, in rehearsals and performances, managing backstage elements. Candidates should have ability to work independently, ability to work with others, computer skills, oral communication skills, organizational skills, personal interest in the field. Duration is 6–8 weeks. Unpaid. Open to recent high school graduates, college freshmen, college sophomores, college juniors, college seniors, recent college graduates, graduate students, career changers, individuals reentering the workforce. International applications accepted.
Benefits On-the-job training, willing to act as a professional reference, willing to complete paperwork for educational credit, willing to provide letters of recommendation, opportunities to attend rehearsals and coachings and to meet with artists and staff.
Contact Write, call, fax, e-mail, or through World Wide Web site Paula Podemski, Production Supervisor, PO Box 9248, Seattle, Washington 98109. Phone: 206-676-5812. Fax: 206-389-7651. E-mail: paula.podemski@seattleopera.org. In-person interview recommended (telephone interview accepted). Applicants must submit a formal organization application, letter of interest, resume, three personal references. Applications are accepted continuously. World Wide Web: http://www.seattleopera.org.

SHADOW BOX THEATRE
325 West End Avenue, 12B
New York, New York 10023

General Information Theater focusing on children's theater and Arts-in-Education for inner-city children, home-based theater, in-school and after-school workshop program, and summer touring group. Established in 1967. Number of employees: 20. Number of internship applications received each year: 20.
Internships Available ▶ *1–2 administrative interns:* responsibilities include assisting with telephone bookings, marketing, publicity, general administrative duties. Candidates should have ability to work independently, ability to work with others, computer skills, office skills, oral communication skills, organizational skills, research skills, written communication skills. Duration is flexible. Unpaid. ▶ *2–4 theater interns:* responsibilities include assisting with technical aspects of theater, house management, box office, and assisting the director. Candidates should have college courses in field, knowledge of field, personal interest in the field, strong interpersonal skills. Duration is flexible. Unpaid. Open to college freshmen, college sophomores, college juniors, college seniors. International applications accepted.
Benefits Willing to complete paperwork for educational credit, willing to provide letters of recommendation, small stipend, local travel/lunch.
Contact Write, call, fax, or e-mail Marlyn Baum, Managing Director. Phone: 212-724-0677. Fax: 212-724-0767. E-mail: sbt@shadowboxtheatre.org. In-person interview required. Applicants must submit a letter of interest, resume, two letters of recommendation. Applications are accepted continuously. World Wide Web: http://www.shadowboxtheatre.org.

SOHO REPERTORY THEATRE
46 Walker Street
New York, New York 10013

General Information Theater specializing in new and avant-garde plays. Established in 1975. Number of employees: 7.
Internships Available ▶ *Administration interns.* Candidates should have computer skills, office skills, oral communication skills, organizational skills, personal interest in the field, self-motivation. Duration is flexible. Unpaid. ▶ *Business interns.* Candidates should have computer skills, office skills, oral communication skills, organizational skills, personal interest in the field, self-motivation. Duration is flexible. Unpaid. ▶ *Development interns.* Candidates should have computer skills, office skills, oral communication skills, organizational skills, personal interest in the field, self-motivation. Duration is flexible. Unpaid. ▶ *Literary interns.* Candidates should have ability to work independently, analytical skills, personal interest in the field, self-motivation, writing skills. Duration is flexible. Unpaid. ▶ *Production interns.* Candidates should have computer skills, office skills, oral communication skills, organizational skills, personal interest in the field, self-motivation. Duration is flexible. Unpaid. Open to college freshmen, college sophomores, college juniors, college seniors, recent college graduates, graduate students, law students, career changers, individuals reentering the workforce.
Benefits Willing to complete paperwork for educational credit, willing to provide letters of recommendation.
Contact Write, call, or fax Alexandra Conley, Executive Director. Phone: 212-941-8632. Fax: 212-941-7148. Applicants must submit a letter of interest, resume. Applications are accepted continuously. World Wide Web: http://www.sohorep.org.

STEPPENWOLF THEATRE COMPANY
758 West North Avenue, 4th floor
Chicago, Illinois 60610

General Information Not-for-profit Tony Award winning theater company. Established in 1976. Number of employees: 70. Number of internship applications received each year: 300.
Internships Available ▶ *1–3 artistic interns:* responsibilities include various activities; see company Web site for complete description. Candidates should have computer skills, oral communication skills, research skills, self-motivation, strong interpersonal skills, written communication skills, strong varied background in theater. Dura-

tion is 3–4 months. Position available as unpaid or at $50 per week. Open to college juniors, college seniors, recent college graduates, graduate students. ▶ *1–2 arts exchange interns:* responsibilities include various activities; see company Web site for complete description. Candidates should have ability to work with others, office skills, oral communication skills, organizational skills, research skills, writing skills, interest in education, strong background in dramatic literature. Duration is 3–4 months. Position available as unpaid or at $50 per week. Open to college freshmen, college sophomores, college juniors, college seniors, recent college graduates, graduate students, career changers, individuals reentering the workforce. ▶ *1 company management intern:* responsibilities include various activities; see company Web site for complete description. Candidates should have computer skills, office skills, oral communication skills, organizational skills, personal interest in the field, strong interpersonal skills, written communication skills. Duration is 3–4 months. Position available as unpaid or at $50 per week. Open to college freshmen, college sophomores, college juniors, college seniors, recent college graduates, graduate students, career changers, individuals reentering the workforce. ▶ *Costuming interns:* responsibilities include various activities; see company Web site for complete description. Candidates should have ability to work with others, experience in the field, oral communication skills, plan to pursue career in field, self-motivation. Duration is 3–12 months. $50–$125 per week. Open to college sophomores, college juniors, college seniors, recent college graduates, graduate students. ▶ *1–2 development interns:* responsibilities include various activities; see company Web site for complete description. Candidates should have ability to work independently, computer skills, oral communication skills, organizational skills, personal interest in the field, self-motivation, strong interpersonal skills, written communication skills. Duration is 3–4 months. Position available as unpaid or at $50 per week. Open to college freshmen, college sophomores, college juniors, college seniors, recent college graduates, graduate students. ▶ *Lighting interns:* responsibilities include various activities; see company Web site for complete description. Candidates should have ability to work with others, experience in the field, oral communication skills, plan to pursue career in field, self-motivation. Duration is 3–12 months. $50–$125 per week. Open to college sophomores, college juniors, college seniors, recent college graduates, graduate students. ▶ *1–2 marketing interns:* responsibilities include various activities; see company Web site for complete description. Candidates should have ability to work with others, office skills, oral communication skills, personal interest in the field, self-motivation, writing skills. Duration is 3–4 months. Position available as unpaid or at $50 per week. Open to college freshmen, college sophomores, college juniors, college seniors, recent college graduates, graduate students, career changers, individuals reentering the workforce. ▶ *1–2 production management interns:* responsibilities include various activities; see company Web site for complete description. Candidates should have computer skills, knowledge of field, oral communication skills, organizational skills, personal interest in the field, written communication skills. Duration is 3–4 months. Position available as unpaid or at $50 per week. Open to college sophomores, college juniors, college seniors, recent college graduates, graduate students. ▶ *Properties interns:* responsibilities include various activities; see company Web site for complete description. Candidates should have ability to work with others, experience in the field, oral communication skills, plan to pursue career in field, self-motivation. Duration is 3–12 months. $50–$125 per week. Open to college sophomores, college juniors, college seniors, recent college graduates, graduate students. ▶ *1–2 publicity interns:* responsibilities include various activities; see company Web site for complete description. Candidates should have ability to work with others, office skills, oral communication skills, personal interest in the field, self-motivation, writing skills. Duration is 3–4 months. Position available as unpaid or at $50 per week. Open to college freshmen, college sophomores, college juniors, college seniors, recent college graduates, graduate students, career changers, individuals reentering the workforce. ▶ *Scenic art interns:* responsibilities include various activities; see company Web site for complete description. Candidates should have ability to work with others, experience in the field, oral communication skills, plan to pursue

career in field, self-motivation. Duration is 3–12 months. $50–$125 per week. Open to college sophomores, college juniors, college seniors, recent college graduates, graduate students. ▶ *Scenic carpentry:* responsibilities include various activities; see company Web site for complete description. Candidates should have ability to work with others, experience in the field, oral communication skills, plan to pursue career in field, self-motivation. Duration is 3–12 months. $50–$125 per week. Open to college sophomores, college juniors, college seniors, recent college graduates, graduate students. ▶ *Sound interns:* responsibilities include various activities; see company Web site for complete description. Candidates should have ability to work with others, experience in the field, oral communication skills, personal interest in the field, self-motivation. Duration is 3–12 months. $50–$125 per week. Open to college sophomores, college juniors, college seniors, recent college graduates, graduate students. ▶ *1–2 special events interns:* responsibilities include various activities; see company Web site for complete description. Candidates should have ability to work with others, office skills, oral communication skills, organizational skills, personal interest in the field, self-motivation, written communication skills. Duration is 3–4 months. Position available as unpaid or at $50 per week. Open to college freshmen, college sophomores, college juniors, college seniors, recent college graduates, graduate students. ▶ *1–2 stage management interns:* responsibilities include various activities; see company Web site for complete description. Candidates should have experience in the field, oral communication skills, organizational skills, plan to pursue career in field, self-motivation, strong interpersonal skills. Duration is several months to full season (1 year). Position available as unpaid or at $50–$125 per week. Open to college juniors, college seniors, recent college graduates, graduate students. International applications accepted.

Benefits Formal training, job counseling, names of contacts, opportunity to attend seminars/workshops, willing to act as a professional reference, willing to complete paperwork for educational credit, willing to provide letters of recommendation, opportunity to attend all productions and events.

Contact Write, call, fax, e-mail, or through World Wide Web site Internship Coordinator, 758 West North Avenue, 4th Floor, Chicago, Illinois 60610. Phone: 312-335-1888 Ext. 5692. Fax: 312-335-0808. E-mail: internships@steppenwolf.org. In-person interview recommended (telephone interview accepted). Applicants must submit a formal organization application, resume, two letters of recommendation, personal statement. Application deadline: February 14 for summer, June 1 for fall, November 1 for winter. World Wide Web: http://www.steppenwolf.org.

TADA!
120 West 28th Street
New York, New York 10001

General Information Nonprofit children's theater ensemble producing high-quality productions performed by children for family audiences. Established in 1984. Number of employees: 10. Number of internship applications received each year: 15.

Internships Available ▶ *1 arts administrative assistant:* responsibilities include assisting in running the office. Candidates should have ability to work with others, experience in the field, office skills, research skills, writing skills. Duration is flexible (minimum 4 weeks). Unpaid. ▶ *1 arts education intern.* Candidates should have ability to work with others, computer skills, knowledge of field, office skills, oral communication skills, organizational skills, self-motivation. Duration is flexible (minimum of 4 weeks). Unpaid. ▶ *1 assistant stage manager:* responsibilities include assisting stage manager with rehearsals and performances. Candidates should have background in technical theater. Duration is 3 months. Paid. ▶ *1 box office intern.* Candidates should have ability to work independently, computer skills, office skills, oral communication skills, organizational skills, strong interpersonal skills. Duration is flexible. Paid. ▶ *1 house manager:* responsibilities include dealing with the audience. Candidates should have experience in the field, oral communication skills, strong interpersonal skills, strong leadership ability. Duration is flexible. Paid. ▶ *1 theater electrician/ board operator:* responsibilities include assisting with technical work and performances. Candidates should have background in techni-

TADA! (continued)

cal theater. Duration is 2 months. Paid. ▶ *1 wardrobe supervisor:* responsibilities include maintaining costumes and working backstage with children. Candidates should have experience in the field. Duration is 2 months. Paid. Open to college freshmen, college sophomores, college juniors, college seniors.

Benefits Names of contacts, willing to complete paperwork for educational credit, willing to provide letters of recommendation.

Contact Write, fax, or e-mail Jody Griffin, Office Manager. Fax: 212-243-6736. E-mail: tada@tadatheater.com. No phone calls. In-person interview recommended (telephone interview accepted). Applicants must submit a letter of interest, resume, letter of recommendation. Application deadline: May 15 for summer; continuous for other positions.

TAMPA BAY BUCCANEERS
1 Buccaneer Place
Tampa, Florida 33607

General Information Professional football team. Established in 1976. Number of employees: 180. Number of internship applications received each year: 300.

Internships Available ▶ *1 communications intern.* Candidates should have ability to work with others, editing skills, knowledge of field, plan to pursue career in field, research skills, written communication skills. Duration is June to February. $5.15 per hour. ▶ *1 marketing intern.* Candidates should have computer skills, knowledge of field, office skills, oral communication skills, organizational skills, plan to pursue career in field, strong interpersonal skills. Duration is June to February. $5.15 per hour. Open to college seniors, recent college graduates, graduate students.

Benefits On-the-job training, possible full-time employment, willing to act as a professional reference, willing to complete paperwork for educational credit, willing to provide letters of recommendation.

Contact Write, fax, or e-mail Gene Magrini, Director of Human Resources. Fax: 813-554-1351. E-mail: magrinig@buccaneers.nfl.com. No phone calls. In-person interview required. Applicants must submit a formal organization application, resume, three writing samples, three personal references, two letters of recommendation. Application deadline: February 15 for summer, June 1 for fall. World Wide Web: http://www.buccaneers.com.

THE THEATER AT MONMOUTH
PO Box 385
Monmouth, Maine 04259

General Information Professional summer theater dedicated to producing classical plays in rotating repertory. Established in 1970. Number of employees: 40. Number of internship applications received each year: 500.

Internships Available ▶ *8–10 actor interns:* responsibilities include acting in mainstage productions and children's show; working backstage; assisting stage manager; and working in office, costume, or scene shop. Candidates should have experience in the field, personal interest in the field. Duration is 12–20 weeks. $50–$150 per week. ▶ *1–3 costume interns:* responsibilities include engaging in all aspects of costumes, including patterning, cutting, stitching, millinery, garment repair, and alterations. Candidates should have knowledge of field, oral communication skills, personal interest in the field, self-motivation, strong interpersonal skills. Duration is 8 weeks. $50–$150 per week. ▶ *1–3 office interns:* responsibilities include staffing box office; house management; concessions and gift shop management; performing customer service and data entry. Candidates should have ability to work independently, ability to work with others, analytical skills, computer skills, knowledge of field, office skills, oral communication skills, organizational skills, personal interest in the field, written communication skills. Duration is 14 weeks. $50–$100 per week. ▶ *2 stage management interns:* responsibilities include assisting stage manager in working backstage and full management of children's show. Candidates should have ability to work independently, analytical skills, knowledge of field, office skills, oral communication skills, organizational skills, personal interest in the field, plan to pursue

career in field, self-motivation, strong interpersonal skills, strong leadership ability, writing skills. Duration is 12 weeks. $50 per week. ▶ *1–3 technical interns:* responsibilities include engaging in all aspects of physical production, including lights and sound, scenery, and props. Candidates should have ability to work with others, oral communication skills, personal interest in the field, self-motivation. Duration is 8–14 weeks. $40–$60 per week. Open to recent high school graduates, college freshmen, college sophomores, college juniors, college seniors, recent college graduates, graduate students, law students, career changers, individuals reentering the workforce. International applications accepted.

Benefits Free housing, free meals, names of contacts, on-the-job training, opportunity to attend seminars/workshops, willing to act as a professional reference, willing to complete paperwork for educational credit, willing to provide letters of recommendation.

Contact Write, e-mail, or through World Wide Web site David Greenham, Producing Manager. E-mail: tamoffice@theateratmonmouth.org. No phone calls. In-person interview recommended (telephone interview accepted). Applicants must submit a letter of interest, resume, three personal references, audition for actor interns. Application deadline: February 1 for summer. World Wide Web: http://www.theateratmonmouth.org.

THEATER FOR THE NEW CITY FOUNDATION, INC.
155 First Avenue
New York, New York 10003

General Information Nonprofit off-off-Broadway theater that presents 44 shows each season. Established in 1970. Number of employees: 10. Number of internship applications received each year: 50.

Internships Available ▶ *Administrative interns:* responsibilities include assisting executive and administrative director. Candidates should have ability to work independently, ability to work with others, analytical skills, office skills, oral communication skills, organizational skills, self-motivation, strong leadership ability, writing skills. Duration is flexible. Unpaid. ▶ *Financial development/fund-raising interns:* responsibilities include writing grants, typing, and performing foundation research and clerical duties. Duration is flexible. Unpaid. ▶ *Technical interns:* responsibilities include assisting technical director. Candidates should have ability to work independently, ability to work with others, analytical skills, office skills, oral communication skills, organizational skills, self-motivation, strong leadership ability, writing skills. Duration is flexible. Unpaid. Open to individuals 17 and older. International applications accepted.

Benefits Possible full-time employment, willing to act as a professional reference, willing to complete paperwork for educational credit, willing to provide letters of recommendation.

Contact Write, call, fax, or e-mail Crystal Field, Executive Director. Phone: 212-254-1109. Fax: 212-979-6570. E-mail: info@theaterforthenewcity.org. In-person interview recommended (telephone interview accepted). Applicants must submit a letter of interest, resume. Applications are accepted continuously. World Wide Web: http://www.theaterforthenewcity.org.

THEATRE OF YUGEN
2840 Mariposa Street
San Francisco, California 94110

General Information Theater that combines Asian theatrical traditions with contemporary themes and electronic media. Established in 1978. Number of employees: 4. Number of internship applications received each year: 6.

Internships Available ▶ *2–4 administrative assistants:* responsibilities include making final reports of grants received, maintaining board meeting minutes, handling membership mailings, scheduling, development, and fund-raising. Candidates should have ability to work with others, office skills, oral communication skills, personal interest in the field, written communication skills. Duration is 3–6 months. Position available as unpaid or paid. Open to college juniors, college seniors, recent college graduates, graduate students, career changers, individuals reentering the workforce. ▶ *1 technical director's assistant:* responsibilities include scheduling rentals, maintaining space and equipment, and running light board and sound equipment. Candidates should have ability to

work with others, computer skills, knowledge of field, organizational skills, personal interest in the field, some background in technical theater (preferred). Duration is 3–6 months. Position available as unpaid or at $10–$12 per hour. Open to college freshmen, college sophomores, college juniors, college seniors, recent college graduates, career changers, individuals reentering the workforce. International applications accepted.
Benefits Willing to act as a professional reference, willing to complete paperwork for educational credit, willing to provide letters of recommendation, complimentary theater tickets, theater discounts, formal training in movement; possible transportation stipend (administrative assistant and technical director's assistant).
Contact Write, fax, or e-mail Libby Zilber, Operations Manager. Fax: 415-621-0223. E-mail: libby@theatreofyugen.org. No phone calls. In-person interview recommended (telephone interview accepted). Applications are accepted continuously. World Wide Web: http://www.theatreofyugen.org.

THE THEATRE-STUDIO, INC.
750 Eighth Avenue, Suite 200
New York, New York 10036

General Information Studio theater that focuses on growth of theater arts for the community. Established in 1980. Number of employees: 10. Number of internship applications received each year: 50.
Internships Available ▶ *1–3 administrative assistant interns:* responsibilities include monitoring daily trafficking schedule and logging phone messages, telephone contact work, correspondence, filing, and organizing and monitoring play scripts. Candidates should have ability to work independently, computer skills, oral communication skills, organizational skills, strong interpersonal skills, written communication skills. Duration is 3–6 months. Unpaid. ▶ *1–5 grant researchers:* responsibilities include researching types of grants available to theater production companies, organizing and presenting findings to artistic director, and selecting and writing grants. Candidates should have ability to work independently, editing skills, knowledge of field, research skills, written communication skills. Position available as unpaid or paid. ▶ *1–3 production assistant interns:* responsibilities include tech crew on two performances per week with various duties including operation of simple sound/light equipment, setting up house, working on set changes and strikes, prop/costume searches, updating fliers and programs, and running errands. Candidates should have ability to work independently, computer skills, knowledge of field, office skills, oral communication skills, organizational skills, personal interest in the field, research skills, self-motivation, strong interpersonal skills, written communication skills. Duration is 3–6 months. Unpaid. Open to high school students, recent high school graduates, college freshmen, college sophomores, college juniors, college seniors, recent college graduates, graduate students, law students, career changers, individuals reentering the workforce.
Benefits Formal training, opportunity to attend seminars/workshops, willing to complete paperwork for educational credit, willing to provide letters of recommendation, opportunity to work in a professional production; opportunity to attend and participate in Artistic Director's Actor/Director/Writer sessions.
Contact Write, call, or fax A. M. Raychel, Producing/Artistic Director. Phone: 212-719-0500. Fax: 212-719-0537. Applicants must submit a letter of interest, resume, two writing samples, three personal references, three letters of recommendation, in-person interview within 2 weeks of receipt of application/letter of interest. Application deadline: February 1 for spring, April 1 for summer, October 1 for winter. World Wide Web: http://www.theatrestudio.org.

THEATRE VIRGINIA
2800 Grove Avenue
Richmond, Virginia 23221

General Information Professional theater producing musicals, dramas, comedies, and classics on its mainstage from September to May; provides numerous educational programs and hosts a young playwrights' and actors' competition called "New Voices

for the Theater". Established in 1954. Number of employees: 45. Number of internship applications received each year: 30.
Internships Available ▶ *12–20 administrative interns and apprenticeships:* responsibilities include working in development, arts administration, ticket operations, marketing/public relations, company management, house management, or education departments. Candidates should have computer skills, oral communication skills, personal interest in the field, self-motivation, strong interpersonal skills, writing skills. Duration is flexible. Position available as unpaid or paid. Open to high school seniors, recent high school graduates, college freshmen, college sophomores, college juniors, college seniors, recent college graduates, graduate students. ▶ *5–10 production interns and apprenticeships:* responsibilities include assisting in area of specialization: production assistance, scenic carpentry, properties, scenic artistry, costume production, wardrobe, electrics, or sound. Candidates should have ability to work independently, ability to work with others, knowledge of field, personal interest in the field, self-motivation. Duration is flexible. Position available as unpaid or paid. Open to recent high school graduates, college freshmen, college sophomores, college juniors, college seniors, recent college graduates, graduate students.
Benefits Job counseling, names of contacts, on-the-job training, possible full-time employment, willing to complete paperwork for educational credit, willing to provide letters of recommendation.
Contact Write, call, fax, e-mail, or through World Wide Web site Raina S. Ames, Director of Education & Outreach. Phone: 804-353-6100. Fax: 804-353-8799. E-mail: rames@theatreva.com. In-person interview recommended (telephone interview accepted). Applicants must submit a letter of interest, resume. Application deadline: March 1 for production positions; continuous for administrative positions. World Wide Web: http://www.theatreva.com.

THEATREWORKS
1100 Hamilton Court
Menlo Park, California 94025

General Information Nationally recognized professional nonprofit theater company presenting high-quality live theater that reflects the diversity of its community. Established in 1970. Number of employees: 37. Number of internship applications received each year: 75.
Internships Available ▶ *5–15 artistic interns:* responsibilities include working in the areas of directing, literary, casting, or musical directing. Candidates should have ability to work with others, oral communication skills, personal interest in the field, research skills, directing experience required for assistant directors, music theory and piano skills required for assistant music directors. Duration is 3-9 months (30 hours per week). Unpaid. Open to college freshmen, college sophomores, college juniors, college seniors, recent college graduates, graduate students, law students, career changers, individuals reentering the workforce. ▶ *3–6 arts management interns:* responsibilities include working in the areas of development/events, outreach, ticket services, marketing, or operations. Candidates should have computer skills, office skills, oral communication skills, organizational skills, personal interest in the field, written communication skills. Duration is 3-9 months (10-30 hours per week). Unpaid. Open to college freshmen, college sophomores, college juniors, college seniors, recent college graduates, graduate students, law students, career changers, individuals reentering the workforce. ▶ *10–15 production interns:* responsibilities include working in the areas of scenic/props, costumes, lighting, sound, stage management, or production management. Candidates should have ability to work with others, experience in the field, oral communication skills, personal interest in the field, plan to pursue career in field, self-motivation. Duration is 3-9 months (35 hours per week). Unpaid. Open to recent high school graduates, college freshmen, college sophomores, college juniors, college seniors, recent college graduates, graduate students, law students, career changers, individuals reentering the workforce.
Benefits Job counseling, names of contacts, on-the-job training, opportunity to attend seminars/workshops, travel reimbursement, willing to act as a professional reference, willing to complete paperwork for educational credit, willing to provide letters of recommendation, complimentary tickets to productions, first option on short-term paid contracts within theater operations.

TheatreWorks (continued)
Contact Write, fax, e-mail, or through World Wide Web site Jodi Corwin, Manager of Intern and Volunteer Programs. Fax: 650-463-1963. E-mail: interns@theatreworks.org. In-person interview recommended (telephone interview accepted). Applicants must submit a formal organization application, letter of interest, resume. Application deadline: March 1 for summer; continuous for all other positions. World Wide Web: http://www.theatreworks.org.

THIRTEENTH STREET REPERTORY COMPANY
50 West 13th Street
New York, New York 10011

General Information Nonprofit off-off-Broadway theater that operates 52 weeks per year and performs full-length plays every 3 months, children's plays every Saturday and Sunday, Sunday Reading Series, and other ongoing projects. Established in 1972. Number of internship applications received each year: 25.

Internships Available ▶ *3 assistants to general manager:* responsibilities include handling scheduling of 60 volunteers, investigating marketing possibilities on Internet, evaluating plays, creating programs for new shows, entering accounting information into computer, running box office, and handling media listings. Candidates should have ability to work independently, computer skills, oral communication skills, organizational skills, written communication skills, Internet skills. Duration is ongoing. Unpaid. Open to high school seniors, recent high school graduates, college freshmen, college sophomores, college juniors, college seniors, recent college graduates, graduate students, career changers, individuals reentering the workforce. ▶ *2 marketing interns.* Candidates should have college courses in field, computer skills, oral communication skills. Duration is ongoing. Unpaid. Open to college freshmen, college sophomores, college juniors, college seniors, recent college graduates, graduate students, career changers. ▶ *2 play evaluations interns:* responsibilities include organizing and cataloging incoming and outgoing plays, organizing play evaluations and entering results in computer, reading and evaluating plays from National Playwriting Contest. Candidates should have computer skills, knowledge of field, oral communication skills, organizational skills, personal interest in the field, college courses in drama criticism. Duration is ongoing. Unpaid. Open to college freshmen, college sophomores, college juniors, college seniors, recent college graduates, graduate students. ▶ *3 publicity interns.* Candidates should have college courses in field, computer skills, oral communication skills. Duration is ongoing. Unpaid. Open to college freshmen, college sophomores, college juniors, college seniors, recent college graduates, graduate students, career changers. ▶ *10–15 stage managers/technicians/assistant directors:* responsibilities include assisting with lights and sound, auditioning, understudying, acting, and assisting play director and artistic director. Candidates should have ability to work independently, ability to work with others, computer skills, knowledge of field, oral communication skills, self-motivation. Duration is several months. Unpaid. Open to high school seniors, recent high school graduates, college freshmen, college sophomores, college juniors, college seniors, recent college graduates, graduate students, career changers, individuals reentering the workforce. International applications accepted.
Benefits Names of contacts, on-the-job training, opportunity to attend seminars/workshops, willing to act as a professional reference, willing to complete paperwork for educational credit, willing to provide letters of recommendation.
Contact Write, call, or e-mail Sandra Nordgren, General Manager. Phone: 917-363-2369. E-mail: sandranord@aol.com. In-person interview recommended (telephone interview accepted). Applicants must submit a formal organization application, letter of interest, resume, two personal references, two letters of recommendation. Applications are accepted continuously.

TRINITY REPERTORY COMPANY
201 Washington Street
Providence, Rhode Island 02903

General Information Professional regional theater engaging the audience as participants. Established in 1964. Number of employees: 120. Number of internship applications received each year: 75.

Internships Available ▶ *3–6 administration interns:* responsibilities include working in, general management, literary management, communications/PR, marketing, and education. Candidates should have computer skills, experience in the field, office skills, oral communication skills, strong interpersonal skills, written communication skills, accounting skills. Duration is August 15 to June 1 (full-time) or one summer. Position available as unpaid or at $60–$75 per week. Open to high school seniors, recent high school graduates, college freshmen, college sophomores, college juniors, college seniors, recent college graduates. ▶ *4–6 production interns:* responsibilities include working in one of several positions in production management, stage management, electrics, scenic carpentry, sound, costume, and props. Candidates should have college courses in field, experience in the field, oral communication skills, plan to pursue career in field, strong interpersonal skills. Duration is August 15 to June1 (full-time) or one summer. $60–$75 per week. Open to recent college graduates. International applications accepted.
Benefits Formal training, job counseling, names of contacts, on-the-job training, opportunity to attend seminars/workshops, possible full-time employment, willing to act as a professional reference, willing to complete paperwork for educational credit, willing to provide letters of recommendation, 2 complimentary tickets for each production, stipend, free housing for year-round interns.
Contact Write, call, fax, or e-mail Jamie Brink Grant, Associate Education Director. Phone: 401-521-1100 Ext. 255. Fax: 401-751-5577. E-mail: jbrinkgrant@trinityrep.com. In-person interview recommended (telephone interview accepted). Applicants must submit a letter of interest, resume, three letters of recommendation, writing sample for education, literary, public relations positions only. Application deadline: June 1 for full-time seasonal interns; continuous for all other positions. World Wide Web: http://www.trinityrep.com.

UNTITLED THEATER COMPANY #61
235 West 102nd Street, Suite 16-S
New York, New York 10025

General Information Nonprofit producer of experimental and philosophic plays off-off-Broadway. Established in 1992. Number of employees: 3. Number of internship applications received each year: 5.

Internships Available ▶ *1–3 artistic associates:* responsibilities include assisting in the directorial and playwriting aspects of theater, including the positions of assistant director and dramaturg. Candidates should have ability to work with others, knowledge of field, oral communication skills, organizational skills, personal interest in the field, research skills, writing skills. Duration is 2 months. Unpaid. Open to college freshmen, college sophomores, college juniors, college seniors, recent college graduates. ▶ *1–5 assistants to the artistic director:* responsibilities include assisting the artistic director in all areas, including publicity, grant writing, and scheduling. Candidates should have ability to work independently, knowledge of field, office skills, oral communication skills, organizational skills, personal interest in the field, research skills, writing skills. Duration is flexible. Unpaid. Open to high school students, recent high school graduates, college freshmen, college sophomores, college juniors, college seniors, recent college graduates. ▶ *1–3 company managers:* responsibilities include organizing performances, readings, and rehearsals. Candidates should have ability to work independently, ability to work with others, knowledge of field, organizational skills. Duration is flexible. Unpaid. Open to college freshmen, college sophomores, college juniors, college seniors, recent college graduates. ▶ *1–5 stage managers:* responsibilities include supervising all the technical aspects of a production including organizing props, light, and sound. Candidates should have knowledge of field, oral communication skills, organizational skills, personal interest in the

field, strong interpersonal skills. Duration is 2 months. Unpaid. Open to high school students, recent high school graduates, college freshmen, college sophomores, college juniors, college seniors, recent college graduates. International applications accepted.
Benefits Names of contacts, on-the-job training, opportunity to attend seminars/workshops, willing to act as a professional reference, willing to complete paperwork for educational credit, willing to provide letters of recommendation.
Contact Write, call, or e-mail Edward Einhorn, Artistic Director, 235 West 102nd Street, Suite 16-S, New York 10025. Phone: 212-866-1073. E-mail: utc61@hotmail.com. In-person interview recommended (telephone interview accepted). Applicants must submit a letter of interest, resume. Applications are accepted continuously. World Wide Web: http://www.untitledtheater.com.

VICTORY GARDENS THEATER
2257 North Lincoln Avenue
Chicago, Illinois 60614

General Information World premiere theater emphasizing the development of Chicago playwrights. Established in 1974. Number of employees: 18. Number of internship applications received each year: 30.
Internships Available ► *1 administrative intern:* responsibilities include assisting managing director, director of development, and marketing director in daily tasks and projects. Candidates should have ability to work independently, analytical skills, college courses in field, computer skills, editing skills, knowledge of field, office skills, oral communication skills, organizational skills, personal interest in the field, research skills, self-motivation, strong interpersonal skills, writing skills. Duration is 3-5 months (variable). Unpaid. Open to college seniors, recent college graduates, graduate students, individuals reentering the workforce. ► *2 artistic interns:* responsibilities include assisting literary manager. Candidates should have ability to work independently, college courses in field, computer skills, editing skills, knowledge of field, office skills, oral communication skills, organizational skills, personal interest in the field, research skills, self-motivation, strong interpersonal skills, writing skills. Duration is 3–6 months. Unpaid. Open to college seniors, recent college graduates, graduate students, career changers, individuals reentering the workforce. ► *3 production interns:* responsibilities include assisting administrative director. Candidates should have ability to work independently, ability to work with others, college courses in field, knowledge of field, plan to pursue career in field, self-motivation, carpentry, electrical, technical theater skills. Duration is 6-8 weeks (variable). Unpaid. Open to recent high school graduates, college freshmen, college sophomores, college juniors, college seniors, recent college graduates, graduate students, law students, career changers, individuals reentering the workforce. International applications accepted.
Benefits Names of contacts, on-the-job training, opportunity to attend seminars/workshops, possible full-time employment, willing to complete paperwork for educational credit, willing to provide letters of recommendation.
Contact Write, fax, or e-mail Andrea Dymond, Executive Assistant, 2257 North Lincoln Avenue, Chicago, Illinois 60614. Fax: 773-549-2779. E-mail: adymond@victorygardens.org. No phone calls. In-person interview recommended (telephone interview accepted). Applicants must submit a letter of interest, resume, two personal references, two letters of recommendation. Applications are accepted continuously. World Wide Web: http://www.victorygardens.org.

VIRGINIA SYMPHONY ORCHESTRA
880 North Military Highway, Suite 1064
Norfolk, Virginia 23518

General Information Symphony orchestra offering 140 performances each season. Established in 1920. Number of employees: 19. Number of internship applications received each year: 12.
Internships Available ► *1–4 departmental assistants:* responsibilities include assisting director in development, marketing, production, or education departments and assisting administration. Candidates should have ability to work independently, ability to work with others, college courses in field, computer skills, personal

interest in the field, self-motivation, dependability and reliability. Duration is flexible. Unpaid. Open to college sophomores, college juniors, college seniors, recent college graduates, graduate students. International applications accepted.
Benefits Possible full-time employment, willing to act as a professional reference, willing to complete paperwork for educational credit, willing to provide letters of recommendation, complimentary admission to all concerts/courses.
Contact Write, fax, or e-mail Marilyn Richardson, Development Office. Fax: 757-466-3046. E-mail: mrichardson@virginiasymphony.org. No phone calls. In-person interview required. Applicants must submit a letter of interest, resume, two personal references, letter of recommendation. Applications are accepted continuously. World Wide Web: http://www.virginiasymphony.org.

VPSTART CROW PRODUCTIONS
9005 Church Street, Suite 203
Manassas, Virginia 20110

General Information Professional nonprofit theater company. Established in 1994. Number of employees: 2. Number of internship applications received each year: 20.
Internships Available ► *1–3 arts administration interns:* responsibilities include working with communications director on publicity, media contacts, advertising; also trained in ticket sales, office duties and others as assigned. Candidates should have ability to work with others, office skills, oral communication skills, personal interest in the field, written communication skills. Duration is 1 semester. Unpaid. Open to high school seniors, recent high school graduates, college freshmen, college sophomores, college juniors, college seniors, recent college graduates, graduate students, career changers, individuals reentering the workforce. ► *1 assistant house manager:* responsibilities include assisting with preparation of theater for audience; trained to operate ticket equipment; running box office, supervising ushers, concession workers, and other duties as assigned. Candidates should have ability to work with others, office skills, oral communication skills, personal interest in the field, strong leadership ability. Duration is 1 semester. Unpaid. Open to high school students, recent high school graduates, college freshmen, college sophomores, college juniors, college seniors, recent college graduates, graduate students, career changers, individuals reentering the workforce. ► *1–3 assistant stage manager/crew interns:* responsibilities include assisting with stage management duties, load-in, prep, and strike of sets, props; assisting stage manager with calling cues, and other duties as assigned. Candidates should have oral communication skills, personal interest in the field, plan to pursue career in field, self-motivation, strong interpersonal skills, strong leadership ability. Duration is 1 semester. Unpaid. Open to high school students, recent high school graduates, college freshmen, college sophomores, college juniors, college seniors, recent college graduates, graduate students, career changers, individuals reentering the workforce. International applications accepted.
Benefits Names of contacts, on-the-job training, willing to act as a professional reference, willing to complete paperwork for educational credit, willing to provide letters of recommendation.
Contact Write, call, e-mail, or through World Wide Web site Diane Wilshere, Volunteer Coordinator. Phone: 703-365-0240. E-mail: information@vpstartcrow.org. In-person interview recommended (telephone interview accepted). Applicants must submit a formal organization application, letter of interest, resume, two letters of recommendation. Applications are accepted continuously. World Wide Web: http://www.vpstartcrow.org.

WALNUT STREET THEATRE
825 Walnut Street
Philadelphia, Pennsylvania 19107

General Information Major regional theater. Established in 1809. Number of employees: 50. Number of internship applications received each year: 250.
Internships Available ► *4 acting interns (including 2 reserved for African Americans):* responsibilities include performing, teaching youth acting classes, understudying mainstage shows and acting as readers at auditions. $280 per week. ► *1–2 casting and literary management interns:* responsibilities include assisting casting direc-

Walnut Street Theatre (continued)

tor in all local and New York auditions; working in literary office reviewing scripts. $280 per week. ▶ *1–2 development interns:* responsibilities include assisting the development manager in grantmanship, responding to volunteers for theater, and fund-raising. $280 per week. ▶ *1 directing intern:* responsibilities include assisting in all areas of the theater including mainstage, studio and education productions. $280 per week. ▶ *1–2 general management interns:* responsibilities include assisting the general manager with space management, housing, building maintenance and agreed contracts. $280 per week. ▶ *1–2 house management interns:* responsibilities include assisting house manager on all mainstage plays, including lobby duty and tickets. $280 per week. ▶ *1–2 marketing interns:* responsibilities include assisting the marketing staff. $280 per week. ▶ *1–2 painting interns:* responsibilities include learning extensive scene-painting techniques in a large paint shop operation and working closely with the charge scenic artist in all phases of scene painting. $280 per week. ▶ *1–2 props interns:* responsibilities include assisting the properties manager in construction and acquisition of props for all productions and learning skills in sewing, upholstery, carpentry, sculpturing, painting, and/or calligraphy. $280 per week. ▶ *1–2 run crew interns:* responsibilities include moving sets, load-ins, and load-outs. $280 per week. ▶ *3–5 stage management interns:* responsibilities include assisting in all facets of rehearsals and productions. $280 per week. ▶ *1–2 subscriptions interns:* responsibilities include phone management, subscription, and ticket exchange. $280 per week. Open to recent college graduates. International applications accepted.
Benefits Formal training, health insurance, opportunity to attend seminars/workshops, possible full-time employment, willing to act as a professional reference, willing to complete paperwork for educational credit, willing to provide letters of recommendation, job placement opportunities.
Contact Write, call, fax, or through World Wide Web site Susan Nicodemus Quinn, Director of Education, 9th and Walnut Streets, Philadelphia, Pennsylvania 19107. Phone: 215-574-3550 Ext. 510. Fax: 215-574-3598. In-person interview recommended (telephone interview accepted). Applicants must submit a formal organization application, letter of interest, resume, three personal references, download application and information at wstonline.org. Application deadline: March 31 for acting interns, June 1 for fall interns. World Wide Web: http://www.wstonline.org.

WESTPORT COUNTRY PLAYHOUSE
PO Box 629
Westport, Connecticut 06881

General Information Professional summer theater in an historic building. Established in 1931. Number of employees: 50. Unit of Connecticut Theatre Foundation, Westport, Connecticut. Number of internship applications received each year: 50.
Internships Available ▶ *10 interns:* responsibilities include working in various areas including scenic design and construction, properties, costume design/wardrobe, lighting, sound, press and marketing, or production/company management. Candidates should have ability to work independently, college courses in field, experience in the field, plan to pursue career in field, strong interpersonal skills. Duration is 3 months in summer. $100 per week. Open to college freshmen, college sophomores, college juniors, college seniors, recent college graduates, graduate students.
Benefits Free housing, names of contacts, on-the-job training, opportunity to attend seminars/workshops, possible full-time employment, willing to act as a professional reference, willing to complete paperwork for educational credit, willing to provide letters of recommendation.
Contact Write, call, fax, e-mail, or through World Wide Web site Hyla Crane, Education Coordinator. Phone: 203-227-5137. Fax: 203-221-7482. E-mail: hcrane@westportplayhouse.org. In-person interview recommended (telephone interview accepted). Applicants must submit a formal organization application, resume, two letters of recommendation, letter of interest stating which internships desired. Application deadline: April 1. World Wide Web: http://www.westportplayhouse.org.

WILLIAMSTOWN THEATER FESTIVAL
1000 Main Street, PO Box 517
Williamstown, Massachusetts 01267

General Information Summer theater presenting productions of revivals of classics and new works by new and established playwrights. Established in 1953. Number of employees: 330. Number of internship applications received each year: 600.
Internships Available ▶ *60–70 acting apprenticeships:* responsibilities include taking acting classes and alternate days of crew work. Candidates should have plan to pursue career in field, self-motivation, strong interpersonal skills, written communication skills. Duration is 1 summer (June-August). Unpaid. Open to high school students, recent high school graduates, college freshmen, college sophomores, college juniors, college seniors, recent college graduates, graduate students, career changers, individuals reentering the workforce, individuals 17 and over. ▶ *60 administrative and technical interns:* responsibilities include working in any of the following areas: scenic design/scenic art, costume design/construction, lighting design/electrics, sound design/production, scenic carpentry, directing, publications/graphic design, photography, general management, production management, company management, house management, box office, publicity, stage management, literary management/dramaturgy, cabaret management/production. Candidates should have knowledge of field, organizational skills, self-motivation, strong interpersonal skills. Duration is 1 summer (June-August). Unpaid. Open to high school students, recent high school graduates, college freshmen, college sophomores, college juniors, college seniors, recent college graduates, graduate students, career changers, individuals reentering the workforce. International applications accepted.
Benefits Formal training, housing at a cost, meals at a cost, names of contacts, on-the-job training, opportunity to attend seminars/workshops, willing to act as a professional reference, willing to complete paperwork for educational credit, willing to provide letters of recommendation, opportunity to work with professionals in field.
Contact Write, call, fax, or e-mail Anne Lowrie, Company Manager, 229 West 42nd Street #801, New York, New York 10036. Phone: 212-395-9090. Fax: 212-395-9099. E-mail: alowrie@wtfestival.org. In-person interview recommended (telephone interview accepted). Applicants must submit a formal organization application, letter of interest, resume, portfolio, two personal references, two letters of recommendation, $30 application fee for acting apprentice workshop only. Application deadline: April 1 for acting apprentices; continuous for other positions. World Wide Web: http://www.wtfestival.org.

THE WILMA THEATER
265 South Broad Street
Philadelphia, Pennsylvania 19107

General Information Nonprofit, professional, innovative theater under the artistic direction of Jiri and Blanka Zizka. Established in 1973. Number of employees: 35. Number of internship applications received each year: 150.
Internships Available ▶ *1 artistic fellow:* responsibilities include assisting artistic directors and literary manager/dramaturg, assistant directing, directing understudies and extras, note-taking for directors, and serving as the artistic directors' personal assistant. Candidates should have ability to work independently, ability to work with others, college degree in related field, experience in the field, organizational skills, writing skills. Duration is full theater season, August to June. $250 per week. Open to recent college graduates, graduate students. ▶ *1–3 development interns:* responsibilities include working with development director on researching new prospects, helping to coordinate fund-raising events, assisting with correspondence, and maintaining development files. Candidates should have ability to work independently, computer skills, office skills, oral communication skills, organizational skills, written communication skills. Duration is flexible. Unpaid. Open to college sophomores, college juniors, college seniors, recent college graduates, graduate students, career changers, individuals reentering the workforce. ▶ *1 education intern:* responsibilities include assisting with administration, registration, and promotion of school; researching; symposium coordination; summer

camp planning; assisting with outreach programming; and publicity for all aspects of the department. Candidates should have ability to work independently, oral communication skills, personal interest in the field, self-motivation, writing skills. Duration is flexible. Unpaid. Open to college sophomores, college juniors, college seniors, recent college graduates, career changers. ▶ *1 graphic design intern:* responsibilities include working with director of communications and director of marketing on all aspects of theater design including the program book, Wilma2advertising, studio school brochure, advertisements, flyers, brochures, and show-specific pieces. Candidates should have ability to work independently, computer skills, experience in the field, plan to pursue career in field, self-motivation, familiarity with Quark XPress, PhotoShop, Word. Duration is 2–6 months (15–20 hours per week). Unpaid. Open to college sophomores, college juniors, college seniors, recent college graduates, graduate students. ▶ *1–2 literary interns:* responsibilities include assisting literary manager/dramaturg with script reading and evaluation, script solicitation, administration, correspondence, and performing dramaturgical research for quarterly newsletter. Candidates should have ability to work independently, analytical skills, editing skills, personal interest in the field, research skills, writing skills. Duration is flexible. Unpaid. Open to college sophomores, college juniors, college seniors, recent college graduates, graduate students, individuals reentering the workforce. ▶ *1–2 marketing interns:* responsibilities include assisting marketing director with various aspects of theater promotion; projects may include subscription, single ticket and group sales marketing; coordination of direct mail campaigns; assisting with graphic design and promotion of printed materials. Candidates should have ability to work independently, ability to work with others, computer skills, oral communication skills, personal interest in the field, written communication skills. Duration is flexible. Unpaid. Open to college sophomores, college juniors, college seniors, recent college graduates, graduate students, career changers, individuals reentering the workforce. ▶ *1–2 marketing/publicity interns:* responsibilities include working with marketing/publicity associates, understudying all aspects of theater promotion, mass mailing, graphic design, editing playbill, photographic archiving, analysis of audience, and development of theater literature. Candidates should have ability to work with others, computer skills, oral communication skills, organizational skills, personal interest in the field, written communication skills. Duration is flexible. Unpaid. Open to college sophomores, college juniors, college seniors, recent college graduates, graduate students, career changers, individuals reentering the workforce. ▶ *1 production fellow:* responsibilities include working closely with the production manager, and technical director. Duties may include set construction, painting, load-in, strike, electrics, lighting, running crew and costume work. Candidates should have ability to work independently, ability to work with others, experience in the field, personal interest in the field, plan to pursue career in field, self-motivation. Duration is full theater season, August to June. $250 per week. Open to recent college graduates, graduate students. ▶ *1 public relations intern:* responsibilities include working with director of communications coordinating varying aspects of community and press relations; projects may include compiling, writing and editing program book; targeting marketing research; writing and editing press releases and updating press contacts. Candidates should have computer skills, knowledge of field, office skills, oral communication skills, written communication skills. Duration is flexible. Unpaid. Open to college sophomores, college juniors, college seniors, recent college graduates, graduate students. ▶ *1 special events intern:* responsibilities include assisting with vital fund-raising portion of annual gala; projects may include creating an ad book and event program; soliciting corporation sponsorships; and assisting during special events. Candidates should have ability to work independently, oral communication skills, organizational skills, self-motivation, written communication skills. Duration is flexible. Unpaid. Open to college sophomores, college juniors, college seniors, recent college graduates, graduate students. ▶ *1–2 stage management fellow:* responsibilities include serving as the assistant to the production stage manager, performing duties including note-taking, cleaning, prepping, serving as a liaison between the actors and PSM, and attending all rehearsals and performances.

Candidates should have experience in the field, organizational skills, personal interest in the field, self-motivation, strong interpersonal skills, ability to thrive under pressure. $250 per week. Open to recent college graduates, graduate students. International applications accepted.

Benefits Job counseling, names of contacts, on-the-job training, possible full-time employment, willing to act as a professional reference, willing to complete paperwork for educational credit, willing to provide letters of recommendation, free tickets, discounts on studio school classes.

Contact Write, fax, e-mail, or through World Wide Web site Deborah Braak, Education Director. Fax: 215-893-0895. E-mail: dlb@wilmatheater.org. No phone calls. In-person interview recommended (telephone interview accepted). Applicants must submit a letter of interest, resume, two writing samples. Applications are accepted continuously. World Wide Web: http://www.wilmatheater.org.

WOLF TRAP FOUNDATION FOR THE PERFORMING ARTS
1624 Trap Road
Vienna, Virginia 22182

General Information Performing arts organization that presents music, dance, theater, opera, and related educational programs. Established in 1971. Number of employees: 70. Number of internship applications received each year: 250.

Internships Available ▶ *1 accounting intern:* responsibilities include assisting in the reporting of all foundation financial activities. Candidates should have ability to work independently, ability to work with others, analytical skills, computer skills, declared college major in field, office skills. Duration is 12 weeks during summer. $210 per week. Open to college freshmen, college sophomores, college juniors, college seniors, recent college graduates, graduate students, career changers. ▶ *6 communications and marketing interns:* responsibilities include working in media relations, advertising, publications, marketing, graphic design, or photography; performing such tasks as research, writing, and editing. Candidates should have ability to work independently, ability to work with others, computer skills, editing skills, knowledge of field, office skills, oral communication skills, organizational skills, personal interest in the field, research skills, self-motivation, strong leadership ability, written communication skills. Duration is dependent upon position. $210 per week. Open to college freshmen, college sophomores, college juniors, college seniors, recent college graduates, graduate students, career changers. ▶ *1–3 development interns:* responsibilities include researching, organizing, and preparing reports on individual, corporate, and foundation prospects. Candidates should have ability to work independently, computer skills, editing skills, office skills, oral communication skills, organizational skills, personal interest in the field, research skills, self-motivation, strong interpersonal skills, writing skills. Duration is 12 weeks during summer, fall, and spring. $210 per week. Open to college freshmen, college sophomores, college juniors, college seniors, recent college graduates, graduate students, career changers. ▶ *1–2 education interns:* responsibilities include assisting with scheduling and coordination of education activities, including artist residencies, field trips, children's performances, and others. Candidates should have ability to work independently, computer skills, editing skills, office skills, oral communication skills, organizational skills, personal interest in the field, self-motivation, strong interpersonal skills, writing skills. Duration is 12 weeks during summer, fall, and spring. $210 per week. Open to college freshmen, college sophomores, college juniors, college seniors, recent college graduates, graduate students, career changers. ▶ *1 food and beverage/catering intern:* responsibilities include assisting with planning and coordination of events and food preparation. Candidates should have experience in the field, oral communication skills, organizational skills, personal interest in the field, strong interpersonal skills. Duration is 12 weeks during summer. $210 per week. Open to college freshmen, college sophomores, college juniors, college seniors, recent college graduates, graduate students, career changers. ▶ *1 group sales/box office intern:* responsibilities include assisting director of group sales in interacting with groups, researching market expansion and creat-

Wolf Trap Foundation for the Performing Arts (continued)

ing marketing materials to boost group sales. Candidates should have computer skills, office skills, oral communication skills, organizational skills, strong interpersonal skills, writing skills. Duration is 12 weeks during summer and spring. $210 per week. Open to college freshmen, college sophomores, college juniors, college seniors, recent college graduates, graduate students, career changers. ▶ *1 human resources intern:* responsibilities include assisting director with employee relations, benefits, policies, and recruiting. Candidates should have ability to work independently, analytical skills, computer skills, editing skills, office skills, oral communication skills, organizational skills, personal interest in the field, research skills, self-motivation, strong interpersonal skills, strong leadership ability, writing skills. Duration is 12 weeks during summer, fall, and spring. $210 per week. Open to college freshmen, college sophomores, college juniors, college seniors, recent college graduates, graduate students, career changers. ▶ *1 information systems intern:* responsibilities include maintaining and repairing all the systems and networks, including network administration, system maintenance, system upgrade, and Internet connectivity. Candidates should have ability to work independently, college courses in field, computer skills, knowledge of field, personal interest in the field, self-motivation, strong interpersonal skills. Duration is 12 weeks during summer. $210 per week. Open to college freshmen, college sophomores, college juniors, college seniors, recent college graduates, graduate students. ▶ *1 opera administration intern (Wolf Trap Opera Company):* responsibilities include attending production meetings, rehearsals, and performances; updating company history, repertoire lists, contact sheets, and mailings lists; and assisting the administrative director and staff in daily office operations. Candidates should have ability to work independently, computer skills, editing skills, office skills, oral communication skills, organizational skills, personal interest in the field, self-motivation, strong interpersonal skills, strong leadership ability, writing skills. Duration is 12 weeks during summer. $210 per week. Open to college freshmen, college sophomores, college juniors, college seniors, recent college graduates, graduate students, career changers. ▶ *1 planning and initiatives intern:* responsibilities include coordinating with staff and outside partners on projects such as planning, government relations, long-term commissions, special productions, new series, and cooperative projects with other arts organizations and community partnerships. Candidates should have ability to work independently, computer skills, oral communication skills, organizational skills, research skills, strong interpersonal skills, written communication skills. Duration is 12 weeks during summer and fall. $210 per week. Open to college freshmen, college sophomores, college juniors, college seniors, recent college graduates, graduate students, career changers. ▶ *1–3 special events interns:* responsibilities include assisting with preparations for special events, organizing volunteers, and assisting the staff with daily office operations. Candidates should have ability to work independently, computer skills, office skills, oral communication skills, organizational skills, personal interest in the field, research skills, self-motivation, strong interpersonal skills, writing skills. Duration is 12 weeks during summer, fall, and spring. $210 per week. Open to college freshmen, college sophomores, college juniors, college seniors, recent college graduates, graduate students, career changers. ▶ *1–3 stage management interns (Wolf Trap Opera Company):* responsibilities include assisting stage management team in all aspects of the rehearsal process and running one side of stage during performance. Candidates should have ability to work independently, experience in the field, oral communication skills, organizational skills, plan to pursue career in field, self-motivation, strong interpersonal skills, ability to read music. Duration is 12 weeks during summer. $210 per week. Open to college freshmen, college sophomores, college juniors, college seniors, recent college graduates, graduate students. ▶ *1–4 technical theater interns (Wolf Trap Opera Company):* responsibilities include working in general technical theater, scenic/prop painting, and costuming, side by side with professional directors, designers, and technicians in mounting and running two operas. Candidates should have ability to work independently, ability to work with others, experience in the field, oral communication skills, organizational skills, self-motivation. Duration is 8-10 weeks during summer. $210 per week. Open to

college freshmen, college sophomores, college juniors, college seniors, recent college graduates, graduate students, career changers. International applications accepted.

Benefits Job counseling, on-the-job training, opportunity to attend seminars/workshops, possible full-time employment, willing to act as a professional reference, willing to complete paperwork for educational credit, willing to provide letters of recommendation, complimentary performance tickets when possible, opportunity to join in 403(b) plan.

Contact Write, call, fax, e-mail, or through World Wide Web site Mia De Mezza, Assistant Director, Education Outreach. Phone: 703-255-1933. Fax: 703-255-1924. E-mail: internships@wolftrap. org. In-person interview recommended (telephone interview accepted). Applicants must submit a letter of interest, resume, two writing samples, two letters of recommendation. Application deadline: March 1 for summer, July 1 for fall, November 1 for spring. World Wide Web: http://www.wolftrap.org.

WOMEN'S PROJECT AND PRODUCTIONS
55 West End Avenue
New York, New York 10023

General Information Nonprofit theater organization that seeks to develop and produce original works written and directed by women in the off-Broadway theater and to promote women in the theater nationally. Established in 1978. Number of employees: 8. Number of internship applications received each year: 100.

Internships Available ▶ *1 administrative intern:* responsibilities include assisting office personnel with general administrative duties and working with the managing director on special projects. Candidates should have ability to work with others, computer skills, office skills, oral communication skills, organizational skills, self-motivation. Duration is flexible. Unpaid. Open to high school students, recent high school graduates, college freshmen, college sophomores, college juniors, college seniors, recent college graduates, graduate students, career changers, individuals reentering the workforce. ▶ *1–2 development assistants:* responsibilities include assisting development director in researching funding sources, drafting development-related correspondence, coordinating mail solicitation, and helping with the ongoing activities of development department. Candidates should have ability to work independently, computer skills, oral communication skills, personal interest in the field, research skills, written communication skills. Duration is 20 hours per week. Unpaid. Open to college freshmen, college sophomores, college juniors, college seniors, recent college graduates, graduate students, career changers, individuals reentering the workforce. ▶ *1–5 education interns:* responsibilities include teaching in New York public schools, creating lesson plans, and assisting with a final production in the Women's Project Theatre. Candidates should have college courses in field, experience in the field, organizational skills, personal interest in the field, strong interpersonal skills. Duration is flexible. Unpaid. Open to college juniors, college seniors, recent college graduates, graduate students, career changers, individuals reentering the workforce. ▶ *2 literary assistants:* responsibilities include reading and evaluating play scripts, assisting in processing scripts and updating artistic files, and assisting literary manager with the reading series and ongoing activities of the literary department. Candidates should have ability to work independently, analytical skills, computer skills, knowledge of field, research skills, written communication skills. Duration is 20 hours per week. Unpaid. Open to college freshmen, college sophomores, college juniors, college seniors, recent college graduates, graduate students, career changers, individuals reentering the workforce. ▶ *1–2 marketing interns:* responsibilities include copywriting for programs, helping to prepare mailings, telemarketing, and assisting in writing newsletter. Candidates should have ability to work independently, computer skills, knowledge of field, oral communication skills, organizational skills. Duration is 6 weeks (minimum). Unpaid. Open to college freshmen, college sophomores, college juniors, college seniors, recent college graduates, graduate students, career changers, individuals reentering the workforce. ▶ *1–5 production interns:* responsibilities include assisting crew during rehearsals or performances of full productions, and possibly serving as general production assistant or assisting the director. Candidates should have ability to work independently, experience in the field, self-motivation, strong interpersonal skills, maturity and ability to handle pressure. Duration is 25 to 35 hours per week. Unpaid. Open to college freshmen, college sophomores, college juniors, college seniors, recent college graduates, graduate students, career changers, individuals reentering the workforce. International applications accepted.

Benefits Names of contacts, possible full-time employment, willing to complete paperwork for educational credit, willing to provide letters of recommendation, complimentary tickets to all performances by WPP and to other New York theaters (when available).

Contact Write, call, fax, or e-mail Cory Hinkle, Assistant to Artistic Director/Intern Coordinator. Phone: 212-765-1706. Fax: 212-765-2024. E-mail: info@womensproject.org. In-person interview recommended (telephone interview accepted). Applicants must submit a letter of interest, resume. Applications are accepted continuously. World Wide Web: http://www.womensproject.org.

PERFORMING ARTS, SPECTATOR SPORTS, AND RELATED INDUSTRIES

AMERICAN DANCE FESTIVAL
Box 90772
Durham, North Carolina 27708

General Information Organization that supports modern dance artists through performance, education, and special programs and works to promote dance consciousness in the American public. Established in 1934. Number of employees: 17. Number of internship applications received each year: 60.

Internships Available ▶ *1 box office intern:* responsibilities include selling single tickets on a computerized box office system (Prologue). Candidates should have ability to work independently, ability to work with others, computer skills, oral communication skills, organizational skills, self-motivation, must have own transportation. Duration is late May through late July. $1100 per duration of internship. Open to college sophomores, college juniors, college seniors, recent college graduates. ▶ *2 facility services interns:* responsibilities include facilitating the technical, studio, housing, food and transportation needs for the entire ADF community; assisting in virtually all aspects of setting up and running an international arts festival. Candidates should have ability to work independently, computer skills, oral communication skills, organizational skills, self-motivation, strong interpersonal skills, video experience (a plus). Duration is late May through late July. $1100 per duration of internship. Open to college freshmen, college sophomores, college juniors, college seniors, recent college graduates, graduate students, law students, career changers. ▶ *1 food and housing intern:* responsibilities include planning and implementing receptions/parties and arranging food/housing requests with Duke University for ADF students and professionals throughout the Festival. Candidates should have ability to work independently, ability to work with others, oral communication skills, organizational skills, self-motivation, evening and weekend work required. Duration is late May through late July. $1100 per duration of internship. Open to college sophomores, college juniors, college seniors, recent college graduates, graduate students. ▶ *1 merchandising intern:* responsibilities include displays, inventory control, ordering, daily cash reports, supervision of the scholarship students and volunteers who work in the store and at the theater. Candidates should have ability to work independently, ability to work with others, oral communication skills, self-motivation, accounting and business skills (helpful) and creative eye for visual display. Duration is late May through July. $1100 per duration of internship. Open to college sophomores, college

juniors, college seniors, recent college graduates, graduate students. ▶ *2 performance interns:* responsibilities include administrative coordination of all activities connected with the professional performing companies. Candidates should have ability to work independently, oral communication skills, organizational skills, personal interest in the field, strong interpersonal skills, written communication skills, ability to handle multiple tasks, attention to detail; must have own transportation. Duration is late May through late July. $950 per duration of internship. Open to college juniors, college seniors, recent college graduates, graduate students, law students, career changers. ▶ *2 press interns:* responsibilities include contacting artists for program information; editing and proofing; design work in newspaper advertisements and invitations. Candidates should have computer skills, editing skills, organizational skills, self-motivation, writing skills, responsibility, attention to detail, ability to work under pressure; must have own transportation. Duration is 8 weeks. $950 per duration of internship. Open to college freshmen, college sophomores, college juniors, college seniors, recent college graduates, graduate students, career changers. ▶ *Production interns:* responsibilities include various assignments including: stage management, wardrobe, sound, electrics, and carpentry. Candidates should have ability to work with others, experience in dance production (preferred). Duration is late May through July. $1100 per duration of internship. Open to college sophomores, college juniors, college seniors, recent college graduates, graduate students. ▶ *2 school interns:* responsibilities include working with an international student body and faculty of over 500 people; maintaining the school's master schedule, as well as publishing the daily and weekly calendars; assisting in academic relationships with Duke University; assisting school VIP's; and assigning jobs to scholarship students. Candidates should have ability to work independently, analytical skills, computer skills, experience in the field, oral communication skills, personal interest in the field, self-motivation, strong interpersonal skills. Duration is 8–9 weeks. $950 per duration of internship. Open to college freshmen, college sophomores, college juniors, college seniors, recent college graduates, graduate students, law students, career changers. ▶ *1 video production intern:* responsibilities include working with the videographer at every video taped event and performance and working with the archive to manage season's videos. Candidates should have ability to work independently, experience with audio visual equipment required. Duration is late May through late July. $950 per duration of internship. Open to college sophomores, college juniors, college seniors, recent college graduates, graduate students, law students. International applications accepted.

Benefits Job counseling, names of contacts, on-the-job training, opportunity to attend seminars/workshops, possible full-time employment, willing to complete paperwork for educational credit, willing to provide letters of recommendation, free dance classes, free admission to dance concerts.

Contact Write, fax, e-mail, or through World Wide Web site Intern Coordinator. Fax: 919-684-5459. E-mail: adf@americandancefestival. org. Telephone interview required. Applicants must submit a formal organization application, letter of interest, resume, two letters of recommendation. Application deadline: February 15 for summer. World Wide Web: http://www.americandancefestival. org.

AMERICAN SYMPHONY ORCHESTRA LEAGUE
33 West 60th Street, 5th Floor
New York, New York 10023

General Information National service organization for symphony, chamber, youth, and university orchestras in America working to ensure the artistic, organizational, and financial strength of American orchestras. Established in 1942. Number of employees: 30. Number of internship applications received each year: 50.

Internships Available ▶ *5 orchestra management fellow:* responsibilities include duties and projects while on rotating 6 to 16-week assignments at American orchestras, including assisting in orchestra operations, marketing, public relations, development, volunteerism, governance, contract negotiations, financial management, long-range planning, artistic administration, education, and outreach. Candidates should have knowledge of field, personal interest in

American Symphony Orchestra League (continued)

the field, plan to pursue career in field, strong interpersonal skills, strong leadership ability. Duration is 1 year. $25,000 stipend. Open to college seniors, recent college graduates, graduate students, law students, career changers, individuals reentering the workforce. International applications accepted.

Benefits Formal training, health insurance, job counseling, names of contacts, on-the-job training, opportunity to attend seminars/ workshops, travel reimbursement, willing to provide letters of recommendation, access to employment services offered by the League.

Contact Write, call, fax, e-mail, or through World Wide Web site Melanie Hausmann, Program Coordinator. Phone: 212-265-5161 Ext. 220. Fax: 212-262-5198. E-mail: mhausmann@symphony.org. In-person interview required. Applicants must submit a formal organization application, resume, academic transcripts, three writing samples, three letters of recommendation. Application deadline: January 1. Fees: $45. World Wide Web: http://www. symphony.org.

ARCADY MUSIC SOCIETY
PO Box 780
Bar Harbor, Maine 04609

General Information Organization that presents high-quality chamber music. Established in 1980. Number of employees: 2. Number of internship applications received each year: 10.

Internships Available ▶ *1–2 summer festival interns:* responsibilities include assisting executive director and regional committees in all logistics of festival presentation including: selling ads, distributing posters, and handling publicity, ticket sales, and artists' housing arrangements. Candidates should have ability to work independently, ability to work with others, computer skills, office skills, oral communication skills, organizational skills, personal interest in the field, self-motivation. Duration is 3–4 months. $1000–$1200 per duration of internship. Open to high school seniors, recent high school graduates, college freshmen, college sophomores, college juniors, college seniors, recent college graduates, graduate students, career changers, individuals reentering the workforce. International applications accepted.

Benefits Free housing, job counseling, names of contacts, on-the-job training, willing to act as a professional reference, willing to complete paperwork for educational credit, willing to provide letters of recommendation, some free meals on concert nights.

Contact Write, call, fax, e-mail, or through World Wide Web site Patricia Ciraulo, Executive Director. Phone: 207-288-2141. Fax: 207-288-2141. E-mail: arcady@arcady.org. In-person interview recommended (telephone interview accepted). Applicants must submit a letter of interest, resume, two personal references. Application deadline: February 1 for summer. World Wide Web: http://www.arcady.org.

ARCHIVE OF CONTEMPORARY MUSIC
54 White Street
New York, New York 10013

General Information Nonprofit music library and research center, with over one million recordings, dedicated to the collection and preservation of all types of popular music from around the world, 1950 to the present. Established in 1986. Number of employees: 3. Number of internship applications received each year: 100.

Internships Available ▶ *12 interns:* responsibilities include assisting in cataloging, filing press clippings, conducting research, and performing general office duties. Candidates should have ability to work with others, computer skills, knowledge of field, office skills, organizational skills, personal interest in the field, research skills, self-motivation. Duration is flexible. Unpaid. Open to high school students, college freshmen, college sophomores, college juniors, college seniors, graduate students. International applications accepted.

Benefits Job counseling, opportunity to attend seminars/ workshops, willing to complete paperwork for educational credit, willing to provide letters of recommendation, computer training, $10 per day for transportation and lunch.

Contact Write, call, fax, e-mail, or through World Wide Web site Mr. Bob George, Director. Phone: 212-226-6967. Fax: 212-226-6540. E-mail: arcmusic@inch.com. In-person interview recommended (telephone interview accepted). Applicants must submit a resume. Applications are accepted continuously. World Wide Web: http://www.arcmusic.org.

BALLET MET
322 Mount Vernon Avenue
Columbus, Ohio 43215

General Information Professional dance company and academy. Established in 1978. Number of employees: 100. Number of internship applications received each year: 150.

Internships Available ▶ *1–4 marketing interns:* responsibilities include working on special events, press coordination, marketing, and some design. Candidates should have ability to work independently, computer skills, editing skills, oral communication skills, written communication skills, design experience helpful. Duration is 3 months. $200 stipend. Open to college sophomores, college juniors, college seniors. International applications accepted.

Benefits Names of contacts, willing to complete paperwork for educational credit, willing to provide letters of recommendation.

Contact Write, call, fax, or e-mail Brandi Pennington, Marketing Communications Associate. Phone: 614-229-4860 Ext. 163. Fax: 614-229-4858. E-mail: bpennington@balletmet.org. In-person interview recommended (telephone interview accepted). Applicants must submit a letter of interest, resume, writing sample. Applications are accepted continuously. World Wide Web: http://www.balletmet.org.

BOWIE BAYSOX
PO Box 1661
Bowie, Maryland 20717

General Information Minor league baseball team affiliated with Baltimore Orioles. Unit of Comcast, Philadelphia, Pennsylvania. Number of internship applications received each year: 300.

Internships Available ▶ *10th Player Program coordinators:* responsibilities include sales and marketing of new program to area businesses via telemarketing and mass direct marketing techniques; aggressive telephone selling. Candidates should have ability to work independently, computer skills, self-motivation, strong interpersonal skills, strong leadership ability, writing skills, ability to work in fast-paced environment. Duration is 1 semester. Unpaid. ▶ *Audio visual interns:* responsibilities include taping and production of pre-recorded AV pieces on Baysox player for broadcast on video board; coordination of all camera operators for in-stadium game broadcast; installation of digital pictures, graphics, and video into click effects program; game-day operation of click effects program in press box for fan entertainment. Candidates should have ability to work independently, computer skills, knowledge of field, oral communication skills, organizational skills, personal interest in the field, research skills, self-motivation, strong interpersonal skills, strong leadership ability, writing skills, ability to work in fast-paced environment. Duration is 1 semester. Unpaid. ▶ *Box office assistants:* responsibilities include assisting ticket manager with daily operations of the ticket box office; taking incoming phone orders for individual game ticket sales; processing ticket orders using select ticketing system; assisting in completing multiple mass mail jobs for renewal of season tickets. Candidates should have ability to work independently, computer skills, oral communication skills, organizational skills, personal interest in the field, self-motivation, strong leadership ability, writing skills, ability to work in fast-paced environment. Duration is 1 semester. Unpaid. ▶ *Group event coordinators:* responsibilities include aggressive selling; helping event coordinator at all times; generating leads through cold calling; servicing clients during events. Candidates should have ability to work independently, ability to work with others, computer skills, knowledge of field, oral communication skills, organizational skills, personal interest in the field, self-motivation, writing skills, ability to work in fast-paced environment. Duration is 1 semester. Unpaid. ▶ *Group events assistants:* responsibilities include assisting full-time group event manager with follow up phone calls, generating leads, coordinating events and servicing clients during events; processing group event orders and mailing group event packages to clients; group database management and maintenance. Candidates should have ability to work independently, computer skills, knowledge of field, oral communication skills, personal interest in the field, strong interpersonal skills, strong leadership ability, written communication skills, ability to work in fast-paced environment. Duration is 1 semester. Unpaid. ▶ *Marketing assistants:* responsibilities include assisting marketing staff with development and implementation of innovative and fun promotions designed to attract fans to the stadium; working with local media to promote the visibility of the Baysox; mass marketing via mailing and pocket schedule distribution. Candidates should have ability to work independently, oral communication skills, organizational skills, strong interpersonal skills, strong leadership ability, writing skills, ability to work in fast-paced environment. Duration is 1 semester. Unpaid. ▶ *Public relation assistants:* responsibilities include assistance with production of Baysox Playbill; dissemination of press releases; assisting director in coordinating media interviews with staff and players; distribution of media credentials; management of press box during games; providing updated scores to wire services; assisting local and national sports media; contacting media with scores. Candidates should have ability to work independently, computer skills, oral communication skills, organizational skills, personal interest in the field, self-motivation, strong interpersonal skills, strong leadership ability, writing skills, ability to work in fast-paced environment. Duration is 1 semester. Unpaid. ▶ *Sponsor sales assistants:* responsibilities include assisting full-time sponsorship sales account managers with follow-up-phone calls; generating leads; coordinating events and serving clients during events; telemarketing and mass direct marketing to area businesses. Candidates should have ability to work independently, computer skills, knowledge of field, oral communication skills, personal interest in the field, self-motivation, strong leadership ability, writing skills, ability to work in fast-paced environment. Duration is 1 semester. Unpaid. ▶ *Theme night assistants:* responsibilities include assisting theme night coordinator with setting up particular nights throughout the season by focusing on targeted audiences with the goals of driving revenues and turnstile attendance on those nights; setting up meetings in and out of office with community groups and organizations; selling pre- and post-game group events. Candidates should have ability to work independently, computer skills, knowledge of field, personal interest in the field, self-motivation, strong interpersonal skills, strong leadership ability, writing skills, ability to work in fast-paced environment. Duration is 1 semester. Unpaid. ▶ *Ticket sales assistants:* responsibilities include aggressive selling, lead generation through cold calling area businesses; use of mass direct marketing techniques to business and residences to sell partial and full-season ticket packages; servicing of clients during events; and box office assistance. Candidates should have ability to work independently, ability to work with others, computer skills, oral communication skills, organizational skills, personal interest in the field, self-motivation, strong leadership ability, writing skills, ability to work in fast-paced environment. Duration is 1 semester. Unpaid. Open to college juniors, college seniors, recent college graduates, graduate students, must be working for academic credits.

Benefits Formal training, on-the-job training, opportunity to attend seminars/workshops, possible full-time employment, willing to act as a professional reference, willing to complete paperwork for educational credit.

Contact Write, call, fax, e-mail, or through World Wide Web site Curt A. Wilson, Recruiter, Human Resources, 3601 South Broad Street, Philadelphia 19148-5290. Phone: 215-389-9502. Fax: 215-389-9413. E-mail: cwilson@comcast-spectacor.com. In-person interview required. Applicants must submit a formal organization application, letter of interest, resume, writing sample, personal reference, letter of recommendation. Applications are accepted continuously. World Wide Web: http://www.baysox.com.

BROOKLYN ACADEMY OF MUSIC
30 Lafayette Avenue
Brooklyn, New York 11217-1486

General Information Internationally recognized performing arts center. Established in 1861. Number of employees: 150. Number of internship applications received each year: 200.

Internships Available ▶ *1–2 fund-raising interns:* responsibilities include writing reports and proposals for grants. Candidates should have ability to work independently, computer skills, office skills, organizational skills, personal interest in the field, writing skills. Duration is flexible. Position available as unpaid or at stipend of $150 per week. ▶ *1 human resources intern:* responsibilities include administrative/clerical duties; (answering phones, filing, possible data entry). Candidates should have ability to work with others, office skills, organizational skills, personal interest in the field, research skills, ability to keep confidential information. Duration is flexible. Unpaid. Open to college freshmen, college sophomores, college juniors, college seniors, recent college graduates, graduate students, law students, career changers. ▶ *1–2 marketing and communications interns:* responsibilities include providing general administrative support services. Candidates should have ability to work independently, computer skills, office skills, oral communication skills, organizational skills, personal interest in the field, written communication skills. Duration is flexible. Position available as unpaid or at stipend of $150 per week. Open to high school seniors, recent high school graduates, college freshmen, college sophomores, college juniors, college seniors, recent college graduates, graduate students, career changers, individuals reentering the workforce. ▶ *1 production intern:* responsibilities include working with stagehands, technical, and wardrobe personnel to provide administrative support. Candidates should have ability to work independently, computer skills, office skills, oral communication skills, organizational skills, personal interest in the field, self-motivation, strong interpersonal skills. Duration is flexible. Unpaid. Open to college freshmen, college sophomores, college juniors, college seniors, recent college graduates, graduate students. ▶ *1 rentals intern:* responsibilities include administrative/clerical duties, answering phones, answering questions about renting the theaters, running errands, and proofreading contracts and schedules. Candidates should have ability to work independently, computer skills, office skills, oral communication skills, self-motivation, strong interpersonal skills. Duration is flexible. Unpaid. Open to college freshmen, college sophomores, college juniors, college seniors, recent college graduates, graduate students, career changers. ▶ *1–2 special events interns:* responsibilities include assisting in fund-raising, planning, and execution of events. Candidates should have computer skills, office skills, organizational skills, personal interest in the field, self-motivation, strong interpersonal skills. Duration is flexible. Position available as unpaid or at stipend of $150 per week. Open to high school students, recent high school graduates, college freshmen, college sophomores, college juniors, college seniors, recent college graduates, graduate students, career changers, individuals reentering the workforce. International applications accepted.

Benefits Names of contacts, possible full-time employment, willing to complete paperwork for educational credit.

Contact Write, fax, or e-mail Katina Jackson, Director of Human Resource, 30 Lafayette Avenue, Brooklyn, New York 11217-1485. Fax: 718-636-4179. E-mail: hrresumes@bam.org. No phone calls. In-person interview required. Applicants must submit a resume, letter of interest specifying which internship requested and dates of availability. Applications are accepted continuously. World Wide Web: http://www.bam.org.

BURNS SPORTS & CELEBRITIES
1007 Church Street, Suite 306
Evanston, Illinois 60201

General Information Sports and entertainment marketing company. Number of employees: 3. Number of internship applications received each year: 400.

Internships Available ▶ *Up to 3 interns:* responsibilities include general office duties, database management, research marketing, travel arrangements, contracts. Candidates should have office skills, oral communication skills, organizational skills, personal interest in the field, self-motivation, strong interpersonal skills. Duration is 1 semester. Position available as unpaid or paid. Open to college freshmen, college sophomores, college juniors, college seniors. International applications accepted.

Burns Sports & Celebrities (continued)

Benefits Possible full-time employment, willing to act as a professional reference, willing to complete paperwork for educational credit, willing to provide letters of recommendation, case-by-case stipend or travel reimbursement.

Contact Write or fax Amy Buckler, Senior Account Executive. Fax: 847-491-9778. E-mail: amyb@burnssports.com. No phone calls. In-person interview recommended (telephone interview accepted). Applicants must submit a letter of interest, resume, three personal references. Applications are accepted continuously. World Wide Web: http://www.burnsports.com.

CARNEGIE HALL
881 Seventh Avenue
New York, New York 10019

General Information Concert hall providing concerts of classical, jazz, and other styles of music. Established in 1891. Number of employees: 270. Number of internship applications received each year: 250.

Internships Available ▶ *Interns:* responsibilities include various possibilities throughout Carnegie Hall (typically in marketing, public affairs, and development). Candidates should have ability to work with others, oral communication skills, written communication skills, MS office skills. Duration is typically 3 to 5 months (may be longer). Position available as unpaid or paid. Open to college freshmen, college sophomores, college juniors, college seniors, recent college graduates, graduate students. International applications accepted.

Benefits On-the-job training, willing to complete paperwork for educational credit, willing to provide letters of recommendation, opportunity to attend concerts.

Contact Write, fax, or e-mail Human Resources. Fax: 212-581-6539. E-mail: humanresources@carnegiehall.org. In-person interview required. Applicants must submit a formal organization application, letter of interest, resume, 1-2 writing samples. Applications are accepted continuously. World Wide Web: http://www.carnegiehall.org.

CHAMBER MUSIC AMERICA
305 Seventh Avenue, 5th Floor
New York, New York 10001-6008

General Information National service organization for professional chamber music ensembles and presenters. Established in 1978. Number of employees: 13. Number of internship applications received each year: 10.

Internships Available ▶ *2–3 Chamber Music Magazine* interns: responsibilities include assisting with editorial and production duties. Candidates should have computer skills, editing skills, organizational skills, writing skills. Duration is flexible. Position available as unpaid or paid. Open to college seniors, recent college graduates, graduate students. ▶ *1 arts administration intern:* responsibilities include assisting with general administration and fund-raising responsibilities. Candidates should have computer skills, office skills, personal interest in the field, written communication skills. Duration is 1–2 semesters. Position available as unpaid or paid. Open to college seniors, recent college graduates, graduate students. ▶ *1 conferences intern:* responsibilities include assisting in administrative duties related to national conference. Candidates should have ability to work with others, analytical skills, office skills, personal interest in the field. Duration is 6–8 weeks. Unpaid. Open to college freshmen, college sophomores, college juniors, college seniors, graduate students. ▶ *4–6 development interns:* responsibilities include assisting in growing development office. Candidates should have written communication skills. Duration is flexible. Position available as unpaid or paid. Open to college seniors, recent college graduates, graduate students. International applications accepted.

Benefits Job counseling, names of contacts, opportunity to attend seminars/workshops, possible full-time employment, willing to complete paperwork for educational credit, possible stipends.

Contact Write, fax, e-mail, or through World Wide Web site Kevin Sky Russell, Director of Administration. Fax: 212-242-7955. E-mail: info@chamber-music.org. No phone calls. In-person interview recommended (telephone interview accepted). Applicants must submit a letter of interest, resume. Applications are accepted continuously. World Wide Web: http://www.chamber-music.org.

CHARLOTTE WILCOX COMPANY
1560 Broadway, Suite 315
New York, New York 10036

General Information Organization managing Broadway, touring-shows, and undertaking various responsibilities including contracts, budgets, taxes, and union rulings. Established in 1976. Number of employees: 5. Number of internship applications received each year: 25.

Internships Available ▶ *1–2 office assistants:* responsibilities include assisting with general office duties including filing, phone work, running errands, computer input, typing, and working on special projects. Candidates should have ability to work independently, computer skills, office skills, oral communication skills, personal interest in the field, plan to pursue career in field, research skills, self-motivation, strong interpersonal skills, writing skills. Duration is flexible. Stipend of $200 per 40-hour week. Open to college freshmen, college sophomores, college juniors, college seniors, recent college graduates. International applications accepted.

Benefits Names of contacts, on-the-job training, possible full-time employment, willing to act as a professional reference, willing to complete paperwork for educational credit, willing to provide letters of recommendation.

Contact Write or fax Charlotte Wilcox, General Manager. Fax: 212-764-5766. No phone calls. In-person interview recommended (telephone interview accepted). Applicants must submit a letter of interest, resume. Applications are accepted continuously.

CITY LIGHTS YOUTH THEATRE
300 West 43rd Street, Suite 402
New York, New York 10036

General Information Nonprofit theater arts education program for students K-12, offering process-oriented classes, workshops, and residencies that engage New York youth from diverse backgrounds in the performance of theater. Established in 1991. Number of employees: 42. Number of internship applications received each year: 25.

Internships Available ▶ *2–3 assistant stage managers:* responsibilities include working closely with the professional stage manager during rehearsals and production of plays that are cast entirely with youth. Candidates should have ability to work independently, ability to work with others, computer skills, oral communication skills, organizational skills, personal interest in the field, self-motivation. Duration is 3–6 months. Unpaid. Open to high school students, recent high school graduates, college freshmen, college sophomores, college juniors, college seniors, recent college graduates, graduate students. ▶ *1 office assistant:* responsibilities include assisting the management team and the office manager; some light bookkeeping; interaction with children, teenagers, and parents necessary. Candidates should have ability to work independently, ability to work with others, computer skills, office skills, oral communication skills, organizational skills, personal interest in the field, self-motivation, word processing and telephone skills. Duration is flexible. Unpaid. Open to high school students, recent high school graduates, college freshmen, college sophomores, college juniors, college seniors, recent college graduates, graduate students. ▶ *6–10 teaching artist assistants:* responsibilities include being matched with a professional theater arts teaching artist for support in the classroom, working with children or teenagers in a theater arts educational setting. Candidates should have ability to work independently, ability to work with others, oral communication skills, personal interest in the field, self-motivation. Duration is 9–15 weeks. Unpaid. Open to recent high school graduates, college freshmen, college sophomores, college juniors, college seniors, recent college graduates, graduate students. International applications accepted.

Benefits On-the-job training, opportunity to attend seminars/workshops, willing to act as a professional reference, willing to complete paperwork for educational credit, willing to provide letters of recommendation.

Contact Write, e-mail, or through World Wide Web site Warren Baumgart, Jr., Artistic Director. Fax: 212-262-1888. E-mail: citylights@clyouththeatre.org. No phone calls. In-person interview required. Applicants must submit a letter of interest, resume, three personal references. Applications are accepted continuously. World Wide Web: http://www.clyouththeatre.org.

COMCAST
3601 South Broad Street
Philadelphia, Pennsylvania 19148-5290

General Information Sports and entertainment company that operates the First Union Spectrum/Center facilities, 3 professional sports franchises, and a cable broadcast sports network. Established in 1967. Number of employees: 3,150. Number of internship applications received each year: 300.

Internships Available ▶ *1 accounting intern:* responsibilities include maintaining data files, preparing bank reconciliations, assisting with payroll functions, analyzing G/L accounts, and entering accounts payable invoices in the accounting system. Candidates should have analytical skills, college courses in field, computer skills, knowledge of field, office skills, Lotus experience (helpful), ability to meet deadlines. Duration is 1 semester in fall, spring, or summer. Unpaid. Open to college juniors and seniors or graduate students working for academic credit. ▶ *1 advertising sales intern:* responsibilities include developing new concepts for advertising venues at the First Union Spectrum/Center, assisting staff with research and design for various projects, handling phone inquiries, coordinating promotions and special events, and assisting with client sponsorship agreements. Candidates should have knowledge of field, oral communication skills, organizational skills, self-motivation, strong interpersonal skills, written communication skills, ability to use Word, WordPerfect, PowerPoint, and Lotus 123 (preferred). Duration is spring or fall semester. Unpaid. Open to college juniors and seniors or graduate students working for academic credit. ▶ *1 building public relations intern:* responsibilities include assisting with generating and pitching story ideas to media; assisting with brainstorming, planning, and executing publicity events; assisting with media tours; handling correspondence and assisting with mailings; and keeping a comprehensive record of events. Candidates should have oral communication skills, organizational skills, research skills, writing skills, good phone skills, ability to use WordPerfect 5.1/6.0. Duration is 1 semester in fall, spring, or summer. Unpaid. Open to college juniors and seniors or graduate students working for academic credit. ▶ *1 electronic media engineering intern:* responsibilities include learning the various computer-controlled systems that operate video, audio, intercom, and electronic message systems throughout the First Union Center; assisting the engineer in event set-up and troubleshooting. Candidates should have analytical skills, college courses in field, computer skills, editing skills, basic understanding of electronic circuit theory including video and audio system signals, component-level understanding of DC electronic (helpful). Duration is 1 semester in fall, spring, or summer. Unpaid. Open to 2nd-year technical school students with audio and television major leading to an associate degree or equivalent. ▶ *1 event production intern:* responsibilities include participating in event-related duties, assisting with coordination of amenities for First Union Center tours, assisting event production staff on various projects, and assisting with coordination of vendor functions. Candidates should have office skills, oral communication skills, strong interpersonal skills, written communication skills, ability to use word processing and spreadsheet applications (Microsoft Word, WordPerfect, Lotus 123, and Excel), good phone skills, and the ability to meet deadlines. Duration is 1 semester in fall, spring, or summer. Unpaid. Open to college juniors and seniors or graduate students working for academic credit. ▶ *1 event public relations intern:* responsibilities include organizing photo files and show files, handling event-related correspondence, helping to plan and execute publicity events, assisting with mailings, and providing support during events. Candidates should have college courses in field, oral communication skills, organizational skills, writing skills, good phone skills, ability to use WordPerfect 5.1/6.0, experience with database management (preferred). Duration is 1 semester in fall, spring, or summer. Unpaid. Open to college

juniors and seniors or graduate students working for academic credit. ▶ *2 event services interns:* responsibilities include assisting in promotion of shows and sporting events to group customers, helping to promote and implement the Public Tour program, processing orders, and customer service. Candidates should have ability to work with others, office skills, oral communication skills, organizational skills, written communication skills, ability to use WordPerfect and Lotus software. Duration is 1 semester in fall, spring, or summer. Unpaid. Open to college juniors and seniors or graduate students working for academic credit. ▶ *2 graphic services interns:* responsibilities include assisting in design, layout, and production of printed materials; maintaining computer files; assisting with production of game-day materials; and participating in brainstorming on proposed graphics projects. Candidates should have college courses in field, knowledge of field, plan to pursue career in field, strong Macintosh computer skills; working knowledge of QuarkXpress, Illustrator, and PhotoShop. Duration is 1 semester in fall, spring, or summer. Unpaid. Open to college juniors and seniors or graduate students working for academic credit. ▶ *1 human resources intern:* responsibilities include working with recruiter to promote and administer the internship program, assisting in orientation of interns, maintaining internship files, and screening incoming employment applications and mailing responses to applicants. Candidates should have oral communication skills, organizational skills, self-motivation, written communication skills, ability to use Microsoft Word (or WordPerfect), Excel, and cc:Mail. Duration is 1 semester in fall, spring, or summer. Unpaid. Open to college juniors and seniors or graduate students working for academic credit. ▶ *2 marketing interns:* responsibilities include promoting shows and sporting events; assisting the security, operations, and promotions departments on days of events, creating post-event marketing summaries, and performing demographic and psychographic market research. Candidates should have college courses in field, oral communication skills, research skills, self-motivation, written communication skills, basic knowledge of word processing and spreadsheet applications, computer graphics experience (helpful). Duration is 1 semester in fall, spring, or summer. Unpaid. Open to college juniors and seniors or graduate students working for academic credit. ▶ *2 operations interns:* responsibilities include assisting with event-related activities, assisting with changeover tasks, and helping to create a production book concerning events held at the First Union Spectrum/Center. Candidates should have analytical skills, knowledge of field, self-motivation, strong interpersonal skills, ability to use WordPerfect, Microsoft Word, and Excel; ability to adapt to a wide variety of projects; ability to meet deadlines. Duration is 1 semester in fall, spring, or summer. Unpaid. Open to college juniors and seniors or graduate students working for academic credit. ▶ *1 tour guide intern:* responsibilities include leading individuals and groups on informative tours of the First Union Center, providing office support, scheduling tours, telemarketing prospective clients, and assisting in marketing and promoting tours. Candidates should have ability to work independently, oral communication skills, self-motivation, strong interpersonal skills, willingness to work some weekends, ability to speak to large groups and to do extensive walking, ability to use WordPerfect and Lotus software. Duration is 1 semester in fall, spring, or summer. Unpaid. Open to college juniors and seniors or graduate students working for academic credit.

Benefits Formal training, names of contacts, on-the-job training, opportunity to attend seminars/workshops, possible full-time employment, willing to act as a professional reference, willing to complete paperwork for educational credit.

Contact Write, call, fax, e-mail, or through World Wide Web site Curt A. Wilson, Human Resources Recruiter, 3601 South Broad Street, Philadelphia, Pennsylvania 19148-5290. Phone: 215-389-9502. Fax: 215-389-9413. E-mail: cwilson@comcast-spectacor.com. In-person interview required. Applicants must submit a formal organization application, resume, letter of recommendation, cover letter indicating reasons for choosing internship and the qualities or attributes that will help make a contribution, faculty recommendation form (sent with application). Applications are accepted continuously. World Wide Web: http://www.comcast-spectacor.com.

CREATIVE EVENT PLANNING
1040 First Avenue, Suite 105
New York, New York 10022

General Information Corporate event planning company. Established in 1989. Number of employees: 2.
Internships Available ▶ *1–2 assistant planners:* responsibilities include general computer work, answering phones, writing proposals, Internet research, and event preparation. Candidates should have ability to work independently, ability to work with others, computer skills, organizational skills, self-motivation, written communication skills. Duration is April to October or beyond. Position available as unpaid or paid. Open to college freshmen, college sophomores, college juniors, college seniors, recent college graduates, graduate students, career changers, individuals reentering the workforce. ▶ *1–2 sales assistants:* responsibilities include calling past clients, finding new clients through warm and cold leads by phone; follow up data, sending marketing materials/press kits; entering information into database. Candidates should have ability to work independently, knowledge of field, oral communication skills, self-motivation, strong interpersonal skills, strong leadership ability. Duration is minimum of 6 months. Position available as unpaid or paid. Open to college juniors, college seniors, recent college graduates, graduate students, career changers, individuals reentering the workforce. International applications accepted.
Contact Write, call, or fax Lynn Silverman, Owner. Phone: 212-421-9080. Fax: 212-421-7838. Applicants must submit a letter of interest, resume.

DELMARVA SHOREBIRDS
6400 Hobbs Road
Salisbury, Maryland 21804

General Information Minor league baseball team affiliated with Baltimore Orioles. Established in 1995. Number of employees: 91. Unit of Comcast, Philadelphia, Pennsylvania. Number of internship applications received each year: 300.
Internships Available ▶ *Graphic design interns:* responsibilities include working with marketing director to create marketing and game day pieces as needed, 4-color art, video board slides; assisting in production and finishing of game and event-related materials; performing other duties as assigned. Candidates should have ability to work independently, ability to work with others, oral communication skills, organizational skills, personal interest in the field, strong leadership ability, writing skills, knowledge of Quark Xpress, PhotoShop and Illustrator necessary; animation experience a plus, ability to work night and weekend events. Duration is 1 semester. Unpaid. ▶ *Marketing and events interns:* responsibilities include working with director of marketing on implementation of corporate marketing strategy; includes media campaigns, implementation of fan survey system, involvement with mascot and community performances, radio, print and television ads, coordination of special events and game day events. Candidates should have ability to work independently, computer skills, oral communication skills, organizational skills, personal interest in the field, self-motivation, strong interpersonal skills, strong leadership ability, writing skills, customer service background, ability to work nights and weekends. Duration is 1 semester. Unpaid.
▶ *Public relations interns:* responsibilities include working with PR director and marketing director in all aspects of promoting the game and events at the park; creating press releases, writing articles, working with media, and keeping game statistics. Candidates should have ability to work independently, computer skills, oral communication skills, organizational skills, personal interest in the field, self-motivation, strong interpersonal skills, strong leadership ability, writing skills, major in public relations, communications or journalism, ability to work nights and weekends. Duration is 1 semester. Unpaid. Open to college juniors, college seniors, recent college graduates, graduate students, must be working for academic credits.
Benefits Formal training, on-the-job training, opportunity to attend seminars/workshops, possible full-time employment, willing to act as a professional reference, willing to complete paperwork for educational credit.

Contact Write, call, fax, e-mail, or through World Wide Web site Curt A. Wilson, Recruiter, Human Resources, 3601 South Broad Street, Philadelphia 19148-5290. Phone: 215-389-9502. Fax: 215-389-9413. E-mail: cwilson@comcast-spectacor.com. Telephone interview required. Applicants must submit a formal organization application, letter of interest, resume, writing sample, letter of recommendation. Applications are accepted continuously. World Wide Web: http://www.dshorebirds.com.

DIXON PLACE
309 East 26th Street
New York, New York 10010

General Information Organization that nurtures theater, performance, dance, and literary artists by encouraging the development of new work and assists emerging and established artists in exploring the creative process by providing a safe, supportive environment. Established in 1986. Number of employees: 10. Number of internship applications received each year: 50.
Internships Available ▶ *1–2 administrative assistants:* responsibilities include preparing monthly calendars, handling press listings and press releases, updating the mailing list, scheduling artists' rehearsal times, and box office management. Candidates should have ability to work independently, computer skills, office skills, personal interest in the field, self-motivation, strong interpersonal skills. Duration is minimum of 3 months. $75–$100 per week.
▶ *1–2 administrative/technical interns:* responsibilities include preparing monthly calendars, press listings, and press releases; updating the mailing list; scheduling artists' rehearsal time; providing technical assistance for artists; working the box office; hosting shows; and opening and closing the theater. Candidates should have computer skills, experience in the field, oral communication skills, self-motivation, strong interpersonal skills. Duration is minimum of 3 months. $75–$100 per week. ▶ *1–2 technical assistants:* responsibilities include providing technical assistance for artists, setting up light, sound, and video; working the box office, opening and closing the theater, and videotaping performances. Candidates should have ability to work independently, experience in the field, oral communication skills, organizational skills, self-motivation, strong interpersonal skills. Duration is minimum of 3 months. $75–$100 per week. Open to college sophomores, college juniors, college seniors, recent college graduates, graduate students, career changers. International applications accepted.
Benefits On-the-job training, opportunity to attend seminars/workshops, willing to complete paperwork for educational credit, willing to provide letters of recommendation.
Contact Write, call, fax, e-mail, or through World Wide Web site Ms. Ellie Covan, Executive Director. Phone: 212-532-1546. Fax: 212-532-1094. E-mail: contact@dixonplace.org. In-person interview recommended (telephone interview accepted). Applicants must submit a letter of interest, resume. Application deadline: April 15 for summer, August 1 for fall, December 1 for winter/spring. World Wide Web: http://www.dixonplace.org.

ELITE MODEL MANAGEMENT, CHICAGO
58 West Huron
Chicago, Illinois 60610

General Information Model management. Established in 1982. Number of employees: 40. Unit of Elite Model Management, New York, New York. Number of internship applications received each year: 100.
Internships Available ▶ *3–5 management assistants:* responsibilities include office duties including filing, fax, phone coverage, and assisting model bookers. Candidates should have ability to work independently, computer skills, office skills, oral communication skills, organizational skills, personal interest in the field, self-motivation, strong interpersonal skills, writing skills. Duration is 2-4 months (flexible). Unpaid. Open to recent high school graduates, college freshmen, college sophomores, college juniors, college seniors, recent college graduates.
Benefits On-the-job training, willing to act as a professional reference, willing to complete paperwork for educational credit, willing to provide letters of recommendation.

Contact Write or fax Shannon E. Hill, New Faces Agent. Fax: 312-943-2590. E-mail: shill@elitechicago.com. No phone calls. Applicants must submit a letter of interest, resume, interview after review of resume. Applications are accepted continuously. World Wide Web: http://www.elitechicago.com.

FREDERICK KEYS
3201 Design Road
Frederick, Maryland 21703

General Information Minor league baseball team affiliated with Baltimore Orioles. Established in 1989. Number of employees: 22. Unit of Comcast, Philadelphia, Pennsylvania. Number of internship applications received each year: 300.
Internships Available ▶ *Box office management trainees:* responsibilities include assisting box office manager in all areas of ticket operations; data entry; processing payments; building accounts; conducting mailings and updating season ticket holders; creating literature; ticket sales promotions; and other special interest projects as needed. Candidates should have ability to work independently, computer skills, office skills, oral communication skills, organizational skills, personal interest in the field, self-motivation, strong interpersonal skills, writing skills, ability to work night and weekends, customer service background (preferred). Duration is 1 semester. Unpaid. ▶ *Group event interns:* responsibilities include customer service; game day and event preparation; assistance with game day reports and mailings; and performing other duties as assigned. Candidates should have ability to work independently, ability to work with others, computer skills, oral communication skills, organizational skills, personal interest in the field, self-motivation, strong leadership ability, writing skills, ability to work nights and weekends; must be enthusiastic with a desire to work hard. Duration is 1 semester. Unpaid. ▶ *Public relations management trainees:* responsibilities include assisting the public relations department with the Keys for Reading Program, Junior Keys Program, and articles for Keys souvenir program; game day duties and special promotional projects as assigned; and assisting in advertising and printing. Candidates should have ability to work independently, computer skills, oral communication skills, organizational skills, personal interest in the field, self-motivation, strong interpersonal skills, strong leadership ability, writing skills, ability to work nights and weekends. Duration is 1 semester. Unpaid. Open to college juniors, college seniors, recent college graduates, graduate students, must be working for academic credits.
Benefits Formal training, on-the-job training, opportunity to attend seminars/workshops, possible full-time employment, willing to act as a professional reference, willing to complete paperwork for educational credit.
Contact Write, call, fax, e-mail, or through World Wide Web site Curt A. Wilson, Recruiter, Human Resources, 3601 South Broad Street, Philadelphia 19148-5290. Phone: 215-389-9502. Fax: 215-389-9413. E-mail: cwilson@comcast-spectacor.com. In-person interview required. Applicants must submit a formal organization application, letter of interest, resume, writing sample, personal reference, letter of recommendation. Applications are accepted continuously. World Wide Web: http://www.frederickkeys.com.

GUS GIORDANO JAZZ DANCE CHICAGO
614 Davis Street
Evanston, Illinois 60201

General Information Nonprofit American jazz dance company that tours internationally and nationally and offers local performances in the Chicago area. Established in 1962. Number of employees: 12. Number of internship applications received each year: 5.
Internships Available ▶ *4 interns:* responsibilities include word processing, writing press releases and dancers' biographies, performing general administrative work, grant writing, and providing research assistance. Candidates should have ability to work independently, ability to work with others, computer skills, office skills, oral communication skills, written communication skills. Duration is 2–6 months. Unpaid. Open to college freshmen, col-

lege sophomores, college juniors, college seniors, recent college graduates, individuals reentering the workforce. International applications accepted.
Benefits On-the-job training, willing to act as a professional reference, willing to complete paperwork for educational credit, willing to provide letters of recommendation.
Contact Write, call, or fax Ben Hodge, Executive Director. Phone: 847-866-6779. Fax: 847-866-9228. E-mail: ggjdc@giordanojazzdance.com. In-person interview recommended (telephone interview accepted). Applicants must submit a letter of interest, resume, two personal references. Applications are accepted continuously.

THE HOUSE FOUNDATION FOR THE ARTS
306 West 38th Street, #401
New York, New York 10018

General Information Foundation that works specifically to raise funds and manage the artistic career of Meredith Monk. Established in 1968. Number of employees: 4. Number of internship applications received each year: 10.
Internships Available ▶ *1–2 archivists:* responsibilities include organizing archive of theatrical, film, opera, dance, and music materials. Candidates should have ability to work independently, computer skills, office skills, organizational skills, personal interest in the field, writing skills. Duration is 3–6 months. Unpaid. ▶ *1–2 assistants to the company manager:* responsibilities include assisting in the production of tours and the New York season, booking, travel arrangements, pre-production, and maintenance of all elements. Candidates should have experience in the field, oral communication skills, organizational skills, personal interest in the field, self-motivation, strong interpersonal skills. Duration is 3–6 months. Unpaid. ▶ *1–3 assistants to the development director:* responsibilities include grant research and fund-raising. Candidates should have ability to work independently, editing skills, office skills, plan to pursue career in field, research skills, writing skills. Duration is 3–6 months. Unpaid. ▶ *1–3 general administrative interns:* responsibilities include answering phones and maintaining correspondence. Candidates should have ability to work independently, computer skills, office skills, organizational skills, personal interest in the field, strong interpersonal skills. Duration is 3–6 months. Unpaid. Open to college juniors, college seniors, recent college graduates, graduate students.
Benefits Possible full-time employment, willing to complete paperwork for educational credit, willing to provide letters of recommendation.
Contact Write or fax Ms. Barbara Dufty, Managing Director. Fax: 212-904-1305. E-mail: monk@meredithmonk.org. In-person interview required. Applicants must submit a letter of interest, resume. Applications are accepted continuously. World Wide Web: http://www.meredithmonk.org.

JACOB'S PILLOW DANCE FESTIVAL, INC.
PO Box 287
Lee, Massachusetts 01238

General Information International festival presenting ten weeks of dance performances and conducting a professional dance school each summer. Established in 1932. Number of employees: 75. Number of internship applications received each year: 100.
Internships Available ▶ *1 archives/preservation assistant:* responsibilities include working alongside the director of preservation in the archives department. Candidates should have ability to work independently, computer skills, oral communication skills, organizational skills, personal interest in the field, research skills, self-motivation. Duration is 3 months or longer. Stipend of $500. Open to college juniors, college seniors, recent college graduates, graduate students, career changers. ▶ *1 business intern:* responsibilities include assisting business manager. Candidates should have computer skills, office skills, organizational skills, personal interest in the field, self-motivation, strong interpersonal skills. Duration is 3 months. Stipend of $500. Open to college juniors, college seniors, recent college graduates, graduate students, career changers. ▶ *2 development interns:* responsibilities include fund-raising and grant writing. Candidates should have ability to work independently, ability to work with others, analytical skills, computer skills, editing skills, oral communication skills,

Jacob's Pillow Dance Festival, Inc. (continued)

organizational skills, personal interest in the field, research skills, self-motivation, writing skills. Duration is 3 months. Stipend of $500. Open to college juniors, college seniors, recent college graduates, graduate students, career changers. ▶ *2 education interns:* responsibilities include assisting education director in the daily operation of school and community programs. Candidates should have ability to work independently, computer skills, knowledge of field, oral communication skills, organizational skills, personal interest in the field, self-motivation, strong interpersonal skills, writing skills. Duration is 3 months. Stipend of $500. Open to college juniors, college seniors, recent college graduates, graduate students, career changers, individuals reentering the workforce. ▶ *3 marketing/press interns:* responsibilities include working to promote the Festival and the school. Candidates should have ability to work independently, ability to work with others, analytical skills, computer skills, editing skills, knowledge of field, oral communication skills, organizational skills, personal interest in the field, research skills, self-motivation, writing skills, design skills. Duration is 3 months. Stipend of $500. Open to college juniors, college seniors, recent college graduates, graduate students, career changers. ▶ *1 operations intern:* responsibilities include managing the day-to-day activities of a multi-theater dance festival. Candidates should have oral communication skills, organizational skills, personal interest in the field, self-motivation, strong interpersonal skills. Duration is 3 months in summer. Stipend of $500. Open to college freshmen, college sophomores, college juniors, college seniors, recent college graduates, graduate students, individuals reentering the workforce. ▶ *1 programming intern:* responsibilities include coordinating audience enrichment programs. Candidates should have analytical skills, computer skills, oral communication skills, organizational skills, personal interest in the field, self-motivation, strong interpersonal skills, writing skills. Duration is 3 months. Stipend of $500. Open to college juniors, college seniors, recent college graduates, graduate students, career changers, individuals reentering the workforce. ▶ *11 technical theater interns:* responsibilities include running crew for 3 theaters and weekly free events. Candidates should have ability to work with others, analytical skills, experience in the field, oral communication skills, personal interest in the field, self-motivation. Duration is 3 months in summer. Stipend of $500. Open to college freshmen, college sophomores, college juniors, college seniors, recent college graduates, graduate students, individuals reentering the workforce. ▶ *2 video/photography interns:* responsibilities include documenting performances and other Festival activities of the season. Candidates should have ability to work independently, ability to work with others, experience in the field, oral communication skills, personal interest in the field, self-motivation. Duration is 3 months in summer. Stipend of $500. Open to college juniors, college seniors, recent college graduates, graduate students, career changers. International applications accepted.

Benefits Free housing, free meals, names of contacts, on-the-job training, opportunity to attend seminars/workshops, possible full-time employment, willing to act as a professional reference, willing to complete paperwork for educational credit, willing to provide letters of recommendation, opportunity to see dance performances.

Contact Write, fax, e-mail, or through World Wide Web site J. R. Glover, Education Programs Director. Phone: 413-637-1322. Fax: 413-243-4744. E-mail: info@jacobspillow.org. Telephone interview required. Applicants must submit a letter of interest, resume, two letters of recommendation, work-related reference, and 2 writing samples (maximum 3 pages) for marketing/press, development, education, and programming applicants. Application deadline: March 6 for summer, September 13 for fall, December 1 for spring. World Wide Web: http://www.jacobspillow.org.

THE JOHN F. KENNEDY CENTER FOR THE PERFORMING ARTS
2700 F Street, NW
Washington, District of Columbia 20566

General Information National performing arts center. Established in 1971. Number of employees: 1,000. Number of internship applications received each year: 700.

Internships Available ▶ *1 Alliance for Arts Education intern:* responsibilities include assisting with national recognition programs for outstanding school administrators and local school boards, administering fellowships, and working with a national network of state organizations. Candidates should have computer skills, knowledge of field, oral communication skills, strong interpersonal skills, writing skills. Duration is 3–4 months. $800 per month. Open to college juniors, college seniors, recent college graduates, graduate students. ▶ *1 American College Theater Festival intern:* responsibilities include assisting with technical coordination of ACTF national festival, responding to telephone inquiries, updating mailing lists, and handling national festival ticket distribution. Candidates should have computer skills, oral communication skills, personal interest in the field, plan to pursue career in field, strong interpersonal skills, writing skills. Duration is 3–4 months. $800 per month. Open to college juniors, college seniors, recent college graduates, graduate students. ▶ *1 Arts Edge intern:* responsibilities include assisting director and staff with research, collection, and organization of information to be disseminated through the Arts Edge Web site. Candidates should have computer skills, knowledge of field, oral communication skills, strong interpersonal skills, writing skills. Duration is 3–4 months. $800 per month. Open to college juniors, college seniors, recent college graduates, graduate students. ▶ *1 Friends of Kennedy Center intern:* responsibilities include working in special events production, volunteer management, retail management, visitor services, and community relations. Candidates should have computer skills, oral communication skills, personal interest in the field, strong interpersonal skills. Duration is 3–4 months. $800 per month. Open to college juniors, college seniors, recent college graduates, graduate students. ▶ *2–4 National Symphony Orchestra interns:* responsibilities include assisting with organization of special concerts for young people, administering training programs and competitions for high school musicians, fielding phone inquiries, researching programming issues, working with volunteers, and compiling material for NSO education programs. Candidates should have computer skills, knowledge of field, oral communication skills, plan to pursue career in field, strong interpersonal skills, writing skills. Duration is 3–4 months. $800 per month. Open to college juniors, college seniors, recent college graduates. ▶ *2 advertising interns:* responsibilities include providing administrative support and dealing with advertising trafficking and placements, broadcast production, editing, and promotional event planning. Candidates should have computer skills, knowledge of field, oral communication skills, plan to pursue career in field, writing skills. Duration is 3–4 months. $800 per month. Open to college juniors, college seniors, recent college graduates, graduate students. ▶ *3–4 development interns:* responsibilities include assisting in administration of fund-raising campaigns and working on project research, special projects, membership services, grants, sponsorship, corporate fund, and Circle Fund. Candidates should have computer skills, oral communication skills, organizational skills, strong interpersonal skills, writing skills. Duration is 3–4 months. $800 per month. Open to college juniors, college seniors, recent college graduates, graduate students. ▶ *6–8 education department interns:* responsibilities include assisting with the administration of arts education events and evaluating programs, workshops, discussions, master classes, and performances. Candidates should have computer skills, oral communication skills, personal interest in the field, plan to pursue career in field, strong interpersonal skills, writing skills. Duration is 3–4 months. $800 per month. Open to college juniors, college seniors, recent college graduates, graduate students. ▶ *1 production intern:* responsibilities include serving as a production or design assistant for shows and events in the Center's six theater and non-theater spaces. Candidates should have computer skills, knowledge of field, oral communication skills, personal interest in the field, strong interpersonal skills. Duration is 3–4 months. $800 per month. Open to college juniors, college seniors, recent college graduates, graduate students. ▶ *1–2 programming interns:* responsibilities include contract preparation, supernumerary coordination, artist hospitality, and special performance event management. Candidates should have ability to work independently, computer skills, organizational skills, plan to pursue career in field, strong interpersonal skills, writing skills. Duration is 3–4 months. $800 per month. Open to college juniors,

college seniors, recent college graduates, graduate students. ▶ *1 special events intern:* responsibilities include assisting with the planning and implementation of all special events including the Kennedy Center Honors, Spring Gala, and cast parties. Candidates should have knowledge of field, organizational skills, personal interest in the field, strong interpersonal skills, writing skills. Duration is 3–4 months. $800 per month. Open to college juniors, college seniors, recent college graduates, graduate students. ▶ *1 youth and family programs intern:* responsibilities include assisting with theater training program, contributing to audience and program development projects, supporting the artistic and production staff, acting as production interns by assisting the stage managers or design assistants, or working with the artistic and production staff. Candidates should have computer skills, knowledge of field, oral communication skills, plan to pursue career in field, writing skills. Duration is 3–4 months. $800 per month. Open to college juniors, college seniors, recent college graduates, graduate students. International applications accepted.
Benefits Formal training, names of contacts, opportunity to attend seminars/workshops, willing to act as a professional reference, willing to complete paperwork for educational credit, willing to provide letters of recommendation, opportunity to attend performances.
Contact Write, call, e-mail, or through World Wide Web site Jennifer Schmidt, Internship Program Coordinator. Phone: 202-416-8821. Fax: 202-416-8853. E-mail: jlschmidt@kennedy-center.org. Applicants must submit a formal organization application, letter of interest, resume, academic transcripts, two letters of recommendation, 1–3 page writing sample. Application deadline: March 1 for summer, June 23 for fall, November 1 for winter/spring. World Wide Web: http://www.kennedy-center.org.

MELLON ARENA
66 Mario Lemieux Place
Pittsburgh, Pennsylvania 15219

General Information Public sports and entertainment facility. Established in 1961. Number of employees: 400. Unit of SMG, Philadelphia, Pennsylvania. Number of internship applications received each year: 50.
Internships Available ▶ *2–4 marketing/group services interns:* responsibilities include preparing and implementing marketing plans for Mellon Arena events; preparing recaps of event sponsorships; maintaining client database; assisting with Web site; field group/corporate sales phone work. Candidates should have ability to work independently, computer skills, oral communication skills, organizational skills, research skills, strong interpersonal skills. Duration is May to August, September to December, or January to April. Position available as unpaid or paid. Open to college sophomores, college juniors, college seniors, recent college graduates, graduate students. International applications accepted.
Benefits Names of contacts, opportunity to attend seminars/workshops, possible full-time employment, willing to act as a professional reference, willing to complete paperwork for educational credit, willing to provide letters of recommendation.
Contact Write, fax, or e-mail Marketing Manager. Fax: 412-391-8454. E-mail: info@mellonarena.com. No phone calls. In-person interview recommended (telephone interview accepted). Applicants must submit a letter of interest, resume. Applications are accepted continuously. World Wide Web: http://www.mellonarena.com.

METROPOLITAN OPERA GUILD EDUCATION DEPARTMENT
70 Lincoln Center Plaza
New York, New York 10023-6593

General Information Program dedicated to furthering music education in schools and communities across the nation through a variety of activities including school residencies, lecture series, backstage tours, multimedia resources, and special performances for students at the Metropolitan Opera House. Established in 1935. Number of employees: 9. Unit of Metropolitan Opera Guild, New York, New York. Number of internship applications received each year: 15.

Internships Available ▶ *4 interns:* responsibilities include performing office tasks, managing the box office, editing and producing study materials, and coordinating students in the Opera House. Candidates should have ability to work independently, computer skills, experience in the field, office skills, oral communication skills, plan to pursue career in field. Duration is 3 months minimum (15 hours minimum per week). Position available as unpaid or paid. Open to college freshmen, college sophomores, college juniors, college seniors, recent college graduates, graduate students. International applications accepted.
Benefits Job counseling, on-the-job training, opportunity to attend seminars/workshops, willing to act as a professional reference, willing to complete paperwork for educational credit, willing to provide letters of recommendation, $500 stipend.
Contact Write, call, fax, e-mail, or through World Wide Web site Ms. Gretchen Weerheim, Family/Schools Coordinator. Phone: 212-769-7022. Fax: 212-769-8519. E-mail: gweerheim@operaed.org. In-person interview required. Applicants must submit a letter of interest, resume, three letters of recommendation. Application deadline: May 1 for summer, July 1 for fall, December 1 for spring. World Wide Web: http://www.operaed.org.

MILWAUKEE BREWERS BASEBALL CLUB
1 Brewers Way
Milwaukee, Wisconsin 53214

General Information Professional sports franchise. Established in 1970. Number of employees: 90. Number of internship applications received each year: 75.
Internships Available ▶ *2–5 media relations interns:* responsibilities include correspondence with fans; research projects; and day-to-day operations in media; writing projects. Candidates should have ability to work independently, computer skills, editing skills, knowledge of field, research skills, writing skills. Duration is 3–4 months (year-round). Unpaid. Open to college sophomores, college juniors, college seniors, graduate students, must be earning college credit. International applications accepted.
Benefits Names of contacts, willing to act as a professional reference, willing to complete paperwork for educational credit, willing to provide letters of recommendation.
Contact Write or fax Jason Parry, Assistant Director, Media Relations, 1 Brewers Way, Milwaukee, Wisconsin 53201-3099. Phone: 414-902-4500. Fax: 414-902-4053. E-mail: jparry@milwaukeebrewers.com. Telephone interview required. Applicants must submit a letter of interest, resume, writing sample, letter of recommendation. Application deadline: February 1 for summer, August 1 for fall, December 1 for spring. World Wide Web: http://www.milwaukeebrewers.com.

MINNESOTA DANCE ALLIANCE
528 Hennepin Avenue, Suite 510
Minneapolis, Minnesota 55403

General Information Service organization for the art of dance in Minnesota. Established in 1979. Number of employees: 2. Number of internship applications received each year: 10.
Internships Available ▶ *Intern assistants to the communications manager:* responsibilities include assisting with publicity and press/artist relations for MDA productions; researching local media, helping with MDA publications and archival folders; working on other projects as needed. Candidates should have editing skills, organizational skills, personal interest in the field, self-motivation, strong interpersonal skills, written communication skills. Duration is flexible. Unpaid. ▶ *Intern assistants to the executive director:* responsibilities include assisting with grant writing and research into funding opportunities, helping prepare final reports, assisting with board meetings and relations, and working on other projects as needed. Candidates should have organizational skills, personal interest in the field, research skills, self-motivation, strong interpersonal skills, written communication skills. Duration is flexible. Unpaid. Open to high school seniors, recent high school graduates, college freshmen, college sophomores, college juniors, college seniors, recent college graduates, graduate students, law students, law school graduates, career changers, individuals reentering the workforce. International applications accepted.

Minnesota Dance Alliance (continued)

Benefits Names of contacts, on-the-job training, opportunity to attend seminars/workshops, possible full-time employment, willing to complete paperwork for educational credit, willing to provide letters of recommendation.
Contact Write, call, or fax Sandra Sullivan, Communications Manager. Phone: 612-340-1900. Fax: 612-340-9919. In-person interview recommended (telephone interview accepted). Applicants must submit a letter of interest, resume, two personal references. Applications are accepted continuously. World Wide Web: http://www.mndancealliance.org.

MISSOURI SYMPHONY SOCIETY
203 South 9th Street
Columbia, Missouri 65201

General Information Private nonprofit corporation dedicated to bringing fine music to central Missouri, educating central Missouri youth about music, and preserving and restoring the historic Missouri Theatre. Established in 1970. Number of employees: 4. Number of internship applications received each year: 10.
Internships Available ▶ *1 marketing intern:* responsibilities include assisting with corporate development and marketing of programs of the professional Missouri Chamber Orchestra and the Historic Missouri Theatre. Candidates should have computer skills, office skills, oral communication skills, organizational skills, writing skills. Duration is 10 weeks (summer, fall, or winter) or 9 months (September to May). Position available as unpaid or paid. Open to college freshmen, college sophomores, college juniors, college seniors, recent college graduates, graduate students, career changers.
Benefits Possible full-time employment, willing to complete paperwork for educational credit, willing to provide letters of recommendation.
Contact Write, fax, or e-mail David A. White, III, Executive Director. Fax: 573-449-4214. E-mail: daw3moss@socket.net. No phone calls. In-person interview recommended (telephone interview accepted). Applicants must submit a letter of interest, resume. Application deadline: March 1 for summer, August 1 for fall, November 1 for winter.

MUSIC MOUNTAIN INC.
PO Box 1739
Sharon, Connecticut 06069

General Information Showcase for string quartets and summer chamber music festival; presents 33 concerts from June through September and offers 8 seminars. Established in 1930.
Internships Available ▶ *1 intern:* responsibilities include working in box office, ticket sales, press, publicity, and artist/seminar participant relations. Candidates should have ability to work independently, ability to work with others, must have own vehicle. Duration is 3 months. $250 per week. Open to college freshmen, college sophomores, college juniors, college seniors, graduate students, career changers, individuals reentering the workforce.
Benefits Free housing, job counseling, names of contacts, opportunity to attend seminars/workshops, willing to provide letters of recommendation, concerts.
Contact Write, call, fax, or e-mail Mr. Nicholas Gordon, President, Board of Managers. Phone: 860-364-2080. Fax: 860-364-2090. E-mail: ngordon@snet.net. In-person interview recommended (telephone interview accepted). Application deadline: April 30 for summer. World Wide Web: http://www.musicmountain.org.

NATIONAL BASKETBALL ASSOCIATION
645 Fifth Avenue
New York, New York 10022

General Information Fully-integrated global sports marketing and entertainment organization. Established in 1946. Number of employees: 1,200. Number of internship applications received each year: 2,000.
Internships Available ▶ *20–30 summer interns:* responsibilities include working in various areas including television production, finance, NBA photos, global merchandising, international public relations, human resources, and events and attractions. Candidates should have ability to work with others, computer skills, oral communication skills, organizational skills, self-motivation. Duration is June to August. Salary competitive with sports and entertainment industries. Open to college sophomores, college juniors. International applications accepted.
Benefits Formal training, job counseling, names of contacts, on-the-job training, opportunity to attend seminars/workshops, possible full-time employment, willing to act as a professional reference, willing to complete paperwork for educational credit, willing to provide letters of recommendation.
Contact Write or e-mail Internship Coordinator. E-mail: collegerecruiting@nba.com. No phone calls. Telephone interview required. Applicants must submit a letter of interest, resume. World Wide Web: http://www.nba.com.

NATIONAL DANCE EDUCATION ORGANIZATION
4948 St. Elmo Avenue, Suite 301
Bethesda, Maryland 20814

General Information National organization serving dance educators teaching Pre-K–12, higher education, private studios, professional preparation programs, and outreach programs of performing arts organizations; offers national/regional conferences, Journal of Dance Education, resources (books, CDs, videos), and technical assistance to individuals, organizations, and departments of education seeking to develop standards/guidelines for dance (content, curriculum, assessments, professional development, certification); membership is individual (professional, student, retiree), institutional, affiliate, or business/corporation. Established in 1997. Number of employees: 5. Number of internship applications received each year: 50.
Internships Available ▶ *2 arts administration/business interns:* responsibilities include helping coordinate 6 divisions (membership, finance, conference, publications and periodicals, grants, and programs); assisting in budget development and running a nonprofit business; liaison with national organizations in dance, arts and education communities; attending national partnership meetings. Candidates should have experience in the field, oral communication skills, personal interest in the field, strong interpersonal skills, strong leadership ability, writing skills. Duration is 1–2 semesters. Unpaid. Open to college seniors, graduate students, law students. ▶ *2 grant procurement and implementation interns:* responsibilities include researching funding sources using electronic databases for Foundation Center and government publications; assisting implementing any grant NDEO is supporting at national, state, and local levels. Candidates should have analytical skills, computer skills, knowledge of field, research skills, self-motivation, writing skills. Duration is 1–2 semesters. Position available as unpaid or paid. Open to college seniors, recent college graduates, graduate students, career changers. ▶ *1 marketing intern:* responsibilities include helping develop new markets and sustain current markets; coordinating activities with press and media; developing innovative ways to promote NDEO and dance education to public, educators and administrators. Candidates should have computer skills, oral communication skills, organizational skills, research skills, self-motivation, written communication skills. Duration is 15–30 weeks. Unpaid. Open to college seniors, recent college graduates, graduate students, career changers. ▶ *1 membership development intern:* responsibilities include developing new programs in membership; coordinating and implementing membership campaigns; interacting with members (new, renewals, and prospective); facilitating all membership services (individual and institutional); maintaining membership database. Candidates should have computer skills, oral communication skills, organizational skills, strong interpersonal skills, strong leadership ability, written communication skills. Duration is 15–30 weeks. Unpaid. Open to college seniors, recent college graduates, graduate students, career changers. ▶ *1 programs intern:* responsibilities include participating in initiating, implementing and maintaining national, state and NDEO programs in dance and arts education. Candidates should have analytical skills, computer skills, organizational skills, strong interpersonal skills, strong leadership ability, writing skills. Duration is 15–30 weeks. Unpaid. Open to college juniors, college seniors, recent college graduates, graduate students. ▶ *2*

research interns: responsibilities include working with key personnel on defining research topic, tools, review of literature, design, methodology, conclusions and recommendations; monitoring initialization, collection, and analysis of data; writing drafts about research in process; seeking funding and support research (commissioned or RFPs). Candidates should have ability to work independently, analytical skills, college courses in field, organizational skills, research skills, writing skills. Duration is 1–2 semesters. Unpaid. Open to college seniors, recent college graduates, graduate students. ▶ *1 standards and curriculum intern:* responsibilities include assisting in the development of national, state, and local school district standards, curricular frameworks, and assessments for teachers and students in dance arts education; assisting in state certification programs. Candidates should have ability to work with others, analytical skills, knowledge of field, organizational skills, writing skills. Duration is 1–2 semesters. Unpaid. Open to college seniors, recent college graduates, graduate students, career changers.

Benefits Formal training, job counseling, names of contacts, on-the-job training, opportunity to attend seminars/workshops, possible full-time employment, willing to act as a professional reference, willing to complete paperwork for educational credit, willing to provide letters of recommendation.

Contact Write, call, fax, e-mail, or through World Wide Web site Dr. Jane Bonbright, Executive Director. Phone: 301-657-2880. Fax: 301-657-2882. E-mail: ndeo@erols.com. In-person interview recommended (telephone interview accepted). Applicants must submit a formal organization application, letter of interest, resume, two writing samples, personal reference, two letters of recommendation. Applications are accepted continuously. World Wide Web: http://www.ndeo.net.

NEW YORK JETS, LLC
1000 Fulton Avenue
Hempstead, New York 11550

General Information Professional football team. Number of employees: 80. Number of internship applications received each year: 150.

Internships Available ▶ *30–35 Jets Fest intern:* responsibilities include running Jets Fest 2002, an interactive football theme park; includes corporate sponsorships and interactions with sponsors and VIP's. Candidates should have personal interest in the field, self-motivation, strong interpersonal skills, strong leadership ability, major in marketing, sports management, or sports marketing. Duration is June to August. $200 per week or school credit. Open to college freshmen, college sophomores, college juniors, college seniors. International applications accepted.

Benefits Free meals, names of contacts, willing to act as a professional reference, willing to complete paperwork for educational credit, willing to provide letters of recommendation.

Contact Write, fax, or e-mail Kenny Zore, Special Events Assistant. Fax: 516-560-8296. E-mail: kzore@jets.nfl.com. No phone calls. In-person interview recommended (telephone interview accepted). Applicants must submit a resume. Application deadline: March 15. World Wide Web: http://www.newyorkjets.com.

NORFOLK CHAMBER MUSIC FESTIVAL–YALE SUMMER SCHOOL OF MUSIC
PO Box 208246
New Haven, Connecticut 06520-8246

General Information Festival that presents high-quality performances of chamber music and other classical music repertoire by world-renowned artists, while providing training and performance opportunities for young professional musicians. Established in 1941. Number of employees: 10. Unit of Yale University, New Haven, Connecticut. Number of internship applications received each year: 150.

Internships Available ▶ *1–2 administrative interns:* responsibilities include general administration and concert hall work. Candidates should have knowledge of field, organizational skills, personal interest in the field, self-motivation, strong interpersonal skills. Duration is June to August. Unpaid. Open to college juniors, college seniors, recent college graduates, career changers. ▶ *1*

artist liaison/facilities manager: responsibilities include handling artist relations and managing housekeepers, concessions workers, and parkers. Candidates should have plan to pursue career in field, self-motivation. Duration is June to August. $2750 per season. Open to recent college graduates, graduate students, career changers, individuals reentering the workforce. ▶ *1 associate administrator:* responsibilities include acting as artist liaison, scheduling, and office work. Candidates should have computer skills, knowledge of field, office skills, organizational skills, self-motivation, strong interpersonal skills. Duration is June to August. $2750 per season. Open to recent college graduates, graduate students, career changers, individuals reentering the workforce. ▶ *1 box office manager:* responsibilities include performing general box office duties. Candidates should have computer skills, organizational skills, self-motivation, strong interpersonal skills. Duration is June to August. $2750 per season. Open to recent college graduates, graduate students, career changers, individuals reentering the workforce. ▶ *1 concert hall manager:* responsibilities include scheduling and performing concert hall management duties. Candidates should have organizational skills, self-motivation, stage management experience. Duration is June to August. $2750 per season. Open to recent college graduates, graduate students, career changers, individuals reentering the workforce. ▶ *1 music librarian:* responsibilities include assisting in the music library. Candidates should have knowledge of field, organizational skills, research skills, strong interpersonal skills. Duration is June to August. $2750 per season. Open to recent college graduates, graduate students, career changers, individuals reentering the workforce. ▶ *1 production intern:* responsibilities include concert production, recording, and festival organization. Candidates should have ability to work with others, organizational skills, personal interest in the field, self-motivation. Duration is June to August. Unpaid. Open to college juniors, college seniors, recent college graduates, career changers. ▶ *1 recording engineer:* responsibilities include recording all festival concerts. Candidates should have computer skills, self-motivation, strong leadership ability, recording experience and knowledge of equipment. Duration is June to August. $2750 per season. Open to recent college graduates, graduate students, career changers, individuals reentering the workforce. International applications accepted.

Benefits Formal training, free housing, free meals, names of contacts, opportunity to attend seminars/workshops, willing to act as a professional reference, willing to complete paperwork for educational credit, willing to provide letters of recommendation, opportunity to attend music performances.

Contact Write, fax, e-mail, or through World Wide Web site Festival Manager. Fax: 203-432-2136. E-mail: norfolk@yale.edu. No phone calls. In-person interview recommended (telephone interview accepted). Applicants must submit a letter of interest, resume, three personal references. Applications are accepted continuously. World Wide Web: http://www.yale.edu/norfolk.

OAKLAND A'S
7677 Oakport Street, #200
Oakland, California 94621

General Information Professional baseball club. Established in 1901. Number of employees: 400. Number of internship applications received each year: 300.

Internships Available ▶ *1–2 FanCard interns:* responsibilities include assisting with ad development and marketing; creating and maintaining point of purchase displays and assisting with the distribution of marketing collateral; updating informational files and accounting/compiling redemption reports; aiding in enrollment of fans; monitoring kiosks and staffing of sign-up tables; providing assistance at FanCard headquarters with reward distribution, point of purchase display maintenance, and customer service; assisting with event planning and fulfillment and monitoring FanCard hot line; and game-day operational support to the ticketing department. Candidates should have ability to work independently, oral communication skills, self-motivation, strong interpersonal skills, written communication skills. Duration is one quarter (year-round). Position available as unpaid or at $500 stipend. Open to college freshmen, college sophomores, college juniors, college seniors, graduate students, law students. ▶ *1–2 baseball operations interns:* responsibilities include updating major

Oakland A's (continued)

and minor league magnetic boards to reflect roster changes, compiling college statistics for amateur draft, entering professional scouting reports, pitcher velocity reports, and minor league pitching statistics. Candidates should have ability to work independently, self-motivation, strong interpersonal skills, written communication skills. Duration is one quarter (year-round). Position available as unpaid or at $500 stipend. Open to college freshmen, college sophomores, college juniors, college seniors, graduate students, law students. ▶ *1–2 community relations interns:* responsibilities include assisting in planning and implementing programs for the baseball season and being a part of the daily activities of the department; assisting with programs including the Little A's, the A's Pitching Pals, and the Read to Succeed Program; assisting in pre-game community activities; responding to requests from local and charitable organizations; assisting community staff in administration of outreach programs; coordinating weekend silent auctions and various game-day activities with supervision from staff; and assisting in graphic publications. Candidates should have ability to work independently, oral communication skills, self-motivation, strong interpersonal skills, written communication skills. Duration is one quarter (year-round). Position available as unpaid or at $500 stipend. Open to college freshmen, college sophomores, college juniors, college seniors, graduate students, law students. ▶ *1–2 corporate sales/marketing interns:* responsibilities include assisting in forming marketing partnerships with corporate sponsors; assisting with contract fulfillment; helping in planning, coordinating, and facilitating of corporate sponsor events; helping implement game-day on-field activities and pregame field visits; assisting with administrative duties and operational issues; forming marketing partnerships with corporate sponsors; helping in planning, coordinating, and facilitating of corporate sponsor events; assisting with administrative duties and operational issues; and assisting in coordination and facilitation of special events. Candidates should have ability to work independently, oral communication skills, self-motivation, strong interpersonal skills, written communication skills. Duration is one quarter (year-round). Position available as unpaid or at $500 stipend. Open to college freshmen, college sophomores, college juniors, college seniors, graduate students, law students. ▶ *1–2 finance interns:* responsibilities include processing and reconciling deposits, researching unpaid suites, updating list of tickets purchased by sponsors, reconciling purchased tickets and ticket account, assisting in Accounts Receivable and Accounts Payable. Candidates should have ability to work independently, oral communication skills, self-motivation, strong interpersonal skills, written communication skills. Duration is one quarter (year-round). Position available as unpaid or at $500 stipend. Open to college freshmen, college sophomores, college juniors, college seniors, graduate students, law students. ▶ *1–2 luxury suites interns:* responsibilities include coordination and facilitation of the A's Birthday Suite Package including scoreboard messages, decorations, food and souvenirs, and trips to the field for pre-game batting practice; preparing ticket packages; adding luxury suite marketing information to the database; learning the BASS ticketing system; conducting surveys in the luxury suite department; spending a total of two weeks as the game day operations department; and other office duties. Candidates should have ability to work independently, oral communication skills, self-motivation, strong interpersonal skills, written communication skills. Duration is one quarter (year-round). Position available as unpaid or at $500 stipend. Open to college freshmen, college sophomores, college juniors, college seniors, graduate students, law students. ▶ *1–2 media relations interns:* responsibilities include assisting at the office and at the Coliseum, assisting in copying game notes, getting starting lineups, scoring the game on the Major League Baseball play-by-play system, operating the SportsTicker, and writing post-game notes, assisting with newspaper clippings, writing magazine notes, preparing statistics packages, and other miscellaneous projects. Candidates should have ability to work independently, oral communication skills, self-motivation, strong interpersonal skills, written communication skills. Duration is one quarter (year-round). Position available as unpaid or at $500 stipend. Open to college freshmen, college sophomores, college juniors, college seniors, graduate students, law students. ▶ *1–2 premium seating and advertising*

interns: responsibilities include providing supporting in the areas of booking orders, database management, marketing, and servicing clientele, supporting advertising and magazine efforts through assisting with maintaining the budget, proofing, and assisting vendors with various needs. Candidates should have ability to work independently, oral communication skills, self-motivation, strong interpersonal skills, written communication skills. Duration is one quarter (year-round). Position available as unpaid or at $500 stipend. Open to college freshmen, college sophomores, college juniors, college seniors, law students. ▶ *1–2 promotions and special events interns:* responsibilities include providing assistance with coordination and facilitation of promotions and special events, assisting in programming including A's Kids Club Mascot Program, the National Anthem Program, and the Promotional Hotline, responding to promotional mail requests, answering phones, and performing other administrative duties for the department. Candidates should have ability to work independently, oral communication skills, self-motivation, strong interpersonal skills, written communication skills, ability to work some nights and weekends. Duration is one quarter (year-round). Position available as unpaid or at $500 stipend. Open to college freshmen, college sophomores, college juniors, college seniors, graduate students, law students. ▶ *1–2 scoreboard operations interns:* responsibilities include camera setup, field to booth messenger, assisting with stat input and paperwork, monitoring satellite games and recording highlights, gathering lineups notes, stats from press box, pulling cable for pre-game ceremonies, keeping score for CG operator, monitoring "B" tape machine and logging highlights, assisting on field camera operators, operating high-home or on-field cameras, assisting in out-of-town scoreboard, breaking down cameras. Candidates should have ability to work independently, oral communication skills, self-motivation, strong interpersonal skills, written communication skills. Duration is one quarter (year-round). Position available as unpaid or at $500 stipend. Open to college freshmen, college sophomores, college juniors, college seniors, graduate students, law students. ▶ *1–2 ticket operations interns:* responsibilities include reconciling media including charges and coupons, assisting in auditing ticket sellers, assisting in ticket distribution and Will Call, generating sales and staffing reports, assisting box office manager and staff accountant in other duties. Candidates should have ability to work independently, oral communication skills, self-motivation, strong interpersonal skills, written communication skills. Duration is one quarter (year-round). Position available as unpaid or at $500 stipend. Open to college freshmen, college sophomores, college juniors, college seniors, graduate students, law students. International applications accepted. **Benefits** On-the-job training, possible full-time employment, willing to act as a professional reference, willing to complete paperwork for educational credit, willing to provide letters of recommendation.
Contact Write, fax, or e-mail Jason Jimenez, Intern Coordinator. Fax: 510-563-2397. E-mail: jjimenez@oaklandathletics.com. No phone calls. In-person interview required. Applicants must submit a formal organization application, resume. Applications are accepted continuously. World Wide Web: http://www.oaklandathletics.com.

OVERLAND ENTERTAINMENT
257 West 52nd Street, 5th Floor
New York, New York 10019

General Information Entertainment company that books and produces private corporate events. Established in 1985. Number of employees: 8. Number of internship applications received each year: 75.
Internships Available ▶ *1–2 entertainment event planning interns:* responsibilities include assisting in the research of event space location and talent availability; maintaining informational computer databases; aiding director of sales in researching new clientele; preparing press packages and informational materials for event proposals. Candidates should have ability to work independently, computer skills, oral communication skills, personal interest in the field, research skills, self-motivation. Duration is 3–5 months.

Unpaid. Open to college freshmen, college sophomores, college juniors, college seniors, recent college graduates, graduate students. International applications accepted.
Benefits Names of contacts, travel reimbursement, willing to complete paperwork for educational credit, willing to provide letters of recommendation, opportunity to attend special entertainment functions.
Contact Write, fax, or e-mail Kelly Brennan, Internship Coordinator. Fax: 212-262-5229. E-mail: kboverland@aol.com. No phone calls. In-person interview required. Applicants must submit a resume, two personal references. Applications are accepted continuously.

PGA TOUR, INC.
100 PGA Tour Boulevard
Ponte Vedra Beach, Florida 32082

General Information Professional Golf Sports Association supporting pro golfers on three tours: PGA Tour, Senior PGA Tour, and Buy.com Tour; manages over 130 tournaments worldwide. Established in 1968. Number of employees: 550. Number of internship applications received each year: 175.
Internships Available ▶ *3–4 communications interns:* responsibilities include working with communications department staff, researching, assisting in press releases, working with sports media; assisting in developing minority intern program yearbook and application. Candidates should have ability to work independently, ability to work with others, analytical skills, computer skills, editing skills, office skills, oral communication skills, organizational skills, research skills, self-motivation, written communication skills. Duration is 9 weeks. $9 per hour. Open to college juniors, college seniors, graduate students, law students. ▶ *4–6 corporate marketing interns:* responsibilities include assisting in marking marketing proposals and promoting to corporate clients, tracking marketing results, attending client meetings; and working with tournaments and sponsors. Candidates should have ability to work independently, analytical skills, computer skills, oral communication skills, research skills, self-motivation, strong interpersonal skills, written communication skills. Duration is 9 weeks. $9 per hour. Open to college juniors, college seniors, graduate students, law students. ▶ *Up to 5 event promotions interns:* responsibilities include working for a sister company, GMR works, traveling to regional golf events promoting GM autos including Buick and Cadillac. Candidates should have ability to work independently, ability to work with others, computer skills, oral communication skills, self-motivation. Duration is 9 weeks. $9 per hour. Open to college juniors, college seniors, graduate students, law students. ▶ *2 television production interns:* responsibilities include working with PGA Tour productions, editing, logging tapes, assisting production staff with post-event shows; may work with TV broadcast staff, analyzing program ratings domestically and internationally. Candidates should have ability to work independently, ability to work with others, analytical skills, computer skills, editing skills, knowledge of field, office skills, oral communication skills, organizational skills, research skills, self-motivation, strong leadership ability, written communication skills. Duration is 9 weeks. $9 per hour. Open to college juniors, college seniors, graduate students. ▶ *6–8 tournament operations interns:* responsibilities include working with sponsors, setting up golf operations, helping with managing the events, scoring, working with volunteers; based either at specific tournament or traveling on a weekly basis. Candidates should have ability to work independently, ability to work with others, office skills, oral communication skills, plan to pursue career in field, self-motivation, strong leadership ability, written communication skills, knowledge or experience in playing golf (preferred). Duration is 9 weeks. $9 per hour. Open to college juniors, college seniors, graduate students, law students.
Benefits Housing at a cost, job counseling, names of contacts, on-the-job training, opportunity to attend seminars/workshops, possible full-time employment, travel reimbursement, willing to act as a professional reference, willing to complete paperwork for educational credit, willing to provide letters of recommendation, temporary membership to golf course.
Contact Write or e-mail Mike Cooney, Director, Human Resources. Phone: 904-273-3520. Fax: 904-273-3588. E-mail: mip@mail.pgatour.com. In-person interview recommended (telephone interview accepted). Applicants must submit a formal organization application, letter of interest, resume, academic transcripts, writing sample, three personal references. Application deadline: March 15 for summer, May 25 for fall. World Wide Web: http://www.pgatour.com.

PHILADELPHIA 76ERS
3601 South Broad Street
Philadelphia, Pennsylvania 19148-5290

General Information Professional basketball team playing in the National Basketball Association. Unit of Comcast, Philadelphia, Pennsylvania. Number of internship applications received each year: 250.
Internships Available ▶ *2 box office interns:* responsibilities include processing contracts, processing and mailing season tickets and game-day tickets, and handling customer questions and complaints. Candidates should have office skills, oral communication skills, organizational skills, strong interpersonal skills, ability to use Windows 95 programs such as Microsoft Excel and WordPerfect. Duration is 1 semester in spring or fall. Unpaid. ▶ *1 community relations intern:* responsibilities include handling phone inquiries; maintaining database files; ordering merchandise for charitable donations; assisting staff with correspondence and special projects; and responding to requests for autographed items, financial donations, tickets, and speaking appearances. Candidates should have oral communication skills, organizational skills, strong interpersonal skills, strong leadership ability, ability to use Microsoft Word, Excel, and WordPerfect (preferred). Duration is 1 semester in fall, spring, or summer. Unpaid. ▶ *2 fan relations interns:* responsibilities include responding to requests for fan club information, selling fan club memberships at home games, and tracking inventory and mailing for fan club. Candidates should have oral communication skills, organizational skills, strong interpersonal skills, ability to work game days outside normal business hours, proficiency in use of the Internet and Microsoft applications (Word, Access, and Excel). Duration is 1 semester in fall or spring. Unpaid. ▶ *1 marketing intern:* responsibilities include following up on promotions/marketing events and advertising, updating the Web site, assisting the director of fan relations, and responding to customer phone inquiries. Candidates should have oral communication skills, strong interpersonal skills, written communication skills, ability to use Microsoft Office and the Internet, experience with PageMaker (desirable), ability to work some game nights and weekends. Duration is 1 semester in fall, spring, or summer. Unpaid. ▶ *1 operations intern:* responsibilities include handling phone inquiries and clerical tasks, assisting coaching and scouting staff, assisting with operation of scouting database, and helping with a variety of duties related to team practices and games. Candidates should have office skills, organizational skills, research skills, strong interpersonal skills, written communication skills, excellent phone skills, ability to use Microsoft Word and Excel. Duration is 1 semester in fall, spring, or summer. Unpaid. ▶ *1 promotions intern:* responsibilities include following up on event promotions and creating post-event marketing summaries, updating computer kiosks, assisting in game operations/promotional events, and scripting advertising that will appear on Arenavision and message boards. Candidates should have oral communication skills, organizational skills, strong interpersonal skills, written communication skills, ability to use Microsoft Office applications, WordPerfect, and Lotus 123; event production background (preferred). Duration is 1 semester in fall, spring, or summer. Unpaid. ▶ *1 public relations intern:* responsibilities include acting as liaison with media, attending home games (including weekends), assisting with publications, organizing team and individual photo files, organizing mass mailings, handling press clippings, and participating in a variety of public relations projects. Candidates should have editing skills, oral communication skills, organizational skills, strong interpersonal skills, writing skills, ability to use PageMaker, MS Word, WordPerfect, or Lotus 123 software. Duration is 1 semester in fall, spring, or summer. Unpaid. ▶ *1–2 sales interns:* responsibilities include assisting in mass marketing campaigns and in prospecting leads for corporate sales managers; coordinating trade shows, open houses, and off-site presentations; helping with clerical duties, customer service, and phone relations.

Philadelphia 76ers (continued)

Candidates should have oral communication skills, organizational skills, research skills, strong interpersonal skills, written communication skills, professional phone skills, attention to detail. Duration is 1 semester in fall, spring, or summer. Unpaid. ▶ *5 statistics interns:* responsibilities include recording, deciphering, and logging box scores; updating individual and team statistics as well as play-by-play records for 76ers and other NBA teams; and assisting staff on various projects. Candidates should have ability to work independently, computer skills, office skills, research skills, self-motivation, attention to detail and accuracy with numbers, interest in basketball statistics (preferred). Duration is 1 semester in fall, spring, or summer. Unpaid. Open to college juniors, college seniors, graduate students, must be working for academic credit. International applications accepted.

Benefits Names of contacts, on-the-job training, possible full-time employment, willing to complete paperwork for educational credit, excellent experience in the sports and entertainment industry.

Contact Write or through World Wide Web site Internship Program, Human Resources Department. In-person interview required. Applicants must submit a formal organization application, resume, cover letter indicating reasons for choosing a particular internship and the qualities/attributes that will help make a contribution; faculty recommendation form (sent with application). Application deadline: at least 2 months prior to intended start date. World Wide Web: http://www.comcast-spectacor.com.

PHILADELPHIA FLYERS
3601 South Broad Street
Philadelphia, Pennsylvania 19148-5290

General Information Professional hockey team in the National Hockey League. Unit of Comcast, Philadelphia, Pennsylvania.

Internships Available ▶ *1 community relations intern:* responsibilities include scheduling and arranging Flyers School program, corresponding with elementary schools, handling charitable donation requests, sorting and answering fan mail, scheduling birthday packages and get well cards, organizing and assisting in team/individual public appearances and promotional events, and data entry. Candidates should have oral communication skills, strong interpersonal skills, written communication skills, ability to use Microsoft Word, WordPerfect, Lotus 123, and Goldmine software (preferred). Duration is 1 semester in fall, spring, or summer. Unpaid. ▶ *1 fan development/youth hockey intern:* responsibilities include assisting fan development staff on research, design, and brainstorming for proposed projects; assisting in coordination of NHL BREAKOUT event, and performing minimal clerical duties. Candidates should have oral communication skills, written communication skills, interest in sports marketing and/or public relations, hockey background (preferred). Duration is June 1 through July 31. Unpaid. ▶ *2 public relations interns:* responsibilities include assisting with production and distribution of game notes for media, obtaining post-game quotes from participants, organizing publications database and photo files, assisting in coordination of NHL All-Star balloting, assisting with press releases and publicity events, and handling daily and weekly press clippings. Candidates should have oral communication skills, organizational skills, written communication skills, ability to use WordPerfect 5.1/6.0, ability with database management (preferred). Duration is 1 semester in fall, spring, or summer. Unpaid. ▶ *1 rink management and development intern:* responsibilities include assisting rink development staff with projects involving facility marketing, public relations, site analysis, and construction-related issues; helping with clerical duties as assigned. Candidates should have oral communication skills, written communication skills, interest in facility management, marketing, group sales and/or public relations, or construction management is preferred. Duration is May 1 through September 1. Unpaid. ▶ *1 sales/marketing intern:* responsibilities include assisting sales/marketing staff with projects and brainstorming sessions, responding to phone inquiries, helping with season ticket database mailings and game-day promotions, maintaining data files, and game-day customer relations. Candidates should have oral communication skills, organizational skills, writ-

ten communication skills, ability to meet deadlines, friendly manner for customer service contacts, knowledge of WordPerfect (required) and Goldmine (helpful), ability to work game nights and game weekends. Duration is 1 semester in fall, spring, or summer. Unpaid. Open to college juniors, college seniors, graduate students, must be working for academic credit.

Benefits Names of contacts, possible full-time employment, willing to complete paperwork for educational credit, excellent experience in the sports and entertainment industry.

Contact Write or through World Wide Web site Internship Program, Human Resources Department. No phone calls. In-person interview required. Applicants must submit a formal organization application, resume, cover letter indicating reasons for choosing internship and qualities/attributes that will help make a contribution, faculty recommendation form (sent with application). Application deadline: at least 2 months prior to intended start date. World Wide Web: http://www.comcast-spectacor.com.

PHILADELPHIA PHANTOMS
3601 South Broad Street
Philadelphia, Pennsylvania 19148-5290

General Information The American Hockey League affiliate of the Philadelphia Flyers. Unit of Comcast, Philadelphia, Pennsylvania. Number of internship applications received each year: 200.

Internships Available ▶ *2 assistants to the ticketing manager:* responsibilities include assisting with phone sales, customer service inquiries, and internal data entry/accounting tasks; distributing Phantoms literature at selected events; and working on a variety of promotional projects. Candidates should have ability to work independently, oral communication skills, strong interpersonal skills, written communication skills, ability to use WordPerfect and Lotus 123 software. Duration is 1 semester in fall, spring, or summer. Unpaid. ▶ *1 marketing intern:* responsibilities include assisting staff with marketing projects, following up event promotions, and creating post-event marketing summaries; writing and handling press releases and statistics; assisting in day-of-event operations; and coordinating media publicity. Candidates should have oral communication skills, self-motivation, strong interpersonal skills, ability to use Word, WordPerfect, and Lotus 123. Duration is 1 semester in fall, spring, or summer. Unpaid. ▶ *1 public relations intern:* responsibilities include writing and handling press releases and statistics, corresponding with season ticket holders, assisting in advertising and printing, coordinating media publicity, and working on various projects with staff. Candidates should have editing skills, oral communication skills, writing skills, ability to use Word, WordPerfect, and Lotus 123. Duration is 1 semester in fall, spring, or summer. Unpaid. Open to college juniors, college seniors, graduate students, must be working for academic credit. International applications accepted.

Benefits Names of contacts, possible full-time employment, willing to complete paperwork for educational credit, excellent experience in the sports and entertainment industry.

Contact Write or through World Wide Web site Internship Program, Human Resources Department. In-person interview required. Applicants must submit a formal organization application, resume, cover letter indicating reasons for choosing a particular internship and the qualities or attributes that will help make a contribution, faculty recommendation form (sent with application). Application deadline: at least 2 months prior to intended start date. World Wide Web: http://www.comcast-spectacor.com.

PHOTOGRAPHY WEST GALLERY
PO Box 5306
Carmel, California 93921

General Information Fine art photography gallery that sells photography, posters, books, and notecards; publisher of 5 major photography books. Established in 1980. Number of employees: 4. Number of internship applications received each year: 20.

Internships Available ▶ *2 gallery interns:* responsibilities include talking to customers about photography, inventorying artwork, answering phones, restocking gallery, clerical work. Candidates should have college courses in field, knowledge of field, oral com-

munication skills, personal interest in the field, strong interpersonal skills, written communication skills. Duration is 3–6 months. $8–$10 per hour. Open to recent high school graduates, college freshmen, college sophomores, college juniors, college seniors, recent college graduates, graduate students.
Benefits Names of contacts, on-the-job training, possible full-time employment, willing to act as a professional reference, willing to complete paperwork for educational credit, willing to provide letters of recommendation.
Contact Write, fax, e-mail, or through World Wide Web site Carol Williams, Owner. Fax: 831-625-1288. No phone calls. In-person interview recommended (telephone interview accepted). Applicants must submit a resume, three personal references. Applications are accepted continuously. World Wide Web: http://www.photographywest.com.

POSEY SCHOOL OF DANCE, INC.
PO Box 254
Northport, New York 11768

General Information Community school of dance offering education and professional training. Established in 1953. Number of employees: 10. Number of internship applications received each year: 25.
Internships Available ▶ *1 studio manager.* Candidates should have oral communication skills, strong interpersonal skills, strong leadership ability, knowledge of dance techniques, ballet, and modern dance. Duration is 10–12 months. Position available as unpaid or at $100–$450 per month. Open to recent college graduates, graduate students, career changers. ▶ *1 summer studio manager.* Candidates should have oral communication skills, strong interpersonal skills, strong leadership ability, written communication skills, knowledge of dance techniques, ballet, and modern dance. Duration is 2–3 months. $250–$300 per duration of internship. Open to recent college graduates, graduate students, career changers, performers entering education field.
Benefits Formal training, job counseling, names of contacts, opportunity to attend seminars/workshops, possible full-time employment, willing to act as a professional reference, willing to complete paperwork for educational credit, willing to provide letters of recommendation, personal introductions.
Contact Write, call, or e-mail Ms. Elsa Posey, President. Phone: 631-757-2700. E-mail: eposey@optonline.net. Telephone interview required. Applicants must submit a letter of interest, resume. Applications are accepted continuously.

RDV SPORTS
8701 Maitland Summit Boulevard
Orlando, Florida 32810

General Information Parent company of the Orlando Magic (NBA), the Orlando Miracle (WNBA), and RDV Sportsplex (health club facility). Established in 1989. Number of employees: 500. Number of internship applications received each year: 650.
Internships Available ▶ *30–40 interns:* responsibilities include duties in one of the following areas: basketball operations/coaching, broadcast/production, broadcast/radio, corporate sales, community relations, creative services, fitness, human resources, team marketing, team media, ticket sales,or team charities. Candidates should have ability to work independently, computer skills, knowledge of field, organizational skills, self-motivation, writing skills. Duration is 1 season (9 months) or 1 semester (4 months). Stipend of $232 bi-weekly. Open to college juniors, college seniors, graduate students, recent college graduates (within 18 months following graduation).
Benefits Job counseling, names of contacts, on-the-job training, opportunity to attend seminars/workshops, possible full-time employment, willing to complete paperwork for educational credit, tickets to games, job-shadowing, athletic club access.
Contact Fax, e-mail, or through World Wide Web site Cindy Anderson, Recruitment Specialist. Fax: 407-916-2884. E-mail: canderson@rdvsports.com. No phone calls. Telephone interview required. Applicants must submit a formal organization application, resume, three writing samples, drug screen, background check required; in-person interview required for finalists; demo tape required for some positions; driver's license check required

for some positions. Application deadline: February 20 for summer, June 30 for fall, October 31 for spring. World Wide Web: http://www.rdvsportsplex.com.

RICHARD FRANKEL PRODUCTIONS
729 7th Avenue, 12th Floor
New York, New York 10019

General Information Independent theatrical production and general management company that manages and produces plays and musicals and acts as general manager for other theatrical producers. Established in 1985. Number of employees: 60. Number of internship applications received each year: 1,000.
Internships Available ▶ *12–15 interns:* responsibilities include assignments under the supervision of the general manager of one show, compiling daily sales figures, assisting company managers at theater, providing production assistant services for shows in rehearsal and pre-production, and implementing grassroots marketing campaigns. Candidates should have ability to work independently, computer skills, oral communication skills, organizational skills, personal interest in the field, self-motivation, strong interpersonal skills, strong leadership ability, written communication skills. Duration is 3-5 months full-time (Monday through Friday 10 AM to 6 PM). Position available as unpaid or at $150 per week. Open to college freshmen, college sophomores, college juniors, college seniors, recent college graduates, graduate students, law students. International applications accepted.
Benefits Formal training, job counseling, names of contacts, on-the-job training, opportunity to attend seminars/workshops, possible full-time employment, willing to act as a professional reference, willing to complete paperwork for educational credit, willing to provide letters of recommendation.
Contact Write, call, fax, e-mail, or through World Wide Web site Lori Steiger-Perry, Internship Coordinator, 729 Seventh Avenue, 12th Floor, New York, New York 10019. Phone: 212-302-5559. Fax: 212-302-8094. E-mail: lori@rfpny.com. In-person interview required. Applicants must submit a letter of interest, resume, academic transcripts. Application deadline: April 15 for summer, July 15 for fall, November 15 for spring. World Wide Web: http://www.rfpny.com.

ROCKPORT CHAMBER MUSIC FESTIVAL
PO Box 312
Rockport, Massachusetts 01966

General Information Four-week festival in June-July presenting chamber music featuring nationally known groups. Established in 1982. Number of employees: 2. Number of internship applications received each year: 10.
Internships Available ▶ *1 summer intern/stage manager:* responsibilities include handling office, selling tickets, and assisting artistic director. Candidates should have ability to work with others, computer skills, knowledge of field, office skills, oral communication skills, personal interest in the field, self-motivation, ability to read music well. Duration is 5 weeks. $200 per week. Open to college freshmen, college sophomores, college juniors, college seniors, recent college graduates. International applications accepted.
Benefits Free housing, job counseling, names of contacts, willing to complete paperwork for educational credit, willing to provide letters of recommendation, opportunity to interact with musicians.
Contact Write, call, fax, e-mail, or through World Wide Web site Laura C. Tapley, General Manager. Phone: 978-548-7391. Fax: 978-546-7391. E-mail: rcmf@shore.net. Telephone interview required. Applicants must submit a letter of interest, resume, two letters of recommendation. Application deadline: April 1 for summer. World Wide Web: http://www.rcmf.org.

SAN DIEGO PADRES BASEBALL CLUB
8880 Rio San Diego Drive, Suite 400
San Diego, California 92108

General Information Professional major league baseball club. Established in 1969. Number of employees: 160. Number of internship applications received each year: 250.

San Diego Padres Baseball Club (continued)

Internships Available ▶ *5–8 interns.* Candidates should have ability to work independently, analytical skills, computer skills, oral communication skills, plan to pursue career in field, self-motivation, strong interpersonal skills, writing skills. Duration is April to October. $7.25–$8.25 per hour. Open to college freshmen, college sophomores, college juniors, college seniors, recent college graduates, graduate students, law students. International applications accepted.

Benefits Names of contacts, on-the-job training, opportunity to attend seminars/workshops, possible full-time employment, willing to act as a professional reference, willing to complete paperwork for educational credit, willing to provide letters of recommendation, some free meals.

Contact Write, call, fax, or e-mail Tim Katzman, Corporate Communications, 8880 Rio San Diego Drive, Suite 400, San Deigo 92108. Phone: 619-881-6539. Fax: 619-497-5338. E-mail: tkatzman@padres.com. In-person interview required. Applicants must submit a letter of interest, resume, writing sample, two personal references. Application deadline: February 15.

SAN FRANCISCO 49ERS
4949 Centennial Boulevard
Santa Clara, California 95054

General Information Professional football team. Established in 1946. Number of employees: 90. Number of internship applications received each year: 100.

Internships Available ▶ *1–2 season interns:* responsibilities include assisting public relations department with interview requests, fan mail requests, and research for publications. Candidates should have ability to work with others, knowledge of field, office skills, oral communication skills, personal interest in the field, written communication skills. Duration is 7–8 months. $7 per hour. Open to college sophomores, college juniors, college seniors, recent college graduates, graduate students. ▶ *2 summer camp interns:* responsibilities include assisting public relations department staff at training camp, handling interview requests, writing features, and general office work. Candidates should have ability to work with others, knowledge of field, oral communication skills, personal interest in the field, written communication skills. Duration is 1 month. $7 per hour. Open to college freshmen, college sophomores, college juniors, college seniors, recent college graduates, graduate students. International applications accepted.

Benefits Names of contacts, on-the-job training, possible full-time employment, willing to act as a professional reference, willing to complete paperwork for educational credit, willing to provide letters of recommendation.

Contact Write Internship Coordinator. Fax: 408-727-2760. No phone calls. Applicants must submit a letter of interest, resume. Application deadline: May 15. World Wide Web: http://www.sf49ers.com.

SOMERSET PATRIOTS
1 Patriots Park
Bridgewater, New Jersey 08807

General Information Member of the Atlantic League of Professional Baseball.

Internships Available ▶ *3 group sales/promotions interns:* responsibilities include assisting directors with data entry, tracking, and organizing day-to-day sales activities; mailings; printing and distribution of tickets. Candidates should have computer skills, organizational skills, management and sales skills, video/scoreboard experience a plus. Duration is April to September. $750 per month or college credit. ▶ *2 operations interns:* responsibilities include assisting director of operations with daily operations of Commerce Bank Ballpark; planning/coordinating game day staff, community use of the facility, and general office work. Candidates should have computer skills, organizational skills, management skills. $750 per month or college credit. ▶ *2 ticketing interns:* responsibilities include assisting director of ticketing with all ticketing aspects at ballpark. Candidates should have oral communication skills, organizational skills, written communication skills, experience with ticketing is a plus, but not required. Duration is April to September. $750 per month or college credit.

Contact Write or fax Chris Bryan, Internship Coordinator. Fax: 908-252-0776. No phone calls. Applicants must submit a resume. Applications are accepted continuously. World Wide Web: http://www.somersetpatriots.com.

SPOLETO FESTIVAL USA
PO Box 157
Charleston, South Carolina 29402-0157

General Information Arts festival that produces and presents world-class opera, dance, theater, chamber music, symphonic music, jazz, visual arts, and experimental multimedia works of all kinds. Established in 1977. Number of employees: 20. Number of internship applications received each year: 200.

Internships Available ▶ *2–3 artist services interns:* responsibilities include assisting with artist transportation, preparing mailings and artist welcome packets, scheduling and set-up of backstage hospitality, answering phones, correspondence, filing, and other administrative tasks. Candidates should have ability to work independently, ability to work with others, computer skills, office skills, organizational skills, self-motivation. Duration is 4–6 weeks. $250 per week. ▶ *9–12 box office interns:* responsibilities include assisting with box office window/telephone sales, program information, ticket collection, and processing mail orders. Candidates should have ability to work with others, computer skills, oral communication skills, strong customer service skills. Duration is 4–5 weeks. $250 per week. ▶ *1–2 business office intern:* responsibilities include assisting with recording cash receipts, preparing and recording disbursements, and personnel and payroll operations. Candidates should have computer skills, organizational skills. Duration is 4–5 weeks. $250 per week. ▶ *2 development interns:* responsibilities include assisting with development report, distribution of contributor benefits, and coordination of special events; extensive phone work; managing invitation mailings and RSVP's. Candidates should have ability to work independently, ability to work with others, organizational skills, self-motivation. Duration is 4–5 weeks. $250 per week. ▶ *15 merchandising interns:* responsibilities include assisting with sales of souvenir merchandise. Candidates should have ability to work with others, oral communication skills, organizational skills, self-motivation, strong customer service skills. Duration is 4–5 weeks. $250 per week. ▶ *6–7 orchestra management interns:* responsibilities include assisting in the transport and setup of equipment and large instruments for rehearsals and performances. Candidates should have ability to work independently, ability to work with others, self-motivation, knowledge of music helpful. Duration is 4–5 weeks. $250 per week. ▶ *30 production interns:* responsibilities include working in stage carpentry and electrics, wardrobe, properties, wigs and makeup, sound, and production administration. Candidates should have ability to work independently, ability to work with others, experience in the field, self-motivation. Duration is 4–5 weeks. $250 per week. ▶ *5 public relations interns:* responsibilities include staffing the press room and assisting the press in obtaining interviews, photos, and story information for print, radio, and television coverage. Candidates should have ability to work with others, computer skills, office skills, writing skills. Duration is 4–5 weeks. $250 per week. Open to college freshmen, college sophomores, college juniors, college seniors, recent college graduates, graduate students. International applications accepted.

Benefits Free housing, possible full-time employment, willing to complete paperwork for educational credit, willing to provide letters of recommendation, access to performances.

Contact Write, fax, e-mail, or through World Wide Web site Apprentice Coordinator. Fax: 843-723-6383. E-mail: apprentice@spoletousa.org. No phone calls. Applicants must submit a formal organization application, letter of interest, resume, two letters of recommendation, 2 writing samples (public relations positions only). Application deadline: February 1. World Wide Web: http://www.spoletousa.org.

THE SUCHIN COMPANY
12747 Riverside Drive, Suite 208
Valley Village, California 91607-3333

General Information   Production/management company that represents actors, writers, singers, comedians; advises and counsels with regard to career aspirations/T.V. product; makeup artists, and costumes. Established in 1979. Number of employees: 5. Number of internship applications received each year: 150.
Internships Available   ▶ *4 assistants:* responsibilities include phones, marketing, computers, filing, script reading and analysis. Candidates should have ability to work independently, office skills, research skills, strong interest in entertainment business. Duration is 3–6 months. Unpaid. Open to college freshmen, college sophomores, college juniors, college seniors, career changers. International applications accepted.
Benefits   Job counseling, names of contacts, on-the-job training, opportunity to attend seminars/workshops, possible full-time employment, willing to act as a professional reference, willing to complete paperwork for educational credit, willing to provide letters of recommendation, chance to be with entertainment industry members.
Contact   Write, fax, or e-mail Milton B. Suchin, President. Phone: 818-505-0044. Fax: 818-505-0110. E-mail: starmgri@aol.com. In-person interview recommended (telephone interview accepted). Applicants must submit a letter of interest, resume. Applications are accepted continuously.

THEATRE BUILDING CHICAGO
1225 West Belmont Avenue
Chicago, Illinois 60657

General Information   Live theater with three-space multiplex that emphasizes new musicals. Established in 1969. Number of employees: 10. Number of internship applications received each year: 20.
Internships Available   ▶ *1–2 "Stages" summer interns:* responsibilities include acting as stage manager or production manager for intense weekend festival of musical; coordinating 12 plays; 36 authors, and 125 performing artists. Candidates should have ability to work with others, oral communication skills, organizational skills, self-motivation, strong leadership ability, written communication skills. Duration is June 17 to August 17. $500 per duration of internship. Open to high school students, recent high school graduates, college freshmen, college sophomores, college juniors, college seniors. ▶ *1–3 box office and marketing interns:* responsibilities include ticketing, phone work, customer service; correspondence and marketing tools including Web site, flyers, programs, and broadsides. Candidates should have ability to work with others, computer skills, office skills, oral communication skills, writing skills. Duration is 1 year (full-time). $500 monthly stipend. Open to recent college graduates, graduate students, career changers, individuals reentering the workforce. ▶ *1–3 marketing and fundraising interns:* responsibilities include assisting executive director in grant writing; individual donor campaigns, marketing and public relations planning for renting their space and for presenting musical productions. Candidates should have ability to work with others, computer skills, organizational skills, self-motivation, writing skills. Duration is 1 year (full-time). $500 monthly stipend. Open to recent college graduates, graduate students, career changers, individuals reentering the workforce. International applications accepted.
Benefits   Health insurance, on-the-job training, opportunity to attend seminars/workshops, willing to act as a professional reference, willing to complete paperwork for educational credit, willing to provide letters of recommendation.
Contact   Write, call, fax, or e-mail Joan Mazzonelli, Executive Director. Phone: 773-929-7367 Ext. 221. Fax: 773-327-1404. E-mail: mazzonelli@aol.com. In-person interview recommended (telephone interview accepted). Applicants must submit a formal organization application, resume. Applications are accepted continuously. World Wide Web: http://www.theatrebuilding.org.

WASHINGTON PERFORMING ARTS SOCIETY
2000 L Street, NW, Suite 510
Washington, District of Columbia 20036-4907

General Information   Nonprofit organization focused on presenting classical music, traditional and contemporary dance, world music, jazz, Latino artforms, gospel, and performance art in concert halls, theaters, schools, senior citizen centers, and embassies throughout the Washington, DC area. Established in 1965. Number of employees: 40. Number of internship applications received each year: 25.
Internships Available   ▶ *1 administrative assistant:* responsibilities include general assistance to the Finance and Administration Department, including general office work, maintenance of databases and spreadsheets, as well as organization and evaluation of new information. Candidates should have computer skills, office skills, organizational skills, research skills, self-motivation, writing skills. Duration is 1–2 semesters. Position available as unpaid or paid. Open to college juniors, college seniors, recent college graduates, graduate students, career changers. ▶ *1 development assistant:* responsibilities include researching corporate, foundation, and individual donors, processing mail, assisting with writing of grants and special events, and general office work; some evening hours required. Candidates should have ability to work with others, computer skills, plan to pursue career in field, research skills, writing skills. Duration is 1 semester. Position available as unpaid or paid. Open to college seniors, recent college graduates, graduate students, career changers. ▶ *1 graphic design assistant.* Candidates should have ability to work with others, computer skills, knowledge of field, personal interest in the field, self-motivation, fluency in Quark, knowledge of PhotoShop. Duration is 1–2 semesters. Position available as unpaid or paid. Open to college juniors, college seniors, recent college graduates, graduate students, career changers. ▶ *1 programming assistant:* responsibilities include transporting artists, coordinating/booking hotel accommodations, assisting with front-of-house and ticketing at performances, and general office work. Candidates should have computer skills, knowledge of field, organizational skills, personal interest in the field, research skills, strong interpersonal skills. Duration is 4–9 months. Position available as unpaid or paid. Open to college seniors, recent college graduates, graduate students, career changers. ▶ *1–2 public relations and marketing assistants:* responsibilities include writing and distributing press releases; writing copy for promotions, sales pieces, and newsletters; assisting with special promotions, direct mail campaigns, list management, and response tracking and analysis; proofing; preparing reviewer kits for concerts; maintaining press kits and department files; and general office work. Candidates should have editing skills, knowledge of field, organizational skills, research skills, self-motivation, writing skills. Duration is 1–2 semesters. Position available as unpaid or paid. Open to college juniors, college seniors, recent college graduates, graduate students, career changers.
Benefits   Names of contacts, willing to complete paperwork for educational credit, willing to provide letters of recommendation.
Contact   Write, call, fax, e-mail, or through World Wide Web site Education Manager. Phone: 202-833-9800. Fax: 202-331-7678. E-mail: wpas@wpas.org. In-person interview recommended (telephone interview accepted). Applicants must submit a letter of interest, resume, writing sample, personal reference. Application deadline: April 15 for summer, July 15 for fall, November 15 for winter/spring. World Wide Web: http://www.wpas.org.

EDUCATIONAL SERVICES

GENERAL

ACADEMIC STUDY ASSOCIATES–ASA
10 New King Street
White Plains, New York 10604

General Information Summer pre-college programs for high school students. Established in 1984. Number of employees: 10. Number of internship applications received each year: 400.
Internships Available ▶ *80–100 resident advisors:* responsibilities include introducing high school students to academic, social, and recreational aspects of college life. Candidates should have ability to work with others, oral communication skills, self-motivation, creativity, flexibility, interest in working with high school students. $300 per week. Open to college juniors, college seniors, recent college graduates, graduate students.
Benefits Free housing, free meals.
International Internships Available in France; Spain; United Kingdom.
Contact Through World Wide Web site Shawna Zelnick, Director of Human Resources. Phone: 800-752-2250. Fax: 914-686-7740. E-mail: szelnick@asaprograms.com. In-person interview required. Applicants must submit a formal organization application, two letters of recommendation. Applications are accepted continuously. World Wide Web: http://www.asaprograms.com.

AIM FOR THE HANDICAPPED
945 Danbury Road
Dayton, Ohio 45420

General Information Educational facility that offers specialized education to handicapped children and adults. Established in 1958. Number of employees: 7. Number of internship applications received each year: 15.
Internships Available ▶ *1–3 education department assistants:* responsibilities include teaching handicapped children and adults, setting up programs in schools, working on the newsletter, and performing general office duties. Candidates should have ability to work with others, office skills, oral communication skills, personal interest in the field, self-motivation, written communication skills. Duration is flexible. Unpaid. Open to high school students, recent high school graduates, college freshmen, college sophomores, college juniors, college seniors, recent college graduates, graduate students, career changers, individuals reentering the workforce. International applications accepted.
Benefits On-the-job training, possible full-time employment, willing to act as a professional reference, willing to complete paperwork for educational credit, willing to provide letters of recommendation, assistance in locating housing.
Contact Write, call, fax, or e-mail Lynn E. Switzer, Education Director. Phone: 937-294-4611. Fax: 937-294-3783. E-mail: aimeducation@hotmail.com. In-person interview recommended (telephone interview accepted). Applicants must submit a letter of interest, resume, three personal references, three letters of recommendation. Applications are accepted continuously.

ALICE PAUL CENTENNIAL FOUNDATION
128 Hooten Road
Mt. Laurel, New Jersey 08054

General Information Nonprofit corporation created to celebrate Alice Paul's birth in 1885; goals are to enhance public aware-ness of the life and work of Alice Paul and to educate women and girls to accept leadership challenges in their lives, communities, and work places. Established in 1984. Number of employees: 3. Number of internship applications received each year: 1.
Internships Available ▶ *1–3 administrative interns/research assistants:* responsibilities include research, assistance with specific programs or events, database management, and education research. Candidates should have ability to work independently, ability to work with others, analytical skills, college courses in field, computer skills, knowledge of field, oral communication skills, organizational skills, personal interest in the field, plan to pursue career in field, research skills, self-motivation, strong leadership ability, writing skills. Duration is flexible. Unpaid. Open to high school students, recent high school graduates, college freshmen, college sophomores, college juniors, college seniors, recent college graduates, graduate students, law students, career changers, individuals reentering the workforce. International applications accepted.
Benefits On-the-job training, opportunity to attend seminars/workshops, willing to act as a professional reference, willing to complete paperwork for educational credit, willing to provide letters of recommendation.
Contact Write, call, fax, e-mail, or through World Wide Web site Rhonda Carboni, President. Phone: 856-231-1885. Fax: 856-231-4223. E-mail: info@alicepaul.org. In-person interview recommended (telephone interview accepted). Applicants must submit a formal organization application, letter of interest, resume, personal reference. Applications are accepted continuously. World Wide Web: http://www.alicepaul.org.

AMERICAN COUNCILS FOR INTERNATIONAL EDUCATION
1776 Massachusetts Avenue, NW, Suite 700
Washington, District of Columbia 20036

General Information Nonprofit organization dealing with educational development and exchange with the former Soviet Union and Eastern Europe. Established in 1975. Number of employees: 80. Number of internship applications received each year: 250.
Internships Available ▶ *10–15 interns:* responsibilities include communications, setting up conferences, clerical work, and general office duties. Candidates should have computer skills, oral communication skills, personal interest in the field, strong interpersonal skills, written communication skills. Duration is May to August. $8–$10 per hour. Open to college sophomores, college juniors, college seniors. International applications accepted.
Benefits Names of contacts, opportunity to attend seminars/workshops, possible full-time employment, willing to act as a professional reference, willing to complete paperwork for educational credit, willing to provide letters of recommendation.
Contact Write, fax, or e-mail Isabel Gomes, Human Resources Officer. Fax: 202-872-9178. E-mail: gomes@actr.org. No phone calls. In-person interview recommended (telephone interview accepted). Applicants must submit a letter of interest, resume, academic transcripts. Applications are accepted continuously. World Wide Web: http://www.actr.org.

AMERICAN INSTITUTE FOR FOREIGN STUDY
River Plaza, 9 West Broad Street
Stamford, Connecticut 06902

General Information Institute providing educational/cultural exchanges for high school and college students and interested adults on 15 campuses in Europe, Asia, Australia, Africa, Russia and South America. Established in 1964. Number of employees: 125. Number of internship applications received each year: 100.

Internships Available ▶ *25–40 interns:* responsibilities include attending classes for 4 weeks and working for 10 weeks full-time in business (marketing, finance, management), communications (media), fine arts (design and lens media), politics, and theater. Candidates should have minimum 2.5 GPA for London and Shizuoka programs; minimum 3.00 GPA for Netherlands program. Duration is 12–15 weeks. Unpaid. Open to college sophomores, college juniors, college seniors. International applications accepted.

Benefits Formal training, opportunity to attend seminars/workshops, possible full-time employment, willing to complete paperwork for educational credit, willing to provide letters of recommendation, health insurance, housing, and meals provided at $11,340 per semester.

International Internships Available in Shizuoka, Japan; Amsterdam, Netherlands; London, United Kingdom.

Contact Write, call, fax, e-mail, or through World Wide Web site Sharman Hedayati, College Division, Director of Admissions. Phone: 800-727-AIFS Ext. 5057. Fax: 203-399-5597. E-mail: info@aifs.org. Applicants must submit a formal organization application, academic transcripts, writing sample, two personal references, tuition payment required upon acceptance. Application deadline: May 15 for fall, November 1 for spring. Fees: $50. World Wide Web: http://www.aifs.org.

AMERICAN UNIVERSITY IN MOSCOW
1800 Connecticut Avenue, NW
Washington, District of Columbia 20009

General Information Educational institute that conducts conferences, seminars, and educational programs for students and leaders in business, politics, and academia in the U.S. and the Commonwealth of Independent States. Established in 1991. Number of employees: 5. Number of internship applications received each year: 50.

Internships Available ▶ *5 assistants to program coordinators:* responsibilities include assisting in all work related to the programs. Candidates should have computer skills, editing skills, office skills, oral communication skills, writing skills. Duration is 1–6 months. Unpaid. Open to recent high school graduates, college freshmen, college sophomores, college juniors, college seniors, recent college graduates. International applications accepted.

Benefits Names of contacts, opportunity to attend seminars/workshops, possible full-time employment, travel reimbursement, willing to complete paperwork for educational credit, willing to provide letters of recommendation.

Contact Write, call, fax, e-mail, or through World Wide Web site Dr. Edward Lozansky, President. Phone: 202-986-6010. Fax: 202-667-4244. E-mail: lozansky@aol.com. Telephone interview required. Applicants must submit a resume. Applications are accepted continuously. World Wide Web: http://www.RussiaHouse.org.

AMERISPAN UNLIMITED
PO Box 40007
Philadelphia, Pennsylvania 19106-0007

General Information Company that specializes in internships, volunteer work, and language programs in Latin America. Established in 1993. Number of employees: 10. Number of internship applications received each year: 200.

Internships Available ▶ *1–4 ESL teachers:* responsibilities include planning and implementing ESL classes for small groups of people of various ages and levels. Candidates should have ability to speak high-intermediate level of Spanish, ESL certification and/or experience, college degree. Duration is 3–6 months. Unpaid. Open to recent college graduates, graduate students. ▶ *10–30 environmental and/or zoological interns:* responsibilities include working in animal rescue and/or conservation; cloud forests, national parks, eco/adventure tourism, orchard gardens, botany, bird and butterfly sanctuaries, and environmental education. Candidates should have experience in the field, ability to speak high-intermediate level of Spanish; experience living in remote areas; good physical condition. Duration is 4 weeks to 6 months. Unpaid. Open to recent high school graduates, college juniors, college

seniors, recent college graduates, graduate students, law students, career changers, individuals reentering the workforce. ▶ *Professional interns:* responsibilities include working in a professional environment in one of the following fields: accounting, banking, economics, education, engineering, government, hotel, law, marketing, medicine, psychology, social work, or tourism. Candidates should have college degree in related field, knowledge of field, organizational skills, plan to pursue career in field, good Spanish skills (oral and written). Duration is 1–6 months. Unpaid. Open to recent college graduates, graduate students, law students, career changers. ▶ *5–20 social work/education/health-care interns:* responsibilities include working with abused, poor and/or street children; addiction counseling; physically and/or mentally disabled children, adults, and elderly; teaching arts and crafts; teaching English; working in rural villages or health clinics/hospitals. Candidates should have ability to speak high-intermediate level of Spanish; related experience and/or certification. Duration is 4 weeks to 6 months. Unpaid. Open to recent high school graduates, college seniors, recent college graduates, graduate students, law students, career changers, individuals reentering the workforce. ▶ *1–4 student services coordinators:* responsibilities include administrative duties, computer work, correspondence, translations, organizing activities, and helping on special projects. Candidates should have computer skills, ability to speak high-intermediate level of Spanish, administrative and customer service experience, college degree. Duration is 3–6 months. Unpaid. Open to recent college graduates, graduate students, law students, career changers, individuals reentering the workforce. International applications accepted.

Benefits Meals at a cost, names of contacts, willing to act as a professional reference, travel insurance; free housing or housing at cost available depending on internship position.

International Internships Available in Argentina; Bolivia; Brazil; Chile; Costa Rica; Ecuador; Guatemala; Mexico; Peru.

Contact Write, call, fax, e-mail, or through World Wide Web site Elizabeth Gregory, Volunteer/Internship Program Director, 117 South 17th Street, Suite 1401, Philadelphia, Pennsylvania 19103. Phone: 800-879-6640. Fax: 215-751-1986. E-mail: info@amerispan.com. Telephone interview required. Applicants must submit a formal organization application, letter of interest, resume, two letters of recommendation, $300 placement fee. Application deadline: 2 months prior to start of internship. Fees: $50. World Wide Web: http://www.amerispan.com.

ARCADIA UNIVERSITY CENTER FOR EDUCATION ABROAD
450 South Easton Road
Glenside, Pennsylvania 19038-3295

General Information University-based study abroad provider that arranges junior and senior year abroad for transfer credit. Established in 1948. Unit of Arcadia University, Glenside, Pennsylvania.

Internships Available ▶ *Australia Parliamentary interns in Canberra:* responsibilities include positions in government or government-related fields in Canberra, Australia's capital city. Candidates should have ability to work independently, college courses in field, oral communication skills, research skills, strong interpersonal skills, written communication skills. Duration is 1 semester. Unpaid. ▶ *Dublin parliamentary interns:* responsibilities include acting as an aide to a member of the Irish Parliament in Dublin. Candidates should have ability to work independently, college courses in field, oral communication skills, research skills, strong interpersonal skills, written communication skills. Duration is 1 semester. Unpaid. ▶ *London interns:* responsibilities include holding positions in public policy, social science, communications, or business. Candidates should have ability to work independently, college courses in field, oral communication skills, strong interpersonal skills, written communication skills. Duration is 1 semester or 1 summer. Unpaid. ▶ *Scottish parliamentary interns:* responsibilities include research project under the direction of a member of the Scottish Parliament. Candidates should have ability to work independently, college courses in field, oral communication skills, research skills, strong interpersonal skills, written communication skills. Duration is 1 semester. Unpaid. ▶ *Sydney interns:* responsibilities include positions in the humanities, arts, business, or social science. Candidates

Arcadia University Center for Education Abroad (continued)
should have ability to work independently, college courses in field, oral communication skills, strong interpersonal skills, written communication skills. Duration is one semester or summer. Unpaid. Open to college juniors, college seniors.
Benefits Health insurance, tuition assistance, willing to complete paperwork for educational credit, guaranteed housing, orientation, ongoing host country support, ISID card, Arcadia University transcript.
International Internships Available in Canberra, Australia; Sydney, Australia; Dublin, Ireland; Edinburgh, United Kingdom; London, United Kingdom.
Contact Write, call, fax, e-mail, or through World Wide Web site Program Coordinators, Arcadia University, 450 South Easton Road, Glenside, Pennsylvania 19038-3295. Phone: 866-927-2234. Fax: 215-572-2174. E-mail: cea@arcadia.edu. In-person interview required. Applicants must submit a formal organization application, resume, academic transcripts, personal reference, letter of recommendation, personal essay. Application deadline: March 10 for summer (London); March 31 for summer (Sydney), April 20 for fall (Sydney, Dublin, London); April 2 for fall (Scotland), October 15 for spring (Sydney, Dublin, London, Scotland), November 15 for spring (Canberra); March 15 for fall (Canberra). Fees: $35. World Wide Web: http://www.arcadia.edu/cea.

ASHAY: EDUCATIONAL RESOURCES FOR A MULTICULTURAL WORLD
1800 South Robertson Boulevard, Suite 408
Los Angeles, California 90035

General Information Organization that develops educational curriculum designed to help people understand and appreciate human differences from race and ethnicity to sexuality, age, and ability. Established in 1995. Number of employees: 2. Number of internship applications received each year: 20.
Internships Available ▶ *1–3 event planning interns:* responsibilities include helping plan and implement programs to expose people to Ashay and cultivate further involvement, working on small receptions in people's homes and larger special events, overseeing logistics, including invitations and food. Candidates should have ability to work independently, organizational skills, self-motivation, strong interpersonal skills, strong leadership ability. Duration is 3–6 months. Position available as unpaid or paid. Open to college seniors, recent college graduates, graduate students, career changers, individuals reentering the workforce. ▶ *1–2 fund-raising interns:* responsibilities include researching, writing for grants and corporate sponsorships, planning/implementing fund-raising events, and helping with direct mail campaign. Candidates should have ability to work independently, computer skills, organizational skills, research skills, self-motivation, written communication skills. Duration is 4–6 months. Position available as unpaid or paid. Open to college seniors, recent college graduates, graduate students, career changers, individuals reentering the workforce. ▶ *1–3 marketing and promotion interns:* responsibilities include helping to plan and implement teachers focus groups, researching leads for multicultural communication game distribution, identifying conferences at which game can be presented, working to have game included in educational resource catalogs. Candidates should have ability to work independently, organizational skills, research skills, self-motivation, strong interpersonal skills, written communication skills. Duration is 3–6 months. Position available as unpaid or paid. Open to college seniors, recent college graduates, graduate students, career changers, individuals reentering the workforce. ▶ *1–3 multicultural communication game interns:* responsibilities include promoting game with schools, camps, and other organizations; facilitating the game with various groups; researching new questions and additional resources. Candidates should have ability to work independently, computer skills, self-motivation, strong interpersonal skills, strong leadership ability. Duration is 4–6 months. Position available as unpaid or paid. Open to college juniors, college seniors, recent college graduates, graduate students, career changers, individuals reentering the workforce. ▶ *1–3 special projects interns:* responsibilities include varied duties depending on intern's skills/interests and project needs. Possible areas include Web master, database design

and maintenance, public speaking, outreach and networking, and graphic design. Candidates should have ability to work independently, ability to work with others, computer skills, organizational skills, research skills, self-motivation. Duration is 4–6 months. Position available as unpaid or paid. Open to college juniors, college seniors, recent college graduates, graduate students, career changers, individuals reentering the workforce. International applications accepted.
Benefits On-the-job training, willing to act as a professional reference, willing to complete paperwork for educational credit, willing to provide letters of recommendation, learning valuable transferable skills, possible stipends.
Contact Write, call, fax, e-mail, or through World Wide Web site Ms. Shifra Teitelbaum, Director, 1800 South Robertson Boulevard, Suite 408, Los Angeles, California 90035. Phone: 310-842-9125. Fax: 310-204-6221. E-mail: shifra@ashay.org. In-person interview recommended (telephone interview accepted). Applicants must submit a letter of interest, resume, two personal references. Applications are accepted continuously. World Wide Web: http://www.ashay.org.

ASSOCIATION FOR EXPERIENTIAL EDUCATION (AEE)
2305 Canyon Boulevard, Suite 100
Boulder, Colorado 80302

General Information Not-for-profit international professional membership association with roots in adventure education, committed to the development, practice, and evaluation of experiential learning in all settings. Established in 1972. Number of employees: 5. Number of internship applications received each year: 100.
Internships Available ▶ *1–5 administrative interns:* responsibilities include duties that are dependent upon the applicant's experience and interests and the needs of AEE. Candidates should have computer skills, office skills, organizational skills, self-motivation, strong interpersonal skills. Duration is 1-6 months (3 months preferred). Unpaid. ▶ *1–3 publications and marketing interns:* responsibilities include various duties dependent on the applicant's interest and experience, as well as on the needs of AEE. Candidates should have editing skills, research skills, self-motivation, writing skills. Duration is 1 to 12 months (3 months preferred). Unpaid. Open to high school students, recent high school graduates, college freshmen, college sophomores, college juniors, college seniors, recent college graduates, graduate students, law students, career changers, individuals reentering the workforce. International applications accepted.
Benefits Formal training, job counseling, names of contacts, on-the-job training, opportunity to attend seminars/workshops, possible full-time employment, willing to act as a professional reference, willing to complete paperwork for educational credit, willing to provide letters of recommendation.
Contact Write, fax, or e-mail Sandy Moore, Membership Director. Fax: 303-440-9581. E-mail: sandy@aee.org. No phone calls. Applicants must submit a formal organization application, letter of interest, resume. Applications are accepted continuously. World Wide Web: http://www.aee.org.

AUDUBON CENTER OF THE NORTH WOODS
PO Box 530
Sandstone, Minnesota 55072

General Information Environmental education center that stresses the positive relationship between people and nature; programs combine natural history, outdoor skills, and ethics and serve youth, college, and adult audiences. Established in 1968. Number of employees: 31. Number of internship applications received each year: 40.
Internships Available ▶ *4–6 environmental education interns:* responsibilities include leading residential programs for children and adults and assisting with eco-tours, outdoor recreation trips, gear care, curriculum development, and maintenance; teaching in an outdoor setting is a strong component. Candidates should have ability to work independently, ability to work with others, college courses in field, knowledge of field, oral communication skills, self-motivation. Duration is 5–12 months. $300–$550 per

month. Open to college seniors, recent college graduates, graduate students. ▶ *4–6 summer environmental education interns:* responsibilities include residential environmental instruction for summer youth camps, dorm supervision, camping/canoeing trips, assistance with teacher workshops and adult/family programs, gear care, and maintenance. Candidates should have ability to work with others, knowledge of field, oral communication skills, personal interest in the field, self-motivation, strong leadership ability. Duration is 3–4 months. $500–$550 per month. Open to college sophomores, college juniors, college seniors, recent college graduates, graduate students. ▶ *1 summer wildlife rehabilitation intern:* responsibilities include care, feeding, and maintenance of education and rehabilitation animals, initial first aid and stabilization of rehabilitation animals, contact with general public. Candidates should have ability to work independently, knowledge of field, organizational skills, self-motivation, strong interpersonal skills. Duration is 3–4 months. $300–$400 per month. Open to college juniors, college seniors, recent college graduates, graduate students. ▶ *1–2 wildlife interns:* responsibilities include care/feeding/training of educational raptors and reptiles, educational programming with captive animals, care/feeding of animals in rehabilitation, development of educational materials, maintenance, and adventure programming. Candidates should have ability to work independently, ability to work with others, experience in the field, oral communication skills, organizational skills, self-motivation. Duration is 6–12 months. $300–$550 per month. Open to college juniors, college seniors, recent college graduates, graduate students. International applications accepted.

Benefits Formal training, free housing, free meals, names of contacts, on-the-job training, opportunity to attend seminars/workshops, possible full-time employment, willing to act as a professional reference, willing to complete paperwork for educational credit, willing to provide letters of recommendation, graduate credits in environmental education.

Contact Write, call, fax, or e-mail Intern Coordinator. Phone: 320-245-2648. Fax: 320-245-5272. E-mail: audubonl@audubon-center.org. In-person interview recommended (telephone interview accepted). Applicants must submit a letter of interest, resume, three personal references. Applications are accepted continuously. World Wide Web: http://www.audubon-center.org.

AURORA UNIVERSITY–LAKE GENEVA CAMPUS
PO Box 210
Williams Bay, Wisconsin 53191

General Information Educational conference center providing outdoor and nontraditional learning experiences and sponsoring regional conferences. Established in 1886. Number of employees: 100. Affiliate of Aurora University, Aurora, Illinois. Number of internship applications received each year: 50.

Internships Available ▶ *6–8 adventure education positions:* responsibilities include facilitating team building and leadership development programs for adolescents, colleges, and adult groups by utilizing trust building, group initiatives, high and low ropes courses, team and individual climbing elements, and off-campus rock climbing. Candidates should have experience in the field, oral communication skills, organizational skills, strong interpersonal skills, strong leadership ability. Duration is March-November. $300–$350 per week. Open to college seniors, recent college graduates, graduate students, career changers. ▶ *1 outdoor recreation position:* responsibilities include coordinating conference groups and leading activities, including sports, games, natural awareness, and orienteering. Candidates should have ability to work independently, ability to work with others, experience in the field, self-motivation, strong leadership ability, waterfront skills, qualified life guard, experience in sailing, canoeing, windsurfing, skiing (downhill or cross country). Duration is 1 summer or 1 winter (12 to 15 weeks each). $200–$250 per week. Open to college seniors, recent college graduates, graduate students. ▶ *7 outdoor/environmental education positions:* responsibilities include coordinating school groups and teaching classes in natural awareness, wetlands, lake study, astronomy, and weather. Candidates should have ability to work with others, organizational skills, personal interest in the field, plan to pursue career in field, self-motivation, strong leadership

ability. Duration is September-May. $200–$250 per week. Open to recent college graduates, graduate students. International applications accepted.

Benefits Formal training, names of contacts, on-the-job training, willing to act as a professional reference, willing to complete paperwork for educational credit, willing to provide letters of recommendation, supplemental medical policy, use of recreational facilities (tennis, golf, waterfront), free room and board for outdoor/environmental education and outdoor recreation positions, room and board at a cost for adventure education positions.

Contact Write, fax, e-mail, or through World Wide Web site Cathy Coster, Associate Director of Adventure Education. Fax: 262-245-8549. E-mail: ccoster@aurora.edu. No phone calls. In-person interview recommended (telephone interview accepted). Applicants must submit a letter of interest, resume, three personal references. Application deadline: February 1 for March positions, April 1 for summer positions, August 1 for September positions, November 1 for winter positions. World Wide Web: http://www.augeowms.org.

BOSTON UNIVERSITY SARGENT CENTER SCHOOL PROGRAM
36 Sargent Camp Road
Hancock, New Hampshire 03449

General Information Program offering environmental and outdoor education, including initiatives, trust activities, and ropes-course work, for 5th- through 8th-graders. Established in 1912. Number of employees: 20. Unit of Boston University, Boston, Massachusetts. Number of internship applications received each year: 50.

Internships Available ▶ *1 nature center coordinator:* responsibilities include assisting in teaching environmental lessons, providing interns with new ideas or facts for lessons, supervising students in the nature center during free time, creating new displays, working on the physical appearance of the nature center, and attending most meals. Candidates should have ability to work independently, knowledge of field, oral communication skills, organizational skills, personal interest in the field, research skills, self-motivation. Duration is 3–9 months. $150–$190 per week. ▶ *15 resident school program interns:* responsibilities include teaching groups of 8-10 students environmental and outdoor education, supervising students, and attending weekly staff meetings. Candidates should have ability to work with others, oral communication skills, personal interest in the field, self-motivation, strong leadership ability. Duration is 3–9 months. $150–$190 per week. Open to recent high school graduates, college freshmen, college sophomores, college juniors, college seniors, recent college graduates, graduate students, law students, career changers, individuals reentering the workforce. International applications accepted.

Benefits Formal training, free housing, free meals, names of contacts, on-the-job training, opportunity to attend seminars/workshops, possible full-time employment, willing to complete paperwork for educational credit, willing to provide letters of recommendation, job lists provided when available.

Contact Write, call, fax, e-mail, or through World Wide Web site Diane Silver, School Program Coordinator. Phone: 603-525-3311. Fax: 603-525-4151. E-mail: school_program@busc.mv.com. In-person interview recommended (telephone interview accepted). Applicants must submit a formal organization application, three letters of recommendation. Application deadline: June 30 for fall, December 12 for winter/spring. World Wide Web: http://www.bu.edu/outdoor.

BRECKENRIDGE OUTDOOR EDUCATION CENTER
Box 697
Breckenridge, Colorado 80424

General Information Education center offering year-round wilderness and adventure programs for individuals of all abilities, as well as team building, leadership development, and adaptive skiing opportunities for individuals with disabilities and other special needs, and team building programs for professionals.

Breckenridge Outdoor Education Center (continued)

Accredited by Association of Experiential Education. Established in 1976. Number of employees: 25. Number of internship applications received each year: 100.

Internships Available ▶ *10–12 summer wilderness interns:* responsibilities include planning, implementation/facilitation/evaluation of wilderness courses, administrative duties, and assisting professional challenge courses. Candidates should have oral communication skills, personal interest in the field, self-motivation, strong interpersonal skills, CPR and first aid certifications. Duration is May 15 to September 15. $50 per month stipend. ▶ *10–12 winter interns:* responsibilities include serving as adaptive ski instructor, assisting on wilderness courses, assisting on professional challenge courses, and administrative duties. Candidates should have ability to work independently, ability to work with others, personal interest in the field, self-motivation, strong leadership ability, CPR and first aid certifications. Duration is November 1 to April 30. $50 per month stipend. Open to individuals at least 21 years old. International applications accepted.

Benefits Formal training, free housing, free meals, names of contacts, possible full-time employment, willing to complete paperwork for educational credit, willing to provide letters of recommendation, ski pass in winter, worker's compensation, athletics club pass.

Contact Write, call, fax, e-mail, or through World Wide Web site Robyn Graber, Internship Coordinator. Phone: 970-453-6422 Ext. 11. Fax: 970-453-4676. E-mail: internship@boec.org. In-person interview recommended (telephone interview accepted). Applicants must submit a letter of interest, resume, formal application (available on Web site). Application deadline: March 1 for summer, September 1 for winter. World Wide Web: http://www.boec.org.

BROOKINGS INSTITUTION–CENTER FOR PUBLIC POLICY EDUCATION (CPPE)
1775 Massachusetts Avenue, NW
Washington, District of Columbia 20036

General Information Nonprofit public policy research organization that designs and conducts executive education programs for corporate and government executives. Established in 1917. Number of employees: 250. Number of internship applications received each year: 50.

Internships Available ▶ *1–2 interns:* responsibilities include working with senior staff members to identify possible topics and speakers for public policy conferences, researching new companies to visit as part of conferences on understanding business policy, working with marketing staff to identify potential companies to attend programs, and performing clerical duties as assigned. Candidates should have computer skills, oral communication skills, organizational skills, research skills, self-motivation, strong interpersonal skills. Duration is one semester or summer. Unpaid. Open to college juniors, college seniors.

Benefits On-the-job training, opportunity to attend seminars/workshops, willing to complete paperwork for educational credit.

Contact Write, fax, or e-mail Rick Henry, Program Associate, 1775 Massachusetts Avenue, NW, Washington, District of Columbia 20036. Fax: 202-797-6319. E-mail: rhenry@brookings.edu. No phone calls. Telephone interview required. Applicants must submit a resume, writing sample, cover letter. Application deadline: March 1 for summer, July 1 for fall, November 1 for spring. World Wide Web: http://www.brookings.edu/execed.

CALIFORNIA ACADEMY OF SCIENCES, CAREERS IN SCIENCE
Golden Gate Park
San Francisco, California 94118

General Information Work-based youth-development program focusing on youth traditionally under-represented in the sciences. Established in 1996. Number of employees: 32. Number of internship applications received each year: 100.

Internships Available ▶ *10–15 level one interns:* responsibilities include teaching science on museum floor and through outreach to community partners; providing administrative assistance to the Education Department, opportunities to assist research scientists

or graduate assistants with original research. Candidates should have ability to work independently, ability to work with others, personal interest in the field, self-motivation. $7–$9.50 per hour. Open to high school students, recent high school graduates, college freshmen, must be between the ages of 14–17.

Benefits Formal training, names of contacts, on-the-job training, opportunity to attend seminars/workshops, tuition assistance, willing to act as a professional reference, willing to provide letters of recommendation, career and educational planning.

Contact Write, call, fax, or e-mail Ashley Conrad–Saydah, Careers in Science Manager. Phone: 415-750-7366. Fax: 415-750-7367. E-mail: cis@calacademy.org. In-person interview required. Applicants must submit a formal organization application. Application deadline: May 1. World Wide Web: http://www.calacademy.org/education/internships.

CAMP FIRE USA GULF WIND COUNCIL
1814 Creighton Road
Pensacola, Florida 32504

General Information Organization that provides informal educational opportunities for young persons. Established in 1910. Number of employees: 40. Unit of Camp Fire USA, Kansas City, Missouri. Number of internship applications received each year: 20.

Internships Available ▶ *1 Special Sitters program coordinator:* responsibilities include developing, implementing, and monitoring Special Sitters project, including performing tasks involving publicity, community outreach, recruitment and training, and matching and referring sitters to families. Candidates should have knowledge of field, oral communication skills, organizational skills, strong leadership ability, written communication skills, experience with special needs children. Duration is 6–12 months. Position available as unpaid or paid. Open to individuals 18 years of age or older. ▶ *1–4 area program managers:* responsibilities include managing, maintaining, and extending program services. Candidates should have oral communication skills, organizational skills, self-motivation, strong interpersonal skills, strong leadership ability, written communication skills. Duration is 11 months. Position available as unpaid or at salary depending on duties and experience. Open to individuals 18 years of age or older. ▶ *5–20 club co-leaders:* responsibilities include facilitating activities tailored to children's needs and interests. Candidates should have ability to work independently, oral communication skills, organizational skills, self-motivation, strong interpersonal skills, strong leadership ability. Duration is 2 semesters. Unpaid. Open to individuals 18 years of age or older. ▶ *1 program assistant intern:* responsibilities include assisting program director in administering youth programs and providing program assistance to program department staff and planning special events. Candidates should have computer skills, knowledge of field, office skills, organizational skills, personal interest in the field, writing skills. Duration is 1–2 semesters. Position available as unpaid or paid. Open to college juniors, college seniors, recent college graduates, graduate students, individuals reentering the workforce, mature individuals of 21 years of age or older. ▶ *5 self-reliance coordinators:* responsibilities include arranging and teaching assigned self-reliance courses. Candidates should have oral communication skills, organizational skills, self-motivation, strong interpersonal skills, strong leadership ability, written communication skills. Duration is 3–12 months. Position available as unpaid or paid. Open to individuals 18 years of age or older. ▶ *1 self-reliance manager:* responsibilities include recruiting course participants and arranging course sites; managing program staff. Candidates should have oral communication skills, organizational skills, strong interpersonal skills, strong leadership ability, written communication skills, management or supervisory experience. Duration is 12 months. Position available as unpaid or paid. Open to recent college graduates, graduate students, career changers, individuals reentering the workforce, individuals 21 years of age or older. International applications accepted.

Benefits Names of contacts, on-the-job training, opportunity to attend seminars/workshops, possible full-time employment, travel reimbursement, willing to complete paperwork for educational credit, willing to provide letters of recommendation.

Contact Write, call, fax, or e-mail La-Vonne Haven, Executive Director. Phone: 850-476-1760. Fax: 850-476-6614. E-mail: cfgulfwind@aol.com. In-person interview required. Applicants must submit a formal organization application, letter of interest, resume, personal and criminal background checks, fingerprint screening, tuberculosis test required. Applications are accepted continuously.

CASA XELAJU
3034 47th Avenue South
Minneapolis, Minnesota 55406

General Information Cultural institute. Established in 1987. Number of employees: 40. Number of internship applications received each year: 75.

Internships Available ▶ *2 business/computer interns:* responsibilities include working on Web site, assisting international coordinator in organizing field trips, translating lectures, and working with banks and local businesses. Candidates should have ability to work independently, college courses in field, self-motivation, written communication skills, ability to speak Spanish. Duration is 6 weeks. Unpaid. Open to college sophomores, college juniors, college seniors. ▶ *6 human rights/labor union interns.* Candidates should have ability to work independently, analytical skills, college courses in field, computer skills, knowledge of field, office skills, oral communication skills, organizational skills, research skills, self-motivation, strong interpersonal skills, strong leadership ability, writing skills, ability to read, write, and speak Spanish. Duration is 6 weeks. Unpaid. Open to college freshmen, college sophomores, college juniors, college seniors, recent college graduates, graduate students, law students. ▶ *6 journalism interns:* responsibilities include working on newspapers on different tasks including photojournalism, business office, layout, news, wire services, reporting. Candidates should have ability to work independently, ability to work with others, analytical skills, editing skills, writing skills, ability to write, read, and speak Spanish. Duration is 6 weeks. Unpaid. Open to college juniors, college seniors, recent college graduates, graduate students. ▶ *5 medical interns:* responsibilities include working with the grassroots organization Clinica Alemana and working in a national hospital as a resident. Candidates should have declared college major in field, oral communication skills, self-motivation, ability to write, read, and speak Spanish. Duration is 6 weeks. Unpaid. Open to college seniors, recent college graduates, graduate students. ▶ *2–4 research community development interns:* responsibilities include working with a rural community in Quetzaltenango, Guatemala; researching issues in the community and developing solutions. Candidates should have ability to work independently, ability to work with others, analytical skills, computer skills, editing skills, knowledge of field, office skills, oral communication skills, organizational skills, personal interest in the field, research skills, self-motivation, strong leadership ability, writing skills. Duration is 6–12 months. Unpaid. Open to college juniors, college seniors, recent college graduates, graduate students, law students, career changers. ▶ *2 senior advisors (Women's Sewing Association):* responsibilities include helping to develop broader markets for selling goods in USA and European countries. Candidates should have ability to work independently, ability to work with others, analytical skills, college courses in field, computer skills, editing skills, office skills, oral communication skills, organizational skills, personal interest in the field, plan to pursue career in field, research skills, self-motivation, strong leadership ability, writing skills. Duration is 6–12 months. Unpaid. Open to college juniors, college seniors, recent college graduates, graduate students, law students. ▶ *4 social work interns:* responsibilities include helping a local women's shelter address domestic violence; helping children with homework; and working with local community. Candidates should have analytical skills, knowledge of field, office skills, oral communication skills, strong interpersonal skills, strong leadership ability, written communication skills, ability to read, write, and speak Spanish. Duration is 7 weeks. Unpaid. Open to college juniors, college seniors, recent college graduates, graduate students. International applications accepted.

Benefits Housing at a cost, opportunity to attend seminars/workshops, possible full-time employment, willing to act as a professional reference, willing to complete paperwork for educational credit, willing to provide letters of recommendation.

International Internships Available in Guatemala.

Contact Write, call, e-mail, or through World Wide Web site Julio E. Batres, Director, 3034 47th Avenue South, Minneapolis, Minnesota 55406. Phone: 888-796-CASA. Fax: 612-729-9264. E-mail: info@casaxelaju.com. Telephone interview required. Applicants must submit a formal organization application, letter of interest, resume, two letters of recommendation. Applications are accepted continuously. Fees: $50. World Wide Web: http://www.casaxelaju.com.

THE CENTER FOR CROSS-CULTURAL STUDY
446 Main Street
Amherst, Massachusetts 01002

General Information Educational institution/study abroad program combining academic coursework and internships in a variety of fields. Established in 1969. Number of employees: 40. Number of internship applications received each year: 10.

Internships Available ▶ *1–2 interns (Seville, Spain):* responsibilities include duties based on type of position and field of study. Candidates should have ability to work with others, knowledge of field, oral communication skills, written communication skills, one semester of college-level Spanish or equivalent; participation in an Upper-Division, CC-CS Semester Academic Program in Seville, Spain. Duration is one semester (10-15 hours per week). Unpaid. Open to college freshmen, college sophomores, college juniors, college seniors. International applications accepted.

Benefits On-the-job training, willing to act as a professional reference, willing to complete paperwork for educational credit, possibility of 3-6 credits per semester for equine science and educational positions.

International Internships Available in Seville, Spain.

Contact Write, call, fax, e-mail, or through World Wide Web site Dr. Judith Ortiz, U.S. Director. Phone: 413-256-0011. Fax: 413-256-1968. E-mail: ortiz@cccs.com. In-person interview required. Applicants must submit a formal organization application, letter of interest, resume, academic transcripts, three letters of recommendation. Application deadline: May 15 for fall, November 15 for spring. Fees: $30. World Wide Web: http://www.StudyinSpain.org.

CENTER FOR TALENTED YOUTH/JOHNS HOPKINS UNIVERSITY
3400 North Charles Street
Baltimore, Maryland 21218

General Information Organization that provides academically talented pre-college students with the opportunity to take rigorous courses in mathematics, science, computer science, humanities, and writing at college campuses in the United States. Established in 1980. Number of employees: 150. Unit of Johns Hopkins University, Baltimore, Maryland. Number of internship applications received each year: 2,500.

Internships Available ▶ *20–25 health assistants:* responsibilities include overseeing medication and medical appointments for live-in, pre-college students; contacting parents when necessary, completing reports. Candidates should have oral communication skills, organizational skills, personal interest in the field, self-motivation, strong interpersonal skills, written communication skills. Duration is late June through early August. $2200 per 6-week internship. Open to college juniors, college seniors, recent college graduates, graduate students, medical or pre-med students. ▶ *20 office managers:* responsibilities include managing an office, overseeing petty cash account, and supervising office staff at a fast-paced, live-in camp for gifted pre-college students. Candidates should have computer skills, experience in the field, office skills, organizational skills, strong interpersonal skills, strong leadership ability. Duration is late June through early August. $3600 per 7-week internship. Open to college juniors, college seniors, recent college graduates, graduate students, business students. ▶ *400 resident assistants:* responsibilities include caring for the needs of live-in, pre-college students, sponsoring and leading daily activities. Candidates should have ability to work with others, oral communication skills, organizational skills, self-motivation, strong leadership ability. Duration is late June through early August.

Center for Talented Youth/Johns Hopkins University (continued)
$2000 per 6-week internship. Open to college freshmen, college sophomores, college juniors, college seniors, recent college graduates. ▶ *40–45 residential program assistants:* responsibilities include answering phones, covering office, purchasing supplies, and conducting recreational activities at a residential camp for gifted pre-college students. Candidates should have computer skills, office skills, oral communication skills, self-motivation, strong interpersonal skills, written communication skills. Duration is late June through early August. $2200 per 6-week internship. Open to college juniors, college seniors, recent college graduates, age 21 and over preferred in order to drive rental vehicles. ▶ *400 teaching assistants/laboratory assistants:* responsibilities include supporting instructor with clerical work for the class, tutoring the students, proctoring study hall, and teaching some lessons. Candidates should have college courses in field, oral communication skills, personal interest in the field, strong interpersonal skills, strong leadership ability, written communication skills. Duration is late June through early August. $1800 per 6-week internship. Open to college freshmen, college sophomores, college juniors, college seniors, recent college graduates, graduate students, law students. International applications accepted.
Benefits Formal training, free housing, free meals, job counseling, names of contacts, on-the-job training, opportunity to attend seminars/workshops, possible full-time employment, willing to act as a professional reference, willing to complete paperwork for educational credit, willing to provide letters of recommendation.
Contact Write, call, fax, e-mail, or through World Wide Web site Summer Employment Opportunities. Phone: 410-516-0053. Fax: 410-516-0093. E-mail: ctysummer@jhu.edu. Telephone interview required. Applicants must submit a formal organization application, letter of interest, resume, academic transcripts, 1-3 letters of recommendation. Application deadline: January 25 for priority deadline. World Wide Web: http://www.jhu.edu/gifted/ctysummer.

CENTRO DE DISENO ARQUITECTURA Y CONTRUCCION
Apartado Postal 3900
Tegucigalpa Honduras

General Information Private university specializing in architecture and design that is committed to investigation and community outreach. Established in 1996. Number of employees: 43. Number of internship applications received each year: 5.
Internships Available ▶ *1 computer services intern:* responsibilities include providing support to users of computer lab; offering training opportunities for students and staff; helping design operational programs; developing database for university operations. Candidates should have ability to work independently, computer skills, knowledge of field, self-motivation, strong interpersonal skills, minimum of intermediate-level Spanish. Duration is 1–3 semesters. Position available as unpaid or paid. Open to college juniors, college seniors, recent college graduates, graduate students, career changers. ▶ *1–2 construction technology interns:* responsibilities include giving workshops on specific construction skills, such as building types, the use of specific materials, and building models. Candidates should have ability to work with others, experience in the field, oral communication skills, personal interest in the field, minimum of intermediate-level Spanish. Duration is 1–12 weeks. Position available as unpaid or paid. Open to college seniors, recent college graduates, graduate students, career changers, individuals reentering the workforce, people with specific construction skills. ▶ *1 environmental issues intern:* responsibilities include researching laws and compliance alternatives, proposing and developing extension courses, organizing environmental events, preparing training and course materials, helping draft proposals for program needs. Candidates should have ability to work independently, knowledge of field, research skills, self-motivation, written communication skills, minimum of intermediate-level Spanish. Duration is 1–3 semesters. Position available as unpaid or paid. Open to college juniors, college seniors, recent college graduates, graduate students, career changers, individuals reentering the workforce, professionals in the field desiring overseas experience or research opportunities. ▶ *1–2 general support personnel:* responsibilities include general support activities for

the academic and research programs; responsibilities vary depending upon needs at the time of the internship; work primarily office/clerical. Candidates should have ability to work independently, computer skills, office skills, research skills, strong interpersonal skills, written communication skills. Duration is 1–12 months. Position available as unpaid or paid. Open to college freshmen, college sophomores, college juniors, college seniors, recent college graduates, graduate students, individuals reentering the workforce. ▶ *1 librarian:* responsibilities include activities to strengthen library services, managing Internet access and monitoring for topics of interest, soliciting additional library resources. Candidates should have ability to work independently, computer skills, knowledge of field, research skills, self-motivation, minimum of intermediate-level Spanish. Duration is 1–3 semesters. Position available as unpaid or paid. Open to college seniors, recent college graduates, graduate students, career changers, individuals reentering the workforce, professionals in the field desiring overseas experience. ▶ *1 marketing intern:* responsibilities include helping design and write public relations and promotional materials, designing ad campaigns, organizing promotional events, working with student admissions process, investigating need for new degree and extension courses. Candidates should have ability to work with others, computer skills, experience in the field, self-motivation, minimum of intermediate-level Spanish. Duration is 2–6 months. Position available as unpaid or paid. Open to college seniors, recent college graduates, graduate students, career changers, individuals reentering the workforce, professionals in the field desiring overseas experience. ▶ *1–2 municipal support interns:* responsibilities include helping develop materials to train municipal employees and elected officials on basic urban planning issues. Candidates should have ability to work independently, declared college major in field, knowledge of field, self-motivation, written communication skills, minimum of intermediate-level Spanish. Duration is 1–3 semesters. Position available as unpaid or paid. Open to college seniors, recent college graduates, graduate students, career changers, individuals reentering the workforce, professionals in the field desiring overseas experience or research opportunities. ▶ *1–3 research interns:* responsibilities include locating and translating background materials; participating in testing, experiments, and design; providing logistical support; helping design final reports, and drafting proposals for additional research projects. Candidates should have ability to work independently, ability to work with others, analytical skills, knowledge of field, research skills, minimum of intermediate-level Spanish. Duration is 1–3 semesters. Position available as unpaid or paid. Open to college juniors, college seniors, recent college graduates, graduate students, career changers, individuals reentering the workforce, professionals in the fields of architecture, design, engineering, or construction desiring overseas experience. ▶ *1–3 teaching assistants:* responsibilities include providing support for teachers in workshop settings, helping prepare exercises and materials, evaluating and proposing teaching methods, proposing and developing new courses, and helping draft proposals for program needs. Candidates should have declared college major in field, knowledge of field, oral communication skills, self-motivation, strong interpersonal skills, minimum of intermediate-level Spanish. Duration is 1–3 semesters. Position available as unpaid or paid. Open to college seniors, recent college graduates, graduate students, career changers, individuals reentering the workforce, architecture or design professionals desiring overseas or teaching experience. ▶ *1–4 urban and regional planning interns:* responsibilities include working with municipal governments to develop plans and offering courses or training on the subject. Candidates should have ability to work with others, declared college major in field, oral communication skills, written communication skills, minimum of intermediate-level Spanish. Duration is 1–12 months. Position available as unpaid or paid. Open to college seniors, recent college graduates, graduate students, individuals reentering the workforce, professionals in the field desiring overseas experience. International applications accepted.

Benefits Housing at a cost, meals at a cost, on-the-job training, opportunity to attend seminars/workshops, possible full-time employment, willing to act as a professional reference, willing to complete paperwork for educational credit, willing to provide letters of recommendation, participation in CEDAC courses free of charge.

International Internships Available in Tegucigalpa, Honduras.

Contact Write, fax, or e-mail Lorette Pellettiere Calix, Internship Coordinator, TGU-00039, PO Box 025387, Miami, Florida 33102-5387. Phone: 011-504-232-4195. Fax: 011-504-231-0729. E-mail: cedac@sdnhon.org.hn. Applicants must submit a letter of interest, resume, academic transcripts, three letters of recommendation, e-mail address if possible. Applications are accepted continuously. World Wide Web: http://www.cedac.edu.hn.

CHINGACHGOOK YMCA OUTDOOR CENTER
1872 Pilot Knob Road
Kattskill Bay, New York 12844

General Information Outdoor environmental and adventure education center in the Adirondacks that teaches school children, college students, families, and adult groups. Established in 1913. Number of employees: 100. Branch of Capital District YMCA, Albany, New York. Number of internship applications received each year: 10.

Internships Available ▶ *2–4 food services staff interns:* responsibilities include preparing meals for the dining room with 3-10 others, serving up to 400 persons per meal. Candidates should have ability to work independently, ability to work with others, knowledge of field. Duration is 7–15 weeks. Position available as unpaid or at $250–$400 per week. Open to recent high school graduates, college freshmen, college sophomores, college juniors, college seniors, recent college graduates, individuals reentering the workforce. ▶ *3–4 outdoor educators:* responsibilities include leading environmental, recreational, adventure, and outdoor classes for school children, families, college students, and adults. Candidates should have knowledge of field, personal interest in the field, strong interpersonal skills, strong leadership ability. Duration is 8–20 weeks. Position available as unpaid or at $125–$200 per week. Open to recent high school graduates, college freshmen, college sophomores, college juniors, college seniors, recent college graduates. International applications accepted.

Benefits Formal training, free housing, free meals, names of contacts, on-the-job training, opportunity to attend seminars/workshops, possible full-time employment, tuition assistance, willing to act as a professional reference, willing to complete paperwork for educational credit.

Contact Write, call, fax, or e-mail Kenis Sweet, Outdoor Education Director. Phone: 518-656-9462 Ext. 14. Fax: 518-656-9362. E-mail: ksweet@cdymca.org. In-person interview recommended (telephone interview accepted). Applicants must submit a letter of interest, resume, three personal references. Application deadline: February 1 for spring, June 1 for fall. World Wide Web: http://www.chingachgook.org.

CHOATE ROSEMARY HALL
333 Christian Street
Wallingford, Connecticut 06492

General Information Secondary school with summer enrichment and credit programs for middle and high school students. Established in 1916. Number of employees: 125. Number of internship applications received each year: 100.

Internships Available ▶ *25–30 teaching interns:* responsibilities include teaching two classes, serving as residential house adviser, and coaching two afternoons per week. Candidates should have ability to work with others, organizational skills, personal interest in the field, plan to pursue career in field, self-motivation, strong leadership ability. Duration is 5 weeks. $2300–$2400 per duration of internship. Open to college juniors, college seniors, recent college graduates, graduate students, career changers. International applications accepted.

Benefits Free housing, free meals, names of contacts, on-the-job training, willing to act as a professional reference, willing to provide letters of recommendation, training with two different senior teachers.

Contact Write, call, fax, e-mail, or through World Wide Web site Jim Irzyk, Director of Summer Programs. Phone: 203-697-2365. Fax: 203-697-2519. E-mail: jirzyk@choate.edu. In-person interview recommended (telephone interview accepted). Applicants must submit a formal organization application, letter of interest, resume, academic transcripts, two letters of recommendation. Application deadline: March 1 for teaching positions (submissions by January encouraged). World Wide Web: http://www.choate.edu/summer.

THE COLLEGE SETTLEMENT OF PHILADELPHIA AND KUHN DAY CAMP
600 Witmer Road
Horsham, Pennsylvania 19044

General Information Resident and day camp that stresses environmental awareness in all activities including rock climbing, backpacking, outpost camping, and ""regular" camping; offers a residential outdoor school program for schools in the Philadelphia area during the fall and spring. Established in 1922. Number of employees: 63. Number of internship applications received each year: 200.

Internships Available ▶ *50–65 counselors:* responsibilities include living with children and directing activities. Candidates should have ability to work independently, experience in the field, oral communication skills, self-motivation, strong interpersonal skills, strong leadership ability. Duration is 9 weeks (summer only). $1800–$2000 per duration of internship. Open to college freshmen, college sophomores, college juniors, college seniors, recent college graduates, graduate students. ▶ *2 health providers:* responsibilities include living at Health Center; providing first day screenings, administering medications, and attending to sick or injured campers and staff. Candidates should have knowledge of field, organizational skills, personal interest in the field, plan to pursue career in field, strong interpersonal skills, RN or BSN required. Duration is 9 weeks (summer only). $3000 per duration of internship. Open to recent college graduates, graduate students. ▶ *3 lifeguards:* responsibilities include instructing swimming and ensuring safety of recreational program participants. Candidates should have knowledge of field, oral communication skills, strong interpersonal skills, strong leadership ability, lifeguard training required; water safety instruction helpful. Duration is 9 weeks (summer only). $2000 per duration of internship. Open to college sophomores, college juniors, college seniors, recent college graduates, graduate students. ▶ *5 teachers/naturalists:* responsibilities include teaching small groups of children and leading large group and environmental activities. Candidates should have experience in the field, oral communication skills, personal interest in the field, strong interpersonal skills, strong leadership ability. Duration is 3 months (spring and fall only). $225 per week. Open to college juniors, college seniors, recent college graduates, graduate students. ▶ *2 teen adventure leaders:* responsibilities include leading adventure trips with 13- and 14-year-olds. Candidates should have experience in the field, oral communication skills, personal interest in the field, self-motivation, strong interpersonal skills, strong leadership ability. Duration is 9 weeks (summer only). $3000 per duration of internship. Open to college seniors, recent college graduates, graduate students, individuals reentering the workforce. International applications accepted.

Benefits Formal training, free housing, free meals, names of contacts, opportunity to attend seminars/workshops, willing to act as a professional reference, willing to complete paperwork for educational credit, willing to provide letters of recommendation.

Contact Write, call, fax, or e-mail Andrew Fielding, Program Director, 600 Winter Road, Horsham, Pennsylvania 19044. Phone: 215-542-7974. Fax: 215-542-7457. E-mail: camps@collegesettlement.org. In-person interview recommended (telephone interview accepted). Applicants must submit a formal organization application, resume, three personal references. Application deadline: January 1 for spring (recommended), May 1 for summer (recommended), August 1 for fall (recommended). World Wide Web: http://www.collegesettlement.org.

CORO
911 Washington Avenue, Suite 510
St. Louis, Missouri 63101

General Information Organization that conducts research, education, and training in public affairs; participants learn from

Coro (continued)

their experiences in field assignments, interviews, and projects with diverse organizations. Established in 1942. Number of employees: 40. Number of internship applications received each year: 300.

Internships Available ▶ *64 Coro Fellows Program in Public Affairs:* responsibilities include working a minimum of 1600 hours over 9.5 months in 5 field assignments of public affairs (government, business, labor unions, non-profit, and political campaigns); dozens of group interviews, 2 projects, 2-3 three-day retreats, and bi-weekly seminars. Candidates should have ability to work independently, analytical skills, oral communication skills, organizational skills, personal interest in the field, self-motivation, strong interpersonal skills, strong leadership ability, writing skills, commitment to public service. Duration is September to June. Position available as unpaid or paid. Open to college seniors, recent college graduates, graduate students, law students, career changers, individuals reentering the workforce. International applications accepted.
Benefits Formal training, names of contacts, on-the-job training, opportunity to attend seminars/workshops, willing to act as a professional reference, willing to complete paperwork for educational credit, willing to provide letters of recommendation, monthly stipends available based on financial need (ranging from $400–$800).
Contact Write, call, fax, e-mail, or through World Wide Web site Matthew Rosen, Fellows Recruiter, 911 Washington Avenue, Suite 510, St. Louis, Missouri 63101. Phone: 314-621-3040 Ext. 11. Fax: 314-621-1874. E-mail: mrosen@coro.org. Applicants must submit a formal organization application, academic transcripts, three writing samples, three letters of recommendation, participation (for finalists) in a series of group "exercises" and interviews in March/April. Application deadline: February 1. Fees: $50. World Wide Web: http://www.coro.org.

CORO CENTER FOR LEADERSHIP
425 Sixth Avenue, Suite 1790
Pittsburgh, Pennsylvania 15212

General Information Leadership training center. Established in 1999. Number of employees: 8. Affiliate of Coro National, San Francisco, California.
Internships Available ▶ *3 Allegheny County Executive Fellows:* responsibilities include complying with specifications set by the county's requirements, attending training, meetings, sessions, and completing assigned projects. Candidates should have ability to work independently, ability to work with others, analytical skills, knowledge of field, oral communication skills, personal interest in the field, self-motivation, strong leadership ability, writing skills. Duration is July to June. $37,500 per year. Open to graduate students, law students, career changers, individuals reentering the workforce. ▶ *16 Coro Community Problem Solving Fellows:* responsibilities include completing field assignments, attending weekly seminars and evening networking events, completing a group project, and conducting leadership interviews. Candidates should have ability to work independently, ability to work with others, oral communication skills, self-motivation, strong leadership ability, written communication skills. Duration is June to August. $2000 stipend. Open to college freshmen, college sophomores, college juniors, college seniors, recent college graduates. ▶ *16 Fellows in Public Affairs:* responsibilities include attending seminars, participating in five multi-sector placements, participating in group and individual projects. Candidates should have ability to work independently, ability to work with others, analytical skills, oral communication skills, personal interest in the field, self-motivation, strong leadership ability, written communication skills. Duration is September to May; full-time. Position available as unpaid or at $7000 to $12,000 stipend based on financial need. Open to recent college graduates, graduate students, law students, career changers, individuals reentering the workforce. ▶ *20–25 Information Technology Fellows:* responsibilities include meeting weekly; attending site visits and related events; conducting interviews with professionals in this field of study. Candidates should have knowledge of field, personal interest in the field, plan to pursue career in

field, self-motivation, strong leadership ability. Duration is June to August. Unpaid. Open to graduate students, career changers. International applications accepted.
Benefits Formal training, names of contacts, on-the-job training, opportunity to attend seminars/workshops, tuition assistance, willing to act as a professional reference, willing to provide letters of recommendation, stipends; possible graduate school credit for Fellows in Public Affairs.
Contact Write, call, fax, e-mail, or through World Wide Web site McCrae Holliday, Outreach Liaison. Phone: 412-201-5772 Ext. 4420. Fax: 412-201-0672. E-mail: mholliday@coro.org. Applicants must submit a formal organization application, resume, academic transcripts, writing sample, personal reference, letter of recommendation, $50 fee for some applications. Application deadline: February for Fellows in Public Affairs, March for Community Problem Solving Fellows, March for Allegheny County Executive Fellows, April for Information Technology Fellows. World Wide Web: http://www.coro.org.

CORO NEW YORK LEADERSHIP CENTER
42 Broadway, 18th Floor
New York, New York 10004

General Information Organization that conducts research, education, and training in public affairs; participants' learning comes from their experiences in field assignments, interviews, and projects with diverse organizations. Established in 1942. Number of employees: 8. Affiliate of Coro Foundation National Organization, San Francisco, California. Number of internship applications received each year: 100.
Internships Available ▶ *12 Coro Fellows in Public Affairs:* responsibilities include working a minimum of 1600 hours over 9.5 months in 6 field assignments in public affairs (government, business, labor unions, nonprofit, media, and political campaigns); dozens of group interviews, individual and group consulting projects, 2-3 three-day retreats, and bi-weekly seminars. Candidates should have ability to work independently, analytical skills, computer skills, editing skills, office skills, oral communication skills, organizational skills, personal interest in the field, research skills, self-motivation, strong interpersonal skills, strong leadership ability, writing skills. Duration is September-June. Position available as unpaid or paid. Open to college seniors, recent college graduates, graduate students, law students, career changers, individuals reentering the workforce. International applications accepted.
Benefits Formal training, health insurance, names of contacts, on-the-job training, opportunity to attend seminars/workshops, possible full-time employment, tuition assistance, willing to act as a professional reference, willing to complete paperwork for educational credit, willing to provide letters of recommendation, need-based financial aid including loan deferments, scholarships, stipends, subsidized housing; graduate credit.
Contact Write, call, fax, e-mail, or through World Wide Web site Joy Sinderbrand, Director of Recruitment/Program Manager, 42 Broadway, 18th Floor, New York, New York 10004. Phone: 212-248-2935 Ext. 230. Fax: 212-248-2970. E-mail: jsinderbrand@coro.org. In-person interview required. Applicants must submit a formal organization application, resume, academic transcripts, three writing samples, three letters of recommendation, participation (for finalists) in a series of group "exercises" and interviews in late March/early April. Application deadline: early February. Fees: $50. World Wide Web: http://www.coro.org.

CORO NORTHERN CALIFORNIA
220 Sansome Street, 4th Floor
San Francisco, California 94104

General Information Organization that conducts research, education, and training in public affairs; participants' learning comes from their experiences in field assignments, interviews, and projects with diverse organizations. Established in 1942. Number of employees: 7. Number of internship applications received each year: 100.
Internships Available ▶ *12 Coro Fellows in Public Affairs:* responsibilities include working a minimum of 1600 hours over 9.5 months in 6 field assignments of public affairs (government, business, labor unions, nonprofit, media, and political campaigns); dozens

of group interviews, 2 projects, 2-3 three-day retreats, bi-weekly seminars, and Focus weeks. Candidates should have ability to work independently, analytical skills, computer skills, editing skills, office skills, oral communication skills, organizational skills, personal interest in the field, research skills, self-motivation, strong interpersonal skills, strong leadership ability, writing skills. Duration is September to June. Up to $15,000 stipend for duration of internship, need-based. Open to college seniors, recent college graduates, graduate students, law students, career changers, individuals reentering the workforce.
Benefits Formal training, names of contacts, on-the-job training, opportunity to attend seminars/workshops, possible full-time employment, willing to act as a professional reference, willing to complete paperwork for educational credit, willing to provide letters of recommendation.
Contact Write, call, fax, e-mail, or through World Wide Web site Scott Peterson, Program Director. Phone: 415-986-0521. Fax: 415-986-5522. E-mail: coronocal@coro.org. Applicants must submit a formal organization application, academic transcripts, three writing samples, three letters of recommendation, participation (for finalists) in a series of group "exercises" and interviews in late March/early April. Application deadline: first week of February. Fees: $50. World Wide Web: http://www.coro.org.

CORO SOUTHERN CALIFORNIA
811 Wilshire Boulevard, Suite 1025
Los Angeles, California 90017-2624

General Information Organization that conducts research, education, and training in public affairs; participants' learning comes from their experiences in field assignments, interviews, and projects with diverse organizations. Established in 1942. Number of employees: 12. Number of internship applications received each year: 100.
Internships Available ▶ *12 Coro Program in Public Affairs fellows:* responsibilities include working a minimum of 1600 hours over 9½ months in 6 field assignments of public affairs (government, business, labor unions, non-profit, media, and political campaigns); dozens of group interviews, 2 projects, 2-3 three-day retreats, and bi-weekly seminars. Candidates should have ability to work independently, analytical skills, computer skills, editing skills, office skills, oral communication skills, organizational skills, personal interest in the field, research skills, self-motivation, strong interpersonal skills, strong leadership ability, writing skills. Duration is September-June. Paid. Open to college seniors, recent college graduates, graduate students, law students, career changers, individuals reentering the workforce. International applications accepted.
Benefits Formal training, names of contacts, on-the-job training, opportunity to attend seminars/workshops, possible full-time employment, willing to act as a professional reference, willing to complete paperwork for educational credit, willing to provide letters of recommendation, monthly stipends available based on financial need (ranging from $800–$1200).
Contact Write, call, fax, e-mail, or through World Wide Web site Malcolm Amado Uno, Program Manager, 811 Wilshire Boulevard, Suite 1025, Los Angeles, California 90017-2624. Phone: 213-623-1234 Ext. 28. Fax: 213-680-0079. E-mail: muno@coro.org. In-person interview required. Applicants must submit a formal organization application, resume, academic transcripts, three writing samples, personal reference, three letters of recommendation, all finalists must participate in a selection event in late March/early April. Application deadline: February 1. Fees: $50. World Wide Web: http://www.coro.org.

CUBAN STUDIES INSTITUTE
Tulane University, Caroline Richardson Building
New Orleans, Louisiana 70118-5698

General Information Organization that promotes academic and cultural collaboration and exchanges with Cuban institutions and scholars. Established in 1995. Number of employees: 3. Unit of Roger Thayer Stone Center for Latin American Studies. Number of internship applications received each year: 4.
Internships Available ▶ *6 development interns:* responsibilities include working side by side with community members on grass-roots development projects. Candidates should have ability to work independently, self-motivation, strong interpersonal skills, basic Spanish highly recommended. Duration is 3 weeks to 1 semester. Unpaid. Open to college freshmen, college sophomores, college juniors, college seniors, recent college graduates, graduate students, law students, career changers, individuals reentering the workforce. International applications accepted.
Benefits Health insurance, housing at a cost, meals at a cost, names of contacts, on-the-job training, opportunity to attend seminars/workshops, willing to act as a professional reference, willing to complete paperwork for educational credit, willing to provide letters of recommendation.
International Internships Available in Cuba; Ecuador.
Contact Write, call, fax, e-mail, or through World Wide Web site Prof. Deborah Ramil, Program Coordinator, Caroline Richardson Building, Tulane University, New Orleans 70118. Phone: 504-862-8629. Fax: 504-862-8678. E-mail: cuba@tulane.edu. In-person interview recommended (telephone interview accepted). Applicants must submit a formal organization application, letter of interest, two letters of recommendation, medical clearance and housing forms; $500 deposit. Application deadline: May 15 for summer interns; continuous for all other positions. World Wide Web: http://www.cuba.tulane.edu.

CULTURE LINK
8201 Peters Road, Suite 1000
Plantation, Florida 33324

General Information Study abroad and exchange programs, international education, and teacher training company. Established in 1996. Number of employees: 4. Number of internship applications received each year: 100.
Internships Available ▶ *2–4 communications (journalism) interns:* responsibilities include assisting regular staff with ongoing duties and special projects. Candidates should have ability to work with others, computer skills, office skills, oral communication skills, organizational skills, personal interest in the field, self-motivation, writing skills, fluency in Spanish. Duration is 8–14 weeks. Unpaid. Open to high school seniors, recent high school graduates, college freshmen, college sophomores, college juniors, college seniors, recent college graduates, graduate students, career changers, individuals reentering the workforce. ▶ *4–6 health care and medical field interns:* responsibilities include hands-on work allowing intern to bring together theoretical knowledge, functional competencies, and skills developed in school. Candidates should have ability to work independently, ability to work with others, college courses in field, computer skills, knowledge of field, organizational skills, personal interest in the field, self-motivation, strong leadership ability, fluency in Spanish. Duration is 8–14 weeks. Unpaid. Open to college sophomores, college juniors, college seniors, recent college graduates, graduate students. ▶ *6–10 international business interns:* responsibilities include work in field projects as assigned. Candidates should have ability to work independently, college courses in field, computer skills, oral communication skills, organizational skills, personal interest in the field, plan to pursue career in field, self-motivation, strong interpersonal skills, strong leadership ability, written communication skills, fluency in Spanish. Duration is 8–14 weeks. Unpaid. Open to high school seniors, recent high school graduates, college freshmen, college sophomores, college juniors, college seniors, recent college graduates, graduate students, career changers, individuals reentering the workforce. ▶ *4–6 marketing interns:* responsibilities include assignments as needed; providing office support according to intern's skills and interests. Candidates should have ability to work independently, ability to work with others, college courses in field, computer skills, knowledge of field, oral communication skills, organizational skills, strong leadership ability, written communication skills. Duration is 8–14 weeks. Unpaid. Open to high school students, recent high school graduates, college freshmen, college sophomores, college juniors, college seniors, recent college graduates, graduate students, career changers, individuals reentering the workforce. International applications accepted.

Culture Link (continued)

Benefits Housing at a cost, meals at a cost, names of contacts, on-the-job training, willing to act as a professional reference, willing to complete paperwork for educational credit, willing to provide letters of recommendation.

International Internships Available in Chile; Venezuela.

Contact Call, e-mail, or through World Wide Web site Beatriz Guzman, President. Phone: 954-432-2355. Fax: 954-916-2601. E-mail: culture@culturelinkusa.org. Applicants must submit a formal organization application, letter of interest, resume, academic transcripts, personal reference, letter of recommendation, (2) photos. Applications are accepted continuously. Fees: $50. World Wide Web: http://www.culturelinkusa.org.

THE CUSHMAN SCHOOL
592 North East 60th Street
Miami, Florida 33137

General Information Non-denominational, non-discriminatory independent school designed for preschool through 8th grade boys and girls of average and above average development and learning ability. Established in 1924. Number of employees: 54. Number of internship applications received each year: 15.

Internships Available ▶ *2–4 educational interns:* responsibilities include helping with small reading groups, assisting in the writing process, and generating thematic projects. Candidates should have knowledge of field, oral communication skills, personal interest in the field, strong interpersonal skills. Duration is 1 semester. Paid. Open to recent college graduates, graduate students. International applications accepted.

Benefits Opportunity to attend seminars/workshops, possible full-time employment, willing to complete paperwork for educational credit, opportunity to teach, stipend of $2000 for U.S. residents, $3000 for foreign residents.

Contact Write, fax, or e-mail Ann Gorman, Internship Coordinator. Fax: 305-757-1632. E-mail: 1234567111@msn.com. No phone calls. Applicants must submit a letter of interest, resume, photo of applicant. Application deadline: May 1 for spring positions for following year, December 5 for fall positions for following year. World Wide Web: http://www.cushmanschool.org.

DAVIS & COMPANY, INC.
11 Harristown Road
Glen Rock, New Jersey 07452

General Information Firm that helps companies improve performance by reaching, engaging, and motivating employees; services include communication consulting, implementation, training/learning, evaluation, and measurement; has extensive experience building awareness about key business issues, including organizational change, business strategy, vision, mission, process improvement, and reward and recognition. Established in 1984. Number of employees: 17. Number of internship applications received each year: 100.

Internships Available ▶ *2 interns:* responsibilities include writing short articles for newsletters, research, organizing media lists, and attending client meetings. It could also entail designing graphics and Web site support. Candidates should have declared college major in field, oral communication skills, plan to pursue career in field, strong interpersonal skills, written communication skills, enthusiasm, good attitude. Duration is 2–3 months. $7–$10 per hour. Open to college juniors, college seniors, recent college graduates, graduate students.

Benefits Job counseling, names of contacts, on-the-job training, opportunity to attend seminars/workshops, possible full-time employment, travel reimbursement, willing to complete paperwork for educational credit, willing to provide letters of recommendation.

Contact Write, fax, or e-mail Ms. Ellen Van Den Heuvel, Director of Human Resources and Administration. Fax: 201-445-5122. E-mail: ellen.vandenheuvel@davisandco.com. No phone calls. In-person interview required. Applicants must submit a letter of interest, resume. Applications are accepted continuously. World Wide Web: http://www.davisandco.com.

DUBLIN INTERNSHIPS
8 Orlagh Lawn, Scholarstown Road
Dublin 16 Ireland

General Information Organization that provides professional-level internships in Dublin, Ireland across the spectrum of majors and career options . Established in 1989. Number of employees: 4. Number of internship applications received each year: 120.

Internships Available ▶ *Interns:* responsibilities include professional level work under supervision in area of intern's interest. Candidates should have ability to work with others, college courses in field, computer skills, knowledge of field, flexibility. Duration is 10 weeks in summer; 15 weeks in fall and spring. Unpaid. Open to college juniors, college seniors, recent college graduates, graduate students, law students, career changers. International applications accepted.

Benefits Housing at a cost, meals at a cost, on-the-job training, opportunity to attend seminars/workshops, tuition assistance, willing to act as a professional reference, willing to complete paperwork for educational credit, willing to provide letters of recommendation, orientation, information, and advice about cultural and historical visits.

International Internships Available.

Contact Write, call, fax, e-mail, or through World Wide Web site Mary H. Rieke, Director. E-mail: mhrieke@eircom.net. Applicants must submit a formal organization application, letter of interest, resume, academic transcripts, two letters of recommendation, photograph. Application deadline: March 1 for summer, May 1 for fall, October 1 for spring. World Wide Web: http://homepage.eircom.net/~dublinternships.

EDUCATE THE CHILDREN
PO Box 414
Ithaca, New York 14851

General Information International development organization. Established in 1991. Number of employees: 3. Number of internship applications received each year: 22.

Internships Available ▶ *6 English teaching interns (Nepal):* responsibilities include teaching and tutoring Nepali children at an English-speaking boarding or government school in Kathmandu. Candidates should have experience in the field, strong interpersonal skills, cross-cultural skills, teaching/tutoring skills. Duration is 3 months. Unpaid. Open to individuals at least 20 years of age. ▶ *1 program assistant (Ithaca):* responsibilities include research, secretarial tasks, newsletter production, and design and execution of promotional campaigns. Candidates should have ability to work independently, computer skills, office skills, oral communication skills, research skills, written communication skills. Duration is flexible. Unpaid. Open to college freshmen, college sophomores, college juniors, college seniors, recent college graduates, graduate students, career changers. International applications accepted.

Benefits On-the-job training, opportunity to attend seminars/workshops, willing to act as a professional reference, willing to complete paperwork for educational credit, willing to provide letters of recommendation, housing and/or meals for some placements in Nepal.

International Internships Available in Kathmandu, Nepal.

Contact Write or e-mail Susanna Pearce, Co-Director. E-mail: info@etc-nepal.org. In-person interview recommended (telephone interview accepted). Applicants must submit a formal organization application, resume, two personal references, $500 application fee for Nepal position; contact organization to inquire about Nepal placement; due to safety concerns, placement in Nepal may not be available. Applications are accepted continuously. World Wide Web: http://www.etc-nepal.org.

EDUCATIONAL TESTING SERVICE
Rosedale Road
Princeton, New Jersey 08541

General Information Private not-for-profit educational measurement institution and leader in educational research, that develops and administers achievement and admission tests. Established in 1948. Number of employees: 2,000. Number of internship applications received each year: 80.

Internships Available ▶ *3 ETS Postdoctoral Fellowship Award Program interns:* responsibilities include conducting intern's own original research at ETS in fields relevant to education, psychology, psychometrics, statistics, computer science, linguistics, testing, minority issues, or policy research. Candidates should have analytical skills, computer skills, knowledge of field, oral communication skills, organizational skills, research skills, written communication skills, academic scholarship with relevance to ETS research mission. Duration is 1 year. $38,000 per internship plus relocation expense reimbursement. Open to doctoral-level scholars. ▶ *1 Sylvia Taylor Johnson Minority Fellowship in Educational Measurement:* responsibilities include carrying out independent research, outlined in 5-page research proposal, under the mentorship of ETS senior scientist. Candidates should have ability to work independently, analytical skills, experience in the field, oral communication skills, research skills, written communication skills. Duration is 1 year. Paid. Open to minority scholars who hold a PhD or EdD; must be U.S. citizen. ▶ *8–12 summer program in research (graduate students):* responsibilities include independent research with access to a mentor in fields relevant to education, psychology, psychometrics, statistics, computer science, linguistics, testing, minority issues, or policy research; participation in seminars and workshops. Candidates should have ability to work with others, computer skills, knowledge of field, oral communication skills, research skills, written communication skills, scholarship with relevance to ETS mission. Duration is 8 weeks. $4000 per duration of internship. Open to doctoral students who have completed one year of full-time graduate study. International applications accepted.
Benefits Housing at a cost, meals at a cost, names of contacts, on-the-job training, opportunity to attend seminars/workshops, possible full-time employment, willing to act as a professional reference, willing to complete paperwork for educational credit, willing to provide letters of recommendation, reimbursement of roundtrip travel expenses (minimal compensation if accompanied by spouse or child).
Contact Write, call, fax, e-mail, or through World Wide Web site Ms. Linda J. DeLauro, Fellowship Program Administrator, Rosedale Road, Mail Stop 09R, Princeton, New Jersey 08541. Phone: 609-734-1806. Fax: 609-734-1755. E-mail: ldelauro@ets.org. Telephone interview required. Applicants must submit a formal organization application, letter of interest, resume, academic transcripts, writing sample, three letters of recommendation, additional requirements vary by program (contact ETS for specifics), 2-3 personal references. Application deadline: February 15 for summer internship and postdoctoral positions. World Wide Web: http://www.ets.org.

EDUCATION AUSTRALIA
PO Box 2233
Amherst, Massachusetts 01004

General Information Educational consultant who advises and recruits students who wish to study or intern in Australia. Established in 1988. Number of employees: 2. Unit of Global Education Designs, Pty. Ltd., Brisbane, Australia. Number of internship applications received each year: 20.
Internships Available ▶ *Interns:* responsibilities include working in areas of interest, including management, marketing, finance and accounting, media, public relations, law, politics, the arts, social work, or biology. Candidates should have ability to work independently, oral communication skills, personal interest in the field, self-motivation, strong interpersonal skills. Duration is 6 weeks to 1 year. Unpaid. Open to high school seniors, recent high school graduates, college freshmen, college sophomores, college juniors, college seniors, recent college graduates, graduate students, law students. International applications accepted.
Benefits On-the-job training, interns placed in homestays which include meals.
International Internships Available in Australia.
Contact Write, call, fax, e-mail, or through World Wide Web site Dr. Maurice A. Howe, Executive Director. Phone: 800-344-6741. Fax: 413-549-0741. E-mail: edaust@rcn.com. Applicants must submit a formal organization application, resume, academic transcripts,

$500 deposit (applied to total cost). Application deadline: 4 months prior to start of internship, March 1 for fall. World Wide Web: http://users.rcn.com/edaust.

EXPERIENCE AMERICA
860 B McAllister Street
San Francisco, California 94102

General Information Internship placement organization for foreign students. Established in 1996. Number of employees: 2. Number of internship applications received each year: 100.
Internships Available ▶ *1–100 Experience America interns:* responsibilities include placements in all professional industries and career fields, based on academic background and work experience. Candidates should have ability to work independently, ability to work with others, analytical skills, computer skills, office skills, oral communication skills, organizational skills, research skills, self-motivation. Duration is 2–12 months. Unpaid. ▶ *10–20 financial services interns:* responsibilities include assisting financial consultants in portfolio asset management, stock market research, marketing, and educational seminars. Candidates should have ability to work independently, ability to work with others, college courses in field, computer skills, office skills, oral communication skills, organizational skills, personal interest in the field, plan to pursue career in field, research skills, self-motivation, proficiency in English. Duration is 2–6 months. Unpaid. Open to foreign nationals age 18–30. International applications accepted.
Benefits Health insurance, housing at a cost, meals at a cost, on-the-job training, opportunity to attend seminars/workshops, willing to act as a professional reference, willing to complete paperwork for educational credit, willing to provide letters of recommendation.
International Internships Available in Australia; Chile; China; France; Germany; Hungary; Ireland; Italy; Thailand; United Kingdom.
Contact Write, call, fax, e-mail, or through World Wide Web site Rebecca Megerssa, Executive Director. Phone: 415-921-3654. Fax: 415-921-3654. E-mail: interns@experienceamerica.com. In-person interview recommended (telephone interview accepted). Applicants must submit a formal organization application, letter of interest, resume, personal reference, letter of recommendation. Applications are accepted continuously. Fees: $250. World Wide Web: http://www.experienceamerica.com.

EXPLORATIONS IN TRAVEL, INC.
2458 River Road
Guilford, Vermont 05301

General Information Organization that provides travel opportunities and volunteer placements for students and adults. Established in 1990. Number of employees: 3. Number of internship applications received each year: 50.
Internships Available ▶ *1–5 agricultural/conservation volunteers (New Zealand):* responsibilities include working on small farms, teaching in schools, working with environmental and conservation organizations. Candidates should have ability to work independently, oral communication skills, self-motivation, strong interpersonal skills. Duration is flexible. Unpaid. Open to high school seniors, recent high school graduates, college freshmen, college sophomores, college juniors, college seniors, recent college graduates, graduate students, career changers, individuals reentering the workforce. ▶ *1–5 agroforestry and rainforest reserve volunteers (Costa Rica):* responsibilities include working with a small rainforest reserve in Costa Rica, including trail maintenance, tree planting, connection with local school and students. Candidates should have ability to work independently, ability to work with others, self-motivation, Spanish language skills. Duration is flexible. Unpaid. Open to recent high school graduates, college freshmen, college sophomores, college juniors, college seniors, recent college graduates, graduate students, career changers, individuals reentering the workforce, retired persons. ▶ *1–5 animal shelter volunteers (Puerto Rico):* responsibilities include working with an animal shelter/clinic in Puerto Rico caring for dogs, cats, and horses, and assisting veterinarian. Candidates should have ability to work independently, ability to work with others, personal interest in the field, self-motivation, Spanish language skills useful. Dura-

Explorations in Travel, Inc. (continued)

tion is flexible. Unpaid. Open to recent high school graduates, college freshmen, college sophomores, college juniors, college seniors, recent college graduates, graduate students, career changers, individuals reentering the workforce, retired persons. ▶ *1–5 conservation interns (Guatemala):* responsibilities include instruction in ecology, agriculture, animal husbandry, environmental education and history; volunteers assist with reforestation projects, trail maintenance, organic gardening, farm animals, and medicinal plants. Candidates should have ability to work independently, oral communication skills, self-motivation, strong interpersonal skills, strong leadership ability, written communication skills. Duration is flexible. Unpaid. Open to recent high school graduates, college freshmen, college sophomores, college juniors, college seniors, recent college graduates, graduate students, career changers, individuals reentering the workforce, retired persons. ▶ *1–5 environmental education/conservation volunteers (Mexico):* responsibilities include teaching environmental education to student and community members in Mexico, assisting with field research on environmental changes to conservation areas. Candidates should have ability to work independently, ability to work with others, self-motivation, Spanish language skills useful. Duration is flexible. Unpaid. Open to recent high school graduates, college freshmen, college sophomores, college juniors, college seniors, recent college graduates, graduate students, career changers, individuals reentering the workforce, retired persons. ▶ *1–5 environmental/ conservation project volunteers (Ecuador):* responsibilities include working on environmental and conservation projects. Candidates should have ability to work independently, ability to work with others, self-motivation, Spanish language skills. Duration is flexible. Unpaid. Open to recent high school graduates, college freshmen, college sophomores, college juniors, college seniors, recent college graduates, graduate students, career changers, individuals reentering the workforce, retired persons. ▶ *1 individual and group projects intern (Nepal):* responsibilities include conservation and community group projects available in 2-week blocks; individual positions in schools and orphanages can also be arranged. Candidates should have ability to work independently, oral communication skills, self-motivation, strong interpersonal skills. Duration is 2 weeks to one year. Unpaid. Open to recent high school graduates, college freshmen, college sophomores, college juniors, college seniors, recent college graduates, graduate students, career changers, individuals reentering the workforce, retired persons. ▶ *1–5 rainforest conservation volunteers (Australia):* responsibilities include working in a tropical research center which focuses on the study, care, and rehabilitation of flying foxes in Australia; rainforest protection activism opportunity also available. Candidates should have ability to work independently, oral communication skills, personal interest in the field, self-motivation, strong interpersonal skills. Duration is flexible. Unpaid. Open to college freshmen, college sophomores, college juniors, college seniors, recent college graduates, graduate students, career changers, individuals reentering the workforce, retired persons. ▶ *1–5 rainforest reserve volunteers (Puerto Rico):* responsibilities include working with a small rainforest reserve in Puerto Rico on trail maintenance, reforestation projects, receiving visiting eco-tourist groups. Candidates should have ability to work independently, self-motivation, strong interpersonal skills. Duration is flexible. Unpaid. Open to high school seniors, recent high school graduates, college freshmen, college sophomores, college juniors, college seniors, recent college graduates, graduate students, career changers, individuals reentering the workforce, retired persons. ▶ *1–5 rainforest/conservation volunteers (Costa Rica):* responsibilities include working on a small rainforest reserve, including trail maintenance, tree planting, and connection with local school and students. Candidates should have ability to work independently, ability to work with others, personal interest in the field, self-motivation, Spanish language skills. Duration is flexible. Unpaid. Open to high school seniors, recent high school graduates, college freshmen, college sophomores, college juniors, college seniors, recent college graduates, graduate students, career changers, individuals reentering the workforce, retired persons. ▶ *1–5 sea turtle project volunteers (Costa Rica and Mexico):* responsibilities include working with an environmental organization that focuses on protecting beaches and monitoring sea turtles, night patrols

of beaches, and documenting turtle activity. Candidates should have ability to work independently, ability to work with others, personal interest in the field, self-motivation, Spanish language skills useful. Duration is flexible (April to August). Unpaid. Open to recent high school graduates, college freshmen, college sophomores, college juniors, college seniors, recent college graduates, graduate students, career changers, individuals reentering the workforce, retired persons. ▶ *1–5 teaching assistant volunteers (Costa Rica):* responsibilities include working with rural elementary and secondary schools in Costa Rica, including teaching English and other subjects and organizing recreational activities. Candidates should have ability to work independently, oral communication skills, self-motivation, strong interpersonal skills, strong leadership ability, written communication skills, Spanish language skills. Duration is flexible. Unpaid. Open to recent high school graduates, college freshmen, college sophomores, college juniors, college seniors, recent college graduates, graduate students, career changers, individuals reentering the workforce, retired persons. ▶ *1–5 teaching assistant volunteers (Ecuador):* responsibilities include working with rural elementary and secondary schools in Ecuador, including teaching English and other subjects and organizing recreational activities. Candidates should have ability to work independently, oral communication skills, self-motivation, strong interpersonal skills, strong leadership ability, written communication skills, Spanish language skills. Duration is flexible. Unpaid. Open to recent high school graduates, college freshmen, college sophomores, college juniors, college seniors, recent college graduates, graduate students, career changers, individuals reentering the workforce, retired persons. ▶ *1–5 teaching assistant volunteers (Mexico):* responsibilities include working with secondary schools in the Yucatan including teaching English and other subjects and organizing recreational activities. Candidates should have ability to work independently, oral communication skills, self-motivation, strong interpersonal skills, strong leadership ability, written communication skills, Spanish language skills. Duration is flexible. Unpaid. Open to recent high school graduates, college freshmen, college sophomores, college juniors, college seniors, recent college graduates, graduate students, career changers, individuals reentering the workforce, retired persons. ▶ *1–5 wildlife rescue volunteers (Costa Rica and Belize):* responsibilities include working with an environmental education center and wildlife rehabilitation. Candidates should have ability to work independently, ability to work with others, self-motivation, Spanish language skills useful (for Costa Rica). Duration is flexible (one month minimum). Unpaid. Open to recent high school graduates, college freshmen, college sophomores, college juniors, college seniors, recent college graduates, graduate students, career changers, individuals reentering the workforce, retired persons. International applications accepted.
Benefits Housing at a cost, meals at a cost, names of contacts, willing to act as a professional reference, willing to complete paperwork for educational credit, willing to provide letters of recommendation, opportunity for language study.
International Internships Available in Belize; Costa Rica; Ecuador; Guatemala; Mexico; Nepal; New Zealand; Puerto Rico.
Contact Write, call, fax, e-mail, or through World Wide Web site John Lee, Volunteer Coordinator. Phone: 802-257-0152. Fax: 802-257-2784. E-mail: explore@volunteertravel.com. Telephone interview required. Applicants must submit a formal organization application, letter of interest, resume, two letters of recommendation, placement fee of $775–$975 upon acceptance. Applications are accepted continuously. Fees: $35. World Wide Web: http://www.volunteertravel.com.

FINANCIAL MARKETS CENTER
PO Box 334
Philomont, Virginia 20131

General Information Nonprofit research and education institute. Established in 1997. Number of employees: 5. Number of internship applications received each year: 75.
Internships Available ▶ *1–2 interns:* responsibilities include data collection and analysis; literature reviews; documents and survey research; preparing reports and summaries; Web site maintenance and promotion; and general office support. Candidates should

have ability to work independently, analytical skills, computer skills, oral communication skills, research skills, writing skills. Duration is 1–3 semesters. $8–$17 per hour. Open to college freshmen, college sophomores, college juniors, college seniors, recent college graduates, graduate students, law students. International applications accepted.

Benefits On-the-job training, opportunity to attend seminars/workshops, possible full-time employment, travel reimbursement, willing to act as a professional reference, willing to provide letters of recommendation, stipend.

Contact Write, e-mail, or through World Wide Web site Tom Schlesinger, Executive Director. Fax: 540-338-7757. E-mail: tom@fmcenter.org. No phone calls. In-person interview recommended (telephone interview accepted). Applicants must submit a letter of interest, resume, writing sample, 3 personal references (for top applicants). Application deadline: March 15 for summer, July 30 for fall, November 30 for spring. World Wide Web: http://www.fmcenter.org.

FLORIDA INTERNATIONAL UNIVERSITY
University Park
Miami, Florida 33199

General Information Large multicampus, multicultural university in Miami-Dade County, Florida. Established in 1965. Number of employees: 4,000. Number of internship applications received each year: 10.

Internships Available ▶ *1–2 health promotion interns:* responsibilities include health promotion program planning, implementation and evaluation; development and dissemination of health communication materials; providing one-on-one health education consultation (e.g. fitness assessments, smoking cessation); and teaching workshops on a variety of subjects for a diverse university population. Candidates should have ability to work independently, college courses in field, computer skills, oral communication skills, strong interpersonal skills. Duration is preferably January to April or August to December. Unpaid. Open to graduate students from Master of Public Health program. ▶ *1–2 health promotion/health education interns:* responsibilities include health promotion planning, implementation and evaluation; development and dissemination of health communication materials; providing one-on-one health consultations, teaching workshops on a variety of topics. Candidates should have ability to work independently, ability to work with others, computer skills, declared college major in field, knowledge of field, oral communication skills, self-motivation, ability to work with diverse population. Duration is preferably January to April, May to August, or August to December. Unpaid. Open to college seniors, recent college graduates. ▶ *1–2 wellness interns:* responsibilities include coordinating special health promotion events; creating and disseminating health promotion materials; conducting one-on-one consultations; and teaching workshops on a variety of health related topics. Duration is flexible (ideally January-April, April-August, or August to December). Unpaid. Open to college freshmen, college sophomores, college juniors, college seniors, recent college graduates, graduate students. International applications accepted.

Benefits Formal training, job counseling, names of contacts, on-the-job training, opportunity to attend seminars/workshops, possible full-time employment, willing to act as a professional reference, willing to complete paperwork for educational credit, willing to provide letters of recommendation.

Contact Write, call, fax, e-mail, or through World Wide Web site Mariela Gabaroni, Wellness Coordinator, University Park, HWC 215, Miami, Florida 33199. Phone: 305-348-4020. Fax: 305-348-6655. E-mail: xgabaron@fiu.edu. Telephone interview required. Applicants must submit a letter of interest, resume. Applications are accepted continuously. World Wide Web: http://http://www.fiu.edu/.

FOOD SERVICE MANAGEMENT INTERNSHIP COMMITTEE
Lawyers Club Dining Service, 551 South State Street
Ann Arbor, Michigan 48109-1208

General Information Educational program whose purpose is to introduce aspiring professionals to the food service industry and to provide on-the-job experience that will better qualify them to assume responsibilities related to college and university food service. Established in 1961. Unit of Association of College and University Housing Officers–International/National Association of College and University Food Services. Number of internship applications received each year: 120.

Internships Available ▶ *55–65 food service management interns:* responsibilities include working with food service employees to develop understanding of personnel, production, service, sanitation, and safety issues; working with professional staff to learn policies and issues affecting decisions in food service, gaining experience in supervision, and planning and coordinating food service functions. Candidates should have ability to work with others, college courses in field, knowledge of field, oral communication skills, organizational skills, personal interest in the field. Duration is 8 weeks. Stipend of $1600. Open to college juniors, college seniors, recent college graduates, graduate students. International applications accepted.

Benefits Free housing, free meals, job counseling, names of contacts, on-the-job training, opportunity to attend seminars/workshops, possible full-time employment, willing to act as a professional reference, willing to complete paperwork for educational credit, willing to provide letters of recommendation.

Contact Write, call, fax, e-mail, or through World Wide Web site Holly Downey, Assistant Manager, 551 South State Street, Ann Arbor, Michigan 48109-1208. Phone: 734-763-5161. Fax: 734-763-6732. E-mail: hkdowney@umich.edu. Telephone interview required. Applicants must submit a formal organization application, letter of interest, resume, academic transcripts, letter of recommendation. Application deadline: January 28 for summer. World Wide Web: http://www.nacufs.org.

THE FULBRIGHT COMMISSION
62 Doughty Street
London WC1N 2JS United Kingdom

General Information Educational exchange between the U.S. and the U.K. Established in 1948. Number of employees: 7. Number of internship applications received each year: 15.

Internships Available ▶ *1–2 information officers:* responsibilities include working in the U.S. Educational Advisory Service providing information and advice about studying in the U.S., project work on events, researching publications and handouts, and some general administrative work. Candidates should have office skills, personal interest in the field, research skills, self-motivation, strong interpersonal skills, written communication skills. Duration is 6 months. $8 per hour. ▶ *4–8 student information officers:* responsibilities include answering inquiries about studying in the U.S., project work on events, information sheets, publications, newsletters, and some general administrative work. Candidates should have ability to work independently, ability to work with others, office skills, oral communication skills, organizational skills, written communication skills. Duration is 3 months. Unpaid. Open to college juniors, college seniors, recent college graduates, graduate students. International applications accepted.

Benefits On-the-job training, willing to act as a professional reference, willing to complete paperwork for educational credit, willing to provide letters of recommendation, possible reimbursement of fee for work visa, free lunch, reimbursement for travel in London.

International Internships Available.

Contact Write, call, fax, or e-mail Josephine Metcalf, Director, U.S. Educational Advisory Service. Phone: 44-20-7404-6994. Fax: 44-20-7404-6874. E-mail: jmetcalf@fulbright.co.uk. In-person interview recommended (telephone interview accepted). Applicants must submit a letter of interest, resume, names and contact details of two referees. Applications are accepted continuously. World Wide Web: http://www.fulbright.co.uk.

THE FUND FOR AMERICAN STUDIES
1706 New Hampshire Avenue, NW
Washington, District of Columbia 20009

General Information Internship coordinating foundation. Number of employees: 20. Number of internship applications received each year: 1,500.

The Fund for American Studies (continued)
Internships Available ▶ *70–85 Institute on Political Journalism interns:* responsibilities include working with media organization and taking classes on ethics and journalism at Georgetown University. Candidates should have computer skills, oral communication skills, plan to pursue career in field, self-motivation, writing skills. Duration is 7 weeks (June-July). Unpaid. Open to college freshmen, college sophomores, college juniors, college seniors, sophomores and juniors preferred. ▶ *40–50 The Bryce Harlow Institute on Business and Government Affairs interns:* responsibilities include working with D.C. firm and taking classes in economics and business. Candidates should have computer skills, office skills, oral communication skills, plan to pursue career in field, self-motivation, written communication skills. Duration is 7 weeks (June-July). Unpaid. Open to college freshmen, college sophomores, college juniors, college seniors, graduate students, law students, sophomores and juniors preferred. ▶ *100–115 The Institute on Comparative Political and Economic Systems interns:* responsibilities include taking classes on corporate politics and economics at Georgetown University and working with political international organization in DC. Candidates should have oral communication skills, plan to pursue career in field, self-motivation, written communication skills. Duration is 7 weeks (June-July). Unpaid. Open to college freshmen, college sophomores, college juniors, college seniors, graduate students, law students, sophomores and juniors preferred. International applications accepted.
Benefits Housing at a cost, names of contacts, on-the-job training, opportunity to attend seminars/workshops, willing to act as a professional reference, willing to provide letters of recommendation, college credit through Georgetown University, tuition assistance (scholarship).
International Internships Available in Prague, Czech Republic; Athens, Greece.
Contact Call, e-mail, or through World Wide Web site Tim Sprinkle, Admissions. Phone: 202-986-0384. Fax: 202-318-0441. E-mail: admissions@tfas.org. Applicants must submit a formal organization application, resume, academic transcripts, two letters of recommendation, essay (writing sample for journalism program). Application deadline: January 15 for summer (preferred); March 15 for final deadline. Fees: $30. World Wide Web: http://www.dcinternships.org.

GIRLS INCORPORATED OF HUNTSVILLE
PO Box 3066
Huntsville, Alabama 35804

General Information Youth agency providing informal education programs, services, and activities to girls ages 5–19. Established in 1975. Number of employees: 17. Unit of Girls Incorporated, New York, New York.
Internships Available ▶ *1–3 Operation Smart volunteers:* responsibilities include facilitating hands-on science and math activities relevant to technology with girls. Candidates should have analytical skills, knowledge of field, personal interest in the field, self-motivation, strong interpersonal skills, experience desirable. Duration is 8 weeks. Unpaid. Open to recent high school graduates, college freshmen, college sophomores, college juniors, college seniors, recent college graduates, graduate students, career changers, high school juniors and seniors. International applications accepted.
Benefits Formal training, names of contacts, on-the-job training, opportunity to attend seminars/workshops, possible full-time employment, willing to complete paperwork for educational credit, willing to provide letters of recommendation.
Contact Write, call, or e-mail Mildred Henderson, Coordinator of Operation Smart. Phone: 256-851-9911. Fax: 256-851-9930. E-mail: smalone@hiwaay.net. In-person interview required. Applicants must submit a letter of interest, resume, three personal references, letter of recommendation, background check required. Application deadline: June 1 for summer; continuous for other positions.

GLOBAL CAMPUS STUDY ABROAD, UNIVERSITY OF MINNESOTA
230 Heller Hall, 271 19th Avenue South
Minneapolis, Minnesota 55455

General Information Study abroad program designed to give students an opportunity to accent program curriculum by working as an intern in a variety of fields. Established in 1972. Number of employees: 30. Number of internship applications received each year: 100.
Internships Available ▶ *35 London interns:* responsibilities include working in one of a variety of fields. Candidates should have college courses in field, oral communication skills, personal interest in the field. Duration is 4 months. Unpaid. Open to college sophomores, college juniors, college seniors, recent college graduates. ▶ *Montpellier interns:* responsibilities include various activities depending upon internship placement; goal of internship is to introduce students to the organization and French working life and is one course in a full-time study program. Candidates should have ability to work with others, knowledge of field, oral communication skills, personal interest in the field, self-motivation, written communication skills, strong French language skills. Duration is 5–10 months. Unpaid. Open to college freshmen, college sophomores, college juniors, college seniors. ▶ *25 Toledo interns:* responsibilities include working in one of a variety of fields. Candidates should have college courses in field, personal interest in the field, strong Spanish language skills. Duration is 4 months. Unpaid. Open to college sophomores, college juniors, college seniors, recent college graduates. International applications accepted.
Benefits Health insurance, housing at a cost, meals at a cost, names of contacts, on-the-job training, opportunity to attend seminars/workshops, willing to complete paperwork for educational credit, willing to provide letters of recommendation, participants earn 15 University of Minnesota semester credits while on the International Program (3 or 6 of those credits go towards the internship).
International Internships Available in Montpellier, France; Toledo, Spain; London, United Kingdom.
Contact Write, call, fax, e-mail, or through World Wide Web site Internship Coordinator. Phone: 612-626-9000. Fax: 612-626-8009. E-mail: umabroad@umn.edu. In-person interview required. Applicants must submit a formal organization application, letter of interest, resume, academic transcripts, writing sample, 1-2 personal references, 1-2 letters of recommendation. Application deadline: April 15 for fall (England); May 15 fall or academic year (France), July 30 for fall or academic year (Spain), October 15 for spring (England), November 15 for spring (Spain and France); March 1 for summer (Spain)). Fees: $50. World Wide Web: http://www.umabroad.umn.edu/.

GLOBAL CAMPUS STUDY ABROAD, UNIVERSITY OF MINNESOTA, MINNESOTA STUDIES IN INTERNATIONAL DEVELOPMENT (MSID)
230 Heller Hall, 271 19th Avenue South
Minneapolis, Minnesota 55455

General Information Study abroad program for students and professionals built around grassroots development internships in Ecuador, India, Kenya, and Senegal; fields include agriculture, education, environment, health, microbusiness development, social services, and women in development. Established in 1982. Number of employees: 25. Unit of University of Minnesota, Twin Cities Campus, Minneapolis, Minnesota. Number of internship applications received each year: 90.
Internships Available ▶ *70–100 interns:* responsibilities include working in a non-governmental organization at the grassroots level in the area of intern's choice and completing related coursework. Candidates should have ability to work independently, analytical skills, personal interest in the field, self-motivation, strong interpersonal skills, intercultural sensitivity and adaptability. Duration is one semester or academic year. Unpaid. Open to college juniors, college seniors, recent college graduates, graduate students, law students, career changers, individuals reentering the workforce. International applications accepted.

Benefits Health insurance, on-the-job training, opportunity to attend seminars/workshops, willing to complete paperwork for educational credit, willing to provide letters of recommendation, up to 16-20 semester credits for the internship and related coursework; support services overseas.
International Internships Available in Ecuador; India; Kenya; Senegal.
Contact Write, call, fax, e-mail, or through World Wide Web site Internship Coordinator. Phone: 612-626-9000. Fax: 612-626-8009. E-mail: umabroad@tc.umn.edu. Applicants must submit a formal organization application, letter of interest, resume, academic transcripts, 250-word autobiography; 1-2 letters of recommendation. Application deadline: February 15 for priority consideration; March 15 final deadline for fall and academic year placements, June 1 for priority consideration; October 15 final deadline for spring semester placements. Fees: $50. World Wide Web: http://www.umabroad.umn.edu/.

GLOBAL SERVICE CORPS
300 Broadway, Suite 28
San Francisco, California 94133

General Information Nonprofit organization providing international cultural immersion and service learning programs in HIV/AIDS prevention, sustainable agriculture, environmental education, health care, and ESL (English as a second language). Established in 1993. Number of employees: 7. Unit of Earth Island Institute, San Francisco, California. Number of internship applications received each year: 125.
Internships Available ▶ *1–15 Buddhism studies/Thailand project interns:* responsibilities include learning about Buddhism through daily interface and conversation with monks at a local monastery, while helping monks with conversational English. Candidates should have ability to work with others, oral communication skills, personal interest in the field, self-motivation, written communication skills. Duration is 3 weeks to 6 months (year-round). Unpaid. Open to recent high school graduates, college freshmen, college sophomores, college juniors, college seniors, recent college graduates, graduate students, law students, career changers, individuals reentering the workforce, retirees. ▶ *1–15 English instructors (Thailand):* responsibilities include assisting Thai teachers; leading classes in conversation, vocabulary, pronunciation, reading, writing, and games and songs. Candidates should have ability to work independently, ability to work with others, oral communication skills, plan to pursue career in field, self-motivation, written communication skills. Duration is 3 weeks to 6 months (year-round). Unpaid. Open to recent high school graduates, college freshmen, college sophomores, college juniors, college seniors, recent college graduates, graduate students, law students, career changers, individuals reentering the workforce, retirees. ▶ *HIV/AIDS awareness and education interns (Tanzania):* responsibilities include teaching and spreading awareness of HIV/AIDS through talks and specific curricula in schools and at community meetings; reporting on this work and successes/failures. Candidates should have ability to work independently, oral communication skills, personal interest in the field, self-motivation, strong interpersonal skills, written communication skills. Duration is 4 weeks to 6 months (year-round). Unpaid. Open to college sophomores, college juniors, college seniors, recent college graduates, graduate students, law students, career changers, individuals reentering the workforce, individuals over 20 years of age. ▶ *Tanzania program assistants (headquarters office):* responsibilities include recruiting, registering, and corresponding with Tanzania program participants, communicating with Tanzania in-country program director, and preparing packets. Candidates should have computer skills, oral communication skills, organizational skills, personal interest in the field, written communication skills, travel and/or work experience in Tanzania or East Africa. Duration is 3–6 months. $200 per month plus local transportation costs. Open to college freshmen, college sophomores, college juniors, college seniors, recent college graduates, graduate students, law students, career changers, individuals reentering the workforce. ▶ *Web marketing assistants (headquarters office):* responsibilities include Web research, Web page linking, search engine positioning, communicating with colleges and universities, and database

administration. Candidates should have ability to work independently, computer skills, experience in the field, personal interest in the field, research skills, written communication skills. Duration is 3–6 months. $200 per month plus local transportation costs. Open to college freshmen, college sophomores, college juniors, college seniors, recent college graduates, graduate students, law students, career changers, individuals reentering the workforce. ▶ *Environmental educators (Thailand):* responsibilities include teaching environmental education classes in English at local schools. Candidates should have ability to work independently, oral communication skills, personal interest in the field, self-motivation, written communication skills. Duration is 3 weeks to 6 months (year-round). Unpaid. Open to recent high school graduates, college freshmen, college sophomores, college juniors, college seniors, recent college graduates, graduate students, law students, career changers, individuals reentering the workforce. ▶ *4–8 headquarters office assistants (special projects):* responsibilities include responding to email, overseeing mailings, assisting with international program administration, assisting with accounting, and special projects. Candidates should have ability to work independently, computer skills, office skills, oral communication skills, organizational skills, written communication skills. Duration is 3–6 months. $200 per month plus local transportation costs. Open to college freshmen, college sophomores, college juniors, college seniors, recent college graduates, graduate students, law students, career changers, individuals reentering the workforce. ▶ *1–15 health-care interns (Thailand):* responsibilities include shadowing doctors at a hospital or nurses at a rural health clinic; presenting conversational English classes. Candidates should have knowledge of field, oral communication skills, plan to pursue career in field, self-motivation, strong interpersonal skills, written communication skills. Duration is 3 weeks to 6 months (year-round). Unpaid. Open to college freshmen, college sophomores, college juniors, college seniors, recent college graduates, graduate students, law students, career changers, individuals reentering the workforce, retirees. ▶ *Sustainable agriculture teachers (Tanzania):* responsibilities include learning the methods and mechanics of biointensive agriculture and organic gardening; teaching biointensive agriculture to others in Tanzania; reporting on work and successes/failures. Candidates should have ability to work independently, oral communication skills, organizational skills, personal interest in the field, self-motivation, strong interpersonal skills. Duration is 4 weeks to 6 months (year-round). Unpaid. Open to college sophomores, college juniors, college seniors, recent college graduates, graduate students, law students, career changers, individuals reentering the workforce, individuals over 20 years of age. International applications accepted.
Benefits Formal training, names of contacts, on-the-job training, possible full-time employment, willing to act as a professional reference, willing to complete paperwork for educational credit, willing to provide letters of recommendation, cost of program includes meals, homestay, travel in country, and project administration; college credits and financial aid through SUNY-Albany.
International Internships Available in Thailand; United Republic of Tanzania.
Contact Write, call, fax, e-mail, or through World Wide Web site Andrea Brooks, Manager of Operations. Phone: 415-788-3666 Ext. 128. Fax: 415-788-7324. E-mail: gsctanzania@earthisland.org. Telephone interview required. Applicants must submit a formal organization application, letter of interest, resume, 1-2 letters of recommendation. Application deadline: January 1 for spring, April 1 for summer, July 1 for fall, October 1 for winter. Fees: $300. World Wide Web: http://www.globalservicecorps.org.

HIDDEN VILLA ENVIRONMENTAL EDUCATION PROGRAM
26870 Moody Road
Los Altos Hills, California 94022

General Information School-year program introducing 4-12 year olds to the wonders and magic of an organic farm and garden and the natural world. Established in 1970. Number of employees: 10. Unit of The Trust for Hidden Villa, Los Altos Hills, California. Number of internship applications received each year: 40.

Hidden Villa Environmental Education Program (continued)

Internships Available ▶ *Environmental education interns:* responsibilities include teaching on a farm, in the wilderness, and in a classroom for 25 hours per week; working on a farm for 10 hours per week; and spending 5 hours per week on special projects and in meetings. Candidates should have oral communication skills, plan to pursue career in field, self-motivation, strong interpersonal skills, strong leadership ability, desire to work outdoors and with children. Duration is September to May. $500 per month. Open to recent high school graduates, college freshmen, college sophomores, college juniors, college seniors, recent college graduates, graduate students, law students, career changers, individuals reentering the workforce. International applications accepted.

Benefits Formal training, free housing, health insurance, job counseling, names of contacts, opportunity to attend seminars/workshops, willing to complete paperwork for educational credit, willing to provide letters of recommendation, reimbursement for mileage, unlimited farm-grown food.

Contact Write, call, fax, or e-mail Claire Elliott, Internship Coordinator. Phone: 650-949-8643. Fax: 650-948-1916. E-mail: hveep@hiddenvilla.org. Telephone interview required. Applicants must submit a formal organization application, letter of interest, resume. Application deadline: April 13. World Wide Web: http://www.hiddenvilla.org.

HIGHER EDUCATION CONSORTIUM FOR URBAN AFFAIRS, INC.
2233 University Avenue, Suite 210
St. Paul, Minnesota 55114-1629

General Information Nonprofit education consortium providing college-level study programs in U.S. and abroad, focusing on strategies to address social inequality; programs include internships, field projects, and independent research. Established in 1971. Number of employees: 15. Number of internship applications received each year: 100.

Internships Available ▶ *25 City Arts interns:* responsibilities include working in one of many Minneapolis-St. Paul arts-related projects combined with seminars that explore the connections between the arts, cultural expression, social change, and the impact of class, race, and gender. Placement based on intern's interests. Candidates should have ability to work with others, oral communication skills, personal interest in the field, self-motivation. Duration is February to May. Position available as unpaid or paid. Open to college sophomores, college juniors, college seniors. ▶ *40–50 Metro Urban Studies Term (MUST) interns:* responsibilities include working in one of many Minneapolis-St.Paul public, nonprofit, or community agencies, combined with seminars that examine issues of social inequality in the urban environment and strategies for change; placement based on intern's interests. Candidates should have ability to work with others, analytical skills, oral communication skills, personal interest in the field, self-motivation, written communication skills. Duration is September to December or February to May. Position available as unpaid or paid. Open to college sophomores, college juniors, college seniors. ▶ *20 Partners Program interns:* responsibilities include working in a nonprofit organization in Minnesota, Wisconsin, and North Dakota. Candidates should have ability to work with others, organizational skills, personal interest in the field, self-motivation, strong leadership ability. Duration is June–August. $8.50 per hour. Open to college freshmen, college sophomores, college juniors. ▶ *15 community internships (Latin America):* responsibilities include working in one of many community agencies based in Quito, Ecuador, combined with seminar and independent project, all focussing on community participation for social change. Placement based on intern's interests. Candidates should have ability to work independently, personal interest in the field, self-motivation, strong interpersonal skills, two years college-level Spanish. Duration is September to December. Unpaid. Open to college sophomores, college juniors, college seniors. ▶ *20 democracy and social change interns (Northern Ireland):* responsibilities include working in one of many organizations in Northern Ireland, combined with seminar and independent project, focusing on democracy, peace and conflict resolution, and social change; place-

ment based on intern's interests. Candidates should have ability to work with others, personal interest in the field, self-motivation, strong leadership ability. Duration is February to May. Unpaid. Open to college sophomores, college juniors, college seniors. International applications accepted.

Benefits Opportunity to attend seminars/workshops, willing to complete paperwork for educational credit, willing to provide letters of recommendation, full semester of academic credit.

International Internships Available in Quito, Ecuador; United Kingdom.

Contact Write, call, fax, e-mail, or through World Wide Web site Michael Eaton, Director of Student Services. Phone: 800-554-1089. Fax: 651-659-9421. E-mail: info@hecua.org. Applicants must submit a formal organization application, resume, academic transcripts, two personal references. Application deadline: March 15 for Community Internships in Latin America, April 15 for Metro Urban Studies Term (fall program), November 1 for Northern Ireland positions, December 1 for City Arts (spring program) and Metro Urban Studies Term (spring program); April 1 for Partners Internship program. Fees: $75. World Wide Web: http://www.hecua.org.

HOPE CHAPEL
Church Office, 300 Ohukai Road, Building C-210
Kihei, Hawaii 96753

General Information Christ-centered interdenominational church with an emphasis on Bible teaching and inspirational worship serving a membership base of 1200 people. Number of employees: 28.

Internships Available ▶ *8 interns:* responsibilities include assignment to a ministry overseer whose gifts and talents compliment those of the intern; ministry areas include pastoral, children's, junior and senior high school, worship/special events, small groups, and administration; comprehensive exposure to all areas of ministry; all projects will be tailored to interest and gifts of intern. Duration is 1 year (August to August); 60 hours per week (40 hours in specialty area and the remainder in other areas). $400 monthly stipend. Open to college-age individuals who are seriously considering full-time vocational ministry. International applications accepted.

Benefits Free housing, paid utilities.

Contact Write, call, fax, e-mail, or through World Wide Web site Jason Spence, Associate Pastor. Phone: 808-879-3853 Ext. 232. Fax: 808-874-2886. E-mail: info@hopemaui.org. Application deadline: May. World Wide Web: http://www.hopemaui.org.

HORIZONS FOR YOUTH
121 Lakeview Street
Sharon, Massachusetts 02067

General Information Residential environmental education center that works with children. Established in 1938. Number of employees: 20. Number of internship applications received each year: 100.

Internships Available ▶ *1–3 field instructor/teachers:* responsibilities include developing and teaching outdoor activities related to ecology, environmental science, and group dynamics. Candidates should have ability to work with others, oral communication skills, personal interest in the field, self-motivation, previous work with children. Duration is 12–17 weeks. $250 per week. Open to college sophomores, college juniors, college seniors, recent college graduates, graduate students, law students, career changers. ▶ *1 kitchen assistant:* responsibilities include working to support a kitchen that serves up to 250 people. Candidates should have ability to work independently, ability to work with others, oral communication skills, organizational skills, personal interest in the field, self-motivation, cooking knowledge. Duration is 12–17 weeks. $250 per week. Open to college sophomores, college juniors, college seniors, recent college graduates, graduate students, career changers. International applications accepted.

Benefits Free housing, free meals, on-the-job training, opportunity to attend seminars/workshops, possible full-time employment, willing to act as a professional reference, willing to complete paperwork for educational credit, willing to provide letters of recommendation.

Contact Write, call, fax, e-mail, or through World Wide Web site Mr. James Barnett, School Program Director. Phone: 781-828-7550. Fax: 781-784-1287. E-mail: outdoors@hfy.org. In-person interview recommended (telephone interview accepted). Applicants must submit a formal organization application, letter of interest, resume, 3 references. Applications are accepted continuously. World Wide Web: http://www.hfy.org.

THE HOSPITALITY MANAGEMENT TRAINING INSTITUTE
760 Market Street, Suite 1009
San Francisco, California 94102

General Information Hotel/restaurant management college teaching certified management classes with diploma programs, internships, and job placement services worldwide. Established in 1991. Number of employees: 16. Affiliate of American Hotel and Motel Association, Washington, District of Columbia. Number of internship applications received each year: 7.

Internships Available ▶ *1–10 hospitality administration interns:* responsibilities include front desk and concierge duties, event planning. Candidates should have ability to work with others, computer skills, oral communication skills, organizational skills, personal interest in the field. Duration is flexible. Position available as unpaid or at $10–$15 per hour. Open to recent high school graduates, college freshmen, college sophomores, college juniors, college seniors, recent college graduates, career changers, individuals reentering the workforce. ▶ *1–10 hospitality operations interns:* responsibilities include front desk duties, concierge positions in hotels, and events planning. Candidates should have ability to work with others, computer skills, oral communication skills, organizational skills, personal interest in the field, writing skills. Duration is flexible. Position available as unpaid or at $12–$15 per hour. Open to recent high school graduates, college freshmen, college sophomores, college juniors, college seniors, recent college graduates, career changers, individuals reentering the workforce. ▶ *2 marketing interns:* responsibilities include placing international phone calls, creating marketing reports, and assisting with update of business plan. Candidates should have ability to work with others, computer skills, oral communication skills, bilingual ability. Duration is flexible. Position available as unpaid or at $7–$10 per hour. Open to college seniors, recent college graduates, graduate students. ▶ *2 preschool teachers:* responsibilities include assisting head teacher with adult teacher certification students. Candidates should have ability to work with others, computer skills, oral communication skills. Duration is flexible. Position available as unpaid or at $7–$10 per hour. Open to college seniors, recent college graduates, graduate students. International applications accepted.
Benefits Formal training, job counseling, names of contacts, on-the-job training, possible full-time employment, willing to act as a professional reference, willing to complete paperwork for educational credit, willing to provide letters of recommendation.
International Internships Available in Australia; Paris, France; Tokyo, Japan; Mexico; London, United Kingdom.
Contact Write, fax, e-mail, or through World Wide Web site Sherris Goodwin, Executive Director. Fax: 415-677-9810. E-mail: hotelscool@aol.com. No phone calls. In-person interview recommended (telephone interview accepted). Applicants must submit a formal organization application, letter of interest, resume, academic transcripts, three personal references, two letters of recommendation, three letters of recommendation. Applications are accepted continuously. World Wide Web: http://www.hotelcollege.com.

IACOCCA INSTITUTE, GLOBAL VILLAGE FOR FUTURE LEADERS OF BUSINESS & INDUSTRY
111 Research Drive
Bethlehem, Pennsylvania 18015

General Information Institution of higher learning. Established in 1988. Number of employees: 56. Division of Lehigh University, Bethlehem, Pennsylvania. Number of internship applications received each year: 200.

Internships Available ▶ *Global Village Iacocca interns:* responsibilities include attending all lectures/seminars and other scheduled learning activities, sharing information about home culture and history with other interns, hosting executive visitors, and producing results on assigned projects. Candidates should have oral communication skills, self-motivation, strong interpersonal skills, strong leadership ability, well-developed personal value system. Duration is 6 weeks (June 24 to August 5). Unpaid. Open to college freshmen, college sophomores, college juniors, college seniors, recent college graduates, graduate students, law students, career changers, young entrepreneurs, family-owned business members, corporate new-hires. International applications accepted.
Benefits Formal training, housing at a cost, job counseling, names of contacts, on-the-job training, opportunity to attend seminars/workshops, willing to act as a professional reference, willing to complete paperwork for educational credit, willing to provide letters of recommendation.
Contact Write, call, fax, e-mail, or through World Wide Web site M. Frances Schurtz-Leon, Candidate Manager, 111 Research Drive, Bethlehem, Pennsylvania 18015. Phone: 610-758-6887. Fax: 610-758-6550. E-mail: mfs2@lehigh.edu. Applicants must submit a formal organization application, letter of interest, resume, academic transcripts, personal reference, two letters of recommendation. Applications are accepted continuously. Fees: $50. World Wide Web: http://www.lehigh.edu/~village/Iacocca/.

INNER QUEST, INC.
34752 Charles Town Pike
Purcellville, Virginia 20132

General Information Outdoor education organization teaching personal growth and skill development through outdoor adventure activities including rock climbing, caving, canoeing, kayaking, and challenge courses. Established in 1979. Number of employees: 20. Number of internship applications received each year: 100.

Internships Available ▶ *10 apprentice instructors:* responsibilities include teaching climbing, caving, canoeing, kayaking, and challenge courses. Candidates should have ability to work with others, oral communication skills, strong leadership ability. Duration is 12 weeks. $1200 per duration of internship. Open to individuals 18 or older.
Benefits Formal training, on-the-job training, possible full-time employment, willing to complete paperwork for educational credit, willing to provide letters of recommendation.
Contact Write, call, fax, or e-mail Sara Smith, Director. Phone: 540-668-6699. Fax: 540-668-6253. E-mail: innerquestinfo@cs.com. In-person interview recommended (telephone interview accepted). Applicants must submit a formal organization application, letter of interest, resume, three personal references. Application deadline: February 1 for spring, April 1 for summer. World Wide Web: http://www.InnerQuestOnline.com.

THE INSTITUTE FOR EARTH EDUCATION
Cedar Cove
Greenville, West Virginia 24945

General Information Designer of educational programs that will help people increase their understanding of, appreciation for, and harmony with the earth's natural systems and communities. Established in 1974. Number of employees: 3. Number of internship applications received each year: 10.

Internships Available ▶ *1–6 earth education interns:* responsibilities include development and maintenance of the center; helping with food production and preservation; and assisting in the international office. Candidates should have oral communication skills, plan to pursue career in field, self-motivation, strong interpersonal skills, written communication skills, willingness to work hard and follow instructions when needed. Duration is 2–12 months. Unpaid. ▶ *1 landcare coordinator:* responsibilities include assisting in master planning, housing rehabilitation, trail design, and establishing teepee and treehouse villages; developing wild cave tours; some basic maintenance. Candidates should have ability to work independently, knowledge of field, oral communication skills, personal interest in the field, self-motivation, strong interpersonal skills. Duration is 2–12 months. Unpaid. ▶ *2–4*

The Institute for Earth Education (continued)
organic gardeners: responsibilities include planning, sowing, harvesting, and preserving organic produce. Candidates should have ability to work independently, ability to work with others, knowledge of field, oral communication skills, personal interest in the field, self-motivation. Duration is 2–12 months. Unpaid. Open to recent high school graduates, college freshmen, college sophomores, college juniors, college seniors, recent college graduates, graduate students, career changers, individuals reentering the workforce. International applications accepted.
Benefits Formal training, free housing, free meals, job counseling, names of contacts, on-the-job training, opportunity to attend seminars/workshops, willing to act as a professional reference, willing to complete paperwork for educational credit, willing to provide letters of recommendation.
Contact Write, call, fax, e-mail, or through World Wide Web site Internship Coordinator. Phone: 304-832-6404. Fax: 304-832-6077. E-mail: iee1@aol.com. Telephone interview required. Applicants must submit a formal organization application, resume, letter of recommendation. Applications are accepted continuously. World Wide Web: http://www.eartheducation.org.

THE INSTITUTE FOR EXPERIENTIAL LEARNING
1776 Massachusetts Avenue, NW, Suite 201
Washington, District of Columbia 20036

General Information Institute that works to advance the theory of experiential education through internship programs for graduate and undergraduate students in all majors. Established in 1990. Number of employees: 9. Number of internship applications received each year: 650.
Internships Available ▶ *80–100 IEL interns:* responsibilities include participating fully in office life by attending meetings and special events, performing research, writing reports, and preparing briefings. Candidates should have ability to work independently, analytical skills, knowledge of field, office skills, oral communication skills, organizational skills, personal interest in the field, research skills, self-motivation, strong interpersonal skills, strong leadership ability, writing skills. Duration is 10-15 weeks, 4 days per week. Position available as unpaid or at $300–$1500 per month. Open to college juniors, college seniors, recent college graduates, graduate students, law students, career changers. International applications accepted.
Benefits Formal training, housing at a cost, job counseling, names of contacts, opportunity to attend seminars/workshops, possible full-time employment, willing to act as a professional reference, willing to complete paperwork for educational credit, willing to provide letters of recommendation, career counseling and professional development.
Contact Write, call, fax, e-mail, or through World Wide Web site Jerrod Wheeler, Program Coordinator, 1776 Massachusetts Avenue, NW Suite 201, Washington, District of Columbia 20036. Phone: 202-833-8580. Fax: 202-833-8581. E-mail: info@ielnet.org. Telephone interview required. Applicants must submit a formal organization application, academic transcripts, three letters of recommendation. Application deadline: April 2 for summer, May 4 for fall, November 24 for spring. Fees: $50. World Wide Web: http://www.ielnet.org.

INSTITUTE FOR INTERNATIONAL COOPERATION AND DEVELOPMENT
PO Box 520
Williamstown, Massachusetts 01267

General Information Nonprofit organization training volunteers for work in Africa and Latin America; involves people from local communities in fields of education, health, and small-scale construction. Established in 1987. Number of employees: 10. Number of internship applications received each year: 3,000.
Internships Available ▶ *15–20 volunteers in Angola:* responsibilities include preventive health care, teaching in schools, and community environmental projects. Candidates should have oral communication skills, personal interest in the field, self-motivation, strong interpersonal skills, strong leadership ability. Duration is 13 months. Unpaid. ▶ *15–20 volunteers in Brazil:* responsibilities

include helping in community construction, collecting information from local people, and working with street children. Duration is 6 months. Unpaid. ▶ *Volunteers in El Salvador:* responsibilities include working with families in rural villages to provide health care, assisting small-scale farmers in improving food production, and HIV prevention. Candidates should have oral communication skills, personal interest in the field, self-motivation, strong interpersonal skills, strong leadership ability. Duration is 12 months. Unpaid. ▶ *15–20 volunteers in Mozambique:* responsibilities include teaching in schools for street kids and in vocational schools, teacher training, and village health campaigns. Candidates should have oral communication skills, personal interest in the field, self-motivation, strong interpersonal skills, strong leadership ability. Duration is 19 months. Unpaid. ▶ *10–15 volunteers in Nicaragua:* responsibilities include working with families in rural villages to provide health care, assisting small-scale farmers in improving food production, and HIV prevention. Candidates should have oral communication skills, personal interest in the field, self-motivation, strong interpersonal skills. Duration is 13 months. Unpaid. ▶ *15–20 volunteers in Zimbabwe:* responsibilities include working with families in rural villages to provide health care, assisting small-scale farmers in improving food production, and HIV prevention. Candidates should have oral communication skills, personal interest in the field, self-motivation, strong interpersonal skills, strong leadership ability. Duration is 13 months. Unpaid. Open to individuals over 18 years old. International applications accepted.
Benefits Formal training, health insurance, job counseling, names of contacts, on-the-job training, opportunity to attend seminars/workshops, possible full-time employment, tuition assistance, willing to act as a professional reference, willing to complete paperwork for educational credit, willing to provide letters of recommendation, housing, meals, and education are provided with tuition.
International Internships Available in Angola; Brazil; Mozambique; Nicaragua; Zimbabwe.
Contact Write, call, fax, e-mail, or through World Wide Web site Uli Stosch, Director. Phone: 413-458-9828. Fax: 413-458-3323. E-mail: info@iicd-volunteer.org. In-person interview recommended (telephone interview accepted). Applicants must submit a formal organization application, letter of interest, resume. Applications are accepted continuously. World Wide Web: http://www.iicd-volunteer.org.

INSTITUTE FOR LEADERSHIP DEVELOPMENT
1810-2 Assiniboine, York University
Toronto, Ontario M3J 1P3 Canada

General Information United Nations Global Partnership Institute that builds leadership skills in young professionals and entrepreneurs in Canada and around the world through skills enhancement programs, distance learning, and work placements. Established in 1995. Number of employees: 10. Affiliate of United Nations, New York, New York. Number of internship applications received each year: 700.
Internships Available ▶ *35–40 interns:* responsibilities include a variety of assignments with UN agencies, international institutions, and private sector organizations. Candidates should have ability to work with others, college degree in related field, computer skills, plan to pursue career in field, strong leadership ability, second language skills often required. Duration is 6 to 10 months on average. $700–$1400 per month. Open to those with a graduate degree or equivalent.
Benefits Health insurance, opportunity to attend seminars/workshops, possible full-time employment, willing to act as a professional reference, willing to provide letters of recommendation, job search support, pre-placement training, housing at a cost/free housing (depending on placement).
International Internships Available in Rio de Janiero, Brazil; Rome, Italy; Beirut, Lebanon; Mexico City, Mexico; Harare, Zimbabwe.
Contact Write, call, fax, or e-mail Muni Ahlawat, Programmes Coordinator, 1810-2 Assiniboine, York University, 4700 Keele Street, Toronto, Ontario M3J 1P3 Canada. Phone: 416-736-2100 Ext. 88704. Fax: 416-736-5693. E-mail: unforum@yorku.ca. In-person interview recommended (telephone interview accepted). Applicants

must submit a letter of interest, resume, two letters of recommendation, formal application (must be submitted by mail or courier; faxes and e-mails are not acceptable). Application deadline: June 30 for fall. World Wide Web: http://www.ildglobal.org.

INSTITUTE FOR THE INTERNATIONAL EDUCATION OF STUDENTS (IES)
33 North LaSalle Street, 15th Floor
Chicago, Illinois 60602-2602

General Information Study abroad program provider. Established in 1950.

Internships Available ▶ *Arts/museum interns:* responsibilities include assignments in England, Ireland, Australia, Austria, Japan, Germany, Spain, and France. Candidates should have ability to work with others, knowledge of field, oral communication skills, personal interest in the field, self-motivation, strong grasp of country's native language (usually needed). Duration is one semester, year, or summer (London and Madrid only). Unpaid. Open to college juniors, college seniors. ▶ *Business and marketing interns:* responsibilities include assignments in Australia, China, Germany, Argentina, Spain, France, Japan, Ireland, England, Austria, and Italy. Candidates should have ability to work with others, knowledge of field, oral communication skills, personal interest in the field, self-motivation, strong grasp of country's native language (usually needed). Duration is one semester, year, or summer. Unpaid. Open to college juniors, college seniors. ▶ *Communications and journalism interns:* responsibilities include assignments in China, Germany, England, Spain, Italy, France, Austria, Australia, and Japan. Candidates should have ability to work with others, knowledge of field, oral communication skills, personal interest in the field, self-motivation, strong grasp of country's native language (usually needed). Duration is one semester, year, or summer (London and Dublin only). Unpaid. Open to college juniors, college seniors. ▶ *Education and teaching interns:* responsibilities include assignments in China, Germany, Argentina, France, Spain, Japan, Austria, and England. Candidates should have ability to work with others, knowledge of field, oral communication skills, personal interest in the field, self-motivation, strong grasp of country's native language (usually needed). Duration is one semester, year, or summer (London only). Unpaid. Open to college juniors, college seniors. ▶ *International relations and government interns:* responsibilities include assignments in Germany, Argentina, England, Spain, France, Japan, Australia, Ireland, and Chile. Candidates should have ability to work with others, knowledge of field, oral communication skills, personal interest in the field, self-motivation, strong grasp of country's native language (usually needed). Duration is one semester, year, or summer (London, Madrid, and Dublin only). Unpaid. Open to college juniors, college seniors. ▶ *2–3 marketing interns (Chicago):* responsibilities include working with vice president of marketing, recruitment, and information systems to review ongoing research projects, developing processes and designs for approaching the marketing questions at hand, and implementing market research projects. Candidates should have ability to work independently, ability to work with others, analytical skills, computer skills, organizational skills, personal interest in the field, strong critical thinking skills. Duration is 2–3 months. $2000 stipend for full-time interns; prorated share for part-time interns. Open to college sophomores, college juniors, college seniors, recent college graduates. ▶ *Science interns:* responsibilities include assignments in Australia, Germany, France, Ireland, Argentina, England, Spain, and Italy. Candidates should have ability to work with others, knowledge of field, oral communication skills, personal interest in the field, self-motivation, strong grasp of country's native language (usually needed). Duration is one semester, year, or summer (London only). Unpaid. Open to college juniors, college seniors. ▶ *Social and political activism interns:* responsibilities include assignments in Australia, China, Germany, France, Ireland, Argentina, England, Spain, Italy, Japan, Austria, Ireland, and Chile. Candidates should have ability to work with others, knowledge of field, personal interest in the field, self-motivation, strong grasp of country's native language (usually needed). Duration is one semester, year, or summer. Unpaid. Open to college juniors, college seniors. ▶ *Theater interns:*

responsibilities include assignments in England, Germany, and Ireland. Candidates should have ability to work with others, knowledge of field, oral communication skills, personal interest in the field, self-motivation, strong grasp of country's native language (usually needed). Duration is one year, semester, or summer (London and Dublin only). Unpaid. Open to college juniors, college seniors. International applications accepted.

International Internships Available.

Contact Call, e-mail, or through World Wide Web site IES Representative. Phone: 800-995-2300. Fax: 312-944-1448. E-mail: info@iesabroad.org. In-person interview required. Applicants must submit a formal organization application, letter of interest, resume, academic transcripts, must be participant in IES study abroad program; program fees vary by placement. Application deadline: March 1 for summer (London), May 1 for spring and summer (except London summer), June 15 for fall. World Wide Web: http://www.iesabroad.org.

INSTITUTE OF INTERNATIONAL EDUCATION– OFFICE FOR LATIN AMERICA
Londres 16, 2nd Floor, Col. Juarez
Mexico City, DF 06600 Mexico

General Information Nonprofit educational exchange organization. Established in 1974. Number of employees: 14. Division of Institute of International Education, New York, New York. Number of internship applications received each year: 15.

Internships Available ▶ *1–3 student advising interns:* responsibilities include advising the public on all aspects of U.S. education, including information about the admissions process and testing programs; working on assigned research projects and possibly assisting with outreach activities. Candidates should have organizational skills, research skills, self-motivation, strong interpersonal skills, proficiency in Spanish. Duration is 3–4 months. $400 per month. Open to college sophomores, college juniors, college seniors, recent college graduates, graduate students. International applications accepted.

Benefits Names of contacts, on-the-job training, opportunity to attend seminars/workshops, possible full-time employment, willing to act as a professional reference, willing to complete paperwork for educational credit, willing to provide letters of recommendation.

International Internships Available.

Contact Write, call, fax, e-mail, or through World Wide Web site Brian Bolton, Coordinator for Educational Services, AmEmbassy Mexico (IIE), PO Box 3087, Laredo, Texas 78044-3087. E-mail: bbolton@pd.state.gov. Applicants must submit a formal organization application, letter of interest, resume, academic transcripts, two letters of recommendation. Application deadline: March 15 for summer, June 15 for fall, October 15 for spring. World Wide Web: http://www.iie.org/latinamerica.

INTERLOCKEN
RFD 2, Box 165
Hillsboro Upper Village, New Hampshire 03244

General Information Experiential learning center that offers educational summer adventures for young people ages 9-18, an international residential summer camp in New Hampshire, and travel programs in the U.S. and abroad. Established in 1961. Number of employees: 9. Number of internship applications received each year: 200.

Internships Available ▶ *25–30 camp counselors:* responsibilities include teaching specialty areas and being responsible for living units. Candidates should have self-motivation, strong interpersonal skills, skills for teaching in particular area and experience working with children. Duration is 9 weeks. $1400–$2000 per duration of internship. Open to college freshmen, college sophomores, college juniors, college seniors, recent college graduates, graduate students. ▶ *25–30 travel interns:* responsibilities include leading a small group travel adventure in the U.S., Europe, Latin America, Africa or Asia. Candidates should have ability to work independently, knowledge of field, self-motivation, strong interpersonal skills, strong leadership ability, experience working with teenagers, willingness to work 24 hours a day 7 days a week.

Interlocken (continued)

Duration is 4–6 weeks. $1550–$2050 per duration of internship. Open to graduate students, minimum age of 24. International applications accepted.

Benefits Free housing, free meals, names of contacts, willing to act as a professional reference, willing to complete paperwork for educational credit, willing to provide letters of recommendation.

International Internships Available in Quebec, Canada; Paris, France; Venice, Italy.

Contact Write, fax, e-mail, or through World Wide Web site Rick Davis, Marketing Director. Fax: 603-478-5260. E-mail: rick@interlocken.org. In-person interview recommended (telephone interview accepted). Applicants must submit a formal organization application, letter of interest, resume, three letters of recommendation. Applications are accepted continuously. World Wide Web: http://www.interlocken.org.

INTERNATIONAL FIELD STUDIES
709 College Avenue
Columbus, Ohio 43209

General Information Nonprofit organization that provides logistical support to get students and educators into the marine biology field. Two programs are offered: marine biology field station in Andros Island, Bahamas, and sailing programs in the northern and central Bahamas. Established in 1970. Number of employees: 6. Number of internship applications received each year: 40.

Internships Available ▶ *1–3 co-directors:* responsibilities include overseeing staff and working with group leaders to coordinate trips. Candidates should have experience in the field, organizational skills, self-motivation, strong interpersonal skills, strong leadership ability. Duration is 1–2 years. $200–$500 per month. Open to graduate students. ▶ *2–6 field station interns:* responsibilities include supporting staff at field station. Candidates should have ability to work with others, experience in the field, personal interest in the field, self-motivation, mechanical abilities desirable. Duration is 1–2 years. $200–$500 per month. Open to recent college graduates, must be 21 or over. ▶ *1–3 sailing first-mates:* responsibilities include supporting crew on sailing program. Candidates should have ability to work with others, personal interest in the field, self-motivation, strong leadership ability, mechanical abilities. Duration is 1–2 years. $200–$500 per month. Open to recent college graduates, must be 21 or over. International applications accepted.

Benefits Free housing, free meals, on-the-job training, opportunity to attend seminars/workshops, possible full-time employment, willing to act as a professional reference, willing to complete paperwork for educational credit, willing to provide letters of recommendation, stipend, transportation to Bahamas (when available).

International Internships Available in Andros Island, Bahamas.

Contact Write, call, fax, e-mail, or through World Wide Web site Internship Coordinator. Phone: 800-962-3805. Fax: 614-235-9744. E-mail: employment@intlfieldstudies.com. In-person interview required. Applicants must submit a formal organization application, letter of interest, resume, two personal references, $595 for on-site interview (one week); reimbursed after 12 months of employment. Applications are accepted continuously. World Wide Web: http://www.intlfieldstudies.com.

THE INTERNATIONAL PARTNERSHIP FOR SERVICE-LEARNING
815 Second Avenue, Suite 315
New York, New York 10017

General Information Organization that administers international graduate and undergraduate study-abroad programs, combining academic study with service-learning/hands-on community service. Established in 1982. Number of employees: 5. Number of internship applications received each year: 150.

Internships Available ▶ *100–200 student program interns:* responsibilities include providing service to communities in need, teaching/tutoring at all levels (preschool–adult), providing rehabilitation for mentally or physically handicapped people, or assisting with health care, counseling, recreation, and community development. Candidates should have oral communication skills, personal interest in the field, strong interpersonal skills, written communication skills, minimum score of 550 on the TOEFL (non-native English speakers). Duration is variable. Unpaid. Open to recent high school graduates, college freshmen, college sophomores, college juniors, college seniors, recent college graduates, graduate students, career changers, individuals reentering the workforce, retirees. International applications accepted.

Benefits Housing at a cost, meals at a cost, on-the-job training, opportunity to attend seminars/workshops, willing to act as a professional reference, willing to complete paperwork for educational credit, willing to provide letters of recommendation, academic study and credit.

International Internships Available in Prague, Czech Republic; Guayaquil and Quito, Ecuador; Montpellier, France; Calcutta, India; Beer-Sheva, Israel; Kingston, Jamaica; Guadalajara, Mexico; Manila, Philippines; Moscow, Russian Federation; London and Glasgow, United Kingdom.

Contact Write, call, fax, e-mail, or through World Wide Web site Director of Student Programs. Phone: 212-986-0989. Fax: 212-986-5039. E-mail: info@ipsl.org. Applicants must submit a formal organization application, academic transcripts, two personal references, two letters of recommendation, $250 deposit as part of program fees. Application deadline: April 15 for summer, July 15 for fall, November 15 for spring. World Wide Web: http://www.ipsl.org.

INTERNATIONAL YMCA
Go Global, 5 West 63rd Street, 2nd Floor
New York, New York 10023

General Information Organization providing global awareness programs for children to promote understanding of international cultures and peoples. Branch of YMCA of Greater New York, New York, New York.

Internships Available ▶ *Diversity workshop leaders:* responsibilities include designing workshop to present to children (ages 5-12); workshop must be inspired by and directly related to intern's personal skills, area of expertise, or cultural background; workshop must be interactive, comparative, and highlight realities of multiculturalism and diversity in the world. Candidates should have ability to work independently, ability to work with others, computer skills, office skills, self-motivation, strong leadership ability, proficiency in an art from, subject, or talent from a country or region in the world; willingness and ability to work with children (prior experience desired but not necessary). Duration is minimum of 3 months; 5 month commitment preferable. Unpaid. Open to recent high school graduates, college freshmen, college sophomores, college juniors, college seniors, recent college graduates, graduate students, law students, career changers. ▶ *Graphic and web site designers:* responsibilities include print and HTML design of outgoing communication and press materials. Candidates should have ability to work independently, ability to work with others, computer skills, editing skills, self-motivation, written communication skills, proficiency in Publisher, Illustrator, PhotoShop, and other design programs; knowledge of HTML and Internet-related database. Duration is 3 months (up to 20 hours per week). Unpaid. Open to college sophomores, college juniors, college seniors, recent college graduates.

Benefits Opportunity to attend seminars/workshops, possible full-time employment, travel reimbursement, willing to act as a professional reference, willing to complete paperwork for educational credit, willing to provide letters of recommendation.

Contact Write, call, or e-mail Leeza Ahmady, Project Coordinator. Phone: 212-727-8800 Ext. 4303. E-mail: lahmady@ymcanyc.org. In-person interview recommended (telephone interview accepted). Applicants must submit a letter of interest, resume. Applications are accepted continuously. World Wide Web: http://www.ymcainternational.org.

INTERNSHIPS IN FRANCOPHONE EUROPE
26 Rue Cmdt. Mouchette J-108
75014 Paris France

General Information Semester-long academic program that includes 12 weeks full-time professional experience in French public life, preceded by 5 weeks of intensive preparation. Established in 1988. Number of employees: 4.

Internships Available ▶ *5–10 interns:* responsibilities include working in various institutions in the public sector and non-governmental organizations. Candidates should have ability to work independently, ability to work with others, analytical skills, self-motivation, adequate command of French. Duration is 12–17 weeks. Unpaid. Open to college sophomores, college juniors, college seniors, recent college graduates, graduate students. International applications accepted.

Benefits Formal training, job counseling, opportunity to attend seminars/workshops, tuition assistance, willing to complete paperwork for educational credit, willing to provide letters of recommendation, faculty advising throughout the internship.

International Internships Available.

Contact Write, call, fax, e-mail, or through World Wide Web site Timothy Carlson, Co-director. Phone: 33-1-43-21-78-07. Fax: 33-1-42-79-94-13. E-mail: ifeparis@worldnet.fr. Applicants must submit a formal organization application, resume, academic transcripts, writing sample, two letters of recommendation, other materials specified on Web site. Application deadline: June 1 for fall, November 1 for spring. Fees: $50. World Wide Web: http://www.ifeparis.org.

I-TO-I USA, INC.
8 East 1st Avenue, Suite 103
Denver, Colorado 80203

General Information 0rganization that sends volunteers abroad to various altruistic projects, provides ESL training online and paid placements. Established in 1992. Number of employees: 25. Unit of i-to-i, Leeds, United Kingdom. Number of internship applications received each year: 750.

Internships Available ▶ *Building interns:* responsibilities include working alongside the local people, assisting in the layout of designs of basic buildings, constructing ovens and installing roofs. Candidates should have ability to work with others, self-motivation. Duration is 3 months. Unpaid. Open to those 17 or older. ▶ *Care work interns:* responsibilities include working in orphanages, schools, residential homes and with street kids; involvement in essential activities from afternoon sports to teaching arts and crafts to deaf children. Candidates should have ability to work with others, oral communication skills, self-motivation. Duration is 2–9 months. Open to those 17 or older. ▶ *Conservation interns:* responsibilities include a range of plant and animal conservation projects from turtle conservation in Costa Rica to reforestation in Australia. Candidates should have ability to work with others, self-motivation. Duration is 2 weeks to one year. Unpaid. Open to those 17 or older. ▶ *Health interns:* responsibilities include shadowing doctors and nurses or, assisting doctors and nurses, according to intern's level of experience. Candidates should have ability to work with others, knowledge of field, self-motivation. Duration is 2 to 6 months. Open to those 17 years or older. ▶ *Interns:* responsibilities include placement in Leeds (UK) in area of intern's background and interest. Candidates should have ability to work with others, computer skills, office skills, oral communication skills, self-motivation, written communication skills. Duration is up to 6 months. $6 per hour. Open to college freshmen, college sophomores, college juniors, college seniors, recent college graduates, graduate students. ▶ *Media interns:* responsibilities include work in journalism, radio and TV. Candidates should have ability to work independently, ability to work with others, computer skills, editing skills, office skills, research skills, self-motivation, writing skills. Duration is 2 weeks to 6 months. Unpaid. Open to those 17 or older. ▶ *Teaching business interns:* responsibilities include assisting in or teaching MBA courses at institutes abroad, according to intern's level of experience. Candidates should have ability to work with others, computer skills, office skills, oral communication skills, research skills, strong leadership ability. Duration is 3 to 6 months . Unpaid. Open to college

juniors, college seniors, recent college graduates, graduate students, law students, career changers. ▶ *Teaching interns:* responsibilities include acting as a teaching assistant or teacher of English in a range of classroom situations from Buddhist monks in Nepal to orphans in Sri Lanka. Candidates should have ability to work independently, ability to work with others, oral communication skills, self-motivation, strong leadership ability, written communication skills. Duration is 2 weeks to one year. Unpaid. Open to those 17 or older. ▶ *Work experience interns:* responsibilities include opportunities to use skills in accounting, business, marketing, advertising. Candidates should have computer skills, knowledge of field, office skills, self-motivation, writing skills. Duration is 2 weeks to 6 months. Open to those 17 years or older. International applications accepted.

Benefits Formal training, health insurance, on-the-job training, opportunity to attend seminars/workshops, willing to act as a professional reference, willing to provide letters of recommendation, teaching interns receive training; some internships include free housing and meals.

International Internships Available in Australia; Bolivia; China; Costa Rica; Ecuador; Ghana; Honduras; India; Ireland; Nepal; Republic of Korea; Russian Federation; Sri Lanka; Thailand.

Contact Write, call, fax, e-mail, or through World Wide Web site Kevin O'Neill, Director. Phone: 303-321-8278. Fax: 303-321-8278. E-mail: info@eliabroad.com. In-person interview recommended (telephone interview accepted). Applicants must submit a formal organization application, resume, writing sample, personal reference. Applications are accepted continuously. Fees: $250. World Wide Web: http://www.i-to-i.com.

JOHN C. CAMPBELL FOLK SCHOOL
One Folk School Road
Brasstown, North Carolina 28902

General Information School with weekend classes and one-week sessions throughout the year that teaches crafts, wood, metal, fiber, painting, song/dance, and musical instruments. Established in 1925. Number of employees: 38. Number of internship applications received each year: 30.

Internships Available ▶ *2 hosts:* responsibilities include supporting programming operations. Candidates should have ability to work independently, oral communication skills, organizational skills, self-motivation, strong interpersonal skills, strong leadership ability. Duration is 6 months. Unpaid. Open to recent high school graduates, college freshmen, college sophomores, college juniors, college seniors, recent college graduates, graduate students, law students, career changers, individuals reentering the workforce. ▶ *3–8 work/study interns:* responsibilities include general indoor and outdoor maintenance. Candidates should have ability to work independently, oral communication skills, self-motivation, strong interpersonal skills, interest in arts and crafts. Duration is 6–12 weeks. Unpaid. Open to recent high school graduates, college freshmen, college sophomores, college juniors, college seniors, recent college graduates, graduate students, law students, law school graduates, career changers, individuals reentering the workforce. International applications accepted.

Benefits Free housing, free meals, opportunity to attend seminars/workshops, tuition assistance, willing to provide letters of recommendation, free classes.

Contact Write, call, fax, or e-mail Hanne Dalsemer, Registrar, 1 Folk School Road, Brasstown, North Carolina 28902. Phone: 828-837-2775. Fax: 828-837-8637. E-mail: hanne@folkschool.org. Telephone interview required. Applicants must submit a formal organization application, two personal references, personal statement (1-2 pages). Applications are accepted continuously. Fees: $35. World Wide Web: http://www.folkschool.org.

JOINT COMMISSION RESOURCES
One Renaissance Boulevard
Oakbrook Terrace, Illinois 60181

General Information Company that continuously improves the safety and quality of care in the U.S. and internationally through the provision of education, publications, consultation services, and international accreditation. Established in 2000. Number of employees: 80. Subsidiary of Joint Commission on Accredita-

Joint Commission Resources (continued)

tion of Healthcare Organizations, Oakbrook Terrace, Illinois. Number of internship applications received each year: 12.

Internships Available ▶ *1 editorial intern:* responsibilities include checking and entering copyedits, checking typeset pages and indexed manuscript, researching for select publications, assisting editors with preparing publications for production, conducting competitive analyses and updating competitor files, coordinating reviews and entering review comments, securing permissions, creating art/table logs; fact-checking, verifying references/bibliographies, compiling bibliographies; checking cross references; attending meetings. Candidates should have editing skills, oral communication skills, organizational skills, plan to pursue career in field, self-motivation, written communication skills. Duration is 2–3 months. $8 per hour. Open to college juniors, college seniors, recent college graduates. International applications accepted.

Benefits On-the-job training, possible full-time employment, willing to act as a professional reference, willing to complete paperwork for educational credit, willing to provide letters of recommendation.

Contact Write, call, or e-mail Ruth Metsch, Associate Director, Human Resources. Phone: 630-792-5615. Fax: 630-792-4615. E-mail: rmetsch@jcaho.org. In-person interview required. Applicants must submit a formal organization application, letter of interest, resume, 2-3 writing samples, 1-2 letters of recommendation. Application deadline: April 30 for summer. World Wide Web: http://www.jcrinc.com.

JUILLIARD SCHOOL
60 Lincoln Center Plaza
New York, New York 10023-6590

General Information Specialized professional school for the performing arts. Established in 1905. Number of employees: 550. Number of internship applications received each year: 200.

Internships Available ▶ *1 concert office intern:* responsibilities include general assistance in box office management, preparation of recital programs/publicity, concert production and scheduling in numerous venues. Candidates should have computer skills, organizational skills, self-motivation, strong interpersonal skills, music background (helpful). Duration is September to May. $241 per week. Open to college freshmen, college sophomores, college juniors, college seniors, recent college graduates, graduate students, career changers, individuals reentering the workforce. ▶ *5 costume shop interns:* responsibilities include constructing costumes, dyeing, painting, and performing alterations and repairs. Candidates should have ability to work with others, knowledge of field, plan to pursue career in field, self-motivation, sewing experience. Duration is September to May. $241 per week. Open to recent high school graduates, college freshmen, college sophomores, college juniors, college seniors, recent college graduates, graduate students, career changers. ▶ *1 dance division intern:* responsibilities include assisting the dance production coordinator who manages the daily and long-term planning of dance productions. Candidates should have ability to work independently, computer skills, experience in the field, oral communication skills, organizational skills, personal interest in the field, self-motivation, strong interpersonal skills. Duration is September to May. $241 per week. Open to college freshmen, college sophomores, college juniors, college seniors, recent college graduates, graduate students, career changers. ▶ *1 drama division intern:* responsibilities include assisting administrative director in daily administrative and production operations. Candidates should have ability to work independently, ability to work with others, computer skills, office skills, oral communication skills, organizational skills, self-motivation, written communication skills. Duration is September to May. $241 per week. Open to recent high school graduates, college freshmen, college sophomores, college juniors, college seniors, recent college graduates, graduate students, career changers. ▶ *2 electrics interns:* responsibilities include reading light plots and assisting master electricians with hanging, focusing, and maintaining equipment. Candidates should have ability to work with others, experience in the field, plan to pursue career in field, self-motivation. Duration is September to May. $241 per week.

Open to recent high school graduates, college freshmen, college sophomores, college juniors, college seniors, recent college graduates, graduate students, career changers. ▶ *1 facilities management intern:* responsibilities include assisting the associate vice president of facilities and engineering. Candidates should have ability to work independently, college courses in field, computer skills, oral communication skills, organizational skills, plan to pursue career in field, self-motivation, strong interpersonal skills, written communication skills. Duration is September to May. $241 per week. Open to college freshmen, college sophomores, college juniors, college seniors, recent college graduates, graduate students, career changers, individuals reentering the workforce. ▶ *1 orchestra library intern:* responsibilities include assisting orchestra librarian with securing and preparing all of the music for Juilliard's Performing Ensembles. Candidates should have ability to work independently, experience in the field, plan to pursue career in field, self-motivation, strong interpersonal skills, music background essential. Duration is September to May. $241 per week. Open to recent college graduates, graduate students, career changers. ▶ *1 orchestra management intern:* responsibilities include management of lab orchestra and assisting orchestra manager. Candidates should have ability to work with others, college degree in related field, experience in the field, oral communication skills, self-motivation, strong leadership ability, written communication skills, music background essential. Duration is September to May. $241 per week. Open to recent college graduates, graduate students, career changers. ▶ *2 production assistants:* responsibilities include working with resident production stage managers on various productions and special events. Candidates should have ability to work independently, ability to work with others, computer skills, oral communication skills, organizational skills, self-motivation. $241 per week. Open to college freshmen, college sophomores, college juniors, college seniors, recent college graduates, graduate students, career changers, individuals reentering the workforce. ▶ *2 props interns:* responsibilities include reviewing script for props breakdown; researching, designing, and constructing prop designs; and running crew assignments. Candidates should have ability to work with others, experience in the field, plan to pursue career in field, self-motivation. Duration is September to May. $241 per week. Open to recent high school graduates, college freshmen, college sophomores, college juniors, college seniors, recent college graduates, graduate students, career changers. ▶ *2 scene painting interns:* responsibilities include assisting design, layout, scene painting, texturing, sculpturing, and paint shop maintenance. Candidates should have ability to work independently, ability to work with others, experience in the field, plan to pursue career in field, self-motivation. Duration is September to May. $241 per week. Open to college seniors, recent college graduates, graduate students, career changers. ▶ *6 stage management interns:* responsibilities include assisting production stage managers on opera, drama, and dance productions. Candidates should have ability to work independently, ability to work with others, knowledge of field, oral communication skills, plan to pursue career in field, self-motivation, written communication skills. Duration is September to May. $241 per week. Open to college sophomores, college juniors, college seniors, recent college graduates, graduate students. ▶ *1 vocal arts intern:* responsibilities include assisting administrative staff with daily operations of vocal arts department. Candidates should have computer skills, oral communication skills, organizational skills, personal interest in the field, self-motivation, strong interpersonal skills, written communication skills. Duration is September to May. $241 per week. Open to college freshmen, college sophomores, college juniors, college seniors, recent college graduates, graduate students, career changers.

Benefits Health insurance, names of contacts, possible full-time employment, willing to complete paperwork for educational credit, willing to provide letters of recommendation.

Contact Write, call, fax, e-mail, or through World Wide Web site Helen Taynton, Intern Director. Phone: 212-799-5000 Ext. 621. Fax: 212-724-0263. E-mail: htaynton@juilliard.edu. In-person interview recommended (telephone interview accepted). Applicants must submit a formal organization application, resume, three letters of recommendation, 250-word statement of expectations of the internship program and how it relates to career goals. Application deadline: June 1. Fees: $15.

LANGLEY AEROSPACE RESEARCH SUMMER SCHOLARS (LARSS)
NASA, Mail Stop 400-LARSS
Hampton, Virginia 23681

General Information Education office that promotes opportunities related to university affairs for students, teachers, and faculty. Division of NASA Langley Research Center, Hampton, Virginia. Number of internship applications received each year: 400.
Internships Available ▶ *125–150 LARSS participants.* Candidates should have computer skills, declared college major in field, knowledge of field, plan to pursue career in field, research skills. Duration is early June to mid-August (40 hours per week). $4500 per duration of internship. Open to rising college juniors, seniors, and graduate students.
Benefits Housing at a cost, on-the-job training, opportunity to attend seminars/workshops, possible full-time employment, willing to act as a professional reference, willing to complete paperwork for educational credit, willing to provide letters of recommendation.
Contact Write, call, fax, e-mail, or through World Wide Web site Heidi Davis, Director, LARSS Program, NASA Mail Stop 400-LARSS, Hampton 23681. Phone: 757-864-5298. Fax: 757-864-9701. E-mail: h.b.davis@larc.nasa.gov. Applicants must submit a formal organization application, letter of interest, resume, academic transcripts, writing sample, two letters of recommendation. Application deadline: February 1. World Wide Web: http://edu.larc.nasa.gov/larss.

LANGUAGE STUDIES ABROAD, INC. (LSA)
1801 Highway 50 East, Suite I
Carson City, Nevada 89701

General Information Company that has established partners in countries outside the U.S.A. to provide opportunities for foreigners to develop an understanding of languages and cultures through education and work experiences. Established in 1985. Number of employees: 4.
Internships Available ▶ *Interns.* Candidates should have ability to work with others, oral communication skills, self-motivation, written communication skills. Unpaid. Open to college freshmen, college sophomores, college juniors, college seniors, recent college graduates, graduate students. International applications accepted.
Benefits Health insurance, housing at a cost, meals at a cost, on-the-job training.
International Internships Available in Vienna, Austria; Paris, France; Berlin, Germany; Florence and Rome, Italy; Cuernavaca and Morelin, Mexico; Madrid, Sevilla, Salamanca, Grenada, and Barcelona, Spain.
Contact Write, call, fax, e-mail, or through World Wide Web site Internship Coordinator. Phone: 800-424-5522. Fax: 775-883-2266. E-mail: info@languagestudiesabroad.com. Applicants must submit a formal organization application. Applications are accepted continuously. Fees: $100. World Wide Web: http://www.languagestudiesabroad.com.

LEARN WELL RESOURCES
3967 Valley Vista
Camino, California 95709

General Information Nonprofit education organization. Established in 1994. Number of employees: 4. Number of internship applications received each year: 3.
Internships Available ▶ *1–2 education program developers:* responsibilities include helping to develop online health and ethics courses. Candidates should have ability to work independently, computer skills, knowledge of field, research skills, self-motivation, writing skills. Duration is 1–2 semesters. Unpaid. Open to graduate students.
Benefits On-the-job training.
Contact Write R. Klimes, President, 3967 Valley Vista, Camino, California 95709. Phone: 530-644-2123. E-mail: edu@learnwell.org. Applicants must submit a formal organization application, resume. Applications are accepted continuously. World Wide Web: http://www.learnwell.org.

LITTLE KESWICK SCHOOL, INC.
Keswick, Virginia 22947

General Information Special education residential school for 30 emotionally disturbed or learning disabled boys ages 10-15. Established in 1963. Number of employees: 35. Number of internship applications received each year: 5.
Internships Available ▶ *1–2 interns:* responsibilities include working as a classroom, recreation, or residential aide. Candidates should have ability to work with others, experience in the field, oral communication skills, personal interest in the field, self-motivation. Duration is 1–2 semesters. Unpaid. Open to college seniors, recent college graduates, graduate students. International applications accepted.
Benefits Formal training, free meals, names of contacts, opportunity to attend seminars/workshops, possible full-time employment, willing to act as a professional reference, willing to complete paperwork for educational credit, willing to provide letters of recommendation.
Contact Write, call, or fax Ms. Terry Columbus, Director, PO Box 24, Keswick, Virginia 22947. Phone: 434-295-0457. Fax: 434-977-1892. E-mail: lks@avenue.org. In-person interview required. Applicants must submit a formal organization application, resume. Applications are accepted continuously. World Wide Web: http://monticello.avenue.org/lks/.

THE LOWELL WHITEMAN SCHOOL
42605 RCR #36
Steamboat Springs, Colorado 80487

General Information College prep boarding and day school for grades 9-12. Established in 1957. Number of employees: 30. Affiliate of National Association of Independent Schools, Washington, District of Columbia. Number of internship applications received each year: 150.
Internships Available ▶ *3–4 interns:* responsibilities include dormitory supervision, activities, and teaching one class. Candidates should have ability to work independently, college degree in related field, oral communication skills, self-motivation, strong interpersonal skills, strong leadership ability. Duration is 2 semesters beginning mid-August. $10,000 per duration of internship. Open to recent college graduates, graduate students. ▶ *4 residential/teaching interns:* responsibilities include assisting dorm parent with residential students and teaching one class. Candidates should have ability to work independently, college degree in related field, oral communication skills, plan to pursue career in field, strong interpersonal skills, strong leadership ability. Duration is August 15-June 1. $10,000 per duration of internship. Open to recent college graduates. International applications accepted.
Benefits Free housing, free meals, health insurance, opportunity to attend seminars/workshops, possible full-time employment, willing to act as a professional reference, willing to complete paperwork for educational credit, willing to provide letters of recommendation.
Contact Write, call, fax, e-mail, or through World Wide Web site Walt Daub, Head of School. Phone: 970-879-1350. Fax: 970-879-0506. E-mail: daubw@whiteman.edu. In-person interview required. Applicants must submit a letter of interest, resume, academic transcripts, three letters of recommendation. Application deadline: May 1. World Wide Web: http://www.whiteman.edu.

MACKINAC CENTER FOR PUBLIC POLICY
140 West Main Street
Midland, Michigan 48640

General Information Nonprofit, non-partisan research and education organization. Established in 1987. Number of employees: 32. Number of internship applications received each year: 75.
Internships Available ▶ *2 Education Reform Leadership Project interns:* responsibilities include assisting with targeted volunteer recruitment and grassroots mobilization efforts to identify and train qualified and interested citizen-leaders to help advance the cause of school choice; providing logistical and administrative support for school choice training seminars and local town hall meetings; assisting with providing liaison support between the Mackinac Center and regional field coordinators and local volunteers;

Mackinac Center for Public Policy (continued)

responding to inquiries from volunteers, education reform and advocates and external constituent groups who seek information about the Education Reform Leadership Project or about school choice in general ; and assisting with maintaining accurate and thorough database of constituents associated with Education Reform Leadership Project; and contributing to developing and maintaining a comprehensive school choice Web site. Candidates should have ability to work independently, ability to work with others, oral communication skills, organizational skills, self-motivation, written communication skills, Web design experience (preferred), marketing and volunteer recruitment skills, and previous customer service experience. Duration is one summer. Paid. Open to high school seniors, college freshmen, college sophomores, college juniors, college seniors, recent college graduates, graduate students, law students. ▶ *3 education research interns:* responsibilities include assisting with the research and writing associated with Michigan Education Report, Michigan Education Digest, education commentaries, and other education-related publications: providing general administrative support to professional education staff including information management and Internet research; assisting staff with preparation of meeting materials, mailings, projects, and events. Candidates should have ability to work with others, computer skills, oral communication skills, organizational skills, personal interest in the field, research skills, writing skills, ability to work in high-performance, fast-paced environment with minimal supervision. Duration is one summer (part-time). Paid. Open to high school seniors, college freshmen, college sophomores, college juniors, college seniors, recent college graduates, graduate students. ▶ *Fiscal policy research interns:* responsibilities include producing two editions of Michigan Privatization Report (MPR), including article selection, assigning of authors, research, writing, and editing, finding or taking photographs for MPR texts, writing "procedure" for producing MPR, general clerical work as needed, identifying and designing creative programs and marketing materials to promote the mission and vision of the Mackinac Center; selling advertisement space in MPR. Candidates should have editing skills, oral communication skills, organizational skills, personal interest in the field, research skills, strong interpersonal skills, writing skills. Duration is one summer (full-time). Paid. Open to college freshmen, college sophomores, college juniors, college seniors, recent college graduates. ▶ *1–2 labor policy research interns:* responsibilities include researching critical emerging employment law issues; educating the public concerning the legal right of workers operating under collective bargaining; working with employees who desire to know or exercise their workplace rights; writing memos and report on assigned labor projects; and assisting in litigation matters as assigned. Candidates should have oral communication skills, organizational skills, research skills, interest in employment law, labor relations, and labor policy issues. Duration is one summer (part-time). Paid. Open to high school students, college freshmen, college sophomores, college juniors, college seniors, recent college graduates, graduate students, law students. International applications accepted.
Benefits Formal training, job counseling, on-the-job training, willing to act as a professional reference, willing to complete paperwork for educational credit, willing to provide letters of recommendation, small stipend.
Contact Write, call, fax, e-mail, or through World Wide Web site Michael D. Lafaive, Intern Coordinator. Phone: 517-631-0900. Fax: 517-631-0964. E-mail: lafaive@mackinac.org. In-person interview recommended (telephone interview accepted). Applicants must submit a letter of interest, resume, two personal references. Application deadline: March 15. World Wide Web: http://www.mackinac.org.

MANHATTAN COUNTRY SCHOOL FARM
Roxbury, New York 12474

General Information Rural Catskill Mountains campus of a New York City independent elementary and junior high school, the Manhattan Country School. Established in 1968. Unit of Manhattan Country School, New York, New York.

Internships Available ▶ *Environmental education interns:* responsibilities include working as member of team of veteran farm educators teaching students from age 8 to 14 in one of main curriculum areas: farming, cooking, textiles, nature study, Catskills studies; intern will also be able to conduct research in area of his or her interest related to farm program; student supervision. Candidates should have interest in teaching children about the environment; valid driver's license. Duration is 1–2 semesters. Monthly stipend. Open to individuals who have completed one or more years of undergraduate study (preferred).
Benefits Free housing, some board provided.
Contact Write, call, or e-mail Ginny Scheer, Farm Director. Phone: 607-326-7049. E-mail: mcsfarm@catskill.net. Applicants must submit a letter of interest, resume. World Wide Web: http://www.manhattancountryschool.org.

MANICE EDUCATION CENTER
68 Savoy Road
Florida, Massachusetts 01247

General Information Environmental/wilderness education program serving economically disadvantaged New York City youth through challenging outdoor adventures. Established in 1897. Number of employees: 15. Unit of Christodora, Inc., New York, New York. Number of internship applications received each year: 25.
Internships Available ▶ *1–3 AmeriCorps Teaching Internships:* responsibilities include work six months in New York City teaching about the environment through hands-on experiences; remaining six months (April-October) will be spent in Massachusetts at the Manice Education Center leading wilderness trips and teaching environmental education to NYC students. Candidates should have ability to work with others, college courses in field, knowledge of field, oral communication skills, strong leadership ability, wilderness camping skills, first aid/CPR; street smarts. Duration is 12 months (November to October). Position available as unpaid or at $160 per week plus educational award. Open to college sophomores, college juniors, college seniors, recent college graduates, graduate students, career changers. ▶ *4 environmental education interns:* responsibilities include teaching ecology, wilderness, and group leadership skills; facilitating environmental debates; leading science labs and cooperative games; and being responsible for the overnight supervision of 6 students, 4 nights per week. Candidates should have knowledge of field, oral communication skills, personal interest in the field, self-motivation, strong interpersonal skills, strong leadership ability. Duration is 2 months in spring or fall. $170–$200 per week. Open to college sophomores, college juniors, college seniors, recent college graduates, graduate students, career changers. ▶ *4 wilderness leadership interns:* responsibilities include co-leading wilderness expeditions; teaching low-impact wilderness travel skills, general ecology, and interpretation; facilitating environmental debates; leading science labs and cooperative games; and supervising students overnight. Candidates should have experience in the field, oral communication skills, personal interest in the field, self-motivation, strong interpersonal skills, strong leadership ability. Duration is June 15 to September 2. $170–$200 per week. Open to college sophomores, college juniors, college seniors, recent college graduates, graduate students. International applications accepted.
Benefits Formal training, free housing, free meals, health insurance, job counseling, names of contacts, on-the-job training, possible full-time employment, willing to act as a professional reference, willing to complete paperwork for educational credit, willing to provide letters of recommendation, job lists provided when available, equipment discounts, wilderness first aid training for summer interns.
Contact Write, fax, e-mail, or through World Wide Web site Ms. Dawn Chávez, Director, One East 53rd Street, 14th floor, New York, New York 10022. Phone: 212-371-5225. Fax: 212-371-2111. E-mail: dawn@christodora.org. In-person interview recommended (telephone interview accepted). Applicants must submit a formal organization application, letter of interest, resume, academic transcripts, two personal references, three letters of recommendation.

Application deadline: February 1 for spring, March 1 for summer, June 1 for fall. World Wide Web: http://www.christodora.org.

MARIST COLLEGE–MARIST INTERNATIONAL PROGRAMS
3399 North Road
Poughkeepsie, New York 12601-1387

General Information Study abroad programs designed to give U.S. undergraduate students the opportunity to participate actively in another culture by combining an internship overseas with coursework at a host institution. Number of internship applications received each year: 100.
Internships Available ▶ *Interns:* responsibilities include working for organization or business as determined by intern's interest. Unpaid. Open to college sophomores, college juniors, college seniors.
Benefits On-the-job training, willing to complete paperwork for educational credit, undergraduate academic credit.
International Internships Available in Sydney, Australia; Dublin, Ireland; Florence, Italy; Madrid, Spain; Leeds, United Kingdom.
Contact Write, call, fax, e-mail, or through World Wide Web site Carol Toufali, Coordinator. Phone: 845-575-3330. Fax: 845-575-3294. E-mail: international@marist.edu. In-person interview required. Applicants must submit a formal organization application, letter of interest, resume, academic transcripts, writing sample, two letters of recommendation. Application deadline: March 15 for fall semester, October 1 for spring semester. Fees: $35. World Wide Web: http://www.marist.edu/international.

MCKEEVER ENVIRONMENTAL LEARNING CENTER
55 McKeever Lane
Sandy Lake, Pennsylvania 16145

General Information Resident environmental education center for grades K-12 that specializes in preservice and in-service teacher education. Established in 1974. Number of employees: 10. Department of Slippery Rock University of Pennsylvania, Slippery Rock, Pennsylvania. Number of internship applications received each year: 15.
Internships Available ▶ *2 co-op interns:* responsibilities include assisting in implementing special programs, supervising student teachers, providing alternate evening coverage, overseeing props and program supplies, providing on-line status with rental group activities, and assisting with office support. Candidates should have ability to work independently, ability to work with others, oral communication skills, organizational skills, strong leadership ability. Duration is 12 months. $8 per hour. Open to recent college graduates. ▶ *1–3 teaching interns:* responsibilities include teaching in the Center's residential environmental education programs. Candidates should have ability to work with others, oral communication skills, organizational skills, desire to work with children in an outdoor setting. Duration is 2 months. $8 per hour. Open to college seniors, recent college graduates. International applications accepted.
Benefits Formal training, free housing, free meals, job counseling, names of contacts, on-the-job training, opportunity to attend seminars/workshops, travel reimbursement, willing to act as a professional reference, willing to provide letters of recommendation.
Contact Write, call, fax, e-mail, or through World Wide Web site Mr. Francis M. Bires, Director. Phone: 724-376-1000. Fax: 724-376-8235. E-mail: info@mckeever.org. In-person interview required. Applicants must submit a formal organization application, letter of interest, resume, academic transcripts, three letters of recommendation. Applications are accepted continuously. World Wide Web: http://www.mckeever.org.

MIDDLE EARTH, INC.
299 Jacksonville Road
Warminster, Pennsylvania 18974

General Information Day treatment center and alternative high school. Established in 1973. Number of employees: 14. Number of internship applications received each year: 12.

Internships Available ▶ *3 criminal justice interns:* responsibilities include conducting informal counseling and working with probation officers. Duration is dependent on university requirements. Unpaid. Open to college sophomores, college juniors, college seniors, recent college graduates, graduate students. ▶ *3 educational interns:* responsibilities include teaching in classroom setting. Duration is flexible. Unpaid. Open to college sophomores, college juniors, college seniors, recent college graduates, graduate students. ▶ *3 psychology interns.* Duration is flexible. Unpaid. Open to college juniors, college seniors, recent college graduates, graduate students. ▶ *3–5 social services interns:* responsibilities include working one-on-one with adolescents. Duration is dependent on university requirements. Unpaid. Open to college sophomores, college juniors, college seniors, recent college graduates, graduate students. Candidates for all positions should have ability to work independently, oral communication skills, organizational skills, personal interest in the field, self-motivation, strong interpersonal skills. International applications accepted.
Benefits Formal training, names of contacts, on-the-job training, opportunity to attend seminars/workshops, possible full-time employment, willing to act as a professional reference, willing to complete paperwork for educational credit, willing to provide letters of recommendation, lunch provided at no cost.
Contact Write, call, or fax Ms. Elizabeth A. Quigley, Director of Educational Programming. Phone: 215-443-0280. Fax: 215-443-0245. In-person interview recommended (telephone interview accepted). Applications are accepted continuously.

MINIWANCA EDUCATION CENTER
8845 West Garfield Road
Shelby, Michigan 49455

General Information Multi-purpose youth center on the shores of Lake Michigan offering retreat, conference, leadership development, team building, and community building services for a variety of populations. Established in 1924. Number of employees: 12. Unit of American Youth Foundation, St. Louis, Missouri. Number of internship applications received each year: 10.
Internships Available ▶ *1–10 program interns:* responsibilities include assisting in program development and implementation for a variety of populations, facilitating ropes courses and other experience-based activities, providing hospitality for retreats and conferences, assisting in support services for all programs, assisting with administration, marketing, public relations, and evaluations of all programs. Candidates should have ability to work independently, ability to work with others, knowledge of field, self-motivation, strong leadership ability, experience working with children; CPR and first aid certification (required); lifeguard training (preferred). Duration is 1–2 semesters. $500 per month. Open to individuals at least 18 years of age. International applications accepted.
Benefits Formal training, free housing, health insurance, job counseling, names of contacts, on-the-job training, opportunity to attend seminars/workshops, willing to complete paperwork for educational credit, willing to provide letters of recommendation, meals (when programs are running).
Contact Write, call, fax, e-mail, or through World Wide Web site Jon Mark Howard, Director Education Services. Phone: 231-861-2262. Fax: 231-861-5244. E-mail: miniwanca.outreach@ayf.com. In-person interview recommended (telephone interview accepted). Applicants must submit a formal organization application, letter of interest, resume, three personal references, letter of recommendation. Applications are accepted continuously. World Wide Web: http://www.ayf.com.

MINNETRISTA CULTURAL CENTER/OAKHURST GARDENS
1200 North Minnetrista Parkway
Muncie, Indiana 47303

General Information Organization that provides lifelong learning experiences for the people of east central Indiana featuring art, history, science and environmental education through

Minnetrista Cultural Center/Oakhurst Gardens (continued)
programs, exhibits, and workshops. Established in 1988. Number of employees: 65. Number of internship applications received each year: 30.

Internships Available ▶ *1 Children's Garden assistant:* responsibilities include maintenance and upkeep of the Children's Garden, developing educational programs and materials, and leading small activities or programs. Candidates should have ability to work independently, ability to work with others, experience in the field, oral communication skills, self-motivation, written communication skills. Duration is minimum of one semester (20 hours per week). Unpaid. Open to college sophomores, college juniors, college seniors, recent college graduates, graduate students, career changers. ▶ *1 assistant archivist (general projects):* responsibilities include arranging and describing archival collections and assisting in reference service and other projects as assigned. Candidates should have ability to work independently, ability to work with others, computer skills, knowledge of field, organizational skills, interest in local history. Duration is minimum of one semester (10 to 20 hours per week). Unpaid. Open to college sophomores, college juniors, college seniors, recent college graduates, graduate students, career changers. ▶ *1–3 collection assistants (specific collections):* responsibilities include researching and cataloging objects; measuring and marking objects; providing a written record of objects prior to storage; overseeing photographing of objects; proper packing and assigning permanent storage location; other duties as assigned. Candidates should have ability to work independently, knowledge of field, self-motivation, ability to lift 30-40 pounds and climb a ladder. Duration is minimum of one semester (30 hours per week). Unpaid. Open to college sophomores, college juniors, college seniors, recent college graduates, graduate students, career changers. ▶ *1 educational resource developer/ assistant:* responsibilities include inventorying cultural artifacts; implementing a system for record keeping and coding using computer resources available; developing educational kits with lesson plans using inventoried items, questionnaire to determine educational kit needs for teachers, and strategy for future kits. Candidates should have ability to work independently, ability to work with others, computer skills, knowledge of field, organizational skills, ability to lift 20-30 pounds. Duration is one semester (minimum of 20 hours per week). Unpaid. Open to college sophomores, college juniors, college seniors, recent college graduates, graduate students, career changers. ▶ *3–5 environmental education assistants:* responsibilities include surveying and research; planning, development, coordination, implementation and documentation of project; leading groups, interacting with visitors, training volunteers, and assisting staff. Candidates should have ability to work independently, oral communication skills, organizational skills, strong interpersonal skills, background in research pertaining to area of study. Duration is minimum one semester or college release time. Open to college sophomores, college juniors, college seniors, recent college graduates, graduate students, career changers. ▶ *2–3 events and promotion assistants (specific events):* responsibilities include development of programs; assisting with planning and promotion; coordination of promotional mailings; making contacts and arrangements; other duties as assigned. Candidates should have ability to work independently, organizational skills, personal interest in the field, strong interpersonal skills, creativity; good marketing background; some event planning experience helpful; average knowledge of Microsoft Office. Duration is varies with event. Unpaid. Open to college sophomores, college juniors, college seniors, recent college graduates, graduate students, career changers. ▶ *1 exhibit design assistant:* responsibilities include assisting in the design of exhibits (working within limitations of space and material); assuring exhibits meet museum standards; and developing a driving tour depending upon subject matter. Candidates should have ability to work independently, ability to work with others, college courses in field, organizational skills, personal interest in the field. Duration is minimum of one semester (10 to 20 hours per week). Unpaid. Open to college sophomores, college juniors, college seniors, recent college graduates, graduate students, career changers. ▶ *Marketing assistants:* responsibilities include developing a marketing plan for a project; providing edited copy, as necessary, to graphics; developing and contacting targeted audience; overseeing and implementing

distribution of pieces; developing measures of effectiveness; preparing and presenting evaluation and summary of project. Candidates should have ability to work independently, ability to work with others, computer skills, declared college major in field, knowledge of field, office skills, oral communication skills, organizational skills, self-motivation, written communication skills. Duration is minimum of one semester (15-40 hours per week). Unpaid. Open to college juniors, college seniors, recent college graduates, graduate students, career changers. ▶ *1 merchandising assistant:* responsibilities include assisting with inventory control, purchasing, displays, sales analysis, and sales during peak periods; analyzing merchandising trends, making projections for future needs; other duties as assigned. Candidates should have ability to work independently, ability to work with others, computer skills, oral communication skills, organizational skills, written communication skills, basic knowledge of retail concepts and merchandising. Duration is minimum one semester (15-20 hours per week). Unpaid. Open to college sophomores, college juniors, college seniors, recent college graduates, graduate students, career changers. ▶ *2 natural resource research assistants:* responsibilities include working with current grid system of plants and animals to update records, monitoring water quality and updating records, working with volunteers to teach data collection, taking photographs for documentation. Candidates should have ability to work independently, ability to work with others, knowledge of field, organizational skills, some experience with a GIS system; knowledge of digital and 35mm cameras necessary. Duration is February to June or June to October (minimum of 10-15 hours per week). Unpaid. Open to college sophomores, college juniors, college seniors, recent college graduates, graduate students, career changers. ▶ *Oral/public historians:* responsibilities include conducting and transcribing tape recorded oral history interviews and providing recordings and written transcripts. Candidates should have ability to work independently, ability to work with others, computer skills, knowledge of field, oral communication skills. Duration is by project, 10-20 hours per interview. Unpaid. Open to college sophomores, college juniors, college seniors, recent college graduates, graduate students, career changers. ▶ *1 professional development program assistant:* responsibilities include schedule making and developing of time lines; event planning, contacting presenters by letter/phone, assisting with development and implementation of the publication of each event, implementation of events, developing and implementing evaluations of event. Candidates should have ability to work independently, ability to work with others, experience in the field, oral communication skills, organizational skills, self-motivation, written communication skills. Duration is minimum of one semester (average of 20 hours per week). Unpaid. Open to college sophomores, college juniors, college seniors, recent college graduates, graduate students, career changers. ▶ *1–3 research analysts/assistants:* responsibilities include marketing research and analysis of information on east central Indiana or a specific area, researching using the library and Internet as well as other appropriate sources, developing a profile of participants in cultural activities and a bench mark as it relates to other cultural institutions, putting all information into a usable format that includes the sources. Candidates should have ability to work independently, ability to work with others, computer skills, knowledge of field, research skills. Duration is one semester (minimum of 20 hours per week). Unpaid. Open to college sophomores, college juniors, college seniors, recent college graduates, graduate students, career changers. ▶ *2–3 research assistants:* responsibilities include assisting with primary documents research on a task-by-task or project-by-project basis; archival and census research; meeting with staff to receive individual assignments; participation in research plan development. Candidates should have ability to work independently, ability to work with others, analytical skills, written communication skills, some archival/ library research experience; attention to detail; experience with primary document research (preferred but not necessary). Duration is dependent on project (minimum 8-10 hours per week). Unpaid. Open to college sophomores, college juniors, college seniors, recent college graduates, graduate students, career changers. International applications accepted.

Benefits Names of contacts, on-the-job training, willing to act as a professional reference, willing to complete paperwork for educational credit, willing to provide letters of recommendation. **Contact** Write, call, fax, e-mail, or through World Wide Web site Judy Rust, Director of Volunteers. Phone: 765-282-4848. Fax: 765-741-5110. E-mail: jrust@mcc.mccoak.org. In-person interview recommended (telephone interview accepted). Applicants must submit a formal organization application, letter of interest, resume, portfolio. Applications are accepted continuously. World Wide Web: http://www.mccoak.org.

MISS PORTER'S SCHOOL
60 Main Street
Farmington, Connecticut 06032

General Information Independent boarding and day school for girls grades 9-12. Established in 1843. Number of employees: 120. Number of internship applications received each year: 100.
Internships Available ▶ *3–4 teaching interns:* responsibilities include teaching 1-2 sections within discipline, acting as Assistant House Director, and coaching or advising the equivalent of two seasons of activity. Candidates should have ability to work independently, ability to work with others, college courses in field, computer skills, oral communication skills, strong interest in working with adolescents. Duration is 2 semesters. $14,000 per internship. Open to recent college graduates, graduate students. International applications accepted.
Benefits Free housing, free meals, health insurance, job counseling, names of contacts, on-the-job training, opportunity to attend seminars/workshops, possible full-time employment, travel reimbursement, willing to act as a professional reference, willing to complete paperwork for educational credit, willing to provide letters of recommendation, mentorship by teacher.
Contact Write, call, fax, e-mail, or through World Wide Web site Alan P. Sherman, Director, New Teacher Program. Phone: 860-409-3500. Fax: 860-409-3515. E-mail: alan_sherman@missporters. org. In-person interview required. Applicants must submit a letter of interest, resume, academic transcripts, two letters of recommendation. Applications are accepted continuously. World Wide Web: http://www.missporters.org.

MOUNTAIN LAKE BIOLOGICAL STATION, UNIVERSITY OF VIRGINIA
238 Gilmer Hall, PO Box 400327
Charlottesville, Virginia 22904-4327

General Information Academic center for teaching and research in field biology. Established in 1929. Number of employees: 6. Academic Research Center/Institute of University of Virginia, Charlottesville, Virginia. Number of internship applications received each year: 150.
Internships Available ▶ *10 REU interns:* responsibilities include supervised independent research. Candidates should have ability to work independently, ability to work with others, analytical skills, college courses in field, computer skills, oral communication skills, personal interest in the field, plan to pursue career in field, self-motivation, writing skills. Duration is June 1 to August 15. $3100 scholarship. Open to college freshmen, college sophomores, college juniors, must be U.S. citizen.
Benefits Free housing, free meals, names of contacts, opportunity to attend seminars/workshops, possible full-time employment, travel reimbursement, tuition assistance, willing to act as a professional reference, willing to complete paperwork for educational credit, willing to provide letters of recommendation.
Contact Write, call, fax, e-mail, or through World Wide Web site Eric Nagy, REU Coordinator, Gilmer Hall Room 238, Charlottesville, Virginia 22904-4327. Phone: 434-982-5486. Fax: 434-982-5626. E-mail: mtlake@virginia.edu. Applicants must submit a formal organization application, academic transcripts, letter of recommendation, essay. Application deadline: March 1. World Wide Web: http://www.virginia.edu/~mtlake.

NAFSA
1307 New York Avenue, NW, 8th Floor
Washington, District of Columbia 20005

General Information Nonprofit membership association that provides training, information, and other educational services to professionals in the field of international educational exchange. Established in 1963. Number of employees: 50. Number of internship applications received each year: 50.
Internships Available ▶ *Interns:* responsibilities include working on a specific project in areas including publications, conference, membership, accounting, human resources, special programs, public policy and press relations. Duration is flexible. Position available as unpaid or paid. Open to college freshmen, college sophomores, college juniors, college seniors, recent college graduates, graduate students, law students, career changers, individuals reentering the workforce. International applications accepted.
Benefits On-the-job training, willing to act as a professional reference.
Contact Write, fax, or e-mail Jill Erbland, Executive Assistant. Fax: 202-737-3657. E-mail: internship@nafsa.org. Applicants must submit a letter of interest, resume. Applications are accepted continuously. World Wide Web: http://www.nafsa.org.

NATIONAL 4-H CENTER
7100 Connecticut Avenue
Chevy Chase, Maryland 20815

General Information Conference center that teaches political awareness and the history of Washington, D.C. Established in 1951. Number of employees: 180. Number of internship applications received each year: 120.
Internships Available ▶ *2–6 fall program assistants for WOW:* responsibilities include participation in 3 to 4 week training period; leading workshops and assemblies; escorting groups; working with a wide range of youth; learning routes; field trip logistics; learning political awareness workshops. Candidates should have ability to work independently, office skills, oral communication skills, organizational skills, research skills, self-motivation, strong interpersonal skills, strong leadership ability, writing skills. Duration is 11–20 weeks. $250–$300 per week. Open to high school seniors, recent high school graduates, college freshmen, college sophomores, college juniors, college seniors, recent college graduates, 18 through 26 year olds. ▶ *4–8 spring program assistants for WOW:* responsibilities include participation in 3 to 4 week training period; learning to teach workshops on political awareness; coordinating field trip logistics; learning routes; leading workshops and assemblies; office work. Candidates should have ability to work independently, computer skills, office skills, oral communication skills, organizational skills, research skills, self-motivation, strong interpersonal skills, strong leadership ability, writing skills. Duration is 17–21 weeks. $250–$300 per week. Open to high school seniors, recent high school graduates, college freshmen, college sophomores, college juniors, college seniors, recent college graduates, 18 through 26 year olds. ▶ *9–15 summer program assistants for CWF:* responsibilities include participation in 3 to 4 week training period; leading workshops and assemblies; escorting groups; working with high school youth; learning routes; field trip logistics; learning political awareness workshops. Candidates should have ability to work independently, office skills, oral communication skills, organizational skills, research skills, self-motivation, strong interpersonal skills, strong leadership ability, writing skills. Duration is 13–17 weeks. $250–$300 per week. Open to high school seniors, recent high school graduates, college freshmen, college sophomores, college juniors, college seniors, recent college graduates, 18 through 26 year olds. ▶ *2–5 summer program assistants for WOW:* responsibilities include participation in 3 to 4 week training period; learning workshops and assemblies; escorting groups; working with a wide range of youth; learning routes; field trip logistics; learning political awareness workshops. Candidates should have ability to work independently, office skills, oral communication skills, organizational skills, research skills, self-motivation, strong interpersonal skills, strong leadership ability, writing skills. Duration is 13–17 weeks. $250–$300 per week. Open to high school students, recent high school graduates, college freshmen,

college sophomores, college juniors, college seniors, recent college graduates, 18 through 26 year olds. International applications accepted.
Benefits Free housing, free meals, opportunity to attend seminars/workshops, willing to provide letters of recommendation.
Contact Write, call, fax, e-mail, or through World Wide Web site Joel Ann Hawthorne, Sales Director. Phone: 301-961-2801. Fax: 301-961-2922. E-mail: jhawthorne@fourhcouncil.edu. Telephone interview required. Applicants must submit a resume, two writing samples, three letters of recommendation, application package available online. Application deadline: January 15 for summer, June 1 for fall, November 1 for spring. World Wide Web: http://www.n4h.org.

NATIONAL COALITION OF ALTERNATIVE COMMUNITY SCHOOLS TEACHER EDUCATION PROGRAM
Upattinas Resource Center, 429 Greenridge Road
Glenmoore, Pennsylvania 19343

General Information Coalition that offers internships in alternative education in grades K-12, public and private, with the possibility of international placement. Established in 1993. Number of employees: 1. Affiliate of National Coalition of Alternative Community Schools (NCACS), Ann Arbor, Michigan. Number of internship applications received each year: 12.
Internships Available ▶ *10 alternative/experiential teaching interns:* responsibilities include teaching at a member school. Candidates should have ability to work independently, oral communication skills, personal interest in the field, self-motivation, strong interpersonal skills. Duration is 1 year. Position available as unpaid or paid. Open to college seniors, recent college graduates, graduate students, career changers, individuals reentering the workforce. International applications accepted.
Benefits Formal training, job counseling, names of contacts, on-the-job training, opportunity to attend seminars/workshops, possible full-time employment, tuition assistance, willing to act as a professional reference, willing to complete paperwork for educational credit, willing to provide letters of recommendation, some housing (depending on placement).
International Internships Available in Yokohama, Japan.
Contact Write, call, fax, e-mail, or through World Wide Web site Ms. Sandra M. Hurst, Director of Teacher Education Program, Upattinas Resource Center, 429 Greenridge Road, Glenmore, Pennsylvania 19343. Phone: 610-458-5138. Fax: 610-458-8688. E-mail: sandy@upattinas.org. In-person interview recommended (telephone interview accepted). Applicants must submit a formal organization application, letter of interest, resume, academic transcripts, personal reference, $3000 fee for tuition upon acceptance. Applications are accepted continuously. Fees: $25. World Wide Web: http://www.ncacs.org.

NATIONAL SOCIETY FOR EXPERIENTIAL EDUCATION
9001 Braddock Road, Suite 380
Springfield, Virginia 22151

General Information Nonprofit education association and resource center that supports colleges and universities, high schools, community agencies, and businesses by helping students learn through meaningful work and service experiences. Established in 1971. Number of employees: 4.
Internships Available ▶ *1 publications intern:* responsibilities include assisting with writing and editing publications and publications order fulfillment. Candidates should have ability to work independently, ability to work with others, computer skills, organizational skills, self-motivation, writing skills. Duration is flexible. Position available as unpaid or paid. ▶ *1 special projects intern:* responsibilities include assisting in a wide variety of duties including logistics for meetings and training institute, fund-raising, and membership services. Candidates should have ability to work independently, ability to work with others, oral communication skills, organizational skills, self-motivation, written communication skills. Duration is flexible. Position available as unpaid or

paid. Open to college freshmen, college sophomores, college juniors, college seniors, recent college graduates, graduate students. International applications accepted.
Benefits Job counseling, names of contacts, willing to complete paperwork for educational credit, willing to provide letters of recommendation, possible membership, publications, stipend.
Contact Write, fax, e-mail, or through World Wide Web site Dennis Boyd, Interim Executive Director. Fax: 703-426-8400. E-mail: info@nsee.org. No phone calls. In-person interview recommended (telephone interview accepted). Applicants must submit a letter of interest, resume, writing sample. Applications are accepted continuously. World Wide Web: http://www.nsee.org.

NEW CANAAN COUNTRY SCHOOL
PO Box 997
New Canaan, Connecticut 06840

General Information Independent elementary school enrolling 575 students in grades pre-K through 9. Established in 1936. Number of employees: 120. Number of internship applications received each year: 200.
Internships Available ▶ *16–18 teaching fellowships:* responsibilities include assisting in all areas of program in a self-contained K-6 homeroom. Candidates should have oral communication skills, personal interest in the field, self-motivation, strong interpersonal skills, written communication skills. Duration is September to June. $16,000 taxable stipend. Open to college seniors, recent college graduates, graduate students, career changers. International applications accepted.
Benefits Formal training, health insurance, housing at a cost, job counseling, names of contacts, opportunity to attend seminars/workshops, possible full-time employment, tuition assistance, willing to provide letters of recommendation.
Contact Write or call Ms. Dana Mallozzi, Fellowship Coordinator. Phone: 203-972-0771. Fax: 203-966-5924. E-mail: dmallozzi@countryschool.net. In-person interview required. Applicants must submit a letter of interest, resume, academic transcripts, three letters of recommendation. Application deadline: April 1. World Wide Web: http://www.nccs.pvt.k12.ct.us.

NEW CANAAN NATURE CENTER
144 Oenoke Ridge
New Canaan, Connecticut 06840

General Information Environmental education center and sanctuary dedicated to helping people of all ages understand, appreciate, and care for the natural world. Established in 1960. Number of employees: 30. Number of internship applications received each year: 150.
Internships Available ▶ *2–3 fall and school year teachers/naturalists:* responsibilities include planning and presenting natural science programs for pre-kindergarten through middle school students, teaching selected public programs, and assisting with animal care. Candidates should have ability to work independently, ability to work with others, knowledge of field, oral communication skills. Duration is 9 months (Labor Day to Memorial Day). $275 per week. Open to recent college graduates, graduate students, career changers, individuals reentering the workforce. ▶ *1–2 spring teachers/naturalists:* responsibilities include planning and presenting natural science programs for pre-kindergarten through middle school students, teaching selected public programs, and assisting with animal care. Candidates should have ability to work independently, ability to work with others, knowledge of field, oral communication skills. Duration is 5 months (January 1-Memorial Day). $275 per week. Open to recent college graduates, graduate students, career changers, individuals reentering the workforce. ▶ *1–15 summer teachers/naturalists:* responsibilities include planning and team-teaching diverse programs that include the study of natural science, nature crafts, sensory awareness, and general environmental education in day camp setting with groups of up to 14 children (pre-K through 4th grade). Candidates should have ability to work independently, ability to work with others, knowledge of field, oral communication skills, personal interest in the field. Duration is 11 weeks. $250 per week. Open to college freshmen, college sophomores, college juniors, college seniors,

recent college graduates, graduate students, career changers, individuals reentering the workforce. International applications accepted.

Benefits Formal training, free housing, job counseling, on-the-job training, opportunity to attend seminars/workshops, possible full-time employment, willing to act as a professional reference, willing to complete paperwork for educational credit, willing to provide letters of recommendation.

Contact Write, fax, or e-mail Ms. Ann Kozlowicz, Director of School Programs. Phone: 203-966-9577 Ext. 38. Fax: 203-966-6536. E-mail: akozlowicz@newcanaannature.org. In-person interview recommended (telephone interview accepted). Applicants must submit a letter of interest, resume, three personal references. Application deadline: January 1 for spring, April 1 for summer, July 1 for fall and school year. World Wide Web: http://www.newcanaannature.org.

NEWFOUND HARBOR MARINE INSTITUTE
1300 Big Pine Avenue
Big Pine Key, Florida 33043

General Information Nonprofit residential education center offering programs in marine environmental education to groups seeking to increase their understanding of the ocean and natural ecosystems. Established in 1965. Number of employees: 80. Number of internship applications received each year: 70.

Internships Available ▶ *10–18 science interns:* responsibilities include teaching, dorm duty, dining hall management, housekeeping, and daily interaction with children. Candidates should have ability to work with others, declared college major in field, oral communication skills, plan to pursue career in field, strong leadership ability. Duration is 3–5 months. $50 per week. Open to college sophomores, college juniors, college seniors, recent college graduates, graduate students, career changers. International applications accepted.

Benefits Formal training, free housing, free meals, job counseling, names of contacts, opportunity to attend seminars/workshops, possible full-time employment, willing to act as a professional reference, willing to complete paperwork for educational credit, willing to provide letters of recommendation.

Contact Write, call, fax, or e-mail Assistant Science Program Director. Phone: 305-872-2331. Fax: 305-872-2555. E-mail: info@nhmi.org. Telephone interview required. Applicants must submit a formal organization application, letter of interest, resume, academic transcripts, three letters of recommendation. Application deadline: April 30 for summer, July 1 for fall, October 15 for spring. World Wide Web: http://www.nhmi.org.

19TH DISTRICT INTERNSHIP ASSOCIATION
PO Box 2731
York, Pennsylvania 17405

General Information Non-political, non-partisan community involvement, good government initiative whose mission is to provide financial sponsorship for college students from the 19th Congressional District to work in the Washington office of the District Congressman each summer. Established in 1977. Number of internship applications received each year: 30.

Internships Available ▶ *6 summer internships:* responsibilities include participating in the routine and not-so-routine duties of the congressional office; students are also given an opportunity to observe government in action and are treated as employees, not student interns. Candidates should have ability to work independently, ability to work with others, analytical skills, computer skills, editing skills, office skills, oral communication skills, organizational skills, research skills, self-motivation, strong leadership ability, writing skills. Duration is 12 weeks from mid-May through mid-August (6 weeks in Washington; 6 weeks in local DTST office). Paid. Open to undergraduate students 18 to 22 years of age, who are legal residents of the 19th Congressional District of Pennsylvania; can attend any college or university.

Benefits Free housing, on-the-job training, opportunity to attend seminars/workshops, possible full-time employment, willing to act as a professional reference, willing to provide letters of recom-

mendation, $200 weekly stipend for basic expenses, free shuttle service to and from Union Station (within walking distance of Congressman's office).

Contact Through World Wide Web site Internship Coordinator. In-person interview recommended (telephone interview accepted). Applicants must submit a formal organization application, in-person interview for semi-finalists. Application deadline: February 15 for summer. World Wide Web: http://www.house.gov/platts.

NORTHFIELD MOUNT HERMON SCHOOL
206 Main Street
Northfield, Massachusetts 01360-1089

General Information Private co-educational boarding school with 1100 students in 9th grade through the post-graduate level. Established in 1879. Number of employees: 500. Number of internship applications received each year: 250.

Internships Available ▶ *6–8 First-Year Teacher Program interns:* responsibilities include working closely with master teacher during fall term; full responsibility for classes during winter and spring terms; coaching two seasons; living in dormitory apartments; serving as advisor to 6-8 students. Duration is September to June. $22,000 per year. ▶ *1–3 administrative interns:* responsibilities include working closely with administrator in a specific program; teaching courses where appropriate; living in dormitory apartments; advising group of 6-8 students; coaching athletic teams if appropriate. Duration is September to June. $16,000 per year. Candidates for all positions should have college degree in related field, oral communication skills, strong interpersonal skills, written communication skills, competitive athletics experience. Open to college seniors, recent college graduates, graduate students. International applications accepted.

Benefits Formal training, free housing, free meals, health insurance, job counseling, names of contacts, on-the-job training, opportunity to attend seminars/workshops, possible full-time employment, willing to act as a professional reference, willing to provide letters of recommendation, life insurance.

Contact Write, call, fax, e-mail, or through World Wide Web site Office of Faculty Recruitment. Phone: 413-498-3410. Fax: 413-498-3054. E-mail: faculty_recruitment@nmhschool.org. In-person interview recommended (telephone interview accepted). Applicants must submit a letter of interest, resume, academic transcripts, two letters of recommendation. Applications are accepted continuously. World Wide Web: http://www.nmhschool.org.

NORTHFIELD MOUNT HERMON SUMMER SESSION
206 Main Street
Northfield, Massachusetts 01360

General Information Summer coeducational boarding school with a curriculum focusing on enrichment for junior and senior high school students; students come from all over the U.S. and the world. Established in 1961. Number of employees: 110. Number of internship applications received each year: 250.

Internships Available ▶ *35–40 teaching interns:* responsibilities include assistant teaching, leading a sport and workshop, assisting with dorm supervision. Candidates should have ability to work independently, college courses in field, organizational skills, personal interest in the field, self-motivation, strong interpersonal skills. Duration is 6 weeks. $2000 per duration of internship. Open to college juniors, college seniors, recent college graduates, graduate students. International applications accepted.

Benefits Formal training, free housing, free meals, job counseling, names of contacts, possible full-time employment, willing to complete paperwork for educational credit, willing to provide letters of recommendation.

Contact Write, call, fax, e-mail, or through World Wide Web site Pamela Lester, Assistant. Phone: 413-498-3290. Fax: 413-498-3112. E-mail: summer_school@nmhschool.org. Applicants must submit a formal organization application, letter of interest, resume, academic transcripts, two letters of recommendation, either in-person or telephone interview. Application deadline: February 1 for summer. World Wide Web: http://www.nmh.northfield.ma.us/summer/.

THE OUTDOORS WISCONSIN LEADERSHIP SCHOOL (OWLS)
350 Constance Boulevard
Williams Bay, Wisconsin 53191-0210

General Information   Leading provider of adventure education in the Midwest focusing on leadership, communication, creativity, risk-taking, trust-building, and problem solving. Unit of Aurora University, Lake Geneva Campus, Williams Bay, Wisconsin.
Internships Available   ▶ *Interns.* Candidates should have some course work in related areas and experience working with people. Paid. Open to college seniors, recent college graduates.
Benefits   Free housing, free meals, supplemental health insurance.
Contact   Write or e-mail Cathy Coster. Phone: 262-245-5531 Ext. 8544. Fax: 262-245-8549. E-mail: owls@idcnet.com. Applicants must submit a letter of interest, resume, names of 3 references. Applications are accepted continuously. World Wide Web: http://www.augeowms.org/owls.html.

PACIFIC AND ASIAN AFFAIRS COUNCIL (PAAC)
1601 East-West Road, 4th Floor
Honolulu, Hawaii 96848

General Information   Nonprofit organization that has been providing global education for over 47 years; member of the World Affairs Council of America and has organized forums featuring speakers including the Dalai Lama and Bob Dole. Established in 1954. Number of employees: 4. Number of internship applications received each year: 15.
Internships Available   ▶ *1–2 assistant program coordinators:* responsibilities include helping to plan educational programs and doing basic office duties. Candidates should have computer skills, office skills, organizational skills, research skills, self-motivation, writing skills. Duration is flexible. Unpaid. Open to college freshmen, college sophomores, college juniors, college seniors, recent college graduates, graduate students, law students, career changers. International applications accepted.
Benefits   Names of contacts, on-the-job training, opportunity to attend seminars/workshops, possible full-time employment, willing to act as a professional reference, willing to complete paperwork for educational credit, willing to provide letters of recommendation.
Contact   Write, call, fax, or e-mail Lisa Maruyama, Executive Director, 1601 East-West Road, 4th Floor, Honolulu, Hawaii 96848. Phone: 808-944-7780. Fax: 808-944-7785. E-mail: paac@aloha.net. In-person interview recommended (telephone interview accepted). Applicants must submit a letter of interest, resume. Applications are accepted continuously. World Wide Web: http://www.aloha.net/~paac.

PARK SCHOOL
171 Goddard Avenue
Brookline, Massachusetts 02445

General Information   Independent day school of more than 500 students from nursery through 9th grade. Established in 1888. Number of employees: 100. Number of internship applications received each year: 150.
Internships Available   ▶ *8–10 teaching interns:* responsibilities include teaching full-time with a mentor teacher in 2 different classroom placements during the year and learning to handle all aspects of teaching, coaching, and play directing. Candidates should have knowledge of field, oral communication skills, personal interest in the field, self-motivation, strong interpersonal skills, written communication skills. Duration is academic year (9 months). $15,000 per internship plus additional pay for coaching, drama, and after school program help. Open to recent college graduates, graduate students, career changers. International applications accepted.
Benefits   Formal training, health insurance, job counseling, names of contacts, on-the-job training, opportunity to attend seminars/workshops, tuition assistance, willing to act as a professional reference, willing to complete paperwork for educational credit, willing to provide letters of recommendation, free lunches.

Contact   Write, fax, or e-mail Linda Knight, Director of Interns. Fax: 617-277-2456. E-mail: linda_knight@parkschool.org. Applicants must submit a letter of interest, resume, academic transcripts, three letters of recommendation, in-person interview (held February to May). Applications are accepted continuously. World Wide Web: http://www.parkschool.org.

PEAK PERFORMANCE
PO Box 1867
Big Bear Lake, California 92315-1867

General Information   Company that designs and delivers experiential adventure learning for businesses, schools, churches, and families. Established in 1994. Number of employees: 25. Number of internship applications received each year: 50.
Internships Available   ▶ *1 marketing intern:* responsibilities include market research, writing copy and releases, maintaining database, conducting presentations, planning special events, and assisting with program delivery. Candidates should have computer skills, oral communication skills, personal interest in the field, research skills, self-motivation, writing skills. Duration is 2–6 months. $50–$100 per week. Open to recent college graduates, graduate students, law students, career changers, individuals reentering the workforce. ▶ *1–4 program specialists:* responsibilities include designing and delivering adventure education programs to varied audiences. Candidates should have ability to work with others, oral communication skills, personal interest in the field, self-motivation, strong leadership ability. Duration is 3–8 months. Position available as unpaid or at $50 per week. Open to college juniors, college seniors, recent college graduates, graduate students, career changers, individuals reentering the workforce. International applications accepted.
Benefits   Formal training, free housing, free meals, job counseling, on-the-job training, opportunity to attend seminars/workshops, possible full-time employment, willing to act as a professional reference, willing to complete paperwork for educational credit, willing to provide letters of recommendation, discounts on equipment.
Contact   Write, fax, e-mail, or through World Wide Web site Mark H. Rowland, President. Fax: 909-866-9004. E-mail: info@peaktraining.com. No phone calls. Telephone interview required. Applicants must submit a letter of interest, resume, three personal references. Applications are accepted continuously. World Wide Web: http://www.peaktraining.com.

THE PHILADELPHIA CENTER
121 South Broad Street, 7th Floor
Philadelphia, Pennsylvania 19107

General Information   Off-campus experiential education program comprised of a full-time internship with opportunities in all disciplines, academic seminars, and independent living. Established in 1967. Number of employees: 10. Affiliate of Great Lakes College Association, Inc., Ann Arbor, Michigan. Number of internship applications received each year: 250.
Internships Available   ▶ *180–200 interns:* responsibilities include working in numerous fields including communications, business, education, law, government, psychology, social service, science and the arts. Duration is 1 semester. Unpaid. Open to college freshmen, college sophomores, college juniors, college seniors, recent college graduates, graduate students. International applications accepted.
Benefits   Formal training, job counseling, names of contacts, on-the-job training, opportunity to attend seminars/workshops, willing to act as a professional reference, willing to complete paperwork for educational credit, willing to provide letters of recommendation, college credit, more than 700 placements from which to choose, program student advisors act as career and academic counselors, networking possibilities.
Contact   Write, call, fax, e-mail, or through World Wide Web site Ilene Baker, Information Manager. Phone: 215-735-7300. Fax: 215-735-7373. E-mail: admin@philactr.edu. Applicants must submit a formal organization application, resume, academic transcripts, two letters of recommendation, proof of eligibility for off-campus study (determined by applicant's school), $8000 tuition cost upon acceptance. Applications are accepted continuously. World Wide Web: http://www.philactr.edu.

PHILLIPS ACADEMY
180 Main Street
Andover, Massachusetts 01810-4161

General Information   Private secondary boarding and day preparatory school. Established in 1778. Number of employees: 550. Number of internship applications received each year: 300.
Internships Available   ▶ *10–12 fellowships:* responsibilities include teaching two sections of a departmental offering, acting as house counselor in dormitory, and participating in athletics. Candidates should have ability to work independently, college courses in field, knowledge of field, oral communication skills, plan to pursue career in field, self-motivation, strong interpersonal skills, strong leadership ability, written communication skills. Duration is September to June. $17,500 per year. Open to college seniors, recent college graduates, graduate students, career changers. ▶ *20 teaching assistants:* responsibilities include assisting the teaching of two courses, running a dormitory, coaching an afternoon activity, chaperoning, and facilitating nearly every facet of boarding school life. Candidates should have ability to work independently, ability to work with others, oral communication skills, plan to pursue career in field, self-motivation, strong leadership ability, writing skills, interest in working with adolescents. Duration is June 21 to August 2. $2400 per duration of internship. Open to recent college graduates, graduate students. ▶ *12–14 teaching assistants (math and science for minority students):* responsibilities include assisting with teaching minority students two courses in mathematics, biology, chemistry, physics, or English; college counseling; running help sessions or study halls; and occasional chaperoning of on- and off-campus activities. Candidates should have declared college major in field, oral communication skills, strong interpersonal skills, written communication skills, interest in working with minority adolescents. Duration is late June to early August. $2400 per duration of internship. Open to college seniors, recent college graduates, graduate students. ▶ *1 teaching fellowship in community service:* responsibilities include serving as assistant director of the community service program, managing various aspects of the program, mentoring, student coordinators, meeting with agency contacts, transporting student volunteers, and participating on the faculty advisory board. Candidates should have ability to work independently, ability to work with others, knowledge of field, oral communication skills, personal interest in the field, plan to pursue career in field, self-motivation, strong leadership ability, written communication skills. Duration is September to June. $17,500 per year. Open to college seniors, recent college graduates, graduate students, career changers, those who have one-year work in service learning environment (preferred). International applications accepted.
Benefits   Free housing, free meals, health insurance, job counseling, names of contacts, on-the-job training, opportunity to attend seminars/workshops, willing to act as a professional reference, willing to provide letters of recommendation, life insurance, dental insurance.
Contact   Write, call, or e-mail Stephen D. Carter, Dean of Faculty. Phone: 978-749-4003. E-mail: ldiamondis@andover.edu. In-person interview required. Applicants must submit a formal organization application, letter of interest, resume, academic transcripts, writing sample, personal reference, two letters of recommendation. Application deadline: February 1 for fellowships (September start), February 15 for teaching assistants (June start). World Wide Web: http://www.andover.edu.

PRESIDENTIAL CLASSROOM
119 Oronoco Street
Alexandria, Virginia 22314-2015

General Information   Nonprofit, nonpartisan educational organization that brings high school students to Washington, D.C. for 1-week experiential government programs. Established in 1968. Number of employees: 15. Number of internship applications received each year: 200.
Internships Available   ▶ *12 program interns:* responsibilities include providing administrative, logistical, and academic support. Candidates should have ability to work independently, oral communication skills, organizational skills, strong interpersonal skills, strong leadership ability. Duration is 6 weeks in summer; 10 weeks in winter.

Unpaid. Open to college sophomores, college juniors, college seniors, recent college graduates, graduate students. International applications accepted.
Benefits   Formal training, free housing, free meals, job counseling, names of contacts, opportunity to attend seminars/workshops, possible full-time employment, willing to act as a professional reference, willing to complete paperwork for educational credit, willing to provide letters of recommendation, small stipend.
Contact   Write, call, fax, e-mail, or through World Wide Web site Lou Digioia, Program Manager. Phone: 800-441-6533. Fax: 703-548-5728. E-mail: intern@presidentialclassroom.org. Telephone interview required. Applicants must submit a formal organization application, two letters of recommendation. Applications are accepted continuously. World Wide Web: http://www. presidentialclassroom.org.

PROJECT USE, URBAN SUBURBAN ENVIRONMENTS
PO Box 837, 76 East Front Street
Red Bank, New Jersey 07701-0837

General Information   Year-round experiential educational center for children and adults from all backgrounds offering one-to-21 day programs for schools, state agencies, service corps, youth groups, and the general public; activities include initiative games, high ropes courses, backpacking, canoeing, kayaking, rock climbing, and environmental education. Established in 1970. Number of employees: 15. Number of internship applications received each year: 3.
Internships Available   ▶ *1–3 field instructors:* responsibilities include preparing for, conducting, and concluding safe wilderness experiences for all courses. Candidates should have ability to work independently, oral communication skills, personal interest in the field, research skills, self-motivation, strong interpersonal skills, written communication skills, love of outdoors and related activities. Duration is 3 months. $100–$150 per week. Open to high school seniors, recent high school graduates, college freshmen, college sophomores, college juniors, college seniors, recent college graduates, graduate students, law students, career changers, individuals reentering the workforce, must be 18 years old. International applications accepted.
Benefits   Formal training, free housing, free meals, names of contacts, opportunity to attend seminars/workshops, possible full-time employment, willing to act as a professional reference, willing to complete paperwork for educational credit, willing to provide letters of recommendation.
Contact   Write, call, fax, e-mail, or through World Wide Web site Nancy Medrow, Program Director. Phone: 732-219-7300. Fax: 732-219-7305. E-mail: projectuse@monmouth.com. In-person interview recommended (telephone interview accepted). Applicants must submit a formal organization application, two personal references. Applications are accepted continuously. World Wide Web: http://www.projectuse.com.

PUBLIC BROADCASTING SERVICE (PBS)
1320 Braddock Place
Alexandria, Virginia 22314

General Information   Nonprofit media, television, and online education corporation. Established in 1969. Number of employees: 500. Number of internship applications received each year: 200.
Internships Available   ▶ *10–15 interns:* responsibilities include working in various departments including accounting, broadcast operations, human resources, information technology, Web site development/editing, program operations, and communications. Duration is 6–12 weeks. $6 per hour. Open to college freshmen, college sophomores, college juniors, college seniors, recent college graduates, graduate students, law students. International applications accepted.
Benefits   On-the-job training, possible full-time employment, willing to complete paperwork for educational credit, willing to provide letters of recommendation.
Contact   Write, fax, or e-mail Internship Program. Fax: 703-739-8689. E-mail: jobs@pbs.org. No phone calls. In-person interview recommended (telephone interview accepted). Applicants must

Public Broadcasting Service (PBS) (continued)

submit a letter of interest, resume. Applications are accepted continuously. World Wide Web: http://www.pbs.org.

PUBLIC LEADERSHIP EDUCATION NETWORK (PLEN)
1001 Connecticut Avenue, NW, Suite 900
Washington, District of Columbia 20036-5507

General Information   National consortium of women's and other colleges that runs public policy programs and places students as interns in organizations working with public policy. Established in 1978. Number of employees: 3. Number of internship applications received each year: 30.
Internships Available   ▶ *12–20 women and public policy interns:* responsibilities include performing various duties, including research, writing reports, and attending hearings. Candidates should have knowledge of field, office skills, oral communication skills, organizational skills, personal interest in the field, research skills, written communication skills. Duration is 1 semester. Position available as unpaid or paid. Open to college freshmen, college sophomores, college juniors, college seniors, recent college graduates, graduate students. International applications accepted.
Benefits   Formal training, job counseling, names of contacts, on-the-job training, opportunity to attend seminars/workshops, willing to act as a professional reference, willing to complete paperwork for educational credit, willing to provide letters of recommendation, opportunity to attend classes focusing on women and public policy, assistance in locating housing.
International Internships   Available in London, United Kingdom.
Contact   Write, call, fax, or e-mail Liz Swanson, Executive Director, 1001 Connecticut Avenue, NW, Suite 900, Washington, District of Columbia 20036-5607. Phone: 202-872-1585. Fax: 202-457-0549. E-mail: plen@plen.org. In-person interview recommended (telephone interview accepted). Applicants must submit a formal organization application, letter of interest, resume, writing sample, letter of recommendation. Application deadline: February 16 for summer, July 15 for fall, November 5 for spring. Fees: $45. World Wide Web: http://www.plen.org.

QUEST–UNIVERSITY FRIENDS MEETING
4001 9th Avenue NE
Seattle, Washington 98105

General Information   Social service/social justice internship program for young adults. Established in 1992. Number of employees: 6. Number of internship applications received each year: 30.
Internships Available   ▶ *6 quest interns:* responsibilities include entry-level positions in social service, social justice, peace and environmental organizations. Candidates should have ability to work independently, ability to work with others, computer skills, oral communication skills, research skills, writing skills. Duration is September 1 to August 31. $100 per month living allowance; $525 exit stipend; $4700 AmeriCorps Education Award. Open to college seniors, recent college graduates, graduate students, young adults age 21-30. International applications accepted.
Benefits   Free housing, free meals, health insurance, on-the-job training, opportunity to attend seminars/workshops, tuition assistance, willing to provide letters of recommendation.
Contact   Write, call, e-mail, or through World Wide Web site Carolyn Stevens, Program Coordinator. Phone: 206-324-8963. E-mail: zenquake@ix.netcom.com. In-person interview recommended (telephone interview accepted). Applicants must submit a formal organization application, resume, two letters of recommendation. Application deadline: March 1 for fall. World Wide Web: http://www.scn.org/spiritual/friends/quest.html.

RESEARCH EXPERIENCE FOR UNDERGRADUATES, BOSTON UNIVERSITY
College of Engineering, 44 Cummington Street, Room 107
Boston, Massachusetts 02215

General Information   Summer research program for undergraduate students; funded by the National Science Foundation, the Boston University Undergraduate Research Opportunities Program, the Biomedical Engineering Department and the College of Engineering. Unit of Boston University, Boston, Massachusetts. Number of internship applications received each year: 300.
Internships Available   ▶ *Summer research undergraduates:* responsibilities include working on a research project with a faculty member; see Web site for list of possible projects. Candidates should have minimum 3.3 GPA (preferred); must have research goals and interests. Duration is June to August. Stipend. Open to upcoming undergraduate juniors and seniors; must be U.S. citizen or permanent resident.
Benefits   Free housing, limited travel subsidies.
Contact   Write, call, fax, e-mail, or through World Wide Web site Internship Coordinator, 44 Cummington Street, Room 107, Boston 02215. Phone: 617-353-6447. Fax: 617-353-7285. E-mail: reu@bu.edu. Online application. Application deadline: March. World Wide Web: http://www.bu.edu/eng/ugrad/programs.html.

RIVER BEND NATURE CENTER
PO Box 186
Faribault, Minnesota 55021

General Information   Provider of environmental and natural education programs to schools and the community. Established in 1980. Number of employees: 8. Number of internship applications received each year: 50.
Internships Available   ▶ *2–4 naturalist interns:* responsibilities include providing natural history programs to the public and children; writing press releases, curriculum, and newsletters; and assisting with land management and maintenance practices. Candidates should have ability to work independently, oral communication skills, plan to pursue career in field, self-motivation, strong interpersonal skills, written communication skills. Duration is seasonal. $140 per week. Open to college juniors, college seniors, recent college graduates, graduate students, career changers. ▶ *4 summer program naturalists:* responsibilities include developing and teaching programs for youth environmental day camps; designing and completing individual project; teaching weekend programs for all ages; assisting with facility management, displays, and publications. Candidates should have oral communication skills, plan to pursue career in field, self-motivation, strong interpersonal skills, strong leadership ability. Duration is 12 weeks. $170 per week. Open to college juniors, college seniors, recent college graduates, graduate students, career changers, individuals reentering the workforce.
Benefits   Formal training, free housing, job counseling, names of contacts, on-the-job training, opportunity to attend seminars/workshops, willing to act as a professional reference, willing to complete paperwork for educational credit, willing to provide letters of recommendation, professional development fund.
Contact   Write, e-mail, or through World Wide Web site John Blackmer, Chief Naturalist. E-mail: blackmer@rbnc.org. No phone calls. In-person interview recommended (telephone interview accepted). Applicants must submit a letter of interest, resume, three personal references, application packet (must be requested). Application deadline: February 15 for summer, May 8 for school-year positions. World Wide Web: http://www.rbnc.org.

ROGERS ENVIRONMENTAL EDUCATION CENTER
2721 State Highway 80
Sherburne, New York 13460

General Information   Group of environmental education centers dedicated to teaching the public about natural resources, environmental issues, natural history, and ecological principles. Established in 1967. Number of employees: 6. Unit of New York State Department of Environmental Conservation, Albany, New York. Number of internship applications received each year: 50.
Internships Available   ▶ *15–20 naturalist interns:* responsibilities include teaching groups, writing articles, and working on special projects. Candidates should have ability to work with others, college courses in field, oral communication skills, personal interest in the field, self-motivation, written communication skills. Duration is 10–12 weeks. $200 per week. Open to college sophomores,

college juniors, college seniors, recent college graduates, graduate students, career changers, individuals reentering the workforce. International applications accepted.

Benefits Formal training, free housing, job counseling, names of contacts, on-the-job training, opportunity to attend seminars/workshops, willing to act as a professional reference, willing to complete paperwork for educational credit, willing to provide letters of recommendation.

Contact Write, call, fax, e-mail, or in person Mr. Fred von Mechow, Environmental Educator II. Phone: 607-674-4017. Fax: 607-674-2655. E-mail: rogers@gw.dec.state.ny.us. In-person interview recommended (telephone interview accepted). Applicants must submit a formal organization application, resume, three personal references. Application deadline: February 15 for summer, May 1 for fall, August 1 for winter, December 1 for spring. World Wide Web: http://www.ascent.net/rogers/.

ST. PAUL'S SCHOOL
325 Pleasant Street
Concord, New Hampshire 03301-2591

General Information Coeducational boarding school offering year-round college preparatory programs. Established in 1856. Number of employees: 200. Number of internship applications received each year: 150.

Internships Available ▶ *30–35 Advanced Studies Program interns:* responsibilities include offering classroom assistance and dormitory supervision and supervising recreational activities. Candidates should have college courses in field, oral communication skills, personal interest in the field, self-motivation, strong interpersonal skills. Duration is 6 weeks in summer. $2000 per duration of internship plus up to $200 in qualifying travel expenses. Open to college juniors, college seniors, recent college graduates. ▶ *2–4 teaching fellows:* responsibilities include teaching, coaching, and supervising students in dormitories. Candidates should have college courses in field, knowledge of field, oral communication skills, self-motivation, strong interpersonal skills. Duration is 9 months. $15,000 per duration of internship. Open to college seniors, recent college graduates. International applications accepted.

Benefits Formal training, free housing, free meals, job counseling, names of contacts, on-the-job training, opportunity to attend seminars/workshops, possible full-time employment, willing to act as a professional reference, willing to provide letters of recommendation, health insurance for academic year interns.

Contact Write, call, fax, e-mail, or through World Wide Web site Mr. Thomas P. Bazos, Director, Apprentice Teaching Programs. Phone: 603-229-4777. Fax: 603-229-4767. E-mail: asp@sps.edu. In-person interview required. Applicants must submit a formal organization application, resume, academic transcripts, three letters of recommendation, 2-page personal statement. Application deadline: January 20 for application resume, personal statement, February 1 for academic transcripts, recommendations. World Wide Web: http://www.sps.edu.

SCHUYLKILL CENTER FOR ENVIRONMENTAL EDUCATION
8480 Hagy's Mill Road
Philadelphia, Pennsylvania 19128-1998

General Information Environmental education facility presenting programming for kindergarten through graduate school with a yearly audience of 80,000. Established in 1965. Number of employees: 16. Number of internship applications received each year: 28.

Internships Available ▶ *2 education interns:* responsibilities include teaching daily class, assisting education staff, and working on projects. Candidates should have ability to work independently, college courses in field, plan to pursue career in field, self-motivation, writing skills, previous experience working with children; natural history background (preferred). Duration is 4–16 weeks. Position available as unpaid or paid. Open to recent high school graduates, college freshmen, college sophomores, college juniors, college seniors, recent college graduates, graduate students, career changers, individuals reentering the workforce. ▶ *2–4 forest restoration ecologists:* responsibilities include accumulating base-

line data for Piedmont Forest restoration; includes some physical labor. Candidates should have ability to work independently, ability to work with others, analytical skills, experience in the field, plan to pursue career in field, research skills. Duration is flexible. Unpaid. Open to college sophomores, college juniors, college seniors, graduate students. International applications accepted.

Benefits Formal training, names of contacts, on-the-job training, opportunity to attend seminars/workshops, willing to complete paperwork for educational credit, willing to provide letters of recommendation.

Contact Write, call, fax, or e-mail Kathy Bright, Director of Education. Phone: 215-482-7300 Ext. 124. Fax: 215-482-8158. E-mail: kbright@schuylkillcenter.org. In-person interview recommended (telephone interview accepted). Applicants must submit a formal organization application, letter of interest, resume, personal reference, letter of recommendation. Applications are accepted continuously. World Wide Web: http://www.schuylkillcenter.org.

SPANISH EDUCATION DEVELOPMENT CENTER
1840 Kalorama Road, NW
Washington, District of Columbia 20009

General Information Hispanic nonprofit organization that offers educational programs for children and adults. Established in 1971. Number of employees: 25.

Internships Available ▶ *20–40 English as a second language teachers:* responsibilities include leading a small group by implementing teacher's lesson plans, observing and learning selected ESL techniques from the teacher, and working with individual students who have been absent or who need extra assistance. Candidates should have ability to work independently, ability to work with others, oral communication skills, self-motivation. Duration is 12 weeks (7:00-9:00 pm Monday through Thursday, or 11:00 am-2:00 pm, Saturday and Sunday. Unpaid. Open to college freshmen, college sophomores, college juniors, college seniors, recent college graduates, graduate students, law students. ▶ *8–10 after school teacher aides (Silver Spring, Maryland):* responsibilities include conducting small group activities with children. Candidates should have ability to work independently, ability to work with others, oral communication skills, self-motivation. Duration is flexible (3:00 pm-6:30 pm, Monday to Friday). Unpaid. Open to high school students, recent high school graduates, college freshmen, college sophomores, college juniors, college seniors, recent college graduates, graduate students, law students. ▶ *10–20 preschool teacher assistants:* responsibilities include helping classroom teacher supervise children; preparing educational materials; interacting with children through stories, games, teaching, and songs; working with children in small group activities designed either by the teacher or the assistant. Candidates should have ability to work independently, ability to work with others, oral communication skills, self-motivation. Duration is flexible (7:00 am-6:00 pm, Monday to Friday). Unpaid. Open to high school students, recent high school graduates, college freshmen, college sophomores, college juniors, college seniors, recent college graduates, graduate students. ▶ *2–5 proposal writing interns:* responsibilities include performing foundation research and proposal writing. Candidates should have computer skills, editing skills, research skills, writing skills. Duration is flexible. Unpaid. Open to college freshmen, college sophomores, college juniors, college seniors, recent college graduates, individuals reentering the workforce. ▶ *6–10 special project assistants:* responsibilities include conducting foundation research, public relations, fund-raising, and material and curriculum development. Candidates should have computer skills, editing skills, research skills, writing skills. Duration is flexible. Unpaid. Open to college freshmen, college sophomores, college juniors, college seniors, recent college graduates, graduate students, individuals reentering the workforce. International applications accepted.

Benefits Formal training, willing to complete paperwork for educational credit, willing to provide letters of recommendation.

Contact Write, call, fax, or e-mail Ms. Doris Ruano, Director, Volunteer Program. Phone: 202-462-8848. Fax: 202-462-6886. E-mail: dorisruano@sedcenter.com. In-person interview recommended (telephone interview accepted). Applicants must submit a resume. Applications are accepted continuously.

SPONSORS FOR EDUCATIONAL OPPORTUNITY (SEO) CAREER PROGRAM
23 Gramercy Park South
New York, New York 10003

General Information Nonprofit organization that provides training, orientation, and summer internships to undergraduate students of color in the areas of accounting, asset management, corporate law, investment banking, management consulting, information technology, media, and philanthropy. Established in 1963. Unit of Sponsors for Educational Opportunity, New York, New York. Number of internship applications received each year: 2,000.

Internships Available ▶ *4–6 San Francisco Investment Banking Program interns.* Candidates should have ability to work independently, ability to work with others, analytical skills, computer skills, knowledge of field, prior financial services experience (preferred). Duration is minimum 10 weeks in summer. Competitive salary. Open to college juniors. ▶ *10–15 accounting interns:* responsibilities include working as full member of auditing teams on client engagements; or working in either internal audit division, the comptroller's office, or on the staff of the chief financial officer at a major investment banking firm. Candidates should have ability to work independently, ability to work with others, analytical skills, college courses in field, computer skills, knowledge of field. Duration is minimum 10 weeks in summer. Competitive salary. Open to college juniors. ▶ *15–20 asset management interns:* responsibilities include working as research assistants to one or more portfolio managers, and in marketing to identify potential clients. Candidates should have ability to work independently, ability to work with others, analytical skills, computer skills, knowledge of field, coursework in economics and finance desirable. Duration is minimum 10 weeks in summer. Competitive salary. Open to college juniors; exceptional sophomores may be considered; seniors who will have one semester to complete at the time of the internship may be considered. ▶ *30–35 corporate law interns:* responsibilities include document indexing, distributions, citation checking and document review, working side- by-side with established attorneys on significant assignments that range from closing of major corporate transactions to pro bono projects. Candidates should have ability to work independently, ability to work with others, analytical skills, oral communication skills, plan to pursue career in field, written communication skills. Duration is minimum 10 weeks in summer. Competitive salary. Open to graduating seniors who plan to attend law school in the fall; exceptional juniors may be considered. ▶ *10–20 information technology interns:* responsibilities include developing, testing, maintaining, installing, and/or deploying third party proprietary technologies. Candidates should have analytical skills, computer skills, research skills, self-motivation, coursework in computer science, engineering, and other quantitative subjects. Duration is minimum 10 weeks in summer. Competitive salary. Open to college freshmen, college sophomores, college juniors. ▶ *125–150 investment banking interns:* responsibilities include working in finance, research, or sales and trading at major investment firm; performing tasks similar to those of full-time analysts. Candidates should have ability to work independently, ability to work with others, analytical skills, computer skills, knowledge of field, coursework in economics and finance desirable. Duration is minimum 10 weeks in summer. Competitive salary. Open to college juniors; exceptional freshmen and sophomores may be considered; seniors who will have one semester to complete at the time of the internship may be considered. ▶ *10–20 management consulting interns:* responsibilities include research for presentations, data analysis, "number crunching" and preparation of presentation documents; interfacing with clients and travel to client offices to conduct on-site analyses. Candidates should have ability to work independently, ability to work with others, analytical skills, knowledge of field, oral communication skills, written communication skills. Duration is minimum 10 weeks in summer. Competitive salary. Open to college juniors; seniors who will have one semester to complete

at the time of the internship may be considered. ▶ *3–6 media interns:* responsibilities include assisting editors on major stories, working with online publication, selling ad space, and analyzing data for strategic marketing plans. Candidates should have ability to work with others, oral communication skills, self-motivation, written communication skills, comfort with financial/business modeling in Excel. Duration is minimum 10 weeks in summer. Competitive salary. Open to college sophomores, college juniors. ▶ *10 philanthropy interns:* responsibilities include site visits, budget preparation, program evaluation, and report writing. Candidates should have oral communication skills, research skills, written communication skills, demonstrated commitment to the nonprofit field. Duration is minimum 10 weeks in summer. Competitive salary. Open to college sophomores, college juniors, college seniors. International applications accepted.

Benefits Formal training, housing at a cost, job counseling, names of contacts, on-the-job training, opportunity to attend seminars/workshops, possible full-time employment, willing to complete paperwork for educational credit.

International Internships Available in Hong Kong, China; London, United Kingdom.

Contact Write, call, e-mail, or through World Wide Web site Career Program. Phone: 212-979-2040. E-mail: careerprogram@seo-ny.org. In-person interview required. Applicants must submit a formal organization application, resume, academic transcripts, writing sample, two letters of recommendation. Application deadline: January 15 for early action deadline, February 15 for final deadline. World Wide Web: http://www.seo-ny.org.

SUMMER AT HAWTHORNE VALLEY FARM CAMP
327 CR 21C
Ghent, New York 12075

General Information Farm and nature camp experience for children aged 9-15 on a commercial biodynamic dairy farm. Established in 1972. Number of employees: 25. Unit of Hawthorne Valley Association, Inc., Ghent, New York. Number of internship applications received each year: 30.

Internships Available ▶ *12–15 summer camp counselors:* responsibilities include working with children in an outdoor nature camp/farm setting in a variety of relevant activities. Candidates should have oral communication skills, personal interest in the field, self-motivation, strong interpersonal skills, strong leadership ability. Duration is end of June to mid-August (8 weeks). $1500 for pre-teen camp program counselors; $1700 for teen camp program counselors. Open to recent high school graduates, college freshmen, college sophomores, college juniors, college seniors, career changers, applicants over 21 years preferred; younger applicants must be mature and experienced with children.

Benefits Formal training, free housing, free meals, job counseling, on-the-job training, opportunity to attend seminars/workshops, willing to act as a professional reference, willing to complete paperwork for educational credit, willing to provide letters of recommendation.

International Internships Available.

Contact Write, call, fax, e-mail, or through World Wide Web site Ruth Bruns, Executive Director. Phone: 518-672-4790. Fax: 518-672-7608. E-mail: vsp@taconic.net. In-person interview recommended (telephone interview accepted). Applicants must submit a formal organization application, letter of interest, resume, references with observations of applicant with children. Application deadline: June 1 for summer camp counselors (hiring begins January and is usually completed by April 15).

SUMMERBRIDGE NATIONAL
361 Oak Street
San Francisco, California 94102

General Information Education program that provides free academic enrichment to 5th-9th graders and teaching, mentorship, and tutoring opportunities to high school and college students. Established in 1991. Number of employees: 14. Number of internship applications received each year: 1,300.

Internships Available ▶ *100–160 master teachers:* responsibilities include mentoring young high school and college teacher interns, supporting lesson planning, providing resources, and monitoring teachers. Candidates should have ability to work with others, oral communication skills, organizational skills, strong leadership ability, written communication skills. Duration is mid-June to August. $500–$1500 per duration of internship. Open to recent college graduates, graduate students, experienced middle school educators. ▶ *500–800 school-year tutors:* responsibilities include providing one-to-one mentoring, teaching, and tutoring to children. Candidates should have ability to work with others, oral communication skills, organizational skills, self-motivation, strong leadership ability, writing skills. Duration is September through May. Position available as unpaid or at $500–$2500 per duration of internship. Open to high school students, college freshmen, college sophomores, college juniors, college seniors, recent college graduates, graduate students. ▶ *800–900 summer teachers:* responsibilities include planning daily lessons, planning and overseeing special events, and acting as mentors. Candidates should have ability to work with others, oral communication skills, organizational skills, self-motivation, strong leadership ability, writing skills. Duration is 2–3 months. Position available as unpaid or at $500-$2000 per internship; stipend enhancement may be possible upon request. Open to high school students, recent high school graduates, college freshmen, college sophomores, college juniors, college seniors, recent college graduates. International applications accepted.

Benefits Formal training, on-the-job training, opportunity to attend seminars/workshops, possible full-time employment, tuition assistance, willing to act as a professional reference, willing to complete paperwork for educational credit, willing to provide letters of recommendation, room and board for out-of-town interns may be available.

International Internships Available in Hong Kong.

Contact Write, call, e-mail, or through World Wide Web site Melissa Jones, Admissions and Assessment Manager. Phone: 415-865-2970 Ext. 102. E-mail: admissions@summerbridge.org. Telephone interview required. Applicants must submit a formal organization application, resume, academic transcripts, general application via Web site. Application deadline: April 10 for summer teachers; continuous for all other positions. World Wide Web: http://www.summerbridge.org.

SUMMER STUDY AT PENN STATE
University Park, Pennsylvania 16802

General Information Pre-collegiate academic summer program. Established in 1991. Number of employees: 83. Unit of Summer Study Programs, Melville, New York. Number of internship applications received each year: 250.

Internships Available ▶ *40–50 staff advisors/enrichment instructors:* responsibilities include teaching one or two enrichment classes per day; organizing and supervising afternoon activities; chaperoning nightly events; residing in dedicated residence halls and chaperoning weekend excursions. Candidates should have ability to work independently, ability to work with others, college courses in field, oral communication skills, organizational skills, plan to pursue career in field, self-motivation, strong leadership ability, interest in teaching high school students. Duration is June 23-August 3 or July 1-July 25. Paid. Open to college juniors, college seniors, recent college graduates, graduate students, law students, individuals reentering the workforce. ▶ *3–5 staff advisors/ office support staff members:* responsibilities include completing office rotations involving performing administrative tasks, scheduling and confirming activities, planning and coordinating special events and chaperoning afternoon, evening, and weekend events. Candidates should have ability to work independently, ability to work with others, computer skills, office skills, oral communication skills, organizational skills, self-motivation, strong leadership ability, writing skills. Duration is June 23-August 3 or July 1-July 25. Paid. Open to college juniors, college seniors, recent college graduates, graduate students, law students, career changers, individuals reentering the workforce. ▶ *10–12 staff advisors/sports clinic instructors:* responsibilities include instructing a sports clinic; organizing and supervising afternoon and evening activities; residing in dedicated residence hall, and chaperoning weekend excursions. Candidates should have ability to work independently, ability to work with others, knowledge of field, oral communica-

tion skills, organizational skills, personal interest in the field, self-motivation, strong leadership ability, athletic ability. Duration is June 23-August 3 or July 1-July 25. Paid. Open to college juniors, college seniors, recent college graduates, graduate students, law students, individuals reentering the workforce.

Benefits Free housing, free meals, willing to act as a professional reference, willing to complete paperwork for educational credit, willing to provide letters of recommendation, ability to develop and instruct courses.

Contact Call or e-mail Lina Yacovelli, Director of Personnel, 900 Walt Whitman Road, Melville, New York 11747. Phone: 631-424-1000. Fax: 631-424-0567. E-mail: lyacovelli@summerstudy.com. In-person interview required. Applicants must submit a formal organization application, resume, academic transcripts, three personal references. Application deadline: April 15. World Wide Web: http://www.summerstudy.com.

SUNY CORTLAND CAREER SERVICES/INTERNSHIP OFFICE
State University of New York
Cortland, New York 13045

General Information 4-year liberal arts college. Established in 1868. Number of employees: 1,000. Unit of State University of New York at Albany, Albany, New York. Number of internship applications received each year: 5.

Internships Available ▶ *1 career services intern:* responsibilities include learning all areas of career service, including counseling, career exploration, event planning and implementation, information/library management, experiential education, recruitment, and job search skills; and interacting with all levels of administration and students. Candidates should have office skills, oral communication skills, organizational skills, personal interest in the field, strong interpersonal skills, writing skills. Duration is flexible. Unpaid. Open to graduate students, career changers. International applications accepted.

Benefits Formal training, job counseling, names of contacts, opportunity to attend seminars/workshops, willing to complete paperwork for educational credit, willing to provide letters of recommendation, housing at reduced rate possible in summer.

Contact Write, fax, or e-mail Mr. John Shirley, Assistant Director. Fax: 607-753-2937. E-mail: johns@em.cortland.edu. No phone calls. In-person interview recommended (telephone interview accepted). Applicants must submit a letter of interest, resume. Applications are accepted continuously. World Wide Web: http://www.cortland.edu/www/career/.

TEACH FOR AMERICA
315 West 36th Street, 6th Floor
New York, New York 10018

General Information National teachers corps. Established in 1989. Unit of Americorps, Washington, District of Columbia. Number of internship applications received each year: 100.

Internships Available ▶ *42 operations coordinators:* responsibilities include implementing and maintaining operational systems at a participating school site, developing and maintaining administrative office systems, staffing school materials rooms at the host university, securing pro bono donations from the local community to support the summer institute program, and assisting with the set-up and take-down of university resources and office systems. Candidates should have ability to work independently, analytical skills, computer skills, editing skills, office skills, oral communication skills, organizational skills, research skills, self-motivation, strong interpersonal skills, strong leadership ability, writing skills, responsibility, achievement, sense of perspective, efficiency. Duration is mid-June to early August. $2500 per duration of internship. Open to college freshmen, college sophomores, college juniors, college seniors, recent college graduates. International applications accepted.

Benefits Free housing, free meals, on-the-job training, travel reimbursement, willing to act as a professional reference, willing to complete paperwork for educational credit, willing to provide letters of recommendation.

Teach for America (continued)

Contact Director of Institute Support. Applicants must submit a formal organization application, letter of interest, resume, personal reference, letter of intent. Application deadline: February 1 for summer. World Wide Web: http://www.teachforamerica.org.

TOUCH OF NATURE ENVIRONMENTAL CENTER
Southern Illinois University, Mailcode 6888
Carbondale, Illinois 62901-6888

General Information Year-round educational, recreational, and service facility specializing in outdoor education, therapeutic recreation, environmental and experiential education, and conference services; supports academic and public service mission of the University. Established in 1949. Number of employees: 80. Unit of Southern Illinois University Carbondale, Carbondale, Illinois. Number of internship applications received each year: 20.

Internships Available ▶ *2–5 Environmental Ed-Ventures apprentices and interns:* responsibilities include lending logistical support to programs; program support to senior staff; co-facilitating environmental activities with groups of all ages in outdoor settings; co-leading travel expeditions with ecological and environmental focus; facilitating evening programs. Candidates should have knowledge of field, oral communication skills, personal interest in the field, strong interpersonal skills, strong leadership ability, flexibility. Duration is 1 month. $250–$1000 per month. Open to college juniors, college seniors, recent college graduates, graduate students, career changers. ▶ *1 Underway Outdoor Program intern:* responsibilities include assisting in field and in the office. Candidates should have ability to work independently, ability to work with others, knowledge of field, organizational skills, self-motivation, writing skills. Duration is May to August. Position available as unpaid or at $500–$800 per month. Open to college freshmen, college sophomores, college juniors, college seniors, recent college graduates, graduate students, individuals reentering the workforce. ▶ *6–12 spectrum interns:* responsibilities include assisting lead and assistant instructors in providing outdoor therapeutic programs for youth at risk. Candidates should have knowledge of field, oral communication skills, plan to pursue career in field, strong interpersonal skills, strong leadership ability, written communication skills. Duration is 3–6 months. $250–$1000 per month. Open to high school students, recent high school graduates, college freshmen, college sophomores, college juniors, college seniors, recent college graduates, graduate students, law students, career changers, individuals reentering the workforce. ▶ *1–5 therapeutic recreation/fieldwork interns:* responsibilities include observing and participating in various facets of Camp operations including camper intake and placement, staff training, camper care and supervision, program planning and presentation, evaluations and reviews; meeting regularly with director to address specific educational requirements. Candidates should have ability to work independently, knowledge of field, personal interest in the field, strong interpersonal skills, strong leadership ability, some coursework and experience in the field is desirable. Duration is May 30 to August 10. $365–$600 per month. Open to college freshmen, college sophomores, college juniors, college seniors, recent college graduates, graduate students. International applications accepted.

Benefits Free housing, on-the-job training, possible full-time employment, willing to complete paperwork for educational credit, willing to provide letters of recommendation, meals during program operation.

Contact Write, call, fax, e-mail, or through World Wide Web site Internship Coordinator. Phone: 618-453-1121. Fax: 618-453-1188. E-mail: tonec@siu.edu. In-person interview recommended (telephone interview accepted). Applicants must submit a formal organization application, letter of interest, resume, three personal references. Applications are accepted continuously. World Wide Web: http://www.pso.siu.edu/tonec.

UNIVERSITY OF CINCINNATI COLLEGE OF MEDICINE
231 Albert Sabin Way, ML 0552
Cincinnati, Ohio 45267-0552

General Information College of medicine. Established in 1819. Number of employees: 3,000. Division of University of Cincinnati, Cincinnati, Ohio. Number of internship applications received each year: 150.

Internships Available ▶ *17 Summer Premedical Enrichment Program (SPEP) interns:* responsibilities include full-time participation in all program events, classes, and activities. Candidates should have college courses in field, plan to pursue career in field, self-motivation, demonstrated interest in career in medicine. Duration is 6 weeks. $1000 per duration of internship. ▶ *4 Summer Research Scholars (SRS):* responsibilities include functioning as full participating member of biomedical research team, preparation and presentation of research results at research symposium at end of program. Candidates should have ability to work independently, ability to work with others, analytical skills, college courses in field, personal interest in the field, research skills. Duration is 8 weeks. $2000 per duration of internship. Open to college sophomores, college juniors, college seniors, recent college graduates, graduate students.

Benefits Free housing, job counseling, on-the-job training, opportunity to attend seminars/workshops, travel reimbursement, willing to act as a professional reference, willing to complete paperwork for educational credit, willing to provide letters of recommendation, stipend; some free meals, other meals at cost.

Contact Write, call, fax, e-mail, or through World Wide Web site Roberta Handwerger, M.A., Director, Recruitment Programs. Phone: 513-558-0693. Fax: 513-558-1165. E-mail: roberta.handwerger@uc.edu. Applicants must submit a formal organization application, letter of interest, academic transcripts, two letters of recommendation, written personal statement regarding motivation for participating in Summer Program. Application deadline: March 1 for priority deadline, April 15 for final deadline. World Wide Web: http://www.med.uc.edu.

UNIVERSITY OF CONNECTICUT SCHOOLS OF MEDICINE, DENTAL MEDICINE, AND GRADUATE SCHOOL
263 Farmington Avenue
Farmington, Connecticut 06030-1905

General Information Medical, dental, and graduate schools. Established in 1968. Number of employees: 4,000. Branch of University of Connecticut, Storrs, Connecticut. Number of internship applications received each year: 150.

Internships Available ▶ *20–30 summer research fellows:* responsibilities include a research enrichment experience and some exposure to clinical medicine or dental medicine; faculty develop and make available suitable project descriptions from which interns may select a research opportunity; intern will meet with faculty sponsor and develop research protocol; 30+ hours per week working on project with faculty sponsor and/or designates; 8-10 hours per week for clinical experientials and enrichments. Candidates should have ability to work independently, ability to work with others, plan to pursue career in field, research skills, self-motivation, completion of some college biology and chemistry (preferably through organic chemistry); previous lab experience is desirable. Duration is June to August (10 weeks). $2500–$3000 per duration of internship. ▶ *6 summer research interns:* responsibilities include a research enrichment experience; a faculty sponsor will be identified for each intern; faculty develop and make available suitable project descriptions; interns will spend 30+ hours per week on project working with faculty sponsor and/or designates; lab positions available in: cell, developmental, molecular, and oral biology, immunology, biochemistry, neuroscience and cellular and molecular pharmacology. Candidates should have ability to work independently, ability to work with others, plan to pursue career in field, research skills, self-motivation, completion of some college biology and chemistry; previous lab experience desirable. Duration is June to August (10 weeks). $3000 per duration of internship. Open to college sophomores, college juniors.

Benefits Job counseling, on-the-job training, willing to complete paperwork for educational credit, willing to provide letters of recommendation.

Contact Write, call, e-mail, or through World Wide Web site Robin Walsh, Director of Student Activities. Phone: 860-679-3971. Fax: 860-679-1282. E-mail: rwalsh@nso1.uchc.edu. In-person interview recommended (telephone interview accepted). Applicants must submit a formal organization application, academic transcripts, writing sample, two letters of recommendation. Application deadline: February 1 for undergraduate summer research internships, April 1 for college summer research fellowships. Fees: $25.

UNIVERSITY OF GEORGIA, MARINE EDUCATION CENTER AND AQUARIUM
30 Ocean Science Circle
Savannah, Georgia 31411

General Information Marine education center and aquarium that emphasizes teaching about the coastal environment. Established in 1970. Number of employees: 19. Unit of University of Georgia, Athens, Georgia. Number of internship applications received each year: 60.

Internships Available ▶ *3–4 marine education interns:* responsibilities include teaching a wide variety of marine-related topics to K-12 students and adults at location on Skidaway Island, Georgia; completing an education project. Candidates should have oral communication skills, personal interest in the field, plan to pursue career in field, self-motivation, strong interpersonal skills, recent college degree in science or science education (completed before start of internship). Duration is 50 weeks. $249 per week. Open to recent college graduates, college seniors who will graduate before start of internship. International applications accepted.

Benefits Formal training, free housing, job counseling, names of contacts, on-the-job training, opportunity to attend seminars/workshops, willing to provide letters of recommendation, some meals provided.

Contact Write, call, fax, e-mail, or through World Wide Web site Dr. Willis B. Hayes, Associate Director for Education, Marine Extension Service. Phone: 912-598-2496. Fax: 912-598-2302. E-mail: hayes@uga.edu. Telephone interview required. Applicants must submit a letter of interest, resume, academic transcripts, three letters of recommendation. Application deadline: April 15 for fall. World Wide Web: http://www.uga.edu/aquarium.

UNIVERSITY OF MICHIGAN, SCHOOL OF PUBLIC HEALTH, POPULATION FELLOWS PROGRAMS
1214 South University, 2nd Floor
Ann Arbor, Michigan 48104-2548

General Information Programs offering internships and fellowships in population, family planning, reproductive health, and population-environment. Established in 1984. Number of employees: 20. Number of internship applications received each year: 300.

Internships Available ▶ *4 HBCU/HSI/TCU graduate interns:* responsibilities include applied internship in international population or population-environment and additional professional development as appropriate. Candidates should have analytical skills, knowledge of field, organizational skills, personal interest in the field, plan to pursue career in field. Duration is 3–6 months. Stipend. Open to individuals with graduate degrees from historically black colleges or universities, Hispanic-serving institutions, or tribal colleges and universities. ▶ *20 HBCU/HSI/TCU undergraduate interns:* responsibilities include entry-level, professional work in international population and population-environment. Candidates should have analytical skills, oral communication skills, organizational skills, personal interest in the field, strong interpersonal skills, written communication skills. Duration is 12 weeks. Professional stipend for duration of internship. Open to juniors and seniors from historically black colleges and universities, Hispanic-serving institutions, or tribal colleges and universities. ▶ *15 population fellows:* responsibilities include population, family planning, and reproductive health programming, including program design, implementation, administration, and evaluation. Candidates should have college degree in related field, experience in the field,

personal interest in the field. Duration is 2 years. Yearly stipend. Open to U.S. citizens or permanent residents with graduate degree in population-related area. ▶ *20–30 population graduate internship funding opportunities:* responsibilities include positions in international population, family planning, and reproductive health or population-environment which are unpaid or require significant additional support (candidate must have identified or secured full-time internship). Candidates should have personal interest in the field, plan to pursue career in field. Duration is 2–4 months. Taxable stipend up to $5000 (overseas internship) or $3000 (U.S.-based internship). Open to U.S. citizens or permanent residents in the first year of graduate program in relevant area. ▶ *5 population-environment fellows:* responsibilities include design, implementation, and evaluation of programs that link population, family planning, and reproductive health service delivery with environmental programming. Candidates should have college degree in related field, knowledge of field, personal interest in the field. Duration is 2 years. Yearly stipend. Open to U.S. citizens or permanent residents with graduate degree and expertise in population/environment fields.

Benefits Health insurance, names of contacts, on-the-job training, opportunity to attend seminars/workshops, travel reimbursement, willing to act as a professional reference, willing to provide letters of recommendation, housing assistance.

International Internships Available.

Contact Write, call, fax, e-mail, or through World Wide Web site Population Fellows Programs. Phone: 734-763-9456. Fax: 734-647-0643. E-mail: pop.fellows@umich.edu. In-person interview recommended (telephone interview accepted). Applicants must submit a formal organization application, letter of interest, resume, academic transcripts, writing sample, three letters of recommendation. Application deadline: February 1 for undergraduate positions, April 1 for fall fellows and HBCU/HSI/TCU graduate interns, April 2 for population graduate internship funding positions, November 1 for spring fellows and HBCU/HSI/TCU graduate interns. World Wide Web: http://www.sph.umich.edu/pfps.

U.S. ENVIRONMENTAL PROTECTION AGENCY, OFFICE OF ENVIRONMENTAL EDUCATION, NNEMS FELLOWSHIP PROGRAM
1200 Pennsylvania Avenue, NW (1704A)
Washington, District of Columbia 20460

General Information The NNEMS Fellowship Program offers undergraduate and graduate students research opportunities nationwide. Established in 1987. Division of Environmental Protection Agency, Washington, District of Columbia. Number of internship applications received each year: 350.

Internships Available ▶ *70–80 national network for environmental management studies fellowship positions:* responsibilities include research in the areas of environmental policy, regulation, and law; environmental management and administration; environmental science; public relations and communications; computer programming and development. Candidates should have ability to work independently, ability to work with others, college courses in field, personal interest in the field, research skills, written communication skills, minimum GPA of 3.0 (undergraduates), enrollment in an academic program directly related to pollution abatement and control, one semester of graduate work (graduate students). Duration is full-time summer or part-time school year. $1900–$3100 per month. Open to college freshmen, college sophomores, college juniors, college seniors, graduate students.

Benefits On-the-job training, opportunity to attend seminars/workshops, willing to act as a professional reference, willing to complete paperwork for educational credit, willing to provide letters of recommendation, work-related travel reimbursement, stipend for fellowship period.

Contact Write, e-mail, or through World Wide Web site Sheri Jojokian, Environmental Education Specialist. E-mail: jojokian.sheri@epa.gov. Telephone interview required. Applicants must submit a formal organization application, resume, academic transcripts, letter of recommendation, 1-page work plan proposal, 1 letter of reference from a professor or advisor, NNEMS Liability Agreement (obtained from Web site or Career Service Center of

U.S. Environmental Protection Agency, Office of Environmental Education, NNEMS Fellowship Program (continued)
participating universities). Application deadline: February 8 for summer. World Wide Web: http://www. epa.gov/enviroed/students.html.

U.S. SERVAS, INC.
11 John Street, Suite 505
New York, New York 10038

General Information Cultural exchange and peace organization created to give people the opportunity to have a short homestay with hosts in other cultures; strives for peace through education and the understanding of cultural differences both in the U.S. and abroad. Established in 1948. Number of employees: 4. Unit of Servas, International, New York, New York. Number of internship applications received each year: 20.
Internships Available ▶ *1–2 administrative interns:* responsibilities include educating potential members about the program, answering members' questions, e-mail, phones, mail, small projects; helping with Web site; some filing and data entry. Candidates should have ability to work independently, ability to work with others, computer skills, oral communication skills, writing skills, personal interest in the field (helpful). Duration is 1–6 months. Unpaid. Open to high school students, recent high school graduates, college freshmen, college sophomores, college juniors, college seniors, recent college graduates, graduate students, law students, career changers, individuals reentering the workforce, senior citizens. ▶ *1–2 development interns:* responsibilities include membership research through computer analysis; conducting demographic surveys, and compiling quantitative data; some data entry and filing required. Candidates should have ability to work independently, ability to work with others, analytical skills, computer skills, personal interest in the field, research skills, self-motivation, college courses in field useful. Duration is 1–6 months. Unpaid. Open to high school students, recent high school graduates, college freshmen, college sophomores, college juniors, college seniors, recent college graduates, graduate students, law students, career changers, individuals reentering the workforce. International applications accepted.
Benefits Names of contacts, on-the-job training, opportunity to attend seminars/workshops, possible full-time employment, willing to act as a professional reference, willing to complete paperwork for educational credit, willing to provide letters of recommendation, $4 per day lunch stipend, $3 per day transportation stipend.
Contact Write, call, fax, or e-mail Gina Mintz, Intern Coordinator/Program Assistant. Phone: 212-267-0252. Fax: 212-267-0292. E-mail: info@usservas.com. In-person interview recommended (telephone interview accepted). Applicants must submit a formal organization application, resume, two personal references. Applications are accepted continuously. World Wide Web: http://www.usservas.org.

VOYAGEUR OUTWARD BOUND SCHOOL
101 East Chapman Street
Ely, Minnesota 55731

General Information Adventure-based school using wilderness experiences to enhance students' self-reliance, compassion, physical fitness, and cooperation. Established in 1964. Number of employees: 135. Unit of Voyageur Outward Bound, Ely, Minnesota. Number of internship applications received each year: 200.
Internships Available ▶ *20–25 interns:* responsibilities include initial field training and support work assignments in all program areas. Candidates should have experience in the field, self-motivation, strong interpersonal skills, flexibility, sense of humor. Duration is 5–8 weeks. $50 per week stipend. Open to college sophomores, college juniors, college seniors, recent college graduates, graduate students, law students, career changers, individuals reentering the workforce, indiiduals age 21 or older (preferred). International applications accepted.

Benefits Free housing, free meals, job counseling, names of contacts, on-the-job training, willing to act as a professional reference, willing to complete paperwork for educational credit, willing to provide letters of recommendation.
Contact Write, fax, e-mail, or through World Wide Web site Staffing Coordinator. Fax: 218-365-7079. E-mail: vobs@vobs.com. No phone calls. Telephone interview required. Applicants must submit a formal organization application, three letters of recommendation. Application deadline: March 1 for summer. World Wide Web: http://www.vobs.com.

WAHSEGA 4-H CENTER
77 Cloverleaf Trail
Dahlonega, Georgia 30533

General Information Outdoor and environmental education center for youth. Established in 1937. Number of employees: 15. Unit of University of Georgia, Athens, Georgia. Number of internship applications received each year: 50.
Internships Available ▶ *8 environmental education instructors:* responsibilities include teaching environmental education classes for students in third through eighth grade from public and private schools throughout Georgia. Candidates should have ability to work independently, oral communication skills, personal interest in the field, self-motivation, strong interpersonal skills, patience and ability to work with youth. Duration is 3–9 months. $225 per week. Open to college sophomores, college juniors, college seniors, recent college graduates, graduate students, law students. International applications accepted.
Benefits Free housing, free meals, health insurance, on-the-job training, willing to act as a professional reference, willing to complete paperwork for educational credit, willing to provide letters of recommendation, certification in American Red Cross Standard First Aid and CPR.
Contact Write, call, fax, or e-mail Paul Coote, Environmental Education Program Coordinator. Phone: 706-864-2050. Fax: 706-867-2901. E-mail: paulc@uga.edu. In-person interview recommended (telephone interview accepted). Applicants must submit a letter of interest, resume. Applications are accepted continuously. World Wide Web: http://www.wahsega4h.org.

WOLF CREEK OUTDOOR SCHOOL/REDWOOD NATIONAL AND STATE PARKS
PO Box 7
Orrick, California 95555

General Information School for students in grades 4-6 offering programs in awareness and value clarification, campfire programs, and old growth, stream, and prairie studies. Established in 1972. Number of employees: 4. Division of Redwood National and State Parks, Orrick, California. Number of internship applications received each year: 30.
Internships Available ▶ *6 environmental education interns:* responsibilities include instructing 4th, 5th, and 6th grade students; leading activities involving environmental education. Candidates should have desire to work with children; camp experience helpful. Duration is 12 weeks. $10 per day. Open to college freshmen, college sophomores, college juniors, college seniors, recent college graduates. International applications accepted.
Benefits Free housing, names of contacts, possible full-time employment, willing to complete paperwork for educational credit, willing to provide letters of recommendation.
Contact Write, call, fax, or through World Wide Web site Debra Savage, Park Ranger/Director. Phone: 707-822-7611 Ext. 5266. Fax: 707-488-2861. Applicants must submit a formal organization application, letter of interest, resume. Applications are accepted continuously. World Wide Web: http://www.nps.gov/redw/index.html.

WOLVERINE CAMPS OUTDOOR EDUCATION CENTER
Wolverine Camps
Wolverine, Michigan 49799

General Information Residential outdoor education program for grades 5-8. Established in 1968. Number of employees: 8. Number of internship applications received each year: 3.
Internships Available ▶ *1–3 instructors:* responsibilities include teaching classes in natural history, pioneer living, orienteering, survival, and ropes course; performing light maintenance duties; and program planning. Candidates should have ability to work with others, declared college major in field, oral communication skills, plan to pursue career in field, self-motivation, willingness to learn new skills. Duration is 6 months. $100–$125 per week. Open to college seniors, recent college graduates. International applications accepted.
Benefits Formal training, free housing, free meals, names of contacts, on-the-job training, opportunity to attend seminars/workshops, possible full-time employment, willing to complete paperwork for educational credit, willing to provide letters of recommendation.
Contact Write, call, fax, e-mail, or through World Wide Web site Mr. Eric Schupbach, Director. Phone: 231-525-8211. Fax: 231-525-6112. E-mail: camps@wolverinecamps.com. In-person interview recommended (telephone interview accepted). Applicants must submit a resume. Applications are accepted continuously. World Wide Web: http://www.wolverinecamps.com.

WOMEN'S SPORTS FOUNDATION
Eisenhower Park
East Meadow, New York 11554

General Information Nonprofit national education organization that promotes sports and fitness opportunities for girls and women. Established in 1974. Number of employees: 35. Number of internship applications received each year: 150.
Internships Available ▶ *17–48 interns:* responsibilities include researching topics in women's sports, staffing the Information Referral Service and toll-free hot line, assisting staff with projects according to abilities and skills, writing for the newsletter, and planning fund-raising projects and events. Duration is 3–12 months. $450–$700 per month. ▶ *2–6 minority interns:* responsibilities include researching topics in women's sports, staffing the Information Referral Service and toll-free hot line, assisting staff with projects according to abilities and skills, writing for newsletter, and planning fund-raising projects and events. Duration is 3–12 months. $1000 per month. Candidates for all positions should have ability to work independently, computer skills, editing skills, knowledge of field, office skills, oral communication skills, organizational skills, personal interest in the field, research skills, self-motivation, strong interpersonal skills, writing skills. Open to recent high school graduates, college freshmen, college sophomores, college juniors, college seniors, recent college graduates, graduate students, law students, career changers, individuals reentering the workforce. International applications accepted.
Benefits Job counseling, names of contacts, on-the-job training, opportunity to attend seminars/workshops, willing to complete paperwork for educational credit, willing to provide letters of recommendation.
Contact Write, call, fax, e-mail, or through World Wide Web site Jennifer Walter, Educational Services Manager. Phone: 516-542-4700. Fax: 516-542-4716. E-mail: wosportjaw@aol.com. In-person interview recommended (telephone interview accepted). Applicants must submit a formal organization application, resume, two letters of recommendation. Applications are accepted continuously. World Wide Web: http://www.womenssportsfoundation.org.

WOMEN'S STUDIES PROGRAM/AFRICAN AND LATIN AMERICAN STUDIES PROGRAM
Colgate University, 13 Oak Drive
Hamilton, New York 13346-1398

General Information Educational services organizatioin. Department of Colgate University, Hamilton, New York. Number of internship applications received each year: 60.

Internships Available ▶ *1 African and Latin American Studies Program Assistant:* responsibilities include assisting the director and secretary in planning and execution of programming (lectures, film series, workshops, study groups); acting as liaison among student groups and faculty members. Candidates should have college courses in field, computer skills, knowledge of field, organizational skills, self-motivation, strong interpersonal skills, must speak and write Spanish well. Duration is August 15 to June 1. $18,000 per duration of internship. ▶ *1 Women's Studies Program assistant:* responsibilities include assisting director of the Women's Study Program in administration of the Center for Women's Studies; programming (film series, workshops, brown bag lunch series, lectures). Candidates should have ability to work independently, college courses in field, computer skills, knowledge of field, self-motivation, strong interpersonal skills. Duration is August 15 to June 1. $18,000 per duration of internship. Open to recent college graduates, graduate students. International applications accepted.
Benefits Health insurance, on-the-job training, opportunity to attend seminars/workshops, travel reimbursement, willing to act as a professional reference, willing to provide letters of recommendation, faculty/staff privileges.
Contact Write, call, or e-mail Mary Keys, Secretary, WMST/ALST Programs, Hamilton 13346-1398. Phone: 315-228-7546. Fax: 315-228-7098. E-mail: mkeys@mail.colgate.edu. Applicants must submit a letter of interest, resume, academic transcripts, portfolio, writing sample, telephone interview followed by in-person interview if appropriate. Application deadline: March 26.

WOODBERRY FOREST SUMMER SCHOOL
Woodberry Station
Woodberry Forest, Virginia 22989

General Information Summer school program that provides developmental, remedial, and advanced credit academic work and enrichment for high school-age students. Established in 1889. Number of employees: 21. Unit of Woodberry Forest School. Number of internship applications received each year: 200.
Internships Available ▶ *20–25 teaching interns:* responsibilities include assisting with classroom instruction, tutoring and reviewing with students, monitoring study hall, supervising dormitories, supervising athletics and fine arts programs, and chaperoning trips. Candidates should have knowledge of field, oral communication skills, self-motivation, strong interpersonal skills, strong leadership ability, written communication skills. Duration is 6–7 weeks. $1700 per duration of internship. Open to college juniors, college seniors, recent college graduates, graduate students, career changers, individuals reentering the workforce. International applications accepted.
Benefits Free housing, free meals, on-the-job training, willing to complete paperwork for educational credit, willing to provide letters of recommendation.
Contact Write, call, fax, or e-mail David McRae, Director. Phone: 540-672-6047. Fax: 540-672-9076. E-mail: wfs_summer@woodberry.org. In-person interview recommended (telephone interview accepted). Applicants must submit a letter of interest, resume, academic transcripts, two personal references. Application deadline: March 15 for summer. World Wide Web: http://www.woodberry.org.

WOODROW WILSON INTERNATIONAL CENTER FOR SCHOLARS
One Woodrow Wilson Plaza, 1300 Pennsylvania Avenue, NW
Washington, District of Columbia 20004-3027

General Information Public policy research institute. Established in 1968. Number of employees: 90. Number of internship applications received each year: 700.
Internships Available ▶ *50–60 research assistants:* responsibilities include searching for source materials at area institutions; analysis and summarization of research materials; compilation of bibliographies; proofreading and editing of written work; clarification of quotations in response to references; and locating and

Woodrow Wilson International Center for Scholars (continued)

transporting of inter-library loan materials. Candidates should have college courses in field, computer skills, editing skills, office skills, research skills, writing skills. Duration is 3–9 months. Position available as unpaid or at $5 per hour stipend. Open to college juniors, college seniors, recent college graduates, graduate students, law students, career changers. International applications accepted.
Benefits Opportunity to attend seminars/workshops, willing to act as a professional reference, willing to complete paperwork for educational credit, willing to provide letters of recommendation.
Contact Write, call, fax, e-mail, or through World Wide Web site Dr. Bahman Amini, Internship Coordinator. Phone: 202-691-4053. Fax: 202-691-4001. E-mail: benamini@wwic.si.edu. In-person interview recommended (telephone interview accepted). Applicants must submit a letter of interest, resume, academic transcripts, two letters of recommendation. Applications are accepted continuously. World Wide Web: http://wwics.si.edu/.

WORLDTEACH
CID–Harvard University, 79 John F. Kennedy Street
Cambridge, Massachusetts 02138

General Information Private, nonprofit organization that sends volunteers to teach in Africa, Asia, and Latin America. Established in 1986. Number of employees: 10. Unit of Center for International Development, Cambridge, Massachusetts. Number of internship applications received each year: 300.
Internships Available ▶ *20–60 summer teachers:* responsibilities include teaching English and taking part in cultural exchange with people of the host country (Ecuador, Costa Rica, China, or Namibia). Candidates should have computer skills, oral communication skills, personal interest in the field, strong interpersonal skills, English fluency, commitment to service. Duration is 8 weeks (June to August). Unpaid. Open to recent high school graduates, college freshmen, college sophomores, college juniors, college seniors, recent college graduates, graduate students, law students, career changers, individuals reentering the workforce.
▶ *250–300 teachers:* responsibilities include primarily teaching English and occasionally science and mathematics to students in developing countries. Candidates should have ability to work independently, oral communication skills, self-motivation, strong interpersonal skills, strong leadership ability, interest in other cultures, commitment to service. Duration is 6–12 months. Small monthly living allowance (varies from country to country). Open to recent college graduates, graduate students, law students, career changers. International applications accepted.
Benefits Formal training, free housing, health insurance, names of contacts, opportunity to attend seminars/workshops, possible full-time employment, willing to provide letters of recommendation, student loans deferrable, possible scholarships to help cover the program fee.
International Internships Available in China; Costa Rica; Ecuador; Guatemala; Honduras; Mexico; Namibia; South Africa.
Contact Write, call, fax, e-mail, or through World Wide Web site Admissions Department, CID-Harvard University, 79 John F. Kennedy Street, Cambridge, Massachusetts 02138. Phone: 800-4-TEACH-0. Fax: 617-495-1599. E-mail: info@worldteach.org. In-person interview recommended (telephone interview accepted). Applicants must submit a formal organization application, resume, 3 essays, 2 personal references or letters of recommendation, academic transcripts for full-year programs. Application deadline: February 1 for April departures, April 1 for summer departures, July 1 for September departures, November 15 for January departures. World Wide Web: http://www.worldteach.org.

WYMAN CENTER
600 Kiwanis Drive
Eureka, Missouri 63025

General Information Youth development organization that focuses on educational readiness, citizenship, self-esteem, self-motivation, leadership, communication, intercultural understanding, environment, and community/relationship building. Established in 1898. Number of employees: 50. Number of internship applications received each year: 25.

Internships Available ▶ *1–8 program interns:* responsibilities include instructing and facilitating groups in environmental and adventure activities including caving, orienteering, high and low challenge courses, evening activities, and training and supervising counselors; participating in presentations and outreach programs; and designing curriculum and teaching materials; community-based programs for youth, other positions available in community-based programs for youth, teens, and families. Candidates should have experience in the field, oral communication skills, personal interest in the field, plan to pursue career in field, self-motivation, strong interpersonal skills. Duration is flexible. $400–$800 per month. Open to recent high school graduates, college freshmen, college sophomores, college juniors, college seniors, recent college graduates, graduate students, law students, career changers, individuals reentering the workforce. International applications accepted.
Benefits Formal training, free housing, free meals, names of contacts, on-the-job training, opportunity to attend seminars/workshops, possible full-time employment, willing to act as a professional reference, willing to complete paperwork for educational credit, willing to provide letters of recommendation.
Contact Write, fax, or through World Wide Web site Cheryl Estwonick, Executive Secretary. Fax: 636-938-5289. No phone calls. In-person interview recommended (telephone interview accepted). Applicants must submit a formal organization application, letter of interest, resume, three personal references, child abuse and criminal background checks required. Application deadline: February 1 for spring, April 15 for summer, August 1 for fall. World Wide Web: http://www.wymancenter.org.

YMCA CAMP BERNIE ENVIRONMENTAL EDUCATION CENTER
327 Turkey Top Road
Port Murray, New Jersey 07865

General Information Resident summer camp and September through June resident outdoor education center where students from New York and New Jersey spend 2–5 days per week in an outdoor setting. Established in 1956. Number of employees: 87. Branch of YMCA of Ridgewood, Ridgewood, New Jersey. Number of internship applications received each year: 7.
Internships Available ▶ *2–5 interns/outdoor educators:* responsibilities include assisting with planning, leading, and supervising instructional and recreational activities for elementary, junior, and high school students; instructing classes in all areas of environmental and outdoor education; and conducting outdoor education planning and training sessions for teachers, students, and parents. Candidates should have college courses in field, oral communication skills, personal interest in the field, strong interpersonal skills, strong leadership ability. Duration is flexible. Unpaid. Open to college juniors, college seniors, recent college graduates, graduate students, career changers. International applications accepted.
Benefits Formal training, free housing, free meals, on-the-job training, opportunity to attend seminars/workshops, possible full-time employment, travel reimbursement, willing to act as a professional reference, willing to complete paperwork for educational credit, willing to provide letters of recommendation.
Contact Write, call, fax, e-mail, or through World Wide Web site Kirk Weber, Director of Environmental Education. Phone: 908-832-5315. Fax: 908-832-9078. E-mail: campbernie@campbernieymca.org. In-person interview recommended. Applicants must submit a formal organization application, letter of interest, resume, three letters of recommendation, 6 personal references. Applications are accepted continuously. World Wide Web: http://www.campbernieymca.org.

YMCA OF GREATER NEW YORK AT GREENKILL OUTDOOR ENVIRONMENTAL EDUCATION CENTER
Big Pond Road, PO Box B
Huguenot, New York 12746

General Information Center that provides outdoor education and other camping/conference-related services to elementary school-age students to help develop teamwork and an understanding of natural resources. Established in 1975. Number of employees: 40. Branch of YMCA of Greater New York, New York, New York. Number of internship applications received each year: 75.

Internships Available ▶ *2–6 naturalists interns:* responsibilities include teaching outdoor environmental education and assisting with operating the residential center. Candidates should have college courses in field, personal interest in the field, plan to pursue career in field, strong interpersonal skills, strong leadership ability. Duration is 8–16 weeks. $50–$100 per week. Open to college juniors, college seniors, recent college graduates, career changers. International applications accepted.

Benefits Formal training, free housing, free meals, names of contacts, on-the-job training, possible full-time employment, willing to complete paperwork for educational credit, willing to provide letters of recommendation, worker's compensation.
Contact Write, call, fax, or e-mail Heather Chadwick, Director. Phone: 845-858-2200. Fax: 845-858-7823. E-mail: camps@ymcanyc. org. In-person interview recommended (telephone interview accepted). Applicants must submit a formal organization application, letter of interest, resume, three personal references. Application deadline: January 15 for spring, March 15 for summer, April 15 for fall, October 15 for winter. World Wide Web: http://www. ymcanyc.org.

FINANCE AND INSURANCE

GENERAL

AETNA
151 Farmington Avenue, RSAH
Hartford, Connecticut 06156

General Information Global insurance and health-care benefits company. Established in 1858. Number of employees: 47,000. Number of internship applications received each year: 2,000.
Internships Available ▶ *50 interns:* responsibilities include performing various duties in actuarial, information technology, accounting, and business areas. Candidates should have college courses in field, computer skills, oral communication skills, personal interest in the field, self-motivation, strong leadership ability, written communication skills, minimum GPA of 3.0. Duration is 1 summer. $10–$15 per hour. Open to college freshmen, college sophomores, college juniors, college seniors.
Benefits Formal training, job counseling, names of contacts, on-the-job training, opportunity to attend seminars/workshops, possible full-time employment, willing to provide letters of recommendation.
Contact Write, e-mail, or through World Wide Web site Lissa Alberto, Intern Coordinator, 151 Farmington Avenue, RSAA, Hartford, Connecticut 06156. E-mail: albertol@aetna.com. No phone calls. In-person interview recommended (telephone interview accepted). Applicants must submit a letter of interest, resume. Application deadline: mid-March. World Wide Web: http://www.aetna.com.

ALTERNATIVES FEDERAL CREDIT UNION
301 West State Street
Ithaca, New York 14850

General Information Community development credit union that focuses services toward low income residents of Tompkins County, New York. Established in 1979. Number of employees: 35. Number of internship applications received each year: 40.
Internships Available ▶ *1 Dollars for Dreams assistant:* responsibilities include assisting the adult adviser with goal projects, fundraising, and motivating youth for this branch credit union run for and by youth under age 19. Candidates should have oral communication skills, strong interpersonal skills. Duration is flexible (approximately 10 hours per week). Unpaid. Open to recent high school graduates, college freshmen, college sophomores, college juniors, college seniors, recent college graduates, graduate students, law students, law school graduates, career changers, individuals reentering the workforce. ▶ *Community partnership lending interns:* responsibilities include working with potential partner lists to promote program to community nonprofit organizations. Candidates should have strong interpersonal skills. Duration is one semester (5-10 hours per week). Unpaid. Open to college freshmen, college sophomores, college juniors, college seniors, recent college graduates, graduate students, law school graduates. ▶ *1 computer instruction intern:* responsibilities include providing one-to-one and small group instruction on basics of Lotus123 Excel, Wordperfect, or other computer programs to assist staff in becoming more proficient. Candidates should have computer skills, oral communication skills, personal interest in the field, strong interpersonal skills. Duration is 200–300 hours. Unpaid. Open to college freshmen, college sophomores, college juniors, college seniors, recent college graduates, graduate students, law school graduates. ▶ *Disaster planning interns:* responsibilities include gathering data and using disaster contingency plan software to expand program. Candidates should have strong interpersonal skills. Duration is one semester (2-4 hours per week). Unpaid. Open to college freshmen, college sophomores, college juniors, college seniors, recent college graduates, graduate students, law school graduates. ▶ *1–3 loan operations clerks:* responsibilities include clerk-level duties allowing intern to gain experience in office procedures, work habits, and corporate structure and process. Candidates should have ability to work with others, self-motivation. Duration is flexible. Unpaid. Open to high school students, recent high school graduates, college freshmen, college sophomores, college juniors, college seniors, recent college graduates, graduate students, law students, law school graduates, career changers, individuals reentering the workforce. ▶ *Loan procedures manual interns:* responsibilities include updating loan procedures manual, including interviewing staff and editing. Candidates should have ability to work independently, business background and loan knowledge (helpful). Duration is one semester (10 hours per week). Unpaid. Open to college freshmen, college sophomores, college juniors, college seniors, recent college graduates, graduate students, law school graduates. ▶ *1–2 micro enterprise development interns:* responsibilities include working on database, videotape classes, research, identifying share ware and other business resources online; collecting anecdotal information and success stories from participants. Candidates should have ability to work independently, college courses in field, computer skills, oral communication skills, organizational skills, personal interest in the field, research skills, self-motivation, strong interpersonal skills, writing skills. Duration is 200–300 hours. Unpaid. Open to college sophomores, college juniors, college seniors, recent college graduates, graduate students, law school graduates, small business owners. ▶ *1 photo opportunity intern:* responsibilities include documenting photographically the credit union for publication, including its successful projects and members. Candidates should have ability to work independently, self-motivation, strong interpersonal skills, photography experience and ability. Duration is flexible. Unpaid. Open to high school students, recent high school graduates, college freshmen, college sophomores, college juniors, college seniors, recent college graduates, graduate students, law students, law school graduates, career changers, individuals reentering the workforce. ▶ *Staff scheduling interns:* responsibilities include researching and testing software options; most research done on Internet. Candidates should have strong interpersonal skills. Duration is one semester (10 hours per week). Unpaid. Open to college freshmen, college sophomores, college juniors, college seniors, recent college graduates, graduate students, law school graduates. ▶ *Student loan products interns:* responsibilities include researching non-guaranteed and other student loan products offered by local lenders. Candidates should have strong interpersonal skills. Duration is one semester (3-5 hours per week). Unpaid. Open to college freshmen, college sophomores, college juniors, college seniors, recent college graduates, graduate students, law school graduates. International applications accepted.

Benefits On-the-job training, possible full-time employment, willing to act as a professional reference, willing to complete paperwork for educational credit, willing to provide letters of recommendation.

Contact Write, call, fax, e-mail, or through World Wide Web site Sharon Kinnan, Human Resource Manager. Phone: 607-273-3582 Ext. 821. Fax: 607-277-6391. E-mail: skinnan@alternatives.org. In-person interview recommended (telephone interview accepted). Applicants must submit a formal organization application, resume, three personal references. Applications are accepted continuously. World Wide Web: http://www.alternatives.org.

APPLIED CARD SYSTEMS
800 Delaware Avenue
Wilmington, Delaware 19801

General Information Credit card service company with offices in Delaware, Kentucky, West Virginia, and Florida. Established in 1987.
Internships Available ▶ *Interns:* responsibilities include positions in various departments including collections, customer service, learning and development, information technology, payment processing, facilities, human resources, credit, audit, and accounting. Duration is 8 weeks. Paid. Open to college freshmen, college sophomores, college juniors, college seniors.
Contact Write, e-mail, or through World Wide Web site Human Resources. E-mail: acshr@appliedcard.com. Applicants must submit a resume. Applications are accepted continuously. World Wide Web: http://www.appliedcard.com.

CAREFIRST BLUECROSS BLUESHIELD
10455 Mill Run Circle
Owings Mills, Maryland 21117

General Information Managed care organization (insurance company). Established in 1937. Number of employees: 1,800. Number of internship applications received each year: 300.
Internships Available ▶ *1–5 interns.* Candidates should have office skills, oral communication skills, personal interest in the field, strong interpersonal skills, written communication skills, Microsoft computer software knowledge (desirable). Duration is full-time in summer, part-time during academic year. $8–$12 per hour depending on experience. Open to college freshmen, college sophomores, college juniors, college seniors, graduate students. International applications accepted.
Benefits On-the-job training, opportunity to attend seminars/workshops, possible full-time employment, willing to complete paperwork for educational credit.
Contact Write, call, fax, or e-mail Tony Davis, Employment Associate. Phone: 410-998-7880. Fax: 410-998-5313. E-mail: tony.davis@carefirst.com. In-person interview required. Applicants must submit a letter of interest, resume. Applications are accepted continuously. World Wide Web: http://www.carefirst.com.

COMMUNITY FINANCIAL SERVICES, LLP
216 Haddon Avenue, Suite 327
Westmont, New Jersey 08108

General Information Firm specializing in debt reduction for corporations. Established in 1987. Number of employees: 6. Unit of Community Financial Management Services, Atlanta, Georgia. Number of internship applications received each year: 25.
Internships Available ▶ *1–4 accounting assistants:* responsibilities include organizing and entering client supplied data into accounting programs, completing routine sales and income tax returns. Candidates should have computer skills, knowledge of field, organizational skills, plan to pursue career in field. Duration is 10–13 weeks. $10–$12 per hour. Open to recent high school graduates, college freshmen, college sophomores, college juniors, graduate students, law students.
Benefits On-the-job training, travel reimbursement, willing to act as a professional reference, willing to complete paperwork for educational credit, willing to provide letters of recommendation.
Contact Write, fax, or e-mail Stephan L. Schneider, National Partner, PO Box 355, Collingswood 08108. Phone: 856-869-4236. Fax: 856-869-4239. E-mail: sschneider1@compuserve.com. In-person interview required. Applicants must submit a letter of interest, resume. Application deadline: April 15 for summer.

FANNIE MAE
3900 Wisconsin Avenue, NW
Washington, District of Columbia 20016

General Information Financial services company, whose mission is to tear down barriers, lower costs, and increase the opportunities for home ownership and affordable rental housing for all Americans. Established in 1938. Number of employees: 4,000. Number of internship applications received each year: 200.
Internships Available ▶ *10–15 corporate interns:* responsibilities include handling professional-level assignments in business units across the company, including financial analysis, market research, and systems testing and development. Candidates should have analytical skills, computer skills, oral communication skills, plan to pursue career in field, written communication skills, 3-5 years of relevant work experience, fluency in English, minimum GPA of 3.3. Duration is 10 weeks. Paid. Open to first-year MBA students specializing in finance, MIS, and/or real estate; first-year MS students specializing in industrial or computer engineering. International applications accepted.
Benefits Formal training, job counseling, on-the-job training, opportunity to attend seminars/workshops, possible full-time employment, willing to complete paperwork for educational credit, assignment to a peer mentor, possible free housing.
Contact Write, fax, or e-mail Sylvia Bailey, Program Manager, 3900 Wisconsin Avenue, NW, Washington, District of Columbia 20016. Fax: 202-752-3804. E-mail: sylvia_bailey@fanniemae.com. No phone calls. Applicants must submit a letter of interest, resume, writing sample. Application deadline: January 31. World Wide Web: http://www.fanniemae.com.

FEDERAL RESERVE BANK OF CHICAGO
230 South LaSalle Street
Chicago, Illinois 60604

General Information Institution that formulates the nation's monetary policy, supervises and regulates member banks and bank holding companies, acts as the government's bank, and operates nationwide payments mechanism for clearing of checks and the transferring of funds. Established in 1913. Number of employees: 2,170. Unit of The Federal Reserve System, Washington, District of Columbia. Number of internship applications received each year: 2,000.
Internships Available ▶ *30–40 summer interns:* responsibilities include working in internal auditing, supervision and regulation, human resources, operations, communications, automation, or economic research departments on projects for the assigned area; projects with the intern group; participating in several seminars, workshops, and outside activities. Candidates should have analytical skills, computer skills, plan to pursue career in field, self-motivation, strong interpersonal skills, ability to learn quickly. Duration is 1 summer. $8.50–$16.50 per hour. Open to recent high school graduates, college freshmen, college sophomores, college juniors, college seniors, recent college graduates, graduate students, law students.
Benefits Job counseling, names of contacts, on-the-job training, opportunity to attend seminars/workshops, possible full-time employment, willing to act as a professional reference, willing to complete paperwork for educational credit, willing to provide letters of recommendation, assistance with resume preparation, interview assistance provided, subsidized meals, networking events.
Contact Write or fax Melissa Lilly, Recruiter, Human Resources Department, 12th Floor, 230 South LaSalle Street, Chicago, Illinois 60604. Fax: 312-913-2682. No phone calls. Applicants must submit a resume, interview if applicant's skills and interests meet needs of the organization. Application deadline: March 1. World Wide Web: http://www.chicagofed.org.

HORSMAN BROTHERS, INC.
139 Sunrise Avenue, Suite 308
Palm Beach, Florida 33480

General Information Financial advisory and marketing firm for hedge funds for wealthy private investors. Established in 1998. Number of employees: 3. Number of internship applications received each year: 40.
Internships Available ▶ *2–6 administrative assistant interns:* responsibilities include assisting in weekly and monthly strategic and tactical trading conferences; assisting in marketing activities, newsletter formatting and production; assisting in seminar presentations and in telephone follow-ups. Candidates should have ability to work

Horsman Brothers, Inc. (continued)

independently, ability to work with others, computer skills, oral communication skills, written communication skills. Duration is 6–18 months. Unpaid. Open to college seniors, recent college graduates, graduate students, law students. International applications accepted.

Benefits Formal training, on-the-job training, opportunity to attend seminars/workshops, willing to act as a professional reference, willing to complete paperwork for educational credit, willing to provide letters of recommendation.

Contact Write or e-mail L. Horsman, Vice President. E-mail: horsmanbrothers@worldnet.att.net. No phone calls. In-person interview recommended (telephone interview accepted). Applicants must submit a formal organization application, letter of interest, sometimes personal references or letters of recommendation. Applications are accepted continuously.

ING AETNA FINANCIAL SERVICES
151 Farmington Avenue, TSB2
Hartford, Connecticut 06156

General Information Global financial services company. Branch of ING, Amsterdam, Netherlands. Number of internship applications received each year: 500.

Internships Available ▶ *35–50 summer interns:* responsibilities include performing various duties in actuarial, information technology, accounting, and business areas. Candidates should have ability to work independently, analytical skills, college courses in field, computer skills, oral communication skills, organizational skills, personal interest in the field, plan to pursue career in field, self-motivation, strong interpersonal skills, strong leadership ability, written communication skills. Duration is June to August. $9–$15 per hour. Open to college freshmen, college sophomores, college juniors, college seniors.

Benefits Formal training, job counseling, names of contacts, on-the-job training, opportunity to attend seminars/workshops, possible full-time employment, travel reimbursement, willing to act as a professional reference, willing to complete paperwork for educational credit, willing to provide letters of recommendation.

Contact Write, fax, or through World Wide Web site Javier Padilla, Staffing, 151 Farmington Avenue, TSB2, Hartford 06156. Fax: 860-273-0804. No phone calls. In-person interview recommended (telephone interview accepted). Applicants must submit a letter of interest, resume, academic transcripts. Application deadline: February 1. World Wide Web: http://ing-usa.com.

INTERNATIONAL MONETARY FUND
700 19th Street, NW
Washington, District of Columbia 20431

General Information International financial institution responsible for monitoring the international monetary system. Established in 1946. Number of employees: 3,000. Number of internship applications received each year: 750.

Internships Available ▶ *37 summer interns:* responsibilities include undertaking a research project on a subject set by the employing department and preparing a paper. Candidates should have ability to work independently, analytical skills, college degree in related field, computer skills, knowledge of field, organizational skills, research skills, self-motivation, writing skills. Duration is 13 weeks. $3650 per month (paid on daily basis). Open to graduate students in international economics or a related field, preferably at end of third or fourth year in PhD program. International applications accepted.

Benefits Health insurance, meals at a cost, opportunity to attend seminars/workshops, possible full-time employment, travel reimbursement.

Contact Write, fax, or through World Wide Web site Summer Intern Program, Recruitment and Staffing Division, 700 19th Street, NW, Washington, District of Columbia 20431. Fax: 202-623-7333. Applicants must submit a letter of interest, resume, academic transcripts, college campus interview during IMF recruitment (desirable); applications should be made online at www.imf.org/recruitment. Application deadline: January 31. World Wide Web: http://www.imf.org.

LILLY BETER CAPITAL GROUP, LTD.
2424 North Federal Highway, Suite 150
Boca Raton, Florida 33431

General Information Financial consulting-investment banking firm. Established in 1970. Number of employees: 20. Number of internship applications received each year: 100.

Internships Available ▶ *1–3 associates/interns:* responsibilities include working in all aspects of investment banking, filing, letter writing, sitting in on meetings, note-taking, making telephone calls, and working on legal documents. Candidates should have ability to work independently, ability to work with others, college courses in field, computer skills, editing skills, knowledge of field, office skills, oral communication skills, organizational skills, personal interest in the field, plan to pursue career in field, research skills, self-motivation, writing skills. Duration is 1–4 months. Unpaid. Open to college freshmen, college juniors, college seniors, graduate students, law students. International applications accepted.

Benefits Free meals, on-the-job training, willing to act as a professional reference, willing to provide letters of recommendation.

Contact Write, fax, e-mail, or through World Wide Web site Richard Kosloske, President. Phone: 561-361-1030. Fax: 561-361-8997. E-mail: rick@lillybetercapitalgroup.com. In-person interview recommended (telephone interview accepted). Applicants must submit a formal organization application, resume, cover letter. Applications are accepted continuously. World Wide Web: http://lillybetercapitalgroup.com.

MERRILL LYNCH
2001 Spring Road
Oak Brook, Illinois 60523

General Information Full-service financial institution that offers services to the public. Number of employees: 50. Division of Merrill Lynch, New York, New York. Number of internship applications received each year: 100.

Internships Available ▶ *5 interns.* Candidates should have ability to work with others, computer skills, office skills, oral communication skills, personal interest in the field, writing skills. Duration is one summer or semester. Unpaid. Open to college sophomores, college juniors, college seniors. International applications accepted.

Benefits Free meals, names of contacts, on-the-job training, opportunity to attend seminars/workshops, possible full-time employment, willing to act as a professional reference, willing to complete paperwork for educational credit, willing to provide letters of recommendation.

Contact Write, call, fax, or e-mail Don Heatherly, Certified Financial Manager. Phone: 630-954-1000. Fax: 630-954-6299. E-mail: donald_heatherly@ml.com. In-person interview recommended (telephone interview accepted). Applicants must submit a letter of interest, resume. Application deadline: June 1 for summer, September 1 for fall, December 1 for spring. World Wide Web: http://www.ml.com.

NATIONAL ASSOCIATION OF PROFESSIONAL SURPLUS LINES OFFICES, LTD.
6405 North Cosby Avenue, #201
Kansas City, Missouri 64151

General Information Trade association representing the surplus lines segment of the insurance industry. Established in 1975. Number of employees: 6. Number of internship applications received each year: 100.

Internships Available ▶ *6–8 summer interns:* responsibilities include placement with NAPSLO member firms across the U.S., 5 weeks working with a company member, 4 weeks working with a surplus lines broker agent member; 4 interns selected to attend the NAPSLO Annual Convention; one intern selected to receive an additional internship in London. Candidates should have ability to work with others, computer skills, oral communication skills, plan to pursue career in field, self-motivation, written communication skills, business, finance, insurance majors (preferred). Duration is 9 weeks. $400 per week. Open to college juniors, college seniors, recent college graduates, graduate students. International applications accepted.

Benefits Free housing, names of contacts, possible full-time employment, travel reimbursement, willing to act as a professional reference, willing to complete paperwork for educational credit, willing to provide letters of recommendation.

International Internships Available in London, United Kingdom.

Contact Write, call, fax, e-mail, or through World Wide Web site Jessica Free, Internship Coordinator. Phone: 816-741-3910. Fax: 816-741-5409. E-mail: internship@napslo.org. Applicants must submit a formal organization application, resume, academic transcripts, two letters of recommendation, selected applicants will be contacted for an interview. Application deadline: February 1. World Wide Web: http://www.napslo.org.

NONPROFIT FINANCIAL CENTER
29 East Madison, Suite 1700
Chicago, Illinois 60602-4415

General Information Comprehensive financial services provider for nonprofit organizations; programming falls into five main areas of service: financing, training, consulting, informational resources, and member services. Established in 1980. Number of employees: 10. Number of internship applications received each year: 25.

Internships Available ▶ *1–2 marketing interns:* responsibilities include assisting marketing director with campaigns, design materials, and overseeing publication production; working with Webmaster to update Web site; and creating new marketing campaigns. Candidates should have ability to work independently, college courses in field, computer skills, oral communication skills, personal interest in the field, written communication skills. Duration is flexible. Unpaid. Open to college freshmen, college sophomores, college juniors, college seniors, recent college graduates, graduate students, individuals reentering the workforce. ▶ *1–2 operations interns:* responsibilities include overseeing internal operations projects; verifying databox information; directing filing projects; creating new forms for databox; and other duties as assigned. Candidates should have office skills, oral communication skills, organizational skills, strong interpersonal skills, written communication skills. Duration is flexible. Unpaid. Open to college sophomores, college juniors, college seniors, recent college graduates, graduate students, individuals reentering the workforce. ▶ *2–4 program services interns:* responsibilities include assisting program services department; coordinating consulting and instructional projects; conducting related research and development duties; attending and coordinating related conferences; and some lending-related duties. Candidates should have ability to work with others, computer skills, oral communication skills, research skills, writing skills. Duration is flexible. Unpaid. Open to college juniors, college seniors, recent college graduates, graduate students, individuals reentering the workforce. International applications accepted.

Benefits Job counseling, opportunity to attend seminars/workshops, willing to act as a professional reference, willing to complete paperwork for educational credit, willing to provide letters of recommendation.

Contact Write, call, fax, e-mail, or through World Wide Web site Ana Gehant, Outreach and Development Director. Phone: 312-252-0420. Fax: 312-252-0099. E-mail: ana@nfconline.org. In-person interview recommended (telephone interview accepted). Applicants must submit a letter of interest, resume. Applications are accepted continuously. World Wide Web: http://www.NFConline.org.

PRINCIPAL FINANCIAL GROUP
711 High Street
Des Moines, Iowa 50392-0550

General Information Organization that provides financial services. Established in 1879. Number of employees: 8,500. Number of internship applications received each year: 200.

Internships Available ▶ *8–12 accounting interns:* responsibilities include assisting on accounting projects in a team environment. Candidates should have declared college major in field, plan to pursue career in field, self-motivation, strong interpersonal skills, strong leadership ability. Duration is 3 months. $11 per hour. Open to college sophomores, college juniors, college seniors, graduate students. ▶ *5–6 actuarial interns:* responsibilities include

assisting in the performance of the actuarial function. Candidates should have analytical skills, college courses in field, plan to pursue career in field, self-motivation, strong interpersonal skills, strong leadership ability. Duration is 3 months. Salary plus housing stipend. Open to college sophomores, college juniors. ▶ *1–2 capital management interns:* responsibilities include researching possible entities of investing and funding. Candidates should have ability to work independently, analytical skills, declared college major in field, plan to pursue career in field, research skills, strong leadership ability. Duration is 3 months. $13–$18 per hour. Open to MBA students. ▶ *8–10 commercial real estate interns:* responsibilities include assisting in purchasing, underwriting, and liquidating corporate owned property. Candidates should have ability to work independently, analytical skills, college courses in field, plan to pursue career in field, strong interpersonal skills, experience in finance and/or real estate (preferred). Duration is 6–9 months. $11.50 to $12.50 per hour plus housing subsidy. Open to college juniors, college seniors. ▶ *30–40 information analyst interns:* responsibilities include application development, database administration, and networking. Candidates should have ability to work independently, declared college major in field, plan to pursue career in field, self-motivation, strong interpersonal skills, strong leadership ability. Duration is 3–12 months. $14 per hour plus housing stipend. Open to college sophomores, college juniors, college seniors.

Benefits Job counseling, on-the-job training, opportunity to attend seminars/workshops, possible full-time employment, willing to act as a professional reference, willing to complete paperwork for educational credit, willing to provide letters of recommendation.

Contact Through World Wide Web site Internship Coordinator. No phone calls. In-person interview recommended (telephone interview accepted). Applicants must submit a letter of interest, resume, academic transcripts. Applications are accepted continuously. World Wide Web: http://www.principal.com/careers.

STATE FARM INSURANCE COMPANIES
3 State Farm Plaza, K-1
Bloomington, Illinois 61791

General Information Insurance company. Established in 1922. Number of employees: 10,000. Number of internship applications received each year: 200.

Internships Available ▶ *15–20 business analyst interns:* responsibilities include two weeks training, 9 weeks assigned to a corporate systems area which includes hands-on projects that provide an excellent opportunity to learn more about State Farm systems operations. Candidates should have oral communication skills, strong interpersonal skills, strong leadership ability, written communication skills, major in accounting, insurance, or finance; 6-9 hours of accounting depending on major; minimum GPA of 3.2 overall and in major. Duration is one summer. $14 per hour. ▶ *9–12 corporate accounting interns:* responsibilities include two weeks training, 9 weeks assigned to a corporate accounting area which includes hands-on projects that provide an excellent opportunity to learn more about State Farm accounting operations. Candidates should have oral communication skills, strong interpersonal skills, strong leadership ability, written communication skills, major in accounting, insurance, or finance with 12 or more hours of accounting; minimum GPA of 3.2 overall, 3.2 in major courses. Duration is one summer. $14 per hour. ▶ *60 programmer/analyst interns:* responsibilities include two weeks training, 9 weeks in an area with real programming assignments; participation in professional and personal development classes. Candidates should have oral communication skills, strong interpersonal skills, strong leadership ability, written communication skills, major in computer science, management information systems, or mathematics; minimum GPA 3.2; 6-9 hours applied computer science classes (at least 3 hours in COBOL, PL/1, PASCAL, C, C++, or other high level languages). Duration is one summer. $14 per hour. Open to college sophomores, college juniors, college seniors.

Benefits Formal training, housing at a cost, meals at a cost, opportunity to attend seminars/workshops, possible full-time employ-

State Farm Insurance Companies (continued)
ment, travel reimbursement, willing to complete paperwork for educational credit, possible 401(k) contribution, assistance with locating housing.

Contact Write, call, e-mail, or through World Wide Web site Leslie Humphries, Human Resources Representative, 3 State Farm Plaza, K—1, Bloomington, Illinois 61791. Phone: 309-763-2553. E-mail: leslie.humphries@statefarm.com. In-person interview required. Applicants must submit a formal organization application, resume, academic transcripts, application may be made through college placement office. Application deadline: February 1 for summer. World Wide Web: http://www.statefarm.com.

STATE TEACHERS RETIREMENT SYSTEM OF OHIO (STRS OHIO)
275 East Broad Street
Columbus, Ohio 43215-3771

General Information One of the largest pension funds in the United States managing assets totaling over $55 billion at market value and providing benefits to more than 400,000 public educators. Established in 1920. Number of employees: 725. Number of internship applications received each year: 2,000.

Internships Available ▶ *1 PC support intern:* responsibilities include performing installations of PC hardware and software/operating systems; performing preventative maintenance, diagnosis, and minor repairs of hardware and software/operating systems configurations. Candidates should have ability to work independently, analytical skills, college courses in field, computer skills, knowledge of field, office skills, oral communication skills, organizational skills, personal interest in the field, self-motivation, strong interpersonal skills, strong leadership ability, writing skills. Duration is 3–4 months. $600–$750 per week. Open to college juniors or seniors seeking degree in computer-related field. ▶ *1 communications/editorial intern:* responsibilities include assisting members of the department in fulfilling their duties; assisting members of the editorial team in writing brochure copy, newsletter articles, Web-based information, news releases, and other communication materials. Candidates should have ability to work independently, college courses in field, declared college major in field, editing skills, office skills, oral communication skills, organizational skills, personal interest in the field, plan to pursue career in field, research skills, self-motivation, strong interpersonal skills, writing skills, proficiency in word processing software, experience with Microsoft Word and Macintosh preferred. Duration is 3-4 months (year-round). $600–$750 per week. Open to college juniors, college seniors, recent college graduates, graduate students. ▶ *1 communications/graphic design intern:* responsibilities include assisting members of the department in fulfilling their duties; assisting members of the design team in the production of print materials, Web-based communication, and multimedia presentations. Candidates should have ability to work independently, college courses in field, editing skills, office skills, oral communication skills, organizational skills, personal interest in the field, plan to pursue career in field, self-motivation, strong interpersonal skills, writing skills, proficiency in word processing software, experience with Microsoft Word and Macintosh preferred. Duration is 3-4 months (year-round). $600–$750 per week. Open to college juniors, college seniors, recent college graduates, graduate students. ▶ *1–2 employer reporting interns:* responsibilities include performing general administrative duties for the accounting department, assisting in other areas of finance on an as-needed basis, responding to telephone inquiries from employers, typing, and distributing correspondence between STRS and employers. Candidates should have ability to work independently, analytical skills, college courses in field, office skills, oral communication skills, organizational skills, personal interest in the field, plan to pursue career in field, self-motivation, strong interpersonal skills, writing skills, knowledge of word processing software and other Windows applications preferred including use of standard spreadsheet. Duration is 3–4 months. $600–$750 per week. Open to college juniors, college seniors, recent college graduates, graduate students. ▶ *1 engineering support intern:* responsibilities include setting up new equipment in computerized maintenance management software system and organizing CAD files. Candidates should have

ability to work independently, analytical skills, college courses in field, computer skills, knowledge of field, office skills, oral communication skills, organizational skills, personal interest in the field, self-motivation, strong interpersonal skills, strong leadership ability, writing skills. Duration is 3–4 months. $600–$750 per week. Open to college juniors and seniors seeking degree in mechanical engineering or information technology. ▶ *1 human resources intern:* responsibilities include performing administrative and various human resources related activities for the Human Resource Services Department. Candidates should have ability to work independently, analytical skills, college courses in field, computer skills, knowledge of field, office skills, oral communication skills, organizational skills, personal interest in the field, self-motivation, strong interpersonal skills, strong leadership ability, writing skills. Duration is 3–4 months. $600–$750 per week. Open to college undergraduate or graduate students contemplating a career in human resources. ▶ *1 programmer intern:* responsibilities include designing, coding, testing, and implementing of computer programs from program specifications. Candidates should have ability to work independently, analytical skills, college courses in field, computer skills, knowledge of field, office skills, oral communication skills, organizational skills, personal interest in the field, self-motivation, strong interpersonal skills, strong leadership ability, writing skills. Duration is 3–4 months. $600–$750 per week. Open to recent college graduates, college juniors or seniors seeking degree in computer-related field. ▶ *1 programmer/developer intern:* responsibilities include designing, coding, testing, modifying, and implementing STRS information systems using Computer Aided Software Engineering (CASE) methodologies. Candidates should have ability to work independently, college courses in field, computer skills, office skills, organizational skills, personal interest in the field, plan to pursue career in field, research skills, self-motivation, strong interpersonal skills, writing skills, experience in information technology preferred. Duration is 3-4 months or year-round part-time (approximately 20 hours per week). $600–$750 per week. Open to college juniors, college seniors, recent college graduates, graduate students. ▶ *1 research assistant/fixed income intern:* responsibilities include compiling and analyzing data to assist the investment staff in making decisions regarding bond and mortgage investments; providing research to aid in analysis of company and industry credit reviews, mortgage pass-through, and treasury securities. Candidates should have ability to work independently, analytical skills, editing skills, office skills, oral communication skills, organizational skills, personal interest in the field, plan to pursue career in field, research skills, self-motivation, strong interpersonal skills, writing skills, minimum GPA of 3.5, knowledge of spreadsheet software preferred; major in finance, accounting, or economics (preferred). Duration is 3–4 months. $600–$750 per week. Open to college juniors, college seniors, recent college graduates, graduate students. ▶ *1 research assistant/real estate intern:* responsibilities include working on assigned projects to assist the investment staff in acquisition disposition, and asset management decisions. Candidates should have ability to work independently, analytical skills, college courses in field, office skills, oral communication skills, organizational skills, personal interest in the field, plan to pursue career in field, research skills, self-motivation, strong interpersonal skills, writing skills, working knowledge of application software for word processing, spreadsheets, and databases. Duration is 3–4 months. $600–$750 per week. Open to graduate students, college juniors, seniors, or recent graduates with real estate major. ▶ *1–2 research assistants/equities interns:* responsibilities include assisting the manager and equity securities analysts in the fundamental research process to ensure high-quality investment decisions. Candidates should have ability to work independently, analytical skills, office skills, oral communication skills, organizational skills, personal interest in the field, plan to pursue career in field, research skills, self-motivation, strong interpersonal skills, strong leadership ability, writing skills, minimum GPA of 3.5, competence in the use of standard spreadsheet and word processing software; major in finance, accounting, or economics (preferred). Duration is 3-4 months or part-time year-round (approximately 20 hours per week). $600–$750 per week. Open to college juniors, college seniors, recent college graduates, graduate students. ▶ *1 research/international assistant intern:* responsibilities include assisting the portfolio manager and country analysts in the fundamental research process to ensure high quality investment decisions. Candidates should have ability to work independently, analytical skills, college courses in field, computer skills, editing skills, office skills, oral communication skills, organizational skills, personal interest in the field, plan to pursue career in field, research skills, self-motivation, strong interpersonal skills, writing skills, minimum GPA of 3.5, competence in the use of standard spreadsheet and word processing software. Duration is 3–4 months. $600–$750 per week. Open to college juniors, college seniors, recent college graduates, graduate students. ▶ *1 service desk intern:* responsibilities include assisting in analysis, problem identification, and support for a variety of technologies and applications via the help desk response line, e-mail, or walk-ins. Candidates should have ability to work independently, analytical skills, college courses in field, computer skills, knowledge of field, office skills, oral communication skills, organizational skills, personal interest in the field, self-motivation, strong interpersonal skills, strong leadership ability, writing skills. Duration is 3–4 months. $600–$750 per week. Open to college juniors and seniors seeking degree in computer-related field. ▶ *1 teaching assistant intern (Child-Care Center):* responsibilities include maintaining safe, positive environment for children between 8 weeks and 6 years of age. Candidates should have ability to work independently, college courses in field, knowledge of field, oral communication skills, personal interest in the field, self-motivation, strong interpersonal skills, strong leadership ability. Duration is 3–4 months. $600–$750 per week.

Open to college juniors and seniors seeking degree in child care. ▶ *1 technical reporting intern:* responsibilities include assisting in providing report and systems development support to the investment and/or real estate user community, under direction of team lead. Candidates should have ability to work independently, analytical skills, college courses in field, computer skills, knowledge of field, office skills, oral communication skills, organizational skills, personal interest in the field, self-motivation, strong interpersonal skills, strong leadership ability, writing skills. Duration is 3–4 months. $600–$750 per week. Open to college juniors and seniors seeking degree in business management and/or computer-related field. International applications accepted.

Benefits Formal training, free housing, job counseling, on-the-job training, opportunity to attend seminars/workshops, possible full-time employment, travel reimbursement, willing to act as a professional reference, willing to complete paperwork for educational credit, willing to provide letters of recommendation, free fitness center membership.

Contact Write, call, fax, e-mail, or through World Wide Web site Marilyn A. Thomas, Staffing Programs Manager, 275 East Broad Street, Columbus, Ohio 43215-3771. Phone: 614-227-2908. Fax: 614-233-8721. E-mail: thomasm@strsoh.org. In-person interview recommended (telephone interview accepted). Applicants must submit a formal organization application, letter of interest, resume, physical and drug screen required, 3 personal/business references. Application deadline: April 30 for summer; continuous for other positions. World Wide Web: http://www.strsoh.org.

HEALTH CARE AND SOCIAL ASSISTANCE

HEALTH-CARE SERVICES

ACCREDITED CARE, INC.
106 West Third Street, Suite 707
Jamestown, New York 14701

General Information Provider of home health-care services. Established in 1979. Number of employees: 50. Number of internship applications received each year: 10.
Internships Available ▶ *1 general intern:* responsibilities include assisting with all aspects of home health care. Duration is flexible; minimum of 2 months. Position available or at $5–$7 per hour. ▶ *1 general office assistant (part-time):* responsibilities include administrative duties. Duration is flexible (minimum of 2 months). Position available as unpaid or at $5–$7 per hour. Candidates for all positions should have oral communication skills, organizational skills, personal interest in the field, strong interpersonal skills, written communication skills. Open to high school students, recent high school graduates, college freshmen, college sophomores, college juniors, college seniors, recent college graduates, graduate students, law students, career changers, individuals reentering the workforce. International applications accepted.
Benefits Formal training, job counseling, on-the-job training, opportunity to attend seminars/workshops, possible full-time employment, willing to act as a professional reference, willing to complete paperwork for educational credit, willing to provide letters of recommendation.
Contact Write, call, or e-mail Mr. Fred Press, Director. Phone: 212-517-8110. E-mail: acihomehealth@aol.com. In-person interview recommended (telephone interview accepted). Applicants must submit a letter of interest, resume. Applications are accepted continuously.

ADVOCATE FITNESS
Northern Trust Fitness Center, 801 South Canal Street, C-P1
Chicago, Illinois 60607

General Information Health-care organization. Established in 1898. Number of employees: 22,000. Branch of Advocate Health Care, Oak Brook, Illinois. Number of internship applications received each year: 100.
Internships Available ▶ *7–8 site interns:* responsibilities include various duties, depending on intern's developmental needs and interests. Candidates should have ability to work independently, college courses in field, knowledge of field, organizational skills, self-motivation, strong interpersonal skills. Duration is 400 hours. Position available as unpaid or at $250–$500 per duration of internship. Open to college juniors, college seniors, recent college graduates, graduate students.
Benefits Names of contacts, on-the-job training, opportunity to attend seminars/workshops, possible full-time employment, willing to act as a professional reference, willing to complete paperwork for educational credit, willing to provide letters of recommendation.

Contact Write, call, fax, or e-mail Eric M. Nelson, Manager, Fitness Programs, Northern Trust Fitness Center, 801 South Canal Street, C-P1, Chicago, Illinois 60607. Phone: 312-557-2201. Fax: 312-557-5707. E-mail: en4@ntrs.com. In-person interview recommended (telephone interview accepted). Applicants must submit a resume. Applications are accepted continuously.

AMERICAN ACADEMY OF PEDIATRICS
Department of Federal Affairs, 601 13th Street, NW, Suite 400 North
Washington, District of Columbia 20005

General Information Organization of 55,000 primary care pediatricians, pediatric medical subspecialists, and pediatric surgical specialists dedicated to the health and well-being of infants, children, adolescents, and young adults. Established in 1930.
Internships Available ▶ *3 Washington Office interns:* responsibilities include include attending and reporting on congressional hearings and Department of Health and Human Services meetings/hearings, research, coalitions, association work, and medical work. Duration is minimum of 4 weeks. Unpaid. Open to college freshmen, college sophomores, college juniors, college seniors, graduate students, medical students, residents, and AAP members and family.
Contact Write, call, or e-mail Mary McGowan, Internship Coordinator. Phone: 202-347-8600. E-mail: mmcgowan@aap.org. Letter of interest; see Web site for details. Applications are accepted continuously. World Wide Web: http://www.aap.org/advocacy/washing/intern.html.

AMERICAN CANCER SOCIETY
1626 Locust Street
Philadelphia, Pennsylvania 19103

General Information Nationwide community-based voluntary health organization dedicated to eliminating cancer as a major health problem by preventing cancer, saving lives, and diminishing suffering from cancer, through research, education, advocacy, and service. Established in 1913. Number of employees: 65. Unit of American Cancer Society, Pennsylvania Division, Hershey, Pennsylvania. Number of internship applications received each year: 20.
Internships Available ▶ *Cancer prevention and detection interns:* responsibilities include vary dependent on program priorities. Candidates should have experience in the field, knowledge of field, organizational skills, research skills, self-motivation, strong interpersonal skills. Duration is 1 semester. Unpaid. ▶ *Patient services interns:* responsibilities include assisting in responding to requests for help from cancer patients and caregivers; working with volunteers involved in program delivery. Candidates should have ability to work independently, oral communication skills, strong interpersonal skills, written communication skills. Duration is flexible. Unpaid. Open to college freshmen, college sophomores, college juniors, college seniors, recent college graduates, graduate students. International applications accepted.
Benefits On-the-job training, opportunity to attend seminars/workshops, possible full-time employment, willing to act as a professional reference, willing to complete paperwork for educational credit, willing to provide letters of recommendation.

Contact Write or fax Theresa McGrath, Regional Director Cancer Control. Fax: 215-985-5406. No phone calls. In-person interview required. Applicants must submit a formal organization application, letter of interest, resume, two letters of recommendation, writing sample occasionally required. Applications are accepted continuously.

AMERICAN LUNG ASSOCIATION OF CENTRAL FLORIDA
1333 West Colonial Drive
Orlando, Florida 32804

General Information Nonprofit health organization. Established in 1904. Number of employees: 10. Affiliate of American Lung Association, New York, New York. Number of internship applications received each year: 20.

Internships Available ▶ *1–2 health sciences interns:* responsibilities include coordinating various programs related to lung disease and assisting program director as needed. Candidates should have ability to work independently, computer skills, knowledge of field, personal interest in the field, self-motivation, strong interpersonal skills. Duration is flexible. Unpaid. Open to high school seniors, recent high school graduates, college freshmen, college sophomores, college juniors, college seniors, recent college graduates, graduate students, career changers, individuals reentering the workforce. ▶ *1–3 public relations interns:* responsibilities include public relations, media relations, special events, fund-raising; assignments made based on intern's talents and interests. Candidates should have ability to work independently, computer skills, oral communication skills, self-motivation, strong interpersonal skills, written communication skills. Duration is flexible, typically semester-long. Unpaid. Open to college freshmen, college sophomores, college juniors, college seniors, recent college graduates.

Benefits Names of contacts, on-the-job training, opportunity to attend seminars/workshops, possible full-time employment, travel reimbursement, willing to act as a professional reference, willing to complete paperwork for educational credit, willing to provide letters of recommendation.

Contact Write, call, fax, or e-mail Cheryl Owens, Program Director, 1333 West Colonial Drive, Orlando, Florida 32804. Phone: 407-425-5864. Fax: 407-425-2876. E-mail: cowens@alacf.org. In-person interview recommended (telephone interview accepted). Applicants must submit a letter of interest, resume. Applications are accepted continuously. World Wide Web: http://www.lungusa.org.

AMERICAN LUNG ASSOCIATION OF THE DISTRICT OF COLUMBIA (ALADC)
475 H Street, NW
Washington, District of Columbia 20001-2617

General Information Voluntary private health association working to prevent lung disease and promote lung health. Established in 1902. Number of employees: 10. Unit of American Lung Association, New York, New York. Number of internship applications received each year: 20.

Internships Available ▶ *1 creative design/special events marketing intern:* responsibilities include assisting in design and production of ALADC's annual report and newsletter, designing graphics, updating Web site, and assisting with design and layout of brochures and other promotional and educational materials; assisting with development and implementation of marketing plans; conducting marketing research and analysis; maintaining marketing contacts database. Candidates should have computer skills, office skills, oral communication skills, strong interpersonal skills, written communication skills, desktop publishing and familiarity with Internet and HTML. Duration is 4 weeks minimum. Unpaid. Open to college sophomores, college juniors, college seniors, recent college graduates, graduate students, career changers. ▶ *2–3 program interns:* responsibilities include providing staff support to lung health, environmental health and tobacco, and asthma education programs; assisting with information research as well as production and distribution of program promotional materials; maintaining program contact records in database, and assisting in the coordination of health fairs. Candidates should have computer skills, office skills, oral communication skills,

organizational skills, strong interpersonal skills, written communication skills. Duration is 2 months. Unpaid. Open to college freshmen, college sophomores, college juniors, college seniors, recent college graduates, graduate students, career changers, individuals reentering the workforce. International applications accepted.

Benefits Names of contacts, on-the-job training, opportunity to attend seminars/workshops, willing to act as a professional reference, willing to complete paperwork for educational credit, willing to provide letters of recommendation, reimbursement of expenses while on official assignments.

Contact Write, fax, or e-mail Mr. Rolando Andrewn, Executive Director. Fax: 202-682-5874. E-mail: randrewn@aladc.org. No phone calls. In-person interview recommended (telephone interview accepted). Applicants must submit a letter of interest, resume, two personal references. Applications are accepted continuously. World Wide Web: http://www.aladc.org.

AMERICAN RED CROSS–GREATER HARTFORD CHAPTER
209 Farmington Avenue
Farmington, Connecticut 06032

General Information Human service organization helping individuals and communities to prevent, prepare for, and respond to emergencies; programs and services include health and safety, emergency services (education and response) and blood services. Established in 1969. Number of employees: 50. Unit of American Red Cross–National Capital Chapter, Washington, District of Columbia. Number of internship applications received each year: 10.

Internships Available ▶ *1–3 communication interns:* responsibilities include researching, writing and editing articles for newsletter "Real Heroes", News for chapter Web site; assisting with public relations on special events and/or at the scene of a disaster. Candidates should have ability to work independently, college courses in field, computer skills, oral communication skills, strong interpersonal skills, written communication skills. Duration is 10–15 weeks (minimum 8 hours a week). Unpaid. Open to college sophomores, college juniors, college seniors, recent college graduates, career changers, individuals reentering the workforce. ▶ *1–3 community outreach interns:* responsibilities include identifying opportunities to promote ARC services and programs within the community; helping with general outreach and network community resources; focusing on Hispanic and African-American organizations and groups, helping recruit volunteers. Candidates should have ability to work independently, oral communication skills, organizational skills, self-motivation, written communication skills, Spanish-speaking ability. Duration is 10–15 weeks, (minimum 8 hours per week). Unpaid. Open to college sophomores, college juniors, college seniors. ▶ *1–2 disaster services interns–planning and preparedness:* responsibilities include working with volunteers and paid staff to increase readiness and ability to respond to meet community disaster needs; assisting with implementation of disaster programs, planning of disaster drills and exercises; coordinating volunteer recruitment, retention and recognition. Candidates should have ability to work with others, computer skills, organizational skills, self-motivation, public speaking skills. Duration is 10–15 or more weeks, (minimum 8 hours a week). Unpaid. Open to college juniors, college seniors, recent college graduates, career changers, individuals reentering the workforce. ▶ *1–2 grant writing interns:* responsibilities include researching potential sources of grant funding, compiling new prospects in system; researching, developing and completing grant proposals to be submitted with the support of chapter staff; tracking and follow-up with existing grants in the community. Candidates should have ability to work independently, oral communication skills, research skills, self-motivation, writing skills, creativity. Duration is 10–15 weeks, or more (minimum 8 hours a week). Unpaid. Open to college juniors, college seniors, recent college graduates, career changers, individuals reentering the workforce. ▶ *1 market research intern–AED Project:* responsibilities include assisting in development of sales and marketing plan for new programs and products, including AED (automated external defibrillator); analyzing program activity, patterns, and audience motivations;

American Red Cross–Greater Hartford Chapter (continued)
establishing communications and collaborations with other agencies. Candidates should have ability to work independently, analytical skills, college courses in field, oral communication skills, organizational skills, written communication skills. Duration is 10–15 weeks. Unpaid. Open to college seniors, career changers, individuals reentering the workforce. ▶ *1 market research intern–Babysitter's Training Program:* responsibilities include establishing Babysitter's Training Program; analyzing program activity, patterns and audience motivations; identifying current customers and competitors in order to increase participation in ARC Health Services Courses; designing and developing a data collection system; analyzing data to provide recommendations for increasing course enrollment. Candidates should have oral communication skills, organizational skills, written communication skills. Duration is 10–15 weeks. Unpaid. Open to college juniors, college seniors, career changers, individuals reentering the workforce. ▶ *1 youth outreach intern:* responsibilities include identifying youth organizations to promote ARC programs and services; organizing special projects involving youth; supporting youth leadership team; providing training; recruiting youth and helping generate interest in ARC programs. Candidates should have ability to work independently, oral communication skills, organizational skills, strong interpersonal skills, written communication skills, public speaking and group facilitation skills. Duration is 10–15 weeks, (minimum 8 hours per week). Unpaid. Open to college juniors, college seniors, career changers, individuals reentering the workforce. International applications accepted.
Benefits Names of contacts, on-the-job training, opportunity to attend seminars/workshops, willing to act as a professional reference, willing to complete paperwork for educational credit, willing to provide letters of recommendation, formal training possibility for certain positions.
Contact Write, call, fax, e-mail, or through World Wide Web site Anouchka Bayard-Blanchard, Manager, Youth Services. Phone: 860-678-2799. Fax: 860-678-5461. E-mail: bayarda@usa.redcross.org. In-person interview recommended (telephone interview accepted). Applicants must submit a formal organization application, resume, two writing samples, two personal references. Applications are accepted continuously. World Wide Web: http://www.greaterhartfordredcross.org.

ARIZONA HEART INSTITUTE MESA
6335 East Main Street, Suite 4
Mesa, Arizona 85205

General Information Outpatient clinic dedicated to prevention and treatment of heart and vascular diseases. Established in 1975. Number of employees: 30. Division of Arizona Heart Institute, Phoenix, Arizona. Number of internship applications received each year: 25.
Internships Available ▶ *6–8 exercise physiology interns (undergraduate):* responsibilities include completing flow chart of experiences and observations; participating in Phase II and III cardiovascular rehabilitation program; patient education, supervision, and follow-up. Candidates should have computer skills, knowledge of field, oral communication skills, strong interpersonal skills, current CPR certification. Duration is 350–700 hours. Unpaid. Open to college seniors, recent college graduates, graduate students. ▶ *2 graduate exercise physiology interns (cardiovascular conditioning):* responsibilities include completing flow chart of clinical observations and experiences, participating in operation of Phase II and III cardiovascular rehabilitation program, and supervising and instructing undergraduate interns. Candidates should have college degree in related field, computer skills, knowledge of field, oral communication skills, strong interpersonal skills, current CPR certification. Duration is September to December or January to April. Unpaid. Open to recent college graduates, graduate students. International applications accepted.
Benefits Formal training, on-the-job training, opportunity to attend seminars/workshops, possible full-time employment, willing to act as a professional reference, willing to complete paperwork for educational credit, willing to provide letters of recommendation, occasional free meals.

Contact Call, fax, or e-mail Denise Gonzales, Program Director, Cardiovascular Conditioning, 6335 East Main Street, Suite 4, Mesa, Arizona 85205. Phone: 602-244-9700. Fax: 602-218-4353. E-mail: dgonzales@azheart.com. In-person interview recommended. Applicants must submit a formal organization application, letter of interest, resume, academic transcripts, two letters of recommendation. Applications are accepted continuously. World Wide Web: http://www.azheart.com.

CAMP LA JOLLA
176 C Avenue
Coronado, California 92118

General Information Fitness and weight loss camp. Established in 1979. Number of employees: 86. Number of internship applications received each year: 75.
Internships Available ▶ *15–20 counselors:* responsibilities include working with campers, teaching three physical activity classes per day, and acting as counselor. Candidates should have ability to work with others, knowledge of field, organizational skills, personal interest in the field, strong leadership ability. Duration is 8–10 weeks. Position available as unpaid or paid. Open to college freshmen, college sophomores, college juniors, college seniors, recent college graduates, graduate students. International applications accepted.
Benefits Free housing, free meals, names of contacts, on-the-job training, willing to complete paperwork for educational credit, willing to provide letters of recommendation.
Contact Write, call, fax, e-mail, or through World Wide Web site Donna Volpe, Director, 176 C Avenue, Coronado, California 92118. Phone: 800-825-8746. Fax: 619-435-8188. E-mail: camplj@aol.com. In-person interview recommended (telephone interview accepted). Applicants must submit a formal organization application, personal reference, letter of recommendation. Application deadline: April 1 for priority deadline; however, applications are accepted on a continuous basis. World Wide Web: http://www.camplajolla.com.

CHILDREN'S HOSPICE INTERNATIONAL
901 North Pitt Street, Suite 230
Alexandria, Virginia 22314

General Information Organization that provides advocacy and outreach services for children with life-threatening conditions and their families. Established in 1983. Number of employees: 4. Number of internship applications received each year: 20.
Internships Available ▶ *1–2 interns:* responsibilities include performing office duties, coordinating resources, disseminating information, and working on special projects. Candidates should have computer skills, oral communication skills, organizational skills, strong interpersonal skills, written communication skills. Duration is flexible. Unpaid. Open to college freshmen, college sophomores, college juniors, college seniors, recent college graduates, graduate students, law students, career changers, individuals reentering the workforce. ▶ *1 receptionist/administrative assistant:* responsibilities include answering information requests, performing general office activities, and preparing mailings. Candidates should have computer skills, editing skills, oral communication skills, organizational skills, research skills, self-motivation. Unpaid. Open to high school students, recent high school graduates, college freshmen, college sophomores, college juniors, college seniors, recent college graduates, graduate students, law students, career changers, individuals reentering the workforce. International applications accepted.
Benefits On-the-job training, opportunity to attend seminars/workshops, possible full-time employment, willing to complete paperwork for educational credit, willing to provide letters of recommendation.
Contact Write, call, fax, or e-mail Ann Armstrong-Dailey, Founding Director. Phone: 703-684-0330. Fax: 703-684-0226. E-mail: chiorg@aol.com. In-person interview recommended (telephone interview accepted). Applicants must submit a letter of interest, resume. Application deadline: March 1 for summer, December 15 for spring. World Wide Web: http://www.chionline.org.

CLINICAL DIRECTORS NETWORK, INC.
54 West 39th Street, 11th Floor
New York, New York 10018

General Information Nonprofit network that arranges conferences, workshops, and training for clinicians research; emphasizes clinical trials, health-care services, research and development, and finding alternative treatments for AIDS through community programs. Established in 1985. Number of employees: 15. Number of internship applications received each year: 75.

Internships Available ▶ *1 AIDS program intern:* responsibilities include gathering and entering information into the database and assisting at a health center. Candidates should have ability to work independently, college courses in field, personal interest in the field, strong interpersonal skills, computer literacy in IBM-compatible programs, interest in public health and/or public administration. Duration is 1 summer to 1 year. Unpaid. Open to recent high school graduates, college freshmen, college sophomores, college juniors, college seniors, recent college graduates, graduate students. ▶ *1–2 administrative interns:* responsibilities include setting up conferences, preparing contacts, making hotel arrangements, data entry, and assisting in fund-raising events. Candidates should have ability to work independently, analytical skills, office skills, oral communication skills, organizational skills, self-motivation, strong interpersonal skills, written communication skills, computer literacy in IBM-related programs, interest in public health and/or public administration. Duration is year-round. Unpaid. Open to recent high school graduates, college freshmen, college sophomores, college juniors, college seniors, recent college graduates, individuals reentering the workforce. ▶ *1–2 asthma/SMART/cardiovascular interns:* responsibilities include assisting Coordinator with health centers. Candidates should have ability to work independently, analytical skills, college courses in field, office skills, oral communication skills, personal interest in the field, research skills, self-motivation, strong interpersonal skills, written communication skills, computer literacy in IBM-related programs, interest in public health and/or public administration. Duration is year-round. Unpaid. Open to recent high school graduates, college freshmen, college sophomores, college juniors, college seniors, recent college graduates, graduate students. ▶ *1–2 marketing interns:* responsibilities include assisting in the marketing department, research for future conference sponsors, and developing marketing tools. Candidates should have ability to work independently, declared college major in field, office skills, oral communication skills, organizational skills, self-motivation, strong interpersonal skills, written communication skills, computer literacy in IBM-compatible programs, interest in public health and/or public administration. Duration is year-round. Unpaid. Open to college freshmen, college sophomores, college juniors, college seniors, recent college graduates. ▶ *4–6 research programs interns:* responsibilities include assisting research program coordinator with administrative and research tasks at office and health centers. Candidates should have ability to work independently, analytical skills, oral communication skills, organizational skills, plan to pursue career in field, research skills, self-motivation, strong interpersonal skills, written communication skills, computer literacy in IBM-compatible programs, interest in public health and/or public administration. Duration is year-round. Unpaid. Open to recent high school graduates, college freshmen, college sophomores, college juniors, college seniors, recent college graduates, graduate students. International applications accepted.

Benefits On-the-job training, opportunity to attend seminars/workshops, willing to act as a professional reference, willing to complete paperwork for educational credit, willing to provide letters of recommendation, networking opportunities.

Contact Write, fax, e-mail, or through World Wide Web site Internship Department, 54 West 39 Street, 11th Floor, New York, New York 10018. Fax: 212-382-0669. E-mail: info@cdnetwork.org. No phone calls. In-person interview required. Applicants must submit a formal organization application, letter of interest, resume. Applications are accepted continuously. World Wide Web: http://www.cdnetwork.org.

COUNCIL ON ALCOHOLISM AND DRUG ABUSE
232 East Canon Perdido
Santa Barbara, California 93101

General Information Organization that actively provides prevention, education, intervention, referral and treatment services throughout Santa Barbara County. Established in 1949. Number of employees: 115. Affiliate of National Council on Alcoholism (NCA). Number of internship applications received each year: 25.

Internships Available ▶ *Perinatal Program interns:* responsibilities include assisting in childcare, daycare, and parenting skills activities and other duties assigned by childcare specialist or perinatal manager. Candidates should have college courses in field, experience in the field, personal interest in the field, strong interpersonal skills, written communication skills. Unpaid. Open to college freshmen, college sophomores, college juniors, college seniors, recent college graduates, graduate students, law students, career changers, individuals reentering the workforce. ▶ *Teen Court Program interns.* Candidates should have ability to work with others, oral communication skills, plan to pursue career in field, self-motivation, written communication skills, ability to work well with at-risk youth. Duration is 6 months (8-10 hours per week). Unpaid. Open to college sophomores, college juniors, college seniors, recent college graduates, graduate students, law students, must be working toward bachelor's degree or have degree in related field. ▶ *1–3 coordinators for special events interns:* responsibilities include coordination of multiple special events for youth and families. Candidates should have ability to work independently, editing skills, office skills, oral communication skills, organizational skills, self-motivation, strong interpersonal skills, writing skills. Duration is flexible. Unpaid. Open to college freshmen, college sophomores, college juniors, college seniors, recent college graduates. ▶ *Information and referral counselors.* Candidates should have knowledge of field, oral communication skills, personal interest in the field, strong interpersonal skills, written communication skills, six months of sobriety required. Duration is 2 hours per week. Position available as unpaid or paid. Open to recent high school graduates, college freshmen, college sophomores, college juniors, college seniors, recent college graduates, graduate students, law students, career changers, individuals reentering the workforce. International applications accepted.

Benefits Job counseling, on-the-job training, opportunity to attend seminars/workshops, possible full-time employment, willing to act as a professional reference, willing to complete paperwork for educational credit, willing to provide letters of recommendation.

Contact Write, call, fax, or e-mail Maria Long, Director of Special Events. Phone: 805-963-1433. Fax: 805-963-4099. E-mail: mariawlong@hotmail.com. In-person interview recommended (telephone interview accepted). Applicants must submit a letter of interest, resume. Applications are accepted continuously. World Wide Web: http://www.sbcada.org.

DR. PAUL SCHWANN APPLIED HEALTH AND RESEARCH CENTRE
3737 Wascana Parkway, University of Regina
Regina, Saskatchewan S4S 0A2 Canada

General Information Health, rehabilitation, and research centre. Established in 1980. Number of employees: 10. Unit of University of Regina, Regina, Saskatchewan, Canada. Number of internship applications received each year: 6.

Internships Available ▶ *Exercise science and research interns:* responsibilities include assisting in ongoing rehabilitation and risk reduction programming in the areas of cardiovascular health, musculoskeletal health, and workplace health; assisting in research projects and general administration of the centre and potential special events. Candidates should have computer skills, declared college major in field, oral communication skills, strong interpersonal skills, strong leadership ability, written communication skills. Duration is flexible. Unpaid. Open to college seniors, recent college graduates, graduate students. International applications accepted.

Benefits On-the-job training, opportunity to attend seminars/workshops, possible full-time employment, willing to act as a

Dr. Paul Schwann Applied Health and Research Centre (continued)
professional reference, willing to complete paperwork for educational credit, willing to provide letters of recommendation, some formal training.
International Internships Available.
Contact Write, call, fax, e-mail, or through World Wide Web site Nancy Turner, Coordinator. Phone: 306-585-5293. Fax: 306-585-5363. E-mail: nancy.turner@uregina.ca. In-person interview recommended (telephone interview accepted). Applicants must submit a letter of interest, resume, academic transcripts sometimes required. Applications are accepted continuously. World Wide Web: http://www.uregina.ca/pasweb/dpsc/.

THE EVANGELICAL LUTHERAN GOOD SAMARITAN SOCIETY
PO Box 5038
Sioux Falls, South Dakota 57117-5038

General Information Society that provides shelter and services to the frail elderly and others in need and operates approximately 250 nursing centers and residential facilities throughout the country. Established in 1922. Number of employees: 270. Number of internship applications received each year: 300.
Internships Available ► *Administrators in training:* responsibilities include operating and administering a long-term care facility. Candidates should have college courses in field, knowledge of field, organizational skills, self-motivation, strong interpersonal skills, strong leadership ability. Duration is 6–12 months. Monthly stipend. Open to college seniors, recent college graduates, graduate students, law students, career changers, individuals reentering the workforce. International applications accepted.
Benefits Formal training, free meals, health insurance, on-the-job training, opportunity to attend seminars/workshops, possible full-time employment, travel reimbursement, willing to complete paperwork for educational credit.
Contact Write, call, fax, or e-mail Dean Mertz, Vice President for Human Resources. Phone: 605-362-3100 Ext. 120. Fax: 605-362-3240. E-mail: dmertz@good-sam.com. In-person interview required. Applicants must submit a formal organization application, letter of interest, resume, academic transcripts, three personal references. Applications are accepted continuously. World Wide Web: http://www.good-sam.com.

EXTENDICARE HEALTH SERVICES, INC.
111 West Michigan Street
Milwaukee, Wisconsin 53203

General Information Nationwide operator of over 200 long-term care, subacute, and assisted living facilities. Established in 1968. Number of employees: 350. Subsidiary of Extendicare, Inc., Markham, Ontario, Canada. Number of internship applications received each year: 100.
Internships Available ► *5 accounting analysts:* responsibilities include working in accounts payable, tax accounts receivable, and general accounting. Candidates should have ability to work with others, office skills, organizational skills, research skills, self-motivation, knowledge of Microsoft Access and Excel (helpful). Duration is May to August. $10–$12 per hour. Open to college juniors, college seniors, recent college graduates. ► *5 administrators in training:* responsibilities include preparing to take the licensure exam to become a nursing home administrator. Candidates should have ability to work independently, analytical skills, oral communication skills, organizational skills, plan to pursue career in field, self-motivation, strong interpersonal skills, strong leadership ability, written communication skills, prior experience in the service or health-care industry (preferred). Duration is 6 months. Paid. Open to college seniors, recent college graduates, graduate students, law students, career changers.
Benefits Possible full-time employment.
Contact Write, call, fax, or e-mail John Goff, National Recruiter. Phone: 414-908-8186. Fax: 414-908-8143. E-mail: jgoff@extendicare.com. Telephone interview required. Applicants must submit a letter of interest, resume, in-person interview (travel expenses paid) for finalists. Application deadline: May 15 for summer. World Wide Web: http://www.extendicare.com.

FAMILY SERVICE BUREAU OF NEWARK
393 Central Avenue
Newark, New Jersey 07103

General Information Behavioral health organization providing counseling to all ages concerning most mental health issues; psychiatrist available; substance abuse programs. Established in 1882. Number of employees: 29. Affiliate of New Community Corporation, Newark, New York. Number of internship applications received each year: 15.
Internships Available ► *2–3 marriage and family therapy interns:* responsibilities include telephone intakes; face-to-face intakes; individual/couple/family/group counseling, working in agency committees; collaborating with other service providers. Candidates should have ability to work independently, ability to work with others, declared college major in field, oral communication skills, self-motivation, written communication skills. Duration is 1 year. Unpaid. Open to graduate students. ► *4–5 master social work interns:* responsibilities include telephone intakes; face-to-face intakes; individual/couple/family/group counseling; participating on agency committees; collaborating with other service providers; administrative track student would work in policy; procedures; grant proposals; strengthening relationships with other service providers. Candidates should have ability to work independently, ability to work with others, declared college major in field, oral communication skills, self-motivation, written communication skills. Duration is 1-2 semesters; may be year-round. Unpaid. Open to graduate students. ► *1–2 substance abuse counselor interns:* responsibilities include assessment and treatment of suspected/known substance abusers of all ages, facilitating groups, working collaboratively with other community service providers, assisting in program development; working with other agency professionals to provide comprehensive services. Candidates should have ability to work independently, ability to work with others, oral communication skills, plan to pursue career in field, self-motivation, written communication skills. Duration is 1 semester. Unpaid. Open to college seniors, graduate students. International applications accepted.
Benefits On-the-job training, opportunity to attend seminars/workshops, possible full-time employment, willing to act as a professional reference, willing to complete paperwork for educational credit, willing to provide letters of recommendation, willing to work in collaboration with intern's academic program.
Contact Write or fax Linda Combs, Training Director. Fax: 732-484-3452. E-mail: lcombs@newcommunity.org. No phone calls. In-person interview required. Applicants must submit a formal organization application, resume, two personal references. Applications are accepted continuously.

FEMINIST HEALTH CENTER OF PORTSMOUTH, INC.
559 Portsmouth Avenue, PO Box 456
Greenland, New Hampshire 03840

General Information Free-standing, nonprofit clinic providing the following services: GYN care, primary care, abortions, STD/HIV counseling and testing, pregnancy testing, birth control, health education, and community outreach. Established in 1980. Number of employees: 20. Number of internship applications received each year: 5.
Internships Available ► *1–5 health-care counselors:* responsibilities include information sharing, client interviewing and assessing, communicating effectively, and utilizing strong interpersonal skills while working as part of a team in the delivery of care. Candidates should have college courses in field, oral communication skills, personal interest in the field, strong interpersonal skills, prochoice views. Position available as unpaid or at $6.50–$9 per hour. Open to college freshmen, college sophomores, college juniors, college seniors, recent college graduates, graduate students, career changers, individuals reentering the workforce.
Benefits Formal training, job counseling, names of contacts, on-the-job training, possible full-time employment, willing to act as a professional reference, willing to complete paperwork for educational credit, willing to provide letters of recommendation.

Contact Write, call, or fax Diana Braun, Executive Director. Phone: 603-436-7588. Fax: 603-431-0451. In-person interview recommended (telephone interview accepted). Applicants must submit a letter of interest, resume, academic transcripts, three personal references, three letters of recommendation. Applications are accepted continuously.

FRONTIER NURSING SERVICE
132 FNS Drive
Wendover, Kentucky 41775

General Information Rural health-care provider and midwife educator. Established in 1925. Number of employees: 300. Number of internship applications received each year: 30.
Internships Available ▶ *4–5 "Courier" volunteers:* responsibilities include delivering supplies, hosting dinners, assisting with office work, participating in various community events, acting as teaching aide in local schools, and accompanying health care professionals during daily routine. Candidates should have ability to work independently, self-motivation, strong interpersonal skills, valid driver's license, access to a car. Duration is 8–12 weeks. Unpaid. Open to recent high school graduates, college freshmen, college sophomores, college juniors, college seniors, recent college graduates, graduate students, law students, career changers, individuals reentering the workforce, individuals at least 18 years old. International applications accepted.
Benefits Housing at a cost, meals at a cost, willing to complete paperwork for educational credit, willing to provide letters of recommendation.
Contact Write, call, fax, e-mail, or through World Wide Web site Barb Gibson, Courier Coordinator. Phone: 606-672-2317. Fax: 606-672-3022. E-mail: courierprogram@yahoo.com. Telephone interview required. Applicants must submit a formal organization application, three letters of recommendation, $250 room and board fee to be paid by applicant or applicant's college/school (upon acceptance). Applications are accepted continuously. World Wide Web: http://www.frontiernursing.org.

GLOBAL HEALTH ACTION
PO Box 15086
Atlanta, Georgia 30333

General Information Organization that sponsors health leadership and management training programs around the globe; community development and empowerment. Established in 1972. Number of employees: 12. Number of internship applications received each year: 150.
Internships Available ▶ *2 development/fund-raising/public relations interns:* responsibilities include participating in development and marketing plan and conducting marketing audit; conducting prospect research; updating donor/prospect files; assisting with special events, the production of collateral materials, correspondence and mailings; and media relations. Candidates should have computer skills, knowledge of field, organizational skills, plan to pursue career in field, research skills, strong interpersonal skills, written communication skills. Duration is May/June to August/September (14 weeks, 20 hours per week). $1500 per duration of internship. Open to college sophomores, college juniors, college seniors, graduate students. ▶ *2 fund-raising/public relations/marketing interns:* responsibilities include conducting prospect research; updating donor/prospect files; assisting with special events, production of collateral materials, correspondence and mailings, and media relations. Candidates should have computer skills, knowledge of field, organizational skills, plan to pursue career in field, research skills, strong interpersonal skills, written communication skills. Duration is January to May or August to December (15 weeks, 10 hours per week). $300–$500 per semester. Open to college sophomores, college juniors, college seniors, graduate students. ▶ *1 health programs spring or fall intern:* responsibilities include analyzing and reporting on participant evaluation data; preparing general correspondence to training program applicants; supporting course participants with identified needs; creating, updating, and sending course-related promotional material; participating in program-related meetings and events; supporting course trainers with materials, classrooms and handouts; coordinating volunteers for GHA course events; conducting

research on topics relevant to GHA course development and special events. Candidates should have computer skills, organizational skills, plan to pursue career in field, research skills, strong interpersonal skills, written communication skills. Duration is January to May or August to December, (15 weeks, 10 hours per week). $300–$500 per semester. Open to college sophomores, college juniors, college seniors, graduate students. ▶ *1 health programs summer intern:* responsibilities include preparing general correspondence to training program applicants; supporting course participants with identified needs; creating, updating, and sending course-related promotional materials; participating in program-related meetings and events; supporting course trainers with materials, classrooms, and handouts; coordinating volunteers for GHA course events; conducting research on topics relevant to GHA course development and special events. Candidates should have computer skills, organizational skills, plan to pursue career in field, research skills, strong interpersonal skills, written communication skills. Duration is May/June to August/September, (14 weeks, 20 hours per week). $1500 per duration of internship. Open to college sophomores, college juniors, college seniors, graduate students. ▶ *1 high school summer intern:* responsibilities include administrative duties, some Web-based research, and assistance with course materials. Candidates should have computer skills, office skills, oral communication skills, organizational skills, self-motivation, written communication skills. Duration is May to August (10 hours per week). Unpaid. Open to high school students, recent high school graduates. International applications accepted.
Benefits On-the-job training, opportunity to attend seminars/workshops, possible full-time employment, willing to act as a professional reference, willing to complete paperwork for educational credit, willing to provide letters of recommendation, work-related travel reimbursement.
Contact Write or fax Virginia M. Thompson, Director of Administration and Finance, PO Box 15086, Atlanta, Georgia 30333. Fax: 404-634-9685. E-mail: gha@globalhealthaction.org. No phone calls. In-person interview recommended (telephone interview accepted). Applicants must submit a letter of interest, resume, one short writing sample. Application deadline: March 31 for summer, June 30 for fall, November 29 for spring. World Wide Web: http://www.globalhealthaction.org.

GOULD FARM
Box 157, Gould Road
Monterey, Massachusetts 01245-0157

General Information Rural residential center providing integrated, structured rehabilitation for adults with psychiatric disorders and a continuum of services through the Boston Area Program. Established in 1913. Number of employees: 45. Number of internship applications received each year: 100.
Internships Available ▶ *1 community resources workleader:* responsibilities include helping clients to improve personal, social, and work skills. Candidates should have ability to work independently, computer skills, office skills, oral communication skills, organizational skills, strong interpersonal skills, strong leadership ability, written communication skills, public relations skills. Duration is 12 months. $250 per month. Open to college juniors, college seniors, recent college graduates, graduate students, career changers. ▶ *1–2 farm workleaders:* responsibilities include making assignments for animal care, field work, haying, and fencing; working with clients; teaching work habits and skills. Candidates should have oral communication skills, personal interest in the field, strong interpersonal skills, strong leadership ability, knowledge in the field and ability to drive farm equipment a plus. Duration is 12 months. $250 per month. Open to college juniors, college seniors, recent college graduates, graduate students. ▶ *1–2 forestry and grounds work leaders :* responsibilities include providing leadership and direction to landscaping and forestry teams, clearing forest trails, mowing lawns, trimming yards and flower gardens. Candidates should have knowledge of field, oral communication skills, organizational skills, self-motivation, strong interpersonal skills, strong leadership ability. Duration is 12 months. $250 per month. Open to college seniors, recent college graduates, graduate students, career changers. ▶ *1–3 gardens workleaders:* responsibilities include making assign-

Gould Farm (continued)

ments for maintaining the grounds and gardens, teaching work habits and skills, helping clients develop social skills. Candidates should have ability to work with others, experience in the field, oral communication skills, personal interest in the field, self-motivation, strong leadership ability. Duration is 3 months in summer. $250 per month. Open to college juniors, college seniors, recent college graduates, graduate students. ▶ *1–3 kitchen and roadside store workleaders:* responsibilities include making assignment for meals and operating restaurant; helping clients to improve work habits, work, and social skills. Candidates should have ability to work independently, experience in the field, oral communication skills, personal interest in the field, strong interpersonal skills, strong leadership ability. Duration is 12 months. $250 per month. Open to college juniors, college seniors, recent college graduates, graduate students, career changers. ▶ *1 maintenance workleader:* responsibilities include leading maintenance work groups for the upkeep/repair of residential facilities. Candidates should have experience in the field, oral communication skills, self-motivation, strong interpersonal skills, strong leadership ability, general handy person skills. Duration is 12 months. $250 per month. Open to college seniors, recent college graduates, career changers, retirees. ▶ *2–3 residential advisors:* responsibilities include working as house advisors in one of three houses; assisting with social skills, medications, goal setting, recreation, and informal counseling. Candidates should have oral communication skills, organizational skills, personal interest in the field, self-motivation, strong interpersonal skills, driver's license, college residential work a plus. Duration is 12 months. $250 per month. Open to college juniors, college seniors, recent college graduates, graduate students, career changers. ▶ *1–2 volunteer case managers (Boston program):* responsibilities include providing support to clients who have moved on from Gould Farm to more independent living, facilitating meal preparation and providing rides, helping with job searches, assisting with medication, attending meetings and training, organizing and leading activities. Candidates should have oral communication skills, personal interest in the field, self-motivation, strong interpersonal skills, strong leadership ability, driver's license required. Duration is 12 months. $250 per month. Open to college juniors, college seniors, recent college graduates, graduate students, career changers.

Benefits Formal training, free housing, free meals, health insurance, on-the-job training, opportunity to attend seminars/workshops, possible full-time employment, willing to complete paperwork for educational credit, willing to provide letters of recommendation, AmeriCorps Education Awards.

Contact Write, call, fax, e-mail, or through World Wide Web site Ms. Cynthia Meyer, Director, Human Resources, Box 157 Gould Road, Monterey, Massachusetts 01245-0157. Phone: 413-528-1804 Ext. 17. Fax: 413-528-5051. E-mail: humanresources@gouldfarm. org. In-person interview recommended (telephone interview accepted). Applicants must submit a letter of interest, resume, total of 3 references or letters of recommendation. Application deadline: February 1 for spring, March 1 for summer, June 1 for fall. World Wide Web: http://www.gouldfarm.org.

GRACIE SQUARE HOSPITAL
420 East 76th Street
New York, New York 10021

General Information   Psychiatric hospital with the following inpatient services: general, geriatric, drug/alcohol detoxification and rehabilitation, Asian, and psychiatric patients. Established in 1958. Number of employees: 400. Unit of New York Presbyterian Hospital Network, New York, New York. Number of internship applications received each year: 100.

Internships Available   ▶ *1–2 psychology externs:* responsibilities include performing psychodiagnostic testing, individual and group psychotherapy, and attending staff meetings and workshops. Duration is September through May. $2000 per duration of internship. Open to graduate students. ▶ *1–2 psychology interns:* responsibilities include attending workshops and staff meetings; doing psychodiagnostic testing and psychotherapy commensurate with skills. Duration is 10 weeks minimum from May to August; start and end dates flexible. $2000 per duration of internship. Open

to college juniors, college seniors, recent college graduates, graduate students. Candidates for all positions should have ability to work independently, ability to work with others, analytical skills, oral communication skills, self-motivation, writing skills.

Benefits On-the-job training, opportunity to attend seminars/workshops, willing to complete paperwork for educational credit, willing to provide letters of recommendation.

Contact Write, call, fax, e-mail, or through World Wide Web site Dr. Fran Luckom-Nurnberg, Director, Department of Psychological Services. Phone: 212-434-5378. Fax: 212-434-5373. E-mail: info@nygsh.org. In-person interview required. Applicants must submit a formal organization application, resume, academic transcripts, writing sample, two letters of recommendation. Application deadline: January 31 for academic year, February 28 for summer. World Wide Web: http://www.nygsh.org.

HARRIS COUNTY PUBLIC HEALTH
2223 West Loop South, #718
Houston, Texas 77027

General Information   Agency that provides health inspection, education, and health care for the county excluding the City of Houston. Established in 1950. Number of employees: 200. Number of internship applications received each year: 5.

Internships Available   ▶ *2–4 environment interns:* responsibilities include monitoring water, air, mosquitoes, and animals; research and other tasks. Candidates should have ability to work independently, computer skills, office skills, research skills, writing skills. Duration is 1 semester. Unpaid. Open to college juniors, college seniors, recent college graduates, graduate students. ▶ *3–6 public health interns:* responsibilities include research; surveys, data entry, according to the division; pollution, animal, mosquito control, community health services, health education, and administration. Candidates should have ability to work independently, ability to work with others, computer skills, oral communication skills, self-motivation, written communication skills. Duration is 200 hours. Unpaid. Open to recent college graduates, graduate students. International applications accepted.

Benefits Names of contacts, on-the-job training, opportunity to attend seminars/workshops, possible full-time employment, willing to act as a professional reference, willing to complete paperwork for educational credit, willing to provide letters of recommendation.

Contact Write, call, fax, e-mail, or through World Wide Web site Lyndall Maxwell, Volunteer and Student Services Coordinator, 2223 West Loop South #718, Houston, Texas 77027. Phone: 713-439-6000. Fax: 713-439-6080. E-mail: lmaxwell@hd.co.harris.tx.us. In-person interview recommended (telephone interview accepted). Applicants must submit a formal organization application, letter of interest, resume. Applications are accepted continuously. World Wide Web: http://www.hd.co.harris.tx.us.

HEALTH CAREER OPPORTUNITY PROGRAM, RUSK INSTITUTE OF REHABILITATION MEDICINE
New York University Medical Center, 560 First Avenue,
Greenberg Hall, Room C-95
New York, New York 10016

General Information   Full-service rehabilitation facility. Established in 1948. Number of employees: 1,000. Unit of New York University Medical Center, New York, New York. Number of internship applications received each year: 1,000.

Internships Available   ▶ *50–150 interns/Reader's Digest Fellows:* responsibilities include performing tasks related to either a research area or a clinical area such as nursing, rehabilitation medicine, recreation therapy, occupational therapy, physical therapy, and horticultural therapy, and attending lectures, films, demonstrations, and presentations on the various careers in rehabilitation. Candidates should have ability to work independently, oral communication skills, personal interest in the field, self-motivation, strong interpersonal skills. Duration is 4 weeks. Unpaid. Open to high school seniors, college freshmen, college sophomores, college juniors, college seniors, career changers. International applications accepted.

Benefits Formal training, meals at a cost, on-the-job training, opportunity to attend seminars/workshops, willing to provide letters of recommendation, housing provided at $575 for the months of June and July.
Contact Write, fax, or e-mail Mr. Glenn Goldfinger, Director, HCOP, New York University Medical Center, 560 First Avenue, Greenberg Hall, C-95, New York, New York 10016. Fax: 212-263-0750. E-mail: glenn.goldfinger@med.nyu.edu. No phone calls. Applicants must submit a formal organization application, letter of interest, resume, writing sample, personal reference, letter of recommendation. Application deadline: March 1 for summer fellows/interns.

HEALTH FITNESS CORPORATION AT GE CORPORATE HEADQUARTERS
3135 Easton Turnpike
Fairfield, Connecticut 06431

General Information Corporate health and fitness facility. Established in 1982. Number of employees: 2. Branch of Health Fitness Corporation, Minneapolis, Minnesota. Number of internship applications received each year: 12.
Internships Available ▶ *1–2 health and fitness interns:* responsibilities include assisting in the daily operation of the fitness facility, including fitness testing, program orientation, one-on-one training, group exercise classes, and development of motivational and health education programs. Candidates should have college courses in field, oral communication skills, personal interest in the field, self-motivation, strong interpersonal skills, CPR certification. Duration is 12–15 weeks. Position available as unpaid or paid. Open to college seniors, recent college graduates, graduate students. International applications accepted.
Benefits Possible full-time employment, willing to act as a professional reference, willing to complete paperwork for educational credit, willing to provide letters of recommendation.
Contact Write, call, fax, or e-mail Audra Scuderi, Program Director/Intern Coordinator. Phone: 203-373-3800. Fax: 203-373-3131. E-mail: scuderia@corporate.ge.com. In-person interview recommended (telephone interview accepted). Applicants must submit a letter of interest, resume. Application deadline: April 1 for summer, July 1 for fall, October 31 for spring.

INDIAN HEALTH SERVICE
801 Thompson
Rockville, Maryland 20852

General Information Provider of health care to over 1.5 million American Indians and Alaska Natives; seeks to elevate health status to the highest level possible. Established in 1955. Number of employees: 375. Unit of Department of Health and Human Services, Washington, District of Columbia. Number of internship applications received each year: 180.
Internships Available ▶ *1–20 COSTEP externs (commissioned corps):* responsibilities include assisting an administrative or health professional in carrying out the program. Candidates should have ability to work independently, ability to work with others, knowledge of field, plan to pursue career in field, self-motivation, strong leadership ability. Duration is 120 days. Salary depends on experience and college credit. Open to college juniors, college seniors. ▶ *180 civil interns:* responsibilities include working in area in health profession related to intern's course of study. Candidates should have ability to work with others, analytical skills, computer skills, knowledge of field, oral communication skills, written communication skills. Duration is 120 days. Paid. Open to college sophomores, college juniors, college seniors.
Benefits Job counseling, names of contacts, on-the-job training, opportunity to attend seminars/workshops, possible full-time employment, willing to complete paperwork for educational credit, tuition assistance for students who receive an Indian Health Service scholarship.
Contact Write, call, fax, or e-mail Vickye M. Santiago, Intern Coordinator. Phone: 301-443-6197. Fax: 301-443-6048. E-mail: vsantiag@hqe.ihs.gov. Applicants must submit a letter of interest, resume, academic transcripts, proof of Indian eligibility (if needed). Application deadline: March 15 for summer, July 15 for winter. World Wide Web: http://www.ihs.gov.

INNISFREE VILLAGE
5505 Walnut Level Road
Crozet, Virginia 22932

General Information Lifesharing community with adults with disabilities. Established in 1971. Number of employees: 12. Number of internship applications received each year: 25.
Internships Available ▶ *5–10 residential counselors:* responsibilities include living in family-style homes with 3–8 coworkers (adults with mental disabilities); caring for personal needs and helping to run the house; assisting in therapeutic workstations of weavery, woodwork, cooking, baking, and gardening. Candidates should have ability to work independently, ability to work with others, oral communication skills, patience, flexibility. Duration is minimum of one year. Unpaid. Open to individuals 21 years old and over. International applications accepted.
Benefits Free housing, free meals, health insurance, on-the-job training, willing to provide letters of recommendation, 15 vacation days paid at $45 per day; $215 monthly stipend.
Contact Write, call, fax, e-mail, or through World Wide Web site Nancy Chappell, Community Coordinator. Phone: 434-823-5400. Fax: 434-823-5027. E-mail: innisfreevillage@prodigy.net. In-person interview recommended (telephone interview accepted). Applicants must submit a formal organization application, three personal references, police record and TB test required. Applications are accepted continuously. World Wide Web: http://www.avenue.org/innisfree.

INSTITUTE FOR MENTAL HEALTH INITIATIVES
2175 K Street, NW, Suite 700
Washington, District of Columbia 20037

General Information Not-for-profit organization that promotes mental health by making the latest research accessible and understandable to the general public and the media industry. Established in 1982. Number of employees: 10. Unit of The George Washington University, Washington, District of Columbia. Number of internship applications received each year: 90.
Internships Available ▶ *1 business intern:* responsibilities include supporting IMHI's staff in general office management as well as fiscal and personnel budgeting and management. Duration is flexible. Unpaid. ▶ *1 community intervention intern:* responsibilities include supporting programs directed toward community interventions including IMHI's RETHINK anger management program and resilience interventions. Duration is flexible. Unpaid. ▶ *1 development intern:* responsibilities include assisting staff in development phase of projects and support IMHI's fund-raising efforts. Duration is flexible. Unpaid. ▶ *1 media intern:* responsibilities include assisting media team in design and implementation of media projects including IMHL's publication "Dialogue" as well as the development of relationships with media professionals. Duration is flexible. Unpaid. Candidates for all positions should have ability to work independently, ability to work with others, oral communication skills, organizational skills, self-motivation, written communication skills. Open to college freshmen, college sophomores, college juniors, college seniors, recent college graduates, graduate students. International applications accepted.
Benefits Names of contacts, opportunity to attend seminars/workshops, possible full-time employment, willing to complete paperwork for educational credit, willing to provide letters of recommendation.
Contact Write, call, fax, e-mail, or through World Wide Web site Intern Coordinator. Phone: 202-467-2285. Fax: 202-467-2289. E-mail: imhi-info@gwumc.edu. In-person interview recommended (telephone interview accepted). Applicants must submit a letter of interest, resume, two personal references, 1–2 page writing sample. Application deadline: April 1 for summer (priority deadline), August 1 for fall, December 1 for spring. World Wide Web: http://www.gwumc.edu/sphhs/imhi.

INTERMOUNTAIN PLANNED PARENTHOOD
721 North 29th Street
Billings, Montana 59101

General Information Organization that serves 18,000 patients per year for birth control, cancer screening, treatment for sexually transmitted diseases, counseling, and education; the organization believes in wanted children, loving and committed parents, decisions based on knowledge, and the right to make those decisions. Established in 1969. Number of employees: 118. Affiliate of Planned Parenthood Federation of America, New York, New York. Number of internship applications received each year: 5.

Internships Available ▶ *Interns:* responsibilities include working in education, development, administration, patient services, or other positions; each position has varying responsibilities, duties, and requirements. Candidates should have ability to work independently, ability to work with others, computer skills, oral communication skills, personal interest in the field, self-motivation. Duration is flexible. Unpaid. Open to high school students, recent high school graduates, college freshmen, college sophomores, college juniors, college seniors, recent college graduates, graduate students, law students, career changers, individuals reentering the workforce. International applications accepted.

Benefits On-the-job training, willing to complete paperwork for educational credit, willing to provide letters of recommendation, basic reproductive healthcare and family planning services provided free after 50 hours of work.

Contact Write, call, fax, e-mail, or through World Wide Web site Diana Baldwin, Human Resource Director. Phone: 406-248-3636 Ext. 20. Fax: 406-254-9330. E-mail: diana.baldwin@ppfa.org. Applicants must submit a formal organization application, letter of interest, resume. Applications are accepted continuously. World Wide Web: http://www.impp.org.

KAIROS DWELLING
2945 Gull Road
Kalamazoo, Michigan 49048

General Information Home for the terminally ill. Established in 1998. Number of employees: 4. Number of internship applications received each year: 4.

Internships Available ▶ *2 personal caregivers.* Candidates should have ability to work independently, personal interest in the field, self-motivation, strong interpersonal skills, loving and compassionate presence, flexibility. Duration is 2 months-1 year (minimum of 40 hours per week). Unpaid. Open to recent high school graduates, college freshmen, college sophomores, college juniors, college seniors, recent college graduates, graduate students, law students, career changers, individuals reentering the workforce, persons out of high school who are looking for a volunteer experience. International applications accepted.

Benefits Free housing, free meals, on-the-job training, opportunity to attend seminars/workshops.

Contact Write, call, fax, or e-mail Sr. Maureen Metty, SSJRN, Director. Phone: 616-381-3688. Fax: 616-388-8016. E-mail: kairosdwelling1@juno.com. In-person interview recommended (telephone interview accepted). Applicants must submit a formal organization application, letter of interest, resume, three personal references, three letters of recommendation. Applications are accepted continuously.

LANCASTER GENERAL CARDIAC AND VASCULAR REHABILITATION
2100 Harrisburg Pike
Lancaster, Pennsylvania 17604

General Information Cardiac and vascular rehabilitation unit combining exercise training to increase strength and stamina, education to reduce risk, and help with lifestyle changes for those who have experienced a cardiac event. Established in 1986. Number of employees: 12. Division of Lancaster General Heart Center, Lancaster, Pennsylvania. Number of internship applications received each year: 30.

Internships Available ▶ *1–2 exercise physiology interns:* responsibilities include participating in the daily activities of the exercise physiologists, observing in other health-care settings, and working in conjunction with registered nurses. Candidates should have ability to work independently, ability to work with others, college degree in related field, oral communication skills, self-motivation. Duration is 10–12 weeks. Unpaid. Open to college seniors, recent college graduates.

Benefits Formal training, names of contacts, on-the-job training, opportunity to attend seminars/workshops, willing to act as a professional reference, willing to complete paperwork for educational credit, willing to provide letters of recommendation.

Contact Write, call, fax, or e-mail D.C. Clark, Exercise Physiologist. Phone: 717-290-3126. Fax: 717-290-3124. E-mail: dfclark@ lancastergeneral.org. In-person interview recommended (telephone interview accepted). Applicants must submit a letter of interest, resume, academic transcripts. Applications are accepted continuously. World Wide Web: http://www.lancastergeneral.org.

L & T HEALTH AND FITNESS
7309 Arlington Boulevard #202
Falls Church, Virginia 22042

General Information Premier provider of innovative health and fitness management services including health fitness programming, facility management, facility design consultation, and health promotional services. Established in 1984. Number of employees: 300. Number of internship applications received each year: 75.

Internships Available ▶ *Fitness specialist interns:* responsibilities include learning all aspects of facility management and operations, assisting staff with creation and implementation of health promotion programs, and supervising group and one-on-one fitness activities. Candidates should have ability to work independently, oral communication skills, personal interest in the field, strong interpersonal skills, writing skills. Duration is flexible. $100 per week stipend based on full-time (40 hours). Open to college sophomores, college juniors, college seniors, graduate students, must be enrolled in health/fitness-related degree program. International applications accepted.

Benefits On-the-job training, opportunity to attend seminars/workshops, possible full-time employment, willing to act as a professional reference, willing to provide letters of recommendation.

Contact Write, call, fax, e-mail, or through World Wide Web site Rose Cooper, Director of Recruiting, 7309 Arlington Boulevard, #202, Falls Church, Virginia 22042. Phone: 703-204-1355 Ext. 33. Fax: 703-204-2332. E-mail: r.cooper@ltwell.com. In-person interview recommended (telephone interview accepted). Applicants must submit a formal organization application, resume. Applications are accepted continuously. World Wide Web: http://www.ltwell.com.

LIGHTHOUSE INTERNATIONAL
111 East 59th Street
New York, New York 10022

General Information The leading resource worldwide on vision impairment and vision rehabilitation. Established in 1905. Number of employees: 400. Number of internship applications received each year: 30.

Internships Available ▶ *15–20 interns:* responsibilities include working in specific professional areas such as social work, vision rehabilitation (O&M, RT), PT, OT, and low vision services as well as research, development (grant writing), computer technology, writing, editing, and human resource and volunteer management. Candidates should have ability to work with others, college courses in field, personal interest in the field, self-motivation, written communication skills, additional requirements for specific internships. Duration is semester (with some flexibility). Unpaid. Open to college sophomores, college juniors, college seniors, graduate students. International applications accepted.

Benefits On-the-job training, opportunity to attend seminars/workshops, travel reimbursement, willing to act as a professional reference, willing to complete paperwork for educational credit, willing to provide letters of recommendation.

Contact Write, call, or e-mail Margaret Rodgers, Director, Volunteer Resources. Phone: 212-821-9405. E-mail: mrodgers@lighthouse.

org. Applicants must submit a letter of interest, resume. Applications are accepted continuously. World Wide Web: http://www.lighthouse.org.

THE MAY INSTITUTE
1 Commerce Way
Norwood, Massachusetts 02062

General Information Organization with over 140 behavioral, health-care, education, and rehabilitation programs serving 8000 individuals and families each year. Established in 1955. Number of employees: 2,000.
Internships Available ▶ *Classroom teachers:* responsibilities include working in a classroom setting providing direct instruction to children, adolescents, and young adults with brain injury, autism, or other developmental disabilities. Candidates should have oral communication skills, personal interest in the field, strong interpersonal skills, written communication skills. Duration is 3 months. $10–$12 per hour. ▶ *Residential teachers:* responsibilities include working in a group home setting providing direct instruction to children, adolescents, and young adults with autism, brain injury, or other developmental disabilities. Candidates should have ability to work with others, oral communication skills, personal interest in the field, written communication skills. Duration is 3 months. $10–$12 per hour. Open to recent high school graduates, college freshmen, college sophomores, college juniors, college seniors, recent college graduates, graduate students, law students, career changers, individuals reentering the workforce.
Benefits Formal training, on-the-job training, possible full-time employment, willing to act as a professional reference, willing to complete paperwork for educational credit, willing to provide letters of recommendation.
Contact Write, call, fax, or e-mail Paula Norton, Senior Recruiter. Phone: 781-440-0400 Ext. 201. Fax: 781-440-0414. E-mail: pnorton@mayinstitute.org. In-person interview required. Applicants must submit a formal organization application, letter of interest, resume, two professional references. Applications are accepted continuously. World Wide Web: http://www.mayinstitute.org.

NATIONAL ASSOCIATION OF ANOREXIA NERVOSA AND ASSOCIATED DISORDERS (ANAD)
PO Box 7
Highland Park, Illinois 60035

General Information National, nonprofit, educational, and self-help association offering a variety of services to aid anorexics, bulimics, compulsive eaters, and their families. Established in 1976. Number of employees: 10. Number of internship applications received each year: 70.
Internships Available ▶ *6 interns:* responsibilities include research, national hot line, correspondence with eating disorders sufferers, organizing a national conference, and coordinating and administering special projects. Candidates should have ability to work independently, oral communication skills, self-motivation, strong interpersonal skills, writing skills. Duration is flexible. Unpaid. Open to college juniors, college seniors, recent college graduates, graduate students.
Benefits On-the-job training, willing to complete paperwork for educational credit, willing to provide letters of recommendation.
Contact Write, call, fax, e-mail, or through World Wide Web site Dawn Ries, Administrator. Phone: 847-831-3438. Fax: 847-433-4632. E-mail: anad20@aol.com. Applicants must submit a letter of interest, resume. Applications are accepted continuously. World Wide Web: http://www.anad.org.

NATIONAL BRAIN TUMOR FOUNDATION
414 13th Street, Suite 700
Oakland, California 94612-2603

General Information Nonprofit health organization. Established in 1981. Number of employees: 10. Number of internship applications received each year: 6.
Internships Available ▶ *1–2 patient services interns:* responsibilities include assistance in staffing patient information line, editing, writing and producing national newsletter, and coordinating resources for national network of support groups. Candidates

should have ability to work independently, knowledge of field, office skills, oral communication skills, organizational skills, plan to pursue career in field, self-motivation, strong interpersonal skills, writing skills. Duration is 3–6 months. Position available as unpaid or at small stipend for graduate social work interns. Open to college juniors, college seniors, recent college graduates, graduate students. International applications accepted.
Benefits Opportunity to attend seminars/workshops, willing to act as a professional reference, willing to complete paperwork for educational credit, willing to provide letters of recommendation.
Contact Write, call, fax, or e-mail Patient Services. Phone: 510-839-9777. Fax: 510-839-9779. E-mail: nbtf@braintumor.org. In-person interview recommended (telephone interview accepted). Applicants must submit a letter of interest, resume. Applications are accepted continuously. World Wide Web: http://www.braintumor.org.

NATIONAL HEALTHY MOTHERS, HEALTHY BABIES
121 North Washington Street, Suite 300
Alexandria, Virginia 22314

General Information Public health education resource coalition promoting and enhancing culturally and linguistically appropriate services for mothers, babies, and families. Established in 1981. Number of employees: 9. Number of internship applications received each year: 100.
Internships Available ▶ *8 interns:* responsibilities include drafting articles for HMHB publications; assisting with Web site and list servers; gathering information from Internet, publications, and direct contacts with members and experts; working on special projects in a core program area; administrative duties as assigned. Candidates should have oral communication skills, organizational skills, strong interpersonal skills, written communication skills, commitment to maternal and child health, knowledge of nonprofit sector, experience working with underserved populations. Duration is 3 months (20-35 hours per week). Unpaid. Open to college freshmen, college sophomores, college juniors, college seniors, recent college graduates, graduate students.
Benefits Job counseling, names of contacts, opportunity to attend seminars/workshops, willing to act as a professional reference, willing to complete paperwork for educational credit, willing to provide letters of recommendation.
Contact Write, call, fax, e-mail, or through World Wide Web site Intern Coordinator. Phone: 703-836-6110 Ext. 234. Fax: 703-836-3470. E-mail: info@hmhb.org. In-person interview recommended (telephone interview accepted). Applicants must submit a resume, cover letter, three personal reference (two must be non-academic). Applications are accepted continuously. World Wide Web: http://www.hmhb.org.

NATIONAL LYMPHEDEMA NETWORK
1611 Telegraph Avenue, Suite 1111
Oakland, California 94612

General Information Nonprofit support and mutual assistance organization for sufferers of lymphedema and their caregivers, providing treatment referrals, educational materials, individual guidance counseling, support groups, and conferences. Established in 1988. Number of employees: 4.
Internships Available ▶ *1–2 program assistants:* responsibilities include working on variety of projects including development of chapter manuals, assisting in setting-up of local NLN chapters, establishment of nationwide speakers bureau, researching possible grant makers/funders. Candidates should have oral communication skills, organizational skills, self-motivation, strong interpersonal skills, written communication skills. Duration is flexible. Unpaid. Open to recent high school graduates, college freshmen, college sophomores, college juniors, college seniors, recent college graduates, graduate students, law students, career changers, individuals reentering the workforce, senior citizens.
▶ *1–3 project development interns:* responsibilities include various projects; development of National Speakers Bureau, grant writing, fund-raising special events, statistical analysis, on-site resource library development. Candidates should have ability to work independently, oral communication skills, research skills, self-motivation, writing skills. Duration is flexible (minimum of 10 hours per week for 8 weeks). Unpaid. Open to high school

National Lymphedema Network (continued)
seniors, recent high school graduates, college freshmen, college sophomores, college juniors, college seniors, recent college graduates, graduate students, law students, career changers, volunteer opportunities for disabled. International applications accepted.
Benefits Names of contacts, on-the-job training, willing to act as a professional reference, willing to complete paperwork for educational credit, willing to provide letters of recommendation.
Contact Write, call, fax, e-mail, or through World Wide Web site Dana Wilcoxen, Outreach Coordinator. Phone: 510-208-3200. Fax: 510-208-3110. E-mail: nln@lymphnet.org. In-person interview required. Applicants must submit a letter of interest, resume, personal reference. Applications are accepted continuously. World Wide Web: http://www.lymphnet.org.

NATIVE AMERICAN HEALTH EDUCATION RESOURCE CENTER
PO Box 572, 809 High Street
Lake Andes, South Dakota 57356-0572

General Information Nonprofit grassroots organization committed to providing education, empowerment skills for women and children, self-help skills, and other resources to the Native American community of the Yankston Sioux Reservation, the surrounding area, and nationwide. Established in 1985. Number of employees: 15. Affiliate of Native American Community Board, Lake Andes, South Dakota. Number of internship applications received each year: 65.
Internships Available ► *1 domestic violence advocate intern:* responsibilities include sheltering, rape advocacy, support groups, outreach projects, court advocacy, referrals to other service agencies, housing referrals, and assistance getting re-established in the community after leaving abusive partners. Candidates should have ability to work independently, knowledge of field, office skills, oral communication skills, self-motivation, strong interpersonal skills. Duration is 3–12 months. $500 per month. Open to college juniors, college seniors, recent college graduates, graduate students. ► *1–2 reproductive health educators:* responsibilities include planning and executing a community-wide reproductive health program designated to provide health education information and workshops on reproductive tract infections (RTI's); writing public service announcements for Native radio; and coordinating focus groups and round tables. Candidates should have ability to work independently, college courses in field, computer skills, personal interest in the field, research skills, self-motivation, strong leadership ability, writing skills. Duration is 6–12 months. $1000 per month for Native Americans; $500 per month for others. Open to college juniors, college seniors, recent college graduates, graduate students, law students, Native Americans preferred. ► *2–4 reproductive health educators/interns:* responsibilities include working with staff to provide support services in the various programs of the Native American Women's Health Education Resource and the Women's Lodge (shelter for battered women); developing health education materials; contributing to the newsletter; and assisting on the 24-hour youth hot line. Candidates should have ability to work independently, college courses in field, computer skills, personal interest in the field, research skills, self-motivation, strong leadership ability, writing skills. Duration is 3–12 months. $500 per month. Open to college juniors, college seniors, recent college graduates, graduate students, law students. International applications accepted.
Benefits Formal training, free housing, on-the-job training, opportunity to attend seminars/workshops, willing to act as a professional reference, willing to provide letters of recommendation, monthly living stipend.
Contact Write, call, fax, e-mail, or through World Wide Web site Karen Tuttle, Administrative Program Coordinator. Phone: 605-487-7072. Fax: 605-487-7964. E-mail: karen@charles-mix.com. Telephone interview required. Applicants must submit a letter of interest, resume, two personal references. Applications are accepted continuously. World Wide Web: http://www.nativeshop.org.

NEW YORK PRESBYTERIAN HOSPITAL, WEILL CORNELL WESTCHESTER
21 Bloomingdale Road
White Plains, New York 10605

General Information Nonprofit and voluntary comprehensive psychiatric facility with inpatient, partial hospitalization, day hospital programs, clinics, and outpatient departments. Established in 1894. Number of employees: 1,000. Division of New York Presbyterian Hospital, New York, New York. Number of internship applications received each year: 100.
Internships Available ► *1–2 administrative volunteers:* responsibilities include working in an administrative office assisting with daily operations. Candidates should have ability to work independently, computer skills, office skills, oral communication skills, organizational skills, strong interpersonal skills, writing skills. Duration is June to August (full-time). Unpaid. ► *10–20 clinical volunteers:* responsibilities include working in an inpatient unit, partial hospitalized program, or day hospital program. Candidates should have ability to work independently, knowledge of field, oral communication skills, personal interest in the field, strong interpersonal skills. Duration is June to August (full-time). Unpaid. ► *8–10 research volunteers:* responsibilities include working on a clinical or scientific research project, collecting data, interviewing subjects, and entering data into computer. Candidates should have analytical skills, computer skills, research skills, background in biology or chemistry. Duration is June to August (full-time). Unpaid. Open to college sophomores, college juniors, college seniors, recent college graduates. International applications accepted.
Benefits Opportunity to attend seminars/workshops, possible full-time employment, willing to complete paperwork for educational credit, willing to provide letters of recommendation, participation in orientation program.
Contact Write, call, or fax Diane A. Clark, Manager, Volunteer and Patient Services. Phone: 914-997-5780. Fax: 914-682-6909. In-person interview recommended (telephone interview accepted). Applicants must submit a formal organization application, resume, one academic and one personal letter of recommendation. Application deadline: April 1 for summer, August 1 for fall.

NORTHWESTERN MEMORIAL HOSPITAL WELLNESS INSTITUTE
251 East Huron Street
Chicago, Illinois 60611

General Information Leading academic medical center serving the entire Chicago area; an organization of caregivers who consistently aspire to high standards of quality and cost effectiveness. Established in 1972. Number of employees: 4,000. Number of internship applications received each year: 75.
Internships Available ► *1 health promotion intern:* responsibilities include assisting in community education seminars, program coordination; development of speaker biographies and researching educational materials; coordinating corporate wellness programs; locating speakers and implementing program logistics; facilitating employee wellness events; assisting with various screenings, incentive programs, blood pressure screenings, nutrition and exercise programs, and mind/body services. Candidates should have ability to work independently, computer skills, declared college major in field, knowledge of field, oral communication skills, self-motivation, written communication skills. Duration is 8–12 weeks. Unpaid. Open to college seniors, recent college graduates, graduate students. International applications accepted.
Benefits Housing at a cost, names of contacts, on-the-job training, opportunity to attend seminars/workshops, possible full-time employment, travel reimbursement, willing to act as a professional reference, willing to complete paperwork for educational credit, willing to provide letters of recommendation.
Contact Write, call, or fax Leigh Ginther, Marketing Coordinator, 150 East Huron Street, Suite 1100, Chicago, Illinois 60611. Phone: 312-926-8895. Fax: 312-926-5444. In-person interview required. Applicants must submit a letter of interest, resume. Applications are accepted continuously. World Wide Web: http://www.NMH.org.

PLANNED PARENTHOOD OF WESTERN PENNSYLVANIA
209 9th Street, Suite 400
Pittsburgh, Pennsylvania 15222

General Information Nonprofit organization that offers services and programs to meet the community's reproductive health care, advocacy, and educational needs. Established in 1930. Number of employees: 28. Affiliate of Planned Parenthood Federation of America, New York, New York. Number of internship applications received each year: 20.

Internships Available ▶ *1–4 general internships.* Candidates should have ability to work independently, ability to work with others, analytical skills, computer skills, office skills, oral communication skills, organizational skills, personal interest in the field, research skills, self-motivation, strong leadership ability, written communication skills, knowledge of field (helpful). Duration is 1–3 semesters. Unpaid. Open to college freshmen, college sophomores, college juniors, college seniors, recent college graduates, graduate students, career changers, individuals reentering the workforce. ▶ *1–2 peer education interns:* responsibilities include refining peer education assessment tools; entering and analyzing pre- and post- test data from outcome evaluations of the peer education program; assisting with agency projects as they arise. Candidates should have ability to work independently, ability to work with others, analytical skills, computer skills, knowledge of field, office skills, oral communication skills, organizational skills, personal interest in the field, self-motivation, writing skills, knowledge of statistical software. Duration is one semester to one academic year. Unpaid. Open to college juniors, college seniors, recent college graduates, graduate students. International applications accepted.

Benefits Opportunity to attend seminars/workshops, willing to act as a professional reference, willing to complete paperwork for educational credit, willing to provide letters of recommendation.

Contact Write, call, fax, e-mail, or through World Wide Web site Volunteer and Intern Coordinator. Phone: 412-434-8969. Fax: 412-434-8974. E-mail: volunteer@ppwp.org. In-person interview required. Applicants must submit a formal organization application, letter of interest, resume, three personal references. Applications are accepted continuously. World Wide Web: http://www.ppwp.org.

RUTH SHEETS ADULT CARE CENTER
228 West Edenton Street
Raleigh, North Carolina 27603

General Information Care center specializing in the care of dementia patients, most of whom have been diagnosed with Alzheimer's disease. Established in 1991. Number of employees: 4. Number of internship applications received each year: 12.

Internships Available ▶ *1–2 social work interns:* responsibilities include performing intake work and keeping progress notes, service notes, and service plans. Candidates should have ability to work independently, oral communication skills, personal interest in the field, self-motivation, strong interpersonal skills, strong leadership ability. Duration is 1 semester. Position available as unpaid or at $220 per month. Open to college freshmen, college sophomores, college juniors, college seniors.

Benefits Job counseling, meals at a cost, names of contacts, opportunity to attend seminars/workshops, possible full-time employment, travel reimbursement, willing to complete paperwork for educational credit, willing to provide letters of recommendation.

Contact Write, call, or fax Judith A. Shotts, Director. Phone: 919-832-7227. Fax: 919-829-5780. In-person interview recommended (telephone interview accepted). Applicants must submit a resume, two personal references, letter of recommendation. Application deadline: November 15 for spring.

SAINT THOMAS HEALTH SERVICES
PO Box 380
Nashville, Tennessee 37202

General Information Catholic, faith-based nonprofit hospital, dedicated to physical, emotional and spiritual healing. Established in 1898. Number of employees: 4,000. Unit of Ascension Health, St. Louis, Missouri. Number of internship applications received each year: 100.

Internships Available ▶ *1–2 marketing and public relations interns:* responsibilities include writing and editing articles for the weekly newsletter; publishing the newsletter to the Intranet; assisting with content review and updates to the Web site; assisting with special events, online research, office administrative-related duties. Candidates should have ability to work independently, computer skills, editing skills, self-motivation, strong interpersonal skills, writing skills. Duration is 12 weeks. Unpaid. Open to college sophomores, college juniors, college seniors. International applications accepted.

Benefits On-the-job training, willing to act as a professional reference, willing to complete paperwork for educational credit, willing to provide letters of recommendation, stipend of $750.

Contact Write, fax, or e-mail Tara Geske, Publications and Web Site Coordinator. Fax: 615-222-4482. E-mail: tgeske@stthomas.org. No phone calls. In-person interview required. Applicants must submit a letter of interest, resume, two writing samples. Applications are accepted continuously. World Wide Web: http://www.saintthomas.org.

SWEDISH MEDICAL CENTER/HUMAN RESOURCES
747 Broadway
Seattle, Washington 98122-4307

General Information Acute medical care facility. Established in 1910. Number of employees: 7,000. Number of internship applications received each year: 50.

Internships Available ▶ *Interns:* responsibilities include assisting in various departments of medical center as needed; positions include epidemiology, nursing (residency), quality improvement, and pastoral care. Candidates should have computer skills, office skills, oral communication skills, personal interest in the field, strong interpersonal skills, health-care experience and knowledge of medical terminology desirable. Duration is flexible. Position available as unpaid or paid. Open to college juniors, college seniors, recent college graduates, graduate students. International applications accepted.

Benefits On-the-job training, possible full-time employment, willing to act as a professional reference, willing to complete paperwork for educational credit, stipends sometimes available for some positions.

Contact Write, call, fax, e-mail, or through World Wide Web site Director of Employment, 747 Broadway, Seattle, Washington 98122-4307. Phone: 206-386-2141. Fax: 206-386-2145. E-mail: jobs@swedish.org. In-person interview recommended (telephone interview accepted). Applicants must submit a formal organization application, letter of interest, resume, 2-4 personal or professional references/letters of recommendation. Applications are accepted continuously. World Wide Web: http://www.swedish.org.

THOMAS JEFFERSON UNIVERSITY
Eleventh and Walnut Streets
Philadelphia, Pennsylvania 19107

General Information Internationally recognized academic health-care center whose mission is to promote state-of-the-art research, quality education, and quality health care. Established in 1824. Number of employees: 11,500. Number of internship applications received each year: 10.

Internships Available ▶ *2 voluntary human resources interns:* responsibilities include rotation of employee relations and employment divisions, data entry, report production and analyses, applicant tracking, reference checks, surveys. Candidates should have ability to work independently, computer skills, declared college major in field, office skills, oral communication skills, organizational skills, personal interest in the field, plan to pursue career in field, self-motivation, strong interpersonal skills. Duration is 1 summer or 1 semester. Unpaid. Open to college juniors, college seniors.

Benefits Job counseling, on-the-job training, opportunity to attend seminars/workshops, possible full-time employment, willing to act as a professional reference, willing to complete paperwork for educational credit, willing to provide letters of recommendation.

Contact Write, fax, or e-mail Kimberly Nichols, Coordinator, Recruitment Systems, 201 South 11th Street, 1st Floor, Martin Building, Philadelphia, Pennsylvania 19107. Phone: 215-503-8219.

Thomas Jefferson University (continued)
Fax: 215-503-2183. E-mail: kimberly.nichols@mail.tju.edu. In-person interview required. Applicants must submit a formal organization application, resume. Application deadline: April 1 for summer, October 1 for spring. World Wide Web: http://http://www.tju.edu/jchp.

TRAVEL NURSES, USA
3215 Guess Road, Suite 212
Durham, North Carolina 27705

General Information Nurse recruitment firm that specializes in matching RNs with positions in the U.S., Canada, and the Caribbean; also sponsors nurses for green card. Established in 2000. Number of employees: 5. Number of internship applications received each year: 70.
Internships Available ▶ *5–10 care plan coordinators:* responsibilities include organizing the patient care of elderly residents with other members of the health-care team. Duration is 1–2 years. $21–$23 per hour. ▶ *10 nurse managers:* responsibilities include overseeing care of elderly residents in a nursing unit; supervising RNs, LPNs, and CNAs. Duration is 1–2 years. $21–$23 per hour. ▶ *5–10 staff development coordinators :* responsibilities include maintaining education of all employees in nursing facility; administering vaccines as needed; inservice for nursing staff. Duration is 1–2 years. $21–$23 per hour. Candidates for all positions should have ability to work with others, experience in the field, oral communication skills, written communication skills, RN licensure. Open to recent college graduates, graduate students, career changers, international graduates. International applications accepted.
Benefits On-the-job training, possible full-time employment, sponsors interns for work permits.
International Internships Available in Canada.
Contact Fax or e-mail Linda McNair, Nurse Recruiter, 3215 Guess Road, Suite 212, Durham, North Carolina 27705. Fax: 919-620-8879. E-mail: sucessful1s@yahoo.com. No phone calls. Telephone interview required. Applicants must submit a resume, academic transcripts, two personal references, RN licensure, CPR card. Applications are accepted continuously. World Wide Web: http://www.travelnurse.bigstep.com.

VILLA MARIA
2300 Dulaney Valley Road
Timonium, Maryland 21093

General Information Organization that provides mental health and special education programs to children, families, and adults. Number of employees: 600. Division of Catholic Charities, Baltimore, Maryland. Number of internship applications received each year: 100.
Internships Available ▶ *15–20 educational treatment assistant interns:* responsibilities include developing and maintaining a therapeutic environment in the classroom; intern is assigned to a class setting where he/she will assist with the preparation and implementation of lesson plans under the direction of the teacher. Candidates should have ability to work independently, declared college major in field, oral communication skills, self-motivation, strong interpersonal skills. Duration is 1 semester. Unpaid. Open to college juniors, college seniors, graduate students, law students, career changers. ▶ *10–15 graduate therapists:* responsibilities include providing individual and family therapy to clients on an assigned caseload under supervision of a licensed practitioner; will be responsible for all case management responsibilities. Candidates should have ability to work independently, oral communication skills, plan to pursue career in field, strong interpersonal skills, written communication skills. Duration is 1 to 2 semesters depending on graduate program requirements. Unpaid. Open to graduate students. ▶ *10–15 residential treatment interns:* responsibilities include helping develop and maintaining a therapeutic environment for children; involves creating opportunities for corrective emotional experiences and socialization as well as fostering relationships that promote development and growth. Candidates should have ability to work independently, declared college major in field, oral communication skills, self-motivation, strong interpersonal

skills. Duration is minimum of 100 hours. Unpaid. Open to college juniors, college seniors, recent college graduates, graduate students, law students, career changers. ▶ *2–4 therapeutic after school program assistants:* responsibilities include assisting in activity programming; transportation and general supervision of children ages 5-13. Candidates should have ability to work independently, college courses in field, oral communication skills, self-motivation, strong interpersonal skills. Duration is 1 semester. Unpaid. Open to college juniors, college seniors, recent college graduates, graduate students, law students, career changers. International applications accepted.
Benefits Formal training, free meals, job counseling, on-the-job training, opportunity to attend seminars/workshops, possible full-time employment, willing to act as a professional reference, willing to complete paperwork for educational credit, willing to provide letters of recommendation.
Contact Write, call, fax, or e-mail Carol Shear, Director of Volunteer Services, 2300 Dulaney Valley Road (Villa Maria), Timonium 21093. Phone: 410-252-4700. Fax: 410-252-3040. E-mail: cshear@catholiccharities-md.org. In-person interview recommended (telephone interview accepted). Applicants must submit a formal organization application, resume, academic transcripts, three personal references, letter of recommendation. Applications are accepted continuously.

VISITING NURSE SERVICE OF NEW YORK
107 East 70th Street
New York, New York 10021

General Information Full-service home health care organization. Established in 1893. Number of employees: 8,000. Number of internship applications received each year: 15.
Internships Available ▶ *1 foundation research and communications intern:* responsibilities include researching and drafting/creating grant proposals and reports for current donors; researching donors (corporations and foundations) through a variety of sources; working internally and externally to increase funding revenue. Candidates should have ability to work independently, computer skills, oral communication skills, research skills, self-motivation, written communication skills. Duration is year-round (minimum of 3 months). Position available as unpaid or paid. Open to college juniors, college seniors, recent college graduates, graduate students, career changers. ▶ *1 marketing and community relations intern:* responsibilities include conducting research on corporate, foundation, and individual donors; preparing donor and prospect profiles; drafting fund-raising correspondence including solicitation materials, acknowledgement letters, and VNSNY fact sheets. Candidates should have computer skills, oral communication skills, personal interest in the field, research skills, self-motivation, written communication skills. Duration is year-round (minimum of 3 months). Position available as unpaid or paid.
Benefits On-the-job training, willing to act as a professional reference, willing to provide letters of recommendation, education grant/stipend.
Contact Write, call, fax, or e-mail Kathryn Harrington, Volunteer Coordinator. Phone: 212-794-6342. Fax: 212-794-6480. E-mail: kharrington@vnsny.org. Applicants must submit a resume, two personal references, two letters of recommendation. Applications are accepted continuously.

YMCA NEW HORIZONS
12831 Newport Avenue, Suite 250
Tustin, California 92780

General Information Organization serving the developmentally disabled in Orange County. Established in 1972. Number of employees: 300. Branch of YMCA of Orange County, Tustin, California. Number of internship applications received each year: 30.
Internships Available ▶ *2–4 counselors :* responsibilities include counseling new horizons participants, supervising clients, initiating program scheduled activities. Candidates should have ability to work with others, oral communication skills, self-motivation, strong leadership ability. Duration is 3–6 months. Unpaid. Open to high school students, recent high school graduates, college

freshmen, college sophomores, college juniors, college seniors, recent college graduates, graduate students, law students, career changers, individuals reentering the workforce, court referral. International applications accepted.

Benefits Free meals, job counseling, possible full-time employment, willing to act as a professional reference, willing to complete paperwork for educational credit, willing to provide letters of recommendation, certification.

Contact Call or e-mail Marc Uy, Internship Coordinator. Phone: 714-838-0181 Ext. 117. Fax: 714-838-6478. E-mail: muy@ymcaoc. net. In-person interview recommended (telephone interview accepted). Applicants must submit a formal organization application. Applications are accepted continuously. World Wide Web: http://www.ymcaoc.org.

SOCIAL ASSISTANCE

AFFILIATED SANTE GROUP AND THE ROCK CREEK FOUNDATION
700 Roeder Road, 4th Floor
Silver Spring, Maryland 20910

General Information Student and volunteer program that meets academic and personal community service needs by helping individuals with disabilities create individualized solutions to their emotional, job, and life-functioning issues in society. Established in 1973. Number of employees: 300. Number of internship applications received each year: 500.

Internships Available ▶ *5 business and nonprofit management interns:* responsibilities include working with director of marketing on development projects and marketing campaigns and managing referral base. Candidates should have ability to work independently, analytical skills, computer skills, declared college major in field, editing skills, knowledge of field, office skills, oral communication skills, organizational skills, personal interest in the field, plan to pursue career in field, research skills, self-motivation, strong interpersonal skills, strong leadership ability, writing skills. Duration is 3 months minimum (2 days weekly). Unpaid. Open to college juniors, college seniors, recent college graduates, graduate students, career changers, individuals reentering the workforce. ▶ *5 computer volunteers/interns:* responsibilities include assessment, management, research, database maintenance, or programming. Candidates should have ability to work independently, ability to work with others, analytical skills, computer skills, editing skills, knowledge of field, office skills, organizational skills, personal interest in the field, self-motivation, writing skills. Duration is 3 months minimum (2 days weekly). Unpaid. Open to high school students, recent high school graduates, college freshmen, college sophomores, college juniors, college seniors, recent college graduates, graduate students, career changers, individuals reentering the workforce. ▶ *5 employment consultants:* responsibilities include assisting adults with disabilities to integrate into the community and on the job. Candidates should have ability to work independently, computer skills, knowledge of field, oral communication skills, organizational skills, personal interest in the field, self-motivation, strong interpersonal skills, strong leadership ability, writing skills. Duration is 3 months minimum (2 days weekly). Unpaid. Open to college juniors, college seniors, recent college graduates, graduate students, individuals reentering the workforce. ▶ *10 leadership/volunteerism/service learning interns:* responsibilities include working with individuals with disabilities. Candidates should have ability to work independently, analytical skills, computer skills, editing skills, experience in the field, organizational skills, personal interest in the field, self-motivation, strong interpersonal skills, strong leadership ability, writing skills. Duration is 3 months minimum (2 days weekly). Unpaid. Open to high school students, recent high school graduates, college freshmen, college sophomores, college juniors, college seniors, recent college graduates, graduate students, law students, career changers, individuals reentering the workforce, participants in community volunteer programs. ▶ *5 organizational development interns:* responsibilities include working with directors and staff to conduct surveys on policy, procedures,

systems of companies, meetings, and infrastructure. Candidates should have ability to work independently, analytical skills, college courses in field, computer skills, editing skills, knowledge of field, office skills, oral communication skills, organizational skills, personal interest in the field, self-motivation, strong interpersonal skills, strong leadership ability, writing skills. Duration is 3 months minimum (2 days weekly). Unpaid. Open to college juniors, college seniors, recent college graduates, graduate students, career changers, individuals reentering the workforce. ▶ *5 psychology interns:* responsibilities include developing and teaching consumer life skills such as community adaptation. Candidates should have ability to work independently, oral communication skills, organizational skills, personal interest in the field, self-motivation, strong interpersonal skills, strong leadership ability, written communication skills. Duration is 3 months minimum (2 days weekly). Unpaid. Open to college sophomores, college juniors, college seniors, recent college graduates, graduate students, career changers, individuals reentering the workforce. ▶ *5 public relations/marketing interns:* responsibilities include marketing duties, technical writing, media networking, and special event planning. Candidates should have ability to work independently, analytical skills, computer skills, editing skills, knowledge of field, oral communication skills, organizational skills, personal interest in the field, plan to pursue career in field, research skills, self-motivation, strong interpersonal skills, strong leadership ability, writing skills, declared major in nonprofit management, mental health management, special event planning, or fund-raising. Duration is 3 months minimum (2 days weekly). Unpaid. Open to college juniors, college seniors, graduate students. ▶ *5 recreation specialists:* responsibilities include facilitating groups and assisting with community integration and special events. Candidates should have ability to work independently, computer skills, knowledge of field, oral communication skills, organizational skills, personal interest in the field, self-motivation, strong interpersonal skills, strong leadership ability, writing skills. Duration is 3 months minimum (2 days weekly). Unpaid. Open to high school seniors, recent high school graduates, college freshmen, college sophomores, college juniors, college seniors, recent college graduates, graduate students, career changers, individuals reentering the workforce, therapeutic recreation majors. ▶ *5 rehabilitation counseling interns:* responsibilities include performing assessments; case management, attending interdisciplinary team meetings; and assisting with vocational goal planning. Candidates should have ability to work independently, analytical skills, college degree in related field, computer skills, oral communication skills, organizational skills, personal interest in the field, plan to pursue career in field, self-motivation, strong interpersonal skills, strong leadership ability, writing skills. Duration is 3 months minimum (2 days weekly). Unpaid. Open to graduate students. ▶ *3 research interns:* responsibilities include performing special research projects in behavioral applications, neuropsychology, human relations, and recreation. Candidates should have ability to work independently, analytical skills, college courses in field, computer skills, editing skills, knowledge of field, office skills, organizational skills, personal interest in the field, plan to pursue career in field, research skills, self-motivation, strong interpersonal skills, strong leadership ability, writing skills, grant writing and/or fund-raising experience (encouraged). Duration is 3 months minimum (2 days weekly). Unpaid. Open to college seniors, recent college graduates, graduate students, career changers. ▶ *10 social work/counseling interns:* responsibilities include case management, facilitating groups and one-on-one, and performing assessments. Candidates should have ability to work independently, college courses in field, knowledge of field, oral communication skills, organizational skills, personal interest in the field, plan to pursue career in field, self-motivation, strong interpersonal skills, strong leadership ability, written communication skills. Duration is 3 months minimum (2 days weekly). Unpaid. Open to college juniors, college seniors, recent college graduates, graduate students, career changers, individuals reentering the workforce. ▶ *5 student/volunteer career counselors:* responsibilities include assisting staff with interviewing students, surveying satisfaction, updating database for community referrals, and attending seminars/community collaborations. Candidates should have ability to work independently, college courses in field, computer skills, editing skills, knowledge of field, office skills, oral com-

Affiliated Sante Group and the Rock Creek Foundation (continued)

munication skills, organizational skills, personal interest in the field, self-motivation, strong interpersonal skills, strong leadership ability, writing skills. Duration is 3 months minimum (2 days weekly). Unpaid. Open to college freshmen, college sophomores, college juniors, college seniors, recent college graduates, graduate students, career changers, individuals reentering the workforce. International applications accepted.

Benefits Formal training, job counseling, names of contacts, on-the-job training, opportunity to attend seminars/workshops, possible full-time employment, willing to act as a professional reference, willing to complete paperwork for educational credit, willing to provide letters of recommendation, possibility of partial parking reimbursement.

Contact Write, call, fax, e-mail, or through World Wide Web site Ms. Beth Albaneze, Director of Students/Volunteers. Phone: 301-589-8303 Ext. 417. Fax: 301-589-5861. E-mail: balbaneze@santegroup.org. In-person interview recommended (telephone interview accepted). Applicants must submit a formal organization application, letter of interest, resume, personal reference, letter of recommendation, learning contract from school, TB/physical required if in direct service; application may be downloaded from Web site. Applications are accepted continuously. World Wide Web: http://www.thesantegroup.org.

ALFRED CAMPANELLI YMCA
300 West Wise Road
Schaumburg, Illinois 60193

General Information Organization providing a safe, clean environment, with well-trained staff and consistent programs to meet the needs and nurture the development of a healthy spirit, mind, and body. Established in 1967. Number of employees: 125. Number of internship applications received each year: 10.

Internships Available ▶ *1–2 aquatics assistants:* responsibilities include assisting in aquatics program and staff scheduling. Candidates should have ability to work with others, oral communication skills, organizational skills, plan to pursue career in field, self-motivation, strong leadership ability, CPR, first aid, and lifeguarding certifications. Duration is 3-6 months (flexible). Position available as unpaid or paid. Open to college juniors, college seniors, recent college graduates, career changers, individuals reentering the workforce. ▶ *1–2 day camp counselors/assistants:* responsibilities include assisting with the day-to-day operation of a large suburban day camp; supervising staff, scheduling activities; maintaining accurate records and budget. Candidates should have knowledge of field, oral communication skills, organizational skills, strong interpersonal skills, strong leadership ability, written communication skills. Duration is early June to mid-August. $7.50–$11 per hour. Open to college freshmen, college sophomores, college juniors, college seniors, recent college graduates, graduate students. ▶ *1–2 marketing assistants:* responsibilities include assisting with membership campaigns, internal/external promotions, and brochure development. Candidates should have ability to work with others, oral communication skills, organizational skills, plan to pursue career in field, self-motivation, strong leadership ability, business/marketing experience (individuals working towards degree in field preferred). Duration is 3-6 months (flexible). Position available as unpaid or paid. Open to college juniors, college seniors, recent college graduates, career changers, individuals reentering the workforce. ▶ *1–2 senior programs assistants:* responsibilities include working with senior citizens in a day center setting, focusing on programs and social activity. Candidates should have college courses in field, organizational skills, personal interest in the field, self-motivation, strong interpersonal skills, written communication skills. Duration is 1-3 months (flexible). Negotiable stipend. Open to college sophomores, college juniors, college seniors, recent college graduates, graduate students, individuals reentering the workforce. ▶ *1–2 sports and fitness assistants:* responsibilities include running sports leagues and exercise incentives; providing health education. Candidates should have ability to work with others, oral communication skills, organizational skills, plan to pursue career in field, self-motivation, strong leadership ability, CPR and first aid certifications; fitness instructor certification is a plus; individuals working towards

degree in related field preferred; experience working with people of all ages. Duration is 3-6 months (flexible). Position available as unpaid or paid. Open to college juniors, college seniors, recent college graduates, career changers, individuals reentering the workforce. ▶ *1–2 teen programs assistants:* responsibilities include working with 7th-9th grade students at a drop-in teen center focusing on mentoring, tutoring, and social programs. Candidates should have college courses in field, knowledge of field, organizational skills, strong interpersonal skills, strong leadership ability. Duration is 1-2 months (flexible). Negotiable stipend. Open to college sophomores, college juniors, college seniors, recent college graduates. International applications accepted.

Benefits Formal training, job counseling, names of contacts, on-the-job training, opportunity to attend seminars/workshops, possible full-time employment, willing to act as a professional reference, willing to complete paperwork for educational credit, willing to provide letters of recommendation.

Contact Write, call, fax, or e-mail Chris Weittenhiller, Sports and Fitness Director. Phone: 847-891-9622. Fax: 847-891-8901. E-mail: chrisw@campanelliymca.org. In-person interview required. Applicants must submit a letter of interest, resume, two personal references, proof of any relevant certifications (such as CPR or first aid). Applications are accepted continuously.

ALLIANCE FOR CHILDREN AND FAMILIES POLICY OFFICE
1701 K Street, NW, Suite 200
Washington, District of Columbia 20006-1503

General Information Organization representing nationwide voluntary nonprofit agencies that provide a wide range of services to children and families. Established in 1911. Number of employees: 6. Division of Alliance for Children and Families, Milwaukee, Wisconsin. Number of internship applications received each year: 60.

Internships Available ▶ *2–3 public policy interns:* responsibilities include monitoring and analyzing proposed legislation on child and family issues; attending congressional hearings and national advocacy coalition meetings; writing issue briefs, policy updates, and articles for monthly newsletter; assisting with planning of annual Public Policy Conference; attending staff meetings and updating office on specific policy issue areas; assisting with national and grassroots advocacy initiatives. Candidates should have ability to work independently, analytical skills, college courses in field, personal interest in the field, writing skills. Duration is flexible. Unpaid. Open to college juniors, college seniors, recent college graduates, graduate students, law students, career changers. International applications accepted.

Benefits Names of contacts, on-the-job training, opportunity to attend seminars/workshops, willing to complete paperwork for educational credit, willing to provide letters of recommendation.

Contact Write, call, fax, or e-mail Carmen Delgado Votaw, Senior Vice President. Phone: 202-223-3447. Fax: 202-331-7476. E-mail: cvotaw@alliance1.org. In-person interview required. Applicants must submit a letter of interest, resume, writing sample. Applications are accepted continuously. World Wide Web: http://www.alliance1.org.

ALTERNATIVE HOUSE
2136 Gallows Road, Suite E
Dunn Loring, Virginia 22027

General Information Shelter and outreach program that builds on the innate strengths and resiliency of children, youth, and families through individual, group, and family interaction. Established in 1972. Number of employees: 25. Unit of Alternative House, Inc., Dunn Loring, Virginia. Number of internship applications received each year: 30.

Internships Available ▶ *1–6 emergency teen shelter interns:* responsibilities include planning and initiating recreational, educational, and group activities for youth ages 13-17; supervising youth; maintaining documentation of activities; and adhering to professional standards. Candidates should have oral communication skills, self-motivation, strong interpersonal skills, strong leadership ability, written communication skills. Duration is 3–12 months. Unpaid.

Open to high school seniors, recent high school graduates, college freshmen, college sophomores, college juniors, college seniors, recent college graduates, graduate students, law students, career changers, individuals reentering the workforce. ▶ *1–3 outreach programs interns:* responsibilities include implementing new programs in outreach and teen center programs; planning and initiating recreational, educational, and group activities for youth ages 13-17; networking with people within the community and other agencies; and adhering to professional standards. Candidates should have ability to work independently, oral communication skills, self-motivation, strong interpersonal skills, strong leadership ability. Duration is 3–12 months. Unpaid. Open to college sophomores, college juniors, college seniors, recent college graduates, graduate students, law students, career changers. International applications accepted.
Benefits Formal training, free meals, possible full-time employment, willing to complete paperwork for educational credit, willing to provide letters of recommendation.
Contact Write, call, or fax Volunteer Coordinator. Phone: 703-820-9039. Fax: 703-820-0788. In-person interview recommended (telephone interview accepted). Applicants must submit a formal organization application, letter of interest, resume, three personal references. Application deadline: April 15 for summer, August 1 for fall, December 15 for spring.

ALTERNATIVES, INC.
4730 North Sheridan Road
Chicago, Illinois 60640

General Information Comprehensive youth-service agency serving the north side of Chicago. Established in 1993. Number of employees: 7. Number of internship applications received each year: 3.
Internships Available ▶ *5–7 interns:* responsibilities include possible positions in administrative, counseling, and programs. Candidates should have ability to work independently, ability to work with others, oral communication skills, personal interest in the field, written communication skills, flexibility. Duration is 3–12 months. Unpaid. Open to recent high school graduates, college freshmen, college sophomores, college juniors, college seniors, recent college graduates, graduate students, law students, career changers, individuals reentering the workforce. International applications accepted.
Benefits On-the-job training, opportunity to attend seminars/workshops, possible full-time employment, willing to act as a professional reference, willing to complete paperwork for educational credit, willing to provide letters of recommendation.
Contact Write, call, fax, or e-mail Zofia Ruzyc, Resource Coordinator. Phone: 773-506-7474. Fax: 773-506-9420. E-mail: zruzyc@alternativesyouth.org. In-person interview required. Applicants must submit a letter of interest, resume, two writing samples, three references. Applications are accepted continuously. World Wide Web: http://www.alternativesyouth.org.

AMAZON-AFRICA AID ORGANIZATION
PO Box 7776
Ann Arbor, Michigan 48107

General Information Organization dedicated to improving the human condition by providing technical and financial aid to impoverished regions around the world.
Internships Available ▶ *1 general office intern:* responsibilities include assisting executive and program directors in overall management and operation of organization; some activities may include volunteer recruitment, fund-raising, public relations, general office management. Candidates should have ability to work independently, written communication skills, computer skills including Microsoft Word, Microsoft Excel, and Netscape Navigator; Web design experience and Portuguese or Spanish a plus, but not required. Duration is flexible. Unpaid.
Benefits Arrangements may be made for free housing in return for a minimum of 40 hours work per month.
Contact Write Daniel Weiss, PhD, Executive Director. Applicants must submit a letter of interest, resume, minimum of 3 references. Applications are accepted continuously. World Wide Web: http://www.amazonafrica.org.

AMERICAN FOUNDATION FOR THE BLIND
11 Penn Plaza, Suite 300
New York, New York 10001

General Information Nonprofit organization with offices in Atlanta, Chicago, Dallas, San Francisco, and Washington, DC that serves as the national resource for the public and for local services for blind and visually-impaired persons. Established in 1921. Number of employees: 150. Number of internship applications received each year: 5.
Internships Available ▶ *1–3 social science research assistants:* responsibilities include conducting policy research and program evaluation. Candidates should have ability to work independently, ability to work with others, computer skills, organizational skills, personal interest in the field, research skills. Duration is 1–2 semesters. Position available as unpaid or at $6-$16 per hour depending on experience (if funding permits). Open to college juniors, college seniors, recent college graduates, graduate students, law students, career changers, individuals reentering the workforce. International applications accepted.
Benefits Job counseling, names of contacts, on-the-job training, opportunity to attend seminars/workshops, possible full-time employment, willing to act as a professional reference, willing to complete paperwork for educational credit, willing to provide letters of recommendation.
Contact Write, call, fax, e-mail, or through World Wide Web site Dr. Corinne Kirchner, Director of Policy Research and Program Evaluation. Phone: 212-502-7640. Fax: 212-502-7773. E-mail: corinne@afb.net. In-person interview recommended (telephone interview accepted). Applicants must submit a resume, 2 personal references or letters of recommendation; one writing sample may be required. Applications are accepted continuously. World Wide Web: http://www.afb.org/afb.

AMERICAN FRIENDS SERVICE COMMITTEE
1501 Cherry Street
Philadelphia, Pennsylvania 19102-1479

General Information Nonprofit organization. Established in 1917. Number of employees: 80. Number of internship applications received each year: 40.
Internships Available ▶ *20 Mexico program volunteers:* responsibilities include volunteer work in rural Mexico. Candidates should have ability to work with others, oral communication skills, self-motivation, Spanish. Duration is July 1 to August 20. Unpaid. Open to recent high school graduates, college freshmen, college sophomores, college juniors, college seniors, recent college graduates, graduate students, law students, law school graduates, individuals reentering the workforce. International applications accepted.
Benefits Housing at a cost, meals at a cost, opportunity to attend seminars/workshops, travel reimbursement, tuition assistance, willing to provide letters of recommendation.
International Internships Available in Xilitla, Mexico.
Contact Call or e-mail Linda Oh, Mexico Summer Project Recruitment Coordinator. Phone: 215-241-7295. Fax: 215-241-7026. E-mail: mexsummer@afsc.org. Applicants must submit a formal organization application, resume, three personal references, three letters of recommendation. Application deadline: March 1. World Wide Web: http://www.afsc.org.

AMERICAN RED CROSS
8111 Gatehouse Road, 6th Floor
Falls Church, Virginia 22042

General Information Humanitarian organization that provides relief to victims of disasters and helps people prevent, prepare for, and respond to emergencies. Established in 1881. Number of employees: 1,000. Number of internship applications received each year: 200.
Internships Available ▶ *10–30 Presidential interns for racial/ethnic minority students:* responsibilities include working in positions throughout NHQ including finance, government relations, biomedical services, international services, communications, HIV/AIDS education, disaster, and the Holland Laboratory. Candidates should have college courses in field, oral communication skills, personal interest in the field, self-motivation, strong interpersonal

American Red Cross (continued)

skills, written communication skills. Duration is 10 weeks. $9.40 per hour. Open to college freshmen, college sophomores, college juniors, college seniors, recent college graduates, graduate students, law students.

Benefits On-the-job training, opportunity to attend seminars/workshops, possible full-time employment, willing to complete paperwork for educational credit, willing to provide letters of recommendation.

Contact Write, call, fax, e-mail, or through World Wide Web site Jennifer Carino, Diversity Associate. Phone: 703-206-8368. Fax: 703-206-8572. E-mail: carinoj@usa.redcross.org. In-person interview recommended (telephone interview accepted). Applicants must submit a letter of interest, resume. Application deadline: March 2 for summer. World Wide Web: http://www.redcross.org.

THE ARCH, INC.
175-43 Hillside Avenue
Jamaica, New York 11432

General Information Organization that provides human services towards a more just, equitable world through diversity education and arts outreach programs; assists at-risk communities, families, and individuals with arts performance/classes/workshops, food distribution, and advocacy. Established in 1998. Number of employees: 10. Number of internship applications received each year: 2,500.

Internships Available ▶ *PC computer experts/graphics designers:* responsibilities include maintaining Web page; designing, producing, formatting newsletter, brochures, posters, letterheads, official letters (written by others); maintaining computer files, address book, e-mail records, and correspondence records. Candidates should have ability to work independently, ability to work with others, organizational skills, self-motivation. Duration is flexible. Unpaid. Open to high school students, recent high school graduates, college freshmen, college sophomores, college juniors, college seniors, recent college graduates, graduate students, law students, career changers, individuals reentering the workforce. ▶ *1–2 accounting interns:* responsibilities include undertaking pro bono or reduced fee work maintaining 'The Arch' accounts, as required of a 501 (C) (3) not-for-profit corporation. Candidates should have strong interpersonal skills. Duration is flexible. Position available as unpaid or at $25–$50 per hour for CPAs. Open to high school students, recent high school graduates, college freshmen, college sophomores, college juniors, college seniors, recent college graduates, graduate students, law students, career changers, individuals reentering the workforce, certified public accountants only. ▶ *Grant writers:* responsibilities include researching information about potential funding sources; taking part in the process of funding, regularly sharing reports with the directors of Arch; providing detailed accounts on requirements for sources, as well as liaison with sources and funders. Duration is flexible. Position available as unpaid or paid. Open to high school students, recent high school graduates, college freshmen, college sophomores, college juniors, college seniors, recent college graduates, graduate students, law students, career changers, individuals reentering the workforce. ▶ *1–2 legal expert/advisors:* responsibilities include advising "The Arch" on legal issues and taking necessary action for "The Arch" only, not for its clients, on a pro bono/reduced fee basis. Candidates should have ability to work independently, personal interest in the field, self-motivation, strong interpersonal skills, strong leadership ability. Duration is flexible. Unpaid. Open to practicing attorneys or law professors only. ▶ *Marketing interns:* responsibilities include assisting in media market research; calling newspaper and magazine editors and radio and T.V. producers to develop a database of media contacts for the organization. Duration is flexible. Position available as unpaid or paid. Open to high school students, recent high school graduates, college freshmen, college sophomores, college juniors, college seniors, recent college graduates, graduate students, law students, career changers, individuals reentering the workforce. ▶ *Media associates:* responsibilities include assisting with development of 5-minute music capsules featuring undiscovered artists for broadcast by college radio stations; archiving/documenting in multimedia. Candidates should have

ability to work independently, ability to work with others, knowledge of field, organizational skills, research skills, self-motivation. Duration is flexible. Unpaid. Open to high school students, recent high school graduates, college freshmen, college sophomores, college juniors, college seniors, recent college graduates, graduate students, law students, career changers, individuals reentering the workforce. ▶ *1–2 office managers:* responsibilities include light bookkeeping: receiving/disbursing funds; maintaining records and files; filing, typing, and maintaining records of correspondence, addresses, E-mail; making telephone calls; interacting with respondents; running errands connected with office work. Candidates should have ability to work independently, office skills, organizational skills, self-motivation, strong interpersonal skills. Duration is 6-12 month commitment (preferred), 20 hours per week. Unpaid. Open to high school students, recent high school graduates, college freshmen, college sophomores, college juniors, college seniors, recent college graduates, graduate students, law students, career changers, individuals reentering the workforce. International applications accepted.

Benefits Formal training, free meals, names of contacts, on-the-job training, opportunity to attend seminars/workshops, possible full-time employment, willing to act as a professional reference, willing to complete paperwork for educational credit, willing to provide letters of recommendation, fruits, vegetables, variety of bread and baked goods provided; free housing or housing at a cost in some cases.

Contact Write, call, fax, e-mail, or through World Wide Web site Craig Kaufman, Director. Phone: 718-523-6900. Fax: 718-262-8234. E-mail: kaufman@thearch.org. Applicants must submit a letter of interest, resume, personal reference. Applications are accepted continuously. World Wide Web: http://www.thearch.org.

AUDUBON YMCA
2460 Boulevard of the Generals
Norristown, Pennsylvania 19403

General Information Organization that provides the community with services that promote healthy spirits, minds, and bodies. Established in 1984. Number of employees: 70. Branch of Phoenixville Area YMCA, Phoenixville, Pennsylvania. Number of internship applications received each year: 4.

Internships Available ▶ *2–5 child-care interns:* responsibilities include assisting with staffing schedules, designing lesson plans for various age groups, assisting in provider care, learning state licensing requirements, developing promotional piece for services offered. Candidates should have oral communication skills, plan to pursue career in field, self-motivation, strong interpersonal skills, strong leadership ability, written communication skills. Duration is summer or 1-3 semesters. Position available as unpaid or paid. Open to high school seniors, college freshmen, college sophomores, college juniors, college seniors, recent college graduates, individuals pursuing child-care certificates. ▶ *1–3 community and family recreation interns:* responsibilities include designing lesson plan for outdoor education, designing youth and/or family special events, creating promotional strategy for youth and/or family programs, assisting in day camp program during summer internship. Candidates should have ability to work independently, oral communication skills, personal interest in the field, self-motivation, strong interpersonal skills, strong leadership ability. Duration is summer or 1-3 semesters. Position available as unpaid or paid. Open to college freshmen, college sophomores, college juniors, college seniors, recent college graduates, PHEAA work-study eligibles. ▶ *1 technology assistant:* responsibilities include assisting with implementing computer use in child-care programs; troubleshooting computer problems in departments and administration areas; assisting with computer upgrades; instructing staff in Word, Excel, and entry-level graphics programs. Candidates should have ability to work independently, computer skills, knowledge of field, oral communication skills, self-motivation, strong interpersonal skills. Duration is 1 summer or 1-3 semesters. Position available as unpaid or paid. Open to college sophomores, college juniors, college seniors, recent college graduates, individuals reentering the workforce. ▶ *5–10 volunteers:* responsibilities include performing office duties and assisting in childcare, administration, physical education, or marketing. Candidates should have ability to work independently, office skills, oral communication skills, personal interest in the field, self-motivation, strong interpersonal skills. Duration is flexible. Unpaid. Open to college freshmen, college sophomores, college juniors, college seniors, recent college graduates, graduate students, career changers.

Benefits Job counseling, names of contacts, on-the-job training, opportunity to attend seminars/workshops, possible full-time employment, willing to complete paperwork for educational credit, willing to provide letters of recommendation.

Contact Write, call, fax, or e-mail Janet Genuardi, Branch Executive Director. Phone: 610-539-0900. Fax: 610-539-2975. E-mail: jlg@net-thing.net. In-person interview recommended (telephone interview accepted). Applicants must submit a letter of interest, resume, two personal references, two letters of recommendation. Applications are accepted continuously. World Wide Web: http://www.phoenixvilleymca.com.

BAILEY HOUSE, INC
275 7th Avenue, 12th Floor
New York, New York 10001

General Information Nonprofit agency that provides housing and supportive services for families living with HIV and AIDS. Established in 1983. Number of employees: 48. Number of internship applications received each year: 12.

Internships Available ▶ *INVEST interns:* responsibilities include working with the INVEST Team to create and maintain innovative services to residents on projects including "The Book Club" and "Back to Work Clothing Closet". Candidates should have ability to work independently, analytical skills, computer skills, editing skills, knowledge of field, office skills, oral communication skills, organizational skills, personal interest in the field, research skills, self-motivation, strong interpersonal skills, strong leadership ability, writing skills. Position available as unpaid or paid. Open to high school seniors, recent high school graduates, individuals reentering the workforce. ▶ *Administrative interns:* responsibilities include providing coverage when necessary to accomplish short-term administrative tasks for all departments including greeting visitors, answering phones, forwarding messages, faxing, and creating documents. Candidates should have ability to work with others, analytical skills, computer skills, editing skills, knowledge of field, office skills, oral communication skills, organizational skills, personal interest in the field, plan to pursue career in field, research skills, self-motivation, strong leadership ability, writing skills. Position available as unpaid or paid. Open to high school seniors, recent high school graduates, college freshmen, college sophomores, college juniors, college seniors, recent college graduates, graduate students, law students, career changers, individuals reentering the workforce. ▶ *Volunteer service interns:* responsibilities include assisting the coordinator of volunteer services with recruitment, interviewing and retention of volunteers and interns; assisting with the production of the volunteer newsletter, creating flyers and organizing mass mailings; helping staff volunteers for special events and agency needs. Candidates should have ability to work independently, analytical skills, computer skills, editing skills, knowledge of field, office skills, oral communication skills, organizational skills, personal interest in the field, plan to pursue career in field, research skills, self-motivation, strong interpersonal skills, strong leadership ability, writing skills. Position available as unpaid or paid. Open to high school seniors, recent high school graduates, college freshmen, college sophomores, college juniors, college seniors, recent college graduates, graduate students, law students, career changers, individuals reentering the workforce. International applications accepted.

Benefits Names of contacts, on-the-job training, travel reimbursement, willing to act as a professional reference, willing to complete paperwork for educational credit, willing to provide letters of recommendation.

Contact Write, call, fax, e-mail, or through World Wide Web site Tamesha Harper, Coordinator of Volunteer Services. Phone: 212-633-2500 Ext. 215. Fax: 212-633-2932. E-mail: tharper@baileyhouse.org. In-person interview required. Applicants must submit a formal organization application, resume, two personal references. Applications are accepted continuously. World Wide Web: http://www.baileyhouse.org.

BERKSHIRE FARM CENTER AND SERVICES FOR YOUTH
Route 22
Canaan, New York 12029

General Information Nonprofit social service agency serving at-risk adolescents of New York State and their families. Established in 1886. Number of employees: 350. Number of internship applications received each year: 15.

Internships Available ▶ *10–15 teaching assistants:* responsibilities include assisting teacher in diverse subjects in public junior and high schools. Candidates should have ability to work independently, ability to work with others, oral communication skills, plan to pursue career in field, self-motivation, strong leadership ability, written communication skills, interest in at-risk adolescents. Duration is flexible. Unpaid. ▶ *Youth counselors/advocates/mentors:* responsibilities include assisting in supervision of troubled adolescents. Candidates should have personal interest in the field, self-motivation, strong interpersonal skills, interest in at-risk adolescents; possible plan to pursue career in field. Duration is flexible. Unpaid. Open to recent high school graduates, college freshmen, college sophomores, college juniors, college seniors, recent college graduates, graduate students, law students, career changers, individuals reentering the workforce. International applications accepted.

Benefits Formal training, free meals, job counseling, names of contacts, on-the-job training, opportunity to attend seminars/workshops, possible full-time employment, willing to act as a professional reference, willing to complete paperwork for educational credit, willing to provide letters of recommendation, opportunity to clarify interest in field by practical experience working with at-risk adolescents.

Contact Write, call, or fax Lawrence "Lari" Brandstein, Director of Volunteer Services. Phone: 518-781-4567 Ext. 322. Fax: 518-781-3710. In-person interview recommended (telephone interview accepted). Applicants must submit a formal organization application, letter of interest, resume, three personal references. Applications are accepted continuously.

BETHESDA LUTHERAN HOMES AND SERVICES, INC.
700 Hoffmann Drive
Watertown, Wisconsin 53094-6204

General Information Facility that provides residential and training services to individuals with developmental disabilities. Established in 1904. Number of employees: 700. Number of internship applications received each year: 21.

Internships Available ▶ *2 Camp Matz interns (co-op positions):* responsibilities include supervising and coordinating all activities for the Servant Event Program at Camp Matz. Candidates should have ability to work independently, ability to work with others, oral communication skills, strong leadership ability, written communication skills, camp experience desirable, Lutheran background. Duration is 12 weeks in summer. $7.50 per hour. ▶ *1 chaplaincy representative (co-op position):* responsibilities include providing spiritual nurture for people with developmental disabilities, leading Bible classes, and serving as a chapel aide. Candidates should have ability to work independently, oral communication skills, personal interest in the field, strong interpersonal skills, Lutheran background. Duration is 12 weeks in summer. $7.50 per hour. ▶ *1 nursing student co-op:* responsibilities include performing nursing duties designed to enhance the student's knowledge of the role of a professional nurse in a facility that provides care and treatment for people who have physical and mental disabilities. Candidates should have ability to work with others, declared college major in field, experience in the field, personal interest in the field, plan to pursue career in field. Duration is 12 weeks in summer. $7.50 per hour. ▶ *1 psychology intern:* responsibilities include assisting in preparing resident annual summaries and psychological assessments, preparing and analyzing data collec-

Bethesda Lutheran Homes and Services, Inc. (continued)

tion materials, assisting in the development of behavior treatment programs. Candidates should have ability to work with others, analytical skills, college courses in field, organizational skills, personal interest in the field. Duration is 12 weeks in summer. $7.50 per hour. ▶ *1 public relations co-op:* responsibilities include writing articles and stories, doing layouts and photographic assignments, constructing displays, giving tours of Bethesda, and assisting with special events as required. Candidates should have ability to work with others, computer skills, editing skills, oral communication skills, plan to pursue career in field, self-motivation, writing skills. Duration is 12 weeks in summer. $7.50 per hour. ▶ *1 student social worker (co-op position):* responsibilities include working directly with residents individually or in groups in social skill development or behavior training; assisting with writing and monitoring Individual Program Plans (in conjunction with an assigned social worker/QMRP). Candidates should have ability to work with others, college courses in field, organizational skills, personal interest in the field, plan to pursue career in field. Duration is 12 weeks in summer. $7.50 per hour. ▶ *1 student teacher (co-op position):* responsibilities include working as a team, assisting in organizing and planning classroom activities, seeking materials and preparing for activities outlines in lesson plans, and assisting with all record keeping as assigned by the supervising teacher. Candidates should have declared college major in field, knowledge of field, personal interest in the field, plan to pursue career in field, strong interpersonal skills, strong leadership ability. Duration is 12 weeks in summer. $7.50 per hour. Open to college juniors, college seniors, graduate students.
Benefits Formal training, free housing, meals at a cost, on-the-job training, opportunity to attend seminars/workshops, possible full-time employment, willing to act as a professional reference, willing to complete paperwork for educational credit, willing to provide letters of recommendation.
Contact Write, call, fax, e-mail, or through World Wide Web site Thomas Heuer, Coordinator, Outreach Programs and Services. Phone: 800-369-4636 Ext. 416. Fax: 920-262-6513. E-mail: theuer@blhs.org. In-person interview recommended (telephone interview accepted). Applicants must submit a formal organization application, two personal references, letter of recommendation, cover letter, resume desirable; preference given to Lutheran students. Application deadline: March 1 for summer co-op positions. World Wide Web: http://www.blhs.org.

BIG BROTHERS BIG SISTERS-NIAGARA COUNTY, INC.
86 Park Avenue
Lockport, New York 14094

General Information Nonprofit organization that matches in-risk children, ages 7-15, from single-parent homes, with a volunteer adult role model to serve as a friend. Established in 1973. Number of employees: 4. Unit of Big Brothers Big Sisters of America, Philadelphia, Pennsylvania. Number of internship applications received each year: 3.
Internships Available ▶ *1 program aide:* responsibilities include assisting with office responsibilities, planning, implementing, and participating in agency events, contributing to newsletters, keeping records, and performing clerical work. Candidates should have ability to work independently, ability to work with others, office skills, oral communication skills, organizational skills, personal interest in the field. Duration is flexible. Unpaid. Open to high school students, college freshmen, college sophomores, college juniors, college seniors, recent college graduates, graduate students, career changers, individuals reentering the workforce. International applications accepted.
Benefits Formal training, job counseling, names of contacts, on-the-job training, willing to act as a professional reference, willing to complete paperwork for educational credit, willing to provide letters of recommendation.
Contact Write, call, fax, or e-mail Annemarie C. Bettino, President. Phone: 716-434-1855. Fax: 716-434-2242. E-mail: bbbsnc@buffnet.net. In-person interview required. Applicants must submit a letter of interest, resume, academic transcripts. Applications are accepted continuously.

BIG BROTHERS/BIG SISTERS OF BEAVER COUNTY
426 Adams Street
Beaver, Pennsylvania 15074

General Information Youth development agency that recruits, screens, and supervises adult volunteers in one-to-one mentoring relationships with disadvantaged school-age youth. Established in 1976. Number of employees: 7. Affiliate of Big Brothers Big Sisters of America, Philadelphia, Pennsylvania. Number of internship applications received each year: 10.
Internships Available ▶ *1–3 caseworker interns:* responsibilities include assisting caseworkers with recruitment, screening, training, supervising volunteers, and fund-raising. Candidates should have ability to work with others, college courses in field, oral communication skills, plan to pursue career in field, self-motivation. Duration is 3 months. Unpaid. Open to college sophomores, college juniors, college seniors, graduate students. International applications accepted.
Benefits Opportunity to attend seminars/workshops, possible full-time employment, travel reimbursement, willing to complete paperwork for educational credit.
Contact Write, call, or fax Pam Webb, Executive Director. Phone: 724-728-4300. Fax: 724-728-3674. In-person interview required. Applicants must submit a letter of interest, resume. Application deadline: August 1 for fall, November 1 for spring.

BIG BROTHERS/BIG SISTERS OF BERRIEN & CASS
1 South Fifth, PO Box 194
Niles, Michigan 49120-0194

General Information Organization that prepares children for the future by enhancing their strengths through new experiences and friendship with qualified mentors. Established in 1967. Number of employees: 3. Unit of Big Brothers Big Sisters of America, Philadelphia, Pennsylvania. Number of internship applications received each year: 4.
Internships Available ▶ *Case work assistants:* responsibilities include supervising unmatched clients, conducting volunteer and client trainings, contributing to the agency newsletter, and membership on the Activities Committee. Candidates should have oral communication skills, plan to pursue career in field, self-motivation, strong interpersonal skills, written communication skills. Duration is flexible. Unpaid. Open to any interested individual. International applications accepted.
Benefits On-the-job training, willing to complete paperwork for educational credit, willing to provide letters of recommendation, approved mileage reimbursement.
Contact Write, call, fax, or e-mail Carol Milburn, Co-Director. Phone: 616-684-1100. Fax: 616-684-1490. In-person interview required. Applicants must submit a formal organization application. Applications are accepted continuously.

BIG BROTHERS/BIG SISTERS OF BUCKS COUNTY
2875 Old York Road
Jamison, Pennsylvania 18929

General Information Organization that provides mentoring services to youth. Established in 1963. Number of employees: 23. Affiliate of Big Brothers Big Sisters of America, Philadelphia, Pennsylvania. Number of internship applications received each year: 4.
Internships Available ▶ *Case manager interns:* responsibilities include recruitment, screening, matching and supervision of volunteers, in addition to screening, matching, and match supervision of youth. Candidates should have ability to work independently, ability to work with others, college courses in field, computer skills, oral communication skills, organizational skills. Duration is year-round. Unpaid. Open to college freshmen, college sophomores, college juniors, college seniors, recent college graduates, graduate students, career changers, individuals reentering the workforce. ▶ *1 recruitment intern:* responsibilities include community recruitment of Big Brothers and Little Sisters. Candidates should have ability to work independently, experience in the field, office skills, oral communication skills, self-motivation, writing skills. Duration is year-round. Unpaid. Open to recent high school graduates, college sophomores, college juniors, college seniors, recent

college graduates, graduate students, career changers, individuals reentering the workforce. International applications accepted.
Benefits Formal training, names of contacts, on-the-job training, opportunity to attend seminars/workshops, possible full-time employment, travel reimbursement, willing to act as a professional reference, willing to complete paperwork for educational credit, willing to provide letters of recommendation.
Contact Write, call, fax, e-mail, or through World Wide Web site Leonette Boiarski, Director of Programs. Phone: 215-343-8260 Ext. 15. Fax: 215-343-8265. E-mail: boiarski@bbbsbc.org. In-person interview required. Applicants must submit a formal organization application, letter of interest, resume, three personal references. Applications are accepted continuously. World Wide Web: http://www.bbbsbc.org.

BIG BROTHERS BIG SISTERS OF CAMDEN AND GLOUCESTER COUNTIES
246 South White Horse Pike
Audubon, New Jersey 08106

General Information Organization with mission to provide positive role models and to enhance the development of youth in need. Established in 1959. Number of employees: 6. Affiliate of Big Brothers Big Sisters of America, Philadelphia, Pennsylvania. Number of internship applications received each year: 5.
Internships Available ▶ *1–3 fund development assistants:* responsibilities include assisting with planning and organizing special events and fund-raising campaigns. Candidates should have office skills, oral communication skills, organizational skills, personal interest in the field, self-motivation, written communication skills. Duration is flexible. Unpaid. Open to recent high school graduates, college freshmen, college sophomores, college juniors, college seniors, recent college graduates, graduate students. ▶ *1–3 grant and program development interns:* responsibilities include assisting in researching and writing grants; also assisting with strategic planning and other initiatives such as program development, public relations, and recruitment. Candidates should have ability to work independently, ability to work with others, editing skills, research skills, writing skills. Duration is flexible. Unpaid. Open to college seniors, recent college graduates, graduate students. ▶ *1–3 program assistants:* responsibilities include assisting with follow-up co-worker activities with existing matches; may participate in screening of potential volunteers and clients; assisting with planning certain programs and campaigns. Candidates should have ability to work with others, college courses in field, oral communication skills, plan to pursue career in field, written communication skills. Duration is flexible. Unpaid. Open to college juniors, college seniors, recent college graduates, graduate students. ▶ *1–3 program coordinators:* responsibilities include assisting in coordinating an aspect of program; interviewing potential volunteers and clients; making and following-up with all mentor matches in the program and assisting in other aspects such as recruiting. Candidates should have ability to work independently, ability to work with others, oral communication skills, organizational skills, written communication skills. Duration is flexible. Unpaid. Open to graduate students.
Benefits Names of contacts, on-the-job training, possible full-time employment, willing to act as a professional reference, willing to complete paperwork for educational credit, willing to provide letters of recommendation.
Contact Write, call, fax, or e-mail Robert Jakubowski, Executive Director. Phone: 856-546-1221. Fax: 856-546-6721. E-mail: bbbscg@snip.net. In-person interview recommended (telephone interview accepted). Applicants must submit a letter of interest, 2-3 personal references. Applications are accepted continuously.

BIG BROTHERS/BIG SISTERS OF CENTRAL SUSQUEHANNA VALLEY
335 Market Street, Suite 2B
Sunbury, Pennsylvania 1780

General Information Program that matches adult volunteers one-to-one with children needing additional adult companionship, support, guidance and understanding; provides group activities for children and youth. Established in 1982. Number of

employees: 2. Affiliate of Big Brothers Big Sisters of America, Philadelphia, Pennsylvania. Number of internship applications received each year: 2.
Internships Available ▶ *1–2 adjunct caseworkers:* responsibilities include contacting clients to monitor progress of client matches; writing and recording case notes reports; maintaining records of clients, cases, volunteers, and parents' inquiries; performing routine clerical work; assisting with social and fund-raising functions; and attending group meetings, staff meetings, and board of director meetings. Candidates should have ability to work independently, oral communication skills, personal interest in the field, strong interpersonal skills, written communication skills. Duration is 1–2 semesters. Unpaid. Open to college freshmen, college sophomores, college juniors, college seniors. International applications accepted.
Benefits Opportunity to attend seminars/workshops, travel reimbursement, willing to act as a professional reference, willing to complete paperwork for educational credit, willing to provide letters of recommendation.
Contact Write, call, fax, or e-mail Peggy Reichenbach, Executive Director, 356 Market Street, Sunbury, Pennsylvania 17801-2338. Phone: 570-286-3127. Fax: 570-286-3150. E-mail: csv_bbbs@msn.com. In-person interview recommended (telephone interview accepted). Applicants must submit a formal organization application, resume, three personal references. Applications are accepted continuously.

BIG BROTHERS/BIG SISTERS OF MIDCOAST MAINE
PO Box 457
Damariscotta, Maine 04543

General Information Youth mentoring organization. Established in 1980. Number of employees: 7. Affiliate of Big Brothers Big Sisters of America, Philadelphia, Pennsylvania. Number of internship applications received each year: 3.
Internships Available ▶ *Mentoring program intern:* responsibilities include proofreading, computer data input and recovery, editing, phone answering. Candidates should have ability to work independently, ability to work with others, computer skills, office skills, personal interest in the field, self-motivation. Duration is May 1 to September 1. Unpaid. Open to college freshmen, college sophomores, college juniors, college seniors, recent college graduates, graduate students, career changers. International applications accepted.
Benefits On-the-job training, willing to act as a professional reference, willing to complete paperwork for educational credit, willing to provide letters of recommendation.
Contact Write, call, or fax Bill Michaud, Executive Director. Phone: 207-563-5599. Fax: 207-563-7124. E-mail: bbbsmcm@lincoln.midcoast.com. In-person interview required. Applicants must submit a formal organization application, letter of interest, resume. Application deadline: May 1.

BIG BROTHERS/BIG SISTERS OF NEVADA
4045 South Spencer, Suite A-57
Las Vegas, Nevada 89119

General Information Organization that matches children ages 6-17, with mature, responsible, caring adults and older high school students. Established in 1973. Number of employees: 20. Affiliate of Big Brothers Big Sisters of America, Philadelphia, Pennsylvania. Number of internship applications received each year: 2.
Internships Available ▶ *1–3 case management and intake interns:* responsibilities include managing a designated case load, interviewing prospective clients and volunteers, and documenting results of interviews. Candidates should have ability to work independently, declared college major in field, oral communication skills, self-motivation, strong interpersonal skills, written communication skills. Duration is 3–12 months. Position available as unpaid or paid. Open to college sophomores, college juniors, college seniors, recent college graduates, graduate students, career changers, individuals reentering the workforce. ▶ *1 youth intervention intern:* responsibilities include interviewing prospective clients and volunteers, documentation. Candidates should have ability to work

independently, declared college major in field, oral communication skills, self-motivation, strong interpersonal skills, written communication skills, Spanish-speaking preferred. Duration is flexible. Position available as unpaid or paid. Open to college freshmen, college sophomores, college juniors, college seniors. International applications accepted.
Benefits Names of contacts, on-the-job training, opportunity to attend seminars/workshops, possible full-time employment, willing to complete paperwork for educational credit, willing to provide letters of recommendation, mileage reimbursement.
Contact Write, fax, or through World Wide Web site Veronica Torres, Program Director. Fax: 702-737-9209. No phone calls. In-person interview recommended (telephone interview accepted). Applicants must submit a letter of interest, resume, academic transcripts, 2-3 letters of recommendation. Applications are accepted continuously. World Wide Web: http://www.bbbssn.org.

BIG BROTHERS/BIG SISTERS OF NORTH ALABAMA
3322 South Memorial Parkway, Suite 617
Huntsville, Alabama 35801

General Information Organization that provides friends and role models for children ages 5-15 and fosters one-to-one mentoring relationships with adult volunteers. Established in 1982. Number of employees: 4. Unit of Big Brothers Big Sisters of America, Philadelphia, Pennsylvania. Number of internship applications received each year: 4.
Internships Available ► *1–4 long-term interns:* responsibilities include observing interviews, home visits, and empowerment training of volunteers, children, and their parents; working with staff to process applications to programs; participating in matching children and volunteers; helping to recruit volunteers; and participating in agency fund-raisers. Candidates should have ability to work independently, ability to work with others, office skills, oral communication skills, plan to pursue career in field, self-motivation, written communication skills, case management experience, background in social science or education. Duration is minimum of 500 hours. Unpaid. Open to college juniors, college seniors. ► *1–4 short-term interns:* responsibilities include observing interviews, home visits, and empowerment training of volunteers, children, and their parents; working with staff to process applications to programs, participating in matching children and volunteers, helping to recruit volunteers, and participating in agency fund-raisers. Candidates should have computer skills, oral communication skills, strong interpersonal skills, written communication skills. Duration is under 500 hours. Unpaid. Open to high school seniors, recent high school graduates, college freshmen, college sophomores, college juniors, college seniors, individuals reentering the workforce. International applications accepted.
Benefits Formal training, names of contacts, on-the-job training, possible full-time employment, willing to complete paperwork for educational credit, willing to provide letters of recommendation.
Contact Write, call, or fax Camille Solley, Executive Director, 3322 South Memorial Parkway Suite 617, Huntsville, Alabama 35801. Phone: 256-880-2123. Fax: 256-880-2177. E-mail: bbbsna@yahoo.com. In-person interview required. Applicants must submit a resume, personal reference. Applications are accepted continuously.

BIG BROTHERS BIG SISTERS OF ORANGE COUNTY
253 South William Street
Newburgh, New York 12550

General Information Human service agency dedicated to youth development through mentoring and life skills programs. Established in 1977. Number of employees: 10. Affiliate of Big Brothers Big Sisters of America, Philadelphia, Pennsylvania. Number of internship applications received each year: 6.
Internships Available ► *2–4 mentoring manager assistants.* Candidates should have computer skills, declared college major in field, organizational skills, personal interest in the field, self-motivation,

strong interpersonal skills. Duration is 4–12 months. Unpaid. ► *1 public relations intern.* Candidates should have computer skills, knowledge of field, oral communication skills, self-motivation, strong interpersonal skills, written communication skills. Duration is 4–12 months. Unpaid. Open to college juniors, college seniors, recent college graduates, graduate students.
Benefits On-the-job training, opportunity to attend seminars/workshops, possible full-time employment, willing to act as a professional reference, willing to complete paperwork for educational credit, willing to provide letters of recommendation.
Contact Write, e-mail, or through World Wide Web site Nancy A. Kosloski, Executive Director. Phone: 845-562-5900. Fax: 845-562-1408. E-mail: bbbsoc@warwick.net. In-person interview required. Applicants must submit a letter of interest, resume, two personal references. Applications are accepted continuously. World Wide Web: http://www.mentorachild.org.

BIG BROTHERS/BIG SISTERS OF ROCK AND WALWORTH COUNTIES
2433 South Riverside Drive
Beloit, Wisconsin 53511

General Information Organization that matches children ages 6-14 from single-parent families with adult role models and provides opportunities for the emotional growth of children. Established in 1971. Number of employees: 7. Affiliate of Big Brothers Big Sisters of America, Philadelphia, Pennsylvania. Number of internship applications received each year: 2.
Internships Available ► *1–2 fund-raising coordinators:* responsibilities include planning annual bowling and golf events, writing grant proposals, and general fund-raising. Candidates should have ability to work independently, knowledge of field, oral communication skills, organizational skills, self-motivation, written communication skills. Duration is flexible. Position available as unpaid or at $5.50–$10.50 per hour. Open to college freshmen, college sophomores, college juniors, college seniors, recent college graduates, graduate students, law students, career changers, individuals reentering the workforce. ► *1–2 general office interns:* responsibilities include billing, data entry, telephoning, and computer input. Candidates should have ability to work with others, computer skills, knowledge of field, office skills, oral communication skills, writing skills. Duration is flexible. Position available as unpaid or at $5.50–$8 per hour. Open to recent high school graduates, college freshmen, college sophomores, college juniors, college seniors, recent college graduates, graduate students, career changers, individuals reentering the workforce. International applications accepted.
Benefits Formal training, names of contacts, opportunity to attend seminars/workshops, travel reimbursement, willing to act as a professional reference, willing to complete paperwork for educational credit, willing to provide letters of recommendation.
Contact Write, call, or e-mail Nancy Mignon, Executive Director. Phone: 608-362-8223. Fax: 608-362-5835. E-mail: bbbsnancy@aol.com. In-person interview required. Applicants must submit a letter of interest, resume, two personal references, two letters of recommendation. Applications are accepted continuously.

BIG BROTHERS BIG SISTERS OF SALEM COUNTY
29 South Main Street
Woodstown, New Jersey 08098

General Information Organization that provides positive opportunities for growth and development for children and at-risk youth through one-to-one matches with volunteers, educational programs, and recreational activities. Established in 1986. Number of employees: 2. Affiliate of Big Brothers Big Sisters of America, Philadelphia, Pennsylvania. Number of internship applications received each year: 1.
Internships Available ► *1 fund developer:* responsibilities include helping plan fund-raisers, distributing flyers, and soliciting door prizes and corporate sponsors. Candidates should have ability to work independently, computer skills, oral communication skills, organizational skills, personal interest in the field, self-motivation, strong interpersonal skills. Duration is 6–12 months. Unpaid. Open to recent high school graduates, college freshmen, college

sophomores, college juniors, college seniors, recent college graduates, graduate students, law students, career changers, individuals reentering the workforce. ▶ *1 program intern:* responsibilities include providing casework services, interviewing children and families, and matching supervision and assistance with recreational and educational activities. Candidates should have ability to work independently, ability to work with others, computer skills, experience in the field, oral communication skills, self-motivation, written communication skills. Duration is 12 months. Unpaid. Open to college freshmen, college sophomores, college juniors, college seniors, recent college graduates, graduate students, law students, career changers, individuals reentering the workforce. ▶ *1 volunteer recruiter:* responsibilities include creating brochures of information to be distributed throughout the county; calling and writing to local businesses asking for volunteers. Candidates should have ability to work independently, ability to work with others, computer skills, oral communication skills, self-motivation, strong leadership ability. Duration is 3–6 months. Unpaid. Open to high school seniors, recent high school graduates, college freshmen, college sophomores, college juniors, college seniors, recent college graduates, graduate students, law students, career changers, individuals reentering the workforce. International applications accepted.
Benefits Formal training, job counseling, names of contacts, on-the-job training, opportunity to attend seminars/workshops, possible full-time employment, travel reimbursement, willing to act as a professional reference, willing to complete paperwork for educational credit, willing to provide letters of recommendation.
Contact Write, call, or fax Lori Tesauro, Executive Director. Phone: 856-769-3556. Fax: 856-769-3566. E-mail: salemcountybbbs@ hotmail.com. In-person interview required. Applicants must submit a letter of interest, resume, personal reference, three letters of recommendation. Applications are accepted continuously.

BIG BROTHERS/BIG SISTERS OF THE FOX VALLEY
158 East Chicago Street
Elgin, Illinois 60120

General Information Youth development agency that provides programs to enrich young people's lives and match adult volunteers with children from single-parent homes. Established in 1980. Number of employees: 9. Unit of Big Brothers Big Sisters of America, Philadelphia, Pennsylvania. Number of internship applications received each year: 12.
Internships Available ▶ *1 case worker intern:* responsibilities include interviewing, training, public speaking, surveying, researching, supervising activities, acting as group co-leader, recruiting youth, and fund-raising. Duration is flexible. Unpaid. Open to college freshmen, college sophomores, college juniors, college seniors, recent college graduates, graduate students, law students, career changers, individuals reentering the workforce. International applications accepted.
Benefits Formal training, names of contacts, possible full-time employment, willing to complete paperwork for educational credit, willing to provide letters of recommendation.
Contact Write or e-mail Ms. Deborah Howe, Executive Director. E-mail: dhowe@bbbsfoxvalley.org. No phone calls. In-person interview required. Applicants must submit a resume. Applications are accepted continuously. World Wide Web: http://www. bbbsfoxvalley.org.

BIG BROTHERS/BIG SISTERS OF THE MARSHFIELD AREA
837 South Central Avenue
Marshfield, Wisconsin 54449-4126

General Information Organization that serves children from single parent families by providing role models, friends, and positive life experiences. Established in 1967. Number of employees: 6. Unit of Big Brothers Big Sisters of America, Philadelphia, Pennsylvania. Number of internship applications received each year: 2.
Internships Available ▶ *1–2 case managers (social work):* responsibilities include screening volunteers, clients, and parents; processing volunteers and clients; writing individual plans; and assisting

in planning and carrying out agency activities and socials. Candidates should have analytical skills, knowledge of field, oral communication skills, self-motivation, strong interpersonal skills, written communication skills. Duration is flexible. Unpaid. Open to college seniors, recent college graduates, graduate students, career changers, individuals reentering the workforce. ▶ *1–2 marketing interns:* responsibilities include developing marketing campaign strategies and various promotional materials, researching various avenues to use as tools for promotion and advertising. Candidates should have college courses in field, editing skills, organizational skills, self-motivation, strong interpersonal skills, written communication skills. Duration is flexible. Unpaid. Open to college juniors, college seniors, recent college graduates, graduate students, career changers, individuals reentering the workforce. ▶ *1–2 program directors:* responsibilities include pursuing advertising, publications, public service announcements and presentations, and developing new ways to promote program. Candidates should have analytical skills, knowledge of field, oral communication skills, self-motivation, strong interpersonal skills, strong leadership ability. Duration is flexible. Unpaid. Open to college juniors, college seniors, recent college graduates, graduate students, career changers, individuals reentering the workforce.
Benefits Job counseling, on-the-job training, opportunity to attend seminars/workshops, travel reimbursement, willing to act as a professional reference, willing to complete paperwork for educational credit, willing to provide letters of recommendation.
Contact Write Ms. Leslie Plechaty, Executive Director. Fax: 715-384-7145. No phone calls. In-person interview required. Applicants must submit a letter of interest, resume, personal reference, two letters of recommendation. Applications are accepted continuously.

BOULDER COUNTY AIDS PROJECT
2118 14th Street
Boulder, Colorado 80302

General Information AIDS service organization. Established in 1984. Number of employees: 14. Number of internship applications received each year: 6.
Internships Available ▶ *2 Latino outreach interns:* responsibilities include assisting coordinator with speaking engagements and other outreach activities. Candidates should have ability to work independently, oral communication skills, self-motivation, strong interpersonal skills, bilingual English/Spanish ability. Duration is flexible. Unpaid. Open to college freshmen, college sophomores, college juniors, college seniors, recent college graduates, graduate students. ▶ *1–3 agency assistants:* responsibilities include administrative assistance to different agency departments. Candidates should have computer skills, office skills, organizational skills, strong interpersonal skills, writing skills. Unpaid. Open to high school seniors, recent high school graduates, college freshmen, college sophomores, college juniors, college seniors, recent college graduates, career changers, individuals reentering the workforce. ▶ *1–3 special events associates:* responsibilities include coordinating special events for fund-raising. Candidates should have ability to work independently, oral communication skills, organizational skills, self-motivation, strong interpersonal skills. Duration is commitment of 1 academic year, but will accept 1 semester. Unpaid. Open to college freshmen, college sophomores, college juniors, college seniors, recent college graduates, career changers, individuals reentering the workforce.
Benefits On-the-job training, opportunity to attend seminars/ workshops, willing to act as a professional reference, willing to complete paperwork for educational credit, willing to provide letters of recommendation.
Contact Write, e-mail, or through World Wide Web site Jenny Schwartz, Intern Coordinator, 2118 14th Street, Boulder, Colorado 80302. E-mail: jaschwartz@worldnet.att.net. No phone calls. In-person interview required. Applicants must submit a letter of interest, resume, two writing samples, two personal references, two letters of recommendation. Applications are accepted continuously. World Wide Web: http://www.bcap.org.

BOYS AND GIRLS CLUB OF BROCKTON, INC.
233 Warren Avenue
Brockton, Massachusetts 02301-4321

General Information Youth development organization that provides guidance and offers programs to serve youth of disadvantaged circumstances. Established in 1988. Number of employees: 30. Unit of Boys and Girls Clubs of America, Atlanta, Georgia. Number of internship applications received each year: 5.

Internships Available ▶ *1 fund-raising intern:* responsibilities include assisting in implementing the annual financial development plan, grant writing, assisting with board and youth fund-raising events, and directing mail campaigns. Candidates should have ability to work independently, analytical skills, organizational skills, personal interest in the field, research skills, self-motivation. Duration is flexible. Unpaid. Open to college sophomores, college juniors, college seniors. ▶ *1–3 health promotion interns:* responsibilities include assisting in supervising teen leaders in planning and implementing prevention programs for peers and younger members. Candidates should have ability to work independently, ability to work with others, oral communication skills, personal interest in the field, self-motivation, strong leadership ability. Unpaid. Open to college juniors, college seniors. ▶ *1–5 learning center interns:* responsibilities include helping to coordinate and implement learning center programs in computer learning, homework assistance, tutoring, SAT preparation, and career awareness activities; and leading field trips, special activities, and programs. Candidates should have ability to work independently, ability to work with others, oral communication skills, self-motivation, strong leadership ability, written communication skills. Duration is flexible. Unpaid. Open to college freshmen, college sophomores, college juniors, college seniors, individuals reentering the workforce. ▶ *1–3 leisure studies interns:* responsibilities include working with the sports programs in basketball, soccer, volleyball, and baseball, working in the games room, and planning special events. Candidates should have ability to work independently, knowledge of field, oral communication skills, personal interest in the field, strong interpersonal skills, strong leadership ability. Duration is flexible. Unpaid. Open to college freshmen, college sophomores, college juniors, college seniors, individuals reentering the workforce. ▶ *1 marketing intern:* responsibilities include promoting club programs, implementing annual marketing plan, maintaining media relations, organizing membership and volunteer recruitment campaigns, planning and implementing regional campaigns, updating brochures, and assisting with annual newsletter and annual report. Candidates should have ability to work independently, analytical skills, computer skills, organizational skills, research skills, self-motivation, writing skills. Duration is flexible. Unpaid. Open to college freshmen, college sophomores, college juniors, college seniors. International applications accepted.

Benefits Formal training, names of contacts, on-the-job training, possible full-time employment, willing to act as a professional reference, willing to complete paperwork for educational credit, willing to provide letters of recommendation.

Contact Write, call, or fax Stephanie Sylvain, Director of Outreach Services. Phone: 508-586-3503. Fax: 508-588-2772. In-person interview required. Applicants must submit a resume, personal reference, two letters of recommendation. Application deadline: August 1 for fall; continuous for remainder of year.

BOYS AND GIRLS CLUB OF CLIFTON
822 Clifton Avenue
Clifton, New Jersey 07013

General Information Youth serving organization for boys and girls ages 2½-17. Established in 1958. Number of employees: 72. Unit of Boys and Girls Clubs of America, Atlanta, Georgia. Number of internship applications received each year: 20.

Internships Available ▶ *9 "School's Out" program supervisors:* responsibilities include implementing care programs from 2:30-6:30 for 35 students ages 6-11. Candidates should have experience in the field, oral communication skills, personal interest in the field, self-motivation, strong interpersonal skills. Duration is 10 months. $7–$8.50 per hour. Open to individuals 18 years or

older. ▶ *6–8 after-school program counselors:* responsibilities include acting as group leader for elementary school children and providing supervision and instruction in the after-school program 3-6:30 daily. Candidates should have experience in the field, oral communication skills, organizational skills, personal interest in the field, self-motivation, strong interpersonal skills. Duration is from September-June. $7–$10 per hour. Open to high school seniors, college freshmen, college sophomores, college juniors, college seniors. ▶ *4–6 lifeguards:* responsibilities include lifeguarding pool for all open swims, lessons, swim team, and adult swims. Candidates should have lifeguard training , first aid/CPR certification. Duration is 12 months. $7.50–$8.50 per hour. ▶ *1 summer assistant program director:* responsibilities include implementing and supervising summer day camp program; working with staff and children (Monday-Friday) to direct summer program activities. Candidates should have experience in the field, oral communication skills, personal interest in the field, self-motivation, strong interpersonal skills, written communication skills. Duration is June to August. $9–$10.50 per hour. Open to college juniors, college seniors, recent college graduates. ▶ *6–10 summer group counselors:* responsibilities include supervising and conducting activities for a group of 25 youngsters ages 6-12, overseeing specific age groups in a highly structured camp-at-home program, and performing administrative duties. Candidates should have experience in the field, oral communication skills, personal interest in the field, self-motivation, strong interpersonal skills, strong leadership ability. Duration is June 25-August 24. $7–$8.50 per hour. Open to high school seniors, college freshmen, college sophomores, college juniors, college seniors. ▶ *1 summer trip program coordinator:* responsibilities include implementing summer trip program for three age groups (6-8, 9-10, 11-16); one trip per week per age group; supervision, chaperoning, and administration of program. Candidates should have ability to work with others, office skills, oral communication skills, personal interest in the field, self-motivation, written communication skills, responsibility, maturity. Duration is June to September. $9–$10.50 per hour. Open to college juniors, college seniors. ▶ *4–6 water safety instructors:* responsibilities include teaching American Red Cross swim lessons levels I-VII plus safety and life saving classes. Candidates should have experience in the field, current WSI, first aid, and CPR certifications. Duration is 12 months. $10.50 per hour. Open to high school seniors, recent high school graduates, college freshmen, college sophomores, college juniors, college seniors, individuals reentering the workforce.

Benefits Formal training, names of contacts, possible full-time employment, willing to complete paperwork for educational credit, willing to provide letters of recommendation, access to Boys and Girls Club of America job listings and career services.

Contact Write, call, fax, e-mail, or through World Wide Web site Robert Foster, Director of Operations. Phone: 973-773-2697 Ext. 19. Fax: 973-773-3103. E-mail: rfoster@bgcclifton.org. In-person interview required. Applicants must submit a resume, two personal references, letter of recommendation. Application deadline: April 15 for summer, August 15 for fall, December 15 for winter/ spring. World Wide Web: http://www.boysandgirlsclbclifton.org.

BOYS AND GIRLS CLUB OF EAST AURORA
24 Paine Street
East Aurora, New York 14052

General Information Youth service organization. Established in 1939. Number of employees: 18. Affiliate of Boys and Girls Club of America, Atlanta, Georgia. Number of internship applications received each year: 1.

Internships Available ▶ *1 fund development director:* responsibilities include applying for grants from local government and foundation resources; assisting with coordination of special events; marketing club through newsletters. Candidates should have computer skills, knowledge of field, oral communication skills, research skills, writing skills. Duration is 3–6 months. Position available as unpaid or at percentage of funds raised. Open to college seniors, recent college graduates, graduate students, career changers. ▶ *1–2 youth development professionals:* responsibilities include organizing, directing and supervising youth in a variety of program settings: athletics, social recreation, social work; drug, alcohol, and sex prevention; mentoring, tutoring, homework help, technology. Candidates should have organizational skills, personal interest in the field, self-motivation, strong interpersonal skills, strong leadership ability. Duration is 3–6 months. Position available as unpaid or at $6–$8 per hour. Open to high school students, recent high school graduates, college freshmen, college sophomores, college juniors, college seniors, recent college graduates, graduate students, career changers. International applications accepted.

Benefits Formal training, job counseling, on-the-job training, opportunity to attend seminars/workshops, possible full-time employment, willing to act as a professional reference, willing to complete paperwork for educational credit, willing to provide letters of recommendation.

Contact Write, call, fax, or e-mail Mr. Gary D. Schutrum, Executive Director. Phone: 716-652-1060. Fax: 716-652-0212. E-mail: gschutrum@bgcea.org. In-person interview required. Applicants must submit a formal organization application, letter of interest, resume, academic transcripts, letter of recommendation. Applications are accepted continuously. World Wide Web: http://www.bgcea.org.

BOYS AND GIRLS CLUB OF LAKELAND, INC.
PO Box 763
Lakeland, Florida 33802

General Information Organization that helps local disadvantaged youth to become responsible citizens and leaders. Established in 1939. Number of employees: 27. Unit of Boys and Girls Clubs of America, Atlanta, Georgia. Number of internship applications received each year: 1.

Internships Available ▶ *1–4 interns:* responsibilities include working with youth ages 6-18 from disadvantaged urban backgrounds. Candidates should have ability to work independently, ability to work with others, oral communication skills, organizational skills, personal interest in the field, self-motivation. Duration is flexible. Unpaid. Open to high school students, recent high school graduates, college freshmen, college sophomores, college juniors, college seniors, recent college graduates, graduate students, career changers, individuals reentering the workforce. International applications accepted.

Benefits Formal training, job counseling, names of contacts, opportunity to attend seminars/workshops, possible full-time employment, willing to complete paperwork for educational credit, willing to provide letters of recommendation.

Contact Write or call Rex Perry, Executive Director. Phone: 863-686-1719. In-person interview recommended (telephone interview accepted). Applicants must submit a letter of interest, resume. Applications are accepted continuously.

BOYS AND GIRLS CLUB OF NASH/EDGECOMBE COUNTIES
405 Raleigh Road
Rocky Mount, North Carolina 27802

General Information Youth development center. Number of employees: 45. Affiliate of Boys and Girls Club of America, Atlanta, Georgia. Number of internship applications received each year: 25.

Internships Available ▶ *5–10 recreation interns:* responsibilities include developing and coordinating programs; participating in fund-raising and marketing; performing administrative duties as required. Candidates should have ability to work with others, declared college major in field, oral communication skills, personal interest in the field, strong leadership ability. Duration is 12 weeks in summer. Position available as unpaid or paid. Open to college freshmen, college sophomores, college juniors, college seniors, recent college graduates, graduate students. International applications accepted.

Benefits Formal training, job counseling, on-the-job training, opportunity to attend seminars/workshops, possible full-time employment, willing to act as a professional reference, willing to complete paperwork for educational credit, willing to provide letters of recommendation.

Contact Write, call, or e-mail Misty L. Miller, Director of Operations, PO Box 1622, Rocky Mount 27802. Phone: 252-977-9924.

Fax: 252-985-0277. E-mail: mmiller@bgcne.org. In-person interview recommended (telephone interview accepted). Applicants must submit a formal organization application, resume, academic transcripts, three personal references. Applications are accepted continuously. World Wide Web: http://www.bgcne.org.

BOYS AND GIRLS CLUB OF PLYMOUTH, INC.
PO Box 3479
Plymouth, Massachusetts 02361

General Information Organization that provides area youth with activities designed to build self-esteem, develop leadership skills, and promote positive life choices. Established in 1911. Number of employees: 12. Unit of Boys and Girls Clubs of America, Atlanta, Georgia. Number of internship applications received each year: 6.

Internships Available ▶ *1 junior staff intern:* responsibilities include interacting with children, handling small amounts of money. Candidates should have ability to work with others, oral communication skills, personal interest in the field, self-motivation, patience. Duration is 10 months. Position available as unpaid or at $6.75 per hour. Open to high school students. ▶ *1–2 youth counselors:* responsibilities include running programs, dealing with children and parents, answering phones, and overseeing recreational activities. Candidates should have ability to work independently, oral communication skills, personal interest in the field, self-motivation, strong interpersonal skills. Duration is 10–30 weeks. Position available as unpaid or at $7 per hour. Open to recent high school graduates, college freshmen, college sophomores, college juniors, college seniors, recent college graduates, graduate students, career changers, individuals reentering the workforce. International applications accepted.

Benefits Names of contacts, on-the-job training, willing to act as a professional reference, willing to complete paperwork for educational credit, willing to provide letters of recommendation.

Contact Write, call, fax, or e-mail Mr. Ron Randall, Executive Director. Phone: 508-746-6070. Fax: 508-746-5953. E-mail: rran676590@aol.com. In-person interview required. Applicants must submit a formal organization application, resume, two letters of recommendation. Applications are accepted continuously.

BOYS AND GIRLS CLUB OF TAMPA BAY, INC.
3020 West Laurel Street
Tampa, Florida 33607

General Information Youth agency with 21 sites in Hillsborough County that serves school-age children after school and all day on school holidays and during the summer by providing educational, athletic, cultural, enrichment, and prevention programs with a focus on the disadvantaged. Established in 1929. Number of employees: 150. Affiliate of Boys and Girls Clubs of America, Atlanta, Georgia. Number of internship applications received each year: 3.

Internships Available ▶ *1–3 career program directors:* responsibilities include working with youth on college and career program development goal setting classes, job readiness, and volunteer activities (community service). Candidates should have oral communication skills, personal interest in the field, self-motivation, strong interpersonal skills, strong leadership ability. Duration is 1–2 semesters. Unpaid. Open to recent high school graduates, college freshmen, college sophomores, college juniors, college seniors, individuals reentering the workforce, individuals 18 years or older with high school diploma or GED. ▶ *2–14 cultural arts specialists:* responsibilities include working with small groups of youth to develop singing, musical instrument, dance, or artistic talents; auditioning students and working on a show group; working with youth in developing skills in painting, sculpting, and related media. Candidates should have ability to work independently, oral communication skills, organizational skills, personal interest in the field, strong interpersonal skills, strong leadership ability. Duration is 1 semester, school year, or summer. Unpaid. Open to recent high school graduates, college freshmen, college sophomores, college juniors, college seniors, recent college graduates, career changers, individuals reentering the workforce, individuals 18 years of age or older. ▶ *2–5 data collection specialists:* responsibilities include obtaining data on club membership, program participa-

Boys and Girls Club of Tampa Bay, Inc. (continued)

tion, and attendance from clubs and schools, and entering data into main system and relating it to grant reports. Candidates should have ability to work independently, computer skills, personal interest in the field, research skills, self-motivation, written communication skills. Duration is 1 semester. Unpaid. Open to college freshmen, college sophomores, college juniors, college seniors, recent college graduates, graduate students, law students, career changers, individuals reentering the workforce, individuals 18 years of age or older. ▶ *10–19 girls' sports coordinators:* responsibilities include planning and implementing athletic events for females only. Candidates should have oral communication skills, organizational skills, personal interest in the field, strong interpersonal skills, strong leadership ability. Duration is 1–2 semesters. Unpaid. Open to recent high school graduates, college freshmen, college sophomores, college juniors, college seniors, recent college graduates, career changers, individuals reentering the workforce, individuals 18 years of age or older. ▶ *1–6 outreach program specialists:* responsibilities include delivering outreach and prevention programs to public and private schools and public housing sites, planning and implementing school outreach programs with educational and athletic activities, and conducting county-wide outreach events. Candidates should have ability to work independently, oral communication skills, organizational skills, personal interest in the field, self-motivation, strong interpersonal skills. Duration is 1 semester, school year, or summer. Unpaid. Open to recent high school graduates, college freshmen, college sophomores, college juniors, college seniors, recent college graduates, graduate students, career changers, individuals reentering the workforce, individuals 18 years of age or older. ▶ *10–19 prevention specialists:* responsibilities include conducting group sessions with school-aged children in violence prevention, drug abuse prevention, AIDS education, peer pressure response, and similar programs. Candidates should have analytical skills, oral communication skills, personal interest in the field, strong interpersonal skills, written communication skills. Duration is 1–2 semesters. Unpaid. Open to recent high school graduates, college freshmen, college sophomores, college juniors, college seniors, recent college graduates, career changers, individuals 18 years of age or older. ▶ *1–3 research associates:* responsibilities include researching grant opportunities, collecting data, and assisting with grant writing and monitoring. Candidates should have ability to work independently, editing skills, plan to pursue career in field, research skills, self-motivation, written communication skills. Duration is 1 semester, school year, or summer. Unpaid. Open to college freshmen, college sophomores, college juniors, college seniors, recent college graduates, graduate students, career changers, individuals reentering the workforce, individuals 18 years of age or older. ▶ *1 special events coordinator:* responsibilities include working with management staff to develop and implement special events and fundraisers for Boys and Girls Clubs of Tampa Bay. Candidates should have ability to work independently, organizational skills, personal interest in the field, self-motivation, strong interpersonal skills. Duration is 1 semester, school year, or summer. Unpaid. Open to college freshmen, college sophomores, college juniors, college seniors, recent college graduates, graduate students, career changers, individuals reentering the workforce, individuals 18 years of age or older. ▶ *2 teen services coordinators:* responsibilities include working directly with teens, developing leadership skills, and enhancing their educational pursuit. Candidates should have oral communication skills, personal interest in the field, strong interpersonal skills, strong leadership ability, written communication skills. Unpaid. Open to recent high school graduates, college freshmen, college sophomores, college juniors, college seniors, recent college graduates, graduate students, career changers, individuals reentering the workforce. ▶ *14–28 tutor/homework assistants:* responsibilities include working with children one-to-one and in small groups to improve their academic achievement. Candidates should have ability to work independently, oral communication skills, personal interest in the field, self-motivation, strong interpersonal skills, written communication skills. Duration is 1–2 semesters. Unpaid. Open to recent high school graduates, college freshmen, college sophomores, college juniors, college seniors, recent college graduates, graduate students, law students, career changers, individuals reentering the work-

force, individuals 18 years of age or older. ▶ *14–56 youth development professionals:* responsibilities include coordinating and leading appropriate activities within a group while acting as program assistant to year-round staff. Candidates should have ability to work independently, oral communication skills, organizational skills, personal interest in the field, self-motivation, strong interpersonal skills. Duration is 1 summer or semester. Unpaid. Open to recent high school graduates, college freshmen, college sophomores, college juniors, college seniors, recent college graduates, graduate students, career changers, individuals reentering the workforce, individuals 18 years of age or older. ▶ *1–3 youth development professionals/aquatics coordinators:* responsibilities include assisting in program areas as designated by club director, working with small groups of children on specific programs, supervising aquatic activities, coaching and managing synchronized swimming team. Candidates should have ability to work independently, oral communication skills, organizational skills, personal interest in the field, self-motivation, strong interpersonal skills, lifeguard and WSI certification. Duration is 2 semesters. Unpaid. Open to recent high school graduates, college freshmen, college sophomores, college juniors, college seniors, recent college graduates, graduate students, career changers, individuals reentering the workforce, individuals 18 years of age or older. International applications accepted.

Benefits Formal training, job counseling, names of contacts, on-the-job training, opportunity to attend seminars/workshops, possible full-time employment, willing to act as a professional reference, willing to complete paperwork for educational credit, willing to provide letters of recommendation, some AmeriCorps positions.

Contact Write, call, fax, or e-mail Lisbeth Moore, Director of Services to Clubs. Phone: 813-875-5771. Fax: 813-875-4428. E-mail: bmoore@bgctampa.org. In-person interview required. Applicants must submit a formal organization application, letter of interest, resume. Applications are accepted continuously. World Wide Web: http://www.bgctampa.org.

BOYS AND GIRLS CLUB OF WORCESTER
2 Ionic Avenue
Worcester, Massachusetts 01608

General Information Organization that provides recreation, physical education, and leadership development activities for youth. Established in 1889. Number of employees: 33. Unit of Boys and Girls Clubs of America, Atlanta, Georgia. Number of internship applications received each year: 3.

Internships Available ▶ *Youth development interns:* responsibilities include assisting staff with delivery of programs. Candidates should have ability to work independently, oral communication skills, organizational skills, plan to pursue career in field, self-motivation, strong interpersonal skills, strong leadership ability. Duration is flexible. Unpaid. Open to college freshmen, college sophomores, college juniors, college seniors, recent college graduates. International applications accepted.

Benefits Job counseling, names of contacts, on-the-job training, possible full-time employment, willing to complete paperwork for educational credit, willing to provide letters of recommendation.

Contact Write, call, fax, e-mail, or through World Wide Web site Ron Hadorn, Executive Director. Phone: 508-754-2686. Fax: 508-754-3635. E-mail: bgcworc@worldnet.att.net. In-person interview recommended (telephone interview accepted). Applicants must submit a letter of interest, resume, academic transcripts, two personal references. Application deadline: April 1 for summer, October 1 for spring. World Wide Web: http://www.worcesterboysandgirls.org.

BOYS AND GIRLS CLUBS OF ALBANY
21 Delaware Avenue
Albany, New York 12210

General Information Organization that promotes the social, educational, and vocational development of at-risk boys and girls by building self-esteem, values, and skills during youth and adolescence. Established in 1891. Number of employees: 35. Affiliate of Boys and Girls Clubs of America, Atlanta, Georgia. Number of internship applications received each year: 10.

Internships Available ▶ *1–10 program assistants:* responsibilities include working with children, implementing activities, supervising children, and working with the site director and coordinator. Candidates should have oral communication skills, personal interest in the field, self-motivation, strong interpersonal skills, strong leadership ability. Duration is flexible. Unpaid. Open to high school students, recent high school graduates, college freshmen, college sophomores, college juniors, college seniors, recent college graduates, graduate students, law students, career changers, individuals reentering the workforce. ▶ *1–5 program counselors:* responsibilities include helping youth to achieve and maintain fitness to acquire a broad range of physical skills; to develop a sense of teamwork, cooperation, and fairness; and to lead healthy, active lifestyles. Candidates should have ability to work independently, ability to work with others, knowledge of field, organizational skills, self-motivation, strong leadership ability. Duration is flexible. Unpaid. Open to high school students, recent high school graduates, college freshmen, college sophomores, college juniors, college seniors, recent college graduates, graduate students, law students, career changers, individuals reentering the workforce, senior citizens. International applications accepted.

Benefits Formal training, names of contacts, on-the-job training, opportunity to attend seminars/workshops, possible full-time employment, willing to act as a professional reference, willing to complete paperwork for educational credit, willing to provide letters of recommendation.

Contact Write, call, or fax Doretha Holmes, Deputy Executive Director. Phone: 518-462-5528. Fax: 518-462-5540. In-person interview required. Applicants must submit a formal organization application, letter of interest, resume, two writing samples, three personal references, three letters of recommendation. Applications are accepted continuously.

BOYS AND GIRLS CLUBS OF CENTRAL WYOMING
353 West 'A' Street
Casper, Wyoming 82601

General Information Youth-serving organization. Established in 1969. Number of employees: 11. Affiliate of Boys and Girls Clubs of America, Atlanta, Georgia.

Internships Available ▶ *1 program coordinator:* responsibilities include working on program sustainability, new programs, and volunteer recruitment. Candidates should have ability to work independently, analytical skills, computer skills, knowledge of field, office skills, oral communication skills, organizational skills, personal interest in the field, self-motivation, strong interpersonal skills, strong leadership ability, writing skills. Duration is 1 semester. Position available as unpaid or paid. Open to college freshmen, college sophomores, college juniors, college seniors, recent college graduates, graduate students.

Benefits Formal training, job counseling, on-the-job training, opportunity to attend seminars/workshops, willing to act as a professional reference, willing to complete paperwork for educational credit, willing to provide letters of recommendation.

Contact Write, call, fax, or e-mail Ashley Bright, Chief Professional Officer. Phone: 307-235-5694. Fax: 307-235-5697. E-mail: bgccw@coffey.com. In-person interview recommended (telephone interview accepted). Applicants must submit a formal organization application, letter of interest, resume, academic transcripts, four personal references, three letters of recommendation.

BOYS AND GIRLS CLUBS OF LARIMER COUNTY
103 Smokey Street
Fort Collins, Colorado 80525

General Information Organization that helps all youth to develop maximum potential by providing personal growth and educational and recreational programs in an environment of mutual trust and respect. Established in 1987. Number of employees: 16. Unit of Boys and Girls Clubs of America, Atlanta, Georgia.

Internships Available ▶ *Gameroom/recreation interns:* responsibilities include supervising and assisting full-time staff with playtime and recreational activities for children ages 6-18. Candidates should have ability to work independently, ability to work with others, personal interest in the field. Duration is flexible. Unpaid.

▶ *Learning-lab/computer technicians:* responsibilities include planning, implementing, and coordinating activities of the computer lab with full-time staff for youth ages 6-18. Duration is flexible. Unpaid. ▶ *Program director interns:* responsibilities include helping full-time staff with the planning and supervision of programs for children ages 6-18. Candidates should have computer skills, knowledge of field, organizational skills, self-motivation, strong interpersonal skills. Duration is flexible. Unpaid. Open to college freshmen, college sophomores, college juniors, college seniors, recent college graduates, graduate students. International applications accepted.

Benefits Names of contacts, opportunity to attend seminars/workshops, possible full-time employment, willing to complete paperwork for educational credit, willing to provide letters of recommendation.

Contact Write, call, or fax Maryjo Morgan, Office Manager. Phone: 970-223-1709. Fax: 970-206-9531. In-person interview recommended (telephone interview accepted). Applicants must submit a formal organization application, background check required. Applications are accepted continuously.

BOYS AND GIRLS CLUBS OF NEWARK
155 Washington Street, Suite 202
Newark, New Jersey 07102-2001

General Information Youth development agency. Established in 1938. Number of employees: 42. Affiliate of Boys and Girls Clubs of America, Atlanta, Georgia. Number of internship applications received each year: 15.

Internships Available ▶ *2 accounting assistants.* Candidates should have analytical skills, declared college major in field, knowledge of field, office skills, self-motivation, strong interpersonal skills. Duration is flexible. Unpaid. Open to college sophomores, college juniors, college seniors, recent college graduates, graduate students. ▶ *2–5 office assistants:* responsibilities include general office help. Candidates should have ability to work with others, computer skills, office skills, self-motivation, writing skills. Duration is flexible. Unpaid. Open to high school students, recent high school graduates, college freshmen, college sophomores, college juniors, college seniors, recent college graduates, graduate students, law students, career changers, individuals reentering the workforce. ▶ *3–6 social workers.* Candidates should have ability to work independently, knowledge of field, oral communication skills, organizational skills, strong interpersonal skills, writing skills. Duration is flexible. Unpaid. Open to college freshmen, college sophomores, college juniors, college seniors, recent college graduates. ▶ *10–30 tutors:* responsibilities include assisting students with homework. Candidates should have oral communication skills, strong interpersonal skills, strong leadership ability. Duration is flexible. Unpaid. Open to high school students, recent high school graduates. International applications accepted.

Benefits Formal training, job counseling, on-the-job training, opportunity to attend seminars/workshops, possible full-time employment, willing to act as a professional reference, willing to complete paperwork for educational credit, willing to provide letters of recommendation.

Contact Write, call, fax, or e-mail Tiana Johnson, Human Resources Director. Phone: 973-242-1200 Ext. 17. Fax: 973-242-8629. E-mail: tjohnson@bgcn.org. In-person interview required. Applicants must submit a formal organization application. Applications are accepted continuously. World Wide Web: http://www.bgcn.org.

BOYS AND GIRLS CLUBS OF TRACY
753 West Lowell Avenue
Tracy, California 95376

General Information Youth service organization providing a safe, supportive, and nurturing environment with programs that enrich the lives of the young people of the community. Established in 1989. Number of employees: 24. Affiliate of Boys and Girls Clubs of America, Atlanta, Georgia.

Internships Available ▶ *Program assistants:* responsibilities include supervising and interacting with children; helping implement and plan special events and programs; assisting with membership tracking; maintaining positive relationship with community. Duration is flexible. Unpaid. Open to college sophomores, college juniors,

Boys and Girls Clubs of Tracy (continued)

college seniors, recent college graduates, graduate students, law students, career changers, individuals reentering the workforce. ▶ *Programmers:* responsibilities include national character and leadership development, educational and career development, health and life skills programs. Duration is flexible. Unpaid. Open to college freshmen, college sophomores, college juniors, college seniors, recent college graduates, graduate students, law students, career changers, individuals reentering the workforce. Candidates for all positions should have ability to work independently, ability to work with others, analytical skills, computer skills, editing skills, knowledge of field, office skills, oral communication skills, organizational skills, personal interest in the field, research skills, self-motivation, strong leadership ability, writing skills. International applications accepted.

Benefits Job counseling, on-the-job training, opportunity to attend seminars/workshops, possible full-time employment, willing to act as a professional reference, willing to complete paperwork for educational credit, willing to provide letters of recommendation.

Contact Write, call, or fax Steven Gough, Director of Operations. Phone: 209-832-2582. Fax: 209-832-4687. In-person interview recommended (telephone interview accepted). Applicants must submit a formal organization application, personal reference. Applications are accepted continuously. World Wide Web: http://bgca. org.

BOYS HOPE GIRLS HOPE NATIONAL OFFICE
12120 Bridgeton Square Drive
Bridgeton, Missouri 63044-2607

General Information National organization that provides family-like homes and college preparatory educational opportunities for at-risk, yet academically capable, boys and girls. Established in 1977. Number of employees: 125. Number of internship applications received each year: 100.

Internships Available ▶ *1–2 administrative interns:* responsibilities include providing administrative support and office support for executive office resource development efforts. Candidates should have ability to work with others, office skills, oral communication skills, personal interest in the field, plan to pursue career in field, written communication skills. Duration is flexible. $200 per month. Open to college juniors, college seniors, recent college graduates, graduate students, career changers. ▶ *50 tutors:* responsibilities include providing tutoring assistance to boys or girls at a local program. Candidates should have oral communication skills, strong interpersonal skills, strong leadership ability. Duration is flexible. $200 per month. Open to recent college graduates, graduate students, career changers. ▶ *30–40 volunteer residential counselors:* responsibilities include living with children and other staff, maintaining a structured and stable home environment for up to 8 boys or girls, assuming a mentoring role, assisting students in academics, assisting houseparents in daily home operation, and exploring college and career opportunities with students. Candidates should have ability to work independently, oral communication skills, self-motivation, strong interpersonal skills, strong leadership ability. Duration is 12 months. $200 per month. Open to recent college graduates, graduate students, career changers.

Benefits Formal training, free housing, free meals, health insurance, on-the-job training, opportunity to attend seminars/workshops, possible full-time employment, travel reimbursement, willing to act as a professional reference, willing to complete paperwork for educational credit, willing to provide letters of recommendation.

Contact Write, call, fax, e-mail, or through World Wide Web site Laurie Keefe, Volunteer Coordinator. Phone: 800-545-2697. Fax: 314-298-1251. E-mail: lkeefe@bhgh.org. In-person interview recommended (telephone interview accepted). Applicants must submit a formal organization application, resume, academic transcripts, three personal references, criminal history background check, physical exam, driver's license. Applications are accepted continuously. World Wide Web: http://www.boyshopegirlshope. org.

BOYS HOPE GIRLS HOPE OF ARIZONA
3443 North Central Avenue, Suite 713
Phoenix, Arizona 85012

General Information Private, nonprofit residential scholarship program working with bright and gifted at-risk youth; provides 100% support for youth in high school and assistance in college. Established in 1989. Number of employees: 11. Affiliate of Boys Hope Girls Hope, St. Louis, Missouri. Number of internship applications received each year: 3.

Internships Available ▶ *1–2 program assistants:* responsibilities include program development and enhancement; community networking and public speaking; recruitment and assessment of potential participants in the program; case management. Candidates should have ability to work independently, oral communication skills, personal interest in the field, plan to pursue career in field, self-motivation, strong interpersonal skills. Duration is flexible. Position available as unpaid or paid. Open to college juniors, college seniors, recent college graduates, graduate students. ▶ *2–3 residential counselors:* responsibilities include direct care and supervision of up to 8 youth; live-in position to support and empower youth to develop intellectually, emotionally, socially, physically and spiritually. Candidates should have ability to work with others, knowledge of field, oral communication skills, organizational skills, personal interest in the field. Duration is one year (August to August). Position available as unpaid or at $200 per month; AmeriCorp stipend at end of service. Open to recent college graduates, graduate students.

Benefits Formal training, free housing, on-the-job training, opportunity to attend seminars/workshops, possible full-time employment, willing to act as a professional reference, willing to complete paperwork for educational credit, willing to provide letters of recommendation, stipend and other benefits negotiable.

Contact Write or call Jennifer Bretz, Program Director. Phone: 602-266-4873. Fax: 602-200-8426. E-mail: jbretz@bhgh.org. In-person interview required. Applicants must submit a formal organization application, letter of interest, resume. Applications are accepted continuously. World Wide Web: http://www.boyshopegirlshope.org.

BREAK THE CYCLE
PO Box 64996
Los Angeles, California 90064

General Information Nonprofit organization whose mission is to end domestic violence by providing preventative education, free legal representation, advocacy, and support to young people ages 12-22. Established in 1995. Number of employees: 11. Number of internship applications received each year: 30.

Internships Available ▶ *1–2 Break-the-Cycle Interns:* responsibilities include providing a wide range of administrative support; assisting in fundraising efforts; performing research and writing on various domestic violence, womens' and youth issues; and conducting various forms of outreach. Candidates should have computer skills, office skills, oral communication skills, self-motivation, strong interpersonal skills, written communication skills. Duration is 1 semester. Unpaid. Open to college freshmen, college sophomores, college juniors, college seniors. ▶ *1–2 law interns:* responsibilities include exposure to a wide range of legal work and experiences, including: performing traditional legal research on public interest law issues that affect the lives and safety of the youth that Break-the-Cycle serves; co-teaching "Ending Violence: A Curriculum for Educating Teens on Domestic Violence and the Law"; and conducting various forms of outreach and client advocacy. Candidates should have computer skills, oral communication skills, personal interest in the field, self-motivation, strong interpersonal skills, written communication skills. Duration is 1 semester. Unpaid. Open to law students. ▶ *2 summer interns:* responsibilities include providing wide range of administrative support to programs; performing research and writing on various domestic violence, youth, and women's issues; assisting in fund-raising, and conducting outreach. Candidates should have computer skills, office skills, oral communication skills, self-motivation, strong interpersonal skills, written communication skills. Duration is June to August with possibility of extension. Unpaid. Open to recent high school graduates, college fresh-

men, college sophomores, college juniors, college seniors, recent college graduates. International applications accepted.
Benefits On-the-job training, opportunity to attend seminars/workshops, possible full-time employment, willing to complete paperwork for educational credit.
Contact Write, call, fax, or e-mail Volunteer Coordinator. Phone: 310-286-3366. Fax: 310-286-3386. E-mail: volunteer@break-the-cycle.org. In-person interview recommended (telephone interview accepted). Applicants must submit a letter of interest, resume. Application deadline: March 1 for summer; continuous for year-round positions. World Wide Web: http://www.break-the-cycle.org.

BRETHREN VOLUNTEER SERVICE
1451 Dundee Avenue
Elgin, Illinois 60120

General Information Volunteer organization with goals that include working for peace, advocating justice, serving basic human needs, and maintaining the integrity of creation. Established in 1948. Number of employees: 4. Unit of Church of the Brethren, Elgin, Illinois. Number of internship applications received each year: 100.
Internships Available ▶ *80–100 domestic volunteers:* responsibilities include performing duties that vary according to project and volunteer's skills, experience, and interest. Duration is 1 year. $60–$80 per month. Open to individuals 18 years or older. ▶ *20–30 overseas volunteers:* responsibilities include possible positions in Europe, Latin America, Japan, and Nigeria; performing duties that vary according to project and volunteer's skills, experience, and interest. Duration is minimum of 2 years. $60–$80 per month. Open to college graduates 21 years or older. International applications accepted.
Benefits Free housing, free meals, health insurance, cost of travel expenses to and from project for U.S. positions; some projects may qualify for educational award.
International Internships Available.
Contact Write, call, fax, e-mail, or through World Wide Web site Brethren Volunteer Service Recruitment. Phone: 800-323-8039 Ext. 454. Fax: 847-742-0278. E-mail: bvs_gb@brethren.org. Applicants must submit a formal organization application, letter of interest, resume, academic transcripts, current photo and essay, $400 for overseas travel. Applications are accepted continuously. World Wide Web: http://www.brethrenvolunteerservice.org.

BUTLER COUNTY RAPE CRISIS CENTER
110 South College Avenue
Oxford, Ohio 45056

General Information Social service agency providing information and support to adult and child survivors of sexual assault as well as community education and prevention services. Established in 1990. Number of employees: 9. Affiliate of Community Counseling and Crisis Center, Oxford, Ohio. Number of internship applications received each year: 20.
Internships Available ▶ *10–30 volunteer victim advocates:* responsibilities include providing crisis counseling and advocacy for a 24-hour service that responds to sexual assault victims by phone or face-to-face in Butler County hospitals and police stations. Candidates should have ability to work independently, oral communication skills, personal interest in the field, self-motivation, strong interpersonal skills. Duration is summer (May start) or fall (September start). Unpaid. Open to recent high school graduates, college freshmen, college sophomores, college juniors, college seniors, recent college graduates, graduate students, law students, career changers, individuals reentering the workforce, must be over age of 18 and living in or near Butler County. International applications accepted.
Benefits Formal training, on-the-job training, opportunity to attend seminars/workshops, willing to act as a professional reference, willing to complete paperwork for educational credit, willing to provide letters of recommendation.
Contact Write, call, or e-mail Jennifer Weigel, Assistant Director. Phone: 513-523-4149. Fax: 513-523-4145. E-mail: rcp@one.net.

In-person interview required. Applicants must submit a formal organization application. Application deadline: April 30 for summer, September 30 for fall.

CABBAGE PATCH SETTLEMENT HOUSE
1413 South Sixth Street
Louisville, Kentucky 40208

General Information Independently funded Christian charity serving inner-city, at-risk clients through day care, family services, recreation, education, and counseling programs. Established in 1910. Number of employees: 30. Number of internship applications received each year: 25.
Internships Available ▶ *2 counselor's assistants:* responsibilities include conducting home visits; assisting with group meetings, field trips, and therapy sessions; behavioral modification sessions with at-risk children. Candidates should have analytical skills, college courses in field, knowledge of field, strong interpersonal skills. Duration is flexible. Unpaid. Open to college seniors, recent college graduates, graduate students. ▶ *1–2 day-care assistants:* responsibilities include assisting in programs and leadership for youth ages 2½ to 6. Candidates should have ability to work with others, knowledge of field, self-motivation, strong leadership ability. Duration is flexible. Position available as unpaid or at $250–$400 per week. Open to college juniors, college seniors, recent college graduates, graduate students, career changers. ▶ *1–5 education aides:* responsibilities include tutoring, supervising study hall for grades 1-12, and teaching college preparation classes for at-risk students; monitoring tutoring lab. Candidates should have college courses in field, computer skills, experience in the field, self-motivation, strong interpersonal skills, written communication skills. Duration is flexible (September to May). Position available as unpaid or at $250–$400 per week. Open to college juniors, college seniors, recent college graduates, graduate students, career changers. ▶ *1 maintenance and housekeeping intern:* responsibilities include developing preventive maintenance systems and bid specifications for repair and renovation projects; minor repairs and light housekeeping. Candidates should have ability to work independently, analytical skills, knowledge of field, organizational skills, self-motivation. Duration is flexible. Position available as unpaid or at $200–$400 per week. Open to recent high school graduates, college freshmen, college sophomores, college juniors, college seniors, recent college graduates, graduate students, law students, career changers, individuals reentering the workforce. ▶ *1–6 recreation assistants:* responsibilities include planning and leading recreation and outdoor camping programs for youth; enforcing discipline. Candidates should have knowledge of field, self-motivation, strong interpersonal skills, strong leadership ability. Duration is 10 weeks to 10 months. Position available as unpaid or at $280–$400 per week. Open to college juniors, college seniors, recent college graduates, graduate students, career changers. ▶ *1–4 social work aides:* responsibilities include developing proactive social work programs for at-risk youth and their families. Candidates should have college courses in field, computer skills, experience in the field, knowledge of field, strong interpersonal skills. Duration is flexible. Position available as unpaid or at $250–$400 per week. Open to college juniors, college seniors, recent college graduates, graduate students, career changers.
Benefits Job counseling, names of contacts, possible full-time employment, willing to act as a professional reference, willing to complete paperwork for educational credit, willing to provide letters of recommendation.
Contact Write, fax, or e-mail W. Rodney Napier, Director of Programs and Facilities. Fax: 502-637-9943. E-mail: rnapier@cabbagepatch.org. No phone calls. In-person interview required. Applicants must submit a letter of interest, resume, academic transcripts, three personal references, three letters of recommendation, criminal records check required. Application deadline: April 30 for summer, August 30 for fall, December 15 for spring.

CAMP COURAGEOUS OF IOWA
12007 190th Street
Monticello, Iowa 52310-0418

General Information Year-round camp holding the belief that individuals with disabilities have the right to opportunities found

Camp Courageous of Iowa (continued)

in the world around them; curriculum challenges these individuals with recreational and educational activities. Established in 1972. Number of employees: 40. Number of internship applications received each year: 30.

Internships Available ▶ *1–15 counselors:* responsibilities include personal care of campers who have disabilities, assisting in leading activities for the same individuals, responsible for health and well-being of the campers. Candidates should have ability to work independently, oral communication skills, self-motivation, strong interpersonal skills, strong leadership ability, ability to work with special needs children and adults of all ages. Duration is year-round. Position available as unpaid or paid. ▶ *1–10 medical, dietary, maintenance interns.* Candidates should have ability to work independently, ability to work with others, knowledge of field, oral communication skills, personal interest in the field, self-motivation. Duration is year-round. Unpaid. Open to high school seniors, recent high school graduates, college freshmen, college sophomores, college juniors, college seniors, recent college graduates, graduate students, career changers, individuals reentering the workforce. International applications accepted.

Benefits Free housing, free meals, on-the-job training, possible full-time employment, willing to act as a professional reference, willing to complete paperwork for educational credit, willing to provide letters of recommendation, worker's compensation, restricted medical plan, possibility of monthly stipend.

Contact Write, call, fax, e-mail, or through World Wide Web site Tom Shank, Internship Coordinator, 12007 190th Street, PO Box 418, Monticello, Iowa 52310-0418. Phone: 319-465-5916 Ext. 204. Fax: 319-465-5919. E-mail: tshank@campcourageous.org. In-person interview recommended (telephone interview accepted). Applicants must submit a formal organization application, three personal references. Application deadline: April 16 for summer. World Wide Web: http://www.campcourageous.org.

CAMP FIRE BOYS AND GIRLS
PO Box 3275
San Diego, California 92163-1275

General Information Nonprofit organization providing clubs, camping, and self-reliance for youth to develop self-esteem and the skills to function as caring, self-directed individuals. Established in 1929. Number of employees: 6. Unit of Camp Fire USA, Kansas City, Missouri. Number of internship applications received each year: 6.

Internships Available ▶ *1 resident camp program coordinator:* responsibilities include coordinating program schedule for summer resident camp for 100 at-risk youth per week; supporting counseling staff and organizing all camp activities and programs. Candidates should have ability to work independently, knowledge of field, oral communication skills, organizational skills, personal interest in the field, self-motivation, strong interpersonal skills, strong leadership ability, desire to work with children in an outdoor setting. Duration is late June to mid-August. Position available as unpaid or at $200–$250 per week (including room and board). Open to college freshmen, college sophomores, college juniors, college seniors, recent college graduates, graduate students. ▶ *3 self-reliance instructors:* responsibilities include working with classroom-sized groups of children to deliver a fun, structured, interactive course on self-reliance; scheduling courses; and keeping applicable records. Candidates should have ability to work independently, college courses in field, oral communication skills, self-motivation, strong interpersonal skills. Duration is 1 semester. Position available as unpaid or paid. Open to college juniors, college seniors, recent college graduates, graduate students.

Benefits Formal training, names of contacts, possible full-time employment, willing to complete paperwork for educational credit, willing to provide letters of recommendation.

Contact Write, call, or fax Nancy Thompson, Administrative Assistant. Phone: 619-291-8985. Fax: 619-291-8988. E-mail: campfiresd@aol.com. In-person interview required. Applicants must submit a resume, three personal references. Applications are accepted continuously.

CAMP FIRE USA GEORGIA COUNCIL
100 Edgewood Avenue, NE, Suite 528
Atlanta, Georgia 30303

General Information Organization that provides fun, experiential programs which enable youth to develop into caring, self-directed, and responsible individuals. Established in 1910. Number of employees: 18. Unit of Camp Fire USA, Kansas City, Missouri. Number of internship applications received each year: 10.

Internships Available ▶ *1 clerical assistant:* responsibilities include entering data from outcome measurement surveys. Candidates should have ability to work independently, computer skills, office skills, organizational skills, written communication skills. Duration is 1 semester. Position available as unpaid or paid. Open to high school seniors, recent high school graduates, college freshmen, college sophomores, college juniors, college seniors. ▶ *1–2 environmental education interns:* responsibilities include assisting with environmental education program at resident camp. Candidates should have college courses in field, oral communication skills, personal interest in the field, self-motivation, strong interpersonal skills, strong leadership ability. Duration is flexible. Position available as unpaid or paid. Open to college juniors, college seniors, recent college graduates, graduate students. ▶ *1–2 program assistants:* responsibilities include assisting program staff in all areas of program delivery in underserved areas. Candidates should have ability to work independently, ability to work with others, oral communication skills, personal interest in the field, self-motivation, strong leadership ability, Spanish language skills helpful. Duration is 1–2 semesters. Unpaid. Open to recent high school graduates, college freshmen, college sophomores, college juniors, college seniors, recent college graduates, graduate students, individuals reentering the workforce. ▶ *1 public relations intern:* responsibilities include writing press releases, designing flyers, and taking photographs. Candidates should have ability to work independently, computer skills, editing skills, writing skills. Duration is 1 semester. Unpaid. Open to college juniors, college seniors, recent college graduates, graduate students, career changers, individuals reentering the workforce.

Benefits Formal training, names of contacts, on-the-job training, opportunity to attend seminars/workshops, willing to complete paperwork for educational credit, willing to provide letters of recommendation, housing and meals (summer only).

Contact Write, call, fax, or e-mail Karen Sullivan, Executive Director. Phone: 404-527-7125 Ext. 135. Fax: 404-527-7139. E-mail: kasullivan@campfireusaga.org. In-person interview recommended (telephone interview accepted). Applicants must submit a letter of interest, resume, three writing samples, personal reference, background check. Applications are accepted continuously. World Wide Web: http://www.campfireusaga.org.

CAMP FIRE USA, IOWANA COUNCIL
3401 Williams Boulevard, SW
Cedar Rapids, Iowa 52404

General Information Organization that provides informal education opportunities for youth to function as caring, self-directed, responsible individuals and seeks to improve conditions in society that affect youth. Established in 1910. Number of employees: 6. Unit of Camp Fire USA, Kansas City, Missouri. Number of internship applications received each year: 1.

Internships Available ▶ *1 alumni search intern:* responsibilities include developing and implementing a plan to locate "lost" Camp Fire alumni in the eastern third of Iowa. Candidates should have ability to work independently, ability to work with others, oral communication skills, organizational skills, self-motivation, written communication skills. Duration is flexible. Unpaid. Open to high school students, recent high school graduates, college freshmen, college sophomores, college juniors, college seniors, recent college graduates, graduate students, law students, career changers, individuals reentering the workforce. ▶ *1–3 club administrators:* responsibilities include recruiting youth and adult volunteers, providing training, and programming. Candidates should have ability to work independently, organizational skills, self-motivation, strong interpersonal skills, strong leadership ability. Duration is 9–12 months. Unpaid. Open to recent high school graduates,

college freshmen, college sophomores, college juniors, college seniors, recent college graduates, graduate students, law students, career changers, individuals reentering the workforce. ▶ *1 grant research intern:* responsibilities include researching grant opportunities for Camp Hitaga and The Iowana Council of Camp Fire; preliminary grant writing. Candidates should have ability to work independently, organizational skills, research skills, self-motivation, written communication skills. Duration is 1–2 semesters. Unpaid. Open to college freshmen, college sophomores, college juniors, college seniors, recent college graduates, graduate students, law students, career changers, individuals reentering the workforce. ▶ *1 marketing (Absolutely Incredible Kid Day) intern:* responsibilities include developing and implementing marketing plan for Absolutely Incredible Kid Day, the 3rd Thursday in March; asking people to write loving letters to children. Candidates should have ability to work independently, organizational skills, self-motivation, strong interpersonal skills, strong leadership ability, written communication skills. Duration is 2–8 months. Unpaid. Open to high school students, recent high school graduates, college freshmen, college sophomores, college juniors, college seniors, recent college graduates, graduate students, law students, career changers, individuals reentering the workforce. ▶ *1–10 program camp directors:* responsibilities include assisting with program development and implementation, facility management, marketing, fund-raising, and volunteer management. Candidates should have ability to work independently, oral communication skills, organizational skills, self-motivation, strong interpersonal skills, written communication skills. Duration is 10–12 weeks. Position available as unpaid or at $1100–$1300 per duration of internship. Open to recent high school graduates, college freshmen, college sophomores, college juniors, college seniors, recent college graduates, graduate students, law students, career changers, individuals reentering the workforce. ▶ *1 self-reliance administrator:* responsibilities include training self-reliance instructors, scheduling courses, and working with schools. Candidates should have ability to work independently, organizational skills, self-motivation, strong interpersonal skills, strong leadership ability. Duration is 9 months. Position available as unpaid or at $7–$9 per hour. Open to recent high school graduates, college freshmen, college sophomores, college juniors, college seniors, recent college graduates, graduate students, law students, career changers, individuals reentering the workforce. ▶ *1–12 summer camp counselors:* responsibilities include assisting children at day/resident camp with activities of daily living, as well as participating in individual and group camping activities. Candidates should have organizational skills, self-motivation, strong interpersonal skills, strong leadership ability. Duration is 2–4 months. $1200–$1800 per duration of internship. Open to high school seniors, recent high school graduates, college freshmen, college sophomores, college juniors, college seniors, recent college graduates, graduate students, law students, career changers, individuals reentering the workforce. International applications accepted.
Benefits Names of contacts, possible full-time employment, travel reimbursement, willing to act as a professional reference, willing to complete paperwork for educational credit, willing to provide letters of recommendation.
Contact Write, call, or fax Dennis W. Clubb, Executive Director, 226 29th Street Drive, SE, Suite E-2, Cedar Rapids, Iowa 52403. Phone: 319-390-6411. Fax: 319-390-6413. In-person interview recommended (telephone interview accepted). Applicants must submit a formal organization application, letter of interest, resume. Application deadline: May 1 for summer; continuous for other positions. World Wide Web: http://www1.cedar-rapids.net/campfire.

CAMP FIRE USA, NORTH OAKLAND COUNCIL
4450 Walton Boulevard, Suite C
Waterford, Michigan 48329

General Information Organization that provides, through a program of informal education, opportunities for youth to realize their potential and to function as caring, self-directed individuals, responsible to themselves and to others. Established in 1910. Number of employees: 4. Unit of Camp Fire USA, Kansas City, Missouri.

Internships Available ▶ *Club leaders:* responsibilities include conducting a Camp Fire program for a group of 5-15 children. Candidates should have oral communication skills, organizational skills, self-motivation, strong interpersonal skills, strong leadership ability. Duration is 2 semesters. Unpaid. Open to recent high school graduates, college freshmen, college sophomores, college juniors, college seniors, recent college graduates, individuals reentering the workforce. ▶ *1–15 day camp counselors:* responsibilities include working with a group of 10 campers in a day camp setting on a pre-planned program. Candidates should have oral communication skills, organizational skills, self-motivation, strong interpersonal skills, strong leadership ability. Duration is 4 weeks in the summer. $125 per week. Open to recent high school graduates, college freshmen, college sophomores, college juniors, college seniors, recent college graduates, graduate students, law students, career changers, individuals reentering the workforce. ▶ *1–4 school club leaders:* responsibilities include conducting a bi-weekly pre-planned Camp Fire meeting for at-risk youth. Candidates should have oral communication skills, organizational skills, plan to pursue career in field, self-motivation, strong interpersonal skills. Duration is 2 semesters. Position available as unpaid or at $7 per hour. Open to high school seniors, recent high school graduates, college freshmen, college sophomores, college juniors, college seniors, recent college graduates, graduate students, law students, career changers, individuals reentering the workforce. International applications accepted.
Benefits Formal training, names of contacts, opportunity to attend seminars/workshops, willing to complete paperwork for educational credit, willing to provide letters of recommendation.
Contact Write, call, fax, e-mail, or through World Wide Web site Ms. Barb Zelinski, Program Director. Phone: 248-618-9050. Fax: 248-618-9052. E-mail: campfireusano@aol.com. In-person interview required. Application deadline: May 1 for summer camp. World Wide Web: http://www.comnet.org/campfirenoc.

CAMP FIRE USA WATHANA COUNCIL
16250 Northland Drive, #301
Southfield, Michigan

General Information Nonprofit youth development organization. Established in 1910. Number of employees: 16. Unit of Camp Fire USA, Kansas City, Missouri.
Internships Available ▶ *1 communications associate:* responsibilities include assisting director of communications with public/media relations, special events, grant writing, newsletter, and Web site development. Candidates should have ability to work independently, ability to work with others, computer skills, office skills, oral communication skills, written communication skills. Duration is 1 semester. Position available as unpaid or at $8.50–$10 per hour. Open to college seniors. ▶ *2–3 summer camp interns:* responsibilities include working with camp director to plan and implement youth programs at summer residential camp in Holly, Michigan. Candidates should have ability to work with others, oral communication skills, self-motivation, strong leadership ability, commitment to work with youth. Duration is June to August. $8.50–$10 per hour. Open to college juniors, college seniors. ▶ *1–2 youth program associates:* responsibilities include working directly with program staff to plan and implement a multi-faceted youth development program. Candidates should have ability to work with others, oral communication skills, plan to pursue career in field, self-motivation, commitment to work with youth. Duration is 1 semester. Position available as unpaid or at $8.50–$10 per hour. Open to college sophomores, college juniors, college seniors.
Benefits Formal training, job counseling, on-the-job training, opportunity to attend seminars/workshops, possible full-time employment, willing to act as a professional reference, willing to complete paperwork for educational credit, willing to provide letters of recommendation.
Contact Write, fax, or e-mail Allen L. Cushing, Executive Director. Fax: 248-599-4307. E-mail: campfirewcalcush@msn.com. No phone calls. In-person interview required. Applicants must submit a letter of interest, resume, three personal references, two letters of recommendation. Applications are accepted continuously.

CAMPHILL SOLTANE
224 Nantmeal Road
Glenmoore, Pennsylvania 19343

General Information Life-sharing community that provides a bridge from youth to adulthood for people with developmental disabilities through community life, further education and training, the arts, and job placement in the surrounding area. Established in 1988. Number of employees: 36. Affiliate of Camphill Association of North America, Hudson, New York. Number of internship applications received each year: 30.
Internships Available ▶ *8–10 interns:* responsibilities include working in positions depending on skills and talents of intern. Candidates should have ability to work independently, ability to work with others, oral communication skills, self-motivation, personal interest in developmental disabilities, alternative lifestyles, and personal growth. Duration is ten to twelve months (late August to late July preferred). Unpaid. Open to recent high school graduates, college freshmen, college sophomores, college juniors, college seniors, recent college graduates, graduate students, career changers, individuals reentering the workforce, must be 19 years of age or older. International applications accepted.
Benefits Formal training, free housing, free meals, names of contacts, on-the-job training, opportunity to attend seminars/workshops, willing to act as a professional reference, willing to complete paperwork for educational credit, willing to provide letters of recommendation, monthly stipend, health insurance (after initial 3 months), vacation funds in July, possibility of continuing involvement, tuition assistance available for AmeriCorps participants.
Contact Write, call, fax, e-mail, or through World Wide Web site Mr. Gregg Davis, Executive Director. Phone: 610-469-0933. Fax: 610-469-1054. E-mail: gdavis@camphillsoltane.org. In-person interview recommended (telephone interview accepted). Applicants must submit a formal organization application, three personal references. Applications are accepted continuously. World Wide Web: http://www.camphillsoltane.org.

CAMP WOODSON
741 Old U.S. Highway 70
Swannanoa, North Carolina 28778

General Information Year-round therapeutic wilderness camping program for juvenile delinquents and/or at-risk youth. Established in 1976. Number of employees: 21. Division of Department of Juvenile Justice and Delinquency Prevention, State of North Carolina, Raleigh, North Carolina. Number of internship applications received each year: 15.
Internships Available ▶ *3–5 fieldwork interns:* responsibilities include hiking, camping, canoeing, horseback riding, and/or rock climbing with students and staff; assisting with office paperwork including documentation, treatment plans, and records; and daily counseling of individuals and groups. Candidates should have ability to work independently, oral communication skills, self-motivation, strong interpersonal skills, strong leadership ability, must have own transportation. Duration is 1–4 months. Unpaid. Open to college freshmen, college sophomores, college juniors, college seniors, recent college graduates, graduate students, law students, career changers, individuals reentering the workforce. International applications accepted.
Benefits Formal training, free meals, job counseling, names of contacts, opportunity to attend seminars/workshops, possible full-time employment, willing to complete paperwork for educational credit, willing to provide letters of recommendation, use of equipment; possible housing.
Contact Write, call, fax, or e-mail Larry Stanley, Internship Coordinator. Phone: 828-686-5411 Ext. 237. Fax: 828-686-7671. E-mail: ncs1555@mindspring.com. In-person interview recommended (telephone interview accepted). Applicants must submit a letter of interest, resume, three personal references. Application deadline: March 1 for spring.

CAPITAL CITY YOUTH SERVICES
2407 Roberts Avenue
Tallahassee, Florida 32310

General Information Nonprofit youth services agency that provides counseling, short-term residential, and community/school outreach to youth and families in crisis. Established in 1974. Number of employees: 43. Number of internship applications received each year: 18.
Internships Available ▶ *1 business intern:* responsibilities include computer data entry, accounts receivable, setting up and using spreadsheets, organizing file system, accounts payable, and some general ledger duties. Candidates should have ability to work with others, analytical skills, college courses in field, organizational skills, personal interest in the field, plan to pursue career in field. Duration is 1–2 semesters. Unpaid. Open to college sophomores, college juniors. ▶ *1 communications intern:* responsibilities include outreach, event planning, designing literature and other PR activities as needed. Candidates should have ability to work independently, oral communication skills, organizational skills, personal interest in the field, strong interpersonal skills, written communication skills. Duration is flexible. Unpaid. Open to college freshmen, college sophomores, college juniors, college seniors, recent college graduates, graduate students, career changers, individuals reentering the workforce. ▶ *1–3 residential program interns:* responsibilities include case management, youth development, follow-ups; direct supervision, crisis calls, program management, educational assistance, and group counseling. Candidates should have ability to work independently, oral communication skills, personal interest in the field, self-motivation, strong interpersonal skills, written communication skills. Duration is flexible. Unpaid. Open to college juniors, college seniors, recent college graduates, graduate students. International applications accepted.
Benefits On-the-job training, opportunity to attend seminars/workshops, possible full-time employment, willing to act as a professional reference, willing to complete paperwork for educational credit, willing to provide letters of recommendation.
Contact Write, call, fax, or e-mail Melanie Carty, Communications Director. Phone: 850-576-6000. Fax: 850-576-2580. E-mail: melanie@ccys.org. In-person interview required. Applicants must submit a formal organization application, letter of interest, resume, two personal references, in-depth background check required. Applications are accepted continuously. World Wide Web: http://www.ccys.org.

CATHOLIC BIG BROTHERS
3300 West Temple Street
Los Angeles, California 90026

General Information Social service organization that provides healthy role models for at-risk youth. Established in 1925. Number of employees: 50. Affiliate of Big Brothers/Big Sisters of America, Inc, Philadelphia, Pennsylvania. Number of internship applications received each year: 3.
Internships Available ▶ *1 development assistant:* responsibilities include assisting director of development, locating foundations, researching criteria for grant applications, and writing letters to donors. Candidates should have computer skills, office skills, oral communication skills, organizational skills, research skills, strong interpersonal skills, written communication skills. Duration is flexible. Unpaid. Open to recent high school graduates, college freshmen, college sophomores, college juniors, college seniors, recent college graduates, graduate students, career changers, individuals reentering the workforce. ▶ *1–8 director's assistants:* responsibilities include assisting director of programs, keeping records, assuring quality, and planning and follow-up. Candidates should have office skills, oral communication skills, personal interest in the field, self-motivation, strong interpersonal skills, written communication skills. Duration is flexible. Unpaid. Open to college freshmen, college sophomores, college juniors, college seniors, recent college graduates, graduate students, career changers, individuals reentering the workforce. ▶ *1 marketing/public relations assistant:* responsibilities include assisting director of marketing/public relations, contacting media, coordinating events, and preparing press releases. Candidates should have oral communication skills, personal interest in the field, self-motivation, strong

interpersonal skills, writing skills. Duration is flexible. Unpaid. ▶ *1–3 school-based mentoring programs assistants:* responsibilities include assisting director of programs, working with youth and volunteers, record keeping and reports, tutoring, and mentoring. Candidates should have oral communication skills, personal interest in the field, self-motivation, strong interpersonal skills, written communication skills. Duration is flexible. Unpaid. Open to recent high school graduates, college freshmen, college sophomores, college juniors, college seniors, recent college graduates, graduate students, career changers, individuals reentering the workforce. ▶ *1–8 social work interns:* responsibilities include assisting directors with programs, case management, working with youth, counseling, tutoring, mentoring youth. Candidates should have office skills, oral communication skills, personal interest in the field, plan to pursue career in field, self-motivation, strong interpersonal skills, written communication skills. Duration is flexible (6 months to 12 months). Unpaid. Open to recent high school graduates, college freshmen, college sophomores, college juniors, college seniors, recent college graduates, graduate students, career changers, individuals reentering the workforce. International applications accepted.

Benefits Formal training, on-the-job training, possible full-time employment, travel reimbursement, willing to act as a professional reference, willing to complete paperwork for educational credit, willing to provide letters of recommendation.

Contact Write, call, fax, e-mail, or through World Wide Web site Douglas Ferraro. Phone: 213-251-9800. Fax: 213-251-9855. E-mail: info@catholicbigbrothers.org. In-person interview required. Applicants must submit a letter of interest, resume, writing sample. Applications are accepted continuously. World Wide Web: http://www.catholicbigbrothers.org.

CATHOLIC CHARITIES DIOCESE OF METUCHEN
319 Maple Street
Perth Amboy, New Jersey 08861

General Information Multi-service agency providing a wide range of quality services to individuals, families, neighborhoods, and communities. Established in 1982. Number of employees: 700. Unit of Catholic Charities USA, Alexandria, Virginia. Number of internship applications received each year: 55.

Internships Available ▶ *10 Bridgewater family services office interns:* responsibilities include conducting assessments and individual, couples, and family therapy; performing administrative duties. Candidates should have ability to work independently, oral communication skills, plan to pursue career in field, strong interpersonal skills, written communication skills. Duration is 2–3 semesters. Unpaid. Open to graduate students, graduate students in the mental health field. ▶ *1–3 East Brunswick child/adolescent partial care interns:* responsibilities include conducting case management, crisis management, intakes, and individual, family, and group counseling with emphasis on group treatment. Candidates should have oral communication skills, personal interest in the field, plan to pursue career in field, strong interpersonal skills, written communication skills. Duration is 2 semesters. Unpaid. Open to graduate students, college seniors in social work program. ▶ *3 East Brunswick mental health center interns:* responsibilities include conducting assessments; case management; individual, couples, family, and group counseling. Candidates should have ability to work independently, oral communication skills, plan to pursue career in field, strong interpersonal skills, written communication skills. Duration is 2 semesters. Unpaid. Open to second-year MSW students. ▶ *1 Edison child/adolescent partial care intern:* responsibilities include conducting case management, crisis management, screenings, and individual, family, and group counseling with emphasis on group treatment. Candidates should have ability to work independently, oral communication skills, personal interest in the field, strong interpersonal skills, written communication skills. Duration is 2 semesters. Unpaid. Open to first- or second-year MSW students. ▶ *3 Edison family services office interns:* responsibilities include conducting assessments, case management, and individual, couples, family, and group counseling. Candidates should have ability to work independently, oral communication skills, personal interest in the field, strong interpersonal skills, written communication skills. Duration is 2 semesters. Unpaid.

Open to second-year MSW students. ▶ *1–12 Flemington family services office interns:* responsibilities include conducting assessments; individual, couples, family, and group counseling; case management, with an emphasis on family therapy. Candidates should have ability to work independently, oral communication skills, plan to pursue career in field, strong interpersonal skills, written communication skills. Duration is 1–3 semesters. Unpaid. Open to graduate students in the mental health field. ▶ *7 Perth Amboy skills training program and inner city counseling program interns:* responsibilities include conducting intakes, assessments, and individual, couples, family, and group counseling; and performing traditional office and in-home services in the areas of child neglect/abuse, sexual abuse, juvenile justice, or foster families. Candidates should have ability to work independently, oral communication skills, personal interest in the field, strong interpersonal skills, written communication skills. Duration is 2 semesters. Unpaid. Open to BSW seniors and first- and second-year MSW students. ▶ *7 Phillipsburg family services office interns:* responsibilities include conducting assessments, and individual, couples, and family counseling. Candidates should have ability to work independently, oral communication skills, personal interest in the field, strong interpersonal skills, written communication skills. Duration is 2 semesters. Unpaid. Open to graduate students in the mental health field. International applications accepted.

Benefits Names of contacts, on-the-job training, opportunity to attend seminars/workshops, possible full-time employment, willing to complete paperwork for educational credit, willing to provide letters of recommendation.

Contact Write, call, or fax Jed Klein, Student Coordinator, 288 Rues Lane, East Brunswick, New Jersey 08816. Phone: 732-257-6100. Fax: 732-651-9834. In-person interview required. Applications are accepted continuously.

CENTER FOR COMMUNITY SOLUTIONS
4508 Mission Bay Drive
San Diego, California 92109

General Information Community center providing services including hospital accompaniment for rape survivors, 24-hour sexual assault and domestic violence crisis prevention and intervention, educational programs, and various counseling services, with focus on domestic violence and sexual assault. Established in 1969. Number of employees: 60. Number of internship applications received each year: 20.

Internships Available ▶ *10–20 crisis line counselors:* responsibilities include working on 24-hour crisis line for survivors of sexual assault and family violence. Candidates should have ability to work independently, college courses in field, knowledge of field, oral communication skills, personal interest in the field, self-motivation. Duration is flexible. Unpaid. Open to college freshmen, college sophomores, college juniors, college seniors. ▶ *1–15 in-person counseling interns/MFT and social work interns:* responsibilities include in-person counseling for men, women, and their families. Candidates should have college degree in related field, knowledge of field, oral communication skills, plan to pursue career in field, strong interpersonal skills, written communication skills. Duration is 1 year. Unpaid. Open to graduate students. ▶ *1–4 legal clinic assistants:* responsibilities include assisting with temporary restraining orders and divorce procedures for battered women. Candidates should have ability to work independently, ability to work with others, oral communication skills, plan to pursue career in field, self-motivation, written communication skills. Position available as unpaid or paid. Open to law students. ▶ *5–10 safehouse assistants:* responsibilities include helping with emergency shelter for victims of violence. Candidates should have ability to work independently, ability to work with others, knowledge of field, oral communication skills, self-motivation, strong leadership ability, written communication skills. Unpaid. Open to college freshmen, college sophomores, college juniors, college seniors, recent college graduates, graduate students, career changers, individuals reentering the workforce. ▶ *5–10 speakers:* responsibilities include speaking on violence against women and other issues. Candidates should have ability to work independently, ability to work with others, knowledge of field, oral communication skills, self-motivation. Unpaid. Open to college freshmen, college sophomores, college

Center for Community Solutions (continued)

juniors, college seniors, recent college graduates, graduate students, law students, career changers, individuals reentering the workforce.
Benefits Formal training, job counseling, names of contacts, on-the-job training, opportunity to attend seminars/workshops, travel reimbursement, willing to act as a professional reference, willing to complete paperwork for educational credit, therapy training and supervision.
Contact Write or call Liza Boyer, Director, Clinical Services. Phone: 858-272-5777 Ext. 26. Fax: 858-272-5361. E-mail: lboyer@ccssd.org. In-person interview required. Applicants must submit a formal organization application, resume, autobiographical statement. Application deadline: June 15 for fall, December 31 for winter/spring.

CENTRAL LAKE YMCA
700 Lakeview Parkway
Vernon Hills, Illinois 60061

General Information Not-for-profit community agency focusing on families, children and communities. Established in 2001. Number of employees: 75. Branch of Lake County Family YMCA, Waukegan, Illinois. Number of internship applications received each year: 2.
Internships Available ▶ *Interns:* responsibilities include assignments based on need of organization and intern. Position available as unpaid or paid. Open to college freshmen, college sophomores, college juniors, college seniors, recent college graduates, graduate students. International applications accepted.
Benefits On-the-job training, possible full-time employment, willing to act as a professional reference, willing to complete paperwork for educational credit, willing to provide letters of recommendation.
Contact Write, call, fax, or e-mail Sara E. Ross, Program Executive. Phone: 847-367-6797. Fax: 847-367-5855. E-mail: selizr@hotmail.com. In-person interview recommended. Applicants must submit a formal organization application, letter of interest, three personal references. Applications are accepted continuously. World Wide Web: http://www.centrallakeymca.org.

CENTRAL VERMONT COUNCIL ON AGING/ NEIGHBOR TO NEIGHBOR AMERICORPS
30 Washington Street
Barre, Vermont 05641

General Information AmeriCorps program hosted by five area agencies on aging that works to connect volunteers to meet the needs of elders in their community; 25 members statewide develop and organize successful programs for the aged. Established in 1975. Number of employees: 30. Number of internship applications received each year: 40.
Internships Available ▶ *25 Neighbor to Neighbor AmeriCorps Members:* responsibilities include working independently or on teams of 6; balancing time between providing direct service to elders and adults with disabilities and recruiting volunteers to meet the needs of clients. Candidates should have ability to work independently, organizational skills, personal interest in the field, self-motivation, strong interpersonal skills. Duration is September to August. $800 per month. Open to college seniors, recent college graduates, graduate students, individuals reentering the workforce.
Benefits Formal training, health insurance, job counseling, names of contacts, on-the-job training, opportunity to attend seminars/workshops, possible full-time employment, travel reimbursement, tuition assistance, willing to act as a professional reference, willing to complete paperwork for educational credit, willing to provide letters of recommendation.
Contact Call, e-mail, or through World Wide Web site Renée Ross, Program Director. Phone: 802-479-0531. Fax: 802-479-4235. E-mail: amccvoca@sover.net. In-person interview recommended (telephone interview accepted). Applicants must submit a formal organization application, letter of interest, resume, 3 personal references or 2 letters of recommendation. Application deadline: August 31. World Wide Web: http://www.americorps.org.

CHESTER APARTMENTS NEIGHBORHOOD NETWORKS COMPUTER TRAINING CENTER
1225 West 9th Street
Chester, Pennsylvania 19013

General Information Company that provides social services to children, adults, and seniors in computer training, vocational training, and life skills to help residents move from welfare to work or career change. Established in 1980. Number of employees: 6. Unit of Inter-State Realty Management, Marlton, New Jersey. Number of internship applications received each year: 5.
Internships Available ▶ *1–2 basic computer class instructors:* responsibilities include teaching basic computer classes to adults, seniors or children, substitute teaching, job readiness courses. Candidates should have knowledge of field, office skills, oral communication skills, strong leadership ability, skills with Windows OS, Microsoft Office, and other office and educational software. Duration is 13-week semester. Unpaid. Open to recent high school graduates, college sophomores, college juniors, college seniors, career changers. ▶ *1–2 social services interns:* responsibilities include tutoring school-aged children, arts and crafts with seniors and children, homework help, exercise classes with seniors and children, local trips, and organization and planning. Candidates should have knowledge of field, oral communication skills, personal interest in the field, self-motivation, strong interpersonal skills. Duration is 6-9 months (2-4 hours per day). Unpaid. Open to high school seniors, recent high school graduates, college freshmen, college sophomores, college juniors, college seniors, recent college graduates, individuals reentering the workforce. International applications accepted.
Benefits Job counseling, on-the-job training, opportunity to attend seminars/workshops, possible full-time employment, willing to act as a professional reference, willing to complete paperwork for educational credit, willing to provide letters of recommendation.
Contact Write, call, or fax Leslie Allen, Training Director. Phone: 610-874-3295. Fax: 610-874-2744. E-mail: chester@snip.net. In-person interview required. Applicants must submit a formal organization application, letter of interest, resume, personal reference, letter of recommendation. Applications are accepted continuously.

CHILD AND FAMILY SERVICES OF NEWPORT COUNTY
19 Valley Road
Middletown, Rhode Island 02842

General Information Nonprofit agency providing services for children, their families, and the communities in which they live. Established in 1867. Number of employees: 275. Number of internship applications received each year: 30.
Internships Available ▶ *1–5 child-care interns:* responsibilities include assisting teachers with classroom management, one-on-one parent contacts. Candidates should have ability to work independently, college courses in field, oral communication skills, self-motivation, strong interpersonal skills. Duration is 1 semester. Unpaid. Open to college sophomores, college juniors, college seniors, graduate students. ▶ *1–4 community-based interns:* responsibilities include assisting staff in the provision of wide range of home-based services to families in process of reunification or seeking to avoid separation. Candidates should have ability to work independently, declared college major in field, oral communication skills, self-motivation, strong interpersonal skills. Duration is 6 months. Unpaid. Open to college sophomores, college juniors, college seniors, graduate students. ▶ *5–15 residential program interns:* responsibilities include working with staff to provide safe, nurturing environment in which youth 6-18 can learn and grow; includes one-on-one and group activities. Candidates should have ability to work independently, ability to work with others, declared college major in field, oral communication skills, personal interest in the field, self-motivation. Duration is minimum of 6 months. Unpaid. Open to college sophomores, college juniors, college seniors, graduate students. ▶ *1–5 school-based interns:* responsibilities include assisting in classroom with special programs; developing group programs; working one-on-one with students needing special attention. Candidates should have ability to work

independently, declared college major in field, oral communication skills, self-motivation, strong interpersonal skills. Duration is 1 semester. Unpaid. Open to college juniors, college seniors, graduate students. International applications accepted.

Benefits On-the-job training, opportunity to attend seminars/workshops, possible full-time employment, willing to act as a professional reference, willing to complete paperwork for educational credit, willing to provide letters of recommendation.

Contact Write, call, or e-mail Martha Parks, Volunteer/Intern Project Director. Phone: 401-848-4210. Fax: 401-848-2336. E-mail: mparks@cfsnewport.org. In-person interview required. Applicants must submit a formal organization application, resume, three personal references. Applications are accepted continuously.

CHILD CARE, INC.
275 7th Avenue
New York, New York 10001

General Information Nonprofit child-care and early education resource organization that offers programs on public policy work, training for child-care providers, and referrals for parents. Established in 1980. Number of employees: 35. Number of internship applications received each year: 50.

Internships Available ▶ *1–3 development interns:* responsibilities include assisting with coordination of memberships, researching prospective funders, writing articles for newsletter, writing and editing correspondence with funders and members. Candidates should have ability to work independently, ability to work with others, computer skills, office skills, personal interest in the field, research skills, self-motivation, writing skills, creative thinking; some awareness of child-care issues (helpful). Duration is 2–3 months in summer; positions during school year negotiable. Position available as unpaid or paid. Open to college freshmen, college sophomores, college juniors, college seniors, recent college graduates, graduate students, career changers. ▶ *1–2 program associates:* responsibilities include assisting in preparing materials and training sessions related to starting and expanding child-care programs; working on editing and preparing resource papers for publication; developing training database; helping in preparing and conducting training sessions. Candidates should have ability to work with others, computer skills, oral communication skills, organizational skills, writing skills. Duration is one semester. Unpaid. Open to recent high school graduates, college sophomores, college juniors, college seniors, recent college graduates, graduate students, career changers, individuals reentering the workforce.

Benefits Names of contacts, on-the-job training, opportunity to attend seminars/workshops, willing to act as a professional reference, willing to complete paperwork for educational credit, willing to provide letters of recommendation, possibility of stipend, transportation reimbursement provided.

Contact Write, fax, or e-mail Elissa Nelson, Development Associate. Fax: 212-929-5785. E-mail: info@childcareinc.org. No phone calls. In-person interview required. Applicants must submit a letter of interest, resume, writing samples for some positions. Applications are accepted continuously. World Wide Web: http://www.childcareinc.org.

CHRYSALIS: A CENTER FOR WOMEN
4432 Chicago Avenue, S
Minneapolis, Minnesota 55407-3522

General Information Multi-service organization serving women and their families; programs include mental health, chemical dependency, legal assistance, family education, resource referral, supportive counseling, and education and support groups. Established in 1974. Number of employees: 50. Number of internship applications received each year: 100.

Internships Available ▶ *2 chemical dependency interns:* responsibilities include developing a caseload of clients in a feminist-based, high quality chemical dependency outreach program. Candidates should have college courses in field, knowledge of field, personal interest in the field, plan to pursue career in field, strong interpersonal skills. Duration is flexible. Unpaid. Open to graduate students, those enrolled in or graduates of chemical dependency certification program. ▶ *2–3 development interns:* responsibilities include assisting development department in areas of fund-raising,

annual appeals, grant writing, and donor research. Candidates should have ability to work independently, computer skills, organizational skills, self-motivation, strong interpersonal skills, writing skills. Duration is 150 hours or more. Unpaid. Open to college freshmen, college sophomores, college juniors, college seniors, recent college graduates, graduate students, career changers, individuals reentering the workforce. ▶ *2–3 family education interns:* responsibilities include providing support in several capacities to children in various stages of development. Candidates should have knowledge of field, oral communication skills, personal interest in the field, self-motivation, strong interpersonal skills. Duration is 150 hours or more. Unpaid. Open to college freshmen, college sophomores, college juniors, college seniors, recent college graduates, career changers, individuals reentering the workforce. ▶ *2–3 legal and resource interns:* responsibilities include helping empower women through education and advocacy; hosting legal education sessions; facilitating legal advice clinics and offering peer support through the resource counseling program. Candidates should have ability to work independently, knowledge of field, oral communication skills, personal interest in the field, strong interpersonal skills. Duration is 150 hours or more. Unpaid. Open to college freshmen, college sophomores, college juniors, college seniors, recent college graduates, graduate students, law students, career changers, individuals reentering the workforce. ▶ *3 mental health clinic interns:* responsibilities include participating in all aspects of clinic operations, including intakes and individual, group, and family therapy. Candidates should have college courses in field, knowledge of field, oral communication skills, plan to pursue career in field, strong interpersonal skills. Duration is 9 month minimum, September through June. Unpaid. Open to graduate students. ▶ *10–15 resource counseling interns:* responsibilities include providing support, resources, and referrals to women who call or walk into the Center. Candidates should have oral communication skills, personal interest in the field, self-motivation, strong interpersonal skills. Duration is 150 hours or more. Unpaid. Open to college freshmen, college sophomores, college juniors, college seniors, recent college graduates, graduate students, law students, career changers, individuals reentering the workforce. International applications accepted.

Benefits Formal training, names of contacts, on-the-job training, opportunity to attend seminars/workshops, possible full-time employment, willing to act as a professional reference, willing to complete paperwork for educational credit, willing to provide letters of recommendation.

Contact Call, e-mail, or through World Wide Web site Ms. Karen Smith, Volunteer Services Coordinator, 4432 Chicago Avenue S, Minneapolis, Minnesota 55407-3522. Phone: 612-870-2420. Fax: 612-870-2403. E-mail: ksmith@chrysaliswomen.org. In-person interview recommended (telephone interview accepted). Applicants must submit a letter of interest, resume, 1 or 2 professional references. Applications are accepted continuously. World Wide Web: http://www.chrysaliswomen.org.

CIRCLE OF NEIGHBORS
One College Center, Box 76000
Colorado Springs, Colorado 80970

General Information Nonprofit community service organization focusing on planning and funding for college-bound students. Established in 1897. Number of employees: 4. Number of internship applications received each year: 25.

Internships Available ▶ *College planning consultants:* responsibilities include explaining the process of college planning and interviewing candidates for assistance. Candidates should have ability to work independently, oral communication skills, personal interest in the field, self-motivation, strong interpersonal skills, strong leadership skills. Duration is flexible. Position available as unpaid or at $100 to $3000 (depending on number of hours worked). Open to high school students, recent high school graduates, college freshmen, college sophomores, college juniors, college seniors, recent college graduates, graduate students, law students, career changers, individuals reentering the workforce, retirees. International applications accepted.

Benefits Formal training, job counseling, names of contacts, on-the-job training, opportunity to attend seminars/workshops,

Circle of Neighbors (continued)

possible full-time employment, tuition assistance, willing to act as a professional reference, willing to complete paperwork for educational credit, willing to provide letters of recommendation. **Contact** Write, call, fax, e-mail, or through World Wide Web site Tom Okuto, Director of Consultants, One College Circle, Box 68832, Tucson, Arizona 85737. Phone: 800-743-4731. Fax: 888-743-4731. E-mail: info@circleofneighbors.org. Applicants must submit a letter of interest, resume, in-person interview recommended, online or telephone interview acceptable. Applications are accepted continuously. World Wide Web: http://www.circleofneighbors.org.

COLUMBUS YOUTH CAMP
12454 West Youth Camp Road
Columbus, Indiana 47201

General Information Nonprofit youth organization. Established in 1928. Number of employees: 3. Division of Foundation for Youth, Columbus, Indiana. Number of internship applications received each year: 10.
Internships Available ▶ *1–2 interpretation interns:* responsibilities include interpretive needs assessment; developing nature trail and signage; researching historical information of camp history. Candidates should have ability to work independently, oral communication skills, organizational skills, personal interest in the field, research skills, written communication skills. Duration is 3 months. $750 per duration of internship. ▶ *2–6 outdoor recreation resource management interns:* responsibilities include assisting in program planning and implementation; supervising seasonal staff; inspection and maintenance of challenge course elements; assisting in leading adventure trips; assisting with administrative responsibilities. Candidates should have ability to work independently, personal interest in the field, self-motivation, strong interpersonal skills, strong leadership ability. Duration is 3 months. $1000 per duration of internship. Open to college sophomores, college juniors, college seniors, recent college graduates, graduate students. International applications accepted.
Benefits Free housing, names of contacts, on-the-job training, opportunity to attend seminars/workshops, possible full-time employment, willing to act as a professional reference, willing to complete paperwork for educational credit, willing to provide letters of recommendation.
Contact Write, call, fax, or e-mail Laura Boggess, Director of Programs. Phone: 812-342-2698. Fax: 812-372-3226. E-mail: laura@columbusyouthcamp.com. In-person interview recommended (telephone interview accepted). Applicants must submit a letter of interest, resume. Application deadline: February 15 for summer, May 15 for fall, December 1 for spring. World Wide Web: http://www.columbusyouthcamp.com.

COMMISSION FOR WOMEN–COUNSELING AND CAREER CENTER
255 North Washington Street, 4th Floor
Rockville, Maryland 20850

General Information Commission that conducts research and advocacy activities for women's issues and operates a counseling and career center primarily for women. Established in 1976. Number of employees: 20. Department of Montgomery County Government, Rockville, Maryland. Number of internship applications received each year: 15.
Internships Available ▶ *1–3 Commission for Women interns:* responsibilities include researching and preparing reports. Candidates should have ability to work independently, analytical skills, computer skills, editing skills, knowledge of field, oral communication skills, organizational skills, personal interest in the field, research skills, self-motivation, strong interpersonal skills, strong leadership ability, writing skills. Duration is 1 year. Unpaid. Open to college seniors, recent college graduates, graduate students, law students, career changers, individuals reentering the workforce. ▶ *1–5 counseling interns:* responsibilities include providing psychosocial and career counseling to adults using short term, problem-solving approach; facilitating workshops/seminar. Candidates should have ability to work with others, analytical skills, college degree in

related field, oral communication skills, plan to pursue career in field, counseling experience (preferred). Duration is 2 semesters (preferred). Unpaid. Open to second-year graduate students enrolled in a master's program for social work or counseling and are using this experience as part of a formal practicum or internship approved by their university for credit. ▶ *5 information and referral specialists:* responsibilities include assisting with information and referral services and providing intake for the counseling center. Candidates should have analytical skills, college degree in related field, computer skills, knowledge of field, oral communication skills, organizational skills, personal interest in the field, research skills, strong interpersonal skills, written communication skills. Duration is 2 semesters (preferred). Unpaid. Open to college juniors, college seniors, recent college graduates, graduate students, career changers. International applications accepted.
Benefits Job counseling, on-the-job training, opportunity to attend seminars/workshops, willing to complete paperwork for educational credit, willing to provide letters of recommendation, supervision for counseling interns and those who need supervision in order to earn certification.
Contact Write, fax, e-mail, or through World Wide Web site Alyssa Philipp, Intake Services Coordinator. Fax: 301-279-1318. E-mail: philia@co.mo.md.us. In-person interview recommended (telephone interview accepted). Applicants must submit a formal organization application, resume, letter of interest including time of availability. Applications are accepted continuously. World Wide Web: http://www.co.mo.md.us/cfw.

COMMON GROUND SANCTUARY
1410 South Telegraph
Bloomfield Hills, Michigan 48302

General Information Comprehensive voluntary counseling and psychiatric assessment services for children, youth, and families; residential and non-residential care for people who are in crisis situations. Established in 1971. Number of employees: 198. Number of internship applications received each year: 60.
Internships Available ▶ *1 accountant:* responsibilities include tracking daily receipts and disbursements, performing general ledger, payroll, budgeting, and budget analysis duties. Candidates should have ability to work independently, analytical skills, computer skills, experience in the field, organizational skills, self-motivation, strong interpersonal skills, written communication skills. Duration is minimum of 1 semester. Unpaid. Open to recent high school graduates, college freshmen, college sophomores, college juniors, college seniors, career changers, individuals reentering the workforce. ▶ *1 business administrator:* responsibilities include assisting in developing business plans, strategic planning, internal information management, and personnel policies. Candidates should have ability to work independently, analytical skills, experience in the field, office skills, oral communication skills, organizational skills, self-motivation, strong interpersonal skills, strong leadership ability, written communication skills. Duration is minimum of 1 semester. Unpaid. Open to college freshmen, college sophomores, college juniors, college seniors, recent college graduates. ▶ *6 counselors:* responsibilities include directing case load of 2-10 youth and families and providing after-care and advocacy counseling. Candidates should have college courses in field, knowledge of field, oral communication skills, personal interest in the field, self-motivation, strong interpersonal skills, writing skills. Duration is 14–52 weeks. Unpaid. ▶ *4–20 direct care workers:* responsibilities include performing daily supervision, intakes, group counseling, recreational supervision, and teen consultation. Candidates should have personal interest in the field, strong interpersonal skills, written communication skills. Duration is minimum of 1 semester. Unpaid. Open to recent high school graduates, college freshmen, college sophomores, college juniors, college seniors, recent college graduates, law students, career changers, individuals reentering the workforce. ▶ *2 marketing and public relations interns:* responsibilities include assisting in development and implementation of a corporate public relations strategic plan, including written, oral, and media relations, as well as marketing publications. Candidates should have ability to work with others, computer skills, knowledge of field, oral communica-

tion skills, personal interest in the field, self-motivation, written communication skills. Duration is 10–52 weeks. Unpaid. Open to high school seniors, recent high school graduates, college freshmen, college sophomores, college juniors, college seniors, recent college graduates, graduate students, individuals reentering the workforce. ▶ *2 victim assistance advocates:* responsibilities include providing advocacy, counseling, and support services to victims of crime, providing education and awareness classes/outreach, and supporting research and statistics. Candidates should have ability to work with others, college courses in field, computer skills, knowledge of field, oral communication skills, research skills, self-motivation, written communication skills. Duration is 12–52 weeks. Unpaid. Open to college freshmen, college sophomores, college juniors, college seniors, graduate students. International applications accepted.

Benefits Free meals, opportunity to attend seminars/workshops, possible full-time employment, travel reimbursement, willing to complete paperwork for educational credit, willing to provide letters of recommendation.

Contact Write, fax, or e-mail James A. Perlaki, Vice President of Community Intervention Services. Fax: 248-456-8147. E-mail: sanctuary6@aol.com. No phone calls. In-person interview required. Applicants must submit a formal organization application, resume, academic transcripts, three personal references. Application deadline: February 1 for spring/summer (recommended), November 1 for winter (recommended). World Wide Web: http://commongroundsanctuary.org.

COMMUNITY CRISIS CENTER
PO Box 1390
Elgin, Illinois 60121

General Information Center providing immediate, twenty-four hour, caring and professional services in response to requests from individuals and families affected by domestic violence, sexual assault, and other crisis situations. Established in 1975. Number of employees: 80. Number of internship applications received each year: 15.

Internships Available ▶ *4–6 case managers:* responsibilities include crisis intervention on the hot line, individual counseling with an assigned shelter resident client, providing information to walk-in clients. Duration is 400 hours. Unpaid. Open to college seniors. ▶ *1–2 children's workers:* responsibilities include assisting Children's Program staff with individual and group activities with the children in the shelter. Duration is 1 semester (20 hours per week). Unpaid. Open to college sophomores. ▶ *2–4 counselors:* responsibilities include crisis intervention via hotline, individual and group counseling with residents and walk-in clients, family counseling with resident adults and their minor children. Duration is September to May. Unpaid. Open to graduate students. ▶ *2–4 shelter workers:* responsibilities include assisting resident case managers in responding to the needs of the women and children in the shelter. Duration is 1 semester (20 hours per week). Unpaid. Open to college sophomores. Candidates for all positions should have college courses in field, oral communication skills, strong interpersonal skills, written communication skills. International applications accepted.

Benefits Formal training, names of contacts, on-the-job training, opportunity to attend seminars/workshops, possible full-time employment, willing to act as a professional reference, willing to complete paperwork for educational credit, willing to provide letters of recommendation.

Contact Call or fax Maureen Manning-Rosenfeld, Director of Client Services. Phone: 847-697-2380. Fax: 847-742-4182. In-person interview required. Applicants must submit a letter of interest, resume. Application deadline: March 1 for summer, April 1 for fall, October 1 for spring.

COMMUNITY HARVEST FOOD BANK
PO Box 10967
Fort Wayne, Indiana 46855

General Information Organization that works to alleviate hunger by collecting and distributing donated foods; operates through a network of 600 agencies in northeast Indiana and Allen County. Established in 1983. Number of employees: 28. Number of internship applications received each year: 2.

Internships Available ▶ *1–2 agency services interns:* responsibilities include working directly with member agencies, handling order placements, invoicing, appointments, and taking care of agency needs; ensuring that office runs smoothly; and helping with on-site monitoring. Candidates should have ability to work independently, ability to work with others, computer skills, office skills, oral communication skills, organizational skills. Duration is ongoing throughout the year. Unpaid. Open to recent high school graduates, college freshmen, college sophomores, college juniors, college seniors, career changers, individuals reentering the workforce. ▶ *1 resource development intern:* responsibilities include maintenance and expansion of 11,000-name database, researching emerging trends in fund-raising (e.g. cause-related marketing), proposal writing and preparation, direct mail newsletter writing, printing and preparation. Candidates should have ability to work independently, computer skills, oral communication skills, personal interest in the field, research skills, written communication skills. Duration is 3–12 months. Unpaid. Open to college freshmen, college sophomores, college juniors, college seniors, recent college graduates, graduate students. ▶ *2–3 warehouse assistants:* responsibilities include keeping records of attendance and product usage and warehouse distribution of food to member agencies. Candidates should have ability to work independently, computer skills, oral communication skills, personal interest in the field, self-motivation, strong interpersonal skills, strong leadership ability, writing skills, ability to perform physical labor (lifting, loading and unloading). Duration is 3 months. Unpaid. Open to recent high school graduates, college freshmen, college sophomores, college juniors, college seniors, recent college graduates, graduate students, law students, career changers, individuals reentering the workforce. International applications accepted.

Benefits On-the-job training, possible full-time employment, willing to act as a professional reference, willing to complete paperwork for educational credit, willing to provide letters of recommendation.

Contact Write, call, fax, or e-mail Carlos Nunez, Resource Development Manager. Phone: 260-447-3696. Fax: 260-447-4859. E-mail: cnunez@secondharvest.org. In-person interview recommended (telephone interview accepted). Applicants must submit a letter of interest, resume. Applications are accepted continuously. World Wide Web: http://www.communityharvest.org.

COMMUNITY MEDIATION CENTER
165 South Main Street, Suite A
Harrisonburg, Virginia 22801

General Information Mediation center providing services to individuals, families, organizations, and communities, as well as mediation and conflict resolution training. Established in 1982. Number of employees: 9. Number of internship applications received each year: 15.

Internships Available ▶ *5 case managers:* responsibilities include interviewing clients referred to mediation (by phone or in court) and scheduling cases for mediation. Candidates should have ability to work independently, college courses in field, oral communication skills, personal interest in the field, self-motivation, strong interpersonal skills, written communication skills. Duration is flexible. Unpaid. Open to college juniors, college seniors, recent college graduates, graduate students, law students, career changers. International applications accepted.

Benefits Formal training, names of contacts, on-the-job training, opportunity to attend seminars/workshops, willing to act as a professional reference, willing to complete paperwork for educational credit, willing to provide letters of recommendation.

Contact Write, call, fax, e-mail, or through World Wide Web site Timothy Ruebke, Director of Mediation Services. Phone: 540-434-0059. Fax: 540-574-0174. E-mail: mediate@rica.net. In-person interview recommended (telephone interview accepted). Applicants must submit a letter of interest, resume. Application deadline: April 1 for summer, July 1 for fall, November 1 for spring. World Wide Web: http://home.rica.net/mediate/.

CORPORATION FOR NATIONAL SERVICE
1201 New York Avenue, NW
Washington, District of Columbia 20525

General Information   Federal government corporation in partnership with state and local governments and nonprofit organizations that administers AmeriCorps, Learn and Serve America, and the National Senior Service Corps. Established in 1994. Number of employees: 350. Number of internship applications received each year: 150.

Internships Available   ▶ *AmeriCorps recruitment, selection, and placement interns:* responsibilities include working on a project designed to improve the methods, efficiency, and evaluation of recruitment efforts. Candidates should have ability to work independently, ability to work with others, analytical skills, oral communication skills, research skills, written communication skills, interest in community service, background working with student organizations or admission offices. Duration is 10 weeks in summer. Unpaid. Open to college freshmen, college sophomores, college juniors, college seniors, recent college graduates, graduate students. ▶ *1 AmeriCorps* NCCC intern:* responsibilities include supporting the production of a quarterly newsletter, acting as liaison to the field for the development of submissions to the contractor responsible for newsletter layout, and helping maintain NCCC project information. Candidates should have ability to work independently, editing skills, organizational skills, self-motivation, writing skills, Microsoft Office experience (useful), area of study in journalism (helpful but not required). Duration is 10 weeks. Unpaid. Open to college freshmen, college sophomores, college juniors, college seniors, recent college graduates, graduate students. ▶ *1 AmeriCorps* State, South Cluster office intern:* responsibilities include identifying efforts made between AmeriCorps*State and other corporation-supported programs to resolve community need, studying interaction between state commissions and their governing bodies, studying state commission feedback on performance and exploring methods of improvement, and gathering and assembling resource guide of program and state commission best practices. Candidates should have ability to work with others, self-motivation, commitment to national service movement, experience in community service helpful, academic background in social work or public administration helpful. Duration is one summer. Unpaid. Open to college freshmen, college sophomores, college juniors, college seniors, recent college graduates, graduate students. ▶ *1–3 AmeriCorps* VISTA interns:* responsibilities include designing, delivering, and tabulating results of evaluations; assisting in the design of training for AmeriCorps*VISTA leaders; recruiting colleges to participate in the VISTA Post-Service Educational Opportunities Program, and expanding the VISTA alumni database. Candidates should have ability to work independently, analytical skills, oral communication skills, organizational skills, personal interest in the field, research skills, strong interpersonal skills, writing skills, knowledge of MS Word helpful. Duration is 10 weeks. Unpaid. Open to college freshmen, college sophomores, college juniors, college seniors, recent college graduates, graduate students. ▶ *1 General Counsel intern:* responsibilities include working on various assignments in the Office of the General Counsel, including legal research, writing memoranda, case preparation, and developing guidelines. Candidates should have experience with legal research and nonprofit service organizations (desirable). Duration is 10 weeks in summer. Unpaid. Open to 1st- and second-year law students only. ▶ *2–5 Learn and Serve America interns:* responsibilities include developing a program director's manual; enhancing the content of information on the Web, preparing articles for publication, researching program issues, reviewing program portfolios and developing profiles, and filling requests for the field. Candidates should have ability to work independently, ability to work with others, personal interest in the field, self-motivation, writing skills, experience with service-learning (preferred). Duration is 10 weeks. Unpaid. Open to college freshmen, college sophomores, college juniors, college seniors, recent college graduates, graduate students. ▶ *National Senior Service Corps interns:* responsibilities include analyzing and mapping service data, researching questions about Senior Corps programs from Congress, developing program enhancements for foster grandparents, senior companions, and the retired and senior volunteers. Candidates should have ability to work independently, oral communication skills, written communication skills. Duration is 10 weeks in summer. Unpaid. Open to college freshmen, college sophomores, college juniors, college seniors, recent college graduates, graduate students. ▶ *1–2 congressional and intergovernmental relations interns:* responsibilities include researching policy matters related to national service, supporting key work related to reauthorization legislation, assisting with preparation of materials for the next appropriations cycle, and responding to congressional inquiries. Candidates should have ability to work independently, analytical skills, knowledge of field, office skills, oral communication skills, written communication skills, ability to handle simple math; academic background in political science, public policy, economics, public administration, law, or English. Duration is flexible. Unpaid. Open to college sophomores, college juniors, college seniors, recent college graduates, graduate students. ▶ *1 evaluation and effective practices interns:* responsibilities include performing research on various policy studies including enrollment and attrition issues in AmeriCorps, gender bias in national service, and how to promote quality programming in a decentralized structure, performance planning, and creating customer service standards. Candidates should have ability to work independently, ability to work with others, analytical skills, college courses in field, knowledge of field, research skills, written communication skills, proficiency in MS Word (required); knowledge of Excel and SPSS (useful). Duration is 10 weeks. Unpaid. Open to college sophomores, college juniors, college seniors, recent college graduates, graduate students. ▶ *Public affairs interns:* responsibilities include writing press releases and feature articles, assisting with special events such as press conferences, assembling press packets, transcribing speeches, and compiling news clips packages for targeted members of Congress. Candidates should have ability to work with others, research skills, writing skills, academic background in journalism, marketing, or communications (useful). Duration is 10 weeks in summer. Unpaid. Open to college freshmen, college sophomores, college juniors, college seniors, recent college graduates, graduate students.
Benefits   On-the-job training, opportunity to attend seminars/workshops, possible full-time employment, willing to act as a professional reference, willing to provide letters of recommendation.
Contact   Write, call, fax, e-mail, or through World Wide Web site Internship Coordinator. Phone: 202-606-5000 Ext. 463. Fax: 202-565-2784. E-mail: internships@cns.gov. Telephone interview required. Applicants must submit a letter of interest, resume. Applications are accepted continuously. World Wide Web: http://www.nationalservice.org/.

COUNTERPOINT SHELTERS AND CRISIS CENTER
715 Inkster Road
Inkster, Michigan 48141

General Information   Social service agency that provides a wide range of services including drug abuse prevention and a runaway shelter. Established in 1975. Number of employees: 30. Unit of Starfish Family Services, Inkster, Michigan. Number of internship applications received each year: 40.
Internships Available   ▶ *6–10 counseling or group work interns:* responsibilities include working with non-adjudicated teens toward family reunification, helping teens with independent living skills, and performing group work; crisis line and crisis drop-in counseling. Candidates should have ability to work with others, college courses in field, knowledge of field, oral communication skills, plan to pursue career in field, self-motivation, written communication skills. Duration is 1–2 semesters. Unpaid. Open to college freshmen, college sophomores, college juniors, college seniors, graduate students, career changers. ▶ *1–3 youth assistance group workers.* Candidates should have ability to work independently, oral communication skills, self-motivation, written communication skills, group work skills. Duration is flexible. Unpaid. Open to college freshmen, college sophomores, college juniors, college seniors, recent college graduates, graduate students, law students, career changers. ▶ *10–15 youth care workers/counselors:* responsibilities include managing floor in residential program for 1-6 adolescents, conducting intakes, performing crisis management and individual, family, and group counseling. Candidates should

have ability to work independently, ability to work with others, knowledge of field, oral communication skills, plan to pursue career in field, written communication skills, background in social work/psychology. Duration is flexible. Unpaid. Open to college freshmen, college sophomores, college juniors, college seniors. International applications accepted.

Benefits Names of contacts, on-the-job training, opportunity to attend seminars/workshops, possible full-time employment, willing to act as a professional reference, willing to complete paperwork for educational credit, willing to provide letters of recommendation.

Contact Write, call, or e-mail Mary Ellen Rehse, Youth Services Director. Phone: 313-277-2450. E-mail: mrehse@sfish.org. In-person interview required. Applicants must submit a formal organization application, personal reference, letter of recommendation, TB tests, criminal records check, drug screening; academic transcripts desirable. Applications are accepted continuously. World Wide Web: http://www.sfishonline.org.

CREATIVE RESPONSE TO CONFLICT AND CHILDREN'S CREATIVE RESPONSE TO CONFLICT
PO Box 271
Nyack, New York 10960

General Information Program established by the New York Quaker Project on Community Conflict to provide specially designed activities in which participants experience ways to examine conflicts and develop solutions. Established in 1972. Number of employees: 6. Number of internship applications received each year: 25.

Internships Available ▶ *2 interns:* responsibilities include facilitating small groups within workshops, helping to gather materials for use with activities, and sharing administrative duties. Candidates should have knowledge of field, oral communication skills, plan to pursue career in field, strong interpersonal skills, ability to work well with children, commitment to nonviolence. Duration is 3–12 months. Unpaid. Open to college seniors, recent college graduates, graduate students, law students, career changers, individuals reentering the workforce, retired teachers. International applications accepted.

Benefits Formal training, on-the-job training, opportunity to attend seminars/workshops, tuition assistance, willing to complete paperwork for educational credit, willing to provide letters of recommendation.

Contact Write, call, fax, or e-mail Priscilla Prutzman, Executive Director. Phone: 845-353-1796. Fax: 845-358-4924. E-mail: ccrcnyack@aol.com. In-person interview recommended (telephone interview accepted). Applicants must submit a letter of interest, resume, personal reference, three letters of recommendation. Applications are accepted continuously. World Wide Web: http://www.ccrcglobal.org.

CRISIS SUPPORT SERVICES
PO Box 9102
Berkeley, California 94709

General Information Nonprofit, volunteer-based agency that operates a 24-hour telephone crisis line, community education and training, grief counseling, in-home senior outreach and therapy group for those who have attempted suicide. Established in 1966. Number of employees: 16. Number of internship applications received each year: 60.

Internships Available ▶ *Counselors:* responsibilities include answering 24-hour crisis line; mental health interns also co-facilitate groups and provide individual and family counseling. Candidates should have ability to work independently, oral communication skills, self-motivation, strong interpersonal skills, written communication skills. Duration is one year (minimum 4 hours per week). Unpaid. Open to adults 19 and over. International applications accepted.

Benefits Formal training, on-the-job training, opportunity to attend seminars/workshops, willing to act as a professional reference, willing to complete paperwork for educational credit, willing to provide letters of recommendation.

Contact Write, call, fax, or through World Wide Web site Chrissy Brewer, Clinical Director. Phone: 510-848-1515. Fax: 510-486-0443. In-person interview required. Applicants must submit a formal organization application, three letters of recommendation. Applications are accepted continuously. World Wide Web: http://www.crisissupport.org.

THE CUBA AMERICA JEWISH MISSION
1442A Walnut Street, #224
Berkeley, California 94709

General Information Nonprofit organization that assists in the revitalization of Jewish life in Cuba by working to improve physical and spiritual well-being and to assist new Cuban settlers in Israel. Established in 1997. Number of employees: 3. Number of internship applications received each year: 2.

Internships Available ▶ *1 executive assistant:* responsibilities include answering requests for information; developing programming; newsletter; coordinating and developing volunteer programs; clerical duties; bookkeeping, and fund-raising. Candidates should have ability to work independently, analytical skills, editing skills, office skills, oral communication skills, organizational skills, personal interest in the field, self-motivation, strong interpersonal skills, strong leadership ability, writing skills, Spanish (helpful); knowledge of Word, Excel, and Quicken. Duration is flexible. Position available as unpaid or at $10 per hour. Open to recent high school graduates, college freshmen, college sophomores, college juniors, college seniors, recent college graduates, graduate students, law students, career changers, individuals reentering the workforce. ▶ *1 grant writer:* responsibilities include grant writing to obtain funding for both administration and programming. Candidates should have analytical skills, computer skills, editing skills, knowledge of field, personal interest in the field, research skills, self-motivation, writing skills, previous experience with grant writing in or out of school. Duration is flexible . Position available as unpaid or paid. Open to college sophomores, college juniors, college seniors, recent college graduates, graduate students, law students, career changers, individuals reentering the workforce. International applications accepted.

Benefits On-the-job training, willing to act as a professional reference, willing to complete paperwork for educational credit, willing to provide letters of recommendation.

Contact Write, fax, e-mail, or through World Wide Web site June Safran, Executive Director. Fax: 510-527-2514. E-mail: june@thecajm.org. No phone calls. In-person interview recommended (telephone interview accepted). Applicants must submit a letter of interest, resume, two writing samples. Applications are accepted continuously. World Wide Web: http://www.thecajm.org.

DANIEL WEBSTER COUNCIL, BOY SCOUTS: OUTDOOR EDUCATION & OUTREACH DIVISION
571 Holt Avenue
Manchester, New Hampshire 03109

General Information Outdoor adventure education/counseling program for troubled youths; national outreach program for at-risk and developmentally disabled youth. Established in 1984. Number of employees: 5. Number of internship applications received each year: 12.

Internships Available ▶ *Adventure program assistants:* responsibilities include designing and implementing outdoor adventure-based counseling programs. Candidates should have ability to work with others, experience in the field, oral communication skills, personal interest in the field, self-motivation, strong leadership ability. Duration is 9.5 months (beginning in fall). $800 per month. Open to recent college graduates, graduate students.

Benefits Formal training, free housing, names of contacts, opportunity to attend seminars/workshops, possible full-time employment, travel reimbursement, willing to act as a professional reference, willing to complete paperwork for educational credit, willing to provide letters of recommendation, stipend and grocery allowance.

Contact Write, call, or e-mail John Rainville, Director of Outdoor Education and Outreach Program. Phone: 603-625-6431. E-mail: jrainvil@bsamail.org. In-person interview recommended (telephone

Daniel Webster Council, Boy Scouts: Outdoor Education & Outreach Division
(*continued*)
interview accepted). Applicants must submit a letter of interest, resume, two personal references. Application deadline: August 15.

D.C. RAPE CRISIS CENTER
PO Box 34125
Washington, District of Columbia 20043

General Information Private nonprofit agency offering 24-hour crisis counseling, companion services, and community education programs on related issues. Established in 1972. Number of employees: 17. Number of internship applications received each year: 50.
Internships Available ▶ *1–2 administration interns:* responsibilities include coordinating the workshop program, database management, and assisting in planning the Center's annual gala. Candidates should have ability to work with others, office skills, oral communication skills, organizational skills, self-motivation, written communication skills. Duration is flexible. Unpaid. Open to high school seniors, recent high school graduates, college freshmen, college sophomores, college juniors, college seniors, recent college graduates, individuals reentering the workforce. ▶ *2 community education interns:* responsibilities include assisting with coordinating Sexual Assault Awareness Month, self-defense classes, and other community education projects; some interns, depending on experience, have the option of being trained to conduct presentations. Candidates should have ability to work with others, knowledge of field, oral communication skills, organizational skills, self-motivation, written communication skills. Duration is flexible (3 months minimum). Unpaid. Open to high school seniors, recent high school graduates, college freshmen, college sophomores, college juniors, college seniors, recent college graduates, graduate students, career changers, individuals reentering the workforce. ▶ *3–5 counseling and advocacy interns:* responsibilities include assisting with volunteer schedule and other volunteer-related projects, attending training sessions for professionals on sexual abuse, and assisting the counseling and advocacy department by working on ongoing projects including updating the referral guide to the library; summer interns can be trained to work on 24-hour crisis hotline. Candidates should have office skills, oral communication skills, organizational skills, personal interest in the field, self-motivation, strong interpersonal skills. Duration is flexible (3 months minimum). Unpaid. Open to high school seniors, recent high school graduates, college freshmen, college sophomores, college juniors, college seniors, recent college graduates, career changers, individuals reentering the workforce. ▶ *2 development interns:* responsibilities include assisting with fund-raising projects, including direct mail, phone-a-thons, and special projects and events. Candidates should have ability to work independently, computer skills, office skills, organizational skills, self-motivation, strong interpersonal skills. Duration is flexible (3 months minimum). Unpaid. Open to high school seniors, recent high school graduates, college freshmen, college sophomores, college juniors, college seniors, recent college graduates, career changers, individuals reentering the workforce. International applications accepted.
Benefits Formal training, names of contacts, opportunity to attend seminars/workshops, travel reimbursement, willing to act as a professional reference, willing to complete paperwork for educational credit, willing to provide letters of recommendation.
Contact Write, call, fax, or e-mail Janice Harper, Administrative Assistant/Internship Coordinator. Phone: 202-232-0789 Ext. 221. Fax: 202-387-3812. E-mail: dcrcc@starpower.net. In-person interview recommended (telephone interview accepted). Applicants must submit a formal organization application, letter of interest, resume. Applications are accepted continuously. World Wide Web: http://www.dcrcc.org.

ECUMENICAL SOCIAL MINISTRIES
201 North Weber Street
Colorado Springs, Colorado 80903

General Information Nonprofit human services agency that provides basic emergency services, food, rental assistance, job

assistance, medicine, and clothing. Established in 1982. Number of employees: 12. Number of internship applications received each year: 20.
Internships Available ▶ *2 accounting interns:* responsibilities include running statistical reports, making out financial statements, working with loan program, and learning data entry, voucher systems, checkbook systems, and the process for acknowledging donations. Candidates should have ability to work independently, computer skills, editing skills, self-motivation, written communication skills. Duration is flexible. Unpaid. Open to high school seniors, college freshmen, college sophomores, college juniors, college seniors. ▶ *1–10 human resource interns:* responsibilities include assisting clients in seeking employment and career opportunities and helping individuals develop interviewing techniques and cover letters. Candidates should have ability to work independently, ability to work with others, knowledge of field, oral communication skills, self-motivation, written communication skills. Duration is flexible. Unpaid. Open to high school seniors, college freshmen, college sophomores, college juniors, college seniors, recent college graduates, graduate students, career changers, individuals reentering the workforce. ▶ *1–10 social work interns:* responsibilities include assisting low-income families in rent or utilities, and working in direct services to provide assistance in counseling, goal setting, and financial planning. Candidates should have ability to work independently, computer skills, personal interest in the field, plan to pursue career in field, self-motivation, strong interpersonal skills. Duration is flexible. Unpaid. Open to high school seniors, college freshmen, college sophomores, college juniors, college seniors, recent college graduates, graduate students, career changers, individuals reentering the workforce. International applications accepted.
Benefits On-the-job training, willing to act as a professional reference, willing to complete paperwork for educational credit, willing to provide letters of recommendation.
Contact Write, call, fax, or e-mail Marcia Hanscom, Volunteer Director. Phone: 719-228-6785. Fax: 719-636-3452. E-mail: esmmarcia@juno.com. In-person interview required. Applicants must submit a formal organization application, letter of interest, resume, two personal references. Applications are accepted continuously.

ELIZABETH STONE HOUSE
PO Box 59
Jamaica Plain, Massachusetts 02130

General Information Emergency shelter for battered women and their children; provides residential mental health alternative for women in emotional distress and their children and transitional housing and economic development programs. Established in 1974. Number of employees: 20. Number of internship applications received each year: 150.
Internships Available ▶ *1–5 administrative/direct service interns:* responsibilities include providing support to outreach coordinator, fund-raiser, administrative coordinator, and direct service staff. Candidates should have ability to work independently, ability to work with others, computer skills, office skills, oral communication skills, organizational skills, personal interest in the field, self-motivation, written communication skills. Duration is flexible. Unpaid. Open to recent high school graduates, college freshmen, college sophomores, college juniors, college seniors, recent college graduates, graduate students, law students, career changers, individuals reentering the workforce. ▶ *Child-care interns:* responsibilities include coordinating children's activities with child-care worker and supervisor. Candidates should have ability to work with others, experience in the field, oral communication skills, plan to pursue career in field, self-motivation. Duration is flexible. Unpaid. Open to college freshmen, college sophomores, college juniors, college seniors, recent college graduates, graduate students, law students, career changers, individuals reentering the workforce. ▶ *5–10 direct service co-advocates:* responsibilities include providing emotional support to women in the program and attending at least one weekly house meeting. Candidates should have ability to work independently, personal interest in the field, self-motivation, strong interpersonal skills, strong leadership ability. Duration is minimum of 6 months. Unpaid. Open to college freshmen, college sophomores, college juniors, college seniors, recent

college graduates, graduate students, law students, career changers, individuals reentering the workforce. ▶ *Donation interns:* responsibilities include creating holding spaces for donations, coordinating all receiving and distribution of donations to residents, and sending appropriate thank you notes. Candidates should have ability to work independently, oral communication skills, personal interest in the field, self-motivation, written communication skills. Duration is flexible. Unpaid. Open to college freshmen, college sophomores, college juniors, college seniors, recent college graduates, graduate students, law students, career changers, individuals reentering the workforce. International applications accepted.

Benefits On-the-job training, opportunity to attend seminars/workshops, willing to act as a professional reference, willing to complete paperwork for educational credit, willing to provide letters of recommendation.

Contact Write, call, or fax Rebecca Mattei, Direct Service Advocate/Volunteer/Intern Coordinator. Phone: 617-522-3659 Ext. 205. Fax: 617-522-0968. E-mail: stonehse@aol.com. In-person interview recommended (telephone interview accepted). Applicants must submit a formal organization application. Application deadline: May 30 for fall.

THE EMPOWER PROGRAM
1312 8th Street, NW
Washington, District of Columbia 20001

General Information Nonprofit educational organization that works with youth, ages 10-21, to prevent gender-based violence, such as sexual harassment, sexual assault, dating violence, and bullying. Established in 1992. Number of employees: 8. Number of internship applications received each year: 25.

Internships Available ▶ *1–2 program assistants/development assistants:* responsibilities include participation in various aspects of organization's program development, fund-raising and research, events planning, and editing publication. Candidates should have ability to work independently, computer skills, editing skills, office skills, oral communication skills, organizational skills, personal interest in the field, research skills, self-motivation, strong interpersonal skills, writing skills. Duration is flexible. Unpaid. Open to high school students, recent high school graduates, college freshmen, college sophomores, college juniors, college seniors, recent college graduates, graduate students, law students, career changers, individuals reentering the workforce. International applications accepted.

Benefits Names of contacts, on-the-job training, opportunity to attend seminars/workshops, possible full-time employment, willing to act as a professional reference, willing to complete paperwork for educational credit, willing to provide letters of recommendation.

Contact Write, call, fax, e-mail, or through World Wide Web site Sydney Campbell, Office Manager, 1312 8th Street, NW, Washington, District of Columbia 20001. Phone: 202-232-8200. Fax: 202-234-1901. E-mail: empower@empowered.org. In-person interview recommended (telephone interview accepted). Applicants must submit a letter of interest, resume, writing sample. Application deadline: March 31 for summer, August 1 for fall, November 30 for spring. World Wide Web: http://www.empowered.org.

FAIR ACRES FAMILY YMCA
2600 Grand Avenue
Carthage, Missouri 64836

General Information Nonprofit organization that promotes family harmony and health. Established in 1990. Number of employees: 55. Number of internship applications received each year: 3.

Internships Available ▶ *1–7 camp counselors:* responsibilities include organizing and supervising activities for a group of 15 school-age children. Candidates should have ability to work with others, knowledge of field, organizational skills, personal interest in the field. Duration is 13 weeks. $5.25–$5.50 per hour. Open to recent high school graduates, college freshmen, college sophomores, college juniors, college seniors. ▶ *1–5 fitness center attendants:* responsibilities include assisting fitness center users in the proper usage of fitness center machines and free weights. Candidates

should have ability to work independently, ability to work with others, oral communication skills, personal interest in the field, knowledge of fitness. Duration is 3–12 months. Position available as unpaid or at $5.30–$6.30 per hour. Open to recent high school graduates, college freshmen, college sophomores, college juniors, college seniors, individuals reentering the workforce. ▶ *1–5 youth coordinators:* responsibilities include creating and coordinating activities for pre-school through school-age youth. Candidates should have ability to work independently, ability to work with others, knowledge of field, oral communication skills, written communication skills. Duration is 3 months. Position available as unpaid or paid. Open to recent high school graduates, college freshmen, college sophomores, college juniors, college seniors, recent college graduates, career changers. International applications accepted.

Benefits Names of contacts, on-the-job training, opportunity to attend seminars/workshops, possible full-time employment, willing to act as a professional reference, willing to complete paperwork for educational credit, willing to provide letters of recommendation.

Contact Write, call, or fax Debby Orr, Business Services Director. Phone: 417-358-1070. Fax: 417-358-1102. In-person interview recommended (telephone interview accepted). Applicants must submit a formal organization application, three personal references, three letters of recommendation. Application deadline: May 15 for summer, August 1 for fall, December 1 for spring.

FAMILY SERVICE AGENCY OF SAN MATEO COUNTY
1870 El Camino Real
Burlingame, California 94010

General Information Agency that provides a full range of counseling including individual, couple, group, and family therapy. Established in 1950. Number of employees: 200. Number of internship applications received each year: 30.

Internships Available ▶ *8 interns:* responsibilities include performing individual, couple, family, and group counseling. Duration is 9 months (September-May). Unpaid. Open to graduate students. ▶ *Non-licensed counselors:* responsibilities include performing individual, couple, family, and group counseling. Duration is unlimited. Position available as unpaid or paid. Open to post-graduate students. Candidates for all positions should have ability to work independently, oral communication skills, self-motivation, strong interpersonal skills, written communication skills. International applications accepted.

Benefits Formal training, willing to complete paperwork for educational credit.

Contact Write, call, or fax Doris J. O'Neal, Managing Supervisor. Phone: 650-692-0555. Fax: 650-363-1401. In-person interview required. Applicants must submit a letter of interest, resume. Application deadline: August 31 for graduate students; continuous for post-graduate students.

FAMILY YMCA
465 West Sixth Avenue
Lancaster, Ohio 43130

General Information Nonprofit organization providing fitness, health, social, and recreational opportunities for children, adults, and families. Established in 1920. Number of employees: 62. Number of internship applications received each year: 1.

Internships Available ▶ *1–2 program interns:* responsibilities include assisting with programs in youth sports, recreation, and childcare. Candidates should have ability to work independently, ability to work with others, oral communication skills, personal interest in the field, self-motivation, strong leadership ability, written communication skills. Duration is flexible. Position available as unpaid or paid. Open to college freshmen, college sophomores, college juniors, college seniors, recent college graduates, graduate students, law students, career changers. International applications accepted.

Benefits Job counseling, names of contacts, on-the-job training, opportunity to attend seminars/workshops, willing to act as a

Family YMCA (continued)

professional reference, willing to complete paperwork for educational credit, willing to provide letters of recommendation, YMCA membership.
Contact Write, call, or fax Randall Au, Director of Youth and Family Services. Phone: 740-654-0616. Fax: 740-654-4206. In-person interview required. Applicants must submit a formal organization application, letter of interest, resume, high school diploma, academic transcripts, and 1-3 personal references for child care positions. Applications are accepted continuously.

FAMILY YMCA OF LOWER BUCKS COUNTY
601 South Oxford Valley Road
Fairless Hills, Pennsylvania 19030

General Information Association that serves the community by providing facilities to promote healthy bodies, minds, and spirits. Established in 1956. Number of employees: 276. Unit of YMCA of the USA, Chicago, Illinois. Number of internship applications received each year: 2.
Internships Available ▶ *Up to 5 aquatics instructors:* responsibilities include teaching aquatics, programming, and lifeguarding. Candidates should have WSI certification. Duration is flexible. Position available as unpaid or at $5.25–$10 per hour. Open to high school students, recent high school graduates, college freshmen, college sophomores, college juniors, college seniors, recent college graduates, graduate students, law students, career changers, individuals reentering the workforce. ▶ *Up to 10 child-care assistants:* responsibilities include assisting in the teaching of children and the administration of child-care programs. Candidates should have personal interest in the field, strong interpersonal skills, strong leadership ability, criminal background check/child abuse clearance required. Duration is flexible. Position available as unpaid or at $5.25–$10 per hour. Open to college freshmen, college sophomores, college juniors, college seniors, recent college graduates, graduate students, law students, career changers, individuals reentering the workforce, recent high school graduates over 18 years old. ▶ *2 communications/public relations interns:* responsibilities include fund-raising, planning events, and media relations (writing press releases, articles, and designing ads). Candidates should have ability to work independently, computer skills, oral communication skills, organizational skills, personal interest in the field, writing skills. Duration is flexible. Position available as unpaid or at $6–$10 per hour. Open to recent high school graduates, college freshmen, college sophomores, college juniors, college seniors, recent college graduates, career changers, individuals reentering the workforce. ▶ *Up to 10 fitness assistants:* responsibilities include assisting the senior physical education director and teaching classes in gymnastics, youth sports, and adult fitness. Candidates should have ability to work with others, knowledge of field, personal interest in the field, self-motivation. Duration is flexible. Position available as unpaid or at $6–$10 per hour. Open to high school students, recent high school graduates, college freshmen, college sophomores, college juniors, college seniors, recent college graduates, graduate students, law students, career changers, individuals reentering the workforce. ▶ *10 membership services:* responsibilities include computer data entry, answering phones, greeting members, and taking new members on tours. Candidates should have computer skills, oral communication skills, organizational skills, self-motivation, strong interpersonal skills. Duration is flexible. Position available as unpaid or at $6–$10 per hour. Open to high school students, recent high school graduates, college freshmen, college sophomores, college juniors, college seniors, recent college graduates, graduate students, law students, career changers, individuals reentering the workforce. ▶ *5 strength training instructors:* responsibilities include assisting with program orientations, assisting members with equipment, assisting physical director with other duties; personal training possibilities. Candidates should have knowledge of field, plan to pursue career in field, self-motivation, strong interpersonal skills, strong leadership ability, national certification preferred (ACE, AFAA, YMCA). Duration is flexible. Position available as unpaid or at $6–$10 per hour. Open to college freshmen, col-

lege sophomores, college juniors, college seniors, career changers, individuals reentering the workforce. International applications accepted.
Benefits Job counseling, names of contacts, on-the-job training, opportunity to attend seminars/workshops, possible full-time employment, travel reimbursement, willing to complete paperwork for educational credit, willing to provide letters of recommendation.
Contact Write, call, fax, or through World Wide Web site Kristina L. Zigenfus, Physical Director. Phone: 215-949-3400 Ext. 25. Fax: 215-946-9329. In-person interview recommended (telephone interview accepted). Applicants must submit a resume, three personal references. Applications are accepted continuously. World Wide Web: http://lowerbucksymca.org.

FEGS (FEDERATION EMPLOYMENT AND GUIDANCE SERVICE)
315 Hudson Street
New York, New York 10013

General Information One of the largest not-for-profit human services organizations in the country, providing vocational, educational, and rehabilitation services for clients with physical, psychiatric, and developmental disabilities; provides employment services, vocational rehabilitation, services for high school drop-out prevention, and services for new immigrants. Established in 1934. Number of employees: 2,700. Number of internship applications received each year: 350.
Internships Available ▶ *150–200 interns:* responsibilities include working on special projects as developed and arranged between the intern and the agency. Candidates should have knowledge of field, oral communication skills, organizational skills, personal interest in the field, plan to pursue career in field, strong interpersonal skills, written communication skills. Duration is flexible (preferably 2 semesters). Unpaid. Open to college freshmen, college sophomores, college juniors, college seniors, recent college graduates, graduate students, law students, career changers, individuals reentering the workforce. International applications accepted.
Benefits Formal training, job counseling, on-the-job training, opportunity to attend seminars/workshops, possible full-time employment, willing to act as a professional reference, willing to complete paperwork for educational credit, willing to provide letters of recommendation, extensive training program.
Contact Write, call, or e-mail Ms. Karen Zuckerman, Director of Student Internship Program, 315 Hudson Street, 9th Floor, New York, New York 10013. Phone: 212-366-8228. E-mail: kzuckerman@fegs.org. In-person interview required. Applicants must submit a formal organization application, letter of interest, resume, two letters of recommendation. Applications are accepted continuously. World Wide Web: http://www.fegs.org.

FLORENCE CRITTENTON CENTER
234 East Avenue 33
Los Angeles, California 90031-1937

General Information Residential treatment center for abused and neglected teenage girls and teen moms and group home for severely emotionally disturbed adolescents; provides residents with educational, vocational, parenting, and life skills. Established in 1892. Number of employees: 105. Number of internship applications received each year: 30.
Internships Available ▶ *5–10 cuddlers:* responsibilities include changing, feeding, playing, supervising, and other duties associated with caring for infants and toddlers in Child Development Center. Candidates should have personal interest in the field, strong interpersonal skills, some knowledge/experience with children preferred. Duration is 2 hours per week for about 3 months. Unpaid. Open to college freshmen, college sophomores, college juniors, college seniors, recent college graduates, graduate students, law students, career changers, individuals reentering the workforce, adults over 18 years of age. ▶ *20–25 mentors:* responsibilities include developing a long term one-on-one relationship with teenage girl who has suffered severe abuse or neglect; acting as a role model and mentor. Candidates should have self-motivation, strong interpersonal skills, strong leadership ability,

ability to handle disturbed behavior. Duration is 8 hours per month for six months to one year. Unpaid. Open to college freshmen, college sophomores, college juniors, college seniors, recent college graduates, graduate students, law students, career changers, individuals reentering the workforce, females over 18 years of age. ▶ *2–3 readers/storytellers:* responsibilities include reading to residents as well as their infants and toddlers one night a week. Candidates should have oral communication skills, personal interest in the field, self-motivation, strong interpersonal skills, ability to handle disturbed behavior. Duration is 1 hour per week for approximately 3 months. Unpaid. Open to college freshmen, college sophomores, college juniors, college seniors, recent college graduates, graduate students, law students, career changers, individuals reentering the workforce, adults over 18 years of age. ▶ *20–25 tutors:* responsibilities include working one-on-one with a resident, tutoring on various high school subjects which include math, literacy, English, history, etc. Candidates should have ability to work with others, oral communication skills, personal interest in the field, self-motivation, ability to handle disturbed behavior. Duration is 1 hour per week for approximately 3 months. Unpaid. Open to recent high school graduates, college freshmen, college sophomores, college juniors, college seniors, recent college graduates, graduate students, law students, career changers, individuals reentering the workforce, adults over 18 years of age. ▶ *4–5 workshop coordinators:* responsibilities include conducting workshops/activities with residents on cultural, artistic, athletic, vocational, or clinical topics, varying according to the interests of the volunteer. Candidates should have oral communication skills, strong interpersonal skills, strong leadership ability, knowledge of topic/activity. Duration is flexible. Unpaid. Open to college freshmen, college sophomores, college juniors, college seniors, recent college graduates, graduate students, law students, career changers, individuals reentering the workforce, adults over 18 years of age. International applications accepted.

Benefits Formal training, on-the-job training, possible full-time employment, willing to act as a professional reference, willing to complete paperwork for educational credit, willing to provide letters of recommendation, experience working with at-risk youth.

Contact Write, call, fax, or e-mail Bianca Perlman, Volunteer Services and Special Projects Coordinator, PO Box 31219, Los Angeles, California 90031-1937. Phone: 323-225-4211 Ext. 209. Fax: 323-225-1602. E-mail: bianca@florencecrittenton.com. In-person interview required. Applicants must submit a formal organization application, three personal references, TB test, criminal clearance check. Applications are accepted continuously. World Wide Web: http://www.florencecrittenton.com.

FOURTH WORLD MOVEMENT
7600 Willow Hill Drive
Landover, Maryland 20785

General Information International organization that develops partnerships between very poor families and other citizens through civic, educational, and cultural projects; projects maintained by culturally diverse corps of full-time, long-term volunteers. Established in 1957. Number of employees: 10. Unit of International Movement ATD Fourth World, Pierrelaye, France. Number of internship applications received each year: 100.

Internships Available ▶ *2–6 FWM volunteers:* responsibilities include working on projects emphasizing education, creative expression, and civic involvement undertaken in partnership with families in persistent poverty. Candidates should have ability to work independently, self-motivation, strong interpersonal skills, sense of commitment and community. Duration is 2–20 years. $3200–$6500 per year. Open to those who have completed 3-month FWM internship. ▶ *4–12 Fourth World interns:* responsibilities include living and working with the full-time volunteers at Washington-area center, with shorter stays at the New York center; participating in office and manual work and in programs with poor children and their families; learning the Movement's history and approach through videos, readings, and discussions; planning and evaluating meetings; writing regular reports about experiences. Candidates should have ability to work independently, ability to work with others, self-motivation, one year employment or college experience, patience, willingness to question one's

knowledge, sense of humor. Duration is 2-3 months (possible 2 year commitment). Unpaid. Open to U.S. citizens 19 years or older, high school graduates. International applications accepted.

Benefits Formal training, free housing, names of contacts, on-the-job training, opportunity to attend seminars/workshops, willing to act as a professional reference, willing to complete paperwork for educational credit, willing to provide letters of recommendation, possibility of long-term international commitment.

Contact Write, e-mail, or through World Wide Web site Denis Jay, Internship Coordinator. E-mail: fourthworld@erols.com. No phone calls. In-person interview recommended (telephone interview accepted). Applicants must submit a formal organization application, letter of interest, resume, three letters of recommendation, self-addressed stamped envelope (55 cents). Application deadline: May 15 for summer, August 15 for fall, December 15 for spring. Fees: $25. World Wide Web: http://www.atd-fourthworld.org.

FRESH YOUTH INITIATIVES
280 Ft. Washington Avenue #5
New York, New York 10032

General Information Youth service organization. Established in 1993. Number of employees: 8. Number of internship applications received each year: 25.

Internships Available ▶ *5 group leaders:* responsibilities include working directly with client population according to intern's talents, interests, and organizational needs. Candidates should have ability to work independently, analytical skills, computer skills, editing skills, office skills, oral communication skills, personal interest in the field, research skills, self-motivation, strong leadership ability, writing skills. Duration is flexible. Unpaid. Open to recent high school graduates, college freshmen, college sophomores, college juniors, college seniors, recent college graduates, graduate students, career changers, individuals reentering the workforce.

Benefits On-the-job training, opportunity to attend seminars/workshops, willing to act as a professional reference, willing to complete paperwork for educational credit, willing to provide letters of recommendation.

Contact Write, fax, or e-mail Rodney M. Fuller, Co-Director. Fax: 212-781-1151. E-mail: info@freshyouth.org. No phone calls. In-person interview recommended (telephone interview accepted). Applicants must submit a letter of interest, resume, personal reference. Applications are accepted continuously. World Wide Web: http://www.freshyouth.org.

GIRL SCOUTS OF PALM GLADES COUNCIL, INC.
2728 Lake Worth Road
Lake Worth, Florida 33461

General Information Organization that strives to instill leadership qualities in young women, to develop their self-esteem, to help them to reach their fullest potential, and to prepare them to be caring, confident, and resourceful citizens. Established in 1912. Number of employees: 25. Unit of Girl Scouts of the USA, New York, New York. Number of internship applications received each year: 5.

Internships Available ▶ *1 accounting assistant:* responsibilities include journal entries, accounts payable, cash receipts, and assistance with bank records. Candidates should have ability to work independently, analytical skills, office skills, research skills, strong interpersonal skills, knowledge of Word and Excel. Duration is flexible (20 hours per week). $8–$10 per hour. Open to college freshmen, college sophomores, college juniors, college seniors, recent college graduates, career changers, individuals reentering the workforce. ▶ *1 marketing/communications intern:* responsibilities include assisting director of communications with all aspects of public relations, publicity, and promotion media. Candidates should have ability to work independently, college courses in field, computer skills, editing skills, oral communication skills, organizational skills, strong interpersonal skills, writing skills. Duration is one semester minimum. Unpaid. Open to college sophomores, college juniors, college seniors. International applications accepted.

Benefits Job counseling, names of contacts, possible full-time employment, willing to complete paperwork for educational credit, willing to provide letters of recommendation.

Girl Scouts of Palm Glades Council, Inc. (continued)
Contact Write, fax, e-mail, or through World Wide Web site Lisa Johnson, Director, Marketing and Communications. Fax: 561-547-2169. E-mail: ljohnson@gspgc.org. In-person interview recommended (telephone interview accepted). Applicants must submit a letter of interest, resume, writing sample. Applications are accepted continuously. World Wide Web: http://gspgc.org.

GIRL SCOUTS OF RIVERLAND COUNCIL
2710 Quarry Road
LaCrosse, Wisconsin 54601

General Information Youth organization. Established in 1943. Number of employees: 15. Unit of Girl Scouts of the USA, New York, New York. Number of internship applications received each year: 3.
Internships Available ▶ *2–4 Girl Scout facilitators:* responsibilities include recruitment of Girl Scouts from target populations and providing programming for troops. Candidates should have ability to work independently, ability to work with others, oral communication skills, self-motivation, strong leadership ability, written communication skills. Duration is 12–26 weeks. Position available as unpaid or at $1500–$3000 per duration of internship. Open to recent high school graduates, college freshmen, college sophomores, college juniors, college seniors, recent college graduates, graduate students, career changers, individuals reentering the workforce. ▶ *1 MIS intern:* responsibilities include assisting in all MIS operations. Candidates should have ability to work independently, computer skills, oral communication skills, organizational skills, personal interest in the field, strong interpersonal skills. Duration is 2 semesters. $5–$6 per hour. ▶ *1–2 program directors:* responsibilities include organization of on-site camp and tripping program for resident campers. Candidates should have ability to work independently, ability to work with others, oral communication skills, strong leadership ability, written communication skills. Duration is 10–13 weeks. $1500–$2000 per duration of internship. Open to college freshmen, college sophomores, college juniors, college seniors, recent college graduates. ▶ *1–3 program specialists:* responsibilities include planning and implementation of Girl Scouting program activities such as badge workshops, Gold and Silver Award Banquet, resident and day camping opportunities. Candidates should have ability to work independently, organizational skills, personal interest in the field, self-motivation, written communication skills. Duration is 12–16 weeks. Position available as unpaid or at $1500–$3000 per semester. Open to college freshmen, college sophomores, college juniors, college seniors, recent college graduates, graduate students, career changers, individuals reentering the workforce. ▶ *1 training assistant:* responsibilities include conducting adult education trainings in the volunteer management system. Candidates should have ability to work independently, computer skills, oral communication skills, organizational skills, self-motivation, strong interpersonal skills, strong leadership ability, written communication skills. Duration is 1–2 semesters. Position available as unpaid or paid. Open to college juniors, recent college graduates. International applications accepted.
Benefits Job counseling, names of contacts, on-the-job training, opportunity to attend seminars/workshops, possible full-time employment, travel reimbursement, willing to act as a professional reference, willing to complete paperwork for educational credit, willing to provide letters of recommendation.
Contact Write, call, or e-mail Sarah Resch, Assistant Executive Director-Program. Phone: 608-784-3693. Fax: 608-784-3613. E-mail: campehawee@yahoo.com. In-person interview recommended (telephone interview accepted). Applicants must submit a letter of interest, resume, personal reference. Applications are accepted continuously. World Wide Web: http://www.gsriverland.com.

GIRL SCOUTS OF SOUTHWESTERN NEW YORK
2661 Horton Road
Jamestown, New York 14701

General Information Organization that provides girls with contemporary developmental experiences to inspire the highest ideals of character and conduct and fosters development

into happy, resourceful, and contributing adult women. Established in 1930. Number of employees: 13. Unit of Girl Scouts of the USA, New York, New York. Number of internship applications received each year: 1.
Internships Available ▶ *1–3 outreach managers:* responsibilities include assisting with the delivery of community outreach programs for girls in underserved areas. Candidates should have oral communication skills, organizational skills, personal interest in the field, self-motivation, strong interpersonal skills, strong leadership ability, writing skills. Unpaid. Open to college freshmen, college sophomores, college juniors, college seniors, recent college graduates, graduate students, law students, career changers, individuals reentering the workforce. ▶ *1–2 program assistants:* responsibilities include assisting with the design and delivery of programs for girls ages 5-17. Candidates should have ability to work with others, oral communication skills, organizational skills, strong leadership ability. Duration is flexible. Unpaid. Open to high school students. ▶ *Summer resident camp interns:* responsibilities include administrative duties, camp direction, unit leading, and a variety of other duties. Candidates should have oral communication skills, organizational skills, personal interest in the field, self-motivation, strong interpersonal skills, strong leadership ability. $6–$9 per hour. Open to high school seniors, recent high school graduates, college freshmen, college sophomores, college juniors, college seniors, recent college graduates, graduate students, law students, career changers. ▶ *1–3 training assistants:* responsibilities include designing and delivering volunteer training to groups of 10-45 adults. Candidates should have oral communication skills, organizational skills, research skills, self-motivation, strong interpersonal skills, strong leadership ability. Unpaid. Open to recent high school graduates, college freshmen, college sophomores, college juniors, college seniors, recent college graduates, graduate students, law students, career changers, individuals reentering the workforce. International applications accepted.
Benefits Names of contacts, opportunity to attend seminars/workshops, possible full-time employment, travel reimbursement, willing to complete paperwork for educational credit, willing to provide letters of recommendation.
Contact Write, call, fax, or e-mail Lisa Lane-Gniewecki, Executive Director. Phone: 716-665-2225. Fax: 716-661-9704. E-mail: gsswny@yahoo.com. In-person interview recommended (telephone interview accepted). Applicants must submit a resume. Applications are accepted continuously.

GIRLS INCORPORATED OF GREATER LOWELL
220 Worthen Street
Lowell, Massachusetts 01852

General Information Nonprofit organization that provides after-school programs for girls ages 6–18 in the greater Lowell area. Established in 1945. Number of employees: 11. Affiliate of Girls Incorporated, New York, New York. Number of internship applications received each year: 2.
Internships Available ▶ *1–2 program counselors:* responsibilities include developing and implementing educational, cultural, and recreational programs for girls at least 6 years old. Candidates should have ability to work independently, personal interest in the field, self-motivation, strong interpersonal skills. Duration is 3–12 months. Position available as unpaid or at $8 per hour. Open to high school seniors, recent high school graduates, college freshmen, college sophomores, college juniors, college seniors, recent college graduates, graduate students, career changers, individuals reentering the workforce, must be 18 or older. International applications accepted.
Benefits Formal training, names of contacts, on-the-job training, opportunity to attend seminars/workshops, willing to act as a professional reference, willing to complete paperwork for educational credit, willing to provide letters of recommendation.
Contact Write, call, fax, or e-mail Carol S. Duncan, Executive Director. Phone: 978-458-6529. Fax: 978-458-4837. E-mail: ggrlowell@aol.com. In-person interview required. Applicants must submit a letter of interest, resume. Applications are accepted continuously.

GIRLS INCORPORATED OF METROPOLITAN DALLAS
2040 Empire Central Drive
Dallas, Texas 75235

General Information Nonprofit agency that strives to assist economically disadvantaged girls ages 6-18. Established in 1968. Number of employees: 60. Affiliate of Girls Incorporated, New York, New York. Number of internship applications received each year: 8.

Internships Available ▶ *1 program assistant:* responsibilities include coordinating programs or Board committees and assisting with executive and management duties. Duration is flexible. Unpaid. Open to college freshmen, college sophomores, college juniors, college seniors, recent college graduates, graduate students, career changers, individuals reentering the workforce. ▶ *1 public relations assistant:* responsibilities include contacting media, writing press releases, maintaining media list, and assisting with special events. Candidates should have computer skills, oral communication skills, organizational skills, strong interpersonal skills, written communication skills. Duration is flexible. Unpaid. Open to college freshmen, college sophomores, college juniors, college seniors, recent college graduates, graduate students, career changers, individuals reentering the workforce. ▶ *1 special events assistant:* responsibilities include working on major fund-raising event and working with volunteers, corporate sponsors, and graphic artists/ printers. Candidates should have computer skills, oral communication skills, organizational skills, strong interpersonal skills, writing skills. Duration is flexible. Unpaid. Open to college freshmen, college sophomores, college juniors, college seniors, recent college graduates, graduate students, career changers, individuals reentering the workforce. ▶ *1 volunteer specialist:* responsibilities include interacting with volunteers on all levels, assisting with special events, using computer skills, attending volunteer fairs, mailing information to prospective volunteers. Candidates should have ability to work independently, ability to work with others, computer skills, office skills, oral communication skills, organizational skills, self-motivation, written communication skills. Duration is flexible. Position available as unpaid or paid. Open to college freshmen, college sophomores, college juniors, college seniors, recent college graduates, career changers, individuals reentering the workforce.

Benefits Names of contacts, opportunity to attend seminars/ workshops, possible full-time employment, travel reimbursement, willing to provide letters of recommendation.

Contact Write, call, fax, or e-mail Lynette Smith, Director of Community Relations. Phone: 214-654-4530. Fax: 214-350-8115. E-mail: lnsmith71@yahoo.com. In-person interview required. Applicants must submit a formal organization application, letter of interest, resume, three personal references, letter of recommendation (optional). Application deadline: May 1 for summer, July 1 for fall, December 1 for spring.

GIRLS INCORPORATED OF ST. LOUIS
4746 Carter Avenue
St. Louis, Missouri 63115

General Information Service organization providing after school and summer programs for girls ages 4–18 years; provides innovative programs to help young women become independent power leaders of the future. Established in 1865. Number of employees: 50. Affiliate of Girls Incorporated, New York, New York. Number of internship applications received each year: 2.

Internships Available ▶ *1–10 Center instructors:* responsibilities include providing workshops for after school and summer participants in the areas of dance, science, art, music, sports, sewing, culinary arts, health, drama, computers, fitness and entrepreneurship; must be proficient in at least two areas. Candidates should have ability to work independently, analytical skills, computer skills, oral communication skills, organizational skills, personal interest in the field, self-motivation, strong interpersonal skills, strong leadership ability, written communication skills. Duration is 10-week summer program (40 hours per week) or one year (September to September). Position available as unpaid or at $7–$10 per hour. Open to college freshmen, college sophomores, college juniors,

college seniors, recent college graduates, graduate students, law students, career changers, individuals reentering the workforce. ▶ *1–3 outreach instructors:* responsibilities include providing workshops for children on various topics relating to drug abuse, pregnancy prevention, and safety session preventing physical abuse. Candidates should have ability to work independently, analytical skills, computer skills, knowledge of field, oral communication skills, organizational skills, personal interest in the field, research skills, self-motivation, strong interpersonal skills, strong leadership ability, written communication skills. Duration is one year (September to September). Position available as unpaid or at $8–$10 per hour. Open to college sophomores, college juniors, college seniors, recent college graduates, graduate students, law students, career changers, individuals reentering the workforce.

Benefits On-the-job training, possible full-time employment, willing to act as a professional reference, willing to provide letters of recommendation.

Contact Write, call, or fax Andriette J. Fields, Program Director. Phone: 314-385-8088. Fax: 314-385-6540. In-person interview recommended (telephone interview accepted). Applicants must submit a letter of interest, resume, personal reference.

GLADNEY CENTER FOR ADOPTION
6300 John Ryan Drive
Fort Worth, Texas 76132-4122

General Information Adoption agency and maternity home. Established in 1887. Number of employees: 65. Number of internship applications received each year: 20.

Internships Available ▶ *1 admissions intern:* responsibilities include answering inquiry calls and making professional assessment of client's needs; direct contact with young women, mostly over the phone, interested in pursuing an adoption plan for their unborn child; admitting birth mothers to the program that is most appropriate for their needs. Candidates should have office skills, oral communication skills, organizational skills, personal interest in the field, strong interpersonal skills. Duration is 1–2 semesters. Unpaid. Open to college juniors, college seniors, graduate students. ▶ *2–4 birth parent services interns:* responsibilities include answering inquiry calls and making professional assessment of client's needs; direct contact with young women and their families planning adoption for their unborn child; attending weekly case management meetings. Candidates should have office skills, oral communication skills, organizational skills, personal interest in the field, strong interpersonal skills. Duration is 1–2 semesters. Unpaid. Open to graduate students. ▶ *1–2 domestic adoption interns:* responsibilities include phone contact and counseling with adoptive families; assisting caseworker with maintaining files to adhere to licensing standards; making home visits to clients in the Metroplex; attending weekly case management meetings. Duration is 1–2 semesters. Unpaid. Open to graduate students. ▶ *1 international program intern:* responsibilities include observing and assisting with international adoption casework including conducting orientations and post-placement supervision; assisting with maintenance of international child registry database, adoptive family pre-adoption education program, international post-placement process and adoptive parent survey process. Candidates should have ability to work with others, office skills, oral communication skills, organizational skills, personal interest in the field. Duration is 1–2 semesters. Unpaid. Open to college freshmen, college sophomores, college juniors, college seniors. ▶ *1 post-adoption intern:* responsibilities include answering post-adoption line and being available to answer post-adoption related questions of birth mothers, adult adoptees, and adoptive parents; co-facilitating a monthly birth parent support group, answering letters from birth parents; coordinating on-going non-identifying communication between adoptive parents and birth parents. Candidates should have oral communication skills, organizational skills, personal interest in the field, strong interpersonal skills, written communication skills. Duration is 1–2 semesters. Unpaid. Open to college sophomores, college juniors, college seniors, graduate students. ▶ *1 transitional care program intern:* responsibilities include assisting transitional care coordinator with recruiting new transitional care families; assuring all current families meet licensing standards; placing children with families; obtaining medical records for

Gladney Center for Adoption (continued)

children; obtaining necessary supplies for families, arranging placement of children with adoptive families. Candidates should have ability to work with others, office skills, oral communication skills, organizational skills, personal interest in the field. Duration is 1–2 semesters. Unpaid. Open to college freshmen, college sophomores, college juniors, college seniors.

Benefits Formal training, on-the-job training, willing to complete paperwork for educational credit, first aid and CPR training provided for some internships.

Contact Write, call, fax, e-mail, or through World Wide Web site Hannah Powell, Human Resources Assistant. Phone: 817-922-6000. Fax: 817-922-5955. E-mail: jobline@gladney.org. In-person interview required. Applicants must submit a formal organization application, resume, personal reference, negative TB-PPD test, rubella screen, drug screen, background check, first aid and CPR training required for some internships. Applications are accepted continuously. World Wide Web: http://www.gladney.org.

GLOBAL CHILDREN'S ORGANIZATION
10524 West Pico Boulevard, Suite 216
Los Angeles, California 90064

General Information Nonprofit organization whose mission is to "restore children to childhood" through providing summer camp program that serve children traumatized by intolerance and violence in Croatia and Los Angeles. Established in 1992. Number of employees: 2. Number of internship applications received each year: 40.

Internships Available ▶ *4–6 interns:* responsibilities include assisting GCO staff in administrative duties regarding camp programs in Croatia and Los Angeles; general clerical duties, Internet research, and drafting correspondence. Candidates should have ability to work independently, computer skills, editing skills, office skills, oral communication skills, personal interest in the field, research skills, self-motivation, written communication skills. Duration is 1–2 semesters. Unpaid. Open to high school students, recent high school graduates, college freshmen, college sophomores, college juniors, college seniors, recent college graduates, graduate students, law students, career changers, individuals reentering the workforce. ▶ *1–2 nonprofit intern for public relations: Web site:* responsibilities include working on press releases, newsletters, promotional materials, managing Web sites. Candidates should have editing skills, oral communication skills, organizational skills, self-motivation, writing skills. Duration is 1–2 semesters. Unpaid. Open to college freshmen, college sophomores, college juniors, college seniors, recent college graduates, graduate students, career changers. ▶ *1–3 nonprofit interns for administration and planning:* responsibilities include working with director or board creating programs, working on administration, funding, proposals, creating curriculum. Candidates should have ability to work independently, ability to work with others, computer skills, editing skills, research skills, self-motivation, writing skills. Duration is 1–2 semesters. Unpaid. Open to high school students, recent high school graduates, college freshmen, college sophomores, college juniors, college seniors, recent college graduates, graduate students, law students. International applications accepted.

Benefits On-the-job training, willing to act as a professional reference, willing to complete paperwork for educational credit, willing to provide letters of recommendation.

International Internships Available in Korcula Island, Croatia.

Contact Write, call, fax, or e-mail Judith Jenya, Executive Director. Phone: 310-842-9235. Fax: 310-842-9236. E-mail: gw@globalchild.org. In-person interview recommended (telephone interview accepted). Applicants must submit a letter of interest, resume, writing sample, personal reference, two letters of recommendation. Application deadline: April 1 for summer, August 1 for fall, November 1 for spring. World Wide Web: http://www.globalchild.org.

GOLDEN CRADLE ADOPTION SERVICES
1050 Kings Highway North, Suite 201
Cherry Hill, New Jersey 08034

General Information Private, nonprofit, New Jersey licensed agency that provides adoption and maternity services to men and women faced with an unplanned pregnancy and to people seeking to build families through adoption. Established in 1980. Number of employees: 12. Number of internship applications received each year: 5.

Internships Available ▶ *1 public relations/marketing intern:* responsibilities include reviewing and revising all marketing materials and developing short-term and long-range marketing plans for the organization. Candidates should have college courses in field, computer skills, plan to pursue career in field, self-motivation, writing skills. Duration is flexible. Unpaid. Open to college juniors, college seniors, recent college graduates, graduate students, career changers. ▶ *1–2 research analysts:* responsibilities include gathering and analyzing data to review services and provide improvements for clients. Candidates should have college courses in field, computer skills, research skills, self-motivation, written communication skills. Duration is flexible. Unpaid. Open to college juniors, college seniors, recent college graduates, graduate students, career changers. ▶ *1–3 social work interns:* responsibilities include handling client caseload by following a birth parent or adoptive parent through the adoption process, following New Jersey regulations regarding adoption. Candidates should have computer skills, declared college major in field, plan to pursue career in field, strong interpersonal skills, writing skills. Duration is flexible. Unpaid. International applications accepted.

Benefits Formal training, names of contacts, on-the-job training, possible full-time employment, travel reimbursement, willing to complete paperwork for educational credit, willing to provide letters of recommendation.

Contact Write, call, fax, e-mail, or through World Wide Web site Jared N. Rolsky, Executive Director. Phone: 856-667-2229. Fax: 856-667-5437. E-mail: info@goldencradle.org. In-person interview required. Applications are accepted continuously. World Wide Web: http://www.goldencradle.org.

GRASSROOTS INTERNATIONAL
179 Boylston Street, 4th Floor
Boston, Massachusetts 02130

General Information Organization that provides cash grants and material aid to community organizations for social change in Haiti, Mexico, Eritrea, Brazil, the West Bank, and Gaza strip. Established in 1983. Number of employees: 9. Number of internship applications received each year: 50.

Internships Available ▶ *1 Brazil program intern:* responsibilities include performing research related to Latin America and the Caribbean. Candidates should have ability to work independently, computer skills, oral communication skills, organizational skills, research skills, writing skills. Duration is 1 semester. Unpaid. ▶ *1 The Middle East and Horn of Africa intern.* Candidates should have ability to work independently, computer skills, oral communication skills, organizational skills, research skills, writing skills. Duration is 1 semester. Unpaid. ▶ *1 communications/media program assistant:* responsibilities include monitoring the international electronic and print media. Candidates should have ability to work independently, analytical skills, computer skills, oral communication skills, organizational skills, research skills, writing skills. Duration is 1 semester. Unpaid. ▶ *1 gender intern.* Candidates should have ability to work independently, computer skills, oral communication skills, organizational skills, research skills, writing skills. Duration is 1 semester. Unpaid. Open to college freshmen, college sophomores, college juniors, college seniors, recent college graduates, graduate students, career changers. International applications accepted.

Benefits Formal training, names of contacts, opportunity to attend seminars/workshops, willing to complete paperwork for educational credit, willing to provide letters of recommendation.

Contact Write, fax, e-mail, or through World Wide Web site Jen Lemire, Internship Coordinator. Fax: 617-524-5525. E-mail: jobs@grassrootsonline.org. In-person interview recommended (telephone interview accepted). Applicants must submit a letter of interest, resume. Applications are accepted continuously. World Wide Web: http://www.grassrootsonline.org.

GREEN CHIMNEYS CHILDREN'S SERVICES, INC.
Caller Box 719, Doansburg Road
Brewster, New York 10509

General Information　Voluntary, nonsectarian multiservice agency and residential treatment center dedicated to basic education for children and daily living skills programs for adults. Established in 1947. Number of employees: 350. Number of internship applications received each year: 30.
Internships Available　▶ *1–6 education interns:* responsibilities include teaching assistant duties in special education classroom setting. Candidates should have ability to work independently, knowledge of field, oral communication skills, personal interest in the field, strong interpersonal skills, written communication skills. Duration is 3–5 months. Position available as unpaid or paid. ▶ *1–6 farm interns:* responsibilities include assisting with farm science, riding, and greenhouse programs; assisting the professional staff with teaching the students while participating in daily chores, daily living skills programs, public programming events, academic studies, horticultural projects, athletics and recreational activities, and other outdoor activities. Candidates should have ability to work independently, experience in the field, oral communication skills, personal interest in the field, strong interpersonal skills, written communication skills. Duration is 3 months minimum; June 1-August 31 for summer, September 1-December 30 for fall, January 3-May 31 for winter/spring. Position available as unpaid or paid. Open to college juniors, college seniors, recent college graduates, graduate students. International applications accepted.
Benefits　Free housing, free meals, opportunity to attend seminars/workshops, possible full-time employment, willing to complete paperwork for educational credit, willing to provide letters of recommendation.
Contact　Write, call, fax, or e-mail Ms. Jackie Ryan, Intern Coordinator. Phone: 845-279-2995 Ext. 158. Fax: 845-279-2714. E-mail: jryan@greenchimneys.org. In-person interview recommended (telephone interview accepted). Applicants must submit a formal organization application, resume, three personal references. Applications are accepted continuously. World Wide Web: http://www.greenchimneys.org.

HABITAT FOR HUMANITY INTERNATIONAL
322 West Lamar Street
Americus, Georgia 31709

General Information　Nonprofit, Christian housing ministry dedicated to the elimination of poverty housing worldwide. Established in 1976. Number of employees: 600. Number of internship applications received each year: 150.
Internships Available　▶ *1 international training intern:* responsibilities include supporting and promoting quality international training and education and designing and presenting training materials. Candidates should have oral communication skills, strong interpersonal skills, writing skills, experience in adult education. Duration is 3–12 months. $450 per month. ▶ *2 summer youth blitz interns:* responsibilities include logistics coordination, media communication, preparing morning reflections, communication with participants, program advisers, and community-team building, discussion facilitation and liaison between all parties. Candidates should have oral communication skills, strong interpersonal skills, strong leadership ability, written communication skills, experience working with youth ages 16-18; travel involved. Duration is May to August. Food stipend of $56 per week. International applications accepted.
Benefits　Free housing, health insurance, possible full-time employment, travel reimbursement, willing to act as a professional reference, willing to provide letters of recommendation.
Contact　Write, call, fax, e-mail, or through World Wide Web site Volunteer Services. Phone: 229-924-6935 Ext. 2377. Fax: 229-924-0641. E-mail: vsd@habitat.org. Applicants must submit a formal organization application, resume, portfolio, writing sample, two personal references. Applications are accepted continuously. World Wide Web: http://habitat.org.

HABITAT FOR HUMANITY LAKE COUNTY, IL
315 North Martin Luther King Jr. Avenue
Waukegan, Illinois 60085

General Information　Nonprofit homebuilder and social service provider. Established in 1989. Number of employees: 7. Affiliate of Habitat for Humanity International, Americus, Georgia.
Internships Available　▶ *1–2 construction manager interns:* responsibilities include assisting construction manager with building homes from permitting through final punch list while working with volunteers; both on-site and office responsibilities; many opportunities to network. Candidates should have ability to work independently, experience in the field, oral communication skills, strong interpersonal skills. Duration is 6 months–1 year. Unpaid. Open to recent college graduates, graduate students, career changers, individuals reentering the workforce. ▶ *Family services interns:* responsibilities include coordinating activities to assist in Family Services Department; includes presenting information at meetings; interpreting documents; coordinating information; writing letters; and meeting with clients. Candidates should have ability to work independently, computer skills, declared college major in field, strong interpersonal skills, written communication skills. Duration is 6 months-1 year. Unpaid. Open to college seniors, recent college graduates, graduate students, career changers. ▶ *1 legal assistant intern:* responsibilities include assisting in real estate closings, corporate law issues, risk management issues, and family law. Candidates should have ability to work independently, college courses in field, experience in the field, self-motivation, written communication skills. Duration is 6 months-1 year. Unpaid. Open to recent college graduates, graduate students, law students, career changers, individuals reentering the workforce. ▶ *1 public relations intern:* responsibilities include assisting resource development director in promoting organization through media, events, and written publications; many opportunities to network with others in field; many "hands-on" and creative opportunities. Candidates should have ability to work independently, computer skills, editing skills, experience in the field, oral communication skills, written communication skills. Duration is 6 months–1 year. Unpaid. Open to college seniors, recent college graduates, graduate students, career changers, individuals reentering the workforce. ▶ *Resource development interns:* responsibilities include researching and writing grants; coordinating and overseeing data entry, mailings; writing manuals for groups working on house with Habitat. Candidates should have computer skills, organizational skills, research skills, strong interpersonal skills, writing skills. Duration is 6 months–1 year. Unpaid. Open to recent college graduates, graduate students, career changers, individuals reentering the workforce. International applications accepted.
Benefits　Formal training, names of contacts, on-the-job training, opportunity to attend seminars/workshops, possible full-time employment, willing to act as a professional reference, willing to complete paperwork for educational credit, willing to provide letters of recommendation, free meals (limited).
Contact　Write, call, fax, e-mail, or through World Wide Web site Julie Donovan, Executive Director, 315 Martin Luther King Jr. Avenue, Waukegan 60085. Phone: 847-623-1020. Fax: 847-623-1038. E-mail: jdonovan@hfh.cncdsl.com. Telephone interview required. Applicants must submit a letter of interest, resume, academic transcripts, writing sample, personal reference. Applications are accepted continuously. World Wide Web: http://www.habitatlc.org.

HARBEL PREVENTION AND RECOVERY CENTER
5807 Harford Road
Baltimore, Maryland 21214

General Information　State-certified substance abuse and treatment program that provides early intervention/prevention services through individual, family, and group counseling, school outreach, and tutoring. Established in 1970. Number of employees: 40. Unit of HARBEL Community Organization, Baltimore, Maryland. Number of internship applications received each year: 15.
Internships Available　▶ *2–3 addiction counselor interns:* responsibilities include providing individual and group counseling in outpatient substance abuse program that serves adults and

HARBEL Prevention and Recovery Center (continued)

adolescents. Candidates should have college courses in field, knowledge of field, plan to pursue career in field, strong interpersonal skills, written communication skills. Duration is 2 semester (required). Unpaid. Open to graduate students. ▶ *Tutors:* responsibilities include providing one-on-one tutoring services to high risk middle/senior high students. Candidates should have ability to work independently, ability to work with others, oral communication skills, personal interest in the field, self-motivation, ability to act as a positive drug-free role model. Duration is flexible; normally minimum of 1 semester. Unpaid. Open to high school students, recent high school graduates, college sophomores, college juniors, college seniors, recent college graduates, graduate students, law students, career changers, individuals reentering the workforce. International applications accepted.

Benefits Names of contacts, opportunity to attend seminars/workshops, willing to act as a professional reference, willing to complete paperwork for educational credit, willing to provide letters of recommendation.

Contact Call Patricia Stabile, Director. Phone: 410-444-2100. Fax: 410-426-1140. E-mail: harbelprc@yahoo.com. In-person interview required. Applicants must submit a formal organization application, letter of interest, resume, tutoring program requires 3 references and in-person interview only. Applications are accepted continuously. World Wide Web: http://phoenix.gouher.edu/~harbellhprc.htm.

HARBOR, INC.
PO Box 1903
Smithfield, North Carolina 27577

General Information Domestic violence/sexual assault/displaced homemaker agency. Established in 1984. Number of employees: 11. Number of internship applications received each year: 5.

Internships Available ▶ *1 crisis counselor.* Candidates should have ability to work independently, analytical skills, college courses in field, computer skills, knowledge of field, organizational skills, research skills, self-motivation, strong interpersonal skills, writing skills, must have car for use at agency. Duration is flexible. Position available as unpaid or paid. Open to college seniors, recent college graduates, graduate students. International applications accepted.

Benefits Names of contacts, on-the-job training, possible full-time employment, travel reimbursement, willing to act as a professional reference, willing to complete paperwork for educational credit, willing to provide letters of recommendation.

Contact Write or e-mail Keri Christensen, Executive Director. Fax: 919-938-4515. E-mail: harborinc2002@aol.com. No phone calls. In-person interview recommended (telephone interview accepted). Applicants must submit a formal organization application, letter of interest, resume, three personal references, car for use at the agency.

HARDEE COUNTY FAMILY YMCA
610 West Orange Street
Wauchula, Florida 33873

General Information Organization that offers programs to help strengthen local families. Number of employees: 25. Unit of Sarasota Family YMCA, Inc., Sarasota, Florida. Number of internship applications received each year: 2.

Internships Available ▶ *8 child-care workers:* responsibilities include supervising children ages 5-12. Duration is 3 months in summer or one semester. Unpaid. Open to high school seniors, recent high school graduates, college freshmen, college sophomores, college juniors, college seniors, recent college graduates, graduate students, law students, career changers, individuals reentering the workforce. ▶ *1 office/administration intern:* responsibilities include working on computer, organization/filing, and front desk. Candidates should have computer skills, office skills, oral communication skills, organizational skills, strong interpersonal skills. Duration is one summer or semester. Unpaid. Open to high school seniors, recent high school graduates, college freshmen, college sophomores, college juniors, college seniors, recent college graduates, graduate students, career changers, individuals

reentering the workforce. ▶ *2 sports/fitness interns:* responsibilities include assisting in youth sports and fitness programs including coordinating programs, maintaining equipment, overseeing fitness floor, and possibly teaching classes. Candidates should have knowledge of field, personal interest in the field, self-motivation, strong interpersonal skills, strong leadership ability, basic computer skills. Duration is one summer or semester. Unpaid. Open to high school seniors, recent high school graduates, college freshmen, college sophomores, college juniors, college seniors, recent college graduates, graduate students, career changers, individuals reentering the workforce. International applications accepted.

Benefits Names of contacts, willing to complete paperwork for educational credit, willing to provide letters of recommendation, free membership in YMCA.

Contact Write or call Executive Director. Phone: 863-773-6445. In-person interview required. Applicants must submit a formal organization application, resume, two personal references, 2 professional references; criminal background check required. Applications are accepted continuously.

HARTFORD FOOD SYSTEM
509 Wethersfield Avenue
Hartford, Connecticut 06114

General Information Community food-advocacy organization that develops and operates food programs designed to assist lower-income families; includes policy, farming, and nutrition. Established in 1978. Number of employees: 7. Number of internship applications received each year: 40.

Internships Available ▶ *1–2 food policy research assistants:* responsibilities include investigating policies and issues related to food, agriculture, or nutrition. Candidates should have computer skills, oral communication skills, personal interest in the field, research skills, self-motivation, writing skills. Duration is 6–12 months. $200–$250 per week. Open to college seniors, recent college graduates, graduate students, law students, career changers. ▶ *4–8 organic farm interns:* responsibilities include general farm duties on a 16-acre community-supported agriculture farm that grows organic produce for and with lower-income urban families. Candidates should have ability to work independently, ability to work with others, oral communication skills, personal interest in the field, self-motivation, ability to perform hard physical labor. Duration is 2–8 months. $150–$200 per week. Open to college freshmen, college sophomores, college juniors, college seniors, recent college graduates, graduate students, career changers. International applications accepted.

Benefits Health insurance, names of contacts, opportunity to attend seminars/workshops, possible full-time employment, travel reimbursement, willing to act as a professional reference, willing to complete paperwork for educational credit, willing to provide letters of recommendation, stipend, possibility of housing.

Contact Write, call, or e-mail Mr. Mark Winne, Executive Director. Phone: 860-296-9325. E-mail: info@hartfordfood.org. In-person interview recommended (telephone interview accepted). Applicants must submit a letter of interest, resume, writing sample, 2-3 personal references. Application deadline: February 1 for farm positions, August 1 for policy positions (fall), December 1 for policy positions (winter/spring). World Wide Web: http://www.hartfordfood.org.

HELP LINE TELEPHONE SERVICES, INC.
3 West 29th Street, 10th Floor
New York, New York 10001

General Information Telephone crisis hot line. Established in 1970. Number of employees: 5. Number of internship applications received each year: 5.

Internships Available ▶ *1–2 database assistants:* responsibilities include assisting in setting up and maintaining databases. Candidates should have ability to work with others, analytical skills, computer skills, experience in the field, oral communication skills, research skills. Duration is flexible. Position available as unpaid or at $10–$12 per hour. Open to college juniors, college seniors, recent college graduates, graduate students, career changers, individuals reentering the workforce. ▶ *1–2 research assistants for fundraising:* responsibilities include assisting the executive director with research necessary to seek funding and writing grants. Candidates should have analytical skills, computer skills, oral communication skills, personal interest in the field, self-motivation, written communication skills. Duration is flexible. Position available as unpaid or at $12 per hour. Open to college juniors, college seniors, graduate students, law students. ▶ *1 visual aides assistant:* responsibilities include assisting in setting up library of videos and tapes, including reviewing, editing, and cataloging. Candidates should have ability to work independently, editing skills, oral communication skills, organizational skills, research skills, self-motivation. Duration is 3–6 months. Unpaid. Open to college sophomores, college juniors, college seniors, recent college graduates, graduate students, career changers, individuals who are knowledgeable based on life experience. International applications accepted.

Benefits Names of contacts, on-the-job training, opportunity to attend seminars/workshops, travel reimbursement, willing to act as a professional reference, willing to complete paperwork for educational credit, willing to provide letters of recommendation, opportunity to work independently with excellent supervision.

Contact Write, call, fax, or e-mail Ina Labiner, Executive Director. Phone: 212-684-4480 Ext. 208. Fax: 212-684-4483. E-mail: info@helpline.org. In-person interview recommended (telephone interview accepted). Applicants must submit a resume, two writing samples. Applications are accepted continuously. World Wide Web: http://www.helpline.org.

HEMLOCK GIRL SCOUT COUNCIL
350 Hale Avenue
Harrisburg, Pennsylvania 17105

General Information Youth services organization that focuses on the growth and development of girls ages 5-17 and the training and support of adults who work with them. Established in 1963. Number of employees: 45. Unit of Girl Scouts of the USA, New York, New York. Number of internship applications received each year: 1.

Internships Available ▶ *1–3 field aides:* responsibilities include supporting adults, promoting the delivery of programs, and providing special activities for girls. Duration is flexible. Unpaid. ▶ *1–10 resident camp counselors:* responsibilities include developing and implementing weekly outdoor thematic programs for girls ages 6-17. Candidates should have ability to work with others, oral communication skills, self-motivation, strong leadership ability. Duration is June 17 through August 12. $165–$220 per week. Open to college sophomores, college juniors, college seniors. International applications accepted.

Benefits Names of contacts, opportunity to attend seminars/workshops, possible full-time employment, travel reimbursement, willing to complete paperwork for educational credit, willing to provide letters of recommendation.

Contact Write, fax, or e-mail Mr. Randall K. Cline, Executive Director. Fax: 717-234-5097. E-mail: rcline@hgsc.org. No phone calls. In-person interview recommended (telephone interview accepted). Applications are accepted continuously. World Wide Web: http://www.hgsc.org.

HERBERT HOOVER BOYS AND GIRLS CLUB
2901 North Grand Avenue
St. Louis, Missouri 63107

General Information Organization that provides educational, sports, personal development, and cultural programs for youth ages 6-18. Established in 1967. Number of employees: 29. Unit of Boys and Girls Clubs of America, Atlanta, Georgia. Number of internship applications received each year: 40.

Internships Available ▶ *1–2 computer instructors:* responsibilities include giving computer instruction to youth and assisting in computer club and resource center. Candidates should have ability to work independently, ability to work with others, computer skills, knowledge of field, oral communication skills. Duration is 12 months. $15–$25 per hour. Open to college seniors, recent college graduates, graduate students. ▶ *1–3 tutors:* responsibilities include providing tutoring and homework assistance in resource center. Candidates should have ability to work with others, computer skills, knowledge of field, oral communication skills,

strong leadership ability. Duration is 9 months. Position available as unpaid or at $6–$11 per hour. Open to college seniors, recent college graduates, graduate students. ▶ *8–20 youth group counselors:* responsibilities include supervising and planning activities of group summer day camp, providing counseling and guidance as needed to include appropriate age-specific programs and support. Candidates should have ability to work independently, college courses in field, oral communication skills, organizational skills, plan to pursue career in field, self-motivation, strong leadership ability, written communication skills. Duration is 3 months. $5.50–$8 per hour. Open to recent high school graduates, college freshmen, college sophomores, college juniors, college seniors, recent college graduates, graduate students, individuals reentering the workforce. International applications accepted.

Benefits Formal training, names of contacts, on-the-job training, possible full-time employment, willing to complete paperwork for educational credit, willing to provide letters of recommendation.

Contact Write, call, fax, or e-mail Debra M. B. Harris, Unit Director. Phone: 314-652-8300. Fax: 314-652-8007. E-mail: debra@hhbgc.org. In-person interview required. Applicants must submit a resume. Application deadline: May 1 for summer, August 1 for fall. World Wide Web: http://www.hhbgc.org.

HILLEL: THE FOUNDATION FOR JEWISH CAMPUS LIFE
1640 Rhode Island Avenue, NW
Washington, District of Columbia 20036

General Information Jewish foundation that promotes religious, social, educational, and recreational student activities, focusing on leadership development. Established in 1923. Number of employees: 68. Number of internship applications received each year: 500.

Internships Available ▶ *1 Arline and David L. Bittker Fellowship:* responsibilities include Jewish identity and awareness programming, networking with Jewish student leaders from around the world, developing leadership programs through conferences, national initiatives, and grants programs; working with students on the Hillel Board of Directors. Candidates should have ability to work independently, oral communication skills, organizational skills, personal interest in the field, plan to pursue career in field, self-motivation, strong interpersonal skills, strong leadership ability, writing skills, creativity. Duration is 1 year. $22,500 per year. ▶ *1 Bronfman Fellow:* responsibilities include serving as personal assistant to the president and international director of Hillel, helping coordinate site visits, working on major fund-raising initiatives, and interaction with major leaders of the Jewish community. Candidates should have ability to work with others, oral communication skills, personal interest in the field, writing skills, multi-tasking ability. Duration is 1 year. $22,500 per year. ▶ *1 Hillel Tzedek Fellow:* responsibilities include overseeing campuses involved in community service initiatives, training and developing new programs for those students and supervisors, planning major Jewish public policy conference as well as social justice programming pieces for other student conferences, and administering grants for student programs. Candidates should have ability to work independently, analytical skills, computer skills, oral communication skills, organizational skills, personal interest in the field, self-motivation, strong interpersonal skills, strong leadership ability, writing skills. Duration is 1 year. $22,500 per year. ▶ *65–100 Hillel's Steinhardt Jewish Campus Service Corps:* responsibilities include promoting Jewish involvement to previously unaffiliated Jewish students on campus; creating involving programs to encourage Jewish students to interact with other Jews in social, educational, or community service settings; working with Jewish leaders on campus to connect them to their Judaism. Candidates should have ability to work independently, computer skills, oral communication skills, self-motivation, strong interpersonal skills, strong leadership ability, written communication skills, creativity. Duration is 11 months. $21,000–$23,000 per duration of internship. ▶ *1 Israel Fellow:* responsibilities include promoting Israel advocacy on campus; assisting students and campus professionals in creating Israel programs and addressing Israel issues on campus. Candidates should have ability to work independently, ability to work with others, computer skills, oral communication skills,

Hillel: The Foundation for Jewish Campus Life (continued)
personal interest in the field, written communication skills, must have spent time in Israel. Duration is 1 year. $22,500 per year. ▶ *1 Iyyun Fellowship:* responsibilities include serving as educational and programming resource to Jewish college students; assisting in development of the Jewish learning component of all Hillel conferences. Candidates should have ability to work independently, ability to work with others, college courses in field, editing skills, knowledge of field, organizational skills, writing skills. Duration is 1 year. $22,500 per year. ▶ *1 Samuel and Helene Soref Fellowship:* responsibilities include Jewish identity and awareness programming; working with Jewish student leaders from small Jewish campus communities; helping create pieces of student conferences; administering grants for student programs. Candidates should have ability to work independently, ability to work with others, oral communication skills, personal interest in the field, written communication skills. Duration is 1 year. $22,500 per year. Open to college seniors, recent college graduates. International applications accepted.
Benefits Formal training, health insurance, names of contacts, on-the-job training, opportunity to attend seminars/workshops, possible full-time employment, willing to act as a professional reference, willing to provide letters of recommendation.
International Internships Available in Montreal, Canada; Toronto, Canada; Vancouver, Canada; Jerusalem, Israel; Tel Aviv, Israel; Montevideo, Uruguay.
Contact Write, call, fax, e-mail, or through World Wide Web site Rachel Gurshman, Assistant Director of Human Resources. Phone: 202-857-6559. Fax: 202-857-6693. E-mail: rgurshman@hillel.org. Telephone interview required. Applicants must submit a formal organization application, resume, academic transcripts, writing sample, two letters of recommendation, Internet application (for Jewish Campus Service Corps), photograph. Application deadline: March 1. Fees: $25. World Wide Web: http://www.hillel.org.

HILLSIDE CHILDREN'S CENTER
1337 East Main Street
Rochester, New York 14609

General Information Local leader in caring for young people with a wide range of emotional, behavioral, or life circumstance problems through a variety of comprehensive, family-centered services. Established in 1837. Number of employees: 5,000. Affiliate of Crestwood Children's Center, Scottsville, New York. Number of internship applications received each year: 50.
Internships Available ▶ *4–8 YFDS interns:* responsibilities include working directly with youth and staff; counseling; being responsible for supervising youth in everyday living situations; observation of staff working with youth. Candidates should have ability to work with others, knowledge of field, oral communication skills, organizational skills, personal interest in the field, plan to pursue career in field, self-motivation, writing skills. Duration is flexible. Unpaid. Open to college sophomores, college juniors, college seniors. ▶ *3–6 education interns:* responsibilities include working with youth in classroom settings; helping with problem subjects; assisting teacher in teaching; tutoring; observation of classroom. Candidates should have ability to work with others, college courses in field, computer skills, knowledge of field, oral communication skills, organizational skills, personal interest in the field, plan to pursue career in field, self-motivation, writing skills. Duration is flexible. Unpaid. Open to college freshmen, college sophomores, college juniors, college seniors. ▶ *1–3 recreation department interns:* responsibilities include helping recreation department; supervising youth and running activities that keep the youth busy and active. Candidates should have ability to work with others, college courses in field, knowledge of field, oral communication skills, organizational skills, personal interest in the field, plan to pursue career in field, self-motivation, written communication skills. Duration is 1 or 2 semesters or summer. Unpaid. Open to college freshmen, college sophomores, college juniors, college seniors, graduate students, career changers. ▶ *Social work interns:* responsibilities include following a BSW, MSW employee, learning the role of a social worker or family service primary; working directly with youth; counseling, working on files, advocating, and observing. Candidates should have ability to work independently, ability to

work with others, college courses in field, computer skills, knowledge of field, oral communication skills, organizational skills, personal interest in the field, plan to pursue career in field, research skills, self-motivation, strong leadership ability, writing skills. Duration is flexible. Unpaid. Open to college juniors, college seniors.
Benefits Formal training, names of contacts, on-the-job training, opportunity to attend seminars/workshops, possible full-time employment, willing to complete paperwork for educational credit, willing to provide letters of recommendation.
Contact Call or e-mail Terry Bourgeois, Intern Specialist. Phone: 716-654-4529. Fax: 716-654-4460. E-mail: tbourgeo@hillside.com. In-person interview required. Applicants must submit a formal organization application, letter of interest, resume, orientation and 2-hour crisis awareness training. Application deadline: April 1 for summer, July 1 for fall, November 1 for spring. World Wide Web: http://www.hillside.com.

THE HOME FOR LITTLE WANDERERS
271 Huntington Avenue
Boston, Massachusetts 02115

General Information Nonprofit child and family welfare organization providing multi-disciplinary services ranging from prevention to residential cares, schools, and home-based support. Established in 1799. Number of employees: 904. Number of internship applications received each year: 25.
Internships Available ▶ *8–15 direct-care interns:* responsibilities include may include mentoring kids with emotional and behavioral issues, running activity groups, tutoring or planning activities for kids (depending on site of position). Candidates should have ability to work with others, experience in the field, oral communication skills, organizational skills, personal interest in the field, self-motivation. Duration is September 1-May 1. Unpaid. Open to college sophomores, college juniors, college seniors, recent college graduates, graduate students, career changers. ▶ *1–3 human resources interns:* responsibilities include helping with recruitment, job fairs, sorting resumes, recruiting database, Web sites, corporate and community relations, orientations, and paper work compliance. Candidates should have ability to work with others, computer skills, organizational skills, personal interest in the field, self-motivation, writing skills. Duration is 10 weeks. Unpaid. Open to college sophomores, college juniors, college seniors, recent college graduates, career changers. ▶ *10–20 school helpers:* responsibilities include helping with elementary-age children in classrooms and with after school programs, tutoring, activities, co-leading after school groups, in-school mentoring, and classroom support. Candidates should have ability to work with others, experience in the field, oral communication skills, organizational skills, personal interest in the field, self-motivation. Duration is 8 months (September-May) on a weekly basis; hours 9-5. Unpaid. Open to college freshmen, college sophomores, college juniors, college seniors, recent college graduates, graduate students, career changers, individuals reentering the workforce. International applications accepted.
Benefits On-the-job training, opportunity to attend seminars/ workshops, possible full-time employment, willing to act as a professional reference, willing to complete paperwork for educational credit, willing to provide letters of recommendation.
Contact E-mail or through World Wide Web site Carolyn Flanagan, Volunteers and Intern Manager. Phone: 617-585-7521. Fax: 617-437-8500. E-mail: cflanagan@thehome.org. In-person interview required. Applicants must submit a formal organization application, resume, three letters of recommendation. Application deadline: April 1 for graduate level (fall to spring) may be direct care or school helper position, August 1 for fall (1 semester), September 1 for undergraduate level (fall to spring) may be direct care or school helper, December 1 for spring (1 semester). World Wide Web: http://www.thehome.org.

HOME FREE
3409 Kilmer Lane
Plymouth, Minnesota 55441

General Information Organization that provides services for battered women and their children including safe temporary housing, advocacy, information, support, and referrals. Established in 1980. Number of employees: 30. Division of Missions, Inc., Plymouth, Minnesota. Number of internship applications received each year: 10.

Internships Available ▶ *1 children's advocate:* responsibilities include providing direct services and recreational activities for children; helping them to express their feelings and needs; assessing children's needs in cooperation with staff and mothers; and modeling non-violent disciplinary options. Candidates should have ability to work independently, plan to pursue career in field, self-motivation, strong interpersonal skills. Duration is flexible. Unpaid. Open to high school seniors, recent high school graduates, college freshmen, college sophomores, college juniors, college seniors, recent college graduates, graduate students, career changers, individuals reentering the workforce. ▶ *1–3 legal advocate interns:* responsibilities include providing crisis support to women who have been assaulted by their partners; accompanying women to Order for Protection filings and hearings in family/criminal court; providing other individual and systems advocacy. Candidates should have ability to work independently, computer skills, oral communication skills, self-motivation, strong interpersonal skills, written communication skills. Duration is flexible. Unpaid. Open to recent high school graduates, college freshmen, college sophomores, college juniors, college seniors, recent college graduates, graduate students, law students, career changers, individuals reentering the workforce. ▶ *1–2 women's advocate interns:* responsibilities include providing advocacy in a battered women's shelter, individual and systems advocacy including the criminal justice system; facilitating cooperative living in the shelter, providing support to shelter residents, and answering the crisis line. Candidates should have ability to work independently, office skills, oral communication skills, self-motivation, strong interpersonal skills, strong leadership ability, written communication skills. Duration is flexible. Unpaid. Open to recent high school graduates, college freshmen, college sophomores, college juniors, college seniors, recent college graduates, graduate students, law students, career changers, individuals reentering the workforce. International applications accepted.

Benefits Formal training, on-the-job training, opportunity to attend seminars/workshops, willing to act as a professional reference, willing to complete paperwork for educational credit, willing to provide letters of recommendation, work-related travel reimbursement.

Contact Write or call Kari Hitchcock, Volunteer Coordinator. Phone: 763-545-7080 Ext. 11. Fax: 763-545-7071. In-person interview required. Applicants must submit a formal organization application, letter of interest, two letters of recommendation. Applications are accepted continuously.

H.O.M.E. INC.
PO Box 10
Orland, Maine 04472-0010

General Information Corporation dedicated to "helping people to help themselves" by providing education, an outlet for the sale of crafts, and health care to low-income individuals in addition to job training and housing. Established in 1970. Number of employees: 50. Number of internship applications received each year: 15.

Internships Available ▶ *1 adult volunteer program intern:* responsibilities include clearing land, gathering hay, painting houses, putting up fences, and working on repairs with low-income families. Candidates should have ability to work independently, oral communication skills, self-motivation, strong interpersonal skills, writing skills. Duration is 6–12 months. Unpaid. Open to high school seniors, recent high school graduates, individuals reentering the workforce. ▶ *2 farm assistants:* responsibilities include working with Cashmere goats, sheep, work horses, and all phases of farm life; training horses to work as team; gardening; cutting hay; general barn duties. Candidates should have ability to work independently, ability to work with others, knowledge of field, oral communication skills, personal interest in the field, self-motivation, written communication skills, flexibility. Duration is 6–12 months. Unpaid. Open to recent high school graduates, recent college graduates, career changers, individuals reentering the workforce. ▶ *2 house construction interns:* responsibilities include learning construction

and carpentry and building homes. Candidates should have ability to work independently, oral communication skills, self-motivation, strong interpersonal skills, willingness to learn and follow instructions. Duration is 3–24 months. Unpaid. Open to recent high school graduates, recent college graduates, career changers, individuals reentering the workforce. ▶ *2 wood harvesting/processing interns:* responsibilities include operating saw and shingle mill and harvesting wood with horses. Candidates should have ability to work independently, oral communication skills, self-motivation, strong interpersonal skills, written communication skills. Duration is 6–24 months. Unpaid. Open to recent high school graduates, individuals reentering the workforce. ▶ *2 woodworking/cabinet makers:* responsibilities include learning cabinetry and woodworking from start to finish. Candidates should have ability to work independently, oral communication skills, self-motivation, strong interpersonal skills, written communication skills. Duration is 6–24 months. Unpaid. Open to recent high school graduates, recent college graduates, career changers, individuals reentering the workforce. International applications accepted.

Benefits Free housing, free meals, opportunity to attend seminars/workshops, possible full-time employment, willing to complete paperwork for educational credit, willing to provide letters of recommendation, possible small stipend after training.

Contact Write, call, or e-mail Fr. Randy Eldridge, OHR, Volunteer Coordinator. Phone: 207-469-7961 Ext. 24. Fax: 207-469-1023. E-mail: padre@acadia.net. Applicants must submit a letter of interest, resume, two personal references, two letters of recommendation. Application deadline: February 1 for summer, July 1 for fall, November 1 for spring. World Wide Web: http://www.homecoop.net.

HOPE FAMILY RESOURCES, INC.
81 Pondfield Road, PMB 353
Bronxville, New York 10708

General Information Comprehensive counseling care and education agency strengthening the well-being of laypersons and clergy/religious with faith and reason through family centers, counselor formation programs, and media. Established in 1985. Number of employees: 8. Number of internship applications received each year: 12.

Internships Available ▶ *2–4 Counseling Enrichment and Practice interns:* responsibilities include field instruction assignments of study and direct counseling service in the New York metropolitan area. Candidates should have ability to work independently, ability to work with others, oral communication skills, organizational skills, plan to pursue career in field, written communication skills. Duration is one year (September to August). Unpaid. Open to college seniors, recent college graduates, graduate students, career changers, students and alumni of faith-based/universities or seminaries preferred. ▶ *2–4 mental health management interns:* responsibilities include coordination, communications, data-entry, paraprofessional counseling, research, fund-raising, and translation (if possible). Candidates should have computer skills, personal interest in the field, plan to pursue career in field, self-motivation, strong interpersonal skills, writing skills, bi-lingual or multi-lingual ability (a plus). Duration is one year (April to March). Unpaid. Open to recent high school graduates, college freshmen, college sophomores, college juniors, college seniors, recent college graduates, graduate students, career changers, students or alumni of faith-based high schools, universities, or seminaries preferred. International applications accepted.

Benefits Formal training, free meals, housing at a cost, job counseling, on-the-job training, opportunity to attend seminars/workshops, possible full-time employment, travel reimbursement, willing to act as a professional reference, willing to complete paperwork for educational credit, vacation time, liability insurance (for counseling positions).

Contact Write, call, or e-mail Dr. Denise Mari, Counseling Director. Phone: 914-793-9508. E-mail: team@hopeforme.org. In-person interview required. Applicants must submit a letter of interest, resume, academic transcripts, two writing samples, three personal references, statement of adequate physical and psychological health; police/background clearance required. Application deadline:

Hope Family Resources, Inc. (continued)
April 1 for mental health management positions, September 1 for counseling positions. Fees: $20. World Wide Web: http://www.hopeforme.org.

HOPE FOR KIDS, INC.
1001 University Drive
State College, Pennsylvania 16804

General Information Therapeutic foster care program. Established in 1997. Number of employees: 9. Number of internship applications received each year: 40.
Internships Available ▶ *1–5 case manager assistants:* responsibilities include assisting with case management, school placements, family visits and interventions, intake meeting, counseling arrangements, and aftercare/transition plans. Candidates should have ability to work independently, college courses in field, computer skills, knowledge of field, office skills, oral communication skills, organizational skills, self-motivation, strong interpersonal skills, written communication skills. Duration is flexible. Unpaid. Open to college seniors. ▶ *1 fund-raiser/event coordinator assistant:* responsibilities include assisting with fund-raising and event coordination. Candidates should have ability to work independently, computer skills, knowledge of field, office skills, oral communication skills, organizational skills, research skills, self-motivation, strong interpersonal skills, writing skills. Duration is flexible. Unpaid. Open to college seniors. ▶ *1–2 missions interns:* responsibilities include assisting with coordination of trips to El Salvador to partake in mission trip to feed the street children. Candidates should have ability to work independently, office skills, oral communication skills, personal interest in the field, strong interpersonal skills, writing skills. Duration is flexible. Unpaid. International applications accepted.
Benefits On-the-job training, travel reimbursement, willing to act as a professional reference, willing to complete paperwork for educational credit, willing to provide letters of recommendation.
International Internships Available in San Salvador, El Salvador.
Contact Write, call, fax, or e-mail Celeste Glass, Clinical Supervisor, PO Box 1331, State College, Pennsylvania 16804. Phone: 814-861-4673. Fax: 814-861-5077. E-mail: bgold1703@aol.com. In-person interview recommended (telephone interview accepted). Applicants must submit a letter of interest, resume, three personal references. Applications are accepted continuously. World Wide Web: http://hopeforkidsinc.net.

HOUSING ASSISTANCE COUNCIL
1025 Vermont Avenue, NW, Suite 606
Washington, District of Columbia 20005

General Information National nonprofit organization concerned with rural low-income housing. Established in 1971. Number of employees: 33. Number of internship applications received each year: 20.
Internships Available ▶ *1–2 interns:* responsibilities include data entry and/or analysis depending on organization's needs. Candidates should have ability to work independently, ability to work with others, analytical skills, personal interest in the field, research skills, writing skills. Duration is 1-2 months (usually summer). Position available as unpaid or at minimum wage or above. Open to high school students, recent high school graduates, college freshmen, college sophomores, college juniors, college seniors, recent college graduates, graduate students, law students, career changers, individuals reentering the workforce. International applications accepted.
Benefits On-the-job training, opportunity to attend seminars/workshops, possible full-time employment, willing to act as a professional reference, willing to complete paperwork for educational credit, willing to provide letters of recommendation.
Contact Through World Wide Web site Internship Coordinator. No phone calls. In-person interview recommended (telephone interview accepted). Applicants must submit a letter of interest, resume, writing sample, three personal references. Applications are accepted continuously. World Wide Web: http://www.ruralhome.org.

IMMIGRATION AND REFUGEE SERVICES OF AMERICA
1717 Massachusetts Avenue, NW, Suite 200
Washington, District of Columbia 20036

General Information Nonsectarian network of nonprofit agencies providing direct services and advocacy for migrant individuals and families of all nationalities. Established in 1922. Number of employees: 55. Number of internship applications received each year: 300.
Internships Available ▶ *1 program development for direct services to refugees intern:* responsibilities include researching international, national, state, and local program opportunities and policy matters in health care, housing, and other immigrant issues; needs assessment; proposal development; program development; administration and evaluation; general administrative support. Candidates should have computer skills, oral communication skills, personal interest in the field, self-motivation, written communication skills, graduate-level course work in social work (preferred). Duration is 12 weeks minimum. $75-$100 monthly stipend. Open to college seniors, recent college graduates, graduate students. ▶ *1 refugee mental health program intern:* responsibilities include assisting in preparation of regional mental health conferences, online research, correspondence and editing reports, and general administrative support. Candidates should have computer skills, oral communication skills, personal interest in the field, self-motivation, writing skills. Duration is 12 weeks minimum. $75-$100 monthly stipend. Open to college freshmen, college sophomores, college juniors, college seniors, recent college graduates, graduate students, career changers. International applications accepted.
Benefits On-the-job training, willing to act as a professional reference, willing to complete paperwork for educational credit, willing to provide letters of recommendation, local travel reimbursement.
Contact Write, fax, or e-mail Madelyn C. Leeke, Esq., Program Officer. Fax: 202-797-2363. E-mail: mleeke@irsa-uscr.org. In-person interview recommended (telephone interview accepted). Applicants must submit a letter of interest, resume, two personal references, one 3- to 5-page writing sample. Application deadline: April 15 for summer, August 1 for fall, December 15 for winter/spring. World Wide Web: http://www.irsa-uscr.org.

INTERNATIONAL RESCUE COMMITTEE–ATLANTA RESETTLEMENT OFFICE
4151 Memorial Drive, Suite 201-C
Decatur, Georgia 30032

General Information Nonsecular refugee settlement organization that helps refugees find jobs and accommodation and adjust during their first 90 days in the U.S. Established in 1933. Number of employees: 52. Branch of International Rescue Committee, New York, New York. Number of internship applications received each year: 40.
Internships Available ▶ *Volunteers:* responsibilities include various tasks working with refugees primarily from Africa, the Middle East, Asia, and Eastern Europe. Candidates should have ability to work independently, ability to work with others, oral communication skills, organizational skills, self-motivation. Duration is flexible. Unpaid. Open to high school students and up. International applications accepted.
Benefits Possible full-time employment, willing to act as a professional reference, willing to complete paperwork for educational credit, willing to provide letters of recommendation.
Contact Write, call, fax, or e-mail Ann Taylor, Volunteer Coordinator, 4151 Memorial Drive, Suite 201-C, Decatur, Georgia 30032. Phone: 404-292-7731 Ext. 26. Fax: 404-292-5325. E-mail: ann@atl.intrescom.org. In-person interview required. Applicants must submit a formal organization application, two personal references. Applications are accepted continuously. World Wide Web: http://www.irc-atlanta.org.

INTERNATIONAL SERVICE EXTENSION OF THE YMCA
6300 Westpark, Suite 600
Houston, Texas 77057

General Information Community service organization with local associations worldwide. Established in 1974. Number of employees: 25. Unit of YMCA of the USA, Chicago, Illinois. Number of internship applications received each year: 40.
Internships Available ▶ *25–30 English teachers:* responsibilities include teaching English in a community-based YMCA in Taiwan. Candidates should have knowledge of field, oral communication skills, personal interest in the field, strong interpersonal skills, written communication skills, willingness to live in another culture for 1 year. Duration is 1 year. NT$26,000–NT$31,000 per month (approximately $795–$950 U.S. dollars). Open to recent college graduates, graduate students, law students, career changers. International applications accepted.
Benefits Free housing, health insurance, names of contacts, possible full-time employment, willing to provide letters of recommendation, orientations in U.S. and Taiwan, paid vacation, airfare reimbursed.
International Internships Available in Taiwan.
Contact Write, call, or e-mail Patty Schnabel, Program Director. Phone: 713-339-9015 Ext. 338. Fax: 281-842-9077. E-mail: kpsmile@flash.net. In-person interview required. Applicants must submit a formal organization application, letter of interest, academic transcripts, three letters of recommendation. Application deadline: April 15 for fall placement. Fees: $50. World Wide Web: http://www.ymca.net.

JEWISH FAMILY AND CHILDREN'S SERVICES
2150 Post Street
San Francisco, California 94115

General Information Multifunction social service and mental health organization that provides multiple programs including counseling, homecare, adoptions, and emigrant resettlement; the oldest ongoing charity west of the Mississippi. Established in 1850.
Internships Available ▶ *Academic year interns:* responsibilities include working in counseling, case management, homecare, adoptions, or emigrant resettlement. Candidates should have enrollment in a clinical training program. Duration is 1 academic year. Unpaid. Open to 2nd-year graduate students or postgraduate students. ▶ *Summer interns:* responsibilities include Jewish communal work. Duration is 10 weeks. $200 per week. Open to Jewish undergraduate students.
Contact Write, call, fax, or e-mail Yael Moses, Supervisor, Adult Services, 2150 Post Street, San Francisco, California 94115. Phone: 415-449-1234. Fax: 415-449-1253. E-mail: yaelm@jfcs.org. Applicants must submit a letter of interest, resume. Application deadline: May 15 for summer, June 30 for academic year. World Wide Web: http://www.jfcs.org.

JOBS FOR YOUTH
50 East Washington, 4th Floor
Chicago, Illinois 60602

General Information Job readiness agency that helps young men and women from low-income families become a part of the economic mainstream and provides the business community with motivated entry-level workers. Established in 1979. Number of employees: 40. Number of internship applications received each year: 40.
Internships Available ▶ *5–10 assessment interns:* responsibilities include overseeing assessment portion of program; providing orientation to all incoming clients; monitoring test taking; and interviewing all prospective clients and enrolling them in a workshop or GED classes. Candidates should have oral communication skills, organizational skills, personal interest in the field, strong interpersonal skills. Duration is flexible. Unpaid. Open to college juniors, college seniors.

Benefits On-the-job training, possible full-time employment, willing to act as a professional reference, willing to complete paperwork for educational credit, willing to provide letters of recommendation.
Contact Call or e-mail Kristin Anderson, Director of Volunteer Services. Phone: 312-499-2929. E-mail: kanderson47@yahoo.com. In-person interview required. Applicants must submit a letter of interest, resume. Applications are accepted continuously. World Wide Web: http://www.jfychicago.org.

JOINT ACTION IN COMMUNITY SERVICE, INC., SAN FRANCISCO REGIONAL OFFICE
71 Stevenson Street, Room 1015
San Francisco, California 94105

General Information National nonprofit organization serving at-risk youth ages 16-24. Established in 1967. Number of employees: 8. Unit of Joint Action in Community Service, Washington, District of Columbia. Number of internship applications received each year: 80.
Internships Available ▶ *1 resource development internship:* responsibilities include researching resources for at-risk youth ages 16-24; creating user friendly resource book and locating contacts at social services agencies. Candidates should have ability to work independently, oral communication skills, research skills, strong interpersonal skills, writing skills. Duration is minimum 1 semester/quarter or summer, 4 hours per week. Unpaid. Open to college sophomores, college juniors, college seniors, recent college graduates, graduate students, career changers, individuals reentering the workforce. ▶ *1–3 youth services interns:* responsibilities include making outreach calls to at-risk youth ages 16-24 and providing support, resources and referrals based on needs, such as job search assistance or locating housing. Candidates should have office skills, oral communication skills, personal interest in the field, plan to pursue career in field, self-motivation, strong interpersonal skills. Duration is minimum 1 semester/quarter or summer, 4–8 hours per week. Unpaid. Open to college juniors, college seniors, recent college graduates, graduate students, career changers, individuals reentering the workforce.
Benefits Formal training, willing to act as a professional reference, willing to complete paperwork for educational credit, willing to provide letters of recommendation, oppourtunity to gain experience in social services.
Contact Write, fax, or e-mail Kristin Graffagnino, Deputy Director. Phone: 415-975-4710. Fax: 415-975-4881. E-mail: kgraffagnino@doleta.gov. In-person interview recommended (telephone interview accepted). Applicants must submit a letter of interest, resume. Applications are accepted continuously. World Wide Web: http://www.jacsinc.org.

JOINT ACTION IN COMMUNITY SERVICE (JACS)
Suite 965W, The Curtis Center, 170 South Independence Mall West
Philadelphia, Pennsylvania 19106-3315

General Information Youth service organization that provides support services to students from the Job Corps program. Established in 1967. Number of employees: 4. Branch of Joint Action in Community Service, Washington, District of Columbia. Number of internship applications received each year: 10.
Internships Available ▶ *1–2 client outreach/office assistants:* responsibilities include contacting former Job Corps students and conducting needs assessments, locating resources for use by staff, and various administrative tasks. Candidates should have ability to work independently, office skills, oral communication skills, self-motivation, strong interpersonal skills, written communication skills. Duration is 2–12 months. Unpaid. Open to college freshmen, college sophomores, college juniors, college seniors, recent college graduates, graduate students, law students, career changers, individuals reentering the workforce, retirees; must be 18 or over. International applications accepted.
Benefits Formal training, job counseling, names of contacts, on-the-job training, opportunity to attend seminars/workshops, willing to act as a professional reference, willing to complete

Joint Action in Community Service (JACS) (continued)

paperwork for educational credit, willing to provide letters of recommendation, stipend for travel and meal expenses.
Contact Write, call, fax, or e-mail Stefanie Eshleman, Deputy Regional Director, Suite 965 W, The Curitis Center, 170 South Independence Mall West, Philadelphia, Pennsylvania 19106-3315. Phone: 215-861-5530. Fax: 215-861-5535. E-mail: seshleman@doleta. gov. In-person interview recommended (telephone interview accepted). Applicants must submit a letter of interest, resume, two personal references. Applications are accepted continuously. World Wide Web: http://www.jacsinc.org.

KOSCIUSKO COMMUNITY YMCA
1401 East Smith Street
Warsaw, Indiana 46580

General Information Organization that provides health, fitness, aquatics, and social services to the community. Established in 1961. Number of employees: 115. Unit of YMCA of the USA, Chicago, Illinois. Number of internship applications received each year: 5.
Internships Available ▶ *1–5 day camp counselors:* responsibilities include working hands-on with children in daily camp. Candidates should have ability to work independently, personal interest in the field, self-motivation, strong interpersonal skills, strong leadership ability. Duration is 5–12 weeks. Position available as unpaid or at $6–$7 per hour. Open to college freshmen, college sophomores, college juniors, college seniors. ▶ *1–5 physical department interns:* responsibilities include organizing classes and programs; marketing, hiring, training, and supervising staff; creating new programs and evaluating current programs; performing other duties in the physical department. Candidates should have ability to work independently, oral communication skills, organizational skills, self-motivation, strong interpersonal skills, written communication skills. Duration is as needed. Position available as unpaid or at $6–$7 per hour. Open to college freshmen, college sophomores, college juniors, college seniors, recent college graduates. International applications accepted.
Benefits Formal training, job counseling, names of contacts, opportunity to attend seminars/workshops, possible full-time employment, willing to complete paperwork for educational credit, willing to provide letters of recommendation.
Contact Write, call, fax, or e-mail Tom Garland, Executive Director. Phone: 574-269-9622. Fax: 574-269-1396. E-mail: tgarland@kcymca. org. In-person interview required. Applicants must submit a resume, three personal references. Application deadline: May 1 for summer. World Wide Web: http://www.kcymca.org.

LACASA/ ZACHARIAS CENTER (LAKE COUNTY COUNCIL AGAINST SEXUAL ASSAULT)
4275 Old Grand Avenue
Gurnee, Illinois 60031

General Information Comprehensive sexual abuse/sexual assault center. Established in 1981. Number of employees: 19. Unit of Illinois Coalition Against Sexual Assault (ICASA), Springfield, Illinois. Number of internship applications received each year: 10.
Internships Available ▶ *1–2 advocacy interns:* responsibilities include medical and court advocacy for survivors of sexual assault in Lake County; includes hotline work and medical advocacy at hospitals. Candidates should have ability to work independently, ability to work with others, computer skills, oral communication skills, organizational skills, personal interest in the field, self-motivation. Duration is 6 months minimum. Unpaid. Open to recent high school graduates, college freshmen, college sophomores, college juniors, college seniors, recent college graduates, graduate students, law students. ▶ *1–3 clinical interns:* responsibilities include providing client-centered, trauma-based individual and group counseling to non-offending survivors of sexual assault and sexual abuse, ages 3 through adult. Candidates should have ability to work independently, ability to work with others, knowledge of field, oral communication skills, personal interest in the field, self-motivation, writing skills, feminist philosophy, trauma-based

model. Duration is 6 months minimum. Unpaid. Open to graduate students. International applications accepted.
Benefits Formal training, names of contacts, on-the-job training, opportunity to attend seminars/workshops, willing to act as a professional reference, willing to complete paperwork for educational credit, willing to provide letters of recommendation.
Contact Call Joanie Dovekas, Director of Clinical Services, 4275 Old Grand Avenue, Gurnee, Illinois 60031. Phone: 847-244-1187 Ext. 32. Fax: 847-244-6380. In-person interview required. Applicants must submit a letter of interest, resume, three personal references, successful completion of state-required volunteer training course (40–60 hours). Applications are accepted continuously. World Wide Web: http://www.info@lacasagurnee.org.

LATIN AMERICAN ART RESOURCE PROJECT
7044 Woodville Road
Mt. Airy, Maryland 21771

General Information Development program that teaches artists, artisans, and art educators in disadvantaged Central American communities how to make art and artisanry with low-cost local resources. Established in 1994. Number of employees: 3. Number of internship applications received each year: 20.
Internships Available ▶ *1–3 development interns:* responsibilities include preparation of indigenous materials for demonstration purposes; organizing workshops and program presentations; project documentation; fund-raising for specific projects; conducted at USA site with possible follow-through in Honduras. Candidates should have office skills, oral communication skills, personal interest in the field, research skills, strong interpersonal skills, written communication skills, emotional maturity. Duration is 1–3 months. Unpaid. Open to recent high school graduates, college freshmen, college sophomores, college juniors, college seniors, recent college graduates, graduate students, law students, career changers, individuals reentering the workforce, social and community workers. ▶ *1–3 studio interns:* responsibilities include preparation of art materials, assistance with art projects, photographic documentation; some office duties, studio maintenance; USA site with possible follow-through in Honduras. Candidates should have ability to work with others, office skills, personal interest in the field, self-motivation, honesty and responsibility, aptitude for manual skills. Duration is 1–3 months. Unpaid. Open to recent high school graduates, college freshmen, college sophomores, college juniors, college seniors, recent college graduates, graduate students, law students, career changers, individuals reentering the workforce, young artists, art students. International applications accepted.
Benefits Housing at a cost, job counseling, meals at a cost, names of contacts, on-the-job training, opportunity to attend seminars/workshops, possible full-time employment, willing to act as a professional reference, willing to complete paperwork for educational credit, willing to provide letters of recommendation, tutorials and classes included in program cost; possibility of reduction of program cost.
International Internships Available in Honduras.
Contact Write, call, e-mail, or through World Wide Web site Mr. William Swetcharnik, Program Director. Phone: 301-831-7286. E-mail: swetcharnik@hood.edu. In-person interview recommended (telephone interview accepted). Applicants must submit a formal organization application, letter of interest, resume, academic transcripts, two personal references, two letters of recommendation, cost ranging from $2200-$4800, depending on number of months of participation. Applications are accepted continuously. Fees: $100. World Wide Web: http://www.hood.edu/academic/art/laarp.

LEON COUNTY VOLUNTEER SERVICES
200 West Park Avenue
Tallahassee, Florida 32301

General Information Organization whose mission is to enhance and expand county services through the recruitment and participation of volunteers and interns as partners in the delivery of quality service. Established in 1991. Number of employees:

3. Division of Leon County Board of County Commissioners, Tallahassee, Florida. Number of internship applications received each year: 180.

Internships Available ▶ *1–2 assistants to volunteer coordinators:* responsibilities include assisting in screening, interviewing, and placing volunteers in county government departments; conducting volunteer orientations and exit interviews; assisting the director of volunteer services in event planning/marketing and other duties as necessary. Candidates should have ability to work independently, ability to work with others, computer skills, office skills, oral communication skills, self-motivation, strong leadership ability, writing skills. Duration is 1 semester. Unpaid. Open to college sophomores, college juniors, college seniors, recent college graduates, graduate students, law students, career changers, individuals reentering the workforce. ▶ *1–3 county administration interns:* responsibilities include conducting research on special projects; preparing written materials based on research in the form of reports and/or Board agenda items; preparing correspondence for county administrator and/or Board; assisting in county's legislative program. Candidates should have analytical skills, computer skills, office skills, oral communication skills, personal interest in the field, research skills, written communication skills. Duration is 1 semester. Unpaid. Open to college juniors, college seniors, recent college graduates, graduate students, law students. ▶ *1–4 courts program assistants:* responsibilities include assisting professional staff and learning coordination systems within state courts system mandated program. Candidates should have computer skills, oral communication skills, research skills, self-motivation, strong interpersonal skills, written communication skills, major in social work, pre-law, criminology, public administration, or communications (preferred). Duration is 1 semester. Unpaid. Open to college sophomores, college juniors, college seniors, recent college graduates, graduate students, law students. ▶ *1–4 human resources associates:* responsibilities include providing professional administrative, research, and technical assistance to the Human Resources Division through short and long-term projects; compiling and organizing data for administrative action; assisting in the preparation and maintenance of statistical records, preparing reports and presentations, preparing salary and classification documents, and with training and staff development events; assisting in data input and telephone surveying, reviewing job applications, and restructuring the Human Resource database; work will be reviewed while in progress and upon completion. Candidates should have computer skills, office skills, oral communication skills, organizational skills, personal interest in the field, strong interpersonal skills. Duration is 1 semester. Unpaid. Open to college freshmen, college sophomores, college juniors, college seniors, recent college graduates, graduate students, law students, career changers. ▶ *1–2 investigative interns:* responsibilities include conducting interviews with defendants; interviewing witnesses and victims; may also include filming, taking crime scene pictures, and gathering evidence or delivering subpoenas to government agencies; intern may view trials, court proceedings, and depositions. Candidates should have experience in the field, oral communication skills, plan to pursue career in field, self-motivation, strong interpersonal skills. Duration is 1 semester. Unpaid. Open to college freshmen, college sophomores, college juniors, college seniors, recent college graduates, graduate students, law students, career changers. ▶ *1–2 management and budget assistants:* responsibilities include assisting in the performance of management analysis studies and analysis of county and non-county departments to determine conformance with the approved budgets and in production and distribution of budget documents. Candidates should have office skills, oral communication skills, strong interpersonal skills, written communication skills, proficiency in Microsoft Word, Excel, and WordPerfect. Duration is 1 semester. Position available as unpaid or paid. Open to college freshmen, college sophomores, college juniors, college seniors, recent college graduates, graduate students, career changers, individuals reentering the workforce. ▶ *1–4 reference librarian assistants:* responsibilities include providing reference assistance to patrons over the telephone and in person. Candidates should have college courses in field, computer skills, oral communication skills, plan to pursue career in field, strong interpersonal skills, familiarity with reference interviewing, database searching. Duration is 1

semester. Unpaid. Open to recent college graduates, graduate students, must be currently enrolled in library science courses or have library degree. ▶ *1–2 youth development marketing assistants:* responsibilities include planning, organizing, implementing, directing, and evaluating marketing plan; establishing and presenting objectives, goals, and plans for learning activities for 4-H youth members. Candidates should have computer skills, office skills, oral communication skills, personal interest in the field, self-motivation, strong leadership ability. Duration is 1 semester. Unpaid. Open to college freshmen, college sophomores, college juniors, college seniors, recent college graduates, graduate students, law students, career changers. International applications accepted.
Benefits Formal training, job counseling, on-the-job training, opportunity to attend seminars/workshops, possible full-time employment, willing to act as a professional reference, willing to complete paperwork for educational credit, willing to provide letters of recommendation, worker's compensation.
Contact Write, call, fax, e-mail, or through World Wide Web site Chris Trent, Internship Coordinator, 200 West Park Avenue, Tallahassee, Florida 32301. Phone: 850-921-3015. Fax: 850-413-9095. E-mail: trentc@mail.co.leon.fl.us. In-person interview required. Applicants must submit a formal organization application, resume, three personal references, criminal history background check required for victim advocate positions. Applications are accepted continuously. World Wide Web: http://www.volunteerleon.org.

THE LINDA FELDMAN RAPE CRISIS CENTRE IN JERUSALEM
POB 2549
Jerusalem 91024 Israel

General Information Sexual violence outreach, aid, education, and prevention centre. Established in 1981. Number of employees: 10. Affiliate of Association of Rape Crisis Centres in Israel, Jerusalem, Israel. Number of internship applications received each year: 10.
Internships Available ▶ *1 fund-raising and resource development intern:* responsibilities include research on funding opportunities; grant-writing and reporting; contact with private donors; and special events planning. Candidates should have ability to work independently, computer skills, personal interest in the field, research skills, self-motivation, written communication skills. Duration is 6–24 months. Unpaid. Open to college juniors, college seniors, recent college graduates, graduate students, law students, career changers, some flexibility on age for exceptional applicants. International applications accepted.
Benefits Formal training, health insurance, on-the-job training, opportunity to attend seminars/workshops, willing to act as a professional reference, willing to complete paperwork for educational credit, willing to provide letters of recommendation, travel stipend within Jerusalem.
International Internships Available.
Contact E-mail Emma Grant-Rosenhead, Director of Fundraising. E-mail: jrcc@netvision.net.il. No phone calls. In-person interview recommended (telephone interview accepted). Applicants must submit a letter of interest, resume, writing sample, personal reference, letter of recommendation. Applications are accepted continuously.

LITTLE BROTHERS–FRIENDS OF THE ELDERLY
355 North Ashland
Chicago, Illinois 60607

General Information National nonprofit voluntary organization committed to relieving isolation and loneliness among the elderly. Established in 1959. Number of employees: 40. Affiliate of International Federation of Little Brothers of the Poor, Paris, France. Number of internship applications received each year: 45.
Internships Available ▶ *1 Spanish-speaking program assistant:* responsibilities include developing and nurturing friendships with diverse Hispanic elderly and planning and executing various social activities. Candidates should have ability to work independently, knowledge of field, oral communication skills, personal interest in the field, self-motivation, strong interpersonal skills, valid

Little Brothers–Friends of the Elderly (continued)

driver's license; fluency in Spanish. Duration is 12 months. $600 monthly stipend. Open to college seniors, recent college graduates, career changers, individuals reentering the workforce. ▶ *1–3 art therapy interns:* responsibilities include facilitating the development of integrated art projects into the Rochelle vacation schedule; developing calendar of art projects for homebound celebrations; maintaining a visiting relationship with a core of elderly who have a desire for artistic expression in their lives; participating in program and evaluation meetings. Candidates should have ability to work independently, knowledge of field, oral communication skills, personal interest in the field, self-motivation, strong interpersonal skills. Duration is 3–12 months. Unpaid. Open to college seniors, recent college graduates, graduate students, career changers, individuals reentering the workforce. ▶ *1–20 intergenerational visiting program interns:* responsibilities include organizing activities for the elderly, giving daily living assistance, driving, and conducting special summer projects. Candidates should have ability to work independently, college courses in field, knowledge of field, oral communication skills, organizational skills, personal interest in the field, self-motivation, strong interpersonal skills. Duration is 9–12 months. Unpaid. Open to college freshmen, college sophomores, college juniors, college seniors, recent college graduates, graduate students, career changers, individuals reentering the workforce. ▶ *1–2 marketing interns:* responsibilities include research, the development of a marketing plan (including a budget) and supporting materials, and implementation of the plan. Candidates should have ability to work independently, oral communication skills, personal interest in the field, research skills, self-motivation, writing skills. Duration is 3–12 months. Unpaid. Open to college freshmen, college sophomores, college juniors, college seniors, recent college graduates, graduate students, career changers. ▶ *1–3 photography interns:* responsibilities include visiting the elderly in their homes during holiday parties and at special gatherings; photographing the elderly who are visited and/or those who attend the celebrations; taking responsibility for the development of the photographs, identifying and cataloging each shot according to date and whether it was an individual shot or taken at a Little Brothers event. Candidates should have ability to work independently, oral communication skills, personal interest in the field, self-motivation, strong interpersonal skills. Duration is 3–12 months. Unpaid. Open to college freshmen, college sophomores, college juniors, college seniors, recent college graduates, graduate students, career changers, individuals reentering the workforce. ▶ *1–4 program assistants:* responsibilities include developing and nurturing friendship with diverse elderly individuals and planning and executing various social activities. Candidates should have ability to work independently, knowledge of field, oral communication skills, personal interest in the field, self-motivation, strong interpersonal skills, valid driver's license. Duration is 12 months. $600 monthly stipend. Open to college juniors, college seniors, recent college graduates, graduate students, career changers, individuals reentering the workforce. ▶ *1–3 public relations interns:* responsibilities include working in the areas of marketing/public relations, and fund-raising. Candidates should have ability to work independently, ability to work with others, editing skills, knowledge of field, oral communication skills, personal interest in the field, research skills, self-motivation, writing skills. Duration is 3–12 months. Unpaid. Open to college freshmen, college sophomores, college juniors, college seniors, recent college graduates, graduate students, career changers, individuals reentering the workforce. ▶ *1–8 summer vacation interns:* responsibilities include creating a family atmosphere for the elderly, organizing activities, giving daily living assistance, and driving in a country setting. Candidates should have oral communication skills, organizational skills, personal interest in the field, self-motivation, strong interpersonal skills. Duration is 7 weeks. $200 stipend. Open to college freshmen, college sophomores, college juniors, college seniors, recent college graduates, graduate students, career changers, individuals reentering the workforce. International applications accepted.

Benefits Health insurance, names of contacts, on-the-job training, opportunity to attend seminars/workshops, possible full-time employment, willing to act as a professional reference, willing to complete paperwork for educational credit, willing to

provide letters of recommendation, room and board for summer vacation interns, room and health insurance for program assistants. **International Internships** Available in France; Berlin, Germany; Dublin, Ireland; Acapulco, Mexico; Barcelona, Spain. **Contact** Write, call, fax, e-mail, or through World Wide Web site Ms. Christine Bertrand, Intergenerational Coordinator. Phone: 312-455-1000. Fax: 312-455-9674. E-mail: cbertrand.chi@littlebrothers. org. In-person interview recommended (telephone interview accepted). Applicants must submit a letter of interest, resume, two personal references, two letters of recommendation, 2-3 writing samples for public relations interns. Applications are accepted continuously. World Wide Web: http://www.littlebrothers.org/chicago.

LIVING IN SAFE ALTERNATIVES, INC.–PLAINVILLE GROUP HOME
50 Bank Street
Plainville, Connecticut 06062-2703

General Information Group home setting in a residential community serving the social, emotional, educational, and therapeutic needs of abused, abandoned, neglected, and adjudicated adolescent females; strong focus on teaching independent living skills. Established in 1972. Number of employees: 17. Division of Living in Safe Alternatives, Inc., Plainville, Connecticut. Number of internship applications received each year: 8.
Internships Available ▶ *1–2 occupational therapy interns:* responsibilities include teaching life skills to clients, assessing and testing client's life skills ability, providing groups and individual life skill counseling, writing and implementing life skill work plan for clients. Candidates should have college courses in field, knowledge of field, oral communication skills, personal interest in the field, plan to pursue career in field, self-motivation, strong interpersonal skills, written communication skills. Duration is 1–2 semesters. Unpaid. Open to college juniors, college seniors, graduate students. ▶ *1–2 social work/counseling interns:* responsibilities include helping provide individual and group counseling to clients, implementing psychological testing to clients, writing and implementing client treatment plans, performing family therapy and monitoring psychotropic medication of clients. Candidates should have knowledge of field, oral communication skills, plan to pursue career in field, self-motivation, strong interpersonal skills, written communication skills, MSW or MA in counseling. Duration is 1–2 semesters. Unpaid. Open to recent college graduates, graduate students. ▶ *1–2 youth worker interns:* responsibilities include interaction with and observation of clients, communication with on-duty staff weekly, participation in supervision, and one self-directed workshop or group with clients. Candidates should have knowledge of field, oral communication skills, personal interest in the field, self-motivation, strong interpersonal skills, written communication skills. Duration is 1–2 semesters. Unpaid. Open to college juniors, college seniors, recent college graduates, graduate students. International applications accepted.
Benefits Formal training, names of contacts, on-the-job training, opportunity to attend seminars/workshops, possible full-time employment, willing to act as a professional reference, willing to complete paperwork for educational credit, willing to provide letters of recommendation.
Contact Write, call, or fax Sonia Cruz, Program Coordinator, 50 Bank Street, Plainville, Connecticut 08062-2703. Phone: 860-747-9930. Fax: 860-793-2231. In-person interview required. Applicants must submit a formal organization application, letter of interest, resume, three personal references, letter of recommendation, current physical exam (including PPD), police and DCF background check required. Application deadline: November 1 for spring.

LUTHERAN VOLUNTEER CORPS
1226 Vermont Avenue, NW
Washington, District of Columbia 20005

General Information Nonprofit organization that places individuals in full-time volunteer assignments; placements include: advocacy, health, legal, environmental, social services, education, and youth child services. Established in 1979. Number of employees: 90. Unit of Luther Place Memorial Church, Washington, District of Columbia. Number of internship applications received each year: 145.

Internships Available ▶ *80–90 volunteers:* responsibilities include various duties according to position; positions available in nine U.S. cities. Candidates should have ability to work independently, ability to work with others, organizational skills, personal interest in the field, self-motivation, flexibility and maturity. Duration is 1–2 years. $85 monthly stipend. Open to college seniors, recent college graduates, career changers, individuals reentering the workforce.

Benefits Free housing, free meals, health insurance, names of contacts, on-the-job training, opportunity to attend seminars/workshops, travel reimbursement, willing to act as a professional reference, willing to complete paperwork for educational credit, willing to provide letters of recommendation, possibility of eligibility for AmeriCorps.

Contact Write, call, fax, e-mail, or through World Wide Web site Joanne Roepke Bode, Recruitment Coordinator, 1226 Vermont Avenue, Washington, District of Columbia 20005. Phone: 202-387-3222. Fax: 202-667-0037. E-mail: staff@lvchome.org. Telephone interview required. Applicants must submit a formal organization application, academic transcripts, three personal references, one essay. Application deadline: applications accepted February 1 to June 1 only. World Wide Web: http://www.lvchome.org.

MAINE CENTERS FOR WOMEN, WORK, AND COMMUNITY
Stoddard House, University of Maine at Augusta, 46 University Drive
Augusta, Maine 04330-9410

General Information Program providing a range of comprehensive support, pre-employment, education, training, self-employment, and employment services and resources designed to assist displaced homemakers and single parents in developing marketable skills and in making the transition to economically viable paid employment. Established in 1978. Number of employees: 35. Unit of The University of Maine at Augusta, Augusta, Maine. Number of internship applications received each year: 3.

Internships Available ▶ *1–10 interns:* responsibilities include working in program planning and direct service, management information systems assistance, self-employment, workforce literacy, economic and leadership development training, and advocacy; may also focus on research and public policy issues relating to women's economic development. Candidates should have ability to work independently, computer skills, knowledge of field, organizational skills, strong interpersonal skills, written communication skills. Duration is 3–12 months. Unpaid. Open to college juniors, college seniors, recent college graduates, graduate students, law students, career changers, individuals reentering the workforce. International applications accepted.

Benefits Job counseling, names of contacts, on-the-job training, opportunity to attend seminars/workshops, willing to act as a professional reference, willing to complete paperwork for educational credit, willing to provide letters of recommendation, reimbursement for job-related travel expenses.

Contact Write, call, fax, or e-mail Ms. Eloise Vitelli, Associate Director. Phone: 207-621-3432. Fax: 207-621-3429. E-mail: evitelli@maine.edu. In-person interview required. Applicants must submit a formal organization application, letter of interest, resume, 2 personal references or letters of recommendation. Applications are accepted continuously. World Wide Web: http://mcwwc.uma.maine.edu.

MAKE-A-WISH FOUNDATION OF CENTRAL AND SOUTHERN ARIZONA
711 East Northern Avenue
Phoenix, Arizona 85020

General Information Nonprofit organization that grants wishes to children age 2½–18 who suffer from life-threatening illnesses. Established in 1980. Number of employees: 6. Unit of Make-A-Wish Foundation of America, Phoenix, Arizona. Number of internship applications received each year: 5.

Internships Available ▶ *1 intern:* responsibilities include assisting staff in all aspects of program administration. Candidates should have ability to work with others, computer skills, oral communication skills, self-motivation, written communication skills, ability to work well with children and to interact with volunteers. Duration is flexible. Unpaid. Open to college freshmen, college sophomores, college juniors, college seniors, recent college graduates, graduate students. International applications accepted.

Benefits Names of contacts, on-the-job training, opportunity to attend seminars/workshops, possible full-time employment, willing to act as a professional reference, willing to complete paperwork for educational credit, willing to provide letters of recommendation, good nonprofit experience.

Contact Write, call, fax, e-mail, or through World Wide Web site Myra Petersen, Volunteer Manager, 711 East Northern Avenue, Phoenix, Arizona 85020. Phone: 602-395-9474 Ext. 132. Fax: 602-395-0722. E-mail: mpetersen@makeawishcsaz.org. In-person interview recommended (telephone interview accepted). Applicants must submit a letter of interest, resume, personal reference, two letters of recommendation. Application deadline: June 1 for fall, October 1 for spring. World Wide Web: http://www.wish.org/centralaz.

MANHATTAN EMERGENCY SHELTER, INC.
831 Leavenworth
Manhattan, Kansas 66502

General Information Temporary emergency shelter and transitional living facility for those in need (homeless). Established in 1985. Number of employees: 11. Number of internship applications received each year: 5.

Internships Available ▶ *1–3 assistant case workers:* responsibilities include assisting client services director in helping guests regain their independence and self-sufficiency. Candidates should have ability to work independently, analytical skills, computer skills, knowledge of field, office skills, oral communication skills, organizational skills, personal interest in the field, plan to pursue career in field, self-motivation, strong interpersonal skills, strong leadership ability, writing skills. Duration is flexible. Unpaid. Open to high school seniors, recent high school graduates, college freshmen, college sophomores, college juniors, college seniors, individuals reentering the workforce. International applications accepted.

Benefits Free meals, names of contacts, on-the-job training, opportunity to attend seminars/workshops, possible full-time employment, willing to act as a professional reference, willing to complete paperwork for educational credit, willing to provide letters of recommendation.

Contact Write, call, fax, or e-mail Junell Norris, Executive Director, PO Box 896, Manhattan, Kansas 66505-0896. Phone: 785-537-3113. Fax: 785-537-1380. E-mail: junellnorris@hotmail.com. In-person interview recommended (telephone interview accepted). Applicants must submit a formal organization application, letter of interest, resume, academic transcripts, portfolio, two personal references, two letters of recommendation. Application deadline: April 1 for summer, December 1 for spring. World Wide Web: http://orion.jmc.ksu.edu/sponsors/mesi/www/.

MARYHAVEN CENTER OF HOPE
1010 Route 112
Port Jefferson Station, New York 11776

General Information Not-for-profit, non-sectarian agency committed to serving both children and adults who are mentally and physically challenged by establishing, maintaining, and operating progressive programs and services which are residential, therapeutic, and vocational in nature; goal is the attainment of normalization in all aspects of life for each individual in its care. Established in 1931. Number of employees: 1,065. Affiliate of Catholic Health Services of Long Island, Melville, New York. Number of internship applications received each year: 40.

Internships Available ▶ *Applied behavior specialist assistants:* responsibilities include following up on behavior plan at sites, reporting to ABS, collecting data, and reporting results. Duration is flexible. Unpaid. ▶ *Applied behavior specialist interns:* responsibilities include data collection, analysis, and functional assessments. Duration is flexible. Position available as unpaid or

Maryhaven Center of Hope (continued)

at $7 per hour. ▶ *Home touch coordinators:* responsibilities include tracking goals, billing sheets for monthly services to consumers, petty cash, mileage for staff; liaison between staff, families, and consumers; reviewing documentation for completion and accuracy. Duration is flexible. Unpaid. ▶ *Human resource specialist interns:* responsibilities include recruiting, clerical tasks, benefit administration, and special projects. Duration is flexible. Position available as unpaid or at $7 per hour. ▶ *Recreational therapist interns:* responsibilities include assisting in running groups, special projects, and outings; needs assessments for individual consumers. Duration is flexible. Unpaid. ▶ *Service coordinators:* responsibilities include consumer contact; overseeing training in work setting, case notes, and observing consumers during free time activities. Duration is flexible. Unpaid. ▶ *Social worker interns:* responsibilities include individual sessions, crisis intervention techniques. Duration is flexible. Unpaid. ▶ *Special education teacher interns:* responsibilities include classroom management; IEP development, leading to special education certification. Duration is flexible. Unpaid. ▶ *Vocational instructor interns:* responsibilities include assisting in running groups, assisting with thrift shop, performing evaluations on consumers, individual assessments for work readiness and skills. Duration is flexible. Unpaid. ▶ *Vocational rehabilitation counselor interns:* responsibilities include consumer contact, overseeing training in work setting, case notes, and observing consumers during free time activities. Duration is flexible. Unpaid. International applications accepted.
Benefits Formal training, names of contacts, on-the-job training, opportunity to attend seminars/workshops, possible full-time employment, willing to act as a professional reference, willing to complete paperwork for educational credit, willing to provide letters of recommendation.
Contact Write, call, fax, or e-mail Elizabeth Schultz, Human Resource Manager. Phone: 631-474-4120 Ext. 277. Fax: 631-474-0826. E-mail: eschultz@maryhaven.org. In-person interview recommended (telephone interview accepted). Applicants must submit a formal organization application, resume, academic transcripts, personal reference, course curriculum, TB testing required upon acceptance. Applications are accepted continuously.

MASSACHUSETTS SOCIETY OF PREVENTION OF CRUELTY TO CHILDREN–CAPE COD
206 Breed's Hill Road
Hyannis, Massachusetts 02601

General Information Child welfare agency that focuses on the prevention of child abuse and neglect. Established in 1878. Number of employees: 60. Unit of MSPCC, Boston, Massachusetts. Number of internship applications received each year: 5.
Internships Available ▶ *2–3 interns:* responsibilities include providing assistance to home visitors and group leaders and working with parents and children on developmental and behavioral issues. Candidates should have personal interest in the field, self-motivation, strong interpersonal skills. Duration is flexible. Unpaid. Open to college freshmen, college sophomores, college juniors, college seniors, recent college graduates, graduate students, law students, career changers, individuals reentering the workforce. ▶ *2–3 social work interns:* responsibilities include visiting homes with families of young children and conducting group and family parenting education. Candidates should have ability to work independently, ability to work with others, personal interest in the field. Duration is 2 semesters. Unpaid. Open to college juniors, college seniors, recent college graduates, graduate students, career changers, individuals reentering the workforce.
Benefits Formal training, opportunity to attend seminars/workshops, possible full-time employment, travel reimbursement, willing to complete paperwork for educational credit, willing to provide letters of recommendation, group and individual supervisory meetings.
Contact Write, call, or fax Nancy L. Roberts, Good Start Director. Phone: 800-272-9722. Fax: 508-790-3988. In-person interview required. Applicants must submit a formal organization application, resume, three personal references, criminal offense record investigation required. Applications are accepted continuously. World Wide Web: http://www.mspcc.org.

MCMAHON SERVICES FOR CHILDREN
305 Seventh Avenue, 9th Floor
New York, New York 10001

General Information Foster care program that provides out-of-home placement services for abused and neglected children and adolescents. Established in 1937. Number of employees: 70. Division of Good Shepherd Services, New York, New York. Number of internship applications received each year: 12.
Internships Available ▶ *3–5 social work assistants:* responsibilities include assisting staff in providing services to children and families and developing arts and crafts projects. Candidates should have ability to work independently, oral communication skills, personal interest in the field, self-motivation, strong interpersonal skills, written communication skills, valid driver's license; Spanish ability; willingness to do field work, use public transportation, and make inner city home visits. Duration is flexible. Unpaid. Open to college juniors, college seniors, recent college graduates, graduate students.
Benefits Job counseling, opportunity to attend seminars/workshops, travel reimbursement, willing to complete paperwork for educational credit, willing to provide letters of recommendation.
Contact Write, call, or fax Sr. Sheila Kelly, Family Activity Supervisor. Phone: 212-243-7070 Ext. 249. Fax: 212-243-8085. In-person interview recommended (telephone interview accepted). Applicants must submit a formal organization application, letter of interest, resume, two personal references, two letters of recommendation, Central State Registry clearance; fingerprinting (depending on position). Application deadline: April 1 for summer.

MEALS ON WHEELS OF SAN FRANCISCO, INC.
1375 Fairfax Avenue
San Francisco, California 94124

General Information Human/social services organization serving nutritious food to homebound elderly of San Francisco. Established in 1970. Number of employees: 50. Affiliate of Meals on Wheels Association of America, Washington, District of Columbia. Number of internship applications received each year: 5.
Internships Available ▶ *1 Web site developer:* responsibilities include developing, designing, and maintaining organization's Web site. Candidates should have computer skills, editing skills, knowledge of field, writing skills. Duration is 1 year. Position available as unpaid or paid. Open to high school seniors, recent high school graduates, college freshmen, college sophomores, college juniors, college seniors, recent college graduates, graduate students, career changers, individuals reentering the workforce. ▶ *1–2 database management interns:* responsibilities include database management/entry for fundraising system. Candidates should have ability to work independently, analytical skills, computer skills, office skills, research skills, self-motivation. Duration is 1 year. Position available as unpaid or paid. Open to recent high school graduates, college freshmen, college sophomores, college juniors, college seniors, career changers. ▶ *1–2 development assistants:* responsibilities include assisting in development/fund-raising office with grant applications, direct mail pieces, special events, public relations, marketing and communications. Candidates should have ability to work independently, ability to work with others, analytical skills, computer skills, oral communication skills, organizational skills, personal interest in the field, self-motivation, written communication skills. Duration is 20-40 hours per week. Position available as unpaid or paid. Open to college juniors, college seniors, recent college graduates, graduate students.
Benefits Free meals, names of contacts, on-the-job training, opportunity to attend seminars/workshops, possible full-time employment, travel reimbursement, willing to act as a professional reference, willing to complete paperwork for educational credit, willing to provide letters of recommendation.
Contact Write, call, fax, or e-mail Michelle Wynne, Director of Marketing and Communications, 1375 Fairfax Avenue, San Francisco, California 94124. Phone: 415-920-1111 Ext. 233. Fax: 415-920-1110. E-mail: mwynne@mowsf.org. Applicants must submit a letter of interest, resume, two personal references. Applications are accepted continuously. World Wide Web: http://www.mowsf.org.

METRO ATLANTA YMCA
100 Edgewood Avenue, NE, Suite 1100
Atlanta, Georgia 30303

General Information Nonprofit agency dedicated to providing programs and services that develop spirit, mind, and body. Established in 1858. Number of employees: 2,500. Number of internship applications received each year: 48.

Internships Available ▶ *Courtesy Center representatives:* responsibilities include front desk, front-line public relations to members. Candidates should have ability to work with others, oral communication skills, organizational skills, strong leadership ability. Duration is 1 semester. Position available as unpaid or paid. Open to recent high school graduates, college freshmen, college sophomores, college juniors, college seniors, recent college graduates, graduate students, law students, career changers, individuals reentering the workforce. ▶ *Aquatics interns:* responsibilities include lifeguarding, swim instruction, program planning, and class organization. Candidates should have ability to work with others, knowledge of field, organizational skills, self-motivation, strong leadership ability, written communication skills. Duration is seasonal. Position available as unpaid or paid. Open to high school seniors, recent high school graduates, college freshmen, college sophomores, college juniors, college seniors, recent college graduates, graduate students, law students, career changers, individuals reentering the workforce. ▶ *Camp interns:* responsibilities include working in arts and crafts, equestrian, environmental studies, and leadership training with 3-16 year olds; working as counselors or bus drivers. Candidates should have ability to work independently, ability to work with others, personal interest in the field, self-motivation, strong leadership ability. Duration is seasonal. Position available as unpaid or paid. Open to high school seniors, recent high school graduates, college freshmen, college sophomores, college juniors, college seniors, recent college graduates, graduate students, law students, career changers, individuals reentering the workforce. ▶ *Clerical interns:* responsibilities include human resources, data entry, filing, organizing, communications, public relations. Candidates should have ability to work with others, editing skills, oral communication skills, writing skills. Position available as unpaid or paid. Open to recent high school graduates, college freshmen, college sophomores, college juniors, college seniors, recent college graduates, graduate students, law students, career changers, individuals reentering the workforce. ▶ *Education interns:* responsibilities include acting as pre-school teacher's assistants, child-care site monitors, after-school enrichment, and tutoring. Candidates should have ability to work with others, college courses in field, knowledge of field, plan to pursue career in field, strong leadership ability, completion at least two years of college or be in process of completing second year of college. Duration is 1 semester. Position available as unpaid or at stipend or minimum wage. Open to college sophomores, college juniors, college seniors, recent college graduates. ▶ *Membership representatives:* responsibilities include signing-up new members, telling the YMCA story, developing relationships with members and organizations. Candidates should have ability to work with others, oral communication skills, self-motivation, strong leadership ability. Duration is 1 semester. Position available as unpaid or paid. Open to recent high school graduates, college freshmen, college sophomores, college juniors, college seniors, recent college graduates, graduate students, law students, career changers, individuals reentering the workforce. ▶ *Sports/recreation interns (coaches, monitors, referees):* responsibilities include climbing wall, ropes course, dance, gymnastics, volleyball, basketball, soccer, tennis, and sports clinic instructors. Candidates should have ability to work independently, ability to work with others, experience in the field, knowledge of field, strong leadership ability. Duration is sports season (includes volleyball, basketball, soccer, gymnastics, tennis). Position available as unpaid or at minimum wage per hour or $1000 stipend. Open to high school seniors, recent high school graduates, college freshmen, college sophomores, college juniors, college seniors, recent college graduates, graduate students, law students, career changers, individuals reentering the workforce. ▶ *Wellness interns:* responsibilities include working as an aerobics instructor, wellness coach, or personal trainer. Candidates should have college courses in field, knowledge of field, personal interest in the field. Duration is 1 semester. Position available as unpaid or paid. Open to recent high school graduates, college freshmen, college sophomores, college juniors, college seniors, recent college graduates, career changers.

Benefits Formal training, on-the-job training, opportunity to attend seminars/workshops, possible full-time employment, willing to act as a professional reference, willing to complete paperwork for educational credit, willing to provide letters of recommendation, minimum wage/stipend.

Contact Fax or e-mail Nicky Rosenbluth, Staff Development Director. Fax: 404-527-7693. E-mail: careers@ymcaatlanta.org. No phone calls. In-person interview recommended (telephone interview accepted). Applicants must submit a formal organization application, letter of interest, resume, personal reference, letter of recommendation, criminal background check required. Applications are accepted continuously. World Wide Web: http://www.ymcaatlanta.org.

METROPOLITAN YMCA OF THE ORANGES
2 Babcock Place
West Orange, New Jersey 07052

General Information Association that seeks to improve the quality of community life by fostering healthful living, developing responsible leaders and citizens, strengthening the family unit, promoting the quality of all persons, protecting the environment, and uniting community members and community organizations to solve contemporary problems. Established in 1886. Number of employees: 10. Number of internship applications received each year: 10.

Internships Available ▶ *2–3 athletics interns:* responsibilities include developing, teaching, and implementing sports programs. Candidates should have experience in the field, organizational skills, personal interest in the field, strong interpersonal skills, strong leadership ability. Duration is flexible. Position available as unpaid or paid. ▶ *2–3 child-care interns:* responsibilities include teaching children ages 6 weeks–5 years. Candidates should have college courses in field, knowledge of field, organizational skills, personal interest in the field, strong interpersonal skills. Duration is flexible. Position available as unpaid or paid. ▶ *2–3 environmental education interns:* responsibilities include developing, teaching, and implementing programs in environmental education. Candidates should have college courses in field, organizational skills, personal interest in the field, strong interpersonal skills, strong leadership ability. Duration is flexible. Position available as unpaid or paid. ▶ *Up to 5 marketing/public relations interns:* responsibilities include working directly with the marketing director to help implement marketing strategies at YMCA branches. Candidates should have ability to work with others, college courses in field, computer skills, editing skills, oral communication skills, writing skills. Duration is 6 months-1 year. Position available as unpaid or paid. Open to college freshmen, college sophomores, college juniors, college seniors, recent college graduates, graduate students, law students, career changers, individuals reentering the workforce. International applications accepted.

Benefits Names of contacts, opportunity to attend seminars/workshops, possible full-time employment, travel reimbursement, willing to complete paperwork for educational credit, willing to provide letters of recommendation.

Contact Write, call, fax, or e-mail Carol Mealy, Marketing Director. Phone: 973-325-8881. Fax: 973-325-8771. E-mail: cmealy@metroymcas.org. In-person interview required. Applicants must submit a resume. Application deadline: March 1 for summer, October 1 for winter. World Wide Web: http://www.metroymcas.org.

METUCHEN–EDISON YMCA
65 High Street
Metuchen, New Jersey 08840

General Information Community-based YMCA that offers membership privileges and programming services to build body, mind, and spirit for all persons in the community. Established in 1921. Number of employees: 200. Number of internship applications received each year: 2.

Metuchen–Edison YMCA (continued)

Internships Available ▶ *2–4 child-care classroom teachers:* responsibilities include assisting in day-care center, kindergarten class, or pre-school program. Candidates should have oral communication skills, personal interest in the field, strong interpersonal skills, strong leadership ability, written communication skills. Duration is 4 weeks (minimum). Paid. Open to high school seniors, recent high school graduates, college freshmen, college sophomores, college juniors, college seniors, recent college graduates, career changers, individuals reentering the workforce. ▶ *1–3 fitness directors:* responsibilities include conducting fitness testing and demonstrating Nautilus, free weight, and cardiorespiratory equipment. Candidates should have knowledge of field, oral communication skills, self-motivation, strong interpersonal skills, strong leadership ability. Duration is flexible. Paid. Open to college freshmen, college sophomores, college juniors, college seniors, recent college graduates, graduate students, career changers, individuals reentering the workforce. International applications accepted.
Benefits Formal training, names of contacts, on-the-job training, opportunity to attend seminars/workshops, possible full-time employment, travel reimbursement, willing to act as a professional reference, willing to complete paperwork for educational credit, willing to provide letters of recommendation, national YMCA job listings provided.
Contact Write, call, fax, or e-mail Megan Powers, Branch Executive Director. Phone: 732-548-2044. Fax: 732-549-0910. E-mail: mpmetedisonymca1@aol.com. In-person interview required. Applicants must submit a formal organization application, resume, two personal references, criminal background check required. Applications are accepted continuously.

MIDDLE EARTH
98 Grove Street
Somerville, New Jersey 08876

General Information Nonprofit community-based organization with a mission to provide adolescents with prevention, intervention, and crisis services to enable them to develop into responsible and productive members of the community. Established in 1972. Number of employees: 15. Number of internship applications received each year: 5.
Internships Available ▶ *Alternative to Incarceration Case Managers:* responsibilities include coordination of all aspects of the participant's case, liaison work with the Probation Division, the schools, involved agencies and the family; providing informal one-to-one counseling, crisis intervention, and development of individual program plans; monitoring progress on the level system and initiating consequences for non-compliance. Candidates should have ability to work with others, college courses in field, oral communication skills, organizational skills, personal interest in the field, self-motivation, strong leadership ability. Duration is 1 semester. Position available as unpaid or paid. Open to college juniors, college seniors, graduate students. ▶ *Agency-wide interns:* responsibilities include supervising mentoring at drop-in-centers, supervising community services projects, and serving the agency where needed. Candidates should have ability to work with others, college courses in field, knowledge of field, oral communication skills, personal interest in the field, research skills, self-motivation, strong leadership ability, writing skills. Duration is 1 semester. Position available as unpaid or paid. Open to college freshmen, college sophomores, college juniors, college seniors, recent college graduates, graduate students, law students. ▶ *Mentors:* responsibilities include spending 2-5 hours per week with each client; services include: outreach to adolescent and or family, mentoring, life skills, 24-hour crisis support and counseling. Candidates should have ability to work with others, college courses in field, knowledge of field, oral communication skills, organizational skills, personal interest in the field, self-motivation, strong leadership ability, writing skills. Duration is 1 semester. Position available as unpaid or paid. Open to college freshmen, college sophomores, college juniors, college seniors, recent college graduates, graduate students.
Benefits On-the-job training, opportunity to attend seminars/workshops, possible full-time employment, travel reimbursement,

willing to act as a professional reference, willing to complete paperwork for educational credit, willing to provide letters of recommendation.
Contact Write, call, or fax Gary Hrynoweski, Senior Case Manager. Phone: 908-725-7223. Fax: 908-722-5411. In-person interview required. Applicants must submit a letter of interest, resume, personal reference. Applications are accepted continuously.

MOHAWK VALLEY COMMUNITY ACTION AGENCY, INC.
207 North James Street
Rome, New York 13440

General Information Community action agency that offers a range of human services programs to benefit low/moderate income families and individuals. Established in 1966. Number of employees: 290. Number of internship applications received each year: 10.
Internships Available ▶ *1–2 public information interns:* responsibilities include working with area news organizations to promote the agency and to educate the public about the various programs and services offered. Candidates should have editing skills, knowledge of field, oral communication skills, research skills, writing skills. Duration is 6–12 months. Unpaid. Open to recent high school graduates, college freshmen, college sophomores, college juniors, college seniors, recent college graduates. International applications accepted.
Benefits Names of contacts, possible full-time employment, travel reimbursement, willing to complete paperwork for educational credit, willing to provide letters of recommendation.
Contact Write, call, or fax Richard E. Weltz, Deputy Director. Phone: 315-339-5640. Fax: 315-339-2981. E-mail: rweltz@mvcaa.com. In-person interview required. Applicants must submit a formal organization application, resume. Applications are accepted continuously. World Wide Web: http://mvcaa.com.

MORRIS AREA GIRL SCOUT COUNCIL
1579 Sussex Turnpike
Randolph, New Jersey 07869

General Information Agency that recruits and retains girls and adults into the Girl Scouting organization and provides fun and interesting programs so that girls can become happy, resourceful citizens. Established in 1912. Number of employees: 50. Unit of Girl Scouts of the USA, New York, New York.
Internships Available ▶ *1–2 clerical aides:* responsibilities include collating and using computer and risograph. Candidates should have ability to work with others, computer skills, office skills, organizational skills, self-motivation, written communication skills. Duration is 3–10 months. Paid. Open to high school seniors, recent high school graduates, college freshmen, college sophomores, college juniors, college seniors, recent college graduates, individuals reentering the workforce. ▶ *2 field aides:* responsibilities include organizing troops, orienting leaders, and giving support to volunteers. Candidates should have oral communication skills, self-motivation, strong interpersonal skills, strong leadership ability, written communication skills. Duration is 3–10 months. Paid. Open to college juniors, college seniors, recent college graduates, individuals reentering the workforce. ▶ *1 fund development intern:* responsibilities include researching funding sources and writing proposals. Candidates should have ability to work independently, computer skills, oral communication skills, research skills, writing skills. Duration is 3–10 months. Unpaid. Open to college juniors, college seniors, recent college graduates, individuals reentering the workforce. ▶ *1–5 special needs aides:* responsibilities include planning programs and conducting meetings for the hearing impaired, physically impaired, and emotionally disturbed. Candidates should have ability to work independently, oral communication skills, organizational skills, personal interest in the field, strong interpersonal skills. Duration is 3–10 months. Paid. Open to college juniors, college seniors, recent college graduates, graduate students, career changers. International applications accepted.

Benefits Formal training, on-the-job training, possible full-time employment, willing to complete paperwork for educational credit, willing to provide letters of recommendation.
Contact Write, call, fax, or e-mail Martha Krall, Membership Services Director. Phone: 973-927-7722. Fax: 973-927-7683. E-mail: gsboard@magsc.org. In-person interview required. Applicants must submit a resume. Applications are accepted continuously. World Wide Web: http://magsc.org.

MY SISTER'S PLACE
PO Box 29596
Washington, District of Columbia 20017

General Information Temporary shelter for battered women and their children; services include children's programs, a 24-hour hot line, support groups, transitional housing, financial assistance, community education, public relations, and administration. Established in 1979. Number of employees: 14. Number of internship applications received each year: 25.
Internships Available ▶ *1 SOS center assistant:* responsibilities include supervising children, screening potential clients over the phone, assisting with case management, accompanying clients to court, assisting with support groups, and performing administrative work. Candidates should have college courses in field, knowledge of field, office skills, oral communication skills, personal interest in the field, plan to pursue career in field, self-motivation, strong interpersonal skills, written communication skills, ability to work in fast-paced environment. Duration is at least one semester. Unpaid. Open to college juniors, college seniors, recent college graduates, graduate students, law students, career changers, individuals reentering the workforce. ▶ *1–2 administration interns:* responsibilities include providing general administrative help. Candidates should have ability to work independently, ability to work with others, office skills, self-motivation. Duration is at least one semester. Unpaid. Open to recent high school graduates, college freshmen, college sophomores, college juniors, college seniors, recent college graduates, graduate students, law students, career changers, individuals reentering the workforce. ▶ *1–2 hot line interns:* responsibilities include answering hot line, assisting residents, and crisis counseling. Candidates should have ability to work independently, ability to work with others, oral communication skills, personal interest in the field, self-motivation. Duration is at least one semester. Unpaid. Open to college juniors, college seniors, recent college graduates, graduate students, law students, career changers, individuals reentering the workforce. ▶ *1–2 public relations interns:* responsibilities include assisting with community education, Latino outreach, events, public speaking, newsletter, governmental research, and public relations. Candidates should have ability to work independently, computer skills, editing skills, office skills, oral communication skills, organizational skills, personal interest in the field, research skills, self-motivation, strong interpersonal skills, writing skills, women's issues background; bilingual ability a plus. Duration is at least one semester. Unpaid. Open to college sophomores, college juniors, college seniors, recent college graduates, graduate students, law students, career changers, individuals reentering the workforce.
Benefits Formal training, job counseling, names of contacts, opportunity to attend seminars/workshops, possible full-time employment, willing to complete paperwork for educational credit, willing to provide letters of recommendation, training in crisis counseling.
Contact Write, call, fax, or e-mail Ali-Sha Pemberton, Volunteer Program Director. Phone: 202-529-5261. Fax: 202-529-5984. E-mail: mspoutreach@aol.com. In-person interview required. Applicants must submit a letter of interest, resume, writing sample (public relations interns). Application deadline: April 1 for summer, July 1 for fall, November 1 for winter.

NATIONAL SPORTS CENTER FOR THE DISABLED
677 Winter Park Drive, PO Box 1290
Winter Park, Colorado 80482

General Information Organization that provides mountain recreational services to children and adults with disabilities. Established in 1970. Number of employees: 54. Unit of Winter Park Recreation Association, Winter Park, Colorado. Number of internship applications received each year: 30.
Internships Available ▶ *5–6 summer instructors:* responsibilities include assessing, planning, implementing, leading, and documenting a wide variety of outdoor recreation activities. Candidates should have knowledge of field, organizational skills, strong interpersonal skills, strong leadership ability, college courses in recreation or related field. Duration is 3 months. Unpaid. ▶ *5 winter instructors:* responsibilities include assessing and evaluating disabled students, teaching skiing one-on-one, assisting with adaptive equipment lab, administering a weekly program, and assisting with special events and projects. Candidates should have ability to work independently, college courses in field, knowledge of field, organizational skills, strong interpersonal skills, strong leadership ability. Duration is 1–20 weeks. Unpaid. Open to college seniors, graduate students, career changers. International applications accepted.
Benefits Names of contacts, opportunity to attend seminars/workshops, possible full-time employment, willing to complete paperwork for educational credit, willing to provide letters of recommendation, season pass to resort, uniform, half-price food at the cafeteria, free transportation, eligibility for employee housing at reasonable cost.
Contact Write, call, fax, e-mail, or through World Wide Web site Ms. Georgianne Glass Dominguez, CTRS Operations Manager, Intern Supervisor. Phone: 970-726-1542. Fax: 970-726-4112. E-mail: gdominguez@nscd.org. In-person interview recommended (telephone interview accepted). Applicants must submit a formal organization application, letter of interest, resume. Application deadline: March 1 for summer, August 1 for winter. World Wide Web: http://www.nscd.org/nscd.

NCO YOUTH AND FAMILY SERVICES
1305 West Oswego Road
Naperville, Illinois 60540

General Information Licensed child welfare agency providing individual, family, and group counseling, prevention services, crisis programs for runaways, and boys group home. Established in 1971. Number of employees: 17. Number of internship applications received each year: 25.
Internships Available ▶ *1 counselor master:* responsibilities include providing individual, family, and group counseling. Candidates should have ability to work independently, analytical skills, college degree in related field, oral communication skills, strong interpersonal skills, written communication skills. Duration is 9 months (fall to spring). Unpaid. Open to second year students in master's program. ▶ *2 youth workers:* responsibilities include working on activities with shelter residents. Candidates should have ability to work independently, declared college major in field, oral communication skills, strong interpersonal skills, strong leadership ability. Duration is flexible. Unpaid. Open to college seniors. International applications accepted.
Benefits Names of contacts, on-the-job training, opportunity to attend seminars/workshops, possible full-time employment, willing to act as a professional reference, willing to complete paperwork for educational credit, willing to provide letters of recommendation.
Contact Write, call, or fax Ms. Beverly Garrett, Executive Director, 1305 West Oswego Road, Naperville, Illinois 60540. Phone: 630-961-2992. Fax: 630-961-7251. In-person interview required. Applicants must submit a letter of interest, resume, three personal references. Application deadline: March 1 for fall counselor masters positions.

NEW HORIZONS FOR COMMUNITY-BOUND INDIVIDUALS, INC.
1340 Southeast 9th Avenue
Hialeah, Florida 33010

General Information Nonprofit organization serving adults with mental retardation by providing recreational, vocational, and medical assistance in a residential setting. Established in 1979. Number of employees: 9.

New Horizons for Community-Bound Individuals, Inc. (continued)

Internships Available ▶ *5 volunteers:* responsibilities include working in administration, direct care, accounts, social work, or art therapy (dependent on the volunteer's interests and skills). Candidates should have ability to work independently, ability to work with others, college courses in field, personal interest in the field, counseling skills (helpful). Duration is flexible. Unpaid. Open to college freshmen, college sophomores, college juniors, college seniors. International applications accepted.
Benefits Possible full-time employment.
Contact Write, call, fax, or e-mail Ed Aldama, Executive Director, 1340 Southeast 9th Avenue, Hialeah, Florida 33010. Phone: 305-887-1535. Fax: 305-887-4948. E-mail: info@nuhorizons.org. Applicants must submit a resume, personal reference. Applications are accepted continuously. World Wide Web: http://www.nuhorizons.org.

OLD FIRST REFORMED CHURCH
4th and Race Streets
Philadelphia, Pennsylvania 19106

General Information Church with strong community outreach component, including homeless shelter, summer day camp, job program for teenagers, and urban workcamp program. Established in 1727. Number of employees: 4. Unit of United Church of Christ, Cleveland, Ohio. Number of internship applications received each year: 15.
Internships Available ▶ *4 summer staff interns:* responsibilities include staffing summer day camp or teen jobs program. Candidates should have oral communication skills, self-motivation, strong interpersonal skills, strong leadership ability, strong ability to work with children. Duration is 2 months. $150 per week. Open to recent high school graduates, college freshmen, college sophomores, college juniors, college seniors, recent college graduates, graduate students, career changers, individuals reentering the workforce. ▶ *1 volunteer:* responsibilities include working with homeless shelter, youth groups, urban workcamp program, summer day camp and youth jobs program; generally serving as welcoming presence for inclusive church community. Candidates should have ability to work independently, computer skills, editing skills, office skills, oral communication skills, organizational skills, personal interest in the field, self-motivation, strong interpersonal skills, strong leadership ability, writing skills. Duration is 1 year. $150 per week. Open to college freshmen, college sophomores, college juniors, college seniors, recent college graduates, graduate students, career changers, individuals reentering the workforce. International applications accepted.
Benefits Free housing, health insurance, job counseling, on-the-job training, opportunity to attend seminars/workshops, willing to act as a professional reference, willing to complete paperwork for educational credit, willing to provide letters of recommendation, catastrophic insurance, free meals for summer interns, AmeriCorps educational credit.
Contact Write, call, fax, or e-mail Rev. Geneva M. Butz, Pastor. Phone: 215-922-4566. Fax: 215-922-6366. E-mail: oldfirst@oldfirstucc.org. In-person interview recommended (telephone interview accepted). Applicants must submit a formal organization application, letter of interest, resume, three personal references, additional application to the United Church of Christ Office of Voluntary Service. Application deadline: May 1 for summer.

OLIVET BOYS AND GIRLS CLUB OF READING AND BERKS COUNTIES
1161 Pershing Boulevard
Reading, Pennsylvania 19611

General Information Youth development agency. Established in 1898. Number of employees: 75. Unit of Boys and Girls Clubs of America, Atlanta, Georgia. Number of internship applications received each year: 10.
Internships Available ▶ *1–3 drug and alcohol education assistants:* responsibilities include assisting with drug and alcohol education programs at the club and in outreach programs, assisting in HIV/AIDS education programs and individual guidance programs at seasonal retreats and at week-long residential camps. Duration is

flexible (usually 10 weeks). Position available as unpaid or paid. Open to college freshmen, college sophomores, college juniors, college seniors. ▶ *1–4 education assistants:* responsibilities include assisting with the planning and operation of homework centers, tutoring and publicizing the center, working with literacy programs, and expanding current computer programs. Candidates should have ability to work with others, computer skills, written communication skills. Duration is flexible (usually 10 weeks). Position available as unpaid or paid. Open to college freshmen, college sophomores, college juniors, college seniors, recent college graduates, graduate students. ▶ *1–3 physical education assistants:* responsibilities include assisting with the planning and implementation of physical education activities for the facilities including gym and fitness rooms, and supervising and maintaining safety levels of all program equipment. Duration is flexible (usually 10 weeks). Position available as unpaid or paid. Open to college freshmen, college sophomores, college juniors, college seniors. ▶ *Program assistants:* responsibilities include assisting in providing recreation, education and guidance programs for children ages 6-18. Candidates should have knowledge of field, personal interest in the field, plan to pursue career in field, self-motivation. Duration is 1 semester. Unpaid. Open to college juniors, college seniors, recent college graduates.
Benefits On-the-job training, opportunity to attend seminars/workshops, possible full-time employment, willing to provide letters of recommendation.
Contact Write Richard G. DeGroote, Vice President, 677 Clinton street, Reading, Pennsylvania 19601. Fax: 610-373-8815. No phone calls. In-person interview required. Applicants must submit a letter of interest, resume. Applications are accepted continuously.

OPERATION BLESSING ARIZONA & FESTIVAL OF HOPE
2543 Boyd Avenue
Fort Worth, Texas 76109

General Information Christian humanitarian organization that feeds the poor and provides clothing assistance; also works with children's home. Established in 1997. Number of employees: 2.
Internships Available ▶ *1–3 program assistants:* responsibilities include setting up recreational program for group home having 8-12 children under 13 years of age; assisting in caring for and helping with homework. Candidates should have ability to work independently, ability to work with others, organizational skills, self-motivation. Duration is 3–6 months. $6–$8 per hour. Open to recent high school graduates, college freshmen, college sophomores, college juniors, college seniors, individuals reentering the workforce. ▶ *1 program director:* responsibilities include managing (with supervision) group home for 8-10 children under 13 years of age. Candidates should have college courses in field, computer skills, office skills, personal interest in the field, plan to pursue career in field, self-motivation. Duration is 2 semesters. $10–$14 per hour. Open to college juniors, college seniors, career changers.
Benefits Free housing, free meals, on-the-job training, possible full-time employment, willing to act as a professional reference, willing to complete paperwork for educational credit, willing to provide letters of recommendation.
Contact Call or e-mail Greg Ayers, Executive Director. Phone: 520-631-7643. E-mail: obarizona@aol.com. In-person interview recommended (telephone interview accepted). Applicants must submit a letter of interest, three personal references, three letters of recommendation. Applications are accepted continuously.

PARENTAL STRESS CENTER
5877 Commerce Street
Pittsburgh, Pennsylvania 15206

General Information Family services organization. Established in 1975. Number of employees: 100. Number of internship applications received each year: 10.
Internships Available ▶ *1–3 MIS interns:* responsibilities include database management, network support, multi-media production, (depends on intern's expertise). Candidates should have ability to work with others, analytical skills, computer skills, experi-

ence in the field, written communication skills. Duration is flexible. Position available as unpaid or paid. Open to college juniors, college seniors, recent college graduates, graduate students, law students, career changers. ▶ *1–2 development/marketing assistants:* responsibilities include development of marketing material, contacts with various media, preparation of fund-raising materials, and personal contact. Candidates should have computer skills, oral communication skills, organizational skills, self-motivation, writing skills. Duration is flexible. Position available as unpaid or paid. Open to college juniors, college seniors, recent college graduates, graduate students, law students, career changers. ▶ *2–6 facilitator of parenting education interns:* responsibilities include supervising, planning, and facilitating various parenting education classes and marketing classes and working with individual families. Candidates should have ability to work with others, computer skills, experience in the field, self-motivation, written communication skills. Duration is flexible. Position available as unpaid or paid. Open to college juniors, college seniors, recent college graduates, graduate students, law students, career changers, individuals reentering the workforce. ▶ *1–4 family support counselors:* responsibilities include providing family support services, parenting education, and counseling. Candidates should have ability to work independently, organizational skills, plan to pursue career in field, self-motivation, strong interpersonal skills, written communication skills. Duration is flexible. Position available as unpaid or paid. Open to college juniors, college seniors, recent college graduates, graduate students, law students, career changers. International applications accepted.

Benefits Formal training, job counseling, names of contacts, on-the-job training, opportunity to attend seminars/workshops, possible full-time employment, willing to act as a professional reference, willing to complete paperwork for educational credit, willing to provide letters of recommendation.

Contact Write, call, fax, e-mail, or through World Wide Web site Timothy P. Snyder, Executive Director. Phone: 412-361-4800. Fax: 412-361-4801. E-mail: pscinc@aol.com. In-person interview recommended (telephone interview accepted). Applicants must submit a letter of interest, resume, academic transcripts, writing sample, three personal references. Applications are accepted continuously. World Wide Web: http://www.pscfamily.net.

PENN LAUREL GIRL SCOUT COUNCIL
1600 Mount Zion Road, PO Box 20159
York, Pennsylvania 17402-0140

General Information Organization that inspires girls with the highest ideals of character, conduct, patriotism, and service to become happy and resourceful citizens. Established in 1961. Number of employees: 50. Unit of Girl Scouts of the USA, New York, New York. Number of internship applications received each year: 250.

Internships Available ▶ *2 business managers:* responsibilities include performing accounting, purchasing, store sales, and marketing functions. Candidates should have ability to work independently, ability to work with others, college courses in field, knowledge of field, office skills, oral communication skills, organizational skills, self-motivation. Duration is June 1 to August 15. $2200–$2600 per duration of internship. Open to college sophomores, college juniors, college seniors, recent college graduates, graduate students. ▶ *30–45 camp counselors:* responsibilities include monitoring the care and well-being of campers and scheduling programs. Candidates should have ability to work independently, organizational skills, personal interest in the field, self-motivation, strong interpersonal skills, strong leadership ability. Duration is June 1 to August 15. $1800–$2300 per duration of internship. Open to recent high school graduates, college freshmen, college sophomores, college juniors, college seniors, recent college graduates, graduate students. ▶ *1–3 camp directors:* responsibilities include interviewing, hiring, and supervising seasonal camp staff, overseeing all aspects of the summer resident camp program. Candidates should have experience in the field, organizational skills, self-motivation, strong interpersonal skills, strong leadership ability. Duration is February 1 to September 30. $4500–$5500 per duration of internship. Open to recent college graduates, graduate students, career changers, individuals reentering the workforce. ▶ *2 nature*

specialists:* responsibilities include developing and implementing camp nature program. Candidates should have knowledge of field, oral communication skills, organizational skills, personal interest in the field, strong interpersonal skills. Duration is June 1 to August 15. $1900–$2300 per duration of internship. Open to college sophomores, college juniors, college seniors, recent college graduates. ▶ *2 nurses:* responsibilities include performing general nursing duties. Candidates should have ability to work independently, college degree in related field, experience in the field, organizational skills, strong interpersonal skills, strong leadership ability. Duration is June 1 to August 15. Salary based on experience and certification/license. Open to recent college graduates, LPN's, RN's, EMT's. ▶ *1–3 program directors:* responsibilities include planning summer camp program activities and badgework. Candidates should have ability to work independently, knowledge of field, organizational skills, self-motivation, strong interpersonal skills, strong leadership ability. Duration is June 1 to August 15. $2200–$2600 per duration of internship. Open to college juniors, college seniors, recent college graduates, graduate students. ▶ *1 riding director:* responsibilities include developing, teaching, and supervising riding program, staff, campers and care of horses. Candidates should have ability to work independently, knowledge of field, organizational skills, self-motivation, strong interpersonal skills, strong leadership ability, CHA certification or equivalent experience in English riding instruction. Duration is June 1 to August 15. $2100–$2500 per duration of internship. Open to college juniors, college seniors, recent college graduates, graduate students. ▶ *3–5 riding instructors:* responsibilities include teaching riding skills, performing stable management duties, and working with campers in their units. Candidates should have ability to work independently, experience in the field, personal interest in the field, self-motivation, strong interpersonal skills. Duration is June 1 to August 15. $1900–$2300 per duration of internship. Open to recent high school graduates, college freshmen, college sophomores, college juniors, college seniors, recent college graduates, graduate students. ▶ *5–6 waterfront assistants:* responsibilities include teaching swimming. Candidates should have experience in the field, oral communication skills, personal interest in the field, self-motivation, strong interpersonal skills, strong leadership ability, American Red Cross Lifeguard course. Duration is June 1 to August 15. $1900–$2300 per duration of internship. Open to recent high school graduates, college freshmen, college sophomores, college juniors, college seniors, recent college graduates, graduate students. ▶ *2 waterfront directors:* responsibilities include teaching, training, and supervising staff and campers; exercising sound judgment in anticipating and preventing accidents. Candidates should have ability to work independently, knowledge of field, organizational skills, self-motivation, strong interpersonal skills, strong leadership ability, current ARC-WSI and lifeguarding certification, high level of responsibility. Duration is June 1 to August 15. $2100–$2500 per duration of internship. Open to college juniors, college seniors, recent college graduates, graduate students. International applications accepted.

Benefits Formal training, free housing, free meals, health insurance, opportunity to attend seminars/workshops, possible full-time employment, willing to complete paperwork for educational credit, willing to provide letters of recommendation.

Contact Write, call, fax, or e-mail Vicky Miley, Outdoor Program Administrator. Phone: 717-757-3561. Fax: 717-755-1550. E-mail: vmiley@plgsc.org. In-person interview recommended (telephone interview accepted). Applicants must submit a formal organization application, three personal references. Application deadline: May 30 for summer. World Wide Web: http://www.pennlaurel.org.

PHOENIXVILLE AREA YMCA
400 East Pothouse Road
Phoenixville, Pennsylvania 19460

General Information Organization that provides the community with services that promote healthy spirits, minds, and bodies. Established in 1952. Number of employees: 200. Number of internship applications received each year: 3.

Internships Available ▶ *1–3 aquatic interns:* responsibilities include teaching preschool, youth, and adult swim programs; conducting

Phoenixville Area YMCA (continued)

aquatic fitness and/or therapeutic program; assisting with staff scheduling; assisting with management of outdoor pool complex during summer internship. Candidates should have experience in the field, oral communication skills, personal interest in the field, self-motivation, strong interpersonal skills, strong leadership ability. Duration is summer or 1-3 semesters. Position available as unpaid or paid. Open to college freshmen, college sophomores, college juniors, college seniors, recent college graduates, graduate students, PHEAA work-study eligibles. ▶ *2–5 child-care interns:* responsibilities include assisting with staffing schedules, designing lesson plans for various age groups, assisting in provider care, learning state licensing requirements, developing a promotional piece for services offered. Candidates should have knowledge of field, plan to pursue career in field, self-motivation, strong interpersonal skills, strong leadership ability, written communication skills. Duration is one summer or 1-3 semesters. Position available as unpaid or paid. Open to high school seniors, college freshmen, college sophomores, college juniors, college seniors, recent college graduates, individuals pursuing child-care certificates. ▶ *1–3 community and family recreation interns:* responsibilities include designing lesson plan for outdoor education, designing youth and/or family special events, creating promotional strategy for youth and/or family programs, assisting in day camp program during summer internship. Candidates should have ability to work independently, oral communication skills, personal interest in the field, self-motivation, strong interpersonal skills, strong leadership ability. Duration is one summer or 1-3 semesters. Position available as unpaid or paid. Open to college freshmen, college sophomores, college juniors, college seniors, recent college graduates, PHEAA work-study eligibles. ▶ *1 corporate office intern:* responsibilities include basic accounting, data entry, answering phones, filing, word processing, spreadsheets. Candidates should have computer skills, office skills, organizational skills, plan to pursue career in field, self-motivation, strong interpersonal skills. Duration is 1 summer or 1 semester. Unpaid. Open to college sophomores, college juniors, college seniors, graduate students, PHEAA work-study eligibles. ▶ *1 financial development intern:* responsibilities include entering data into donor database, assisting with fund-raising events, assisting with organizing annual appeal, researching and writing grant proposals. Candidates should have ability to work independently, computer skills, personal interest in the field, research skills, strong interpersonal skills, writing skills. Duration is 1–3 semesters. Position available as unpaid or paid. Open to college juniors, college seniors, graduate students, PHEAA work-study eligibles. ▶ *1–3 health and fitness interns:* responsibilities include designing individualized fitness programs, orienting clients on equipment use, developing fitness-related bulletin boards, developing and implementing fitness incentive program, fitness testing. Candidates should have knowledge of field, organizational skills, plan to pursue career in field, self-motivation, strong interpersonal skills, strong leadership ability. Duration is one summer or 1-3 semesters. Unpaid. Open to high school seniors, college juniors, college seniors, recent college graduates, graduate students, PHEAA work-study elegibles. ▶ *1–2 member services representatives:* responsibilities include greeting members, parents, guests; taking payments; taking class registrations; dispensing information; assisting with security issues; answering phones. Candidates should have ability to work independently, computer skills, oral communication skills, self-motivation, strong interpersonal skills, strong leadership ability. Duration is 1 summer or 1-3 semesters. Position available as unpaid or paid. Open to recent high school graduates, college freshmen, college sophomores, college juniors, college seniors, recent college graduates, individuals reentering the workforce, PHEAA work-study eligibles. ▶ *1 public relations intern:* responsibilities include writing press releases, duplication of public relations materials, design of fliers, sign painting and special event decorations. Candidates should have computer skills, editing skills, knowledge of field, self-motivation, strong interpersonal skills, written communication skills. Duration is summer or 1-3 semesters. Unpaid. Open to college sophomores, college juniors, college seniors, recent college graduates, graduate students, PHEAA work-study eligibles. ▶ *1 youth sports assistant:* responsibilities include assisting in organizing youth sports leagues; entering registration into league database;

coordinating use of fields/facilities; working in sports camps during summer; monitoring league activities and standings. Candidates should have knowledge of field, oral communication skills, personal interest in the field, self-motivation, strong interpersonal skills, strong leadership ability. Duration is 1-3 semesters or 1 summer. Position available as unpaid or paid. Open to PHEAA work-study eligibles.

Benefits Job counseling, names of contacts, on-the-job training, opportunity to attend seminars/workshops, possible full-time employment, willing to complete paperwork for educational credit, willing to provide letters of recommendation.

Contact Write, call, fax, or e-mail Linda S. Petrecca, Human Resources Director, 2460 Boulevard of the Generals, Norristown, Pennsylvania 19403. Phone: 610-539-9190. Fax: 610-539-8650. E-mail: lpetrecca@phoenixvilleareaymca.org. In-person interview recommended (telephone interview accepted). Applicants must submit a letter of interest, resume, two personal references, two letters of recommendation. Applications are accepted continuously. World Wide Web: http://www.phoenixvilleareaymca.org.

POWER OF HOPE
1337 Lincoln Street, Suite 2
Bellingham, Washington 98226

General Information Arts-based program that empowers teens to live positive, engaged lives through discovery of their own sense of purpose and creative potential. Established in 1996. Number of employees: 5. Branch of Whidbey Institute, Clinton, Washington. Number of internship applications received each year: 15.

Internships Available ▶ *Administration and fund-raising interns:* responsibilities include nonprofit administrative tasks, general fund-raising, and event fund-raising. Candidates should have ability to work independently, ability to work with others, computer skills, office skills, organizational skills. Duration is flexible. Position available as unpaid or paid. Open to college juniors, college seniors, recent college graduates, graduate students, individuals reentering the workforce. ▶ *School-year interns:* responsibilities include outreach into schools, program leadership, facilitating meetings with youth 14-18 years old, tracking youth projects, follow-up on youth project needs, organizing projects, and giving direction to participants. Candidates should have ability to work independently, ability to work with others, computer skills, oral communication skills, organizational skills, self-motivation. Duration is flexible. Position available as unpaid or paid. Open to college freshmen, college sophomores, college juniors, college seniors, recent college graduates, graduate students. ▶ *Summer interns:* responsibilities include participating and assisting in an arts-based youth camp and programs, working with artists and youth 14-18 from diverse backgrounds. Candidates should have ability to work independently, ability to work with others, strong leadership ability, experience working with youth, camping/outdoor, kitchen, and teamwork skills. Duration is May to September. Position available as unpaid or paid. Open to recent high school graduates, college freshmen, college sophomores, college juniors, college seniors, recent college graduates, individuals reentering the workforce.

Benefits Formal training, on-the-job training, opportunity to attend seminars/workshops, willing to act as a professional reference, willing to complete paperwork for educational credit, willing to provide letters of recommendation, housing assistance may be available (depending on length of internship).

Contact Write, call, e-mail, or through World Wide Web site Sue Anderson, Co-Director. Phone: 360-671-7390. Fax: 360-671-7580. E-mail: poh@powerofhope.org. In-person interview recommended (telephone interview accepted). Applicants must submit a formal organization application, letter of interest, resume, three personal references, background check for criminal history. Applications are accepted continuously. World Wide Web: http://www.powerofhope.org.

PRESBYTERIAN CHILD WELFARE AGENCY
116 Buckhorn Lane
Buckhorn, Kentucky 41721

General Information Agency that provides residential care for abused children. Established in 1902. Number of employees: 385.

Internships Available ▶ *2–4 case workers:* responsibilities include working with abused and neglected children. Candidates should have ability to work independently, computer skills, oral communication skills, self-motivation, strong interpersonal skills, strong leadership ability, written communication skills. Duration is 6 months to 2 years. Paid. Open to college juniors, college seniors, recent college graduates, graduate students, career changers. ▶ *3–5 child-care specialists or social workers:* responsibilities include performing diverse child-care duties. Candidates should have ability to work independently, analytical skills, college courses in field, computer skills, experience in the field, office skills, oral communication skills, plan to pursue career in field, self-motivation, strong interpersonal skills, strong leadership ability, written communication skills. Duration is 6 months to 2 years. Paid. Open to college juniors, college seniors, recent college graduates, graduate students, career changers. ▶ *1–3 therapists:* responsibilities include supervising case workers and house parents. Candidates should have ability to work independently, college courses in field, computer skills, knowledge of field, oral communication skills, organizational skills, self-motivation, strong interpersonal skills, strong leadership ability, written communication skills. Duration is 1–2 years. Paid. Open to college seniors, recent college graduates, graduate students. International applications accepted.

Benefits Free housing, job counseling, names of contacts, opportunity to attend seminars/workshops, possible full-time employment, willing to complete paperwork for educational credit, willing to provide letters of recommendation, reimbursement for some expenses.

Contact Write, call, fax, or e-mail Patty Wilder, Human Resources Coordinator. Phone: 606-398-7000. Fax: 606-398-7912. E-mail: patty.wilder@buckhorn.org. In-person interview required. Applicants must submit a resume, personal reference. Applications are accepted continuously. World Wide Web: http://www.buckhornchildren.org.

PRISONERS AID ASSOCIATION OF MARYLAND, INC.
204 East 25th Street
Baltimore, Maryland 21218

General Information Social service agency primarily working with inmates and ex-offenders who are usually destitute and homeless . Established in 1869. Number of employees: 15. Number of internship applications received each year: 10.

Internships Available ▶ *1–5 client advocates:* responsibilities include working closely with clients to contact social service programs, keep appointments, stay on their schedules, and become stable and self sufficient. Candidates should have ability to work independently, computer skills, oral communication skills, strong interpersonal skills, written communication skills. Duration is year-round (minimum 6-week commitment). Unpaid. Open to college freshmen, college sophomores, college juniors, college seniors, recent college graduates, graduate students, law students, career changers, individuals reentering the workforce. ▶ *Counselors:* responsibilities include counseling for behavior and life style changes. Candidates should have computer skills, oral communication skills, personal interest in the field, self-motivation, strong interpersonal skills, written communication skills. Duration is year-round (minimum 6-week commitment). Unpaid. Open to college juniors, college seniors, recent college graduates, graduate students, law students, career changers, individuals reentering the workforce. ▶ *Junior case managers:* responsibilities include helping clients establish goals, get into treatment programs, and follow through on goal achievement. Candidates should have ability to work independently, oral communication skills, self-motivation, strong interpersonal skills, written communication skills. Duration is year-round (minimum 6-week commitment). Unpaid. Open to college sophomores, college juniors, college

seniors, recent college graduates, graduate students, law students, career changers, individuals reentering the workforce. International applications accepted.

Benefits Names of contacts, possible full-time employment, willing to act as a professional reference, willing to complete paperwork for educational credit, willing to provide letters of recommendation.

Contact Write, call, fax, e-mail, or through World Wide Web site Malinda Miles, Executive Director. Phone: 410-662-0359. Fax: 410-662-0358. E-mail: prisonersaid@hotmail.com. In-person interview recommended (telephone interview accepted). Applicants must submit a resume. Applications are accepted continuously. World Wide Web: http://www.prisonersaid.org.

PROGRAM FOR AID TO VICTIMS OF SEXUAL ASSAULT, INC. (PAVSA)
Building for Women, 32 East First Street, Suite 200
Duluth, Minnesota 55802

General Information Program offering crisis intervention and support advocacy to victims/survivors of sexual assault and their friends and family and sexual assault education to the community, professionals, and schools. Established in 1975. Number of employees: 5. Number of internship applications received each year: 15.

Internships Available ▶ *1–3 advocate interns:* responsibilities include assisting in crisis intervention, assisting in coordinating volunteers, one-to-one advocacy, and systems advocacy; will design a project for term of the internship in conjunction with agency needs. Candidates should have ability to work independently, oral communication skills, organizational skills, personal interest in the field, self-motivation, strong interpersonal skills. Duration is 3–12 months. Unpaid. Open to college sophomores, college juniors, college seniors, recent college graduates, graduate students, law students, career changers. ▶ *1–2 researchers:* responsibilities include initiating and completing research project under supervision of staff members and presenting results to staff and community. Candidates should have ability to work independently, analytical skills, computer skills, research skills, self-motivation, strong interpersonal skills, written communication skills. Duration is 3–12 months. Unpaid. Open to college juniors, college seniors, recent college graduates, graduate students, law students, career changers. International applications accepted.

Benefits Formal training, job counseling, names of contacts, opportunity to attend seminars/workshops, willing to act as a professional reference, willing to complete paperwork for educational credit, willing to provide letters of recommendation, mileage reimbursement for work-related activities.

Contact Write, call, fax, or e-mail Beth Olson, Program Coordinator. Phone: 218-726-1442. Fax: 218-720-4890. E-mail: pavsa@cp.duluth.mn.us. In-person interview recommended (telephone interview accepted). Applicants must submit a formal organization application, resume, three personal references, criminal history background check required; participation in 40 hours of training in either March or October. Applications are accepted continuously. World Wide Web: http://www.cpinternet.com/~pavsa.

THE RAPE CRISIS CENTER OF CENTRAL MASSACHUSETTS, INC.
146 West Boylston Drive
Worcester, Massachusetts 01606

General Information Program providing comprehensive services to survivors of sexual assault and their concerned others as well as education geared toward ending violence against women. Established in 1973. Number of employees: 18. Number of internship applications received each year: 10.

Internships Available ▶ *Counselors:* responsibilities include providing legal and medical advocacy, on-call hot line coverage, face-to-face counseling, and opportunity for facilitating support groups. Duration is 6–12 months. Unpaid. Open to individuals 18 or older. International applications accepted.

The Rape Crisis Center of Central Massachusetts, Inc. (continued)

Benefits Formal training, names of contacts, opportunity to attend seminars/workshops, possible full-time employment, travel reimbursement, willing to complete paperwork for educational credit, willing to provide letters of recommendation.
Contact Write, call, or fax Director of Counseling Services. Phone: 508-852-7600. Fax: 508-852-7870. In-person interview required. Volunteer questionnaire. Application deadline: February 10 for spring, August 31 for fall.

THE RAPE CRISIS CENTER OF CENTRAL MASSACHUSETTS, INC.
275 Nichols Road
Fitchburg, Massachusetts 01420

General Information Program providing comprehensive services to survivors of sexual assault and their concerned others as well as education geared toward ending violence against women. Established in 1973. Number of employees: 14. Number of internship applications received each year: 10.
Internships Available ▶ *10 counselors:* responsibilities include providing legal and medical advocacy, on-call hotline coverage, and face-to-face counseling; opportunity for facilitating support groups. Duration is 6 months minimum. Unpaid. Open to individuals at least 18 years of age. International applications accepted.
Benefits Formal training, names of contacts, opportunity to attend seminars/workshops, possible full-time employment, travel reimbursement, willing to complete paperwork for educational credit, willing to provide letters of recommendation.
Contact Write, call, or fax Director of Counseling Services. Phone: 978-343-5683. Fax: 978-343-5478. In-person interview required. Volunteer questionnaire. Application deadline: March 31 for spring, August 31 for fall.

REFUGEE AND IMMIGRATION SERVICES
1615 Kecoughtan Road
Hampton, Virginia 23661

General Information Nonprofit organization providing accommodation for refugee housing, employment, and ESL tutoring; refugees are assisted in acquiring a variety of services. Established in 1975. Number of employees: 14. Unit of Catholic Diocese of Richmond, Richmond, Virginia. Number of internship applications received each year: 2.
Internships Available ▶ *1–6 ESL interns:* responsibilities include ESL tutoring, teaching ESL work site classes, office work, assistance in preparing ESL training workshops, or publishing a newsletter. Candidates should have ability to work with others, college courses in field, office skills, organizational skills, personal interest in the field, plan to pursue career in field, self-motivation. Duration is 1–12 months. Unpaid. Open to college sophomores, college juniors, college seniors, recent college graduates, graduate students, career changers, individuals reentering the workforce. ▶ *1–4 law interns:* responsibilities include assisting immigration lawyer. Candidates should have college courses in field, computer skills, office skills, oral communication skills, plan to pursue career in field, written communication skills. Duration is 1–12 months. Unpaid. Open to college sophomores, college seniors, recent college graduates, graduate students, law students, individuals reentering the workforce. ▶ *1–6 social science interns:* responsibilities include assisting caseworkers in providing social services for refugees, including counseling, transportation, and possibly interpreting. Candidates should have ability to work independently, college courses in field, office skills, organizational skills, plan to pursue career in field, strong interpersonal skills. Duration is 1–12 months. Unpaid. Open to college freshmen, college sophomores, college juniors, college seniors, recent college graduates, graduate students, career changers, individuals reentering the workforce. International applications accepted.
Benefits Job counseling, on-the-job training, opportunity to attend seminars/workshops, possible full-time employment, willing to act as a professional reference, willing to complete paperwork for educational credit, willing to provide letters of recommendation.
Contact Write, call, fax, or e-mail Karen Kurilko, Regional Director. Phone: 757-247-3600. Fax: 757-247-1070. E-mail: kkurilko@hrris.

org. In-person interview recommended (telephone interview accepted). Applicants must submit a formal organization application, resume, two personal references, two letters of recommendation. Applications are accepted continuously. World Wide Web: http://www.richmonddiocese.org/ris/.

REGINA RESCUE MISSION, INC.
2076 Scarth Street
Regina, Saskatchewan S4P 3H1 Canada

General Information Nonprofit organization that exists to rescue people from poverty, addiction, and sin, by offering emergency help, life changing recovery programs, and the Gospel message. Established in 2000. Number of employees: 4. Unit of Association of Gospel Rescue Missions, North Kansas City, Missouri. Number of internship applications received each year: 1.
Internships Available ▶ *2–4 interns:* responsibilities include learning all aspects of rescue mission work from vision to implementation, administration, development (fund-raising), chaplaincy work, budgeting, short range and long range planning, and building operations/kitchen, maintenance, janitorial, vehicle, security, volunteerism, human resources). Candidates should have ability to work independently, organizational skills, personal interest in the field, self-motivation, strong interpersonal skills. Duration is flexible. $100 per month. Open to college freshmen, college sophomores, college juniors, college seniors, recent college graduates, graduate students, law students, career changers, individuals reentering the workforce, must be a born-again Christian. International applications accepted.
Benefits Formal training, free housing, free meals, on-the-job training, willing to act as a professional reference, willing to complete paperwork for educational credit, willing to provide letters of recommendation, participation in "Rescue College" (see www.agrm.org).
International Internships Available.
Contact Write, fax, or e-mail Michelle Porter, Associate Director, PO Box 3356 Stn Main, Regina, Saskatchewan S4P 3H1 Canada. Fax: 425-740-7738. E-mail: porter@sprint.ca. No phone calls. In-person interview recommended (telephone interview accepted). Applicants must submit a letter of interest, resume, two personal references, must be able to sign doctrinal statement, 2 letters of recommendation (1 from pastor, 1 from college). Applications are accepted continuously. World Wide Web: http://www.agrm.org/.

RESOURCE CENTER FOR WOMEN
1301 Seminole Boulevard, Suite 150
Largo, Florida 33770

General Information Displaced homemaker and single parent organization providing Pinellas and Pasco County clients with personal and career counseling, preemployment training, personal growth and assertiveness training, decision-making and problem-solving techniques, parenting classes, professional career placement services, and referrals for other services. Established in 1977. Number of employees: 15. Number of internship applications received each year: 10.
Internships Available ▶ *3 assistant intake counselors:* responsibilities include screening clients, scheduling intake counseling appointments, referring clients to available community services, and assisting with case management and clerical tasks. Candidates should have ability to work independently, ability to work with others, oral communication skills, organizational skills, personal interest in the field, written communication skills, ability to work under multiple demands of clients undergoing stress and remain calm; sense of humor. Duration is flexible. Unpaid. Open to college seniors, recent college graduates, graduate students, retired professionals. ▶ *1 community development/media representative:* responsibilities include assisting with public relations, preparing news releases and public service announcements, and maintaining speaker's bureau. Candidates should have ability to work independently, ability to work with others, computer skills, editing skills, knowledge of field, oral communication skills, personal interest in the field, plan to pursue career in field, research skills, writing skills. Duration is flexible. Unpaid. Open to college seniors,

recent college graduates, graduate students. ▶ *3 community/agency outreach interns:* responsibilities include visiting community sites and interviewing potential clients, distributing material, and providing information and referrals for various needs of clients. Candidates should have ability to work independently, ability to work with others, computer skills, editing skills, oral communication skills, self-motivation, writing skills. Duration is flexible. Unpaid. Open to college seniors, recent college graduates, graduate students, professional volunteers. ▶ *3 job developer interns:* responsibilities include developing and maintaining a network of job/employment contacts and monitoring placement services files. Candidates should have editing skills, oral communication skills, organizational skills, personal interest in the field, research skills, self-motivation, strong interpersonal skills, written communication skills, human resources knowledge, knowledge of business/employment field. Duration is flexible. Unpaid. Open to college seniors, recent college graduates, graduate students, professional volunteers. ▶ *3 personal growth counselor interns:* responsibilities include intake interviews, serving as teaching assistant in career and personal growth classes, referrals to other agencies, short-term individual counseling assistance, and short-term group experience. Candidates should have ability to work independently, ability to work with others, college courses in field, knowledge of field, oral communication skills, personal interest in the field, plan to pursue career in field, self-motivation, written communication skills. Duration is flexible. Unpaid. Open to recent college graduates, graduate students. ▶ *1 research assistant:* responsibilities include conducting statistical/demographic research (national/state/local), grant and subject research, and setting up libraries. Candidates should have ability to work independently, analytical skills, computer skills, editing skills, office skills, organizational skills, research skills, self-motivation, writing skills. Duration is flexible. Unpaid. Open to college seniors, recent college graduates, graduate students, retired professionals/volunteers. International applications accepted.

Benefits Formal training, job counseling, names of contacts, on-the-job training, opportunity to attend seminars/workshops, possible full-time employment, travel reimbursement, willing to act as a professional reference, willing to complete paperwork for educational credit, willing to provide letters of recommendation.

Contact Write or fax Ms. Dolores K. Benjamin, Executive Director. Phone: 727-586-1110. Fax: 727-585-4089. In-person interview recommended (telephone interview accepted). Applicants must submit a letter of interest, resume, three personal references, three letters of recommendation, background check. Applications are accepted continuously.

ROCKY MOUNTAIN VILLAGE
2644 Alvarado Road
Empire, Colorado 80438

General Information Nonprofit organization that provides services for children and adults with physical and/or mental disabilities. Established in 1951. Number of employees: 10. Program of Easter Seals Colorado, Lakewood, Colorado. Number of internship applications received each year: 5.

Internships Available ▶ *1–10 camp counselors:* responsibilities include responsible for the health, safety, and happiness of 1-3 people with developmental disabilities. Candidates should have ability to work with others, knowledge of field, oral communication skills, personal interest in the field. Duration is 1 summer. $200 per week plus bonus if entire season completed. Open to high school seniors, recent high school graduates, college freshmen, college sophomores, college juniors, college seniors, recent college graduates, graduate students, law students, career changers, individuals reentering the workforce. ▶ *1 office assistant:* responsibilities include assisting with answering phones, camp paperwork, and other office work. Candidates should have ability to work independently, ability to work with others, computer skills, office skills, oral communication skills, written communication skills. Duration is 1 summer. $200 per week plus bonus if entire season completed. Open to high school seniors, recent high school graduates, college freshmen, college sophomores, college juniors, college seniors, recent college graduates, graduate students, law students, career changers, individuals reentering the

workforce. ▶ *1 program intern:* responsibilities include working with the assistant director to coordinate, develop, and implement programs for summer residential coed camp for people with disabilities. Candidates should have experience in the field, organizational skills, personal interest in the field, strong interpersonal skills, strong leadership ability. Duration is 1 summer. $200 per week with $300 bonus if entire season completed. Open to college freshmen, college sophomores, college juniors, college seniors, recent college graduates, graduate students. ▶ *1 public relations intern:* responsibilities include working with computer specialist to develop weekly camp newsletter, developing press releases, and working with director of communications for Easter Seals. Candidates should have ability to work independently, ability to work with others, computer skills, experience in the field, writing skills, newsletter/layout skills. Duration is 1 summer. Position available as unpaid or at $200 per week with $200 bonus if entire season completed. Open to recent high school graduates, college freshmen, college sophomores, college juniors, college seniors, recent college graduates, graduate students. International applications accepted.

Benefits Free housing, free meals, on-the-job training, willing to act as a professional reference, willing to complete paperwork for educational credit, willing to provide letters of recommendation.

Contact Write, call, fax, e-mail, or through World Wide Web site Ms. Melissa Huber, Assistant Director, 2644 Alvarado Road, PO Box 115, Empire, Colorado 80438. Phone: 303-569-2333. Fax: 303-569-3857. E-mail: huberm@cess.org. In-person interview recommended (telephone interview accepted). Applicants must submit a formal organization application, letter of interest, resume, three letters of recommendation. Applications are accepted continuously. World Wide Web: http://www.eastersealsco.org.

SAFEHOUSE DENVER, INC.
1649 Downing Street
Denver, Colorado 80218

General Information Domestic violence outreach and shelter facility, serving women and children who are victims of domestic violence. Established in 1977. Number of employees: 26. Number of internship applications received each year: 10.

Internships Available ▶ *1–3 outreach advocates:* responsibilities include answering the crisis line, facilitating groups, working on indirect projects, attending staff meetings, and participating in supervisions. Candidates should have ability to work independently, computer skills, oral communication skills, organizational skills, self-motivation, strong interpersonal skills, written communication skills. Duration is 16–52 weeks. Unpaid. ▶ *2–3 shelter advocates:* responsibilities include answering the 24-hour crisis line, maintaining a safe and secure residential facility, and individual case management and advocacy. Candidates should have college courses in field, knowledge of field, self-motivation. Duration is year-round. Unpaid. Open to college seniors, recent college graduates, graduate students, career changers. International applications accepted.

Benefits Formal training, on-the-job training, opportunity to attend seminars/workshops, willing to act as a professional reference, willing to provide letters of recommendation.

Contact Write, call, or fax Mollie Hill, Director of Outresearch Services, PO Box 19888, Denver, Colorado 80218. Phone: 303-318-9959. Fax: 303-318-9979. E-mail: safhsedenver@earthlink.net. In-person interview required. Applicants must submit a letter of interest, resume, personal reference. Applications are accepted continuously. World Wide Web: http://www.safehouse-denver.com.

ST. ELIZABETH SHELTER
804 Alarid Street
Sante Fe, New Mexico 87505

General Information Homeless shelter providing services to individuals and families. Established in 1986. Number of employees: 26. Number of internship applications received each year: 10.

Internships Available ▶ *6 direct-service interns:* responsibilities include taking in homeless guests, supervising evening operation of shelter, maintenance of facilities, and assisting with case

St. Elizabeth Shelter (continued)

management. Candidates should have ability to work independently, personal interest in the field, self-motivation, strong interpersonal skills. Duration is 6–12 months. $60–$90 per week. Open to college freshmen, college sophomores, college juniors, college seniors, recent college graduates, graduate students, law students, career changers, individuals reentering the workforce. International applications accepted.

Benefits Free housing, free meals, health insurance, names of contacts, on-the-job training, opportunity to attend seminars/ workshops, possible full-time employment, willing to act as a professional reference, willing to complete paperwork for educational credit, willing to provide letters of recommendation.

Contact Write, call, fax, e-mail, or through World Wide Web site Mr. Del Bomberger, Executive Director. Phone: 505-982-6611. Fax: 505-982-5347. E-mail: director@saintelizabethshelter.org. Telephone interview required. Applicants must submit a formal organization application, letter of interest, resume, three personal references. Applications are accepted continuously. World Wide Web: http://www.saintelizabethshelter.org.

SAN DIEGO YOUTH AND COMMUNITY SERVICES
3255 Wing Street
San Diego, California 92110

General Information Local social service agency that provides innovative responses to emerging social problems including support services for at-risk children and their families. Established in 1970. Number of employees: 180. Number of internship applications received each year: 70.

Internships Available ▶ *5 AOD interns specialists:* responsibilities include planning, implementing, and supervising peer education, mediation, and after-school recreational activities for at-risk youth. Candidates should have ability to work independently, ability to work with others, oral communication skills, personal interest in the field, self-motivation. Duration is 3–6 months. Unpaid. Open to college freshmen, college sophomores, college juniors, college seniors, recent college graduates, graduate students, law students, career changers, individuals reentering the workforce. ▶ *3–6 HIV prevention and education interns:* responsibilities include co-facilitating group discussion of HIV/AIDS and related prevention issues; assisting in coordinating and implementing HIV/ AIDS related group activities; providing input toward maintaining a dynamic curriculum. Candidates should have ability to work with others, knowledge of field, oral communication skills, personal interest in the field, written communication skills. Duration is 3–6 months. Unpaid. Open to college juniors, college seniors, recent college graduates, graduate students. ▶ *2–3 case manager interns:* responsibilities include providing assistance to agency social workers and case managers for youth in probation group home or teen recovery center. Candidates should have ability to work independently, oral communication skills, self-motivation, strong interpersonal skills, writing skills. Duration is 3–6 months. Unpaid. Open to college juniors, college seniors, recent college graduates, graduate students. ▶ *10–11 community development specialist interns:* responsibilities include assisting in neighborhood locations frequented by youth; creating opportunities for youth to receive education on drug and alcohol abuse and treatment, HIV/ AIDS and other STI's, and information and referrals. Duration is 3–6 months. Unpaid. Open to recent high school graduates, college freshmen, college sophomores, college juniors, college seniors, recent college graduates, graduate students, law students, career changers, individuals reentering the workforce. ▶ *1–4 counselor interns:* responsibilities include providing general counseling and advocacy services to those in need and maintaining client records; facilitating off-site counseling groups as assigned. Candidates should have ability to work independently, oral communication skills, personal interest in the field, self-motivation, strong interpersonal skills, written communication skills. Duration is 9–12 months. Unpaid. Open to those working toward MFT license. ▶ *5–6 emergency teen shelter interns:* responsibilities include supervising shelter residents in milieu and recreational trips, group therapy, and assessing case files. Candidates should have ability to work independently, oral communication skills, personal interest in the field, self-motivation, strong interpersonal skills, writ-

ten communication skills. Duration is 3–6 months. Unpaid. Open to college freshmen, college sophomores, college juniors, college seniors, recent college graduates, graduate students, law students, career changers, individuals reentering the workforce. ▶ *10–20 foster and adoptions interns:* responsibilities include mentoring and tutoring foster and adopted students in reading and math and working with youth during after school program; co-facilitating groups and assisting on developing life plan goals. Candidates should have ability to work independently, oral communication skills, personal interest in the field, self-motivation, strong interpersonal skills, written communication skills. Duration is 3–6 months. Unpaid. Open to recent high school graduates, college freshmen, college sophomores, college juniors, college seniors, recent college graduates, graduate students, law students, career changers, individuals reentering the workforce. ▶ *1–4 mobile health clinic volunteers:* responsibilities include counseling HIV-positive youth, collecting data, and developing and distributing promotional and educational materials. Candidates should have ability to work independently, ability to work with others, oral communication skills, self-motivation, written communication skills. Duration is 3–6 months. Unpaid. Open to recent high school graduates, college freshmen, college sophomores, college juniors, college seniors, recent college graduates, graduate students, law students, career changers, individuals reentering the workforce. International applications accepted.

Benefits Formal training, job counseling, names of contacts, on-the-job training, opportunity to attend seminars/workshops, possible full-time employment, willing to act as a professional reference, willing to complete paperwork for educational credit, willing to provide letters of recommendation, free meals (depending on center where intern works).

Contact Write, call, fax, e-mail, or through World Wide Web site Tammy del Cano, Volunteer Services Administrator, 3255 Wing Street, San Diego, California 92110. Phone: 619-221-8600 Ext. 271. Fax: 619-221-8611. E-mail: volunteer@sdycs.org. In-person interview recommended (telephone interview accepted). Applicants must submit a formal organization application, letter of interest, resume, three personal references, TB test and background check required. Applications are accepted continuously. World Wide Web: http:// www.sdycs.org.

SAN DIEGUITO BOYS AND GIRLS CLUBS
PO Box 615
Solana Beach, California 92075

General Information Organization dedicated to sponsoring activities that promote the health, self-esteem, and welfare of youth. Established in 1968. Number of employees: 75. Unit of Boys and Girls Clubs of America, Atlanta, Georgia. Number of internship applications received each year: 5.

Internships Available ▶ *1 arts and crafts program assistant:* responsibilities include supervising children, facilitating arts and crafts activities. Candidates should have personal interest in the field, self-motivation, strong interpersonal skills, strong leadership ability. Duration is 1 summer. Position available as unpaid or paid. Open to high school seniors, recent high school graduates, college freshmen, college sophomores, college juniors, college seniors, recent college graduates, graduate students, law students, career changers, individuals reentering the workforce. ▶ *1 education assistant:* responsibilities include teaching children to operate computer programs and supervising children in tutoring programs. Candidates should have ability to work with others, computer skills, self-motivation, writing skills. Duration is 1 summer. Position available as unpaid or paid. Open to high school seniors, recent high school graduates, college freshmen, college sophomores, college juniors, college seniors, recent college graduates, graduate students, law students, career changers, individuals reentering the workforce. ▶ *1 games room assistant:* responsibilities include supervising children; supervising social recreation games, pool, football, and Ping Pong; answering phones and dealing with people needing assistance. Candidates should have personal interest in the field, self-motivation, strong interpersonal skills, strong leadership ability. Duration is 1 summer. Position available as unpaid or paid. Open to high school seniors, recent high school graduates, college freshmen, college sophomores, col-

lege juniors, college seniors, recent college graduates, graduate students, law students, career changers, individuals reentering the workforce. ▶ *1 marketing/public relations intern:* responsibilities include producing and publishing bimonthly program brochure, and marketing programs through schools and press releases. Candidates should have ability to work independently, computer skills, editing skills, office skills, oral communication skills, research skills, strong interpersonal skills, writing skills. Duration is 1 summer. Position available as unpaid or paid. Open to recent high school graduates, college freshmen, college sophomores, college juniors, college seniors, recent college graduates, graduate students, law students, career changers, individuals reentering the workforce. ▶ *1 physical education assistant:* responsibilities include supervising children and physical education activities. Candidates should have ability to work with others, personal interest in the field, self-motivation, strong leadership ability. Duration is 1 summer. Position available as unpaid or paid. Open to high school seniors, recent high school graduates, college freshmen, college sophomores, college juniors, college seniors, recent college graduates, graduate students, law students, career changers, individuals reentering the workforce. International applications accepted.
Benefits Names of contacts, opportunity to attend seminars/workshops, possible full-time employment, willing to complete paperwork for educational credit, willing to provide letters of recommendation.
Contact Write, fax, or e-mail Kathy Walker, Director of Operations. Fax: 858-755-0138. E-mail: kwalker@bgcsdto.org. No phone calls. In-person interview required. Applicants must submit a formal organization application, letter of interest, resume, personal reference, two letters of recommendation. Applications are accepted continuously.

SARAH HEINZ HOUSE
One Heinz Street
Pittsburgh, Pennsylvania 15212

General Information Youth recreation center for children ages 7-18. Established in 1901. Number of employees: 55. Unit of Boys and Girls Clubs of America, Atlanta, Georgia. Number of internship applications received each year: 15.
Internships Available ▶ *1–7 day camp counselors:* responsibilities include supervising children, planning and implementing programs or activities, and counseling children. Duration is June to August. $1000 per duration of internship. ▶ *1–10 resident camp counselors:* responsibilities include supervising children, planning and implementing programs or activities, and counseling children. Duration is June to July (boys), July to August (girls). $900–$1000 per duration of internship. Candidates for all positions should have ability to work independently, personal interest in the field, self-motivation, strong interpersonal skills, strong leadership ability. Open to high school seniors, recent high school graduates, college freshmen, college sophomores, college juniors, college seniors, recent college graduates, graduate students, law students, career changers, individuals reentering the workforce.
Benefits Formal training, on-the-job training, willing to act as a professional reference, willing to complete paperwork for educational credit, willing to provide letters of recommendation, free housing, meals, and health insurance available at resident camp only.
Contact Write, call, fax, or e-mail Jennifer L. Roberts, Program Director. Phone: 412-231-2377. Fax: 412-231-2428. E-mail: roberts@sarahheinzhouse.com. In-person interview required. Applicants must submit a formal organization application, resume, three personal references. Application deadline: May 31. World Wide Web: http://www.sarahheinzhouse.org.

SERVICE LEAGUE OF SAN MATEO COUNTY
727 Middlefield Road
Redwood City, California 94063

General Information Organization that provides services to San Mateo jail inmates, their families, and those released from jail. Established in 1961. Number of employees: 11. Number of internship applications received each year: 6.
Internships Available ▶ *1 assistant release counselor:* responsibilities include interviewing and assisting former inmates and their families with counseling and emergency needs and maintaining

computer client records and statistics. Candidates should have computer skills, oral communication skills, organizational skills, plan to pursue career in field, self-motivation, strong interpersonal skills. Duration is 6 months minimum; flexible hours (minimum 8 hours per week). Unpaid. Open to college juniors, college seniors, recent college graduates. ▶ *1 assistant to jail coordinator:* responsibilities include assisting jail coordinators, responding to inmate requests in county jail as appropriate, acting as liaison between inmate and family. Candidates should have ability to work independently, declared college major in field, oral communication skills, organizational skills, self-motivation, strong interpersonal skills, personal interest or knowledge of field, strong sense of self. Duration is 9 months (school year); flexible hours (minimum 8 hours per week). Unpaid. Open to college sophomores, college juniors, college seniors, recent college graduates, individuals age 21 or older.
Benefits On-the-job training, willing to act as a professional reference, willing to complete paperwork for educational credit, willing to provide letters of recommendation.
Contact Write or call Ernestine Gemmet, Volunteer Director. Phone: 650-364-4664. Fax: 650-365-6817. E-mail: servl@aol.com. Applicants must submit a formal organization application, letter of interest, three letters of recommendation. Applications are accepted continuously.

SOUTHEAST PREVENTION SERVICES
7 Church Street
Statesboro, Georgia 30458

General Information Center that acts as a lending library, produces newsletters, holds workshops and conferences related to substance abuse prevention as it relates to risk and protective factors, and provides research-based prevention programs for youth. Established in 1991. Number of employees: 2. Subsidiary of Pineland MH/MR/SA Community Service Board, Statesboro, Georgia. Number of internship applications received each year: 8.
Internships Available ▶ *2 health educator/evaluator specialists:* responsibilities include developing and presenting educational offerings, assisting with survey implementation and tabulation of results, serving on planning committee for educational workshops or conferences, assisting with gathering data for programs. Candidates should have oral communication skills, personal interest in the field, research skills, self-motivation, written communication skills. Duration is August to December, January to May, and May to August. $500 per semester. Open to college seniors, graduate students. International applications accepted.
Benefits Names of contacts, on-the-job training, opportunity to attend seminars/workshops, travel reimbursement, willing to provide letters of recommendation.
Contact Write or e-mail Charlotte Mallard, Program Manager, 7 Church Street, Statesboro, Georgia 30458. E-mail: cmallard75@hotmail.com. In-person interview required. Applicants must submit a letter of interest, resume. Application deadline: May 1 for summer, August 1 for fall, December 1 for spring.

SOUTH WOOD COUNTY YMCA
211 Wisconsin River Drive
Port Edwards, Wisconsin 54469

General Information Fellowship based on Christian values with a mission to provide facilities, programs, and services that enhance the health and physical well-being of all persons and improve the quality of life for the citizens of southern Wood County. Established in 1958. Number of employees: 125. Number of internship applications received each year: 6.
Internships Available ▶ *1 aquatics assistant:* responsibilities include performing various tasks in the pool area. Candidates should have ability to work independently, experience in the field, oral communication skills, personal interest in the field, self-motivation, strong interpersonal skills, strong leadership ability. Duration is flexible. Position available as unpaid or paid. Open to high school students, recent high school graduates, college freshmen, college sophomores, college juniors, college seniors, recent college graduates, individuals reentering the workforce. ▶ *1 assistant maintenance intern.* Candidates should have ability to work

South Wood County YMCA (continued)

independently, ability to work with others, personal interest in the field, self-motivation. Unpaid. Open to high school students, recent high school graduates, college freshmen, college sophomores, college juniors, college seniors, individuals reentering the workforce.
▶ *1 day-care assistant:* responsibilities include caring for children. Candidates should have oral communication skills, organizational skills, personal interest in the field, self-motivation, strong interpersonal skills. Duration is flexible. Position available as unpaid or paid. Open to recent high school graduates, college freshmen, college sophomores, college juniors, college seniors, recent college graduates, individuals reentering the workforce.
▶ *1 office area assistant:* responsibilities include performing various office-related duties. Candidates should have ability to work independently, computer skills, office skills, oral communication skills, personal interest in the field, self-motivation, strong interpersonal skills, writing skills. Unpaid. Open to high school seniors, recent high school graduates, college freshmen, college sophomores, college juniors, college seniors, recent college graduates, individuals reentering the workforce. ▶ *1 physical fitness assistant:* responsibilities include conducting fitness classes and testing. Candidates should have ability to work independently, knowledge of field, oral communication skills, organizational skills, personal interest in the field, self-motivation, strong interpersonal skills, strong leadership ability. Duration is flexible. Position available as unpaid or paid. Open to recent high school graduates, college freshmen, college sophomores, college juniors, college seniors, recent college graduates, individuals reentering the workforce. ▶ *1–2 summer camp assistants:* responsibilities include performing camp-related duties. Candidates should have oral communication skills, personal interest in the field, self-motivation, strong interpersonal skills, strong leadership ability. Duration is flexible. Unpaid. Open to high school students, recent high school graduates, college freshmen, college sophomores, college juniors, college seniors, recent college graduates. ▶ *1 summer special events assistant coordinator.* Candidates should have ability to work independently, oral communication skills, personal interest in the field, research skills, self-motivation, strong interpersonal skills, strong leadership ability, written communication skills. Duration is flexible. Unpaid. Open to high school students, recent high school graduates, college freshmen, college sophomores, college juniors, college seniors, recent college graduates, individuals reentering the workforce. ▶ *1 youth director assistant:* responsibilities include working in youth sports. Candidates should have ability to work independently, oral communication skills, organizational skills, personal interest in the field, self-motivation, strong interpersonal skills, strong leadership ability. Unpaid. Open to high school seniors, recent high school graduates, college freshmen, college sophomores, college juniors, college seniors, recent college graduates, individuals reentering the workforce. International applications accepted.
Benefits Formal training, names of contacts, on-the-job training, opportunity to attend seminars/workshops, possible full-time employment, willing to act as a professional reference, willing to complete paperwork for educational credit, willing to provide letters of recommendation, national YMCA job listings provided, YMCA membership.
Contact Write, call, or fax Donald Franklin, Executive Director. Phone: 715-887-3240. Fax: 715-887-3262. In-person interview recommended (telephone interview accepted). Applicants must submit a letter of interest, resume, two personal references. Applications are accepted continuously.

SPRING LAKE RANCH, INC.
Spring Lake Road
Cuttingsville, Vermont 05738

General Information Therapeutic community for emotionally disturbed adults. Established in 1933. Number of employees: 35. Number of internship applications received each year: 20.
Internships Available ▶ *1–6 work leaders/house advisers:* responsibilities include leading work crews in a safe manner so that residents will have a challenging, meaningful, enjoyable experience; overseeing practical aspects of house residents' lives and giving them support and guidance in reaching their goals; and participating

in and contributing to the ranch community. Candidates should have oral communication skills, organizational skills, personal interest in the field, self-motivation, strong interpersonal skills. Duration is 6 months or longer. $193 per week. Open to recent college graduates, graduate students, career changers, individuals reentering the workforce, individuals 21 or older (college degree not necessary).
Benefits Free housing, free meals, health insurance, on-the-job training, opportunity to attend seminars/workshops, possible full-time employment, willing to provide letters of recommendation, vacation and sick time.
Contact Write, call, or e-mail Ms. Lynn McDermott, Personnel Director, PO Box 310, Cuttingsville, Vermont 05738. Phone: 802-492-3322. E-mail: lynnslr@mindspring.com. In-person interview recommended (telephone interview accepted). Applicants must submit a resume. Applications are accepted continuously.

STARLIGHT CHILDREN'S FOUNDATION OF NY*NJ*CT
1560 Broadway, Suite 600
New York, New York 10036

General Information Organization that brightens the lives of seriously ill children between the ages of 4 and 18 through a variety of programs, including wish granting and various activities in and out of hospital pediatric wards. Established in 1985. Number of employees: 8. Unit of Starlight Children's Foundation International, Los Angeles, California. Number of internship applications received each year: 100.
Internships Available ▶ *1–3 children's services interns:* responsibilities include maintaining hospital party and outpatient activities programs, scheduling parties and entertainment for parties, distributing outpatient tickets, maintaining donor correspondence, and assisting with granting of wishes. Duration is 3 months minimum. Unpaid. ▶ *1–2 marketing and event interns:* responsibilities include working closely with fund-raising associate by assisting with the planning and implementation of special events, maintaining donor correspondence, and soliciting various items and donations; also assists with promotions, newsletters, and marketing. Duration is 3 months minimum. Unpaid. Candidates for all positions should have office skills, oral communication skills, organizational skills, self-motivation, strong interpersonal skills, written communication skills. Open to college sophomores, college juniors, college seniors, recent college graduates. International applications accepted.
Benefits Formal training, on-the-job training, willing to complete paperwork for educational credit, willing to provide letters of recommendation.
Contact Write, call, fax, or e-mail Michele Hall, Marketing and Volunteer Coordinator. Phone: 212-354-2878. Fax: 212-354-2977. E-mail: michele@starlightnyc.org. In-person interview recommended (telephone interview accepted). Applicants must submit a formal organization application, letter of interest, resume, three personal references. Application deadline: March 31 for summer; continuous for fall and winter. World Wide Web: http://www.starlight.org.

STRIDES THERAPEUTIC RIDING
PO Box 572455
Tarzana, California 91357-2455

General Information Organization providing therapeutic horsemanship for the disabled. Established in 1987. Number of employees: 2. Unit of North American Riding for the Handicapped Association (NARHA), Denver, Colorado. Number of internship applications received each year: 15.
Internships Available ▶ *2–3 program assistants:* responsibilities include assisting with lessons for disabled riders, horse and tack care, and horse training (if qualified). Candidates should have ability to work independently, ability to work with others, oral communication skills, self-motivation, strong leadership ability, riding experience (preferred). Duration is 2–4 months. Unpaid. Open to high school seniors, recent high school graduates, college freshmen, college sophomores, college juniors, college seniors, recent college graduates, graduate students, law students, career

changers, individuals reentering the workforce, elderly persons in good physical condition. International applications accepted.
Benefits Formal training, job counseling, names of contacts, on-the-job training, opportunity to attend seminars/workshops, possible full-time employment, willing to act as a professional reference, willing to complete paperwork for educational credit, willing to provide letters of recommendation, insurance for accident or injury on the job.
Contact Write, call, fax, e-mail, or through World Wide Web site Nora Fischbach, Program Director. Phone: 818-371-4953. Fax: 818-705-2201. E-mail: strides@onebox.com. In-person interview recommended (telephone interview accepted). Applicants must submit a formal organization application, letter of interest, resume, two personal references. Applications are accepted continuously. World Wide Web: http://www.strides.org.

TAHIRIH JUSTICE CENTER
PO Box 7638
Falls Church, Virginia 22040

General Information Nonprofit human rights organization aiding women who are fleeing gender persecution and are seeking asylum in the United States. Established in 1997. Number of employees: 6. Number of internship applications received each year: 30.
Internships Available ▶ *1–2 VAWA legal and outreach interns:* responsibilities include legal research; legal writing including memos, affidavits and client-related correspondence; outreach to immigrants and domestic violence communities. Candidates should have ability to work independently, computer skills, office skills, organizational skills, personal interest in the field, plan to pursue career in field, research skills, self-motivation, writing skills. Unpaid. Open to graduate students, law students. ▶ *1–2 human rights legal interns:* responsibilities include interviewing clients, gathering evidence, drafting affidavits and legal memoranda, researching legal and country conditions. Candidates should have analytical skills, editing skills, knowledge of field, personal interest in the field, strong interpersonal skills, writing skills. Duration is 3–4 months. Unpaid. Open to law students, career changers. ▶ *Office administration interns:* responsibilities include general office administration duties; research; representation of organization at conferences; and speaking engagements. Candidates should have ability to work with others, office skills, oral communication skills, personal interest in the field, research skills, writing skills. Unpaid. Open to high school students, recent high school graduates, college freshmen, college sophomores, college juniors, college seniors, recent college graduates, graduate students, law students. International applications accepted.
Benefits Names of contacts, on-the-job training, opportunity to attend seminars/workshops, possible full-time employment, willing to act as a professional reference, willing to provide letters of recommendation.
Contact Write, call, fax, e-mail, or through World Wide Web site Katy Parsi-Boetig, Director of Programming. Phone: 703-237-4554. Fax: 703-237-4574. E-mail: justice@tahirih.org. In-person interview recommended (telephone interview accepted). Applicants must submit a letter of interest, resume, writing sample. Applications are accepted continuously. World Wide Web: http://www.tahirih.org.

TEEN LINE
PO Box 48750
Los Angeles, California 90048

General Information Organization that provides teen-to-teen hot line and associated community outreach services. Established in 1981. Number of employees: 5. Unit of Cedars-Sinai Medical Center, Los Angeles, California. Number of internship applications received each year: 20.
Internships Available ▶ *2–4 administrative interns:* responsibilities include assisting program manager with all administrative tasks. Candidates should have ability to work independently, computer skills, organizational skills, self-motivation, strong interpersonal skills, written communication skills. Duration is flexible (minimum of 12 weeks in summer and minimum of 6 months during the year). Unpaid. Open to high school students, recent

high school graduates, college freshmen, college sophomores, college juniors, college seniors, recent college graduates. ▶ *6 resource associates:* responsibilities include facilitating meetings of adolescents and supervising their work on teen hot line. Candidates should have analytical skills, knowledge of field, oral communication skills, organizational skills, personal interest in the field, strong interpersonal skills. Duration is 6 months. Unpaid. Open to graduate students. International applications accepted.
Benefits Formal training, on-the-job training, opportunity to attend seminars/workshops, possible full-time employment, willing to complete paperwork for educational credit, willing to provide letters of recommendation.
Contact Write, call, fax, or e-mail Jenni Kim-Harris, Program Manager. Phone: 310-423-3401 Ext. 2. Fax: 310-423-0456. E-mail: teenlineca@aol.com. In-person interview recommended (telephone interview accepted). Applicants must submit a resume. Applications are accepted continuously. World Wide Web: http://www.teenlineonline.org.

TEEN RESPONSE, INC.
6758 Bramble Avenue
Cincinnati, Ohio 45227

General Information Nonprofit youth-serving community organization engaged in building leadership skills and positive self-esteem in youth 10-16 years of age. Established in 1993. Number of employees: 5. Number of internship applications received each year: 100.
Internships Available ▶ *1–2 youth social workers:* responsibilities include working directly with youth and engaging them in productive activities to foster personal growth and build positive self-esteem and developing activities for this process; working as a role-model/mentor for youth in group and one-on-one settings. Candidates should have ability to work independently, oral communication skills, personal interest in the field, self-motivation, strong interpersonal skills, written communication skills. Duration is 3–12 months. Unpaid. Open to college freshmen, college sophomores, college juniors, college seniors, recent college graduates. International applications accepted.
Benefits Free housing, names of contacts, on-the-job training, opportunity to attend seminars/workshops, willing to act as a professional reference, willing to complete paperwork for educational credit, willing to provide letters of recommendation.
Contact Write, call, or e-mail Mark Wooten, Administrative Assistant, PO Box 9555, Cincinnati, Ohio 45209-0555. Phone: 513-272-8222. Fax: 513-272-8222. E-mail: teenresponseinc@netzero. net. In-person interview recommended (telephone interview accepted). Applicants must submit a formal organization application, letter of interest, resume, writing sample, three personal references. Applications are accepted continuously. World Wide Web: http://www.teenresponseinc.com.

TEXAS ALLIANCE FOR HUMAN NEEDS
1016 East 12th Street
Austin, Texas 78702

General Information Independent statewide coalition concerned with issues affecting low- and moderate-income individuals in Texas. Established in 1982. Number of employees: 3. Number of internship applications received each year: 80.
Internships Available ▶ *2 basic money management interns:* responsibilities include assisting field organizers in developing meetings and literature on low-income/poverty issues, specifically financial education issues, aid in setting up and teaching classes. Candidates should have ability to work independently, oral communication skills, organizational skills, research skills, self-motivation, strong interpersonal skills, strong leadership ability. Duration is 6–12 months. Unpaid. Open to college juniors, college seniors, recent college graduates, graduate students, law students, career changers, individuals reentering the workforce. ▶ *3–6 combination interns:* Candidates should have ability to work independently, ability to work with others, analytical skills, computer skills, oral communication skills, written communication skills. Duration is 3–6 months. Position available as unpaid or paid. Open to college juniors, college seniors, recent college graduates, graduate students, law students, career changers, individuals reentering the workforce.

Texas Alliance for Human Needs (continued)

▶ *1–3 development interns:* responsibilities include direct mail, major donor solicitation, and grant-writing projects. Candidates should have ability to work independently, computer skills, oral communication skills, organizational skills, research skills, self-motivation, strong interpersonal skills, writing skills. Duration is 3–6 months. Position available as unpaid or at commission (percentage of funds raised). Open to college juniors, college seniors, recent college graduates, graduate students, law students, career changers, individuals reentering the workforce. ▶ *1–3 education interns:* responsibilities include writing and distributing educational pieces on poverty issues. Candidates should have ability to work independently, computer skills, oral communication skills, research skills, self-motivation, written communication skills. Duration is 3–6 months. Unpaid. Open to high school seniors, recent high school graduates, college freshmen, college sophomores, college juniors, college seniors, recent college graduates, graduate students, law students, career changers, individuals reentering the workforce. ▶ *1 minority issues intern:* responsibilities include organizing and documenting issues impacting the minority communities, serving as liaison to Texas Minority Health Network, and coordinating newsletters and interns. Candidates should have ability to work independently, ability to work with others, editing skills, office skills, oral communication skills, organizational skills, personal interest in the field, research skills, self-motivation, strong leadership ability, writing skills. Duration is 6–9 months. $300 per month. Open to recent college graduates, graduate students, law students, career changers, individuals reentering the workforce. ▶ *1–3 newsletter interns:* responsibilities include assisting in preparation of newsletter by researching and writing articles. Candidates should have ability to work independently, analytical skills, computer skills, editing skills, organizational skills, research skills, self-motivation, writing skills. Duration is 3–6 months. Unpaid. Open to college freshmen, college sophomores, college juniors, college seniors, recent college graduates, graduate students, law students, career changers, individuals reentering the workforce. ▶ *1–3 office interns:* responsibilities include answering phone, filing, responding to letters, assembling information packets, and maintaining the computer mailing list. Candidates should have ability to work independently, ability to work with others, computer skills, office skills, oral communication skills, organizational skills, research skills, self-motivation, writing skills. Duration is 3–6 months. Unpaid. Open to college freshmen, college sophomores, college juniors, college seniors, recent college graduates, graduate students, law students, career changers, individuals reentering the workforce. ▶ *2–3 research/poverty interns:* responsibilities include researching poverty issues and attending legislative hearings. Candidates should have ability to work independently, analytical skills, computer skills, research skills, self-motivation, writing skills. Duration is 3–6 months. Unpaid. Open to recent high school graduates, college freshmen, college sophomores, college juniors, college seniors, recent college graduates, graduate students, law students, career changers, individuals reentering the workforce. International applications accepted.

Benefits Free housing, job counseling, names of contacts, on-the-job training, opportunity to attend seminars/workshops, willing to act as a professional reference, willing to complete paperwork for educational credit, willing to provide letters of recommendation, health insurance for minority issues interns.

Contact Write, call, fax, e-mail, or through World Wide Web site Ms. Jude Filler, Executive Director. Phone: 512-474-5019. Fax: 512-474-5058. E-mail: volunteer@texasneeds.org. Telephone interview required. Applicants must submit a letter of interest, resume. Applications are accepted continuously. World Wide Web: http://www.txalliance.org.

THISTLEDEW CAMP
62741 County Road 551
Togo, Minnesota 55723

General Information Residential correctional camp for juvenile males that offers short-term program for nonserious offenders including a special education program, work experience, recreation, and a comprehensive high-adventure portion. Established in 1955. Number of employees: 57. Unit of Min-

nesota Department of Corrections, St. Paul, Minnesota. Number of internship applications received each year: 15.

Internships Available ▶ *2–6 challenge interns:* responsibilities include assisting director of high adventure challenge program including training of students on high ropes course, rock climbing, helping in supervision of a 3-day solo experience, and participating in 2- or 3-week long wilderness treks; possible modes of travel are canoeing, backpacking, or cross-country skiing. Candidates should have ability to work with others, personal interest in the field. Duration is 12 weeks. $412 per duration of internship. Open to college juniors, college seniors. ▶ *2–6 residential interns:* responsibilities include assisting professional staff with counseling and report writing, working some afternoons and evenings helping to supervise students in work and recreational activities; also includes involvement in a week-long wilderness expedition with a graduating group. Candidates should have ability to work with others, personal interest in the field. Duration is 12 weeks. $412 per duration of internship. Open to college juniors, college seniors. ▶ *2–3 school interns:* responsibilities include assisting professional staff in providing treatment and education for juvenile boys ages 13 to 17 years; can also fulfill student teaching requirements at Thistledew. Candidates should have ability to work independently, ability to work with others, oral communication skills, personal interest in the field, written communication skills. Duration is 12 weeks. $412 per duration of internship. Open to college juniors, college seniors. ▶ *1–6 therapeutic adventure interns:* responsibilities include assisting professional staff in the facilitation of rock climbing, solo, wilderness travel skills and expedition; extensive wilderness travel and rigorous physical activity required. Candidates should have ability to work independently, oral communication skills, personal interest in the field, self-motivation, strong interpersonal skills, written communication skills. Duration is minimum of 3 months. $412 per duration of internship. Open to college juniors, college seniors, graduate students. International applications accepted.

Benefits Formal training, free housing, free meals, names of contacts, on-the-job training, opportunity to attend seminars/workshops, possible full-time employment, willing to complete paperwork for educational credit, willing to provide letters of recommendation.

Contact Write, call, fax, or e-mail Christine Phillips, Personnel Officer. Phone: 218-376-4411. Fax: 218-376-4679. E-mail: cphillips@dac.thd.state.mn.us. In-person interview recommended (telephone interview accepted). Applicants must submit a formal organization application, letter of interest, resume, two personal references, Mantoux Test (TB) plus a physical exam and background check. Applications are accepted continuously. World Wide Web: http://www.thistledewcamp.com.

TRAVELERS AID
60 Walton Street, #200
Atlanta, Georgia 30303

General Information Nonprofit social service agency working with people in crisis, preventing homelessness. Established in 1900. Number of employees: 16. Unit of Travelers Aid International, Washington, District of Columbia. Number of internship applications received each year: 10.

Internships Available ▶ *1–3 development associates:* responsibilities include assisting with fund-raising and working on annual campaign. Candidates should have ability to work independently, oral communication skills, personal interest in the field, research skills, self-motivation, written communication skills. Duration is 6–12 months. Position available as unpaid or paid. Open to college freshmen, college sophomores, college juniors, college seniors, graduate students. ▶ *1–4 social work interns:* responsibilities include intake assessment, case management, crisis intervention, resource development with a variety of client populations. Candidates should have ability to work independently, oral communication skills, strong interpersonal skills, written communication skills, must be enrolled in BSW or MSW program. Duration is flexible. Unpaid. Open to college juniors, college seniors, graduate students. ▶ *1–3 volunteer coordinator associates:* responsibilities include helping to coordinate the volunteer program. Candidates should have experience in the field, oral communication skills, self-motivation,

strong interpersonal skills, written communication skills. Duration is 6–12 months. Unpaid. Open to college freshmen, college sophomores, college juniors, college seniors, recent college graduates, graduate students. International applications accepted.
Benefits Names of contacts, on-the-job training, opportunity to attend seminars/workshops, possible full-time employment, travel reimbursement, willing to act as a professional reference, willing to complete paperwork for educational credit, willing to provide letters of recommendation.
Contact Call, fax, or e-mail Kay Bernier, Associate Director, 60 Walton Street, #200, Atlanta, Georgia 30303. Phone: 404-817-7070 Ext. 14. Fax: 404-817-9922. E-mail: kaybernier@hotmail.com. Applicants must submit a resume, two writing samples, 3 personal references or letters of recommendation, in-person or telephone interview. Application deadline: May 1 for summer, November 1 for January.

UCSF AIDS HEALTH PROJECT
Box 0884
San Francisco, California 94143-0884

General Information HIV education, prevention, and counseling organization. Established in 1984. Number of employees: 90. Unit of University of California, San Francisco, San Francisco, California. Number of internship applications received each year: 80.
Internships Available ▶ *1 AHP Services Center operations intern:* responsibilities include assisting with production and dissemination of forms, flyers, notices, and manuals; assisting with data compilation for monthly statistical reports. Candidates should have ability to work with others, computer skills, office skills. Duration is one year beginning in July. Unpaid. Open to college graduates with interest in health professions, social services, or nonprofit management. ▶ *3 HIV counseling and testing program interns:* responsibilities include fielding calls from individuals needing appointments or basic information; meeting clients at AHP test sites throughout San Francisco; recording client data in database (training provided). Candidates should have computer skills, strong interpersonal skills, ability to do accurate data entry. Duration is one year beginning in July. Unpaid. Open to recent college graduates, graduate students, law students, career changers, individuals reentering the workforce, college graduates with interest in health professions, social services, or nonprofit management. ▶ *1 Risk Evaluation and Counseling for Health (REACH) intern:* responsibilities include assisting in all daily activities of unit; assisting in design of publicity for specialized workshops, forums, and other community events and production of brochures, newsletters, and other public relations materials. Candidates should have computer skills, strong interpersonal skills. Duration is one year beginning in July. Unpaid. Open to college graduates with interest in health professions, social services, or nonprofit management. ▶ *1 psychological support services intern:* responsibilities include assisting with daily administrative tasks; assuring that clinical staff receive needed support; training provided. Candidates should have computer skills, strong interpersonal skills. Duration is one year beginning in July. Unpaid. Open to college graduates with interest in health professions, social services, or nonprofit management. ▶ *1 publications program intern:* responsibilities include serving as staff level research assistant and writer for FOCUS and PERSPECTIVES; works with other agency staff on special research, writing, and editorial projects as needed. Candidates should have computer skills, strong interpersonal skills, written communication skills. Duration is one year beginning in July. Unpaid. Open to college graduates with interest in health professions, social services, or related management. ▶ *1 research program interns:* responsibilities include assisting in writing, editing, and proofreading grant proposals; assisting in recruiting research subjects and attending monthly meetings with researchers; assisting with entering, cleaning, and coding research project data, and generating reports. Candidates should have computer skills, strong interpersonal skills. Duration is one year beginning in July. Unpaid. Open to college graduates with interest in health professions, social services, or nonprofit management. ▶ *1 training program intern:* responsibilities include researching current information regarding HIV-related statistics, psychological and legal issues, and medication updates;

assisting administrators in preparation for trainings; delivering training modules under guidance of program's trainees. Candidates should have computer skills, strong interpersonal skills. Duration is one year beginning in July. Unpaid. Open to college graduates with interest in health professions, social services, or nonprofit management. International applications accepted.
Benefits On-the-job training, opportunity to attend seminars/workshops, willing to act as a professional reference, willing to complete paperwork for educational credit, willing to provide letters of recommendation, $800 monthly housing stipend.
Contact Write, call, fax, e-mail, or through World Wide Web site Carol Music, Staffing Coordinator. Phone: 415-476-3890. Fax: 415-476-3613. E-mail: cmusic@itsa.ucsf.edu. Telephone interview required. Applicants must submit a formal organization application, resume, 2 writing samples (publications position). Application deadline: March 31. World Wide Web: http://www.ucsf-ahp.org.

UNITED WAY OF WACO
PO Box 2027
Waco, Texas 76703

General Information Clearinghouse for pledges that are allocated to member agencies. Established in 1923. Number of employees: 1. Number of internship applications received each year: 4.
Internships Available ▶ *1 intern:* responsibilities include recordkeeping, sending out press notices, and assisting in the placing of volunteers in member agencies. Candidates should have computer skills (helpful). Duration is flexible. Unpaid. Open to high school students, recent high school graduates, college freshmen, college sophomores, college juniors, college seniors, recent college graduates, graduate students, law students, career changers, individuals reentering the workforce. International applications accepted.
Benefits Names of contacts, possible full-time employment, willing to complete paperwork for educational credit, willing to provide letters of recommendation.
Contact Write, call, or fax Dorothy Wienecke, Communication Coordinator/Volunteer Center Director. Phone: 254-752-2753. Fax: 254-752-2769. In-person interview recommended (telephone interview accepted). Applicants must submit a resume. Applications are accepted continuously.

UNIVERSITY FOR THE STUDY OF HUMAN GOODNESS/HUMAN SERVICE ALLIANCE
3983 Old Greensboro Road
Winston-Salem, North Carolina 27101

General Information Organization whose mission is to expand others' capacity to serve. Established in 1987. Number of internship applications received each year: 100.
Internships Available ▶ *10–30 service learning interns:* responsibilities include working in various areas including nonprofit management; restaurant management/marketing; video production; volunteer management; and public speaking. Candidates should have ability to work independently, ability to work with others, oral communication skills, self-motivation, strong leadership ability, written communication skills. Duration is January-December or July-June; co-ops and summer internships also available. Unpaid. Open to recent high school graduates, college freshmen, college sophomores, college juniors, college seniors, recent college graduates, graduate students, law students, career changers, individuals reentering the workforce, retirees. International applications accepted.
Benefits Free housing, free meals, job counseling, on-the-job training, opportunity to attend seminars/workshops, willing to act as a professional reference, willing to provide letters of recommendation, free tuition for program.
Contact Write, call, fax, e-mail, or through World Wide Web site Joanna White, Dean of Admissions. Phone: 336-761-8745. Fax: 336-722-7882. E-mail: jwhite@ufhg.org. In-person interview recommended. Applicants must submit a formal organization application, three personal references, questionnaire, full-length

photo. Application deadline: June 1 for mid-July entry, December 1 for January entry. World Wide Web: http://www.ufhg.org.

UPPER BUCKS YMCA
151 South 14th Street
Quakertown, Pennsylvania 18951

General Information   Social service organization that provides programs in health, fitness, aquatics, and child care. Established in 1969. Number of employees: 100. Number of internship applications received each year: 1.
Internships Available   ▶ *1 camp counselor:* responsibilities include planning activities and ensuring safety and welfare of campers ages 5-12. Candidates should have oral communication skills, strong interpersonal skills, written communication skills, declared major in education or human services. Duration is 3½ months. $6–$7 per hour. ▶ *2 child-care interns:* responsibilities include working in a team-teaching situation and caring for the safety of the children. Candidates should have college courses in field, oral communication skills, plan to pursue career in field, strong interpersonal skills, strong leadership ability, background in early childhood, human services, or education. Duration is 3 months. $6 per hour. ▶ *1 physical instructor:* responsibilities include setting up weight training and fitness programs, supervising workout programs, and coaching children in sports. Candidates should have ability to work independently, ability to work with others, knowledge of field, oral communication skills, personal interest in the field. Duration is flexible. Unpaid. Open to college freshmen, college sophomores, college juniors, college seniors, recent college graduates, graduate students, law students, career changers, individuals reentering the workforce. International applications accepted.
Benefits Names of contacts, opportunity to attend seminars/workshops, possible full-time employment, travel reimbursement, willing to complete paperwork for educational credit, willing to provide letters of recommendation, CPR and first aid training, YMCA membership.
Contact Write, call, or fax Pat Hess, Child Care Director. Phone: 215-536-8409. Fax: 215-538-2943. In-person interview required. Application deadline: May 1 for summer, August 1 for fall, December 1 for winter. Fees: $20.

U.S. COMMITTEE FOR REFUGEES
1717 Massachusetts Avenue, NW, Suite 200
Washington, District of Columbia 20036

General Information Sister agency of Immigration and Refugee Services of America, working primarily to insure that the protection and assistance needs of refugees and internally displaced persons overseas are met.
Internships Available ▶ *1 communication intern:* responsibilities include assisting communications officer in forging links with print, radio, and television media; assisting media database management; tracking organization in the news; answering inquiries about organization. Candidates should have editing skills, knowledge of field, oral communication skills, personal interest in the field, writing skills. Duration is 12 weeks minimum. $75–$100 monthly stipend . Open to college juniors, college seniors, recent college graduates, graduate students, career changers. ▶ *1 fund-raising/development intern:* responsibilities include researching potential funding sources, assisting direct mailing campaigns, tracking IRSA organization in the news, answering inquiries about IRSA work, attending meetings on behalf of development staff, working with donor management database. Candidates should have ability to work independently, computer skills, personal interest in the field, writing skills, enthusiasm, positive attitude. Duration is 12 week minimum. $75–$100 monthly stipend. Open to college freshmen, college sophomores, college juniors, college seniors, recent college graduates, graduate students, career changers. ▶ *1 government liaison intern:* responsibilities include drafting correspondence and making calls related to advocacy efforts; providing written summaries of bills and regulations; drafting informational memos and action alerts to partner agencies; attending congressional hearings, mark-ups, and briefings; researching legal issues on migra-

tion; arranging meetings with congressional staff; providing clerical support. Candidates should have knowledge of field, personal interest in the field, research skills, writing skills, ability to work well under pressure, graduate-level course work in law (preferred). Duration is 12 weeks minimum. $75–$100 monthly stipend. Open to college seniors, recent college graduates, graduate students, law students. ▶ *6 research interns:* responsibilities include researching current refugee situations for newsletter articles, reports. and annual survey; areas of research are: Africa, Latin America, Asia, North America, Europe, the former Soviet Union, and the Middle East; other responsibilities include attending meetings of relevance to region, responding to public inquiries, and some clerical support. Candidates should have ability to work independently, computer skills, editing skills, research skills, writing skills. Duration is 12 weeks minimum. $75–$100 monthly stipend. Open to college juniors, college seniors, recent college graduates, graduate students, career changers.
Benefits On-the-job training, willing to act as a professional reference, willing to complete paperwork for educational credit, willing to provide letters of recommendation.
Contact Write, fax, or e-mail Marisa Olivo, Program Assistant. Fax: 202-347-3418. E-mail: molivo@irsa-uscr.org. Applicants must submit a letter of interest, resume, writing sample of 3-5 pages; 2 references (names and contact information only). Application deadline: April 15 for summer, August 1 for fall, December 10 for spring. World Wide Web: http://www.refugees.org.

VALLEY YOUTH HOUSE
520 Walnut Street
Allentown, Pennsylvania 18101

General Information Youth house that provides preventative and responsive services for troubled young people and families; offers emergency shelter, long-term care, counseling, guidance, information, preparation for adulthood, and referral. Established in 1973. Number of employees: 186. Number of internship applications received each year: 40.
Internships Available ▶ *3 administration interns:* responsibilities include performing program audits, assisting in the planning and execution of the Project Child Conference (community conference on child abuse), coordinating community resources, completing agency research, and assisting in agency grant writing. Candidates should have declared college major in field, oral communication skills, organizational skills, self-motivation, strong interpersonal skills, written communication skills. Duration is 1–2 semesters. Unpaid. Open to college seniors, graduate students. ▶ *8–10 bachelor's-level clinical counseling interns:* responsibilities include becoming familiar with the policies, practices, and protocols of the agency; conducting entry and intake interviews with clients; providing individual counseling; participating in family counseling as an observer; providing ongoing behavior management and client supervision; accompanying clients to appointments and activities; providing direct in-person client services; providing all appropriate and required timely documentation; performing case management; and participating in weekly undergraduate intern group supervision. Candidates should have declared college major in field, oral communication skills, self-motivation, strong interpersonal skills, written communication skills. Duration is 1–2 semesters. Unpaid. Open to college juniors, college seniors. ▶ *10–15 master's-level clinical counseling interns:* responsibilities include performing direct, in-person client service; successfully engaging and maintaining clients through the treatment process; completing adolescent and parent intake interviews and their subsequent dictation; providing individual, parent, family, and group counseling services within the context of office-based or outreach services according to treatment plans; providing ongoing case coordination; assessing and collecting client fees; completing necessary documentation; participating in weekly supervision and biweekly group supervision. Candidates should have ability to work independently, declared college major in field, oral communication skills, self-motivation, strong interpersonal skills, written communication skills. Duration is 2 semesters. Unpaid. Open to graduate students. International applications accepted.

Benefits Names of contacts, opportunity to attend seminars/workshops, possible full-time employment, travel reimbursement, willing to act as a professional reference, willing to complete paperwork for educational credit, willing to provide letters of recommendation.
Contact Write, call, or fax Marcella Kraybill, Internship Coordinator. Phone: 610-432-6481. Fax: 610-432-6648. In-person interview required. Applicants must submit a formal organization application, resume. Application deadline: April 30 for summer, July 30 for fall (until slots are filled).

VILLAGE ATLANTA (ATLANTA UNION MISSION)
3965 Roosevelt Highway
College Park, Georgia 30349

General Information Christian rehabilitation program for homeless women and their children, providing each family with their own 2-room efficiency apartment during their 6-month stay, a 4-phase therapeutic program to help mothers move towards self-sufficiency and independent living, and a therapeutic child development center. Established in 1938. Number of employees: 20. Unit of Atlanta Union Mission, Atlanta, Georgia. Number of internship applications received each year: 10.
Internships Available ▶ *1–3 child-care providers:* responsibilities include supervising and caring for children in child development center (nursery, preschool, or after school), preparing developmentally appropriate lessons and teaching art and educational activities, and acting as a role model by demonstrating positive interactions and social behavior. Candidates should have ability to work with others, experience in the field, oral communication skills, organizational skills, personal interest in the field, strong leadership ability. Duration is 3–12 months. Unpaid. Open to high school seniors, recent high school graduates, college freshmen, college sophomores, college juniors, college seniors, recent college graduates, graduate students, career changers, individuals reentering the workforce. ▶ *1–3 counseling/social work interns:* responsibilities include providing therapeutic activities that promote the welfare of the clients and/or their children such as recordkeeping, case management, intake, group, individual therapy, and educational classes. Candidates should have college courses in field, knowledge of field, oral communication skills, strong interpersonal skills, strong leadership ability, written communication skills. Duration is 6–12 months. Unpaid. Open to college seniors, recent college graduates, graduate students, career changers, individuals reentering the workforce. International applications accepted.
Benefits Free housing, free meals, names of contacts, on-the-job training, opportunity to attend seminars/workshops, possible full-time employment, willing to act as a professional reference, willing to complete paperwork for educational credit, willing to provide letters of recommendation.
Contact Write, call, fax, e-mail, or through World Wide Web site Terry Freeman, Program Director. Phone: 404-669-0138. Fax: 404-762-0240. E-mail: terry.freeman@myaum.org. In-person interview recommended (telephone interview accepted). Applicants must submit a resume. Applications are accepted continuously. World Wide Web: http://www.aumcares.org.

VINCENTIAN SERVICE CORPS–CENTRAL
7800 Natural Bridge
St. Louis, Missouri 63121

General Information Faith-based volunteer program for lay women and men who want to work with those at an economic disadvantage while living in a community with other members and experiencing a simple lifestyle. Established in 1984. Number of employees: 2. Affiliate of Vincentian Service Corps, New York, New York. Number of internship applications received each year: 12.
Internships Available ▶ *4 child-care workers (infant to kindergarten):* responsibilities include developing relationships with the children and their parents; assisting in planning and executing the daily activities designed for emotional, social, educational, and physical development of assigned children. Candidates should have ability to work with others, knowledge of field, oral communication skills, personal interest in the field, self-motivation. Duration

is 1 year (full-time). $100 monthly stipend. Open to college seniors, recent college graduates, career changers, individuals reentering the workforce, individuals interested in young children. ▶ *1–2 high school instructors:* responsibilities include teaching 5 periods a day, preparing for assemblies, group sessions, guiding students, and completing paper work for class. Candidates should have ability to work independently, analytical skills, experience in the field, oral communication skills, organizational skills, self-motivation, strong interpersonal skills, strong leadership ability, writing skills. Duration is 1–2 years. $100 monthly stipend. Open to recent college graduates, graduate students. ▶ *1–2 outreach ministry for inner city children interns:* responsibilities include tutoring, coaching sports/recreational activities, summer camp, and teaching. Candidates should have oral communication skills, organizational skills, self-motivation, strong interpersonal skills, strong leadership ability. Duration is 1–2 years. $100 monthly stipend. Open to recent college graduates. ▶ *1 shelter assistant:* responsibilities include assisting women in moving from an abusive situation and attaining job and parenting skills; helping them learn how to handle conflict and live in positive relationships. Candidates should have knowledge of field, oral communication skills, personal interest in the field, strong interpersonal skills, strong leadership ability. Duration is August to August. $100 monthly stipend. Open to recent college graduates, graduate students, law students, career changers. ▶ *6–12 skills trainers:* responsibilities include training and direct care for clients regarding everyday activities, plus helping to maintain the daily household operations; helping clients build social skills. Candidates should have ability to work with others, oral communication skills, personal interest in the field, self-motivation. Duration is 1 year (full-time). $100 monthly stipend. Open to college seniors, recent college graduates, graduate students, law students, career changers, individuals reentering the workforce, anyone able to work with handicapped people. ▶ *10–20 volunteers:* responsibilities include working with parishes, schools, clinics, and social service agencies in urban areas. Candidates should have ability to work with others, oral communication skills, self-motivation, written communication skills, desire to experience community. Duration is 1 year. $100 monthly stipend. Open to college seniors, recent college graduates, graduate students, career changers.
Benefits Free housing, health insurance, opportunity to attend seminars/workshops, possible full-time employment, travel reimbursement, tuition assistance, willing to complete paperwork for educational credit.
Contact Write, call, fax, e-mail, or through World Wide Web site Sr. Mary Catherine Dunn, D.C., Director. Phone: 314-382-2800 Ext. 291. Fax: 314-382-8392. E-mail: vsccentral@juno.com. Telephone interview required. Applicants must submit a formal organization application, academic transcripts, 5 personal references. Application deadline: May 31 for fall. World Wide Web: http://www.vscorps.org.

VISITING NEIGHBORS, INC.
611 Broadway, 5th Floor, Suite 510
New York, New York 10012

General Information Organization that fosters independence for senior citizens living in their homes through neighbor assistance and an escort and shopping program. Established in 1972. Number of employees: 11. Number of internship applications received each year: 6.
Internships Available ▶ *1–6 psychology interns:* responsibilities include working with professional staff on small caseload while providing mental stimulation, encouragement, and physical independence to people over 60. Candidates should have analytical skills, oral communication skills, personal interest in the field, strong interpersonal skills, written communication skills. Duration is 6–12 months. Unpaid. Open to college sophomores, college juniors, college seniors, recent college graduates, graduate students, career changers, individuals reentering the workforce. ▶ *1–6 public relations and communications interns:* responsibilities include working on newsletter and putting together press kit. Candidates should have ability to work independently, oral communication skills, self-motivation, strong interpersonal skills, writing skills. Duration is flexible. Unpaid. Open to college sophomores,

Visiting Neighbors, Inc. (continued)

college juniors, college seniors, recent college graduates, graduate students, career changers, individuals reentering the workforce. ▶ *1–6 social work interns:* responsibilities include working in office, in field with clients, and managing a caseload in size corresponding to intern's level of experience and maturity. Candidates should have ability to work independently, oral communication skills, personal interest in the field, self-motivation, strong interpersonal skills, writing skills, communication skills. Duration is flexible. Unpaid. Open to high school students, recent high school graduates, college freshmen, college sophomores, college juniors, college seniors, recent college graduates, graduate students, law students, career changers, individuals reentering the workforce. International applications accepted.

Benefits On-the-job training, willing to act as a professional reference, willing to complete paperwork for educational credit, willing to provide letters of recommendation.

Contact Write, call, or fax Ms. Cynthia Maurer, Executive Director. Phone: 212-260-6200. Fax: 212-260-2962. In-person interview required. Applicants must submit a formal organization application, letter of interest, 2 personal references and/or letters of recommendation. Applications are accepted continuously.

VOLUNTEERS OF AMERICA
1660 Duke Street
Alexandria, Virginia 22314

General Information National, nonprofit, spiritually-based organization providing comprehensive human services and affordable housing for families, the elderly, and people with disabilities. Established in 1896. Number of internship applications received each year: 25.

Internships Available ▶ *1–3 international services interns:* responsibilities include program development, research, grant writing, representation at international agency briefings. Candidates should have ability to work independently, analytical skills, knowledge of field, research skills, written communication skills. Duration is flexible. Unpaid. Open to college seniors, recent college graduates, graduate students, individuals reentering the workforce, exchange students. ▶ *1–3 public policy interns:* responsibilities include attending hearings on Capitol Hill, attending coalition meetings, contributing articles to monthly newsletter, and a variety of other tasks. Candidates should have ability to work with others, analytical skills, knowledge of field, research skills, self-motivation, written communication skills. Duration is flexible. Unpaid. Open to college juniors, college seniors, recent college graduates, graduate students, law students. International applications accepted.

Benefits Travel reimbursement, willing to complete paperwork for educational credit.

Contact Write, call, or e-mail Christine Fall, Public Policy Assistant. Phone: 703-341-5000. Fax: 703-341-7000. E-mail: cfall@voa.org. Telephone interview required. Applicants must submit a resume, writing sample. Applications are accepted continuously. World Wide Web: http://www.volunteersofamerica.org.

WASHINGTON COMMUNITY YMCA/YWCA
121 East Main Street
Washington, Iowa 52353

General Information Organization that provides health, recreation, and social programs including full-service child care. Established in 1925. Number of employees: 50.

Internships Available ▶ *1 child caregiver:* responsibilities include providing child care. Duration is flexible. Unpaid. ▶ *1 health/fitness intern:* responsibilities include working with individuals and groups on health and wellness. Duration is 6–12 weeks. Position available as unpaid or paid. ▶ *2 summer camp/school age child-care interns.* Duration is one summer. Paid. ▶ *1–2 youth physical programs interns:* responsibilities include setting up, administering, and implementing youth sports for kindergarten through sixth grades. Duration is 6–12 weeks. Unpaid. Candidates for all positions should have oral communication skills, creativity. Open to college freshmen, college sophomores, college juniors, college seniors. International applications accepted.

Benefits Possible full-time employment, willing to complete paperwork for educational credit, willing to provide letters of recommendation.

Contact Write, call, or fax Chris Detrick, Executive Director. Phone: 319-653-2141. Fax: 319-653-2142. In-person interview required. Applicants must submit a formal organization application, letter of interest, resume, three letters of recommendation. Application deadline: 4-6 weeks prior to start of internship.

WASHINGTON COUNTY YOUTH SERVICES BUREAU
38 Elm Street, PO Box 627
Montpelier, Vermont 05601

General Information Alcohol/drug abuse outpatient treatment program for youth; provides individual/family counseling programs. Established in 1970. Number of employees: 50. Number of internship applications received each year: 4.

Internships Available ▶ *1–3 after-school programs counselors:* responsibilities include helping to facilitate group activities for adolescents. Candidates should have knowledge of field, oral communication skills, self-motivation, strong interpersonal skills, an interest in working with youth. Duration is 10–12 months. Unpaid. Open to college juniors, college seniors, recent college graduates, graduate students, individuals reentering the workforce. ▶ *1 drug counselor:* responsibilities include counseling individuals and families where drug use/abuse is an issue. Candidates should have ability to work independently, ability to work with others, college courses in field, knowledge of field, oral communication skills, organizational skills, self-motivation, an interest in working with youth. Duration is 10 to 12 months (20 hours a week). Unpaid. Open to college seniors, recent college graduates, graduate students, career changers. ▶ *1–2 individual/family counselors:* responsibilities include working with the family counselor and youth on a variety of issues. Candidates should have college courses in field, knowledge of field, oral communication skills, self-motivation, strong interpersonal skills, an interest in working with youth. Duration is 10 to 12 months (20 hours a week). Unpaid. Open to recent college graduates, graduate students, individuals reentering the workforce. International applications accepted.

Benefits Formal training, on-the-job training, opportunity to attend seminars/workshops, possible full-time employment, travel reimbursement, willing to act as a professional reference, willing to complete paperwork for educational credit, willing to provide letters of recommendation.

Contact Write, call, or fax Dawn Poitras, Clinical Director. Phone: 802-229-9151. Fax: 802-229-2508. In-person interview required. Applicants must submit a letter of interest, resume, three letters of recommendation. Applications are accepted continuously.

WATERVILLE AREA BOYS AND GIRLS CLUB
126 North Street
Waterville, Maine 04901

General Information Nonprofit youth agency that provides social, educational, and recreational activities to persons ages 6–20. Established in 1924. Number of employees: 90. Number of internship applications received each year: 5.

Internships Available ▶ *1–3 Teen Center counselors:* responsibilities include individual and group programming with at-risk teens. Candidates should have oral communication skills, personal interest in the field, strong interpersonal skills, strong leadership ability. Duration is September 1 to June 30. Unpaid. Open to high school students, recent high school graduates, college freshmen, college sophomores, college juniors, college seniors, recent college graduates, graduate students, career changers, individuals reentering the workforce. ▶ *1 aquatics director assistant:* responsibilities include teaching swimming, coaching swim team, and maintaining indoor pools. Candidates should have ability to work independently, personal interest in the field, strong interpersonal skills, strong leadership ability, writing skills. Duration is September 1 to June 30. Unpaid. Open to recent high school graduates, college freshmen, college sophomores, college juniors, college seniors, recent college graduates, career changers, individuals reentering the workforce. ▶ *1 arts and crafts instructor:* responsibilities include teaching an art curriculum. Candidates should have knowledge of field, oral communication skills, personal interest in the field, strong interpersonal skills, strong leadership ability. Duration is September 1 to June 30. Unpaid. Open to high school students, recent high school graduates, college freshmen, college sophomores, college juniors, college seniors, recent college graduates, graduate students, career changers, individuals reentering the workforce. ▶ *1 assistant athletic director:* responsibilities include organizing athletic games, activities, and teams. Candidates should have college courses in field, knowledge of field, personal interest in the field, strong interpersonal skills. Duration is 12 months. Unpaid. Open to recent high school graduates, college freshmen, college sophomores, college juniors, college seniors, recent college graduates, career changers, individuals reentering the workforce. ▶ *1 sports management intern:* responsibilities include assisting the assistant executive director. Candidates should have ability to work independently, oral communication skills, self-motivation, strong interpersonal skills, written communication skills. Duration is September 1 to June 30. Unpaid. Open to recent high school graduates, college freshmen, college sophomores, college juniors, college seniors, recent college graduates, career changers, individuals reentering the workforce. International applications accepted.

Benefits Formal training, job counseling, names of contacts, on-the-job training, opportunity to attend seminars/workshops, possible full-time employment, willing to complete paperwork for educational credit, willing to provide letters of recommendation.

Contact Write, call, fax, or e-mail Vaughn Clark, Volunteer Coordinator. Phone: 207-873-0684. Fax: 207-861-8016. E-mail: ymca@mint.net. In-person interview recommended (telephone interview accepted). Applicants must submit a letter of interest, resume, academic transcripts, three personal references. Application deadline: January 1 for spring, April 1 for summer, July 1 for fall, November 1 for winter. World Wide Web: http://www. aplaceforkidstogo.com.

WAYNESBORO YMCA
810 East Main Street
Waynesboro, Pennsylvania 17268

General Information Worldwide fellowship united by a common loyalty to Jesus Christ for the purpose of building Christian personality and a Christian society. Established in 1915. Number of employees: 50. Number of internship applications received each year: 1.

Internships Available ▶ *1–3 assistant aquatic supervisors:* responsibilities include teaching programs for 6-36 month olds, 3-5 year olds, 6-12 year olds; teaching water exercise for adults and seniors, conducting arthritis water program, performing administrative duties, supervising housekeeping of pool area, maintaining records of swimming lesson participants, and keeping monthly statistical summaries. Candidates should have ability to work independently, knowledge of field, personal interest in the field, self-motivation, strong interpersonal skills, certification in CPR, first aid, and lifeguard. Duration is 3–12 months. Position available as unpaid or at $5.75–$6.50 per hour. Open to college freshmen, college sophomores, college juniors, college seniors, recent college graduates, graduate students, career changers, individuals reentering the workforce. ▶ *1–3 day camp counselors:* responsibilities include directing small group of youth ages 6-12; organizing and implementing daily activities and special events. Candidates should have ability to work with others, organizational skills, personal interest in the field, strong leadership ability, CPR and first aid training (provided). Duration is June to August. Position available as unpaid or at $5.65–$6 per hour. Open to high school seniors, recent high school graduates, college freshmen, college sophomores, college juniors, college seniors, recent college graduates, graduate students. ▶ *1–2 fitness consultants:* responsibilities include assessing members' fitness status and needs and designing an exercise program to meet those needs; cleaning equipment; and overseeing fitness center. Candidates should have ability to work independently, analytical skills, oral communication skills, personal interest in the field, self-motivation, strong interpersonal skills. Duration is flexible. Unpaid. Open to college freshmen, college sophomores, college juniors, college seniors, recent college graduates, graduate students, individuals reentering the workforce.

▶ *1–2 group supervisors:* responsibilities include overseeing and assisting in the operation of an after-school program for school-age children. Candidates should have ability to work independently, experience in the field, oral communication skills, plan to pursue career in field, strong interpersonal skills, interest in aiding children socially and emotionally. Duration is 9 months. Position available as unpaid or at $5.65–$5.85 per hour. Open to high school seniors, recent high school graduates, college freshmen, college sophomores, college juniors, college seniors, recent college graduates, individuals reentering the workforce. ▶ *1 sport coordinator:* responsibilities include organizing, planning and implementing sport leagues and camps in the summer; responsible for adult and youth sport programs. Candidates should have knowledge of field, oral communication skills, organizational skills, self-motivation, strong leadership ability. Duration is May to August. Unpaid. Open to college juniors, college seniors, recent college graduates, graduate students. ▶ *1–2 summer playground supervisors:* responsibilities include organizing, planning, and implementing daily activities for youth 5 years to 6th grade (held off-site at several community sites); responsible for children during their scheduled time. Candidates should have oral communication skills, organizational skills, personal interest in the field, self-motivation, strong interpersonal skills. Duration is early June to early August (8 weeks). Position available as unpaid or at $5.65–$7.50 per hour. Open to high school seniors, recent high school graduates, college freshmen, college sophomores, college juniors, college seniors, recent college graduates. International applications accepted.

Benefits Names of contacts, on-the-job training, opportunity to attend seminars/workshops, possible full-time employment, travel reimbursement, willing to complete paperwork for educational credit, willing to provide letters of recommendation.

Contact Write, call, or fax H. Alan Smith, Senior Program Director. Phone: 717-762-6012. Fax: 717-762-4368. In-person interview required. Applicants must submit a letter of interest, resume, three personal references. Application deadline: April 1 for summer, October 1 for winter. World Wide Web: http://www.WboY.org.

WEDIKO CHILDREN'S SERVICES
266 Beacon Street
Boston, Massachusetts 02116

General Information Organization that operates a 45-day summer Residential Treatment Program for emotionally disturbed children in southern New Hampshire; located on a 450-acre camp-like setting. Established in 1934. Number of employees: 10. Division of Wediko Children's Services, Boston, Massachusetts. Number of internship applications received each year: 300.

Internships Available ▶ *70–100 activity assistants:* responsibilities include working in a residential psycho-educational treatment program serving children and adolescents (ages 7-18) with serious emotional and behavioral disabilities. Candidates should have organizational skills, self-motivation, strong interpersonal skills, strong leadership ability, strong desire to work with special needs children. Duration is late June to late August. $1100–$1700 per duration of internship. ▶ *70–100 direct-care staff:* responsibilities include working as part of a team of 6-8 adults; each team is responsible for a group of 8-10 children/adolescents. Candidates should have oral communication skills, self-motivation, strong interpersonal skills, strong leadership ability, strong desire to work with special needs children. Duration is late June to late August. $1100–$1700 per duration of internship. ▶ *70–100 direct-care/ teaching assistants:* responsibilities include planning and implementing active, learner-centered language arts, math and science curricula. Candidates should have oral communication skills, self-motivation, strong interpersonal skills, strong leadership ability, written communication skills. Duration is late June to late August. $1100–$1700 per duration of internship. Open to college sophomores, college juniors, college seniors, recent college graduates, graduate students, law students, career changers. International applications accepted.

Benefits Formal training, free housing, free meals, job counseling, on-the-job training, opportunity to attend seminars/workshops,

Wediko Children's Services (continued)
possible full-time employment, willing to act as a professional reference, willing to provide letters of recommendation, AmeriCorps education award ($1150).
Contact Write, call, or e-mail Sarah K. Lotchin, Manager, NH Summer Program, 266 Beacon Street, Boston, Massachusetts 02116. Phone: 617-536-2747. Fax: 617-536-9489. E-mail: slotchin@wediko.org. In-person interview recommended (telephone interview accepted). Applicants must submit a formal organization application, letter of recommendation. Applications are accepted continuously. World Wide Web: http://www.wediko.org.

WITTENBRAKER YMCA
1201 Church Street
New Castle, Indiana 47362

General Information Community service center offering all types of activities, educational services, and community events. Established in 1924. Number of employees: 100. Branch of YMCA of the USA, Chicago, Illinois. Number of internship applications received each year: 10.
Internships Available ▶ *1–5 aquatics staff interns:* responsibilities include pool maintenance, swim lesson instruction, lifeguarding, water aerobics instruction, special event planning, and working with youth. Candidates should have ability to work independently, ability to work with others, knowledge of field, oral communication skills, self-motivation. Position available as unpaid or paid. Open to college sophomores, college juniors, college seniors, recent college graduates, graduate students. ▶ *1–5 fitness staff interns:* responsibilities include fitness assessments, personal training, developing workout programs, helping with special events, and working with youth. Candidates should have ability to work independently, knowledge of field, oral communication skills, self-motivation, strong interpersonal skills, written communication skills. Position available as unpaid or paid. Open to college freshmen, college sophomores, college juniors, college seniors, recent college graduates, graduate students. ▶ *1–5 sports programs interns:* responsibilities include working with adults and youth; developing sports programs, supervising and organizing programs for YMCA sports director. Candidates should have ability to work independently, ability to work with others, computer skills, knowledge of field, oral communication skills, organizational skills, self-motivation, writing skills. Position available as unpaid or paid. Open to college freshmen, college sophomores, college juniors, college seniors, recent college graduates, graduate students. International applications accepted.
Benefits Formal training, job counseling, names of contacts, on-the-job training, opportunity to attend seminars/workshops, possible full-time employment, willing to act as a professional reference, willing to complete paperwork for educational credit, willing to provide letters of recommendation.
Contact Write Chris Williams, Executive Director. Phone: 765-529-3804. Fax: 765-529-4575. In-person interview recommended (telephone interview accepted). Applicants must submit a letter of interest, resume, three personal references. Applications are accepted continuously.

WOMEN IN COMMUNITY SERVICE
1111 3rd Avenue, Room 800
Seattle, Washington 98101

General Information Organization that strives to reduce poverty by promoting self-reliance. Established in 1964. Number of employees: 4. Unit of Women in Community Service, Alexandria, Virginia. Number of internship applications received each year: 20.
Internships Available ▶ *2–4 student interns:* responsibilities include guiding former Job Corps students (ages 16-24) in making life transitions. Candidates should have ability to work independently, computer skills, oral communication skills, organizational skills, self-motivation, written communication skills. Duration is 2–6 months. Unpaid. Open to recent high school graduates, college freshmen, college sophomores, college juniors, college seniors,

recent college graduates, graduate students, career changers, individuals reentering the workforce. International applications accepted.
Benefits On-the-job training, opportunity to attend seminars/workshops, willing to act as a professional reference, willing to complete paperwork for educational credit, willing to provide letters of recommendation.
Contact Write, call, fax, e-mail, or through World Wide Web site Hope O'Brien, Specialist, Volunteer Support, 1111 3rd Avenue, Room 800, Seattle, Washington 98101. Phone: 206-553-2082. Fax: 206-553-6151. E-mail: wicsregx@aol.com. In-person interview recommended (telephone interview accepted). Applicants must submit a formal organization application, two personal references. Applications are accepted continuously. World Wide Web: http://www.wics.org.

THE WOMEN'S CENTER
133 Park Street, NE
Vienna, Virginia 22180

General Information Private nonprofit group of professionals offering individual counseling and psychotherapy, career counseling, separation and divorce services, support and therapy groups, legal and financial education, workshops, and educational programs. Established in 1974. Number of employees: 95. Number of internship applications received each year: 20.
Internships Available ▶ *1–2 career services interns:* responsibilities include helping to implement career programs, researching, and assisting with the annual conference and the mentoring program. Candidates should have ability to work independently, ability to work with others, office skills, oral communication skills, organizational skills, written communication skills. Duration is 3–6 months. Unpaid. Open to college freshmen, college sophomores, college juniors, college seniors, recent college graduates, graduate students, career changers. ▶ *2 development interns:* responsibilities include assisting with fund-raising and proposal writing, foundation research, and corporate solicitation. Candidates should have ability to work with others, oral communication skills, personal interest in the field, written communication skills. Duration is 3–6 months. Unpaid. Open to college freshmen, college sophomores, college juniors, college seniors, recent college graduates, graduate students, career changers. ▶ *3–6 information/intake interns:* responsibilities include assisting callers by providing information and referrals to meet needs, making counseling appointments, and researching community resources. Candidates should have ability to work independently, oral communication skills, strong interpersonal skills, interest in psychology, social work, and/or women's studies. Duration is 3–12 months. Unpaid. Open to college juniors, college seniors, recent college graduates, graduate students, career changers. ▶ *3 public relations interns:* responsibilities include assisting with developing and implementing marketing strategies, publicity, and media contacts for special events; performing research; making press calls; promoting programs; and participating in program planning. Candidates should have ability to work with others, oral communication skills, personal interest in the field, written communication skills. Duration is flexible. Unpaid. Open to college freshmen, college sophomores, college juniors, college seniors, recent college graduates, graduate students, career changers. ▶ *14 therapy/clinical interns:* responsibilities include individual and group therapy and assisting with workshop presentation. Some interns also provide counseling. Duration is 8 months. Unpaid. Open to individuals completing master's degree in social work or professional counseling or a doctorate degree in psychology. International applications accepted.
Benefits On-the-job training, opportunity to attend seminars/workshops, willing to act as a professional reference, willing to complete paperwork for educational credit, willing to provide letters of recommendation.
Contact Write, call, fax, or e-mail Ms. Gale Gearhart, Director of Administration. Phone: 703-281-4928 Ext. 244. Fax: 703-242-1454. E-mail: ggearhart@thewomenscenter.org. In-person interview recommended (telephone interview accepted). Applicants must submit a letter of interest, resume. Applications are accepted continuously. World Wide Web: http://www.thewomenscenter.org.

YAI/NATIONAL INSTITUTE FOR PEOPLE WITH DISABILITIES
460 West 34th Street
New York, New York 10001

General Information Social services agency working with people with mental retardation and/or developmental disabilities in a variety of settings to promote independence and inclusion. Established in 1957. Number of employees: 4,500. Number of internship applications received each year: 150.
Internships Available ▶ *20–30 counselors:* responsibilities include working with adults with developmental disabilities in a residential group home; teaching daily living skills and providing informal counseling. Candidates should have ability to work independently, ability to work with others, personal interest in the field, plan to pursue career in field, related experience a plus but not required. Duration is flexible. Position available as unpaid or paid. Open to recent high school graduates, college freshmen, college sophomores, college juniors, college seniors, recent college graduates, graduate students, career changers, individuals reentering the workforce. ▶ *2–4 human resources interns:* responsibilities include working in fast-paced office with recruitment or benefits team to assist in human resources functions for large not-for-profit agency. Candidates should have ability to work independently, ability to work with others, computer skills, office skills, personal interest in the field. Duration is flexible. Unpaid. Open to college freshmen, college sophomores, college juniors, college seniors, recent college graduates, individuals reentering the workforce. ▶ *10–20 job coaches:* responsibilities include working with adults with mental retardation; providing job training skills and follow-up counseling. Candidates should have ability to work independently, ability to work with others, computer skills, knowledge of field, personal interest in the field, plan to pursue career in field. Duration is flexible. Unpaid. Open to college freshmen, college sophomores, college juniors, college seniors, recent college graduates, graduate students, career changers, individuals reentering the workforce. ▶ *20–30 teacher/teacher assistants:* responsibilities include working with adults with mental retardation in a classroom-setting; providing hands on teaching of daily living skills and community integration. Candidates should have ability to work independently, ability to work with others, personal interest in the field, plan to pursue career in field, experience a plus but not required. Duration is flexible. Position available as unpaid or paid. Open to recent high school graduates, college freshmen, college sophomores, college juniors, college seniors, recent college graduates, graduate students, career changers, individuals reentering the workforce. International applications accepted.
Benefits Formal training, job counseling, on-the-job training, opportunity to attend seminars/workshops, possible full-time employment, willing to act as a professional reference, willing to complete paperwork for educational credit, willing to provide letters of recommendation.
Contact Write, call, fax, e-mail, or through World Wide Web site Human Resources. Phone: 212-273-6165. Fax: 212-563-4836. E-mail: careers@yai.org. In-person interview recommended (telephone interview accepted). Applicants must submit a formal organization application, letter of interest, resume. Applications are accepted continuously. World Wide Web: http://www.yai.org.

YMCA/MENTOR DULUTH
302 West First Street
Duluth, Minnesota 55802

General Information Program that works with youth and families (usually low income, single parent households) to provide adult mentors for children. Established in 1882. Number of employees: 120. Number of internship applications received each year: 5.
Internships Available ▶ *6–8 human services interns:* responsibilities include working with families using interviewing skills; performing casework; maintaining contact with adult volunteers and families; and planning, implementing, and evaluating special programs/activities. Candidates should have ability to work independently, college degree in related field, oral communica-

tion skills, self-motivation, strong interpersonal skills. Duration is 6–12 months. Unpaid. Open to graduate students. International applications accepted.
Benefits Names of contacts, possible full-time employment, travel reimbursement, willing to complete paperwork for educational credit, willing to provide letters of recommendation, free YMCA membership.
Contact Write, call, or e-mail Mr. Blair Gagne, Program Director. Phone: 218-722-4745 Ext. 125. E-mail: bgagne@duluthymca.org. In-person interview required. Applicants must submit a resume, three personal references. Applications are accepted continuously.

YMCA OF METROPOLITAN MOBILE, INC.
PO Box 2272
Mobile, Alabama 36652

General Information Organization that provides instruction and assistance in the areas of health/wellness, community service, youth and adult sports, aquatics programming, and child care. Established in 1856. Number of employees: 400. Number of internship applications received each year: 15.
Internships Available ▶ *2–4 administrative interns:* responsibilities include assisting executive director in developing membership appreciation special events, dealing with member service issues, leading customer service training for staff. Candidates should have oral communication skills, organizational skills, self-motivation, strong interpersonal skills, written communication skills. Duration is as required by intern's school. Unpaid. Open to college freshmen, college sophomores, college juniors, college seniors, recent college graduates, graduate students. ▶ *1–14 child-care/summer day camp interns:* responsibilities include assisting with administration and planning of summer day camp and child-care programs. Candidates should have ability to work with others, oral communication skills, organizational skills. Unpaid. Open to high school students, recent high school graduates, college freshmen, college sophomores, college juniors, college seniors, recent college graduates, graduate students, law students, career changers, individuals reentering the workforce. ▶ *2–4 fitness interns:* responsibilities include assisting fitness director in fitness testing, program implementation, and senior and women's programs. Candidates should have knowledge of field, oral communication skills, self-motivation, strong interpersonal skills, written communication skills. Duration is as required by intern's school. Unpaid. Open to college freshmen, college sophomores, college juniors, college seniors, recent college graduates, graduate students. ▶ *2–14 youth sports interns:* responsibilities include assisting in planning and administration of YMCA youth sports programs. Candidates should have ability to work independently, ability to work with others, analytical skills, knowledge of field, oral communication skills, organizational skills, personal interest in the field, plan to pursue career in field, self-motivation, strong leadership ability, writing skills. Duration is fall, spring, or summer semesters. Unpaid. Open to high school students, recent high school graduates, college freshmen, college sophomores, college juniors, college seniors, recent college graduates, graduate students, law students, career changers, individuals reentering the workforce. International applications accepted.
Benefits On-the-job training, possible full-time employment, willing to act as a professional reference, willing to complete paperwork for educational credit, willing to provide letters of recommendation.
Contact Write, fax, or e-mail Patrick Davenport, Vice President of Operations/COO, PO Box 2272, Mobile, Alabama 36652. Fax: 251-438-1174. E-mail: ymetro@zebra.net. No phone calls. In-person interview recommended (telephone interview accepted). Applicants must submit a formal organization application, letter of interest, resume, personal reference, drug test, criminal background check. Applications are accepted continuously.

YMCA OF THE PIKES PEAK REGION
207 North Nevada
Colorado Springs, Colorado 80903

General Information Organization that runs adult, youth, and children's programs designed to promote personal growth, enhance family relationships, improve physical and mental health,

YMCA of the Pikes Peak Region (continued)

foster leadership abilities, develop specific skills, and to have fun. Established in 1885. Number of employees: 650. Number of internship applications received each year: 25.

Internships Available ▶ *Communications/marketing interns:* responsibilities include developing materials for community-wide celebration of the arts on New Year's Eve, public speaking, and volunteer recruitment. Duration is 8–12 weeks. $200 per month stipend. ▶ *Day camp interns:* responsibilities include developing program for summer day camp. Candidates should have college courses in field, experience in the field, oral communication skills, personal interest in the field, strong interpersonal skills. Duration is 10–12 weeks. $200 per month stipend. ▶ *Fitness/wellness interns:* responsibilities include administering corporate cup program which involves various corporations locally in sports challenges, developing schedules, awards banquets, and events. Candidates should have oral communication skills, personal interest in the field, plan to pursue career in field, self-motivation, strong interpersonal skills, written communication skills. Duration is 8–12 weeks. $200 per month stipend. ▶ *Fund-raisers:* responsibilities include developing database of donors through research and technical information regarding foundations and grants. Candidates should have knowledge of field, office skills, oral communication skills, research skills, strong interpersonal skills, written communication skills. Duration is flexible. $200 per month stipend. Open to college juniors, college seniors. ▶ *1 human resource intern:* responsibilities include developing central directory of updated job descriptions; reviewing and updating all current job descriptions, ensuring most recent YMCA regulatory format is used. Candidates should have oral communication skills, organizational skills, personal interest in the field, self-motivation, strong interpersonal skills, written communication skills. Duration is 2–3 months. $200 per month stipend. Open to college seniors. ▶ *Resident camp program interns:* responsibilities include developing program for resident camp. Candidates should have experience in the field, personal interest in the field, strong interpersonal skills, strong leadership ability. Duration is 8–10 weeks. $200 per month stipend. Open to college juniors, college seniors. ▶ *Youth sports interns:* responsibilities include developing and coordinating youth sports programs for the association or branch. Candidates should have ability to work independently, experience in the field, knowledge of field, personal interest in the field, self-motivation, strong interpersonal skills. Duration is flexible. $200 per month stipend. International applications accepted.

Benefits Possible full-time employment, willing to complete paperwork for educational credit, willing to provide letters of recommendation, free room and board for summer resident camping positions.

Contact Write, fax, or e-mail Lisa Austin, Director of Training and Development. Fax: 719-471-1723. E-mail: laustin@ppymca. org. No phone calls. In-person interview recommended (telephone interview accepted). Applicants must submit a formal organization application, letter of interest, resume, academic transcripts, three personal references, three letters of recommendation. Applications are accepted continuously.

YMCA SAFE PLACE SERVICES
1410 South First Street
Louisville, Kentucky 40208

General Information Agency that provides emergency shelter care to teens with serious family problems. Established in 1974. Number of employees: 35. Unit of YMCA of Greater Louisville, Louisville, Kentucky. Number of internship applications received each year: 25.

Internships Available ▶ *2 administrative interns:* responsibilities include assisting in the development of grant and foundation proposals and performing quality assurance studies. Candidates should have computer skills, editing skills, office skills, organizational skills, research skills, writing skills. Duration is 1–2 semesters. Unpaid. Open to college freshmen, college sophomores, college juniors, college seniors, recent college graduates. ▶ *1–2 clerical interns:* responsibilities include filing, typing, and performing computer work. Candidates should have analytical skills, computer

skills, office skills, research skills, self-motivation, writing skills. Duration is 1 semester. Unpaid. Open to recent high school graduates, college freshmen, college sophomores, college juniors, college seniors, recent college graduates, graduate students, career changers. ▶ *2–4 social workers/counselors:* responsibilities include counseling individuals, groups, and families; presenting life skills; and conducting informal discussions with youth. Candidates should have ability to work independently, oral communication skills, self-motivation, strong interpersonal skills, written communication skills. Duration is 1–2 semesters. Unpaid. Open to graduate students working toward master's degree in social work-related field. ▶ *4–6 youth workers:* responsibilities include supervising 8-10 youths in meal preparation, chores, and recreation. Candidates should have oral communication skills, self-motivation, strong interpersonal skills, strong leadership ability, written communication skills. Duration is 1 semester. Position available as unpaid or at $8–$9 per hour. Open to high school graduates (at least associate degree desirable); must be 21 or over. International applications accepted.

Benefits Formal training, free meals, names of contacts, opportunity to attend seminars/workshops, possible full-time employment, willing to complete paperwork for educational credit, willing to provide letters of recommendation.

Contact Write, fax, or e-mail John M. Papanek, Director of Counseling Services. Fax: 502-635-1443. E-mail: jpapanek@ ymcalouisville.org. No phone calls. In-person interview required. Applications are accepted continuously. World Wide Web: http:// www.ymcalouisville.org.

YOUTH AND SHELTER SERVICES, INC.
420 Kellogg, PO Box 1628
Ames, Iowa 50010

General Information Organization that exists to help children, youth, and families solve problems, grow, and become self-sufficient, responsible, contributing members of society. Established in 1976. Number of employees: 170. Number of internship applications received each year: 20.

Internships Available ▶ *Administrative interns:* responsibilities include duties in various departments including public relations, conference planning, or general administration. Candidates should have ability to work with others, college courses in field, computer skills, editing skills, office skills, organizational skills. Duration is 1 semester or 1 summer. Unpaid. ▶ *Human services interns:* responsibilities include assisting with various programs including foster care, residential center, drug treatment, and day care. Candidates should have college courses in field, personal interest in the field, plan to pursue career in field, strong interpersonal skills. Duration is 1 semester or 1 summer. Unpaid. Open to college freshmen, college sophomores, college juniors, college seniors. International applications accepted.

Benefits Formal training, names of contacts, opportunity to attend seminars/workshops, possible full-time employment, willing to complete paperwork for educational credit, willing to provide letters of recommendation.

Contact Write, call, fax, e-mail, or through World Wide Web site Phyllis Craig, Volunteer Coordinator. Phone: 515-233-3141. Fax: 515-233-2440. E-mail: pcraig@yss.ames.ia.us. In-person interview recommended (telephone interview accepted). Applicants must submit a formal organization application, letter of interest, resume, 2-3 personal references. Application deadline: May 1 for summer, December 30 for spring. World Wide Web: http://www.yss. ames.ia.us.

YOUTH ENRICHMENT SERVICES (YES)
PO Box 105
West Islip, New York 11795

General Information Youth services organization. Established in 1987. Number of employees: 35. Number of internship applications received each year: 10.

Internships Available ▶ *2–5 bookkeeper/administrative assistant interns:* responsibilities include working under the direction of executive director and administrative assistant; grant development, bookkeeping, fiscal responsibilities, vouchering. Candidates should have ability to work independently, analytical skills, computer skills, organizational skills, self-motivation, written communication skills. Duration is flexible. Unpaid. Open to high school seniors, recent high school graduates, college freshmen, college sophomores, college juniors, college seniors, recent college graduates, individuals reentering the workforce. ▶ *1–2 executive director interns:* responsibilities include working with the executive director: budgeting, planning, fiscal implementation, grant writing, program development, monitoring, evaluation, community liaison, meetings, special initiatives. Candidates should have ability to work independently, college courses in field, computer skills, plan to pursue career in field, strong interpersonal skills, plan to pursue career in field, strong interpersonal skills, strong leadership ability. Duration is flexible. Unpaid. Open to college juniors, college seniors, recent college graduates, graduate students, law students, career changers, individuals reentering the workforce. ▶ *2–5 program coordinator interns:* responsibilities include assisting and training with the staff program coordinators and the executive director; outreach, delivery of direct services, community liaison. Candidates should have ability to work with others, computer skills, oral communication skills, self-motivation, strong leadership ability. Duration is flexible. Unpaid. Open to high school students, recent high school graduates, college freshmen, college sophomores, college juniors, college seniors, recent college graduates, graduate students, law students, career changers, individuals reentering the workforce. ▶ *1–2 senior program coordinator interns:* responsibilities include overseeing programs; some budgeting, staff training and supervision; community liaison, outreach, meetings, program scheduling; all under Senior Program Coordinator's direction. Candidates should have ability to work with others, computer skills, oral communication skills, self-motivation, strong leadership ability. Duration is flexible. Unpaid. Open to college sophomores, college juniors, college seniors, recent college graduates, graduate students, law students, career changers, individuals reentering the workforce. International applications accepted.

Benefits Formal training, names of contacts, on-the-job training, opportunity to attend seminars/workshops, possible full-time employment, willing to act as a professional reference, willing to complete paperwork for educational credit, willing to provide letters of recommendation.

Contact Write, call, fax, or e-mail Mary Ann Pfeiffer, Executive Director. Phone: 631-587-5172. Fax: 631-661-2973. E-mail: yesletters@aol.com. In-person interview recommended (telephone interview accepted). Applicants must submit a formal organization application, letter of interest, resume, academic transcripts, three personal references. Applications are accepted continuously. World Wide Web: http://www.yesnews.org.

YOUTH OPPORTUNITIES UPHELD
172 Lincoln Street
Worcester, Massachusetts 01605

General Information Nonprofit organization that provides troubled adolescents and families with opportunities to deal with problems in ways that promote development as individuals and as contributing members of society. Established in 1970. Number of employees: 20. Number of internship applications received each year: 150.

Internships Available ▶ *10–35 court mentor program interns:* responsibilities include working as an outreach counselor for "court-involved" or at-risk adolescents who are struggling with individual or family problems, filing weekly/monthly reports, attending weekly staff meeting, and organizing activities. Candidates should have ability to work independently, self-motivation, strong interpersonal skills, strong leadership ability. Duration is 6–12 months. Unpaid. Open to college freshmen, college sophomores, college juniors, college seniors, graduate students. ▶ *Educational counselors:* responsibilities include working in an alternative school for troubled adolescents, tutoring, participating in sports or activities, and monitoring behaviors on a daily point sheet. Candidates should have ability to work with others, oral communication skills, organizational skills, personal interest in the field, writing skills. Duration is one academic year. Unpaid. Open to college freshmen, college sophomores, college juniors, college seniors, graduate students. ▶ *8 graduate clinical interns:* responsibilities include performing individual/family counseling, assessments, observa-

tions, and therapy sessions. Candidates should have analytical skills, college degree in related field, plan to pursue career in field, strong interpersonal skills. Duration is one academic year. Unpaid. Open to graduate students. ▶ *Residential counselors:* responsibilities include working in a residential home for troubled adolescents, attending group meetings, working as an advocate to youth, and participating in activities that are set up for youth. Candidates should have oral communication skills, personal interest in the field, self-motivation, strong interpersonal skills. Duration is one academic year. Unpaid. Open to college freshmen, college sophomores, college juniors, college seniors, graduate students. ▶ *2 teen parent counselors:* responsibilities include assisting staff in planning group activities, spending time with teenage mothers, assisting in weekly menu planning, and participating as a positive role model. Candidates should have oral communication skills, personal interest in the field, strong interpersonal skills, written communication skills. Duration is one academic year. Unpaid. Open to college freshmen, college sophomores, college juniors, college seniors, graduate students. International applications accepted.

Benefits Formal training, names of contacts, opportunity to attend seminars/workshops, possible full-time employment, travel reimbursement, willing to act as a professional reference, willing to complete paperwork for educational credit, willing to provide letters of recommendation.

Contact Write, call, or fax Lenore Johnson, Coordinator of Mentoring and Prevention Services. Phone: 508-770-0511 Ext. 114. Fax: 508-770-0875. E-mail: johnsonl@youinc.org. In-person interview required. Applicants must submit a formal organization application, letter of interest, resume, three letters of recommendation, criminal records check required. Applications are accepted continuously. World Wide Web: http://www.youinc.org.

YWCA/DOMESTIC VIOLENCE PREVENTION CENTER
626 Church Street
Lynchburg, Virginia 24504

General Information Organization that serves battered women and their children and seeks to eliminate abuse. Established in 1978. Number of employees: 20. Unit of YWCA of the USA, New York, New York. Number of internship applications received each year: 5.

Internships Available ▶ *3–6 interns:* responsibilities include providing casework assistance with both children and adults. Candidates should have ability to work independently, ability to work with others, computer skills, office skills, oral communication skills, personal interest in the field, self-motivation, written communication skills. Duration is 1 semester. Unpaid. Open to college seniors, graduate students, individuals reentering the workforce. International applications accepted.

Benefits Formal training, on-the-job training, opportunity to attend seminars/workshops, possible full-time employment, travel reimbursement, willing to act as a professional reference, willing to complete paperwork for educational credit, willing to provide letters of recommendation.

Contact Write, call, or fax Sheila Andrews, DVPC Director. Phone: 434-528-1041. Fax: 434-847-2529. In-person interview required. Applicants must submit a resume. Applications are accepted continuously.

YWCA OF DAYTON OHIO
141 West Third Street
Dayton, Ohio 45402

General Information Organization whose mission is to provide the tools for women to achieve self-sufficiency and create a safer environment; programs include shelter services for domestic violence, homeless, pregnant/parent teens and childcare and teen services. Established in 1870. Number of employees: 89. Affiliate of YWCA of the USA, New York, New York. Number of internship applications received each year: 20.

Internships Available ▶ *1–2 Girls Inc. summer interns:* responsibilities include assisting with teaching Girls Inc. curriculum, "day camp" activities, and field trips; for more information on Girls

Inc., refer to National Web site, www.girlsinc.org. Candidates should have ability to work independently, ability to work with others, oral communication skills, plan to pursue career in field, major in education, human service, or social service related field. Duration is 8–12 weeks. Position available as unpaid or at $8–$8.50 per hour. Open to college juniors, college seniors. International applications accepted.

Benefits On-the-job training, possible full-time employment, willing to act as a professional reference, willing to complete paperwork for educational credit, willing to provide letters of recommendation.

Contact Call, fax, or e-mail Kristen Burgess, Teen Services Administrator. Phone: 937-461-5550 Ext. 124. Fax: 937-222-0610. E-mail: kburgess@ywcadayton.org. In-person interview required. Applicants must submit a formal organization application, letter of interest, resume, three personal references. Application deadline: May 15. World Wide Web: http://www.ywcadayton.org.

YWCA OF GREATER HARRISBURG
1101 Market Street
Harrisburg, Pennsylvania 17103

General Information Organization that actively serves as an advocate and resource to the community on issues that impact women and children and provides services to empower women, including violence intervention and prevention, child care, and housing. Established in 1894. Number of employees: 100.

Internships Available ▶ *8 advocate interns:* responsibilities include working the hot line, attending emergency hospital and preliminary hearing in sexual assault and domestic violence cases, research, case management, and documentation. Duration is flexible (spring, summer, and fall programs). Unpaid. Open to high school seniors, recent high school graduates, college freshmen, college sophomores, college juniors, college seniors, recent college graduates, graduate students, law students, career changers, individuals reentering the workforce, must be 18 years or older. ▶ *1–4 assistant group supervisors:* responsibilities include assisting in classroom management; providing interesting, challenging educational opportunities for children ages 2 months to 12 years; writing lesson plans; producing displays; interacting with children; and meeting with teachers. Duration is flexible (spring, summer, and fall programs). Unpaid. Open to recent high school graduates, college freshmen, college sophomores, college juniors, college seniors, recent college graduates, graduate students, law students, career changers, individuals reentering the workforce. ▶ *1 education specialist:* responsibilities include grant writing and responding to community organizations' requests for information and training in the areas of sexual assault, domestic violence, and anti-violence. Duration is flexible (spring, summer, and fall programs). Unpaid. Open to high school students, recent high school graduates, college freshmen, college sophomores, college juniors, college seniors, recent college graduates, graduate students, law students, career changers, individuals reentering the workforce. International applications accepted.

Benefits Formal training, names of contacts, possible full-time employment, willing to complete paperwork for educational credit, willing to provide letters of recommendation.

Contact Write or call Jennifer Cooper, Assistant Director of Violence and Prevention Services. Phone: 717-234-7931. Fax: 717-234-1779. E-mail: ywca3@igateway.com. In-person interview required. Applicants must submit a resume. Applications are accepted continuously.

YWCA OF ST. PAUL
198 Western Avenue North
St. Paul, Minnesota 55102-1790

General Information Nonprofit membership-based organization governed by women and dedicated to the advancement of women and families. Established in 1907. Number of employees: 117. Affiliate of YWCA of the USA, New York, New York. Number of internship applications received each year: 15.

Internships Available ▶ *1–3 case manager interns:* responsibilities include providing case management and direction to homeless women by helping them develop plans to eliminate barriers to their self-sufficiency, through education/employment and stabilized housing. Candidates should have ability to work independently, college courses in field, oral communication skills, personal interest in the field, strong interpersonal skills. Duration is 3 months (minimum). Unpaid. Open to college juniors, college seniors, recent college graduates, graduate students. ▶ *1–3 child enrichment center interns:* responsibilities include participating in the children's program by developing and implementing activities appropriate to the curriculum and providing support to the child development specialists. Candidates should have ability to work independently, analytical skills, experience in the field, personal interest in the field, self-motivation, strong interpersonal skills. Duration is 3 months (minimum). Unpaid. Open to college freshmen, college sophomores, college juniors, college seniors, recent college graduates, graduate students, career changers, individuals reentering the workforce. ▶ *1 child-care intern:* responsibilities include assisting in the preparation, implementation, and evaluation of a school-age child-care program. Candidates should have oral communication skills, organizational skills, personal interest in the field, strong interpersonal skills, strong leadership ability, written communication skills. Duration is 3 months (minimum). Unpaid. Open to college freshmen, college sophomores, college juniors, college seniors, recent college graduates, graduate students, career changers. ▶ *1–2 health and fitness intern:* responsibilities include orienting clients to resources, assisting staff with personal training, and representing the health and fitness center. Candidates should have ability to work independently, experience in the field, oral communication skills, personal interest in the field, self-motivation, strong interpersonal skills. Duration is 3 months (minimum). Unpaid. Open to college juniors, college seniors, recent college graduates, graduate students. ▶ *1 housing intake intern:* responsibilities include assisting the director of housing and support services in maintaining a quality comprehensive program for homeless women with dependent children, through efficient management of services, case management, reporting, and full utilization of facilities. Candidates should have ability to work independently, oral communication skills, personal interest in the field, strong interpersonal skills, written communication skills. Duration is 3 months (minimum). Unpaid. Open to college freshmen, college sophomores, college juniors, college seniors, recent college graduates, graduate students, career changers. ▶ *1 mentor/tutor intern:* responsibilities include assisting in the preparation, implementation, and evaluation of a school-age mentoring program. Candidates should have oral communication skills, organizational skills, personal interest in the field, self-motivation, strong interpersonal skills, written communication skills. Duration is 3 months (minimum). Unpaid. Open to college sophomores, college juniors, college seniors, recent college graduates, graduate students. ▶ *1 mentoring project intern:* responsibilities include assisting in the development of family intervention mentoring project for families in transition. Candidates should have ability to work independently, ability to work with others, analytical skills, computer skills, experience in the field, office skills, oral communication skills, organizational skills, self-motivation, strong leadership ability, written communication skills. Duration is 3 months (minimum). Unpaid. Open to college sophomores, college juniors, college seniors, recent college graduates, graduate students, career changers, individuals reentering the workforce. ▶ *1 support services intern:* responsibilities include assisting in monitoring the school attendance of elementary-age students who are part of a family intervention project and maintaining accurate information pertaining to their progress. Candidates should have ability to work independently, college courses in field, computer skills, experience in the field, office skills, oral communication skills, personal interest in the field, self-motivation, strong interpersonal skills, written communication skills. Duration is 3 months (minimum). Unpaid. Open to college juniors, college seniors, recent college graduates, graduate students, career changers, individuals reentering the workforce. ▶ *1 volunteer coordinator intern:* responsibilities include recruiting, screening, and training potential volunteers, and assisting with volunteer program management. Candidates should have ability to work independently, computer skills, office skills, oral communication skills, organizational skills, personal interest in the field, strong interpersonal skills, written communication skills. Duration is 3 months (minimum). Unpaid. Open to college freshmen, college sophomores, college juniors, college seniors, recent college graduates, career changers, individuals reentering the workforce. ▶ *1 youth achievers intern:* responsibilities include helping facilitate an after-school program, developing and implementing behavior management techniques, and implementing individual service plans for youth and families. Candidates should have personal interest in the field, plan to pursue career in field. Duration is 3 months (minimum). Unpaid. Open to college sophomores, college juniors, college seniors, recent college graduates, graduate students. International applications accepted.

Benefits Names of contacts, on-the-job training, opportunity to attend seminars/workshops, possible full-time employment, travel reimbursement, willing to act as a professional reference, willing to complete paperwork for educational credit, willing to provide letters of recommendation.

Contact Write, call, fax, or e-mail Sandra Peterson, Volunteer Services Coordinator. Phone: 651-265-0722. Fax: 651-222-6307. E-mail: volunteer@ywcaofstpaul.org. In-person interview recommended (telephone interview accepted). Applicants must submit a formal organization application, letter of interest, resume, three personal references, letter of recommendation, criminal background check required (paid for by YWCA). Applications are accepted continuously.

YWCA OF WESTERN NEW YORK
190 Franklin Street
Buffalo, New York 14202

General Information Membership movement of women of diverse beliefs, faiths, and values committed to the empowerment of women. Established in 1870. Number of employees: 300. Number of internship applications received each year: 5.

Internships Available ▶ *2 assistant case managers:* responsibilities include conducting intake interviews, documenting files, scheduling presentations, and facilitating workshops. Candidates should have experience in social service setting. Duration is flexible. Unpaid. Open to individuals with at least associate degree. ▶ *1–5 child-care assistants:* responsibilities include assisting in planning activities for children ages 6 weeks-5 years and working cooperatively with teachers and parents. Duration is flexible. Position available as unpaid or paid. ▶ *2 child-care curriculum developers:* responsibilities include developing a curriculum for children ages 6 weeks-12 years in science, math, health, safety, and social studies. Candidates

should have minimum one year of experience working with children. Duration is flexible. Unpaid. Open to individuals with associate degree in early childhood education. ▶ *15 extended day program aides:* responsibilities include developing weekly program plans for children ages 5-12; researching reference articles and organizations; establishing a library system of articles, games, and crafts; and working with children. Candidates should have minimum one year of experience with school-age children. Position available as unpaid or paid. ▶ *1–2 grant research assistants:* responsibilities include researching funding opportunities and compiling required data. Candidates should have written communication skills. Duration is flexible. Unpaid. Open to individuals with high school diploma. ▶ *1 health and wellness assistant:* responsibilities include teaching fitness classes; marketing programs, outreach events, and demonstrations; and assisting with mailings and filing. Duration is 8–10 weeks. Unpaid. Open to individuals with high school diploma. ▶ *1 residence program aide:* responsibilities include performing crisis management, coordinating resident services, recording behavioral data, directing facility supervision services, monitoring medications, and alternating as group team leader. Candidates should have experience in residence community setting. Unpaid. Open to individuals with at least associate degree. ▶ *1–2 special events/public relations interns:* responsibilities include assisting in the arrangement and promotion of special events and helping with publicity. Candidates should have ability to work independently, computer skills, oral communication skills, organizational skills, research skills, self-motivation, strong interpersonal skills, written communication skills. Duration is flexible. Unpaid. Open to individuals with high school diploma. ▶ *4 teen center program aide interns:* responsibilities include performing outreach, facilitating group discussion and workshops, and communicating with teens about available services. Duration is flexible. Unpaid. Open to individuals with at least 2 years of postsecondary education. International applications accepted.

Benefits Formal training, opportunity to attend seminars/workshops, possible full-time employment, willing to complete paperwork for educational credit, willing to provide letters of recommendation.

Contact Write, call, or fax Donna Mostiller, Human Resources Manager. Phone: 716-852-6120. Fax: 716-852-1629. In-person interview required. Applicants must submit a letter of interest, resume, writing sample, three letters of recommendation. Applications are accepted continuously.

INFORMATION

GENERAL

ACCURACY IN MEDIA
4455 Connecticut Avenue, NW, Suite 330
Washington, District of Columbia 20008

General Information Nonprofit educational organization whose purpose is to monitor bias and inaccuracies in the news media through a newsletter and news column. Established in 1969. Number of employees: 10. Number of internship applications received each year: 50.

Internships Available ▶ *1 assistant MIS manager:* responsibilities include assisting MIS chief with maintenance of office computer systems. Candidates should have ability to work independently, computer skills, office skills, organizational skills, personal interest in the field, self-motivation, strong interpersonal skills. Duration is 3–6 months. Position available as unpaid or at $125 per week. Open to high school students, recent high school graduates, college freshmen, college sophomores, college juniors, college seniors, recent college graduates, graduate students, law students, career changers, individuals reentering the workforce. ▶ *1 assistant Web master:* responsibilities include assisting Web master with maintaining and designing Web sites. Candidates should have ability to work independently, analytical skills, computer skills, editing skills, organizational skills, personal interest in the field, research skills, self-motivation, strong interpersonal skills, strong leadership ability, writing skills. Duration is 3–12 months. Position available as unpaid or at $125 per week. Open to high school students, recent high school graduates, college freshmen, college sophomores, college juniors, college seniors, recent college graduates, graduate students, law students, career changers, individuals reentering the workforce. ▶ *1 graphic artist:* responsibilities include creating and designing advertising and marketing materials. Candidates should have ability to work independently, ability to work with others, computer skills, editing skills, personal interest in the field, plan to pursue career in field, self-motivation, writing skills. Duration is 3–12 months. $125 per week. Open to recent high school graduates, college freshmen, college sophomores, college juniors, college seniors, recent college graduates, graduate students. ▶ *1–2 marketing assistants:* responsibilities include assisting with marketing, public relations, and advertising for the organization, with a focus on the Internet. Candidates should have ability to work independently, analytical skills, computer skills, editing skills, oral communication skills, organizational skills, personal interest in the field, plan to pursue career in field, self-motivation, strong interpersonal skills, writing skills. Duration is 3–6 months. Position available as unpaid or at $125 per week. Open to high school students, recent high school graduates, college freshmen, college sophomores, college juniors, college seniors, recent college graduates, graduate students, law students, career changers, individuals reentering the workforce. ▶ *1 researcher:* responsibilities include researching particular topics and producing a study or report on findings. Candidates should have ability to work independently, analytical skills, computer skills, editing skills, personal interest in the field, research skills, self-motivation, strong interpersonal skills, writing skills. Duration is 3–6 months. Position available as unpaid or at $125 per week. Open to high school students, recent high school graduates, college freshmen, college sophomores, college juniors, college seniors, recent college graduates, graduate students, law students, career changers, individuals reentering the workforce.

▶ *1–2 writers:* responsibilities include researching and writing articles for the organization's Web site. Candidates should have ability to work independently, analytical skills, computer skills, editing skills, organizational skills, personal interest in the field, research skills, self-motivation, strong interpersonal skills, writing skills. Duration is 3–6 months. Position available as unpaid or at $125 per week. Open to high school students, recent high school graduates, college freshmen, college sophomores, college juniors, college seniors, recent college graduates, graduate students, law students, career changers, individuals reentering the workforce. International applications accepted.

Benefits On-the-job training, opportunity to attend seminars/workshops, possible full-time employment, willing to act as a professional reference, willing to complete paperwork for educational credit, willing to provide letters of recommendation.

Contact Write, fax, e-mail, or through World Wide Web site Mr. Don Irvine, Executive Director. Fax: 202-364-4098. E-mail: intern@aim.org. No phone calls. In-person interview recommended (telephone interview accepted). Applicants must submit a formal organization application, letter of interest, resume, academic transcripts, two writing samples. Application deadline: March 31 for summer, August 15 for fall, October 31 for spring. World Wide Web: http://www.aim.org/.

BLOOMBERG L.P.
499 Park Avenue
New York, New York 10022

General Information Information services, news and media company serving customers around the world. Established in 1981.

Internships Available ▶ *Interns:* responsibilities include possible positions in various areas including advertising news, operations and broadcast, administration and human resources; internships in New York, Princeton, San Francisco, Dallas, Atlanta, Los Angeles, Singapore, Tokyo, and Hong Kong. Candidates should have personal interest in the field, strong academic background. Duration is summer. Position available as unpaid or paid. Open to college freshmen, college sophomores, college juniors, college seniors, recent college graduates, graduate students.

International Internships Available in Tokyo, Japan.

Contact Through World Wide Web site Internship Coordinator. Phone: 212-318-2000. Fax: 212-980-4585. Online application; see Web site for details. Applications are accepted continuously. World Wide Web: http://www.bloomberg.com.

CENTER FOR INVESTIGATIVE REPORTING, INC.
131 Steuart Street, Suite 600
San Francisco, California 94105

General Information Nonprofit organization producing television and print media reports on national and international issues including the environment, science, public health, constitutional government-freedom of information, social justice, international affairs, economic and financial issues, and the public trust. Established in 1977. Number of employees: 10. Number of internship applications received each year: 100.

Internships Available ▶ *4–6 interns:* responsibilities include working closely with staff reporters on tasks including research, information organization, story development, and production. Candidates should have analytical skills, oral communication skills, personal interest in the field, plan to pursue career in field, self-motivation, written communication skills. Duration is 5 months. Monthly stipend of $500. Open to college freshmen, college sophomores, college juniors, college seniors, recent college graduates, graduate students, law students, career changers, individuals reentering the workforce. International applications accepted.

Benefits Names of contacts, opportunity to attend seminars/workshops, possible full-time employment, willing to complete paperwork for educational credit, willing to provide letters of recommendation.

Contact Write, call, fax, e-mail, or through World Wide Web site Intern Coordinator. Phone: 415-543-1200. Fax: 415-543-8311. E-mail: center@cironline.org. Applicants must submit a letter of interest, resume, 2-3 writing samples. Application deadline: May 1 for summer/fall (July to November), December 1 for winter/spring (February to June). World Wide Web: http://www.muckraker.org.

FORT WORTH PUBLIC LIBRARY
500 West 3rd Street
Fort Worth, Texas 76102

General Information Library. Established in 1901. Number of employees: 225. Number of internship applications received each year: 4.

Internships Available ▶ *1–4 archival assistants:* responsibilities include processing and organizing historical document collections and creating inventory list and summary. Candidates should have ability to work independently, organizational skills, personal interest in the field, research skills, self-motivation. Unpaid. Open to college seniors, recent college graduates, graduate students, career changers. ▶ *1–5 children's program assistants.* Candidates should have strong interpersonal skills. Position available as unpaid or paid. Open to high school students, recent high school graduates, college sophomores, college juniors, college seniors, recent college graduates, graduate students, career changers, individuals reentering the workforce. ▶ *1–5 computer monitors:* responsibilities include overseeing library computers for use by patrons. Candidates should have oral communication skills, strong interpersonal skills. Position available as unpaid or paid. Open to high school students, recent high school graduates, college freshmen, college sophomores, college juniors, college seniors, recent college graduates, graduate students, career changers, individuals reentering the workforce. ▶ *1–5 documents assistants:* responsibilities include helping process materials in the periodicals and Government Documents Department; duties include typing, writing, and shelf reading. Candidates should have ability to work independently, computer skills. Unpaid. Open to high school students, recent high school graduates, college freshmen, college sophomores, college juniors, college seniors, recent college graduates, career changers, individuals reentering the workforce. ▶ *1–3 genealogy interns:* responsibilities include assisting patrons in the Library Genealogy Department with organizing and preparing lineage charts. Candidates should have knowledge of field, oral communication skills, personal interest in the field, research skills, strong interpersonal skills. Unpaid. Open to college seniors, recent college graduates, graduate students, career changers, individuals reentering the workforce. ▶ *1 intern:* responsibilities include working in a Gang Prevention Program; helping prepare program statistics and reports; monitoring computers; and tutoring program participants. Candidates should have computer skills, organizational skills, strong interpersonal skills, strong leadership ability, Spanish-speaking (preferred). Unpaid. Open to college sophomores, college juniors, college seniors, recent college graduates, graduate students, career changers, individuals reentering the workforce. ▶ *1–2 storytime interns:* responsibilities include planning and conducting storytime for children visiting the Library; planning and instructing crafts. Candidates should have oral communication skills, self-motivation, strong interpersonal skills. Unpaid. Open to college sophomores, college juniors, college seniors, recent college graduates, graduate students, career changers, individuals reentering the workforce. International applications accepted.

Benefits On-the-job training, possible full-time employment, willing to act as a professional reference, willing to complete paperwork for educational credit, willing to provide letters of recommendation.

Contact Write, call, fax, e-mail, or through World Wide Web site Miste Anders-Taylor, Volunteer Coordinator. Phone: 817-871-7703. Fax: 817-871-7734. E-mail: manders@fortworthlibrary.org. In-person interview recommended (telephone interview accepted). Applications are accepted continuously. World Wide Web: http://www.fortworthlibrary.org.

JAZBO PRODUCTIONS
185 Pier Avenue, Suite 106
Santa Monica, California 90405

General Information Feature film, television, Internet, and live stage production company involved in the development of feature films and made-for-television productions for the networks and major studios. Established in 1985. Number of employees: 1. Number of internship applications received each year: 150.

Internships Available ▶ *1–2 assistants to the president:* responsibilities include assisting with general office duties and management of scripts, videotapes, and concept treatments; story analysis of scripts; screening potential projects; Web research and content design, and production back-up. Candidates should have ability to work independently, computer skills, oral communication skills, organizational skills, self-motivation, written communication skills. Duration is 4–6 months. Unpaid. Open to college sophomores, college juniors, college seniors, recent college graduates, graduate students, law students, career changers, individuals reentering the workforce.

Benefits Job counseling, names of contacts, on-the-job training, opportunity to attend seminars/workshops, possible full-time employment, willing to act as a professional reference, willing to complete paperwork for educational credit, willing to provide letters of recommendation.

Contact Write, call, fax, or e-mail Ms. Jill Marti, President, 185 Pier Avenue Suite 106, Santa Monica, California 90405. Phone: 310-664-6004. Fax: 310-664-3656. E-mail: jazboinc@aol.com. In-person interview recommended. Applicants must submit a formal organization application, letter of interest, resume, 2-3 professional references, 1–2 personal references. Applications are accepted continuously.

NAPLES FREE-NET
2655 Northbrooke Drive
Naples, Florida 34119

General Information Community-oriented free Internet service provider, homeport for local nonprofit organizations, provider of introductory education on how to use the Internet. Established in 1994. Number of internship applications received each year: 30.

Internships Available ▶ *1–5 Web page development interns:* responsibilities include working with local nonprofit organizations to develop and implement their Web sites and acting as a liaison between the organizations and the Free Net. Candidates should have ability to work with others, computer skills, oral communication skills, self-motivation, written communication skills, HTML experience. Duration is flexible. Unpaid. Open to high school students, recent high school graduates, college freshmen, college sophomores, college juniors, college seniors, recent college graduates, graduate students, career changers, individuals reentering the workforce. ▶ *1–4 help team members:* responsibilities include staffing the service window for ISP, signing up new members, maintaining records, and answering technical questions about set-up and computer operations. Candidates should have ability to work with others, computer skills, experience in the field, office skills, oral communication skills. Duration is flexible (1/2 day once a week required). Unpaid. Open to high school students, recent high school graduates, college freshmen, college sophomores, college juniors, college seniors, recent college graduates, career changers, individuals reentering the workforce. ▶ *1–2 marketing/fundraising interns:* responsibilities include assisting in developing and implementing a community-oriented marketing plan to raise awareness of service and raise funds to support the operation. Candidates should have ability to work independently, knowledge of field, oral communication skills, personal interest in the field, strong interpersonal skills, writing skills. Duration is flexible. Unpaid. Open to college freshmen, college sophomores, college

Naples Free-Net (continued)

juniors, college seniors, recent college graduates, graduate students, career changers, individuals reentering the workforce. ▶ *1 technical team member:* responsibilities include working under the direction of the technical chair to maintain the operational integrity of the system. Candidates should have ability to work independently, ability to work with others, computer skills, oral communication skills, personal interest in the field, self-motivation. Duration is flexible. Unpaid. Open to high school students, recent high school graduates, college freshmen, college sophomores, college juniors, college seniors, recent college graduates, graduate students, career changers, individuals reentering the workforce. International applications accepted.

Benefits Formal training, job counseling, names of contacts, on-the-job training, opportunity to attend seminars/workshops, willing to act as a professional reference, willing to complete paperwork for educational credit, willing to provide letters of recommendation.

Contact Write, fax, or e-mail Dr. Melody Hainsworth, Intern Committee Chair. Fax: 941-513-9696. E-mail: intern@naples.net. No phone calls. Telephone interview required. Applicants must submit a letter of interest, resume, two personal references, description of computer and Internet courses taken and/or knowledge. Applications are accepted continuously. World Wide Web: http://www.naples.net.

MOTION PICTURE AND SOUND RECORDING INDUSTRIES

ASSISTANT DIRECTORS TRAINING PROGRAM
14724 Ventura Boulevard, Suite 775
Sherman Oaks, California 91403

General Information Training program that provides 400 days of paid, on-the-job training, supplemented by classroom seminars, in the work of second assistant directors. Established in 1965. Number of employees: 3. Unit of Directors Guild–Producer Training Plan, Sherman Oaks, California. Number of internship applications received each year: 800.

Internships Available ▶ *15–25 assistant director trainees:* responsibilities include assisting with administrative procedures in motion picture and television production, attending regular seminars that cover subjects pertinent to second assistant director work, and working with various studio and production companies. Candidates should have ability to work independently, oral communication skills, organizational skills, self-motivation, strong interpersonal skills, stamina. Duration is 400 days. $504–$619 per week. Open to college sophomores, college juniors, college seniors, recent college graduates, graduate students, law students, career changers, individuals reentering the workforce, high school graduates with at least 2 years work experience. International applications accepted.

Benefits Formal training, health insurance, job counseling, names of contacts, on-the-job training, opportunity to attend seminars/workshops, possible full-time employment.

Contact Write, call, e-mail, or through World Wide Web site R. John Slosser, Administrator. Phone: 818-386-2545. E-mail: mail@trainingplan.org. In-person interview required. Applicants must submit a formal organization application, resume, academic transcripts, writing sample. Application deadline: November 15 for internship beginning following June. Fees: $75. World Wide Web: http://www.dgptp.org.

ASSOCIATION OF INDEPENDENT VIDEO AND FILMMAKERS–FOUNDATION FOR INDEPENDENT VIDEO AND FILM
304 Hudson Street, 6th Floor
New York, New York 10013

General Information Trade association of 5000 independent media professionals that provides advocacy and information services; also an educational nonprofit organization offering informational and networking events for filmmakers, and the publisher of a national magazine, *The Independent.* Established in 1975. Number of employees: 10. Number of internship applications received each year: 100.

Internships Available ▶ *1 editorial intern:* responsibilities include assisting the Independent Film and Video Monthly editorial staff; researching and writing. Candidates should have ability to work independently, ability to work with others, computer skills, editing skills, knowledge of field, office skills, research skills, self-motivation, written communication skills. Duration is year-round. $100 per month. Open to college juniors, college seniors, recent college graduates, graduate students, career changers. ▶ *2–4 information services interns:* responsibilities include assisting with research, filing, and data entry in Filmmaker Resource Library; assisting with seminar and event coordination. Candidates should have ability to work independently, computer skills, knowledge of field, office skills, oral communication skills, organizational skills, personal interest in the field, research skills, self-motivation, strong interpersonal skills, written communication skills. Duration is year-round (up to 16 hours per week). $100 per month. Open to high school seniors, recent high school graduates, college freshmen, college sophomores, college juniors, college seniors, recent college graduates, graduate students, career changers, individuals reentering the workforce. ▶ *1–2 membership interns:* responsibilities include assisting with research and mailings, including database maintenance. Candidates should have ability to work independently, computer skills, knowledge of field, office skills, research skills, writing skills. Duration is year-round (up to 16 hours per week). Unpaid. Open to college freshmen, college sophomores, college juniors, college seniors, recent college graduates, graduate students, individuals reentering the workforce. International applications accepted.

Benefits Job counseling, names of contacts, opportunity to attend seminars/workshops, willing to act as a professional reference, willing to complete paperwork for educational credit, willing to provide letters of recommendation, membership in AIVF, selection of free publications in library, stipend of $100 a month with a 10-hour Web commitment.

Contact Write, fax, e-mail, or through World Wide Web site Bo Mehrad, Information Services Associate. Fax: 212-463-8519. E-mail: bo@aivf.org. No phone calls. In-person interview required. Applicants must submit a formal organization application, letter of interest, resume. Applications are accepted continuously. World Wide Web: http://www.aivf.org.

BARWOOD FILMS
40 West 57th Street, 18th Floor
New York, New York 10019

General Information Film company. Established in 1984. Number of employees: 3. Number of internship applications received each year: 200.

Internships Available ▶ *1–6 interns:* responsibilities include reading and writing coverage on screenplays, plays, and manuscripts; assisting in developing casting lists for upcoming projects; maintaining database; reading trade publications; and sharing in office work. Candidates should have ability to work independently, organizational skills, personal interest in the field, self-motivation, writing skills. Duration is 1 semester. Unpaid. Open to college freshmen, college sophomores, college juniors, college seniors, recent college graduates, graduate students. International applications accepted.

Benefits Free meals, job counseling, names of contacts, on-the-job training, travel reimbursement, willing to act as a professional reference, willing to complete paperwork for educational credit, willing to provide letters of recommendation.

Contact Write, fax, or e-mail Gina Biscotti, Internship Coordinator, c/o ICM 40 West 57th Street, 18th Floor, New York 10019. Phone: 212-556-6700. Fax: 212-556-6701. E-mail: lilycor@aol.com. In-person interview recommended (telephone interview accepted). Applicants must submit a resume, writing sample. Applications are accepted continuously.

BEACH ASSOCIATES
200 North Glebe Road, Suite 720
Arlington, Virginia 22203

General Information Video production company that specializes in organizational communications. Established in 1979. Number of employees: 10. Number of internship applications received each year: 20.

Internships Available ▶ *1 new media intern:* responsibilities include digitizing and editing video, designing and developing WWW pages and CD-ROMS, working on live Webcast events and designing and maintaining promotional materials. Candidates should have ability to work independently, analytical skills, computer skills, declared college major in field, organizational skills, self-motivation. Duration is 1 semester. Unpaid. Open to students who will receive college credit for internships. ▶ *1 production assistant intern:* responsibilities include entering scripts, answering the phone, logging and labeling tapes, gripping on ENG and EFP shoots, operating teleprompter, editing, running errands, dubbing, typing, making travel arrangements, faxing, copying, bulking tapes, shipping packages, and filing. Candidates should have ability to work with others, college courses in field, computer skills, knowledge of field, office skills, oral communication skills, organizational skills, personal interest in the field, self-motivation, written communication skills. Duration is 1 semester. Unpaid. Open to college sophomores, college juniors, college seniors, recent college graduates.

Benefits Formal training, names of contacts, on-the-job training, opportunity to attend seminars/workshops, willing to complete paperwork for educational credit, willing to provide letters of recommendation, free parking.

Contact Write, call, fax, e-mail, or through World Wide Web site Ms. Kay Leonard, Executive Vice President, General Manager. Phone: 703-812-8813. Fax: 703-812-9710. E-mail: kleonard@beachassociates.com. Telephone interview required. Applicants must submit a letter of interest, resume. Applications are accepted continuously. World Wide Web: http://www.beachassociates.com.

BUZZCO ASSOCIATES, INC.
33 Bleecker Street
New York, New York 10012

General Information Traditional animation company specializing in all forms of 2-D animation with projects ranging from corporate sales films, cable network IDs, network public service announcements, and national and regional commercials. Established in 1985. Number of employees: 5. Number of internship applications received each year: 25.

Internships Available ▶ *1–3 interns:* responsibilities include performing production research and assisting film editorial staff. Candidates should have ability to work with others, plan to pursue career in field, self-motivation. Duration is 1–6 months. Unpaid. Open to high school seniors, recent high school graduates, college freshmen, college sophomores, college juniors, college seniors, recent college graduates, individuals reentering the workforce.

Benefits Job counseling, names of contacts, possible full-time employment, willing to complete paperwork for educational credit, willing to provide letters of recommendation, access to facilities.

Contact Write, call, fax, e-mail, or through World Wide Web site Ms. Candy Kugel, Director, Producer. Phone: 212-473-8800. Fax: 212-473-8891. E-mail: info@buzzco.com. In-person interview required. Applicants must submit a letter of interest. Application deadline: 6 weeks prior to start of internship. World Wide Web: http://www.buzzzco.com.

EUROPA CORPORATION
1411 5th Street, Suite 405
Santa Monica, California 90401

General Information Feature film production company. Established in 1995. Number of employees: 1. Subsidiary of Europa Corporation, Paris, France. Number of internship applications received each year: 30.

Internships Available ▶ *3–5 development interns.* Candidates should have analytical skills, computer skills, office skills, oral communication skills, writing skills. Duration is flexible. Unpaid. Open to college freshmen, college sophomores, college juniors, college seniors. International applications accepted.

Benefits Free meals, names of contacts, on-the-job training, opportunity to attend seminars/workshops, willing to act as a professional reference, willing to complete paperwork for educational credit, willing to provide letters of recommendation.

Contact Fax India Osborne, Vice President of Production. Fax: 310-395-2890. E-mail: indiao@seasideprods.com. No phone calls. In-person interview recommended (telephone interview accepted). Applicants must submit a letter of interest, resume. Applications are accepted continuously.

FILMWORKS LABORATORY, INC.
523 Colorado Avenue
Santa Monica, California 90401

General Information Post production boutique offering lab, telecine, editing, sound, and duplication. Established in 1996. Number of employees: 10. Number of internship applications received each year: 100.

Internships Available ▶ *2–4 post production interns:* responsibilities include breaking down film lab rolls and prepping film for telecine; dubs; addressing mailers; answering phones; ordering lunches; and client services. Candidates should have ability to work independently, college courses in field, organizational skills, personal interest in the field, plan to pursue career in field, strong interpersonal skills. Duration is 1–2 semesters. $6.75 per hour. Open to college freshmen, college sophomores, college juniors, college seniors, recent college graduates.

Benefits Job counseling, possible full-time employment, willing to act as a professional reference, willing to complete paperwork for educational credit, willing to provide letters of recommendation.

Contact Write or fax Victoria English, Vice President. Fax: 310-451-2660. E-mail: post@filmworkslaboratory.com. No phone calls. In-person interview required. Applicants must submit a resume. Applications are accepted continuously. World Wide Web: http://www.filmworkslaboratory.com.

HISTORIC FILMS
211 Third Street
Greenport, New York 11944

General Information Historic stock footage library specializing in archival film and musical performances. Established in 1991. Number of employees: 9. Number of internship applications received each year: 50.

Internships Available ▶ *1–2 research assistants:* responsibilities include video research, logging of images, tape to tape transfer, and various other duties. Candidates should have ability to work independently, analytical skills, office skills, organizational skills, personal interest in the field, research skills. Duration is 6–12 weeks. Unpaid. Open to recent high school graduates, college freshmen, college sophomores, college juniors, college seniors, recent college graduates, graduate students. International applications accepted.

Benefits Names of contacts, on-the-job training, possible full-time employment, willing to act as a professional reference, willing to complete paperwork for educational credit, willing to provide letters of recommendation.

Contact Write, call, fax, e-mail, or through World Wide Web site Kevin Rice, Research Director/Internship Coordinator. Phone: 631-477-9700. Fax: 631-477-9800. E-mail: kevin@historicfilms.com. In-person interview recommended (telephone interview accepted).

Historic Films (continued)
Applicants must submit a letter of interest, resume. Applications are accepted continuously. World Wide Web: http://www.historicfilms.com.

HYBRID FILMS
116 University Place, Suite 2
New York, New York 10003

General Information Independent documentary film and television production company; films have been broadcast internationally on networks including A&E, Court TV, and the BBC. Established in 1995. Number of employees: 3. Number of internship applications received each year: 100.
Internships Available ▶ *1–5 production/edit interns:* responsibilities include logging, transcribing, and digitizing video material; production assistance; general office duties; research for future projects. Candidates should have ability to work independently, computer skills, office skills, personal interest in the field, research skills, self-motivation. Duration is at least 3 months. Unpaid. Open to college freshmen, college sophomores, college juniors, college seniors, recent college graduates, graduate students, career changers. International applications accepted.
Benefits Job counseling, names of contacts, on-the-job training, possible full-time employment, travel reimbursement, willing to act as a professional reference, willing to complete paperwork for educational credit, willing to provide letters of recommendation.
Contact Write, call, fax, or e-mail Courtney Reilly, Production Manager. Phone: 212-463-9908. Fax: 212-675-6344. E-mail: internships@hybridfilms.tv. In-person interview recommended (telephone interview accepted). Applicants must submit a letter of interest, resume. Applications are accepted continuously. World Wide Web: http://hybridfilms.tv.

LEFRAK PRODUCTIONS, INC.
40 West 57th Street, Suite 409
New York, New York 10019

General Information Film and television development company headed by an independent producer. Established in 1980. Number of employees: 5. Number of internship applications received each year: 50.
Internships Available ▶ *5–7 interns:* responsibilities include performing general office work, attending the theater, and looking for new project ideas. Candidates should have ability to work independently, computer skills, knowledge of field, office skills, oral communication skills, organizational skills, plan to pursue career in field, research skills, self-motivation, strong interpersonal skills, written communication skills. Duration is 3 months (full-time or part-time). Unpaid. Open to college freshmen, college sophomores, college juniors, college seniors, recent college graduates, graduate students, law students, career changers. International applications accepted.
Benefits Formal training, job counseling, on-the-job training, possible full-time employment, willing to act as a professional reference, willing to complete paperwork for educational credit, willing to provide letters of recommendation.
Contact Call, fax, or e-mail Melissa Sarrocco, Internship Coordinator. Phone: 212-541-9444. Fax: 212-974-8205. E-mail: lfp@aol.com. In-person interview recommended (telephone interview accepted). Applicants must submit a resume. Application deadline: February 1 for spring, May 1 for summer, November 1 for winter.

LIGHTHOUSE PRODUCTIONS
120 El Camino Drive, Suite 212
Beverly Hills, California 90212

General Information Feature film and television production company. Established in 1974. Number of employees: 2. Number of internship applications received each year: 150.
Internships Available ▶ *2–4 story development interns:* responsibilities include script coverage and general assistant responsibilities (phone, fax, copy machine). Candidates should have analytical skills, office skills, oral communication skills, plan to pursue career in field, writing skills. Duration is 10–15 weeks. Unpaid. Open to

college juniors, college seniors, recent college graduates, graduate students. International applications accepted.
Benefits Formal training, job counseling, willing to complete paperwork for educational credit, willing to provide letters of recommendation.
Contact Write or fax Hugh Miles, Internship Coordinator. Fax: 310-859-7511. No phone calls. In-person interview recommended (telephone interview accepted). Applicants must submit a formal organization application, resume, writing sample. Application deadline: February 1 for spring, May 1 for summer and fall, December 1 for winter.

LIGHTSTORM ENTERTAINMENT, INC.
919 Santa Monica Boulevard
Santa Monica, California 90401

General Information Development and production of feature films and television shows. Established in 1990. Number of employees: 20. Unit of Twentieth Century Fox Film Corp., Los Angeles, California. Number of internship applications received each year: 100.
Internships Available ▶ *4–5 development interns:* responsibilities include script analysis, data entry, research assistance, and general office support. Candidates should have ability to work independently, analytical skills, college courses in field, computer skills, office skills, oral communication skills, organizational skills, personal interest in the field, research skills, self-motivation, strong interpersonal skills, writing skills. Duration is 3–4 months. Unpaid.
▶ *4–5 production interns:* responsibilities include inventory and archiving of production-related materials; research assistance. Candidates should have ability to work independently, college courses in field, computer skills, office skills, oral communication skills, organizational skills, plan to pursue career in field, research skills, self-motivation, strong interpersonal skills, written communication skills. Duration is 3–4 months. Unpaid. Open to college juniors, college seniors, graduate students. International applications accepted.
Benefits Job counseling, on-the-job training, willing to act as a professional reference, willing to complete paperwork for educational credit, willing to provide letters of recommendation.
Contact Write, fax, or e-mail Tom Cohen, Creative Executive. Fax: 310-656-6102. E-mail: tomc@lightstormla.com. No phone calls. In-person interview recommended (telephone interview accepted). Applicants must submit a letter of interest, resume, two writing samples, two personal references, analytical writing sample required for development applicants. Application deadline: April 1 for summer, July 1 for fall, December 1 for spring.

LOVETT PRODUCTIONS, INC.
155 Sixth Avenue, 10th Floor
New York, New York 10013

General Information Independent production company that produces documentary and reality programming, video news releases, industrials, and independent films. Established in 1989. Number of employees: 5. Number of internship applications received each year: 100.
Internships Available ▶ *4–6 production office assistants:* responsibilities include assisting in all aspects of pre- and post-production, research, writing, logging, labeling, videotaping, dubbing, and phones. Candidates should have ability to work independently, ability to work with others, oral communication skills, personal interest in the field, plan to pursue career in field, self-motivation, written communication skills. Duration is 3–4 months. Unpaid. Open to high school seniors, recent high school graduates, college freshmen, college sophomores, college juniors, college seniors, recent college graduates, graduate students, law students, career changers, individuals reentering the workforce. International applications accepted.
Benefits Willing to act as a professional reference, willing to complete paperwork for educational credit, stipend for food and transportation ($13 per day), willing to provide references and recommendations based on performance.
Contact Write, call, or fax Brian Glazer, Internship Coordinator/Production Manager. Phone: 212-242-8999. Fax: 212-242-7347. In-person interview recommended (telephone interview accepted).

Applicants must submit a letter of interest, resume. Applications are accepted continuously. World Wide Web: http://www.lovettproductions.com.

LUCAS DIGITAL LTD.
PO Box 2459
San Rafael, California 94912

General Information Company dedicated to the digital needs of the entertainment industry for visual effects and audio post production; comprised of Industrial Light and Magic (ILM) and Skywalker Sound. Established in 1975. Number of employees: 1,000. Number of internship applications received each year: 700.

Internships Available ▶ *1–3 Skywalker Sound production assistants:* responsibilities include production assistant duties. Candidates should have declared college major in field, knowledge of field, oral communication skills, personal interest in the field, plan to pursue career in field, written communication skills. Duration is winter (7 months part-time); summer (2 months full-time). $9 per hour. ▶ *1 Web development intern:* responsibilities include assisting projects in Internet or interactive areas. Candidates should have college courses in field, computer skills, oral communication skills, organizational skills, written communication skills, graphics design experience. Duration is winter (7 months part-time); summer (2 months full-time). $9 per hour. ▶ *1–3 art department interns:* responsibilities include production assistant and art assistant duties. Candidates should have ability to work with others, computer skills, declared college major in field, oral communication skills, personal interest in the field, plan to pursue career in field. Duration is winter (7 months part-time); summer (2 months full-time). $9 per hour. ▶ *1–3 commercials production assistants:* responsibilities include production assistant duties in a commercial production office. Candidates should have ability to work with others, declared college major in field, oral communication skills, plan to pursue career in field, written communication skills, production experience. Duration is winter (7 months part-time); summer (2 months full-time). $9 per hour. ▶ *2 computer graphics training interns:* responsibilities include editing training class videos, running camera during classes, updating CG tutorials, maintaining library and database. Candidates should have computer skills, oral communication skills, organizational skills, plan to pursue career in field, strong interpersonal skills, written communication skills. Duration is winter (7 months part-time); summer (2 months full-time). $9 per hour. ▶ *2 editorial interns:* responsibilities include production assistant/editorial assistant duties. Candidates should have computer skills, knowledge of field, oral communication skills, plan to pursue career in field, written communication skills, production experience. Duration is winter (7 months part-time); summer (2 months full-time). $9 per hour. ▶ *2 human resources interns:* responsibilities include various human resources projects and research. Candidates should have computer skills, declared college major in field, oral communication skills, plan to pursue career in field, strong interpersonal skills, written communication skills. Duration is winter (7 months part-time); summer (2 months full-time). $9 per hour. ▶ *1 media library intern:* responsibilities include working in media library, tracking, maintaining, and organizing film archives. Candidates should have computer skills, office skills, organizational skills, personal interest in the field, research skills, library studies. Duration is winter (7 months part-time); summer (2 months full-time). $9 per hour. Open to college juniors, college seniors, graduate students. International applications accepted.

Benefits On-the-job training, opportunity to attend seminars/workshops, possible full-time employment, willing to complete paperwork for educational credit.

Contact Write, fax, e-mail, or through World Wide Web site Internship Coordinator. Fax: 415-448-2850. E-mail: interns@lucasdigital.com. No phone calls. In-person interview recommended (telephone interview accepted). Applicants must submit a formal organization application, resume, academic transcripts, two letters of recommendation, questionnaire. Application deadline: April 12 for summer, August 2 for fall/winter. World Wide Web: http://www.ilm.com.

LUCASFILM LTD. AND LUCAS LICENSING LTD.
PO Box 2009
San Rafael, California 94912

General Information Company that provides business services for productions by Lucasfilm. Established in 1971. Number of employees: 300. Number of internship applications received each year: 200.

Internships Available ▶ *8–12 summer interns:* responsibilities include assisting in engineering, marketing, licensing (publishing, merchandising, product development), graphic design, human resources, finance, ITSS ranch operations departments, or archives. Duration is 10 weeks (40 hours per week). $9 per hour. ▶ *5–10 winter interns:* responsibilities include assisting in engineering, marketing, licensing (publishing, merchandising, product development), graphic design, human resources, finance, ITSS ranch operations departments, or archives. Duration is 26 weeks (16-24 hours per week). $9 per hour. Candidates for all positions should have ability to work independently, computer skills, office skills, personal interest in the field, self-motivation. Open to college juniors, college seniors, graduate students, law students.

Benefits Job counseling, on-the-job training, opportunity to attend seminars/workshops, willing to complete paperwork for educational credit, willing to provide letters of recommendation.

Contact Through World Wide Web site Brenda Hodges, Intern Coordinator. Fax: 415-662-2460. No phone calls. Telephone interview required. Applicants must submit a formal organization application, resume, academic transcripts, two letters of recommendation, answers to questionnaire. Application deadline: April 15 for summer, August 31 for winter. World Wide Web: http://www.lucasfilm.com.

MCT MANAGEMENT/BOLD! MARKETING AND PROMOTION
333 West 52nd Street, Suite 1003
New York, New York 10019

General Information Music management and promotion company. Established in 1987. Number of employees: 8. Number of internship applications received each year: 100.

Internships Available ▶ *Artist management assistants:* responsibilities include general office responsibilities and music duplication. Candidates should have computer skills, experience in the field, office skills, oral communication skills, self-motivation, some technical competence. Duration is flexible. Unpaid. ▶ *Promotion assistants:* responsibilities include promotion details, including calls to radio stations, generation of reports, and general office responsibilities. Candidates should have computer skills, oral communication skills, personal interest in the field, self-motivation, strong interpersonal skills. Duration is flexible. Unpaid. Open to college seniors, recent college graduates, career changers. International applications accepted.

Benefits On-the-job training, possible full-time employment, willing to act as a professional reference, willing to complete paperwork for educational credit, willing to provide letters of recommendation, unique experience in music industry.

Contact Write or fax Gregg DeMammos, Human Resource Manager. Fax: 212-315-4601. No phone calls. In-person interview required. Applicants must submit a resume. Applications are accepted continuously.

MD WAX/ COURIER FILMS
1560 Broadway, Room 706
New York, New York 10036

General Information Distributor of foreign and independent films. Established in 1983. Number of employees: 2. Unit of Morton Dennis Wax, New York, New York. Number of internship applications received each year: 50.

Internships Available ▶ *1–3 marketing assistants:* responsibilities include creating and implementing marketing plans for films, writing advertising and promotional releases, contacting exhibitors, and providing general office assistance. Candidates should have ability to work independently, computer skills, office skills, oral communication skills, self-motivation, writing skills. Duration is

MD Wax/ Courier Films (continued)

1–6 months. Unpaid. Open to college freshmen, college sophomores, college juniors, college seniors. International applications accepted.
Benefits On-the-job training, willing to act as a professional reference, willing to complete paperwork for educational credit, willing to provide letters of recommendation.
Contact Write or fax Ms. Sandra Wax, Vice President. Fax: 212-302-5364. No phone calls. Applicants must submit a letter of interest, resume, academic reference. Application deadline: April 1 for summer, October 1 for winter.

METRO-GOLDWYN-MAYER/UNITED ARTISTS
1350 Sixth Avenue, 24th Floor
New York, New York 10019

General Information Movie company that releases first-run films into the domestic market. Established in 1924. Number of employees: 5. Number of internship applications received each year: 200.
Internships Available ▶ *3–5 interns:* responsibilities include working in publicity and promotions departments. Duration is 1 semester. Unpaid. Open to college freshmen, college sophomores, college juniors, college seniors. International applications accepted.
Benefits Names of contacts, willing to complete paperwork for educational credit, willing to provide letters of recommendation.
Contact Write, call, or fax Intern Coordinator. Phone: 212-708-0300. Fax: 212-582-2846. In-person interview required. Applicants must submit a letter of interest, resume. Applications are accepted continuously. World Wide Web: http://www.mgm.com.

MIND OVER MEDIA
2425 Liberty Avenue
Pittsburgh, Pennsylvania 15222

General Information Organization that engages in production of corporate industrial videos and some broadcast videos. Established in 1981. Number of employees: 40. Number of internship applications received each year: 50.
Internships Available ▶ *1–3 production interns:* responsibilities include learning equipment and company operation, performing some duties of a production assistant and associate producer, operating teleprompter, running tapes, getting food for clients, and helping with daily administrative and production tasks. Candidates should have computer skills, knowledge of field, organizational skills, plan to pursue career in field, self-motivation, strong interpersonal skills. Duration is 2 months (with a review and possible rollover). Position available as unpaid or paid. Open to college freshmen, college sophomores, college juniors, college seniors, recent college graduates. International applications accepted.
Benefits Formal training, opportunity to attend seminars/workshops, possible full-time employment, travel reimbursement.
Contact Write, fax, or e-mail Diane Rankin, Client Services Manager. Fax: 412-391-0185. E-mail: careers@momlistens.com. No phone calls. In-person interview required. Applicants must submit a letter of interest, resume. Applications are accepted continuously. World Wide Web: http://www.momknows.com.

NASSAU COUNTY OFFICE OF CINEMA AND TELEVISION PROMOTION
1550 Franklin Avenue, Suite 207
Mineola, New York 11501

General Information Film commission that scouts locations and facilitates film production, commercials, videos, and still photography; also runs the Long Island International Film Expo. Established in 1989. Number of employees: 6. Unit of Nassau County Department of Commerce and Industry, Mineola, New York. Number of internship applications received each year: 40.
Internships Available ▶ *1 data entry intern:* responsibilities include updating and entering data into film database. Candidates should have ability to work with Office Suite program. Duration is flexible. Unpaid. Open to high school seniors, recent high school graduates, college freshmen, college sophomores, college juniors, college seniors, recent college graduates, graduate students, law students, career changers, individuals reentering the workforce.

▶ *1–4 film coordinators:* responsibilities include contacting clients by phone, scouting locations, researching, updating files, following up on film shoots, assisting with permit procedures, and helping with Long Island International Film Expo. Candidates should have ability to work independently, oral communication skills, personal interest in the field, self-motivation, strong interpersonal skills. Duration is flexible. Unpaid. Open to high school seniors, recent high school graduates, college freshmen, college sophomores, college juniors, college seniors, recent college graduates, graduate students, law students, career changers, individuals reentering the workforce. ▶ *3 location photographers:* responsibilities include photographing locations, mansions, and parks. Candidates should have personal interest in the field. Duration is flexible. Unpaid. Open to recent high school graduates, college freshmen, college sophomores, college juniors, college seniors, recent college graduates, graduate students, law students, career changers, individuals reentering the workforce.
Benefits Formal training, names of contacts, willing to complete paperwork for educational credit, willing to provide letters of recommendation.
Contact Write, call, fax, or e-mail Ms. Debra Markowitz, Director. Phone: 516-571-3168. Fax: 516-571-4161. E-mail: debfilm@aol.com. In-person interview recommended (telephone interview accepted). Applicants must submit a resume. Applications are accepted continuously. World Wide Web: http://www.co.nassau.ny.us/tv.html.

OPEN CITY FILMS/ BLOW UP PICTURES
44 Hudson Street, 2nd Floor
New York, New York 10013

General Information Independent film production company. Established in 1993. Number of employees: 8. Number of internship applications received each year: 200.
Internships Available ▶ *4–6 interns:* responsibilities include assisting in all areas of office operations including phones, script reading, research, development, and production. Candidates should have ability to work independently, computer skills, office skills, personal interest in the field, research skills, written communication skills. Duration is 3–4 months. Unpaid. Open to college freshmen, college sophomores, college juniors, college seniors. International applications accepted.
Benefits Willing to act as a professional reference, willing to complete paperwork for educational credit, willing to provide letters of recommendation.
Contact Write, fax, or e-mail Robyn Alcock, Office Manager. Fax: 212-587-1950. E-mail: oc@opencityfilms.com. No phone calls. Applicants must submit a letter of interest, resume. Applications are accepted continuously. World Wide Web: http://www.blowuppictures.com.

PUBLIC INTEREST VIDEO NETWORK
6308 Tone Drive
Bethesda, Maryland 20817

General Information Media center producing public television documentaries and assisting issue-oriented nonprofit organizations and government agencies in using the media. Established in 1979. Number of employees: 3. Number of internship applications received each year: 10.
Internships Available ▶ *2 production assistants:* responsibilities include assisting producer/director in field production, research, editing, graphics, distribution, and office-related matters. Candidates should have ability to work independently, ability to work with others, computer skills, editing skills, office skills, research skills, self-motivation, written communication skills, Media-100 video editing, PhotoShop, After Affects, and Mac computer experience a plus. Duration is 3 or more months. Unpaid. Open to college sophomores, college juniors, college seniors, recent college graduates, graduate students, career changers. International applications accepted.
Benefits Job counseling, names of contacts, on-the-job training, possible full-time employment, travel reimbursement, willing to act as a professional reference, willing to complete paperwork for educational credit, willing to provide letters of recommendation, filming on location across the U.S.

Contact Write, call, fax, e-mail, or through World Wide Web site Mr. Arlen Slobodow, Director. Phone: 301-263-1110. Fax: 301-320-4929. E-mail: info@publicinterestvideo.com. In-person interview recommended (telephone interview accepted). Applicants must submit a letter of interest, resume, three personal references. Application deadline: March 1 for summer (recommended deadline); continuous for academic year positions. World Wide Web: http://www.publicinterestvideo.com.

RADIO & TELEVISION NEWS DIRECTORS FOUNDATION
1600 K Street, NW, #700
Washington, District of Columbia 20006

General Information Nonprofit foundation. Number of employees: 10. Unit of Radio & Television News Directors Foundation, Washington, District of Columbia. Number of internship applications received each year: 150.
Internships Available ▶ *2 Capitol Hill interns:* responsibilities include following newsworthy congressional activities and helping to coordinate broadcast coverage of these activities. Candidates should have college courses in field, knowledge of field, personal interest in the field, plan to pursue career in field, self-motivation, written communication skills. Duration is March to May or June to August. $1000 per month. Open to recent college graduates. International applications accepted.
Benefits Names of contacts, on-the-job training, opportunity to attend seminars/workshops, possible full-time employment.
Contact Write, call, e-mail, or through World Wide Web site Karen Jackson Bullitt, Program Coordinator, 1600 K Street, NW, #700, Washington, District of Columbia 20006. Phone: 202-467-5218. E-mail: karenb@rtndf.org. Applicants must submit a formal organization application, resume, three letters of recommendation. Application deadline: January 18 for spring, April 1 for summer. World Wide Web: http://www.rtndf.org.

SIMON & GOODMAN PICTURE COMPANY
2095 Broadway, Suite 402
New York, New York 10023

General Information Documentary film company. Established in 1987. Number of employees: 5. Number of internship applications received each year: 200.
Internships Available ▶ *3–6 interns:* responsibilities include assisting producers and editors on film shoots, logging tapes, research, and miscellaneous office duties. Candidates should have ability to work with others, college courses in field, knowledge of field, office skills, self-motivation, strong interest in documentary films. Duration is 1 semester. Unpaid. Open to undergraduate or graduate film students, recent graduates. International applications accepted.
Benefits Names of contacts, on-the-job training, opportunity to attend seminars/workshops, possible full-time employment, willing to act as a professional reference, willing to complete paperwork for educational credit, willing to provide letters of recommendation, possible attendance at film shoots.
Contact Write, fax, or e-mail Internship Coordinator. Fax: 212-721-0922. E-mail: sgpic@aol.com. No phone calls. In-person interview recommended (telephone interview accepted). Applicants must submit a letter of interest, resume. Applications are accepted continuously. World Wide Web: http://www.sgpic.com.

S.O.S. PRODUCTIONS, INC.
753 Harmon Avenue
Columbus, Ohio 43223

General Information Film, audio, video, and postproduction facility that makes television commercials and corporate videos. Established in 1981. Number of employees: 26. Number of internship applications received each year: 50.
Internships Available ▶ *1 audio post-production intern:* responsibilities include recording, editing, and working in sound design. Candidates should have college courses in field, oral communication skills, personal interest in the field, self-motivation, strong interpersonal skills, students must be receiving college credit, must have own vehicle and valid driver's license. Duration is 1 semester.

$50 per week. ▶ *1–2 production interns:* responsibilities include setting-up and wrapping video film equipment; understanding the purpose of each production service and the planning and execution phases of the production process; and assisting in building, lighting, and striking sets. Candidates should have college courses in field, oral communication skills, plan to pursue career in field, self-motivation, strong interpersonal skills, students must be receiving college credit, must have own vehicle and valid driver's license. Duration is 10 weeks. $50 per week. Open to college freshmen, college sophomores, college juniors, college seniors.
Benefits Names of contacts, on-the-job training, possible full-time employment, willing to act as a professional reference, willing to complete paperwork for educational credit, willing to provide letters of recommendation.
Contact Write, fax, or e-mail Virginia Hayes, Production Manager. Fax: 614-221-3836. E-mail: vhayes@sostv.com. No phone calls. In-person interview required. Applicants must submit a letter of interest, resume. Applications are accepted continuously.

WALL STREET MUSIC
28545 Greenfield, Suite 200
Southfield, Michigan 48076

General Information Record company and distributor specializing in the marketing, promotion, and sales of various musical genres. Established in 1985. Number of employees: 10. Branch of Wall Street Productions, Atlanta, Georgia. Number of internship applications received each year: 100.
Internships Available ▶ *1–2 engineering/production interns:* responsibilities include learning the inner workings of the music production industry using Digidesign random-access multitrack recording software, digital soundfile editors, digital multitrack tape machines, video/audio machine control interfacing, and digital sequencing software during all stages of the audio production chain, and exercising organizational skills. Candidates should have computer skills, declared college major in field, experience in the field, oral communication skills, organizational skills, plan to pursue career in field. Duration is 15–20 weeks. Unpaid. Open to college freshmen, college sophomores, college juniors, college seniors, recent college graduates, graduate students, law students. ▶ *1–2 marketing interns:* responsibilities include assisting in maintaining databases for each marketing area, contacting and negotiating with mailing list brokers, helping prepare international direct-mail campaigns, composing press releases for international newswires, and disseminating press kits for radio, television, and print. Candidates should have ability to work independently, computer skills, oral communication skills, organizational skills, plan to pursue career in field, written communication skills. Duration is 15–20 weeks. Unpaid. Open to college freshmen, college sophomores, college juniors, college seniors, recent college graduates, graduate students, law students. ▶ *1–2 promotions interns:* responsibilities include assisting in contacting radio, retail, press, and record pools to maintain status and contact reports on computer, providing advance notice of new releases, coordinating promotional mailings, determining need for promotional products, informing of artists' activities, mediating with venues regarding promotional events, exploring advertising opportunities, seeking out additional contacts, and troubleshooting problems. Candidates should have ability to work independently, computer skills, oral communication skills, organizational skills, plan to pursue career in field, written communication skills. Duration is 15–20 weeks. Unpaid. Open to college freshmen, college sophomores, college juniors, college seniors, recent college graduates, graduate students. ▶ *1–2 public relations interns:* responsibilities include writing news releases, biographies, and fact sheets; compiling and packaging press kits; acquiring performance information regarding artist tours and assisting in promotional mailings to magazines and press; arranging for interviews and promotional events and requesting and cataloging tearsheets from press; electronically pasting up press coverage for press kits, tracking inventory of artists' promotional materials, assisting in follow-up of targeted media personnel, exploring media advertising based upon media plan, helping coordinate record release parties, and interacting with Wall Street artists on all promotional issues. Candidates should have ability to work independently, computer

Wall Street Music (continued)

skills, oral communication skills, organizational skills, plan to pursue career in field, written communication skills. Duration is 15–20 weeks. Unpaid. Open to college freshmen, college sophomores, college juniors, college seniors, recent college graduates, graduate students, law students. International applications accepted.
Benefits Job counseling, names of contacts, opportunity to attend seminars/workshops, possible full-time employment, willing to act as a professional reference, willing to complete paperwork for educational credit, willing to provide letters of recommendation, use of company computers for resumes and mass mailings.
Contact Write or e-mail Ms. Colleen Collins, Internship Coordinator. Phone: 248-395-2770. Fax: 248-395-2773. E-mail: info@wallstreetmusic. com. In-person interview recommended (telephone interview accepted). Applicants must submit a formal organization application, letter of interest, resume, two writing samples. Applications are accepted continuously. World Wide Web: http://www. wallstreetmusic.com.

WOMEN MAKE MOVIES, INC.
462 Broadway, 5th Floor
New York, New York 10013

General Information National women's media organization that facilitates the production, promotion, and distribution of films and videotapes by and about women. Established in 1972. Number of employees: 13. Number of internship applications received each year: 60.
Internships Available ▶ *1–5 distribution assistants:* responsibilities include working in distribution department, maintenance of database and mailing lists, upkeep of in-house video library, working in shipping room, and maintaining promotional files. Candidates should have ability to work with others, computer skills, office skills, oral communication skills, organizational skills, personal interest in the field, plan to pursue career in field, written communication skills. Duration is 1 semester. Unpaid. ▶ *1 general office assistant:* responsibilities include working with assistant office manager updating and maintaining lists on computer database, general office duties, and responding to general information requests. Candidates should have computer skills, office skills, oral communication skills, plan to pursue career in field, strong interpersonal skills, written communication skills. Duration is 1 semester. Unpaid. ▶ *1–2 graphic production assistants:* responsibilities include producing one-sheets and other promotional pieces from templates. Candidates should have ability to work with others, knowledge of field, office skills, oral communication skills, personal interest in the field, research skills, written communication skills, knowledge of Macintosh based Quark Xpress and PhotoShop and PC based Front Page. Duration is 1 semester. Unpaid. ▶ *1–2 production assistants:* responsibilities include researching and updating grant files and other filmmaker resources, assisting with management of project files and program databases, and assisting with media workshops. Candidates should have ability to work independently, ability to work with others, computer skills, knowledge of field, office skills, oral communication skills, plan to pursue career in field, written communication skills. Duration is 1 semester. Unpaid. ▶ *1–3 promotions assistants:* responsibilities include assisting sales and marketing staff with outreach to community-based and academic organizations, assisting with production and mailing of promotional materials, designing fliers, and doing on-line research. Candidates should have ability to work with others, computer skills, editing skills, office skills, oral communication skills, writing skills, knowledge of Internet and/or desktop publishing. Duration is 1 semester. Unpaid. Open to college freshmen, college sophomores, college juniors, college seniors, recent college graduates, graduate students. International applications accepted.
Benefits Names of contacts, opportunity to attend seminars/ workshops, travel reimbursement, willing to complete paperwork for educational credit, willing to provide letters of recommendation, access to film collection, resource files, and independent filmmaking network, invitations to screenings and receptions.
Contact Write, fax, e-mail, or through World Wide Web site Talar Attarian, Office Manager. Fax: 212-925-2052. E-mail: info@wmm.

com. No phone calls. In-person interview recommended (telephone interview accepted). Applicants must submit a formal organization application, letter of interest, resume, writing sample. Applications are accepted continuously. World Wide Web: http://www. wmm.com.

NEWSPAPER PUBLISHERS

THE ADVOCATE
PO Box 588
Baton Rouge, Louisiana 70821

General Information Publisher of daily newspaper. Established in 1907. Number of employees: 571. Number of internship applications received each year: 20.
Internships Available ▶ *2 reporter interns:* responsibilities include reporting the news. Candidates should have ability to work with others, computer skills, experience in the field, personal interest in the field, self-motivation, writing skills. Duration is 2 years. $11. 10–$13.53 per hour. Open to college seniors, recent college graduates. International applications accepted.
Benefits Health insurance, possible full-time employment, travel reimbursement, willing to act as a professional reference, willing to provide letters of recommendation.
Contact Write, call, fax, e-mail, or through World Wide Web site Candace Knight, Human Resources Director. Phone: 225-388-0171. Fax: 225-388-0397. E-mail: cknight@theadvocate.com. In-person interview required. Applicants must submit a formal organization application, resume, portfolio, writing sample, three personal references. Applications are accepted continuously. World Wide Web: http://www.theadvocate.com.

AMERICAN PRESS
PO Box 2893
Lake Charles, Louisiana 70602

General Information Daily independent and family-owned newspaper. Established in 1895. Number of employees: 200. Number of internship applications received each year: 50.
Internships Available ▶ *1 editorial intern:* responsibilities include newswriting, reporting, feature writing, and working with top editors. Candidates should have declared college major in field, personal interest in the field, plan to pursue career in field, self-motivation, written communication skills. Duration is 2-3 months in summer. $7.50 per hour. Open to college freshmen, college sophomores, college juniors, college seniors. International applications accepted.
Benefits Formal training, on-the-job training, possible full-time employment, willing to act as a professional reference, willing to complete paperwork for educational credit, willing to provide letters of recommendation, opportunity to work with top editors.
Contact Write, fax, e-mail, or through World Wide Web site Mr. Brett Downer, Editor. Fax: 337-494-4070. E-mail: bdowner@ americanpress.com. No phone calls. Applicants must submit a letter of interest, resume, 5 writing samples. Application deadline: March 30. World Wide Web: http://www.americanpress.com.

AMERICAN YOUTH WORK CENTER/YOUTH TODAY
1200 17th Street, NW, 4th Floor
Washington, District of Columbia 20036

General Information National monthly newspaper for professionals concerned with youth, especially at-risk, out-of-school youth; topics may include child welfare, juvenile justice, child labor, and substance abuse. Established in 1983. Number of employees: 9. Number of internship applications received each year: 100.
Internships Available ▶ *1–3 reporter interns:* responsibilities include gathering and analyzing information, writing short articles, preparing regular features and proofreading copy, covering meetings

on Capitol Hill and meetings sponsored by public policy organizations, and performing some administrative duties. Candidates should have ability to work independently, college courses in field, computer skills, editing skills, knowledge of field, office skills, oral communication skills, organizational skills, plan to pursue career in field, research skills, self-motivation, strong interpersonal skills, writing skills. Duration is full-time summer or part-time or full-time year-round. $5.15 per hour. Open to high school students, recent high school graduates, college freshmen, college sophomores, college juniors, college seniors, recent college graduates, graduate students, career changers. International applications accepted.
Benefits Names of contacts, on-the-job training, opportunity to attend seminars/workshops, possible full-time employment, willing to act as a professional reference, willing to complete paperwork for educational credit, willing to provide letters of recommendation.
International Internships Available in Jamaica.
Contact Write, call, fax, or e-mail Patrick Boyle, Editor. Phone: 202-785-0764. Fax: 202-728-0657. E-mail: pboyle@youthtoday.org. In-person interview recommended (telephone interview accepted). Applicants must submit a letter of interest, resume, two writing samples. Applications are accepted continuously.

ANCHORAGE DAILY NEWS
PO Box 149001
Anchorage, Alaska 99514

General Information General circulation daily newspaper. Established in 1946. Number of employees: 530. Unit of The McClatchy Company, Sacramento, California. Number of internship applications received each year: 400.
Internships Available ▶ *1 copy editor intern:* responsibilities include layout, headlines, editing. Candidates should have computer skills, editing skills, experience in the field, organizational skills, writing skills, ability to meet deadlines. Duration is 12 weeks, June 1-August 31. $9.50 per hour. Open to college juniors, college seniors, recent college graduates, graduate students, career changers, individuals reentering the workforce. ▶ *1 photographer intern:* responsibilities include acting as general assignment photographer; reporting to photo editor; 40 hours/week, overtime as needed on occasion. Candidates should have ability to work independently, experience in the field, oral communication skills, strong interpersonal skills, written communication skills. Duration is 12 weeks, June 1-August 31 (slightly flexible start/stop dates). $9.50 per hour. Open to college sophomores, college juniors, college seniors, recent college graduates, graduate students, career changers, individuals reentering the workforce. ▶ *2 reporting interns:* responsibilities include acting as general assignment reporter, 40 hours/week plus overtime as occasionally needed; reporting, writing, meeting deadlines; reports to metro or feature editor. Candidates should have college courses in field, experience in the field, oral communication skills, research skills, strong interpersonal skills, writing skills. Duration is 12 weeks. $9.50 per hour. Open to college juniors, college seniors, recent college graduates, graduate students, career changers, individuals reentering the workforce.
Benefits Job counseling, names of contacts, on-the-job training, opportunity to attend seminars/workshops, possible full-time employment, travel reimbursement, willing to complete paperwork for educational credit, small grant toward getting to and returning from Anchorage, assistance in finding lodging.
Contact Write, call, or e-mail Ms. Kathleen Macknicki, Internship Coordinator. Phone: 907-257-4453. Fax: 907-258-2157. E-mail: kmacknicki@adn.com. Applicants must submit a letter of interest, resume, portfolio, at least 6 writing samples. Application deadline: January 1 for summer. World Wide Web: http://www.adn.com.

ANN ARBOR NEWS
340 East Huron
Ann Arbor, Michigan 48106-1147

General Information Daily newspaper publisher. Established in 1838. Number of employees: 400. Unit of Newhouse Newspapers. Number of internship applications received each year: 60.

Internships Available ▶ *1–2 photographers:* responsibilities include taking photographs and working in studio. Candidates should have computer skills, knowledge of field, plan to pursue career in field. Duration is 3–6 months. $450 per week. Open to college juniors, college seniors, recent college graduates, graduate students. ▶ *1–2 reporters/copy editors:* responsibilities include performing copy desk work, covering breaking news, and interviewing for features. Candidates should have ability to work with others, college courses in field, editing skills, experience in the field, plan to pursue career in field, writing skills. Duration is 3 months. $450–$500 per week. Open to college sophomores, college juniors, college seniors, recent college graduates, graduate students. ▶ *1–2 sales representatives:* responsibilities include selling classified or display advertising space to contract advertisers and acting as salespersons during summer. Candidates should have ability to work independently, oral communication skills, personal interest in the field, self-motivation, strong interpersonal skills, written communication skills. Duration is 3 months. $12–$15 per hour. Open to college sophomores, college juniors, college seniors.
Benefits Formal training, on-the-job training, possible full-time employment, willing to act as a professional reference, willing to complete paperwork for educational credit.
Contact Write, call, or e-mail Richard W. Fitzgerald, Managing Editor/Ypsilanti, 301 West Michigan Avenue, Suite 201, Ypsilanti, Michigan 48197. Phone: 734-482-4863. Fax: 734-482-2096. E-mail: rfitzgerald@annarbornews.com. Applicants must submit a letter of interest, resume, four writing samples, two personal references, 2 writing references. Application deadline: January 15 for summer. World Wide Web: http://aa.mlive.com.

THE ANNISTON STAR
PO Box 189
Anniston, Alabama 36202

General Information Newspaper. Established in 1883. Number of employees: 100. Number of internship applications received each year: 100.
Internships Available ▶ *1–2 copy editors.* Candidates should have ability to work with others, college courses in field, computer skills, editing skills, written communication skills. Duration is 12 weeks. $350 per week. ▶ *1–2 photo interns.* Duration is 12 weeks (June-August). $350 per week. ▶ *3–4 reporters:* responsibilities include beginning journalism working as a reporter or copy editor. Candidates should have ability to work with others, computer skills, personal interest in the field, writing skills. Duration is 12 weeks (June-August). $350 per week. Open to college juniors, college seniors, recent college graduates, graduate students. International applications accepted.
Benefits Job counseling, on-the-job training, possible full-time employment, willing to complete paperwork for educational credit, willing to provide letters of recommendation.
Contact Write, fax, or e-mail Troy Turner, Managing Editor. Fax: 256-235-3535. E-mail: tturner@annistonstar.com. No phone calls. Applicants must submit a letter of interest, resume, 3-5 writing samples. Application deadline: January 30. World Wide Web: http://www.annistonstar.com.

ARKANSAS DEMOCRAT-GAZETTE
121 East Capitol Avenue
Little Rock, Arkansas 72201

General Information Daily statewide newspaper. Number of employees: 500. Subsidiary of Wehco Media, Little Rock, Arkansas. Number of internship applications received each year: 400.
Internships Available ▶ *2–4 photography, graphics, design, copyediting interns.* Candidates should have editing skills, knowledge of field, plan to pursue career in field, writing skills. Duration is May/June to August/September. Paid. Open to college sophomores, college juniors, college seniors. ▶ *4–6 reporting interns:* responsibilities include reporting in the news, features, business, or sports department. Candidates should have college courses in field, experience in the field, oral communication skills, plan to pursue career in field, research skills, writing skills. Duration is May/June to August/September. Paid. Open to college sophomores, college juniors, college seniors, graduate students. International applications accepted.

Arkansas Democrat-Gazette (continued)

Benefits Names of contacts, on-the-job training, possible full-time employment, willing to act as a professional reference, willing to provide letters of recommendation, opportunity to gain experience.

Contact Write or e-mail Linda Friedlieb, Manager of Editorial Recruitment, 121 East Capitol Avenue, Little Rock, Arkansas 72201. E-mail: linda_friedlieb@adg.ardemgaz.com. Applicants must submit a letter of interest, resume, three personal references, 8-10 work samples (articles, graphics, photos). Application deadline: November 1. World Wide Web: http://www.ardemgaz.com.

ASIAN AMERICAN JOURNALISTS ASSOCIATION
1182 Market Street, Suite 320
San Francisco, California 94102

General Information National nonprofit organization that encourages Asian-American students to pursue journalism careers, seeks to increase employment of and provide support for Asian-American journalists, and promotes fair and accurate coverage of Asian-American issues. Established in 1981. Number of employees: 6.

Internships Available ▶ *3 Stanford Chen interns:* responsibilities include working in small to medium-sized newspapers or broadcast stations throughout the U.S.; one position awarded to resident of Pacific Northwest. Candidates should have oral communication skills, personal interest in the field, plan to pursue career in field, self-motivation, writing skills. Duration is flexible. $1500 per duration of internship. Open to college juniors, college seniors. ▶ *2 interns:* responsibilities include assisting in administration of annual convention, assisting staff in providing job referral and other services to AAJA's nearly 1900 members, and providing administrative support. Duration is year-round. Unpaid.

Benefits Job counseling, names of contacts, willing to complete paperwork for educational credit, willing to provide letters of recommendation, opportunity to attend annual convention.

Contact Write or e-mail Mr. Rene Estudillo, Executive Director. Phone: 415-346-2051. Fax: 415-346-6343. E-mail: national@aaja.org. In-person interview recommended (telephone interview accepted). Applicants must submit a formal organization application, academic transcripts, two personal references. Application deadline: April 15 for summer. World Wide Web: http://www.aaja.org.

THE ATLANTA JOURNAL AND CONSTITUTION
72 Marietta Street, NW
Atlanta, Georgia 30303

General Information Major daily metropolitan newspaper. Number of internship applications received each year: 500.

Internships Available ▶ *News interns:* responsibilities include working in department that matches an intern's area of skill or experience, such as reporting, copy editing, photography, or graphic arts. Candidates should have previous professional daily experience with deadlines, preferably on a newspaper; must have worked on campus newspaper or other publications. Duration is 10 weeks in summer, winter positions possible. $550 per week. Open to college juniors, college seniors, recent college graduates, graduate students.

Benefits Job counseling, opportunity to attend seminars/workshops, possible full-time employment, willing to complete paperwork for educational credit, willing to provide letters of recommendation, mentor system that aids professional growth.

Contact Write, e-mail, or through World Wide Web site Angela Tuck, News Personnel Manager. E-mail: atuck@ajc.com. No phone calls. Applicants must submit a resume, personal reference, 500-word essay (see Web site or write for details), copies of 5-10 news clips or samples of photos/graphics/headlines. Application deadline: December 15 for summer. World Wide Web: http://www.ajc.com/specials/internships.

THE BIRMINGHAM NEWS
2200 Fourth Avenue North
Birmingham, Alabama 35203

General Information Newspaper recognized regionally and nationally for its reporting and commentary. Established in 1888. Number of employees: 643. Unit of Advance Publications, Staten Island, New York. Number of internship applications received each year: 100.

Internships Available ▶ *2 fall sports interns:* responsibilities include working as a beginning sports reporter. Candidates should have ability to work independently, ability to work with others, college courses in field, computer skills, knowledge of field, plan to pursue career in field, research skills, self-motivation, writing skills, minimum B average in course work. Duration is 16 weeks. $375 per week. Open to college sophomores, college juniors, college seniors. ▶ *3 summer advertising interns:* responsibilities include working as a beginning/regular salesperson. Candidates should have ability to work independently, office skills, oral communication skills, self-motivation, writing skills. Duration is 10–12 weeks. $6 per hour. Open to college sophomores, college juniors. ▶ *4 summer news interns:* responsibilities include working as a beginning reporter. Candidates should have ability to work independently, ability to work with others, college courses in field, computer skills, knowledge of field, plan to pursue career in field, research skills, writing skills, minimum B average in course work. Duration is 10–12 weeks. $375 per week. Open to college sophomores, college juniors.

Benefits Formal training, job counseling, on-the-job training, possible full-time employment, travel reimbursement, willing to complete paperwork for educational credit, willing to provide letters of recommendation.

Contact Write, call, or fax Mr. Randy Henderson, Assistant Managing Editor (for news internships). Phone: 205-325-2210. Fax: 205-325-2283. Applicants must submit a letter of interest, resume, 8-10 writing samples. Application deadline: January 15 for summer, April 1 for fall. World Wide Web: http://www.al.com.

BIRMINGHAM POST-HERALD
2200 Fourth Avenue, North
Birmingham, Alabama 35203-3802

General Information Daily afternoon newspaper in Birmingham, Alabama. Established in 1921. Number of employees: 58. Subsidiary of Scripps Howard Company, Cincinnati, Ohio. Number of internship applications received each year: 80.

Internships Available ▶ *1 photographic intern:* responsibilities include working as a beginning photographer. Candidates should have ability to work independently, ability to work with others, college courses in field, knowledge of field, plan to pursue career in field. Duration is 12 weeks. $300 per week. Open to college freshmen, college sophomores, college juniors. ▶ *2 reporting interns:* responsibilities include working as a beginning reporter. Candidates should have ability to work independently, college courses in field, computer skills, oral communication skills, plan to pursue career in field, strong interpersonal skills, writing skills. Duration is 12 weeks. $300 per week. Open to college sophomores, college juniors.

Benefits On-the-job training, possible full-time employment, willing to act as a professional reference, willing to complete paperwork for educational credit, willing to provide letters of recommendation.

Contact Write, fax, or e-mail Becky Gallagher, Public Service Director. Fax: 205-325-2410. E-mail: mailbox@postherald.com. No phone calls. Applicants must submit a letter of interest, resume, three personal references, five writing samples. Application deadline: January 31 for summer, June 1 for fall. World Wide Web: http://www.postherald.com.

THE BOSTON GLOBE
135 Morrissey Boulevard
Boston, Massachusetts 02107

General Information Newspaper. Established in 1872. Number of employees: 2,200. Subsidary of The New York Times, New York, New York. Number of internship applications received each year: 200.

Internships Available ▶ *2 business summer interns:* responsibilities include accounts payable and payroll (accounting intern); advertising sales (advertising intern). Candidates should have ability to work independently, analytical skills, computer skills, knowledge of field, office skills, oral communication skills, organizational skills, personal interest in the field, self-motivation, strong interpersonal skills, written communication skills. Duration is 13 weeks. $570 per week. Open to college sophomores, college juniors. ▶ *2 one-year interns:* responsibilities include advertising sales or advertising design. Candidates should have ability to work independently, analytical skills, college degree in related field, computer skills, knowledge of field, office skills, oral communication skills, organizational skills, plan to pursue career in field, self-motivation, strong interpersonal skills, written communication skills. Duration is 1 year. $24,000–$41,000 per year. Open to recent college graduates. ▶ *15 summer editorial interns:* responsibilities include general assignment reporting for 13 interns; editorial design position and photography position also available. Candidates should have editing skills, writing skills, experience with school newspaper, previous internship at a daily or weekly newspaper. $601 per week. Open to college sophomores, college juniors.

Benefits On-the-job training, opportunity to attend seminars/workshops, health insurance for one-year internship.

Contact Write, fax, e-mail, or through World Wide Web site Tia Purnell, Assistant Manager of College Relations, Human Resources, PO Box 2378, Boston, Massachusetts 02107. Phone: 617-929-2021. Fax: 617-929-3376. E-mail: collegerecruiting@globe.com. Applicants must submit a formal organization application, letter of interest, resume, in-person interview (if selected). Application deadline: February 25 for business summer and one-year positions, November 5 for summer editorial positions. World Wide Web: http://www.boston.com/extranet.

BUCKS COUNTY COURIER TIMES
8400 Route 13
Levittown, Pennsylvania 19057

General Information Suburban Philadelphia newspaper with a circulation of over 70,000. Established in 1910. Number of employees: 300. Unit of Calkins Media, Inc., Levittown, Pennsylvania. Number of internship applications received each year: 100.

Internships Available ▶ *1 copy editor:* responsibilities include copyediting daily newspaper copy. Candidates should have ability to work with others, analytical skills, computer skills, editing skills, knowledge of field, written communication skills. Duration is 12 weeks (June to August). $365 per week. ▶ *1 feature writer:* responsibilities include writing and editing features. Candidates should have analytical skills, computer skills, editing skills, research skills, strong interpersonal skills, writing skills. Duration is 12 weeks (June to August). $365 per week. ▶ *1 photographer/graphics person:* responsibilities include photo or graphic (computer) work. Candidates should have analytical skills, organizational skills, personal interest in the field, self-motivation, strong interpersonal skills. Duration is 12 weeks (June to August). $365 per week. ▶ *Reporters:* responsibilities include reporting for daily newspaper. Candidates should have analytical skills, personal interest in the field, research skills, self-motivation, strong interpersonal skills, writing skills. Duration is 12 weeks (June to August). $365 per week. ▶ *1 sports writer:* responsibilities include writing features covering sports events, and editing. Candidates should have analytical skills, computer skills, editing skills, personal interest in the field, research skills, strong interpersonal skills, writing skills. Duration is 12 weeks (June to August). $365 per week. Open to college juniors, college seniors, recent college graduates, graduate students.

Benefits Names of contacts, willing to complete paperwork for educational credit, willing to provide letters of recommendation, car expenses.

Contact Write, call, fax, or e-mail Carolyn Per, Internship Coordinator. Phone: 215-949-4185. Fax: 215-949-4177. E-mail: cper@phillyburbs.com. In-person interview recommended (telephone interview accepted). Applicants must submit a formal organization application, letter of interest, resume, published writing samples. Application deadline: February 1 for summer. World Wide Web: http://www.bcct-gpn.com.

BUFFALO NEWS
1 News Plaza, PO Box 100
Buffalo, New York 14240

General Information Publisher of daily newspaper. Established in 1880. Number of employees: 1,000. Unit of Berkshire Hathaway, Inc., Omaha, Nebraska. Number of internship applications received each year: 100.

Internships Available ▶ *Copy editors:* responsibilities include editing news stories and verifying facts and grammar. Candidates should have college courses in field, editing skills, knowledge of field, writing skills, experience on school newspaper. Duration is one summer (usually 3 months). $335 per week. Open to college sophomores, college juniors, college seniors, graduate students. ▶ *Photographers:* responsibilities include replacing vacationing staffer. Candidates should have knowledge of field, oral communication skills, written communication skills, experience on school newspaper. Duration is one summer (usually 3 months). $335 per week. Open to college sophomores, college juniors, college seniors, graduate students. ▶ *Reporters:* responsibilities include replacing vacationing staffer. Candidates should have computer skills, oral communication skills, writing skills, experience on school newspaper. Duration is 3 months. $335 per week. Open to college sophomores, college juniors, college seniors, graduate students. ▶ *3–4 salespeople:* responsibilities include selling retail advertising. Candidates should have ability to work independently, analytical skills, college courses in field, knowledge of field, office skills, oral communication skills, organizational skills, personal interest in the field, self-motivation, strong interpersonal skills, written communication skills. Duration is June-August. $235 per week. Open to college freshmen, college sophomores, college juniors, college seniors.

Benefits Willing to complete paperwork for educational credit, willing to provide letters of recommendation.

Contact Write Stephen W. Bell, Managing Editor. E-mail: sbell@buffnews.com. No phone calls. In-person interview required. Applicants must submit a formal organization application, letter of interest, resume, 4-6 writing samples. Application deadline: December 1 for summer. World Wide Web: http://www.buffalo.com.

THE BULLETIN
PO Box 6020
Bend, Oregon 97708-6020

General Information Flagship newspaper in group of 9 papers (5 daily and 4 weekly) located in Oregon and California. Established in 1903. Number of employees: 300. Unit of Western Communications Inc., Bend, Oregon. Number of internship applications received each year: 100.

Internships Available ▶ *Copy editors:* responsibilities include entry-level copyediting and page layout. Candidates should have college courses in field, computer skills, editing skills, plan to pursue career in field, writing skills. Duration is 1 summer (June to September). $7.50 per hour. ▶ *Interns:* responsibilities include substituting for vacationing regular staff members. Candidates should have analytical skills, college courses in field, computer skills, organizational skills, plan to pursue career in field, writing skills. Duration is 1 summer (June to September). $7.50 per hour. ▶ *Photographers:* responsibilities include entry-level news photography. Candidates should have college courses in field, computer skills, experience in the field, organizational skills, plan to pursue career in field, writing skills, published work samples. Duration is 1 summer (June to September). $7.50 per hour. ▶ *Reporters:* responsibilities include entry-level news reporting. Candidates should have

The Bulletin *(continued)*

college courses in field, computer skills, organizational skills, plan to pursue career in field, research skills, writing skills. Duration is 1 summer (June to September). $7.50 per hour. Open to college sophomores, college juniors, college seniors, recent college graduates, graduate students. International applications accepted.
Benefits Job counseling, names of contacts, on-the-job training, opportunity to attend seminars/workshops, willing to act as a professional reference, willing to complete paperwork for educational credit, willing to provide letters of recommendation.
Contact Write Heather Clark, Newsroom Administrator. No phone calls. Telephone interview required. Applicants must submit a letter of interest, resume, 4-8 writing samples. Application deadline: April 1. World Wide Web: http://www.bendbulletin.com.

CALLER-TIMES
820 Lower North Broadway
Corpus Christi, Texas 78401

General Information Daily newspaper providing coverage in a 10-county area in southern Texas. Established in 1883. Number of employees: 400. Unit of EW Scripps, Cincinnati, Ohio. Number of internship applications received each year: 40.
Internships Available ► *3 newsroom interns.* Candidates should have editing skills, research skills, self-motivation, strong interpersonal skills, written communication skills. Duration is 10 weeks. $280–$300 per week. Open to college sophomores, college juniors, college seniors.
Benefits Names of contacts, possible full-time employment, willing to provide letters of recommendation.
Contact Write, call, fax, e-mail, or through World Wide Web site Mr. Nick Jimenez, Editorial Page Editor, PO Box 9136, Corpus Christi, Texas 78469. Phone: 361-886-3787. Fax: 361-886-3732. E-mail: jimenezn@caller.com. In-person interview recommended (telephone interview accepted). Applicants must submit a letter of interest, resume, writing sample. Application deadline: April 30 for summer. World Wide Web: http://www.caller.com.

CHATTANOOGA TIMES FREE PRESS
400 East 11th Street
Chattanooga, Tennessee 37403

General Information Daily newspaper with a daily circulation or 80,000. Number of employees: 100. Unit of Wehco Media, Little Rock, Arkansas. Number of internship applications received each year: 50.
Internships Available ► *2–4 newsroom interns:* responsibilities include writing and reporting articles for newspaper. Candidates should have analytical skills, college courses in field, plan to pursue career in field, self-motivation, writing skills. Duration is 6 months. $9750 per duration of internship. ► *2 photography interns :* responsibilities include completing assignments for publication in newspaper. Candidates should have computer skills, declared college major in field, plan to pursue career in field, self-motivation. Duration is 6 months. $9750 per duration of internship. Open to college juniors, college seniors.
Benefits Job counseling, on-the-job training, opportunity to attend seminars/workshops, possible full-time employment, willing to act as a professional reference, willing to complete paperwork for educational credit, willing to provide letters of recommendation.
Contact Write or e-mail Mark Kennedy, Features Editor. E-mail: mkennedy@timesfreepress.com. No phone calls. Telephone interview required. Applicants must submit a letter of interest, resume, 3–5 writing samples, 2–4 personal references, 1–3 letters of recommendation. Applications are accepted continuously. World Wide Web: http://www.timesfreepress.com.

COLUMBIA JOURNALISM REVIEW
Journalism Building, Columbia University
New York, New York 10027

General Information National monitor of the news media. Established in 1961. Number of employees: 11. Number of internship applications received each year: 100.
Internships Available ► *6 interns:* responsibilities include research and other duties as needed. Candidates should have ability to work independently, ability to work with others, computer skills, oral communication skills, plan to pursue career in field, research skills, written communication skills. Duration is 3–5 months. $8 per hour. Open to college freshmen, college sophomores, college juniors, college seniors, recent college graduates, graduate students, career changers, individuals reentering the workforce. International applications accepted.
Benefits Opportunity to attend seminars/workshops, willing to act as a professional reference, willing to complete paperwork for educational credit, willing to provide letters of recommendation.
Contact Write, call, fax, or e-mail Brent Cunningham, Managing Editor. Phone: 212-854-1882. Fax: 212-854-8580. E-mail: cjr@columbia.edu. Applicants must submit a letter of interest, resume, three writing samples, two letters of recommendation or two reference contacts. Applications are accepted continuously. World Wide Web: http://www.cjr.org.

COLUMBUS LEDGER–ENQUIRER
17 West 12th Street
Columbus, Georgia 31901

General Information Newspaper. Established in 1828. Number of employees: 250. Unit of Knight Ridder, San Jose, California. Number of internship applications received each year: 75.
Internships Available ► *1–4 news or features reporters:* responsibilities include working as a professional journalist writing on deadline. Candidates should have ability to work independently, editing skills, oral communication skills, plan to pursue career in field, writing skills. Duration is 10–12 weeks. Position available as unpaid or paid. Open to recent high school graduates, college freshmen, college sophomores, college juniors, college seniors, graduate students.
Benefits Housing at a cost, job counseling, names of contacts, on-the-job training, opportunity to attend seminars/workshops, possible full-time employment, willing to act as a professional reference, willing to complete paperwork for educational credit, willing to provide letters of recommendation.
Contact Write or e-mail Susan Catron, Managing Editor. Phone: 706-571-8557. Fax: 706-576-6290. E-mail: scatron@ledger-enquirer.com. In-person interview recommended (telephone interview accepted). Applicants must submit a formal organization application, letter of interest, resume, portfolio, personal reference, 10 writing samples. Application deadline: January 15 for summer. World Wide Web: http://www.ledger-enquirer.com.

CONNECTICUT POST
410 State Street
Bridgeport, Connecticut 06604

General Information Daily newspaper. Established in 1883. Number of employees: 525. Subsidiary of Media News Group, Inc., Denver, Colorado. Number of internship applications received each year: 60.
Internships Available ► *Interns:* responsibilities include performing the duties of a reporter; also copy desk and photography work. Candidates should have computer skills, editing skills, oral communication skills, plan to pursue career in field, research skills, writing skills. Duration is based on school guidelines. Unpaid. Open to college freshmen, college sophomores, college juniors, college seniors, high school students over age 16.
Benefits On-the-job training, willing to act as a professional reference, willing to complete paperwork for educational credit, willing to provide letters of recommendation.
Contact Write, call, fax, or e-mail Cindy Simoneau, Assistant Managing Editor, 410 State Street, Bridgeport, Connecticut 06604. Phone: 203-330-6391. Fax: 203-367-8158. E-mail: csimoneau@ctpost.com. In-person interview recommended (telephone interview accepted). Applicants must submit a resume, three writing samples, letter of recommendation, 1 personal reference from an academic advisor. Applications are accepted continuously.

COURIER-JOURNAL
525 West Broadway, PO Box 740031
Louisville, Kentucky 40201-7431

General Information Newspaper serving the state of Kentucky and southern Indiana. Established in 1868. Number of employees: 1,000. Unit of Gannett Co., Inc., McLean, Virginia. Number of internship applications received each year: 250.
Internships Available ▶ *Artists:* responsibilities include helping with layouts, graphics, and illustrations. Candidates should have computer skills, knowledge of field, oral communication skills, personal interest in the field, writing skills, familiarity with desktop publishing applications. Duration is 12 weeks in summer. $400 per week. ▶ *Photographers/photo editors:* responsibilities include photographing news stories and helping with design layout, editing, and developing. Candidates should have ability to work with others, editing skills, oral communication skills, personal interest in the field, research skills, writing skills. Duration is 12 weeks in summer. $400 per week. ▶ *Reporters and copy editors:* responsibilities include attending weekly meetings and working in all aspects of news reporting. Candidates should have ability to work independently, ability to work with others, computer skills, office skills, oral communication skills, personal interest in the field, research skills, writing skills. Duration is 12 weeks in summer. $400 per week. Open to college freshmen, college sophomores, college juniors, college seniors, recent college graduates, graduate students. International applications accepted.
Benefits Job counseling, names of contacts, on-the-job training, opportunity to attend seminars/workshops, possible full-time employment, travel reimbursement, willing to act as a professional reference, willing to complete paperwork for educational credit, willing to provide letters of recommendation.
Contact Write or call Mr. Mervin Aubespin, Associate Editor/Development, PO Box 740031, 525 West Broadway, Louisville, Kentucky 40201-7431. Phone: 502-582-4191. Fax: 502-582-4610. E-mail: maubespin@courier-journal.com. Applicants must submit a letter of interest, resume, academic transcripts, at least 6 writing samples for reporting and copyediting positions; portfolio for design and photography positions. Application deadline: November 15 for summer. World Wide Web: http://www.courier-journal.com.

THE DAILY PRESS
7505 Warwick Boulevard
Newport News, Virginia 23607

General Information Daily newspaper. Established in 1896. Number of employees: 575. Unit of Tribune Company, Chicago, Illinois. Number of internship applications received each year: 300.
Internships Available ▶ *4–5 interns:* responsibilities include writing, copyediting, or performing photographic or graphic art, or broadcasting duties. Candidates should have ability to work independently, analytical skills, college courses in field, computer skills, editing skills, knowledge of field, oral communication skills, organizational skills, personal interest in the field, plan to pursue career in field, research skills, self-motivation, strong interpersonal skills, writing skills. Duration is 10 weeks. $410 per week. Open to college sophomores, college juniors, college seniors, recent college graduates, graduate students, career changers.
Benefits Formal training, job counseling, names of contacts, on-the-job training, opportunity to attend seminars/workshops, possible full-time employment, travel reimbursement, willing to act as a professional reference, willing to complete paperwork for educational credit, willing to provide letters of recommendation, mentoring.
Contact Write, call, fax, e-mail, or through World Wide Web site Sheila R. Solomon, Staff Development Editor. Phone: 757-247-4646. Fax: 757-244-7437. E-mail: srsolomon@dailypress.com. Telephone interview required. Applicants must submit a letter of interest, resume, academic transcripts, portfolio, three personal references, essay, 5 writing samples. Application deadline: December 1 for summer. World Wide Web: http://www.dailypress.com.

THE DALLAS MORNING NEWS
508 Young Street
Dallas, Texas 75202

General Information Newspaper with daily circulation of 520,000 and Sunday circulation of 785,000. Established in 1885. Number of employees: 2,000. Unit of Belo Corporation, Dallas, Texas. Number of internship applications received each year: 400.
Internships Available ▶ *4 copy editors.* Candidates should have analytical skills, college courses in field, editing skills, experience in the field, plan to pursue career in field, writing skills. Duration is 12 weeks. $535 per week. ▶ *1–2 graphic artists.* Candidates should have ability to work with others, college courses in field, computer skills, knowledge of field, self-motivation. Duration is 12 weeks. $535 per week. ▶ *2 photographers.* Candidates should have ability to work with others, college courses in field, knowledge of field, plan to pursue career in field, self-motivation. Duration is 12 weeks. $535 per week. ▶ *7–10 reporters.* Candidates should have analytical skills, college courses in field, editing skills, experience in the field, plan to pursue career in field, writing skills. Duration is 12 weeks. $535 per week. Open to college freshmen, college sophomores, college juniors, college seniors, recent college graduates, graduate students.
Benefits Job counseling, on-the-job training, opportunity to attend seminars/workshops, willing to act as a professional reference, willing to complete paperwork for educational credit, willing to provide letters of recommendation.
Contact Write or through World Wide Web site Sue F. Smith, Deputy Managing Editor, Communications Center, PO Box 655237, Dallas, Texas 75265. Applicants must submit a letter of interest, resume, portfolio, three personal references, 6-10 writing samples, cover letter. Application deadline: December 1 for summer. World Wide Web: http://www.dallasnews.com.

DELAWARE COUNTY DAILY TIMES
500 Mildred Avenue
Primos, Pennsylvania 19018

General Information Seven-day-per-week newspaper serving Delaware County. Established in 1876. Number of employees: 140. Unit of The Journal Register Company, Trenton, New Jersey. Number of internship applications received each year: 50.
Internships Available ▶ *1–3 reporters:* responsibilities include covering fires, school board meetings, corporate events, and features. Candidates should have ability to work independently, ability to work with others, computer skills, personal interest in the field, self-motivation, writing skills. Duration is 3 months. $332 per week. Open to college freshmen, college sophomores, college juniors, college seniors, recent college graduates.
Benefits Possible full-time employment, travel reimbursement, willing to act as a professional reference, willing to complete paperwork for educational credit, willing to provide letters of recommendation.
Contact Write, call, fax, or e-mail Linda DeMeglio, Managing Editor. Phone: 610-622-8817. Fax: 610-622-8887. E-mail: ldemeglio@delcotimes.com. In-person interview recommended (telephone interview accepted). Applicants must submit a letter of interest, resume, 3 to 6 writing samples. Application deadline: March 1 for summer. World Wide Web: http://www.delcotimes.com.

DEMOCRAT AND CHRONICLE
55 Exchange Boulevard
Rochester, New York 14614

General Information Newspaper that serves the Rochester, New York area. Number of employees: 1,000. Unit of Gannett Co., Inc., Arlington, Virginia.
Internships Available ▶ *1 business reporting intern.* Candidates should have analytical skills, organizational skills, research skills, self-motivation, written communication skills, valid driver's license. Duration is 10 weeks during summer. $500 per week. ▶ *1 copyediting intern.* Candidates should have analytical skills, editing skills, organizational skills, research skills, self-motivation, written communication skills, valid driver's license. Duration is 10 weeks during summer. $500 per week.

Democrat and Chronicle (continued)

Benefits On-the-job training, willing to complete paperwork for educational credit.

Contact Write Dow Jones Newspaper Fund (through college placement office). No phone calls. Drug test; apply through college placement office. Application deadline: Deadlines, set by the DOW Jones Newspaper Fund, may be obtained through college placement director. World Wide Web: http://www.democratandchronicle.com.

DENVER POST CORPORATION
1560 Broadway
Denver, Colorado 80202

General Information Publisher of general circulation newspaper. Established in 1892. Unit of Media News Group, Inc., Denver, Colorado. Number of internship applications received each year: 300.

Internships Available ► *3–7 interns:* responsibilities include reporting news, editing copy, graphics, or photography in a department commensurate with intern's skills and interests. Candidates should have computer skills, experience in the field, oral communication skills, organizational skills, plan to pursue career in field, self-motivation, strong interpersonal skills, writing skills. Duration is 10 weeks. $460 per week. Open to students who have completed their junior year of college (minimum). International applications accepted.

Benefits On-the-job training, possible full-time employment, willing to act as a professional reference, willing to complete paperwork for educational credit, willing to provide letters of recommendation, reimbursement for travel while on assignment, health insurance after 30 days.

Contact Write or e-mail Internship Recruiter. E-mail: living@denverpost.com. No phone calls. Telephone interview required. Applicants must submit a letter of interest, resume, list of three personal references; reporting applicants should include a portfolio of no more than 5 clips; photography applicants should provide a portfolio with primarily color slides and a self-addressed stamped envelope for return of slides. Application deadline: November 1 for summer. World Wide Web: http://www.denverpost.com.

DES MOINES REGISTER
715 Locust Street
Des Moines, Iowa 50309

General Information Daily and Sunday statewide newspaper. Established in 1826. Unit of Gannett Co., Inc., Arlington, Virginia. Number of internship applications received each year: 200.

Internships Available ► *1 art intern:* responsibilities include producing informational graphics for the daily and Sunday newspaper. Candidates should have ability to work with others, college courses in field, plan to pursue career in field, self-motivation, written communication skills, Macintosh skills. Duration is 12 weeks in summer. $10.62 per hour. ► *3 copy editor interns:* responsibilities include editing copy and stories, writing headlines and doing layouts (2 nightside news copy desk positions; 1 sports copy desk position). Candidates should have ability to work with others, college courses in field, computer skills, editing skills, plan to pursue career in field, self-motivation, layout/design skills. Duration is 12 weeks in summer. $10.62 per hour. ► *1 photo intern:* responsibilities include shooting photos on deadline and for enterprise stories. Candidates should have ability to work with others, college courses in field, computer skills, plan to pursue career in field, self-motivation, strong visual skills. Duration is 12 weeks in summer. $10.62 per hour. ► *5 reporting interns:* responsibilities include reporting stories, both breaking news and enterprise, for the daily and Sunday Register. Candidates should have ability to work with others, college courses in field, plan to pursue career in field, research skills, writing skills. Duration is 12 weeks in summer. $10.62 per hour. ► *1 sports reporter:* responsibilities include providing coverage of high school and collegiate sports. Candidates should have ability to work with others, college courses in field,

plan to pursue career in field, research skills, writing skills. Duration is 12 weeks in summer. $10.62 per hour. Open to college juniors, college seniors.

Benefits Formal training, names of contacts, on-the-job training, opportunity to attend seminars/workshops, possible full-time employment, willing to complete paperwork for educational credit, willing to provide letters of recommendation, reimbursement of work-related travel expenses.

Contact Write or e-mail Diane E. Graham, Managing Editor/Staff Development, PO Box 957, Des Moines, Iowa 50311. E-mail: dgraham@dmreg.com. No phone calls. Applicants must submit a letter of interest, resume, 8-10 work samples, 2-3 personal references. Application deadline: December 1. World Wide Web: http://www.desmoinesregister.com.

DETROIT FREE PRESS
600 West Fort Street
Detroit, Michigan 48226

General Information One of the nation's 20 largest newspapers; winner of 8 Pulitzer Prizes. Established in 1831. Number of employees: 300. Unit of Knight Ridder, San Jose, California. Number of internship applications received each year: 450.

Internships Available ► *1 Web editor.* Duration is 12 weeks. $530 per week. ► *1 business writer.* Duration is 12 weeks. $530 per week. ► *2 city desk interns.* Duration is 12 weeks. $530 per week. ► *1 entertainment writer.* Duration is 12 weeks. $530 per week. ► *1 features copy editor.* Duration is 12 weeks. $530 per week. ► *1 graphics intern.* Duration is 12 weeks. $530 per week. ► *1 health writer.* Duration is 12 weeks. $530 per week. ► *1 lifestyles writer.* Duration is 12 weeks. $530 per week. ► *1 news copy editor.* Duration is 12 weeks. $530 per week. ► *1 photography intern.* Duration is 12 weeks. $530 per week. ► *1 sports copy editor.* Duration is 12 weeks. $530 per week. ► *1 sports writer.* Duration is 12 weeks. $530 per week. Open to college sophomores, college juniors, college seniors, recent college graduates, graduate students, career changers.

Benefits Formal training, job counseling, names of contacts, on-the-job training, opportunity to attend seminars/workshops, possible full-time employment, willing to complete paperwork for educational credit, willing to provide letters of recommendation.

Contact Write, call, fax, e-mail, or through World Wide Web site Mr. Joe Grimm, Recruiting and Development Editor. Phone: 313-222-6490. Fax: 313-222-5981. E-mail: grimm@freepress.com. In-person interview recommended (telephone interview accepted). Applicants must submit a letter of interest, resume, portfolio, three personal references, 6 work samples. Application deadline: December 1 for summer. World Wide Web: http://www.freep.com/jobspage.

DOW JONES NEWSPAPER FUND
PO Box 300
Princeton, New Jersey 08543-0300

General Information Private foundation that promotes journalism careers. Established in 1959. Number of employees: 4. Number of internship applications received each year: 600.

Internships Available ► *12 business reporting interns:* responsibilities include attending a training program; working at a daily newspaper as a business reporter. Candidates should have ability to work independently, ability to work with others, college courses in field, oral communication skills, personal interest in the field, writing skills. Duration is 11-12 weeks in summer (includes one week of training). $325 per week minimum. Open to college sophomores, college juniors. ► *100 editing interns:* responsibilities include attending a 1- to 2-week training program and working as a copy editor at daily newspapers, on-line newspapers, and real-time financial news services. Candidates should have ability to work with others, analytical skills, college courses in field, computer skills, editing skills, personal interest in the field, plan to pursue career in field, writing skills. Duration is 10 weeks in summer (includes 1-2 weeks of training). $325 per week minimum. Open to college juniors, college seniors, graduate students.

Benefits Formal training, $1000 scholarship for those returning to college following the internship, some travel reimbursement.

Contact Write, call, fax, e-mail, or through World Wide Web site Editing Intern Program. Phone: 609-452-2820. Fax: 609-520-5804. E-mail: newsfund@wsj.dowjones.com. Telephone interview required.

Applicants must submit a formal organization application, resume, academic transcripts, two personal references, essay and a test. Application deadline: November 1. World Wide Web: http://www.dowjones.com/newsfund.

ELYRIA CHRONICLE–TELEGRAM
225 East Avenue
Elyria, Ohio 44035

General Information Daily and Sunday newspaper. Established in 1829. Number of employees: 50. Number of internship applications received each year: 60.
Internships Available ▶ *1 copy desk intern:* responsibilities include design, pagination, copyediting, and writing headlines. Candidates should have college courses in field, computer skills, editing skills, knowledge of field, self-motivation, writing skills. Duration is 3 months. $325 per week. Open to college freshmen, college sophomores, college juniors, college seniors. ▶ *2–3 newsroom interns:* responsibilities include reporting and writing. Candidates should have ability to work independently, ability to work with others, plan to pursue career in field, research skills, self-motivation, writing skills. Duration is 3–4 months. $325 per week. Open to college freshmen, college sophomores, college juniors, college seniors. ▶ *1 photo department intern:* responsibilities include taking photos for paper. Candidates should have ability to work independently, ability to work with others, college courses in field, knowledge of field, plan to pursue career in field, self-motivation. Duration is 3 months. $325 per week. Open to college freshmen, college sophomores, college juniors, college seniors, recent college graduates. International applications accepted.
Benefits Job counseling, names of contacts, possible full-time employment, travel reimbursement, willing to act as a professional reference, willing to provide letters of recommendation.
Contact Write, fax, or e-mail Mr. Rudy Dicks, Managing Editor. Fax: 440-329-7282. E-mail: rdicks@chronicletelegram.com. In-person interview required. Applicants must submit a letter of interest, resume, three personal references, 8-10 writing samples. Application deadline: February 15 for summer. World Wide Web: http://www.chronicletelegram.com.

EMPIRE STATE WEEKLIES
2010 Empire Boulevard
Webster, New York 14580

General Information Group of weekly community newspapers serving eastern Monroe and western Wayne counties. Established in 1863. Number of employees: 25. Number of internship applications received each year: 8.
Internships Available ▶ *2 editorial interns:* responsibilities include assisting with general editorial duties. Candidates should have ability to work independently, computer skills, editing skills, oral communication skills, personal interest in the field, self-motivation, strong interpersonal skills, writing skills. Duration is 3–6 months. Unpaid. Open to high school seniors, recent high school graduates, college freshmen, college sophomores, college juniors, college seniors, recent college graduates. International applications accepted.
Benefits Job counseling, on-the-job training, possible full-time employment, willing to complete paperwork for educational credit, willing to provide letters of recommendation.
Contact Write, call, or e-mail Michael B. Sorenson, Managing Editor. Phone: 585-671-1533. Fax: 585-671-7067. E-mail: eswwp@aol.com. In-person interview recommended (telephone interview accepted). Applicants must submit a letter of interest, resume, three writing samples, three personal references. Application deadline: February 15 for spring, April 15 for summer, July 15 for fall.

THE FRESNO BEE
1626 E Street
Fresno, California 93786

General Information Newspaper. Established in 1926. Number of employees: 145. Branch of The McClatchy Company, Sacramento, California. Number of internship applications received each year: 75.

Internships Available ▶ *2–3 general assignment reporters:* responsibilities include general assignment reporting, probably including police, city government, and feature stories. Candidates should have ability to work with others, computer skills, plan to pursue career in field, self-motivation, writing skills. Duration is 12 weeks (June to August). $400 per week. Open to college sophomores, college juniors, college seniors, recent college graduates, not open to those who have had previous internships at Fresno Bee. ▶ *1 photography intern:* responsibilities include general assignments including sports. Candidates should have ability to work with others, college courses in field, computer skills, plan to pursue career in field, self-motivation, photographic skills. Duration is 12 weeks (June to August). $400 per week. Open to college sophomores, college juniors, college seniors, recent college graduates.
Benefits On-the-job training, possible full-time employment, willing to act as a professional reference, willing to complete paperwork for educational credit, willing to provide letters of recommendation.
Contact Write, call, e-mail, or through World Wide Web site Rich Marshall, Senior Editor. Phone: 559-441-6443. Fax: 559-441-6640. E-mail: rmarshal@fresnobee.com. Telephone interview required. Applicants must submit a letter of interest, resume, 3-5 writing samples. Application deadline: January 10. World Wide Web: http://www.fresnobee.com.

THE GAZETTE
30 South Prospect Street
Colorado Springs, Colorado 80903

General Information Daily newspaper. Established in 1872. Number of employees: 500. Unit of Freedom Communications, Irvine, California. Number of internship applications received each year: 100.
Internships Available ▶ *1 photo intern:* responsibilities include all tasks of a staff photographer. Candidates should have ability to work independently, ability to work with others, computer skills, knowledge of field, oral communication skills, personal interest in the field, self-motivation, writing skills. Duration is 3 months. $10 per hour. Open to college freshmen, college sophomores, college juniors, college seniors, recent college graduates, graduate students. ▶ *6–8 writing interns:* responsibilities include various duties from year to year; please refer to Web site for information on number of openings, pay, and types of internships available. Candidates should have ability to work independently, ability to work with others, computer skills, experience in the field, oral communication skills, plan to pursue career in field, self-motivation, writing skills. Duration is 10 weeks. $10 per hour. Open to college juniors, college seniors, recent college graduates, graduate students. International applications accepted.
Benefits Formal training, job counseling, on-the-job training, opportunity to attend seminars/workshops, possible full-time employment, willing to complete paperwork for educational credit.
Contact Write, e-mail, or through World Wide Web site Connie Steele, Newsroom Administrator, 30 South Prospect Street, Colorado Springs, Colorado 80903. Fax: 719-636-0202. E-mail: csteele@gazette.com. No phone calls. Applicants must submit a letter of interest, resume, writing sample, 6 writing samples. Application deadline: December 31 for summer; continuous for photo positions. World Wide Web: http://www.gazette.com/gaz/intern.html.

GAZETTE COMMUNICATIONS
PO Box 511
Cedar Rapids, Iowa 52406

General Information Multimedia company publishing regional newspaper. Established in 1883. Number of employees: 610. Unit of Gazette Communications, Cedar Rapids, Iowa. Number of internship applications received each year: 300.
Internships Available ▶ *2–3 KCRG-TV News interns:* responsibilities include shadowing reporters, assignment editors, photographers, and producers through the television new gathering process; will learn all aspects of news gathering process, but will also focus on intern's interest. Candidates should have ability to work independently, ability to work with others, college courses in field,

Gazette Communications (continued)

oral communication skills, organizational skills, self-motivation. Duration is 1 semester. Unpaid. Open to college juniors, college seniors. ▶ *2 advertising interns:* responsibilities include working with display and classified advertising; planning and conducting sales presentations; coordinating ad design and layouts. Candidates should have ability to work independently, ability to work with others, college courses in field, computer skills, oral communication skills, organizational skills, personal interest in the field, plan to pursue career in field, self-motivation, written communication skills. Duration is May to August. $7.50 per hour. Open to college sophomores, college juniors. ▶ *3–4 news reporting interns:* responsibilities include general reporting responsibilities. Candidates should have ability to work independently, college courses in field, computer skills, knowledge of field, oral communication skills, plan to pursue career in field, self-motivation, writing skills. Duration is 3 months in fall, spring, or summer. $8 per hour. Open to college sophomores, college juniors, college seniors. ▶ *3–4 photo interns:* responsibilities include taking photos for stories in newspaper. Candidates should have ability to work independently, ability to work with others, declared college major in field, knowledge of field, oral communication skills, plan to pursue career in field, self-motivation. Duration is 3 months in fall, spring, or summer. $8 per hour. Open to college sophomores, college juniors, college seniors, recent college graduates. ▶ *1 public relations intern:* responsibilities include assisting with "Newspaper in Education" projects and events, attending Editor's coffees, assisting with "In your Neighborhood" projects, in-house promotions, and other related efforts. Candidates should have ability to work independently, computer skills, knowledge of field, oral communication skills, personal interest in the field, self-motivation, strong interpersonal skills, written communication skills. Duration is 1 summer. $7–$7.50 per hour. Open to college sophomores, college juniors.
Benefits Possible full-time employment, willing to complete paperwork for educational credit, willing to provide letters of recommendation.
Contact Write, fax, or e-mail Patricia Thoms, Employment Manager. Fax: 319-368-8834. E-mail: gazcohr@fyiowa.com. No phone calls. In-person interview recommended (telephone interview accepted). Applicants must submit a letter of interest, resume, 6 news clips, photo portfolio. Application deadline: January 1 for summer (reporters and photographers), March 15 for advertising and public relations (summer term only), July 1 for fall (reporters and photographers); May 1 for fall (reporters and photographers), October 1 for winter (reporters and photographers). World Wide Web: http://www.gazettecommunications.com.

HIGH COUNTRY NEWS
Box 1090
Paonia, Colorado 81428

General Information Paper that covers the communities and environment of the Rocky Mountain West, the Great Basin, and the Pacific Northwest; circulation is 19,000. Established in 1970. Number of employees: 25. Number of internship applications received each year: 75.
Internships Available ▶ *6 interns:* responsibilities include writing news briefs and stories for Western Roundup section, looking for story leads in news releases and newspapers, sorting mail, and answering telephone calls. Candidates should have research skills, self-motivation, strong interpersonal skills, writing skills, knowledge of High Country news and the West. Duration is 4 months. Stipend of $250 per month. Open to recent high school graduates, college freshmen, college sophomores, college juniors, college seniors, recent college graduates, graduate students, law students, career changers, individuals reentering the workforce.
Benefits Free housing, names of contacts, on-the-job training, opportunity to attend seminars/workshops, travel reimbursement, willing to complete paperwork for educational credit, willing to provide letters of recommendation.
Contact Write, call, e-mail, or through World Wide Web site Rebecca Clarren, Assistant Editor, PO Box 1090, Paonia, Colorado 81428. Phone: 970-527-4898. E-mail: rebecca@hcn.org. Telephone interview required. Applicants must submit a letter of interest,

resume, three writing samples. Application deadline: March 1 for summer (May 1-August 31), June 1 for fall (September 1-December 14), October 1 for spring (January 1-April 30). World Wide Web: http://www.hcn.org.

HONOLULU ADVERTISER
Box 3110
Honolulu, Hawaii 96802

General Information Morning/afternoon newspaper with circulation of 150,000. Established in 1856. Number of employees: 150. Affiliate of Gannett Co., Inc., McLean, Virginia. Number of internship applications received each year: 110.
Internships Available ▶ *2–3 interns:* responsibilities include working in the newsroom learning various reporting and editing techniques. Candidates should have ability to work with others, experience in the field, plan to pursue career in field, self-motivation, writing skills. Duration is 10–13 weeks. $10 per hour. Open to college freshmen, college sophomores, college juniors, college seniors, recent college graduates, graduate students.
Benefits On-the-job training, possible full-time employment, willing to act as a professional reference.
Contact Write, call, or e-mail Shauna Goya, Internship Coordinator. Phone: 808-535-2425. Fax: 808-525-8037. E-mail: sgoya@honoluluadvertiser.com. Applicants must submit a letter of interest, resume, three personal references, 6 writing samples; test will be arranged for finalists. Application deadline: December 31 for summer. World Wide Web: http://www.honoluluadvertiser.com.

LANCASTER NEWSPAPERS
8 West King Street, PO Box 1328
Lancaster, Pennsylvania 17608-1328

General Information Community newspaper with a circulation of 100,000 daily and 110,000 Sunday. Established in 1794. Number of employees: 550. Number of internship applications received each year: 75.
Internships Available ▶ *1–2 advertising/marketing interns:* responsibilities include selling advertising and working on marketing projects. Candidates should have ability to work with others, computer skills, knowledge of field, oral communication skills, plan to pursue career in field, written communication skills. Duration is 13 weeks from May to August. Salary commensurate with experience. ▶ *1 information services intern:* responsibilities include PC and Macintosh system support, installation, and troubleshooting. Candidates should have ability to work independently, ability to work with others, analytical skills, computer skills, knowledge of field, plan to pursue career in field. Duration is 13 weeks. $7.50 per hour. ▶ *6–9 reporters:* responsibilities include general assignment reporting. Candidates should have computer skills, editing skills, knowledge of field, writing skills. Duration is 13 weeks. $7.50–$9 per hour. Open to college freshmen, college sophomores, college juniors, college seniors.
Benefits Formal training, possible full-time employment, travel reimbursement, willing to provide letters of recommendation.
Contact Write, fax, or e-mail Randall Yoder, Human Resources Manager. Phone: 717-291-8680. Fax: 717-293-4311. E-mail: humanresources@lnpnews.com. Applicants must submit a letter of interest, resume, three writing samples. Application deadline: December 31 for summer. World Wide Web: http://www.lancasteronline.com.

LEXINGTON HERALD-LEADER
100 Midland Avenue
Lexington, Kentucky 40508

General Information Pulitzer prize-winning newspaper covering central and eastern Kentucky with daily circulation of about 120,000 and Sunday circulation of about 165,000. Number of employees: 520. Unit of Knight Ridder, San Jose, California. Number of internship applications received each year: 200.
Internships Available ▶ *1 copyediting intern:* responsibilities include editing copy and writing headlines. Candidates should have college courses in field, computer skills, editing skills, knowledge of field, writing skills, must have own transportation. Duration is 10 weeks in summer (40 hours per week). $425 per week. Open to

college freshmen, college sophomores, college juniors, college seniors. ▶ *1 design desk intern:* responsibilities include layout and design. Candidates should have ability to work independently, college courses in field, computer skills, knowledge of field, personal interest in the field, must have own transportation. Duration is 10 weeks in summer (40 hours per week). $425 per week. Open to college freshmen, college sophomores, college juniors, college seniors, recent college graduates. ▶ *1 photo intern.* Candidates should have ability to work independently, ability to work with others, knowledge of field, personal interest in the field, self-motivation, must have own transportation. Duration is 10 weeks in summer (40 hours per week). $425 per week. Open to college freshmen, college sophomores, college juniors, college seniors, recent college graduates, graduate students. ▶ *4 reporting interns:* responsibilities include reporting and writing stories. Candidates should have college courses in field, experience in the field, oral communication skills, personal interest in the field, writing skills, must have own transportation. Duration is 10 weeks in summer. $425 per week. Open to college freshmen, college sophomores, college juniors, college seniors, recent college graduates. International applications accepted.

Benefits On-the-job training, opportunity to attend seminars/workshops, possible full-time employment, willing to act as a professional reference, willing to complete paperwork for educational credit, willing to provide letters of recommendation, reimbursement for mileage and other job-related expenses while on assignment.

Contact Write Jill Nevel-Saun, Internship Coordinator. Applicants must submit a letter of interest, resume, 5-10 writing samples, telephone interview (for finalists). Application deadline: November 15 for summer. World Wide Web: http://www.kentucky.com.

LIMA NEWS
3515 Elida Road, PO Box 690
Lima, Ohio 45802-0690

General Information Newspaper. Number of employees: 36. Unit of Freedom Communications, Irvine, California. Number of internship applications received each year: 50.

Internships Available ▶ *2 photographers.* Candidates should have ability to work independently, knowledge of field, plan to pursue career in field, self-motivation, strong interpersonal skills. Duration is 3 months (year-round). $300 per week. Open to college freshmen, college sophomores, college juniors, college seniors.

Benefits On-the-job training, possible full-time employment, willing to act as a professional reference, willing to complete paperwork for educational credit.

Contact Write or e-mail Craig Orosz, Photo Editor. E-mail: corosz@limanews.com. No phone calls. In-person interview required. Applicants must submit a letter of interest, resume, three personal references, three letters of recommendation, 6-10 writing clips. Applications are accepted continuously. World Wide Web: http://www.limanews.com.

MIDWEST SUBURBAN PUBLISHING
6901 West 159th Street
Tenley Park, Illinois 60477

General Information Publisher of Daily Southtown and Star Publications. Established in 1901. Unit of Hollinger International, Toronto, Canada. Number of internship applications received each year: 75.

Internships Available ▶ *Interns.* Duration is 12 weeks in summer. Paid. Open to college freshmen, college sophomores, college juniors, college seniors, graduate students. International applications accepted.

Benefits Possible full-time employment, willing to complete paperwork for educational credit, willing to provide letters of recommendation, possible travel reimbursement.

Contact Write, fax, or e-mail John Hector, Metro Editor. Fax: 708-633-5999. E-mail: jhector@dailysouthtown.com. No phone calls. In-person interview recommended (telephone interview accepted). Applicants must submit a letter of interest, resume, writing clips. Applications are accepted continuously. World Wide Web: http://www.dailysouthtown.com.

MILWAUKEE JOURNAL SENTINEL
333 West State Street
Milwaukee, Wisconsin 53203

General Information Publisher of largest newspaper in Wisconsin with daily circulation of 278,300 and Sunday circulation of 461,000. Established in 1837. Number of employees: 1,500. Subsidiary of Journal Communications, Milwaukee, Wisconsin. Number of internship applications received each year: 500.

Internships Available ▶ *2–3 copy editing interns:* responsibilities include copy editing and writing news and feature stories. Candidates should have ability to work independently, ability to work with others, college courses in field, computer skills, editing skills, experience in the field, plan to pursue career in field, research skills, written communication skills. Duration is 12 weeks. $450 per week. ▶ *Entertainment reporting interns.* Candidates should have ability to work independently, ability to work with others, college courses in field, computer skills, editing skills, experience in the field, research skills. Duration is 12 weeks. $450 per week. ▶ *1 graphics intern:* responsibilities include completing infographics and illustrations. Candidates should have ability to work independently, ability to work with others, college courses in field, computer skills, editing skills, experience in the field, plan to pursue career in field, research skills, self-motivation. Duration is 12 weeks. $450 per week. ▶ *6–7 local news reporting interns:* responsibilities include writing news and feature stories. Candidates should have ability to work independently, ability to work with others, analytical skills, college courses in field, computer skills, editing skills, experience in the field, plan to pursue career in field, research skills, self-motivation, written communication skills. Duration is 12 weeks. $450 per week. ▶ *News design interns.* Candidates should have ability to work independently, ability to work with others, college courses in field, computer skills, editing skills, experience in the field, research skills. Duration is 12 weeks. $450 per week. ▶ *1 photography intern:* responsibilities include taking news and feature photos. Candidates should have ability to work independently, ability to work with others, college courses in field, experience in the field, plan to pursue career in field, self-motivation. Duration is 12 weeks. $450 per week. ▶ *Sports reporting interns.* Candidates should have ability to work independently, ability to work with others, college courses in field, computer skills, editing skills, experience in the field, research skills. Duration is 12 weeks. $450 per week. Open to college juniors, college seniors, recent college graduates, graduate students. International applications accepted.

Benefits Job counseling, on-the-job training, opportunity to attend seminars/workshops, possible full-time employment, willing to act as a professional reference, willing to complete paperwork for educational credit, willing to provide letters of recommendation, reimbursement for mileage and other job-related expenses while on assignment.

Contact Write or e-mail Marilyn Krause, Senior Editor/Administration. E-mail: mkrause@onwis.com. No phone calls. Applicants must submit a resume, portfolio, cover letter, 5-6 writing clips, in-person or telephone interview. Application deadline: November 1 for summer. World Wide Web: http://www.jsonline.com.

NATIONAL JOURNALISM CENTER
800 Maryland Avenue, NE
Washington, District of Columbia 20002

General Information Organization that provides training to reporters in order to improve the field of investigative reporting. Established in 1977. Number of employees: 9. Unit of Education and Research Institute, Washinton, District of Columbia. Number of internship applications received each year: 300.

Internships Available ▶ *10–30 interns:* responsibilities include researching and writing articles for the Center and acting as reporters on staff at Washington Metropolitan-area media outlets. Candidates should have analytical skills, oral communication skills, plan to pursue career in field, research skills, strong interpersonal skills, written communication skills. Duration is 1–3 months. $100 per week. Open to college juniors, college seniors, recent college graduates. ▶ *75–80 journalism interns:* responsibilities include researching, reporting, writing, and some administrative tasks.

National Journalism Center (continued)

Candidates should have ability to work independently, analytical skills, editing skills, organizational skills, plan to pursue career in field, research skills, self-motivation, strong interpersonal skills, writing skills. Duration is 12 weeks. $100 per week. Open to college juniors, college seniors, recent college graduates, career changers.

Benefits Housing at a cost, job counseling, names of contacts, opportunity to attend seminars/workshops, willing to act as a professional reference, willing to complete paperwork for educational credit, willing to provide letters of recommendation, access to in-house job bank, resume referral provided.

Contact Write, call, fax, or e-mail Mr. Malcolm A. Kline, Editor. Phone: 202-544-1333. Fax: 202-546-3489. E-mail: mal@ nationaljournalismcenter.org. In-person interview recommended (telephone interview accepted). Applicants must submit a formal organization application, letter of interest, resume, 2-3 writing samples. Application deadline: February 1 for spring, May 1 for summer, September 1 for fall, November 26 for winter. World Wide Web: http://www.nationaljournalismcenter.org.

THE NEWS & OBSERVER
215 South McDowell Street, PO Box 191
Raleigh, North Carolina 27601

General Information Newspaper. Established in 1894. Number of employees: 1,000. Number of internship applications received each year: 300.

Internships Available ▶ *2 fall visual internships:* responsibilities include page design and creation of graphic elements for daily newspaper. Candidates should have ability to work independently, ability to work with others, experience in the field, personal interest in the field, plan to pursue career in field, self-motivation. Duration is 12 weeks. $450 per week. Open to college sophomores, college juniors, college seniors, recent college graduates, graduate students. ▶ *10 newsroom reporters, copy editors, and graphic artists:* responsibilities include reporting, editing, or designing for the daily newspaper. Candidates should have knowledge of field, personal interest in the field, self-motivation, strong interpersonal skills. Duration is 10 weeks. $450 per week. Open to college sophomores, college juniors, college seniors, recent college graduates, graduate students, career changers.

Benefits Formal training, job counseling, on-the-job training, opportunity to attend seminars/workshops, willing to act as a professional reference, willing to complete paperwork for educational credit, willing to provide letters of recommendation.

Contact Write, call, fax, or e-mail Susan Spring, Newsroom Administrator. Phone: 919-829-4860. Fax: 919-836-5911. E-mail: sspring@nando.com. Applicants must submit a formal organization application, letter of interest, resume, personal reference, 500-word autobiography, 6 writing samples. Application deadline: July 1 for fall, December 1 for summer. World Wide Web: http://www.nando.net/nao.

THE NEWS-COURIER
PO Box 670
Athens, Alabama 35612

General Information Newspaper. Number of employees: 30. Unit of Community Newspaper Holdings, Inc., Birmingham, Alabama. Number of internship applications received each year: 8.

Internships Available ▶ *1 reporter:* responsibilities include interviews, meeting coverage, writing stories, and some photography. Candidates should have editing skills, organizational skills, plan to pursue career in field, self-motivation, written communication skills. Duration is 3 months. $5.30–$5.75 per hour. International applications accepted.

Benefits On-the-job training, possible full-time employment.

Contact Write or fax Sonny Turner, Editor, PO Box 670, Athens, Alabama 35612. Fax: 256-233-7753. No phone calls. In-person interview recommended (telephone interview accepted). Applicants must submit a letter of interest, resume, three personal references, 5 writing samples. Applications are accepted continuously.

NEWSDAY
235 Pinelawn Road
Melville, New York 11747-4250

General Information Nation's sixth largest daily newspaper with a circulation of over 650,000. Established in 1945. Number of employees: 1,000. Subsidiary of The Tribune Company, Chicago, Illinois. Number of internship applications received each year: 200.

Internships Available ▶ *40 reporters, librarians, photographers, graphic interns, and copy editors:* responsibilities include covering spot news, writing features, reporting, taking photographs, library work, on-line Internet research, and artwork. Duration is 10 weeks in summer (full-time); spring and fall positions part-time (2 days per week). Position available as unpaid or at $525 per week for summer positions; spring and fall positions unpaid. Open to college juniors, college seniors, graduate students.

Benefits Opportunity to attend seminars/workshops, willing to complete paperwork for educational credit, willing to provide letters of recommendation, travel reimbursement while on assignment.

Contact Write, call, or e-mail Walter Middlebrook, Associate Editor for Recruitment. Phone: 631-843-2637. E-mail: jobs@newsday. com. Applicants must submit a formal organization application, letter of interest, resume, academic transcripts, three letters of recommendation, writing test (included on application); portfolio (graphics and photography interns), writing samples (reporters, librarians, or editors); Dow Jones test for copyeditors (recommended). Application deadline: May 31 for fall, November 15 for summer, November 8 for spring. World Wide Web: http://www.newsday.com/about/jobs/jobinter/htm.

THE NEWS-SENTINEL
600 West Main Street
Fort Wayne, Indiana 46801

General Information Newspaper published in the afternoon Monday through Saturday. Unit of Knight Ridder, San Jose, California. Number of internship applications received each year: 200.

Internships Available ▶ *1–2 general assignment reporter interns.* Candidates should have computer skills, organizational skills, plan to pursue career in field, self-motivation, writing skills. Duration is 10–12 weeks. $400 per week. Open to college sophomores, college juniors, college seniors, recent college graduates, graduate students, career changers. ▶ *1–2 photographer interns.* Candidates should have computer skills, organizational skills, plan to pursue career in field, self-motivation, writing skills, some photography experience (preferred). Duration is 10–12 weeks. $400 per week. Open to college sophomores, college juniors, college seniors, graduate students, career changers.

Benefits Formal training, job counseling, on-the-job training, opportunity to attend seminars/workshops, possible full-time employment, travel reimbursement, willing to act as a professional reference, willing to complete paperwork for educational credit, willing to provide letters of recommendation.

Contact Write or e-mail Eunice Trotter, Associate Editor. Phone: 260-461-8289. Fax: 260-461-8817. E-mail: etrotter@news-sentinel. com. In-person interview recommended (telephone interview accepted). Applicants must submit a letter of interest, resume, portfolio, 6-8 writing samples. Application deadline: December 1 for summer. World Wide Web: http://www.news-sentinel.com.

OMAHA WORLD-HERALD COMPANY
1334 Dodge Street
Omaha, Nebraska 68102

General Information Mass circulation newspaper. Established in 1865. Number of employees: 800. Number of internship applications received each year: 100.

Internships Available ▶ *4 advertising interns:* responsibilities include sales, production, and special projects. Candidates should have computer skills, declared college major in field, knowledge of field, personal interest in the field, self-motivation, writing skills. Duration is 12 weeks. $400 per week. ▶ *4–6 news interns:* responsibilities include writing news and feature stories and editing copy. Candidates should have analytical skills, editing skills, personal interest in the field, self-motivation, writing skills. Duration is 12 weeks. $400 per week. Open to college juniors, college seniors. International applications accepted.

Benefits Formal training, job counseling, on-the-job training, opportunity to attend seminars/workshops, possible full-time employment, willing to act as a professional reference, willing to complete paperwork for educational credit, willing to provide letters of recommendation, some mentoring, $1000 scholarship.

Contact Write, call, fax, or e-mail Jeff Gauger. Phone: 800-284-6397. Fax: 402-345-0183. E-mail: jgauger@owh.com. In-person interview recommended (telephone interview accepted). Applicants must submit a letter of interest, resume, 4-6 examples of work. Application deadline: November 1 for summer.

ORLANDO SENTINEL
633 North Orange Avenue
Orlando, Florida 32801

General Information Newspaper. Established in 1876. Number of employees: 1,500. Subsidiary of Tribune Company, Chicago, Illinois. Number of internship applications received each year: 250.

Internships Available ▶ *6–8 interns:* responsibilities include working in various areas including reporting, editing, photography, or graphic arts. Candidates should have ability to work with others, analytical skills, experience in the field, plan to pursue career in field, research skills, writing skills. Duration is 10–12 weeks. $500 per week. Open to college juniors, college seniors, graduate students, individuals with previous internships in journalism.

Benefits On-the-job training, opportunity to attend seminars/workshops, possible full-time employment, willing to act as a professional reference, willing to complete paperwork for educational credit.

Contact Write, e-mail, or through World Wide Web site Mr. Dana S. Eagles, Recruitment and Staff Development Editor. E-mail: deagles@orlandosentinel.com. No phone calls. Applicants must submit a letter of interest, resume, three personal references, five work samples. Application deadline: November 15 for summer. World Wide Web: http://www.orlandosentinel.com.

PHILADELPHIA INQUIRER
400 North Broad Street
Philadelphia, Pennsylvania 19130

General Information Major metropolitan newspaper that offers a strong investigative approach to issues and a solid national and foreign report. Established in 1829. Unit of Knight Ridder, San Jose, California. Number of internship applications received each year: 200.

Internships Available ▶ *7 Art Peters Programs interns:* responsibilities include training on copy desk, reporting. Candidates should have ability to work independently, editing skills, plan to pursue career in field, self-motivation, strong interpersonal skills, written communication skills. Duration is 1 summer. $633 per week. Open to college freshmen, college sophomores, college juniors, college seniors, graduate students (between semesters). ▶ *2 Knight Ridder Minority Specialty Development Program interns:* responsibilities include working with editors and reporters. Candidates should have ability to work independently, computer skills, oral communication skills, research skills, self-motivation, strong interpersonal skills, strong leadership ability, written communication skills. Duration is 1 year. $785 per week. Open to recent college graduates, graduate students. ▶ *Suburban Reporting Program interns:* responsibilities include working in geographic beat areas to provide stories on government, schools, police, courts, and features. Candidates should have oral communication skills, plan to pursue career in field, self-motivation, strong interpersonal skills, written communication skills. Duration is 2 years. $565 per week. Open to college seniors, recent college graduates, graduate students, working journalists with limited experience. ▶ *1 minority graphics intern:* responsibilities include graphics and page design. Candidates should have computer skills, oral communication skills, self-motivation, strong interpersonal skills, written communication skills. Duration is 10 weeks. $633 per week. Open to college freshmen, college sophomores, college juniors, college seniors, recent college graduates, graduate students. ▶ *1 minority photojournalism*

intern: responsibilities include shooting assignments in news, features, and sports. Candidates should have ability to work independently, analytical skills, experience in the field, oral communication skills, plan to pursue career in field, self-motivation, strong interpersonal skills, strong leadership ability, written communication skills. Duration is 1 summer. $633 per week. Open to college freshmen, college sophomores, college juniors, college seniors, graduate students. International applications accepted.

Benefits Formal training, job counseling, names of contacts, opportunity to attend seminars/workshops, possible full-time employment, willing to act as a professional reference, willing to complete paperwork for educational credit, willing to provide letters of recommendation, ongoing evaluations.

Contact Write Director of Internships. In-person interview recommended (telephone interview accepted). Applicants must submit a resume, portfolio, three personal references, 10 writing samples. World Wide Web: http://www.phillynews.com.

THE PULLIAM FELLOWSHIPS
307 North Pennsylvania Street
Indianapolis, Indiana 46204

General Information Journalism work-study program for college students serious about pursuing a career in journalism. Established in 1974. Number of employees: 2. Unit of Gannett Co., Inc., Arlington, Virginia. Number of internship applications received each year: 160.

Internships Available ▶ *20 Pulliam fellowships:* responsibilities include reporting and copy editing. Candidates should have ability to work independently, ability to work with others, editing skills, plan to pursue career in field, self-motivation, writing skills. Duration is 10 weeks. $6000 stipend. Open to college sophomores, college juniors, college seniors. International applications accepted.

Benefits Job counseling, names of contacts, on-the-job training, opportunity to attend seminars/workshops, possible full-time employment, travel reimbursement, willing to act as a professional reference, willing to provide letters of recommendation, 2 lunches and 1 dinner provided weekly.

Contact Write, call, fax, e-mail, or through World Wide Web site Russell B. Pulliam, Fellowship Director. Phone: 317-444-6001. Fax: 317-444-6750. E-mail: russell.pulliam@indystar.com. Applicants must submit a formal organization application, academic transcripts, three letters of recommendation, editorial (400-600 words) on any topic, photo of self suitable for reproduction, 5-10 writing samples. Application deadline: March 1 for final entries; other early admissions applicants will be considered with later entries, November 15 for early admissions applicants; up to five winners will be notified by December 15. World Wide Web: http://www.indystar.com/pjf.

REGIONAL NEWS
12243 South Harlem Avenue
Palos Heights, Illinois 60463

General Information Weekly suburban newspaper. Established in 1941. Number of employees: 30. Number of internship applications received each year: 20.

Internships Available ▶ *1 display advertising/outside sales intern:* responsibilities include performing primarily outside and some telephone sales. Candidates should have ability to work independently, college courses in field, experience in the field, oral communication skills, personal interest in the field, self-motivation, strong interpersonal skills. Duration is 11–13 weeks. $8.50 per hour plus commission. Open to college juniors, college seniors, recent college graduates, graduate students, career changers with sales experience.

Benefits Formal training, job counseling, names of contacts, on-the-job training, possible full-time employment, travel reimbursement, willing to act as a professional reference, willing to complete paperwork for educational credit, willing to provide letters of recommendation, phone and car allowances.

Contact Write Mr. Charles Richards, Publisher. Fax: 708-448-4012. No phone calls. In-person interview required. Applicants must submit a formal organization application, letter of interest, resume. Application deadline: March 1 for summer.

THE REPORTER
PO Box 630
Fond du Lac, Wisconsin 54936-0630

General Information Daily newspaper. Established in 1870. Number of employees: 110. Unit of Gannett Co., Inc., Arlington, Virginia. Number of internship applications received each year: 25.
Internships Available ▶ *1 news intern:* responsibilities include newswriting duties. Candidates should have ability to work independently, ability to work with others, analytical skills, college courses in field, computer skills, self-motivation, writing skills. Duration is 12 weeks. $8 per hour. Open to college sophomores, college juniors, college seniors, recent college graduates, graduate students.
Benefits On-the-job training, possible full-time employment, willing to act as a professional reference, willing to complete paperwork for educational credit, willing to provide letters of recommendation.
Contact Write, call, fax, or e-mail Mr. Harley Buchholz, Editor. Phone: 920-922-4600. Fax: 920-922-5388. E-mail: hbuchholz@smgpo.gannett.com. In-person interview recommended (telephone interview accepted). Applicants must submit a letter of interest, resume, portfolio, 5-7 writing samples, 2-3 personal references. Application deadline: March 1 for summer. World Wide Web: http://www.fdlreporter.com.

RICHMOND TIMES-DISPATCH
300 East Franklin Street
Richmond, Virginia 23219

General Information Newspaper with daily circulation of approximately 210,000 and Sunday circulation of 240,000. Established in 1850. Number of employees: 900. Unit of Media General, Richmond, Virginia. Number of internship applications received each year: 180.
Internships Available ▶ *1 graphics intern:* responsibilities include using PC graphics illustration and free-hand illustration in news department. Candidates should have ability to work independently, computer skills, personal interest in the field, self-motivation, strong interpersonal skills, writing skills. Duration is 10 weeks (May to August). $435 per week. ▶ *6 news department editorial interns:* responsibilities include writing, reporting, editing, and processing information. Candidates should have analytical skills, editing skills, plan to pursue career in field, self-motivation, strong interpersonal skills, writing skills. Duration is 10 weeks (May to August). $435 per week. ▶ *1 photo intern:* responsibilities include taking news and feature photographs and conducting photo lab work. Candidates should have ability to work independently, computer skills, knowledge of field, plan to pursue career in field, strong interpersonal skills, writing skills. Duration is 10 weeks (September to November). $435 per week. Open to college juniors, college seniors, recent college graduates, graduate students.
Benefits Job counseling, names of contacts, on-the-job training, possible full-time employment, willing to provide letters of recommendation, opportunity to attend periodic intern meetings that include speakers from the newsroom and other departments.
Contact Write or e-mail Mr. John A. Dillon, Deputy Managing Editor, PO Box 85333, Richmond, Virginia 23293. E-mail: jdillon@timesdispatch.com. In-person interview recommended (telephone interview accepted). Applicants must submit a letter of interest, resume, 5-8 writing samples, 2-3 personal references. Application deadline: January 10 for summer positions, June 12 for photo position, December 10 for spring positions. World Wide Web: http://www.timesdispatch.com.

ROLL CALL
50 F Street, NW, Suite 700
Washington, District of Columbia 20001

General Information Twice-weekly newspaper covering Capitol Hill. Established in 1955. Number of employees: 40. Unit of The Economist, London, United Kingdom. Number of internship applications received each year: 50.
Internships Available ▶ *3 editorial interns:* responsibilities include assisting editors and reporters with research and reporting; some independent reporting and writing; some general office duties. Candidates should have computer skills, plan to pursue career in field, research skills, self-motivation, writing skills. Duration is one summer or semester. Unpaid. Open to college freshmen, college sophomores, college juniors, college seniors, recent college graduates, graduate students. International applications accepted.
Benefits On-the-job training, possible full-time employment, willing to act as a professional reference, willing to complete paperwork for educational credit, willing to provide letters of recommendation.
Contact Write, call, fax, or e-mail Doug Fruehling, Managing Editor. Phone: 202-824-6831. Fax: 202-824-0902. E-mail: dwf@rollcall.com. Telephone interview required. Applicants must submit a letter of interest, resume, two writing samples. Application deadline: March 1 for summer, July 31 for fall, November 15 for spring. World Wide Web: http://www.rollcall.com.

THE SAGINAW NEWS
203 South Washington Avenue
Saginaw, Michigan 48607

General Information Newspaper with a circulation of 50,000 evening and 63,000 Sunday papers in eastern and mid-Michigan. Established in 1859. Number of internship applications received each year: 100.
Internships Available ▶ *1–2 news interns.* Candidates should have ability to work independently, oral communication skills, self-motivation, strong interpersonal skills, writing skills. Duration is 3–4 months. $10.12 per hour. Open to college freshmen, college sophomores, college juniors, college seniors, recent college graduates.
Benefits Names of contacts, on-the-job training, possible full-time employment, willing to act as a professional reference.
Contact Write or e-mail Jodi McFarland, Assistant Metro Editor. Phone: 989-776-9675. Fax: 989-752-3115. E-mail: jmcfarland@thesaginawnews.com. In-person interview required. Applicants must submit a letter of interest, resume, three personal references, 6 writing samples. Applications are accepted continuously.

ST. PETERSBURG TIMES
490 First Avenue South
St. Petersburg, Florida 33701-4204

General Information Independent metropolitan daily newspaper covering west-central Florida. Established in 1884. Number of employees: 1,500. Number of internship applications received each year: 500.
Internships Available ▶ *12–18 summer interns:* responsibilities include working either in the newsroom, design and graphics, or business departments performing hands-on newspaper tasks. Candidates should have ability to work with others, analytical skills, experience in the field, oral communication skills, organizational skills, written communication skills. Duration is 10–12 weeks. $450 per week. Open to college sophomores, college juniors, college seniors, recent college graduates.
Benefits On-the-job training, possible full-time employment, willing to act as a professional reference, willing to provide letters of recommendation, scholarships available for returning students.
Contact Write, call, or e-mail Nancy Waclawek, Director of Corporate Giving, PO Box 1121, St. Petersburg, Florida 33731. Phone: 727-893-8780. Fax: 727-892-2257. E-mail: waclawek@sptimes.com. Applicants must submit a letter of interest, resume, three personal references, 5-6 clips (reporting interns), portfolio samples (art/design/photography interns). Application deadline: December 1 for news and marketing interns; February 15 for all other departments. World Wide Web: http://www.sptimes.com/internship.

SAN FRANCISCO BAY GUARDIAN
520 Hampshire Street
San Francisco, California 94110

General Information San Francisco-based liberal alternative news and arts/entertainment weekly paper. Established in 1966. Number of employees: 100. Number of internship applications received each year: 175.

Internships Available ▶ *3 arts and entertainment journalism interns:* responsibilities include sorting mail and faxes, compiling and writing "superlists," becoming a staff writer for the calendar section, writing preview blurbs and short reviews by pitch or on assignment. Candidates should have ability to work independently, computer skills, oral communication skills, plan to pursue career in field, research skills, self-motivation, strong interpersonal skills, writing skills, demonstrable or background; interest in either music, theater, or film; knowledge of San Francisco area (helpful). Duration is 4 months (2 days per week). Unpaid. Open to recent high school graduates, college freshmen, college sophomores, college juniors, college seniors, recent college graduates, graduate students. ▶ *1 culture intern:* responsibilities include writing, editing, research, fact-checking, and light office work. Candidates should have ability to work with others, editing skills, oral communication skills, plan to pursue career in field, research skills, self-motivation, writing skills, sense of humor, knowledge of San Francisco area. Duration is 4 months (2 days per week). Unpaid. Open to recent high school graduates, college freshmen, college sophomores, college juniors, college seniors, recent college graduates, graduate students, law students, career changers, individuals reentering the workforce. ▶ *4 news interns:* responsibilities include writing, researching, checking facts, and assisting in the newsroom. Candidates should have ability to work independently, analytical skills, computer skills, oral communication skills, personal interest in the field, research skills, self-motivation, writing skills, knowledge of San Francisco area. Duration is 4 months (2 days per week). Unpaid. Open to recent high school graduates, college freshmen, college sophomores, college juniors, college seniors, recent college graduates, graduate students, law students, career changers, individuals reentering the workforce. ▶ *1 online department intern:* responsibilities include writing and researching stories and working on Web site. Candidates should have ability to work independently, analytical skills, computer skills, editing skills, knowledge of field, oral communication skills, personal interest in the field, research skills, self-motivation, strong interpersonal skills, strong leadership ability, writing skills, design and/or html skills. Duration is 4 months (2 days per week). Unpaid. Open to high school seniors, recent high school graduates, college freshmen, college sophomores, college juniors, college seniors, recent college graduates, graduate students, law students, career changers, individuals reentering the workforce. International applications accepted.
Benefits Job counseling, names of contacts, on-the-job training, opportunity to attend seminars/workshops, willing to act as a professional reference, willing to complete paperwork for educational credit, willing to provide letters of recommendation.
Contact Through World Wide Web site Camille T. Taiara, Editorial Coordinator. Phone: 415-255-3100. E-mail: camille@sfbg.com. In-person interview recommended (telephone interview accepted). Applicants must submit a resume, three writing samples, cover letter. Application deadline: April 15 for summer, August 15 for fall, December 15 for spring. World Wide Web: http://www.sfbg.com.

SAN FRANCISCO CHRONICLE
901 Mission Street
San Francisco, California 94103-2988

General Information Nationally prominent newspaper with daily circulation of 475,000 and Sunday circulation of 592,000. Established in 1865. Number of employees: 640. Unit of The Hearst Corporation, New York, New York. Number of internship applications received each year: 800.
Internships Available ▶ *2-year interns:* responsibilities include reporting, copyediting, photography, graphics and design, or library assignments depending on skills and experience; working as part of regular staff following a brief orientation. $31,000 the first year; $38,000 the second year. Open to college graduates who have been out of school no longer than 1 year prior to start of internship. ▶ *Summer interns:* responsibilities include reporting, copy editing, photography, graphics and design, or library assignments depending on the applicant's skills and experience; working as part of regular staff following a brief orientation. Duration is 12 weeks beginning in mid-June. $521 per week. Open to college students or college graduates who have been out of school

no longer than 1 year prior to start of internship. Candidates for all positions should have computer skills, editing skills, knowledge of field, plan to pursue career in field, writing skills. International applications accepted.
Benefits Hands-on experience system of mentors.
Contact Write, e-mail, or through World Wide Web site Rebecca Markowitz, Editorial Hiring Assistant, 901 Mission Street, San Francisco, California 94103-2988. Fax: 415-495-3843. E-mail: rmarkowitz@sfchronicle.com. No phone calls. Applicants must submit a letter of interest, resume, 3 professional references, clippings, portfolio, or examples of work (dependent upon position). Application deadline: November 15 for summer. World Wide Web: http://www.sfgate.com/chronicle/internships/.

SOCIETY OF PROFESSIONAL JOURNALISTS
3909 North Meridian Street
Indianapolis, Indiana 46208

General Information Organization that serves the professional needs of journalists and students pursuing careers in journalism. Established in 1909. Number of employees: 20. Number of internship applications received each year: 25.
Internships Available ▶ *2 Pulliam/Kilgore interns:* responsibilities include researching and writing about freedom of information issues. Candidates should have ability to work independently, computer skills, editing skills, research skills, writing skills. Duration is 10 weeks in summer. $400 per week. Open to college juniors, college seniors, recent college graduates, graduate students, law students. International applications accepted.
Benefits Names of contacts, opportunity to attend seminars/workshops, possible full-time employment, willing to complete paperwork for educational credit.
Contact Write, call, fax, or e-mail Jeff Mohl, Magazine Editor. Phone: 317-927-8000. Fax: 317-920-4789. E-mail: jmohl@spj.org. Applicants must submit a formal organization application, letter of interest, resume, 5 writing samples. World Wide Web: http://www.spj.org.

SOUTH FLORIDA SUN-SENTINEL
200 East Las Olas Boulevard
Fort Lauderdale, Florida 33301

General Information Daily newspaper. Unit of Tribune Company, Chicago, Illinois. Number of internship applications received each year: 400.
Internships Available ▶ *2–3 copy editors.* Candidates should have computer skills, editing skills, oral communication skills, plan to pursue career in field, writing skills. Duration is 10 weeks. $500 per week. Open to college sophomores, college juniors, college seniors, recent college graduates, graduate students. ▶ *1–2 graphic artists.* Candidates should have computer skills, oral communication skills, plan to pursue career in field, research skills, self-motivation, writing skills. Duration is 10 weeks. $500 per week. Open to college sophomores, college juniors, college seniors, recent college graduates, graduate students. ▶ *1–2 photographers.* Candidates should have ability to work independently, computer skills, oral communication skills, plan to pursue career in field, self-motivation, written communication skills. Duration is 10 weeks. $500 per week. Open to college sophomores, college juniors, college seniors, graduate students. ▶ *5–7 reporters.* Candidates should have analytical skills, experience in the field, oral communication skills, plan to pursue career in field, research skills, writing skills. Duration is 10 weeks. $500 per week. Open to college sophomores, college juniors, college seniors, recent college graduates, graduate students.
Benefits On-the-job training, opportunity to attend seminars/workshops, possible full-time employment, willing to act as a professional reference, willing to complete paperwork for educational credit, willing to provide letters of recommendation.
Contact Write Kathleen Pellegrino, Recruitment Editor. Phone: 954-356-4536. Fax: 954-356-4609. E-mail: kpellegrino@sun-sentinel.com. In-person interview recommended (telephone interview accepted). Applicants must submit a letter of interest, resume, three personal references, 8-10 writing samples. Application deadline: December 1 for summer. World Wide Web: http://sun-sentinel.com.

THE STATE NEWSPAPER
PO Box 1333
Columbia, South Carolina 29202

General Information Newspaper that serves South Carolina with a daily circulation of 120,000. Established in 1891. Number of employees: 500. Unit of Knight Ridder, San Jose, California. Number of internship applications received each year: 150.
Internships Available ▶ *1 copy editor:* responsibilities include editing copy and writing headlines. Candidates should have ability to work independently, college courses in field, editing skills, oral communication skills, plan to pursue career in field, written communication skills. Duration is 10–12 weeks. $375 per week. Open to college sophomores, college juniors. ▶ *1–2 reporting interns:* responsibilities include covering events and writing stories. Candidates should have ability to work independently, oral communication skills, organizational skills, plan to pursue career in field, writing skills. Duration is 10-12 weeks in summer. $375 per week. Open to college freshmen, college sophomores, college juniors. International applications accepted.
Benefits Job counseling, names of contacts, on-the-job training, opportunity to attend seminars/workshops, possible full-time employment, willing to complete paperwork for educational credit, willing to provide letters of recommendation.
Contact Write John Drescher, Managing Editor. Fax: 803-771-8407. No phone calls. Applicants must submit a letter of interest, resume, three personal references, five writing samples. Application deadline: January 1 for summer. World Wide Web: http://www.thestate.com.

THE TAMPA TRIBUNE
200 South Parker Street
Tampa, Florida 33606

General Information Newspaper that publishes a morning edition, Monday to Sunday, with a circulation of about 265,000. Number of employees: 500. Unit of Media General, Richmond, Virginia. Number of internship applications received each year: 200.
Internships Available ▶ *1 copyeditor intern.* Candidates should have experience in copyediting (AP style grammar and English). Duration is 12 weeks in summer. $400 per week. ▶ *4 interns:* responsibilities include reporting and handling all aspects of news gathering and writing. Duration is 12 weeks. $400 per week. Open to college freshmen, college sophomores, college juniors, college seniors, graduate students.
Benefits On-the-job training, willing to act as a professional reference, willing to provide letters of recommendation, professional experience.
Contact Write or call Beverly Dominick, News Recruiting and Training Manager, PO Box 191, Tampa, Florida 33601. Phone: 813-259-7763. Applicants must submit a formal organization application, letter of interest, resume, three personal references, 6-10 writing samples, at least 1 letter of recommendation. Application deadline: December 1. World Wide Web: http://www.tampatrib.com.

TIMES LEADER
15 North Main Street
Wilkes-Barre, Pennsylvania 18711

General Information Newspaper. Number of employees: 200. Unit of Knight Ridder, San Jose, California. Number of internship applications received each year: 24.
Internships Available ▶ *2–6 interns:* responsibilities include reporting, copy editing, photography, or page design, depending on intern's interests. Candidates should have knowledge of field, plan to pursue career in field, self-motivation, strong interpersonal skills, written communication skills. Duration is 6–12 weeks. Position available as unpaid or at $300 per week. Open to college freshmen, college sophomores, college juniors, college seniors, recent college graduates, graduate students.
Benefits On-the-job training.
Contact Write, fax, or e-mail Pamela C. Turfa, Intern Coordinator, 15 North Main Street, Wilkes-Barre, Pennsylvania 18711. Phone: 570-829-7177. Fax: 570-970-7446. E-mail: pamt@leader.

net. Applicants must submit a letter of interest, resume, 3 to 5 writing samples. Applications are accepted continuously. World Wide Web: http://www.timesleader.com.

TOLEDO BLADE
541 North Superior Street
Toledo, Ohio 43660

General Information Publisher of newspaper with daily circulation of 145,000 and Sunday circulation of 200,000. Established in 1836. Number of employees: 750. Division of Block Communications, Inc., Toledo, Ohio. Number of internship applications received each year: 300.
Internships Available ▶ *4 city desk reporters:* responsibilities include general assignment reporting. Candidates should have ability to work independently, ability to work with others, college courses in field, computer skills, editing skills, knowledge of field, oral communication skills, plan to pursue career in field, research skills, written communication skills. Duration is 13 weeks in summer only. $503 per week. ▶ *4 photographers:* responsibilities include taking, processing, and printing pictures. Candidates should have ability to work independently, ability to work with others, college courses in field, computer skills, oral communication skills, personal interest in the field, plan to pursue career in field, written communication skills, advanced photography skills, accuracy a must. Duration is 1 semester. $503 per week. Open to college juniors, college seniors, recent college graduates, graduate students.
Benefits On-the-job training, possible full-time employment, willing to act as a professional reference, willing to complete paperwork for educational credit, willing to provide letters of recommendation.
Contact Write or e-mail Luann Sharp, Assistant Managing Editor. E-mail: luannsharp@theblade.com. No phone calls. Telephone interview required. Applicants must submit a formal organization application, letter of interest, resume, three personal references, writing samples. Application deadline: January 15 for city desk positions; continuous for photographer positions. World Wide Web: http://www.toledoblade.com.

THE TUSCALOOSA NEWS
2001 6th Street
Tuscaloosa, Alabama 35401

General Information Daily newspaper. Number of employees: 200. Subsidiary of The New York Times, New York, New York. Number of internship applications received each year: 200.
Internships Available ▶ *Reporting interns:* responsibilities include general reporting responsibilities. Candidates should have ability to work independently, ability to work with others, computer skills, research skills, self-motivation, writing skills. Duration is flexible. Paid. Open to college freshmen, college sophomores, college juniors, college seniors, recent college graduates, graduate students, law students, career changers, individuals reentering the workforce. International applications accepted.
Benefits On-the-job training, opportunity to attend seminars/ workshops, possible full-time employment, willing to act as a professional reference, willing to provide letters of recommendation.
Contact Write or e-mail Greg Retsinas, City Editor. Fax: 205-349-0802. E-mail: greg.retsinas@tuscaloosanews.com. No phone calls. Applicants must submit a letter of interest, resume, three writing samples. Applications are accepted continuously. World Wide Web: http://tuscaloosanews.com.

THE VILLAGE VOICE
36 Cooper Square
New York, New York 10003

General Information Weekly newspaper that covers the arts. Established in 1955. Number of employees: 250. Number of internship applications received each year: 200.
Internships Available ▶ *15–30 interns:* responsibilities include researching, editing, and answering telephones and the mail. Candidates should have ability to work independently, computer skills, editing skills, knowledge of field, plan to pursue career in field, research skills, written communication skills. Duration is 3 months (year-round). Unpaid. Open to high school students,

recent high school graduates, college freshmen, college sophomores, college juniors, college seniors, recent college graduates, graduate students, law students, career changers, individuals reentering the workforce. International applications accepted.

Benefits Formal training, on-the-job training, opportunity to attend seminars/workshops, possible full-time employment, willing to complete paperwork for educational credit, willing to provide letters of recommendation.

Contact Write, call, e-mail, or through World Wide Web site Alana Forbes, Intern Coordinator. Phone: 212-475-3300 Ext. 2002. Fax: 212-475-8944. E-mail: editor@villagevoice.com. Applicants must submit a formal organization application, letter of interest, resume, 2-3 writing samples (no poetry or fiction), 1-2 personal references or letters of recommendation. Application deadline: January 31 for spring, March 31 for summer, July 31 for fall, November 30 for winter. World Wide Web: http://www.villagevoice.com.

THE VINDICATOR
PO Box 780
Youngstown, Ohio 44501-0780

General Information Daily newspaper with circulation of about 78,000. Established in 1869. Number of employees: 400. Number of internship applications received each year: 35.

Internships Available ▶ *6 copy editors:* responsibilities include editing stories for content, spelling, grammar, accuracy, and style, writing headlines; learning basics of design and pagination. Candidates should have ability to work independently, computer skills, editing skills, strong interpersonal skills, writing skills. Duration is 12–15 weeks. $300 per week. Open to college sophomores, college juniors, college seniors. ▶ *5 general assignment reporters:* responsibilities include substantive contributions to the daily work of a newspaper in the following areas: reporting, copy desk, photography, and design/graphics. Candidates should have ability to work independently, ability to work with others, computer skills, editing skills, knowledge of field, writing skills. Duration is 12 weeks. $300 per week. Open to college sophomores, college juniors, college seniors. ▶ *1 page designer:* responsibilities include design and pagination. Candidates should have ability to work independently, computer skills, knowledge of field, organizational skills, strong interpersonal skills. Duration is 12 weeks. $300 per week. Open to college sophomores, college juniors, college seniors, recent college graduates.

Benefits On-the-job training, possible full-time employment, willing to complete paperwork for educational credit.

Contact Write, call, or e-mail Ernest A. Brown, Jr., Assistant Regional Editor/Intern Coordinator, PO Box 780, Youngstown, Ohio 44501-0780. Phone: 330-747-1471 Ext. 304. Fax: 330-747-6712. E-mail: vindinews@cboss.com. In-person interview required. Applicants must submit a letter of interest, resume, three writing samples, two personal references. Application deadline: March 31 for summer; contact for deadlines for other positions.

THE WALL STREET JOURNAL
PO Box 300
Princeton, New Jersey 08543-0300

General Information Global daily business paper with circulation of nearly 2 million and a news staff of 500. Established in 1889. Number of employees: 8,500. Unit of Dow Jones & Co., New York, New York. Number of internship applications received each year: 500.

Internships Available ▶ *18 summer news reporting interns:* responsibilities include reporting and writing on a daily basis; positions located at bureaus throughout the country. Candidates should have computer skills, office skills, research skills, self-motivation, written communication skills. Duration is 10 weeks in June, July, and August. $700 per week. Open to college freshmen, college sophomores, college juniors, college seniors, recent college graduates, graduate students. International applications accepted.

Benefits Willing to provide letters of recommendation.

International Internships Available in Brussels, Belgium; Hong Kong, China; Tokyo, Japan; London, United Kingdom.

Contact Write Cathy Panagoulias, Assistant Managing Editor. E-mail: jobs@wsj.com. No phone calls. Applicants must submit a resume, cover letter, 12 byline clips on legal-size paper; interview for applicants accepted or final consideration. Application deadline: November 1.

THE WASHINGTON POST
1150 15th Street, NW
Washington, District of Columbia 20071

General Information Newspaper publisher. Established in 1877. Number of employees: 3,500. Unit of The Washington Post Co., Washington, District of Columbia. Number of internship applications received each year: 600.

Internships Available ▶ *3–4 copy editors:* responsibilities include working on foreign, national, metro, sports, and business copy desks. Candidates should have ability to work with others, computer skills, editing skills, knowledge of field, personal interest in the field, writing skills. Duration is 12 weeks (June to August). $894.75 per week. ▶ *1 news artist:* responsibilities include designing pages and producing graphics and maps. Candidates should have ability to work with others, computer skills, editing skills, knowledge of field, research skills, writing skills. Duration is 12 weeks (June to August). $813.40 per week. ▶ *1 page designer:* responsibilities include designing pages for news and features sections. Candidates should have ability to work with others, computer skills, editing skills, knowledge of field, oral communication skills, writing skills. Duration is 12 weeks (June to August). $894.75 per week. ▶ *1 photographer:* responsibilities include shooting photos and working inside the photo department. Candidates should have ability to work independently, ability to work with others, experience in the field, oral communication skills, personal interest in the field. Duration is 12 weeks (June to August). $813.40 per week. ▶ *12–14 reporters:* responsibilities include reporting and writing stories for metro, business, sports, and style sections. Candidates should have ability to work independently, knowledge of field, research skills, strong interpersonal skills, writing skills. Duration is 12 weeks (June to August). $813.40 per week. Open to college juniors, college seniors, graduate students. International applications accepted.

Benefits Formal training, job counseling, names of contacts, opportunity to attend seminars/workshops, possible full-time employment, willing to act as a professional reference, willing to provide letters of recommendation, reimbursement of work-related travel expenses.

Contact Write, e-mail, or through World Wide Web site Cheryl G. Butler, Summer News Program. E-mail: butlerc@washpost.com. No phone calls. In-person interview required. Applicants must submit a formal organization application, resume, academic transcripts, portfolio, two letters of recommendation, 6-8 writing samples or photo/graphics portfolio. Application deadline: November 1. World Wide Web: http://www.washingtonpost.com/intern.

WINSTON-SALEM JOURNAL
PO Box 3159
Winston-Salem, North Carolina 27102

General Information Daily newspaper serving 9 counties in northwestern North Carolina. Established in 1897. Number of employees: 463. Unit of Media General, Richmond, Virginia. Number of internship applications received each year: 75.

Internships Available ▶ *1 advertising salesperson:* responsibilities include selling and laying out ads and customer relations. Candidates should have college courses in field, experience in the field, organizational skills, plan to pursue career in field, strong interpersonal skills. Duration is flexible. $275 per week. ▶ *1 marketing and creative services intern:* responsibilities include assisting marketing department with creative services special projects. Duration is flexible. $300 per week. ▶ *3–4 newspaper reporters:* responsibilities include general assignment reporting. Candidates should have college courses in field, experience in the field, plan to pursue career in field, self-motivation, writing skills. Duration is 10–12 weeks. $375 per week. ▶ *1 photographer:* responsibilities include taking photos, performing general assignments, and developing and printing film. Candidates should have ability to work independently, college courses in field, experience in the field,

Winston-Salem Journal (continued)

plan to pursue career in field. Duration is flexible. $375 per week. Open to college juniors, college seniors returning to school in the fall. International applications accepted.
Benefits Formal training, possible full-time employment, travel reimbursement.
Contact Write, call, fax, or e-mail Randy Noftle, Director of Human Resources. Phone: 336-727-7330. Fax: 336-727-4096. E-mail: rnoftle@wsjournal.com. In-person interview recommended (telephone interview accepted). Applicants must submit a formal organization application, letter of interest, resume, academic transcripts, two letters of recommendation. Application deadline: December 1 for summer. World Wide Web: http://www.wsjournal.com.

NEWSPAPER, PERIODICAL, BOOK, AND DATABASE PUBLISHERS

AGORA, INC.
14 West Mt. Vernon Place
Baltimore, Maryland 21201

General Information International publisher of investment, travel, and health-related consumer publications with affiliated offices in Florida, New Mexico, London, Paris, and Ireland. Established in 1979. Number of employees: 180. Number of internship applications received each year: 400.
Internships Available ▶ *Copy writers:* responsibilities include working with promotional advertising material, brochures, newsletter articles, special reports, and bulletins. Candidates should have ability to work independently, computer skills, editing skills, research skills, writing skills. Duration is 3–6 months. $10 to $15 per day, or $6 per hour. ▶ *Editorial associates:* responsibilities include research, fact checking, correcting copy, and administrative duties. Candidates should have ability to work independently, ability to work with others, computer skills, oral communication skills, written communication skills. Duration is 3–6 months. $10 to $15 per day, or $6 per hour. ▶ *Graphic design interns.* Candidates should have ability to work independently, college courses in field, knowledge of field, office skills, personal interest in the field, self-motivation, knowledge of Quark, Illustrator, PhotoShop, PageMaker, and Word. Duration is 3–6 months. $10 to $15 per day, or $6 per hour. ▶ *Marketing interns:* responsibilities include print buying, customer correspondence, and general administrative duties. Candidates should have ability to work independently, ability to work with others, computer skills, oral communication skills, written communication skills. Duration is 3–6 months. $10 to $15 per day, or $6 per hour. Open to college freshmen, college sophomores, college juniors, college seniors, graduate students. International applications accepted.
Benefits Opportunity to attend seminars/workshops, possible full-time employment, willing to complete paperwork for educational credit, willing to provide letters of recommendation, free housing for out-of-state and international interns.
International Internships Available in France; Waterford, Ireland.
Contact Write, fax, or e-mail Elizabeth Massing, Personnel Specialist. Phone: 410-230-1263. Fax: 410-783-8455. E-mail: emassing@agora-inc.com. Applicants must submit a letter of interest, resume, cover letter indicating placement preference. Applications are accepted continuously. World Wide Web: http://www.agora-inc.com.

AMEDIA/AMAGAZINE
677 Fifth Avenue, Third Floor
New York, New York 10022

General Information National lifestyle magazine for Asian Americans. Established in 1990. Number of employees: 8. Subsidiary of Click 2 Asia, Los Angeles, California. Number of internship applications received each year: 50.

Internships Available ▶ *1–3 editorial interns:* responsibilities include writing and reporting stories; library and online research; assisting in editorial planning; helping manage the administrative workflow of editorial department. Candidates should have oral communication skills, personal interest in the field, plan to pursue career in field, research skills, writing skills. Duration is 15 hours per week (fall, spring or summer). Unpaid. Open to college juniors, college seniors, must be Asian American including South Asian.
Benefits Willing to act as a professional reference, willing to complete paperwork for educational credit, willing to provide letters of recommendation.
Contact Write, call, fax, or e-mail Jennifer Abbasi, Assistant Editor. Phone: 212-593-8089 Ext. 261. Fax: 212-593-8082. E-mail: jabbasi@amediainc.com. In-person interview required. Applicants must submit a letter of interest, resume, two writing samples. Application deadline: April 1 for summer, August 1 for fall, December 1 for spring.

ARCHAE EDITIONS
Box 444, Prince Street Station
New York, New York 10012-0008

General Information Nonprofit organization that produces alternative materials and literature (books, prints, audios, videos, and film). Established in 1977. Number of employees: 1. Number of internship applications received each year: 50.
Internships Available ▶ *5–10 collaborative assistants.* Duration is flexible. Unpaid. Open to college juniors, college seniors, recent college graduates, graduate students. ▶ *8–10 interns:* responsibilities include collaborating with a productive full-time artist/writer (usually Richard Kostelanetz) in the project-centered production of books, videotapes, films, holograms, and audiotapes for exhibition and production. Candidates should have ability to work independently, computer skills, editing skills, plan to pursue career in field, self-motivation, desire to complete a project that should prominently display the intern's name. Duration is flexible. Unpaid. Open to college sophomores, college juniors, college seniors, recent college graduates, career changers. International applications accepted.
Benefits Job counseling, names of contacts, on-the-job training, possible full-time employment, willing to complete paperwork for educational credit, willing to provide letters of recommendation, projects on which interns can put their names.
Contact Write or e-mail Mr. Richard Kostelanetz, Director of Literature and Media. E-mail: rkostelanetz@bigfoot.com. No phone calls. In-person interview recommended (telephone interview accepted). Applicants must submit a letter of interest, resume. Applications are accepted continuously.

ART PAPERS MAGAZINE
PO Box 5748
Atlanta, Georgia 31107

General Information Nonprofit organization and publisher of ART PAPERS Magazine Hot brings readers diverse, independent and award-winning coverage within a dialogue of international contemporary art. Established in 1977. Number of employees: 6. Number of internship applications received each year: 50.
Internships Available ▶ *1 advertising interns:* responsibilities include organizing and researching information for potential current advertisers; creating strategic sales campaign; contacting potential advertisers. Candidates should have ability to work independently, analytical skills, computer skills, editing skills, office skills, oral communication skills, organizational skills, research skills, self-motivation, writing skills, strong interest in sales and marketing (experience preferred). Duration is 1 semester (minimum). Unpaid. ▶ *2 editorial interns:* responsibilities include assisting editors with correspondence and communication with contributing writers; copy editing; assisting in management of articles through production; updating and maintaining records and archives. Candidates should have ability to work independently, computer skills, editing skills, knowledge of field, research skills, writing skills. Duration is 1 semester (minimum); 6-12 month residency available. Unpaid. ▶ *1 finance and operations intern:* responsibilities include researching contacts for potential sponsors and donors; assisting

with grant writing and editing; assisting with basic accounting functions; working to create beneficial partnerships with other organizations. Candidates should have ability to work independently, college courses in field, computer skills, experience in the field, organizational skills, research skills, writing skills, Quickbooks and Excel. Duration is 1 semester (minimum). Unpaid. ▶ *1 marketing and development intern:* responsibilities include developing marketing campaigns to reach new vendors and subscribers; researching, identifying, and contacting potential subscribers; developing, marketing and implementing circulation expansion projects; researching and identifying potential advertisers. Candidates should have ability to work independently, computer skills, organizational skills, research skills, writing skills, background or experience in marketing, database experience a plus. Duration is 1 semester (minimum). Unpaid. Open to college juniors, college seniors, recent college graduates, graduate students.
Benefits Willing to act as a professional reference, willing to complete paperwork for educational credit, willing to provide letters of recommendation.
Contact Write, call, fax, or e-mail Development Manager. Phone: 404-588-1837 Ext. 11. Fax: 404-588-1836. E-mail: circulation@ artpapers.org. In-person interview recommended (telephone interview accepted). Applicants must submit a letter of interest, resume, academic transcripts, three personal references, two letters of recommendation, 1 writing sample (editorial intern); portfolio (graphic intern). Applications are accepted continuously. World Wide Web: http://www.artpapers.org.

BARRICADE BOOKS
185 Bridge Plaza North, Suite 308A
Fort Lee, New Jersey 07024

General Information Publishing company. Established in 1991. Number of employees: 10. Number of internship applications received each year: 100.
Internships Available ▶ *1–2 publisher's assistants:* responsibilities include general office support and entry-level editorial and publicity tasks. Candidates should have office skills, oral communication skills, personal interest in the field, self-motivation, writing skills. Duration is 3 months. $25 per day. Open to college sophomores, college juniors, college seniors, recent college graduates, graduate students. International applications accepted.
Benefits On-the-job training, willing to act as a professional reference, willing to complete paperwork for educational credit, willing to provide letters of recommendation.
Contact Write, call, fax, e-mail, or through World Wide Web site Jeff Nordstedt, Internship Coordinator. Phone: 201-944-7600. Fax: 201-944-6363. E-mail: jeff@barricadebooks.com. Applicants must submit a letter of interest, resume. Application deadline: May 1 for summer, December 1 for spring. World Wide Web: http://www.barricadebooks.com.

BEACON PRESS
25 Beacon Street
Boston, Massachusetts 02108

General Information Publisher of trade and scholarly nonfiction. Established in 1854. Number of employees: 30. Unit of Unitarian Universalist Association, Boston, Massachusetts. Number of internship applications received each year: 300.
Internships Available ▶ *Interns:* responsibilities include working in various departments including marketing, publicity, editing, and business. Candidates should have ability to work independently, analytical skills, computer skills, office skills, oral communication skills, organizational skills, self-motivation, written communication skills, editing and research skills (helpful). Duration is flexible. Unpaid. Open to college freshmen, college sophomores, college juniors, college seniors, recent college graduates, graduate students, career changers, individuals reentering the workforce. International applications accepted.
Benefits Job counseling, names of contacts, on-the-job training, possible full-time employment, willing to complete paperwork for educational credit, willing to provide letters of recommendation.
Contact Write, fax, or e-mail Christopher Vyce, Assistant to the Director. Fax: 617-723-3097. E-mail: cvyce@beacon.org. No phone

calls. Applicants must submit a letter of interest, resume, cover letter. Application deadline: March 1 for summer, June 1 for fall, October 1 for winter, December 1 for spring.

BEAVER COUNTY TIMES
400 Fair Avenue
Beaver, Pennsylvania 15009

General Information County-wide newspaper with a weekday circulation of 43,000 and a Sunday circulation of 52,000.
Internships Available ▶ *Copy editor interns:* responsibilities include duties essentially the same as staff members. Candidates should have knowledge of pagination. ▶ *Photography intern:* responsibilities include duties essentially the same as those performed by regular staff members. Duration is 13 weeks.
Contact Write Internship Coordinator. Phone: 724-775-3200. Fax: 724-775-4180. Samples of work. World Wide Web: http://www.timesonline.com.

BIBLICAL ARCHAEOLOGY SOCIETY
4710 41st Street, NW
Washington, District of Columbia 20016

General Information Nonprofit nondenominational, educational organization publishing 3 magazines and producing other media and tours on archaeology and the Bible. Established in 1975. Number of employees: 25. Number of internship applications received each year: 50.
Internships Available ▶ *1–2 editorial assistants:* responsibilities include clerical duties, letter writing, photo searches, proofreading, corrections to publications, and correspondence. Candidates should have ability to work with others, computer skills, office skills, oral communication skills, research skills, written communication skills. Duration is minimum of one summer or one semester. Position available as unpaid or at $7–$8 per hour. Open to college freshmen, college sophomores, college juniors, college seniors, recent college graduates, graduate students, career changers, individuals reentering the workforce. International applications accepted.
Benefits Names of contacts, on-the-job training, possible full-time employment, travel reimbursement, willing to act as a professional reference, willing to complete paperwork for educational credit, willing to provide letters of recommendation.
Contact Write, fax, or e-mail Celeste Pickard, Personnel Manager, 4710 41st Street, NW, Washington, District of Columbia 20016. Fax: 202-364-2636. E-mail: operations@bib-arch.org. In-person interview recommended (telephone interview accepted). Applicants must submit a letter of interest, resume, writing sample. Applications are accepted continuously. World Wide Web: http://www.biblicalarchaeology.org.

BOSTON MAGAZINE
300 Massachusetts Avenue
Boston, Massachusetts 02115

General Information Publisher of city/regional magazine. Established in 1962. Number of employees: 50. Unit of Metrocorp, Inc., Philadelphia, Pennsylvania. Number of internship applications received each year: 300.
Internships Available ▶ *3 advertising sales interns:* responsibilities include assisting account executives and sales assistant with client contact and management of materials, including soliciting and preparing media packets. Candidates should have ability to work independently, computer skills, office skills, oral communication skills, personal interest in the field, strong interpersonal skills. Duration is 1 semester. Unpaid. ▶ *1–2 art interns:* responsibilities include assisting art director and associate with monthly productions, extensive photo research, and trafficking artwork. Candidates should have computer skills, oral communication skills, personal interest in the field, self-motivation, strong interpersonal skills, writing skills. Duration is 1 semester. Unpaid. ▶ *5–10 editorial interns:* responsibilities include working in direct positions with writers and editors, performing basic research, tracking and calling sources for information, and working on story development. Candidates should have ability to work with others, computer skills, research skills, self-motivation, writing skills. Duration is 1 semester.

Unpaid. ▶ *2 marketing interns:* responsibilities include assisting in event coordination, sales materials preparation, working with advertising clients, proofreading and writing marketing sections of the magazine. Candidates should have ability to work with others, computer skills, office skills, personal interest in the field, writing skills. Duration is 1 semester. Unpaid. ▶ *2 promotions/ special projects interns:* responsibilities include helping in organizing functions sponsored by the magazine, working with the production manager, helping service the various advertising and promotion needs of the manager, and compiling and writing monthly press reports. Candidates should have ability to work independently, computer skills, office skills, organizational skills, personal interest in the field, strong interpersonal skills. Duration is 1–4 months. Unpaid. Open to college freshmen, college sophomores, college juniors, college seniors, recent college graduates.

Benefits Names of contacts, opportunity to attend seminars/ workshops, possible full-time employment, willing to complete paperwork for educational credit, willing to provide letters of recommendation.

Contact Write, fax, or e-mail Carly Geeza, Executive Coordinator. Fax: 617-262-4925. E-mail: cgeeza@bostonmagazine.com. No phone calls. Applicants must submit a letter of interest, resume, 2-3 writing samples for editorial positions. Application deadline: March 15 for summer, August 1 for fall, November 21 for spring. World Wide Web: http://www.bostonmagazine.com.

THE BUREAU OF NATIONAL AFFAIRS, INC.
1250 23rd Street, NW, 4th Floor
Washington, District of Columbia 20037-1164

General Information Private publisher of print and electronic news and specialized news and information services covering developments in business, economics, law, taxation, employee relations, environmental protection, and other public policy issues. Established in 1947. Number of employees: 1,600. Number of internship applications received each year: 100.

Internships Available ▶ *2 editorial interns:* responsibilities include clipping the wire service, copyediting, proofreading, and reporting. Candidates should have ability to work with others, analytical skills, editing skills, research skills, self-motivation, writing skills. Duration is 15 to 18 hours per week in spring and fall; 37.5 hours per week in summer. $11.34 per hour. Open to college juniors, college seniors. ▶ *2 legal editorial interns:* responsibilities include proofreading, writing headnotes, and writing cases. Candidates should have ability to work with others, analytical skills, editing skills, research skills, writing skills. Duration is 12 weeks in summer. $11.34 per hour. Open to law students. ▶ *Technical tools interns:* responsibilities include providing end user technical support; researching and writing technical documentation code; maintaining computer programs; developing knowledge of programming and document procedures. Candidates should have ability to work with others, oral communication skills, plan to pursue career in field, research skills, writing skills, knowledge of SGML, C, C++, HTML, UNIX, and search engine configuration. Duration is one semester or longer. $10–$15 per hour. Open to college freshmen, college sophomores, college juniors, college seniors. International applications accepted.

Benefits Formal training, possible full-time employment, willing to complete paperwork for educational credit.

Contact Write, call, fax, or e-mail Anthony A. Harris, Employment Director. Phone: 202-261-1566. Fax: 202-261-1583. E-mail: tharris@bna.com. In-person interview recommended (telephone interview accepted). Applicants must submit a letter of interest, resume, 4 newsclips (preferably published). Application deadline: February 1 for summer, May 1 for fall, November 1 for spring. World Wide Web: http://www.bna.com.

CHARLESBRIDGE PUBLISHING
85 Main Street
Watertown, Massachusetts 02472

General Information Publisher of school books that help children use reason and creative thinking to learn and solve problems, as well as trade fiction and nonfiction picture books. Established in 1979. Number of employees: 30. Number of internship applications received each year: 100.

Internships Available ▶ *4 editorial assistants:* responsibilities include researching, editing, proofreading, writing, and revising manuscripts. Candidates should have analytical skills, editing skills, oral communication skills, organizational skills, research skills, writing skills. Duration is 1 semester. Unpaid. Open to college juniors, college seniors, recent college graduates, graduate students, career changers, individuals reentering the workforce. ▶ *1 graphic arts assistant:* responsibilities include creating illustrations, designing layouts, communicating with editors, evaluating the graphic potential of stories, and researching accuracy of illustrations. Candidates should have ability to work independently, ability to work with others, oral communication skills, research skills, self-motivation, experience in graphic arts, sensitivity to text/art interface in children's picture books. Duration is 1 semester. Unpaid. Open to college sophomores, college juniors, college seniors, recent college graduates, graduate students, individuals reentering the workforce. ▶ *1 marketing intern:* responsibilities include researching, writing, compiling data, planning, surveying, e-mail campaign analysis, communicating with sales, editorial and administration. Candidates should have computer skills, oral communication skills, self-motivation, strong interpersonal skills, written communication skills. Duration is 1 semester. Unpaid. Open to college sophomores, college juniors, college seniors, recent college graduates, graduate students, law students, career changers.

Benefits On-the-job training, opportunity to attend seminars/ workshops, willing to act as a professional reference, willing to complete paperwork for educational credit, willing to provide letters of recommendation.

Contact Write or e-mail Ms. Elena Dworkin Wright, Managing Editor. E-mail: schooleditorial@charlesbridge.com. No phone calls. In-person interview recommended (telephone interview accepted). Applicants must submit a letter of interest, resume, 2-3 art samples (graphic art interns), 1 writing sample (editorial interns). Applications are accepted continuously. World Wide Web: http://www. charlesbridge.com.

CHILDREN'S PRESSLINE
227 West 29th Street, 14th Floor
New York, New York 10001

General Information Nonprofit youth journalism program. Established in 2001. Number of employees: 3. Number of internship applications received each year: 10.

Internships Available ▶ *1 developmental associate:* responsibilities include helping bureau director write grant proposals. Candidates should have ability to work independently, analytical skills, knowledge of field, organizational skills, plan to pursue career in field, research skills, writing skills. Duration is flexible. Unpaid. Open to recent high school graduates, college sophomores, college juniors, college seniors, recent college graduates, career changers, individuals reentering the workforce. ▶ *2 editorial assistants:* responsibilities include editing, working with kids, and some office support. Candidates should have ability to work independently, computer skills, editing skills, oral communication skills, organizational skills, personal interest in the field, plan to pursue career in field, research skills, self-motivation, strong interpersonal skills, strong leadership ability, writing skills. Duration is flexible. Unpaid. Open to recent high school graduates, college freshmen, college sophomores, college juniors, college seniors, recent college graduates, graduate students, law students, career changers, individuals reentering the workforce. ▶ *1 youth worker:* responsibilities include working with kids (at-risk and others) in a journalism/deadline-driven atmosphere. Candidates should have computer skills, knowledge of field, oral communication skills, personal interest in the field, writing skills. Duration is flexible. Unpaid. Open to recent high school graduates, college juniors, college seniors, recent college graduates, graduate students, career changers, individuals reentering the workforce. International applications accepted.

Benefits Job counseling, names of contacts, on-the-job training, opportunity to attend seminars/workshops, possible full-time employment, travel reimbursement, willing to act as a profes-

sional reference, willing to complete paperwork for educational credit, willing to provide letters of recommendation, possibility of part-time employment.
Contact Write, call, fax, or e-mail Katina Paron, Program Director. Phone: 212-760-2772. Fax: 212-760-1142. E-mail: katinaparon@ yahoo.com. In-person interview required. Applicants must submit a letter of interest, resume, writing sample, two personal references, letter of recommendation. Applications are accepted continuously. World Wide Web: http://www.cenews.org.

THE CHRONICLE OF THE HORSE
108 The Plains Road, PO Box 46
Middleburg, Virginia 20118

General Information Weekly sport horse magazine with primary focus on news and additional articles on horse care, rider profiles, and how-to information on all English horse sports and breeding. Established in 1937. Number of employees: 20. Number of internship applications received each year: 25.
Internships Available ▶ *3–4 editorial interns:* responsibilities include proofreading, editing, writing, and working on special projects/ assignments. Candidates should have ability to work with others, editing skills, oral communication skills, personal interest in the field, research skills, self-motivation, writing skills, knowledge of horse sports. Duration is 3–4 months. $6.50 per hour. Open to recent high school graduates, college freshmen, college sophomores, college juniors, college seniors, recent college graduates. International applications accepted.
Benefits Names of contacts, on-the-job training, possible full-time employment, travel reimbursement, willing to act as a professional reference, willing to complete paperwork for educational credit, willing to provide letters of recommendation.
Contact Write, call, e-mail, or through World Wide Web site Beth Rasin, Assistant Editor. Phone: 540-687-6341. Fax: 540-687-3937. E-mail: bethr@chronofhorse.com. In-person interview required. Applicants must submit a resume, writing sample, letter of interest including equestrian background. Applications are accepted continuously. World Wide Web: http://www.chronofhorse.com.

CITY LIMITS
120 Wall Street, 20th Floor
New York, New York 10005

General Information New York's urban affairs news magazine. Established in 1976. Number of employees: 11. Unit of City Limits Community Information Service, New York, New York. Number of internship applications received each year: 30.
Internships Available ▶ *1–3 editorial interns:* responsibilities include research, reporting, and writing for City Limits magazine and the City Limits weekly bulletin. Candidates should have ability to work independently, research skills, self-motivation, writing skills, reporting experience preferred. Duration is 3–5 months. Unpaid. Open to college freshmen, college sophomores, college juniors, college seniors, recent college graduates, career changers. International applications accepted.
Benefits Job counseling, names of contacts, on-the-job training, possible full-time employment, willing to act as a professional reference, willing to complete paperwork for educational credit, willing to provide letters of recommendation.
Contact Write, call, fax, or e-mail Matt Pacenza, Associate Editor. Phone: 212-479-3351. Fax: 212-344-6457. E-mail: matt@citylimits. org. In-person interview recommended (telephone interview accepted). Applicants must submit a letter of interest, resume, three writing samples. Applications are accepted continuously. World Wide Web: http://www.citylimits.org.

CONGRESSIONAL QUARTERLY, INC.
1414 22nd Street, NW
Washington, District of Columbia 20037

General Information Company that publishes accurate, timely, and objective information on Congress and national politics; services include a weekly magazine and research reports, daily, weekly, and annual publications, and an online product "CQ. com" as well as books and directories. Established in 1945.

Number of employees: 275. Subsidiary of Times Publishing Company, St. Petersburg, Florida. Number of internship applications received each year: 200.
Internships Available ▶ *Interns:* responsibilities include working on the news media service and performing duties in the editorial, marketing, and advertising departments. Candidates should have computer skills, knowledge of field, office skills, oral communication skills, strong interpersonal skills, writing skills. Duration is 3 months. Position available as unpaid or paid. Open to college juniors, college seniors, recent college graduates, graduate students, law students. International applications accepted.
Benefits Names of contacts, opportunity to attend seminars/ workshops, willing to complete paperwork for educational credit, willing to provide letters of recommendation.
Contact Write, fax, or e-mail Annette M. Billings, Human Resources Manager. Fax: 202-293-1487. E-mail: abillings@cq.com. No phone calls. Applicants must submit a letter of interest, resume, three writing samples. Applications are accepted continuously.

CONNECTICUT MAGAZINE
35 Nutmeg Drive
Trumbull, Connecticut 06611

General Information General interest regional magazine with a circulation of 90,000. Established in 1971. Number of employees: 26. Unit of Journal Register Company, Trenton, New Jersey. Number of internship applications received each year: 75.
Internships Available ▶ *2–4 editorial interns:* responsibilities include working on monthly calendar and dining guide sections, checking facts, researching, typing correspondence, answering phones, and taking responsibility for various special projects. Candidates should have editing skills, oral communication skills, organizational skills, personal interest in the field, self-motivation, writing skills. Duration is 1 semester. Unpaid. Open to college freshmen, college sophomores, college juniors, college seniors, recent college graduates, graduate students, career changers, individuals reentering the workforce. International applications accepted.
Benefits Job counseling, names of contacts, willing to act as a professional reference, willing to complete paperwork for educational credit, willing to provide letters of recommendation.
Contact Write, call, fax, e-mail, or through World Wide Web site Fran Holden, Editorial Assistant. Phone: 203-380-6600 Ext. 329. Fax: 203-380-6612. E-mail: fholden@connecticutmag.com. In-person interview recommended (telephone interview accepted). Applicants must submit a letter of interest, resume, 2-3 writing samples. Applications are accepted continuously. World Wide Web: http:// www.connecticutmag.com.

DAVID R. GODINE, PUBLISHER, INC.
9 Hamilton Place
Boston, Massachusetts 02108

General Information Book publisher specializing in high-quality books on art, typography, and photography, as well as poetry, fiction, reprints of classics, and children's literature; publishes 25 titles per year. Established in 1970. Number of employees: 6. Number of internship applications received each year: 50.
Internships Available ▶ *3 interns:* responsibilities include general office work to assist with publicity, editing, and sales duties. Candidates should have editing skills, oral communication skills, organizational skills, plan to pursue career in field, written communication skills, Quark Xpress, PhotoShop, and HTML skills. Duration is 4 months minimum (20-25 hours per week minimum). Unpaid. Open to college juniors, college seniors, recent college graduates, graduate students. International applications accepted.
Benefits Formal training, job counseling, names of contacts, on-the-job training, opportunity to attend seminars/workshops, willing to act as a professional reference, willing to complete paperwork for educational credit, willing to provide letters of recommendation, accessible by subway.
Contact Write or e-mail Carl W. Scarbrough, Director of Publicity. Phone: 617-451-9600 Ext. 24. E-mail: info@godine.com. In-person interview recommended (telephone interview accepted). Applicants must submit a letter of interest, resume. Application deadline: March 1 for summer, June 1 for fall, October 1 for spring. World Wide Web: http://www.godine.com.

DULUTH NEWS TRIBUNE
424 West First Street
Duluth, Minnesota 55802

General Information Daily morning newspaper. Number of employees: 300. Division of Knight Ridder, San Jose, California. Number of internship applications received each year: 400.
Internships Available ► *11 Ridder Fellows:* responsibilities include positions available in news, sports, and features reporting; photography, graphic arts, copy editing, and page design. Candidates should have ability to work independently, ability to work with others, oral communication skills, self-motivation, written communication skills. Duration is summer (8 weeks). $440 per week. Open to college freshmen, college sophomores, college juniors, college seniors. International applications accepted.
Benefits Free housing, names of contacts, on-the-job training, opportunity to attend seminars/workshops, possible full-time employment, willing to act as a professional reference, willing to complete paperwork for educational credit, willing to provide letters of recommendation.
Contact Write, call, or e-mail Holly Gruber, Intern Coordinator. Phone: 218-720-4106. Fax: 218-720-4120. E-mail: hgruber@ duluthnews.com. Telephone interview required. Applicants must submit a letter of interest, resume, portfolio, four personal references, an essay (1-2 pages) on motivation for internship; 10-15 writing samples. Application deadline: December 1.

EARL G. GRAVES, LTD./BLACK ENTERPRISE MAGAZINE
130 Fifth Avenue
New York, New York 10011

General Information Publishing and ancillary products company. Established in 1970. Number of employees: 100. Number of internship applications received each year: 400.
Internships Available ► *4–6 editorial interns:* responsibilities include receiving assignments from the section editor and working as staff writer. Candidates should have analytical skills, editing skills, experience in the field, oral communication skills, personal interest in the field, plan to pursue career in field, research skills, writing skills. Duration is 10 weeks. Paid. Open to college sophomores, college juniors, college seniors, graduate students. International applications accepted.
Benefits Job counseling, names of contacts, on-the-job training, opportunity to attend seminars/workshops, possible full-time employment, willing to act as a professional reference, willing to complete paperwork for educational credit, willing to provide letters of recommendation.
Contact Write or e-mail Natalie M. Hibbert, Employment and Benefits Programs Manager. E-mail: careers@blackenterprise.com. No phone calls. In-person interview recommended (telephone interview accepted). Applicants must submit a formal organization application, letter of interest, resume, as many writing samples as possible. Application deadline: February 1 for summer. World Wide Web: http://www.blackenterprise.com.

ELSEVIER HEALTH SCIENCE
11830 Westline Industrial Drive
St. Louis, Missouri 63146

General Information Publisher of medical/health science textbooks, reference books, and journals and producer of videos, multimedia products, and seminars/conferences. Established in 1906. Number of employees: 850. Subsidiary of Harcourt Health Sciences, Chestnut Hill, Massachusetts. Number of internship applications received each year: 50.
Internships Available ► *Editorial interns:* responsibilities include reviewing manuscripts, phone surveying reviewers and synopsizing comments, obtaining copyright permissions, arranging for freelance photographers, and working for an editor responsible for developing a manuscript for a text or reference book in the health science field. Candidates should have editing skills, oral communication skills, plan to pursue career in field, research skills, writing skills. Duration is flexible. $7.50 per hour. ► *Marketing interns:* responsibilities include copywriting and/or editing. Candidates should have editing skills, oral communication skills, plan to

pursue career in field, research skills, writing skills. Duration is flexible. $7.50 per hour. ► *Production interns:* responsibilities include dealing with print vendors, cost containment, quality control, and electronic product development. Candidates should have computer skills, editing skills, oral communication skills, plan to pursue career in field, writing skills. Duration is flexible. Paid. Open to college freshmen, college sophomores, college juniors, college seniors. International applications accepted.
Benefits Possible full-time employment, willing to complete paperwork for educational credit.
Contact Write, fax, or through World Wide Web site Human Resources. Fax: 314-432-0779. No phone calls. In-person interview required. Applicants must submit a formal organization application, letter of interest, resume. Applications are accepted continuously. World Wide Web: http://www.mosby.com.

ENERGIZE, INC.
5450 Wissahickon Avenue
Philadelphia, Pennsylvania 19144

General Information Training, consulting, and publishing firm that specializes in volunteerism and assists international, national, state, and local organizations in developing citizen participation programs; publishes and distributes more than 65 books via a direct mailing catalog and a major Web site. Established in 1977. Number of employees: 5. Number of internship applications received each year: 10.
Internships Available ► *1–2 marketing assistants:* responsibilities include print and cyberspace marketing and research, editorial, and reporting duties. Candidates should have computer skills, personal interest in the field, research skills, written communication skills. Duration is flexible. Unpaid. Open to college freshmen, college sophomores, college juniors, college seniors, recent college graduates, graduate students, career changers, individuals reentering the workforce. International applications accepted.
Benefits Job counseling, names of contacts, on-the-job training, opportunity to attend seminars/workshops, willing to act as a professional reference, willing to complete paperwork for educational credit, willing to provide letters of recommendation.
Contact Write or e-mail Ms. Susan J. Ellis, President. Phone: 215-438-8342. Fax: 215-438-0434. E-mail: susan@energizeinc.com. In-person interview required. Applicants must submit a letter of interest, resume. Applications are accepted continuously. World Wide Web: http://www.energizeinc.com.

ENTERTAINMENT DESIGN AND LIGHTING DIMENSIONS MAGAZINES
32 West 18th Street, 11th Floor
New York, New York 10011-4612

General Information Publisher of leading trade magazines for the entertainment technology industry, covering all aspects of sound, lighting, set design, costume, architectural and themed entertainment applications. Established in 1967. Number of employees: 30. Division of Intertec Publishing Corporation, Overland Park, Kansas. Number of internship applications received each year: 35.
Internships Available ► *1 publishing/editorial intern:* responsibilities include supporting promotions and marketing projects, assisting with production, circulation, and advertising activities, and providing support for editorial projects and activities. Candidates should have computer skills, office skills, oral communication skills, personal interest in the field, strong interpersonal skills, writing skills. Duration is 8–10 weeks. Minimum wage to $10 per hour. ► *6–12 technical theater interns at BLMC:* responsibilities include technical assistance with production of Broadway Lighting Master Classes Seminar; hanging and focusing lights, running A/V equipment; related preparatory administrative and office work. Candidates should have ability to work with others, office skills, personal interest in the field, theater lighting experience (a strong preference). Position available as unpaid or paid. Open to recent high school graduates, college freshmen, college sophomores, college juniors, college seniors, recent college graduates, graduate students, individuals reentering the workforce.

Benefits Names of contacts, on-the-job training, willing to complete paperwork for educational credit.

Contact Write, fax, or e-mail Florence Dobransky, Internship Coordinator. Fax: 212-206-3798. E-mail: fdobransky@ primediabusiness.com. No phone calls. In-person interview recommended (telephone interview accepted). Applicants must submit a letter of interest, letter of recommendation, resume (if applicable). Application deadline: May 15 for summer. World Wide Web: http://www.etecnyc.net.

ENTERTAINMENT WEEKLY
1675 Broadway
New York, New York 10019

General Information Weekly magazine covering popular entertainment. Established in 1990. Number of employees: 200. Subsidiary of Time, Inc., New York, New York. Number of internship applications received each year: 750.

Internships Available ▶ *1 art intern:* responsibilities include assisting design editors in various tasks and maintaining art archives. Candidates should have ability to work independently, ability to work with others, college courses in field, computer skills, knowledge of field, office skills, oral communication skills, organizational skills, personal interest in the field, plan to pursue career in field, self-motivation. Duration is 3–5 months. $10 per hour. Open to college juniors, college seniors, recent college graduates, graduate students. ▶ *3 editorial interns:* responsibilities include assisting editors in various tasks, such as inputting stories, transcribing interviews, running copy, and handling reader mail. Candidates should have ability to work independently, ability to work with others, college courses in field, computer skills, editing skills, knowledge of field, office skills, oral communication skills, organizational skills, personal interest in the field, plan to pursue career in field, research skills, self-motivation, writing skills, love of entertainment. Duration is 3–5 months. $10 per hour. Open to college juniors, college seniors, recent college graduates, graduate students. ▶ *2 ew.com interns:* responsibilities include updating editorial databases; performing research; inputting database changes. Candidates should have ability to work independently, computer skills, office skills, oral communication skills, research skills, written communication skills. Duration is 5–6 months. $10 per hour. Open to college seniors, recent college graduates, graduate students. ▶ *1 photo intern:* responsibilities include assisting photo editors in various tasks including obtaining photos, contacting photographers, and maintaining archives. Candidates should have ability to work independently, ability to work with others, college courses in field, computer skills, knowledge of field, office skills, oral communication skills, organizational skills, personal interest in the field, plan to pursue career in field, self-motivation. Duration is 3 months (approximate). $10 per hour. Open to college juniors, college seniors, recent college graduates, graduate students.

Benefits On-the-job training, possible full-time employment, willing to act as a professional reference, willing to complete paperwork for educational credit.

Contact Write, call, or fax Ms. Annabel Bentley, Director of Research Services. Phone: 212-522-1864. Fax: 212-522-6104. In-person interview required. Applicants must submit a letter of interest, resume, 4-5 previously published clips; 5 writing samples. Application deadline: February 15 for summer, June 15 for fall, October 15 for spring. World Wide Web: http://ew.com.

E/THE ENVIRONMENTAL MAGAZINE
28 Knight Street
Norwalk, Connecticut 06851

General Information Magazine serving as a clearinghouse of information, news, and commentary on environmental issues, geared toward both the general public and dedicated environmentalists for the purpose of promoting environmental awareness and activism. Established in 1990. Number of employees: 6. Number of internship applications received each year: 50.

Internships Available ▶ *4 advertising interns:* responsibilities include assisting in advertisement sales, handling mailings, proofing ads, and computer work. Duration is flexible. Unpaid. Open to college freshmen, college sophomores, college juniors, college seniors, recent college graduates, graduate students, career changers. ▶ *4 editorial interns:* responsibilities include keying articles, proofreading, responding to editorial phone calls, correspondence, and performing library and phone research; will have opportunity to write and publish articles, possible travel for stories, Internet research, and conducting product reviews. Duration is 2 months minimum. Unpaid. Open to recent high school graduates, college freshmen, college sophomores, college juniors, college seniors, recent college graduates, graduate students, career changers, individuals reentering the workforce. Candidates for all positions should have ability to work independently, oral communication skills, self-motivation, strong interpersonal skills, written communication skills. International applications accepted.

Benefits Job counseling, names of contacts, opportunity to attend seminars/workshops, possible full-time employment, willing to act as a professional reference, willing to complete paperwork for educational credit, willing to provide letters of recommendation, some free meals.

Contact Write, call, fax, e-mail, or through World Wide Web site Brian Howard, Managing Editor. Phone: 203-854-5559 Ext. 109. Fax: 203-866-0602. E-mail: info@emagazine.com. In-person interview recommended (telephone interview accepted). Applicants must submit a letter of interest, resume, two writing samples. Applications are accepted continuously. World Wide Web: http://www. emagazine.com.

F & W PUBLICATIONS, INC.
4700 East Galbraith Road
Cincinnati, Ohio 45236

General Information Book and magazine publisher of self-help materials in the art, writing, crafts, design, and woodworking fields. Established in 1910. Number of employees: 300. Number of internship applications received each year: 150.

Internships Available ▶ *4–10 editorial assistants:* responsibilities include copyediting, proofreading, researching, writing and editorial planning. Candidates should have ability to work with others, college courses in field, computer skills, editing skills, organizational skills, plan to pursue career in field, research skills, self-motivation, writing skills. Duration is 10–12 weeks. $350 per week. ▶ *2 graphic design assistants:* responsibilities include working on basic design assignments on MAC software, contributing to book and magazine layouts. Candidates should have ability to work independently, ability to work with others, declared college major in field, oral communication skills, organizational skills, plan to pursue career in field, experience with Quark Xpress, Illustrator and PhotoShop packages required. Duration is 10-12 weeks (May to August or June to September). $350 per week. ▶ *2 marketing/conference assistants:* responsibilities include analysis, financial, or copywriting, researching, and planning mailings. Candidates should have ability to work with others, analytical skills, computer skills, oral communication skills, organizational skills, plan to pursue career in field, research skills, self-motivation, writing skills. Duration is 10-12 weeks (May to August or June to September). $350 per week. Open to college juniors, graduate students, students returning to school after internship ends (required).

Benefits Job counseling, on-the-job training, possible full-time employment, willing to act as a professional reference, willing to complete paperwork for educational credit.

Contact Write, e-mail, or through World Wide Web site Debbie Carroll, Human Resources Recruiter. Fax: 513-531-0293. E-mail: debbie.carroll@fwpubs.com. No phone calls. In-person interview recommended (telephone interview accepted). Applicants must submit a letter of interest, resume, 1-3 samples of work (design interns), 2-3 writing samples. Application deadline: January 15 for summer. World Wide Web: http://www.fwpublications.com.

FANTAGRAPHICS BOOKS, INC.
7563 Lake City Way, NE
Seattle, Washington 98115

General Information Publisher of original comic books and book collections, book collections of classic comic strips and underground comic books, and a trade magazine about the comics industry. Established in 1976. Number of employees: 50. Number of internship applications received each year: 50.

Fantagraphics Books, Inc. (continued)

Internships Available ▶ *3–4 editorial interns:* responsibilities include typesetting, proofreading, copyediting, writing copy, and assisting in promotional work. Duration is variable. Unpaid. ▶ *1–2 promotion/ marketing interns:* responsibilities include writing press releases and general office work related to publicity, public relations, and marketing. Duration is 2–3 months. Unpaid. Candidates for all positions should have computer skills, editing skills, knowledge of field, office skills, organizational skills, personal interest in the field, written communication skills. Open to recent high school graduates, college freshmen, college sophomores, college juniors, college seniors, recent college graduates, graduate students, law students, career changers, individuals reentering the workforce, must be 18 or older. International applications accepted.

Benefits Names of contacts, possible full-time employment, willing to complete paperwork for educational credit, willing to provide letters of recommendation.

Contact Write, fax, or e-mail Anthony Pulsipher, Internship Coordinator. Fax: 206-524-2104. E-mail: anthony@eroscomix.com. No phone calls. Applicants must submit a letter of interest, resume. Applications are accepted continuously. World Wide Web: http://www.fantagraphics.com.

FARRAR, STRAUS, AND GIROUX
19 Union Square West
New York, New York 10003

General Information General trade book publisher. Established in 1946. Number of employees: 100. Number of internship applications received each year: 250.

Internships Available ▶ *Interns:* responsibilities include working in different departments. Candidates should have ability to work with others, computer skills, office skills, oral communication skills, personal interest in the field, written communication skills. Duration is flexible. Unpaid. Open to college freshmen, college sophomores, college juniors, college seniors, recent college graduates, graduate students, career changers. International applications accepted.

Benefits Possible full-time employment, willing to complete paperwork for educational credit, willing to provide letters of recommendation.

Contact Call Ms. Peggy Miller, Coordinator of Interns. Phone: 212-741-6900. In-person interview required. Applicants must submit a resume. Applications are accepted continuously.

FOREIGN AFFAIRS MAGAZINE
58 East 68th Street
New York, New York 10021

General Information Bimonthly journal devoted to international affairs and U.S. foreign policy. Established in 1922. Number of employees: 15. Division of Council on Foreign Relations, New York, New York. Number of internship applications received each year: 400.

Internships Available ▶ *1 academic-year intern:* responsibilities include editing, proofreading, and layout for articles to be published in magazine; research and fact checking; writing press releases; assisting with art acquisition; archiving; screening unsolicited manuscripts. Candidates should have analytical skills, editing skills, personal interest in the field, self-motivation, strong interpersonal skills, writing skills. Duration is 10 months. $450 per week. Open to college seniors, recent college graduates, graduate students, law students. ▶ *2 semester interns:* responsibilities include copyediting and proofreading, fact-checking, screening unsolicited manuscripts, and assisting editors. Candidates should have ability to work independently, editing skills, personal interest in the field, research skills, strong interpersonal skills, writing skills. Duration is 3 months. Unpaid. Open to college juniors, college seniors, recent college graduates, graduate students, law students. ▶ *1 summer intern:* responsibilities include editing, proofreading, and layout for articles to be published in magazine, research and fact checking, writing press releases, assisting with art acquisition, archiving, and screening unsolicited manuscripts. Candidates should have analytical skills, editing skills, oral communication skills, personal interest in the field, strong interpersonal

skills, writing skills. Duration is 10 weeks. $300 per week. Open to college juniors, college seniors, recent college graduates, graduate students, law students. International applications accepted.

Benefits Formal training, health insurance, names of contacts, on-the-job training, opportunity to attend seminars/workshops, possible full-time employment, willing to act as a professional reference, willing to provide letters of recommendation, attendance at Council on Foreign Relations events.

Contact Write or call Editorial Assistant. Phone: 212-434-9507. Applicants must submit a letter of interest, resume, three writing samples, three letters of recommendation. Application deadline: mid-March for summer and academic year, early December for spring semester interns, end of academic year (late May) for fall semester interns. World Wide Web: http://www.foreignaffairs. org.

FOREIGN POLICY MAGAZINE
1779 Massachusetts Avenue, NW
Washington, District of Columbia 20036

General Information Bimonthly magazine on global politics, economics, and ideas. Established in 1970. Number of employees: 25. Unit of Carnegie Endowment for International Peace, Washington, District of Columbia.

Internships Available ▶ *1–3 editorial assistants:* responsibilities include research, reviewing manuscripts, fact checking and proofreading articles for publication, and assisting in all aspects of magazine publication. Candidates should have computer skills, research skills, writing skills, strong research skills in a foreign language desirable. Duration is 3–4 months. Unpaid. Open to college juniors, college seniors, recent college graduates, graduate students, law students. International applications accepted.

Benefits Opportunity to attend seminars/workshops, willing to complete paperwork for educational credit, willing to provide letters of recommendation, reimbursement of local travel expenses.

Contact Through World Wide Web site Volunteer Internship Coordinator. Phone: 202-939-2230. Fax: 202-483-4430. E-mail: editor@ceip.org. In-person interview recommended (telephone interview accepted). Applicants must submit a letter of interest, resume, one writing sample, or various clips, totaling 5-10 pages. Application deadline: April 1 for summer, August 1 for fall, November 1 for spring. World Wide Web: http://www.foreignpolicy. com.

FRIENDS JOURNAL
1216 Arch Street 2A
Philadelphia, Pennsylvania 19107

General Information Monthly religious periodical with emphasis on social action, spiritual nurturing, news/features, poetry, and book reviews. Established in 1955. Number of employees: 6. Number of internship applications received each year: 25.

Internships Available ▶ *1–3 editorial assistants:* responsibilities include editing, proofreading, writing, working on the computer, possible Web site work, and office tasks. Candidates should have ability to work independently, computer skills, editing skills, organizational skills, self-motivation, written communication skills. Duration is flexible. Unpaid. ▶ *1–3 office assistants:* responsibilities include assisting with development and circulation tasks, and assisting editors. Candidates should have ability to work independently, ability to work with others, computer skills, office skills, organizational skills, self-motivation. Duration is flexible. Unpaid. Open to college freshmen, college sophomores, college juniors, college seniors, recent college graduates, graduate students, career changers, individuals reentering the workforce. International applications accepted.

Benefits Names of contacts, on-the-job training, possible full-time employment, willing to act as a professional reference, willing to complete paperwork for educational credit, willing to provide letters of recommendation.

Contact Write, call, fax, e-mail, or through World Wide Web site Susan Corson-Finnerty, Publisher and Executive Editor, 1216 Arch Street, 2A, Philadelphia, Pennsylvania 19107. Phone: 215-563-8629. Fax: 215-568-1377. E-mail: publisher_exec_ed@friendsjournal. org. In-person interview recommended (telephone interview accepted). Applicants must submit a letter of interest, resume, three personal references, 2-3 writing samples. Applications are accepted continuously. World Wide Web: http://www.friendsjournal.org.

HARPER'S MAGAZINE FOUNDATION
666 Broadway, 11th Floor
New York, New York 10012

General Information   Magazine publisher. Established in 1850. Number of employees: 35. Number of internship applications received each year: 100.

Internships Available   ▶ *4 editorial interns:* responsibilities include assisting a section editor (Readings, Forum, or Articles and Annotations), participating in the general tasks required to run a magazine, and working on the Harper's Index. Candidates should have computer skills, oral communication skills, organizational skills, personal interest in the field, research skills, writing skills. Duration is summer (3 months), fall (4 months), or winter (5 months). Unpaid. Open to college freshmen, college sophomores, college juniors, college seniors, recent college graduates, graduate students, law students, career changers, individuals reentering the workforce. International applications accepted.

Benefits   Formal training, names of contacts, on-the-job training, possible full-time employment, willing to complete paperwork for educational credit, willing to provide letters of recommendation, transportation within New York City (unlimited Metro Card).

Contact   Write, call, fax, e-mail, or through World Wide Web site Elizabeth Giddens, Associate Editor. Phone: 212-420-5720. Fax: 212-228-5889. E-mail: elizabeth@harpers.org. In-person interview required. Applicants must submit a formal organization application, resume. Application deadline: February 15 for summer, June 15 for fall, October 15 for winter. World Wide Web: http://www.harpers.org.

HILL STREET PRESS
191 East Broad Street, Suite 209
Athens, Georgia 30601-2848

General Information   Independent publisher of literary and trade fiction and nonfiction related to the diverse American South. Established in 1998. Number of employees: 4. Number of internship applications received each year: 40.

Internships Available   ▶ *4–5 editorial interns:* responsibilities include evaluating unsolicited manuscripts, proofreading, editorial research, technical preparation of manuscripts, drafting rejection letters, general office duties, and product development. Candidates should have ability to work independently, computer skills, editing skills, office skills, research skills, self-motivation, interest in the literature of the American South. Duration is 1 semester. Unpaid. ▶ *2 marketing assistants:* responsibilities include maintaining databases and Web sites, developing review lists, production of advertising copy, mass mailings, special events publicity. Candidates should have computer skills, office skills, organizational skills, research skills, strong interpersonal skills, writing skills. Duration is 1 semester. Unpaid. Open to college sophomores, college juniors, college seniors, recent college graduates, graduate students, career changers.

Benefits   Names of contacts, on-the-job training, willing to act as a professional reference, willing to complete paperwork for educational credit, willing to provide letters of recommendation.

Contact   Write Judy J. Long, Vice President/Editor-in-Chief, 191 East Broad Street, Suite 209, Athens, Georgia 30601-2848. Fax: 706-613-7204. No phone calls. In-person interview recommended (telephone interview accepted). Applicants must submit a letter of interest, resume, two writing samples. Applications are accepted continuously. World Wide Web: http://www.hillstreetpress.com.

HISPANIC LINK JOURNALISM FOUNDATION
1420 N Street, NW
Washington, District of Columbia 20005

General Information   News service based in Washington, D.C., that publishes the national newsweekly *Hispanic Link Weekly Report* (in English), and syndicates 3 columns weekly (in English and Spanish) through the Los Angeles Times syndicate to approximately 70 newspapers and magazines in the U.S. and Latin America. Established in 1980. Number of employees: 5. Number of internship applications received each year: 40.

Internships Available   ▶ *1–2 fellowships:* responsibilities include writing for *Hispanic Link Weekly Report* and other media outlets. Candidates should have analytical skills, oral communication skills, plan to pursue career in field, research skills, written communication skills. Duration is 1 year. $21,000 stipend for duration of internship. ▶ *2–3 reporting interns:* responsibilities include a variety of tasks ranging from office and basic media training to full reporting, editing, and marketing training. Candidates should have personal interest in the field, plan to pursue career in field. Duration is flexible. Unpaid. Open to anyone interested regardless of education. International applications accepted.

Benefits   Formal training, health insurance, job counseling, names of contacts, on-the-job training, travel reimbursement, willing to act as a professional reference, willing to complete paperwork for educational credit, willing to provide letters of recommendation, direct contact with potential employers provided (for paid interns only).

Contact   Write, call, fax, or e-mail Hector Ericksen-Mendoza, Executive Director. Phone: 202-238-0705. Fax: 202-238-0706. E-mail: hector@hispaniclink.org. Telephone interview required. Applicants must submit a formal organization application, letter of interest, resume, three personal references, 3-10 writing clips. Application deadline: January 1 for winter/spring, May 1 for summer/fall. World Wide Web: http://www.hispaniclink.org.

HOUGHTON MIFFLIN COMPANY
222 Berkeley Street
Boston, Massachusetts 02116-3764

General Information   Publisher of college textbooks and educational software. Established in 1834. Number of employees: 1,196. Unit of Vivendi Universal, Paris, France.

Internships Available   ▶ *12 interns:* responsibilities include working in editorial, marketing, and advertising, production art and design, production, rights and permissions, custom publishing, or software development. Candidates should have computer skills, oral communication skills, written communication skills. Duration is 3 months (June-August), 35 hours per week. $9 per hour. Open to college sophomores, college juniors. International applications accepted.

Benefits   Opportunity to attend seminars/workshops, possible full-time employment, willing to complete paperwork for educational credit.

Contact   Write or through World Wide Web site Monica Herrera, Senior Administrative Coordinator. No phone calls. Telephone interview required. Applicants must submit a letter of interest, resume. Application deadline: March 31. World Wide Web: http://www.hmco.com.

HUNTER HOUSE, INC., PUBLISHERS
PO Box 2914
Alameda, California 94501

General Information   Independent book publishing company that specializes in health, social issues, self-help/psychology, and women's issues. Established in 1978. Number of employees: 8. Number of internship applications received each year: 20.

Internships Available   ▶ *1–4 editorial interns:* responsibilities include copyediting manuscripts, proofreading page proofs, confirming resource information for particular books, compiling contacts, drafting letters, soliciting endorsements for upcoming books, logging and helping to evaluate manuscript submissions, and conducting library and bookstore research. Candidates should have computer skills, editing skills, plan to pursue career in field, research skills, written communication skills. Duration is 3 months minimum, 16-20 hours per week. Unpaid. Open to college freshmen, college sophomores, college juniors, college seniors, recent college graduates, career changers. ▶ *1 editorial/marketing intern:* responsibilities include following one project through editorial finalization and then working on the same book in marketing and publicity. Candidates should have ability to work independently, ability to work with others, computer skills, editing skills, experience in the field, personal interest in the field, research skills,

Hunter House, Inc., Publishers (continued)
written communication skills. Duration is 3 months minimum, 16-20 hours per week. Unpaid. Open to college freshmen, college sophomores, college juniors, college seniors, individuals reentering the workforce. ▶ *1 marketing intern:* responsibilities include compiling lists of contacts who will review the book, researching direct mail lists, writing promotional copy, updating marketing database, organizing direct mailings. Candidates should have analytical skills, computer skills, oral communication skills, self-motivation, strong interpersonal skills, written communication skills. Duration is 3 months minimum, 16-20 hours per week. Unpaid. Open to college juniors, college seniors, recent college graduates, individuals reentering the workforce. ▶ *1 publicity intern:* responsibilities include writing, designing, and mailing promotional new book announcement fliers; choosing relevant media for newly released books and mailing review copies to this list; assisting with book, radio, television, and print interviews for authors; helping to write and mail press kits; contacting book stores to schedule and organize author events and signings. Candidates should have computer skills, experience in the field, oral communication skills, self-motivation, written communication skills. Duration is 3 months minimum, 16-20 hours per week. Unpaid. Open to college sophomores, college juniors, college seniors, recent college graduates, individuals reentering the workforce. ▶ *1 publisher's assistant intern:* responsibilities include assisting the publisher with business analysis and modeling, long-term plans and project schedules, and with daily activities related to operations and book acquisitions. Candidates should have ability to work with others, analytical skills, office skills, organizational skills, research skills, literacy with either spreadsheets, databases, and scheduling software, or Internet and HTML. Duration is 3 months minimum, 16-20 hours per week. Unpaid. Open to college seniors, recent college graduates, graduate students, career changers, individuals reentering the workforce. International applications accepted.
Benefits Names of contacts, on-the-job training, willing to complete paperwork for educational credit, willing to provide letters of recommendation.
Contact Write, fax, e-mail, or through World Wide Web site Internship Coordinator, PO Box 2914, Alameda, California 94501-0914. Fax: 510-865-4295. E-mail: hhi@hunterhouse.com. No phone calls. In-person interview recommended (telephone interview accepted). Applicants must submit a formal organization application, letter of interest, resume, two personal references. Applications are accepted continuously. World Wide Web: http://www.hunterhouse.com/.

ISLAND PRESS
1718 Connecticut Avenue, NW, Suite 300
Washington, District of Columbia 20009

General Information Nonprofit publisher of books about the environment for professionals, students, and general readers. Established in 1978. Number of employees: 26. Number of internship applications received each year: 100.
Internships Available ▶ *1–2 IT interns :* responsibilities include assisting IT and New Media with managing network and maintaining and upgrading PCs. Candidates should have ability to work with others, computer skills, knowledge of field, oral communication skills. Duration is 3–4 months. $10 per hour. Open to college juniors, college seniors, recent college graduates, graduate students, law students. ▶ *1 general intern:* responsibilities include handling all communications through front office and general/operational support for all departments as needed. Candidates should have computer skills, office skills, oral communication skills, organizational skills, self-motivation, interest in publishing and/or environment preferred. Duration is 20 hours per week (flexible). $10 per hour. Open to recent high school graduates, college freshmen, college sophomores, college juniors, college seniors, recent college graduates, graduate students, law students, career changers, individuals reentering the workforce. ▶ *1 marketing interns:* responsibilities include assisting marketing staff with exhibit preparation, mailings, and contacting vendors. Candidates should have ability to work independently, computer skills, office skills, oral communication skills, plan to pursue career in field, written communication skills. Duration is 3–4 months. $10 per

hour. Open to college juniors, college seniors, recent college graduates, graduate students. ▶ *1–3 publicity intern:* responsibilities include assisting in all steps of publicity campaign execution; responsible for all book review receipts and distribution in-house and to authors; general department support. Candidates should have ability to work independently, computer skills, oral communication skills, organizational skills, self-motivation, written communication skills, ability to juggle multiple tasks. Duration is 3-4 months minimum (longer preferred); 20 hours per week (flexible). $10 per hour. Open to recent high school graduates, college freshmen, college sophomores, college juniors, college seniors, recent college graduates, individuals reentering the workforce. International applications accepted.
Benefits On-the-job training, possible full-time employment, willing to act as a professional reference, willing to complete paperwork for educational credit, willing to provide letters of recommendation, small stipend.
Contact Write, e-mail, or through World Wide Web site Bill Malone, Director of Human Resources, 1718 Connecticut Avenue, NW, Suite 300, Washington, District of Columbia 20009. E-mail: resumes@islandpress.org. No phone calls. In-person interview recommended (telephone interview accepted). Applicants must submit a letter of interest, resume, two writing samples. Applications are accepted continuously. World Wide Web: http://www.islandpress.org.

IVAN R. DEE, PUBLISHER
1332 North Halsted Street
Chicago, Illinois 60622-2694

General Information Book publisher. Established in 1987. Number of employees: 9. Unit of Rowman & Littlefield Publishing Group, Lanham, Maryland. Number of internship applications received each year: 375.
Internships Available ▶ *2–4 general internships in publishing:* responsibilities include proofreading, general operational duties, marketing, and production. Candidates should have ability to work independently, analytical skills, oral communication skills, personal interest in the field, self-motivation, written communication skills. Duration is 1 semester. Unpaid. ▶ *1 information systems intern:* responsibilities include maintaining databases, updating information, and editing and assisting with Web site. Candidates should have ability to work independently, analytical skills, computer skills, knowledge of field, self-motivation, experience with Microsoft Access and Excel. Duration is 1 semester. $6–$10 per hour. ▶ *1–2 publicity interns:* responsibilities include assisting publicist with special projects including research, correspondence, and assisting with author events. Candidates should have office skills, oral communication skills, personal interest in the field, research skills, strong interpersonal skills, writing skills. Duration is 1 semester. Unpaid. Open to college juniors, college seniors, recent college graduates, graduate students. International applications accepted.
Benefits Opportunity to attend seminars/workshops, willing to act as a professional reference, willing to complete paperwork for educational credit, willing to provide letters of recommendation, $10 per day to cover lunch and transportation costs.
Contact Write, fax, or e-mail Vicki Hsu, Production Editor. Fax: 312-787-6269. E-mail: elephant@ivanrdee.com. No phone calls. In-person interview recommended (telephone interview accepted). Applicants must submit a letter of interest, resume. Applications are accepted continuously. World Wide Web: http://www.ivanrdee.com.

JOHN WILEY & SONS, INC.
111 River Street
Hoboken, New Jersey 07030

General Information Largest and oldest independent publishing company in North America. Established in 1807. Number of employees: 950. Number of internship applications received each year: 300.
Internships Available ▶ *2–3 editorial assistants:* responsibilities include assisting product development, conducting market research and comparative analysis on competing books, and contacting professors as potential reviewers for manuscripts. Candidates should have ability to work independently, analytical skills,

computer skills, knowledge of field, office skills, oral communication skills, organizational skills, personal interest in the field, research skills, self-motivation, strong interpersonal skills, written communication skills. Duration is 9 weeks in summer. $300 per week. ▶ *1–2 finance assistants:* responsibilities include assisting in corporate finance department and working in several areas including accounts payable, royalties, and payroll. Candidates should have analytical skills, computer skills, experience in the field, office skills, organizational skills, personal interest in the field, ability to work with numbers. Duration is 9 weeks in summer. $300 per week. ▶ *2–4 information technology interns:* responsibilities include software/hardware trouble shooting, basic network wiring, light applications development, and basic support call responding. Candidates should have ability to work independently, declared college major in field, experience in the field, office skills, oral communication skills, plan to pursue career in field, self-motivation, strong interpersonal skills, writing skills, knowledge of Word, Lotus, NT/Novell Server, Sun Solaris, Unix, and databases. Duration is 9 weeks in summer. $350 per week. ▶ *2–3 marketing assistants:* responsibilities include building a database of target sales opportunities, conducting telephone research, assisting in preparation of material for national sales meeting, and Internet marketing. Candidates should have ability to work independently, analytical skills, computer skills, office skills, oral communication skills, organizational skills, plan to pursue career in field, research skills, self-motivation, strong interpersonal skills, writing skills. Duration is 9 weeks in summer. $300 per week. ▶ *1–3 new media assistants:* responsibilities include assisting with research, development, and/or pilot implementation including new publishing technologies; Internet research, Web development, project tracking, and Web site quality assurance. Candidates should have ability to work independently, analytical skills, college courses in field, computer skills, knowledge of field, office skills, oral communication skills, organizational skills, plan to pursue career in field, research skills, self-motivation, strong interpersonal skills, writing skills. Duration is 9 weeks in summer. $300 per week. Open to college juniors.

Benefits Names of contacts, on-the-job training, opportunity to attend seminars/workshops, possible full-time employment, willing to act as a professional reference, willing to provide letters of recommendation, stipend.

Contact Write, e-mail, or through World Wide Web site Internship Coordinator. E-mail: opportunities@wiley.com. No phone calls. In-person interview required. Applicants must submit a letter of interest, resume, professional/academic reference. Application deadline: March 1. World Wide Web: http://www.wiley.com.

LIBRARY JOURNAL MAGAZINE
245 West 17th Street
New York, New York 10011-5300

General Information Trade magazine that provides news and book reviews for public and academic libraries. Established in 1876. Number of employees: 25. Division of Cahners Business Information, New York, New York. Number of internship applications received each year: 20.

Internships Available ▶ *1–4 book review interns:* responsibilities include processing and fact-checking book reviews and special articles; assisting with everyday duties such as opening and sorting mail, calling publishers, and answering status queries. Candidates should have ability to work independently, ability to work with others, computer skills, editing skills, office skills, oral communication skills, organizational skills, self-motivation, writing skills. Duration is 3–4 months. Position available as unpaid or at $6–$8 per hour. ▶ *1 news intern:* responsibilities include assisting the four-person news department; time will be divided between writing short news items for the Web site and the magazine proper, as well as performing administrative work such as preparing mailings. Candidates should have ability to work independently, ability to work with others, computer skills, office skills, oral communication skills, organizational skills, self-motivation, writing skills. Duration is 3–4 months. Position available as unpaid or at $6–$8 per hour. Open to college freshmen, college sophomores, college juniors, college seniors.

Benefits On-the-job training, possible full-time employment, willing to act as a professional reference, willing to complete paperwork for educational credit, willing to provide letters of recommendation, opportunity to write book reviews and news briefs with a published byline.

Contact Call, fax, or e-mail Rachel Collins, Book Room Assistant, 245 West 17th Street, New York, New York 10011-5300. Phone: 212-463-6818. Fax: 212-463-6734. E-mail: rcollins@cahners.com. In-person interview required. Applicants must submit a letter of interest, resume, two writing samples. Applications are accepted continuously. World Wide Web: http://www.libraryjournal.com.

LOS ANGELES MAGAZINE
5900 Wilshire Boulevard, 10th Floor
Los Angeles, California 90036

General Information City magazine that focuses on local issues, problems, people, trends, events, and lifestyles, and highlights options and opportunities available in the southern California area. Established in 1960. Number of employees: 50. Unit of Emmis Communications, Indianapolis, Indiana. Number of internship applications received each year: 50.

Internships Available ▶ *4–6 editorial interns:* responsibilities include fact checking, researching, and performing basic clerical duties. Candidates should have ability to work independently, oral communication skills, plan to pursue career in field, research skills, writing skills. Duration is 2–3 months. Unpaid. Open to college juniors, college seniors.

Benefits Willing to complete paperwork for educational credit, willing to provide letters of recommendation.

Contact Write, fax, or e-mail Mr. Eric Mercado, Research Editor. Fax: 323-801-0105. E-mail: emercado@lamag.com. No phone calls. In-person interview recommended (telephone interview accepted). Applicants must submit a letter of interest, resume, writing sample. Application deadline: April 1 for summer, July 31 for fall, October 31 for winter, December 1 for spring. World Wide Web: http://www.lamag.com.

MAD MAGAZINE
1700 Broadway
New York, New York 10019

General Information Magazine/publishing company. Established in 1952. Number of employees: 12. Number of internship applications received each year: 80.

Internships Available ▶ *2–4 summer interns:* responsibilities include attending and participating in brainstorming sessions, working on article conception and development; also includes filing and photocopying. Candidates should have ability to work with others, writing skills. Duration is June 5 to July 14 and July 17 to August 25. Unpaid. Open to college freshmen, college sophomores, college juniors.

Benefits Willing to complete paperwork for educational credit, opportunity to do freelance writing.

Contact Write Amy Vozeolas, Associate Editor. Phone: 212-506-4850. Applicants must submit writing sample. Application deadline: April 24.

METRO NEW MEDIA, INC.
55 Perry Street, #1M
New York, New York 10014

General Information Company that publishes New York Theatre Wire (www.nytheatre-wire.com) and Curator's Choice (www.nymuseums.com). Established in 1996. Number of employees: 2. Number of internship applications received each year: 70.

Internships Available ▶ *1 Web design intern:* responsibilities include general Web design and systems development. Duration is 1–2 semesters. Unpaid. ▶ *1 assistant editor/general cultural reporter:* responsibilities include working directly with publisher and leading New York theater journalists and editors. Candidates should have Web expertise. Duration is 1–2 semesters. Unpaid.

Benefits On-the-job training, opportunity to attend seminars/workshops, willing to act as a professional reference, willing to complete paperwork for educational credit, willing to provide letters of recommendation.

Metro New Media, Inc. (continued)

Contact E-mail Internship Coordinator. E-mail: metro@nytheatre-wire.com. No phone calls. Applicants must submit a letter of interest, resume. Applications are accepted continuously. World Wide Web: http://www.nytheatre-wire.com.

MIDDLE EAST RESEARCH AND INFORMATION PROJECT, INC. (MERIP)
1500 Massachusetts Avenue, NW, Suite 119
Washington, District of Columbia 20005

General Information Nonprofit organization seeking to educate the public about the contemporary Middle East in such areas as peace, human rights, politics, and social justice; major program is the Middle East Report, a quarterly magazine that provides an independent look at the region and U.S. policy. Established in 1971. Number of employees: 4. Number of internship applications received each year: 80.

Internships Available ▶ *1 editorial intern:* responsibilities include assisting the editorial staff in producing the Middle East Report; may include light research, proofreading, inputting copy, making corrections, and formatting articles for typesetting. Candidates should have background in journalism or publications. Duration is flexible. Unpaid. Open to college juniors, college seniors, recent college graduates, career changers, individuals reentering the workforce. ▶ *1 educational outreach intern:* responsibilities include organizing outreach program to teachers and students. Duration is flexible. Unpaid. ▶ *1 media outreach intern:* responsibilities include helping media outreach director prepare material for journalists, maintaining database of media professionals, and assisting with conference preparations. Candidates should have experience in the field. Duration is flexible. Unpaid. International applications accepted.

Benefits Job counseling, names of contacts, opportunity to attend seminars/workshops, willing to act as a professional reference, willing to complete paperwork for educational credit, willing to provide letters of recommendation, opportunity to hear summer lunch speakers.

Contact Write, fax, e-mail, or through World Wide Web site Intern Coordinator. Fax: 202-223-3604. E-mail: ctoensing@merip.org. In-person interview recommended (telephone interview accepted). Applicants must submit a letter of interest, resume, writing sample. Applications are accepted continuously. World Wide Web: http://www.merip.org.

MILWAUKEE MAGAZINE
417 East Chicago Street
Milwaukee, Wisconsin 53202

General Information Magazine that entertains readers, keeps them informed on important regional issues, and helps them get the most from their city. Established in 1979. Number of employees: 35. Subsidiary of Quad/Graphics Inc., Sussex, Wisconsin. Number of internship applications received each year: 25.

Internships Available ▶ *1–3 editorial interns:* responsibilities include researching special projects, reporting, and some writing. Candidates should have analytical skills, experience in the field, self-motivation, strong interpersonal skills, written communication skills, demonstrated interest in magazine journalism (highly recommended). Duration is 1 semester or summer. Unpaid. Open to college sophomores, college juniors, college seniors, recent college graduates, graduate students, career changers.

Benefits Names of contacts, on-the-job training, willing to act as a professional reference, willing to complete paperwork for educational credit, willing to provide letters of recommendation, possibility of part-time or freelance employment.

Contact Write or e-mail Natalie Dorman, Assistant Editor. E-mail: natalie.dorman@qg.com. No phone calls. In-person interview recommended (telephone interview accepted). Applicants must submit a letter of interest, resume, 3-5 writing samples; 2-3 personal references. Application deadline: January 1 for spring, March 1 for summer. World Wide Web: http://www.milwaukeemagazine.com.

MOMENT MAGAZINE
4710 41st Street, NW
Washington, District of Columbia 20016

General Information Independent Jewish bimonthly magazine that covers political, artistic, social, religious, and cultural issues affecting the Jewish world. Established in 1975. Number of employees: 20. Unit of Jewish Educational Ventures. Number of internship applications received each year: 40.

Internships Available ▶ *1–2 editorial assistants:* responsibilities include proofreading, writing, performing administrative tasks, research, and fact checking. Candidates should have ability to work independently, ability to work with others, computer skills, office skills, oral communication skills, personal interest in the field, research skills, written communication skills. Duration is 3 months minimum (15-20 hours per week). Position available as unpaid or paid. Open to college sophomores, college juniors, college seniors, recent college graduates. International applications accepted.

Benefits Names of contacts, willing to complete paperwork for educational credit, willing to provide letters of recommendation.

Contact Write, call, fax, or e-mail Celeste Pickard, Personnel Manager. Phone: 202-364-3300. Fax: 202-364-2636. E-mail: operations@bib-arch.org. In-person interview recommended (telephone interview accepted). Applicants must submit a letter of interest, resume, writing samples (helpful). Applications are accepted continuously. World Wide Web: http://www.momentmag.com.

MOTHER JONES MAGAZINE
731 Market Street, Suite 600
San Francisco, California 94103

General Information Magazine that specializes in investigative reporting and political analysis. Established in 1976. Number of employees: 50. Number of internship applications received each year: 500.

Internships Available ▶ *6–10 editorial interns:* responsibilities include fact checking and reporting support, research, and reporting assistance on investigative research projects for both magazine and Web site. Candidates should have editing skills, research skills, writing skills. Duration is 4 months (minimum). $100 per month stipend; after 4 months, interns are reviewed for the Mother Jones fellowship which requires an additional 4–8-month commitment and pays a larger stipend. Open to recent college graduates, graduate students. International applications accepted.

Benefits Names of contacts, opportunity to attend seminars/workshops, willing to complete paperwork for educational credit, willing to provide letters of recommendation.

Contact Write, fax, e-mail, or through World Wide Web site Internship Coordinator. Fax: 415-665-6696. E-mail: intern@motherjones.com. No phone calls. In-person interview recommended (telephone interview accepted). Applicants must submit a letter of interest, resume, three writing samples, names and phone numbers of 3 personal references. Applications are accepted continuously. World Wide Web: http://www.motherjones.com.

MS. MAGAZINE
433 South Beverly Drive
Beverly Hills, California 90212

General Information Feminist magazine with focus on international news, health, arts, work, and books. Established in 1972. Number of employees: 25. Subsidiary of Feminist Majority Foundation, Beverly Hills, California. Number of internship applications received each year: 200.

Internships Available ▶ *3–4 editorial interns:* responsibilities include answering phones, responding to e-mails, doing research for editors, attending weekly editorial meetings, some writing. Candidates should have ability to work with others, knowledge of field, oral communication skills, research skills, self-motivation, written communication skills. Duration is one fall, spring, or summer. Unpaid. Open to college sophomores, college juniors, college seniors, career changers, individuals reentering the workforce. ▶ *3–4 marketing interns:* responsibilities include supporting the Marketing Circulation Department in marketing and promotion activities.

Candidates should have ability to work independently, ability to work with others, analytical skills, computer skills, office skills, oral communication skills, organizational skills, personal interest in the field, research skills, self-motivation, written communication skills. Duration is one fall, spring, or summer. Unpaid. Open to recent high school graduates, college sophomores, college juniors, college seniors, graduate students, career changers, individuals reentering the workforce. International applications accepted.
Benefits On-the-job training, willing to act as a professional reference, willing to complete paperwork for educational credit, willing to provide letters of recommendation, academic credit.
Contact Write or through World Wide Web site Internship Coordinator. Fax: 310-556-2514. No phone calls. In-person interview recommended (telephone interview accepted). Applicants must submit a letter of interest, resume, writing sample. Applications are accepted continuously. World Wide Web: http://www.msmagazine.com.

NATIONAL NEWS BUREAU
PO Box 43039
Philadelphia, Pennsylvania 19129

General Information Organization that handles the syndication of feature materials for newspapers, periodicals, and magazines. Established in 1979. Number of employees: 14. Number of internship applications received each year: 200.
Internships Available ▶ *4–8 interns:* responsibilities include interviewing and reviewing and writing travel stories. Candidates should have ability to work independently, self-motivation, strong interpersonal skills. Duration is 1 semester. Paid. Open to recent high school graduates, college freshmen, college sophomores, college juniors, college seniors, recent college graduates, graduate students, career changers. International applications accepted.
Benefits Formal training, free housing, health insurance, names of contacts, on-the-job training, opportunity to attend seminars/workshops, possible full-time employment, travel reimbursement, willing to complete paperwork for educational credit, willing to provide letters of recommendation.
International Internships Available.
Contact Write or e-mail Mr. Harry Jay Katz, Publisher. Fax: 215-893-5394. E-mail: hjaykatz@aol.com. No phone calls. In-person interview required. Applicants must submit a letter of interest, resume, copy of valid passport and/or driver's license. Applications are accepted continuously. World Wide Web: http://www.nationalnewsbureau.com.

THE NATION INSTITUTE
33 Irving Place, 8th Floor
New York, New York 10003

General Information Nonprofit foundation, affiliated with The Nation magazine, that supports research, conferences, seminars, educational programs, and independent media with an emphasis on social justice, civil liberties, cultural politics, and peace. Established in 1966. Number of employees: 5. Affiliate of The Nation Magazine, New York, New York. Number of internship applications received each year: 400.
Internships Available ▶ *24 interns:* responsibilities include checking facts; research; reading and evaluating manuscripts; assisting the advertising, circulation, and the promotional staff; filing; photocopying; and running errands. Candidates should have ability to work with others, computer skills, knowledge of field, personal interest in the field, plan to pursue career in field, research skills, writing skills. Duration is 1 semester. $150 per week. Open to recent high school graduates, college freshmen, college sophomores, college juniors, college seniors, recent college graduates, graduate students, law students, career changers, individuals reentering the workforce. International applications accepted.
Benefits Job counseling, names of contacts, on-the-job training, opportunity to attend seminars/workshops, willing to act as a professional reference, willing to complete paperwork for educational credit, willing to provide letters of recommendation, small stipend provided.
Contact Write, call, or e-mail Richard Kim, Internship Director. Phone: 212-209-5400. E-mail: rkim@thenation.com. Applicants

must submit a letter of interest, resume, two writing samples, two letters of recommendation. Application deadline: March 22 for summer, July 19 for fall, November 8 for winter/spring. World Wide Web: http://www.thenation.com.

NEW MOON PUBLISHING
PO Box 3620
Duluth, Minnesota 55803-3620

General Information Magazine publishing. Established in 1992. Number of employees: 8. Number of internship applications received each year: 12.
Internships Available ▶ *1–2 business administration interns:* responsibilities include database entry, telephone, assisting with day to day management at small publishing company. Duration is one spring, fall, summer. Unpaid. Open to high school seniors, college freshmen, college sophomores, college juniors, college seniors. ▶ *1–3 editorial interns:* responsibilities include some writing, researching, editing, and acquiring material; maintaining files; inputting submissions; researching and securing artwork; working with Girls Editorial Board; working with adult and girl contributors; contributing to planning and organizing of upcoming issues. Candidates should have ability to work independently, analytical skills, computer skills, editing skills, oral communication skills, organizational skills, personal interest in the field, research skills, self-motivation, strong interpersonal skills, strong leadership ability, writing skills, commitment to girls' and women's issues. Duration is fall, spring, or summer semester. Unpaid. Open to high school students, recent high school graduates, college freshmen, college sophomores, college juniors, college seniors, recent college graduates, graduate students, career changers, individuals reentering the workforce. ▶ *1 general communications intern:* responsibilities include developing communications and administrative systems via sources research; development, and organization. Candidates should have ability to work independently, computer skills, knowledge of field, office skills, organizational skills, research skills. Duration is one spring, fall, summer. Unpaid. Open to college sophomores, college juniors, college seniors, recent college graduates, graduate students. ▶ *1–2 marketing/e-commerce interns:* responsibilities include researching and implementing traffic-building strategies; continual development of site based on customer feedback; assisting in all administrative functions of on-line catalog. Candidates should have ability to work independently, computer skills, office skills, organizational skills, strong interpersonal skills, knowledge of Web design, HTML, and on-line marketing. Duration is flexible. Unpaid. Open to college juniors, college seniors, recent college graduates, graduate students. ▶ *1–2 public relations interns:* responsibilities include researching media outlets, writing and distributing press releases, developing fact sheet and brochures. Candidates should have ability to work independently, analytical skills, college courses in field, computer skills, knowledge of field, oral communication skills, organizational skills, personal interest in the field, research skills, self-motivation, strong interpersonal skills, writing skills, commitment to girls' and women's issues. Duration is fall, spring, or summer semester. Unpaid. Open to college juniors, college seniors, recent college graduates, graduate students, career changers. ▶ *1–2 social science/research/advocacy interns:* responsibilities include engaging in action projects that have critical strategic contacts and raise awareness of equality issues. Candidates should have ability to work independently, analytical skills, computer skills, personal interest in the field, research skills, writing skills. Duration is one fall, summer, spring. Unpaid. Open to college juniors, college seniors, recent college graduates, graduate students. ▶ *1–3 turn beauty inside out interns:* responsibilities include fund raising, outreach, planning, community project organizing, and researching funders. Candidates should have ability to work independently, office skills, oral communication skills, organizational skills, research skills, writing skills. Duration is one spring, fall, summer. Unpaid. Open to college sophomores, college juniors, college seniors, recent college graduates, graduate students, career changers. International applications accepted.
Benefits Names of contacts, on-the-job training, willing to act as a professional reference, willing to complete paperwork for educational credit, willing to provide letters of recommendation.

New Moon Publishing (continued)

Contact Write, call, fax, or e-mail Deb Mylin, Managing Editor. Phone: 218-728-5507 Ext. 21. Fax: 218-728-0314. E-mail: girl@ newmoon.org. In-person interview recommended (telephone interview accepted). Applicants must submit a letter of interest, resume, three writing samples. Application deadline: February 1 for summer, May 1 for fall, October 1 for spring. World Wide Web: http://www.newmoon.org.

THE NEW REPUBLIC
1331 H Street, NW, Suite 700
Washington, District of Columbia 20005

General Information Weekly journal of opinion. Established in 1914. Number of employees: 30. Number of internship applications received each year: 200.

Internships Available ▶ *3–5 reporters/researchers:* responsibilities include reading unsolicited manuscripts, proofreading, checking facts, handling editor's correspondence, periodic phone coverage, running errands, and writing short articles and editorials. Candidates should have ability to work independently, analytical skills, editing skills, office skills, oral communication skills, personal interest in the field, research skills, self-motivation, strong interpersonal skills, writing skills, journalism background (preferred). Duration is one summer or one academic year. $300 per week. Open to college freshmen, college sophomores, college juniors, college seniors, recent college graduates, graduate students, law students. International applications accepted.

Benefits Health insurance, job counseling, names of contacts, possible full-time employment, willing to act as a professional reference, willing to provide letters of recommendation, opportunity to attend lunches with prominent political figures.

Contact Write or e-mail Internship Coordinator. E-mail: tnr@aol. com. No phone calls. Applicants must submit a letter of interest, resume, two letters of recommendation, in-person or telephone interview for finalists, 3-5 writing samples. Application deadline: March 1. World Wide Web: http://www.thenewrepublic.com.

NEWSWEEK
251 West 57th Street
New York, New York 10019

General Information Major weekly news magazine. Established in 1933. Number of employees: 400. Unit of Washington Post Company, Washington, District of Columbia.

Internships Available ▶ *10–12 editorial interns:* responsibilities include fact-checking, researching, reporting, and copy flow tasks. Candidates should have ability to work independently, ability to work with others, personal interest in the field, research skills, experience on school paper or other internships, writing and reporting skills. Duration is 13 weeks. $540 per week. ▶ *2 photo interns:* responsibilities include conducting Internet searches for published photos. Candidates should have knowledge of field, organizational skills, personal interest in the field, self-motivation, strong interpersonal skills. Duration is 13 weeks. $540 per week. ▶ *1 public relations intern:* responsibilities include writing press releases, fielding media calls, and updating biographies of editors and correspondents; working with PR department staff on assignments (as directed); writing news stories for internal newsletter. Candidates should have ability to work independently, ability to work with others, computer skills, organizational skills, personal interest in the field, writing skills. Duration is 13 weeks. $540 per week. Open to college juniors, college seniors, recent college graduates, graduate students. International applications accepted.

Benefits On-the-job training, possible full-time employment, opportunity to attend editorial meetings and luncheons with editors.

Contact Write Mark Miller, Chief of Correspondents. Applicants must submit a resume, cover letter, names and phone numbers of 2 references, 5 published writing samples (editorial positions), 2 writing samples (public relations positions). Application deadline: January 10 for summer. World Wide Web: http://www.newsweek. com.

THE NEW YORK TIMES
229 West 43rd Street
New York, New York 10036

General Information Newspaper. Established in 1851. Number of employees: 4,000. Number of internship applications received each year: 300.

Internships Available ▶ *3 copy editors:* responsibilities include editing stories and writing headlines for publication. Candidates should have ability to work independently, analytical skills, computer skills, editing skills, knowledge of field, oral communication skills, plan to pursue career in field, research skills, self-motivation, strong interpersonal skills, writing skills. Duration is end of May to beginning of August. $700 per week. Open to college juniors, college seniors, graduate students. ▶ *1 design intern:* responsibilities include producing page layouts for publication. Candidates should have ability to work independently, computer skills, knowledge of field, oral communication skills, organizational skills, plan to pursue career in field, self-motivation, writing skills. Duration is end of May to beginning of August. $700 per week. Open to college juniors, college seniors, graduate students. ▶ *1 graphics intern:* responsibilities include producing graphics for publication. Candidates should have ability to work independently, analytical skills, computer skills, knowledge of field, oral communication skills, organizational skills, plan to pursue career in field, research skills, self-motivation, strong interpersonal skills, writing skills. Duration is end of May to beginning of August . $700 per week. Open to college juniors, college seniors, graduate students. ▶ *1 photographer.* Candidates should have ability to work independently, knowledge of field, oral communication skills, plan to pursue career in field, strong interpersonal skills, written communication skills. Duration is end of May to beginning of August. $700 per week. Open to college juniors, college seniors, graduate students. ▶ *4 reporters:* responsibilities include reporting and writing stories for publication. Candidates should have ability to work independently, analytical skills, computer skills, knowledge of field, oral communication skills, plan to pursue career in field, research skills, self-motivation, strong interpersonal skills, writing skills. Duration is end of May to beginning of August. $700 per week. Open to college seniors, graduate students. International applications accepted.

Benefits Job counseling, names of contacts, on-the-job training, opportunity to attend seminars/workshops, possible full-time employment, travel reimbursement, willing to act as a professional reference, willing to complete paperwork for educational credit, willing to provide letters of recommendation, $300 monthly housing subsidy.

Contact Write, call, or e-mail Sheila Rule, Senior Manager, Recruiting. Phone: 212-556-4143. E-mail: rulesh@nytimes.com. Applicants must submit a letter of interest, resume, portfolio, 8-10 writing samples; previous internship required. Application deadline: November 15. World Wide Web: http://www.nytimes.com.

PENGUIN PUTNAM, INC.
375 Hudson Street
New York, New York 10014

General Information Adult and children's trade book publisher. Established in 1838. Number of employees: 800. Division of Pearson plc, London, United Kingdom. Number of internship applications received each year: 300.

Internships Available ▶ *5–8 art department interns:* responsibilities include paste and mechanical work, light design work, corrections, and packaging of originals; also some light clerical work involved in the day-to-day operations of the office. Candidates should have computer skills, office skills, oral communication skills, personal interest in the field, self-motivation, strong interpersonal skills. Duration is 1 summer or semester. Paid. ▶ *8–10 editorial interns:* responsibilities include reading and evaluating unsolicited manuscripts, drafting and sending rejection letters, and research. Candidates should have editing skills, oral communication skills, personal interest in the field, self-motivation, strong interpersonal skills, writing skills. Duration is 1 summer or semester. Paid. ▶ *4–6 marketing interns:* responsibilities include special projects within the department and general office support. Candidates should have office skills, oral communication skills, personal interest in the field, self-motivation, strong interpersonal skills, writing skills. Duration is 1 summer or semester. Paid. ▶ *4–6 publicity interns:* responsibilities include special projects within the department and general office support. Candidates should have office skills, oral communication skills, personal interest in the field, self-motivation, strong interpersonal skills, writing skills. Duration is 1 summer or semester. Paid. ▶ *15–20 publishing interns:* responsibilities include working in a department such as editorial, art, marketing, online, production, sales, subsidiary rights, contracts, and publicity. Candidates should have office skills, oral communication skills, personal interest in the field, self-motivation, strong interpersonal skills, writing skills. Duration is 1 summer or semester. Paid. Open to college freshmen, college sophomores, college juniors, college seniors, graduate students, law students. International applications accepted.

Benefits On-the-job training, willing to complete paperwork for educational credit.

Contact Write, fax, or e-mail Debbie Schokett, Human Resources Associate. Fax: 212-366-2930. E-mail: jobs@penguinputnam.com. In-person interview required. Applicants must submit a letter of interest, resume. Application deadline: January 15 for spring, February 28 for summer; continuous for other positions, August 31 for fall. World Wide Web: http://www.penguinputnam.com.

PENOBSCOT BAY PRESS
PO Box 36
Stonington, Maine 04681

General Information Publisher of books, computer graphics, and 3 weekly newspapers. Established in 1964. Number of employees: 20. Number of internship applications received each year: 40.

Internships Available ▶ *1 advertising intern:* responsibilities include assisting with sales, research, filing, and design. Candidates should have ability to work independently, ability to work with others, oral communication skills, organizational skills, personal interest in the field, self-motivation. Duration is June to August. Position available as unpaid or at minimum wage or stipend. Open to high school seniors, recent high school graduates, college freshmen, college sophomores, college juniors, college seniors. ▶ *1 editorial intern:* responsibilities include writing, researching, filing, photographing, and performing production and clerical duties. Candidates should have ability to work independently, ability to work with others, organizational skills, personal interest in the field, self-motivation, writing skills. Duration is June to August. Stipend. Open to high school students, recent high school graduates, college freshmen, college sophomores, college juniors, college seniors.

Benefits Names of contacts, on-the-job training, opportunity to attend seminars/workshops, possible full-time employment, willing to act as a professional reference, willing to complete paperwork for educational credit, willing to provide letters of recommendation.

Contact Write, fax, or e-mail Mr. Nat Barrows, Publisher. Fax: 207-367-6397. E-mail: cis@penobscotbaypress.com. No phone calls. In-person interview recommended (telephone interview accepted). Applicants must submit a letter of interest, resume, portfolio, two personal references, two letters of recommendation, 6 writing samples. Applications are accepted continuously.

PHILADELPHIA MAGAZINE
1818 Market Street, 36th Floor
Philadelphia, Pennsylvania 19103

General Information City magazine covering local politics, news, and entertainment. Established in 1908. Number of employees: 50. Unit of Metro Corporation, New York, New York. Number of internship applications received each year: 150.

Internships Available ▶ *2–3 art interns:* responsibilities include assisting designers, photographers, and stylists. Candidates should have ability to work independently, computer skills, knowledge of field, organizational skills, strong interpersonal skills. Duration is 1 semester or summer. Unpaid. Open to high school seniors, college freshmen, college sophomores, college juniors, college seniors, recent college graduates. ▶ *6–7 editorial interns:* responsibilities include assisting writers with research, function-

ing as a general editorial assistant, fact checking, reporting, and writing brief articles. Candidates should have ability to work independently, analytical skills, oral communication skills, organizational skills, research skills, strong interpersonal skills. Duration is 1 semester or summer. Unpaid. Open to college freshmen, college sophomores, college juniors, college seniors, recent college graduates, graduate students, career changers. International applications accepted.

Benefits Job counseling, names of contacts, possible full-time employment, willing to act as a professional reference, willing to complete paperwork for educational credit, willing to provide letters of recommendation.

Contact Write or e-mail Erin Alden, Research Editor/Intern Coordinator. Fax: 215-656-3502. E-mail: ealden@phillymag.com. No phone calls. In-person interview recommended (telephone interview accepted). Applicants must submit a letter of interest, resume, 3-5 writing samples. Application deadline: March 1 for summer, August 15 for fall, December 1 for spring. World Wide Web: http://www.phillymag.com.

POHLY & PARTNERS
27 Melcher Street, Floor 2
Boston, Massachusetts 02210

General Information Custom publisher of magazines and online content. Established in 1987. Number of employees: 35. Number of internship applications received each year: 100.

Internships Available ▶ *1–2 ad sales/marketing interns:* responsibilities include supporting ad sales department, client contacts, and maintaining database. Candidates should have ability to work independently, ability to work with others, computer skills, oral communication skills, research skills, written communication skills, must be receiving academic credit. Duration is 1 semester. Unpaid. ▶ *2–3 editorial interns:* responsibilities include fact-checking; writing, as assigned. Candidates should have ability to work independently, oral communication skills, plan to pursue career in field, self-motivation, writing skills, must be receiving academic credit. Duration is 1 semester. Unpaid. ▶ *1 marketing intern:* responsibilities include supporting marketing communications program, maintaining database, and doing analysis. Candidates should have ability to work independently, oral communication skills, research skills, strong interpersonal skills, writing skills, must be receiving academic credit. Duration is 1 semester. Unpaid. Open to college juniors, college seniors, graduate students. International applications accepted.

Benefits On-the-job training, possible full-time employment, willing to act as a professional reference, willing to complete paperwork for educational credit, willing to provide letters of recommendation.

Contact Write, e-mail, or through World Wide Web site Karen English, Senior Editor. E-mail: karene@pohlypartners.com. No phone calls. In-person interview recommended (telephone interview accepted). Applicants must submit a letter of interest, resume, writing samples for editorial internship. Applications are accepted continuously. World Wide Web: http://www.pohlypartners.com.

PRINTED MATTER, INC.
535 West 22nd Street
New York, New York 10011

General Information Nonprofit arts organization whose mission is to foster the appreciation, dissemination, and understanding of artists' books and related publications by artists. Established in 1976. Number of employees: 5. Number of internship applications received each year: 10.

Internships Available ▶ *1–4 interns:* responsibilities include assisting with daily and ongoing operations including exhibits and special events. Candidates should have ability to work independently, ability to work with others, oral communication skills, organizational skills, personal interest in the field, self-motivation. Duration is minimum of 3 months. Unpaid. Open to college freshmen, college sophomores, college juniors, college seniors, recent college graduates, graduate students, law students, career changers. International applications accepted.

Printed Matter, Inc. (continued)

Benefits On-the-job training, willing to act as a professional reference, willing to complete paperwork for educational credit, willing to provide letters of recommendation.

Contact Write, call, fax, or e-mail Max Schumann, Manager. Phone: 212-925-0325. Fax: 212-925-0464. E-mail: mschumann@printedmatter.org. In-person interview recommended (telephone interview accepted). Applicants must submit a letter of interest, resume. Applications are accepted continuously. World Wide Web: http://www.printedmatter.org.

PSYCHOLOGY TODAY
49 East 21st Street, 11th Floor
New York, New York 10010

General Information Magazine publishing company. Established in 1991. Number of employees: 30. Number of internship applications received each year: 100.

Internships Available ▶ *3–4 editorial interns:* responsibilities include writing at least 2 stories, fact-checking, proofreading, and light clerical duties. Candidates should have editing skills, organizational skills, plan to pursue career in field, research skills, writing skills, major in psychology or journalism (preferred). Duration is 1 semester. Unpaid. Open to college sophomores, college juniors, college seniors, recent college graduates, graduate students. International applications accepted.

Benefits On-the-job training, willing to act as a professional reference, willing to complete paperwork for educational credit, willing to provide letters of recommendation, small stipend.

Contact Write, call, fax, or e-mail Kaja Perina, Internship Coordinator. Fax: 212-260-7445. E-mail: kaja@pychologytoday.com. In-person interview recommended (telephone interview accepted). Applicants must submit a resume, clips from previous work and cover letter all in Word format. Applications are accepted continuously.

RANDOM HOUSE, INC.
1540 Broadway
New York, New York 10036

General Information General trade book publisher. Established in 1925. Number of employees: 1,800. Division of Bertelsmann, Gutersloh, Germany. Number of internship applications received each year: 1,000.

Internships Available ▶ *25–30 summer interns:* responsibilities include working in one of the major publishing groups or functional areas. Candidates should have knowledge of field, office skills, oral communication skills, personal interest in the field, self-motivation, written communication skills. Duration is 10 weeks. $300 per week. Open to college juniors. International applications accepted.

Benefits Job counseling, opportunity to attend seminars/workshops, possible full-time employment.

Contact Write, fax, e-mail, or through World Wide Web site Internship Coordinator. Fax: 212-782-8450. E-mail: internship@randomhouse.com. No phone calls. In-person interview required. Applicants must submit a letter of interest, resume. Application deadline: March 31. World Wide Web: http://www.randomhouse.com.

RODALE INC.
33 East Minor Street
Emmaus, Pennsylvania 18098

General Information International publisher of healthy active living content; magazine titles include *Prevention, Men's Health,* and *Runner's World;* book titles include *Dr. Shapiro's Picture Perfect Weight Loss.* Established in 1930. Number of employees: 1,150. Number of internship applications received each year: 1,000.

Internships Available ▶ *40–50 summer interns:* responsibilities include writing, editing, editorial research, marketing, public relations, graphic design, and Web development. Candidates should have computer skills, experience in the field, oral communication skills, organizational skills, self-motivation, strong interpersonal skills, written communication skills. Duration is 11 weeks (typically early June through mid-August). Position available as unpaid or at $425 per week (undergraduate level); $600 per week (gradu-

ate level). Open to college sophomores, college juniors, college seniors, recent college graduates, graduate students. International applications accepted.

Benefits Formal training, job counseling, meals at a cost, names of contacts, on-the-job training, opportunity to attend seminars/workshops, possible full-time employment, willing to act as a professional reference, willing to complete paperwork for educational credit, willing to provide letters of recommendation, free health club access, discounted publications.

Contact Write, fax, e-mail, or through World Wide Web site Internship Program Manager, 33 East Minor Street, Emmaus, Pennsylvania 18098. Fax: 610-967-9209. E-mail: hr3@rodale.com. No phone calls. In-person interview recommended (telephone interview accepted). Applicants must submit a letter of interest, resume, three writing samples, portfolio if applicable. Application deadline: February 1. World Wide Web: http://www.rodale.com.

ROSIE MAGAZINE
375 Lexington Avenue, 9th Floor
New York, New York 10017

General Information Monthly women's magazine. Established in 2001. Number of employees: 50. Unit of G & J USA Publishing, New York, New York. Number of internship applications received each year: 100.

Internships Available ▶ *1–2 articles interns:* responsibilities include helping editors with research, story proposals, and title and caption writing, as well as administrative duties. Candidates should have editing skills, office skills, personal interest in the field, research skills, writing skills, English or journalism majors (preferred). Duration is 3 months. Unpaid. Open to college freshmen, college sophomores, college juniors. ▶ *1–2 beauty interns:* responsibilities include calling in products, organizing press releases, speaking with public relations companies about upcoming stories, and brainstorming for future story ideas. Candidates should have ability to work independently, ability to work with others, office skills, oral communication skills, organizational skills, self-motivation. Unpaid. Open to high school students, recent high school graduates, college freshmen, college sophomores, college juniors, college seniors, graduate students. ▶ *1–2 fashion interns:* responsibilities include calling in and preparing merchandise for shoots and keeping track of market trends. Candidates should have ability to work independently, ability to work with others, office skills, oral communication skills, organizational skills, self-motivation. Unpaid. Open to college freshmen, college sophomores, college juniors, college seniors, graduate students. ▶ *1–2 food interns:* responsibilities include assisting in test kitchens, researching recipes, and administrative duties. Candidates should have ability to work independently, ability to work with others, office skills, oral communication skills, organizational skills, personal interest in the field, self-motivation, written communication skills. Unpaid. Open to college freshmen, college sophomores, college juniors, college seniors, recent college graduates, graduate students. International applications accepted.

Benefits Names of contacts, on-the-job training, willing to complete paperwork for educational credit, willing to provide letters of recommendation, reimbursement of travel expenses and free lunch in lieu of hourly pay.

Contact Write Emily Berdell, Recruiting and Compensation Assistant. No phone calls. In-person interview recommended (telephone interview accepted). Applicants must submit a letter of interest, resume, 2-3 writing samples. Application deadline: March 1 for summer, October 1 for spring; continuous for year-round positions. World Wide Web: http://www.rosie.magazine.com.

RUGGED LAND
276 Canal Street, 5th Floor
New York, New York 10013

General Information Book publishing and film development company. Established in 2001. Number of employees: 4.

Internships Available ▶ *1–3 interns:* responsibilities include research, writing, office work; exposure to all aspects of book publishing and film production including editorial, marketing,

publicity, and subsidiary rights. Candidates should have ability to work independently, oral communication skills, research skills, strong interpersonal skills, writing skills, journalism experience preferred, but not essential. Duration is fall (September to December), spring (January to April), or summer (May to August) minimum 3 days per week. Unpaid. Open to college freshmen, college sophomores, college juniors, college seniors, recent college graduates. International applications accepted.
Benefits Names of contacts, willing to act as a professional reference, willing to complete paperwork for educational credit, willing to provide letters of recommendation.
Contact Write, fax, e-mail, or through World Wide Web site Chris Min, Associate Editor. Fax: 212-334-5749. E-mail: cmin@ruggedland. com. No phone calls. In-person interview recommended (telephone interview accepted). Applicants must submit a letter of interest, resume, writing sample. Applications are accepted continuously. World Wide Web: http://www.ruggedland.com.

RUNNING PRESS
125 South 22nd Street
Philadelphia, Pennsylvania 19103

General Information General book publisher mainly of nonfiction, children's titles, art, and gift books. Established in 1972. Number of employees: 80. Number of internship applications received each year: 30.
Internships Available ▶ *1–2 assistants to associate publisher:* responsibilities include working with the associate publisher as well as with the editorial, sales, production, legal, and publicity departments. Candidates should have computer skills, personal interest in the field, research skills, strong interpersonal skills, writing skills. Duration is flexible. Unpaid. Open to college freshmen, college sophomores, college juniors, college seniors, recent college graduates. ▶ *2 design interns:* responsibilities include developing design concepts, scanning artwork, layout and design for book pages, and researching illustrator/photographer candidates. Candidates should have college courses in field, computer skills, oral communication skills, personal interest in the field, self-motivation, knowledge of Quark Xpress and PhotoShop. Duration is flexible. Unpaid. Open to college sophomores, college juniors, college seniors. ▶ *3–4 editorial interns:* responsibilities include assisting with general editorial work. Candidates should have computer skills, editing skills, oral communication skills, personal interest in the field, research skills, writing skills. Duration is flexible. Unpaid. Open to college sophomores, college juniors, college seniors, recent college graduates, graduate students. ▶ *1 production intern:* responsibilities include assisting in daily administrative duties in the production department including some communication with vendors; distribution and/or trafficking materials; coordinating bound galleys; some data entry on computer. Candidates should have ability to work with others, computer skills, office skills, organizational skills, personal interest in the field, writing skills. Duration is 3–4 months. Unpaid. Open to college sophomores, college juniors, college seniors, recent college graduates, graduate students, law students. ▶ *2–3 publicity interns:* responsibilities include providing support to publicity director, publicist and publicity assistant; handling publicity campaign for assigned title(s); drafting pitch letters, press releases, organizing mailing, making follow-up calls to media to pitch title(s), and clipping and filing reviews. Candidates should have computer skills, oral communication skills, personal interest in the field, self-motivation, strong interpersonal skills, written communication skills. Duration is 12 weeks. Unpaid. Open to college sophomores, college juniors, college seniors, recent college graduates, graduate students. ▶ *1–2 special sales interns:* responsibilities include assisting with day-to-day operations of the special sales department including order taking, customer service, and computer work. Candidates should have computer skills, oral communication skills, personal interest in the field, self-motivation, writing skills. Duration is 12 weeks. Unpaid. Open to college sophomores, college juniors, college seniors, recent college graduates, graduate students. International applications accepted.
Benefits Names of contacts, on-the-job training, possible full-time employment, willing to act as a professional reference, will-

ing to complete paperwork for educational credit, willing to provide letters of recommendation, hands-on experience.
Contact Write, call, fax, or e-mail Melissa Wagner, Editor. Phone: 215-567-5080 Ext. 266. Fax: 215-568-2919. E-mail: mwagner@ runningpress.com. In-person interview recommended (telephone interview accepted). Applicants must submit a letter of interest, resume, writing sample. Applications are accepted continuously. World Wide Web: http://www.runningpress.com.

ST. PAUL PIONEER PRESS
345 Cedar Street
St. Paul, Minnesota 55101

General Information Award-winning daily newspaper covering the Twin Cities area. Established in 1849. Number of employees: 1,000. Unit of Knight Ridder, San Jose, California. Number of internship applications received each year: 300.
Internships Available ▶ *1 Native American newsroom intern.* Duration is 12 weeks. $580 per week. ▶ *3–5 newsroom interns:* responsibilities include positions available in reporting, copy editing, graphic design, new media, photography, page design/layout. Duration is 10 weeks. $400 per week. Candidates for all positions should have ability to work independently, ability to work with others, knowledge of field, self-motivation, writing skills. Open to college sophomores, college juniors, college seniors, recent college graduates, graduate students.
Benefits Job counseling, on-the-job training, opportunity to attend seminars/workshops, possible full-time employment, travel reimbursement, willing to act as a professional reference, willing to provide letters of recommendation.
Contact Write, call, or e-mail Rubèn Rosario, Columnist/Internship Coordinator. Phone: 651-228-5454. Fax: 651-228-2159. E-mail: rrosario@pioneerpress.com. In-person interview recommended (telephone interview accepted). Applicants must submit a letter of interest, resume, portfolio, three personal references, 2–page personal essay; 6–8 writing samples. Application deadline: December 30. World Wide Web: http://www.pioneerplanet.com.

SAN DIEGO COMMUNITY NEWSPAPER GROUP
4645 Cass Street
San Diego, California 92169

General Information Publisher of six community newspapers and assorted specialty publications. Established in 1988. Number of employees: 30. Division of Mannis Communications, Inc., San Diego, California. Number of internship applications received each year: 100.
Internships Available ▶ *12 editorial interns:* responsibilities include researching and compiling information for editorials and articles, putting together calendars and obituaries, occasionally gathering editorial information for the senior editor, and writing news and feature articles. Candidates should have ability to work independently, ability to work with others, computer skills, office skills, oral communication skills, written communication skills, knowledge of Associated Press style guidelines. Duration is 9–12 weeks. Unpaid. Open to college freshmen, college sophomores, college juniors, college seniors, recent college graduates, career changers, individuals reentering the workforce. International applications accepted.
Benefits Names of contacts, on-the-job training, possible full-time employment, willing to act as a professional reference, willing to complete paperwork for educational credit, willing to provide letters of recommendation.
Contact Write, call, fax, or e-mail John Gregory, Editor-in-Chief, PO Box 9550, San Diego, California 92169. Phone: 858-270-3103 Ext. 142. Fax: 858-270-9325. E-mail: mail@sdnews.com. In-person interview recommended (telephone interview accepted). Applicants must submit a formal organization application, letter of interest, resume, 1-3 writing samples, 1-3 personal references, letter of recommendation (optional). Applications are accepted continuously. World Wide Web: http://www.sdnews.com.

SAN DIEGO DAILY TRANSCRIPT
2131 Third Avenue
San Diego, California 92101

General Information Newspaper and Web-based publisher of business information and content. Established in 1886. Number of employees: 80. Unit of Transcript Publishing Co., San Diego, California. Number of internship applications received each year: 50.

Internships Available ▶ *1–2 editorial interns:* responsibilities include writing, reporting, and researching business topics. Candidates should have plan to pursue career in field, research skills, self-motivation, writing skills, major in journalism. Duration is 3 months. Minimum wage. Open to college seniors, recent college graduates, graduate students, law students, career changers. International applications accepted.

Benefits On-the-job training, opportunity to attend seminars/workshops, possible full-time employment, willing to act as a professional reference, willing to provide letters of recommendation.

Contact Write, call, or e-mail Adriana Gutierrez, Human Resources Manager. Phone: 619-232-4381. Fax: 619-236-8126. E-mail: gutierrez@sddt.com. In-person interview recommended (telephone interview accepted). Applicants must submit a formal organization application, letter of interest, resume, three writing samples, three personal references. Application deadline: one month prior to start of semester. World Wide Web: http://www.sddt.com.

THE SAN DIEGO UNION-TRIBUNE
350 Camino de la Reina
San Diego, California 92108

General Information Publishing and information services. Number of employees: 1,500. Unit of Copley Newspapers, Inc., La Jolla, California. Number of internship applications received each year: 250.

Internships Available ▶ *1 intern:* responsibilities include working as professional reporter, photographer, page designer, and copyeditor. Candidates should have experience in the field, plan to pursue career in field, research skills, self-motivation, writing skills, fluency in a second language that is spoken in San Diego (a plus). Duration is 10–12 weeks. Position available as unpaid or at $460 per week for summer interns; academic-year interns unpaid . Open to college juniors, college seniors, recent college graduates, graduate students.

Benefits On-the-job training, opportunity to attend seminars/workshops, willing to complete paperwork for educational credit.

Contact Write, call, or e-mail Carol Goodhue, Training and Development Coordinator, PO Box 120191, San Diego, California 92112-0191. Phone: 619-293-1261. E-mail: carol.goodhue@uniontrib.com. Telephone interview required. Applicants must submit a letter of interest, resume, 6 samples of published newspaper stories. Application deadline: November 15 for summer; continuous for unpaid academic positions during school year. World Wide Web: http://www.uniontrib.com.

SCHNEIDER PUBLISHING
11835 West Olympic Boulevard, Suite 1265
Los Angeles, California 90064

General Information Magazine publisher. Established in 1988. Number of employees: 9. Number of internship applications received each year: 50.

Internships Available ▶ *1–3 office assistants:* responsibilities include flexible duties depending on the intern's interest and experience; general assistance with office tasks. Candidates should have ability to work independently, analytical skills, editing skills, office skills, oral communication skills, organizational skills, personal interest in the field, research skills, self-motivation, strong interpersonal skills, writing skills, experience with computers (desirable). Duration is flexible. Position available as unpaid or at $6 per hour. Open to high school seniors, recent high school graduates, college freshmen, college sophomores, college juniors, college seniors, recent college graduates, graduate students. International applications accepted.

Benefits On-the-job training, possible full-time employment, willing to act as a professional reference, willing to complete paperwork for educational credit, willing to provide letters of recommendation, small stipend.

Contact Write, fax, or e-mail Ann Shepphird, Managing Editor, 11835 West Olympic Boulevard, Suite 1265, Los Angeles, California 90064. Fax: 310-577-3715. E-mail: ann@schneiderpublishing.com. No phone calls. In-person interview recommended (telephone interview accepted). Applicants must submit a letter of interest, resume. Applications are accepted continuously.

SCIENCE MAGAZINE
1200 New York Avenue, NW
Washington, District of Columbia 20005

General Information Nonprofit educational magazine. Established in 1880. Number of employees: 120. Subsidiary of American Association for the Advancement of Science, Washington, District of Columbia. Number of internship applications received each year: 40.

Internships Available ▶ *1 intern:* responsibilities include news writing and editing. Candidates should have ability to work with others, analytical skills, editing skills, oral communication skills, research skills, self-motivation, writing skills, knowledge of science. Duration is January 1 to June 30 or July 1 to December 31. $400 per week. Open to college seniors, recent college graduates, graduate students, career changers. International applications accepted.

Benefits Opportunity to attend seminars/workshops, travel reimbursement, willing to act as a professional reference, willing to provide letters of recommendation.

International Internships Available in Cambridge, United Kingdom.

Contact Write, call, fax, or e-mail Eliot Marshall, Senior Writer. Phone: 202-326-6589. Fax: 202-371-9227. E-mail: emarshal@aaas.org. Applicants must submit a letter of interest, resume, two personal references, 3-5 writing samples. Application deadline: April 1 for summer, November 1 for winter. World Wide Web: http://www.sciencemag.org.

SCIENCE NEWS MAGAZINE
1719 N Street, NW
Washington, District of Columbia 20036

General Information Weekly newsmagazine covering science. Established in 1922. Number of employees: 20. Unit of Science Service, Inc., Washington, District of Columbia. Number of internship applications received each year: 80.

Internships Available ▶ *3 science writer interns:* responsibilities include researching and writing short news stories and longer features for weekly magazine. Candidates should have ability to work independently, college courses in field, plan to pursue career in field, research skills, self-motivation, writing skills. Duration is 3–4 months. $1800 per month. Open to college seniors, recent college graduates, graduate students, career changers. International applications accepted.

Benefits Job counseling, names of contacts, on-the-job training, willing to act as a professional reference, willing to complete paperwork for educational credit, willing to provide letters of recommendation, opportunity to write/publish stories.

Contact Write or e-mail Keith Haglund, Internship Coordinator. Fax: 202-659-0365. E-mail: scinews@sciserv.org. No phone calls. Applicants must submit a letter of interest, resume, at least 3 examples of journalistic writing. Application deadline: February 1 for summer, June 15 for fall, October 15 for spring. World Wide Web: http://www.sciencenews.org.

THE SEATTLE TIMES
1120 John Street, PO Box 70
Seattle, Washington 98111

General Information Newspaper. Established in 1896. Number of employees: 2,000. Number of internship applications received each year: 300.

Internships Available ▶ *Residency interns:* responsibilities include reporting, photography, copy desk, and arts/graphics. Candidates should have computer skills, editing skills, experience in the field, plan to pursue career in field, writing skills. Duration is 3 years.

$500 per week. Open to recent college graduates, journalists with limited daily newspaper experience. ▶ *12 summer interns:* responsibilities include reporting, photography, arts/graphics, and copy desk duties. Candidates should have computer skills, editing skills, knowledge of field, plan to pursue career in field, research skills, writing skills. Duration is 12 weeks. $450 per week. Open to college freshmen, college sophomores, college juniors, college seniors, recent college graduates, graduate students.
Benefits Job counseling, on-the-job training, possible full-time employment, willing to act as a professional reference, willing to provide letters of recommendation, possibility of health insurance.
Contact Write, call, fax, e-mail, or through World Wide Web site Danyelle Lesch, Internship Coordinator. Phone: 206-464-2414. Fax: 206-464-2261. E-mail: newsinternships@seattletimes.com. Applicants must submit a formal organization application, letter of interest, resume, 5-7 samples of published work. Application deadline: November 1 for summer interns; contact for deadlines for other positions. World Wide Web: http://seattletimes.com.

SMITHSONIAN INSTITUTION PRESS
750 Ninth Street, NW, #4300
Washington, District of Columbia 20560-0950

General Information Publishing arm of the Smithsonian Institution that annually produces 80–100 publications relating to Smithsonian collections and research interests. Established in 1846. Number of employees: 38. Unit of Smithsonian Institution, Washington, District of Columbia. Number of internship applications received each year: 20.
Internships Available ▶ *1–2 Smithsonian Contributions and Studies series interns:* responsibilities include proofing, editing, and coding files for upload to Web site, as well as proofing and editing of manuscripts in progress. Candidates should have college courses in field, computer skills, editing skills, knowledge of field, self-motivation, written communication skills. Duration is 8–12 weeks. Unpaid. Open to college sophomores, college juniors, college seniors, recent college graduates, graduate students. ▶ *1–2 acquisitions interns:* responsibilities include working on development of books on scholarly subjects for adults, researching the locations of outstanding photographs and illustrations for manuscripts, assisting with the correlation and preparation for publication of book projects. Candidates should have computer skills, office skills, personal interest in the field, research skills, strong interpersonal skills, written communication skills. Duration is 8–12 weeks. Unpaid. Open to college sophomores, college juniors, college seniors, recent college graduates. ▶ *1–2 marketing interns:* responsibilities include assisting marketing staff with preparing print advertisements, flyers, and brochures for direct mail, publicity kits, sales kits, and jacket copy; sending books out for review by media and course adoption. Candidates should have ability to work with others, computer skills, office skills, oral communication skills, writing skills. Duration is 8–12 weeks. Unpaid. Open to college sophomores, college juniors, college seniors, recent college graduates.
Benefits Job counseling, names of contacts, opportunity to attend seminars/workshops, possible full-time employment, willing to complete paperwork for educational credit, willing to provide letters of recommendation, one-on-one professional mentor/student involvement.
Contact Write or e-mail Ms. Anne Garvey, Internship Coordinator, 750 Ninth Street, NW #4300, Washington, District of Columbia 20560-0950. E-mail: agarvey@sipress.si.edu. In-person interview recommended (telephone interview accepted). Applicants must submit a formal organization application, resume, academic transcripts, two letters of recommendation, personal essay. Application deadline: April 1 for summer, July 1 for fall, October 1 for spring. World Wide Web: http://www.sipress.si.edu.

SOUTH CAROLINA PRESS ASSOCIATION FOUNDATION
PO Box 11429
Columbia, South Carolina 29211

General Information One of the nation's oldest state press associations; members include all daily newspapers and nearly every weekly newspaper in South Carolina. Established in 1875.

Internships Available ▶ *3 summer interns:* responsibilities include working in either editorial, advertising, or photography positions. Candidates should have ability to work independently, computer skills, personal interest in the field, research skills, self-motivation, written communication skills, previous newspaper experience and working knowledge of newspaper software and/or camera equipment, darkroom, computer photo experience beneficial; preference given to journalism, advertising or communications majors. Duration is 10 weeks. $3000 per duration of internship. Open to any South Carolina college or university student who has completed the sophomore year by the start of internship.
Benefits On-the-job training, approved travel expenses involved in work assignments and additional work will be funded by intern's host newspaper.
Contact Call or through World Wide Web site Internship Coordinator. Phone: 888-SCPRESS. Applicants must submit a formal organization application, resume, academic transcripts, letter of recommendation from college advisor (communication or journalism department director of communication/journalism major); maximum of 6 newspaper work samples; list of college activities; list of college scholarships or awards received; statement of interest (maximum 250 words). Application deadline: December. World Wide Web: http://www.scpress.org.

SOUTHERN PROGRESS CORPORATION
PO Box 2581
Birmingham, Alabama 35202

General Information Magazine and book publisher that specializes in lifestyle publications. Established in 1886. Number of employees: 1,300. Subsidiary of AOL Time Warner, Inc., New York, New York. Number of internship applications received each year: 500.
Internships Available ▶ *1–2 accounting interns:* responsibilities include general accounting functions. Candidates should have analytical skills, computer skills, declared college major in field, knowledge of field, organizational skills. Duration is 3–5 months. $10 per hour. ▶ *4–6 advertising interns:* responsibilities include writing ad copy, selecting promotional items, assisting sales team with sales calls. Candidates should have ability to work independently, ability to work with others, college courses in field, organizational skills, personal interest in the field, written communication skills. Duration is 3–5 months. $10 per hour. ▶ *9–12 editorial interns:* responsibilities include writing, proofreading, editing, and research. Candidates should have ability to work with others, editing skills, experience in the field, personal interest in the field, research skills, writing skills. Duration is 3–5 months. $10 per hour. ▶ *2–3 graphic design interns:* responsibilities include designing promotional material for advertising department. Candidates should have ability to work independently, computer skills, declared college major in field, knowledge of field, organizational skills. Duration is 3–5 months. $10 per hour. ▶ *1 information systems intern:* responsibilities include working on help desk, computer programming. Candidates should have ability to work with others, analytical skills, college courses in field, computer skills, knowledge of field. Duration is 3–5 months. $10 per hour. ▶ *2–4 marketing interns:* responsibilities include maintaining vendor performance records, report tracking, and special research projects. Candidates should have analytical skills, computer skills, knowledge of field, organizational skills, personal interest in the field, research skills. Duration is 3–5 months. $10 per hour. ▶ *2 new media interns:* responsibilities include designing and updating magazine Internet sites. Candidates should have ability to work with others, computer skills, knowledge of field, plan to pursue career in field, self-motivation, written communication skills, familiarity with HTML; graphic design or new media majors a plus. Duration is 3–5 months. $10 per hour. ▶ *1–2 test kitchens interns:* responsibilities include preparing recipes for taste testing and photography. Candidates should have ability to work independently, ability to work with others, knowledge of field, culinary arts degree preferred. Duration is 8–10 weeks. $10 per hour. Open to college juniors, college seniors, recent college graduates, graduate students.
Benefits Job counseling, names of contacts, on-the-job training, opportunity to attend seminars/workshops, possible full-time

Southern Progress Corporation (continued)

employment, willing to complete paperwork for educational credit, willing to provide letters of recommendation, reimbursement of work-related travel expenses.

Contact Write, fax, or through World Wide Web site Holly Hughey, Student Intern Coordinator. Fax: 205-455-6750. No phone calls. In-person interview required. Applicants must submit a letter of interest, resume, letter of recommendation, design samples, at least 5 writing samples. Application deadline: February 15 for summer, June 15 for fall, September 15 for winter/spring. World Wide Web: http://www.southernprogress.com.

SURFACE MAGAZINE
70 Washington Street, #807
Brooklyn, New York 11201

General Information National lifestyle magazine exploring emerging trends in fashion, interiors, architecture, art, graphics, film, and music. Established in 1994. Number of employees: 15. Number of internship applications received each year: 200.

Internships Available ▶ *1–4 advertising/promotions interns:* responsibilities include updating and managing databases; conducting media research; planning and execution of promotional events. Candidates should have ability to work independently, computer skills, oral communication skills, self-motivation, writing skills. Duration is 3–6 months. Unpaid. Open to college freshmen, college sophomores, college juniors, college seniors, recent college graduates, graduate students. ▶ *1–2 editorial interns:* responsibilities include researching, developing, writing, and editing editorial content. Candidates should have ability to work independently, computer skills, editing skills, plan to pursue career in field, research skills, writing skills. Duration is 3–6 months. Unpaid. Open to college juniors, college seniors, recent college graduates, graduate students.

Benefits Formal training, on-the-job training, willing to act as a professional reference, willing to complete paperwork for educational credit, willing to provide letters of recommendation.

Contact Fax or e-mail Elizabeth Birkenbuel, Publisher's Assistant. Fax: 718-488-0651. E-mail: ebirkenbuel@surfacemag.com. No phone calls. In-person interview required. Applicants must submit a letter of interest, resume, three personal references. Application deadline: February 1 for spring, May 1 for summer, August 1 for fall, November 1 for winter.

TEACHER MAGAZINE
6935 Arlington Road, Suite 100
Bethesda, Maryland 20814-5281

General Information National magazine that covers K-12 education and reports on the teaching profession, school policy and culture, and the people who influence education. Established in 1989. Number of employees: 10. Unit of Editorial Projects in Education, Inc., Bethesda, Maryland. Number of internship applications received each year: 50.

Internships Available ▶ *1 editorial intern:* responsibilities include researching and writing "Calendar" section; writing short articles and sidebars; proofreading and fact-checking articles; and assisting staff with special projects. Candidates should have ability to work independently, editing skills, oral communication skills, research skills, writing skills, attention to detail. Duration is 12-15 weeks (15 hours per week). $6 per hour. Open to college sophomores, college juniors, college seniors, recent college graduates, graduate students, teachers. International applications accepted.

Benefits On-the-job training, willing to act as a professional reference, willing to complete paperwork for educational credit, opportunity to write and publish short articles.

Contact Write or e-mail Samantha Stainburn, Managing Editor. E-mail: sstain@epe.org. No phone calls. Telephone interview required. Applicants must submit a resume, three writing samples, cover letter. Application deadline: May 1 for summer, August 1 for fall, November 15 for spring. World Wide Web: http://www.teachermagazine.org.

THIEME
333 7th Avenue
New York, New York 10001

General Information Publisher of medical and scientific books and journals, as well as electronic products. Established in 1979. Number of employees: 35. Subsidiary of Georg Thieme Verlag, Stuttgart, Germany. Number of internship applications received each year: 500.

Internships Available ▶ *1–2 Internet interns:* responsibilities include Web site maintenance, Internet research, some trouble shooting. Candidates should have college courses in field, computer skills, knowledge of field, strong interpersonal skills. Duration is 10–26 weeks. $70 per week. ▶ *1–2 accounting interns:* responsibilities include budgeting, long-term planning, currency hedging, acquisitions, credit risk-management. Candidates should have analytical skills, college courses in field, computer skills, knowledge of field. Duration is 10–26 weeks. $70 per week. ▶ *1–2 editorial interns:* responsibilities include book planning, research, author relations, permissions, special projects. Candidates should have ability to work with others, computer skills, personal interest in the field, written communication skills. Duration is 10–26 weeks. $70 per week. ▶ *1–2 marketing interns:* responsibilities include medical advertising, promotional material, market research, direct mail, review copies. Candidates should have computer skills, oral communication skills, personal interest in the field, strong interpersonal skills, written communication skills. Duration is 10–26 weeks. $70 per week. ▶ *1–2 production interns:* responsibilities include book production from manuscript to finished book including copy editing, proofreading, correspondence with contributors, copying, faxing, and dealing with freelancers. Candidates should have computer skills, editing skills, oral communication skills, research skills, strong interpersonal skills, written communication skills. Duration is 10–26 weeks. $70 per week. ▶ *1–2 sales interns:* responsibilities include advance book information, planning and organizing medical exhibits, distributor relations. Candidates should have ability to work with others, computer skills, organizational skills, personal interest in the field. Duration is 10–26 weeks. $70 per week. Open to college juniors, college seniors, recent college graduates, graduate students, career changers. International applications accepted.

Benefits On-the-job training, willing to act as a professional reference, willing to complete paperwork for educational credit, willing to provide letters of recommendation, stipend to cover lunch and transportation to work.

Contact Write, fax, or e-mail Internship Coordinator. Fax: 212-947-1112. E-mail: intern@thieme.com. No phone calls. In-person interview recommended (telephone interview accepted). Applicants must submit a formal organization application, resume, list of 3 professional references. Applications are accepted continuously. World Wide Web: http://www.thieme.com.

TIKKUN MAGAZINE
2107 Van Ness Avenue, Suite 302
San Francisco, California 94109

General Information Bimonthly Jewish critique of politics, culture, and society; influence is not limited to the Jewish population. Established in 1986. Number of employees: 4. Unit of Institute for Labor and Mental Health, Oakland, California. Number of internship applications received each year: 30.

Internships Available ▶ *3–6 editorial, production, and publishing interns:* responsibilities include reading unsolicited manuscripts, writing evaluations and rejection letters, handling author correspondence, proofreading galleys, performing independent research project; assisting with production of magazine, soliciting advertising, organizing outside conferences, lectures, seminars, and teach-ins; assisting in office administration. Candidates should have ability to work independently, editing skills, office skills, oral communication skills, personal interest in the field, self-motivation, strong interpersonal skills, written communication skills. Duration is flexible; prefer a commitment of at least three months. Unpaid. Open to college freshmen, college sophomores, college juniors, college seniors, recent college graduates, graduate students, law students, career changers, individuals reentering the workforce. International applications accepted.

Benefits Job counseling, names of contacts, on-the-job training, possible full-time employment, willing to act as a professional reference, willing to complete paperwork for educational credit, willing to provide letters of recommendation, free books, free admission to local cultural events including films, lectures, and readings.
Contact Write, call, or e-mail Liat Weingart, Assistant Editor. Phone: 415-575-1200. Fax: 415-575-1434. E-mail: magazine@tikkun. org. In-person interview recommended (telephone interview accepted). Applicants must submit a letter of interest, resume. Applications are accepted continuously. World Wide Web: http://www.tikkun.org.

WASHINGTONIAN MAGAZINE
1828 L Street, NW, Suite 200
Washington, District of Columbia 20036

General Information General interest magazine that focuses on the people and issues of Washington, DC. Established in 1965. Number of employees: 60. Number of internship applications received each year: 250.
Internships Available ▶ *1–3 advertising/account executive interns:* responsibilities include phone sales and updating and researching ad files. Candidates should have ability to work independently, computer skills, office skills, oral communication skills, personal interest in the field, self-motivation, strong interpersonal skills, written communication skills. Duration is 3–5 months. Approximately $5 per hour (tax free). Open to undergraduates receiving college credit. ▶ *1–2 art interns:* responsibilities include assisting with production and in-house design assignments using PhotoShop and Quark Xpress. Candidates should have college courses in field, computer skills, oral communication skills, personal interest in the field, strong interpersonal skills. Duration is 2–3 months. Unpaid. Open to college freshmen, college sophomores, college juniors, college seniors, graduate students. ▶ *4 editorial/interns:* responsibilities include fact checking, research, and writing. Candidates should have ability to work independently, experience in the field, organizational skills, personal interest in the field, research skills, self-motivation, writing skills. Duration is 3–5 months. $6.15 per hour. Open to college freshmen, college sophomores, college juniors, college seniors, recent college graduates, graduate students, career changers. International applications accepted.
Benefits Names of contacts, opportunity to attend seminars/workshops, willing to act as a professional reference, willing to complete paperwork for educational credit, willing to provide letters of recommendation.
Contact Write, call, fax, or e-mail Cindy Rich, Internship Coordinator. Phone: 202-296-3600. Fax: 202-862-3526. E-mail: crich@washingtonian. com. In-person interview recommended (telephone interview accepted). Applicants must submit a letter of interest, resume, three writing samples. Application deadline: March 1 for summer positions, November 1 for January positions. World Wide Web: http://www.washingtonian.com.

WATERBURY REPUBLICAN-AMERICAN
389 Meadow Street
Waterbury, Connecticut 06702

General Information Newspaper publishing daily and Sunday editions. Established in 1844. Number of employees: 320. Number of internship applications received each year: 50.
Internships Available ▶ *1–2 advertising sales interns:* responsibilities include selling advertising to clients. Candidates should have ability to work independently, oral communication skills, plan to pursue career in field, self-motivation, strong interpersonal skills, written communication skills, must have own transportation. Duration is 2–3 months. Paid. ▶ *1–2 graphics designers:* responsibilities include creating advertisements for clients. Candidates should have ability to work independently, ability to work with others, college courses in field, computer skills, plan to pursue career in field, self-motivation, prior graphics course work/experience preferred; (Adobe Illustrator, other graphics software); multi-ad creator. Duration is 2–3 months. Paid. ▶ *1–2 photographers:* responsibilities include photographing news-related events and people. Candidates should have ability to work independently, ability to work with others, declared college major in field, experience in the field,

plan to pursue career in field. Duration is 2–4 months. Paid. ▶ *1–3 reporters:* responsibilities include collecting and reporting news. Candidates should have ability to work independently, computer skills, declared college major in field, oral communication skills, plan to pursue career in field, writing skills. Duration is 2–4 months. Paid. Open to college sophomores, college juniors, college seniors, graduate students.
Benefits On-the-job training, opportunity to attend seminars/workshops, possible full-time employment, willing to act as a professional reference, willing to complete paperwork for educational credit, willing to provide letters of recommendation.
Contact Write, fax, or e-mail Patricia D. Nagle, Personal Manager. Fax: 203-573-9432. E-mail: pnagle@rep-am.com. No phone calls. In-person interview required. Applicants must submit a formal organization application, letter of interest, resume, portfolio (if applicable). Applications are accepted continuously.

WEIDER PUBLICATIONS–MEN'S FITNESS MAGAZINE
21100 Erwin Street
Woodland Hills, California 91367

General Information National fitness magazine. Established in 1975. Number of employees: 260. Number of internship applications received each year: 75.
Internships Available ▶ *1–2 art interns:* responsibilities include working in the Art Department with art and photo assistants, helping to organize the art library, working with contributors, and assisting in the general monthly production cycle of the magazine. Candidates should have ability to work with others, college courses in field, computer skills, organizational skills, personal interest in the field, plan to pursue career in field, experience with Macs, PhotoShop, and Quark a plus. Duration is 3–4 months. Unpaid. Open to college freshmen, college sophomores, college juniors, college seniors, student must be receiving school credit for internship (preference given to students from Los Angeles area).
Benefits Possible full-time employment, willing to act as a professional reference, willing to complete paperwork for educational credit, willing to provide letters of recommendation.
Contact Fax or e-mail Charlie Knudtson, Art Assistant, 21100 Erwin Street, Woodland Hills, California 91367. Phone: 818-226-0105. Fax: 818-883-9286. E-mail: cknudtso@weiderpub.com. In-person interview recommended (telephone interview accepted). Applicants must submit a letter of interest, resume. Applications are accepted continuously. World Wide Web: http://www.mensfitness.com.

WILSON QUARTERLY
1 Woodrow Wilson Plaza, 1300 Pennsylvania Avenue, NW
Washington, District of Columbia 20004-3027

General Information General interest quarterly magazine focusing on humanities-related topics and providing a comprehensive survey of the latest scholarly research in a broad range of subject areas. Established in 1976. Number of employees: 6. Subsidiary of Woodrow Wilson International Center for Scholars, Washington, District of Columbia. Number of internship applications received each year: 200.
Internships Available ▶ *1–3 editorial interns:* responsibilities include fact checking, background and art research, phone work, and some basic office duties, including delivering packages and photocopying. Candidates should have ability to work independently, office skills, oral communication skills, organizational skills, research skills, written communication skills. Duration is 4–12 months. $400–$800 per month. Open to college sophomores, college juniors, college seniors, recent college graduates, graduate students.
Benefits Job counseling, names of contacts, willing to act as a professional reference, willing to complete paperwork for educational credit, willing to provide letters of recommendation, reimbursement of expenses related to editorial research.
Contact Write Mr. James Carman, Managing Editor. Applicants must submit a letter of interest, resume, three writing samples,

Wilson Quarterly (continued)

list of personal references. Application deadline: March 15 for summer, July 15 for fall, October 15 for spring. World Wide Web: http://www.wilsonquarterly.com.

WIRED MAGAZINE
520 Third Street, Third Floor
San Francisco, California 94107

General Information Magazine. Established in 1993. Number of employees: 80. Division of Conde Nast Publications, New York, New York. Number of internship applications received each year: 300.

Internships Available ▶ *1 editorial intern:* responsibilities include reporting articles for publication, administrative duties, and research. Candidates should have ability to work independently, analytical skills, computer skills, editing skills, knowledge of field, office skills, oral communication skills, organizational skills, personal interest in the field, research skills, self-motivation, strong interpersonal skills, writing skills. Duration is 4 months. $10 per hour. ▶ *1 products intern.* Duration is 4 months. $10 per hour. ▶ *1 research intern:* responsibilities include researching and fact checking articles in the magazine, story idea generation, and writing and reporting stories for publications. Candidates should have ability to work independently, ability to work with others, analytical skills, computer skills, editing skills, knowledge of field, office skills, organizational skills, personal interest in the field, research skills, self-motivation, writing skills. Duration is 4 months. $10 per hour. Open to recent college graduates, graduate students, individuals reentering the workforce. International applications accepted.

Benefits Meals at a cost, on-the-job training, possible full-time employment.

Contact Write or fax Jason Edwards, Research Editor. Fax: 415-276-5100. In-person interview required. Applicants must submit a letter of interest, resume, two personal references, professional references, 2-3 writing samples. Application deadline: February 1 for spring, June 1 for summer, October 1 for winter. World Wide Web: http://www.wired.com/wired.

WOMEN EXPRESS, INC.
PO Box 120-027
Boston, Massachusetts 02112-0027

General Information Publisher of *Teen Voices* and Teen Voices Online, a teen feminist magazine. Established in 1988. Number of employees: 11. Number of internship applications received each year: 200.

Internships Available ▶ *2–3 advertising interns:* responsibilities include researching leads; preparing letters and media kit; maintaining contacts and database; assisting in quarterly advertising drives; implementing advertising campaign and strategy. Candidates should have ability to work independently, college degree in related field, computer skills, experience in the field, knowledge of field, oral communication skills, organizational skills, research skills, self-motivation, written communication skills, sales experience (preferred); knowledge of ACT! helpful, but will train. Duration is 4-6 months (12-16 hours per week). Unpaid. Open to college freshmen, college sophomores, college juniors, college seniors, recent college graduates, graduate students, career changers, individuals reentering the workforce. ▶ *2–3 business management/human resources interns:* responsibilities include assisting in daily operation of organization; setting up and improving administrative systems; help recruiting volunteers and interns; managing hours compliance; coordinating staff and related events. Candidates should have ability to work independently, ability to work with others, college courses in field, computer skills, knowledge of field, office skills, oral communication skills, organizational skills, personal interest in the field, plan to pursue career in field, self-motivation, strong leadership ability, written communication skills, time management skills; initiative and high level of responsibility. Duration is 4-6 months (12-16 hours per week). Unpaid. Open to college freshmen, college sophomores, college juniors, college seniors, recent college graduates, graduate students, career changers, individuals reentering the workforce.

▶ *1–2 business/accounting interns:* responsibilities include assisting in financial oversight of Women Express; working with executive director and audit committee of Board of Directors to prepare expense reports; helping manage accounts payable and receivable; collections, deposits. Candidates should have ability to work independently, ability to work with others, college degree in related field, computer skills, declared college major in field, experience in the field, knowledge of field, office skills, oral communication skills, organizational skills, written communication skills, knowledge of Peachtree preferred but will train if necessary. Duration is 4-6 months (12-16 hours per week). Unpaid. Open to college juniors, college seniors, recent college graduates, graduate students, law students, career changers, individuals reentering the workforce. ▶ *2–3 circulation/marketing interns:* responsibilities include coordinating customer service, fulfillment of subscriptions and direct mail; helping conceptualize a renewal service and other ways to retain subscribers and attract new ones. Candidates should have ability to work independently, ability to work with others, computer skills, office skills, oral communication skills, organizational skills, research skills, self-motivation, written communication skills, knowledge of databases and postal system (helpful). Duration is 4-6 months (12-16 hours per week). Unpaid. Open to college freshmen, college sophomores, college juniors, college seniors, recent college graduates, graduate students, law students, career changers, individuals reentering the workforce. ▶ *2–3 editorial assistants:* responsibilities include working with managing editor to manage editorial process; arranging editorial meetings; ensuring deadlines are met; managing submissions; writing editorials; acting as a liaison to teen writers. Candidates should have ability to work independently, ability to work with others, computer skills, editing skills, knowledge of field, organizational skills, personal interest in the field, research skills, writing skills. Duration is 4-6 months (12-16 hours per week). ▶ *10–15 editorial mentors:* responsibilities include working directly with low-skilled teens on the teen editorial board as a mentor and resource; helping teens to research and write sections of the magazines; compiling resources; fact checking, content and development; communicating with writers. Candidates should have ability to work independently, editing skills, experience in the field, knowledge of field, oral communication skills, organizational skills, personal interest in the field, research skills, self-motivation, strong interpersonal skills, strong leadership ability, written communication skills, experience working with at-risk teens (helpful). Duration is 4-6 months (6-10 hours per week). Unpaid. Open to college sophomores, college juniors, college seniors, recent college graduates, graduate students, law students, career changers, individuals reentering the workforce. ▶ *1–2 graphic design interns:* responsibilities include designing materials including flyers, invitations, brochures, posters for Teen Voices, fund-raising and teen programs; special supplements in the magazine, program books. Candidates should have ability to work independently, college degree in related field, computer skills, declared college major in field, experience in the field, knowledge of field, organizational skills, personal interest in the field, plan to pursue career in field, Quark Express essential. Duration is 4-6 months (12-16 hours per week). Unpaid. Open to college freshmen, college sophomores, college juniors, college seniors, recent college graduates, graduate students, law students, career changers, individuals reentering the workforce. ▶ *1–2 public relations interns:* responsibilities include promoting WE/Teen Voices magazine on a local and national level; coordinating public relations for national and local media; writing press releases, attending press conferences; managing media contacts and database. Candidates should have ability to work independently, ability to work with others, experience in the field, oral communication skills, organizational skills, self-motivation, strong leadership ability, written communication skills. Duration is 4–6 months. Unpaid. Open to college juniors, college seniors, recent college graduates, graduate students, law students, career changers, individuals reentering the workforce. ▶ *1–2 publishing interns:* responsibilities include assisting in marketing Teen Voices to bookstores and consumers; researching advertising leads; assessing costs and benefits; writing copy for advertisements; manage a distribution and newsstand sales; working closely with distribution. Candidates should have ability to work independently, ability to work with others, analytical skills, knowledge of field, oral com-

munication skills, organizational skills, research skills, self-motivation, written communication skills, marketing, sales or publishing experience (preferred). Duration is 4-6 months (12-16 hours per week). Unpaid. Open to college freshmen, college sophomores, college juniors, college seniors, recent college graduates, graduate students, career changers, individuals reentering the workforce. ▶ *4–5 special events/fund-raising interns:* responsibilities include assisting with all fund-raising activities including foundation research, grant writing, donor management and special campaigns and events; working with fund-raising committee of the Board of Directors. Candidates should have analytical skills, experience in the field, knowledge of field, oral communication skills, organizational skills, research skills, self-motivation, strong leadership ability, written communication skills, professional presentation skills. Duration is 4-6 months (12-16 hours per week). Unpaid. Open to college freshmen, college sophomores, college juniors, college seniors, recent college graduates, graduate students, law students, career changers, individuals reentering the workforce. ▶ *1–2 teen programs interns:* responsibilities include working with and supervising high-risk adolescent girls in three programs; teaching life and job skills; working with families, logistics, transportation; scheduling training sessions; supporting mentors; providing crisis intervention. Candidates should have ability to work independently, experience in the field, knowledge of field, oral communication skills, organizational skills, self-motivation, strong interpersonal skills, strong leadership ability, written communication skills, Masters level social work (preferred), experience in working with teens strongly recommended. Duration is 4-6 months (12-16 hours per week). Unpaid. Open to college freshmen, college sophomores, college juniors, college seniors, recent college graduates, graduate students, individuals reentering the workforce. International applications accepted.
Benefits Names of contacts, on-the-job training, opportunity to attend seminars/workshops, possible full-time employment, willing to act as a professional reference, willing to complete paperwork for educational credit, willing to provide letters of recommendation, assistance in locating housing.
Contact Write, call, fax, e-mail, or through World Wide Web site Sreevidya Purushothaman, Volunteer Coordinator, 515 Washington Street, 6th Floor, Boston, Massachusetts 02111. Phone: 617-426-5505. Fax: 617-426-5577. E-mail: womenexp@teenvioces.com. In-person interview recommended (telephone interview accepted). Applicants must submit a letter of interest, resume, portfolio for graphic design position; writing sample for editorial position. Applications are accepted continuously. World Wide Web: http://www.teenvoices.com.

RADIO BROADCASTING

KEUN/KJJB RADIO
330 West Laurel Avenue
Eunice, Louisiana 70535

General Information Radio and cable television programming. Established in 1952. Number of employees: 10. Number of internship applications received each year: 5.
Internships Available ▶ *1 intern:* responsibilities include radio work and public relations. Candidates should have ability to work independently, computer skills, plan to pursue career in field, self-motivation, writing skills. Duration is 3–12 months. Unpaid. Open to college freshmen, college sophomores, college juniors, college seniors, recent college graduates, graduate students, individuals reentering the workforce. International applications accepted.
Benefits Job counseling, names of contacts, opportunity to attend seminars/workshops, possible full-time employment, willing to complete paperwork for educational credit, willing to provide letters of recommendation.
Contact Write, fax, or e-mail Mr. Karl Rene De Rouen, President and General Manager. Fax: 337-457-3081. E-mail: karl@keunworldwide.com. No phone calls. Applicants must submit a

formal organization application, resume. Application deadline: 6 months prior to start of internship. World Wide Web: http://www.keunworldwide.com.

KFAN RADIO
7900 Xerxes Avenue South, Suite 102
Minneapolis, Minnesota 55431

General Information All sports-talk station in the Twin Cities and surrounding areas. Established in 1991. Number of employees: 300. Subsidiary of Clear Channel Communications, San Antonio, Texas. Number of internship applications received each year: 50.
Internships Available ▶ *10 promotions assistants:* responsibilities include working with programming and on-air talent, live remotes, broadcasts, contesting/merchandising, public relations, client relations, event planning and implementation, and writing opportunities. Candidates should have ability to work independently, ability to work with others, computer skills, office skills, oral communication skills, organizational skills, personal interest in the field, self-motivation, strong leadership ability. Duration is January to May; May to August; August to December. Unpaid. Open to high school students, college freshmen, college sophomores, college juniors, college seniors, recent college graduates, must be working for academic credit. International applications accepted.
Benefits Names of contacts, on-the-job training, opportunity to attend seminars/workshops, possible full-time employment, travel reimbursement, willing to act as a professional reference, willing to complete paperwork for educational credit, willing to provide letters of recommendation.
Contact Write, call, fax, e-mail, or through World Wide Web site Jeremy Stender, Promotions Coordinator. Phone: 952-820-4314. Fax: 952-820-4241. E-mail: jeremystender@clearchannel.com. Applicants must submit a letter of interest, resume. Applications are accepted continuously. World Wide Web: http://www.kfan.com.

KJNP AM-FM RADIO-TV
2501 Mission Road, PO Box 56359
North Pole, Alaska 99705-1359

General Information Christian radio and television station spreading the gospel of Jesus Christ throughout Alaska and the Northern Hemisphere. Established in 1967. Unit of Evangelistic Missionary Fellowship, Lakewood, Colorado. Number of internship applications received each year: 4.
Internships Available ▶ *1 TV technician:* responsibilities include taking meter readings on transmitter; airing prerecorded programs (entails cueing and rewinding tapes before airing) directly off the satellite, commercials, public service announcements, and interlude tapes between programs; maintaining TV log; and monitoring all equipment in control room during air time. Candidates should have ability to work independently, ability to work with others, self-motivation. Duration is minimum of 3 months. Unpaid. Open to recent high school graduates, college freshmen, college sophomores, college juniors, college seniors, recent college graduates, graduate students, law students, career changers, individuals reentering the workforce. ▶ *1 camera operator:* responsibilities include operating cameras for live public service format program, preparing set to go on the air, escorting guests to the set, and helping out in other areas of the station. Candidates should have ability to work with others. Duration is flexible. Unpaid. Open to high school students, recent high school graduates, college freshmen, college sophomores, college juniors, college seniors, recent college graduates, graduate students, law students, career changers, individuals reentering the workforce. ▶ *Engineering interns:* responsibilities include maintaining electronic equipment and calibrating transmitters. Candidates should have ability to work independently, ability to work with others, self-motivation. Duration is flexible. Unpaid. Open to recent high school graduates, college freshmen, college sophomores, college juniors, college seniors, recent college graduates, graduate students, law students, career changers, individuals reentering the workforce. ▶ *Maintenance interns:* responsibilities include maintaining grounds and buildings, cutting wood, removing snow in winter, and some carpentry work. Candidates should have ability to work independently,

KJNP AM-FM Radio-TV (continued)

ability to work with others, self-motivation. Duration is flexible. Unpaid. Open to high school students, recent high school graduates, college freshmen, college sophomores, college juniors, college seniors, recent college graduates, graduate students, law students, career changers, individuals reentering the workforce. ▶ *1 radio technician:* responsibilities include making sure stations are on the air, following and keeping logs for both the AM and FM stations, answering the lobby telephone, and helping in other areas of the station. Candidates should have ability to work with others, oral communication skills. Duration is 1 year. Unpaid. Open to high school seniors, recent high school graduates, college freshmen, college sophomores, college juniors, college seniors, recent college graduates, graduate students, law students, career changers, individuals reentering the workforce. ▶ *1 receptionist intern:* responsibilities include answering 5 incoming telephone lines and intercom calls, greeting guests and tourists, directing calls to proper departments, monitoring AM/FM/TV, answering 2-way system, keeping coffee and hot water supplied, keeping lobby area clean, typing Trapline Chatter messages that are aired over radio, and performing office work. Candidates should have ability to work with others, oral communication skills, self-motivation, written communication skills. Duration is flexible. Unpaid. Open to recent high school graduates, college freshmen, college sophomores, college juniors, college seniors, recent college graduates, graduate students, law students, career changers, individuals reentering the workforce. International applications accepted.

Benefits Free housing, on-the-job training, willing to complete paperwork for educational credit, willing to provide letters of recommendation.

Contact Write, call, fax, or e-mail Ms. Julie K. Beaver, Secretary to President. Phone: 907-488-2216. Fax: 907-488-5246. E-mail: kjnp@mosquitonet.com. Applicants must submit a formal organization application, letter of interest, three professional or personal references. Applications are accepted continuously. World Wide Web: http://www.mosquitonet.com/~kjnp.

NEWS RADIO WGST
1819 Peachtree Road, Suite 700
Atlanta, Georgia 30309

General Information News/talk radio station. Established in 1929. Number of employees: 100. Unit of Sunrise Television Corporation, St. Petersburg, Florida. Number of internship applications received each year: 10.

Internships Available ▶ *1 news department intern:* responsibilities include taking in network feeds; carting, labeling, and channeling the feeds appropriately; taking in reporter feeds; making police and fire checks; pursuing news tape; and writing news copy. Candidates should have organizational skills, news writing skills, availability for work odd hours. Duration is 1 semester. Unpaid. ▶ *2–3 programming department interns:* responsibilities include assisting on remote broadcasts, dubbing public service announcements, helping to disseminate programming information to other departments, and screening calls for talk show. Candidates should have knowledge of field, oral communication skills, research skills, self-motivation, writing skills. Duration is 3 months. Unpaid. ▶ *2–3 promotions department interns:* responsibilities include writing public service and promotional announcements, working on database projects, contacting contest winners, and assisting with weekend and evening remote broadcasts. Candidates should have organizational skills. Duration is 3 months. Unpaid. Open to high school students, recent high school graduates, college freshmen, college sophomores, college juniors, college seniors, recent college graduates, graduate students. International applications accepted.

Benefits Possible full-time employment, willing to complete paperwork for educational credit, willing to provide letters of recommendation.

Contact Write or fax Paul Mann, News Director. Fax: 404-367-6401. No phone calls. In-person interview required. Applicants must submit a letter of interest, resume. Applications are accepted continuously. World Wide Web: http://www.wgst.com.

93XRT
4949 West Belmont Avenue
Chicago, Illinois 60641

General Information Major commercial radio stations. Established in 1972. Number of employees: 130. Number of internship applications received each year: 200.

Internships Available ▶ *5 FM93 XRT programming department intern:* responsibilities include maintaining the record library, maintaining weekly trade publications, and assisting in special events. Candidates should have ability to work independently, college courses in field, computer skills, office skills, oral communication skills, research skills, self-motivation, strong interpersonal skills, written communication skills. Duration is flexible. Unpaid. ▶ *5 promotions department interns:* responsibilities include gaining experience in promotions, marketing, public relations, and special event management. Candidates should have college courses in field, oral communication skills, strong interpersonal skills, written communication skills. Duration is flexible. Unpaid. ▶ *1–3 sales interns:* responsibilities include gaining experience in all areas of sales and marketing; accompanying reps on sales calls; general office duties. Candidates should have computer skills, oral communication skills, organizational skills, self-motivation, strong interpersonal skills, written communication skills. Duration is 3 months. Unpaid. Open to college freshmen, college sophomores, college juniors, college seniors. International applications accepted.

Benefits Names of contacts, on-the-job training, possible full-time employment, willing to complete paperwork for educational credit, willing to provide letters of recommendation.

Contact Write, fax, e-mail, or through World Wide Web site Jennifer Manyluk, Programming Assistant. Fax: 773-427-3543. E-mail: manyluk@wxrtwscr.cbs.com. No phone calls. In-person interview recommended (telephone interview accepted). Applicants must submit a letter of interest, resume. Application deadline: March 15 for summer, August 1 for fall, November 1 for winter. World Wide Web: http://www.wxrt.com.

SHADOW BROADCAST SERVICES
201 Route 17 North, 9th Floor
Rutherford, New Jersey 07070

General Information Traffic, news, sports, weather, and programming services. Established in 1977. Number of employees: 100. Division of Westwood One Radio Network, Mutual Broadcasting System, Arlington, Virginia. Number of internship applications received each year: 30.

Internships Available ▶ *7 sports interns:* responsibilities include keeping up on sports scores and stats, faxing stations, and informing announcers of sports information. Candidates should have ability to work independently, ability to work with others, oral communication skills, personal interest in the field, writing skills. Duration is 6-week program throughout the year. $50 per duration of internship. ▶ *7–14 traffic interns:* responsibilities include phone calls, faxing, writing, collecting information, and listening for information. Candidates should have ability to work independently, oral communication skills, personal interest in the field, strong interpersonal skills. Duration is 1 semester. $50 per duration of internship. Open to college freshmen, college sophomores, college juniors, college seniors, graduate students. International applications accepted.

Benefits Possible full-time employment, willing to act as a professional reference, willing to complete paperwork for educational credit, willing to provide letters of recommendation, $50 one-time fee at end of internship.

Contact Write, call, fax, or e-mail Sal Cowan, Intern Coordinator, 201 Route 17 North, 9th Floor, Rutherford, New Jersey 07070. Phone: 201-939-1888. Fax: 201-939-1043. E-mail: sal_cowan@ metronetworks.com. In-person interview required. Applicants must submit a resume. Application deadline: May 1 for summer, December 1 for winter/spring.

WALK FM/AM
66 Colonial Drive
Patchogue, New York 11772

General Information Commercial FM/AM radio station offering programming to Long Island's adult audiences. Established in 1951. Number of employees: 40. Unit of Clear Channel Communications, Dallas, Texas. Number of internship applications received each year: 30.

Internships Available ▶ *1–2 engineering department interns:* responsibilities include assisting the chief engineer and ITM manager with studio, station, and computer operations. Candidates should have ability to work independently, ability to work with others, analytical skills, college courses in field, computer skills, office skills, oral communication skills, organizational skills, personal interest in the field, plan to pursue career in field, self-motivation. Duration is 1 semester. Unpaid. Open to college freshmen, college sophomores, college juniors, college seniors, must receive academic credit for internship. ▶ *2–5 news department interns:* responsibilities include assisting with information gathering, news writing, and traffic coordination. Candidates should have ability to work independently, ability to work with others, analytical skills, computer skills, editing skills, knowledge of field, oral communication skills, organizational skills, personal interest in the field, research skills, self-motivation, writing skills. Duration is 8–12 weeks. Unpaid. Open to college freshmen, college sophomores, college juniors, college seniors, graduate students, law students, must receive academic credit for internship. ▶ *2–4 programming interns:* responsibilities include assisting the program director on a daily basis with music, scheduling, airshift scheduling, contesting, and cross-promotions. Candidates should have ability to work independently, ability to work with others, computer skills, editing skills, office skills, oral communication skills, organizational skills, plan to pursue career in field, self-motivation, writing skills. Duration is 1 semester. Unpaid. Open to high school students, recent high school graduates, college freshmen, college sophomores, college juniors, college seniors, must receive academic credit for internship. ▶ *2–12 promotion department interns:* responsibilities include assisting at station and with public appearances, meeting and greeting, and helping set up and breakdown sound equipment. Candidates should have oral communication skills, personal interest in the field, self-motivation, strong interpersonal skills, clean personal appearance; must be available to work weekends. Duration is 6–8 weeks. Unpaid. Open to college freshmen, college sophomores, college juniors, college seniors, graduate students, law students, must receive academic credit for internship. International applications accepted.

Benefits Formal training, job counseling, names of contacts, on-the-job training, possible full-time employment, willing to act as a professional reference, willing to complete paperwork for educational credit, willing to provide letters of recommendation.

Contact Write, call, fax, e-mail, or through World Wide Web site Bill Terry, Intern Coordinator, PO Box 230, Patchogue, New York 11772. Phone: 631-475-5200. Fax: 631-475-9016. E-mail: bterry@walkradio.com. In-person interview recommended (telephone interview accepted). Applicants must submit a resume. Application deadline: April 30 for summer; continuous for positions during academic year. World Wide Web: http://www.WALKRADIO.com.

WCEV-AM
5356 West Belmont Avenue
Chicago, Illinois 60641

General Information Multi-ethnic radio station broadcasting in 12 languages. Established in 1979. Number of internship applications received each year: 30.

Internships Available ▶ *1 programming intern:* responsibilities include performing on-air duties in English and providing general assistance in programming department. Candidates should have computer skills, oral communication skills, organizational skills, personal interest in the field, strong interpersonal skills, written communication skills. Duration is 3 months. Unpaid. Open to college freshmen, college sophomores, college juniors, college seniors, recent college graduates, graduate students, law students, career changers. ▶ *1 sales intern:* responsibilities include working with station sales manager on campaigns and station promotions. Candidates should have oral communication skills, personal interest in the field, strong interpersonal skills, written communication skills. Duration is 3 months. Unpaid. Open to college juniors, college seniors, recent college graduates, graduate students, law students, career changers. International applications accepted.

Benefits Job counseling, on-the-job training, possible full-time employment, willing to act as a professional reference, willing to complete paperwork for educational credit, willing to provide letters of recommendation.

Contact Write or call Ms. Lucyna Migala, Vice President and Program Director. Phone: 773-282-6700. In-person interview required. Applicants must submit a resume. Applications are accepted continuously.

WCTC-AM/WMGQ-FM
78 Veronica Avenue
Somerset, New Jersey 08873

General Information WCTC-AM is a news/talk station serving the central New Jersey area. WMGQ-FM is a stereo music station featuring adult contemporary programming. Established in 1946. Number of employees: 50. Unit of Greater Media, Inc., New Brunswick, New Jersey. Number of internship applications received each year: 40.

Internships Available ▶ *10–15 marketing and promotions interns:* responsibilities include writing marketing proposals and attending events. Candidates should have ability to work independently, office skills, oral communication skills, organizational skills, self-motivation, strong interpersonal skills, written communication skills. Duration is flexible (need summer interns). Unpaid. Open to recent high school graduates, college freshmen, college sophomores, college juniors, college seniors, recent college graduates. ▶ *1 news reporter:* responsibilities include gathering and writing news stories. Duration is one semester (24 hours per week). Unpaid. Open to college juniors, college seniors, recent college graduates, graduate students.

Benefits Formal training, job counseling, names of contacts, possible full-time employment, willing to act as a professional reference, willing to complete paperwork for educational credit, willing to provide letters of recommendation.

Contact Write, call, fax, or e-mail Cheryl Carlisle, Director of Marketing. Phone: 732-249-2600. Fax: 732-249-9010. E-mail: ccarlisle@greaterrvb.com. In-person interview required. Applicants must submit a letter of interest, resume. Applications are accepted continuously.

THE WESTWOOD ONE RADIO NETWORKS
524 West 57th Street, 1st Floor
New York, New York 10019

General Information America's largest radio network providing over 150 news, sports, music, talk, and entertainment programs; features; live events; 24-hour formats; and Shadow Broadcast services. Number of employees: 125. Number of internship applications received each year: 20.

Internships Available ▶ *2–4 artist relations/programming interns:* responsibilities include working in the programming and production departments; contacting artist representatives, including publicists and record company personnel; researching the artists being interviewed, including assembling and reviewing artist biographies and other source material. Candidates should have office skills, oral communication skills, organizational skills, self-motivation, strong interpersonal skills, written communication skills, broadcast experience in radio/entertainment (helpful). Unpaid. Open to college freshmen, college sophomores, college juniors, college seniors, must be earning academic credit.

Benefits Job counseling, names of contacts, possible full-time employment, willing to act as a professional reference, willing to complete paperwork for educational credit, willing to provide letters of recommendation, $50 stipend.

Contact Write, call, or fax Pam Green, Senior Director of Artist Relations. Phone: 212-975-2106. Fax: 212-262-3960. In-person interview required. Applicants must submit a letter of interest, resume. Applications are accepted continuously.

WGN-RADIO 720
435 North Michigan Avenue
Chicago, Illinois 60611

General Information Radio station featuring a progressive and flexible full-service news/talk and sports format. Established in 1924. Number of employees: 120. Unit of Tribune Company, Chicago, Illinois. Number of internship applications received each year: 2,000.

Internships Available ▶ *2 news interns:* responsibilities include answering phones, researching and writing stories, taking feeds, and assisting with major event coverage. Candidates should have analytical skills, computer skills, editing skills, plan to pursue career in field, self-motivation, written communication skills. Duration is 14 weeks. $75 per week. Open to college sophomores, college juniors, college seniors, recent college graduates, graduate students, law students, career changers, individuals reentering the workforce. ▶ *2 programming interns:* responsibilities include booking guests, generating ideas, screening phones, producing audio, editing, completing promotional and programming paperwork, maintaining computerized music library, and completing special projects. Candidates should have editing skills, experience in the field, plan to pursue career in field, research skills, strong interpersonal skills, written communication skills. Duration is 14 weeks. $75 per week. Open to college sophomores, college juniors, college seniors, recent college graduates, graduate students, law students, career changers, individuals reentering the workforce. ▶ *1 promotion intern:* responsibilities include preparing weekly press releases, writing and scheduling promotional announcements, working promotional events, writing for monthly listener newsletter, and compiling and editing community calendar newspaper column. Candidates should have ability to work independently, computer skills, knowledge of field, plan to pursue career in field, strong interpersonal skills, writing skills. Duration is 14 weeks. $75 per week. Open to college sophomores, college juniors, college seniors, recent college graduates, graduate students, career changers, individuals reentering the workforce. ▶ *1 sales intern:* responsibilities include preparation of sales presentations, training in strategies, prospecting, follow-up, promotional/marketing activities, and research. Candidates should have computer skills, oral communication skills, plan to pursue career in field, research skills, self-motivation, strong interpersonal skills. Duration is 14 weeks. Unpaid. Open to college seniors, recent college graduates, graduate students, law students, career changers, individuals reentering the workforce. ▶ *1 sports intern:* responsibilities include covering sports events; answering phones; and researching, writing, and producing stories. Candidates should have editing skills, experience in the field, plan to pursue career in field, research skills, self-motivation, strong interpersonal skills. Duration is 14 weeks. $75 per week. Open to college sophomores, college juniors, college seniors, recent college graduates, graduate students, law students, career changers, individuals reentering the workforce. International applications accepted.

Benefits Formal training, job counseling, names of contacts, opportunity to attend seminars/workshops, possible full-time employment, willing to act as a professional reference, willing to complete paperwork for educational credit, willing to provide letters of recommendation.

Contact Write, fax, e-mail, or through World Wide Web site Kurt Vanderah, Producer, 435 North Michigan, Chicago, Illinois 60611. Fax: 312-222-3072. E-mail: kurtvanderah@wgnradio.com. No phone calls. In-person interview required. Applicants must submit a letter of interest, resume. Application deadline: January 1 for spring, April 1 for summer, July 1 for fall, October 1 for winter. World Wide Web: http://wgnradio.com.

WJXA 92.9 FM/WMAK 96.3 FM
504 Rosedale Avenue
Nashville, Tennessee 37211

General Information Commercial radio station featuring soft rock and oldies music. Established in 1948. Number of employees: 50. Division of South Central Communications, Evansville, Indiana. Number of internship applications received each year: 50.

Internships Available ▶ *2 accounting/general business interns:* responsibilities include working on spreadsheets, filing, accounts payable, accounts receivable, and word processing. Duration is flexible. Unpaid. Open to recent high school graduates, college freshmen, career changers. ▶ *2 promotions interns:* responsibilities include assisting promotions director with internal and external sales promotions and station-involved events. Candidates should have ability to work with others, oral communication skills, personal interest in the field, self-motivation, written communication skills. Duration is flexible. Unpaid. Must be enrolled in credit-bearing program. ▶ *2 retail marketing interns:* responsibilities include assisting retail marketing director. Candidates should have ability to work independently, ability to work with others, computer skills, editing skills, oral communication skills, personal interest in the field, research skills, written communication skills. Unpaid. International applications accepted.

Benefits Names of contacts, on-the-job training, possible full-time employment, willing to complete paperwork for educational credit, willing to provide letters of recommendation.

Contact Write Sarah Robison, Business Manager, PO Box 40596, Nashville, Tennessee 37204. Fax: 615-259-4594. No phone calls. In-person interview recommended (telephone interview accepted). Applicants must submit a formal organization application, resume, writing sample, two personal references, two letters of recommendation, evidence of enrollment in credit-bearing program. Applications are accepted continuously.

WKXL–AM/FM RADIO AND WOTX 102.3 FM
37 Redington Road, PO Box 875
Concord, New Hampshire 03302-0875

General Information Commercial radio stations with full-service format serving the over-30 audience in the capital city region of south central New Hampshire with a heavy emphasis on news, talk, sports, and community affairs. Established in 1946. Number of employees: 10. Unit of Vox Radio Group, Claremont, New Hampshire.

Internships Available ▶ *1 news department intern:* responsibilities include assisting in covering, writing, editing, and rewriting local and state news. Candidates should have ability to work with others, college courses in field, oral communication skills, personal interest in the field, writing skills. Duration is 3 months minimum. Unpaid. ▶ *1 sales department intern:* responsibilities include assisting sales manager with sales, research, sales service, and promotions. Candidates should have oral communication skills, plan to pursue career in field, self-motivation, strong interpersonal skills, written communication skills, major in communications, marketing or business. Duration is 3 months minimum. Unpaid. Open to college sophomores, college juniors, college seniors, recent college graduates, graduate students.

Benefits Job counseling, names of contacts, on-the-job training, willing to complete paperwork for educational credit, willing to provide letters of recommendation.

Contact Write, fax, e-mail, or through World Wide Web site Bob Lipman. Fax: 603-224-6404. E-mail: wkxl@conknet.com. No phone calls. In-person interview required. Applicants must submit a letter of interest, resume, two letters of recommendation. Applications are accepted continuously.

WMMR-FM
1 Bala Plaza
Bala-Cynwyd, Pennsylvania 19004

General Information Album-oriented rock station providing entertainment, music, news, and public affairs programming to eastern Pennsylvania, New Jersey, and Delaware. Established in 1968. Number of employees: 45. Unit of Greater Media, Inc., New Brunswick, New Jersey. Number of internship applications received each year: 200.

Internships Available ▶ *5–7 programming/promotions interns:* responsibilities include pulling and filing music, assisting the traffic and continuity department, answering correspondence, handling phone requests and giveaways, and preparing broadcast packs for remote broadcasts. Candidates should have ability to work independently, computer skills, office skills, oral communication

skills, self-motivation, strong interpersonal skills. Duration is flexible. Unpaid. Open to individuals receiving college credit.
Benefits Names of contacts, possible full-time employment, willing to complete paperwork for educational credit, willing to provide letters of recommendation.
Contact Write, call, fax, or e-mail Mike von Flotow, Intern Coordinator. Phone: 610-771-9752. Fax: 610-771-9710. E-mail: djs@wmmr.com. In-person interview required. Applicants must submit a letter of interest, resume. Applications are accepted continuously. World Wide Web: http://www.wmmr.com.

WOPP-AM
1101 Cameron Road
Opp, Alabama 36467

General Information Commercial radio station broadcasting music, news, weather, and sports. Established in 1980. Number of employees: 9. Number of internship applications received each year: 20.
Internships Available ▶ *2 news interns:* responsibilities include gathering news. Candidates should have computer skills, oral communication skills, plan to pursue career in field, research skills, strong interpersonal skills, written communication skills. Duration is 3 months. Unpaid. ▶ *1 production intern:* responsibilities include producing promos and some commercials. Candidates should have ability to work independently, computer skills, editing skills, oral communication skills, personal interest in the field, writing skills. Unpaid. ▶ *1 sales intern:* responsibilities include selling and writing ads. Candidates should have knowledge of field, office skills, plan to pursue career in field, self-motivation, writing skills. Commission of 25%. Open to college seniors. International applications accepted.
Benefits On-the-job training, opportunity to attend seminars/workshops, willing to act as a professional reference, willing to complete paperwork for educational credit, willing to provide letters of recommendation, sales interns earn commission and are reimbursed gas money.
Contact Write, fax, or e-mail Mr. Robert H. Boothe, General Manager. Fax: 334-493-4546. E-mail: wopp@wopp.com. No phone calls. Applicants must submit a resume, four personal references. Applications are accepted continuously. World Wide Web: http://www.wopp.com.

WOR RADIO
1440 Broadway
New York, New York 10018

General Information Radio station. Established in 1989. Number of employees: 150. Division of Buckley Broadcasting, Greenwich, Connecticut. Number of internship applications received each year: 50.
Internships Available ▶ *8–10 radio station interns:* responsibilities include assisting station personnel with hands-on jobs in any of the following departments: programming, engineering, or marketing. Candidates should have college courses in field, knowledge of field, self-motivation, strong interpersonal skills, writing skills. Duration is 1 semester (requires 2 full days per week in fall and spring semesters and 3 full days per week in summer). $10 per day. Open to college juniors, college seniors.
Benefits Opportunity to attend seminars/workshops, possible full-time employment, willing to act as a professional reference, willing to complete paperwork for educational credit, willing to provide letters of recommendation.
Contact Write, call, fax, or e-mail Ms. Weleskie Dias, Internship Coordinator. Phone: 212-642-4538. Fax: 212-642-4486. E-mail: wdias@wor710.com. In-person interview required. Applicants must submit a letter of interest, resume. Applications are accepted continuously. World Wide Web: http://www.wor710.com.

WRQX FM MIX 107.3
4400 Jenifer Street, NW
Washington, District of Columbia 20015

General Information Organization that includes three radio stations. WRQX-FM is an adult contemporary station; WJZW-FM is a jazz station; WMAL-AM is a major market news station featur-

ing news, talk, weather, and traffic reporting. Established in 1990. Number of employees: 150. Division of Disney–ABC, Inc., New York, New York. Number of internship applications received each year: 20.
Internships Available ▶ *2–3 advertising sales interns:* responsibilities include assisting with proposals, researching clients, organizing and producing proposals, and accompanying sales staff on presentations. Candidates should have ability to work independently, computer skills, office skills, oral communication skills, strong interpersonal skills, written communication skills. Duration is 1 semester. Unpaid. Open to college juniors, college seniors. ▶ *1–3 marketing/promotion interns:* responsibilities include coordinating contests, assisting with the execution of promotions, researching promotional opportunities, and attending promotions. Candidates should have ability to work independently, computer skills, office skills, oral communication skills, organizational skills, personal interest in the field, plan to pursue career in field, self-motivation, strong interpersonal skills. Duration is 1 semester. Unpaid. Open to college juniors, college seniors. ▶ *2–3 morning show interns:* responsibilities include helping the morning show producer with day-to-day operations; must be available from 5:30 a.m. to at least 10:00 a.m. Candidates should have ability to work with others, college courses in field, office skills, oral communication skills, organizational skills, plan to pursue career in field. Duration is 1 semester. Unpaid. Open to college juniors, college seniors, graduate students. ▶ *2–3 news interns:* responsibilities include operating newsroom computer system, conducting research and story checks, performing telephone interviews, and typing. Candidates should have ability to work independently, computer skills, editing skills, research skills, strong interpersonal skills, written communication skills. Duration is 1 semester. Unpaid. Open to college juniors, college seniors. International applications accepted.
Benefits Names of contacts, possible full-time employment, willing to act as a professional reference, willing to complete paperwork for educational credit.
Contact Write, call, fax, e-mail, or through World Wide Web site Renee Sharrow, Promotion and Marketing Assistant. Phone: 202-895-2405. Fax: 202-686-3070. E-mail: renee.l.sharrow@abc.com. In-person interview required. Applicants must submit a formal organization application, letter of interest, resume, two letters of recommendation, example of work (for WMAL position). Applications are accepted continuously. World Wide Web: http://www.mix1073FM.com.

SOFTWARE PUBLISHERS

ELECTRONIC ARTS
209 Redwood Shores Parkway
Redwood City, California 94065-1175

General Information Interactive entertainment software company. Established in 1982. Number of internship applications received each year: 1,000.
Internships Available ▶ *6–12 computer graphic artists:* responsibilities include producing bit map graphics, 3D shapes, and computer animation by creating new art and/or retouching existing art. Candidates should have ability to work with others, college courses in field, computer skills, knowledge of field, self-motivation, knowledge of 3D graphics programs. Duration is 3 months for summer interns; 6 months for co-ops. $2050–$2306.25 per month. Open to college sophomores, college juniors, college seniors, graduate students. ▶ *2 online developers.* Candidates should have knowledge of field, plan to pursue career in field, self-motivation, strong interpersonal skills, knowledge of JAVA, HTML, JAVA Script, PERL, and CGI. Duration is 3 months for summer interns; 6 months for co-ops. $2562.50–$2989.58 per month. Open to college freshmen, college sophomores, college juniors, college seniors, recent college graduates. ▶ *15–25 software engineers:* responsibilities include programming specific features into the game; testing, debugging, and documenting code contributions. Candidates should have ability to work with others, analytical skills, college courses in field, computer skills, plan to pursue career in field,

Electronic Arts (continued)

knowledge of C and C++, gaming industry experience. Duration is 3 months for summer interns, 6 months for co-ops. $2562.50–$2989.58 per month. Open to college sophomores, college juniors, college seniors, graduate students, those with one year remaining in school.

Benefits On-the-job training, opportunity to attend seminars/workshops, willing to act as a professional reference, willing to complete paperwork for educational credit, willing to provide letters of recommendation, mandated disability plan, health club membership, housing stipend, reimbursement for bike and helmet.

Contact E-mail or through World Wide Web site Anita Stokes, University Relations Manager, 209 Redwood Shores Parkway, Redwood City, California 94065-1175. E-mail: interns@ea.com. In-person interview recommended (telephone interview accepted). Applicants must submit a resume, portfolio, additional requirements located on Web site. Application deadline: February 28 for summer. World Wide Web: http://www.jobs.ea.com.

EMC CORPORATION
9 Technology Drive
Westboro, Massachusetts 01580

General Information Major supplier of storage and enterprise computing solutions; products include CLARiiON full fiber channel storage systems, high-end NT and UNIX- based AViiON servers, and related software and services. Established in 1968. Number of employees: 19,000. Number of internship applications received each year: 3,000.

Internships Available ▶ *5–10 engineering co-ops:* responsibilities include code and test development and expanding product's compatibility with various operating systems running on AViiON hardware. Candidates should have ability to work independently, analytical skills, college courses in field, computer skills, knowledge of field, oral communication skills, strong interpersonal skills. Duration is 3–6 months. $14–$35 per hour. Open to college sophomores, college juniors, college seniors, recent college graduates, graduate students. ▶ *2–4 firmware development interns:* responsibilities include developing NT qualification test plans, automating firmware qualification to expedite process, integrating test process with Data General/UX and/or NT based application, and developing firmware for integration testing on new PCI controllers. Candidates should have ability to work independently, analytical skills, college courses in field, computer skills, knowledge of field, oral communication skills, strong interpersonal skills. Duration is 3–6 months. $14–$35 per hour. Open to college sophomores, college juniors, college seniors, recent college graduates, graduate students. ▶ *1–3 mechanical engineering co-ops:* responsibilities include using 3D CAD to design various casting, plastics, and sheet metal parts; tasks include thermal and structural analysis to ensure design integrity, and engineering tests and prototype builds. Candidates should have ability to work with others, analytical skills, college courses in field, computer skills, knowledge of field, office skills, oral communication skills, personal interest in the field, plan to pursue career in field, self-motivation, written communication skills. Duration is 6 months. $14–$35 per hour. Open to college sophomores, college juniors, college seniors. ▶ *3–7 software development interns:* responsibilities include working on projects involving coding, testing, Web page development, and network management; position located at Research Triangle Park, NC. Candidates should have ability to work independently, ability to work with others, analytical skills, college courses in field, computer skills, knowledge of field, oral communication skills, plan to pursue career in field. Duration is 3–6 months. $14–$35 per hour. Open to college sophomores, college juniors, college seniors, recent college graduates, graduate students. ▶ *2–4 software quality assurance interns:* responsibilities include integrating a variety of hardware and software. Candidates should have ability to work independently, college courses in field, computer skills, knowledge of field, strong interpersonal skills. Duration is 3–6 months. $14–$35 per hour. Open to college sophomores, college juniors, college seniors, recent college graduates, graduate students. ▶ *2–5 systems engineering interns:* responsibilities include working on schematic capture; simulation; systems configuration; loading, running, and debugging bios; diagnostic programs; and NT and UNIX operating systems. Candidates should have ability to work independently, analytical skills, college courses in field, computer skills, knowledge of field, self-motivation, strong interpersonal skills. Duration is 3–6 months. $14–$35 per hour. Open to college sophomores, college juniors, college seniors, recent college graduates, graduate students. International applications accepted.

Benefits Formal training, on-the-job training, opportunity to attend seminars/workshops, possible full-time employment, willing to complete paperwork for educational credit, sick time, paid holidays.

Contact Through World Wide Web site Internship Coordinator. No phone calls. In-person interview recommended (telephone interview accepted). Applicants must submit a letter of interest, resume. Application deadline: April 1 for summer interns; continuous for all other positions. World Wide Web: http://www.emc.com.

PPP INFOTECH LIMITED
No. 9/1, Manjolai First Street, Kalaimagal Nagar, Ekkaduthangal
Chennai (Madras), Tamil Nadu 600 097 India

General Information Software company developing software technologies for computer networking, Internet, and Intranet for more than 10,000 customers in 80 countries with substantial sales in America and Europe. Established in 1995. Number of employees: 25. Number of internship applications received each year: 5.

Internships Available ▶ *2–4 consultant-marketing interns:* responsibilities include promoting and marketing software products; talking to several organizations over Internet chat, phone and email, meeting decision makers of companies, may also take part in media campaigns for the locality. Candidates should have ability to work independently, office skills, oral communication skills, personal interest in the field, strong leadership ability, written communication skills. Payment will be made on commission basis. Open to college freshmen, college sophomores, recent college graduates, graduate students, career changers, individuals reentering the workforce. International applications accepted.

Benefits Housing at a cost, job counseling, meals at a cost, names of contacts, on-the-job training, tuition assistance, willing to act as a professional reference, willing to complete paperwork for educational credit, willing to provide letters of recommendation.

International Internships Available.

Contact Call or e-mail B. Parameshwar Babu, Director. E-mail: pbabu@pppindia.com. Telephone interview required. Applicants must submit a letter of interest, resume, interview over e-mail and Internet chat is preferred. Applications are accepted continuously. World Wide Web: http://www.pppinfotech.com.

TELECOMMUNICATIONS

ARKANSAS EDUCATIONAL TELECOMMUNICATIONS NETWORK (AETN)
PO Box 1250
Conway, Arkansas 72033

General Information Organization whose mission is to offer lifelong learning to all Arkansans by supplying instructional programs to schools; also presents high-quality public television service.

Internships Available ▶ *Interns:* responsibilities include working in one of several departments: communications, development, operations, production, programming, and finance/administration. Candidates should have ability to work with others, computer skills, oral communication skills, personal interest in the field, written communication skills, flexibility, professional attitude/cooperative spirit, punctuality. Duration is one spring (January to May); summer (June to August); fall (September to December). Unpaid.

Contact Write, call, or e-mail Mechelle Williams, Volunteer Coordinator. Phone: 800-682-4159. E-mail: mwilliams@aetn.org. World Wide Web: http://www.aetn.org.

AT&T
200 Laurel Avenue, Room D32B03
Middletown, New Jersey 07748

General Information Telecommunication company. Established in 1885. Number of internship applications received each year: 1,000.

Internships Available ▶ *100–150 interns.* Candidates should have study in computer science, computer engineering, or electrical engineering; GPA of 3.0 or above. Duration is 12 weeks in summer. Salary depends on intern's level of education . Open to college sophomores, college juniors, college seniors, graduate students. International applications accepted.

Benefits On-the-job training, opportunity to attend seminars/workshops, travel reimbursement, willing to act as a professional reference, willing to provide letters of recommendation, opportunity to work with renowned scientist.

Contact Through World Wide Web site Connie Rose, Staff Manager. Telephone interview required. Applicants must submit a formal organization application, letter of interest, resume, academic transcripts, personal reference, letter of recommendation. Application deadline: April 15. World Wide Web: http://www.att.com.

BLACK ENTERTAINMENT TELEVISION
1235 W Street, NE
Washington, District of Columbia 20018

General Information Telecommunications company consisting of cable network channel, 2 magazines, pay per view channel, and other venues of mass communication. Established in 1980. Number of employees: 530. Number of internship applications received each year: 600.

Internships Available ▶ *40–60 interns:* responsibilities include various duties according to departmental needs. Candidates should have computer skills, oral communication skills, organizational skills, plan to pursue career in field, strong interpersonal skills. Duration is 1 semester. Unpaid. Open to high school seniors, college freshmen, college sophomores, college juniors, college seniors, graduate students, law students. International applications accepted.

Benefits On-the-job training, possible full-time employment, willing to complete paperwork for educational credit.

Contact Write or fax Nikki Gainey, Internship Coordinator. Fax: 202-608-2589. E-mail: nikki.gainey@bet.net. In-person interview recommended (telephone interview accepted). Applicants must submit a formal organization application, letter of interest, resume, academic transcripts, three letters of recommendation, verification from school that internship is for academic credit. Application deadline: March 27 for summer, July 3 for fall, November 13 for spring. World Wide Web: http://www.bet.com.

GEOSPATIAL INFORMATION AND TECHNOLOGY ASSOCIATION (GITA)
14456 East Evans Avenue
Aurora, Colorado 80014-1409

General Information Educational association serving professionals using geospatial information and technology in infrastructure-based industries (utilities, telecommunications, oil and gas pipeline, local government). Established in 1979. Number of employees: 11. Number of internship applications received each year: 20.

Internships Available ▶ *Up to 9 interns:* responsibilities include working with GITA corporate members, using their geospatial information and technology skills in the workplace at their facilities. Interns may also find their own internship opportunities. Candidates should have college courses in field, computer skills, knowledge of field, personal interest in the field, plan to pursue career in field, self-motivation. Duration is dependent on internship arranged. Paid. Open to college juniors, college seniors, graduate students. International applications accepted.

Benefits Names of contacts, on-the-job training, possible full-time employment.

International Internships Available.

Contact Write, call, fax, e-mail, or through World Wide Web site Rosemarie Seemann, 14456 East Evans Avenue, Aurora, Colorado 80014. Phone: 303-337-0513. Fax: 303-337-1001. E-mail: rseemann@gita.org. Applicants must submit a formal organization application, letter of interest, academic transcripts, three personal references, three letters of recommendation. Application deadline: January 31 for summer. World Wide Web: http://www.gita.org.

SBC/AMERITECH
2000 West Ameritech Center Drive
Hoffman Estates, Illinois 60196

General Information Organization responsible for the planning, designing, construction, and maintenance of the telecommunication network and installing and maintaining communication services to customers. Number of internship applications received each year: 200.

Internships Available ▶ *Management trainees:* responsibilities include telecommunications engineering, installation, switch technologies, and operator services (both technical and supervisory). Candidates should have analytical skills, oral communication skills, personal interest in the field, self-motivation, strong interpersonal skills, strong leadership ability. Duration is 3 months. $1650 per month (minimum). Open to college sophomores, college juniors, graduate students, college juniors preferred.

Benefits Job counseling, names of contacts, on-the-job training, opportunity to attend seminars/workshops, possible full-time employment, travel reimbursement.

Contact Write, fax, or through World Wide Web site A. T. Draftz, Senior Recruiting/Sourcing Consultant, Ameritech Management Staffing Center, 2000 Ameritech Drive, Room 2F48, Hoffman Estates, Illinois 60195. Fax: 847-248-9029. No phone calls. In-person interview recommended (telephone interview accepted). Applicants must submit a formal organization application, resume, academic transcripts. Applications are accepted continuously. World Wide Web: http://www.sbc.com.

VERIZON WIRELESS
180 Washington Valley Road
Bedminster, New Jersey 07921

General Information Communication business and headquarters for a cellular phone company. Established in 1987. Number of employees: 30,000. Number of internship applications received each year: 50.

Internships Available ▶ *6–12 health and fitness specialists:* responsibilities include opening and closing the facility; stress testing, creating motivational programs for the achievement of a healthy lifestyle, and orientations; positions available in New Jersey, New York, Pennsylvania, South Carolina, Maryland, Georgia, California, Utah, and Ohio. Candidates should have college courses in field, oral communication skills, plan to pursue career in field, self-motivation, strong interpersonal skills. Duration is 3 to 6 months (flexible). $1000 per duration of internship. Open to college juniors, college seniors, recent college graduates, graduate students, career changers. International applications accepted.

Benefits Formal training, job counseling, on-the-job training, possible full-time employment, willing to act as a professional reference, willing to complete paperwork for educational credit, willing to provide letters of recommendation.

Contact Write, call, fax, e-mail, or through World Wide Web site Mark Monteyne, Health Promotion Wellness Director/Head Coach, 180 Washington Valley Road, Bedminster, New Jersey 07921. Phone: 908-306-7198. Fax: 908-306-4229. E-mail: mark.monteyne@verizonwireless.com. Telephone interview required. Applicants must submit a resume, academic transcripts, three personal references. Applications are accepted continuously.

TELEVISION BROADCASTING

ABC NEWS NIGHTLINE
1717 DeSales Street, NW
Washington, District of Columbia 20036

General Information Television news, broadcast journalism company. Established in 1980. Number of employees: 30. Number of internship applications received each year: 400.
Internships Available ▶ *4–6 interns:* responsibilities include helping to manage the enormous flow of information that comes into the office every day; participating in all editorial conferences with access to all areas of the broadcast. Candidates should have oral communication skills, personal interest in the field, self-motivation, strong interpersonal skills, written communication skills. Duration is 1 semester (flexible). Unpaid. Open to college juniors, college seniors, graduate students, law students. International applications accepted.
Benefits Names of contacts, on-the-job training, opportunity to attend seminars/workshops, willing to act as a professional reference, willing to complete paperwork for educational credit, willing to provide letters of recommendation, occasional free meals, some travel reimbursement.
Contact Write, call, e-mail, or through World Wide Web site Intern Coordinator, 1717 DeSales Street, NW, Washington, District of Columbia 20036. Phone: 202-222-7000. Fax: 202-222-7976. E-mail: niteline@abcnews.com. Telephone interview required. Applicants must submit a formal organization application, letter of interest, resume, academic transcripts, two letters of recommendation, letter from university confirming eligibility to receive credit. Application deadline: March 15 for summer, July 1 for fall, October 1 for winter, November 15 for spring semester I; February 1 for spring semester II. World Wide Web: http://www.abcnews.com.

ACADEMY OF TELEVISION ARTS AND SCIENCES
5220 Lankershim Boulevard
North Hollywood, California 91601-3109

General Information Service and awards organization that presents the annual primetime Emmy awards; provides activities for television industry members; and fosters competition for college students in the form of a paid summer internship program which places students with Los Angeles-based television stations, production companies, studios, and other television-related venues. Established in 1946. Number of employees: 52. Number of internship applications received each year: 1,050.
Internships Available ▶ *27–29 interns:* responsibilities include working as an intern in one of 27 categories: Agency, Traditional Animation, Computer Generated Animation, Art Direction, Broadcast Advertising and Promotion, Business Affairs, Casting, Children's Programming and Development, Cinematography, Commercials, Costume Design, Development, Documentary/Reality Production, Editing, Entertainment News, Episodic Series, Movies for Television, Music, Network Programming Management, Production Management, Public Relations and Publicity, Sound, Syndication/Distribution, Television Directing-Single Camera, Television Directing–Multi-Camera, Television Scriptwriting, and Videotape Post Production. Candidates should have college courses in field, knowledge of field, oral communication skills, plan to pursue career in field, self-motivation, written communication skills, employment authorization and a social security card to receive stipend (if international student). Duration is 8 weeks. $2500 per duration of internship. Open to college freshmen, college sophomores, college juniors, college seniors, recent college graduates, graduate students, law students. International applications accepted.
Benefits Job counseling, opportunity to attend seminars/workshops, willing to act as a professional reference, willing to provide letters of recommendation, $500 housing/travel supplement for non-L.A. County residents.
Contact Write, call, fax, e-mail, or through World Wide Web site Internships. Phone: 818-754-2830. Fax: 818-761-8524. E-mail:

internships@emmys.org. Applicants must submit a formal organization application, letter of interest, resume, academic transcripts, writing sample, three letters of recommendation, videotaped interview if selected as a finalist, portfolio may be required (depending on category). Application deadline: March 15 for summer. World Wide Web: http://www.emmys.tv.

AMERICA'S MOST WANTED/STF PRODUCTIONS, INC.
5151 Wisconsin Avenue, NW
Washington, District of Columbia 20016

General Information Major television production company. Subsidiary of Fox Television Stations, Inc., Los Angeles, California.
Internships Available ▶ *Hot line interns:* responsibilities include attending weekly show meeting; assisting in Hot line department; opportunities to interact with personnel in all major aspects of production, cross-train between departments, and "pitch" a story. Candidates should have ability to work independently, ability to work with others, oral communication skills, personal interest in the field, research skills, self-motivation, writing skills. Duration is one semester (15-20 hours per week). Unpaid. ▶ *Missing children interns:* responsibilities include attending weekly show meeting; assisting in Missing Children Department; opportunities to interact with personnel in all major aspects of production, cross-train between departments, and "pitch" a story. Duration is one semester (15-20 hours per week). ▶ *News interns:* responsibilities include attending weekly show meeting; assisting in News Department; opportunities to identify, research and "pitch" a story and assist in its development and final production, if selected; interacting with personnel in all major aspects of television production; cross-training opportunities. Candidates should have ability to work independently, ability to work with others, personal interest in the field, research skills, self-motivation, writing skills. Duration is one semester (15-20 hours per week). Unpaid. ▶ *Production interns:* responsibilities include attending weekly show meeting, assisting in production; opportunities to pitch stories for production, interact with personnel in all major aspects of television production, and cross-training between production and News, Publicity, Hot line and Missing Children. Candidates should have ability to work independently, ability to work with others, personal interest in the field, research skills, self-motivation, writing skills. Duration is one semester (15-20 hours per week). Unpaid. ▶ *Publicity interns:* responsibilities include attending weekly show meeting; assisting in Publicity Department; opportunities to assist in development and final production, interact with personnel in all major aspects of television production, cross-train between departments, and pitch a story. Candidates should have ability to work independently, ability to work with others, personal interest in the field, research skills, self-motivation, writing skills. Duration is one semester (15-20 hours per week). Unpaid. Open to college sophomores, college juniors, college seniors.
Benefits On-the-job training, willing to complete paperwork for educational credit.
Contact Write or call Steve McDowall, Intern Coordinator. Phone: 202-204-2600. E-mail: smcdowall@amw.com. Applicants must submit a formal organization application, resume, writing sample, signed letter from college or university indicating that academic credit will be received for the internship. Applications are accepted continuously.

ARKANSAS EDUCATIONAL TELECOMMUNICATIONS NETWORK
PO Box 1250
Conway, Arkansas 72033

General Information Public television station providing PBS programs, educational shows and materials; also produces local programming. Established in 1961. Number of employees: 100. Number of internship applications received each year: 80.
Internships Available ▶ *4 K-12 services interns:* responsibilities include video library review and update and researching, designing, and writing summaries for teacher's guides. Candidates should have ability to work independently, ability to work with others, analytical skills, computer skills, research skills, writing skills. Dura-

tion is 1 semester. Unpaid. Open to college freshmen, college sophomores, college juniors, college seniors, recent college graduates, graduate students, career changers, individuals reentering the workforce. ▶ *1–2 accounting office assistant interns:* responsibilities include assisting with researching invoices, keying and processing payable vouchers, and reconciling fund records; helping reconcile monthly bank statements and preparing monthly trade account statements. Candidates should have college courses in field, computer skills, knowledge of field, office skills, good typing skills, good math skills. Duration is 1 semester. Unpaid. Open to college sophomores, college juniors, college seniors, recent college graduates, graduate students, career changers, individuals reentering the workforce. ▶ *1 broadcast management intern:* responsibilities include general administration duties and research assistance (labor law questions, political concerns, grant applications, donor prospects). Candidates should have analytical skills, computer skills, organizational skills, research skills, strong leadership ability, writing skills. Duration is 1 semester. Unpaid. Open to college sophomores, college juniors, college seniors, recent college graduates, graduate students, law students, career changers, individuals reentering the workforce. ▶ *1–2 development interns:* responsibilities include assisting with events, with mailings to members and volunteers, updating computer files, research assistance on special projects, and providing administrative and clerical support. Candidates should have ability to work independently, ability to work with others, computer skills, editing skills, office skills, oral communication skills, organizational skills, research skills, self-motivation, writing skills. Duration is 1 semester. Unpaid. Open to high school students, recent high school graduates, college freshmen, college sophomores, college juniors, college seniors, recent college graduates, graduate students, law students, career changers, individuals reentering the workforce. ▶ *1–2 general business interns:* responsibilities include performing general finance/administration office duties; assisting in accounting processes, personnel/payroll duties, and purchasing activities. Candidates should have college courses in field, computer skills, knowledge of field, office skills, oral communication skills, written communication skills. Duration is 1 semester. Unpaid. Open to college freshmen, college sophomores, college juniors, college seniors, recent college graduates, graduate students, career changers, individuals reentering the workforce. ▶ *2 graphics interns:* responsibilities include programming research for monthly Program Guide; layout and design for brochures, flyers, and newsletters; photography, assisting with assembly of scenery for AETN productions; and assisting Web designer. Candidates should have college courses in field, knowledge of field, personal interest in the field, research skills, familiarity with computer graphic programs. Duration is 1 semester. Unpaid. Open to college freshmen, college sophomores, college juniors, college seniors, recent college graduates, graduate students, career changers, individuals reentering the workforce. ▶ *1 human resource intern:* responsibilities include assisting with annual employee performance evaluations, scheduling employee training, composing job advertisements, collecting/reporting applicant statistics, and contracts for professional services. Candidates should have computer skills, office skills, oral communication skills, organizational skills, writing skills. Duration is 1 semester. Unpaid. Open to college sophomores, college juniors, college seniors, recent college graduates, graduate students, law students, career changers, individuals reentering the workforce. ▶ *2 membership interns:* responsibilities include data entry, telephone customer service, handling member correspondence, running weekly mailings and reports, packaging and mailing premiums, and sorting and labeling bulk mailings. Candidates should have ability to work independently, ability to work with others, computer skills, editing skills, office skills, oral communication skills, organizational skills, self-motivation, ability to follow directions, good ability with numbers. Duration is 1 semester. Unpaid. Open to high school students, recent high school graduates, college freshmen, college sophomores, college juniors, college seniors, recent college graduates, graduate students, law students, career changers, individuals reentering the workforce. ▶ *2 outreach/publicist interns:* responsibilities include research, writing program features and news/press releases, preparing and mailing outreach information packets, and assisting in preparation of outreach events. Candidates should have computer skills, editing

skills, personal interest in the field, research skills, writing skills. Duration is 1 semester. Unpaid. Open to recent high school graduates, college freshmen, college sophomores, college juniors, college seniors, recent college graduates, graduate students, career changers, individuals reentering the workforce. ▶ *3 postsecondary services interns:* responsibilities include designing multimedia presentations; evaluating technology training; and analyzing basic skills needs. Candidates should have ability to work independently, ability to work with others, analytical skills, organizational skills, self-motivation. Duration is 1 semester. Unpaid. Open to college freshmen, college sophomores, college juniors, college seniors, recent college graduates, graduate students, career changers, individuals reentering the workforce. ▶ *6 production assistant interns:* responsibilities include operating studio cameras under supervision, arranging studio sets, lighting sets, floor directing, assistant directing, and assisting videographics in the field. Candidates should have ability to work with others, knowledge of field, oral communication skills, plan to pursue career in field. Duration is 1 semester. Unpaid. Open to college sophomores, college juniors, college seniors, recent college graduates, graduate students. ▶ *5 production interns:* responsibilities include assisting in business aspects of production, preparing programs for broadcast, and with phone supervision during live broadcasts; screening and transcribing video tapes. Candidates should have analytical skills, computer skills, office skills, personal interest in the field, research skills, strong interpersonal skills. Duration is 1 semester. Unpaid. Open to college freshmen, college sophomores, college juniors, college seniors, recent college graduates, graduate students. ▶ *2 program assistant interns:* responsibilities include performing general office duties; working in video library, preparing film and videotape programs for shipping, and maintaining program records in database. Candidates should have ability to work independently, analytical skills, computer skills, office skills, organizational skills, must be good with numbers. Duration is 1 semester. Unpaid. Open to college freshmen, college sophomores, college juniors, college seniors, recent college graduates, graduate students, career changers, individuals reentering the workforce. ▶ *1 purchasing intern:* responsibilities include assisting in keying updates to vendor database, writing specifications for sealed bids, research and proposals, lease and land management, and risk management/ insurance. Candidates should have ability to work independently, organizational skills, writing skills, good math and customer service skills. Duration is 1 semester. Unpaid. Open to college freshmen, college sophomores, college juniors, college seniors, recent college graduates, graduate students, career changers, individuals reentering the workforce. ▶ *2 viewer services assistant interns:* responsibilities include performing general office duties, working on department files, and preparing responses to viewer inquiries. Candidates should have computer skills, office skills, oral communication skills, research skills, strong interpersonal skills, written communication skills. Duration is 1 semester. Unpaid. Open to recent high school graduates, college freshmen, college sophomores, college juniors, college seniors, recent college graduates, graduate students, career changers, individuals reentering the workforce. International applications accepted.

Benefits On-the-job training, willing to act as a professional reference, willing to complete paperwork for educational credit, willing to provide letters of recommendation.

Contact Write, call, fax, or e-mail Martha A. Perry, Interim Volunteer and Intern Coordinator. Phone: 800-662-2386 Ext. 43. Fax: 501-852-2280. E-mail: mperry@aetn.org. In-person interview recommended (telephone interview accepted). Applicants must submit a formal organization application, resume, letter of recommendation, writing samples (for communications and programming positions). Application deadline: April 1 for summer, June 15 for fall, October 30 for spring. World Wide Web: http://www.aetn.org.

AT&T BROADBAND–CHANNEL 26
1111 Anderson Drive
San Rafael, California 94901

General Information Public access and local origination facility where professional and nonprofessional community programming is produced. Established in 1976. Number of employees:

5. Department of AT&T Broadband, San Rafael, California. Number of internship applications received each year: 20.
Internships Available ▶ *4–8 access interns:* responsibilities include assisting access coordinator and programming. Candidates should have ability to work independently, ability to work with others, knowledge of field, office skills, organizational skills, personal interest in the field. Duration is flexible; minimum of 140 hours per semester required. Unpaid. ▶ *4–6 productions interns:* responsibilities include working for staff productions, overseeing automated playback system, office maintenance, and working as part of crew on public access productions. Candidates should have ability to work independently, ability to work with others, office skills, organizational skills, personal interest in the field. Duration is flexible; minimum of 140 hours per semester. Unpaid. Open to recent high school graduates, college freshmen, college sophomores, college juniors, college seniors, recent college graduates, graduate students, career changers, individuals reentering the workforce.
Benefits Job counseling, opportunity to attend seminars/ workshops, willing to complete paperwork for educational credit, willing to provide letters of recommendation, informal training in television production.
Contact Write or call Ms. Jennifer Kloepping, Producer/Director. Phone: 415-459-5333 Ext. 1242. In-person interview recommended (telephone interview accepted). Applicants must submit a formal organization application, two personal references. Application deadline: May 15 for summer, August 15 for fall, December 15 for spring. World Wide Web: http://communityprogramming. marin.org.

BAY NEWS 9 RADIO
7901 66th Street North
Pinellas Park, Florida 33781

General Information Television news station serving the Bay area of Florida. Unit of AOL Time Warner, Inc., New York, New York.
Internships Available ▶ *Interns.* Unpaid. Open to students of journalism, television production, or graphic arts, in junior year (minimum) or 4 year program or having completed one year of technical training.
Contact Write or fax Human Resource Manager. Fax: 727-437-2031. No phone calls. Applicants must submit a letter of interest, resume, evidence of college credit for internship. World Wide Web: http://www.baynews9.com.

BLASTRO
906 East 5th Street, Suite 103
Austin, Texas 78702

General Information Internet television network. Established in 2000. Number of employees: 6. Number of internship applications received each year: 50.
Internships Available ▶ *New media interns:* responsibilities include hands-on experience in the internet television industry, training in media compression for streaming video, basic non-linear editing and 2-D animation Web development with HTML, Javascript, and Flash. Candidates should have ability to work independently, ability to work with others, computer skills, ability to learn quickly. Unpaid. Open to college freshmen, college sophomores, college juniors. International applications accepted.
Benefits On-the-job training, willing to complete paperwork for educational credit, willing to provide letters of recommendation.
Contact E-mail Rob Campanell, Director. Fax: 612-485-3149. E-mail: contact@blastro.com. No phone calls. Applicants must submit a letter of interest, resume. Application deadline: April 20 for summer, August 20 for fall and spring. World Wide Web: http://www. blastro.com.

BNNTV/CAMERAPLANET
253 Fifth Avenue, Seventh Floor
New York, New York 10016

General Information Television, film, Web, and news production company. Established in 1983. Number of employees: 30. Number of internship applications received each year: 50.

Internships Available ▶ *1–3 Camera Planet interns:* responsibilities include working with CameraPlanet.com staff to develop and upload user video to Web site. Candidates should have ability to work independently, ability to work with others, analytical skills, office skills, oral communication skills, organizational skills, self-motivation, written communication skills. Duration is 3 months. Unpaid. Open to college sophomores, college juniors, college seniors, recent college graduates, graduate students, career changers, individuals reentering the workforce. ▶ *1–3 development interns:* responsibilities include working with TV and film development division to research and develop story ideas. Candidates should have ability to work independently, ability to work with others, analytical skills, oral communication skills, research skills, self-motivation, writing skills. Duration is 3 months. Unpaid. Open to college freshmen, college sophomores, college juniors, college seniors, recent college graduates, career changers, individuals reentering the workforce. International applications accepted.
Benefits On-the-job training, opportunity to attend seminars/ workshops, possible full-time employment, willing to act as a professional reference, willing to complete paperwork for educational credit, willing to provide letters of recommendation.
Contact Call, fax, or e-mail Ben Pickup, Intern Coordinator. Phone: 212-779-0500. Fax: 212-532-5554. E-mail: ben.pickup@ bnntv.com. In-person interview recommended (telephone interview accepted). Applicants must submit a formal organization application, resume. Application deadline: January 28 for spring, May 28 for summer, September 28 for fall. World Wide Web: http:// www.bnntv.com.

CABLEVISION OF RARITAN VALLEY
275 Centennial, CN 6805
Piscataway, New Jersey 08855-6805

General Information Cable company providing an assortment of cable services to its local community. Established in 1973. Number of employees: 450. Unit of Cablevision, Bethpage, New York. Number of internship applications received each year: 15.
Internships Available ▶ *2–4 production interns:* responsibilities include assisting on productions in studio and out in field; gaining experience on camera, audio, and tape equipment; learning process of packaging stories on non-linear editing system. Candidates should have ability to work independently, ability to work with others, oral communication skills, plan to pursue career in field, self-motivation. Duration is 1 semester. Unpaid. Open to college freshmen, college sophomores, college juniors, college seniors. International applications accepted.
Benefits On-the-job training, possible full-time employment, willing to act as a professional reference, willing to complete paperwork for educational credit, willing to provide letters of recommendation, hands-on experience.
Contact Write, call, or e-mail Angela D. Greene, Operations Supervisor. Phone: 732-317-7053. Fax: 732-317-7066. E-mail: agreene@cablevision.com. In-person interview recommended (telephone interview accepted). Applicants must submit a letter of interest, resume, school's guidelines for internships. Application deadline: May 1 for summer, August 1 for fall, December 1 for spring.

CABLEVISION OF SOUTHERN WESTCHESTER
47 Purdy Street
Harrison, New York 10528

General Information Company that provides local programming for cable in Westchester, broadcasting news, sports, talk shows, and medical shows in the studio and on location. Number of employees: 325. Unit of Cablevision, Bethpage, New York. Number of internship applications received each year: 250.
Internships Available ▶ *Interns.* Candidates should have college courses in field, knowledge of field, plan to pursue career in field, strong interpersonal skills. Duration is 1 semester. Unpaid. Open to college freshmen, college sophomores, college juniors, college seniors. International applications accepted.
Benefits On-the-job training, possible full-time employment, willing to complete paperwork for educational credit, willing to provide letters of recommendation.

Contact Write, call, fax, or e-mail Dan Cecconie, Area Manager, Westchester, Rockland, Hudson Valley. Phone: 914-835-5543. Fax: 914-835-5098. E-mail: dcecconi@cablevision.com. In-person interview recommended (telephone interview accepted). Applicants must submit a letter of interest, resume. Applications are accepted continuously.

CBS, INC.
1170 Soldiers Field Road
Boston, Massachusetts 02134

General Information Broadcast television and AM–FM radio stations serving the Boston area. Established in 1921. Number of employees: 300. Affiliate of CBS, Inc., New York, New York. Number of internship applications received each year: 200.

Internships Available ▶ *1–2 BZ Productions interns:* responsibilities include learning how commercials and promotional spots are made, field and studio production skills, post- production techniques, and an overview of writing, directing, producing and editing; learning the terminology and uses of production equipment, logging and labeling tapes, and organizing production office, working closely with the TV Sales Department; needed Monday to Friday. Candidates should have knowledge of field, oral communication skills, organizational skills, personal interest in the field, self-motivation, strong interpersonal skills. Duration is 1 semester. Unpaid. ▶ *1–3 WBZ Newsradio: news interns:* responsibilities include assisting WBZ Newsradio news department in news gathering, writing, audio production, and administration. Days needed: Monday-Friday 8am-11pm, plus possible weekend work (flexible). Candidates should have oral communication skills, personal interest in the field, research skills, self-motivation, strong interpersonal skills, written communication skills. Duration is 1 semester. Unpaid. ▶ *1–3 WBZ Newsradio: programming interns:* responsibilities include assisting with radio programming administrative tasks, working on special projects, learning use of radio broadcast equipment. Days needed: Monday-Friday 9:30am-6pm (flexible), some weekend work. Candidates should have oral communication skills, organizational skills, personal interest in the field, research skills, self-motivation, written communication skills. Duration is 1 semester. Unpaid. ▶ *1–4 WBZ-TV News: Assignment Desk interns:* responsibilities include assisting assignment editors, reporters, and producers in gathering news stories, pre-interviewing, researching, viewing/logging tapes, and extensive phone work to help cultivate news stories. Days needed: weekdays, nights, weekends (varies). Candidates should have oral communication skills, personal interest in the field, research skills, self-motivation, strong interpersonal skills, ability to work in a hectic environment. Duration is 1 semester. Unpaid. ▶ *1–3 WBZ-TV News: I-Team interns:* responsibilities include documenting research, pre-interviewing subjects, taking telephone tips, researching and developing tips, and logging tapes. Days needed: Monday-Friday. Candidates should have ability to work independently, computer skills, office skills, oral communication skills, personal interest in the field, research skills, strong interpersonal skills, written communication skills. Duration is 1 semester. Unpaid. ▶ *1–3 WBZ-TV:promotions/creative services interns:* responsibilities include learning how a TV station uses their own air to achieve strategic marketing goals and objectives; learning the logistics and language of promotion; gaining a working knowledge of television production, from the creative writing process, to field producing, to post production in the edit room; learning how to develop and execute news topicals, news serials, and public service announcement. Days needed: Monday-Friday. Candidates should have computer skills, office skills, oral communication skills, personal interest in the field, strong interpersonal skills, writing skills. Duration is 1 semester. Unpaid. ▶ *1 management information systems intern:* responsibilities include working with the director of information technology who designs, installs, and maintains computers and network operations for WBZ-TV, WBZ NewsRadio, and WODS-FM; assisting in "help desk" type functions; installing PCs, supporting sales and news users on software/hardware problems or questions; learning computer hardware/software, some networking components and theory, and end-user support skills. Days needed: Monday-Friday. Candidates should have computer skills, knowledge of field, organizational skills, personal interest in the

field, self-motivation, strong interpersonal skills. Duration is 1 semester. Unpaid. ▶ *1 news media (Web) intern:* responsibilities include assisting Webmaster in site development, design, and upkeep; learning how Web site content is maintained and updated; using HTML; helping design graphics for the site; learning how ad space is used by the sales departments; answering or forwarding numerous daily e-mail requests; developing skills in current Web design/publishing software, including Adobe PhotoShop, Allair HomeSite, Netscape Navigator/Communicator, Microsoft Internet Explorer, and Microsoft Office. Days needed: Monday-Friday. Candidates should have computer skills, knowledge of field, personal interest in the field, self-motivation, strong interpersonal skills, HTML experience. Duration is 1 semester. Unpaid. ▶ *1–2 public relations/affairs interns:* responsibilities include writing and maintaining updated biographies, photos, and press materials; tracking station press coverage for monthly reports; scheduling speaking engagements for talent; coordinating publicity elements of special events and broadcasts including telethons, network, and syndication talent visits; assisting in planning and execution of photo shoots; distributing press releases to media and maintaining the media database; updating and coordinating materials for the station's Web site with the Webmaster. Days needed: Monday—Friday. Candidates should have ability to work independently, computer skills, oral communication skills, personal interest in the field, strong interpersonal skills, written communication skills. Duration is 1 semester. Unpaid. Open to college sophomores, college juniors, college seniors, graduate students. International applications accepted.

Benefits Opportunity to attend seminars/workshops, willing to complete paperwork for educational credit, willing to provide letters of recommendation.

Contact Write, call, fax, e-mail, or through World Wide Web site Andrea Goldstein, Internship Program Manager. Phone: 617-787-7113. Fax: 617-787-7275. E-mail: agoldste@boston.cbs.com. In-person interview recommended (telephone interview accepted). Applicants must submit a resume, academic transcripts, formal application (portion of which must be completed by intern/faculty advisor). Application deadline: March 15 for summer, July 15 for fall, November 15 for spring. World Wide Web: http://www.wbz.com.

CBS NEWS, INC.
524 West 57th Street
New York, New York 100019

General Information World-wide news organization serving the CBS Television and Radio Networks with regularly scheduled news, public affairs broadcasts, and special reports. Established in 1966. Subsidiary of Viacom, Pittsburgh, Pennsylvania. Number of internship applications received each year: 900.

Internships Available ▶ *40–60 production interns:* responsibilities include working in various broadcast and support departments, including CBS This Morning, Evening News, 48 Hours, public relations, CBS promotions, CBS production, Sunday Morning/Weekend News, NewsPath, and Up to the Minute. Candidates should have ability to work with others, computer skills, knowledge of field, oral communication skills, written communication skills. Duration is 1 semester. Unpaid. Open to college juniors, college seniors, graduate students, law students. International applications accepted.

Benefits Job counseling, on-the-job training, opportunity to attend seminars/workshops, possible full-time employment, willing to act as a professional reference, willing to complete paperwork for educational credit, willing to provide letters of recommendation.

Contact Write, call, fax, or e-mail Ms. Eldra Rodriguez-Gillman, Director of Professional Advancement and Internships, 524 West 57th Street, New York, New York 10019. Phone: 212-975-4321. Fax: 212-975-6699. E-mail: eig@cbsnews.com. In-person interview recommended (telephone interview accepted). Applicants must submit a letter of interest, resume, academic transcripts, writing sample, two letters of recommendation. Application deadline: February 1 for summer; continuous for fall and spring positions.

CHARLIE ROSE SHOW
499 Park Avenue, 11th Floor
New York, New York 10022

General Information Nightly television program featuring one-on-one interviews and roundtable discussions. Established in 1991. Number of employees: 15. Unit of Bloomberg, New York, New York. Number of internship applications received each year: 150.

Internships Available ▶ *9–11 production interns:* responsibilities include helping with research for upcoming guests, meeting and greeting guests, maintaining the green room and studio, and basic office duties. Candidates should have computer skills, knowledge of field, organizational skills, self-motivation, strong interpersonal skills. Duration is 1 semester. Unpaid. Open to college juniors, college seniors, recent college graduates, graduate students. International applications accepted.

Benefits Possible full-time employment, willing to act as a professional reference, willing to complete paperwork for educational credit, willing to provide letters of recommendation, on-site shoots, free snacks/food, contact with celebrities.

Contact Write or fax Shelley Hoffmann, Producer/Internship Coordinator. Phone: 212-940-1600. Fax: 212-940-1909. In-person interview required. Applicants must submit a letter of interest, resume. Applications are accepted continuously. World Wide Web: http://www.pbs.org/charlierose.

CHARTER COMMUNICATIONS
95 Higgins Street
Worcester, Massachusetts 01606

General Information Cable company servicing 22 central Massachusetts communities. Established in 1975. Number of employees: 400. Unit of Charter Communications, St. Louis, Missouri. Number of internship applications received each year: 30.

Internships Available ▶ *4–5 advertising production assistants:* responsibilities include lighting, setting up equipment, editing, producing, scriptwriting, and maintaining sets. Candidates should have ability to work with others, declared college major in field, plan to pursue career in field, self-motivation. Duration is flexible. Unpaid. Open to college juniors, college seniors. ▶ *1 community affairs assistant:* responsibilities include writing newsletters, conducting company tours, attending meetings, writing press releases, and dealing with the public. Candidates should have computer skills, editing skills, oral communication skills, plan to pursue career in field, strong interpersonal skills, written communication skills. Duration is flexible. Unpaid. Open to college juniors, college seniors. ▶ *2–4 production assistants for news:* responsibilities include running camera and audio, writing scripts, editing, co-producing, directing, and floor directing. Candidates should have ability to work with others, college courses in field, computer skills, experience in the field, oral communication skills, personal interest in the field, self-motivation. Duration is 1 semester. Unpaid. Open to college juniors, college seniors, recent college graduates. ▶ *2–4 production assistants for programming production:* responsibilities include hands-on experience in all phases of television production (studio and remotes). Candidates should have declared college major in field, oral communication skills, plan to pursue career in field, self-motivation, strong interpersonal skills, ability to work days, nights, or weekends. Duration is one semester (minimum 18 hours per week). Unpaid. Open to college juniors, college seniors, recent college graduates, graduate students. International applications accepted.

Benefits On-the-job training, possible full-time employment, willing to complete paperwork for educational credit.

Contact Write, call, fax, or e-mail Bill Jackson, Production Manager. Phone: 508-853-1515. Fax: 508-854-5065. E-mail: bjackson@greatermediaworc.com. In-person interview recommended (telephone interview accepted). Applicants must submit a formal organization application, letter of interest, resume. Application deadline: May 1 for summer, August 1 for fall, December 1 for spring; first come, first serve for all deadlines. World Wide Web: http://www.chartercom.com.

CNN AMERICA, INC.
820 1st Street, NE
Washington, District of Columbia 20002

General Information Cable news network offering 24 hours of news and information programming daily. Established in 1980. Number of employees: 300. Unit of AOL Time Warner, Inc., New York, New York. Number of internship applications received each year: 500.

Internships Available ▶ *15–20 departmental interns:* responsibilities include assisting with production needs, conducting research, and learning about booking guests and show research. Duration is 12–15 weeks. Unpaid. ▶ *5–10 rotation interns:* responsibilities include assisting writers, producers, video librarians, and field crews. Duration is 12–15 weeks. Unpaid. Candidates for all positions should have ability to work independently, college courses in field, oral communication skills, plan to pursue career in field, self-motivation, strong interpersonal skills. Open to college juniors, college seniors, graduate students. International applications accepted.

Benefits Formal training, names of contacts, opportunity to attend seminars/workshops, willing to complete paperwork for educational credit.

International Internships Available in London, United Kingdom.

Contact Write, call, e-mail, or through World Wide Web site Shanda Taylor, Human Resources Coordinator. Phone: 202-515-2916. E-mail: shanda.taylor@turner.com. Applicants must submit a formal organization application, letter of interest, resume, academic transcripts, two letters of recommendation, 1–2 page essay. Application deadline: March 1 for summer, July 1 for fall, November 1 for spring. World Wide Web: http://www.turnerjobs.com.

COMCAST SPORTSNET
3601 South Broad Street
Philadelphia, Pennsylvania 19148

General Information Cable television sports network. Established in 1997. Number of employees: 120. Unit of Comcast, Philadelphia, Pennsylvania. Number of internship applications received each year: 100.

Internships Available ▶ *2–4 marketing interns.* Candidates should have oral communication skills, organizational skills, self-motivation, writing skills, ability to use MS Word (or WordPerfect), MS Excel, and cc:Mail. Duration is 1 semester in fall, spring, or summer. Unpaid. ▶ *2–4 programming/production interns:* responsibilities include screening and logging taped programming to prepare for editing; detail work to procure footage from external sources; helping to line up guests for appearances; preparing, copying, and distributing programming information internally; and researching background and details and statistical information for local shows. Candidates should have oral communication skills, organizational skills, written communication skills, ability to use word processing and spreadsheet applications. Duration is 1 semester in fall, spring, or summer. Unpaid. Open to college juniors, college seniors, graduate students, must be working for academic credit. International applications accepted.

Benefits Names of contacts, on-the-job training, possible full-time employment, willing to act as a professional reference, willing to complete paperwork for educational credit, willing to provide letters of recommendation, excellent experience in the sports and entertainment industry.

Contact Write, fax, e-mail, or through World Wide Web site Kerri Barber, Internship Program, Human Resources Department. Fax: 215-952-5996. E-mail: kbarber@comcastsportsnet.com. No phone calls. In-person interview required. Applicants must submit a formal organization application, resume, cover letter indicating reasons for choosing a particular internship and the qualities or attributes that will help make a contribution; faculty recommendation form (sent with application). Application deadline: at least 2 months prior to intended start date. World Wide Web: http://www.comcastsportsnet.com.

COMEDY CENTRAL
1775 Broadway, 10th Floor
New York, New York 10019

General Information Advertiser-supported basic cable comedy service. Established in 1991. Number of employees: 300. Unit of Time Warner and Viacom, New York, New York. Number of internship applications received each year: 800.
Internships Available ▶ *1–2 accounts payable interns:* responsibilities include providing basic office support; assisting with batching and inputting vendor invoices and employee expense reports; maintaining vendor information; and filing invoices, reports, and federal ID letters. Candidates should have computer skills, office skills. Duration is 1 semester. Unpaid. Open to college freshmen, college sophomores, college juniors, college seniors. ▶ *1–2 advertising/marketing interns:* responsibilities include occasionally attending radio record sessions, assisting off-air producer on various tape projects, maintaining advertising portfolio and radio tape library, processing bills, and organizing budget book. Candidates should have computer skills, office skills. Duration is 1 semester. Unpaid. Open to college freshmen, college sophomores, college juniors, college seniors. ▶ *1–2 affiliate marketing interns:* responsibilities include updating database for quarterly mailing and fax broadcasting; working with video library to fulfill dubbing requests; contacting talent agencies and management for updated press materials on comedians; ordering and maintaining supply of Comedy Central premiums. Candidates should have computer skills, office skills. Duration is 1 semester. Unpaid. Open to college freshmen, college sophomores, college juniors, college seniors. ▶ *1–2 affiliate relations interns:* responsibilities include supporting affiliate sales group. Candidates should have computer skills, oral communication skills, self-motivation, strong interpersonal skills, written communication skills. Duration is 1 semester. Unpaid. Open to college freshmen, college sophomores, college juniors, college seniors. ▶ *1–2 affiliate revenue interns:* responsibilities include assisting managers and analysts with special projects as needed; working with billing system to update subscribers; applying cash; and tracking all payments made by cable systems. Candidates should have computer skills, office skills. Duration is 1 semester. Unpaid. Open to college freshmen, college sophomores, college juniors, college seniors. ▶ *2 corporate communication/public relations interns:* responsibilities include assisting in day-to-day public relations effort/events, maintaining network press digest, updating press releases and executive and talent bio photo files, maintaining press tape library, general office support, and coordinating press kits. Candidates should have office skills, writing skills. Duration is 1 semester. Unpaid. Open to college freshmen, college sophomores, college juniors, college seniors. ▶ *1–2 finance interns.* Duration is 1 semester. Unpaid. ▶ *1 human resources intern:* responsibilities include assisting in development of human resources administrative filing system, assisting in various human resources projects, providing general office support, and assisting in development of recruitment database. Candidates should have computer skills, office skills. Duration is 1 semester. Unpaid. Open to college freshmen, college sophomores, college juniors, college seniors. ▶ *1–2 off-air creative interns.* Duration is 1 semester. Unpaid. ▶ *1–2 on-air creative interns:* responsibilities include providing general office support, assisting at external shoots and screenings, helping production assistants, and assisting on occasional off-lining. Candidates should have strong interpersonal skills, flexible schedule. Duration is 1 semester. Unpaid. Open to college freshmen, college sophomores, college juniors, college seniors. ▶ *Online/enterprise interns:* responsibilities include assisting in updating games horoscopes, videoclips; basic HTML site maintenance, media acquisition of video images, and providing ideas/feedback in site maintenance and development. Candidates should have written communication skills, knowledge of Word, Excel, Explorer, Netscape, HTML, and PhotoShop; some experience in JAVA script and Premiere (preferred). Duration is 1 semester. Unpaid. Open to college freshmen, college sophomores, college juniors, college seniors. ▶ *2–3 production interns:* responsibilities include providing basic office support, copying and labeling various programs for other departments, helping organize program cart sheets, and maintaining prop closet and reel library. Candidates should have ability to work independently, computer skills, oral

communication skills, self-motivation, strong interpersonal skills, written communication skills. Duration is 1 semester. Unpaid. Open to college freshmen, college sophomores, college juniors, college seniors. ▶ *1–2 sales research interns:* responsibilities include providing basic office support and working with Nielsen database. Candidates should have computer skills, office skills. Duration is 1 semester. Unpaid. Open to college freshmen, college sophomores, college juniors, college seniors. ▶ *Talent development interns (New York and Los Angeles):* responsibilities include assisting in evaluating current series scripts, unsolicited submissions, and writing samples. Candidates should have sense of humor and interest in comedy (helpful). Duration is 1 semester. Unpaid. Open to college freshmen, college sophomores, college juniors, college seniors.
Benefits On-the-job training, possible full-time employment, willing to act as a professional reference, willing to complete paperwork for educational credit, willing to provide letters of recommendation, small travel stipend, opportunity to attend show tapings and planned intern trips.
Contact Write, fax, or e-mail Human Resources Coordinator. Fax: 212-767-4257. E-mail: interns@comedycentral.com. No phone calls. In-person interview required. Applicants must submit a letter of interest, resume, verification of school credit for internship. Applications are accepted continuously. World Wide Web: http://www.comedycentral.com.

C-SPAN
400 North Capitol Street, NW, Suite 650
Washington, District of Columbia 20001

General Information Provides audience access to live gavel-to-gavel proceedings of the U.S. House of Representatives, the U.S. Senate, and to other forums where public policy is discussed, debated, and decided, without editing, commentary, or analysis and with a balanced presentation of points-of-view. Established in 1979. Number of employees: 280. Number of internship applications received each year: 300.
Internships Available ▶ *1–3 "Washington Journal" interns:* responsibilities include developing specific live and taped programs for morning program, *The Washington Journal*; greeting guests, setting up studio/green room, follow-up with guests, and research. Candidates should have ability to work independently, computer skills, oral communication skills, personal interest in the field, self-motivation, strong interpersonal skills. Duration is 10–12 weeks. Unpaid. ▶ *1–2 affiliate relations interns:* responsibilities include maintaining and improving carriage of C-SPAN networks among cable affiliates through affiliate promotions and relationships with cable contacts at the corporate level. Candidates should have ability to work independently, computer skills, oral communication skills, personal interest in the field, strong interpersonal skills, written communication skills. Duration is 10–12 weeks. Unpaid. ▶ *1–2 book TV interns:* responsibilities include working with book TV on C-SPAN2 which explores the world of nonfiction books including recently published biographies and historical works, older history books, politics or culture, books about current events and public issues. Candidates should have analytical skills, computer skills, organizational skills, personal interest in the field, research skills, self-motivation. Duration is 10–12 weeks. Unpaid. ▶ *1 community relations intern:* responsibilities include supporting targeted community marketing efforts to cable companies across the country; developing educational materials and outreach programs. Candidates should have ability to work independently, computer skills, oral communication skills, personal interest in the field, strong interpersonal skills, written communication skills. Duration is 10–12 weeks. Unpaid. ▶ *1–2 engineering interns:* responsibilities include being responsible for overall technical quality of C-SPAN's products; working with other departments to purchase and repair technical equipment; tracking new technologies and recommending ways C-SPAN can use these technologies. Candidates should have ability to work independently, ability to work with others, computer skills, editing skills, oral communication skills, organizational skills, personal interest in the field, research skills, self-motivation, writing skills. Duration is 10–12 weeks. Unpaid. ▶ *1–2 field producers:* responsibilities include developing programming ideas by researching specific areas of government, its history and the process, as well as coordinating logistical aspects required in production.

C-SPAN (continued)

Candidates should have analytical skills, computer skills, organizational skills, personal interest in the field, research skills, self-motivation. Duration is 10–12 weeks. Unpaid. ▶ *Field production interns:* responsibilities include handling audio, lighting, and camera operation for events that take place in and around Washington D.C. and executing set-up and breakdown of equipment. Candidates should have ability to work independently, personal interest in the field, self-motivation, strong interpersonal skills, strong leadership ability. Duration is 10 weeks. Unpaid. ▶ *1–2 human resources interns:* responsibilities include working in benefits, employee records, payroll, and employee relations. Candidates should have ability to work independently, computer skills, editing skills, experience in the field, oral communication skills, organizational skills, research skills, self-motivation, strong interpersonal skills, writing skills. Duration is 10–12 weeks. Unpaid. ▶ *1–2 marketing interns:* responsibilities include providing creative direction and developing support materials that promote the network to cable operators, educators, and viewers; generating ads and publications. Candidates should have computer skills, editing skills, organizational skills, personal interest in the field, self-motivation, writing skills. Duration is 10–12 weeks. Unpaid. ▶ *1–2 media relations interns:* responsibilities include communicating C-SPAN's mission, programming, style, and content to national media outlets. Candidates should have computer skills, office skills, organizational skills, personal interest in the field, research skills, self-motivation. Duration is 10–12 weeks. Unpaid. ▶ *1–2 new media interns:* responsibilities include developing and managing contracts and initiating business relationships relating to C-SPAN products, videotapes, transcripts, and online services. Candidates should have computer skills, editing skills, experience in the field, organizational skills, research skills, writing skills. Duration is 10–12 weeks. Unpaid. ▶ *1–2 programming operations editorial interns:* responsibilities include working with producers in developing daily schedule, tracking House and Senate floor debate, script-writing, voiceovers, scheduling breaks, coordinating final programming that airs on C-SPAN. Candidates should have computer skills, oral communication skills, personal interest in the field, self-motivation, strong interpersonal skills. Duration is 10 weeks. Unpaid. ▶ *1–2 programming operations technical interns:* responsibilities include technical aspects of setting the networks on-air, including program direction, master control, camera, lighting, audio and on-air promotions. Candidates should have ability to work with others, knowledge of field, oral communication skills, personal interest in the field, self-motivation, strong leadership ability. Duration is 10 weeks. Unpaid. ▶ *1–2 radio interns:* responsibilities include broadcasting a mix of daily programs similar in style to those found on the C-SPAN television networks, including congressional hearings, speeches, debates, and forum discussions. Candidates should have ability to work independently, computer skills, editing skills, oral communication skills, organizational skills, personal interest in the field, research skills, self-motivation, strong interpersonal skills, writing skills. Duration is 10–12 weeks. Unpaid. Open to college juniors, college seniors. International applications accepted.

Benefits Job counseling, names of contacts, possible full-time employment, willing to complete paperwork for educational credit.

Contact Write, call, fax, e-mail, or through World Wide Web site Angela P. Seldon, Human Resources Senior Specialist. Phone: 202-626-4868. Fax: 202-737-3323. E-mail: aseldon@c-span.org. In-person interview recommended (telephone interview accepted). Applicants must submit a letter of interest, resume, interactive application available. Applications are accepted continuously. World Wide Web: http://www.c-span.org.

E! ENTERTAINMENT TELEVISION NETWORKS
5750 Wilshire Boulevard
Los Angeles, California 90036

General Information Cable television network(s) and entertainment-related Web site. Established in 1990. Number of employees: 700. Number of internship applications received each year: 250.

Internships Available ▶ *1–2 benefits intern:* responsibilities include assisting with preparation for benefit meetings and events; assisting with safety programs/trainings; reviewing paperwork for online processes for benefits administration; assisting with update of Workers Comp OSHA log, ordering and maintaining benefit and compliance materials, administrative and research duties as needed. Candidates should have ability to work with others, college courses in field, office skills, personal interest in the field, plan to pursue career in field. Duration is 2–3 months. Unpaid. Open to college sophomores, college juniors, college seniors, graduate students, law students. ▶ *1–2 human resources recruitment interns:* responsibilities include providing general support for Recruitment team, administrative and research duties as needed; assisting with recruitment research including recruiting and finding next intern; shadowing each recruitment team member and assisting in creation of recruitment manual; assisting in ordering/maintaining new hire and temporary employee materials; creating new hire packets. Candidates should have ability to work with others, college courses in field, office skills, personal interest in the field, plan to pursue career in field, previous experience in office environment or customer service position preferred. Duration is 2–3 months. Unpaid. Open to college sophomores, college juniors, college seniors, graduate students, law students. ▶ *20–40 interns:* responsibilities include working in production (Los Angeles and New York City offices); Web site support and production (Los Angeles); international development (Los Angeles); and advertising sales (Los Angeles, New York, and Chicago). Candidates should have ability to work with others, college courses in field, office skills, personal interest in the field, plan to pursue career in field. Duration is summer, fall, or spring semesters/quarters; 15 to 40 hours per week for 3 months. Unpaid. Open to college juniors, college seniors, graduate students. ▶ *1–2 program planning interns:* responsibilities include assisting in fielding calls, handling on-air schedule questions, and ratings requests; pulling Nielsen Ratings with Galaxy Explorer; assist in weekly ratings reports, gathering program information, maintaining databases, scheduling E! style and E! radio; evaluating programming for Standards and Practices. Candidates should have ability to work with others, college courses in field, office skills, personal interest in the field, plan to pursue career in field, experience with PC platform, MS Excel and Word; experience with Filemaker Pro, Powerpoint and Galaxy Explorer a plus. Duration is 2–3 months. Unpaid. Open to college juniors, college seniors, recent college graduates, graduate students. International applications accepted.

Benefits On-the-job training, possible full-time employment, willing to complete paperwork for educational credit.

Contact Write, fax, or e-mail Human Resources, Internship Coordinator. Fax: 323-954-2888. E-mail: hr@eentertainment.com. No phone calls. In-person interview required. Applicants must submit a letter of interest, resume, letter from school (on school letterhead) verifying eligibility for school credit. Applications are accepted continuously. World Wide Web: http://www.eonline.com.

HOME BOX OFFICE
1100 Avenue of the Americas
New York, New York 10036

General Information Subscriber-based cable television channel. Established in 1972. Number of employees: 2,000. Unit of AOL Time Warner, Inc., New York, New York. Number of internship applications received each year: 1,500.

Internships Available ▶ *50–75 communications interns:* responsibilities include duties relating to all areas of communications including production, original programming, advertising, marketing, finance, computers, human resources, public relations, accounting, and photography. Candidates should have computer skills, office skills, oral communication skills, personal interest in the field, strong interpersonal skills, writing skills. Duration is 10–12 weeks. $500 per duration of internship. ▶ *2–4 human resources interns:* responsibilities include recruiting, reviewing resumes, and conducting phone interviews. Candidates should have ability to work independently, computer skills, office skills, oral communication skills, organizational skills, strong interpersonal skills. Duration is 10–12 weeks. $500 per duration of internship. Open to college sophomores, college juniors, college seniors. International applications accepted.

Benefits Possible full-time employment, willing to complete paperwork for educational credit, willing to provide letters of recommendation.

Contact Write or through World Wide Web site Internship Coordinator. No phone calls. In-person interview required. Applicants must submit a letter of interest, resume, formal letter from college or university stating that intern will receive academic credit. Applications are accepted continuously. World Wide Web: http://www.HBO.com.

THE JERRY SPRINGER SHOW
454 North Columbus Drive
Chicago, Illinois 60611

General Information One-hour daily syndicated talk show working its 10th season as one of America's most popular talk shows. Established in 1991. Number of employees: 60. Number of internship applications received each year: 800.

Internships Available ▶ *6–12 production interns:* responsibilities include researching and interviewing prospective guests for the show, researching possible show topics on the Internet and over the phone, being involved in all show day procedures, and working with guests who will be appearing on the program. Candidates should have ability to work with others, oral communication skills, organizational skills, plan to pursue career in field, research skills. Duration is minimum of 3 months (30 hours per week). Unpaid. Open to recent high school graduates, college freshmen, college sophomores, college juniors, college seniors, recent college graduates, graduate students, career changers. ▶ *1 technical intern:* responsibilities include assisting in the control room during taping, working closely with the assistant director on various production elements, production paperwork, assisting the director/assistant director, stage managers, delivering shows for satellite transmission when necessary. Candidates should have college courses in field, oral communication skills, organizational skills, plan to pursue career in field. Duration is minimum of 3 months (24 hours per week). Unpaid. Open to college freshmen, college sophomores, college juniors, college seniors, recent college graduates. ▶ *10–15 universal interns:* responsibilities include working in various areas including research, audience, production, business office, editing, and viewer mail. Candidates should have ability to work with others, office skills, oral communication skills, plan to pursue career in field. Duration is minimum of 3 months (24 hours per week). Unpaid. Open to recent high school graduates, college freshmen, college sophomores, college juniors, college seniors, recent college graduates. International applications accepted.

Benefits On-the-job training, possible full-time employment, willing to act as a professional reference, willing to complete paperwork for educational credit, willing to provide letters of recommendation.

Contact Write, call, fax, or e-mail Nathan Kotterman, Internship Coordinator. Phone: 312-321-5390. Fax: 312-321-5353. E-mail: springerpa@hotmail.com. In-person interview recommended (telephone interview accepted). Applicants must submit a formal organization application, letter of interest, resume. Applications are accepted continuously. World Wide Web: http://www.jerryspringer.com.

KCRA-TV
3 Television Circle
Sacramento, California 95814

General Information Commercial broadcast television station. Established in 1945. Number of employees: 230. Unit of Hearst-Argyle Television, Inc., New York, New York. Number of internship applications received each year: 100.

Internships Available ▶ *2 commercial production assistants:* responsibilities include production of commercial spots, promotions, public service announcements, and some special programming. Candidates should have college courses in field, computer skills, editing skills, personal interest in the field, research skills, self-motivation. Duration is 1 semester. Unpaid. Open to college sophomores, college

juniors, college seniors, recent college graduates, graduate students. ▶ *2 community relations assistants:* responsibilities include providing clerical support for public relations functions and KCRA-TV scholarship program, preparing community calendar, and assisting in production of public affairs programming. Candidates should have ability to work independently, computer skills, office skills, organizational skills, personal interest in the field, strong interpersonal skills, writing skills. Duration is 1 semester. Unpaid. Open to college sophomores, college juniors, college seniors, recent college graduates, graduate students. ▶ *1 consumer reporter assistant:* responsibilities include researching stories, setting up locations, accompanying reporters on assignment, and researching case files and records. Candidates should have college courses in field, computer skills, personal interest in the field, research skills, self-motivation, written communication skills. Duration is 1 semester. Unpaid. Open to college juniors, college seniors, recent college graduates, graduate students. ▶ *3 editing assistants:* responsibilities include working with the engineering supervisor and staff in transferring video and audio reports to master library tapes. Candidates should have ability to work with others, computer skills, oral communication skills, organizational skills, personal interest in the field, self-motivation. Duration is 1 semester. Unpaid. Open to college sophomores, college juniors, college seniors, recent college graduates, graduate students. ▶ *6 general news assistants:* responsibilities include working at the assignment desk answering reporters' phones, researching stories, accompanying reporters and/or photographers on assignments, and assisting news producers with production chores. Candidates should have college courses in field, computer skills, editing skills, personal interest in the field, research skills, written communication skills. Duration is 1 semester. Unpaid. Open to college sophomores, college juniors, college seniors, recent college graduates, graduate students. ▶ *1 graphics assistant:* responsibilities include working with art department in non-broadcast artwork including sales prices, printwork, set building and design, and computer graphics. Candidates should have college courses in field, computer skills, editing skills, plan to pursue career in field, self-motivation. Duration is 1 semester. Unpaid. Open to college sophomores, college juniors, college seniors, recent college graduates, graduate students. ▶ *1 maintenance engineer assistant:* responsibilities include helping troubleshoot and repair electronic broadcast equipment; helping install and remove equipment; observing the operation of the television station from a technical viewpoint. Candidates should have ability to work independently, ability to work with others, knowledge of field, organizational skills, plan to pursue career in field, self-motivation. Duration is 1 semester. Unpaid. Open to college seniors, recent college graduates, graduate students. ▶ *3 news producer assistants:* responsibilities include performing news production functions including tearing scripts, recording and logging news feeds, answering telephones, researching news stories, and writing. Candidates should have ability to work with others, computer skills, personal interest in the field, research skills, self-motivation, written communication skills. Duration is 1 semester. Unpaid. Open to college sophomores, college juniors, college seniors, recent college graduates, graduate students. ▶ *2 news special projects interns:* responsibilities include researching story ideas and assisting reporters and photographers in researching information for series and special projects. Candidates should have computer skills, organizational skills, personal interest in the field, research skills, self-motivation, written communication skills. Duration is 1 semester. Unpaid. Open to college sophomores, college juniors, college seniors, recent college graduates, graduate students. ▶ *1 promotions assistant:* responsibilities include assisting with production of on-air promotional spots including field, studio, and post production work; creating outside media work (newspaper ads and radio spots); and producing public service announcements. Candidates should have ability to work with others, college courses in field, computer skills, plan to pursue career in field, self-motivation. Duration is 1 semester. Unpaid. Open to college sophomores, college juniors, college seniors, recent college graduates, graduate students. ▶ *2 sales marketing assistant:* responsibilities include working on sales research, typing rough formats for sales promotion information; opportunities to accompany account executives on sales calls. Candidates should have computer skills, office skills, organizational

KCRA-TV (continued)

skills, personal interest in the field, self-motivation, strong interpersonal skills, writing skills. Duration is 1 semester. Unpaid. Open to college sophomores, college juniors, college seniors, recent college graduates, graduate students. ▶ *1–3 sports assistants:* responsibilities include compiling scores, researching stories and game information, monitoring televised games, and accompanying reporter and photographer in the field. Duration is 1 semester. Unpaid. Open to college sophomores, college juniors, college seniors, recent college graduates, graduate students.

Benefits On-the-job training, possible full-time employment, willing to complete paperwork for educational credit.

Contact Write, call, fax, or e-mail Julia Seabourn, Newsroom/Internship Program Administrative Assistant. Phone: 916-325-3287. Fax: 916-554-4663. E-mail: jseabourn@hearst.com. In-person interview recommended (telephone interview accepted). Applicants must submit a formal organization application, letter of interest, resume. Application deadline: April 8 for summer, July 15 for fall, November 25 for spring. World Wide Web: http://www.thekcrachannel.com.

KGO TELEVISION ABC, INC.
900 Front Street
San Francisco, California 94111

General Information Television station. Number of employees: 230. Affiliate of Disney–ABC, Inc., New York, New York. Number of internship applications received each year: 100.

Internships Available ▶ *News Research/"Seven On Your Side" interns:* responsibilities include assisting staff with research, collecting information from online services, maintaining news database, following up viewer letters, and other duties as assigned. Candidates should have ability to work independently, oral communication skills, plan to pursue career in field, research skills, written communication skills. Duration is 1 semester. $6.75 per hour. ▶ *Accounting/finance interns:* responsibilities include spreadsheet work; general office support; opportunities to assist with preparation of operation plan, capital budget, and/or annual and quarterly forecasts. Candidates should have ability to work independently, computer skills, knowledge of field, oral communication skills, organizational skills, written communication skills, familiarity with MS Office (helpful). Duration is 1 semester. $6.75 per hour. ▶ *Graphics interns:* responsibilities include visual research; general office support. Candidates should have ability to work independently, computer skills, knowledge of field, oral communication skills, written communication skills, creative talent, sense of humor. Duration is 1 semester. $6.75 per hour. ▶ *Human resources interns:* responsibilities include assisting in daily operations; may include projects in benefits, compensation, and/or recruitment. Candidates should have ability to work independently, oral communication skills, organizational skills, personal interest in the field, strong interpersonal skills, written communication skills, knowledge of MS Word and Excel (helpful). Duration is 1 semester. $6.75 per hour. ▶ *Information systems interns:* responsibilities include providing internal support for desktop applications, operating systems, and network troubleshooting. Candidates should have ability to work independently, analytical skills, computer skills, personal interest in the field, strong interpersonal skills, knowledge of operating systems and Novell NetWare. Duration is 1 semester. $6.75 per hour. ▶ *Marketing research interns:* responsibilities include working with Nielsen overnight reports, keeping track of ratings, creating new graphs, updating programming schedules, and general office duties. Candidates should have ability to work independently, computer skills, oral communication skills, personal interest in the field, written communication skills, attention to detail; knowledge of MS Office (helpful); marketing/research major (preferred). Duration is 1 semester. $6.75 per hour. ▶ *News/assignment desk interns:* responsibilities include monitoring news sources; screening, answering, and following up phone calls; updating source lists, and other duties as assigned. Candidates should have ability to work independently, ability to work with others, oral communication skills, plan to pursue career in field, written communication skills. Duration is 1 semester. $6.75 per hour. ▶ *News/weather interns:* responsibilities include assisting staff with preparation of on-air graphics and information. Candidates

should have ability to work independently, computer skills, declared college major in field, oral communication skills, plan to pursue career in field, written communication skills, familiarity with DIFAX products, domestic data bulletins, and Netscape a plus. Duration is 1 semester. $6.75 per hour. ▶ *On-air promotions interns:* responsibilities include assisting with pre-production duties such as logging tapes, searching for footage, and setting up promo shots; performing supervised edit sessions; assisting as assigned on location; other duties. Candidates should have ability to work independently, knowledge of field, personal interest in the field, strong interpersonal skills, energy and enthusiasm; ability to work well under pressure. Duration is 1 semester. $6.75 per hour. ▶ *Public affairs interns:* responsibilities include assisting community relations manager and director of public affairs; general office correspondence; selecting and writing 10 Second Community Calendar announcements; other duties as assigned. Candidates should have ability to work independently, oral communication skills, personal interest in the field, strong interpersonal skills, writing skills. Duration is 1 semester. $6.75 per hour. ▶ *Sales interns:* responsibilities include assisting in daily operations of broadcast sales office; general office support. Candidates should have ability to work independently, computer skills, oral communication skills, personal interest in the field, written communication skills, attention to detail; knowledge of Windows (helpful); marketing/communications major (preferred). Duration is 1 semester. $6.75 per hour. ▶ *Sports interns:* responsibilities include assisting the staff in daily operations, which may include watching and logging televised games, reviewing sports footage, and general office support. Candidates should have knowledge of field, oral communication skills, organizational skills, personal interest in the field, strong interpersonal skills, written communication skills. Duration is 1 semester. $6.75 per hour. Open to college juniors, college seniors, graduate students. International applications accepted.

Benefits On-the-job training, willing to complete paperwork for educational credit.

Contact Call Carrie L. Hess, Human Resources Administrator. Phone: 415-954-7774. Fax: 415-954-7514. E-mail: carrie.hess@abc.com. In-person interview required. Applicants must submit a formal organization application, letter of interest, resume, academic transcripts, two letters of recommendation. Applications are accepted continuously. World Wide Web: http://www.abc7news.com.

KIDSNET
6856 Eastern Avenue, NW, Suite 208
Washington, District of Columbia 20012

General Information Informational clearinghouse for children's electronic media. Established in 1983. Number of employees: 4. Number of internship applications received each year: 40.

Internships Available ▶ *2–3 research interns:* responsibilities include marketing, fulfilling subscriber requests, updating and maintaining computer database, preparing, editing, and distributing monthly publication; working with on-line services, assisting in grant application process, preparing for participation in national, regional, and local conferences, workshops, and charter member and board meetings. Candidates should have analytical skills, computer skills, editing skills, oral communication skills, organizational skills, written communication skills. Duration is 2–4 months. Unpaid. Open to college sophomores, college juniors, college seniors. International applications accepted.

Benefits Opportunity to attend seminars/workshops, possible full-time employment, willing to act as a professional reference, willing to complete paperwork for educational credit, willing to provide letters of recommendation.

Contact Write, call, fax, e-mail, or through World Wide Web site Karrie Johnston, Research Manager. Phone: 202-291-1400. Fax: 202-882-7315. E-mail: editor@kidsnet.org. In-person interview recommended (telephone interview accepted). Applicants must submit a letter of interest, resume, writing sample. Applications are accepted continuously. World Wide Web: http://www.kidsnet.org.

KQED INC.
2601 Mariposa Street
San Francisco, California 94110

General Information Public broadcasting company that includes KQED-TV and KQED-FM. Established in 1954. Number of employees: 230. Number of internship applications received each year: 100.

Internships Available ▶ *1 KQED Media Education Project intern:* responsibilities include working at the Center for Education and Lifelong Learning on such tasks as writing/editing publications, researching media, dubbing videotapes, and developing educational workshops. Candidates should have ability to work independently, computer skills, oral communication skills, research skills, written communication skills, minimum GPA of 2.5, experience with PC or Macintosh word processing and desktop publishing applications, Spanish skills a plus. Duration is flexible, minimum of 15 hours per week. Unpaid. ▶ *1 KQED TV Web intern:* responsibilities include participating in maintenance and development of the CELL Web site, researching and updating content, assisting program development staff and Web manager. Candidates should have ability to work independently, oral communication skills, organizational skills, written communication skills, minimum GPA of 2.5, strong computer skills including HTML programming, desktop publishing, and telecommunications. Duration is flexible, typically 4 months in spring, fall, or summer. Unpaid. ▶ *1 KQED TV program publicity intern:* responsibilities include assisting the publicist, filing program information and press clips, proofreading, research, writing, and organizing and preparing mailings. Candidates should have oral communication skills, organizational skills, self-motivation, strong interpersonal skills, writing skills, minimum GPA of 2.5, attention to detail, flexibility, Macintosh and/or PC proficiency, humor and enthusiasm. Duration is 1 semester (15-20 hours per week). Unpaid. ▶ *2 KQED educational services interns:* responsibilities include working in KQED's Center for Education and Lifelong Learning, writing and editing publications, doing audience research, developing educational content, and facilitating outreach activities. Candidates should have ability to work independently, computer skills, oral communication skills, research skills, self-motivation, written communication skills, major in education or related experience (preferred), Spanish skills a plus, knowledge of word processing and desktop publishing desirable, minimum GPA of 2.5. Duration is flexible, minimum of 15 hours. Unpaid. ▶ *1 KQED human resources intern:* responsibilities include developing effective communication techniques, HTML Web maintenance, events planning, employee relations, diversity training, benefits administration, recruiting, and customer services. Candidates should have computer skills, oral communication skills, organizational skills, self-motivation, writing skills, minimum GPA of 2.5, major in liberal arts, strong English/grammatical skills. Duration is flexible (16-24 hours per week); typically 4 months in spring, fall, or summer. Unpaid. ▶ *2 KQED-FM news interns:* responsibilities include researching, reporting, sound gathering, producing news and feature stories, and attending seminars and workshops on a variety of topics. Candidates should have oral communication skills, strong interpersonal skills, written communication skills, minimum GPA of 2.5; major in journalism, communications, or broadcasting or strong writing experience. Duration is 4 months, minimum of 16-24 hours per week. Unpaid. Open to college juniors, college seniors, graduate students. International applications accepted.

Benefits Formal training, job counseling, names of contacts, opportunity to attend seminars/workshops, willing to complete paperwork for educational credit.

Contact Write, fax, e-mail, or through World Wide Web site Katherine Yamamoto, Labor Relations Manager. Fax: 415-553-2183. E-mail: hr@kqed.org. No phone calls. In-person interview recommended (telephone interview accepted). Applicants must submit a letter of interest, resume, proof of eligibility to receive college credit; women and minorities strongly encouraged to apply. Applications are accepted continuously. World Wide Web: http://www.kqed.org/HR.

KSDK NEWS CHANNEL 5
1000 Market Street
St. Louis, Missouri 63101

General Information NBC-affiliated news source for St. Louis. Established in 1947. Number of employees: 155. Unit of Gannett, Arlington, Virginia. Number of internship applications received each year: 400.

Internships Available ▶ *1 assignment desk intern:* responsibilities include answering phones and making calls, primary story research. Candidates should have ability to work independently, college courses in field, computer skills, knowledge of field, oral communication skills, organizational skills, personal interest in the field, plan to pursue career in field, research skills, self-motivation, strong interpersonal skills, written communication skills. Duration is flexible by semester. Unpaid. Open to college freshmen, college sophomores, college juniors, college seniors, graduate students. ▶ *1 community relations/news intern:* responsibilities include working on projects for community relations department as well as news. Candidates should have ability to work independently, analytical skills, college courses in field, computer skills, knowledge of field, oral communication skills, organizational skills, personal interest in the field, plan to pursue career in field, research skills, self-motivation, strong interpersonal skills, strong leadership ability, written communication skills. Duration is flexible. Unpaid. Open to college freshmen, college sophomores, college juniors, college seniors. ▶ *1 program/magazine show intern:* responsibilities include assisting with production of *Show Me St. Louis*. Candidates should have ability to work independently, ability to work with others, college courses in field, computer skills, knowledge of field, oral communication skills, organizational skills, personal interest in the field, plan to pursue career in field, research skills, self-motivation, strong leadership ability, written communication skills. Duration is flexible. Unpaid. Open to college freshmen, college sophomores, college juniors, college seniors, graduate students. ▶ *1 research/special projects intern:* responsibilities include working on various stories, working as reporters' assistants, and working with producers. Candidates should have ability to work independently, ability to work with others, college courses in field, computer skills, knowledge of field, oral communication skills, organizational skills, personal interest in the field, plan to pursue career in field, research skills, self-motivation, written communication skills. Duration is flexible by semester. Unpaid. Open to college freshmen, college sophomores, college juniors, college seniors, graduate students. ▶ *1 sports intern:* responsibilities include researching sports stories and tracking games. Candidates should have ability to work independently, ability to work with others, college courses in field, computer skills, knowledge of field, oral communication skills, organizational skills, personal interest in the field, research skills, self-motivation, written communication skills. Duration is flexible by semester. Unpaid. Open to college freshmen, college sophomores, college juniors, college seniors, graduate students. International applications accepted.

Benefits Formal training, job counseling, names of contacts, on-the-job training, opportunity to attend seminars/workshops, possible full-time employment, willing to act as a professional reference, willing to complete paperwork for educational credit, willing to provide letters of recommendation, mileage reimbursement while on assignment.

Contact Write, call, fax, e-mail, or through World Wide Web site Ava Ehrlich, Executive Producer. Phone: 314-444-5120. Fax: 314-444-5164. E-mail: aehrlich@ksdk.gannett.com. In-person interview recommended (telephone interview accepted). Applicants must submit a letter of interest, resume, academic transcripts, 3 writing samples (broadcast). Application deadline: April 15 for fall, April 15 for summer, December 1 for winter. World Wide Web: http://ksdk.com.

KUED-TV
101 Wasatch Drive, University of Utah
Salt Lake City, Utah 84112

General Information Television station whose goal is to be a vital community resource in the areas of public discourse, education, community service, and the arts by providing alternative, noncommercial television programs that educate, enlighten, and

KUED-TV (continued)

entertain. Established in 1958. Number of employees: 107. Unit of University of Utah, Salt Lake City, Utah. Number of internship applications received each year: 10.

Internships Available ▶ *1 intern:* responsibilities include performing studio and field production lighting, audio work, off- and on-line editing; and rotating among administrative, development, and creative services departments. Candidates should have personal interest in the field. Duration is 1 summer. $1500 per duration of internship. Open to college juniors, college seniors. International applications accepted.

Benefits Formal training.

Contact Write or e-mail Christy Dunn, Human Resources Officer. E-mail: cdunn@media.utah.edu. No phone calls. In-person interview required. Applicants must submit a letter of interest, resume. Application deadline: April 24 for summer. World Wide Web: http://www.media.utah.edu.

LATE SHOW WITH DAVID LETTERMAN
1697 Broadway
New York, New York 10019

General Information Nightly talk/comedy/variety program. Established in 1993. Number of employees: 90. Unit of Worldwide Pants Incorporated, New York, New York. Number of internship applications received each year: 750.

Internships Available ▶ *14–15 interns:* responsibilities include working with specific departments including writing, production, talent, research, music, finance, and audience development, mailroom/audio department and as a floater. Candidates should have office skills, oral communication skills, organizational skills, plan to pursue career in field, strong interpersonal skills. Duration is approximately 3-4 months (depending on semester). Unpaid. Open to college sophomores, college juniors, college seniors. International applications accepted.

Benefits Names of contacts, on-the-job training, possible full-time employment, willing to act as a professional reference, willing to complete paperwork for educational credit, willing to provide letters of recommendation, exposure to a nationally-aired TV production.

Contact Write, call, or fax Janice Penino, Director, Human Resources. Phone: 212-975-5806. Fax: 212-975-4734. In-person interview required. Applicants must submit a resume, must be receiving college credit. Application deadline: March 1 for summer, June 1 for fall, October 1 for spring. World Wide Web: http://www.cbs.com.

MEDIA ONE
27800 Franklin Road
Southfield, Michigan 48034

General Information Cable television local programming department producing local origination programming. Established in 1981. Number of employees: 15. Division of Comcast, Philadelphia, Pennsylvania. Number of internship applications received each year: 15.

Internships Available ▶ *2–4 newsmaker interns:* responsibilities include learning video production, editing, and camera work. Candidates should have knowledge of field, oral communication skills, plan to pursue career in field, strong interpersonal skills, writing skills. Duration is minimum of 3 to 4 months. Unpaid. Open to college freshmen, college sophomores, college juniors, college seniors, recent college graduates, graduate students, law students, career changers, individuals reentering the workforce. International applications accepted.

Benefits Formal training, opportunity to attend seminars/workshops, possible full-time employment, willing to act as a professional reference, willing to complete paperwork for educational credit, willing to provide letters of recommendation.

Contact Write, call, fax, or e-mail Trista Pogue, Producer. Phone: 248-359-6526. Fax: 248-359-6750. E-mail: trista_pogue@cable.comcast.com. In-person interview required. Applicants must submit a letter of interest, resume. Application deadline: January 5 for spring, March 1 for summer, October 1 for winter.

MSNBC
One MSNBC Plaza
Secaucus, New Jersey 07094

General Information News network providing full coverage of the day's events, updates on breaking stories, and in-depth reports.

Internships Available ▶ *Interns:* responsibilities include positions in dayside newsroom, editing, fitness center, human resources, with "Imus in the Morning," marketing advertising and promotion, media relations, with "The News with Brian Williams," on-air graphics, planning/editorial, and production. Candidates should have ability to work independently, ability to work with others, analytical skills, computer skills, oral communication skills, research skills, self-motivation, written communication skills. Duration is 1 semester (minimum 16 hours per week). Unpaid.

Contact Write, fax, or e-mail Jeff Meade, Internship Coordinator. Fax: 201-583-5819. E-mail: employment@msnbc.com. Applicants must submit a resume, materials as specified on Web site. World Wide Web: http://www.msnbc.com.

MTV NETWORKS
1515 Broadway
New York, New York 10036

General Information Global entertainment cable television company comprising several channels including Music Television, VH1, Nickelodeon, TVLAND, TNN, CMT, and The Digital Suite. Established in 1981. Division of Viacom, Inc., New York, New York. Number of internship applications received each year: 6,000.

Internships Available ▶ *Interns:* responsibilities include working in various MTV Network channels in areas ranging from creative to corporate. Candidates should have computer skills, oral communication skills, written communication skills, flexibility and good work ethic; major in production, marketing, psychology, English, or broadcast journalism (preferred). Duration is 10 weeks (minimum of 2 full days per week). Unpaid. Open to college juniors, college seniors, some sophomores considered; must be receiving academic credit for internship. International applications accepted.

Benefits Formal training, job counseling, on-the-job training, opportunity to attend seminars/workshops, possible full-time employment, willing to act as a professional reference, willing to complete paperwork for educational credit, willing to provide letters of recommendation.

International Internships Available.

Contact Write, fax, e-mail, or through World Wide Web site Suzanne Lumerman, Internship Recruiter. Fax: 212-846-1473. E-mail: internships@mtvn.com. No phone calls. In-person interview recommended (telephone interview accepted). Applicants must submit a resume, cover letter indicating areas of interest and preferred semester. Applications are accepted continuously. World Wide Web: http://www.mtv.com.

NBC4
30 Rockefeller Plaza, Suite 687–E1
New York, New York 10112

General Information Television broadcasting station. Established in 1941. Number of employees: 35. Number of internship applications received each year: 35.

Internships Available ▶ *20 NEWS-4 interns:* responsibilities include gathering information, researching stories, working in the field on remotes, and performing field and library research; positions at assignment desk, specials unit, investigative/political, sports, meteorology, consumer news, Long Island and New Jersey bureaus, news and entertainment. Candidates should have ability to work independently, ability to work with others, oral communication skills, organizational skills, personal interest in the field, self-motivation, writing skills. Duration is spring, summer, or fall. Unpaid. Open to college sophomores, college juniors, college seniors, graduate students. ▶ *Creative services interns:* responsibilities include assisting on-air administrator, producers/writers, managers, and directors in all facets of pre- and post-production; tagging network and syndicated promotions, and assisting with major campaign work. Candidates should have ability to work independently, oral communication skills, organizational skills, personal interest in the field, self-motivation, written communication skills. Duration is spring, summer, or fall. Unpaid. Open to college freshmen, college sophomores, college juniors, college seniors, graduate students. ▶ *1 marketing intern.* Candidates should have ability to work with others, oral communication skills, organizational skills, research skills, self-motivation, writing skills. Duration is spring, summer, or fall. Unpaid. Open to college sophomores, college juniors, college seniors, graduate students. ▶ *Research interns:* responsibilities include analyzing daily station ratings and sweeps rating books; assisting sales department with special projects, and helping to develop sales promotions. Candidates should have ability to work independently, oral communication skills, personal interest in the field, research skills, writing skills. Duration is one spring, summer, or fall. Unpaid. Open to college freshmen, college sophomores, college juniors, college seniors, graduate students. ▶ *Sales interns.* Candidates should have ability to work independently, oral communication skills, personal interest in the field, self-motivation, writing skills. Duration is spring, summer, or fall. Unpaid. Open to college freshmen, college sophomores, college juniors, college seniors. ▶ *Station relations interns:* responsibilities include organizing and producing daily public service announcements and assisting in the production of studio and remote shows. Candidates should have ability to work with others, oral communication skills, organizational skills, personal interest in the field, research skills, written communication skills. Duration is spring, summer, or fall. Unpaid. Open to college freshmen, college sophomores, college juniors, college seniors, graduate students.

Benefits Opportunity to attend seminars/workshops, willing to act as a professional reference, willing to complete paperwork for educational credit, willing to provide letters of recommendation, reimbursement of reasonable travel expenses, opportunity to interact with professionals in all departments.

Contact Write, fax, or e-mail Ms. Millie Quiles, Internship Recruiter, 30 Rockefeller Plaza, Suite 687-E1, New York, New York 10012. Fax: 212-664-6449. E-mail: millie.quiles@nbc.com. No phone calls. In-person interview required. Applicants must submit a letter of interest, resume, some documentation showing academic credit will be received for the internship experience. Applications are accepted continuously.

NJN, THE NEW JERSEY NETWORK
25 South Stockton Street, PO Box 777
Trenton, New Jersey 08625-0777

General Information Public television company. Established in 1970. Number of employees: 160. Number of internship applications received each year: 50.

Internships Available ▶ *2 news assistants:* responsibilities include researching and setting up field reports, working the news desk and crew logistics, news video compiling and archiving, and interviewing newsmakers in the field (for advanced interns). Candidates should have ability to work independently, college courses in field, computer skills, office skills, oral communication skills, personal interest in the field, plan to pursue career in field, self-motivation, strong interpersonal skills, written communication skills. Duration is flexible, usually 15 hours per week. Unpaid. Open to college sophomores, college juniors, college seniors, must be earning college credit. International applications accepted.

Benefits On-the-job training.

Contact Write, call, fax, or e-mail Mike Curtis, Producer. Phone: 609-777-5193. Fax: 609-633-2927. E-mail: mcurtis@njn.org. Applicants must submit a letter of interest, resume, in-person interview recommended. Applications are accepted continuously. World Wide Web: http://www.njn.net.

SESAME WORKSHOP
One Lincoln Plaza
New York, New York 10023

General Information Not-for-profit company using media to educate children and families worldwide; sponsors programs for traditional and new media; engages in publishing, product licensing, and community outreach; producer of Sesame Street. Established in 1969. Number of employees: 350. Number of internship applications received each year: 500.

Internships Available ▶ *10–20 interns:* responsibilities include working in book publishing, graphic design, administrative, and various production departments. Candidates should have ability to work independently, ability to work with others, analytical skills, college courses in field, computer skills, editing skills, knowledge of field, office skills, oral communication skills, organizational skills, personal interest in the field, plan to pursue career in field, research skills, self-motivation, strong leadership ability, writing skills, knowledge of Microsoft Word. Duration is 3 months. Unpaid. Open to college freshmen, college sophomores, college juniors, college seniors, graduate students, law students, must be currently enrolled in college or university. International applications accepted.

Benefits Opportunity to attend seminars/workshops, possible full-time employment, willing to act as a professional reference, willing to complete paperwork for educational credit, willing to provide letters of recommendation, daily stipend.

Contact Write, fax, or e-mail Internship Coordinator, One Lincoln Plaza, Fourth Floor, New York, New York 10023. Fax: 212-875-6113. E-mail: human.resources@sesameworkshop.org. No phone calls. In-person interview recommended (telephone interview accepted). Applicants must submit a letter of interest, resume, letter from advisor confirming school enrollment. Application deadline: April 1 for summer, August 1 for fall, December 1 for spring/winter. World Wide Web: http://www.sesameworkshop.org.

THINKTVNETWORK/GREATER DAYTON PUBLIC TELEVISION
110 South Jefferson Street
Dayton, Ohio 45402-2415

General Information Television station comprising 2 public broadcasting stations: WPTD and WPTO. Established in 1959. Number of employees: 50. Number of internship applications received each year: 15.

Internships Available ▶ *3–4 interns:* responsibilities include working in areas of production, engineering, or marketing/administration. Candidates should have ability to work independently, computer skills, editing skills, office skills, oral communication skills, organizational skills, personal interest in the field, plan to pursue career in field, research skills, self-motivation, strong interpersonal skills, writing skills, experience or college courses in field. Duration is flexible. $6–$7 per hour. Open to college juniors, college seniors. International applications accepted.

Benefits Formal training, names of contacts, possible full-time employment, willing to complete paperwork for educational credit, willing to provide letters of recommendation.

Contact Write, fax, or through World Wide Web site Ms. Jennifer Chisiaghi, Office and Personnel Manager. Fax: 937-220-1642. E-mail: jennifer_chisiaghi@wptd.pbs.org. No phone calls. In-person interview required. Applicants must submit a formal organization application, letter of interest, resume. Applications are accepted continuously. World Wide Web: http://www.thinktv.org.

WCAU-TV, CHANNEL 10 TELEVISION, INVESTIGATIVE UNIT
10 Monument Road
Bala Cynwyd, Pennsylvania 19004

General Information Investigative unit that prepares reports for television and helps people with complaints about products, services, and institutions. Number of employees: 3. Unit of NBC 10, Bala Cynwyd, Pennsylvania. Number of internship applications received each year: 50.

Internships Available ▶ *1–5 researcher interns:* responsibilities include researching and setting up news stories; coming up with story ideas, handling viewer communication, logging tapes, and assisting in investigations. Candidates should have ability to work independently, ability to work with others, oral communication skills, organizational skills, research skills, self-motivation. Dura-

WCAU-TV, Channel 10 Television, Investigative Unit (continued)
tion is 1 semester. Unpaid. Open to college juniors, college seniors, must be receiving college credit. International applications accepted.
Benefits Formal training, possible full-time employment, willing to complete paperwork for educational credit, willing to provide letters of recommendation.
Contact Write, call, fax, or through World Wide Web site Producer. Phone: 610-668-5645. Fax: 610-668-5649. Applicants must submit a letter of interest, resume, application (available on Web site). Applications are accepted continuously. World Wide Web: http://www.nbc10.com.

WCHS-TV
1301 Piedmont Road
Charleston, West Virginia 25301

General Information Commercial television station broadcasting in a competitive top-50 market. Established in 1958. Number of employees: 100. Unit of Sinclair Broadcast Group, Baltimore, Maryland. Number of internship applications received each year: 40.
Internships Available ► *6–15 news interns:* responsibilities include performing off-air reporting duties such as gathering and writing news stories and running the teleprompter. Candidates should have college courses in field, computer skills, editing skills, plan to pursue career in field, strong interpersonal skills, writing skills. Duration is 200 hours. Unpaid. Open to college freshmen, college sophomores, college juniors, college seniors, recent college graduates, graduate students, law students, career changers, individuals reentering the workforce. International applications accepted.
Benefits Willing to complete paperwork for educational credit, willing to provide letters of recommendation.
Contact Write, call, or fax Ms. Jessica Worstell, News Administrative Assistant. Phone: 304-345-4115. Fax: 304-345-1849. In-person interview recommended (telephone interview accepted). Applicants must submit a resume. Applications are accepted continuously. World Wide Web: http://www.wchstv.com.

WCNC-TV/NBC6
1001 Wood Ridge Center Drive
Charlotte, North Carolina 28217

General Information TV station. Number of employees: 200. Subsidiary of BECO Coporation, Dallas, Texas. Number of internship applications received each year: 200.
Internships Available ► *Interns:* responsibilities include weekly evaluation; participation in intern newscasts; workshops; completion of beat calls and projects; specific positions available in reporting, producing, new media, assignment desk, editing, photography, sports, weather, sales, art, promotions and community affairs. Candidates should have ability to work independently, oral communication skills, plan to pursue career in field, research skills, self-motivation, written communication skills. Duration is 1–2 semesters. Unpaid. Open to college juniors, college seniors, graduate students. International applications accepted.
Benefits Names of contacts, willing to act as a professional reference, willing to complete paperwork for educational credit, willing to provide letters of recommendation.
Contact E-mail Greg Shepperd, Planning Editor. Fax: 704-357-4975. E-mail: gshepperd@nbc6.com. No phone calls. In-person interview recommended (telephone interview accepted). Applicants must submit a formal organization application, letter of interest, resume, letter of recommendation. Applications are accepted continuously. World Wide Web: http://www.nbc6.com.

WDAF-TV
3030 Summit
Kansas City, Missouri 64108

General Information FOX affiliate that provides diverse programming, including sports and entertainment, with emphasis on local news. Established in 1949. Number of employees: 215. Unit of News Corporation, Los Angeles, California. Number of internship applications received each year: 40.

Internships Available ► *1–2 art/graphics interns:* responsibilities include working on AVA Paintbox or Macintosh. Candidates should have ability to work independently, college courses in field, computer skills, oral communication skills, self-motivation. Duration is one summer or one semester. Unpaid. ► *1–2 community relations/public relations interns:* responsibilities include writing and producing public service announcements, helping with events, writing press releases, assisting in field and studio shoots, and performing clerical responsibilities. Candidates should have ability to work independently, college courses in field, computer skills, organizational skills, strong interpersonal skills, writing skills. Duration is one summer or one semester. Unpaid. ► *1–3 creative services interns:* responsibilities include writing on-air voice-over copy, assisting in field and studio shoots, editing, producing audio carts, and performing various other duties. Candidates should have ability to work independently, college courses in field, computer skills, oral communication skills, self-motivation, writing skills. Duration is 1 semester. Unpaid. ► *3–5 news interns.* Candidates should have computer skills, oral communication skills, plan to pursue career in field, self-motivation, strong interpersonal skills, writing skills. Duration is one summer or one semester. Unpaid. ► *1–2 sales interns:* responsibilities include assisting account executives, going on sales calls, and performing various other duties. Candidates should have computer skills, knowledge of field, oral communication skills, self-motivation, strong interpersonal skills, writing skills. Duration is one summer or one semester. Unpaid. Open to college juniors, college seniors. International applications accepted.
Benefits Job counseling, names of contacts, on-the-job training, possible full-time employment, willing to complete paperwork for educational credit, willing to provide letters of recommendation.
Contact Write or fax Gail Lang, Human Resources Director. Fax: 816-932-9193. In-person interview required. Applicants must submit a letter of interest, resume, three personal references, three letters of recommendation. Applications are accepted continuously. World Wide Web: http://www.wdaftv4.com.

WDBJ TELEVISION, INC.
2001 Colonial Avenue
Roanoke, Virginia 24015

General Information CBS affiliate with a potential viewing audience of over 1 million each week in portions of Virginia, West Virginia, and North Carolina. Established in 1955. Number of employees: 130. Unit of Schurz Communications, Inc., South Bend, Indiana. Number of internship applications received each year: 25.
Internships Available ► *1 engineering intern:* responsibilities include assisting with master control and maintenance observation. Candidates should have ability to work independently, ability to work with others, declared college major in field, self-motivation. Duration is flexible. Unpaid. Open to college juniors, college seniors. ► *1–2 news interns:* responsibilities include assisting with reporting and producing. Candidates should have ability to work independently, ability to work with others, computer skills, declared college major in field, self-motivation, writing skills. Duration is flexible. Unpaid. Open to college juniors, college seniors. ► *1–2 production interns:* responsibilities include learning camera techniques, lighting, audio, tape editing, studio set-up, electronic field production, and character generator. Candidates should have ability to work independently, ability to work with others, computer skills, declared college major in field. Duration is flexible. Unpaid. Open to college juniors, college seniors. ► *1 sales intern:* responsibilities include working with business community to sell broadcast air time. Candidates should have computer skills, declared college major in field, oral communication skills, strong interpersonal skills, written communication skills. Duration is flexible. Unpaid. International applications accepted.
Benefits Possible full-time employment, willing to complete paperwork for educational credit.
Contact Write, fax, e-mail, or through World Wide Web site Ms. Monica L. Taylor, Personnel Manager. Fax: 540-344-5097. E-mail: mtaylor@wdbj7.com. No phone calls. In-person interview required. Applicants must submit a formal organization application, letter

of interest, resume, letter of recommendation. Applications are accepted continuously. World Wide Web: http://www.wdbj7.com.

WDCQ-TV
1961 Delta Road
University Center, Michigan 48710

General Information   Professional TV and radio stations (PBS and NPR) providing academic preparation for work in telecommunications industry. Established in 1964. Number of employees: 30. Unit of Delta College, University Center, Michigan.
Internships Available ▶ *1–2 TV field/studio production interns:* responsibilities include assisting in producing and editing on-air productions. Duration is 4–6 months. Position available as unpaid or paid. ▶ *1 radio intern:* responsibilities include on-air programming, fund-raising on-air, and assisting with production of audio tapes. Duration is 4–6 months. Position available as unpaid or paid. Candidates for all positions should have ability to work independently, computer skills, knowledge of field, oral communication skills, written communication skills. Open to college freshmen, college sophomores, college juniors, college seniors.
Benefits   Formal training, job counseling, names of contacts, willing to complete paperwork for educational credit, willing to provide letters of recommendation.
Contact   Write, call, or e-mail Mr. Kent Wieland, Production Manager, Delta Broadcasting. Phone: 517-686-9350. E-mail: kwwielan@alpha.delta.edu. Applicants must submit a letter of interest, resume. Applications are accepted continuously. World Wide Web: http://www.delta.edu/~tvradio.

WDIV-TV
550 West Lafayette Boulevard
Detroit, Michigan 48226

General Information   Commercial television station. Number of employees: 200. Unit of Post-Newsweek Stations, Detroit, Michigan. Number of internship applications received each year: 250.
Internships Available ▶ *5–8 news department interns:* responsibilities include assisting in various areas including assignment desk, sports, and special projects. Candidates should have ability to work with others, college courses in field, oral communication skills, plan to pursue career in field, self-motivation, written communication skills. Duration is 1 semester. Unpaid. ▶ *2–3 programming department interns:* responsibilities include assisting producers with field and studio shoots, research, writing scripts, screening and logging tapes, audience booking, organizing edit sessions, and researching and gathering materials for editorials and documentaries. Candidates should have college courses in field, oral communication skills, plan to pursue career in field, self-motivation, writing skills. Duration is 1 semester. Unpaid. ▶ *1 research department intern:* responsibilities include creating sales onesheets; maintaining research wall, weekly sweeps tracking report, and news promotable ratings/calendars; recording and viewing of competitors' newscast promotables; assisting in assembly or presentations; typing various reports and assisting in analysis; miscellaneous projects. Candidates should have ability to work with others, college courses in field, computer skills, oral communication skills, plan to pursue career in field, self-motivation, written communication skills. Duration is 1 semester. Unpaid. ▶ *1 sales department intern:* responsibilities include maintenance of matrix sales software; monitoring daily newspapers and radio to establish new leading sourcing; monitoring local TV competitors to establish new promotional ideas; maintenance of client contracts and weekly updates of sales sports for account executives; assisting in writing sales orders, on client calls, with development of client news packages, and with sales rating seminar. Candidates should have ability to work with others, college courses in field, computer skills, oral communication skills, plan to pursue career in field, self-motivation, written communication skills. Duration is 1 semester. Unpaid. Open to college juniors, college seniors, graduate students.
Benefits   On-the-job training, willing to complete paperwork for educational credit.
Contact   Write, call, or fax Barbara Zielinski, Human Resources Administrator. Phone: 313-222-0468. Fax: 313-222-0471. In-person

interview required. Applicants must submit a formal organization application, resume. Application deadline: April 1 for summer, October 1 for winter.

WEWB-TV
14 Corporate Woods Boulevard
Albany, New York 12211

General Information   WEWB-TV (WB45) is the capital region's affiliate for Warner Brothers Television (The 'WB') and Tribune Broadcasting. Established in 1999. Number of employees: 13. Unit of Tribune Broadcasting Company, Chicago, Illinois. Number of internship applications received each year: 50.
Internships Available ▶ *2–3 marketing/sales interns:* responsibilities include working in the fast-paced environment of a growing TV station; participating in station events, assisting station staff and learning how WB affiliate operates. Candidates should have computer skills, office skills, oral communication skills, strong interpersonal skills, writing skills. Duration is 1 semester. Unpaid. Open to college freshmen, college sophomores, college juniors, college seniors.
Benefits   On-the-job training, willing to act as a professional reference, willing to complete paperwork for educational credit, willing to provide letters of recommendation.
Contact   Fax or e-mail Dan Sher, Marketing/Public Relations Director. Fax: 518-431-3155. E-mail: dsher@tribune.com. No phone calls. In-person interview recommended (telephone interview accepted). Applicants must submit a letter of interest, resume. Applications are accepted continuously. World Wide Web: http://www.wb45.com.

WEWS-TV 5
3001 Euclid Avenue
Cleveland, Ohio 44115

General Information   Television station. Established in 1947. Number of employees: 187. Unit of Scripps Howard Company, Cincinnati, Ohio. Number of internship applications received each year: 175.
Internships Available ▶ *1 Akron News Bureau intern:* responsibilities include working as the assignment desk editor in Akron. Candidates should have ability to work independently, oral communication skills, self-motivation, strong interpersonal skills, written communication skills. Duration is 1 quarter or semester. Unpaid. Open to college sophomores, college juniors, graduate students, law students. ▶ *1–3 Good Morning Cleveland interns:* responsibilities include hands-on experience in the production of a live daily morning news/talk show; duties range from researching topics, helping viewers, and assisting at assignment desk to keeping show records. Candidates should have ability to work independently, ability to work with others, computer skills, oral communication skills, organizational skills, research skills, self-motivation, strong leadership ability. Duration is 1 quarter or semester. Unpaid. Open to college juniors, college seniors, graduate students. ▶ *3–6 Team 5 investigators:* responsibilities include conducting phone work, giving referrals to viewers who call helpline, accompanying field reporters, and assisting the investigative team with research. Candidates should have ability to work independently, oral communication skills, organizational skills, research skills, self-motivation, strong interpersonal skills, strong leadership ability, written communication skills, interest in investigative and consumer reporting and producing. Duration is 1 quarter or semester. Unpaid. Open to college juniors, college seniors, graduate students, law students. ▶ *1 editing intern:* responsibilities include working with editors, receiving and cataloging video materials from all over the world, and learning to edit stories that are to appear on the air. Candidates should have ability to work independently, oral communication skills, organizational skills, self-motivation, strong interpersonal skills. Duration is 1 quarter or semester. Unpaid. Open to college juniors, college seniors, graduate students, law students. ▶ *6–8 news assignment desk interns:* responsibilities include answering phone calls, placing calls to local law enforcement or story contacts, and communicating with field news crews. Candidates should have ability to work independently, computer skills, oral communication skills, organizational skills, research skills, self-motivation, strong

WEWS-TV 5 (continued)

interpersonal skills, strong leadership ability. Duration is 1 quarter or semester. Unpaid. Open to college juniors, college seniors, graduate students, law students. ▶ *1–2 news producing interns:* responsibilities include working with producers, overseeing newscasts as they are being formatted to the final seconds of the broadcast; student will leave with a portfolio of writing samples and newscasts. Candidates should have ability to work independently, ability to work with others, computer skills, oral communication skills, organizational skills, research skills, self-motivation, strong leadership ability, writing skills, a strong interest in becoming a producer. Duration is 1 quarter or semester. Unpaid. Open to college juniors, college seniors, graduate students. ▶ *1 production intern.* Candidates should have oral communication skills, self-motivation, strong interpersonal skills. Duration is 1 quarter or semester. Unpaid. Open to college juniors, college seniors, graduate students. ▶ *2 promotion interns:* responsibilities include assisting with the coordination of station events and special projects, answering viewer calls and letters, sending out promotional materials, writing movie promos, scheduling and maintaining public service announcements, and performing general office duties. Candidates should have ability to work independently, computer skills, oral communication skills, organizational skills, plan to pursue career in field, self-motivation, strong interpersonal skills, strong leadership ability, written communication skills. Duration is 1 quarter or semester. Unpaid. Open to college juniors, college seniors, graduate students. ▶ *1–3 sales interns:* responsibilities include typing, filing, checking sales orders, assisting the sales managers on special projects, assisting the account executives, and occasionally accompanying account executives on sales calls. Candidates should have computer skills, office skills, oral communication skills, organizational skills, self-motivation, strong interpersonal skills, written communication skills. Duration is 1 quarter or semester. Unpaid. Open to college juniors, college seniors, graduate students. ▶ *3 sports interns:* responsibilities include clearing the sports wires, shot-sheeting and timing interviews, monitoring afternoon sports feeds, helping keep the sports director informed on breaking events, and periodically accompanying the sports producer on stories. Candidates should have ability to work independently, oral communication skills, self-motivation, strong interpersonal skills, written communication skills, knowledge of sports helpful. Duration is 1 quarter or semester. Unpaid. Open to college juniors, college seniors, graduate students, law students. International applications accepted.

Benefits Possible full-time employment, willing to complete paperwork for educational credit, hands-on experience.

Contact Write or fax Ms. Moreen Bailey Frater, Community Affairs Director. Phone: 216-431-5555. Fax: 216-361-1762. E-mail: bailey@wews.com. In-person interview required. Applicants must submit a letter of interest, resume. Applications are accepted continuously. World Wide Web: http://www.newsnet5.com.

WGAL 8 (TV)
1300 Columbia Avenue
Lancaster, Pennsylvania 17604-7127

General Information Television station, affiliated with NBC, emphasizing news, public affairs, and programming. Established in 1949. Number of employees: 150. Unit of Hearst-Argyle Television, Inc., New York, New York. Number of internship applications received each year: 100.

Internships Available ▶ *1–2 creative services interns:* responsibilities include working as production assistant on commercial, promotional, and public service announcement shoots and updating Web site data. Candidates should have computer skills, declared college major in field, oral communication skills, organizational skills, personal interest in the field, self-motivation, strong interpersonal skills, writing skills, audio and video editing skills, knowledge of field cameras. Duration is 1 semester. Unpaid. Open to college juniors, college seniors, graduate students, applicants must attend school or have home residence in viewing area. ▶ *4–6 news interns:* responsibilities include accompanying reporters and assisting the assignment editor and newscast producers. Candidates should have ability to work independently, oral communication skills, organizational skills, strong leadership ability, writing skills.

Duration is 1 semester. Unpaid. Open to college juniors, college seniors, graduate students, applicants must be attending school or have home residence in viewing area. ▶ *1–2 sports interns:* responsibilities include assisting department staff. Candidates should have ability to work independently, declared college major in field, knowledge of field, oral communication skills, personal interest in the field, self-motivation, strong interpersonal skills, writing skills, video editing skills. Duration is 1 semester. Unpaid. Open to college juniors, college seniors, graduate students, applicants must attend school or have home residence in viewing area. ▶ *1–2 weather interns:* responsibilities include preparing weather data and learning about broadcasting. Candidates should have ability to work independently, ability to work with others, analytical skills, computer skills, declared college major in field, oral communication skills, organizational skills, self-motivation, written communication skills. Duration is 1 semester. Unpaid. Open to college juniors, college seniors, graduate students, applicants must attend school or have home residence in viewing area.

Benefits On-the-job training, possible full-time employment, willing to complete paperwork for educational credit.

Contact Write, call, fax, e-mail, or through World Wide Web site Juliet Finkey, Internship Coordinator. Phone: 717-393-5851 Ext. 255. Fax: 717-393-9484. E-mail: news8@wgal.com. In-person interview required. Applicants must submit a letter of interest, resume. Application deadline: up to one year in advance, particularly for summer positions. World Wide Web: http://www.thewgalchannel.com.

WHYY, INC.
Independence Mall West, 150 North Sixth Street
Philadelphia, Pennsylvania 19106

General Information Public television and radio station. Established in 1954. Number of employees: 221. Number of internship applications received each year: 200.

Internships Available ▶ *1–2 Radio Times interns:* responsibilities include assisting staff with radio production duties and with library research relating to upcoming interview guests on the local public affairs program produced by WHYY-FM. Candidates should have ability to work independently, ability to work with others, college courses in field, computer skills, editing skills, research skills. Duration is 1 semester. Unpaid. Open to college sophomores, college juniors, college seniors. ▶ *1–3 TV news interns for "Twelve Tonight":* responsibilities include assisting the news and editorial staff with monitoring scanners and 2-way radio calls, performing clerical duties, and preparing stories to air in the Wilmington, Delaware office. Candidates should have ability to work with others, college courses in field, computer skills, research skills, writing skills. Duration is 1 semester. Unpaid. Open to college sophomores, college juniors, college seniors. ▶ *2–5 TV production interns:* responsibilities include assisting staff with library research and related duties, assisting with operating character generator/teleprompter, logging tapes, typing and filing scripts, and performing general office duties. Candidates should have ability to work with others, college courses in field, computer skills, editing skills, research skills, self-motivation, writing skills. Duration is 1 semester. Unpaid. Open to college sophomores, college juniors, college seniors. ▶ *1–2 Voices in the Family interns.* Candidates should have college courses in field, computer skills, editing skills, research skills, strong interpersonal skills. Duration is 1 semester. Unpaid. Open to college sophomores, college juniors, college seniors. ▶ *2–3 WHYY-FM news interns:* responsibilities include assisting reporters with writing broadcast copy, handling phone calls, setting up interviews, and gathering research material and sound bites for broadcast. Candidates should have ability to work independently, college courses in field, computer skills, editing skills, research skills, writing skills. Duration is 1 semester. Unpaid. Open to college juniors, college seniors. ▶ *1–3 development/fundraising interns:* responsibilities include assisting staff with choosing premiums for pledge drives, calling to obtain samples, writing and designing premium brochures, assisting with market research, and updating reports using Lotus 123. Candidates should have ability to work independently, ability to work with others, computer skills, office skills, oral communication skills, writing skills. Duration is 1 semester. Unpaid. Open to college sophomores, college juniors, college seniors. ▶ *1 foundation/grants research intern:* responsibilities include assisting grants writer in establishing a coordinated and unified approach to soliciting support for WHYY, researching the many funding services to which WHYY could apply, and composing brief profiles of potential donors. Candidates should have ability to work independently, computer skills, research skills, self-motivation, writing skills. Duration is 1 semester. Unpaid. Open to college sophomores, college juniors, college seniors. ▶ *1 human resources assistant:* responsibilities include assisting staff with administrative, recruitment, benefits, and training needs. Candidates should have college courses in field, computer skills, oral communication skills, personal interest in the field, plan to pursue career in field, strong interpersonal skills. Duration is 1 semester. Unpaid. Open to college sophomores, college juniors, college seniors. ▶ *1 marketing intern:* responsibilities include assisting marketing/sales representatives with database research for client presentations, performing market research and audience research projects, and assisting with administrative duties as needed. Candidates should have ability to work independently, ability to work with others, computer skills, office skills, oral communication skills, research skills. Duration is 1 semester. Unpaid. ▶ *1–2 member services interns:* responsibilities include responding to member service calls and requests, assisting with premium shipments and inventory maintenance, assisting with fund-raisers, and performing general office duties. Candidates should have ability to work independently, ability to work with others, computer skills, oral communication skills, self-motivation, writing skills. Duration is 1 semester. Unpaid. Open to college sophomores, college juniors, college seniors. ▶ *1–2 public information/public relations interns:* responsibilities include assisting publicists with writing press releases and pieces for company newsletter, updating mailing lists and press clips, and assisting with special events and promotional activities. Candidates should have ability to work with others, college courses in field, computer skills, editing skills, writing skills. Duration is 1 semester. Unpaid. Open to college sophomores, college juniors, college seniors.

Benefits Possible full-time employment, willing to complete paperwork for educational credit.

Contact Write, call, fax, e-mail, or through World Wide Web site Ms. Sandra Chatfield, Community Relations Manager. Phone: 215-351-1261. Fax: 215-574-1477. E-mail: schatfield@whyy.org. In-person interview required. Applicants must submit a formal organization application, letter of interest, resume, writing sample. Applications are accepted continuously. World Wide Web: http://www.whyy.org.

WLRN PUBLIC RADIO AND TELEVISION
172 Northeast 15th Street
Miami, Florida 33132

General Information Public radio and television station. Established in 1951. Number of employees: 100. Division of Miami-Dade County Public Schools, Miami, Florida. Number of internship applications received each year: 10.

Internships Available ▶ *1 instructional television intern:* responsibilities include assisting with the selection, purchase, and promotion of instructional television programming and outreach programming. Candidates should have ability to work independently, ability to work with others, computer skills, self-motivation, available between the hours of 8:00 am and 4:30 pm. Duration is 3 months to 1 year. Unpaid. Open to college freshmen, college sophomores, college juniors, college seniors. ▶ *3–5 interns:* responsibilities include working in TV production, radio, public relations, and technical aspects of radio and TV. Candidates should have ability to work independently, ability to work with others, college courses in field, self-motivation, available between the hours of 8:00 am and 4:30 pm. Duration is 1-2 semesters; up to 1 year. Unpaid. Open to college freshmen, college sophomores, college juniors, college seniors, must be local student. ▶ *1–2 production interns:* responsibilities include operating studio cameras, assisting with set construction and breakdown and assisting with remote productions; may also assist with stage managing, and video tape recording. Candidates should have ability to work independently, ability to work with others, knowledge of field,

self-motivation, available between the hours of 8:00 am and 4:30 pm. Duration is 1 semester. Unpaid. Open to college freshmen, college sophomores, college juniors, college seniors, graduate students. ▶ *1 programming intern:* responsibilities include conducting research to help with the selection of programming for air; helping with scheduling programs. Candidates should have ability to work independently, ability to work with others, computer skills, organizational skills, self-motivation, available between the hours of 8:00 am to 4:30 pm. Duration is 3 months to 1 year. Unpaid. Open to college freshmen, college sophomores, college juniors, college seniors. ▶ *1 public information intern:* responsibilities include writing press releases, preparing promotional material, and assisting with the distribution of these materials; other day-to-day press office activities. Candidates should have ability to work independently, ability to work with others, knowledge of field, self-motivation, written communication skills. Duration is 3 months to 1 year. Unpaid. Open to college freshmen, college sophomores, college juniors, college seniors. International applications accepted.

Benefits On-the-job training, possible full-time employment, willing to complete paperwork for educational credit.

Contact Write, call, fax, e-mail, or through World Wide Web site Ramiro Cruz, Internship Coordinator. Phone: 305-995-2267. Fax: 305-995-2226. E-mail: rcruz@wlrn.org. In-person interview recommended (telephone interview accepted). Applicants must submit a letter of interest, resume, academic transcripts. Applications are accepted continuously. World Wide Web: http://www.wlrn.org.

WMAR-TV
6400 York Road
Baltimore, Maryland 21212

General Information Television station affiliate of ABC network. Established in 1947. Number of employees: 200. Unit of Scripps Howard Company, Cincinnati, Ohio. Number of internship applications received each year: 150.

Internships Available ▶ *1 creative services intern:* responsibilities include assisting promotion producers for news and entertainment promotion. Duration is 1 semester. Unpaid. Open to college juniors, college seniors, graduate students, applicants must be eligible for course credit for internship. ▶ *3 news interns:* responsibilities include assisting in all aspects of news, reporting, producing, writing, and assignment functions. Duration is 1 semester. Unpaid. Open to college juniors, college seniors, graduate students, applicants must be eligible for course credit for internship. ▶ *1 production intern:* responsibilities include directing show preparation including pre-production of video packages, writing, editing, and post production. Duration is 1 semester. Unpaid. Open to college juniors, college seniors, graduate students. ▶ *1 public affairs intern:* responsibilities include assisting with public service announcements and production of local public affairs programs. Duration is 1 semester. Unpaid. Open to college juniors, college seniors, graduate students, applicants must be eligible for course credit for internship. ▶ *1 sales intern:* responsibilities include working on development of sales promotions and presentations and possibly in research. Duration is 1 semester. Unpaid. Open to college juniors, college seniors, graduate students, applicants must be eligible for course credit for internship. ▶ *1 sports production intern:* responsibilities include covering area sports events. Duration is 1 semester. Unpaid. Open to college juniors, college seniors, graduate students, applicants must be eligible for course credit for internship. Candidates for all positions should have ability to work independently, college courses in field, computer skills, oral communication skills, strong interpersonal skills, writing skills.

Benefits Willing to complete paperwork for educational credit.

Contact Write Ms. Brenda O. Mustian, Internship Coordinator. No phone calls. In-person interview required. Applicants must submit a formal organization application, writing sample. Application deadline: January 1 for spring, May 1 for summer, September 1 for fall.

WNYW-FOX TELEVISION
205 East 67th Street
New York, New York 10021

General Information Television station with a hands-on training program for individuals interested in obtaining experience in various fields of TV broadcasting. Established in 1986. Number of employees: 250. Unit of Fox, Inc., Los Angeles, California. Number of internship applications received each year: 600.
Internships Available ▶ *35–40 interns:* responsibilities include working in one of the following departments depending on intern's interest: human resources, sales, traffic, 10 o'clock/evening news, "Good Day New York", programming, or newsroom. Duration is flexible. Unpaid. Open to college juniors, college seniors. International applications accepted.
Benefits Opportunity to attend seminars/workshops, willing to complete paperwork for educational credit, $5 per day travel stipend.
Contact Write or call Ms. Iris Sierra, Human Resources Director. Phone: 212-452-5700. In-person interview required. Applicants must submit a letter of interest, resume. Applications are accepted continuously.

WPEC-TV 12
1100 Fairfield Drive
West Palm Beach, Florida 33407

General Information CBS affiliate television station. Established in 1973. Number of employees: 100. Unit of Freedom Communications, West Palm Beach, Florida. Number of internship applications received each year: 40.
Internships Available ▶ *Interns:* responsibilities include performing tasks similar to entry-level positions in newsroom, some graphic artwork, and community relations. Candidates should have ability to work with others, reliability. Duration is flexible. Unpaid. Open to college freshmen, college sophomores, college juniors, college seniors, must be earning school credit for internship. International applications accepted.
Benefits Names of contacts, possible full-time employment, willing to complete paperwork for educational credit, willing to provide letters of recommendation.
Contact Write, call, or fax Rob Hubler, Executive Producer. Phone: 561-844-1212 Ext. 1310. Fax: 561-881-0731. In-person interview recommended (telephone interview accepted). Applicants must submit a formal organization application, letter of interest, resume. Applications are accepted continuously.

WPRI-TV/WNAC-TV
25 Catamore Boulevard
East Providence, Rhode Island 02914

General Information Broadcast television station that handles news, commercial production, and promotion. Established in 1954. Number of employees: 123. Affiliate of Sunrise Television Corporation, St. Petersburg, Florida. Number of internship applications received each year: 50.
Internships Available ▶ *1 business intern:* responsibilities include billing, filing, copying payables and collections, organizing files, handling incoming and outgoing mail, and distributing traffic logs and faxes. Candidates should have ability to work independently, computer skills, knowledge of field, office skills, organizational skills, research skills, self-motivation, strong interpersonal skills, writing skills. Duration is 1 semester. Unpaid. ▶ *1–2 engineering interns:* responsibilities include operation of videotape machines and audio equipment; dubbing commercials, television shows, and public service announcements. Candidates should have ability to work independently, ability to work with others, computer skills, declared college major in field, editing skills, knowledge of field, organizational skills, self-motivation. Duration is 1 semester. Unpaid. ▶ *4–8 news interns:* responsibilities include assisting producer in newsroom work. Candidates should have computer skills, editing skills, knowledge of field, oral communication skills, plan to pursue career in field, research skills, self-motivation, strong interpersonal skills, writing skills. Duration is 3–4 months. Unpaid. ▶ *4–8 production interns:* responsibilities include working in studio and assisting with lighting, sets, and camera work. Candidates should have

college courses in field, computer skills, plan to pursue career in field, research skills, self-motivation, strong interpersonal skills, writing skills. Duration is 1 semester. Unpaid. ▶ *1–2 production producer interns:* responsibilities include rough scriptwriting for commercials. Candidates should have ability to work independently, computer skills, editing skills, knowledge of field, organizational skills, research skills, self-motivation, strong interpersonal skills, writing skills. Duration is 1 semester. Unpaid. ▶ *Programming interns:* responsibilities include organizing tapes for daily air on both stations, maintaining the film library, organizing incoming information from both networks, and distributing and answering viewer mail. Candidates should have ability to work independently, analytical skills, computer skills, editing skills, knowledge of field, organizational skills, plan to pursue career in field, research skills, self-motivation, strong interpersonal skills, writing skills. Duration is 1 semester. Unpaid. ▶ *2–4 promotion interns:* responsibilities include assisting producer and writing. Candidates should have ability to work independently, computer skills, knowledge of field, research skills, self-motivation, strong interpersonal skills, writing skills. Duration is 1 semester. Unpaid. ▶ *1–2 public affairs interns:* responsibilities include researching and writing public service announcements; updating the Web site; and reviewing incoming public service announcements and doing post-production on them. Candidates should have ability to work independently, computer skills, editing skills, knowledge of field, office skills, research skills, self-motivation, strong interpersonal skills, writing skills. Duration is 1 semester. Unpaid. ▶ *1–2 research and marketing interns:* responsibilities include preparing charts and graphs using Neilsen information for sales and station use, preparing presentations for account executives. Candidates should have ability to work independently, computer skills, editing skills, office skills, organizational skills, research skills, strong interpersonal skills, writing skills. Duration is 1 semester. Unpaid. ▶ *3–5 sports interns:* responsibilities include learning to write for sports broadcasting, editing and archiving sports highlights, and charting games and incoming video feeds. Candidates should have ability to work independently, computer skills, editing skills, knowledge of field, office skills, organizational skills, plan to pursue career in field, strong interpersonal skills, writing skills. Duration is 1 semester. Unpaid. Open to college freshmen, college sophomores, college juniors, college seniors. International applications accepted.
Benefits Formal training, on-the-job training, possible full-time employment, willing to complete paperwork for educational credit, willing to provide letters of recommendation.
Contact Write, call, fax, e-mail, or through World Wide Web site Mr. Richard Lynch, Internship Coordinator. Phone: 401-438-7200. Fax: 401-434-3761. E-mail: rlynch@wpri.com. In-person interview required. Applicants must submit a letter of interest, resume, 2-3 writing samples. Application deadline: January 1 for spring, May 1 for summer, September 1 for fall. World Wide Web: http://www.wpri.com.

WPVI-TV
4100 City Line Avenue
Philadelphia, Pennsylvania 19131

General Information Television station that broadcasts local news 4 hours per day and an additional 4 to 6 hours weekly of other local shows. Established in 1948. Number of employees: 220. Unit of American Broadcasting Company, Inc., New York, New York. Number of internship applications received each year: 100.
Internships Available ▶ *1–2 "Sunday Live" interns:* responsibilities include booking guests and generating theme for weekly show. Duration is 1 semester. Unpaid. Open to college juniors, college seniors. ▶ *1–2 creative services interns:* responsibilities include assisting with press releases, program schedules, and on-air promotions. Duration is 1 semester. Unpaid. Open to college juniors, college seniors. ▶ *6–8 news department interns:* responsibilities include serving as production assistants to newscast, segment producers, and assignment editor. Duration is 1 semester. Unpaid. Open to college juniors, college seniors. ▶ *3–5 public affairs department interns:* responsibilities include working as production assistants to producers, photographers, and editors working on the magazine shows

"Prime Time", "Visions", "Fast Forward", and a variety of other studio programs. Duration is 1 semester. Unpaid. Open to college juniors, college seniors, graduate students. Candidates for all positions should have personal interest in the field, self-motivation, strong interpersonal skills, eligibility to receive academic credit.
Benefits Job counseling, names of contacts, willing to complete paperwork for educational credit, willing to provide letters of recommendation.
Contact Write, call, or fax Ms. Linda Munich, Director of Public Affairs. Phone: 215-878-9700. Fax: 215-581-4515. In-person interview required. Applicants must submit a formal organization application, letter of interest, resume, signature of academic advisor or school representative. Applications are accepted continuously. World Wide Web: http://www.wpvi.com.

WRDW-TV
1301 Georgia Avenue
North Augusta, South Carolina 29841

General Information Broadcast commercial CBS-network affiliate television station. Established in 1954. Number of employees: 85. Unit of Gray Communications, Inc., Albany, Georgia. Number of internship applications received each year: 10.
Internships Available ▶ *News-production interns:* responsibilities include news writing, story setup, field interviews, telephone interviews, videotape editing. Candidates should have declared college major in field, oral communication skills, plan to pursue career in field, self-motivation, strong interpersonal skills, written communication skills. Duration is 6–9 weeks. Unpaid. Open to college juniors, college seniors.
Benefits Job counseling, willing to act as a professional reference, willing to complete paperwork for educational credit, willing to provide letters of recommendation.
Contact Write or e-mail Estelle Parsley, Director of News and Operations, PO Box 1212, Augusta, Georgia 30903. Fax: 803-279-8316. E-mail: estelle.parsley@wrdw.com. No phone calls. In-person interview recommended (telephone interview accepted). Applicants must submit a letter of interest, resume, drug screening required. Applications are accepted continuously. World Wide Web: http://www.wrdw.com.

WTIU-TV
Radio-TV Building, Indiana University
Bloomington, Indiana 47405

General Information Public television station serving south central Indiana with a full schedule of national and local programming. Established in 1969. Number of employees: 40. Unit of Indiana University Bloomington, Bloomington, Indiana.
Internships Available ▶ *1–4 local production assistants:* responsibilities include assisting with production of local programs in public affairs, business, and sports. Candidates should have ability to work with others, computer skills, oral communication skills, organizational skills, written communication skills. Duration is flexible. Unpaid. ▶ *1–2 promotions assistants:* responsibilities include assisting with on-air promotion production. Candidates should have ability to work independently, computer skills, editing skills, organizational skills, strong interpersonal skills, written communication skills. Duration is flexible. Unpaid. ▶ *1 public information assistant:* responsibilities include assisting with publications and non-broadcast promotion. Candidates should have computer skills, editing skills, oral communication skills, organizational skills, research skills, written communication skills. Duration is flexible. Unpaid. ▶ *1–2 videographers:* responsibilities include assisting with field shoots and studio productions. Candidates should have ability to work independently, computer skills, editing skills, self-motivation. Duration is flexible. Unpaid. Open to college sophomores, college juniors, college seniors.
Benefits Job counseling, names of contacts, on-the-job training, possible full-time employment, willing to complete paperwork for educational credit, willing to provide letters of recommendation.
Contact Write, fax, or through World Wide Web site Phil Meyer, Station Manager. Fax: 812-855-2970. No phone calls. In-person interview required. Applicants must submit a letter of interest, resume, writing sample, two letters of recommendation. Applications are accepted continuously. World Wide Web: http://www.wtiu.indiana.edu.

WTVF NEWS
474 James Robertson Parkway
Nashville, Tennessee 37219

General Information CBS television affiliate that produces and airs local newscasts, current events, entertainment, and public service shows. Number of employees: 200. Unit of Landmark Community, Norfolk, Virginia. Number of internship applications received each year: 60.
Internships Available ▶ *1–4 Newschannel 5+ interns:* responsibilities include scheduling guests, camera operation, some editing, answering phones, greeting guests, limited writing, switcher operation, graphics and audio tasks. Candidates should have ability to work independently, editing skills, oral communication skills, plan to pursue career in field, strong interpersonal skills. Duration is 1 semester. Unpaid. Open to college sophomores, college juniors, college seniors. ▶ *4–5 Talk of the Town interns:* responsibilities include answering viewer calls and letters, assisting with studio floor direction, typing daily show lists, assisting guests on outside remotes, and filling recipe requests. Candidates should have oral communication skills, organizational skills, strong interpersonal skills. Duration is 1 semester. Unpaid. Open to college freshmen, college sophomores, college juniors, college seniors. ▶ *7–10 news department interns:* responsibilities include answering phones, making beat calls, calling to verify facts, writing stories and logging video feeds, going out with reporters and photographers on stories, editing videotape, and ripping scripts. Candidates should have oral communication skills, plan to pursue career in field, self-motivation, strong interpersonal skills, written communication skills. Duration is length of school term. Unpaid. Open to college freshmen, college sophomores, college juniors, college seniors. International applications accepted.
Benefits Names of contacts, possible full-time employment, willing to act as a professional reference, willing to complete paperwork for educational credit, willing to provide letters of recommendation.
Contact Write, call, or fax Ms. Neysa Ellery, Assignment Editor. Phone: 615-248-5281. Fax: 615-244-9883. In-person interview recommended (telephone interview accepted). Applicants must submit a letter of interest, resume. Applications are accepted continuously. World Wide Web: http://www.newchannel5.com.

WWSB
1477 Tenth Street
Sarasota, Florida 34236

General Information ABC affiliate, television news and programming. Established in 1971. Number of employees: 100. Division of Southern Broadcasting Corporation, Sarasota, Florida. Number of internship applications received each year: 30.
Internships Available ▶ *News interns.* Candidates should have ability to work independently, college courses in field, oral communication skills, plan to pursue career in field, self-motivation, strong interpersonal skills. Duration is 1 semester. Unpaid. Open to college students with at least 6 credit hours of communication or journalism. International applications accepted.
Benefits On-the-job training, possible full-time employment, willing to act as a professional reference, willing to provide letters of recommendation.
Contact Write, fax, or e-mail Kay Miller, News Director. Phone: 941-923-8840. Fax: 941-923-8709. E-mail: kmiller@wwsb.com. In-person interview required. Applicants must submit a letter of interest, resume, at least 6 hours of college communication courses; must be receiving college credit. Applications are accepted continuously.

WXIX-TV 19
19 Broadcast Plaza, 635 West 7th Street
Cincinnati, Ohio 45203

General Information Broadcasting station offering the Cincinnati TV market a variety of entertainment programming, includ-

WXIX-TV 19 *(continued)*

ing the Fox network and local programming and news. Established in 1968. Number of employees: 130. Unit of Raycom Media, Inc., Montgomery, Alabama. Number of internship applications received each year: 100.

Internships Available ▶ *3–4 news interns:* responsibilities include shadowing reporters and photographers on news stories, updating assignment desk files, making beat calls to police and fire departments, following up on news stories, and tape dubbing on VHS machines. Candidates should have coursework in journalism, broadcasting, communications, or public relations. Duration is minimum of 10 hours per week. Unpaid. Open to college juniors, college seniors, must be earning college credit. ▶ *Sales promotion interns:* responsibilities include assisting in sales promotion and event execution; assisting with various client-related projects and reports; assisting in coordination of commercial production; updating and maintaining sales promotion event calendar; attending weekly sales and promotion meetings. Candidates should have coursework in related areas of study. Duration is minimum of 10 hours per week. Unpaid. Open to college juniors, college seniors, must be earning college credit. ▶ *Sports interns:* responsibilities include logging videotape of games and sporting events; accompanying photographers to gather sound for stories; gathering score and sporting event information; tape dubbing on VHS and Beta machines; assisting in preparation for Ten O'clock News and Sports Wrap . Candidates should have coursework in related areas of study. Duration is minimum of 4 weeks. Unpaid. Open to college juniors, college seniors, must be earning college credit. ▶ *Weather interns:* responsibilities include helping prepare daily weather show; making forecasts; drawing graphics; performing weather analysis by plotting maps; research through Internet and National Weather Service; searching for weather scenes on BASYS computer system. Candidates should have course work in meteorology or related areas. Duration is minimum of 10 hours per week. Unpaid. Open to college juniors, college seniors.

Benefits Names of contacts, possible full-time employment, willing to complete paperwork for educational credit, willing to provide letters of recommendation.

Contact Write, fax, e-mail, or through World Wide Web site Ms. Jenny Wagner, Human Resources Supervisor. Fax: 513-421-0341. E-mail: hr@fox19.com. No phone calls. Applicants must submit a resume, cover letter. Applications are accepted continuously. World Wide Web: http://www.fox19.com.

MANUFACTURING

GENERAL

APPLE COMPUTER, INC.
1 Infinite Loop, MS 84-3CE
Cupertino, California 95014

General Information Computer company whose mission is to bring the best personal computing products and support to students, educators, designers, scientists, engineers, business persons, and consumers in 140 countries around the world. Established in 1977. Number of employees: 9,000. Number of internship applications received each year: 6,000.
Internships Available ▶ *Finance interns.* Candidates should have ability to work independently, ability to work with others, analytical skills, college courses in field, experience in the field, oral communication skills, written communication skills. Duration is 3 months. Paid. Open to college juniors, college seniors, graduate students, MBA students. ▶ *Hardware engineering interns.* Candidates should have ability to work independently, ability to work with others, college courses in field, computer skills, experience in the field, organizational skills, self-motivation. Duration is 3 months. Paid. Open to college sophomores, college juniors, graduate students, college seniors enrolled in graduate programs. ▶ *Information systems and technology interns.* Candidates should have ability to work independently, ability to work with others, college courses in field, computer skills, experience in the field, oral communication skills. Duration is 3 months. Paid. Open to college sophomores, college juniors, graduate students, college seniors enrolled in graduate programs. ▶ *Marketing interns.* Candidates should have ability to work independently, ability to work with others, computer skills, experience in the field, oral communication skills, written communication skills. Duration is 3 months. Paid. Open to college seniors, graduate students, MBA students. ▶ *Systems software engineering interns.* Candidates should have ability to work independently, ability to work with others, college courses in field, computer skills, experience in the field, oral communication skills, self-motivation. Duration is 3 months. Paid. Open to college sophomores, college juniors, graduate students, college seniors enrolled in graduate programs. International applications accepted.
Benefits Health insurance, housing at a cost, opportunity to attend seminars/workshops, possible full-time employment, travel reimbursement, willing to act as a professional reference, willing to provide letters of recommendation, training, competitive salary.
Contact E-mail or through World Wide Web site University Relations. Fax: 408-974-5957. E-mail: applejobs@apple.com. No phone calls. Telephone interview required. Applicants must submit a resume. Applications are accepted continuously. World Wide Web: http://www.apple.com.

BIC CORPORATION
500 Bic Drive
Milford, Connecticut 06460

General Information Manufacturer of writing instruments, lighters, and shavers. Established in 1958. Number of employees: 950. Subsidiary of Societe Bic, Clichy, France. Number of internship applications received each year: 100.
Internships Available ▶ *3–4 interns:* responsibilities include assisting in various departments (marketing, manufacturing, engineering, information technology, or accounting/finance) according to intern's abilities and departmental needs. Candidates should have analytical skills, computer skills, knowledge of field, oral com-munication skills, organizational skills, self-motivation, strong interpersonal skills, strong leadership ability, written communica-tion skills. Duration is flexible. Paid. ▶ *2–3 sales/marketing interns:* responsibilities include assisting in marketing department accord-ing to intern's abilities and departmental needs. Candidates should have analytical skills, computer skills, knowledge of field, oral com-munication skills, organizational skills, research skills, self-motivation, strong interpersonal skills, strong leadership ability, written communication skills. Duration is flexible. Paid. Open to college juniors, college seniors, recent college graduates, gradu-ate students.
Benefits Health insurance, job counseling, on-the-job training, possible full-time employment, travel reimbursement, access to company store and company activities, breakfast and lunch at cost.
Contact Write, fax, e-mail, or through World Wide Web site Paul Moyher, Corporate Human Resources Manager. Fax: 203-783-2200. E-mail: jobs@bicworld.com. No phone calls. In-person interview required. Applicants must submit a letter of interest, resume, three personal references. Applications are accepted continuously. World Wide Web: http://www.bicworld.com.

THE BOEING COMPANY
PO Box 3707, MS 6H-PR
Seattle, Washington 98124

General Information Largest aerospace company in the world, a global enterprise that designs, produces, and supports com-mercial airplanes, defense systems, and civil and defense space systems. Established in 1916. Number of employees: 78,200. Number of internship applications received each year: 10,000.
Internships Available ▶ *50–100 business interns:* responsibilities include procurement, finance, and accounting. Candidates should have ability to work independently, analytical skills, computer skills, knowledge of field, oral communication skills, organizational skills, personal interest in the field, strong interpersonal skills, writing skills, major in business-related field. Duration is 1 summer; 6 months for co-ops. Paid. Open to college juniors, college seniors, graduate students. ▶ *15–60 computer science interns:* responsibili-ties include computer systems programming and software analysis. Candidates should have ability to work independently, ability to work with others, computer skills, oral communication skills, personal interest in the field, writing skills, major in computing, information technology, or computer engineering. Duration is 1 summer for interns; 6 months for co-ops. Paid. Open to college sophomores, college juniors, college seniors and graduate students who are not graduating following semester. ▶ *200–500 engineer-ing interns:* responsibilities include working with a lead engineer in design, engineering labs, or supporting manufacturing. Candidates should have analytical skills, knowledge of field, oral communica-tion skills, personal interest in the field, strong interpersonal skills, writing skills, major in engineering. Duration is 1 summer for interns; 6 months for co-ops. Paid. Open to college juniors, col-lege seniors, college seniors and graduate students who are not graduating following semester. International applications accepted.
Benefits Formal training, health insurance, housing at a cost, opportunity to attend seminars/workshops, possible full-time employment, travel reimbursement, tuition assistance, access to recreation and fitness facilities.
Contact Through World Wide Web site Internship Program. No phone calls. In-person interview recommended (telephone interview accepted). Applicants must submit a formal organization applica-

The Boeing Company (continued)

tion, resume, application materials as specified on Web site: www.boeing.com/employment. Applications are accepted continuously. World Wide Web: http://www.boeing.com.

THE BOEING COMPANY–ST. LOUIS
PO Box 516, Mailcode S2761740
St. Louis, Missouri 63166-0516

General Information   Defense contractor and producer of military aircraft and missiles. Number of employees: 20,000. Division of The Boeing Company, Seattle, Washington. Number of internship applications received each year: 3,000.
Internships Available ▶ *5–25 business administration interns:* responsibilities include working on a variety of assignments including accounting contracts and pricing, logistics, estimating, and business operations. Candidates should have analytical skills, computer skills, oral communication skills, personal interest in the field, self-motivation, written communication skills. Duration is 10–13 weeks. Paid. ▶ *Electrical engineering/computer science/computer engineering interns:* responsibilities include working on a variety of assignments such as mission systems software designing programs, testing operational flight programs for avionic systems, and supporting flight test and hardware integration. Candidates should have ability to work with others, analytical skills, college courses in field, computer skills, oral communication skills, self-motivation. Duration is 10–13 weeks. Paid. ▶ *5–10 industrial engineering interns:* responsibilities include working on a variety of assignments including production methods engineering, liaison engineering, human factors, and strategic modernization. Candidates should have analytical skills, oral communication skills, organizational skills, personal interest in the field, self-motivation, strong interpersonal skills. Duration is 10–13 weeks. Paid. ▶ *10–30 mechanical/aerospace engineering interns:* responsibilities include working on a variety of assignments including flight test engineering, structural definition, liaison engineering, and design development. Candidates should have ability to work with others, analytical skills, computer skills, declared college major in field, oral communication skills, organizational skills, personal interest in the field, plan to pursue career in field, self-motivation. Duration is 10–13 weeks. Paid. Open to college juniors, college seniors.
Benefits   Formal training, free housing, health insurance, job counseling, on-the-job training, opportunity to attend seminars/workshops, possible full-time employment, travel reimbursement, tuition assistance, willing to complete paperwork for educational credit, relocation assistance.
Contact   Through World Wide Web site Internship Coordinator. Electronic application: www.boeing.com/employment/college/internshipdetails.html#types. Application deadline: February 1 for summer, April 1 for fall, September 1 for spring. World Wide Web: http://www.boeing.com.

CAROLYN RAY
578 Nepperhan Avenue
Yonkers, New York 10701

General Information   Manufacturer of fabrics and wallcoverings for interior designers and architects. Established in 1979. Number of employees: 4. Number of internship applications received each year: 20.
Internships Available ▶ *1–2 general assistants:* responsibilities include sample-making, clerical duties, customer service, studio production, maintenance, and organization. Candidates should have ability to work independently, ability to work with others, oral communication skills, organizational skills, personal interest in the field, self-motivation. Duration is flexible. Unpaid. Open to high school students, recent high school graduates, college freshmen, college sophomores, college juniors, college seniors, recent college graduates, graduate students, career changers, individuals reentering the workforce. International applications accepted.
Benefits   Job counseling, names of contacts, on-the-job training, opportunity to attend seminars/workshops, possible full-time employment, willing to act as a professional reference, willing to

complete paperwork for educational credit, willing to provide letters of recommendation, reimbursement of local travel expenses.
Contact   Write, fax, or e-mail Carolyn Schulz, Internship Coordinator. Fax: 914-476-0677. E-mail: carolyn-ray@msn.com. In-person interview recommended (telephone interview accepted). Applicants must submit a letter of interest, resume, portfolio, two letters of recommendation. Applications are accepted continuously.

CATERPILLAR, INC.
100 NE Adams Street
Peoria, Illinois 61629-1490

General Information   Fortune 100 company and the world's largest manufacturer of construction and mining equipment, diesel and natural gas engines, and industrial gas turbines.
Internships Available ▶ *Interns:* responsibilities include possible experiences in wide range of business and/or technical fields related to the intern's academic studies; working in teams to solve problems in accounting, computer information systems, engineering/research manufacturing, technical marketing. Candidates should have minimum GPA 2.8; must be U.S. citizen, permanent resident, refugee or asylee. Duration is 12 weeks (summer); 16 weeks (fall/spring). Paid. Open to individuals who have completed at least one year of full-time undergraduate work at a four-year institution.
Benefits   Possible full-time employment.
Contact   Write Corporate Professional Employment, 100 Northeast Adams Street, Peoria 61629-1490. No phone calls. Applicants must submit a letter of interest, resume, academic transcripts. Applications are accepted continuously. World Wide Web: http://www.cat.com.

CNH GLOBAL N.V.
7 South 600 County Line Road
Burr Ridge, Illinois 60521

General Information   Manufacturer of agricultural and industrial equipment. Established in 1999. Number of employees: 500. Unit of Fiat, Turin, Italy. Number of internship applications received each year: 1,000.
Internships Available ▶ *50–100 interns:* responsibilities include working in field of interest: accounting, engineering, finance, human resources, logistics, product evaluation, programming, purchasing, sales, service, or service parts. Candidates should have computer skills, oral communication skills, strong interpersonal skills, written communication skills, personal transportation; agricultural background a plus. Duration is 3 months (average). $400–$450 per week. Open to college sophomores, college juniors, college seniors, graduate students. International applications accepted.
Benefits   Housing at a cost, on-the-job training, opportunity to attend seminars/workshops, possible full-time employment, travel reimbursement, willing to act as a professional reference, willing to complete paperwork for educational credit, willing to provide letters of recommendation.
Contact   Write, fax, e-mail, or through World Wide Web site Glenn E. Kubat, Manager, Employment and Staffing. Fax: 630-877-2334. E-mail: glenn.kubat@cnh.com. No phone calls. In-person interview recommended (telephone interview accepted). Applicants must submit a formal organization application, letter of interest, resume, academic transcripts. Applications are accepted continuously. World Wide Web: http://www.cnh.com.

ELIZABETH DOW
155 6th Avenue, 4th Floor
New York, New York 10013

General Information   Manufacturer of handpainted wallcoverings and interior decorative painting. Established in 1992. Number of employees: 10. Number of internship applications received each year: 750.
Internships Available ▶ *10–12 interns:* responsibilities include sampling, painting, studio work (art and design internships); Macintosh skills, database entry, followup (marketing/managerial internships). Candidates should have ability to work independently, ability to work with others, oral communication skills, organizational skills, personal interest in the field, self-motivation. Duration is

flexible. Position available as unpaid or at minimum wage. Open to high school students, recent high school graduates, college freshmen, college sophomores, college juniors, college seniors, recent college graduates, graduate students, career changers, individuals reentering the workforce. International applications accepted.

Benefits Possible full-time employment, willing to act as a professional reference, willing to complete paperwork for educational credit, willing to provide letters of recommendation.

Contact Write, call, fax, or e-mail Xavier Santana, Internship Coordinator. Phone: 212-463-0144. Fax: 212-463-0824. E-mail: edowltd@aol.com. In-person interview recommended (telephone interview accepted). Applicants must submit a letter of interest, resume, personal reference, two letters of recommendation, portfolio (optional). Application deadline: continuous, but as early as possible for summer. World Wide Web: http://www.elizabethdow.com.

GENERAL MILLS
Number One General Mills Boulevard
Minneapolis, Minnesota 55426

General Information 13.5 billion dollar consumer foods company. Established in 1928. Number of employees: 10,500.

Internships Available ► *4–6 financial analyst interns:* responsibilities include special projects and financial analysis. Candidates should have analytical skills, declared college major in field, oral communication skills, personal interest in the field, strong interpersonal skills, strong leadership ability. Duration is 12 weeks in summer. $3000–$3200 per month. Open to college sophomores, college juniors. ► *10–12 information systems interns.* Candidates should have ability to work independently, computer skills, declared college major in field, oral communication skills, plan to pursue career in field, strong interpersonal skills. Duration is 12 weeks in summer. $2800–$3000 per month. Open to college sophomores, college juniors. ► *4–8 packaging interns:* responsibilities include interacting with product developers, process engineers, and packaging engineers; developing new product packaging. Candidates should have ability to work independently, ability to work with others, analytical skills, experience in the field, strong leadership ability. Duration is 12 weeks in summer. $3000–$4000 per month. Open to college sophomores, college juniors. ► *4–8 quality associate interns:* responsibilities include projects supporting quality operations in manufacturing plant; problem solving and analyzing quality problems; working with teams to develop quality improvement initiatives. Candidates should have ability to work with others, analytical skills, college courses in field, knowledge of field, personal interest in the field, self-motivation, strong leadership ability. Duration is 12 weeks. $2900–$4000 per month. Open to college sophomores, college juniors, graduate students. ► *10–20 research and development summer interns:* responsibilities include working with team to create new products and improve quality of existing products. Candidates should have analytical skills, knowledge of field, research skills, self-motivation, strong interpersonal skills, strong leadership ability. Duration is 12 weeks. $2900–$4000 per month. Open to college sophomores, college juniors, graduate students. ► *5 senior financial analyst interns:* responsibilities include special projects and financial analysis. Candidates should have analytical skills, declared college major in field, knowledge of field, personal interest in the field, strong interpersonal skills, strong leadership ability. Duration is 12 weeks in summer. $5400 per month. Open to first-year graduate students.

Benefits Formal training, housing at a cost, job counseling, names of contacts, on-the-job training, opportunity to attend seminars/workshops, possible full-time employment, travel reimbursement, willing to complete paperwork for educational credit.

Contact Write, call, fax, e-mail, or through World Wide Web site Marilyn Callaway, Campus Event Coordinator. Phone: 763-764-3393. Fax: 763-764-2445. E-mail: marilyn.callaway@genmills.com. In-person interview required. Applicants must submit a formal organization application, resume, academic transcripts. World Wide Web: http://www.generalmills.com.

HALLMARK CARDS, INC.
2501 McGee, #112, Box 419580
Kansas City, Missouri 64141

General Information Personal expression company that designs, manufactures, and distributes greeting cards as well as albums, ornaments, collectibles, gift wrap, partyware, and related products. Established in 1910. Number of employees: 6,000. Number of internship applications received each year: 1,500.

Internships Available ► *1–5 financial analysts:* responsibilities include assisting with cash management, financial plans, forecasts, internal auditing, and other projects that may be individual or team-based. Candidates should have analytical skills, college courses in field, computer skills, plan to pursue career in field, self-motivation, strong interpersonal skills. Duration is 10-12 weeks in summer. Paid. Open to college juniors, graduate students. ► *10–12 information technology analysts:* responsibilities include applying technical training (including programming) to solve problems in specific business area: trouble-shooting, implementation, needs analysis, design/program minor systems; some Web development opportunities. Candidates should have college courses in field, oral communication skills, organizational skills, strong interpersonal skills, strong leadership ability. Duration is 10-12 weeks in summer. Paid. Open to college juniors. ► *5–10 manufacturing interns:* responsibilities include working with industrial, mechanical, and electrical engineering staff; assisting in productivity improvement efforts in a variety of plant operations. Candidates should have analytical skills, college courses in field, oral communication skills, plan to pursue career in field, strong interpersonal skills, strong leadership ability. Duration is 10–12 weeks. Paid. Open to college sophomores, college juniors. ► *1–8 marketing associates:* responsibilities include assisting with strategic product development and product management by gathering, analyzing, and evaluating information. Candidates should have analytical skills, college courses in field, computer skills, oral communication skills, plan to pursue career in field, strong interpersonal skills, strong leadership ability. Duration is 10-12 weeks in summer. Paid. Open to college juniors, graduate students.

Benefits Job counseling, on-the-job training, possible full-time employment, travel reimbursement, 50% discount on most Hallmark products in company store (20% discount at Halls Plaza, Halls Crown Center, and associated stores), business travel accident insurance, paid holidays.

Contact Write, fax, or e-mail College Relations. Fax: 816-274-4299. E-mail: hcolle1@hallmark.com. No phone calls. In-person interview recommended (telephone interview accepted). Applicants must submit a formal organization application, letter of interest, resume, academic transcripts, two personal references. Application deadline: January 15 for summer. World Wide Web: http://www.hallmark.com.

INTERNATIONAL PAPER
6400 Poplar Avenue, Department PI
Memphis, Tennessee 38197

General Information Paper manufacturer and producer of products including paper, forest products, business communications, specialty industrial, photographic, commercial and magazine printing papers; food packaging; corrugated containers; pulp; also involved in oil and gas exploration. Established in 1898. Number of employees: 2,500. Unit of International Paper, Stamford, Connecticut. Number of internship applications received each year: 800.

Internships Available ► *15–20 African–American finance fellowships.* Candidates should have ability to work independently, analytical skills, college courses in field, plan to pursue career in field, strong interpersonal skills, strong leadership ability. Duration is 3–6 months. Paid. ► *85 engineering interns:* responsibilities include working in manufacturing facilities; placements available in various U.S. locations. Candidates should have ability to work independently, declared college major in field, plan to pursue career in field, strong interpersonal skills, strong leadership ability. Duration is 3–6 months. Paid. ► *15–25 information technology interns.* Candidates should have ability to work independently, computer skills, declared college major in field, plan to pursue career in field, strong interpersonal skills, strong leadership ability. Duration is 3–6 months. Paid. Open to college freshmen, college sophomores, college juniors, college seniors, graduate students. International applications accepted.

Benefits Formal training, free housing, job counseling, meals at a cost, names of contacts, on-the-job training, opportunity to attend seminars/workshops, possible full-time employment, travel reimbursement, willing to act as a professional reference, willing to complete paperwork for educational credit, willing to provide letters of recommendation, paid holidays for summer interns.

Contact Through World Wide Web site Internship Coordinator, 6400 Poplar Avenue, Memphis, Tennessee 38197. No phone calls. In-person interview recommended (telephone interview accepted). Applicants must submit a letter of interest, resume. Applications are accepted continuously. World Wide Web: http://www.ipaper. com.

KIMBERLY-CLARK CORPORATION
2100 Winchester Road
Neenah, Wisconsin 54956-0999

General Information Manufacturer of personal care, tissue, and health-care products. Established in 1872. Number of employees: 5,100. Number of internship applications received each year: 800.

Internships Available ▶ *15–20 MIS interns (business systems):* responsibilities include modifying and maintaining production outputs; maintaining the project team documentation library which includes screen hierarchies, program index list, JCL index list, production support call lists, and program library; performing program moves to the production environment; developing test data, executing tests, and verifying test results; developing personal computer solutions to business problems; and applying Windows 95 knowledge to accomplish tasks; positions available in Neenah (WI), Roswell (GA), and Knoxville (TN). Candidates should have ability to work independently, college courses in field, computer skills, oral communication skills, plan to pursue career in field, research skills, self-motivation, strong interpersonal skills, strong leadership ability, written communication skills, working knowledge of at least one programming language; minimum GPA of 3.0. Duration is 3 months in summer. $18 per hour. Open to college juniors. ▶ *15–20 MIS interns (computer services):* responsibilities include testing new desktop and server software; evaluating various desktop, server, and network configurations and performance; developing applications to improve productivity of support teams; assisting with the administration of Netware file servers; documenting LAN/WAN network configurations; generating Internet/ Intranet statistical reports; positions available in Neenah (WI), Roswell (GA), and Knoxville (TN). Candidates should have ability to work independently, college courses in field, oral communication skills, plan to pursue career in field, research skills, self-motivation, strong interpersonal skills, strong leadership ability, written communication skills, working knowledge of Windows 95, NT, UNIX, or Novell, minimum GPA of 3.0. Duration is 3 months in summer. $18 per hour. Open to college juniors. ▶ *35– 45 electrical engineering co-ops:* responsibilities include application of electrical engineering skills to a manufacturing environment working with automated manufacturing equipment including programmable controllers, analog and digital motor controllers, and discrete control hardware. Candidates should have declared college major in field, oral communication skills, self-motivation, strong interpersonal skills, written communication skills, minimum GPA of 3.0, completed basic circuits course. Duration is 3–6 months. $15.85–$21.70 per hour. Open to college sophomores, college juniors, college seniors. ▶ *16 finance interns:* responsibilities include working on various projects including cost and financial analysis, budgeting and forecasting, and financial controls. Candidates should have analytical skills, college courses in field, oral communication skills, plan to pursue career in field, self-motivation, strong interpersonal skills, strong leadership ability, written communication skills, minimum overall GPA of 3.2. Duration is 3 months in summer. $17 per hour. Open to college juniors, college seniors. ▶ *15–25 logistics interns:* responsibilities include supporting logistics and the supply chain by controlling materials from the vendor to and through the production facil-

ity, to the warehouse, and to the customer. Candidates should have analytical skills, oral communication skills, organizational skills, self-motivation, strong interpersonal skills, written communication skills. Duration is 3–6 months. $17–$19 per hour. Open to college sophomores, college juniors, college seniors. ▶ *35–45 mechanical engineering co-ops:* responsibilities include applying mechanical engineering skills to a manufacturing environment through CAD design, familiarization with plant safety, documentation, and participation on a project team. Candidates should have declared college major in field, oral communication skills, self-motivation, strong interpersonal skills, written communication skills, minimum GPA of 3.0, completed basic drafting course. Duration is 3–6 months. $16.35–$21.70 per hour. Open to college sophomores, college juniors, college seniors. ▶ *25–35 research and development co-ops:* responsibilities include product, process, or materials development. Candidates should have college courses in field, oral communication skills, self-motivation, strong interpersonal skills, written communication skills, minimum GPA of 3.0. Duration is 3–6 months. $15.85–$21.70 per hour. Open to college sophomores, college juniors, college seniors. ▶ *5–10 research and development interns:* responsibilities include product, process, or materials development. Candidates should have college courses in field, oral communication skills, self-motivation, strong interpersonal skills, written communication skills, minimum GPA of 3.0. Duration is 3–6 months. $15.85– $21.70 per hour. Open to college juniors.

Benefits Formal training, on-the-job training, opportunity to attend seminars/workshops, possible full-time employment, travel reimbursement.

Contact Write, call, fax, e-mail, or through World Wide Web site Kay Keberlein, Recruiting Assistant. Phone: 920-721-2602. Fax: 920-721-4219. E-mail: kkeber@kcc.com. In-person interview recommended (telephone interview accepted). Applicants must submit a letter of interest, resume, academic transcripts. Application deadline: February 1 for summer; continuous for co-op positions. World Wide Web: http://www.kimberly-clark.com.

MATTEL, INC.
333 Continental Boulevard
El Segundo, California 90245

General Information Worldwide leader in the design, manufacture, and marketing of family products. Established in 1945. Number of employees: 2,200. Number of internship applications received each year: 250.

Internships Available ▶ *8–12 marketing interns:* responsibilities include assisting with the management of the product development process from concept to retail distribution; recommending marketing actions for assigned brand based on evaluation of product analysis, testing, and sales performance. Candidates should have college degree in related field, oral communication skills, plan to pursue career in field, self-motivation, strong leadership ability, written communication skills. Duration is 10-12 weeks in summer. $900–$1100 per week. ▶ *2–4 senior financial analyst interns:* responsibilities include financial planning and analysis at corporate level, comprehensive financial forecasting, analysis of actual results, analysis of new business ventures and divestitures, capital expenditure analysis, preparation of presentations to senior management and special reports. Candidates should have analytical skills, oral communication skills, plan to pursue career in field, self-motivation, strong interpersonal skills, written communication skills. Duration is 10-12 weeks in summer. $900–$1100 per week. Open to graduate students. International applications accepted.

Benefits Names of contacts, on-the-job training, opportunity to attend seminars/workshops, possible full-time employment, travel reimbursement, willing to act as a professional reference, willing to complete paperwork for educational credit, willing to provide letters of recommendation, on-site fitness center, half-day Fridays, "picnics in the park," toy discounts.

Contact Write or e-mail Corporate Staffing, Attn: Internships. E-mail: corpstaf@mattel.com. No phone calls. In-person interview required. Applicants must submit a letter of interest, resume. Application deadline: March 1. World Wide Web: http://www. mattel.com.

MOTOROLA (ARIZONA SEMICONDUCTOR PRODUCTS SECTOR)
2200 West Broadway Road, MD: M375/AZ09
Mesa, Arizona 85202

General Information Electronics manufacturing company. Established in 1989. Number of employees: 6,500. Division of Motorola, Schaumburg, Illinois. Number of internship applications received each year: 40.

Internships Available ▶ *3–5 health promotion/wellness interns:* responsibilities include design, development, marketing, implementation, and evaluation of wellness programs for 8,000 Motorola SPS employees, and assisting with day-to-day wellness program activities. Candidates should have ability to work with others, college courses in field, computer skills, personal interest in the field, plan to pursue career in field, an understanding of wellness as a healthy balance of optimal physical, emotional, social, intellectual, occupational, and spiritual well-being. Duration is flexible. Unpaid. ▶ *3–5 recreation and fitness interns.* Candidates should have ability to work independently, ability to work with others, computer skills, organizational skills, plan to pursue career in field, an understanding of basic fitness concepts; an overall interest in the wellness and health field. Duration is flexible. Unpaid. Open to college seniors, recent college graduates, graduate students.

Benefits Formal training, meals at a cost, names of contacts, on-the-job training, opportunity to attend seminars/workshops, willing to act as a professional reference, willing to complete paperwork for educational credit, willing to provide letters of recommendation.

Contact Write, call, fax, or e-mail Alison McAleer, Premier Employee Services Account Manager, 2200 West Broadway Road, MD: M375/AZ09, Mesa, Arizona 85202. Phone: 480-655-2105. Fax: 480-655-3837. E-mail: a.mcaleer@motorola.com. Telephone interview required. Applicants must submit a letter of interest, resume. Application deadline: April 1 for summer, July 1 for fall, November 1 for spring.

NATIONAL STARCH AND CHEMICAL COMPANY
10 Finderne Avenue
Bridgewater, New Jersey 08807

General Information Leading manufacturer of adhesives, specialty chemicals, resins, electronic materials, specialty food, and industrial starches. Established in 1895. Number of employees: 1,200. Unit of Imperial Chemical Industries, Bridgewater, New Jersey. Number of internship applications received each year: 1,000.

Internships Available ▶ *15–20 summer interns:* responsibilities include working at World Headquarters in Bridgewater, NJ, or at one of major manufacturing plants in Indiana, Illinois, North Carolina, South Carolina, or Missouri. Candidates should have analytical skills, computer skills, oral communication skills, organizational skills, personal interest in the field, research skills, self-motivation, strong interpersonal skills, strong leadership ability, written communication skills, major in chemistry, chemical engineering, food science, MIS/CIS, polymer science, or material science. Duration is 3 months. Competitive salary. Open to college sophomores, college juniors, college seniors, graduate students.

Benefits On-the-job training, opportunity to attend seminars/workshops, possible full-time employment, travel reimbursement.

Contact Write, fax, or e-mail Colleen Twill, Graduate Development Manager, 10 Finderne Avenue, Bridgewater, New Jersey 08807. Fax: 908-685-6956. E-mail: colleen.twill@nstarch.com. No phone calls. In-person interview required. Applicants must submit a letter of interest, resume, academic transcripts. Application deadline: February 28. World Wide Web: http://www.nationalstarch.com.

OSHKOSH B'GOSH, INC.
112 Otter Avenue, PO Box 300
Oshkosh, Wisconsin 54902

General Information Manufacturer, marketer, and retailer of children's wear and menswear. Established in 1895. Number of employees: 405. Number of internship applications received each year: 200.

Internships Available ▶ *1–3 associate merchandisers:* responsibilities include coordinating and developing new and existing sales aids; assisting merchandise manager in development of seasonal lot numbers forecasts, analysis of seasonal product costing, and working with designers and artists in all aspects of line development. Candidates should have ability to work independently, ability to work with others, analytical skills, college courses in field, computer skills, oral communication skills, plan to pursue career in field, self-motivation, written communication skills. Duration is 10–12 weeks. Paid. Open to college juniors, college seniors, recent college graduates, graduate students. ▶ *1 import associate:* responsibilities include working with factory, agent, and mill to replicate desired fabric; implementing and maintaining tracking system; ensuring on-time delivery of salesman samples. Candidates should have ability to work independently, ability to work with others, analytical skills, college courses in field, computer skills, office skills, oral communication skills, organizational skills, plan to pursue career in field, self-motivation, written communication skills. Duration is 10–12 weeks. Paid. Open to college juniors, college seniors, recent college graduates, graduate students. ▶ *1 product development associate:* responsibilities include gathering information needed from suppliers; completing purchasing and shipping tasks; organizing and maintaining all fabric, color, and documentation systems. Candidates should have ability to work independently, ability to work with others, analytical skills, college courses in field, computer skills, office skills, oral communication skills, organizational skills, plan to pursue career in field, research skills, self-motivation, writing skills. Duration is 10–12 weeks. Paid. Open to college juniors, college seniors, recent college graduates. ▶ *1 programmer intern:* responsibilities include coding, testing, and debugging programs under direct supervision; maintaining and documenting programs. Candidates should have ability to work independently, ability to work with others, analytical skills, college courses in field, computer skills, editing skills, knowledge of field, oral communication skills, organizational skills, plan to pursue career in field, research skills, writing skills. Duration is 10–12 weeks. Paid. Open to college juniors, college seniors.

Benefits Free housing, on-the-job training, opportunity to attend seminars/workshops, possible full-time employment, travel reimbursement, willing to act as a professional reference, willing to complete paperwork for educational credit, willing to provide letters of recommendation.

Contact Write, fax, e-mail, or through World Wide Web site Brent Frederick, Corporate Recruiter, 112 Otter Avenue, PO Box 300, Oshkosh 54903. Fax: 920-232-2744. E-mail: jobs@bgosh.com. Telephone interview required. Applicants must submit a letter of interest, resume, portfolio, personal reference. Applications are accepted continuously. World Wide Web: http://www.oshkoshbgosh.com.

OWENS CORNING WORLD HEADQUARTERS
One Owens Corning Parkway
Toledo, Ohio 43659

General Information Manufacturing company providing complete building material systems and advanced glass fiber used in more than 40,000 composite end-use applications. Established in 1938. Number of employees: 1,000. Number of internship applications received each year: 1,500.

Internships Available ▶ *1–6 finance interns:* responsibilities include working in the area of audit, business analysis, tax, external reporting, and corporate accounting. Candidates should have ability to work independently, ability to work with others, analytical skills, computer skills, knowledge of field, oral communication skills, organizational skills, plan to pursue career in field, self-motivation, writing skills, major in accounting or finance. Duration is one summer. $13–$16 per hour. Open to college juniors, college seniors. ▶ *1–3 human resources interns:* responsibilities include assist-

Owens Corning World Headquarters (continued)

ing with training and development programs; supporting compensation and benefits projects. Candidates should have ability to work independently, computer skills, knowledge of field, oral communication skills, organizational skills, self-motivation, strong interpersonal skills, major in human resources. Duration is one summer. $12.19–$15 per hour. Open to college juniors, college seniors. ► *1–5 information systems interns:* responsibilities include working on analysis, design, technology application, and release testing/deployment activities. Candidates should have ability to work independently, ability to work with others, analytical skills, computer skills, declared college major in field, oral communication skills, organizational skills, personal interest in the field, self-motivation. Duration is one summer. $14–$17 per hour. Open to college juniors, college seniors. ► *1–4 leadership development interns:* responsibilities include working on various projects including planning, new product implementation, materials and management, corporate development, market research, and profit improvement. Candidates should have analytical skills, computer skills, oral communication skills, organizational skills, self-motivation, strong interpersonal skills, strong leadership ability, written communication skills. Duration is one summer. $5600 per month. Open to graduate students. ► *1–5 manufacturing engineer interns:* responsibilities include working in chemical, mechanical, ceramic, and manufacturing technology. Candidates should have ability to work independently, analytical skills, college courses in field, computer skills, oral communication skills, organizational skills, plan to pursue career in field, self-motivation, strong interpersonal skills, written communication skills, technical expertise. Duration is one summer. $15.60–$19.20 per hour. Open to college juniors, college seniors. ► *1–3 sales/marketing interns:* responsibilities include working in specific geographic area within 200-300 miles radius of Toledo, analyzing the market, identifying major general contractors, determining products they are purchasing and why they are purchasing them. Candidates should have ability to work independently, analytical skills, college courses in field, computer skills, knowledge of field, oral communication skills, organizational skills, self-motivation, strong interpersonal skills, written communication skills, ability to establish relationships. Duration is one summer. $10.63–$13.08 per hour. Open to college juniors, college seniors.

Benefits On-the-job training, opportunity to attend seminars/workshops, possible full-time employment, travel reimbursement, possibility of relocation or housing assistance.

Contact Through World Wide Web site Elizabeth Polak, University Relations Leader, One Owens Corning Parkway, Toledo, Ohio 43659. E-mail: resume@owenscorning.com. No phone calls. In-person interview required. Applicants must submit a formal organization application, resume. Application deadline: March 1. World Wide Web: http://www.owenscorning.com.

PELLA CORPORATION
102 Main Street
Pella, Iowa 50219

General Information One of the largest manufacturer of Pella windows and doors. Established in 1925. Number of employees: 7,500. Number of internship applications received each year: 1,000.

Internships Available ► *Accounting interns:* responsibilities include estimating costs, pricing products, analyzing profits, annual financial statements, budgeting processes, financial analysis, and financial statement preparation. Candidates should have analytical skills, computer skills, declared college major in field, oral communication skills, organizational skills, written communication skills, technical skills, MS Excel. Duration is flexible. $2300–$2600 per duration of internship. Open to college juniors, college seniors. ► *30–40 engineering interns.* Candidates should have computer skills, declared college major in field, organizational skills, strong interpersonal skills, strong leadership ability, experience in fixture-machine design, auto-CAD. Duration is flexible. $2400–$3000 per duration of internship. Open to college sophomores, college juniors, college seniors. ► *2 human resource co-ops:* responsibilities include recruitment, selection, benefits compensation, and training and development. Candidates should

have knowledge of field, oral communication skills, organizational skills, strong interpersonal skills, strong leadership ability. Duration is flexible. $2300–$2600 per duration of internship. Open to college juniors, college seniors. ► *12–15 information technology interns:* responsibilities include supporting user-requested changes to database; reports. Candidates should have ability to work with others, analytical skills, computer skills, programming and design experience a plus. Duration is flexible. $2500–$2800 per duration of internship. Open to college juniors, college seniors. ► *2 international sales co-ops:* responsibilities include researching potential new global markets, reporting market information, and compiling market segmentation for identified countries. Candidates should have ability to work with others, computer skills, oral communication skills, research skills, strong leadership ability, written communication skills, ability to speak a language other than English (helpful); experience living in another culture a plus. Duration is flexible. $2300–$2600 per duration of internship. Open to college juniors, college seniors. ► *3 marketing interns:* responsibilities include marketing communications, merchandising, market research, customer satisfaction programs, market support services, technical publications, and/or product line management. Candidates should have analytical skills, declared college major in field, oral communication skills, organizational skills, strong interpersonal skills, written communication skills, Excel and Word proficiency, understanding of spreadsheets and regression analysis, presentation skills. Duration is flexible (May-August). $2200–$2600 per duration of internship. Open to college juniors, college seniors. International applications accepted.

Benefits Housing at a cost, on-the-job training, opportunity to attend seminars/workshops, possible full-time employment, travel reimbursement, tuition assistance, willing to act as a professional reference, willing to complete paperwork for educational credit, willing to provide letters of recommendation, health and dental insurance, holiday pay, vacation pay.

Contact Write, fax, e-mail, or through World Wide Web site Alison Van Vark, College Relations Coordinator, 102 Main Street, Pella, Iowa 50219. Fax: 641-621-6684. E-mail: advvark@pella.com. No phone calls. In-person interview required. Applicants must submit a resume, academic transcripts. Applications are accepted continuously. World Wide Web: http://www.pella.com.

SGI (SILICON GRAPHICS, INC.)
1600 Amphitheatre Parkway
Mountain View, California 94043-1351

General Information Leading supplier of high-performance interactive computing systems; offers a broad range of products from desktop workstations to servers and high-end supercomputers. Established in 1982. Number of employees: 4,500. Number of internship applications received each year: 1,500.

Internships Available ► *Business development interns:* responsibilities include identifying strategic alliances; negotiation and management of partner contracts; conducting research and competitive analysis. Paid. ► *Financial analyst interns:* responsibilities include budgeting, expense control and accounting, cost accounting, and revenue planning. Paid. ► *Hardware engineering interns:* responsibilities include microprocessor design, logic design, mask layout, CAD, computer systems design, or mechanical engineering. Paid. ► *Human resources interns:* responsibilities include planning and implementing wage reviews, meetings, focus groups, management reports, recruiting, and training. Paid. ► *Information systems interns:* responsibilities include opportunities to work as a business analyst, programming analyst, network analyst, database administrator, desktop support, or systems administrator. Paid. ► *Manufacturing interns:* responsibilities include forecasting and analyzing product transitions, developing material plan, strategizing and implementing processes throughout the manufacturing cycle. Paid. ► *Marketing interns:* responsibilities include opportunities in areas of product, strategic, service, and/or technical marketing. Paid. ► *Software engineering interns:* responsibilities include working on operating systems, applications, supercomputing applications, compiler design, or graphics system software. Paid. ► *Support/service interns:* responsibilities include UNIX and/or NT technical product support. Paid. Candidates for all positions should have computer skills, declared college major in field, experience in the field,

self-motivation, strong interpersonal skills. Open to college sophomores, college juniors, college seniors, graduate students.
Benefits Names of contacts, on-the-job training, opportunity to attend seminars/workshops, possible full-time employment, travel reimbursement, willing to act as a professional reference, willing to complete paperwork for educational credit, willing to provide letters of recommendation, internal marketing of strong performers to hiring managers, housing subsidy, paid holidays, access to fitness facilities.
Contact Write, fax, e-mail, or through World Wide Web site Intern Program Manager. Fax: 650-932-0820. E-mail: krohna@sgi.com. No phone calls. In-person interview recommended (telephone interview accepted). Applicants must submit a letter of interest, resume. Applications are accepted continuously. World Wide Web: http://www.sgi.com.

SUSQUEHANNA PFALTZGRAFF COMPANY
140 East Market Street
York, Pennsylvania 17401

General Information Privately-held, diversified media and dinnerware manufacturing company. Established in 1811. Number of employees: 2,000. Number of internship applications received each year: 40.
Internships Available ▶ *1–5 accounting interns:* responsibilities include assisting in preparing financial statements, business forecasting, product costing, and the monthly closing. Candidates should have analytical skills, computer skills, declared college major in field, oral communication skills, strong interpersonal skills, written communication skills. Duration is 10–12 weeks. $8.50 per hour. ▶ *1–3 computer programmers:* responsibilities include writing computer programs for various projects and needs. Candidates should have ability to work independently, analytical skills, computer skills, declared college major in field, plan to pursue career in field. Duration is 12 weeks. $8.50 per hour. ▶ *1 human resources intern:* responsibilities include exposure to all facets of a human resources department (recruiting, benefits, payroll, HRIS, compensation, training). Candidates should have college courses in field, computer skills, office skills, oral communication skills, plan to pursue career in field, strong interpersonal skills. Duration is 10–12 weeks. $8.50 per hour. ▶ *1–3 marketing interns:* responsibilities include assisting marketing manager with special projects. Candidates should have computer skills, declared college major in field, oral communication skills, strong interpersonal skills, written communication skills. Duration is 12 weeks. $8.50 per hour. Open to college juniors, college seniors, recent college graduates. International applications accepted.
Benefits On-the-job training, possible full-time employment, willing to act as a professional reference, willing to complete paperwork for educational credit.
Contact Write, fax, or e-mail Corporate Human Resources, 140 East Market Street, York, Pennsylvania 17401. Fax: 717-852-2594. E-mail: corp.hr@suspfz.com. No phone calls. In-person interview required. Applicants must submit a letter of interest, resume. Application deadline: April 1 for summer.

TRACY WATTS , INC.
305 West 20th Street
New York, New York 10011

General Information Millinery studio that produces hat collections for high-end retailers and custom costumes work. Established in 1993. Number of employees: 2. Number of internship applications received each year: 30.
Internships Available ▶ *2 intern/assistants:* responsibilities include assisting in all aspects of the business; dealing with buyers and stylists, hand-finishing production, running errands to garment district, and answering telephone. Candidates should have ability to work independently, computer skills, personal interest in the field, self-motivation, strong interpersonal skills, design or art background. Duration is 12 weeks (summer, fall, or spring). Unpaid. Open to college freshmen, college sophomores, college juniors, college seniors, recent college graduates, graduate students, career changers. International applications accepted.
Benefits Job counseling, names of contacts, on-the-job training, opportunity to attend seminars/workshops, possible full-time employment, willing to act as a professional reference, willing to complete paperwork for educational credit, willing to provide letters of recommendation, exposure to retail buyers, designers, and fashion magazine editors; learning custom techniques of millinery production; free lunch daily; free hats.
Contact Write or e-mail Ms. Tracy Watts, President. E-mail: tracywatts@rcn.com. In-person interview required. Applicants must submit a letter of interest, resume, portfolio, letter of recommendation, cover letter, work samples. Applications are accepted continuously. World Wide Web: http://www.tracywatts.com.

TRANS-LUX CORPORATION
110 Richards Avenue
Norwalk, Connecticut 06854

General Information Leading manufacturer, distributor, and servicer of real-time electronic information displays for use in both the indoor and outdoor markets; owner of movie theater chain in southwest United States. Established in 1920. Number of employees: 225. Number of internship applications received each year: 400.
Internships Available ▶ *1–3 PC support interns:* responsibilities include performing a variety of PC support duties; supporting the user community through troubleshooting, upgrades, and installations. Candidates should have ability to work independently, experience in the field, self-motivation, strong interpersonal skills. Duration is flexible. Position available as unpaid or at $10–$15 per hour. Open to college juniors, college seniors. ▶ *3–6 accounting interns:* responsibilities include assisting the accounting department with general accounting duties which may include account analysis, consolidation of bank requisitions, and preparation of property tax returns. Candidates should have analytical skills, college courses in field, computer skills, knowledge of field, personal interest in the field, retail-oriented background. Duration is flexible. Position available as unpaid or at $8–$10 per hour. Open to college sophomores, college juniors, college seniors, recent college graduates, graduate students. ▶ *1–3 business development internship:* responsibilities include assisting the sales and marketing departments with business development work, including identifying contacts and sources for key markets; duties may also include development of database. Candidates should have computer skills, knowledge of field, oral communication skills, personal interest in the field, research skills, strong interpersonal skills. Duration is flexible. Position available as unpaid or at $10–$12 per hour. Open to college sophomores, college juniors, college seniors, graduate students. ▶ *6–9 engineering department interns:* responsibilities include assisting the engineering department with hardware and software design projects, design completion, prototyping, and other functions or special projects. Candidates should have ability to work independently, ability to work with others, analytical skills, college courses in field, computer skills, knowledge of field, oral communication skills, organizational skills, personal interest in the field, self-motivation, specific programming experience for software positions. Duration is flexible. Position available as unpaid or at $12–$15 per hour. Open to college juniors, college seniors, recent college graduates, graduate students. ▶ *1–3 human resources department interns:* responsibilities include assisting a busy human resources department by performing a variety of entry-level professional duties. Candidates should have ability to work independently, analytical skills, computer skills, office skills, oral communication skills, organizational skills, personal interest in the field, research skills, self-motivation, strong interpersonal skills, writing skills. Duration is flexible. Position available as unpaid or at $10–$12 per hour. Open to college juniors, college seniors, recent college graduates, graduate students. ▶ *1–3 manufacturing timestudy interns:* responsibilities include determining standards for the subassemblies and final assemblies of manufacturing process; other duties may include serving as back-up bidder for FC's. Candidates should have ability to work with others, analytical skills, knowledge of field, personal interest in the field, research skills. Duration is flexible. Position available as unpaid or at $12–$15 per hour. Open to college juniors, college seniors, recent college graduates, graduate students. ▶ *1–3 programming interns:* responsibilities include assisting the MIS Department's application development staff in modifying programs written in RPG400. Candidates should have

Trans-Lux Corporation (continued)

college courses in field, computer skills, knowledge of field. Duration is flexible. Position available as unpaid or at $10–$15 per hour. Open to college sophomores, college juniors, college seniors, graduate students. ▶ *1–3 sales and marketing intern:* responsibilities include working with sales and marketing professionals, as well as other departments, on a variety of projects including development of sales training programs and redesign of systems. Candidates should have analytical skills, oral communication skills, organizational skills, personal interest in the field, strong interpersonal skills, written communication skills. Duration is flexible. Position available as unpaid or at $10–$12 per hour. Open to college juniors, college seniors, recent college graduates, graduate students. International applications accepted.

Benefits Job counseling, names of contacts, on-the-job training, opportunity to attend seminars/workshops, possible full-time employment, willing to act as a professional reference, willing to complete paperwork for educational credit, willing to provide letters of recommendation.

Contact Write, fax, or e-mail Lisa Charest, Human Resources Generalist. Fax: 203-857-0299. E-mail: internships@trans-lux.com. In-person interview recommended (telephone interview accepted). Applicants must submit a formal organization application, letter of interest, resume. Application deadline: January 30 for spring, May 30 for summer, September 30 for fall. World Wide Web: http://www.trans-lux.com.

WEYERHAEUSER
PO Box 9777
Federal Way, Washington 98063-9777

General Information One of the world's largest integrated forest product companies. Established in 1900. Number of employees: 45,000.

Internships Available ▶ *Interns:* responsibilities include positions available in various disciplines; visit organization Web site for specific information about positions. Candidates should have ability to work with others, computer skills, declared college major in field, plan to pursue career in field, self-motivation. Duration is 3–6 months. $12–$15 per hour. Open to college juniors, college seniors, graduate students.

Benefits Formal training, job counseling, names of contacts, on-the-job training, opportunity to attend seminars/workshops, possible full-time employment, travel reimbursement, willing to act as a professional reference, willing to complete paperwork for educational credit, willing to provide letters of recommendation.

International Internships Available in Canada.

Contact Write, e-mail, or through World Wide Web site Debra Barton, College Recruiting Consultant, PO Box 9777, Federal Way, Washington 98063. Phone: 800-525-5440. Fax: 253-924-2602. E-mail: debra.barton@weyerhaeuser.com. Applicants must submit a resume, academic transcripts. Applications are accepted continuously. World Wide Web: http://www.weyerhaeuser.com.

PHARMACEUTICAL AND MEDICINE MANUFACTURING

ABBOTT LABORATORIES
College Relations, Department 39K, Building AP51, 200 Abbott Park Road
Abbott Park, Illinois 60064-6208

General Information Global, diversified company dedicated to the discovery, development, manufacture, and marketing of health-care products and services. Established in 1888. Number of employees: 57,000. Number of internship applications received each year: 5,000.

Internships Available ▶ *Computing and information science interns:* responsibilities include supporting day-to-day responsibilities related to: application development, technical support, data processing operations, and business systems. Duration is May to August. $10.50–$14.50 per hour. Open to college freshmen, college sophomores, college juniors, college seniors, graduate students. ▶ *Engineering interns:* responsibilities include supporting day-to-day operations in areas of engineering including chemical, software, manufacturing, hazardous waste, telecommunications, hardware, mechanical, electrical, materials or environmental development, and support of production processes and systems. Duration is May to August. $10.50–$14.50 per hour. Open to college freshmen, college sophomores, college juniors, college seniors, graduate students. ▶ *Finance and accounting interns:* responsibilities include supporting day-to-day responsibilities in corporate, division, or plant-level financial planning and analysis; manufacturing or general accounting or financial reporting. Duration is May to August. $10.50–$14.50 per hour. Open to college freshmen, college sophomores, college juniors, college seniors, graduate students. ▶ *Human resources interns:* responsibilities include supporting day-to-day responsibilities in areas including compensation and benefits, employee relations, training and development, staffing, and work/family life and diversity. Duration is May to August. $10.50–$14.50 per hour. Open to college freshmen, college sophomores, college juniors, college seniors, graduate students. ▶ *Production/operations management interns:* responsibilities include supporting day-to-day operations in areas including scale-up, process development, quality control, production planning, or packaging of products and instrument systems. Duration is May to August. $10.50–$14.50 per hour. Open to college freshmen, college sophomores, college juniors, college seniors, graduate students. ▶ *Sales and marketing interns:* responsibilities include supporting day-to-day responsibilities in marketing. Duration is May to August. $10.50–$14.50 per hour. Open to college freshmen, college sophomores, college juniors, college seniors, graduate students, MBA students. ▶ *70–90 science and research development interns:* responsibilities include supporting day-to-day operations in synthetic organic chemistry, analytical chemistry, molecular biology, virology, immunology, pharmacology, pharmacy, physiology, biochemistry, toxicology, pathology, research data management, or analytical services. Duration is May to August. $10.50–$14.50 per hour. Open to college freshmen, college sophomores, college juniors, college seniors, graduate students. International applications accepted.

Benefits Formal training, free housing, free meals, names of contacts, on-the-job training, opportunity to attend seminars/workshops, possible full-time employment, travel reimbursement for interns outside 40-mile radius of site.

Contact Through World Wide Web site Amy Alderson, Corporate Senior College Relations Specialist, College Relations Department 39K, Building AP51, 200 Abbott Park Road, Abbott Park, Illinois 60064-6208. Phone: 847-935-3707. Fax: 847-937-9646. E-mail: amy.alderson@abbott.com. In-person interview recommended (telephone interview accepted). Applicants must submit a resume. Application deadline: March 1. World Wide Web: http://www.abbott.com.

ALZA CORPORATION
1900 Charleston Road, PO Box 7210
Mountain View, California 94039-7210

General Information Company that is leading the next generation of drug delivery with the world's broadest array of technology platforms, including oral, transdermal, implantable and liposomal technologies; applies its delivery technology to develop and manufacture pharmaceutical products with enhanced therapeutic value for many of the world's leading pharmaceutical companies. Established in 1968. Number of employees: 2,000. Subsidiary of Johnson and Johnson, New Brunswick, New Jersey. Number of internship applications received each year: 300.

Internships Available ▶ *15 summer interns:* responsibilities include working in biology, chemical engineering, chemistry, computer science, or business (MBAs); for more information refer to the Web site. Duration is 3 months. Paid. Open to college freshmen, college sophomores, college juniors, college seniors, graduate students. International applications accepted.

Benefits Meals at a cost, on-the-job training, opportunity to attend seminars/workshops, possible full-time employment, willing to act as a professional reference, willing to complete paperwork for educational credit, willing to provide letters of recommendation.
Contact Write, call, fax, e-mail, or through World Wide Web site Human Resources, 1900 Charleston Road, PO Box 7210, Mountain View 94039-7210. Phone: 650-564-5319. Fax: 650-564-5656. E-mail: jobs@alza.com. In-person interview recommended (telephone interview accepted). Applicants must submit a letter of interest, resume. Applications are accepted continuously. World Wide Web: http://www.alza.com.

MERCK RESEARCH LABORATORIES
Summneytown Pike, WP-42, PO Box 4
West Point, Pennsylvania 19486

General Information Pharmaceutical corporation dedicated to the discovery and development of drugs to benefit the population. Established in 1890. Number of employees: 5,000. Division of Merck & Company, Inc., Rahway, New Jersey. Number of internship applications received each year: 500.
Internships ▶ *75–100 summer interns:* responsibilities include hands-on research throughout research labs. Candidates should have ability to work independently, declared college major in field, oral communication skills, plan to pursue career in field, research skills, self-motivation, strong interpersonal skills, strong leadership ability. Duration is 12–14 weeks. $500–$600 per week. Open to college juniors, graduate students.
Benefits Housing at a cost, meals at a cost, on-the-job training, opportunity to attend seminars/workshops, possible full-time employment, travel reimbursement.
Contact Write, fax, or e-mail Meredith Keilty, Human Resources Representative, Summneytown Pike, WP-42, PO Box 4, West Point, Pennsylvania 19486. Fax: 215-652-7376. E-mail: meredith_keilty@merck.com. No phone calls. Telephone interview required. Applicants must submit a formal organization application, letter of interest, resume, academic transcripts. Application deadline: December 31. World Wide Web: http://www.merck.com.

WYETH-AYERST PHARMACEUTICALS
555 East Lancaster Avenue
St. Davids, Pennsylvania 19087

General Information Company that develops pharmaceutical, vaccine, and nutritional products. Established in 1926. Division of American Home Products Corporation, Madison, New Jersey. Number of internship applications received each year: 1,000.
Internships Available ▶ *1–3 finance interns:* responsibilities include providing support to different areas of global financial operations. Candidates should have ability to work independently, ability to work with others, analytical skills, computer skills, declared college major in field, self-motivation. Duration is 3–4 months. Paid. Open to college sophomores, college juniors, college seniors, graduate students. ▶ *1–2 human resources interns:* responsibilities include working in the areas of global strategy, staff-employee relations, and the corporate office of the senior vice president of human resources. Candidates should have ability to work independently, college courses in field, office skills, self-motivation, strong interpersonal skills. Duration is 3–4 months. Paid. Open to college sophomores, college juniors, college seniors, graduate students. ▶ *1–5 industrial engineering interns:* responsibilities include assisting with various logistics and process improvement projects. Candidates should have ability to work independently, ability to work with others, analytical skills, computer skills, declared college major in field, self-motivation. Duration is 3–4 months. Paid. Open to college sophomores, college juniors, college seniors, graduate students. ▶ *15–20 information technology interns:* responsibilities include working on special projects in the areas of applications development, client server development, data security, or Web design. Candidates should have ability to work independently, ability to work with others, analytical skills, computer skills, declared college major in field, self-motivation. Duration is 3–4 months. Paid. Open to college sophomores, college juniors, college seniors, graduate students. ▶ *15–20 marketing interns:* responsibilities include working on special projects involving market research and marketing databases. Candidates should have computer skills, declared college major in field, research skills, self-motivation, strong interpersonal skills, written communication skills. Duration is 3–4 months. Paid. Open to college sophomores, college juniors, college seniors, graduate students. ▶ *1 public policy intern:* responsibilities include assisting in conducting quantitative and qualitative public policy research on topics related to the pharmaceutical industry. Candidates should have analytical skills, declared college major in field, research skills, self-motivation, strong interpersonal skills, writing skills. Duration is 3–4 months. Paid. Open to graduate students. ▶ *1–3 public relations interns:* responsibilities include providing support for a broad range of projects including media relations activities, strategic planning, special events, and development of marketing communications plans. Candidates should have college courses in field, oral communication skills, plan to pursue career in field, self-motivation, strong interpersonal skills, written communication skills. Duration is 3–4 months. Paid. Open to college sophomores, college juniors, college seniors. International applications accepted.
Benefits On-the-job training, possible full-time employment, willing to act as a professional reference, willing to complete paperwork for educational credit, willing to provide letters of recommendation.
Contact E-mail College Relations Manager, PO Box 7886, Philadelphia 19101-7886. Fax: 610-995-4812. E-mail: interns@labs.wyeth.com. No phone calls. In-person interview recommended (telephone interview accepted). Applicants must submit a resume. Applications are accepted continuously. World Wide Web: http://www.wyethjobs.com.

OTHER SERVICES

BUSINESS, PROFESSIONAL, LABOR, POLITICAL, AND OTHER ORGANIZATIONS

ALASKA CIVIL LIBERTIES UNION
PO Box 201844
Anchorage, Alaska 99520-1844

General Information Nonprofit, non-partisan organization dedicated to protecting the guarantees of civil liberties in the Bill of Rights and Alaska Constitution through public education, litigation, and political lobbying. Established in 1983. Number of employees: 3. Affiliate of American Civil Liberties Union, New York, New York. Number of internship applications received each year: 4.

Internships Available ▶ *1 law clerk:* responsibilities include researching and drafting legal memoranda, assisting volunteer attorneys with filing pleadings, monitoring legislative committee hearings, and researching/ drafting testimony and position papers on legislation affecting civil liberties. Candidates should have ability to work independently, analytical skills, oral communication skills, personal interest in the field, research skills, writing skills. Duration is one quarter, semester, or summer (flexible). Unpaid. Open to graduate students, law students. International applications accepted.

Benefits Names of contacts, willing to act as a professional reference, willing to complete paperwork for educational credit, willing to provide letters of recommendation, free housing (when available).

Contact Write, fax, or e-mail Jennifer Rudinger, Executive Director, PO Box 201844, Anchorage, Alaska 99520-1844. Fax: 907-258-0288. E-mail: akclu@alaska.net. No phone calls. Telephone interview required. Applicants must submit a letter of interest, resume, academic transcripts. Applications are accepted continuously. World Wide Web: http://www.aclu.org.

AMERICAN ASSOCIATION OF ADVERTISING AGENCIES
405 Lexington Avenue, 18th Floor
New York, New York 10174-1801

General Information National trade association of the advertising industry with more than 575 members nationwide. Established in 1917. Number of employees: 100. Number of internship applications received each year: 450.

Internships Available ▶ *70–90 multicultural advertising interns:* responsibilities include performing duties in account management, art direction, interactive technologies, copywriting, research, broadcast production, graphic design, traffic, print product, and media in New York, Chicago, Boston, Detroit, Dallas, Seattle, Philadelphia, Portland, Los Angeles, or San Francisco. Candidates should have ability to work independently, ability to work with others, analytical skills, computer skills, knowledge of field, oral communication skills, organizational skills, personal interest in the field, plan to pursue career in field, research skills, self-motivation, writing skills. Duration is 10 weeks. $350–$400 per week. Open to college juniors, college seniors, graduate students.

Benefits Names of contacts, opportunity to attend seminars/ workshops, possible full-time employment, willing to act as a professional reference, willing to complete paperwork for educational credit, willing to provide letters of recommendation, 60% payment of housing and transportation costs.

Contact Write, call, fax, e-mail, or through World Wide Web site Tiffany R. Warren, Manager of Diversity Programs. Phone: 800-676-9333. Fax: 212-573-8968. E-mail: maip@aaaa.org. In-person interview required. Applicants must submit a formal organization application, resume, academic transcripts, two letters of recommendation, 2-3 writing or creative samples (for art/ copywriting positions). Application deadline: February 1 for summer 2002. World Wide Web: http://www.aaaa.org.

AMERICAN ASSOCIATION OF UNIVERSITY WOMEN EDUCATIONAL FOUNDATION
1111 16th Street, NW
Washington, District of Columbia 20036-4873

General Information Foundation that provides funding for educational programs that directly benefit women and girls; groundbreaking research on gender bias in schools; fellowships and grants for outstanding women from around the globe; and vital community action projects. Established in 1881. Number of employees: 90. Unit of AAUW, Washington, District of Columbia. Number of internship applications received each year: 30.

Internships Available ▶ *1 Eleanor Roosevelt teacher fellowships and community action grants intern:* responsibilities include assisting with the management and assessment of funding programs. Duration is flexible. Unpaid. ▶ *1 communications intern:* responsibilities include assisting the coordinator with monitoring and managing the flow of materials between the two staffs; editing and writing articles, press releases, and creative briefs for meetings; and other programmatic, technical, and administrative projects. Duration is flexible. Unpaid. ▶ *2 development interns:* responsibilities include working with the staff to analyze contribution systems, determine donor trends, research potential funders, and write text for proposals, donor profiles, and publications. Duration is flexible. Unpaid. ▶ *1 gender equity research intern:* responsibilities include assisting in the coordination of commissioned research reports currently in production. Duration is flexible. Unpaid. ▶ *1 higher education fellowships intern:* responsibilities include working with the senior program officer on program assessment projects and the development of a major Colleges of Teacher Education initiative. Duration is flexible. Unpaid. ▶ *1 international fellowships intern:* responsibilities include assisting the senior program officer with assessment and evaluation efforts. Duration is flexible. Unpaid. ▶ *1 multicultural initiatives and higher education intern:* responsibilities include assisting the associate director and coordinator of multicultural initiatives and the program officer for career development grants and selected professions fellowships to assess grant programs; researching and writing articles on minority women in higher education; and coordinating conferences and meetings. Duration is flexible. Unpaid. Open to college freshmen, college sophomores, college juniors, college seniors, recent college graduates, graduate students.

Benefits Formal training, job counseling, names of contacts, opportunity to attend seminars/workshops, possible full-time employment, willing to complete paperwork for educational

credit, willing to provide letters of recommendation, small stipend, computer courses on all levels, career development lunches, networking opportunities.
Contact Write, call, fax, or e-mail Jai Fawn Burrello, Internship Coordinator. Phone: 202-785-7700. Fax: 202-872-1413. E-mail: aauwjobs@aauw.org. In-person interview recommended (telephone interview accepted). Applicants must submit a letter of interest, resume, writing sample. Applications are accepted continuously. World Wide Web: http://www.aauw.org.

AMERICAN COUNCIL FOR THE UNITED NATIONS UNIVERSITY
4421 Garrison Street, NW
Washington, District of Columbia 20016

General Information Nonprofit corporation that provides support for the United Nations University, an autonomous organization of the United Nations that focuses intellectual resources on world problems; global, decentralized, non-degree granting, postgraduate research institution; manages the Millennium Project on futures research and global change. Established in 1976. Number of employees: 3. Affiliate of United Nations University, Tokyo, Japan. Number of internship applications received each year: 100.
Internships Available ▶ *5–8 Millennium Project interns:* responsibilities include assisting with research and editing in social and technological fields, entering data, attending meetings and conferences, reviewing and reading documents, helping develop studies, and Web site improvements. Candidates should have analytical skills, computer skills, editing skills, organizational skills, research skills, writing skills. Duration is 2½ months to 1 year (preferably full-time). Unpaid. Open to college juniors, college seniors, recent college graduates, graduate students, law students, career changers, individuals reentering the workforce, preference given to graduate students. ▶ *1–2 Web master's assistants:* responsibilities include maintaining and improving Web site, assisting global research on future of global change, attending conferences, and finding the best ideas and experts. Candidates should have analytical skills, computer skills, editing skills, organizational skills, research skills, writing skills. Duration is 2½ months to 1 year (preferably full-time for 1 semester). Unpaid. Open to college juniors, college seniors, recent college graduates, graduate students, career changers, individuals reentering the workforce. ▶ *1–2 general interns:* responsibilities include providing liaison services between U.S. research institutions and the United Nations University programs. Candidates should have computer skills, editing skills, office skills, oral communication skills, organizational skills, self-motivation. Duration is flexible (preferably full-time for one semester). Unpaid. Open to college juniors, college seniors, recent college graduates, graduate students, law students, career changers, individuals reentering the workforce, preference given to graduate students. ▶ *2–3 video interns:* responsibilities include scanning Internet and other sources for images and video footage; assisting in editing and production for documentaries on global change. Candidates should have analytical skills, computer skills, editing skills, organizational skills, video skills. Duration is 2½ months to 1 year (preferably full-time for 1 semester). Unpaid. Open to college juniors, college seniors, recent college graduates, graduate students, career changers, individuals reentering the workforce. International applications accepted.
Benefits Formal training, job counseling, names of contacts, on-the-job training, opportunity to attend seminars/workshops, possible full-time employment, willing to act as a professional reference, willing to complete paperwork for educational credit, willing to provide letters of recommendation, work-related travel reimbursement.
International Internships Available in Buenos Aires, Argentina; Beijing, China; Cairo, Egypt; Maduri, India; Rome, Italy; Tokyo, Japan; Moscow, Russian Federation; London, United Kingdom.
Contact Write, call, fax, e-mail, or through World Wide Web site Jerome C. Glenn, Executive Director. Phone: 202-686-5179. Fax: 202-686-5179. E-mail: jglenn@igc.org. In-person interview recommended (telephone interview accepted). Applicants must submit a letter of interest, resume. Applications are accepted continuously. World Wide Web: http://www.millennium-project.org.

THE AMERICAN ENTERPRISE INSTITUTE (AEI)
1150 17th Street, NW
Washington, District of Columbia 20036

General Information Public policy making organization. Established in 1943. Number of employees: 150. Number of internship applications received each year: 600.
Internships Available ▶ *40 interns:* responsibilities include opportunities in the following areas: economic policy, foreign and defense studies, political and social studies, public relations, The American Enterprise magazine, communications, seminars and conferences, publications, publications marketing, information systems, marketing, and accounting. Candidates should have computer skills, personal interest in the field, research skills, self-motivation, written communication skills. Duration is flexible (usually one semester). Unpaid. Open to college juniors, college seniors, graduate students, law students. International applications accepted.
Benefits Free meals, names of contacts, opportunity to attend seminars/workshops, possible full-time employment, willing to act as a professional reference, willing to provide letters of recommendation.
Contact Write or fax Intern Coordinator. Phone: 202-862-5800. Fax: 202-862-7171. Applicants must submit a letter of interest, resume, academic transcripts, 500-word writing sample. Application deadline: April 1 for summer, September 15 for fall, December 1 for spring. World Wide Web: http://www.aei.org.

AMERICAN FEDERATION OF TEACHERS
555 New Jersey Avenue, NW
Washington, District of Columbia 20001

General Information Public employee labor union. Established in 1916. Number of employees: 350. Number of internship applications received each year: 150.
Internships Available ▶ *Interns:* responsibilities include research, writing, support for policy development and resources for affiliates. Candidates should have ability to work independently, knowledge of field, organizational skills, strong interpersonal skills, writing skills. $280 per week. Open to college sophomores, college juniors, college seniors, recent college graduates, graduate students, law students. International applications accepted.
Benefits On-the-job training, opportunity to attend seminars/workshops, willing to complete paperwork for educational credit, willing to provide letters of recommendation, health insurance (if necessary).
Contact Write, fax, or e-mail Patricia Olshefski, Director, PSRP Department. Fax: 202-879-4597. E-mail: intern@aft.org. No phone calls. Applicants must submit a resume, academic transcripts, writing sample, letter of recommendation, letter of interest indicating type of experience desired and reason for applying. Application deadline: March 1 for summer, July 1 for fall, November 1 for winter. World Wide Web: http://www.aft.org.

AMERICAN FOREIGN SERVICE ASSOCIATION
2101 E Street, NW
Washington, District of Columbia 20037

General Information Professional association and labor union representing members of the U.S. Foreign Service in labor-management relations, in promoting and advancing the diplomatic profession, and securing popular support for an active and effective U.S. foreign policy. Established in 1924. Number of employees: 25.
Internships Available ▶ *1 advocacy and legislative affairs intern:* responsibilities include drafting letters to Congress and opinion leaders, calling congressional staff members, and working with community leaders. Candidates should have ability to work independently, ability to work with others, computer skills, self-motivation, writing skills. Duration is 1 semester (16 hours per week, minimum). Paid. Open to college freshmen, college sophomores, college juniors, college seniors. ▶ *Corporate affairs interns:* responsibilities include working under direct supervision of AFSA's director for corporate relations, primarily with local representative offices of U.S. companies and with USG foreign affairs agencies; duties will include coordination of luncheons and events, research on U.S. firms to support recruitment of new IA

members, and contact with USG officials to support program events and objectives and to assist with specific problems. Candidates should have ability to work independently, computer skills, strong interpersonal skills, writing skills, Microsoft Word, Access and Excel; some background in international business practices and issues. Duration is minimum of 16 hours per week; flexible scheduling. ▶ *1 editorial/research assistant (Foreign Service Journal):* responsibilities include editing, writing, fact-checking and proofreading for the Foreign Service Journal; opportunity to write an article for the Journal in addition to some administrative work. Candidates should have computer skills, writing skills, knowledge of HTML is welcome; native-level fluency in English is required; interest in international affairs, preferably with coursework in the field; publications experience is a plus. Duration is 1 semester. $300 stipend (fall and spring interns); $500 stipend (summer interns). Open to college freshmen, college sophomores, college juniors, college seniors. ▶ *1 legislative affairs intern:* responsibilities include helping maintain database, analyzing and summarizing legislation, attending hearings, working with grassroots and coalition organizations, and helping develop and implement legislative strategy. Candidates should have analytical skills, computer skills, editing skills, organizational skills, research skills, self-motivation, writing skills, general understanding of the legislative process and politics in general. Duration is 1 semester. Paid. Open to college freshmen, college sophomores, college juniors, college seniors. ▶ *1 public affairs intern:* responsibilities include interviewing Foreign Service personnel, drafting articles and other materials, and placing articles in newspapers and magazines. Candidates should have ability to work independently, editing skills, oral communication skills, self-motivation, strong interpersonal skills, writing skills, some exposure to international affairs is desirable. Duration is 1 semester. Paid. Open to college freshmen, college sophomores, college juniors, college seniors. ▶ *1 publications marketing/advertising intern (Foreign Service Journal):* responsibilities include helping design and operate a marketing campaign; gaining experience in promoting a supplement, print advertising, direct mailing, phone skills, as well as overall production, circulation, and distribution of magazine. Candidates should have computer skills, hard-working and dependable; detail-oriented; general understanding of marketing and advertising. Duration is 1 semester (16-24 hours per week). Paid. Open to college freshmen, college sophomores, college juniors, college seniors. International applications accepted.
Benefits Willing to act as a professional reference, willing to complete paperwork for educational credit, willing to provide letters of recommendation, stipends available.
Contact Write, call, fax, e-mail, or through World Wide Web site Intern Coordinator. Phone: 202-338-4045. Fax: 202-338-6820. E-mail: afsa@afsa.org. In-person interview recommended (telephone interview accepted). Applicants must submit a letter of interest, resume, writing sample. Applications are accepted continuously. World Wide Web: http://www.afsa.org.

AMERICAN ISRAEL PUBLIC AFFAIRS COMMITTEE (AIPAC)
440 First Street, NW, Suite 600
Washington, District of Columbia 20001

General Information Bipartisan organization that lobbies Congress and the Administration on legislation that affects the U.S.-Israel relationship. Established in 1954. Number of employees: 100. Number of internship applications received each year: 300.
Internships Available ▶ *10–25 interns:* responsibilities include a variety of tasks and positions, including research, writing, public relations, legislative work, and event planning. Candidates should have computer skills, office skills, oral communication skills, research skills, writing skills, knowledge of/interest in the Middle-East. Duration is one semester (minimum of 16 hours per week) or summer (full-time). Unpaid. Open to college freshmen, college sophomores, college juniors, college seniors, recent college graduates, graduate students.
Benefits Job counseling, opportunity to attend seminars/workshops, willing to act as a professional reference, willing to

complete paperwork for educational credit, willing to provide letters of recommendation, stipend for summer positions (full-time).
International Internships Available in Jerusalem, Israel.
Contact Write, call, fax, e-mail, or through World Wide Web site Joel Barkin, Internship Coordinator. Phone: 202-639-5327. Fax: 202-347-4918. E-mail: joel_barkin@aipac.org. Applicants must submit a letter of interest, resume, writing sample, two letters of recommendation, passport size photo. Application deadline: January 15 for spring, April 1 for summer, September 15 for fall, December 1 for winter. World Wide Web: http://www.aipac.org.

AMERICAN JUDICATURE SOCIETY
180 North Michigan Avenue, Suite 600
Chicago, Illinois 60601

General Information Society that strives to maintain and enhance the independence and effectiveness of the judicial system. Established in 1913. Number of employees: 15. Number of internship applications received each year: 50.
Internships Available ▶ *1–2 law clerks:* responsibilities include legal research and writing and assisting in the publication of various journals/newsletters. Candidates should have ability to work independently, analytical skills, computer skills, editing skills, research skills, writing skills. Duration is 2–3 months. Unpaid. Open to law students. ▶ *1–2 research assistants:* responsibilities include library research, writing reports, and collating and cataloging information. Candidates should have analytical skills, college courses in field, computer skills, office skills, research skills, writing skills. Duration is 2–3 months. Unpaid. Open to college juniors, college seniors. International applications accepted.
Benefits On-the-job training, possible full-time employment, willing to act as a professional reference, willing to complete paperwork for educational credit, willing to provide letters of recommendation, opportunity to develop legal and social science research skills.
Contact Write, e-mail, or through World Wide Web site Malia Reddick, Director of Research. E-mail: mreddick@ajs.org. No phone calls. In-person interview required. Applicants must submit a letter of interest, resume, writing sample, three personal references. Application deadline: April 1 for summer, August 1 for fall, December 1 for spring. World Wide Web: http://www.ajs.org.

AMERICAN OUTLOOK MAGAZINE
5395 Emerson Way
Indianapolis, Indiana 46226

General Information Nonprofit futurist public policy think tank. Established in 1961. Number of employees: 54. Division of Hudson Institute, Indianapolis, Indiana. Number of internship applications received each year: 5.
Internships Available ▶ *2–3 editorial assistants:* responsibilities include assisting with production of American Outlook&OR magazine and other Hudson Institute publications. Candidates should have analytical skills, computer skills, editing skills, research skills, writing skills. Duration is 3–4 months. Unpaid. Open to college seniors, recent college graduates, graduate students. International applications accepted.
Benefits On-the-job training, willing to act as a professional reference, willing to complete paperwork for educational credit, willing to provide letters of recommendation.
Contact Write, fax, or e-mail Sam Karnick, Editor-in-Chief. Fax: 317-545-9639. E-mail: samk@hudson.org. No phone calls. In-person interview required. Applicants must submit a letter of interest, resume, three writing samples. Application deadline: January 1 for spring, May 1 for summer, August 1 for fall. World Wide Web: http://www.americanoutlook.org.

THE AMERICAN-SCANDINAVIAN FOUNDATION
58 Park Avenue
New York, New York 10016

General Information Nonprofit organization founded to develop and promote educational and cultural exchange between the United States and the Scandinavian countries of Denmark,

Finland, Iceland, Norway, and Sweden. Established in 1910. Number of employees: 22. Number of internship applications received each year: 60.

Internships Available ▶ *5–10 TEFOL positions (Finland):* responsibilities include teaching English as a foreign language to Finns at a variety of age levels in Finnish public schools, institutes, or private firms. Candidates should have declared college major in field, experience in the field, plan to pursue career in field, English, education, ESL, or related major. Duration is 3–10 months. $750–$900 per month. Open to college juniors, college seniors, recent college graduates, graduate students. ▶ *20–30 engineering interns (Scandinavia):* responsibilities include computer programming, performing entry-level engineering fieldwork, and assisting with projects. Candidates should have declared college major in field, knowledge of field, self-motivation, openness to a cross-cultural experience. Duration is 2–6 months. $775–$1110 per month. Open to college juniors, college seniors, graduate students.

Benefits Health insurance, on-the-job training, international cultural experience, assistance in obtaining work permits for those who have found their own internships.

International Internships Available in Finland; Sweden.

Contact Write, call, e-mail, or through World Wide Web site Exchange Division. Phone: 212-879-9779. Fax: 212-686-2115. E-mail: trainscan@amscan.org. Applicants must submit a formal organization application, resume, academic transcripts, letter of recommendation. Application deadline: January 1 for engineering positions, March 1 for TEFOL positions. Fees: $50. World Wide Web: http://www.amscan.org.

AMERICAN SOCIETY OF COMPOSERS, AUTHORS, AND PUBLISHERS
1 Lincoln Plaza, Floor 6
New York, New York 10023-7129

General Information Membership organization of over 70,000 composers, songwriters, lyricists, and music publishers; ASCAP's function is to protect the rights of its members by licensing and paying royalties for the public performances of their copyrighted works. Established in 1914. Number of employees: 700. Number of internship applications received each year: 30.

Internships Available ▶ *10–20 interns:* responsibilities include diverse tasks structured to reflect the intern's interests, talents, and skills level. Candidates should have analytical skills, computer skills, oral communication skills, strong interpersonal skills, written communication skills. Duration is flexible. Unpaid. Open to high school students, recent high school graduates, college freshmen, college sophomores, college juniors, college seniors, recent college graduates, graduate students, law students, career changers, individuals reentering the workforce. International applications accepted.

Benefits Possible full-time employment, willing to complete paperwork for educational credit, willing to provide letters of recommendation.

Contact Write or e-mail Yndrhis Santana, Human Resources Administrator. Fax: 212-874-8480. E-mail: jobline@ascap.com. No phone calls. In-person interview required. Applicants must submit a letter of interest, resume. Applications are accepted continuously. World Wide Web: http://www.ascap.com.

AMERICAN SOCIETY OF INTERNATIONAL LAW
2223 Massachusetts Avenue, NW
Washington, District of Columbia 20008

General Information Professional organization that engages in the exploration of international legal issues, including economic and private transactions, the environment, armed conflicts, human rights, dispute resolution, space, and the United Nations system. Established in 1906. Number of employees: 18. Number of internship applications received each year: 150.

Internships Available ▶ *1–3 financial office assistants:* responsibilities include assisting the controllers office with accounting functions. Candidates should have computer skills, knowledge of field, office skills, organizational skills, self-motivation. Duration is 8–10 weeks. Unpaid. Open to college freshmen, college sophomores, college juniors. ▶ *1 library/research assistant:* responsibili-

ties include helping to maintain the ASIL Web site; assisting staff and the Washington legal community with their information needs; and general library activities. Candidates should have ability to work independently, ability to work with others, computer skills, office skills, oral communication skills, research skills, writing skills. Duration is one semester or summer. Unpaid. Open to college sophomores, college juniors, college seniors, graduate students, law students. ▶ *1 meetings assistant:* responsibilities include database development, correspondence with panelists and exhibitors, Internet research on panelists and exhibitors, assisting with CLE administration for the Annual Meeting, and other administrative functions associated with the meeting planning. Candidates should have ability to work independently, computer skills, office skills, oral communication skills, organizational skills, research skills, self-motivation, strong interpersonal skills, writing skills. Duration is one semester or summer. Unpaid. Open to college juniors, college seniors, graduate students, law students. ▶ *1 publications intern:* responsibilities include bluebooking citations, desktop publishing, and formatting text for ASIL publications including ITProceedings of the Annual Meeting and IT Studies in Transnational Legal Policy series. Candidates should have ability to work independently, computer skills, editing skills, organizational skills, research skills, strong bluebooking and citation checking skills. Duration is one semester or summer. Unpaid. Open to law students. ▶ *1 research assistant—American Journal of International Law.* Duration is one semester or one summer (minimum). Position available as unpaid or paid. Open to second- and third-year law students. ▶ *1–3 sales and marketing assistants:* responsibilities include assisting in the promotion of the Society's programs and publications; conducting market research; assisting in the development and implementation of marketing strategies. Candidates should have computer skills, oral communication skills, organizational skills, research skills, strong interpersonal skills, written communication skills. Duration is 1 semester or summer. Unpaid. Open to college juniors, college seniors, graduate students, law students. International applications accepted.

Benefits Opportunity to attend seminars/workshops, possible full-time employment, willing to act as a professional reference, willing to complete paperwork for educational credit, willing to provide letters of recommendation, assistance with development of legal analysis skills available for some positions.

Contact Write or fax Internship Coordinator. Fax: 202-797-7133. No phone calls. In-person interview recommended (telephone interview accepted). Applicants must submit a letter of interest, resume, list of three references (one work, one academic, one personal reference) with telephone numbers. Application deadline: April 1 for summer, August 1 for fall, December 1 for spring. World Wide Web: http://www.asil.org.

AMERICAN SOCIETY OF MAGAZINE EDITORS
919 Third Avenue, 22nd Floor
New York, New York 10022

General Information Professional society for magazine editors that provides a forum for the discussion of matters of mutual concern. Established in 1963. Number of employees: 3. Unit of Magazine Publishers of America, New York, New York. Number of internship applications received each year: 175.

Internships Available ▶ *40 editorial interns:* responsibilities include performing entry-level editorial tasks. Candidates should have college courses in field, editing skills, knowledge of field, plan to pursue career in field, writing skills, previous magazine experience. Duration is 10 weeks in summer. Stipend of $325 per week. Open to college juniors. International applications accepted.

Benefits Housing at a cost, opportunity to attend seminars/workshops, willing to act as a professional reference, willing to provide letters of recommendation, distribution of resumes to ASME members.

Contact Write, fax, e-mail, or through World Wide Web site Marlene Kahan, Executive Director. Fax: 212-906-0128. E-mail: asme@magazine.org. No phone calls. Applicants must submit a formal organization application, letter of interest, resume, three writing samples, letter of recommendation. Application deadline: November 15. World Wide Web: http://www.asme.magazine.org.

AMIDEAST
1730 M Street, NW, Suite 1100
Washington, District of Columbia 20036

General Information Private nonprofit organization promoting cooperation and understanding between Americans and the people of the Middle East and North Africa through education and development programs. Established in 1951. Number of employees: 53. Number of internship applications received each year: 100.

Internships Available ► *1 editorial research intern:* responsibilities include assisting in writing, researching, and marketing of quarterly professional periodical and other resources for overseas educational advisers and organizing and maintaining advising resource collections. Duration is flexible. Paid. ► *1 intern for special projects-short-term training:* responsibilities include researching short-term training programs, responding to trainees' requests, maintaining accurate records, corresponding with trainers and the field offices, and providing general program support. Candidates should have ability to work independently, ability to work with others, computer skills, office skills, oral communication skills, written communication skills. Duration is 1 month. Paid. ► *1 public relations/fund-raising intern:* responsibilities include researching international companies and compiling information to support fund-raising, public relations, and marketing products and services; researching, writing, and proofreading newsletters, annual report, flyers, and press releases; updating computerized mailing/donor lists. Candidates should have ability to work independently, ability to work with others, computer skills, office skills, oral communication skills, written communication skills. Duration is flexible. Paid. ► *2 publications interns:* responsibilities include researching, writing, editing, and producing educational materials; processing publications orders; and developing and implementing marketing activities. Candidates should have ability to work independently, ability to work with others, computer skills, office skills, oral communication skills, written communication skills. Duration is flexible (3 months minimum). Paid. ► *1 study abroad intern:* responsibilities include researching markets, developing advertisements and promotional materials, preparing mass mailings, and responding to requests for information. Candidates should have ability to work independently, ability to work with others, computer skills, office skills, oral communication skills, written communication skills. Duration is 1 semester. Paid. Open to college freshmen, college sophomores, college juniors, college seniors. International applications accepted.

Benefits Willing to complete paperwork for educational credit, willing to provide letters of recommendation.

Contact Write, call, e-mail, or through World Wide Web site Shawnte Jefferies, Personnel Assistant. Phone: 202-776-9600. E-mail: personnel@amideast.org. In-person interview recommended (telephone interview accepted). Applicants must submit a letter of interest, resume. Applications are accepted continuously. World Wide Web: http://www.amideast.org.

ARTHRITIS FOUNDATION, NORTHERN CALIFORNIA CHAPTER
657 Mission Street, Suite 603
San Francisco, California 94105

General Information Foundation that seeks to improve lives through leadership in the prevention, control, and cure of arthritis and related diseases. Established in 1948. Number of employees: 20. Unit of Arthritis Foundation, Atlanta, Georgia. Number of internship applications received each year: 40.

Internships Available ► *6–8 summer science fellowship interns:* responsibilities include working on arthritis research in laboratory. Candidates should have ability to work with others, knowledge of field, personal interest in the field, plan to pursue career in field. Duration is 8 weeks. $1500–$2000 per duration of internship. Open to high school seniors, recent high school graduates, college freshmen, college sophomores, college juniors, college seniors, high school juniors. International applications accepted.

Benefits Stipend, hands-on laboratory experience.

Contact Write, fax, or e-mail Molly Klarman, Patient and Community Services, 657 Mission Street Suite 603, San Francisco, California 94105. Fax: 415-356-1240. E-mail: mklarman@arthritis.org. No phone calls. Applicants must submit a formal organization application, academic transcripts, three letters of recommendation. Application deadline: February 11. World Wide Web: http://www.arthritis.org.

ASHOKA: INNOVATORS FOR THE PUBLIC
1700 North Moore Street, Suite 2000
Arlington, Virginia 22209-1903

General Information International nonprofit organization presenting fellowships to individuals with creative ideas for social change in Asia, Latin America, Central Europe, Africa, and North America. Established in 1980. Number of employees: 52. Number of internship applications received each year: 100.

Internships Available ► *Interns:* responsibilities include working in areas of development, recruitment and selection of fellows, fellowship support services, environmental education, citizen-based initiative, social marketing, finance, research, computers, and administration; working in offices dealing with Latin America, Asia, Central Europe, Africa, and North America. Candidates should have ability to work independently, ability to work with others, computer skills, oral communication skills, research skills, self-motivation, writing skills, language ability (French, Spanish, Portuguese, Thai or other Asian language a plus); should have entrepreneurial spirit. Duration is flexible (minimum of 12 hours per week preferred). Unpaid. Open to college freshmen, college sophomores, college juniors, college seniors, recent college graduates, graduate students, law students, career changers, individuals reentering the workforce. International applications accepted.

Benefits Names of contacts, opportunity to attend seminars/workshops, possible full-time employment, willing to complete paperwork for educational credit, willing to provide letters of recommendation.

Contact Write, fax, e-mail, or through World Wide Web site Elizabeth Nelson, Program Manager. Phone: 703-527-8300. Fax: 703-527-8383. E-mail: enelson@ashoka.org. In-person interview recommended (telephone interview accepted). Applicants must submit a letter of interest, resume, cover letter. Applications are accepted continuously. World Wide Web: http://www.ashoka.org.

ASIAN AMERICAN ECONOMIC DEVELOPMENT ENTERPRISES, INC. (AAEDE)
216 West Garvey Avenue, Unit E
Monterey Park, California 91754

General Information Nonprofit organization aiding small business owners in the community via workshops and individual consultation and providing the community with job fairs and volunteer opportunities. Established in 1977. Number of employees: 4. Number of internship applications received each year: 40.

Internships Available ► *1–2 community liaisons:* responsibilities include contacting various media and community organizations by sending out press releases, compiling press kits, arranging radio and television interviews, and making new media and association contacts for AAEDE. Candidates should have oral communication skills, organizational skills, self-motivation, writing skills. Duration is 8-12 hours per week. Position available as unpaid or paid. ► *2–3 conference coordinator assistants:* responsibilities include participating in all aspects of conference planning, including design and selection of invitations, sponsorship, speaker arrangements, lecture materials, lecture hall preparation, volunteer recruitment, and room set-up planning. Candidates should have ability to work with others, oral communication skills, organizational skills, self-motivation, creative and detail-oriented nature. Duration is 8-12 hours per week. Position available as unpaid or paid. ► *2–3 newsletter publication assistants:* responsibilities include gathering and evaluating information for newsletter, writing articles, editing submissions, reporting on community events, supporting design and layout, compiling graphic boards, interacting with the printer, and assisting with bulk mail. Candidates should have ability to work independently, ability to work with others, computer skills, editing skills, research skills, writing skills. Duration is 8-12 hours per week. Unpaid. ► *2–3 research/special project assistants:*

responsibilities include gathering and evaluating business and/or demographic information for programs and grant applications, attending community meetings, evaluating proposals, and interacting with small business clients. Candidates should have analytical skills, computer skills, oral communication skills, research skills, writing skills, foreign language skills and business experience helpful. Duration is 8-12 hours per week. Unpaid. Open to college freshmen, college sophomores, college juniors, college seniors, recent college graduates, graduate students.

Benefits Opportunity to attend seminars/workshops, willing to act as a professional reference, willing to complete paperwork for educational credit, willing to provide letters of recommendation.

Contact Write, call, fax, e-mail, or through World Wide Web site Van Truong, Program Manager, 216 West Garvey Avenue, Unit E, Monterey Park, California 91754. Phone: 626-572-7021. Fax: 626-572-6533. E-mail: vt@aaede.org. In-person interview recommended (telephone interview accepted). Applicants must submit a letter of interest, resume. Applications are accepted continuously. World Wide Web: http://www.aaede.org.

ASIAN PACIFIC AMERICAN DISPUTE RESOLUTION CENTER
1145 Wilshire Boulevard, Suite 100
Los Angeles, California 90017

General Information Center that provides mediation and conciliation services to individuals, organizations, and businesses that are interested in resolving disputes outside the court system. Established in 1989. Number of employees: 7. Number of internship applications received each year: 100.

Internships Available ▶ *5 AmeriCorps VISTA Interns:* responsibilities include serving in one of five API social service agencies; creating an outreach strategy in their own agency and for the entire collaborative, as well as having choice to write grants, develop volunteer programs, or develop curriculum. Candidates should have oral communication skills, organizational skills, personal interest in the field, self-motivation, strong interpersonal skills, strong leadership ability. Duration is one year (40 hours per week). $700 per month. Open to college sophomores, college juniors, college seniors, recent college graduates, graduate students, law students, career changers, individuals reentering the workforce. ▶ *1 development specialist:* responsibilities include assisting in the creation of a database with contact information on community organizations as well as corporations in the local area; assisting with grant writing for the Center; supporting the day-to-day activities and special projects. Candidates should have ability to work independently, organizational skills, research skills, self-motivation, strong interpersonal skills, writing skills. Duration is 10–12 weeks. Unpaid. Open to college juniors, college seniors, recent college graduates, graduate students, law students, career changers, individuals reentering the workforce. ▶ *Language specialists:* responsibilities include translating casework (applications, evaluations), outreach materials (flyers, presentations, brochures) and recruitment materials (flyers, paperwork) into language of expertise. Candidates should have editing skills, written communication skills, competence in a foreign language (especially in an Asian language). Duration is 8–10 weeks. Unpaid. Open to college juniors, college seniors, recent college graduates, graduate students, law students, career changers. ▶ *1 peer mediation intern:* responsibilities include assisting in compiling and packaging of Peer Mediation curriculum, researching and networking with other programs, and other projects assigned by the Peer Mediation Coordinator; after training, intern will assist at local high school. Candidates should have oral communication skills, organizational skills, personal interest in the field, self-motivation, strong interpersonal skills. Duration is 4 months (10-12 hours per week). Unpaid. Open to college juniors, college seniors, recent college graduates, graduate students, law students, career changers, individuals reentering the workforce. ▶ *1–5 social service interns:* responsibilities include conducting intake interviews, interacting with clients, and performing casework; observing and participating in mediation (with completed training provided by Center); assisting with community education, public presentations, and outreach programs. Candidates should have oral communication skills, organizational skills, personal interest in the field, self-

motivation, strong interpersonal skills, written communication skills. Duration is 16 weeks (12-15 hours per week). Unpaid. Open to college juniors, college seniors, recent college graduates, graduate students, law students, career changers. International applications accepted.

Benefits Formal training, on-the-job training, opportunity to attend seminars/workshops, willing to complete paperwork for educational credit, willing to provide letters of recommendation, parking validation.

Contact Write, call, fax, or e-mail Volunteer Coordinator. Phone: 213-250-8190. Fax: 213-250-8195. E-mail: apadrc@sbcglobal.net. In-person interview recommended (telephone interview accepted). Applicants must submit a letter of interest, resume, application form. Applications are accepted continuously.

THE ASSOCIATION OF FUNDRAISING PROFESSIONALS
1101 King Street, Suite 700
Alexandria, Virginia 22314-2967

General Information Organization that advocates development and growth of fund-raising professionals working to advance philanthropy and volunteerism and to promote high ethical standards in the fund-raising profession. Established in 1960. Number of employees: 50. Number of internship applications received each year: 10.

Internships Available ▶ *1–2 resource center interns:* responsibilities include researching and performing data entry, daily tracking of requests; processing book, periodicals, and tapes; maintaining library database; greeting visitors and assisting with inquiries; some phone work. Candidates should have computer skills, office skills, oral communication skills, organizational skills, research skills, strong interpersonal skills. Duration is nine months to one year (minimum 15 hours per week suggested). Unpaid. Open to recent high school graduates, college freshmen, college sophomores, college juniors, college seniors, career changers, individuals reentering the workforce.

Benefits Names of contacts, possible full-time employment, willing to complete paperwork for educational credit, willing to provide letters of recommendation.

Contact Write, call, fax, or e-mail Jan Alfieri, Manager AFP Resource Center. Phone: 703-519-8458. Fax: 703-684-0540. E-mail: jalfieri@afpnet.org. In-person interview required. Applicants must submit a resume, cover letter. Applications are accepted continuously. World Wide Web: http://www.afpnet.org.

ASTA FOUNDATION, INC.
1101 King Street
Alexandria, Virginia 22314

General Information Organization that encourages professionalism in the travel and tourism industry by offering financial aid to students and funding research in the tourism field. Established in 1982. Number of employees: 1. Affiliate of American Society of Travel Agents, Inc., Alexandria, Virginia. Number of internship applications received each year: 5.

Internships Available ▶ *1–3 David J. Hallissey interns:* responsibilities include assisting ASTA's research department with projects related to the travel industry. Candidates should have ability to work independently, ability to work with others, computer skills, oral communication skills, personal interest in the field, written communication skills, background in statistics and social research (at minimum one college-level course). Duration is 3–6 months. $1000–$1500 per duration of internship. Open to undergraduate and graduate students from Washington, DC Metro area colleges and universities who are pursuing studies in travel/tourism; students who reside in DC area but attend school elsewhere will be considered for summer internships only. ▶ *1 Fernando R. Ayuso Scholarship Fellow:* responsibilities include attending a travel and trade show in Madrid, Spain for 10 days, utilizing knowledge of the Spanish language in order to interview Spanish tourism officials and to facilitate show functions. Candidates should have college courses in field, experience in the field, oral communication skills, plan to pursue career in field, written communication skills, ability to speak and read Spanish at a working level. Dura-

ASTA Foundation, Inc. (continued)

tion is 10 days in January/February. Unpaid. Open to college juniors, college seniors, recent college graduates, graduate students, individuals with at least 2 years of college credit or work experience in the travel and tourism industry.

Benefits Free housing, free meals, opportunity to attend seminars/workshops, travel reimbursement, expenses for 10-day Ayuso position reimbursed.

International Internships Available in Madrid, Spain.

Contact Write, call, fax, or through World Wide Web site Internship Coordinator. Phone: 703-739-2782. Fax: 703-684-8319. Materials as outlined on Web site. Application deadline: July for both positions. World Wide Web: http://www.astanet.com.

ATLANTIC COUNCIL OF THE UNITED STATES
910 17th Street, NW, Suite 1000
Washington, District of Columbia 20006

General Information National, nonprofit, nonpartisan center for the formation of foreign policy. Established in 1961. Number of employees: 40. Number of internship applications received each year: 250.

Internships Available ▶ *15–20 John A. Baker interns:* responsibilities include scholarly research, administrative and/or office tasks, computer entry and application, weekly Intern Discussion Series roundtables, and a research project. Candidates should have computer skills, knowledge of field, office skills, personal interest in the field, research skills, written communication skills. Duration is 1 summer or semester. Unpaid. Open to college freshmen, college sophomores, college juniors, college seniors, recent college graduates, graduate students. International applications accepted.

Benefits Job counseling, names of contacts, opportunity to attend seminars/workshops, possible full-time employment, willing to complete paperwork for educational credit, willing to provide letters of recommendation, weekly Intern Discussion Series roundtables.

Contact Write, fax, e-mail, or through World Wide Web site Internship Coordinator. Fax: 202-463-7241. E-mail: internships@acus.org. Telephone interview required. Applicants must submit a letter of interest, resume, academic transcripts, writing sample, two letters of recommendation. Application deadline: March 30 for summer (priority); however, applications are received on a continuous basis, November 15 for spring (priority). World Wide Web: http://www.acus.org.

BENTON FOUNDATION
1625 K Street, NW
Washington, District of Columbia 20006

General Information Private, nonpartisan foundation whose goal is to promote public interest in communications tools, applications, and policies. Established in 1948. Number of employees: 30. Number of internship applications received each year: 50.

Internships Available ▶ *1–3 communications policy and practice interns:* responsibilities include assisting in the publication of Benton's daily on-line news service and other reports and publications. Candidates should have ability to work independently, computer skills, knowledge of field, research skills, self-motivation, written communication skills. Duration is 1 semester. Paid. Open to graduate students. International applications accepted.

Benefits On-the-job training, opportunity to attend seminars/workshops, willing to act as a professional reference, willing to complete paperwork for educational credit, willing to provide letters of recommendation.

Contact Write or e-mail Rachel Anderson, Communications Policy and Practice Senior Associate. E-mail: rachel@benton.org. No phone calls. In-person interview recommended (telephone interview accepted). Applicants must submit a letter of interest, resume, writing sample. Applications are accepted continuously. World Wide Web: http://www.benton.org.

BRAZILIAN-AMERICAN CHAMBER OF COMMERCE, INC.
509 Madison Avenue, 3rd Floor
New York, New York 10022

General Information Bilateral trade association aiming at fostering better business relations between Brazil and the U.S. Established in 1969. Number of employees: 5. Number of internship applications received each year: 6.

Internships Available ▶ *2–3 membership marketing interns:* responsibilities include contacting potential members over the phone, researching for annual publication, and handling business information requests. Candidates should have oral communication skills, organizational skills, self-motivation, strong interpersonal skills, written communication skills. Duration is one spring, summer, or fall (minimum 25 hours per week). $600 stipend per month. Open to college seniors, graduate students.

Benefits Job counseling, names of contacts, on-the-job training, opportunity to attend seminars/workshops, willing to act as a professional reference, willing to complete paperwork for educational credit, willing to provide letters of recommendation.

Contact Write, fax, or e-mail Sueli Bonaparte, Executive Director, 509 Madison Avenue, 3rd Floor, New York, New York 10022. Fax: 212-751-7692. E-mail: membership@brazilcham.com. No phone calls. In-person interview recommended (telephone interview accepted). Applicants must submit a letter of interest, resume, academic transcripts, writing sample, letter of recommendation. Application deadline: May 15. World Wide Web: http://www.brazilcham.com.

BUSINESS INFORMATION SERVICE FOR NEWLY INDEPENDENT STATES (BISNIS)
1401 Constitution Avenue, NW, Ronald Reagan Building
Washington, District of Columbia 20230

General Information U.S. government-funded organization that assists U.S. companies seeking to export U.S. products or services or to establish business cooperation in the former Soviet Union. Established in 1992. Number of employees: 15. Unit of United States Department of Commerce, Washington, District of Columbia. Number of internship applications received each year: 15.

Internships Available ▶ *1–3 interns:* responsibilities include answering public inquiries on NIS commercial issues; researching and writing reports and/or articles; assisting with trade events and visiting delegations; and administrative support. Candidates should have ability to work independently, computer skills, editing skills, oral communication skills, personal interest in the field, research skills, writing skills. Duration is one semester (20 hours per week). Unpaid. Open to college freshmen, college sophomores, college juniors, college seniors, graduate students, law students, must be U.S. citizen.

Benefits Names of contacts, opportunity to attend seminars/workshops, willing to act as a professional reference, willing to complete paperwork for educational credit, willing to provide letters of recommendation, language class participation.

Contact Write, call, fax, or e-mail Joan Morgan, Intern Coordinator. Phone: 202-482-2709. Fax: 202-482-2293. E-mail: bisnis@ita.doc.gov. In-person interview recommended (telephone interview accepted). Applicants must submit a letter of interest, resume, academic transcripts, 1-2 writing samples. Applications are accepted continuously. World Wide Web: http://www.bisnis.doc.gov.

CAMARA DE COMERCIO E INDUSTRIA BOLIVIANO-ALEMANA
Avenue Ecuador 2277
La Paz Bolivia

General Information Organization working in the field of commerce and industry by offering different services for members and others who have a relationship between Bolivia and Germany. Number of employees: 10. Number of internship applications received each year: 6.

Internships Available ▶ *30 interns:* responsibilities include placement in Bolivian firms according to area of interest. Duration is

3–6 months. Unpaid. ▶ *1–2 law/business administration interns:* responsibilities include answering questions from members, writing articles for magazine, and preparing special events. Duration is 3–4 months. Unpaid. Candidates for all positions should have ability to work independently, ability to work with others, computer skills, self-motivation, written communication skills, must speak and write Spanish and German. Open to high school students, recent high school graduates, graduate students, law students.
Benefits Housing at a cost, names of contacts, willing to provide letters of recommendation.
International Internships Available.
Contact E-mail Armin Talke, Internship Coordinator. Phone: 591-2-411774. Fax: 591-2-413321. E-mail: talke@ahkbol.com. Applicants must submit a letter of interest, academic transcripts, formal application in German. Applications are accepted continuously. Fees: $120.

CAMPAIGN FOR U.N. REFORM
420 7th Street, Suite C
Washington, District of Columbia 20003

General Information Political lobbying organization. Established in 1975. Number of employees: 3. Number of internship applications received each year: 100.
Internships Available ▶ *3–8 research associates/interns:* responsibilities include attending coalition meetings; writing press releases; analyzing voting patterns of Congress in regards to UN related votes; document duplication and distribution on Capitol Hill; researching UN related issues. Candidates should have ability to work independently, ability to work with others, computer skills, oral communication skills, writing skills. Duration is 1–4 months. $5 per day. Open to college freshmen, college sophomores, college juniors, college seniors, recent college graduates, graduate students. International applications accepted.
Benefits Formal training, names of contacts, on-the-job training, opportunity to attend seminars/workshops, travel reimbursement, willing to act as a professional reference, willing to complete paperwork for educational credit, willing to provide letters of recommendation.
Contact Write, fax, or e-mail Don Kraus, Executive Director, 420 7th Street, Suite C, Washington, District of Columbia 20003. Fax: 202-546-8703. E-mail: draus@cunr.org. In-person interview recommended (telephone interview accepted). Applicants must submit a letter of interest, resume, writing sample. Applications are accepted continuously. World Wide Web: http://www.cunr.org.

CANADIAN EMBASSY
501 Pennsylvania Avenue, NW
Washington, District of Columbia 20001

General Information Embassy that provides students the opportunity for involvement in governmental affairs in order to gain a general understanding of the Canada/U.S. bilateral relationship. Established in 1936. Number of employees: 250. Number of internship applications received each year: 400.
Internships Available ▶ *2–5 economics interns:* responsibilities include working in various areas, including energy, trade, science, defense, and OLIFI. Candidates should have computer skills, oral communication skills, organizational skills, research skills, strong interpersonal skills, writing skills, U.S. or Canadian citizenship. Duration is January to December. Unpaid. Open to college sophomores, college juniors, college seniors, recent college graduates, graduate students, law students. ▶ *2–5 politics interns:* responsibilities include working in congressional relations and the environment. Candidates should have ability to work with others, computer skills, oral communication skills, organizational skills, research skills, writing skills, U.S. or Canadian citizenship. Duration is January to December. Unpaid. Open to college juniors, college seniors, recent college graduates, graduate students, law students. ▶ *5 public affairs interns:* responsibilities include working in various areas, including relations, special events, cultural relations, press, and publications. Candidates should have ability to work with others, computer skills, oral communication skills, organizational skills, research skills, writing skills, U.S. or Canadian citizenship. Duration is 1 semester. Unpaid. Open to college

sophomores, college juniors, college seniors, recent college graduates, graduate students. International applications accepted.
Benefits Job counseling, names of contacts, opportunity to attend seminars/workshops, willing to complete paperwork for educational credit, willing to provide letters of recommendation, networking opportunities, access to gym.
Contact Write, call, fax, e-mail, or through World Wide Web site Ingrid S. Summa, Internship Coordinator. Phone: 202-682-1740 Ext. 7530. Fax: 202-682-7791. E-mail: ingrid.summa@dfait-maeci. gc.ca. Telephone interview required. Applicants must submit a letter of interest, resume, academic transcripts, writing sample, three letters of recommendation. Application deadline: March 15 for summer, July 15 for fall, November 15 for winter/spring. World Wide Web: http://www.canadianembassy.org.

CARIBBEAN LATIN AMERICAN ACTION
1818 N Street, NW, Suite 500
Washington, District of Columbia 20036

General Information Organization that promotes economic development in the Caribbean basin countries. Established in 1978. Number of employees: 12. Number of internship applications received each year: 35.
Internships Available ▶ *1–4 interns:* responsibilities include researching, writing, editing, conference planning, acting as a congressional liaison, and making regional contacts. Candidates should have ability to work independently, oral communication skills, research skills, self-motivation, written communication skills, Spanish fluency a plus. Duration is 1 semester. Unpaid. Open to college freshmen, college sophomores, college juniors, college seniors, graduate students. International applications accepted.
Benefits Names of contacts, possible full-time employment, willing to complete paperwork for educational credit, willing to provide letters of recommendation.
Contact E-mail Internship Coordinator. E-mail: info@claa.org. In-person interview recommended (telephone interview accepted). Applicants must submit a formal organization application, letter of interest, resume, academic transcripts, writing sample. Applications are accepted continuously. World Wide Web: http://www. claa.org.

CAUX SCHOLARS PROGRAM
1156 15th Street, NW, Suite 910
Washington, District of Columbia 20005

General Information Program that trains young adults in the theory and practice of conflict transformation in the international context. Established in 1991. Number of employees: 8. Unit of MRA/Initiatives of Change, Washington, District of Columbia. Number of internship applications received each year: 30.
Internships Available ▶ *1–10 Caux Scholars:* responsibilities include attending course held in Switzerland in conflict transformation at a cost of $2000; working 10 hours per week in practical conference support. Candidates should have oral communication skills, personal interest in the field, self-motivation, strong interpersonal skills. Duration is 1 month (July to August). Unpaid. Open to college juniors, college seniors, recent college graduates, graduate students, law students, career changers. ▶ *1 Caux Scholars Program intern:* responsibilities include mailing information, working on production of reports and brochures, helping with mailings, maintaining database, handling phone and written inquiries, and attending Executive Committee and Advisory Board meetings. Candidates should have ability to work independently, computer skills, research skills, self-motivation, strong interpersonal skills, written communication skills. Duration is flexible (generally fall to summer). Unpaid. Open to college juniors, college seniors, recent college graduates, graduate students. ▶ *1 IC intern:* responsibilities include answering telephone, responding to inquiries, mailings, conference/meeting arrangements, database maintenance, and arranging programs for international guests. Candidates should have ability to work with others, computer skills, office skills, oral communication skills, self-motivation, written communication skills. Duration is flexible. Unpaid. Open to college juniors, college seniors, recent college graduates, graduate students. International applications accepted.

Caux Scholars Program (continued)

Benefits Job counseling, names of contacts, opportunity to attend seminars/workshops, travel reimbursement, willing to complete paperwork for educational credit, willing to provide letters of recommendation, housing may be provided at no cost.
International Internships Available in Australia; United Kingdom.
Contact Write, call, fax, e-mail, or through World Wide Web site Ms. N. Sherman, Program Director. Phone: 202-872-9077. Fax: 202-872-9137. E-mail: cauxsp@aol.com. In-person interview recommended (telephone interview accepted). Applicants must submit a formal organization application, letter of interest, resume, essay, either 2 personal references or 2 letters of recommendation. Application deadline: April 1 for summer. Fees: $25. World Wide Web: http://www.cauxscholars.org.

CDS INTERNATIONAL, INC.
871 United Nations Plaza, 15th Floor
New York, New York 10017-1814

General Information Organization that prepares college students and recent graduates for the challenges of international business by combining in-depth language training with on-the-job experience in another country; programs currently offered for Americans wishing to go to Germany/Switzerland/Turkey/Argentina and for internationals seeking experience in the U.S. Established in 1968. Number of employees: 20. Number of internship applications received each year: 500.
Internships Available ▶ *10 Bayer summer program interns:* responsibilities include working in chemistry and engineering fields. Candidates should have ability to work independently, ability to work with others, declared college major in field, knowledge of field, oral communication skills, plan to pursue career in field. Duration is 2–3 months. DM 2500 per month (approximate); limited stipends available for 1-month language course. Open to college freshmen, college sophomores, college juniors, college seniors. ▶ *60–80 Congress-Bundestag Youth Exchange for Young Professionals participants:* responsibilities include 2 months of German language training, 4 months at an institution of higher education, and a 5-month internship; interns live with host families in Germany. Candidates should have knowledge of field, plan to pursue career in field, sincere intercultural interest paired with interest, goals, and experience in a business, technical, agricultural, or vocational field; individuals in other fields invited to apply. Duration is 1 year (July-July). Position available as unpaid or paid. Open to recent high school graduates, college freshmen, college sophomores, college juniors, college seniors, recent college graduates, U.S. citizens between 18 and 24 years old (no former CBYX high school scholarship recipients). ▶ *Independent work abroad program interns:* responsibilities include assignments negotiated between intern and company. Candidates should have declared college major in field, experience in the field, oral communication skills, self-motivation, strong interpersonal skills, intercultural interest. Duration is 1–18 months. Position available as unpaid or paid. Open to college freshmen, college sophomores, college juniors, college seniors, recent college graduates, graduate students, young professionals. ▶ *Interns.* Candidates should have ability to work independently, declared college major in field, experience in the field, oral communication skills, plan to pursue career in field, strong interpersonal skills. Duration is 6–18 months. DM 1500 per month (average); limited stipends available for one-month language course. Open to college juniors, college seniors, recent college graduates, graduate students, young professionals. ▶ *Summer program interns.* Candidates should have college courses in field, knowledge of field, oral communication skills, strong interpersonal skills, intercultural interest. Duration is 2–3 months. DM 1000 per month (approximate); limited stipends available for 1-month language course. Open to college freshmen, college sophomores, college juniors, college seniors, graduate students.
Benefits Housing at a cost, on-the-job training, willing to provide letters of recommendation, opportunity to live and work in another country; assistance in securing necessary work and residency permits, scholarships for some programs, health insurance for some programs.
International Internships Available in Argentina; Germany; Switzerland; Turkey.

Contact Write, call, fax, e-mail, or through World Wide Web site Isabell Kowalk, Program Officer. Phone: 212-497-3500. Fax: 212-497-3535. E-mail: info@cdsintl.org. In-person interview recommended (telephone interview accepted). Applicants must submit a formal organization application, letter of interest, academic transcripts, two letters of recommendation, resume; contact for program-specific application materials. Application deadline: February 1 for summer interns; continuous for other positions, December 1 for Congress-Bundestag Youth Exchange for Young Professionals. World Wide Web: http://www.cdsintl.org.

CENTER FOR COMMUNICATION, INC.
271 Madison Avenue, Suite 700
New York, New York 10016

General Information Nonprofit organization that encourages university students to meet professionals in communications industries by sponsoring seminars featuring workers in print and broadcast journalism, book and magazine publishing, advertising, public relations, and new technologies. Established in 1980. Number of employees: 6. Number of internship applications received each year: 100.
Internships Available ▶ *Interns:* responsibilities include researching senior topics; collecting newsclips; compiling suggested reading lists; helping to promote, support, and publicize activities; and participating in all aspects of production of seminars. Candidates should have ability to work independently, computer skills, research skills, self-motivation, strong interpersonal skills, strong career interest in the arts. Position available as unpaid or at $250 per spring or fall internship (2 days per week); $500 per summer internship (4 days per week). Open to college sophomores, college juniors, college seniors, recent college graduates, graduate students. International applications accepted.
Benefits Names of contacts, opportunity to attend seminars/workshops, willing to act as a professional reference, willing to complete paperwork for educational credit, willing to provide letters of recommendation.
International Internships Available in London, United Kingdom.
Contact Write, call, fax, e-mail, or through World Wide Web site Frank Argllier, Director of Student Affairs. Phone: 212-686-5005 Ext. 13. Fax: 212-686-6393. E-mail: frank@cencom.org. In-person interview required. Applicants must submit a letter of interest, resume, two personal references, 1 or 2 letters of recommendation. Applications are accepted continuously. World Wide Web: http://www.cencom.org.

CENTER FOR FOLKLIFE & CULTURAL HERITAGE
750 9th Street, NW, Suite 4100
Washington, District of Columbia 20560

General Information Center that engages in cultural conservation and representation activities that promote continuity, integrity, and equity for traditional ethnic, tribal, regional, minority, and working-class cultures in the U.S. and abroad through scholarly research, professional advocacy, and public programs. Established in 1967. Number of employees: 45. Unit of Smithsonian Institution, Washington, District of Columbia. Number of internship applications received each year: 200.
Internships Available ▶ *1–25 interns:* responsibilities include organizing and handling written, audio and visual documentation and logistics for public programs, educational resources, publications, and recordings; performing computer input for archivist; following up field work by organizing and compiling reports and documentation; following up with potential participants by securing necessary information related to festival presentation; and acquiring and disseminating information from and to festival staff. Candidates should have ability to work with others, office skills, organizational skills, personal interest in the field, self-motivation. Duration is 1–12 months. Unpaid. Open to high school students, recent high school graduates, college freshmen, college sophomores, college juniors, college seniors, recent college graduates, graduate students, law students, career changers, individuals reentering the workforce. International applications accepted.

Benefits Names of contacts, on-the-job training, opportunity to attend seminars/workshops, willing to act as a professional reference, willing to complete paperwork for educational credit, willing to provide letters of recommendation.

Contact Write, call, fax, or e-mail Ms. Arlene Reiniger, Program Specialist, Intern Coordinator. Phone: 202-275-1180. Fax: 202-275-1119. E-mail: arlene@folklife.si.edu. Applicants must submit a formal organization application, academic transcripts, writing sample, two letters of recommendation. Application deadline: March 15 for summer; continuous for other seasons. World Wide Web: http://sss.si.edu/folklife.

CENTER FOR STRATEGIC & INTERNATIONAL STUDIES
1800 K Street, NW
Washington, District of Columbia 20006

General Information Public policy research organization dedicated to analysis and policy impact. Established in 1962. Number of employees: 180. Number of internship applications received each year: 600.

Internships Available ▶ *2 Anne Armstrong Leadership Awards:* responsibilities include research, data collection, and administrative duties. Candidates should have declared college major in field, oral communication skills, research skills, strong leadership ability, writing skills, minimum GPA of 3.5 in area of concentration. Duration is 3 months. $3000 per duration of internship. Open to college sophomores, college juniors, college seniors, recent college graduates. ▶ *60–70 interns:* responsibilities include research, data collection, and administrative duties. Candidates should have ability to work independently, college courses in field, computer skills, editing skills, knowledge of field, organizational skills, personal interest in the field, research skills, writing skills. Duration is 10–15 weeks. Position available as unpaid or paid. Open to college juniors, college seniors, recent college graduates, graduate students, law students. International applications accepted.

Benefits Job counseling, opportunity to attend seminars/ workshops, possible full-time employment, travel reimbursement, willing to complete paperwork for educational credit, willing to provide letters of recommendation.

Contact Write, call, fax, or e-mail Shav Howard, Intern Coordinator, 1800 K Street, NW, Suite 400, Washington, District of Columbia 20006. Phone: 202-775-3223. Fax: 202-466-5141. E-mail: internships@csis.org. Applicants must submit a letter of interest, resume, 1 writing sample (10 pages or less). Application deadline: March 1 for summer, July 1 for fall, November 1 for spring. World Wide Web: http://www.csis.org.

CENTER FOR STUDENT MISSIONS
27302 Calle Arroyo
San Juan Capistrano, California 92675

General Information Organization that facilitates Christian mission and service trips in several urban locations throughout the U.S. and Canada. Established in 1988. Number of employees: 2. Number of internship applications received each year: 100.

Internships Available ▶ *40–50 city hosts:* responsibilities include hosting and leading suburban and rural church youth groups during short-term mission and service trips (two to six days) in the inner-cities of Chicago, Washington, DC, Houston, Los Angeles, Toronto, San Francisco, Nashville, Philadelphia, and Seattle. Candidates should have ability to work independently, oral communication skills, strong interpersonal skills, strong leadership ability, youth ministry experience or desire for experience, strong Christian faith. Duration is 3–11 months. Paid. Open to college freshmen, college sophomores, college juniors, college seniors, recent college graduates, graduate students, career changers.

Benefits Free housing, free meals, on-the-job training, possible full-time employment, willing to act as a professional reference, willing to complete paperwork for educational credit, willing to provide letters of recommendation.

International Internships Available in Toronto, Canada.

Contact Write, call, fax, e-mail, or through World Wide Web site Kyle Becchetti, Vice President of Operations, 27302 Calle Arroyo, San Juan Capistrano, California 92675. Phone: 949-248-8200. Fax:

949-248-7753. E-mail: info@csm.org. In-person interview required. Applicants must submit a formal organization application, four personal references. Applications are accepted continuously. World Wide Web: http://www.csm.org.

CENTER FOR THE NEW WEST
1625 Broadway, Suite 720
Denver, Colorado 80202

General Information Public policy research organization. Established in 1989. Number of employees: 5. Number of internship applications received each year: 50.

Internships Available ▶ *1 Web site intern:* responsibilities include maintaining, updating, and marketing Web site; assisting with list serve database; sending bulk e-mail as directed. Candidates should have ability to work independently, computer skills, experience in the field, office skills, organizational skills, personal interest in the field, self-motivation. Duration is flexible. Paid. Open to high school students, college freshmen, college sophomores, college juniors, college seniors, graduate students. ▶ *1–2 public policy research interns:* responsibilities include providing assistance to director of research for speeches, forums, reports, and published articles; assisting in forum preparation. Candidates should have ability to work independently, ability to work with others, college courses in field, computer skills, oral communication skills, organizational skills, plan to pursue career in field, research skills, written communication skills. Duration is flexible. Position available as unpaid or paid. Open to college juniors, college seniors, graduate students, law students. International applications accepted.

Benefits Opportunity to attend seminars/workshops, travel reimbursement, willing to act as a professional reference, willing to complete paperwork for educational credit, willing to provide letters of recommendation.

Contact Write, fax, e-mail, or through World Wide Web site John Maddox, Director, Research and Special Projects. Fax: 303-572-5499. E-mail: cnwinfo@newwest.org. No phone calls. In-person interview required. Applicants must submit a resume, letter of interest as described on Web site. Applications are accepted continuously. World Wide Web: http://www.newwest.org.

CENTER OF CONCERN
1225 Otis Street, NE
Washington, District of Columbia 20017

General Information Social justice research organization. Established in 1971. Number of employees: 15. Number of internship applications received each year: 100.

Internships Available ▶ *2–3 Global Women's Project interns:* responsibilities include research and communication on women's activities and policies affecting women around the world. Candidates should have ability to work independently, college courses in field, knowledge of field, office skills, research skills, written communication skills. Duration is flexible. Unpaid. Open to college juniors, college seniors, recent college graduates, graduate students. ▶ *2–3 foreign aid and international financial institutions project interns:* responsibilities include monitoring relevant congressional activities, drafting memos summarizing legislative developments, attending meetings, and assisting with library research and general support work. Candidates should have ability to work independently, college courses in field, knowledge of field, research skills, self-motivation, written communication skills. Duration is flexible. Unpaid. Open to college juniors, college seniors, recent college graduates, graduate students, law students. ▶ *1 global justice education intern:* responsibilities include assisting with outreach to schools and dissemination of educational materials for elementary and secondary schools. Candidates should have ability to work independently, computer skills, oral communication skills, organizational skills, writing skills. Duration is flexible. Unpaid. Open to college juniors, college seniors, recent college graduates, graduate students, career changers. ▶ *2–3 international economics research interns:* responsibilities include surveying literature, assisting with research, networking, and general support on economic issues. Candidates should have ability to work independently, college courses in field, knowledge of field, research skills, self-

Center of Concern (continued)

motivation, written communication skills. Duration is flexible. Unpaid. Open to college seniors, recent college graduates, graduate students.

Benefits Free meals, names of contacts, opportunity to attend seminars/workshops, willing to act as a professional reference, willing to complete paperwork for educational credit, willing to provide letters of recommendation, exposure to international networks and Washington, D.C. international development community, possibility of travel reimbursement.

Contact Write, fax, e-mail, or through World Wide Web site Candy Warner, Director of Administration. Fax: 202-832-9494. E-mail: cwarner@coc.org. No phone calls. Telephone interview required. Applicants must submit a letter of interest, resume, writing sample. Applications are accepted continuously. World Wide Web: http://www.coc.org.

CENTER ON POLICY ATTITUDES
1779 Massachusetts Avenue, NW, Suite 510
Washington, District of Columbia 20036

General Information Research organization, think tank, and public opinion polling organization devoted to the study of public and elite attitudes on foreign and domestic public policy. Established in 1992. Number of employees: 8. Affiliate of University of Maryland, College Park, College Park, Maryland. Number of internship applications received each year: 125.

Internships Available ▶ *1–2 Web site interns:* responsibilities include assisting the Webmaster in maintaining and updating COPA's Web site, and assisting in small research tasks as needed. Candidates should have ability to work independently, ability to work with others, college courses in field, computer skills, editing skills, research skills, writing skills. Duration is 1 semester. $10 per hour. Open to college juniors, college seniors, recent college graduates. ▶ *1–2 office interns:* responsibilities include assisting in office support by filing; maintaining database mailing lists and press lists; and assisting on small research projects as needed. Candidates should have ability to work with others, computer skills, office skills, organizational skills, personal interest in the field, research skills. Duration is 1–2 semesters. $7 per hour. Open to college sophomores, college juniors, college seniors, recent college graduates, graduate students. International applications accepted.

Benefits Travel reimbursement, willing to act as a professional reference, willing to provide letters of recommendation.

Contact Write or fax Research Associate, 1779 Massachusetts Avenue, NW, Suite 510, Washington, District of Columbia 20036. Fax: 202-232-1159. In-person interview recommended (telephone interview accepted). Applicants must submit a letter of interest, resume. Applications are accepted continuously. World Wide Web: http://www.policyattitudes.org.

CITIZENS FOR PARTICIPATION IN POLITICAL ACTION (CPPAX)
43 Winter Street, 7th Floor
Boston, Massachusetts 02108

General Information Multi-issue, progressive grassroots political organization with a current focus on economic democracy, including fair taxes, adequate human services, cuts in military budget, economic and labor rights issues, campaign finance reform, reform of managed health-care system, and public education funding. Established in 1962. Number of employees: 5. Number of internship applications received each year: 60.

Internships Available ▶ *1–2 economic democracy interns:* responsibilities include researching, writing, and organizing for a fair economy and assisting with campaign for single-payer national health-care plan. Duration is flexible. Unpaid. ▶ *1–2 electoral action interns:* responsibilities include researching and organizing candidates and ballot questions, concentrating on campaign finance reform. Duration is flexible. Unpaid. ▶ *1–2 events planning interns:* responsibilities include planning annual membership convention and other events throughout the year. Duration is flexible. Unpaid. ▶ *1–2 fund-raising interns:* responsibilities include aiding development staff in all areas of grassroots fund-raising and researching and writing grant proposals. Duration is flexible. Unpaid. ▶ *Nonprofit man-*

agement interns: responsibilities include assisting with database management, learning rudimentary bookkeeping, recruiting and training volunteers, and helping with strategic planning. Duration is flexible. Unpaid. ▶ *1–2 peace and new priorities interns:* responsibilities include performing congressional research, member organizing for peace, and organizing campaign for the rights of oppressed people in Burma. Duration is flexible. Unpaid. ▶ *1–2 publications interns:* responsibilities include researching, writing, and producing publications. Duration is flexible. Unpaid. Open to high school students, recent high school graduates, college freshmen, college sophomores, college juniors, college seniors, recent college graduates, graduate students, law students, career changers, individuals reentering the workforce. International applications accepted.

Benefits On-the-job training, travel reimbursement, willing to act as a professional reference, willing to complete paperwork for educational credit, willing to provide letters of recommendation.

Contact Write, call, fax, or e-mail Megan McMamara, Office Manager/Outreach Coordinator. Phone: 617-426-3040. Fax: 617-426-8389. E-mail: cppax@cppax.org. In-person interview recommended (telephone interview accepted). Applicants must submit a letter of interest, resume. Applications are accepted continuously. World Wide Web: http://www.cppax.org.

CLIENTLOGIC
3102 West End Avenue, Suite 1000
Nashville, Tennessee 37203

General Information International provider of customer management solutions, including customer care, fulfillment, and marketing services with operations in nine countries. Established in 1998. Number of employees: 80. Number of internship applications received each year: 500.

Internships Available ▶ *1–3 Flash/HTML designers:* responsibilities include creation of Flash demos and animations, Web programming and design (HTML), graphics creation. Candidates should have ability to work independently, computer skills, editing skills, organizational skills, personal interest in the field, self-motivation, skilled Flash and HTML programmer with an eye for design, inquisitive learner, Web experience, proficient in Net research. Duration is 3–9 months. Unpaid. Open to recent high school graduates, college freshmen, college sophomores, college juniors, college seniors, recent college graduates, graduate students, law students, career changers, individuals reentering the workforce. ▶ *1–3 Web programming and design analysts:* responsibilities include web programming and design (HTML), graphics creation, online research, competitor Web site analysis/tracking. Candidates should have computer skills, organizational skills, personal interest in the field, skilled HTML programmer with an eye for design, Web experience, inquisitive learner, proficient in Net research. Duration is 3–9 months. Unpaid. Open to college freshmen, college sophomores, college juniors, college seniors, recent college graduates, graduate students, law students, career changers, individuals reentering the workforce. ▶ *1–3 events and trade show planners:* responsibilities include event planning, conference evaluation, trade show coordination (giveaways, collateral, booth), business report composition. Candidates should have ability to work with others, computer skills, office skills, oral communication skills, organizational skills, personal interest in the field, detail-oriented, skilled planner, inquisitive learner, proficient in Net research, event experience preferred but not required. Duration is 3–9 months. Unpaid. Open to recent high school graduates, college freshmen, college sophomores, college juniors, college seniors, recent college graduates, graduate students, law students, career changers, individuals reentering the workforce. ▶ *1–2 marketing support (high school helpers):* responsibilities include support for marketing and PR team including organization, research, promotions, events, and trade show preparation. Candidates should have computer skills, office skills, organizational skills, self-motivation, strong interpersonal skills. Duration is 3–9 months. Unpaid. Open to high school students, recent high school graduates. ▶ *1–2 media relations analysts:* responsibilities include media outreach, press release composition, online research, market monitoring, media planning, business report composition. Candidates should have experience in the field, oral communication skills, organizational skills, personal interest in the field, strong interpersonal skills, written communication skills, PR/MarCom/media experience, avid reader, inquisitive learner, proficient in Net research. Duration is 3–9 months. Unpaid. Open to college freshmen, college sophomores, college juniors, college seniors, recent college graduates, graduate students, law students, career changers, individuals reentering the workforce. ▶ *1–4 public relations/marketing analysts:* responsibilities include press releases, award applications, sales presentations, online research, PR outreach, copywriting, market monitoring, media planning, business report composition. Candidates should have office skills, oral communication skills, organizational skills, personal interest in the field, strong interpersonal skills, written communication skills, PR experience, avid reader, inquisitive learner, proficient in Net research. Duration is 3–9 months. Unpaid. Open to college freshmen, college sophomores, college juniors, college seniors, recent college graduates, graduate students, law students, career changers, individuals reentering the workforce. ▶ *1–2 sales information analysts:* responsibilities include sales presentations, proposal log, online prospecting database, sales support. Candidates should have ability to work with others, computer skills, office skills, organizational skills, self-motivation. Duration is 3–9 months. Unpaid. Open to high school seniors, recent high school graduates, college freshmen, college sophomores, college juniors, college seniors, recent college graduates, graduate students, law students, career changers, individuals reentering the workforce. ▶ *1–3 strategic research analysts (business intelligence):* responsibilities include online research, business outreach, market and trend analysis, product planning, and business report composition. Candidates should have analytical skills, organizational skills, personal interest in the field, research skills, writing skills, avid reader, inquisitive learner, proficient in Net research. Duration is 3–9 months. Unpaid. Open to college freshmen, college sophomores, college juniors, college seniors, recent college graduates, graduate students, law students, career changers, individuals reentering the workforce. International applications accepted.

Benefits Job counseling, names of contacts, on-the-job training, opportunity to attend seminars/workshops, possible full-time employment, willing to act as a professional reference, willing to complete paperwork for educational credit, willing to provide letters of recommendation, substantive work, fun/relaxed environment, business travel reimbursement, team outings, networking, flexible schedules.

International Internships Available in The Hague, Netherlands.
Contact Write, fax, or e-mail Ms. Channing Rollo, Manager of Business Intelligence. Phone: 615-301-7100. Fax: 615-301-7150. E-mail: internship@clientlogic.com. In-person interview recommended (telephone interview accepted). Applicants must submit a letter of interest, resume, writing sample. Applications are accepted continuously. World Wide Web: http://www.clientlogic.com.

COALITION FOR AMERICAN LEADERSHIP ABROAD
AFSA Building, 2101 E Street, NW
Washington, District of Columbia 20037

General Information Association whose goal is to promote American engagement in world affairs and act as resource for foreign affairs. Established in 1996. Number of employees: 4.
Internships Available ▶ *2–3 advocacy and legislative affairs interns:* responsibilities include drafting letters to Congress, working with local community leaders, and grassroots campaign work. Candidates should have ability to work independently, ability to work with others, computer skills, editing skills, writing skills. Duration is (minimum of 16 hours per week) one summer or semester. Position available as unpaid or at $200–$300 per duration of internship. Open to college sophomores, college juniors, college seniors, recent college graduates, graduate students, law students. International applications accepted.
Benefits Job counseling, opportunity to attend seminars/workshops, willing to act as a professional reference, willing to complete paperwork for educational credit, willing to provide letters of recommendation.
Contact Write, call, fax, e-mail, or through World Wide Web site Harry Blaney, President. Phone: 202-944-5519. Fax: 202-338-6820.

E-mail: colead@afsa.org. In-person interview recommended. Applicants must submit a letter of interest, resume with grade average. Application deadline: March 15 for summer, July 15 for fall, October 15 for spring. World Wide Web: http://www.colead.org.

COMMITTEE FOR ECONOMIC DEVELOPMENT
2000 L Street, NW, Suite 700
Washington, District of Columbia 20036

General Information Nonprofit, nonpartisan, business-sponsored policy organization involving 250 of the nation's business and education leaders; develops in-depth studies that are distributed to Congress, the Administration, and state, local, and public- and private-sector leaders. Established in 1942. Number of employees: 12. Number of internship applications received each year: 75.
Internships Available ▶ *2–4 research interns:* responsibilities include researching prospective legislation, attending and summarizing meetings and hearings, and compiling statistics and other data in connection with CED publications and studies in progress. Candidates should have analytical skills, computer skills, research skills, writing skills, college courses in economics. Duration is flexible. $1000 per duration of internship. Open to college sophomores, college juniors, college seniors, recent college graduates. International applications accepted.
Benefits Opportunity to attend seminars/workshops, travel reimbursement, willing to complete paperwork for educational credit, willing to provide letters of recommendation, opportunity to attend congressional hearings and other events.
Contact Write, call, fax, e-mail, or through World Wide Web site Chris Dreibelbis, Intern Coordinator. Phone: 202-296-5860. Fax: 202-223-0776. E-mail: chris.dreibelbis@ced.org. Applicants must submit a letter of interest, resume, academic transcripts, writing sample. Application deadline: March 20 for summer; continuous for all other positions. World Wide Web: http://www.ced.org.

THE CONGRESSIONAL INSTITUTE, INC.
316 Pennsylvania Avenue, SE, Suite 403
Washington, District of Columbia 20003

General Information Public policy educational and research organization. Established in 1987. Number of employees: 6. Number of internship applications received each year: 24.
Internships Available ▶ *2–3 general interns:* responsibilities include research, meeting planning, database entry, general office tasks; Web site research, layout, and design. Candidates should have computer skills, office skills, oral communication skills, organizational skills, strong interpersonal skills, writing skills. Duration is 1 semester. Position available as unpaid or at $6.50–$8 per hour. Open to recent high school graduates, college freshmen, college sophomores, college juniors, college seniors, recent college graduates.
Benefits Free meals, names of contacts, on-the-job training, opportunity to attend seminars/workshops, possible full-time employment, willing to act as a professional reference, willing to complete paperwork for educational credit, willing to provide letters of recommendation.
Contact Write, call, fax, or e-mail Karen Bronson, Executive Director. Phone: 202-547-4600. Fax: 202-547-3556. E-mail: change_leader@conginst.org. In-person interview recommended (telephone interview accepted). Applicants must submit a letter of interest, resume, writing sample, three personal references, two letters of recommendation. Application deadline: March 15 for summer, August 1 for fall, December 1 for spring. World Wide Web: http://www.conginst.org.

CONGRESSMAN JOHN T. DOOLITTLE
U.S. House of Representatives, 2410 Rayburn House Office Building
Washington, District of Columbia 20515

General Information Congressional office.

Congressman John T. Doolittle (continued)

Internships Available ▶ *Interns:* responsibilities include assisting members of Congressman Doolittle's staff with daily responsibilities in either the Washington, DC office or the Roseville, CA office. Unpaid.

Contact Write, call, fax, or through World Wide Web site Intern Coordinator. Phone: 202-225-2511. Fax: 202-225-5444. World Wide Web: http://www.house.gov/doolittle/.

COUNCIL ON FOREIGN RELATIONS
58 East 68th Street
New York, New York 10021

General Information National nonpartisan membership organization and think tank dedicated to fostering America's understanding of other nations through study and debate. Established in 1921. Number of employees: 140. Number of internship applications received each year: 500.

Internships Available ▶ *1 Franklin Williams intern:* responsibilities include program coordination, substantive and business writing, research, and budget management; encouraged to attend Council's extensive meetings programs. Candidates should have organizational skills, plan to pursue career in field, research skills, strong interpersonal skills, writing skills. Duration is 1 semester. Paid. Open to college juniors, college seniors, graduate students, minorities, especially African-Americans, encouraged to apply. ▶ *1–3 Washington, D.C. interns:* responsibilities include supporting staff members with day-to-day office duties, providing research support which can be geared towards intern's academic interests. Candidates should have ability to work independently, computer skills, declared college major in field, office skills, oral communication skills, organizational skills. Duration is 1 semester. Unpaid. Open to college freshmen, college sophomores, college juniors, college seniors. ▶ *1–2 corporate program interns:* responsibilities include researching companies that may be interested in joining the Corporate Program, setting up appointments with potential members, assisting with conference planning, and database maintenance. Candidates should have computer skills, declared college major in field, office skills, research skills, strong interpersonal skills, written communication skills. Duration is 1 semester. Unpaid. Open to college freshmen, college sophomores, college juniors, college seniors. ▶ *1 custom anthology program intern:* responsibilities include researching articles to be used in anthologies; preparing articles for the printer; securing purchase orders from bookstores; fulfilling requests for information on the program; possible marketing/promotion opportunities. Candidates should have computer skills, office skills, oral communication skills, organizational skills, strong interpersonal skills. Duration is 1 semester. $300 per month. Open to college sophomores, college juniors, college seniors. ▶ *1–2 executive office interns:* responsibilities include word processing; proofreading; preparing mailings; communicating with members, Board of Directors, and staff, including scheduling appointments, making confirmation calls for meetings, handling telephone requests, and greeting visitors; assisting with writing, editing, and proofreading articles and reports. Candidates should have computer skills, declared college major in field, editing skills, office skills, oral communication skills, strong interpersonal skills. Duration is 1 semester. Unpaid. Open to college sophomores, college juniors, college seniors. ▶ *1 human resources intern:* responsibilities include providing administrative support to human resources department, maintaining files and records, assembling orientation packets; scheduling interviews; providing information to staff. Candidates should have ability to work with others, office skills, oral communication skills, organizational skills, personal interest in the field. Duration is 1 semester. Unpaid. Open to college sophomores, college juniors, college seniors, recent college graduates, graduate students. ▶ *1 meetings program intern:* responsibilities include assisting staff in all facets of event/meeting preparation; making confirmation calls to participants and correspondence tracking; providing research and administrative support. Candidates should have ability to work with others, oral communication skills, organizational skills. Duration is 1 semester. Unpaid. Open to college freshmen, college sophomores, college juniors, college seniors. ▶ *1–2 office of communications interns:* responsibilities include assisting with the

development and maintenance of media contact database; responding to public inquiries about the Council and requests for publications; assisting with editing news releases; providing general administrative support. Candidates should have computer skills, declared college major in field, editing skills, office skills, oral communication skills, organizational skills. Duration is 1 semester. Unpaid. Open to college sophomores, college juniors, college seniors. ▶ *1 publications intern:* responsibilities include all aspects of editorial and production process, editing and proofreading, help in maintaining the publications on the Council's Web site, and some clerical work. Candidates should have ability to work independently, declared college major in field, editing skills, office skills, organizational skills, writing skills. Duration is 1 semester. Unpaid. Open to college freshmen, college sophomores, college juniors, college seniors. ▶ *1–3 studies department interns:* responsibilities include providing general administrative support, preparing materials for meetings (including invitations), assisting with research. Candidates should have declared college major in field, editing skills, office skills, organizational skills, research skills, written communication skills. Duration is 1 semester. Unpaid. Open to college sophomores, college juniors, college seniors. International applications accepted.

Benefits Names of contacts, possible full-time employment, travel reimbursement, willing to complete paperwork for educational credit, willing to provide letters of recommendation, access to Council's private library and opportunity to sit in on foreign policy discussion groups.

Contact Write, fax, e-mail, or through World Wide Web site Internship Coordinator. Fax: 212-434-9893. E-mail: humanresources@cfr.org. No phone calls. In-person interview required. Applicants must submit a letter of interest, resume. Applications are accepted continuously. World Wide Web: http://www.cfr.org.

COUNCIL ON HEMISPHERIC AFFAIRS
1444 I Street, NW, Suite 211
Washington, District of Columbia 20005

General Information Research and information organization that analyzes and monitors diplomatic, economic, social, human rights, political, trade, development, environmental, social justice, drug, and military trends in U.S.-Latin American and U.S.-Canadian relations. Established in 1975. Number of employees: 19. Number of internship applications received each year: 500.

Internships Available ▶ *2–4 Canadian-U.S. relations research associates:* responsibilities include researching U.S.-Canadian political and economic relations, as well as Canadian-Latin American relations; drafting and publishing articles that spotlight bilateral issues. Candidates should have ability to work independently, editing skills, knowledge of field, oral communication skills, organizational skills, strong leadership ability, writing skills. Duration is 18 weeks or 14 weeks in summer. Unpaid. Open to high school seniors, recent high school graduates, college freshmen, college sophomores, college juniors, college seniors, recent college graduates, graduate students, law students, career changers, individuals reentering the workforce. ▶ *2–4 Caribbean Affairs research associates:* responsibilities include monitoring, researching, and preparing draft articles for publication on U.S.-Caribbean economic and political issues; researching Caribbean basic developmental and democracy-building projects. Candidates should have ability to work independently, analytical skills, computer skills, editing skills, oral communication skills, research skills, strong leadership ability, written communication skills. Duration is 18 weeks or 14 weeks in summer. Paid. Open to high school seniors, recent high school graduates, college freshmen, college sophomores, college juniors, college seniors, recent college graduates, graduate students, law students, career changers, individuals reentering the workforce. ▶ *10–15 U.S.-Latin American relations research associates:* responsibilities include research, writing, and by-line publishing of articles on pressing regional topics, as well as some light administrative duties. Candidates should have ability to work independently, ability to work with others, analytical skills, computer skills, editing skills, knowledge of field, oral communication skills, personal interest in the field, research skills, self-motivation, strong leadership ability, writing skills. Duration is 18 weeks or 14 weeks in summer. Unpaid. Open to high school seniors, recent high school graduates, college freshmen, college sophomores, college juniors, college seniors, recent college graduates, graduate students, law students, career changers, individuals reentering the workforce, academics on sabbatical, retirees. ▶ *1–2 computer-based research associates:* responsibilities include taking a leadership position in both creating literature on hemispheric substantive issues and distributing them via the Internet; supervising e-mail flow, and editing the organization's Web site. Candidates should have ability to work independently, analytical skills, computer skills, editing skills, oral communication skills, organizational skills, written communication skills. Duration is 18 weeks or 14 weeks in summer. Unpaid. Open to high school seniors, recent high school graduates, college freshmen, college sophomores, college juniors, college seniors, recent college graduates, graduate students, law students, career changers, individuals reentering the workforce. ▶ *3–5 economic affairs research associates:* responsibilities include monitoring economic indicators, interviewing international and regional lending agency officers, and drafting and publishing professional economic analyses and op-ed articles for the media. Candidates should have ability to work independently, ability to work with others, analytical skills, computer skills, editing skills, oral communication skills, writing skills. Duration is 18 weeks or 14 weeks in summer. Unpaid. Open to high school seniors, recent high school graduates, college freshmen, college sophomores, college juniors, college seniors, recent college graduates, graduate students, law students, career changers, individuals reentering the workforce. ▶ *1–2 freedom of press research associates:* responsibilities include monitoring issues of freedom of the press and media responsibility throughout the hemisphere. Candidates should have ability to work independently, ability to work with others, experience in the field, oral communication skills, writing skills. Duration is 18 weeks or 14 weeks in summer. Unpaid. Open to high school seniors, recent high school graduates, college freshmen, college sophomores, college juniors, college seniors, recent college graduates, graduate students, law students, career changers, individuals reentering the workforce. ▶ *2–4 hemispheric security affairs research associates :* responsibilities include monitoring U.S. and Canadian military sales policies to Latin America; evaluating patterns of the Pentagon's cooperation with Latin American military institutions and the relationship of hemispheric armed forces with their civilian governments. Candidates should have ability to work independently, ability to work with others, analytical skills, editing skills, oral communication skills, research skills. Duration is 18 weeks or 14 weeks in summer. Unpaid. Open to high school seniors, recent high school graduates, college freshmen, college sophomores, college juniors, college seniors, recent college graduates, graduate students, law students, career changers, individuals reentering the workforce. ▶ *Hemispheric trade research associates:* responsibilities include research, preparing reports, publishing by-line articles. Candidates should have ability to work independently, computer skills, editing skills, oral communication skills, organizational skills, self-motivation, strong interpersonal skills, writing skills. Duration is 18 weeks or 14 weeks in summer. Unpaid. Open to high school seniors, recent high school graduates, college freshmen, college sophomores, college juniors, college seniors, recent college graduates, graduate students, law students, career changers, individuals reentering the workforce. ▶ *2–4 institutional affairs research associates:* responsibilities include representing the organization's interests and positions to other organizations and the media. Candidates should have ability to work independently, analytical skills, computer skills, editing skills, oral communication skills, writing skills. Duration is 18 weeks or 14 weeks in summer. Unpaid. Open to high school seniors, recent high school graduates, college freshmen, college sophomores, college juniors, college seniors, recent college graduates, graduate students, law students, career changers, individuals reentering the workforce. ▶ *2–4 public analysis and information research associates:* responsibilities include public writing; political and economic themes for publication in print and electronic media. Candidates should have ability to work independently, analytical skills, computer skills, editing skills, knowledge of field, oral communication skills, organizational skills, strong interpersonal skills, writing skills, journalism background (helpful). Duration is 18 weeks or 14 weeks in summer. Open to high school seniors, recent high school graduates, college freshmen, college sophomores,

college juniors, college seniors, recent college graduates, graduate students, law students, career changers, individuals reentering the workforce. International applications accepted.
Benefits Formal training, job counseling, names of contacts, on-the-job training, opportunity to attend seminars/workshops, possible full-time employment, willing to act as a professional reference, willing to complete paperwork for educational credit, willing to provide letters of recommendation, occasional meals and recreational trips.
Contact Write, call, fax, e-mail, or through World Wide Web site Secretary for Internships. Phone: 202-216-9261. Fax: 202-216-9193. E-mail: coha@coha.org. In-person interview recommended (telephone interview accepted). Applicants must submit a formal organization application, letter of interest, resume, academic transcripts, writing sample, two personal references, two letters of recommendation. Applications are accepted continuously. World Wide Web: http://www.coha.org.

CROHN'S AND COLITIS FOUNDATION OF AMERICA
386 Park Avenue South
New York, New York 10016

General Information Foundation whose mission is to stimulate and encourage innovative basic biomedical and clinical research of inflammatory bowel disease. Established in 1967. Number of employees: 39. Number of internship applications received each year: 12.
Internships Available ▶ *1–16 student research fellowship awards:* responsibilities include conducting full-time research with mentor investigating a subject relevant to inflammatory bowel disease. Candidates should have major in a medical field. Duration is 10 weeks in the spring. $2500 per duration of internship. Open to college juniors, college seniors, recent college graduates, graduate students.
Benefits Opportunity to attend seminars/workshops, willing to act as a professional reference, willing to complete paperwork for educational credit, willing to provide letters of recommendation.
Contact Write, call, fax, e-mail, or through World Wide Web site Carol Cox, Manager of Research Programs. Phone: 800-932-2423. Fax: 212-779-4098. E-mail: info@ccfa.org. Applicants must submit a formal organization application. Application deadline: March 15. World Wide Web: http://www.ccfa.org.

CSEA
143 Washington Avenue
Albany, New York 12210

General Information Political lobbying organization working on behalf of 265,000 public, private, and active retired labor union members. Established in 1912. Number of employees: 250. Affiliate of AFSCME Local 1000, AFL-CIO. Number of internship applications received each year: 30.
Internships Available ▶ *2–3 legislative and political action interns.* Candidates should have ability to work independently, ability to work with others, analytical skills, self-motivation, writing skills. Duration is January to June. Paid. Open to college freshmen, college sophomores, college juniors, college seniors, recent college graduates. International applications accepted.
Benefits Formal training, on-the-job training, opportunity to attend seminars/workshops, possible full-time employment, willing to act as a professional reference, willing to complete paperwork for educational credit, willing to provide letters of recommendation.
Contact Write, call, fax, or e-mail Michael J. Neidl, III, Legislative Coordinator. Phone: 518-436-8622. Fax: 518-427-1677. E-mail: neidl@cseainc.org. In-person interview required. Applicants must submit a letter of interest, resume, writing sample, (in special circumstances telephone interview considered). Application deadline: November 15. World Wide Web: http://www.csea.net.

DEMOCRATIC SENATORIAL CAMPAIGN COMMITTEE
430 South Capitol Street, SE
Washington, District of Columbia 20003

General Information Organization that supports and assists Democratic candidates running for the U.S. Senate. Established in 1959. Number of employees: 40. Branch of Democratic National Committee, Washington, District of Columbia. Number of internship applications received each year: 200.

Internships Available ▶ *3–6 interns:* responsibilities include providing administrative support to the political, finance, research, or press departments. Candidates should have ability to work independently, computer skills, oral communication skills, research skills, strong interpersonal skills, written communication skills. Duration is 1 semester or summer. Unpaid. Open to college freshmen, college sophomores, college juniors, college seniors, recent college graduates. International applications accepted.

Benefits Names of contacts, opportunity to attend seminars/workshops, possible full-time employment, willing to act as a professional reference, willing to complete paperwork for educational credit, willing to provide letters of recommendation.

Contact Write, call, fax, e-mail, or through World Wide Web site Bradley Katz, Research Assistant. Phone: 202-224-2447. Fax: 202-485-3120. E-mail: katz@dscc.org. Telephone interview required. Applicants must submit a letter of interest, resume, writing sample, letter of recommendation. Applications are accepted continuously. World Wide Web: http://www.dscc.org.

ECONOMIC STRATEGY INSTITUTE
1401 H Street, NW, Suite 560
Washington, District of Columbia 20005

General Information Nonprofit public policy research organization specializing in international trade issues. Established in 1989. Number of employees: 15. Number of internship applications received each year: 150.

Internships Available ▶ *1–4 research assistants:* responsibilities include assisting research associates and senior staff with trade policy research, performing general office duties, and assisting with publications. Candidates should have ability to work independently, ability to work with others, computer skills, oral communication skills, research skills, writing skills. Duration is 3-4 months in summer or anytime during the academic year. Unpaid. Open to college sophomores, college juniors, college seniors, recent college graduates, graduate students, law students, career changers, individuals reentering the workforce. International applications accepted.

Benefits Opportunity to attend seminars/workshops, possible full-time employment, willing to act as a professional reference, willing to complete paperwork for educational credit, willing to provide letters of recommendation, work-related travel reimbursement.

Contact Write, call, fax, or e-mail Riki Swanson, Research Associate. Phone: 202-326-8547. Fax: 202-289-1319. E-mail: rswanson@econstrat.org. In-person interview recommended (telephone interview accepted). Applicants must submit a letter of interest, resume, writing sample, letter of recommendation. Applications are accepted continuously. World Wide Web: http://www.econstrat.org.

ELIZABETH GLASER PEDIATRIC AIDS FOUNDATION
2950 31st Street, Suite 125
Santa Monica, California 90405

General Information Foundation providing funds for research programs related to pediatric HIV/AIDS and motivating participants to consider future careers in this field. Established in 1989. Number of employees: 25. Branch of Elizabeth Glaser Pediatric AIDS Foundation, New York, New York. Number of internship applications received each year: 100.

Internships Available ▶ *50 interns:* responsibilities include performing independent research in basic medical, clinical, epidemiological, or psychosocial areas relating to pediatric AIDS. Candidates should have minimum 3.0 GPA if high school or college student

(not required for medical or graduate students). Duration is 320 hours (minimum of 4 hours per week). $2000 stipend upon completion of internship. Open to high school seniors, college freshmen, college sophomores, college juniors, college seniors, graduate students, medical school students. International applications accepted.

Benefits Job counseling, names of contacts.

International Internships Available.

Contact Write, call, fax, e-mail, or through World Wide Web site Mr. Chris Hudnall, Program Coordinator. Phone: 310-314-1459. Fax: 310-314-1469. E-mail: chris@pedaids.org. Applicants must submit a formal organization application, resume, academic transcripts, letter of sponsorship from MD, PhD, or LCSW who has expertise in pediatric HIV/AIDS; statement of purpose from applicant, documentation from school registrar of full-time educational status, abbreviated curriculum vitae of sponsor. Application deadline: mid-March. World Wide Web: http://www.pedaids.org.

EMBASSY OF FRANCE, ASSISTANT PROGRAM, CULTURAL SERVICES DEPARTMENT
4101 Reservoir Road, NW
Washington, District of Columbia 20007

General Information Diplomatic mission representing France in the United States.

Internships Available ▶ *1,500 teaching assistantships:* responsibilities include teaching in French primary and secondary schools. 890 euros, minus approximately 60 euros for social security (medical insurance). Open to college freshmen, college sophomores, college juniors, college seniors, graduate students, must be U.S. citizen under 30 years of age majoring or minoring in French.

Benefits Free introductory courses provided to facilitate assistants' integration and introduction to their jobs.

International Internships Available in France.

Contact Write, fax, e-mail, or through World Wide Web site Ambassade de France aux Etats-Unis, Assistant Program, Service Culturel/SCULE, Washington 20007. Fax: 202-944-6043. E-mail: assistant@frenchculture.org. Applicants must submit a formal organization application, academic transcripts, 2 academic recommendations, 1 copy of medical certificate, 2 passport or ID photos. Application deadline: January. World Wide Web: http://www.info-france-usa.org/visitingfrance/teach.asp.

EMIGRE MEMORIAL GERMAN INTERNSHIP PROGRAMS
PO Box 345
Durham, New Hampshire 03824

General Information Program sending students from non-German speaking countries to work, live and study in German Parliaments. Established in 1965. Number of internship applications received each year: 25.

Internships Available ▶ *Up to 6 Deutscher Bundestag interns (Berlin):* responsibilities include work-study in the administrative, legislative research, and political areas of the Parliament. Candidates should have ability to work independently, analytical skills, college courses in field, computer skills, editing skills, knowledge of field, oral communication skills, organizational skills, personal interest in the field, plan to pursue career in field, research skills, self-motivation, strong interpersonal skills, writing skills, high fluency in German. Duration is 3 months. $1000–$2500 per duration of internship. Open to college sophomores, college juniors, college seniors, recent college graduates, graduate students, law students, young professionals. ▶ *5 Landtag interns:* responsibilities include work-study in German state legislatures. Candidates should have ability to work independently, analytical skills, college courses in field, computer skills, editing skills, knowledge of field, office skills, oral communication skills, organizational skills, personal interest in the field, research skills, self-motivation, strong interpersonal skills, written communication skills, fluency in German. Duration is 1–2 months. Position available as unpaid or at stipend of $200 to $1000 per internship. Open to college sophomores, college juniors, college seniors, recent college graduates, graduate students, law students. International applications accepted.

Benefits Names of contacts, on-the-job training, opportunity to attend seminars/workshops, willing to act as a professional reference, willing to provide letters of recommendation, possibility of subsidized housing.

International Internships Available in Berlin, Germany; Dresden, Germany; Erfurt, Germany; Mainz, Germany; Schwerin, Germany; Wiesbaden, Germany.

Contact Write Prof. George K. Romoser, Director. No phone calls. In-person interview recommended (telephone interview accepted). Applicants must submit a formal organization application, letter of interest, resume, academic transcripts, three letters of recommendation, in-person interview required for finalists. Application deadline: February 11. Fees: $125.

THE EURASIA FOUNDATION
1350 Connecticut Avenue, NW, Suite 1000
Washington, District of Columbia 20036

General Information Nonprofit grantmaking foundation. Established in 1993. Number of employees: 300. Number of internship applications received each year: 40.

Internships Available ▶ *2 development interns:* responsibilities include background research on prospective funders and outreach opportunities; helping to maintain database; assisting in logistics for events; helping to maintain/update Web site; providing writing support. Duration is 1–4 semesters. $8 per hour. ▶ *1 government relations intern:* responsibilities include background research on political figures and offices; helping to maintain database; scheduling and some correspondence for director of government relations; helping with logistics in hosting events. Duration is 1–2 years. $8 per hour. Candidates for all positions should have ability to work independently, ability to work with others, computer skills, editing skills, office skills, oral communication skills, personal interest in the field, research skills, self-motivation, writing skills. Open to college juniors, college seniors, graduate students.

Benefits Job counseling, names of contacts, on-the-job training, opportunity to attend seminars/workshops, willing to act as a professional reference, willing to complete paperwork for educational credit, willing to provide letters of recommendation.

Contact Write, fax, or e-mail Martin Varghese, HR Assistant. Fax: 202-234-7377. E-mail: resumes@eurasia.org. No phone calls. In-person interview required. Applicants must submit a letter of interest, resume, writing sample. Applications are accepted continuously. World Wide Web: http://www.eurasia.org.

FARM SANCTUARY
3100 Aikens Road
Watkins Glen, New York 14891

General Information National nonprofit organization dedicated to ending animal agriculture abuses through public education programs, legislation, farm animal cruelty investigations, and campaigns, in addition to running shelters that provide 24-hour emergency rescue, rehabilitation, and permanent care for hundreds of animals. Established in 1986. Number of employees: 25. Number of internship applications received each year: 200.

Internships Available ▶ *6 interns:* responsibilities include farm chores/barn cleaning, office work, and conducting educational tours. Candidates should have ability to work independently, ability to work with others, personal interest in the field, self-motivation, commitment to vegetarianism. Duration is 1–3 months. Unpaid. Open to high school students, recent high school graduates, college freshmen, college sophomores, college juniors, college seniors, recent college graduates, graduate students, law students, career changers, individuals reentering the workforce. International applications accepted.

Benefits Free housing, job counseling, names of contacts, possible full-time employment, willing to complete paperwork for educational credit, willing to provide letters of recommendation.

Contact Write, call, fax, e-mail, or through World Wide Web site Michelle Waffner, Education Coordinator, PO Box 150, Watkins Glen, New York 14891. Phone: 607-583-4512. Fax: 607-583-4349. E-mail: education@farmsanctuary.org. Telephone interview required.

Applicants must submit a formal organization application, two letters of recommendation. Applications are accepted continuously. World Wide Web: http://www.farmsanctuary.org.

FEDERAL BUREAU OF INVESTIGATION (FBI) HEADQUARTERS
J. Edgar Hoover Building, 935 Pennsylvania Avenue, NW
Washington, District of Columbia 20535-0001

General Information Principal investigative arm of the U.S. Department of Justice with the authority and responsibility to investigate specific crimes assigned to it and to provide other law enforcement agencies with cooperative services. Established in 1908.

Internships Available ▶ *Honors Internship Program:* responsibilities include working with Special Agents and Professional Support personnel on important cases and procedures; initial orientation followed by assignment to a division based on intern's academic discipline, potential contribution, and the needs of the Bureau. Candidates should have minimum GPA of 3.0; students must be returning to their campus following the program. Duration is early June to mid-August. Unpaid. Open to undergraduates enrolled in junior year at time of application; graduate-level students must be enrolled in school and attending full time; must be U.S. citizen. ▶ *Presidential Management (PMI) Interns.* Candidates should have clear interest and commitment to a career in analysis and management of public policies and programs. Duration is initital two-year full -time service appointment after which individual is eligible for permanent federal government position. Open to graduate students from variety of disciplines who are completing or expecting to complete a master's or doctoral-level degree during the current academic year.

Benefits Travel expenses to and from Washington, DC , information and assistance on housing (Honors Program).

Contact Through World Wide Web site Internship Coordinator. Materials as specified on Web site: www.fbi.gov/employment/intern.htm. World Wide Web: http://www.fbi.gov.

FERGUSON ENTERPRISES, INC.
618 Bland Boulevard
Newport News, Virginia 23605

General Information Supply company with nearly 700 locations in 47 states, the District of Columbia, Puerto Rico, and Mexico, serving contractors, large industrial businesses, manufacturers, and municipalities. Established in 1953.

Internships Available ▶ *Interns:* responsibilities include rotational assignments: warehouse operations, counter sales, purchasing/operations, inside/outside sales, and branch operations. Duration is 8 to 14 weeks during the summer between college junior and senior years. Position available as unpaid or paid. Open to rising college seniors.

Contact E-mail or through World Wide Web site Internship Coordinator. E-mail: resumes@ferguson.com. Application deadline: February-April time frame during junior year in college. World Wide Web: http://www.ferguson.com.

FOOD AND ALLIED SERVICE TRADES DEPARTMENT, AFL-CIO
1925 K Street, NW, Suite 400
Washington, District of Columbia 20006-1132

General Information Labor organization that provides research support services for affiliated unions. Established in 1975. Number of employees: 15. Unit of AFL-CIO, Washington, District of Columbia. Number of internship applications received each year: 100.

Internships Available ▶ *3 interns:* responsibilities include gathering and analyzing information on public and private organizations; researching to assist affiliated unions in organizing and bargaining programs; research is based on a wide range of sources including the Internet, CD data, information sources, publications, and publicly available information from a host of government sources. Candidates should have ability to work independently, personal interest in the field, research skills, writing skills, com-

Food and Allied Service Trades Department, AFL-CIO (continued)
mitment to social justice. Duration is 1–14 weeks. $150 per week. Open to college freshmen, college sophomores, college juniors, college seniors, graduate students, law students. International applications accepted.
Benefits Job counseling, names of contacts, on-the-job training, opportunity to attend seminars/workshops, possible full-time employment, willing to act as a professional reference, willing to complete paperwork for educational credit, willing to provide letters of recommendation.
Contact Write, fax, or e-mail Mr. Gene Bruskin, Secretary/Treasurer. Fax: 202-737-7208. E-mail: genebruskin@fastaflcio.org. Applicants must submit a letter of interest, resume, writing sample. Applications are accepted continuously. World Wide Web: http://www.fastaflcio.org.

FOOD FIRST/ INSTITUTE FOR FOOD AND DEVELOPMENT POLICY
398 60th Street
Oakland, California 94618-1212

General Information Nonprofit people's think tank. Established in 1975. Number of employees: 9. Number of internship applications received each year: 35.
Internships Available ▶ *1–2 membership and development assistants:* responsibilities include assisting with keeping track of members, member relations, and correspondence. Candidates should have computer skills, office skills, oral communication skills, personal interest in the field, plan to pursue career in field, written communication skills. Duration is 3–12 months. Unpaid. Open to college juniors, college seniors, recent college graduates, career changers, individuals reentering the workforce. ▶ *1 publishing intern:* responsibilities include all aspects of publishing. Candidates should have computer skills, editing skills, office skills, plan to pursue career in field, self-motivation, written communication skills. Duration is 3–12 months. Unpaid. Open to college juniors, college seniors, recent college graduates, graduate students, career changers, individuals reentering the workforce. ▶ *5–10 research interns:* responsibilities include library and Internet research on issues of hunger and poverty. Candidates should have ability to work independently, analytical skills, research skills, self-motivation, writing skills. Duration is 3-12 months (10 hours per week minimum). Unpaid. Open to college sophomores, college juniors, college seniors, recent college graduates, graduate students, law students, career changers, individuals reentering the workforce. International applications accepted.
Benefits Free meals, names of contacts, on-the-job training, willing to act as a professional reference, willing to complete paperwork for educational credit, willing to provide letters of recommendation.
Contact Write, call, fax, e-mail, or through World Wide Web site Marilyn Borchardt, Development Director. Phone: 510-654-4400. Fax: 510-654-4551. E-mail: marbor@foodfirst.org. Telephone interview required. Applicants must submit a formal organization application, letter of interest, resume, writing sample, two personal references. Applications are accepted continuously. World Wide Web: http://www.foodfirst.org.

FOREIGN POLICY ASSOCIATION
470 Park Avenue South, 2nd Floor, North
New York, New York 10016-6819

General Information National, nonprofit organization that educates Americans about significant world issues by providing impartial, nonpartisan publications, programs, and forums to increase public awareness of international matters. Established in 1918. Number of employees: 30. Number of internship applications received each year: 450.
Internships Available ▶ *1–2 editorial interns:* responsibilities include assisting with fact checking, resource lists, and updates for publications and performing minimal clerical tasks. Candidates should have ability to work independently, computer skills, personal interest in the field, self-motivation, writing skills. Duration is 8–10 weeks. Unpaid. Open to college juniors, college seniors, recent college graduates. ▶ *1–2 sales and fulfillment interns:* responsibili-

ties include data entry with Microsoft Access, assistance with promotional mailings, and minimal clerical tasks. Candidates should have ability to work independently, analytical skills, computer skills, organizational skills, self-motivation. Duration is flexible. Position available as unpaid or paid. Open to college freshmen, college sophomores, career changers, individuals reentering the workforce. International applications accepted.
Benefits Job counseling, names of contacts, on-the-job training, possible full-time employment, travel reimbursement, willing to act as a professional reference, willing to complete paperwork for educational credit, willing to provide letters of recommendation, free admission to events and free publications.
Contact Write, fax, or through World Wide Web site Director of appropriate department. Fax: 212-481-9275. No phone calls. In-person interview recommended (telephone interview accepted). Applicants must submit a letter of interest, resume. Applications are accepted continuously. World Wide Web: http://www.fpa.org.

FOREIGN POLICY RESEARCH INSTITUTE
1528 Walnut Street, Suite 610
Philadelphia, Pennsylvania 19102

General Information Independent nonprofit organization devoted to scholarly research and public education on international affairs; publishes an academic quarterly journal. Established in 1955. Number of employees: 10. Number of internship applications received each year: 100.
Internships Available ▶ *1–2 administrative assistants:* responsibilities include general office assistance, conference preparation, public relations, development. Candidates should have computer skills, knowledge of field, office skills, organizational skills, personal interest in the field. Duration is 1 semester. Position available as unpaid or paid. Open to recent high school graduates, college freshmen, college sophomores, college juniors, college seniors, recent college graduates, graduate students. ▶ *1 editorial assistant:* responsibilities include proofreading, fact-checking, assisting in publication of Orbis, FPRI's journal of world affairs. Candidates should have computer skills, editing skills, knowledge of field, organizational skills, personal interest in the field, research skills. Duration is 1 semester. Position available as unpaid or paid. Open to college freshmen, college sophomores, college juniors, college seniors, recent college graduates, graduate students. ▶ *4–6 research assistants:* responsibilities include maintaining data files, conducting literature searches, compiling indices, general office/research help. Candidates should have computer skills, knowledge of field, organizational skills, personal interest in the field, research skills, writing skills. Duration is 1 semester. Position available as unpaid or paid. Open to college freshmen, college sophomores, college juniors, college seniors, recent college graduates, graduate students. International applications accepted.
Benefits Opportunity to attend seminars/workshops, willing to complete paperwork for educational credit, willing to provide letters of recommendation, use of library resources, salary for those eligible for Pennsylvania state work-study only.
Contact Write, fax, or e-mail Internship Coordinator. Fax: 215-732-4401. E-mail: intern@fpri.org. No phone calls. Applicants must submit a letter of interest, resume, writing sample, two letters of recommendation. Application deadline: April 1 for summer, December 1 for spring. World Wide Web: http://www.fpri.org.

GERMAN-AMERICAN BUSINESS COUNCIL
1524 18th Street, Suite 2
Washington, District of Columbia 20036

General Information Nonprofit organization offering seminars and workshops on German-American business relations. Established in 1990. Number of employees: 2. Number of internship applications received each year: 50.
Internships Available ▶ *1–2 administrative interns:* responsibilities include organizing seminars/workshops, membership correspondence and a variety of administrative tasks. Candidates should have ability to work independently, computer skills, office skills, organizational skills, research skills, written communication skills, must be able to speak German. Duration is 3–12 months. Unpaid. Open to college freshmen, college sophomores,

college juniors, college seniors, recent college graduates, graduate students. International applications accepted.

Benefits On-the-job training, opportunity to attend seminars/workshops, willing to complete paperwork for educational credit, willing to provide letters of recommendation.

Contact Write or call Sabine Creamer, Office Manager. Phone: 202-332-7700. E-mail: gabc.creamer@worldnet.att.net. In-person interview recommended (telephone interview accepted). Applications are accepted continuously.

THE HANSARD SOCIETY FOR PARLIAMENTARY GOVERNMENT
St. Philips Building North, Sheffield Street
London WC2A 2EX United Kingdom

General Information Program that brings overseas students into contact with the political process in Britain and enables them to meet and learn from its leading figures. Established in 1944. Number of employees: 11. Number of internship applications received each year: 70.

Internships Available ▶ *16 research assistants (political):* responsibilities include acting as research assistant to member of Parliament, lobby group, or associated political organization. Candidates should have college courses in field, oral communication skills, personal interest in the field, self-motivation, strong interpersonal skills, written communication skills. Duration is 1 or 2 semesters, 3 days per week. Unpaid. Open to college freshmen, college sophomores, college juniors, college seniors, recent college graduates, graduate students. International applications accepted.

Benefits Housing at a cost, opportunity to attend seminars/workshops, willing to act as a professional reference, willing to complete paperwork for educational credit, willing to provide letters of recommendation, academic credit, London Travelcard, calendar of study visits and cultural events.

International Internships Available.

Contact Write, call, fax, e-mail, or through World Wide Web site Melanie Rimmer, Programme Coordinator, St. Phillips Building North, Sheffield Street, London WC2A 2EX United Kingdom. Phone: 44-020-7955-7713. Fax: 44-020-7955-7492. E-mail: study@hansard.lse.ac.uk. Applicants must submit a formal organization application, letter of interest, resume, academic transcripts, writing sample, personal reference, letter of recommendation. Applications are accepted continuously. World Wide Web: http://www.hansardsociety.org.uk.

HERBERT SCOVILLE, JR. PEACE FELLOWSHIP
110 Maryland Avenue, NE, Suite 409
Washington, District of Columbia 20002

General Information Fellowship named for the late Dr. Herbert Scoville Jr., a longtime nuclear arms control activist in both government and private life, who devoted special attention to encouraging young people interested in arms control and disarmament issues; brings 2-4 fellows per semester to Washington, D.C., to serve as project assistants at one of 23 arms control/disarmament groups. Established in 1987. Number of employees: 1. Number of internship applications received each year: 60.

Internships Available ▶ *2–4 Scoville Peace fellows:* responsibilities include serving as special project assistant and working on research and/or advocacy in the field of peace and security. Candidates should have ability to work with others, oral communication skills, personal interest in the field, plan to pursue career in field, research skills, written communication skills. Duration is 6–9 months. Stipend of $1800 per month. Open to recent college graduates, graduate students, career changers.

Benefits Health insurance, travel reimbursement.

Contact Call, e-mail, or through World Wide Web site Mr. Paul Revsine, Program Director. Phone: 202-543-4100 Ext. 124. E-mail: scoville@clw.org. In-person interview required. Applicants must submit a letter of interest, resume, two personal references, two letters of recommendation, 2 essays with requirements that can be obtained by accessing Web site or calling for information. Application deadline: February 1 for fall, October 15 for spring. World Wide Web: http://www.scoville.org.

THE HILLELS OF NEW YORK
426 West 58th Street
New York, New York 10019-1102

General Information Jewish university student organization. Number of employees: 7. Division of Hillel, The Foundation for Jewish Campus Life, Washington, District of Columbia. Number of internship applications received each year: 225.

Internships Available ▶ *Jewish communal service interns.* Candidates should have ability to work independently, computer skills, oral communication skills, organizational skills, self-motivation, strong interpersonal skills, strong leadership ability, written communication skills. Duration is first week of June through first week of August. $1300–$1500 per duration of internship. Open to college freshmen, college sophomores, college juniors. ▶ *Accounting interns.* Candidates should have ability to work independently, computer skills, self-motivation, strong interpersonal skills, strong leadership ability, written communication skills. Duration is first week of June through first week of August. $1300–$1500 per duration of internship. Open to college freshmen, college sophomores, college juniors. ▶ *Education interns.* Candidates should have ability to work independently, computer skills, oral communication skills, self-motivation, strong interpersonal skills, strong leadership ability, writing skills. Duration is first week of June through first week of August. $1300–$1500 per duration of internship. Open to college freshmen, college sophomores, college juniors. ▶ *Event planning interns.* Candidates should have ability to work independently, computer skills, oral communication skills, self-motivation, strong interpersonal skills, strong leadership ability, written communication skills. Duration is first week of June through first week of August. $1300–$1500 per duration of internship. Open to college freshmen, college sophomores, college juniors. ▶ *Finance interns.* Candidates should have ability to work independently, computer skills, oral communication skills, self-motivation, strong interpersonal skills, strong leadership ability. Duration is first week of June through first week of August. $1300–$1500 per duration of internship. ▶ *Information systems interns.* Candidates should have ability to work independently, computer skills, self-motivation, strong interpersonal skills, strong leadership ability, written communication skills. Duration is first week of June through first week of August. $1300–$1500 per duration of internship. Open to college freshmen, college sophomores, college juniors. ▶ *Journalism interns.* Candidates should have ability to work independently, computer skills, editing skills, oral communication skills, self-motivation, strong interpersonal skills, strong leadership ability, written communication skills. Duration is first week of June through first week of August. $1300–$1500 per duration of internship. Open to college freshmen, college sophomores, college juniors. ▶ *Law interns.* Candidates should have ability to work independently, computer skills, research skills, self-motivation, strong interpersonal skills, strong leadership ability, written communication skills. Duration is first week of June through first week of August. $1300–$1500 per duration of internship. Open to college freshmen, college sophomores, college juniors. ▶ *Museum interns.* Candidates should have ability to work independently, computer skills, oral communication skills, self-motivation, strong interpersonal skills, strong leadership ability, written communication skills. Duration is first week of June through first week of August. $1300–$1500 per duration of internship. Open to college freshmen, college sophomores, college juniors. ▶ *Psychology interns.* Candidates should have ability to work independently, computer skills, oral communication skills, strong interpersonal skills, strong leadership ability, written communication skills. Duration is first week of June through first week of August. $1300–$1500 per duration of internship. Open to college freshmen, college sophomores, college juniors. ▶ *Public relations/marketing interns.* Candidates should have ability to work independently, computer skills, oral communication skills, self-motivation, strong interpersonal skills, strong leadership ability, written communication skills. Duration is first week of June through first week of August. $1300–$1500 per duration of internship. Open to college freshmen, college sophomores, college juniors. ▶ *Social work interns.* Candidates should have ability to work independently, computer skills, oral communication skills, self-motivation, strong interpersonal skills, strong leadership ability, written communica-

The Hillels of New York (continued)

tion skills. Duration is first week of June through first week of August. $1300–$1500 per duration of internship. Open to college freshmen, college sophomores, college juniors.
Benefits Formal training, job counseling, names of contacts, on-the-job training, opportunity to attend seminars/workshops, possible full-time employment, willing to act as a professional reference, willing to complete paperwork for educational credit, willing to provide letters of recommendation, leadership training.
Contact Write, call, e-mail, or through World Wide Web site Wendy Miller-Gamer, Director of Regional Programs. Phone: 212-957-2030 Ext. 19. E-mail: wmillergamer@hillels-ny.org. In-person interview required. Applicants must submit a formal organization application, resume, academic transcripts, two writing samples, two letters of recommendation. Application deadline: April 15. World Wide Web: http://www.hillels-ny.org.

HOUSTON INTERNATIONAL PROTOCOL ALLIANCE
901 Bagby, Suite 100
Houston, Texas 77002

General Information Nonprofit organization that serves as the protocol office for the city of Houston, working closely with the mayor's office to serve the local consular corps, visiting dignitaries, and the Sister City program. Established in 1983. Number of employees: 6. Department of Greater Houston Convention & Visitors Bureau, Houston, Texas. Number of internship applications received each year: 40.
Internships Available ▶ *7–10 protocol interns:* responsibilities include research, event coordination, day-to-day administrative tasks, special projects, and drafting correspondence. Candidates should have organizational skills, personal interest in the field, research skills, self-motivation, strong interpersonal skills, written communication skills. Duration is 3-6 months with option of extending past six months. Unpaid. Open to college freshmen, college sophomores, college juniors, college seniors, recent college graduates, graduate students. International applications accepted.
Benefits Job counseling, names of contacts, willing to act as a professional reference, willing to complete paperwork for educational credit, willing to provide letters of recommendation, free parking.
Contact Write, call, or fax Diana Santana, Protocol Officer. Phone: 713-227-3395. Fax: 713-227-3399. E-mail: dsantana@ghcvb.org. In-person interview recommended (telephone interview accepted). Applicants must submit a letter of interest, resume, writing sample. Application deadline: April 15 for summer, July 15 for fall, November 15 for spring.

INSTITUTE FOR POLICY STUDIES
733 15th Street, NW, Suite 1020
Washington, District of Columbia 20005

General Information Progressive, nonprofit, public policy research institute that conducts research and public outreach on a range of domestic and foreign policy issues. Established in 1963. Number of employees: 24. Number of internship applications received each year: 200.
Internships Available ▶ *1 Drug Policy Project intern:* responsibilities include helping to foster a paradigm shift replacing the punitive and coercive "social control model" of drug policy with a public health and community economic development model. Candidates should have ability to work independently, computer skills, editing skills, organizational skills, research skills, self-motivation, writing skills. Duration is flexible. Unpaid. Open to college freshmen, college sophomores, college juniors, college seniors. ▶ *1 Global Economy Project intern:* responsibilities include producing policy papers related to the international division of labor, global job crisis, and the enforcement of international labor rights; monitoring the social and economic impact of the North American Free Trade Agreement. Candidates should have ability to work independently, ability to work with others, editing skills, oral communication skills, personal interest in the field, research skills, self-motivation, writing skills. Unpaid. Open to college freshmen, college sophomores, college juniors, college seniors, gradu-

ate students, law students. ▶ *1 Human Rights Award Event intern:* responsibilities include marketing and planning the annual fall event marking the presentation of the international and domestic human rights award to a distinguished group or individual, engaging in extensive networking with the human rights community in Washington, D.C. Candidates should have ability to work independently, oral communication skills, organizational skills, personal interest in the field, self-motivation, strong interpersonal skills, strong leadership ability, writing skills. Duration is flexible. Unpaid. Open to college freshmen, college sophomores, college juniors, college seniors, graduate students, law students. ▶ *1 Miriam Pemberton Economic Conversion Project intern:* responsibilities include research, writing, organizing, and dealing with administrative hassles related to the conversion of military resources to civilian use. Candidates should have ability to work independently, ability to work with others, computer skills, editing skills, office skills, oral communication skills, research skills, writing skills. Duration is flexible. Unpaid. Open to college freshmen, college sophomores, college juniors, college seniors, recent college graduates, graduate students, law students, career changers. ▶ *1 Pathways to the 21st Century intern:* responsibilities include outlining analysis of this century and helping to prepare the foundation for the next. Candidates should have ability to work independently, ability to work with others, computer skills, editing skills, oral communication skills, organizational skills, self-motivation, writing skills. Duration is flexible. Unpaid. Open to college freshmen, college sophomores, college juniors, college seniors, recent college graduates, graduate students, law students. ▶ *1 Progressive Challenge intern:* responsibilities include participating in progressive politics and debates. Candidates should have ability to work independently, ability to work with others, computer skills, editing skills, organizational skills, personal interest in the field, research skills, self-motivation, writing skills, knowledge of Internet (a plus). Duration is flexible. Unpaid. Open to college freshmen, college sophomores, college juniors, college seniors, graduate students, law students. ▶ *1 Social Action Leadership School for Activists intern:* responsibilities include coordinating training sessions and engaging in extensive outreach to the activist community. Candidates should have ability to work with others, oral communication skills, organizational skills, personal interest in the field, strong leadership ability, writing skills. Duration is flexible. Unpaid. Open to college freshmen, college sophomores, college juniors, college seniors, graduate students, law students. ▶ *1 Sustainable Energy and Economy Network intern:* responsibilities include researching and writing independent projects. Candidates should have ability to work independently, personal interest in the field, research skills, self-motivation, writing skills, background in gender studies, environmental issues, micro credit, or activities of the Bretton Woods Institutions. Duration is flexible. Unpaid. Open to college freshmen, college sophomores, college juniors, college seniors, graduate students, law students. ▶ *1 United Nations Project intern:* responsibilities include research and assisting in crafting memos and op-eds to reverse anti-UN policies. Candidates should have ability to work with others, computer skills, editing skills, oral communication skills, research skills, self-motivation, writing skills. Duration is flexible. Unpaid. Open to college freshmen, college sophomores, college juniors, college seniors, recent college graduates, graduate students, law students. ▶ *1 campaign for migrant and domestic workers intern:* responsibilities include publicizing the plight of domestic and migrant workers and producing literature on workers' legal rights. Candidates should have computer skills, editing skills, organizational skills, personal interest in the field, research skills, writing skills. Duration is flexible. Unpaid. Open to college freshmen, college sophomores, college juniors, college seniors, recent college graduates, graduate students, law students. ▶ *1 corporate accountability/national tax policy/feminist agenda project intern:* responsibilities include assisting in writing briefing papers and articles intended to apply a liberal analysis to tax policy, to promote more responsible corporate behavior with respect to pay equity and prevention of sexual harassment, and working jointly with Center for Advancement of Public Policy on these issues. Candidates should have ability to work independently, ability to work with others, oral communication skills, personal interest in the field, research skills, writing skills. Duration is flexible. Unpaid. Open to college freshmen, college sophomores, college juniors, college seniors, graduate students, law students. ▶ *1 press/ public relations intern:* responsibilities include assisting the media office in developing databases and media outreach strategies, helping respond to inquiries from the press as well as in outreach to Congress, the media, grassroots groups, and other policy-making organizations. Candidates should have ability to work independently, computer skills, editing skills, office skills, oral communication skills, organizational skills, research skills, writing skills. Duration is flexible. Unpaid. Open to college freshmen, college sophomores, college juniors, college seniors, graduate students, law students. International applications accepted.

Benefits Job counseling, names of contacts, opportunity to attend seminars/workshops, possible full-time employment, willing to complete paperwork for educational credit, willing to provide letters of recommendation.

Contact Write, fax, e-mail, or through World Wide Web site Ms. Dorian Lipscombe, Director of Administration. Fax: 202-387-7915. E-mail: dorian@igc.org. No phone calls. Applicants must submit a formal organization application, letter of interest, resume, academic transcripts, writing sample, two letters of recommendation. Application deadline: April 15 for summer. World Wide Web: http://www.ips-dc.org.

INSTITUTE OF CULTURAL AFFAIRS
4220 North 25th Street, Suite 4
Phoenix, Arizona 85016

General Information Nonprofit organization promoting social innovation through participation and community building with ICA's technology of participation (ToP Trademark) approach to leadership with organizations, neighborhoods, and schools. Established in 1973. Number of employees: 14. Unit of Institute of Cultural Affairs International, Brussels, Belgium. Number of internship applications received each year: 6.

Internships Available ▶ *1–2 Hispanic services interns:* responsibilities include assisting the Director in Small Community Development along the Arizona-Mexico border; assisting with neighborhood project implementation, facilitation, and fund-raising. Candidates should have ability to work with others, computer skills, personal interest in the field, self-motivation, bilingual English/Spanish required, flexibility to work some evenings and/or weekends. Duration is 1–2 years. Position available as unpaid or at stipend of $900–$1000 per month. Open to college juniors, college seniors, recent college graduates, graduate students. ▶ *2–3 community youth development interns:* responsibilities include gathering interest by working with national and international participants to focus, conference, recruit, and register participants; establishing and leading events. Candidates should have ability to work with others, oral communication skills, personal interest in the field, strong leadership ability, writing skills. Duration is 3–18 months. Position available as unpaid or at stipend of $900–$1000 per month. Open to college juniors, college seniors, recent college graduates, graduate students. ▶ *1–2 neighborhood partnership interns:* responsibilities include working to assist senior staff in developing neighborhood partnerships in Phoenix, project administration and documentation, supporting local project implementation, helping with facilitation work with nonprofit neighborhood groups, recruiting participants, and helping with fund-raising. Candidates should have ability to work with others, computer skills, personal interest in the field, self-motivation, bilingual English/Spanish preferred, flexibility to work some evenings and/or weekends. Duration is 6–24 months. Position available as unpaid or at stipend of $900–$1000 per month. Open to college juniors, college seniors, recent college graduates, graduate students. ▶ *2 short-term interns:* responsibilities include working to support ICA trainers, facilitators, and field office representatives in marketing, fund-raising, program set-up and documentation, and administration in various locations across the U.S. Candidates should have ability to work with others, computer skills, oral communication skills, plan to pursue career in field, self-motivation, written communication skills. Duration is 3 months minimum. Unpaid. Open to college sophomores, college juniors, college seniors, recent college graduates, graduate students. International applications accepted.

Benefits Formal training, housing at a cost, meals at a cost, names of contacts, on-the-job training, opportunity to attend seminars/workshops, possible full-time employment, willing to act as a professional reference, willing to complete paperwork for educational credit, willing to provide letters of recommendation, opportunity to develop skills with facilitation methods.

Contact Write, call, fax, e-mail, or through World Wide Web site Tim Hedger, Educational Partnership Coordinator. Phone: 800-742-4032. Fax: 602-954-0563. E-mail: opportunities@ica-usa.org. In-person interview recommended (telephone interview accepted). Applicants must submit a letter of interest, resume. Applications are accepted continuously. World Wide Web: http://www.ica-usa.org.

INTERHEMISPHERIC RESOURCE CENTER
PO Box 2178
Silver City, New Mexico 88062

General Information Private, nonprofit research and analysis policy institute producing books, policy reports, and periodicals on U.S. foreign policy, U.S.–Mexico-relations. Established in 1979. Number of employees: 9. Number of internship applications received each year: 50.

Internships Available ▶ *1–4 research interns:* responsibilities include working with staff writers compiling information on U.S. foreign policy and the U.S.-Mexico border; positions also available in Albuquerque. Candidates should have ability to work independently, ability to work with others, computer skills, knowledge of field, organizational skills, personal interest in the field, research skills, written communication skills. Duration is 3 months. Unpaid. Open to recent high school graduates, college freshmen, college sophomores, college juniors, college seniors, recent college graduates, graduate students, career changers. International applications accepted.

Benefits Free housing, names of contacts, on-the-job training, opportunity to attend seminars/workshops, possible full-time employment, willing to complete paperwork for educational credit, willing to provide letters of recommendation.

Contact Write, fax, e-mail, or through World Wide Web site Siri Khalsa, Administrative Assistant. Fax: 505-388-0619. E-mail: siri@irc-online.org. No phone calls. Telephone interview required. Applicants must submit a letter of interest, resume, three writing samples, 3 letters of recommendation, including 2 from professors. Applications are accepted continuously. World Wide Web: http://www.irc-online.org.

INTERNATIONAL CENTER
731 8th Street, SE
Washington, District of Columbia 20003

General Information Nonprofit organization dedicated to promoting good governance and development through direct contacts with all levels of governments, institutions, and individuals; has established major initiatives in settling regional conflicts, fostering bilateral relations, and supporting democratic movements and has provided seeds for reforestation projects in over 130 countries; has recently started water purification projects in Central America and Ghana. Established in 1977. Number of employees: 12. Number of internship applications received each year: 200.

Internships Available ▶ *2–4 Korea Project: kioson interns:* responsibilities include providing journalists, academics, NGO staff, and government officials of South Korea with information on several issues including regional security of the Korea peninsula and northeast Asia. Candidates should have ability to work independently, analytical skills, editing skills, research skills, written communication skills. Duration is 4–12 months. Unpaid. Open to college juniors, college seniors, recent college graduates, graduate students. ▶ *4–10 Russia Commission interns:* responsibilities include assisting with all programs of the Commission on U.S.-Russian relations, hosting foreign visitors, conducting translations, assisting with international business and marketing projects, editing electronic newsletters, conducting research, and managing databases. Candidates should have ability to work independently, ability to work with others, analytical skills, editing skills, written communication skills. Duration is 3–4 months. Unpaid. Open to college

juniors, college seniors, recent college graduates, graduate students, law students. ▶ *2–3 Viet Nam Trade Council interns:* responsibilities include assisting with all aspects of the U.S.-Vietnam Trade Council, hosting foreign officials in D.C., organizing meetings and conferences, conducting research, and compiling statistics for briefing books. Candidates should have ability to work independently, ability to work with others, computer skills, knowledge of field, oral communication skills, organizational skills, personal interest in the field, strong leadership ability, writing skills. Duration is 4–12 months. Unpaid. Open to college juniors, college seniors, recent college graduates, graduate students. ▶ *4–8 new forests project interns:* responsibilities include conducting research, writing project proposals, translating documents into Spanish/French, packaging tree seeds for worldwide distribution, assisting with fund-raising projects, edition of electronic newsletters, managing databases, and project coordination. Candidates should have ability to work independently, ability to work with others, computer skills, editing skills, oral communication skills, organizational skills, personal interest in the field, research skills, self-motivation, written communication skills. Duration is 4–12 months. Unpaid. Open to college freshmen, college sophomores, college juniors, college seniors, recent college graduates, graduate students, law students. International applications accepted.

Benefits Names of contacts, opportunity to attend seminars/workshops, possible full-time employment, travel reimbursement, willing to complete paperwork for educational credit, willing to provide letters of recommendation.

Contact Write, call, fax, e-mail, or through World Wide Web site Erick Toledo, Intern Coordinator. Phone: 202-547-3800. Fax: 202-546-4784. E-mail: icnfp@erols.com. In-person interview recommended (telephone interview accepted). Applicants must submit a letter of interest, resume, writing sample. Application deadline: March 31 for summer, June 15 for fall, November 15 for spring. World Wide Web: http://www.internationalcenter.com.

INTERNATIONAL FOUNDATION OF EMPLOYEE BENEFIT PLANS
18700 West Bluemound Road, PO Box 69
Brookfield, Wisconsin 53008-0069

General Information Nonprofit educational association serving the employee benefits industry as an information clearinghouse. Established in 1954. Number of employees: 148. Number of internship applications received each year: 1,000.

Internships Available ▶ *200 interns:* responsibilities include assisting with diverse duties in employee benefits and benefit administration. Candidates should have ability to work independently, computer skills, oral communication skills, personal interest in the field, strong interpersonal skills, written communication skills. Duration is usually 2 consecutive summers (between sophomore/junior year and junior/senior year); open to discussing availability. $7–$12 per hour. Open to college sophomores. International applications accepted.

Benefits Formal training, job counseling, opportunity to attend seminars/workshops, possible full-time employment, willing to complete paperwork for educational credit, willing to provide letters of recommendation, use of all services of the Foundation, including the library.

International Internships Available in Toronto, Canada.

Contact Write, call, fax, e-mail, or through World Wide Web site Dorothy Ellis, Administrative Assistant, 18700 West Bluemound Road, PO Box 69, Brookfield, Wisconsin 53008-0069. Phone: 262-786-6710 Ext. 8218. Fax: 262-786-8670. E-mail: dorothye@ifebp.org. In-person interview required. Application deadline: March 30. World Wide Web: http://www.ifebp.org.

INTERNATIONAL LABOR OFFICE
1828 L Street, NW, Suite 600
Washington, District of Columbia 20036

General Information Specialized agency of the United Nations that brings together governments, workers, and employers to improve working conditions, generate employment, and promote human rights. Established in 1919. Number of employees: 10. Number of internship applications received each year: 250.

Internships Available ▶ *Marketing/publications interns:* responsibilities include composing marketing brochures and flyers, writing book notices, selecting media to solicit book reviews, and creating awareness of ILO publications as part of the Marketing/Publications Unit. Duration is flexible. Unpaid. Open to college freshmen, college sophomores, college juniors, college seniors during fall semester. ▶ *Technical information/library interns:* responsibilities include drafting replies to inquiries, assisting in the maintenance of information documents and publications collection, and providing materials to constituency and the general public. Duration is flexible. Unpaid. Open to college freshmen, college sophomores, college juniors, college seniors.

Benefits Opportunity to attend seminars/workshops, travel reimbursement, willing to complete paperwork for educational credit.

Contact Write or through World Wide Web site Ms. Karen Dogan, Recruitment Officer, 1828 L Street, NW, Washington, District of Columbia 20036. No phone calls. Applicants must submit a resume, letter of interest stating dates of availability. Applications are accepted continuously. World Wide Web: http://www.us.ilo.org.

INTERNATIONAL RADIO AND TELEVISION SOCIETY FOUNDATION, INC.
420 Lexington Avenue, Suite 1601
New York, New York 10170

General Information Organization providing a forum for all segments of the communication industry, as a business that entertains, informs, educates, and serves the American public in a meaningful way. Number of internship applications received each year: 600.

Internships Available ▶ *Summer fellows:* responsibilities include extensive one-week orientation to broadcasting, cable, advertising, and new media; taking a number of related field trips and learning networking skills by attending industry social events; eight weeks of full-time "real world" experience through placements with NY-based corporations in a variety of areas. Candidates should have major in communications or demonstrated strong interest in field through extracurricular activities or other practical experience. Duration is nine weeks (June to August). Unpaid. Open to college juniors, college seniors, graduate students, must be attending school full-time.

Benefits All expenses paid.

Contact Write, call, or through World Wide Web site Internship Coordinator. Phone: 212-867-6650. Fax: 212-867-6653. Applicants must submit a formal organization application. World Wide Web: http://www.irts.org.

INTERNATIONAL TRADE ADMINISTRATION
14th Street and Constitution Avenue, NW, Room 7417
Washington, District of Columbia 20230

General Information International trade organization that assists small and medium-sized businesses in exporting overseas and formulates and implements U.S. foreign trade policy. Established in 1980. Number of employees: 1,745. Unit of United States Department of Commerce, Washington, District of Columbia. Number of internship applications received each year: 300.

Internships Available ▶ *1 student career experience program intern:* responsibilities include assisting with advising on international economic policy, administering international trade treaties, monitoring imports and exports, promoting exports, and many other trade-related functions. Candidates should have ability to work with others, computer skills, oral communication skills, written communication skills, U.S. citizenship. Duration is 4–24 months. $9.17–$12.71 per hour. ▶ *1 student temporary employment program intern:* responsibilities include assisting with advising on international economic policy, administering international trade treaties, monitoring imports and exports, promoting exports, and many other trade-related functions. Candidates should have ability to work with others, computer skills, oral communication skills, written communication skills, U.S. citizenship. Duration is 3–12 months. $9.17–$12.71 per hour. ▶ *30–40 volunteer interns:* responsibilities include assisting with advising on international economic policy, administering international trade treaties, monitoring imports and exports, promoting exports, and many other trade-related functions. Candidates should have U.S. citizenship. Duration is flexible. Unpaid. Open to high school students, college freshmen, college sophomores, college juniors, college seniors, graduate students, law students.

Benefits Formal training, health insurance, possible full-time employment, willing to complete paperwork for educational credit, willing to provide letters of recommendation.

Contact Fax or e-mail Tina James, Human Resources Specialist. Fax: 202-482-1903. E-mail: tina_james@ita.doc.gov. No phone calls. Applicants must submit a resume, academic transcripts. Applications are accepted continuously.

INTERNATIONAL VOLUNTARY SERVICES, INC.
1625 K Street, NW, Suite 102
Washington, District of Columbia 20006

General Information Private voluntary organization that provides technical assistance to local organizations in the developing world. Established in 1953. Number of employees: 5. Number of internship applications received each year: 150.

Internships Available ▶ *1–2 Andes program interns:* responsibilities include keeping track of field activities, summarizing reports, and fund-raising. Duration is 1–9 months. Unpaid. Open to college juniors, college seniors, recent college graduates, graduate students, law students. ▶ *1 program intern:* responsibilities include keeping track of field activities, summarizing reports, and fund-raising. Duration is 3–6 months. Unpaid. Open to college juniors, college seniors, recent college graduates, graduate students. Candidates for all positions should have ability to work independently, computer skills, oral communication skills, personal interest in the field, writing skills, fluency in Spanish (preferred). International applications accepted.

Benefits Job counseling, names of contacts, on-the-job training, opportunity to attend seminars/workshops, willing to act as a professional reference, willing to complete paperwork for educational credit, willing to provide letters of recommendation, small transportation stipend.

Contact Write or e-mail Anne Shirk, Executive Director. E-mail: ivs.inc@erols.com. No phone calls. In-person interview recommended (telephone interview accepted). Applicants must submit a letter of interest, resume, personal reference. Applications are accepted continuously.

INVESTOR RESPONSIBILITY RESEARCH CENTER
1350 Connecticut Avenue, NW, Suite 700
Washington, District of Columbia 20036-1701

General Information Research organization that reports to nearly 400 institutional investors on a wide range of questions relating to the role of business in society. Established in 1972. Number of employees: 86. Number of internship applications received each year: 100.

Internships Available ▶ *6–8 CGS interns:* responsibilities include extracting data from proxy materials filed by U.S. corporations and writing related analysis. Candidates should have computer skills, research skills, self-motivation, writing skills. Duration is 2–3 months. Unpaid. Open to college freshmen, college sophomores, college juniors, college seniors. ▶ *3–5 GSS interns.* Candidates should have analytical skills, plan to pursue career in field, research skills, writing skills, attention to detail, experience with databases and MS Word (preferred), major in business, finance, economics, international relations, or languages. Duration is year-round (minimum of 30 hours per week and a 6-month commitment). Unpaid. Open to college freshmen, college sophomores, college juniors, college seniors, recent college graduates, graduate students, law students, career changers. ▶ *1–2 corporate benching service interns.* Candidates should have research skills, self-motivation, writing skills, attention to detail, familiarity with Lexis/Nexis and experience working with databases a plus, interest in role of business in society. Duration is flexible (at least 20 hours per week part-time, 35 hours per week full-time). $10 per hour. Open to college fresh-

men, college sophomores, college juniors, college seniors, recent college graduates, graduate students, law students, career changers. ▶ *Research analyst interns:* responsibilities include writing reports or articles; compiling databases on selected topics; and working on surveys concerning stockholders, questions relating to social responsibility, and corporate governance issues. Candidates should have analytical skills, personal interest in the field, research skills, self-motivation, writing skills, attention to detail, experience with databases and MS Word (preferred), major in business, finance, economics, or general liberal arts. Duration is year-round (minimum of 20-30 hours per week and at least 2-6 month commitment). Position available as unpaid or at $10 per hour (students receiving academic credit are not paid). Open to college freshmen, college sophomores, college juniors, college seniors, recent college graduates, graduate students, law students, career changers. International applications accepted.

Benefits On-the-job training, possible full-time employment, willing to act as a professional reference, willing to complete paperwork for educational credit, willing to provide letters of recommendation.

Contact Write, fax, e-mail, or through World Wide Web site Charine Adams, Director, Human Resources, 1350 Connecticut Avenue, NW Suite 700, Washington, District of Columbia 20036-1701. Fax: 202-833-3555. E-mail: c.adams@irrc.org. No phone calls. In-person interview recommended (telephone interview accepted). Applicants must submit a letter of interest, resume, writing sample. Application deadline: January 15 for spring, corporate benching service interns. World Wide Web: http://irrc.org.

ISAR: INITIATIVE FOR SOCIAL ACTION AND RENEWAL EURASIA
1601 Connecticut Avenue, NW, Suite 301
Washington, District of Columbia 20009

General Information Nonprofit, nongovernmental organization that supports environmental groups and projects in the former Soviet Union. Established in 1983. Number of employees: 11. Number of internship applications received each year: 75.

Internships Available ▶ *Interns:* responsibilities include focusing on individual projects, answering telephones, filing, entering data, and processing requests for information. Candidates should have editing skills, knowledge of field, office skills, personal interest in the field, writing skills. Duration is 3–6 months. Position available as unpaid or paid. Open to college freshmen, college sophomores, college juniors, college seniors, recent college graduates, graduate students. International applications accepted.

Benefits Job counseling, names of contacts, opportunity to attend seminars/workshops, possible full-time employment, willing to complete paperwork for educational credit, willing to provide letters of recommendation, office training, reimbursement of local travel expenses to and from ISAR.

Contact Write or through World Wide Web site Alice Hengesbach, Office Manager. Fax: 202-667-3291. E-mail: alice@isar.org. No phone calls. In-person interview recommended (telephone interview accepted). Applicants must submit a letter of interest, resume. Applications are accepted continuously. World Wide Web: http://www.isar.org.

JAMESTOWN FOUNDATION
4516 43rd Street, NW
Washington, District of Columbia 20016

General Information Nonprofit organization specializing in increasing Western understanding of the former Soviet Union and China through the monitoring of political, economic, and social trends. Established in 1983. Number of employees: 10. Number of internship applications received each year: 30.

Internships Available ▶ *1–4 research assistants:* responsibilities include providing administrative and research support for Foundation staff. Candidates should have ability to work independently, computer skills, office skills, research skills, writing skills, Russian or central Asian language skills (helpful). Duration is 1 semester. Unpaid. Open to college freshmen, college sophomores, college juniors, college seniors, graduate students. International applications accepted.

Jamestown Foundation (continued)

Benefits Job counseling, on-the-job training, opportunity to attend seminars/workshops, willing to complete paperwork for educational credit, willing to provide letters of recommendation.
Contact Write, call, fax, e-mail, or through World Wide Web site Tamara Stuchlak, Intern Coordinator. Phone: 202-483-8888. Fax: 202-483-8337. E-mail: stuchlak@jamestown.org. In-person interview recommended (telephone interview accepted). Applicants must submit a letter of interest, resume, application materials and procedures available on Web site. Applications are accepted continuously. World Wide Web: http://www.jamestown.org.

JAPAN-AMERICA SOCIETY OF WASHINGTON, DC
1020 19th Street, LL #40
Washington, District of Columbia 20036

General Information Organization dedicated to promoting a better understanding between Japan and the United States through programs and services. Established in 1957. Number of employees: 5. Affiliate of National Association of Japan America Societies, Washington, District of Columbia. Number of internship applications received each year: 20.
Internships Available ▶ *2–3 interns:* responsibilities include various office duties in membership programs and services. Candidates should have ability to work independently, office skills, oral communication skills, organizational skills, self-motivation, written communication skills. Duration is minimum of 8 weeks. Unpaid. Open to college freshmen, college sophomores, college juniors, college seniors, graduate students. International applications accepted.
Benefits Job counseling, names of contacts, opportunity to attend seminars/workshops, possible full-time employment, willing to complete paperwork for educational credit, willing to provide letters of recommendation, travel reimbursement related to internship assignments.
Contact Write, fax, or e-mail Internship Coordinator. Fax: 202-833-2456. E-mail: jaswdc@intr.net. No phone calls. In-person interview recommended (telephone interview accepted). Applicants must submit a letter of interest, resume. Application deadline: March 31 for summer, July 31 for fall, November 30 for spring. World Wide Web: http://www.us-japan.org.

JAPAN–AMERICA STUDENT CONFERENCE, INC.
2nd Floor, 606 18th Street, NW
Washington, District of Columbia 20006-5202

General Information 30-day exchange program for 30-40 Japanese and 30-40 American university students; alternates annually between Japan and the United States; freshman to PhD levels. Established in 1934. Number of employees: 3. Number of internship applications received each year: 5.
Internships Available ▶ *1–3 interns:* responsibilities include fundraising, general administrative duties, coordinating alumni activities, acting as university liaison, working with database and other computer systems, and archival research. Candidates should have ability to work with others, computer skills, office skills, organizational skills, personal interest in the field, research skills, self-motivation. Duration is flexible. Unpaid. Open to college freshmen, college sophomores, college juniors, college seniors, recent college graduates, graduate students, law students, career changers, individuals reentering the workforce. International applications accepted.
Benefits On-the-job training, opportunity to attend seminars/workshops, willing to act as a professional reference, willing to complete paperwork for educational credit, willing to provide letters of recommendation.
Contact Write, call, fax, or e-mail Ms. Gretchen Hobbs Donaldson, Executive Director, 606 18th Street, NW, 2nd Floor, Washington, District of Columbia 20006-5202. Phone: 202-289-4231. Fax: 202-789-8265. E-mail: jascinc@jasc.org. In-person interview required. Applicants must submit a letter of interest, resume, two personal references. Applications are accepted continuously. World Wide Web: http://www.jasc.org.

JUNIOR ACHIEVEMENT OF ORANGE COUNTY/ INLAND EMPIRE
301 East 17th Street, Suite 202
Costa Mesa, California 92627

General Information Nonprofit organization dedicated to educating and inspiring young people to value free enterprise, business, and economics to improve the quality of their lives. Established in 1919. Number of employees: 4. Division of Junior Achievement of Southern California, Inc., Los Angeles, California.
Internships Available ▶ *1–2 marketing/development interns:* responsibilities include assisting executive director in marketing and fundraising, community outreach, newsletter, and special events. Candidates should have computer skills, oral communication skills, personal interest in the field, research skills, self-motivation, strong interpersonal skills, presentation skills. Duration is flexible. Unpaid. ▶ *1–2 program interns:* responsibilities include assisting program managers with recruiting, training, monitoring volunteers; administration and data entry. Candidates should have computer skills, oral communication skills, organizational skills, personal interest in the field, strong interpersonal skills, presentation skills. Duration is flexible. Unpaid. Open to college juniors, college seniors, recent college graduates, graduate students.
Benefits On-the-job training, possible full-time employment, willing to act as a professional reference, willing to complete paperwork for educational credit, willing to provide letters of recommendation.
Contact Write, fax, or e-mail Christine Shewbridge, Director of Education. Fax: 949-515-2508. E-mail: cshewbridge@jasocal.org. No phone calls. In-person interview required. Applicants must submit a letter of interest, resume, two personal references. Applications are accepted continuously. World Wide Web: http://www.ja.org.

KENNAN INSTITUTE FOR ADVANCED RUSSIAN STUDIES
1300 Pennsylvania Avenue, NW
Washington, District of Columbia 20004

General Information Institute that sponsors domestic and foreign scholars to conduct research in residence on topics related to the former Soviet Union. Established in 1974. Number of employees: 10. Unit of Woodrow Wilson International Center for Scholars, Washington, District of Columbia. Number of internship applications received each year: 80.
Internships Available ▶ *10–15 research interns:* responsibilities include providing research assistance for a scholar in residence, conducting research, translating, editing, some photocopying, summarizing research articles, compiling bibliographies, and writing reports. Candidates should have ability to work independently, editing skills, knowledge of field, organizational skills, research skills, Russian language ability. Duration is 3–9 months. $3.50–$6 per hour. Open to college juniors, college seniors, recent college graduates, graduate students, law students. ▶ *1 staff intern:* responsibilities include providing assistance to various staff members, organizing and maintaining library, and researching assignments. Candidates should have ability to work independently, college courses in field, office skills, organizational skills, research skills, Russian or Ukrainian language skills. Duration is 3 months minimum. $3.50–$6 per hour. Open to recent college graduates, graduate students. International applications accepted.
Benefits Opportunity to attend seminars/workshops, willing to complete paperwork for educational credit, willing to provide letters of recommendation, subsidy for using Washington, DC metro.
Contact Write, call, fax, or e-mail Mr. Joseph Dresen, Intern Coordinator, 1300 Pennsylvania Avenue, NW, Washington, District of Columbia 20004. Phone: 202-691-4245. Fax: 202-691-4247. E-mail: dresenjo@wwic.si.edu. In-person interview recommended (telephone interview accepted). Applicants must submit a letter of interest, resume. Applications are accepted continuously. World Wide Web: http://wwics.si.edu/PROGRAMS/REGION/KENNAN/ KENNAN.HTM.

KOREA ECONOMIC INSTITUTE OF AMERICA
1101 Vermont Avenue, Suite 401
Washington, District of Columbia 20005

General Information Institute that promotes an understanding with respect to economic relations between the United States and the Republic of Korea. Established in 1982. Number of employees: 7. Affiliate of Korea Institute for International Economics Policy, Seoul, Republic of Korea.
Internships Available ▶ *2 operations and research interns:* responsibilities include attending Korea-related conferences, programs, and hearings in the Washington Area; preparing short reports for transmission to Korea; assisting with preparation of conferences and programs, helping to prepare daily news summary, maintaining library organization, responding to information requests from within U.S. and abroad; researching publication requests, and assisting with correspondence. Candidates should have computer skills, office skills, organizational skills, writing skills, background in political science and/or economics, interest in the Asia-Pacific, attention to detail, professional demeanor. Duration is year-round (minimum of 30 hours per week). Unpaid. Open to college sophomores, college juniors, college seniors, graduate students. International applications accepted.
Benefits Names of contacts, opportunity to attend seminars/workshops, willing to act as a professional reference, willing to complete paperwork for educational credit, willing to provide letters of recommendation, reimbursement of work-related meals and travel.
Contact Write, fax, or e-mail Ms. Caroline G. Cooper, Director of Congressional Affairs and Trade Policy. Fax: 202-371-0692. E-mail: cgc@keia.org. No phone calls. *Applicant must submit an application and recommendation form which may be downloaded from organization Web site; a brief writing sample. Application deadline: April 15 for summer, June 15 for fall, November 1 for spring. World Wide Web: http://www.keia.org.

LAWYERS ALLIANCE FOR WORLD SECURITY /COMMITTEE FOR NATIONAL SECURITY
1901 Pennsylvania Avenue, NW, Suite 201
Washington, District of Columbia 20006

General Information Non-governmental organization focusing on arms control and international security. Established in 1981. Number of employees: 7. Number of internship applications received each year: 100.
Internships Available ▶ *2–3 project assistants/associates:* responsibilities include research, editing, some administrative duties, assisting with preparation and follow-up of projects, and correspondence. Candidates should have computer skills, organizational skills, research skills, written communication skills, some experience and college-level courses in international relations/arms control (desirable); some experience with HTML (desirable). Duration is 3 to 4 months or a semester. Unpaid. Open to college sophomores, college juniors, college seniors, recent college graduates, graduate students.
Benefits Job counseling, names of contacts, on-the-job training, opportunity to attend seminars/workshops, possible full-time employment, willing to act as a professional reference, willing to complete paperwork for educational credit, willing to provide letters of recommendation.
Contact Write, call, fax, e-mail, or through World Wide Web site Ms. Stephanie Powell, Program Manager. Phone: 202-745-2450. Fax: 202-667-0444. E-mail: spowell@lawscns.org. In-person interview recommended (telephone interview accepted). Applicants must submit a letter of interest, resume, academic transcripts, 3–5-page writing sample. Applications are accepted continuously. World Wide Web: http://www.lawscns.org.

LEGACY INTERNATIONAL'S GLOBAL YOUTH VILLAGE
1020 Legacy Drive
Bedford, Virginia 24523

General Information International youth training program in a camp setting that focuses on cross-cultural understanding and leadership training and offers workshops in conflict resolution, the arts, ESOL, international relations, and other programs. Established in 1979. Number of employees: 9. Unit of Legacy International, Bedford, Virginia. Number of internship applications received each year: 40.
Internships Available ▶ *8–12 counselors/program specialists:* responsibilities include live-in cabin counseling plus other duties pending on the intern's skills. Candidates should have ability to work with others, oral communication skills, organizational skills, personal interest in the field, strong leadership ability, cross-cultural communication skills. Duration is 4 weeks (July to August). Position available as unpaid or at $900–$1200 per duration of internship. Open to college juniors, college seniors, recent college graduates, graduate students, career changers, individuals reentering the workforce, must be 21 years or older. ▶ *6 food service interns:* responsibilities include learning how a food service operation works while serving as a prep cook in Legacy's vegetarian kitchen; meals prepared using whole foods, served family style, with an international flare. Candidates should have ability to work independently, ability to work with others, oral communication skills, personal interest in the field, self-motivation. Duration is 4 weeks (July—August). $900–$1200 per duration of internship. Open to college sophomores, college juniors, college seniors, recent college graduates, graduate students, career changers, individuals reentering the workforce, must be 20 years or older. International applications accepted.
Benefits Formal training, free housing, free meals, health insurance, names of contacts, on-the-job training, possible full-time employment, willing to act as a professional reference, willing to complete paperwork for educational credit, willing to provide letters of recommendation, laundry service, stipend based on qualifications.
Contact Write, fax, e-mail, or through World Wide Web site Leila Baz, Staff Coordinator. Fax: 540-297-1860. E-mail: staff@legacyintl.org. No phone calls. In-person interview recommended (telephone interview accepted). Applicants must submit a formal organization application, resume, 2-3 professional references with phone/fax numbers. Applications are accepted continuously. World Wide Web: http://www.globalyouthvillage.org.

MELPOMENE INSTITUTE FOR WOMEN'S HEALTH RESEARCH
1010 University Avenue
St. Paul, Minnesota 55104

General Information Organization helping girls and women of all ages to link physical activity and health through research, education, and publication. Established in 1982. Number of employees: 15. Number of internship applications received each year: 50.
Internships Available ▶ *3–6 interns:* responsibilities include a variety of assignments in health research, marketing/public relations, or computer projects depending on intern's background and interests. Candidates should have ability to work independently, ability to work with others, oral communication skills, personal interest in the field, writing skills, experience with PC's (helpful). Duration is 13-15 weeks (10-12 hours per week). Unpaid. Open to college freshmen, college sophomores, college juniors, college seniors, recent college graduates, graduate students, career changers, individuals reentering the workforce. International applications accepted.
Benefits Names of contacts, on-the-job training, opportunity to attend seminars/workshops, willing to act as a professional reference, willing to complete paperwork for educational credit, willing to provide letters of recommendation, opportunity to contribute to research on women's health, small stipend.
Contact Write, call, fax, e-mail, or through World Wide Web site Maureen Moo-Dodge, Director of Internships, 1010 University Avenue, St. Paul, Minnesota 55104. Phone: 651-642-1951. Fax: 651-642-1871. E-mail: health@melpomene.org. In-person interview recommended (telephone interview accepted). Applicants must submit a formal organization application, letter of interest, resume, two writing samples, three personal references, outline of expectations for internship. Application deadline: April 1 for summer, June 1 for fall, October 1 for winter. World Wide Web: http://www.melpomene.org.

MERIDIAN INTERNATIONAL CENTER–EDUCATIONAL AND VISITOR SERVICES
1630 Crescent Place, NW
Washington, District of Columbia 20009

General Information Service promoting international understanding through exchange of people, ideas, and the arts; Educational and Visitor Services division offers training, conferences, and services for international visitors and Americans sponsored by the U.S. and foreign governments or private corporations. Established in 1960. Number of employees: 100. Number of internship applications received each year: 50.

Internships Available ▶ *1–2 Resources Center interns:* responsibilities include maintaining and developing information for programming of international visitors; conducting research on several different subjects, and distributing program information for resource forums; escorting international visitors to DC appointments. Candidates should have computer skills, office skills, oral communication skills, organizational skills, research skills, self-motivation, written communication skills. Duration is 6–12 months. Unpaid. Open to college juniors, college seniors, recent college graduates, graduate students. ▶ *1 The Hospitality Information Service (THIS) intern:* responsibilities include assisting in maintaining database with assistants and volunteers; administrative duties; and assisting in program coordination for diplomats. Candidates should have ability to work with others, computer skills, office skills, oral communication skills, self-motivation, foreign language skills (helpful). Duration is 1–3 months. Unpaid. Open to college freshmen, college sophomores, college juniors, college seniors, graduate students. ▶ *2–3 arts and communications interns:* responsibilities include helping with press and public relations; planning cultural programs and receptions; assisting staff with exhibitions; and monitoring galleries. Candidates should have ability to work independently, ability to work with others, computer skills, experience in the field, oral communication skills, plan to pursue career in field, written communication skills. Duration is 2–3 months. Unpaid. Open to college juniors, college seniors, recent college graduates, graduate students. ▶ *2–3 development interns:* responsibilities include assisting in planning large fund-raising galas and other special events; assisting with public relations and media relations; providing support for all development staff. Candidates should have computer skills, office skills, oral communication skills, self-motivation, strong interpersonal skills, written communication skills, must have excellent English language skills. Duration is 3–12 months. Unpaid. Open to college sophomores, college juniors, college seniors, recent college graduates, graduate students. ▶ *1–2 international classroom interns:* responsibilities include assisting with creating, improving, and expanding Meridian's collection of curriculum aids for use by D.C. public school educators instructing students about international issues and events. Candidates should have ability to work independently, computer skills, office skills, oral communication skills, personal interest in the field, research skills, strong interpersonal skills, written communication skills. Duration is 3–6 months. Unpaid. Open to college sophomores, college juniors, college seniors. ▶ *1–2 visitor services assistants:* responsibilities include working with volunteer corps, acting as a liaison between international visitors and volunteers, scheduling cultural events, assisting in conferences and workshops, and maintaining records. Candidates should have ability to work independently, ability to work with others, computer skills, office skills, oral communication skills, written communication skills. Duration is flexible. Unpaid. Open to high school students, recent high school graduates, college freshmen, college sophomores, college juniors, college seniors, recent college graduates, graduate students. ▶ *1 world affairs intern:* responsibilities include assisting in conference registration; coordinating variety of lectures, briefings, discussions, and seminars with an international theme. Candidates should have office skills, oral communication skills, organizational skills, personal interest in the field, plan to pursue career in field, written communication skills, data entry skills. Duration is 1–3 months. Unpaid. Open to high school students, college freshmen, college sophomores, college juniors, college seniors, recent college graduates, graduate students. International applications accepted.

Benefits Formal training, job counseling, names of contacts, on-the-job training, opportunity to attend seminars/workshops, possible full-time employment, willing to act as a professional reference, willing to complete paperwork for educational credit, willing to provide letters of recommendation.
Contact Write, fax, or through World Wide Web site Intern Coordinator. Fax: 202-667-1475. No phone calls. Telephone interview required. Applicants must submit a letter of interest, resume. Applications are accepted continuously. World Wide Web: http://www.meridian.org.

THE MIDDLE EAST INSTITUTE
1761 N Street, NW
Washington, District of Columbia 20036

General Information Nonprofit organization dedicated to improving public knowledge and understanding of the politics, economics, cultures, languages, and religions of the Middle East, North Africa, Caucasus, and Central Asia; publishing the Middle East Journal; teaching Arabic, Hebrew, Persian, and Turkish languages; presenting cultural and political programs; and operating the Keiser Library. Established in 1946. Number of employees: 15. Number of internship applications received each year: 100.

Internships Available ▶ *1 development intern:* responsibilities include helping maintain records, increasing fund-raising activities, and writing articles about MEI lectures. Candidates should have ability to work independently, computer skills, editing skills, office skills, organizational skills, research skills, strong interpersonal skills, writing skills. Duration is 1 semester. Unpaid. Open to college freshmen, college sophomores, college juniors, college seniors, recent college graduates. ▶ *1–2 library interns:* responsibilities include compiling bibliographies, researching topics for patrons, answering telephone inquiries on the Middle East, and writing for the Institute's Web site. Candidates should have ability to work independently, computer skills, office skills, oral communication skills, organizational skills, research skills, strong interpersonal skills, writing skills. Duration is 1 semester. Unpaid. Open to college freshmen, college sophomores, college juniors, college seniors, recent college graduates. ▶ *2–3 programs interns:* responsibilities include research for conferences and seminars, helping to administer public events, correspondence, and writing articles about MEI. Candidates should have ability to work independently, oral communication skills, research skills, strong interpersonal skills, writing skills. Duration is 1 semester. Unpaid. Open to college freshmen, college sophomores, college juniors, college seniors, recent college graduates, graduate students. ▶ *3–4 publication interns:* responsibilities include proofreading book reviews, helping compile the journal's "Bibliography of Periodical Literature," drafting book annotations for publication in the Middle East Journal, maintaining two databases, and writing articles about MEI lectures. Candidates should have ability to work independently, computer skills, editing skills, organizational skills, plan to pursue career in field, research skills, writing skills. Duration is 1 semester. Unpaid. Open to college freshmen, college sophomores, college juniors, college seniors, recent college graduates, graduate students. International applications accepted.

Benefits Names of contacts, opportunity to attend seminars/workshops, willing to complete paperwork for educational credit, willing to provide letters of recommendation, 1 language course tuition-free, 1 year free membership in organization, reimbursement of local travel expenses.
Contact Write, call, fax, e-mail, or through World Wide Web site Talal Belrhiti, Internship Coordinator. Phone: 202-785-0191. Fax: 202-452-8876. E-mail: ast-ed@mideasti.org. In-person interview recommended (telephone interview accepted). Applicants must submit a letter of interest, resume, academic transcripts, writing sample, letter of recommendation. Applications are accepted continuously. World Wide Web: http://www.mideasti.org.

NATIONAL ASSOCIATION FOR COMMUNITY MEDIATION
1527 New Hampshire Avenue, NW
Washington, District of Columbia 20036

General Information An organization of community mediation programs and volunteer mediations whose goals are to provide a compelling voice in policy making, legislative arenas, and network support. Established in 1994. Number of employees: 4. Number of internship applications received each year: 20.

Internships Available ▶ *2–3 interns:* responsibilities include research, information gathering, networking, maintaining communication with related national organizations, creating a profile of state mediation associations and activities in their states, and additional administrative and clerical tasks as needed. Candidates should have ability to work independently, computer skills, oral communication skills, research skills, strong interpersonal skills, written communication skills, background or experience in mediation or conflict resolution. Duration is 3–6 months. Position available as unpaid or paid. Open to college juniors, college seniors, recent college graduates, graduate students, law students, law school graduates, career changers. International applications accepted.

Benefits Names of contacts, on-the-job training, opportunity to attend seminars/workshops, travel reimbursement, willing to act as a professional reference, willing to complete paperwork for educational credit, willing to provide letters of recommendation, possibility of stipend.

Contact Write, fax, or e-mail Craig Coletta, Coordinator, 1527 New Hampshire Avenue, NW, Washington, District of Columbia 20036. Fax: 202-667-8629. E-mail: nafcm@nafcm.org. No phone calls. Telephone interview required. Applicants must submit a letter of interest, resume, three personal references. Applications are accepted continuously. World Wide Web: http://www.nafcm.org.

NATIONAL ASSOCIATION OF COLLEGIATE DIRECTORS OF ATHLETICS (NACDA)
24651 Detroit Road
Westlake, Ohio 44145

General Information Largest association of collegiate athletics administrators with a membership of more than 6,100 individuals and more than 1,600 institutions throughout the United States, Canada, and Mexico. Established in 1965. Number of employees: 10. Number of internship applications received each year: 50.

Internships Available ▶ *3–4 administrative interns:* responsibilities include assisting with a wide range of activities and duties, including one of NACDA's main undertakings, its annual convention, which requires months of preparation to make the event successful. Candidates should have computer skills, oral communication skills, plan to pursue career in field, self-motivation, strong interpersonal skills, written communication skills. Duration is one summer (May to August) or 10 months (September-July 1). $100 per week. Open to college freshmen, college sophomores, college juniors, college seniors, recent college graduates, graduate students, career changers, individuals reentering the workforce. International applications accepted.

Benefits Willing to act as a professional reference, willing to complete paperwork for educational credit, willing to provide letters of recommendation.

Contact Write, call, fax, or e-mail Becky Parke, Assistant Administrator/Association Liaison, PO Box 16428, Cleveland, Ohio 44116. Phone: 440-892-4000. Fax: 440-892-4007. E-mail: bparke@nacda.com. In-person interview recommended (telephone interview accepted). Applicants must submit a letter of interest, resume. Applications are accepted continuously. World Wide Web: http://www.nacda.com.

NATIONAL ASSOCIATION OF ELECTED AND APPOINTED OFFICIALS (NALEO) EDUCATIONAL FUND
5800 South Eastern Avenue, Suite 365
Los Angeles, California 90040

General Information Nonprofit organization that promotes participation in the American political process. Established in 1981. Number of internship applications received each year: 300.

Internships Available ▶ *Up to 10 Ford Motor Company Fellows:* responsibilities include working with a member of the House of Representative in Washington, D.C. Candidates should have ability to work independently, analytical skills, computer skills, research

skills, self-motivation, writing skills. Duration is June 25 to August 3. Stipend of $1200. Open to graduate students, college seniors graduating in May. ▶ *Up to 14 Shell Legislative Internship (SLIP):* responsibilities include participating in the legislative process with an elected or appointed official from intern's home state. Candidates should have ability to work independently, analytical skills, computer skills, editing skills, office skills, oral communication skills, organizational skills, research skills, self-motivation, strong interpersonal skills, strong leadership ability, writing skills. Duration is June 25 to August 3 . Stipend of $1500. Open to college juniors, college seniors.

Benefits Free housing, free meals, names of contacts, opportunity to attend seminars/workshops, possible full-time employment, travel reimbursement, willing to act as a professional reference, willing to provide letters of recommendation.

Contact Write, call, fax, e-mail, or through World Wide Web site Edith Castillo-Kuncewicki, Director of Leadership Programs. Phone: 323-720-1932 Ext. 122. Fax: 323-720-9519. E-mail: ecastillo@naleo. org. Telephone interview required. Applicants must submit a formal organization application, resume, academic transcripts, two writing samples, two letters of recommendation. Application deadline: March 7 for Internship Program, March 28 for Ford Fellows Program. World Wide Web: http://www.naleo.org.

THE NATIONAL CENTER FOR PUBLIC POLICY RESEARCH
777 North Capitol Street, NE, Suite 803
Washington, District of Columbia 20002-4294

General Information Resource center for conservative activists, journalists, and policymakers that seeks to promote enlightened and reasoned debate on diverse public policy issues; dedicated to the principles of a strong defense, free competitive enterprise, and individual liberty. Established in 1982. Number of employees: 7. Number of internship applications received each year: 100.

Internships Available ▶ *3–5 research assistants:* responsibilities include researching a topic of interest concerning U.S. domestic policy and/or international relations and general office support. Candidates should have ability to work independently, office skills, organizational skills, research skills, self-motivation, writing skills. Duration is flexible (37.5 hours per week). $6–$7 per hour. Open to college freshmen, college sophomores, college juniors, college seniors, recent college graduates, graduate students.

Benefits Job counseling, names of contacts, on-the-job training, opportunity to attend seminars/workshops, possible full-time employment, willing to complete paperwork for educational credit, willing to provide letters of recommendation.

Contact Write, fax, or e-mail David Almasi, Executive Director. Fax: 202-408-7773. E-mail: dalmasi@nationalcenter.org. No phone calls. Telephone interview required. Applicants must submit a formal organization application, letter of interest, resume, writing sample, personal reference. Applications are accepted continuously. World Wide Web: http://www.nationalcenter.org.

NATIONAL FOUNDATION FOR WOMEN LEGISLATORS
910 16th Street, NW, Suite 100
Washington, District of Columbia 20005

General Information 501(c)(3) nonprofit, nonpartisan foundation providing leadership training and issue education to women who hold and/or run for elected office at all state and federal levels. Established in 1938. Number of employees: 9. Number of internship applications received each year: 30.

Internships Available ▶ *15 general interns.* Candidates should have ability to work independently, analytical skills, computer skills, editing skills, office skills, oral communication skills, organizational skills, research skills, self-motivation, strong interpersonal skills, strong leadership ability, writing skills, team player. Duration is year-round. Position available as unpaid or paid. Open to college juniors, college seniors, recent college graduates, graduate students, law students, career changers, individuals reentering the workforce. International applications accepted.

Benefits Names of contacts, on-the-job training, opportunity to attend seminars/workshops, possible full-time employment, will-

National Foundation for Women Legislators (continued)

ing to act as a professional reference, willing to complete paperwork for educational credit, willing to provide letters of recommendation.

Contact Write, call, fax, e-mail, or through World Wide Web site Robin Read, President/CEO, 910 16th Street, NW Suite 100, Washington 20005. Phone: 202-337-3565. Fax: 202-337-3566. E-mail: nfwl@erols.com. In-person interview recommended (telephone interview accepted). Applicants must submit a letter of interest, resume. Applications are accepted continuously. World Wide Web: http://www.womenlegislators.org.

NATIONAL INSTITUTE FOR PUBLIC POLICY
3031 Javier Road, Suite 300
Fairfax, Virginia 22031

General Information Organization that provides historically-based strategic analysis, policy research, and education in the international security field. Established in 1981. Number of employees: 20. Number of internship applications received each year: 50.

Internships Available ▶ *1–2 research support interns:* responsibilities include researching and writing educational materials, assisting with editing the journal *Comparative Strategy*, and assisting with organizing conferences. Candidates should have college courses in field, knowledge of field, personal interest in the field, research skills. Duration is flexible. Position available as unpaid or paid. Open to recent college graduates, graduate students.

Benefits Job counseling, names of contacts, opportunity to attend seminars/workshops, possible full-time employment, willing to complete paperwork for educational credit, willing to provide letters of recommendation.

Contact Write, call, or fax Mr. John J. Kohout, III, Vice President. Phone: 703-698-0563. Fax: 703-698-0566. E-mail: john.kohout@nipp.org. In-person interview required. Applicants must submit a letter of interest, resume, writing sample. Applications are accepted continuously. World Wide Web: http://www.nipp.org.

NATIONAL OPINION RESEARCH CENTER
1155 East 60th Street
Chicago, Illinois 60637

General Information Social science research center that studies health, education, labor, alcohol and drug abuse, and other areas of public policy interest; located at University of Chicago. Established in 1941. Number of employees: 500. Number of internship applications received each year: 175.

Internships Available ▶ *12–15 summer interns:* responsibilities include assisting project staff in coding, editing, and data entry of questionnaires; preparing interviewer training materials; sampling; questionnaire design; and instrument testing. Candidates should have ability to work independently, ability to work with others, analytical skills, personal interest in the field, written communication skills. Duration is 10 weeks. $9.50–$11.50 per hour. Open to college juniors, college seniors, recent college graduates, graduate students. International applications accepted.

Benefits Formal training, names of contacts, on-the-job training, opportunity to attend seminars/workshops, possible full-time employment, willing to act as a professional reference, willing to complete paperwork for educational credit, willing to provide letters of recommendation.

Contact Write, fax, e-mail, or through World Wide Web site Ms. Rupa Datta, Senior Survey Director. Fax: 773-753-7886. E-mail: norc-intern@norcmail.uchicago.edu. Telephone interview required. Applicants must submit a letter of interest, resume, 5-page writing sample. Application deadline: April 15 for summer. World Wide Web: http://www.norc.uchicago.edu.

NATIONAL SECURITY ARCHIVE, THE GEORGE WASHINGTON UNIVERSITY
Gelman Library, Suite 701, 2130 H Street, NW
Washington, District of Columbia 20037

General Information Nonprofit research institute, library, and publisher providing scholars, journalists, librarians, students, and other researchers with unclassified and declassified government

documents for research and informed debate. Established in 1985. Number of employees: 25. Number of internship applications received each year: 150.

Internships Available ▶ *5–10 interns:* responsibilities include performing library and archival research; building chronology of events; obtaining, ordering, and cataloging government documents; and entering computer data. Candidates should have ability to work independently, college courses in field, computer skills, knowledge of field, research skills, writing skills. Duration is 2 months. Unpaid. Open to college freshmen, college sophomores, college juniors, college seniors, recent college graduates, graduate students. International applications accepted.

Benefits Possible full-time employment, willing to complete paperwork for educational credit, willing to provide letters of recommendation.

Contact Write, call, fax, or e-mail Ms. Sue Bechtel, Administrator. Phone: 202-994-7000. Fax: 202-994-7005. E-mail: sbechtel@gwu.edu. Applicants must submit a letter of interest, resume, writing sample. Application deadline: March 15 for summer (suggested), July 15 for fall (suggested), December 1 for spring (suggested). World Wide Web: http://www.gwu.edu/~nsarchiv.

NETWORK IN SOLIDARITY WITH THE PEOPLE OF GUATEMALA
1830 Connecticut Avenue, NW
Washington, District of Columbia 20009

General Information Organization that educates North Americans to work for justice in Guatemala, to support Guatemala's grassroots movement, and to reorient U.S. policy towards Guatemala. Established in 1981. Number of employees: 6. Number of internship applications received each year: 30.

Internships Available ▶ *10–15 human rights monitors:* responsibilities include monitoring human rights in Guatemalan villages and acting as a link to U.S. sister communities. Candidates should have ability to work independently, analytical skills, self-motivation, strong interpersonal skills, strong leadership ability, Spanish speaking ability. Duration is 6–12 months. $250 per month. Open to college freshmen, college sophomores, college juniors, college seniors, recent college graduates, graduate students, law students, career changers, individuals reentering the workforce. ▶ *1 human rights network intern:* responsibilities include alerting individuals, local committees, and national organizations to human rights emergencies in Guatemala and activating network to generate faxes, telexes, and phone calls. Candidates should have ability to work independently, ability to work with others, editing skills, written communication skills. Duration is 1–6 semesters. Unpaid. Open to college sophomores, college juniors, college seniors, recent college graduates, graduate students, law students, career changers, individuals reentering the workforce. ▶ *1–6 legislative work interns:* responsibilities include monitoring U.S. government activity related to Guatemala and promoting grassroots initiatives toward a positive U.S. relationship with Guatemala. Candidates should have analytical skills, computer skills, editing skills, knowledge of field, writing skills. Duration is 1–6 semesters. Unpaid. Open to college freshmen, college sophomores, college juniors, college seniors, recent college graduates, graduate students, career changers, individuals reentering the workforce. ▶ *1–6 solidarity update interns:* responsibilities include preparing the bulletin that provides news, action suggestions, and resources to get involved in supporting the people of Guatemala. Candidates should have analytical skills, computer skills, editing skills, organizational skills, writing skills. Duration is 1–6 semesters. Unpaid. Open to college sophomores, college juniors, college seniors, recent college graduates, graduate students, career changers, individuals reentering the workforce. ▶ *1–2 tour interns:* responsibilities include bringing representatives of Guatemala's popular movement to speak to communities across the United States, coordinating national speaking tours, developing promotional resources, tracking and distributing material aid raised (fall only). Candidates should have computer skills, knowledge of field, office skills, oral communication skills, organizational skills, written communication skills. Duration is August to December. Unpaid. Open to college freshmen, college sophomores, college juniors, college seniors, recent college graduates, graduate students.

Benefits Names of contacts, on-the-job training, opportunity to attend seminars/workshops, travel reimbursement, willing to act as a professional reference, willing to complete paperwork for educational credit, willing to provide letters of recommendation, additional benefits for human rights monitors (in Guatemala): health insurance, free housing, free meals, formal training.
International Internships Available in Guatemala.
Contact Write, call, fax, e-mail, or through World Wide Web site Heather Dean, G.A.P. Coordinator. Phone: 202-265-8713. Fax: 202-223-8221. E-mail: nisguagap@igc.org. Telephone interview required. Applicants must submit a formal organization application, resume, writing sample, three personal references. Application deadline: January 2 for February training, May 1 for June training, September 1 for October training. World Wide Web: http://www.nisgua.org.

NEW YORK COMMITTEE FOR OCCUPATIONAL SAFETY AND HEALTH
275 Seventh Avenue
New York, New York 10001

General Information Organization of labor unions and safety and health activists that provides training programs, educational materials, and technical assistance. Established in 1979. Number of employees: 12. Number of internship applications received each year: 20.
Internships Available ▶ *Interns:* responsibilities include performing duties in the areas of research, legislative work, training, and technical assistance. Candidates should have ability to work independently, computer skills, organizational skills, research skills, self-motivation, written communication skills. Unpaid. Open to college juniors, college seniors, recent college graduates, graduate students.
Benefits Job counseling, names of contacts, opportunity to attend seminars/workshops, possible full-time employment, travel reimbursement, willing to provide letters of recommendation.
Contact Write, call, fax, or e-mail Joel Shufro, Director. Phone: 212-627-3900 Ext. 15. Fax: 212-627-9812. E-mail: jshufro@nycosh.org. In-person interview recommended (telephone interview accepted). Applicants must submit a letter of interest, resume, writing sample, two personal references. Applications are accepted continuously.

NEW YORK UNION SEMESTER, QUEENS COLLEGE
25 West 43rd Street, 19th Floor
New York, New York 10036

General Information Program that provides students with the opportunity to intern with a union for a semester while studying at Queens College. Established in 1999. Number of employees: 1. Unit of Queens College Labor Resource Center, New York, New York. Number of internship applications received each year: 50.
Internships Available ▶ *20–50 interns:* responsibilities include working with unions, typically writing articles for a union newsletter, advocating on behalf of the legal rights of immigrant workers, assisting in anti-sweatshop campaigns, investigating occupational health and safety violations, or working in a community outreach center. Candidates should have ability to work independently, oral communication skills, personal interest in the field, strong interpersonal skills, written communication skills. Duration is August to December. Stipend of $210 per week. Open to college sophomores, college juniors, college seniors, recent college graduates. International applications accepted.
Benefits Formal training, job counseling, names of contacts, on-the-job training, opportunity to attend seminars/workshops, possible full-time employment, tuition assistance, willing to act as a professional reference, willing to complete paperwork for educational credit, willing to provide letters of recommendation.
Contact Write, call, fax, e-mail, or through World Wide Web site Sara Nichols, Program Coordinator, 25 West 43rd Street, 19th Floor, New York, New York 10036. Phone: 212-827-0200. Fax: 212-827-5955. E-mail: unionsemester@qc.edu. Telephone interview required. Applicants must submit a formal organization applica-tion, academic transcripts, three personal references, essay (assigned). Application deadline: June 15. World Wide Web: http://www.qc.edu/unionsemester.

NON-PROFIT HOUSING ASSOCIATION OF NORTHERN CALIFORNIA
369 Pine Street, Suite 350
San Francisco, California 94104

General Information Association of nonprofit housing developers in northern California. Established in 1979. Number of employees: 5. Number of internship applications received each year: 10.
Internships Available ▶ *1 writer/researcher:* responsibilities include researching relevant housing issues such as child development, education, and need for affordable housing, and producing written work on the subject. Candidates should have ability to work independently, analytical skills, college courses in field, computer skills, editing skills, experience in the field, office skills, oral communication skills, organizational skills, plan to pursue career in field, research skills, self-motivation, strong interpersonal skills, writing skills. Duration is dependent upon availability. Position available as unpaid or at a variable stipend. Open to recent college graduates, graduate students. International applications accepted.
Benefits On-the-job training, opportunity to attend seminars/workshops, possible full-time employment, travel reimbursement, willing to act as a professional reference, willing to complete paperwork for educational credit, willing to provide letters of recommendation, commuter benefit.
Contact Write, call, or e-mail Dianne J. Spaulding, Executive Director. Phone: 415-989-8160. Fax: 415-989-8166. E-mail: dianne@nonprofithousing.org. In-person interview required. Applicants must submit a letter of interest, resume. Applications are accepted continuously. World Wide Web: http://www.nonprofithousing.org.

NORTHEAST–MIDWEST INSTITUTE
218 D Street, SE
Washington, District of Columbia 20003

General Information Nonprofit research and public education organization that develops public policy, provides technical assistance, sponsors regional conferences, and distributes publications. Established in 1977. Number of employees: 20. Number of internship applications received each year: 25.
Internships Available ▶ *2 interns:* responsibilities include working in various departments including Brownfields, Energy, Great Lakes/Ecosystems, Smart Growth, Trade and Transportation, and Upper Mississippi. Candidates should have oral communication skills, organizational skills, writing skills. Duration is one summer. Unpaid. International applications accepted.
Benefits Names of contacts, opportunity to attend seminars/workshops, willing to provide letters of recommendation.
Contact Write or fax Heather Lockridge, Administrative Assistant. Fax: 202-544-0043. No phone calls. In-person interview recommended (telephone interview accepted). Applicants must submit a letter of interest, resume, academic transcripts, writing sample. Application deadline: May 1. World Wide Web: http://www.nemw.org.

OHIO LEGISLATIVE SERVICE COMMISSION, RIFFE CENTER FOR GOVERNMENT AND THE ARTS
77 South High Street, 9th Floor
Columbus, Ohio 43215-6136

General Information Non-partisan organization providing the members of the Ohio General Assembly with legal, bill-drafting, research, and other support services. Established in 1953. Number of employees: 135. Unit of Ohio General Assembly, Columbus, Ohio. Number of internship applications received each year: 200.
Internships Available ▶ *27 legislative interns:* responsibilities include providing general staff assistance to elected officials including assisting with constituent work; performing legislative research; writing press releases, newspaper columns, and speeches; attend-

Ohio Legislative Service Commission, Riffe Center for Government and the Arts (continued)

ing committee meetings. Candidates should have ability to work independently, analytical skills, oral communication skills, self-motivation, strong interpersonal skills, written communication skills. Duration is 13 months (December 1 to December 31 of the following year). $24,500–$25,500 per year. ▶ 2 telecommunications interns: responsibilities include working in Ohio State House telecommunications studio; working as production assistants for production of televised legislative sessions and with video production, editing, audio, floor directing, and lighting; and conducting studio tours for the public. Candidates should have college degree in related field, oral communication skills, self-motivation, strong interpersonal skills, written communication skills, video production experience. Duration is 13 months (December 1 to December 31 of the following year). $24,500–$25,500 per year. Open to individuals with at least a bachelor's degree by start of internship. International applications accepted.

Benefits Formal training, health insurance, names of contacts, on-the-job training, opportunity to attend seminars/workshops, possible full-time employment, willing to act as a professional reference, willing to provide letters of recommendation, leave time.

Contact Write, call, e-mail, or through World Wide Web site Rachel Faherty, Internship Coordinator. Phone: 614-466-3615. E-mail: rfaherty@lsc.state.oh.us. In-person interview required. Applicants must submit a formal organization application, resume, academic transcripts, three letters of recommendation, 2-4-page typewritten autobiographical statement. Application deadline: April 15 for legislative positions, May 31 for telecommunications positions. World Wide Web: http://www.lsc.state.oh.us.

PARLIAMENTARY MONITORING GROUP (PMG)
122 Longmarket Street
Cape Town, Western Cape 8001 South Africa

General Information Independent not-for-profit organization that monitors parliamentary committees and provides summary reports of committee meetings on the Internet. Established in 1995. Number of employees: 9. Affiliate of Institute for Democracy in South Africa (IDASA), Cape Town, South Africa. Number of internship applications received each year: 50.

Internships Available ▶ 1 parliamentary monitor: responsibilities include attendance at daily parliamentary committee meeting and writing detailed reports of the proceedings which are published on Web site. Candidates should have ability to work with others, analytical skills, computer skills, personal interest in the field, self-motivation, writing skills. Duration is February to June or August to November. Unpaid. Open to recent college graduates, graduate students, law students. International applications accepted.

Benefits On-the-job training, willing to act as a professional reference, willing to complete paperwork for educational credit, willing to provide letters of recommendation.

International Internships Available.

Contact E-mail Ms. Gaile Moogmann, Managing Editor, 307 Westminster House, 122 Long Market Street, Cape Town 8001 South Africa. Phone: 27-21- 4241816. Fax: 27-21-4241814. E-mail: info@pmg.org.za. Applicants must submit a letter of interest, resume, two letters of recommendation. Applications are accepted continuously. World Wide Web: http://www.pmg.org.za.

PRESBYTERIAN CHURCH (USA), PRESBYTERIAN HISTORICAL SOCIETY
425 Lombard Street
Philadelphia, Pennsylvania 19147-1516

General Information Archives that collect and preserve official records and personal papers of the Presbyterian Church, serve the administrative needs of the Presbyterian Church, and provide access to academic and other researchers. Established in 1852. Number of employees: 25. Unit of Presbyterian Church (USA), Louisville, Kentucky. Number of internship applications received each year: 1.

Internships Available ▶ 1 archives intern: responsibilities include processing archival collections and assisting with reference questions. Candidates should have ability to work independently,

college courses in field, organizational skills, personal interest in the field, research skills, written communication skills. Duration is flexible. Position available as unpaid at $7.50–$9 per hour. Open to college freshmen, college sophomores, college juniors, college seniors, graduate students, career changers. International applications accepted.

Benefits On-the-job training, willing to act as a professional reference, willing to complete paperwork for educational credit, willing to provide letters of recommendation.

Contact Write, fax, or e-mail Margery N. Sly, Deputy Director. Fax: 215-627-0509. E-mail: msly@history.pcusa.org. No phone calls. In-person interview recommended (telephone interview accepted). Applicants must submit a letter of interest, resume, three personal references. Applications are accepted continuously. World Wide Web: http://www.history.pcusa.org.

PUBLIC FORUM INSTITUTE
2300 M Street, NW, Suite 900
Washington, District of Columbia 20037

General Information Nonpartisan, independent public policy group specializing in the development of public forums to debate major issues on the national agenda and maintaining a strong emphasis on social security and budget issues, trade, energy, and economic policy. Established in 1978. Number of employees: 14. Number of internship applications received each year: 200.

Internships Available ▶ 2–4 congressional policy forum interns: responsibilities include researching speakers issued for policy forums, attending congressional hearings, and working on survey reports. Candidates should have ability to work independently, computer skills, organizational skills, personal interest in the field, self-motivation, strong interpersonal skills. Duration is flexible. Unpaid. Open to college freshmen, college sophomores, college juniors, college seniors, individuals reentering the workforce. ▶ 1–2 media associates: responsibilities include reporting to communication director, press conferences, pitching position development, public policy editorial development, and writing press/reporter research. Candidates should have computer skills, plan to pursue career in field, self-motivation, strong interpersonal skills, written communication skills. Duration is 2–3 months. Unpaid. Open to college freshmen, college sophomores, college juniors, college seniors, recent college graduates, graduate students, law students, career changers, individuals reentering the workforce. ▶ 1–2 public affairs associates: responsibilities include working with senior vice president for business development; proposal writing, team presentations, corporate research, and new ideas creation. Candidates should have oral communication skills, plan to pursue career in field, self-motivation, strong interpersonal skills, written communication skills. Duration is 1–3 months. Unpaid. Open to college freshmen, college sophomores, college juniors, college seniors, recent college graduates, graduate students, career changers, business school students. ▶ 4 summer associates: responsibilities include joining a team of 3 professional staff and being fully integrated into the activities of that team; working primarily on national public policy summits. Candidates should have ability to work independently, computer skills, organizational skills, personal interest in the field, self-motivation, strong interpersonal skills. Duration is flexible. Unpaid. Open to college freshmen, college sophomores, college juniors, college seniors, individuals reentering the workforce. ▶ 2–3 summer project associates: responsibilities include public policy event planning for congressional summits on topical issues; grassroots public relations and outreach work (no phone answering/mail handling). Candidates should have computer skills, oral communication skills, organizational skills, self-motivation, strong interpersonal skills. Duration is 2–3 months. Unpaid. Open to college freshmen, college sophomores, college juniors.

Benefits Names of contacts, on-the-job training, opportunity to attend seminars/workshops, possible full-time employment, willing to act as a professional reference, willing to complete paperwork for educational credit, willing to provide letters of recommendation.

Contact Write, e-mail, or through World Wide Web site Anne C. Neel, Vice President of Personnel. E-mail: anne@pfidc.org. No phone calls. In-person interview recommended (telephone interview accepted). Applicants must submit a formal organization application, letter of interest, two personal references. Application deadline: March 31 for summer, August 31 for fall, November 30 for January term, December 31 for spring. World Wide Web: http://www.publicforuminstitute.com.

QUAKER UNITED NATIONS OFFICE
777 United Nations Plaza, 5th Floor
New York, New York 10017

General Information　Organization that represents the world body of the Religious Society of Friends (Quakers) at the United Nations. Established in 1948. Number of employees: 8. Number of internship applications received each year: 65.
Internships Available　▶ *2 interns:* responsibilities include providing program and administrative office support for staff by following the schedule of meetings and stream of documents around the activities of the General Assembly; monitoring, researching, and interpreting one or more substantial issues of interest to intern and QUNO; and assisting with office tasks, including mailings, filing, phones, and assisting visitors. Candidates should have college courses in field, office skills, oral communication skills, organizational skills, personal interest in the field, writing skills. Duration is 1 year. $16,000 per year. Open to recent college graduates. International applications accepted.
Benefits　Health insurance, opportunity to attend seminars/workshops, travel reimbursement, willing to act as a professional reference, willing to provide letters of recommendation, 10 days vacation.
Contact　Write, call, fax, e-mail, or through World Wide Web site Internship Coordinator. Phone: 212-682-2745. Fax: 212-983-0034. E-mail: qunony@pipeline.com. In-person interview recommended (telephone interview accepted). Applicants must submit writing sample, application (available by e-mail), 4 personal references and/or letters of recommendation. Application deadline: February 8. World Wide Web: http://www.quno.org.

REASON PUBLIC POLICY INSTITUTE
3415 South Sepulveda Boulevard, Suite 400
Los Angeles, California 90035

General Information　Public policy research institute/think tank. Number of employees: 20. Division of Reason Foundation, Los Angeles, California. Number of internship applications received each year: 150.
Internships Available　▶ *1–5 policy interns:* responsibilities include research, writing, analyzing policy issues. Candidates should have ability to work independently, analytical skills, oral communication skills, research skills, self-motivation, writing skills. Duration is flexible. Position available as unpaid or at $1000–$5000. Open to college seniors, recent college graduates, graduate students, law students. International applications accepted.
Benefits　Formal training, possible full-time employment, willing to act as a professional reference, willing to complete paperwork for educational credit, willing to provide letters of recommendation, publications.
Contact　Fax or e-mail Geoff Segal, Policy Analyst. Fax: 310-391-4395. E-mail: gsegal@rppi.org. No phone calls. In-person interview recommended (telephone interview accepted). Applicants must submit a letter of interest, resume, 2 or 3 writing samples. Applications are accepted continuously. World Wide Web: http://www.rppi.org.

REPORTERS COMMITTEE FOR FREEDOM OF THE PRESS
1815 North Fort Myer Drive, Suite 900
Arlington, Virginia 22209

General Information　Organization that helps reporters around the country gather and cover the news and advises them about First Amendment and freedom of information rights. Established in 1970. Number of employees: 10. Number of internship applications received each year: 75.
Internships Available　▶ *1 journalism intern (broadcast):* responsibilities include covering media law issues that affect broadcasters such as cameras in courtrooms. Part-time applicants will be considered. Duration is 1 semester. Unpaid. ▶ *1 journalism intern (news gathering):* responsibilities include assisting in editing publications, covering legal issues that involve journalists but do not fall within traditional media law categories, and covering legal problems encountered by American journalists abroad. Duration is flexible. Unpaid. Open to college juniors, college seniors, recent college graduates, graduate students, law students, career changers. Candidates for all positions should have editing skills, personal interest in the field, self-motivation, strong interpersonal skills, writing skills. International applications accepted.
Benefits　Formal training, on-the-job training, opportunity to attend seminars/workshops, willing to act as a professional reference, willing to complete paperwork for educational credit, willing to provide letters of recommendation, stipend available.
Contact　Write, call, or e-mail Ms. Rebecca Daugherty, Internship Coordinator. Phone: 703-807-2100. E-mail: rcfp@rcfp.org. Applicants must submit a letter of interest, resume, writing sample. Application deadline: January 31 for summer, March 31 for fall, October 31 for winter/spring. World Wide Web: http://www.rcfp.org.

ROBERT BOSCH FOUNDATION FELLOWSHIP PROGRAM, CDS INTERNATIONAL, INC.
871 United Nations Plaza, 15th Floor
New York, New York 10017

General Information　Fellowship program in Germany for American citizens in the fields of business, economics, journalism, law, mass communications, political science, and public affairs/public policy. Established in 1968. Number of employees: 23. Number of internship applications received each year: 130.
Internships Available　▶ *20 executive level interns:* responsibilities include performing various duties dependent upon field of specialization. Candidates should have ability to work independently, analytical skills, experience in the field, oral communication skills, personal interest in the field, strong leadership ability. Duration is 6–12 months. Paid. Open to recent college graduates, graduate students, law students.
Benefits　Health insurance, opportunity to attend seminars/workshops, travel reimbursement, tuition assistance, German language training; stipend of 1800 euros per month.
International Internships　Available in Germany.
Contact　Through World Wide Web site Mr. Martin Black, Program Officer. Phone: 212-497-3518. Fax: 212-497-3535. E-mail: mblack@cdsintl.org. In-person interview required. Applicants must submit a formal organization application, letter of interest, resume, academic transcripts, two letters of recommendation, statement of purpose. Application deadline: October 15 for September of the following year. World Wide Web: http://www.cdsintl.org.

SEARCH FOR COMMON GROUND
1601 Connecticut Avenue, NW, Suite 200
Washington, District of Columbia 20009

General Information　Nonprofit organization that specializes in domestic and international conflict resolution. Established in 1982. Number of employees: 60. Number of internship applications received each year: 500.
Internships Available　▶ *5–10 interns:* responsibilities include planning conferences; making travel arrangements; administrative support; and researching, writing, editing, and proofreading on any of the following programs: Search for Common Ground in Macedonia, Burundi, Angola, Democratic Republic of Congo, the Middle East, Ukraine, West Africa, or U.S.; Common Ground Productions, arts and culture, communications, Web editing. Candidates should have editing skills, office skills, oral communication skills, organizational skills, personal interest in the field, research skills, self-motivation, strong interpersonal skills, writing skills, experience living in a mentioned international area or speaking its language is helpful. Duration is 3–4 months. Unpaid. Open to college freshmen, college sophomores, college juniors, college seniors, recent college graduates, graduate students, career changers. International applications accepted.
Benefits　Names of contacts, on-the-job training, opportunity to attend seminars/workshops, possible full-time employment, travel

Search for Common Ground (continued)
reimbursement, willing to complete paperwork for educational credit, willing to provide letters of recommendation.
International Internships Available in Brussels, Belgium.
Contact Write, fax, e-mail, or through World Wide Web site Nancy Toubia, Human Resources Generalist. Fax: 202-232-6718. E-mail: search@sfcg.org. No phone calls. In-person interview recommended (telephone interview accepted). Applicants must submit a letter of interest, resume, two writing samples. Application deadline: February 1 for summer, April 1 for fall, September 1 for spring. World Wide Web: http://www.sfcg.org.

SHORE FACTS MARKETING RESEARCH
PO Box 1759
Ocean City, Maryland 21843

General Information Firm that provides market research for clients in resort retail industries by using psychographic and demographic data, focus group interviews, videotape analysis, and extensive mail and personal interviews. Established in 1987. Number of employees: 5. Number of internship applications received each year: 65.
Internships Available ▶ *2 Internet researchers:* responsibilities include using the Web to conduct research. Candidates should have ability to work independently, ability to work with others, computer skills, personal interest in the field, research skills, self-motivation. Duration is flexible. Unpaid. Open to high school seniors, recent high school graduates, college freshmen, college sophomores, college juniors, college seniors, recent college graduates, graduate students, law students, career changers, individuals reentering the workforce. ▶ *2 administrative assistants:* responsibilities include working with small business owner to facilitate running of market research firm. Candidates should have ability to work independently, organizational skills, personal interest in the field, self-motivation, strong interpersonal skills. Duration is flexible. Unpaid. Open to high school seniors, recent high school graduates, college freshmen, college sophomores, college juniors, college seniors, recent college graduates, graduate students, law students, career changers, individuals reentering the workforce. ▶ *3 computer analysis interns:* responsibilities include collecting, processing, and interpreting market research data on IBM and Macintosh computers. Candidates should have ability to work independently, ability to work with others, computer skills, oral communication skills, personal interest in the field, self-motivation. Duration is flexible. Unpaid. Open to high school seniors, recent high school graduates, college freshmen, college sophomores, college juniors, college seniors, recent college graduates, graduate students, law students, career changers, individuals reentering the workforce. ▶ *4 interviewers:* responsibilities include interviewing subjects on a variety of research topics and writing summations of the findings. Candidates should have ability to work independently, oral communication skills, research skills, self-motivation, strong interpersonal skills. Duration is flexible. Unpaid. Open to college freshmen, college sophomores, college juniors, college seniors, recent college graduates, graduate students, law students, career changers. ▶ *1–2 management major interns:* responsibilities include organizing and structuring work flow at busy market research firm. Candidates should have office skills, oral communication skills, organizational skills, personal interest in the field, strong interpersonal skills. Duration is flexible. Unpaid. Open to college freshmen, college sophomores, college juniors, college seniors, recent college graduates, graduate students, law students, career changers, individuals reentering the workforce. ▶ *2–3 videographers:* responsibilities include videotaping market research sessions and editing film. Candidates should have ability to work independently, ability to work with others, knowledge of field, personal interest in the field, self-motivation, video skills. Duration is flexible. Unpaid. Open to high school seniors, recent high school graduates, college freshmen, college sophomores, college juniors, college seniors, recent college graduates, graduate students, law students, career changers, individuals reentering the workforce. International applications accepted.
Benefits Formal training, job counseling, names of contacts, opportunity to attend seminars/workshops, willing to act as a

professional reference, willing to complete paperwork for educational credit, willing to provide letters of recommendation, health club membership.
Contact Write, call, or fax Mr. Paul D. Jankovic, Owner/Publisher. Phone: 410-524-5351. Fax: 302-539-1232. E-mail: ecprg@aol.com. Applicants must submit a letter of interest, resume. Applications are accepted continuously. World Wide Web: http://www.ecusa.com.

SOCIALIST PARTY USA
339 Lafayette Street, Room 303
New York, New York 11001

General Information Political party. Established in 1901. Number of employees: 3. Number of internship applications received each year: 15.
Internships Available ▶ *1–2 campaign clearinghouse interns:* responsibilities include press relations, fund-raising, light paperwork; will provide on-the-spot training. Candidates should have office skills, oral communication skills, personal interest in the field, self-motivation, strong leadership ability, written communication skills. Duration is one summer or semester. Unpaid. Open to high school students, college freshmen, college sophomores, college juniors, college seniors, graduate students.
Benefits Free meals, opportunity to attend seminars/workshops, travel reimbursement, willing to complete paperwork for educational credit, willing to provide letters of recommendation.
Contact Write, call, fax, e-mail, or through World Wide Web site Greg Pason, National Secretary. Phone: 212-982-4586. Fax: 212-982-4586. E-mail: natsec@sp-usa.org. In-person interview recommended (telephone interview accepted). Applicants must submit a letter of interest. Applications are accepted continuously. World Wide Web: http://www.votesocialist.org.

SOCIETY FOR INTERNATIONAL DEVELOPMENT–WASHINGTON CHAPTER
1875 Connecticut Avenue, NW, Suite 720
Washington, District of Columbia 20009-5728

General Information Nonpolitical, nonprofit membership organization with over 65 chapters around the world providing ways in which those interested in development can exchange ideas, information, and experiences with others. Established in 1957. Number of employees: 5. Unit of Society for International Development International, Rome, Italy. Number of internship applications received each year: 200.
Internships Available ▶ *2–4 interns:* responsibilities include writing for newsletter, serving as liaison with SID work groups, organizing program and events, attending informational and educational programs, promoting SID among prospective members, and assisting with general office duties. Candidates should have oral communication skills, strong interpersonal skills, writing skills. Duration is 1 semester. Unpaid. Open to college sophomores, college juniors, college seniors, recent college graduates, graduate students. International applications accepted.
Benefits Names of contacts, opportunity to attend seminars/workshops, willing to complete paperwork for educational credit, willing to provide letters of recommendation.
Contact Write, call, fax, or e-mail Alina Zyszkowski, Executive Director. Phone: 202-884-8590. Fax: 202-884-8499. E-mail: sid@aed.org. In-person interview recommended (telephone interview accepted). Applicants must submit a resume, writing sample, three personal references. Applications are accepted continuously. World Wide Web: http://www.sidw.org.

SPORTING GOODS MANUFACTURERS ASSOCIATION
1150 17th Street, NW, Suite 407
Washington, District of Columbia 20036

General Information Trade association that promotes sports participation for all people and fosters sports products industry growth. Established in 1906. Number of employees: 4. Number of internship applications received each year: 15.
Internships Available ▶ *1 intern:* responsibilities include performing legislative research, attending congressional hearings, handling

oral and written public inquiries, and event planning. Candidates should have ability to work independently, ability to work with others, computer skills, knowledge of field, office skills, oral communication skills, writing skills. Duration is 2–5 months. Paid. Open to college sophomores, college juniors, college seniors.
Benefits Opportunity to attend seminars/workshops, travel reimbursement, willing to complete paperwork for educational credit, willing to provide letters of recommendation.
Contact Write, call, or fax John Loving, Manager of Government Relations. Phone: 202-775-1762. Fax: 202-296-7462. In-person interview recommended (telephone interview accepted). Applicants must submit a resume, cover letter. Applications are accepted continuously. World Wide Web: http://www.sgma.com.

TIBET JUSTICE CENTER
2288 Fulton #312
Berkeley, California 94704

General Information Nonprofit membership group promoting self-determination for the Tibetan people and advocating human rights, environmental protection, and peaceful resolution through legal research, analysis, and education. Established in 1989. Number of employees: 2. Number of internship applications received each year: 30.
Internships Available ▶ *Interns:* responsibilities include general organizational assistance, research, writing, and editing. Candidates should have ability to work independently, organizational skills, personal interest in the field, research skills, writing skills. Duration is flexible; full time in summer, part time during school semester. Unpaid. Open to college freshmen, college sophomores, college juniors, college seniors, recent college graduates, graduate students, law students. International applications accepted.
Benefits Job counseling, names of contacts, willing to act as a professional reference, willing to complete paperwork for educational credit, willing to provide letters of recommendation.
Contact Write, call, fax, or e-mail Minnie Cancellaro, Executive Director. Phone: 510-486-0588. Fax: 510-548-3785. E-mail: minnie@tibetjustice.org. In-person interview recommended (telephone interview accepted). Applicants must submit a resume, 1 writing sample (optional). Applications are accepted continuously. World Wide Web: http://www.tibetjustice.org.

TUITION PAINTERS
1201 Braddock Place, Suite 605
Alexandria, Virginia 22314

General Information Entrepreneurial development company. Established in 1996. Number of employees: 200. Number of internship applications received each year: 1,000.
Internships Available ▶ *80–150 management/marketing interns:* responsibilities include running own small business, receiving training and support from the company, but bearing responsibility for all marketing and sales, employee management and supervision, and public relations. Candidates should have ability to work independently, oral communication skills, organizational skills, self-motivation, strong interpersonal skills, strong leadership ability. Duration is March to August. Salary commission-based. Open to college freshmen, college sophomores, college juniors.
Benefits Formal training, job counseling, names of contacts, on-the-job training, opportunity to attend seminars/workshops, possible full-time employment, willing to act as a professional reference, willing to complete paperwork for educational credit, willing to provide letters of recommendation.
Contact Through World Wide Web site Barry Lake, President. Phone: 800-393-4521. Fax: 703-684-3414. E-mail: barrylake2@aol.com. In-person interview required. Application deadline: February 15. World Wide Web: http://www.tuitionpainters.com.

UNITED NATIONS ASSOCIATION OF THE USA
801 2nd Avenue
New York, New York 10017

General Information Nonprofit, nonpartisan, national organization dedicated to strengthening the United Nations system and to enhancing U.S. participation in the UN and other international institutions. Established in 1964. Number of employees:

40. Affiliate of United Nations, New York, New York. Number of internship applications received each year: 200.
Internships Available ▶ *Adopt-A-Minefield interns:* responsibilities include extensive research and writing related to landmines. Candidates should have ability to work independently, computer skills, research skills, written communication skills. Duration is minimum of 6 weeks. Unpaid. Open to college freshmen, college sophomores, college juniors, college seniors, recent college graduates. ▶ *2–4 American NGO Coalition for the International Criminal Court interns:* responsibilities include researching ICC issues in the U.S.; writing reports, briefs, and letters. Candidates should have ability to work independently, personal interest in the field, plan to pursue career in field, research skills, writing skills. Duration is minimum of 6 weeks. Unpaid. Open to college freshmen, college sophomores, college juniors, college seniors, recent college graduates, graduate students, law students. ▶ *2–4 Business Council for the UN interns:* responsibilities include establishing a partnership between the business community and the UN. Candidates should have ability to work independently, computer skills, office skills, oral communication skills, research skills, strong interpersonal skills, writing skills. Duration is minimum of 4 weeks. Unpaid. Open to college freshmen, college sophomores, college juniors, college seniors, recent college graduates, graduate students, individuals reentering the workforce. ▶ *1 Council of Organizations intern:* responsibilities include assisting the liaison of the UNAUSA and performing research. Candidates should have computer skills, office skills, organizational skills, clerical skills. Duration is flexible. Unpaid. Open to college freshmen, college sophomores, college juniors, college seniors. ▶ *1–2 Executive office interns:* responsibilities include providing research and analysis on issues of global significance and preparing materials for meetings and conferences. Candidates should have ability to work independently, ability to work with others, computer skills, office skills, oral communication skills, organizational skills, research skills, writing skills. Duration is minimum of 6 weeks. Unpaid. Open to college seniors, recent college graduates, graduate students. ▶ *1–2 Global Health Initiative interns:* responsibilities include research, writing, preparing outreach, and maintaining Web site. Candidates should have ability to work independently, personal interest in the field, research skills, written communication skills. Duration is minimum of 6 weeks. Unpaid. Open to college juniors, college seniors, recent college graduates, graduate students, career changers, individuals reentering the workforce. ▶ *6 Model UN and education interns:* responsibilities include researching the global issues and the work of the United Nations and adapting this information for use by the public; collecting materials for distribution to chapters, preparing responses to public inquiries, or assisting with outreach programs; researching and writing background papers about international issues; and assisting with the development of international affairs-related programs for youth. Candidates should have ability to work independently, editing skills, oral communication skills, research skills, strong leadership ability, writing skills. Duration is flexible. Unpaid. Open to high school students, recent high school graduates, college freshmen, college sophomores, college juniors, college seniors, recent college graduates, graduate students. ▶ *4 communication department interns:* responsibilities include writing, fact-checking, proofreading, and monitoring new developments in the U.N. Candidates should have computer skills, editing skills, oral communication skills, research skills, strong interpersonal skills, writing skills. Duration is flexible. Unpaid. Open to college freshmen, college sophomores, college juniors, college seniors, recent college graduates, graduate students. ▶ *2–4 development interns:* responsibilities include assisting in identifying potential speakers and guests for chairman's council members and researching and writing profiles of individuals, foundations, and other funding sources. Candidates should have computer skills, oral communication skills, organizational skills, research skills, strong interpersonal skills, written communication skills. Duration is minimum of 6 weeks. Unpaid. Open to college freshmen, college sophomores, college juniors, college seniors, recent college graduates, graduate students. ▶ *2–3 media relations and public affairs interns:* responsibilities include research on U.N. issues; distributing documents and press releases; writing on both internal and external publications. Candidates should have ability to work independently, editing skills, oral communication skills, organizational

United Nations Association of the USA (continued)
skills, personal interest in the field, written communication skills. Duration is minimum of 6 weeks. Unpaid. Open to high school seniors, recent high school graduates, college freshmen, college sophomores, college juniors, college seniors, recent college graduates, graduate students. ▶ *2–4 national membership interns:* responsibilities include assisting with training and support to network of community-based chapters and statewide divisions, especially in areas of board development. fund-raising, and recruitment. Candidates should have ability to work independently, computer skills, office skills, oral communication skills, organizational skills, written communication skills. Duration is flexible. Unpaid. Open to high school seniors, recent high school graduates, college freshmen, college sophomores, college juniors, college seniors, recent college graduates, graduate students. ▶ *4 policy studies department interns:* responsibilities include performing independent research, maintaining correspondence with other organizations, and public outreach. Candidates should have ability to work independently, computer skills, editing skills, oral communication skills, research skills, writing skills. Duration is flexible (20-35 hours per week). Unpaid. Open to college seniors, recent college graduates, graduate students, law students. International applications accepted.
Benefits Opportunity to attend seminars/workshops, willing to act as a professional reference, willing to complete paperwork for educational credit, willing to provide letters of recommendation, U.N. Headquarters passes.
Contact Write or through World Wide Web site Veronica Wayner, Intern Coordinator. No phone calls. Telephone interview required. Applicants must submit a formal organization application, letter of interest, resume, writing sample, two letters of recommendation. Application deadline: March 15 for summer; continuous for other positions. World Wide Web: http://www.unausa.org.

UNITED NATIONS HEADQUARTERS INTERNSHIP PROGRAM, OFFICE OF HUMAN RESOURCES MANAGEMENT
United Nations Secretariat, Room S-2570
New York, New York 10017

General Information Organization that promotes understanding of major problems confronting the world and how the United Nations attempts to find solutions. Established in 1945. Number of employees: 14,000. Number of internship applications received each year: 2,000.
Internships Available ▶ *120 interns:* responsibilities include carrying out an assignment in the department or office of the Secretariat that has selected the intern. Candidates should have analytical skills, computer skills, personal interest in the field, research skills, self-motivation. Duration is 2 months in spring, summer, or fall. Unpaid. Open to law students, graduate students under the age of 30. International applications accepted.
Benefits Meals at a cost, opportunity to attend seminars/workshops, willing to provide letters of recommendation, opportunity to attend meetings.
Contact Write, e-mail, or through World Wide Web site Internship Coordinator, United Nations Secretariat, Room S-2590D, New York, New York 10017. Phone: 212-963-7522. Fax: 212-963-3683. E-mail: ohrm_interns@un.org. Applicants must submit a resume, academic transcripts, 2 copies of formal application in English or French, short essay in English or French stating reason for seeking the internship. Application deadline: four to twelve months prior to start of internship. World Wide Web: http://www.un.org.

UNITED NATIONS POPULATION FUND
220 East 42nd Street, 16th Floor
New York, New York 10017

General Information Nonprofit organization that is part of the UN common system. Established in 1969. Number of employees: 300. Number of internship applications received each year: 60.
Internships Available ▶ *Interns:* responsibilities include working under supervision of senior staff member in multilateral population activities. Candidates should have personal interest in the field, proficiency in English; fluency in French, Spanish or Arabic

a plus. Duration is year-round. Unpaid. Open to individuals with first year master's level degree in social science field with concentration in population studies. International applications accepted.
Benefits On-the-job training, opportunity to attend seminars/workshops, willing to act as a professional reference, willing to provide letters of recommendation.
Contact Write, call, fax, e-mail, or through World Wide Web site Bertha del Carpio, Personnel Assistant, 220 East 42nd Street 16th Floor, New York, New York 10017. Phone: 212-297-5356. Fax: 212-297-4908. E-mail: carpio@unfpa.org. Applicants must submit a formal organization application, letter of interest, resume, proof of medical insurance. Applications are accepted continuously. World Wide Web: http://www.unfpa.org.

THE URBAN INSTITUTE
2100 M Street, NW
Washington, District of Columbia 20037

General Information Private nonprofit, nonpartisan public policy research organization. Established in 1968. Number of employees: 417. Number of internship applications received each year: 500.
Internships Available ▶ *5–15 temporary research assistants:* responsibilities include assisting senior researchers in public policy research, data gathering, literature reviews, telephone survey work, and statistical analyses using a software package such as SAS or SPSS. Candidates should have analytical skills, college courses in field, computer skills, plan to pursue career in field, research skills, writing skills. Duration is flexible. $9–$14 per hour. Open to college freshmen, college sophomores, college juniors, college seniors, graduate students. International applications accepted.
Benefits On-the-job training, opportunity to attend seminars/workshops, possible full-time employment, willing to act as a professional reference, willing to complete paperwork for educational credit, willing to provide letters of recommendation.
Contact Write, fax, e-mail, or through World Wide Web site Irene Marchuk, Internship Coordinator, Human Resources. Fax: 202-887-5189. E-mail: resumes@ui.urban.org. No phone calls. In-person interview recommended (telephone interview accepted). Applicants must submit a formal organization application, letter of interest, resume, academic transcripts, writing sample, three personal references. Applications are accepted continuously. World Wide Web: http://www.urban.org.

U.S. OLYMPIC COMMITTEE
One Olympic Plaza
Colorado Springs, Colorado 80909-5760

General Information Nonprofit sports organization promoting sports in the U.S. and sending teams to the Olympics. Established in 1978. Number of employees: 500. Number of internship applications received each year: 750.
Internships Available ▶ *25 Colorado Springs interns:* responsibilities include working in broadcasting, sports administration, sport science, accounting, journalism and public relations, computer science, or marketing department. Candidates should have ability to work independently, college courses in field, computer skills, knowledge of field, plan to pursue career in field, written communication skills. Duration is 1 semester. Housing, meals, and pay combined equal $8.50 per hour. ▶ *3 Lake Placid interns:* responsibilities include working in sports administration or sport science department. Candidates should have ability to work independently, college courses in field, computer skills, knowledge of field, oral communication skills, plan to pursue career in field, written communication skills. Duration is 1 semester. Housing, meals and pay combined equal $8.50 per hour. ▶ *3 San Diego interns:* responsibilities include working in sports administration or sport science department. Candidates should have ability to work independently, college courses in field, computer skills, knowledge of field, oral communication skills, plan to pursue career in field, written communication skills. Duration is 1 semester. Housing, meals, and pay combined $8.50 per hour. Open to college juniors, college seniors, graduate students.
Benefits On-the-job training, opportunity to attend seminars/workshops, possible full-time employment, willing to complete paperwork for educational credit.

Contact Write, call, fax, or e-mail Manager of Intern Program, One Olympic Plaza, Colorado Springs, Colorado 80909. Phone: 719-632-5551 Ext. 2597. Fax: 719-578-4817. E-mail: internprog@ usoc.org. Telephone interview required. Applicants must submit a formal organization application, letter of interest, resume, 6 writing samples for journalism positions; official academic transcripts (unofficial printouts are not acceptable), up to 3 letters of recommendation. Application deadline: February 15 for summer, June 1 for fall, October 1 for winter/spring. World Wide Web: http://www.usolympicteam.com.

U.S. POULTRY & EGG ASSOCIATION
1530 Cooledge Road
Tucker, Georgia 30084-7303

General Information Organization dedicated to the growth, progress, and welfare of the poultry industry. Established in 1947. Number of employees: 18.
Internships Available ▶ *1 communications intern:* responsibilities include writing press releases, research, designing promotional materials, developing and creating press kits. Candidates should have computer skills, oral communication skills, self-motivation, writing skills, public relations, journalism, or communications major (helpful). Duration is flexible. Position available as unpaid or paid. Open to college freshmen, college sophomores, college juniors, college seniors, recent college graduates, graduate students, individuals reentering the workforce. International applications accepted.
Benefits Names of contacts, on-the-job training, willing to act as a professional reference, willing to complete paperwork for educational credit, willing to provide letters of recommendation.
Contact Write, fax, e-mail, or through World Wide Web site Vice President of Communications. Fax: 770-493-9257. E-mail: promo@ poultryegg.org. No phone calls. Applicants must submit a letter of interest, resume, two writing samples. Applications are accepted continuously. World Wide Web: http://www.poultryegg.org.

U.S. TERM LIMITS
10 G Street, NE, Suite 410
Washington, District of Columbia 20002

General Information Non-partisan issue advocacy organization. Established in 1992. Number of employees: 15. Number of internship applications received each year: 30.
Internships Available ▶ *4–5 interns:* responsibilities include research to USTL's political staff, assistance to media relations director, and some clerical chores including preparing mass mailings. Candidates should have computer skills, oral communication skills, personal interest in the field, research skills, writing skills. Duration is flexible. $800 per month (full-time), $400 per month (part-time). Open to college freshmen, college sophomores, college juniors, college seniors. International applications accepted.
Benefits On-the-job training, opportunity to attend seminars/ workshops, willing to act as a professional reference, willing to complete paperwork for educational credit, willing to provide letters of recommendation.
Contact Write, call, fax, e-mail, or through World Wide Web site Kurt A. Gardinier, Intern Coordinator/Media Relations Director, 10 G Street, NE, Suite 410, Washington, District of Columbia 20002. Phone: 202-379-3000 Ext. 109. Fax: 202-379-3010. E-mail: kagardinier@ustermlimits.org. Applicants must submit a letter of interest, resume, writing sample. Applications are accepted continuously. World Wide Web: http://www.ustermlimits.org.

US-UKRAINE FOUNDATION
733 15th Street, NW, Suite 1026
Washington, District of Columbia 20005

General Information Nonprofit non-governmental organization established to facilitate democratic development, free market reform, and to enhance human rights in the Ukraine. Established in 1991. Number of employees: 13. Number of internship applications received each year: 40.
Internships Available ▶ *1–4 interns:* responsibilities include reporting on congressional hearings and other events, Web site maintenance, office management, and program support; other responsibilities depend upon interests and skills of intern. Candidates should have ability to work with others, computer skills, office skills, personal interest in the field, self-motivation, written communication skills. Duration is flexible (usually one summer or one semester). Unpaid. Open to college freshmen, college sophomores, college juniors, college seniors, recent college graduates, graduate students, law students, career changers. International applications accepted.
Benefits On-the-job training, opportunity to attend seminars/ workshops, willing to act as a professional reference, willing to complete paperwork for educational credit, willing to provide letters of recommendation.
Contact Write, fax, e-mail, or through World Wide Web site Motrya Mac, Intern Coordinator, 733 15th Street, NW, Suite 1026, Washington, District of Columbia 20005. Fax: 202-347-4267. E-mail: usuf@usukraine.org. No phone calls. In-person interview recommended (telephone interview accepted). Applicants must submit a letter of interest, resume. Applications are accepted continuously. World Wide Web: http://www.usukraine.org.

VAULT
150 West 22nd Street
New York, New York 10011

General Information Career services firm. Established in 1996. Number of employees: 40. Number of internship applications received each year: 600.
Internships Available ▶ *5–7 content summer associates:* responsibilities include working on various business-oriented writing projects; some research is also required. Candidates should have ability to work with others, computer skills, organizational skills, research skills, writing skills. Position available as unpaid or paid. Open to college freshmen, college sophomores, college juniors, college seniors, recent college graduates, graduate students, law students. International applications accepted.
Benefits Names of contacts, on-the-job training, possible full-time employment, travel reimbursement, willing to act as a professional reference, willing to complete paperwork for educational credit, willing to provide letters of recommendation.
Contact Write, call, fax, or e-mail Mary Lerner, Director of Content. Phone: 212-366-4212. Fax: 212-366-6117. E-mail: mlerner@ staff.vault.com. In-person interview required. Applicants must submit a letter of interest, resume. Applications are accepted continuously. World Wide Web: http://www.vault.com.

VIA
PO Box 20266
Stanford, California 94309

General Information Private, nonprofit, nonsectarian organization dedicated to increasing understanding between the United States and Asia. Established in 1963. Number of employees: 10. Number of internship applications received each year: 40.
Internships Available ▶ *2–4 volunteer English resources in Indonesia:* responsibilities include assisting non-government organization, editing brochures and periodicals in English, providing English language support to the organization. Candidates should have ability to work independently, ability to work with others, experience in the field, personal interest in the field, self-motivation. Duration is 1–2 years. Living stipend varies by post. Open to recent college graduates, graduate students, career changers, must have bachelor's degree. ▶ *20–30 volunteer English teachers in Asia:* responsibilities include teaching English language instruction at university level to government officials, social science researchers, students in schools for the handicapped, and at orphanages. Candidates should have ability to work independently, ability to work with others, personal interest in the field, self-motivation, at least one course in language of host country, ESL training. Duration is 1–2 years. Living stipend varies by post. Open to recent college graduates, career changers, must have bachelor's degree. International applications accepted.
Benefits Formal training, health insurance, possible full-time employment, willing to provide letters of recommendation, scholarships to cover participation fee, transportation to host country, stipend to cover cost of living including room and board.

VIA (continued)

International Internships Available in China; Indonesia; Lao People's Democratic Republic; Viet Nam.
Contact Write, call, fax, e-mail, or through World Wide Web site Ann Le, Program Director. Phone: 650-723-3228. Fax: 650-725-1805. E-mail: info@viaprograms.org. In-person interview required. Applicants must submit a formal organization application, participation fee upon acceptance of $1350 for 1 year, $950 for 2 years, participation in training program in San Francisco and on Internet. Application deadline: February 15 for June/July departure. World Wide Web: http://www.viaprograms.org.

VISIONS IN ACTION
2710 Ontario Road, NW
Washington, District of Columbia 20009

General Information Nonprofit organization that places volunteers with other nonprofit organizations, development organizations, research institutes, health centers, and the progressive press in the countries of Uganda, Tanzania, South Africa, Zimbabwe, and Mexico. Established in 1988. Number of employees: 8. Number of internship applications received each year: 100.
Internships Available ▶ *10–20 Mexico summer program volunteers:* responsibilities include participation in group project supporting local community development efforts in the state of Oaxaca; participation in various learning and cultural activities in Oaxaca and Chiapas. Candidates should have ability to work with others, personal interest in the field. Duration is seven to nine weeks (mid-June to mid-August). Unpaid. Open to high school seniors, recent high school graduates, college freshmen, college sophomores, college juniors, college seniors, recent college graduates, graduate students, law students, career changers, individuals reentering the workforce, must be 18 years of age or older. ▶ *10–20 Tanzania summer program volunteers:* responsibilities include participation in a group project involving appropriate technology, learning how to build solar cookers, biogas systems, and participation in a five-day safari to the Serengeti and Ngorongoro Crater. Candidates should have ability to work with others, personal interest in the field. Duration is seven to nine weeks (mid-June to mid-August). Unpaid. Open to high school seniors, recent high school graduates, college freshmen, college sophomores, college juniors, college seniors, recent college graduates, graduate students, law students, career changers, individuals reentering the workforce, must be 18 years of age or older. ▶ *20–30 U.S. office interns:* responsibilities include working in areas of recruitment, international administration, public relations, finance, fund-raising, research, Internet, newsletter, or conference organizing. Candidates should have computer skills, office skills, oral communication skills, organizational skills, research skills, written communication skills. Duration is 3 months. Unpaid. Open to college freshmen, college sophomores, college juniors, college seniors, recent college graduates, graduate students, law students, career changers, individuals reentering the workforce. ▶ *50–100 community development workers:* responsibilities include working with communities in low-income areas. Candidates should have oral communication skills, organizational skills, personal interest in the field, strong interpersonal skills, written communication skills. Duration is 6–12 months. Unpaid. Open to college juniors, college seniors, recent college graduates, graduate students, law students, career changers. ▶ *10–20 democratization trainers/election monitors:* responsibilities include training voters on their rights and voting procedures, monitoring elections, leading voting workshops, and observing ballot counting. Candidates should have analytical skills, oral communication skills, organizational skills, personal interest in the field, strong interpersonal skills, written communication skills. Duration is 6–12 months. Unpaid. Open to college juniors, college seniors, recent college graduates, graduate students, law students, career changers. ▶ *30–60 health professionals:* responsibilities include working in a clinic, lab, or hospital. Candidates should have analytical skills, knowledge of field, personal interest in the field, strong interpersonal skills. Duration is 6–12 months. Unpaid. Open to college juniors, college seniors, recent college graduates, graduate students, law students, career changers. ▶ *30–60 journalists:* responsibilities include working for a newspaper, magazine, or radio/television station. Candidates should have abil-

ity to work independently, knowledge of field, oral communication skills, research skills, written communication skills. Duration is 6–12 months. Unpaid. Open to college juniors, college seniors, recent college graduates, graduate students, law students, career changers. ▶ *10–20 microfinance specialists:* responsibilities include working with local microfinance institutions providing small loans for income-generating projects. Candidates should have computer skills, experience in the field, office skills, strong leadership ability. Duration is 1–2 years. Unpaid. Open to recent college graduates, graduate students, law students. ▶ *50–100 program assistants:* responsibilities include writing, research, administration and organizing office-based assistance in areas of human rights, environment, children, women, housing, social work, or democratization. Candidates should have ability to work with others, computer skills, office skills, oral communication skills, personal interest in the field, written communication skills. Duration is 6–12 months. Unpaid. Open to college juniors, college seniors, recent college graduates, graduate students, law students, career changers. ▶ *40–80 project managers:* responsibilities include managing rural and urban development projects. Candidates should have knowledge of field, oral communication skills, organizational skills, strong leadership ability, written communication skills. Duration is 6–12 months. Unpaid. Open to college juniors, college seniors, recent college graduates, graduate students, law students, career changers. ▶ *40–80 public health educators:* responsibilities include performing research, educating, and designing communication material. Candidates should have office skills, oral communication skills, personal interest in the field, strong interpersonal skills, written communication skills. Duration is 6–12 months. Unpaid. Open to college juniors, college seniors, recent college graduates, graduate students, law students, career changers. ▶ *40–80 researchers:* responsibilities include assisting with research in either a natural or social science discipline. Candidates should have analytical skills, computer skills, office skills, research skills, writing skills. Duration is 6–12 months. Unpaid. Open to college juniors, college seniors, recent college graduates, graduate students, law students, career changers. ▶ *30–60 youth group coordinators:* responsibilities include leading community service projects, sports, and vocational training. Candidates should have ability to work with others, oral communication skills, organizational skills, personal interest in the field, self-motivation, strong leadership ability. Duration is 6–12 months. Unpaid. Open to college juniors, college seniors, recent college graduates, graduate students, law students, career changers. International applications accepted.
Benefits Formal training, job counseling, names of contacts, on-the-job training, opportunity to attend seminars/workshops, possible full-time employment, willing to act as a professional reference, willing to complete paperwork for educational credit, willing to provide letters of recommendation, monthly stipend of $50–$100 for international placements.
International Internships Available in Mexico; South Africa; Uganda; United Republic of Tanzania; Zimbabwe.
Contact Write, call, fax, e-mail, or through World Wide Web site Program Coordinator. Phone: 202-625-7402. Fax: 202-588-9344. E-mail: visions@igc.org. Telephone interview required. Applicants must submit a formal organization application, resume, two letters of recommendation. Application deadline: April 1 for July 10th departure (South Africa, Mexico, Tanzania), April 1 for Tanzania and Mexico 7-9 week summer programs, June 1 for September 1st departure (Uganda), October 1 for January 10th departure (South Africa, Zimbabwe, Mexico). Fees: $45. World Wide Web: http://www.visionsinaction.org.

THE WINANT AND CLAYTON VOLUNTEERS, INC.
109 East 50th Street
New York, New York 10022

General Information International reciprocal exchange program between the U.S. and the U.K. Established in 1948. Number of employees: 1. Affiliate of St. Bartholomew's Church, New York, New York. Number of internship applications received each year: 75.
Internships Available ▶ *20 volunteers:* responsibilities include working in youth clubs, centers for the homeless, rehabilitation and drug-crisis centers, programs for the elderly, and early child-

hood day care. Candidates should have ability to work independently, oral communication skills, self-motivation, strong interpersonal skills, strong leadership ability, maturity and flexibility. Duration is 9 weeks (7 weeks volunteering; 2 weeks independent travel). Unpaid. Open to U.S. citizens 18 or older.

Benefits Free housing, 2 weeks independent travel, opportunity to see United Kingdom and live and work in another culture, small stipend available (paid in British pounds); applicant is responsible for airfare.

International Internships Available in United Kingdom.

Contact Write, call, or fax Ms. Nanette Rousseau, Coordinator of Volunteers. Phone: 212-378-0271. Fax: 212-378-0281. In-person interview recommended (telephone interview accepted). Applicants must submit a formal organization application, letter of interest, resume, two writing samples, five personal references. Application deadline: January 31 for summer. Fees: $35.

WOMEN'S CAMPAIGN FUND
734 15th Street, Suite 500
Washington, District of Columbia 20005

General Information Political action committee. Established in 1974. Number of employees: 4. Number of internship applications received each year: 75.

Internships Available ▶ *1 communications intern:* responsibilities include political research and writing, developing and updating the Web page, writing press releases, and providing follow-up to media contacts. Candidates should have computer skills, editing skills, office skills, oral communication skills, plan to pursue career in field, research skills, self-motivation, written communication skills. Duration is 3 months. Unpaid. Open to college freshmen, college sophomores, college juniors, college seniors, recent college graduates, graduate students, law students. ▶ *1–2 development interns:* responsibilities include assisting development department with all aspects of fund-raising, including event planning and high donor solicitation, maintaining and updating contributor lists and databases, and processing of contributions. Candidates should have computer skills, office skills, organizational skills, personal interest in the field, strong interpersonal skills, written communication skills. Duration is 3 months. Unpaid. Open to college freshmen, college sophomores, college juniors, college seniors, recent college graduates. ▶ *3–4 political interns:* responsibilities include political research and tracking, event planning, list development for candidate fund-raising activities, and providing administrative support. Candidates should have ability to work independently, ability to work with others, office skills, oral communication skills, personal interest in the field, writing skills. Duration is 3 months. Unpaid. Open to college freshmen, college sophomores, college juniors, college seniors, recent college graduates, graduate students, law students. International applications accepted.

Benefits On-the-job training, possible full-time employment, willing to act as a professional reference, willing to complete paperwork for educational credit, willing to provide letters of recommendation.

Contact Write, call, fax, or e-mail Monica Cash, Office Manager, 734 15th Street, Suite 500, Washington, District of Columbia 20005. Phone: 202-393-8164. Fax: 202-393-0649. E-mail: monica@wcfonline.org. In-person interview recommended (telephone interview accepted). Applicants must submit a letter of interest, resume, personal reference. Applications are accepted continuously. World Wide Web: http://www.wcfonline.org.

WOMEN'S INSTITUTE FOR FREEDOM OF THE PRESS
1940 Calvert Street, NW
Washington, District of Columbia 20009-1502

General Information Institute dedicated to researching and publishing new ideas and perspectives on expanding the communications system to make it more democratic, especially to increase the communication of women with each other and with the general public. Established in 1972. Number of employees: 1. Number of internship applications received each year: 12.

Internships Available ▶ *2 archives interns:* responsibilities include categorizing historic women's papers for research. Candidates should have ability to work independently, analytical, organizational skills, personal interest in the field, written communication skills. Duration is flexible. Unpaid. Open to high school students, recent high school graduates, college freshmen, college sophomores, college juniors, college seniors, recent college graduates, graduate students, law students, career changers, individuals reentering the workforce. ▶ *2–4 computer/online specialists:* responsibilities include surveying current uses of electronic communications for women's issues and equality, including management of Web site and new uses of computer video and audio. Candidates should have ability to work independently, analytical skills, computer skills, knowledge of field, organizational skills, personal interest in the field. Duration is flexible. Unpaid. Open to high school students, recent high school graduates, college freshmen, college sophomores, college juniors, college seniors, recent college graduates, graduate students, law students, career changers, individuals reentering the workforce, computer technologists. ▶ *1–2 editors:* responsibilities include editing an issue of associates newsletter. Candidates should have ability to work independently, computer skills, editing skills, personal interest in the field, self-motivation, writing skills. Duration is flexible. Unpaid. Open to high school students, recent high school graduates, college freshmen, college sophomores, college juniors, recent college graduates, graduate students, law students, career changers, individuals reentering the workforce. ▶ *2–4 organizational liaisons:* responsibilities include acting as WIFP liaison with other women's groups and media change/democracy organizations; attending meetings, conferences, and press conferences. Candidates should have ability to work independently, computer skills, editing skills, personal interest in the field, self-motivation, writing skills. Duration is flexible. Unpaid. Open to high school students, recent high school graduates, college freshmen, college sophomores, college juniors, college seniors, recent college graduates, graduate students, law students, career changers, individuals reentering the workforce. ▶ *1–5 writers:* responsibilities include writing articles on WIFP work and ongoing projects. Candidates should have analytical skills, organizational skills, personal interest in the field, self-motivation, written communication skills. Duration is flexible. Unpaid. Open to high school students, recent high school graduates, college freshmen, college sophomores, college juniors, college seniors, recent college graduates, graduate students, law students, career changers, individuals reentering the workforce. International applications accepted.

Benefits Opportunity to attend seminars/workshops, willing to act as a professional reference, willing to complete paperwork for educational credit, willing to provide letters of recommendation.

Contact Write, e-mail, or through World Wide Web site Dr. Martha Leslie Allen, Director. Fax: 202-986-6355. E-mail: director@wifp.org. No phone calls. Applicants must submit a letter of interest, resume. Applications are accepted continuously. World Wide Web: http://www.wifp.org.

WOMEN'S POLICY, INC.
409 12th Street, SW, Suite 310
Washington, District of Columbia 20024

General Information Public policy research and publications organization that monitors congressional action affecting women and children. Established in 1995. Number of employees: 5. Affiliate of The George Washington University, Washington, District of Columbia. Number of internship applications received each year: 30.

Internships Available ▶ *2 interns:* responsibilities include attending congressional hearings, writing articles and fact sheets, other duties associated with newsletter publications, and miscellaneous clerical duties. Candidates should have ability to work independently, ability to work with others, analytical skills, computer skills, office skills, oral communication skills, organizational skills, research skills, written communication skills. Duration is flexible. Unpaid. Open to college sophomores, college juniors, college seniors, recent college graduates, graduate students.

Benefits Names of contacts, on-the-job training, opportunity to attend seminars/workshops, willing to act as a professional refer-

Women's Policy, Inc. (continued)

ence, willing to complete paperwork for educational credit, willing to provide letters of recommendation, opportunity to attend projects and events with congressional caucus for women's issues. **Contact** Write, call, fax, e-mail, or through World Wide Web site Mary Anne Leary, Internship Coordinator, 409 12th Street, SW, Suite 310, Washington, District of Columbia 20024. Phone: 202-554-2323. Fax: 202-554-2346. E-mail: webmaster@womenspolicy. org. In-person interview recommended (telephone interview accepted). Applicants must submit a letter of interest, resume, writing sample, three personal references, telephone interview recommended. Application deadline: April 1 for summer, August 1 for fall, November 15 for winter/spring. World Wide Web: http://www.womenspolicy.org.

WORLD AFFAIRS COUNCILS OF AMERICA
1800 K Street, Suite 1014
Washington, District of Columbia 20006

General Information Nongovernmental, nonprofit, nonpartisan organization composed of over 80 independent world affairs councils and affiliated educational institutions located throughout the U.S. whose purpose is to improve the quality of citizen education in international affairs. Established in 1960. Number of employees: 3. Number of internship applications received each year: 25.

Internships Available ▶ *1 general intern:* responsibilities include locating speakers on a wide range of topics connected with world affairs (foreign policy, environmental issues, and defense), maintaining records on World Affairs Councils and updating information on an ongoing basis, handling telephone inquiries regarding the work of the WACs, and updating the database of information, embassies, and think tanks. Candidates should have ability to work with others, computer skills, editing skills, organizational skills, personal interest in the field, writing skills. Duration is one semester or summer. Unpaid. Open to college sophomores, college juniors, college seniors.
Benefits Job counseling, names of contacts, willing to complete paperwork for educational credit, willing to provide letters of recommendation.
Contact Write, call, or e-mail Francesca Martonffy, Internship Coordinator. Phone: 202-833-4557. Fax: 202-833-4555. E-mail: ncwao@aol.com. Applicants must submit a letter of interest, resume, writing sample. Applications are accepted continuously. World Wide Web: http://www.worldaffairscouncils.org.

WORLD FEDERALIST ASSOCIATION
418 7th Street, SE
Washington, District of Columbia 20003

General Information Organization working to transform the United Nations into a democratic world federation capable of protecting the environment, abolishing war, and protecting human rights. Established in 1947. Number of employees: 13. Number of internship applications received each year: 100.
Internships Available ▶ *1 alternative advocacy intern:* responsibilities include involvement with grassroots community relations; congressional relations; media relations; information, education, and outreach; advocacy network support. Candidates should have oral communication skills, written communication skills, background in international issues and legislative affairs (desirable). Duration is minimum of 2 months (preferred); 3 months for summer. $10 per day. ▶ *1 environmental advocacy interns:* responsibilities include research, NGO and other meetings, and some communications work; working with grassroots outreach program. Candidates should have oral communication skills, written communication skills. Duration is minimum of 2 months (preferred); 3 months for summer. $10 per day. ▶ *2 grassroots organizing and campus outreach interns:* responsibilities include assisting with writing and research of field materials; organizing numbers of activist program on media and legislative work; assisting in selecting districts to target for organizing and advocacy. Candidates should have oral communication skills, personal interest in the field, written communication skills, background in international issues (preferred). Duration is minimum of 2 months (preferred); 3

months for summer. $10 per day. ▶ *1 media and public relations interns:* responsibilities include updating national Web site; reviewing developments reported by major news outlets. Candidates should have personal interest in the field, written communication skills. Duration is minimum of 2 months (preferred); 3 months for summer. $10 per day. ▶ *1 online marketing and foundations outreach interns:* responsibilities include traveling to DC Foundation Center for training and research; helping select direct marketing mailing lists; and assisting with writing of grant proposals. Candidates should have oral communication skills, written communication skills. Duration is minimum of 2 months (preferred); 3 months for summer . $10 per day. ▶ *2 research and legislative interns:* responsibilities include research, writing briefs and fact sheets, updating Web pages, calling congressional offices, participating in lobby visits, and attending and summarizing meetings. Candidates should have research skills, writing skills. Duration is minimum of 2 months (preferred); 3 months for summer. $10 per day. Open to college freshmen, college sophomores, college juniors, college seniors, recent college graduates, graduate students, law students. International applications accepted.
Benefits Opportunity to attend seminars/workshops, possible full-time employment, willing to act as a professional reference, willing to complete paperwork for educational credit, willing to provide letters of recommendation, networking with other peace/justice organizations both nationally and internationally.
Contact Write, call, fax, or e-mail Christian W. Hansson, Internship Coordinator, 418 Seventh Street, SE, Washington, District of Columbia 20003. Phone: 800-WFA-0123. Fax: 202-546-3749. E-mail: chansson@wfa.org. In-person interview recommended (telephone interview accepted). Applicants must submit a letter of interest, resume, writing sample. Applications are accepted continuously. World Wide Web: http://www.wfa.org.

WORLD FEDERALIST MOVEMENT
United Nations Office, 777 United Nations Plaza, 12th Floor
New York, New York 10017

General Information Educational organization dedicated to promoting international order and an effective United Nations. Established in 1947. Number of employees: 18. Number of internship applications received each year: 100.
Internships Available ▶ *1 Betsy Dana scholar:* responsibilities include assisting with office work and research, gathering United Nations documents, writing reports, and meeting with nongovernmental representatives and United Nations officials and personnel. Candidates should have ability to work independently, analytical skills, computer skills, knowledge of field, office skills, research skills, self-motivation, writing skills. Duration is 10 weeks. $1000 per duration of internship. Open to college juniors, college seniors, recent college graduates, graduate students. International applications accepted.
Benefits Names of contacts, on-the-job training, opportunity to attend seminars/workshops, willing to complete paperwork for educational credit, willing to provide letters of recommendation.
Contact Write, call, fax, e-mail, or through World Wide Web site Victoria Clarke, Program Associate. Phone: 212-599-1320. Fax: 212-599-1332. E-mail: wfm@igc.apc.org. In-person interview recommended (telephone interview accepted). Applicants must submit a letter of interest, resume, two writing samples. Application deadline: April 30. World Wide Web: http://www.wfm.org.

YOUTH SERVICE AMERICA
1101 15th Street, NW, Suite 200
Washington, District of Columbia 20005-5002

General Information Resource center and the premier alliance of 200+ organizations committed to increasing the quantity and quality of opportunities for young Americans to serve locally, nationally, or globally. Established in 1986. Number of employees: 12. Number of internship applications received each year: 200.
Internships Available ▶ *2–4 National Service Members interns:* responsibilities include assisting in writing and editing the National Service Briefing, recruiting new members, helping to organize the Faces of Youth Service national speakers' bureau, and assist-

ing with the development policy and funding section of SERVEnet. Candidates should have computer skills, oral communication skills, organizational skills, research skills, writing skills, interest in community service and youth involvement, ability to manage several tasks at once, sense of humor. Duration is flexible. Unpaid. ▶ *1–2 National Youth Service Day interns:* responsibilities include assisting with public relations strategy development, putting together media kits, development of the Toolkit (Web site section of SERVEnet), outreach to thousands of communities and local organizations, and marketing outreach to other national nonprofit organizations. Candidates should have computer skills, oral communication skills, organizational skills, research skills, written communication skills, interest in community service and youth involvement, ability to manage several tasks at once, sense of humor. Duration is flexible. Unpaid. ▶ *1–2 President's Student Service Awards interns:* responsibilities include developing a database of activities and implementation, writing news articles to promote the program, assisting in the development of marketing strategies, making outreach calls, and maintaining the Web site for awards. Candidates should have computer skills, oral communication skills, organizational skills, research skills, written communication skills, interest in community service and youth involvement, ability to manage several tasks at once, sense of humor. Duration is flexible. Unpaid. ▶ *2–4 SERVEnet interns:* responsibilities include assisting the managing editor and Webmaster with building Web site content and graphics, writing articles for various sections of SERVEnet, conducting research, developing marketing plans, and helping to organize the SERVEnet ambassadors/community mapping initiative. Candidates should have computer skills, oral communication skills, organizational skills, research skills, written communication skills, interest in community service and youth involvement, ability to manage several tasks at once, sense of humor. Duration is flexible. Unpaid. ▶ *2–4 development interns:* responsibilities include producing monthly YSA updates for board members, funders, and major donors; researching potential funders; responding to requests for information; and administrative support. Candidates should have computer skills, oral communication skills, organizational skills, research skills, writing skills, interest in community and youth involvement, ability to manage several tasks at once, sense of humor. Duration is flexible. Unpaid. ▶ *1–2 finance/administrative interns:* responsibilities include inputting AR and AP data, tracking invoices, and performing administrative tasks for accounting activities. Candidates should have computer skills, office skills, oral communication skills, organizational skills, writing skills, interest in community and youth involvement, ability to manage several tasks at once, sense of humor. Duration is flexible. Unpaid. Open to recent high school graduates, college freshmen, college sophomores, college juniors, college seniors, recent college graduates, graduate students. International applications accepted.
Benefits Names of contacts, on-the-job training, opportunity to attend seminars/workshops, possible full-time employment, willing to act as a professional reference, willing to complete paperwork for educational credit, willing to provide letters of recommendation, possible stipend.
Contact Fax or e-mail Sharon Brender, Chief Operating Officer, 1101 15th Street, NW, Suite 200, Washington, District of Columbia 20005-5002. Fax: 202-296-4030. E-mail: sbrender@ysa.org. In-person interview required. Applicants must submit a letter of interest, resume, two writing samples. Applications are accepted continuously. World Wide Web: http://www.servenet.org.

ENVIRONMENT, CONSERVATION, AND WILDLIFE ORGANIZATIONS

ALLIANCE FOR THE WILD ROCKIES
PO Box 8731
Missoula, Montana 59807

General Information Organization whose aim is to preserve and protect the remaining wilderness and biodiversity of the Northern Rockies bio-region by empowering regional conservationists and informing the public about the loss of wildlands. Established in 1988. Number of employees: 3. Number of internship applications received each year: 50.
Internships Available ▶ *1–2 ecosystem defense interns:* responsibilities include administering the Forest Watch program that includes reviewing timber sales, mining, and other development proposals; and filing written appeals when necessary. Candidates should have computer skills, knowledge of field, office skills, oral communication skills, research skills, self-motivation, writing skills, legal background. Duration is 1–2 semesters. Position available as unpaid or paid. ▶ *1–3 outreach/education interns:* responsibilities include staffing AWR office, supervising volunteers, and public outreach. Candidates should have ability to work independently, ability to work with others, computer skills, editing skills, knowledge of field, office skills, oral communication skills, personal interest in the field, self-motivation, writing skills. Duration is 1-2 semesters (15-20 hours per week). Position available as unpaid or paid. Open to high school students, recent high school graduates, college freshmen, college sophomores, college juniors, college seniors, recent college graduates, graduate students, law students, career changers, individuals reentering the workforce. International applications accepted.
Benefits Formal training, job counseling, names of contacts, on-the-job training, opportunity to attend seminars/workshops, possible full-time employment, travel reimbursement, willing to complete paperwork for educational credit, willing to provide letters of recommendation, possibility of stipend or college credit.
Contact Write, call, fax, or e-mail Outreach Director. Phone: 406-721-5420. Fax: 406-721-9917. E-mail: awr@wildrockiesalliance.org. In-person interview recommended (telephone interview accepted). Applicants must submit a letter of interest, resume, writing sample, three personal references. Application deadline: April 15 for spring, August 15 for fall, December 15 for winter. World Wide Web: http://www.wildrockiesalliance.org.

THE AMERICAN FLORAL ENDOWMENT
11 Glen-Ed Professional Park
Glen Carbon, Illinois 62034

General Information National research foundation established to secure contributions for funding research and education relevant to floriculture, the results of which benefit the industry and general public. Established in 1961. Number of employees: 10. Number of internship applications received each year: 50.
Internships Available ▶ *1–50 Mosmiller internships.* Candidates should have ability to work independently, knowledge of field, oral communication skills, self-motivation, strong interpersonal skills, strong leadership ability, written communication skills, must have an interest in a career as a retail florist or wholesaler and demonstrate an understanding of the basic skills required for a career in either and/or both career paths. Duration is 10–16 weeks. $2000 scholarship upon completion of internship. Open to college freshmen, college sophomores, college juniors, college seniors, recent college graduates, graduate students. ▶ *5–50 Vic and Margaret Ball internships.* Candidates should have ability to work independently, knowledge of field, oral communication skills, self-motivation, strong interpersonal skills, strong leadership ability, written communication skills, must be interested in a

The American Floral Endowment (continued)

career as a commercial grower and demonstrate a basic understanding of the fundamental skills. Duration is 3–6 months. $4000 scholarship upon completion of 4-month internship; $6000 scholarship upon completion of 6-month internship; 3-month summer experience ($1500). Open to college freshmen, college sophomores, college juniors, college seniors, graduate students.
Benefits Paid internship in addition to scholarships up to $6000.
International Internships Available.
Contact Write, call, e-mail, or through World Wide Web site Steven F. Martinez, Executive Vice President. Phone: 618-692-0045. Fax: 618-692-4045. E-mail: afe@endowment.org. Applicants must submit a formal organization application, letter of interest, academic transcripts, letter of recommendation from advisor. Application deadline: March 1 for fall/winter, November 1 for summer/spring. World Wide Web: http://www.emdowment.org.

AMERICAN FORESTS
910 17th Street, NW, Suite 600
Washington, District of Columbia 20006

General Information Organization dedicated to ensuring the benefits of trees and forests for future generations. Established in 1875. Number of employees: 30. Number of internship applications received each year: 300.
Internships Available ▶ *1 communications/publications intern:* responsibilities include research and writing articles and press releases. Duration is flexible. $50 per week. ▶ *1 marketing intern (DC):* responsibilities include developing partnerships for tree planting. Duration is flexible. $50 per week. ▶ *1–2 policy interns:* responsibilities include writing and research. Duration is flexible. $50 per week. ▶ *1 policy research intern:* responsibilities include assisting with planning of policy and workshops. Duration is 8–10 weeks. $50 per week. ▶ *2 program services interns:* responsibilities include developing partnerships for tree planting. Duration is flexible. $50 per week. ▶ *1 urban forestry intern:* responsibilities include research and acting as community liaison. Duration is flexible. $50 per week. Open to college sophomores, college juniors, college seniors, recent college graduates, graduate students. International applications accepted.
Benefits Opportunity to attend seminars/workshops, possible full-time employment, willing to complete paperwork for educational credit, willing to provide letters of recommendation, opportunity to write for publications and present own seminar.
Contact Write or fax Lu Rose, Vice President of Administration. Fax: 202-955-4588. No phone calls. In-person interview recommended (telephone interview accepted). Applicants must submit a letter of interest, resume, writing sample. Applications are accepted continuously. World Wide Web: http://www.amfor.org.

AMERICAN HIKING SOCIETY
1422 Fenwick Lane
Silver Spring, Maryland 20910

General Information National organization dedicated to serving and working with the hiking community to promote and protect foot trails and the hiking experience. Established in 1976. Number of employees: 10. Number of internship applications received each year: 100.
Internships Available ▶ *1–2 conservation and policy intern:* responsibilities include tracking and analyzing legislation, attending and reporting on congressional hearings, surveying member organizations, developing outreach events, recreation research, mailings; working with conservation coalitions and other organization support tools. Candidates should have ability to work independently, college courses in field, knowledge of field, organizational skills, research skills, written communication skills. Duration is 2–3 months. Position available as unpaid or at $500 per duration of internship. Open to college freshmen, college sophomores, college juniors, college seniors, recent college graduates, graduate students, law students. ▶ *1 corporate relations intern:* responsibilities include assisting the director of corporate relations with business development, co-promotions and cause-related marketing; supporting National Trails Day Program development; producing corporate sponsorship reports; fulfilling sponsorship informa-

tion requests, grant research; partnership planning, sponsor benefit fulfillment; and development of promotions. Candidates should have ability to work independently, editing skills, experience in the field, written communication skills. Duration is 2–3 months. Position available as unpaid or at $500 per duration of internship. Open to college sophomores, college juniors, college seniors, recent college graduates. International applications accepted.
Benefits On-the-job training, opportunity to attend seminars/workshops, possible full-time employment, willing to act as a professional reference, willing to complete paperwork for educational credit, willing to provide letters of recommendation.
Contact Write, call, or e-mail Office Manager. Phone: 301-565-6704. Fax: 301-565-6714. E-mail: info@americanhiking.org. Telephone interview required. Applicants must submit a letter of interest, resume, writing sample. Application deadline: April 15 for summer, August 15 for fall, December 15 for spring. World Wide Web: http://www.americanhiking.org.

AMERICAN HORTICULTURAL SOCIETY
7931 East Boulevard Drive
Alexandria, Virginia 22308-1300

General Information Society that promotes excellence in horticulture through information, education, training, publications, and leadership. Established in 1922. Number of employees: 20. Number of internship applications received each year: 25.
Internships Available ▶ *6–8 horticultural interns:* responsibilities include maintaining plant collections, displays, and test gardens and working in gardening information offices. Candidates should have ability to work independently, plan to pursue career in field, research skills, self-motivation, strong interpersonal skills. Duration is 3–9 months. $8 per hour. Open to college freshmen, college sophomores, college juniors, college seniors, recent college graduates, graduate students, career changers.
Benefits Job counseling, names of contacts, on-the-job training, opportunity to attend seminars/workshops, willing to act as a professional reference, willing to complete paperwork for educational credit, willing to provide letters of recommendation, job lists provided when available.
Contact Write, call, fax, e-mail, or through World Wide Web site Janet Walker, Director of Horticulture. Phone: 703-768-5700 Ext. 112. Fax: 703-768-8700. E-mail: jwalker@ahs.org. In-person interview recommended (telephone interview accepted). Applicants must submit a formal organization application, resume, academic transcripts, three personal references. Applications are accepted continuously. World Wide Web: http://www.ahs.org.

AMERICAN RIVERS
1025 Vermont Avenue, NW #720
Washington, District of Columbia 20005

General Information Nonprofit membership organization that represents 22,000 members nationwide and is dedicated to protecting and restoring America's river systems and fostering a river stewardship ethic by seeking federal and state protection for rivers through legal and legislation advocacy; covers nationally significant rivers, hydropower policy reform, western water issues, urban rivers, and clean water issues. Established in 1973. Number of employees: 30. Number of internship applications received each year: 75.
Internships Available ▶ *4 communications interns:* responsibilities include working as a media intern with the Media Affairs Campaign involving production of promotional materials, press releases, media correspondence; monitoring the news; maintaining slides, photos, videotapes, and the media database, or working as a Web assistant with American Rivers Online Campaign, assisting with daily Web site maintenance, coding graphics design, content development, and brainstorming new ways to use the Internet to communicate organizational message. Candidates should have computer skills, editing skills, oral communication skills, plan to pursue career in field, writing skills. Duration is 3 months (approximately 30 hours per week). $1500 stipend. ▶ *6–12 conservation interns:* responsibilities include legislative research, grassroots organizing through contact with national environmental and river groups, working on various conservation programs, responding to requests from river activists, researching American Rivers issues

in preparation of written materials, and various long term projects; may work with Corps Reform Campaign, Hydropower Campaign, Legislative/Public Policy Campaign, Rivers Unplugged Campaign, or Wild and Scenic Rivers Campaign. Candidates should have analytical skills, computer skills, knowledge of field, personal interest in the field, research skills, writing skills. Duration is 3 months (approximately 30 hours per week). $1500 stipend. Open to college sophomores, college juniors, college seniors, recent college graduates, graduate students, law students. International applications accepted.
Benefits Names of contacts, opportunity to attend seminars/workshops, willing to act as a professional reference, willing to complete paperwork for educational credit, willing to provide letters of recommendation, opportunity to work with senior-level staff and have significant impact on important projects.
Contact Write, call, fax, or e-mail Internship Coordinator. Phone: 202-347-7550. Fax: 202-347-9240. E-mail: ahoffert@amrivers.org. Applicants must submit a letter of interest, resume, writing sample, three personal references. Applications are accepted continuously. World Wide Web: http://www.amrivers.org.

ANACOSTIA WATERSHED SOCIETY
4302 Baltimore Avenue
Bladensburg, Maryland 20710

General Information Small environmental group whose purpose is to restore the Anacostia River, an urban river in Washington, D.C., by organizing volunteers to perform stream cleanups, tree planting, and water quality monitoring. Established in 1989. Number of employees: 7. Number of internship applications received each year: 15.
Internships Available ▶ *1–2 assistant project managers:* responsibilities include organizing volunteers to perform stream cleanups, water quality monitoring, newsletter writing, and tree planting. Candidates should have ability to work independently, ability to work with others, computer skills, office skills, personal interest in the field, writing skills. Duration is 1–3 semesters. Unpaid. Open to college sophomores, college juniors, college seniors, recent college graduates, graduate students. International applications accepted.
Benefits On-the-job training, opportunity to attend seminars/workshops, willing to act as a professional reference, willing to complete paperwork for educational credit, willing to provide letters of recommendation.
Contact Write, call, fax, e-mail, or through World Wide Web site Mr. James Connolly, Executive Director. Phone: 301-699-6204. Fax: 301-699-3317. E-mail: jim@anacostiaws.org. In-person interview recommended (telephone interview accepted). Applicants must submit a letter of interest, resume. Applications are accepted continuously. World Wide Web: http://www.anacostiaws.org.

ANIMAL LEGAL DEFENSE FUND
127 Fourth Street
Petaluma, California 94952-3005

General Information National nonprofit public interest law organization dedicated to protecting animals and establishing their legal rights through litigation. Established in 1979. Number of employees: 20. Number of internship applications received each year: 100.
Internships Available ▶ *2 Eleanor Seiling Legal Clerkship interns:* responsibilities include legal research and preparation of pleadings in cases currently being handled by ALDF; placement is in ALDF's Rockville, Maryland office. Candidates should have analytical skills, computer skills, writing skills, administrative law coursework, previous law clerking experience. Duration is 10 weeks in summer. $3500 per duration of internship. Open to second-year law students only.
Benefits On-the-job training, possible full-time employment, willing to act as a professional reference, willing to provide letters of recommendation.
Contact Write, call, fax, e-mail, or through World Wide Web site Pamela Miller, Office Administrator, 6930 Carroll Avenue, Suite 800, Takoma Park, Maryland 20912. Phone: 301-891-6790. Fax: 301-891-6707. E-mail: pmiller@aldf.org. Applicants must submit a

resume, writing sample, three personal references. Application deadline: November 30. World Wide Web: http://www.aldf.org.

THE ANTARCTICA PROJECT
1630 Connecticut Avenue, NW, 3rd Floor
Washington, District of Columbia 20009

General Information Organization working to preserve Antarctica and its flora and fauna by educating the public and governments on Antarctic conservation. Established in 1982. Number of employees: 3. Unit of Antarctic and Southern Ocean Coalition (ASOC), Washington, District of Columbia. Number of internship applications received each year: 30.
Internships Available ▶ *1–2 interns:* responsibilities include conducting research and writing on a variety of conservation issues, attending relevant meetings, helping communicate with members, and some administrative duties. Candidates should have ability to work independently, ability to work with others, declared college major in field, knowledge of field, oral communication skills, research skills, self-motivation, written communication skills. Duration is 1–4 months. Unpaid. Open to college sophomores, college juniors, college seniors, recent college graduates, graduate students, law students. International applications accepted.
Benefits On-the-job training, opportunity to attend seminars/workshops, willing to complete paperwork for educational credit, willing to provide letters of recommendation.
Contact Write, fax, or e-mail Beth Clark, Director. Phone: 202-234-2480. Fax: 202-387-4823. E-mail: antarctica@igc.org. In-person interview recommended (telephone interview accepted). Applicants must submit a letter of interest, resume, writing sample. Applications are accepted continuously. World Wide Web: http://www.asoc.org.

APPALACHIAN MOUNTAIN CLUB, VOLUNTEER TRAILS PROGRAM
PO Box 298
Gorham, New Hampshire 03581

General Information Recreation/conservation organization that sponsors weekly volunteer-based camps, providing backcountry service projects in New York, New England, and other locations. Established in 1876. Number of employees: 100. Unit of Appalachian Mountain Club, Boston, Massachusetts. Number of internship applications received each year: 250.
Internships Available ▶ *Trail crew leaders:* responsibilities include leading trail crews of people 50 years of age or older, teen programs, and women's programs (inquire for other special groups). Candidates should have oral communication skills, organizational skills, self-motivation, strong interpersonal skills, strong leadership ability. Duration is mid-May to late August. Paid. ▶ *200 week-long and weekend volunteers:* responsibilities include maintaining and brushing trails; strenuous physical work to stabilize the treadway through the use of water bars, step stones, and drainage cleaning; positions located at worksites in the northeastern U.S. Candidates should have self-motivation, strong interpersonal skills. Duration is 1 to 2 weeks (mid-June through September). Unpaid. Open to individuals ages 16 and up.
Benefits Willing to complete paperwork for educational credit.
Contact Write, call, fax, or e-mail Kim Marion, North Country Volunteer Coordinator. Phone: 603-466-2721 Ext. 192. Fax: 603-466-2822. E-mail: kmarion@amcinfo.org. Applicants must submit a formal organization application. Application deadline: April 1 for trail crew leaders; continuous for all other positions. World Wide Web: http://www.outdoors.org.

ARLINGTONIANS FOR A CLEAN ENVIRONMENT (ACE)
3308 South Stafford Street
Arlington, Virginia 22206

General Information Organization working to improve the environment of Arlington County, Virginia together with local government and community organizations to achieve and maintain a clean and sustainable community. Established in 1978.
Internships Available ▶ *ACE Project Watershed Watch program assistants:* responsibilities include recruiting volunteers, organiz-

Arlingtonians for a Clean Environment (ACE) (continued)

ing and implementing volunteer projects including stream cleanups, invasive plant removal, storm drain marking, organizing and delivering classroom and community presentations about watersheds, documenting outcome of events, and office work. Candidates should have ability to work with others, organizational skills, computer skills including experience with Microsoft Work and Access, multi-tasking, and public speaking experience; interest and/or experience with environmental or outdoor education and Spanish speaking ability (desirable). Duration is 12 weeks (approximately 20 hours per week) beginning mid-May. Stipend. **Contact** Fax or through World Wide Web site Elenor Hodges, Executive Director. Phone: 703-228-6427. Fax: 703-228-6407. Applicants must submit a letter of interest, resume. World Wide Web: http://www.arlingtonenvironment.org.

ASPEN CENTER FOR ENVIRONMENTAL STUDIES
100 Puppy Smith Street
Aspen, Colorado 81611

General Information Private nonprofit environmental education center located within the Hallam Lake Nature Preserve whose mission is to inspire a life-long commitment to the preservation of the natural world by educating for environmental stewardship, conserving and restoring the balance of natural communities, and advancing the ethic that the earth must be respected and nurtured. Established in 1968. Number of employees: 12. Number of internship applications received each year: 150.
Internships Available ▶ *12 summer naturalist interns:* responsibilities include leading off-site interpretive hikes at the Maroon Bells, Snowmass, and on top of Aspen Mountain, teaching environmental education programs for children and adults, maintaining trails, assisting with cutthroat trout project, and caring for resident birds of prey. Candidates should have ability to work with others, college courses in field, experience in the field, oral communication skills, personal interest in the field, self-motivation. Duration is June through September. $125 per week. Open to college juniors, college seniors, recent college graduates, graduate students. International applications accepted.
Benefits Formal training, free housing, on-the-job training, opportunity to attend seminars/workshops, possible full-time employment, willing to act as a professional reference, willing to complete paperwork for educational credit, willing to provide letters of recommendation, tuition-free participation in Natural Field School courses.
Contact Write, call, fax, e-mail, or through World Wide Web site Internship Coordinator. Phone: 970-925-5756. Fax: 970-925-4819. E-mail: aces@aspennature.org. Applicants must submit a formal organization application, resume, in-person or telephone interview for qualified applicants. Application deadline: March 1. World Wide Web: http://www.aspennature.org.

ASSATEAGUE ISLAND NATIONAL SEASHORE
7206 National Seashore Lane
Berlin, Maryland 21811

General Information National seashore committed to preservation and interpretation of the natural environment. Established in 1965. Number of employees: 50. Unit of United States National Park Service, Washington, District of Columbia. Number of internship applications received each year: 70.
Internships Available ▶ *1–2 environmental education interns:* responsibilities include providing information to visitors, creating and presenting environmental education programs on and off-site to grade levels kindergarten through middle-school. Candidates should have oral communication skills, self-motivation, strong interpersonal skills, biology or education major. Duration is end of August through October. Unpaid. ▶ *1–4 interpretive naturalists:* responsibilities include providing information to visitors through guided walks, recreational demonstrations, campfires, illustrated evening programs, aquarium duty, children's activities, and visitor center duty. Candidates should have oral communication skills, self-motivation, strong interpersonal skills, biology or education major. Duration is early June to late August. Unpaid.

▶ *1–2 resource management interns:* responsibilities include providing service to researchers, scientists, or park biologists in a variety of activities. Candidates should have ability to work with others, declared college major in field, self-motivation, ability to work under physically demanding circumstances. Duration is early June to late August. Unpaid. Open to college sophomores, college juniors, college seniors, recent college graduates, graduate students, career changers.
Benefits Formal training, free housing, job counseling, on-the-job training, opportunity to attend seminars/workshops, willing to complete paperwork for educational credit, willing to provide letters of recommendation, information on the application process for seasonal employment, worker's compensation, uniform provided, $12 per day provided for food.
Contact Write, fax, or e-mail Ms. Liz Davis, Park Ranger. Fax: 410-641-1099. E-mail: liz_davis@nps.gov. No phone calls. Telephone interview required. Applicants must submit a letter of interest, resume, academic transcripts, two letters of recommendation. Applications are accepted continuously. World Wide Web: http://www.nps.gov/asis/.

AUDUBON NATURALIST SOCIETY
8940 Jones Mill Road
Chevy Chase, Maryland 20815

General Information Independent, nonprofit, environmental education and conservation organization serving the metropolitan Washington, D.C. region. Established in 1897. Number of employees: 30. Number of internship applications received each year: 100.
Internships Available ▶ *5–10 environmental education interns:* responsibilities include co-teaching children's classes in environmental education, maintaining a classroom, assisting with the upkeep of a 40-acre wildlife sanctuary, and undertaking an independent project. Candidates should have ability to work independently, ability to work with others, personal interest in the field, self-motivation, strong leadership ability, experience working with children. Duration is 3 months in summer. $1200–$2400 per duration of internship. Open to college freshmen, college sophomores, college juniors, college seniors, recent college graduates, graduate students, career changers. International applications accepted.
Benefits Formal training, free housing, names of contacts, on-the-job training, opportunity to attend seminars/workshops, willing to act as a professional reference, willing to complete paperwork for educational credit, willing to provide letters of recommendation.
Contact Write, call, fax, or e-mail Andy Vernor, Children's and Family Program Coordinator. Phone: 301-652-9188 Ext. 15. Fax: 301-951-7179. E-mail: avernor@audubonnaturalist.org. In-person interview recommended (telephone interview accepted). Applicants must submit a formal organization application, letter of interest, resume, three personal references, two letters of recommendation. Application deadline: March 31.

AULLWOOD AUDUBON CENTER AND FARM
1000 Aullwood Road
Dayton, Ohio 45414

General Information Nature center and organic farm dedicated to educating the public about environmental issues through the presentation of formal and informal tours. Established in 1957. Number of employees: 16. Division of National Audubon Society, New York, New York. Number of internship applications received each year: 70.
Internships Available ▶ *Administrative assistant interns:* responsibilities include fiscal planning; networking with other Audubon groups; tracking projects; teaching; and participating in meetings, activities, and special events. Candidates should have computer skills, office skills, oral communication skills, written communication skills. Duration is flexible. $110 per week. Open to college sophomores, college juniors, college seniors, recent college graduates, graduate students. ▶ *Environmental education interns:* responsibilities include teaching youth and school groups, assisting with educational program development and teaching materials preparation, and involvement with all aspects of operations. Candidates should have college courses in field, experience in the field, oral communication skills, organizational skills, written communica-

tion skills. Duration is flexible. $110 per week. Open to college sophomores, college juniors, college seniors, recent college graduates, graduate students. ▶ *Maintenance interns:* responsibilities include working in close contact with the maintenance staff in dealing with special problems of the sanctuary. Candidates should have knowledge of field, experience with power equipment and vehicle maintenance. Duration is flexible. $110 per week. Open to college sophomores, college juniors, college seniors, recent college graduates. ▶ *Museum store interns:* responsibilities include contacts with suppliers and assisting with daily store operations. Candidates should have ability to work independently, computer skills, office skills, oral communication skills, organizational skills. Duration is flexible. $110 per week. Open to college sophomores, college juniors, college seniors, recent college graduates, graduate students. ▶ *Organic agriculture interns:* responsibilities include involvement in all aspects of farm work, including farm chores, organic vegetable garden, marketing, and record keeping. Candidates should have ability to work independently, oral communication skills, organizational skills, personal interest in the field, self-motivation, ability to lift 40–60 pounds repeatedly. Duration is flexible. $110 per week. Open to college sophomores, college juniors, college seniors, recent college graduates, graduate students. International applications accepted.

Benefits Formal training, free housing, job counseling, names of contacts, opportunity to attend seminars/workshops, possible full-time employment, willing to complete paperwork for educational credit, willing to provide letters of recommendation.

Contact Write, call, e-mail, or through World Wide Web site Ms. Alison J. Verey, Intern Coordinator. Phone: 937-890-7360. E-mail: averey@audubon.org. Telephone interview required. Applicants must submit a formal organization application, resume, three personal references. Applications are accepted continuously. World Wide Web: http://www.aullwood.center.audubon.org.

BARRIER ISLAND ENVIRONMENTAL EDUCATION CENTER
2810 Seabrook Island Road
John's Island, South Carolina 29455-6219

General Information Resident environmental education center serving elementary and middle school students in 3- or 5-day sessions; subjects include marine biology, forest ecology, sensory awareness, and Indian life. Established in 1981. Number of employees: 15. Division of Saint Christopher Camp and Conference Center, John's Island, South Carolina. Number of internship applications received each year: 50.

Internships Available ▶ *13 naturalist interns:* responsibilities include performing tasks similar to those of regular teaching staff in the morning and afternoon, leading afternoon recreation activities, running evening programs, and working on a news curriculum. Candidates should have ability to work independently, college courses in field, computer skills, experience in the field, oral communication skills, organizational skills, plan to pursue career in field, self-motivation, strong interpersonal skills, strong leadership ability, writing skills, BA/BS in education or biology/science-related field. Duration is August to May. Paid. Open to recent college graduates, graduate students. International applications accepted.

Benefits Free housing, free meals, names of contacts, on-the-job training, possible full-time employment, willing to complete paperwork for educational credit, willing to provide letters of recommendation, temporary health insurance/medical allowance program.

Contact Write, call, fax, e-mail, or through World Wide Web site Director. Phone: 843-768-1337. Fax: 843-768-0918. E-mail: bieec@aol.com. Applicants must submit a formal organization application, resume (including educational and employment histories) and a recent photo. Applications are accepted continuously. World Wide Web: http://www.stchristopher.org.

BLACKWATER NATIONAL WILDLIFE REFUGE
2145 Key Wallace Drive
Cambridge, Maryland 21613

General Information Refuge providing a resting and feeding area for migratory waterfowl, habitat for threatened and endangered species (bald eagle, Delmarva fox squirrel), and wildlife-oriented recreation for the public. Established in 1933. Number of employees: 25. Unit of Fish & Wildlife Service Region V, Hadley, Massachusetts. Number of internship applications received each year: 20.

Internships Available ▶ *1 fall or spring intern:* responsibilities include greeting the public, answering questions, showing films in the auditorium, acting as cashier, giving orientation talks to youth groups, assisting with wetland environmental education programs, preparing and presenting refuge slide program, guiding bus and trail tours, and answering letters and information requests. Duration is 3–6 months. Stipend of $25 per day. ▶ *1 summer or winter intern:* responsibilities include greeting the public, answering questions, showing films in the auditorium, acting as cashier, giving orientation talks to youth groups, assisting with wetland environmental education programs, preparing and presenting refuge slide program, guiding bus and trail tours, and answering letters and information requests. Duration is 12–16 weeks. Stipend of $25 per day. Candidates for all positions should have ability to work independently, ability to work with others, computer skills, oral communication skills, self-motivation, written communication skills. Open to college freshmen, college sophomores, college juniors, college seniors, recent college graduates, graduate students, career changers, individuals reentering the workforce. International applications accepted.

Benefits Free housing, names of contacts, on-the-job training, opportunity to attend seminars/workshops, willing to act as a professional reference, willing to complete paperwork for educational credit, willing to provide letters of recommendation.

Contact Write, call, fax, or e-mail Ms. Maggie Briggs, Outdoor Recreation Planner. Phone: 410-228-2677. Fax: 410-221-7738. E-mail: maggie_briggs@fws.gov. In-person interview recommended (telephone interview accepted). Applicants must submit a formal organization application, resume, three personal references. Application deadline: March 31 for summer, June 30 for fall, December 30 for spring. World Wide Web: http://www.blackwater.fws.gov/.

BLUE OCEAN SOCIETY FOR MARINE CONSERVATION
PO Box 44, 50 Piscataqua Street
New Castle, New Hampshire 03854

General Information Nonprofit organization dedicated to promoting marine conservation through public education, information resources, and marine research in New England focusing on the Gulf of Maine. Established in 2000. Number of employees: 4. Number of internship applications received each year: 15.

Internships Available ▶ *3–6 research assistant interns:* responsibilities include working with naturalists aboard whale watch boats, collecting data, and educating passengers; assisting in data analysis, event planning and fund-raising. Candidates should have ability to work with others, knowledge of field, oral communication skills, self-motivation, written communication skills. Duration is May to August, September or October; fall, winter, spring positions also available; suggested commitment for all is 10-12 weeks. Unpaid. Open to college freshmen, college sophomores, college juniors, college seniors, recent college graduates, graduate students, individuals reentering the workforce, high school seniors and recent high school graduates who live locally. International applications accepted.

Benefits Formal training, job counseling, names of contacts, on-the-job training, opportunity to attend seminars/workshops, willing to act as a professional reference, willing to complete paperwork for educational credit, willing to provide letters of recommendation.

Contact Call or through World Wide Web site Jen Hafner, Vice President, PO Box 44, New Castle, New Hampshire 03854. Phone: 603-433-7320. E-mail: info@blueoceansociety.org. In-person interview recommended (telephone interview accepted). Applicants must submit a formal organization application, letter of interest, resume, 2 provided recommendation forms. Application deadline: March 1 for summer; continuous for fall, winter, and spring. World Wide Web: http://www.blueoceansociety.org.

BOWMAN'S HILL WILDFLOWER PRESERVE
PO Box 685, 1635 River Road
New Hope, Pennsylvania 18938-0685

General Information   Natural preserve that grows, cares for, and exhibits a living collection of Pennsylvania's native plants and provides educational programs, exhibits, and literature centered on regional flora. Established in 1934. Number of employees: 9. Number of internship applications received each year: 60.

Internships Available   ▶ *1–3 preserve interns:* responsibilities include leading tours and field trips, growing wildflowers, assisting with nursery operations, collecting and storing seeds, maintaining plant collection and trail system, completing an assigned project, maintaining a daily journal, weeding, planting, pruning, and performing trail work. Candidates should have ability to work independently, knowledge of field, oral communication skills, plan to pursue career in field, self-motivation, strong interpersonal skills. Duration is 10 weeks (extensions possible). $7 per hour. Open to college sophomores, college juniors, college seniors, recent college graduates, graduate students, career changers, individuals reentering the workforce. International applications accepted.

Benefits   Formal training, names of contacts, on-the-job training, opportunity to attend seminars/workshops, possible full-time employment, willing to act as a professional reference, willing to complete paperwork for educational credit, willing to provide letters of recommendation.

Contact   Write, call, fax, e-mail, or through World Wide Web site Gabrielle Sivitz, Intern Coordinator, PO Box 685, New Hope, Pennsylvania 18938-0685. Phone: 215-862-2924. Fax: 215-862-1846. E-mail: bhwp@bhwp.org. In-person interview recommended (telephone interview accepted). Applicants must submit a formal organization application, resume, three personal references. Application deadline: February 16 for summer. World Wide Web: http://www.bhwp.org.

BRUKNER NATURE CENTER
5995 Horseshoe Bend Road
Troy, Ohio 45373

General Information   Nature center whose mission is to provide environmental education and wildlife rehabilitation. Established in 1974. Number of employees: 9. Number of internship applications received each year: 75.

Internships Available   ▶ *2–3 education/wildlife rehabilitation assistants:* responsibilities include learning and participating in all phases of operation, assisting in the care of native Ohio wildlife, and providing programs for schools using live animals. Candidates should have ability to work independently, oral communication skills, personal interest in the field, self-motivation, strong interpersonal skills. Duration is 3–9 months. $75 per week. Open to college juniors, college seniors, recent college graduates, graduate students. International applications accepted.

Benefits   Free housing, job counseling, names of contacts, on-the-job training, opportunity to attend seminars/workshops, possible full-time employment, willing to act as a professional reference, willing to complete paperwork for educational credit, willing to provide letters of recommendation.

Contact   Write or e-mail Ms. Debra K. Brill, Administrative Director. Phone: 937-698-6493. Fax: 937-698-4619. E-mail: brukner@juno.com. Telephone interview required. Applicants must submit a letter of interest, resume. Applications are accepted continuously.

BUREAU OF LAND MANAGEMENT, UPPER MISSOURI RIVER BREAKS NATIONAL MONUMENT
Airport Road
Lewistown, Montana 59457

General Information   Area maintaining 150-mile scenic, historic, and natural resource along the Missouri River which includes a major part of the Lewis and Clark National Historic Trail as well as the Nez Perce National Historic Trail. Established in 1946. Number of employees: 30. Unit of Bureau of Land Management, Lewiston, Montana. Number of internship applications received each year: 20.

Internships Available   ▶ *1–2 campground hosts:* responsibilities include imparting rules and knowledge to visitors, performing light maintenance, and providing emergency assistance. Duration is May to September. Unpaid. Open to college freshmen, college sophomores, college juniors, college seniors, recent college graduates, graduate students, law students, career changers, individuals reentering the workforce, retired personnel. ▶ *6 river rangers:* responsibilities include staffing visitor center and remote river launch points, registering river boaters, providing visitor services including resource interpretation, conducting river patrols, and maintaining recreation sites. Duration is 14 weeks. Unpaid. Open to college freshmen, college sophomores, college juniors, college seniors, recent college graduates, graduate students, law students, career changers, retired personnel. ▶ *1–2 visitor center hosts:* responsibilities include protecting resources, running slide programs, and operating visitor services including resource interpretation. Duration is April to September. Unpaid. Open to college freshmen, college sophomores, college juniors, college seniors, recent college graduates, graduate students, law students, career changers, individuals reentering the workforce, retired personnel. Candidates for all positions should have ability to work independently, oral communication skills, personal interest in the field, self-motivation, strong interpersonal skills.

Benefits   Free housing, on-the-job training, willing to complete paperwork for educational credit, willing to provide letters of recommendation, reimbursement for living expenses.

Contact   Write or call Sandra M. Padilla, Lead Park Ranger, Airport Road, Lewiston, Montana 59457. Phone: 406-538-7461. Fax: 406-538-1904. E-mail: spadilla@mt.blm.gov. Telephone interview required. Applicants must submit a formal organization application, letter of interest, academic transcripts. Application deadline: April 1 for summer. World Wide Web: http://www.mt.blm.gov/ldo.

CANYONLANDS FIELD INSTITUTE
PO Box 68
Moab, Utah 84532

General Information   Nonprofit, outdoor and environmental education organization. Established in 1984. Number of internship applications received each year: 10.

Internships Available   ▶ *1 marketing and fund-raising intern:* responsibilities include processing information inquiries; grant writing and reporting; front desk and phone coverage; press release and flyer design; assisting with one field program; and other projects as needed. Candidates should have ability to work independently, ability to work with others, computer skills, oral communication skills, writing skills. Duration is 2–3 months. $200 per month. Open to college juniors, college seniors, recent college graduates, graduate students, career changers. International applications accepted.

Benefits   Free housing, on-the-job training, opportunity to attend seminars/workshops, willing to act as a professional reference, willing to complete paperwork for educational credit, willing to provide letters of recommendation, some meals provided for field program; outdoor recreation opportunities (hiking, biking, rafting, climbing).

Contact   Write, call, e-mail, or through World Wide Web site John Geiger, Program Coordinator. Phone: 435-259-7750. Fax: 435-259-2335. E-mail: cfiinfo@canyonlandsfieldinst.org. Telephone interview required. Applicants must submit a letter of interest, resume, three personal references. Applications are accepted continuously. World Wide Web: http://canyonlandsfieldinst.org.

CAPE LOOKOUT NATIONAL SEASHORE
131 Charles Street
Harkers Island, North Carolina 28531

General Information   Organization dedicated to preservation and protection of Cape Lookout National Seashore through interpretation, education, resource protection, and maintenance of the park. Established in 1966. Number of employees: 25. Unit of United States National Park Service, Washington, District of Columbia. Number of internship applications received each year: 15.

Internships Available ▶ *1–2 natural resource assistants:* responsibilities include conducting daily monitoring and protection activities for shorebirds and sea turtles; activities include posting areas, excavating and monitoring nests, and recording data; must live on island for 5-day work week. Candidates should have ability to work independently, personal interest in the field, self-motivation, ability to work outdoors under variable weather conditions. Duration is 12–16 weeks. Unpaid. Open to college freshmen, college sophomores, college juniors, college seniors, recent college graduates, graduate students. ▶ *3–4 visitor services interns:* responsibilities include assisting at visitor center, answering questions, orienting visitors to park; designing and writing interpretive brochures; assisting in maintenance of exhibits; presenting interpretive programs on/off site; assisting with education programs; working periodically at Cape Lookout Lighthouse; may be required to spend nights at the seashore. Duration is minimum of 1 month. Unpaid. Open to high school students, recent high school graduates, college freshmen, college sophomores, college juniors, college seniors, recent college graduates, graduate students, law students, career changers, individuals reentering the workforce. International applications accepted.

Benefits Formal training, free housing, job counseling, names of contacts, on-the-job training, opportunity to attend seminars/workshops, possible full-time employment, willing to complete paperwork for educational credit, willing to provide letters of recommendation.

Contact Write, call, fax, or e-mail Superintendent. Phone: 252-728-2250. Fax: 252-728-2160. E-mail: calo_administration@nps.gov. Applicants must submit a letter of interest, resume. Applications are accepted continuously. World Wide Web: http://www.nps.gov/calo.

CARIBBEAN CONSERVATION CORPORATION
4424 Northwest 13th Street, Suite A1
Gainesville, Florida 32609

General Information Organization that is dedicated to the conservation of sea turtles and related marine and coastal wildlife through research, training, advocacy, education, and protection of natural areas. Established in 1959. Number of employees: 8. Number of internship applications received each year: 200.

Internships Available ▶ *4–6 birding research assistants:* responsibilities include study of migrant and neotropical birds, working with volunteer groups including supervising and educating volunteers in avian behavior and research methodology. Candidates should have oral communication skills, organizational skills, research skills, strong interpersonal skills, background/experience with birds preferred. Duration is minimum of 2 months. Unpaid. ▶ *8 green turtle research assistants:* responsibilities include assisting scientists with research on the green turtle, monitoring turtle nesting beach, tagging turtles and recording data, working with volunteer groups on turtle projects, and educating tourists about turtles. Candidates should have oral communication skills, plan to pursue career in field, research skills, strong interpersonal skills, background/experience with turtles preferred. Duration is minimum of 2 months, beginning in June, ending in late October. Unpaid. ▶ *4–6 leatherback turtle research assistants:* responsibilities include assisting scientists with research on the leatherback turtle, monitoring turtle nesting beach, tagging turtles and recording data, working with volunteer groups on turtle projects, and educating tourists about turtles. Candidates should have oral communication skills, plan to pursue career in field, research skills, strong interpersonal skills, background/experience with turtles preferred, ability to speak English and Spanish at conversational levels. Duration is 2 months or more, beginning in March, ending in late May. Unpaid. Open to college freshmen, college sophomores, college juniors, college seniors, recent college graduates, graduate students, career changers. International applications accepted.

Benefits Formal training, free housing, free meals, willing to complete paperwork for educational credit, willing to provide letters of recommendation.

International Internships Available in Costa Rica.

Contact Write, fax, or e-mail Dan Evans, Field Program Coordinator. Fax: 352-375-2449. E-mail: resprog@cccturtle.org. No phone calls. Telephone interview required. Applicants must submit a formal

organization application, letter of interest, resume, three personal references. Application deadline: April 1 for green turtle research assistants, December 31 for leatherback turtle research assistants; continuous for birding research assistants. World Wide Web: http://www.cccturtle.org.

CAROLINA RAPTOR CENTER, INC.
PO Box 16443
Charlotte, North Carolina 28297

General Information Nonprofit organization that exists to provide public education and contribute research on the importance of raptors and to care for sick, injured, and orphaned raptors. Established in 1981. Number of employees: 15. Number of internship applications received each year: 30.

Internships Available ▶ *3–5 environmental educators:* responsibilities include assisting with the care of trained birds of prey, presenting programs at site and elsewhere, and helping with displays and exhibits. Candidates should have ability to work independently, computer skills, oral communication skills, organizational skills, personal interest in the field, strong interpersonal skills, writing skills. Duration is minimum of 120 hours. Unpaid. Open to high school students, recent high school graduates, college freshmen, college sophomores, college juniors, college seniors, recent college graduates, graduate students, career changers. ▶ *3–5 raptor care interns:* responsibilities include caring for, feeding, and training nonreleasable raptors. Candidates should have ability to work independently, ability to work with others, organizational skills, personal interest in the field, self-motivation. Duration is minimum of 120 hours. Unpaid. Open to high school students, recent high school graduates, college freshmen, college sophomores, college juniors, college seniors, recent college graduates, graduate students, career changers, individuals reentering the workforce. ▶ *5–7 raptor rehabilitators:* responsibilities include assisting with care, feeding, and releasing to the wild injured and orphaned raptors. Candidates should have ability to work independently, ability to work with others, organizational skills, personal interest in the field, self-motivation, written communication skills. Duration is minimum of 120 hours. Unpaid. Open to high school students, recent high school graduates, college freshmen, college sophomores, college juniors, college seniors, recent college graduates, graduate students, career changers, individuals reentering the workforce. International applications accepted.

Benefits Names of contacts, on-the-job training, opportunity to attend seminars/workshops, willing to complete paperwork for educational credit, willing to provide letters of recommendation.

Contact Write, fax, e-mail, or through World Wide Web site Lori Sparkman, Director of Volunteer Programs. Fax: 704-875-8814. E-mail: lorisparkman@mindspring.com. No phone calls. In-person interview recommended (telephone interview accepted). Applicants must submit a formal organization application, letter of interest, resume, three personal references. Applications are accepted continuously. World Wide Web: http://www.birdsofprey.org.

CARRYING CAPACITY NETWORK
2000 P Street, NW, Suite 310
Washington, District of Columbia 20036

General Information Informational network striving to make the public aware of such issues as environmental degradation, resource conservation, and population stabilization. Established in 1989. Number of employees: 4. Number of internship applications received each year: 50.

Internships Available ▶ *1–2 staff/program assistants:* responsibilities include providing general office support, giving telephone assistance, maintaining the database, offering membership and research support, working on independent projects, and assisting with staff projects. Candidates should have ability to work independently, computer skills, oral communication skills, personal interest in the field, research skills, self-motivation, writing skills. Duration is minimum of 3 months. $7–$8.50 per hour. Open to high school seniors, recent high school graduates, college freshmen, college sophomores, college juniors, college seniors, recent college graduates, graduate students, law students, career changers, individuals reentering the workforce. International applications accepted.

Carrying Capacity Network (continued)

Benefits Opportunity to attend seminars/workshops, possible full-time employment, willing to complete paperwork for educational credit, willing to provide letters of recommendation.

Contact Write, call, fax, e-mail, or through World Wide Web site Robin Lazaro, Network Coordinator. Phone: 202-296-4548. Fax: 202-296-4609. E-mail: ccn@us.net. In-person interview recommended (telephone interview accepted). Applicants must submit a letter of interest, resume. Applications are accepted continuously. World Wide Web: http://www.carryingcapacity.org.

CENTER FOR ENVIRONMENTAL HEALTH
528 61st Street, Suite A
Oakland, California 94609

General Information Nonprofit environmental and public health organization. Established in 1996. Number of employees: 6. Number of internship applications received each year: 35.

Internships Available ▶ *1–2 interns:* responsibilities include assistance in various programmatic, administrative, and fundraising projects. Candidates should have oral communication skills, organizational skills, research skills, strong interpersonal skills, written communication skills. Duration is 2–12 months. $300 per month. Open to college freshmen, college sophomores, college juniors, college seniors, recent college graduates, graduate students, law students, individuals reentering the workforce. ▶ *1 project coordinator assistant:* responsibilities include assisting Health Care Without Harm (HCWH) project coordinator in local and national coalition work with research, networking, and general assistance. Candidates should have ability to work with others, computer skills, office skills, oral communication skills, organizational skills, self-motivation. Duration is 3–12 months. $300 per month. Open to college sophomores, college juniors, college seniors, recent college graduates, graduate students. ▶ *1 staff scientist assistant:* responsibilities include assisting staff scientist with programmatic research and reporting; assisting in day-to-day office activities. Candidates should have ability to work with others, computer skills, oral communication skills, organizational skills, research skills, written communication skills. Duration is 3–12 months. $300 per month. Open to college freshmen, college sophomores, college juniors, college seniors, recent college graduates, graduate students, law students, career changers, individuals reentering the workforce. International applications accepted.

Benefits Names of contacts, on-the-job training, opportunity to attend seminars/workshops, possible full-time employment, travel reimbursement, willing to act as a professional reference, willing to complete paperwork for educational credit, willing to provide letters of recommendation.

Contact Write, call, fax, e-mail, or through World Wide Web site Michael Green, Executive Director. Phone: 510-594-9864. Fax: 510-594-9863. E-mail: ceh@cehca.org. In-person interview required. Applicants must submit a letter of interest, resume, writing sample, three personal references. Application deadline: January 20 for spring, May 20 for summer. World Wide Web: http://www.cehca.org.

CENTER FOR HEALTH, ENVIRONMENT, AND JUSTICE
PO Box 6806
Falls Church, Virginia 22040-6806

General Information Organization that assists grassroots citizens' groups in the fight against pollution. Established in 1981. Number of employees: 15. Number of internship applications received each year: 75.

Internships Available ▶ *1–2 development interns:* responsibilities include assisting with all aspects of development including grant writing, prospect research, and major donor activities. Candidates should have ability to work independently, editing skills, knowledge of field, oral communication skills, organizational skills, personal interest in the field, plan to pursue career in field, self-motivation, strong interpersonal skills, strong leadership ability, writing skills. Duration is flexible. Unpaid. Open to college seniors, recent college graduates, graduate students, career changers, individuals reentering the workforce. ▶ *1–5 grassroots organizing interns:*

responsibilities include assisting with a variety of tasks including communication with local communities and answering phone inquiries. Candidates should have ability to work independently, analytical skills, oral communication skills, organizational skills, plan to pursue career in field, self-motivation, strong interpersonal skills, strong leadership ability. Duration is flexible. Position available as unpaid or paid. Open to college freshmen, college sophomores, college juniors, college seniors, recent college graduates, graduate students, career changers, individuals reentering the workforce. ▶ *1–2 journalism interns:* responsibilities include researching and updating a guidebook, working with editor of quarterly magazine. Candidates should have ability to work independently, computer skills, editing skills, organizational skills, personal interest in the field, plan to pursue career in field, self-motivation, strong interpersonal skills, strong leadership ability, writing skills. Duration is flexible. Unpaid. Open to college juniors, college seniors, graduate students, career changers, individuals reentering the workforce. ▶ *4–6 national campaign organizing interns:* responsibilities include working on and helping with organizing two national campaigns: Stop Dioxin Exposure Campaign and Health Care Without Harm Campaign. Candidates should have ability to work independently, analytical skills, computer skills, editing skills, office skills, oral communication skills, organizational skills, plan to pursue career in field, research skills, self-motivation, strong interpersonal skills, strong leadership ability, writing skills. Duration is flexible. Paid. Open to college juniors, college seniors, recent college graduates, graduate students, law students, career changers, individuals reentering the workforce. ▶ *1–3 nonprofit management interns:* responsibilities include assisting with a variety of tasks including marketing, public relations, schedule coordinating, and other activities. Candidates should have ability to work independently, computer skills, office skills, oral communication skills, organizational skills, plan to pursue career in field, self-motivation, strong interpersonal skills, strong leadership ability. Duration is flexible. Unpaid. Open to college seniors, recent college graduates, graduate students, career changers, individuals reentering the workforce. ▶ *1–4 research interns:* responsibilities include researching, compiling, and distributing information to activists in response to written and telephone inquiries. Candidates should have ability to work independently, analytical skills, computer skills, organizational skills, plan to pursue career in field, research skills, self-motivation, strong interpersonal skills, strong leadership ability, writing skills. Duration is flexible. Unpaid. Open to college sophomores, college juniors, college seniors, recent college graduates, graduate students, career changers, individuals reentering the workforce. ▶ *1–5 science interns:* responsibilities include compiling toxicity profiles on common chemicals found at contaminated sites. Candidates should have ability to work independently, ability to work with others, analytical skills, computer skills, plan to pursue career in field, research skills, self-motivation, written communication skills. Duration is flexible. Paid. Open to college juniors, college seniors, recent college graduates, graduate students, career changers, individuals reentering the workforce. International applications accepted.

Benefits Formal training, job counseling, names of contacts, opportunity to attend seminars/workshops, possible full-time employment, willing to complete paperwork for educational credit, willing to provide letters of recommendation, small transportation stipend.

Contact Write, e-mail, or through World Wide Web site Ms. Sharon Franklin, Administrator. Fax: 703-237-8389. E-mail: sfranklin@chej.org. No phone calls. In-person interview recommended (telephone interview accepted). Applicants must submit a letter of interest, resume. Application deadline: March 15 for summer, October 31 for winter, December 15 for spring. World Wide Web: http://www.chej.org.

CENTER FOR URBAN HORTICULTURE/ WASHINGTON PARK ARBORETUM
University of Washington, Box 354115
Seattle, Washington 98195-4115

General Information Division within college whose mission is research, teaching, and public service in urban horticulture with programs that center on urban plant selection, placement, restoration, and management. Number of employees: 40. Unit of College of Forest Resources, University of Washington, Seattle, Washington. Number of internship applications received each year: 20.

Internships Available ▶ *1 curatorial intern:* responsibilities include field inventory and mapping, label making and placement, plant records data entry, and herbarium documentation. Candidates should have oral communication skills, written communication skills, computer literacy, attention to detail, working knowledge of botanical nomenclature and systematic botany, interest in woody ornamental plants. Duration is 3–6 months. $7–$8 per hour. ▶ *1–2 public education for adults interns:* responsibilities include planning, coordinating, and implementing public symposium and outreach curriculum; writing and editing newsletters, developing interpretive displays, leading tours, and co-instructing public courses. Candidates should have plan to pursue career in field, background in horticulture, knowledge of Web software (helpful). Duration is 8–12 weeks. $8 per hour. ▶ *1 youth education assistant:* responsibilities include assisting with development, promotion, instruction, and evaluation of educational programs for youth, families, adults, and the general public which includes group tours, workshops, and summer camps. Candidates should have self-motivation, major in education, horticulture, or ecological studies. Duration is 3–5 months. $7–$9 per hour. Open to college freshmen, college sophomores, college juniors, college seniors, graduate students. International applications accepted.

Benefits Formal training, opportunity to attend seminars/workshops, possible full-time employment, willing to complete paperwork for educational credit, willing to provide letters of recommendation.

Contact Write, call, or fax Sue Nicol, Outreach Coordinator. Phone: 206-685-8033. Fax: 206-325-8893. Applicants must submit a resume, two personal references, letter of interest indicating which position desired. Application deadline: March 31. World Wide Web: http://depts.washington.edu/urbhort/.

CENTRAL WISCONSIN ENVIRONMENTAL STATION/UNIVERSITY OF WISCONSIN–STEVENS POINT
10186 County Road MM
Amherst Junction, Wisconsin 54407

General Information Environmental station that provides a foundation for appreciation and understanding of the environment and develops the skills and attitudes needed to deal with present and future environmental problems. Established in 1975. Number of employees: 15. Unit of University of Wisconsin–Stevens Point, Stevens Point, Wisconsin. Number of internship applications received each year: 20.

Internships Available ▶ *3–4 environmental education interns:* responsibilities include providing instruction in environmental studies for groups of K-12 students, directing K-12 programs one day per week, being involved in a variety of administrative responsibilities, working with weekend groups, and performing other duties as necessary. Candidates should have oral communication skills, personal interest in the field, self-motivation, strong interpersonal skills, written communication skills, understanding of ecological concepts. Duration is 1 semester. $1800 per semester. Open to college juniors, college seniors, recent college graduates, graduate students, career changers, must be Wisconsin resident or attending Wisconsin state university.

Benefits Formal training, on-the-job training, opportunity to attend seminars/workshops, willing to act as a professional reference, willing to complete paperwork for educational credit, willing to provide letters of recommendation, some meals provided, possible housing allowance.

Contact E-mail Rebecca Clarke, Program Manager. E-mail: bclarke@uwsp.edu. In-person interview recommended (telephone interview accepted). Applicants must submit a formal organization application, letter of interest, resume, academic transcripts, three personal references. Application deadline: July 1 for fall, December 1 for spring. World Wide Web: http://www.uwsp.edu/cnr/cwes.

CHATTAHOOCHEE/OCONEE NATIONAL FOREST
1755 Cleveland Highway
Gainesville, Georgia 30501

General Information Forest service whose purpose is caring for the land and serving the people. Number of employees: 160. Unit of United States Forest Service, Washington, District of Columbia. Number of internship applications received each year: 5.

Internships Available ▶ *2 interpreters:* responsibilities include providing visitors with information. Candidates should have ability to work independently, declared college major in field, oral communication skills, plan to pursue career in field, research skills, strong interpersonal skills. Duration is 10 weeks. Unpaid. ▶ *2 recreation assistants:* responsibilities include developing recreational programs. Candidates should have ability to work independently, ability to work with others, college courses in field, oral communication skills, plan to pursue career in field, self-motivation, major in outdoor education. Duration is 10 weeks. Unpaid. Open to college freshmen, college sophomores, college juniors, college seniors. International applications accepted.

Benefits Formal training, free housing, names of contacts, opportunity to attend seminars/workshops, possible full-time employment, willing to complete paperwork for educational credit, willing to provide letters of recommendation, small fee for travel and meals.

Contact Write, call, or fax Ms. Luana W. Kitchens, Human Resources Program Manager. Phone: 770-297-3016. Fax: 770-534-4411. In-person interview recommended (telephone interview accepted). Applicants must submit a letter of interest, resume. Application deadline: April 1 for summer. World Wide Web: http://www.fs.fed.us.

CHEQUAMEGON NATIONAL FOREST, THE GREAT DIVIDE DISTRICT
PO Box 896
Hayward, Wisconsin 54843

General Information National forest focusing on natural resource management and emphasizing multiple use and conservation of resources including wildlife, recreation, timber, wilderness, water, and soil. Established in 1905. Number of employees: 35. Unit of United States Forest Service, Washington, District of Columbia. Number of internship applications received each year: 30.

Internships Available ▶ *1–2 biological assistants:* responsibilities include working outdoors in all types of weather with biological technician gathering field information, doing maintenance work, being able to work with chainsaws, brush saws, and drive a tractor. Candidates should have ability to work independently, ability to work with others, experience in the field, personal interest in the field, plan to pursue career in field, self-motivation. Duration is June to August. $250–$330 per week. Open to college sophomores, college juniors, college seniors, recent college graduates, graduate students. ▶ *1–2 recreation interns:* responsibilities include assisting recreation technician with campground maintenance, trail maintenance, working with the public, giving accurate information. Candidates should have ability to work independently, ability to work with others, personal interest in the field, self-motivation. Duration is June to September. Position available as unpaid or at $9–$12 per hour. Open to college sophomores, college juniors, college seniors, recent college graduates, graduate students. ▶ *1 wilderness ranger intern:* responsibilities include working in the Rainbow Lake and Porcupine Wilderness areas, meeting with the public, constructing new trails, maintaining campsites, and engaging in other resource management projects. Candidates should have ability to work independently, ability to work with others, knowledge of field, oral communication skills, personal interest in the field, self-motivation, strong leadership ability, map reading skills, outdoor experience. Duration is June to September. Position available as unpaid or at $100–$125 per week. Open to college juniors, college seniors, recent college graduates, graduate students. International applications accepted.

Chequamegon National Forest, The Great Divide District (continued)

Benefits Formal training, names of contacts, on-the-job training, opportunity to attend seminars/workshops, willing to act as a professional reference, willing to complete paperwork for educational credit, willing to provide letters of recommendation, stipend $20–$25/ per day for meals or hourly pay of $9.

Contact Write, call, fax, or e-mail Ms. Kathy M. Moe, Biological Technician. Phone: 715-634-4821. Fax: 715-634-3769. E-mail: kmoe@fs.fed.us. Telephone interview required. Applicants must submit a letter of interest, resume, two personal references, two letters of recommendation. Application deadline: February 28 for summer.

CHESAPEAKE WILDLIFE SANCTUARY
17308 Queen Anne Bridge Road
Bowie, Maryland 20716-9053

General Information Nonprofit wildlife rehabilitation center that rescues and treats an average of 10,000 injured and orphaned animals annually, providing intensive, hands-on training and experience to individuals who wish to pursue a career in wildlife, veterinary medicine, or related fields. Established in 1980. Number of employees: 13. Number of internship applications received each year: 150.

Internships Available ▶ *1–3 administration interns:* responsibilities include preparation of grant proposals to support our land trust, oiled wildlife, or intern and volunteer programs; fundraising; and computer training. Candidates should have ability to work independently, computer skills, office skills, oral communication skills, organizational skills, self-motivation, strong interpersonal skills, written communication skills. Duration is 3–12 months. Unpaid. Open to recent high school graduates, college freshmen, college sophomores, college juniors, college seniors, recent college graduates, graduate students, law students, career changers, individuals reentering the workforce. ▶ *5–25 avian interns:* responsibilities include recordkeeping, rehabilitation, cleaning cages and equipment, and rearing of a variety of birds; assisting with the sanctuary's regional oiled wildlife emergency response program. Candidates should have ability to work independently, oral communication skills, personal interest in the field, self-motivation, strong interpersonal skills, professional attitude. Duration is 3–12 months. Unpaid. Open to high school seniors, recent high school graduates, college freshmen, college sophomores, college juniors, college seniors, recent college graduates, graduate students, law students, career changers, individuals reentering the workforce, individuals 16 or older. ▶ *2–5 large mammals interns:* responsibilities include recordkeeping, rehabilitation, rearing, feeding, cleaning, health checks, and medical treatment of white-tailed deer. Candidates should have ability to work independently, ability to work with others, oral communication skills, personal interest in the field, self-motivation, professional attitude. Duration is 3–12 months. Unpaid. Open to high school seniors, recent high school graduates, college freshmen, college sophomores, college juniors, college seniors, recent college graduates, graduate students, career changers. ▶ *2–4 small mammals interns:* responsibilities include recordkeeping, cleaning, feeding, and rehabilitation focusing on hand-rearing and care of small mammals (squirrels, rabbits, opossums, groundhogs, and other animals). Candidates should have ability to work independently, ability to work with others, oral communication skills, personal interest in the field, self-motivation, professional attitude. Duration is 3–12 months. Unpaid. Open to high school seniors, recent high school graduates, college freshmen, college sophomores, college juniors, college seniors, recent college graduates, graduate students, law students, career changers, individuals reentering the workforce. ▶ *1–3 veterinary interns:* responsibilities include recordkeeping and treatment of injured wildlife, medical treatment of trauma cases, and design of treatment protocols. Candidates should have ability to work independently, ability to work with others, knowledge of field, oral communication skills, strong leadership ability, written communication skills. Duration is 1 month to 1 year. Unpaid. Open to 3rd- or 4th-year veterinary students. ▶ *1–5 wildlife education interns:* responsibilities include design and presentation of on- and off-site educational programs for the public, and docent training programs. Candidates should have ability to work

independently, ability to work with others, oral communication skills, personal interest in the field, self-motivation, written communication skills. Duration is 3–12 months. Unpaid. Open to college freshmen, college sophomores, college juniors, college seniors, recent college graduates, graduate students. International applications accepted.

Benefits Formal training, housing at a cost, job counseling, names of contacts, on-the-job training, opportunity to attend seminars/workshops, possible full-time employment, willing to act as a professional reference, willing to complete paperwork for educational credit, willing to provide letters of recommendation, possibility of merit-based scholarship following internship.

Contact Write, call, fax, e-mail, or through World Wide Web site Marjorie Hewitt, Intern Coordinator, 17308 Queen Anne Bridge Road, Bowie, Maryland 20716-9033. Phone: 301-390-7011. Fax: 301-249-3511. E-mail: bowiecws@yahoo.com. Telephone interview required. Applicants must submit a formal organization application, resume, academic transcripts, two letters of recommendation, 2-page essay stating goals for internship; a self-addressed stamped envelope requesting application form. Applications are accepted continuously. World Wide Web: http://www.chesapeakewildlife.org.

CHEWONKI FOUNDATION, INC.
485 Chewonki Neck Road
Wiscasset, Maine 04578

General Information Year-round environmental education center offering summer camp, wilderness expeditions, trips and workshops for families, individuals, and school programs; located on the coast of Maine. Established in 1915. Number of employees: 60. Number of internship applications received each year: 25.

Internships Available ▶ *2–4 camp counselors:* responsibilities include serving as resident counselor in cabin with 8–10 boys, activity instructor, and assistant wilderness trip leader. Candidates should have knowledge of field, personal interest in the field, self-motivation, strong interpersonal skills, strong leadership ability. Duration is 8-10 weeks in summer. $975–$2500 per duration of internship. Open to high school students, recent high school graduates, college freshmen, college sophomores, college juniors, college seniors, recent college graduates, graduate students. ▶ *2–4 environmental education interns:* responsibilities include working in wilderness encampments with school groups; teaching camping and related wilderness skills and natural history. Candidates should have college courses in field, oral communication skills, personal interest in the field, self-motivation, strong interpersonal skills, strong leadership ability. Duration is 12–15 weeks. $100–$250 per week. Open to college seniors, graduate students, career changers, individuals reentering the workforce. International applications accepted.

Benefits Free housing, free meals, names of contacts, on-the-job training, possible full-time employment, willing to act as a professional reference, willing to complete paperwork for educational credit, willing to provide letters of recommendation.

Contact Write, call, fax, e-mail, or through World Wide Web site Dick Thomas, Camp Director. Phone: 207-882-7323. Fax: 207-882-4074. E-mail: info@chewonki.org. In-person interview recommended (telephone interview accepted). Applicants must submit a formal organization application, resume, 3 personal references or letters of recommendation. Applications are accepted continuously. World Wide Web: http://www.chewonki.org.

CHINCOTEAGUE NATIONAL WILDLIFE REFUGE
PO Box 62, 8231 Beach Road
Chincoteague, Virginia 23336

General Information Wildlife refuge located on a barrier island off the Eastern Shore of Virginia that has 14,000 acres of beach, saltmarsh, freshwater marsh, and maritime forest; migrating and wintering area for waterfowl; home or stopover for 1 endangered and 2 threatened species. Established in 1943. Number of employees: 20. Division of U.S. Fish and Wildlife Service, Department of the Interior, Washington, District of Columbia. Number of internship applications received each year: 50.

Internships Available ▶ *1 fall biology intern:* responsibilities include assisting with wildlife population censuses and surveys, vegeta-

tion sampling, operating deer hunter check station, and assisting in other routine duties. Candidates should have ability to work independently, college courses in field, knowledge of field, plan to pursue career in field, self-motivation, written communication skills. Duration is 8–12 weeks. $100 per week (variable). ▶ *1–2 spring and fall environmental education interns:* responsibilities include developing and conducting environmental education programs for various school groups, assisting with development of environmental education materials for teachers, and assisting with teacher workshops. Candidates should have ability to work independently, college courses in field, oral communication skills, organizational skills, personal interest in the field, writing skills. Duration is 10–13 weeks. $100 per week (variable). ▶ *2–6 spring and summer biology interns:* responsibilities include assisting with wildlife population censuses and surveys, collecting and recording information in support of the refuge's piping plover program, studying adult arrival and nest survey data, assisting in routing piping plover management including construction of predator exclosures, and other routine duties. Candidates should have ability to work independently, college courses in field, knowledge of field, personal interest in the field, strong interpersonal skills, written communication skills. Duration is 8–12 weeks. $100 per week (variable). ▶ *2 spring, summer and fall interpretive interns:* responsibilities include staffing the visitor center, developing and conducting interpretive programs as well as other informational materials. Candidates should have ability to work independently, knowledge of field, oral communication skills, organizational skills, personal interest in the field, written communication skills. Duration is 10–13 weeks. $100 per week (variable). Open to college juniors, college seniors, recent college graduates, graduate students. International applications accepted.
Benefits Free housing, names of contacts, willing to complete paperwork for educational credit, willing to provide letters of recommendation.
Contact Write or e-mail Mr. John D. Schroer, Refuge Manager. Phone: 757-336-6122. Fax: 757-336-5273. E-mail: r5rw_chnwr@mail.fws.gov. Applicants must submit a letter of interest, resume, telephone interview for finalists. Application deadline: January 15 for spring, March 15 for summer, July 15 for fall. World Wide Web: http://chinco.fws.gov.

CINCINNATI NATURE CENTER
4949 Tealtown Road
Milford, Ohio 45150

General Information Private nonprofit environmental education center with three sites, including farms and large natural area totaling 1,425 acres. Established in 1966. Number of employees: 40. Number of internship applications received each year: 20.
Internships Available ▶ *6 environmental education interns:* responsibilities include teaching youth from pre-school through high school about environmental concepts in a natural or farm setting using a hands-on, experiential approach; assisting with special events; developing and conducting programs for the general public; helping with grounds work, chores, and other tasks related to operating a nature center and/or educational farm. Candidates should have college courses in field, oral communication skills, personal interest in the field, self-motivation, strong interpersonal skills, written communication skills. Duration is one semester (40 hours per week with the possibility of an extension). $105 per week. Open to college freshmen, college sophomores, college juniors, college seniors, recent college graduates, graduate students, career changers, individuals reentering the workforce. ▶ *1–2 farm interns:* responsibilities include assisting with chores on an educational farm including care and maintenance of crops, livestock, and gardens. Candidates should have ability to work independently, ability to work with others, personal interest in the field, self-motivation. Duration is flexible. $105 per week. Open to college freshmen, college sophomores, college juniors, college seniors, graduate students, individuals reentering the workforce.
Benefits Free housing, on-the-job training, opportunity to attend seminars/workshops, willing to act as a professional reference, willing to complete paperwork for educational credit, willing to

provide letters of recommendation, $15 per week gas reimbursement if the internship takes place at a site other than where housing is offered.
Contact Write, call, fax, or e-mail Connie Brockman, Education Director, 4949 Tealtown Road, Milford, Ohio 45150. Phone: 513-831-1711 Ext. 27. Fax: 513-831-8052. E-mail: cbrockman@cincynature.org. In-person interview recommended (telephone interview accepted). Applicants must submit a letter of interest, resume, two letters of recommendation, one essay on personal environmental ethnic. Applications are accepted continuously. World Wide Web: http://www.cincynature.org.

CISPUS LEARNING CENTER
2142 Cispus Road
Randle, Washington 98377-9305

General Information Outdoor education learning facility used by school groups for environmental education; offers teacher training and a challenge course. Established in 1981. Number of employees: 20. Unit of Association of Washington School Principals, Olympia, Washington. Number of internship applications received each year: 24.
Internships Available ▶ *1–3 challenge course facilitators:* responsibilities include facilitating groups on the challenge ropes course. Candidates should have ability to work independently, oral communication skills, organizational skills, personal interest in the field, strong interpersonal skills, strong leadership ability, experience with youth. Duration is 12–16 weeks. $500 per month. Open to college juniors, college seniors, recent college graduates, graduate students, career changers, individuals reentering the workforce. International applications accepted.
Benefits Formal training, free housing, free meals, names of contacts, on-the-job training, opportunity to attend seminars/workshops, willing to act as a professional reference, willing to complete paperwork for educational credit, willing to provide letters of recommendation, orientation.
Contact Write, call, e-mail, or through World Wide Web site Kelly Johnston, Challenge Course Manager. Phone: 360-497-7131. E-mail: cispusropes@myhome.net. Telephone interview required. Applicants must submit a formal organization application, letter of interest, resume, three personal references. Applications are accepted continuously. World Wide Web: http://www.cispus.org.

CLARKE MOSQUITO CONTROL
159 North Garden Avenue
Roselle, Illinois 60172

General Information Largest and oldest professional mosquito control contractor in the world. Established in 1946. Number of employees: 150. Number of internship applications received each year: 200.
Internships Available ▶ *50 biology interns:* responsibilities include a variety of field-related duties which may include inspection, treatment collection of blood samples, or lab work. Candidates should have ability to work independently, self-motivation, strong interpersonal skills, must have valid driver's license and good driving record. Duration is April to September (approximately). $9–$11 per hour. Open to anyone 18 years of age or older. ▶ *4 environmental science interns:* responsibilities include stocking of mosquitofish and performing inspections. Candidates should have ability to work independently, self-motivation, strong interpersonal skills, good map-reading skills, valid driver's license, and good driving record. Duration is April to September (approximately). $9–$11 per hour. Open to anyone 18 years of age or older. ▶ *10 geography interns:* responsibilities include possibility of a variety of field and/or office duties. Candidates should have ability to work independently, self-motivation, strong interpersonal skills, must have valid driver's license and good driving record. Duration is April to September (approximately). $9–$11 per hour. Open to anyone 18 years of age or older. ▶ *20 life science interns:* responsibilities include collecting adult and larval mosquito for identification and monitoring of mosquito populations; may involve lab and/or field work. Candidates should have ability to work independently, self-motivation, strong interpersonal skills, must have valid driver's license and good driving record. Duration is April to September (approximately). $9–$11 per hour. Open to

Clarke Mosquito Control (continued)

anyone 18 years of age or older. ► *12–14 light trap runners:* responsibilities include collecting and identifying tmosquito samples. Candidates should have ability to work independently, oral communication skills, self-motivation, strong interpersonal skills, valid driver's license, good driving record, must be able to use own vehicle (with reimbursement). Duration is April to September (3 days per week part-time or full-time). $10 per hour. Open to anyone over 18 years of age. ► *10 natural resources interns:* responsibilities include possibility of a variety of field-related duties, such as field inspection and treatment. Candidates should have ability to work independently, personal interest in the field, strong interpersonal skills, ability to read and understand maps, hike/walk through uneven terrain, valid driver's license, and good driving record. Duration is April to September (approximately). $9–$11 per hour. Open to anyone over 18 years of age. ► *2 research and development interns:* responsibilities include assisting with the testing of products and equipment, as well as field research projects. Candidates should have ability to work independently, self-motivation, strong interpersonal skills, must have valid driver's license and good driving record. Duration is April to September (approximately). $10 per hour. Open to anyone over 18 years of age.

Benefits Possible full-time employment, willing to complete paperwork for educational credit, willing to provide letters of recommendation.

Contact Write, call, fax, e-mail, or through World Wide Web site Jennifer Burrus, Human Resources Coordinator. Phone: 800-323-5727. Fax: 800-832-9344. E-mail: humanresources@clarkemosquito.com. In-person interview required. Applicants must submit a formal organization application. Application deadline: May 1 for summer. World Wide Web: http://www.clarkemosquito.com.

CLIMATE INSTITUTE
333½ Pennsylvania Avenue, SE
Washington, District of Columbia 20003

General Information Organization serving as a link between scientists and policymakers on the issues of climate change and stratospheric ozone depletion. Established in 1986. Number of employees: 8. Number of internship applications received each year: 30.

Internships Available ► *2–5 research assistants:* responsibilities include assisting with projects and office operations and supporting fund-raising activities. Candidates should have ability to work independently, ability to work with others, office skills, research skills, writing skills. Duration is flexible. Unpaid. Open to high school students, recent high school graduates, college freshmen, college sophomores, college juniors, college seniors, recent college graduates, graduate students, law students, career changers, individuals reentering the workforce. International applications accepted.

Benefits Job counseling, names of contacts, opportunity to attend seminars/workshops, possible full-time employment, willing to act as a professional reference, willing to complete paperwork for educational credit, willing to provide letters of recommendation.

Contact Write, fax, or e-mail Michelle Lennox, Intern Coordinator, 333½ Pennsylvania Avenue, SE, Washington, District of Columbia 20003-1148. Fax: 202-547-0111. E-mail: info@climate.org. In-person interview recommended (telephone interview accepted). Applicants must submit a letter of interest, resume, writing sample. Applications are accepted continuously. World Wide Web: http://www.climate.org.

CLINIC FOR THE REHABILITATION OF WILDLIFE (C.R.O.W.)
PO Box 150
Sanibel Island, Florida 33957

General Information Nonprofit wildlife rehabilitation center and veterinary hospital dedicated to the care of injured, ill, and orphaned native and migratory wildlife of Lee County. Established in 1968. Number of employees: 5. Number of internship applications received each year: 100.

Internships Available ► *2–4 externs:* responsibilities include participating on rehabilitative team. Candidates should have ability to work with others, personal interest in the field, self-motivation, background in natural science and/or veterinary field (recommended); willingness to participate with staff in manual labor (a must). Duration is 6–8 weeks. Unpaid. Open to college sophomores, college juniors, college seniors, recent college graduates, graduate students, career changers. ► *1–2 fellows:* responsibilities include organizing and supporting volunteers and externs with daily cleaning, feeding, and rehabilitation of wildlife patients in outside compounds; assisting veterinarian as needed with clinic duties. Candidates should have oral communication skills, organizational skills, personal interest in the field, self-motivation, strong interpersonal skills, prior externship with C.R.O.W. (preferred); background in natural science or experience with animals, willingness to perform manual labor. Duration is 6 months. Stipend of $500 per month. Open to college freshmen, college sophomores, college juniors, college seniors, recent college graduates, graduate students, career changers.

Benefits Free housing, on-the-job training, willing to act as a professional reference, willing to complete paperwork for educational credit, willing to provide letters of recommendation.

Contact Write, call, or e-mail Dr. PJ Deitschel, Externships. Phone: 941-472-3644. E-mail: crowclinic@aol.com. Telephone interview required. Applicants must submit a formal organization application, letter of interest, resume, academic transcripts, 2 recommendations (1 must be from a veterinarian if vet student). Applications are accepted continuously. World Wide Web: http://www.crowclinic.org.

CLYDE E. BUCKLEY WILDLIFE SANCTUARY
1305 Germany Road
Frankfort, Kentucky 40601

General Information Sanctuary working to teach the public about the environment through hands-on experience, and to encourage the potential of native flora and fauna through sound wildlife management. Established in 1967. Number of employees: 3. Unit of National Audubon Society, New York, New York. Number of internship applications received each year: 30.

Internships Available ► *6 sanctuary operations interns:* responsibilities include assisting with nature interpretation, environmental education, wildlife management, research, caretaking, maintenance, administration, exhibits, photography, gift shop operations, fundraising, and creative writing. Candidates should have ability to work independently, ability to work with others, computer skills, knowledge of field, oral communication skills, self-motivation. Duration is 10 weeks. $100 per week. Open to college freshmen, college sophomores, college juniors, college seniors, recent college graduates, graduate students, career changers, individuals reentering the workforce.

Benefits Formal training, free housing, opportunity to attend seminars/workshops, willing to complete paperwork for educational credit, worker's compensation, utilities, uniforms.

Contact Write, call, fax, or e-mail Mr. Timothy Williams, Sanctuary Manager. Phone: 859-873-5711. Fax: 859-873-5711. E-mail: twilliams@audubon.org. Applicants must submit a resume, two personal references, letter describing reason for internship and potential contribution to programs (include interests and hobbies). Application deadline: February 15 for spring, May 15 for summer, August 15 for fall.

COLORADO WILDLIFE FEDERATION
445 Union Boulevard, Suite 302
Lakewood, Colorado 80228-1243

General Information Conservation education organization that focuses on issues affecting Colorado's wildlife and conservation programs for children. Established in 1953. Number of employees: 5. Affiliate of National Wildlife Federation, Vienna, Virginia. Number of internship applications received each year: 40.

Internships Available ► *1 conservation advocacy intern:* responsibilities include assisting staff and Board of Directors by working on various conservation advocacy campaigns, including off-road vehicles and mule deer herd health. Candidates should have ability to work independently, analytical skills, college courses in field, computer skills, editing skills, knowledge of field, office skills, oral communication skills, organizational skills, personal interest in the field, research skills, self-motivation, strong interpersonal skills, writing skills. Duration is year-round. Position available as unpaid or at $7–$10 per hour. Open to college freshmen, college sophomores, college juniors, college seniors, recent college graduates, graduate students, law students, career changers. ▶ *1–4 education interns:* responsibilities include visiting 2nd through 8th grade classrooms in the Denver metropolitan area to bring conservation education programming to students, and leading outdoor education programs for the students at Two Ponds National Wildlife Refuge in Arvada, Colorado. Candidates should have ability to work independently, knowledge of field, oral communication skills, personal interest in the field, research skills, self-motivation, strong interpersonal skills, ability to work with children. Duration is September to June. Position available as unpaid or at $8 per hour. Open to recent high school graduates, college freshmen, college sophomores, college juniors, college seniors, recent college graduates, graduate students, law students, career changers, individuals reentering the workforce. International applications accepted.

Benefits Job counseling, names of contacts, on-the-job training, opportunity to attend seminars/workshops, willing to complete paperwork for educational credit, willing to provide letters of recommendation, mileage reimbursement for delivering programs.

Contact Write, call, fax, e-mail, or through World Wide Web site Michael Brogan, Director of Education. Phone: 303-987-0400. Fax: 303-987-0200. E-mail: education@coloradowildlife.org. In-person interview recommended (telephone interview accepted). Applicants must submit a letter of interest, resume. Applications are accepted continuously. World Wide Web: http://www.coloradowildlife.org.

COMMUNITY ENVIRONMENTAL CENTER
43-10 11th Street
Long Island City, New York 11101

General Information Not-for-profit energy conservation and environmental education center. Established in 1994. Number of employees: 40. Number of internship applications received each year: 40.

Internships Available ▶ *1–2 construction management interns (technical services):* responsibilities include developing construction management documentation, quality management, and performing field inspections. Candidates should have ability to work independently, computer skills, experience in the field, oral communication skills, self-motivation, writing skills, major or degree in construction management or related field; must be able to travel. Duration is 3–6 months. Position available as unpaid or at $12 per hour. Open to college seniors, recent college graduates, graduate students. ▶ *1–2 energy interns (technical services):* responsibilities include developing heating distribution and system specifications, performing building performance analyses, assisting in construction management and designing, and conducting energy audits. Candidates should have ability to work independently, oral communication skills, organizational skills, personal interest in the field, writing skills, degree or major in energy or mechanical engineering or related field; experience in doing energy audits on buildings; must be able to travel. Duration is 3–6 months. Position available as unpaid or at $12 per hour. Open to college seniors, recent college graduates, graduate students. ▶ *1–2 fundraising support/office support interns:* responsibilities include research of urban environmental issues; preparation of informational materials, including writing, editing, and layout; miscellaneous projects (e.g., educational programs, technical analyses, policy). Candidates should have ability to work independently, ability to work with others, editing skills, personal interest in the field, research skills, writing skills. Duration is one semester or one summer. Position available as unpaid or at $8 per hour. Open to high school students, recent high school graduates, college freshmen, college sophomores, college juniors, college seniors, individuals reentering the workforce. International applications accepted.

Benefits On-the-job training, opportunity to attend seminars/workshops, possible full-time employment, willing to act as a professional reference, willing to complete paperwork for educational credit, willing to provide letters of recommendation.

Contact Write, call, fax, or e-mail Lynn Grace, Director of the Learning Center/Outreach, 43-10 11th Street, Long Island City, New York 11101. Phone: 718-784-1444 Ext. 107. Fax: 718-784-8347. E-mail: cecenter@earthlink.net. In-person interview required. Applicants must submit a letter of interest, resume. Applications are accepted continuously.

THE CONSERVANCY OF SOUTHWEST FLORIDA
1450 Merrihue Drive
Naples, Florida 34102

General Information Locally based, nonprofit conservation organization whose efforts are primarily focused on ecological research, environmental protection, and environmental education; operates 2 nature centers, a wildlife rehabilitation clinic, and offers many environment programs and activities for the public. Established in 1964. Number of employees: 48. Number of internship applications received each year: 200.

Internships Available ▶ *2 Museum of Natural History/Naples Nature Center Conservation Associates:* responsibilities include working in museum research and exhibit interpretation and design, outdoors on nature trails, and delivering programs. Candidates should have ability to work independently, computer skills, knowledge of field, oral communication skills, personal interest in the field, self-motivation, strong interpersonal skills. Duration is 6–9 months. $125 per week. Open to college juniors, college seniors, recent college graduates, graduate students. ▶ *1 environmental land acquisition conservation associate:* responsibilities include assisting in purchasing conservation land; conducting research; coordinating responses and commentary on land acquisition issues. Candidates should have ability to work independently, oral communication skills, personal interest in the field, research skills, self-motivation, strong interpersonal skills, written communication skills. Duration is 3–9 months. $125 per week. Open to college seniors, recent college graduates, graduate students, law students. ▶ *1 environmental policy conservation associate:* responsibilities include assisting in all aspects of research and investigations of environmental issues. Candidates should have ability to work independently, ability to work with others, oral communication skills, personal interest in the field, self-motivation, written communication skills. Duration is 3–9 months. $125 per week. Open to recent college graduates, graduate students, law students. ▶ *1 environmental science conservation associate:* responsibilities include working on current field and/or office projects. Candidates should have analytical skills, college degree in related field, oral communication skills, plan to pursue career in field, research skills, written communication skills. Duration is 3–9 months. $125 per week. Open to recent college graduates, graduate students, law students. ▶ *1 grassroots advocacy conservation associate.* Candidates should have ability to work independently, college courses in field, computer skills, oral communication skills, organizational skills, personal interest in the field, self-motivation, strong interpersonal skills, written communication skills. Duration is 3–9 months. $125 per week. Open to college seniors, recent college graduates, graduate students, law students. ▶ *2–4 naturalist conservation associates (Briggs):* responsibilities include teaching marine and estuarine ecology programs as well as environmental education programs for summer programs and adult visitors; assisting in development of and implementation of summer programs and community outreach programs; supervising nature center; leading outdoor excursions, guided local-tour and canoe trips within Rookery Bay National Estuarine Reserve and other south Florida ecosystems. Candidates should have ability to work independently, college courses in field, knowledge of field, oral communication skills, organizational skills, personal interest in the field, self-motivation, strong interpersonal skills, physical ability to hike and canoe. Duration is 3–9 months. $125 per week. Open to college juniors, college seniors, recent college graduates, graduate students. ▶ *1 school programs conservation associate:* responsibilities include teaching the natural science of Florida ecology to preschool and elementary school children; providing field trips for children focusing on south Florida ecology and environmental science; planning day-long and occasional week-long children's events; assisting staff in developing new programs including ecotourism and community education for all ages. Candidates should have ability to work independently, ability to

The Conservancy of Southwest Florida (continued)

work with others, college courses in field, computer skills, oral communication skills, organizational skills, personal interest in the field, self-motivation, experience with children. Duration is 6–9 months. $125 per week. Open to college juniors, college seniors, recent college graduates, graduate students. ▶ *4 sea turtle research conservation associates:* responsibilities include monitoring and recording loggerhead sea turtle nesting information, measuring and tagging nesting turtles, securing the nest, and relocating when necessary. Candidates should have ability to work independently, declared college major in field, oral communication skills, personal interest in the field, self-motivation, strong interpersonal skills, ability to work in hot, buggy conditions. Duration is 3–5 months. $125 per week. Open to college seniors, recent college graduates, graduate students. ▶ *4 summer camp conservation associates:* responsibilities include teaching the natural science of Florida ecology to preschool, elementary, and middle school students; some outdoor work in hot and buggy conditions; assisting staff with developing camp curricula. Candidates should have ability to work independently, college courses in field, oral communication skills, personal interest in the field, self-motivation, strong interpersonal skills, favorable attitude towards children. Duration is 3 months. $125 per week. Open to college juniors, college seniors, recent college graduates, graduate students. ▶ *4 wildlife rehabilitation conservation associates:* responsibilities include assisting in care and treatment of injured, sick, and orphaned Florida wildlife and cleaning and maintaining facilities. Candidates should have ability to work independently, college courses in field, experience in the field, personal interest in the field, self-motivation, strong interpersonal skills. Duration is 6–9 months. $125 per week. Open to college juniors, college seniors, recent college graduates, graduate students. International applications accepted.

Benefits Formal training, free housing, job counseling, names of contacts, on-the-job training, opportunity to attend seminars/workshops, possible full-time employment, willing to act as a professional reference, willing to complete paperwork for educational credit, willing to provide letters of recommendation, uniform shirts furnished, accident insurance at no cost.

Contact Write, call, fax, e-mail, or through World Wide Web site Sharon L. Truluck, Human Resources Director, 1450 Merrihue Drive, Naples, Florida 34102. Phone: 941-262-0304. Fax: 941-262-0672. E-mail: humanresources@conservancy.org. Telephone interview required. Applicants must submit a formal organization application, letter of interest, resume, academic transcripts, three personal references, three letters of recommendation. Applications are accepted continuously. World Wide Web: http://www.conservancy.org.

CORAL CAY CONSERVATION, LTD.
The Tower, 13th Floor, 125 High Street, Colliers Wood London SW19 2JG United Kingdom

General Information Coral reef and tropical forest conservation organization. Established in 1986. Number of employees: 20. Number of internship applications received each year: 20.

Internships Available ▶ *1 chief technical advisor (Philippines Marine Projects):* responsibilities include managing science program from 2 Philippines projects, teaching, survey planning, data management, and report writing are all required. Duration is 6–12 months. Position available as unpaid or paid. Open to graduate students. ▶ *2–4 chief technical advisors (Honduras):* responsibilities include management of scientific program for Caribbean coral reef conservation project; reporting to UK office and liaison with host country counterparts. Candidates should have college degree in related field, experience in the field, oral communication skills, research skills, self-motivation, strong interpersonal skills. Duration is 6–12 months. Position available as unpaid or paid. Open to recent college graduates, graduate students. ▶ *1–3 chief technical advisors (South Pacific Marine Projects):* responsibilities include managing the science program from marine survey projects involving teaching, data analysis, report writing, and survey diving. Duration is 6–12 months. Position available as unpaid or paid. Open to graduate students. ▶ *1–2 head office research assistants:* responsibilities include data management, report production, administra-

tion, teaching (presentations), and statistical analysis. Duration is 6–12 months. Position available as unpaid or paid. Open to graduate students. ▶ *2 marine conservation project leaders (Philippines):* responsibilities include managing, administering, and leading a major conservation project site with up to 35 volunteers and local staff. Candidates should have experience in the field, organizational skills, personal interest in the field, self-motivation, strong interpersonal skills, strong leadership ability. Duration is 6 months. $150 per month (local subsistence wage only). Open to graduate students, law students, career changers, individuals reentering the workforce, management professionals. ▶ *3 medical officers (Honduras, Philippines):* responsibilities include serving on a remote conservation project site; responsible for care of up to 35 volunteers and local staff. Candidates should have ability to work independently, college degree in related field, organizational skills, strong interpersonal skills, strong leadership ability. Duration is 4 months. Unpaid. Open to recent college graduates, graduate students, career changers, must be nurse, doctor, or paramedic. ▶ *2 project leaders (Honduras):* responsibilities include managing, administering, and leading a major conservation project site in Roatan, Honduras. Candidates should have organizational skills, personal interest in the field, self-motivation, strong interpersonal skills, strong leadership ability, diving experience essential. Duration is 6 months. $150 per month (local subsistence wage only). Open to graduate students, law students, career changers, individuals reentering the workforce, management professionals. ▶ *2 project leaders (Philippines):* responsibilities include managing, administering, and leading a major conservation project site with up to 35 volunteers and local staff. Candidates should have experience in the field, organizational skills, personal interest in the field, self-motivation, strong interpersonal skills, strong leadership ability. Duration is 6 months. $150 per month (local subsistence wage only). Open to graduate students, law students, career changers, individuals reentering the workforce, management professionals. ▶ *2 rainforest conservation project leaders (Philippines):* responsibilities include managing, administering, and leading a major conservation project site with up to 35 volunteers and local staff. Candidates should have experience in the field, organizational skills, personal interest in the field, self-motivation, strong interpersonal skills, strong leadership ability. Duration is 6 months. $150 per month (local subsistence wage only). Open to graduate students, law students, career changers, individuals reentering the workforce, management professionals. ▶ *4–8 science officers (Honduras):* responsibilities include coordinating day-to-day scientific program for Caribbean coral reef conservation project; training volunteer divers in marine ecology; and organizing survey work. Candidates should have college degree in related field, experience in the field, oral communication skills, research skills, self-motivation, strong interpersonal skills. Duration is 3–6 months. Unpaid. Open to recent college graduates, graduate students. ▶ *3 science officers (Honduras, Philippines):* responsibilities include conducting and coordinating surveying activities in a remote conservation project site with up to 35 volunteers. Candidates should have ability to work with others, oral communication skills, research skills, strong leadership ability, written communication skills, must have relevant scientific degree. Duration is 4 months. Unpaid. Open to recent college graduates, graduate students, career changers, individuals reentering the workforce. ▶ *3 scuba instructors (Philippines):* responsibilities include diving instruction and coordination of safe diving activity in remote marine conservation site. Candidates should have knowledge of field, oral communication skills, organizational skills, strong interpersonal skills, strong leadership ability, must have relevant scuba certification. Duration is 4 months. Unpaid. Open to recent high school graduates, college freshmen, college sophomores, college juniors, college seniors, recent college graduates, graduate students, law students, career changers, individuals reentering the workforce. International applications accepted.

Benefits Free housing, free meals, health insurance, job counseling, names of contacts, on-the-job training, opportunity to attend seminars/workshops, possible full-time employment, travel reimbursement, willing to act as a professional reference, willing to complete paperwork for educational credit, willing to provide letters of recommendation.

International Internships Available in Fiji; Honduras; Malaysia; Philippines; Samoa; London, United Kingdom.
Contact E-mail Peter Raines, Managing Director. Fax: 44-20-7498-8447. E-mail: psr@coralcay.org. No phone calls. In-person interview recommended (telephone interview accepted). Applicants must submit a formal organization application, letter of interest, resume, academic transcripts, portfolio, two personal references, two letters of recommendation. Applications are accepted continuously. World Wide Web: http://www.coralcay.org.

CORKSCREW SWAMP SANCTUARY
375 Sanctuary Road
Naples, Florida 34120

General Information 11,000-acre wilderness area in southwest Florida providing preservation, protection, and public education; home to old-growth bald cypress forest and Florida's largest nesting colony of endangered wood storks. Established in 1954. Number of employees: 23. Unit of National Audubon Society, New York, New York. Number of internship applications received each year: 200.
Internships Available ▶ *2–4 naturalist educators:* responsibilities include environmental education and interpretation tasks, program development and staffing, and maintenance of visitor center. Candidates should have ability to work independently, ability to work with others, oral communication skills, some experience in environmental area, education background recommended. Duration is 6-8 months (start late August/early September). $150 per week. Open to college juniors, college seniors, recent college graduates, graduate students, career changers. ▶ *2–4 resource management team members:* responsibilities include resource management fieldwork, exotic plant removal, trail maintenance, staffing and maintenance of visitor center and grounds. Candidates should have ability to work independently, ability to work with others, personal interest in the field. Duration is 6 months. $150 per week. Open to college freshmen, college sophomores, college juniors, college seniors, recent college graduates, graduate students, career changers.
Benefits Formal training, free housing, job counseling, names of contacts, on-the-job training, willing to complete paperwork for educational credit, willing to provide letters of recommendation, job lists provided when available, $50 allowance for necessary clothing/uniform.
Contact Write, fax, or e-mail Laurel Chaplin, Education Director. Fax: 941-348-9155. E-mail: lchaplin@audubon.org. No phone calls. Telephone interview required. Applicants must submit a letter of interest, resume, three personal references. Applications are accepted continuously. World Wide Web: http://www.audubon.org/local/sanctuary/corkscrew.

DEEP PORTAGE CONSERVATION RESERVE
2197 Nature Center Drive, NW
Hackensack, Minnesota 56452

General Information 6000-acre forest and conservation education center that conducts programs in environmental education. Established in 1973. Number of employees: 22. Number of internship applications received each year: 40.
Internships Available ▶ *5–10 instructor interns:* responsibilities include teaching environmental education. Candidates should have ability to work with others, oral communication skills, organizational skills, personal interest in the field, written communication skills. Duration is 3–6 months. $175-$225 per week for summer positions; $250 per week for other positions. Open to college freshmen, college sophomores, college juniors, college seniors, graduate students, career changers, individuals reentering the workforce. International applications accepted.
Benefits Formal training, free housing, free meals, job counseling, names of contacts, opportunity to attend seminars/workshops, possible full-time employment, willing to complete paperwork for educational credit, willing to provide letters of recommendation.
Contact Write, call, fax, e-mail, or through World Wide Web site Dale Yerger, Director. Phone: 218-682-2325. Fax: 218-682-3121. E-mail: portage@uslink.net. In-person interview recommended (telephone interview accepted). Applicants must submit a resume, three personal references. Applications are accepted continuously. World Wide Web: http://www.deep-portage.org.

DELAWARE NATURE SOCIETY (ASHLAND NATURE CENTER)
PO Box 700, Brackenville and Barley Mill Road
Hockessin, Delaware 19707

General Information Environmental education and advocacy organization. Established in 1964. Number of employees: 70. Number of internship applications received each year: 5.
Internships Available ▶ *1–3 environmental education interns:* responsibilities include teaching and co-teaching children's classes and leading or assisting with field trips. Candidates should have ability to work with others, computer skills, knowledge of field, oral communication skills, personal interest in the field, ability to work with children, outdoor skills. Duration is 1–12 months. Position available as unpaid or paid. Open to college juniors, college seniors, recent college graduates, graduate students, career changers. International applications accepted.
Benefits Formal training, on-the-job training, opportunity to attend seminars/workshops, possible full-time employment, willing to act as a professional reference, willing to complete paperwork for educational credit, willing to provide letters of recommendation.
Contact Write, call, fax, e-mail, or through World Wide Web site Karen Travers, Members Programs Coordinator, PO Box 700, Hockessin, Delaware 19707. Phone: 302-239-2334 Ext. 15. Fax: 302-239-2473. E-mail: karen@dnsashland.org. In-person interview required. Applicants must submit a formal organization application, letter of interest, resume, two personal references, two letters of recommendation. Applications are accepted continuously. World Wide Web: http://www.delawarenaturesociety.org.

DELAWARE WATER GAP NATIONAL RECREATION AREA
294 Old Milford Road
Milford, Pennsylvania 18337

General Information Organization devoted to conserving scenery, natural and historic objects, and wildlife for the enjoyment of future generations. Established in 1965. Number of employees: 128. Unit of United States National Park Service, Washington, District of Columbia. Number of internship applications received each year: 15.
Internships Available ▶ *1 geographic information systems laboratory assistant:* responsibilities include developing and implementing various software tools to facilitate spatial data creation, managing and analyzing within a GIS, assisting in development of GIS analytical procedure, and assisting in development of network communications. Candidates should have ability to work independently, ability to work with others, college courses in field, computer skills, organizational skills, self-motivation. Duration is 12–14 weeks. Unpaid. Open to college sophomores, college juniors, college seniors, recent college graduates, graduate students, career changers, individuals reentering the workforce. ▶ *1 resource assistant:* responsibilities include assisting with divisional activities that may include wildlife, fisheries, vegetation monitoring/management, trails development, water resources planning, wetland studies, and cultural landscape. Candidates should have ability to work independently, ability to work with others, college courses in field, computer skills, knowledge of field, oral communication skills, self-motivation, written communication skills. Duration is 3 months minimum. Unpaid. Open to college juniors, college seniors, recent college graduates, graduate students. ▶ *2 water quality assistants:* responsibilities include measuring water quality in streams and rivers, maintaining and calibrating equipment, performing data entry, and analyzing data. Candidates should have ability to work independently, ability to work with others, analytical skills, computer skills, knowledge of field, organizational skills. Duration is 12 weeks. Unpaid. Open to college juniors, college seniors, recent college graduates, graduate students. International applications accepted.

Delaware Water Gap National Recreation Area (continued)

Benefits Free housing, job counseling, names of contacts, willing to complete paperwork for educational credit, willing to provide letters of recommendation, worker's compensation, potential stipend.

Contact Write or fax Patrick J. Lynch, Chief, Division of Research and Resource Planning. Fax: 570-296-4706. E-mail: patrick_lynch@ nps.gov. No phone calls. In-person interview recommended (telephone interview accepted). Applicants must submit a letter of interest, resume. Application deadline: February 15 for spring/ summer, November 1 for winter. World Wide Web: http://www. nps.gov/dewa.

DOLPHIN RESEARCH CENTER
58901 Overseas Highway
Grassy Key, Florida 33050-6019

General Information Organization dedicated to teaching, learning, and caring for marine mammals and the environment. Established in 1984. Number of employees: 70. Number of internship applications received each year: 100.

Internships Available ▶ *1 animal care and training intern:* responsibilities include assisting trainers during dolphin and sea lion training sessions; conducting segments of public sessions or workshops; assisting with data collection for research, repair, and maintenance of training equipment; food preparation; assisting with husbandry procedures. Candidates should have ability to work with others, knowledge of field, oral communication skills, organizational skills, personal interest in the field, self-motivation. Duration is 3–4 months. Unpaid. Open to college freshmen, college sophomores, college juniors, college seniors, recent college graduates, career changers. ▶ *1 animal husbandry/medical intern:* responsibilities include food and vitamin prep; stocking and inventorying food and husbandry supplies; fish delivery assistance; training and supervising other volunteers/interns; maintaining husbandry and medical files; assisting with medical procedures and observations; assisting with data collection for on-going research. Candidates should have ability to work independently, experience in the field, oral communication skills, organizational skills, plan to pursue career in field, strong interpersonal skills. Duration is 3–4 months. Unpaid. Open to college sophomores, college juniors, college seniors, recent college graduates, career changers. ▶ *1 dolphin/ child therapy intern:* responsibilities include supporting dolphin-assisted therapy staff; preparation and maintenance of session equipment; assisting program participants and families; recording session notes and maintaining records; preparing program folders; assisting with data collection for ongoing research. Candidates should have ability to work with others, college courses in field, knowledge of field, oral communication skills, plan to pursue career in field. Duration is 3–4 months. Unpaid. Open to college freshmen, college sophomores, college juniors, college seniors, recent college graduates, career changers. ▶ *1–2 education interns:* responsibilities include supporting education staff; assisting with coordination of students in week-long DolphinLab classes; handling information requests and correspondence; preparing DolphinLab participant notebooks; assisting and/or teaching seminars and community outreach presentations; recording minutes for department meetings. Candidates should have college courses in field, oral communication skills, personal interest in the field, plan to pursue career in field, strong interpersonal skills. Duration is 3–4 months. Unpaid. Open to college sophomores, college juniors, college seniors, recent college graduates, career changers. ▶ *1 guest programs intern:* responsibilities include assisting with educating and entertaining guests; narrating training sessions; teaching workshops; photographing program participants; food preparation; and other responsibilities. Candidates should have ability to work with others, oral communication skills, organizational skills, personal interest in the field, self-motivation. Duration is 3–4 months. Unpaid. Open to college freshmen, college sophomores, college juniors, college seniors, recent college graduates, graduate students, career changers. ▶ *1–2 research interns:* responsibilities include preparation and maintenance of research equipment; coordinating and assisting with data collection for on-going research; summarizing and analyzing research data; maintaining records; training and supervising other volunteers/

interns in data collection. Candidates should have ability to work independently, ability to work with others, computer skills, knowledge of field, oral communication skills, plan to pursue career in field. Duration is 3–4 months. Unpaid. Open to college sophomores, college juniors, college seniors, recent college graduates, graduate students. International applications accepted.

Benefits Formal training, on-the-job training, opportunity to attend seminars/workshops, possible full-time employment, willing to act as a professional reference, willing to complete paperwork for educational credit, willing to provide letters of recommendation.

Contact Write, call, fax, e-mail, or through World Wide Web site Merrell Williams, Volunteer Resources Director. Phone: 305-289-1121 Ext. 230. Fax: 305-743-7627. E-mail: drc-vr@dolphins.org. Telephone interview required. Applicants must submit a formal organization application, resume, academic transcripts, two letters of recommendation, volunteer application with the intern application. Application deadline: February 1 for summer, June 1 for fall, October 1 for winter. World Wide Web: http://www. dolphins.org.

EDUCATIONAL COMMUNICATIONS, INC.;ECONEWS TELEVISION;ENVIRONMENTAL DIRECTIONS RADIO;ECOLOGY CENTER OF SOUTHERN CALIFORNIA;PROJECT ECOTOURISM,COMPENDIUM
PO Box 351419
Los Angeles, California 90035-9119

General Information Environmental broadcasting, cablecasting and conservation organization specializing in ecological activism and audio/video production and distribution; also promotes ecotourism. Established in 1958. Unit of Educational Communications, Idyllwild, California. Number of internship applications received each year: 50.

Internships Available ▶ *Interns:* responsibilities include working in a variety of areas including ecological and environmental activism, administration, networking, organizing research, fund-raising, public speaking, membership development, writing, producing, editing, directing television and radio productions, distribution, publishing, journalism, and broadcasting. Candidates should have ability to work independently, ability to work with others, editing skills, personal interest in the field, writing skills, English speaking/ understanding ability. Duration is flexible (prefer 3 days per week). Unpaid. Open to high school students, recent high school graduates, college freshmen, college sophomores, college juniors, college seniors, recent college graduates, graduate students, law students, career changers, individuals reentering the workforce. International applications accepted.

Benefits Job counseling, names of contacts, on-the-job training, opportunity to attend seminars/workshops, willing to act as a professional reference, willing to complete paperwork for educational credit, willing to provide letters of recommendation, referrals provided, opportunity to produce and host own television and radio shows, possible travel reimbursement.

International Internships Available.

Contact Write, call, or e-mail Leslie Lewis, Administrative Assistant. Phone: 310-559-9160. E-mail: ecnp@aol.com. Telephone interview required. Applicants must submit a letter of interest, personal reference, demo tape (television editing position) if available. Applications are accepted continuously. World Wide Web: http:// www.ecoprojects.org.

EL MALPAIS NATIONAL CONSERVATION AREA AND NATIONAL MONUMENT
2001 East Santa Fe Avenue
Grants, New Mexico 87020

General Information Area designated by Congress to preserve the natural geology and cultural resources surrounding Grant's Lava Flows; land includes 2 wilderness areas. Number of employees: 5. Unit of Bureau of Land Management, Albuquerque Field Office, Albuquerque, New Mexico. Number of internship applications received each year: 12.

Internships Available ▶ *1–2 backcountry rangers:* responsibilities include patrolling NCA backcountry/wilderness by vehicle or on foot, keeping a written patrol log, writing reports, providing visitors with accurate information, giving guided tours, assisting with maintenance, and staffing visitor center. Duration is 3 months (flexible). Unpaid. ▶ *1–2 visitor information specialists:* responsibilities include staffing the visitor center desk, responding to visitor questions, selling Cooperating Association books and materials, patrolling NCA by vehicle or on foot, keeping a written patrol log, writing reports as necessary, giving guided tours, and assisting with maintenance. Duration is 3 months (flexible). Unpaid. Candidates for all positions should have computer skills, oral communication skills, personal interest in the field, strong interpersonal skills, written communication skills.
Benefits Free housing, willing to complete paperwork for educational credit, willing to provide letters of recommendation.
Contact Write or call Ms. Karen Davis, Volunteer Coordinator/Park Ranger. Phone: 505-287-7911. Fax: 505-285-5041. E-mail: karen_davis@blm.gov. Applicants must submit a formal organization application, resume, two personal references. Applications are accepted continuously.

ENDANGERED SPECIES COALITION
1101 14th Street, NW, Suite 1001
Washington, District of Columbia 20005

General Information Environmental organization working to protect endangered species and the Endangered Species Act. Established in 1982. Number of employees: 6. Number of internship applications received each year: 60.
Internships Available ▶ *1–3 organizing internships:* responsibilities include contacting activists and environmental groups via phone, e-mail, or fax on endangered species issues; keeping up with legislation on endangered species issues; assisting with daily office activities and database maintenance; helping answer requests for information. Candidates should have ability to work independently, ability to work with others, knowledge of field, oral communication skills, organizational skills, personal interest in the field, self-motivation, strong leadership ability, writing skills. Duration is 1 semester. Position available as unpaid or paid. Open to college freshmen, college sophomores, college juniors, college seniors, recent college graduates. International applications accepted.
Benefits On-the-job training, willing to act as a professional reference, willing to complete paperwork for educational credit, willing to provide letters of recommendation.
Contact Write, fax, or e-mail Eileen Brancale, Northeast Organizer. Phone: 202-772-3234. Fax: 202-756-2804. E-mail: ebrancale@stopextinction.org. In-person interview recommended (telephone interview accepted). Applicants must submit a letter of interest, resume, one-page writing sample. Applications are accepted continuously. World Wide Web: http://www.stopextinction.org.

ENVIRONMENTAL AND ENERGY STUDY INSTITUTE
122 C Street, NW, Suite 700
Washington, District of Columbia 20001-2109

General Information Nonpartisan public policy research and analysis organization that strives to produce better informed congressional debate and to generate credible and innovative policies for environmentally sustainable development. Established in 1984. Number of employees: 11. Number of internship applications received each year: 120.
Internships Available ▶ *1 Legislative intern:* responsibilities include researching energy and environmental issues for fund-raising proposals, assisting with writing proposals and grant reports, attending meetings and reporting on proceedings, helping prepare annual report, and performing administrative tasks. Duration is flexible. Unpaid. ▶ *3 public policy interns:* responsibilities include researching for institute reports, publications, and projects; attending congressional hearings and other meetings; reporting on proceedings to EESI staff and assisting in administrative work; setting up and attending meetings with other organizations and congressional offices; and assisting with congressional briefings

on water quality and efficiency, climate change, energy efficiency, and transportation. Candidates should have oral communication skills, personal interest in the field, self-motivation, strong interpersonal skills, written communication skills. Duration is flexible. Unpaid. Open to college freshmen, college sophomores, college juniors, college seniors, graduate students. International applications accepted.
Benefits Names of contacts, possible full-time employment, willing to complete paperwork for educational credit, willing to provide letters of recommendation, leadership skills.
Contact Write, call, fax, or through World Wide Web site Intern Coordinator. Phone: 202-628-1400. Fax: 202-628-1825. In-person interview recommended (telephone interview accepted). Applicants must submit a letter of interest, resume. Applications are accepted continuously. World Wide Web: http://www.eesi.org.

ENVIRONMENTAL DEFENSE FUND
257 Park Avenue South
New York, New York 10010

General Information Nonprofit national advocacy organization with over 300,000 members working to develop economical and viable solutions to tough environmental problems. Established in 1967. Number of employees: 80. Number of internship applications received each year: 100.
Internships Available ▶ *4–6 legal interns:* responsibilities include working on issues involving fisheries management, land use issues integrated with issues of air pollution and traffic congestion, legislative issues, policy/legal research, and policy analysis. Duration is May to August. Position available as unpaid or at $450–$500 per week. ▶ *4–6 program recruiters:* responsibilities include working on issues involving fisheries management, land use issues integrated with issues of air pollution and traffic congestion, legislation issues, policy/legal research, and policy analysis. Duration is May to August. Position available as unpaid or at $450–$500 per week. Candidates for all positions should have ability to work independently, computer skills, declared college major in field, oral communication skills, plan to pursue career in field, research skills, writing skills. Open to recent college graduates, graduate students, law students, career changers.
Benefits Names of contacts, opportunity to attend seminars/workshops, travel reimbursement, willing to act as a professional reference, willing to complete paperwork for educational credit, willing to provide letters of recommendation.
Contact Call, fax, or e-mail Maxine Adams, Intern Recruiter. Phone: 212-505-2100. Fax: 212-533-6748. E-mail: maxineadams@environmentaldefense.org. In-person interview recommended (telephone interview accepted). Applicants must submit a letter of interest, resume, academic transcripts, writing sample, two letters of recommendation. Application deadline: March 31 for summer.

ENVIRONMENTAL RESOURCE CENTER
PO Box 819, 411 East Sixth Street
Ketchum, Idaho 83340

General Information Nonprofit organization dedicated to providing resources and educational programs to the public about local, regional, and global environmental issues; acts as umbrella organization for local groups such as Sun Valley Avalanche Center, Wood River Valley Conservation Forum, and the Wood River Action Plan. Established in 1989. Number of employees: 2. Number of internship applications received each year: 30.
Internships Available ▶ *1–2 environmental educators:* responsibilities include helping with teaching environmental education classes, working on individual projects such as the organization of summer events, volunteers, and press work; and researching and writing environmental "fact sheets". Candidates should have ability to work with others, computer skills, oral communication skills, personal interest in the field, written communication skills. Duration is 10 weeks in summer (minimum 20 hours per week). Position available as unpaid or paid. Open to college freshmen, college sophomores, college juniors, college seniors, recent college

Environmental Resource Center (continued)
graduates, graduate students, law students, career changers, individuals reentering the workforce. International applications accepted.
Benefits Formal training, job counseling, names of contacts, on-the-job training, opportunity to attend seminars/workshops, possible full-time employment, willing to act as a professional reference, willing to complete paperwork for educational credit, willing to provide letters of recommendation, assistance in finding housing.
Contact Write, call, fax, or e-mail Craig Barry, Executive Director. Phone: 208-726-4333. Fax: 208-726-1531. E-mail: erc@ercsv.org. In-person interview recommended. Applicants must submit a letter of interest, resume, personal reference. Application deadline: April 1. World Wide Web: http://www.ercsv.org.

EXOTIC FELINE BREEDING COMPOUND, INC.
HCR 1, Box 84
Rosamond, California 93560

General Information Nonprofit organization dedicated to the preservation and propagation of rare and endangered felines through breeding, research, and education. Established in 1977. Number of employees: 5. Number of internship applications received each year: 3.
Internships Available ▶ *1–3 keepers:* responsibilities include cleaning cages, behavioral observation, completion of health charts, dietary preparation, assisting in medical procedures, educational talks with public, and office procedures. Candidates should have ability to work independently, ability to work with others, analytical skills, declared college major in field, personal interest in the field, plan to pursue career in field. Duration is flexible. Unpaid. Open to college freshmen, college sophomores, college juniors, college seniors, recent college graduates, graduate students. International applications accepted.
Benefits Housing at a cost, on-the-job training, willing to act as a professional reference, willing to complete paperwork for educational credit, willing to provide letters of recommendation.
Contact Write, call, fax, or e-mail Sandra Masek, Director/General Manager, HCR 1, Box 84, Rosamond, California 93560. Phone: 661-256-3793. Fax: 661-256-6867. E-mail: info@cathouse-fcc.org. Applicants must submit a letter of interest, resume, letter of recommendation. Applications are accepted continuously. World Wide Web: http://www.cathouse-fcc.org.

FAIRVIEW LAKE ENVIRONMENTAL EDUCATION
CENTER–YMCA
1035 Fairview Lake Road
Newton, New Jersey 07860

General Information Residential facility that offers a hands-on approach to education and presents all-age courses dealing with life sciences, ecology, and technical wilderness skills. Established in 1915. Number of employees: 40. Branch of Metropolitan YMCA of the Oranges, West Orange, New Jersey. Number of internship applications received each year: 10.
Internships Available ▶ *1–3 naturalist interns:* responsibilities include participating in training, observing courses, teaching, aiding in maintenance, designing displays, and submitting paperwork. Duration is 3 months (fall); 5 months (spring). $150 per week. Open to college juniors, college seniors, recent college graduates, graduate students. ▶ *2 recreational interns:* responsibilities include teaching, participating in training including team building, challenge, boating, archery, and hiking. Duration is 3 months. $150 per week. Open to college freshmen, college sophomores, college juniors, college seniors, recent college graduates, graduate students. Candidates for all positions should have ability to work with others, college courses in field, oral communication skills, personal interest in the field. International applications accepted.
Benefits Formal training, free housing, free meals, opportunity to attend seminars/workshops, possible full-time employment, willing to complete paperwork for educational credit, willing to provide letters of recommendation, opportunity to receive certifications in first aid, CPR, and lifeguarding.

Contact Write, call, fax, or e-mail Ms. Christina Henriksen, Environmental Education Director. Phone: 973-383-9282. Fax: 973-383-6386. E-mail: fairviewlake@nac.net. In-person interview recommended (telephone interview accepted). Applicants must submit a letter of interest, resume. Application deadline: March 1 for spring, September 1 for fall.

FARM AND WILDERNESS FOUNDATION
263 Farm and Wilderness Road
Plymouth, Vermont 05056

General Information Quaker-based foundation operating 6 summer camps, a retreat center, a school-year outdoor education program, and a year-round work crew. Established in 1939. Number of employees: 200. Number of internship applications received each year: 30.
Internships Available ▶ *2–3 carpentry interns:* responsibilities include working in maintenance and carpentry. Candidates should have ability to work independently, ability to work with others, knowledge of field, personal interest in the field, self-motivation, some experience helpful. Duration is 3–8 months. $155–$175 per week. Open to college freshmen, college sophomores, college juniors, college seniors, recent college graduates, graduate students, career changers, individuals reentering the workforce. ▶ *2–3 farm interns:* responsibilities include working in organic farming and gardening. Candidates should have ability to work independently, ability to work with others, oral communication skills, personal interest in the field, self-motivation. Duration is 3–8 months. $155–$175 per week. Open to college freshmen, college sophomores, college juniors, college seniors, recent college graduates, graduate students, individuals reentering the workforce. ▶ *2 maintenance interns:* responsibilities include opening, maintaining, and closing seasonal utilities, vehicle fleet, and buildings of an extensive physical plant. Candidates should have ability to work independently, ability to work with others, knowledge of field, organizational skills, personal interest in the field, self-motivation, some experience helpful. Duration is 3–8 months. $155–$175 per week. Open to college freshmen, college sophomores, college juniors, college seniors, recent college graduates, graduate students, career changers, individuals reentering the workforce. ▶ *4–8 outdoor education interns:* responsibilities include instructing outdoor education day programs, school groups, and some adult special-need groups. Candidates should have oral communication skills, organizational skills, plan to pursue career in field, strong interpersonal skills, strong leadership ability, interest in teaching ages 3 to adult. Duration is 10 weeks. $155–$175 per week. Open to college sophomores, college juniors, college seniors, recent college graduates, graduate students, individuals reentering the workforce. ▶ *1–2 retreat center caretakers:* responsibilities include responding to needs of groups in residence, scheduling and outreach to interested groups, and caretaking facilities. Candidates should have ability to work independently, office skills, oral communication skills, self-motivation, strong interpersonal skills, ability to keep facilities clean and orderly. Duration is 10 weeks. $155–$175 per week. Open to college juniors, college seniors, recent college graduates, graduate students, career changers, individuals reentering the workforce. International applications accepted.
Benefits Free housing, free meals, on-the-job training, willing to complete paperwork for educational credit, willing to provide letters of recommendation, worker's compensation.
Contact Write or e-mail Taz Squire, Facilities Managers. E-mail: taz@fandw.org. No phone calls. Telephone interview required. Applicants must submit a formal organization application, letter of interest, resume, two personal references. Application deadline: January 1 for spring/fall; continuous for outdoor education positions. World Wide Web: http://www.fandw.org.

FENTON RANCH
26473 Highway 126
Jemez Springs, New Mexico 87025

General Information Residential facility that houses the environmental education program for a Manzano Day School, a private elementary school. Established in 1974. Number of employees: 5. Unit of Manzano Day School, Albuquerque, New Mexico. Number of internship applications received each year: 80.

Internships Available ▶ *1–2 environmental education interns:* responsibilities include teaching environmental education programs to elementary-aged children, designing curriculums, facilitating free time, keeping journals, supervising meals, and playing with children outdoors. Candidates should have ability to work independently, ability to work with others, oral communication skills, organizational skills, personal interest in the field, self-motivation, strong leadership ability. Duration is 7 weeks (early April to mid- May) or 11 weeks (mid-August to late October). $200 per week. Open to college sophomores, college juniors, college seniors, recent college graduates, graduate students, career changers.

Benefits Free housing, free meals, on-the-job training, travel reimbursement, willing to act as a professional reference, willing to complete paperwork for educational credit, willing to provide letters of recommendation.

Contact Write, call, or e-mail Kestrel Mandras, Fenton Director, 1801 Central Avenue NW, Albuquerque 87104. Phone: 505-243-6659. Fax: 505-243-4711. E-mail: km@mds.k12.nm.us. Telephone interview required. Applicants must submit a formal organization application, letter of interest, resume, three personal references. Application deadline: March 1 for spring, July 15 for fall. World Wide Web: http://www.mds.k12.nm.us/programs/fenton/fenton.html.

FERNWOOD NATURE CENTER
13988 Range Line Road
Niles, Michigan 49120

General Information Nature Center and botanical garden working to educate people about the natural environment and to create environmental awareness and appreciation. Established in 1963. Number of employees: 15. Number of internship applications received each year: 15.

Internships Available ▶ *1 seasonal naturalist:* responsibilities include leading nature walks for children, teaching classes, and maintaining trails and displays. Candidates should have college courses in field, experience in the field, oral communication skills, personal interest in the field, strong interpersonal skills, experience or interest in working with children. Duration is 8 months (March to November). $220–$250 per week. Open to college juniors, college seniors, recent college graduates, graduate students, career changers, individuals reentering the workforce.

Benefits Formal training, free housing, job counseling, names of contacts, on-the-job training, opportunity to attend seminars/workshops, travel reimbursement, willing to act as a professional reference, willing to complete paperwork for educational credit, willing to provide letters of recommendation.

Contact Write, call, or e-mail Ms. Wendy E. Jones, Head Naturalist. Phone: 616-695-6491. E-mail: nature@remc11.k12.mi.us. In-person interview recommended (telephone interview accepted). Applicants must submit a letter of interest, resume, three personal references. Application deadline: February 1. World Wide Web: http://www.fernwoodbotanical.org.

FIVE RIVERS ENVIRONMENTAL EDUCATION CENTER
5 Rivers Center, Game Farm Road
Delmar, New York 12054

General Information Environmental center providing education programs to the public and schools. Established in 1973. Number of employees: 5. Unit of New York State Department of Environmental Conservation, Albany, New York. Number of internship applications received each year: 75.

Internships Available ▶ *8 naturalist interns:* responsibilities include teaching environmental programs and conducting other projects. Candidates should have oral communication skills, personal interest in the field, self-motivation, strong interpersonal skills, written communication skills. Duration is 10–12 weeks. $200 per week.

Open to college freshmen, college sophomores, college juniors, college seniors, recent college graduates, graduate students, career changers, individuals reentering the workforce.

Benefits Formal training, free housing, job counseling, names of contacts, on-the-job training, opportunity to attend seminars/workshops, travel reimbursement, willing to act as a professional reference, willing to complete paperwork for educational credit, willing to provide letters of recommendation, worker's compensation. **Contact** Write, call, or e-mail Ms. Anita Sanchez, Senior Environmental Educator. Phone: 518-475-0291. E-mail: amsanche@gw.dec.state.ny.us. In-person interview recommended (telephone interview accepted). Applicants must submit a formal organization application, resume, three personal references. Applications are accepted continuously.

FIVE RIVERS METROPARKS
1375 East Siebenthaler Avenue
Dayton, Ohio 45414

General Information Park agency with a total of 11,000 acres and annual visitation of approximately 5 million people that manages 24 facilities for public education, outdoor recreation, and protection of natural resources. Established in 1963. Number of employees: 170. Number of internship applications received each year: 30.

Internships Available ▶ *1–2 Adventure Central apprentices:* responsibilities include assisting in all phases of programming, animal care, and equipment upkeep. Candidates should have ability to work independently, knowledge of field, oral communication skills, personal interest in the field, self-motivation, strong interpersonal skills, ability and interest in working with inner-city youth. Duration is 12 months. $7 per hour (32 hours per week). ▶ *1 Carriage Hill agriculture intern/apprentice:* responsibilities include assisting with farm chores, animal care, agricultural work, and general park maintenance. Candidates should have ability to work independently, ability to work with others, oral communication skills, personal interest in the field, self-motivation. Duration is 3–9 months. $7 per hour (32 hours per week). ▶ *1 Carriage Hill restoration intern:* responsibilities include conducting major and minor repairs to historic structures and reconstructions and assisting with general farm maintenance and farm chores. Candidates should have ability to work independently, ability to work with others, personal interest in the field, research skills, self-motivation. Duration is 3–9 months. $7 per hour (32 hours per week). ▶ *1 Cox Arboretum apprentice:* responsibilities include planning and implementing educational programs, monitoring plant hot line, and working with staff and volunteers on horticulturally related projects. Candidates should have ability to work independently, oral communication skills, personal interest in the field, self-motivation, strong interpersonal skills, written communication skills. Duration is 12 months. $7 per hour (32 hours per week). ▶ *1 Germantown MetroPark apprentice:* responsibilities include working in all phases of nature center programming and facility upkeep; conducting walks, workshops, and tours; and staffing the nature center. Candidates should have ability to work independently, ability to work with others, knowledge of field, oral communication skills, personal interest in the field, self-motivation. Duration is 9–12 months. $7 per hour (32 hours per week). ▶ *1 North MetroPark apprentice:* responsibilities include leading natural history-oriented interpretive walks, workshops, and school programs; assisting with special events; and caring for some wild animals, primarily reptiles. Candidates should have ability to work independently, ability to work with others, knowledge of field, oral communication skills, personal interest in the field, self-motivation. Duration is 12 months. $7 per hour (32 hours per week). ▶ *1 Possum Creek farm apprentice:* responsibilities include leading tours of nature trail, barn, and farm animal area; assisting with weekend programs and special events; caring for farm animals; and performing some farm maintenance. Candidates should have ability to work independently, ability to work with others, oral communication skills, personal interest in the field, self-motivation, written communication skills. Duration is 12 months. $7 per hour (32 hours per week). ▶ *1 Wegerzyn adult education intern:* responsibilities include assisting chief of horticultural education in planning and implementing adult gardening programs, special seminars,

Five Rivers MetroParks (continued)

workshops, and professional horticulture training programs. Candidates should have ability to work independently, ability to work with others, oral communication skills, personal interest in the field, self-motivation, written communication skills. Duration is 3–9 months. $7 per hour (32 hours per week). ▶ *1 Wegerzyn youth program apprentice:* responsibilities include developing educational materials and activities; planning and presenting programs for youth, school groups, and families; maintaining the Children's Discovery Garden. Candidates should have ability to work independently, oral communication skills, personal interest in the field, self-motivation, strong interpersonal skills, written communication skills. Duration is 12 months. $7 per hour (32 hours per week). Open to college freshmen, college sophomores, college juniors, college seniors, recent college graduates, graduate students, career changers, individuals reentering the workforce. **Benefits** Job counseling, names of contacts, on-the-job training, opportunity to attend seminars/workshops, possible full-time employment, willing to act as a professional reference, willing to complete paperwork for educational credit, housing provided at some sites.
Contact Write Ms. Lyn Modic, Assistant Director, Education and Programming. Phone: 937-278-8231. Fax: 937-278-8849. E-mail: lmodic@metroparks.org. In-person interview recommended (telephone interview accepted). Applicants must submit a formal organization application, letter of interest, resume, three personal references. Applications are accepted continuously. World Wide Web: http://www.metroparks.org.

FRANCIS BEIDLER FORREST
336 Sanctuary Road
Harleyville, South Carolina 29448

General Information Nonprofit environmental organization. Established in 1977. Number of employees: 10. Unit of National Audubon Society, New York, New York. Number of internship applications received each year: 30.
Internships Available ▶ *Naturalist interns:* responsibilities include leading interpretive walks for all ages on 1-1/2 mile boardwalk through virgin swamp forest; leading half-day canoe trips; running visitor center desk; wildlife and sanctuary management as needed; independent project; assisting with ongoing special events and research; maintenance. Candidates should have ability to work independently, declared college major in field, oral communication skills, plan to pursue career in field, self-motivation, strong interpersonal skills. Duration is 3 months. $150 per week. Open to college juniors, college seniors, recent college graduates, graduate students, career changers, individuals reentering the workforce.
Benefits Free housing, on-the-job training, willing to act as a professional reference, willing to complete paperwork for educational credit, willing to provide letters of recommendation.
Contact Write, call, fax, e-mail, or in person Michael Dawson, Center Director. Phone: 843-462-2150. Fax: 843-462-2713. E-mail: mdawson@audubon.org. Telephone interview required. Applicants must submit a letter of interest, resume, three personal references. Application deadline: January 15 for spring, April 15 for summer, July 15 for fall. World Wide Web: http://www.pride-net.com/swamp/.

FRIENDS OF THE EARTH
1025 Vermont Avenue, NW, Suite 300
Washington, District of Columbia 20005

General Information Independent global advocacy organization working to protect the Earth from environmental disaster, preserve biological, cultural, and ethnic diversity, and empower citizens and help them develop an effective voice in decisions affecting their environment and lives. Established in 1969. Number of employees: 35. Number of internship applications received each year: 250.
Internships Available ▶ *6 fellowships:* responsibilities include working with project directors from Eco-Team, Global Team, Journalism, Communications and Marketing, and Protect the Planet Team in researching, writing, lobbying, and assisting with administrative support on a variety of topics, including taxation and consump-

tion, corporate accountability, water resource protection, ozone layer protection, Northwest rivers and wetlands, and trade and international banking/monetary policy. Duration is 6 months. $1200 per month. Open to recent college graduates, graduate students, law students. ▶ *5–10 interns:* responsibilities include working with project directors from Eco-Team, Global Team, Journalism, Communications and Marketing, and Protect the Planet Team in researching, writing, lobbying, and assisting with administrative support on a variety of topics, including consumption and taxation, corporate accountability, water resource protection, ozone layer protection, Northwest rivers and wetlands, and trade and international banking/monetary policy. Duration is 3–6 months. Unpaid. Open to college seniors, recent college graduates, graduate students, law students. Candidates for all positions should have ability to work independently, computer skills, knowledge of field, oral communication skills, research skills, written communication skills. International applications accepted.
Benefits Names of contacts, on-the-job training, opportunity to attend seminars/workshops, travel reimbursement, willing to complete paperwork for educational credit, willing to provide letters of recommendation.
Contact Write, fax, or e-mail Lisa Martin, Executive Assistant. Fax: 202-783-0444. E-mail: jobs@foe.org. No phone calls. Applicants must submit a letter of interest, resume, one 3-page writing sample. Applications are accepted continuously. World Wide Web: http://www.foe.org/FOE.

FUND FOR ANIMALS, INC.
8121 Georgia Avenue, Suite 301
Silver Spring, Maryland 20910

General Information Nonprofit animal protection organization that focuses on companion animal and wildlife issues. Established in 1967. Number of employees: 13. Unit of The Fund for Animals, New York, New York. Number of internship applications received each year: 30.
Internships Available ▶ *1–5 interns:* responsibilities include performing a variety of tasks in the legal, legislative, outreach, campaign, and administrative departments. Candidates should have strong interest in animal advocacy. Duration is minimum of 3 months. Position available as unpaid or at $500 per internship or academic credit. Open to high school students, recent high school graduates, college freshmen, college sophomores, college juniors, college seniors, recent college graduates, graduate students, law students, career changers, individuals reentering the workforce. International applications accepted.
Benefits Formal training, opportunity to attend seminars/workshops, willing to complete paperwork for educational credit, willing to provide letters of recommendation, reimbursement for work-related travel expenses.
Contact Write, call, fax, or e-mail Jennifer Allen, Program Coordinator. Phone: 301-585-2591 Ext. 206. Fax: 301-585-2595. E-mail: jallen@fund.org. In-person interview recommended (telephone interview accepted). Applicants must submit a letter of interest, resume, writing sample, two letters of recommendation, completed questionnaire. Applications are accepted continuously. World Wide Web: http://www.fund.org.

GENESEE VALLEY OUTDOOR LEARNING CENTER
1717 Rayville Road
Parkton, Maryland 21120

General Information Experiential learning center that offers ropes course and environmental programs for school children, those with special needs, at-risk youth, and corporations. Number of employees: 20. Number of internship applications received each year: 10.
Internships Available ▶ *10–15 challenge course interns:* responsibilities include educating groups, maintenance, and other educational requirements as needed; 5–6 day work week; occasional evenings. Candidates should have ability to work independently, personal interest in the field, self-motivation, strong interpersonal skills, strong leadership ability, current first aid and CPR certifications. Duration is minimum of 3 months. $180–$250 per week. Open to high school students, recent high school graduates, college freshmen, college sophomores, college juniors, college seniors,

recent college graduates, graduate students, law students, career changers, individuals reentering the workforce. ▶ *8–10 instructors:* responsibilities include educating groups, maintenance and other educational requirements as needed; 5-6 day work week, some evenings. Candidates should have ability to work independently, oral communication skills, personal interest in the field, self-motivation, strong interpersonal skills, strong leadership ability, current first aid and CPR certifications. Duration is minimum of 3 months. $180–$250 per week. Open to recent high school graduates, college freshmen, college sophomores, college juniors, college seniors, recent college graduates, graduate students, law students, career changers, individuals reentering the workforce. ▶ *1 youth camp director:* responsibilities include directing 7 and 8 year-old camp (day), overseeing instructors and CITs and program; 5-day work week; educational requirements as needed. Candidates should have experience in the field, oral communication skills, personal interest in the field, self-motivation, strong interpersonal skills, strong leadership ability. Duration is June 17 to August 30. $180 to $250 per week, depending on experience level . Open to college freshmen, college sophomores, college juniors, college seniors, recent college graduates, graduate students, law students, career changers, individuals reentering the workforce. International applications accepted.
Benefits Formal training, free housing, free meals, on-the-job training, possible full-time employment, willing to act as a professional reference, willing to complete paperwork for educational credit, willing to provide letters of recommendation, health insurance assistance.
Contact Write, call, fax, e-mail, or through World Wide Web site Marcia Denmark, Supervisor of Program and Personnel, 1717 Rayville Road, Parkton, Maryland 21120. Phone: 410-343-0101. Fax: 410-343-1451. E-mail: genouted@bcpl.net. In-person interview recommended (telephone interview accepted). Applicants must submit a formal organization application, letter of interest, resume, three personal references. Application deadline: March 15 for spring, May 31 for summer, August 23 for fall. World Wide Web: http://www.geneseevalley.org.

GEORGE WASHINGTON & JEFFERSON NATIONAL FORESTS
5162 Valleypointe Parkway
Roanoke, Virginia 24019-3050

General Information Organization responsible for the management of the George Washington and Jefferson National Forests, including recreation, wildlife, timber, wilderness, watershed, range, and cultural resources. Established in 1940. Number of employees: 364. Number of internship applications received each year: 15.
Internships Available ▶ *Interns:* responsibilities include working in cultural resources, range, recreation, timber, or wildlife. Candidates should have ability to work independently, knowledge of field, oral communication skills, plan to pursue career in field, self-motivation, strong interpersonal skills. Duration is 1–3 months. Unpaid. Open to college freshmen, college sophomores, college juniors, college seniors, recent college graduates, graduate students.
Benefits On-the-job training, willing to complete paperwork for educational credit, willing to provide letters of recommendation.
Contact Write, call, or fax Dave Collins, Program Coordinator. Phone: 540-265-5166. Fax: 540-265-5145. In-person interview recommended (telephone interview accepted). Applications are accepted continuously.

GEORGIA 4-H ENVIRONMENTAL EDUCATION PROGRAM
350 Rock Eagle Road
Eatonton, Georgia 31024

General Information Environmental education center that services school-age children from the Southeast during the school year, instructing students and teachers in science and outdoor education. Established in 1979. Number of employees: 50. Unit of University of Georgia, College of Agricultural and Environmental Science, Athens, Georgia, Athens, Georgia. Number of internship applications received each year: 10.

Internships Available ▶ *1–4 environmental education instructors:* responsibilities include teaching environmental/outdoor education classes to primarily 4th-8th grade students, including ecology, living history, outdoor skills; night classes, and team-building; other duties (lab work, trail maintenance) as assigned. Candidates should have ability to work independently, oral communication skills, organizational skills, personal interest in the field, self-motivation, strong interpersonal skills, strong leadership ability, written communication skills. Duration is fall or spring seasons (usually 12-15 weeks). $180 per week. Open to college juniors, college seniors, recent college graduates.
Benefits Formal training, free housing, free meals, health insurance, names of contacts, on-the-job training, possible full-time employment, willing to complete paperwork for educational credit, willing to provide letters of recommendation.
Contact Write, call, fax, or e-mail Mr. Steve Dorsch, Environmental Education Coordinator. Phone: 706-484-2862. Fax: 706-484-2888. E-mail: sdorsch@uga.edu. Applicants must submit a letter of interest, resume, three personal references. Application deadline: December 15 for spring.

GLACIER INSTITUTE
PO Box 7457
Kalispell, Montana 59904

General Information Outdoor education organization dedicated to raising awareness for and appreciation of Glacier National Park and its surroundings. Established in 1983. Number of employees: 5. Number of internship applications received each year: 50.
Internships Available ▶ *1 assistant program director:* responsibilities include assisting in management of the environmental education facility including overseeing food preparation and purchase and some teaching. Candidates should have ability to work independently, oral communication skills, organizational skills, self-motivation, strong interpersonal skills, strong leadership ability. Duration is 7–8 months. $600–$700 per month. Open to recent college graduates, graduate students, career changers. ▶ *2–3 interns:* responsibilities include providing administrative and field backup to instructors teaching college-level courses in and around Glacier National Park and teaching a basic outdoor education curriculum in a day camp setting. Candidates should have oral communication skills, organizational skills, personal interest in the field, self-motivation, strong interpersonal skills, strong leadership ability. Duration is 3–7 months. $200–$500 per month. Open to college juniors, college seniors, recent college graduates, graduate students, career changers. ▶ *5–6 interns/teachers:* responsibilities include teaching an environmental education curriculum to fifth and sixth graders in a residential setting, or working with adults on day-long or multiple day courses. Candidates should have ability to work with others, oral communication skills, personal interest in the field, self-motivation, strong leadership ability, written communication skills. Duration is 2-3 months in spring, fall, or summer. $200–$600 per month. Open to college juniors, college seniors, recent college graduates, graduate students, career changers. ▶ *2–3 teachers/naturalists:* responsibilities include teaching an environmental education curriculum to fifth and sixth graders in a residential setting; and assisting in instruction and administrative duties for summer camps, elderhostels, writing workshops, and teacher training workshops. Candidates should have ability to work independently, ability to work with others, oral communication skills, personal interest in the field, self-motivation. Duration is 7–8 months. $500–$600 per month. Open to college juniors, college seniors, recent college graduates, graduate students, career changers. International applications accepted.
Benefits Formal training, free housing, free meals, names of contacts, on-the-job training, opportunity to attend seminars/workshops, possible full-time employment, willing to act as a professional reference, willing to complete paperwork for educational credit, willing to provide letters of recommendation.
Contact Write, call, fax, e-mail, or through World Wide Web site R. J. Devitt, Program Director. Phone: 406-755-1211. Fax: 406-755-7154. E-mail: glacinst@digisys.net. In-person interview recommended (telephone interview accepted). Applicants must submit a formal organization application, letter of interest, resume, writ-

Glacier Institute (continued)

ing sample, three personal references. Application deadline: January 20 for spring and summer, March 1 for fall. World Wide Web: http://www.glacierinstitute.org.

GLEN HELEN OUTDOOR EDUCATION CENTER
1075 State Route 343
Yellow Springs, Ohio 45387

General Information Residential environmental education center for elementary school-age children. Established in 1956. Number of employees: 6. Unit of Antioch University, Yellow Springs, Ohio. Number of internship applications received each year: 100.

Internships Available ▶ 10 naturalist interns: responsibilities include planning and leading small groups of elementary school-age students in residential environmental education programs; opportunity to care for a bird of prey at raptor center. Candidates should have ability to work independently, personal interest in the field, self-motivation, strong interpersonal skills, strong leadership ability. Duration is mid-August to mid-December or early January to early June. $250 per month. Open to college juniors, college seniors, recent college graduates, graduate students, career changers. International applications accepted.

Benefits Formal training, free housing, free meals, names of contacts, on-the-job training, opportunity to attend seminars/workshops, tuition assistance, willing to complete paperwork for educational credit, willing to provide letters of recommendation, opportunity to purchase health insurance, 12 undergraduate credits or 10 graduate credits through Antioch University.

Contact Write, call, fax, or e-mail Sue Feller, Assistant Director. Phone: 937-767-7648. Fax: 937-767-6655. E-mail: sfeller@antioch-college.edu. In-person interview recommended (telephone interview accepted). Applicants must submit a formal organization application, academic transcripts, three personal references. Applications are accepted continuously. World Wide Web: http://www.glenhelen.org.

GLOBAL RESPONSE
PO Box 7490, 3546 Old Pearl Street
Boulder, Colorado 80306-7490

General Information Environmental action and education network. Established in 1990. Number of employees: 3. Number of internship applications received each year: 20.

Internships Available ▶ 1–3 Webmasters: responsibilities include maintaining and updating Web site on an ongoing basis, developing strategies for fund-raising on the Internet, and publicizing Web site. Candidates should have ability to work independently, computer skills, self-motivation. Duration is minimum of 1 year (at least 8 hours per month). Unpaid. ▶ 1–3 administrative assistants: responsibilities include organizing and maintaining files on environmental topics, organizations, and monthly publications; answering phones; preparing materials for board members; maintaining membership database; and generating spreadsheets. Candidates should have ability to work independently, computer skills, office skills, oral communication skills, organizational skills, self-motivation, written communication skills. Duration is minimum of 3 months (at least 8 hours per week). Unpaid. ▶ 1–3 assistant volunteer coordinators: responsibilities include organizing volunteers for temporary and long-term tasks; recruiting, interviewing, and evaluating volunteers; supervising volunteer activities; assisting in scheduling volunteers for special events; and working closely with volunteer organizations. Candidates should have ability to work independently, oral communication skills, self-motivation, strong interpersonal skills, strong leadership ability, written communication skills. Duration is minimum of 3 months (at least 8 hours per week). Unpaid. ▶ 1–3 e-mail administrators: responsibilities include managing Listserv account, facilitating member subscriptions and unsubscriptions, investigating direct e-mail possibilities, and coordinating treatment of e-mail and conventional membership. Candidates should have computer skills, organizational skills. Duration is minimum of 3 months (at least 8 hours per week). Unpaid. ▶ 1–3 freelance journalists: responsibilities include writing articles about Global Response members and activities and submitting them to a variety of periodicals for publication. Candidates should have ability to work independently, editing skills, research skills, self-motivation, writing skills. Duration is minimum of 3 months (at least 8 hours per week). Unpaid. ▶ 1–3 fund-raising assistants: responsibilities include assisting Executive Director with grant proposals, research, and follow-up; developing strategies and materials for generating corporate donations; assisting in membership donation appeals; and organizing special gift planning. Candidates should have ability to work independently, oral communication skills, organizational skills, research skills, self-motivation, strong interpersonal skills, writing skills. Duration is minimum of 3 months (at least 8 hours per week). Unpaid. ▶ 1–3 materials editors: responsibilities include reviewing and editing the organization's marketing, education, and in-house documents. Candidates should have ability to work independently, editing skills, research skills, self-motivation, writing skills. Duration is minimum of 3 months (at least 8 hours per day). Unpaid. ▶ 1–3 outreach coordinators: responsibilities include writing press releases and articles, and developing and publicizing materials for the purpose of outreach and fostering collaboration with three target groups: youth, high school students, and adults. Candidates should have ability to work independently, oral communication skills, self-motivation, strong interpersonal skills, strong leadership ability, written communication skills. Duration is minimum of 3 months (at least 8 hours per day). Unpaid. ▶ 1–3 research associates: responsibilities include researching environmental topics (such as deforestation, nuclear energy, oceans, and mining) in order to develop new actions or researching past actions and campaigns to update membership and the board; and developing strategies to gauge effectiveness of letter-writing. Candidates should have ability to work independently, research skills, self-motivation, writing skills. Duration is minimum of 3 months (at least 8 hours per week). Unpaid. ▶ 1–3 special events coordinators: responsibilities include compiling a calendar of outreach events, developing strategies for outreach, and cultivating contacts with collaborating organizations to develop events. Candidates should have ability to work independently, oral communication skills, organizational skills, self-motivation, strong interpersonal skills, strong leadership ability, written communication skills. Duration is minimum of 3 months (at least 8 hours per week). Unpaid. Open to high school students, recent high school graduates, college freshmen, college sophomores, college juniors, college seniors, recent college graduates, graduate students, law students, career changers, individuals reentering the workforce. International applications accepted.

Benefits On-the-job training, willing to act as a professional reference, willing to complete paperwork for educational credit, willing to provide letters of recommendation.

Contact Write, call, fax, e-mail, or through World Wide Web site Mariella Colvin, Intern Recruitment Coordinator, PO Box 7490, 3546 Old Pearl Street, Boulder, Colorado 80306-7490. Phone: 303-444-0306. Fax: 303-449-9794. E-mail: action@globalresponse.org. In-person interview recommended (telephone interview accepted). Applicants must submit a letter of interest, resume, writing sample, GPA (if applicable). Applications are accepted continuously. World Wide Web: http://www.globalresponse.org.

GOLDEN GATE NATIONAL RECREATION AREA
Fort Mason, Building 201
San Francisco, California 94123

General Information Organization that seeks to conserve the scenery, cultural objects, and wildlife near San Francisco for the enjoyment of future generations. Established in 1972. Number of employees: 500. Unit of United States National Park Service, Washington, District of Columbia. Number of internship applications received each year: 100.

Internships Available ▶ 2–5 community outreach interns: responsibilities include inspiring others to become involved with Golden Gate National Recreation Area by recruiting volunteers from diverse communities or giving presentations to community groups; helping create and distribute volunteer newsletters, updating volunteer database, and helping with special events. Candidates should have ability to work independently, oral communication skills, self-motivation, strong interpersonal skills, written communication skills. Duration is 6–8 months. $15 per day (for out-of-pocket expenses). Open to individuals 18 or older. ▶ *5–10 environmental education interns:* responsibilities include assisting park rangers in presenting education programs to visiting school children and researching topics for programs. Candidates should have ability to work independently, ability to work with others, oral communication skills, personal interest in the field, self-motivation. Duration is 3-9 months (no summers). $15 per day (for out-of-pocket expenses). Open to college freshmen, college sophomores, college juniors, college seniors, recent college graduates, graduate students, individuals reentering the workforce, individuals 18 or older. ▶ *10–20 historical/cultural interpretation interns:* responsibilities include assisting park rangers in roving patrols, spot interpretation, researching and developing individual program, collecting weather data, and operating visitor center; selected sites have period costume interpretation possibilities. Candidates should have ability to work independently, ability to work with others, oral communication skills, personal interest in the field, self-motivation, ability to relate to a diverse visiting public. Duration is 9 months. $15 per day (for out-of-pocket expenses). Open to recent high school graduates, recent college graduates, career changers, individuals reentering the workforce, individuals 18 or older. ▶ *10–20 natural resource management interns:* responsibilities include restoring habitats, monitoring vegetation and wildlife, assisting in native plant nursery operations, and performing duties pertaining to aquatics and hydrology. Candidates should have ability to work independently, ability to work with others, personal interest in the field, self-motivation, enthusiasm, willingness to work with small groups, willingness to work occasionally around children. Duration is 6–12 months. $15 per day (for out-of-pocket expenses). Open to individuals 18 or older. ▶ *1–4 public relations/communication interns:* responsibilities include assisting with press releases and weekly electronic newsletter; designing and updating park fact sheets; arranging press interviews and news filming within the park, as well as dealing with the public. Candidates should have ability to work independently, computer skills, oral communication skills, personal interest in the field, self-motivation, written communication skills. Duration is 6–8 months. $15 per day (for out-of-pocket expenses). Open to individuals 18 or older. ▶ *1–2 roads and trails interns:* responsibilities include controlling erosion, building trail structures (crib walls, water bars, cable steps) and hauling materials as a trail worker; trail inventory to measure and describe "social trails" (unofficial trails cut by the visiting public). Candidates should have personal interest in the field, self-motivation, strong interpersonal skills, enthusiasm, strong body. Duration is 6–8 months. $15 per day (for out-of-pocket expenses). Open to individuals 18 or older. International applications accepted.

Benefits Formal training, names of contacts, opportunity to attend seminars/workshops, possible full-time employment, willing to complete paperwork for educational credit, willing to provide letters of recommendation, out-of-pocket expenses provided on limited basis, free housing for full-time interns.

Contact Write, call, fax, or e-mail Theresa Kreidler, Volunteer Manager. Phone: 415-561-4756. Fax: 415-561-4750. E-mail: goga_volunteers@nps.gov. In-person interview recommended (telephone interview accepted). Applicants must submit a formal organization application, cover letter and resume recommended. Applications are accepted continuously. World Wide Web: http://www.nps.gov/goga/vip/.

GREAT VALLEY NATURE CENTER
PO Box 82
Devault, Pennsylvania 19432

General Information Center that provides environmental education and recreational experience for school children, organized groups, and the general public. Established in 1974. Number of employees: 9. Number of internship applications received each year: 40.

Internships Available ▶ *1 animal caretaker/educator:* responsibilities include taking care of large animal collection used for educational programs. Candidates should have ability to work independently, ability to work with others, knowledge of field, self-motivation. Duration is flexible. $125–$175 per week. Open

to high school seniors, recent high school graduates, college freshmen, college sophomores, college juniors, college seniors, recent college graduates, graduate students, career changers, individuals reentering the workforce. ▶ *1 marketing/public relations intern:* responsibilities include marketing all facets of Nature Center, including making contacts, brochures, television, newspapers, and radio promotion. Candidates should have ability to work independently, ability to work with others, editing skills, oral communication skills, self-motivation, writing skills. Duration is flexible. $125–$175 per week. ▶ *5–10 teachers:* responsibilities include teaching educational programs to school groups and the general public, proposing exhibits, and caring for the animals; possibility of leading adventure programs (canoeing, rock climbing). Candidates should have ability to work independently, ability to work with others, knowledge of field, oral communication skills, personal interest in the field. Duration is flexible. $125–$175 per week. Open to recent high school graduates, college freshmen, college sophomores, college juniors, college seniors, recent college graduates, graduate students, career changers, individuals reentering the workforce. International applications accepted.

Benefits On-the-job training, opportunity to attend seminars/workshops, possible full-time employment, willing to act as a professional reference, willing to complete paperwork for educational credit, willing to provide letters of recommendation.

Contact Write, call, fax, or e-mail Heidi Malizia, Outreach/Intern Coordinator. Phone: 610-935-9777. Fax: 610-935-0130. E-mail: gvncee@nni.com. In-person interview recommended (telephone interview accepted). Applicants must submit a formal organization application, letter of interest, resume. Application deadline: April 30 for summer, November 30 for winter/spring.

GREEN MOUNTAIN CLUB
4711 Waterbury-Stowe Road
Waterbury Center, Vermont 05677

General Information Organization that promotes hiking in the Green Mountains, maintains trails, and protects the Long Trail Corridor. Established in 1910. Number of employees: 12. Number of internship applications received each year: 100.

Internships Available ▶ *12–18 Long Trail patrol interns:* responsibilities include building hiking trails with simple hand tools; learning techniques for constructing with stone and logs; working closely with a small crew. Candidates should have ability to work independently, personal interest in the field, self-motivation, strong interpersonal skills, willingness to live outdoors for a week at a time. Duration is flexible (opportunities available June through September). $200–$240 per week. Open to recent high school graduates, college freshmen, college sophomores, college juniors, college seniors, recent college graduates, career changers, individuals reentering the workforce, individuals 18 years and older. ▶ *15–20 backcountry caretakers:* responsibilities include educating public on mountain ecology and safety; maintaining wilderness campsites and hiking trails. Candidates should have ability to work independently, oral communication skills, personal interest in the field, self-motivation, strong interpersonal skills. Duration is flexible (opportunities available May through October). $200–$240 per week. Open to recent high school graduates, college freshmen, college sophomores, college juniors, college seniors, recent college graduates, graduate students, career changers, individuals reentering the workforce, individuals 18 years and older. ▶ *3 education programs interns:* responsibilities include developing displays, brochures, presentations, and slide shows on the social, ecological, and physical aspects of the Long Trail System and its management. Candidates should have computer skills, editing skills, experience in the field, office skills, organizational skills, self-motivation, writing skills. Duration is 1–6 months. Unpaid. Open to recent high school graduates, college freshmen, college sophomores, college juniors, college seniors, recent college graduates, graduate students, career changers, individuals reentering the workforce. ▶ *2 outdoor leadership interns:* responsibilities include apprenticeship with professional leaders to help run groups of volunteers who camp in the Vermont mountains; building primitive hiking trails. Candidates should have ability to work with others, personal interest in the field, self-motivation. Duration is July to September (full-time). Unpaid. Open to individuals 17 years

Green Mountain Club (continued)

and older. ▶ *5–10 recreation/resource management interns.* Candidates should have ability to work independently, personal interest in the field, self-motivation, strong interpersonal skills. Duration is flexible (year-round). Position available as unpaid or paid. Open to recent high school graduates, college freshmen, college sophomores, college juniors, college seniors, recent college graduates, graduate students, career changers, individuals reentering the workforce. International applications accepted.
Benefits Free housing, job counseling, names of contacts, on-the-job training, opportunity to attend seminars/workshops, possible full-time employment, travel reimbursement, tuition assistance, willing to act as a professional reference, willing to complete paperwork for educational credit, willing to provide letters of recommendation, office space, computer use; free board for outdoor leadership interns.
Contact Write, call, or e-mail Mr. Dave Hardy, Director of Field Programs. Phone: 802-244-7037. E-mail: dave@greenmountainclub.org. In-person interview recommended (telephone interview accepted). Applicants must submit a letter of interest, resume, two personal references. Applications are accepted continuously. World Wide Web: http://www.greenmountainclub.org.

HAWK MOUNTAIN SANCTUARY
1700 Hawk Mountain Road
Kempton, Pennsylvania 19529

General Information Privately supported wildlife preserve maintaining a 2500-acre Appalachian mountain reserve visited by 80,000 people per year, including 8,000 children in organized groups. Established in 1934. Number of employees: 16. Number of internship applications received each year: 60.
Internships Available ▶ *2 biological survey and monitoring interns:* responsibilities include assisting with census of flora and fauna populations, maintaining databases, analyzing and preparing technical and nontechnical reports, participating in some interpretative activities for visitors, conducting an independent research project including final report. Duration is 4 months. $500 per month. ▶ *4 ecological research interns:* responsibilities include designing and implementing research project with research staff, assisting with ongoing projects, and public speaking. Duration is 4 months. $500 per month. ▶ *4 science education interns:* responsibilities include becoming involved in outdoor education/environmental education for organized school groups, the visiting public pertaining to raptor conservation, the northern Appalachian ecosystem, and public speaking. Duration is 4 months. $500 per month. Candidates for all positions should have ability to work with others, personal interest in the field. Open to college juniors, college seniors, recent college graduates, graduate students. International applications accepted.
Benefits Formal training, free housing, job counseling, names of contacts, opportunity to attend seminars/workshops, willing to complete paperwork for educational credit, willing to provide letters of recommendation.
Contact Write, call, or e-mail Kyle McCarty, Intern Coordinator. Phone: 610-756-6961. Fax: 610-756-4468. E-mail: mccarty@hawkmountain.org. In-person interview recommended (telephone interview accepted). Applicants must submit a formal organization application, letter of interest, resume, self-addressed envelope. Application deadline: February 15 for spring, June 15 for fall. World Wide Web: http://www.hawkmountain.org.

HAWTHORNE VALLEY FARM VISITING STUDENTS PROGRAM
327CR 21C
Ghent, New York 12075

General Information Residential farm/environmental education program that follows the Waldorf educational philosophy; biodynamic dairy farm with commercial processing dairy, bakery, full health food store, gardens and CSA and K-12 Waldorf School. Established in 1972. Number of employees: 11. Branch of Hawthorne Valley Association, Inc., Ghent, New York. Number of internship applications received each year: 20.

Internships Available ▶ *3–4 interns:* responsibilities include planning and implementing outdoor programs for elementary school children including baking bread, pressing cider, gardening, and feeding animals. Candidates should have oral communication skills, organizational skills, personal interest in the field, self-motivation, strong interpersonal skills, strong leadership ability, maturity, experience working with children (helpful). Duration is 3–18 months. $200 per month stipend. Open to college freshmen, college sophomores, college juniors, college seniors, recent college graduates, graduate students, career changers, individuals reentering the workforce.
Benefits Formal training, free housing, free meals, opportunity to attend seminars/workshops, possible full-time employment, willing to act as a professional reference, willing to complete paperwork for educational credit, willing to provide letters of recommendation, opportunity to observe Waldorf school classes K-12, participate in biodynamic agriculture and community cultural events.
Contact Write, call, fax, e-mail, or through World Wide Web site Ruth Bruns, Executive Director, 327 Route 21C, Ghent, New York 12075. Phone: 518-672-4790. Fax: 518-672-7608. E-mail: vsp@taconic.net. In-person interview recommended (telephone interview accepted). Applicants must submit a formal organization application, letter of interest, resume, 3 personal references showing work with children. Applications are accepted continuously. World Wide Web: http://www.camppage.com/hawthorne.

IDAHO RIVERS UNITED
PO Box 633
Boise, Idaho 83701

General Information Citizens' nonprofit river conservation organization working on wild and scenic rivers, water policy, and salmon restoration. Established in 1987. Number of employees: 7. Number of internship applications received each year: 10.
Internships Available ▶ *1–4 conservation assistants:* responsibilities include duties related to intern's interests and abilities, primarily helping staff with hydropower, wild and scenic issues, and salmon restoration. Candidates should have ability to work independently, ability to work with others, analytical skills, personal interest in the field, research skills, written communication skills, organization/campaign mobilization skills. Duration is 1 summer, spring or fall. Position available as unpaid or paid. Open to college freshmen, college sophomores, college juniors, college seniors, recent college graduates, graduate students, law students, career changers, individuals reentering the workforce.
Benefits Names of contacts, on-the-job training, opportunity to attend seminars/workshops, possible full-time employment, travel reimbursement, willing to act as a professional reference, willing to complete paperwork for educational credit, willing to provide letters of recommendation.
Contact Write, fax, or e-mail Dan Skinner, Conservation Organizer. Fax: 208-343-9376. E-mail: iru@idahorivers.org. No phone calls. In-person interview recommended (telephone interview accepted). Applicants must submit a resume, letter of interest (can be e-mailed). Applications are accepted continuously. World Wide Web: http://www.idahorivers.org.

INSTITUTE FOR AGRICULTURE AND TRADE POLICY (IATP)
Environment and Agriculture Program, 2105 First Avenue South
Minneapolis, Minnesota 55404-2505

General Information Institute promoting resilient family farms, rural communities, and ecosystems around the world through research and education, science and technology, and advocacy.
Internships Available ▶ *Interns:* responsibilities include conducting research on environmental, agricultural, and trade policy issues, developing "how-to" literature on organizing forestry cooperatives, and design and maintenance of Web pages; intern may work on any of a variety of ongoing projects. Duration is minimum of 3 months (full- or part-time). Unpaid.

Benefits Names of contacts, willing to act as a professional reference, willing to complete paperwork for educational credit, some positions may offer small stipends.
Contact Write, call, fax, e-mail, or through World Wide Web site Internship Coordinator. Phone: 612-870-3411. Fax: 612-870-4846. E-mail: iatp@iatp.org. World Wide Web: http://www.iatp.org.

INTERNATIONAL CRANE FOUNDATION
PO Box 447
Baraboo, Wisconsin 53913

General Information Nonprofit foundation dedicated to the preservation of cranes and the wetlands on which they depend. Established in 1973. Number of employees: 30. Number of internship applications received each year: 200.
Internships Available ▶ *2 aviculture associates:* responsibilities include caring for and breeding cranes, completing one independent project under the supervision of a full-time employee, and supervising the volunteer chick parent program with emphasis on chick rearing. Candidates should have ability to work independently, ability to work with others, computer skills, knowledge of field, oral communication skills, personal interest in the field, research skills, self-motivation, writing skills. Duration is 6 months. $650 per month. ▶ *3 aviculture interns:* responsibilities include caring for and breeding cranes and completing an independent project under the supervision of a full-time employee. Candidates should have ability to work independently, ability to work with others, computer skills, knowledge of field, oral communication skills, personal interest in the field, self-motivation. Duration is 6 months. $350 per month. Open to college juniors, college seniors, recent college graduates. International applications accepted.
Benefits Free housing, names of contacts, on-the-job training, possible full-time employment, willing to act as a professional reference, willing to complete paperwork for educational credit, willing to provide letters of recommendation.
Contact Write or e-mail Kelly Maguire, Aviculturist. E-mail: kelly@savingcranes.org. No phone calls. Applicants must submit a letter of interest, resume, three letters of recommendation, telephone interview if selected as a finalist. Applications are accepted continuously. World Wide Web: http://www.savingcranes.org.

JACKSON HOLE CONSERVATION ALLIANCE
PO Box 2728
Jackson, Wyoming 83001

General Information Local nonprofit membership organization dedicated to protecting Jackson Hole's wildlife, scenery, and open spaces through land-use planning, citizen involvement, and natural resource conservation. Established in 1979. Number of employees: 11. Number of internship applications received each year: 75.
Internships Available ▶ *2–3 project interns:* responsibilities include working on an independent project of mutual interest to both the intern and the Alliance; helping with the day-to-day office administration of a nonprofit grassroots organization; assisting at meetings and special events; coordinating volunteers; maintaining community contacts; working on land-use planning and resource conservation issues; organizing fund-raising events, educational forums, and field trips. Candidates should have ability to work independently, computer skills, oral communication skills, organizational skills, strong interpersonal skills, written communication skills. Duration is 3–4 months. $650 per month. Open to college juniors, college seniors, recent college graduates, graduate students, law students, career changers, individuals reentering the workforce. International applications accepted.
Benefits Names of contacts, opportunity to attend seminars/workshops, possible full-time employment, travel reimbursement, willing to act as a professional reference, willing to complete paperwork for educational credit, willing to provide letters of recommendation.
Contact Write, call, fax, e-mail, or through World Wide Web site Kathy Berry, Outreach Director. Phone: 307-733-9417. Fax: 307-733-9008. E-mail: kathy@jhalliance.org. In-person interview recommended (telephone interview accepted). Applicants must submit

a letter of interest, resume, two personal references. Application deadline: April 1 for summer, October 15 for winter. World Wide Web: http://www.jhalliance.com.

JACKSON HOLE LAND TRUST
PO Box 2897
Jackson, Wyoming 83001

General Information Trust organized to protect open space on private land in Jackson Hole through voluntary nongovernmental means. Established in 1981. Number of employees: 12. Number of internship applications received each year: 60.
Internships Available ▶ *4 interns:* responsibilities include office work, research, errands, field work, GIS, public relations. Candidates should have ability to work with others, oral communication skills, research skills, self-motivation, writing skills. Duration is June 1 through August 31; September 1 through November 30; December 1 through February 28; March 1 through May 31. $5.15 per hour. Open to college freshmen, college sophomores, college juniors, college seniors, recent college graduates, graduate students, law students, career changers, individuals reentering the workforce.
Benefits Names of contacts, on-the-job training, opportunity to attend seminars/workshops, possible full-time employment, travel reimbursement, willing to act as a professional reference, willing to complete paperwork for educational credit, willing to provide letters of recommendation.
Contact Write, call, fax, e-mail, or through World Wide Web site Susan Hall, Intern Coordinator. Phone: 307-733-4707. Fax: 307-733-4144. E-mail: susan@jhlandtrust.org. In-person interview recommended (telephone interview accepted). Applicants must submit a letter of interest, resume, writing sample. Applications are accepted continuously. World Wide Web: http://www.jhlandtrust.org.

KAUA'I NATIONAL WILDLIFE REFUGE COMPLEX
PO Box 1128
Kilauea, Hawaii 96754

General Information Complex of refuges that promote conservation of wildlife, wildlife habitat, and cultural resources through environmental education and interpretation. Established in 1985. Number of employees: 9. Unit of Hawaiian and Pacific Islands National Wildlife Refuge Complex, Honolulu, Hawaii. Number of internship applications received each year: 30.
Internships Available ▶ *1–2 visitor services interns:* responsibilities include greeting, orienting, and educating visiting public and school groups; performing daily maintenance tasks, including opening and closing the refuge; counting fee monies. Candidates should have ability to work independently, oral communication skills, plan to pursue career in field, research skills, strong interpersonal skills, writing skills. Duration is 3–5 months. $125 per week. Open to college juniors, college seniors, recent college graduates, graduate students, individuals reentering the workforce.
Benefits Formal training, free housing, job counseling, names of contacts, on-the-job training, travel reimbursement, willing to act as a professional reference, willing to complete paperwork for educational credit, willing to provide letters of recommendation.
Contact Write, call, fax, or e-mail Kathy Batha, Supervisory Park Ranger, PO Box 1125, Kilauea, Hawaii 96754. Phone: 808-828-1413. Fax: 808-828-6634. E-mail: kathy_batha@fws.gov. In-person interview recommended (telephone interview accepted). Applicants must submit a letter of interest, resume, two personal references. Application deadline: March 31 for summer, June 30 for fall, November 15 for winter.

LAND TRUST ALLIANCE
1331 H Street, NW, Suite 400
Washington, District of Columbia 20005-4734

General Information National organization of local and regional land conservation groups providing information, education, technical assistance, public policy advocacy, and public education. Established in 1982. Number of employees: 45. Number of internship applications received each year: 50.

Land Trust Alliance (continued)

Internships Available ▶ *1 Land Trust Research intern:* responsibilities include researching and providing a wide array of information products and services to constituents. Candidates should have ability to work with others, oral communication skills, personal interest in the field, research skills, self-motivation, written communication skills. Duration is one semester or year. Unpaid. Open to college seniors, recent college graduates, graduate students, law students, career changers, individuals reentering the workforce. ▶ *Interns:* responsibilities include database research, networking with land trusts in the United States and Canada, library research, culling and organizing information into marketable formats, responding to requests for information from individuals and organizations, land trust database management and organization. Candidates should have ability to work with others, oral communication skills, personal interest in the field, research skills, self-motivation, written communication skills. Duration is flexible. Small stipend occasionally available for special projects. Open to college seniors, recent college graduates, graduate students, law students, career changers, individuals reentering the workforce. ▶ *Public policy interns:* responsibilities include working with the public policy director on policy issues of concern to land conservationists. Candidates should have oral communication skills, written communication skills. Position available as unpaid or paid.
Benefits Job counseling, names of contacts, on-the-job training, opportunity to attend seminars/workshops, possible full-time employment, willing to act as a professional reference, willing to complete paperwork for educational credit, willing to provide letters of recommendation.
Contact Write, fax, e-mail, or through World Wide Web site Rob Aldrich, Director of Information Services. Phone: 202-638-4725. Fax: 202-638-4730. E-mail: raldrich@lta.org. In-person interview recommended (telephone interview accepted). Applicants must submit a letter of interest, resume, 3-4 personal references, writing sample for advanced candidates. Applications are accepted continuously. World Wide Web: http://www.lta.org.

LEAGUE OF CONSERVATION VOTERS
1920 L Street, NW, Suite 800
Washington, District of Columbia 20036

General Information Bipartisan political arm of the environmental community. Established in 1970. Number of employees: 38. Number of internship applications received each year: 500.
Internships Available ▶ *1–5 Education Fund interns:* responsibilities include researching, assisting with training, coordinating trips, grassroots programming. Candidates should have ability to work independently, ability to work with others, computer skills, editing skills, oral communication skills, organizational skills, research skills, self-motivation, writing skills, Training, organizing, grassroots organizing, state outreach, local outreach. Duration is 3–6 months. $1100 monthly stipend. Open to college freshmen, college sophomores, college juniors, college seniors, recent college graduates. ▶ *1–2 communications interns:* responsibilities include researching stories for news reporters, drafting press releases, and assisting with media relations and media plans. Candidates should have ability to work independently, ability to work with others, college courses in field, computer skills, editing skills, oral communication skills, personal interest in the field, plan to pursue career in field, research skills, self-motivation, writing skills. Duration is 3–6 months. $1160 monthly stipend. Open to college juniors, college seniors, recent college graduates. ▶ *1–5 political interns:* responsibilities include researching congressional voting records and environmental legislation, studying and reporting on congressional candidates. Candidates should have ability to work independently, ability to work with others, college courses in field, personal interest in the field, plan to pursue career in field, research skills, written communication skills. Duration is 6 months. $1100 monthly stipend. Open to recent college graduates. International applications accepted.
Benefits Opportunity to attend seminars/workshops, possible full-time employment, willing to act as a professional reference, willing to provide letters of recommendation.

Contact Write, call, fax, or e-mail Allyson Woods, Intern Coordinator. Fax: 202-835-0491. E-mail: allyson_woods@lcv.org. Applicants must submit a letter of interest, resume, writing sample, three personal references, telephone or in-person interview. Application deadline: February 1 for spring, April 1 for summer, December 1 for winter. World Wide Web: http://www.lcv.org.

LINSLY OUTDOOR CENTER
2425 Route 168
Georgetown, Pennsylvania 15043

General Information Outdoor center that builds teamwork, self-esteem, and trust through a variety of programs that provide adventure, environmental education, and a unique outdoor experience for groups of all ages. Established in 1987. Number of employees: 8. Unit of Linsly School, Wheeling, West Virginia. Number of internship applications received each year: 100.
Internships Available ▶ *6 instructors/interns:* responsibilities include teaching and developing adventure, challenge, and environmental education programs for all age groups, supervising day and evening programs, and assisting in daily operations. Candidates should have ability to work independently, ability to work with others, organizational skills, self-motivation, strong leadership ability. Duration is 3-4 months in spring, summer, or fall. $180–$210 per week. Open to college freshmen, college sophomores, college juniors, college seniors, recent college graduates, graduate students, career changers.
Benefits Formal training, free housing, names of contacts, possible full-time employment, willing to act as a professional reference, willing to complete paperwork for educational credit, willing to provide letters of recommendation, some free meals.
Contact Write, call, e-mail, or through World Wide Web site Jeff Hasis, Director. Phone: 724-899-2100. E-mail: loc1@timesnet.net. In-person interview recommended (telephone interview accepted). Applicants must submit a formal organization application, letter of interest, resume, three personal references. Applications are accepted continuously. World Wide Web: http://www.linsly.org.

LONG LAKE CONSERVATION CENTER
28952 438th Lane
Palisade, Minnesota 56469

General Information Residential conservation/environmental education facility providing activities and learning units designed to heighten and enhance students' appreciation of and sensitivity toward the environment. Established in 1963. Number of employees: 18. Unit of Aitkin County Parks Commission, Aitkin, Minnesota. Number of internship applications received each year: 50.
Internships Available ▶ *4–8 naturalist interns:* responsibilities include teaching, leading adolescents in environmental education programs and activities, and supervising groups of students. Candidates should have ability to work independently, oral communication skills, organizational skills, personal interest in the field, strong interpersonal skills, written communication skills. Duration is 3–12 months. $100 per week. Open to college freshmen, college sophomores, college juniors, college seniors, recent college graduates, graduate students, career changers, individuals reentering the workforce. International applications accepted.
Benefits Free housing, free meals, job counseling, names of contacts, on-the-job training, willing to act as a professional reference, willing to complete paperwork for educational credit, willing to provide letters of recommendation.
Contact Write, call, fax, or e-mail Pam Carlson, Administration Coordinator. Phone: 800-450-5522. Fax: 218-768-2309. E-mail: llcc@mlecmn.net. Applicants must submit a formal organization application, letter of interest, resume, academic transcripts, letter of recommendation. Applications are accepted continuously. World Wide Web: http://www.llcc.org.

MANTI–LA SAL NATIONAL FOREST, MONTICELLO RANGER DISTRICT
PO Box 820
Monticello, Utah 84535

General Information Ranger district located on the Colorado Plateau near Moab, Utah, that manages numerous Anasazi ruins and the Dark Canyon Wilderness. Established in 1906. Number of employees: 15. Unit of Manti–La Sal National Forest, Price, Utah. Number of internship applications received each year: 15.

Internships Available ▶ *2–3 archaeological assistants:* responsibilities include assisting with office and fieldwork including surveying, identifying, and recording archaeological sites and ruins; projects and tasks undertaken can be negotiated depending on interests and skills. Candidates should have ability to work with others, college courses in field, computer skills, office skills, self-motivation, writing skills, driver's license. Duration is 2–4 months. Unpaid. Open to recent high school graduates, college freshmen, college sophomores, college juniors, college seniors, recent college graduates, graduate students, career changers, individuals reentering the workforce, seniors/retirees. ▶ *2–3 recreation site maintenance interns:* responsibilities include making public contacts, collecting and evaluating visitor use data, and assisting with recreation/trails/campground maintenance programs. Candidates should have ability to work independently, ability to work with others, oral communication skills, driver's license, physical fitness (lifting, hiking). Duration is 2–4 months. Position available as unpaid or paid. Open to individuals 18 years or older. ▶ *2 wilderness rangers:* responsibilities include making public contacts, providing information, and collecting and evaluating visitor use data. Candidates should have ability to work independently, ability to work with others, self-motivation, good physical condition (hiking), outdoor skills (map reading, backpacking, 4x4 driving). Unpaid. Open to college freshmen, college sophomores, college juniors, college seniors, recent college graduates, graduate students, career changers, individuals reentering the workforce, seniors/retirees. International applications accepted.

Benefits Free housing, job counseling, on-the-job training, travel reimbursement, willing to complete paperwork for educational credit, willing to provide letters of recommendation, possible subsistence reimbursement.

Contact Write, call, or e-mail Donald Irwin, District Heritage Manager. Phone: 435-587-2041. E-mail: dcirwin@fs.fed.us. Informal application. Application deadline: April 30 for summer.

MAX MCGRAW WILDLIFE FOUNDATION
PO Box 9
Dundee, Illinois 60118

General Information Private, not-for-profit organization dedicated to wildlife research, education, and conservation; educational department reaches over 14,000 people through programs and events. Established in 1962. Number of employees: 47. Number of internship applications received each year: 50.

Internships Available ▶ *1–2 conservation education assistants:* responsibilities include planning and presenting programs for children and adults, leading tours, creating educational materials, and assisting education staff as needed. Candidates should have computer skills, knowledge of field, office skills, oral communication skills, organizational skills, personal interest in the field, self-motivation, strong interpersonal skills, writing skills, coursework in the biological/environmental sciences. Duration is February through November. $1000–$1150 per month. Open to college juniors, college seniors, recent college graduates, graduate students, career changers, individuals reentering the workforce. International applications accepted.

Benefits Formal training, free housing, job counseling, names of contacts, on-the-job training, opportunity to attend seminars/workshops, willing to act as a professional reference, willing to complete paperwork for educational credit, willing to provide letters of recommendation.

Contact Write, call, fax, or e-mail Colleen Kulesza, Conservation Education Coordinator. Phone: 847-428-2240. Fax: 847-741-8157. E-mail: colleenkulesza@aol.com. Applicants must submit a letter of interest, resume. Application deadline: December 10. World Wide Web: http://www.mcgrawwildlife.org.

MERCK FAMILY FUND
303 Adams Street
Milton, Massachusetts 02186-4253

General Information Private grantmaking foundation committed to the preservation of the environment through protection of eastern ecosystems and sustainable economics and a concern for socially and economically disadvantaged people; supports youth and organizes urban greening projects in Boston, Providence, and New York. Established in 1954. Number of employees: 3. Number of internship applications received each year: 100.

Internships Available ▶ *1 foundation intern:* responsibilities include conducting extensive written and phone outreach with nonprofit groups; assisting with office administration; and participating in research projects related to sustainable economics, eastern forest ecosystems, urban greening, and youth organizing. Candidates should have organizational skills, research skills, self-motivation, strong interpersonal skills, written communication skills, familiarity with the Foundation's program areas; familiarity with Macintosh computers and Internet research. Duration is 3–8 months. $1200 per month for 4-day work week or $10 per hour for fewer hours. Open to college seniors, recent college graduates, graduate students, law students, career changers.

Benefits Job counseling, names of contacts, on-the-job training, opportunity to attend seminars/workshops, willing to act as a professional reference, willing to complete paperwork for educational credit, willing to provide letters of recommendation.

Contact Write, fax, e-mail, or through World Wide Web site Betsy Caruso, Fund Administrator. Fax: 617-696-7262. E-mail: merck@merckff.org. No phone calls. In-person interview required. Applicants must submit a letter of interest, resume, writing sample, list of 3 references. Application deadline: March 1 for summer, June 1 for fall, October 1 for spring. World Wide Web: http://www.merckff.org.

MERCK FOREST AND FARMLAND CENTER
Box 86, Route 315
Rupert, Vermont 05768

General Information Center that teaches about land stewardship and sustainability by providing programs, access, and demonstrations on over 3130 acres of working farm and forest land. Established in 1950. Number of employees: 12. Number of internship applications received each year: 50.

Internships Available ▶ *1–4 resource assistants:* responsibilities include environmental education, farm chores, forest and trail management, Visitor Center duties, and seasonal work including maple sugaring, lambing, organic gardening, and public programs. Candidates should have ability to work independently, ability to work with others, personal interest in the field, self-motivation. Duration is 4 months. $65 per week. Open to recent high school graduates, college freshmen, college sophomores, college juniors, college seniors, recent college graduates, graduate students, law students, career changers, individuals reentering the workforce, must be 18 or older. International applications accepted.

Benefits Free housing, on-the-job training, opportunity to attend seminars/workshops, willing to complete paperwork for educational credit, willing to provide letters of recommendation, free organic farm products.

Contact Write, call, fax, or e-mail Ken Smith, Executive Director. Phone: 802-394-7836. Fax: 802-394-2519. E-mail: merck@vermontel.net. In-person interview recommended (telephone interview accepted). Applicants must submit a letter of interest, resume. Applications are accepted continuously. World Wide Web: http://www.merckforest.org.

MONONGAHELA NATIONAL FOREST, WHITE SULPHUR DISTRICT
410 East Main Street
White Sulphur Springs, West Virginia 24986

General Information National forest dedicated to land management and public services. Established in 1920. Number of employees: 2. Unit of Monongahela National Forest, Elkins, West Virginia. Number of internship applications received each year: 1.

Internships Available ▶ *1–2 gate attendants/hosts:* responsibilities include greeting campers, maintaining grounds, and cleaning. Candidates should have ability to work independently, ability to work with others, oral communication skills, personal interest in the field, self-motivation. Duration is May to August. Unpaid. Open to recent high school graduates, college freshmen, college sophomores, college juniors, college seniors, recent college graduates, graduate students, law students, career changers, individuals reentering the workforce. ▶ *1–2 naturalists:* responsibilities include providing environmental education programs for campers and developing and conducting a variety of nature programs for all ages. Candidates should have ability to work with others, college courses in field, oral communication skills, personal interest in the field, self-motivation. Duration is June to August. Unpaid. Open to college freshmen, college sophomores, college juniors, college seniors, recent college graduates, graduate students. International applications accepted.

Benefits Free housing, on-the-job training, willing to complete paperwork for educational credit.

Contact Write or fax Tim Henry, Assistant Ranger, PO Box 210, Marlinton, West Virginia 24954. Fax: 304-799-6820. E-mail: tlhenry@ fs.fed.us. No phone calls. Telephone interview required. Applicants must submit a letter of interest, resume, two personal references, two letters of recommendation. Application deadline: May 1.

MOUNTAIN TRAIL OUTDOOR SCHOOL
PO Box 250
Hendersonville, North Carolina 28793-0250

General Information Outdoor school that educates and inspires students of all ages to protect the natural and human environment. Established in 1991. Number of employees: 15. Unit of Kanuga Conference Center, Hendersonville, North Carolina. Number of internship applications received each year: 50.

Internships Available ▶ *2–4 outdoor environmental education interns:* responsibilities include teaching natural history classes, environmental awareness, and adventure activities, and assisting with training and program development. Candidates should have knowledge of field, oral communication skills, organizational skills, personal interest in the field, strong interpersonal skills, strong leadership ability, experience and/or desire to work with youth. Duration is 4–5 months. $200 per week. Open to college freshmen, college sophomores, college juniors, college seniors, recent college graduates, graduate students. International applications accepted.

Benefits Formal training, free housing, free meals, job counseling, names of contacts, on-the-job training, opportunity to attend seminars/workshops, possible full-time employment, willing to act as a professional reference, willing to complete paperwork for educational credit, willing to provide letters of recommendation, limited health insurance.

Contact Write, call, e-mail, or through World Wide Web site Paul Bockoven, Director, Outdoor Education. Phone: 828-692-9136. Fax: 828-696-3589. E-mail: mtos@kanuga.org. Telephone interview required. Applicants must submit a formal organization application, letter of interest, resume, three letters of recommendation. Application deadline: January 1 for spring, June 1 for fall. World Wide Web: http://www.kanuga.org/mtos.htm.

NACUL CENTER FOR ECOLOGICAL ARCHITECTURE
592 Main Street
Amherst, Massachusetts 01002

General Information Center that researches and develops ecological architecture designs including sustainable communities, solar buildings, and other socially responsible projects. Established in 1970. Number of employees: 4. Number of internship applications received each year: 25.

Internships Available ▶ *3–6 architectural interns:* responsibilities include drafting, researching, model building, office work, photography, and design. Candidates should have ability to work with others, college courses in field, computer skills, office skills, personal interest in the field, research skills, self-motivation. Duration is 3–12 months. Unpaid. Open to college freshmen, college sophomores, college juniors, college seniors, recent college graduates, graduate students. International applications accepted.

Benefits Formal training, on-the-job training, opportunity to attend seminars/workshops, possible full-time employment, willing to act as a professional reference, willing to complete paperwork for educational credit, willing to provide letters of recommendation.

Contact Write, call, fax, e-mail, or through World Wide Web site Tullio Inglese, Director. Phone: 413-256-8025. Fax: 413-253-2451. E-mail: info@nacul.com. In-person interview recommended (telephone interview accepted). Applicants must submit a formal organization application, resume, portfolio. Applications are accepted continuously. World Wide Web: http://nacul.com.

NATIONAL AQUARIUM IN BALTIMORE
Pier 3, 501 East Pratt Street
Baltimore, Maryland 21202

General Information State-of-the-art aquatic institution dedicated to the conservation and preservation of the environment. Established in 1981. Number of employees: 350. Number of internship applications received each year: 240.

Internships Available ▶ *20–40 interns:* responsibilities include working in horticulture, marine education, herpetology, membership, public relations, marine mammal training, library, water quality, development, marketing, aquarists, aviculturists, or information systems; interns work with staff on daily duties and special events. Candidates should have ability to work with others, college courses in field, knowledge of field, oral communication skills, personal interest in the field, plan to pursue career in field. Duration is 120 hours. Unpaid. Open to college freshmen, college sophomores, college juniors, college seniors. International applications accepted.

Benefits Names of contacts, on-the-job training, opportunity to attend seminars/workshops, willing to act as a professional reference, willing to complete paperwork for educational credit, willing to provide letters of recommendation, uniform, 30% discount at gift shop and on food service.

Contact Write, call, fax, e-mail, or through World Wide Web site Donna Gartner, Internship Coordinator. Phone: 410-576-3888. Fax: 410-659-0116. E-mail: intern@aqua.org. Telephone interview required. Applicants must submit a formal organization application, letter of interest, academic transcripts, email interview if necessary (international students). Application deadline: April 1 for summer and fall, November 1 for winter and spring. World Wide Web: http://www.aqua.org.

NATIONAL PARKS CONSERVATION ASSOCIATION
1300 19th Street, NW, Suite 300
Washington, District of Columbia 20036

General Information National environmental organization dedicated to protecting and enhancing the national park system. Established in 1919. Number of employees: 120. Number of internship applications received each year: 75.

Internships Available ▶ *1–3 policy interns:* responsibilities include researching issues pertaining to natural and cultural resource policies and providing research support for staff. Candidates should have oral communication skills, personal interest in the field, research skills, self-motivation, strong interpersonal skills, written communication skills. Duration is 10–14 weeks. $8.57–$11.43 per hour. Open to college seniors, recent college graduates, graduate students, law students, career changers. International applications accepted.

Benefits Names of contacts, opportunity to attend seminars/ workshops, possible full-time employment, willing to act as a professional reference, willing to complete paperwork for educational credit, willing to provide letters of recommendation.

Contact Write, call, fax, or e-mail Scott E. Edwards, Program Manager, 1300 19th Street, NW Suite 300, Washington, District of Columbia 20036. Phone: 202-454-3349 Ext. 117. Fax: 202-659-8183. E-mail: sedwards@npca.org. In-person interview recommended (telephone interview accepted). Applicants must submit a letter of interest, resume, academic transcripts, writing sample, three personal references. Application deadline: March 15 for summer, July 15 for fall, October 1 for winter. World Wide Web: http://www.npca.org.

NATIONAL WILDLIFE FEDERATION
11100 Wildlife Center Drive
Reston, Virginia 20190

General Information Nation's largest nonprofit conservation education organization. Established in 1936. Number of internship applications received each year: 500.

Internships Available ▶ *8–15 interns:* responsibilities include researching environmental policy issues; attending congressional hearings, briefings, and seminars; lobbying on environmental legislation; and routine office work; areas covered include endangered habitat, water quality, wetlands, land stewardship, international development, and sustainable communities. Candidates should have ability to work with others, college degree in related field, experience in the field, oral communication skills, writing skills, interest in environmental issues, volunteer experience valued. Duration is 20–24 weeks. $303 per week. Open to college seniors, recent college graduates, graduate students, law students. International applications accepted.

Benefits Formal training, health insurance, names of contacts, willing to act as a professional reference, willing to complete paperwork for educational credit, willing to provide letters of recommendation.

Contact Write, fax, e-mail, or through World Wide Web site Aline Brito, Internship Coordinator. E-mail: brito@nwf.org. No phone calls. In-person interview recommended (telephone interview accepted). Applicants must submit a letter of interest, resume, writing sample, 3-5 academic or professional references. Application deadline: March 15 for July positions, October 15 for January positions. World Wide Web: http://www.nwf.org/nwf.

NATIONAL WILDLIFE FEDERATION CAMPUS ECOLOGY PROGRAM
11100 Wildlife Center Drive
Reston, Virginia 20190-5362

General Information Organization that supports practical conservation projects on college and university campuses by assisting with project implementation, providing training, and documenting lessons learned nationally. Established in 1936. Number of employees: 250. Number of internship applications received each year: 60.

Internships Available ▶ *12 campus ecology fellowships:* responsibilities include identifying environmental sustainable projects/program on intern's campus, determining the best action to achieve identified goals, and taking steps to implement this action plan. Candidates should have ability to work independently, ability to work with others, computer skills, oral communication skills, organizational skills, personal interest in the field, self-motivation, written communication skills. Duration is one academic year. Stipends up to $1200 per semester. Open to college freshmen, college sophomores, college juniors, college seniors, graduate students, law students. ▶ *5–10 program interns:* responsibilities include working in backyard wildlife habitat, NatureLink, school yard habitats, and as habitat stewards; assisting staff; offering presentations; sending information and responding to e-mail/phone/mail requests from general public. Candidates should have ability to work independently, oral communication skills, organizational skills, personal interest in the field, strong interpersonal skills, written communication skills. Duration is 6 months (full-time). $275 per week. Open to recent college graduates, graduate students. ▶ *2–4 special projects interns:* responsibilities include assistance with various projects, possibly including resource develop-

ment, research, database development, and Web maintenance. Candidates should have ability to work independently, office skills, personal interest in the field, research skills, writing skills. Duration is flexible. Unpaid. Open to high school students, recent high school graduates, college freshmen, college sophomores, college juniors, college seniors, recent college graduates, graduate students, law students, career changers, individuals reentering the workforce. International applications accepted.

Benefits On-the-job training, opportunity to attend seminars/workshops, possible full-time employment, willing to act as a professional reference, willing to complete paperwork for educational credit, willing to provide letters of recommendation.

Contact Write or e-mail Kathy Cacciola, Coordinator, 11100 Wildlife Center Drive, Reston, Virginia 20190-5362. Fax: 703-438-6468. E-mail: cacciola@nwf.org. No phone calls. Telephone interview required. Applicants must submit a formal organization application, resume, two personal references, three letters of recommendation. Applications are accepted continuously. World Wide Web: http://www.nwf.org/campus ecology.

THE NATURE CONSERVANCY AT THE NAGS HEAD WOODS PRESERVE
701 West Ocean Acres Drive
Kill Devil Hills, North Carolina 27948

General Information Nature preserve whose mission is to protect and preserve the diversity of plants, animals, and natural communities in maritime forest preserve. Established in 1977. Number of employees: 6. Branch of The Nature Conservancy, Arlington, Virginia. Number of internship applications received each year: 50.

Internships Available ▶ *2 naturalist/outdoor education interns:* responsibilities include designing and implementing an interpretive program that targets the educational needs of the preserve, guiding kayak and field trips, leading sessions of EcoCamp, maintaining and assisting in the development of interpretive exhibits and publications. Candidates should have ability to work independently, experience in the field, oral communication skills, strong interpersonal skills, good physical condition desirable; first aid and CPR certification. Duration is late May to early September. $7–$9 per hour. Open to college juniors, college seniors, recent college graduates, graduate students. International applications accepted.

Benefits Free housing, names of contacts, on-the-job training, willing to complete paperwork for educational credit, willing to provide letters of recommendation.

Contact Write, call, fax, or e-mail Ms. Rhana S. Paris, Education Coordinator. Phone: 252-441-2525 Ext. 23. Fax: 252-441-1271. E-mail: rparis@tnc.org. Applicants must submit a letter of interest, resume, two personal references. Application deadline: February 15. World Wide Web: http://www.nature.org.

NATURE CONSERVANCY, NORTH CAROLINA CHAPTER
4705 University Drive, Suite 290
Durham, North Carolina 27707

General Information Conservation organization that seeks to preserve plants, animals, and natural communities by protecting lands and waters. Established in 1977. Number of employees: 40. Number of internship applications received each year: 70.

Internships Available ▶ *1–2 Nags Head Woods environmental education interns:* responsibilities include leading educational field trips, assisting with an environmental education camp for K-12 children, maintaining and repairing trails, preparing reports, assisting with monitoring, posting boundaries, removing invasive species, assisting with prescribed fires, interacting with the public, and generally contributing to the maintenance and security of one or more nature preserves (the Mountains District of Western North Carolina, the Southeast Coastal Plain District, or the Nags Head Woods preserve on the Outer Banks; an internship report is required at the end of the term of employment. Duration is 6 months (May through October). $7–$8.50 per hour. Open to college juniors, college seniors, recent college graduates, graduate students. International applications accepted.

Nature Conservancy, North Carolina Chapter (continued)

Benefits Formal training, names of contacts, travel reimbursement, willing to complete paperwork for educational credit, willing to provide letters of recommendation.
Contact Write, fax, e-mail, or through World Wide Web site Dan Bell, Internship Coordinator. Fax: 919-403-0379. E-mail: dbell@tnc.org. No phone calls. Materials as posted on Web site. Application deadline: March 1 for summer. World Wide Web: http://www.nature.org.

NEW ENGLAND SMALL FARM INSTITUTE/ NORTHEAST WORKERS ON ORGANIC FARMS
PO Box 608, 275 Jackson Street
Belchertown, Massachusetts 01007

General Information Small farm demonstration and training center that manages public farmland and advocates sustainable agriculture in New England. Established in 1978. Number of employees: 10. Number of internship applications received each year: 200.
Internships Available ▶ *80–100 farm apprentices/Northeast Workers on Organic Farms (NEWOOF):* responsibilities include farm work; specific responsibilities vary at each farm. Candidates should have ability to work independently, ability to work with others, personal interest in the field, self-motivation, ability to do hard physical work and work with flexible schedule. Duration is 1 growing season, or other as negotiated. Position available as unpaid or paid. Open to recent high school graduates, college freshmen, college sophomores, college juniors, college seniors, recent college graduates, graduate students, career changers, individuals reentering the workforce.
Benefits Names of contacts, on-the-job training, other benefits negotiated with individual farms.
Contact Write, call, fax, e-mail, or through World Wide Web site Michelle Wiggins, Program Manager, NEWOOF. Phone: 413-323-4531. Fax: 413-323-9594. E-mail: newoof@smallfarm.org. Applicants must submit a formal organization application, additional application materials may be required depending on position. Applications are accepted continuously. Fees: $10. World Wide Web: http://www.smallfarm.org.

NEW ENGLAND WILD FLOWER SOCIETY
180 Hemenway Road
Framingham, Massachusetts 01701-2699

General Information Private nonprofit botanical garden dedicated to the conservation of temperate North American plants; offers programs in education, horticulture, research, habitat preservation, and conservation advocacy. Established in 1900. Number of employees: 30. Number of internship applications received each year: 30.
Internships Available ▶ *2 education interns:* responsibilities include assisting with children's and family programs, leading tours, curriculum development, exhibit preparation, special projects, and community outreach. Candidates should have ability to work independently, ability to work with others, experience in the field, oral communication skills, personal interest in the field, U.S. citizenship. Duration is mid-May to August 31. Position available as unpaid or at $8–$10 per hour. Open to college juniors, college seniors, recent college graduates. ▶ *1 native plant horticulture intern:* responsibilities include general maintenance duties in a garden setting, rigorous physical labor, native plant identification, and standard horticultural practices. Candidates should have ability to work independently, ability to work with others, experience in the field, personal interest in the field, self-motivation, U.S. citizenship. Duration is 3 months (May 15-August 15) or 6 months (March 19-August 31). $230 per week. Open to college juniors, college seniors, recent college graduates, graduate students, career changers, individuals reentering the workforce. ▶ *2 plant conservation fellows:* responsibilities include gaining experience in plant conservation program activities on and off-site, including both administrative and field work activities such as natural areas management, assisting with regional rare plant monitoring program, and record-keeping. Candidates should have ability to work independently, ability to work with others, experience in

the field, personal interest in the field, self-motivation, U.S. citizenship. Duration is 6 months (March to August). $230 per week. Open to college juniors, college seniors, recent college graduates, graduate students, career changers, individuals reentering the workforce. ▶ *1 propagation and nursery management intern:* responsibilities include native plant identification, native plant propagation, seed collection, record-keeping, production and sales, and public information duties. Candidates should have ability to work independently, ability to work with others, knowledge of field, personal interest in the field, self-motivation, U.S. citizenship. Duration is 6 months (March-August). $230 per week. Open to college juniors, college seniors, recent college graduates, graduate students, career changers, individuals reentering the workforce.
Benefits Formal training, free housing, names of contacts, opportunity to attend seminars/workshops, willing to complete paperwork for educational credit, willing to provide letters of recommendation, worker's compensation.
Contact Write, call, fax, e-mail, or through World Wide Web site Tom Smarr, Horticulturist. Phone: 508-877-7630 Ext. 3404. Fax: 508-877-3658. E-mail: tsmarr@newfs.org. In-person interview recommended (telephone interview accepted). Applicants must submit a formal organization application, resume, two letters of recommendation, application can be downloaded from Web site. Application deadline: February 10 for spring/summer interns, March 15 for summer intern. World Wide Web: http://www.newfs.org/~newfs/.

NICOLET NATIONAL FOREST, EAGLE RIVER-FLORENCE RANGER DISTRICT
PO Box 1809
Eagle River, Wisconsin 54521

General Information District providing management and administration of recreation areas and wilderness. Established in 1897. Number of employees: 35. Number of internship applications received each year: 25.
Internships Available ▶ *2 trails coordinator-wilderness ranger interns:* responsibilities include assisting in the operation and maintenance of all recreation trails inside and outside of the three designated wildernesses, conducting trail condition surveys, and recommending trail rehabilitation and other actions needed to provide for public safety and enjoyment of the trails. Candidates should have ability to work independently, ability to work with others, personal interest in the field, self-motivation. Duration is 3 months in summer. $30 per day stipend. Open to high school students, recent high school graduates, college freshmen, college sophomores, college juniors, college seniors, recent college graduates, graduate students, law students, career changers, individuals reentering the workforce.
Benefits Free housing, on-the-job training, willing to act as a professional reference, willing to complete paperwork for educational credit, willing to provide letters of recommendation, uniform provided, work-related travel expenses reimbursed.
Contact Write, call, fax, e-mail, or through World Wide Web site Mr. Jeff Herrett, Assistant District Ranger. Phone: 715-479-2827. Fax: 715-479-6407. E-mail: jherrett@fs.fed.us. Applicants must submit a letter of interest, resume. Application deadline: March 24. World Wide Web: http://www.fs.fed.us/r9/cnnf.

NORRIS SQUARE NEIGHBORHOOD PROJECT, INC.
2141 North Howard Street
Philadelphia, Pennsylvania 19122

General Information Urban environmental education center that works with children and families to improve Norris Square community. Established in 1973. Number of employees: 11. Number of internship applications received each year: 3.
Internships Available ▶ *1–2 administrative assistants:* responsibilities include assisting executive director with development research. Candidates should have ability to work with others, computer skills, research skills, writing skills. Duration is flexible. Unpaid. Open to college freshmen, college sophomores, college juniors, college seniors, recent college graduates, graduate students, law students, career changers, individuals reentering the workforce. ▶ *1–2 group leaders/teachers:* responsibilities include working with

other NS staff to provide after school activities for children in kindergarten to grade 10; developing lessons, leading children in science, computer, or arts and crafts activities. Candidates should have ability to work independently, ability to work with others, self-motivation. Duration is August 15 to June 15. Unpaid. Open to recent high school graduates, college freshmen, college sophomores, college juniors, college seniors, recent college graduates, graduate students, law students, career changers, individuals reentering the workforce. ▶ *1–2 summer day camp leaders:* responsibilities include leading children in day camp activities in theme based summer camp such as environmental education, or arts and crafts. Candidates should have ability to work independently, ability to work with others, oral communication skills, self-motivation, outdoor/camp experience. Duration is June 15 to August 30 (Monday to Friday, 8:30 am-4:30 pm). Unpaid. Open to recent high school graduates, college sophomores, college juniors, college seniors, recent college graduates, individuals reentering the workforce. International applications accepted.

Benefits Job counseling, names of contacts, on-the-job training, opportunity to attend seminars/workshops, possible full-time employment, willing to act as a professional reference, willing to complete paperwork for educational credit, willing to provide letters of recommendation, possibility of travel reimbursement and some free meals.

Contact Write, call, fax, or e-mail Carol Keck, Executive Director. Phone: 215-426-4631. Fax: 215-426-8031. E-mail: ckeck@hotmail.com. In-person interview recommended (telephone interview accepted). Applicants must submit a formal organization application, letter of interest, resume, academic transcripts, two personal references, two letters of recommendation. Application deadline: April 1 for summer (preferred), July 15 for fall (preferred). World Wide Web: http://www.nsnp.org.

NORTH CAROLINA BOTANICAL GARDEN
Campus Box 3375, Totten Center, UNC-CH
Chapel Hill, North Carolina 27599-3375

General Information Regional center for research, conservation, and interpretation of plants, particularly those native to the southeastern U.S., as well as horticultural plants with traditional uses or those of special botanical interest. Established in 1960. Number of employees: 25. Unit of The University of North Carolina at Chapel Hill, Chapel Hill, North Carolina. Number of internship applications received each year: 35.

Internships Available ▶ *1 garden collections and native plant propagation intern:* responsibilities include horticultural maintenance, development, and interpretation of display collections focusing on native plants in Garden Commons, Plant Families Garden, wildflower borders and nature trail system; seed collecting, cleaning, and processing; native plant propagation; and working with volunteers. Candidates should have ability to work independently, computer skills, personal interest in the field, self-motivation, strong interpersonal skills. Duration is 3–12 months. $8.21 per hour. ▶ *1 herb garden and education outreach intern:* responsibilities include horticultural maintenance, development and interpretation of the Mercer Reeves Hubbard Herb Garden; planning and implementing horticultural therapy programs for persons with special needs; assisting in environmental education outreach programs in public schools; and working with volunteers. Candidates should have ability to work independently, computer skills, personal interest in the field, self-motivation, strong interpersonal skills. Duration is 3–12 months. $8.21 per hour. ▶ *1 native habitat gardens and plant records intern:* responsibilities include horticultural maintenance, development and interpretation of Native Habitat Gardens that highlight native southeast U.S. flora; implementing weekly "What's In Bloom?" interpretive display; assisting with plant label and records database; assisting with overall Garden interpretation strategy; and working with volunteers. Candidates should have ability to work independently, computer skills, knowledge of field, personal interest in the field, self-motivation, strong interpersonal skills. Duration is 3–12 months. $8.21 per hour. ▶ *1 public education and tour guide intern:* responsibilities include assessment of existing programs and development of additional on-site education programs for pre- and school-age children; planning and preparing pre- and post-visit materials; and working with volunteer

tour guide training, scheduling, and program presentations. Candidates should have ability to work independently, computer skills, personal interest in the field, self-motivation, strong interpersonal skills. Duration is 3–12 months. $8.21 per hour. Open to recent high school graduates, college freshmen, college sophomores, college juniors, college seniors, recent college graduates, graduate students, career changers, individuals reentering the workforce. International applications accepted.

Benefits Job counseling, names of contacts, on-the-job training, opportunity to attend seminars/workshops, possible full-time employment, willing to act as a professional reference, willing to complete paperwork for educational credit, willing to provide letters of recommendation, flexible start and end dates.

Contact Write, call, fax, or e-mail Mr. James L. Ward, Curator. Phone: 919-962-0522. Fax: 919-962-3531. E-mail: wardjl@email.unc. edu. In-person interview recommended (telephone interview accepted). Applicants must submit a formal organization application, letter of interest, resume, three personal references. Applications are accepted continuously. World Wide Web: http://www. unc.edu/depts/ncbg.

NORTH CASCADES INSTITUTE
810 State Route 20
Sedro Woolley, Washington 98284-9394

General Information Environmental education organization dedicated to increasing understanding and appreciation of the natural, historical, and cultural landscapes of the Pacific Northwest through field seminars, school programs, watershed education, summer camps, and other programs. Established in 1986. Number of employees: 12. Number of internship applications received each year: 40.

Internships Available ▶ *1–2 administrative interns:* responsibilities include assisting program coordinator or director and writing, editing, telephoning, mailing, and database work. Candidates should have ability to work independently, ability to work with others, oral communication skills, personal interest in the field, self-motivation, written communication skills. Duration is 3 months. Unpaid. ▶ *6–12 environmental education interns:* responsibilities include teaching in environmental education programs for youth. Candidates should have ability to work independently, oral communication skills, personal interest in the field, self-motivation, strong interpersonal skills, written communication skills, current first aid and CPR certification. Duration is 7–10 weeks. Unpaid. ▶ *1–2 program interns:* responsibilities include assisting program coordinator with admissions, enrollment, registration, and publicity. Candidates should have ability to work independently, oral communication skills, self-motivation, strong interpersonal skills, written communication skills. Duration is 2–4 months. Unpaid. Open to college juniors, college seniors, recent college graduates, graduate students. International applications accepted.

Benefits Formal training, job counseling, names of contacts, on-the-job training, opportunity to attend seminars/workshops, willing to act as a professional reference, willing to complete paperwork for educational credit, willing to provide letters of recommendation, housing and meals provided for environmental education internships ("Mountain School" program only); training, materials, and college credit for environmental education internships.

Contact Write, call, fax, e-mail, or through World Wide Web site Christie L. Fairchild, School Programs Coordinator. Phone: 360-856-5700 Ext. 202. Fax: 360-856-1934. E-mail: nci@ncascades.org. In-person interview recommended (telephone interview accepted). Applicants must submit a formal organization application, letter of interest, resume, three personal references. Application deadline: January 15 for spring, June 15 for fall. World Wide Web: http://ncascades.org/nci/.

NORTHWEST COALITION FOR ALTERNATIVES TO PESTICIDES
PO Box 1393
Eugene, Oregon 97440

General Information Nonprofit 5-state grassroots membership organization that works to protect people and the environment

Northwest Coalition for Alternatives to Pesticides (continued)
by advancing healthy solutions to pest problems. Established in 1977. Number of employees: 9. Number of internship applications received each year: 15.

Internships Available ▶ *1–2 information services/program assistants:* responsibilities include assisting with NCAP's program work including researching and writing articles for NCAP's quarterly Journal of Pesticide Reform and responding to requests for information; each intern has a special project, depending on skills and interests. Candidates should have ability to work independently, computer skills, office skills, oral communication skills, organizational skills, personal interest in the field, research skills, self-motivation, strong interpersonal skills, writing skills. Duration is flexible. Unpaid. Open to high school students, recent high school graduates, college freshmen, college sophomores, college juniors, college seniors, recent college graduates, graduate students, law students, career changers, individuals reentering the workforce. International applications accepted.

Benefits Names of contacts, on-the-job training, willing to complete paperwork for educational credit, willing to provide letters of recommendation.

Contact Write, call, or e-mail Megan Kemple, Public Education Coordinator. Phone: 541-344-5044 Ext. 20. Fax: 541-344-6923. E-mail: info@pesticide.org. In-person interview recommended (telephone interview accepted). Applicants must submit a letter of interest, resume. Applications are accepted continuously. World Wide Web: http://www.pesticide.org.

NUCLEAR INFORMATION AND RESOURCE SERVICE
1424 16th Street, NW, Suite 404
Washington, District of Columbia 20036

General Information Organization that assists citizens and communities concerned with the dangers of nuclear power and radioactive waste by promoting safe energy and energy alternatives. Established in 1978. Number of employees: 7. Number of internship applications received each year: 75.

Internships Available ▶ *1 communications intern:* responsibilities include helping run and improve Web site, improving and operating e-mail and Internet capabilities, designing and building databases, updating press contacts, and writing information sheets. Candidates should have computer skills, personal interest in the field, strong interpersonal skills. Duration is flexible. Unpaid. ▶ *1 radiation and health hazard intern.* Candidates should have ability to work with others, oral communication skills, research skills, writing skills. Duration is flexible. Unpaid. ▶ *Radioactive waste interns.* Candidates should have ability to work independently, experience in the field, oral communication skills, personal interest in the field, strong interpersonal skills, written communication skills. Duration is flexible. Unpaid. ▶ *1 reactor watchdog intern.* Candidates should have ability to work independently, ability to work with others, oral communication skills, personal interest in the field. Duration is flexible. Unpaid. Open to high school students, recent high school graduates, college freshmen, college sophomores, college juniors, college seniors, recent college graduates, graduate students, law students, career changers, individuals reentering the workforce.

Benefits Names of contacts, opportunity to attend seminars/workshops, possible full-time employment, willing to complete paperwork for educational credit, willing to provide letters of recommendation.

Contact Write, fax, or e-mail Don Keesing, Administrative Coordinator. Fax: 202-462-2183. E-mail: nirsnet@nirs.org. No phone calls. Applicants must submit a resume, writing sample. Applications are accepted continuously. World Wide Web: http://www.nirs.org.

THE OJAI FOUNDATION
9739 Ojai-Santa Paula Road
Ojai, California 93023

General Information Nonprofit organization whose purpose is to offer a center for education, renewal, and the honoring of life's many passages. Established in 1974. Number of employees: 8. Number of internship applications received each year: 10.

Internships Available ▶ *1–2 center management interns:* responsibilities include acting as administrative assistant to the leadership council; attendance at meetings and events both on and off the land; special project on completion of program. Candidates should have experience in the field, oral communication skills, organizational skills, self-motivation, strong leadership ability, written communication skills. Duration is 6–7 months. Unpaid. Open to recent high school graduates, college freshmen, college sophomores, college juniors, college seniors, recent college graduates, graduate students, career changers, individuals reentering the workforce, those interested in business management or starting their own center. ▶ *1–2 land stewardship interns:* responsibilities include participation in meetings and staff councils; hands-on activities and projects on the land; research assignments; special project on completion of program. Candidates should have ability to work independently, ability to work with others, experience in the field, oral communication skills, personal interest in the field, self-motivation. Duration is 6–7 months. Unpaid. Open to recent high school graduates, college freshmen, college sophomores, college juniors, college seniors, recent college graduates, graduate students, career changers, individuals reentering the workforce, those interested in alternative gardening, landscaping, land management, and community practices. International applications accepted.

Benefits Free housing, on-the-job training, opportunity to attend seminars/workshops, willing to act as a professional reference, willing to provide letters of recommendation, living in community close to the earth.

Contact Write, fax, or e-mail Marlow Hotchkiss, Director. Phone: 805-646-8343 Ext. 104. Fax: 805-646-2456. E-mail: ojaifdn@jetlink.net. Applicants must submit a letter of interest, resume, two personal references, in-person interview for finalists. Applications are accepted continuously. World Wide Web: http://ojaifoundation.org.

OREGON ENVIRONMENTAL COUNCIL
520 SW 6th Avenue, Suite 940
Portland, Oregon 97204-1535

General Information Nonprofit environmental organization. Established in 1968. Number of employees: 11.

Internships Available ▶ *2–3 environmental policy research assistants:* responsibilities include researching environmental policy issues, writing reports and summaries, and assisting OEC program staff. Candidates should have ability to work independently, computer skills, personal interest in the field, research skills, writing skills. Duration is 2–3 months. Unpaid. Open to college freshmen, college sophomores, college juniors, college seniors, recent college graduates, graduate students, law students. International applications accepted.

Benefits Willing to act as a professional reference, willing to complete paperwork for educational credit, willing to provide letters of recommendation.

Contact Write, fax, e-mail, or through World Wide Web site Clare Naber, Volunteer/Internship Coordinator. Fax: 503-222-1405. E-mail: clare@orcouncil.org. No phone calls. Telephone interview required. Applicants must submit a letter of interest, resume, personal reference. Applications are accepted continuously. World Wide Web: http://www.orcouncil.org.

OREGON MUSEUM OF SCIENCE AND INDUSTRY SCIENCE CAMPS
508 Southwest 13th Street
Redmond, Oregon 97756

General Information Organization that teaches natural history, outdoor skills, and environmental science to students of all ages in a residential camp setting in the desert, the Cascade Mountains, and on the Pacific coast. Established in 1951. Number of employees: 50. Division of Oregon Museum of Science and Industry, Portland, Oregon. Number of internship applications received each year: 30.

Internships Available ▶ *2 administration interns:* responsibilities include assisting with office administration, data presentation, and

other duties as necessary to help facilitate the smooth operation of an educational facility. Candidates should have ability to work independently, computer skills, knowledge of field, office skills, research skills, writing skills. Duration is 3 months. $15–$20 per day. ▶ *8 naturalist interns:* responsibilities include reviewing available curriculum and becoming proficient in teaching those subjects, developing and organizing program materials and displays, aiding in logistics for field programs, and being a positive role model for students. Candidates should have knowledge of field, organizational skills, personal interest in the field, self-motivation, strong interpersonal skills, strong leadership ability. Duration is 3 months. $15–$20 per day. Open to college juniors, college seniors, recent college graduates, graduate students. International applications accepted.
Benefits Free housing, free meals, on-the-job training, opportunity to attend seminars/workshops, possible full-time employment, willing to act as a professional reference, willing to complete paperwork for educational credit, willing to provide letters of recommendation.
Contact Write, call, fax, or e-mail Kayla Chitwood, Programming Coordinator. Phone: 541-504-2538. Fax: 541-504-2538. E-mail: sciencecamps@omsi.edu. In-person interview recommended (telephone interview accepted). Applicants must submit a formal organization application, letter of interest, resume, three personal references, letter of recommendation. Applications are accepted continuously. World Wide Web: http://www.omsi.com.

PACIFIC ENVIRONMENT AND RESOURCES CENTER
1440 Broadway, Suite 306
Oakland, California 94612

General Information Nonprofit organization that employs grassroots activism and environmental advocacy and is committed to global environmental improvement projects around the Pacific Rim. Established in 1987. Number of employees: 11. Number of internship applications received each year: 20.
Internships Available ▶ *1 administrative intern:* responsibilities include letter writing, typing, organizing files and information, answering phones, filling requests for information, assisting with mailings and databases, and helping with other miscellaneous tasks. Candidates should have ability to work independently, ability to work with others, computer skills, office skills, oral communication skills, organizational skills, research skills, writing skills. Duration is 3 months. Unpaid. ▶ *1–5 independent project interns:* responsibilities include working with a project director on an issue that relates to a PERC project. Candidates should have ability to work independently, analytical skills, oral communication skills, research skills, self-motivation, writing skills. Duration is 4 months. Unpaid. ▶ *1–3 project assistants:* responsibilities include researching and summarizing information on a particular subject of interest to the intern and relevant to a PERC project. Candidates should have ability to work independently, oral communication skills, organizational skills, research skills, self-motivation, written communication skills. Duration is 3–9 months. Unpaid. Open to college freshmen, college sophomores, college juniors, college seniors, recent college graduates, graduate students, career changers, individuals reentering the workforce. International applications accepted.
Benefits Job counseling, names of contacts, possible full-time employment, willing to act as a professional reference, willing to complete paperwork for educational credit, willing to provide letters of recommendation, opportunity to work with experts, structured supervision, opportunity to learn about global environmental issues.
Contact Write, fax, e-mail, or through World Wide Web site David Gordon, Director of Programs. Fax: 510-251-8838. E-mail: info@pacificenvironment.org. No phone calls. In-person interview recommended (telephone interview accepted). Applicants must submit a formal organization application, letter of interest, resume. Applications are accepted continuously. World Wide Web: http://www.pacificenvironment.org.

PAYETTE NATIONAL FOREST, MCCALL RANGER DISTRICT
PO Box 1026
McCall, Idaho 83638

General Information Forest service that cares for the land and serves the people. Established in 1905. Number of employees: 30. Number of internship applications received each year: 5.
Internships Available ▶ *2 recreation assistants:* responsibilities include assisting with campground, trailhead, and dispersed site maintenance. Duration is 3-4 months in summer. $50–$60 per week. Open to recent high school graduates, college freshmen, college sophomores, college juniors, college seniors, recent college graduates, graduate students, law students, individuals reentering the workforce. ▶ *1–3 trail maintenance volunteers:* responsibilities include working with small crew constructing and maintaining trails in steep terrain while camping out. Duration is 3-4 months in summer. Position available as unpaid or at $60–$80 per week. Open to recent high school graduates, college freshmen, college sophomores, college juniors, college seniors, recent college graduates, graduate students, law students, career changers, individuals reentering the workforce. Candidates for all positions should have ability to work independently, ability to work with others, self-motivation. International applications accepted.
Benefits Free housing, on-the-job training, willing to act as a professional reference, willing to provide letters of recommendation.
Contact Write, call, fax, or e-mail Jeff Gildehaus, Recreation Planner. Phone: 208-634-0400. Fax: 208-634-0433. E-mail: payette/r4@fs.fed.us. Applicants must submit a resume. Applications are accepted continuously. World Wide Web: http://www.mccall.net/pnf.

PEACE VALLEY NATURE CENTER
170 Chapman Road
Doylestown, Pennsylvania 18901

General Information Center that promotes environmental awareness through a variety of educational experiences; serves as a wildlife sanctuary where citizens of southeast Pennsylvania can enjoy natural beauty. Established in 1975. Number of employees: 4. Unit of Bucks County Department of Parks and Recreation, Langhorne, Pennsylvania. Number of internship applications received each year: 25.
Internships Available ▶ *2 naturalist interns:* responsibilities include observing and teaching environmental education programs to children of all ages, completing and presenting an approved project, writing a newsletter article on a natural history topic, filling out weekly diary, assisting in all aspects of nature center operations. Candidates should have ability to work independently, knowledge of field, oral communication skills, personal interest in the field, plan to pursue career in field, self-motivation, strong interpersonal skills, strong leadership ability, writing skills. Duration is 10–12 weeks. $5.15 per hour. Open to college freshmen, college sophomores, college juniors, college seniors, recent college graduates, graduate students, career changers.
Benefits Formal training, free housing, names of contacts, on-the-job training, opportunity to attend seminars/workshops, willing to act as a professional reference, willing to complete paperwork for educational credit, willing to provide letters of recommendation.
Contact Write, call, fax, or e-mail Gail Hill, Environmental Education Director. Phone: 215-345-7860. Fax: 215-345-4529. E-mail: pvnceed@nni.com. In-person interview recommended (telephone interview accepted). Applicants must submit a formal organization application, letter of interest, resume, two personal references. Application deadline: April 15 for summer.

PEOPLE FOR THE ETHICAL TREATMENT OF ANIMALS (PETA)
501 Front Street
Norfolk, Virginia 23510

General Information International animal rights group whose motto is "Animals are not ours to eat, wear, experiment on, or to use for entertainment". Established in 1980. Number of employees: 90. Number of internship applications received each year: 50.

People for the Ethical Treatment of Animals (PETA) (continued)

Internships Available ▶ *6–8 interns:* responsibilities include helping with grassroots outreach activities including stunts, demonstrations, and tabling events; office work; attending demonstrations; preparing mailings; creating props; and working on special projects. Candidates should have ability to work with others, oral communication skills, personal interest in the field. Duration is flexible. $50 per week. Open to individuals at least 18 years of age. International applications accepted.

Benefits Free housing, free meals, on-the-job training, possible full-time employment, travel reimbursement, willing to act as a professional reference, willing to complete paperwork for educational credit.

Contact Write, call, fax, e-mail, or through World Wide Web site Vicki Carey, Human Resources Manager, 501 Front Street, Norfolk, Virginia 23510. Phone: 757-622-7382 Ext. 1416. Fax: 757-628-0789. E-mail: vickic@fsap.org. Applicants must submit a formal organization application, letter of interest, resume, three letters of recommendation, 2-page essay discussing interest in animal rights and expectations of internship. Applications are accepted continuously. World Wide Web: http://www.peta-online.org.

PILOT MOUNTAIN STATE PARK
1792 Pilot Knob Park Road
Pinnacle, North Carolina 27043-9201

General Information State park that preserves North Carolina's natural heritage and provides recreation opportunities for park visitors. Established in 1968. Number of employees: 14. Unit of North Carolina Department of ENR, Division of Parks and Recreation, Raleigh, North Carolina. Number of internship applications received each year: 4.

Internships Available ▶ *2–5 park interns:* responsibilities include participating in park operation, environmental education programs, resource management, trail work, visitor contact, and outdoor projects. Candidates should have ability to work independently, ability to work with others, oral communication skills, personal interest in the field, self-motivation, written communication skills. Duration is arranged with academic institution. Unpaid. Open to recent high school graduates, college freshmen, college sophomores, college juniors, college seniors, recent college graduates, graduate students, law students, career changers, individuals reentering the workforce, must be age 18 or older. International applications accepted.

Benefits Names of contacts, on-the-job training, willing to act as a professional reference, willing to complete paperwork for educational credit, willing to provide letters of recommendation, recreational opportunities (hiking, canoeing, and rock climbing).

Contact Write, call, fax, or e-mail Janet Pearson, Volunteer Manager. Phone: 336-325-2355. Fax: 336-325-2751. E-mail: pilotmtn@surry.net. In-person interview recommended (telephone interview accepted). Applicants must submit a letter of interest, three personal references. Applications are accepted continuously. World Wide Web: http://ils.unc.edu/parkproject/pimo.html.

PLANET DRUM FOUNDATION
PO Box 31251
San Francisco, California 94131

General Information Nonprofit ecological education organization promoting the ideas of bioregionalism and urban sustainability through publications, workshops, lectures, performances, and hands-on environmental work. Established in 1973. Number of employees: 5.

Internships Available ▶ *Ecuador Restoration Project assistants:* responsibilities include assisting in various areas of urban sustainability in Ecuador's coastal cities with projects including re-vegetation of hillsides, water supply and purity, ecology education, alternative energy and more. Duration is year-round. Unpaid. ▶ *Administrative assistants:* responsibilities include running Planet Drum's office, acting as assistant to the Director, arranging appointments, conducting research, sorting archival materials, organizing the library, responding to telephone requests, and leading bulk mail parties. Duration is 3 months minimum (20 hours per week). Unpaid. ▶ *Art and design assistants:* responsibilities include helping with

the design and layout for flyers, notices to members, project photo albums, displays for tabling, and Web page; taking photos. Candidates should have sense of humor. Duration is 3 months minimum (20 hours per week). Unpaid. ▶ *Bioregional association assistants:* responsibilities include expanding outreach and helping design a publicity campaign, assisting in planning a membership or Board of Directors' meeting, working on documenting and disseminating the results of this meeting, helping to organize a resources database. Duration is 3 months minimum (20 hours per week). Unpaid. ▶ *Editorial assistants:* responsibilities include helping with the Planet Drum Pulse newsletter and other publications. Candidates should have ability to work independently, ability to work with others, editing skills, writing skills. Duration is 3 months minimum (20 hours per week). Unpaid. ▶ *Event coordinator assistants:* responsibilities include helping to plan benefit events or the Shasta Bioregional Gathering (a long-weekend event); includes obtaining donations; promotion to media and attendees; and scheduling workshops, speakers, and entertainment. Duration is 3 months minimum (20 hours per week). Unpaid. International applications accepted.

Benefits Names of contacts, on-the-job training, opportunity to attend seminars/workshops, willing to complete paperwork for educational credit, willing to provide letters of recommendation, access to library, small stipend for local travel, opportunity to complete a project.

International Internships Available in Bahia de Caraquez, Ecuador.

Contact Write, call, fax, or e-mail Judy Goldhaft, Managing Director. Phone: 415-285-6556. Fax: 415-285-6563. E-mail: planetdrum@igc.org. In-person interview recommended (telephone interview accepted). Applicants must submit a formal organization application, resume. Applications are accepted continuously. World Wide Web: http://www.planetdrum.org.

POCONO ENVIRONMENTAL EDUCATION CENTER
RR 2, Box 1010
Dingmans Ferry, Pennsylvania 18328

General Information Center that advances environmental awareness, knowledge, and skills through education. Established in 1968. Number of employees: 24. Number of internship applications received each year: 300.

Internships Available ▶ *1 development intern:* responsibilities include assisting director of development with management of membership and volunteer services, coordinating special events, and researching funding sources. Candidates should have ability to work independently, ability to work with others, analytical skills, computer skills, knowledge of field, office skills, organizational skills, personal interest in the field, research skills, self-motivation, written communication skills. Duration is 6–10 months. Position available as unpaid or at $500–$800 per month. Open to college juniors, college seniors, recent college graduates, graduate students, career changers, individuals reentering the workforce. ▶ *6–10 environmental education instructors:* responsibilities include teaching environment/outdoor education to people of all ages, developing programs and activities, performing daily operations and procedures, and assisting with support services. Candidates should have ability to work independently, ability to work with others, college courses in field, computer skills, knowledge of field, office skills, organizational skills, personal interest in the field, self-motivation. Duration is 6–10 months. Position available as unpaid or at $700–$800 per month. Open to recent college graduates, graduate students. ▶ *2–4 environmental education interns:* responsibilities include teaching environment/outdoor education/recreation opportunities to all visitors and guests, assisting in all daily operations and support services. Candidates should have ability to work with others, knowledge of field, office skills, oral communication skills, personal interest in the field, self-motivation. Duration is 3–6 months. $500–$700 per month. Open to college juniors, college seniors, recent college graduates, graduate students, law students, career changers, individuals reentering the workforce. ▶ *1–2 program planning interns:* responsibilities include scheduling group's program/activities, coordinating cabins, facilities, staff, and food-service arrangements; designing weekly schedules, and teaching environment/outdoor education to people of all ages. Candidates should have ability to work independently, ability to

work with others, analytical skills, knowledge of field, office skills, oral communication skills, organizational skills, personal interest in the field, self-motivation, written communication skills. Duration is 6–10 months. Position available as unpaid or at $500–$800 per month. Open to college juniors, college seniors, recent college graduates, graduate students. ▶ *1 public relations intern:* responsibilities include writing press releases, designing layout for promotional materials, maintaining a darkroom, and assisting with programs and activities. Candidates should have ability to work independently, computer skills, editing skills, knowledge of field, office skills, oral communication skills, personal interest in the field, self-motivation, strong interpersonal skills, writing skills. Duration is 6–10 months. Position available as unpaid or at $500–$800 per month. Open to college juniors, college seniors, recent college graduates, graduate students. International applications accepted.
Benefits Formal training, free housing, free meals, job counseling, names of contacts, on-the-job training, opportunity to attend seminars/workshops, tuition assistance, willing to act as a professional reference, willing to complete paperwork for educational credit, willing to provide letters of recommendation.
Contact Write, call, fax, e-mail, or through World Wide Web site Ms. Florence Mauro, Director of Education. Phone: 570-828-2319. Fax: 570-828-9695. E-mail: fmauro@peec.org. In-person interview recommended (telephone interview accepted). Applicants must submit a letter of interest, resume, two personal references, 2 writing samples for public relations intern applicants. Application deadline: February 1 for summer, June 1 for fall, October 1 for winter/spring. World Wide Web: http://www.peec.org.

POK-O-MACCREADY OUTDOOR EDUCATION CENTER
112 Reber Road North
Willsboro, New York 12996

General Information Outdoor education center in the Adirondacks that allows children in grades 5–12 to participate in activities including pond study, pioneer living, rock climbing, cross-country skiing, winter camping, environmental study, and overnight hikes. Established in 1905. Number of employees: 9. Number of internship applications received each year: 12.
Internships Available ▶ *2–4 outdoor educator interns:* responsibilities include teaching and facilitating groups of middle-school children in different aspects of outdoor education, work projects as necessary. Candidates should have ability to work independently, oral communication skills, personal interest in the field, self-motivation, strong interpersonal skills, experience in outdoor activities; working with children a plus. Duration is 2 months. $100–$150 per month. Open to recent high school graduates, college freshmen, college sophomores, college juniors, college seniors, recent college graduates. International applications accepted.
Benefits Formal training, free housing, free meals, possible full-time employment, willing to complete paperwork for educational credit, worker's compensation.
Contact Write, call, fax, or e-mail John Patla, Director. Phone: 518-963-7967. Fax: 518-963-4165. E-mail: pmoec@willex.com. Applicants must submit a letter of interest, resume. Applications are accepted continuously. World Wide Web: http://www.pokomac.com.

POWDER RIVER BASIN RESOURCE COUNCIL
23 North Scott, Suite 19
Sheridan, Wyoming 82801

General Information Nonprofit membership conservation/agriculture organization promoting stewardship of Wyoming's natural resources and quality of life through organizing, public education, and lobbying. Established in 1973. Number of employees: 6. Affiliate of Western Organization Resource Council, Billings, Montana. Number of internship applications received each year: 50.
Internships Available ▶ *1–2 project assistants:* responsibilities include assisting with research; compiling information; drafting materials connected with resource issues such as water develop-

ment, energy development, waste management, and sustainable agriculture; evaluating conservation policies; and increasing citizen involvement in decision making. Candidates should have ability to work independently, ability to work with others, research skills, self-motivation, writing skills. Duration is 3 months. $200–$250 per month. Open to college freshmen, college sophomores, college juniors, college seniors, recent college graduates, graduate students, law students, career changers, individuals reentering the workforce. International applications accepted.
Benefits Formal training, housing at a cost, meals at a cost, names of contacts, willing to complete paperwork for educational credit, willing to provide letters of recommendation, staff car for travel.
Contact Write, call, fax, e-mail, or through World Wide Web site Kevin Lind, Director. Phone: 307-672-5809. Fax: 307-672-5800. E-mail: klind@powderriverbasin.org. In-person interview recommended (telephone interview accepted). Applicants must submit a letter of interest, resume, three personal references, one-page writing sample. Applications are accepted continuously. World Wide Web: http://www.web.vcn.com/prbrc.

QUEENS COLLEGE CENTER FOR ENVIRONMENTAL TEACHING AND RESEARCH
Caumsett State Park, 31 Lloyd Harbor Road
Huntington, New York 11743

General Information Residential environmental and outdoor education and research center. Established in 1979. Number of employees: 19. Department of Queens College of the City University of New York, Flushing, New York. Number of internship applications received each year: 75.
Internships Available ▶ *2 interns:* responsibilities include preparing and presenting lessons in environmental education to all age groups, presenting live animal presentation and outreach programs, visiting other environmental centers, and caring for in-house raptors and reptiles. Candidates should have knowledge of field, oral communication skills, personal interest in the field, strong interpersonal skills, strong leadership ability. Duration is one summer or semester. $50 per week; $100 per week (summer interns). Open to college freshmen, college sophomores, college juniors, college seniors, recent college graduates, graduate students, law students. ▶ *1–5 naturalist interns:* responsibilities include teaching environmental and outdoor education topics to various ages/grade levels during residential overnight programs, day programs, and classroom visits; animal care; and house support. Candidates should have oral communication skills, organizational skills, personal interest in the field, plan to pursue career in field, strong interpersonal skills, strong leadership ability, written communication skills. Duration is one summer or semester. $50 per week; $100 per week (summer interns). Open to college sophomores, college juniors, college seniors, recent college graduates, graduate students, career changers. International applications accepted.
Benefits Free housing, free meals, job counseling, names of contacts, on-the-job training, opportunity to attend seminars/workshops, possible full-time employment, willing to complete paperwork for educational credit, willing to provide letters of recommendation.
Contact Write, fax, or e-mail Program Director. Fax: 631-421-3557. E-mail: peter.schmidt@rcn.com. No phone calls. Applicants must submit a letter of interest, resume, three personal references. Application deadline: March 1 for summer, July 1 for fall, October 1 for winter, December 1 for spring.

RANDALL DAVEY AUDUBON CENTER
PO Box 9314
Santa Fe, New Mexico 87504

General Information Environmental education center that advocates environmental issues that affect the southwest United States. Established in 1983. Number of employees: 5. Unit of National Audubon Society, New York, New York. Number of internship applications received each year: 30.
Internships Available ▶ *1–3 environmental education interns:* responsibilities include assisting in planning and teaching environmental education classes for students, staffing the visitor center, leading interpretive walks, assisting with the maintenance

of building and grounds, and assisting with newsletter writing and production. Candidates should have ability to work independently, oral communication skills, organizational skills, personal interest in the field, plan to pursue career in field, strong interpersonal skills. Duration is 3 months. $125 per week. Open to college freshmen, college sophomores, college juniors, college seniors, recent college graduates, graduate students, career changers, individuals reentering the workforce.

Benefits Formal training, free housing, job counseling, names of contacts, on-the-job training, opportunity to attend seminars/workshops, willing to act as a professional reference, willing to complete paperwork for educational credit, willing to provide letters of recommendation.

Contact Write, call, fax, or e-mail Lauren Parmelee, Director of Education. Phone: 505-983-4609. Fax: 505-983-2355. E-mail: lparmelee@audubon.org. Telephone interview required. Applicants must submit a letter of interest, resume, 2-3 personal references or letters of recommendation. Application deadline: February 15 for summer, June 24 for fall, November 15 for spring. World Wide Web: http://www.audubon.org.

THE RAPTOR CENTER AT THE VERMONT INSTITUTE OF NATURAL SCIENCE
27023 Church Hill Road
Woodstock, Vermont 05091-9720

General Information Living museum of birds of prey and rehabilitation facility for all birds. Established in 1987. Number of employees: 4. Number of internship applications received each year: 100.

Internships Available ▶ *1–2 wildlife care interns:* responsibilities include assisting with medical care of rehabilitation birds and providing captive management and husbandry for over 70 birds and reptiles used for education. Candidates should have ability to work independently, knowledge of field, oral communication skills, organizational skills, personal interest in the field, self-motivation, strong interpersonal skills, must be 18 years or older, have valid driver's license, able to climb stairs and lift up to 40 pounds, work in all weather conditions. Duration is 3–5 months (40 hours per week). Unpaid. Open to college freshmen, college sophomores, college juniors, college seniors, recent college graduates, graduate students, law students, career changers, individuals reentering the workforce. International applications accepted.

Benefits Formal training, free housing, names of contacts, on-the-job training, opportunity to attend seminars/workshops, willing to act as a professional reference, willing to complete paperwork for educational credit, willing to provide letters of recommendation, food allowance ($400 per month).

Contact Write, call, fax, or e-mail Mike Pratt, Director, Wildlife Services. Phone: 802-457-2779 Ext. 125. Fax: 802-457-1053. E-mail: mpratt@vinsweb.org. Telephone interview required. Applicants must submit a letter of interest, resume, two letters of recommendation. Application deadline: March 15 for summer (May-August), July 1 for fall (September-December), December 1 for winter and spring. World Wide Web: http://www.vinsweb.org.

RIVERBEND ENVIRONMENTAL EDUCATION CENTER
1950 Spring Mill Road
Gladwyne, Pennsylvania 19035

General Information Environmental education center emphasizing awareness, appreciation, and understanding of the environment. Established in 1974. Number of employees: 6. Number of internship applications received each year: 150.

Internships Available ▶ *3 Riverbend Exploration Camp environmental education interns:* responsibilities include attending one-week training session, assisting staff with summer day camp, greeting and speaking with public visitors, leading nature walks, assisting with upkeep and cleaning of facilities. Candidates should have ability to work independently, personal interest in the field, self-motivation, strong interpersonal skills, knowledge of basic environmental concepts; experience with children. Duration is

13 weeks (June to August). Salary commensurate with qualifications. Open to college sophomores, college juniors, college seniors, recent college graduates, graduate students, career changers. ▶ *3 development interns:* responsibilities include assisting staff with all administrative facets of fund-raising including membership, special events, foundation and corporate research, grantwriting, and reporting. Candidates should have ability to work with others, computer skills, office skills, organizational skills, research skills, writing skills. Unpaid. Open to college sophomores, college juniors, college seniors, recent college graduates, graduate students, career changers. ▶ *7–10 environmental educators:* responsibilities include planning and leading week-long day camp programs for children ages 4-14. Candidates should have ability to work with others, oral communication skills, personal interest in the field, self-motivation, knowledge of environmental concepts; experience educating children. Duration is June to August. Salary commensurate with qualifications. Open to college seniors, recent college graduates, graduate students, career changers, individuals reentering the workforce, individuals with experience equivalent to college degree (acceptable). ▶ *3 seasonal environmental education interns:* responsibilities include teaching classes in schools, organized groups, and public; maintaining teaching areas; planning and preparing classes and public programs from assigned environmental concepts; assisting in developing and revising classes and programs; maintaining small animal cages; assisting with promotion of programs via press releases, newsletter, and articles; assisting with development and implementation of large public events; and assisting with office duties. Candidates should have ability to work independently, personal interest in the field, plan to pursue career in field, self-motivation, strong interpersonal skills, knowledge of basic environmental concepts. Duration is January-June, June-September, or September-December (40 hours per week). Salary commensurate with qualifications. Open to college sophomores, college juniors, college seniors, recent college graduates, career changers, individuals reentering the workforce. ▶ *3–10 summer junior interns:* responsibilities include assisting with day-to-day operations of summer day camp with environmental themes, including working with groups of children. Candidates should have ability to work with others, oral communication skills, personal interest in the field, self-motivation. Duration is June to August (dates flexible). Unpaid. Open to high school seniors, recent high school graduates, college freshmen, college sophomores, college juniors, college seniors, recent college graduates, graduate students, law students, career changers, individuals reentering the workforce. International applications accepted.

Benefits Formal training, job counseling, names of contacts, on-the-job training, opportunity to attend seminars/workshops, possible full-time employment, willing to act as a professional reference, willing to complete paperwork for educational credit, willing to provide letters of recommendation, introduction to administration of other environmental centers, opportunity to visit other environmental centers in the region, possibility of free housing.

Contact Write, call, fax, e-mail, or through World Wide Web site Jeanne Braha, Camp Director. Phone: 610-527-5234. Fax: 610-527-1161. E-mail: riverbendcamp@aol.com. In-person interview recommended (telephone interview accepted). Applicants must submit a letter of interest, resume, three personal references. Applications are accepted continuously. World Wide Web: http://www.gladwyne.com/riverbend/.

SALT RIVER PROJECT (SRP)–PROJECT EMPLOYEES RECREATION ASSOCIATION (PERA)
PO Box 52025
Phoenix, Arizona 85072-2025

General Information Private club for Salt River Project employees and their immediate families. Established in 1952. Number of employees: 50. Division of Salt River Project, Tempe, Arizona. Number of internship applications received each year: 15.

Internships Available ▶ *Recreation interns:* responsibilities include working in the fitness center; assisting with facility booking, snack bar operations, maintenance, bartending, and special events; assembling 2 educational classes; working on promotional flyers and billings; overseeing the recreational aids; and assisting with

swimming pool. Candidates should have ability to work with others, computer skills, knowledge of field, organizational skills, plan to pursue career in field, self-motivation. Duration is flexible. $75 per week. Open to college seniors, recent college graduates, graduate students, career changers, individuals reentering the workforce. International applications accepted.
Benefits Formal training, job counseling, names of contacts, opportunity to attend seminars/workshops, possible full-time employment, willing to complete paperwork for educational credit, willing to provide letters of recommendation, use of facility (store, fitness, pool).
Contact Write, call, or fax John Madden, Activities Supervisor. Phone: 602-236-5782. Fax: 602-236-5920. In-person interview recommended (telephone interview accepted). Applicants must submit a formal organization application, letter of interest, resume. Applications are accepted continuously.

SARETT NATURE CENTER
2300 Benton Center Road
Benton Harbor, Michigan 49022

General Information Nature center designed to provide environmental education for the surrounding school districts, as well as an outlet for natural history education of the general public. Established in 1970. Number of employees: 8. Unit of Michigan Audubon Society, Lansing, Michigan. Number of internship applications received each year: 20.
Internships Available ▶ *2 naturalist interns:* responsibilities include teaching diverse natural history programs to school groups, primarily preschool through sixth grade; leading interpretive nature walks; and teaching cross-country skiing. Candidates should have ability to work independently, ability to work with others, college courses in field, knowledge of field, oral communication skills. Duration is 3–5 months. $6 per hour. Open to college sophomores, college juniors, college seniors, recent college graduates.
Benefits Free housing, job counseling, names of contacts, on-the-job training, opportunity to attend seminars/workshops, willing to complete paperwork for educational credit, willing to provide letters of recommendation.
Contact Write, call, fax, or e-mail Dianne Braybrook, Chief Naturalist. Phone: 616-927-4832. Fax: 616-927-2742. E-mail: sarett@sarett.com. Applicants must submit a letter of interest, resume, three personal references. Applications are accepted continuously. World Wide Web: http://www.sarett.com.

SAVE AMERICA'S FORESTS
4 Library Court, SE
Washington, District of Columbia 20003

General Information Environmental and forest protection education and lobbying organization. Established in 1989. Number of employees: 8.
Internships Available ▶ *2–4 interns:* responsibilities include research, writing, office tasks, lobbying, organizing for legislation. Candidates should have analytical skills, knowledge of field, office skills, oral communication skills, strong interpersonal skills, writing skills. Duration is 1 semester. Stipend available. Open to college sophomores, college juniors, college seniors, recent college graduates, graduate students, law students, career changers.
Benefits On-the-job training, possible full-time employment, willing to act as a professional reference, willing to complete paperwork for educational credit, willing to provide letters of recommendation.
Contact Write, call, e-mail, or through World Wide Web site Internship Coordinator, 4 Library Court, SE, Washington, District of Columbia 20003. Phone: 202-544-9219. E-mail: intern@saveamericasforests.org. Telephone interview required. Applicants must submit a letter of interest, resume, two writing samples, 2 personal references or letters of recommendation. Applications are accepted continuously. World Wide Web: http://www.saveamericasforests.org.

SAVE THE SOUND, INC.
20 Marshall Street
Norwalk, Connecticut 06854

General Information Environmental, nonprofit organization dedicated to the protection, restoration, and appreciation of Long Island Sound and its watershed through programs in education, research, and advocacy. Established in 1972. Number of employees: 8. Number of internship applications received each year: 60.
Internships Available ▶ *2 education interns:* responsibilities include assisting in development of new programs, creating support materials, and teaching programs. Candidates should have ability to work independently, ability to work with others, oral communication skills, organizational skills, strong leadership ability, written communication skills. Duration is flexible. Unpaid. Open to college freshmen, college sophomores, college juniors, college seniors, recent college graduates, graduate students. ▶ *1 habitat restoration field intern:* responsibilities include conducting field surveys (from land and water) at selected sites around the Long Island Sound to identify stormwater and sewer outfalls and other sources of pollution and habitat degradation, and collecting data to assess the impact of those sources on nearby coastal habitats. Candidates should have computer skills, BS degree in marine science, biology, ecology, environmental science or a related field preferred; upper-level undergraduates with appropriate coursework/work experience will be considered; must have valid driver's license, transportation, and valid Connecticut or New York Safe Boating Certificate. Duration is 10 weeks from May to September (20 to 30 hours per week). Unpaid. ▶ *1 marketing assistants:* responsibilities include assisting in the development of a three-year public relations plan. Candidates should have ability to work with others, computer skills, office skills, oral communication skills, writing skills. Duration is flexible. Unpaid. Open to college freshmen, college sophomores, college juniors, college seniors, recent college graduates, graduate students, career changers. ▶ *1 membership database assistant:* responsibilities include inputting membership data into the database and maintaining current membership information. Candidates should have ability to work independently, computer skills, office skills, organizational skills, self-motivation. Duration is flexible. Unpaid. Open to high school seniors, recent high school graduates, college freshmen, college sophomores, college juniors, college seniors, career changers. ▶ *1 nonprofit management intern:* responsibilities include assisting in the expansion of the fund-raising capabilities; specific projects will be geared toward intern's experience. Candidates should have ability to work with others, college courses in field, computer skills, editing skills, office skills, organizational skills, writing skills. Duration is flexible. Unpaid. Open to college juniors, college seniors, recent college graduates, graduate students. ▶ *1 volunteer coordinator assistant:* responsibilities include helping recruit and place volunteers, assembling support materials, and coordinating volunteer activities. Candidates should have ability to work with others, computer skills, office skills, oral communication skills, strong leadership ability, writing skills, basic understanding of lab skills and science-related topics. Duration is flexible. Unpaid. Open to high school seniors, college freshmen, college sophomores, college juniors, college seniors, recent college graduates, career changers. ▶ *1–2 water quality research interns:* responsibilities include identifying algae from water samples in lab and analyzing pigment content and nutrients of samples to track algae blooms. Candidates should have ability to work independently, analytical skills, knowledge of field, personal interest in the field, basic understanding of lab skills and science-related topics. Duration is flexible. Unpaid. Open to college freshmen, college sophomores, college juniors, college seniors, recent college graduates, graduate students, career changers.
Benefits Opportunity to attend seminars/workshops, willing to act as a professional reference, willing to complete paperwork for educational credit, willing to provide letters of recommendation.
Contact Write, fax, or e-mail Leah Lopez, Staff Attorney. Phone: 203-354-0036. Fax: 203-354-0041. E-mail: llopez@savethesound.org. In-person interview recommended (telephone interview accepted). Applicants must submit a formal organization application, letter of interest, resume, writing sample, 3 references, list

Save the Sound, Inc. (continued)

of applicable coursework for habitat restoration and water quality positions. Application deadline: May 1 for habitat restoration and water quality field interns; continuous for all other positions. World Wide Web: http://www.savethesound.org.

SCENIC AMERICA
801 Pennsylvania Avenue, SE, #300
Washington, District of Columbia 20003

General Information   Organization that educates the public about the need to protect and improve the visual environment through research and technical assistance to local and state activists and concerned citizens. Established in 1978. Number of employees: 7. Number of internship applications received each year: 60.

Internships Available   ► *1 policy intern:* responsibilities include research on billboard control and other issues; preparing and follow-up on scenic news e-newsletter; meetings with other nonprofits and government officials; improving resource center and databases. Candidates should have ability to work independently, ability to work with others, oral communication skills, research skills, writing skills, professionalism and a genuine interest in policy issues. Duration is 10–18 weeks. $100 per week. ► *1 program intern:* responsibilities include working on scenic conservation projects; research and writing correspondence; attending meetings. Candidates should have ability to work independently, ability to work with others, computer skills, oral communication skills, research skills, written communication skills, genuine interest in organization's issues. Duration is 10–18 weeks. $100 per week. Open to college freshmen, college sophomores, college juniors, college seniors, graduate students, law students. International applications accepted.

Benefits   Names of contacts, on-the-job training, opportunity to attend seminars/workshops, willing to act as a professional reference, willing to complete paperwork for educational credit, willing to provide letters of recommendation.

Contact   Write, call, fax, or e-mail Tom Pelikan, Director of Policy. Phone: 202-543-6200 Ext. 16. Fax: 202-543-9130. E-mail: pelikan@scenic.org. In-person interview recommended (telephone interview accepted). Applicants must submit a letter of interest, resume, writing sample, three personal references. Applications are accepted continuously. World Wide Web: http://www.scenic.org.

SEATTLE AUDUBON SOCIETY
8050 35th Avenue, NE
Seattle, Washington 98115

General Information   Society protecting birds and the natural environment by involving volunteers and the community in education, advocacy, preservation, science, and enjoyment. Established in 1916. Number of employees: 14. Unit of National Audubon Society, New York, New York. Number of internship applications received each year: 10.

Internships Available   ► *1 Northwest Shade-Grown Coffee Campaign intern:* responsibilities include researching various facets of coffee industry, consumer habits, and market trends to determine best cities in which to spread the word about shade-grown coffee; doing public outreach and marketing for the campaign; and communicating with campaign members, media, and the public. Candidates should have oral communication skills, research skills, self-motivation, strong interpersonal skills, writing skills. Duration is 10 weeks (20 hours per week) or 200 hours within a similar time period. Unpaid. Open to college seniors, recent college graduates, graduate students, law students, career changers, individuals reentering the workforce. ► *1 birdweb intern:* responsibilities include researching ornithology, data entry, managing databases, processing digital images. Candidates should have ability to work independently, computer skills, office skills, oral communication skills, personal interest in the field, research skills, writing skills. Duration is flexible. Unpaid. Open to college freshmen, college sophomores, college juniors, college seniors, recent college graduates, graduate students, career changers, individuals reentering the workforce. ► *1 communications intern:* responsibilities include assisting with efforts to publicize events, initiatives and programs; assisting with the maintenance of media database

and news clip file; general writing and research to support programs, events, and initiatives. Candidates should have ability to work independently, ability to work with others, college courses in field, organizational skills, plan to pursue career in field, writing skills. Duration is 10 weeks (20 hours per week). Unpaid. Open to college juniors, college seniors, recent college graduates, graduate students, career changers, individuals reentering the workforce. ► *1 conservation intern:* responsibilities include projects in at least two of the following areas: urban habitat, aquatics, forests, shade-grown coffee, and wildlife and salmon recovery. Candidates should have analytical skills, computer skills, oral communication skills, personal interest in the field, self-motivation, written communication skills. Duration is 10 weeks (20 hours per week). Unpaid. Open to college seniors, recent college graduates, graduate students, law students, career changers. ► *1 education intern:* responsibilities include assisting with at least one of the following programs: Summer Nature Camp or Spring Curriculum Planning for Nature Camp; school-based program for 3rd-5th graders; clubs for high schoolers; and educational kit programs. Candidates should have knowledge of field, oral communication skills, organizational skills, strong interpersonal skills, strong leadership ability. Duration is 10 weeks (20 hours per week). Unpaid. Open to college seniors, recent college graduates, graduate students, law students, career changers. ► *1 shade coffee intern:* responsibilities include coordinating special projects; public outreach; research and writing; working with public and nonprofit coffee companies; consumer polling. Candidates should have ability to work with others, computer skills, organizational skills, personal interest in the field, self-motivation, written communication skills. Duration is 3–6 months. Unpaid. Open to college juniors, college seniors, recent college graduates, graduate students, law students, career changers, individuals reentering the workforce. ► *1 technology intern:* responsibilities include assisting the technology committee chair in overseeing the operations of computer software and hardware, and maintaining Web site. Candidates should have ability to work independently, analytical skills, computer skills, experience in the field, self-motivation. Duration is 10 weeks (20 hours per week). Unpaid. Open to recent college graduates, graduate students, career changers. ► *1 volunteer and development programs intern:* responsibilities include assisting the volunteer coordinator and Volunteer Program Committee with multiple elements of program: recruiting, screening, orientation, training, recognizing, communicating, publicizing, managing the database, and budgeting; helping schedule and train nature shop volunteer ambassadors; assisting the executive director with development projects. Candidates should have ability to work independently, computer skills, oral communication skills, plan to pursue career in field, strong interpersonal skills, writing skills. Duration is 10 weeks (20 hours per week). Unpaid. Open to college seniors, recent college graduates, graduate students, law students, career changers. International applications accepted.

Benefits   Job counseling, names of contacts, on-the-job training, opportunity to attend seminars/workshops, possible full-time employment, willing to act as a professional reference, willing to complete paperwork for educational credit, willing to provide letters of recommendation.

Contact   Write, call, fax, e-mail, or through World Wide Web site Lorraine Hartmann, Volunteer Coordinator. Phone: 206-523-8243 Ext. 12. Fax: 206-528-7779. E-mail: lorraineh@seattleaudubon.org. In-person interview recommended (telephone interview accepted). Applicants must submit a formal organization application, letter of interest, resume, two personal references, letters of recommendation preferred. Applications are accepted continuously. World Wide Web: http://www.seattleaudubon.org.

SHARON AUDUBON CENTER
325 Cornwall Bridge Road
Sharon, Connecticut 06069

General Information   1200-acre sanctuary providing environmental education, wildlife rehabilitation, and nature enjoyment. Established in 1961. Number of employees: 6. Unit of National Audubon Society, New York, New York. Number of internship applications received each year: 100.

Internships Available ▶ *1–2 bird banding interns (M.A.P.S. project):* responsibilities include operating mist-netting and banding (MAPS Monitoring Avian Productivity and Survivorship) stations in Connecticut and New York, following two weeks of intensive training. Candidates should have ability to work independently, knowledge of field, organizational skills, personal interest in the field, research skills, strong interpersonal skills, birding skills. Duration is 12 weeks. $100–$200 per week. Open to college juniors, college seniors, recent college graduates. ▶ *2 environmental education interns:* responsibilities include teaching a wide variety of environmental and natural history topics to on-site and outreach audiences, assisting with curriculum development and exhibits, rehabilitating injured and orphaned birds, and participating in many other facets of a nature center's day-to-day operations. Candidates should have oral communication skills, personal interest in the field, self-motivation, strong interpersonal skills, strong leadership ability. Duration is 3 months. $100 per week. Open to college juniors, college seniors, recent college graduates, graduate students. ▶ *1–3 research apprentices:* responsibilities include assisting in ongoing projects, including breeding bird census, biological monitoring, data entering, habitat management and researching/writing management plans for tracts of land. Candidates should have personal interest in the field, plan to pursue career in field, research skills, self-motivation, strong interpersonal skills. Duration is 8–12 weeks. $100 per week. Open to college juniors, college seniors, recent college graduates, graduate students. ▶ *1–2 summer naturalists:* responsibilities include teaching and designing curriculum for week-long summer nature programs for children ages 4 -14. Candidates should have experience in the field, oral communication skills, personal interest in the field, self-motivation, strong interpersonal skills, strong leadership ability. Duration is 11–12 weeks. $1000–$1800 per duration of internship. Open to college juniors, college seniors, recent college graduates, graduate students. International applications accepted.

Benefits Free housing, names of contacts, opportunity to attend seminars/workshops, willing to act as a professional reference, willing to complete paperwork for educational credit, willing to provide letters of recommendation, worker's compensation, Audubon Summer Camp scholarship eligibility.

Contact Write, call, fax, or e-mail Mr. Joseph Markow, Environmental Education Specialist. Phone: 860-364-0520. Fax: 860-364-5792. E-mail: jmarkow@audubon.org. In-person interview recommended (telephone interview accepted). Applicants must submit a letter of interest, resume, three personal references. Applications are accepted continuously. World Wide Web: http://www.audubon.org/local/sanctuary/sharon.

SHAVER'S CREEK ENVIRONMENTAL CENTER, PENNSYLVANIA STATE UNIVERSITY
508A Keller Building
University Park, Pennsylvania 16802

General Information Center providing exemplary day and residential environmental education and outdoor adventure programming. Established in 1976. Number of employees: 20. Unit of Division of Continuing and Distance Education, Pennsylvania State University, University Park, Pennsylvania. Number of internship applications received each year: 75.

Internships Available ▶ *4–6 environmental education interns:* responsibilities include participating in all aspects of the center's operation which may include summer camps, school programs, visitor center operations, live animal care and handling, public natural and cultural history walks, volunteer training and supervision, adventure and recreational programs, weekend festivals and events, teacher and pre-teacher workshops, team building programs, curriculum and program development, and writing articles for newsletter. Candidates should have organizational skills, plan to pursue career in field, self-motivation, strong interpersonal skills, strong leadership ability, background in education or natural sciences helpful. Duration is January to May, June to August, or September to December. $150–$175 per week. Open to college freshmen, college sophomores, college juniors, college seniors, recent college graduates, career changers. International applications accepted.

Benefits Formal training, free housing, on-the-job training, opportunity to attend seminars/workshops, willing to act as a professional reference, willing to complete paperwork for educational credit, willing to provide letters of recommendation, assistance with resume preparation, access to the Internet, meals during residential programs.

Contact Write, call, fax, e-mail, or through World Wide Web site Doug Wentzel, Intern Coordinator. Phone: 814-863-2000. Fax: 814-865-2706. E-mail: shaverscreek@outreach.psu.edu. Telephone interview required. Applicants must submit a formal organization application, letter of interest, resume, three personal references, 3 letters of recommendation (international applicants only). Application deadline: March 1 for summer, July 1 for fall, November 1 for spring. World Wide Web: http://www.shaverscreek.org.

SIERRA CLUB
408 C Street, NE
Washington, District of Columbia 20002

General Information Organization dedicated to the preservation and enjoyment of the environment. Established in 1892. Number of employees: 40. Unit of Sierra Club, San Francisco, California. Number of internship applications received each year: 200.

Internships Available ▶ *6–10 issue-oriented interns:* responsibilities include performing research on a specific environmental issue (public lands and wilderness, toxics and environmental quality, energy and global warming, population, human rights, trade) to be used in the education of the public and Congress; attending congressional hearings, meetings with other environmental groups, and other strategy sessions; and other administrative duties. Candidates should have ability to work independently, computer skills, oral communication skills, personal interest in the field, research skills, writing skills, ability to work in a busy office. Duration is 1 semester. Unpaid. Open to college freshmen, college sophomores, college juniors, college seniors, recent college graduates, graduate students, law students, career changers. ▶ *1–3 media interns:* responsibilities include helping set up press conferences, issuing press releases, and ensuring that journalists receive timely information; writing op-ed articles for newspapers on environmental issues. Candidates should have ability to work independently, computer skills, editing skills, oral communication skills, personal interest in the field, writing skills, ability to work in a busy office. Duration is 1 semester. Unpaid. Open to college freshmen, college sophomores, college juniors, college seniors, recent college graduates, graduate students. ▶ *1–3 political interns:* responsibilities include helping with the endorsement process of individuals running for Congress and checking voting records. Candidates should have ability to work independently, computer skills, oral communication skills, personal interest in the field, research skills, strong interpersonal skills, writing skills. Duration is 1 semester. Unpaid. Open to college freshmen, college sophomores, college juniors, college seniors, recent college graduates, graduate students, law students. International applications accepted.

Benefits Names of contacts, opportunity to attend seminars/workshops, possible full-time employment, willing to act as a professional reference, willing to complete paperwork for educational credit, willing to provide letters of recommendation, 4 summer college stipends.

Contact Write, fax, or e-mail Joanne Tait, Executive Coordinator. Fax: 202-547-6009. E-mail: dc-internships@sierraclub.org. No phone calls. Applicants must submit a letter of interest, resume, writing sample. Application deadline: March 15 for summer. World Wide Web: http://www.sierraclub.org.

SLIDE RANCH
2025 Shoreline Highway
Muir Beach, California 94965

General Information Environmental farm and wilderness-based teaching center; serves wide variety of schools, organizations, and families from both the local affluent area and also from low-income, urban, under-served populations. Established in 1970. Number of employees: 14. Number of internship applications received each year: 100.

Slide Ranch (continued)

Internships Available ▶ *6 teachers-in-residence:* responsibilities include planning lessons and teaching groups and families, gardening, caring for various farm animals, and various community responsibilities. Candidates should have ability to work with others, oral communication skills, personal interest in the field, self-motivation, experience and interest in community living situation, educational skills. Duration is February 1 to December 20. $300 per month. Open to anyone with interest in outdoor education (do not need college degree). International applications accepted.

Benefits Formal training, free housing, free meals, names of contacts, on-the-job training, opportunity to attend seminars/ workshops, possible full-time employment, willing to act as a professional reference, willing to complete paperwork for educational credit, willing to provide letters of recommendation.

Contact Write, call, fax, e-mail, or through World Wide Web site Program Coordinator. Phone: 415-381-6155. Fax: 415-381-5762. E-mail: admin@slideranch.org. In-person interview recommended (telephone interview accepted). Applicants must submit a letter of interest, resume, three personal references, personal statement. Application deadline: September 30. World Wide Web: http:// www.slideranch.org.

SOCIETY OF AMERICAN FORESTERS
5400 Grosvenor Lane
Bethesda, Maryland 20814

General Information Professional organization founded to advance the science, education, technology, and practice of forestry. Established in 1900. Number of employees: 29. Number of internship applications received each year: 8.

Internships Available ▶ *2 Henry Clepper Forest Policy interns:* responsibilities include preparing background reports on current resource issues; assisting, preparing, and developing recommendations to Congress; monitoring federal environmental and natural resources legislation; providing liaison support with environmental and natural resource organizations. Candidates should have ability to work independently, knowledge of field, oral communication skills, research skills, self-motivation, written communication skills. Duration is 6 months starting July or January. $1000 per month. Open to college seniors, recent college graduates, graduate students. International applications accepted.

Benefits Names of contacts, opportunity to attend seminars/ workshops, willing to provide letters of recommendation, association with established professionals in SAF and other organizations.

Contact Write, call, fax, or e-mail Michael T. Goergen, Director. Phone: 301-897-8720 Ext. 116. Fax: 301-897-3690. E-mail: goergenm@ safnet.org. Applicants must submit a letter of interest, resume, academic transcripts, writing sample, 1-3 personal references. Application deadline: April 15 for fall, October 15 for spring. World Wide Web: http://www.safnet.org.

SOMERSET COUNTY PARK COMMISSION
ENVIRONMENTAL EDUCATION CENTER
190 Lord Stirling Road
Basking Ridge, New Jersey 07920

General Information Environmental education center/park providing leisure learning opportunities for the public, schools, and scouting groups. Established in 1971. Number of employees: 15. Division of Somerset County Park Commission, North Branch, New Jersey. Number of internship applications received each year: 50.

Internships Available ▶ *3-4 maintenance crew:* responsibilities include assisting the maintenance department with trail maintenance and repair, landscaping, and various outdoor assignments within an outdoor park setting. Candidates should have ability to work with others, personal interest in the field, self-motivation, trailwork experience and experience with hand tools preferred. Duration is 8 weeks. $7.65 per hour. Open to high school seniors, recent high school graduates, college freshmen, college sophomores, college juniors, college seniors, recent college graduates, graduate students, career changers, individuals reentering the workforce.

▶ *7 seasonal naturalist assistants:* responsibilities include assisting in presentation of environmental projects and teaching various kinds of environmental education programs to all age ranges of public. Candidates should have experience in the field, oral communication skills, personal interest in the field, strong interpersonal skills, environmental education background preferred. Duration is 10–11 weeks. $8.65 per hour. Open to college freshmen, college sophomores, college juniors, college seniors, recent college graduates, graduate students, career changers, individuals reentering the workforce.

Benefits Job counseling, names of contacts, on-the-job training, possible full-time employment, willing to act as a professional reference, willing to complete paperwork for educational credit, willing to provide letters of recommendation.

Contact Write, call, fax, e-mail, or through World Wide Web site Kurt Bender, Environmental Science Supervisor. Phone: 908-766-2489 Ext. 332. Fax: 908-766-2687. E-mail: kbbender@parks.co. somerset.nj.us. In-person interview recommended (telephone interview accepted). Applicants must submit a formal organization application, letter of interest, resume. Application deadline: April 30 for summer. World Wide Web: http://www.park.co. somerset.nj.us.

SOUTHERN RESEARCH STATION
200 W.T. Weaver Boulevard, PO Box 2680
Asheville, North Carolina 28802

General Information One of seven forest service research stations in the U.S. that manages forest land and conducts research in biology, forestry, global warming, and forest genetics and economics. Established in 1905. Number of employees: 125. Unit of USDA Forest Service, Asheville, North Carolina.

Internships Available ▶ *20–24 conservation education interns:* responsibilities include teaching children in inner cities about conservation concepts, recycling, and water quality. Candidates should have knowledge of field, organizational skills, self-motivation, strong interpersonal skills, declared college major in natural science, agriculture, forestry, urban forestry, or education; ability to work with children. Duration is June 1 through August 15. $8.32–$9.60 per hour. Open to college freshmen, college sophomores, college juniors, college seniors, graduate students, individuals currently enrolled in a college program.

Benefits Travel reimbursement, willing to act as a professional reference, willing to complete paperwork for educational credit, willing to provide letters of recommendation.

Contact Write, call, fax, e-mail, or through World Wide Web site Rodney C. Kindlund, Public Affairs Officer. Phone: 828-259-0560. Fax: 828-257-4838. E-mail: rkindlund@fs.fed.us. Applicants must submit a resume, academic transcripts, two letters of recommendation. Application deadline: January 15. World Wide Web: http://www.srs.fs.fed.us.

STUDENT CONSERVATION ASSOCIATION (SCA)
PO Box 550, 687 River Road
Charlestown, New Hampshire 03603

General Information Nonprofit organization that places interns year-round in expense-paid conservation projects in national parks, national historic sites, forests, and wildlife refuges nationwide. Established in 1957. Number of employees: 75. Number of internship applications received each year: 5,000.

Internships Available ▶ *75–100 Northeast residential interns:* responsibilities include outdoor conservation projects including trail construction, erosion control, maintenance, conducting environmental education programs in local schools and community groups (winter months). Candidates should have ability to work with others, oral communication skills, self-motivation, written communication skills, qualifications as specified on web site. Duration is 3–10 months. $50 per week; education award of up to $4725. Open to recent high school graduates, college freshmen, college sophomores, college juniors, college seniors, recent college graduates, must be between 18–25. ▶ *1,500 environmental and cultural resource management interns:* responsibilities include resource management duties ranging from backcountry patrol, wildlife ecology, forestry, and environmental education to archaeology and historical interpretation. Candidates should have ability

to work independently, oral communication skills, organizational skills, self-motivation, strong interpersonal skills, qualifications as specified on Web site. Duration is 12–52 weeks. $50–$250 per week. Open to recent high school graduates, college freshmen, college sophomores, college juniors, college seniors, recent college graduates, graduate students, law students, career changers, individuals reentering the workforce, individuals at least 18 years of age. ▶ *150–200 outdoor leaders:* responsibilities include managing all aspects of month-long high school trail crew, training and leading 6-10 high school youth in national park or forest. Candidates should have ability to work independently, experience in the field, oral communication skills, strong interpersonal skills, strong leadership ability, qualifications as specified on Web site. Duration is 1-3 months in summer. $300–$525 per week. Open to college seniors, recent college graduates, graduate students, law students, career changers, individuals reentering the workforce, must be 21 or older. International applications accepted.
Benefits Formal training, free housing, health insurance, names of contacts, on-the-job training, opportunity to attend seminars/workshops, possible full-time employment, travel reimbursement, tuition assistance, willing to complete paperwork for educational credit, uniform stipend, weekly living allowance, eligibility for AmeriCorps educational awards, loan deferment.
Contact Write, call, fax, e-mail, or through World Wide Web site Recruitment Office. Phone: 603-543-1700. Fax: 603-543-1828. E-mail: internships@sca-inc.org. Telephone interview required. Applicants must submit a formal organization application, academic transcripts, three letters of recommendation, additional requirements available on Web site; $20 application fee (U.S., Canada, and Mexico); $40 application fee (other international). Applications are accepted continuously. World Wide Web: http://www.sca-inc.org.

SULLYS HILL NATIONAL GAME PRESERVE
PO Box 286
Fort Totten, North Dakota 58335

General Information National wildlife refuge system, part of the larger national system of lands totaling 93 million acres; manages wildlife, habitat and people for a variety of opportunities. Established in 1904. Number of employees: 4. Unit of Devils Lake Wetland Management District Complex, Devils Lake, North Dakota. Number of internship applications received each year: 20.
Internships Available ▶ *1–5 environmental education interns:* responsibilities include environmental education, public recreation, wildlife management. Candidates should have ability to work independently, ability to work with others, oral communication skills, personal interest in the field, self-motivation, written communication skills. Duration is flexible. Unpaid. Open to recent high school graduates, college freshmen, college sophomores, college juniors, college seniors, recent college graduates, graduate students, career changers, individuals reentering the workforce. ▶ *1 park or refuge ranger intern:* responsibilities include visitor relations, wildlife refuge management and maintenance, assisting in events and workshops. Candidates should have ability to work independently, ability to work with others, knowledge of field, oral communication skills, organizational skills, personal interest in the field. Unpaid. Open to college sophomores, college juniors, college seniors, recent college graduates, graduate students, individuals reentering the workforce. ▶ *2–3 wildlife biologist interns:* responsibilities include wildlife surveys, habitat inventories, wildlife studies, species management. Candidates should have ability to work independently, computer skills, oral communication skills, personal interest in the field, plan to pursue career in field, strong interpersonal skills. Duration is flexible. Unpaid. Open to college freshmen, college sophomores, college juniors, college seniors, recent college graduates, graduate students. International applications accepted.
Benefits Formal training, free housing, job counseling, names of contacts, on-the-job training, travel reimbursement, willing to act as a professional reference, willing to complete paperwork for educational credit, willing to provide letters of recommendation, food stipend.

Contact Write, call, fax, or e-mail Brian Vose, Refuge Manager, PO Box 908, Devils Lake, North Dakota 58301. Phone: 701-662-8611. Fax: 701-662-8612. E-mail: brian_vose@fws.gov. Telephone interview required. Applicants must submit a letter of interest, resume, three personal references. Application deadline: April 30 for summer, August 15 for fall, December 1 for spring.

SURFRIDER FOUNDATION
122 South El Camino Real, #67
San Clemente, California 92672

General Information Nonprofit environmental organization dedicated to the protection, preservation, and restoration of the world's oceans, waves, and beaches through conservation, activism, research, and education. Established in 1984. Number of employees: 14. Number of internship applications received each year: 50.
Internships Available ▶ *Chapter interns/volunteers:* responsibilities include working in local communities with chapter leaders on local issues; areas available include administrative, public relations/media, legal counsel, membership services, events/fund-raisers, literature distribution, newsletter publication, research. Candidates should have oral communication skills, organizational skills, personal interest in the field, strong interpersonal skills, strong leadership ability. Duration is flexible. Unpaid. Open to high school seniors, recent high school graduates, college freshmen, college sophomores, college juniors, college seniors, recent college graduates, law students. ▶ *4–5 national interns/volunteers:* responsibilities include working in Southern California area in administrative chapter development, events/fund-raisers, legislative analysis, program research, cataloging and archiving, public speaking, report writing, newsletter, or membership development. Candidates should have ability to work with others, computer skills, office skills, oral communication skills, organizational skills, written communication skills. Duration is flexible. Unpaid. Open to high school seniors, recent high school graduates, college freshmen, college sophomores, college juniors, college seniors, recent college graduates, graduate students, law students.
Benefits Possible full-time employment, willing to act as a professional reference, willing to complete paperwork for educational credit, willing to provide letters of recommendation.
Contact Write or e-mail Michelle Kremer, Deputy Executive Director. E-mail: mkremer@surfrider.org. No phone calls. Telephone interview required. Applicants must submit a letter of interest, resume, three writing samples. Applications are accepted continuously. World Wide Web: http://www.surfrider.org.

THREE LAKES NATURE CENTER AND AQUARIUM
400 Sausiluta Drive
Richmond, Virginia 23227

General Information Facility providing environmental education in many areas through visitation, public and school programs, and group tours. Established in 1992. Number of employees: 4. Subsidiary of Henrico County Division of Recreation and Parks, Richmond, Virginia. Number of internship applications received each year: 10.
Internships Available ▶ *2 nature center interns:* responsibilities include participating in all aspects of nature center operation including program planning and implementation, exhibit design and fabrication, and animal care and maintenance. Candidates should have ability to work independently, oral communication skills, organizational skills, personal interest in the field, self-motivation, strong leadership ability. Duration is flexible. Unpaid. Open to college freshmen, college sophomores, college juniors, college seniors, graduate students. International applications accepted.
Benefits Formal training, names of contacts, willing to provide letters of recommendation.
Contact Write, call, fax, or e-mail Mr. Tom Thorp, Nature Program Coordinator. Phone: 804-261-8230. Fax: 804-266-6938. E-mail: tt-threelakes@juno.com. In-person interview recommended (telephone interview accepted). Applicants must submit a letter of interest, resume. Applications are accepted continuously. World Wide Web: http://www.co.henrico.va.us/rec/31nature.htm.

TREES FOR TOMORROW NATURAL RESOURCES EDUCATION CENTER
519 Sheridan Street East
Eagle River, Wisconsin 54521

General Information Natural resource education center teaching fourth graders through adults about the wise use and management of forests, wildlife, water, and soil resources. Established in 1944. Number of employees: 23. Number of internship applications received each year: 50.
Internships Available ▶ *4 naturalist interns:* responsibilities include teaching student groups ranging from fourth graders to adults about the importance of conserving natural resources (forests, wildlife, water, soil, and energy) through hands-on activities and guided tours of managed forest areas and industries. Candidates should have ability to work with others, oral communication skills, self-motivation, strong leadership ability, written communication skills. Duration is 9 months (August 26-June 1). $700–$750 per month. Open to college juniors, college seniors, recent college graduates, graduate students, law students, career changers, individuals reentering the workforce. ▶ *1 outreach naturalist:* responsibilities include presenting natural resource programs to resorts and campgrounds on behalf of Trees For Tomorrow and the U.S. Forest Service. Candidates should have ability to work independently, college courses in field, knowledge of field, oral communication skills, self-motivation. Duration is May to August. $650 per month. Open to college seniors, recent college graduates, graduate students. International applications accepted.
Benefits Formal training, free housing, free meals, health insurance, job counseling, names of contacts, on-the-job training, opportunity to attend seminars/workshops, possible full-time employment, willing to act as a professional reference, willing to complete paperwork for educational credit, willing to provide letters of recommendation.
Contact Write, call, fax, e-mail, or through World Wide Web site Ms. Sandy Lotto, Intern Coordinator. Phone: 800-838-9472. Fax: 715-479-2318. E-mail: trees@nnex.net. Telephone interview required. Applicants must submit a letter of interest, resume, three personal references. Application deadline: May 15 for nine-month position. World Wide Web: http://www.treesfortomorrow.com.

TREES NEW YORK
51 Chambers Street, Suite 1412 A
New York, New York 10007

General Information Nonprofit organization dedicated to the preservation, improvement, and increase of New York's urban forest, through advocacy education, publishing, and direct community service. Established in 1979. Number of employees: 7. Number of internship applications received each year: 50.
Internships Available ▶ *1–2 interns:* responsibilities include projects relating to organization's programs, general office duties, some desktop publishing and computer work. Candidates should have ability to work independently, computer skills, organizational skills, self-motivation, written communication skills, interest in urban forestry, forestry, nonprofit management, and environmental studies (these applicants will be given priority); teaching experience. Duration is flexible. Unpaid. Open to college freshmen, college sophomores, college juniors, college seniors, recent college graduates, graduate students, career changers, individuals reentering the workforce. International applications accepted.
Benefits Names of contacts, willing to complete paperwork for educational credit, willing to provide letters of recommendation.
Contact Write, call, fax, e-mail, or through World Wide Web site Leslie Fitzpatrick. Phone: 212-227-1887. Fax: 212-732-5325. E-mail: treesny@treesny.com. In-person interview required. Applicants must submit a resume, cover letter indicating preference in time frame. Applications are accepted continuously. World Wide Web: http://www.treesny.com.

TRUSTEES OF RESERVATIONS, WESTERN REGION
PO Box 792
Stockbridge, Massachusetts 01262

General Information Organization that preserves properties of scenic, historical, and ecological value throughout Massachusetts for public use and enjoyment. Established in 1891. Number of employees: 11. Unit of Trustees of Reservations, Beverly, Massachusetts. Number of internship applications received each year: 30.
Internships Available ▶ *1–3 historic site interns:* responsibilities include working with the historic resources manager to gain professional experience in the daily administration of historic properties and collections management. Candidates should have ability to work independently, oral communication skills, self-motivation, strong interpersonal skills, written communication skills, availability to work weekends. Duration is 10–15 weeks. Position available as unpaid or at $300 per week.
Benefits Free housing, willing to act as a professional reference, willing to complete paperwork for educational credit, willing to provide letters of recommendation.
Contact Write Will Garrison, Historic Resources Manager. E-mail: wgarrison@ttor.org. No phone calls. In-person interview recommended (telephone interview accepted). Applicants must submit a letter of interest, resume. Application deadline: March 15 for summer. World Wide Web: http://www.thetrustees.org.

TURTLE MOUNTAIN ENVIRONMENTAL LEARNING CENTER
#2 Lake Metigoshe State Park
Bottineau, North Dakota 58318

General Information Environmental education program for diverse age groups that emphasizes learning in an outdoor environment. Established in 1985. Number of employees: 1. Unit of Lake Metigoshe State Park, Bottineau, North Dakota. Number of internship applications received each year: 20.
Internships Available ▶ *2 naturalist interns:* responsibilities include facilitating group activities and discussions in teaching environmental awareness. Candidates should have ability to work independently, ability to work with others, oral communication skills, personal interest in the field, self-motivation, desire to share nature with all age groups. Duration is April 1 to June 5, May 25 to September 5, August 25 to November 1. $160 per week. Open to college freshmen, college sophomores, college juniors, college seniors, recent college graduates, career changers, individuals reentering the workforce. International applications accepted.
Benefits Free housing, names of contacts, on-the-job training, opportunity to attend seminars/workshops, willing to act as a professional reference, willing to complete paperwork for educational credit, willing to provide letters of recommendation, reimbursement of work-related travel expenses, uniforms provided.
Contact Write, call, fax, e-mail, or through World Wide Web site Greg Hansen, TMELC Coordinator. Phone: 701-263-4514. Fax: 701-263-4648. E-mail: tmelc@state.nd.us. Applicants must submit a letter of interest, resume, academic transcripts, three personal references, telephone interview if selected. Application deadline: February 28 for spring, April 1 for summer, August 1 for fall. World Wide Web: http://www.state.nd.us/ndparks/Parks/Metigoshe/TMELC.htm.

UNIVERSITY OF RHODE ISLAND, ENVIRONMENTAL EDUCATION CENTER
W. Alton Jones Campus, 401 Victory Highway
West Greenwich, Rhode Island 02817

General Information Organization dedicated to educating school-age children about the environment, ecology, cultural history, farming, and group building. Established in 1964. Number of employees: 20. Department of University of Rhode Island, Kingston, Rhode Island. Number of internship applications received each year: 15.
Internships Available ▶ *1 animal and garden manager:* responsibilities include overseeing the day-to-day functions of an historic, working farm including facilities maintenance, animal care, chores, and gardening, carrying out all duties in a manner that makes the farm, animals, and gardens as safe and accessible as possible to children. Candidates should have ability to work independently, knowledge of field, personal interest in the field, self-motivation, strong interpersonal skills, previous experience caring for farm animals and gardens. Duration is mid-March to mid-September.

$250–$300 per week. Open to college freshmen, college sophomores, college juniors, college seniors, recent college graduates, graduate students. ▶ *3–5 field teachers/naturalists:* responsibilities include planning and teaching outdoor lessons in forest and wetland ecology, team building, outdoor skills, environmental issues, farming, and Native American and pioneer history on 2300-acre wilderness campus; teaching outdoor lessons in farming, animal care, gardening, and pioneer history on 300-acre historic farm. Candidates should have knowledge of field, oral communication skills, personal interest in the field, strong interpersonal skills, strong leadership ability. Duration is 4–9 months. Minimum stipend of $250 per week . Open to college freshmen, college sophomores, college juniors, college seniors, recent college graduates, graduate students. ▶ *1 student camp nurse/EMT:* responsibilities include assisting RN in injury and illness assessment, dispensing medication, and operating camp infirmary. Candidates should have declared college major in field, knowledge of field, oral communication skills, self-motivation, strong interpersonal skills. Duration is mid-June to mid-August. $300–$350 per week. Open to college sophomores, college juniors, college seniors, recent college graduates, graduate students, nursing students or EMT's. ▶ *16 summer camp naturalists/counselors:* responsibilities include leading campers ages 8-13 during seven six-day residential camping programs; counselors may teach up to seven themes or lead natural and cultural history and sensory awareness, canoeing, no-trace camping and survival skills, conservation activities, and new games. Candidates should have ability to work with others, knowledge of field, oral communication skills, strong leadership ability, CPR and first aid. Duration is 9 weeks (mid-June to mid-August). Stipend of approximately $185 per week. Open to high school seniors, recent high school graduates, college freshmen, college sophomores, college juniors, college seniors, recent college graduates, graduate students. ▶ *10–12 teen expedition leaders:* responsibilities include leading week-long sessions of the Teen Expeditions program; planning and implementing canoeing, kayaking, backpacking, and rock climbing trips for participants ages 12-17. Candidates should have ability to work with others, experience in the field, oral communication skills, organizational skills, self-motivation, strong leadership ability, strong skills in at least one of the following: canoeing, kayaking, backpacking, or rock climbing. Duration is mid-June to late August. Minimum stipend of $200 per week. Open to college juniors, college seniors, recent college graduates, graduate students. International applications accepted.
Benefits Formal training, free housing, free meals, on-the-job training, willing to act as a professional reference, willing to complete paperwork for educational credit, willing to provide letters of recommendation.
Contact Write, call, fax, e-mail, or through World Wide Web site Mr. John Jacques, Manager. Phone: 401-397-3304 Ext. 6043. Fax: 401-397-3293. E-mail: urieec@etal.uri.edu. In-person interview recommended (telephone interview accepted). Applicants must submit a formal organization application, letter of interest, resume, two personal references. Application deadline: January 15 for spring, May 15 for summer, July 15 for fall, November 15 for winter. World Wide Web: http://www.uri.edu/ajc/eec.

UPHAM WOODS 4-H ENVIRONMENTAL CENTER
N194 County Road North
Wisconsin Dells, Wisconsin 53965

General Information Youth camp and environmental education facility where youth and adults gain first-hand experience in natural sciences, citizenship, and group living. Established in 1941. Number of employees: 7. Subsidiary of University of Wisconsin Extension/Youth Development, Madison, Wisconsin. Number of internship applications received each year: 20.
Internships Available ▶ *3–5 teaching naturalists:* responsibilities include teaching all ages of youth environmental education and youth development skills. Candidates should have computer skills, oral communication skills, organizational skills, personal interest in the field, strong interpersonal skills, strong leadership ability. Duration is 4–12 months. $250–$300 per week depending on certifications such as for lifeguarding or completion of degree(s).

Open to college juniors, college seniors, recent college graduates, graduate students, career changers. International applications accepted.
Benefits Free housing, job counseling, names of contacts, willing to complete paperwork for educational credit, willing to provide letters of recommendation, most meals provided.
Contact Write, call, fax, or e-mail Bob Nichols, Director. Phone: 608-254-6461. Fax: 608-253-7140. E-mail: bob.nichols@ces.uwex.edu. In-person interview recommended (telephone interview accepted). Applicants must submit a letter of interest, resume. Application deadline: February 1 for spring, March 1 for summer, November 1 for winter.

U.S. FISH AND WILDLIFE SERVICE
103 East Plumtree Road
Sunderland, Massachusetts 01375

General Information Federal agency conserving the nation's natural resources. Established in 1871. Number of employees: 2. Unit of U.S. Fish and Wildlife Service Northeast Regional Office, Hadley, Massachusetts. Number of internship applications received each year: 6.
Internships Available ▶ *1 environmental database manager:* responsibilities include managing and updating databases on the management activities of the Connecticut River Migratory Fish Restoration Program. Candidates should have ability to work independently, computer skills, organizational skills, personal interest in the field, self-motivation, experience with data. Duration is flexible (year-round). Unpaid. Open to high school students, recent high school graduates, college freshmen, college sophomores, college juniors, college seniors, recent college graduates, graduate students, law students, career changers, individuals reentering the workforce, retirees. ▶ *1–5 migratory fish count coordinators:* responsibilities include assembling and reporting daily migratory fish counts by calling seven dams and recording their data on migratory fish. Candidates should have ability to work independently, ability to work with others, computer skills, office skills, oral communication skills, organizational skills. Duration is May 1 to August 1. Unpaid. Open to high school students, recent high school graduates, college freshmen, college sophomores, college juniors, college seniors, recent college graduates, graduate students, law students, career changers, individuals reentering the workforce, retirees. ▶ *1 technical assistant:* responsibilities include assisting field technician with a wide variety of duties related to fisheries management; some field work available. Candidates should have ability to work independently, ability to work with others, oral communication skills, organizational skills, personal interest in the field, self-motivation. Duration is flexible (year-round). Unpaid. Open to college freshmen, college sophomores, college juniors, college seniors, recent college graduates, graduate students, law students, career changers, individuals reentering the workforce, retirees. International applications accepted.
Benefits Job counseling, names of contacts, on-the-job training, willing to act as a professional reference, willing to complete paperwork for educational credit, willing to provide letters of recommendation.
Contact Write, call, e-mail, or through World Wide Web site Janice N. Rowan, Coordinator. Phone: 413-548-9138. Fax: 413-548-9622. E-mail: jan_rowan@fws.gov. In-person interview recommended (telephone interview accepted). Applicants must submit a letter of interest, resume. Applications are accepted continuously. World Wide Web: http://www.fws.gov/r5crc.

U.S. FOREST SERVICE, PIKE AND SAN ISABEL FORESTS, SOUTH PARK DISTRICT
PO Box 219
Fairplay, Colorado 80440

General Information National forest district with 4 broad missions: research, international forestry, state and private forestry, and managing forest resources in a way that will best meet the needs of its visitors without impairing the productivity of the land. Established in 1905. Number of employees: 40. Unit of Pike & San Isabel National Forests, Pueblo, Colorado. Number of internship applications received each year: 40.

U.S. Forest Service, Pike and San Isabel Forests, South Park District (continued)

Internships Available ▶ *1–2 hosts (Wilkerson Pass Visitor Center).* Candidates should have ability to work independently, ability to work with others, knowledge of field, oral communication skills, self-motivation, strong leadership ability. Duration is May through September or longer depending on weather (40 hours per week). Position available as unpaid or at $70 per week. Open to recent high school graduates, college freshmen, college sophomores, college juniors, college seniors, recent college graduates, graduate students, career changers, individuals reentering the workforce, retirees. ▶ *2–4 naturalists/interpreters:* responsibilities include developing and conducting interpretive programs at Wilkerson Pass and 21 campgrounds; writing news releases; assisting with the maintenance of interpretive center; operating book sales outlet; providing visitor information; and conducting various independent projects including creating publications, fliers, children's programs, photography exhibits, and district projects. Candidates should have ability to work independently, computer skills, oral communication skills, organizational skills, plan to pursue career in field, self-motivation, strong interpersonal skills, writing skills. Duration is end of May-end of September (2 months minimum). Position available as unpaid or at $70 per week (40 hours per week). Open to recent high school graduates, college freshmen, college sophomores, college juniors, college seniors, recent college graduates, graduate students, law students, career changers, individuals reentering the workforce, individuals 18 years or older. International applications accepted.

Benefits Formal training, free housing, job counseling, names of contacts, opportunity to attend seminars/workshops, tuition assistance, willing to complete paperwork for educational credit, willing to provide letters of recommendation, specific information on USFS hiring methods and applications.

International Internships Available in United Kingdom.

Contact Write, call, or e-mail Rebecca J. Anderson, Interpretive Specialist. Phone: 719-836-3852. E-mail: banderson05@fs.fed.us. Applicants must submit a letter of interest, resume, writing sample, volunteer application. Application deadline: March applications preferred. World Wide Web: http://www.fs.fed.us/r2/psicc/sopa.

U.S. FOREST SERVICE, STANISLAUS NATIONAL FOREST
#1 Pinecrest Lake Road
Pinecrest, California 95364

General Information Land management agency. Established in 1906. Number of employees: 60. Unit of United States Department of Agriculture, National Forest Service, Washington, District of Columbia. Number of internship applications received each year: 50.

Internships Available ▶ *1–10 natural resource interpretive assistants:* responsibilities include researching, preparing, presenting, and evaluating programs including guided walks, talks, or campfire programs; assisting other interpreters of natural resources with set-up and children's activities; working with a wide variety of audiences. Candidates should have ability to work independently, knowledge of field, oral communication skills, self-motivation, strong interpersonal skills, written communication skills. Duration is usually June-September (other times throughout the year may be available). $17 per day. Open to high school students, recent high school graduates, college freshmen, college sophomores, college juniors, college seniors, recent college graduates, graduate students, law students, career changers, individuals reentering the workforce, retirees. ▶ *1 recreation technician:* responsibilities include assisting in developing a recreation program; cleaning restrooms, picking up trash and litter, installing stoves, picnic tables and sign posts; describing rules, regulations, and recreational opportunities to the public. Candidates should have ability to work independently, ability to work with others, oral communication skills, ability to work on feet for extended periods; ability to lift and carry 40 pounds. Duration is 10–14 weeks. $17 per day. Open to high school students, recent high school graduates, college freshmen, college sophomores, college juniors, college seniors, recent college graduates, graduate students, law students, career changers, individuals reentering the workforce. ▶ *4–8 wilderness interns:* responsibilities include wilderness monitoring work requir-

ing multiple day trips into the wilderness backcountry to gather the data needed to restore and protect these special lands. Candidates should have ability to work independently, ability to work with others, analytical skills, experience in the field, personal interest in the field, writing skills, must have own backpacking equipment, be physically fit, and skilled at map and compass use and reconnaissance. Duration is mid-June to mid-August. $17 per day. Open to college freshmen, college sophomores, college juniors, college seniors. ▶ *1 writer/editor/graphics designer:* responsibilities include completing annual newsletter, Junior Ranger newsletter, and information displays, brochures, and handouts. Candidates should have ability to work independently, computer skills, editing skills, knowledge of field, writing skills, experience with IBM computer graphics programs. Duration is flexible. $17 per day. Open to high school students, recent high school graduates, college freshmen, college sophomores, college juniors, college seniors, recent college graduates, graduate students, law students, career changers, individuals reentering the workforce, retirees. International applications accepted.

Benefits Formal training, free housing, job counseling, names of contacts, on-the-job training, opportunity to attend seminars/workshops, willing to act as a professional reference, willing to complete paperwork for educational credit, willing to provide letters of recommendation.

Contact Write, call, fax, or e-mail Joy Barney, Interpretive Specialist/Environmental Education Coordinator, #1 Pinecrest Lake Road, Pinecrest, California 95364. Phone: 209-965-3434. Fax: 209-965-3372. E-mail: jbarney@fs.fed.us. In-person interview recommended (telephone interview accepted). Applicants must submit a formal organization application, two personal references. Applications are accepted continuously.

VOLUNTEERS FOR OUTDOOR COLORADO
600 South Marion Parkway
Denver, Colorado 80209

General Information Organization that seeks to instill a personal sense of responsibility for the stewardship of Colorado's public lands, working in partnership with federal, state, and local land management agencies and other nonprofits to organize volunteers on projects statewide, year-round. Established in 1984. Number of employees: 8. Number of internship applications received each year: 35.

Internships Available ▶ *200–250 VOC Network interns:* responsibilities include working for federal, state, and local management agencies or other nonprofit agencies in Colorado backcountry, environmental education, recreation, botany, and research/field work. Candidates should have personal interest in the field. Duration is flexible. Position available as unpaid or paid. Open to high school students, recent high school graduates, college freshmen, college sophomores, college juniors, college seniors, recent college graduates, graduate students, law students, career changers, individuals reentering the workforce. International applications accepted.

Benefits Names of contacts, on-the-job training, willing to complete paperwork for educational credit, possible stipend and housing/training reimbursement for VOC Network interns.

Contact Write, call, fax, e-mail, or through World Wide Web site Cory Lampert, Administrative Assistant/VOC Network. Phone: 303-715-1010. Fax: 303-715-1212. E-mail: voc@voc.org. In-person interview recommended (telephone interview accepted). Applicants must submit a letter of interest, resume, personal reference, writing sample for clearinghouse interns. Applications are accepted continuously. World Wide Web: http://www.voc.org.

WETLANDS INSTITUTE
1075 Stone Harbor Boulevard
Stone Harbor, New Jersey 08247-1424

General Information Private nonprofit organization dedicated to public education and scientific research concerning intertidal salt marshes and other coastal ecosystems. Established in 1969. Number of employees: 15. Number of internship applications received each year: 60.

Internships Available ▶ *2 aquarist interns:* responsibilities include maintaining aquariums in exhibit building, collecting specimens,

and interpreting exhibits for visitors. Candidates should have ability to work independently, college courses in field, knowledge of field, personal interest in the field, self-motivation. Duration is one summer. Unpaid. Open to college freshmen, college sophomores, college juniors, college seniors, recent college graduates, graduate students, individuals reentering the workforce.
▶ *2–6 environmental education interns:* responsibilities include teaching summer nature classes and assisting with public programs. Candidates should have knowledge of field, oral communication skills, personal interest in the field, self-motivation, strong interpersonal skills, written communication skills. Duration is 3 months. Unpaid. Open to college freshmen, college sophomores, college juniors, college seniors, recent college graduates, graduate students, career changers, individuals reentering the workforce.
▶ *2 horticulture interns:* responsibilities include maintaining, improving, and cataloging gardens on the grounds; identifying indigenous salt marsh plants; educating visitors. Candidates should have ability to work independently, ability to work with others, college courses in field, oral communication skills, personal interest in the field, self-motivation, strong leadership ability. Duration is 3 months. Unpaid. Open to college freshmen, college sophomores, college juniors, college seniors, recent college graduates, graduate students. ▶ *10–20 research interns:* responsibilities include assisting visiting researchers with projects. Candidates should have college courses in field, computer skills, knowledge of field, personal interest in the field, self-motivation. Duration is May to August/September. Stipend. Open to college freshmen, college sophomores, college juniors, college seniors, recent college graduates, graduate students. International applications accepted.
Benefits Formal training, opportunity to attend seminars/workshops, willing to act as a professional reference, willing to complete paperwork for educational credit, willing to provide letters of recommendation, limited housing.
Contact Write, call, fax, or through World Wide Web site Intern Coordinator. Phone: 609-368-1211. Fax: 609-368-3871. In-person interview recommended (telephone interview accepted). Applicants must submit a formal organization application, resume, academic transcripts, letter stating personal goals, one academic reference. Application deadline: March 15 for summer, September 1 for fall, December 1 for spring. World Wide Web: http://www.wetlandsinstitute.org.

WILDLIFE CONSERVATION SOCIETY/BRONX ZOO
Education Department, 2300 Southern Boulevard
Bronx, New York 10460-1099

General Information Society devoted to the conservation of wildlife and habitats through conservation, education, and science. Established in 1895. Number of employees: 600. Number of internship applications received each year: 200.
Internships Available ▶ *1–2 distance learning interns:* responsibilities include helping set up, coordinate and breakdown videoconferencing equipment; helping administer and deliver distance learning programs for K-12 classrooms. Candidates should have oral communication skills, organizational skills, personal interest in the field, strong interpersonal skills, written communication skills. Duration is 1 semester. Position available as unpaid or at $8–$10 per hour. ▶ *4 fall/spring teaching interns:* responsibilities include assisting staff in teaching school groups who come to the zoo by teaching principles of zoology, ecology, and conservation science. Candidates should have knowledge of field, oral communication skills, strong interpersonal skills, experience working with children. Duration is 18–20 weeks. $8–$10 per hour. ▶ *10–12 summer teaching interns:* responsibilities include helping to run conservation-based summer camp at the zoo, leading children in crafts, games, songs, and demonstrating live animals. Candidates should have knowledge of field, oral communication skills, strong interpersonal skills, experience working with children. Duration is 11 weeks. $8–$10 per hour. Open to college juniors, college seniors, recent college graduates, graduate students. International applications accepted.
Benefits Formal training, on-the-job training.
Contact Write, fax, e-mail, or through World Wide Web site Ms. Ilyssa Gillman, Intern Coordinator. Fax: 718-365-3300. E-mail: igillman@wcs.org. No phone calls. In-person interview required.

Applicants must submit a letter of interest, resume, letter of recommendation, application from Web site (preferred). Applications are accepted continuously. World Wide Web: http://www.wcs.org.

WILDLIFE SOCIETY
5410 Grosvenor Lane
Bethesda, Maryland 20814-2197

General Information Society whose mission is to enhance the scientific, technical, managerial, and educational capabilities and achievements of wildlife professionals. Established in 1937. Number of employees: 12. Number of internship applications received each year: 15.
Internships Available ▶ *2 policy interns:* responsibilities include researching conservation issues, preparing background information for use in testimony or comments, attending briefings and hearings, writing for and assisting with the preparation of publications, and assisting with the routine activities of the society. Candidates should have knowledge of field, research skills, self-motivation, writing skills, course work in wildlife, natural resources, biology, or management (preferred). Duration is 6 months. $1000 per month. Open to college seniors, recent college graduates, graduate students. International applications accepted.
Benefits Willing to provide letters of recommendation.
Contact Write, call, fax, e-mail, or through World Wide Web site Thomas M. Franklin, Wildlife Policy Director. Phone: 301-897-9770. Fax: 301-530-2471. E-mail: tws@wildlife.org. In-person interview recommended (telephone interview accepted). Applicants must submit a letter of interest, resume, academic transcripts, two writing samples, three personal references. Applications are accepted continuously. World Wide Web: http://www.wildlife.org.

WOLF RIDGE ENVIRONMENTAL LEARNING CENTER
6282 Cranberry Road
Finland, Minnesota 55603

General Information Residential environmental school for students of all ages whose mission is to teach stewardship, promote a quality environment through educational programs, and awaken the natural curiosity of the human mind. Established in 1971. Number of employees: 45. Number of internship applications received each year: 50.
Internships Available ▶ *16 student naturalists:* responsibilities include teaching ecology, cultural history, and recreation classes; participating in diplomatic liaison relationships; participating in seminars; conducting formal evening slide presentations; enrolling in a post-baccalaureate program in environmental education offered through the University of Minnesota, Duluth. Candidates should have ability to work independently, analytical skills, college degree in related field, knowledge of field, oral communication skills, organizational skills, personal interest in the field, plan to pursue career in field, research skills, self-motivation, strong interpersonal skills, strong leadership ability, written communication skills, desire to learn, willingness and ability to work alone and engage in physical activity. Duration is 9 months. Stipend of $3000. Open to recent college graduates, graduate students, career changers. International applications accepted.
Benefits Formal training, free housing, free meals, job counseling, names of contacts, on-the-job training, opportunity to attend seminars/workshops, tuition assistance, willing to act as a professional reference, willing to complete paperwork for educational credit, willing to provide letters of recommendation, post-baccalaureate certificate in environmental education through University of Minnesota, Duluth.
Contact Write, call, fax, e-mail, or through World Wide Web site Joe Walewski, Director of Naturalist Training. Phone: 218-353-7414. Fax: 218-353-7762. E-mail: mail@wolf-ridge.org. Telephone interview required. Applicants must submit a formal organization application, letter of interest, resume, academic transcripts, three personal references, program cost of up to $2500 if accepted. Application deadline: March 31. World Wide Web: http://www.wolf-ridge.org.

WOOD LAKE NATURE CENTER
6710 Lake Shore Drive
Richfield, Minnesota 55423

General Information Natural area with 150 acres of fields, woods, marsh, and restored prairie preserved by the city of Richfield to give children and adults a place to explore, observe, and learn about the natural world. Established in 1970. Number of employees: 8. Division of City of Richfield, Recreation Services, Richfield, Minnesota. Number of internship applications received each year: 50.
Internships Available ▶ *1–3 naturalist interns:* responsibilities include leading environmental education activities for individuals of all ages. Candidates should have college courses in field, knowledge of field, oral communication skills, plan to pursue career in field, self-motivation, strong interpersonal skills. Duration is flexible (10 weeks or more). Position available as unpaid or paid. Open to college juniors, college seniors, recent college graduates, graduate students, law students, career changers, individuals reentering the workforce. ▶ *1–4 summer interns:* responsibilities include teaching classes, supervising volunteers, exhibit design, and animal care. Candidates should have ability to work independently, knowledge of field, oral communication skills, plan to pursue career in field, self-motivation, strong interpersonal skills. Duration is June through August. Position available as unpaid or paid. Open to college juniors, college seniors, recent college graduates, graduate students, career changers, individuals reentering the workforce.
Benefits Formal training, job counseling, names of contacts, on-the-job training, opportunity to attend seminars/workshops, willing to act as a professional reference, willing to complete paperwork for educational credit, willing to provide letters of recommendation.
Contact Write, call, fax, e-mail, or through World Wide Web site Mr. Tom Moffatt, Naturalist/Intern Coordinator. Phone: 612-861-9365. Fax: 612-861-9367. E-mail: tmoffatt@ci.richfield.mn.us. In-person interview recommended (telephone interview accepted). Applicants must submit a formal organization application, letter of interest, resume, academic transcripts, three personal references. Application deadline: February 1 for spring, April 1 for summer, August 1 for fall, December 1 for winter. World Wide Web: http://www.ci.richfield.mn.us/RecreationServices/WoodLake/.

YMCA BECKET–CHIMNEY CORNERS OUTDOOR CENTER
748 Hamilton Road
Becket, Massachusetts 01223

General Information 1200-acre outdoor center in Berkshire Mountains serving over 10,000 guests annually in retreat, environmental education, adventure, and family camp programs. Established in 1903. Number of employees: 350. Number of internship applications received each year: 30.
Internships Available ▶ *Program instructors:* responsibilities include leading recreation and education programs; providing general support and administrative procedures specific to the outdoor center programs. Candidates should have ability to work with others, personal interest in the field, strong leadership ability. Duration is 2–12 months. $270 per week. Open to recent high school graduates, college freshmen, college sophomores, college juniors, college seniors, recent college graduates, career changers, individuals reentering the workforce. International applications accepted.
Benefits Formal training, free housing, free meals, job counseling, names of contacts, on-the-job training, opportunity to attend seminars/workshops, possible full-time employment, willing to act as a professional reference, willing to complete paperwork for educational credit, willing to provide letters of recommendation, free use of the facility when not working.
Contact Write, call, fax, or e-mail Eric Grimes, Director of Outdoor Environmental Education. Phone: 413-623-8991. Fax: 413-623-5890. E-mail: egrimes@bccymca.org. Telephone interview required. Applicants must submit a formal organization application, letter of interest, resume, three personal references. Applications are accepted continuously. World Wide Web: http://www.bccymca.org.

YMCA CAMP KERN
5291 State Route 350
Oregonia, Ohio 45054

General Information Camp operating as a residential outdoor education center. Established in 1910. Number of employees: 35. Branch of Dayton YMCA, Dayton, Ohio. Number of internship applications received each year: 5.
Internships Available ▶ *Naturalist interns:* responsibilities include teaching and leading activities dealing with natural history, pioneer, and Native American topics. Candidates should have oral communication skills, personal interest in the field, self-motivation, strong interpersonal skills, desire to work with children. Duration is one fall or spring. $100 per week. Open to high school students, recent high school graduates, college freshmen, college sophomores, college juniors, college seniors, recent college graduates, graduate students, law students, career changers, individuals reentering the workforce. International applications accepted.
Benefits Free housing, free meals, names of contacts, opportunity to attend seminars/workshops, possible full-time employment, willing to complete paperwork for educational credit, willing to provide letters of recommendation.
Contact Write, call, fax, or e-mail Dave Moran, Director of Outdoor Education. Phone: 513-932-3756. Fax: 513-932-8607. E-mail: dmoran@daytonymca.org. In-person interview recommended (telephone interview accepted). Applicants must submit a letter of interest, resume. Applications are accepted continuously. World Wide Web: http://www.campkern.org.

YMCA CAMP WIDJIWAGAN'S ENVIRONMENTAL EDUCATION PROGRAM
3788 North Arm Road
Ely, Minnesota 55731-9604

General Information Educational facility that uses a wilderness-based program to teach about the environment. Established in 1973. Number of employees: 18. Unit of YMCA of Greater St. Paul, St. Paul, Minnesota. Number of internship applications received each year: 15.
Internships Available ▶ *2–4 naturalist interns:* responsibilities include leading students in grades 4-9, helping co-lead small group activities for 10 students, serving in program support roles, and assisting with curriculum as part of independent intern project development. Candidates should have oral communication skills, organizational skills, personal interest in the field, self-motivation, strong interpersonal skills. Duration is 1 semester. $120–$160 per month. Open to college sophomores, college juniors, college seniors, recent college graduates.
Benefits Free meals, willing to complete paperwork for educational credit, willing to provide letters of recommendation, extensive training and staff development, possibility of seasonal, full-time employment.
Contact Write or call Ms. Karen Pick, Senior Program Director–Camp Widjiwagan. Phone: 218-365-2117. Fax: 218-365-2018. Applicants must submit a formal organization application, resume, personal reference, letter of recommendation. Application deadline: June 10 for fall, August 15 for winter. World Wide Web: http://www.mtn.org/widji.

ZERO POPULATION GROWTH
1400 16th Street, NW, Suite 320
Washington, District of Columbia 20036

General Information National nonprofit membership organization that works to mobilize broad public support for a sustainable balance of the earth's people, environment, and resources. Established in 1968. Number of employees: 30. Number of internship applications received each year: 70.
Internships Available ▶ *1–2 Planet Pop Radio interns:* responsibilities include assisting with programming, responding to audience mail, assisting with technical operation, and possibly some on-air work. Candidates should have computer skills, editing skills, knowledge of field, oral communication skills, organizational skills, personal interest in the field. Duration is flexible. Unpaid. Open to college freshmen, college sophomores, college juniors, col-

lege seniors, recent college graduates, graduate students. ▶ *1 field and outreach fellow:* responsibilities include grassroots organizing, coordinating exhibits, and public speaking. Candidates should have ability to work independently, computer skills, editing skills, oral communication skills, organizational skills, personal interest in the field, self-motivation, strong interpersonal skills. Duration is January 1 to June 15 or July 1 to December 15. $600 bi-weekly. Open to recent college graduates, graduate students. ▶ *1–2 government relations fellows:* responsibilities include monitoring legislation and influencing public policy. Candidates should have ability to work independently, ability to work with others, analytical skills, computer skills, oral communication skills, personal interest in the field, self-motivation, written communication skills. Duration is January to June and July to December. $600 bi-weekly. Open to recent college graduates, graduate students. ▶ *1–2 media/ communications fellows:* responsibilities include researching, writing, and marketing publications and general media work. Candidates should have computer skills, editing skills, office skills, personal interest in the field, research skills, writing skills. Duration is January to June and July to December. $600 bi-weekly. Open to recent college graduates, graduate students. ▶ *1–2 population education fellows:* responsibilities include developing and marketing teaching materials and teacher training. Candidates should have ability to work independently, computer skills, editing skills, organizational skills, personal interest in the field, research skills, written communication skills. Duration is January to June and July to December. $600 bi-weekly. Open to recent college graduates, graduate students. ▶ *1–2 research interns:* responsibilities include researching and writing reports. Candidates should have ability to work independently, analytical skills, computer skills, editing skills, research skills, writing skills. Duration is flexible. Unpaid. Open to recent college graduates. International applications accepted.

Benefits Job counseling, on-the-job training, possible full-time employment, willing to act as a professional reference, willing to complete paperwork for educational credit, willing to provide letters of recommendation, health insurance for paid fellowships.

Contact Write, call, fax, e-mail, or through World Wide Web site Jay Keller, Internship/Fellowship Coordinator, 1400 15th Street, NW, Suite 320, Washington, District of Columbia 20036. Phone: 202-323-2200. Fax: 202-332-2302. E-mail: jay@zpg.org. Applicants must submit a letter of interest, resume, three reference names, titles, and phone numbers, two writing samples (totaling 3-5 pages). Application deadline: April 15 for July-December paid fellowships, October 1 for January-June paid fellowships; continuous for all unpaid positions. World Wide Web: http://www.zpg. org.

SOCIAL ADVOCACY ORGANIZATIONS

ACADEMY FOR EDUCATIONAL DEVELOPMENT
1825 Connecticut Avenue, NW
Washington, District of Columbia 20009

General Information Nonprofit organization committed to solving critical social issues within the U.S. and around the world through education, social marketing, research, training, policy analysis, and innovative program design and management. Established in 1961. Number of employees: 400. Number of internship applications received each year: 200.

Internships Available ▶ *Interns:* responsibilities include research, writing, coordination of itineraries and meeting schedules for consultants, visitors, and students; proposal preparation and production. Candidates should have editing skills, oral communication skills, organizational skills, written communication skills, demonstrated proficiency in Word Perfect 8 and/or Microsoft Word. Duration is 1–6 months. Position available as unpaid or at wage based on academic status, work experience, and project budget; non-paid internships provide academic credit and/or work experience. Open to high school students, college freshmen, col-

lege sophomores, college juniors, college seniors, graduate students, retirees with 5-10 years of academic and/or work experience; college graduates, depending on academic accomplishment and work experience. International applications accepted.

Benefits On-the-job training, possible full-time employment, willing to act as a professional reference, willing to complete paperwork for educational credit.

Contact E-mail Diana Akasa, Human Resources Coordinator. Phone: 202-884-8502. Fax: 202-884-8709. E-mail: employ@aed. org. In-person interview recommended (telephone interview accepted). Applicants must submit a letter of interest, resume. Applications are accepted continuously. World Wide Web: http:// www.aed.org.

ACCURACY IN ACADEMIA
4455 Connecticut Avenue
Washington, District of Columbia 20008

General Information Nonprofit organization dedicated to fighting political correctness and defending free speech on college campuses nationwide. Established in 1985. Number of employees: 3. Number of internship applications received each year: 20.

Internships Available ▶ *2 writer/research interns:* responsibilities include writing and research for newspaper the "Campus Report" and for Web page; assisting with conference planning on an as needed basis. Candidates should have ability to work independently, analytical skills, computer skills, editing skills, knowledge of field, office skills, oral communication skills, organizational skills, personal interest in the field, plan to pursue career in field, research skills, self-motivation, strong interpersonal skills, writing skills. Duration is 8–16 weeks. $25 per day. Open to high school students, recent high school graduates, college freshmen, college sophomores, college juniors, college seniors, recent college graduates, graduate students, law students, career changers, individuals reentering the workforce. International applications accepted.

Benefits On-the-job training, opportunity to attend seminars/ workshops, possible full-time employment, willing to act as a professional reference, willing to complete paperwork for educational credit, willing to provide letters of recommendation.

Contact Write, fax, or e-mail Dan Flynn, Executive Director, 4455 Connecticut Avenue, Washington, District of Columbia 20008. Phone: 202-364-3085. Fax: 202-364-4098. E-mail: dan@academia. org. In-person interview recommended (telephone interview accepted). Applicants must submit a formal organization application, letter of interest, resume, two writing samples, two letters of recommendation. Application deadline: April 15 for summer, November 15 for winter. World Wide Web: http://www.academia. org.

THE ACTIVISM CENTER AT WETLANDS PRESERVE
New York, New York

General Information Multi-issue activism organization that uses public education and creative protest to challenge the abuse of animals, the environment, and human beings by corporations and governments worldwide. Established in 1989. Number of internship applications received each year: 200.

Internships Available ▶ *Earth and animal liberation political prisoner support interns:* responsibilities include generate media attention, public support, and legal assistance for people unjustly jailed for involvement in environmental and animal rights activism. Candidates should have ability to work with others, oral communication skills, research skills, self-motivation, written communication skills. Duration is flexible. ▶ *Animal rights legislative internship:* responsibilities include lobbying legislators and consulates on local, state, federal, and international animal rights issues; conducting research; organizing voters in critical legislative districts; acting as group liaison to organizations working on local, state, federal, and international animal rights issues. Candidates should have ability to work independently, editing skills, organizational skills, research skills, self-motivation, writing skills. Duration is flexible. Unpaid. ▶ *Animal rights resource and outreach interns:* responsibilities include serving as resource librarian to resource center of hundreds of books, videos, and informational files on animal rights issues; writing articles on organization's animal rights activities for "Wet-

The Activism Center at Wetlands Preserve (continued)
lands Works" newsletter; contacting student groups to arrange presentations at schools. Candidates should have organizational skills, personal interest in the field, writing skills. Duration is flexible. Unpaid. ▶ *Anti-fur interns:* responsibilities include working with staff and volunteers to organize anti-fur protests and other events, and developing educational materials for activists and the public, including a boycott/protest target list of stores that sell fur in NYC; conducting extensive research and developing detailed files on the NYC fur industry, working on legislative campaigns and ballot initiatives to ban the sale of fur and to ban fur farming and trapping. Candidates should have ability to work independently, ability to work with others, computer skills, organizational skills, personal interest in the field, research skills. Duration is flexible. Unpaid. ▶ *Anti-sweatshop interns:* responsibilities include working with the Global Sweatshop Coalition on direct solidarity campaign with workers on the bottom rung of the global economic ladder to defend fair wages and decent working conditions and uphold the rights of workers, both within the U.S. and abroad to organize and unionize. Candidates should have oral communication skills, organizational skills, personal interest in the field, self-motivation, strong leadership ability, writing skills. Duration is flexible. Unpaid. ▶ *1–4 computer maintenance interns:* responsibilities include maintain and administer small network of Macintosh, Windows, and Linux machines; troubleshoot all machines; install new hardware and software, secure donations of new equipment. Candidates should have ability to work independently, computer skills, knowledge of field, self-motivation. Duration is flexible. Unpaid. ▶ *1–10 data managers:* responsibilities include preparing written instructions for use with all databases; instructing high school interns in data entry; supervising and assessing work of assistants; and completing several hours of data entry weekly. Candidates should have ability to work with others, computer skills, editing skills, knowledge of field, office skills, organizational skills, knowledge of Microsoft Excel, Filemaker Pro, Access (strongly preferred), knowledge of MYSQL also helpful. Duration is flexible. Unpaid. ▶ *Fund-raising/development interns:* responsibilities include researching and implementing fund-raising and organizational development strategies to support human rights, animal rights, and environmental projects. Candidates should have knowledge of field, office skills, organizational skills, research skills, strong interpersonal skills, strong leadership ability. Unpaid. ▶ *Graphic designer and/or Web designer:* responsibilities include laying out brochures, reports, posters, and pamphlets; creating logos; designing and/or coding websites on human, animal, and environmental justice issues. Candidates should have ability to work independently, computer skills, experience in the field, self-motivation, artistic/graphic design skills. Duration is flexible. Unpaid. ▶ *Indigenous rights interns:* responsibilities include working with interns, volunteers, and staff on organizing demonstrations, rallies, and marches against corporations involved in the destruction of indigenous homelands in Colombia, Ecuador, and Burma; organizing educational forums on a broad range of indigenous rights issues; networking with local, national, and international human rights and environmental groups. Candidates should have ability to work with others, oral communication skills, personal interest in the field, self-motivation, strong leadership ability, writing skills. Duration is flexible. Unpaid. ▶ *1–6 internship outreach/recruitment assistants:* responsibilities include processing internship applications; responding to intern inquiries; posting information on internship program to internship Web sites and activism listservs; arranging, coordinating, and staffing information booths at concerts, street fairs, and other events to publicize Wetlands internships; coordinating mailings to high school and college internship programs and student organizations. Candidates should have office skills, oral communication skills, organizational skills, research skills, strong interpersonal skills. Duration is flexible. Unpaid. ▶ *Media relations interns:* responsibilities include maintaining database of contact information for over 600 news organizations; drafting media advisories and news releases; conducting interviews with media; and pitching stories to media through oral communication. Candidates should have ability to work independently, computer skills, editing skills, oral communication skills, personal interest in the field, writing skills. Duration is flexible. Unpaid. ▶ *Novice activist interns for the environment and*

human and animal rights: responsibilities include working on a variety of projects as the need arises in order to gain exposure to a wide range of issues and tasks, issues will include fighting sweatshop labor, working for legislation against animal cruelty, defending rainforests, and campaigning against the first trade. Candidates should have ability to work independently, ability to work with others, personal interest in the field, self-motivation. Duration is flexible. Unpaid. ▶ *Protest photographers/videographers:* responsibilities include attending conferences, rallies, marches, demonstrations and other events, taking photos and/or short video to be used by mainstream and independent media to document protest activities; videographers may also develop produced programs for video and public access TV. Candidates should have ability to work independently, knowledge of field, personal interest in the field, self-motivation. ▶ *1–6 protest/direct action/civil disobedience interns:* responsibilities include working with an affinity group in organizing direct actions, protests, and street theater events; taking on responsibilities including researching issues and targets; scouting locations; researching, building and/or acquiring special equipment, creating banners, signs, literature, press releases, and press packets; recruiting participants for the action and supporting roles; alerting media to the upcoming event. Candidates should have ability to work with others, personal interest in the field, self-motivation, strong leadership ability. Duration is flexible. Unpaid. Open to any interested person. International applications accepted.

Benefits Names of contacts, on-the-job training, opportunity to attend seminars/workshops, willing to act as a professional reference, willing to complete paperwork for educational credit, willing to provide letters of recommendation.

International Internships Available.

Contact Call, fax, e-mail, or through World Wide Web site Adam Weissman, Internship Program Coordinator. Phone: 212-947-7744. Fax: 212-947-7773. E-mail: adam@wetlands-preserve.org. In-person interview recommended (telephone interview accepted). Applicants must submit a formal organization application. Applications are accepted continuously. World Wide Web: http://www.wetlands-preserve.org/activismcenter.html.

ADC RESEARCH INSTITUTE
4201 Connecticut Avenue, NW, Suite 300
Washington, District of Columbia 20008

General Information Grassroots civil rights organization that defends the rights of Arab-Americans, promotes Arab heritage, and addresses Middle East issues. Established in 1980. Number of employees: 13.

Internships Available ▶ *1 American Committee on Jerusalem intern:* responsibilities include assisting on projects and campaigns which defend the rights of Palestinians, Muslims and Christians; educating the public and policymakers for a balanced viewpoint in Jerusalem. Candidates should have knowledge of field, writing skills. Duration is 1 summer or semester. Position available as unpaid or at $800 for graduate students; $500 for undergraduates for summer; prorated for semesters. Open to college sophomores, college juniors, college seniors, recent college graduates, graduate students. ▶ *2 education and outreach interns:* responsibilities include working closely with director of educational programs in mobilizing grassroots network of ADC activists; campaigning for Arab-American issues; responding to requests from educators and activists; developing lesson plans; working with peace and human rights organizations on Middle East issues, Palestinian rights, and the humanitarian crisis in Iraq; writing articles for ADC newsletter. Candidates should have writing skills, knowledge of Arab world or Arab-American community. Duration is 1-2 semesters or 10-week summer term. Position available as unpaid or at $800 for graduate students; $500 for undergraduates during summer term; prorated during semester. Open to college sophomores, college juniors, college seniors, recent college graduates, graduate students. ▶ *Government affairs interns:* responsibilities include assisting government affairs director in monitoring Congress and administration on Arab-American issues (Middle East and civil rights), researching legislation, attending hearings, and writing for ADC newsletter. Candidates should have knowledge of field, research skills, writing skills. Duration is 1-2 semesters or one summer (10 weeks). Position available as unpaid or at $800 for graduate students; $500 for undergraduates for summer; prorated for semesters. Open to college juniors, college seniors, recent college graduates, graduate students, law students, career changers. ▶ *1–2 information systems interns:* responsibilities include organizing Internet workshop and assisting in all aspects of registration process for national convention. Candidates should have ability to work independently, oral communication skills, research skills, extensive knowledge/willingness to learn, and good computer instincts. Duration is flexible (full-time during summer). $800 stipend for graduate students; $500 for undergraduates during summer; prorated during semester. Open to college sophomores, college juniors, college seniors, recent college graduates, graduate students. ▶ *4 legal interns:* responsibilities include working closely with attorney on immigration law, civil and human rights law, international law, and treaties; screening new cases as they come into the office; legal research; drafting client letters and press releases. Candidates should have ability to work independently, analytical skills, research skills, writing skills, 1-2 years of law school, strong commitment to civil rights and diversity. Duration is 1-2 semesters or 10-week summer term. Position available as unpaid or at $800 for 10-week summer term; prorated during semester. Open to graduate students, law students. ▶ *4 media and publications interns:* responsibilities include writing articles for ADC Times; conducting research; producing and/or updating publications; helping write, edit, and design Annual Activity Report; maintaining video book library and filing system; monitoring media; responding to public and media information requests. Candidates should have knowledge of field, research skills, writing skills. Duration is 1-2 semesters or 10-week summer term. Position available as unpaid or at $800 for graduate students; $500 for undergraduates during summer term; prorated for semesters. Open to college sophomores, college juniors, college seniors, recent college graduates, graduate students. ▶ *2 organizing and special events interns:* responsibilities include assisting the director with work involving the national network of local chapters, organizing regional conferences, and monitoring and mobilizing activists to work on projects. Candidates should have computer skills, knowledge of field, oral communication skills, organizational skills, written communication skills. Duration is 1-2 semesters or 10-week summer term. Position available as unpaid or at $800 for graduate students; $500 for undergraduates during summer; prorated for semesters. Open to college sophomores, college juniors, college seniors, recent college graduates, graduate students. ▶ *15 summer interns:* responsibilities include attending meetings and conferences of government officials; emphasis on educational programs located around Washington, D.C.; working with legal, media, education, and organizing departments in relation to projects and campaigns; working with ADC programs and campaigns in legal, education, media, and political action. Candidates should have knowledge of field, writing skills. Duration is 10 weeks. Position available as unpaid or at $500 stipend for undergraduates; $800 stipend for graduate and law students. Open to college sophomores, college juniors, college seniors, recent college graduates, graduate students, law students. International applications accepted.

Benefits Names of contacts, on-the-job training, opportunity to attend seminars/workshops, willing to complete paperwork for educational credit, willing to provide letters of recommendation, one day per week of leadership development skills for summer interns, introduction to Washington, assistance with locating roommates and/or housing, opportunity to attend meetings with Congress, administration officials, Arab embassies, and American organizations.

Contact Write, call, fax, or e-mail Mr. Marvin Wingfield, Director of Education and Outreach. Phone: 202-244-2990. Fax: 202-244-3196. E-mail: marvinw@adc.org. Applicants must submit a letter of interest, resume, academic transcripts, two letters of recommendation, 2-page essay. Application deadline: March 1 for summer; continuous for fall and spring. World Wide Web: http://www.adc.org.

ADVOCATES FOR YOUTH
1025 Vermont Avenue, NW, Suite 200
Washington, District of Columbia 20005

General Information National organization dedicated exclusively to the advancement of adolescent sexual and reproductive health.

Internships Available ▶ *Interns.* Duration is 3 month (minimum of 35 hours per week) part-time positions may be available. Position available as unpaid or paid.

Contact Write Director of Internships. Applicants must submit a letter of interest, resume. Applications are accepted continuously. World Wide Web: http://www.advocatesforyouth.org.

AIDS ACTION
1906 Sunderland Place, NW
Washington, District of Columbia 20036

General Information National organization devoted solely to lobbying the federal government for AIDS policy, legislation, and funding. Established in 1984. Number of employees: 17. Number of internship applications received each year: 25.

Internships Available ▶ *1–3 Pedro Zamora fellows:* responsibilities include updating/writing policy briefs on various issues; researching variety of health and civil rights issues related to HIV; attending congressional hearings and coalition meetings; monitoring voting records. Candidates should have ability to work with others, analytical skills, knowledge of field, oral communication skills, research skills, self-motivation, written communication skills. Duration is 10–24 weeks. Position available as unpaid or at $300 per week. Open to recent high school graduates, college freshmen, college sophomores, college juniors, college seniors, recent college graduates, graduate students. International applications accepted.

Benefits Names of contacts, opportunity to attend seminars/workshops, possible full-time employment, willing to act as a professional reference, willing to complete paperwork for educational credit.

Contact Write, call, fax, e-mail, or through World Wide Web site Scott Brawley, Fellowship Coordinator. Phone: 202-530-8030 Ext. 3047. Fax: 202-530-8031. E-mail: sbrawley@aidsaction.org. In-person interview required. Applicants must submit a formal organization application, letter of interest, resume, two personal references, letter of recommendation. Application deadline: April 15 for summer, July 15 for fall, December 1 for spring. World Wide Web: http://www.aidsaction.org.

ALBANY COUNTY SAFE PROJECT
312 Steele
Laramie, Wyoming 82070

General Information Project that advocates for victims of domestic violence and sexual assault. Established in 1980. Number of employees: 5. Unit of Wyoming Coalition Against Domestic Violence and Sexual Assault/Wyoming State Division of Victim Services, Laramie, Wyoming. Number of internship applications received each year: 5.

Internships Available ▶ *2–5 SAFE project interns:* responsibilities include assisting staff with office management; presentations; shelter coverage. Candidates should have ability to work independently, ability to work with others, computer skills, oral communication skills, written communication skills, completion of 40 hours of training, depending on agency involvement. Duration is 1–2 semesters. Position available as unpaid or paid. Open to high school seniors, recent high school graduates, college freshmen, college sophomores, college juniors, college seniors, recent college graduates, graduate students, law students, career changers, individuals reentering the workforce. ▶ *2–5 volunteer interns:* responsibilities include working with staff to determine a new project, developing the project, and implementing it in the community; direct service projects available. Candidates should have ability to work independently, oral communication skills, self-motivation, strong interpersonal skills, written communication skills, completion of SAFE Project 40-hour training or equivalent (for hot line coverage). Duration is 1–2 semesters. Unpaid. Open

Albany County SAFE Project (continued)
to college freshmen, college sophomores, college juniors, college seniors, recent college graduates, graduate students, law students. International applications accepted.
Benefits Formal training, names of contacts, on-the-job training, opportunity to attend seminars/workshops, possible full-time employment, willing to act as a professional reference, willing to complete paperwork for educational credit, willing to provide letters of recommendation, work-related travel reimbursement.
Contact Write, call, fax, or e-mail Linda J. Torres, Executive Director. Phone: 307-742-7273. Fax: 307-745-4510. E-mail: safeproject@qwest.net. In-person interview required. Applicants must submit a letter of interest, resume, three personal references. Applications are accepted continuously.

ALLIANCE FOR GLOBAL JUSTICE
1247 E Street, SE
Washington, District of Columbia 20003

General Information Progressive, grassroots organization that works for social change through a variety of projects; brings together different organizations to promote a cross-fertilization of ideas and build a broader base of support to work together to defend the human and economic rights of people throughout the world. Established in 1998. Number of employees: 18. Number of internship applications received each year: 30.
Internships Available ▶ *2–3 program interns:* responsibilities include writing and researching articles for newsletters, lobbying work, monitoring campaigns, organizing conferences, attending meetings, and some general office and clerical tasks. Candidates should have ability to work independently, analytical skills, computer skills, knowledge of field, organizational skills, personal interest in the field, self-motivation, strong interpersonal skills, written communication skills, knowledge of Latin American issues; Spanish ability helpful. Duration is flexible (8 weeks minimum). Unpaid. Open to college sophomores, college juniors, college seniors, recent college graduates, graduate students. International applications accepted.
Benefits On-the-job training, opportunity to attend seminars/workshops, willing to act as a professional reference, willing to complete paperwork for educational credit, willing to provide letters of recommendation.
Contact Write, call, fax, e-mail, or through World Wide Web site Kathy Hoyt, Intern Coordinator, 1247 E Street, SE, Washington, District of Columbia 20003. Phone: 202-544-9355. Fax: 202-544-9359. E-mail: agj@afgj.org. Telephone interview required. Applicants must submit a letter of interest, resume, writing sample, two personal references. Applications are accepted continuously. World Wide Web: http://www.afgj.org.

ALLIANCE FOR HEALTH REFORM
1444 Eye Street, NW, Suite 910
Washington, District of Columbia 20005

General Information Nonpartisan, not-for-profit organization that strives to educate news media, congressional staff, and others about issues in health reform. Established in 1991. Number of employees: 7. Number of internship applications received each year: 50.
Internships Available ▶ *2–3 interns:* responsibilities include helping with seminar logistics; performing research on all aspects of health reform; carrying out general administrative duties; and working closely with experienced policy professionals, congressional staffers, administrators, journalists, and other members of the policy community. Candidates should have ability to work with others, college courses in field, oral communication skills, organizational skills, personal interest in the field, research skills, written communication skills. Duration is 2 months minimum. Position available as unpaid or paid. Open to college freshmen, college sophomores, college juniors, college seniors, recent college graduates, graduate students, law students, career changers, individuals reentering the workforce. International applications accepted.

Benefits Opportunity to attend seminars/workshops, willing to complete paperwork for educational credit, willing to provide letters of recommendation.
Contact Write, fax, e-mail, or through World Wide Web site Ms. Nancy Peavy, Director of Operations. Fax: 202-789-2233. E-mail: npeavy@allhealth.org. In-person interview recommended (telephone interview accepted). Applicants must submit a letter of interest, resume, academic transcripts, writing sample, two personal references. Application deadline: March 1 for summer, November 1 for winter. World Wide Web: http://www.allhealth.org.

ALLIANCE FOR JUSTICE
11 Dupont Circle, NW, 2nd Floor
Washington, District of Columbia 20036

General Information Association of national, regional, and local organizations working for the public interest to provide equal access to government forums for all groups and individuals. Established in 1979. Number of employees: 30. Number of internship applications received each year: 200.
Internships Available ▶ *3–4 Everett interns:* responsibilities include general office duties, working mostly with First Monday Coordinator on First Monday event (held the first Monday in October of each year). Candidates should have ability to work with others, computer skills, oral communication skills, organizational skills, research skills, written communication skills. Duration is May to August. $210 per week. Open to college freshmen, college sophomores, college juniors, college seniors, graduate students, law students. ▶ *1–2 fellowship interns:* responsibilities include researching records of judicial nominees, providing technical assistance on laws governing lobbying and electoral activities by nonprofits, organizing national "First Monday" conferences promoting public interest work, and analyzing legal issues that affect the public interest community. Candidates should have computer skills, oral communication skills, organizational skills, research skills, writing skills. Duration is August to September. $32,000 per year. Open to law school graduates. ▶ *Winter interns:* responsibilities include general office duties. Candidates should have computer skills, oral communication skills, organizational skills, research skills, writing skills. Duration is October to May. Unpaid. Open to college freshmen, college sophomores, college juniors, college seniors, graduate students, law students. International applications accepted.
Benefits Names of contacts, on-the-job training, opportunity to attend seminars/workshops, willing to act as a professional reference, willing to complete paperwork for educational credit, willing to provide letters of recommendation.
Contact Write, fax, or e-mail Alicia Holmes, Director of Administration. Fax: 202-822-6068. E-mail: alliance@afj.org. No phone calls. In-person interview recommended (telephone interview accepted). Applicants must submit a letter of interest, resume, writing sample. Application deadline: February 1 for summer, October 1 for winter. World Wide Web: http://www.afj.org.

AMERICAN CIVIL LIBERTIES UNION
125 Broad Street, 18th Floor
New York, New York 10004

General Information Public interest nonprofit organization. Number of internship applications received each year: 250.
Internships Available ▶ *1–2 college interns:* responsibilities include various research projects for attorneys in legal department, as well as other projects assigned by paralegal including intake correspondence. Candidates should have computer skills, personal interest in the field, research skills, self-motivation, strong interpersonal skills, written communication skills. Duration is 10–12 weeks. Unpaid. Open to recent high school graduates, college freshmen, college sophomores, college juniors, college seniors, recent college graduates. International applications accepted.
Benefits Opportunity to attend seminars/workshops, willing to act as a professional reference, willing to complete paperwork for educational credit.
Contact Write or call David Baluarte, Internship Coordinator. Phone: 212-549-2610. Fax: 212-549-2651. E-mail: dbaluarte@aclu.org. Applicants must submit a letter of interest, resume, 5-page

non-fiction writing sample. Application deadline: March 1 for summer, August 1 for fall, November 1 for spring. World Wide Web: http://www.aclu.org.

AMERICAN FORUM IN WASHINGTON
National Press Building, 529 14th Street, NW, Suite 840
Washington, District of Columbia 20045

General Information   Progressive nonprofit media organization that publishes articles on quality of life issues and provides a resource for progressives to disseminate social commentary to the media. Established in 1981. Number of employees: 5. Number of internship applications received each year: 60.
Internships Available   ▶ *2–3 editorial assistants:* responsibilities include editing and proofing of articles and related research; contacting authors and tracking in-office article status; developing press releases, PSAs and audio and video scripts. Candidates should have ability to work independently, ability to work with others, editing skills, office skills, writing skills. Duration is 1 semester (minimum 14 hours per week). Unpaid. ▶ *2–4 media interns:* responsibilities include surveying media; researching and writing reports; analyzing usage data; preparing media packets for print, broadcast, and online media outlets. Candidates should have ability to work independently, computer skills, personal interest in the field, research skills, strong interpersonal skills, writing skills. Duration is 1 semester minimum (14 hours per week). Unpaid. ▶ *1–3 state organizers:* responsibilities include developing reports, board volunteer events, organizational affiliations, policy updates and related information, assisting with state meeting and member building. Candidates should have ability to work with others, oral communication skills, organizational skills, strong leadership ability, written communication skills. Duration is minimum 14 hours per week. Unpaid. Open to recent high school graduates, college freshmen, college sophomores, college juniors, college seniors, recent college graduates, graduate students, career changers. International applications accepted.
Benefits   Names of contacts, opportunity to attend seminars/workshops, possible full-time employment, willing to complete paperwork for educational credit, willing to provide letters of recommendation.
Contact   Write, call, fax, or e-mail Lutrecia N. Borders, Intern Coordinator. Phone: 202-638-1431. Fax: 202-638-1434. E-mail: forum@mediaforum.org. In-person interview recommended (telephone interview accepted). Applicants must submit a letter of interest, resume. Applications are accepted continuously. World Wide Web: http://www.mediaforum.org.

AMERICAN FRIENDS SERVICE COMMITTEE–ARIZONA AREA PROGRAM
931 North Fifth Avenue
Tucson, Arizona 85705

General Information   Nonprofit social justice and peace organization. Established in 1917. Branch of American Friends Service Committee, Philadelphia, Pennsylvania. Number of internship applications received each year: 10.
Internships Available   ▶ *1 community intern:* responsibilities include contributing to current projects; planning, publicizing, and facilitating conferences and workshops; supporting coalitions and other groups; helping maintain area program office in Tucson; creating a personal project in consultation with program coordinator; promoting peace and justice. Candidates should have ability to work independently, analytical skills, computer skills, oral communication skills, organizational skills, personal interest in the field, self-motivation, strong interpersonal skills, writing skills. Duration is 9 to 12 months. $650–$800 per month. Open to recent high school graduates, recent college graduates. International applications accepted.
Benefits   Health insurance, names of contacts, on-the-job training, opportunity to attend seminars/workshops, travel reimbursement, willing to act as a professional reference, willing to complete paperwork for educational credit, willing to provide letters of recommendation.
Contact   Write, call, fax, or e-mail Caroline Isaacs, Program Coordinator, 931 North Fifth Avenue, Tucson, Arizona 85705.

Phone: 520-623-9141. Fax: 520-623-5901. E-mail: afscazcj@azstarnet.com. In-person interview recommended (telephone interview accepted). Applicants must submit a resume, writing sample, three personal references. Application deadline: April 1. World Wide Web: http://www.afsc.org/az.htm.

AMERICAN HUMANE ASSOCIATION
63 Inverness Drive East
Englewood, Colorado 80112

General Information   National organization dedicated to identifying and preventing animal and child abuse and neglect; provides advocacy, research, training, technical assistance, and other services in the areas of animal and child protection. Established in 1877. Number of employees: 60. Number of internship applications received each year: 10.
Internships Available   ▶ *1 marketing intern:* responsibilities include project management of a range of existing cause marketing programs with corporate sponsors, evaluating market opportunities, and creating proposals. Candidates should have ability to work independently, computer skills, oral communication skills, research skills, written communication skills. Duration is flexible. Position available as unpaid or paid. ▶ *1 public relations intern:* responsibilities include preparing press releases and articles, contacting media, using on-line services to create mailing lists, and participating in campaign/event planning. Candidates should have ability to work independently, analytical skills, oral communication skills, research skills, strong interpersonal skills, written communication skills. Duration is flexible. Position available as unpaid or paid. Open to college juniors, college seniors, recent college graduates.
Benefits   Possible full-time employment, willing to act as a professional reference, willing to complete paperwork for educational credit, willing to provide letters of recommendation, stipend may be available.
Contact   Write, fax, e-mail, or through World Wide Web site Linda Konstan, Vice President of Human Resources. Fax: 303-792-5333. E-mail: linda@americanhumane.org. No phone calls. In-person interview recommended (telephone interview accepted). Applicants must submit a letter of interest, resume, 2 personal references/letters of recommendation. Applications are accepted continuously. World Wide Web: http://www.americanhumane.org.

AMERICAN JEWISH CONGRESS, GOVERNMENTAL AND PUBLIC AFFAIRS OFFICE
1001 Connecticut Avenue, NW, Suite 407
Washington, District of Columbia 20036

General Information   National community relations organization dedicated to protecting the religious, civil, political, and economic rights of all Americans. Established in 1918. Number of employees: 3. Unit of American Jewish Congress, New York, New York. Number of internship applications received each year: 50.
Internships Available   ▶ *3–4 legislative interns:* responsibilities include attending and reporting on congressional committee hearings and interest group coalition meetings and performing administrative duties. Candidates should have ability to work with others, office skills, oral communication skills, personal interest in the field, self-motivation, written communication skills. Duration is 3 months minimum. Unpaid. ▶ *1 public policy institute intern:* responsibilities include helping with development activities of regional office; writing policy papers generated from regional public policy institute; and administrative activities. Candidates should have oral communication skills, personal interest in the field, self-motivation, strong interpersonal skills, written communication skills. Duration is year-round. Unpaid. Open to college freshmen, college sophomores, college juniors, college seniors, recent college graduates. International applications accepted.
Benefits   Names of contacts, opportunity to attend seminars/workshops, possible full-time employment, travel reimbursement, willing to act as a professional reference, willing to complete paperwork for educational credit, willing to provide letters of recommendation.
International Internships   Available in Jerusalem, Israel.

American Jewish Congress, Governmental and Public Affairs Office (continued)
Contact Write, call, or fax Charles D. Brooks, Director. Phone: 202-466-9661. Fax: 202-466-9665. E-mail: washrep@ajcongress. org. Telephone interview required. Applicants must submit a formal organization application, letter of interest, resume, writing sample. Applications are accepted continuously. World Wide Web: http://www.ajcongress.org.

AMERICANS FOR DEMOCRATIC ACTION
1625 K Street, NW, Suite 210
Washington, District of Columbia 20006

General Information Nation's oldest liberal lobbying group that combines grassroots organizing with lobbying on various issues at local, state, and national levels. Established in 1947. Number of employees: 10. Number of internship applications received each year: 100.
Internships Available ▶ *4–10 legislative interns:* responsibilities include researching, writing, helping with mailings, and following one or two issues on Capitol Hill. Candidates should have ability to work independently, analytical skills, computer skills, editing skills, knowledge of field, office skills, organizational skills, personal interest in the field, research skills, self-motivation, strong interpersonal skills, writing skills. Duration is flexible. Unpaid. Open to high school students, recent high school graduates, college freshmen, college sophomores, college juniors, college seniors, recent college graduates, graduate students, law students, career changers, individuals reentering the workforce. International applications accepted.
Benefits Names of contacts, opportunity to attend seminars/ workshops, possible full-time employment, willing to act as a professional reference, willing to complete paperwork for educational credit, willing to provide letters of recommendation.
Contact Write, call, fax, e-mail, or through World Wide Web site Valerie Dulk-Jacobs, Special Assistant to the Director. Phone: 202-785-5980. Fax: 202-785-5969. E-mail: adaction@ix.netcom.com. In-person interview recommended (telephone interview accepted). Applicants must submit a resume, one-page letter of interest indicating legislative issues important and career plans. Application deadline: May 1 for summer, August 1 for fall, December 1 for spring. World Wide Web: http://www.adaction.org.

AMNESTY INTERNATIONAL, MIDWEST REGION
53 West Jackson, Suite 731
Chicago, Illinois 60604-3607

General Information Grassroots international human rights organization that trains and organizes membership, functions as a liaison with the media, and organizes fund-raising and special events. Established in 1961. Number of employees: 12. Unit of Amnesty International USA, New York, New York. Number of internship applications received each year: 50.
Internships Available ▶ *1–2 OUTFRONT human rights interns:* responsibilities include coordination of various outreach projects promoting international LGBT human rights and the work of the OUTFRONT Program. Candidates should have ability to work independently, ability to work with others, computer skills, editing skills, office skills, oral communication skills, organizational skills, personal interest in the field, research skills, self-motivation, written communication skills. Duration is 1–12 months. Unpaid. Open to high school students, recent high school graduates, college freshmen, college sophomores, college juniors, college seniors, recent college graduates. ▶ *1 death penalty abolition intern:* responsibilities include working with deputy director on death penalty related projects in region. Candidates should have ability to work independently, computer skills, editing skills, office skills, oral communication skills, organizational skills, personal interest in the field, research skills, self-motivation, strong interpersonal skills, strong leadership ability, writing skills. Duration is flexible. Unpaid. Open to high school students, recent high school graduates, college freshmen, college sophomores, college juniors, college seniors, recent college graduates, graduate students, law students. ▶ *1–2 membership development interns:* responsibilities include maintaining and recruiting members by managing lists, phone, and e-mail; developing and sending membership information; contacting

group coordinators; data entry; and assisting in event planning. Candidates should have ability to work independently, computer skills, editing skills, office skills, oral communication skills, organizational skills, personal interest in the field, research skills, self-motivation, strong interpersonal skills, writing skills. Duration is 3–6 months. Unpaid. Open to high school students, recent high school graduates, college freshmen, college sophomores, college juniors, college seniors, recent college graduates, graduate students, law students. ▶ *1–2 office/ general administrative interns:* responsibilities include working in a not-for-profit office environment, organizing various information including international reports, country specific materials (written and audio-visual) and other office duties. Candidates should have ability to work independently, ability to work with others, analytical skills, computer skills, editing skills, office skills, oral communication skills, organizational skills, personal interest in the field, self-motivation, writing skills. Duration is 3 to 6 months (2-3 days a week). Unpaid. Open to high school students, recent high school graduates, college freshmen, college sophomores, college juniors, college seniors. ▶ *1 torture campaign intern* . Candidates should have computer skills, office skills, organizational skills, research skills, self-motivation, written communication skills. Duration is flexible. Unpaid. Open to high school students, recent high school graduates, college freshmen, college sophomores, college juniors, college seniors, recent college graduates, career changers, individuals reentering the workforce. ▶ *1 women's human rights intern:* responsibilities include attending Women's Convention Coalition meetings, assisting in passing resolution through City Council, arranging Alderman visits, outreach to ally organizations, answering general requests, mailings help, and general office work. Candidates should have ability to work independently, computer skills, office skills, oral communication skills, organizational skills, personal interest in the field, research skills, self-motivation, strong interpersonal skills, written communication skills. Duration is 1–6 months. Unpaid. Open to college freshmen, college sophomores, college juniors, college seniors, recent college graduates, graduate students, law students, career changers. International applications accepted.
Benefits Opportunity to attend seminars/workshops, willing to complete paperwork for educational credit, willing to provide letters of recommendation.
International Internships Available.
Contact Write, call, fax, or through World Wide Web site Office Administrator. Phone: 312-427-2060. Fax: 312-427-2589. In-person interview recommended (telephone interview accepted). Applicants must submit a formal organization application, letter of interest, resume, two personal references, 1-2 letters of recommendation for interns 3 months or longer. Applications are accepted continuously. World Wide Web: http://www.amnesty-usa.org.

AMNESTY INTERNATIONAL USA, WASHINGTON OFFICE
600 Pennsylvania Avenue, SE, 5th Floor
Washington, District of Columbia 20003

General Information Organization conducting a worldwide movement working impartially for the release of prisoners of conscience, fair and prompt trials for political prisoners, and an end to torture and executions. Established in 1961. Number of employees: 45. Unit of Amnesty International USA, New York, New York. Number of internship applications received each year: 500.
Internships Available ▶ *2 African affairs interns:* responsibilities include monitoring and providing information on developments in the region, participating in projects that promote human rights policy in the region. Candidates should have ability to work independently, computer skills, office skills, oral communication skills, organizational skills, personal interest in the field, research skills, strong interpersonal skills, writing skills. Duration is minimum of 3 months. Unpaid. Open to college freshmen, college sophomores, college juniors, college seniors, recent college graduates, graduate students, law students, career changers. ▶ *2 Asian affairs interns:* responsibilities include monitoring and providing information on developments in the region, participating in projects that promote human rights policy in the region. Candidates should have abil-

ity to work independently, computer skills, office skills, oral communication skills, organizational skills, personal interest in the field, research skills, strong interpersonal skills, writing skills. Duration is minimum of 3 months. Unpaid. Open to college freshmen, college sophomores, college juniors, college seniors, recent college graduates, graduate students, law students, career changers. ▶ *4 European/Middle Eastern affairs interns:* responsibilities include monitoring and providing information on developments in the region, participating in projects that promote human rights policy in the region. Candidates should have ability to work independently, computer skills, office skills, oral communication skills, organizational skills, personal interest in the field, research skills, strong interpersonal skills, writing skills. Duration is minimum of 3 months. Paid. Open to college freshmen, college sophomores, college juniors, college seniors, recent college graduates, graduate students, law students, career changers. ▶ *2 Latin American affairs interns:* responsibilities include monitoring and providing information on developments in the region, participating in projects that promote human rights policy in the region. Candidates should have ability to work independently, computer skills, office skills, oral communication skills, organizational skills, personal interest in the field, research skills, strong interpersonal skills, writing skills. Duration is minimum of 3 months. Unpaid. Open to college freshmen, college sophomores, college juniors, college seniors, recent college graduates, graduate students. ▶ *1–2 Program to Abolish the Death Penalty interns:* responsibilities include assisting in creating training materials for organizing against the death penalty, and providing research on the death penalty and related issues in the U.S. and internationally. Candidates should have ability to work independently, computer skills, office skills, oral communication skills, organizational skills, personal interest in the field, research skills, strong interpersonal skills, writing skills. Duration is minimum of 3 months. Unpaid. Open to college freshmen, college sophomores, college juniors, college seniors, recent college graduates, graduate students. ▶ *3 campaign interns:* responsibilities include assisting with all aspects of campaigns and crisis response including planning, materials preparation, event coordination, and evaluation. Candidates should have ability to work independently, computer skills, office skills, oral communication skills, organizational skills, personal interest in the field, research skills, strong interpersonal skills, writing skills. Duration is minimum of 3 months. Unpaid. Open to college freshmen, college sophomores, college juniors, college seniors, recent college graduates, graduate students. ▶ *2–3 country specialists:* responsibilities include assisting in the recruitment, training, and servicing of volunteer country specialists. Candidates should have ability to work independently, computer skills, office skills, oral communication skills, organizational skills, personal interest in the field, strong interpersonal skills, writing skills. Duration is minimum of 3 months. Unpaid. Open to college freshmen, college sophomores, college juniors, college seniors, recent college graduates, graduate students. ▶ *1 grassroots advocacy intern:* responsibilities include assisting in promoting the legislative priorities of AIUSA; providing information to AISUA members and groups that are lobbying the congressional representatives assisting in developing online human rights actions. Candidates should have ability to work independently, computer skills, office skills, oral communication skills, organizational skills, personal interest in the field, research skills, strong interpersonal skills, writing skills. Duration is minimum of 3 months. Unpaid. Open to college freshmen, college sophomores, college juniors, college seniors, recent college graduates, graduate students, law students, career changers. ▶ *2 human rights and the environment interns:* responsibilities include providing research on cases involving environmental and human rights violations and assisting in grassroots organizing strategies. Candidates should have ability to work independently, computer skills, office skills, oral communication skills, organizational skills, personal interest in the field, research skills, strong interpersonal skills, writing skills. Duration is minimum of 3 months. Unpaid. Open to college freshmen, college sophomores, college juniors, college seniors, recent college graduates, graduate students. ▶ *1 media relations intern:* responsibilities include assisting the press officer with all aspects of work to ensure media coverage of human rights issues. Candidates should have ability to work independently, computer skills, office skills, oral communication skills, organizational skills,

personal interest in the field, strong interpersonal skills, writing skills. Duration is minimum of 3 months. Unpaid. Open to college freshmen, college sophomores, college juniors, college seniors, recent college graduates, graduate students. ▶ *3–4 mid-Atlantic regional office interns:* responsibilities include working to mobilize, motivate and support AIUSA members in their efforts to publicize and eliminate worldwide human rights abuses. Candidates should have ability to work independently, computer skills, office skills, oral communication skills, organizational skills, personal interest in the field, research skills, strong interpersonal skills, writing skills. Duration is minimum of 3 months. Unpaid. Open to college freshmen, college sophomores, college juniors, college seniors, recent college graduates, graduate students. ▶ *3–4 national field program interns:* responsibilities include assisting in the coordination of national training programs and the development of activists tools and assisting in grassroots organizing strategies. Candidates should have ability to work independently, office skills, oral communication skills, organizational skills, personal interest in the field, research skills, strong interpersonal skills, writing skills. Duration is minimum of 3 months. Unpaid. Open to college freshmen, college sophomores, college juniors, college seniors, recent college graduates, graduate students. ▶ *1 new media Web site intern:* responsibilities include updating Web pages; creating new pages including graphic work; helping produce online events; site maintenance; and running log file reports. Candidates should have ability to work independently, ability to work with others, computer skills, oral communication skills, organizational skills, personal interest in the field, writing skills, Web development skills (preferred). Duration is minimum of 3 months . Unpaid. Open to high school seniors, college freshmen, college sophomores, college juniors, college seniors, recent college graduates, graduate students. ▶ *1–2 refugee interns:* responsibilities include providing research and documentation to be used to support asylum claims; maintaining resource materials and database files; responding to information requests. Candidates should have ability to work independently, ability to work with others, office skills, oral communication skills, organizational skills, personal interest in the field, research skills, writing skills. Duration is minimum of 3 months. Unpaid. Open to college freshmen, college sophomores, college juniors, college seniors, recent college graduates, graduate students. ▶ *1 women's program intern:* responsibilities include representing Women's Program at events, meetings and networking opportunities, conducting outreach to women's organizations; maintaining events calendar; research; and compilation of materials. Candidates should have ability to work independently, ability to work with others, office skills, oral communication skills, organizational skills, personal interest in the field, research skills, writing skills. Duration is minimum of 3 months. Unpaid. Open to college freshmen, college sophomores, college juniors, college seniors, recent college graduates, graduate students. International applications accepted.

Benefits Job counseling, names of contacts, opportunity to attend seminars/workshops, travel reimbursement, willing to act as a professional reference, willing to complete paperwork for educational credit, willing to provide letters of recommendation.

Contact Write, call, fax, or e-mail Oneida Khalsa, Office Manager. Phone: 202-544-0200. Fax: 202-546-7142. E-mail: okhalsa@aiusa. org. Telephone interview required. Applicants must submit a letter of interest, resume, writing sample, two letters of recommendation. Application deadline: February 15 for spring, April 15 for summer, August 15 for fall, November 30 for winter. World Wide Web: http://amnesty-usa.org.

ANIMAL PROTECTION INSTITUTE
1122 S Street
Sacramento, California 95814

General Information Animal advocacy organization. Established in 1968. Number of employees: 19. Number of internship applications received each year: 40.

Internships Available ▶ *1–2 animal advocacy interns:* responsibilities include assisting program and legal staff with advocacy campaigns by conducting research, writing publications, drafting member action alerts, and lobbying public officials. Candidates should have ability to work independently, analytical skills, plan

Animal Protection Institute (continued)

to pursue career in field, research skills, strong interpersonal skills, written communication skills. Duration is 40 hours per week during summer; variable during school year. Position available as unpaid or at $7-$12 per hour (for summer positions only). Open to college juniors, college seniors, recent college graduates, graduate students, law students. ▶ *2–6 animal care (primates) interns:* responsibilities include animal care at the Texas Snow Monkey Sanctuary in Dilley, Texas; physical labor for rescued primates (vervets, baboons, and snow monkeys). Candidates should have ability to work with others, college courses in field, experience in the field, personal interest in the field, plan to pursue career in field, self-motivation. Duration is 2–6 months. Unpaid. Open to college juniors, college seniors, graduate students.
Benefits On-the-job training, opportunity to attend seminars/workshops, possible full-time employment, willing to act as a professional reference, willing to complete paperwork for educational credit, willing to provide letters of recommendation, housing provided for animal care positions.
Contact Write, fax, or e-mail Alan Berger, Executive Director, PO Box 22505, Sacramento, California 95822. Fax: 916-447-3070. E-mail: ahberger@earthlink.net. No phone calls. In-person interview recommended (telephone interview accepted). Applicants must submit a letter of interest, resume, writing sample, three personal references. Application deadline: March 15 for summer; continuous for school-year positions. World Wide Web: http://www.api4animals.org.

ARAB AMERICAN INSTITUTE
1600 K Street, NW, Suite 601
Washington, District of Columbia 20006

General Information Organization that nurtures and encourages direct participation of Arab Americans in political and civic life in the U.S. Established in 1985. Number of employees: 15. Number of internship applications received each year: 75.
Internships Available ▶ *3–4 interns:* responsibilities include assisting in Public Affairs or Organizing Departments, setting up meetings, assisting with logistics of special events, helping the Institute build its action network; some clerical work, research, and writing. Candidates should have ability to work independently, college courses in field, computer skills, knowledge of field, research skills, writing skills. Duration is minimum 6 weeks in winter, spring, summer, or fall. $500–$1000 per month. Open to college freshmen, college sophomores, college juniors, college seniors, recent college graduates, graduate students. International applications accepted.
Benefits Opportunity to attend seminars/workshops, possible full-time employment, willing to complete paperwork for educational credit, willing to provide letters of recommendation.
Contact Write, call, fax, or e-mail Dianne L. Davidson, Office Manager. Phone: 202-429-9210. Fax: 202-429-9214. E-mail: ddavidson@aaiusa.org. In-person interview recommended (telephone interview accepted). Applicants must submit a letter of interest, resume, writing sample. Application deadline: April 15 for summer, August 9 for fall, December 13 for spring. World Wide Web: http://www.aaiusa.org.

THE ARMS CONTROL ASSOCIATION
1726 M Street, NW, Suite 201
Washington, District of Columbia 20036

General Information Independent research organization dedicated to raising public knowledge of arms control and related national security issues. Established in 1971. Number of employees: 8. Number of internship applications received each year: 200.
Internships Available ▶ *2–4 foreign affairs/national security interns:* responsibilities include research support and clerical duties. Candidates should have ability to work with others, analytical skills, computer skills, office skills, personal interest in the field, research skills, self-motivation. Duration is 1 semester. Unpaid. Open to college freshmen, college sophomores, college juniors, college seniors, recent college graduates, graduate students.
Benefits Job counseling, meals at a cost, names of contacts, on-the-job training, opportunity to attend seminars/workshops, possible

full-time employment, travel reimbursement, willing to act as a professional reference, willing to complete paperwork for educational credit, willing to provide letters of recommendation, $10 per day lunch stipend.
Contact Write, call, fax, e-mail, or through World Wide Web site Alex Wagner, Research Analyst and Intern Coordinator. Phone: 202-463-8270 Ext. 102. Fax: 202-463-8273. E-mail: awagner@armscontrol.org. In-person interview recommended (telephone interview accepted). Applicants must submit a letter of interest, resume, 1 writing sample (3-5 pages). Application deadline: April 15 for summer, August 15 for fall, December 15 for winter/spring. World Wide Web: http://www.armscontrol.org.

ASIAN PACIFIC AMERICAN INSTITUTE FOR CONGRESSIONAL STUDIES (APAICS)
1001 Connecticut Avenue, Suite 835
Washington, District of Columbia 20036

General Information Non-partisan, non-profit, educational organization whose mission is to promote the participation of Asian American and Pacific Islanders in the political process.
Internships Available ▶ *Interns:* responsibilities include obtaining updates on legislation, regulations, and court decisions affecting the Asian American and Pacific Islander communities; research, writing political briefings, program administration,and general office work. Duration is flexibe (year-round). Unpaid. Open to college freshmen, college sophomores, college juniors, college seniors, graduate students. ▶ *Summer interns (Washington DC):* responsibilities include placements in Congress, federal agencies, and institutions that further the mission of APAICS. Candidates should have oral communication skills, personal interest in the field, strong leadership ability, written communication skills, minimum GPA of 3.3. $2500 stipend. Open to college freshmen, college sophomores, college juniors, college seniors, recent college graduates, minimum 18 years of age.
Benefits Willing to complete paperwork for educational credit.
Contact Call, fax, or e-mail Internship Coordinator. Phone: 202-296-9200. Fax: 202-296-9236. E-mail: apaics@apaics.org. Materials as specified on Web site. Application deadline: mid February for summer; continuous for all other positions. World Wide Web: http://www.apaics.org.

ASSOCIATION FOR CHILDHOOD EDUCATION INTERNATIONAL
17904 Georgia Avenue, Suite 215
Olney, Maryland 20832

General Information Not-for-profit professional membership association of educators concerned with children from infancy through early adolescence. Established in 1892. Number of employees: 14. Number of internship applications received each year: 5.
Internships Available ▶ *2 office interns.* Candidates should have computer skills, oral communication skills, personal interest in the field, self-motivation, strong interpersonal skills, written communication skills. Duration is 3–6 weeks. Position available as unpaid or paid. Open to college juniors, college seniors, recent college graduates, graduate students, career changers, individuals reentering the workforce. International applications accepted.
Benefits Names of contacts, on-the-job training, willing to act as a professional reference, willing to complete paperwork for educational credit, willing to provide letters of recommendation.
Contact Fax, e-mail, or through World Wide Web site Mynor Gonzales, Branch Relations Manager. Fax: 301-570-2212. E-mail: aceimemb@aol.com. No phone calls. In-person interview recommended (telephone interview accepted). Applicants must submit a formal organization application, letter of interest. Applications are accepted continuously. World Wide Web: http://www.acei.org.

ASSOCIATION FOR WOMEN IN SCIENCE (AWIS)
1200 New York Avenue, NW, Suite 650
Washington, District of Columbia 20005

General Information Nonprofit organization whose mission is to expand education and employment opportunities in science for girls and women. Established in 1971. Number of employees: 7. Number of internship applications received each year: 150.

Internships Available ▶ *Interns:* responsibilities include helping to develop chapter activities and plan AWIS events; assisting with grant proposal writing; legislative analysis; assisting with magazine production, membership services, and research; and/or obtaining resources/statistics on issues of women in science, Web site maintenance. Candidates should have ability to work independently, office skills, research skills, strong interpersonal skills, written communication skills. Duration is flexible. Paid. Open to college freshmen, college sophomores, college juniors, college seniors, recent college graduates, graduate students. International applications accepted.

Benefits Opportunity to attend seminars/workshops, willing to complete paperwork for educational credit, willing to provide letters of recommendation.

Contact Write or e-mail Intern Coordinator. E-mail: awis@awis. org. Applicants must submit a letter of interest, resume. Applications are accepted continuously. World Wide Web: http://www. awis.org.

THE AUDRE LORDE PROJECT
85 South Oxford Street
Brooklyn, New York 11217

General Information Lesbian, gay, bisexual, two spirits, and transgender people of color center for community organizing in the New York City area that works for community wellness and progressive social and economic justice. Established in 1993. Number of employees: 8. Number of internship applications received each year: 25.

Internships Available ▶ *1 community organizing assistant:* responsibilities include working directly with the executive director to help with community organizing campaigns, research, and administrative duties. Candidates should have oral communication skills, organizational skills, strong interpersonal skills, written communication skills, commitment to organization's mission and principles. Duration is minimum 24 hours per week for 3 months. Unpaid. Open to high school students, recent high school graduates, college freshmen, college sophomores, college juniors, college seniors, recent college graduates, graduate students, career changers. ▶ *1 development assistant:* responsibilities include working directly with executive director and fund-raising committee to develop and implement creative strategies for sustainable fundraising; includes correspondence with donors, researching prospective funding streams, and donor data management. Candidates should have ability to work independently, computer skills, oral communication skills, strong interpersonal skills, writing skills, commitment to organization's mission and principles. Duration is minimum of 24 hours per week for 3 months. Unpaid. Open to high school students, recent high school graduates, college freshmen, college sophomores, college juniors, college seniors, recent college graduates, graduate students, career changers, individuals reentering the workforce.

Benefits Names of contacts, opportunity to attend seminars/workshops, willing to act as a professional reference, willing to complete paperwork for educational credit, willing to provide letters of recommendation, hands-on community organizing experience.

Contact Write, call, or e-mail Desmond Rudder, Volunteer and Outreach Program Coordinator, 85 South Oxford Street, Brooklyn, New York 11217. Phone: 718-596-0342 Ext. 14. E-mail: drudder@alp.org. In-person interview required. Applicants must submit a formal organization application, resume, writing sample, three personal references. Application deadline: January 2 for spring, April 15 for summer, October 1 for winter. World Wide Web: http://www.alp.org.

BASTROP CHILDREN'S ADVOCACY CENTER
1002 Chestnut Street
Bastrop, Texas 78602

General Information Private, nonprofit, community site providing forensic interviewing, individual, group, and family counseling for abuse survivors and their families; also coordinates agencies involved in civic and criminal investigation of child abuse. Established in 1992. Number of employees: 5. Affiliate of

Children's Advocacy Centers of Texas, Austin, Texas. Number of internship applications received each year: 5.

Internships Available ▶ *2-3 clinical interns:* responsibilities include individual, group, and family counseling; outreach activities including community and in-school presentations; home visits; advocacy; basic office work; computer work. Candidates should have ability to work independently, analytical skills, declared college major in field, knowledge of field, oral communication skills, plan to pursue career in field, self-motivation, strong interpersonal skills, writing skills, must provide own transportation. Duration is as educational contract requires. Unpaid. Open to college seniors, recent college graduates, graduate students, post graduates seeking contact hours for licensure.

Benefits On-the-job training, opportunity to attend seminars/workshops, willing to act as a professional reference, willing to complete paperwork for educational credit, willing to provide letters of recommendation, mileage reimbursement to/from home in neighboring counties.

Contact Write, call, or e-mail Tracey Chance, Clinical Director, PO Box 1098, Bastrop 78602. Phone: 512-321-6161. Fax: 512-303-3985. E-mail: tchancebcac@yahoo.com. In-person interview required. Applicants must submit a letter of interest, resume, academic transcripts, 1-2 recommendations (may be from professors). Applications are accepted continuously. World Wide Web: http://www.childrensadvocacycenter.org.

BETTER GOVERNMENT ASSOCIATION
28 East Jackson Boulevard, Suite 1900
Chicago, Illinois 60604

General Information Nationally recognized public interest organization that collaborates with local and national print and broadcast news organizations to investigate waste, corruption, and inefficiency in government. Established in 1923. Number of employees: 7. Number of internship applications received each year: 150.

Internships Available ▶ *7-10 interns:* responsibilities include conducting background research, interviews, litigation searches, surveillance, and administrative duties. Candidates should have ability to work independently, analytical skills, research skills, self-motivation, strong interpersonal skills, desire to work in the public interest. Duration is flexible. Unpaid. Open to college juniors, college seniors, recent college graduates, graduate students, law students. ▶ *1-3 legal interns:* responsibilities include researching, analyzing, and developing legal theory; investigating waste, fraud, and corruption in government; and performing general office duties. Candidates should have ability to work independently, analytical skills, organizational skills, personal interest in the field, research skills, self-motivation, written communication skills. Duration is flexible. Unpaid. Open to law students. International applications accepted.

Benefits Job counseling, names of contacts, opportunity to attend seminars/workshops, possible full-time employment, willing to act as a professional reference, willing to complete paperwork for educational credit, willing to provide letters of recommendation, leadership skills.

Contact Write, call, fax, e-mail, or through World Wide Web site Jay E. Stewart, Staff Attorney. Phone: 312-427-8330. Fax: 312-427-8340. E-mail: jayestew@hotmail.com. Applicants must submit a letter of interest, resume. Application deadline: January 15 for spring, May 30 for summer, September 1 for fall. World Wide Web: http://www.bettergov.org.

BIRTHING THE FUTURE
PO Box 830
Durango, Colorado 81302

General Information Organization dedicated to inspiring, fostering, and advocating vision and practical models for the healing and well being of life on the planet through birth activism.

Internships Available ▶ *2 interns:* responsibilities include office work including phone, writing, e-mail, and Web work; supervised, independent work on a project of intern's choosing that supports organization's mission. Candidates should have skills in marketing and sales, research, Web design, graphics, or creative

Birthing the Future (continued)

writing, video production, design, and photography skills would be beneficial, but are not required. Duration is minimum of 8 weeks (25 to 30 hours per week).

Benefits Free housing, covering of food expenses (negotiable), hands-on experience in organizational, financial, and day-to-day aspects of doing birth activism.

Contact Write, call, fax, or e-mail Suzanne Arms, President. Phone: 970-884-4090. Fax: 970-884-9141. E-mail: suzanne@birthingthefuture.com. Resume focusing on relevant skills and experience; a personal letter about oneself, including interest, availability, and length of internship desired; photo of applicant. Applications are accepted continuously. World Wide Web: http://www.birthingthefuture.com.

BREAD FOR THE WORLD AND BREAD FOR THE WORLD INSTITUTE
50 F Street NW, Suite 500
Washington, District of Columbia 20001

General Information Nonprofit anti-hunger advocacy organization that addresses U.S. public policy affecting the hungry. Established in 1974. Number of employees: 60. Number of internship applications received each year: 100.

Internships Available ▶ *1–2 annual hunger report interns:* responsibilities include assisting with publishing a major reference guide on global hunger. Candidates should have ability to work independently, analytical skills, computer skills, editing skills, knowledge of field, oral communication skills, organizational skills, personal interest in the field, research skills, self-motivation, strong interpersonal skills, strong leadership ability, writing skills. Duration is 3 months or 1-2 years. Unpaid. Open to college sophomores, college juniors, college seniors, recent college graduates, graduate students. ▶ *1 church relations intern:* responsibilities include carrying out promotional efforts to churches and denominational representatives in support of BFW legislation. Candidates should have ability to work independently, computer skills, knowledge of field, office skills, oral communication skills, organizational skills, personal interest in the field, self-motivation, strong interpersonal skills, writing skills. Duration is 8–10 weeks. Unpaid. Open to college freshmen, college sophomores, college juniors, college seniors, recent college graduates. ▶ *1–3 development interns:* responsibilities include assisting with fund-raising for both the general budget and special projects. Candidates should have ability to work independently, computer skills, office skills, oral communication skills, personal interest in the field, self-motivation, strong interpersonal skills, writing skills. Duration is 3 months or 1-2 years. Unpaid. Open to college freshmen, college sophomores, college juniors, college seniors, recent college graduates. ▶ *1 domestic hunger issues intern:* responsibilities include assisting with developing and communicating policy and legislative strategy on domestic hunger issues. Candidates should have ability to work independently, analytical skills, college courses in field, computer skills, editing skills, knowledge of field, oral communication skills, personal interest in the field, research skills, self-motivation, strong interpersonal skills, writing skills. Duration is 3 months or 1-2 years. Unpaid. Open to college freshmen, college sophomores, college juniors, college seniors, recent college graduates. ▶ *1 human resources intern.* Candidates should have ability to work independently, college courses in field, computer skills, oral communication skills, organizational skills, plan to pursue career in field, research skills, self-motivation, strong interpersonal skills, writing skills. Duration is 3 months or 1 year. Unpaid. Open to college freshmen, college sophomores, college juniors, college seniors, recent college graduates, graduate students, career changers. ▶ *1 international hunger issues intern:* responsibilities include assisting with research and lobbying support. Candidates should have ability to work independently, computer skills, editing skills, knowledge of field, oral communication skills, organizational skills, personal interest in the field, plan to pursue career in field, research skills, self-motivation, strong interpersonal skills, strong leadership ability, writing skills. Duration is 3 months or 1-2 years. Unpaid. Open to college sophomores, college juniors, college seniors, recent college graduates, graduate students. ▶ *1 media intern:* responsibilities include using a variety of media to fulfill objectives. Candidates

should have ability to work independently, computer skills, knowledge of field, oral communication skills, personal interest in the field, self-motivation, strong interpersonal skills, writing skills. Duration is 3 months or 1-2 years. Unpaid. Open to college freshmen, college sophomores, college juniors, college seniors, recent college graduates. ▶ *1–3 organizing interns:* responsibilities include assisting with building a strong grassroots lobbying network by working on specific projects or in a specific region of the country. Candidates should have ability to work independently, computer skills, knowledge of field, oral communication skills, organizational skills, personal interest in the field, self-motivation, strong interpersonal skills, writing skills. Duration is 3 months or 1-2 years. Unpaid. Open to college freshmen, college sophomores, college juniors, college seniors, recent college graduates. ▶ *1–5 stipend interns:* responsibilities include serving in any capacity where needed in any of the above positions. Candidates should have ability to work independently, computer skills, office skills, oral communication skills, personal interest in the field, self-motivation, strong interpersonal skills, written communication skills. Duration is 1 year. $17,595 per year plus medical and dental benefits. Open to recent college graduates, graduate students, career changers. International applications accepted.

Benefits Job counseling, names of contacts, opportunity to attend seminars/workshops, possible full-time employment, willing to complete paperwork for educational credit, willing to provide letters of recommendation, reimbursement of work-related travel expenses.

Contact Write, call, fax, e-mail, or through World Wide Web site Ms. Katherine Simmons, Human Resources Manager. Phone: 202-639-9400. Fax: 202-639-9401. E-mail: human.resources@bread.org. Applicants must submit a formal organization application, letter of interest, resume, academic transcripts, writing sample, three letters of recommendation. Application deadline: April 1 for summer, July 1 for fall, November 1 for winter and spring. World Wide Web: http://www.bread.org.

CALIFORNIA NATIONAL ORGANIZATION FOR WOMEN
926 J Street, Suite 820
Sacramento, California 95814

General Information Women's rights organization working primarily on legislation in the state of California. Established in 1972. Number of employees: 6. Branch of National Organization for Women (National Action Center), Washington, District of Columbia. Number of internship applications received each year: 5.

Internships Available ▶ *1–3 California NOW interns:* responsibilities include communication with local chapters, specific short- or long-term projects as assigned, depending on intern's interests. Candidates should have ability to work independently, computer skills, oral communication skills, research skills, writing skills. Duration is flexible. Unpaid. Open to high school students, recent high school graduates, college freshmen, college sophomores, college juniors, college seniors, recent college graduates, graduate students, law students, career changers, individuals reentering the workforce. International applications accepted.

Benefits On-the-job training, opportunity to attend seminars/workshops, travel reimbursement, willing to act as a professional reference, willing to complete paperwork for educational credit, willing to provide letters of recommendation.

Contact Write, call, fax, or e-mail Mandy Benson, Field Director. Phone: 916-442-3414. Fax: 916-442-6942. E-mail: fielddir@canow.org. In-person interview recommended (telephone interview accepted). Applicants must submit a letter of interest. Applications are accepted continuously. World Wide Web: http://www.canow.org.

CAMPAIGN FOR TOBACCO-FREE KIDS
1400 Eye Street, NW, Suite 1200
Washington, District of Columbia 20005

General Information Organization dedicated to protecting children from tobacco addiction and exposure to secondhand smoke.

Internships Available ▶ *Interns:* responsibilities include assisting on substantive projects in a variety of areas, including constituency relations, and research. Candidates should have writing skills, attention to detail; responsibility, strong writing skills, ability to multi-task. Duration is minimum 12 weeks, 15 hours per week (fall interns). Paid.
Benefits Willing to complete paperwork for educational credit.
Contact Fax Internship Coordinator. Fax: 202-296-5427. E-mail: jobs@tobaccofreekids.org. No phone calls. Applicants must submit a letter of interest, resume, two writing samples, 2 references. Applications are accepted continuously. World Wide Web: http://tobaccofreekids.org.

CARAL–CALIFORNIA ABORTION & REPRODUCTIVE RIGHTS ACTION LEAGUE
32 Monterey Boulevard
San Francisco, California 94131

General Information Political lobbying, educational organization dedicated to creating and sustaining a constituency that uses the political process to guarantee the full range of reproductive rights to all women. Established in 1978. Number of employees: 9. Affiliate of National Abortion and Reproductive Rights Action League, Washington, District of Columbia. Number of internship applications received each year: 25.
Internships Available ▶ *1–3 grassroots organizing interns:* responsibilities include coordinating volunteers, supervising and directing campaign strategy implementation, legislative alert organizing, event work, and writing. Candidates should have ability to work independently, ability to work with others, oral communication skills, personal interest in the field, self-motivation, written communication skills, MAC computer skills (preferred), ability to work in busy environment, be a team player, access to a car. Duration is 15-20 hours per week. Unpaid. Open to high school students, recent high school graduates, college freshmen, college sophomores, college juniors, college seniors, recent college graduates, graduate students, law students, individuals reentering the workforce. ▶ *Legislative interns:* responsibilities include tracking local, state, and national legislation on abortion and other reproductive health issues; designing fact sheets, writing newsletter articles, and developing other educational material on existing and pending legislation. Candidates should have MAC computer skills (preferred). Duration is 10 hours per week. Unpaid. ▶ *Political interns:* responsibilities include helping with electoral strategy, public education, and candidate endorsements for elections; participation in grassroots efforts surrounding targeted races of CARAL-endorsed candidates. Candidates should have MAC computer skills (preferred). Duration is 20 hours per week. Unpaid.
Benefits Formal training, names of contacts, on-the-job training, opportunity to attend seminars/workshops, possible full-time employment, willing to act as a professional reference, willing to complete paperwork for educational credit, willing to provide letters of recommendation, work and travel stipends.
Contact Write, call, fax, e-mail, or through World Wide Web site Kody Hilton, Administrative Coordinator, 32 Monterey Boulevard, San Francisco, California 94131. Phone: 415-334-1502 Ext. 305. Fax: 415-334-6510. E-mail: caral@aol.com. Applicants must submit a letter of interest, resume. Applications are accepted continuously. World Wide Web: http://www.caral.org or www.choice.org.

THE CARTER CENTER
One Copenhill, 453 Freedom Parkway
Atlanta, Georgia 30307

General Information Nonprofit organization, founded by Jimmy and Rosalynn Carter, dedicated to resolving conflicts, promoting democracy, and fighting disease, hunger, poverty, and oppression throughout the world. Established in 1982. Number of employees: 150. Unit of Emory University, Atlanta, Georgia. Number of internship applications received each year: 300.
Internships Available ▶ *Graduate assistants:* responsibilities include duties focusing on issues concerning democratization and development, global health, and urban revitalization. Candidates should have ability to work independently, college courses in field, knowledge of field, research skills, writing skills. Duration is 10

weeks (40 hours per week). Stipend of $3000. Open to graduate and professional students who have completed at least one year of graduate study. ▶ *Interns:* responsibilities include duties focusing on issues concerning democratization and development, global health, and urban revitalization, including some office administration. Candidates should have college courses in field, computer skills, research skills, writing skills, interest in contemporary international and domestic issues. Duration is at least 15 weeks (minimum of 20 hours per week). Unpaid. Open to college juniors, college seniors, recent college graduates, graduate students. International applications accepted.
Benefits Formal training, job counseling, names of contacts, opportunity to attend seminars/workshops, willing to complete paperwork for educational credit, willing to provide letters of recommendation, possibility of financial aid.
Contact Write, call, fax, or through World Wide Web site Director, Educational Program. Phone: 404-420-5151. Fax: 404-420-5196. Applicants must submit a formal organization application, resume, academic transcripts, writing sample, two letters of recommendation, short essay describing interest in field. Application deadline: March 15 for summer, June 15 for fall, October 15 for spring. World Wide Web: http://www.cartercenter.org.

CENTER FOR EQUAL OPPORTUNITY
14 Pidgeon Hill Drive, Suite 500
Sterling, Virginia 20165

General Information Nonprofit research organization specializing in race, ethnicity, language issues, and assimilation. Established in 1995. Number of employees: 10. Number of internship applications received each year: 12.
Internships Available ▶ *3–6 research assistants:* responsibilities include conducting research for senior staff, contributing to reports, and other writing assignments. Candidates should have ability to work with others, personal interest in the field, research skills, self-motivation, writing skills. Duration is 2–3 months. Unpaid. Open to college freshmen, college sophomores, college juniors, college seniors, recent college graduates, graduate students, law students.
Benefits Names of contacts, opportunity to attend seminars/workshops, willing to act as a professional reference, willing to complete paperwork for educational credit, willing to provide letters of recommendation.
Contact Write, call, fax, e-mail, or through World Wide Web site David Gersten, Executive Director. Phone: 703-421-5443. Fax: 703-421-6401. E-mail: comment@ceousa.org. Telephone interview required. Applicants must submit a letter of interest, resume, writing sample. Applications are accepted continuously. World Wide Web: http://www.ceousa.org.

CENTER FOR NONPROLIFERATION STUDIES
Monterey Institute of International Studies, 425 Van Buren
Monterey, California 93940

General Information Largest nongovernmental organization in U.S. devoted exclusively to research and training in nonproliferation issues; striving to combat the spread of weapons of mass destruction through training and information dissemination. Established in 1989. Number of employees: 60. Unit of Monterey Institute of International Studies, Monterey, California.
Internships Available ▶ *Nonproliferation internships (DC office):* responsibilities include researching chemical and biological weapons nonproliferation issues; monitoring events in Congress, administration, and media; collecting documents and testimony; assisting with outreach activities. Candidates should have computer skills, office skills, research skills. Duration is 5 months. $7–$9 per hour. Open to college seniors, recent college graduates, graduate students. ▶ *5–10 summer undergraduate internships in nonproliferation studies:* responsibilities include research assistance for one of the following projects: East Asia Nonproliferation; Monitoring Proliferation Threats; Newly Independent States Nonproliferation; Chemical and Biological Nonproliferation; Education. Candidates should have ability to work independently, personal

Center for Nonproliferation Studies (continued)
interest in the field, research skills, writing skills. Duration is 2–4 months. $7 per hour. Open to college juniors, college seniors. International applications accepted.
Benefits On-the-job training, opportunity to attend seminars/ workshops.
Contact E-mail or through World Wide Web site Fred Wehling, Education Coordinator. Fax: 831-647-6522. E-mail: fwehling@miis. edu. Applicants must submit a letter of interest, resume, academic transcripts, letter of recommendation. Application deadline: February 15 for summer (Monterey), June 29 for fall (DC), November 12 for winter/spring (DC). World Wide Web: http://cns.miis. edu.

CENTER FOR WOMEN POLICY STUDIES (CWPS)
1211 Connecticut Avenue, NW, Suite 312
Washington, District of Columbia 20036

General Information Public policy research and advocacy organization that advances the rights of women. Established in 1972. Number of employees: 12. Number of internship applications received each year: 150.
Internships Available ▶ *1–3 policy research/program assistants:* responsibilities include assisting with library research, fact checking, data entry, and supporting various programs; working on policy analysis and advocacy programs. Candidates should have ability to work with others, computer skills, knowledge of field, research skills, writing skills. Duration is 2–3 months. Unpaid. Open to college seniors, recent college graduates, graduate students, law students, career changers, individuals reentering the workforce. International applications accepted.
Benefits Opportunity to attend seminars/workshops, willing to complete paperwork for educational credit, willing to provide letters of recommendation.
Contact Write, fax, e-mail, or through World Wide Web site Leslie R. Wolfe, President. Fax: 202-296-8962. E-mail: cwps@ centerwomenpolicy.org. No phone calls. In-person interview recommended (telephone interview accepted). Applicants must submit a letter of interest, resume. Applications are accepted continuously. World Wide Web: http://www.centerwomenpolicy.org.

CHICAGO FOUNDATION FOR WOMEN
230 West Superior, Suite 400
Chicago, Illinois 60610-3536

General Information Foundation dedicated to increasing resources and opportunities for women and girls; the Foundation has awarded over $8 million to hundreds of programs serving women and girls in the greater Chicago area. Established in 1985. Number of employees: 17. Affiliate of Women's Funding Network, San Francisco, California. Number of internship applications received each year: 50.
Internships Available ▶ *1 Jessica Eve Patt intern:* responsibilities include assisting with special projects and administrative support in development department, interacting with leaders in women's philanthropic and social service advocacy community. Candidates should have computer skills, office skills, oral communication skills, organizational skills, personal interest in the field, strong interpersonal skills. Duration is 12–24 months. $10 per hour. Open to high school students, recent high school graduates, college freshmen, college sophomores, college juniors, college seniors, recent college graduates, graduate students, law students, career changers, individuals reentering the workforce. ▶ *1 communications intern:* responsibilities include assisting communications department with development of materials for large annual fund-raising event; conducting outreach and marketing around event. Candidates should have computer skills, oral communication skills, personal interest in the field, research skills, strong interpersonal skills, written communication skills. Duration is 4–5 months. $8–$10 per hour. Open to college freshmen, college sophomores, college juniors, college seniors, recent college graduates, graduate students, career changers, individuals reentering the workforce. ▶ *1 program/public policy intern:* responsibilities include providing administrative support to grant-making and technical assistance programs; research projects coordinated with grantee organiza-

tions and peers in philanthropic field. Candidates should have analytical skills, college courses in field, organizational skills, research skills, self-motivation, strong interpersonal skills. Duration is 3–5 months. $1000–$2000 per duration of internship. Open to recent college graduates, graduate students. ▶ *1 staff/development intern:* responsibilities include providing administrative support to development department; assisting with execution of special events. Candidates should have ability to work with others, computer skills, office skills. Duration is 4–12 months. $8–$10 per hour. Open to recent high school graduates, college freshmen, college sophomores, college juniors, college seniors, recent college graduates, career changers, individuals reentering the workforce. International applications accepted.
Benefits Names of contacts, opportunity to attend seminars/ workshops, possible full-time employment, travel reimbursement, willing to complete paperwork for educational credit, willing to provide letters of recommendation.
Contact Write, fax, or e-mail Erin Hustings, Internship Coordinator/ Executive Assistant to the Directors, 230 West Superior, Suite 400, Chicago, Illinois 60610-3636. Fax: 312-266-0990. E-mail: ehustings@ cfw.org. No phone calls. In-person interview required. Applicants must submit a letter of interest, resume. Applications are accepted continuously. World Wide Web: http://www.cfw.org.

CHILDREN NOW
1212 Broadway, 5th Floor
Oakland, California 94612

General Information Independent, nonpartisan research and action organization dedicated to improving children's lives.
Internships Available ▶ *1 Internet intern:* responsibilities include working with Internet coordinator to develop and implement a strategic marketing plan for organization's Web sites; developing outreach materials; helping to develop and promote collateral media opportunities at Web portals and related commercial Web sites; re-purpose and repairage content using Macromedia Dream Weaver and Adobe PhotoShop tools. Candidates should have ability to work independently, computer skills, organizational skills, writing skills, willingness to comply with established file-naming schemes; commitment to children's advocacy issues; experience with basic HTML. Duration is 10 weeks in summer (40 hours per week). $300 weekly stipend. ▶ *1 children and the media intern:* responsibilities include assisting in organization and coordination of events, briefings, and convenings; updating database; researching content for staff; assisting Internet coordinator in content development; writing letters to industry leaders, academics, and advocates; assisting department with mailings, proofreading, and reports. Candidates should have ability to work independently, computer skills, organizational skills, research skills, writing skills. Duration is 10 weeks in summer (40 hours per week). $300 weekly stipend. ▶ *1 nonprofit fund-raising intern:* responsibilities include researching and reporting on prospective sources of funding; participating in general department planning and fund-raising efforts. Candidates should have ability to work independently, computer skills, organizational skills, research skills, writing skills, interest in children's issues; desire to learn about non-profit fund-raising. Duration is 10 weeks in summer (40 hours per week). $300 weekly stipend. ▶ *1 policy intern I:* responsibilities include two main components: Child Indicators Project and Easy Care and Education Project; conducting on-line and library research and data collection about factors influencing child well-being; writing fact sheets and/or papers; developing advocacy tools for Children Now's family of Web sites. Candidates should have ability to work independently, computer skills, organizational skills, research skills, writing skills, strong background in college-level statistics or public health research; Microsoft Excel, attention to detail. Duration is 10 weeks in summer (40 hours per week). $300 weekly stipend. ▶ *1 policy intern II:* responsibilities include work focusing on the link between young children's medical care and their school readiness; on-line and library researching; writing annotated bibliographies, brief reports, and/or fact sheets; helping to coordinate an advisory committee; planning/developing statewide initiative; contributions to other projects, as needed. Candidates should have ability to work independently, computer skills, organizational skills, strong

skills in researching/writing about maternal and child health issues, preferably with experience in early childhood development. Duration is 10 weeks in summer (40 hours per week). $300 weekly stipend. Open to candidate enrolled in MPH, MPP, JD and other related masters-level programs (strongly preferred). ▶ *1–2 policy interns III:* responsibilities include work focusing on one of the following three projects: Access to Care for Undocumented Children, Health Policy and the 2002 Election, or Tax policy. Candidates should have ability to work independently, computer skills, organizational skills, research skills, writing skills. Duration is 10 weeks in summer (40 hours per week). $300 weekly stipend. Open to candidates enrolled in MPH, MPP, JD or other related masters-level programs (strongly preferred); undergraduate with coursework in public policy and/or health policy may also apply. **Contact** Write, fax, or e-mail Internship Coordinator. Fax: 510-763-1974. E-mail: ajones@childrennow.org. World Wide Web: http://www.childrennow.org.

CHILDREN'S DEFENSE FUND
25 E Street, NW
Washington, District of Columbia 20001

General Information Advocacy organization that exists to provide a strong voice for children; goals are achieved by educating the public about children's needs and encouraging preventive investment in children before they get sick, get into trouble, drop out of school, or suffer from family breakdown. Established in 1969. Number of employees: 110. Number of internship applications received each year: 450.
Internships Available ▶ *60–100 interns:* responsibilities include duties from general office tasks to extensive researching and writing. Candidates should have ability to work with others, computer skills, office skills, research skills, writing skills, flexibility. Duration is flexible. Unpaid. Open to high school students, recent high school graduates, college freshmen, college sophomores, college juniors, college seniors, recent college graduates, graduate students, law students, career changers, individuals reentering the workforce. International applications accepted.
Benefits On-the-job training, opportunity to attend seminars/workshops, possible full-time employment, travel reimbursement, willing to act as a professional reference, willing to complete paperwork for educational credit, willing to provide letters of recommendation.
Contact Write, call, fax, or e-mail Herman Piper, Internship Coordinator. Phone: 202-662-3797. Fax: 202-662-3570. E-mail: hpiper@childrensdefense.org. Telephone interview required. Applicants must submit a formal organization application, letter of interest, resume, three personal references. Applications are accepted continuously. World Wide Web: http://www.childrensdefense.org.

CITIZEN ADVOCACY CENTER
238 North York Road
Elmhurst, Illinois 60126

General Information Organization that educates citizens about civil tools to initiate actions to stimulate citizen awareness and involvement, monitor local government, help citizens on issues of public significance, and litigate on behalf of citizens to sustain access to justice. Established in 1994. Number of employees: 4. Number of internship applications received each year: 75.
Internships Available ▶ *4–10 interns:* responsibilities include writing articles and brochures, researching local government issues, attending meetings, facilitating community programs and grassroots activism. Candidates should have ability to work independently, ability to work with others, personal interest in the field, research skills, self-motivation, writing skills. Duration is 8–10 weeks. Unpaid. Open to high school students, recent high school graduates, college freshmen, college sophomores, college juniors, college seniors, recent college graduates, graduate students, law students, career changers, individuals reentering the workforce. International applications accepted.
Benefits On-the-job training, willing to act as a professional reference, willing to complete paperwork for educational credit, willing to provide letters of recommendation.

Contact Write, call, fax, or e-mail Ms. Terry Pastika, Community Lawyer, PO Box 420, Elmhurst, Illinois 60126. Phone: 630-833-4080. Fax: 630-833-4083. E-mail: tpastika@essential.org. In-person interview recommended (telephone interview accepted). Applicants must submit a letter of interest, resume. Application deadline: March 1 for summer; continuous for other positions. World Wide Web: http://www.citizenadvocacycenter.org.

CITIZENS AGAINST GOVERNMENT WASTE
1301 Connecticut Avenue, NW
Washington, District of Columbia 20036

General Information One million member private, nonpartisan, nonprofit organization dedicated to educating Americans about waste, fraud, and abuse in the federal government. Established in 1984. Number of employees: 16. Number of internship applications received each year: 60.
Internships Available ▶ *2 corporate development/membership interns:* responsibilities include providing support for fund-raising activities including helping research potential corporate and individual donors. Candidates should have ability to work independently, computer skills, oral communication skills, strong interpersonal skills, written communication skills. Duration is flexible. Unpaid. ▶ *1 finance/accounting intern:* responsibilities include aiding finance/human resources department in payroll and accounting issues. Candidates should have ability to work with others, computer skills, office skills, oral communication skills, organizational skills. Duration is flexible. Unpaid. ▶ *2 government affairs interns:* responsibilities include monitoring hearings, summarizing essential testimony and votes taken during committee meetings, tracking legislation, and attending hearings on the Hill. Candidates should have ability to work independently, computer skills, oral communication skills, strong interpersonal skills, written communication skills. Duration is flexible. Unpaid. ▶ *2 grassroots interns:* responsibilities include visiting Capitol Hill, attending coalition meetings, writing articles for bi-weekly grassroots newsletter, and keeping abreast of the current political agenda. Candidates should have ability to work independently, computer skills, oral communication skills, strong interpersonal skills, written communication skills. Duration is flexible. Unpaid. ▶ *1 health and science policy intern:* responsibilities include assisting director of health and science with research, trading legislation, writing regarding medicare, health savings accounts, prescription drugs and price controls. Candidates should have ability to work independently, computer skills, research skills, writing skills. Duration is flexible. Unpaid. ▶ *2 media interns:* responsibilities include assisting in answering press and public information requests, producing and distributing press releases, and maintaining media database. Candidates should have ability to work independently, computer skills, oral communication skills, research skills, writing skills. Duration is flexible. Unpaid. ▶ *2 research interns:* responsibilities include formulating policy papers and collecting data for original investigative studies, researching and writing for annual "Pig Book", "Prime Cuts", and special projects. Candidates should have ability to work independently, computer skills, oral communication skills, research skills, strong interpersonal skills, written communication skills. Duration is flexible. Unpaid. Open to college freshmen, college sophomores, college juniors, college seniors, recent college graduates. International applications accepted.
Benefits Names of contacts, opportunity to attend seminars/workshops, willing to act as a professional reference, willing to complete paperwork for educational credit, willing to provide letters of recommendation.
Contact Write, fax, or e-mail Kerrie N. Rezac, Intern Coordinator. Phone: 202-467-5300. Fax: 202-467-4253. E-mail: interns@cagw.org. Telephone interview required. Applicants must submit a letter of interest, resume, writing sample. Applications are accepted continuously. World Wide Web: http://www.cagw.org.

CITIZENS FOR A SOUND ECONOMY AND CSE FOUNDATION
1250 H Street, NW, Suite 700
Washington, District of Columbia 20005

General Information Organization working to educate and mobilize citizens to promote market-based solutions for public

Citizens for a Sound Economy and CSE Foundation (continued)

policy issues such as tax and budget policy, trade policy, and regulatory policy. Established in 1984. Number of employees: 40. Number of internship applications received each year: 200.
Internships Available ▶ *1 information technology intern:* responsibilities include assisting with lower-level support desk calls, computer repair and troubleshooting, and performing technical research. Candidates should have ability to work with others, computer skills, knowledge of field, personal interest in the field. Duration is flexible. Unpaid. Open to high school seniors, recent high school graduates, college freshmen, college sophomores, college juniors, college seniors. ▶ *1–3 internships with Jim Miller:* responsibilities include researching and drafting documents regarding economic growth, budget, and regulatory issues, as well as providing general administrative support. Candidates should have ability to work independently, office skills, research skills, self-motivation, writing skills. Duration is flexible. Unpaid. Open to college sophomores, college juniors, college seniors, recent college graduates. ▶ *1 public affairs intern:* responsibilities include assisting with press conferences, special events, op-ed and article placement, and event follow-up. Candidates should have oral communication skills, personal interest in the field, self-motivation, strong interpersonal skills, writing skills. Duration is flexible. Unpaid. Open to college freshmen, college sophomores, college juniors, college seniors. ▶ *1–2 research interns:* responsibilities include assisting with the researching, writing; and editing of organizational reports and publications. Candidates should have ability to work independently, editing skills, research skills, self-motivation, writing skills. Duration is flexible. Unpaid. Open to college sophomores, college juniors, college seniors. International applications accepted.
Benefits Opportunity to attend seminars/workshops, willing to complete paperwork for educational credit, willing to provide letters of recommendation.
Contact Write, call, fax, or e-mail Nicole Thompson, Intern Coordinator. Phone: 202-783-3870. Fax: 202-783-4687. E-mail: nthompson@cse.org. In-person interview recommended (telephone interview accepted). Applicants must submit a formal organization application, letter of interest, resume, writing sample, letter of recommendation. Applications are accepted continuously. World Wide Web: http://www.cse.org.

CITIZENS FOR TAX JUSTICE
1311 L Street, NW
Washington, District of Columbia 20005

General Information Research and advocacy organization. Established in 1979. Number of employees: 9. Number of internship applications received each year: 100.
Internships Available ▶ *2 research interns:* responsibilities include research, writing, representing organization at coalition meetings. Candidates should have ability to work independently, analytical skills, computer skills, editing skills, knowledge of field, office skills, oral communication skills, organizational skills, personal interest in the field, research skills, self-motivation, strong interpersonal skills, strong leadership ability, writing skills. Duration is 10 weeks during summer. $225 per week. Open to college freshmen, college sophomores, college juniors, college seniors, recent college graduates, (college sophomores and juniors preferred).
Benefits Opportunity to attend seminars/workshops, possible full-time employment, willing to act as a professional reference, willing to complete paperwork for educational credit, willing to provide letters of recommendation.
Contact Write, fax, e-mail, or through World Wide Web site Fiona Hsu, Intern Coordinator, 1311 L Street, NW, Washington, District of Columbia 20005. Fax: 202-638-3486. E-mail: fiona@ctj.org. No phone calls. Telephone interview required. Applicants must submit a letter of interest, resume, writing sample, three personal references. Application deadline: March 1. World Wide Web: http://www.ctj.org.

CITIZENS' NETWORK FOR FOREIGN AFFAIRS (CNFA)
1111 19th Street, NW, Suite 900
Washington, District of Columbia 20036

General Information Nonprofit, nonpartisan organization dedicated to stimulating international economic growth in developing and emerging world markets. Established in 1986. Number of employees: 17. Number of internship applications received each year: 500.
Internships Available ▶ *4–5 interns:* responsibilities include staff support and researching, attending, and reporting on meetings. Candidates should have ability to work independently, computer skills, knowledge of field, research skills, self-motivation, written communication skills. Duration is 5 months in spring, 4 months in fall, 3 months in summer. $1000 per month. Open to college juniors, college seniors, recent college graduates. International applications accepted.
Benefits Formal training, job counseling, names of contacts, on-the-job training, opportunity to attend seminars/workshops, possible full-time employment, willing to complete paperwork for educational credit, willing to provide letters of recommendation.
Contact Write, call, fax, e-mail, or through World Wide Web site Ms. Ashley Dopson, Internship Coordinator. Phone: 202-296-3920. Fax: 202-296-3948. E-mail: intern@cnfa.org. Applicants must submit a letter of interest, resume, writing sample, three letters of recommendation. Application deadline: April 1 for summer, July 1 for fall, November 1 for spring. World Wide Web: http://www.cnfa.org.

COMMON CAUSE
1250 Connecticut Avenue, NW
Washington, District of Columbia 20036

General Information Nonprofit, nonpartisan citizens' lobbying group working to promote honesty, accountability, and ethics in government. Established in 1970. Number of employees: 40. Number of internship applications received each year: 150.
Internships Available ▶ *1 Web/Internet Communications intern:* responsibilities include working the design and maintenance of the Common Cause web site, working on writing and sending CauseNet alerts. Candidates should have computer skills, editing skills, knowledge of field, research skills, writing skills. Unpaid. Open to high school seniors, recent high school graduates, college freshmen, college sophomores, college juniors, college seniors, recent college graduates. ▶ *3 campaign finance research intern:* responsibilities include helping staff collect and analyze reports of political contributions to candidates and political parties, and gathering research materials regarding PACs and other large political donors. Candidates should have ability to work independently, computer skills, knowledge of field, organizational skills, research skills, self-motivation. Unpaid. Open to high school seniors, college freshmen, college sophomores, college juniors, college seniors, recent college graduates, graduate students. ▶ *20–25 grassroots interns:* responsibilities include organizing grassroots effort, research, public relations, legislation. Candidates should have ability to work independently, oral communication skills, self-motivation, strong interpersonal skills, written communication skills. Unpaid. Open to high school students, recent high school graduates, college freshmen, college sophomores, college juniors, college seniors, recent college graduates, graduate students, law students. ▶ *1 issue mail intern:* responsibilities include issuing mail correspondence and assisting the governing board representative. Candidates should have ability to work independently, computer skills, editing skills, oral communication skills, writing skills. Unpaid. Open to college freshmen, college sophomores, college juniors, college seniors, recent college graduates, graduate students. ▶ *2–3 legislative policy interns:* responsibilities include assisting lobbying staff and researching issues development. Candidates should have analytical skills, computer skills, oral communication skills, organizational skills, strong interpersonal skills, written communication skills. Unpaid. Open to college freshmen, college sophomores, college juniors, college seniors, recent college graduates, graduate students, law students. ▶ *3 media communication interns:* responsibilities include assisting in producing, proofing,

and editing press releases; booking radio talk shows; answering requests for information. Candidates should have editing skills, oral communication skills, personal interest in the field, strong interpersonal skills. Unpaid. Open to college freshmen, college sophomores, college juniors, college seniors, recent college graduates, graduate students. ▶ *1 membership and fund-raising intern:* responsibilities include assisting membership/fund-raising staff. Candidates should have ability to work with others, office skills, oral communication skills, personal interest in the field. Unpaid. Open to college freshmen, college sophomores, college juniors, college seniors, recent college graduates, graduate students. ▶ *2 state issues interns:* responsibilities include assisting 43 state organizations and activists across the country in grassroots campaigns and legislative battles. Candidates should have ability to work independently, oral communication skills, research skills, strong interpersonal skills, written communication skills. Unpaid. Open to recent high school graduates, college freshmen, college sophomores, college juniors, college seniors. International applications accepted.

Benefits Job counseling, opportunity to attend seminars/workshops, willing to act as a professional reference, willing to complete paperwork for educational credit, willing to provide letters of recommendation, daily travel expenses paid.

Contact Write, call, fax, e-mail, or through World Wide Web site Laura Williams, Youth Outreach Coordinator. Phone: 202-833-1200. Fax: 202-659-3716. E-mail: lwill@commoncause.org. Applicants must submit a formal organization application, resume, writing sample. Applications are accepted continuously. World Wide Web: http://www.commoncause.org.

THE CONGRESSIONAL HUNGER CENTER
229½ Pennsylvania Avenue, SE
Washington, District of Columbia 20003

General Information National nonprofit organization that develops leaders in the fight against hunger. Established in 1993. Number of employees: 9. Number of internship applications received each year: 150.

Internships Available ▶ *20–24 Mickey Leland–Bill Emerson Hunger Fellows:* responsibilities include working at field site (6 months) and policy site (6 months) addressing hunger and poverty from a grassroots local and national policy level. Candidates should have ability to work with others, organizational skills, personal interest in the field, research skills, strong leadership ability, writing skills. Duration is 1 year beginning in August. $10,000 per year. Open to college freshmen, college sophomores, college juniors, college seniors, recent college graduates, graduate students, law students, career changers, individuals reentering the workforce. ▶ *10–12 Mickey Leland–Bill Emerson International Hunger Fellows:* responsibilities include working at field site (12 months) and policy site (12 months) addressing hunger and poverty from a grassroots local and national policy level. Candidates should have ability to work with others, experience in the field, oral communication skills, plan to pursue career in field, strong leadership ability, written communication skills. Duration is summer 2003 to summer 2005. Stipend of $1000 per month. Open to recent college graduates, graduate students, law students, career changers, (graduate students given preference). ▶ *Interns:* responsibilities include working on one of several projects, depending on the intern's interests. Duration is flexible. Position available as unpaid or paid. Open to individuals 18 years of age or older.

Benefits Formal training, free housing, health insurance, names of contacts, on-the-job training, opportunity to attend seminars/workshops, travel reimbursement, tuition assistance, willing to act as a professional reference, willing to provide letters of recommendation, stipend.

International Internships Available.

Contact Call, fax, e-mail, or through World Wide Web site John Kelley, Co-Director, 229½ Pennsylvania Avenue, SE, Washington, District of Columbia 20003. Phone: 202-547-7022 Ext. 16. Fax: 202-547-7575. E-mail: fellows@hungercenter.org. In-person interview required. Applicants must submit a formal organization application, resume, essay. Application deadline: January 31 for fellows program. World Wide Web: http://www.hungercenter.org.

CONSERVATION LAW FOUNDATION
62 Summer Street
Boston, Massachusetts 02110-1016

General Information Nonprofit regional environmental advocacy organization.

Internships Available ▶ *Environmental interns:* responsibilities include maintaining news clippings, helping staff with record keeping and occasional mailings, assisting advocates with library or Internet research in CLF project areas; additional positions possible in information systems and development and communications. Candidates should have computer proficiency is a plus. Duration is minimum of 3 months (10–14 hours per week). Unpaid. Open to college freshmen, college sophomores, college juniors, college seniors.

Contact Write, fax, or e-mail Lily Orr, Volunteer Coordinator. Fax: 617-350-4030. E-mail: lorr@clf.org. Applicants must submit a letter of interest, resume. Applications are accepted continuously. World Wide Web: http://www.clf.org.

THE CONSERVATIVE CAUCUS, INC.
450 Maple Avenue East, Suite 309
Vienna, Virginia 22180

General Information Organization dedicated to grassroots lobbying for conservative policies at the federal level. Established in 1974. Number of employees: 25. Number of internship applications received each year: 10.

Internships Available ▶ *1–2 interns:* responsibilities include researching government documents, helping set up press conferences, or working on petitions. Candidates should have ability to work independently, office skills, personal interest in the field, research skills, written communication skills. Duration is flexible. Unpaid. Open to high school students, recent high school graduates, college freshmen, college sophomores, college juniors, college seniors, recent college graduates, graduate students, law students, career changers, individuals reentering the workforce. International applications accepted.

Benefits Names of contacts, on-the-job training, opportunity to attend seminars/workshops, possible full-time employment, willing to complete paperwork for educational credit, willing to provide letters of recommendation.

Contact Write, fax, or e-mail Mr. Charles Orndorff, Administrative Vice Chairman. Fax: 703-281-4108. E-mail: corndorf@cais.com. Applicants must submit a formal organization application, resume, two personal references. Application deadline: March 15 for summer, July 15 for fall, October 15 for winter. World Wide Web: http://www.conservativeusa.org.

CONSUMER ENERGY COUNCIL OF AMERICA
2000 L Street, NW, Suite 802
Washington, District of Columbia 20036

General Information Research and policy organization that promotes consumer interests in policy issues, conducts research, and builds coalitions between public and private sectors; issues include utility industry restructuring, energy distribution in the developing world, telecommunications policy, and pricing policies. Established in 1973. Number of employees: 7. Number of internship applications received each year: 200.

Internships Available ▶ *2–4 research assistants:* responsibilities include researching policies, drafting letters, tracking legislation, reviewing literature, compiling and analyzing data, preparing tables and charts, editing, proofreading, assisting in drafting proposals, assisting in project development, and some general office work. Candidates should have ability to work independently, analytical skills, computer skills, editing skills, office skills, oral communication skills, organizational skills, research skills, self-motivation, strong interpersonal skills, strong leadership ability, writing skills. Duration is flexible (usually 3 months). Position available as unpaid or paid. Open to college sophomores, college juniors, college seniors, recent college graduates, graduate students. International applications accepted.

Benefits Job counseling, names of contacts, on-the-job training, opportunity to attend seminars/workshops, possible full-time employment, travel reimbursement, willing to act as a profes-

sional reference, willing to complete paperwork for educational credit, willing to provide letters of recommendation, stipends may be available based on project funding.
Contact Write, fax, e-mail, or through World Wide Web site Internship Coordinator. Phone: 202-659-0404. Fax: 202-659-0407. E-mail: outreach@cecarf.org. In-person interview recommended. Applicants must submit a letter of interest, resume, academic transcripts or GPA, 3 in-depth writing samples, 3 letters of recommendation from professors or employers. Applications are accepted continuously. World Wide Web: http://www.cecarf.org.

CONSUMER FEDERATION OF AMERICA
1424 16th Street, NW, Suite 604
Washington, District of Columbia 20036

General Information Nonprofit public interest organization seeking to advocate consumer interest in the areas of product safety, telecommunications, protection against consumer scams, advertising, insurance, real estate, banking, health care, and utility deregulation before Congress, federal regulatory agencies, and the courts. Established in 1967. Number of employees: 15. Number of internship applications received each year: 50.
Internships Available ▶ *2 general interns:* responsibilities include research, working on legislation, attending occasional coalition meetings and briefings on Capitol Hill, as well as working with regulatory agencies. Candidates should have ability to work independently, office skills, organizational skills, personal interest in the field, research skills, written communication skills. Duration is 1 semester. $25 weekly stipend for undergraduates working full-time, $50 weekly stipend for graduates and law students working full-time; salary negotiable. Open to college freshmen, college sophomores, college juniors, college seniors, recent college graduates, graduate students, law students. International applications accepted.
Benefits Names of contacts, opportunity to attend seminars/workshops, travel reimbursement, willing to act as a professional reference, willing to complete paperwork for educational credit, willing to provide letters of recommendation.
Contact Write, call, or through World Wide Web site Susan Peschin, Project Director. Phone: 202-387-6121. Fax: 202-265-7987. E-mail: speschin@consumerfed.org. Applicants must submit a letter of interest, resume, writing sample. Applications are accepted continuously. World Wide Web: http://www.consumerfed.org.

COUNCIL FOR A LIVABLE WORLD
110 Maryland Avenue, NE, Suite 409
Washington, District of Columbia 20002

General Information Organization founded by Leo Szilard and other pioneers of nuclear weapons to stop the nuclear arms race; has prepared an agenda for action advocating the reduction of danger posed by weapons of mass destruction, the strengthening and reform of multilateral conflict resolution and peacekeeping, and the revision of the military budget to meet current circumstances. Established in 1980. Number of employees: 18. Number of internship applications received each year: 90.
Internships Available ▶ *2 interns:* responsibilities include assisting with research, writing factsheets, networking at meetings, attending debates, and sharing daily administrative duties. Candidates should have ability to work independently, analytical skills, computer skills, editing skills, knowledge of field, office skills, personal interest in the field, self-motivation, written communication skills. Duration is 3–6 months. $1000 per month. Open to college sophomores, college juniors, college seniors, recent college graduates, graduate students, law students, career changers, individuals reentering the workforce. International applications accepted.
Benefits Job counseling, opportunity to attend seminars/workshops, travel reimbursement, willing to complete paperwork for educational credit, willing to provide letters of recommendation.
Contact Write, call, fax, e-mail, or through World Wide Web site Eva Blaszczynski, Intern Coordinator/Policy Analyst. Phone: 202-543-4100. Fax: 202-543-6297. E-mail: evab@clw.org. In-person interview recommended (telephone interview accepted). Applicants must submit a letter of interest, resume, writing sample, two letters of recommendation. Application deadline: March 15 for summer positions; continuous for other positions. World Wide Web: http://www.clw.org/clw/intern.html.

THE DEVELOPMENT GAP
927 15th Street, NW, Fourth Floor
Washington, District of Columbia 20005

General Information Organization that works for grassroots input into economic policymaking, and organizes opposition to imposition of economic policy from Washington. Established in 1977. Number of employees: 7. Number of internship applications received each year: 60.
Internships Available ▶ *4–8 interns:* responsibilities include conducting research and writing reports on the impact of World Bank/IMF programs; assisting with organizing events. Candidates should have experience in the field, oral communication skills, personal interest in the field, research skills, self-motivation, written communication skills. Duration is flexible. Unpaid. Open to recent college graduates, graduate students, career changers. International applications accepted.
Benefits Names of contacts, on-the-job training, opportunity to attend seminars/workshops, willing to act as a professional reference, willing to complete paperwork for educational credit, willing to provide letters of recommendation, reimbursement of local transportation expenses.
Contact Write or e-mail Karen Hansen-Kuhn, Internship Coordinator. E-mail: khk@developmentgap.org. Applicants must submit a letter of interest, resume, writing sample. Applications are accepted continuously. World Wide Web: http://www.developmentgap.org.

EQUALITY FLORIDA
1222 South Dale Mabry, #652
Tampa, Florida 33629

General Information State-wide education and advocacy organization that works to achieve social, political, and economic justice and is dedicated to ending discrimination based on sexual orientation, race, class, and gender. Established in 1997. Number of employees: 11. Number of internship applications received each year: 10.
Internships Available ▶ *1–2 communications interns:* responsibilities include drafting press releases, writing for newsletter, being included in Media Watch project which monitors and responds to bias and bigotry in press coverage. Candidates should have ability to work with others, computer skills, editing skills, research skills, writing skills, strong personal commitment to diversity and to advancing lesbian, gay, bisexual, and transgender rights. Duration is one semester and summer. Position available as unpaid or at $1300 per semester. Open to college freshmen, college sophomores, college juniors, college seniors, recent college graduates, graduate students, law students, career changers. ▶ *1–2 development interns:* responsibilities include working closely with the director of development on creating membership appeals and soliciting support from major donors. Candidates should have computer skills, organizational skills, strong leadership ability, written communication skills, strong personal commitment to diversity and advancing lesbian, gay, bisexual and transgender rights. Duration is one semester or summer. Position available as unpaid or at $1300 per semester. Open to college freshmen, college sophomores, college juniors, college seniors, recent college graduates, graduate students, law students, career changers. ▶ *1–2 field interns:* responsibilities include working on ongoing voter registration and identification efforts within Florida's LGBT community and will be especially involved in all electoral mobilization efforts. Candidates should have ability to work with others, oral communication skills, organizational skills, written communication skills, strong personal commitment to diversity and to advancing lesbian, gay, bisexual, and transgender rights. Duration is one semester and summer. Position available as unpaid or at $1300 per semester. Open to college freshmen, college sophomores, college juniors, college seniors, recent college graduates, graduate students, law students, career changers. ▶ *1–2 leadership develop-*

ment interns: responsibilities include working with director of operations to plan, implement, and conduct leadership conferences at the local community level and at the statewide level. Candidates should have computer skills, office skills, organizational skills, self-motivation, strong interpersonal skills, strong leadership ability. Duration is one semester or summer. Position available as unpaid or at $1300 per semester. Open to college freshmen, college sophomores, college juniors, college seniors, recent college graduates, graduate students, career changers. ▶ *1–2 legislative interns:* responsibilities include assignment in Tallahassee and working in lobbying and legislative research. Candidates should have analytical skills, oral communication skills, research skills, written communication skills, strong personal commitment to diversity and to advancing lesbian, gay, transgender, and bisexual rights. Duration is one semester or summer. Position available as unpaid or at $1300 per semester. Open to college freshmen, college sophomores, college juniors, college seniors, recent college graduates, graduate students, law students, career changers. ▶ *1–2 operations (infrastructure/human resources) interns:* responsibilities include working with director of operations to organize and coordinate all project management, accounting, legal, computer systems, physical site (office), and human resources needs. Candidates should have computer skills, office skills, organizational skills, self-motivation, strong interpersonal skills, writing skills. Duration is one semester or summer. Position available as unpaid or at $1300 per semester. Open to college freshmen, college sophomores, college juniors, college seniors, recent college graduates, graduate students, career changers. International applications accepted.

Benefits Names of contacts, on-the-job training, opportunity to attend seminars/workshops, willing to act as a professional reference, willing to complete paperwork for educational credit, willing to provide letters of recommendation.

Contact Write, call, fax, e-mail, or through World Wide Web site Ted Howard, Director of Operations. Phone: 813-870-3735 Ext. 206. Fax: 813-870-1499. E-mail: ted@eqfl.org. In-person interview recommended (telephone interview accepted). Applicants must submit a formal organization application, letter of interest, resume, three personal references, two letters of recommendation. Applications are accepted continuously. World Wide Web: http://www.eqfl.org.

EQUAL JUSTICE USA/QUIXOTE CENTER
3502 Varnum Street
Brentwood, Maryland 20722

General Information Grassroots campaign for human rights in the U.S. legal system; sponsors Moratorium Now! campaign that mobilizes support nationwide for an immediate halt to executions. Established in 1990. Number of employees: 5. Number of internship applications received each year: 5.

Internships Available ▶ *1–3 fund-raising interns:* responsibilities include assisting development coordinator; writing thank you cards; assisting with mailings; organizing house parties; assisting grants writer; organizing major donor information. Candidates should have ability to work independently, ability to work with others, computer skills, oral communication skills, self-motivation, writing skills. Duration is flexible. Position available as unpaid or paid. ▶ *1–3 general office interns:* responsibilities include general office help; fulfilling information requests; special projects; assisting with mailings (writings, editing and/or stuffing); maintaining media contacts list; organizing filing system. Candidates should have computer skills, office skills, oral communication skills, organizational skills, self-motivation, strong interpersonal skills. Duration is flexible. Position available as unpaid or paid. ▶ *1–3 grassroots organizing intern:* responsibilities include recruiting groups to pass moratorium resolutions; making follow-up calls and e-mails to activists; developing strategies to reach new groups; assisting with collecting stories for newsletters. Candidates should have ability to work independently, ability to work with others, computer skills, oral communication skills, self-motivation, written communication skills. Duration is flexible. Position available as unpaid or paid. Open to high school students, recent high school graduates, college freshmen, college sophomores, college juniors, col-

lege seniors, recent college graduates, graduate students, law students, career changers, individuals reentering the workforce. International applications accepted.

Benefits Names of contacts, on-the-job training, opportunity to attend seminars/workshops, willing to act as a professional reference, willing to complete paperwork for educational credit, willing to provide letters of recommendation.

Contact Call, fax, e-mail, or through World Wide Web site Trisha Kendall, Organizer, PO Box 5206, Hyattsville, Maryland 20782. Phone: 301-699-0042. Fax: 301-864-2182. E-mail: trishak@quixote.org. In-person interview recommended (telephone interview accepted). Applicants must submit a letter of interest, resume, writing sample. Applications are accepted continuously. World Wide Web: http://www.quixote.org/ej.

FAMILIES U.S.A. FOUNDATION
1334 G Street, NW, 3rd Floor
Washington, District of Columbia 20005

General Information National health-care consumer advocacy organization engaged in the fight for affordable health and long-term care for all American families, in areas including policy research, field organizing, lobbying, and media operations. Established in 1982. Number of employees: 30. Number of internship applications received each year: 300.

Internships Available ▶ *1 field organizing intern:* responsibilities include working with more than 200 state and local organizations that are involved in consumer health issues, helping provide a wide array of technical assistance on issues such as Medicaid and managed care, using innovative on-line and teleconferencing techniques to communicate with these groups. Candidates should have ability to work independently, oral communication skills, organizational skills, personal interest in the field, self-motivation, written communication skills. Duration is one semester (possibly longer if internship successful). $6.15 per hour. Open to college juniors, college seniors, recent college graduates, graduate students, law students, individuals reentering the workforce. ▶ *2 health policy interns:* responsibilities include engaging in health policy research on issues such as consumer protections in managed care, the devolution of federal health programs such as Medicare and Medicaid, access and affordability issues, and analysis of federal and state health-care legislation. Candidates should have ability to work independently, editing skills, personal interest in the field, research skills, self-motivation, written communication skills. Duration is one semester (possibly longer if internship successful). $6.15 per hour. Open to college seniors, recent college graduates, graduate students. ▶ *2 media interns:* responsibilities include contacting media, interviewing individuals with health-care stories, helping with media events, and monitoring media. Candidates should have ability to work independently, oral communication skills, organizational skills, personal interest in the field, strong interpersonal skills, written communication skills. Duration is one semester (possibly longer if internship successful). $6.15 per hour. Open to college sophomores, college juniors, college seniors, recent college graduates, career changers, individuals reentering the workforce. International applications accepted.

Benefits On-the-job training, opportunity to attend seminars/workshops, willing to act as a professional reference, willing to complete paperwork for educational credit, willing to provide letters of recommendation.

Contact Write, fax, e-mail, or through World Wide Web site Internship Program Coordinator. Fax: 202-347-2417. E-mail: intern@familiesusa.org. No phone calls. Telephone interview required. Applicants must submit a letter of interest, resume, writing sample (2-3 pages). Application deadline: March 15 for summer, July 15 for fall, December 1 for winter/spring. World Wide Web: http://www.familiesusa.org.

FARM SANCTUARY–WEST
19080 Newville Road
Orland, California 95963

General Information National nonprofit organization dedicated to ending animal agricultural abuses through public education programs, legislation, farm animal cruelty investigations and campaigns, in addition to providing shelters for rescuing,

Farm Sanctuary–West (continued)

rehabilitating, and providing permanent care for hundreds of animals. Established in 1993. Number of employees: 6. Branch of Farm Sanctuary, Watkins Glen, New York. Number of internship applications received each year: 200.

Internships Available ▶ *4 interns:* responsibilities include farm chores/barn cleaning, and conducting educational tours. Candidates should have ability to work with others, personal interest in the field, self-motivation, commitment to vegetarianism. Duration is 1–3 months. Unpaid. Open to high school students, recent high school graduates, college freshmen, college sophomores, college juniors, college seniors, recent college graduates, graduate students, law students, career changers, individuals reentering the workforce. International applications accepted.

Benefits Free housing, job counseling, names of contacts, possible full-time employment, willing to complete paperwork for educational credit, willing to provide letters of recommendation.

Contact Write, call, fax, e-mail, or through World Wide Web site Michelle Waffner, Education Coordinator, PO Box 150, Watkins Glen, New York 14891. Phone: 607-583-4512. Fax: 607-583-4349. E-mail: education@farmsanctuary.org. Telephone interview required. Applicants must submit a formal organization application, two letters of recommendation. Applications are accepted continuously. World Wide Web: http://www.farmsanctuary.org.

FEDERATION FOR AMERICAN IMMIGRATION REFORM (FAIR)
1666 Connecticut Avenue, NW, Suite 400
Washington, District of Columbia 20009

General Information Nonprofit public education organization. Established in 1979. Number of employees: 25. Number of internship applications received each year: 100.

Internships Available ▶ *Web site development intern:* responsibilities include reporting to director of special projects and working with Webmaster; helping to develop e-mail database into an automated information system designed to inform an interested public on immigration issues and to identify activists; may also work on Web site redesign and updating. Candidates should have self-motivation, word processing and database program experience, experience with Internet searches and e-mail communications desirable; HTML knowledge would be an asset. Duration is 3-months (at least 32 hours per week). $8 per hour. ▶ *1 government relations intern:* responsibilities include tracking and analyzing legislation; conducting research; distributing information to Hill staff; assisting with Hill mailings; attending, taking notes, and reporting on Hill committee hearings; filing, faxing, and some general office duties. Candidates should have ability to work independently, knowledge of field, oral communication skills, personal interest in the field, self-motivation, written communication skills, MS Word experience, familiarity and comfort with goals of organization. Duration is 12-16 weeks (flexible full-time hours); position generally available year-round. $8 per hour. Open to college sophomores, college juniors, college seniors, recent college graduates, graduate students, law students. ▶ *1 law intern:* responsibilities include heavy research, primarily in the areas of immigration law, constitutional law, and administrative law; writing briefs, editing, and cite checking law review articles. Candidates should have ability to work independently, analytical skills, college courses in field, organizational skills, research skills, written communication skills, student status in a JD program, demonstrated or strong interest in helping citizens fight illegal immigration and control mass immigration. Duration is 12-16 weeks during summer. Minimum $10 per hour depending on experience. Open to law students. ▶ *1 media relations intern:* responsibilities include updating the media database, scheduling radio shows, faxing background material to television, radio, and print press; maintaining the video library, attending and helping plan press conferences, filing and writing articles for the newsletter. Candidates should have ability to work independently, computer skills, organizational skills, personal interest in the field, self-motivation, written communication skills, familiarity and comfort with goals of organization. Duration is usually a 6-month position but can be flexible. $8 per hour. Open to college freshmen, college sophomores, college juniors, college seniors, recent college graduates, graduate students,

law students. ▶ *1 membership development/fund-raising intern:* responsibilities include coordination and production of 6-month appreciation gift mailings, assisting with round table meeting planning, drafting articles for the monthly newsletter, assisting with major donor mailings, and foundation research. Candidates should have ability to work independently, office skills, organizational skills, plan to pursue career in field, self-motivation, written communication skills, Internet experience, MS Word. Duration is 12-16 weeks (flexible full-time hours). $8 per hour. Open to recent high school graduates, college freshmen, college sophomores, college juniors, college seniors, recent college graduates. International applications accepted.

Benefits Job counseling, on-the-job training, opportunity to attend seminars/workshops, possible full-time employment, travel reimbursement, willing to act as a professional reference, willing to complete paperwork for educational credit, willing to provide letters of recommendation.

Contact Write, fax, e-mail, or through World Wide Web site Intern Coordinator. Fax: 202-387-3447. E-mail: jobs@fairus.org. In-person interview recommended (telephone interview accepted). Applicants must submit a letter of interest, resume, writing sample, 2–3 personal references, academic transcripts (helpful). Application deadline: April 30 for summer, July 1 for fall; continuous for winter/spring positions. World Wide Web: http://www.fairus.org.

FEDERATION OF AMERICAN SCIENTISTS
1717 K Street NW, Suite 209
Washington, District of Columbia 20036

General Information Nonprofit, privately funded organization engaged in analysis and advocacy on the consequences of science and technology on public policy. Established in 1945. Number of employees: 16. Number of internship applications received each year: 150.

Internships Available ▶ *Interns:* responsibilities include assisting project director with various projects of intern's choice and some administrative work; consult Web site for more information. Candidates should have ability to work independently, computer skills, knowledge of field, oral communication skills, research skills, strong interpersonal skills. Duration is flexible. Position available as unpaid or paid. Open to high school seniors, recent high school graduates, college freshmen, college sophomores, college juniors, college seniors, recent college graduates, graduate students, law students, career changers. International applications accepted.

Benefits On-the-job training, opportunity to attend seminars/workshops, willing to act as a professional reference, willing to complete paperwork for educational credit, willing to provide letters of recommendation, stipend depending on hours per week worked and funding availability.

Contact Write, fax, or e-mail Karen Kelley, Organization Manager, 1717 K Street NW, Suite 209, Washington, District of Columbia 20036. Fax: 202-675-1010. E-mail: fas@fas.org. No phone calls. In-person interview required. Applicants must submit a letter of interest, resume, writing sample, personal reference, three personal references. Applications are accepted continuously. World Wide Web: http://www.fas.org.

FELLOWSHIP OF RECONCILIATION
PO Box 271
Nyack, New York 10960

General Information National interfaith peace and justice organization committed to active nonviolence as a means of personal, and social change. Established in 1915. Number of employees: 27. Number of internship applications received each year: 50.

Internships Available ▶ *1 disarmament and racial economic justice intern:* responsibilities include helping staff person coordinate/ facilitate workshops, assisting with outreach, and helping with special events and media coverage. Candidates should have ability to work independently, ability to work with others, computer skills, experience in the field, oral communication skills, organizational skills. Duration is September to August 15. $650 per month. Open to individuals 21 and over. ▶ *1 international issues intern:* responsibilities include working with a staff person

on organizing national campaigns and promoting local support for other national efforts. Candidates should have ability to work independently, computer skills, knowledge of field, organizational skills, self-motivation, written communication skills. Duration is September to August 15. $650 per month. Open to individuals 21 and over. ▶ *1 local group organizing intern:* responsibilities include working with FOR's network of 80 local groups and affiliates, helping in the formation of new groups, preparing informational mailing and resources, organizing gatherings, helping plan nationwide Stop the Violence vigils, and carrying out other projects to strengthen local FOR organizing. Candidates should have computer skills, office skills, organizational skills, self-motivation, strong interpersonal skills, written communication skills. Duration is September to August 15. $650 per month. Open to individuals age 21 and over. ▶ *1 nonviolence training intern:* responsibilities include assisting training coordinator in providing training and support for trainers; working with an FOR task force; updating and publishing FOR Trainers Directory; organizing training events and facilitating workshops; revising curriculum. Candidates should have computer skills, office skills, oral communication skills, organizational skills, self-motivation, strong interpersonal skills. Duration is September to August 15. $650 per month. Open to individuals 21 and over. ▶ *1 publications intern:* responsibilities include working with staff of "Fellowship" (oldest continuously published peace journal in the U.S.), developing essentials in publications, engaging in media outreach for FOR program, maintaining and updating media list and press packet, sending press releases, assisting with Web page, keyboarding, proofreading, handling correspondence, and conducting research. Candidates should have ability to work independently, computer skills, editing skills, experience in the field, research skills, writing skills. Duration is September to August 15. $650 per month. Open to individuals 21 and over.
Benefits Free housing, health insurance, on-the-job training, opportunity to attend seminars/workshops, willing to act as a professional reference, willing to complete paperwork for educational credit, willing to provide letters of recommendation, 4 weeks vacation and paid holidays.
Contact Write, call, fax, e-mail, or through World Wide Web site Yvonne Royster, Administrative Assistant. Phone: 845-358-4601. Fax: 845-358-4924. E-mail: for@forusa.org. Telephone interview required. Applicants must submit a formal organization application, resume, personal reference, three personal references. Application deadline: March 31. World Wide Web: http://www.forusa.org.

FEMINIST MAJORITY AND FEMINIST MAJORITY FOUNDATION (CALIFORNIA OFFICE)
8105 West Third Street
Los Angeles, California 90048

General Information Nonprofit research and advocacy organizations dedicated to promoting equality for women. Established in 1987. Number of employees: 20. Number of internship applications received each year: 300.
Internships Available ▶ *5–10 interns:* responsibilities include researching, writing, analyzing policy, organizing demonstrations and pro-choice rock-and-roll concerts, and clinic defense. Candidates should have ability to work independently, ability to work with others, knowledge of field, self-motivation, strong leadership ability, written communication skills. Duration is 2 months minimum. Unpaid. Open to college freshmen, college sophomores, college juniors, college seniors, recent college graduates, graduate students, law students.
Benefits Job counseling, names of contacts, on-the-job training, possible full-time employment, willing to act as a professional reference, willing to complete paperwork for educational credit, willing to provide letters of recommendation.
Contact Write, call, fax, e-mail, or through World Wide Web site Diana Garcia, Internship Coordinator. Phone: 323-651-0495. Fax: 323-653-2689. E-mail: dgarcia@feminist.org. Applicants must submit a letter of interest, resume, writing sample, two personal references, two letters of recommendation, telephone or in-person interview for finalists. Applications are accepted continuously. World Wide Web: http://www.feminist.org.

FEMINIST MAJORITY AND FEMINIST MAJORITY FOUNDATION (VIRGINIA OFFICE)
1600 Wilson Boulevard, Suite 801
Arlington, Virginia 22209

General Information Nonprofit research and advocacy organization dedicated to promoting equality for women. Established in 1987. Number of employees: 30. Number of internship applications received each year: 150.
Internships Available ▶ *4–10 interns:* responsibilities include monitoring press conferences and congressional hearings; researching, writing, and analyzing policy; organizing demonstrations; constructing and updating Web site; advocacy on women's rights violations outside of the U.S. Candidates should have ability to work independently, ability to work with others, oral communication skills, self-motivation, written communication skills. Duration is minimum of 2 months. Stipend of $80 per week. Open to college freshmen, college sophomores, college juniors, college seniors. International applications accepted.
Benefits Names of contacts, willing to complete paperwork for educational credit, willing to provide letters of recommendation, computer training provided.
Contact Write, call, e-mail, or through World Wide Web site Sirena Riley, Coordinator, Campus Program. Phone: 703-522-2214. Fax: 703-522-2219. E-mail: sriley@feminist.org. Telephone interview required. Applicants must submit a letter of interest, resume, writing sample, two personal references. Applications are accepted continuously. World Wide Web: http://www.feminist.org.

FIGHT CRIME: INVEST IN KIDS
2000 P Street, NW, Suite 240
Washington, District of Columbia 20036

General Information Nonprofit, bipartisan anti-crime and child advocacy organization led by police chiefs, sheriffs, prosecutors and victims of violence. Established in 1996. Number of employees: 20. Number of internship applications received each year: 50.
Internships Available ▶ *1–3 interns:* responsibilities include possible positions in media, federal policy, state policy, outreach, and research; please see Web site for openings. Candidates should have ability to work with others, knowledge of field, oral communication skills, personal interest in the field, written communication skills. Duration is flexible (usually semester). $125 per week. Open to college freshmen, college sophomores, college juniors, college seniors. International applications accepted.
Benefits Willing to act as a professional reference, willing to complete paperwork for educational credit, willing to provide letters of recommendation, opportunity to attend events on Capitol Hill.
Contact Write, fax, or e-mail Intern Coordinator, 2000 P Street, NW Suite 240, Washington 20036. Fax: 202-776-0110. E-mail: info@fightcrime.org. No phone calls. Telephone interview required. Applicants must submit a letter of interest, resume, writing sample. Application deadline: March 15 for summer, August 1 for fall, November 15 for winter/spring. World Wide Web: http://www.fightcrime.org.

FIRST CHANCE/ Y-CHOW, INC.
1800 Western Avenue, Suite 104
San Bernardino, California 92411

General Information Nonprofit prevention/outreach education organization. Established in 1988. Number of employees: 5. Number of internship applications received each year: 2.
Internships Available ▶ *1–5 community health outreach workers:* responsibilities include outreach education in traditional and nontraditional settings, group presentations, documentation, general office and reception duties, meeting attendance and participation. Candidates should have ability to work independently, oral communication skills, personal interest in the field, self-motivation, strong interpersonal skills, written communication skills. Duration is flexible. Unpaid. Open to college freshmen, college sophomores, college juniors, college seniors, recent college graduates, graduate students, law students, career changers, individuals reentering the workforce. ▶ *1–5 youth-to-youth com-*

First Chance/ Y-CHOW, Inc. (continued)
munity health outreach workers: responsibilities include outreach education of peers, group presentations, documentation, general office skills, and special event participation (training provided). Candidates should have ability to work independently, oral communication skills, personal interest in the field, self-motivation, strong interpersonal skills. Duration is flexible. Unpaid. Open to high school students, recent high school graduates, college freshmen, college sophomores, college juniors, college seniors, recent college graduates, individuals aged 12-24 years.
Benefits On-the-job training, willing to act as a professional reference, willing to complete paperwork for educational credit, willing to provide letters of recommendation.
Contact Write or e-mail Faith Bolton, Programs Administrator, 466 Orange Street, #338, Redlands 92374. Fax: 909-473-0881. E-mail: ychows@gte.net. No phone calls. In-person interview required. Applicants must submit a resume, writing sample. Applications are accepted continuously.

FRIENDS COMMITTEE ON NATIONAL LEGISLATION
245 Second Street, NE
Washington, District of Columbia 20002

General Information Lobbying organization guided by Quaker religious beliefs that attempts to bring spiritual values to public policy decisions. Established in 1943. Number of employees: 22. Number of internship applications received each year: 30.
Internships Available ▶ *3 legislative interns:* responsibilities include attending coalition meetings, answering constituent phone calls and letters, contributing to FCNL's newsletter, writing issue papers, drafting documents and letters for legislative advocacy, preparing FCNL's weekly legislative action message, and performing general administrative work. Candidates should have ability to work independently, analytical skills, computer skills, editing skills, office skills, oral communication skills, organizational skills, personal interest in the field, research skills, self-motivation, strong interpersonal skills, writing skills. Duration is 11 months. $1100 per month. Open to recent college graduates, graduate students, law students. International applications accepted.
Benefits Health insurance, on-the-job training, opportunity to attend seminars/workshops, possible full-time employment, willing to act as a professional reference, willing to complete paperwork for educational credit, willing to provide letters of recommendation.
Contact Write, fax, e-mail, or through World Wide Web site Internship Coordinator. Fax: 202-547-6019. E-mail: fcnl@fcnl.org. No phone calls. Telephone interview required. Applicants must submit a formal organization application, academic transcripts, four personal references. Application deadline: applicants for September through July position must apply between January 1 and March 1. World Wide Web: http://www.fcnl.org.

FRIENDS FOR A NON-VIOLENT WORLD
1050 Selby Avenue
St. Paul, Minnesota 55104

General Information Organization that provides education about non-violence and peacemaking. Established in 1981. Number of employees: 3. Number of internship applications received each year: 15.
Internships Available ▶ *2 summer peace interns:* responsibilities include coordinating one major project such as organizing our week-long summer camp; office work; participation in study group. Candidates should have knowledge of field, office skills, organizational skills, self-motivation, strong interpersonal skills, passion for non-violence. Duration is June 15-August 30. $1575 per duration of internship. Open to college freshmen, college sophomores, college juniors, college seniors, recent college graduates, graduate students, law students, career changers, individuals reentering the workforce.
Benefits Formal training, on-the-job training, opportunity to attend seminars/workshops, willing to act as a professional reference, willing to complete paperwork for educational credit, willing to provide letters of recommendation, support from mentors.

Contact Write, call, fax, e-mail, or through World Wide Web site Executive Director, 1050 Selby Avenue, St. Paul, Minnesota 55104. Phone: 651-917-0383. Fax: 651-917-0379. E-mail: info@fnvw.org. In-person interview recommended (telephone interview accepted). Applicants must submit a letter of interest, resume, three personal references. Application deadline: April 1 for summer; continuous for fall/spring. World Wide Web: http://www.fnvw.org.

FRIENDS OF THE THIRD WORLD
611 West Wayne Street
Fort Wayne, Indiana 46802-2167

General Information Organization that advocates nonviolent voluntary action against the root causes of poverty. Established in 1972. Number of employees: 3.
Internships Available ▶ *1–2 event organizers:* responsibilities include editing and writing; media work, supervision of other local volunteers; contacting for recruitment and contributions; events including student workday, World Food Day event, and international festival. Candidates should have ability to work independently, oral communication skills, self-motivation, strong interpersonal skills, written communication skills. Duration is 6–12 months. Unpaid. Open to high school seniors, recent high school graduates, college freshmen, college sophomores, college juniors, college seniors, recent college graduates, graduate students, law students, career changers, individuals reentering the workforce. ▶ *1–2 graphic artist editor/printers:* responsibilities include working with unskilled trainees and community volunteers to produce newsletters, catalogs, and event materials. Candidates should have computer skills, self-motivation, strong interpersonal skills, writing skills, artistic ability. Duration is 6 months to 2 years. Unpaid. Open to college sophomores, college juniors, college seniors, recent college graduates, graduate students, law students, career changers, individuals reentering the workforce. ▶ *1–2 handicraft marketing interns:* responsibilities include communicating with low-income producers of handmade crafts, writing and presenting information, developing and implementing marketing displays. Candidates should have ability to work independently, oral communication skills, personal interest in the field, written communication skills. Duration is 2 months to 2 years. Unpaid. Open to high school students, recent high school graduates, college freshmen, college sophomores, college juniors, college seniors, recent college graduates, graduate students, law students, career changers, individuals reentering the workforce. International applications accepted.
Benefits On-the-job training, opportunity to attend seminars/workshops, willing to act as a professional reference, willing to complete paperwork for educational credit, willing to provide letters of recommendation, free housing and meals and small stipend with commitment of at least 3 months; possibility of student loan deferment.
Contact Marian Waltz, Volunteer Coordinator. Phone: 260-422-6821. Fax: 260-422-1650. E-mail: fotw@igc.org. Telephone interview required. Applicants must submit a formal organization application, personal reference. Applications are accepted continuously. World Wide Web: http://www.friendsofthethirdworld.org.

GAY AND LESBIAN VICTORY FUND
1705 DeSales Street, NW, Suite 500
Washington, District of Columbia 20036

General Information National donor network committed to electing qualified, openly gay and lesbian candidates to public office. Established in 1991. Number of employees: 15. Number of internship applications received each year: 40.
Internships Available ▶ *3 interns:* responsibilities include duties coincident with interest and experience of intern; positions available in the areas of media relations, fund-raising, campaign management, and research. Candidates should have ability to work independently, ability to work with others, computer skills, oral communication skills, organizational skills, personal interest in the field, self-motivation, written communication skills. Duration is flexible. Position available as unpaid or at $400–$800 per month. Open to college sophomores, college juniors, college seniors, recent college graduates, graduate students, law students, career changers, individuals reentering the workforce.

Benefits Job counseling, names of contacts, possible full-time employment, willing to act as a professional reference, willing to complete paperwork for educational credit, willing to provide letters of recommendation, networking opportunities, stipend.
Contact Write, call, fax, e-mail, or through World Wide Web site Meghan Duffy, Intern Coordinator, 1705 DeSales Street NW, Suite 500, Washington, District of Columbia 20036. Phone: 202-842-8679. Fax: 202-289-3863. E-mail: mduffy@victoryfund.org. In-person interview recommended (telephone interview accepted). Applicants must submit a formal organization application, letter of interest, resume, two personal references, application can be downloaded through Web site. World Wide Web: http://www.victoryfund.org.

GLOBAL EXCHANGE
2017 Mission Street, Room 303
San Francisco, California 94110

General Information Nonprofit research, education, action center devoted to international human rights. Established in 1988. Number of employees: 45. Number of internship applications received each year: 400.
Internships Available ▶ *2 alternative trade interns:* responsibilities include overseeing craft booth at Bay Area fairs and festivals, and researching and writing materials about country conditions and alternative trade. Candidates should have ability to work independently, oral communication skills, personal interest in the field, self-motivation, strong interpersonal skills. Duration is 4–12 weeks. Unpaid. Open to college freshmen, college sophomores, college juniors, college seniors, recent college graduates, career changers. ▶ *4 campaign program interns:* responsibilities include organizing and promoting campaign to end Cold War against Cuba and campaign to promote peace in Mexico. Candidates should have ability to work independently, analytical skills, editing skills, organizational skills, research skills, self-motivation, strong leadership ability, writing skills. Duration is 4–12 weeks. Unpaid. Open to college seniors, recent college graduates, graduate students. ▶ *1–2 fund-raising interns:* responsibilities include researching private and corporate foundations, developing ways to reach new members, and cultivating existing members. Candidates should have computer skills, office skills, oral communication skills, organizational skills, personal interest in the field, research skills, self-motivation, writing skills. Duration is 8–12 weeks. Unpaid. Open to college freshmen, college sophomores, college juniors, college seniors, recent college graduates, graduate students. ▶ *4 human rights interns:* responsibilities include organizing around the issues of human rights, corporate accountability, and the global economy. Candidates should have ability to work independently, analytical skills, organizational skills, personal interest in the field, plan to pursue career in field, research skills, self-motivation, strong interpersonal skills, strong leadership ability, written communication skills. Duration is 8–12 weeks. Unpaid. Open to recent college graduates, graduate students, law students. ▶ *2 media interns:* responsibilities include writing and distributing promotional articles on the work of Global Exchange, developing media contacts, developing and distributing promotional materials for Global Exchange Speakers Bureau. Candidates should have computer skills, editing skills, oral communication skills, research skills, strong interpersonal skills, writing skills. Duration is 8–10 weeks. Unpaid. Open to college juniors, college seniors, recent college graduates, graduate students, career changers. ▶ *2–10 reality tours interns:* responsibilities include developing information packets about areas to be visited (Cuba, Mexico, Central America), inputting data, producing flyers, answering phones, typing, and mailing. Candidates should have computer skills, office skills, oral communication skills, organizational skills, research skills, writing skills. Duration is 1–6 months. Unpaid. Open to college sophomores, college juniors, recent college graduates. ▶ *2 research interns:* responsibilities include researching role of global corporations and economic institutions such as WTO, World Bank, and IMF in the global economy; researching and writing about GMO's, high tech industries, and China in the global economy. Candidates should have analytical skills, computer skills, office skills, research skills, self-motivation, writing skills.

Duration is 4–12 weeks. Unpaid. Open to college seniors, recent college graduates, graduate students. International applications accepted.
Benefits Names of contacts, on-the-job training, opportunity to attend seminars/workshops, willing to act as a professional reference, willing to complete paperwork for educational credit, willing to provide letters of recommendation.
International Internships Available in San Cristobal de las Casas, Mexico.
Contact Write, call, e-mail, or through World Wide Web site Fred Braley, Intern Coordinator. Phone: 415-255-7296 Ext. 227. E-mail: fred@globalexchange.org. Telephone interview required. Applicants must submit a formal organization application, letter of interest, resume, academic transcripts, two letters of recommendation. Application deadline: April 1 for summer positions; continuous for other positions. World Wide Web: http://www.globalexchange.org.

HADASSAH, THE WOMEN'S ZIONIST ORGANIZATION
5100 Wisconsin Avenue, NW, Suite 250
Washington, District of Columbia 20016

General Information Political lobbying organization that promotes women's rights and the security of Israel. Established in 1912. Number of employees: 3. Branch of Hadassah Zionist Women's Organization of America, New York, New York. Number of internship applications received each year: 15.
Internships Available ▶ *1–4 interns:* responsibilities include representing Hadassah at Coalition meetings, congressional hearings, and events; reporting in writing to Hadassah staff about events attended. Candidates should have ability to work independently, ability to work with others, knowledge of field, oral communication skills, personal interest in the field, writing skills. Duration is summer or school semester(s). Unpaid. Open to recent high school graduates, college freshmen, college sophomores, college juniors, college seniors.
Benefits Job counseling, names of contacts, opportunity to attend seminars/workshops, possible full-time employment, travel reimbursement, willing to act as a professional reference, willing to complete paperwork for educational credit, willing to provide letters of recommendation.
International Internships Available in Jerusalem, Israel.
Contact Write, fax, or e-mail Marla Gilson, Director. Phone: 202-363-4600. Fax: 202-363-4651. E-mail: mgilson@hadassah.org. In-person interview recommended (telephone interview accepted). Applicants must submit a letter of interest, resume, writing sample. Applications are accepted continuously. World Wide Web: http://www.hadassah.org.

HEARTS AND MINDS NETWORK
3074 Broadway
New York, New York 10027

General Information Nonprofit organization addressing poverty, the environment, human rights, addictions, and other major issues, and providing a clearinghouse for information to the public, nationwide, and beyond. Established in 1996. Number of employees: 20. Number of internship applications received each year: 100.
Internships Available ▶ *5 Web site design and development interns:* responsibilities include Web site editing, design, management, promotion, Web site hosting, software. Candidates should have ability to work independently, ability to work with others, computer skills, knowledge of field, personal interest in the field, self-motivation. Duration is 4 weeks (minimum). Unpaid. Open to high school students, recent high school graduates, college freshmen, college sophomores, college juniors, college seniors, recent college graduates, graduate students, law students, career changers, individuals reentering the workforce. ▶ *3 accounting and financial management interns:* responsibilities include bookkeeping, accounting, analysis and reporting, or socially-responsible investing. Candidates should have ability to work independently, ability to work with others, computer skills, knowledge of field, personal interest in the field, self-motivation. Duration is 4 weeks

Hearts and Minds Network (continued)

(minimum). Unpaid. Open to high school students, recent high school graduates, college freshmen, college sophomores, college juniors, college seniors, recent college graduates, graduate students, law students, career changers, individuals reentering the workforce. ▶ *3 carpentry and interior design interns:* responsibilities include designing and drafting improvements for Hearts and Minds office space. Duration is 4 weeks (minimum). Unpaid. ▶ *4 computers/ technical support interns:* responsibilities include providing technical support for computers, printers, software, phones, and Web site. Candidates should have ability to work independently, computer skills, personal interest in the field, self-motivation, strong interpersonal skills. Duration is 4 weeks (minimum). Unpaid. Open to high school students, recent high school graduates, college freshmen, college sophomores, college juniors, college seniors, recent college graduates, graduate students, law students, career changers, individuals reentering the workforce. ▶ *19 creative and graphic design interns:* responsibilities include arts management, creative writing, fine art, illustration, or photography for Web site, campaigns, or print publications (5 positions); art direction and graphic design for Web site, ad campaigns, or print publications (5 positions); or doing promotional writing for Web site, ad campaigns, or print publications (4 positions); copywriting (4 positions). Candidates should have ability to work independently, knowledge of field, self-motivation, design skills or artistic ability. Duration is 4 weeks (minimum). Unpaid. Open to high school students, recent high school graduates, college freshmen, college sophomores, college juniors, college seniors, recent college graduates, graduate students, law students, career changers, individuals reentering the workforce. ▶ *5 education interns:* responsibilities include teaching economically disadvantaged high school students writing, art, and Web site design. Candidates should have ability to work independently, personal interest in the field, self-motivation, strong interpersonal skills. Duration is 4 weeks (minimum). Unpaid. Open to high school students, recent high school graduates, college freshmen, college sophomores, college juniors, college seniors, recent college graduates, graduate students, law students, law school graduates, career changers, individuals reentering the workforce. ▶ *5 fund-raising/events planning/ad sales interns:* responsibilities include fund-raising through direct mailing, corporate, foundation, or personal solicitation; planning cultural and fund-raising events; may also include selling ads for Web site and/or print publications. Candidates should have ability to work independently, computer skills, oral communication skills, personal interest in the field, self-motivation, strong interpersonal skills. Duration is 4 weeks (minimum). Unpaid. Open to high school students, recent high school graduates, college freshmen, college sophomores, college juniors, college seniors, recent college graduates, graduate students, law students, career changers, individuals reentering the workforce. ▶ *8–10 general interns:* responsibilities include working in any combination of other position offerings. Candidates should have ability to work independently, ability to work with others, organizational skills, personal interest in the field, self-motivation. Duration is 4 weeks (minimum). Unpaid. Open to high school students, recent high school graduates, college freshmen, college sophomores, college juniors, college seniors, recent college graduates, graduate students, law students, career changers, individuals reentering the workforce. ▶ *15 journalism interns:* responsibilities include research, writing, and editing articles. Candidates should have ability to work independently, computer skills, personal interest in the field, self-motivation, strong interpersonal skills, writing skills. Duration is 4 weeks (minimum). Unpaid. Open to high school students, recent high school graduates, college freshmen, college sophomores, college juniors, college seniors, recent college graduates, graduate students, law students, career changers, individuals reentering the workforce. ▶ *5 law and regulatory compliance interns:* responsibilities include possible employee, volunteer, member, and government relations; advice on copyrights; avoiding libel, liability, and other legal exposure; regulatory compliance. Candidates should have ability to work independently, knowledge of field, self-motivation, strong interpersonal skills. Duration is 4 weeks (minimum). Unpaid. Open to high school students, recent high school graduates, college freshmen, college sophomores, college juniors, college seniors,

recent college graduates, graduate students, law students, career changers, individuals reentering the workforce. ▶ *7 marketing and publishing interns:* responsibilities include strategy planning; circulation promotion; production, direct mailing, and/or other marketing activities. Candidates should have ability to work independently, computer skills, personal interest in the field, self-motivation, strong interpersonal skills. Duration is 4 weeks (minimum). Unpaid. Open to high school students, recent high school graduates, college freshmen, college sophomores, college juniors, college seniors, recent college graduates, graduate students, law students, career changers, individuals reentering the workforce. ▶ *4 marketing/research interns:* responsibilities include strategic planning, surveys, and focus groups to evaluate effectiveness of organization; research and reporting on social issues. Candidates should have ability to work independently, analytical skills, computer skills, personal interest in the field, strong interpersonal skills. Duration is 4 weeks (minimum). Unpaid. Open to high school students, recent high school graduates, college freshmen, college sophomores, college juniors, college seniors, recent college graduates, graduate students, law students, career changers, individuals reentering the workforce. ▶ *7 office interns:* responsibilities include office management, phone calls, photocopying, running errands, faxing, word processing, and desk top publishing. Candidates should have ability to work independently, ability to work with others, computer skills, personal interest in the field, self-motivation. Duration is 4 weeks (minimum). Unpaid. Open to high school students, recent high school graduates, college freshmen, college sophomores, college juniors, college seniors, recent college graduates, graduate students, law students, career changers, individuals reentering the workforce. ▶ *3 personnel/ volunteer recruitment and relations interns:* responsibilities include recruiting, communicating with, and supervising volunteers and interns at the office and all over the world (via phone and e-mail). Candidates should have ability to work independently, computer skills, personal interest in the field, self-motivation, strong interpersonal skills. Duration is 4 weeks (minimum). Unpaid. Open to high school students, recent high school graduates, college freshmen, college sophomores, college juniors, college seniors, recent college graduates, graduate students, law students, career changers, individuals reentering the workforce. ▶ *5 public relations/ advertising interns:* responsibilities include working on public service ad campaigns regarding the environment, homelessness, addictions, child abuse, and other important issues; working on campaigns to promote Hearts and Minds publications; or contacting major media and writing press releases and other marketing materials. Candidates should have oral communication skills, personal interest in the field, self-motivation, strong interpersonal skills, written communication skills. Duration is 4 weeks (minimum). Unpaid. Open to high school students, recent high school graduates, college freshmen, college sophomores, college juniors, college seniors, recent college graduates, graduate students, law students, career changers, individuals reentering the workforce. International applications accepted.

Benefits Job counseling, on-the-job training, opportunity to attend seminars/workshops, willing to act as a professional reference, willing to complete paperwork for educational credit, willing to provide letters of recommendation, advice on resume and cover letter, cooperation for independent study; local (commuting) travel may be reimbursed.

Contact Write, call, fax, e-mail, or through World Wide Web site Volunteer/Internship Manager. Phone: 212-280-0333. Fax: 212-280-0336. E-mail: help@change.net. In-person interview recommended (telephone interview accepted). Applicants must submit a letter of interest, resume, three personal references, portfolio helpful (for graphic design, writing, art, and photography applicants). Applications are accepted continuously. World Wide Web: http://www.change.net.

INFACT
46 Plympton Street
Boston, Massachusetts 02118

General Information National grassroots nonprofit organization whose purpose is to stop life-threatening abuses of transnational corporations and increase their accountability to people around

the world. Established in 1977. Number of employees: 20. Number of internship applications received each year: 200.
Internships Available ▶ *1–2 media assistants:* responsibilities include working with media organizers on outreach to targeted areas; tracking and monitoring developments in the campaign issues; helping prepare reports; letters to the editor and other written and verbal media outreach. Candidates should have oral communication skills, personal interest in the field, strong interpersonal skills, written communication skills. Duration is one summer. Position available as unpaid or paid. ▶ *1–10 organizing assistants:* responsibilities include organizing activists at the local, regional, and national level; responding to requests for information; design and layout of organizing materials; and outreach to targeted constituencies. Candidates should have oral communication skills, personal interest in the field, self-motivation, strong interpersonal skills. Duration is one summer. Position available as unpaid or paid. ▶ *1–2 research assistants:* responsibilities include compiling and analyzing information for Infact's campaigns; project management and implementation; monitoring business publications; assisting with research reports; utilizing library and Internet skills; and gathering information and providing support. Candidates should have personal interest in the field, research skills, self-motivation, strong interpersonal skills, written communication skills. Duration is one summer. Position available as unpaid or paid. Open to high school seniors, recent high school graduates, college freshmen, college sophomores, college juniors, college seniors, recent college graduates, graduate students, law students, career changers, individuals reentering the workforce. International applications accepted.
Benefits Possible full-time employment, willing to act as a professional reference, willing to complete paperwork for educational credit, willing to provide letters of recommendation.
Contact Write, call, fax, e-mail, or through World Wide Web site Rachael Running, Internship Coordinator, 46 Plympton Street, Boston, Massachusetts 02118. Phone: 617-695-2525. Fax: 617-695-2626. E-mail: rachael@infact.org. In-person interview recommended (telephone interview accepted). Applicants must submit a letter of interest, resume, three personal references. Applications are accepted continuously. World Wide Web: http://www.infact.org.

INSTITUTE FOR WOMEN'S POLICY RESEARCH
1707 L Street, NW, Suite 750
Washington, District of Columbia 20036

General Information Nonprofit research organization that works primarily on issues related to equal opportunity and economic and social justice for women. Established in 1987. Number of employees: 24. Number of internship applications received each year: 200.
Internships Available ▶ *1 communications intern:* responsibilities include handling requests for information; layout and design, editing, and proofreading; maintaining Web page. Candidates should have computer skills, editing skills, office skills, oral communication skills, personal interest in the field, written communication skills. Duration is 10–12 weeks. Position available as unpaid or paid. Open to college freshmen, college sophomores, college juniors, college seniors, recent college graduates, graduate students, individuals reentering the workforce. ▶ *1 development intern:* responsibilities include assisting director of development and membership coordinator with grant research, preparing reports and proposals, direct mail, special events, and outreach efforts. Candidates should have computer skills, office skills, oral communication skills, personal interest in the field, written communication skills. Duration is 10–12 weeks. Position available as unpaid or paid. Open to college freshmen, college sophomores, college juniors, college seniors, recent college graduates, graduate students, individuals reentering the workforce. ▶ *2–4 research interns:* responsibilities include performing literature reviews, collecting data and resources, preparing reports and summaries, attending relevant meetings and congressional hearings, and providing general office support. Candidates should have ability to work independently, ability to work with others, computer skills, office skills, oral communication skills, organizational skills, personal interest in the field, research skills, self-motivation, writ-

ing skills. Duration is 10–12 weeks. Position available as unpaid or paid. Open to college freshmen, college sophomores, college juniors, college seniors, recent college graduates, graduate students, law students, individuals reentering the workforce. International applications accepted.
Benefits Opportunity to attend seminars/workshops, travel reimbursement, willing to act as a professional reference, willing to complete paperwork for educational credit, willing to provide letters of recommendation.
Contact E-mail or through World Wide Web site Danielle Hayot, Research Program Coordinator. Fax: 202-833-4362. E-mail: hayot@iwpr.org. No phone calls. Telephone interview required. Applicants must submit a letter of interest, resume, writing sample, three personal references. Application deadline: March 10 for summer positions; continuous for fall and spring positions. World Wide Web: http://www.iwpr.org.

INTERNATIONAL ECONOMIC DEVELOPMENT COUNCIL
734 15th Street, NW, Suite 800
Washington, District of Columbia 20005

General Information Nonprofit membership association that serves public and private sector practitioners in economic development and provides information to its members to help improve local economies. Established in 1967. Number of employees: 30. Number of internship applications received each year: 35.
Internships Available ▶ *5–8 interns:* responsibilities include assisting with research project on urban economic-related topics, tracking legislation, writing newsletter articles, and completing survey analyses. Candidates should have ability to work independently, organizational skills, plan to pursue career in field, research skills, strong interpersonal skills, writing skills. Duration is flexible (minimum commitment of 2 months). Position available as unpaid or at $8.50–$10.50 per hour. Open to college juniors, college seniors, recent college graduates, graduate students, PhD candidates. International applications accepted.
Benefits Names of contacts, on-the-job training, opportunity to attend seminars/workshops, possible full-time employment, willing to act as a professional reference, willing to complete paperwork for educational credit, willing to provide letters of recommendation, practical work experience, opportunity to have work published.
Contact Write, fax, or e-mail Mary Reynolds, Internship Coordinator/Economic Development Associate, 734 15th Street, NW, Suite 900, Washington, District of Columbia 20005. Phone: 202-223-7800. Fax: 202-223-4745. E-mail: mreynolds@iedconline.org. Applicants must submit a letter of interest, resume, writing sample. Application deadline: first week of March for summer; continuous for other seasons. World Wide Web: http://www.iedonline.org.

INTERNATIONAL HUMAN RIGHTS LAW GROUP
1200 18th Street, NW, Suite 602
Washington, District of Columbia 20036

General Information Nonprofit organization of human rights and legal professionals engaged in human rights advocacy, litigation, and training around the world. Established in 1978. Number of employees: 28. Number of internship applications received each year: 200.
Internships Available ▶ *6–8 legal/graduate interns:* responsibilities include assisting attorneys in program work; legal research projects; writing, summarizing, and analyzing reports. Candidates should have ability to work independently, analytical skills, experience in the field, research skills, self-motivation, writing skills. Duration is 10–12 weeks. Unpaid. Open to graduate students, law students, career changers. ▶ *2–3 undergraduate interns:* responsibilities include researching, writing, and administrative duties. Candidates should have oral communication skills, personal interest in the field, research skills, self-motivation, strong interpersonal skills, writing skills. Duration is 10–12 weeks. Unpaid. Open to college sophomores, college juniors, college seniors, recent college graduates. International applications accepted.
Benefits Names of contacts, opportunity to attend seminars/workshops, willing to act as a professional reference, willing to

International Human Rights Law Group (continued)
complete paperwork for educational credit, willing to provide letters of recommendation, opportunity to learn how human rights organization works.
International Internships Available in Bosnia and Herzegovina; Burundi; Cambodia; D.R.C., Congo; Morocco; Nigeria.
Contact Write, fax, e-mail, or through World Wide Web site Internship Coordinator, 1200 18th Street, NW, Suite 602, Washington, District of Columbia 20036. Fax: 202-822-4606. E-mail: humanrights@hrlawgroup.org. No phone calls. Telephone interview required. Applicants must submit a letter of interest, resume, three letters of recommendation, 5-page writing sample. Application deadline: March 1 for summer, August 31 for fall, December 31 for spring. World Wide Web: http://www.hrlawgroup.org.

INTERNS FOR PEACE
475 Riverside Drive, Room 240
New York, New York 10115-0109

General Information Organization that trains for conflict resolution through community work in Israel and the Middle East. Established in 1976. Number of employees: 20. Number of internship applications received each year: 120.
Internships Available ▶ *12 interns:* responsibilities include performing duties designed to bring groups together through community work in Israel and the Middle East; helping to design community development activities that meet mutual interests of Jews and Arabs in six principal areas: women, education, sports, arts, community, and business. Candidates should have plan to pursue a career in intergroup relations, advanced language skills in Hebrew or Arabic. Duration is 12 months. $500 stipend per month. Open to recent college graduates, individuals reentering the workforce. International applications accepted.
Benefits Formal training, free housing, health insurance, job counseling, names of contacts, opportunity to attend seminars/workshops, possible full-time employment, willing to complete paperwork for educational credit, willing to provide letters of recommendation, reimbursement of work-related travel expenses.
Contact Write, call, or fax Karen Wald Cohen, International Co-Director. Phone: 212-870-2226. Fax: 212-870-2911. In-person interview required. Applicants must submit a letter of interest, resume. Applications are accepted continuously.

JAPAN PACIFIC RESOURCE NETWORK
310 8th Street #305
Oakland, California 94607

General Information Nonprofit educational organization promoting nonprofit activities, civil rights, and corporate social responsibility in the U.S. and Japan. Established in 1985. Number of employees: 4. Number of internship applications received each year: 20.
Internships Available ▶ *Administrative interns:* responsibilities include assisting executive director and administrative assistant with office work and the organization's projects. Candidates should have computer skills, office skills, oral communication skills, self-motivation, strong interpersonal skills, writing skills. Duration is minimum 3 months (8-10 hours per week). Unpaid. Open to college freshmen, college sophomores, college juniors, college seniors, recent college graduates, graduate students, law students, career changers, individuals reentering the workforce. ▶ *Research interns:* responsibilities include assisting a senior researcher and other staff with research projects. Candidates should have ability to work with others, computer skills, editing skills, research skills, self-motivation, writing skills. Duration is minimum 3 months (8-10 hours per week). Unpaid. Open to college freshmen, college sophomores, college juniors, college seniors, recent college graduates, graduate students, law students, career changers. International applications accepted.
Benefits On-the-job training, opportunity to attend seminars/workshops, possible full-time employment, willing to complete paperwork for educational credit, willing to provide letters of recommendation.
Contact Write, call, fax, e-mail, or through World Wide Web site Hiroshi Kashiwagi, Executive Director. Phone: 510-891-9045. Fax:

510-891-9047. E-mail: jprn@igc.apc.org. In-person interview recommended (telephone interview accepted). Applicants must submit a letter of interest, resume, one writing sample recommended. Applications are accepted continuously. World Wide Web: http://www.jprn.org.

JOBS WITH JUSTICE
501 Third Street, NW
Washington, District of Columbia 20001-2797

General Information National coalition of labor unions and religious, civil rights, women's, student, farm, and community organizations working together at the local level to defend and expand the rights of working people. Established in 1987. Number of employees: 9.
Internships Available ▶ *2–3 interns:* responsibilities include organizing student-labor outreach, assisting national staff in providing support services to local coalitions, helping in preparation for trainings, and general administrative support. Candidates should have ability to work independently, ability to work with others, computer skills, office skills, self-motivation, interest in the labor movement and/or issues affecting working people; desktop publishing, database, and Web experience a plus. Duration is summer, spring, winter, or fall semester (full- or part-time). Position available as unpaid or paid. Open to high school students, recent high school graduates, college freshmen, college sophomores, college juniors, college seniors, recent college graduates, graduate students, career changers, individuals reentering the workforce. International applications accepted.
Benefits Job counseling, willing to act as a professional reference, willing to complete paperwork for educational credit, willing to provide letters of recommendation, small stipend (depending on need).
Contact Write, call, fax, e-mail, or through World Wide Web site Alison Fletcher, Office Coordinator, 501 Third Street, NW, Washington, District of Columbia 20001. Phone: 202-434-1106. Fax: 202-434-1477. E-mail: allison@jwj.org. Applicants must submit a letter of interest, resume. Applications are accepted continuously. World Wide Web: http://www.jwj.org.

JUSTICEWORKS COMMUNITY, INC.
1012 Eighth Avenue
Brooklyn, New York 11215

General Information Nonprofit agency whose mission is to effect more humane criminal justice policy through public education, advocacy, and community organizing. Established in 1992. Number of employees: 6. Number of internship applications received each year: 8.
Internships Available ▶ *1 community organizing intern:* responsibilities include making educational presentations recruiting community members to public actions and the larger social justice movement. Candidates should have computer skills, oral communication skills, personal interest in the field, strong interpersonal skills, writing skills. Duration is September to June (2 semesters). Unpaid. Open to recent college graduates, graduate students, law students, career changers. ▶ *3 national campaign assistants:* responsibilities include contacting national public education sites primarily by telephone; mailings to same sites; research for additional sites. Candidates should have ability to work independently, computer skills, oral communication skills, organizational skills, research skills, written communication skills. Duration is one semester to one year. Unpaid. Open to college freshmen, college sophomores, college juniors, college seniors, recent college graduates, graduate students, law students. ▶ *1 research intern:* responsibilities include research, primarily on the Internet, on the current status of mandatory minimum sentencing laws (state-by-state) as well as the existence of alternatives to incarceration (state-by-state). Candidates should have ability to work independently, analytical skills, computer skills, research skills, written communication skills, ability to access and maximize information on the Internet. Duration is one semester to one year. Unpaid. Open to college seniors, graduate students, law students. International applications accepted.

Benefits Names of contacts, opportunity to attend seminars/ workshops, willing to act as a professional reference, willing to complete paperwork for educational credit, willing to provide letters of recommendation.

Contact Write, call, fax, or e-mail Mary-Elizabeth Fitzgerald, Executive Director. Phone: 718-499-6704. Fax: 718-832-2832. E-mail: justiceworks@msn.com. In-person interview required. Applicants must submit a letter of interest, resume, academic transcripts, writing sample, three letters of recommendation. Applications are accepted continuously. World Wide Web: http://www.justiceworks.org.

KANSANS FOR LIFE
2501 East Central
Wichita, Kansas 67214-4511

General Information Not-for-profit educational organization, charitable organization, and political action committee dedicated to education, organization, registration and selecting of political candidates to eliminate abortion, euthanasia, and infanticide. Established in 1981. Number of employees: 4. Affiliate of National Right to Life Committee, Washington, District of Columbia. Number of internship applications received each year: 5.

Internships Available ► *1 church coordinator:* responsibilities include developing and maintaining contact with all churches in the state regarding pro-life issues. Candidates should have ability to work independently, computer skills, office skills, oral communication skills, organizational skills, self-motivation, strong interpersonal skills, writing skills. Duration is 1 year. Unpaid. Open to college juniors, college seniors, graduate students, individuals reentering the workforce. ► *1 graphic design intern:* responsibilities include designing promotional materials. Candidates should have graphic design experience. Duration is flexible. Unpaid. Open to high school students, recent high school graduates, college freshmen, college sophomores, college juniors, college seniors, recent college graduates, graduate students, law students, career changers, individuals reentering the workforce. ► *1 grassroots coordinator:* responsibilities include contacting volunteers to organize active participaion in grassroots political efforts; telephone work and direct contact with volunteers. Candidates should have ability to work independently, ability to work with others, oral communication skills, organizational skills, personal interest in the field, self-motivation, strong leadership ability. Duration is May to August. Unpaid. Open to college seniors. ► *1 legislative intern:* responsibilities include research and writing on legislation pertaining to abortion, euthanasia, and infanticide. Candidates should have ability to work independently, analytical skills, knowledge of field, personal interest in the field, research skills, self-motivation, writing skills. Duration is 1 semester. Unpaid. Open to law students. ► *1 program producer:* responsibilities include programming, planning, supervising production of annual radio telethon. Candidates should have ability to work independently, oral communication skills, organizational skills, strong interpersonal skills, written communication skills, broadcast experience. Duration is 1 year. Unpaid. Open to graduate students, individuals reentering the workforce.

Benefits Free housing, travel reimbursement, willing to act as a professional reference, willing to complete paperwork for educational credit, willing to provide letters of recommendation.

Contact Write Joan Hawkins, Executive Director. Fax: 316-687-0303. E-mail: kfl@kfl.org. No phone calls. In-person interview recommended (telephone interview accepted). Applicants must submit a formal organization application, letter of interest, resume, academic transcripts, three writing samples, three personal references, three letters of recommendation. Application deadline: April 1 for summer; continuous for other positions, November 1 for legislative positions. World Wide Web: http://www.kfl.org.

KOREAN AMERICAN COALITION
3727 West 6th Street, Suite 515
Los Angeles, California 90020

General Information Nonprofit community advocacy organization. Established in 1983. Number of employees: 15. Number of internship applications received each year: 80.

Internships Available ► *4–6 corporate interns:* responsibilities include working with KAC and a designated multinational corporation. Candidates should have college courses in field, knowledge of field, oral communication skills, self-motivation, strong interpersonal skills, written communication skills. Duration is 2 months. $1000 per duration of internship. Open to college sophomores, college juniors, non-graduating college seniors. ► *1–4 legal interns:* responsibilities include working in law office 4 days per week and KAC office 1 day per week. Candidates should have computer skills, knowledge of field, office skills, oral communication skills, personal interest in the field, self-motivation, strong interpersonal skills, written communication skills. Duration is 2 months. $1000 per duration of internship. Open to college freshmen, college sophomores, college juniors. ► *2–5 media interns:* responsibilities include working with KAC and local news service. Candidates should have knowledge of field, office skills, oral communication skills, strong interpersonal skills, writing skills. Duration is 2 months. $1000 per duration of internship. Open to college freshmen, college sophomores, college juniors, non-graduating college seniors. ► *2–4 political interns:* responsibilities include working with KAC and a local political office in various functions. Candidates should have knowledge of field, office skills, oral communication skills, self-motivation, strong interpersonal skills, writing skills. Duration is 2 months. $1000 per duration of internship. Open to college freshmen, college sophomores, college juniors, non-graduating college seniors. International applications accepted.

Benefits Names of contacts, opportunity to attend seminars/ workshops, possible full-time employment, willing to act as a professional reference, willing to complete paperwork for educational credit, willing to provide letters of recommendation.

Contact Write, call, fax, or e-mail Graise Lee, Program Coordinator. Phone: 213-365-5999. Fax: 213-380-7990. E-mail: kac_program_coordinator@hotmail.com. Telephone interview required. Applicants must submit a formal organization application, resume, academic transcripts, two letters of recommendation, 2 essays. Application deadline: February 23 for summer. Fees: $10.

LAWYERS' COMMITTEE FOR CIVIL RIGHTS UNDER LAW
1401 New York Avenue, NW, Suite 400
Washington, District of Columbia 20005

General Information Civil rights litigation and advocacy organization. Established in 1963. Number of employees: 40. Number of internship applications received each year: 300.

Internships Available ► *Graduate interns:* responsibilities include assisting in public policy research, locating experts, and other project-related activities. Candidates should have analytical skills, college courses in field, organizational skills, research skills, writing skills. Duration is flexible. Unpaid. Open to graduate students. ► *10–15 law student interns:* responsibilities include legal research and writing, assisting attorneys with case investigation and trial preparation, working with civil rights and/or community based organizations, interviewing clients and witnesses. Candidates should have ability to work independently, ability to work with others, personal interest in the field, research skills, writing skills, evidence of community service or civil rights interest. Duration is flexible. Unpaid. Open to law students. ► *Undergraduate interns:* responsibilities include assisting administrative and attorney employees with administrative tasks, desktop publishing, non-legal writing and research, filing, and some clerical work. Candidates should have ability to work independently, ability to work with others, office skills, personal interest in the field, self-motivation, evidence of community service or civil rights interest. Duration is flexible. Unpaid. Open to college freshmen, college sophomores, college juniors, college seniors, recent college graduates, graduate students, career changers, individuals reentering the workforce. International applications accepted.

Benefits Names of contacts, on-the-job training, opportunity to attend seminars/workshops, possible full-time employment, travel reimbursement, willing to act as a professional reference, willing to complete paperwork for educational credit, willing to provide letters of recommendation.

Contact Write, call, fax, e-mail, or through World Wide Web site Kathy Coates, Intern Coordinator. Phone: 202-662-8600. Fax: 202-783-0857. E-mail: kcoates@lawyerscomm.org. In-person interview

Lawyers' Committee for Civil Rights under Law (continued)
recommended (telephone interview accepted). Applicants must submit a letter of interest, resume, writing sample, three personal references. Applications are accepted continuously. World Wide Web: http://www.lawyerscomm.org.

MARCH OF DIMES BIRTH DEFECTS FOUNDATION, OFFICE OF GOVERNMENT AFFAIRS
1146 19th Street, NW, 6th Floor
Washington, District of Columbia 20036

General Information Nonprofit organization that is dedicated to the prevention of birth defects through research, public health education, advocacy, and community service. Established in 1938. Number of employees: 11. Unit of National Office March of Dimes, White Plains, New York. Number of internship applications received each year: 25.
Internships Available ▶ *School-year interns:* responsibilities include assisting with monitoring, tracking, and reporting on public policy issues; researching and drafting letters, position papers, testimony, and legislative updates; attending and monitoring congressional hearings, markups, and meetings; and providing general office support. Candidates should have knowledge of field, personal interest in the field, research skills, self-motivation, strong interpersonal skills, writing skills. Duration is one semester or summer. Position available as unpaid or paid. Open to college sophomores, college juniors, college seniors, recent college graduates, graduate students.
Benefits Willing to complete paperwork for educational credit.
Contact Write, call, fax, or e-mail Susan Langley, Office Manager, 1146 19th Street NW 6th Floor, Washington, District of Columbia 20036. Phone: 202-659-1800. Fax: 202-296-2964. E-mail: slangley@marchofdimes.com. In-person interview recommended (telephone interview accepted). Applicants must submit a letter of interest, resume, writing sample, three letters of recommendation. Applications are accepted continuously. World Wide Web: http://www.modimes.org.

MASSACHUSETTS PUBLIC INTEREST RESEARCH GROUPS
29 Temple Place
Boston, Massachusetts 02111-1305

General Information Nonprofit, nonpartisan organization involved in research, organizing, and advocacy for statewide environmental and consumer protection reforms. Established in 1972. Number of employees: 40. Number of internship applications received each year: 70.
Internships Available ▶ *2–5 program interns:* responsibilities include conducting research; preparing investigative reports; drafting public education materials; working with media and coalition groups to build support for issues through public education programs; representing MASSPIRG on specific issues to coalition and other local organizations; and preparing testimony for government hearings on pending legislation. Candidates should have ability to work independently, ability to work with others, computer skills, oral communication skills, organizational skills, personal interest in the field, self-motivation, writing skills. Duration is flexible. Position available as unpaid or paid. Open to college freshmen, college sophomores, college juniors, college seniors, recent college graduates, graduate students, law students, career changers. International applications accepted.
Benefits Names of contacts, on-the-job training, opportunity to attend seminars/workshops, possible full-time employment, willing to act as a professional reference, willing to complete paperwork for educational credit, willing to provide letters of recommendation, small stipend.
Contact Write, call, fax, e-mail, or through World Wide Web site Tara Hudson, Program Administrator. Phone: 617-292-4800. Fax: 617-292-8057. E-mail: tara@masspirg.org. In-person interview recommended (telephone interview accepted). Applicants must submit a letter of interest, resume. Applications are accepted continuously. World Wide Web: http://www.masspirg.org.

METRO FAMILY YMCA
2831 Southwest Barbur Boulevard
Portland, Oregon 97201

General Information Organization that promotes Christian principles through programs that build healthy bodies, minds, and spirits for all. Established in 1977. Number of employees: 140. Unit of YMCA of Columbia-Willamette, Portland, Oregon. Number of internship applications received each year: 12.
Internships Available ▶ *4 adult health/fitness/cardiac rehabilitation interns:* responsibilities include teaching land and water classes and overseeing weight room, cardiovascular and health education, social events, and program operations. Candidates should have college courses in field, oral communication skills, personal interest in the field, plan to pursue career in field, strong interpersonal skills. Duration is 10 weeks or 1 semester (36-40 hours per week). Unpaid. Open to college freshmen, college sophomores, college juniors, college seniors, recent college graduates, graduate students, career changers. ▶ *4 child-care program interns:* responsibilities include assisting teachers, teaching students, and performing administrative duties. Candidates should have declared college major in field, experience in the field, personal interest in the field, strong interpersonal skills, strong leadership ability. Duration is 10 weeks or 1 semester. Unpaid. Open to college sophomores, college juniors, college seniors. ▶ *1 corporate site intern:* responsibilities include assisting program directors at corporate health and fitness sites; teaching fitness; and conducting weight orientations, health education, and incentive programs. Candidates should have college courses in field, experience in the field, oral communication skills, self-motivation, strong interpersonal skills, strong leadership ability. Duration is 1 semester. Unpaid. Open to college juniors, college seniors. ▶ *4 youth sports and aquatics interns:* responsibilities include assisting program director in youth sports program and with special events; coordinating programs; performing administrative duties; and teaching. Candidates should have college courses in field, oral communication skills, personal interest in the field, strong interpersonal skills, strong leadership ability. Duration is 10 weeks or 1 semester. Unpaid. Open to college freshmen, college sophomores, college juniors, college seniors, recent college graduates, graduate students. International applications accepted.
Benefits Formal training, job counseling, names of contacts, on-the-job training, opportunity to attend seminars/workshops, possible full-time employment, willing to complete paperwork for educational credit, willing to provide letters of recommendation.
Contact Write or e-mail Erika Johnson, Program Director. E-mail: enathman@ymca-portland.org. No phone calls. In-person interview recommended (telephone interview accepted). Applicants must submit a letter of interest, resume. Application deadline: March 1 for spring, May 1 for summer, August 1 for fall, November 1 for winter.

METRO JUSTICE OF ROCHESTER
36 St. Paul Street, Room 112
Rochester, New York 14604

General Information Multi-issue community organization focusing on economic justice, antiracism, Latin American solidarity, health care, labor, women's issues, and environmental issues. Established in 1965. Number of employees: 2. Number of internship applications received each year: 10.
Internships Available ▶ *2–3 interns:* responsibilities include assisting with a substantial research project that aids the community in some way. Candidates should have ability to work independently, ability to work with others, oral communication skills, research skills, self-motivation, written communication skills. Duration is 1–2 semesters. Unpaid. Open to college sophomores, college juniors, college seniors, recent college graduates, graduate students, law students.
Benefits Willing to complete paperwork for educational credit, willing to provide letters of recommendation.
Contact Write, call, fax, or e-mail Mr. William Appel, Organizer. Phone: 585-325-2560. Fax: 585-325-2561. E-mail: metroj@frontiernet.net. In-person interview recommended (telephone interview

accepted). Applicants must submit a letter of interest, resume. Applications are accepted continuously. World Wide Web: http://www.ggw.org/MetroJustice.

MID-SOUTH PEACE AND JUSTICE CENTER
1000 South Cooper Street
Memphis, Tennessee 38104

General Information Grassroots organization that advocates and educates people in peace and justice issues. Established in 1982. Number of employees: 2. Number of internship applications received each year: 10.
Internships Available ▶ *Alternative public spending outreach coordinators:* responsibilities include working with community organizations and general public about the need to change federal spending priorities. Duration is flexible. Unpaid. Open to individuals age 18 or older. ▶ *1–2 community gardens interns.* Duration is flexible. Unpaid. ▶ *Environmental justice interns:* responsibilities include researching impact of toxics, pollution, and waste on Memphis, particularly on the African-American community, creating educational materials, and helping to design an outreach program. Duration is flexible. Unpaid. Open to individuals age 18 or older. ▶ *1–2 fair trade coordinators.* Duration is flexible. Unpaid. ▶ *1–2 fair trade store and market coordinators.* Duration is flexible. Unpaid. ▶ *Human rights interns:* responsibilities include working in human rights area with an economic focus. Duration is flexible. Unpaid. Open to individuals age 18 or older. ▶ *1–2 living wage coordinators.* Duration is flexible. Unpaid. ▶ *Media watch interns:* responsibilities include performing an in-depth analysis of news coverage. Duration is flexible. Unpaid. Open to individuals age 18 or older. ▶ *Nonviolence interns:* responsibilities include working with pledge of nonviolence in public schools and community. Duration is flexible. Unpaid. Open to individuals age 18 or older. ▶ *Office manager interns:* responsibilities include coordinating the overall operations of the office. Duration is flexible. Unpaid. Open to individuals age 18 or older. ▶ *Tax reform interns:* responsibilities include working with community groups for fair taxation and educating the public about the current regressive structure of the Tennessee tax system. Duration is flexible. Unpaid. Open to individuals age 18 or older. International applications accepted.
Benefits On-the-job training, willing to act as a professional reference, willing to complete paperwork for educational credit, willing to provide letters of recommendation, assistance in finding affordable housing.
Contact Write, call, fax, or e-mail Julie Rogers, Coordinator, PO Box 11428, Memphis, Tennessee 38111-0428. Phone: 901-725-4990. Fax: 901-725-7858. E-mail: pandjcenter@aol.com. Applicants must submit a formal organization application, three personal references. Applications are accepted continuously. World Wide Web: http://www.members.aol.com/PandJcenter/peace.html.

MOTHERS' VOICES
165 West 46th Street, Suite 701
New York, New York 10036

General Information The only national, grassroots, nonprofit organization working to mobilize parents to educate and advocate sexual health and HIV/AIDS prevention. Established in 1991. Number of employees: 7. Number of internship applications received each year: 25.
Internships Available ▶ *1–2 community programs associates:* responsibilities include assisting community programs director in the planning, assessment, implementation, and evaluation of sexual health and HIV prevention education and advocacy programs; community organizing and networking. Candidates should have ability to work independently, oral communication skills, self-motivation, strong interpersonal skills, written communication skills, basic understanding of sexual health and HIV. Duration is flexible. Unpaid. Open to college freshmen, college sophomores, college juniors, college seniors, recent college graduates, graduate students, career changers, individuals reentering the workforce. International applications accepted.

Benefits Job counseling, on-the-job training, opportunity to attend seminars/workshops, willing to act as a professional reference, willing to complete paperwork for educational credit, willing to provide letters of recommendation.
Contact Write, call, fax, or e-mail Giokazta Molina, Director of Community Programs. Phone: 212-730-2777 Ext. 223. Fax: 212-730-4378. E-mail: gm@mvoices.org. In-person interview required. Applicants must submit a letter of interest, resume, writing sample, three personal references. Applications are accepted continuously. World Wide Web: http://www.mvoices.org.

NATIONAL ABORTION AND REPRODUCTIVE RIGHTS ACTION LEAGUE OF OHIO
614 West Superior Avenue, Suite 608
Cleveland, Ohio 44113

General Information Political lobbying and grassroots organization and education foundation. Established in 1979. Number of employees: 2. Affiliate of National Abortion and Reproductive Rights Action League, Washington, District of Columbia. Number of internship applications received each year: 5.
Internships Available ▶ *1–3 interns:* responsibilities include assisting with educational, grassroots organizing and lobbying projects; providing staff support as needed. Candidates should have ability to work independently, organizational skills, personal interest in the field, research skills, strong interpersonal skills, writing skills. Duration is flexible. Unpaid. Open to high school seniors, recent high school graduates, college freshmen, college sophomores, college juniors, college seniors, recent college graduates.
Benefits On-the-job training, opportunity to attend seminars/workshops, willing to act as a professional reference, willing to complete paperwork for educational credit, willing to provide letters of recommendation.
Contact Call, fax, or e-mail Intern Coordinator, 614 West Superior Avenue, Suite 608, Cleveland, Ohio 44113. Phone: 216-522-0169. Fax: 216-522-0044. E-mail: choice@naralohio.org. In-person interview required. Applicants must submit a letter of interest, resume. Applications are accepted continuously. World Wide Web: http://www.naralohio.org.

NATIONAL ASIAN PACIFIC AMERICAN LEGAL CONSORTIUM
1140 Connecticut Avenue, NW, Suite 1200
Washington, District of Columbia 20036

General Information Civil rights organization that advances the legal and civil rights of Asian-Pacific Americans through litigation, advocacy, public education, and public policy development. Established in 1991. Number of employees: 12. Number of internship applications received each year: 100.
Internships Available ▶ *1–2 communications interns:* responsibilities include assisting the communications staff and program staff with implementing media strategies; writing press releases and media alerts; assisting with writing and editing of newsletter and other publications; arranging and implementing press conferences; performing some administrative work. Candidates should have ability to work with others, computer skills, editing skills, research skills, writing skills. Duration is 1 semester. Unpaid. Open to high school seniors, recent high school graduates, college freshmen, college sophomores, college juniors, college seniors, recent college graduates, graduate students, career changers, individuals reentering the workforce. ▶ *1–2 development interns:* responsibilities include researching grant opportunities, assisting with proposal writing, and assisting with individual donors program as needed. Candidates should have ability to work independently, oral communication skills, organizational skills, self-motivation, strong interpersonal skills, written communication skills. Duration is January to June or June to November/December. Unpaid. Open to college seniors, graduate students, career changers. ▶ *1–10 law student interns:* responsibilities include assisting the executive director and legal staff on special research projects; writing policy statements, legislative alerts, and news articles; reviewing and assisting in preparation of amicus briefs; attending congressional hearings and representing NAPALC at coalition meetings; some administrative work. Candidates should have analytical skills,

National Asian Pacific American Legal Consortium (continued)

computer skills, editing skills, organizational skills, research skills, writing skills. Duration is 1 semester. Unpaid. Open to law students. ▶ *1–10 undergraduate and graduate interns:* responsibilities include assisting consortium's executive director, associate director, and legal staff on special research projects; writing legislative alerts, press releases, and news articles; attending congressional hearings and representing NAPALC at coalition meetings; some administrative work. Candidates should have ability to work with others, computer skills, editing skills, research skills, writing skills. Duration is 10 weeks or 1 semester. Unpaid. Open to college juniors, college seniors, graduate students.

Benefits Job counseling, names of contacts, on-the-job training, opportunity to attend seminars/workshops, possible full-time employment, travel reimbursement, willing to act as a professional reference, willing to complete paperwork for educational credit, willing to provide letters of recommendation.

Contact Write, call, fax, e-mail, or through World Wide Web site Mr. Vincent Eng, Legal Director. Phone: 202-296-2300. Fax: 202-296-2318. E-mail: veng@napalc.org. Telephone interview required. Applicants must submit a letter of interest, resume, one 2–5 page writing sample. Applications are accepted continuously. World Wide Web: http://www.napalc.org.

NATIONAL ASSOCIATION FOR EQUAL OPPORTUNITY IN HIGHER EDUCATION
8701 Georgia Avenue, Suite 200
Silver Spring, Maryland 20910

General Information Organization whose objective is to implement programs and policies which affect minority student enrollment, using diverse strategies to ensure an increase of Black students into HBCU establishments. Established in 1969. Number of employees: 36. Number of internship applications received each year: 300.

Internships Available ▶ *Interns:* responsibilities include policy writing, research, computer services. Candidates should have ability to work independently, ability to work with others, analytical skills, college courses in field, computer skills, office skills, oral communication skills, personal interest in the field, research skills, self-motivation, written communication skills. Duration is 10 weeks in summer (various hours during the fall and spring). $500–$550 per week. Open to college freshmen, college sophomores, college juniors, college seniors, graduate students, law students, medical students. International applications accepted.

Benefits Housing at a cost, job counseling, names of contacts, on-the-job training, opportunity to attend seminars/workshops, possible full-time employment, travel reimbursement, willing to act as a professional reference, willing to complete paperwork for educational credit, willing to provide letters of recommendation.

Contact Write, call, fax, or through World Wide Web site Dr. Jacquelyn Madry-Taylor, Director of the Internship Program, 8701 Georgia Avenue, Suite 200, Silver Spring, Maryland 20910. Phone: 301-650-2440. Fax: 301-495-3306. E-mail: jtaylor@nafeo.org. Telephone interview required. Applicants must submit a formal organization application, resume, academic transcripts, writing sample, two letters of recommendation. Application deadline: March 31 for summer. World Wide Web: http://www.nafeo.org.

NATIONAL CENTER FOR FAIR AND OPEN TESTING (FAIRTEST)
342 Broadway
Cambridge, Massachusetts 02139

General Information Public education and advocacy organization fighting race, gender, and class bias in standardized exams and promoting assessment methods that are fair, accurate, and educationally sound. Established in 1985. Number of employees: 6. Number of internship applications received each year: 25.

Internships Available ▶ *1–2 Denise Carty-Bennia interns:* responsibilities include researching and writing for a current project or campaign related to civil rights and educational testing, preparing a report on test coaching, and researching challenges to tests and test misuses. Duration is 1 summer. Position available as unpaid or at small stipend. Open to college juniors, college seniors, graduate students, individuals re-entering the workforce with BA or higher.

Benefits Names of contacts, willing to complete paperwork for educational credit, willing to provide letters of recommendation.

Contact Write Internship Coordinator. Applicants must submit a letter of interest, resume, writing sample. Applications are accepted continuously.

NATIONAL CENTER FOR LESBIAN RIGHTS
870 Market Street, Suite 570
San Francisco, California 94102

General Information Legal and advocacy organization for LGBT communities, including immigration, full civil and human rights; provides litigation, legal resources, and community education to more than 1,500 LGBT members nationwide. Established in 1977. Number of employees: 9. Number of internship applications received each year: 20.

Internships Available ▶ *1–3 law clerks:* responsibilities include contact with inquiring calls and e-mails made by nationwide members of gay, lesbian, and transgender communities; issues vary from adoption by same sex couples, second parent adoptions, and LGBT rights in the workplace, and human rights; proofreading existing manuals with law resources/cases/information on the above-mentioned. Candidates should have college courses in field, editing skills, knowledge of field, oral communication skills, research skills, writing skills. Duration is 1 semester. Work-study available. Open to law students.

Benefits On-the-job training.

Contact Write Courtney Joslin, Staff Attorney. Fax: 415-239-8442. E-mail: joslin@nclrights.org. No phone calls. Applicants must submit a formal organization application, letter of interest, resume. Applications are accepted continuously. World Wide Web: http://www.nclrights.org.

NATIONAL COALITION FOR CHILD PROTECTION REFORM
325 Broadway, Suite 201
New York, New York 10007

General Information Nonprofit organization dedicated to improving the child welfare system through public education and litigation. Established in 1992. Number of employees: 1. Unit of National Coalition for Child Protection Reform, Alexandria, Virginia. Number of internship applications received each year: 12.

Internships Available ▶ *1–2 law student interns:* responsibilities include drafting position papers, assisting with class action litigation, providing assistance to other attorneys litigating child welfare issues. Duration is minimum of 10 hours per week. Unpaid. Open to recent college graduates, graduate students, law students. ▶ *1–2 summer associates:* responsibilities include drafting position papers, assisting with class action litigation, providing assistance to attorneys litigating child welfare issues. Duration is June to August. Unpaid. Open to law students. Candidates for all positions should have analytical skills, personal interest in the field, research skills, strong interpersonal skills, writing skills. International applications accepted.

Benefits Free meals, names of contacts, on-the-job training, opportunity to attend seminars/workshops, travel reimbursement, willing to act as a professional reference, willing to complete paperwork for educational credit, willing to provide letters of recommendation.

Contact Write, call, fax, e-mail, or through World Wide Web site Carolyn Kubitschek, Vice President. Phone: 212-349-0900. Fax: 212-349-0694. E-mail: ckubitschek@lanskub.com. In-person interview recommended (telephone interview accepted). Applicants must submit a letter of interest, resume, writing sample. Applications are accepted continuously. World Wide Web: http://www.nccpr.org.

NATIONAL COMMITTEE FOR RESPONSIVE PHILANTHROPY
2001 S Street, NW, Suite 620
Washington, District of Columbia 20009

General Information Organization committed to making philanthropy more responsive to the economically, socially, and politically disenfranchised. Established in 1976. Number of employees: 11. Number of internship applications received each year: 150.

Internships Available ▶ *2–4 research interns:* responsibilities include public interest research, organizing and policy advocacy; assisting with information gathering, data analysis, and report writing; helping with administrative tasks; accountability for self-directed research; duties are 85% program/15% administrative. Candidates should have ability to work independently, analytical skills, computer skills, personal interest in the field, research skills, self-motivation, writing skills. Duration is 3-12 months. $10 per hour. Open to college freshmen, college sophomores, college juniors, college seniors, recent college graduates, graduate students. International applications accepted.

Benefits On-the-job training, opportunity to attend seminars/workshops, possible full-time employment, willing to act as a professional reference, willing to complete paperwork for educational credit, willing to provide letters of recommendation.

Contact Write, call, fax, e-mail, or through World Wide Web site Almudena Ocejo, Research Coordinator. Phone: 202-387-9177. Fax: 202-332-5084. E-mail: almudena@ncrp.org. In-person interview recommended (telephone interview accepted). Applicants must submit a letter of interest, resume, writing sample, three personal references. Applications are accepted continuously. World Wide Web: http://www.ncrp.org.

NATIONAL CONSUMERS LEAGUE
1701 K Street, NW, Suite 1200
Washington, District of Columbia 20006

General Information Private nonprofit membership consumer advocacy organization. Established in 1899. Number of employees: 26. Number of internship applications received each year: 50.

Internships Available ▶ *1 communications intern:* responsibilities include writing consumer-friendly articles, drafting press releases, developing press outreach materials and lists, marketing publications, assisting in Web design and publication layout. Candidates should have ability to work independently, ability to work with others, editing skills, oral communication skills, self-motivation, writing skills. Duration is minimum of 8 weeks (20 hours per week). Unpaid. Open to college juniors, college seniors, recent college graduates, graduate students, career changers, individuals reentering the workforce. ▶ *1 events coordinator intern:* responsibilities include planning and expediting events, communicating with speakers and attendees, developing and implementing event budgets, negotiating event contracts, working on site with hotel and catering staff, maintaining accurate records and files. Candidates should have ability to work independently, ability to work with others, oral communication skills, organizational skills, self-motivation, written communication skills. Duration is minimum 8 weeks (20 hours per week). Unpaid. Open to college juniors, college seniors, recent college graduates, graduate students, career changers, individuals reentering the workforce. ▶ *2–3 public policy interns:* responsibilities include working on issues in food and drug safety, health care, child labor, consumer fraud, financial services, telecommunications, or e-commerce. Candidates should have ability to work independently, ability to work with others, computer skills, oral communication skills, self-motivation, written communication skills. Duration is minimum of 8 weeks (20 hours per week). Unpaid. Open to college juniors, college seniors, recent college graduates, graduate students, law students, career changers, individuals reentering the workforce. International applications accepted.

Benefits Job counseling, names of contacts, opportunity to attend seminars/workshops, willing to act as a professional reference, willing to complete paperwork for educational credit, willing to provide letters of recommendation, opportunity to contribute to League publications.

Contact Write, call, fax, or e-mail Ms. Sara Cooper, Executive Vice President. Phone: 202-835-3323 Ext. 111. Fax: 202-835-0747. E-mail: intern@nclnet.org. Telephone interview required. Applicants must submit a formal organization application, letter of interest, resume, writing sample, letter of recommendation on supplied form. Applications are accepted continuously. World Wide Web: http://www.nclnet.org.

NATIONAL COUNCIL FOR RESEARCH ON WOMEN
11 Hanover Square
New York, New York 10005

General Information Working alliance of centers and individuals actively involved in feminist research, policy analysis, advocacy, and innovative programs for women and girls. Established in 1981. Number of employees: 9. Number of internship applications received each year: 50.

Internships Available ▶ *3–5 interns:* responsibilities include administrative duties, including database maintenance, fulfilling orders, mail merges, and organization; networking with others in the field, getting an introduction to nonprofits, and gaining access to women-centered goings-on around the world; depending on skills and experience, intern will take on substantive projects. Candidates should have ability to work independently, oral communication skills, personal interest in the field, strong interpersonal skills, written communication skills. Duration is 3 months (at least 2-3 days per week). $10 per day for subway and lunch. Open to recent high school graduates, college freshmen, college sophomores, college juniors, college seniors, recent college graduates, graduate students, law students, career changers. International applications accepted.

Benefits On-the-job training, opportunity to attend seminars/workshops, willing to act as a professional reference, willing to complete paperwork for educational credit, willing to provide letters of recommendation.

Contact Write, call, fax, or e-mail Elizabeth Horton, Director of Administration, 11 Hanover Square, 20th Floor, New York, New York 10005. Phone: 212-785-7335. Fax: 212-785-7350. E-mail: lhorton@ncrw.org. In-person interview recommended (telephone interview accepted). Applicants must submit a resume, writing sample, two personal references. Applications are accepted continuously. World Wide Web: http://www.ncrw.org.

NATIONAL COUNCIL OF JEWISH WOMEN– LEGISLATIVE OFFICE
1707 L Street, NW, Suite 950
Washington, District of Columbia 20036

General Information Legislative branch office of a large membership organization with a service and advocacy mission. Established in 1893. Number of employees: 6. Branch of National Council of Jewish Women, New York, New York. Number of internship applications received each year: 20.

Internships Available ▶ *2 legislative interns:* responsibilities include assisting staff with substantive hands-on lobbying and tracking legislative issues. Candidates should have analytical skills, computer skills, personal interest in the field, research skills, writing skills, progressive stance on social issues. Duration is flexible. Unpaid. Open to college sophomores, college juniors, college seniors, recent college graduates, graduate students. International applications accepted.

Benefits Job counseling, on-the-job training, opportunity to attend seminars/workshops, travel reimbursement, willing to act as a professional reference, willing to complete paperwork for educational credit, willing to provide letters of recommendation.

International Internships Available in Israel.

Contact Write, call, fax, e-mail, or through World Wide Web site Jody Rabhan, Associate Director, 1707 L Street, NW, Suite 950, Washington, District of Columbia 20036. Phone: 202-296-2588. Fax: 202-331-7792. E-mail: action@ncjwdc.org. In-person interview recommended (telephone interview accepted). Applicants must submit a letter of interest, resume, writing sample, personal reference. Application deadline: February 1 for summer, November 1 for spring. World Wide Web: http://www.ncjw.org.

NATIONAL CRIME PREVENTION COUNCIL
1000 Connecticut Avenue, NW, 13th Floor
Washington, District of Columbia 20036

General Information Organization that helps focus the power of the individual and the community in the fight against crime. Established in 1980. Number of employees: 70. Number of internship applications received each year: 200.

Internships Available ▶ *6 interns:* responsibilities include working in any of the following programs: communities, research, press relations, public service, policing, prevention, education, state services, human resources, finance, and production. Candidates should have ability to work independently, ability to work with others, computer skills, knowledge of field, office skills, oral communication skills, personal interest in the field, research skills, self-motivation, writing skills. Duration is one summer. $8 per hour. Open to high school students, college freshmen, college sophomores, college juniors, college seniors, recent college graduates, graduate students, law students.

Benefits Opportunity to attend seminars/workshops, possible full-time employment, travel reimbursement, willing to act as a professional reference, willing to complete paperwork for educational credit, willing to provide letters of recommendation.

Contact Write, call, fax, or e-mail Vernell Banks, Human Resources Assistant. Phone: 202-466-6272. Fax: 202-296-1356. E-mail: vbanks@ncpc.org. Telephone interview required. Applicants must submit a letter of interest, resume, writing sample. Application deadline: March 31. World Wide Web: http://www.ncpc.org.

NATIONAL CRIMINAL JUSTICE ASSOCIATION
720 7th Street, NW, Third Floor
Washington, District of Columbia 20001-3716

General Information Nonprofit, membership-based criminal justice association representing state and local government interests in public safety and crime control to Congress, federal executive, and private and public agencies. Established in 1971. Number of employees: 8. Number of internship applications received each year: 100.

Internships Available ▶ *1 graduate intern:* responsibilities include researching, writing, and developing a quarterly policy report; and assisting staff with other projects. Candidates should have analytical skills, editing skills, knowledge of field, oral communication skills, research skills, self-motivation, writing skills. Duration is fall, spring, or summer. Unpaid. Open to graduate students. ▶ *1–2 undergraduate interns:* responsibilities include researching and writing articles for the monthly association newsletter; attending hearings, press conferences, and Supreme Court sessions; possibly assisting staff with grant projects. Candidates should have ability to work independently, analytical skills, editing skills, personal interest in the field, research skills, self-motivation, writing skills. Duration is fall, spring, or summer. Unpaid. Open to college sophomores, college juniors, college seniors. International applications accepted.

Benefits On-the-job training, opportunity to attend seminars/workshops, willing to act as a professional reference, willing to complete paperwork for educational credit, willing to provide letters of recommendation, opportunity to attend congressional hearing, Supreme Court briefings and Justice Department meetings.

Contact Write, call, fax, e-mail, or through World Wide Web site Linda Lee, Staff Associate/Editor, 720 7th Street, NW, 3rd Floor, Washington, District of Columbia 20001-3716. Phone: 202-628-8550. Fax: 202-628-0080. E-mail: llee@ncja.org. Telephone interview required. Applicants must submit a letter of interest, resume, academic transcripts, writing sample, two personal references, two letters of recommendation. Applications are accepted continuously. World Wide Web: http://www.ncja.org.

NATIONAL ORGANIZATION FOR VICTIM ASSISTANCE (NOVA)
1730 Park Road, NW
Washington, District of Columbia 20010

General Information Private, nonprofit, 501(c)(3) organization of victim and witness assistance programs and practitioners, criminal justice agencies and professionals, mental health professionals, researchers, former victims and survivors, and others committed to the recognition and implementation of victim rights and services. Established in 1975. Number of employees: 8. Number of internship applications received each year: 30.

Internships Available ▶ *1–5 conference assistants:* responsibilities include assisting the conference coordinator with logistics of preparing a national victims conference of approximately 2000 participants. Candidates should have computer skills, office skills, oral communication skills, strong interpersonal skills, written communication skills. Duration is flexible. Unpaid. Open to high school students, recent high school graduates, college freshmen, college sophomores, college juniors, college seniors, recent college graduates, graduate students, law students, career changers, individuals reentering the workforce. ▶ *1 legislative assistants/ lobbyist:* responsibilities include assisting in monitoring proposed federal and state legislation and promoting passage of designated bills to assist victims of crime. Candidates should have ability to work with others, oral communication skills, personal interest in the field, research skills, self-motivation, written communication skills. Duration is flexible. Unpaid. Open to college freshmen, college sophomores, college juniors, college seniors, recent college graduates, graduate students, law students, career changers, individuals reentering the workforce. ▶ *Office assistants:* responsibilities include assisting in general office duties including answering phones and victim letters; mailings; special projects. Candidates should have office skills, personal interest in the field, strong interpersonal skills, writing skills. Duration is flexible. Unpaid. Open to high school students, recent high school graduates, college freshmen, college sophomores, college juniors, college seniors, recent college graduates, graduate students, law students, career changers, individuals reentering the workforce. ▶ *Victim advocates/ crisis intervenors:* responsibilities include working directly with victims of crime by phone, mail, or in person; possibility of participating in a 40-hour training to learn crisis intervention. Candidates should have ability to work independently, oral communication skills, personal interest in the field, strong interpersonal skills, writing skills. Duration is flexible. Unpaid. Open to high school students, recent high school graduates, college freshmen, college sophomores, college juniors, college seniors, recent college graduates, graduate students, law students, career changers, individuals reentering the workforce. International applications accepted.

Benefits Formal training, names of contacts, on-the-job training, opportunity to attend seminars/workshops, willing to act as a professional reference, willing to complete paperwork for educational credit, willing to provide letters of recommendation, flexible hours, input in designing the internship, development of long-lasting skills, free housing (when available).

Contact Write, call, fax, e-mail, or through World Wide Web site Cheryl Guidry Tyiska, Director of Victim Services, 1730 Park Road, NW, Washington, District of Columbia 20010. Phone: 202-232-6682. Fax: 202-462-2255. E-mail: cheryl@try-nova.org. In-person interview recommended (telephone interview accepted). Applicants must submit a letter of interest, resume, personal reference. Applications are accepted continuously. World Wide Web: http://www.try-nova.org.

NATIONAL ORGANIZATION FOR WOMEN (NATIONAL ACTION CENTER)
733 15th Street, NW, 2nd Floor
Washington, District of Columbia 20005

General Information Feminist organization working to ensure full equality for women and to end discrimination. Established in 1966. Number of employees: 35. Number of internship applications received each year: 200.

Internships Available ▶ *1–2 Internet/LAN interns:* responsibilities include assisting in programming and maintaining NOW's Web page and working with membership services. Candidates should have ability to work with others, computer skills, experience in the field, organizational skills, research skills, self-motivation. Duration is 1 semester. Unpaid. Open to college freshmen, college sophomores, college juniors, college seniors, recent college graduates, graduate students. ▶ *1 comptroller assistant:* responsibilities include maintaining a nonprofit organization's cash flow by assisting comptroller in daily book maintenance and organizing for yearly audit. Candidates should have ability to work independently, analytical skills, college courses in field, computer skills, office skills, organizational skills. Duration is 1 semester. Unpaid. Open to college sophomores, college juniors, college seniors, recent college graduates. ▶ *1–2 direct mail/fund-raising/development interns:* responsibilities include researching, writing, creating ads, working on product catalog, grant writing and research. Candidates should have ability to work independently, computer skills, research skills, strong interpersonal skills, written communication skills. Duration is 1 semester. Unpaid. Open to college sophomores, college juniors, college seniors, recent college graduates, graduate students, individuals reentering the workforce. ▶ *1–4 field organizing interns:* responsibilities include working on special projects in areas including welfare rights, lesbian rights, racial diversity, violence against women, and state and chapter development. Candidates should have ability to work with others, oral communication skills, organizational skills, personal interest in the field, written communication skills. Duration is 1 semester. Unpaid. Open to high school seniors, recent high school graduates, college freshmen, college sophomores, college juniors, college seniors, recent college graduates, graduate students. ▶ *1–3 government relations interns:* responsibilities include lobbying, attending meetings, and performing legislative research and writing. Candidates should have ability to work independently, analytical skills, organizational skills, self-motivation, strong interpersonal skills, written communication skills. Duration is 14 weeks. Unpaid. Open to college sophomores, college juniors, college seniors, recent college graduates, graduate students. ▶ *1–3 legal interns:* responsibilities include researching, writing, analysis, and policy drafts. Candidates should have analytical skills, knowledge of field, oral communication skills, organizational skills, research skills, self-motivation. Duration is 8–10 weeks. Unpaid. Open to law students. ▶ *1–2 political action interns:* responsibilities include assisting NOW in PAC organizing, meeting with candidates, candidate research, processing endorsement requests, and managing Federal Election Commission materials. Candidates should have analytical skills, computer skills, organizational skills, self-motivation, strong interpersonal skills, written communication skills. Duration is 1 semester. Unpaid. Open to college freshmen, college sophomores, college juniors, college seniors, recent college graduates. ▶ *2–4 press/communications interns:* responsibilities include researching and writing articles for the *National NOW Times*, assisting in maintaining press clippings, drafting press releases. Candidates should have editing skills, research skills, self-motivation, strong interpersonal skills, writing skills. Duration is 1 semester. Unpaid. Open to college freshmen, college sophomores, college juniors, college seniors, recent college graduates, graduate students, individuals reentering the workforce. International applications accepted.

Benefits Names of contacts, on-the-job training, opportunity to attend seminars/workshops, possible full-time employment, willing to act as a professional reference, willing to complete paperwork for educational credit, willing to provide letters of recommendation, formal training in grassroots organizing, field trips.

Contact Write, call, fax, e-mail, or through World Wide Web site Intern Coordinator. Phone: 202-628-8669. Fax: 202-785-8576. E-mail: nowinterns@aol.com. Telephone interview required. Applicants must submit a formal organization application, letter of interest, resume, 1-2 letters of recommendation. Application deadline: March 15 for summer, July 30 for fall, November 20 for spring. World Wide Web: http://www.now.org.

NATIONAL PARTNERSHIP FOR WOMEN AND FAMILIES
1875 Connecticut Avenue, NW, Suite 650
Washington, District of Columbia 20009

General Information Nonprofit, nonpartisan organization that uses public education and advocacy to promote fairness in the workplace, quality health care, and policies that help women and men meet the dual demands of work and family. Founded as the Women's Legal Defense Fund, the National Partnership has grown from a small group of volunteers into one of the nation's most powerful and effective advocates for women and families; works with business, government, unions, nonprofit organizations, and the media, and is a voice of fairness, a source for solutions, and a force for change. Established in 1971. Number of employees: 28. Number of internship applications received each year: 250.

Internships Available ▶ *1 Action Council and membership intern:* responsibilities include membership recruitment and fund-raising; expanding the National Partnership's membership in the Action Council through implementation of small fund-raising events, creation of fund-raising solicitations, follow-up of pledges, and administrative duties associated with the daily operations of the development department; conducting research regarding current and potential major donors. Candidates should have ability to work independently, computer skills, oral communication skills, organizational skills, research skills, written communication skills. Duration is 8-10 weeks (10-20 hours per week during academic year; full-time during summer). Unpaid. Open to college freshmen, college sophomores, college juniors, college seniors, recent college graduates, graduate students. ▶ *1 annual luncheon intern:* responsibilities include assisting in the production of the annual luncheon, including coordinating invitation and follow-up mailings to guests, tracking responses, assisting with logistics, and other luncheon related duties. Candidates should have ability to work independently, computer skills, oral communication skills, organizational skills, research skills, written communication skills. Duration is 8-10 weeks (10-20 hours per week during academic year; full-time during summer). Unpaid. Open to college freshmen, college sophomores, college juniors, college seniors, recent college graduates, graduate students. ▶ *Up to 2 communications interns:* responsibilities include researching, writing, and assisting with quarterly newsletter production; attending inside and outside meetings and press events; responding to requests for information from the media and public; producing and distributing daily clip packets; and maintaining filing systems. Candidates should have ability to work independently, computer skills, oral communication skills, organizational skills, research skills, written communication skills. Duration is 8-10 weeks (10-20 hours per week during academic year; full-time during summer). Unpaid. Open to college freshmen, college sophomores, college juniors, college seniors, recent college graduates, graduate students. ▶ *1–2 law clerks for Health Program:* responsibilities include assisting with the National Partnership's advocacy efforts to improve women's access to affordable, quality health care; researching and analyzing women's health issues, monitoring federal and state legislation, and attending and reporting back to staff about relevant congressional hearings, briefings, and other meetings. Candidates should have ability to work independently, editing skills, research skills, self-motivation, writing skills, background in women's health. Duration is 8-10 weeks (10-20 hours per week during academic year; full time during summer). Unpaid. Open to graduate students, law students. ▶ *1–2 law clerks for Work and Family Program:* responsibilities include assisting the National Partnership's advocacy efforts in the areas of equal employment opportunities, family friendly workplace policy, expansion of the Family and Medical Leave Act, and employment barriers affecting low-income women; working on ensuring effective enforcement of federal agencies responsible for enforcing anti-discrimination laws, and attending and reporting back to staff about relevant congressional hearings, briefings, and other meetings. Candidates should have ability to work independently, editing skills, research skills, self-motivation, writing skills. Duration is 8-10 weeks (10-20 hours per week during academic year; full-time during summer). Unpaid. Open to law students. ▶ *1–2 law clerks for workplace fairness:* responsibilities include assisting the National Partnership's advocacy efforts in the areas of equal employment opportunities, employment barriers affecting low-income women, and the civil rights impact of welfare reform; legal research and writing in support of monitoring of EEO enforcement; advocacy of broader laws and legal interpretations; amicus litigation; coalition advocacy; and public education about laws and proposals in this area. Candidates should have ability to work independently, editing skills, research skills, self-motivation, writing skills. Duration is 8-10 weeks (10-20 hours per week during academic year; full-time during summer). Unpaid. Open to law students. ▶ *1–2 work and family interns:* responsibilities include assisting with the National Partnership's

National Partnership for Women and Families (continued)

advocacy efforts in the areas of equal employment opportunities, family-friendly workplace policy, expansion of the Family and Medical Leave Act, and barriers affecting low-income women; ensuring effective enforcement of federal agencies responsible for enforcing anti-discrimination laws, monitoring and developing legislative initiatives on employment issues, and public education. Candidates should have ability to work independently, computer skills, oral communication skills, organizational skills, research skills, written communication skills. Duration is 8-10 weeks (10-20 hours per week during academic year; full-time during summer). Unpaid. Open to college freshmen, college sophomores, college juniors, college seniors, recent college graduates, graduate students. ▶ *1–2 workplace fairness interns:* responsibilities include assisting with the National Partnership's advocacy efforts in the areas of equal employment opportunities, such as affirmative action, employment barriers affecting low-income women, particularly welfare recipients, and the civil rights impact of welfare policy changes at the national and state levels. Interns will also assist in monitoring enforcement of federal anti-discrimination laws, advocating for legislation on employment issues, representation of the National Partnership in coalitions, research and writing, and educating the public about laws and proposals in the area, including developing fact sheets and other informational materials. Candidates should have ability to work independently, computer skills, office skills, oral communication skills, organizational skills, research skills, written communication skills. Duration is 8-10 weeks (10-20 hours per week during academic year; full time during summer). Unpaid. Open to college freshmen, college sophomores, college juniors, college seniors, recent college graduates, graduate students. International applications accepted.

Benefits Job counseling, names of contacts, on-the-job training, opportunity to attend seminars/workshops, willing to act as a professional reference, willing to complete paperwork for educational credit, willing to provide letters of recommendation.

Contact Write, call, fax, or e-mail Ms. Helen Seery McBride, Director of Administration. Phone: 202-986-2600. Fax: 202-986-2539. E-mail: hmcbride@nationalpartnership.org. Applicants must submit a letter of interest, resume, academic transcripts, writing sample, references. Application deadline: February 15 for summer law clerks; rolling for spring/fall, March 15 for summer undergraduates; rolling for spring/fall. World Wide Web: http://www.nationalpartnership.org.

NATIONAL PEACE FOUNDATION
666 11th Street, NW, Suite 202
Washington, District of Columbia 20001

General Information Grassroots network of women who are dedicated to a peaceful future, locally and globally. Established in 1982. Number of employees: 6. Number of internship applications received each year: 40.

Internships Available ▶ *Interns.* Duration is one summer or semester. Small stipend. Open to graduate students. International applications accepted.

Contact Write, call, or fax Kathleen Lansing, Deputy Director. Phone: 202-783-7030. Fax: 202-783-7040. In-person interview recommended (telephone interview accepted). Applicants must submit a resume, writing sample, cover letter. Application deadline: early August for fall, April 15 for summer, December 1 for spring. World Wide Web: http://www.nationalpeace.org.

NATIONAL STUDENT CAMPAIGN AGAINST HUNGER AND HOMELESSNESS
233 North Pleasant Street, Suite 32
Amherst, Massachusetts 01002

General Information Coalition of student and community members who are working to end hunger and homelessness through education, service, and organizing; trains students to create or improve service programs, promotes campus and community collaborations, and initiates programs to fight poverty. Established in 1985. Number of employees: 4. Unit of Center for Public Interest Research, Boston, Massachusetts. Number of internship applications received each year: 50.

Internships Available ▶ *2–4 Annual Hunger Cleanup interns:* responsibilities include publicizing community service work-a-thon to campuses across the country and coordinating fundraising efforts for the cleanup. Candidates should have oral communication skills, personal interest in the field, self-motivation, strong interpersonal skills. Duration is flexible (at least one semester). Unpaid. Open to high school seniors, recent high school graduates, college freshmen, college sophomores, college juniors, college seniors, recent college graduates, graduate students, law students, career changers, individuals reentering the workforce. ▶ *1–2 Internet interns:* responsibilities include updating and expanding existing Web site; building list serve, utilizing Internet to build network student participants. Candidates should have ability to work independently, computer skills, personal interest in the field, self-motivation, written communication skills, creativity. Duration is 1 semester. Unpaid. Open to high school seniors, recent high school graduates, college freshmen, college sophomores, college juniors, college seniors, recent college graduates, graduate students, career changers, individuals reentering the workforce. ▶ *2 National Conference interns:* responsibilities include helping to organize the annual national student conference held each October. Candidates should have ability to work independently, oral communication skills, personal interest in the field, self-motivation, strong interpersonal skills. Duration is flexible; at least fall semester; summer internships also available. Unpaid. Open to high school seniors, recent high school graduates, college freshmen, college sophomores, college juniors, college seniors, recent college graduates, graduate students, law students, career changers, individuals reentering the workforce. ▶ *2 food salvage interns:* responsibilities include developing food salvage programs that ensure unused high school and college campus cafeteria food will go to those members of the local community who are in need of it. Candidates should have oral communication skills, personal interest in the field, self-motivation, strong interpersonal skills, written communication skills. Duration is flexible; at least one semester. Unpaid. Open to high school seniors, recent high school graduates, college freshmen, college sophomores, college juniors, college seniors, recent college graduates, graduate students, career changers, individuals reentering the workforce. ▶ *1–3 public policy interns:* responsibilities include developing network around local and national legislation that addresses the problems of hunger and homelessness, researching current legislation, and writing monthly action alert. Candidates should have ability to work independently, editing skills, personal interest in the field, research skills, writing skills. Duration is at least 1 semester/quarter. Unpaid. Open to high school seniors, recent high school graduates, college freshmen, college sophomores, college juniors, college seniors, recent college graduates, graduate students, law students, career changers, individuals reentering the workforce. ▶ *2 publication interns:* responsibilities include updating project manuals and developing a series of fact sheets on hunger and homelessness. Candidates should have ability to work independently, ability to work with others, editing skills, research skills, writing skills. Duration is flexible; at least one semester. Unpaid. Open to high school seniors, recent high school graduates, college freshmen, college sophomores, college juniors, college seniors, recent college graduates, graduate students, career changers, individuals reentering the workforce. International applications accepted.

Benefits Job counseling, names of contacts, on-the-job training, opportunity to attend seminars/workshops, possible full-time employment, willing to act as a professional reference, willing to complete paperwork for educational credit, willing to provide letters of recommendation, opportunity for meaningful project experience, chance to make a difference in lives of others; possibility of free housing for National Conference interns.

Contact Write, call, fax, e-mail, or through World Wide Web site Jennifer Hecker, Organizing Director. Phone: 800-664-8647. Fax: 413-256-6435. E-mail: nscah@aol.com. In-person interview recommended (telephone interview accepted). Applicants must submit a letter of interest, resume. Applications are accepted continuously. World Wide Web: http://www.studentsagainsthunger.org.

NATIONAL TRAINING AND INFORMATION CENTER
810 North Milwaukee
Chicago, Illinois 60622

General Information Resource center for grassroots neighborhood groups that provides training in community organizing and focuses on issues including housing, reinvestment, safe neighborhoods, and education. Established in 1972. Number of employees: 18. Number of internship applications received each year: 30.

Internships Available ▶ *2 community organizing/policy interns:* responsibilities include researching domestic policy, attending night and weekend meetings in Chicago neighborhoods, writing, and supporting staff as directed. Candidates should have oral communication skills, personal interest in the field, research skills, strong interpersonal skills, strong leadership ability, writing skills. Duration is 3–12 months. Unpaid. Open to high school students, recent high school graduates, college freshmen, college sophomores, college juniors, college seniors, recent college graduates, graduate students, law students, career changers, individuals reentering the workforce. ▶ *1–6 street organizer/policy research interns:* responsibilities include working with community organizations to develop local residents' leadership capacity; organizing public meetings; carrying out one-on-one interviews with neighborhood residents; developing strategies to address issues of concern to those residents. Candidates should have ability to work independently, oral communication skills, personal interest in the field, strong interpersonal skills, strong leadership ability. Duration is 2–8 months. Unpaid. Open to college sophomores, college juniors, college seniors, recent college graduates, career changers. International applications accepted.

Benefits Formal training, job counseling, names of contacts, on-the-job training, opportunity to attend seminars/workshops, possible full-time employment, willing to act as a professional reference, willing to complete paperwork for educational credit, willing to provide letters of recommendation.

Contact Write, fax, or e-mail Joseph W. Mariano, Staff Director. Fax: 312-243-7044. E-mail: mariano@ntic-us.org. No phone calls. In-person interview recommended (telephone interview accepted). Applicants must submit a letter of interest, resume. Applications are accepted continuously. World Wide Web: http://www.ntic.us.org.

NATIONAL WHISTLEBLOWER CENTER
3238 P Street, NW
Washington, District of Columbia 20007

General Information Nonprofit educational and advocacy organization committed to environmental protection, nuclear safety, government accountability, and protecting the rights of employee whistle blowers. Established in 1988. Number of employees: 6. Number of internship applications received each year: 100.

Internships Available ▶ *Law clerks:* responsibilities include significant legal research and writing projects, assisting at trials, and performing all the work of an associate attorney. Duration is 10 weeks (minimum). Unpaid. Open to college freshmen, college sophomores, college juniors, college seniors, law students. International applications accepted.

Benefits Opportunity to attend seminars/workshops, willing to act as a professional reference, willing to complete paperwork for educational credit, willing to provide letters of recommendation, one-on-one supervision from an attorney.

Contact Write, call, fax, or e-mail Joyce Claro, Internship Coordinator, 3238 P Street, NW, Washington, District of Columbia 20007. Phone: 202-342-6980. Fax: 202-342-6984. E-mail: whistle@whistleblowers.org. Telephone interview required. Applicants must submit a letter of interest, resume. Application deadline: March 1 for summer, September 1 for January positions, December 1 for spring. World Wide Web: http://www.whistleblowers.org.

NATIONAL WOMEN'S HEALTH NETWORK
514 10th Street, NW, Suite 400
Washington, District of Columbia 20004

General Information Organization that provides information on women's health issues and advocates for women's health by functioning as a watchdog over federal agencies. Established in 1975. Number of employees: 5. Number of internship applications received each year: 200.

Internships Available ▶ *5 women's health advocacy interns:* responsibilities include working in the clearinghouse and on special projects, attending meetings and conferences. Candidates should have oral communication skills, organizational skills, personal interest in the field, research skills, self-motivation, strong interpersonal skills, writing skills. Duration is 10 weeks (minimum). Position available as unpaid or at $160 per week for spring/fall only; no summer stipend. Open to college freshmen, college sophomores, college juniors, college seniors, recent college graduates, graduate students, law students, career changers, individuals reentering the workforce. International applications accepted.

Benefits Names of contacts, opportunity to attend seminars/workshops, willing to act as a professional reference, willing to complete paperwork for educational credit, willing to provide letters of recommendation.

Contact Write, call, or fax Stephanie Donne, Clearinghouse Coordinator. Phone: 202-347-1140. Fax: 202-347-1168. Telephone interview required. Applicants must submit a letter of interest, resume, writing sample. Application deadline: continuous for spring and fall, March 15 for summer. World Wide Web: http://www.womenshealthnetwork.org.

NATIONAL WOMEN'S JUSTICE COALITION, INC.
GPO Box 3148
Canberra ACT 2601 Australia

General Information Organization that provides networking, capacity building, and lobbying to promote women's legal equality in Australia. Established in 1995. Number of employees: 4. Number of internship applications received each year: 50.

Internships Available ▶ *1–4 interns.* Candidates should have ability to work independently, analytical skills, computer skills, editing skills, experience in the field, office skills, oral communication skills, organizational skills, personal interest in the field, research skills, self-motivation, strong interpersonal skills, strong leadership ability, writing skills. Duration is 1–2 semesters. Unpaid. Open to graduate students, law students.

Benefits Names of contacts, on-the-job training, willing to act as a professional reference, willing to complete paperwork for educational credit, willing to provide letters of recommendation.

International Internships Available.

Contact E-mail Intern Coordinator, GPO Box 3148, Canberra 2601 Australia. Fax: 61-2-6257-3070. E-mail: nwjc@nwjc.org.au. No phone calls. Telephone interview required. Applicants must submit a formal organization application, resume, academic transcripts, two writing samples, two personal references. Applications are accepted continuously. World Wide Web: http://www.nwjc.org.au.

NATIONAL WOMEN'S POLITICAL CAUCUS
1630 Connecticut Avenue, NW, Suite 201
Washington, District of Columbia 20009

General Information National bipartisan grassroots organization dedicated to the advancement of women through appointed and elected public office; operates a nonprofit, leadership development, education, and research arm and conducts extensive training seminars designed to train women for potential candidacy. Established in 1971. Number of employees: 3. Number of internship applications received each year: 100.

Internships Available ▶ *1–2 interns:* responsibilities include working in media and communications, political and electoral politics, membership, grassroots organizing, or development and fundraising. Candidates should have ability to work independently, computer skills, office skills, oral communication skills, strong interpersonal skills, written communication skills. Duration is 1

National Women's Political Caucus (continued)

semester. Unpaid. Open to college freshmen, college sophomores, college juniors, college seniors, recent college graduates, graduate students.
Benefits Names of contacts, on-the-job training, opportunity to attend seminars/workshops, willing to act as a professional reference, willing to complete paperwork for educational credit, willing to provide letters of recommendation, opportunity to gain leadership skills.
Contact Write, call, fax, or e-mail Katherine Minarik, Political Director/Intern Coordinator. Phone: 202-785-1100. Fax: 202-785-3605. E-mail: info@nwpc.org. Telephone interview required. Applicants must submit a letter of interest, resume, writing sample. Applications are accepted continuously. World Wide Web: http://www.nwpc.org.

NATIONAL YOUTH & MILITARISM PROGRAM, AMERICAN FRIENDS SERVICE COMMITTEE
1501 Cherry Street
Philadelphia, Pennsylvania 19102

General Information Quaker organization committed to peace and social justice; conducts public education campaigns and supports grassroots organizing on issues involving youth, war, and peace. Established in 1917. Number of employees: 70. Unit of American Friends Service Committee, Philadelphia, Pennsylvania. Number of internship applications received each year: 40.
Internships Available ▶ *1 Jim Bristol Youth and Militarism Fellow:* responsibilities include working for social change on a national level. Candidates should have ability to work with others, computer skills, experience in the field, oral communication skills, personal interest in the field, written communication skills. Duration is 9 months. $10 per hour.
Benefits Health insurance, on-the-job training, opportunity to attend seminars/workshops, travel reimbursement, willing to act as a professional reference.
Contact Write, fax, or e-mail Program Coordinator, 1501 Cherry Street, Philadelphia, Pennsylvania 19102. Fax: 215-241-7177. E-mail: youthmil@afsc.org. No phone calls. In-person interview required. Applicants must submit a formal organization application, letter of interest, resume. World Wide Web: http://www.afsc.org/youthmil.htm.

NETWORK
801 Pennsylvania Avenue, SE, Suite 460
Washington, District of Columbia 20003

General Information National Catholic social justice lobby whose members seek to influence national legislation for healthcare reform, affordable housing, economic conversion, deficit reduction, and global collaboration for equitable and sustainable development. Established in 1971. Number of employees: 12. Number of internship applications received each year: 20.
Internships Available ▶ *3 associates:* responsibilities include representing staff at coalition meetings, conveying legislative information to staff, lobbying, activating grassroots organizing, and assisting with administrative work. Candidates should have ability to work with others, computer skills, oral communication skills, personal interest in the field, self-motivation, written communication skills. Duration is 11 months. $7700 per duration of internship. Open to recent college graduates, career changers, individuals reentering the workforce.
Benefits Names of contacts, on-the-job training, opportunity to attend seminars/workshops, possible full-time employment, willing to complete paperwork for educational credit, willing to provide letters of recommendation, full health benefits for paid internships.
Contact Write, call, fax, e-mail, or through World Wide Web site Ms. Linda Rich, Associate Coordinator. Phone: 202-547-5556. Fax: 202-547-5510. E-mail: lrich@networklobby.org. Telephone interview required. Applicants must submit a formal organization application, resume, two personal references. Application deadline: February 1. World Wide Web: http://www.networklobby.org.

NEW YORK ASSOCIATION FOR VOLUNTEER ADMINISTRATION
PO Box 659, Grand Central Station
New York, New York 10163

General Information Membership organization whose purpose is to promote professionalism and strengthen leadership in volunteerism. Established in 1996. Affiliate of Association for Volunteer Administration, Richmond, Virginia. Number of internship applications received each year: 3.
Internships Available ▶ *1–4 volunteer management apprentices:* responsibilities include varied tasks based on match of apprentice and agency; position includes program planning, training, recruitment, placement and retention and volunteer staff relations as well as special projects. Candidates should have ability to work independently, oral communication skills, plan to pursue career in field, strong interpersonal skills, strong leadership ability, written communication skills. Duration is 3–4 months. Unpaid. Open to college seniors, recent college graduates, graduate students, career changers, individuals reentering the workforce. International applications accepted.
Benefits Formal training, job counseling, on-the-job training, opportunity to attend seminars/workshops, willing to act as a professional reference, willing to provide letters of recommendation, possible stipend.
Contact Write, call, or e-mail Rhoda White, Chair-Apprentice Committee, 300 East 74th Street 32F, New York, New York 10021. Phone: 212-535-1747. E-mail: rhora59@hotmail.com. In-person interview required. Applicants must submit a formal organization application, letter of interest, resume, letter of recommendation. Applications are accepted continuously.

NORTH CAROLINA CENTER FOR PUBLIC POLICY RESEARCH
PO Box 430
Raleigh, North Carolina 27602

General Information Public policy research center that studies state government policies and procedures and attempts to educate the public. Established in 1977. Number of employees: 6.
Internships Available ▶ *2 research interns:* responsibilities include keeping up with legislation, writing and researching articles, and performing data entry. Candidates should have personal interest in the field, plan to pursue career in field, research skills, writing skills. Duration is 10 weeks. Paid. Open to college juniors, college seniors, recent college graduates, graduate students. International applications accepted.
Benefits Willing to act as a professional reference, willing to complete paperwork for educational credit, willing to provide letters of recommendation.
Contact Write, call, fax, or e-mail Policy Analyst. Phone: 919-832-2839. Fax: 919-832-2847. E-mail: rosebud@ncppr.org. In-person interview recommended (telephone interview accepted). Applicants must submit a resume, academic transcripts, writing sample. Application deadline: March 31 for summer; continuous for all other positions. World Wide Web: http://www.ncinsider.com/nccppr.

NORTHWEST FEDERATION OF COMMUNITY ORGANIZATIONS
1905 South Jackson Street
Seattle, Washington 98144

General Information Regional network of statewide nonprofit citizen advocacy and action organizations. Established in 1993. Number of employees: 7. Number of internship applications received each year: 25.
Internships Available ▶ *1–5 research and policy interns:* responsibilities include research on current issues; writing reports, fact sheets, or flyers based on research; some field work/travel may be involved; working with local grassroots activists/organizers; playing a role in campaign development, outreach, education, and training. Candidates should have analytical skills, computer skills, personal interest in the field, research skills, writing skills. Dura-

tion is 10-week minimum. Unpaid. Open to college sophomores, college juniors, college seniors, recent college graduates, graduate students, law students. International applications accepted.
Benefits Formal training, on-the-job training, opportunity to attend seminars/workshops, possible full-time employment, willing to act as a professional reference, willing to complete paperwork for educational credit, willing to provide letters of recommendation.
Contact Write, call, fax, or e-mail Bryan Hall, Intern Coordinator. Phone: 206-568-5400. Fax: 206-568-5444. E-mail: bryan@nwfco.org. Telephone interview required. Applicants must submit a letter of interest, resume, writing sample. Applications are accepted continuously. World Wide Web: http://www.nwfco.org.

OCTOBER 22 COALITION TO STOP POLICE BRUTALITY
PO Box 2627
New York, New York 10009

General Information Community-based nonprofit group fighting police brutality. Established in 1996. Number of employees: 4. Number of internship applications received each year: 6.
Internships Available ▶ *2 office assistants:* responsibilities include communication with local grassroots organizations, families of people killed by police, lawyers, and researchers on police. Candidates should have ability to work with others, oral communication skills, personal interest in the field. Duration is 1 semester. Unpaid. Open to college freshmen, college sophomores, college juniors, college seniors. International applications accepted.
Benefits On-the-job training, willing to act as a professional reference, willing to complete paperwork for educational credit, willing to provide letters of recommendation.
Contact Write, call, or e-mail Kathryn Lee, Managing Director, 263 East 10th Street, Apartment 1, New York, New York 10009. Phone: 212-477-8062. E-mail: no1022@aol.com. In-person interview recommended (telephone interview accepted). Applicants must submit a letter of interest. Applications are accepted continuously. World Wide Web: http://www.october22.org.

OHIO CITIZEN ACTION
614 West Superior, Suite 1200
Cleveland, Ohio 44113

General Information State's largest environmental, consumer advocacy and nonprofit grassroots group. Established in 1975. Number of employees: 85. Number of internship applications received each year: 30.
Internships Available ▶ *10–30 community organizers/grassroots organizers:* responsibilities include educating and involving the public on environmental and political issues through petitioning, fundraising, and letter writing campaigns. Candidates should have ability to work independently, ability to work with others, oral communication skills, organizational skills, personal interest in the field, self-motivation, strong leadership ability. Duration is flexible. $350–$425 per week. Open to high school seniors, recent high school graduates, college freshmen, college sophomores, college juniors, college seniors, recent college graduates, graduate students, law students, career changers, individuals reentering the workforce. International applications accepted.
Benefits Formal training, free housing, health insurance, job counseling, names of contacts, on-the-job training, opportunity to attend seminars/workshops, possible full-time employment, travel reimbursement, willing to act as a professional reference, willing to complete paperwork for educational credit, willing to provide letters of recommendation.
Contact Write, call, fax, e-mail, or through World Wide Web site Kendall E. Jackson, Staff Director. Phone: 216-861-5200. Fax: 216-694-6904. E-mail: kjackson@ohiocitizen.org. In-person interview recommended (telephone interview accepted). Applicants must submit a formal organization application, resume, call 216-623-3952 for interview. Applications are accepted continuously. World Wide Web: http://ohiocitizen.org.

OPERATION CROSSROADS AFRICA
34 Mount Morris Park
New York, New York 10027

General Information International nonprofit, nongovernmental volunteer organization. Established in 1957. Number of employees: 2. Number of internship applications received each year: 250.
Internships Available ▶ *150–200 Crossroads volunteers (Africa or Brazil):* responsibilities include living and working with group of 8-10 volunteers in rural African village or in Salvador, Bahia (Brazil) performing agriculture, education, community health, construction, or women's development projects. Candidates should have knowledge of field, oral communication skills, personal interest in the field, strong interpersonal skills, willingness to experience another culture. Duration is mid-June to mid-August. Unpaid. Open to high school seniors, recent high school graduates, college freshmen, college sophomores, college juniors, college seniors, recent college graduates, graduate students, individuals reentering the workforce, must be at least 17 years of age. ▶ *12–14 Crossroads volunteers (Namibia):* responsibilities include living and working with group of 12–15 volunteers in Namibia, southern Africa; community service, language and culture study, and travel in-country. Candidates should have ability to work with others, oral communication skills, personal interest in the field, interest in Africa and African diaspora. Duration is September 15 to December 15 or January 15 to April 15. Unpaid. Open to high school seniors, recent high school graduates, college freshmen, college sophomores, college juniors, college seniors, recent college graduates, graduate students. International applications accepted.
Benefits Free housing, free meals, health insurance, on-the-job training, travel reimbursement, willing to act as a professional reference, willing to complete paperwork for educational credit, willing to provide letters of recommendation, limited number of scholarships available.
International Internships Available in Gambia; Ghana; Kenya; Malawi; Senegal; South Africa; Uganda; United Republic of Tanzania.
Contact Write, call, e-mail, or through World Wide Web site Kate Shackford, Director of Program Services. Phone: 212-289-1949. Fax: 212-289-2526. E-mail: oca@igc.org. Applicants must submit a formal organization application, three letters of recommendation, participation fee of $3500 upon acceptance. Application deadline: February 1 for summer, July 30 for fall (Namibia), October 31 for spring (Namibia). Fees: $25. World Wide Web: http://www.igc.org/oca.

ORGANIZATION OF CHINESE AMERICANS
1001 Connecticut Avenue, NW, Suite 601
Washington, District of Columbia 20036

General Information National nonprofit advocacy organization of concerned Chinese Americans dedicated to securing social justice, equal opportunity, and equal treatment of Chinese Americans. Established in 1973. Number of employees: 10. Number of internship applications received each year: 120.
Internships Available ▶ *1–4 congressional interns:* responsibilities include attending subcommittee hearings, tracking legislation, research, writing articles and press releases, and office duties. Candidates should have ability to work independently, ability to work with others, analytical skills, computer skills, editing skills, office skills, oral communication skills, research skills, self-motivation, strong leadership ability, writing skills. Duration is 10 weeks. Paid. ▶ *1–4 government interns:* responsibilities include attending subcommittee hearings, tracking legislation, research, writing articles and press releases, and office duties. Candidates should have ability to work independently, ability to work with others, analytical skills, computer skills, editing skills, office skills, oral communication skills, research skills, self-motivation, strong leadership ability, writing skills. Duration is 10 weeks. Paid. ▶ *1–4 national office interns:* responsibilities include writing press releases and articles; attending meetings. Candidates should have ability to work independently, analytical skills, computer skills, editing skills, office skills, oral communication skills, organizational skills, research skills, self-motivation, strong interpersonal skills, writing

skills. Duration is 10 weeks. Paid. Open to college freshmen, college sophomores, college juniors, college seniors.
Benefits Opportunity to attend seminars/workshops, willing to act as a professional reference, willing to complete paperwork for educational credit, willing to provide letters of recommendation, stipend of $2000.
Contact Write, call, fax, or e-mail Keith McAllister, Director of Technology. Phone: 202-223-5500. Fax: 202-296-0540. E-mail: oca@ocanatl.org. Telephone interview required. Applicants must submit a formal organization application, resume, academic transcripts, writing sample, two personal references, cover letters, essay (typed and double-spaced) explaining interest in internship. Application deadline: March 24 for summer, July 15 for fall, November 15 for spring. World Wide Web: http://www.ocanatl.org.

OVARIAN CANCER NATIONAL ALLIANCE
910 17th Street, NW, Suite 413
Washington, District of Columbia 20006

General Information Nonprofit organization working at the national level to increase public and professional understanding of ovarian cancer and to advocate for increased research for more effective diagnostics and treatment. Established in 1997. Number of employees: 8. Number of internship applications received each year: 10.
Internships Available ▶ *1–2 staff assistants:* responsibilities include working closely with the public education director and communications coordinator; handling consumer correspondence, data entry, statistics, and information gathering; outreach; writing and working with constituent groups. Candidates should have ability to work independently, computer skills, personal interest in the field, writing skills, interest in women's and health issues. Duration is one summer or semester. Stipend. Open to college freshmen, college sophomores, college juniors, college seniors, recent college graduates, career changers.
Benefits On-the-job training, opportunity to attend seminars/workshops, willing to act as a professional reference, willing to complete paperwork for educational credit, willing to provide letters of recommendation, stipend available.
Contact Write, call, fax, e-mail, or through World Wide Web site Sheri Diorio, Director of Finance and Administration. Phone: 202-331-1332. Fax: 202-331-2292. E-mail: ocna@ovariancancer.org. In-person interview recommended (telephone interview accepted). Applicants must submit a resume, writing sample, two personal references. Applications are accepted continuously. World Wide Web: http://www.ovariancancer.org.

OWL: THE VOICE OF MIDLIFE AND OLDER WOMEN
666 11th Street, NW, Suite 700
Washington, District of Columbia 20001

General Information National membership organization that strives to improve the status and quality of life for women, midlife and older. Established in 1980. Number of employees: 8. Number of internship applications received each year: 15.
Internships Available ▶ *1 communications/public relations intern.* Candidates should have analytical skills, editing skills, oral communication skills, research skills, strong interest in women's issues, positive attitude; computer skills helpful. Duration is flexible (3 month minimum, 16 hours per week). Unpaid. ▶ *1 development/fund-raising intern.* Candidates should have oral communication skills, organizational skills, research skills, strong interpersonal skills, written communication skills, strong interest in women's issues, positive attitude; computer skills helpful. Duration is flexible (3 month minimum, 16 hours per week). Unpaid. ▶ *1 organizing and advocacy intern.* Candidates should have analytical skills, oral communication skills, organizational skills, self-motivation, writing skills, strong interest in women's issues, positive attitude; computer skills helpful. Duration is flexible (3 month minimum, 16 hours per week). Unpaid. ▶ *1 public policy and research intern.* Candidates should have ability to work independently, analytical skills, oral communication skills, research skills, writing skills, strong interest in women's issues, positive attitude; computer skills

helpful. Duration is flexible (3 month minimum, 16 hours per week). Unpaid. Open to college sophomores, college juniors, college seniors, recent college graduates, graduate students, law students, career changers, individuals reentering the workforce, non-traditional students. International applications accepted.
Benefits Opportunity to attend seminars/workshops, possible full-time employment, travel reimbursement, willing to act as a professional reference, willing to complete paperwork for educational credit, willing to provide letters of recommendation, willing to design special projects to match intern's academic targets.
Contact Write, call, fax, or e-mail Laurie M. Young, Executive Director, 666 11th Street, NW, Suite 700, Washington, District of Columbia 20001. Phone: 800-825-3695. Fax: 202-638-2356. E-mail: lyoung@owl-national.org. In-person interview recommended (telephone interview accepted). Applicants must submit a letter of interest, resume, two writing samples, personal reference, letter of recommendation. Applications are accepted continuously. World Wide Web: http://www.owl-national.org.

PARTNERS FOR LIVABLE COMMUNITIES
1429 21st Street, NW
Washington, District of Columbia 20036

General Information Nonprofit organization working to improve the livability of communities by promoting quality of life, economic development, and social equity. Established in 1978. Number of employees: 8. Number of internship applications received each year: 25.
Internships Available ▶ *1–2 Creative City Public Policy Writers:* responsibilities include public policy research and documentation for Partners' publication on the Creative City; documenting best practices in participating cities; analyzing and documenting success of Creative City initiatives. Candidates should have ability to work independently, computer skills, editing skills, research skills, writing skills. Duration is flexible. Position available as unpaid or paid. Open to recent college graduates, graduate students, career changers, individuals reentering the workforce. ▶ *2–4 interns:* responsibilities include assisting in research, writing, event coordinating, and information management. Candidates should have ability to work independently, ability to work with others, computer skills, editing skills, organizational skills, personal interest in the field, research skills, self-motivation, written communication skills. Duration is flexible. Position available as unpaid or at stipend. Open to college freshmen, college sophomores, college juniors, college seniors, recent college graduates, graduate students, law students, career changers, individuals reentering the workforce.
Benefits Names of contacts, opportunity to attend seminars/workshops, willing to act as a professional reference, willing to complete paperwork for educational credit, willing to provide letters of recommendation, possibility of stipend for Creative City Public Policy Writers.
Contact Write, call, fax, or e-mail Laura Durham, Senior Program Officer. Phone: 202-887-5990. Fax: 202-466-4845. E-mail: partners@livable.com. In-person interview recommended (telephone interview accepted). Applicants must submit a letter of interest, resume, writing sample, dates available, goals for internship experience. Applications are accepted continuously. World Wide Web: http://www.livable.com.

PEACE ACTION AND PEACE ACTION EDUCATION FUND
1819 H Street, NW, Room 425
Washington, District of Columbia 20006

General Information Grassroots peace and justice organization that seeks to promote global security by converting to a peace economy and stopping the nuclear arms race and conventional arms trade. Established in 1957. Number of employees: 16. Number of internship applications received each year: 100.
Internships Available ▶ *1–2 organizing department interns:* responsibilities include assisting with event organizing, research, writing, desk top publishing, Web publishing, some administrative work. Duration is 3 months. Small stipend. ▶ *1–2 policy department interns:* responsibilities include research, writing, desktop and Web publish-

ing, coalition meetings, some event organizing, and administrative work. Duration is 3 months. Small stipend. Candidates for all positions should have ability to work independently, ability to work with others, computer skills, organizational skills, personal interest in the field, written communication skills. Open to high school seniors, recent high school graduates, college freshmen, college sophomores, college juniors, college seniors, recent college graduates, graduate students, law students, career changers, individuals reentering the workforce. International applications accepted.

Benefits Names of contacts, on-the-job training, opportunity to attend seminars/workshops, possible full-time employment, travel reimbursement, willing to act as a professional reference, willing to complete paperwork for educational credit, willing to provide letters of recommendation.

Contact Write, call, fax, e-mail, or through World Wide Web site Carie Benzschawel, Internship Coordinator. Phone: 202-862-9740 Ext. 3041. Fax: 202-862-9762. E-mail: cbenzschawel@peace-action. org. Telephone interview required. Applicants must submit a letter of interest, resume, 2-3 personal references. Applications are accepted continuously. World Wide Web: http://www.peace-action. org.

PENNSYLVANIA LESBIAN AND GAY TASKFORCE
1616 Walnut Street, Suite 1005
Philadelphia, Pennsylvania 19103-5310

General Information Public interest organization dedicated to the civil, human, and constitutional rights of lesbian and gay people, focusing on research, public policy, advocacy, direct service, and litigation. Established in 1978. Number of employees: 2. Number of internship applications received each year: 6.

Internships Available ▶ *2 education interns:* responsibilities include performing research and statistical analysis and offering clerical support. Candidates should have ability to work independently, ability to work with others, computer skills, office skills, oral communication skills, research skills, written communication skills, library skills. Duration is ongoing. Unpaid. Open to college seniors, recent college graduates, graduate students, law students. ▶ *2 law interns:* responsibilities include performing research and offering clerical support. Candidates should have ability to work independently, computer skills, declared college major in field, office skills, oral communication skills, research skills, writing skills. Duration is ongoing. Unpaid.

Benefits Names of contacts, on-the-job training, opportunity to attend seminars/workshops, possible full-time employment, travel reimbursement, willing to provide letters of recommendation.

Contact Write, call, fax, or e-mail Ms. Rita Addessa, Executive Director. Phone: 215-772-2000. Fax: 215-772-2004. E-mail: plgtf@ plgtf.org. In-person interview required. Applicants must submit a letter of interest, resume, writing sample. Applications are accepted continuously. World Wide Web: http://plgtf.org.

PEOPLE FOR THE AMERICAN WAY FOUNDATION
2000 M Street, NW, #400
Washington, District of Columbia 20036

General Information Nonprofit, 300,000-member, progressive, nonpartisan, constitutional liberties organization. Established in 1980. Number of employees: 65. Number of internship applications received each year: 300.

Internships Available ▶ *5–6 Everett Public Service Internships:* responsibilities include writing, research, grassroots organizing, congressional monitoring. Candidates should have ability to work with others, computer skills, oral communication skills, research skills, writing skills. Duration is 10 weeks. $220–$250 per week. Open to college freshmen, college sophomores, college juniors, college seniors, recent college graduates, graduate students, law students. ▶ *5–10 interns:* responsibilities include writing, grassroots organizing, researching, monitoring legislation, performing media relations, marketing, and development work. Candidates should have ability to work with others, computer skills, knowledge of field, oral communication skills, plan to pursue career in field, written communication skills. Duration is 2–12 months. Position available as unpaid or at $7.50–$10 per hour. Open to high school students, recent high school graduates, college freshmen, col-

lege sophomores, college juniors, college seniors, recent college graduates, graduate students, law students, career changers, individuals reentering the workforce. International applications accepted.

Benefits Job counseling, opportunity to attend seminars/ workshops, possible full-time employment, willing to act as a professional reference, willing to complete paperwork for educational credit, willing to provide letters of recommendation.

Contact Write, call, fax, e-mail, or through World Wide Web site Ms. Judy Green, Senior Vice President for Personnel. Phone: 202-467-2306. Fax: 202-293-2672. E-mail: jgreen@pfaw.org. Telephone interview required. Applicants must submit a letter of interest, resume. Application deadline: April 30 for summer. World Wide Web: http://www.pfaw.org.

PEOPLE MAKING A DIFFERENCE THROUGH COMMUNITY SERVICE, INC.
PO Box 120189
Boston, Massachusetts 02112-0189

General Information Organization that involves and engages people through meaningful, hands-on work that meets the needs of charities in Greater Boston. Established in 1992. Number of employees: 1. Number of internship applications received each year: 3.

Internships Available ▶ *1–2 development assistants:* responsibilities include assisting board development committee with biannual appeals and special events for grassroots support. Candidates should have ability to work independently, ability to work with others, computer skills, knowledge of field, office skills, organizational skills, research skills, self-motivation. Duration is flexible. Unpaid. Open to college seniors, recent college graduates, graduate students, career changers. ▶ *1–3 program project coordinators:* responsibilities include assisting with all aspects of service program: volunteer recruitment, project development, planning, evaluation, participation, and fund-raising. Candidates should have ability to work with others, computer skills, experience in the field, organizational skills, personal interest in the field, self-motivation. Duration is flexible. Unpaid. Open to college juniors, college seniors, recent college graduates, graduate students. ▶ *1 strategic business plan writer:* responsibilities include working with executive director and Board to develop, research, and write 5-year strategic business plan. Candidates should have ability to work independently, analytical skills, college degree in related field, computer skills, editing skills, knowledge of field, organizational skills, personal interest in the field, research skills, self-motivation, writing skills. Position available as unpaid or paid. Open to business school students or graduates.

Benefits Names of contacts, on-the-job training, opportunity to attend seminars/workshops, willing to act as a professional reference, willing to complete paperwork for educational credit, willing to provide letters of recommendation.

Contact Write or e-mail Lori Tsuruda, Founder and Executive Director. E-mail: lori@pmd.org. No phone calls. In-person interview required. Applicants must submit a letter of interest, resume, academic transcripts, three personal references, two letters of recommendation, participation in at least one PMD community service project prior to application (offered on a weekly basis). Applications are accepted continuously. World Wide Web: http:// www.pmd.org.

PHYSICIANS FOR HUMAN RIGHTS
100 Boylston Street, Suite 702
Boston, Massachusetts 02116

General Information Organization that examines health effects of human rights violations and applies methods of medical research to the documentation of those violations. Established in 1986. Number of employees: 30. Number of internship applications received each year: 30.

Internships Available ▶ *5–7 interns (in Boston and DC offices):* responsibilities include possibility of researching cases of health professionals and others whose international human rights are violated, assisting in organization of advocacy actions and educational events on health and human rights, drafting letters and background

Physicians for Human Rights (continued)

materials, and researching topics of special interest to the organization in the field of health and human rights. Candidates should have ability to work independently, ability to work with others, computer skills, personal interest in the field, writing skills. Duration is minimum of 2 months. Unpaid. Open to recent high school graduates, college freshmen, college sophomores, college juniors, college seniors, recent college graduates. International applications accepted.
Benefits Names of contacts, opportunity to attend seminars/workshops, willing to complete paperwork for educational credit.
Contact Write, fax, or e-mail Kathleen Carspecken, Internship Coordinator. Phone: 617-695-0041 Ext. 201. Fax: 617-695-0307. E-mail: kathcars@phrusa.org. In-person interview recommended (telephone interview accepted). Applicants must submit a letter of interest, resume, writing sample. Applications are accepted continuously. World Wide Web: http://www.phrusa.org/.

PHYSICIANS FOR SOCIAL RESPONSIBILITY
1875 Connecticut Avenue, #1012
Washington, District of Columbia 20009

General Information Organization of health-care professionals and other concerned citizens working to prevent nuclear war and dedicated to the elimination of weapons of mass destruction, the preservation of a sustainable environment, and the reduction of violence and its causes; recipient of 1985 Nobel Peace Prize. Established in 1961. Number of employees: 20. Number of internship applications received each year: 200.
Internships Available ▶ *1 environmental health intern:* responsibilities include researching and writing on various national and international environmental health issues including global climate change and persistent toxic pollutants. Candidates should have ability to work independently, oral communication skills, research skills, self-motivation, strong interpersonal skills, written communication skills. Duration is 3 months or more (6 months to 1 year preferred). $200 per week. Open to college juniors, college seniors, recent college graduates, graduate students. ▶ *1 medical student coordinator.* Candidates should have ability to work independently, computer skills, organizational skills, research skills, self-motivation, writing skills. Duration is 3 months or longer. $200 per week. Open to college juniors, college seniors, graduate students, medical students. ▶ *1–2 security program interns:* responsibilities include research, writing, and related tasks in the field of nuclear weapons. Candidates should have analytical skills, computer skills, personal interest in the field, research skills, self-motivation, writing skills. Duration is 3 months or more. $200 per week. Open to college freshmen, college sophomores, college juniors, college seniors, recent college graduates, graduate students, law students. ▶ *1 violence prevention intern:* responsibilities include research into violence, especially gun violence, from both public health and criminal justice perspectives; outreach to physicians, medical students, other health professionals; updating and developing activist materials and Web site . Candidates should have ability to work independently, computer skills, oral communication skills, research skills, self-motivation, strong interpersonal skills, written communication skills, familiarity with/interest in public health and public policy. Duration is 3 months or more. $200 per week. Open to college juniors, college seniors, recent college graduates, graduate students. International applications accepted.
Benefits Names of contacts, possible full-time employment, willing to complete paperwork for educational credit, willing to provide letters of recommendation.
Contact Write, fax, or e-mail Alyson Michael, Coordinator, 1875 Connecticut Avenue #1012, Washington, District of Columbia 20009. Fax: 202-667-4261. E-mail: psrnatl@igc.apc.org. No phone calls. Telephone interview required. Applicants must submit a letter of interest, resume, writing sample. Application deadline: March 15 for summer, July 15 for fall, November 15 for spring. World Wide Web: http://www.psr.org.

PHYSICIANS FOR SOCIAL RESPONSIBILITY–LOS ANGELES
3250 Wilshire Boulevard, Suite 1400
Los Angeles, California 90010

General Information Organization that works toward creating a world free of nuclear weapons, global environmental pollution, and gun violence. Established in 1970. Number of employees: 5. Unit of Physicians for Social Responsibility, Washington, District of Columbia. Number of internship applications received each year: 8.
Internships Available ▶ *3 assistant environmental/health care policy organizers:* responsibilities include media outreach, creating publications and databases, organizing public events, research, promoting computer networks, and building grassroots support. Candidates should have computer skills, office skills, organizational skills, personal interest in the field, research skills, written communication skills. Duration is flexible. Unpaid. International applications accepted.
Benefits On-the-job training, opportunity to attend seminars/workshops, possible full-time employment, travel reimbursement, willing to act as a professional reference, willing to complete paperwork for educational credit, willing to provide letters of recommendation, paid parking.
Contact E-mail Johanna Congleton, Public Health Organizer. Phone: 213-386-4901. Fax: 213-386-4184. E-mail: congleton@psr.org. In-person interview recommended (telephone interview accepted). Applicants must submit a letter of interest, resume. Applications are accepted continuously. World Wide Web: http://www.psrla.org.

POINTS OF LIGHT FOUNDATION
1400 I Street, NW
Washington, District of Columbia 20005

General Information Nonprofit, nonpartisan organization that strives to engage more people more effectively in volunteer community service to help solve serious social problems. Established in 1990. Number of employees: 125. Number of internship applications received each year: 100.
Internships Available ▶ *5 summer interns:* responsibilities include working in one of the following program areas: External Relations, The Institute, Positioning and Public Awareness, Local Infrastructure, Development, and Partnerships for National Service. Candidates should have college courses in field, editing skills, oral communication skills, plan to pursue career in field, research skills, written communication skills. Duration is 10 weeks. $225 per week. Open to college freshmen, college sophomores, college juniors, college seniors, graduate students, law students. International applications accepted.
Benefits Opportunity to attend seminars/workshops, willing to complete paperwork for educational credit, willing to provide letters of recommendation.
Contact Write, fax, e-mail, or through World Wide Web site Human Resources Manager. Fax: 202-729-3225. E-mail: ldavis@pointsoflight.org. No phone calls. In-person interview recommended (telephone interview accepted). Applicants must submit a letter of interest, resume. Application deadline: May 3. World Wide Web: http://www.pointsoflight.org.

THE POPULATION INSTITUTE
107 2nd Street, NE
Washington, District of Columbia 20002

General Information Nonprofit grassroots organization specializing in the link between international population and environmental issues. Established in 1969. Number of employees: 18. Number of internship applications received each year: 50.
Internships Available ▶ *1 World Population Awareness Week coordinator:* responsibilities include organizing events and establishing network of contacts for this officially sponsored week. Candidates should have ability to work independently, computer skills, editing skills, oral communication skills, organizational skills, self-motivation, strong interpersonal skills, strong leadership ability, writing skills. Duration is 1 year. $2000 per month. ▶ *1–2 field coordinators:* responsibilities include planning and implementing

trips around the nation for the president of the Institute and maintaining contact with educators and community organizations. Candidates should have ability to work independently, computer skills, office skills, oral communication skills, organizational skills, self-motivation, strong interpersonal skills, strong leadership ability, writing skills. Duration is 1 year. $2000 per month. ▶ *1 media fellow:* responsibilities include maintaining a press list, acting as liaison with media, writing, reporting, proofreading, and editing. Candidates should have ability to work independently, college degree in related field, computer skills, editing skills, oral communication skills, research skills, self-motivation, strong interpersonal skills, writing skills. Duration is 1 year. $2000 per month. ▶ *1–2 public policy fellows:* responsibilities include assisting with legislative alerts and informing legislators and key staff about population issues. Candidates should have ability to work independently, analytical skills, college courses in field, computer skills, oral communication skills, organizational skills, self-motivation, strong interpersonal skills, strong leadership ability. Duration is 1 year. $2000 per month. Open to college freshmen, college sophomores, college juniors, college seniors, recent college graduates, graduate students, those 21 to 25 years old only.

Benefits Formal training, names of contacts, on-the-job training, opportunity to attend seminars/workshops, willing to act as a professional reference, willing to complete paperwork for educational credit, willing to provide letters of recommendation, health and dental coverage, paid vacation, sick leave.

Contact Write, call, fax, e-mail, or through World Wide Web site Education Coordinator. Phone: 202-544-3300. Fax: 202-544-0068. E-mail: web@populationinstitute.org. In-person interview required. Applicants must submit a letter of interest, resume, academic transcripts, three letters of recommendation. Application deadline: April 15. World Wide Web: http://www.populationinstitute.org.

PROGRESSIVE ACTION NETWORK (EAST COAST AND MIDWEST INTERNS)
1341 G Street, NW, Suite 600
Washington, District of Columbia 20005

General Information Network providing stable funding for progressive political organizations, mobilizing mass numbers of people to participate in the political process, and developing activism and membership development careers. Established in 1978. Number of employees: 2. Number of internship applications received each year: 50.

Internships Available ▶ *25–50 field and phone outreach staff interns:* responsibilities include educating and fund-raising by phone or by doing neighborhood outreach; positions available in New Jersey, Minnesota, Washington, Iowa, Wisconsin, and Indiana. Candidates should have analytical skills, oral communication skills, personal interest in the field, self-motivation, strong interpersonal skills, ability to learn quickly, desire to work with people. Duration is minimum of 2 months. $9–$11 per hour, plus bonus (either full-time or part-time). Open to high school seniors, recent high school graduates, college freshmen, college sophomores, college juniors, college seniors, recent college graduates, graduate students, law students, career changers, individuals reentering the workforce.

Benefits Formal training, health insurance, opportunity to attend seminars/workshops, possible full-time employment, willing to act as a professional reference, willing to complete paperwork for educational credit, willing to provide letters of recommendation, relocation opportunity, career placement, reimbursement for job-related travel expenses.

Contact Write, fax, or e-mail Barbara Helmick, Executive Director. Phone: 202-624-1720. Fax: 202-737-9197. In-person interview recommended (telephone interview accepted). For more information visit Web site. Applications are accepted continuously. World Wide Web: http://www.progressiveaction.org.

PUBLIC CITIZEN'S CONGRESS WATCH
215 Pennsylvania Avenue, SE
Washington, District of Columbia 20003

General Information Consumer organization concerned with lobbying, organizing, and researching consumer rights and government and corporate accountability. Established in 1971.

Number of employees: 16. Unit of Public Citizen, Washington, District of Columbia. Number of internship applications received each year: 50.

Internships Available ▶ *2 field/grassroots interns.* Duration is 3–4 months. Unpaid. ▶ *1–2 research interns:* responsibilities include researching legislation, making phone calls to Congress, organizing conferences and rallies, and assisting with office duties. Candidates should have organizational skills, research skills. Duration is 3–4 months. Unpaid. Open to college freshmen, college sophomores, college juniors, college seniors, recent college graduates, graduate students, law students. International applications accepted.

Benefits Formal training, possible full-time employment, willing to complete paperwork for educational credit.

Contact Write, call, or fax Natalie Brandon, Legislative Assistant. Phone: 202-454-5186. Fax: 202-547-7392. In-person interview recommended (telephone interview accepted). Applicants must submit a letter of interest, resume, writing sample. Applications are accepted continuously. World Wide Web: http://www.citizen.org.

PUBLIC CITIZEN'S CRITICAL MASS ENERGY PROJECT
215 Pennsylvania Avenue, SE
Washington, District of Columbia 20003

General Information Project that opposes nuclear power and promotes cleaner, safer energy alternatives, and sustainable agriculture; researches and writes studies on energy issues, food irradiation, and nuclear waste; lobbies Congress; monitors relevant federal and state agencies; initiates litigation; and works with press and citizen groups. Established in 1974. Number of employees: 8. Unit of Public Citizen, Washington, District of Columbia. Number of internship applications received each year: 40.

Internships Available ▶ *2–4 interns:* responsibilities include researching and writing reports on energy-related policy or legal matters, helping in a lobbying campaign, working with the media and/or providing assistance to local safe energy organizations, performing some administrative tasks, and helping with organizing. Candidates should have ability to work independently, computer skills, oral communication skills, organizational skills, personal interest in the field, research skills, self-motivation, strong interpersonal skills, strong leadership ability, writing skills, commitment to progressive causes. Duration is flexible. Position available as unpaid or paid. Open to college sophomores, college juniors, college seniors, recent college graduates, graduate students, law students, career changers, individuals reentering the workforce. International applications accepted.

Benefits Names of contacts, on-the-job training, opportunity to attend seminars/workshops, willing to complete paperwork for educational credit, willing to provide letters of recommendation.

Contact Write, fax, e-mail, or through World Wide Web site Patricia Lovera, Organizing Director. Fax: 202-547-7392. E-mail: cmep@citizen.org. No phone calls. In-person interview recommended (telephone interview accepted). Applicants must submit a letter of interest, resume, writing sample. Applications are accepted continuously. World Wide Web: http://www.citizen.org/cmep.

PUBLIC POLICY DEPARTMENT OF THE GENERAL FEDERATION OF WOMEN'S CLUBS
1734 N Street, NW
Washington, District of Columbia 20036-0246

General Information Advocacy branch of GFWC. Number of employees: 1. Number of internship applications received each year: 45.

Internships Available ▶ *1–2 research assistants:* responsibilities include researching resolutions (issue positions) and gathering relevant materials; findings will be used by GFWC national committee to determine if resolutions need to be amended and updated; attending meetings with the department director. Candidates should have ability to work independently, analytical skills, computer skills, organizational skills, research skills, self-motivation, writing skills, strong background in political science.

Public Policy Department of the General Federation of Women's Clubs (continued)
Duration is 1 semester. Unpaid. Open to college freshmen, college sophomores, college juniors, college seniors, recent college graduates, graduate students, law students, individuals reentering the workforce. International applications accepted.
Benefits Job counseling, names of contacts, on-the-job training, possible full-time employment, travel reimbursement, willing to act as a professional reference, willing to complete paperwork for educational credit, willing to provide letters of recommendation, small stipend commensurate with experience and availability.
Contact Call, fax, or e-mail Sarah Albert, Public Policy Director. Phone: 202-347-3168. Fax: 202-835-0246. E-mail: legislation@gfwc.org. Applicants must submit a letter of interest, resume, two personal references. Applications are accepted continuously. World Wide Web: http://www.gfwc.org.

QUAKER PEACE CENTRE
3 Rye Road
Cape Town 7700 South Africa

General Information Peace centre. Established in 1988. Number of employees: 26. Number of internship applications received each year: 20.
Internships Available ▶ *Administrative/fieldwork interns.* Candidates should have computer skills, knowledge of field, office skills, organizational skills, personal interest in the field, strong interpersonal skills. Duration is 6 months. Unpaid. Open to recent college graduates, career changers. International applications accepted.
Benefits Opportunity to attend seminars/workshops, willing to act as a professional reference, willing to provide letters of recommendation.
International Internships Available.
Contact Write Mr. Jeremy Routledge. E-mail: jeremy@qpc.org.za. No phone calls. Applications are accepted continuously. World Wide Web: http://www.quaker.org/capetown/.

RAINFOREST RELIEF
338 Prospect Place
Brooklyn, New York 11238

General Information Rainforest preservation/conservation organization working to reduce the demand for rainforest-destructive materials through education and direct action. Established in 1989. Number of internship applications received each year: 20.
Internships Available ▶ *1–10 Banana Co-Op interns:* responsibilities include working with Banana Project coordinator to assist four Wöes in Talamanca, Costa Rica, with stabilizing their production and processing of organic, shade-grown bananas and banana products and finding markets. Candidates should have ability to work with others, oral communication skills, organizational skills, knowledge of Spanish helpful. Duration is 1–12 months. Unpaid. Open to high school seniors, recent high school graduates, college freshmen, college sophomores, college juniors, college seniors, recent college graduates, graduate students, law students, career changers, individuals reentering the workforce. ▶ *National Waterfronts interns:* responsibilities include research planned and started waterfront construction projects around the country to prevent use of uncertified rainforest woods; contacting architects, planners, and municipal officials to help generate long-term policies. Candidates should have ability to work independently, computer skills, oral communication skills, research skills, self-motivation, written communication skills. Duration is 12 months. Unpaid. Open to college freshmen, college sophomores, college juniors, college seniors, recent college graduates, graduate students, law students, career changers, individuals reentering the workforce. ▶ *1 New Jersey waterfronts campaign assistant:* responsibilities include contacting all waterfront towns in NJ and working to convince them to pass policies to ban the use of unsustainable rainforest woods for boardwalking, piers, pilings, and bulkheads; organizing with other groups. Candidates should have ability to work independently, oral communication skills, organizational skills, self-motivation, strong interpersonal skills, written communication skills. Duration is 3–6 months. Unpaid. Open to recent high

school graduates, college freshmen, college sophomores, college juniors, college seniors, recent college graduates, graduate students, career changers, individuals reentering the workforce. ▶ *1–3 New York City: Campaign Assistants:* responsibilities include assisting director with campaign to end the use of unsustainable rainforest woods by NYC; organizing in schools; projects; letter campaigns; outreach; meetings. Candidates should have ability to work independently, oral communication skills, organizational skills, strong interpersonal skills, strong leadership ability. Duration is 6–12 months. Unpaid. Open to recent high school graduates, college freshmen, college sophomores, college juniors, college seniors, recent college graduates, graduate students, career changers, individuals reentering the workforce. ▶ *1–2 graphics interns:* responsibilities include working with director to design, produce, and print brochures, pamphlets, buttons, stickers, and other graphic pieces. Candidates should have ability to work independently, ability to work with others, computer skills, experience in the field, self-motivation, graphic and design. Duration is 3–12 months. Unpaid. Open to high school students, recent high school graduates, college freshmen, college sophomores, college juniors, college seniors, recent college graduates, graduate students, career changers, individuals reentering the workforce. ▶ *1 import-export data intern:* responsibilities include compiling and organizing data obtained through imports database on rainforest wood imports by company name, location, species, and products; generating reports. Candidates should have ability to work independently, computer skills, organizational skills, research skills, self-motivation, writing skills. Duration is 3–6 months. Unpaid. Open to high school seniors, recent high school graduates, college freshmen, college sophomores, college juniors, college seniors, recent college graduates, graduate students, career changers, individuals reentering the workforce. ▶ *1 media intern:* responsibilities include assisting director in "marketing" positions on rainforest destruction to newspapers, magazines, home improvement programs, and other media; keeping track of articles/videotapes. Candidates should have ability to work independently, oral communication skills, research skills, self-motivation, strong interpersonal skills, written communication skills. Duration is 3–6 months. Unpaid. Open to recent high school graduates, college freshmen, college sophomores, college juniors, college seniors, recent college graduates, graduate students, career changers, individuals reentering the workforce. ▶ *1–2 office manager's assistants:* responsibilities include clerical work, organizing the office, light bookkeeping, responding to information requests, organizing meetings, scheduling and booking presentations. Candidates should have computer skills, office skills, oral communication skills, strong interpersonal skills, written communication skills. Duration is 6–12 months. Unpaid. Open to high school seniors, recent high school graduates, college freshmen, college sophomores, college juniors, college seniors, recent college graduates, graduate students, career changers, individuals reentering the workforce. ▶ *1–2 presentations coordinators:* responsibilities include assisting director (and later other presenters) in outreach for presentations in schools, colleges, and community groups; keeping track of scheduled presentations and donations. Candidates should have oral communication skills, organizational skills, self-motivation, strong interpersonal skills, written communication skills. Duration is 3–12 months. Unpaid. Open to high school students, recent high school graduates, college freshmen, college sophomores, college juniors, college seniors, recent college graduates, graduate students, career changers, individuals reentering the workforce. ▶ *4 set construction interns:* responsibilities include researching and identifying rainforest plywood used for set construction in NYC and school theaters nationwide; working with construction unions, producers, and directors to end the practice. Candidates should have ability to work independently, computer skills, oral communication skills, self-motivation, strong interpersonal skills, written communication skills. Duration is 6–12 months. Unpaid. Open to high school students, recent high school graduates, college freshmen, college sophomores, college juniors, college seniors, recent college graduates, graduate students, career changers, individuals reentering the workforce. ▶ *2–3 special events assistants:* responsibilities include working with director and development staff to help coordinate special events; marketing events via the media and outreach to businesses, the community, and donors; organizing

volunteers for the event. Candidates should have ability to work with others, computer skills, oral communication skills, self-motivation, strong leadership ability. Duration is 6–12 months. Unpaid. Open to high school seniors, recent high school graduates, college freshmen, college sophomores, college juniors, college seniors, recent college graduates, career changers, individuals reentering the workforce. ▶ *1–5 telephone outreach interns:* responsibilities include calling people who have expressed an interest in organization and converting them to "Member" status. Candidates should have ability to work independently, ability to work with others, oral communication skills, self-motivation, good phone skills. Duration is 1–12 months. Position available as unpaid or paid. Open to high school students, recent high school graduates, college freshmen, college sophomores, college juniors, college seniors, recent college graduates, career changers, individuals reentering the workforce. International applications accepted.
Benefits Names of contacts, on-the-job training, opportunity to attend seminars/workshops, possible full-time employment, travel reimbursement, willing to act as a professional reference, willing to complete paperwork for educational credit, willing to provide letters of recommendation, possibility of part-time employment, free meals at office.
International Internships Available in Costa Rica; Quito, Ecuador; Kalimantan, Indonesia; Milan, Italy.
Contact Write, call, fax, or e-mail Tim Keating, Executive Director, PO Box 150566, Brooklyn, New York 11215. Phone: 718-398-3760. Fax: 718-398-3760. E-mail: relief@igc.org. In-person interview recommended (telephone interview accepted). Applicants must submit a letter of interest, resume. Applications are accepted continuously. World Wide Web: http://www.rainforestrelief.org.

RELIGIOUS ACTION CENTER OF REFORM JUDAISM
2027 Massachusetts Avenue, NW
Washington, District of Columbia 20036

General Information Organization that advocates social justice and religious liberty, serves as a Reform Jewish movement advocate in the nation's capital, and monitors legislation of concern to American Jewish communities. Established in 1961. Number of employees: 20. Unit of Union of American Hebrew Congregations, New York, New York. Number of internship applications received each year: 30.
Internships Available ▶ *7 legislative assistants:* responsibilities include representing the Center in various coalitions, monitoring legislation, participating in visits to offices of senators and representatives, preparing educational and programmatic materials for congregations, and performing administrative work. Candidates should have ability to work with others, personal interest in the field, plan to pursue career in field, self-motivation, strong leadership ability, written communication skills. Duration is 1 year. $19,000 per year. Open to college seniors, recent college graduates. International applications accepted.
Benefits Health insurance, names of contacts, opportunity to attend seminars/workshops, travel reimbursement, willing to act as a professional reference, willing to provide letters of recommendation.
Contact Write, call, fax, e-mail, or through World Wide Web site Mark Pelavin, Associate Director. Phone: 202-387-2800. Fax: 202-667-9070. E-mail: mpelavin@uahc.org. Applicants must submit a formal organization application, resume, academic transcripts, writing sample, two letters of recommendation. Application deadline: March 15. World Wide Web: http://www.rac.org.

RESOURCE CENTER FOR NONVIOLENCE
515 Broadway
Santa Cruz, California 95060

General Information Organization that offers a wide-ranging educational program in the history, theory, methodology, and current practice of nonviolence as a source for personal and social change. Established in 1976. Number of employees: 7. Unit of Eschaton Foundation, Santa Cruz, California. Number of internship applications received each year: 20.

Internships Available ▶ *2–6 interns:* responsibilities include engaging in personal study, planning and directing the program, participating in events, and working on community education in the theory and practice of nonviolence. Candidates should have ability to work independently, analytical skills, computer skills, knowledge of field, oral communication skills, organizational skills, personal interest in the field, self-motivation, strong interpersonal skills, strong leadership ability, written communication skills. Duration is flexible. Unpaid. Open to college sophomores, college juniors, college seniors, recent college graduates, graduate students, career changers. International applications accepted.
Benefits Job counseling, names of contacts, on-the-job training, opportunity to attend seminars/workshops, willing to act as a professional reference, willing to complete paperwork for educational credit, willing to provide letters of recommendation.
Contact Write, call, fax, e-mail, or through World Wide Web site Intern Coordinator. Phone: 831-423-1626. Fax: 831-423-8716. E-mail: rcnv@rcnv.org. In-person interview recommended (telephone interview accepted). Applicants must submit a formal organization application, two letters of recommendation, essay question. Applications are accepted continuously. World Wide Web: http://www.rcnv.org.

RESULTS
440 First Street, NW, Suite 450
Washington, District of Columbia 20001

General Information Grassroots citizens lobbying group working to create the political will to end hunger and poverty. Established in 1980. Number of employees: 20. Number of internship applications received each year: 50.
Internships Available ▶ *1 administrative intern:* responsibilities include office support, communications, lobbying, and research. Candidates should have ability to work independently, ability to work with others, analytical skills, computer skills, editing skills, office skills, organizational skills, research skills, self-motivation, writing skills. Duration is flexible. Unpaid. ▶ *1 conference intern:* responsibilities include supporting the annual Washington conference for volunteers. Candidates should have computer skills, office skills, organizational skills, self-motivation, strong interpersonal skills, writing skills. Duration is 1 summer or spring. Position available as unpaid or paid. ▶ *1 development intern:* responsibilities include research into fund-raising and compiling material for donors. Candidates should have computer skills, office skills, oral communication skills, organizational skills, writing skills. Duration is flexible. Unpaid. ▶ *1 domestic legislative intern:* responsibilities include researching and grass roots support. Candidates should have ability to work with others, computer skills, editing skills, oral communication skills, organizational skills, research skills, writing skills. Duration is flexible. Position available as unpaid or paid. ▶ *1 global legislative intern:* responsibilities include research and grassroots support. Candidates should have ability to work with others, computer skills, editing skills, oral communication skills, organizational skills, research skills, writing skills. Duration is flexible. Unpaid. Open to college freshmen, college sophomores, college juniors, college seniors, graduate students. International applications accepted.
Benefits Formal training, on-the-job training, travel reimbursement, willing to act as a professional reference, willing to complete paperwork for educational credit, willing to provide letters of recommendation, possible health insurance, possibility of small stipend.
Contact Write, call, fax, e-mail, or through World Wide Web site Melessa Rogers, Operations Manager, 440 First Street, NW, Suite 450, Washington, District of Columbia 20001. Phone: 202-783-7100. Fax: 202-783-2818. E-mail: results@resultsusa.org. Applicants must submit a letter of interest, resume, writing sample. Applications are accepted continuously. World Wide Web: http://www.resultsusa.org.

THE RUTHERFORD INSTITUTE
PO Box 7482
Charlottesville, Virginia 22906-7482

General Information Nonprofit, legal, and educational civil liberties organization specializing in the defense of constitutional

The Rutherford Institute (continued)

and human rights. Established in 1982. Number of employees: 20. Number of internship applications received each year: 65.

Internships Available ▶ *5 summer interns:* responsibilities include participation in an intensive course in constitutional law, and providing research and writing for litigation in state and federal courts and for educational resources. Candidates should have ability to work independently, analytical skills, computer skills, editing skills, organizational skills, personal interest in the field, plan to pursue career in field, research skills, self-motivation, written communication skills. Duration is 8–10 weeks. Position available as unpaid or at $200–$400 per week. Open to law students.

Benefits On-the-job training, travel reimbursement, willing to act as a professional reference, willing to complete paperwork for educational credit, willing to provide letters of recommendation, housing stipend of $300 per month.

Contact Write, call, fax, or e-mail Candice Mills Jones, Internship Program Coordinator, PO Box 7482, Charlottesville, Virginia 22906-7482. Phone: 434-978-3888. Fax: 434-978-1789. E-mail: candicej@rutherford.org. Applicants must submit a letter of interest, resume, writing sample, two personal references. Application deadline: February 15 for 1st-year law students, November 15 for 2nd- and 3rd-year law students. World Wide Web: http://www.rutherford.org.

SEATTLE YOUTH INVOLVEMENT NETWORK
2017 East Spruce Street
Seattle, Washington 98122

General Information Organization that advocates for youth in order to create positive changes in the community through civic involvement, leadership development, and volunteer service. Established in 1992. Number of employees: 7. Number of internship applications received each year: 5.

Internships Available ▶ *1–2 fund-raising interns:* responsibilities include assisting with grant writing, special events, and other fund-raising activities. Candidates should have ability to work independently, computer skills, office skills, organizational skills, strong interpersonal skills, writing skills, some interest or experience in fund-raising. Duration is flexible. $7 per hour. ▶ *1 program intern:* responsibilities include working with youth to design and implement forums, service projects, publications, and activities in the community. Candidates should have ability to work independently, computer skills, organizational skills, strong interpersonal skills, strong leadership ability, written communication skills. Duration is flexible. $7 per hour. Open to high school students.

Benefits Names of contacts, on-the-job training, possible full-time employment, willing to act as a professional reference, willing to complete paperwork for educational credit, willing to provide letters of recommendation.

Contact Write, fax, e-mail, or through World Wide Web site Liz Vivian, Executive Director, 2017 East Spruce Street, Seattle, Washington 98122. Fax: 206-323-8731. E-mail: liz@seattleyouth.org. No phone calls. In-person interview recommended (telephone interview accepted). Applicants must submit a letter of interest, resume, criminal records check required. Applications are accepted continuously. World Wide Web: http://www.seattleyouth.org.

SOCIETY FOR HEALTH, ENVIRONMENT AND WOMEN DEVELOPMENT
GPO 8975, EPC 2121
Kathmandu Nepal

General Information Nonprofit organization that promotes community development, computer education, environmental, health, and women's issues. Established in 1998. Number of employees: 3. Number of internship applications received each year: 12.

Internships Available ▶ *Community development interns.* Candidates should have plan to pursue career in field, research skills, self-motivation, strong interpersonal skills. Duration is 2–4 months. Unpaid. Open to high school seniors, college seniors, career changers, individuals reentering the workforce. ▶ *Environment and health interns:* responsibilities include helping conduct program

in all areas of Nepal. Candidates should have ability to work independently, computer skills, knowledge of field, organizational skills, self-motivation, strong interpersonal skills. Duration is 2–6 months. Unpaid. Open to high school seniors, college sophomores, college seniors, graduate students, career changers, individuals reentering the workforce. ▶ *Women's development interns:* responsibilities include helping conduct programs that help women. Candidates should have computer skills, knowledge of field, organizational skills, self-motivation, strong interpersonal skills. Duration is 2–6 months. Unpaid. Open to high school seniors, college seniors, graduate students, career changers, individuals reentering the workforce. International applications accepted.

Benefits Housing at a cost, meals at a cost, names of contacts, on-the-job training, willing to provide letters of recommendation.

International Internships Available.

Contact Write, e-mail, or through World Wide Web site Shree Krishna Maharjan, President. E-mail: info@shewd.org. Applicants must submit a formal organization application, resume, academic transcripts, $75 donation. Applications are accepted continuously. World Wide Web: http://www.shewd.org.

SOUTHEAST ASIA RESOURCE ACTION CENTER (SEARAC)
1628 16th Street, NW, 3rd Floor
Washington, District of Columbia 20009-3099

General Information National capacity-building and advocacy organization for Americans of Cambodian, Laotian, and Vietnamese descent. Established in 1979. Number of employees: 6. Number of internship applications received each year: 20.

Internships Available ▶ *1 intern:* responsibilities include conducting research, assisting public education and advocacy efforts, responding to requests for information, attending public meetings, contributing articles for publication, and administrative duties. Candidates should have computer skills, research skills, self-motivation, strong interpersonal skills, written communication skills, multicultural sensitivity, interest in community and public service, knowledge of Southeast Asia, knowledge of immigrant issues. Duration is 1–2 semesters. Unpaid. Open to college sophomores, college juniors, college seniors, recent college graduates, graduate students, law students, career changers, individuals reentering the workforce. International applications accepted.

Benefits Job counseling, names of contacts, on-the-job training, opportunity to attend seminars/workshops, willing to act as a professional reference, willing to complete paperwork for educational credit, willing to provide letters of recommendation.

Contact Write, call, fax, e-mail, or through World Wide Web site Ms. Eloise Needleman, Administrative Manager. Phone: 202-667-4690. Fax: 202-667-6449. E-mail: searac@searac.org. In-person interview recommended (telephone interview accepted). Applicants must submit a formal organization application, letter of interest, resume, academic transcripts, writing sample. Applications are accepted continuously. World Wide Web: http://www.searac.org.

SPEAK OUT
PO Box 99096
Emeryville, California 94662

General Information Nonprofit national speakers and artists agency providing 200 speakers and artists who address issues of social, economic, and political justice, working primarily through campuses and community groups. Established in 1990. Number of employees: 5. Affiliate of Institute for Democratic Education and Culture, Oakland, California. Number of internship applications received each year: 10.

Internships Available ▶ *2 interns:* responsibilities include working alongside staff members on specific projects, setting up speaking engagements, coordinating tour schedules, working on publicity campaigns and grant writing, and performing some basic office work. Candidates should have ability to work independently, computer skills, office skills, oral communication skills, writing skills. Duration is minimum of one month commitment. Unpaid. Open to high school students, recent high school graduates, college freshmen, college sophomores, college juniors, college seniors.

Benefits Names of contacts, on-the-job training, willing to act as a professional reference, willing to complete paperwork for educational credit, willing to provide letters of recommendation.
Contact Write, call, fax, e-mail, or through World Wide Web site Lolan Sevilla, Program Coordinator. Phone: 510-601-0182. Fax: 510-601-0183. E-mail: speakout@igc.org. Applicants must submit a formal organization application, letter of interest, resume, writing sample, letter of recommendation. Applications are accepted continuously. World Wide Web: http://www.speakersandartists.org.

STUDENT PUGWASH USA
2029 P Street, Suite 301
Washington, District of Columbia 20036

General Information National nonprofit educational organization that provides a wide range of activities for university and select high school students to promote the socially responsible application of science and technology. Established in 1979. Number of employees: 2. Number of internship applications received each year: 15.
Internships Available ▶ *1–2 interns:* responsibilities include helping plan and organize national conference; researching science, technology, and society issues; providing general support for nationwide chapter program; possibility of publishing issue brief. Candidates should have computer skills, knowledge of field, research skills, self-motivation, strong interpersonal skills, written communication skills. Duration is 3–4 months (year-round). Unpaid. Open to college freshmen, college sophomores, college juniors, college seniors, recent college graduates, graduate students, law students.
Benefits Formal training, job counseling, names of contacts, opportunity to attend seminars/workshops, possible full-time employment, willing to complete paperwork for educational credit, willing to provide letters of recommendation.
Contact Write, call, fax, e-mail, or through World Wide Web site Susan Veres, Executive Director. Phone: 202-429-8900. Fax: 202-429-8905. E-mail: spusa@spusa.org. In-person interview recommended (telephone interview accepted). Applicants must submit a letter of interest, resume, writing sample. Application deadline: May 15 for summer, August 16 for fall, December 13 for spring. World Wide Web: http://www.spusa.org/pugwash/.

THIRD MILLENNIUM: ADVOCATES FOR THE FUTURE, INC.
Empire State Building, 350 Fifth Avenue, Suite 5809
New York, New York 10118

General Information National, nonprofit advocacy and educational organization started by young Americans concerned about the long-term future of the U.S.; purpose is to redirect America's political focus from the next election cycle to the next generation cycle, addressing the issues of the national debt, crime, the environment, race relations, and health care from a generational perspective. Established in 1993. Number of employees: 3. Number of internship applications received each year: 15.
Internships Available ▶ *2 general interns:* responsibilities include researching grants, writing press releases, researching congressional testimony, and administrative work. Candidates should have ability to work independently, oral communication skills, personal interest in the field, research skills, self-motivation, written communication skills. Duration is flexible. Unpaid. Open to college freshmen, college sophomores, college juniors, college seniors, recent college graduates.
Benefits Names of contacts, opportunity to attend seminars/workshops, possible full-time employment, travel reimbursement, willing to act as a professional reference, willing to complete paperwork for educational credit, willing to provide letters of recommendation, opportunity to write op-ed pieces and meet future leaders.
Contact Write, call, fax, or e-mail Cindy Ng, Director of Operations. Phone: 212-760-4240. Fax: 212-760-2795. E-mail: cindyng@thirdmil.org. Applicants must submit a letter of interest, resume. Applications are accepted continuously. World Wide Web: http://www.thirdmil.org.

TOXICS ACTION CENTER
29 Temple Place
Boston, Massachusetts 02111

General Information Organization that provides organizing assistance to neighborhood groups battling toxics and pollution in their communities. Number of employees: 5. Number of internship applications received each year: 35.
Internships Available ▶ *1–3 Nuke-Free New England interns:* responsibilities include working to pressure utility and government officials to close down nuclear power plants. (Internships also available in Portland, ME and West Hartford, CT). Candidates should have oral communication skills, organizational skills, personal interest in the field, self-motivation, strong interpersonal skills, written communication skills. Duration is flexible. Position available as unpaid or paid. Open to college freshmen, college sophomores, college juniors, college seniors, recent college graduates, graduate students, law students. ▶ *1 Sooty Six intern:* responsibilities include working to organize citizens to pressure the CT government to clean up CT oil and coal power plants. (Available in West Hartford, CT office). Candidates should have oral communication skills, organizational skills, personal interest in the field, self-motivation, strong interpersonal skills, written communication skills. Duration is flexible. Position available as unpaid or paid. Open to college freshmen, college sophomores, college juniors, college seniors, recent college graduates, graduate students, law students. ▶ *1 Web page intern:* responsibilities include helping set up and manage organization's Web page, establishing links to other sites and publicizing resources to grassroots groups. Candidates should have computer skills, oral communication skills, organizational skills, personal interest in the field, self-motivation, written communication skills. Duration is flexible. Position available as unpaid or paid. Open to college freshmen, college sophomores, college juniors, college seniors, recent college graduates, graduate students, law students. ▶ *3 conference interns:* responsibilities include working with staff to set up training conferences for local activists in MA, CT, and ME, (internships also available in Portland, ME and West Hartford, CT). Candidates should have ability to work with others, oral communication skills, personal interest in the field, self-motivation, written communication skills. Duration is flexible. Position available as unpaid or paid. Open to college freshmen, college sophomores, college juniors, college seniors, recent college graduates, graduate students, law students. ▶ *1 legal manual intern:* responsibilities include researching and preparing a manual to guide over 400 neighborhood groups (that are battling toxic pollution in their communities) in legal and organizational matters. Candidates should have ability to work independently, organizational skills, personal interest in the field, self-motivation, writing skills. Duration is flexible. Position available as unpaid or paid. Open to graduate students, law students. ▶ *1–3 pesticides interns:* responsibilities include working with community activists to help stop pesticide exposure from agricultural sources, right-of-way spraying, and use by municipalities; (internships also available in Portland, ME and West Hartford (CT). Candidates should have oral communication skills, organizational skills, personal interest in the field, self-motivation, strong interpersonal skills, written communication skills. Duration is flexible. Position available as unpaid or paid. Open to college freshmen, college sophomores, college juniors, college seniors, recent college graduates, graduate students, law students. ▶ *1–2 recycling interns:* responsibilities include working with residents to develop and implement effective municipal recycling campaigns. Candidates should have oral communication skills, organizational skills, personal interest in the field, self-motivation, strong interpersonal skills, written communication skills. Duration is flexible. Position available as unpaid or paid. Open to college freshmen, college sophomores, college juniors, college seniors, recent college graduates, graduate students, law students. International applications accepted.
Benefits Names of contacts, on-the-job training, opportunity to attend seminars/workshops, possible full-time employment, willing to act as a professional reference, willing to complete paperwork for educational credit, willing to provide letters of recommendation, possibility of small stipend.

Toxics Action Center (continued)

Contact Write, call, fax, or through World Wide Web site Tara Hudson, Administrator. Phone: 617-292-4821. Fax: 617-292-8057. Applicants must submit a letter of interest, resume. Applications are accepted continuously. World Wide Web: http://www.toxicsaction.org.

TRAPROCK PEACE CENTER
103A Keets Road
Deerfield, Massachusetts 01342

General Information Local and regional peace education center. Established in 1979. Number of internship applications received each year: 5.

Internships Available ▶ *1–2 community organizer interns:* responsibilities include phone calls, flyering, planning and organizing events, general office work, maintenance, visiting schools and festivals. Candidates should have ability to work independently, computer skills, oral communication skills, personal interest in the field, strong interpersonal skills, written communication skills. Duration is 3 months. Unpaid. Open to college freshmen, college sophomores, college juniors, college seniors, career changers, individuals reentering the workforce. International applications accepted.

Benefits Free housing, names of contacts, on-the-job training, opportunity to attend seminars/workshops, willing to act as a professional reference, willing to provide letters of recommendation.

Contact Write Sunny Miller, Director. Phone: 413-773-7427. In-person interview required. Applicants must submit a letter of interest, resume, 4 letters of recommendation (2 from employers, 2 from housemates). Applications are accepted continuously. World Wide Web: http://www.traprockpeace.org.

20/20 VISION
1828 Jefferson Place, NW
Washington, District of Columbia 20036

General Information Nonprofit lobbying and citizen education organization whose goal is to revitalize democracy by creating persistent, strategic citizen action, persuading decision-makers to protect the earth by reducing militarism, and preserving the environment. Established in 1986. Number of employees: 8. Number of internship applications received each year: 200.

Internships Available ▶ *1–3 interns:* responsibilities include assisting with general office responsibilities and working on specific projects within the legislation, media, field, development, promotion, and membership departments as priorities dictate. Candidates should have ability to work independently, editing skills, knowledge of field, oral communication skills, personal interest in the field, research skills, self-motivation, strong interpersonal skills, writing skills. Duration is 2-3 months minimum. Position available as unpaid or paid. Open to college freshmen, college sophomores, college juniors, college seniors, recent college graduates, graduate students. International applications accepted.

Benefits Job counseling, names of contacts, travel reimbursement, willing to complete paperwork for educational credit, willing to provide letters of recommendation.

Contact Write, call, fax, e-mail, or through World Wide Web site Erik Olsen, Campaign Coordinator. Phone: 202-833-2020. Fax: 202-833-5307. E-mail: erik@2020vision.org. In-person interview recommended (telephone interview accepted). Applicants must submit a letter of interest, resume, writing sample, personal reference. Applications are accepted continuously. World Wide Web: http://www.2020vision.org.

UNITED NATIONS INTERNATIONAL RESEARCH AND TRAINING INSTITUTE FOR THE ADVANCEMENT OF WOMEN (INSTRAW)
Calle Cesar Nicolas Penson 102-A, La Esperilla
Santo Domingo Dominican Republic

General Information Policy research, training, information, and networking on gender equality and women's advancement.

Established in 1976. Number of employees: 10. Unit of United Nations, New York, New York. Number of internship applications received each year: 35.

Internships Available ▶ *Research interns:* responsibilities include doing bibliographic searches, reading and summarizing documents, database inputting, proofreading. Candidates should have knowledge of field, organizational skills, research skills, self-motivation, writing skills. Duration is 3 months. Unpaid. Open to those with BA degree or more advanced degree. International applications accepted.

Benefits Opportunity to attend seminars/workshops, willing to provide letters of recommendation.

International Internships Available.

Contact E-mail or through World Wide Web site Julia Tavares, Associate Social Affairs Officer. Fax: 809-685-2117. E-mail: instraw.hq.sd@codetel.net.do. No phone calls. Applicants must submit a formal organization application, letter of interest, resume, letter of recommendation. Applications are accepted continuously. World Wide Web: http://www.un-instraw.org.

U.S.–ASIA INSTITUTE
232 East Capitol Street, NE
Washington, District of Columbia 20003

General Information Private, non-governmental organization that promotes dialogue on international issues of common interest to the United States and participating Asian nations. Established in 1979. Number of employees: 5. Number of internship applications received each year: 80.

Internships Available ▶ *1–2 staff assistants:* responsibilities include assisting staff in organizing various programs, performing research and office work, and attending and reporting on congressional hearings, seminars, and workshops. Candidates should have editing skills, knowledge of field, office skills, personal interest in the field, research skills, self-motivation. Duration is 3 months minimum (preferred). Unpaid. Open to college juniors, college seniors, recent college graduates, graduate students. International applications accepted.

Benefits Opportunity to attend seminars/workshops, willing to complete paperwork for educational credit, willing to provide letters of recommendation.

Contact Write, call, fax, e-mail, or through World Wide Web site Mary Sue Bissell, Vice President. Phone: 202-544-3181. Fax: 202-543-1748. E-mail: usasiai@aol.com. In-person interview recommended (telephone interview accepted). Applicants must submit a resume, academic transcripts, cover letter, 1 writing sample (1–2 pages). Application deadline: March 15 for spring/summer, July 15 for fall, November 15 for winter. World Wide Web: http://www.usasiainstitute.com.

U.S. PUBLIC INTEREST RESEARCH GROUP (PIRG)
218 D Street, SE
Washington, District of Columbia 20003

General Information National lobbying office for network of statewide consumer, environmental, and campaign finance reform public interest watchdog organizations. Established in 1983. Number of employees: 35. Number of internship applications received each year: 100.

Internships Available ▶ *1–2 administrative interns:* responsibilities include working with administrative director on day-to-day management of organization, including computer systems, filing systems, publications, and other administrative tasks. Candidates should have ability to work independently, ability to work with others, computer skills, office skills, oral communication skills, written communication skills. Duration is 1 semester. Unpaid. Open to college freshmen, college sophomores, college juniors, college seniors, recent college graduates. ▶ *1–3 campaign interns:* responsibilities include coordinating media events, coordinating grassroots campaign activities, and working with campaign offices across the United States. Candidates should have ability to work independently, oral communication skills, organizational skills, strong interpersonal skills, written communication skills. Duration is 1 semester. Unpaid. Open to college freshmen, college sophomores, college juniors, college seniors, recent college graduates. ▶ *4–8 legislative interns:* responsibilities include conducting research, preparing investigative reports, coordinating media events, coordinating grassroots campaigns, monitoring legislation, coordinating coalitions. Candidates should have ability to work independently, ability to work with others, oral communication skills, organizational skills, self-motivation, written communication skills. Duration is 1 semester. Unpaid. Open to college freshmen, college sophomores, college juniors, college seniors, recent college graduates, graduate students, law students. International applications accepted.

Benefits Opportunity to attend seminars/workshops, possible full-time employment, willing to act as a professional reference, willing to complete paperwork for educational credit, willing to provide letters of recommendation, various training sessions, brown bag lunch discussions; will be part of campus work-study programs.

Contact Write, call, fax, or e-mail Rick Trilsch, Intern Coordinator. Phone: 202-546-9707. Fax: 202-546-2461. E-mail: uspirg@pirg. org. In-person interview recommended (telephone interview accepted). Applicants must submit a letter of interest, resume, 1–3 page writing sample. Applications are accepted continuously. World Wide Web: http://www.uspirg.org.

VANGUARD COMMUNICATIONS
2121 K Street, NW, Suite 300
Washington, District of Columbia 20037

General Information Company that develops and implements advocacy communications campaigns to help resolve the world's most pressing problems, such as the environment, energy, healthcare, issues concerning women and children, human rights, civil liberties, reproductive choice, and education. Established in 1987. Number of employees: 31. Number of internship applications received each year: 50.

Internships Available ▶ *Interns:* responsibilities include drafting and distributing press releases, monitoring client news coverage, media database maintenance, assisting in news release production, contacting reporters, editing correspondence, and assisting office personnel. Candidates should have office skills, oral communication skills, strong interpersonal skills, written communication skills, previous work/internships experience and knowledge of Microsoft Word preferred; major in mass communications, public relations, journalism, or related subject required. Duration is 6–8 weeks. Unpaid. Open to college freshmen, college sophomores, college juniors, college seniors, graduate students. International applications accepted.

Benefits On-the-job training, willing to complete paperwork for educational credit, reimbursement for Metro expenses.

Contact Write, fax, or e-mail Stacey St. Holder, Internship Coordinator. Fax: 202-331-9420. E-mail: sstholder@vancomm.com. No phone calls. In-person interview recommended (telephone interview accepted). Applicants must submit a resume, two writing samples, cover letter. Applications are accepted continuously. World Wide Web: http://www.vancomm.com.

THE VEGETARIAN RESOURCE GROUP
PO Box 1463
Baltimore, Maryland 21203

General Information Public interest group that educates the public about the various aspects of vegetarianism, including health, environment, and ethics. Established in 1982. Number of employees: 8. Number of internship applications received each year: 20.

Internships Available ▶ *1–4 interns:* responsibilities include writing for *The Vegetarian Journal* and performing research, Web-related activities, outreach work, and clerical duties. Candidates should have ability to work independently, ability to work with others, computer skills, organizational skills, personal interest in the field, self-motivation, writing skills. Duration is 1–16 weeks. Unpaid. Open to high school students, recent high school graduates, college freshmen, college sophomores, college juniors, college seniors, recent college graduates, graduate students, law students, career changers, individuals reentering the workforce. International applications accepted.

Benefits Free housing, names of contacts, on-the-job training, opportunity to attend seminars/workshops, possible full-time

employment, travel reimbursement, willing to act as a professional reference, willing to complete paperwork for educational credit, willing to provide letters of recommendation.

Contact Write or e-mail Mr. Charles Stahler. Phone: 410-366-8343. E-mail: vrg@vrg.org. In-person interview recommended (telephone interview accepted). Applicants must submit a letter of interest, resume, writing sample. Applications are accepted continuously. World Wide Web: http://www.vrg.org.

VOICES FOR CHILDREN
2851 Meadow Lark Drive
San Diego, California 92123

General Information Nonprofit children's advocacy for those in foster care. Established in 1980. Number of employees: 19. Affiliate of National Court Appointed Special Advocate Association, Seattle, Washington. Number of internship applications received each year: 200.

Internships Available ▶ *20 IEP educational surrogates:* responsibilities include reviewing and evaluating progress of foster children within the school site; interviewing child, teachers, and staff; attending individual education program meetings. Candidates should have ability to work independently, ability to work with others, oral communication skills, research skills, written communication skills, ability to maintain objectivity. Duration is one year (after training). Unpaid. Open to college juniors, college seniors, recent college graduates, graduate students, law students, career changers, individuals reentering the workforce, must be 21 years or older. ▶ *20 case assessment program interns:* responsibilities include reading, reviewing, and summarizing court case files of foster children and making recommendations as to type of advocate needed. Candidates should have ability to work independently, analytical skills, research skills, written communication skills, ability to make objective recommendations. Duration is as needed. Unpaid. Open to recent college graduates, graduate students, law students, career changers, individuals reentering the workforce, must be 21 years or older. ▶ *150–200 court-appointed special advocates:* responsibilities include advocacy for abused and neglected children in foster care through juvenile court system, providing continuity and support; interviewing all parties; preparing written reports for the court. Candidates should have ability to work independently, oral communication skills, personal interest in the field, research skills, strong interpersonal skills, written communication skills. Duration is 1 year (after training). Unpaid. Open to college juniors, college seniors, recent college graduates, graduate students, law students, career changers, individuals reentering the workforce, must be 21 years or older. ▶ *50 court-appointed special monitors:* responsibilities include monitoring and evaluating the progress of dependent children of juvenile court (in foster care); interviewing parties; preparing written reports for court. Candidates should have ability to work independently, oral communication skills, personal interest in the field, research skills, strong interpersonal skills, written communication skills. Duration is one year (after training). Unpaid. Open to college juniors, college seniors, recent college graduates, graduate students, law students, career changers, individuals reentering the workforce, must be 21 years or older.

Benefits Formal training, on-the-job training, opportunity to attend seminars/workshops, travel reimbursement, willing to act as a professional reference, willing to complete paperwork for educational credit, 44-hour training on social services and juvenile court law and court procedures.

Contact Write, call, e-mail, or through World Wide Web site Gary B. Cagle, Volunteer Recruitment Coordinator. Phone: 858-569-2096 Ext. 227. Fax: 858-569-7151. E-mail: garyc@voices4children. com. In-person interview required. Applicants must submit a formal organization application, three personal references, criminal background check required. Applications are accepted continuously. World Wide Web: http://www.voices4children.com.

WASHINGTON OFFICE ON AFRICA
212 East Capitol Street
Washington, District of Columbia 20003

General Information Progressive ecumenical advocacy organization for a just U.S. policy toward Africa. Established in 1972. Number of employees: 2. Number of internship applications received each year: 40.

Internships Available ▶ *1–2 research and advocacy interns:* responsibilities include engaging with other Africa-related advocacy organizations on advocacy strategy; drafting briefing documents for grassroots constituency; Capitol Hill lobbying; and related office work. Candidates should have ability to work independently, ability to work with others, analytical skills, oral communication skills, personal interest in the field, written communication skills. Duration is 2–6 months. Unpaid. Open to college sophomores, college juniors, college seniors, graduate students. International applications accepted.

Benefits Opportunity to attend seminars/workshops, willing to act as a professional reference, willing to complete paperwork for educational credit, willing to provide letters of recommendation, reimbursement of work-related travel expenses.

Contact Write, fax, or e-mail Leon P. Spencer, Executive Director. Phone: 202-547-7503. Fax: 202-547-7505. E-mail: woa@igc.org. In-person interview recommended (telephone interview accepted). Applicants must submit a formal organization application, letter of interest, resume, writing sample, two letters of recommendation. Applications are accepted continuously. World Wide Web: http://www.woaafrica.org.

WASHINGTON OFFICE ON LATIN AMERICA
1630 Connecticut Avenue, NW
Washington, District of Columbia 20009

General Information Nongovernmental organization aiming to help shape foreign policy that advances human rights and political and economic development in Latin America. Established in 1974. Number of employees: 18. Number of internship applications received each year: 150.

Internships Available ▶ *7 interns:* responsibilities include monitoring U.S. foreign policy and events in the region, assisting administrative staff with clerical duties, and actively participating in day-to-day operations of human rights organization. Candidates should have college courses in field, knowledge of field, office skills, personal interest in the field, research skills, writing skills, must be Spanish-speaking. Duration is 1 semester or summer. Unpaid. Open to college freshmen, college sophomores, college juniors, college seniors, recent college graduates. International applications accepted.

Benefits Job counseling, names of contacts, possible full-time employment, willing to complete paperwork for educational credit, willing to provide letters of recommendation.

Contact Write, call, fax, or e-mail Jana Kurtz, Internship Coordinator. Phone: 202-797-2171. Fax: 202-797-2172. E-mail: wola@wola.org. Telephone interview required. Applicants must submit a letter of interest, resume, writing sample, two personal references, telephone interview for finalists only. Application deadline: March 15 for summer, August 1 for fall, December 1 for spring. World Wide Web: http://www.wola.org.

WASHINGTON PEACE CENTER
1801 Columbia Road, NW, Suite 104
Washington, District of Columbia 20009

General Information Multi-issue, grassroots, anti-racist organization working for nonviolent social change through education and action. Established in 1963. Number of employees: 2. Number of internship applications received each year: 100.

Internships Available ▶ *1–3 interns:* responsibilities include developing programs and materials in support of educational events and direct actions; community outreach and development to further social justice initiatives such as economic literacy, anti-racism education, and anti-military campaigns. Candidates should have ability to work independently, ability to work with others, computer skills, strong leadership ability, writing skills, commitment to social justice. Duration is 1 semester. Unpaid. Open to

high school seniors, recent high school graduates, college freshmen, college sophomores, college juniors, college seniors, recent college graduates, graduate students. International applications accepted.

Benefits Opportunity to attend seminars/workshops, willing to act as a professional reference, willing to complete paperwork for educational credit, willing to provide letters of recommendation.

Contact Write, call, fax, or e-mail Maria Ramos, Coordinator. Phone: 202-234-2000. Fax: 202-234-7064. E-mail: wpc@igc.org. In-person interview recommended (telephone interview accepted). Applicants must submit a letter of interest, resume, personal history in social justice activism and/or social service projects. Application deadline: April 1 for summer, November 1 for spring; continuous for remainder of year. World Wide Web: http://www.washingtonpeacecenter.org.

WEST VIRGINIA KIDS COUNT FUND
1031 Quarrier Street, Suite 313
Charleston, West Virginia 25301

General Information Advocacy group that seeks to improve the lives of West Virginia's at-risk children by mobilizing the private and public sectors to create prevention and early intervention programs, policies, and strategies; creates and maintains a statewide network of child advocates; and collects, analyzes, and disseminates information about at-risk children to the public through the media. Established in 1989. Number of employees: 3. Number of internship applications received each year: 2.

Internships Available ▶ *1 communications intern:* responsibilities include writing fact sheets, media releases, compiling information, organizing media contacts, compiling media results, working on desktop publishing and Web site maintenance. Candidates should have ability to work with others, analytical skills, computer skills, oral communication skills, plan to pursue career in field, research skills, written communication skills. Duration is flexible. Unpaid. Open to college juniors, college seniors, graduate students. International applications accepted.

Benefits Names of contacts, opportunity to attend seminars/workshops, travel reimbursement, willing to complete paperwork for educational credit, willing to provide letters of recommendation, networking opportunities with professionals in the field.

Contact Write, call, fax, or e-mail Missy Menefee, Director of Communications. Phone: 304-345-2101. Fax: 304-345-2102. E-mail: missymenefee@wvkidscountfund.org. In-person interview recommended (telephone interview accepted). Applications are accepted continuously. World Wide Web: http://www.wvkidscountfund.org.

WIDER OPPORTUNITIES FOR WOMEN, INC.
815 15th Street, NW, Suite 916
Washington, District of Columbia 20005-3104

General Information Organization that works nationally and in Washington, D.C., to achieve economic self-sufficiency for women through public policy advocacy and program service delivery. Established in 1964. Number of employees: 5. Number of internship applications received each year: 100.

Internships Available ▶ *2–4 Nontraditional Occupations for Women Project interns:* responsibilities include case management, evaluation, administration, and organizing. Candidates should have ability to work with others, computer skills, oral communication skills, organizational skills, personal interest in the field, self-motivation. Duration is one summer. Unpaid. Open to college freshmen, college sophomores, college juniors, college seniors, graduate students. ▶ *1–3 public policy interns:* responsibilities include researching and analyzing public policies for their impact on women's employment and training; representing WOW at briefings, hearings, and other meetings relating to legislative agenda; State Organizing for Family Economic Self-Sufficiency Projects; updating grassroots network of women's employment training organizations on legislation and soliciting their support when necessary. Candidates should have analytical skills, computer skills, personal interest in the field, research skills, self-motivation, written communication skills. Duration is one summer. Unpaid. Open to college freshmen, college sophomores, college juniors, college seniors, graduate students. ▶ *1–3 resource development interns:* responsibilities include newsletter writing and layout; maintaining resource library; developing graphic/photo stock library of women performing non-traditional jobs; researching, writing, and layout to update existing publications. Candidates should have computer skills, personal interest in the field, research skills, self-motivation, writing skills. Duration is one summer. Unpaid. Open to college freshmen, college sophomores, college juniors, college seniors, recent college graduates, graduate students. International applications accepted.

Benefits Job counseling, names of contacts, willing to complete paperwork for educational credit, willing to provide letters of recommendation, assistance with resume preparation, stipend of $10 per day to cover transportation and lunch.

Contact Write, fax, e-mail, or through World Wide Web site Vivian Staples, Office Manager. Fax: 202-638-4885. E-mail: info@w-o-w. org. In-person interview recommended (telephone interview accepted). Applicants must submit a resume, writing sample, cover letter. Applications are accepted continuously. World Wide Web: http://www.w-o-w.org.

WOMEN'S ACTION FOR NEW DIRECTIONS/ WOMEN LEGISLATORS' LOBBY
110 Maryland Avenue, NE, Suite 205
Washington, District of Columbia 20002

General Information National membership organization aiming to empower women to get politically involved. Established in 1980. Number of employees: 4. Number of internship applications received each year: 50.

Internships Available ▶ *1 assistant to WILL director:* responsibilities include researching, assisting with lobbying, preparing and editing reports on issues related to violence against women, and women's issues in general; mailing press and member communications; organizing conference and seminars for women state legislators; phoning women state legislators; offering general office support. Duration is 3–12 months. Small stipend. ▶ *1 assistant to director of policy and program:* responsibilities include researching, assisting and supporting lobbying; preparing and editing reports on issues related to arms control, military budget, and nuclear issues; mailing press and member communications, attending congressional hearings, and offering general office support. Duration is 3–12 months. Small stipend. Candidates for all positions should have computer skills, oral communication skills, organizational skills, self-motivation, strong interpersonal skills, written communication skills. International applications accepted.

Benefits Formal training, job counseling, names of contacts, opportunity to attend seminars/workshops, willing to act as a professional reference, willing to complete paperwork for educational credit, willing to provide letters of recommendation.

Contact Write or e-mail Kimberly Robson, Director of Policy and Programs. E-mail: wand@wand.org. No phone calls. In-person interview recommended (telephone interview accepted). Applicants must submit a resume, writing sample. Applications are accepted continuously. World Wide Web: http://www.wand.org.

WOMEN'S INTERNATIONAL LEAGUE FOR PEACE AND FREEDOM
1213 Race Street
Philadelphia, Pennsylvania 19107-1691

General Information Organization devoted to ending sexism, racism, classism, oppression, militarism, and all forms of violence. Established in 1915. Number of employees: 8. Division of Women's International League for Peace and Freedom, Geneva, Switzerland. Number of internship applications received each year: 100.

Internships Available ▶ *1–3 communications interns:* responsibilities include maintaining the content and design of the organization's Web site; researching and linking to other online political and peace activist resources. Candidates should have ability to work independently, computer skills, organizational skills, research skills, writing skills. Duration is 12 weeks (minimum 20 hours per week). Position available as unpaid or at $117 per week. Open to high school seniors, recent high school graduates, college freshmen,

college sophomores, college juniors, college seniors, recent college graduates, law students, career changers, individuals reentering the workforce. ▶ *1–2 development interns:* responsibilities include working with development director and staff on funding WILPF national political campaign; includes coordinating, fund-raising, appeal letters, and grant research. Candidates should have ability to work independently, ability to work with others, oral communication skills, organizational skills, research skills, writing skills. Duration is 12 weeks (minimum 20 hours per week). Position available as unpaid or at $117 per week. Open to high school seniors, recent high school graduates, college freshmen, college sophomores, college juniors, college seniors, recent college graduates, graduate students, law students, career changers, individuals reentering the workforce. ▶ *1–3 membership assistants:* responsibilities include helping members organize new branches and strengthen existing branches and participating in all phases of campaigning from keeping records to bringing in new members. Candidates should have ability to work independently, oral communication skills, self-motivation, strong interpersonal skills, strong leadership ability, written communication skills. Duration is 12 weeks (minimum 20 hours per week). Position available as unpaid or at $117 per week. Open to high school seniors, recent high school graduates, college freshmen, college sophomores, college juniors, college seniors, recent college graduates, graduate students, law students, career changers, individuals reentering the workforce. ▶ *1–3 national program assistants:* responsibilities include working with branches around the country; tracking legislation; working with program coordinator to develop and implement national programs. Candidates should have ability to work independently, ability to work with others, oral communication skills, research skills, self-motivation, writing skills. Duration is 12 weeks (minimum 20 hours per week). Position available as unpaid or at $117 per week. Open to high school seniors, recent high school graduates, college freshmen, college sophomores, college juniors, college seniors, recent college graduates, graduate students, law students, career changers, individuals reentering the workforce. ▶ *1 publications assistant:* responsibilities include assisting the editor in locating and soliciting copy, editing news, researching and writing stories, checking facts, and using desktop publishing programs. Candidates should have ability to work independently, computer skills, editing skills, oral communication skills, research skills, writing skills. Duration is 12 weeks (minimum 20 hours per week). Position available as unpaid or at $117 per week. Open to college freshmen, college sophomores, college juniors, college seniors, recent college graduates, graduate students, career changers, individuals reentering the workforce. International applications accepted.

Benefits Formal training, on-the-job training, opportunity to attend seminars/workshops, possible full-time employment, willing to act as a professional reference, willing to complete paperwork for educational credit, willing to provide letters of recommendation.

International Internships Available in Geneva, Switzerland.

Contact Write, call, fax, e-mail, or through World Wide Web site Jody Dodd, Leadership/Outreach Coordinator. Phone: 215-563-7110. Fax: 215-563-5527. E-mail: jdodd@wilpf.org. In-person interview recommended (telephone interview accepted). Applicants must submit a letter of interest, resume, writing sample. Application deadline: May 1 for summer, August 1 for fall, December 1 for spring. World Wide Web: http://www.wilpf.org.

WORLD HUNGER ECUMENICAL ARIZONA TASK FORCE (WHEAT)
4423 North 24th Street, Suite 540
Phoenix, Arizona 85016

General Information Nonprofit organization that educates, advocates, and empowers individuals to action in the fight against hunger. Established in 1979. Number of employees: 5. Number of internship applications received each year: 19.

Internships Available ▶ *1–2 communication interns:* responsibilities include assisting in all stages of disseminating WHEAT reports and analyses to news media; establishing and maintaining relationship with print, broadcast and electronic media. Candidates should have ability to work independently, oral communication skills,

World Hunger Ecumenical Arizona Task Force (WHEAT) (continued)
strong interpersonal skills, written communication skills, attention to detail. Duration is flexible. Unpaid. Open to high school seniors, recent high school graduates, college freshmen, college sophomores, college juniors, college seniors, recent college graduates, graduate students, law students, career changers, individuals reentering the workforce. ▶ *1–2 local and global food security issues interns:* responsibilities include assisting in researching, preparing, and distributing information on how legislative proposals would affect families, the federal budget, states, and third world countries. Candidates should have ability to work independently, computer skills, oral communication skills, organizational skills, self-motivation, strong leadership ability, strong Internet skills, familiarity with tax and budget concepts, fluency in a foreign language (helpful), quantitative analytic skills (required). Duration is flexible. Unpaid. ▶ *Nonprofit event planning interns:* responsibilities include scheduling, set up, and content of various events; gathering appropriate materials for use as hand outs; helping maintain contacts with state civic, religious, and community action organizations; helping plan annual conference workshops and seminars. Candidates should have ability to work independently, analytical skills, oral communication skills, organizational skills, self-motivation, strong leadership ability. Duration is flexible. Unpaid. Open to high school seniors, recent high school graduates, college freshmen, college sophomores, college juniors, college seniors, recent college graduates, graduate students, law students, career changers, individuals reentering the workforce. ▶ *1–2 nonprofit fund-raising interns:* responsibilities include identifying potential contributors, preparing reports and proposals to funders, and maintaining information on grants to WHEAT; conducting research on foundations and new funding sources. Candidates should have ability to work independently, computer skills, oral communication skills, organizational skills, self-motivation, strong leadership ability. Duration is flexible. Unpaid. Open to high school seniors, recent high school graduates, college freshmen, college sophomores, college juniors, college seniors, recent college graduates, graduate students, law students, career changers, individuals reentering the workforce. ▶ *1–2 nonprofit management interns:* responsibilities include assisting with staff recruitment process; preparing reconciliations of bi-weekly time sheets; ordering supplies and coding invoices; assisting staff with computer and/or software-related problems and doing preventive maintenance. Candidates should have ability to work independently, computer skills, oral communication skills, organizational skills, self-motivation, strong leadership ability. Duration is flexible. Unpaid. Open to high school seniors, recent high school graduates, college freshmen, college sophomores, college juniors, college seniors, recent college graduates, graduate students, law students, career changers, individuals reentering the workforce.

▶ *1–2 nonprofit marketing and promotion interns:* responsibilities include developing materials for use in press kits and corporate information packets; researching specific subjects; assisting in preparation of materials for presentations; collecting and analyzing data from range of sources to track state economics and finances. Candidates should have ability to work independently, computer skills, oral communication skills, organizational skills, self-motivation, strong leadership ability. Duration is flexible. Unpaid. Open to high school seniors, recent high school graduates, college freshmen, college sophomores, college juniors, college seniors, recent college graduates, graduate students, law students, career changers, individuals reentering the workforce. ▶ *1–2 outreach campaigns interns:* responsibilities include helping maintain communication with partner groups and others; tracking use of creative outreach strategies; helping develop new materials; helping research state and local policies affecting ability of individuals to obtain economic security. Candidates should have ability to work independently, computer skills, oral communication skills, organizational skills, self-motivation, strong leadership ability. Duration is flexible. Unpaid. Open to high school seniors, recent high school graduates, college freshmen, college sophomores, college juniors, college seniors, recent college graduates, graduate students, law students, career changers, individuals reentering the workforce. ▶ *1–2 state/federal policy watch interns:* responsibilities include following process of legislative proposals; responding to requests for information on WHEAT projects; assisting in monitoring federal budget process and implications of budget proposals on programs involving low-income families and individuals. Candidates should have ability to work independently, computer skills, oral communication skills, organizational skills, self-motivation, strong leadership ability. Duration is flexible. Unpaid. Open to high school seniors, recent high school graduates, college freshmen, college sophomores, college juniors, college seniors, recent college graduates, graduate students, law students, career changers, individuals reentering the workforce. International applications accepted.

Benefits Formal training, names of contacts, on-the-job training, opportunity to attend seminars/workshops, possible full-time employment, travel reimbursement, willing to act as a professional reference, willing to complete paperwork for educational credit, willing to provide letters of recommendation.

Contact Write, call, fax, e-mail, or through World Wide Web site Dr. Tamera Zivic, Executive Director. Phone: 602-955-5076. Fax: 602-955-5290. E-mail: wheat@hungerhurts.org. In-person interview recommended (telephone interview accepted). Applicants must submit a formal organization application, letter of interest, resume, academic transcripts, two personal references, two letters of recommendation. Applications are accepted continuously. World Wide Web: http://www.hungerhurts.org.

PROFESSIONAL, SCIENTIFIC, AND TECHNICAL SERVICES

GENERAL

ACOLYTE SYSTEMS, INC.
363 Seventh Avenue, 21st Floor
New York, New York 10001

General Information Developer, designer, and marketer of wireless lighting systems and devices that can be customized for a wide variety of applications.

Internships Available ▶ *Accounting interns:* responsibilities include assisting financial officer; assisting with general accounting tasks; keeping notes on meetings and interviews; working with supervisor to create project based on student's educational objective; clerical and office tasks as needed. Candidates should have college level accounting knowledge, skills, and abilities; knowledge of general accounting software; typing skills; punctuality; professionalism. Duration is 3 to 6 months (flexible to school schedule). ▶ *Business administration interns:* responsibilities include assisting chief executive officer; scheduling meetings; handling corporate correspondence; keeping notes on meetings and interviews; working with supervisor to create project based on student's educational objective; clerical and office tasks as needed. Candidates should have organizational skills, knowledge of general office software and typing skills; punctuality; professionalism. Duration is 3-6 months (flexible to school schedule) 30 to 40 hours per week. ▶ *Publicity interns (public relations department):* responsibilities include assisting publicity staff; creating and maintaining information databases; helping write and distribute press releases; keeping notes on meetings and interviews; writing with supervisor to create project based on studen's educational objective; clerical and office tasks as needed. Candidates should have organizational skills, knowledge of general office software, typing skills, punctuality, professionalism. Duration is 3 to 6 months (flexible to school schedule) 30-40 hours per week. Unpaid.

Benefits Possible full-time employment, travel stipend.

Contact Fax or e-mail Internship Coordinator. Phone: 888-ACOLYTE. Fax: 212-629-6931. E-mail: info@888acolyte.com. Resume (faxed) to the attention of staff member listed on Web site as contact for position of interest or e-mail resume. Applications are accepted continuously. World Wide Web: http://www.smartlyte.com.

A. E. SCHWARTZ & ASSOCIATES
PO Box 79228
Waverley, Massachusetts 02479-0228

General Information Comprehensive training and consulting organization offering over 40 management and professional training programs to managers and support staff nationally and internationally. Established in 1982. Number of employees: 12. Number of internship applications received each year: 1,200.

Internships Available ▶ *1 HTML/JAVA/CGI programmer:* responsibilities include assisting in programming and managing commercial Web sites: trainingconsortium.com and aeschwartz.com. Candidates should have ability to work independently, ability to work with others, college courses in field, computer skills, oral communication skills, organizational skills, personal interest in the field, self-motivation, written communication skills, Internet knowledge and experience. Duration is flexible (minimum 16-24 hours weekly). Position available as unpaid or paid. Open to college juniors, college seniors, recent college graduates, graduate students, career changers, individuals reentering the workforce. ▶ *3 IBM software specialists:* responsibilities include learning and teaching all Windows software packages, converting and constructing databases (Internet emphasis), performing desktop publishing using graphics software, and researching new products. Candidates should have ability to work independently, computer skills, declared college major in field, oral communication skills, organizational skills, personal interest in the field, self-motivation, written communication skills, Internet knowledge and experience. Duration is flexible (minimum 16-24 hours weekly). Position available as unpaid or paid. Open to college sophomores, college juniors, college seniors, recent college graduates, graduate students, career changers, individuals reentering the workforce. ▶ *1 Internet marketing intern:* responsibilities include assisting in managing and creating marketing venues of commercial Web sites, including bulk e-mail, preferred business partnerships, auto-responders, and bounty agreements. Candidates should have ability to work independently, ability to work with others, computer skills, oral communication skills, organizational skills, personal interest in the field, self-motivation, written communication skills, Internet knowledge and experience. Duration is flexible (minimum 16-24 hours weekly). Position available as unpaid or paid. Open to college sophomores, college juniors, college seniors, recent college graduates, graduate students, career changers. ▶ *3-5 business technology interns:* responsibilities include developing new version of commercial Web site; maintaining and posting new data; researching and installing new software/hardware; creating solutions and generating information for end-users, partners, and registrants; developing systems for tracking and project management; managing corporate e-mail and autoresponders. Candidates should have ability to work independently, computer skills, oral communication skills, organizational skills, written communication skills, Internet knowledge and experience. Duration is flexible (minimum 16-24 hours weekly). Position available as unpaid or paid. Open to college sophomores, college juniors, college seniors, recent college graduates, graduate students, career changers. ▶ *3-5 graphic designers:* responsibilities include creating new design concepts; designing flyers, book covers, sales materials, catalog, and exhibit materials including specialty and promotional items; writing, editing, and copyediting; providing camera-ready output and overseeing printing; Internet Web design. Candidates should have ability to work independently, analytical skills, computer skills, declared college major in field, oral communication skills, organizational skills, written communication skills, Internet knowledge and experience. Duration is flexible (minimum 16-24 hours weekly). Position available as unpaid or paid. Open to college sophomores, college juniors, college seniors, recent college graduates, graduate students, career changers, individuals reentering the workforce. ▶ *2 public relations interns:* responsibilities include arranging media coverage; networking with organizations to arrange media coverage for special projects; writing letters, articles, and press releases; and placing advertisements and directory listings. Candidates should have ability to work independently, computer skills, oral communication skills, organizational skills, personal interest in the field, self-motivation, strong interpersonal skills, written communication skills, Internet knowledge and experience. Duration

A. E. Schwartz & Associates (continued)

is flexible (minimum 16-24 hours weekly). Position available as unpaid or paid. Open to college sophomores, college juniors, college seniors, recent college graduates, graduate students, career changers, individuals reentering the workforce. ▶ *3–5 publishing interns:* responsibilities include coordinating marketing and placement of new releases online; researching supplemental information; editing, developing, writing, and evaluating new and existing materials. Candidates should have ability to work independently, ability to work with others, analytical skills, computer skills, editing skills, oral communication skills, organizational skills, written communication skills, Internet knowledge and experience. Duration is flexible (minimum 16-24 hours weekly). Position available as unpaid or paid. Open to college sophomores, college juniors, college seniors, recent college graduates, graduate students, career changers, individuals reentering the workforce. ▶ *3–5 sales/ marketing interns:* responsibilities include developing strategies and new distribution outlets, networking with sponsoring organizations to arrange programs, developing contacts, researching new distribution avenues (Internet emphasis), developing and maintaining computer systems for mail projects, placing advertisements, and handling correspondence. Candidates should have ability to work independently, ability to work with others, oral communication skills, organizational skills, personal interest in the field, self-motivation, Internet knowledge and experience. Duration is flexible (minimum 16-24 hours weekly). Position available as unpaid or paid. Open to college sophomores, college juniors, college seniors, recent college graduates, graduate students, career changers, individuals reentering the workforce. ▶ *3–5 video production/ voice overs interns:* responsibilities include video and voice over projects that will require production, graphic design, animation, recording, and file conversion. Candidates should have ability to work independently, computer skills, oral communication skills, organizational skills, written communication skills, Internet knowledge and experience. Duration is Flexible (minimum 16–24 hours weekly). Position available as unpaid or paid. Open to college sophomores, college juniors, college seniors, recent college graduates, graduate students, career changers. ▶ *3–5 writers/ editors:* responsibilities include assisting in the writing, editing, and copyediting of new and existing materials (on- and offline); researching supplemental information; writing articles for training and management journals; and compiling, writing, and editing manuscripts and training manuals. Candidates should have ability to work independently, ability to work with others, analytical skills, computer skills, editing skills, oral communication skills, organizational skills, written communication skills, Internet knowledge and experience. Duration is flexible (minimum 16-24 hours weekly). Position available as unpaid or paid. Open to college sophomores, college juniors, college seniors, recent college graduates, graduate students, career changers, individuals reentering the workforce. International applications accepted.

Benefits Formal training, on-the-job training, possible full-time employment, willing to act as a professional reference, willing to complete paperwork for educational credit, willing to provide letters of recommendation, opportunity to attend seminars/workshops/ meetings, travel stipend for some positions.

Contact Write, fax, or e-mail Mr. Andrew E. Schwartz, CEO. Fax: 617-926-0660. E-mail: interns@aeschwartz.com. In-person interview recommended (telephone interview accepted). Applicants must submit a letter of interest, resume, two writing samples, 3 personal and professional references (names and phone numbers). Applications are accepted continuously. World Wide Web: http://www. aeschwartz.com.

AMERICAN PSYCHOLOGICAL ASSOCIATION
750 First Street, NE
Washington, District of Columbia 20002-4242

General Information Scientific and professional organization that represents psychology in the U.S.; the largest association of psychologists worldwide, with a membership greater than 155,000.
Internships Available ▶ *4 Congressional Fellows:* responsibilities include working as legislative assistant on the staff of a member of Congress or congressional committee; conducting legislative or oversight work, assisting in hearings and debates, preparing

briefs, and writing speeches. Candidates should have ability to work independently, ability to work with others, oral communication skills, written communication skills, demonstrated competence in scientific and/or professional psychology. Duration is 1 year. Stipend ranging from $48,500 to $63,100 depending upon years of post-doctoral experience. Open to APA members (or applicants for membership) with a doctorate in psychology at the time of application, minimum of 2 years post-doctoral experience (preferred). ▶ *1 Science Policy Fellow:* responsibilities include working as special assistant in an executive branch research funding/ coordinating office. Candidates should have ability to work independently, ability to work with others, oral communication skills, written communication skills, demonstrated competence in scientific psychology, sensitivity toward policy issues, and a strong interest in applying psychological knowledge to national science policy issues. Duration is 1 year. $52,900. Open to APA members (or applicants for membership) with a doctorate in psychology with one year post-doctoral experience. ▶ *Public interest policy interns:* responsibilities include working on public interest issues pertaining to children, women, ethnic minorities, HIV/AIDS, disabilities, aging, lesbian/bisexual concerns, media, and/or violence. Duration is 15-20 hours per wee (minimum). $14.50 per hour. Open to doctoral students in psychology or related field in at least second year of training.
Benefits Up to $3000 per fellow for relocation to Washington DC and travel expenses during year.
Contact Through World Wide Web site Internship Coordinator. Phone: 800-374-2721. Materials as detailed on Web site. Application deadline: mid-December for Science Fellowship Program, late December for Congressional Fellowship Program, late March for Public Interest Policy Program. World Wide Web: http://www.apa. org.

ANIMAL BEHAVIOR CENTER OF NEW YORK
89-10 Eliot Avenue
Rego Park, New York 11374

General Information Not-for-profit applied animal behavior treatment and teaching center. Established in 1992. Number of employees: 15. Subsidiary of American Foundation for Animal Rescue, Inc., Rego Park, New York. Number of internship applications received each year: 100.
Internships Available ▶ *24 canine behavior counselors (CBC):* responsibilities include lectures, case studies, videotape, training dogs, instruction (private and group), rounds, off-site trips to veterinarian hospitals and shelters. Candidates should have ability to work independently, analytical skills, oral communication skills, personal interest in the field, plan to pursue career in field, strong interpersonal skills. Duration is 1–3 months. Unpaid. Open to recent high school graduates, college freshmen, college sophomores, college juniors, college seniors, recent college graduates, graduate students, career changers, individuals reentering the workforce. International applications accepted.
Benefits Formal training, housing at a cost, job counseling, on-the-job training, opportunity to attend seminars/workshops, possible full-time employment, willing to act as a professional reference, willing to complete paperwork for educational credit, willing to provide letters of recommendation.
Contact Write, call, fax, e-mail, or through World Wide Web site Robert DeFranco, Executive Director, 89-10 Elitot Avenue, Rego Park, New York 11374. Phone: 718-205-0200. Fax: 718-205-3962. E-mail: abcny@canines.com. In-person interview recommended (telephone interview accepted). Applicants must submit a formal organization application, $3000 program fee upon acceptance. Applications are accepted continuously. Fees: $50. World Wide Web: http://www.canines.com.

AUTOMOTIVE RESTORATION, INC.
1785 Barnum Avenue
Stratford, Connecticut 06614

General Information Antique and classic automobile restoration shop that performs panel fabrication, woodwork, upholstery, body, paint, and mechanical work; includes management, appraisal, and evaluation. Established in 1977. Number of employees: 38. Number of internship applications received each year: 50.

Internships Available ▶ *1–2 general office interns:* responsibilities include bookkeeping, invoicing, research, documentation, and business management. Candidates should have ability to work with others, computer skills, office skills, oral communication skills, research skills, written communication skills. Duration is flexible. $6 to $15 per hour commensurate with experience and ability. Open to recent high school graduates, college freshmen, college sophomores, college juniors, college seniors, recent college graduates, graduate students, law students, career changers, individuals reentering the workforce, must be 18 or older. ▶ *4 restoration apprentices:* responsibilities include assisting tradespeople in areas including panel fabrication, photography, research, documentation, upholstery, older vehicle mechanics, vintage race mechanics, paint/body, assembly/detail, and woodwork. Candidates should have ability to work with others, analytical skills, oral communication skills, self-motivation, written communication skills, technical interests and educational background. Duration is flexible. $6 to $15 per hour commensurate with experience and ability. Open to high school seniors, recent high school graduates, college freshmen, college sophomores, college juniors, college seniors, recent college graduates, graduate students, career changers, individuals reentering the workforce, must be 18 or older. International applications accepted.

Benefits Names of contacts, on-the-job training, opportunity to attend seminars/workshops, possible full-time employment, travel reimbursement, willing to act as a professional reference, willing to complete paperwork for educational credit, willing to provide letters of recommendation.

Contact Write, call, fax, e-mail, or through World Wide Web site Mrs. Denise Cutrone, Human Resources, 1785 Barnum Avenue, Stratford, Connecticut 06497. Phone: 203-377-6745. Fax: 203-386-0486. E-mail: kent@auto-restore.com. In-person interview recommended (telephone interview accepted). Applicants must submit a letter of interest, resume. Applications are accepted continuously. World Wide Web: http://www.automotiverestorations.com.

BATTELLE MEMORIAL INSTITUTE
505 King Avenue
Columbus, Ohio 43201

General Information Provider of innovative science and technology solutions for government and commercial customers worldwide and management of three national laboratories for the U.S. Department of Energy. Established in 1923.

Internships Available ▶ *Co-ops:* responsibilities include working on an assignment directly related to intern's field of study. Duration is one academic term (full-time). Paid. ▶ *Internships:* responsibilities include assignments that may or may not be directly related to intern's college major. Duration is 3 months to 3 years; part- or full-time. Paid. Open to college freshmen, college sophomores, college juniors, college seniors.

Benefits Possible full-time employment.

Contact Through World Wide Web site Internship Coordinator. Phone: 614-424-6424. Materials as specfied on Web site. Applications are accepted continuously. World Wide Web: http://www.battelle.org.

BENETECH
480 California Avenue, Suite 201
Palo Alto, California 94306-1609

General Information Nonprofit developer of technology to address social needs. Established in 1989. Number of employees: 15. Number of internship applications received each year: 100.

Internships Available ▶ *1–3 software interns:* responsibilities include programming and testing for reading systems and other adaptive tools for people with disabilities. Candidates should have analytical skills, computer skills, personal interest in the field, research skills, self-motivation, programming experience. Duration is 1 summer or 1 semester. Position available as unpaid or at $8–$15 per hour. Open to college sophomores, college juniors, college seniors, recent college graduates, graduate students, individuals with disabilities are encouraged to apply. ▶ *1–3 technology for social needs*

interns: responsibilities include researching social applications of technology, analyzing needs, and developing funding applications. Candidates should have ability to work independently, oral communication skills, research skills, self-motivation, strong interpersonal skills, written communication skills. Duration is 1 summer or 1 semester. Position available as unpaid or at $8–$12 per hour. Open to recent high school graduates, college sophomores, college juniors, college seniors, graduate students, law students. International applications accepted.

Benefits On-the-job training, possible full-time employment, willing to act as a professional reference, willing to provide letters of recommendation.

Contact Write, fax, or e-mail Jane Simchuk, Manager of Administration, 480 California Avenue, Suite 201, Palo Alto, California 94306-1609. Fax: 650-603-8887. E-mail: jane@benetech.org. No phone calls. Telephone interview required. Applicants must submit a letter of interest, resume, writing sample, letter of recommendation. Application deadline: May 15 for summer. World Wide Web: http://www.benetech.org.

THE BOSPAS FOREST FARM
c/o Familia Pepe Davila, Hotel Imbabura, Calle Oviedo 9 33
Ibarra Ecuador

General Information Farm dedicated to growing a variety of crops and trees organically and sustainably, focussing on diversity rather than on mono culture, using agroforestry and permaculture techniques. Established in 1999. Number of employees: 4. Unit of The International Vetiver Network, Leesburg, Virginia. Number of internship applications received each year: 5.

Internships Available ▶ *1–2 Bospas Arboretum establishment assistants:* responsibilities include researching the tree species in the area, setting up an inventory of tree species, making descriptions of trees, preparing and painting signs. Candidates should have ability to work independently, ability to work with others, knowledge of field, personal interest in the field, basic Spanish. Duration is 1 month. Unpaid. ▶ *1–2 general farm activities assistants:* responsibilities include planting trees, compost making, general maintenance, construction work, irrigation system, machete work. Candidates should have ability to work with others, knowledge of field, basic Spanish. Duration is 1 month. Unpaid. Open to college seniors, recent college graduates, graduate students. International applications accepted.

Benefits Housing at a cost, meals at a cost, names of contacts, on-the-job training, willing to provide letters of recommendation.

International Internships Available.

Contact Write or e-mail Piet P. Sabbe, c/o Familia Pepe Davila-Hotel Imbabura, Calle Oviedo 9 33, Ibarra Ecuador. E-mail: bospas22@hotmail.com. No phone calls. Applicants must submit a letter of interest, two writing samples, two letters of recommendation. Applications are accepted continuously. World Wide Web: http://www.ecuativer.com/bospas.

CENTER FOR COASTAL STUDIES, INC.
59 Commercial Street, PO Box 1036
Provincetown, Massachusetts 02657

General Information Marine mammal/habitat/coastal ecology and research organization. Established in 1976. Number of employees: 15. Number of internship applications received each year: 50.

Internships Available ▶ *2–4 research interns:* responsibilities include data collection, entry, and some analysis; an independent project. Candidates should have ability to work independently, ability to work with others, computer skills, research skills, self-motivation, written communication skills. Duration is 3–5 months. $500 per month. Open to college juniors, college seniors, recent college graduates, graduate students, must be pursuing career in marine animal research. International applications accepted.

Contact Write, e-mail, or through World Wide Web site Internship Coordinator. Phone: 508-487-3622. Fax: 508-487-4495. E-mail: ccs@coastalstudies.org. In-person interview recommended (telephone interview accepted). Applicants must submit a letter of interest, resume, academic transcripts, two letters of recommendation.

Center for Coastal Studies, Inc. (continued)

Application deadline: January 31 for summer and fall, October 31 for winter. Fees: $10. World Wide Web: http://www.coastalstudies.org.

CLEANEVENT USA, INC.
8350 Parkline Boulevard, Suite 100
Orlando, Florida 32809

General Information Provider of cleaning and waste management services to venues and events. Established in 1997. Number of employees: 40. Number of internship applications received each year: 100.

Internships Available ▶ *1–4 event coordinators:* responsibilities include assisting in event planning, administration, payroll, dispatching, recruiting, and job costing. Candidates should have ability to work independently, ability to work with others, computer skills, oral communication skills, high energy level. Duration is 5–12 months. $1000 per month. Open to college juniors, college seniors, recent college graduates. International applications accepted.

Benefits Names of contacts, on-the-job training, possible full-time employment, willing to act as a professional reference, willing to complete paperwork for educational credit, willing to provide letters of recommendation, travel, meals, and lodging provided (during events).

Contact Write, fax, or e-mail Caroline Peach, Human Resource Manager. Fax: 407-856-0131. E-mail: cpeach@cleaneventusa.com. No phone calls. Telephone interview required. Applicants must submit a letter of interest, resume. Application deadline: June 2 for fall, November 30 for spring.

CONSUMER ELECTRONICS ASSOCIATION
2500 Wilson Boulevard
Arlington, Virginia 22201

General Information Association representing 650 companies that make the products that give consumers access to entertainment, education, and information; producer, sponsor and manager of the world's biggest consumer technology event—the International Consumer Electronics show. Established in 1924. Number of employees: 120. Number of internship applications received each year: 2,500.

Internships Available ▶ *1–2 Web services interns:* responsibilities include managing and maintaining new and existing content on various CEA Web sites; facilitating the creation of new web-based content management tools using SQL, ASP, and HTML, and assisting with day-to-day management and maintenance of CEA's Web sites. Candidates should have ability to work with others, computer skills, knowledge of field, oral communication skills, knowledge of HTML and Javascript. Duration is summer (May to August) and/or 6-month period. Paid. Open to college sophomores, college juniors, college seniors, recent college graduates, graduate students, career changers. ▶ *1 communications intern:* responsibilities include writing press releases and other promotional materials, assisting with the scheduling of press conferences for CES, assisting with maintaining the PR contact database, researching new media contacts, and providing general support for the communications staff. Candidates should have experience in the field, oral communication skills, organizational skills, plan to pursue career in field, writing skills. Duration is summer (May to August). Paid. Open to college sophomores, college juniors, college seniors. ▶ *1 editorial intern:* responsibilities include writing short articles for Vision Magazine, helping edit copy, and helping collect artwork for Vision, researching information on potential Hall of Fame candidates, and writing biographies for Hall of Fame nominees. Candidates should have editing skills, experience in the field, oral communication skills, research skills, writing skills. Duration is summer (May to August). Paid. Open to college sophomores, college juniors, college seniors. ▶ *1 graphics intern:* responsibilities include assisting staff with day-to-day graphics requests, such as small design projects, camera-ready materials, and scanning of needed graphics. Candidates should have ability to work independently, computer skills, experience in the field, oral communication skills, plan to pursue career in field, knowledge of

Quark Xpress, Adobe Photoshop, and Adobe Illustrator. Duration is summer (May to August) and/or fall semester. Paid. Open to college sophomores, college juniors, college seniors. ▶ *1–2 information technology interns :* responsibilities include providing hands-on end-user PC/technical support, trouble-shooting network, and assisting with e-mail and PC problems; working with staff to assess needs and to identify and implement solutions. Candidates should have ability to work with others, computer skills, experience in the field, oral communication skills, plan to pursue career in field, customer service skills. Duration is summer (May to August) and/or 6-month period. Paid. Open to college sophomores, college juniors, college seniors, recent college graduates. ▶ *1 library intern:* responsibilities include answering in-depth reference questions; contributing to daily current awareness listing, database management, indexing and abstracting, cataloging, and online searching of information services; day-to-day library functions including shelving, checking-in magazines, and answering ready-reference questions. Candidates should have computer skills, experience in the field, plan to pursue career in field, research skills, customer service skills and Web knowledge. Duration is summer (May to August), fall or spring semester. Paid. Open to recent college graduates, graduate students. ▶ *1 marketing intern:* responsibilities include working closely with the marketing department staff on marketing strategy, promotion campaigns for CEA/CES events and writing promotional copy; also coordinating design work with graphics staff, coordinating mail house and printing processes, and assisting in staffing in local CEA events. Candidates should have ability to work with others, knowledge of field, office skills, oral communication skills, organizational skills, written communication skills. Duration is summer (May to August) and/or fall semester. Paid. Open to college juniors, college seniors, recent college graduates, graduate students. ▶ *1 technology policy intern:* responsibilities include supporting and working on federal technology issues; monitoring events and hearings, tracking state and federal legislation; researching and writing; Web site support; drafting position papers; issues will include broadband, privacy, digital download, and recording rights. Candidates should have knowledge of field, oral communication skills, personal interest in the field, research skills, writing skills. Duration is summer (May to August). Paid. Open to college juniors, college seniors, graduate students, law students. International applications accepted.

Benefits Formal training, names of contacts, on-the-job training, opportunity to attend seminars/workshops, possible full-time employment, willing to act as a professional reference, willing to complete paperwork for educational credit, willing to provide letters of recommendation.

Contact E-mail or through World Wide Web site Amy Hegeman, Human Resources Specialist. Fax: 703-907-7056. E-mail: ceajobs@ce.org. No phone calls. In-person interview required. Applicants must submit a resume, three personal references, 2 writing samples for communications and editorial positions. Application deadline: June 1 for summer; continuous for other positions. World Wide Web: http://www.ce.org.

CREATIVE PRODUCERS GROUP
4818 Washington Boulevard
St. Louis, Missouri 63108

General Information Marketing communications company specializing in meetings, video, events, and Web for Fortune 500 firms. Established in 1985. Number of employees: 35. Number of internship applications received each year: 30.

Internships Available ▶ *1–2 graphic design interns:* responsibilities include logo design, print work, Web design. Candidates should have computer skills, declared college major in field, knowledge of field, oral communication skills, self-motivation, written communication skills. Duration is 1 semester. Unpaid. ▶ *1 production intern:* responsibilities include assisting producers and project managers with the production of major meetings, tours, and events. Candidates should have knowledge of field, oral communication skills, organizational skills, plan to pursue career in field, self-motivation, written communication skills. Duration is 1 semester. Unpaid. ▶ *1–2 sales and marketing interns:* responsibilities include research, writing press releases, assisting sales people with proposals and presentations. Candidates should have analytical skills, declared college major in field, knowledge of field, oral communication skills, self-motivation, written communication skills. Duration is 1 semester. Unpaid. ▶ *1–3 video interns:* responsibilities include dubs, video library assistance, production assistance, Media 100 editing, stock footage location. Candidates should have declared college major in field, knowledge of field, oral communication skills, organizational skills, self-motivation, written communication skills. Duration is 1 semester. Unpaid. Open to college sophomores, college juniors, college seniors.

Benefits On-the-job training, willing to act as a professional reference, willing to complete paperwork for educational credit, willing to provide letters of recommendation.

Contact Write, e-mail, or through World Wide Web site Amy M. J. Elz, Manager, Marketing and Special Projects. Fax: 314-367-5510. E-mail: internships@getcreative.com. No phone calls. In-person interview required. Applicants must submit a formal organization application, letter of interest, resume. Applications are accepted continuously. World Wide Web: http://www.getcreative.com.

DELOITTE & TOUCHE
10 Westport Road
Wilton, Connecticut 06897

General Information One of the world's leading professional services firms that provides accounting and auditing, management consulting, and tax services. Established in 1895. Number of employees: 300. Unit of Deloitte Touche Tohmatsu, New York, New York. Number of internship applications received each year: 10,000.

Internships Available ▶ *400–600 assurance interns:* responsibilities include preparation of audit workpapers, communicating with the client, and analysis of issues pertaining to specific areas of an audit; special projects as assigned. Candidates should have ability to work with others, analytical skills, oral communication skills, organizational skills, written communication skills. Duration is 10–12 weeks. $600–$1200 per week. Open to college juniors, college seniors, graduate students. ▶ *60–80 enterprise risk services interns:* responsibilities include providing support to large corporate clients in a range of industry and technology control consulting services including control assessments, network and PC systems security, and business process and application control implementation; providing internal audit services. Candidates should have ability to work with others, analytical skills, computer skills, oral communication skills, organizational skills, written communication skills. Duration is 10–12 weeks. $750–$1000 per week. Open to college juniors, college seniors, graduate students. ▶ *15–25 financial advisory services interns:* responsibilities include working with a team of consultants to provide support in the areas of corporate finance, valuation, reorganization, mergers and acquisitions, and dispute consulting. Candidates should have ability to work with others, analytical skills, oral communication skills, research skills, strong leadership ability, written communication skills. Duration is 10–12 weeks. $750–$1000 per week. Open to college juniors, college seniors, graduate students. ▶ *10–30 human capital advisory services interns:* responsibilities include working with a team of consultants providing consultant services to Fortune 500 companies in areas of human resources strategies, compensation, human resources communications, actuarial, benefits, and global human resources strategies. Candidates should have ability to work with others, analytical skills, computer skills, oral communication skills, organizational skills, written communication skills. Duration is 10–12 weeks. $750–$1000 per week. Open to college juniors, college seniors, graduate students. ▶ *Up to 10 solutions interns:* responsibilities include working with team of consultants providing consulting services to middle-market and emerging growth companies in areas of information management, operations management, and financial services consulting. Candidates should have ability to work with others, analytical skills, computer skills, oral communication skills, organizational skills, written communication skills. Duration is 10–12 weeks. $750–$1200 per week. Open to college juniors, college seniors, graduate students. ▶ *250–300 tax interns:* responsibilities include working within tax career tracks of generalist, specialist, and creative tax services consultant; working with tax teams. Candidates should have ability to

work with others, analytical skills, computer skills, oral communication skills, research skills, written communication skills. Duration is 10–12 weeks. $650–$1300 per week. Open to college juniors, college seniors, graduate students, law students, applicants must not have completed coursework at time of internship. International applications accepted.

Benefits Formal training, on-the-job training, opportunity to attend seminars/workshops, possible full-time employment, travel reimbursement, willing to complete paperwork for educational credit, holiday and illness pay, networking, building of technical skills; laptop computer provided; tuition assistance and free housing are offered only in select locations.

International Internships Available in Australia; Canada; France; Germany; Netherlands; United Kingdom.

Contact Write, fax, or through World Wide Web site Internship Coordinator. No phone calls. In-person interview required. Applicants must submit a resume, candidates should contact their career placement center to sign-up for an interview, participate in on-campus recruiting program, or apply online. Applications are accepted continuously. World Wide Web: http://www.deloitte.com.

ENVIROTROL, INC.
432 Green Street
Sewickley, Pennsylvania 15143

General Information Company specializing in reactivation services and activated carbon services. Established in 1970. Number of employees: 24. Number of internship applications received each year: 300.

Internships Available ▶ *1 E-Business and Internet Group intern (Sewickley, PA):* responsibilities include development of new Web pages relevant to Envirotrol's new business offerings; assisting in the E-commerce development activities using MS Frontpage with the StoreFront 2000 add-in; assisting in developing automated Web pages which allow for customer interactivity including Microsoft Active Server Pages; learnings to manage remote NT Web Server which houses Envirotrol Web and E-commerce site; assisting in developing database driven Internet applications using Microsoft Access, Microsoft SQL Server and Microsoft's Internet Information Server. Candidates should have ability to work independently, ability to work with others, college courses in field, computer skills, knowledge of field, office skills, oral communication skills, organizational skills, personal interest in the field, plan to pursue career in field, self-motivation, writing skills, must be in final semester of a degree or diploma of credited courses. Duration is 1 semester. Unpaid. ▶ *1 MIS intern (Sewickley, PA):* responsibilities include creating a database of information and locating equipment for inventory listing; projects may include the following: converting forms to PDFs for use on the Web, creating HTML pages for the Internet, software installation and troubleshooting, programming automatic HTML reports using Front Page 2000, maintaining MS Exchange Server installation, General Access 2000 visual basic programming, MS SQL Query Building. Candidates should have ability to work independently, ability to work with others, college courses in field, computer skills, knowledge of field, office skills, oral communication skills, organizational skills, personal interest in the field, plan to pursue career in field, self-motivation, strong leadership ability, writing skills, must be in final semester of degree or diploma of credited courses. Duration is 1 semester (will work around student's school work schedule). Unpaid. ▶ *1 lab intern (Darlington, PA):* responsibilities include performing experiments and evaluation tests in support of research and development activities for activated carbon and other materials; experiments will involve preparation of reagents, weighing of materials, experimental data taking and recording, testing of resultant products, and set up and breakdown of experimental equipment; reports of findings and tests will be generated by the intern as instructed. Candidates should have ability to work independently, ability to work with others, analytical skills, computer skills, declared college major in field, editing skills, knowledge of field, office skills, oral communication skills, organizational skills, personal interest in the field, plan to pursue career in field, research skills, self-motivation, writing skills, must be in final semester of a degree or diploma of credited courses.

Envirotrol, Inc. (continued)

Duration is 1 semester (will work around student's school and work schedule). Unpaid. ▶ *1 safety intern (Darlington, PA):* responsibilities include updating and entering entries of MSDS's; safety inspections; assisting with monthly safety meetings; assisting with workplace monitoring; inventory personal protection equipment; development of job safety procedures; one-on-one safety training; inventory laboratory chemicals; conducting tailgate safety meetings; conducting respirator fit testing; participating in employee and manager safety committees; assisting in accident/incident investigation; assisting in the development of new and review existing safety program. Candidates should have ability to work independently, ability to work with others, analytical skills, college courses in field, computer skills, knowledge of field, oral communication skills, organizational skills, plan to pursue career in field, self-motivation, writing skills, must be able to wear a half-mask respirator. Duration is 1 semester (will work around student's school and work schedule). Unpaid. Open to college seniors.

Benefits On-the-job training, opportunity to attend seminars/workshops, willing to act as a professional reference, willing to complete paperwork for educational credit, willing to provide letters of recommendation.

Contact Write, fax, or e-mail Trina N. Suttelle, Internship Coordinator, 432 Green Street, PO Box 61, Sewickley 15143. Fax: 412-741-2670. E-mail: trina@envirotrol.com. No phone calls. In-person interview required. Applicants must submit a letter of interest, resume, academic transcripts, internship is for credited courses only; intern must be in final semester before graduation. Applications are accepted continuously. World Wide Web: http://www.envirotrol.com.

FEDERAL BUREAU OF INVESTIGATION, FBI ACADEMY
Quantico, Virginia 22135

General Information Academy that trains FBI personnel and other members of the law enforcement community and is viewed as one of the world's premier law enforcement institutions of higher learning.

Internships Available ▶ *FBI Academy interns:* responsibilities include assignments by individual traning unit; tasks will vary with background and education of student, needs of unit, and work assigned. Frequently duties involve research development and updating work projects, usually related to student's educational endeavors. Duration is minimum of 14 weeks beginning in late August or early January; full-time 8:00 am to 4:30 pm Monday to Friday unless otherwise specified. Unpaid. Open to U.S. citizens at least 18 years old; college juniors, college seniors, or graduate students (preferred). ▶ *National Center for the Analysis of Violent Crime (NCAVC) interns:* responsibilities include work related to violent crime research of the NCAVC; obtaining case materials, reviewing case files and coding information onto a research instrument; assisting in analysis and reporting of research data, or developing and extending resource materials; observing case consultations, auditing classes taught to police; occasional clerical tasks. Duration is minimum of 14 weeks beginning the first week in September (after Labor Day) or the second week in January; 8:15 am to 5:00 pm, Monday to Friday. Unpaid. Open to college juniors and above; must have student status during internship. Candidates for all positions should have analytical skills, computer skills, writing skills, ability to qualify under FBI employee standards; minimum GPA 3.0; pass a polygraph and drug test as part of background investigation.

Contact Through World Wide Web site Internship Coordinator. Materials as specified on Web site: www.fbi.gov/employment/intern.htm. Application deadline: March 1 for positions starting in January, November 1 for positions starting in August or September. World Wide Web: http://www.fbi.gov/hq/td/academy/academy.htm.

FUJITSU IT HOLDINGS, INC.
1250 East Argues
Sunnyvale, California 94088-3470

General Information Corporation providing integrated computing solutions to meet the needs of many of the largest users of information technology in the world.

Internships Available ▶ *Interns.* Duration is flexible. Paid. Open to individuals enrolled in an accredited community college or university, who have completed freshman year, and are at least 18 years old.

Benefits Health insurance, fitness subsidy, 401(K) savings plan, paid holidays, numerous intern events (e.g. tours, briefings).

Contact Write College Relations, 1250 East Arques Avenue, MS 300, Sunnyvale 94088. Materials as specified on Web site. Applications are accepted continuously. World Wide Web: http://www.fih.fujitsu.com/fih/employment/index.html.

GENSYS MULTIMEDIA PRODUCTIONS, INC.
10850 Wilshire Boulevard, Suite 380
Los Angeles, California 90024

General Information Multimedia production company providing complete production and multimedia services including 3D, CBT, interactive, and the Internet to clients worldwide. Established in 1994.

Internships Available ▶ *AVID interns:* responsibilities include gaining real-world experience on a variety of video/interactive and film productions; working hands-on on real projects with deadlines under senior supervisors; a highly creative environment with hi-end equipment, and software. Candidates should have ability to work independently, ability to work with others, personal interest in the field, self-motivation, minimum six months of prior AVID experience. Duration is 24-48 weeks (40 hours per week). Unpaid. Open to recent high school graduates, college seniors, recent college graduates, graduate students, international English speaking post-graduate students encouraged to apply. ▶ *Lightwave 3D internships:* responsibilities include gaining real world experience in Lightwave 3D and variety of software and platforms; working on projects with deadlines under senior supervisors in a highly creative environment with Hi-end equipment and software. Candidates should have ability to work independently, ability to work with others, personal interest in the field, self-motivation, minimum six months of prior Lightwave 3D experience. Duration is 24-48 weeks (40 hours per week). Unpaid. Open to recent high school graduates, college seniors, recent college graduates, graduate students, international English speaking post-graduate students encouraged to apply. ▶ *1 assistant producer internship:* responsibilities include gaining real world experience in the area of production; working on real projects with deadlines under supervision in a highly creative environment. Candidates should have ability to work independently, ability to work with others, analytical skills, oral communication skills, organizational skills, written communication skills, minimum 6 months of related production experience; above average grades; desire to help produce, design, implement, and cultivate GMP's projects. Duration is 24–48 weeks (40 hours per week). Unpaid. Open to recent high school graduates, college seniors, recent college graduates, graduate students, international English-speaking post-graduate students encouraged to apply. ▶ *1 multimedia marketing specialist internship:* responsibilities include designing a marketing plan, identifying suitable markets, targeting potential clients, and implementing step-by-step advertising and public relations campaign; working on real projects with deadlines under senior supervisors. Candidates should have ability to work independently, analytical skills, oral communication skills, personal interest in the field, self-motivation, strong interpersonal skills, written communication skills, above average grades; desire to design, implement, and cultivate GMP's projects; 6 months minimum of prior marketing experience. Duration is 24-48 weeks (40 hours per week). Unpaid. Open to recent high school graduates, college seniors, recent college graduates, graduate students, international English speaking post-graduate students encouraged to apply. ▶ *New media multimedia specialist internship:* responsibilities include gaining real world experience in multimedia Web design, Flash, and variety of software and platforms; working on real projects with deadlines

under senior supervisors in a highly creative environment with hi-end equipment. Candidates should have ability to work independently, ability to work with others, personal interest in the field, self-motivation, minimum 6 months of prior HTML, Flash, Scripting, Web design experience. Duration is 24-48 weeks (40 hours per week). Unpaid. Open to recent high school graduates, college seniors, recent college graduates, graduate students, international English speaking post-graduate students encouraged to apply. International applications accepted.
Benefits On-the-job training.
Contact Write, call, fax, e-mail, or through World Wide Web site David Victory. Phone: 310-441-2556. Fax: 310-441-2558. E-mail: dpv@vrset.com. Applicants must submit a resume, reels for AVID internship; CD/reels for Lightware 3D internship; CD-ROM or weblinks for New Media multimedia specialist. Applications are accepted continuously. World Wide Web: http://www.gensysmultimedia.com.

HERITAGE FOUNDATION
214 Massachusetts Avenue, NE
Washington, District of Columbia 20002

General Information Conservative think tank whose mission is to formulate and promote public policies based on the principles of free enterprise, limited government, individual freedom, traditional American values, and a strong national defense. Established in 1973. Number of employees: 180. Number of internship applications received each year: 700.
Internships Available ▶ *40–50 academic year interns:* responsibilities include performing a variety of research and administrative assignments, attending public lectures and conferences, and assisting with computer and other projects. Duration is 1–10 weeks. $10 per day expense stipend (spring and fall); $50 per day (summer). Open to college sophomores, college juniors, college seniors, recent college graduates, graduate students. ▶ *40–50 summer interns:* responsibilities include performing a variety of research and administrative assignments, attending public lectures and conferences, and assisting with computer and other projects. Duration is 10 weeks. Position available as unpaid or at $250 per week. Open to college juniors, college seniors, recent college graduates. Candidates for all positions should have ability to work independently, ability to work with others, computer skills, research skills, self-motivation, writing skills. International applications accepted.
Benefits Formal training, job counseling, names of contacts, opportunity to attend seminars/workshops, possible full-time employment, willing to complete paperwork for educational credit, willing to provide letters of recommendation.
Contact Write, call, or through World Wide Web site Intern Coordinator. Phone: 202-608-6172. Applicants must submit a formal organization application, letter of interest, resume, writing sample, two letters of recommendation. Application deadline: March 1 for summer; continuous for fall and spring. World Wide Web: http://www.heritage.org/internships.

HEWITT ASSOCIATES LLC
100 Half Day Road
Lincolnshire, Illinois 60069

General Information Consulting firm specializing in human resource solutions that help clients get the most from design, financing, communication, administration, delivery of human resources, compensation, and benefit plans. Established in 1940. Number of employees: 13,000. Number of internship applications received each year: 1,000.
Internships Available ▶ *12–20 actuarial consultants:* responsibilities include using analytical and communication skills to help clients address various employee benefit issues, pension valuations, merger and acquisition strategy, union negotiation support, design of executive retirement plans, and financial analysis of health-care benefits. Candidates should have ability to work independently, analytical skills, plan to pursue career in field, self-motivation, strong interpersonal skills. Duration is 10–12 weeks. Paid. ▶ *10–25 business analysts:* responsibilities include working on teams delivering pension, 401(k), or health and welfare benefits to clients' employees; testing the computer systems that support the benefit plans; researching client problems; benefit calculations; and analyzing data. Candidates should have ability to work independently, ability to work with others, analytical skills, self-motivation, detail orientation and flexibility. Duration is 10–12 weeks. Paid. ▶ *3–5 information systems interns:* responsibilities include formulating and recommending strategies for the use of computer and communications technology to support all of the practices within Hewitt Associates, including Peoplesoft, Lotus Notes, and internal systems. Candidates should have ability to work independently, ability to work with others, analytical skills, knowledge of field, SQL, C++, Visual Basic, Windows NT, Access, networking, and database administration experience. Duration is 10–12 weeks. Paid. ▶ *8–10 programmer analysts:* responsibilities include working on teams to deliver the technology that administers clients' benefit plans, tailoring Hewitt's customized systems and software to clients' requirements, developing system specifications, customizing programs, converting data, and designing and implementing interactive systems including voice-response and Internet. Candidates should have ability to work independently, ability to work with others, analytical skills, self-motivation, COBOL, JCL knowledge. Duration is 10–12 weeks. Paid. Open to individuals entering senior year of college. International applications accepted.
Benefits Free housing, free meals, on-the-job training, opportunity to attend seminars/workshops, possible full-time employment, willing to act as a professional reference, willing to complete paperwork for educational credit, willing to provide letters of recommendation.
Contact Write, fax, or through World Wide Web site Kathy Hancock, Recruiting Consultant, 100 Half Day Road, Lincolnshire, Illinois 60069. Fax: 847-575-1178. E-mail: careers@hewitt.com. No phone calls. In-person interview required. Applicants must submit a letter of interest, resume, academic transcripts. Application deadline: January 15 for summer. World Wide Web: http://www.hewitt.com.

JEFFERSON GOVERNMENT RELATIONS
1615 L Street, NW, Suite 650
Washington, District of Columbia 20036

General Information Professional services firm bringing talent and depth to many areas, including congressional relations, regulatory affairs, health care, federal marketing, crisis communications, infrastructure, cities, state, and local public affairs, and e-commerce. Established in 1987. Number of employees: 25. Number of internship applications received each year: 500.
Internships Available ▶ *1–4 interns:* responsibilities include reporting to group supervisors, conducting professional and administrative duties, and conducting research for current clients or new business activity; depending upon internship selected, opportunities exist for entry-level accounting duties, human resource management, government relations, and health care. Candidates should have analytical skills, oral communication skills, plan to pursue career in field, research skills, written communication skills, an interest in public policy, government, politics, regulatory and environmental issues, or personnel and human resources. Duration is usually 2 to 4 months; renewable. Unpaid. Open to college freshmen, college sophomores, college juniors, college seniors, recent college graduates, graduate students, law students. International applications accepted.
Benefits Names of contacts, willing to act as a professional reference, willing to complete paperwork for educational credit, willing to provide letters of recommendation, $150 per month transportation reimbursement.
Contact Write, call, fax, or e-mail Ms. Andrea Whetzel, Executive Assistant. Phone: 202-626-8227. Fax: 202-626-8593. E-mail: awhetzel@jeffersongr.com. In-person interview recommended (telephone interview accepted). Applicants must submit a letter of interest, resume, academic transcripts, writing sample. Applications are accepted continuously. World Wide Web: http://www.jeffersongr.com.

LM SERVICES, LLC
131 West 33rd Street
New York, New York 10001

General Information Global company that designs, sources, and distributes infants' and children's clothing under the brands Little Me and Ralph Lauren. Established in 1914. Number of employees: 620. Subsidiary of S. Schwab Company, Inc. Number of internship applications received each year: 150.

Internships Available ▶ *2–6 Little Me design interns:* responsibilities include setting up merchandise approval and design package system; working with the merchandising staff or all licensed products; maintaining color system, and participating in showroom preps for line reviews. Candidates should have ability to work independently, ability to work with others, college courses in field, oral communication skills, organizational skills, personal interest in the field, self-motivation, strong leadership ability, must be earning academic credit. Duration is spring, summer, or fall semesters. Unpaid. Open to college freshmen, college sophomores, college juniors, college seniors. ▶ *Little Me merchandising interns:* responsibilities include assisting designers in making presentation boards; tabbing colors for prints and stripes; copying materials used for recordkeeping, file submits; attending design meetings as well as tracking samples needed from showrooms. Candidates should have ability to work independently, ability to work with others, college courses in field, oral communication skills, organizational skills, personal interest in the field, self-motivation, strong leadership ability. Duration is spring, summer, or fall semesters. Unpaid. ▶ *1–2 Ralph Lauren Childrenswear merchandising interns:* responsibilities include assisting the merchandising staff with daily maintenance of the line list, communications with design on fabric approvals/trimsheet updates, sample tracking and price comparisons. Candidates should have ability to work independently, ability to work with others, computer skills, oral communication skills, organizational skills, personal interest in the field, self-motivation, strong leadership ability, must be earning academic credit. Duration is spring, summer, or fall semester. Unpaid. Open to college sophomores, college juniors, college seniors. ▶ *2–3 Ralph Lauren Childrenswear retail analysis interns:* responsibilities include assisting the department with management meeting packets, database administration, analyzing end of month reports, developing various reports/spreadsheets and general day to day analytical activities. Candidates should have ability to work independently, ability to work with others, analytical skills, computer skills, knowledge of field, office skills, oral communication skills, organizational skills, personal interest in the field, self-motivation, strong leadership ability, written communication skills, finance and economic majors; must be earning academic credit. Duration is spring, summer, or fall semester. Unpaid. ▶ *30–40 Ralph Lauren Childrenswear retail merchandising interns:* responsibilities include managing, marketing, and merchandising the Ralph Lauren Childrenswear in-store shop presentations with the guidance and supervision of a merchandise coordinator. Candidates should have ability to work independently, ability to work with others, oral communication skills, organizational skills, personal interest in the field, self-motivation, strong leadership ability, must be earning academic credit. Duration is spring, summer, or fall semester. Unpaid. Open to college sophomores, college juniors, college seniors. ▶ *3–4 Ralph Lauren Childrenswear showroom sales interns:* responsibilities include assisting key account managers with market preparation; coordinating pamphlets and setting up showrooms for appointments; tracking weekly orders, data entry, and other projects relating to the retail business. Candidates should have ability to work independently, ability to work with others, computer skills, office skills, oral communication skills, organizational skills, personal interest in the field, self-motivation, strong leadership ability, must be earning academic credit. Duration is spring, summer, or fall semester. Unpaid. Open to college sophomores, college juniors, college seniors. ▶ *2–3 marketing interns (Ralph Lauren Childrenswear and Little Me):* responsibilities include maintaining periodical library; updating competitive binder; conducting product research; signing samples in and out for editorial purposes; assisting in the coordination of the sample room (when needed), and developing various spreadsheets requiring data entry. Candidates should have ability to work independently, ability to work with others,

college courses in field, computer skills, knowledge of field, office skills, oral communication skills, organizational skills, self-motivation, strong leadership ability, writing skills, must be earning academic credit. Duration is spring, summer or fall semester. Unpaid. Open to college sophomores, college juniors, college seniors.

Benefits Names of contacts, on-the-job training, possible full-time employment, willing to act as a professional reference, willing to complete paperwork for educational credit, willing to provide letters of recommendation.

Contact Write, fax, or e-mail Ruby Hovsepian, Internship Manager. Fax: 212-643-2790. E-mail: rhovsepian@sschwab.com. No phone calls. In-person interview recommended (telephone interview accepted). Applicants must submit a letter of interest, resume, verification letter from school. Applications are accepted continuously.

THE NATIONAL ACADEMIES
2101 Constitution Avenue, NW
Washington, District of Columbia 20418

General Information Non-governmental science, engineering, and medical policy organization. Established in 1863. Number of employees: 1,100. Number of internship applications received each year: 200.

Internships Available ▶ *15–20 Christine Mirzayan National Academies Interns:* responsibilities include involvement with analysis and creation of science and technology policy and familiarization with interaction of science, technology, and government by working on a science and technology policy study. Candidates should have ability to work independently, oral communication skills, personal interest in the field, self-motivation, strong interpersonal skills, written communication skills. Duration is 10 weeks (summer); 12 weeks (winter). $4700–$5600 per duration of internship. Open to recent college graduates, graduate students, law students, those currently or about to enroll or recent graduates from graduate degree program (MS, MBA, JD, MD, PhD, DVM). International applications accepted.

Benefits Opportunity to attend seminars/workshops, travel reimbursement.

Contact E-mail or through World Wide Web site Deborah D. Stine, Program Director. Phone: 202-334-2455. Fax: 202-334-1667. E-mail: nrc-ip@nas.edu. Applicants must submit a formal organization application, personal reference. Application deadline: March 1 for summer interns, November 1 for winter interns. World Wide Web: http://www.nationalacademies.org/internship.

ORGANIZERS' COLLABORATIVE
PO Box 400897
Cambridge, Massachusetts 02140

General Information Collaborative that develops Web sites and publishes information to help social change organizations become more effective in their use of electronic mail, databases, and the world-wide web. Established in 1999. Number of employees: 1. Number of internship applications received each year: 25.

Internships Available ▶ *1–2 Internet organizers/Web site managers:* responsibilities include acting as issue specialists (housing, rights, peace) using email to recruit editors for national online directory of social change resources. Candidates should have ability to work independently, computer skills, oral communication skills, self-motivation, strong interpersonal skills. Duration is 2 months (start September, January, or June). Unpaid. Open to high school students, recent high school graduates, college freshmen, college sophomores, college juniors, college seniors, recent college graduates, graduate students, law students, career changers, individuals reentering the workforce. ▶ *1–2 Web site programmers:* responsibilities include developing Web-based national directory of social change-related e-mail lists. Candidates should have ability to work independently, oral communication skills, self-motivation, strong interpersonal skills, Web development experience and experience with PHP, PERL, JAVA script, Visual Basic, Filemaker, or HTML. Duration is 2–9 months (start September, January, or June). Position available as unpaid or paid. Open to high school students, recent high school graduates, college freshmen, college sophomores, college juniors, college seniors, graduate students, law students, career changers, individuals reentering the workforce. ▶ *1 development associate:* responsibilities include prospect research on potential donors, media work, and organizing annual fund-raising event. Candidates should have ability to work independently, oral communication skills, self-motivation, written communication skills. Duration is 2–9 months (start September, January or June). Unpaid. ▶ *1–2 graphic designers (Web):* responsibilities include helping produce art work and graphics for Web site, brochures, and publications. Candidates should have ability to work independently, oral communication skills, self-motivation, strong interpersonal skills, experience with PhotoShop, Fireworks, Quark Xpress, or Illustrator helpful. Duration is 2–9 months (start September, January, or June). Unpaid. Open to high school students, recent high school graduates, college freshmen, college sophomores, college juniors, college seniors, recent college graduates, graduate students, law students, career changers, individuals reentering the workforce. International applications accepted.

Benefits Travel reimbursement, willing to act as a professional reference, willing to complete paperwork for educational credit, willing to provide letters of recommendation, some stipends available.

Contact Write or e-mail Rich Cowan, President. Phone: 617-426-1228 Ext. 108. Fax: 617-695-1295. E-mail: oc@organizenow.net. Applicants must submit a resume, brief cover letter indicating how many hours available to work and relevant experience with computers, politics, or social change activism. Application deadline: April 10 for summer, August 1 for fall, November 10 for winter, December 1 for spring. World Wide Web: http://organizenow.net.

PERFORMANCE RESEARCH
25 Mill Street, Queen Anne Square
Newport, Rhode Island 02840

General Information Market research firm specializing in quantitatively and qualitatively evaluating the effectiveness of sports and special event sponsorships. Established in 1986. Number of employees: 30. Number of internship applications received each year: 400.

Internships Available ▶ *1–2 market research interns:* responsibilities include travel and data collecting at sporting events, conducting personal interviews, performing data entry, designing surveys, and generating reports. Candidates should have ability to work independently, oral communication skills, research skills, self-motivation, strong interpersonal skills, writing skills, some experience with word processing and graphics applications on the computer (preferred). Duration is 12–15 weeks. $2000 stipend. Open to college juniors, college seniors, recent college graduates, graduate students. International applications accepted.

Benefits Job counseling, names of contacts, possible full-time employment, willing to act as a professional reference, willing to complete paperwork for educational credit, willing to provide letters of recommendation, stipend paid upon completion of internship, work-related travel reimbursement.

Contact Write, fax, e-mail, or through World Wide Web site Mr. Doug Snow, Internship Coordinator. Fax: 401-848-0110. E-mail: reports@performanceresearch.com. In-person interview required. Applicants must submit a letter of interest, resume, writing sample. Application deadline: February 15 for spring, April 15 for summer, July 15 for fall, November 15 for winter. World Wide Web: http://www.performanceresearch.com.

PIONEER HI-BRED INTERNATIONAL
400 Locust Street, Suite 700, PO Box 14454
Des Moines, Iowa 50306-3454

General Information World leader in the discovery, development, and delivery of elite crop genetics. Established in 1926. Number of employees: 1,500. Subsidiary of DuPont, Wilmington, Delaware. Number of internship applications received each year: 1,000.

Internships Available ▶ *35–40 product advancement trial interns.* Candidates should have ability to work independently, college courses in field, knowledge of field, oral communication skills, personal interest in the field, plan to pursue career in field, self-motivation, strong interpersonal skills, strong leadership ability,

written communication skills. Duration is 6 months. $9–$12 per hour plus a $1000 stipend upon successful completion of internship. Open to college sophomores, college juniors, college seniors, recent college graduates. ▶ *50 professional interns:* responsibilities include participating in development activities organized by Pioneer and completing and presenting a project at the end of the internship. Candidates should have analytical skills, college courses in field, computer skills, experience in the field, oral communication skills, strong interpersonal skills, strong leadership ability, written communication skills. Duration is 3 months. $9–$12 per hour plus a $1000 stipend if returning to school. Open to college sophomores, college juniors, college seniors. International applications accepted.

Benefits Formal training, free meals, job counseling, on-the-job training, opportunity to attend seminars/workshops, possible full-time employment, travel reimbursement, tuition assistance, willing to act as a professional reference, willing to complete paperwork for educational credit, willing to provide letters of recommendation.

International Internships Available.

Contact Write, e-mail, or through World Wide Web site Carla Cain, Employment Services Manager. Fax: 515-334-6555. E-mail: carla.cain@pioneer.com. No phone calls. In-person interview recommended (telephone interview accepted). Applicants must submit a formal organization application, letter of interest, academic transcripts, portfolio, writing sample, personal reference, letter of recommendation, resume that can be scanned. Applications are accepted continuously. World Wide Web: http://www.pioneer.com.

SMITHSONIAN INSTITUTION, OFFICE OF THE CHIEF TECHNOLOGY OFFICER
Arts and Industries Building, 900 Jefferson Drive, SW, Room 2224
Washington, District of Columbia 20560-0433

General Information Unit that provides the Smithsonian's central computing and telecommunications services and training as well as leadership in information technology. Established in 1846. Number of employees: 170. Unit of Smithsonian Institution, Washington, District of Columbia. Number of internship applications received each year: 50.

Internships Available ▶ *Interns:* responsibilities include providing technical support to several mainframe systems and network servers doing computer training, helping to maintain e-mail and Web services, assisting with image scanning and the development of multimedia documents. Candidates should have computer skills, knowledge of field, interest in computer help desk operations, e-mail, programming languages, or network design. Duration is flexible. Position available as unpaid or paid. Open to high school students, recent high school graduates, college freshmen, college sophomores, college juniors, college seniors, recent college graduates, graduate students, law students, career changers, individuals reentering the workforce, must be 16 years or older. International applications accepted.

Benefits On-the-job training, opportunity to attend seminars/workshops, willing to complete paperwork for educational credit, willing to provide letters of recommendation, practical experience with an information technology services unit.

Contact Write, fax, or through World Wide Web site Sherri Manning, Internship Coordinator, Arts and Industries Building 900 Jefferson Drive, SW, Room 2225, Washington, District of Columbia 20560-0433. Fax: 202-633-9466. No phone calls. Applicants must submit a formal organization application, letter of interest, resume, academic transcripts, personal reference, essay. Applications are accepted continuously. World Wide Web: http://www.si.edu/organiza/offices/oit/start.htm.

SQUIER KNAPP OCHS DUNN
511 Second Street, NE
Washington, District of Columbia 20002

General Information Political consulting firm specializing in communications/media; Communications Company (affiliate)

Squier Knapp Ochs Dunn (continued)

does consulting for corporations and associations. Established in 1969. Number of employees: 18. Number of internship applications received each year: 50.

Internships Available ▶ *Staff assistants:* responsibilities include assisting in production, candidate, issue, and media research; light administrative work. Candidates should have ability to work independently, office skills, oral communication skills, research skills, strong interpersonal skills. Duration is 1 semester. $6.15 per hour. Open to college freshmen, college sophomores, college juniors, college seniors. International applications accepted.

Benefits On-the-job training, possible full-time employment, willing to act as a professional reference, willing to complete paperwork for educational credit, willing to provide letters of recommendation.

Contact Write or fax Andrew Shipley, Production Coordinator. Fax: 202-543-6911. No phone calls. In-person interview recommended (telephone interview accepted). Applicants must submit a letter of interest, resume, writing sample, 1-2 personal references. Applications are accepted continuously.

TOXIKON
15 Wiggins Avenue
Bedford, Massachusetts 01730

General Information Environmental chemistry and toxicology (mammalion and in vitro) contract testing labs. Established in 1977. Number of employees: 90. Number of internship applications received each year: 35.

Internships Available ▶ *2–3 assistant environmental chemistry lab technicians:* responsibilities include extracting and analyzing inorganic, environmental samples, including oil and grease and total petroleum hydrocarbons, according to method and within the framework of Toxikon SOP's and QAP and in a timely manner; analyses include nitrates, nitrites, sulfates, acidity, alkalinity, turbidity, conductivity, pH, DO, Suspended Solids, Total Solids, BOD; maintaining complete and thorough records of all extractions, sample preparations and analysis; entering analyses data into SAM as soon as they are complete; maintaining a current work order due table; ensuring proper method validation and performance within all required QA/QC, EPA and GLP guidelines. Duration is 40 hours per week in summer (May—August). $10 per hour plus overtime potential. Open to college juniors, college seniors, recent college graduates. ▶ *1 assistant in vitro lab technician:* responsibilities include setting up and conducting various tests for in vitro studies conducted under FDA, ISO/EN, GLP and other guidelines for the department; Ames Assays, water testing, microbial penetration; this position supports the microbiology and cell culture labs; responsible for all equipment utilized and assigned, including calibration and maintenance logs. Duration is 40 hours per week in summer (May—August). $10 per hour plus overtime potential. Open to college juniors, college seniors, recent college graduates. ▶ *1 assistant in vivo lab technician:* responsibilities include animal testing (small rodents such as mice, guinea pigs, hamsters) conducted under appropriate guidelines (FDA, EPA, GLP, ISO) for medical product registration; includes preparation of reagents and testing solutions as well as maintaining complete documentation testing data; working with mice, rats, hamsters, rabbits, guinea pigs and dogs under the direction of a senior lab technician. Duration is 40 hours per week in summer (May—August). $10 per hour plus overtime potential. Open to college juniors, college seniors, recent college graduates, individuals experienced with animal handling. ▶ *1 log-in assistant:* responsibilities include receiving and logging samples on the computer; assisting with sample return and disposal; reviewing contracts and filing; preparing bottle orders for environmental chemistry division and assisting with the toxicology log-in, including microbiology and cell culture departments. Duration is 40 hours per week in summer (May—August). $10 per hour plus overtime potential. Open to college juniors, college seniors, recent college graduates. Candidates for all positions should have ability to work independently, ability to work with others, college courses in field, knowledge of field, organizational

skills, plan to pursue career in field, self-motivation, ability to work in a fast-paced production lab environment while meeting or exceeding project due dates.

Benefits Formal training, job counseling, names of contacts, on-the-job training, possible full-time employment, willing to act as a professional reference, willing to complete paperwork for educational credit, willing to provide letters of recommendation.

Contact Write, fax, e-mail, or through World Wide Web site Susan Brosman, Human Resources Generalist. Fax: 781-271-1137. E-mail: hr@toxikon.com. No phone calls. In-person interview recommended (telephone interview accepted). Applicants must submit a formal organization application, letter of interest, resume, academic transcripts, portfolio, three personal references. Applications are accepted continuously. World Wide Web: http://www.toxikon.com.

VINTAGE RACING SERVICES, INC.
1785 Barnum Avenue
Stratford, Connecticut 06614

General Information Company that performs vintage race car restoration, sales, maintenance, and track support. Established in 1985.

Internships Available ▶ *1–2 general office interns:* responsibilities include bookkeeping, invoicing, research, documentation, and business management. Candidates should have ability to work with others, computer skills, office skills, oral communication skills, research skills, written communication skills. Duration is flexible. $6 to $15 per hour commensurate with experience and ability. Open to recent high school graduates, college freshmen, college sophomores, college juniors, college seniors, recent college graduates, graduate students, law students, career changers, individuals reentering the workforce, must be 18 or older. ▶ *3 race car technicians:* responsibilities include vintage race car preparation, trackside maintenance, system design, component repair/design and fabrication, repair and maintenance. Candidates should have ability to work with others, analytical skills, personal interest in the field, self-motivation, written communication skills, willingness to travel within U.S. Duration is flexible. $7 to $25 per hour commensurate with experience and ability. Open to high school seniors, recent high school graduates, college freshmen, college sophomores, college juniors, college seniors, recent college graduates, graduate students, law students, career changers, individuals reentering the workforce, must be 18 years or older. International applications accepted.

Benefits Names of contacts, on-the-job training, opportunity to attend seminars/workshops, possible full-time employment, travel reimbursement, willing to act as a professional reference, willing to complete paperwork for educational credit, willing to provide letters of recommendation.

Contact Write, call, fax, e-mail, or through World Wide Web site Mrs. Denise Cutrone, Human Resources. Phone: 203-377-6745. Fax: 203-386-0486. E-mail: kent@auto-restore.com. In-person interview recommended (telephone interview accepted). Applicants must submit a letter of interest, resume. Applications are accepted continuously. World Wide Web: http://www.vintageracingservices.com.

ADVERTISING AND PUBLIC RELATIONS

THE ADVERTISING CLUB
235 Park Avenue South, Sixth Floor
New York, New York 10003

General Information Association that strives to elevate the understanding of marketing and advertising communications by providing a common forum for members of the industry to address mutual interests; this is accomplished through education, community service, and career development. Established in 1896. Number of employees: 9. Unit of American Advertising Federation, Washington, District of Columbia. Number of internship applications received each year: 500.

Internships Available ▶ *Account management interns:* responsibilities include assisting account executives in serving clients; coordinating all aspects of campaigns; acting as liaison between agency and clients; planning ads for publication. Candidates should have computer skills, oral communication skills, strong interpersonal skills, writing skills. Duration is 10 weeks. Position available as unpaid or paid. ▶ *Creative interns:* responsibilities include assisting art directors and designers; copywriting (for some positions). Candidates should have computer skills, proficiency in QuarkXpress and Adobe PhotoShop; comprehension of stats, mock-ups, film production, and mechanical production helpful. Duration is 10 weeks. Position available as unpaid or paid. ▶ *Media interns:* responsibilities include assisting media planners with preparation of general advertising plans; exploring alternative media options including interactive media. Candidates should have analytical skills, computer skills, mathematical skills, good presentation skills. Duration is 10 weeks. Position available as unpaid or paid. ▶ *New media/interactive interns.* Duration is 10 weeks. Position available as unpaid or paid. ▶ *Production interns:* responsibilities include working with creative departments to produce print, television, and radio advertisements. Candidates should have organizational skills, high level of energy and enthusiasm; experience in field (helpful). Duration is 10 weeks. Position available as unpaid or paid. ▶ *Publishing interns:* responsibilities include assisting promotion/marketing staff with trade shows/events, creation of collateral materials, presentation and in-house marketing duties. Candidates should have oral communication skills, organizational skills, written communication skills, knowledge of Word, Excel, Powerpoint, Quark. Duration is 10 weeks. Position available as unpaid or paid. Open to college juniors, college seniors.

Benefits Names of contacts, opportunity to attend seminars/workshops.

Contact Write, call, fax, e-mail, or through World Wide Web site Cathryn Weber-Gonyo, Program Manager. Phone: 212-533-8080 Ext. 210. Fax: 212-533-1929. E-mail: cathryn@adclubny.org. In-person interview recommended (telephone interview accepted). Applicants must submit a formal organization application, resume, academic transcripts, writing sample, two letters of recommendation, portfolio (for creative internship positions). Application deadline: March 6 for summer. World Wide Web: http://www.adclubny.org.

AIGNER ASSOCIATES PR INC./SPECIAL EVENTS, INC.
250 Everett Street
Boston, Massachusetts 02134

General Information Public relations and strategic marketing company. Established in 1984. Number of employees: 8. Number of internship applications received each year: 80.

Internships Available ▶ *2 account coordinators:* responsibilities include assisting with media contacts, office support, writing, and helping with special event production. Duration is 1 semester. Unpaid. Open to college freshmen, college sophomores, college juniors, college seniors.

Benefits Names of contacts, possible full-time employment, willing to complete paperwork for educational credit, willing to provide letters of recommendation.

Contact Write, call, or fax Intern Coordinator. Phone: 617-254-9500. Fax: 617-254-3700. In-person interview required. Applicants must submit a letter of interest, resume, two writing samples. Application deadline: January 1 for spring, May 1 for summer, August 1 for fall. World Wide Web: http://www.aignerassoc.com.

AIRVERTISE, LLC
300 Saunders Road, Suite 100
Riverwoods, Illinois 60015

General Information Advertising firm specializing in wireless advertising solutions for companies in the field of new media and emerging technology.

Internships Available ▶ *Interns:* responsibilities include positions in sales and marketing, public relations, consumer profiling, advertising market research and reporting, and technology analysis.

Contact Through World Wide Web site Internship Coordinator. Phone: 847-205-5200. Fax: 847-556-0182. E-mail: info@airvertise.com. Resume through Web site. World Wide Web: http://www.airvertise.com.

ALTICOR, INC. FAMILY OF COMPANIES
7575 Fulton Street East
Ada, Michigan 49355-0001

General Information One of the world's largest network marketing companies, marketing products and services through independent distributors in the U.S. and more than 60 other countries and territories. Established in 1959. Number of employees: 5,000. Number of internship applications received each year: 600.

Internships Available ▶ *15–30 summer interns:* responsibilities include working in any of the following departments: accounting, marketing, chemistry, biology, chemical and electrical engineering, and/or purchasing. Candidates should have declared college major in field, minimum GPA of 3.0. Duration is 12-13 weeks. Minimum of $11 per hour. Open to college juniors, graduate students, college seniors with term or semester remaining.

Benefits Travel reimbursement, willing to complete paperwork for educational credit, discounts on Amway products.

Contact Write, fax, or e-mail Barb Halstead, Recruiter. Fax: 616-787-5675. E-mail: barb.halstead@altcor.com. No phone calls. In-person interview required. Applicants must submit a letter of interest, resume, academic transcripts. Application deadline: January 31 for January 31 (recommended). World Wide Web: http://www.amway.com.

AT&T MEDIA SERVICES
1030 Higgins Road, Suite 100
Park Ridge, Illinois 60068

General Information Cable advertising company that sells local air time on cable networks such as CNN, ESPN, and BET, and produces commercials. Number of employees: 140. Unit of AT&T Broadband, Denver, Colorado. Number of internship applications received each year: 40.

Internships Available ▶ *6 TV production interns:* responsibilities include assisting in location and studio production of commercials, set-up and breakdown of all equipment, and audio monitoring. Candidates should have ability to work with others, college courses in field, computer skills, knowledge of field, plan to pursue career in field. Duration is flexible. Unpaid. ▶ *6 copywriting interns:* responsibilities include assisting producers and writing ad copy. Candidates should have college courses in field, computer skills, knowledge of field, personal interest in the field, plan to pursue career in field, writing skills. Duration is 3–6 months. Unpaid. ▶ *Marketing and sales research interns:* responsibilities include implementing and producing advertising proposals, developing sales presentations, marketing related products, and promotional events. Candidates should have college courses in field, computer skills, organizational skills, plan to pursue career in field, research skills, writing skills. Duration is flexible. Unpaid. Open to college juniors, college seniors, recent college graduates, graduate students.

Benefits Willing to complete paperwork for educational credit, willing to provide letters of recommendation.

Contact Write, fax, or e-mail Mr. Terry Cantwell, Production Manager. Fax: 847-292-0164. E-mail: cantwell.terry@broadband.att.com. No phone calls. In-person interview required. Applicants must submit a resume. Applications are accepted continuously.

BERNSTEIN-REIN ADVERTISING
4600 Madison, Suite 1500
Kansas City, Missouri 64112

General Information Full-service advertising agency. Established in 1964. Number of employees: 340. Number of internship applications received each year: 200.

Bernstein-Rein Advertising (continued)

Internships Available ▶ *1–2 account management interns:* responsibilities include attending internal strategy meetings, coordinating daily operations of accounts, and writing conference reports. Candidates should have college courses in field, knowledge of field, office skills, oral communication skills, organizational skills, personal interest in the field, plan to pursue career in field, written communication skills. Duration is June to August. $8 per hour. ▶ *1–2 creative interns:* responsibilities include working as a copywriter or art director; conceiving and executing print, outdoor, and broadcast advertising; creating logos and taglines; selecting talent; and attending commercial shoots and edits. Candidates should have ability to work with others, college courses in field, computer skills, knowledge of field, personal interest in the field, writing skills, graphic design/art experience. Duration is June to August. $8 per hour. ▶ *1 database/direct mail marketing intern.* Candidates should have analytical skills, computer skills, knowledge of field, oral communication skills, research skills, writing skills. Duration is June to August. $8 per hour. ▶ *1 market research intern:* responsibilities include designing questionnaires, observing focus groups and field data collection, researching secondary sources, obtaining bids from vendors, and assisting in report generation. Candidates should have analytical skills, computer skills, knowledge of field, oral communication skills, research skills, writing skills. Duration is June to August. $8 per hour. ▶ *1–2 media interns:* responsibilities include researching media, targeting markets, developing budgets, projecting ratings, assisting in post-buy analyses, attending meetings with national media representatives, and researching new media trends. Candidates should have analytical skills, computer skills, knowledge of field, office skills, organizational skills, research skills. Duration is June to August. $8 per hour. Open to college students entering their senior year.
Benefits On-the-job training, possible full-time employment, willing to complete paperwork for educational credit.
Contact Write, fax, or e-mail Shannan McKee, Manager of Human Resources. Fax: 816-531-5708. E-mail: shannan_mckee@bradv. com. No phone calls. In-person interview required. Applicants must submit a formal organization application, letter of interest, resume, writing sample, three personal references. Application deadline: March 1.

BOZELL & JACOBS, LLC
13801 FNB Parkway
Omaha, Nebraska 68154

General Information Full-service advertising and public relations firm. Established in 1921. Number of employees: 50. Number of internship applications received each year: 100.
Internships Available ▶ *5–8 advertising and public relations interns:* responsibilities include working closely with advertising and public relations professionals, assisting with client projects, and working on a team to develop a complete campaign for client. Candidates should have ability to work with others, knowledge of field, oral communication skills, personal interest in the field, self-motivation, written communication skills, relevant course work or professional experience. Duration is 12 weeks in summer. $7 per hour. Open to college sophomores, college juniors, college seniors, recent college graduates, graduate students. International applications accepted.
Benefits Possible full-time employment, willing to complete paperwork for educational credit, willing to provide letters of recommendation.
Contact Write, fax, or e-mail Katy Briggs, Internship Coordinator. Fax: 402-965-4308. E-mail: kbriggs@bozelljacobs.com. No phone calls. In-person interview recommended (telephone interview accepted). Applicants must submit a formal organization application, letter of interest, resume, academic transcripts, writing sample, letter of recommendation, portfolio for creative positions. Application deadline: March 1. World Wide Web: http://www. bozelljacobs.com/summerintern.

BRETT SINGER & ASSOCIATES, LLC/DAVID GERSTEN & ASSOCIATES, INC.
240 West 44th Street
New York, New York 10036

General Information Entertainment publicity office focusing mostly on theater (Broadway, off-Broadway, tours). Established in 1995. Number of employees: 5. Number of internship applications received each year: 25.
Internships Available ▶ *1–3 publicity interns:* responsibilities include clerical work (copying, filing, typing), Internet research, and heavy phone work. Candidates should have ability to work with others, office skills, oral communication skills, organizational skills, personal interest in the field. Duration is flexible. Position available as unpaid or at $50 per week. Open to high school students, recent high school graduates, college freshmen, college sophomores, college juniors, college seniors, recent college graduates, graduate students, (college student/recent graduates preferred). International applications accepted.
Benefits Job counseling, names of contacts, on-the-job training, opportunity to attend seminars/workshops, possible full-time employment, travel reimbursement, willing to act as a professional reference, willing to complete paperwork for educational credit, willing to provide letters of recommendation.
Contact Write, fax, or e-mail Brett Singer, President. Phone: 212-575-0263. Fax: 212-575-2240. E-mail: interns@brettsinger.com. In-person interview recommended (telephone interview accepted). Applicants must submit a letter of interest, resume. Applications are accepted continuously. World Wide Web: http://www.brettsinger. com.

BROADCAST ADVERTISING CLUB OF CHICAGO
325 West Huron Street
Chicago, Illinois 60610

General Information Club made up of 800 broadcast media executives. Established in 1950. Number of employees: 4. Number of internship applications received each year: 150.
Internships Available ▶ *6–10 assistant time buyer/planner/broadcast station sales interns.* Candidates should have ability to work with others, college courses in field, computer skills, oral communication skills, personal interest in the field, plan to pursue career in field, written communication skills. Duration is 10 weeks in summer (full-time). Stipend of $2000. Open to college juniors, college seniors. International applications accepted.
Benefits Job counseling, names of contacts, on-the-job training, opportunity to attend seminars/workshops, possible full-time employment, willing to act as a professional reference, willing to complete paperwork for educational credit, willing to provide letters of recommendation.
Contact Write, call, or fax Joyce R. Saxon, Chairperson, Academic Committee, 235 West Eugenie Street, Chicago, Illinois 60614-5774. Phone: 312-642-7805. Fax: 312-440-1970. E-mail: office325@ aol.com. In-person interview required. Applicants must submit a formal organization application, resume, 500-word essay on specified topic. Application deadline: February 1.

BROWN-MILLER COMMUNICATIONS
1114 Jones Street
Martinez, California 94553

General Information Full-service public relations agency serving the health food and agriculture industries; emphasizes creativity, strong writing skills, thorough research, and persistent work. Established in 1987. Number of employees: 8. Number of internship applications received each year: 50.
Internships Available ▶ *1 account coordinator:* responsibilities include writing press releases and magazine articles, answering phones and making media calls, coordinating special events, preparing monthly activity reports, supervising account timelines, tracking press clippings, coordinating product mailing, performing database updates, running errands, researching, and filing. Candidates should have computer skills, oral communication skills, personal interest in the field, self-motivation, writing skills. Duration is 1 semester. Unpaid. Open to individuals with two years of

college-related course experience in public relations, journalism, English, or communications. International applications accepted.
Benefits Job counseling, travel reimbursement, willing to complete paperwork for educational credit, willing to provide letters of recommendation, writing and editing skills enhancement, exposure to media relations.
Contact Write, fax, or e-mail Amy Woodman, Internship Coordinator. Fax: 925-370-9811. E-mail: bmc@brownmillerpr.com. No phone calls. In-person interview recommended (telephone interview accepted). Applicants must submit a letter of interest, resume, two writing samples. Applications are accepted continuously. World Wide Web: http://www.brownmillerpr.com.

BRYAN FARRISH RADIO PROMOTION
14230 Ventura Boulevard
Sherman Oaks, California 91423

General Information Music and talk show marketing firm. Established in 1998. Number of employees: 7. Number of internship applications received each year: 50.
Internships Available ▶ *1–7 music airplay promotion interns.* Duration is flexible. Unpaid. Open to individuals over age 21.
Benefits Job counseling, names of contacts, on-the-job training, opportunity to attend seminars/workshops, possible full-time employment, willing to act as a professional reference, willing to complete paperwork for educational credit, willing to provide letters of recommendation, CDs and passes to artist performances.
Contact Call Jo Jo Roberto, Office Assistant. Phone: 818-905-8038 Ext. 16. Fax: 818-905-9149. E-mail: jojo@radio-media.com. In-person interview required. Applications are accepted continuously. World Wide Web: http://www.radio-media.com.

CAIRNS & ASSOCIATES
3 Park Avenue, 14th Floor
New York, New York 10016

General Information Full-service public relations and integrated marketing agency. Established in 1983. Number of employees: 45. Number of internship applications received each year: 1,000.
Internships Available ▶ *2–6 interns:* responsibilities include preparing media lists and coordinating press mailings, contacting editors and television producers, maintaining press clippings, preparing client reports, writing press materials, and conducting research projects. Candidates should have knowledge of field, oral communication skills, personal interest in the field, research skills, self-motivation, written communication skills. Duration is 1 semester. Position available as unpaid or at minimum wage or for academic credit. Open to college sophomores, college juniors, college seniors.
Benefits Job counseling, names of contacts, on-the-job training, opportunity to attend seminars/workshops, possible full-time employment, willing to complete paperwork for educational credit, willing to provide letters of recommendation, participation in mentor program.
Contact Write, call, or fax Jen Agoado, Associate Account Executive. Phone: 212-413-0503. Fax: 212-413-0792. In-person interview required. Applicants must submit a letter of interest, resume. Applications are accepted continuously.

CANAAN PUBLIC RELATIONS
75 South Broadway, Suite 470
White Plains, New York 10601

General Information Full-service public relations firm with two major divisions: travel, hospitality, and entertainment; beauty, health, and fitness. Established in 1977. Number of employees: 8. Number of internship applications received each year: 50.
Internships Available ▶ *1–3 interns:* responsibilities include assisting account executive, preparing press kits, editing, writing, and helping plan events. Candidates should have office skills, oral communication skills, organizational skills, self-motivation, strong interpersonal skills, written communication skills. Duration is flexible. $15 per day. Open to college seniors, recent college graduates, graduate students. International applications accepted.

Benefits Formal training, names of contacts, opportunity to attend seminars/workshops, possible full-time employment, travel reimbursement, willing to complete paperwork for educational credit, willing to provide letters of recommendation.
International Internships Available.
Contact Write, fax, or e-mail Jed Canaan, President, 75 South Broadway, Suite 470, White Plains, New York 10601. Phone: 914-304-4080. Fax: 914-304-4083. E-mail: jedc@canaanpr.com. In-person interview required. Applicants must submit a letter of interest, resume. Applications are accepted continuously. World Wide Web: http://www.canaanpr.com.

COLE HENDERSON DRAKE
426 Marietta Street
Atlanta, Georgia 30313

General Information Advertising agency. Established in 1969. Number of employees: 30. Number of internship applications received each year: 30.
Internships Available ▶ *1 account planning intern:* responsibilities include overall view of account planning; developing and presenting a project; assisting planner. Candidates should have ability to work independently, analytical skills, plan to pursue career in field, self-motivation, strong leadership ability. Duration is 1 semester. $500 per duration of internship. ▶ *1–2 client services interns:* responsibilities include overview of account management; developing and presenting a project; assisting account manager in analysis, recommendations, and client programs. Candidates should have ability to work with others, plan to pursue career in field, self-motivation, strong leadership ability. Duration is 1 semester. $500 per duration of internship. ▶ *1 creative intern:* responsibilities include assisting creative department. Candidates should have ability to work independently, computer skills, declared college major in field, experience in the field, plan to pursue career in field, solid knowledge of Photoshop, QuarkXpress and Illustrator. Duration is 1 semester. $500 per duration of internship. ▶ *1 media planning intern:* responsibilities include overview of media planning; developing and presenting a project; assisting planners. Candidates should have ability to work independently, declared college major in field, plan to pursue career in field, self-motivation, strong leadership ability, writing skills. Duration is 1 semester. $500 per duration of internship. Open to college juniors, college seniors, recent college graduates, graduate students. International applications accepted.
Benefits Willing to act as a professional reference, willing to complete paperwork for educational credit, willing to provide letters of recommendation.
Contact Write, call, fax, or e-mail April Voris, Client Services Manager. Phone: 404-892-4500. Fax: 404-892-4522. E-mail: avoris@chdatlanta.com. In-person interview recommended (telephone interview accepted). Applicants must submit a letter of interest, resume, portfolio. Application deadline: March 28 for summer, July 31 for fall, October 31 for spring. World Wide Web: http://www.chdatlanta.com.

COLLEGE CONNECTIONS/ HALSTEAD COMMUNICATIONS
329 East 82nd Street
New York, New York 10027

General Information Company providing public relations for education and nonprofit organizations. Established in 1980. Number of employees: 7. Number of internship applications received each year: 250.
Internships Available ▶ *1 public relations intern:* responsibilities include writing pitch letters and press releases, pitching stories to print and broadcast media, word processing, compiling and updating databases, generating mailing lists, and conducting mailings. Candidates should have computer skills, office skills, oral communication skills, organizational skills, personal interest in the field, self-motivation, writing skills, creativity and flexibility, knowledge of MS-Office (preferred). Duration is flexible; (about 40 hours per week). Position available as unpaid or at $10–$12 per hour. Open to college juniors, college seniors, recent college graduates.

College Connections/ Halstead Communications (continued)
Benefits Job counseling, names of contacts, on-the-job training, opportunity to attend seminars/workshops, possible full-time employment, travel reimbursement, willing to act as a professional reference, willing to complete paperwork for educational credit, willing to provide letters of recommendation.
Contact Write, call, fax, or e-mail Heidi Reinholdt, Internship Coordinator. Phone: 212-734-2190. Fax: 212-517-7284. E-mail: halstead@halsteadpr.com. Applicants must submit a resume, cover letter stating interest and availability. Application deadline: Call for deadlines. World Wide Web: http://www.halsteadpr.com.

CONE
90 Canal Street
Boston, Massachusetts 02114

General Information Public relations/communications firm that seeks to find true alignments between companies and their customers and to create programs and communications to build image, understanding, and sales. Established in 1980. Number of employees: 60. Number of internship applications received each year: 100.
Internships Available ▶ *10–15 account management interns:* responsibilities include engaging in all aspects of strategic marketing communications while linked to a team through which the intern will be exposed to all areas of account management. Candidates should have ability to work with others, college courses in field, computer skills, plan to pursue career in field, self-motivation, written communication skills. Duration is 3 months. Unpaid. Open to college freshmen, college sophomores, college juniors, college seniors, graduate students. ▶ *1 human resources intern:* responsibilities include performing diverse human resources functions including, intern/employee development training and workshops, employee benefits, intern administration, scanning and reviewing resumes, sitting in on interviews, and other administrative duties. Candidates should have ability to work independently, computer skills, oral communication skills, organizational skills, plan to pursue career in field, strong interpersonal skills, written communication skills. Duration is 3 months. Unpaid. Open to college freshmen, college sophomores, college juniors, college seniors. International applications accepted.
Benefits Formal training, job counseling, names of contacts, opportunity to attend seminars/workshops, willing to complete paperwork for educational credit, willing to provide letters of recommendation, assistance with resume preparation and interviews, networking opportunities.
Contact Write, call, fax, or e-mail Wendy Krampf, Human Resources Assistant. Phone: 617-227-2111 Ext. 8305. Fax: 617-523-3955. E-mail: hr@coneinc.com. In-person interview required. Applicants must submit a letter of interest, resume. Application deadline: April 1 for summer, June 1 for fall, November 1 for spring. World Wide Web: http://www.coneinc.com.

COOPER COMMUNICATIONS, INC.
5350 Topanga Canyon Boulevard
Woodland Hills, California 91364-1718

General Information Marketing/public relations firm specializing in corporate public relations, strategic planning, marketing, and media relations. Established in 1982. Number of employees: 8. Number of internship applications received each year: 50.
Internships Available ▶ *Public relations interns:* responsibilities include composing correspondence, creating media lists, placing media follow-up calls, assembling press kits, database work, research, and general office support. Candidates should have ability to work with others, declared college major in field, editing skills, oral communication skills, organizational skills, writing skills, knowledge of Microsoft Word for windows 95 or 98; ability to work under deadline and handle several tasks at once. Duration is 15-20 hours per week. Minimum wage after 30 days. Open to college freshmen, college sophomores, college juniors, college seniors. International applications accepted.

Benefits On-the-job training, possible full-time employment, willing to act as a professional reference, willing to complete paperwork for educational credit, willing to provide letters of recommendation.
Contact Write, call, or fax Abby Sturgeon, Account Executive. Phone: 818-348-8030. Fax: 818-348-8230. In-person interview recommended (telephone interview accepted). Applicants must submit a letter of interest, resume. Applications are accepted continuously. World Wide Web: http://coopercommunications.net.

C. PAUL LUONGO COMPANY, PUBLIC RELATIONS AND MARKETING
441 Stuart Street
Boston, Massachusetts 02116

General Information Public relations firm and marketing agency that offers corporate, product, and financial publicity consulting and marketing communications services throughout the U.S. and Canada. Established in 1964. Number of employees: 6. Number of internship applications received each year: 100.
Internships Available ▶ *1–2 assistant to president interns:* responsibilities include new business and media research, telephone contacts. Duration is 3–6 months. Unpaid. Open to recent high school graduates, college freshmen, college sophomores, college juniors, college seniors, recent college graduates, graduate students, law students, career changers, individuals reentering the workforce. ▶ *1 intern:* responsibilities include performing a variety of public relations activities. Duration is 3 months minimum. Unpaid. Open to high school seniors, recent high school graduates, college freshmen, college sophomores, college juniors, college seniors, recent college graduates, graduate students, law students, career changers, individuals reentering the workforce. Candidates for all positions should have ability to work independently, analytical skills, computer skills, editing skills, office skills, oral communication skills, organizational skills, research skills, self-motivation, strong interpersonal skills, strong leadership ability, writing skills. International applications accepted.
Benefits Formal training, job counseling, names of contacts, on-the-job training, possible full-time employment, willing to act as a professional reference, willing to complete paperwork for educational credit, willing to provide letters of recommendation.
Contact Write, call, fax, e-mail, or through World Wide Web site Mr. C. Paul Luongo, President. Phone: 617-266-4210. Fax: 617-266-2211. E-mail: cpaul@cpaulluongo.com. In-person interview recommended (telephone interview accepted). Applicants must submit a letter of interest, resume. Applications are accepted continuously. World Wide Web: http://www.cpaulluongo.com.

CREATIVE MANAGEMENT SERVICES
906 D Street, NE
Washington, District of Columbia 20002

General Information Modeling and casting agency and communications company producing advertising, marketing, public relations, and event planning for large and small companies and the government. Established in 1980. Number of employees: 2. Number of internship applications received each year: 100.
Internships Available ▶ *1 special assistant to the president:* responsibilities include interviewing talent; handling client bookings; making arrangements for travel and wardrobe; accompanying owner to photo shoots, TV bookings, fashion shows, and parties; and assisting with events planning and writing/advertising services. Candidates should have ability to work independently, ability to work with others, analytical skills, computer skills, office skills, oral communication skills, organizational skills, self-motivation, strong leadership ability, writing skills. Duration is 3 months or 1 semester. Unpaid. Open to high school students, recent high school graduates, college freshmen, college sophomores, college juniors, college seniors, recent college graduates, graduate students, law students, career changers, individuals reentering the workforce.
Benefits Job counseling, names of contacts, on-the-job training, willing to act as a professional reference, willing to complete paperwork for educational credit, willing to provide letters of recommendation, lunch provided.

Contact Write, call, or e-mail Ms. Anne Schwab, President. Phone: 202-333-3560. Fax: 202-544-2856. E-mail: crmgtser@aol.com. In-person interview recommended (telephone interview accepted). Applicants must submit a letter of interest, resume. Applications are accepted continuously.

CROMARTY AND COMPANY
246 West End Avenue, Suite 12A
New York, New York 10023

General Information Theatrical press agency serving a wide range of Broadway, off-Broadway, music, and dance clients by handling publicity needs. Established in 1987. Number of employees: 5. Number of internship applications received each year: 200.
Internships Available ▶ *1–2 interns:* responsibilities include assisting press agents in all aspects of publicity, including writing and mailing press releases and other materials, attending opening nights and interviews, and assisting in the office. Candidates should have ability to work independently, college courses in field, computer skills, editing skills, knowledge of field, office skills, oral communication skills, organizational skills, personal interest in the field, plan to pursue career in field, self-motivation, strong interpersonal skills, strong leadership ability, writing skills. Duration is 4 months. $50–$100 per week. Open to college freshmen, college sophomores, college juniors, college seniors, recent college graduates, graduate students, career changers, individuals reentering the workforce. International applications accepted.
Benefits Names of contacts, possible full-time employment, travel reimbursement, willing to complete paperwork for educational credit, willing to provide letters of recommendation, reimbursement for lunch on work days, small stipend.
Contact Write, e-mail, or through World Wide Web site Peter Cromarty, Internship Coordinator, PO Box 237154, New York, New York 10023. E-mail: peterc@cromarty.com. No phone calls. In-person interview recommended (telephone interview accepted). Applicants must submit a letter of interest, resume, writing sample. Application deadline: April 1 for summer, September 1 for fall, November 1 for winter. World Wide Web: http://www.cromarty.com.

DYE ,VAN MOL, AND LAWRENCE
209 Seventh Avenue North
Nashville, Tennessee 37219

General Information Full-service marketing and communications firm that specializes in national, regional, and local public relations and community activities. Established in 1980. Number of employees: 70. Number of internship applications received each year: 50.
Internships Available ▶ *1–2 interns:* responsibilities include research and writing, arranging special events and meetings, and calling the media. Candidates should have ability to work with others, oral communication skills, organizational skills, research skills, self-motivation, writing skills. Duration is 3-5 months in fall, spring, or summer. $7 per hour. Open to college juniors, college seniors, recent college graduates, graduate students.
Benefits Formal training, names of contacts, willing to complete paperwork for educational credit, willing to provide letters of recommendation.
Contact Write, fax, or e-mail Katy Francisco, Internship Coordinator. Phone: 615-244-1818. Fax: 615-780-3303. E-mail: katy.francisco@dvl.com. In-person interview required. Applicants must submit a letter of interest, resume, formal application (available online). Application deadline: February 28 for summer, June 30 for fall, October 1 for spring. World Wide Web: http://www.dvl.com.

DYKEMAN ASSOCIATES, INC.
4115 Rawlins
Dallas, Texas 75219

General Information Full-service marketing, public relations, and video production firm. Established in 1974. Number of employees: 5. Number of internship applications received each year: 75.

Internships Available ▶ *3–4 interns:* responsibilities include assisting with production of collateral materials, video production, and ad preparation; compiling media lists; contacting media; setting up programs for speakers; creating proposals for business prospects; and monitoring presentations to clients. Candidates should have analytical skills, college courses in field, computer skills, organizational skills, plan to pursue career in field, self-motivation, writing skills, dependability. Duration is 1 semester to 1 year. $12 per hour in barter dollars. Open to college juniors, college seniors, recent college graduates, graduate students. International applications accepted.
Benefits Formal training, job counseling, names of contacts, on-the-job training, opportunity to attend seminars/workshops, possible full-time employment, willing to complete paperwork for educational credit, willing to provide letters of recommendation, job listings, barter dollars (in lieu of cash) for salary.
Contact Write, fax, or e-mail Ms. Alice Dykeman, President/CEO. Fax: 214-528-0241. E-mail: adykeman@airmail.net. No phone calls. In-person interview recommended (telephone interview accepted). Applicants must submit a letter of interest, resume, four writing samples, two personal references, two letters of recommendation. Application deadline: March 15 for summer, June 15 for fall, November 15 for spring. World Wide Web: http://www.dykemanassoc.com.

EAST COAST PROMOTION AND RESEARCH GROUP
PO Box 1759
Ocean City, Maryland 21843

General Information Broad-based marketing and research business. Established in 1976. Number of employees: 10.
Internships Available ▶ *2 accounting interns:* responsibilities include tracking billing and financial records of busy advertising agency. Unpaid. ▶ *2 administrative assistants:* responsibilities include helping coordinate agency activities. Unpaid. ▶ *2 advertising interns:* responsibilities include helping develop advertising campaigns for new and existing advertising clients. Duration is 1–3 semesters. Unpaid. ▶ *2 computer science interns:* responsibilities include laying out and designing advertising campaigns on IBM and Macintosh computers. Duration is 8–10 weeks. Unpaid. ▶ *2 copy writers:* responsibilities include developing a theme and writing copy for advertising campaign. Unpaid. ▶ *3 graphic design interns:* responsibilities include developing a concept for an advertising campaign and laying out and designing ads on Macintosh and IBM computers. Unpaid. ▶ *1 human resource intern:* responsibilities include scheduling and updating personnel-related information. Unpaid. ▶ *2 management intern.* Unpaid. ▶ *4 marketing research interns:* responsibilities include conducting market research projects. Unpaid. ▶ *2 photography interns:* responsibilities include shooting black-and-white and color photographs for advertising and public relations campaigns. Unpaid. ▶ *3 public relations interns:* responsibilities include creating, writing, and servicing public relations campaigns for agency clients. Unpaid. ▶ *2 public relations writers:* responsibilities include developing marketing and sales promotion projects for advertising agency clients. Unpaid. International applications accepted.
Benefits Job counseling, names of contacts, opportunity to attend seminars/workshops, possible full-time employment, willing to complete paperwork for educational credit, willing to provide letters of recommendation, health club membership available, orientation program.
Contact Write, call, fax, or e-mail Mr. Paul Jankovic, President. Phone: 410-524-5351. Fax: 302-539-1232. E-mail: ecprg@aol.com. Applicants must submit a letter of interest, resume. Applications are accepted continuously. World Wide Web: http://www.ecusa.com.

THE EDELMAN GROUP
420 Lexington Avenue, Suite 1706
New York, New York 10170

General Information Firm that specializes in design, advertising, and marketing for corporate clients. Established in 1982. Number of employees: 9. Number of internship applications received each year: 200.

The Edelman Group (continued)

Internships Available ▶ *1 accounting assistant:* responsibilities include invoicing, billing, and reconciling accounts. Candidates should have ability to work independently, computer skills, oral communication skills, organizational skills, personal interest in the field. Duration is 1 semester. Unpaid. Open to college freshmen, college sophomores, college juniors, college seniors, recent college graduates. ▶ *1–2 graphic design interns:* responsibilities include photo research, preparing artwork for presentation, and some design work. Candidates should have ability to work independently, ability to work with others, personal interest in the field, plan to pursue career in field, self-motivation, previous study of design and/or fine art. Duration is flexible. Unpaid. Open to college freshmen, college sophomores, college juniors, college seniors, recent college graduates. ▶ *1 receptionist/office intern:* responsibilities include answering telephone calls from clients and using fax and copying machines. Candidates should have ability to work with others, computer skills, office skills, oral communication skills, personal interest in the field, written communication skills. Duration is 1 semester. Unpaid. Open to college freshmen, college sophomores, college juniors, college seniors. ▶ *1 sales assistant:* responsibilities include assisting salesperson with research, lead qualification, and telemarketing. Candidates should have computer skills, oral communication skills, personal interest in the field, research skills, self-motivation, strong interpersonal skills. Duration is flexible. Unpaid. Open to college freshmen, college sophomores, college juniors, college seniors. International applications accepted.

Benefits Formal training, possible full-time employment, willing to complete paperwork for educational credit, willing to provide letters of recommendation.

Contact Write or e-mail Sandy Gibbs, Office Administrator, 420 Lexington Avenue,, Suite 1706, New York, New York 10170. Fax: 212-490-5985. E-mail: sandy@edelmangroup.com. No phone calls. In-person interview recommended (telephone interview accepted). Applicants must submit a resume, two personal references, portfolio (graphic design positions). Applications are accepted continuously. World Wide Web: http://www.edelmangroup.com.

EISNER, PETROU, AND ASSOCIATES
927 15th Street, NW, Suite 900
Washington, District of Columbia 20005

General Information Full-service marketing communications agency specializing in technology, travel/tourism/hospitality, health care, business-to-business public relations, and special events. Established in 1986. Number of employees: 22. Affiliate of Eisner Communications, Baltimore, Maryland. Number of internship applications received each year: 50.

Internships Available ▶ *1–3 public relations interns (Baltimore office):* responsibilities include performing research, special events planning and implementation, and assisting with media relations and client contact. Candidates should have knowledge of field, oral communication skills, organizational skills, strong interpersonal skills, written communication skills, major in public relations/communications, previous public relations class work or internship experience. Duration is 1 semester. Position available as unpaid or paid. ▶ *1–3 public relations interns (Washington office):* responsibilities include performing research, special events planning and implementation, and assisting in media relations and client contact. Candidates should have ability to work independently, knowledge of field, oral communication skills, organizational skills, strong interpersonal skills, written communication skills, major in public relations/journalism, previous public relations class work or internship experience. Duration is 1 semester. Position available as unpaid or paid. Open to college juniors, college seniors, recent college graduates. International applications accepted.

Benefits Names of contacts, opportunity to attend seminars/workshops, possible full-time employment, travel reimbursement, willing to complete paperwork for educational credit, willing to provide letters of recommendation, possible college credit and/or stipend, Metro card.

Contact Write, fax, e-mail, or through World Wide Web site Ms. Lisa Miles, Internship Coordinator. Fax: 202-682-9028. E-mail: info@eisnerpetrou.com. No phone calls. In-person interview

recommended (telephone interview accepted). Applicants must submit a letter of interest, resume, writing sample. Application deadline: April 15 for summer, July 15 for fall, November 15 for spring. World Wide Web: http://www.eisnerpetrou.com.

FENTON COMMUNICATIONS
1320 18th Street, NW
Washington, District of Columbia 20036

General Information Issue-oriented public relations firm committed to representing socially responsible clients. Established in 1981. Number of employees: 30. Number of internship applications received each year: 200.

Internships Available ▶ *2–4 public relations interns:* responsibilities include program work (campaign strategy brainstorming, writing, conducting research, organizing press conferences); administrative work; developing media lists; monitoring media coverage. Candidates should have experience in the field, office skills, oral communication skills, personal interest in the field, writing skills. Duration is one semester (full-time). Position available as unpaid or at $1200 per month. Open to college freshmen, college sophomores, college juniors, college seniors, recent college graduates, graduate students. International applications accepted.

Benefits Formal training, job counseling, opportunity to attend seminars/workshops, possible full-time employment, willing to complete paperwork for educational credit, willing to provide letters of recommendation, opportunity to attend press conferences; YMCA membership; Metro passes.

Contact Write, fax, e-mail, or through World Wide Web site Mary Duppler, Human Resource Manager, 1320 18th Street, NW, Washington, District of Columbia 20030. Fax: 202-822-4787. E-mail: fenton@fenton.com. No phone calls. Telephone interview required. Applicants must submit a letter of interest, resume, 2-3 writing samples. Applications are accepted continuously. World Wide Web: http://www.fenton.com.

FORTUNE PUBLIC RELATIONS
2319 California Street
Berkeley, California 94703

General Information Restaurant and food products public relations firm. Established in 1986. Number of employees: 2. Number of internship applications received each year: 20.

Internships Available ▶ *1 publicist trainee:* responsibilities include copywriting, client contact, press kit design and production, media list development, media follow-up calls, and general office duties. Candidates should have ability to work independently, knowledge of field, oral communication skills, writing skills, IBM or PC computer skills. Duration is flexible. Unpaid. Open to college seniors, recent college graduates, graduate students, career changers, individuals reentering the workforce. International applications accepted.

Benefits Job counseling, names of contacts, on-the-job training, opportunity to attend seminars/workshops, willing to act as a professional reference, willing to complete paperwork for educational credit, willing to provide letters of recommendation, possibility of part-time employment.

Contact Write, call, fax, or e-mail Tom Walton, Co-owner. Phone: 510-548-1097. Fax: 510-841-7006. E-mail: fortunepr@aol.com. In-person interview recommended (telephone interview accepted). Applicants must submit a resume. Applications are accepted continuously. World Wide Web: http://www.fortunepublicrelations.com.

HILL AND KNOWLTON, INC.
466 Lexington Avenue, 3rd Floor
New York, New York 10017

General Information Headquarters of global public relations firm. Established in 1927. Number of employees: 150. Number of internship applications received each year: 700.

Internships Available ▶ *Fall/winter interns:* responsibilities include working on assignments and attending regular employee seminars and office events; internships available in New York City, Washington (DC), Chicago, Houston, Los Angeles, San Francisco, Sacramento, Tampa, and Ft. Lauderdale. Candidates should have oral com-

munication skills, organizational skills, personal interest in the field, written communication skills, previous academic or work experience in public relations or communications field helpful. Duration is flexible. $10 per hour. ▶ *6–12 summer interns:* responsibilities include working with one or two supervisors as part of account teams; exposure to practice specialties within the public relations profession such as media relations, financial relations, marketing and crisis communications, and health care; researching; preparing and presenting proposals; internships available in New York City, Washington (DC), Chicago, Houston, Los Angeles, San Francisco, Sacramento, Tampa, and Ft. Lauderdale. Candidates should have oral communication skills, organizational skills, personal interest in the field, written communication skills, previous academic or work experience in public relations or communication field helpful. Duration is mid-June to mid-August (8-10 week minimum). $10 per hour. Open to college juniors, college seniors, recent college graduates, graduate students. International applications accepted.
Benefits Formal training, opportunity to attend seminars/workshops, possible full-time employment, willing to complete paperwork for educational credit, willing to provide letters of recommendation.
Contact E-mail or through World Wide Web site Donna Renella, Senior Managing Director, Recruitment. E-mail: careers@hillandknowlton.com. Telephone interview required. Applicants must submit a letter of interest, resume, 1 specified essay. Application deadline: March 1 for summer, July 30 for fall, October 15 for winter. World Wide Web: http://www.hillandknowlton.com.

HWH PUBLIC RELATIONS/NEW MEDIA
1414 Avenue of the Americas
New York, New York 10019

General Information Public relations agency. Established in 1980. Number of employees: 25. Number of internship applications received each year: 100.
Internships Available ▶ *5–7 public relations interns:* responsibilities include writing press releases, researching and compiling media lists, phone pitching, arranging media appointments, administrative tasks. Candidates should have ability to work independently, ability to work with others, computer skills, knowledge of field, office skills, oral communication skills, writing skills. Duration is 1 semester; (minimum of 15 hours per week required). Unpaid. Open to college juniors, college seniors.
Benefits Willing to act as a professional reference, willing to complete paperwork for educational credit, willing to provide letters of recommendation.
Contact Write, call, fax, e-mail, or through World Wide Web site Michael Zorek, Intern Coordinator. Phone: 212-355-5049. Fax: 212-593-0065. E-mail: michaelz@hwhpr.com. In-person interview recommended (telephone interview accepted). Applicants must submit a letter of interest, resume, writing sample. Application deadline: March 31 for summer, June 30 for fall, October 31 for spring. World Wide Web: http://www.hwhpr.com.

JACKSINA COMPANY
1501 Broadway, Suite 1508
New York, New York 10036

General Information Publicity, public relations, and marketing company whose expertise is concentrated in the entertainment field with specific attention to the promoting, publicizing, and marketing of Broadway shows and films; also works in the music industry. Established in 1978. Number of employees: 3. Number of internship applications received each year: 50.
Internships Available ▶ *2 assistants to account executives:* responsibilities include working in areas that include public relations, marketing, film production, and television development. Candidates should have office skills, oral communication skills, organizational skills, personal interest in the field, strong interpersonal skills, written communication skills. Duration is 3–6 months. Unpaid. Open to college sophomores, college juniors, college seniors, recent college graduates, graduate students. ▶ *1–2 general assistants:* responsibilities include assisting in all areas within the organization. Candidates should have ability to work independently, office skills, oral communication skills, personal interest in the field, self-

motivation, strong interpersonal skills, written communication skills. Duration is 3–6 months. Unpaid. Open to college freshmen, college sophomores, college juniors, college seniors. International applications accepted.
Benefits Free meals, job counseling, on-the-job training, opportunity to attend seminars/workshops, possible full-time employment, travel reimbursement, willing to act as a professional reference, willing to complete paperwork for educational credit, willing to provide letters of recommendation.
Contact Write, call, or fax Judy Jacksina, President. Phone: 212-221-8361. Fax: 212-221-8369. In-person interview recommended (telephone interview accepted). Applicants must submit a resume. Applications are accepted continuously.

KCSA PUBLIC RELATIONS WORLDWIDE
800 Second Avenue
New York, New York 10017

General Information Public relations agency specializing in public and investor relations, corporate communications, and marketing communications. Established in 1969. Number of employees: 71. Number of internship applications received each year: 350.
Internships Available ▶ *3–5 public relations interns:* responsibilities include working with various groups. Candidates should have ability to work with others, computer skills, oral communication skills, personal interest in the field, self-motivation, written communication skills. Duration is flexible. Unpaid. Open to college sophomores, college juniors, college seniors. International applications accepted.
Benefits Formal training, job counseling, on-the-job training, possible full-time employment, travel reimbursement, willing to complete paperwork for educational credit, willing to provide letters of recommendation.
Contact Write, fax, or e-mail Deborah Radman, Managing Partner. Fax: 212-697-0910. E-mail: dradman@kcsa.com. In-person interview required. Applicants must submit a letter of interest, resume. Applications are accepted continuously. World Wide Web: http://www.kcsa.com.

KELMAN AND COMPANY
118½ South La Brea Avenue
Los Angeles, California 90036

General Information Public relations firm representing a variety of entertainment and tourism accounts, including international resorts and hotels and airlines. Established in 1992. Number of employees: 6. Number of internship applications received each year: 100.
Internships Available ▶ *1–3 public relations assistants:* responsibilities include writing, researching, and performing telephone follow-up. Candidates should have ability to work independently, computer skills, office skills, oral communication skills, organizational skills, personal interest in the field, research skills, self-motivation, strong interpersonal skills, written communication skills. Duration is 2–12 months. Unpaid. Open to college freshmen, college sophomores, college juniors, college seniors, recent college graduates, graduate students, career changers, individuals reentering the workforce. International applications accepted.
Benefits Job counseling, names of contacts, on-the-job training, willing to act as a professional reference, willing to complete paperwork for educational credit, willing to provide letters of recommendation.
Contact Write, call, fax, or e-mail Ms. Deborah Kelman, President. Phone: 323-932-6262. Fax: 323-932-1425. E-mail: kelmanco@pacbell.net. In-person interview recommended (telephone interview accepted). Applicants must submit a letter of interest, resume, 1-2 writing samples. Applications are accepted continuously.

LEVINE COMMUNICATIONS OFFICE
10333 Ashton Avenue
Los Angeles, California 90024

General Information Entertainment public relations firm. Established in 1983. Number of employees: 4. Number of internship applications received each year: 500.

Levine Communications Office (continued)

Internships Available ▶ *1–25 interns:* responsibilities include writing press releases, assembling media lists, writing pitch letters, pitching stories to media, working events, administrative duties, research. Candidates should have oral communication skills, organizational skills, self-motivation, strong interpersonal skills, writing skills. Duration is 295 total hours. Unpaid. Open to high school students, recent high school graduates, college freshmen, college sophomores, college juniors, college seniors, recent college graduates, graduate students, law students, career changers, individuals reentering the workforce. International applications accepted.

Benefits Job counseling, names of contacts, on-the-job training, opportunity to attend seminars/workshops, willing to act as a professional reference, willing to complete paperwork for educational credit, willing to provide letters of recommendation.

Contact Write, call, fax, e-mail, or through World Wide Web site Jeff Veal, Internship Coordinator. Phone: 310-248-6222 Ext. 14. Fax: 310-248-6227. E-mail: jeff@levinepr.com. In-person interview recommended (telephone interview accepted). Applicants must submit a formal organization application, letter of interest, resume. Applications are accepted continuously. World Wide Web: http://www.levinepr.com.

LEVIN PUBLIC RELATIONS & MARKETING, INC.
30 Glenn Street
White Plains, New York 10603

General Information Public relations firm. Established in 1984. Number of employees: 6. Number of internship applications received each year: 50.

Internships Available ▶ *1–3 junior account executives:* responsibilities include tracking client projects, calling reporters/clients, writing, report generation, client contact, Web research, and e-mail. Candidates should have ability to work independently, computer skills, office skills, oral communication skills, organizational skills, writing skills. Duration is 1 month to 1 year. $10–$12 per hour. Open to college freshmen, college sophomores, college juniors, college seniors, recent college graduates, career changers, individuals reentering the workforce.

Benefits Health insurance, job counseling, names of contacts, on-the-job training, opportunity to attend seminars/workshops, possible full-time employment, willing to act as a professional reference, willing to complete paperwork for educational credit, willing to provide letters of recommendation.

Contact Write, call, fax, e-mail, or through World Wide Web site Don Levin, President. Phone: 914-993-0900. Fax: 914-993-9589. E-mail: levin@levinpr.com. Telephone interview required. Applicants must submit a letter of interest, resume. Applications are accepted continuously. World Wide Web: http://www.levinpr.com.

LIGGETT-STASHOWER PUBLIC RELATIONS
1228 Euclid Avenue
Cleveland, Ohio 44115

General Information Public relations division of one of the largest communications firms in the Midwest serving clients nationwide. Established in 1980. Number of employees: 150. Unit of Liggett-Stashower Inc., Cleveland, Ohio. Number of internship applications received each year: 100.

Internships Available ▶ *1–2 public relations interns:* responsibilities include assisting with media relations, contacting print editors and broadcast journalists on telephone, and assisting on general assignments as needed. Candidates should have computer skills, knowledge of field, oral communication skills, plan to pursue career in field, writing skills, formal education in public relations; membership in PRSSA (a plus). Duration is 1 summer or fall semester. Minimum wage stipend. Open to college juniors, college seniors.

Benefits Formal training, names of contacts, on-the-job training, opportunity to attend seminars/workshops, willing to act as a professional reference, willing to complete paperwork for educational credit, willing to provide letters of recommendation.

Contact Write, fax, or e-mail Ms. Marilyn Casey, Vice President. Fax: 216-736-8118. E-mail: mcasey@liggett.com. No phone calls.

In-person interview required. Applicants must submit a letter of interest, resume, portfolio, three writing samples. Application deadline: March 1 for summer, July 1 for fall. World Wide Web: http://www.liggett.com.

LINDY PROMOTIONS, INC.
4343 Montgomery Avenue, Suite 5
Bethesda, Maryland 20814

General Information Promotions and event planning company. Number of employees: 3. Number of internship applications received each year: 400.

Internships Available ▶ *1–4 marketing interns:* responsibilities include various administrative duties, grassroots marketing in the D.C. metropolitan area, writing press releases, helping with planning and execution of events, assisting with mailings, advertising sales for monthly newsletter. Candidates should have ability to work independently, computer skills, office skills, organizational skills, personal interest in the field, research skills, self-motivation, strong interpersonal skills, strong leadership ability, writing skills. Duration is 3–4 months. Unpaid. Open to college sophomores, college juniors, college seniors.

Benefits Names of contacts, on-the-job training, possible full-time employment, willing to act as a professional reference, willing to complete paperwork for educational credit, willing to provide letters of recommendation.

Contact Write, fax, or e-mail Landa Bierenbaum, Event Coordinator, 4343 Montgomery Avenue, Suite 5, Bethesda, Maryland 20814. Fax: 301-652-7714. E-mail: landa@lindypromo.com. In-person interview recommended (telephone interview accepted). Applicants must submit a letter of interest, resume. World Wide Web: http://www.lindypromo.com.

LORD, SULLIVAN & YODER PUBLIC RELATIONS
250 Old Wilson Bridge Road
Columbus, Ohio 43085

General Information Full-service marketing communications and public relations firm. Established in 1965. Number of employees: 90. Number of internship applications received each year: 20.

Internships Available ▶ *1 intern:* responsibilities include writing news releases, Web site copy, assisting management in new business and client research; developing media lists and editorial calendars; media relations; attending internal and client meetings; others tasks as appropriate. Candidates should have computer skills, organizational skills, research skills, self-motivation, writing skills, (preference is given to communications majors). Duration is flexible. $10 per hour. Open to college sophomores, college juniors, college seniors. International applications accepted.

Benefits Job counseling, on-the-job training, opportunity to attend seminars/workshops, possible full-time employment, travel reimbursement, willing to act as a professional reference, willing to complete paperwork for educational credit, willing to provide letters of recommendation, $1500 scholarship.

Contact Call, e-mail, or through World Wide Web site Melissa Kennedy, Account Associate. Phone: 614-825-1734. Fax: 614-846-2780. E-mail: mkennedy@lsy.com. Applicants must submit a formal organization application, letter of interest, resume, three writing samples, two letters of recommendation, completed case study. Application deadline: March 15 for summer. World Wide Web: http://www.lsy.com.

MAGNET COMMUNICATIONS
110 Fifth Avenue
New York, New York 10011

General Information Public relations agency providing full-service communications services including media relations, special events, strategic planning and research, creative services, corporate management, and crisis management. Established in 2000. Number of employees: 150. Division of Havas Advertising, Paris, France. Number of internship applications received each year: 500.

Internships Available ▶ *5–10 interns:* responsibilities include writing press materials, pitching stories, researching and fact-checking, and coordinating special events. Candidates should have ability to work with others, oral communication skills, plan to pursue career in field, self-motivation, written communication skills. Duration is 3 months in fall, summer, or spring. $7–$10 per hour. Open to college juniors, college seniors, recent college graduates. International applications accepted.

Benefits Formal training, names of contacts, on-the-job training, opportunity to attend seminars/workshops, possible full-time employment, willing to complete paperwork for educational credit, willing to provide letters of recommendation.

Contact Write, e-mail, or through World Wide Web site Intern Coordinator. E-mail: hrjobs@magnetcom.com. No phone calls. In-person interview required. Applicants must submit a formal organization application, letter of interest, resume, three writing samples. Application deadline: February 28 for summer; continuous for other positions. World Wide Web: http://www.magnetcom.com.

MANNING, SELVAGE & LEE
1170 Peachtree Street, Suite 400
Atlanta, Georgia 30309

General Information International global public relations firm.
Internships Available ▶ *Summer interns (Georgia)*. Candidates should have overall GPA of 3.0 or higher. Duration is 1 summer. ▶ *Summer interns (New York):* responsibilities include assignment to work in a specific practice group and also to work with other interns to complete a public relations program for a client; completion of a basic training program. Candidates should have declared college major in field, overall GPA of 3.0 or higher. Duration is 8 weeks (full-time). $10 per hour. Open to individuals who have completed junior or senior year of college.
Contact Through World Wide Web site Internship Coordinator. Electronic application and other materials as specified on Web site. Application deadline: late February (Georgia), May (New York). World Wide Web: http://www.mslpr.com.

MAXIMUM EXPOSURE PR
50 Tice Boulevard
Woodcliff Lake, New Jersey 07677

General Information Public relations firm servicing a wide variety of interests including consumer products, professionals, business-to-business services, and nonprofit organizations. Established in 1986. Number of employees: 5.
Internships Available ▶ *Public relations interns:* responsibilities include assisting account executives in all aspects of public relations and performing clerical work. Candidates should have ability to work independently, computer skills, office skills, oral communication skills, organizational skills, plan to pursue career in field, self-motivation, strong interpersonal skills, written communication skills. Duration is year-round. Unpaid. Open to college freshmen, college sophomores, college juniors, college seniors. International applications accepted.
Benefits On-the-job training, willing to act as a professional reference, willing to complete paperwork for educational credit, willing to provide letters of recommendation.
Contact Write or e-mail Andrea Pass, Vice President. E-mail: andrea@maximumexposurepr.com. No phone calls. In-person interview required. Applicants must submit a resume, three writing samples. Applications are accepted continuously. World Wide Web: http://www.maximumexposurepr.com.

MITCH SCHNEIDER ORGANIZATION
14724 Ventura Boulevard, Suite 410
Sherman Oaks, California 91403

General Information Music public relations company. Established in 1995. Number of employees: 15. Number of internship applications received each year: 150.
Internships Available ▶ *5–10 interns:* responsibilities include assisting in writing news items, organizing mailings, making follow-up phone calls, updating computer database information, and researching media and various business contacts. Candidates should have ability to work with others, office skills, oral communication skills, plan to pursue career in field, self-motivation,

written communication skills. Duration is 3 months (15 hours minimum per week). Unpaid. Open to college freshmen, college sophomores, college juniors, college seniors, graduate students.
Benefits Job counseling, names of contacts, opportunity to attend seminars/workshops, possible full-time employment, willing to act as a professional reference, willing to complete paperwork for educational credit, willing to provide letters of recommendation, opportunity to attend music-related events and receive company products.
Contact Write, fax, e-mail, or through World Wide Web site Heather Morales, Internship Coordinator. Fax: 818-380-0430. E-mail: msoorg@aol.com. No phone calls. In-person interview recommended (telephone interview accepted). Applicants must submit a letter of interest, resume, completed internship application. Applications are accepted continuously. World Wide Web: http://www.msopr.com.

MORTON DENNIS WAX & ASSOCIATES, INC.
1560 Broadway
New York, New York 10036

General Information Organization that provides public relations/marketing for entertainment, communications, and allied industries. Established in 1956. Number of employees: 2. Number of internship applications received each year: 40.
Internships Available ▶ *2–4 film distribution/marketing interns:* responsibilities include writing and researching press releases, stories, and media marketing plans; contacting clients and the media; researching the marketing of foreign films; creating marketing mailing lists; and performing general office duties. Duration is 2–6 months. Unpaid. ▶ *3–4 public relations/marketing interns:* responsibilities include writing and researching press releases, stories, and media marketing plans; and contacting clients and media. Duration is 1–6 months. Unpaid. Candidates for all positions should have ability to work independently, computer skills, office skills, oral communication skills, self-motivation, writing skills. Open to college freshmen, college sophomores, college juniors, college seniors. International applications accepted.
Benefits Names of contacts, possible full-time employment, willing to act as a professional reference, willing to complete paperwork for educational credit, willing to provide letters of recommendation.
Contact Write Ms. Sandra Wax, Vice President, 1560 Broadway #706, New York, New York 10036. No phone calls. Applicants must submit a letter of interest, resume. Application deadline: April 30 for spring/summer, September 1 for fall.

M. SILVER ASSOCIATES, INC.
747 Third Avenue, 23rd Floor
New York, New York 10017-2803

General Information Public relations/marketing communications consultants to travel, consumer, and tourism industries worldwide. Established in 1960. Number of employees: 28. Number of internship applications received each year: 100.
Internships Available ▶ *2–4 fall/winter/spring interns:* responsibilities include assisting account group with daily workload necessary to serving clients, attending staff/creative meetings, conducting on-line research, writing press releases, preparing and disseminating press releases, press kits, and photographs; using ACT database to initiate, track, and report on media contact; assisting with press trip invitations, itineraries, and trips. Duration is 1 semester. $6–8 per hour depending on experience. Open to college sophomores, college juniors, college seniors, only those studying toward a public relations/communications degree or having completed other PR internship. ▶ *2–3 summer interns:* responsibilities include assisting account group with daily work load necessary to serving clients; attending staff/creative meetings; conducting on-line research; writing press releases; preparing and disseminating press releases, press kits, and photographs; using ACT database to initiate, track, and report on media contact; assisting with press trip invitations, itineraries, and trips. Duration is end of May semester through mid-August. $200 per week. Open to college sophomores, college juniors, only those studying toward public relations/communications degree or having completed

M. Silver Associates, Inc. (continued)

other PR internship. Candidates for all positions should have college courses in field, computer skills, experience in the field, oral communication skills, organizational skills, written communication skills.

Benefits Job counseling, names of contacts, on-the-job training, possible full-time employment, willing to act as a professional reference, willing to complete paperwork for educational credit, willing to provide letters of recommendation, opportunity to attend staff meetings/creative sessions and to be a fully participating accounts group member; stipend for travel and lunch.

Contact Write, call, fax, e-mail, or through World Wide Web site Vivian DiMare, Operations Administrator/Internship Coordinator. Phone: 212-754-6500 Ext. 204. Fax: 212-754-6698. E-mail: vivian@msilver-pr.com. In-person interview recommended (telephone interview accepted). Applicants must submit a letter of interest, resume, 1 or 2 letters of recommendation. Applications are accepted continuously. World Wide Web: http://www.msilver-pr.com.

NATIONAL CANCER INSTITUTE, OFFICE OF COMMUNICATIONS
Building 31, Room 10A28, 31 Center Drive, MSC 2580
Bethesda, Maryland 20892-2580

General Information Organization responsible for developing and managing communications activities of the National Cancer Institute and disseminating information to the public, the press, and health professionals. Established in 1937. Number of employees: 5,000. Unit of National Institute of Health, Bethesda, Maryland. Number of internship applications received each year: 50.

Internships Available ▶ *1–5 health communication interns:* responsibilities include planning, developing, evaluating, and promoting education and information programs to target audiences; preparing and carrying out national education campaigns; and pretesting and evaluating health education materials. Candidates should have computer skills, knowledge of field, oral communication skills, organizational skills, self-motivation, written communication skills. Duration is 6 months-1 year. $1500–$2100 per month. ▶ *1–3 science writing interns:* responsibilities include handling inquiries from reporters, writing news and feature articles and fact sheets for the press and public, and attending scientific meetings. Candidates should have analytical skills, oral communication skills, organizational skills, writing skills, knowledge of science. Duration is 6 months-1 year. $1500–$2100 per month. Open to graduate students.

Benefits Formal training, health insurance, on-the-job training, opportunity to attend seminars/workshops, willing to complete paperwork for educational credit, reimbursement of on-the-job travel expenses, free parking, paid government holidays.

Contact Write, e-mail, or through World Wide Web site Internship Director. Fax: 301-496-7096. E-mail: nciinterndirector@mail.nih.gov. No phone calls. Telephone interview required. Applicants must submit a formal organization application, letter of interest, resume, academic transcripts, two writing samples, letter of recommendation, 1 personal reference from advisor/Dean stating student status and expected date of graduation. Application deadline: March 15 for July—December term, September 15 for January—June term. World Wide Web: http://internship.cancer.gov.

NORTH CAROLINA AMATEUR SPORTS
PO Box 12727
Research Triangle Park, North Carolina 27709

General Information Organization that promotes the Olympic movement through amateur sports, produces the State Games of North Carolina and Cycle North Carolina, sponsors state conferences on the Olympic movement and amateur sports, and attracts national and international events and conferences to North Carolina. Established in 1983. Number of employees: 5. Number of internship applications received each year: 30.

Internships Available ▶ *1 Cycle North Carolina Assistant Ride Director:* responsibilities include assisting with event management, equipment procurement and distribution, recruitment, scheduling and supervising of volunteers, coordinating logistics, assisting with event promotion, processing entries, and distributing entry confirmations. Candidates should have ability to work with others, oral communication skills, organizational skills, self-motivation, strong leadership ability, written communication skills. Duration is August through October. Paid. Open to college juniors, college seniors, recent college graduates, graduate students, career changers. ▶ *1 competition intern:* responsibilities include State Games of North Carolina equipment procurement, venue set-up, temporary warehouse organization, communications planning and implementation. Candidates should have ability to work independently, ability to work with others, oral communication skills, organizational skills, self-motivation. Duration is mid-May through mid-July. $200 per week. Open to college freshmen, college sophomores, college juniors, college seniors, recent college graduates, graduate students. ▶ *Data services intern:* responsibilities include State Games of North Carolina entry processing, validation and roster verification, weekly entry summary reports, and registration reports. Candidates should have ability to work independently, ability to work with others, computer skills, oral communication skills, organizational skills, written communication skills. Duration is mid-May through mid-July. $200 per week. Open to college freshmen, college sophomores, college juniors, college seniors, recent college graduates, graduate students. ▶ *1 marketing intern:* responsibilities include marketing and media/promotions for the State Games of North Carolina including sponsor fulfillment, signage, merchandise and ticket distribution, sports information, and event results. Candidates should have ability to work independently, computer skills, oral communication skills, organizational skills, writing skills. Duration is mid-May through mid-July. $200 per week. Open to college freshmen, college sophomores, college juniors, college seniors, recent college graduates, graduate students. ▶ *1 special events intern:* responsibilities include planning, organizing, and implementing special programs and projects associated with the State Games of North Carolina, including Celebration of Athletes, VIP Reception, Sportsmanship Program, and Host Hotel Program. Candidates should have ability to work independently, ability to work with others, oral communication skills, organizational skills, personal interest in the field, strong leadership ability, written communication skills. Duration is mid-May through mid-July. $200 per week. Open to college freshmen, college sophomores, college juniors, college seniors, recent college graduates, graduate students. ▶ *1 volunteer coordinator:* responsibilities include recruiting, training, supervising, and assigning 1000-2000 volunteers who work with the State Games. Candidates should have computer skills, oral communication skills, organizational skills, self-motivation, strong interpersonal skills, written communication skills. Duration is 8–10 weeks. $150–$200 per week. Open to college freshmen, college sophomores, college juniors, college seniors, recent college graduates, graduate students. ▶ *Volunteer services intern:* responsibilities include recruiting, training, supervising, and assigning volunteers for the State Games of North Carolina. Candidates should have ability to work independently, computer skills, oral communication skills, organizational skills, self-motivation, written communication skills. Duration is mid-May through mid-July. $200 per week. Open to college freshmen, college sophomores, college juniors, college seniors, recent college graduates, graduate students.

Benefits Job counseling, names of contacts, on-the-job training, opportunity to attend seminars/workshops, possible full-time employment, travel reimbursement, willing to act as a professional reference, willing to complete paperwork for educational credit, willing to provide letters of recommendation.

Contact Write, call, fax, e-mail, or through World Wide Web site Amy Rose, Director of Operations. Phone: 919-361-1133 Ext. 2. Fax: 919-361-2559. E-mail: ncas1@mindspring.com. In-person interview recommended (telephone interview accepted). Applicants must submit a formal organization application, letter of interest, resume, three personal references. Application deadline: July 1 for Cycle North Carolina position; February 15 for other positions. World Wide Web: http://www.ncsports.org.

OCEAN CITY ADVERTISING AGENCY
PO Box 1759
Ocean City, Maryland 21843

General Information Full-service advertising agency that serves the resort area by providing advertising, public relations, sales promotion, photography, and market research services. Established in 1976. Number of employees: 10. Number of internship applications received each year: 100.

Internships Available ▶ *2 accounting interns:* responsibilities include tracking billing and financial records of busy advertising agency. Candidates should have computer skills, knowledge of field, personal interest in the field, self-motivation, strong interpersonal skills. Duration is 1–2 semesters. Unpaid. ▶ *2 advertising interns:* responsibilities include helping develop advertising campaigns for new and existing advertising clients. Candidates should have computer skills, oral communication skills, personal interest in the field, self-motivation, strong interpersonal skills, strong leadership ability. Duration is flexible. Unpaid. ▶ *2 computer science interns:* responsibilities include laying out and designing advertising campaigns on IBM and Macintosh computers. Candidates should have ability to work independently, computer skills, knowledge of field, personal interest in the field, self-motivation, strong interpersonal skills. Duration is 1–2 semesters. Unpaid. ▶ *2 copy writers:* responsibilities include developing a theme and writing copy for advertising campaign. Candidates should have computer skills, personal interest in the field, self-motivation, writing skills. Duration is 1–2 semesters. Unpaid. ▶ *3 graphic design interns:* responsibilities include developing a concept for an advertising campaign and laying out and designing ads on Macintosh and IBM computers. Candidates should have ability to work independently, college courses in field, computer skills, knowledge of field, personal interest in the field, self-motivation. Duration is 1–2 semesters. Unpaid. ▶ *2 human resources interns:* responsibilities include scheduling personnel records. Candidates should have ability to work with others, office skills, organizational skills, personal interest in the field, self-motivation, strong leadership ability. Duration is flexible. Unpaid. ▶ *2 management interns:* responsibilities include helping control functional aspects of a growing business. Candidates should have ability to work independently, organizational skills, personal interest in the field, self-motivation, strong interpersonal skills, strong leadership ability. Duration is 1–2 semesters. Unpaid. ▶ *4 marketing research interns:* responsibilities include conducting market research projects. Candidates should have ability to work independently, computer skills, oral communication skills, organizational skills, personal interest in the field, strong interpersonal skills. Duration is 1–2 semesters. Unpaid. ▶ *2 photography interns:* responsibilities include shooting black-and-white and color photographs for advertising and public relations campaigns. Candidates should have ability to work independently, knowledge of field, organizational skills, personal interest in the field, self-motivation, strong interpersonal skills. Duration is 1–2 semesters. Unpaid. ▶ *3 public relations interns:* responsibilities include creating, writing, and servicing public relations campaigns for agency clients. Candidates should have ability to work independently, computer skills, self-motivation, strong interpersonal skills, writing skills. Duration is 1–2 semesters. Unpaid. ▶ *2 public relations writers:* responsibilities include writing press releases for advertising agency clients. Candidates should have ability to work with others, computer skills, editing skills, personal interest in the field, writing skills. Duration is flexible. Unpaid. ▶ *2 videographers:* responsibilities include helping to shoot video. Candidates should have ability to work independently, ability to work with others, experience in the field, personal interest in the field, self-motivation, photo skills. Duration is 1–2 semesters. Unpaid. Open to college freshmen, college sophomores, college juniors, college seniors, recent college graduates, graduate students, law students, career changers. International applications accepted.

Benefits Formal training, job counseling, names of contacts, opportunity to attend seminars/workshops, possible full-time employment, willing to act as a professional reference, willing to complete paperwork for educational credit, willing to provide letters of recommendation, health club membership available.

Contact Write or fax Mr. Paul Jankovic, President. Phone: 410-524-5351. Fax: 302-539-1232. E-mail: ecprg@aol.com. Applicants must submit a letter of interest, resume. Applications are accepted continuously. World Wide Web: http://www.ecusa.com.

PERFORMANCE MARKETING
3122 Fire Road, Suite 200
Egg Harbor Township, New Jersey 08234

General Information Advertising and marketing consulting company. Established in 2001. Number of employees: 4. Number of internship applications received each year: 30.

Internships Available ▶ *1–4 marketing interns:* responsibilities include assisting in the planning and execution of advertising campaigns; press release distribution and writing; scheduling and organization of special events; and other duties as assigned. Candidates should have computer skills, oral communication skills, personal interest in the field, self-motivation, written communication skills. Duration is flexible. Paid. Open to college freshmen, college sophomores, college juniors, college seniors, recent college graduates, graduate students.

Benefits On-the-job training, possible full-time employment, willing to act as a professional reference, willing to complete paperwork for educational credit, willing to provide letters of recommendation, stipend for travel and lunch.

Contact Write, call, fax, or e-mail Glenn Davila, Director of Client Services. Phone: 609-646-0414. Fax: 609-646-1350. E-mail: gdavila@callpm.com. In-person interview required. Applicants must submit a letter of interest, resume. Applications are accepted continuously.

THE PETE SANDERS GROUP
230 West 41st Street, Suite 1802
New York, New York 10036

General Information Public relations firm specializing in entertainment with clients including Broadway musicals "Chicago," and "Annie Get Your Gun". Established in 1990. Number of employees: 7. Number of internship applications received each year: 40.

Internships Available ▶ *2 press interns:* responsibilities include direct contact with the media, setting up and supervising press interviews, editing press releases, assisting in special events planning, and general office duties. Candidates should have ability to work independently, computer skills, editing skills, office skills, oral communication skills, personal interest in the field, self-motivation, strong interpersonal skills, writing skills, major in communications, journalism, theater, or English. Duration is 8 weeks minimum (generally 1 semester or winter break). Unpaid. Open to college sophomores, college juniors, college seniors, recent college graduates. International applications accepted.

Benefits Free meals, on-the-job training, opportunity to attend seminars/workshops, possible full-time employment, travel reimbursement, willing to act as a professional reference, willing to complete paperwork for educational credit, willing to provide letters of recommendation, some complimentary theater tickets.

Contact Write, call, fax, or e-mail Glenna Freedman, Internship Supervisor, 230 West 41st Street, Suite 1802, New York, New York 10036. Phone: 212-730-0067. Fax: 212-730-0394. E-mail: gbfpress@ aol.com. In-person interview recommended (telephone interview accepted). Applicants must submit a letter of interest, resume. Applications are accepted continuously.

PMK PUBLIC RELATIONS
650 5th Avenue, 33rd Floor
New York, New York 10019

General Information Entertainment public relations/publicists. Number of employees: 28. Unit of Momentum, New York, New York. Number of internship applications received each year: 200.

Internships Available ▶ *2–5 internships.* Candidates should have ability to work independently, computer skills, office skills, oral communication skills, organizational skills, personal interest in the field, self-motivation, strong interpersonal skills. Duration is one semester or summer. Unpaid. Open to college freshmen, college sophomores, college juniors, college seniors. International applications accepted.

PMK Public Relations (continued)

Benefits Names of contacts, possible full-time employment, willing to act as a professional reference, willing to complete paperwork for educational credit, willing to provide letters of recommendation.
Contact Write, fax, or e-mail Jennifer Plante, Intern Coordinator. Phone: 212-582-1111. Fax: 212-582-6666. E-mail: jennifer.plante@ pmkhbh.com. In-person interview recommended (telephone interview accepted). Applicants must submit a letter of interest, resume. Applications are accepted continuously.

PORTER NOVELLI
220 East 42nd Street
New York, New York 10017

General Information Marketing-based public relations firm with divisions for health-care, consumer, business-to-business, and media relations. Established in 1972. Number of employees: 200. Unit of Omnicon-New York, New York, New York. Number of internship applications received each year: 400.
Internships Available ▶ *1–5 interns:* responsibilities include media contact, press materials, researching special events, brainstorming, media coverage, and administrative duties. Candidates should have ability to work independently, ability to work with others, oral communication skills, plan to pursue career in field, written communication skills, major in communications or public relations (preferred). Duration is 3 months. $375 per week. Open to college juniors, college seniors, recent college graduates, graduate students. International applications accepted.
Benefits On-the-job training, opportunity to attend seminars/ workshops, possible full-time employment, travel reimbursement, willing to complete paperwork for educational credit.
Contact Write, fax, e-mail, or through World Wide Web site Lisa Fiestal, Associate, Human Resources. Fax: 212-601-8101. E-mail: lfiestal@porternovelli.com. No phone calls. In-person interview required. Applicants must submit a letter of interest, resume, two writing samples, two personal references, writing test. Application deadline: January 31 for summer. World Wide Web: http:// www.porternovelli.com.

QUALLY AND COMPANY, INC.
2238 Central Street
Evanston, Illinois 60201-5724

General Information Integrated advertising agency specializing in new product development, new product introductions, and repositioning of existing products and services. Established in 1979. Number of employees: 4. Number of internship applications received each year: 175.
Internships Available ▶ *2–3 art directors:* responsibilities include performing art, design, production, and general tasks. Candidates should have ability to work independently, analytical skills, computer skills, editing skills, experience in the field, organizational skills, plan to pursue career in field, self-motivation. Duration is 3–9 months. Unpaid. ▶ *2 copy writers:* responsibilities include performing various writing assignments and general tasks. Candidates should have ability to work independently, ability to work with others, analytical skills, college courses in field, computer skills, editing skills, knowledge of field, organizational skills, plan to pursue career in field, research skills, self-motivation, writing skills. Duration is 3–6 months. Unpaid. Open to college juniors, college seniors, recent college graduates, graduate students, law students, career changers. ▶ *2–3 graphic designers:* responsibilities include assisting with art direction and computer production and performing general tasks. Candidates should have ability to work independently, ability to work with others, analytical skills, college courses in field, computer skills, knowledge of field, organizational skills, plan to pursue career in field, self-motivation. Duration is 3–6 months. Unpaid. Open to college juniors, college seniors, recent college graduates, graduate students, career changers. ▶ *2 new business development interns:* responsibilities include assisting with new business development, direct mail, account service, and public relations. Candidates should have ability to work independently, analytical skills, computer skills, knowledge of field, office skills, oral communication skills, personal

interest in the field, research skills, self-motivation, strong interpersonal skills, written communication skills. Duration is 3–6 months. Unpaid. Open to college juniors, college seniors, recent college graduates, graduate students, law students, career changers. ▶ *1 research intern:* responsibilities include researching for new and existing businesses and performing general tasks. Candidates should have analytical skills, computer skills, declared college major in field, editing skills, knowledge of field, organizational skills, personal interest in the field, research skills, self-motivation, writing skills. Duration is 3–6 months. Unpaid. Open to college juniors, college seniors, recent college graduates, graduate students, law students, career changers. International applications accepted.
Benefits Formal training, job counseling, names of contacts, on-the-job training, opportunity to attend seminars/workshops, possible full-time employment, willing to act as a professional reference, willing to complete paperwork for educational credit, willing to provide letters of recommendation, networking opportunities.
Contact Write, call, or e-mail Mr. Robert Qually, President/ Creative Director. Phone: 847-864-0785. E-mail: quallycompany@ hotmail.com. In-person interview recommended (telephone interview accepted). Applicants must submit a letter of interest, resume, portfolio, three personal references, three letters of recommendation, 10 writing samples (copywriter position). Application deadline: nine months in advance of desired internship.

QUIET RESORTS PUBLIC RELATIONS
PO Box 505
Bethany Beach, Delaware 19930

General Information Public relations firm operating weekly and seasonal newspapers in local resort towns and providing publicity services. Established in 1989. Number of employees: 6. Number of internship applications received each year: 45.
Internships Available ▶ *2 Internet graduate student interns:* responsibilities include designing Web page layout. Candidates should have ability to work independently, ability to work with others, analytical skills, computer skills, personal interest in the field, self-motivation. Duration is flexible. Unpaid. Open to graduate students. ▶ *2–3 Web page designers:* responsibilities include performing Web design duties. Candidates should have ability to work independently, ability to work with others, computer skills, organizational skills, personal interest in the field. Duration is flexible. Unpaid. Open to high school seniors, recent high school graduates, college freshmen, college sophomores, college juniors, college seniors, recent college graduates, graduate students, law students, career changers, individuals reentering the workforce. ▶ *2 administrative assistants:* responsibilities include working with owner, publisher, and editor. Candidates should have ability to work independently, office skills, oral communication skills, self-motivation, strong interpersonal skills. Duration is 1–2 semesters. Unpaid. Open to high school seniors, recent high school graduates, college freshmen, college sophomores, college juniors, college seniors, recent college graduates, graduate students, law students, career changers, individuals reentering the workforce. ▶ *3 advertising layout interns:* responsibilities include creating comprehensive campaigns and performing typesetting duties. Candidates should have ability to work independently, computer skills, personal interest in the field, self-motivation, strong interpersonal skills, strong leadership ability. Duration is 1–2 semesters. Unpaid. Open to college freshmen, college sophomores, college juniors, college seniors, recent college graduates, graduate students, law students, career changers, individuals reentering the workforce. ▶ *4 advertising/sales interns:* responsibilities include developing sales leads in a local territory; contact with local businesses by mail, phone, and personal interviews; and creating advertising ideas for the clients. Candidates should have ability to work independently, oral communication skills, self-motivation, strong interpersonal skills, written communication skills. Duration is 1–2 semesters. Unpaid. Open to college freshmen, college sophomores, college juniors, college seniors, recent college graduates, graduate students, law students, career changers. ▶ *2 circulation interns:* responsibilities include overseeing the organization and distribution of newsletters, pamphlets, and magazines to the local market and by direct mail. Candidates should have ability to work independently, analytical skills,

computer skills, organizational skills, self-motivation, strong interpersonal skills. Duration is flexible. Unpaid. Open to high school seniors, recent high school graduates, college freshmen, college sophomores, college juniors, college seniors, graduate students, law students, career changers, individuals reentering the workforce. ▶ *2 editorial interns:* responsibilities include developing newsworthy topics, interviewing subjects, writing stories, and helping with production and organization. Candidates should have personal interest in the field, self-motivation, strong interpersonal skills, writing skills. Duration is flexible. Unpaid. Open to recent high school graduates, college freshmen, college sophomores, college juniors, college seniors, recent college graduates, graduate students, law students, career changers, individuals reentering the workforce. ▶ *2 photography interns:* responsibilities include developing photographic opportunities. Candidates should have ability to work independently, ability to work with others, knowledge of field, personal interest in the field, self-motivation, photo skills. Duration is 1–2 semesters. Unpaid. Open to high school seniors, recent high school graduates, college freshmen, college sophomores, college juniors, college seniors, recent college graduates, graduate students, law students, career changers, individuals reentering the workforce. ▶ *3 production interns:* responsibilities include designing, typesetting, and pasting-up ads and articles for newsletters, newspapers, and brochures. Candidates should have ability to work independently, computer skills, office skills, personal interest in the field, strong interpersonal skills. Duration is 1–2 semesters. Unpaid. Open to college freshmen, college sophomores, college juniors, college seniors, recent college graduates, graduate students, law students, career changers. ▶ *4 reporters:* responsibilities include developing and following up on news and feature topics of local interest. Candidates should have ability to work with others, computer skills, editing skills, oral communication skills, writing skills. Duration is 1–2 semesters. Unpaid. Open to recent high school graduates, college freshmen, college sophomores, college juniors, college seniors, recent college graduates, graduate students, law students, career changers. ▶ *2 typesetters:* responsibilities include designing, laying out, and composing advertisements on Macintosh or IBM-compatible computers. Candidates should have ability to work independently, computer skills, office skills, organizational skills, personal interest in the field, self-motivation, strong interpersonal skills. Duration is flexible. Unpaid. Open to recent high school graduates, college freshmen, college sophomores, college juniors, college seniors, recent college graduates, graduate students, law students, career changers, individuals reentering the workforce. International applications accepted.
Benefits Formal training, names of contacts, opportunity to attend seminars/workshops, possible full-time employment, willing to act as a professional reference, willing to complete paperwork for educational credit, willing to provide letters of recommendation, health club membership available.
Contact Write, call, fax, or e-mail Mr. Paul D. Jankovic, Publisher and Owner. Phone: 410-524-5351. Fax: 302-539-1232. E-mail: ecprg@aol.com. Applicants must submit a letter of interest, resume. Applications are accepted continuously. World Wide Web: http://www.ecusa.com.

THE ROCKEY COMPANY
2121 Fifth Avenue
Seattle, Washington 98121

General Information Public relations and public affairs firm that provides counsel to a wide range of industries including retail, real estate technology, banking, and health care. Established in 1962. Number of employees: 27. Division of Hill & Knowlton. Number of internship applications received each year: 80.
Internships Available ▶ *1 public relations intern:* responsibilities include working directly with account executives on various public relations and public affairs projects. Candidates should have ability to work with others, knowledge of field, oral communication skills, organizational skills, self-motivation, writing skills. Duration is 10–12 weeks. $8 per hour. Open to college juniors, college seniors, recent college graduates.
Benefits On-the-job training, opportunity to attend seminars/workshops, possible full-time employment, travel reimbursement,

willing to act as a professional reference, willing to complete paperwork for educational credit, willing to provide letters of recommendation.
Contact Write, call, or e-mail Katy Strausborger, Internship Coordinator. Phone: 206-728-1100. E-mail: kstrausborger@rockey-seattle.com. In-person interview required. Applicants must submit a letter of interest, resume, two writing samples. Applications are accepted continuously. World Wide Web: http://www.rockey-seattle.com.

ROSEN GROUP
30 West 26th Street
New York, New York 10010

General Information Public relations firm specializing in media, publishing, and liquor promotions. Established in 1984. Number of employees: 10. Number of internship applications received each year: 50.
Internships Available ▶ *2 office interns:* responsibilities include writing, copying, and performing phone work and research. Candidates should have ability to work with others, oral communication skills, personal interest in the field, plan to pursue career in field, writing skills. Duration is 1 semester. $6–$7 per hour. Open to college juniors, college seniors, recent college graduates.
Benefits On-the-job training, possible full-time employment, willing to complete paperwork for educational credit, willing to provide letters of recommendation.
Contact Write, call, or e-mail Ms. Lori Rosen, President. Phone: 212-255-8455. E-mail: lori@rosengrouppr.com. In-person interview required. Applicants must submit a letter of interest, resume. Applications are accepted continuously. World Wide Web: http://www.rosengrouppr.com.

SALLY FISCHER PUBLIC RELATIONS
330 West 58th Street, Suite 509
New York, New York 10019

General Information Small public relations firm specializing in the areas of design, fashion, food, publishing, and entertainment. Established in 1989. Number of employees: 10. Number of internship applications received each year: 75.
Internships Available ▶ *3–4 interns:* responsibilities include direct involvement in all aspects of public relations, including special events, media relations, client relations, and writing. Candidates should have editing skills, oral communication skills, personal interest in the field, research skills, strong interpersonal skills, writing skills. Duration is flexible. Unpaid. Open to high school seniors, college freshmen, college sophomores, college juniors, college seniors, recent college graduates, graduate students, career changers, individuals reentering the workforce. ▶ *2–4 junior publicist trainees:* responsibilities include direct hands-on experience, working with clients as well as a team with employees, planning strategies, writing press releases, contacting the media. Candidates should have editing skills, oral communication skills, personal interest in the field, plan to pursue career in field, research skills, writing skills. Duration is flexible. Unpaid. Open to high school seniors, recent high school graduates, college freshmen, college sophomores, college juniors, college seniors, recent college graduates, career changers, individuals reentering the workforce. International applications accepted.
Benefits Names of contacts, possible full-time employment, travel reimbursement, willing to act as a professional reference, willing to complete paperwork for educational credit, willing to provide letters of recommendation.
Contact Write, call, fax, or e-mail Susanna Forde, Assistant to President/Intern Coordinator. Phone: 212-246-2977. Fax: 212-246-8116. E-mail: susannah@sallyfischerpr.com. In-person interview recommended (telephone interview accepted). Applicants must submit a letter of interest, resume. Application deadline: January 1 for spring, May 1 for summer. World Wide Web: http://www.sallyfpr.com.

SHIRLEY HERZ ASSOCIATES
165 West 46th Street, Suite 910
New York, New York 10036

General Information Public relations firm for Broadway and off-Broadway shows, projects, and institutions. Established in 1972. Number of employees: 5. Number of internship applications received each year: 200.

Internships Available ▶ *3–5 interns:* responsibilities include aiding five press agents, answering phones, and writing press releases. Candidates should have ability to work independently, ability to work with others, computer skills, editing skills, office skills, oral communication skills, organizational skills, research skills, self-motivation, writing skills. Duration is 1 semester. Unpaid. Open to college freshmen, college sophomores, college juniors, college seniors. International applications accepted.

Benefits Formal training, possible full-time employment, willing to complete paperwork for educational credit, willing to provide letters of recommendation.

Contact Write, call, or fax James Shubert, Intern Coordinator. Phone: 212-221-8466. Fax: 212-921-8023. In-person interview required. Applicants must submit a letter of interest, resume. Applications are accepted continuously.

SILVERMAN MEDIA & MARKETING GROUP, INC.
Woodbury, New York

General Information Media and marketing company specializing in public relations, integrated marketing, special event creation and management, celebrity representation, and Internet communications; focuses on sports, entertainment, nonprofit, travel, special events, TV shows, home video, automotive, and new product publicity and promotion. Established in 1984. Number of employees: 6. Number of internship applications received each year: 200.

Internships Available ▶ *1–3 public relations/special events assistants:* responsibilities include assisting with media research and contact, phone work, event and account coordination, writing of press releases, and general office duties. Candidates should have office skills, oral communication skills, plan to pursue career in field, self-motivation, strong interpersonal skills, written communication skills. Duration is 3–4 months. Unpaid. Open to college freshmen, college sophomores, college juniors, college seniors, recent college graduates, graduate students, law students, career changers, individuals reentering the workforce.

Benefits Job counseling, names of contacts, on-the-job training, possible full-time employment, willing to act as a professional reference, willing to complete paperwork for educational credit, willing to provide letters of recommendation, $15 per day travel reimbursement.

Contact Write, call, fax, or e-mail Morgan Futch, Assistant to the President. Phone: 212-686-5983. Fax: 212-686-8742. E-mail: smmg4hits@aol.com. In-person interview required. Applicants must submit a letter of interest, resume, photo at time of interview to attach to resume, proof of lodging in the Long Island area prior to interview. Applications are accepted continuously. World Wide Web: http://www.silvermanmedia.com.

SMITHSONIAN OFFICE OF PUBLIC AFFAIRS
1000 Jefferson Drive, SW, Room 354
Washington, District of Columbia 20560-0033

General Information Office of the Smithsonian that informs the public and staff through publications and media relations about exhibitions, programs, and research activities. Number of employees: 16. Unit of Smithsonian Institution, Washington, District of Columbia.

Internships Available ▶ *Media relations interns:* responsibilities include updating mailing lists of journalists, newspapers, and magazines; organizing materials and filling information kits for journalists; and writing news releases and other informational materials. Duration is flexible. Unpaid. ▶ *Publications interns:* responsibilities include writing features, news stories, and column items. Candidates should have research skills, writing skills, interviewing skills. Duration is flexible. Unpaid. Open to high school students, college freshmen, college sophomores, college juniors, college seniors, recent college graduates, graduate students. International applications accepted.

Benefits Willing to act as a professional reference, willing to complete paperwork for educational credit.

Contact Write, call, or fax Bill Holmes, Administrative Officer, 1000 Jefferson Drive, SW Room 354, Washington, District of Columbia 20560-0033. Phone: 202-357-2627. Fax: 202-357-3346. Applicants must submit a formal organization application, academic transcripts, personal reference, essay, by-lined writing samples for publications positions. Applications are accepted continuously. World Wide Web: http://www.si.edu.

TERRIE WILLIAMS AGENCY
1500 Broadway, Suite 502
New York, New York 10036

General Information Full-service firm that specializes in public relations, media relations, and special event planning for entertainment, sports, political, and corporate figures and conglomerates in the United States and abroad. Established in 1988. Number of employees: 5. Number of internship applications received each year: 200.

Internships Available ▶ *1–3 public relations interns:* responsibilities include writing and researching for newsletters and press releases, developing press kits, and assisting with campaigns. Candidates should have ability to work independently, ability to work with others, analytical skills, computer skills, editing skills, knowledge of field, office skills, oral communication skills, organizational skills, research skills, self-motivation, writing skills. Duration is 12 weeks. Unpaid. Open to college freshmen, college sophomores, college juniors, college seniors, recent college graduates, graduate students, law students, career changers, individuals reentering the workforce. International applications accepted.

Benefits Job counseling, names of contacts, on-the-job training, possible full-time employment, travel reimbursement, willing to act as a professional reference, willing to complete paperwork for educational credit, willing to provide letters of recommendation.

Contact Write, fax, or e-mail Terrie Williams, President. Phone: 212-220-4333 Ext. 225. Fax: 212-220-4299. E-mail: tmwms@terriewilliams.com. In-person interview recommended (telephone interview accepted). Applicants must submit a letter of interest, resume, two personal references, 2-3 writing samples. Applications are accepted continuously.

UNIVERSITY DIRECTORIES
PO Box 8830
Chapel Hill, North Carolina 27515

General Information Publisher of campus telephone directories. Established in 1974. Number of employees: 30. Unit of The Village Companies, Chapel Hill, North Carolina. Number of internship applications received each year: 1,100.

Internships Available ▶ *350 sales interns.* Candidates should have ability to work independently, oral communication skills, self-motivation, strong interpersonal skills, strong leadership ability. Duration is 10 weeks. Commission. Open to college freshmen, college sophomores, college juniors, college seniors, recent college graduates, graduate students. International applications accepted.

Benefits Formal training, job counseling, names of contacts, opportunity to attend seminars/workshops, possible full-time employment, willing to complete paperwork for educational credit, willing to provide letters of recommendation.

Contact Write, call, fax, e-mail, or through World Wide Web site Yvonne Knutson, National Recruiting Manager. Phone: 800-743-5556 Ext. 143. Fax: 919-968-8513. E-mail: yknutson@vilcom.com. In-person interview recommended (telephone interview accepted). Applicants must submit a letter of interest, resume. Application deadline: April 15 for summer. World Wide Web: http://www.universitydirectories.com.

WEBER SHANDWICK
640 5th Avenue
New York, New York 10019

General Information   Full-service communications agency. Established in 1980. Number of employees: 250. Division of InterPublic Group, New York, New York. Number of internship applications received each year: 500.
Internships Available   ▶ *6–10 public relations interns:* responsibilities include writing, researching, and performing media relations activities. Candidates should have ability to work independently, ability to work with others, plan to pursue career in field, research skills, self-motivation, written communication skills. Duration is 10 weeks. $10 and up per hour. Open to college juniors, college seniors, recent college graduates, graduate students. International applications accepted.
Benefits Job counseling, names of contacts, on-the-job training, opportunity to attend seminars/workshops, possible full-time employment, willing to act as a professional reference, willing to complete paperwork for educational credit, willing to provide letters of recommendation.
Contact Write, fax, or e-mail Kate Ophals, Assistant Human Resources Manager. Fax: 212-445-8095. E-mail: kophals@ webershandwick.com. No phone calls. In-person interview recommended (telephone interview accepted). Applicants must submit a letter of interest, resume, writing sample. Application deadline: March 31 for summer. World Wide Web: http://www. webershandwick.com.

WEBER SHANDWICK
676 North St. Clair, Suite 1000
Chicago, Illinois 60611-3110

General Information   Consumer public relations firm. Number of employees: 120. Subsidiary of Weber Shandwick Worldwide, Minneapolis, Minnesota. Number of internship applications received each year: 500.
Internships Available   ▶ *14–18 interns:* responsibilities include working on 2-3 accounts, compiling media lists, pitching, market research, vendor coordination, writing, editing, and daily clip reports. Candidates should have oral communication skills, plan to pursue career in field, strong interpersonal skills, written communication skills, major in journalism, communications, public relations, or related fields. Duration is 3 months. Paid. Open to college juniors, college seniors, recent college graduates, graduate students, career changers. International applications accepted.
Benefits Names of contacts, on-the-job training, possible full-time employment, willing to act as a professional reference, willing to complete paperwork for educational credit, willing to provide letters of recommendation.
Contact E-mail Intern Coordinator, 676 North St. Clair, Suite 1000, Chicago, Illinois 60611-3110. E-mail: internships@ webershandwick.com. No phone calls. In-person interview required. Applicants must submit a letter of interest, resume, test for writing and proofreading skills. Applications are accepted continuously. World Wide Web: http://www.webershandwick.com.

WIDMEYER COMMUNICATIONS
1825 Connecticut Avenue, NW, Fifth Floor
Washington, District of Columbia 20009

General Information   Public relations firm. Established in 1987. Number of employees: 70. Number of internship applications received each year: 150.
Internships Available   ▶ *1–3 fellows.* Candidates should have oral communication skills, self-motivation, strong interpersonal skills, writing skills. Duration is September to December, January to May, and June to August. $10 per hour. Open to recent college graduates. International applications accepted.
Benefits Health insurance.
Contact Write or e-mail Laura Hamra, Human Resources. Phone: 202-667-0901. Fax: 202-667-0902. E-mail: jobs@widmeyer.com. Applicants must submit a letter of interest, resume, two writing samples. Application deadline: April 15 for summer fellows, August 1 for fall fellows, December 1 for winter fellows. World Wide Web: http://www.widmeyer.com.

ARCHITECTURAL, ENGINEERING, AND DESIGN SERVICES

AMERICAN & INTERNATIONAL DESIGNS, INC.
900 South Avenue
Staten Island, New York 10314

General Information   Interior design firm that specializes in restaurant, health-care, medical, corporate facilities and the luxury home market. Established in 1980. Number of employees: 5. Number of internship applications received each year: 400.
Internships Available   ▶ *3–4 CAD operator/3/0 modeling operators:* responsibilities include developing space plans; drawing floor plans, furniture plans, tile plans, window elevations, and general drafting and plotting. Candidates should have college courses in field, computer skills, experience in the field, organizational skills, plan to pursue career in field. Duration is 8–10 weeks. Unpaid. Open to college juniors, college seniors, recent college graduates, graduate students. ▶ *2–4 administrative interns:* responsibilities include working directly with the administrator, assisting in minutes of meetings, project management, and expediting and tracking interior design projects. Candidates should have ability to work independently, computer skills, office skills, oral communication skills, organizational skills, written communication skills. Unpaid. Open to high school seniors, recent high school graduates. ▶ *1 advertising assistant:* responsibilities include preparing and coordinating media kits for distribution on TV Magazine Books; editorials of current interior design projects. Candidates should have computer skills, declared college major in field, experience in the field, knowledge of field, personal interest in the field, writing skills. Duration is 3–8 weeks. Unpaid. Open to college juniors, college seniors, recent college graduates, graduate students. ▶ *2 bookkeeper/accounting assistants:* responsibilities include assisting in maintaining financial books for 3 divisions, preparing budgets, and keeping intern time sheets. Candidates should have ability to work independently, college courses in field, experience in the field, office skills, organizational skills, plan to pursue career in field. Duration is 6–10 weeks. Unpaid. Open to college sophomores, college juniors, college seniors, recent college graduates, graduate students. ▶ *2 computer and technical information interns:* responsibilities include researching new products, assisting in training on new software, installing updates, reviewing all equipment and new contracts, maintaining supplies, and Web site development. Candidates should have ability to work with others, experience in the field, office skills, plan to pursue career in field, research skills. Duration is 8–10 weeks. Unpaid. Open to college juniors, college seniors, recent college graduates, graduate students. ▶ *3 graphic design interns:* responsibilities include designing graphics for collateral materials, brochures, inserts, press kits, tear sheets, Web site, mailings, and presentations. Candidates should have ability to work independently, computer skills, experience in the field, organizational skills, plan to pursue career in field, research skills, writing skills. Duration is 8–12 weeks. Unpaid. Open to college sophomores, college juniors, college seniors, recent college graduates, graduate students, individuals reentering the workforce. ▶ *5–10 junior interior designer interns:* responsibilities include working with design team to develop and administrate interior design projects. Candidates should have college courses in field, computer skills, office skills, organizational skills, plan to pursue career in field, 3D skills, auto CAD, rendering drafting skills. Duration is 6–8 weeks. Unpaid. Open to college juniors, college seniors, recent college graduates, graduate students. ▶ *2 librarian interns:* responsibilities include maintaining product libraries, updating all literature, coordinating samples, distributing information to all in-house staff, updating presentation boards, and maintaining photo library. Candidates should have ability to work independently, computer skills, office skills, organizational skills, self-motivation, strong interpersonal skills. Duration is 6 weeks. Unpaid. Open to high school seniors, recent high school graduates, college freshmen, college sophomores, col-

American & International Designs, Inc. (continued)

lege juniors, college seniors, recent college graduates. ▶ *2–4 marketing information interns:* responsibilities include launching new design trends and services for the hospitality industries, organizing and developing press kits, attending trade shows and local seminars, coordinating and purchasing mailing lists, assisting in the development of collateral material for information requests. Candidates should have ability to work independently, college courses in field, computer skills, oral communication skills, plan to pursue career in field, strong interpersonal skills. Duration is 8–10 weeks. Unpaid. Open to college juniors, college seniors, recent college graduates, graduate students. ▶ *2 personnel assistants:* responsibilities include maintaining and updating procedures manual, reviewing general procedures with staff, reviewing time sheets, developing daily schedules, preparing letters of recommendation, assisting in job placements, and working with principles. Candidates should have computer skills, office skills, oral communication skills, research skills, strong interpersonal skills, strong leadership ability. Duration is 8–10 weeks. Unpaid. Open to recent high school graduates, college freshmen, college juniors, college seniors. ▶ *4 photographer interns:* responsibilities include photographing projects in progress in several mediums; digital black and white for marketing media; press shots; Web site publication. Candidates should have ability to work independently, analytical skills, college courses in field, computer skills, editing skills, experience in the field, plan to pursue career in field. Duration is 3–12 weeks. Unpaid. Open to college sophomores, college seniors, recent college graduates, graduate students. ▶ *4 public relations interns:* responsibilities include organizing and developing case studies of recent completed jobs, writing public relations news about company and products, vendor public relations, and attending and promoting grand openings. Candidates should have ability to work independently, computer skills, oral communication skills, plan to pursue career in field, research skills, written communication skills. Duration is 6–8 weeks. Unpaid. Open to college juniors, college seniors, recent college graduates, graduate students.

Benefits Formal training, free meals, job counseling, on-the-job training, opportunity to attend seminars/workshops, possible full-time employment, travel reimbursement, willing to act as a professional reference, willing to complete paperwork for educational credit, willing to provide letters of recommendation.

Contact Write, fax, or through World Wide Web site Alex Reyes, Internship Coordinator. Fax: 718-568-3585. E-mail: susan_harann@ aol.com. No phone calls. In-person interview recommended (telephone interview accepted). Applicants must submit a formal organization application, resume, personal reference, portfolio (occasionally). Application deadline: January 30 for spring, May 1 for summer, July 15 for fall, September 15 for winter. World Wide Web: http://www.designamericanyc.com.

AMERICAN STANDARDS TESTING BUREAU, INC.
40 Water Street
New York, New York 10004

General Information Technical and management consulting firm. Established in 1916. Number of employees: 900. Number of internship applications received each year: 1,000.

Internships Available ▶ *3–6 interns:* responsibilities include performing duties consistent with intern's interests and skills. Candidates should have computer skills, organizational skills, self-motivation, strong interpersonal skills, writing skills, declared college major in project accounting, international business, or engineering (particularly welcome). Duration is 1 semester. Position available as unpaid or paid. Open to college juniors, college seniors, recent college graduates, graduate students, law students, career changers, individuals reentering the workforce. ▶ *6–10 management or marketing trainees.* Candidates should have oral communication skills, organizational skills, plan to pursue career in field, research skills, strong interpersonal skills, written communication skills. Duration is 6–12 months. Position available as unpaid or paid. Open to college seniors, recent college graduates, graduate students, law students, career changers, individuals reentering the workforce. International applications accepted.

Benefits Health insurance, possible full-time employment, willing to complete paperwork for educational credit, willing to provide letters of recommendation.

International Internships Available in Brazil; Greece; Republic of Korea; Russian Federation; Spain.

Contact Write, fax, or e-mail Dr. John Zimmerman, Director of Professional Staffing, PO Box 583, New York, New York 10274. Fax: 212-825-2250. E-mail: worldteck@aol.com. No phone calls. In-person interview required. Applicants must submit a formal organization application, resume, three personal references, letter of recommendation. Applications are accepted continuously.

APPLIED RECYCLING INC./INTERMED
162 Washington Street
Belmont, Massachusetts 02478

General Information Engineering and technology company that remanufactures recyclables arising from the factory floors or the waste stream. Established in 1996. Number of employees: 11.

Internships Available ▶ *3–5 analysts:* responsibilities include entry-level duties to learn skills required to work in various operating areas of the company's business. Candidates should have ability to work independently, analytical skills, college courses in field, computer skills, knowledge of field, oral communication skills, personal interest in the field, research skills, self-motivation, strong interpersonal skills, writing skills. Duration is 1 year. $30,000–$50,000 per year. Open to recent college graduates, graduate students. ▶ *8 analysts/technical specialists:* responsibilities include analysis of medical statistics, chronic disease management, and mathematical modeling. Candidates should have analytical skills, computer skills, research skills, written communication skills. Duration is 1 year. $40,000–$60,000 per year. Open to graduate students or recent graduates with major in mathematics, statistics, physics, chemistry, or computer science. International applications accepted.

Benefits Health insurance, possible full-time employment, willing to act as a professional reference, willing to provide letters of recommendation.

International Internships Available in Portugal; Russian Federation.

Contact Write, call, or e-mail Dr. Richard Rosen, CEO, 162 Washington Street, Belmont, Massachusetts 02478. Phone: 781-863-2800. Fax: 781-674-9997. E-mail: richardapplied@netscape. net. In-person interview required. Applicants must submit a letter of interest, resume, academic transcripts, 2 personal references and/or letters of recommendation. Applications are accepted continuously.

BAE SYSTEMS/INFORMATION AND ELECTRONIC WARFARE SECTOR
95 Canal Street, PO Box 2029
Nashua, New Hampshire 03061-2029

General Information Designer and developer of advanced defense electronics. Established in 1951. Number of employees: 4,500.

Internships Available ▶ *Co-ops:* responsibilities include performing various tasks to meet the needs of the organization; positions available in missile/weapon systems development, software engineering, programming, Web development, database/applications development, communications engineering, and circuit analysis. Duration is 4-6 months; generally 1 semester (full-time); may include summer or winter break and return on an alternating semester basis. Position available as unpaid or paid. ▶ *Interns:* responsibilities include performing various tasks to meet the needs of the organization; positions available in missile/weapon systems development, software engineering, programming, Web development, database/applications development, communications engineering, and circuit analysis. Duration is summer or winter break (full-time). Position available as unpaid or paid. Candidates for all positions should have ability to work with others, computer skills, oral communication skills, written communication skills, major in computer science, electrical engineering, computer engineering, electronics, information systems, and finance. Open to college juniors, college seniors.

Benefits Partial benefits for co-ops.

Contact Through World Wide Web site Internship Coordinator. Applications are accepted continuously. World Wide Web: http://www.na.baesystems.com.

BURNS AND MCDONNELL
9400 Ward Parkway
Kansas City, Missouri 64114

General Information Consulting firm for engineering, architectural, and environmental projects. Established in 1898. Number of employees: 1,500. Number of internship applications received each year: 50.
Internships Available ▶ *1–3 architectural interns:* responsibilities include assisting architects on different projects. Duration is 1 summer. Paid. ▶ *3–5 civil engineering interns:* responsibilities include assisting senior engineers with projects. Duration is 1 summer. Paid. ▶ *3–5 electrical engineering interns:* responsibilities include assisting senior electrical engineers with lighting, electrical instruments and control, and a variety of other duties. Duration is 1 summer. Paid. ▶ *1–3 environmental engineer interns:* responsibilities include assisting senior engineer with waste management and water and air pollution control projects. Duration is 1 summer. Paid. ▶ *3–5 mechanical engineering interns:* responsibilities include assisting senior mechanical engineers with projects. Duration is 1 summer. Paid. Candidates for all positions should have computer skills, oral communication skills, organizational skills, plan to pursue career in field, strong interpersonal skills, written communication skills. Open to college freshmen, college sophomores, college juniors, college seniors. International applications accepted.
Benefits Job counseling, names of contacts, on-the-job training, opportunity to attend seminars/workshops, possible full-time employment, travel reimbursement, willing to complete paperwork for educational credit, willing to provide letters of recommendation.
Contact Write, call, fax, e-mail, or through World Wide Web site Melissa Lavin, College Recruiter. Phone: 816-822-3441. Fax: 816-822-3516. E-mail: mlavin@burnsmcd.com. Applicants must submit a resume, academic transcripts. Applications are accepted continuously. World Wide Web: http://www.burnsmcd.com.

COSANTI FOUNDATION-ARCOSANTI WORKSHOP
HC 74, Box 4136
Mayer, Arizona 86333

General Information Nonprofit, public educational foundation devoted to the support of Paolo Soleri's architectural and urban planning research, called "Arcology". Established in 1965. Number of employees: 70. Number of internship applications received each year: 135.
Internships Available ▶ *1–6 Arcosanti woodworking interns:* responsibilities include fabrication of cabinetry and furniture, assisting in ongoing construction of prototype arcology, and leading new workshop participants in daily projects. Candidates should have ability to work independently, personal interest in the field, self-motivation, strong interpersonal skills, mathematical aptitude. Duration is 3–6 months. Unpaid. Open to individuals over 18 years. ▶ *1–7 agriculture/landscaping interns:* responsibilities include application of organic gardening and landscaping and permaculture on a 25.5-acre site, leading new workshop participants in daily activities, and site assessment and design. Candidates should have ability to work independently, ability to work with others, oral communication skills, personal interest in the field, self-motivation, strong leadership ability. Duration is 1–6 months. Unpaid. Open to individuals over 18 years. ▶ *1–3 archivist/network assistants:* responsibilities include photography, photographic and data preservation, and audio/visual presentations. Candidates should have ability to work independently, analytical skills, editing skills, office skills, oral communication skills, organizational skills, personal interest in the field, research skills, self-motivation, strong interpersonal skills, writing skills, willingness to learn; use of MAC/PC platforms and related software. Duration is flexible. Unpaid. Open to college juniors, college seniors, recent college graduates, graduate students, law students, career changers. ▶ *1–6 construction crew leaders/interns:* responsibilities include assisting in all phases of construction of prototype arcology and leading a small construction crew of workshop participants in designing/building the on-site operation. Candidates should have ability to

work with others, experience in the field, oral communication skills, organizational skills, self-motivation, strong leadership ability. Duration is 3–6 months. Unpaid. Open to individuals over 18 years. ▶ *Planning department interns:* responsibilities include drafting of structural and architectural details both on paper and computer, some designing/building, and working in a small designing/building office. Candidates should have ability to work with others, computer skills, oral communication skills, self-motivation, written communication skills, drafting experience. Duration is 3–6 months. Unpaid. Open to individuals over 18 years. ▶ *1–30 workshop participants:* responsibilities include helping in the construction of Arcosanti, a prototype for an energy-efficient town combining architectural and ecological concepts. Candidates should have ability to work independently, oral communication skills, organizational skills, personal interest in the field, self-motivation, strong interpersonal skills, strong leadership ability. Duration is 1–5 weeks. Unpaid. Open to individuals over 18 years. International applications accepted.
Benefits Formal training, names of contacts, on-the-job training, opportunity to attend seminars/workshops, possible full-time employment, willing to complete paperwork for educational credit, willing to provide letters of recommendation, partial stipend for meals; possibility of free housing or housing at cost.
Contact Write, call, fax, e-mail, or through World Wide Web site William W. R. Ozier, Workshop Coordinator. Phone: 520-632-7135. Fax: 520-632-6229. E-mail: workshop@arcosanti.ws. Applicants must submit a formal organization application, letter of interest, resume, three personal references, $950 for 5-week workshop before internship begins. Application deadline: 2 weeks before workshop or 5 weeks before internship. Fees: $50. World Wide Web: http://www.arcosanti.org.

ENGINEERING MINISTRIES INTERNATIONAL
110 South Weber, Suite 104
Colorado Springs, Colorado 80903

General Information Provider of free engineering and architecture services to missionaries in developing countries; nonprofit Christian ministry whose mission is to involve design professionals in missions. Established in 1981. Number of employees: 22. Number of internship applications received each year: 60.
Internships Available ▶ *4–6 architectural missionary interns:* responsibilities include a 2-week missions trip for conceptual design of a ministry facility; office duties such as programming master plans and construction documents; raising support to cover intern's expenses. Candidates should have ability to work with others, declared college major in field. Duration is 3–8 months. Unpaid. ▶ *4–8 architectural overseas missionary interns:* responsibilities include designing and drawing missionary facilities in India or Guatemala; design, AutoCad, and travel; raising support to cover intern's expenses. Candidates should have ability to work with others, computer skills, declared college major in field. Duration is 3–6 months. Unpaid. ▶ *5–6 civil engineering missionary interns:* responsibilities include a 2-week missions trip/site visit to a developing country; helping a missionary by designing a water, wastewater, or drainage system or road; raising support to cover intern's expenses. Candidates should have ability to work with others, declared college major in field. Duration is 3–8 months. Unpaid. ▶ *4–12 construction management missionary interns:* responsibilities include overseeing construction of a needed ministry facility in India or Guatemala for a missionary; budgeting, scheduling, conflict resolution, managing both work teams and nationals; intern must raise own support. Candidates should have ability to work with others, declared college major in field. Duration is 3–12 months. Unpaid. ▶ *6–10 engineering overseas missionary interns:* responsibilities include designing needed facilities for missionaries in India or Guatemala; structural or water resources engineering design; raising support to cover intern's expenses. Candidates should have ability to work independently, ability to work with others, declared college major in field. Duration is 3–6 months. Unpaid. ▶ *1 network administrator/web master intern:* responsibilities include network administration for a 25-computer network running Windows NT small business server; Web page design and updating; raising support to cover intern's expenses. Candidates should have ability to work independently, college courses in field,

Engineering Ministries International (continued)

computer skills, knowledge of field, self-motivation. Duration is 3–8 months. Unpaid. ▶ *4–6 structural engineering missionary interns:* responsibilities include a 2-week missions trip/site visit to conceptually design a ministry facility; office duties such as structural design of small buildings and drawing construction documents; raising support to cover intern's expenses. Candidates should have ability to work with others, declared college major in field. Duration is 3–8 months. Unpaid. ▶ *2–4 surveying missionary interns (overseas):* responsibilities include surveying property for missionary facilities in India or Guatemala; AutoCad, and raising support to cover intern's expenses. Candidates should have ability to work with others, declared college major in field. Duration is 3–8 months. Unpaid. Open to college juniors, college seniors, recent college graduates, graduate students, career changers, individuals reentering the workforce. International applications accepted.
Benefits Housing at a cost, job counseling, names of contacts, on-the-job training, opportunity to attend seminars/workshops, willing to act as a professional reference, willing to complete paperwork for educational credit, willing to provide letters of recommendation, international travel, mentoring.
International Internships Available in Guatemala City, Guatemala; Mussoorie, India.
Contact Write, call, e-mail, or through World Wide Web site Christy Taylor, Intern Director. Phone: 719-633-2078. Fax: 719-633-2970. E-mail: intern@emiusa.org. Telephone interview required. Applicants must submit a formal organization application, letter of interest, resume, written Christian testimony. Application deadline: February 15 for summer, May 20 for fall, September 15 for spring. World Wide Web: http://www.emiusa.org.

GENSLER
One Rockefeller Plaza, Suite 500
New York, New York 10020

General Information Architecture and design firm offering a full range of services including strategic consulting, master planning, and program management.
Internships Available ▶ *Summer or school-year interns:* responsibilities include positions available in 24 global offices; see Web site for details.
Contact Through World Wide Web site Internship Coordinator. Applicants must submit a resume, cover letter; (do not include portfolio or work samples). Application deadline: between March 1 and April 30 for summer; continuous for school year positions. World Wide Web: http://www.gensler.com.

GME CONSULTANTS
14000 21st Avenue North
Minneapolis, Minnesota 55447

General Information Geotechnical materials and environmental engineering consulting firm. Established in 1981. Number of employees: 85. Number of internship applications received each year: 10.
Internships Available ▶ *4–6 field services technicians:* responsibilities include working with civil engineering technicians. Candidates should have ability to work independently, knowledge of field, personal interest in the field, self-motivation, strong interpersonal skills, writing skills. Duration is 4–6 months. $11–$12 per hour. Open to college freshmen, college sophomores, college juniors, college seniors, recent college graduates, graduate students, individuals reentering the workforce. International applications accepted.
Benefits Formal training, on-the-job training, opportunity to attend seminars/workshops, possible full-time employment, willing to act as a professional reference, willing to complete paperwork for educational credit, willing to provide letters of recommendation.
Contact Write, fax, or e-mail Tammy Hakanson, Field Services Manager, 14000 21st Avenue North, Minneapolis, Minnesota 55447. Fax: 763-559-0720. E-mail: thakanson@gmeconsultants. com. No phone calls. In-person interview recommended (telephone interview accepted). Applicants must submit a resume. Applications are accepted continuously. World Wide Web: http://www. gmeconsultants.com.

HARLEYELLIS
26913 Northwestern Highway, Suite 200
Southfield, Michigan 48034-3476

General Information Full-service, planning, architecture, engineering, management, and interiors firm that serves corporate, university, health care, science and research, automotive, and industrial clients throughout the Midwest. Established in 1909. Number of employees: 300. Number of internship applications received each year: 150.
Internships Available ▶ *1–2 architecture co-ops:* responsibilities include opportunity to gain exposure and familiarity with basic construction materials and methods through CADD, training, and field observation and opportunities. Candidates should have ability to work with others, analytical skills, computer skills, declared college major in field, oral communication skills, plan to pursue career in field. Duration is 3 months (minimum). $11–$14 per hour. ▶ *1–2 civil engineer co-ops:* responsibilities include assisting in designing site layouts, grading and utilities including storm and sanitary sewers and watermains, CADD drafting and field measuring. Candidates should have ability to work with others, analytical skills, computer skills, declared college major in field, oral communication skills, personal interest in the field. Duration is 3 months (minimum). $11–$15 per hour. ▶ *1–2 electrical engineer co-ops:* responsibilities include assisting engineers in field data collection, calculations, code research, and other design engineering tasks; preparing CAD generated documents. Candidates should have ability to work with others, analytical skills, computer skills, declared college major in field, oral communication skills, personal interest in the field. Duration is 3 months (minimum). $11–$15 per hour. ▶ *2 facilities management co-ops:* responsibilities include performing basic CAD/CAFM design applications (AutoCAD), assisting in preparing limited calculations (e.g. building areas, space/department allocations), and gathering dimensionally accurate on-site data for CAD applications. Candidates should have ability to work with others, computer skills, oral communication skills, self-motivation, declared college major in architecture, interior architecture, facilities management, or interior design. Duration is 3 months (minimum). $11–$15 per hour. ▶ *2 mechanical engineer co-ops:* responsibilities include developing basic understanding of building design as it relates to mechanical engineering, performing limited mechanical engineering design calculations, developing familiarity with engineering drawings and specifications, CADD, and field measurement. Candidates should have ability to work with others, analytical skills, computer skills, declared college major in field, oral communication skills, personal interest in the field. Duration is 3 months (minimum). $11–$15 per hour. ▶ *1–2 structural engineer co-ops:* responsibilities include assisting in preparation of project structural analysis and design, construction documents (CAD generated), and project written documentation; assisting in gathering on-site data and developing an understanding of the design process. Candidates should have ability to work with others, analytical skills, computer skills, declared college major in field, oral communication skills, personal interest in the field. Duration is 3 months (minimum). $11–$15 per hour. Open to college juniors, college seniors.
Benefits On-the-job training, opportunity to attend seminars/workshops, possible full-time employment, willing to act as a professional reference, willing to complete paperwork for educational credit, willing to provide letters of recommendation, flextime work schedule.
Contact Write, fax, e-mail, or through World Wide Web site Carolyn C. Palmer, Principal. Fax: 248-262-1552. E-mail: ccpalmer@harleyellis.com. In-person interview recommended (telephone interview accepted). Applicants must submit a letter of interest, resume, academic transcripts. Applications are accepted continuously. World Wide Web: http://www.harleyellis.com.

PROGRAM FOR WOMEN IN SCIENCE AND ENGINEERING
Iowa State University, 210 Lab of Mechanics
Ames, Iowa 50011-2131

General Information Program working to increase the number of women in science and engineering. Established in 1986. Number of employees: 5. Unit of Iowa State University of Science and Technology, Ames, Iowa. Number of internship applications received each year: 140.

Internships Available ▶ *20–40 high school interns:* responsibilities include working on an independent research project under the supervision of science or engineering faculty or staff. Candidates should have ability to work with others, analytical skills, oral communication skills, personal interest in the field, plan to pursue career in field, self-motivation, written communication skills. Duration is 6 weeks. $1500 per duration of internship. Open to individuals between junior and senior year in high school. ▶ *30–45 undergraduate interns:* responsibilities include working on an independent research project under the supervision of science or engineering faculty or staff. Candidates should have ability to work with others, analytical skills, college courses in field, knowledge of field, oral communication skills, organizational skills, personal interest in the field, plan to pursue career in field, self-motivation, written communication skills. Duration is 8 weeks. $3000 per duration of internship. Open to college freshmen, college sophomores, college juniors. International applications accepted.

Benefits Housing at a cost, meals at a cost, opportunity to attend seminars/workshops, willing to provide letters of recommendation, opportunity to be part of state-of-the-art scientific research.

Contact Write, call, fax, e-mail, or through World Wide Web site Karen Zunkel, Director. Phone: 515-294-0966. Fax: 515-294-8627. E-mail: pwse@iastate.edu. Applicants must submit a formal organization application, academic transcripts, writing sample, two personal references, two letters of recommendation. Application deadline: February 1 for summer. World Wide Web: http://www.iastate.edu/~pwse_info/.

SHIVE-HATTERY, INC.
115 3rd Street, SE, 9th Floor
Cedar Rapids, Iowa 52401

General Information Engineering and architectural consulting firm. Established in 1962. Unit of Shive-Hattery, Inc., Cedar Rapids, Iowa. Number of internship applications received each year: 20.

Internships Available ▶ *5–10 architect interns:* responsibilities include working under the guidance of a registered professional architect to learn the intricacies of architecture from concept through construction. Candidates should have ability to work independently, ability to work with others, analytical skills, college courses in field, computer skills, knowledge of field, oral communication skills, organizational skills, personal interest in the field, plan to pursue career in field, research skills, self-motivation, strong leadership ability, writing skills. Duration is flexible. Salary dependent on level of education and experience. Open to college sophomores, college juniors, college seniors, recent college graduates. ▶ *5–10 engineering interns:* responsibilities include working under the guidance of a registered professional engineer. Candidates should have ability to work independently, ability to work with others, analytical skills, college courses in field, computer skills, experience in the field, knowledge of field, oral communication skills, organizational skills, personal interest in the field, plan to pursue career in field, research skills, self-motivation, strong leadership ability, writing skills. Duration is flexible. Salary dependent on level of education and experience. Open to college sophomores, college juniors, college seniors, recent college graduates, individuals reentering the workforce. ▶ *5–10 landscape architect interns:* responsibilities include working in any of the following engineering areas: civil, mechanical, electrical, or architectural; duties may include land survey, CAD design, or going to actual job sites. Candidates should have ability to work independently, analytical skills, college courses in field, computer skills, editing skills, knowledge of field, oral communica-

tion skills, organizational skills, personal interest in the field, plan to pursue career in field, research skills, self-motivation, strong leadership ability, writing skills. Duration is flexible. Salary dependent on level of education and experience. Open to college sophomores, college juniors, college seniors, recent college graduates.

Benefits On-the-job training, opportunity to attend seminars/workshops, possible full-time employment, travel reimbursement, willing to complete paperwork for educational credit, worker's compensation.

Contact Write, fax, e-mail, or through World Wide Web site Gloria J. Frost, Vice President/Director of Human Resources, 115 3rd Street, SE, 9th Floor, Box 1599, Cedar Rapids, Iowa 52401. Fax: 800-854-8270. E-mail: gfrost@shive-hattery.com. No phone calls. In-person interview recommended (telephone interview accepted). Applicants must submit a formal organization application, resume. Applications are accepted continuously. World Wide Web: http://www.shive-hattery.com.

WALDEN ASSOCIATES
16 Spring Street
Oyster Bay, New York 11771

General Information Environmental/civil engineering consulting firm. Established in 1995. Number of employees: 10. Number of internship applications received each year: 5.

Internships Available ▶ *1–2 environmental engineers or geologists:* responsibilities include field work, investigations, writing reports, CADD, GIS, project work. Candidates should have ability to work independently, computer skills, oral communication skills, personal interest in the field, self-motivation, written communication skills. Duration is flexible. $10–$18 per hour. Open to college freshmen, college sophomores, college juniors, college seniors, recent college graduates, graduate students. International applications accepted.

Benefits On-the-job training, opportunity to attend seminars/workshops, possible full-time employment, willing to act as a professional reference, willing to complete paperwork for educational credit, willing to provide letters of recommendation.

Contact Write, call, fax, or e-mail Bob Keane, Project Manager. Phone: 516-624-7200. Fax: 516-624-3219. E-mail: jobs@walden-assoc.com. Telephone interview required. Applicants must submit a resume. Applications are accepted continuously. World Wide Web: http://www.walden-assoc.com.

WASHINGTON INTERNSHIPS FOR STUDENTS OF ENGINEERING (WISE)
40 AICHE, 1300 Ete Street NW, Suite 1090, East Tower
Washington, District of Columbia 20005-3314

General Information Program set-up to match engineering students with suitable internships. The seven engineering societies that sponsor WISE are: ANS, ASCE, ASME, IEEE, NSPE and SAE and AIChE (which acts as the program administrator). Established in 1980. Number of internship applications received each year: 75.

Internships Available ▶ *13–15 WISE interns:* responsibilities include researching and completing a paper on a current and topical engineering-related public policy issue; meeting with congressional committees, executive office departments, and corporate government affairs offices daily. Candidates should have ability to work independently, research skills, self-motivation, strong leadership ability, writing skills, membership in an engineering society (required by most of the sponsoring societies). Duration is June to August (10 weeks). $1800 stipend. Open to college juniors, college seniors, recent graduates beginning study in an engineering policy-related master's program.

Benefits Free housing, travel reimbursement, interaction with leaders in Congress and administration, industry, and prominent non-governmental organizations.

Contact Write, call, fax, e-mail, or through World Wide Web site Monisha Banerjee, Program Administrator, AIChE, 1300 Eye Street, NW, Suite 1090, East Tower, Washington, District of Columbia 20005-3314. Phone: 202-962-8690. Fax: 202-962-8699. E-mail: monib@aiche.org. Applicants must submit a formal

Washington Internships for Students of Engineering (WISE) (continued)
organization application, academic transcripts, two writing samples, two personal references, two letters of recommendation. Application deadline: December 1. World Wide Web: http://www.wise-intern.org.

WOLF CREEK NUCLEAR OPERATING CORPORATION
1550 Oxen Lane, PO Box 411
Burlington, Kansas 66839-0411

General Information   Commercial nuclear electric power generating station. Established in 1987. Number of employees: 1,000. Number of internship applications received each year: 20.
Internships Available   ▶ *1–4 engineering trainees:* responsibilities include assisting engineers in daily operations of nuclear power plant; assigned projects as needed to complete mission of work group. Candidates should have ability to work with others, analytical skills, college courses in field, computer skills, oral communication skills, personal interest in the field, self-motivation, written communication skills. Duration is 7 months. $13.50 per hour. Open to college juniors, college seniors.
Benefits   On-the-job training, opportunity to attend seminars/workshops, possible full-time employment, travel reimbursement.
Contact   Write, fax, or e-mail David O. Reynolds, Human Resources Staff Specialist. Fax: 620-364-4186. E-mail: dareyno@wcnoc.com. No phone calls. Applicants must submit a letter of interest, resume, academic transcripts. Application deadline: February 28 for summer/fall, September 30 for spring/summer.

LEGAL SERVICES

ACLU-NATIONAL OFFICE
125 Broad Street, 18th Floor
New York, New York 10004

General Information   Nonprofit nonpartisan public interest organization devoted to upholding civil liberties for all Americans and extending them to groups that have traditionally been denied them.
Internships Available   ▶ *1–4 interns:* responsibilities include factual and legal research into race, poverty, women's rights, and lesbian/gay issues (among others), trial preparation, and providing information to affiliate offices. Candidates should have ability to work independently, ability to work with others, analytical skills, computer skills, office skills, organizational skills, plan to pursue career in field, research skills, writing skills, demonstrated commitment to social and legal issues. Duration is one semester or one summer. Unpaid. Open to college freshmen, college sophomores, college juniors, college seniors.
Benefits   Willing to act as a professional reference, willing to complete paperwork for educational credit, willing to provide letters of recommendation.
Contact   Write, call, or fax Internship Coordinator. Phone: 212-549-2610. Fax: 212-549-2651. Applicants must submit a letter of interest, resume, one 5-page nonfiction writing sample, in-person interview required for some finalists. Application deadline: March 1 for summer, September 1 for fall, November 1 for spring. World Wide Web: http://www.aclu.org.

AMERICAN BAR ASSOCIATION
740 15th Street, NW
Washington, District of Columbia 20005

General Information   National voluntary association of attorneys with primary goals of professional and public service as well as the improvement of the judicial system. Established in 1878. Number of employees: 180. Unit of American Bar Association, Chicago, Illinois.
Internships Available   ▶ *2–4 Center for Immigration Law and Representation interns:* responsibilities include doing various tasks in immigration benefits and procedures including interviewing,

legal research, and case preparation, in either Washington, D.C. or Harlingen, Texas. Duration is 1 semester or 1 summer (for Washington, DC interns) 2-3 months (Harlingen, TX interns). Position available as unpaid or paid. Open to law students.
▶ *Central and East European Law Initiative interns:* responsibilities include researching, writing, and legal assessments (lawyers). Candidates should have ability to work independently, self-motivation, strong interpersonal skills, writing skills, training/experience in international affairs (preferred). Duration is 15 hours per week minimum during school year; full-time in summer. Unpaid. Open to college freshmen, college sophomores, college juniors, college seniors, law students, attorneys. ▶ *6 Commission on Mental and Physical Disability Law interns.* Duration is fall, spring, or summer semester. Position available as unpaid or paid. Open to college freshmen, college sophomores, college juniors, college seniors, law students. ▶ *1 Division for Media Relations and Public Affairs intern:* responsibilities include participating in press briefings, news conferences, strategic planning, event publicity, interview placements, and other duties. Candidates should have demonstrated interest in public relations. Duration is one academic term (part-time). Unpaid. Open to college sophomores, college juniors, college seniors. ▶ *6 Government Public Sector Lawyers Division interns:* responsibilities include helping with the division's publications, assisting in award program, and a wide variety of clerical and administrative tasks. Candidates should have self-motivation, strong leadership ability. Duration is 1 semester or 1 summer. Unpaid. Open to college juniors, college seniors, law students. ▶ *1–3 Governmental Affairs Office interns:* responsibilities include working with the staff, conducting research, and writing memoranda on legislative and policy issues. Candidates should have research skills, writing skills. Duration is part-time during school year; full-time during summer. Unpaid. Open to college freshmen, college sophomores, college juniors, college seniors. ▶ *1 Immigration and Pro Bono Development intern.* Candidates should have immigration law experience/coursework. Duration is 10-20 hours per week for length of school year. Unpaid. Open to law students in second or third year. ▶ *1–5 Public Services Division interns:* responsibilities include compiling information for directories and other databases; coordinating survey development, distribution, and results; assisting with mailings, copying, and faxing. Duration is 8–10 weeks. Position available as unpaid or paid. Open to college freshmen, college sophomores, college juniors, college seniors, undergraduates and first-year law students (project internships only); second and third-year law students (eligible for 1 Public Service Summer Internship). ▶ *6 Section of Dispute Resolution interns:* responsibilities include various tasks in mediation, arbitration, and other non-litigious forms of dispute resolution. Unpaid. Open to college freshmen, college sophomores, college juniors, college seniors. ▶ *1–4 Section of Individual Rights and Responsibilities interns:* responsibilities include conducting legal research; assisting in monitoring state and federal legislative developments on various civil rights, civil liberties, and human rights issues; and writing newsletter articles for the Section newsletter. Candidates should have personal interest in the field, research skills, writing skills. Duration is 1 semester. Unpaid. Open to college juniors, college seniors, law students. ▶ *1–4 Section of International Law and Practice interns:* responsibilities include conducting legal research; assisting in monitoring state and federal legislative developments on various civil rights, civil liberties, and human rights issues; and writing newsletter articles for the Section. Candidates should have personal interest in the field. Duration is 1 academic term or summer. Unpaid. Open to college freshmen, college sophomores, college juniors, college seniors. ▶ *1 Standing Committee on Law and National Security intern:* responsibilities include assisting with daily operation of standing committee business, responding to requests, organizing monthly breakfast meeting, and other tasks as necessary. Duration is 2-3 days per week. Unpaid. Open to college freshmen, college sophomores, college juniors, college seniors, graduate students. International applications accepted.
Benefits   Opportunity to attend seminars/workshops, possible full-time employment, willing to act as a professional reference, willing to complete paperwork for educational credit, willing to provide letters of recommendation.
Contact   Write, call, fax, or through World Wide Web site Internship Coordinator. Phone: 202-662-1010. Fax: 202-662-1032. Applicants

must submit a letter of interest, resume. Applications are accepted continuously. World Wide Web: http://www.abanet.org.

AMERICAN BAR ASSOCIATION–CENTRAL AND EAST EUROPEAN LAW INITIATIVE (CEELI)
740 15th Street, NW
Washington, District of Columbia 20005-1022

General Information Program that provides legal reform in Central and Eastern Europe and the former Soviet states. Established in 1990. Number of employees: 35. Unit of American Bar Association, Chicago, Illinois. Number of internship applications received each year: 400.

Internships Available ▶ *Criminal Law Reform Project interns:* responsibilities include drafting updates on legal reform, organized crime, and criminal law by monitoring the Central European and NIS press; researching issues related to criminal law and procedure in U.S. and Europe; assisting in preparing briefing materials for CEELI liaisons and legal specialists, the U.S. Department of Justice, and selected government agencies. Candidates should have ability to work independently, self-motivation, strong interpersonal skills, training or experience in international affairs (preferred). Duration is minimum of one semester (12-20 hours per week) or one summer (full-time). Unpaid. Open to college freshmen, college sophomores, college juniors, college seniors, law students, attorneys. ▶ *4 legal assessments and research analysts:* responsibilities include organizing and managing legal assessment projects. Specifically, analysts will organize panels of legal experts to comment on draft legislation from CEE and NIS governments, and will draft comprehensive analysis of the legislation based on experts' comments. Candidates should have ability to work independently, self-motivation, strong interpersonal skills, training and/or experience in international affairs (preferred). Duration is minimum of one semester (12-20 hours per week) or one summer (full-time). Unpaid. Open to law students, attorneys. International applications accepted.

Benefits Opportunity to attend seminars/workshops, willing to act as a professional reference, willing to complete paperwork for educational credit, willing to provide letters of recommendation, access to internal ABA job postings for full-time employment.

Contact Write, fax, or e-mail Simon R. Contè, Associate Director, Legal Assessments and Research. Fax: 202-662-1597. E-mail: sconte@abaceeli.org. No phone calls. In-person interview recommended (telephone interview accepted). Applicants must submit a letter of interest, resume, brief writing sample (5 page maximum). Applications are accepted continuously. World Wide Web: http://www.abanet.org/ceeli.

ASSOCIATION OF LEGAL AID ATTORNEYS/UAW 2325
568 Broadway, Room 702A
New York, New York 10012-3225

General Information Oldest and largest major union of lawyers in the U.S., who each year represent some 300,000 indigent New Yorkers in criminal, civil, and juvenile cases. Established in 1969. Number of employees: 650.

Internships Available ▶ *Interns:* responsibilities include exposure to wide variety of activities including HQ administration, criminal law, criminal justice policy (e.g. police abuse, drug law reform), political action, union meetings, and collective bargaining. Duration is one fall, spring and/or summer. Unpaid.

Benefits Willing to complete paperwork for educational credit.

Contact E-mail Michael Letwin, President. Phone: 212-343-0708. E-mail: letwin@alaa.org. Resume and cover letter indicating time of year desired (via e-mail only). Applications are accepted continuously. World Wide Web: http://www.alaa.org.

AYUDA, INC.
1736 Columbia Road, NW
Washington, District of Columbia 20009

General Information Nonprofit community-based agency that provides legal assistance on immigration and domestic violence matters to the low-income, foreign-born population of Washington,

DC metropolitan area. Established in 1971. Number of employees: 15. Number of internship applications received each year: 350.

Internships Available ▶ *4–6 domestic violence legal assistants:* responsibilities include conducting initial interviews with battered women, drafting legal documents, preparing clients for trial, conducting case investigations, assisting at counsel table during trial, attending community outreach activities. Candidates should have ability to work independently, computer skills, experience in the field, office skills, oral communication skills, organizational skills, plan to pursue career in field, research skills, strong interpersonal skills, writing skills, proficiency in Spanish required. Duration is 10–12 weeks. Unpaid. Open to college sophomores, college juniors, college seniors, recent college graduates, graduate students, law students, individuals reentering the workforce. ▶ *5–8 immigration legal assistants:* responsibilities include working in areas of political asylum, naturalization, relative petition, adjustment of status, advance parole, and suspension of deportation. Candidates should have ability to work independently, organizational skills, plan to pursue career in field, self-motivation, strong interpersonal skills, writing skills, proficiency in Spanish required; proficiency in French desired. Duration is 10–12 weeks. Unpaid. Open to college freshmen, college sophomores, college juniors, college seniors, recent college graduates, graduate students, law students, career changers, individuals reentering the workforce. ▶ *1–2 public relations interns:* responsibilities include drafting grant proposals, creating annual report, developing media contacts, and working on fund-raising projects. Candidates should have ability to work independently, computer skills, editing skills, office skills, organizational skills, research skills, self-motivation, strong interpersonal skills, writing skills. Duration is 10–12 weeks. Unpaid. Open to college freshmen, college sophomores, college juniors, college seniors, recent college graduates, graduate students, law students. International applications accepted.

Benefits Opportunity to attend seminars/workshops, willing to act as a professional reference, willing to complete paperwork for educational credit, willing to provide letters of recommendation, help in obtaining fellowships.

Contact Write, call, fax, or e-mail Lauren Butler, Volunteer Coordinator. Phone: 202-387-2870 Ext. 33. Fax: 202-387-0324. E-mail: lbutler@ayudainc.org. In-person interview recommended (telephone interview accepted). Applicants must submit a formal organization application, letter of interest, resume, 2–3 personal references. Application deadline: January 15 for spring, March 15 for summer, September 10 for fall.

BET TZEDEK LEGAL SERVICES
145 South Fairfax Avenue, Suite 200
Los Angeles, California 90036

General Information Legal services organization providing free legal services to poor and low-income residents of Los Angeles County, focusing primarily on senior citizens. Established in 1973. Number of employees: 44. Number of internship applications received each year: 100.

Internships Available ▶ *1–2 marketing/development interns:* responsibilities include assisting in special event production, direct mail solicitation, and telephone follow-up. Candidates should have ability to work independently, computer skills, office skills, organizational skills, strong interpersonal skills, writing skills, good phone skills, high-energy, and people-oriented disposition. Duration is 10-12 weeks (20 hours per week during summer; 8 hours per week during academic year). Unpaid. Open to college sophomores, college juniors, college seniors, recent college graduates, graduate students, career changers. ▶ *1–2 nonprofit fund accounting interns:* responsibilities include working hands-on with computerized accounts payable and receivable documentation, assisting in the input and accounting functions specific to nonprofit organizations with multiple funding sources, receiving training in the use and function of spreadsheet applications, organizing data for review and taking part in the data analysis process. Candidates should have ability to work with others, office skills, oral communication skills, organizational skills, general accounting and/or bookkeeping background (helpful), 10-key experience, moderate typing skills, familiarity with computers. Duration is 10-12 weeks (8 hours per week). Unpaid. Open to college freshmen, college

Bet Tzedek Legal Services (continued)

sophomores, college juniors, college seniors, recent college graduates, graduate students, career changers, individuals reentering the workforce. ▶ *7–9 prescreeners/legal assistants:* responsibilities include prescreening clients by phone for financial and case type eligibility, making appropriate referrals, conducting in-person interviews, writing letters on behalf of clients, and other client advocacy under the direction of supervising attorneys. Candidates should have ability to work independently, analytical skills, oral communication skills, plan to pursue career in field, strong interpersonal skills, written communication skills, demonstrable commitment to community service, understanding of the problems of the poor. Duration is 11-12 weeks (20 hours per week during summer, 8 hours per week during academic year). Unpaid. Open to college freshmen, college sophomores, college juniors, recent college graduates, college seniors (during academic year only).

Benefits Formal training, on-the-job training, willing to act as a professional reference, willing to complete paperwork for educational credit, willing to provide letters of recommendation.

Contact Write, call, fax, or e-mail Ms. Robin Sommerstein, Human Resource Director/Volunteer Coordinator. Phone: 323-549-5814. Fax: 323-939-1040. E-mail: rsommerstein@bettzedek.org. In-person interview recommended (telephone interview accepted). Applicants must submit a letter of interest, resume. Application deadline: April 15 for summer, September 10 for fall. World Wide Web: http://www.bettzedek.org.

CALIFORNIA RURAL LEGAL ASSISTANCE
21 Carr Street
Watsonville, California 95076

General Information Law office funded by federal, state, county, and city government, providing free legal advice to qualifying low-income people in the areas of unemployment, housing, welfare law, debtor rights, and education. Established in 1968. Number of employees: 13. Number of internship applications received each year: 50.

Internships Available ▶ *12 legal interns:* responsibilities include handling case work, conducting client intake, advising and referral, preparing legal materials, and working closely with staff attorneys; special research projects are also possible. Candidates should have ability to work with others, analytical skills, computer skills, oral communication skills, research skills, self-motivation, writing skills. Duration is 2 quarters. Unpaid. Open to college freshmen, college sophomores, college juniors, college seniors, recent college graduates, graduate students, law students. International applications accepted.

Benefits Willing to complete paperwork for educational credit, willing to provide letters of recommendation, 3-4 hours of lectures on law and forms, one-on-one supervision by an attorney.

Contact Write, fax, or e-mail Shirley Conner, Intern Coordinator. Fax: 831-724-7530. E-mail: watsonville@crla.org. No phone calls. In-person interview recommended (telephone interview accepted). Applicants must submit a letter of interest, resume. Applications are accepted continuously.

COUNCIL FOR COURT EXCELLENCE
1717 K Street, Suite 510
Washington, District of Columbia 20036

General Information Nonprofit, nonpartisan civic organization working to improve the administration of justice in local and federal courts through studies of aspects of judicial branch performance and advocacy of related reforms, and through public education about courts. Established in 1982. Number of employees: 6. Number of internship applications received each year: 60.

Internships Available ▶ *3 interns:* responsibilities include assisting in development and progress of priority projects related to court performance in areas such as criminal justice, child abuse and neglect, and civil justice and community education about the courts. Candidates should have computer skills, office skills, research skills, self-motivation, strong interpersonal skills, writing skills. Duration is 1 semester. Unpaid. Open to college freshmen, college sophomores, college juniors, college seniors, recent col-

lege graduates, graduate students, law students, individuals reentering the workforce. International applications accepted.

Benefits Job counseling, names of contacts, on-the-job training, opportunity to attend seminars/workshops, possible full-time employment, travel reimbursement, willing to act as a professional reference, willing to complete paperwork for educational credit, willing to provide letters of recommendation.

Contact Write, call, fax, e-mail, or through World Wide Web site Ms. Priscilla Skillman, Assistant Director, 1717 K Street, NW, Suite 510, Washington, District of Columbia 20036. Phone: 202-785-5917. Fax: 202-785-5922. E-mail: skillman@courtexcellence.org. In-person interview recommended (telephone interview accepted). Applicants must submit a letter of interest, resume, writing sample. Applications are accepted continuously. World Wide Web: http://www.courtexcellence.org.

DISABILITY RIGHTS ADVOCATES
449 15th Street, Suite 303
Oakland, California 94612

General Information Legal advocacy organization that supports the rights of persons with disabilities in litigation relating to the Americans with Disabilities Act. Number of employees: 21. Number of internship applications received each year: 50.

Internships Available ▶ *Fall law clerks.* Candidates should have ability to work independently, ability to work with others, analytical skills, computer skills, oral communication skills, personal interest in the field, writing skills. Duration is 1 semester. Position available as unpaid or paid. Open to law students. ▶ *1–8 law clerks.* Candidates should have ability to work independently, ability to work with others, analytical skills, computer skills, personal interest in the field, writing skills. Duration is June 1 to August 31. Position available as unpaid or at $8–$12 per hour. Open to recent college graduates, graduate students, law students. International applications accepted.

Benefits On-the-job training, possible full-time employment, willing to complete paperwork for educational credit, willing to provide letters of recommendation, travel to and from work reimbursed.

Contact Write, fax, or e-mail Caroline Amimo, Office Administrator. Fax: 510-451-8511. E-mail: carolinea@dralegal.org. No phone calls. Applicants must submit a resume, writing sample, 5-page writing sample. Application deadline: April 1. World Wide Web: http://www.dralegal.org.

GEORGETOWN UNIVERSITY LAW CENTER–CRIMINAL JUSTICE CLINIC
111 F Street, NW
Washington, District of Columbia 20001-2095

General Information Clinic providing representation to indigent criminal defendants in District of Columbia. Established in 1989. Number of employees: 18. Number of internship applications received each year: 400.

Internships Available ▶ *10 investigative interns:* responsibilities include meeting investigative needs of 2 clinic attorneys in all aspects of investigations, including assessing government's cases, interviewing potential witnesses, gathering relevant paperwork, serving subpoenas, collecting evidence, and other field work. Candidates should have oral communication skills, organizational skills, self-motivation, strong interpersonal skills, strong leadership ability, written communication skills. Duration is 1 semester or summer. Unpaid. Open to college freshmen, college sophomores, college juniors, college seniors, recent college graduates, graduate students, law students. International applications accepted.

Benefits Formal training, job counseling, names of contacts, on-the-job training, opportunity to attend seminars/workshops, travel reimbursement, willing to act as a professional reference, willing to complete paperwork for educational credit, willing to provide letters of recommendation, membership in fitness center.

Contact Write, call, fax, e-mail, or through World Wide Web site Rebecca O'Brien, Investigations Supervisor. Phone: 202-662-9589. Fax: 202-662-9681. E-mail: obrienra@law.georgetown.edu. Telephone interview required. Applicants must submit a formal organization application, two personal references. Application deadline:

March 15 for 1st round fall, April 1 for summer, July 1 for 2nd round fall, December 1 for spring. World Wide Web: http://www.law.georgetown.edu/clinics/cjc/iip.html.

JUDICIAL INTERNSHIP PROGRAM, SUPREME COURT OF THE UNITED STATES
Office of the Administrative Assistant to the Chief Justice, Room 5
Washington, District of Columbia 20543

General Information   Office that assists the Chief Justice in fulfilling non-adjudicatory responsibilities. Established in 1972. Number of employees: 350. Number of internship applications received each year: 150.
Internships Available   ▶ *1–3 judicial interns:* responsibilities include routine office tasks; monitoring research on the federal judicial system; helping prepare memoranda, correspondence, background research for articles and speeches; monitoring and summarizing benefits with international judicial visitors. Candidates should have ability to work with others, analytical skills, oral communication skills, research skills, self-motivation, written communication skills, some course work in constitutional law or the Supreme Court (preferred). Duration is 1 semester. Unpaid. Open to college juniors, college seniors. International applications accepted.
Benefits   Opportunity to attend seminars/workshops, willing to act as a professional reference, willing to complete paperwork for educational credit, willing to provide letters of recommendation, $1000 stipend may be available for interns who are returning to academic studies.
Contact   Write, call, or fax Judicial Fellow. Phone: 202-479-3415. Fax: 202-479-3484. Telephone interview required. Applicants must submit a formal organization application, resume, academic transcripts, writing sample, three letters of recommendation, candidate statement describing experience, skills, and reason for application, and essay of 2 pages or more. Application deadline: March 10 for summer, June 1 for fall, October 20 for winter. World Wide Web: http://www.supremecourtus.gov.

KOHN, KOHN AND COLAPINTO, P.C.
3233 P Street, NW
Washington, District of Columbia 20007-2756

General Information   Public interest law firm specializing in representation of whistle-blowers; represents numerous employees who were fired or retaliated against for making disclosures regarding nuclear safety, corporate or government misconduct, environmental protection, or health and safety violations. Established in 1988. Number of employees: 7. Number of internship applications received each year: 100.
Internships Available   ▶ *6–8 legal interns:* responsibilities include significant legal research and writing projects, assisting at trials, and performing all the work of an associate attorney. Candidates should have ability to work independently, ability to work with others, analytical skills, oral communication skills, research skills, written communication skills. Duration is 10 weeks in summer; flexible at other times of year. Unpaid. Open to college juniors, college seniors, recent college graduates, graduate students, law students. International applications accepted.
Benefits   Willing to act as a professional reference, willing to complete paperwork for educational credit, willing to provide letters of recommendation, one-on-one supervision from an attorney.
Contact   Write, call, fax, e-mail, or through World Wide Web site Joyce Claro, Internship Coordinator. Phone: 202-342-6980. Fax: 202-342-6984. E-mail: jc@kkc.com. Telephone interview required. Applicants must submit a resume, cover letter. Application deadline: March 1 for summer, June 1 for fall, September 1 for January positions, December 1 for spring. World Wide Web: http://www.whistleblowers.org.

LAMBDA LEGAL DEFENSE AND EDUCATION FUND, INC.
6030 Wilshire Boulevard, Suite 200
Los Angeles, California 90036-3617

General Information   National organization committed to achieving full recognition of the civil rights of lesbians, gay men, bisexuals, transgenders, and people with HIV/AIDS through impact litigation, education, and public policy work. Established in 1973. Number of employees: 10. Branch of Lambda Legal Defense and Education Fund, Inc., New York, New York. Number of internship applications received each year: 30.
Internships Available   ▶ *1–3 interns:* responsibilities include handling intake of callers, researching legal matters and classifying them into subject-matter files, utilizing programs such as Lexis or Westlaw. Candidates should have ability to work with others, computer skills, personal interest in the field, research skills, self-motivation, writing skills. Duration is summer, fall, or winter/spring semester. Unpaid. Open to law students. International applications accepted.
Benefits   Opportunity to attend seminars/workshops, travel reimbursement, willing to act as a professional reference, willing to complete paperwork for educational credit, willing to provide letters of recommendation.
Contact   Write Stefan Johnson, Intake Coordinator. Phone: 323-937-2728. Fax: 323-937-0601. E-mail: sjohnson@lambdalegal.org. Applicants must submit a letter of interest, resume, writing sample. Application deadline: February 15 for summer, August 15 for fall, November 15 for winter/spring. World Wide Web: http://www.lambdalegal.org.

LAMBDA LEGAL DEFENSE AND EDUCATION FUND, INC.
Southern Regional Office, 1447 Peachtree Street, Suite 1004
Atlanta, Georgia 30309

General Information   National organization committed to achieving full recognition of the civil right of lesbians, gay men, bisexuals, and the transgender, and people with HIV/AIDS through impact litigation, education, and public policy work. Established in 1973. Number of employees: 5. Unit of Lambda Legal–Headquarters, New York, New York. Number of internship applications received each year: 50.
Internships Available   ▶ *1–3 academic year interns:* responsibilities include research, writing, client intake, and special projects. Duration is 3–6 months. Up to $10 per hour. ▶ *1–3 summer interns:* responsibilities include research, writing, client intake, and special projects. Duration is June to August. Unpaid. Candidates for all positions should have analytical skills, college courses in field, personal interest in the field, research skills, writing skills. Open to law students. International applications accepted.
Benefits   Formal training, job counseling, names of contacts, on-the-job training, opportunity to attend seminars/workshops, willing to act as a professional reference, willing to complete paperwork for educational credit, willing to provide letters of recommendation.
Contact   Write Greg Nevins, Staff Attorney. Phone: 404-897-1880. Fax: 404-897-1884. In-person interview recommended (telephone interview accepted). Applicants must submit a letter of interest, resume, academic transcripts, writing sample. Application deadline: April 30 for summer; continuous for academic-year positions. World Wide Web: http://www.lambdalegal.org.

LAMBDA LEGAL DEFENSE AND EDUCATION FUND, INC. (MIDWEST REGION)
11 East Adams, Suite 1008
Chicago, Illinois 60603-6303

General Information   National organization committed to achieving full recognition of the civil rights of lesbians, gay men, and people with HIV/AIDS through impact litigation, education, and public policy work. Established in 1973. Number of employees: 9. Branch of Lambda Legal Defense and Education Fund, Inc., New York, New York.

Lambda Legal Defense and Education Fund, Inc. (Midwest Region) (continued)
Internships Available ▶ *1 fund-raising intern:* responsibilities include assisting with the functions of the fund-raising department; donor research, heavy clerical work and data entry; assisting in planning and execution of special events. Candidates should have ability to work independently, computer skills, office skills, oral communication skills, organizational skills, self-motivation, strong interpersonal skills, written communication skills. Duration is June to August or November. Unpaid. Open to college seniors, recent college graduates, graduate students, career changers. ▶ *1–2 legal help desk interns:* responsibilities include speaking with callers about potential legal issues, assisting them in identifying key facts, and recording vital information for attorneys to review; connecting callers to legal and social services in their area as appropriate. Candidates should have computer skills, oral communication skills, personal interest in the field, self-motivation, strong interpersonal skills, written communication skills. Duration is 6 hours per week (variable number of weeks). Unpaid. Open to college sophomores, college juniors, college seniors, recent college graduates, graduate students, career changers. ▶ *1–3 legal interns:* responsibilities include working with lawyers on legal research projects, preparing written memoranda of work, and assisting in briefs and filings for state and federal courts. Candidates should have ability to work independently, analytical skills, oral communication skills, personal interest in the field, research skills, written communication skills. Duration is 10–12 weeks. Position available as unpaid or at $10 per hour for school-year interns; summer intern stipends vary depending on available funding. Open to law students. International applications accepted.
Benefits Names of contacts, on-the-job training, willing to act as a professional reference, willing to provide letters of recommendation, completion of paperwork for educational credit (for legal internship only).
Contact Write, call, fax, e-mail, or through World Wide Web site RoiAnn Phillips, Program Associate. Phone: 312-663-4413. Fax: 312-663-4307. E-mail: lldefmro@lambdalegal.org. In-person interview required. Applicants must submit a letter of interest, resume, 1 writing sample required for legal internship only; 2–3 personal references. Application deadline: January 1 for summer legal interns; continuous for help desk interns, May 1 for fund-raising interns, July 1 for fall legal interns. World Wide Web: http://www.lambdalegal.org.

LANSNER AND KUBITSCHEK
325 Broadway, Suite 201
New York, New York 10007

General Information Public interest law firm in the areas of family law, civil rights, and social security. Established in 1991. Number of employees: 20. Number of internship applications received each year: 500.
Internships Available ▶ *3–4 fall/spring interns:* responsibilities include interviewing clients, drafting briefs, researching legal issues, tracking down witnesses, and attending court hearings. Candidates should have analytical skills, personal interest in the field, research skills, strong interpersonal skills, writing skills. Duration is one semester (minimum of 10 hours per week). Unpaid. Open to college seniors, recent college graduates, graduate students, law students. ▶ *6–8 summer associates:* responsibilities include interviewing clients, drafting briefs, researching legal issues, tracking down witnesses, attending court hearings, tracking client files, and conducting social security hearings. Candidates should have analytical skills, research skills, strong interpersonal skills, written communication skills. Duration is June to August. Unpaid. Open to law students. ▶ *8–10 winter interns:* responsibilities include drafting briefs, researching legal issues, attending court hearings, and preparing client files. Candidates should have analytical skills, personal interest in the field, research skills, strong interpersonal skills, writing skills. Duration is 3 weeks in January (full-time). Unpaid. Open to college sophomores, college juniors, college seniors. International applications accepted.
Benefits Free meals, names of contacts, on-the-job training, opportunity to attend seminars/workshops, willing to act as a profes-

sional reference, willing to complete paperwork for educational credit, willing to provide letters of recommendation, possibility of academic credit for summer associates.
Contact Write, call, e-mail, or through World Wide Web site Sarah J. Dash, Paralegal. Phone: 212-349-0900. E-mail: sdash@lanskub.com. In-person interview recommended (telephone interview accepted). Applicants must submit a letter of interest, resume, writing sample. Applications are accepted continuously. World Wide Web: http://www.lansmerkubitschek.com.

THE LEGAL AID SOCIETY, CRIMINAL DEFENSE DIVISION
49 Thomas Street, 2nd Floor
New York, New York 10013

General Information Organization that provides free legal assistance to indigent clients in all areas of the law including criminal defense, juvenile, appeals, and civil. Established in 1876. Number of employees: 200. Division of Legal Aid Society, New York, New York. Number of internship applications received each year: 200.
Internships Available ▶ *30–40 investigator interns:* responsibilities include locating, interviewing, and taking written statements from witnesses in the field; background checks and research; serving subpoenas; and assisting attorneys in preparing for court. Candidates should have ability to work independently, oral communication skills, personal interest in the field, strong interpersonal skills, written communication skills, commitment to community service and advocacy for the indigent. Duration is 1–2 semesters. Unpaid. Open to college sophomores, college juniors, college seniors, recent college graduates, graduate students, law students. International applications accepted.
Benefits Formal training, job counseling, opportunity to attend seminars/workshops, possible full-time employment, willing to act as a professional reference, willing to complete paperwork for educational credit, willing to provide letters of recommendation.
Contact Write, call, fax, or e-mail Peter Lane, Intern Coordinator. Phone: 212-298-5001. Fax: 212-693-1149. E-mail: plane@legal-aid.org. In-person interview recommended (telephone interview accepted). Applicants must submit a formal organization application, resume, two personal references, two letters of recommendation. Application deadline: February 1 for spring, March 15 for summer, September 15 for fall. World Wide Web: http://www.legal-aid.org.

LEGAL AID SOCIETY, JUVENILE RIGHTS DIVISION
90 Church Street, 15th Floor
New York, New York 10007

General Information Division representing children in neglect, abuse, and juvenile delinquency proceedings in city's five borough Family Courts. Established in 1962. Number of employees: 273. Division of Legal Aid Society, New York, New York. Number of internship applications received each year: 400.
Internships Available ▶ *Child advocacy interns:* responsibilities include assisting with monitoring compliance with court orders; gathering records from social workers, foster parents, schools, and health professionals; writing letters, drafting motions and orders; serving subpoenas. Duration is flexible. Unpaid. Open to high school seniors, college freshmen, college sophomores, college juniors, college seniors, recent college graduates. ▶ *Clerical interns:* responsibilities include clerical duties as needed. Duration is flexible. Unpaid. Open to high school students, college freshmen, college sophomores, college juniors, college seniors, recent college graduates. ▶ *Legal interns:* responsibilities include being paired with attorneys to help prepare cases for court; drafting motions and orders; conducting legal research and writing briefs; assisting with client interviews. Duration is flexible. Unpaid. Open to law students. ▶ *Paralegal interns:* responsibilities include assisting with monitoring compliance with court orders, writing letters, drafting motions and orders, and serving supoenas. Duration is flexible. Unpaid. Open to college freshmen, college sophomores, college juniors, college seniors, individuals in paralegal program at school. Candidates for all positions should

have ability to work independently, ability to work with others, oral communication skills, organizational skills, written communication skills. International applications accepted.

Benefits Names of contacts, on-the-job training, opportunity to attend seminars/workshops, possible full-time employment, willing to act as a professional reference, willing to complete paperwork for educational credit, willing to provide letters of recommendation.

Contact Fax, e-mail, or through World Wide Web site Veronique Questel, Intern Coordinator, 90 Church Street, 15th Floor, New York, New York 10007. Fax: 718-250-4244. E-mail: questelv@legal-aid.org. In-person interview recommended (telephone interview accepted). Applicants must submit a formal organization application, letter of interest, resume, confidentiality agreement. Applications are accepted continuously. World Wide Web: http://www.legal-aid.org.

LEGAL SERVICES FOR PRISONERS WITH CHILDREN
100 McAllister Street
San Francisco, California 94102

General Information Organization that provides training, technical assistance, advocacy, and litigation support to legal service offices and to prisoners, their families, and advocates throughout California. Established in 1978. Number of employees: 9. Number of internship applications received each year: 75.

Internships Available ▶ *Interns:* responsibilities include handling client intake, responding to requests for assistance from prisoners and their families, conducting legal research, and writing. Candidates should have ability to work independently, ability to work with others, oral communication skills, personal interest in the field, research skills, written communication skills. Duration is flexible. Unpaid. Open to college juniors, college seniors, recent college graduates, graduate students, law students. International applications accepted.

Benefits Job counseling, names of contacts, travel reimbursement, willing to act as a professional reference, willing to complete paperwork for educational credit, willing to provide letters of recommendation.

Contact Write or e-mail Lauren Leslie, Intern Coordinator. Fax: 415-552-3150. E-mail: info@prisonerswithchildren.org. No phone calls. Applicants must submit a letter of interest, resume, writing sample. Applications are accepted continuously. World Wide Web: http://www.prisonerswithchildren.org.

MIGRANT LEGAL ACTION PROGRAM
1001 Connecticut Avenue, NW, Suite 915
Washington, District of Columbia 20036

General Information National support and advocacy center providing legal representation to migrant and seasonal farm workers nationwide concerning employment conditions, health, housing, education, wages, public benefits, and general welfare. Established in 1970. Number of employees: 5. Number of internship applications received each year: 120.

Internships Available ▶ *2-4 law student interns:* responsibilities include legal research and writing under the supervision of a staff attorney. Duration is 1-2 semesters or 1 summer. Unpaid. Open to law students. ▶ *1 undergraduate intern:* responsibilities include assisting staff in a variety of research, writing, and some clerical duties. Duration is 1-2 semesters or 1 summer. Unpaid. Open to college sophomores, college juniors, college seniors, recent college graduates. Candidates for all positions should have ability to work independently, ability to work with others, oral communication skills, research skills, self-motivation, written communication skills.

Benefits Names of contacts, opportunity to attend seminars/workshops, willing to complete paperwork for educational credit, willing to provide letters of recommendation.

Contact Write Mr. Roger C. Rosenthal, Executive Director. In-person interview recommended (telephone interview accepted). Applicants must submit a letter of interest, resume, writing sample,

two personal references. Application deadline: March 1 for summer, August 15 for fall, November 15 for spring. World Wide Web: http://www.mlap.org.

MONTGOMERY COUNTY COMMUNITY CORRECTIONS
11651 Nebel Street
Rockville, Maryland 20852

General Information Agency that provides effective community correctional alternatives between probation/parole supervision and security confinement for male and female adult offenders. Established in 1972. Number of employees: 70. Unit of Montgomery County Department of Corrections and Rehabilitation, Rockville, Maryland. Number of internship applications received each year: 50.

Internships Available ▶ *2 CART interns:* responsibilities include working in the Community Accountability and Treatment Services Program, verifying participant's whereabouts, collecting and testing urine, assisting in group treatment facilitation of life skills and substance-abuse education, performing crisis intervention, and assisting in home visits in the community. Candidates should have ability to work independently, declared college major in field, oral communication skills, personal interest in the field, self-motivation, strong interpersonal skills. Duration is minimum 4 months, maximum 1 year. $5.15 per hour (24 hours per week). ▶ *6 PreRelease Center interns:* responsibilities include supervising adult offenders residing in a community correctional facility preparing for release and recreational trips, collecting and testing urine, coordinating employment, performing resident verifications, and participating as a treatment team member. Candidates should have declared college major in field, oral communication skills, personal interest in the field, self-motivation, strong interpersonal skills, written communication skills. Duration is 4–12 months. $5.15 per hour. Open to college juniors, college seniors, recent college graduates, graduate students, law students, career changers, individuals reentering the workforce. International applications accepted.

Benefits Formal training, job counseling, on-the-job training, opportunity to attend seminars/workshops, possible full-time employment, willing to act as a professional reference, willing to complete paperwork for educational credit, willing to provide letters of recommendation, room and board option.

Contact Write, call, or fax Supervisor of Administration and Training. Phone: 301-468-4200. Fax: 301-468-4420. In-person interview recommended (telephone interview accepted). Applicants must submit a formal organization application. Applications are accepted continuously. World Wide Web: http://www.montgomerycountyjobs.com.

NATIVE AMERICAN RIGHTS FUND
1506 Broadway
Boulder, Colorado 80302

General Information Nonprofit law firm that represents tribes and individuals on tribal issues including land, water, and recognition. Established in 1970. Number of employees: 40. Number of internship applications received each year: 30.

Internships Available ▶ *5 law clerks:* responsibilities include conducting legal research and writing projects on issues of Indian law, procedure, and policy (work setting is either Boulder, Colorado; Anchorage, Alaska; or Washington, DC). Candidates should have ability to work with others, college courses in field, plan to pursue career in field, research skills, written communication skills, background in Native American issues (preferred). Duration is 10–12 weeks. $15 per hour. Open to second-year law students. International applications accepted.

Benefits Formal training, names of contacts, on-the-job training, travel reimbursement, willing to act as a professional reference, willing to complete paperwork for educational credit, willing to provide letters of recommendation.

Contact Write, call, fax, or e-mail Ms. Lorna Babby. Phone: 303-447-8760. Fax: 303-443-7776. E-mail: babby@narf.org. Applicants must submit a letter of interest, resume, academic transcripts, writing sample, three letters of recommendation. Application deadline: October 15 for summer law clerks; continuous for all other positions. World Wide Web: http://www.narf.org.

NEW YORK STATE BAR ASSOCIATION
One Elk Street
Albany, New York 12207

General Information Official organization of lawyers in New York that strives to aid the administration of justice, promote legal reforms, and apply legal knowledge and experience for public benefit. Established in 1876. Number of employees: 115. Number of internship applications received each year: 20.

Internships Available ▶ *1 public relations intern:* responsibilities include writing news releases, preparing backgrounders, scripting broadcast public service announcements, assisting with special events, learning how to conduct research through databases, handling requests for materials produced by the department and available to the public, writing news and feature stories for the monthly newspaper and the staff publication, and assisting with photography. Candidates should have ability to work independently, computer skills, knowledge of field, office skills, personal interest in the field, research skills, writing skills, major in journalism or public relations. Duration is 10 weeks. $8 per hour for summer interns. Open to college juniors and seniors who are residents of the northeastern United States.

Benefits Formal training, job counseling, opportunity to attend seminars/workshops, travel reimbursement, willing to complete paperwork for educational credit, willing to provide letters of recommendation.

Contact Write or e-mail Mr. Brad Carr, Director of Media Services and Public Affairs. Fax: 518-463-4276. E-mail: bcarr@nysba.org. No phone calls. In-person interview required. Applicants must submit a letter of interest, resume, three writing samples. Application deadline: April 1 for summer; continuous for all other positions. World Wide Web: http://www.nysba.org.

OFFICE OF GENERAL COUNSEL
1600 Defense, Pentagon
Washington, District of Columbia 20301-1600

General Information Office that advises high-level policymakers in the Office of the Secretary of Defense and works closely with the military, the Departments of Justice, State, Treasury, and other government agencies. Number of employees: 80. Unit of Office of the Secretary of Defense, Washington, District of Columbia. Number of internship applications received each year: 200.

Internships Available ▶ *10–13 honors legal interns:* responsibilities include assisting with drafting and commenting on legislation, regulations, congressional testimony, litigation materials, and legal opinions, and assisting with the formulation of Department of Defense legal policy on topics of current interest. Candidates should have ability to work independently, ability to work with others, oral communication skills, plan to pursue career in field, research skills, written communication skills. Duration is 10–13 weeks in summer. $470–$575 per week. Open to first and second-year law students.

Benefits Job counseling, names of contacts, willing to complete paperwork for educational credit, willing to provide letters of recommendation.

Contact Write, call, or e-mail Kimberly M. Lenzer, Internship Coordinator. Phone: 703-614-6852. E-mail: lenzerk@osdgc.osd. mil. Applicants must submit a letter of interest, resume, writing sample, form (OF)6-12, statement of class rank and law school transcripts for 2nd-year law students, undergraduate transcripts for both 1st and 2nd-year law students. Application deadline: January 7 for first-year law students, November 20 for second-year law students.

PUBLIC DEFENDER SERVICE FOR THE DISTRICT OF COLUMBIA
633 Indiana Avenue, NW
Washington, District of Columbia 20004

General Information Independent government agency that provides criminal defense for indigent clients of the District of Columbia. Established in 1970. Number of employees: 200. Number of internship applications received each year: 600.

Internships Available ▶ *25–30 case assistants:* responsibilities include working with a staff trial attorney, interviewing witnesses, taking statements, photographing crime scenes, and assisting attorney with trial preparations. Candidates should have analytical skills, oral communication skills, organizational skills, personal interest in the field, strong interpersonal skills. Duration is 12 weeks. Unpaid. Open to college freshmen, college sophomores, college juniors, college seniors, recent college graduates, graduate students, law students, career changers, individuals reentering the workforce. ▶ *5 fellowship investigators:* responsibilities include working with a staff trial attorney, interviewing witnesses, taking statements, photographing crime scenes, and assisting attorney with trial preparations. Candidates should have ability to work independently, experience in the field, oral communication skills, self-motivation, strong interpersonal skills, written communication skills, Spanish speaking ability and writing fluency. Duration is 16 weeks. $1000–$2500 per duration of internship. Open to college juniors, college seniors, recent college graduates, graduate students, law students, career changers, individuals reentering the workforce. ▶ *40 investigators:* responsibilities include working with a staff trial attorney, interviewing witnesses, taking statements, and assisting the attorney with trial preparations. Candidates should have ability to work independently, analytical skills, personal interest in the field, self-motivation, strong interpersonal skills, written communication skills. Duration is 12–16 weeks. Unpaid. Open to college freshmen, college sophomores, college juniors, college seniors, recent college graduates, graduate students, law students, career changers, individuals reentering the workforce. International applications accepted.

Benefits Formal training, housing at a cost, job counseling, names of contacts, on-the-job training, opportunity to attend seminars/workshops, possible full-time employment, travel reimbursement, willing to act as a professional reference, willing to complete paperwork for educational credit, willing to provide letters of recommendation.

Contact Write, call, fax, e-mail, or through World Wide Web site Kesha Taylor, Internship Coordinator. Phone: 800-341-2582. Fax: 202-626-8437. E-mail: internship@pdsdc.org. In-person interview recommended (telephone interview accepted). Applicants must submit a formal organization application, letter of interest, resume, essay, 2 personal references or 2 letters of recommendation. Application deadline: February 1 for spring quarter (priority), April 1 for summer (priority), July 1 for fall (priority), December 1 for spring semester(priority). World Wide Web: http://pdsdc. org.

PUBLIC DEFENDER SERVICE FOR THE DISTRICT OF COLUMBIA, MENTAL HEALTH DIVISION
St. Elizabeths Hospital, Cottage 2
Washington, District of Columbia 20032

General Information Independent government public interest law office that specializes in representing indigent clients facing civil and criminal commitment to D.C. area mental institutions. Established in 1970. Number of employees: 12. Division of Public Defender Service for the District of Columbia, Washington, District of Columbia. Number of internship applications received each year: 70.

Internships Available ▶ *14 investigators:* responsibilities include interviewing clients and witnesses, helping attorneys prepare cases for court, documenting all investigations, gathering and organizing medical and legal records, executing subpoenas, and testifying in court. Candidates should have ability to work independently, analytical skills, oral communication skills, organizational skills, personal interest in the field, self-motivation, strong interpersonal skills, writing skills. Duration is 10-12 weeks minimum (at least 2

days per week during academic year; at least 3 days per week in summer). Unpaid. ▶ *2 social work interns:* responsibilities include assisting social worker in securing necessary social services for clients. Candidates should have ability to work independently, oral communication skills, organizational skills, personal interest in the field, self-motivation, strong interpersonal skills, writing skills. Duration is 10-12 weeks minimum (2 days per week to full-time). Unpaid. Open to college freshmen, college sophomores, college juniors, college seniors, recent college graduates, graduate students, law students, career changers. International applications accepted.
Benefits Formal training, on-the-job training, opportunity to attend seminars/workshops, willing to act as a professional reference, willing to complete paperwork for educational credit, willing to provide letters of recommendation, reimbursement of work-related travel expenses.
Contact Write, call, fax, or e-mail Carolyn Slenska, Chief Investigator. Phone: 202-645-4999. Fax: 202-645-7761. E-mail: cslenska@pdsdc.org. In-person interview recommended (telephone interview accepted). Applicants must submit a letter of interest, resume, two letters of recommendation, one 3–4 page writing sample. Application deadline: March 30 for summer; continuous for all other positions.

PUBLIC INTEREST CLEARINGHOUSE
100 McAllister Street, 2nd Floor
San Francisco, California 94102

General Information Support organization for legal services throughout California and Nevada. Established in 1979. Number of employees: 6.
Internships Available ▶ *1–2 interns:* responsibilities include working with attorneys and staff to provide general support for the organization. Candidates should have ability to work independently, computer skills, office skills, organizational skills, self-motivation. Duration is one semester or summer. Unpaid. Open to college sophomores, college juniors, college seniors, recent college graduates. ▶ *1–2 legal interns:* responsibilities include working with attorneys on the Coordination Project, the Public Interest Law Program, and the Technology Project; interns will research and write on issues with state wide implications for legal service programs and provide general support to their supervising attorney; responsibilities will vary depending on project. Candidates should have ability to work independently, oral communication skills, personal interest in the field, strong interpersonal skills, written communication skills. Duration is one semester (varies according to school schedule). Unpaid. Open to law students. International applications accepted.
Benefits Job counseling, on-the-job training, opportunity to attend seminars/workshops, willing to act as a professional reference, willing to complete paperwork for educational credit, willing to provide letters of recommendation.
Contact Write, fax, or e-mail Amy Hamill, Public Interest Law Program Director. Fax: 415-255-3042. E-mail: ahamill@pic.org. No phone calls. In-person interview required. Applicants must submit a letter of interest, resume, three personal references. Applications are accepted continuously. World Wide Web: http://www.pic.org.

RICHARD P. DIEGUEZ, ATTORNEY AND COUNSELLOR AT LAW
192 Garden Street, Suite 2
Roslyn Heights, New York 11577-1012

General Information Entertainment law practice and entertainment industry educational organization. Established in 1987. Number of internship applications received each year: 200.
Internships Available ▶ *1 law clerk:* responsibilities include assisting with client intake, file maintenance, legal research, investigation, negotiation, and contract review. Candidates should have analytical skills, office skills, oral communication skills, organizational skills, research skills, writing skills. Duration is flexible. Unpaid. Open to college juniors, college seniors, recent college graduates, graduate students, law students, career changers. ▶ *2–4 management assistants:* responsibilities include developing and implementing marketing and promotional campaigns for entertainment

industry educational organizations; industry research; phone contact with producers, publishers, recording artists, managers, agents, and media. Candidates should have ability to work independently, oral communication skills, organizational skills, self-motivation, strong interpersonal skills, strong leadership ability. Duration is flexible. Unpaid. Open to high school students, recent high school graduates, college freshmen, college sophomores, college juniors, college seniors, recent college graduates, graduate students, career changers, individuals reentering the workforce. International applications accepted.
Benefits Job counseling, names of contacts, on-the-job training, opportunity to attend seminars/workshops, willing to act as a professional reference, willing to complete paperwork for educational credit, willing to provide letters of recommendation, hands-on experience.
Contact Richard P. Dieguez, Esq., Attorney, 192 Garden Street, Suite 2, Roslyn Heights, New York 11877-1012. Phone: 516-621-6424. E-mail: rpdieguez@rpdieguez.com. In-person interview recommended (telephone interview accepted). Applicants must submit a letter of interest, resume, academic transcripts, writing sample, three personal references, additional requirements found on Web site at http://www.rpdieguez.com/rpd_internships.html. Applications are accepted continuously. World Wide Web: http://www.rpdieguez.com.

SONOMA COUNTY LEGAL SERVICES FOUNDATION
1212 4th Street, #I
Santa Rosa, California 95404

General Information Foundation that provides legal education, referrals, and services to youth and families, especially on the lower end of the economic scale. Established in 1973. Number of employees: 2. Number of internship applications received each year: 4.
Internships Available ▶ *1–3 legal education assistants:* responsibilities include contacting schools and community groups to arrange speakers on legal topics, contacting attorneys to schedule their participation, providing appropriate resource materials, and follow-up. Unpaid. ▶ *1–3 legal program assistants:* responsibilities include working with clients who have legal issues to help them resolve these with local resources, on their own, or by referral to attorneys; contacting attorneys regarding these cases, recruiting attorneys, and following-up with clients. Duration is flexible (minimum of 3 months desirable). Unpaid. Candidates for all positions should have ability to work independently, ability to work with others, office skills, oral communication skills, personal interest in the field, self-motivation. Open to high school students, recent high school graduates, college freshmen, college sophomores, college juniors, college seniors, recent college graduates, graduate students, law students, career changers, individuals reentering the workforce, seniors. International applications accepted.
Benefits Names of contacts, on-the-job training, opportunity to attend seminars/workshops, travel reimbursement, willing to act as a professional reference, willing to complete paperwork for educational credit, willing to provide letters of recommendation.
Contact Write, call, fax, or e-mail Toni Novak, Executive Director. Phone: 707-546-2924. Fax: 707-546-0263. E-mail: sclsf@sonic.net. In-person interview recommended (telephone interview accepted). Applicants must submit a letter of interest, resume. Applications are accepted continuously.

SOUTHERN CENTER FOR HUMAN RIGHTS
83 Poplar Street, NW
Atlanta, Georgia 30303

General Information Nonprofit law office. Established in 1979. Number of employees: 23. Number of internship applications received each year: 100.
Internships Available ▶ *5–10 human rights interns:* responsibilities include legal research and writing for death penalty and prisoner's rights cases; case investigation. Candidates should have personal interest in the field, research skills, self-motivation, strong

Southern Center for Human Rights (continued)

interpersonal skills, writing skills. Duration is 2–6 months. Unpaid. Open to college seniors, recent college graduates, law students. International applications accepted.

Benefits Job counseling, on-the-job training, opportunity to attend seminars/workshops, travel reimbursement, willing to act as a professional reference, willing to complete paperwork for educational credit, willing to provide letters of recommendation.

Contact Write, e-mail, or through World Wide Web site Ty Alper, Staff Attorney. Phone: 404-688-1202. Fax: 404-688-9440. E-mail: rights@schr.org. Telephone interview required. Applicants must submit a letter of interest, resume, writing sample, three personal references. Applications are accepted continuously. World Wide Web: http://www.schr.org.

STUDENT PRESS LAW CENTER
1815 North Fort Myer Drive, Suite 900
Arlington, Virginia 22209

General Information   Nonprofit corporation that provides free legal assistance to student journalists and advisers and publishes materials explaining students' First Amendment rights. Established in 1974. Number of employees: 4. Number of internship applications received each year: 85.

Internships Available   ▶ *2–3 legal newswriting interns:* responsibilities include writing, editing, and laying out magazine. Candidates should have ability to work with others, editing skills, organizational skills, personal interest in the field, writing skills, student media experience (preferred). Duration is 1 semester or summer. $2500 stipend for full-semester interns; $1800 stipend for summer interns plus possible $600 scholarship. Open to college sophomores, college juniors, college seniors, recent college graduates, graduate students. ▶ *1–2 media law interns:* responsibilities include researching and writing opinions and articles and making client contact. Candidates should have ability to work independently, analytical skills, personal interest in the field, research skills, strong interpersonal skills, written communication skills. Duration is 1 semester or summer. $500 per week for full-time interns; $10 per hour for part-time interns. Open to law students. International applications accepted.

Benefits Job counseling, opportunity to attend seminars/workshops, willing to act as a professional reference, willing to complete paperwork for educational credit, willing to provide letters of recommendation.

Contact Write, e-mail, or through World Wide Web site Mr. Mark Goodman, Executive Director. E-mail: splc@splc.org. Applicants must submit a letter of interest, resume, two personal references, newswriting clips (for journalism applicants); legal writing sample (law applicants). Application deadline: February 1 for summer (suggested date), June 1 for fall (suggested date), November 1 for spring (suggested date). World Wide Web: http://www.splc.org.

VICTIM-WITNESS ASSISTANCE PROGRAM–OFFICE OF THE DISTRICT ATTORNEY, COUNTY OF LOS ANGELES
Volunteer Services, 3204 Rosemead Boulevard, Suite 200
El Monte, California 91731

General Information   Provides a broad range of services to victims and witnesses of crime. Established in 1977. Number of employees: 94. Number of internship applications received each year: 125.

Internships Available   ▶ *30–40 student interns/volunteers:* responsibilities include contacting victims; providing resource referrals; explaining court procedures; providing court escort; providing case status and disposition; notifying families; assisting victims with information about obtaining crime reports, witness fees, property return; arranging for restitution or translation; assisting children, elderly, and handicapped. Candidates should have analytical skills, oral communication skills, personal interest in the field, self-motivation, strong interpersonal skills, written communication skills. Duration is 1 summer, 6 months, or 1 year. Unpaid. Open to college freshmen, college sophomores, college juniors, col-

lege seniors, recent college graduates, graduate students, law students, career changers, individuals over 18 years of age. International applications accepted.

Benefits Formal training, job counseling, names of contacts, opportunity to attend seminars/workshops, possible full-time employment, willing to complete paperwork for educational credit, willing to provide letters of recommendation.

Contact Write, call, fax, or e-mail Floyd Wyatt, Assistant Program Director. Phone: 626-927-2500. Fax: 626-569-9541. E-mail: fwyatt@da.co.la.ca.us. In-person interview required. Applicants must submit a formal organization application, two personal references. Applications are accepted continuously.

VOLUNTEER LEGAL SERVICES PROGRAM
465 California Street, Suite 1100
San Francisco, California 94104

General Information   Legal services program. Established in 1977. Number of employees: 25. Affiliate of Bar Association of San Francisco, San Francisco, California. Number of internship applications received each year: 20.

Internships Available   ▶ *1–2 media interns:* responsibilities include identifying and developing news stories; interviewing clients, staff, and volunteers; writing and distributing press releases; organizing and maintaining media archive; writing and editing articles for various internal publications. Candidates should have ability to work independently, oral communication skills, personal interest in the field, self-motivation, writing skills. Duration is flexible. Unpaid. Open to college seniors, recent college graduates, graduate students, law students, career changers. International applications accepted.

Benefits Opportunity to attend seminars/workshops, willing to act as a professional reference, willing to complete paperwork for educational credit, willing to provide letters of recommendation.

Contact Write, fax, or e-mail Sabrina Smith, Development Associate. Fax: 415-477-2390. E-mail: ssmith@sfbar.org. No phone calls. In-person interview required. Applicants must submit a letter of interest, resume, writing sample. Applications are accepted continuously. World Wide Web: http://www.sfbar.org/vlsp.

WASHINGTON AREA LAWYERS FOR THE ARTS
815 15th Street, NW, Suite 900
Washington, District of Columbia 20005

General Information   Organization that provides legal assistance to artists. Established in 1983. Number of employees: 4. Number of internship applications received each year: 100.

Internships Available   ▶ *2–3 art law interns:* responsibilities include counseling artists/clients by telephone and helping them discern their legal needs; preparing summaries of facts, issues, and applicable laws for the director of legal services, possibly sitting in on client consultations, and organizing workshops and symposia on legal issues and the arts. Candidates should have ability to work independently, college courses in field, computer skills, knowledge of field, oral communication skills, research skills, copyright background (helpful). Duration is 1–4 months. Unpaid. Open to law students. ▶ *1–2 marketing interns.* Candidates should have interest in media relations and arts management, event production skills. Duration is flexible. Unpaid. Open to college freshmen, college sophomores, college juniors, college seniors.

Benefits Formal training, job counseling, on-the-job training, opportunity to attend seminars/workshops, willing to act as a professional reference, willing to complete paperwork for educational credit, willing to provide letters of recommendation.

Contact Write, call, fax, or e-mail John D. Malloy, Director of Legal Services. Phone: 202-393-2826. Fax: 202-393-4444. E-mail: legalservices@thewala.org. In-person interview required. Applicants must submit a letter of interest, resume, academic transcripts, one 1- to 5- page writing sample. Application deadline: January 8 for spring, March 1 for summer, September 1 for fall. World Wide Web: http://www.thewala.org.

WASHINGTON LEGAL FOUNDATION
2009 Massachusetts Avenue, NW
Washington, District of Columbia 20036

General Information Public interest law firm advocating free enterprise and working to restore balance to the judiciary through original litigation and distribution of multiple publications. Established in 1977. Number of employees: 20. Number of internship applications received each year: 100.

Internships Available ▶ *1 legal policy intern:* responsibilities include production of nationally distributed legal policy publications; monitoring and analysis of developments in federal and state courts, legislatures, and regulatory agencies; assisting in setting up and promoting bi-weekly press briefing events; assisting with outreach to and expansion of Foundation's national pro bono network. Candidates should have oral communication skills, research skills, writing skills, interest in intersection between law and public policy. Duration is flexible (minimum 15 hours per week during spring semester). Competitive salary. ▶ *1–5 public affairs interns:* responsibilities include researching, marketing, entering data, filing, and donor correspondence. Candidates should have ability to work with others, computer skills, organizational skills, self-motivation, written communication skills. Duration is flexible. Position available as unpaid or paid. Open to college sophomores, college juniors, college seniors, graduate students. International applications accepted.

Benefits Names of contacts, possible full-time employment, willing to complete paperwork for educational credit, willing to provide letters of recommendation.

Contact Write or e-mail Ms. Constance Claffey Larcher, President. E-mail: administration@wlf.org. No phone calls. In-person interview required. Applicants must submit a letter of interest, resume, writing sample (legal policy position). Applications are accepted continuously. World Wide Web: http://www.wlf.org.

WOMEN'S LAW PROJECT
125 South 9th Street, Suite 300
Philadelphia, Pennsylvania 19107

General Information Nonprofit feminist public interest law firm. Established in 1974. Number of employees: 9. Number of internship applications received each year: 40.

Internships Available ▶ *10–15 telephone counselors:* responsibilities include performing telephone counseling including interviewing callers to identify legal problems; counseling callers on strategies for solving legal problems; providing information; recording information in database. Candidates should have ability to work with others, analytical skills, computer skills, oral communication skills, self-motivation. Duration is minimum of one semester (fall, spring, summer). Unpaid. Open to recent high school graduates, college freshmen, college sophomores, college juniors, college seniors, recent college graduates, graduate students, career changers, individuals reentering the workforce. International applications accepted.

Benefits On-the-job training, willing to act as a professional reference, willing to complete paperwork for educational credit, willing to provide letters of recommendation.

Contact Write or e-mail Debra L. Rubin, Program Manager. Fax: 215-928-9848. E-mail: drubin@womenslawproject.org. No phone calls. In-person interview recommended (telephone interview accepted). Applicants must submit a formal organization application, letter of interest, resume. Applications are accepted continuously.

SCIENTIFIC RESEARCH AND DEVELOPMENT SERVICES

AMERICAN ASSOCIATION FOR THE ADVANCEMENT OF SCIENCE
1200 New York Avenue, NW, #102
Washington, District of Columbia 20005

General Information Nonprofit scientific association, publisher of SCIENCE Magazine. Established in 1848. Number of employees: 400. Number of internship applications received each year: 200.
Internships Available ▶ *Interns:* responsibilities include various positions depending on specific needs of the department. Candidates should have computer skills, knowledge of field, oral communication skills, personal interest in the field, strong interpersonal skills, written communication skills. Duration is 3–5 months. Position available as unpaid or paid. Open to college seniors, recent college graduates, graduate students, individuals reentering the workforce.
Benefits Opportunity to attend seminars/workshops, possible full-time employment, willing to act as a professional reference, willing to complete paperwork for educational credit, willing to provide letters of recommendation, paid holidays when they fall on regularly scheduled work day.
Contact Write or through World Wide Web site Yvette Robinson, Personnel Assistant. Fax: 202-682-1630. No phone calls. In-person interview required. Applicants must submit a letter of interest, resume, 2-3 writing samples, 2-3 letters of recommendation. Application deadline: April 1 for summer, November 1 for fall. World Wide Web: http://www.aaas.org.

AMERICAN GEOGRAPHICAL SOCIETY
120 Wall Street, Suite 100
New York, New York 10005

General Information Organization that encourages geographical research and field work and makes it available to policy makers, the media, and the public to reduce geographical illiteracy in the United States; publishes a scholarly journal, a magazine, and a newsletter; maintains programs of educational travel, volunteer teaching, economic geography, and geographic information service and speakers. Established in 1851. Number of employees: 4. Number of internship applications received each year: 35.
Internships Available ▶ *3–6 editorial, research, and/or administrative interns.* Candidates should have ability to work independently, computer skills, oral communication skills, self-motivation, strong interpersonal skills, writing skills. Duration is 10 weeks minimum. Unpaid. Open to college freshmen, college sophomores, college juniors, college seniors, recent college graduates, graduate students, exceptional high school seniors. International applications accepted.
Benefits Formal training, job counseling, names of contacts, on-the-job training, opportunity to attend seminars/workshops, willing to act as a professional reference, willing to complete paperwork for educational credit, willing to provide letters of recommendation.
Contact Write, call, fax, e-mail, or through World Wide Web site Ms. Mary Lynne Bird, Executive Director. Phone: 212-422-5456. Fax: 212-422-5480. E-mail: amgeosoc@earthlink.net. In-person interview recommended (telephone interview accepted). Applicants must submit a letter of interest, resume, writing sample, two letters of recommendation. Applications are accepted continuously. World Wide Web: http://amergeog.org.

AMERICAN PARKINSON DISEASE ASSOCIATION
2100 Pfingsten Road
Glenview, Illinois 60025

General Information Association dedicated to fund-raising for research, patient education and support, and Parkinson's disease awareness and advocacy. Established in 1961. Number of

American Parkinson Disease Association (continued)

employees: 2. Unit of American Parkinson Disease Association, Staten Island, New York. Number of internship applications received each year: 3.

Internships Available ▶ *1 Parkinson's Disease Information and Referral Center assistant :* responsibilities include phone contact with patients and service providers; office work including computer (Word, Access). Candidates should have ability to work independently, computer skills, office skills, self-motivation. Unpaid. Open to high school students, recent high school graduates, college freshmen, college sophomores, college juniors, college seniors.

Benefits On-the-job training, opportunity to attend seminars/ workshops, willing to act as a professional reference, willing to complete paperwork for educational credit, willing to provide letters of recommendation.

Contact Write, call, fax, e-mail, or through World Wide Web site Susan Reese, Director. Phone: 847-657-5787. Fax: 847-657-5708. E-mail: apdaypd@aol.com. In-person interview recommended (telephone interview accepted). Applicants must submit a letter of interest, resume, two personal references, two letters of recommendation. Applications are accepted continuously. World Wide Web: http://www.apdaparkinson.com.

ASPRS: THE IMAGING AND GEOSPATIAL INFORMATION SOCIETY
5410 Grosvenor Lane, Suite 210
Bethesda, Maryland 20814-2160

General Information Scientific association serving over 7,000 professional members around the world, with a mission to advance knowledge and improve understanding of mapping sciences and to promote responsible applications of photogrammetry, remote sensing, GIS, and supporting technologies. Established in 1934.

Internships Available ▶ *LH systems internships:* responsibilities include carrying out a small research project of intern's choice or working on existing LH systems project as a team member; submission of final report upon completion of internship. Candidates should have ability to work with others, research skills, self-motivation, enrollment in an accredited college or university and membership of ASPRS. Duration is 8 weeks. $2500 stipend plus allowance for travel and living expenses for period of internship. Open to graduate students of photogrammetry and remote sensing.

Benefits Allowance for travel and living expenses for the period of the internship.

International Internships Available in Heerbrugg, Switzerland.

Contact Write, e-mail, or through World Wide Web site ASPRS Scholarship Administrator. Phone: 301-493-0290. Fax: 301-493-0208. E-mail: scholarships@asprs.org. Applicants must submit a formal organization application, academic transcripts, a research proposal (maximum 1000 words) stating significance of the research, proposed methodology, expected results and schedule. Application deadline: early December. World Wide Web: http://www.asprs.org.

BAXTER INTERNATIONAL
1 Baxter Parkway
Deerfield, Illinois 60015

General Information Worldwide leader in critical therapies for people with life-threatening conditions. Established in 1931. Number of employees: 1,300. Number of internship applications received each year: 1,000.

Internships Available ▶ *40–60 interns:* responsibilities include working in finance, engineering, human resources, research and development, marketing, and strategy. Candidates should have ability to work independently, analytical skills, computer skills, oral communication skills, organizational skills, self-motivation, strong interpersonal skills, strong leadership ability, writing skills. Duration is 3 months (May to August). Salary depends on year at school, field, or degree. Open to college sophomores, college juniors, recent college graduates, graduate students, individuals reentering the workforce.

Benefits Housing at a cost, meals at a cost, on-the-job training, opportunity to attend seminars/workshops, possible full-time employment, travel reimbursement, willing to complete paperwork for educational credit, willing to provide letters of recommendation.

Contact Write, fax, e-mail, or through World Wide Web site Ana M. Trbojevich, Manager, Global College Relations. Fax: 847-948-4494. E-mail: internships@baxter.com. No phone calls. In-person interview required. Applicants must submit a letter of interest, resume, academic transcripts. Application deadline: March 1. World Wide Web: http://www.baxter.com.

BERMUDA BIOLOGICAL STATION FOR RESEARCH, INC.
17 Biological Lane
Ferry Reach, St. George's GE01 Bermuda

General Information Research and education center for oceanography, marine biology, and global climate change. Established in 1903. Number of employees: 100. Number of internship applications received each year: 300.

Internships Available ▶ *10 graduate interns:* responsibilities include conducting research with technical staff or independently. Candidates should have acceptance into graduate program by recognized university; thesis proposal must have been approved by advisor at that university; must have faculty supervisor at BBSR and approved funding. Duration is 3 months to 3 years. Unpaid. Open to graduate students. ▶ *8 undergraduate research interns:* responsibilities include conducting independent research project. Candidates should have ability to work independently, college courses in field, knowledge of field, research skills, strong interpersonal skills. Duration is August to November only. Room and board is deducted from salary of approximately $265 per week. Open to college juniors, college seniors. ▶ *Volunteer interns:* responsibilities include working 40 hours per week in lab of scientist who pays intern's room and board. Candidates should have computer skills, knowledge of field, organizational skills, personal interest in the field, self-motivation, strong interpersonal skills. Duration is 3-4 months; 3-5 positions per session, 3 sessions per year. Unpaid. Open to college juniors, college seniors, recent college graduates, graduate students. International applications accepted.

Benefits Opportunity to attend seminars/workshops, possible full-time employment, willing to act as a professional reference, willing to complete paperwork for educational credit, willing to provide letters of recommendation, free room and board for volunteer interns.

International Internships Available.

Contact E-mail or through World Wide Web site Helle Patterson, Education Officer, 17 Biological Lane, Ferry Reach, St. George's GEO1 Bermuda. E-mail: hpatt@sargasso.bbsr.edu. No phone calls. Applicants must submit a formal organization application, letter of interest, resume. Application deadline: February 1 for summer, March 15 for research experience (fall); no application deadline for graduate interns, June 1 for fall, October 1 for spring. World Wide Web: http://www.bbsr.edu/.

BROOKHAVEN NATIONAL LABORATORY
Building 438
Upton, New York 11973-5000

General Information Multidisciplinary scientific laboratory. Established in 1947. Number of employees: 3,000. Unit of United States Department of Energy, Washington, District of Columbia.

Internships Available ▶ *40–70 energy research undergraduate laboratory fellowships:* responsibilities include working in variety of scientific/engineering fields. Candidates should have minimum GPA of 2.5. Duration is one summer (10 weeks) or one semester (16 weeks). $400 per week. Open to college freshmen, college sophomores, college juniors, college seniors, must be U.S. citizen or permanent resident and at least 18 years old.

Benefits Opportunity to attend seminars/workshops, travel reimbursement, willing to complete paperwork for educational credit, housing assistance.

Contact Call or e-mail Todd Clark. Phone: 202-586-7174. E-mail: todd.clark@science.doe.gov. Electronic application: https://applicationlink.labworks.org/applicationlink/default.htm. Application deadline: January for spring, February for summer, August for fall. World Wide Web: http://www.scied.science.doe.gov.

CARNEGIE INSTITUTION OF WASHINGTON
5251 Broad Branch Road, NW
Washington, District of Columbia 20015

General Information Science research organization. Established in 1902. Number of employees: 100. Number of internship applications received each year: 80.
Internships Available ▶ *10–15 interns in geoscience:* responsibilities include research. Candidates should have ability to work independently, analytical skills, college courses in field, oral communication skills, research skills, self-motivation. Duration is June to August (10 weeks). $3000 per duration of internship. Open to college freshmen, college sophomores, college juniors.
Benefits Free housing, on-the-job training, opportunity to attend seminars/workshops, travel reimbursement, willing to act as a professional reference, willing to provide letters of recommendation.
Contact E-mail or through World Wide Web site Dr. Bill Minarik, Summer Education Coordinator. Fax: 202-478-5901. E-mail: minarik@gl.ciw.edu. No phone calls. Applicants must submit a formal organization application, resume, academic transcripts, three letters of recommendation. Application deadline: March 14. World Wide Web: http://www.gl.ciw.edu/interns.

CENTER FOR STRATEGIC AND BUDGETARY ASSESSMENTS
1730 Rhode Island Avenue, NW, Suite 912
Washington, District of Columbia 20036

General Information Organization that analyzes the defense budget, military strategy and policies, and other issues and educates the media, government, and public on these issues. Established in 1983. Number of employees: 12. Number of internship applications received each year: 200.
Internships Available ▶ *1–3 research assistants:* responsibilities include supporting staff research, performing office and administrative tasks. Candidates should have ability to work independently, computer skills, knowledge of field, office skills, oral communication skills, written communication skills. Duration is 10–12 weeks. $300–$400 per week. Open to college juniors, college seniors.
Benefits Names of contacts, opportunity to attend seminars/workshops, willing to complete paperwork for educational credit, willing to provide letters of recommendation.
Contact Write, call, fax, or through World Wide Web site Intern Coordinator. Phone: 202-331-7990. Fax: 202-331-8019. E-mail: info@csbaonline.org. Applicants must submit a letter of interest, resume, writing sample (3-4 pages). Application deadline: April 15 for summer, August 1 for fall, November 15 for spring. World Wide Web: http://www.csbaonline.org.

CIIT CENTERS FOR HEALTH RESEARCH
6 Davis Drive, PO Box 12137
Research Triangle Park, North Carolina 27709-2137

General Information Not-for-profit scientific research institute dedicated to providing an improved scientific basis for understanding and assessing the potential adverse effects of chemicals, pharmaceuticals, and consumer products on human health. Established in 1976. Number of employees: 150. Number of internship applications received each year: 200.
Internships Available ▶ *10–15 summer interns:* responsibilities include working in research laboratories on projects under the direction of a CIIT scientist; conducting an independent research project and presenting findings in a seminar. Candidates should have ability to work independently, ability to work with others, college courses in field, oral communication skills, research skills, self-motivation. Duration is 12–15 weeks. $440–$500 per week. Open to college sophomores, college juniors, college seniors. International applications accepted.
Benefits Formal training, on-the-job training, opportunity to attend seminars/workshops, travel reimbursement, willing to act as a professional reference, willing to complete paperwork for educational credit, willing to provide letters of recommendation.

Contact Write or e-mail Rusty Bramlage, Director, Human Resources. Phone: 919-558-1331. Fax: 919-558-1430. E-mail: bramlage@ciit.org. Telephone interview required. Applicants must submit a formal organization application, three letters of recommendation. Application deadline: March 1. World Wide Web: http://www.ciit.org.

CROW CANYON ARCHAEOLOGICAL CENTER
23390 Road K
Cortez, Colorado 81321

General Information Archaeological center that initiates and conducts significant archaeological research in the Southwest and shares the results through innovative public and professional education, open communication with Native Americans, and partnerships with institutions having common interests. Established in 1983. Number of employees: 50. Number of internship applications received each year: 100.
Internships Available ▶ *3–6 education interns:* responsibilities include assisting in teaching lay participants ranging in age from 4th graders to senior citizens about anthropological/archaeological concepts and methods, serving as docent at excavation sites, assisting in planning and implementing field trips, and developing lesson plan or research project. Candidates should have knowledge of field, oral communication skills, plan to pursue career in field, research skills, self-motivation, strong interpersonal skills. Duration is 8–11 weeks. Unpaid. ▶ *4–6 field interns:* responsibilities include excavating and recording architectural and non-architectural contexts, mapping with a total station, site photography, instructing and supervising lay participants in basic excavation techniques and archaeological concepts. Candidates should have ability to work independently, ability to work with others, experience in the field, oral communication skills, organizational skills, research skills. Duration is 11–12 weeks. Unpaid. ▶ *4 lab interns:* responsibilities include processing, cataloging, and analyzing a variety of archaeological samples, artifacts, maps and other records; collections and database management; maintenance of a small research library; instructing and supervising lay participants ranging in age from 4th graders to senior citizens in laboratory research. Candidates should have analytical skills, computer skills, experience in the field, organizational skills, research skills, strong interpersonal skills. Duration is 11–12 weeks. Unpaid. Open to college juniors, college seniors, recent college graduates, graduate students.
Benefits Free housing, free meals, names of contacts, on-the-job training, travel reimbursement, willing to act as a professional reference, willing to complete paperwork for educational credit, willing to provide letters of recommendation, modest weekly stipend, training in archaeological field and laboratory techniques, experiential teaching program.
Contact Write, e-mail, or through World Wide Web site Human Resources. E-mail: interns@crowcanyon.org. No phone calls. Telephone interview required. Applicants must submit a formal organization application, three personal references, three letters of recommendation. Application deadline: February 15 for education positions, March 1 for research positions. World Wide Web: http://www.crowcanyon.org.

HARVARD SCHOOL OF PUBLIC HEALTH, DIVISION OF BIOLOGICAL SCIENCES
665 Huntington Avenue, Building 1-1204-A
Boston, Massachusetts 02115-6021

General Information Molecular biology research training center. Established in 1923. Number of employees: 2. Division of Harvard University, Cambridge, Massachusetts. Number of internship applications received each year: 130.
Internships Available ▶ *10–16 summer interns:* responsibilities include laboratory-based molecular biology research. Candidates should have analytical skills, college courses in field, knowledge of field, plan to pursue career in field, self-motivation, strong interpersonal skills. Duration is June 10 to August 16. $3100 per duration of internship. Open to minority students at college junior or senior level; must be U.S. citizen or permanent resident.

Harvard School of Public Health, Division of Biological Sciences (continued)
Benefits Free housing, travel reimbursement, graduate-level training for research careers.
Contact Write, call, fax, e-mail, or through World Wide Web site Ruth Kenworthy, Administrator. Phone: 617-432-4470. Fax: 617-432-0433. E-mail: kenworthy@cvlab.harvard.edu. Applicants must submit a formal organization application, letter of interest, academic transcripts, two letters of recommendation. Application deadline: February 15. World Wide Web: http://www.hsph.harvard.edu/sip.

HEALTH AND MEDICINE POLICY RESEARCH GROUP
29 East Madison Street, Suite 602
Chicago, Illinois 60602

General Information Nonprofit organization that performs policy research work on health-care issues affecting the poor, women, children, and the general population. Established in 1980. Number of employees: 6. Number of internship applications received each year: 30.
Internships Available ▶ *1–4 policy interns:* responsibilities include policy research, policy writing, office administration, and conference development. Candidates should have ability to work independently, analytical skills, college courses in field, computer skills, editing skills, knowledge of field, office skills, oral communication skills, organizational skills, personal interest in the field, plan to pursue career in field, research skills, self-motivation, strong interpersonal skills, writing skills. Duration is dependent on intern's availability. Unpaid. Open to college freshmen, college sophomores, college juniors, college seniors, recent college graduates, graduate students, law students. International applications accepted.
Benefits Names of contacts, on-the-job training, opportunity to attend seminars/workshops, willing to act as a professional reference, willing to provide letters of recommendation.
Contact Write, call, fax, or e-mail Margie Schaps, Executive Director, 29 East Madison Street, Suite 602, Chicago, Illinois 60602. Phone: 312-372-4292. Fax: 312-372-2753. E-mail: info@hmprg.org. In-person interview recommended (telephone interview accepted). Applicants must submit a letter of interest, resume, writing sample, personal reference. Application deadline: January 1 for spring, April 1 for summer, October 1 for winter. World Wide Web: http://www.hmprg.org.

INSTITUTE OF ECOSYSTEM STUDIES (IES)
Box R
Millbrook, New York 12545-0178

General Information Ecological research and education institute. Established in 1983. Number of employees: 120. Number of internship applications received each year: 200.
Internships Available ▶ *8–10 research experiences for undergraduates interns:* responsibilities include working closely with a mentor scientist, developing and conducting an independent ecological research project and writing a paper for an Institute publication, and presenting results at a formal symposium. Duration is 12 weeks. $3000 per duration of internship. Open to college freshmen, college sophomores, college juniors, first semester seniors.
Benefits Housing at a cost, names of contacts, opportunity to attend seminars/workshops, possible full-time employment, willing to complete paperwork for educational credit, willing to provide letters of recommendation.
Contact Write, call, fax, e-mail, or through World Wide Web site Heather Dahl, REU Program Assistant. Phone: 845-677-7600 Ext. 326. Fax: 845-677-6455. E-mail: dahlh@ecostudies.org. Applicants must submit a formal organization application, resume, online application at www.ecostudies.org/education/reu/reu1.html. Application deadline: February 15 for summer. World Wide Web: http://www.ecostudies.org.

INTERNATIONAL RESEARCH AND EVALUATION
21098 IRE Control Center
Eagan, Minnesota 55121-0098

General Information Private, nonpartisan, interdisciplinary research company that collects, indexes, stores, synthesizes, retrieves, and disseminates information online and on-demand. Established in 1972. Number of employees: 137. Number of internship applications received each year: 53.
Internships Available ▶ *3–8 interactive multimedia platform interns:* responsibilities include securing input and scanning and embedding data into user-friendly multimedia platforms. Candidates should have analytical skills, computer skills, knowledge of field, plan to pursue career in field, self-motivation, writing skills. Duration is 3 months. $9–$20 per hour. Open to recent high school graduates, college freshmen, college sophomores, college juniors, college seniors, recent college graduates, graduate students. International applications accepted.
Benefits Formal training, health insurance, opportunity to attend seminars/workshops, possible full-time employment, willing to complete paperwork for educational credit.
Contact Write Valantina Voight, Internship Director. Fax: 952-888-9124. E-mail: ireittn@gte.net. No phone calls. In-person interview required. Applicants must submit a letter of interest, academic transcripts. Applications are accepted continuously. World Wide Web: http://www.ire-ittn.com.

LAMONT-DOHERTY EARTH OBSERVATORY
Room 103A Oceanography
Palisades, New York 10964

General Information Organization involved in geological, oceanographic, environmental, and climatic research. Established in 1948. Number of employees: 550. Unit of Columbia University, New York, New York. Number of internship applications received each year: 170.
Internships Available ▶ *14–20 summer interns:* responsibilities include undertaking research projects in oceanography, marine geophysics, geochemistry, geology, and environmental science. Candidates should have analytical skills, computer skills, knowledge of field, personal interest in the field, written communication skills, 2 semesters of calculus. Duration is 10 weeks. $2530 per duration of internship. Open to college sophomores, college juniors.
Benefits Free housing, names of contacts, opportunity to attend seminars/workshops, willing to complete paperwork for educational credit, willing to provide letters of recommendation, travel reimbursement (for travel over 200 miles).
Contact Write or e-mail Dr. Dallas Abbott, Summer Internship Program Director. E-mail: dallas@ldeo.columbia.edu. No phone calls. Applicants must submit a formal organization application, letter of interest, academic transcripts, writing sample, three letters of recommendation. Application deadline: March 10 for summer. World Wide Web: http://www.ldeo.columbia.edu/~dallas/abbott_sum.html.

LAWRENCE LIVERMORE NATIONAL LABORATORY, UNDERGRADUATE SUMMER INSTITUTE
PO Box 808, L-371
Livermore, California 94551-0808

General Information Research facility providing scientific and technological expertise; dedicated to global security, the environment, and the future scientific needs of the nation. Established in 1985. Number of employees: 9,000. Number of internship applications received each year: 100.
Internships Available ▶ *25 interns:* responsibilities include attending lectures on fusion, lasers, computational modeling, physics, chemistry, engineering, and national security. Candidates should have major in applied science field, experience in a lab science setting in previous summers (preferred). Duration is 12 weeks. Paid. Open to college juniors, college seniors, must be returning to college in the fall following the internship.
Benefits Opportunity to attend seminars/workshops, travel reimbursement, opportunity to work on small research projects.
Contact Write, call, fax, e-mail, or through World Wide Web site Linda Allen, Secretary. Phone: 925-422-1748. Fax: 925-424-5205.

E-mail: allen48@llnl.gov. Applicants must submit a formal organization application, letter of interest, resume, academic transcripts, two personal references. Application deadline: January 31. World Wide Web: http://www.llnl.gov/usi/.

LINCOLN LABORATORY, MASSACHUSETTS INSTITUTE OF TECHNOLOGY
244 Wood Street
Lexington, Massachusetts 02420-9108

General Information Research and development center whose primary focus is in the field of advanced electronics; research includes space surveillance, tactical systems, satellite communications, and radar and air traffic control systems. Established in 1951. Number of employees: 2,300. Branch of Massachusetts Institute of Technology, Cambridge, Massachusetts. Number of internship applications received each year: 40.

Internships Available ▶ *15 summer technical assistants:* responsibilities include designing hardware, conducting scientific programming, and offering technical support. Candidates should have analytical skills, computer skills, plan to pursue career in field, research skills, minimum 3.0 GPA, major in physics or mathematics. Duration is 10 weeks. Paid. Open to college juniors and seniors who are minority members (African Americans, Puerto Ricans, Mexican Americans, Native Americans).

Benefits Formal training, housing at a cost, job counseling, on-the-job training, opportunity to attend seminars/workshops, possible full-time employment, travel reimbursement, willing to provide letters of recommendation.

Contact Write, call, fax, e-mail, or through World Wide Web site Mr. Paul F. Hezel, Human Resources Representative. Phone: 781-981-7048. Fax: 781-981-7086. E-mail: hezel@ll.mit.edu. Applicants must submit a formal organization application, letter of interest, resume, academic transcripts, two letters of recommendation. Application deadline: March 1 for summer. World Wide Web: http://www.ll.mit.edu.

LUNAR AND PLANETARY INSTITUTE
3600 Bay Area Boulevard
Houston, Texas 77058-1113

General Information Institute whose goal is to facilitate methods for the distribution of results of current planetary science research to the worldwide scientific community. Established in 1968. Number of employees: 60. Unit of Universities Space Research Association, Columbia, Maryland. Number of internship applications received each year: 166.

Internships Available ▶ *10–12 interns:* responsibilities include participating actively in lunar/planetary research with scientists at the Institute and the NASA Johnson Space Center in such areas as cosmic dust characterization, meteorite fall statistics, planetary rigolith studies, Mars soil analog chemistry, trace element partitioning studies, volcano morphology characterization, planetary volcanism and thermal histories, thermal and mechanical modeling of planetary interiors, database management systems, and search for micro-organisms in geologic samples, and astrobiology. Candidates should have ability to work independently, college courses in field, computer skills, experience in the field, plan to pursue career in field, 50 semester hours of credit. Duration is 10 weeks. $500 per week. Open to college sophomores, college juniors, college seniors. International applications accepted.

Benefits Housing at a cost, opportunity to attend seminars/workshops, up to $1000 travel allowance.

Contact Write, fax, or e-mail Ms. Jodi J. Jordan, Executive Administrator. Fax: 281-486-2173. E-mail: jordan@lpi.usra.edu. No phone calls. Applicants must submit a letter of interest, academic transcripts, three letters of recommendation, biographical sketch including goals, career plans, scientific interests, reason for application, major field of study. Application deadline: February 5 for summer. World Wide Web: http://www.lpi.usra.edu/lpiintern.html.

MARIA MITCHELL OBSERVATORY
3 Vestal Street
Nantucket, Massachusetts 02554

General Information Observatory that runs an active, diverse program in astronomical research and an educational outreach program. Established in 1908. Number of employees: 7. Unit of Maria Mitchell Association, Nantucket, Massachusetts. Number of internship applications received each year: 100.

Internships Available ▶ *6 summer research assistants:* responsibilities include performing scientific research and participating in public and educational programs. Candidates should have ability to work independently, ability to work with others, computer skills, oral communication skills, personal interest in the field, plan to pursue career in field, research skills, self-motivation, written communication skills. Duration is 10–15 weeks. $1300 per month. Open to college freshmen, college sophomores, college juniors, college seniors, must be U.S. citizen or have permanent residency.

Benefits Free housing, job counseling, names of contacts, on-the-job training, opportunity to attend seminars/workshops, travel reimbursement, tuition assistance, willing to complete paperwork for educational credit, willing to provide letters of recommendation.

Contact Write, call, fax, or e-mail Dr. Vladimir Strelnitski, Director. Phone: 508-228-9273. Fax: 508-228-1031. E-mail: vladimir@mmo.org. Telephone interview required. Applicants must submit a formal organization application, letter of interest, resume, academic transcripts, three letters of recommendation. Application deadline: February 15 for summer. World Wide Web: http://www.mmo.org.

MOTE MARINE LABORATORY
1600 Ken Thompson Parkway
Sarasota, Florida 34236

General Information Independent nonprofit organization dedicated to research in marine and environmental sciences. Established in 1955. Number of employees: 200. Number of internship applications received each year: 300.

Internships Available ▶ *2–5 business interns:* responsibilities include business and financial duties, including bookkeeping, accounts payable, and accounts receivable. Candidates should have ability to work independently, ability to work with others, computer skills, office skills, organizational skills, plan to pursue career in field, self-motivation. Duration is 8–16 weeks. Unpaid. Open to college juniors, college seniors. ▶ *2–3 communications interns:* responsibilities include press release writing, preparation of articles for newsletters and magazines, and office assistance. Candidates should have ability to work with others, college courses in field, computer skills, editing skills, written communication skills. Duration is 8–16 weeks. Unpaid. Open to college sophomores, college juniors, college seniors, recent college graduates. ▶ *2–5 development office interns:* responsibilities include administrative duties in marketing/development office. Candidates should have ability to work independently, college courses in field, computer skills, office skills, oral communication skills, plan to pursue career in field, self-motivation, strong interpersonal skills, written communication skills. Duration is 8–16 weeks. Unpaid. Open to college juniors, college seniors. ▶ *2–5 education interns:* responsibilities include assisting as instructors and designing education program. Candidates should have ability to work independently, ability to work with others, college courses in field, oral communication skills, plan to pursue career in field, strong leadership ability. Duration is 8–16 weeks. Unpaid. Open to college sophomores, college juniors, college seniors, recent college graduates. ▶ *20–50 research interns:* responsibilities include various duties depending on assigned research area including tissue processing, sediment and water analysis, animal monitoring, data entry, and report writing. Candidates should have ability to work independently, plan to pursue career in field, research skills, self-motivation. Duration is 8–16 weeks. Unpaid. Open to recent high school graduates, college sophomores, college juniors, college seniors. International applications accepted.

Benefits Housing at a cost, on-the-job training, opportunity to attend seminars/workshops, willing to act as a professional reference, willing to complete paperwork for educational credit, will-

Mote Marine Laboratory (continued)

ing to provide letters of recommendation, free aquarium admission, gift shop discount, a few scholarships available at $150 per week.
Contact Write, call, fax, or e-mail Andrea Davis, Coordinator of Volunteer/Intern Services. Phone: 941-388-4441. Fax: 941-388-4312. E-mail: adavis@mote.org. Applicants must submit a formal organization application, academic transcripts, writing sample. Applications are accepted continuously. World Wide Web: http://www.mote.org.

NATIONAL ASTRONOMY AND IONOSPHERE CENTER (NAIC)
Cornell University, 504 Space Sciences Building
Ithaca, New York 14853-6801

General Information Center for atmospheric sciences, radar, and radio astronomy that operates the world's largest single dish radio telescope (located in Puerto Rico). Established in 1963. Number of employees: 13. Unit of Cornell University. Number of internship applications received each year: 150.
Internships Available ▶ *8–10 summer research assistants:* responsibilities include participation in research projects including searches for pulsars; studies of galaxies, giant stars, or interstellar medium; investigation of ionized portions of the earth's atmosphere; mapping planets or other members of the solar system; and developing projects for instrumentation or software. Candidates should have ability to work independently, ability to work with others, college courses in field, computer skills, knowledge of field, research skills, self-motivation. Duration is 10 weeks. $1600 per month. Open to college freshmen, college sophomores, college juniors, college seniors, first- or second -year graduate students. International applications accepted.
Benefits Formal training, housing at a cost, meals at a cost, opportunity to attend seminars/workshops, travel reimbursement, willing to complete paperwork for educational credit, willing to provide letters of recommendation.
Contact Write, fax, e-mail, or through World Wide Web site Ms. Jill Morrison, Assistant to the Director. Phone: 607-255-3735. Fax: 607-255-8803. E-mail: jtm14@cornell.edu. Applicants must submit a formal organization application, letter of interest, academic transcripts, three letters of recommendation. Application deadline: February 5. World Wide Web: http://www.naic.edu.

NATIONAL CENTER FOR TOXICOLOGICAL RESEARCH (NCTR)
3900 NCTR Road
Jefferson, Arkansas 72079

General Information Center that conducts peer-reviewed biological research relevant to the current and future needs of the Food and Drug Administration. Established in 1971. Number of employees: 600. Unit of Food and Drug Administration, Rockville, Maryland. Number of internship applications received each year: 55.
Internships Available ▶ *8–10 student interns:* responsibilities include participating part-time on-site at NCTR in biological research experiments under the mentorship of an NCTR scientist (while full-time student at an accredited college or university). Candidates should have ability to work independently, ability to work with others, analytical skills, college courses in field, editing skills, oral communication skills, plan to pursue career in field, research skills, self-motivation, writing skills. Duration is 1 year. $12,800–$20,735 stipend per year (part-time). Open to college sophomores, college juniors, college seniors, graduate students, must be from local area. ▶ *15–19 summer student research program interns:* responsibilities include conducting biological research studies (may involve laboratory animals, probably rodents), preparing written reports, and making an oral presentation of research results under mentorship of an NCTR scientist. Candidates should have ability to work independently, ability to work with others, analytical skills, college courses in field, oral communication skills, personal interest in the field, research skills, self-motivation, writing skills. Duration is 10 weeks. $1455–$2770 per month. Open to college fresh-

men, college sophomores, college juniors, college seniors, recent college graduates, graduate students, pre-postdoctoral students.
Benefits On-the-job training, opportunity to attend seminars/workshops.
Contact Write, call, fax, e-mail, or through World Wide Web site Linda McCamant, Program Manager, Oak Ridge Institute for Science and Education (ORISE), Oak Ridge 37831-0117. Phone: 865-576-1089. Fax: 860-241-5219. E-mail: mccamanl@orau.org. In-person interview required. Applicants must submit a formal organization application, letter of interest, academic transcripts, writing sample, three personal references, three letters of recommendation. Application deadline: February 15 for summer student research program; continuous for student interns. World Wide Web: http://www.nctr.fda.gov.

NATIONAL SPACE SOCIETY
600 Pennsylvania Avenue, SE, Suite 201
Washington, District of Columbia 20003

General Information Independent international educational nonprofit organization dedicated to the creation of a spacefaring civilization with 50 chapters and members in more than 35 countries. Established in 1974. Number of employees: 5. Number of internship applications received each year: 10.
Internships Available ▶ *1 journalism intern:* responsibilities include assisting editor of AD ASTRA with publication tasks, selection of images, and maintenance of AD ASTRA index; updating the media contacts database. Candidates should have ability to work independently, computer skills, editing skills, personal interest in the field, research skills, writing skills, minimum GPA of 3.0. Duration is June 1 to August 1 . Unpaid. ▶ *1 public outreach intern:* responsibilities include assisting with responding to inquiries from members and the public and contributing to the planning and coordination of NSS outreach events and programs. Candidates should have ability to work independently, computer skills, oral communication skills, organizational skills, research skills, written communication skills, minimum GPA of 3.0. Duration is June 1 to August 1. Unpaid. ▶ *1 public policy intern:* responsibilities include attending congressional briefings and assisting NSS staff with organization and distribution of testimony, tracking legislation, and political action events. Candidates should have ability to work independently, computer skills, oral communication skills, organizational skills, research skills, written communication skills, minimum GPA of 3.0. Duration is June 1 to August 1. Unpaid. Open to college sophomores, college juniors. International applications accepted.
Benefits Names of contacts, on-the-job training, opportunity to attend seminars/workshops, willing to act as a professional reference, willing to complete paperwork for educational credit, willing to provide letters of recommendation.
Contact Write, fax, e-mail, or through World Wide Web site Internship Coordinator, 600 Pennsylvania Avenue, SE Suite 201, Washington, District of Columbia 20003. Phone: 202-543-1900. Fax: 202-546-4189. E-mail: nsshq@nss.org. Applicants must submit a formal organization application, letter of interest, resume, academic transcripts, letter of recommendation. Application deadline: March 15 for summer; continuous for academic-year positions. World Wide Web: http://www.nss.org.

OAK RIDGE INSTITUTE FOR SCIENCE AND EDUCATION (ORISE)
MS36, PO Box 117
Oak Ridge, Tennessee 37831-0117

General Information Organization that conducts multidisciplinary science and engineering internships. Established in 1946. Number of employees: 300. Unit of United States Department of Energy, Washington, District of Columbia.
Internships Available ▶ *Project Education Research Experiences (HERE) interns:* responsibilities include participating in research in sciences and engineering technology. Candidates should have ability to work independently, ability to work with others, analytical skills, computer skills, research skills, writing skills. Duration is 3–12 months. $350 per week (undergraduates); $400 per week (graduates). Open to college freshmen, college sophomores, col-

lege juniors, college seniors, graduate students. ▶ *Professional interns (graduate students):* responsibilities include participating in fossil energy-related research in the areas of chemistry, computer science, engineering, environmental sciences, geology, mathematics, physics, and statistics at any of the following sites: Savannah River, National Energy Laboratory Center at Pittsburgh (PA) or Morgantown (WV). Duration is 3–18 months. $350–$871 per week. Open to graduate students. ▶ *Professional interns (undergraduate):* responsibilities include participating in fossil energy-related research in the areas of chemistry, computer science, engineering, environmental sciences, geology, mathematics, physics, and statistics at any of the following sites: Savannah River, National Energy Laboratory Center at Pittsburgh (PA) or Morgantown (WV). Duration is 3–18 months. $250–$703 per week. Open to college freshmen, college sophomores, college juniors, college seniors, college graduates with BS received no longer than 2 years ago. ▶ *Technology interns:* responsibilities include research in the areas of chemistry, physics, engineering, mathematics, computer science, safety, and health at National Energy Laboratory Center at Pittsburgh (PA). Duration is 3–18 months. $300 per week. Open to college sophomores at 2-year colleges.
Benefits Travel reimbursement, possible tuition assistance for off-campus students only.
Contact Write, call, fax, e-mail, or through World Wide Web site Kathy Ketner, Project Manager. Phone: 865-576-3427. Fax: 865-241-5220. E-mail: ketnerk@orau.gov. Applicants must submit a formal organization application, academic transcripts, two letters of recommendation. Application deadline: February 15 for summer, February 1 for HERE positions, June 1 for fall, October 1 for spring. World Wide Web: http://www.orau.gov/orise.htm.

PRINCETON PLASMA PHYSICS LABORATORY
PO Box 451, MS-40
Princeton, New Jersey 08543-0451

General Information Research (experimental and theoretical) collaborative national center for science and innovation leading to an attractive energy source. Established in 1950. Number of employees: 600. Unit of Princeton University, Princeton, New Jersey. Number of internship applications received each year: 300.
Internships Available ▶ *25 National Undergraduate Fellowship Program interns:* responsibilities include scientific research (experimental or theoretical) depending on intern's interest. Candidates should have analytical skills, college courses in field, computer skills, plan to pursue career in field, research skills. Duration is 10 weeks in summer. $4800 per duration of internship. Open to college juniors.
Benefits Housing at a cost, meals at a cost, names of contacts, opportunity to attend seminars/workshops, travel reimbursement, willing to act as a professional reference, willing to provide letters of recommendation, one-week introductory course in plasma physics.
Contact Write, e-mail, or through World Wide Web site James Morgan, Program Administrator. Fax: 609-243-2112. E-mail: jmorgan@pppl.gov. Applicants must submit a formal organization application, academic transcripts, two letters of recommendation, personal statement indicating research interests. Application deadline: February 1. World Wide Web: http://www.pppl.gov.

PROCTER & GAMBLE COMPANY
Miami Valley Laboratories, Box 538707
Cincinnati, Ohio 45253-8707

General Information International, technically-based company engaged in the research, development, manufacture, and sale of consumer products in seven Global Business Units: health care, feminine protection, baby care, beauty care, fabric and home care, tissue and towel, and food and beverage. Established in 1837. Unit of Procter and Gamble, Cincinnati, Ohio. Number of internship applications received each year: 100.
Internships Available ▶ *20–30 doctoral summer interns:* responsibilities include performing duties as full-time researcher at one corporate technical center in Cincinnati. Candidates should have ability to work with others, analytical skills, knowledge of field,

oral communication skills, plan to pursue career in field, strong leadership ability, written communication skills. Duration is 10–12 weeks. $850 per week for graduating seniors; salary for graduate students commensurate with schooling. Open to graduate students, graduating seniors going on to graduate school.
Benefits Formal training, on-the-job training, opportunity to attend seminars/workshops, local transportation from housing to work site, affordable university housing available.
Contact E-mail or through World Wide Web site Brenda Cromer, Recruiting Coordinator. Fax: 513-627-2266. E-mail: doctoral.im@pg.com. No phone calls. Telephone interview required. Applicants must submit a letter of interest, resume, two letters of recommendation, application as posted on Web site. Application deadline: March 1 for summer. World Wide Web: http://www.pg.com/careers.

RAND
1700 Main Street, PO Box 2138
Santa Monica, California 90407-2138

General Information Private, nonprofit institution for research and analysis on issues affecting national security and the public welfare. Established in 1948. Number of employees: 1,100. Number of internship applications received each year: 400.
Internships Available ▶ *20–25 summer associates:* responsibilities include conducting research related to dissertation and discussing problems of mutual interest with RAND researchers. Positions available in Santa Monica, CA, Arlington, VA, and Pittsburgh, PA. Candidates should have ability to work independently, ability to work with others, analytical skills, oral communication skills, research skills, written communication skills. Duration is 3 months. Paid. Open to graduate students. International applications accepted.
Benefits Names of contacts, on-the-job training, opportunity to attend seminars/workshops, possible full-time employment, travel reimbursement, willing to complete paperwork for educational credit, willing to provide letters of recommendation, opportunity to use self-written report for future portfolio/vitae.
Contact Write, fax, e-mail, or through World Wide Web site Edward G. Keating, Director, Graduate Student Summer Associate Program. Phone: 310-393-0411 Ext. 6546. Fax: 310-393-4818. E-mail: summerdirector@rand.org. Applicants must submit a letter of interest, resume, names and e-mail addresses of 3 academic references. Application deadline: February 1. World Wide Web: http://www.rand.org.

SMITHSONIAN ENVIRONMENTAL RESEARCH CENTER
647 Contees Wharf Road, PO Box 28
Edgewater, Maryland 21037

General Information Research facility that advances stewardship of the biosphere through interdisciplinary research and educational outreach; SERC's scientists study a variety of interconnected ecosystems at the Center's primary research site in Maryland and at affiliated sites around the world. Established in 1965. Number of employees: 100. Branch of Smithsonian Institution, Washington, District of Columbia. Number of internship applications received each year: 200.
Internships Available ▶ *1–4 environmental and ecology education interns:* responsibilities include conducting nature trail tours on Center's trails, leading group on canoe trips along tidal wetlands, assisting education staff with teacher workshops and environmental education programs. Candidates should have ability to work with others, college courses in field, computer skills, oral communication skills, plan to pursue career in field, self-motivation. Duration is 10–16 weeks. $290–$350 per week. Open to college sophomores, college juniors, college seniors, recent college graduates, graduate students. ▶ *1–4 environmental engineering interns:* responsibilities include assisting SERC engineers in the fields of computers, micrometeorology, nutrient and water flows, and light in ecosystems. Candidates should have ability to work independently, ability to work with others, analytical skills, college courses in field, computer skills, research skills. Duration is 10–16 weeks. $290–$350 per week. Open to college freshmen, college sophomores,

Smithsonian Environmental Research Center (continued)

college juniors, college seniors, recent college graduates, graduate students. ▶ *Environmental research interns:* responsibilities include working on a specific project under the supervision of the Center's professional staff; projects include terrestrial and estuarine environmental research and are tailored to provide the maximum educational benefit to each participant. Candidates should have ability to work independently, ability to work with others, analytical skills, college courses in field, computer skills, research skills. Duration is 10–16 weeks. $290–$350 per week. Open to college freshmen, college sophomores, college juniors, college seniors, recent college graduates, graduate students. International applications accepted.

Benefits Housing at a cost, names of contacts, on-the-job training, opportunity to attend seminars/workshops, possible full-time employment, willing to complete paperwork for educational credit, willing to provide letters of recommendation, access to the Smithsonian Institution.

Contact Write, call, e-mail, or through World Wide Web site Ms. Kim Sproat, Fellowship Coordinator, PO Box 28, Edgewater, Maryland 21037. Phone: 443-482-2217. Fax: 443-482-2380. E-mail: intern@serc.si.edu. Applicants must submit a formal organization application, academic transcripts, two letters of recommendation, personal essay. Application deadline: February 1 for summer (priority consideration), November 15 for spring (priority consideration). World Wide Web: http://www.serc.si.edu/internship/index.htm.

SMITHSONIAN TROPICAL RESEARCH INSTITUTE
1100 Jefferson Drive, Suite 3123
Washington, District of Columbia 20560-0705

General Information Center for basic research on tropical ecosystems that includes modern labs and a network of field stations located in the Republic of Panama. Unit of Smithsonian Institution, Washington, District of Columbia. Number of internship applications received each year: 300.

Internships Available ▶ *Interns:* responsibilities include working at marine or terrestrial research stations on projects that match intern's interests and future career goals. Candidates should have college courses in field, knowledge of field, personal interest in the field, plan to pursue career in field. Duration is flexible. Position available as unpaid or at stipend support available occasionally on a limited basis. Open to individuals completing undergraduate studies or beginning graduate studies in areas related to the interests of STRI staff. International applications accepted.

Benefits Opportunity to attend seminars/workshops, willing to complete paperwork for educational credit.

International Internships Available in Panama.

Contact Write Internship Coordinator, Office of Education, PO Box 37012, Quad, Suite 3123, 705, Washington, District of Columbia 20013-7012. Applicants must submit a formal organization application, resume, academic transcripts, personal reference, letter outlining interests, qualifications, and how travel to Panama and room and board expenses while working there will be paid. Applications are accepted continuously. World Wide Web: http://www.si.edu/stri.

SOUTHWEST RESEARCH INSTITUTE (SWRI)
6220 Culebra Road
San Antonio, Texas 78238-5166

General Information Institute that researches and develops technology in science and engineering fields. Established in 1947. Number of employees: 2,800. Number of internship applications received each year: 1,000.

Internships Available ▶ *20–40 student analysts:* responsibilities include assisting senior-level analysts on current projects. Candidates should have ability to work independently, college courses in field, computer skills, oral communication skills, plan to pursue career in field, self-motivation, strong interpersonal skills, strong leadership ability. Duration is flexible. $10–$20 per hour. ▶ *20–40 student engineers:* responsibilities include assisting senior-level engineers on current projects. Candidates should have ability to work independently, college courses in field, computer skills, oral com-

munication skills, strong interpersonal skills, written communication skills. Duration is flexible. $11–$20 per hour. ▶ *10–15 student scientists:* responsibilities include assisting senior-level scientists on current projects. Candidates should have ability to work independently, computer skills, oral communication skills, strong interpersonal skills, written communication skills, major in physical science. Duration is flexible. $11–$17 per hour. Open to college sophomores, college juniors, college seniors, graduate students.

Benefits Formal training, job counseling, names of contacts, possible full-time employment, travel reimbursement, willing to complete paperwork for educational credit, willing to provide letters of recommendation, competitive salaries based on semester hours completed; free housing for summer positions for students outside the San Antonio area.

Contact Write, call, fax, e-mail, or through World Wide Web site Ernest C. Gomez, Student Employment Coordinator. Phone: 210-522-3503. Fax: 210-522-3990. E-mail: egomez@swri.org. Applicants must submit a formal organization application, academic transcripts, resume recommended. Applications are accepted continuously. World Wide Web: http://www.swri.org.

UNIVERSITY OF CALIFORNIA, LAWRENCE LIVERMORE NATIONAL LABORATORY
PO Box 808
Livermore, California 94551

General Information Government research and development agency. Established in 1952. Number of employees: 7,000. Number of internship applications received each year: 1,500.

Internships Available ▶ *6–12 ASCI Pipeline interns:* responsibilities include individual project designed according to the student's abilities and skills within the discipline of high-performance computing, programming, network administration, graphics, and database management. Candidates should have ability to work independently, ability to work with others, computer skills, plan to pursue career in field, self-motivation, major in computer science. Duration is May to October. $18–$24 per hour. Open to college sophomores, college juniors, college seniors, graduate students, U.S. citizenship required. ▶ *30–40 High-Energy-Density Physics Program (HEDP) interns:* responsibilities include preparatory work for experimental, theoretical, and computational research in hydrodynamics; atomic, plasma, and inertial confinement physics; and radiation/particle transport as applied to the evolution of complex systems. Candidates should have ability to work independently, ability to work with others, analytical skills, declared college major in field, plan to pursue career in field, self-motivation. Duration is May to October. $18–$24 per hour. Open to college juniors, college seniors, graduate students, U.S. citizenship required. ▶ *3–20 Interns for Defense Technologies (IDT):* responsibilities include work in nuclear, mechanical, electrical, and materials engineering. Candidates should have ability to work independently, ability to work with others, analytical skills, declared college major in field, plan to pursue career in field, self-motivation. Duration is May to October. $18–$24 per hour. Open to college sophomores, college juniors, college seniors, graduate students, U.S. citizenship required. ▶ *20–30 Internships in Terascale Simulation Technology (ITST):* responsibilities include preparation for employment as computational scientists. Candidates should have ability to work independently, ability to work with others, college degree in related field, computer skills, plan to pursue career in field, self-motivation. Duration is May to October. $4480–$5860 per month. Open to advanced undergraduate and preferably graduate students; computer science (visualization, modeling, graphics) and mathematics majors; must be U.S. citizen. ▶ *6–10 LLNL College Cyber Defenders (CCD) Program:* responsibilities include learning the concepts and gaining skills in information technologies and protection in a distributed environment (such as the Internet). Candidates should have ability to work independently, ability to work with others, college courses in field, computer skills, self-motivation. Duration is May to October. $15–$24 per hour. Open to college sophomores, college juniors, college seniors, graduate students, U.S. citizenship required; also computer related 2-4 year degrees. ▶ *Laser Science and Technology Student Program (LSTSP):* responsibilities include hands-on experi-

ence in laser and optics projects. Candidates should have ability to work independently, ability to work with others, analytical skills, plan to pursue career in field, self-motivation, major in laser science, optics, or optical engineering. Duration is May to October. $20–$30 per hour. Open to college juniors, college seniors, graduate students, U.S. citizenship required. ▶ *Nuclear Science Internship Program:* responsibilities include training and access to unique nuclear science expertise, equipment, and facilities, by establishing collaborations with key academic institutions. Candidates should have ability to work independently, ability to work with others, computer skills, declared college major in field, plan to pursue career in field, self-motivation. Duration is May to October. $20–$30 per hour. Open to college juniors, college seniors, graduate students, U.S. citizenship required; Actinide, material, and/or nuclear science majors. ▶ *300–400 Scholars Employment Program interns:* responsibilities include working in state of the art facilities at a National Security laboratory in a variety of science and engineering programs. Candidates should have ability to work independently, college courses in field, computer skills, plan to pursue career in field, self-motivation. Duration is May to October. $15–$24 per hour. Open to college freshmen, college sophomores, college juniors, college seniors, recent college graduates, graduate students, U.S. citizenship required.
Benefits Health insurance, opportunity to attend seminars/workshops, possible full-time employment, travel reimbursement.
Contact Through World Wide Web site Toni Scott, Summer Employment Manager, PO Box 808 L-275, Livermore, California 94551. Fax: 925-423-0984. E-mail: scott1@llnl.gov. No phone calls. Applicants must submit a formal organization application, resume, academic transcripts, company designed interest form. Application deadline: February 28 for summer. World Wide Web: http://step.llnl.gov/idt.

UNIVERSITY RESEARCH EXPEDITIONS PROGRAM (UREP)
1 Shields Avenue, University of California
Davis, California 95616-8813

General Information Organization that brings together members of the general public with University of California academics on field research projects worldwide. Established in 1976. Number of employees: 7. Unit of University of California, Davis, Davis, California. Number of internship applications received each year: 250.
Internships Available ▶ *200–300 field researchers:* responsibilities include assisting project leaders in a host of activities including observation, excavation, measurement, data collection, data entry, documentation, and specimen capture. Candidates should have ability to work with others, personal interest in the field, good overall health. Duration is 2–3 weeks. Unpaid. Open to recent high school graduates, college freshmen, college sophomores, college juniors, college seniors, recent college graduates, graduate students, law students, career changers, individuals reentering the workforce, individuals 16 years of age and older. International applications accepted.
Benefits Formal training, housing at a cost, meals at a cost, willing to provide letters of recommendation.
International Internships Available.
Contact Write, call, fax, e-mail, or through World Wide Web site Susan Warren-Alef, Manager, University of California, One Shields Avenue, Davis, California 95616-8813. Phone: 530-757-3529. Fax: 530-757-3537. E-mail: urep@ucdavis.edu. Applicants must submit a formal organization application, program fees range from $675–$1790. Applications are accepted continuously. Fees: $200. World Wide Web: http://www.urep.ucdavis.edu.

WASHINGTON INSTITUTE FOR NEAR EAST POLICY
1828 L Street, NW, Suite 1050
Washington, District of Columbia 20036

General Information Research institute that analyzes U.S. policy in the Middle East. Established in 1985. Number of employees: 35. Number of internship applications received each year: 250.
Internships Available ▶ *5–6 research assistants:* responsibilities include preparing reports and assisting with seminars and conferences. Candidates should have ability to work with others, analytical skills, college courses in field, research skills, written communication skills. Duration is 1 year. $23000–$27000 per year plus extensive benefits. Open to recent college graduates. ▶ *1–8 research interns:* responsibilities include carrying out directed research and administrative duties (including seminars). Duration is flexible (at least 4 days per week preferred). Position available as unpaid or paid. Open to college freshmen, college sophomores, college juniors, college seniors, recent college graduates, graduate students. International applications accepted.
Benefits On-the-job training, opportunity to attend seminars/workshops, possible full-time employment, willing to act as a professional reference, willing to complete paperwork for educational credit, willing to provide letters of recommendation, health insurance and job counseling for research assistants, opportunity to attend Institute events.
Contact Write, fax, e-mail, or through World Wide Web site Patrick Clawson, Deputy Director. Phone: 202-452-0650. Fax: 202-223-5364. E-mail: patrickc@washingtoninstitute.org. In-person interview recommended (telephone interview accepted). Applicants must submit a letter of interest, resume, writing sample, explanation of knowledge of Middle East (suggested). Application deadline: February 1 for research assistants, March 1 for interns (summer). World Wide Web: http://www.washingtoninstitute.org.

WHITNEY LABORATORY
9505 Ocean Shore Boulevard
St. Augustine, Florida 32086

General Information Marine biomedical research laboratory. Established in 1975. Number of employees: 50. Unit of University of Florida, Gainesville, Florida. Number of internship applications received each year: 150.
Internships Available ▶ *10–12 Whitney Summer Undergraduate Research Program interns:* responsibilities include participating in research training in cell, molecular, and neuro biology using marine organisms; planning and executing research program. Candidates should have ability to work independently, ability to work with others, analytical skills, personal interest in the field, plan to pursue career in field, self-motivation. Duration is 10 weeks. $250 per week. Open to college freshmen, college sophomores, college juniors, college seniors. International applications accepted.
Benefits Formal training, free housing, job counseling, names of contacts, opportunity to attend seminars/workshops, travel reimbursement, willing to act as a professional reference, willing to provide letters of recommendation.
Contact Write, call, fax, e-mail, or through World Wide Web site William R. Buzzi, Education Coordinator. Phone: 904-461-4011. Fax: 904-461-4008. E-mail: wrb@whitney.ufl.edu. Applicants must submit a formal organization application, letter of interest, resume, academic transcripts, two letters of recommendation, prioritized list of research interests. Application deadline: February 28 for summer, July 1 for fall, November 1 for winter/spring. World Wide Web: http://http://www.whitney.ufl.edu.

PUBLIC ADMINISTRATION

GENERAL

ALASKA STATE PARKS
550 West 7th Avenue, Suite 1380
Anchorage, Alaska 99501-3561

General Information State agency that maintains parks and provides outdoor recreation facilities. Established in 1970. Number of employees: 194. Division of State of Alaska Department of Natural Resources, Anchorage, Alaska. Number of internship applications received each year: 100.
Internships Available ▶ *15–20 volunteer interns:* responsibilities include various duties at park facilities depending on current needs and intern's abilities. Candidates should have ability to work independently, ability to work with others, college courses in field, knowledge of field, personal interest in the field, self-motivation. Duration is 1 summer. Unpaid. Open to college freshmen, college sophomores, college juniors, college seniors, recent college graduates, graduate students, career changers, individuals reentering the workforce, individuals age 18 or older.
Benefits Free housing, on-the-job training, willing to complete paperwork for educational credit, expense allowance to cover food costs.
Contact Write, call, fax, e-mail, or through World Wide Web site Lynn Blessington, Volunteer Coordinator. Phone: 907-269-8708. Fax: 907-269-8907. E-mail: volunteer@dnr.state.ak.us. Telephone interview required. Applicants must submit a formal organization application, letter of interest, resume, academic transcripts, personal reference, three letters of recommendation. Application deadline: April 1 for summer, August 1 for winter. World Wide Web: http://www.alaskastateparks.org.

AUSTRALIAN EMBASSY
1601 Massachusetts Avenue, NW
Washington, District of Columbia 20036

General Information Diplomatic mission representing Australia in the United States. Established in 1946. Number of employees: 350. Unit of Department of Foreign Affairs and Trade, Canberra, Australia. Number of internship applications received each year: 50.
Internships Available ▶ *1 ANZACC (Australian, New Zealand, American Chamber of Commerce) intern:* responsibilities include assisting with the planning and organizing of ANZACC's annual conference, performing research and answering questions from the regional Chambers, assisting with the production of the ANZACC newsletter, performing general administrative duties. Candidates should have ability to work independently, organizational skills, personal interest in the field, research skills, self-motivation, writing skills. Duration is one semester or summer. Unpaid. Open to college juniors, college seniors, recent college graduates, graduate students. ▶ *1 congressional liaison intern:* responsibilities include research on U.S. domestic and foreign trade policy and on congressional activities of relevance to Australia; reporting on hearings and legislative developments; performing general administrative duties including database usage. Candidates should have ability to work independently, organizational skills, personal interest in the field, research skills, strong interpersonal skills, writing skills, knowledge of Access database desirable. Duration is one semester or summer. Unpaid. Open to college sophomores, college juniors, college seniors, recent college graduates, graduate students. ▶ *1–2 public affairs interns:* responsibilities include assisting with writing Embassy news briefs and features for posting on the Embassy's Website; assisting with writing for Embassy's quarterly newsletter, the Australia Report; composing press releases, compiling embassy fact sheets, library and internet research; daily scanning of US papers for Australia-related clippings; completing mail-outs and parcel/package pick-up; organizational and event liaison assistance as required. Candidates should have ability to work independently, experience in the field, personal interest in the field, research skills, strong interpersonal skills, written communication skills. Duration is one semester or summer. Unpaid. Open to college sophomores, college juniors, college seniors. International applications accepted.
Benefits Willing to complete paperwork for educational credit, willing to provide letters of recommendation.
Contact Write, fax, or e-mail Counselor (Public Affairs). Fax: 202-797-3414. E-mail: public.affairs@austemb.org. In-person interview required. Applicants must submit a letter of interest, resume, three writing samples. Application deadline: April 1 for summer, July 1 for fall, December 1 for spring. World Wide Web: http://www.austemb.org/.

BUREAU OF LAND MANAGEMENT, COOS BAY DISTRICT, UMPQUA RESOURCE AREA
1300 Airport Lane
North Bend, Oregon 97459

General Information Federal agency that manages natural resources on over 270 million acres of public lands for the people of the United States; employs people in many fields including natural resources, administration, and computer resources. Established in 1946. Number of employees: 200. Unit of Bureau of Land Management, Washington, District of Columbia. Number of internship applications received each year: 10.
Internships Available ▶ *1–2 interpretive education interns:* responsibilities include developing and implementing interpretive and environmental education programs; developing interpretive exhibit, brochures, and panels; and assisting staff. Candidates should have ability to work independently, ability to work with others, oral communication skills, organizational skills, personal interest in the field, writing skills. Duration is May to September (40 hours per week). Unpaid. ▶ *2–4 seasonal recreation technical interns:* responsibilities include operating the park entrance station, performing day-to-day maintenance, giving group tours and formal presentations to the public. Candidates should have ability to work independently, ability to work with others, oral communication skills, organizational skills, personal interest in the field, written communication skills. Duration is May to September (40 hours per week). Unpaid. ▶ *1–6 summer natural resource interns:* responsibilities include giving small group tours and presentations, working in the gift shop, developing educational programs, creating displays, and maintaining site. Candidates should have ability to work with others, oral communication skills, personal interest in the field, self-motivation, written communication skills. Duration is May to September (40 hours per week). Unpaid. Open to recent high school graduates, college freshmen, college sophomores, college juniors, college seniors, recent college graduates, graduate students, law students, career changers, individuals reentering the workforce, must be 18 years or older. International applications accepted.
Benefits Formal training, free housing, job counseling, names of contacts, on-the-job training, opportunity to attend seminars/workshops, willing to act as a professional reference, willing to

complete paperwork for educational credit, willing to provide letters of recommendation, reimbursement of on-site travel expenses; $75 stipend per week; preference to volunteers for regular positions.
Contact Write, call, fax, or e-mail Robert Golden, Park Ranger. Phone: 541-756-0100. Fax: 541-751-4303. E-mail: robert_golden@ or.blm.gov. Applicants must submit a letter of interest, resume, three personal references. Application deadline: May 1.

BUREAU OF LAND MANAGEMENT, MONTICELLO FIELD OFFICE
PO Box 7
Monticello, Utah 84535

General Information Federal agency responsible for multiple use management of public lands. Established in 1946. Number of employees: 20. Number of internship applications received each year: 20.
Internships Available ▶ *1–3 Grand Gulch ranger assistants:* responsibilities include providing information to visitors in the Grand Gulch area, conducting foot patrols into remote canyons, light clean-up and maintenance of campsites and ranger station, and assisting with the protection of Anasazi archaeological sites by providing visitors with information on site stewardship and the value of archaeological sites. Duration is 4 weeks minimum. Unpaid. ▶ *1–3 San Juan River ranger assistants:* responsibilities include contacting boaters at launch areas for the San Juan River, accompanying river rangers on rafting patrols of the river, light clean-up and maintenance at launch areas and along the river, and assisting with inventories of resource conditions along the river. Duration is 4 weeks minimum. Unpaid. Candidates for all positions should have ability to work independently, ability to work with others, oral communication skills. Open to recent high school graduates, college freshmen, college sophomores, college juniors, college seniors, recent college graduates, graduate students, law students, career changers, individuals reentering the workforce.
Benefits Formal training, free housing, job counseling, names of contacts, on-the-job training, willing to complete paperwork for educational credit, willing to provide letters of recommendation, opportunity to work in a scenic area with rich archaeological resources, food allowance of $12 per day.
Contact Write, call, fax, or e-mail Kay Wilson, Volunteer Coordinator. Phone: 435-587-1504. Fax: 435-587-1518. E-mail: kwilson@ut.blm.gov. In-person interview recommended (telephone interview accepted). Applicants must submit a resume. Applications are accepted continuously. World Wide Web: http://www.blm.gov/utah/monticello.

BUREAU OF LAND MANAGEMENT, PRICE FIELD OFFICE
125 South, 600 West
Price, Utah 84501

General Information Federal agency responsible for managing and administering the use of public lands located primarily in the western United States and Alaska. Established in 1946. Number of employees: 30. Unit of Bureau of Land Management, Salt Lake City, Utah. Number of internship applications received each year: 4.
Internships Available ▶ *2–4 recreation/archaeology interns:* responsibilities include taking inventory of use and users of Nine Mile Canyon, developing and providing interpretive information to visitors, participating in inventory and recording of cultural sites, monitoring impact of visitation on cultural sites, light maintenance of recreation facilities, and identifying need for facilities development. Candidates should have ability to work independently, oral communication skills, personal interest in the field, research skills, self-motivation. Duration is 5 weeks or 6 months beginning in April. Unpaid. Open to college freshmen, college sophomores, college juniors, college seniors, recent college graduates, graduate students, career changers, individuals reentering the workforce.
▶ *2 recreation/paleontology interns:* responsibilities include taking inventory of recreation use and users, developing and providing educational information to visitors, participating in discovery and recording of fossil sites, monitoring impacts of visitation on paleontological sites, performing light maintenance of recreation facilities, identifying future development needs, and working with CEU Prehistoric Museum in laboratory and field preparation of specimens. Candidates should have ability to work independently, ability to work with others, oral communication skills, personal interest in the field, self-motivation, written communication skills. Duration is Easter through Labor Day (or 8-week time frames). Unpaid. Open to college freshmen, college sophomores, college juniors, college seniors, recent college graduates, graduate students, career changers, individuals reentering the workforce, retirees. ▶ *2–6 river ranger/recreation interns:* responsibilities include conducting compliance checks of private and commercial river runners and monitoring resource conditions. Candidates should have ability to work independently, analytical skills, oral communication skills, self-motivation, strong interpersonal skills, writing skills. Duration is 2–6 months. Unpaid. Open to college freshmen, college sophomores, college juniors, college seniors, recent college graduates, graduate students, career changers, individuals reentering the workforce, retirees. International applications accepted.
Benefits Free housing, job counseling, names of contacts, on-the-job training, opportunity to attend seminars/workshops, possible full-time employment, willing to act as a professional reference, willing to complete paperwork for educational credit, willing to provide letters of recommendation, worker's compensation.
Contact Write, call, fax, or e-mail Mr. Dennis J. Willis, Outdoor Recreation Planner, 125 South 600 West, Price, Utah 84501. Phone: 435-636-3600. Fax: 435-636-3657. E-mail: dennis_willis@ blm.gov. Telephone interview required. Applicants must submit a formal organization application, letter of interest. Applications are accepted continuously. World Wide Web: http://www.blm.gov/price/index.html.

CALIFORNIA EXECUTIVE FELLOWS, JUDICIAL ADMINISTRATION FELLOWS, CALIFORNIA SENATE FELLOWS, CALIFORNIA ASSEMBLY FELLOWS
Center for California Studies, CSU Sacramento, 6000 J Street
Sacramento, California 95819-6081

General Information Public policy, public service, and curricular support unit devoted to promoting the understanding of California's history, cultures, and public policies. Established in 1984. Number of employees: 15. Unit of California State University, Sacramento, Sacramento, California. Number of internship applications received each year: 1,000.
Internships Available ▶ *18 Assembly Fellows:* responsibilities include assuming the role of a professional staff team member in Assembly branch of California's state government. Duration is 11 months. $1882 per month. ▶ *18 Executive Fellows:* responsibilities include assuming the role of a professional staff team member in the Executive branch of California's state government. Duration is 11 months. $1882 per month. ▶ *10 Judicial Administration Fellows:* responsibilities include assuming the role of a professional staff team member in Judicial branch of California's state government. Duration is 11 months. $1882 per month. ▶ *18 Senate Fellows:* responsibilities include assuming the role of a professional staff team member in Senate branch of California's state government. Duration is 11 months. $1882 per month. Candidates for all positions should have ability to work with others, knowledge of field, oral communication skills, personal interest in the field, written communication skills. Open to college seniors, recent college graduates, graduate students, law students, career changers, must have completed 4-year degree by August. International applications accepted.
Benefits Formal training, health insurance, opportunity to attend seminars/workshops, dental and vision care, 12 units of graduate credit for fellows who fulfill academic requirements.
Contact Write, call, fax, e-mail, or through World Wide Web site David DeLuz, Outreach Coordinator, Center for California Studies CSU Sacramento, 6000 J Street, Sacramento, California 95819-6081. Phone: 916-278-6906. Fax: 916-278-5199. E-mail: calstudies@ csus.edu. In-person interview required. Applicants must submit a formal organization application, academic transcripts, writing sample, three letters of recommendation. Application deadline: February. World Wide Web: http://www.csus.edu/calst.

CENTER FOR CALIFORNIA STUDIES
6000 J Street
Sacramento, California 95819-6081

General Information Applied research institute at California State University, Sacramento. Established in 1984. Number of employees: 75. Division of California State University, Sacramento, Sacramento, California. Number of internship applications received each year: 1,000.
Internships Available ▶ *64 Capital Fellows:* responsibilities include working as full-time paid staff assistant to senior executive branch staff, judicial administration officials, and members of the California Assembly and Senate. Candidates should have analytical skills, personal interest in the field, research skills, strong interpersonal skills, strong leadership ability, writing skills. Duration is one year (September/October to August/September). $1882 per month. Open to college seniors, recent college graduates, graduate students, law students, career changers. International applications accepted.
Benefits Formal training, on-the-job training, opportunity to attend seminars/workshops, possible full-time employment, tuition assistance, willing to act as a professional reference, willing to complete paperwork for educational credit, willing to provide letters of recommendation, health and dental benefits, enrollment fees provided, 12 graduate credits from the Government and Public Policy Departments at CSUS.
Contact Write, call, fax, e-mail, or through World Wide Web site David B. DeLuz, Outreach Coordinator. Phone: 916-278-6906. Fax: 916-278-5199. E-mail: calstudies@csus.edu. In-person interview required. Applicants must submit a formal organization application, academic transcripts, two writing samples, two letters of recommendation. Application deadline: February 27. World Wide Web: http://www.csus.edu/calst.

CENTER FOR NATIONAL POLICY
1 Massachusetts Avenue, NW, Suite 333
Washington, District of Columbia 20001-1401

General Information Public policy organization dedicated to advancing America's common goals. Established in 1981. Number of employees: 15. Number of internship applications received each year: 200.
Internships Available ▶ *1–2 communications interns:* responsibilities include assisting with event planning and management of databases; assisting with press research and publicity. Candidates should have computer skills, editing skills, oral communication skills, organizational skills, self-motivation, written communication skills. Duration is 3 months. Unpaid. ▶ *1–2 domestic policy interns:* responsibilities include assisting in policy research; attending seminars/conferences; assisting with general office and administrative work, event planning, and database management. Candidates should have analytical skills, computer skills, oral communication skills, research skills, self-motivation, written communication skills. Duration is 3 months. Unpaid. ▶ *1–2 foreign policy interns:* responsibilities include assisting in policy research, event planning, publicity, general office support work, and database management. Candidates should have ability to work independently, ability to work with others, analytical skills, oral communication skills, organizational skills, research skills, written communication skills. Duration is 3 months. Unpaid. Open to college freshmen, college sophomores, college juniors, college seniors. International applications accepted.
Benefits Job counseling, names of contacts, opportunity to attend seminars/workshops, willing to act as a professional reference, willing to complete paperwork for educational credit, willing to provide letters of recommendation, possibility of stipend.
Contact Write, fax, or e-mail Emily Cooney, Events Coordinator. Fax: 202-682-1818. E-mail: emilyc@cnponline.org. No phone calls. Telephone interview required. Applicants must submit a letter of interest, resume, academic transcripts, writing sample. Applications are accepted continuously. World Wide Web: http://www.cnponline.org.

CENTRAL INTELLIGENCE AGENCY
PO Box 4090
Reston, Virginia 20195

General Information Agency involved in information collection, processing, analysis, and reporting. Established in 1947.
Internships Available ▶ *Graduate studies interns:* responsibilities include becoming acquainted with professional intelligence analysts and participating in substantive agency work. Candidates should have analytical skills, declared college major in field, oral communication skills, self-motivation, strong leadership ability, written communication skills. Duration is flexible. $17.55–$23.64 per hour. Open to college seniors, graduate students. ▶ *Student trainees:* responsibilities include participating in substantive agency assignments commensurate with intern's academic training and ability. Candidates should have analytical skills, declared college major in field, oral communication skills, self-motivation, strong leadership ability, written communication skills. Duration is 3 semesters. $14.16–$17.55 per hour. Open to college sophomores. ▶ *Summer internships:* responsibilities include working with professionals and viewing the role of the agency while gaining work experience. Candidates should have analytical skills, declared college major in field, oral communication skills, self-motivation, strong interpersonal skills, written communication skills. Duration is 2 summers (minimum of 90 days), or 1 summer and 1 semester. $14.16–$17.55 per hour. Open to college sophomores, college juniors.
Benefits Formal training, health insurance, names of contacts, on-the-job training, opportunity to attend seminars/workshops, possible full-time employment, travel reimbursement, willing to complete paperwork for educational credit, willing to provide letters of recommendation, vacation and sick days accrual.
Contact Write or through World Wide Web site Personnel Representative. No phone calls. Applicants must submit a letter of interest, resume, formal application provided following review of cover letter/resume. Application deadline: April 1 for fall, August 1 for spring, November 1 for summer. World Wide Web: http://www.cia.gov.

CITY OF CHICAGO, DEPARTMENT OF PERSONNEL
City Hall, Room 1100, 121 North LaSalle Street
Chicago, Illinois 60602

General Information Municipal government. Number of employees: 42,000. Number of internship applications received each year: 600.
Internships Available ▶ *140–160 summer interns:* responsibilities include performing duties (under supervision) required to assist in various city departments; specific duties vary depending upon individual department's needs. Candidates should have ability to work independently, analytical skills, college courses in field, computer skills, editing skills, knowledge of field, office skills, oral communication skills, organizational skills, plan to pursue career in field, research skills, self-motivation, strong interpersonal skills, strong leadership ability, writing skills. Duration is 10 weeks. $6.50–$9.50 per hour. Open to college freshmen, college sophomores, college juniors, college seniors, graduate students, law students. International applications accepted.
Benefits Formal training, job counseling, on-the-job training, opportunity to attend seminars/workshops, possible full-time employment, willing to act as a professional reference, willing to complete paperwork for educational credit, willing to provide letters of recommendation.
Contact Write, e-mail, or through World Wide Web site Celeste Wright-Harris, Director of Recruitment. E-mail: personnel@cityofchicago.org. In-person interview required. Applicants must submit a formal organization application, letter of interest, resume, academic transcripts, writing samples required for the Office of Special Events position. Applications are accepted continuously. World Wide Web: http://www.cityofchicago.org/personnel.

CITY OF DETROIT–OUTREACH ACTIVITIES UNIT
2 Woodward Avenue, Suite 314, Coleman A. Young Municipal Center
Detroit, Michigan 48226

General Information Internship program that offers college students an opportunity to receive paid work experience in their area of study. Unit of City of Detroit–Human Resources Department, Detroit, Michigan. Number of internship applications received each year: 60.
Internships Available ▶ *1–20 interns:* responsibilities include performing varied tasks depending upon position and department requirements. Candidates should have computer skills, declared college major in field, oral communication skills, plan to pursue career in field, research skills, written communication skills. Duration is 9–10 weeks. Position available as unpaid or at $10–$14 per hour. Open to college juniors, college seniors, graduate students. International applications accepted.
Benefits Opportunity to attend seminars/workshops, possible full-time employment, willing to complete paperwork for educational credit, willing to provide letters of recommendation.
Contact Write or fax Enid White Cyrus, Internship Coordinator, 2 Woodward Avenue, Suite 314, Coleman A. Young Building, Detroit, Michigan 48226. Fax: 313-224-3410. In-person interview required. Applicants must submit a letter of interest, resume, academic transcripts. Application deadline: April 15 for summer. World Wide Web: http://www.ci.detroit.mi.us.

CITY OF LONG BEACH, DEPARTMENT OF HUMAN RESOURCES
333 West Ocean Boulevard, 13th Floor
Long Beach, California 90802

General Information Municipal government consisting of 22 city departments including a health department, oil properties, harbor, gas department, and municipal marina. Established in 1897. Number of employees: 5,400. Number of internship applications received each year: 50.
Internships Available ▶ *1–3 management assistants:* responsibilities include assignments as described on Web site www.ci_long-beach.ca.us/human/manage.htm. Candidates should have oral communication skills, strong interpersonal skills, written communication skills. Duration is 1 year (July to July). $3270 per month. Open to graduate students, must complete master's degree in public administration, business administration, or related field by July. International applications accepted.
Benefits Health insurance, possible full-time employment, executive leave (5 days per calendar year), life insurance.
Contact Write, call, fax, e-mail, or through World Wide Web site Ernie Hernandez, Personnel Analyst, 333 West Ocean Boulevard 13th Floor, Long Beach, California 90802. Phone: 562-570-6915. Fax: 562-570-6666. E-mail: lymccra@ci.long-beach.ca.us. Applicants must submit a resume, academic transcripts, three personal references, 3-5 page statement describing career goals and the reason for application. Application deadline: February 8. World Wide Web: http://www.ci.long-beach.ca.us.

CITY OF NEW YORK/PARKS & RECREATION
830 Fifth Avenue, Room 309
New York, New York 10021

General Information Local government agency responsible for 28,000 acres of green space; oversees cultural, athletic, and social events. Established in 1934. Number of employees: 2,200. Number of internship applications received each year: 1,000.
Internships Available ▶ *100–200 interns:* responsibilities include working in the areas of public administration, recreation, environmental science, computer operations, photography, architecture, landscape architecture, engineering, urban planning, revenue, accounting, commissioner's staff, recruiting, historical signs program, press/marketing, and forestry; locations in all five boroughs. Candidates should have oral communication skills, organizational skills, self-motivation, strong interpersonal skills, written communication skills. Duration is flexible. Position available as unpaid or paid. Open to high school students, recent high school graduates, college freshmen, college sophomores, college juniors, college seniors, recent college graduates, graduate students, law students, individuals reentering the workforce. International applications accepted.
Benefits On-the-job training, opportunity to attend seminars/workshops, possible full-time employment, willing to act as a professional reference, willing to complete paperwork for educational credit, willing to provide letters of recommendation, participation in monthly speaker series; some stipends available for federal work-study participants, travel reimbursement (for unpaid positions).
Contact Write, call, fax, e-mail, or through World Wide Web site Sarah Kay, Director of Recruitment and Internships. Phone: 212-360-1349. Fax: 212-360-1387. E-mail: sarah.kay@parks.nyc.gov. In-person interview required. Applicants must submit a letter of interest, resume, 1-3 writing samples (on specific occasions). Applications are accepted continuously. World Wide Web: http://www.nyc-gov/parks.

CITY OF PHOENIX, BUDGET AND RESEARCH DEPARTMENT
200 West Washington Street, 14th Floor
Phoenix, Arizona 85003-1611

General Information Department that assists in allocation of city resources to provide efficient, effective, and economical municipal services; develops the city's annual budget and capital improvement program by monitoring expenditures and revenues; and conducts management research analysis. Established in 1913. Number of employees: 30. Department of City of Phoenix, Phoenix, Arizona. Number of internship applications received each year: 90.
Internships Available ▶ *3–4 management interns:* responsibilities include conducting municipal research and analysis of administrative and organizational problems, policies, and practices; and providing staff assistance for city council and subcommittees. Candidates should have analytical skills, oral communication skills, plan to pursue career in field, research skills, written communication skills, satisfactory completion of all courses for a master's degree in public or business administration or a closely related field by July 1. Duration is 1 year. $30,552–$43,362 per year. Open to graduate students, law students, career changers, individuals reentering the workforce. International applications accepted.
Benefits Formal training, health insurance, job counseling, names of contacts, opportunity to attend seminars/workshops, possible full-time employment, tuition assistance, dental insurance.
Contact Write Cecile Pettle, Budget and Research Director. In-person interview required. Applicants must submit a formal organization application, letter of interest, resume, academic transcripts, writing sample, three letters of recommendation. Application deadline: January 31 for internships beginning in July (recruitment is generally November-January). World Wide Web: http://phoenix.gov.

CONGRESSIONAL MANAGEMENT FOUNDATION
513 Capitol Court, NE, Suite 300
Washington, District of Columbia 20002

General Information Nonprofit, nonpartisan organization dedicated to helping Congress become a better-managed, more effective institution by tailoring private sector management tools to the congressional environment. Established in 1977. Number of employees: 7. Number of internship applications received each year: 100.
Internships Available ▶ *2–4 interns:* responsibilities include assisting professional staff in all aspects of current projects including research, writing, survey tabulation and analysis, and general office support. Candidates should have computer skills, oral communication skills, personal interest in the field, self-motivation, strong interpersonal skills, written communication skills. Duration is minimum of 3 months. Unpaid. Open to college sophomores, college juniors, college seniors, recent college graduates, graduate students. International applications accepted.
Benefits Job counseling, names of contacts, on-the-job training, opportunity to attend seminars/workshops, willing to act as a professional reference, willing to complete paperwork for educational credit, willing to provide letters of recommendation.

Congressional Management Foundation (continued)

Contact Write, call, or fax Sheree Beverly, Intern Coordinator. Phone: 202-546-0100. Fax: 202-547-0936. Telephone interview required. Applicants must submit a letter of interest, resume, writing sample. Application deadline: March 15 for summer, July 1 for fall, November 1 for spring. World Wide Web: http://www.cmfweb.org.

CONGRESSMAN BILL THOMAS
2208 Rayburn House Office Building
Washington, District of Columbia 20515

General Information Republican U.S. Congressman serving the 21st Congressional District of California; Chairman of Committee on Ways and Means. Number of employees: 8. Number of internship applications received each year: 150.
Internships Available ▶ *10 interns:* responsibilities include legislative research and basic office duties. Candidates should have office skills. Duration is minimum of 6 weeks. Position available as unpaid or paid. Open to college freshmen, college sophomores, college juniors, college seniors. International applications accepted.
Benefits Opportunity to attend seminars/workshops, possible full-time employment, willing to complete paperwork for educational credit.
Contact Write, call, or fax Mary Sue Englund, Intern Coordinator. Phone: 202-225-2915. Fax: 202-225-2908. Applicants must submit a letter of interest, resume, writing sample. Applications are accepted continuously. World Wide Web: http://www.house.gov/billthomas.

CONGRESSMAN MICHAEL BILIRAKIS
2269 Rayburn House Office Building
Washington, District of Columbia 20515

General Information Congressional office. Established in 1982. Number of employees: 9. Number of internship applications received each year: 20.
Internships Available ▶ *1–3 legislative interns:* responsibilities include assisting legislative staff with daily operations from running errands to attending legislative hearings. Candidates should have ability to work with others, computer skills, research skills, self-motivation, writing skills. Duration is 6 weeks minimum. Unpaid. Open to college freshmen, college sophomores, college juniors, college seniors, recent college graduates, graduate students, law students. International applications accepted.
Benefits Names of contacts, opportunity to attend seminars/workshops, willing to complete paperwork for educational credit, willing to provide letters of recommendation.
Contact Write, call, or fax Carrie Melvin, Staff Assistant, 2369 Rayburn House Office Building, Washington, District of Columbia 20515. Phone: 202-225-5755. Fax: 202-225-4085. Applicants must submit a letter of interest, resume, writing sample, 3 letters of recommendation or personal references; telephone interview accepted. Application deadline: January 15 for spring, April 15 for summer, August 15 for fall. World Wide Web: http://www.house.gov/bilirakis.

CONGRESSWOMAN SLAUGHTER
2347 Rayburn House Office Building, (NY-28)
Washington, District of Columbia 20515

General Information Democratic member of the United States House of Representatives. Established in 1986. Number of employees: 10. Unit of United States House of Representatives, Washington, District of Columbia. Number of internship applications received each year: 20.
Internships Available ▶ *1–2 interns:* responsibilities include drafting constituent letters, attending committee hearings, administrative duties, research projects. Candidates should have oral communication skills, organizational skills, research skills, strong interpersonal skills, writing skills, interest in government/legislative process. Duration is flexible. Unpaid. Open to college sophomores, college juniors, college seniors, recent college graduates. International applications accepted.

Benefits Opportunity to attend seminars/workshops, willing to complete paperwork for educational credit, willing to provide letters of recommendation.
Contact Write, call, fax, or through World Wide Web site Mary Beth Walker, Office Manager. Phone: 202-225-3615. Fax: 202-225-7822. Telephone interview required. Applicants must submit a formal organization application, letter of interest, resume, academic transcripts, writing sample, two letters of recommendation. Application deadline: January 5 for spring, March 30 for summer, July 31 for fall, November 3 for winter. World Wide Web: http://www.house.gov/slaughter/.

DEMOCRATIC CAUCUS OF THE HOUSE OF REPRESENTATIVES
Room 4A-4 State House, 200 West Washington Street
Indianapolis, Indiana 46204-2786

General Information Group consisting of the collective membership of state representatives affiliated with the Democratic Party of the House of Representatives. Number of employees: 75. Unit of State of Indiana, Indiana. Number of internship applications received each year: 70.
Internships Available ▶ *15–20 constituent/caucus services interns:* responsibilities include working with a full-time legislative assistant in support of 3 or 4 state representatives, drafting constituent letters, conducting legislative and constituent problem research, attending committee meetings, summarizing legislation, and preparing material for newsletters. Candidates should have ability to work with others, oral communication skills, personal interest in the field, strong leadership ability, written communication skills. Duration is 3–4 months. $275 per week. ▶ *3 media services interns:* responsibilities include working with the caucus media director in assisting all Democratic state representatives with media relations, research, writing news releases, setting up press conferences, taping and sending radio feeds, and coordinating photograph sessions with visiting constituents. Candidates should have oral communication skills, personal interest in the field, strong interpersonal skills, writing skills. Duration is 3–4 months. $275 per week. ▶ *1–2 ways and means intern:* responsibilities include assisting the Democratic fiscal analyst in working for the chief Democratic member of the Ways and Means Committee and following meetings of the Committee. Candidates should have analytical skills, oral communication skills, personal interest in the field, written communication skills. Duration is 3–4 months. $275 per week. Open to college juniors, college seniors, recent college graduates, graduate students.
Benefits Possible full-time employment, willing to complete paperwork for educational credit.
Contact Write, call, fax, e-mail, or through World Wide Web site Carrie Stiers, Internship Director, Room 4A-4, State House, 200 West Washington Street, Indianapolis, Indiana 46204-2786. Phone: 317-232-9830. Fax: 317-232-9795. E-mail: cstiers@iga.state.in.gov. In-person interview required. Applicants must submit a formal organization application, letter of interest, resume, academic transcripts, two letters of recommendation. Application deadline: October 16. World Wide Web: http://www.state.in.us/legislative/house_democrats.

ECONOMIC RESEARCH SERVICE, US DEPARTMENT OF AGRICULTURE
1800 M Street, NW
Washington, District of Columbia 20036-5831

General Information Federal agency that provides economic and social science research and analysis for use by decision makers in areas relating to agriculture, food, natural resources, and rural America. Established in 1961. Number of employees: 450. Unit of United States Department of Agriculture, Washington, District of Columbia. Number of internship applications received each year: 150.
Internships Available ▶ *1–3 computer specialists:* responsibilities include assisting in development of agency Internet or Intranet services; assisting in development of Windows database application programs; assisting in the development and validation of relational databases; and assisting in the development of standard

system operating procedures. Candidates should have analytical skills, declared college major in field, organizational skills, personal interest in the field, plan to pursue career in field, knowledge of Internet technologies, client-server databases, or Visual C++, database, and spreadsheet software. Duration is flexible within period of May to August. $9-$10 per hour, depending on education level. Open to college sophomores, college juniors, college seniors, must be continuing students (enrolled in school in fall).
▶ *10–15 economics assistants/economists:* responsibilities include assisting economists in developing and presenting economic research and analysis, conducting literature searches, collecting and analyzing information using a variety of software packages to develop spreadsheets, creating graphics and text for documents. Candidates should have analytical skills, college courses in field, computer skills, knowledge of field, plan to pursue career in field, research skills. Duration is flexible within period of May to August. $10–$20 per hour, depending on education level. Open to college sophomores, college juniors, college seniors, graduate students, must be continuing students (enrolled in school in fall).
Benefits On-the-job training, opportunity to attend seminars/workshops, willing to act as a professional reference, willing to complete paperwork for educational credit, computer training, public transit subsidy.
Contact Write, call, fax, or e-mail Victoria Smith, Assistant to the Administrator, 1800 M Street, NW, Room 4151, Washington, District of Columbia 20036-5831. Phone: 202-694-5004. Fax: 202-694-5757. E-mail: vsmith@ers.usda.gov. Applicants must submit a formal organization application, resume, academic transcripts, list of references, application form available on Web site. Application deadline: March 1. World Wide Web: http://www.ers.usda.gov.

FEDERAL RESERVE BANK OF NEW YORK
33 Liberty Street
New York, New York 10045

General Information One of the 12 regional banks which along with the Federal Reserve Board in Washington, D.C. comprise the Federal Reserve System, and are responsible for implementing the nation's monetary policy through a variety of techniques including buying and selling U.S. Government securities in the open market. Established in 1913. Number of employees: 3,500. Number of internship applications received each year: 2,500.
Internships Available ▶ *12 graduate summer analysts:* responsibilities include assignment to one particular department for the summer, but will have frequent opportunities to complete projects by collaboration with other analysts and employers around the banks; examples of past assignments include participation in risk examinations, developing reports and databases, and conducting economic research with senior level economists. Candidates should have analytical skills, computer skills, oral communication skills, plan to pursue career in field, written communication skills, strong academic record. Duration is 12–14 weeks. $1250 per week. Open to students pursuing master's degree in business, economics, finance, public policy, or related disciplines. ▶ *12 undergraduate summer interns:* responsibilities include assignment to one particular department for the summer, but have frequent opportunities to complete projects by collaborating with other analysts and employees from around the banks; examples of past assignments include participating in risk examinations, developing reports and databases, and conducting economic research with senior level economists. Candidates should have analytical skills, computer skills, oral communication skills, plan to pursue career in field, research skills, self-motivation, background in business, finance, or related field, strong academic record. Duration is 12–14 weeks. $400–$600 per week. Open to students who have completed junior year of college by beginning of internship.
Benefits Formal training, meals at a cost, on-the-job training, opportunity to attend seminars/workshops, possible full-time employment, willing to act as a professional reference, willing to complete paperwork for educational credit.
Contact Write, e-mail, or through World Wide Web site Internship Coordinator. E-mail: campus@ny.frb.org. No phone calls. In-person interview recommended (telephone interview accepted). Applicants must submit a formal organization application, letter

of interest, resume, academic transcripts, writing sample. Application deadline: January 31 for summer. World Wide Web: http://www.newyorkfed.org.

FINNEGAN FOUNDATION
3600 Raymond Street
Reading, Pennsylvania 19605

General Information Foundation that provides practical training in government and politics by offering internships in Harrisburg, Pennsylvania. Established in 1961. Number of employees: 1. Number of internship applications received each year: 50.
Internships Available ▶ *5–10 interns:* responsibilities include various positions in the many departments of state government. Candidates should have ability to work independently, ability to work with others, analytical skills, research skills, self-motivation, writing skills. Duration is 8–10 weeks. Paid. Open to college freshmen, college sophomores, college juniors, college seniors.
Benefits Opportunity to attend seminars/workshops, willing to act as a professional reference, willing to complete paperwork for educational credit, willing to provide letters of recommendation.
Contact Write, call, fax, e-mail, or through World Wide Web site William C. Baer, Administrator. Phone: 610-929-4582. Fax: 610-921-3075. E-mail: bbam200@aol.com. Applicants must submit a formal organization application, letter of interest, academic transcripts, personal reference, letter of recommendation, essay on varied topics. Application deadline: February for summer. World Wide Web: http://members.aol.com/JAFINNEGAN.

GEOSCIENTISTS-IN-THE-PARKS PROGRAM, GEOLOGIC RESOURCES DIVISION, NATIONAL PARK SERVICE
12795 West Almeda Parkway
Lakewood, Colorado 80228

General Information The Geologic Resources Division provides geologic expertise to National Parks and coordinates the Geologist-in-the-Parks Program. Established in 1995. Number of employees: 900. Division of United States National Park Service, Washington, District of Columbia. Number of internship applications received each year: 300.
Internships Available ▶ *1–4 earth scientists/geologists:* responsibilities include interpreting area geology, producing educational materials, or assisting in resource management. Candidates should have ability to work independently, knowledge of field, oral communication skills, self-motivation, strong interpersonal skills. Duration is flexible. Unpaid. Open to college juniors, college seniors, recent college graduates, graduate students. ▶ *1 geologist or geology intern:* responsibilities include assisting in evaluating and coordinating growing geoscience program. Candidates should have college courses in field, oral communication skills, self-motivation, strong interpersonal skills, written communication skills. Duration is negotiable for summer. Unpaid. Open to college juniors, college seniors, recent college graduates, graduate students. ▶ *1 geologist/guide (park interpreter):* responsibilities include presenting volcano talks, staffing visitor center, interpretive roving, collecting park entrance fees, special projects on geologic interpretation and resource management. Candidates should have ability to work independently, college courses in field, knowledge of field, oral communication skills, self-motivation, interest and/or experience in interpretation and/or education. Duration is May-August. Position available as unpaid or at stipend of $7 per day up to $2500 for 12 weeks. Open to college juniors, college seniors, recent college graduates, graduate students. ▶ *20–100 geologist/hydrologists/air quality specialists:* responsibilities include basic interpretation of the area's physical and integrated natural resources to park visitors; conducting inventories and monitoring geologic features and sites; identifying, cataloging, and caring for geologic specimens; incorporating geology (e.g., information, protection of special features, resource management, hazards) into park actions and planning documents; summarizing scientific literature; developing informative museum or visitor displays; writing teacher guides; mapping geologic resources; and conducting research (e.g., in stratigraphy, slope stability, sedimentology, volcanology, paleontology, caves, soil). Candidates should have

Geoscientists-in-the-Parks Program, Geologic Resources Division, National Park Service (continued)

ability to work independently, college courses in field, oral communication skills, self-motivation, strong interpersonal skills, written communication skills. Duration is 1–9 months. Position available as unpaid or paid. Open to college freshmen, college sophomores, college juniors, college seniors, recent college graduates, graduate students. ▶ *1 interpreter (park guide):* responsibilities include providing technical paleontological assistance on paleo projects, excavations, inventories, monitoring, curation, measuring stratigraphic sections, and paleo databases. Candidates should have ability to work independently, ability to work with others, declared college major in field, organizational skills, self-motivation. Duration is one summer. Unpaid. Open to college juniors, college seniors, recent college graduates, graduate students. ▶ *1 physical science/geology intern:* responsibilities include providing assistance with one or more physical science projects which vary from year to year; may include geologic mapping, paleontological sampling, glacier data collection, water quality monitoring, and evaluating impacts from air pollution. Candidates should have ability to work independently, ability to work with others, analytical skills, declared college major in field, organizational skills, self-motivation. Duration is early May to late September. Position available as unpaid or paid. Open to college juniors, college seniors, recent college graduates, graduate students. ▶ *1 researcher/resource manager:* responsibilities include conducting research projects in stratigraphy, slope stability, sedimentology, groundwater hydrology, geomorphology, or volcanology. Candidates should have ability to work independently, ability to work with others, declared college major in field, knowledge of field, research skills, self-motivation. Duration is flexible. Stipend of $7 per day up to $2500 for 12 weeks of work. Open to graduate students. International applications accepted.
Benefits Free housing, willing to complete paperwork for educational credit.
Contact Through World Wide Web site Judy Geniac, Environmental Protection Specialist. Phone: 303-969-2015. Fax: 303-987-6792. E-mail: judy_geniac@nps.gov. Materials as detailed on Web site. World Wide Web: http://www2.nature.nps.gov/grd/geojob.

HOUSE EDUCATIONAL PROGRAMS
45A State Office Building
St. Paul, Minnesota 55155

General Information Office that provides educational experiences in the legislative process. Established in 1975. Number of employees: 1. Unit of Minnesota House of Representatives, St. Paul, Minnesota. Number of internship applications received each year: 75.
Internships Available ▶ *25–50 legislative interns:* responsibilities include research, corresponding, writing news releases, designing or compiling surveys, telephoning, providing constituent services, monitoring committee meetings, or following the status of a bill. Candidates should have ability to work with others, office skills, oral communication skills, organizational skills, personal interest in the field, research skills, written communication skills. Duration is 3–5 months. Unpaid. Open to college freshmen, college sophomores, college juniors, college seniors, recent college graduates, graduate students, law students, career changers, individuals reentering the workforce. International applications accepted.
Benefits On-the-job training, opportunity to attend seminars/ workshops, willing to act as a professional reference, willing to complete paperwork for educational credit, willing to provide letters of recommendation.
Contact Write, call, fax, or e-mail Josh D. Gackle, 2nd Assistant Sergeant-at-Arms. Phone: 651-296-7452. Fax: 651-215-3903. E-mail: josh.gackle@house.leg.state.mn.us. In-person interview recommended (telephone interview accepted). Applicants must submit a formal organization application, resume. Application deadline: October 1. World Wide Web: http://www.house.leg.state.mn.us.

ILLINOIS LEGISLATIVE STAFF INTERNSHIP PROGRAM
University of Illinois, PO Box 19243
Springfield, Illinois 62794-9243

General Information Program providing experience in a legislative environment. Established in 1963. Number of employees: 254. Number of internship applications received each year: 100.
Internships Available ▶ *45–55 graduate public service interns.* Candidates should have ability to work independently, ability to work with others, computer skills, oral communication skills, writing skills. Duration is 21 months. $850 per month during the academic months; $1700 per month during the summer. Open to recent college graduates, graduate students, law students. ▶ *20 partisan staff interns:* responsibilities include researching issues, drafting bills, analyzing bills and agency budget requests to prepare for committee and floor action; providing general staff work for the party they serve. Candidates should have oral communication skills, writing skills. Duration is August to June (10½ months). $2026 per month. Open to college seniors, recent college graduates, graduate students, law students. ▶ *3 research interns:* responsibilities include researching a variety of questions on public issues for legislators. Candidates should have oral communication skills, research skills, writing skills. Duration is August to June. $2026 per month. Open to college seniors, recent college graduates, graduate students, law students. ▶ *1 science writing intern:* responsibilities include answering a variety of inquiries from legislators and publishing articles on scientific topics in legislative newsletter. Candidates should have oral communication skills, research skills, writing skills. Duration is August to June (10½ months). $2026 per month. Open to college seniors, recent college graduates, graduate students, law students.
Benefits Health insurance, opportunity to attend seminars/ workshops, possible full-time employment, tuition assistance, willing to complete paperwork for educational credit, 8 hours of graduate credit.
Contact Write, call, fax, e-mail, or through World Wide Web site Ms. Gia Simmons, Director of Graduate Intern Programs. Phone: 217-206-6602. Fax: 217-206-6542. E-mail: aldrich.ann@uis.edu. In-person interview required. Applicants must submit a formal organization application, resume, academic transcripts, writing sample, three letters of recommendation. Application deadline: February 1. World Wide Web: http://ilsip.uis.edu.

INTERNATIONAL BUSINESS–GOVERNMENT COUNSELORS, INC. (IBC)
818 Connecticut Avenue, NW, 12th Floor
Washington, District of Columbia 20006

General Information International government relations firm that provides research and analysis to clients from major international corporations; also manages several trade associations. Established in 1972. Number of employees: 20. Number of internship applications received each year: 30.
Internships Available ▶ *1 association management intern:* responsibilities include assisting with membership development, meeting planning, publications, correspondence, Web page and database management, and research. Candidates should have ability to work independently, computer skills, office skills, oral communication skills, self-motivation, strong interpersonal skills. Duration is 3 months (flexible). Unpaid. ▶ *3 interns:* responsibilities include attending congressional hearings and other trade-related meetings, performing basic research on a variety of issues, and providing written summaries. Candidates should have ability to work independently, computer skills, knowledge of field, research skills, self-motivation, written communication skills. Duration is 3 months (flexible). Unpaid. Open to college sophomores, college juniors, college seniors. International applications accepted.
Benefits Job counseling, on-the-job training, opportunity to attend seminars/workshops, willing to act as a professional reference, willing to complete paperwork for educational credit, willing to provide letters of recommendation.
Contact Write or e-mail Ms. Mary Fromyer, Intern Supervisor. Phone: 202-872-8181. Fax: 202-872-8696. E-mail: mfromyer@ibgc. com. Telephone interview required. Applicants must submit a let-

ter of interest, resume, academic transcripts, writing sample. Applications are accepted continuously. World Wide Web: http://www.ibgc.com.

INTERNATIONAL CITY/COUNTY MANAGEMENT ASSOCIATION
777 North Capitol Street, NE, Suite 500
Washington, District of Columbia 20002-4201

General Information Association that promotes and supports professional management of local governments; advocates the council-manager form of government and collects and publishes data and information on local government, primarily in the U.S. Established in 1914. Number of employees: 115. Number of internship applications received each year: 200.
Internships Available ▶ *Environmental program interns:* responsibilities include working on grant- and contract-funded environmental projects; assisting with meetings, workshops, and conference planning; and preparing articles and case studies on local government environmental issues. Candidates should have college courses in field, computer skills, oral communication skills, self-motivation, written communication skills. Duration is flexible. $9–$11 per hour. ▶ *Inquiry service interns:* responsibilities include receiving and responding to requests for information, reading and abstracting new documents to be added to database, and working on special research, writing, and general projects involving other departments. Candidates should have computer skills, oral communication skills, personal interest in the field, research skills, self-motivation, written communication skills. Duration is flexible. $9–$11 per hour. ▶ *International interns:* responsibilities include assisting with recruiting for overseas assignments; researching and writing for quarterly newsletter, arranging seminars, study tours, and on-the-job training for overseas officials. Duration is flexible. $9–$11 per hour. ▶ *Management information publications/urban management interns:* responsibilities include researching and writing brief descriptions of local government programs, making phone calls to collect information for the Software Reference Guide, and helping assemble mailings. Candidates should have computer skills, oral communication skills, research skills, self-motivation, written communication skills. Duration is flexible. $9–$11 per hour. Open to college freshmen, college sophomores, college juniors, college seniors, graduate students. International applications accepted.
Benefits Opportunity to attend seminars/workshops, willing to act as a professional reference, willing to complete paperwork for educational credit, willing to provide letters of recommendation.
Contact Write or e-mail Intern Coordinator, 777 North Capitol Street, NE Suite 500, Washington, District of Columbia 20002-4201. No phone calls. In-person interview recommended (telephone interview accepted). Applicants must submit a letter of interest, resume. Application deadline: March 1 for summer, July 31 for fall, November 1 for spring. World Wide Web: http://icma.org.

INTERNATIONAL TRADE ADMINISTRATION, U.S. AND FOREIGN COMMERCIAL SERVICE
2012 HCHB, 14th and Constitution Avenue, NW
Washington, District of Columbia 20230

General Information International network of commercial specialists in 70 countries that promotes the export of U.S. goods and services. Established in 1980. Number of employees: 100. Unit of United States Department of Commerce, Washington, District of Columbia. Number of internship applications received each year: 50.
Internships Available ▶ *1 certified trade missions intern:* responsibilities include working with private sector organizers of trade missions to provide promotion and logistical support overseas. Candidates should have ability to work independently, computer skills, oral communication skills, research skills, strong interpersonal skills, written communication skills. Duration is year-round (flexible). Unpaid. ▶ *2 international buyer program interns:* responsibilities include assisting project officer to coordinate worldwide promotion of selected U.S. trade shows. Candidates should have ability to work with others, computer skills, oral communication skills, personal interest in the field, written communication skills. Duration is year-round (flexible). Unpaid. ▶ *4 matchmaker program*

interns: responsibilities include assisting project managers to plan, organize, and recruit small to medium size U.S. companies for participation in overseas trade missions. Candidates should have ability to work independently, computer skills, oral communication skills, research skills, strong interpersonal skills, written communication skills. Duration is year-round (flexible). Unpaid. ▶ *2–3 multi-state/catalog exhibition program interns:* responsibilities include assisting project managers to plan, organize, and recruit small to medium size U.S. companies to participate in catalog show exhibitions designed to penetrate foreign markets. Candidates should have ability to work independently, computer skills, oral communication skills, research skills, strong interpersonal skills, written communication skills. Duration is year-round (flexible). Unpaid. ▶ *2 trade fair certification interns:* responsibilities include helping program staff review and select international trade shows for support by U.S. Department of Commerce overseas staff and coordinating domestic promotion of shows to potential exhibitors. Candidates should have analytical skills, computer skills, oral communication skills, research skills, strong interpersonal skills, written communication skills. Duration is year-round (flexible). Unpaid. Open to college freshmen, college sophomores, college juniors, college seniors, graduate students, must be U.S. citizen.
Benefits On-the-job training, willing to act as a professional reference, willing to complete paperwork for educational credit, willing to provide letters of recommendation, international marketing experience.
Contact Write, call, fax, or e-mail Ms. Molly Costa, Manager Matchmaker Program FCS/EPS. Phone: 202-482-0692. Fax: 202-482-0178. E-mail: molly.costa@mail.doc.gov. Telephone interview required. Applicants must submit a formal organization application, letter of interest. Applications are accepted continuously. World Wide Web: http://www.ita.doc.gov/doctm/doctm.html.

MASSACHUSETTS OFFICE OF CONSUMER AFFAIRS AND BUSINESS REGULATION
10 Park Plaza, Suite 5170
Boston, Massachusetts 02116

General Information State's watchdog charged with educating and informing consumers; oversees nine state agencies including the divisions of banks, insurance, telecommunications, and energy. Established in 1969. Number of employees: 44. Number of internship applications received each year: 100.
Internships Available ▶ *1–5 consumer information specialists:* responsibilities include receiving training in consumer protection laws, assisting in research, staffing consumer hotline, answering consumer e-mails and written correspondence. Candidates should have ability to work independently, analytical skills, computer skills, office skills, oral communication skills, organizational skills, research skills, self-motivation, strong interpersonal skills, strong leadership ability, writing skills. Duration is 6 months. Position available as unpaid or at $10 per hour. Open to college freshmen, college sophomores, college juniors, college seniors, graduate students, law students. International applications accepted.
Benefits On-the-job training, opportunity to attend seminars/workshops, willing to act as a professional reference, willing to complete paperwork for educational credit, willing to provide letters of recommendation.
Contact Write, call, fax, or e-mail Jocelyn Carr, Consumer Hotline Manager. Phone: 617-973-8700. Fax: 617-973-8799. E-mail: jocelyn.carr@state.ma.us. In-person interview recommended (telephone interview accepted). Applicants must submit a letter of interest, resume. Application deadline: March 15 for summer interns (recommended), July 1 for fall interns (recommended), November 15 for winter interns (recommended). World Wide Web: http://www.state.ma.us/consumer/.

MICHIGAN HOUSE OF REPRESENTATIVES–REPUBLICAN CAUCUS SERVICES
South House Office Building, 7th Floor
Lansing, Michigan 48909-7514

General Information State legislative office that provides services in media relations, research, legislative analysis, and planning events. Established in 1833. Number of employees: 250. Unit of

Michigan House of Representatives–Republican Caucus Services (continued)
Michigan Legislature, Lansing, Michigan, Lansing, Michigan.
Number of internship applications received each year: 100.
Internships Available ▶ *5 central staff interns:* responsibilities
include answering constituent concerns, assisting with district
events and media relations, and performing detailed analysis of
legislation. Candidates should have ability to work independently,
ability to work with others, computer skills, office skills, oral communication skills, personal interest in the field, written communication skills. Duration is 1 semester. Unpaid. ▶ *1–30 representative staff interns:* responsibilities include scheduling, tracking
legislation, and performing general office duties. Candidates
should have office skills, oral communication skills, personal interest in the field, self-motivation, strong interpersonal skills, written communication skills. Duration is 1 semester. Unpaid. Open
to high school students, recent high school graduates, college
freshmen, college sophomores, college juniors, college seniors,
graduate students. International applications accepted.
Benefits Names of contacts, possible full-time employment, willing to complete paperwork for educational credit, willing to
provide letters of recommendation.
Contact Write, call, or fax Derek Bajema, Communications Analyst.
Phone: 517-373-4932. Fax: 517-373-8402. In-person interview recommended (telephone interview accepted). Applicants must submit
a formal organization application, letter of interest, resume.
Applications are accepted continuously.

MISSOURI LEGISLATIVE INTERN PROGRAM
State Capitol
Jefferson City, Missouri 65101

General Information Program that selects the best students in
related fields at Missouri institutions of higher education and
provides interns an opportunity to gain valuable practical experience in the government process. Established in 1972. Unit of
Missouri State Government, Jefferson City, Missouri. Number
of internship applications received each year: 125.
Internships Available ▶ *100–125 legislative interns:* responsibilities include working with legislators and their staff. Candidates
should have ability to work with others, computer skills, oral communication skills, research skills, written communication skills.
Duration is 1 semester (part-time and full-time); January to mid-
May. Unpaid. Open to college juniors, college seniors, recent college graduates, graduate students, law students. International
applications accepted.
Benefits Opportunity to attend seminars/workshops, willing to
act as a professional reference, willing to complete paperwork
for educational credit, willing to provide letters of recommendation.
Contact Write, call, or fax Representative Deleta Williams, at 573-
751-2272 or Representative Judy Berkstresser at 573-751-1503. Fax:
573-526-7381. In-person interview recommended (telephone
interview accepted). Applicants must submit a formal organization application, letter of interest, resume, academic transcripts,
three letters of recommendation. Application deadline: December
1 for spring.

MONTANA LEGISLATIVE COUNCIL
PO Box 201706
Helena, Montana 59620-1706

General Information Council that provides legislating services.
Established in 1957. Number of employees: 55. Unit of Montana
Legislature, Helena, Montana. Number of internship applications received each year: 11.
Internships Available ▶ *11 interns:* responsibilities include assisting legislators. Duration is January to April (in odd-numbered
years). Unpaid. Open to college juniors, college seniors, must be
enrolled in a Montana school.
Benefits On-the-job training, willing to complete paperwork for
educational credit.
Contact Write, call, fax, or e-mail David D. Bohyer, Director,
Research and Policy Analysis. Phone: 406-444-3064. Fax: 406-444-
3036. E-mail: dbohyer@state.mt.us. Materials to intern coordina-

tor at the college or university. Application deadline: November
1 of even-numbered year (preferred). World Wide Web: http://
www.leg.state.mt.us.

MONTGOMERY COUNTY COMMISSION FOR WOMEN
255 North Washington Street
Rockville, Maryland 20850

General Information Government unit that conducts research
and advocacy activities for women's issues and operates a counseling and career center primarily for women. Established in 1976.
Number of employees: 20. Department of Montgomery County
Government, Rockville, Maryland. Number of internship applications received each year: 15.
Internships Available ▶ *6–7 counseling interns:* responsibilities
include providing individual psychosocial or career counseling
to adults, co-leading groups, special projects. Candidates should
have college degree in related field, knowledge of field, plan to
pursue career in field, self-motivation, strong interpersonal skills.
Duration is 2 semesters (20 hours per week). Unpaid. Open to
individuals enrolled in a graduate-level program for counseling
or social work and are using this experience as part of a formal
practicum or internship approved by their university for credit.
▶ *4–6 information and referral specialists:* responsibilities include
providing intake for counseling center; making referrals to local
resources; assisting individuals in person and by phone to find
information and resources to meet their needs. Candidates should
have computer skills, oral communication skills, personal interest in the field, research skills, strong interpersonal skills. Duration is 1–2 semesters. Unpaid. Open to college seniors, recent
college graduates, career changers, individuals reentering the
workforce. International applications accepted.
Benefits Formal training, on-the-job training, opportunity to
attend seminars/workshops, willing to act as a professional reference, willing to complete paperwork for educational credit, willing to provide letters of recommendation, supervision for
university-based practica and internships.
Contact Write, fax, or e-mail Janice Herold, Clinical Supervisor,
255 North Washington Street, Rockville, Maryland 20850. Phone:
301-279-1800. Fax: 301-279-1318. E-mail: herolj@co.mo.md.us.
In-person interview required. Applicants must submit a resume,
personal reference, letter of interest that indicates time of
availability. Applications are accepted continuously. World Wide
Web: http://www.co.mo.md.us/cfw.

NATIONAL ARCHIVES AND RECORD ADMINISTRATION
National Archives and Records Administration, 8601
Adelphi Road, Room 1200
College Park, Maryland 20740-6001

General Information Custodian of noncurrent federal government records of continuing value, relating to all federal government activities from 1789 to the present. Established in 1935.
Number of employees: 2,000. Unit of United States Federal
Government, Washington, District of Columbia. Number of
internship applications received each year: 35.
Internships Available ▶ *1–20 archival interns:* responsibilities
include working with documents including photographs, motion
pictures, maps, and electronic records; performing basic preservation activities; preparing finding aids; responding to reference
inquiries; or developing outreach programs/products. Candidates
should have ability to work independently, ability to work with
others, oral communication skills, organizational skills, research
skills, written communication skills. Duration is 160 hours
minimum. Unpaid. Open to college freshmen, college sophomores,
college juniors, college seniors, recent college graduates, graduate students. ▶ *1–5 nonarchival interns:* responsibilities include a
variety of administrative functions including facilities management,
policy development, and auditing activities. Candidates should
have ability to work independently, ability to work with others,
oral communication skills, written communication skills. Dura-

tion is 160 hours minimum. Unpaid. Open to college freshmen, college sophomores, college juniors, college seniors, graduate students. International applications accepted.
Benefits On-the-job training, willing to complete paperwork for educational credit, willing to provide letters of recommendation.
Contact Write, call, or fax Student Intern Program, National Archives at College Park, 8601 Adelphi Road, Room 1200, College Park, Maryland 20740-6001. Phone: 301-713-7390 Ext. 260. Fax: 301-713-7342. Telephone interview required. Applicants must submit a letter of interest, resume, academic transcripts, letter of recommendation. Applications are accepted continuously. World Wide Web: http://www.nara.gov/professional/intern/intern.html.

NATIONAL SECURITY AGENCY
9800 Savage Road
Fort George G. Meade, Maryland 20755-6779

General Information Federal government agency that provides foreign signals intelligence to decision-makers and protects U.S. national security information systems. Established in 1952. Number of internship applications received each year: 1,800.
Internships Available ▶ *10–25 computer science interns:* responsibilities include performing a variety of programming and analysis functions, including systems design, computer security research, systems programming, computer security systems design, applications analysis, application, and evaluation. Candidates should have ability to work independently, ability to work with others, college courses in field, knowledge of field, personal interest in the field, minimum GPA of 3.0 preferred. Duration is June through August 31. $2354.42 per month. Open to college juniors, graduate students. ▶ *10–15 electrical or computer engineering interns:* responsibilities include working as part of a small team to develop advanced communication security and foreign signals intelligence collection and processing systems, including fundamental research through advanced development, small to large system design and prototype development, developmental test and evaluation, field installation, and operational support. Candidates should have ability to work independently, ability to work with others, college courses in field, minimum GPA of 3.0 preferred. Duration is June through August 31. $2354.42 per month. Open to college juniors, graduate students. ▶ *25–35 mathematics interns:* responsibilities include using advanced concepts to solve cryptologic problems and helping develop and evaluate code and cipher systems. Candidates should have ability to work independently, ability to work with others, college courses in field, personal interest in the field, minimum 3.5 GPA. Duration is June through August 31. $13–$19 per hour. Open to college juniors, graduate students, exceptional mathematics students in their freshman or sophomore year of college.
Benefits Opportunity to attend seminars/workshops, possible full-time employment, travel reimbursement, willing to complete paperwork for educational credit, annual and sick leave.
Contact Write, fax, e-mail, or through World Wide Web site Cecile O'Connor, Summer Program Manager, 9800 Savage Road, Attention: MB3, Suite 6779, PO Box 1661, Fort George G. Meade, Maryland 20755-6779. Phone: 800-669-0703. Fax: 410-854-4593. E-mail: cmoconn@nsa.gov. In-person interview required. Applicants must submit a resume, academic transcripts, security processing required, 2 letters of recommendation (for mathematics interns). Application deadline: October 15 for summer mathematics interns, November 15 for all other positions. World Wide Web: http://www.nsa.gov.

NEW YORK DEPARTMENT OF CITYWIDE ADMINISTRATIVE SERVICES
1 Center Street, 24th Floor, Rooms 24-25
New York, New York 10007

General Information Program addressing issues in New York City government. Established in 1969. Number of employees: 6. Division of New York City Government, New York, New York. Number of internship applications received each year: 250.
Internships Available ▶ *25 government scholars program interns:* responsibilities include assisting with administrative problem solving, research and policy consultation; planning direct service

delivery; and attending weekly seminars that examine crucial issues facing city government. Duration is 10 weeks. $3500 per duration of internship. Open to college sophomores, college juniors, college seniors. ▶ *25 urban fellows program interns:* responsibilities include assisting with policy analysis and review, direct service delivery, fieldwork, and computer applications; and working in areas such as human services, criminal justice, health, housing, transportation, and economic development. Duration is 9 months. $25,000 per duration of internship. Open to recent college graduates, graduate students, individuals within 2 years of college graduation. Candidates for all positions should have ability to work independently, computer skills, oral communication skills, personal interest in the field, self-motivation, strong interpersonal skills, strong leadership ability, writing skills.
Benefits Job counseling, names of contacts, opportunity to attend seminars/workshops, possible full-time employment, willing to provide letters of recommendation.
Contact Write, call, fax, or through World Wide Web site Ms. Barbara Simmons, Director of Fellowship Programs. Phone: 212-669-3695. Fax: 212-669-3688. Applicants must submit a formal organization application, letter of interest, resume, academic transcripts, two writing samples, two letters of recommendation, application available via Web site. Application deadline: January 3 for government scholars, January 10 for urban fellows. World Wide Web: http://www.ci.nyc.ny.us/html/dcas/html/intern/html.

NEW YORK STATE ASSEMBLY INTERNSHIP PROGRAM
104-A Legislative Office Building
Albany, New York 12248

General Information Program that seeks to provide experiential learning for students and services to elected members and staff of the New York State Assembly. Established in 1971. Number of employees: 6. Unit of New York State Assembly, Albany, New York. Number of internship applications received each year: 190.
Internships Available ▶ *10 graduate interns:* responsibilities include performing research necessary to the development of legislative issues for standing committees and commission offices. Candidates should have C+ average, strong interest in state government. Duration is January to June. $11,500 per duration of internship. Open to students within one year of graduating from graduate school and recent graduates from graduate school. ▶ *150 session interns:* responsibilities include participating in the daily operation of a state legislator's office; attending Assembly sessions, committee meetings, and public hearings; and researching proposed legislation and constituent problems. Candidates should have C+ average, interest in state government. Duration is January to mid-May. $3500 per duration of internship. Open to college juniors, college seniors, college sophomores of exceptional academic standing. International applications accepted.
Benefits Health insurance, names of contacts, on-the-job training, opportunity to attend seminars/workshops, possible full-time employment, willing to complete paperwork for educational credit, willing to provide letters of recommendation.
Contact Write, call, fax, e-mail, or through World Wide Web site James A. Murphy, Director. Phone: 518-455-4704. Fax: 518-455-4705. E-mail: intern@assembly.state.ny.us. Applicants must submit a formal organization application, letter of interest, resume, academic transcripts, writing sample, 3 letters of recommendation (including 1 personal). Application deadline: November 1. World Wide Web: http://assembly.state.ny.us/internship/.

NEW YORK STATE COUNCIL ON THE ARTS
175 Varick Street
New York, New York 10014

General Information State agency engaged in the funding of nonprofit cultural organizations. Established in 1960. Number of employees: 40. Unit of State of New York, Albany, New York. Number of internship applications received each year: 15.
Internships Available ▶ *Staff support services interns:* responsibilities include a variety of clerical work, including writing, drafting, and data entry; directing staff support services; recruiting and working with placement institutions; and serving as staff representa-

tive to agency and outside entities. Duration is flexible. Unpaid. Open to college freshmen, college sophomores, college juniors, college seniors, graduate students, individuals reentering the workforce.
Benefits Willing to complete paperwork for educational credit.
Contact Write, call, or fax Ms. Marnee Geller, Personnel Associate. Phone: 212-627-4455. Fax: 212-620-5911. In-person interview required. Applicants must submit a letter of interest, resume. Applications are accepted continuously. World Wide Web: http://www.nysca.org.

NEW YORK STATE SENATE STUDENT PROGRAMS OFFICE
State Capitol, Room 416, 90 South Swan Street
Albany, New York 12247

General Information Program promoting public service career options with the legislature. Established in 1965. Number of employees: 2. Unit of New York State Senate-The State Legislature, Albany, New York. Number of internship applications received each year: 120.
Internships Available ▶ *1 James L. Biggane Finance Fellow:* responsibilities include placement with senate finance/fiscal studies, working among a strong group of fiscal analysts, acquiring skills, and employing the previous life skills of the fellow. Candidates should have self-motivation. Duration is approximately 10 months (September through late July). $29,500 stipend for duration of fellowship. Open to persons at mid-career, at least 35 years of age at time of application. ▶ *1 Richard J. Roth Journalism Fellow:* responsibilities include researching and writing in Senate press office. Candidates should have analytical skills, editing skills, oral communication skills, research skills, writing skills, New York residency or enrollment at a New York state college or university. Duration is approximately 10 months (September through late July). $29,500 stipend for duration of fellowship. Open to college seniors, recent college graduates, graduate students. ▶ *1 Richard Wiebe Public Service Fellow:* responsibilities include expert-level participation in the routines and specialty areas of a legislative office, including research, analysis, synthesis, and legislative and/or constituent casework. Candidates should have analytical skills, editing skills, oral communication skills, research skills, written communication skills, New York residency or enrollment in a New York university. Duration is approximately 10 months (September through late July). $29,500 stipend for duration of fellowship. Open to graduate students, law students. ▶ *9 legislative fellows:* responsibilities include expert-level participation in the routines and specialty areas of a legislative office, including research, analysis, synthesis, and legislative and/or constituent casework. Candidates should have analytical skills, editing skills, oral communication skills, research skills, written communication skills, New York residency or enrollment in a New York university. Duration is approximately 10 months (September through late July). $29,500 stipend for duration of fellowship. Open to graduate students, law students. ▶ *61 session assistants:* responsibilities include assisting with legislative routines, analyses, and representation. Candidates should have analytical skills, editing skills, oral communication skills, research skills, written communication skills, New York residency or enrollment in a New York college or university. Duration is approximately 4 months (January through late April/early May). $3500 stipend for duration of internship. Open to college sophomores, college juniors, college seniors.
Benefits Formal training, health insurance, job counseling, names of contacts, on-the-job training, opportunity to attend seminars/workshops, possible full-time employment, willing to complete paperwork for educational credit, willing to provide letters of recommendation, willing to complete any necessary paperwork for an intern to receive a loan deferment (where possible).
Contact Write, call, fax, or e-mail Dr. Russell J. Williams, Director. Phone: 518-455-2611. Fax: 518-426-6827. E-mail: students@senate.state.ny.us. In-person interview required. Applicants must submit a formal organization application, resume, academic transcripts, four writing samples, three letters of recommendation, indication of preferred areas of placement, 3 academic references.

Application deadline: May 4 for graduate fellows, October 26 for undergraduates. World Wide Web: http://www.senate.state.ny.us.

OFFICE OF LEGISLATIVE RESEARCH AND GENERAL COUNSEL
436 State Capitol Building
Salt Lake City, Utah 84114

General Information Office that provides professional staff sources to the state legislature. Established in 1948. Number of employees: 53. Unit of Utah State Legislature, Salt Lake City, Utah. Number of internship applications received each year: 75.
Internships Available ▶ *45–65 legislative interns:* responsibilities include providing staff and research services to individual legislators. Candidates should have analytical skills, college courses in field, computer skills, oral communication skills, research skills, strong interpersonal skills, writing skills. Duration is 45 days. $1800 per duration of internship. Open to college juniors, college seniors, recent college graduates, preference given to students from Utah colleges.
Benefits Willing to act as a professional reference, willing to provide letters of recommendation, class credit.
Contact Write, fax, or e-mail Jerry D. Howe, Intern Coordinator, 436 State Capitol Building, Salt Lake City, Utah 89114. Fax: 801-538-1712. E-mail: jhowe@le.state.ut.us. No phone calls. Applicants must submit a resume, academic transcripts, writing sample, three personal references. Application deadline: December 1.

OFFICE OF THE ATTORNEY GENERAL OF MARYLAND, CONSUMER PROTECTION DIVISION
200 St. Paul Place
Baltimore, Maryland 21202

General Information State government agency. Number of employees: 46. Number of internship applications received each year: 300.
Internships Available ▶ *Mediation interns:* responsibilities include mediation of disputes filed by consumer against business entities such as retailers, repair shops, service providers, landlords and home builders. Candidates should have ability to work with others, computer skills, oral communication skills, personal interest in the field, written communication skills. Duration is 1 semester. Position available as unpaid or paid. Open to college freshmen, college sophomores, college juniors, college seniors, graduate students, law students, career changers.
Benefits Willing to act as a professional reference, willing to complete paperwork for educational credit, willing to provide letters of recommendation, educational credit or $9 per day stipend.
Contact Call Ronnie Sanderson, Mediation Supervisor. Phone: 410-576-6355. Fax: 410-576-7040. In-person interview required. Applicants must submit a formal organization application, letter of interest, 2-3 personal references. Applications are accepted continuously. World Wide Web: http://www.oag.state.md.us.

OFFICE OF THE SPEAKER OF THE HOUSE
H-232 The Capitol
Washington, District of Columbia 20515

General Information Congressional Leadership Office including press, public affairs, administration, strategic planning, information technology, and executive scheduling departments. Number of employees: 35. Number of internship applications received each year: 200.
Internships Available ▶ *5–9 Congressional interns:* responsibilities include critical research; preparing memos and press releases; attending hearings, briefings, and lectures; performing administrative duties; shadowing staffers to meetings; accompanying the Speaker to meetings; designing and improving computer systems. Candidates should have ability to work independently, ability to work with others, computer skills, oral communication skills, research skills, self-motivation. Duration is 6 weeks to 3 months (180 working days maximum). Unpaid. Open to recent high school graduates, college freshmen, college sophomores, college

juniors, college seniors, recent college graduates, graduate students, law students, juniors and seniors preferred. International applications accepted.
Benefits Job counseling, names of contacts, on-the-job training, opportunity to attend seminars/workshops, willing to act as a professional reference, willing to complete paperwork for educational credit, willing to provide letters of recommendation, meetings with Speaker, lecture series, photo opportunities, attendance at hearings and joint sessions of Congress.
Contact Call Kristina Moore, Administrative Assistant. Phone: 202-225-0600. Fax: 202-226-1996. E-mail: kristina.moore@mail.house.gov. In-person interview recommended (telephone interview accepted). Applicants must submit a formal organization application, letter of interest, resume, two personal references, two letters of recommendation. Application deadline: April 15 for summer (recommended), July 15 for fall (recommended), November 15 for spring (recommended).

OFFICE OF U.S. SENATOR JEFF BINGAMAN
United States Senate
Washington, District of Columbia 20510

General Information U.S. Senate office. Number of employees: 50. Number of internship applications received each year: 30.
Internships Available ▶ *3–6 fall and spring interns:* responsibilities include writing letters, conducting research, and greeting constituents. Duration is 4 months. Unpaid. ▶ *10–16 summer interns:* responsibilities include wiring letters, conducting research, and greeting constituents. Duration is 5–6 weeks. Position available as unpaid or at $600 per duration of internship. Candidates for all positions should have computer skills, office skills, oral communication skills, self-motivation, strong interpersonal skills, writing skills. Open to undergraduates who are residents of or attending college in New Mexico.
Benefits On-the-job training, opportunity to attend seminars/workshops, willing to act as a professional reference, willing to complete paperwork for educational credit, willing to provide letters of recommendation, possibility of paid housing (summer interns).
Contact Write, call, fax, e-mail, or through World Wide Web site David Pike, Intern Coordinator. Phone: 202-224-5521. Fax: 202-224-2852. E-mail: david_pike@bingaman.senate.gov. Applicants must submit a formal organization application, resume, writing sample, three letters of recommendation. Application deadline: March 31 for summer; continuous for fall and spring. World Wide Web: http://www.senate.gov/~bingaman.

OHIO STATE PARKS
1952 Belcher, Building C-3
Columbus, Ohio 43224

General Information State agency overseeing the operation of 73 state parks. Established in 1949. Number of employees: 5,700. Division of Ohio Department of Natural Resources, Columbus, Ohio.
Internships Available ▶ *100–200 adopt-a-trail volunteers:* responsibilities include adopting a trail to maintain on a regular basis. Candidates should have ability to work independently, ability to work with others, knowledge of field, oral communication skills, personal interest in the field, self-motivation. Duration is flexible, up to 1 year. Unpaid. Open to high school students, recent high school graduates, college freshmen, college sophomores, college juniors, college seniors, recent college graduates, graduate students, law students, career changers. ▶ *100–300 campground hosts:* responsibilities include welcoming people, performing public relations work, helping maintain campgrounds, and leading group activities. Candidates should have ability to work independently, analytical skills, oral communication skills, organizational skills, personal interest in the field, self-motivation, strong interpersonal skills, strong leadership ability. Duration is up to 6 months (April 1 to October 31). Unpaid. Open to college juniors, college seniors, recent college graduates, career changers, retired people, avid campers. ▶ *Green teens:* responsibilities include working in state parks, assisting staff with interpretive programs, trail maintenance, leading youth groups on hiking trips, and light maintenance. Candidates should have ability to work independently, oral com-

munication skills, personal interest in the field, self-motivation, strong interpersonal skills. Duration is flexible; can be year-round depending on projects. Unpaid. Open to high school students, individuals 12 to 18 years of age with parental permission. ▶ *200–400 groups volunteers:* responsibilities include working with various groups including the camera club, garden club, horseman's groups, and scouts in trail maintenance and park beautification. Candidates should have ability to work independently, knowledge of field, oral communication skills, personal interest in the field, self-motivation, strong interpersonal skills, strong leadership ability. Duration is flexible, up to 1 year. Unpaid. Open to high school students, recent high school graduates, college freshmen, college sophomores, college juniors, college seniors, recent college graduates, graduate students, law students, career changers. ▶ *Individual volunteers-in-parks:* responsibilities include a wide variety of work opportunities in state parks and nature centers designed to meet the needs of the individual and the park/nature center. Candidates should have ability to work independently, knowledge of field, oral communication skills, personal interest in the field, self-motivation, strong interpersonal skills. Duration is flexible; can be year-round. Unpaid. Open to recent high school graduates, college freshmen, college sophomores, college juniors, college seniors, recent college graduates, graduate students, career changers, individuals reentering the workforce. International applications accepted.
Benefits Formal training, housing at a cost, job counseling, on-the-job training, opportunity to attend seminars/workshops, willing to act as a professional reference, willing to complete paperwork for educational credit, willing to provide letters of recommendation, worker's compensation, opportunity to learn first-hand about careers in natural resources and parks.
Contact Write, call, fax, or e-mail Mr. Jim Henahan, Community Services Manager. Phone: 614-265-6561. Fax: 614-261-8407. E-mail: jim.henahan@dnr.state.oh.us. In-person interview recommended (telephone interview accepted). Applicants must submit a formal organization application, letter of interest, resume, three letters of recommendation. Applications are accepted continuously. World Wide Web: http://www.state.ohio.us/odnr/parks.

PROJECT VOTE SMART
One Common Ground
Philipsburg, Montana 59858

General Information National library of political information on over 13,000 candidates and elected officials per election cycle. Established in 1988. Number of employees: 20. Number of internship applications received each year: 100.
Internships Available ▶ *12–17 National Political Awareness Test assistants:* responsibilities include conducting ongoing research of political issues to be included in the presidential, congressional, gubernatorial, and state legislative National Political Awareness Tests; administering NPATs to campaigns and candidates. Candidates should have ability to work independently, ability to work with others, oral communication skills, organizational skills, research skills, written communication skills. Duration is 10 weeks. Unpaid. Open to recent high school graduates, college freshmen, college sophomores, college juniors, college seniors, recent college graduates, graduate students, law students. ▶ *2–5 Web researchers:* responsibilities include researching new and changed links, reviewing link suggestions from the Web site, and entering new links and descriptions into the database. Candidates should have ability to work independently, computer skills, editing skills, knowledge of field, office skills, organizational skills. Duration is 10 weeks. Unpaid. Open to high school seniors, college freshmen, college sophomores, college juniors, college seniors, recent college graduates, graduate students, law students. ▶ *10 facilities assistants:* responsibilities include assisting in all areas including lodge and kitchen management and general maintenance. Candidates should have ability to work independently, oral communication skills, self-motivation, strong interpersonal skills, strong leadership ability. Unpaid. Open to recent high school graduates, college freshmen, college sophomores, college juniors, college seniors, recent college graduates, graduate students. ▶ *1 management assistant:* responsibilities include assisting in all areas of managing a nonprofit organization. Candidates should have ability to work independently,

Project Vote Smart (continued)

computer skills, office skills, oral communication skills, organizational skills, strong interpersonal skills. Duration is 10 weeks. Unpaid. Open to recent high school graduates, college freshmen, college sophomores, college juniors, college seniors, recent college graduates, graduate students, law students. ▶ *2 membership assistants:* responsibilities include working in all aspects of the membership department; includes data entry, bulk mailing, research, and statistical analysis; contacting members and vendors; and processing special requests. Candidates should have analytical skills, editing skills, office skills, oral communication skills, research skills, strong interpersonal skills. Duration is 10 weeks. Unpaid. Open to recent high school graduates, college freshmen, college sophomores, college juniors, college seniors, recent college graduates, graduate students, law students. ▶ *2 performance evaluation assistants:* responsibilities include maintaining and updating evaluations by special interest groups; researching new interest groups and adding new ratings. Candidates should have ability to work independently, editing skills, office skills, oral communication skills, personal interest in the field, research skills. Duration is 10 weeks. Unpaid. Open to recent high school graduates, college freshmen, college sophomores, college juniors, college seniors, recent college graduates, graduate students, law students. ▶ *2 public information/media assistants:* responsibilities include maintaining contacts with national media; publicizing PVS through news releases and presentations. Candidates should have editing skills, office skills, oral communication skills, organizational skills, strong interpersonal skills, written communication skills. Duration is 10 weeks. Unpaid. Open to recent high school graduates, college freshmen, college sophomores, college juniors, college seniors, recent college graduates, graduate students, law students. International applications accepted.

Benefits Formal training, free housing, free meals, on-the-job training, possible full-time employment, willing to act as a professional reference, willing to complete paperwork for educational credit, willing to provide letters of recommendation, scholarships available.

Contact Write, call, fax, e-mail, or through World Wide Web site John Russell, Internship Coordinator. Phone: 406-859-VOTE. Fax: 406-859-8680. E-mail: intern@vote-smart.org. Telephone interview required. Applicants must submit a formal organization application, resume, three personal references. Application deadline: May 1 for summer, June 30 for fall, November 30 for spring. World Wide Web: http://www.vote-smart.org.

SAN MATEO COUNTY PLANNING AND BUILDING DIVISION
455 County Center
Redwood City, California 94063

General Information Government division that regulates land use and development in unincorporated San Mateo county. Established in 1856. Number of employees: 50. Division of County of San Mateo, Redwood City, California. Number of internship applications received each year: 5.

Internships Available ▶ *1–2 planning interns:* responsibilities include assisting and coordinating various current planning research projects. Candidates should have ability to work independently, analytical skills, declared college major in field, oral communication skills, research skills, writing skills. Duration is flexible; coordinating various research projects related to current planning. Unpaid. Open to college freshmen, college sophomores, college juniors, college seniors, recent college graduates. ▶ *3–5 research interns:* responsibilities include assisting with literature and telephone surveys, organizing and interpreting data, writing letters and reports, and some clerical work on a variety of projects in Long Range Planning and Current Planning departments. Candidates should have ability to work with others, analytical skills, oral communication skills, personal interest in the field, research skills, written communication skills. Duration is 10 weeks to 1 year. Unpaid. Open to college juniors, college seniors, recent college graduates, graduate students, career changers. International applications accepted.

Benefits Names of contacts, on-the-job training, opportunity to attend seminars/workshops, willing to complete paperwork for educational credit, willing to provide letters of recommendation.
Contact Write, call, or fax Dave Holbrook, Senior Planner/ Internship Coordinator. Phone: 650-363-4161. Fax: 650-363-4849. In-person interview recommended (telephone interview accepted). Applicants must submit a letter of interest, resume. Applications are accepted continuously. World Wide Web: http://www.co.sanmateo.ca.us/planning.

SECURITIES AND EXCHANGE COMMISSION
450 5th Street, NW, M/S 0103
Washington, District of Columbia 20549

General Information Commission that regulates national securities markets, stockbrokers, investment companies, and investment advisors, and prescribes certain disclosure requirements for companies that issue stocks and securities to the public. Number of employees: 2,800. Number of internship applications received each year: 200.

Internships Available ▶ *Advanced commitment program interns:* responsibilities include providing legal research and other assistance to staff attorneys. Candidates should have ability to work independently, analytical skills, knowledge of field, oral communication skills, personal interest in the field, plan to pursue career in field, writing skills. Duration is maximum of 14 months. Paid. Open to third-year law students, recent law student graduates without Bar membership. ▶ *Research assistants:* responsibilities include providing research and other assistance to professional staff members. Duration is 8-12 weeks in summer. Paid. Open to college freshmen, college sophomores, college juniors, college seniors. ▶ *Student observer program interns:* responsibilities include assisting attorneys in research and memoranda of legal cases. Candidates should have ability to work independently, analytical skills, oral communication skills, plan to pursue career in field, research skills, written communication skills. Duration is 10 weeks. Unpaid. Open to third-year law students. ▶ *Summer honors program interns:* responsibilities include participating in topical seminars on various aspects of federal securities laws, taking part in a series of educational lectures and meetings, and working with an assigned attorney on a variety of projects. Candidates should have ability to work independently, analytical skills, personal interest in the field, research skills, writing skills. Duration is 10 weeks. Paid. Open to first- and second-year law students. International applications accepted.

Benefits Formal training, job counseling, names of contacts, opportunity to attend seminars/workshops, possible full-time employment, travel reimbursement, willing to complete paperwork for educational credit, willing to provide letters of recommendation.
Contact Write, call, e-mail, or through World Wide Web site Jill Kirson, Recruiter. Phone: 202-942-7320. E-mail: recruit@sec.gov. In-person interview recommended (telephone interview accepted). Applicants must submit a formal organization application, letter of interest, resume, academic transcripts, three personal references, one 5-10 page writing sample. Application deadline: March 1 for summer honors program; 7 to 8 weeks before start of semester for student observer program; continuous for other positions. World Wide Web: http://www.sec.gov/asec/secjobs. htm.

SENATE REPUBLICAN POLICY COMMITTEE
347 Russell Senate Office Building
Washington, District of Columbia 20510

General Information Committee that assists U.S. Senators and their staffs in aspects of the legislative process, distributes legislative background papers, and provides closed-circuit broadcasting of Senate floor activities. Established in 1946. Number of employees: 17. Unit of United States Senate, Washington, District of Columbia. Number of internship applications received each year: 50.

Internships Available ▶ *3-4 legislative interns:* responsibilities include assisting the RPC staff with a full range of office tasks; answering phones and providing general clerical assistance, as well as conducting legislative research to assist in the compilation of policy papers and other timely projects. Candidates should

have computer skills, editing skills, knowledge of field, office skills, organizational skills, personal interest in the field, research skills, self-motivation, strong interpersonal skills, writing skills, verbal communication skills. Duration is 1–2 semesters. $1000 per month. Open to recent high school graduates, college freshmen, college sophomores, college juniors, college seniors, recent college graduates, graduate students, law students. International applications accepted.
Benefits Names of contacts, opportunity to attend seminars/workshops, possible full-time employment, willing to act as a professional reference, willing to complete paperwork for educational credit, willing to provide letters of recommendation.
Contact Write, call, e-mail, or through World Wide Web site Craig Cheney, Administrative Director. Phone: 202-224-2946. E-mail: mailbox@rpc.senate.gov. Telephone interview required. Applicants must submit a formal organization application, letter of interest, resume, three letters of recommendation, one 3-to 5-page writing sample. Application deadline: March 15 for summer, July 1 for fall, November 30 for spring. World Wide Web: http://rpc.senate.gov.

SENATOR JAMES M. INHOFE
453 Russell Senate Office Building
Washington, District of Columbia 20510

General Information Congressional office representing the State of Oklahoma. Established in 1994. Number of employees: 24. Number of internship applications received each year: 30.
Internships Available ▶ *2–4 spring/fall interns:* responsibilities include administrative duties, correspondence, attending hearings, preparing reports, and running errands. Duration is 10 weeks. Unpaid. Open to college sophomores, college juniors, college seniors, recent college graduates, graduate students, law students, career changers. ▶ *10–12 summer interns:* responsibilities include meeting constituent requests, correspondence, attending hearings and briefings, research, and assisting Senator and staff as needed. Duration is 6 weeks. Position available as unpaid or at $1000 per duration of internship. Open to college sophomores, college juniors, college seniors, recent college graduates. Candidates for all positions should have oral communication skills, personal interest in the field, research skills, strong interpersonal skills, strong leadership ability, writing skills. International applications accepted.
Benefits Opportunity to attend seminars/workshops, willing to act as a professional reference, willing to complete paperwork for educational credit, willing to provide letters of recommendation.
Contact Write, call, e-mail, or through World Wide Web site Drew Mosley, Intern Coordinator. Phone: 202-224-4721. E-mail: drew_mosley@inhofe.senate.gov. Applicants must submit a formal organization application, letter of interest, resume, academic transcripts, writing sample, three personal references, three letters of recommendation. Application deadline: March 15 for summer, August 15 for fall, December 15 for spring. World Wide Web: http://www.senate.gov/~inhofe/.

SENATOR LARRY E. CRAIG
United States Senate
Washington, District of Columbia 20510-1203

General Information Personal office of Republican Senator from Idaho. Number of employees: 22. Number of internship applications received each year: 30.
Internships Available ▶ *5–6 legislative interns:* responsibilities include working with legislative correspondent to research issues; composing correspondence; attending committee hearings; sitting in and taking notes on meetings; and completing small projects; may also include opening, sorting, and delivering mail; answering phone; greeting constituents; running errands; and other clerical duties. Candidates should have ability to work independently, computer skills, oral communication skills, organizational skills, personal interest in the field, research skills, self-motivation, strong interpersonal skills, written communication skills. Duration is 1 semester. $850 per month. Open to college freshmen, college sophomores, college juniors, college seniors, recent college graduates, graduate students, law students, preference given to Idahoans or students attending Idaho institutions.

Benefits On-the-job training, willing to act as a professional reference, willing to complete paperwork for educational credit, willing to provide letters of recommendation, DC political experience for Idaho students.
Contact Write, call, e-mail, or through World Wide Web site Ann Robertson, Intern Coordinator. Phone: 202-224-2752. E-mail: ann_robertson@craig.senate.gov. In-person interview recommended (telephone interview accepted). Applicants must submit a formal organization application, letter of interest, resume, academic transcripts, 1-2 writing samples, 2-3 personal references. Application deadline: March 15 for summer (May-August), July 1 for fall (September-December), November 15 for spring (January-May). World Wide Web: http://craig.senate.gov.

SONOMA COUNTY ECONOMIC DEVELOPMENT BOARD
401 College Avenue, Suite D
Santa Rosa, California 95401-5119

General Information Public agency charged with developing policies and programs to enhance the local economy and quality of life. Established in 1957. Number of employees: 10. Department of County of Sonoma, Santa Rosa, California. Number of internship applications received each year: 600.
Internships Available ▶ *2 public policy fellowships:* responsibilities include researching the following areas: technology/connectivity policy, sustainable business practices, and high tech industry support policies and programs. Candidates should have ability to work independently, oral communication skills, self-motivation, strong interpersonal skills, writing skills. Duration is one year (beginning in summer). $36,600 per year. Open to college seniors, recent college graduates, graduate students, law students. International applications accepted.
Benefits Formal training, job counseling, names of contacts, on-the-job training, opportunity to attend seminars/workshops, willing to act as a professional reference, willing to complete paperwork for educational credit, willing to provide letters of recommendation, opportunity to work with leaders in business, government, and education.
Contact Write Ben G. Stone, Coordinator, 401 College Avenue, Suite D, Santa Rosa, California 95401-5148. E-mail: edb@sonoma-county.org. No phone calls. In-person interview required. Applicants must submit a letter of interest, resume. Application deadline: January 31. World Wide Web: http://www.sonoma-co.org.

SOUTH DAKOTA LEGISLATURE–LEGISLATIVE RESEARCH COUNCIL
500 East Capitol
Pierre, South Dakota 57501-5070

General Information Legislative service agency that provides nonpartisan research and legal services to the 105 members of the South Dakota legislature. Established in 1951. Number of employees: 25. Number of internship applications received each year: 40.
Internships Available ▶ *22 legislative interns:* responsibilities include serving as partisan staff to legislators, conducting research on issues facing the legislature, tracking and responding to legislators' constituent requests, monitoring and summarizing legislative meetings and legislation, and performing general office administration. Candidates should have office skills, organizational skills, research skills, self-motivation, strong interpersonal skills, writing skills. Duration is 7–8 weeks during January-March legislative session. $3200 per duration of internship. Open to college freshmen, college sophomores, college juniors, college seniors, graduate students, law students. International applications accepted.
Benefits Names of contacts, willing to act as a professional reference, willing to complete paperwork for educational credit, willing to provide letters of recommendation.
Contact Write or call Mr. David Ortbahn, Principal Research Analyst. Phone: 605-773-3251. In-person interview recommended (telephone interview accepted). Applicants must submit a formal organization application, academic transcripts, three letters of

South Dakota Legislature–Legislative Research Council (continued)

recommendation. Application deadline: October 15 for winter (January to March). World Wide Web: http://www.lgis.state.sd.us.

STATE OF ILLINOIS, OFFICE OF THE GOVERNOR
107 William G. Stratton Building
Springfield, Illinois 62706

General Information Governing agency of Illinois. Number of internship applications received each year: 150.
Internships Available ▶ *8–16 James H. Dunn, Jr. Memorial Fellowships:* responsibilities include gaining experience in various areas including policy analysis and program administration as part of a public sector management training program. Candidates should have ability to work with others, computer skills, office skills, oral communication skills, personal interest in the field, self-motivation. Duration is August 1 to July 31. $26,700 per year. Open to individuals possessing a bachelor's degree. ▶ *100 Michael Curry summer interns:* responsibilities include working in the Governor's Office and in various agencies under the Governor's jurisdiction learning, firsthand, the operations of Illinois State Government; placements in Springfield and Chicago. Candidates should have ability to work with others, computer skills, office skills, oral communication skills, writing skills. Duration is 10 weeks. $1200 per month. Open to college juniors, college seniors, recent college graduates, graduate students, law students, must be Illinois resident. ▶ *2 Vito Marzullo Internships:* responsibilities include gaining experience in various areas including policy analysis and program administration as part of public sector management training program. Candidates should have ability to work with others, computer skills, office skills, oral communication skills, personal interest in the field, self-motivation. Duration is August 1 to July 31. $26,700 per year. Open to Illinois residents possessing a bachelor's degree. International applications accepted.
Benefits Health insurance, on-the-job training, possible full-time employment, travel reimbursement, willing to act as a professional reference, willing to complete paperwork for educational credit, willing to provide letters of recommendation, life insurance, paid holidays, sick and vacation days.
Contact Write, call, fax, e-mail, or through World Wide Web site Tammy L. Payne, Internship Program Director, 107 William G. Stratton Building, Springfield, Illinois 62706. Phone: 217-782-5213. Fax: 217-524-1677. E-mail: tammy_payne@gov.state.il.us. In-person interview recommended (telephone interview accepted). Applicants must submit a formal organization application, academic transcripts, two writing samples, three letters of recommendation. Application deadline: January 31. World Wide Web: http://www.state.il.us/gov/officeinternship.htm.

STATE OF MINNESOTA, DEPARTMENT OF EMPLOYEE RELATIONS
200 Centennial Office Building, 658 Cedar Street
St. Paul, Minnesota 55155

General Information Department that oversees the State Employee Health Promotion Program which provides consultation and resources to help state agencies develop policies/programs that promote healthy lifestyles and better health among employees and their families. Number of employees: 200. Number of internship applications received each year: 50.
Internships Available ▶ *1 Minnesota State Employee Health Promotion Program intern.* Candidates should have ability to work independently, ability to work with others, computer skills, oral communication skills, personal interest in the field, self-motivation, written communication skills, ability to handle multiple tasks, enthusiasm; major in exercise science, community health, or health education (preferred). Duration is flexible. Unpaid. Open to college juniors, college seniors, recent college graduates, graduate students, must be receiving academic credit. International applications accepted.
Benefits Opportunity to attend seminars/workshops, willing to act as a professional reference, willing to complete paperwork

for educational credit, willing to provide letters of recommendation, parking expenses covered, travel reimbursement (mileage).
Contact Write, call, fax, e-mail, or through World Wide Web site Julie Coe, Health Promotion Consultant. Phone: 651-296-5843. Fax: 651-296-5445. E-mail: julie.coe@state.mn.us. In-person interview recommended (telephone interview accepted). Applicants must submit a letter of interest, resume, three personal references. Application deadline: 3 months prior to start of internship. World Wide Web: http://www.doer.state.mn.us/ei-sehpp.htm.

UNITED STATES SECRET SERVICE
950 H Street, NW, Suite 7400
Washington, District of Columbia 20223

General Information Government office of investigative and protective operations. Established in 1865. Number of employees: 5,600. Unit of United States Department of Treasury, Washington, District of Columbia. Number of internship applications received each year: 130.
Internships Available ▶ *10–15 student volunteer interns:* responsibilities include assisting agents with various tasks and administrative duties. Candidates should have ability to work with others, college courses in field, office skills, oral communication skills, plan to pursue career in field, self-motivation. Duration is 1 semester. Unpaid. Open to college freshmen, college sophomores, college juniors, college seniors.
Benefits Job counseling, names of contacts, on-the-job training, possible full-time employment, willing to complete paperwork for educational credit, willing to provide letters of recommendation.
Contact Write or fax Trumaine Mathis, Human Resources Specialist. Fax: 202-406-5613. No phone calls. In-person interview recommended (telephone interview accepted). Applicants must submit a letter of interest, resume, background check required. Application deadline: January 15 for summer, April 15 for fall, August 15 for spring. World Wide Web: http://www.jobweb.org/employer/ussecret.htm.

U.S. SENATOR DIANNE FEINSTEIN
11111 Santa Monica Boulevard, Suite 915
Los Angeles, California 90025

General Information One of the four district offices representing Senator Feinstein in the state of California. Established in 1992. Number of employees: 8. Number of internship applications received each year: 20.
Internships Available ▶ *6–8 interns:* responsibilities include working with staff members, answering constituent inquiries, assisting with correspondence, and special projects. Candidates should have ability to work independently, ability to work with others, knowledge of field, office skills, oral communication skills, organizational skills, research skills, self-motivation, writing skills. Duration is May through August/September. Unpaid. Open to college freshmen, college sophomores, college juniors, college seniors. International applications accepted.
Benefits Names of contacts, on-the-job training, opportunity to attend seminars/workshops, possible full-time employment, willing to act as a professional reference, willing to complete paperwork for educational credit, willing to provide letters of recommendation.
Contact Write or call Olyvia Rodriguez, Intern Coordinator, 11111 Santa Monica Boulevard, Suite 915, Los Angeles, California 90025. Phone: 310-914-7300. In-person interview recommended (telephone interview accepted). Applicants must submit a formal organization application, letter of interest, resume, writing sample, three personal references. Application deadline: April 20. World Wide Web: http://www.feinstein.senate.gov.

U.S. SENATOR MAX BAUCUS
511 Hart Building
Washington, District of Columbia 20510

General Information Represents state of Montana in U.S. Senate. Established in 1978. Number of employees: 30.
Internships Available ▶ *6 legislative interns:* responsibilities include writing statements, attending hearings and briefings, and research-

ing legislation. Candidates should have ability to work with others, organizational skills, personal interest in the field, research skills, self-motivation, writing skills. Duration is 1 semester or 1 summer. Unpaid. Open to college freshmen, college sophomores, college juniors, college seniors, recent college graduates, graduate students, law students.
Benefits Job counseling, on-the-job training, opportunity to attend seminars/workshops, possible full-time employment, willing to act as a professional reference, willing to complete paperwork for educational credit, willing to provide letters of recommendation.
Contact Write or call Ms. Nancy Hadley, Intern Coordinator. Phone: 202-224-2651. Applicants must submit a formal organization application, writing sample, two personal references. Applications are accepted continuously.

WILLIAM AND MARY JOHNSON YOUTH CENTER
1 Harbor Drive, PO Box 357
Hoonah, Alaska 99829

General Information   Parks and recreation department running youth-oriented programs. Established in 1997. Number of employees: 3. Number of internship applications received each year: 30.
Internships Available   ▶ *1 youth recreation assistant:* responsibilities include working one-on-one with youth at a drop-in recreation center and other sites, both indoor and outdoor sports and crafts activities; prevention education, working with at-risk, native youth. Candidates should have ability to work independently, ability to work with others, college courses in field, knowledge of field, oral communication skills. Duration is 12–14 weeks. $350 per month. Open to college freshmen, college sophomores, college juniors, college seniors, recent college graduates, graduate students, law students, career changers, individuals reentering the workforce. International applications accepted.
Benefits Free housing, free meals, names of contacts, on-the-job training, travel reimbursement, willing to act as a professional reference, willing to complete paperwork for educational credit, willing to provide letters of recommendation.

Contact Write, call, fax, or e-mail Richard Keown, Director, PO Box 357, Hoohan, Alaska 99829. Phone: 907-945-3450. Fax: 907-945-3780. E-mail: fish5699@yahoo.com. Telephone interview required. Applicants must submit a formal organization application, letter of interest, resume. Application deadline: April 1 for summer, September 1 for winter, November 1 for spring.

YOUTH ADVOCACY AND INVOLVEMENT OFFICE, NORTH CAROLINA DEPARTMENT OF ADMINISTRATION
1319 Mail Service Center
Raleigh, North Carolina 27699-1319

General Information   State government agency that serves as an advocate for children and youth; seeks to enhance the quality of life for North Carolina's children and youth through policy reviews, legislative recommendations, and positive intervention through leadership educational opportunities. Established in 1969. Number of employees: 12. Division of North Carolina Department of Administration, Raleigh, North Carolina. Number of internship applications received each year: 350.
Internships Available   ▶ *100 interns.* Candidates should have knowledge of field, oral communication skills, personal interest in the field, strong interpersonal skills, written communication skills. Duration is 10 weeks. $6.75 per hour. Open to college freshmen, college sophomores, college juniors, college seniors, graduate students, must be North Carolina resident.
Benefits Formal training, job counseling, names of contacts, opportunity to attend seminars/workshops, willing to complete paperwork for educational credit, willing to provide letters of recommendation.
Contact Write, call, fax, e-mail, or through World Wide Web site Karen Bass, Internship Coordinator. Phone: 919-733-9296. Fax: 919-733-1461. E-mail: karen.bass@ncmail.net. In-person interview recommended. Applicants must submit a formal organization application, letter of interest, resume, academic transcripts. Application deadline: February 2 for summer. World Wide Web: http://www.doa.state.nc.us/doa/yaio/intern.htm.

REAL ESTATE AND RENTAL AND LEASING

GENERAL

AVIS RENT A CAR SYSTEM, INC.
6 Sylvan Way
Parsippany, New Jersey 07054

General Information Global leader in car rental services, with a worldwide reputation for excellence in customer satisfaction, quality performance, employee involvement, financial strength and innovation; covers over 140 nations through more than 4800 worldwide locations. Established in 1946. Number of employees: 350. Unit of Cendant Corporation, New York, New York. Number of internship applications received each year: 50.

Internships Available ▶ *Account managers:* responsibilities include planning sales strategies, negotiating rates and contract terms, and leading project work that will involve research, documentation, and presentations. Candidates should have computer skills, oral communication skills, self-motivation, strong interpersonal skills, strong leadership ability, written communication skills. Duration is minimum of one year. $8–$12 per hour. Open to college sophomores, college juniors, college seniors. ▶ *5–10 general interns:* responsibilities include various duties based on requesting department. Candidates should have analytical skills, oral communication skills, organizational skills, personal interest in the field, self-motivation, strong interpersonal skills, strong leadership ability. Duration is flexible. $8–$12 per hour. Open to college freshmen, college sophomores, college juniors, college seniors, graduate students. ▶ *1–4 management interns:* responsibilities include all basic rental and car preparation responsibilities in all operations including indirect supervision of employees. Candidates should have oral communication skills, personal interest in the field, self-motivation, strong interpersonal skills, strong leadership ability. Duration is minimum of one year. $8–$12 per hour. Open to college sophomores, college juniors, college seniors.

Benefits Formal training, health insurance, job counseling, on-the-job training, opportunity to attend seminars/workshops, possible full-time employment, willing to act as a professional reference, willing to complete paperwork for educational credit, willing to provide letters of recommendation, travel-related discounts.

Contact Write, fax, e-mail, or through World Wide Web site Melissa Eckstein, Human Resources, 6 Sylvan Way, Parsippany, New Jersey 07054. Fax: 973-496-7584. E-mail: staffing@avis.com. No phone calls. In-person interview required. Applicants must submit a formal organization application, letter of interest, resume, three personal references, letter of recommendation, 1 writing sample may be required. Application deadline: March 1 for summer, December 1 for spring. World Wide Web: http://www.avis.com.

CROWN CAPITAL FINANCIAL
540 Pacific Avenue
San Francisco, California 94133

General Information Commercial real estate/real estate merchant and mortgage banking organization. Established in 1977. Number of internship applications received each year: 200.

Internships Available ▶ *1–2 interns:* responsibilities include working directly for owner principals, assisting in commercial real estate investment and mortgage banking business. Candidates should have analytical skills, computer skills, personal interest in the field, self-motivation, strong interpersonal skills, writing skills. Duration is 3–12 months. $500–$1000 per month. Open to college sophomores, college juniors, college seniors, recent college graduates.

Benefits On-the-job training, possible full-time employment, travel reimbursement, willing to act as a professional reference, willing to complete paperwork for educational credit, willing to provide letters of recommendation, working directly with senior principals of the company.

Contact Write, fax, or e-mail David W. Yancey, President. Phone: 415-398-6330 Ext. 349. Fax: 415-398-6057. E-mail: dyancey@crowncapital.com. Telephone interview required. Applicants must submit a letter of interest, resume, academic transcripts, SAT scores. Application deadline: February 1 for spring, April 1 for summer, July 1 for fall, November 1 for winter. World Wide Web: http://crowncapital.com.

HARVEY PROPERTY MANAGEMENT COMPANY, INC.
6931 Arlington Road, Suite 410
Bethesda, Maryland 20814

General Information Commercial property management and development company. Established in 1987. Number of employees: 10. Number of internship applications received each year: 10.

Internships Available ▶ *1 commercial property management intern:* responsibilities include interaction with tenants, government officials, contractors and owners; researching and establishing databases; learning all aspects of the property management business including legal and financial. Candidates should have ability to work independently, office skills, oral communication skills, personal interest in the field, plan to pursue career in field, research skills, written communication skills. Duration is 12–52 weeks. Unpaid. Open to high school students, college freshmen, college sophomores, college juniors, graduate students.

Benefits On-the-job training, opportunity to attend seminars/workshops, possible full-time employment, willing to act as a professional reference, willing to complete paperwork for educational credit, willing to provide letters of recommendation.

Contact Write, fax, or e-mail Avi Halpert, Vice President, Property Management. Fax: 301-907-0394. E-mail: avih@harveycompanies.com. No phone calls. In-person interview recommended (telephone interview accepted). Applicants must submit a resume, 2 business letters. Applications are accepted continuously.

PENNSYLVANIA REAL ESTATE INVESTMENT TRUST
200 South Broad Street
Philadelphia, Pennsylvania 19102

General Information Real estate management/development of commercial, multi-family, and retail properties. Established in 1960. Number of employees: 125. Number of internship applications received each year: 50.

Internships Available ▶ *2–3 accounting interns:* responsibilities include assisting controllers with various accounting functions. Candidates should have ability to work independently, computer skills, knowledge of field, oral communication skills, organizational skills, personal interest in the field, plan to pursue career in field, strong interpersonal skills, written communication skills. Duration is flexible (mainly the summer months May to August). $10–$12 per hour. Open to college sophomores, college juniors, college seniors. ▶ *1–2 associate interns/financial analysts:* responsibilities include working on specific projects as assigned by the CFO, using analytical abilities. Candidates should have ability to work independently, analytical skills, computer skills, oral communication skills, personal interest in the field, strong interpersonal skills, written communication skills, bachelor's degree (minimum) required. Duration is flexible. Paid. Open to recent college gradu-

ates, graduate students, career changers, individuals reentering the workforce. International applications accepted.

Benefits On-the-job training, possible full-time employment, willing to act as a professional reference, willing to complete paperwork for educational credit, willing to provide letters of recommendation.

Contact Write, fax, or e-mail Jacquelyne Berry Batista, Human Resources Generalist. Fax: 215-735-5286. E-mail: batistaj@preit.com. No phone calls. In-person interview required. Applicants must submit a letter of interest, resume. Applications are accepted continuously. World Wide Web: http://www.preit.com.

RETAIL TRADE

GENERAL

BMW OF NORTH AMERICA, INC.
300 Chestnut Ridge Road
Woodcliff Lake, New Jersey 07677-7731

General Information Sales and marketing of automobiles, motorcycles, and parts. Established in 1976. Number of employees: 1,100. Subsidiary of BMW, AG, Munich, Germany. Number of internship applications received each year: 500.

Internships Available ▶ *10–12 interns:* responsibilities include positions in sales, engineering, finance, distribution, marketing, administration, service, MIS, and legal. Candidates should have analytical skills, college courses in field, computer skills, organizational skills, self-motivation, strong interpersonal skills, written communication skills. Duration is 3 months (minimum), usually summer, but possible opportunities throughout the year. $1076 bi-weekly. Open to college juniors, college seniors, law students. International applications accepted.

Benefits Formal training, job counseling, names of contacts, on-the-job training, travel reimbursement, willing to complete paperwork for educational credit, willing to provide letters of recommendation.

Contact Write, fax, or e-mail Intern Coordinator. Fax: 201-307-0992. E-mail: internships@bmwna.com. No phone calls. Applicants must submit a letter of interest, resume, in-person interview for U.S. applicants; telephone interview for international applicants. Application deadline: at least 4 months before desired start date. World Wide Web: http://www.bmwusa.com.

CELEBRATION FIREWORKS II, INC.
5860 North Michigan Road
Indianapolis, Indiana 46228

General Information Wholesale/retail fireworks sales company. Established in 1989. Number of employees: 900. Number of internship applications received each year: 1,000.

Internships Available ▶ *87 store managers:* responsibilities include managing every aspect of running the store: hiring, firing, training, balancing, selling, and marketing. Candidates should have ability to work independently, analytical skills, office skills, oral communication skills, organizational skills, self-motivation, strong interpersonal skills. Duration is 6-8 weeks (May—July 15). $2500 per internship or 6% of gross sales. Open to recent high school graduates, college freshmen, college sophomores, college juniors, college seniors.

Benefits Formal training, housing at a cost, on-the-job training, willing to act as a professional reference, willing to complete paperwork for educational credit, willing to provide letters of recommendation.

Contact Write, call, fax, or e-mail Elizabeth Howard, Personnel. Phone: 800-762-8286. Fax: 317-257-9448. E-mail: elizhoward@celebrationinc.com. In-person interview recommended (telephone interview accepted). Applicants must submit a resume, two personal references. Application deadline: May 1. World Wide Web: http://www.celebrationinc.com.

THE COCA-COLA COMPANY
PO Box 1734
Atlanta, Georgia 30301

General Information World's largest manufacturer, marketer, and distributor of non-alcoholic beverage concentrates and syrups, with nearly 240 brands. Established in 1886.

Internships Available ▶ *50 The College Fund/Coca-Cola Corporate Interns.* Candidates should have analytical skills, oral communication skills, written communication skills, minimum 3.0 GPA; must be sophomore majoring in chemistry, engineering, finance, human resources, information technology, journalism and communications, marketing, or business management (sales interest); documents that prove legal right to work in the U.S. $2500 per month; $10,000 scholarship upon successful internship performance. Open to African American, Hispanic American, Asian American, and American Indian students attending participating colleges and universities. ▶ *Beverage supply chain operations interns:* responsibilities include contributing to ongoing business critical projects; may include creation of databases, operational analysis, data and records management, development of training and orientation activities, research network simulation modeling, and manufacturing line simulations. Candidates should have analytical skills, organizational skills, project management skills, interest and background in supply chain activities such as manufacturing, logistics engineering, finance, human resources, and quality control. Duration is one summer. Position available as unpaid or paid. Open to college freshmen, college sophomores, college juniors, college seniors, graduate students. ▶ *Consumer brand management interns:* responsibilities include active membership in a specific brand or life stage team; managing up to three projects; assignments will expose intern to a variety of marketing elements; one major marketing project ending with a final presentation to senior management. Candidates should have analytical skills, strong leadership ability, previous business experience (for most management positions); 2 or more years of marketing experience with a major consumer packaged goods company (preferred). Position available as unpaid or paid. Open to individuals currently enrolled in a top MBA program having finished the first year. ▶ *Fountain operations interns:* responsibilities include assigned project in mechanical repair, beverage quality, account management, products and services marketing, fountain equipment technology, supply chain management, customer service. Position available as unpaid or paid. Open to individuals who have completed one year of MBA program and have 3-5 years of business experience (preferred). ▶ *Quality and technical services engineering co-ops:* responsibilities include managing one to six projects; providing project updates, giving formal presentations, creating final reports, interacting heavily with internal and external customers. Candidates should have proficiency in English; graduate degree is a plus; previous work experience and proficiency in languages other than English (favorable but not required). Duration is typically 5-6 months (full-time). Position available as unpaid or paid. Open to individuals enrolled for BS degree in a science or engineering discipline.

Benefits Possible full-time employment, other benefits depending on position and posted on Web site.

Contact Through World Wide Web site General Recruiting. Materials as specified on Web site. World Wide Web: http://www.coca-colaoncampus.com.

GRANDY FARM MARKET
PO Box 673
Grandy, North Carolina 27939

General Information Retail outlet for fruits and vegetables, frozen yogurt, and baked goods. Established in 1987. Number of employees: 25.

Internships Available ▶ *2–4 retail produce interns:* responsibilities include creating product displays, stocking, acting as rotation cashier, and providing customer service. Candidates should have ability to work independently, ability to work with others, oral communication skills, personal interest in the field, self-motivation. Duration is 4–6 months. $5.50–$6.50 per hour. Open to high school seniors, recent high school graduates, college freshmen, college sophomores, college juniors, college seniors, recent college graduates, graduate students. ▶ *2 retail produce trainees:* responsibilities include carrying out various tasks and responsibilities involved in the retail of fresh produce and baked goods; duties are similar to those in a supermarket, but in a farm market atmosphere. Candidates should have personal interest in the field, self-motivation, strong interpersonal skills. Duration is flexible (prefer 6 months). $5.15–$5.50 per hour. Open to recent high school graduates, college freshmen, college sophomores, college juniors, college seniors, recent college graduates. International applications accepted.

Benefits Free housing, meals at a cost, on-the-job training, willing to act as a professional reference, willing to complete paperwork for educational credit, willing to provide letters of recommendation.

Contact Write, call, or e-mail Colon Grandy, Jr., Owner. Phone: 252-453-2658. E-mail: grandyfarmmkt@hotmail.com. Telephone interview required. Applicants must submit a formal organization application, resume, academic transcripts, three personal references, letter of recommendation. Application deadline: May 15.

THE HOME DEPOT, CORPORATE OFFICE
2455 Paces Ferry Road
Atlanta, Georgia 30339

General Information Retailer of hardware, home improvement, and garden/patio supplies. Established in 1979. Number of employees: 4,000. Number of internship applications received each year: 40.

Internships Available ▶ *8–12 Building Better Health Interns:* responsibilities include assisting in coordination of wellness events, facility supervision, instruction of fitness and nutrition classes, writing articles for newsletters, promoting wellness program through incentive and motivational programs, and coordinating community resources in the field. Candidates should have ability to work independently, knowledge of field, oral communication skills, self-motivation, strong interpersonal skills, written communication skills. Duration is 15 weeks, (40 hours per week). Position available as unpaid or at up to $500 stipend at end of 15-week internship. Open to college juniors, college seniors, recent college graduates, graduate students, career changers. International applications accepted.

Benefits Free meals, job counseling, on-the-job training, willing to act as a professional reference, willing to complete paperwork for educational credit, willing to provide letters of recommendation, stipend opportunity.

Contact Write, call, fax, or e-mail Derek Taylor, Wellness Coordinator, 2455 Paces Ferry Road, Atlanta, Georgia 30339. Phone: 770-433-8211 Ext. 17133. Fax: 770-384-4123. E-mail: derek_taylor@ homedepot.com. In-person interview recommended (telephone interview accepted). Applicants must submit a formal organization application, resume, letter of recommendation. Application deadline: March 15 for summer, October 1 for spring.

INTERIOR DESIGN COLLECTIONS
39 East 12th Street, Suite 205
New York, New York 10003

General Information Multi-line sales company representing high-end interior product lines selling to interior designers and architects. Established in 1990. Number of employees: 3. Number of internship applications received each year: 60.

Internships Available ▶ *1–4 IDC associates:* responsibilities include client interaction on phone and at field/sales meetings; administration duties; computer work for customer contact; new client lists and rating; sample coordinating. Candidates should have ability to work independently, computer skills, office skills, oral communication skills, organizational skills, self-motivation, strong interpersonal skills. Duration is 6-12 weeks (2-4 days per week). Unpaid. Open to college sophomores, college juniors, college seniors, recent college graduates, graduate students, career changers. International applications accepted.

Benefits Formal training, job counseling, names of contacts, on-the-job training, opportunity to attend seminars/workshops, possible full-time employment, willing to act as a professional reference, willing to complete paperwork for educational credit, willing to provide letters of recommendation, in-town travel reimbursement; most lunch and job expenses paid.

Contact Write, call, or fax Xenia Psihas. Phone: 212-995-9154. Fax: 212-995-8288. Telephone interview required. Applicants must submit a letter of interest, resume. Application deadline: February 28 for spring, March 30 for summer, July 30 for fall, November 30 for winter.

JC PENNEY COMPANY, INC.
6501 Legacy Drive
Plano, Texas 75024-3698

General Information Multi-billion dollar organization with retail department stores, a catalog business, Eckerd Drug stores, and JC Penney Direct Marketing Services. Established in 1902. Number of employees: 3,600. Number of internship applications received each year: 5,000.

Internships Available ▶ *12 summer assistant buyer interns:* responsibilities include completion of weekly project assignments and participation in field trips, which will provide a realistic overview of store operations, merchandising, and the buying process; final oral presentation to buying executives at a Home Office Buying Unit in Dallas, TX. Candidates should have oral communication skills, plan to pursue career in field, strong interpersonal skills, 3.0 minimum GPA preferred. Duration is 9 weeks. $11.50 per hour. ▶ *4 summer brand design interns:* responsibilities include developing and designing artwork, including prints, patterns, and graphic designs, to be utilized in a private brand strategy. Candidates should have college courses in field, oral communication skills, plan to pursue career in field, strong interpersonal skills, minimum 3.0 GPA preferred; familiarity with U4ia textile design software a plus. Duration is 10 weeks. $11.50 per hour. ▶ *12–18 summer information systems interns:* responsibilities include Internet technology, client/server technology, relational databases, and object-oriented technology. Candidates should have college courses in field, declared college major in field, plan to pursue career in field, minimum 3.0 GPA preferred; experience with Visual Basic, C++, JAVA, HTML, and COBOL. Duration is 10 weeks. $14.42 per hour. ▶ *100 summer merchandise management interns:* responsibilities include participating in decision-making involving customer service, inventory flow, marketing, presentation, and merchandise. Candidates should have personal interest in the field, plan to pursue career in field, strong interpersonal skills, strong leadership ability, 3.0 minimum GPA preferred; retail experience a plus. Duration is 10 weeks. $11.50 per hour. Open to college juniors, college seniors. International applications accepted.

Benefits Formal training, opportunity to attend seminars/ workshops, possible full-time employment, travel reimbursement and free housing for some positions.

Contact Write, call, fax, or through World Wide Web site Michael Silipo, College Relations Manager, PO Box 10001, Dallas 75301-8115. Phone: 972-431-2316. Fax: 972-431-2320. In-person interview required. Applicants must submit a formal organization application, letter of interest, resume, portfolio required for some positions. Application deadline: April 1. World Wide Web: http:// www.jcpenney.com.

LANDS' END
5 Lands' End Lane
Dodgeville, Wisconsin 53595

General Information Direct merchant/e-commerce merchant of traditionally-styled classic casualwear for the family and products for bed and bath; accessories are offered to customers through regular mailing of catalogs and through the Internet. Established in 1963. Number of employees: 6,000. Number of internship applications received each year: 1,500.

Internships Available ▶ *1–2 Web design interns:* responsibilities include working with the Internet team in creating daily and weekly feature content for the business divisions or special projects, including banners, product page images, or content for affiliate programs; and designing Internet-ready graphics, including GIFs, JPEGs, and animated GIFs. Candidates should have ability to work independently, college courses in field, computer skills, self-motivation, strong interpersonal skills, strong leadership ability. Duration is 3–6 months. $15–$20 per hour. ▶ *1–2 apparel design interns:* responsibilities include working with seasoned designers to learn how to design and develop product by interpreting concepts into themes, developing color, fabrication, silhouettes, and mood for upcoming seasons; conducting market research; and drawing flat sketches and illustrations. Candidates should have ability to work independently, college courses in field, strong interpersonal skills, understanding of textile construction; ability to do flat drawings and sketches. Duration is 3 months. $12 per hour. ▶ *2–3 art direction interns:* responsibilities include learning the process behind designing, developing and producing, and selling concepts and layouts; editing film and working with layout revisions; gaining exposure to the process behind a photo shoot. Candidates should have ability to work independently, college courses in field, experience in the field, self-motivation, strong interpersonal skills, strong leadership ability. Duration is 3–6 months. $12 per hour. ▶ *3 corporate fitness interns:* responsibilities include assisting with adult recreation leagues, tournaments, and wellness programs; teaching aerobics classes (land and water), doing fitness evaluations; supervising floor and pool area of the Activity Center; and educating employees on a variety of health-related topics. Candidates should have college courses in field, knowledge of field, self-motivation, strong interpersonal skills, strong leadership ability. Duration is 3 months. Paid. ▶ *1–2 employee services interns:* responsibilities include developing and implementing campus recruitment plans, attending job fairs, townhall events and open houses, and planning special events to attract segments of the population that would be interested in seasonal employment opportunities. Candidates should have ability to work independently, college courses in field, knowledge of field, strong interpersonal skills, strong leadership ability. Duration is June to December. $12 per hour. ▶ *4–6 information services interns:* responsibilities include developing programs and documentation, coding, testing, and debugging programs, and developing specifications and test plans. Candidates should have college courses in field, computer skills, self-motivation, strong interpersonal skills, strong leadership ability. Duration is 3–6 months. $15 per hour. ▶ *2–4 inventory interns:* responsibilities include pre-season planning and forecasting, extensive sales trend analysis, learning inventory concepts and strategies for direct marketing, and tracking the manufacturing process. Candidates should have ability to work independently, analytical skills, self-motivation, strong interpersonal skills, strong leadership ability. Duration is 3 months. $12 per hour. ▶ *1–2 marketing interns:* responsibilities include forecasting circulation, response, demand, advertising costs, and profits across multiple channels; and collecting, reporting, and analyzing data related to understanding customer behavior. Candidates should have analytical skills, college courses in field, computer skills, research skills, self-motivation, strong interpersonal skills. Duration is 3 months. $12–$15 per hour. ▶ *1–2 media relations interns:* responsibilities include working with either the product team or corporate team on public relations campaigns; developing and maintaining relationships with major national and business media; researching and writing public relation materials including fact sheets, captions, press releases, memos, and cover letters; and developing a media list and learning how to "pitch" a story to the media. Candidates should have ability to work with others, college courses in field, self-motivation, writing skills. Duration is 3 months. $12 per hour. ▶ *2–4 merchandising interns:* responsibilities include assisting merchants in driving specific categories through product development, developing competitive analysis for team reviews, and understanding the levers that affect the business. Candidates should have analytical skills, college courses in field, computer skills, knowledge of field, plan to pursue career in field, self-motivation, strong interpersonal skills. Duration is 3 months. $12 per hour. ▶ *3–5 operations management interns:* responsibilities include providing managerial support in distribution centers, taking on a leadership role within call centers operations, and coaching and developing an internal work force. Candidates should have ability to work independently, college courses in field, self-motivation, strong interpersonal skills, strong leadership ability. Duration is June to December. $12 per hour. ▶ *3–4 quality interns:* responsibilities include assisting with product and specification development, fit evaluation, and testing of fabrics. Candidates should have ability to work independently, college courses in field, self-motivation, strong interpersonal skills, strong leadership ability, background in clothing and textiles. Duration is 3 months. $12 per hour. ▶ *2–4 retail store management interns:* responsibilities include assisting with store operations including merchandising, monitoring inventory levels, accountability for overall operations, and setting up and executing store and advertising plans. Candidates should have ability to work independently, experience in the field, self-motivation, strong interpersonal skills, strong leadership ability. Duration is 3 months. $12 per hour. Open to college juniors, college seniors.

Benefits Formal training, job counseling, names of contacts, on-the-job training, opportunity to attend seminars/workshops, possible full-time employment, travel reimbursement, willing to act as a professional reference, willing to complete paperwork for educational credit, willing to provide letters of recommendation, clothing/merchandise discounts, access to on-site fitness facility, payment of housing security deposit.

Contact Write, call, fax, or through World Wide Web site Regina Lord, Intern Coordinator, 5 Lands' End Lane, Dodgeville, Wisconsin 53595. Phone: 608-935-4928. Fax: 608-935-4831. In-person interview recommended (telephone interview accepted). Applicants must submit a resume, portfolio, video conference (where applicable), on-line application, 2-3 writing samples (for certain positions). Application deadline: March 1 for summer, August 1 for fall, December 1 for spring. World Wide Web: http://www.landsend.com.

QVC, INC.
1200 Wilson Drive
West Chester, Pennsylvania 19380

General Information Electronic retailing/e-commerce company. Established in 1986. Number of employees: 2,800. Subsidiary of Comcast Corporation, Philadelphia, Pennsylvania. Number of internship applications received each year: 200.

Internships Available ▶ *MIS interns:* responsibilities include programming/application development with client server and Web technologies. Candidates should have ability to work with others, declared college major in field, oral communication skills, self-motivation, knowledge of C, C++, or Visual Basic. Duration is 3–6 months. Paid. Open to college sophomores, college juniors, college seniors, graduate students. ▶ *Broadcasting interns:* responsibilities include working backstage, in the control room, or in video production. Candidates should have college courses in field, experience in the field, plan to pursue career in field, self-motivation, strong interpersonal skills. Duration is 3–6 months. Paid. Open to college sophomores, college juniors, college seniors. ▶ *Communications interns:* responsibilities include coordinating internal communication projects, researching and gathering information, participating in the management of various communication vehicles. Candidates should have ability to work with others, declared college major in field, research skills, self-motivation, writing skills. Duration is 3–6 months. Paid. Open to college sophomores, college juniors, college seniors, graduate students. ▶ *Human resources interns:* responsibilities include assisting with projects in human resources. Candidates should have computer skills, knowledge of field, office skills, self-motivation,

strong interpersonal skills. Duration is 3–6 months. Paid. Open to college sophomores, college juniors, college seniors, graduate students. ▶ *Merchandising interns:* responsibilities include working directly with QVC buyers in order to learn the product procurement process. Candidates should have organizational skills, plan to pursue career in field, self-motivation, strong interpersonal skills, strong leadership ability. Duration is 3–6 months. Paid. Open to college sophomores, college juniors, college seniors, graduate students. International applications accepted.
Benefits Names of contacts, on-the-job training, opportunity to attend seminars/workshops, possible full-time employment, willing to complete paperwork for educational credit, discount on product purchases.
Contact Write, fax, or e-mail College Relations Recruiter. Fax: 610-701-1150. E-mail: collegerelations@qvc.com. No phone calls. In-person interview required. Applicants must submit a letter of interest, resume, two personal references. Application deadline: March 31 for summer, August 1 for fall, November 15 for spring. World Wide Web: http://www.qvc.com.

RICH'S/LAZARUS/GOLDSMITH'S DEPARTMENT STORES
223 Perimeter Center Parkway
Atlanta, Georgia 30346

General Information Traditional retail department store that emphasizes dynamic store environments, diverse merchandise selection, and superior customer service. Established in 1867. Number of employees: 20,000. Unit of Federated Department Stores, Inc., Cincinnati, Ohio. Number of internship applications received each year: 600.
Internships Available ▶ *50 sales management interns:* responsibilities include management, visual merchandising, human resources, business analysis, and store-line support exposure. Candidates should have ability to work with others, knowledge of field, oral communication skills, organizational skills, self-motivation, strong leadership ability. Duration is 10 weeks. $13 per hour. Open to college sophomores, college juniors, college seniors. International applications accepted.
Benefits Formal training, on-the-job training, possible full-time employment, willing to act as a professional reference, willing to complete paperwork for educational credit, willing to provide letters of recommendation.
Contact Write, fax, e-mail, or through World Wide Web site Kate Coon-Linard, Manager, New Talent. Fax: 770-913-5114. E-mail: kcoon@fds.com. No phone calls. In-person interview required. Applicants must submit a resume. Application deadline: April 1 for summer. World Wide Web: http://www.federated-fds.com.

SAKS FIFTH AVENUE
611 Fifth Avenue
New York, New York 10022

General Information Retail company. Established in 1924. Number of employees: 1,400. Division of Saks, Inc., Birmingham, Alabama. Number of internship applications received each year: 3,500.
Internships Available ▶ *7–27 New York store interns.* Candidates should have analytical skills, knowledge of field, oral communication skills, strong interpersonal skills, strong leadership ability, problem-solving and decision-making skills. Duration is one spring (March to May); one fall (September to January); one summer (June to August). $10 per hour. Open to college juniors, college seniors, recent college graduates.

Benefits Formal training, housing at a cost, job counseling, meals at a cost, names of contacts, on-the-job training, opportunity to attend seminars/workshops, possible full-time employment, willing to act as a professional reference, willing to complete paperwork for educational credit, willing to provide letters of recommendation.
Contact Write, call, fax, or e-mail Peter Goldschmidt, Recruiter/Internship Coordinator. Phone: 212-940-4910. Fax: 212-940-2992. E-mail: peter_goldschmidt@s5a.com. In-person interview required. Applicants must submit a letter of interest, resume, academic transcripts, two personal references. Application deadline: March 1 for fall, November 1 for spring, December 1 for summer.

SHERWIN-WILLIAMS
10440 East Northwest Highway
Dallas, Texas 75238

General Information Division that distributes Sherwin-Williams branded architectural coatings, industrial maintenance products, industrial finishes, and related items. Established in 1866. Number of employees: 100. Division of The Sherwin-Williams Company, Cleveland, Ohio. Number of internship applications received each year: 500.
Internships Available ▶ *1–100 summer co-op interns:* responsibilities include working with customer service, merchandising, credit, and sales areas; assisting store manager in maintaining good customer relations, market development, and inventory management. Candidates should have oral communication skills, organizational skills, personal interest in the field, self-motivation, strong interpersonal skills, strong leadership ability. Duration is 9–12 weeks. $8–$8.50 per hour. Open to college sophomores, college juniors, college seniors. International applications accepted.
Benefits Formal training, names of contacts, on-the-job training, opportunity to attend seminars/workshops, possible full-time employment, willing to complete paperwork for educational credit, willing to provide letters of recommendation.
Contact Write, call, fax, e-mail, or through World Wide Web site Ron Novak, Area Human Resources Manager. Phone: 214-553-3938. Fax: 214-553-3937. E-mail: rdnovak@sherwin.com. In-person interview required. Applicants must submit a formal organization application, letter of interest, resume. Applications are accepted continuously. World Wide Web: http://www.sherwin-williams.com.

THE SOUTHWESTERN COMPANY
PO Box 305140
Nashville, Tennessee 37230

General Information Summer work program for college students. Established in 1868. Number of employees: 75.
Internships Available ▶ *Student sales interns.* Candidates should have ability to work independently, oral communication skills, willingness to work hard. Duration is 12–14 weeks. Paid. Open to college freshmen, college sophomores, college juniors, college seniors, graduate students. International applications accepted.
Benefits Formal training, job counseling, names of contacts, possible full-time employment, willing to complete paperwork for educational credit, willing to provide letters of recommendation, access to full-service placement office.
Contact Write, call, fax, or through World Wide Web site Trey Campbell, Promotions Coordinator. Phone: 615-391-2801. Fax: 615-391-2703. In-person interview recommended (telephone interview accepted). Applicants must submit a formal organization application, letter of interest, resume. Application deadline: June 1. World Wide Web: http://www.southwestern.com.

TRANSPORTATION

GENERAL

AMERICA WEST AIRLINES
4000 East Sky Harbor Boulevard
Phoenix, Arizona 85034

General Information Major U.S. carrier. Established in 1983. Number of employees: 11,000. Number of internship applications received each year: 200.
Internships Available ▶ *Interns:* responsibilities include working in public relations, communications, marketing, sales, or finance. Candidates should have analytical skills, college courses in field, computer skills, written communication skills. Duration is flexible. Position available as unpaid or paid. Open to college freshmen, college sophomores, college juniors, college seniors, graduate students.
Benefits Willing to complete paperwork for educational credit, travel stipend.
International Internships Available.
Contact Write, fax, or e-mail Connie Razza, Internship Coordinator, 4000 East Sky Harbor Boulevard, Phoenix, Arizona 55034. Fax: 480-693-8813. E-mail: employment@americawest.com. No phone calls. In-person interview required. Applicants must submit a letter of interest, resume. Applications are accepted continuously. World Wide Web: http://www.americawest.com.

ARKANSAS BEST CORPORATION
PO Box 10048
Fort Smith, Arkansas 72917-0048

General Information Holding company with subsidiaries engaged in worldwide freight transportation and distribution services, truck tire remanufacturing, and information services. Established in 1935. Number of employees: 15,055. Number of internship applications received each year: 200.
Internships Available ▶ *4–8 programmers/analysts:* responsibilities include analyzing, designing, and programming computer applications systems. Candidates should have analytical skills, college courses in field, computer skills, oral communication skills, strong interpersonal skills. Duration is flexible. $2600–$2800 per month. Open to college juniors, college seniors, graduate students. International applications accepted.
Benefits Formal training, on-the-job training, opportunity to attend seminars/workshops, possible full-time employment, travel reimbursement, willing to act as a professional reference, willing to complete paperwork for educational credit.
Contact Write, fax, e-mail, or through World Wide Web site DTC Recruiting. Fax: 501-784-8599. E-mail: resumes@data-tronics.com. No phone calls. In-person interview recommended (telephone interview accepted). Applicants must submit a formal organization application, letter of interest, resume, academic transcripts. Applications are accepted continuously. World Wide Web: http://www.arkbest.com.

UTILITIES

GENERAL

MINNESOTA POWER
30 West Superior Street
Duluth, Minnesota 55802

General Information Diversified electric utility company that uses fossil fuel and hydro power to generate electricity; has interests in power marketing, telecommunications, coal mining, and natural gas. Established in 1923. Number of employees: 1,500. Number of internship applications received each year: 100.

Internships Available ▶ *15–25 interns:* responsibilities include working in information technology, engineering, or accounting, drafting, financial, power trading, or telecommunications. Candidates should have ability to work with others, college courses in field, computer skills, writing skills, minimum GPA of 3.0. Duration is 6–12 months. Paid. Open to college freshmen, college sophomores, college juniors, college seniors, vocational students.

Benefits Willing to complete paperwork for educational credit.

Contact Through World Wide Web site Kay Ernst, Human Resource Analyst. No phone calls. Application materials as specified on Web site during available periods only. Application deadline: consult Web site for deadlines. World Wide Web: http://www.mnpower.com.

FIELD OF INTEREST INDEX

Artists and Related Workers

Business and Financial Operations

Farming, Fishing, and Forestry

Food Preparation and Serving

Health

Life, Physical, and Social Sciences

Social Scientists and Related Workers

Office and Administration

Personal Care and Service

Transportation, Tourism, and Lodging Attendants

Production

Sales

Transportation and Material Moving Occupations

GEOGRAPHIC INDEX

INTERNATIONAL INTERNSHIPS INDEX

ACADEMIC LEVEL REQUIRED INDEX

COLLEGE SENIORS

RECENT COLLEGE GRADUATES

INTERNATIONAL APPLICANTS ACCEPTED INDEX

PAID INTERNSHIPS INDEX

POSSIBILITY OF PERMANENT EMPLOYMENT INDEX

EMPLOYER INDEX

Notes

Notes

Notes

Notes

Notes

Notes

Notes

Notes

Notes

Notes

Notes

Notes